FREE CD-ROM!

The **NetActivities** CD-ROM turns your classroom computer into an interactive exploration tool that helps students develop their research skills. With **NetActivities**, students can investigate eight different topics related to those studied in *World History: Patterns of Interaction* including:

Interactive technology that takes you beyond the textbook!

- **Cave Art**
- **Chinese Healing Arts**
- **The Parthenon**
- **Counting: Calendars and Cords**

- **The French Revolution**
- **Mass Entertainment**
- **The Roaring Twenties**
- **The Environment**

Everything your students need to begin using **NetActivities** is contained on one CD-ROM; no Internet connection is needed. Students using computers equipped with Internet access will be able to extend their explorations with live links to online resources.

McDougal Littell
A HOUGHTON MIFFLIN COMPANY

P40537

McDougal Littell

WORLD HISTORY

ANNOTATED TEACHER'S EDITION

ISBN 0-395-87275-8
Printed in the United States of America.
    4 5 6 7 8 9–VJM–03 02 01 00 99

Table of Contents

Program Overview

World History: Patterns of Interaction is a highly integrated program that provides teachers with a practical and motivational approach to teaching world history and to helping students think critically and reflectively. (For more information on each element, see pages T6–T32.)

Motivating and Captivating Students

History comes alive for students when they are actively involved in their own learning. Through interactive situations and lively encounters with people and ideas, students can begin to make personal connections to the past. *World History: Patterns of Interaction* provides those lively encounters and personal connections—from a situation demanding personal involvement at the beginning of each chapter, to connections with people, both great and ordinary, from the past.

1 ## Interact with History

In an interactive, imagined situation in each chapter, students encounter the difficult problems and decisions faced by real people of the past. As students put themselves in a key historical situation, they will analyze the issues, explore their options, and become decision-makers.

2 ## History Makers

Focusing on people can make history human and fascinating. These short biographies allow students to see the great men and women of world history as individuals in both triumph and adversity.

3 ## A Voice from the Past

Authentic primary sources scattered throughout the text resonate with the passions and sharp personal observations of people who lived through the historical periods discussed. These real voices from the past help students see that history is human and accessible.

HISTORY MAKERS

**Hatshepsut
reigned 1472–1458 B.C.**

Hatshepsut was an excellent ruler of outstanding achievement who made Egypt more prosperous. As pharaoh, she sent traders down the Red Sea to bring back gold, ebony, baboons, and myrrh trees.

As male pharaohs had done, Hatshepsut planned a tomb for herself in the Valley of the Kings. Carved reliefs on the walls of the temple reveal the glories of her reign.

The inscription from Hatshepsut's obelisk (tall stone shaft) at Karnak trumpets her glory and her feelings about herself:

"I swear as Re loves me, as my father Amon favors me, as my nostrils are filled with satisfying life, as I wear the white crown, as I appear in the red crown, . . . as I rule this land like the son of Isis . . ."

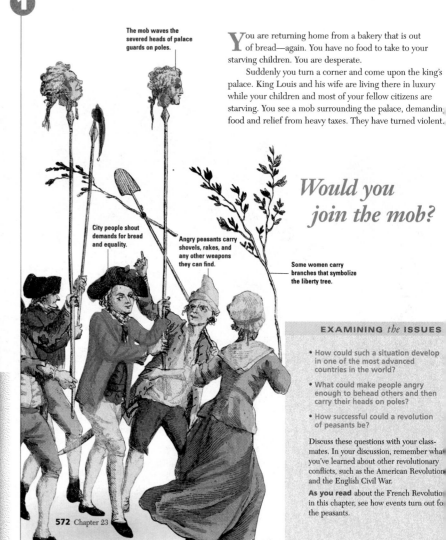

Interact *with* History

1

The mob waves the severed heads of palace guards on poles.

You are returning home from a bakery that is out of bread—again. You have no food to take to your starving children. You are desperate.

Suddenly you turn a corner and come upon the king's palace. King Louis and his wife are living there in luxury while your children and most of your fellow citizens are starving. You see a mob surrounding the palace, demanding food and relief from heavy taxes. They have turned violent.

City people shout demands for bread and equality.

Angry peasants carry shovels, rakes, and any other weapons they can find.

Some women carry branches that symbolize the liberty tree.

Would you join the mob?

EXAMINING *the* ISSUES

- How could such a situation develop in one of the most advanced countries in the world?
- What could make people angry enough to behead others and then carry their heads on poles?
- How successful could a revolution of peasants be?

Discuss these questions with your classmates. In your discussion, remember what you've learned about other revolutionary conflicts, such as the American Revolution and the English Civil War.

As you read about the French Revolution in this chapter, see how events turn out for the peasants.

572 Chapter 23

3

A VOICE FROM THE PAST

I am a griot . . . master in the art of eloquence. . . . we are vessels of speech, we are the repositories [storehouses] which harbor secrets many centuries old. . . . without us the names of kings would vanish. . . . we are the memory of mankind; by the spoken word we bring to life the deeds . . . of kings for younger generations. . . . for the world is old, but the future springs from the past.

DJELI MAMADOU KOUYATE, from *Sundiata, an Epic of Old Mali*

1 Revolution Threatens the French King

MAIN IDEA

Economic and social inequalities in the Old Regime helped cause the French Revolution.

WHY IT MATTERS NOW

Throughout history, economic and social inequalities have at times led peoples to revolt against their governments.

TERMS & NAMES
- Old Regime
- estate
- Louis XVI
- Marie Antoinette
- Estates-General
- National Assembly
- Tennis Court Oath
- Great Fear

SETTING THE STAGE In the 1700s, France was considered the most advanced country of Europe. It was the center of the Enlightenment. It had a large population and a prosperous foreign trade. France's culture was widely praised and emulated by the rest of the world. However, the appearance of success was deceiving. There was great unrest in France, caused by high prices, high taxes, and disturbing questions raised by the Enlightenment ideas of Rousseau and Voltaire.

The Old Regime

In the 1770s, the system of feudalism left over from the Middle Ages—called the **Old Regime**—remained in place. The people of France were still divided into three large social classes, or **estates.**

The Privileged Estates Two of the estates had privileges, including access to high offices and exemptions from paying taxes, that were not granted to the members of the third.

The Roman Catholic Church, whose clergy formed the First Estate, owned 10 percent of the land in France. It provided education and relief services to the poor and contributed about 2 percent of its income to the government.

The Second Estate was made up of rich nobles, much of whose wealth was in land. Although they made up only 2 percent of the population, the nobles owned 20 percent of the land and paid almost no taxes. The majority of the clergy and the nobility scorned Enlightenment ideas as radical notions that threatened their status and power as privileged persons.

Vocabulary
bourgeoisie: the middle class. (The term derives from the walled cities, or *bourgs*, in which the middle class began to develop in the 1200s.)

The Third Estate About 98 percent of the people belonged to the Third Estate. The three groups that made up this estate differed greatly in their economic conditions.

The first group—the bourgeoisie (BUR-zhwah-ZEE)—were merchants and artisans. They were well-educated and believed strongly in the Enlightenment ideals of liberty and equality. Although some of the bourgeoisie were as rich as nobles, they paid high taxes and lacked privileges like the other members of the Third Estate. Many felt that their wealth entitled them to a greater degree of social status and political power.

The workers of France's cities—cooks, servants, and others—formed the second group within the Third Estate, a group poorer than the bourgeoisie. Paid low wages and frequently out of work, they often went hungry. If the cost of bread rose, mobs of these workers might attack carts of grain and bread to steal what they needed.

Peasants formed the largest group within the Third Estate—more than 80 percent of France's 2... ...ir income in dues to nobles, tithes to the ... ...en paid taxes on such basic staples as sal... ...the clergy and the nobles for their pri... ...d and discontented Third Estate wa...

This medallion bears the image of King Louis XVI of France.

Daily Life

A Scholar's Fingernails

Many scholar-officials eventually adopted the fashion of growing their fingernails long. A two-inch fingernail showed clearly that the owner did no manual labor. However, long nails did not prevent the scholar from following the pursuits of the gentry, such as writing poetry, painting, or practicing calligraphy. The photograph above is of a Chinese doctor in the late 19th century.

SCIENCE & TECHNOLOGY

Castles and Siege Weapons

Attacking armies carefully planned how to capture a castle. Engineers would inspect the castle walls for weak points in the stone. Then enemy soldiers would try to ram the walls, causing them to collapse. At the battle site, attackers often constructed the heavy and clumsy weapons shown here.

Siege Tower
- had a platform on top that lowered like a drawbridge
- could support weapons and soldiers

Mantlet
- shielded soldiers

Battering Ram
- made of heavy timber with a sharp metal tip
- swung like a pendulum to crack castle walls or to knock down drawbridge

Trebuchet
- worked like a giant slingshot
- propelled objects up to a distance of 980 feet

Tortoise
- moved slowly on wheels
- sheltered soldiers from falling arrows

An Array of High-Flying Missiles

Using the **trebuchet**, enemy soldiers launched a wide variety of missiles over the castle walls:
- pots of burning lime
- boulders
- severed human heads
- captured soldiers
- diseased cows
- dead horses

Mangonel
- flung huge rocks that crashed into castle walls
- propelled objects up to a distance of 1,300 feet

Connect to History

Making Inferences How do these siege weapons show that their designers knew the architecture of a castle well?

SEE SKILLBUILDER HANDBOOK, PAGE 1005

Connect to Today

Researching Modern technology has made warfare far less personal than it was during the Middle Ages. Find examples of recent weapons. Describe how they affect the way war is conducted.

---

4 Main Idea and Why It Matters Now

By answering the old question, "Why does it matter now?" students begin to understand that historical events have influenced their own lives. Every section of *World History: Patterns of Interaction* clearly tells students the key concept of the section and explains why it matters.

5 Science & Technology

High-interest features such as Science & Technology involve students in learning how early plumbing worked, how the Roman Colosseum managed crowd control, how the Panama Canal was built, and other fascinating technological marvels. Students learn about the impact of science on history through the combination of pictures and words in these engaging and interactive features.

6 Daily Life

A sure way to get students motivated and involved is to show them how people really lived. The Daily Life features describe how people worked and played and provide some thought-provoking facts about their lives.

Finding Support for Reading and Understanding

Providing the resources for students to read critically and reflectively is a key aspect of *World History: Patterns of Interaction*. Many resources help all students and every learning style:

- inner-column notes and questions
- graphics combining visual and verbal information
- assessment questions based on critical-thinking strategies
- visual summaries

❶ Vocabulary

Vocabulary notes define difficult words just when a reader might need help—at point of use.

❷ Graphs

State-of-the-art graphs throughout the text present information and build critical-thinking skills through thought-provoking questions.

❸ Background

Occasionally enhancing and extending the text, the background notes provide that little bit of additional information that helps readers comprehend.

❹ Visual Summary

A visual summary of the most important ideas and events ends each chapter. Some are cause-and-effect flow charts, others are time lines, still others are topical and thematic charts—all give visual learners and others another path to understanding.

---

❶ Vocabulary
edible: safe to eat

❸ Background
Dogs were probably the first domesticated animals, serving as pets and hunting companions. The oldest discovery of human and dog fossils found together dates back to roughly 8000 B.C.

The Neolithic Revolution

For thousands upon thousands of years, humans survived by hunting game and gathering edible plants. They lived in bands of no more than two to three dozen people. The men almost certainly did the hunting. The women gathered fruits, berries, roots, and grasses. Then about 10,000 years ago, some of the women may have scattered seeds near a regular campsite. When they returned the next season, they may have found new crops growing. This discovery would usher in the **Neolithic Revolution,** or the agricultural revolution—the far-reaching changes in human life resulting from the beginnings of farming. The shift from food-gathering to food-producing culture represents one of the great breakthroughs in history.

Causes of the Agricultural Revolution Scientists do not know exactly why the agricultural revolution occurred during this period. Change in climate was probably a key factor. Rising temperatures worldwide provided longer growing seasons and drier land for cultivating wild grasses. A rich supply of grain helped support a small population boom. As populations slowly rose, hunter-gatherers felt pressure to find new food sources. Farming offered an attractive alternative. Unlike hunting, farming provided a steady source of food.

Vocabulary
edible: safe to eat

Background
The agricultural revolution caused a dramatic change in human diet. Hunter-gatherers consumed about 80 percent meat and 20 percent plant foods. The agricultural revolution reversed these percentages.

Agricultural Revolution

SKILLBUILDER: Interpreting Charts
1. How was the agricultural revolution linked to a change in temperature?
2. What effect did the agricultural revolution have on population growth? Why?

Early Farming Methods Some groups practiced **slash-and-burn farming,** in which they cut trees or grasses and burned them to clear a field. The remaining ashes fertilized the soil. Farmers planted crops for a year or two. Then they moved on to another area of land. After several years, the trees and grass grew back, and other farmers repeated the process of slashing and burning.

Domestication of Animals Food gatherers' understanding of plants probably spurred the development of farming. Meanwhile, hunters' expert knowledge of wild animals likely played a key role in the **domestication,** or the taming of animals. They tamed horses, dogs, goats, and pigs. Like farming, domestication of animals came slowly. Stone Age hunters may have driven herds of animals into rocky ravines to be slaughtered. It was then a small step to drive herds into human-made enclosures. From there, farmers could keep the animals as a constant source of food and gradually tame them.

Not only farmers domesticated animals. Pastoral nomads, or wandering herders, tended sheep, goats, camels, or other animals. These herders moved their animals to new pastures and watering places.

Background
Dogs were probably the first domesticated animals, serving as pets and hunting companions. The oldest discovery of human and dog fossils found together dates back to roughly 8000 B.C.

Revolution in Jarmo Today the eroded and barren rolling foothills of the Zagros Mountains in northeastern Iraq seem an unlikely site for the birthplace of agriculture.

14 Chapter 1

Visual Summary

❹ The Peopling of the World

Social Organization

Hunting-Gathering Bands	Growth of Villages	Rise of Cities
Beginning about 2 million B.C.	Beginning about 8000 B.C.	Beginning about 3000 B.C.

Achievements

Key Achievements	Key Achievements	Key Achievements
• Invention of tools • Mastery over fire • Development of language • Creation of art	• Development of agriculture • Domestication of animals • Breakthroughs in farming technology • Food surpluses	• Specialized workers • Record keeping • Complex institutions • Advanced technology

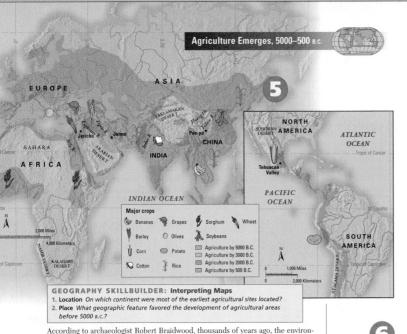

Agriculture Emerges, 5000–500 B.C.

Major crops

- Bananas
- Barley
- Corn
- Cotton
- Grapes
- Olives
- Potato
- Rice
- Sorghum
- Soybeans
- Wheat

- ☐ Agriculture by 5000 B.C.
- ☐ Agriculture by 3000 B.C.
- ☐ Agriculture by 2000 B.C.
- ☐ Agriculture by 500 B.C.

2,000 Miles
4,000 Kilometers

0   1,000 Miles
0   2,000 Kilometers

GEOGRAPHY SKILLBUILDER: Interpreting Maps
1. **Location** *On which continent were most of the earliest agricultural sites located?*
2. **Place** *What geographic feature favored the development of agricultural areas before 5000 B.C.?*

According to archaeologist Robert Braidwood, thousands of years ago, the environmental conditions of this region favored the development of agriculture. Wild wheat and barley, along with wild goats, pigs, sheep, and horses, had once thrived near the Zagros Mountains.

During the early 1950s, Braidwood conducted an archaeological dig at a site called Jarmo. He concluded that its residents first established this agricultural settlement about 9,000 years ago:

A VOICE FROM THE PAST

We found weights for digging sticks, hoe-like [tools], flint-sickle blades, and a wide variety of milling stones. . . . We also discovered several pits that were probably used for the storage of grain. Perhaps the most important evidence of all was animal bones and the impressions left in the mud by cereal grains. . . . The people of Jarmo were adjusting themselves to a completely new way of life, just as we are adjusting ourselves to the consequences of such things as the steam engine. What they learned about living in a revolution may be of more than academic interest to us in our troubled times.

ROBERT BRAIDWOOD, quoted in *Scientific American*

The farmers at Jarmo, and others like them in places as far apart as Mexico and Thailand, were pioneering a new way of life. Villages such as Jarmo marked the beginning of a new era and laid the foundation for modern life.

Villages Grow and Prosper

The changeover from hunting and gathering to farming and herding took place not once, but many times. Neolithic people in many parts of the world independently developed agriculture.

The Peopling of the World **15**

THINK THROUGH HISTORY

B. Making Inferences
What evidence discovered at Jarmo shows how farming created new technological needs?

THINK THROUGH HISTORY

B. Making Inferences
What evidence discovered at Jarmo shows how farming created new technological needs?

---

⑤ Maps

Several hundred maps, developed with the latest computer technology, work together with the text to explain historical events and to help students explore their meanings

⑥ Think Through History

These questions in the inner columns of the text help students both check their comprehension and think critically about historical events.

⑦ Section Assessments

Section and chapter assessments explicitly draw on various critical-thinking strategies to help students focus on the crucial process of becoming proficient thinkers. Among the strategies used are identifying and defining key concepts, using graphics to organize information, answering various critical-thinking questions, and analyzing and applying themes.

---

⑦

Section **2** Assessment

1. TERMS & NAMES

Identify
- nomad
- hunter-gatherer
- Neolithic Revolution
- slash-and-burn farming
- domestication

2. TAKING NOTES

Using a web diagram like the one below, show the effects of the development of agriculture.

Development of Agriculture

Choose one effect and write a paragraph about it.

3. HYPOTHESIZING

Why do you think the development of agriculture occurred around the same time in several different places?

THINK ABOUT
- the migrations of early peoples
- changes in the earth's climate
- a rise in human population

4. THEME ACTIVITY

Science and Technology
Create a chart explaining new tools, utensils, and other artifacts that archaeologists would likely find at the site of a permanent farming settlement. Use information from the text on Jarmo and Catal Huyuk to make your list of objects.

Discovering Connections Across Time and Place

History becomes meaningful when students make connections between the past and the present, when they consider how historical events have influenced their lives, and when they discover some of the fascinating recurring patterns of history across the centuries. *World History: Patterns of Interaction* provides many ways to make connections—both around the world and across time—from high-interest features like Global Impact and Something in Common to the sweeping themes of history.

1 Chapter Openers

A two-page map giving the time and place of each chapter's content, along with images of people and events from the chapter and short anecdotes, offer a richly tempting introduction to the history to come. The connections among geography, history, and themes are firmly established.

2 Previewing Themes

Themes emphasized throughout the text make the connections across time and place vividly real. The eight themes include Power and Authority, Religious and Ethical Systems, Revolution, Interaction with Environment, Economics, Cultural Interaction, Empire Building, and Science and Technology.

3 Internet Connection

The McDougal Littell internet address leads students to a rich web site where they can learn more about the people and events featured in the chapter.

4 Global Impact

These features, which occur in every unit, use pictures and words to help students see how certain major events or movements can have a great impact on history.

5 Video

Eight videos developed especially for *World History: Patterns of Interaction* portray the passions, conflicts, controversies, and triumphs of a developing world. By helping your students make connections across time and place, the videos make the patterns of history comprehensible.

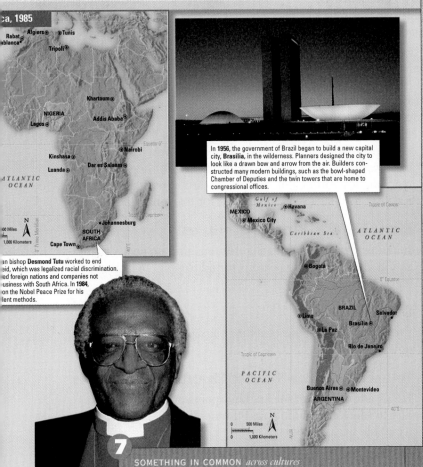

In 1956, the government of Brazil began to build a new capital city, **Brasília**, in the wilderness. Planners designed the city to look like a drawn bow and arrow from the air. Builders constructed many modern buildings, such as the bowl-shaped Chamber of Deputies and the twin towers that are home to congressional offices.

...an bishop **Desmond Tutu** worked to end ...eid, which was legalized racial discrimination. ...ed foreign nations and companies not ...usiness with South Africa. In **1984**, ...on the Nobel Peace Prize for his ...lent methods.

6 Patterns of Change

Important sections called Patterns of Change provide case studies of large historical trends that caused great changes in people's ways of thinking and living. Focusing on one example of a large trend helps students see the patterns reflected in the lives of individuals not unlike themselves.

7 Something in Common

Weddings, sports, burials, healing arts, and entertainment are among the common threads that connect people across time and place. Special features in every unit use text and pictures to show students these common patterns.

8 Connect to History and Connect to Today

Each special feature in the text helps students make connections to the past and to the present.

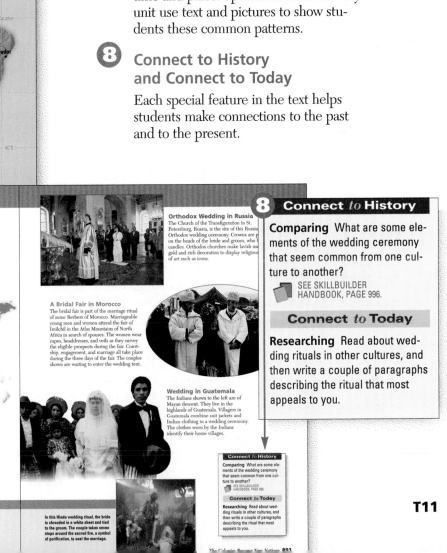

SOMETHING IN COMMON *across cultures*

Wedding Rituals

In cultures throughout the world, people get married. They do so for a variety of reasons: to share life with a loved one, to raise a family, to gain social position, to gain independence, to carry on values and customs. In India, an elaborate wedding ritual has evolved within the Hindu tradition. That ritual expresses Hindus' deepest beliefs about the relationship between men and women, the importance of the family, and the role of the spiritual in the significant moments of life. Other cultures have different rituals with which they surround the wedding ceremony.

Hindu Wedding in India
Hindus traditionally bestow jewelry on brides. This bride is from West Bengal. She is bedecked with gold, silver, and enamel jewelry inlaid with precious stones. Her sari is from Benares and is made of fine silk and gold brocade. The colors of red and gold symbolize life and good luck. The design on the bride's hands is painted in henna. This traditional pattern is believed to keep away evil spirits.

Orthodox Wedding in Russia
The Church of the Transfiguration in St. Petersburg, Russia, is the site of this Russian Orthodox wedding ceremony. Crowns are ... on the heads of the bride and groom, who ... candles. Orthodox churches make lavish use ... gold and rich decoration to display religious ... of art such as icons.

A Bridal Fair in Morocco
The bridal fair is part of the marriage ritual of some Berbers of Morocco. Marriageable young men and women attend the fair of Imilchil in the Atlas Mountains of North Africa in search of spouses. The women wear capes, headdresses, and veils as they survey the eligible prospects during the fair. Courtship, engagement, and marriage all take place during the three days of the fair. The couples shown are waiting to enter the wedding tent.

Wedding in Guatemala
The Indians shown to the left are of Mayan descent. They live in the highlands of Guatemala. Villagers in Guatemala combine suit jackets and Indian clothing in a wedding ceremony. The clothes worn by the Indians identify their home villages.

A gold necklace called a thali is placed around the bride's neck. This necklace contains a medallion with the three symbols of the Hindu trinity—a conch shell, a trident, and a ring.

In this Hindu wedding ritual, the bride is shrouded in a white sheet and tied to the groom. The couple takes seven steps around the sacred fire, a symbol of purification, to seal the marriage.

a **closer look** HINDU RITUALS

8 Connect *to* History

Comparing What are some elements of the wedding ceremony that seem common from one culture to another?

SEE SKILLBUILDER HANDBOOK, PAGE 996.

Connect *to* Today

Researching Read about wedding rituals in other cultures, and then write a couple of paragraphs describing the ritual that most appeals to you.

Connect *to* History

Comparing What are some elements of the wedding ceremony that seem common from one culture to another?
SEE SKILLBUILDER HANDBOOK, PAGE 996.

Connect *to* Today

Researching Read about wedding rituals in other cultures, and then write a couple of paragraphs describing the ritual that most appeals to you.

The Colonies Become New Nations 891

Teacher's Resource Materials

From block scheduling to teaching students acquiring English, teachers are structuring their history lessons to make them work in today's classrooms. *World History: Patterns of Interaction* provides a full range of options to help you teach our shared heritage in ways that meet the needs of your students.

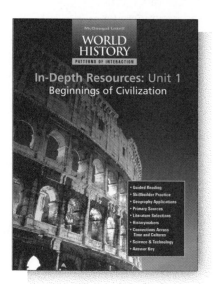

In-Depth Unit Resources

One book for each unit, organized by chapter, includes the following complete set of options for reinforcement, practice, enrichment, and extension:

- **Guided Reading** worksheets develop essential reading skills.

- **Skillbuilder Practice** worksheets supplement the Skillbuilder Handbook in the pupil edition.

- **Geography Application** worksheets provide practice in geography skills.

- **Primary Source** materials feature political cartoons, historical documents, diary entries, letters, and much more.

- **Literature Selection** pages let your students experience history through relevant works of literature.

- **History Maker** pages provide additional short biographies to augment those in each chapter.

- **Connections Across Time and Cultures** provide links between different eras by comparing similar events and developments in different times and places.

- **Science & Technology** worksheets develop, extend, and build upon the ten Science & Technology features in the Pupil's Edition.

Lesson Plans

Provides a two-page lesson plan per section of the Pupil's Edition. Each lesson plan incorporates print and electronic ancillaries, and Internet references. Each plan provides customizing options for teaching less-proficient readers, for students acquiring English, for block scheduling, and for teaching thematically.

Planning for Block Schedules

Includes a pacing guide, chapter teaching models, organization charts, and suggestions for addressing multiple learning styles.

Outline Maps

Provides blackline masters for geography skills development.

Telescoping the Times: Chapter Summaries

Helps address different reading speeds, time constraints due to block scheduling, and the need to reteach. Available in Spanish.

Access for Students Acquiring English: Spanish Translations

Provides strategies for teaching ESL students and Spanish translations of Chapter Summaries and of Guided Reading, Skillbuilder Practice, and Geography Application worksheets.

Writing for Social Studies

Offers support for writing research papers, historical narratives, essays, interviews, oral histories, book reviews, and short reports.

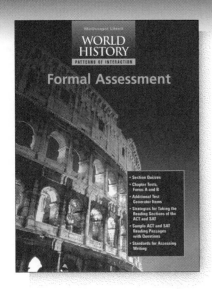

Formal Assessment

Includes the following:

- Section Quizzes
- Chapter Tests, Forms A and B
- Additional Test Questions
- ACT/SAT Test Practice
- Standards for Evaluating Writing

Alternative Assessment

Provides explanations and forms for a variety of assessment options, including cooperative learning, group discussion, role-playing, oral presentation, peer assessment, self-assessment, and portfolio assessment.

Test Generator

Includes all questions in the Section Quizzes and Chapter Tests, forms A and B—plus ten new test items for each chapter, leveled for basic and advanced students.

History from Visuals: Transparencies

Enliven lessons with three volumes of transparencies focusing on Critical Thinking, Geography, and World Art and Cultures.

Warm-Up Transparencies

Five-minute warm-up activities help introduce each section of a chapter.

Video Series and Technology

World History: Patterns of Interaction enables you to expand students' understanding by offering a wide array of technology, including an integrated video series.

Patterns of Interaction Video Series

The eight-video *Patterns of Interaction* series relates to the *Global Impact* features in the text. These videos help students see how cultural interactions have shaped our world and how patterns in history continue to the present day. Each video is 10-12 minutes in length. The *Patterns of Interaction* Resource Book provides you with all the pre-teaching and post-teaching activities you need. Following are the eight videos in the series:

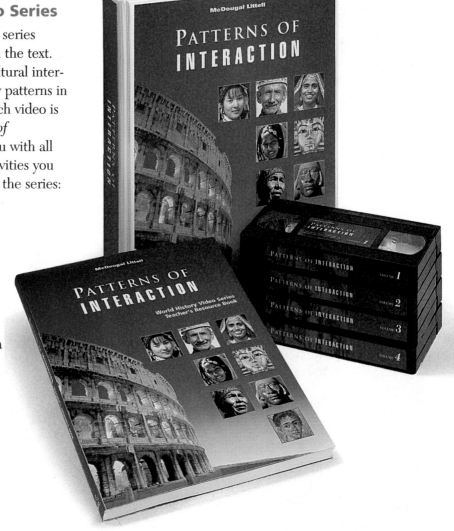

VIDEOS

Volume 1

- **Building Empires:**
  The Rise of the Persians and the Inca

- **Trade Connects the World:**
  Silk Roads and the Pacific Rim

Volume 2

- **The Spread of Epidemic Disease:**
  Bubonic Plague and Smallpox

- **The Geography of Food:**
  The Impact of Potatoes and Sugar

Volume 3

- **Struggling Toward Democracy:** Revolutions in Latin America and South Africa

- **Technology Transforms an Age:** The Industrial and Electronic Revolutions

Volume 4

- **Arming for War:** Modern and Medieval Weapons

- **Cultural Crossroads:** The United States and the World

McDougal Littell World History Curriculum Center

Visit **www.mlworldhistory.com** and click on the World History Curriculum Center for a wide range of information and activities you can put to immediate use. Handy point-and-click icons show the way to a world of possibilities:

- **World History Activities** integrate the Internet with sections of the textbook.
- **Professional Development Links** provide instant access to supplemental teaching and professional development resources.
- **Discussion Groups** encourage teacher-to-teacher exchanges on topics surrounding the teaching of world history.
- **The Diverse Classroom** focuses discussions on management techniques and teaching tools to maintain a successfully inclusive classroom.

CD-ROMS

World History: Electronic Library of Primary Sources on CD-ROM
These primary source selections are correlated with every lesson in the text and include background information and reading comprehension questions.

Battles of the World on CD-ROM
Includes reenactments of main battles, a 4,000-year time line, a comprehensive war database, and analysis of military strategy.

Religions of the World on CD-ROM
Explore the beliefs and practices of the world's religions with over 1,000 photographs, maps, and illustrations.

AUDIOCASSETTES

Chapter Summaries on Audiocassette
Reinforce learning with recorded reading of each chapter summary. Available in English and Spanish.

COMPUTER DISKS

Test Generator
Includes all questions in the formal assessment book, indexed by difficulty level. Available for Macintosh® and Windows®.

VIDEODISC

The Western Civilization Videodisc
Enhance any lesson with still images, maps, and historical film footage.

Chapter Planning Guide

A convenient two-page planning guide can be found at the beginning of every chapter in the teacher's edition of *World History: Patterns of Interaction*. The guide offers invaluable information and options to help you devise the most effective course of instruction.

1 Key Ideas

A chronological, section-by-section summary listing of the key ideas in each chapter. Each column of key ideas connects to the unifying theme for the whole chapter.

2 Copy Masters

A complete listing of reproducible materials for each section reveals the depth of resource material that is available.

3 Assessment

This column locates pages on which quizzes and tests are available for the section or chapter. Alternative assessment guidelines are also noted.

PLANNING GUIDE

CHAPTER 23

The French Revolution and Napoleon

	1 Key Ideas	**2 COPY MASTERS**	**3 ASSESSMENT**
SECTION 1 Revolution Threatens the French King pp. 573–576	Members of the Third Estate demand a more representative government. The fall of the Bastille and the king's removal from Versailles signal the beginning of the French Revolution.	*In-Depth Resources: Unit 5* • **Guided Reading,** p. 37 • **Literature:** from *A Tale of Two Cities,* p. 49 • **History Makers:** Marie Antoinette, p. 52	PE *Section 1 Assessment,* p. 576 *Formal Assessment* • Section Quiz, p. 264 *Alternative Assessment Book* • Standards for Evaluating a Product or Performance
SECTION 2 Revolution Brings Reform and Terror pp. 577–583	The Legislative Assembly faces war and internal divisions. The king is executed, and Robespierre inaugurates the Reign of Terror. A third constitution puts power in the hands of the upper middle class.	*In-Depth Resources: Unit 5* • **Guided Reading,** p. 38 • **Geography Application,** p. 43 • **Primary Sources,** pp. 45, 46, 47 • **History Makers:** Robespierre, p. 53 • **Across Time and Place,** p. 54 • **Science and Technology**	PE *Section 2 Assessment,* p. 583 *Formal Assessment* • Section Quiz, p. 265 *Alternative Assessment Book* • Standards for Evaluating a Cooperative Activity
SECTION 3 Napoleon Forges an Empire pp. 584–588	A brilliant general, Napoleon Bonaparte, becomes emperor of France and assumes broad powers. Through military victories, he establishes mastery over most of Europe.	*In-Depth Resources: Unit 5* • **Guided Reading,** p. 39 • **Primary Source:** Napoleon's Proclamation at Austerlitz, p. 48	PE *Section 3 Assessment,* p. 588 *Formal Assessment* • Section Quiz, p. 266 *Alternative Assessment Book* • Standards for Evaluating a Cooperative Activity
SECTION 4 Napoleon's Empire Collapses pp. 589–592	Napoleon makes political and military mistakes as he tries to increase his power. He is defeated, returns, is defeated again, and finishes his life in exile.	*In-Depth Resources: Unit 5* • **Guided Reading,** p. 40 • **Skillbuilder Practice:** Interpreting Maps, p. 42	PE *Section 4 Assessment,* p. 592 *Formal Assessment* • Section Quiz, p. 267 *Alternative Assessment Book* • Standards for Evaluating a Product or Performance
SECTION 5 The Congress of Vienna Convenes pp. 593–597	Following the plan of Metternich, the Congress of Vienna reestablishes stability in Europe after the defeat of Napoleon.	*In-Depth Resources: Unit 5* • **Guided Reading,** p. 41	PE *Section 5 Assessment,* p. 596 *Formal Assessment* • Section Quiz, p. 268 *Alternative Assessment Book* • Standards for Evaluating a Cooperative Activity
CHAPTER RESOURCES 569A	**Chapter Overview** Revolution leads to the overthrow and execution of the French king. After a period of instability, Napoleon takes control of France and of most of Europe. Napoleon's thirst for power leads to his downfall, and European leaders craft a lasting peace.	*Telescoping the Times* • Chapter Summary, pp. 89–91 *Planning for Block Schedules*	PE *Chapter Assessment,* pp. 598–599 *Chapter Activities,* p. 599 *Formal Assessment* • Chapter Test, forms A and B, pp. 269–274 *Test Generator* *Alternative Assessment Book*

1789–1815

④ TECHNOLOGY

- Warm-Up Transparency 23
- Geography Transparencies
  - G23 Early Sites of the French Revolution, 1789
- World Art and Cultures Transparencies
  - AT50 Portrait of Marie Antoinette
- Electronic Library of Primary Sources
  - from Memoirs of Élisabeth Vigée-Lebrun
- INTERNET RESOURCES
  www.mlworldhistory.com

- Warm-Up Transparency 23
- Electronic Library of Primary Sources
  - from "Execution by Guillotine"
- INTERNET RESOURCES
  www.mlworldhistory.com

- Warm-Up Transparency 23
- World Art and Cultures Transparencies
  - AT51 Napoleon Crossing the St. Bernard Pass
- Electronic Library of Primary Sources
  - from The Letters of Napoleon I
- Battles of the World
  - The Battle of Austerlitz
- INTERNET RESOURCES
  www.mlworldhistory.com

- Warm-Up Transparency 23
- Electronic Library of Primary Sources
  - "The Battle of Waterloo: The Finale"
- INTERNET RESOURCES
  www.mlworldhistory.com

- Warm-Up Transparency 23
- Critical Thinking Transparencies
  - CT23 The French Revolution
- Electronic Library of Primary Sources
  - from Memoirs of Metternich
  - from "Frenchmen, Is This What You Want?"
- INTERNET RESOURCES
  www.mlworldhistory.com

- Chapter Summaries on Audiocassette in English and Spanish
- INTERNET RESOURCES
  www.mlworldhistory.com

⑤ Block Scheduling (90 MINUTES)

Day 1
Section 1, pp. 573–576

Section 2, pp. 577–583

COOPERATIVE ACTIVITY
Debating an Issue,
p. 578 (Teacher's Edition)

Section Assessments,
pp. 576, 583

Day 2
Section 3, pp. 584–588

COOPERATIVE ACTIVITY
Researching Napoleon
and Nelson, p. 587
(Teacher's Edition)

Section 4, pp. 589–592

Section Assessments,
pp. 588, 592

Day 3
Section 5, pp. 593–597

COOPERATIVE ACTIVITY
Investigating World
Peace Organizations,
p. 595 (Teacher's Edition)

Section Assessment, p. 596

Chapter Assessment,
pp. 598–599

Yearly Pacing Chapter 23 Total: 3 days Yearly Total: 85 days

Planning for Block Schedules

⑥ Customizing for Special Needs

Students Acquiring English

Access for Students Acquiring English

- **Guided Reading** for Sections 1–5 (Spanish), pp. 229–233
- **Chapter Summary** (Spanish), pp. 226–228
- **Skillbuilder Practice** Interpreting Maps (Spanish), p. 234
- **Geography Application** The French Revolution Under Siege (Spanish), p. 235

Chapter Summaries on Audiocassette in English and Spanish

INTERNET RESOURCES
www.mlworldhistory.com
The Diverse Classroom.

Less Proficient Readers

In-Depth Resources: Unit 5

- **Guided Reading** for Sections 1–5, pp. 37–41
- **Skillbuilder Practice** Interpreting Maps, p. 42
- **Geography Application** The French Revolution Under Siege, p. 43

Telescoping the Times
- Chapter Summary, pp. 89–91

Chapter Summaries on Audiocassette

Gifted and Talented Students

In-Depth Resources: Unit 5

Primary Sources:
- from A Declaration of the Rights of Man and of the Citizen, 1789, p. 45
- "La Marseillaise," p. 45
- from The Execution of Louis XVI, p. 47
- Napoleon's Proclamation at Austerlitz, 1805, p. 48

History Makers
- Marie Antoinette, p. 52
- Maximilien Robespierre, p. 53

⑦ Connections to Literature READINGS FOR STUDENTS

In-Depth Resources: Unit 5
Literature: from A Tale of Two Cities by Charles Dickens, p. 48

Enrichment Reading

- Sherwood, Frances
  Vindication
  New York: Penguin, 1994

  Mary Wollstonecraft, author of A Vindication of the Rights of Woman, is portrayed vividly in this fictionalized treatment of her life and times.

McDougal Littell Literature Connections
- Dickens, Charles
  A Tale of Two Cities
  (with related readings)

  A classic tale of the French Revolution, with themes of love and self-sacrifice, heroes and quests.

PE = Pupil's Edition	= Overhead Transparency	= Software	= Video
= Copy Master	= CD-ROM	= Audiocassette	= Internet

569B

---

④ Technology

Technology listed for each section ranges from a wealth of transparency choices to videos to CD-ROMs to the Internet.

⑤ Block Scheduling

This pacing guide for block scheduling also lists optional cooperative activities from the teacher's edition.

⑥ Customizing for Special Needs

Here are suggested resources for teaching students acquiring English, less proficient readers, and gifted and talented students. From worksheets and chapter summaries in Spanish to lists of primary-source material, these suggestions offer practical help for basic classroom needs.

⑦ Connections to Literature

Literature Connections from McDougal Littell are stand-alone books with related readings that offer in-depth literary supplements. A SourceBook provides student support materials for each selection. Other reading suggestions refer to ancillary materials or to outside sources.

Teacher's Edition Lesson Support

The *World History: Patterns of Interaction* teacher's edition supports instruction from practical helps for dealing with maps and other graphics to abundant suggestions for classroom activities.

Side columns focus on core instruction with optional suggestions and teaching activities featured at the bottom of the pages.

1 History from Visuals

These notes provide a variety of learning strategies and extension activities to help students make the most of maps, charts, graphs, political cartoons, and key historical photographs.

2 Key Ideas

A listing of key ideas identifies the main points students need to understand in order to meet specific section objectives.

3 More About . . .

These terrific nuggets of information occur often to supplement the text.

4 Teaching Options

Options at the bottom of pages offer a range of choices from connections to many subject areas to cooperative activities to strategies for multiple learning styles.

---

1 History from Visuals

The Three Estates

Interpreting the Cartoon Ask students why the clergyman and the nobleman are standing on a stone rather than standing directly on the fallen man. *Possible Response: The stone represents the taxes and obligations that kept the members of the Third Estate subservient to the nobility and the clergy.*

Extension Activity Have students make lists of adjectives describing the feelings and attitudes of the people depicted in the cartoon.

SKILLBUILDER Answers
1. The Third Estate was oppressed because it paid 50% of its income in taxes to support the most privileged 2% of the French population.
2. They had no reason to desire change, since they already had privileges and wealth.

IN-DEPTH RESOURCES: UNIT 5
Literature: from *A Tale of Two Cities*, p. 49

OBJECTIVE 2 INSTRUCT

2 The Forces of Change

Key Ideas
- New ideas about the power of the people take hold.
- Poor harvests, heavy taxes, and government debt cause instability in France.
- Louis XVI finally calls a meeting of the Estates-General to deal with the crisis.

---

3 MORE ABOUT . . .
Louis XVI

Louis XVI was a lethargic, somewhat fat, rather dull man who was more interested in hunting and tinkering with locks than in governing France. On the day the Bastille fell in Paris, the king wrote only Rien ("Nothing") in his diary—a reference to his lack of success in the hunt.

The Three Estates

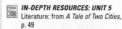

■ First Estate
- made up of clergy of Roman Catholic Church
- scorned Enlightenment ideas

■ Second Estate
- made up of rich nobles
- held highest offices in government
- disagreed about Enlightenment ideas

■ Third Estate
- included bourgeoisie, urban lower class, and peasant farmers
- had no power to influence government
- embraced Enlightenment ideas

Population of France, 1787

98% (Third Estate)
less than 1% (First Estate)
2% (Second Estate)

Percent of Income Paid in Taxes

2% (First Estate)
0% (Second Estate)
50% (Third Estate)

0% 20% 40% 60% 80% 100%

SKILLBUILDER: Interpreting Charts and Political Cartoons
The Third Estate intensely resented the wealthy First and Second Estates.
1. *How do the chart and the graphs help explain the political cartoon?*
2. *Why might the First and Second Estates be opposed to change?*

The Forces of Change

In addition to the growing resentment of the lower classes, other factors were contributing to the revolutionary mood in France.

Enlightenment Ideas New views about power and authority in government were spreading among the Third Estate. The people began questioning long-standing notions about the structure of society and using words like *equality, liberty,* and *democracy.* The success of the American Revolution inspired them, and they discussed the radical ideas of Rousseau and Voltaire. Many shared the beliefs of the Comte d'Antraigues, a friend of Rousseau's:

Background
The ideas of Rousseau and Voltaire are also reflected in the United States Constitution.

A VOICE FROM THE PAST
The Third Estate is the People and the People is the foundation of the State; it is in fact the State itself; the other orders are merely political categories while by the *immutable laws of nature* the People is everything. Everything should be subordinated to it. . . . It is in the People that all national power resides and for the People that all states exist.
COMTE D'ANTRAIGUES, quoted in *Citizens: A Chronicle of the French Revolution*

Economic Woes France's once prosperous economy was failing. The population was expanding rapidly, as were trade and production. However, the heavy burden of taxes made it impossible to conduct business profitably within France. The cost of living rose for everyone. In addition, bad weather in the 1780s caused widespread crop failures, resulting in a severe shortage of grain. The price of bread doubled in 1789, and many people faced starvation.

During this period, France's government sank deeply into debt. Extravagant spending by the king and queen was part of the problem. **Louis XVI**, who became king in 1774, inherited part of the debt from his predecessors. He also borrowed heavily in order to help the American revolutionaries in their war against Great Britain—France's chief rival—thereby nearly doubling the government's debt. When bankers, in 1786, refused to lend the government any more money, Louis faced serious problems.

A Weak Leader Strong leadership might have prevented the coming crisis, but Louis XVI was indecisive and allowed matters to drift. He paid little attention to his government advisers, preferring to spend his time hunting or tinkering with locks rather than attending to the details of governing.

574 Chapter 23

---

4 TEACHING OPTIONS

EXPLORING PRIMARY SOURCES		CONNECTIONS ACROSS THE CURRICULUM	
A Voice from the Past The Comte d'Antraigues, whose statement about the Third Estate became one of the most popular axioms of the Revolution, was from an old aristocratic family. Believing that the feudal noble families should have more power, he initially supported change and even	went as far as agreeing that the nobles should no longer be exempt from taxes. But when the people wanted to reduce all aristocrats to ordinary citizens, he became a counter revolutionary and worked diligently against further changes. Ask students to research the lives of other French aristocrats, such as the Marquis de Lafayette.	**Economics** Taxes and debt are problems faced by most governments. In France at this time, most of the taxes were paid by the poorest people while wealthy nobles paid no taxes. Ask students to propose economic solutions to this situation. Then ask, What might	be the political consequences of your solutions? What happens today when the U.S. government wants to raise taxes to pay off debts or to implement new programs?

574 Chapter 23

Louis had married his wife, **Marie Antoinette,** when he was 15 and she was 14. Because Marie was a member of the royal family of Austria, France's long-time enemy, she became unpopular as soon as she set foot in France. As queen, Marie spent so much money on gowns, jewels, and gifts that she became known as Madame Deficit.

Rather than cutting expenses and increasing taxes, Louis put off dealing with the emergency until France faced bankruptcy. Then, when he tried to tax aristocrats, the Second Estate forced him to call a meeting of the **Estates-General**—an assembly of representatives from all three estates—to get approval for the tax reform. He had the meeting—the first in 175 years—on May 5, 1789, at Versailles.

Revolution Dawns

The clergy and the nobles had dominated the Estates-General throughout the Middle Ages and expected to do so in the 1789 meeting. Under the assembly's medieval rules, each estate's delegates met in a separate hall to vote, and each estate had one vote. The two privileged estates could always outvote the Third Estate.

The National Assembly The Third Estate delegates, mostly members of the bourgeoisie whose views had been shaped by the Enlightenment, were eager to make changes in the government. They insisted that all three estates meet together and that each delegate have a vote. This would give the advantage to the Third Estate, which had as many delegates as the other two estates combined.

Siding with the nobles, the king ordered the Estates-General to follow the medieval rules. The delegates of the Third Estate, however, became more and more determined to wield power. A leading spokesperson for their viewpoint was a clergyman sympathetic to their cause, the Abbé Sieyès (AB-AY syay-YEHS), who argued, "What is the Third Estate? Everything. What has it been up to now in the political order? Nothing. What does it demand? To become something herein." In a dramatic speech, he suggested that the Third Estate delegates name themselves the **National Assembly** and pass laws and reforms in the name of the French people.

**Marie Antoinette
1755–1793**

Marie Antoinette was a pretty, lighthearted, charming woman. However, she was unpopular with the French because of her spending and her involvement in controversial court affairs. She referred to Louis as "the poor man" and sometimes set the clock forward an hour to be rid of his presence.

Marie refused to wear the tight-fitting clothing styles of the day and introduced a loose cotton dress for women. The elderly, who viewed the dress as an undergarment, thought that Marie's clothing was scandalous. The French silk industry was equally angry.

In constant need of entertainment, Marie often spent her time playing cards. One year she lost the equivalent of $1.5 million by gambling in card games.

---

⑤ HISTORYMAKERS

Marie Antoinette

Marie Antoinette was only a teenager when she came to France. Although her behavior made her many enemies, she did have some redeeming qualities. Ask students to investigate Marie Antoinette's life and to list some of her actions that might be considered foolish, as well as some that might be considered admirable.

📰 *IN-DEPTH RESOURCES: UNIT 5*
History Makers: Marie Antoinette, p. 52

🏛 ***WORLD ART AND CULTURES TRANSPARENCIES***
Portrait of Marie Antoinette with Her Children

OBJECTIVE ③ INSTRUCT

Revolution Dawns

Key Ideas

• Third Estate delegates in the Estates-General demand more rights.

• In the first deliberate act of revolution, the Third Estate delegates vote to establish the National Assembly.

• Peasants overthrow the Bastille on July 14, 1789, and the Revolution begins in earnest.

🎞 *GEOGRAPHY TRANSPARENCIES*
GT23 Early Sites of the French Revolution, 1789

💿 ***ELECTRONIC LIBRARY OF PRIMARY SOURCES***
from *Memoirs of Élisabeth Vigée-Lebrun*

HISTORY THROUGH ART: Fine Art

The gap between rich and poor in 18th-century France is clear in these portraits. David, painter of the Revolution, depicted a common woman (*left*) whose appearance displays none of the luxury of the French court (*right*).

Connect *to* History

Comparing What details of the women's expressions and clothing most clearly show the contrasts in lives?

📖 SEE SKILLBUILDER HANDBOOK, PAGE 996.

Connect *to* Today

Contrasting How would you visually convey the gap between rich and poor in your country?

A Woman of the Revolution [La maraîchère] (1795), Jacques Louis David

Marie Antoinette, Jacques Gautier d'Agoty

The French Revolution and Napoleon **575**

---

⑤ History Makers

Short features in the Pupil's Edition text are supplemented with additional information and suggested activities.

⑥ References to Resource Materials

Specific references identify where to find additional support for teaching each section.

	Connect *to* History			⑦	Connect *to* Today	

Comparing

Suggest that students make a chart like the one here to compare the two portraits.

	Woman of the Revolution	Marie Antoinette
Clothing		
Expression		
Posture		

Contrasting You may wish to suggest the following strategies for showing the gap between rich and poor today:

• Look for magazine images of homeless people, victims of floods or tornadoes, and richly dressed people in elegant homes.

• Check the Internet for census statistics showing percentages of people at various income levels. Check also for reports on wealth and poverty.

⑦ Connect to History and Connect to Today

These offer answers and strategies for responding to the questions and activities on the pupil's edition page.

Teacher's Edition Notes may also include:

• Cooperative Activities
• Customizing for Special Needs
• Multiple Learning Styles
• Exploring Primary Sources
• Connections Across the Curriculum
• Special Application Activities
• Skillbuilder Mini-Lessons
• Connections Across Time and Place
• Assessment Suggestions
• Critical Thinking Activities

Reading History

The best learners are active and engaged readers. Successful readers connect what they are reading with what they already know. These readers:
- build associations among ideas
- create visual images of what they are reading
- continually revise their interpretations as they gather more information.

Supporting Readers

World History: Patterns of Interaction uses many strategies to help students become active and engaged readers.

Visual Summary

The Struggle for Independence

The time line shows the dates on which various countries in Asia and Africa achieved their independence after World War II. It also shows (in parentheses) the countries from which they achieved independence.

1946
Philippines (United States)
1947
India, Pakistan (Great Britain)
1948
Israel (Great Britain)
1949
Indonesia (The Netherlands)

1957
Federation of Malaya, Ghana (Great Britain)

1960
Zaire (Belgium)
1962
Algeria (France)
1963
Kenya (Great Britain)
1965
Singapore (Great Britain, Malaya)

1971
Bangladesh (Pakistan)

1975
Angola (Portugal)

Various Learning Styles We know that readers have different styles of understanding—some rely heavily on verbal input and discussion, some need visual supports, and some need to make notes and drawings or create graphic organizers as they learn. *World History: Patterns of Interaction* addresses various learning styles and stimulates learning by posing problems, comparing and contrasting ideas, and presenting different points of view on issues.

Visual Information Many readers rely on visual information when reading unfamiliar material. Pictures make abstractions of time and space more real; photos and artifacts create a context for new ideas; maps help readers associate and compare ideas. In addition, charts of ideas and events in each chapter summarize and clarify information. A visual summary at the end of each chapter provides another way for remembering important ideas and events.

Inner-Column Notes Inner-column notes in *World History: Patterns of Interaction* help students read the text. Vocabulary notes explain and define words and phrases. Background notes provide additional information about a person, idea, or event. Think Through History questions help students to read critically.

Personal Connections Personal stories and human connections can help to bring a subject such as history alive. *World History: Patterns of Interaction* uses personal voices throughout to support student learning.

A VOICE FROM THE PAST
This great Nation will endure as it has endured, will revive and will prosper. . . . let me assert my firm belief that the only thing we have to fear is fear itself—nameless, unreasoning, unjustified terror which paralyzes needed efforts to convert retreat into advance.
FRANKLIN ROOSEVELT, *First Inaugural Address*

Students Acquiring English Second-language learners need to have information and ideas presented to them in multiple ways. Being able to "see" history helps make it real for them. *World History: Patterns of Interaction* uses illustrations and visuals to present information to students in a variety of ways.

Evolving Forms of Reading

Students today need to be able to read in new ways.

Nonlinear Materials Today's students must:
- gather ideas from multiple sources—resource books, magazines, computerized databases, CD-ROMS, the Internet
- know how to evaluate these sources and make decisions about their content
- find their way through nonlinear materials, such as by deciding which area of a computer screen contains the information they want
- make decisions about what level of knowledge and elaboration they need.

Graphic Layouts Today's readers must deal with informational materials that come in various formats:
- multiple columns of text with many pictures, graphs, and maps
- single-column texts with large marginal areas used for illustrations, highlighted information, and thought-provoking ideas
- combination of layouts

The Teacher's Role

Are your students prepared with strategies for reading and learning in the 21st century? Are they able to shift from one form of text presentation to another easily? Do they know how to construct meaning from multiple sources?

Strategies for Teachers You can help your students become active, engaged, and confident readers. Here are some strategies you might try:

- Ask students how they read.
- Do a "think aloud" as students begin to read a text. Ask them to tell you where they look on the page; when they look at the charts, maps, and pictures; and when they read the headings and titles.

- Introduce the text layout and features, and discuss students' options for reading.
- Show students that all material on a page does not have to be read in order.
- Have students experiment with reading the graphics first before reading the text on a page.
- Demonstrate how headings and subheadings can help readers find specific information.
- Use graphic organizers and reading guides to help students gain confidence.

Reading and discussing different types of written material and material expressing different points of view will help students learn to think critically about what they read.

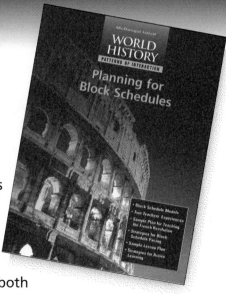

Block Schedules

Today block schedules provide new opportunities and challenges for teachers. *World History: Patterns of Interaction* offers help for teaching in the block throughout both the pupil's edition and the teacher's edition. In addition, *Planning for Block Schedules,* found in the teacher's resource materials, includes a wealth of information and strategies.

Block Scheduling Strategies

The longer class period in a block schedule provides an on-going opportunity for challenging classroom activities. *World History: Patterns of Interaction* offers a variety of cooperative activities and strategies in both the pupil's edition and in the teacher's edition.

Pupil's Edition

- Each chapter begins with an **Interact with History** feature, which can be used as a collaborative activity.

- Each **Section Assessment** provides opportunities for collaborative learning, including a note-taking activity and frequent theme activities.

- **Chapter Assessments** include a variety of chapter activities including **Connect to Today**, a cooperative activity.

- **Unit Portfolio Projects** found on the unit time lines pages provide a variety of options for collaborative activities.

Teacher's Edition

- The **Planning Guide** includes a special section on block scheduling including suggestions for pacing and cooperative activities.

- **Technology Resources** listed in the Planning Guide lists many resources that are useful for cooperative activities.

- **Cooperative Activities** described on the teacher's edition pages offer abundant suggestions for a variety of activities. In addition, Skillbuilder Mini-Lessons, and many other activities presented on the teacher's edition pages help teachers find ideas to make their instruction active and engaging.

Pupil's Edition

> **2. CONNECT TO TODAY: Cooperative Learning**
>
> **THEME POWER AND AUTHORITY** The Muslim empires you have studied based their rule on the Islamic religion. Islam remains an important social and political force in modern Turkey, Iran, India, and Pakistan.
>
> Work with a team to find out the status of Muslims in one of these countries today. Then collaborate with the other teams to create a summary chart of these modern Muslim countries.
>
> Using the Internet or other reference sources, determine the status of Muslims in your team's country.
>
> - What role do Muslims play in the government?
> - Do the country's leaders promote religious tolerance? Explain.
> - What is the overall economic status of Muslims?

Teachers' Edition

TEACHING OPTION	BLOCK SCHEDULING	COOPERATIVE ACTIVITY: Researching Napoleon and Nelson	CLASS TIME 30 MINUTES

Task: Student groups will research the careers of Napoleon Bonaparte and Horatio Nelson and present to the class reports comparing the two men.

Purpose: To learn more about these two leaders.

Activity: Divide the class into groups of four. In each group, pairs of students should research the lives of the two men, paying special attention to the way each man interacted with his troops and to the

specific military strategies that made each so successful. In reports to the class, students should also compare the two men, focusing on their similarities and differences.

Building a Portfolio If the report is among their best work, students should add it to their portfolio.

ALTERNATIVE ASSESSMENT BOOK
Standards for Evaluating a Cooperative Activity

Standards for Evaluation
Reports should . . .

- clearly convey the characteristics of Nelson and Napoleon
- compare the qualities of the two men
- show evidence of thorough research

Assessment Resources

World History: Patterns of Interaction provides you with material that allows you to customize assessment to best fit the activities and structure of your particular classroom. With options for informal, formal, and alternative assessment, these resources furnish you with all the support you need.

Formal Assessment

- Asks, "What do you know?"
- Pencil-and-paper tests in standardized formats such as true-false and multiple choice
- Used to measure students' achievement against other students; report students' achievement; make instructional and grouping decisions

Informal Assessment

- Ongoing assessment
- Primarily based on recurring elements such as Think Through History inner-column questions and section assessments
- Done as students work their way through a chapter section by section

Types of Assessment

Alternative Assessment

- Asks, "What can you do?" and "How do you do it?"
- Implemented under 3 main headings:
   1. Process Assessment—observing students as they work
   2. Product and Performance Assessment—focusing on the end result of students' work
   3. Portfolio Assessment—reviewing and evaluating students' work together

Assessment Options for *World History: Patterns of Interaction*

Assessment Type	Pupil's Edition	Teacher's Edition	Ancillaries
1. Informal	• **Think Through History** • **Skillbuilder questions** • **Geography Skillbuilder** • **Section Assessment** • **Chapter Assessment**		• *In-Depth Resources* **Guided Reading, Skillbuilder Practice, and Geography Application**
2. Formal			• *Formal Assessment* **Section Quizzes, Chapter Tests (Forms A and B), and ACT/SAT Practice** • **Test Generator (software)**
3. Alternative	• **Chapter Activities** • **Skillbuilder Handbook exercises** • **Living History Portfolio Projects** • **Theme Activities**	• **Cooperative Activities** • **Skillbuilder Mini-Lessons** • **Suggested activities throughout the Teacher's Edition**	• *In-Depth Resources* **Primary Sources, Literature Selections** • **Alternative Assessment Book**

Students' Learning Styles

It is probably no surprise to you that every student is unique. Each has not only an individual personality, interests, and abilities, but also a special way of learning. According to Harvard psychologist Howard Gardner, there are seven types of intelligences—linguistic, logical-mathematical, spatial or visual, kinesthetic, interpersonal, intrapersonal, and musical. Each student uses a unique combination of these intelligences, so one teaching method will not promote optimal learning for all students all the time. The following chart can help you recognize your individual students' learning styles so you can teach them most effectively.

Student Characteristics	Learning Style	Classroom Activities
Has good verbal and auditory skills, thinks in words, likes to read and write	Linguistic	Creative and expository writing, debates, speeches, oral reports, dramatic readings, storytelling
Thinks conceptually, abstractly, and logically	Logical-mathematical	Graphic organizers, charts, graphs, time lines, models, prediction exercises
Thinks in visual images, enjoys drawing, designing, and inventing	Spatial or visual	Drawings, maps, flow charts, murals, dioramas, collages, photography
Has good fine-motor coordination and body sense, communicates through body language	Kinesthetic	Demonstrations, role-playing, impersonations
Understands other people, communicates and socializes well	Interpersonal	Discussions, cooperative and collaborative projects, interviews, peer response
Prefers working alone, is intuitive, independent, and self-motivated	Intrapersonal	Response and dialogue journals, learning logs, written reports
Is sensitive to sound and rhythm, enjoys singing, playing, and listening and moving to music	Musical	Interpretive dances, rap songs, musical plays, rhyming games

The teacher's edition of *World History: Patterns of Interaction* provides numerous teaching options that address these learning styles. Support materials for the program, including videos, transparencies, copy masters, and CD-ROMs, offer numerous opportunities to reach the special abilities of all your students.

Teaching Geography Through History

It is impossible to understand historical events without examining both where and when they occur. Geography is more than just the static setting for history, however. Just as the land shapes the people who inhabit it, their history continues to shape the land.

Each chapter in *World History: Patterns of Interaction* begins with a two-page map that locates students firmly in time and place. Other maps within chapters help students visualize places and events they read about. Many of these maps contain several layers of information that provide a better understanding of how and why events in history occurred.

Five Themes

In *World History: Patterns of Interaction*, the importance of the reciprocal relationship between history and geography is emphasized by a focus on five recurrent geographical themes:

- location
- place
- region
- movement
- human/environment interaction

Vegetation Regions of Africa

Widely scattered acacia trees dot the flat, grassy plains of the savanna. Giraffes especially like the acacia leaves, which most other animals cannot reach.

The dense trees and lack of edible vegetation in the humid rain forest make it an unwelcome environment for most people.

Rain forest
Savanna
Desert
Mediterranean

GEOGRAPHY SKILLBUILDER: Interpreting Maps
1. **Location** *About what percent of Africa is desert? savanna?*
2. **Region** *If you were to fold a map of Africa in half along the equator, what do you notice about the similar vegetation zones above and below the fold?*

194 Chapter 8

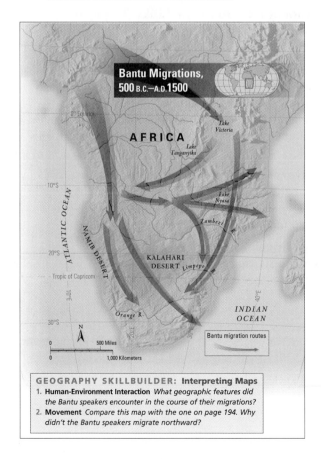

Bantu Migrations, 500 B.C.–A.D. 1500

Bantu migration routes

GEOGRAPHY SKILLBUILDER: Interpreting Maps
1. **Human-Environment Interaction** *What geographic features did the Bantu speakers encounter in the course of their migrations?*
2. **Movement** *Compare this map with the one on page 194. Why didn't the Bantu speakers migrate northward?*

Maps in the Text

There are hundreds of maps in the pupil's edition that work together with the text to further explain historical events and their meaning. Maps can help clarify what is in the text or provide additional information that supplements the text. For example, the map above places students in a particular area of the world, while the map to the left pinpoints a particular area within the broader map above.

Skillbuilder Questions

Skillbuilder questions based on the five themes of geography accompany each map in the book, giving students a chance to develop their sensitivity to the themes, their awareness of geography in general, and their ability to interpret geographical information. To help you access this information easily, the front of the teacher's edition lists every map in the book.

Internet Resources

McDougal Littell's World History Web site—**www.mlworldhistory.com**—offers you an opportunity to become part of a nationwide community of teachers and students using *World History: Patterns of Interaction*. With a user-friendly format, our world history curriculum center helps you meet the challenges of teaching in today's diverse classroom by providing access to a wide range of resources related to the chapters of the textbook.

World History Activities Engage your students in interactive activities and projects that allow them to explore world history topics in a thoroughly modern way.

General World History Links Our editors have gathered some of the best links on the Internet to help you extend lessons, expand your research, and boost your own creativity. These links are keyed to the table of contents for *World History: Patterns of Interaction*.

Professional Development Links This feature enables you to link to the homepages of professional social studies organizations around the globe.

Discussion Groups Exchange ideas, brainstorm, or network with your colleagues. Join the History Discussion Group to post or answer history- or program-related questions. Check out the Idea Exchange Discussion Group for more general teaching strategies and topics.

The Diverse Classroom Chat with educators, find links to a great variety of relevant Web sites, and read abstracts of articles from professional journals—all related to maintaining an inclusive classroom.

Monthly Special Feature Author profiles, web-site guests, and other special events are all part of this monthly feature.

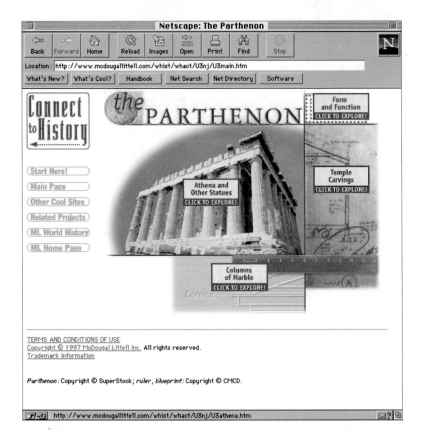

Pacing Guide

The following pacing guide shows how the chapters in *World History: Patterns of Interaction* can be adapted to fit your specific course needs. The Guide is based on 170 days of instruction during the school year. For **block schedules**, see *Planning for Block Schedules* in the teacher's resource materials.

	World Survey	Western Civilization	Non-Western Civilization	Pre-1900 History
UNIT 1 BEGINNINGS OF CIVILIZATION 4 MILLION BC–200 BC				
Chapter 1 The Peopling of the World Beginnings–3500 BC	(days)	(days)	(days)	(days)
1. Human Origins in Africa	1	1	1	2
2. Humans Try to Control Nature	1	1	1	2
3. Patterns of Change: Civilization	2	1	1	2
Chapter 2 Early River Valley Civilizations 3500 BC–450 BC				
1. City-States in Mesopotamia	1	1	1	2
2. Pyramids on the Nile	2	2	2	3
3. Planned Cities on the Indus	1	1	2	3
4. River Dynasties in China	1	1	2	3
Chapter 3 People and Ideas on the Move 3500 BC–259 BC				
1. Indo-European Migrations	1	1	.5	2
2. Roots of Hinduism and Buddhism	1	1	2	2
3. Seafaring Traders Extend Boundaries	1	1	.5	2
4. The Religion of the Hebrews	1	1	1	2
Chapter 4 First Age of Empires 1570 BC–200 BC				
1. The Empires of Egypt and Nubia Collide	1	1	2	2
2. Assyria Dominates the Fertile Crescent	1	1	1	2
3. Persia Unites Many Lands	1	1	1	2
4. An Empire Unifies China	1	1	2	2
Total Days for Unit 1	**17**	**16**	**20**	**33**
UNIT 2 NEW DIRECTIONS IN GOVERNMENT AND SOCIETY 2000 BC–AD 550				
Chapter 5 Classical Greece 2000 BC–300 BC				
1. Cultures of the Mountains and the Sea	1	1	1	2
2. Warring City-States	1	1	1	2
3. Democracy and Greece's Golden Age	1	2	1	2
4. Alexander—Empire-Builder	1	1	1	2
5. The Spread of Hellenistic Culture	1	2	1	2

For **block schedules**, see *Planning for Block Schedules* in the teacher's resource materials.

	World Survey	Western Civilization	Non-Western Civilization	Pre-1900 History
Chapter 6 Ancient Rome and Early Christianity 500 BC–AD 500	(days)	(days)	(days)	(days)
1. The Romans Create a Republic	1	2	1	2
2. The Roman Empire Brings Change	1	2	1	2
3. The Rise of Christianity	1	2	1	2
4. The Decline of the Roman Empire	1	2	1	2
5. Rome and the Roots of Western Civilization	1	2	1	2
Chapter 7 India and China Establish Empires 300 BC–AD 550				
1. First Empires of India	1	.5	1	1
2. Trade Spreads Indian Religion and Culture	1	.5	2	1
3. Han Emperors in China	1	1	2	2
Chapter 8 African Civilizations 1200 BC–AD 500				
1. Diverse Societies in Africa	2	1	2	2
2. The Kingdom of Aksum and East African Trade	1	.5	1	2
3. Patterns of Change: Migration	1	.5	1	2
Chapter 9 The Americas: A Separate World 40,000 BC–AD 700				
1. Hunters and Farmers in the Americas	1	1	1	2
2. Early Mesoamerican Civilizations	1	1	2	2
3. Early Civilizations of the Andes	1	1	2	2
Total Days for Unit 2	**20**	**24**	**24**	**36**
UNIT 3 AN AGE OF EXCHANGE AND ENCOUNTER 500–1500				
Chapter 10 The Muslim World 600–1250				
1. The Rise of Islam	1	1	2	1
2. The Spread of Islam	1	1	2	2
3. Muslim Achievement	1	1	2	2
World Religions: Buddhism, Christianity, Hinduism, Islam, Judaism, Confucianism	2	2	2	2
Chapter 11 Byzantines, Russians, and Turks Interact 500–1500				
1. Byzantium Becomes the New Rome	1	1	1	1
2. Russians Adapt Byzantine Culture	1	1	1	2
3. Turkish Empires Rise in Anatolia	1	1	2	1
Chapter 12 Empires in East Asia 600–1350				
1. Two Great Dynasties in China	1	1	2	2
2. The Mongol Conquests	1	.5	1	2
3. Empire of the Great Khan	1	.5	1	1
4. Feudal Powers in Japan	1	.5	2	2
5. Kingdoms of Southeast Asia and Korea	1	.5	2	1

For **block schedules**, see *Planning for Block Schedules* in the teacher's resource materials.

	World Survey	Western Civilization	Non-Western Civilization	Pre-1900 History
Chapter 13 European Middle Ages 500–1200	(days)	(days)	(days)	(days)
1. Germanic Kingdoms Unite Under Charlemagne	1	2	1	1
2. Feudalism in Europe	2	2	1	2
3. The Age of Chivalry	2	2	1	2
4. The Church Wields Power	1	1	1	2
Chapter 14 The Formation of Western Europe 800–1500				
1. Church Reform and the Crusades	1	2	1	2
2. Trade, Towns, and Financial Revolution	1	2	1	1
3. England and France Develop	1	2	1	2
4. A Century of Turmoil	1	2	1	2
Chapter 15 Societies and Empires of Africa 800–1500				
1. North and Central African Societies	1	.5	1	1
2. West African Empires and Civilizations	1	1	2	2
3. Eastern City-States and Southern Empires	1	.5	1	1
Total Days for Unit 3	**26**	**28**	**32**	**38**
UNIT 4 CONNECTING HEMISPHERES 900–1800				
Chapter 16 Peoples and Empires in the Americas 900–1500				
1. Diverse Societies of North America	2	1	1	2
2. Mayan Kings and Cities	1	1	1	2
3. The Aztecs Control Central Mexico	1	1	1	2
4. The Incas Create a Mountain Empire	2	1	1	2
Chapter 17 European Renaissance and Reformation 1300–1600				
1. Italy: Birthplace of the Renaissance	2	2	1	3
2. The Northern Renaissance	1	2	1	2
3. Luther Starts the Reformation	1	2	1	2
4. The Reformation Continues	1	2	1	2
Chapter 18 The Muslim World Expands 1300–1700				
1. The Ottomans Build a Vast Empire	1	1	2	1
2. Patterns of Change: Cultural Blending	1	1	2	2
3. The Mughals Establish an Empire in India	2	1	2	2
Chapter 19 An Age of Exploration and Isolation 1400–1800				
1. Europeans Explore the East	2	2	2	2
2. China Rejects European Outreach	1	1	2	1
3. Japan Limits Western Contacts	1	1	2	1

For **block schedules**, see *Planning for Block Schedules* in the teacher's resource materials.

	World Survey	Western Civilization	Non-Western Civilization	Pre-1900 History
Chapter 20 The Atlantic World 1492–1800	(days)	(days)	(days)	(days)
1. Spanish Conquests in the Americas	1	1	1	2
2. Competing Claims in North America	1	1	1	2
3. The Atlantic Slave Trade	1	1	1	1
4. The Columbian Exchange and Global Trade	2	1	2	3
Total Days for Unit 4	**24**	**23**	**25**	**34**
UNIT 5 ABSOLUTISM TO REVOLUTION 1500–1900				
Chapter 21 Absolute Monarchs 1500–1800				
1. Spain's Empire and European Absolutism	1	1	1	1
2. France's Ultimate Monarch	2	2	1	2
3. Central European Monarchs Clash	1	1	.5	1
4. Russian Czars Increase Power	2	2	2	2
5. Parliament Limits the English Monarchy	1	1	.5	2
Chapter 22 Enlightenment and Revolution 1550–1789				
1. The Scientific Revolution	2	2	1	2
2. The Enlightenment in Europe	1	2	.5	2
3. The Spread of Enlightenment Ideas	1	1	.5	2
4. American Revolution: The Birth of a Republic	2	2	1	2
Chapter 23 French Revolution and Napoleon 1789–1815				
1. Revolution Threatens the French King	1	1	.5	1
2. Revolution Brings Reform and Terror	2	1	.5	2
3. Napoleon Forges an Empire	1	1	.5	2
4. Napoleon's Empire Collapses	1	1	.5	1
5. The Congress of Vienna Convenes	1	1	.5	2
Chapter 24 Revolutions Sweep The Americas and Europe 1789–1900				
1. Latin American Peoples Win Independence	1	1	1.5	2
2. Revolutions Disrupt Europe	1	1	1	1
3. Patterns of Change: Nationalism	1	1	1	1
4. Revolutions in Art and Philosophy	1	1	1	1
Total Days for Unit 5	**23**	**23**	**15**	**29**
UNIT 6 INDUSTRIALISM AND THE RACE FOR EMPIRE 1700–1917				
Chapter 25 The Industrial Revolution 1700–1900				
1. The Beginnings of Industrialization	1	2	1	
2. Patterns of Change: Industrialization	2	1	1	
3. Industrialism Spreads	1	1	1	
4. An Age of Reforms	2	1	1	

For **block schedules**, see *Planning for Block Schedules* in the teacher's resource materials.

	World Survey (days)	Western Civilization (days)	Non-Western Civilization (days)	Pre-1900 History (days)
Chapter 26 An Age of Democracy and Progress 1815–1914				
1. Political Reform and Activism	1	1	.5	
2. Self-Rule for British Colonies	1	1	.5	
3. Expansion and Crisis in the United States	1	1	.5	
4. Progress at the End of the Century	1	1	.5	
Chapter 27 The New Imperialism 1850–1914				
1. Imperialists Divide Africa	2	1	2	
2. Patterns of Change: Imperialism	1	1	1	
3. Muslim Lands Fall to Imperialist Demands	1	1	1	
4. British Imperialism in India	2	1	1	
5. Western Powers Rule Southeast Asia	1	1	2	
Chapter 28 Transformations Around the Globe 1800–1914				
1. China Responds to Pressure from the West	1	1	.5	
2. Japan Modernizes	1	.5	1	
3. U.S. Economic Imperialism in Latin America	1	1	.5	
4. The Mexican Revolution	1	.5	1	
Total Days for Unit 6	**21**	**17.5**	**15**	
UNIT 7 THE WORLD AT WAR 1914–1945				
Chapter 29 The World at War 1914–1918				
1. The Stage is Set for War	1	2	1	
2. War Consumes Europe	2	2	1	
3. War Affects the World	2	2	1	
4. A Flawed Peace	1	2	1	
Chapter 30 Revolution and Nationalism 1900–1939				
1. Revolutions in Russia	1	1	1	
2. Patterns of Change: Totalitarianism	1	1	1	
3. Collapse of Chinese Imperial Rule	1	1	2	
4. Nationalism in India and Southwest Asia	2	1	2	
Chapter 31 Years of Crisis 1919–1939				
1. An Age of Uncertainty	1	1	.5	
2. A Global Depression	1	1	1	
3. Fascism Rises in Europe	1	1	1	
4. Aggressors on the March	1	1	.5	

For **block schedules**, see *Planning for Block Schedules* in the teacher's resource materials.

	World Survey	Western Civilization	Non-Western Civilization	Pre-1900 History
Chapter 32 World War II 1939–1945	(days)	(days)	(days)	(days)
1. Hitler's Lightning War	1	2	2	
2. Japan Strikes in Asia	1	2	2	
3. The Holocaust	1	2	1	
4. The Allies are Victorious	2	1	1	
5. The Devastation in Europe and Japan	1	1	1	
Total Days for Unit 7	**21**	**24**	**20**	
UNIT 8 PERSPECTIVES ON THE PRESENT 1945–PRESENT				
Chapter 33 Restructuring the Postwar World 1945–Present				
1. Two Superpowers Face Off	1	1	1	
2. Communists Triumph in China	1	.5	1	
3. War in Korea and Vietnam	1	1	1	
4. Cold War Around the World	1	1	1	
5. The Cold War Thaws	1	1	1	
Chapter 34 The Colonies Become New Nations 1945–Present				
1. The Indian Subcontinent Gains Independence	1	1	2	
2. Southeast Asian Nations Gain Independence	1	1	1	
3. New Nations in Africa	1	1	2	
4. Conflicts in the Middle East	1	1	2	
Chapter 35 Struggles for Democracy 1945–Present				
1. Patterns of Change: Democracy	1	1.5	1	
2. Democracy Challenges in African Nations	1	.5	2	
3. Gorbachev Moves Toward Democracy	1	.5	.5	
4. Collapse of the Soviet Union	1	1	.5	
5. China Follows Its Own Path	1	.5	1	
Chapter 36 Global Interdependence 1960–Present				
1. Science and Technology Shape Human Outlook	1	.5	.5	
2. Global Economic Development	1	.5	.5	
3. Continuing Political Challenges Around the World	1	.5	.5	
4. Culture and Values in the Information Age	1	.5	.5	
Total Days for Unit 8	**18**	**14.5**	**19**	

McDougal Littell

WORLD HISTORY

PATTERNS OF INTERACTION

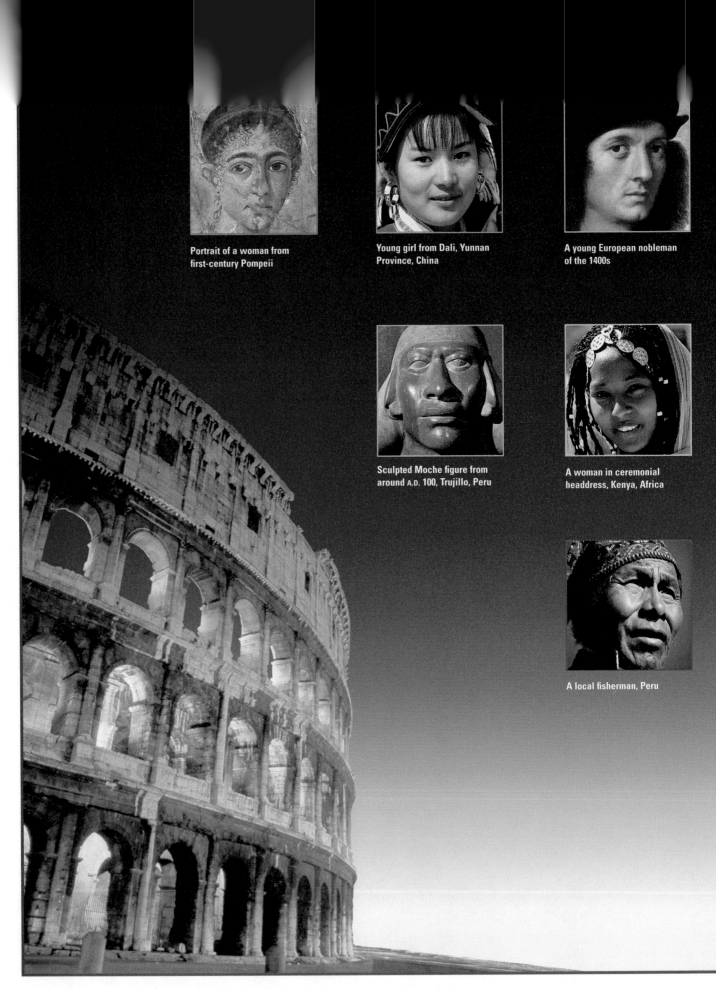

Portrait of a woman from first-century Pompeii

Young girl from Dali, Yunnan Province, China

A young European nobleman of the 1400s

Sculpted Moche figure from around A.D. 100, Trujillo, Peru

A woman in ceremonial headdress, Kenya, Africa

A local fisherman, Peru

Funerary mask, Tomb of
Tutankhamen, around 1300 B.C.

A farmer in Turkey

A woman in traditional dress,
Rajasthan, India

"The history of
civilizations, in fact,
is the history of
continual mutual
borrowings over many
centuries."

—Fernand Braudel

McDougal Littell

WORLD
HISTORY

PATTERNS OF INTERACTION

Roger B. Beck

Linda Black

Larry S. Krieger

Phillip C. Naylor

Dahia Ibo Shabaka

McDougal Littell
A HOUGHTON MIFFLIN COMPANY

Evanston, Illinois • Boston • Dallas

Senior Consultants

Roger B. Beck, Ph.D.

Roger B. Beck is a Professor of African History, World History, History of the Third World, and Social Studies Methods at Eastern Illinois University. He is also a Social Studies Student Teacher Supervisor at that university. Dr. Beck recently served as Associate Dean of the Graduate School and International Programs at Eastern Illinois University. In addition to his distinguished teaching career at high school, college, and graduate school levels, Dr. Beck is a contributing author to several books and has written numerous articles, reviews, and papers. He is also an active member of the National Council for the Social Studies, the World History Association, and the African Studies Association. Dr. Beck was a key contributor to the National Standards for World History.

Linda Black, B.A., M.Ed.

Linda Black teaches World History at Cypress Falls High School in Houston, Texas, and has had a distinguished career in education as a teacher of world history, American history, and Texas history. In 1993–1994, Mrs. Black was named an Outstanding Secondary Social Studies Teacher in the United States by the National Council for the Social Studies. In 1996, she was elected to the Board of Directors of the National Council for the Social Studies. As an active member of that Council, the Texas Council for the Social Studies, the Texas Humanities Alliance, and the World History Association, Mrs. Black frequently presents and directs workshops at the local, state, and national levels.

Larry S. Krieger, B.A., M.A., M.A.T.

Larry S. Krieger is the Social Studies Supervisor for Grades K-12 in Montgomery Township Public Schools in New Jersey. For 26 years he has taught world history in public schools. He has also introduced many innovative in-service programs, such as "Putting the Story Back in History," and has co-authored several successful history textbooks. Mr. Krieger earned his B.A. and M.A.T. from the University of North Carolina and his M.A. from Wake Forest University.

Phillip C. Naylor, Ph.D.

Phillip C. Naylor is an Associate Professor of History at Marquette University and teaches Modern European and non-Western history courses on both graduate and undergraduate levels. He is also the Director of the Western Civilization Program at Marquette University. He has co-authored and co-edited several books, including *State and Society in Algeria* and *Western Receptions/Perceptions: A Trans-Cultural Anthology*. In addition, Dr. Naylor is a contributing author to several history texts and study programs and has published numerous articles, papers, reviews, and CD-ROM projects. In 1996, Dr. Naylor received the Reverend John P. Raynor, S.J., Faculty Award for Teaching Excellence at Marquette University. In 1992, he received the Edward G. Roddy Teaching Award at Merrimack College.

Dahia Ibo Shabaka, B.A., M.A., Ed.S.

Dahia Ibo Shabaka is the Director of Social Studies and African-Centered Education in the Detroit Public Schools system. She has an extensive educational and scholarly background in the disciplines of history, political science, economics, law, and reading, and also in secondary education, curriculum development, and school administration and supervision. Ms. Shabaka has been a teacher, a curriculum coordinator, and a supervisor of Social Studies in the Detroit Secondary Schools. In 1991 she was named Social Studies Educator of the Year by the Michigan Council for the Social Studies. Ms. Shabaka is the recipient of a Fulbright Fellowship at the Hebrew University in Israel and has served as an executive board member of the National Social Studies Supervisors Association.

Copyright © 1999 by McDougal Littell Inc. All rights reserved.
Warning: No part of this work may be reproduced or transmitted in any form or by any means, electronic or mechanical, including photocopying and recording, or by any information storage or retrieval system without prior written permission of McDougal Littell Inc. unless such copying is expressly permitted by federal copyright law. Address inquiries to Manager, Rights and Permissions, McDougal Littell Inc., P.O. Box 1667, Evanston, IL 60204.
Acknowledgments begin on page 1072.
ISBN 0-395-87274-X
Printed in the United States of America.
1 2 3 4 5 6 7 8 9–DWO–03 02 01 00 99 98

This text contains material that appeared originally in *World History: Perspectives on the Past* (D.C. Heath and Company) by Larry S. Krieger, Kenneth Neill, and Dr. Edward Reynolds.

Consultants and Reviewers

Content Consultants

The content consultants reviewed the manuscript for historical depth and accuracy and for clarity of presentation.

Jerry Bentley
Department of History
University of Hawaii
Honolulu, Hawaii

Marc Brettler
Department of Near Eastern
 and Judaic Studies
Brandeis University
Waltham, Massachusetts

Steve Gosch
Department of History
University of Wisconsin at Eau Claire
Eau Claire, Wisconsin

Don Holsinger
Department of History
Seattle Pacific University
Seattle, Washington

Patrick Manning
World History Center
Department of History
Northeastern University
Boston, Massachusetts

Richard Saller
Department of History
University of Chicago
Chicago, Illinois

Wolfgang Schlauch
Department of History
Eastern Illinois University
Charleston, Illinois

Susan Schroeder
Department of History
Loyola University of Chicago
Chicago, Illinois

Scott Waugh
Department of History
University of California, Los Angeles
Los Angeles, California

Multicultural Advisory Board Consultants

The multicultural advisors reviewed the manuscript for appropriate historical content.

Pat A. Brown
Director of the Indianapolis
 Public Schools
 Office of African Centered
 Multicultural Education
Indianapolis Public Schools
Indianapolis, Indiana

Ogle B. Duff
Associate Professor of English
University of Pittsburgh
Pittsburgh, Pennsylvania

Mary Ellen Maddox
Black Education Commission
 Director
Los Angeles Unified School District
Los Angeles, California

Jon Reyhner
Associate Professor and Coordinator of
 the Bilingual Multicultural
 Education Program
Northern Arizona University
Flagstaff, Arizona

Ysidro Valenzuela
Fresno High School
Fresno, California

Teacher Review Panels

The following educators provided ongoing review during the development of prototypes, the table of contents, and key components of the program.

Texas Teacher Panel

Patrick Adams
Pasadena High School
Pasadena, Texas

Ellen Bell
Bellaire High School
Bellaire, Texas

Craig Grace
Lanier High School
Austin, Texas

Katie Ivey
Dimmit High School
Dimmitt, Texas

Pat Knapp
Burgess High School
El Paso, Texas

Eric R. Larson
Clark High School
Plano, Texas

Linda Marrs
Naaman Forest High School
Garland, Texas

Terry McRae
Robert E. Lee High School
Tyler, Texas

Sherrie Prahl
The Woodlands High School
The Woodlands, Texas

Dorothy Schulze
Health Careers High School
San Antonio, Texas

Liz Silva
Townview Magnet Center
Dallas, Texas

Linda Stevens
Central High School
San Angelo, Texas

Midwest Teacher Panel

Bruce Bekemeyer
Marquette High School
Chesterfield, Missouri

Margaret Campbell
Central High School
St. Louis, Missouri

Nancy Coates
Belleville East High School
Belleville, Illinois

Kim Coil
Francis Howell North High School
St. Charles, Missouri

Gary Kasprovich
Granite City High School
Granite City, Illinois

Harry McCown
Hazelwood West High School
Hazelwood, Missouri

Joseph Naumann
McCluer North High School
Florissant, Missouri

Leonard Sullivan
Pattonville High School
Maryland Hts., Missouri

Carole Weeden
Fort Zumwalt South High School
St. Peters, Missouri

Rita Wylie
Parkway West Sr. High School
Ballwin, Missouri

Teacher Reviewers

Glenn Bird
Springville High School
Springville, Utah

Michael Cady
North High School
Phoenix, Arizona

William Canter
Guilford High School
Rockford, Illinois

Nancy Coates
Belleville East High School
Belleville, Illinois

Paul Fitzgerald
Estancia High School
Costa Mesa, California

Tom McDonald
Phoenix Union HSD
Phoenix, Arizona

Myras Osman
Homewood Flossmoor High School
Flossmoor, Illinois

Dorothy Schulze
Health Careers High School
Dallas, Texas

Reviewers (continued)

Student Board

The following students reviewed prototype materials for the textbook.

LaShaunda Allen
Weston High School
Greenville, MS

Brandy Andreas
Rayburn High School
Pasadena, TX

Adam Bishop
Jordan High School
Sandy, UT

Jennifer Bragg
Midlothian High School
Midlothian, VA

Nicole Fevry
Midwood High School
Brooklyn, NY

Phillip Gallegos
Hilltop High School
Chula Vista, CA

Matt Gave
Stevenson Senior High School
Sterling Heights, MI

Blair Hogan
Leesville Road High School
Raleigh, NC

Ngoc Hong
Watkins Mill Senior High School
Gaithersburg, MD

Iman Jalali
Glenbrook North High School
Northbrook, IL

Vivek Makhijani
Durfee High School
Fall River, MA

Todd McDavitt
Derby High School
Derby, KS

Teniqua Mitchell
Linden-McKinley High School
Columbus, OH

Cicely Nash
Edmond Memorial High School
Edmond, OK

Brian Nebrensky
Hillsboro High School
Hillsboro, OR

Jesse Neumyer
Cumberland Valley High School
Mechanicsburg, PA

Nora Patronas
Alba High School
Bayou La Batre, LA

Lindsey Petersen
Stoughton High School
Stoughton, WI

Nicholas Price
Central Lafourche Senior
High School
Mathews, LA

Ben Richey
Fort Vancouver High School
Vancouver, WA

Karen Ryan
Silver Creek High School
San Jose, CA

Matt Shaver
Weatherford High School
Weatherford, TX

Richie Spitler
Atlantic High School
Port Orange, FL

Jessie Stoneberg
Burnsville High School
Burnsville, MN

Kelly Swick
Ocean Township High School
Oakhurst, NJ

Jason Utzig
Kenmore East High School
Tonawanda, NY

Justin Woodly
North Cobb High School
Kennesaw, GA

vii

Beginnings of Civilization

viii

New Directions in Government and Society

ix

Unit 3
500–1500

An Age of Exchange and Encounter

x

xi

Unit 4
900–1800

Connecting Hemispheres

xii

xiii

xiv

The World at War

XV

Unit 8
1945–Present

Perspectives on the Present

xvi

Skillbuilder Handbook

The Skillbuilder Handbook is at the back of the book on pages 990–1014. Refer to it when you need help in answering Think Through History questions, doing the activities entitled Interact with History, or answering questions in Section Assessments and Chapter Assessments.

Patterns of Interaction **Video Series**

VIDEO Each video in the series *Patterns of Interaction* relates to a *Global Impact* feature in the text. These eight exciting videos show how cultural interactions have shaped our world and how patterns in history continue to the present day.

Volume 1

Building Empires
The Rise of the Persians and the Inca
Watch the Persian and Incan empires expand and rule other peoples, with unexpected results for both conquered and conquering cultures.

Trade Connects the World
Silk Roads and the Pacific Rim
Explore the legendary trade routes of the Silk Roads and the modern trade of the Pacific Rim, and notice how both affected much more than economics.

Volume 2

The Spread of Epidemic Disease
Bubonic Plague and Smallpox
Look for sweeping calamities and incredible consequences when interacting peoples bring devastating diseases to one another.

The Geography of Food
The Impact of Potatoes and Sugar
Notice how the introduction of new foods to a region provides security to some and spells disaster for millions.

Volume 3

Struggling Toward Democracy
Revolutions in Latin America and South Africa
Examine the impact of democratic ideas that incite people to join revolutions in 19th century Latin America and 20th century South Africa.

Technology Transforms an Age
The Industrial and Electronic Revolutions
See how another kind of revolution, caused by inventions in industry and communication, affects people not only a century ago but today as well.

Volume 4

Arming for War
Modern and Medieval Weapons
Watch how warring peoples' competition in military technology has resulted in a dangerous game of bigger, better, and faster throughout the ages.

Cultural Crossroads
The United States and the World
Observe how universal enjoyments like music, sports, and fashion become instruments of cultural blending across the world.

VIDEO The Video Icon in the *Global Impact* feature provides you with a link to the *Patterns of Interaction* video series.

xviii

Major Features

xix

Features

Daily Life

Global Impact

Spotlight On

xx

CONNECT *to* TODAY

HISTORY THROUGH ART

Fresco detail by José Clemente Orozco

Marie Antoinette, Jacques Gautier d'Agoty

The sphinx of Nubia's King Taharqa

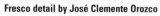

xxi

Features

HISTORY MAKERS

**Padre José Morelos
1765–1815**

Born into poverty, Padre José Morelos did not begin to study for the priesthood until he was 25. In his parish work, he mainly served poor Indians and mestizos. In 1811, he joined Father Hidalgo, along with his parishioners. After Hidalgo's death, Morelos took skillful command of the peasant army.

By 1813, his army controlled all of southern Mexico except for the largest cities. Morelos then called a Mexican congress to set up a democratic government. The supporters of Spain, however, finally caught up with the congress. As the rebels fled, Morelos stayed behind to fight. The Spanish finally captured and shot Morelos in 1815. Napoleon knew of this priest-revolutionary and said: "Give me three generals like him and I can conquer the world."

Historical and Political Maps

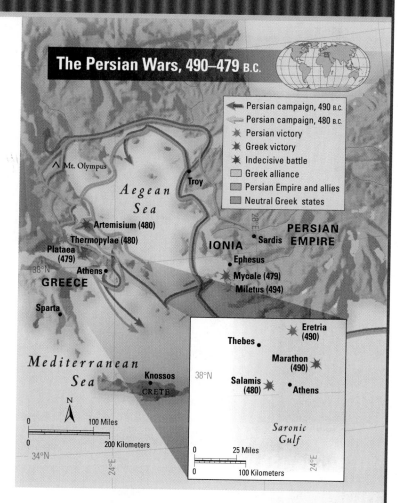

xxiii

Historical and Political Maps

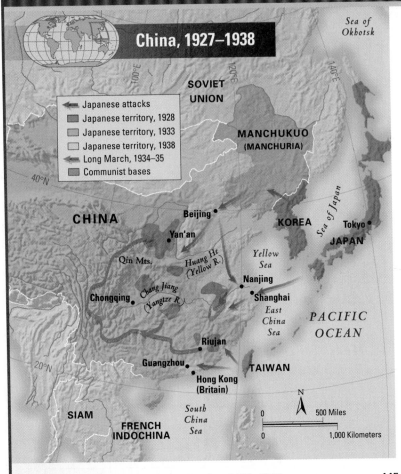

China, 1927–1938

Japanese attacks
Japanese territory, 1928
Japanese territory, 1933
Japanese territory, 1938
Long March, 1934–35
Communist bases

Charts, Graphs, and Time Lines

xxv

Infographics and Focus On

Primary Sources and Personal Voices

VOICE FROM THE PAST
. . . one who has been an emperor
cannot endure to be a fugitive.
THEODORA, quoted in *History of the Wars*

Primary Sources and Personal Voices

VOICE FROM THE PAST
For even though some of the Western methods are different from our own, and may even be an improvement, there is little about them that is new.

KANGXI, quoted in *Emperor of China: Self-Portrait of K'ang-hsi*

xxviii

xxix

While historical events are unique, they often are driven by similar, repeated forces. In telling the history of our world, this book pays special attention to eight significant and recurring themes. These themes are presented to show that from America, to Africa, to Asia, people are more alike than they realize. Throughout history humans have confronted similar obstacles, have struggled to achieve similar goals, and continually have strived to better themselves and the world around them.

Power and Authority

History is often made by the people and institutions in power. As you read about the world's powerful people and governments, try to answer several key questions.

• Who holds the power?
• How did that person or group get power?
• What system of government provides order in this society?
• How does the group or person in power keep or lose power?

Religious and Ethical Systems

Throughout history, humans around the world have been guided by, as much as anything else, their religious and ethical beliefs. As you examine the world's religious and ethical systems, pay attention to several important issues.

• What beliefs are held by a majority of people in a region?
• How do these major religious beliefs differ from one another?
• How do the various religious groups interact with one another?
• How do religious groups react toward nonmembers?

Revolution

Often in history, great change has been achieved only through force. As you read about the continuous overthrow of governments, institutions, and even ideas throughout history, examine several key questions.

• What long-term ideas or institutions are being overthrown?
• What caused people to make this radical change?
• What are the results of the change?

Interaction with Environment

Since the earliest of times, humans have had to deal with their surroundings in order to survive. As you read about our continuous interaction with the environment, keep in mind several important issues.

• How do humans adjust to the climate and terrain where they live?
• How have changes in the natural world forced people to change?
• What positive and negative changes have people made to their environment?

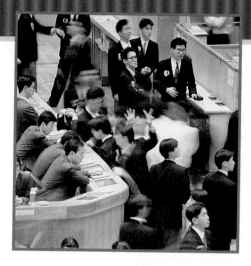

Economics

Economics has proven to be a powerful force in human history. From early times to the present, human cultures have been concerned with how to use their scarce resources to satisfy their needs. As you read about different groups, note several key issues regarding the role of economics in world history.

• What goods and services does a society produce?
• Who controls the wealth and resources of a society?
• How does a society obtain more goods and services?

Cultural Interaction

Today, people around the world share many things, from music, to food, to ideas. Human cultures actually have interacted with each other since ancient times. As you read about how different cultures have interacted, note several significant issues.

• How have cultures interacted (trade, migration, or conquest)?
• What items have cultures passed on to each other?
• What political, economic, and religious ideas have cultures shared?
• What positive and negative effects have resulted from cultural interaction?

Empire Building

Since the beginning of time, human cultures have shared a similar desire to grow more powerful—often by dominating other groups. As you read about empire building through the ages, keep in mind several key issues.

• What motivates groups to conquer other lands and people?
• How does one society gain control of others?
• How does a dominating society control and rule its subjects?

Science and Technology

All humans share an endless desire to know more about their world and to solve whatever problems they encounter. The development of science and technology has played a key role in these quests. As you read about the role of science and technology in world history, try to answer several key questions.

• What tools and methods do people use to solve the various problems they face?
• How do people gain knowledge about their world? How do they use that knowledge?
• How do new discoveries and inventions change the way people live?

xxxi

Geography is the study of the earth and its features. It is also an important part of human history. Since the beginning of time, all civilizations have had to control their surroundings in order to survive. In addition, geography has played a vital role in many historical events. Like history itself, geography reflects several key themes. These themes help us to understand the different ways in which geography has helped shape the story of world history.

Location

Location tells us where in the world a certain area is. Geographers describe location in two ways: *absolute* location and *relative* location. An area's absolute location is its point of latitude and longitude. Latitude is the distance in degrees north or south of the equator. Longitude is the degree distance east or west of an imaginary vertical line that runs through Greenwich, England, called the prime meridian. An area's relative location describes where it is in terms of other areas.

In absolute terms, the middle of Singapore lies at 1°20' north latitude and 103°50' east longitude. This information allows you to pinpoint Singapore on a map. In relative terms, Singapore is an island country on the southern tip of the Malay Peninsula near where the South China Sea and the Indian Ocean meet. How might Singapore's location on the sea have helped it develop into an economic power?

Human/Environment Interaction

Throughout history, humans have changed and have been changed by their environment. Because they live on an island, the people of Singapore have built a bridge in order to travel more easily to mainland Malaysia. In addition, Singapore residents have carved an inviting harbor out of parts of its coastline in order to accommodate the island's busy ocean traffic.

Singapore is one of the most densely populated countries in the world. Many of its nearly three million citizens live in the capital city, Singapore. The country's population density is about 12,000 persons per square mile. In contrast, the United States has a population density of 71 persons per square mile. What environmental challenges does this situation pose?

Singapore

Region

A region is any area that has common characteristics. These characteristics may include physical factors, such as landforms or climate. They also may include cultural aspects, such as language or religion. Singapore is part of a region known as Southeast Asia. The countries of this region share such characteristics as rich, fertile soil, as well as a strong influence of Buddhism and Islam.

Because regions share similar characteristics, they often share similar concerns. In 1967, Singapore joined with the other countries of Southeast Asia to form the Association of Southeast Asian Nations. This body was created to address the region's concerns. What concerns might Singapore have that are unique?

Place

Place, in geography, indicates what an area looks like in both physical and human terms. The physical setting of an area—its landforms, soil, climate, and resources—are aspects of place. So are the different cultures which inhabit an area.

The physical characteristics of Singapore include a hot, moist climate with numerous rain forests. In human terms, Singapore's population is mostly Chinese. How does Singapore's human characteristic tie it to other countries?

Movement

In geography, movement is the transfer of people, goods, and ideas from one place to another. In many ways, history is the story of movement. Since early times, people have migrated in search of better places to live. They have traded with distant peoples to obtain new goods. And they have spread a wealth of ideas from culture to culture.

Singapore, which is a prosperous center of trade and finance, attracts numerous people in search of greater wealth and new goods. What about Singapore's geography makes it the ideal place for the trading of goods?

xxxiii

While history is the story of people, it is also the examination of when events occurred. Keeping track of the order of historical events will help you to better retain and understand the material. To help you remember the order and dates of important events in history, this book contains numerous time lines. Below is some instruction on how to read a time line, as well as a look at some terms associated with tracking time in history.

How to Read a Time Line

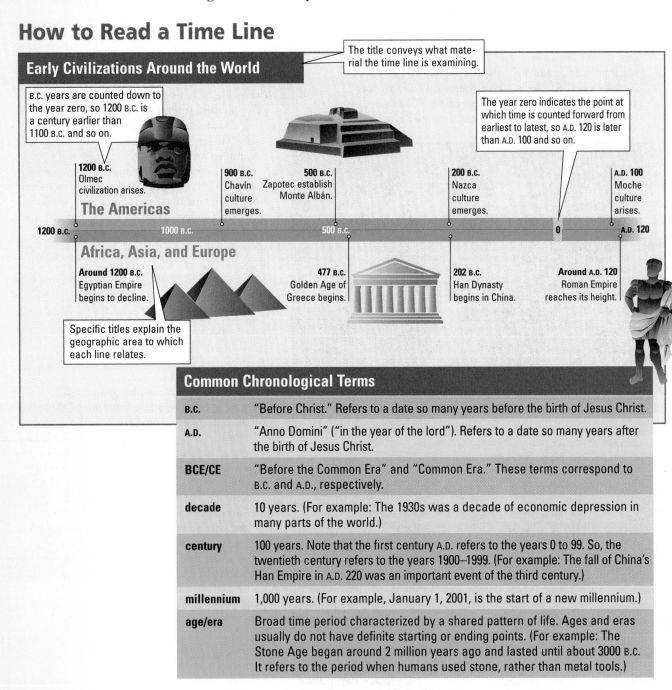

The title conveys what material the time line is examining.

Early Civilizations Around the World

B.C. years are counted down to the year zero, so 1200 B.C. is a century earlier than 1100 B.C. and so on.

The year zero indicates the point at which time is counted forward from earliest to latest, so A.D. 120 is later than A.D. 100 and so on.

The Americas

1200 B.C. Olmec civilization arises.

900 B.C. Chavín culture emerges.

500 B.C. Zapotec establish Monte Albán.

200 B.C. Nazca culture emerges.

A.D. 100 Moche culture arises.

| 1200 B.C. | 1000 B.C. | 500 B.C. | | 0 | A.D. 120 |

Africa, Asia, and Europe

Around 1200 B.C. Egyptian Empire begins to decline.

477 B.C. Golden Age of Greece begins.

202 B.C. Han Dynasty begins in China.

Around A.D. 120 Roman Empire reaches its height.

Specific titles explain the geographic area to which each line relates.

Common Chronological Terms

B.C.	"Before Christ." Refers to a date so many years before the birth of Jesus Christ.
A.D.	"Anno Domini" ("in the year of the lord"). Refers to a date so many years after the birth of Jesus Christ.
BCE/CE	"Before the Common Era" and "Common Era." These terms correspond to B.C. and A.D., respectively.
decade	10 years. (For example: The 1930s was a decade of economic depression in many parts of the world.)
century	100 years. Note that the first century A.D. refers to the years 0 to 99. So, the twentieth century refers to the years 1900–1999. (For example: The fall of China's Han Empire in A.D. 220 was an important event of the third century.)
millennium	1,000 years. (For example, January 1, 2001, is the start of a new millennium.)
age/era	Broad time period characterized by a shared pattern of life. Ages and eras usually do not have definite starting or ending points. (For example: The Stone Age began around 2 million years ago and lasted until about 3000 B.C. It refers to the period when humans used stone, rather than metal tools.)

xxxiv

You are about to examine not only thousands of years of history, but nearly every region of the globe. To help you visualize the faraway places you read about, this book contains numerous maps. Many of these maps contain several layers of information that provide a better understanding of how and why events in history occurred. Below is a look at how to read a map in order to obtain all of the rich information it offers.

How to Read a Map

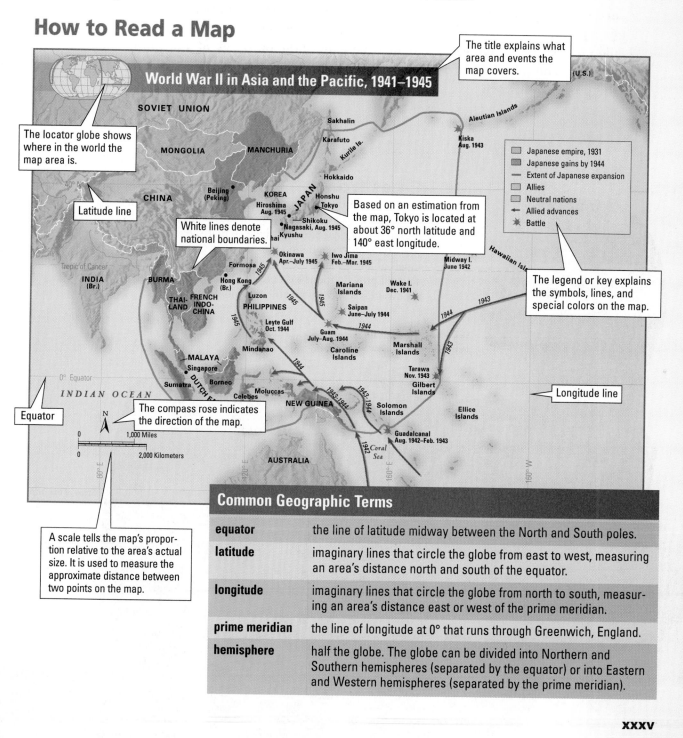

The title explains what area and events the map covers.

The locator globe shows where in the world the map area is.

Latitude line

White lines denote national boundaries.

Based on an estimation from the map, Tokyo is located at about 36° north latitude and 140° east longitude.

The legend or key explains the symbols, lines, and special colors on the map.

World War II in Asia and the Pacific, 1941–1945

Japanese empire, 1931
Japanese gains by 1944
Extent of Japanese expansion
Allies
Neutral nations
Allied advances
Battle

Equator

The compass rose indicates the direction of the map.

A scale tells the map's proportion relative to the area's actual size. It is used to measure the approximate distance between two points on the map.

Longitude line

Common Geographic Terms

equator	the line of latitude midway between the North and South poles.
latitude	imaginary lines that circle the globe from east to west, measuring an area's distance north and south of the equator.
longitude	imaginary lines that circle the globe from north to south, measuring an area's distance east or west of the prime meridian.
prime meridian	the line of longitude at 0° that runs through Greenwich, England.
hemisphere	half the globe. The globe can be divided into Northern and Southern hemispheres (separated by the equator) or into Eastern and Western hemispheres (separated by the prime meridian).

XXXV

Do you like puzzles? If so, you are in luck. You are about to encounter the greatest puzzle there is: history. The study of history is much more than the recollection of dates and names. It is an attempt to answer a continuous and puzzling question: what really happened?

In their effort to solve this puzzle, historians and researchers use a variety of methods. From digging up artifacts, to uncovering eyewitness accounts, experts collect and analyze mountains of data in numerous ways. As a result, the history books you read more accurately depict what life was like in a culture 5,000 years ago, or what caused the outbreak of a devastating war. The following two pages examine some of the pieces used to solve the puzzle of history.

Clues from an Ancient Girl

In 1995, an anthropologist discovered the mummified and frozen remains of a teenage girl in the Andes Mountains of South America. Scientists believe that she is about 500 years old and was a member of the Inca Empire. Because much of her remains are well preserved, scientists hope she will provide them with new information about one of the Americas' most powerful ancient cultures.

An analysis of her stomach content may provide information about the Inca diet.

Her clothing, believed to belong to the upper class, should shed new light on how noble Inca women dressed.

Some of her DNA remains intact, which will help scientists determine whether she has any living descendants.

Modern Science

The ever-improving field of science has lent its hand in the search to learn more about the past. Using everything from microscopes to computers, researchers have shed new light on many historical mysteries. Here, a researcher uses computer technology to determine what the owner of a prehistoric human skull may have looked like.

Written Sources

Historians often look to written documents for insight into the past. There are various types of written sources. Documents written during the same time period as an event are known as *primary* sources. They include such things as diaries and newspapers. They also include drawings, such as the one shown here by Italian painter and inventor, Leonardo da Vinci. His rough sketch of a helicopter-type machine tells us that as early as the late 1400s, humans considered mechanical flight. Material written about an event later, such as books, are known as *secondary* sources. Some written sources began as oral tradition—legends, myths, and beliefs passed on by spoken word from generation to generation.

Digging Up History

Researchers have learned much about the past by discovering the remains of ancient societies. Spearheads like these, which date back to around 9,500 B.C., were found throughout North America. They tell us among other things that the early Americans were hunters. These spearheads were once considered to be the earliest evidence of humankind in the Americas. However, as an example of how history continues to change, scientists recently found evidence of human life in South America as early as 10,500 B.C.

xxxvii

UNIT 1

Beginnings of Civilization
4 million B.C. to 200 B.C.

The Pyramids of Giza

Stone meets sky in this contemporary photograph of two of the three major pyramids at Giza, near Cairo, in Egypt. These magnificent monuments are a testament to the glory of ancient Egyptian civilization.

The pyramids were constructed about 4,500 years ago as burial chambers for Egyptian pharaohs. Pictured are the pyramids of Khufu (or Cheops, in Greek) and Khafre (or Chephren). Khufu and Khafre were the second and third pharaohs of the Fourth Dynasty and ruled Egypt in the 2500s B.C.

The pyramids are marvels of ancient engineering. In a civilization that did not yet know the wheel, giant blocks of stone, some weighing as much as nine tons, were brought over desert sands, and sometimes also across the Nile, to be used in the construction.

The pyramid of Khufu, pictured on the left, is the oldest and largest. When built it was 481 feet high (now 449 feet) and remained the tallest structure in the world until the A.D. 1800s—more than 4,300 years.

These pyramids are a demonstration of the success of ancient peoples at confronting and mastering their environment.

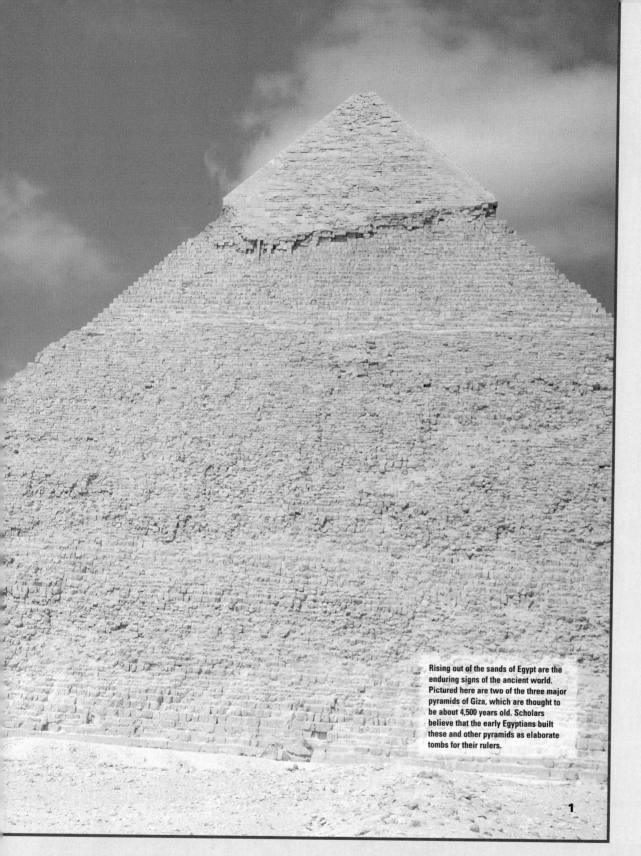

Rising out of the sands of Egypt are the enduring signs of the ancient world. Pictured here are two of the three major pyramids of Giza, which are thought to be about 4,500 years old. Scholars believe that the early Egyptians built these and other pyramids as elaborate tombs for their rulers.

1

This unit covers a grand sweep of history. It describes the beginnings of civilization from the appearance of the earliest hominids in East Africa about 3.6 million B.C. to the establishment of powerful empires in Africa and Asia some 2,000 years ago.

As early humans evolve, they solve the basic problems of survival, and human society develops. Civilization begins to spread throughout the world.

The first civilizations are established in river valleys in Southwest Asia, Egypt, India, and China. Their complex social and economic systems grow. Laws, centralized government, written languages, and technology develop.

The production of surplus food leads to the beginnings of trade. Migrations and trade networks carry new ideas, languages, and cultures throughout the Mediterranean region and as far east as South Asia.

All of these early civilizations share a concern for the afterlife, and different systems of belief evolve into organized religions. During this period, Hinduism, Buddhism, and Judaism emerge.

A series of empires, each one larger than the last, arise from the river valley civilizations. Included among them are the Egyptian, Nubian, Assyrian, and Persian empires. Meanwhile, to the far east, China unites as an empire under the Qin dynasty.

Beginnings of Civilization

Teaching Strategies

The Unit Time Lines in *World History: Patterns of Interaction* are designed to allow students a visual means of comparing events and patterns occurring at the same time in different cultures. The time lines are divided into separate strands, each of which traces the major events of a specific chapter in the unit.

Reading the Time Line For key events within a chapter, students can follow events chronologically by reading from left to right. Comparisons among cultures during the same period can be made by reading from top to bottom.

Dates in the Time Line You might remind students that for early history, the lack of accurate accounts of events often necessitates approximations for dates.

Occasionally, developments do not fall within the chronological divisions of a time line. When that occurs, a separate box displays the events that are outside the time line. In Unit 1, the box highlights events from 4,000,000 B.C. to 8000 B.C.

B.C. and A.D. Review the pattern in which B.C. years move in descending order to 1, while A.D. years move in ascending order from 1. Explain how some books use the abbreviations B.C.E. (Before the Common Era) instead of B.C. (Before Christ) and C.E. (Common Era) instead of A.D. (*Anno Domini* or "In the Year of Our Lord"). Some authors prefer these alternatives because they incorporate less of a Western perspective.

Assessment Finally, point out to the class that as part of the assessment activities in every chapter, there is a question based on the Unit Time Line.

	3500 B.C.	3000 B.C.	2500 B.C.	2000 B.C.

CHAPTER 1 Prehistory to 2500 B.C.
The Peopling of the World

4,000,000 B.C. to 8000 B.C.

4,000,000 B.C. Africa Early hominids appear

2,500,000 B.C. Paleolithic Age begins

1,600,000 B.C. Africa, Asia, Europe Homo erectus appears

200,000 B.C. Europe, Southwest Asia Neanderthals appear

40,000 B.C. Europe Cro-Magnons appear

8000 B.C. Last Ice Age ends; Neolithic Age begins

8000 B.C. Africa, Asia Agriculture begins

3000 B.C. Mesopotamia Bronze Age begins

3000 B.C. Mesopotamia Civilization emerges in Sumer

2600 B.C. *Mesopotamia* ▶

CHAPTER 2 3500 B.C.–450 B.C.
Early River Valley Civilizations

3100 B.C. Egypt Upper and Lower Egypt unite

2600 B.C. Egypt Great Pyramid is built

3000 B.C. Mesopotamia City-states rise in Sumer

2500 B.C. Indus Valley Planned cities rise

2350 B.C. Mesopotamia Sargon of Akkad builds empire

2080 B.C. Egypt Middle Kingdom begins

◀ 2600 B.C. *Egypt*

CHAPTER 3 3500 B.C.–259 B.C.
People and Ideas on the Move

CHAPTER 4 1570 B.C.–200 B.C.
First Age of Empires

	3500 B.C.	3000 B.C.	2500 B.C.	2000 B.C.

MULTIPLE LEARNING STYLES

Visual Learners The time lines for each unit feature art from the pupil's edition selected to represent a civilization, an important historical movement, a crucial event, or an age.

Have visual learners work individually or in groups to find their own representative graphic material for the time line. Such

art may be found in histories of art in the library or on the Web sites of museums or photo houses. Ask students to trace or sketch their graphic choices and insert them on a copy of the time line. Ask them to explain the origin of the art and their reasons for choosing it.

CUSTOMIZING FOR SPECIAL NEEDS

Gifted and Talented Students For the early stages of human history, we know more about developments than about individuals. To add the element of personality to the study of early humans and their cultures, you might ask your gifted students to do research on individuals mentioned in the time line.

For example, in the Unit 1 time line, students might focus on figures such as

Hatshepsut or Shi Huangdi to learn more about their personalities and accomplishments. They might also study *how* historians know what they do about these individuals (monuments, chronicles, legends). The History Makers biographies of Hammurabi, the Buddha, and Hatshepsut in the In-Depth Resources books might help students begin their work.

2000 B.C. China
Xia Dynasty emerges

1790 B.C. Mesopotamia
Hammurabi codifies laws

1640 B.C. Egypt
Hyksos invade Egypt

1532 B.C. China
Shang Dynasty begins

1500 B.C. Indus Valley
Indus Valley cities decline

1027 B.C. China
Zhou Dynasty begins

771 B.C. China
Nomads sack Hao, Zhou capital; dynasty moves to Luoyang

256 B.C. China
Zhou dynasty ends

2000 B.C. Anatolia
Hittites settle

1700 B.C. Asian Steppes
Indo-Europeans begin massive migrations

1500 B.C. India
Aryans move into Indus River Valley

1100 B.C. Mediterranean
Phoenicians begin to dominate trade

1020 B.C. Canaan
King Saul unites Hebrews

922 B.C. Canaan
Hebrew kingdom divides into Israel and Judah

750–550 B.C. India
Hindus compose the *Upanishads*

722 B.C. Mesopotamia
Assyrians conquer Israel

445 B.C. Canaan
Jews rebuild walls of Jerusalem

483 B.C. India
The Buddha dies

◀ Statue of
Dying Buddha

2000 B.C. Nubia
First Nubian kingdom, Kerma, arises

1570 B.C. Egypt
New Kingdom arises

◀ 521 B.C. Persia

1472 B.C. Egypt
Hatshepsut becomes pharoah

1285 B.C. Egypt
Battle of Kadesh between Egyptians and Hittites

850 B.C. Assyria Assyria builds a large empire

751 B.C. Kush Kushite king Piankhi conquers Egypt

550 B.C. Persia Cyrus builds Persian Empire

538 B.C. Persia Cyrus allows Jews to return to Jerusalem

521 B.C. Persia Darius claims throne of Persia

479 B.C. China
Confucius dies

250 B.C. Africa Kingdom of Meroë prospers

221 B.C. China
Shi Huangdi becomes emperor

202 B.C. China
Han Dynasty replaces Qin Dynasty

Living History
Unit 1 Portfolio Project

THEME Interaction with Environment

Your portfolio for this unit will track the ways early humans adjusted to survive in their many environments, as well as the changes they made to those environments. You will show the earliest peoples' surroundings and the technology they created to help them solve basic problems of survival.

Living History Project Choices
Each Chapter Assessment offers you choices of ways to show how the early humans interacted with their environment in that chapter. Activities include the following:

Chapter ❶ field notes, bio board, top 10 list

Chapter ❷ interviews, poems, maps

Chapter ❸ map, dialogue, myth

Chapter ❹ mural, map, short story

Portfolio Project

What Is a Portfolio? A portfolio of student projects arranged chapter-by-chapter provides alternative ways of assessing performance, especially with students whose strengths lie in areas other than memorization or multiple-choice tests. A portfolio is a classroom-based form of assessment that can be more reliable because it adds to the ways of evaluating historical understanding and traces achievement over time.

The portfolio projects for each chapter provide activities that may involve drawings, illustrations, audio or video recordings of group work, or dramatic presentations of student writing. As students collect their individual projects into a portfolio, they may wish to assemble them in folders, bound notebooks, or loose-leaf binders.

Unit and Chapter Themes The portfolio projects for each chapter in a unit are based on the unit theme. The unit theme, along with the two additional themes for each chapter, is important, because the context it provides gives conceptual meaning and organization to diverse factual material.

Portfolio Project The Living History Portfolio Project to the right of each Unit Time Line explains to students the significance of the unit theme. (Refer the class to the World History Theme pages at the front of the book for further discussion of each theme.) Living History then summarizes the formats from which students can choose to demonstrate their understanding of that theme.

Evaluation Encourage students to vary the media in which they work. If students always produce artwork or interviews, they will not provide an adequate basis for assessment. To assist in evaluation, assessment rubrics for portfolio projects accompany each chapter assessment in the teacher's edition.

 The Western Civilization Videodisc

SECTION A: Early Middle Eastern Civilizations to 500 B.C.

 Side One:
Frame 9088

 Universal Play
Button

See Master Guide, Page 1 for Section A

The Peopling of the World

	Key Ideas	**COPY MASTERS**	**ASSESSMENT**
SECTION 1 **Human Origins in Africa** pp. 7–11	The first hominids emerge in East Africa about 3.6 million years ago. They gradually develop large brains and learn to make tools and use fire, which allows them to spread over the earth.	**In-Depth Resources: Unit 1** • **Guided Reading,** p. 1 • **Skillbuilder Practice:** Interpreting Maps, p. 4 • **Primary Source:** from *Lucy: The Beginnings of Humankind,* p. 7 • **Literature:** from *The Clan of the Cave Bear,* p. 11	PE *Section 1 Assessment,* p. 11 *Formal Assessment* • Section Quiz, p. 5 *Alternative Assessment Book* • Standards for Evaluating a Cooperative Activity
SECTION 2 **Humans Try to Control Nature** pp. 12–16	People gradually give up hunting and gathering and learn to cultivate crops, domesticate animals, and live in settled villages. Some villages grow and prosper, developing complex social and economic systems that set the stage for the development of civilization.	**In-Depth Resources: Unit 1** • **Guided Reading,** p. 2 • **Geography Application:** Catal Huyuk, p. 5 • **Primary Sources:** Lascaux Cave Painting, p. 9; "Window on the Stone Age," p. 10 • **History Makers:** The Iceman, p. 15	PE *Section 2 Assessment,* p. 16 *Formal Assessment* • Section Quiz, p. 6 *Alternative Assessment Book* • Standards for Evaluating a Cooperative Activity
SECTION 3 **Civilization Patterns of Change** pp. 17–21	Large cities develop well-defined social systems and powerful institutions. Eventually they develop the five characteristics of civilization. One of the first cities to develop civilization is Ur in Sumer.	**In-Depth Resources: Unit 1** • **Guided Reading,** p. 3 • **Connections Across Time and Cultures:** From Ancient to Modern Communities, p. 16	PE *Section 3 Assessment,* p. 21 *Formal Assessment* • Section Quiz, p. 7 *Alternative Assessment Book* • Standards for Evaluating a Cooperative Activity
CHAPTER RESOURCES	**Chapter Overview** Human beings first emerge in East Africa. As they evolve, they develop complex technology and spread over most of the world. In some areas, people develop agriculture and settled villages, some of which eventually grow into complex cities and develop the five traits of civilization.	*Telescoping the Times* • Chapter Summary, pp. 1–3 *Planning for Block Schedules*	PE *Chapter Assessment,* pp. 22–23 *Chapter Activities,* p. 23 *Formal Assessment* • Chapter Test, forms A and B, pp. 8–13 *Test Generator* *Alternative Assessment Book*

TECHNOLOGY

 Warm-Up Transparency 1

 Electronic Library of Primary Sources
• from "The Cro-Magnons"
 INTERNET RESOURCES
www.mlworldhistory.com

 Warm-Up Transparency 1

 World Art and Cultures Transparencies
• A1 French cave art

 Critical Thinking Transparencies
• CT1 Patterns of Living: Paleolithic Period
to the Neolithic Revolution

 Electronic Library of Primary Sources
• from "Iceman"
 INTERNET RESOURCES
www.mlworldhistory.com

 Warm-Up Transparency 1

 Geography Transparencies
• GT1 Cities of the Ancient Middle East

 World Art and Cultures Transparencies
• AT2 Upper Sumerian artifacts

 Critical Thinking Transparencies
• CT 37 Chapter 1 Visual Summary

 Electronic Library of Primary Sources
• from "The Royal Cemetery at Ur"

 Chapter Summaries on Audiocassette in
English and Spanish
 INTERNET RESOURCES
www.mlworldhistory.com

Block Scheduling (90 MINUTES)

Day 1
Section 1, pp. 7–11

 COOPERATIVE ACTIVITY
Researching Advances in
Stone-Tool Technology,
p. 9 (Teacher's Edition)

Section 2, pp. 12–16

 COOPERATIVE ACTIVITY
Researching the
Development of
Agriculture, p. 15
(Teacher's Edition)

Section Assessments,
pp. 11, 16

Day 2
Section 3, pp. 17–21

 COOPERATIVE ACTIVITY
Researching Pyramids and
Temple Mounds, p. 20
(Teacher's Edition)

Section Assessment, p. 21

Chapter Assessment,
pp. 22–23

Yearly Pacing *Chapter 1 Total:* 2 days *Yearly Total:* 85 days

 Planning for Block Schedules

Customizing for Special Needs

Students Acquiring English

 Access for Students Acquiring English
• **Guided Reading** for Sections 1–3 (Spanish), pp. 14–16
• **Chapter Summary** (Spanish), pp. 11–13
• **Skillbuilder Practice** Interpreting Maps (Spanish), p. 17
• **Geography Application** Catal Huyuk (Spanish), pp. 18–19

 Chapter Summaries on Audiocassette in English and Spanish

 INTERNET RESOURCES
www.mlworldhistory.com
The Diverse Classroom.

Less Proficient Readers

 In-Depth Resources: Unit 1
• **Guided Reading** for Sections 1–3, pp. 1–3
• **Skillbuilder Practice** Interpreting Maps, p. 4
• **Geography Application** Catal Huyuk, p. 5

 Telescoping the Times
• Chapter Summary, pp. 1–3

 Chapter Summaries on Audiocassette

Gifted and Talented Students

 In-Depth Resources: Unit 1
Primary Sources:
• from *Lucy: the Beginnings of Humankind*, p. 7
• Lascaux Cave Painting, p. 9
• "Window on the Stone Age," p. 15

History Maker:
• The Iceman, p. 15

Connections to Literature READINGS FOR STUDENTS

 In-Depth Resources: Unit 1
• from *The Clan of the Cave Bear* by Jean M. Auel, p. 11

Enrichment Reading
• **Golding, William**
The Inheritors
New York: Harcourt, 1995

In an unnamed land, a family of Neanderthal characters encounter members of the new Homo Sapien race.

• **Kurtén, Björn**
Dance of the Tiger: A Novel of the Ice Age
New York: Pantheon, 1980

Tiger, son of the chief of a peaceful village of Homo Sapiens survives a savage attack and is rescued by a Neanderthal clan. In this action-filled story, a leading scholar of the Ice Age offers an answer to the puzzling mystery of why Neanderthals disappeared from the face of the earth.

 = Pupil's Edition   = Overhead Transparency   = Software   = Video

= Copy Master   = CD-ROM   = Audiocassette   = Internet

The Peopling of the World, Prehistory— 2500 b.c.

Predicting and Making Inferences

- Have students read the caption accompanying each picture. Then ask them how they think the life of a prehistoric hunter differed from that of a citizen of Ur.

- Ask students how they think the chapter will explain the change from the hunter's way of life to the city dweller's.

Recognizing Sequences

- Point out to students that the pictures and captions on this spread represent stages in human development. Ask students to create a time line showing the order in which these stages occurred.

Geography Connection

Ask students what the colored areas on the map represent.

- What do these areas have in common?

- Why might the first civilizations have developed there?

CHAPTER
1

The Peopling of the World, Prehistory—2500 B.C.

PREVIEWING THEMES

Interaction with Environment

As early humans spread out over the world, they adapted to each environment they encountered. They learned to fashion tools, to master fire, and to make clothing from animal skins. As time progressed, they learned to harness natural resources.

Science and Technology

Even the earliest prehistoric peoples came up with new ideas, tools, and inventions to solve problems of survival. As people began to live in settlements, they continued to develop new technology to control the environment.

Economics

Early humans hunted animals and gathered wild plant foods. Then about 10,000 years ago, they learned to tame animals and to plant crops. Gradually, more complex economies developed. Extra food supplies freed some people to learn special crafts and to become traders.

INTERNET CONNECTION

Visit us at **www.mlworldhistory.com** to learn more about human prehistory, the development of civilization, and related topics.

PREHISTORIC WORLD TO 2500 B.C.

ATLANTIC OCEAN

Mediterranean Sea

Black Sea

Caspian Sea

Catal Huyuk

UKRAINE

Ur

Red Sea

Nile River

AFRICA

Niger River

ETHIOPIA

Bones from mammoths—gigantic woolly creatures—made unique building materials. Around **20,000 B.C.**, prehistoric hunters in the **Ukraine** used such bones to construct an elaborate hut weighing 23 tons. A pair of huge tusks formed a curved entranceway.

4

GEOGRAPHY THEMES

Place

Ask students to look at the map and captions and locate where the earliest upright-walking creatures lived. Point out that Lucy's ancestors were tree dwellers who lived in a heavily forested region but that the region gradually changed to open grasslands with scattered forested areas. Creatures such as Lucy may have evolved into upright walkers in these grasslands. Ask students to describe how the geography of this place might have influenced the evolution of upright-walking creatures. *Possible responses: They could move from one forested area to another more easily by walking upright; standing* upright allowed them to watch for danger in the open grasslands.

Human-Environment Interaction

Ask students to look at the captions for Ur and the Ukraine. The people of these two areas interacted with their environment in specific, different ways. Ask students to explain which group affected its environment more, and how it did so. *Possible responses: The people of Ur probably affected their environment more. They mined gold and built a city; they probably farmed and may have cut down trees. The people of the Ukraine hunted mammoths and used the bones to build shelters. These practices probably had little impact on the environment.*

ADDITIONAL RESOURCES

Books for the Teacher

- Johanson, Donald C. *Ancestors: In Search of Human Origins.* New York: Villard, 1994.

- Lewin, Roger. *Bones of Contention.* New York: Simon, 1987. Disagreements among the Leakeys and other scholars about human origins.

- Smith, Bruce D. *The Emergence of Agriculture.* New York: Freeman, 1995.

Books for the Student

- Killingray, David. *The Neolithic Revolution.* San Diego: Greenhaven, 1980.

- Warburton, Lois. *Human Origins.* San Diego: Lucent, 1992.

Videos

- *The Agricultural Revolution.* Social Studies School Service, 1985. 800-421-4246.

- *The Beginning Is in the End.* Altschul Group, 1992. 800-323-9084. First civilizations, focusing on Sumer.

- *The Fire and the Stone.* Altschul Group, 1991. 800-323-9084. The role of stone tools and fire in prehistory.

Software

- *Origins of Mankind.* CD-ROM. Society for Visual Education, 1994. 800-829-1900. Travel back in time to meet our prehistoric ancestors.

ASIA

PACIFIC OCEAN

40°N

Around **2600 B.C.** in **Ur**, an ancient city located in present-day Iraq, the queen went to her grave in style. Buried in a royal tomb, she wore a magnificent gold headdress that would show her power in the next life. Her large hoop earrings were a fashion trend among Ur's wealthy women.

INDIAN OCEAN

Equator 0°

In **1974**, Donald Johanson discovered a 3.5 million-year-old fossil, nicknamed **Lucy**. He explained Lucy's claim to fame: "She is the oldest, most complete, best-preserved skeleton of any erect-walking human ancestor that has ever been found." About 47 of her 207 bones made up her reconstructed skeleton.

Tropic of Capricorn

☐ Early civilizations

0   1000 Miles
0   2000 Kilometers

N

5

HISTORY THROUGH ART

Headdress and Jewelry from Ur

The headdress and jewelry shown above include realistic gold "leaves" and beads of gold, lapis lazuli, and carnelian. They came from the Royal Cemetery of Ur, which has given the most complete picture of life in one of the world's first cities. Buried with the royal families and their jewels were the families'

guards and attendants, along with all their clothing, jewelry, and weapons; chariots and the donkeys and oxen that pulled them; elaborately decorated harps and lyres; drums, tambourines, and reed pipes; and even board games.

Interpreting the Art Ask students what they think such artifacts might show about the people of Ur.

Possible responses: People believed in life after death (everything a royal family might need in an afterlife was buried with them); some people attained great wealth and ruled over others; people had developed high technical skill as artisans; people made music and played games; people had learned to domesticate animals and use them for transportation.

This Interact with History feature motivates students by inviting them to put themselves in a key historical situation—the discovery of prehistoric tools. As students imagine themselves handling these tools, they will analyze the issues, explore their options, and become decision-makers.

Purpose
- To set the stage for studying early human development
- To help students understand early humans' need to survive and how they met that need

Teaching Strategy
Thinking Critically After students have imagined themselves in the situation described on this page, have them answer the key questions and give reasons for their decisions.

EXAMINING *the* ISSUES

Following are suggestions for addressing each bulleted question.

1 Ask students what they would need to do to survive in the wild. *Possible responses: Build a shelter; hunt for food.*

2 Ask students what tools they use often. What do the tools help them do? *Possible responses: a needle to sew clothing, a knife to cut meat.*

3 What toolmaking materials would probably be most readily available in the wild? *Possible responses: stones and plants.*

4 Ask students to list tools found in their homes. Which of these tools might prehistoric people have found useful? *The list might include shovels, hatchets, knives, needles, scissors, screwdrivers, and can openers. Prehistoric people would probably have found all but the last two useful.*

Making Connections Ask students to discuss how the needs met by modern tools and inventions resemble and differ from those met by early tools.

Interact *with* History

You have joined a team of scientists on an expedition to an ancient site where early humans once lived. The scientists' goal is to search for evidence that might unlock the mysteries of the past.

You're an eyewitness to their astounding discovery—human-made tools around 5,000 years old.

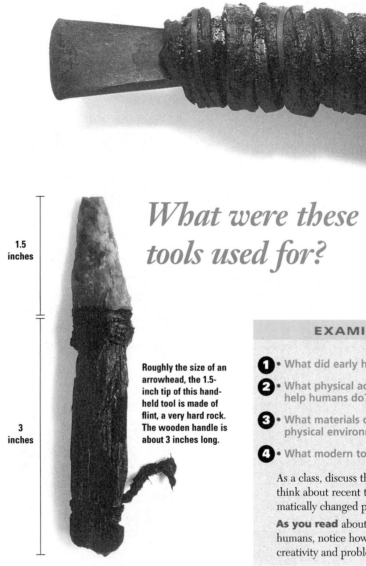

This small sharp-tipped tool is made of bone.

X-rays indicate that the wedge-shaped blade of this tool is made of copper. Birch tar, a gummy substance from the bark of a tree, binds the blade to a 2-foot-long wooden handle partially wrapped with strips of animal hide.

What were these tools used for?

1.5 inches

3 inches

Roughly the size of an arrowhead, the 1.5-inch tip of this hand-held tool is made of flint, a very hard rock. The wooden handle is about 3 inches long.

EXAMINING *the* ISSUES

1 • What did early humans need to do to survive?

2 • What physical actions would these tools help humans do?

3 • What materials did early humans use from their physical environment to make these tools?

4 • What modern tools do these early tools resemble?

As a class, discuss these questions. In your discussion, think about recent tools and inventions that have dramatically changed people's daily lives.

As you read about the ancestors of present-day humans, notice how early toolmakers applied their creativity and problem-solving skills.

Follow-Up
A feature of the chapter assessment will ask students to reevaluate their responses to the situation presented on this page.

Human Origins in Africa

MAIN IDEA

Fossil evidence shows that the earliest humans originated in Africa.

WHY IT MATTERS NOW

Early humans' discoveries helped them survive, grow in numbers, and spread across the globe.

SETTING THE STAGE What were the earliest humans like? Many people have asked themselves this question. Because there are no written records of prehistoric peoples, scientists have to piece together information about the past. Teams of scientists use a variety of research methods and techniques to learn more about how, where, and when early humans developed. Interestingly, recent discoveries provide the most knowledge about human origins and the way prehistoric people lived. Yet the picture of prehistory is still far from complete.

Scientists Search for Human Origins

Written documents provide a window to the distant past. For several thousand years, people have recorded information about their beliefs, activities, and important events. Prehistory, however, dates back to the time before the invention of writing—roughly 5,000 years ago. Without access to written records, scientists investigating the lives of prehistoric peoples face special challenges.

Scientists Discover Clues Specially trained scientists work like detectives to uncover the story of prehistoric peoples. Archaeologists are scientists who learn about early people by excavating and studying the traces of early settlements. An excavated site, called an archaeological dig, provides one of the richest sources of clues to the prehistoric way of life. Archaeologists sift through the dirt in a small plot of land. They analyze all existing evidence, such as bones and artifacts. Bones might reveal what the people looked like, how tall they were, and how long they lived. **Artifacts** are remains, such as tools, jewelry, and other human-made objects. These items might hint at how people dressed, what work they did, or how they worshiped.

Scientists called anthropologists study **culture,** or people's unique way of life. Anthropologists examine the artifacts at archaeological digs. From these, they re-create a picture of early people's cultural behavior, including customs, family life, and social relationships.

Other scientists, called paleontologists, study fossils—evidence of early life preserved in rocks. Human fossils often consist of small fragments of teeth, skulls, or other bones. Paleontologists use complex techniques to date ancient fossil remains and rocks. Archaeologists, anthropologists, paleontologists, and other scientists work as a team to make new discoveries about how prehistoric people lived.

Mary Leakey Finds Footprints In the mid-1970s, Mary Leakey, an archaeologist, led a scientific expedition to the region of Laetoli in Tanzania, an East African nation. There she and her team looked for new clues about human origins. In 1978, they made an amazing discovery. They found prehistoric footprints that resembled those of modern humans. These footprints were made by humanlike beings now called australopithecines (aw·STRAY·loh·PIHTH·ih·SYNZ). Humans and other creatures that walk

Vocabulary
excavating: uncovering by digging

THINK THROUGH HISTORY
A. Making Inferences Why are scientists who study prehistory so important in providing knowledge about the distant past?
A. Possible Answer Using various research methods, they analyze clues that help explain what life was like before written records.

This artifact from around 200,000 B.C. is a hand ax made of flint. An all-purpose tool, the hand ax was probably a hunting weapon, chopper, scraper, and slicer.

SECTION 1 RESOURCES

PRINT RESOURCES

IN-DEPTH RESOURCES: UNIT 1
Guided Reading, p. 1
Skillbuilder Practice: Interpreting Maps, p. 4
Primary Source: from *Lucy: the Beginnings of Humankind,* p. 7
Literature: from *The Clan of the Cave Bear,* p. 11

ACCESS FOR STUDENTS ACQUIRING ENGLISH
Guided Reading (Spanish), p. 14
Skillbuilder Practice (Spanish), p. 17

FORMAL ASSESSMENT
Section Quiz, p. 5

ALTERNATIVE ASSESSMENT BOOK

TECHNOLOGY RESOURCES

CD-ROM
Electronic Library of Primary Sources

INTERNET www.mlworldhistory.com

Hominid Development

Interpreting the Time Line Ask students to carefully compare the hominid skulls and describe the major differences between the skull shape of the australopithecine and that of the Cro-Magnon. *Cro-Magnon has a larger brain case, a flatter face, a more prominent chin, and a less prominent brow ridge.*

Extension Activity Ask students to examine the facts about each hominid. Have them write a statement explaining what important physical change seems to relate to a change in abilities. *Increased brain capacity leads to more-complex abilities.*

HISTORY MAKERS
Mary Leakey

Mary Leakey is best known for discovering the footprints at Laetoli, but she made other major finds. In the 1930s, in the Olduvai Gorge of East Africa, she and Louis Leakey found the oldest group of stone tools then known. These remains led the Leakeys to identify the hominid fossil they found nearby as *Homo habilis.* Ask students to find out more about these tools and present their findings to the class.

OBJECTIVE 2 INSTRUCT

Progress During the Old Stone Age

Key Ideas
- During the Paleolithic Age, people learn to make tools, use fire, and use language.
- The hominid *Homo habilis* appears about 2.5 million years ago in Africa and may be the first to make stone tools.
- A more intelligent hominid, *Homo erectus,* becomes the first to use fire and to migrate from Africa.

Hominid Development

Australopithecines
- 4 million to 1 million B.C.
- found in southern and eastern Africa
- brain size 500 cm³ (cubic centimeters)
- first humanlike creature to walk upright

Homo habilis
- 2.5 million to 1.5 million B.C.
- found in East Africa
- brain size 700 cm³
- first to make stone tools

4 million years ago	3 million years ago
Australopithecines	Homo habilis

HISTORY MAKERS

Mary Leakey
1913–1996

Born in London, England, Mary Leakey left a remarkable legacy in the fields of archaeology and anthropology. "She was one of the world's great originals," said a scientist who worked with the Leakey family on fossil hunts. Mary earned respect for her excavations and well-documented findings.

At 22, she made her first visit to East Africa. In her autobiography she reflected on her experiences there:

"I am lucky enough to have been involved for half a century with work, mostly in East Africa, that very much belongs to everyone, since it concerns the human origins that are common to the whole human race."

upright, such as australopithecines, are called **hominids.** The Laetoli footprints provided striking evidence about the origins of humans:

A VOICE FROM THE PAST
What do these footprints tell us? First, . . . that at least 3,600,000 years ago, what I believe to be man's direct ancestor walked fully upright with a . . . free-striding gait. Second, that the form of the foot was exactly the same as ours. . . . [The footprints produced] a kind of poignant time wrench. At one point, . . . she [the female hominid] stops, pauses, turns to the left to glance at some possible threat or irregularity, and then continues to the north. This motion, so intensely human, transcends time. . . .

MARY LEAKEY, quoted in *National Geographic*

Johanson Discovers "Lucy" While Mary Leakey was working in East Africa, American anthropologist Donald Johanson and his team were also searching for fossils. They were exploring sites in Ethiopia, 1,000 miles to the north. In 1974, Johanson's team made a remarkable find—an unusually complete skeleton of an adult female hominid. They nicknamed her "Lucy" after the Beatles song "Lucy in the Sky with Diamonds." She had lived around 3.5 million years ago—the oldest hominid found to date.

Hominids in Motion Lucy and the hominids who left their footprints in East Africa were species of australopithecines. Walking upright helped them travel distances more easily. They were also able to spot threatening animals and carry food and children.

These early hominids had already developed the opposable thumb. This means that the tip of the thumb can cross the palm of the hand. The opposable thumb was crucial for tasks such as picking up small objects and making tools. (To see its importance, try picking up a coin with just the index and middle fingers. Imagine all the other things that cannot be done without the opposable thumb.)

THINK THROUGH HISTORY
B. Drawing Conclusions
Why were the discoveries of hominid footprints and "Lucy" important?
B. Possible Answer
Provided clues about human prehistory and evidence that earliest hominids may have lived in Africa.

Progress During the Old Stone Age

The invention of tools, mastery over fire, and the development of language are some of the most impressive achievements in human history. These occurred during the prehistoric period known as the Stone Age. It spanned an enormous length of time. The earlier and longer part of the Stone Age, called the Old Stone Age or **Paleolithic Age,** lasted from about 2.5 million to 8000 B.C. The oldest stone chopping tools date back to this era. The New Stone Age, or **Neolithic Age,** began about 8000 B.C. and ended as early as 3000 B.C. in some areas. People who lived during this second phase of the Stone Age learned to polish stone tools, make pottery, grow crops, and raise animals.

Much of the Paleolithic Age occurred during the period in the earth's history known as the Ice Age. During this time, glaciers alternately advanced and retreated as many as 18 times. The last of these ice ages ended about 10,000 years ago. By the beginning of the Neolithic Age, glaciers had retreated to roughly the same area they now occupy.

Vocabulary
glaciers: huge masses of slowly moving ice

8 Chapter 1

CONNECTIONS ACROSS THE CURRICULUM

Science Scientists use various methods to determine the age of prehistoric remains. One way of dating organic remains (including material from dead animals and plants) is radiocarbon dating. Every living thing absorbs a small amount of radioactive carbon (C-14). When it dies, it stops absorbing C-14, and what was absorbed begins to decay. By measuring how much C-14 in organic remains has decayed compared with the C-14 present in air, scientists can learn when the animal or plant died. For dating remains more than 35,000 years old, scientists must measure the rate of decay of chemical elements other than carbon.

EXPLORING PRIMARY SOURCES

A Voice from the Past Mary Leakey wrote about her life and her experiences in Africa in her autobiography, *Disclosing the Past.* Encourage students to read all or part of the book and bring excerpts to class. Have students read aloud several passages and discuss them in class as time permits.

Homo erectus
- 1.6 million to 30,000 B.C.
- found in Africa, Asia, and Europe
- brain size 1,000 cm^3

Neanderthal
- 200,000 to 30,000 B.C.
- found in Europe and Southwest Asia
- brain size 1,450 cm^3
- first to have ritual burials

Cro-Magnon
- 40,000 to 8000 B.C.
- found in Europe
- brain size 1,400 cm^3
- fully modern humans
- created art

million years ago

Homo erectus

1 million years ago

Present

Neanderthal

Cro-Magnon

Homo Habilis: The First Toolmaker? Before the australopithecines eventually vanished, new hominids appeared in East Africa around 2.5 million years ago. In 1960, Mary Leakey and her husband, Louis, discovered a hominid fossil at Olduvai (OHL-duh-VY) Gorge in northern Tanzania. The Leakeys named the fossil *Homo habilis,* which means "man of skill." Scientists jokingly called this hominid "Handy Man." The Leakeys and other researchers found tools made of lava rock. They believed *Homo habilis* used these tools to cut meat and crack open bones. Modern archaeologists have shown that these stone blades could butcher elephant meat.

Homo Erectus Is More Intelligent About 1.6 million years ago, before *Homo habilis* left the scene, another species of hominids appeared in East Africa. This species is now known as *Homo erectus,* or "upright man." Some anthropologists believe *Homo erectus* was a more intelligent and adaptable species than *Homo habilis. Homo erectus* people used intelligence to develop **technology**—ways of applying knowledge, tools, and inventions to meet their needs. Tools made the task of survival easier. These hominids gradually became skillful hunters and invented more sophisticated tools for digging, scraping, and cutting. They also eventually became the first hominids to migrate, or to move, from Africa. Fossils and stone tools show that bands of *Homo erectus* hunters settled in India, China, Southeast Asia, and Europe.

According to anthropologists, *Homo erectus* was the first to use fire. Fire provided warmth in cold climates, cooked food, and frightened away attacking animals. A band of hunters may have carried torches to drive herds of animals into marshes in order to slaughter them. The control of fire also probably helped *Homo erectus* settle new lands.

Homo erectus might also have developed the beginnings of spoken language. Language, like technology, probably gave *Homo erectus* greater control over the environment and boosted chances for survival. The teamwork needed to plan hunts and cooperate in other tasks probably relied on language. *Homo erectus* might have named objects, places, animals, and plants and exchanged ideas.

The Dawn of Modern Humans

Many scientists believe *Homo erectus* eventually developed into **Homo sapiens**—the species name for modern humans. *Homo sapiens* means "wise men." While they physically resembled *Homo erectus, Homo sapiens* had much larger brains. Scientists have traditionally classified Neanderthals and Cro-Magnons as early groups of *Homo sapiens.* However, in 1997, DNA tests on a Neanderthal skeleton indicated that Neanderthals were not ancestors of modern humans. They were, however, affected by the arrival of Cro-Magnons, who may have competed with Neanderthals for land and food.

Neanderthals' Way of Life In 1856, as quarry workers were digging for limestone in the Neander Valley in Germany, they spotted fossilized bone fragments. These were the remains of Neanderthals, whose bones were discovered elsewhere in

CONNECT *to* TODAY

Cheddar Man

In 1997, scientists at Oxford University tested samples of DNA from a Stone Age skeleton nicknamed "Cheddar Man." This young hunter from around 7150 B.C. was found buried in the Cheddar Caves in England.

Scientists then compared the skeleton's samples to samples from people whose families had lived in the area for generations. The results of the genetic tests surprised Adrian Targett, a 42-year-old history teacher who participated in the study. He discovered that Cheddar Man was his ancient relative. Cheddar Man's and Targett's DNA were nearly identical. Scientists believe that the DNA match also proves that Britain's native population is descended from Stone Age humans.

The Peopling of the World **9**

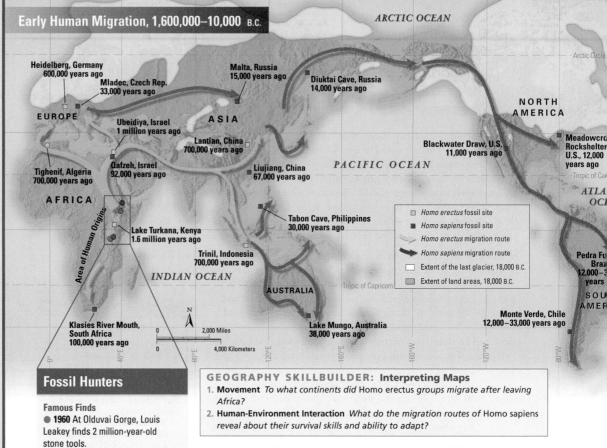

Early Human Migration, 1,600,000–10,000 B.C.

Heidelberg, Germany 600,000 years ago
Mladec, Czech Rep. 33,000 years ago
Malta, Russia 15,000 years ago
Diuktai Cave, Russia 14,000 years ago
EUROPE
Ubeidiya, Israel 1 million years ago
ASIA
Lantian, China 700,000 years ago
Tighenif, Algeria 700,000 years ago
Qafzeh, Israel 92,000 years ago
Liujiang, China 67,000 years ago
AFRICA
Lake Turkana, Kenya 1.6 million years ago
Area of Human Origins
Trinil, Indonesia 700,000 years ago
Tabon Cave, Philippines 30,000 years ago
INDIAN OCEAN
AUSTRALIA
PACIFIC OCEAN
ARCTIC OCEAN
NORTH AMERICA
Blackwater Draw, U.S. 11,000 years ago
Meadowcroft Rockshelter U.S., 12,000 years ago
Pedra Furada Brazil 12,000–33,000 years ago
Klasies River Mouth, South Africa 100,000 years ago
Lake Mungo, Australia 38,000 years ago
Monte Verde, Chile 12,000–33,000 years ago

☐ *Homo erectus* fossil site
■ *Homo sapiens* fossil site
Homo erectus migration route
Homo sapiens migration route
☐ Extent of the last glacier, 18,000 B.C.
▨ Extent of land areas, 18,000 B.C.

0 ___ 2,000 Miles
0 ___ 4,000 Kilometers

Fossil Hunters

Famous Finds

● **1960** At Olduvai Gorge, Louis Leakey finds 2 million-year-old stone tools.

● **1974** In Ethiopia, Donald Johanson finds "Lucy," a 3.5 million-year-old hominid skeleton.

● **1978** At Laetoli, Mary Leakey finds 3.6-million-year-old hominid footprints.

● **1994** In Ethiopia, an international team of scientists finds 2.33 million-year-old hominid jaw.

GEOGRAPHY SKILLBUILDER: Interpreting Maps
1. **Movement** *To what continents did* Homo erectus *groups migrate after leaving Africa?*
2. **Human-Environment Interaction** *What do the migration routes of* Homo sapiens *reveal about their survival skills and ability to adapt?*

Europe and Southwest Asia. These people were powerfully built. They had heavy slanted brows, well-developed muscles, and thick bones. To many people, the name "Neanderthal" calls up the comic-strip image of a club-carrying caveman. However, archaeological discoveries reveal a more realistic picture of these early hominids, who lived between 200,000 and 30,000 years ago.

Evidence suggests that Neanderthals tried to explain and control their world. They developed religious beliefs and performed rituals. About 60,000 years ago, Neanderthals held a funeral for a man in Shanidar Cave, located in northeastern Iraq. Archaeologists theorize that during the funeral, the Neanderthal's family covered his body with flowers. The prehistoric funeral points to a belief in a world beyond the grave. Fossil hunter Richard Leakey, the son of Mary and Louis Leakey, wrote about the meaning of this Neanderthal burial:

> **A VOICE FROM THE PAST**
> The Shanidar events . . . speak clearly of a deep feeling for the spiritual quality of life. A concern for the fate of the human soul is universal in human societies today, and it was evidently a theme of Neanderthal society too. There is also reason to believe that the Neanderthals cared for the old and the sick of their group. A number of individuals buried at the Shanidar Cave, for instance, showed signs of injury during life, and in one case a man was severely crippled. . . . These people lived for a long time, although they needed constant support and care to do so.
> **RICHARD E. LEAKEY,** *The Making of Mankind*

10 Chapter 1

Neanderthals were also resourceful. They survived harsh Ice Age winters by living in caves or temporary shelters made of wood and animal skins. Animal bones found with fossils of Neanderthals indicate their ability to hunt in subarctic regions of Europe. To cut up and skin their prey, Neanderthals fashioned stone blades, scrapers, and other tools.

The Neanderthals survived for some 170,000 years and then vanished about 30,000 years ago. Their disappearance remains a mystery.

Cro-Magnons Emerge About 40,000 years ago, a group of prehistoric humans called Cro-Magnons appeared. Their skeletal remains show that they are identical to modern humans.

Unlike the Neanderthals, Cro-Magnons planned their hunts. They studied animals' habits and stalked their prey. Evidently, Cro-Magnons' superior hunting strategies allowed them to survive more easily. This may have caused Cro-Magnon populations to grow at a slightly faster rate and eventually replace the Neanderthals. Cro-Magnons' advanced skill in spoken language may also have helped them to plan more difficult projects. This cooperation perhaps gave them an edge over the Neanderthals.

Recent Findings Add New Knowledge The story of human origins is constantly changing with new discoveries. Reports of such findings continue to update when and where various species of hominids are believed to have originated. In 1994, two fossil hunters in Ethiopia found a 2.33 million-year-old jaw. It was the oldest fossil belonging to the species that includes modern humans. They also unearthed stone tools at the same site. This find suggests that the first toolmakers emerged earlier than previously thought.

In 1996, a team of researchers from Canada and the United States, including a high school student from New York, dated a Neanderthal bone flute. They believe it is between 43,000 and 82,000 years old. This discovery hints at a previously unknown talent of the Neanderthals—their gift of musical expression.

Each new scientific discovery helps add further details to the still sketchy picture of human prehistory. As time progressed, early humans' skills and tools for surviving and adapting to their environment became more sophisticated. These technological advances would help launch a revolution in the way people lived.

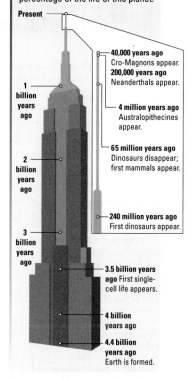

SPOTLIGHT ON

Time Line of Planet Earth
Imagine the 102 stories of the Empire State Building as a scale for a time line of the earth's history. Each story represents about 40 million years. Modern human beings have existed for just a tiny percentage of the life of this planet.

Present

1 billion years ago

2 billion years ago

3 billion years ago

40,000 years ago Cro-Magnons appear.
200,000 years ago Neanderthals appear.

4 million years ago Australopithecines appear.

65 million years ago Dinosaurs disappear; first mammals appear.

240 million years ago First dinosaurs appear.

3.5 billion years ago First single-cell life appears.

4 billion years ago

4.4 billion years ago Earth is formed.

Section 1 Assessment

1. TERMS & NAMES

Identify
- artifact
- culture
- hominid
- Paleolithic Age
- Neolithic Age
- technology
- *Homo sapiens*

2. TAKING NOTES

Create a chart like the one below, showing the advances, discoveries, and inventions of hominids.

Australo-pithecines	*Homo erectus*	Nean-derthals	Cro-Magnons

3. SYNTHESIZING

How do recent findings keep revising knowledge of the prehistoric past?

THINK ABOUT
- modern scientific methods
- the way various species of hominids are classified
- dates relating to hominids

4. ANALYZING THEMES

Interaction with Environment Which of the following skills—toolmaking, the use of fire, or the development of language—do you think gave hominids the most control over their environment? Why?

THINK ABOUT
- the kinds of tools early humans developed
- the various uses of fire
- the benefits of language

The Peopling of the World **11**

Section 2 Overview

OBJECTIVES

1. To describe technological and artistic achievements of the Paleolithic Age.

2. To define and describe the Neolithic Revolution.

3. To give examples of the growth of farming villages.

SKILLBUILDERS

- Interpreting Charts, p. 14
- Interpreting Maps: location, place, p. 15

CRITICAL THINKING

- Making inferences, pp. 12 and 15
- Evaluating, p. 16
- Hypothesizing, p. 16

FOCUS
5-Minute Warm-Up

▶ **Perceiving Effects**
To help students understand the importance of agriculture, have them answer these questions.

1. Before agriculture developed, how did people get food?

2. Read A Voice from the Past on page 15. What new tools did farming encourage people to develop?

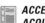 **WARM-UP TRANSPARENCY 1**

OBJECTIVE ① INSTRUCT

Achievements in Technology and Art

▶ **Key Ideas**
- Paleolithic hunter-gatherers develop sophisticated tool kits.
- Stone Age artists create paintings and engravings and carve decorative objects.

IN-DEPTH RESOURCES: UNIT 1
Guided Reading, p. 2

ACCESS FOR STUDENTS ACQUIRING ENGLISH
Guided Reading (Spanish), p. 15

---

2 Humans Try to Control Nature

TERMS & NAMES
- nomad
- hunter-gatherer
- Neolithic Revolution
- slash-and-burn farming
- domestication

MAIN IDEA
The development of agriculture spurred an increase in population and the growth of a settled way of life.

WHY IT MATTERS NOW
New methods for obtaining food and the development of technology laid the foundations for modern civilizations.

SETTING THE STAGE By about 40,000 years ago, human beings had become fully modern in their physical appearance. With a shave, a haircut, and a suit, a Cro-Magnon man would have looked like a businessman. However, over the following thousands of years, the human way of life underwent incredible changes. People developed new technology, artistic skills, and most importantly, agriculture.

Achievements in Technology and Art

Early modern humans quickly distinguished themselves from their ancestors, who had devoted most of their time to the task of survival. As inventors and artists, more advanced humans stepped up the pace of cultural changes.

A New Tool Kit For thousands of years, men and women of the Old Stone Age were nomads. **Nomads** wander from place to place, rather than making permanent settlements. These highly mobile people were always searching for new sources of food. Nomadic groups whose food supply depends on hunting animals and collecting plant foods are called **hunter-gatherers.** Prehistoric hunter-gatherers, such as roving bands of Cro-Magnons, increased their food supply by inventing tools. For example, hunters crafted special spears that enabled them to kill game at greater distances. Digging sticks helped food gatherers pry plants loose at the roots.

Early modern humans had launched a technological revolution. They skillfully used stone, bone, and wood to fashion more than 100 different tools. These expanded tool kits included knives to kill and butcher game and fish hooks and harpoons to catch fish. A chisel-like cutter was designed to make other tools. Cro-Magnons used bone needles to sew clothing made of animal hides.

Paleolithic Art The tools of early modern humans explain how they met their survival needs. Yet their world best springs to life through their artistic creations. Necklaces of seashells, lion teeth, and bear claws adorned both men and women. People ground mammoth tusks into polished beads. They also carved small realistic sculptures of animals that inhabited their world.

The best-known Stone Age works of art are the paintings on the walls and ceilings of European caves, mainly in France and Spain. Here early artists drew lifelike images of wild animals. Cave artists made colored paints from charcoal, mud, and animal blood. In Africa, early artists engraved pictures on rocks or painted scenes in caves or rock shelters. In Australia, they created paintings on large rocks.

THINK THROUGH HISTORY
A. Making Inferences How did Cro-Magnons' new tool kit make the task of survival easier?
A. Possible Answer Improved hunting-and-gathering tools helped Cro-Magnons increase their food supply.

SPOTLIGHT ON

The Iceman's Tool Kit
In 1991, a German couple made an accidental discovery. It gave archaeologists a firsthand look at the technology of early toolmakers. Near the border of Austria and Italy, the two hikers spotted the mummified body of a prehistoric traveler, preserved in ice for some 5,000 years.

Nicknamed the "Iceman," this early human was not empty-handed. The tool kit found with him included a six-foot longbow and a deerskin case with 14 arrows. It also contained a stick with an antler tip for sharpening flint blades, a small flint dagger in a woven sheath, and a copper ax. Unfortunately, officials damaged both Iceman's belongings and his body as they tried to remove him from the ice.

12 Chapter 1

SECTION 2 RESOURCES

PRINT RESOURCES

 IN-DEPTH RESOURCES: UNIT 1
Guided Reading, p. 2
Geography Application: Catal Huyuk, p. 5
Primary Sources: Cave Painting, p. 9; " Stone Age," p. 10
History Maker: The Iceman, p. 15

ACCESS FOR STUDENTS ACQUIRING ENGLISH
Guided Reading (Spanish), p. 15
Geography Application (Spanish), pp. 18–19

FORMAL ASSESSMENT
Section Quiz, p. 6

TECHNOLOGY RESOURCES

 WORLD ART AND CULTURES TRANSPARENCIES
AT1, French cave art

 CRITICAL THINKING TRANSPARENCIES
CT1 Patterns of Living

 CD-ROM
Electronic Library of Primary Sources

 INTERNET www.mlworldhistory.com

Cave Painting

Prehistoric paintings probably served a more meaningful role than just showing vivid scenes from daily life. They may have represented religious beliefs. Early artists may have also hoped their images had magical power that would bring hunters good luck. Perhaps some paintings acted as a kind of textbook to help young hunters identify various animals. The use of pictures to communicate information represents an important first step in the development of writing.

Algeria

Farming and herding gradually replaced hunting as a means of getting food. This African cave painting from Algeria shows women and children tending cattle. The white rings—symbols for huts—illustrate an early version of signs used in writing.

France

Stampeding wild horses and bison seem to come alive in this prehistoric painting below from Lascaux Cave in France. After viewing such striking scenes, the world-famous, 20th-century artist Picasso reportedly said, "We have learned nothing."

Australia

This rock painting from Australia features two humanlike figures holding up their hands. Early artists used stencils to create these outstretched hands, which commonly appear in Australian rock art.

Connect to History

Comparing What do you think is the purpose of each of these paintings?

 SEE SKILLBUILDER HANDBOOK, PAGE 996.

Connect to Today

Analyzing Motives Prehistoric artists painted images on the walls of caves. What motives do you think compel today's artists to paint murals on the walls of city buildings?

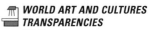 **INTERNET CONNECTION**

Visit us at **www.mlworldhistory.com** to learn more about cave and rock paintings.

 SPOTLIGHT ON
The Iceman's Tool Kit

Students can find out more about the Iceman—what he was doing alone in the Alps, how he died, what kinds of tools he carried—by researching using the keyword *Iceman*. A full-color layout about the Iceman appears in the June 1993 issue of *National Geographic*.

IN-DEPTH RESOURCES: UNIT 1
History Maker: The Iceman, p. 15

ELECTRONIC LIBRARY OF PRIMARY SOURCES
from "Iceman"

MORE ABOUT . . .
African Art

Many of the rock paintings in Algeria were completed in prehistoric times, when large animals, such as the elephants, rhinoceroses, and giraffes depicted in some of the paintings, roamed what is now the Sahara. The region was much wetter then than it is today. It was covered with lakes, streams, forests, and grasslands, which enabled such animals to thrive there.

MORE ABOUT . . .
Cave Painting

Prehistoric artists made their paint from natural sources. They used three basic colors—yellow, black, and red—which they obtained from clay, charcoal, and minerals such as iron. The artists often chose natural swellings or protrusions on the cave walls on which to paint animals, giving the pictures a three-dimensional effect.

WORLD ART AND CULTURES TRANSPARENCIES
AT1 French cave art

 INTERNET
Click *World History* at
www.mlworldhistory.com

Connect to History

Comparing
Possible Responses: Algeria— to record people's lives; to magically increase the herds; Australia—to represent religious beliefs or rituals; to represent a magical act; France— to bring hunters good luck; to help young hunters identify specific animals; to represent religious beliefs.

Connect to Today

Analyzing Motives
Murals are often painted on the walls of inner cities. Students may respond that modern murals are painted to beautify the neighborhood, to make a statement about the lives of people in the inner city, or to inspire the residents of the city.

The Neolithic Revolution

▶ Key Ideas

- A warming climate and a growing population help lead to the Neolithic Revolution.
- Early farmers practice slash-and-burn farming and begin to domesticate animals.
- Environmental conditions near the Zagros Mountains of Iraq spur development of one of the earliest farming settlements.

🏛 CRITICAL THINKING TRANSPARENCIES
CT1 Patterns of Living: Paleolithic Period to the Neolithic Revolution

---

History from Visuals

Agricultural Revolution

Interpreting the Graphs Have students compare the vertical and horizontal axes of the graphs and notice that each graph displays different information about the same time span. Then ask students what correlation exists between the graphs. *The increase in population correlates with a rise in average temperature.*

Extension Activity The change from hunting and gathering to agriculture provided a steady supply of food—but at a cost. Have students research the hardships farmers had to face that hunter-gatherers did not. *Possible response: Farmers had to work hard to plant, tend, harvest, and protect their crops. As agriculture expanded and groups of people grew, diseases spread more easily.*

SKILLBUILDER Answers
1. It began when average temperature rose above 55° F.
2. Population rose sharply because of increased food supply.

The Neolithic Revolution

For thousands upon thousands of years, humans survived by hunting game and gathering edible plants. They lived in bands of no more than two dozen to three dozen people. The men almost certainly did the hunting. The women gathered fruits, berries, roots, and grasses. Then about 10,000 years ago, some of the women may have scattered seeds near a regular campsite. When they returned the next season, they may have found new crops growing. This discovery would usher in the **Neolithic Revolution,** or the agricultural revolution—the far-reaching changes in human life resulting from the beginnings of farming. The shift from food-gathering to food-producing culture represents one of the great breakthroughs in history.

Causes of the Agricultural Revolution Scientists do not know exactly why the agricultural revolution occurred during this period. Change in climate was probably a key factor. Rising temperatures worldwide provided longer growing seasons and drier land for cultivating wild grasses. A rich supply of grain helped support a small population boom. As populations slowly rose, hunter-gatherers felt pressure to find new food sources. Farming offered an attractive alternative. Unlike hunting, farming provided a steady source of food.

Agricultural Revolution

SKILLBUILDER: Interpreting Charts
1. *How was the agricultural revolution linked to a change in temperature?*
2. *What effect did the agricultural revolution have on population growth? Why?*

Early Farming Methods Some groups practiced **slash-and-burn farming,** in which they cut trees or grasses and burned them to clear a field. The remaining ashes fertilized the soil. Farmers planted crops for a year or two. Then they moved on to another area of land. After several years, the trees and grass grew back, and other farmers repeated the process of slashing and burning.

Domestication of Animals Food gatherers' understanding of plants probably spurred the development of farming. Meanwhile, hunters' expert knowledge of wild animals likely played a key role in the **domestication,** or the taming of animals. They tamed horses, dogs, goats, and pigs. Like farming, domestication of animals came slowly. Stone Age hunters may have driven herds of animals into rocky ravines to be slaughtered. It was then a small step to drive herds into human-made enclosures. From there, farmers could keep the animals as a constant source of food and gradually tame them.

Not only farmers domesticated animals. Pastoral nomads, or wandering herders, tended sheep, goats, camels, or other animals. These herders moved their animals to new pastures and watering places.

Revolution in Jarmo Today the eroded and barren rolling foothills of the Zagros Mountains in northeastern Iraq seem an unlikely site for the birthplace of agriculture.

14 Chapter 1

Vocabulary
edible: safe to eat

Background
The agricultural revolution caused a dramatic change in human diet. Hunter-gatherers consumed about 80 percent meat and 20 percent plant foods. The agricultural revolution reversed these percentages.

Background
Dogs were probably the first domesticated animals, serving as pets and hunting companions. The oldest discovery of human and dog fossils found together dates back to roughly 8000 B.C.

CUSTOMIZING FOR SPECIAL NEEDS

Less Proficient Readers
Understanding the Graphs
Pair a less proficient reader with a more proficient one. Ask them to work together to interpret the Agricultural Revolution graphs on this page. They might begin by discussing the elements of the horizontal and vertical axes of

each graph to make sure they agree on what the elements mean. They might then ask each other questions about the graphs—for example, What was the population of the earth 5,000 years ago? What was the average temperature 10,000 years ago? Once they have a firm grasp of each graph's content, they might then work together to answer the Skillbuilder questions.

CUSTOMIZING FOR SPECIAL NEEDS

Gifted and Talented Students
Analyzing Motives Many people
did not begin farming for thousands of years after agriculture began. Others, like some Native American groups in North and South America, never developed agriculture, even though they were acquainted with the practice. Have students work in pairs or small groups to research a group of people

that did not develop agriculture. Have students then write a brief report explaining why they think the people of this group continued as hunter-gatherers. Encourage students to look at geography, climate, availability of food sources, and other factors that might have influenced the people's decision not to farm.

Major crops

Bananas	Grapes	Sorghum	Wheat
Barley	Olives	Soybeans	
Corn	Potato	Agriculture by 5000 B.C.	
		Agriculture by 3000 B.C.	
Cotton	Rice	Agriculture by 2000 B.C.	
		Agriculture by 500 B.C.	

GEOGRAPHY SKILLBUILDER: Interpreting Maps
1. **Location** On which continent were most of the earliest agricultural sites located?
2. **Place** What geographic feature favored the development of agricultural areas before 5000 B.C.?

According to archaeologist Robert Braidwood, thousands of years ago, the environmental conditions of this region favored the development of agriculture. Wild wheat and barley, along with wild goats, pigs, sheep, and horses, had once thrived near the Zagros Mountains.

During the early 1950s, Braidwood conducted an archaeological dig at a site called Jarmo. He concluded that its residents first established this agricultural settlement about 9,000 years ago:

A VOICE FROM THE PAST
We found weights for digging sticks, hoe-like [tools], flint-sickle blades, and a wide variety of milling stones. . . . We also discovered several pits that were probably used for the storage of grain. Perhaps the most important evidence of all was animal bones and the impressions left in the mud by cereal grains. . . . The people of Jarmo were adjusting themselves to a completely new way of life, just as we are adjusting ourselves to the consequences of such things as the steam engine. What they learned about living in a revolution may be of more than academic interest to us in our troubled times.
ROBERT BRAIDWOOD, quoted in *Scientific American*

THINK THROUGH HISTORY
B. Making Inferences
What evidence discovered at Jarmo shows how farming created new technological needs?
B. Possible Answer Early farmers invented digging sticks, hoes, sickles, and other tools for clearing the land, cultivating the soil, and reaping harvests; dug pits for storing grain; used milling stones for grinding grains.

The farmers at Jarmo, and others like them in places as far apart as Mexico and Thailand, were pioneering a new way of life. Villages such as Jarmo marked the beginning of a new era and laid the foundation for modern life.

Villages Grow and Prosper

The changeover from hunting and gathering to farming and herding took place not once, but many times. Neolithic people in many parts of the world independently developed agriculture.

The Peopling of the World **15**

History from Visuals

Agriculture Emerges, 5000–500 B.C.

Interpreting the Map Point out the information in the map key. Then ask students to identify the rivers along which agriculture first developed and to name the major crop in each area. *Nile—wheat; Euphrates and Tigris—barley; Indus—rice; Huang He—soybeans.* Where else did agriculture develop before 5000 B.C.? *Tehuacán Valley in North America.*

Extension Activity Have students find out what animals were domesticated at the earliest agricultural sites. Suggest that they consult a historical atlas for the information. *Nile, Euphrates, and Tigris—cattle, sheep, goats, pigs; Huang He—pigs, dogs.*

SKILLBUILDER Answers
1. Asia.
2. A major river.

MORE ABOUT . . .
Early Agriculture

In 1968, archaeologists were excavating a 7,000-year-old farming village in the Zagros Mountains. In the kitchen of one of the mud-brick homes, they uncovered several long-necked, narrow-mouthed clay jars that they thought had probably contained milk or yogurt. The jars were filed away in a museum until 1996, when an archaeological chemist tested the liquid residue and found that it was wine—the oldest wine ever discovered.

OBJECTIVE ③ INSTRUCT

Villages Grow and Prosper

▶ *Key Ideas*
• Farming develops in many regions around the world as farmers learn to cultivate a variety of plants.

(continued on next page)

TEACHING OPTION | BLOCK SCHEDULING | **COOPERATIVE ACTIVITY: Research the Development of Agriculture** | CLASS TIME 30 MINUTES

Task: Students will investigate an early agricultural site and develop a brief report about it.

Purpose: To learn how agriculture developed.

Activity: Divide the class into groups of three to five students, and have each group choose one of the agricultural sites from the map on this page. Students should research how agriculture developed at their site and then write a brief report on (1) the geography of the area and how it influenced the development of farming, (2) the types of crops and domesticated animals first associated with the site, and (3) the people who first farmed there. Have students create visuals for their report, such as a map, pictures of artifacts, or pictures of the crops grown.

📁 **Building a Portfolio** Students may want to add their report to their portfolio.

▤ **ALTERNATIVE ASSESSMENT BOOK** Standards for Evaluating a Cooperative Activity

Standards for Evaluation
Reports should . . .

• describe the geography of the region and explain how it was suitable for farming
• demonstrate an understanding of how agriculture developed
• include appropriate visuals

(continued from page 15)

- The village of Catal Huyuk exemplifies some of the early farming villages that prospered and supported skilled workers and a varied cultural life.

 IN-DEPTH RESOURCES: UNIT 1
Geography Application: Catal Huyuk, p. 5

ASSESS & RETEACH

Section 2 Assessment
Have students work individually to answer the questions. Then have them check their answers with a partner.

 FORMAL ASSESSMENT
Section Quiz, p. 6

Reteaching Activity
CLASS TIME: 10 MINUTES

Review the graphs on page 14 and the map on page 15 to help students understand the development of agriculture.

CLOSE ACTIVITY

CLASS TIME: 15 MINUTES

Making Inferences
Ask students how they think life today would be different had agriculture never developed. Suggest that they discuss such topics as population, settlement, housing, food procurement, diet, clothing, technology, social relationships, and people's relationship to the natural world.

Farming Develops in Many Places Within a few thousand years, people in many other regions worldwide, especially in fertile river valleys, turned to farming:

- **Africa** The Nile River Valley developed into an important agricultural center for growing wheat, barley, and other crops.
- **China** About 8,000 years ago, farmers along the middle stretches of the Huang He cultivated a grain called millet. About 1,000 years later, Neolithic farmers first domesticated wild rice in the Chang Jiang River delta.
- **Mexico and Central America** Farmers cultivated corn, beans, and squash.
- **Peru** Farmers in the Central Andes were the first to grow tomatoes, sweet potatoes, and white potatoes.

From these early centers of agriculture, farming spread to surrounding regions.

These cooking utensils—a pot, a bone spatula, and a fork—are from a kitchen in Catal Huyuk. They provide a glimpse of the settled life in new agricultural communities.

Catal Huyuk The agricultural village now known as Catal Huyuk (chuh·TUL hoo·YOOK) was located on a fertile plain in south-central Turkey. The village showed the benefits of settled life. Farmers there produced large crops of wheat, barley, and peas. Villagers also raised sheep and cattle.

Many highly skilled workers, such as potters and weavers, worked in Catal Huyuk. The village was best known for its obsidian products. This dark volcanic rock looks like glass. It was used to make mirrors, jewelry, and knives for trade.

At its peak 8,000 years ago, Catal Huyuk was home to about 6,000 people. Its prosperity supported a varied cultural life. Archaeologists have uncovered colorful wall paintings depicting animals and hunting scenes. Many religious shrines were dedicated to a mother goddess. According to her worshipers, she controlled the supply of grain.

The new settled way of life also had its drawbacks. Floods, fire, drought, and other natural disasters could destroy a village. Diseases spread easily among people living close together. Jealous neighbors and roving nomadic bands might attack and loot a wealthy village like Catal Huyuk.

Despite these problems, some early villages expanded into cities that would become the setting for more complex cultures.

THINK THROUGH HISTORY
C. Evaluating
What advantages did farming and herding have over hunting and gathering?
C. Possible Answer
Steadier food supply; safer, more stable way of life; more leisure time.

Vocabulary
shrines: places where sacred relics are kept

Section ② Assessment

1. TERMS & NAMES
Identify
- nomad
- hunter-gatherer
- Neolithic Revolution
- slash-and-burn farming
- domestication

2. TAKING NOTES
Using a web diagram like the one below, show the effects of the development of agriculture.

Development of Agriculture

Choose one effect and write a paragraph about it.

3. HYPOTHESIZING
Why do you think the development of agriculture occurred around the same time in several different places?

THINK ABOUT
- the migrations of early peoples
- changes in the earth's climate
- a rise in human population

4. THEME ACTIVITY
Science and Technology
Create a chart explaining new tools, utensils, and other artifacts that archaeologists would likely find at the site of a permanent farming settlement. Use information from the text on Jarmo and Catal Huyuk to make your list of objects.

16 Chapter 1

ANSWERS

1. TERMS & NAMES
nomad, p. 12
hunter-gatherer, p. 12
Neolithic Revolution, p. 14
slash-and-burn farming, p. 14
domestication, p. 14

2. TAKING NOTES
Possible Responses: More available food, rise in population, new farming tools, emergence of farming villages, more stable communities, more cultural developments.
Paragraphs will vary but should reflect the main ideas in the text.

3. HYPOTHESIZING
Possible Responses: Global warming trends resulted in longer growing seasons; a rich supply of grain helped support a population boom. A rise in population placed pressure on hunter-gatherers, who had migrated throughout the world, to find new sources of food.

4. THEME ACTIVITY
Standards for Evaluation
A chart should
- draw information for a list of artifacts from textbook paragraphs on Jarmo and Catal Huyuk
- explain the use or significance of the artifacts

TERMS & NAMES
- civilization
- specialization
- artisan
- institution
- scribe
- cuneiform
- Bronze Age
- barter
- ziggurat

❸ Civilization

PATTERNS OF CHANGE

CASE STUDY: Ur in Sumer

MAIN IDEA

Prospering agricultural villages, food surpluses, and new technology led to the rise of civilizations.

WHY IT MATTERS NOW

Contemporary civilizations share the same characteristics typical of ancient civilizations.

SETTING THE STAGE Agriculture marked a dramatic change in how people lived together. They began dwelling in larger, more organized communities, such as farming villages and towns. Gradually, from some of these permanent settlements, cities emerged, forming the backdrop of a much more complex way of life—civilization.

Villages Grow into Cities

Over the centuries, people settled in stable communities that were based on agriculture. Domesticated animals became more common. The invention of new tools—hoes, sickles, and plow sticks—made the task of farming easier. As people gradually developed the technology to control their natural environment, they reaped larger harvests. Settlements with a plentiful supply of food could support more heavily populated communities.

As the population of some early farming villages increased, social relationships became more complex. The change from a nomadic hunting-gathering way of life to settled village life took a long time. Likewise, the change from village life to city life was a gradual process that spanned several generations.

Economic Changes To cultivate more land and to produce extra crops, ancient people in larger villages built elaborate irrigation systems. The resulting food surpluses freed some villagers to pursue other jobs and to develop skills besides farming. Individuals who learned to become craftspeople created valuable new products, such as pottery, metal objects, and woven cloth. In turn, people who became traders profited from a broader range of goods to exchange—craftwork, grains, and many raw materials. Two important inventions also fostered the expanded trade between villages. The wheel and the sail enabled traders to transport more goods over longer distances.

Social Changes A more complex and prosperous economy affected the social structure of village life. For example, building and operating large irrigation systems required the cooperation and labor of many people. As other special groups of workers formed, social classes with varying wealth, power and influence began to emerge. A system of social classes would later become more clearly defined as cities grew.

Religion also became more organized. During the Old Stone Age, prehistoric

This photograph shows the well-preserved remains of Skara Brae. This small agricultural village emerged around 3000 B.C. It is located on an island off the coast of northern Scotland.

Section 3 Overview

OBJECTIVES

① To explain how agricultural villages grew into cities.

② To list the characteristics of civilization.

③ To describe how the city of Ur exemplifies early civilization.

SKILLBUILDER
- Interpreting Charts, p. 19

CRITICAL THINKING
- Drawing conclusions, p. 18
- Analyzing causes, p. 20
- Making inferences, p. 21

FOCUS
5-Minute Warm-Up

▶ *Making Inferences*
Answering these questions will help students understand a key trait of civilization.

1. Read Spotlight On The Inca's System of Record Keeping on page 18. How did the Inca use the *quipu* to help them keep records?

2. Why might the Inca have needed special officials to keep records?

 WARM-UP TRANSPARENCY 1

OBJECTIVE ① INSTRUCT

Villages Grow into Cities

▶ *Key Ideas*
- Advances in technology yield a surplus food supply, which frees some people to become specialized workers and to trade with other villages.

- The social structure of early cities becomes more complex, giving rise to social classes and organized religion.

📖 *IN-DEPTH RESOURCES: UNIT 1*
Guided Reading, p. 3
Connections Across Time and Cultures: From Ancient to Modern Communities, p. 16

📖 *ACCESS FOR STUDENTS ACQUIRING ENGLISH*
Guided Reading (Spanish), p. 16

SECTION 3 RESOURCES

PRINT RESOURCES

📖 *IN-DEPTH RESOURCES: UNIT 1*
Guided Reading, p. 3
Connections Across Time and Cultures: From Ancient to Modern Communities, p. 16

📖 *ACCESS FOR STUDENTS ACQUIRING ENGLISH*
Guided Reading (Spanish), p. 16

📖 *FORMAL ASSESSMENT*
Section Quiz, p. 7

TECHNOLOGY RESOURCES

🗺 *GEOGRAPHY TRANSPARENCIES*
GT1 Cities of the Ancient Middle East, 7000–3000 B.C.

🗺 *WORLD ART AND CULTURES TRANSPARENCIES*
AT2 Upper Sumerian artifacts

💿 **CD-ROM**
Electronic Library of Primary Sources

🌐 **INTERNET** www.mlworldhistory.com

What Is Civilization?

Key Ideas

Civilization first arises in Sumer and is marked by the following five characteristics:

- **advanced cities** that are the center of trade for a region
- **specialized occupations** made possible by a surplus food supply
- **complex institutions,** such as government, religion, and an economy
- **record-keeping systems** developed and used by professional record keepers
- **advanced technology** that makes life easier and work more efficient

SPOTLIGHT ON
The Inca's System of Record Keeping

The Incan civilization was unusual in other ways besides the way it kept records. The Inca's greatest cities grew high in the Andes Mountains, and although they had a fine system of roads, they never used the wheel for transportation. Ask students to research the Inca to find details about Incan life that illustrate the other four characteristics of civilization: advanced cities, specialized workers, complex institutions, and advanced technology.

---

peoples' religious beliefs centered around nature, animal spirits, and some idea of an afterlife. During the New Stone Age, farming peoples worshiped the many gods and goddesses who they believed had power over the rain, wind, and other forces of nature. Early city dwellers developed rituals founded on these earlier religious beliefs. As populations grew, common spiritual values became lasting religious traditions.

What Is Civilization?

Most historians believe that one of the first civilizations arose in Sumer, a region that is now part of modern Iraq. Sumer was located in Mesopotamia. Just what set the Sumerians apart from their neighbors? Most scholars define **civilization** as a complex culture with these five characteristics: (1) advanced cities, (2) specialized workers, (3) complex institutions, (4) record keeping, and (5) advanced technology.

Advanced Cities Cities were the birthplaces of the first civilizations. In fact, the word *civilization* comes from the Latin word for *city*. A city is more than a large group of people living together. The size of the population alone does not distinguish a village from a city. One of the key differences is that a city is a center of trade for a larger area. Like their modern-day counterparts, ancient city dwellers depended on trade. Farmers, merchants, and traders brought goods to market in the cities. The city dwellers themselves produced a variety of goods for exchange.

Specialized Workers As cities grew, so did the need for more specialized workers, such as traders, government officials, and priests. Food surpluses provided the opportunity for **specialization**—the development of skills in a specific kind of work. An abundant food supply allowed some people to become expert at jobs besides farming. In early civilizations, some city dwellers became **artisans**—skilled workers who make goods by hand. Specialization helped artisans develop their skill at designing jewelry, fashioning metal tools and weapons, or making pottery. The wide range of crafts that artisans produced helped cities become thriving centers of trade.

Complex Institutions The soaring populations of early cities made government, or a system of ruling, necessary. In civilizations, leaders emerged to maintain order among people and to establish laws. Government is an example of an **institution**—a long-lasting pattern of organization in a community. Complex institutions, such as government, religion, and the economy, are another characteristic of civilization.

With the growth of cities, religion became a formal institution. Most cities had great temples where dozens of priests took charge of religious duties. Sumerians believed that every city belonged to a god who lived in the temple and governed the city's activities. The temple became the hub of both government and religious affairs. It also served as the city's economic center. There food and trade items were distributed to the city's residents.

Record Keeping As government, religion, and the economy became more complex and structured, people recognized the need to keep records. In early civilizations, government officials had to document tax collections, the passage of laws, and the storage of grain. Priests needed some way to keep track of the yearly calendar and important rituals. Merchants had to record accounts of debts and payments.

Most civilizations developed a system of writing, though some devised other methods of record keeping. Around 3000 B.C., Sumerian **scribes**—or professional record keepers—invented a system of writing called **cuneiform** (KYOO·nee·uh·FAWRM), which means "wedge-shaped." (Earlier versions of Sumerian writing consisted of signs called pictographs—symbols of the objects or things

SPOTLIGHT ON
The Inca's System of Record Keeping

The empire of the ancient Inca civilization stretched along the western coast of South America. Though the Inca had no writing system, they kept records using a *quipu,* a complicated set of colored strings tied with different-sized knots at various intervals. Each knot represented a certain amount or its multiple. The colors of each cord represented the item being counted: people, animals, land, and so on.

The *quipucamayoc,* special officials who knew how to use the *quipu,* kept records of births, deaths, marriages, crops, and even important historical events.

18 CHAPTER 1

---

they represented.) The scribe's tool, called a stylus, was a sharpened reed with a wedge-shaped point. It was pressed into moist clay to create symbols. Scribes baked their clay tablets in the sun to preserve the writing.

People soon began to use writing for other purposes besides record keeping. They also wrote about their cities' dramatic events—wars, natural disasters, the reign of kings. Thus, the beginning of civilization in Sumer also signaled the beginning of written history.

Advanced Technology New tools and techniques are always needed to solve the problems that emerge when large groups of people live together. In early civilizations, some farmers began to harness the powers of animals and nature. For example, they used ox-drawn plows to turn the soil. They created elaborate irrigation systems to expand planting areas.

Artisans relied on new technology to make their tasks easier. Around 3500 B.C., Sumerian artisans first used the potter's wheel to shape jugs, plates, and bowls. Sumerian metalworkers discovered that melting together certain amounts of copper and tin made bronze. After 2500 B.C., skilled metalworkers in Sumer's cities turned out bronze spearheads by the thousands. The period called the **Bronze Age** refers to the time when people began using bronze, rather than copper and stone, to fashion tools and weapons. The Bronze Age began in Sumer around 3000 B.C., but the starting date varied in different parts of Europe and Asia.

Background
Toolmakers discovered how to combine copper with a small amount of tin to make bronze. Bronze is harder than copper.

The wedge-shaped symbols of cuneiform are visible in this close-up of a clay tablet.

PATTERNS OF CHANGE: Key Traits of Civilizations

Characteristics	Examples from Sumer			
Advanced Cities	• Uruk—population of about 10,000, which doubled in two centuries • Lagash—population of about 19,000 • Umma—population of about 16,000			
Specialized Workers	• priests • metalworkers • scribes • weavers • merchants • government officials	• soldiers • potters	• teachers • farmers	
Complex Institutions	• Formal governments with officials and laws • Priests with both religious and political power • A rigorous education system for training of scribes			
Record Keeping	• Cuneiform tablets—records of business transactions, historical events, customs, and traditions			
Advanced Technology	By around 3000 B.C.: • The wheel, the plow, and the sailboat probably in daily use • Bronze weapons and body armor that gave Sumerians a military advantage over their enemies			

SKILLBUILDER: Interpreting Charts
1. *Based on the chart, what is one important feature of a city?*
2. *What kinds of social behavior are basic to the five characteristics of civilizations?*

MORE ABOUT . . .
Cuneiform
Early writing took the form of pictographs—pictures expressing words. A picture of a star stood for the word *star*. But this system was limited. What if a scribe wanted to write *slave woman*? The solution was to combine signs. Sumerians got most of their slaves from the mountains, so they combined the signs for "mountain" and "woman" to represent "slave woman."

In time, signs came to represent ideas. The sign for "star" could also mean "sky," "heaven," or "god." Eventually, scribes devised a system in which signs stood for sounds. The word for "water" sounded the same as the word for "in," so scribes used the sign for "water" to express "in." Despite this progress, writing took many years to master. Only professional scribes learned the whole system.

History from Visuals

Key Traits of Civilizations
Interpreting the Chart Have students identify which column lists the key traits of all civilizations and which lists specific examples of each trait.

Extension Activity Point out that the traits are interrelated and that each has an impact on the others. For example, specialized workers create goods for trade, and trade requires the keeping of records. Have students form small groups to list other ways in which the characteristics are interrelated.

SKILLBUILDER Answers
1. A large population.
2. Cooperation and organization.

TEACHING OPTION

CONNECTIONS ACROSS THE CURRICULUM

Literature An ancient Sumerian king is the hero of one of the oldest epic poems in world literature, the *Epic of Gilgamesh*. Parts of the poem were composed in Mesopotamia before 2000 B.C., and for centuries the poem was well-known throughout the region. The library of King Ashurbanipal of Assyria (668–627 B.C.) contained the most complete version of the story.

As the epic opens, Gilgamesh is a powerful Sumerian king who oppresses his people. The people cry to the gods for relief, so the gods create the champion Enkidu to help the people. Enkidu challenges Gilgamesh to a contest of strength and fighting skill. When Gilgamesh wins, the two become friends. After many adventures together, Enkidu dies and Gilgamesh goes in search of immortality. The epic includes a story of a great flood similar to the biblical story of the flood that Noah survives.

Have students research the *Epic of Gilgamesh* and bring their favorite parts of the poem to class. You may want to have student volunteers perform dramatic readings of certain passages.

Civilization Emerges in Ur

▶ Key Ideas
- Ur, a Sumerian city of 30,000 people, is one of the earliest cities to develop a sophisticated civilization.
- By 3000 B.C., Ur has developed the five characteristics of civilization.
- Ur's people practice a complex religion and believe in an afterlife.

 GEOGRAPHY TRANSPARENCIES
GT1 Cities of the Ancient Middle East, 7000–3000 B.C.

WORLD ART AND CULTURES TRANSPARENCIES
AT2 Upper Sumerian artifacts

ELECTRONIC LIBRARY OF PRIMARY SOURCES
from "The Royal Cemetery at Ur"

MORE ABOUT . . .
The Excavation of Ur

As archaeologist Leonard Woolley was excavating at the site of Ur, he uncovered geological evidence that the area once suffered a great flood. This flood might have been the basis of the biblical story of the great flood, from which Noah escaped by building the ark.

The City of Ur

1 **Ziggurat** A massive temple

2 **Court of Nanna** Sacred place of Ur's moon god

3 **Home of the High Priestess** Place where a woman with great religious authority lived

4 **Surrounding Wall** Defense for protecting Ur residents

5 **Temple and Treasury** Administrative centers in Ur

6 **Royal Cemetery** Burial site of the queen and king of Ur

The white lines indicate the shape of the original structure, which once rose as high as 80 feet.

Aerial photograph of Ur taken in 1930.

The underlying photograph at the right shows how the temple mound looked after Leonard Woolley excavated it during the 1920s and 1930s

---

CASE STUDY: Ur in Sumer

Civilization Emerges in Ur

Ur, one of the earliest cities in Sumer, stood on the banks of the Euphrates River in what is now southern Iraq. Some 30,000 people once lived in this ancient city. Ur was the site of a highly sophisticated civilization.

After a series of excavations from 1922 to 1934, English archaeologist Leonard Woolley and his team unraveled the mystery of this long-lost civilization. Woolley's archaeological dig at Ur revealed important clues about Ur's past. Woolley concluded that around 3000 B.C., Ur was a flourishing urban civilization. People in Ur lived in well-defined social classes. Priests and rulers wielded great power. Wealthy merchants profited from foreign trade. Artists and artisans created many extraordinary works, such as lavish ornaments and jewelry, musical instruments, and gold helmets and daggers. Woolley's finds have enabled historians to reconstruct scenes illustrating Ur's advanced culture.

An Agricultural Economy Imagine a time nearly 5,000 years ago. Outside the mud-brick walls surrounding Ur, ox-driven plows cultivate the fields. People are working barefoot in the irrigation ditches that run between patches of green plants. With stone hoes, the workers widen the ditches. The ditches carry water into their fields from the reservoir a mile away. The people of Ur have developed this large-scale irrigation system to provide Ur with food surpluses, which keep the economy thriving. The government officials who plan and direct this public works project ensure its smooth operation.

A Glimpse of City Life A broad dirt road leads from the fields up to the city's wall. Inside the city gate, the city dwellers go about their daily lives. Most people live in small, windowless, one-story, boxlike houses packed tightly together along the street. However, a few wealthy families live in two-story houses with an inner courtyard.

Down another street, accomplished artisans work full-time in their shops. A metalworker makes bronze by carefully mixing molten copper with just the right quantity of tin. Later he will hammer the bronze to make sharp spears—weapons to help Ur's well-organized armies defend the city. As a potter spins his potter's wheel, he expertly shapes the moist clay into a large bowl. These artisans and other craftworkers produce trade goods that help the city of Ur prosper.

THINK THROUGH HISTORY
B. Analyzing Causes
How did Ur's agricultural way of life foster the development of civilization there?
B. Possible Answer
Food surpluses freed Ur residents to develop specialized skills other than farming; sparked a need for advanced technology such as irrigation systems; allowed Ur's economy to flourish; provided a wide range of goods for trade.

20 CHAPTER 1

Task: Students will research cultures in the Americas that built large pyramids or temple mounds.

Purpose: To learn how other cultures shared the same religious aspirations as the Sumerians and expressed them in similar ways.

Activity: Divide the class into groups of three to five students. Assign each group one of these

cultures: Mississippian, Mochica of Peru, Maya, Toltec, Aztec, or city of Teotihuacán. Have students write a report describing (1) the culture's ways of life, (2) its religious practices and beliefs, if known, and (3) the structure and use of its pyramids or mounds. Students might enhance their report with images.

Building a Portfolio Students may want to add their report to their portfolio.

ALTERNATIVE ASSESSMENT BOOK
Standards for Evaluating a Cooperative Activity

Standards for Evaluation
Reports should . . .

- clearly describe the cultural practices of the group
- describe the mounds or pyramids built by the group and explain how they were used

Ur's Thriving Trade The narrow streets open out into a broad avenue where merchants squat under their awnings and trade farmers' crops and artisans' crafts. This is the city's bazaar, or marketplace. People do not use coins to make purchases because money has not yet been invented. However, merchants and their customers know roughly how many pots of grain a farmer must give to buy a jug of wine. This way of trading goods and services without money is called **barter.** More complicated trades require the services of a scribe. He carefully forms cuneiform signs on a clay tablet. The signs show how much barley one farmer owes a merchant for a donkey.

The Temple: Center of City Life Farther down the main avenue stands Ur's tallest and most important building—the temple. Like a city within a city, the temple is surrounded by a heavy wall. Within the temple gate, a massive, tiered structure towers over the city. This pyramid-shaped monument is called a **ziggurat** (ZIHG·uh·RAT), which means "mountain of god." On the exterior of the ziggurat, a flight of perhaps 100 mud-brick stairs leads to the top. At the peak, priests conduct rituals to worship the city god who looms over Ur. Every day, priests with shaved heads climb these stairs. They often drag a plump goat or sheep for a sacrifice. The temple also houses storage areas for grains, woven fabrics, and gems—offerings to the city's god.

A Religious Ritual Recorded A poem preserved in cuneiform tablets reveals Sumerians' burial rituals and their belief in an afterlife. The following is a lament for a young woman's lover who was killed in a distant land. These lines describe what foods she will provide for his spirit when his body is returned home for his funeral:

> **A VOICE FROM THE PAST**
> I will offer him cakes and herbs of the grove,
> I will provide him with the fruits of the field,
> I will provide him with roasted barley and dates . . .
> I will provide him with grapes on the vine,
> I will provide him with apples of the wide earth,
> I will provide him with figs of the wide earth . . .
> I will provide him with dates on their cluster.
> Quoted in *From the Poetry of Sumer* by Samuel Kramer

The fruits, grains, and other foods mentioned in these lines also suggest the wide range of crops that Sumerians either grew themselves or received as trade goods.

The first early cities such as Ur represent a model of civilizations that continued to arise throughout history. While the Sumerians were advancing their culture, civilizations were also developing in Egypt, China, and other countries in Asia.

CONNECT to TODAY

Ziggurat's Role in Persian Gulf War

After 4,000 years, the city of Ur is still making history. During the Persian Gulf War in 1991, the Iraqi military established an air base near the site of the city of Ur. The ziggurat there had been reconstructed.

Hoping that U.S. and Allied forces would not risk destroying the ancient ziggurat, Iraqi forces parked aircraft next to the structure at Ur for protection. However, enemy planes targeted the city of Ur. Exploding bombs caused large craters at the site. Machine-gun attacks from enemy planes also left many bullet holes in the sides of the ziggurat itself.

MORE ABOUT . . .
The Religion of Ur

The Sumerians worshiped many gods, and each Sumerian city had its own patron god. Ur was the earthly home of the moon god, Nanna. Ur also was the birthplace of the biblical patriarch Abraham, who laid foundations for the first monotheistic religion, Judaism.

ASSESS & RETEACH

Section 3 Assessment
Have students work in small groups to discuss the questions and review one another's responses.

 FORMAL ASSESSMENT
Section Quiz, p. 7

Reteaching Activity
CLASS TIME: 10 MINUTES

Use the Guided Reading Worksheet for Section 3 to help review the main ideas of this section.

 IN-DEPTH RESOURCES: UNIT 1
Guided Reading, p. 3

CRITICAL THINKING TRANSPARENCIES
CT37 Chapter 1 Visual Summary

CLOSE ACTIVITY

CLASS TIME: 15 MINUTES

Role Playing
Divide the class into groups of four, and have each group write and perform a short skit set in the ancient city of Ur. Each character in the skit should embody one of these characteristics of civilization: specialization, complex institutions, record keeping, advanced technology.

Section 3 Assessment

1. TERMS & NAMES

Identify
- civilization
- specialization
- artisan
- institution
- scribe
- cuneiform
- Bronze Age
- barter
- ziggurat

2. TAKING NOTES

Create a two-column chart like the one below. List the five characteristics of civilization and give an example from Ur.

Characteristics of Civilization	Example from Ur
1.	
2.	
3.	
4.	
5.	

3. MAKING INFERENCES

In what ways does the ziggurat of Ur reveal that Sumerians had developed an advanced civilization?

THINK ABOUT
- the skills required to build the monument
- the various purposes of the ziggurat
- its location

4. THEME ACTIVITY

Economics Role-play a character from Ur who has a specialized skill, such as an artisan, a trader, or a scribe. Write a monologue explaining how you contribute to the economic welfare of the city.

ANSWERS

1. TERMS & NAMES

- civilization, p. 18
- specialization, p. 18
- artisan, p. 18
- institution, p. 18
- scribe, p. 18
- cuneiform, p. 18
- Bronze Age, p. 19
- barter, p. 21
- ziggurat, p. 21

2. TAKING NOTES

Possible Responses: Advanced Cities—Ur's population of about 30,000 people. Specialized Workers—traders, artisans, and scribes. Complex Institutions—religion under the authority of priests. Record Keeping—cuneiform tablets. Advanced Technology—irrigation systems.

3. MAKING INFERENCES

Possible Responses: Builders and engineers in Ur had the advanced technology to design a complex building; religion played an important role in people's lives; Ur was an advanced city.

4. THEME ACTIVITY

Standards for Evaluation
Monologues of various specialized workers should highlight their roles in supporting Ur's trade and providing goods or services for the economy.

Chapter 1 Assessment

TERMS & NAMES

1. artifact, p. 7
2. culture, p. 7
3. technology, p. 9
4. hunter-gatherer, p. 12
5. Neolithic Revolution, p. 14
6. domestication, p. 14
7. civilization, p.18
8. specialization, p.18
9. institution, p.18
10. Bronze Age, p.19

REVIEW QUESTIONS

11. Archaeologists and anthropologists study bones and ancient artifacts, and paleontologists analyze fossils.

12. Upright posture gave hominids greater mobility and freed their hands to carry objects. The opposable thumb allowed hominids to pick up objects and make tools.

13. People used stone to fashion tools and weapons.

14. In Shanidar Cave, located in northeastern Iraq, archaeologists discovered a body that Neanderthals had buried during a funeral about 60,000 years ago. This ceremony suggests that Neanderthals held religious beliefs.

15. While men in hunting-gathering bands hunted, women gathered plant foods. The women may have scattered seeds near a regular campsite and found new crops growing when they returned the next season.

16. Hunter-gatherers moved when their food supply was exhausted. Farmers grew their own food, could rely on a more stable food supply, and tended to stay in one location, which led to more permanent settlements.

17. Southwest Asia, the Nile Valley in Africa, China, Mexico, and Central America.

18. Food surpluses freed some villagers to pursue jobs other than farming; trade increased.

19. The soaring populations of cities created a need for a system of ruling and a code of laws to maintain order.

20. As government, religion, and the economy grew more complex, people saw a need to organize and keep records of such things as laws, events, and transactions.

Chapter 1 Assessment

TERMS & NAMES

Briefly explain the importance of each of the following to human prehistory.

1. artifact
2. culture
3. technology
4. hunter-gatherer
5. Neolithic Revolution
6. domestication
7. civilization
8. specialization
9. institution
10. Bronze Age

Interact *with* History

On page 6, you played the role of an amateur archaeologist as you tried to figure out the uses of three prehistoric tools. Now that you've read the chapter, what new clues have you discovered that would help you unravel the mystery of who made the tool with the wedge-shaped blade, and why? What evidence can you use to support your conclusions about its purpose? Discuss your ideas with a small group.

REVIEW QUESTIONS

SECTION 1 *(pages 7–11)*
Human Origins in Africa

11. What kinds of evidence do archaeologists, anthropologists, and paleontologists study to find out how prehistoric people lived?

12. Why did the ability to walk upright and the development of the opposable thumb represent important breakthroughs for early hominids?

13. Why is the prehistoric period called the Stone Age?

14. What evidence supports archaeologists' beliefs that Neanderthals developed a form of religion?

SECTION 2 *(pages 12–16)*
Humans Try to Control Nature

15. Why do some archaeologists believe that women were the first farmers?

16. What role did the food supply play in shaping the nomadic life of hunter-gatherers and the settled life of farmers?

17. In what areas of the world did agriculture first develop?

SECTION 3 *(pages 17–21)*
PATTERNS OF CHANGE: CIVILIZATION

18. What economic changes resulted from food surpluses in agricultural villages?

19. Why did the growth of civilization make government necessary?

20. Why did a system of record keeping develop in civilizations?

Visual Summary

The Peopling of the World

Social Organization

Hunting-Gathering Bands	Growth of Villages	Rise of Cities
Beginning about 2 million B.C.	Beginning about 8000 B.C.	Beginning about 3000 B.C.

Achievements

Key Achievements
- Invention of tools
- Mastery over fire
- Development of language
- Creation of art

Key Achievements
- Development of agriculture
- Domestication of animals
- Breakthroughs in farming technology
- Food surpluses

Key Achievements
- Specialized workers
- Record keeping
- Complex institutions
- Advanced technology

Interact *with* History

Possible Responses: The tool is 5,000 years old, which dates it to the late Neolithic period, so it was made by a fully modern human being well after the initial development of agriculture. The tool's elegance and economy of form and its metal blade suggest that it was made by a skilled artisan. The wedge shape of the blade and the size and angle of the tool suggest that it was used by a farmer for breaking up soil and forming furrows in preparation for sowing.

CRITICAL THINKING

1. EFFECTS OF TRADE

THEME ECONOMICS What impact did trade have on the development of civilization?

2. STONE AGE CULTURES

Create a comparison chart like the one below to show the differences between Paleolithic and Neolithic cultures.

	Paleolithic	Neolithic
Source of food		
Means of living		
Technology		
Type of community		

3. THE ROLE OF RELIGION

What trends occurred in religious beliefs over the course of the Stone Age? Consider the religious practices of the Neanderthals, the villagers of Catal Huyuk, and the city dwellers of Ur.

4. ANALYZING PRIMARY SOURCES

The following quotation from Richard Leakey's book *The Making of Mankind* explains how archaeologists learn about the past. Read the paragraph and answer the questions that follow.

A VOICE FROM THE PAST

Litter of the past is the basis of archaeology. The coins, the pottery, the textiles and the buildings of bygone eras offer us clues as to how our [early ancestors] behaved, how they ran their economy, what they believed in and what was important to them. What archaeologists retrieve from excavations are images of past lives. . . . [These images] are pieced together slowly and painstakingly from the information contained in objects found.

- Why is the "litter" that humans leave behind so valuable to archaeologists?

- If archaeologists inspected a week's worth of your family's household trash, what conclusions might they draw about your way of life?

CHAPTER ACTIVITIES

1. LIVING HISTORY: Unit Portfolio Project

THEME INTERACTION WITH ENVIRONMENT Your unit portfolio project focuses on showing the ways in which hominids interacted with the environment. For Chapter 1, you might use one of the following ideas to add to your portfolio:

- Make a poster featuring how early humans adapted to the changing environment. Draw a series of pictures or cartoons showing how they used fire, built shelters, made clothing, and found new sources of food.

- Write a "Top 10" list of important steps that early humans took to control their environment. Read them aloud to your class. Be prepared to explain your rankings.

- Imagine you are an archaeologist working on the first dig of Ur at Sumer. Your job is to organize the artifacts and to discuss how Sumerians may have used them to adapt to their environment. Write your findings as field notes.

2. CONNECT TO TODAY: Cooperative Learning

THEME SCIENCE AND TECHNOLOGY In early civilizations, ox-drawn plows turned the soil, and elaborate irrigation systems expanded planting areas. Today, breakthroughs in technology continue to revolutionize farming methods in the United States and other countries.

Work with a team to create a chart explaining the latest high-tech equipment and machines used on a modern industrialized farm.

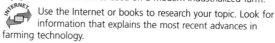 Use the Internet or books to research your topic. Look for information that explains the most recent advances in farming technology.

- Find diagrams that illustrate how farm machines work. You may wish to focus on computerized farm equipment.

- Make comparisons between these labor-saving farm machines and the simple farming tools and methods of early farmers.

3. INTERPRETING A TIME LINE

Revisit the unit time line on pages 2–3. Think of two or more events to add to the Chapter 1 segment of the time line.

FOCUS ON FINE ART

Study this cave painting created during the Stone Age in Argentina.

- What is depicted in the painting?

- What do you think the hands represent?

Connect to History Do you think the painting portrays a scene from daily life, represents religious beliefs, or shows an illustrated story about an important event? Support your answer with reasons.

CHAPTER ACTIVITIES

1. LIVING HISTORY

Standards for Evaluation
A poster should meet these criteria:

- Displays early humans in the environment described in the text.
- Presents examples of early men, women, and children engaged in daily activities.
- Shows causal links among activities (from making a fire to cooking and eating, from hunting to making clothing from skins, etc.).

Standards for Evaluation
A list should meet these criteria:

- Displays an understanding of major survival problems for early humans.
- Contains steps related to various aspects of the environment (weather, land forms, wild animals, etc.).
- Shows evidence of the thought process used to rank choices.
- Is clearly and neatly presented.

Standards for Evaluation
Field notes should meet these criteria:

- Clearly categorize and label artifacts.
- Indicate the materials and methods used to make artifacts, if known.
- Explain how the artifacts may have been used and back the explanation with evidence.

2. CONNECT TO TODAY

Standards for Evaluation
A chart should meet these criteria:

- Presents visual and verbal information that clearly explains how each farm machine works.
- Compares modern and early farming technology and methods, including their pros and cons.

3. INTERPRETING A TIME LINE

Possible Responses: 7000 B.C.— Jarmo, one of the first farming villages, is established in the Zagros Mountains of Iraq; 3000 B.C.— Sumerian scribes invent the cuneiform writing system.

FOCUS ON FINE ART

Answer: The painting depicts wild animals, people, and hands.
Possible Answer: Each hand may signify "I was here."

Connect to History Students' interpretations will vary but should be supported with reasons.

CRITICAL THINKING

1. EFFECTS OF TRADE
Possible Responses: Trade encouraged specialization, growth of cities as economic centers, and development of record keeping for business transactions.

2. STONE AGE CULTURES
Possible Responses: Source of Food— (Paleo) wild game and edible plants; (Neo) crops and livestock. Means of Living—

(Paleo) hunting and gathering; (Neo) farming, herding, specialized craftwork. Technology—(Paleo) hunting-and-gathering tools; (Neo) farming tools, pottery, metalwork. Type of Community—(Paleo) nomadic bands; (Neo) farming villages.

3. THE ROLE OF RELIGION
Possible Responses: Religious beliefs became more complex, and rituals more elaborate and organized.

4. ANALYZING PRIMARY SOURCES
Possible Responses: By examining the litter of the past, archaeologists piece together the history of early peoples. Archaeologists' conclusions about a family's way of life will vary but should be based on specific examples of household garbage.

PLANNING GUIDE
Early River Valley Civilizations

	Key Ideas	**COPY MASTERS**	**ASSESSMENT**
SECTION 1 City-States in Mesopotamia *pp. 27–32*	*Working together to overcome environmental challenges leads to the development of centralized government and cities in Mesopotamia. The Sumerian civilization influences later civilizations.*	*In-Depth Resources: Unit 1* • **Guided Reading**, p. 17 • **Primary Sources:** Assyrian Letters, p. 24; from *The Code of Hammurabi*, p. 25 • **Literature:** Ancient Proverbs, p. 28; from *The Epic of Gilgamesh*, p. 29 • **History Makers:** Hammurabi, p. 31	*Section 1 Assessment,* p. 32 *Formal Assessment* • Section Quiz, p. 16 *Alternative Assessment Book* • Standards for Evaluating a Cooperative Activity
SECTION 2 Pyramids on the Nile *pp. 33–41*	*Egyptian civilization develops along the Nile River. Upper and lower Egypt are united into a kingdom and ruled by pharaohs, who are believed to be gods. Egyptian customs for preparing and burying the bodies of the dead include mummification and burying pharaohs in pyramids.*	*In-Depth Resources: Unit 1* • **Guided Reading,** p. 18 • **Skillbuilder Practice:** Interpreting Visual Sources, p. 21 • **Geography Application:** Egypt and the Nile Delta, p. 22 • **Primary Source:** Sphinx of Amenemhet III, p. 27 • **History Makers:** Tutankhamen, p. 32	*Section 2 Assessment,* p. 39 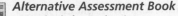 *Formal Assessment* • Section Quiz, p. 17 *Alternative Assessment Book* • Standards for Evaluating a Cooperative Activity
SECTION 3 Planned Cities on the Indus *pp. 42–45*	*The Indus Valley people build planned cities with sophisticated sewage and plumbing systems. Archaeological evidence suggests the Indus civilization is stable and prosperous. Indus Valley culture ends mysteriously.*	*In-Depth Resources: Unit 1* • **Guided Reading,** p. 19 • **Science and Technology:** Early Water Engineering, p. 34	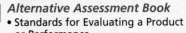 *Section 3 Assessment,* p. 45 *Formal Assessment* • Section Quiz, p. 18 *Alternative Assessment Book* • Standards for Evaluating a Product or Performance
SECTION 4 River Dynasties in China *pp. 46–51*	*Ancient Chinese civilization is ruled by powerful family dynasties. Just rulers are believed to have divine approval. In Chinese culture, family is central to society and religion. Improvements are made in technology and trade. Feudalism is established.*	*In-Depth Resources: Unit 1* • **Guided Reading,** p. 20 • **Connections Across Time and Cultures:** River Civilizations in the Ancient World, p. 33	*Section 4 Assessment,* p. 51 *Formal Assessment* • Section Quiz, p. 19 *Alternative Assessment Book* • Standards for Evaluating a Cooperative Activity
CHAPTER RESOURCES	**Chapter Overview** *The river valley civilizations develop from small farming villages. The civilizations create laws, centralized governments, writing systems, and advanced technologies. The process of trade spreads new ideas to and from these civilizations.*	*Telescoping the Times* • Chapter Summary, pp. 5–7 *Planning for Block Schedules*	*Chapter Assessment,* pp. 52–53 *Chapter Activities,* p. 53 *Formal Assessment* • Chapter Test, forms A and B, pp. 20–25 *Test Generator* *Alternative Assessment Book*

TECHNOLOGY

 Warm-Up Transparency 2

 Geography Transparencies
- GT2 Fertile Crescent Civilizations, 4000–1750 B.C.

 Electronic Library of Primary Sources
- from The Code of Hammurabi

INTERNET RESOURCES
www.mlworldhistory.com

 Warm-Up Transparency 2

 World Art and Cultures Transparencies
- AT3 Great Sphinx
- AT4 Egyptian tomb painting

 Electronic Library of Primary Sources
- from The Tomb of Tutankhamen

INTERNET RESOURCES
www.mlworldhistory.com

 Warm-Up Transparency 2

 Electronic Library of Primary Sources
- from "Indus Culture"

INTERNET RESOURCES
www.mlworldhistory.com

 Warm-Up Transparency 2

 Critical Thinking Transparencies
- CT2 Environmental Factors Shape River Valley Civilizations

World Art and Cultures Transparencies
- AT5 Chinese bronze

 Electronic Library of Primary Sources
- "Building a Town," from Shih ching

INTERNET RESOURCES
www.mlworldhistory.com

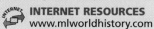 **Chapter Summaries on Audiocassette** in English and Spanish

INTERNET RESOURCES
www.mlworldhistory.com

Block Scheduling (90 MINUTES)

Day 1
Section 1, pp. 27–32

 COOPERATIVE ACTIVITY
Comparing and Contrasting Schools, p. 31 (Teacher's Edition)

Section Assessment, p. 32

Day 2
Section 2, pp. 33–41

 COOPERATIVE ACTIVITY
Building the Pyramids, p. 35 (Teacher's Edition)

Section 3, pp. 42–45

Section Assessments, pp. 29, 45

Day 3
Section 4, pp. 46–51

COOPERATIVE ACTIVITY
Displaying Ancient Chinese Inventions, p. 48 (Teacher's Edition)

Section Assessment, p. 51

Chapter Assessment, pp. 52–53

Yearly Pacing *Chapter 2 Total:* 3 days *Yearly Total:* 85 days

 Planning for Block Schedules

Customizing for Special Needs

Students Acquiring English

 Access for Students Acquiring English
- **Guided Reading** for Sections 1–4 (Spanish), pp. 23–26
- **Chapter Summary** (Spanish), pp. 20–22
- **Skillbuilder Practice** Interpreting Visual Sources (Spanish), p. 27
- **Geography Application** Egypt and the Nile Delta (Spanish), p. 28

 Chapter Summaries on Audiocassette in English and Spanish

INTERNET RESOURCES
www.mlworldhistory.com
The Diverse Classroom

Less Proficient Readers

 In-Depth Resources: Unit 1
- **Guided Reading** for Sections 1–4, pp. 17–20
- **Skillbuilder Practice** Interpreting Visual Sources, p. 21
- **Geography Application** Egypt and the Nile Delta, p. 22

Telescoping the Times
- Chapter Summary, pp. 5–7

 Chapter Summaries on Audiocassette

Gifted and Talented Students

 In-Depth Resources: Unit 1

Primary Sources:
- Assyrian Letters, p. 24
- from The Code of Hammurabi, p. 25
- Sphinx of Amenemhet III, p. 27

History Makers:
- Hammurabi, p. 31
- Tutankhamen, p. 32

Connections to Literature READINGS FOR STUDENTS

 In-Depth Resources: Unit 1
- Ancient Proverbs, p. 28
- from The Epic of Gilgamesh, p. 29

Enrichment Reading

- **MacDonald, Fiona**
  The World in the Time of Tutankhamen
  Persippany, NJ: Dillon, 1997

  King Tut's rule comes vividly to life in this illustrated volume.

- **Rawson, Jessica, ed.**
  Chinese Art
  London: Thames, 1992

  A spectacular collection showing the splendor of Chinese art.

 = Pupil's Edition   = Overhead Transparency   = Software   = Video

 = Copy Master   = CD-ROM   = Audiocassette   = Internet

Early River Valley Civilizations, 3500 B.C.-450 B.C.

Accessing Prior Knowledge

- Ask students to read the captions accompanying the artifacts and share what they know about the civilizations that produced them.

Making Inferences

- Ask students if the artifacts look like they came from the same place or from different places. Explain.

- Have students figure out the age of each artifact. Then ask students if they think the civilizations that produced these artifacts will have anything in common with the modern world.

Geography Connection

Ask students to study the location of the four civilizations.

- Why might these civilizations have made contact with each other?

- What are some routes between the different areas of civilization that might have been used?

CHAPTER 2 Early River Valley Civilizations, 3500 B.C.–450 B.C.

PREVIEWING THEMES

Interaction with Environment

The earliest civilizations formed on river plains. While fertile, these lands also presented challenges, such as seasonal flooding and a limited growing area. To deal with these problems, people created irrigation systems, which produced surplus food. Surpluses supported the rise of cities.

Power and Authority

Projects such as irrigation systems required planning, leadership, and laws—the beginnings of organized government. In some societies, priests controlled the first governments. Over time, power and authority shifted to military leaders and kings.

Science and Technology

Early civilizations depended on breakthroughs in science and technology, including bronze tools, the wheel, the sail, the plow, writing, and mathematics. These innovations spread from one civilization to the next through trade, wars, and the movement of peoples.

INTERNET CONNECTION

Visit us at **www.mlworldhistory.com** to learn more about ancient Sumer, Egypt, India, and China.

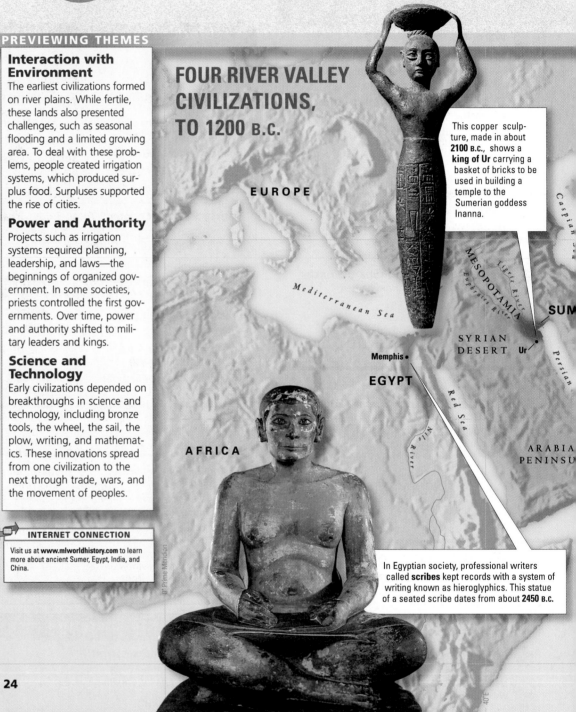

FOUR RIVER VALLEY CIVILIZATIONS, TO 1200 B.C.

EUROPE

Mediterranean Sea

Caspian Sea

MESOPOTAMIA

Tigris River

Euphrates River

SUM

SYRIAN DESERT Ur

Memphis

EGYPT

AFRICA

Red Sea

Nile River

ARABIA PENINSU

This copper sculpture, made in about **2100 B.C.**, shows a **king of Ur** carrying a basket of bricks to be used in building a temple to the Sumerian goddess Inanna.

In Egyptian society, professional writers called **scribes** kept records with a system of writing known as hieroglyphics. This statue of a seated scribe dates from about **2450 B.C.**

24

GEOGRAPHY THEMES

Region

Ask students to look at the regions where the civilizations are located. Do students notice any similarities between these regions? Then ask students to describe the location of cities within each region. Have students speculate about why all the cities are located near rivers. *Similarities: near a large body of water, rivers run through them; cities are located by rivers; rivers provide fresh water.*

Place

Tell students that the natural resources of an area affect the way a society develops there. Ask students to think about this question as they read: Why did each civilization eventually develop a system of trade?

ADDITIONAL RESOURCES

Books for the Teacher

• Cotterell, Arthur. *The Penguin Encyclopedia of Ancient Civilizations.* New York: Viking Penguin, 1988.

• Kramer, S. N. *History Begins at Sumer.* Philadelphia: U of Pennsylvania P, 1981. Cites 39 "firsts" in human history.

Books for the Student

• Cairns, Trevor. *The Coming of Civilization.* New York: Cambridge UP, 1986. The rise of the earliest civilizations.

• Lerner Geography Department. *Street Smart!: Cities of Ancient Worlds.* Minneapolis: Lerner Group, 1994.

Videos

• *Iraq: Cradle of Civilization.* Ambrose Video, 1992. 800-526-4663. The rise of Mesopotamia.

• *The Birth of Civilization: 6000 B.C.-2000 B.C.* Social Studies School Service, 1985. 800-421-4246. Rise and fall of early civilizations in Southwest Asia and China.

Software

• *Cradles of Civilization.* CD-ROM. Society for Visual Education, 1995. 800-624-1678. Human achievements through Mesopotamian and Egyptian civilizations.

• *Pyramid: Challenge of the Pharaoh's Dream.* CD-ROM. Society for Visual Education, 1996. 800-624-1678.

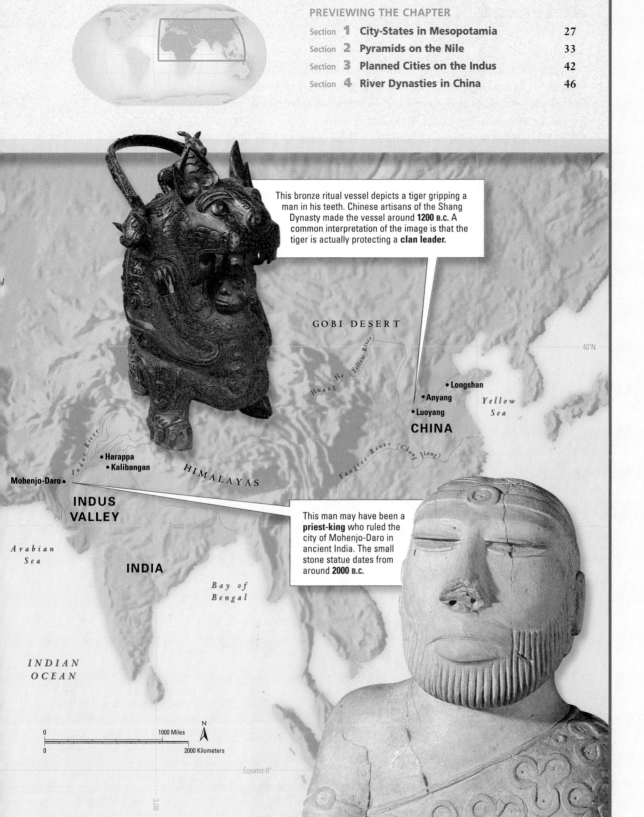

This bronze ritual vessel depicts a tiger gripping a man in his teeth. Chinese artisans of the Shang Dynasty made the vessel around **1200 B.C.** A common interpretation of the image is that the tiger is actually protecting a **clan leader**.

This man may have been a **priest-king** who ruled the city of Mohenjo-Daro in ancient India. The small stone statue dates from around **2000 B.C.**

GOBI DESERT

• Longshan
• Anyang
• Luoyang
CHINA

Yellow Sea

Huang He (Yellow River)

Yangtze River (Chang Jiang)

HIMALAYAS

• Harappa
• Kalibangan
Mohenjo-Daro •

INDUS VALLEY

Indus River

Arabian Sea

INDIA

Bay of Bengal

Tropic of Cancer

INDIAN OCEAN

Equator 0°

0 — 1000 Miles
0 — 2000 Kilometers

N

40°N

HISTORY THROUGH ART

Ancient Art and Artists

The ancient artists who created these works were not expressing their own individual feelings. Instead, they were creating religious, spiritual, and cultural images that were recognizable to the people living within a particular civilization.

The works of ancient artists usually had specific purposes. For example, the writing on the Sumerian figure of Inanna gives credit to a Sumerian king for building a great temple. This figure (along with others like it) was buried in the foundation of the temple. The Chinese tiger figure is actually a vessel, or container, that was used in religious ceremonies. Both the Egyptian and the ancient Indian figures are believed to pay tribute to high-ranking officials in those civilizations.

Interpreting the Art In what ways are these works of art different from modern works of art? Where might you find religious art or art that commemorates public figures in the United States? *Modern art: expresses artist's feelings and ideas, may be abstract. Religious art: churches and museums. Commemorative art: parks, museums, government buildings.*

Interact *with* History

This Interact with History feature motivates students by inviting them to put themselves in a key historical situation—a citizen of the Babylonian Empire. As students imagine themselves living in ancient Babylon, they will debate the righteousness of Hammurabi's code and analyze the purpose of laws in a society.

Purpose

• to prepare students for studying ancient civilizations

• to help students understand daily life in ancient times

• to help students make connections with people and events they will study in this chapter

Teaching Strategy

Thinking Critically After students have imagined themselves in the situation described on this page, have them answer the key questions and give reasons for their decision.

EXAMINING *the* **ISSUES**

Following are suggestions for addressing each bulleted question.

❶ What is the difference between justice and revenge? Does Mummar's punishment fit his crime?

❷ Can laws change behavior? Do people obey the law only because they don't want to be punished?

❸ What problems might a community face if it did not have laws? *Possible answers: lots of crime, people would move away, people wouldn't trust each other.*

Making Connections Ask students to discuss why advanced cities were important to the growth of ancient civilizations.

Follow Up

A feature on the chapter assessment will ask students to reevaluate their responses to the situation presented on this page.

Interact *with* History

It has been a tough year ever since the harvest failed. Many times, you've cursed the name of Mummar, the government official responsible for overseeing the harvest. But now that you've heard about the king's punishment for Mummar, you're not sure what to think.

The law of the Babylonian Empire—Hammurabi's Code—holds people responsible for their actions. It usually applies retaliation as punishment. That is, if you put out the eye of another, your own eye will be put out. Mummar had hired a substitute to handle the harvest this year, and the harvest was a disaster. Because of Mummar's decision, your city has suffered through a serious food shortage. Some people may die. Therefore, the king has sentenced Mummar to die.

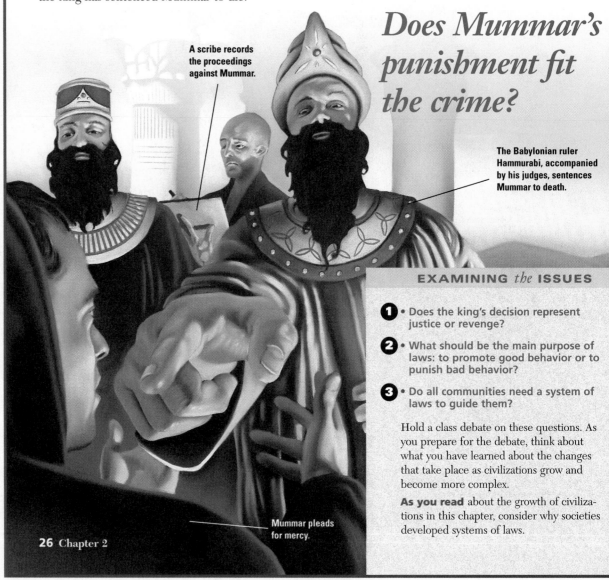

Does Mummar's punishment fit the crime?

A scribe records the proceedings against Mummar.

The Babylonian ruler Hammurabi, accompanied by his judges, sentences Mummar to death.

Mummar pleads for mercy.

26 Chapter 2

EXAMINING *the* **ISSUES**

❶ • Does the king's decision represent justice or revenge?

❷ • What should be the main purpose of laws: to promote good behavior or to punish bad behavior?

❸ • Do all communities need a system of laws to guide them?

Hold a class debate on these questions. As you prepare for the debate, think about what you have learned about the changes that take place as civilizations grow and become more complex.

As you read about the growth of civilizations in this chapter, consider why societies developed systems of laws.

1 City-States in Mesopotamia

TERMS & NAMES
- Fertile Crescent
- silt
- irrigation
- city-state
- dynasty
- cultural diffusion
- polytheism
- empire
- Hammurabi

MAIN IDEA

The earliest civilization in Asia arose in Mesopotamia and organized into city-states.

WHY IT MATTERS NOW

The development of this civilization reflects a pattern that has occurred repeatedly throughout history.

SETTING THE STAGE Two rivers flow from the mountains of what is now Turkey, down through Syria and Iraq, and finally to the Persian Gulf. Six thousand years ago, the waters of these rivers provided the lifeblood that allowed the formation of farming settlements. These grew into villages and then cities. This pattern would also occur along other river systems in northern Africa, India, and China, as the world's first civilizations developed.

Geography of the Fertile Crescent

A desert climate dominates the landscape between the Persian Gulf and the Mediterranean Sea in Southwest Asia. Yet within this dry region lies an arc of land that provides some of the best farming in Southwest Asia. The region's curved shape and the richness of its land led scholars to call it the **Fertile Crescent.**

The Zagros Mountains in Iran lie to the east of Mesopotamia. Melting snows from this and other ranges swelled the Tigris and Euphrates rivers each spring.

Fertile Plains In the eastern part of the Fertile Crescent, the Tigris (TY·grihs) and Euphrates (yoo·FRAY·teez) rivers flow southeastward to the Persian Gulf. (See the map on page 28.) Between them lies a plain that became known as Mesopotamia (MEHS·uh·puh·TAY·mee·uh), which in Greek means "land between the rivers."

The Tigris and Euphrates rivers flooded Mesopotamia at least once a year. As the floodwater receded, it left a thick bed of mud called **silt.** In this rich, new soil, farmers could plant and harvest enormous quantities of wheat and barley. The surpluses from their harvests allowed villages to grow.

THINK THROUGH HISTORY
A. Clarifying Why was silt so important to the inhabitants of Mesopotamia?
A. Answer A new bed of fertile soil each year, it produced surplus harvests and allowed villages to grow.

Environmental Challenges People first began to settle and farm in southern Mesopotamia before 4500 B.C. Around 3500 B.C., the people called the Sumerians, whom you read about in Chapter 1, arrived on the scene. The Sumerians mixed with the local farmers, and their language became dominant in the region. No one knows for sure where the Sumerians came from. Good soil was the advantage that attracted these settlers to the flat, swampy land of Sumer. There were, however, three disadvantages to their new environment.

Early River Valley Civilizations **27**

SECTION 1 RESOURCES

PRINT RESOURCES

 IN-DEPTH RESOURCES: UNIT 1
Guided Reading, p. 17
Primary Sources: Assyrian Letters, p. 24; from *The Code of Hammurabi,* p. 25
Literature: Proverbs, p. 28; from *Gilgamesh,* p. 29
History Makers: Hammurabi, p. 31

 ACCESS FOR STUDENTS ACQUIRING ENGLISH
Guided Reading (Spanish), p. 23

FORMAL ASSESSMENT
Section Quiz, p. 16

TECHNOLOGY RESOURCES

GEOGRAPHY TRANSPARENCIES
GT2 Fertile Crescent Civilizations, 4000–1750 B.C.

CD-ROM
Electronic Library of Primary Sources

INTERNET www.mlworldhistory.com

OBJECTIVES

1. To summarize how geography affected cultural development in the Fertile Crescent.

2. To describe city-states and how other cultures learned about them.

3. To describe Sumerian religious beliefs, social structure, and technology.

4. To explain the influence of Sumer on later civilizations.

SKILLBUILDER

- Interpreting maps: place, human-environment interaction, p. 28

CRITICAL THINKING

- Clarifying, pp. 27, 28
- Analyzing causes, p. 29
- Contrasting, p. 31
- Recognizing effects, p. 32
- Making inferences, p. 32
- Analyzing themes, p. 32

FOCUS
5-Minute Warm-Up

▶ *Making Generalizations*
To understand the importance of cities in the development of civilizations, have students answer these questions.
1. What cities do you know about or have you visited?
2. What can you see in these cities that you would not see in a small town or village?

WARM-UP TRANSPARENCY 2

OBJECTIVE ① INSTRUCT

Geography of the Fertile Crescent

▶ *Key Ideas*
- Living in Mesopotamia has disadvantages as well as benefits.
- The Sumerians work together to overcome these disadvantages.
- Solving problems together is the beginning of Sumerian organized government.

IN-DEPTH RESOURCES: UNIT 1
Guided Reading, p. 17

ACCESS FOR STUDENTS ACQUIRING ENGLISH
Guided Reading (Spanish), p. 23

The Fertile Crescent, 2500 B.C.

Interpreting the Map Tell students to compare the two maps and name the present-day countries that now exist in the area that was Mesopotamia. Ask students what they know about Iran, Iraq, and Kuwait. Also have students find the approximate location of Sumer on the smaller map.

Extension Activity Have students list the different geographic regions pictured on the map. Then discuss with students why the region in which Mesopotamia is located is unique. *Regions: mountain, desert, plains, coastal; unique because it has rivers and rich soil.*

SKILLBUILDER Answers
1. Tigris and Euphrates.
2. Fertile soil and access to mountains and deserts.

MORE ABOUT . . .
Sumerian Building Materials

The first Sumerian houses were simple structures made from reed bundles. Later on, Sumerians built their houses out of sun-dried mud bricks. Sumerians were constantly repairing their houses because the mud bricks became worn down by rain. People made sturdier bricks by baking them in an oven, but even these could not stand up to the effects of nature and time.

The Fertile Crescent, 2500 B.C.

Sumer
Fertile Crescent
Direction of flow of the Tigris and Euphrates

Present-day Persian Gulf

In 2500 B.C. the Persian Gulf was larger than it is today. Over time the Tigris and Euphrates have joined together and filled in this shallow area. The ancient coastline is shown above with a dotted blue line.

GEOGRAPHY SKILLBUILDER: Interpreting Maps
1. **Place** *What major rivers flow through the Fertile Crescent?*
2. **Human-Environment Interaction** *What were some advantages of Sumer's location?*

First, the flooding of the rivers was unpredictable. Sometimes it came as early as April, sometimes as late as June. After the flood receded, the hot sun quickly dried out the mud. Little or no rain fell, and the land became almost a desert. How could Sumerian farmers water their fields during the dry summer months in order to make their barley grow?

Second, Sumer was a small region, only about the size of Massachusetts. The villages were little clusters of reed huts standing in the middle of an open plain. With no natural barriers for protection, a Sumerian village was almost defenseless. How could the villagers protect themselves?

Third, the natural resources of Sumer were extremely limited. Without a good supply of stone, wood, and metal, what were the Sumerians to use for tools or buildings?

Creating Solutions Over a long period of time, the people of Sumer created solutions to deal with these problems. To provide water, they dug **irrigation** ditches that carried river water to their fields and allowed them to produce a surplus of crops. For defense, they built city walls with mud bricks. Finally, Sumerians traded with the peoples of the mountains and the desert for the products they lacked. Sumerians traded their grain, cloth, and crafted tools for the stone, wood, and metal they needed to make their tools and buildings.

These activities required organization, cooperation, and leadership. It took many people working together, for example, for the Sumerians to construct their large irrigation systems. Leaders were needed to plan the projects and supervise the digging. These projects also created a need for laws to settle disputes over how land and water would be distributed. These leaders and laws were the beginning of organized government.

THINK THROUGH HISTORY
B. Clarifying How did the Sumerians overcome their lack of resources?
B. Answer: Through trade.

28 Chapter 2

CONNECTIONS ACROSS TIME AND PLACE

Irrigation Methods Irrigation methods haven't changed much since their early development. Sumerians built canals and ditches leading from the Tigris and Euphrates rivers to holding areas. When the rivers rose, water poured into the canals and ditches and flowed to the holding areas. The resulting supply of water was used throughout the growing season. More canals and ditches brought the water from the holding areas to the fields.

Modern irrigation systems use pumps to bring underground well water to the surface. People also dam rivers to create reservoirs for water storage. Water is carried to fields from wells and reservoirs through a system of pipelines or cement canals. Once the water has reached the field, farmers may flood the entire field, use a sprinkler system, let water slowly drip from pipes into the soil, or run the pipes under the roots of the plants. Ask students to find examples of irrigation in their community, such as lawn sprinklers at a golf course.

Sumerians Create City-States

The Sumerians stand out in history as one of the first groups of people to form a civilization. Five key characteristics set Sumer apart from earlier human societies: (1) advanced cities, (2) specialized workers, (3) complex institutions, (4) record keeping, and (5) advanced technology. All the later peoples who lived in this region of the world built upon the innovations of Sumerian civilization.

By 3000 B.C., the Sumerians had built a number of cities, each surrounded by fields of barley and wheat. Although these cities shared the same culture, they developed their own governments, each with its own rulers. Each city and the surrounding land it controlled formed a **city-state.** A city-state functioned much as an independent country does today. Sumerian city-states included Uruk, Kish, Lagash, Umma, and Ur. As in Ur, which Chapter 1 describes, the center of all Sumerian cities was the walled temple with a ziggurat at its center. There the priests appealed to the gods for the well-being of the city-state.

The Power of Priests Sumer's earliest governments were controlled by the temple priests. The farmers believed that the success of their crops depended upon the blessings of the gods, and the priests acted as go-betweens with the gods. In addition to being a place of worship, the ziggurat was like a city hall. From the ziggurat the priests managed the irrigation system. They also demanded a portion of every farmer's crop as taxes.

Monarchs Take Control In time of war, however, the priests did not lead the city. Instead, the men of the city chose a tough fighter who could command the city's soldiers. At first, a commander's power ended as soon as the war was over. After 3000 B.C., wars between cities became more and more frequent. Gradually, Sumerian priests and people gave commanders permanent control of standing armies.

In time, some military leaders became full-time rulers, or monarchs. These rulers usually passed their power on to their sons, who eventually passed it on to their own heirs. Such a series of rulers from a single family is called a **dynasty.** Between 3000 and 2500 B.C., many Sumerian city-states came under the rule of dynasties.

The Spread of Cities Sumer's city-states grew prosperous from the surplus food produced on their farms. These surpluses allowed Sumerians to increase long-distance trade, exchanging the extra food and other goods for items they needed but did not have.

As their population and trade expanded, the Sumerians came into contact with other peoples, and their ideas—such as living in cities—spread. By 2500 B.C., new cities were arising all over the Fertile Crescent, in what is now Syria, northern Iraq, and Turkey. So, too, did the Sumerians absorb ideas such as religious beliefs from neighboring cultures. This process of a new idea or a product spreading from one culture to another is called **cultural diffusion.**

Sumerian Culture

The belief systems, social structure, technology, and arts of the Sumerians reflected their civilization's triumph over its harsh environment.

A Religion of Many Gods Like many peoples in the Fertile Crescent, the Sumerians believed that many different gods controlled the various forces in nature. The belief in many gods is called **polytheism** (PAHL·ee·thee·IHZ·uhm). Enlil, the god of clouds and air, was among the most powerful gods. Sumerians feared him as "the raging flood that has no rival." Lowest of all the gods were demons known as Wicked Udugs, who caused disease, misfortune, and every kind

The writing on this Sumerian copper figurine from about 2100 B.C. tells that a king of Ur erected a temple for the goddess Inanna.

THINK THROUGH HISTORY
C. Analyzing Causes How did monarchs gain power in the city-states?
C. Answer Frequent wars led Sumerians to give military leaders control of standing armies; these leaders eventually took political power.

Early River Valley Civilizations **29**

CONNECTIONS ACROSS TIME AND PLACE

Cultural Diffusion The process that spread the concept of city-states from Sumeria to other cultures also spread the fashion trend known as grunge from Seattle, Washington, to Europe. Cultural diffusion continues today, but at a much faster pace than in 2500 B.C. Today, television, satellites, and computers have made it possible for people in the most remote

areas to receive news and information at the same rate as city-dwellers.

The information superhighway, as the Internet has been called, is the modern version of Mesopotamian trade routes. It can deliver an ever-widening range of information to homes, schools, and businesses.

Similarly, live TV coverage of important events can be broadcast instantaneously around the world, using satellite transmission. Have students identify other examples of cultural diffusion in sports, fashion, music, or other areas.

History from Visuals

The Standard of Ur

Interpreting the Art Have students examine the panel and read the caption. Ask students to determine what kinds of animals Sumerians might have raised for food.

Extension Activity Explain to students that the panel is part of a larger piece called the Standard of Ur. Have students conduct research to find five facts about the Standard of Ur. *Possible responses: It is a wooden box; found in a grave in the city of Ur; inlaid with shells and lapis lazuli; about 4,500 years old; shows battle and banquet scenes.*

MORE ABOUT . . .
Sumerian Gods and Goddesses

Two other important Sumerian deities were Enki and Ninhursag. Enki, the god of wisdom, helped Enlil arrange the earth. Enlil made general decisions, but the creative and resourceful Enki handled the details. Ninhursag was the mother-goddess and the earth goddess who protected all living things.

This panel made of shells and stone comes from the Sumerian city of Ur. It shows people and livestock captured in war being presented to the victorious king.

of human trouble. Altogether, the Sumerians believed in roughly 3,000 gods.

Sumerians described their gods as doing many of the same things humans do—falling in love, having children, quarreling, and so on. Yet the Sumerians also believed that their gods were both immortal and all-powerful. Humans were nothing but their servants. At any moment, the mighty anger of the gods might strike, sending a fire, a flood, or an enemy to destroy a city. To keep the gods happy, the Sumerians built impressive ziggurats for them and offered rich sacrifices of animals, food, and wine.

Sumerians worked hard to earn the gods' protection in this life. Yet they expected little help from the gods after death. The Sumerians believed that the souls of the dead went to the "land of no return," a dismal, gloomy place between the earth's crust and the ancient sea. No joy awaited souls there. A passage in a Sumerian poem describes the fate of dead souls: "Dust is their fare and clay their food."

Some of the richest accounts of Mesopotamian myths and legends appear in a long poem called the *Epic of Gilgamesh*. It is one of the earliest works of literature in the world. Through the heroic adventures of Gilgamesh, a legendary king, the narrative offers a glimpse into the beliefs and concerns of the ancient Sumerians. The epic tells of Gilgamesh's unsuccessful quest for immortality, a theme that recurs in ancient literature.

Vocabulary
epic: a long heroic poem that tells the story of a historical or legendary figure.

A VOICE FROM THE PAST
Gilgamesh, whither are you wandering?
Life, which you look for, you will never find.
For when the gods created man, they let
Death be his share, and withheld life
In their own hands.
Epic of Gilgamesh

Sumerian beliefs and legends such as those in the *Epic of Gilgamesh* greatly influenced other ancient cultures, including the Hebrews and the Greeks.

Life in Sumerian Society With civilization came greater differences between groups in society, or the beginning of what we call social classes. Priests and kings made up the highest level in Sumerian society. Wealthy merchants ranked next. The vast majority of ordinary Sumerian people worked with their hands in fields and workshops. At the lowest level of Sumerian society were the slaves. Some slaves were foreigners who had been captured in war. Others were Sumerians who had been sold into slavery as children to pay the debts of their poor parents. By working obediently day and night, Sumerian slaves could hope to earn freedom.

Social class affected the lives of both men and women. On the whole, Sumerian women could pursue most of the occupations of city life, from merchant to farmer to artisan. They could hold property in their own name. Women could also join the lower ranks of the priesthood. However, Sumer's written records mention few female

30 Chapter 2

CUSTOMIZING FOR SPECIAL NEEDS

Gifted and Talented Students
Analyzing Poetry Ask students to reread the excerpt from the *Epic of Gilgamesh* and write a paragraph explaining what is happening in the excerpt. You might suggest that students think about who is speaking, the speaker's tone, and what the speaker's

words reveal about Gilgamesh. Invite interested students to use these same ideas to analyze the longer excerpt from *The Epic of Gilgamesh* in the Teacher's Resources.

 IN-DEPTH RESOURCES: UNIT 1
Literature: from *The Epic of Gilgamesh*, p. 29

CUSTOMIZING FOR SPECIAL NEEDS

Less Proficient Readers *Making a Summary Chart* To help students understand the class divisions in Sumerian society, have them complete a chart like the one here.

Order	Who They Were	What They Did
Highest Class	priests and kings	ruled
Second Group		bought and sold goods
Third Group	most Sumerians	
Lowest Class	slaves	

scribes. Therefore, scholars have concluded that girls were not allowed to attend the schools where upper-class boys learned to read and write. Even so, Sumerian women had more rights than women in many later civilizations.

Sumerian Science and Technology

Sumerians invented the wheel, the sail, and the plow; they were the first to use bronze; and they developed the first system of writing, cuneiform. Cuneiform tablets provide evidence of other Mesopotamian innovations. One of the first known maps was made on a clay tablet in about 2300 B.C. Other tablets contain some of the oldest written records of scientific investigations in the areas of astronomy, chemical substances, and symptoms of disease.

Many other new ideas arose from the Sumerians' practical needs. In order to erect city walls and buildings, plan irrigation systems, and survey flooded fields, they needed arithmetic and geometry. They developed a number system in base 60, from which stem the modern units for measuring time (60 seconds = 1 minute) and the 360 degrees of a circle. Sumerian building techniques, including the use of mud bricks and mortar, made the most of the resources available. Their architectural innovations—such as arches, columns, ramps, and the pyramid-shaped design of the ziggurat—permanently influenced Mesopotamian civilization.

The First Empire Builders

From 3000 to 2000 B.C., the city-states of Sumer were almost constantly at war with one another. The weakened city-states could no longer ward off attacks from the peoples of the surrounding deserts and hills. Although the Sumerians never recovered from the attacks on their cities, their civilization did not die. Succeeding sets of rulers adapted the basic ideas of Sumerian culture to meet their own needs.

Sargon of Akkad About 2350 B.C., a conqueror named Sargon defeated the city-states of Sumer. Sargon led his army from Akkad (AK·ad), a city-state north of Sumer. Unlike the Sumerians, the Akkadians were a Semitic (suh·MIHT·ihk) people—that is, they spoke a language related to Arabic and Hebrew. The Akkadians had long before adopted most aspects of Sumerian culture. Sargon's conquests helped to spread that culture even farther, beyond the Tigris-Euphrates Valley.

By taking control of both northern and southern Mesopotamia, Sargon created the world's first empire. An **empire** brings together several peoples, nations, or previously independent states under the control of one ruler. At its height, the Akkadian Empire extended from the Mediterranean Coast in the west to present-day Iran in the east. Sargon's dynasty lasted only about 200 years, after which it declined due to internal fighting, invasions, and a severe famine.

Babylonian Empire In about 2000 B.C., nomadic warriors known as Amorites, another Semitic group, invaded Mesopotamia. Within a short time, the Amorites overwhelmed the Sumerians and established their capital at Babylon, on the Euphrates River. The Babylonian Empire reached its peak during the reign of **Hammurabi,** from 1792 B.C. to 1750 B.C. Hammurabi's most enduring legacy is the code of laws he put together.

This bronze head depicts Sargon of Akkad, who created the world's first empire.

THINK THROUGH HISTORY
D. Contrasting How does an empire differ from a city-state?
D. Answer Both are independent political units. However, a city-state controls only a city and its surrounding territory, whereas an empire controls many peoples, nations, or states.

Early River Valley Civilizations **31**

MORE ABOUT . . .
Cuneiform Tablets

Archaeologists have found whole libraries of cuneiform tablets among Sumerian ruins. Some of the recovered tablets are early grammar and biology textbooks. Others are engraved with epic tales, love poems, laws, a farmer's manual, medical treatments, hymns, proverbs, and essays.

IN-DEPTH RESOURCES: UNIT 1
Literature: Ancient Proverbs, p. 28

OBJECTIVE 4 INSTRUCT

The First Empire Builders

Key Ideas
- Sargon of Akkad creates the first empire by uniting the city-states under his rule.
- Amorites create a new empire in Mesopotamia with Babylon as the capital.
- A harsh code of laws known as the Code of Hammurabi is used to govern Babylonia.
- Sumerian advances influence the groups that dominate the Fertile Crescent over the years.

MORE ABOUT . . .
Sargon of Akkad

Sargon of Akkad was a renowned military leader and ruler who became the subject of epic tales and poems. One of the tales tells how he became king: Sargon's mother was too poor to take care of her son, so she put him in a basket and let him drift down the Euphrates River. Sargon was rescued by an irrigator, who raised him and trained him to be a gardener. A goddess fell in love with Sargon and made him king.

TEACHING OPTION | BLOCK SCHEDULING | **COOPERATIVE ACTIVITY: Comparing and Contrasting Schools** | CLASS TIME 30 MINUTES

Task: Pairs will research Sumerian schools and present diagrams comparing Sumerian schools with schools in the United States today.

Purpose: To learn about Sumerian schools.

Activity: Brainstorm with students a list of questions they have about Sumerian schools. Questions might concern what students studied and the length of the school year. Next, have partners research Sumerian schools and use a Venn diagram to compare Sumerian schools with schools in the U.S. today. In reports to the class, partners should present one element from their charts. Ask partners to share their personal responses to Sumerian schools.

Building a Portfolio: Students who feel that their report and chart are among their best work should add them to their portfolio.

ALTERNATIVE ASSESSMENT BOOK
Standards for Evaluating a Cooperative Activity

Standards for Evaluation
Reports and charts should . . .

- clearly convey information about Sumerian schools
- compare and contrast Sumerian schools and present-day schools in the U.S.
- show evidence of research using a variety of sources

Teacher's Edition **31**

Many of the punishments in the Code of Hammurabi are severe. For example, one law states that a surgeon who accidentally kills a patient during surgery should have his hands cut off. Ask students to do research to find more laws from the code of Hammurabi. Then have students write a paragraph explaining why they think the idea of "an eye for an eye" is a good or poor basis for making laws.

 IN-DEPTH RESOURCES: UNIT 1
Primary Source: from *The Code of Hammurabi*, p. 25
History Makers: Hammurabi, p. 31

 ELECTRONIC LIBRARY OF PRIMARY SOURCES
from The Code of Hammurabi

ASSESS & RETEACH

Section 1 Assessment
Have pairs of students help each other answer the questions. Then invite students to share their diagrams for item 2 with the class.

Section Quiz

 FORMAL ASSESSMENT
Section Quiz, p. 16

Reteaching Activity
CLASS TIME: 20 MINUTES

Divide the class into four groups and assign each group one of the four main parts of the section. Have group members summarize the main ideas and supporting details in each part. Then have groups present this information to the class.

CLOSE ACTIVITY

CLASS TIME: 20 MINUTES

Problems, Solutions, and Effects
Create a chart on the board for students to copy. The chart should have three columns, labeled "Problems," "Solutions," and "Effects." Have students use the chart to record three problems the environment presented for Sumerians, how they solved these problems, and how the solutions helped the Sumerian civilization to develop.

Hammurabi
? –1750 B.C.
The noted lawgiver Hammurabi was also an able military leader, diplomat, and administrator of a vast empire. Hammurabi himself described some of his accomplishments:

When [the gods] Anu and Bel gave me the land of Sumer and Akkad to rule, . . . I dug out the Hammurabi-canal named Nuhus-nisi, which bringeth abundance of water unto the land of Sumer and Akkad. Both the banks thereof I changed to fields for cultivation, and I garnered piles of grain, and I procured unfailing water for the land. . . .
As for the land of Sumer and Akkad, I collected the scattered peoples thereof, and I procured food and drink for them. In abundance and plenty I pastured them, and I caused them to dwell in peaceful habitation.

Hammurabi's Code Although individual Sumerian cities had developed codes of laws, Hammurabi recognized that a single, uniform code would help to unify the diverse groups within his empire. He therefore collected existing rules, judgments, and laws into the Code of Hammurabi. Hammurabi had the code engraved in stone, and copies were placed all over his empire.

The code lists 282 specific laws dealing with everything that affected the community, including family relations, business conduct, and crime. The laws tell us a great deal about the Mesopotamians' beliefs and what they valued. Since many were merchants and traders, for example, many of the laws related to property issues.

Although the code applied to everyone, it set different punishments for rich and poor and for men and women. It frequently applied the principle of retaliation (an eye for an eye and a tooth for a tooth) to punish crimes. Following are two of the laws:

A VOICE FROM THE PAST
- If a man has stolen an ox, a sheep, a pig, or a boat that belonged to a temple or palace, he shall repay thirty times its cost. If it belonged to a private citizen, he shall repay ten times. If the thief cannot pay, he shall be put to death.
- If a woman hates her husband and says to him "You cannot be with me," the authorities in her district will investigate the case. If she has been chaste and without fault, even though her husband has neglected or belittled her, she will be held innocent and may return to her father's house. . . . If the woman is at fault, she shall be thrown into the river.

Code of Hammurabi, adapted from a translation by L. W. King

Despite its severity, Hammurabi's Code carried forward an important idea in Mesopotamian civilization. It reinforced the principle that government had a responsibility for what occurred in society. For example, if a man was robbed and the thief was not caught, the government was required to compensate the victim for his loss.

Two centuries after Hammurabi's reign, the Babylonian Empire fell to nomadic warriors. Over the years, new groups dominated the Fertile Crescent. Yet many ideas of the early Sumerians would be adopted by the later peoples, including the Assyrians, Phoenicians, and Hebrews. Meanwhile, a similar pattern of development, rise, and fall, was taking place to the west, along the Nile River in Egypt. Egyptian civilization is described in Section 2.

THINK THROUGH HISTORY
E. Recognizing Effects How did Hammurabi's law code advance civilization?
E. Possible Answers It established a uniform law code for all the groups in his empire; it reinforced the principle that government had a responsibility to its citizens.

Section ❶ Assessment

1. TERMS & NAMES
Identify
- Fertile Crescent
- silt
- irrigation
- city-state
- dynasty
- cultural diffusion
- polytheism
- empire
- Hammurabi

2. TAKING NOTES
Recreate the chart below on your paper. List three environmental challenges the Sumerians faced and their solutions to these challenges.

Challenges	Solutions
→	
→	
→	

3. MAKING INFERENCES
What advantages did living in cities offer the people of ancient Mesopotamia? Do modern cities offer any of the same advantages? Support your answer with references to the text.

THINK ABOUT
- characteristics of Sumer's city-states
- characteristics of Sumer's economy and society
- development of organized government

4. ANALYZING THEMES
Interaction with Environment
Do you think that living in a river valley with little rainfall helped or hurt the development of civilization in Mesopotamia? Explain your response.

ANSWERS

1. TERMS & NAMES
Fertile Crescent, p. 27
silt, p. 27
irrigation, p. 28
city-state, p. 29
dynasty, p. 29
cultural diffusion, p. 29
polytheism, p. 29

empire, p. 31
Hammurabi, p. 31

2. TAKING NOTES
Challenges: unpredictable flooding, defenselessness, limited resources. Solutions: irrigation, walled cities, trade.

3. MAKING INFERENCES
Possible Responses: Opportunity for wealth; diversity of work available; government that promotes laws, manages economy, and provides assistance; better housing; city walls and armies for protection; proximity to temple; more social contact. Cities today offer many of these advantages.

4. ANALYZING THEMES
Possible Response: It helped, because the Sumerians had to develop the technology and organization to get water to the fields. This led to the development of organized government.

② Pyramids on the Nile

TERMS & NAMES
- cataract
- delta
- Menes
- pharaoh
- theocracy
- pyramid
- mummification
- hieroglyphics
- papyrus

MAIN IDEA

Along the Nile River, civilization emerged in Egypt and became united into a kingdom ruled by pharaohs.

WHY IT MATTERS NOW

Many of the monuments built by the Egyptians stand as a testament to their ancient civilization.

Section 2 Overview

OBJECTIVES

① To summarize how geography affected the development of Egyptian culture.

② To explain the importance of pharaohs, pyramids, and trade in the Old Kingdom.

③ To describe ancient Egyptian religion, social structure, and technology.

④ To explain the shift from the Old Kingdom to the New Kingdom.

SKILLBUILDER

- Interpreting maps: movement, location, p. 34

CRITICAL THINKING

- Contrasting, p. 34
- Making inferences, p. 35
- Analyzing motives, p. 37
- Comparing , p. 38
- Summarizing, p. 39
- Drawing conclusions, p. 39
- Recognizing effects, p. 41

SETTING THE STAGE To the west of the Fertile Crescent in Africa, another river makes its way to the sea. While Sumerian civilization was on the rise, a similar process took place along the banks of this river, the Nile in Egypt. Yet the Egyptian civilization turned out to be very different from the collection of city-states in Mesopotamia. Early on, Egypt was united into a single kingdom, which allowed it to enjoy a high degree of unity, stability, and cultural continuity over a period of 3,000 years.

The Geography of Egypt

From the highlands of east-central Africa to the Mediterranean Sea, the Nile River flows northward for over 4,100 miles, making it the longest river in the world. (See the map on page 34.) A thin ribbon of water in a parched desert land, the great river brings its water to Egypt from distant mountains, plateaus, and lakes in present-day Burundi, Tanzania, Uganda, and Ethiopia.

Egypt's settlements arose along the Nile on a narrow strip of land made fertile by the river. The change from fertile soil to desert—from the Black Land to the Red Land—was so abrupt that a person could stand with one foot in each.

The Gift of the Nile As in Mesopotamia, yearly flooding brought the water and rich soil that allowed settlements to grow. Every year in July, rains and melting snow from the mountains of east-central Africa caused the Nile River to rise and spill over its banks. When the river receded in October, it left behind a rich deposit of fertile black mud.

Before the scorching sun could dry out the soil, the peasants would hitch their cattle to plows and prepare their fields for planting. All fall and winter, they tended the wheat and barley plants. They watered their crops from an intricate network of irrigation ditches. At last came the welcome harvest. This cycle repeated itself year after year—flood, plant, harvest; flood, plant, harvest.

In an otherwise parched land, the abundance brought by the Nile was so great that the Egyptians worshiped it as a god who gave life and seldom turned against them. As the ancient Greek historian Herodotus (hih·RAHD·uh·tuhs) remarked in the fifth century B.C., Egypt was the "gift of the Nile."

A traditional sailboat sails the Nile River in Egypt.

Upper Egypt and Lower Egypt For most of their history, ancient Egyptians knew only the lower part of the Nile—the last 750 miles before the river empties north into the Mediterranean Sea. Their domain ended at a point where jagged granite cliffs and boulders turn the river into churning rapids called a **cataract** (KAT·uh·rakt). Riverboats could not pass this spot, known as the First Cataract, to continue upstream to the south.

Early River Valley Civilizations **33**

FOCUS

5-Minute Warm-Up

▶ **Making Inferences**
Answering these questions will help students understand the role of pyramids in ancient Egyptian life.

1. Study the image of the pyramids on page 36. What are some adjectives that describe the pyramids?

2. How might the rooms in the pyramids have been used?

 WARM-UP TRANSPARENCY 2

OBJECTIVE ① INSTRUCT

The Geography of Egypt

▶ **Key Ideas**
- The predictable flooding of the Nile creates rich soil good for crops.
- The Nile provides a reliable transportation system that promotes trade.
- The geography of Egypt presents drawbacks as well as benefits.

IN-DEPTH RESOURCES: UNIT 1
Guided Reading, p. 18

ACCESS FOR STUDENTS ACQUIRING ENGLISH
Guided Reading (Spanish), p. 24

SECTION 2 RESOURCES

PRINT RESOURCES

IN-DEPTH RESOURCES: UNIT 2
Guided Reading, p. 18
Skillbuilder Practice: Interpreting Visual Sources, p. 21
Geography Application: Egypt and the Nile Delta, p. 22
Primary Source: Sphinx of Amenemhet III, p. 27
History Makers: Tutankhamen, p. 32

ACCESS FOR STUDENTS ACQUIRING ENGLISH
Guided Reading (Spanish), p. 24
Skillbuilder Practice: (Spanish), p. 27

Geography Application: (Spanish), p. 28

FORMAL ASSESSMENT
Section Quiz, p. 17

TECHNOLOGY RESOURCES

WORLD ART AND CULTURES TRANSPARENCIES
AT3 Great Sphinx
AT4 Egyptian tomb painting

CD-ROM
Electronic Library of Primary Sources

Ancient Egypt, 3000–2000 B.C.

Interpreting the Map Ask students to read the map key and use it to locate the Great Pyramids region and the Nile Valley on the map. Then have them use the key to determine the direction in which the prevailing winds blow and the river current flows.

Extension Activity Have students use the scale to measure the distance from the Mediterranean to the First Cataract. Ask why the scale can't be used to accurately measure the Nile's length. Next, ask why a comparison of the length of the Nile's course with the width of the United States is helpful. *The Nile's curves make it longer than the distance from source to mouth. Comparison makes it easier to see the size of the area being discussed.*

SKILLBUILDER Answers
1. North.
2. Upper Egypt lies to the south, Lower Egypt to the north.

MORE ABOUT . . .
Upper and Lower Egypt

The terms Upper Egypt and Lower Egypt can be confusing because of the location of these regions. *Upper* and *lower* refer to land elevation. The region of Upper Egypt was at a high elevation. Lower Egypt was at a low elevation, closer to the Mediterranean Sea.

 IN-DEPTH RESOURCES: UNIT 2
Geography Application: Egypt and the Nile Delta, p. 22

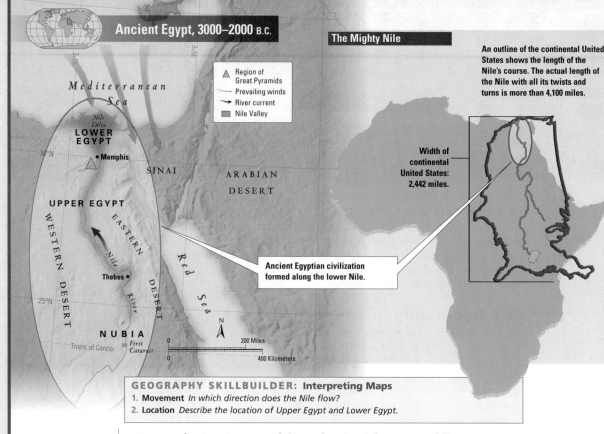

Ancient Egypt, 3000–2000 B.C.

The Mighty Nile

An outline of the continental United States shows the length of the Nile's course. The actual length of the Nile with all its twists and turns is more than 4,100 miles.

- ▲ Region of Great Pyramids
- — Prevailing winds
- → River current
- ▨ Nile Valley

Width of continental United States: 2,442 miles.

Ancient Egyptian civilization formed along the lower Nile.

GEOGRAPHY SKILLBUILDER: Interpreting Maps
1. **Movement** *In which direction does the Nile flow?*
2. **Location** *Describe the location of Upper Egypt and Lower Egypt.*

Between the First Cataract and the Mediterranean lay two very different regions. Upper Egypt (to the south) was a skinny strip of land from the First Cataract to the point where the river starts to fan out into many branches. Lower Egypt (to the north, near the sea) consisted of the Nile **delta** region, which begins about 100 miles before the river enters the Mediterranean. The delta is a broad, marshy, triangular area of land formed by deposits of silt at the mouth of the river. This rich land provided a home for many birds and wild animals.

The Nile provided a reliable system of transportation between Upper and Lower Egypt. The Nile flows north, so northbound boats simply drifted with the current. Southbound boats hoisted a wide sail. The prevailing winds of Egypt blow from north to south, carrying sailboats against the river current. The ease of contact made possible by this watery highway helped unify Egypt's villages and promote trade.

Environmental Challenges Egyptian farmers were much more fortunate than the villagers of Mesopotamia. Compared to the unpredictable Tigris and Euphrates rivers, the Nile was as regular as clockwork. Even so, life in Egypt had its risks. If the Nile's floodwaters were just a few feet lower than normal, the amount of fresh silt and water for crops was greatly reduced. Thousands of people might starve. If the floodwaters were a few feet higher than usual, the water would spread beyond the fields to the mud-brick villages nearby. The unwanted water might destroy houses, granaries, and the precious seeds that farmers needed for planting.

The vast and forbidding deserts on either side of the Nile acted as natural barriers between Egypt and other lands. They forced Egyptians to stay close to the river, their lifeline, which reduced their interaction with other peoples. At the same time, the deserts also shut out invaders. For much of its early history, Egypt was spared the constant warfare that plagued the Fertile Crescent.

THINK THROUGH HISTORY
A. Contrasting
What was the main difference between the flooding of the Nile and that of the rivers in Mesopotamia?
A. Answer Nile flooding occurred with greater regularity than the flooding of the Tigris and Euphrates.

34 Chapter 2

CUSTOMIZING FOR SPECIAL NEEDS

Students Acquiring English
Previewing Vocabulary Pair students acquiring English with proficient readers to preview the vocabulary for this section. First have students take turns reading the words aloud. Then have them look up the words in the glossary at the back of

their books. Proficient readers should make sure students acquiring English understand the definitions. (Note: The student book glossary is in Spanish and English.)

MULTIPLE LEARNING STYLES

Logical-Mathematical Learners *Making a Comparison Chart*
Suggest students use a chart like the one here to compare the geography of Sumeria and Egypt.

	Climate	Rivers	Benefits	Drawbacks
Sumeria	hot, dry			
Egypt	hot, dry			

Movement of Goods and Ideas By 3200 B.C., Egyptians were coming into contact with the people of Mesopotamia. Caravans loaded with goods for trade were traveling between the two regions. By about 2000 B.C., Egyptian traders were also traveling up the Nile on barges to the lands of Nubia and Kush to the south. They were in search of such goods as gold, ivory, cattle, and granite blocks for their massive temples and tombs.

Whole groups of people seem to have moved freely from one region to another in search of better land for farming or grazing. The early Egyptians may have borrowed some ideas from the Mesopotamians in the early development of their cities and in their system of writing. However, the period of Mesopotamian influence ended quickly. From then on, Egypt followed its own cultural path, which was very different from Mesopotamia's. Egypt blended the cultures of the Nile Valley peoples with the cultures of peoples who migrated into the valley from other parts of Africa and from the Fertile Crescent. Egypt thus was a land of cultural, ethnic, and racial diversity throughout its 3,000-year history.

Egypt Unites into a Kingdom

Egyptians lived in farming villages as far back as 5000 B.C., perhaps even earlier. Each village had its own rituals, gods, and chieftain. By 3200 B.C., the villages of Egypt were under the rule of two separate kingdoms, Lower Egypt and Upper Egypt.

According to legend, the king of Lower Egypt wore a red crown, and the king of Upper Egypt wore a tall white crown shaped like a bowling pin. About 3100 B.C., a strong-willed king of Upper Egypt named **Menes** (MEE·neez) united all of Egypt. As a symbol of his united kingdom, Menes created a double crown from the red and white crowns. Menes shrewdly established his capital, Memphis, near the spot where Upper and Lower Egypt met, and established the first Egyptian dynasty. Eventually, the history of ancient Egypt would consist of 31 dynasties, spanning 2,600 years.

Little is known of Egypt's first two dynasties, but records improve with the Third Dynasty. The Third Dynasty begins the period historians call the Old Kingdom, which lasted from 2660 to 2180 B.C. The Old Kingdom set the pattern for Egypt's great civilization.

Pharaohs Rule as Gods The role of the king was one striking difference between Egypt and Mesopotamia. In Mesopotamia, kings were considered to be representatives of the gods. To the Egyptians, kings *were* gods, almost as splendid and powerful as the gods of the heavens. The Egyptian god-kings came to be called **pharaohs** (FAIR·ohz).

The pharaoh stood at the center of Egypt's religion as well as its government and army. This type of government in which the ruler is a divine figure is called a **theocracy.** Egyptians believed that the pharaoh bore full responsibility for the kingdom's well-being. It was the pharaoh who caused the sun to rise, the Nile to flood, and the crops to grow. It was the pharaoh's duty to promote truth and justice.

Builders of the Pyramids Egyptians believed that their king ruled even after his death. He had an eternal spirit, or *ka* (kah), which continued to take part in the governing of Egypt. In the Egyptian's mind, the *ka* remained much like a living king in its needs and pleasures. Since kings expected to reign forever, their tombs were even more important than their palaces. For the kings of the Old Kingdom, the resting place after death was an immense structure called a **pyramid.** The Old Kingdom was the great age of pyramid building in ancient Egypt.

THINK THROUGH HISTORY
B. Making Inferences Why were Egypt's pharaohs unusually powerful rulers?
B. Answer They were believed to be gods as well as temporal rulers.

HISTORY MAKERS

Menes

Who was Menes? Did he exist at all? Historians cannot answer these questions, because the evidence of this early period is very limited. Written accounts of Menes' accomplishments were recorded hundreds or even thousands of years later. By then, Menes had become a legendary hero.

In the retelling, Menes' deeds became imaginary myths. According to one story, Menes finally died after a long and triumphant reign when he was carried off and killed by a hippopotamus.

crown of
Upper Egypt   crown of Upper
and Lower Egypt   crown of
Lower Egypt

Early River Valley Civilizations **35**

OBJECTIVE ② INSTRUCT

Egypt Unites into a Kingdom

▶ **Key Ideas**
- Pharaohs, believed to be gods, rule the Old Kingdom.
- The pyramids, which were tombs for the pharaohs, reflect the strength of the Egyptian culture.
- Trade and migration create cultural, ethnic, and racial diversity in Egypt.

 IN-DEPTH RESOURCES: UNIT 1
Amenemhet III, p. 27
Primary Source: Sphinx of
History Makers: Tutankhamen, p. 32

 WORLD ART AND CULTURES TRANSPARENCIES
AT3 Great Sphinx

 ELECTRONIC LIBRARY OF PRIMARY SOURCES from *The Tomb of Tutankhamen*

HISTORY MAKERS
Menes

Very little is known about Menes. He is believed to have been the first pharaoh of Egypt and to have established the world's first national government.

TEACHING OPTION   BLOCK SCHEDULING   **COOPERATIVE ACTIVITY: Building the Pyramids**   CLASS TIME 30 MINUTES

Task: Partners will research how pyramids were built and create a comic strip showing this process.

Purpose: To learn more about how the Egyptians built the pyramids.

Activity: Have pairs of students research how the Egyptians built their pyramids and list the important steps involved in construction. Then have partners create a comic strip showing these steps. Before they begin to draw, partners should decide how many

individual pictures they will need to create and what each picture will show. Partners should include brief descriptions of the action in each frame, using captions, thought balloons, and speech balloons. Encourage partners to share their comic strips with the class and display them in the classroom.

📁 ***Building a Portfolio:*** Students who feel that their comic strip is among their best work should add it to their portfolio.

 ALTERNATIVE ASSESSMENT BOOK
Standards for Evaluating a Cooperative Activity

Standards for Evaluation
Comic strips should . . .

- use text and pictures to clearly explain the process of pyramid building
- show evidence of thorough research

Teacher's Edition **35**

Great Pyramid at Giza

Interpreting the Visual Ask students to read the diagram and then categorize the different areas inside the pyramid. *Categories: gallery, chambers, passages, air shaft.*

Extension Activity Ask interested students to check current guidebooks to Egypt. How easy is it for tourists to visit the pyramids? *The Pyramids of Giza are on the outskirts of Cairo. Every day buses bring thousands of tourists to the site.*

Daily *Life*

Builders of the Pyramids

Pyramid building was dangerous and grueling work. Laborers risked being crushed by huge stones or falling off the sides of the pyramid. Suggest students read the article titled "Age of Pyramids: Egypt's Old Kingdom" in the January 1995 issue of *National Geographic* to find out more about the pyramid builders.

OBJECTIVE ③ INSTRUCT

Egyptian Culture

▶ **Key Ideas**
- Egyptians believe in many gods. They make elaborate preparations for the afterlife.
- A flexible class structure allows Egyptians in the lower classes to gain status.
- Egyptians develop a writing system called hieroglyphics.
- Egyptians make advances in math, architecture, medicine, and calendar systems.

   WORLD ART AND CULTURES TRANSPARENCIES
   AT4 Egyptian tomb painting

The largest of the pyramids is the Great Pyramid (right background) at Giza, completed about 2556 B.C. The diagram shows how the interior of a pyramid looks.

- King's chamber
- Air shaft
- Grand gallery
- Queen's chamber
- Ascending passage
- Escape passage
- Unfinished chamber

Daily *Life*

Builders of the Pyramids

Etched into some of the stones of the pyramids are the nicknames of the teams of workers who built them—"the Victorious Gang," "the Enduring Gang," and "the Craftsman Gang," for example. Just as construction workers today leave their marks on the skyscrapers they build, the pyramid builders scratched messages for the ages inside the pyramids.

Who were the pyramid builders? The ancient Greek historian Herodotus claimed that the pharaohs worked an army of laborers to death. However, it was actually peasants who provided most of the labor. They had to work for the government when the Nile was in flood and they could not farm. In return for their service, the country provided the workers with food and housing during this period.

These magnificent monuments were remarkable engineering achievements, built by people who had not even begun to use the wheel. Unlike the Sumerians, however, the Egyptians did have a good supply of stone, both granite and limestone. For the Great Pyramid of Giza, for example, the limestone facing was quarried 400 miles upriver. Each perfectly cut stone block weighed at least 2 1/2 tons. Some weighed 15 tons. More than 2 million of these blocks were stacked with precision to a height of 481 feet. The entire structure covered more than 13 acres.

The pyramids also reflect the strength of the Egyptian civilization. They show that Old Kingdom dynasties had developed the economic strength to support massive public works projects, as well as the leadership and government organization to carry them out.

Egyptian Culture

With nature so much in their favor, Egyptians tended to approach life more confidently and optimistically than their neighbors in the Fertile Crescent.

Religion and Life Like the Mesopotamians, the early Egyptians were polytheistic, believing in many gods. The most important gods were Ra, the sun god, and Horus, the god of light. The most important goddess was Isis, who represented the ideal mother and wife. In all, Egyptians worshiped more than 2,000 gods and goddesses. They built huge temples to honor the major deities.

36 Chapter 2

WRITING ACTIVITY

Task: Students will write about daily life in ancient Egypt from the point of view of an Egyptian citizen.

Materials Needed: Writing materials; books and articles on Egypt, if available.

Activity: Have students write a brief description of the life of a pharaoh or a laborer from that

individual's point of view. To help students get started, you might suggest the following first sentences: "As pharaoh, I am the ruler of all Egypt"; "For five years I have been helping to build the pyramid at Giza." Encourage students to include information about the physical, mental, and emotional states of the individual they write about.

Conclusion: Invite students to read their descriptions aloud to the class.

In contrast to the Mesopotamians, with their bleak view of death, Egyptians believed in an afterlife, a life that continued after death. Egyptians believed they would be judged for their deeds when they died. Osiris (oh·SY·rihs), the powerful god of the dead, would weigh each dead person's heart. To win eternal life, the heart could be no heavier than a feather. If the heart tipped the scale, showing that it was heavy with sin, a fierce beast known as the Devourer of Souls would pounce on the impure heart and gobble it up. But if the soul passed this test for purity and truth, it would live forever in the beautiful Other World.

People of all classes planned for their burials, so that they might safely reach the Other World. Kings and queens built great tombs, such as the pyramids, and other Egyptians built smaller tombs. Egyptians preserved a dead person's body by **mummification**—embalming and drying the corpse to prevent it from decaying. (See Something in Common, pages 40–41.) Scholars still accept Herodotus' description of the process of mummification.

A VOICE FROM THE PAST
First, they draw out the brains through the nostrils with an iron hook. . . . Then with a sharp stone they make an incision in the side, and take out all the bowels. . . . Then, having filled the belly with pure myrrh, cassia, and other perfumes, they sew it up again; and when they have done this they steep it in natron [a mineral salt], leaving it under for 70 days. . . . At the end of 70 days, they wash the corpse, and wrap the whole body in bandages of waxen cloth.
HERODOTUS, *The History of Herodotus*

Attendants placed the mummy in a coffin inside a tomb. Then they filled the tomb with items the dead person could use in the afterlife, such as clothing, food, cosmetics, and jewelry. Many Egyptians purchased scrolls that contained hymns, prayers, and magic spells intended to guide the soul in the afterlife. This collection of texts is known as the *Book of the Dead.* These texts often contained declarations intended to prove the soul was worthy of eternal life.

A VOICE FROM THE PAST
Behold, I have come to you, I have brought you truth, I have repelled falsehood for you. I have not done falsehood against men, I have not impoverished my associates, I have done no wrong in the Place of Truth, I have not learnt that which is not, I have done no evil. . . . I have not caused pain, I have not made hungry, I have not made to weep, I have not killed, I have not commanded to kill, I have not made suffering for anyone. . . . I am pure, pure, pure, pure!
Book of the Dead, translated by Raymond O. Faulkner

Life in Egyptian Society Like the grand monuments to the kings, Egyptian society formed a pyramid. The king, queen, and royal family stood at the top. Below them were the other members of the upper class, which included wealthy landowners, government officials, priests, and army commanders. The next tier of the pyramid was the middle class, which included merchants and artisans. At the base of the pyramid was the lower class, by far the largest class. It consisted of peasant farmers and unskilled laborers.

In the later periods of Egyptian history, slavery became a widespread source of labor. Slaves, usually captives from foreign wars, served in the homes of the rich or toiled endlessly in the gold mines of Upper Egypt.

The Egyptians were not locked into their social classes. Lower- and middle-class Egyptians could gain higher status through

Daily *Life*

Egyptian Cosmetics
The dark-lined eyes that look out at us from the artwork of ancient Egypt were the height of fashion 3,000 years ago. Men and women applied the makeup, called kohl, to their eyes with small sticks. They made kohl from powdered minerals mixed with water.

The Egyptians also wore lipstick, made from powdered red ocher (iron oxide) mixed with oil. They soaked flowers and fragrant woods in oil and rubbed the oil into their skin. Sometimes they decked their hairdos with cones of scented wax, which melted slowly in the heat.

These cosmetics were more than just beauty aids. The dark eye makeup softened the glare of the desert sun. The oils protected skin, lips, and hair from the dry desert air. Egyptians kept their cosmetics in chests such as the one shown above, which was found in an Egyptian tomb.

Early River Valley Civilizations **37**

SPOTLIGHT ON
The Rosetta Stone

According to popular history, Jean François Champollion vowed at age 11 that he would be the first to read hieroglyphics. He kept his vow 21 years later, after having become a talented linguist. Ask students to compare reading hieroglyphics to breaking a code. Ask if they can think of other examples of codes. *military codes, Braille, various kinds of passwords*

MORE ABOUT . . .
Hieroglyphics

Egyptians first encountered written language while trading with the Sumerians. However, they did not acknowledge that cuneiform writing might have influenced the development of their own writing system. Instead they credited Thoth, the Egyptian god of learning, with the invention of writing. Egyptians believed that words had magic powers from the gods.

SPOTLIGHT ON

The Rosetta Stone

Although it lasted more than 2,500 years, Egyptian civilization eventually declined. Soon after, the ability to read hieroglyphics was lost and remained so for many centuries.

In 1799, near the delta village of Rosetta, some French soldiers found a polished black stone inscribed with a message in three languages. One version was written in hieroglyphics (top inset). A second version was in a simpler form of hieroglyphics and the third was in Greek (both are shown in the bottom inset).

Since ancient Greek was a well-known language, it provided clues to the meaning of the hieroglyphics. Still, deciphering the Rosetta Stone took many years. In 1822, a French scholar named Jean François Champollion (shahm·paw·LYAWN) finally broke the code of the hieroglyphics.

marriage or success in their jobs. Even some slaves could hope to earn their freedom as a reward for their loyal service. To win the highest positions, people had to be able to read and write. Once a person had these skills, many careers were open in the army, the royal treasury, the priesthood, and the king's court.

Women in Egypt held many of the same rights as men. For example, a wealthy or middle-class woman could own and trade property. She could propose marriage or seek divorce. If she were granted a divorce, she would be entitled to one-third of the couple's property.

Egyptian Writing As in Mesopotamia, the development of writing was one of the keys to the growth of Egyptian civilization. Crude pictographs were the earliest form of writing in Egypt, but scribes quickly developed a more flexible writing system called **hieroglyphics** (HY·ur·uh·GLIHF·ihks). This term comes from the Greek words *hieros* and *gluphē*, meaning "sacred carving."

As with Sumerian cuneiform writing, in the earliest form of hieroglyphics a picture stood for an idea. For instance, a picture of a man stood for the idea of a man; a picture of a bird stood for the idea of a bird. In time, the system changed so that pictures stood for sounds as well as ideas. The owl, for example, stood for an *m* sound. Hieroglyphics could be used almost like letters of the alphabet.

Although hieroglyphics were first written on stone and clay, as in Mesopotamia, the Egyptians soon invented a better writing surface. They used another gift of the Nile, the tall stalks of the **papyrus** (puh·PY·ruhs) reeds that grew in the marshy delta. The Egyptians split the reeds into narrow strips, dampened them, and then pressed them. As the papyrus dried, the plant's sap glued the strips together into a paperlike sheet.

Egyptian Science and Technology Practical needs led to many Egyptian inventions. In order to assess and collect taxes, the Egyptians developed a system of written numbers for counting, adding, and subtracting. Farmers used an early form of geometry to survey and reset property boundaries after the annual floods.

Mathematical knowledge helped Egypt's skillful engineers and architects as well. Builders needed to make accurate calculations and measurements to construct their remarkable pyramids and palaces. Egyptian architects were also the first to use stone columns in homes, palaces, and temples.

To help them keep track of the time between floods and plan their planting season, the Egyptians developed a calendar. Egyptian priests had

THINK THROUGH HISTORY
D. Comparing How was the status of women similar in Egyptian and Sumerian society?
D. Answer Women in both societies could own property and had many rights.

TEACHING OPTION • BLOCK SCHEDULING

SKILLBUILDER MINILESSON: Interpreting Visual Sources
CLASS TIME 20 MINUTES

Explaining the Skill: Visual sources such as the detail from the tomb painting on this page reveal much about the times in which they were created. Images in the painting give information about ancient Egyptian culture.

Applying the Skill: Have students examine the tomb paintings at the top of this page and the next

page and read the caption. Then ask these questions:

1. What activities are being performed in the painting? *Cutting, raking wheat; carrying wheat in baskets; threshing; resting under a tree; driving oxen.*

2. How many different classes are represented by the figures in the painting? Explain. *Two; one man is dressed differently, and a worker is giving him something.*

3. What other details about ancient Egypt does the tomb painting reveal? *How people dressed, that women did not work in the fields, the tools Egyptians used.*

 IN-DEPTH RESOURCES: UNIT 1
Skillbuilder Practice: Interpreting Visual Sources, p. 21

observed that a very bright star, now known as Sirius, began to appear above the eastern horizon just before the floods came. The time between one rising of Sirius and the next was 365 days. They divided this year into 12 months of 30 days each and added five days for holidays and feasting. This calendar was so accurate that it fell short of the true solar year by only six hours.

This detail from a tomb painting shows how the Egyptians grew their grain.

Egyptian medicine was also famous in the ancient world. Although Egyptian medical writings contain all sorts of magic charms and chants, Egyptian doctors also relied on practical knowledge. They knew how to check a person's heart rate by feeling for a pulse in different parts of the body. They set splints for broken bones and had effective treatments for wounds and fevers. They also used surgery to treat some conditions. All in all, the Egyptians approached their study of medicine in a remarkably scientific way.

THINK THROUGH HISTORY
E. Summarizing
What were the main achievements of the ancient Egyptians?
E. Possible Answer
System of written numbers, hieroglyphics, geometry, pyramids, stone columns, accurate calendar, medicine.

Chariot Riders Invade Egypt

The power of the pharaohs declined about 2180 B.C., marking the end of the Old Kingdom. Historians call the period of weakness and turmoil that followed the First Intermediate Period. Strong pharaohs regained control during the Middle Kingdom (2080–1640 B.C.) and restored law and order. They improved trade and transportation by having a canal dug from the Nile to the Red Sea. With the wealth from new trade, the kings undertook other public projects. They had huge dikes built to trap and channel the Nile's floodwaters for irrigation. They also created thousands of new acres of farmland by draining the swamps of Lower Egypt.

The prosperity of the Middle Kingdom did not last. In about 1640 B.C., a group of Asian nomads swept across the Isthmus of Suez into Egypt in horse-drawn chariots. These chariot-riders were the Hyksos (HIHK·sahs), which meant "the rulers of the uplands." The Hyksos ruled much of Egypt from 1640 to 1570 B.C. This 70-year period is sometimes called the Second Intermediate Period.

Egypt fell to the Hyksos at roughly the same time other nomads were invading Mesopotamia and the Indus Valley farther to the east. But Egypt would rise again for a new period of power and glory, the New Kingdom, which is discussed in Chapter 4.

Section 2 Assessment

1. TERMS & NAMES
Identify
• cataract
• delta
• Menes
• pharaoh
• theocracy
• pyramid
• mummification
• hieroglyphics
• papyrus

2. TAKING NOTES
Recreate the web below on your paper and fill in examples related to the main idea in the center.

Egyptian Achievements

Which would you consider most important? Why?

3. DRAWING CONCLUSIONS
Look at the map on page 34. Three natural features determined the boundaries of ancient Egyptian civilization: the Nile River, the First Cataract, and the surrounding desert. In your judgment, which of these features was most important to Egypt's history? Explain your conclusion.

4. THEME ACTIVITY
Interaction with Environment
Using information from Sections 1 and 2, create a chart, sketch, or drawing to show how Sumerians and Egyptians made use of their environment. Then tell which group you think made better use of what they had. Be prepared to defend your opinions.

Early River Valley Civilizations **39**

OBJECTIVE 4 INSTRUCT

Chariot Riders Invade Egypt

▶ *Key Ideas*
• The Old Kingdom ends as the power of the pharaohs declines.
• Strong pharaohs and new irrigation projects revive Egypt during the Middle Kingdom.
• The Middle Kingdom falls to Asian nomads.

ASSESS & RETEACH

Section 2 Assessment
Have students answer the questions and then compare answers with another student.

Section Quiz
FORMAL ASSESSMENT
Section Quiz, p. 17

Reteaching Activity
CLASS TIME: 15 MINUTES

Read aloud items from the list of terms and names one at a time. Have students discuss how each term or name is important to the section they just read.

CLOSE ACTIVITY

CLASS TIME: 30 MINUTES

Identifying Main Ideas
Distribute four index cards to pairs of students and have them label each card using these phrases: Effects of Geography, Kingdoms and Pharaohs, Egyptian Culture, The Old Kingdom Ends. Have partners review Section 2 and list on the cards the main ideas about each topic. Partners can use the cards to quiz each other.

ANSWERS

1. TERMS & NAMES
cataract, p. 33
delta, p. 34
Menes, p. 35
pharaoh, p. 35
theocracy, p. 35
pyramid, p. 35
mummification, p. 37
hieroglyphics, p. 38
papyrus, p. 38

2. TAKING NOTES
Possible Responses: Pyramids, mummification, hieroglyphics, written numbers, calendar, advances in medicine.

3. DRAWING CONCLUSIONS
Possible Responses: The Nile River—it provided fertile soil, a predictable growing season, and easy transportation within Egypt. The First Cataract—it presented an obstacle to trade and communication with peoples on the upper Nile. The deserts—they limited outside contact but also prevented invasions.

4. THEME ACTIVITY
Standards for Evaluation
Visual presentations should meet the following criteria:
• Cover both sections
• Demonstrate knowledge of human interaction with the environment
• Are carefully thought out

Teacher's Edition 39

Dealing with Death

All humans face death. Anthropologists believe that religious beliefs grew out of humanity's attempts to explain what happens after death. The Egyptians wrapped their dead as mummies to preserve the body for an afterlife. The ways other cultures treat their dead reveal their own beliefs about God and the soul. As you compare and contrast the customs on these pages, look for how they are influenced by the religious beliefs of the people who practice them.

Ireland

United States

Egypt

Bali

Ancient Egypt
Among the first people to believe in life after death, the ancient Egyptians mummified the body so the soul could return to it later. Embalmers used chemicals to dry out the body. Then they wrapped the mummy in fine linen and adorned it with jewelry. Egyptian embalmers were so skillful that modern archaeologists have found mummies that still have hair, skin, and teeth thousands of years after burial.

9th-Century Ireland
Christians believe that the dead will be resurrected—brought back to life—before the time of final judgment. Until modern times, therefore, the Roman Catholic Church discouraged cremation. Since the first century A.D., Christians have buried their dead in cemeteries and marked each grave with a stone, a monument, or a cross. The carvings on this 9th-century Irish cross reflect Christian symbolism.

a closer look EGYPTIAN MUMMIES

The Egyptians also mummified the pets of the deceased. These are mummies of a cat and a dog.

These clay vessels are called Canopic jars. After preparing the mummy, embalmers placed the brain, liver, and other internal organs of the mummy in these jars.

40 Chapter 2

Modern Bali

Hindus cremate, or burn, their dead. They consider the body as just a container for a soul that never dies. After a person dies, they believe the soul is reborn in another person. Hindu cremations are sacred rituals. On the Indonesian island of Bali, these rituals involve an elaborate celebration. Several bodies are put in a tall tower made of wood and bamboo, such as the one pictured at right. The whole tower is burned and the ashes scattered in the ocean.

19th-Century Native Americans

Just as Native American languages and lifestyles varied widely, so did Native American customs for dealing with the dead. Many 19th-century Plains Indians, such as the Sioux and the Blackfeet (pictured below), placed their dead on raised platforms. This protected the bodies from wild animals and also lifted the dead closer to the sky, where many spirits were believed to dwell.

This solid gold death mask of the pharaoh Tutankhamen covered the head of his mummy. The mask, which weighs 22.5 pounds, is part of a popular exhibit in the Egyptian Museum in Cairo, Egypt.

Connect *to* History

Recognizing Effects Which groups believed in preserving the body after death? How did those religious beliefs affect their customs?

SEE SKILLBUILDER HANDBOOK, PAGE 995

Connect *to* Today

Reporting Find out about modern Jewish and Muslim burial practices. Illustrate each of these with a picture and a caption like those above. Then write a paragraph comparing them to either Christian or Hindu practices.

Early River Valley Civilizations **41**

OBJECTIVES

1. To describe the impact of geography on the Indus Valley culture.
2. To characterize Indus Valley cities and culture.
3. To list theories about the decline of the Indus Valley civilization.

SKILLBUILDER

- Interpreting Maps: location, human-environment interaction, p. 42

CRITICAL THINKING

- Identifying problems, p. 43
- Making inferences, p. 44
- Analyzing causes, p. 45
- Drawing conclusions, p. 45

FOCUS
5-Minute Warm-Up

▶ *Predicting*
Have students answer these questions to explore the role of artifacts in understanding ancient cultures.

1. What are three artifacts you've read about that helped scientists learn about the past?
2. What three artifacts would you put in a time capsule to help future scientists learn about life in the 20th century?

 WARM-UP TRANSPARENCY 2

OBJECTIVE ① INSTRUCT

The Geography of South Asia

▶ *Key Ideas*
- The Indus and Ganges Rivers create a fertile plain.
- Geography and climate present challenges and opportunities for the Indus Valley people.

 IN-DEPTH RESOURCES: UNIT 1
Guided Reading, p. 19

ACCESS FOR STUDENTS ACQUIRING ENGLISH
Guided Reading (Spanish), p. 25

History from Visuals

Ancient India, 2500–1500 B.C.

Interpreting the Map Have students study the topography of ancient India. What was the geography of the Indus Valley like? *mountains, rivers, plains*
(continued on next page)

TERMS & NAMES
- subcontinent
- monsoon

3 Planned Cities on the Indus

MAIN IDEA	WHY IT MATTERS NOW
The first Indian civilization built well-planned cities on the banks of the Indus River.	The culture of India today has it roots in the civilization of the early Indus cities.

SETTING THE STAGE The great civilizations of Mesopotamia and Egypt rose and fell. They left behind rich histories, but the current cultures in those areas have few links to their predecessors' ancient glories. Farther east, in India, another civilization arose about 2500 B.C. Historians know less about its origins and the reasons for its eventual decline than they do about the origins and decline of Mesopotamia and Egypt. Yet many characteristics of modern Indian culture can be traced to that early civilization.

The Geography of South Asia

A wall of mountains—the Hindu Kush, Karakoram, and Himalaya ranges—separates South Asia from the rest of the continent. As a result, geographers often refer to the land mass that includes what is now India, Pakistan, Nepal, and Bangladesh as a **subcontinent**—the Indian subcontinent.

Rivers, Mountains, and Monsoons The mountains guard an enormous flat and fertile plain formed by two rivers—the Indus and the Ganges (GAN·jeez). These two rivers and the lands they water make up a large area that stretches 1,500 miles across northern India and is called the Indus-Ganges Plain. Below this plain, the southern part of the subcontinent is a peninsula that thrusts south into the Indian Ocean. The center of the peninsula is a high plateau cut by twisting rivers. This region is called the Deccan (DEK·uhn). A narrow border of lush, tropical land lies along the coasts of southern India.

Seasonal winds called **monsoons** dominate India's climate. From October to May, winter monsoons from the northeast blow dry air across the country. Then, in the middle of June, the winds shift. Spring monsoons blow from the southwest, carrying moisture from the ocean in great rain clouds.

Ancient India, 2500–1500 B.C.

- ➡ Dry monsoon winds (October to May)
- ➡ Wet monsoon winds (June to September)
- ▨ Indus Valley civilization

HINDU KUSH MTS.
KARAKORAM MTS.
KHYBER PASS
BOLAN PASS
Harappa
Kalibangan
Mohenjo-Daro
Indus
HIMALAYA MOUNTAINS
INDUS-GANGES PLAIN
Ganges River
Brahmaputra R.
THAR DESERT
Narmada River
INDIA
Arabian Sea
Godavari River
DECCAN PLATEAU
Krishna River
WESTERN GHATS
EASTERN GHATS
Bay of Bengal
INDIAN OCEAN

0 ——— 250 Miles
0 ——— 500 Kilometers

GEOGRAPHY SKILLBUILDER: Interpreting Maps
1. **Location** *From what mountain ranges do the Indus River and its branches flow?*
2. **Human-Environment Interaction** *What landforms presented natural barriers around the Indus Valley?*

SECTION 3 RESOURCES

PRINT RESOURCES

 IN-DEPTH RESOURCES: UNIT 1
Guided Reading, p. 19
Science and Technology: Early Water Engineering, p. 34

ACCESS FOR STUDENTS ACQUIRING ENGLISH
Guided Reading (Spanish), p. 25

FORMAL ASSESSMENT
Section Quiz, p. 18

 ALTERNATIVE ASSESSMENT BOOK

TECHNOLOGY RESOURCES

 CD-ROM
Electronic Library of Primary Sources

 INTERNET www.mlworldhistory.com

THINK THROUGH HISTORY
A. Identifying Problems What environmental challenge did the farmers of the Indus Valley face that the Sumerians and Egyptians did not?
A. Answer floods were unpredictable, river changed course, monsoons

Environmental Challenges The civilization that emerged along the Indus River faced many of the same challenges as the ancient Mesopotamian and Egyptian civilizations. The Indus River flows southwest from the Himalayas to the Arabian Sea. As in Mesopotamia and Egypt, yearly floods spread deposits of rich soil over a wide area. Unlike the Nile floods, however, the floods along the Indus were unpredictable. The river sometimes changed its course. Unlike both the Mesopotamians and the Egyptians, the people of the Indus Valley had to cope with the cycle of wet and dry seasons brought by the monsoon winds. If there was too little rain, plants withered in the fields and people went hungry. Too much rain, and floods swept away whole villages.

The world's tallest mountains to the north and a large desert to the west presented natural boundaries between the Indus Valley and other areas. As in Egypt, the natural barriers helped protect the Indus Valley from invasion. At the same time, the Indus River provided a link to the sea. The river allowed valley inhabitants to develop trade with distant peoples, including the Mesopotamians.

Civilization Emerges on the Indus

Historians know less about the civilization in the Indus Valley than about those to the west. They have not yet deciphered the Indus system of writing. Evidence comes largely from archaeological digs, although many sites remain unexplored, and floods probably washed away others long ago. At its height, however, the civilization of the Indus Valley influenced an area much larger than either Mesopotamia or Egypt.

Earliest Arrivals No one is sure how human settlement began in India. Perhaps people who arrived by sea from Africa settled the south. Northern migrants may have made their way through the Khyber Pass in the Hindu Kush mountains. Archaeologists have found evidence in the highlands of agriculture and domesticated sheep and goats dating to about 7000 B.C. By about 3200 B.C., people were farming in villages along the Indus River.

Planned Cities Around 2500 B.C., while Egyptians were building pyramids, people in the Indus Valley were laying the bricks for India's first cities. Archaeologists have found the ruins of more than 100 settlements along the Indus. The largest cities were Kalibangan, Mohenjo-Daro, and Harappa. (Indus Valley civilization is sometimes called Harappan civilization, because of the many archaeological discoveries made at that site.)

One of the most remarkable achievements of the Indus Valley people was their sophisticated city planning. The cities of the early Mesopotamians were a jumble of buildings connected by a maze of winding streets. In contrast, the people of the Indus laid out their cities on a precise grid system. Cities featured a fortified area called a citadel, which contained the major buildings of the city. There were also separate residential districts. Buildings were constructed of oven-baked bricks cut in standard

The citadel arises out of the ruins of Mohenjo-Daro.

(continued from page 42)
Extension Activity Have pairs of students go through the first half of the section titled "The Geography of South Asia." Partners should locate on the map the different areas mentioned in the text.
SKILLBUILDER Answers
1. Himalayas, Karakorum, and Hindu Kush.
2. Mountain ranges, Thar Desert.

OBJECTIVE ② INSTRUCT

Civilization Emerges on the Indus

▶ ***Key Ideas***
• Early Indus Valley settlers develop farming villages along the Indus River.
• Indus Valley cities are well planned and have plumbing and sewage systems.
• Ruins reveal the character and trading patterns of the Indus Valley civilization.

 ELECTRONIC LIBRARY OF PRIMARY SOURCES from "Indus Culture"

CRITICAL THINKING ACTIVITY
CLASS TIME: 15 MINUTES

Making an Analysis Chart
To help students understand Indus Valley culture, have them complete a chart like the one below using information from the "Culture and Trade" section on page 45.

Archaeological Evidence	What it Reveals
uniform planning and construction of cities	strong central government

MORE ABOUT . . .
Domesticated Animals
The Indus Valley people were among the first in the world to have domesticated animals. These animals included chickens, dogs, buffalo, and humped cattle.

CONNECTIONS ACROSS TIME AND PLACE

Urban Planning Tell students that urban planners design and improve cities to accommodate the needs of the people who live in them. Today, urban planners have more and different elements to consider in order to make cities functional on a variety of levels. For example, cities no longer need defensive walls around them, but they do need lots of space for parking cars. Have students use a Venn diagram to list the needs an Indus Valley urban planner might have had to consider and those a modern planner might have to consider.

Indus Valley City — Both — Modern City

protection from invaders

streets

parking areas

At about the time the Indus Valley people were developing their sewage and plumbing systems, people living in a Stone Age village on the Orkney Islands off the coast of Scotland were building bathrooms. The toilets in the Stone Age bathrooms were not as neatly designed as those in the Indus Valley. Bathroom facilities did exist in Mesopotamia, but they were communal, not private.

 IN-DEPTH RESOURCES: UNIT 1
Science and Technology: Early Water Engineering, p. 34

MORE ABOUT . . .
The Great Bath

The central bathing area of the Great Bath was 39 feet by 23 feet and 8 feet deep. Because the pool is similar to the ritual purification pools of later Indian society, some scholars believe it was used in religious ceremonies. Bathing part or all of the body as part of a ceremony is important in some modern traditions in the Hindu, Buddhist, Jewish, Christian, and Muslim religions, among others.

Plumbing in Mohenjo-Daro

From the time people began living in cities, they have faced the problem of plumbing: how to obtain clean water and remove human wastes? In most ancient cities, people retrieved water from the river or a central well. They dumped wastes into open drainage ditches or carted them out of town. Only the rich had separate bathrooms in their homes.

By contrast, the Indus peoples built extensive and modern-looking plumbing systems. In Mohenjo-Daro, almost every house had a private bathroom and toilet. No other civilization achieved this level of convenience until the 19th and 20th centuries. The toilets were neatly built of brick with a wooden seat. Pipes connected to each house carried wastewater into an underground sewer system.

The swimming pool–sized Great Bath in Mohenjo-Daro was probably used for ritual bathing or other religious purposes. Private dressing rooms, some with their own toilets, surrounded the pool.

In their private baths, people took showers by pouring pitchers of water over their head.

Plumbing Facts

- The ancient Romans also built sophisticated plumbing and sewage systems. Aqueducts supplied Roman cities with water.

- In the 17th century, engineers installed a series of water wheels to pump water for the fountains of Versailles, the palace of French king Louis XIV. The water was pumped from a river ten miles away. This was the first water-supply system powered by machine rather than gravity.

- The first flush toilet was patented in 1775 by Alexander Cumming, a British mathematician and watchmaker.

Wastes drained though clay pipes into brick sewers running below the streets. These sewers had manholes, through which sanitation workers could inspect the drains and clean out the muck.

Connect *to* History

Making Inferences What does the attention the Indus people gave to the plumbing and sewer systems suggest about their culture?

 SEE SKILLBUILDER HANDBOOK, PAGE 1005

Connect *to* Today

Researching Find out how water is supplied and wastewater disposed of in your home or community. Is your home connected to a municipal system? If so, when was this system built and how does it function? If not, how does your home system work? How does the system in your home or community compare to what was used in Mohenjo-Daro?

Connect *to* History

Making Inferences The Indus people valued personal cleanliness and social sanitation. They realized that establishing a citywide waste disposal system would be more effective than leaving waste disposal up to individuals. They may have known that poor sanitation could spread disease. Proper sanitation was made available to all classes, not exclusively to the wealthy. This may mean that the Indus Valley people felt the government had some responsibility to provide services for citizens. The neatly built toilets in private bathrooms may suggest that the Indus Valley people valued privacy.

Connect *to* Today

Researching Encourage students to contact the local water department or sewage facility to find answers to the questions. They may also find answers by contacting local building contractors or plumbers. Encourage students to create diagrams to compare the water and waste systems in their community and in Mohenjo-Daro.

sizes, unlike the simpler, irregular, sun-dried mud bricks of the Mesopotamians. Early engineers also created sophisticated plumbing and sewage systems. These systems could rival any urban drainage systems built before the 19th century. The uniformity in the cities' planning and construction suggests that the Indus peoples had developed a strong central government.

Culture and Trade Archaeological evidence shows that Indus civilization was generally stable. The uniform housing suggests that social divisions in the society were not great. Artifacts such as clay and wooden children's toys suggest a relatively prosperous society that could afford to produce nonessential goods. Finally, few weapons of warfare have been found, suggesting that conflict was limited.

Religious artifacts reveal links to modern Hindu culture. Figures show what may be early representations of Shiva, a major Indian god. Other figures relate to a mother goddess, fertility images, and the worship of cattle. All of these became part of later Indian civilization.

Stamps and seals made of carved stone were probably used by Indus merchants to identify their goods. These show that the Indus peoples conducted long-distance trade. Indus seals found in Sumer, and Sumerian objects found in the Indus Valley ruins, reveal that the two civilizations traded a great deal. Trading began as early as the reign of Sargon of Akkad, around 2350 B.C., and continued until 2000 B.C.

Many Indus seals depict animals, especially cattle. This seal depicts a long-horned bull.

Mysterious End to Indus Valley Culture

Around 1750 B.C., the quality of building in the Indus Valley cities declined. Gradually, the great cities fell into decay. What happened? Some historians think that the Indus River changed course, as it tended to do, so that its floods no longer fertilized the fields near the cities. Other scholars suggest that people wore out the valley's land. They overgrazed it, overfarmed it, and overcut its trees, brush, and grass.

As the Indus Valley civilization neared its end, around 1500 B.C., a sudden catastrophe may have helped cause the cities' downfall. Archaeologists have found the remains of 38 bodies in the ruins of Mohenjo-Daro, seemingly never buried. Their presence suggests that residents may have abandoned the city after a natural disaster or an attack from human enemies. As Chapter 3 explains, the Aryans, a nomadic people from north of the Hindu Kush mountains, swept into the Indus Valley at about this time. Whether they caused the collapse of the first Indus civilization or followed later is not known.

Indian civilization would later grow again under the influence of these nomads. At this same time, farther to the east, another civilization was arising. It too was isolated from outside influences, as you will learn in Section 4.

Section 3 Assessment

1. TERMS & NAMES
Identify
• subcontinent
• monsoon

2. TAKING NOTES
Create a two-column chart like the one below. In the left column, list the environmental conditions faced by the people of the Indus Valley. Next to each condition, in the right column, put a plus sign (+) if it was a benefit or a minus sign (–) if it was a drawback.

Environmental Condition	Benefit or Drawback

3. DRAWING CONCLUSIONS
What evidence has led historians to the following beliefs about Indus civilization?

(a) The cities were run by a strong central government.

(b) Indus people carried on trade with Sumer.

(c) Society was generally peaceful and stable.

Choose one of these conclusions and provide a different explanation based on the evidence.

4. THEME ACTIVITY
Science and Technology
Create a "Wall of Remarkable Indus Valley Achievements." Working in teams, write a paragraph about how your team's designated achievement simplified or complicated the Indus people's lives. Include an illustration or a cartoon.

Early River Valley Civilizations **45**

---

46 Chapter 2

Section 4 Overview

OBJECTIVES

① To explain the effects of geography on cultural development in China.

② To describe the growth and structure of the Shang Dynasty.

③ To describe Shang family structure, religion, and technology.

④ To summarize the rise and fall of the Zhou Dynasty.

SKILLBUILDER

• Interpreting maps: location, region, p. 47

CRITICAL THINKING

• Comparing, p. 48
• Recognizing effects, p. 49
• Synthesizing, p. 50
• Analyzing, p. 51
• Analyzing themes, p. 51

FOCUS

5-Minute Warm-Up

▶ *Drawing Conclusions*
To help students understand the effects of geography on the development of Chinese culture, have them answer these questions.

1. Study the map of China on page 47. What geographic features might have isolated China from other cultures?

2. Which rivers do you think were most important to the development of civilization in China?

 WARM-UP TRANSPARENCY 2

OBJECTIVE ① INSTRUCT

The Geography of China

▶ *Key Ideas*
• Geography isolates China and dictates where early settlements will develop.
• Early settlers face challenges as a result of China's geography.

 IN-DEPTH RESOURCES: UNIT 1
Guided Reading, p. 20

ACCESS FOR STUDENTS ACQUIRING ENGLISH
Guided Reading (Spanish), p. 26

---

④ River Dynasties in China

TERMS & NAMES
• loess
• oracle bone
• Mandate of Heaven
• dynastic cycle
• feudalism

MAIN IDEA
The early rulers introduced ideas about government and society that shaped Chinese civilization.

WHY IT MATTERS NOW
The culture that took root during ancient times still affects Chinese ways of life today.

SETTING THE STAGE The walls of China's first cities were built 1,500 years after the walls of Ur, 1,000 years after the great pyramids of Egypt, and 1,000 years after the planned cities of the Indus valley. Though a late starter, the civilization that began along one of China's river systems 3,500 years ago continues to thrive today. The reason for this endurance lies partly in China's geography.

Background
With a few exceptions, this book uses the Pinyin system for writing Chinese names, which is now standard in most publications.

The Geography of China

Natural barriers isolated ancient China from all other civilizations. To China's east lay the Pacific Ocean. To the west lay the Taklimakan (TAH·kluh·muh·KAHN) desert and the icy 14,000-foot Plateau of Tibet. To the southwest were the Himalaya Mountains. And to the north was the desolate Gobi Desert and the Mongolian Plateau. Two major river systems flow from the mountainous west to the Pacific Ocean. They are the Huang He (hwahng·HUH) in the north and the Yangtze (yang·SEE), in central China.

China's Heartland China's geography helps explain why early settlements developed along these main river systems. Mountain ranges and deserts dominate about two-thirds of China's land mass. About 90 percent of the remaining land that is suitable for farming lies within the comparatively small plain between the Huang He and Yangtze in eastern China. This plain was China's heartland.

Throughout China's long history, its political boundaries have expanded and contracted depending on the strength or weakness of its ruling families. Yet China remained a center of civilization. In the Chinese view, people who lived outside of Chinese civilization were barbarians. Because the Chinese saw their country as the center of the civilized world, their own name for China was the Middle Kingdom.

Background
The Yangtze is also called the Chang Jiang (chahng jyahng).

Environmental Challenges Like the other ancient civilizations in this chapter, China's first civilization arose in a river valley. Then as now, the Huang He, whose name means "yellow river," deposited huge amounts of dusty yellowish silt when it overflowed its banks. This silt is actually fertile soil called **loess** (LOH·uhs) that is blown by the winds from deserts to the west. Like the Tigris, Euphrates, and Indus, the Huang He's floods could be generous or ruinous. At its worst, the floods devoured whole villages, earning the river the nickname "China's Sorrow." (One great flood in A.D. 1887 killed nearly a million people.)

Because of China's relative geographic isolation, early settlers had to supply their own goods rather than trading with outside peoples. However, China's natural boundaries did not completely protect these settlers from outsiders. Invasions from the west and north occurred again and again in Chinese history.

CONNECT *to* TODAY

Three Gorges Project
The world's largest dam is being built between the dramatic granite cliffs that overlook the Yangtze River in central China. When it is completed, the dam promises to provide China with electrical power equivalent to ten nuclear power plants. However, no one is certain how control of the river's flooding will affect the plains downstream from the dam, which provide one-third of China's food.

Chinese officials hail the dam as an engineering achievement that ranks with the 2,000-year-old Great Wall of China. Yet its impact will affect both the future and the past. The lake created by the dam will displace more than a million Chinese whose ancestors farmed along the river for thousands of years. It will also drown forever the archaeological sites of some of China's earliest settlements.

The Huang He, or Yellow River, is so-called for the color of its silt. This silt nurtured early development of Chinese civilization and is still a vital resource today.

Ancient China, 2000–200 B.C.

MONGOLIA

GOBI DESERT

TAKLAMAKAN DESERT

CHINA

NORTH CHINA PLAIN

KOREA

JAPAN

Yellow Sea

Anyang
Zhengzhou
Luoyang
Hao
Yangzhou
QIN LING

Huang He (Yellow)

River

Panlongcheng

Yangtze (Chang Jiang)

PLATEAU OF TIBET

HIMALAYA MOUNTAINS

Ganges River

INDU River

INDIA

Xi Jiang (West)

PACIFIC OCEAN

☐ Extent of Shang Dynasty (Approximate)
☐ Extent of Zhou Dynasty (Approximate)
— Border of modern China

500 Miles
1,000 Kilometers

GEOGRAPHY SKILLBUILDER: Interpreting Maps
1. **Location** *Describe the location of the Huang He and Yangtze River in terms of where they rise and end.*
2. **Region** *What area did the Shang and Zhou dynasties control?*

Civilization Emerges in Shang Times

Although Chinese civilization arose later than the others discussed in this chapter, humans have inhabited China for about a million years. Fossil remains show that ancestors of modern humans lived in southwest China about 1.7 million years ago. In northern China near Beijing, a *Homo erectus* skeleton was found. Known as Peking man, his remains show that people settled the river valley about 500,000 years ago.

The First Dynasties Even before the Sumerians settled in southern Mesopotamia, early Chinese cultures were building farming settlements along the Huang He. Around 2000 B.C., some of these settlements grew into China's first cities. According to legend, the first Chinese dynasty, the Xia (shyah) Dynasty, emerged about this time. Its leader was an engineer and mathematician named Yu. Yu's flood-control and irrigation projects helped tame the Huang He and its tributaries so settlements could grow. Since there are no written records from this period, the actual events of this time are unknown. During this period, however, farm surpluses allowed cities to grow. However, the legend of Yu reflects the level of technology of a society making the transition to civilization.

About the time the civilizations of Mesopotamia, Egypt, and the Indus Valley fell to outside invaders, a people called the Shang rose to power in northern China. The Shang Dynasty, which lasted from about 1532 to 1027 B.C., became the first family of rulers to leave written records. The Shang kings also built elaborate palaces and tombs that have been uncovered by archaeologists. Artifacts found among the remains have revealed a great deal about Shang society.

Early Cities Among the oldest and most important Shang cities was Anyang (ahn-YAHNG), one of the capitals of the Shang Dynasty. Unlike the cities of the Indus Valley or Fertile Crescent, Anyang was built mainly of wood. The city stood in a forest

Early River Valley Civilizations **47**

History from Visuals

Ancient China, 2000–200 B.C.
Interpreting the Map Have students study the map of ancient China. Why is the area of the Shang and Zhou dynasties striped? *The area is striped to show that both dynasties ruled here.*

Extension Activity Ask students which geographic features might have prevented trade between China and the Indus Valley and which did not completely protect China from invaders. *Prevented trade: Himalaya Mountains, Plateau of Tibet; did not protect: Gobi Desert, Taklamakan Desert.*

SKILLBUILDER Answers
1. They rise in the western mountains and flow east across the North China plain to the Pacific Ocean.
2. Eastern China between the Huang He and the Yangtze River.

 CRITICAL THINKING TRANSPARENCIES
CT2 Environmental Factors Shape River Valley Civilizations

OBJECTIVE ② INSTRUCT

Civilization Emerges in Shang Times

▶ *Key Ideas*
• According to legend, the first Chinese dynasty is the Xia, which predates the first Sumerian settlements.
• Shang kings build palaces and leave written records. Shang cities are protected by massive earthen walls.
• Shang society is divided between ruling nobles and peasant farmers.

IN-DEPTH RESOURCES: UNIT 1
Connections Across Time and Cultures: River Civilizations in the Ancient World, p. 33

Lady Hao led an unusual life for a woman in ancient China. Would it be unusual for a modern woman to do what Lady Hao did? Ask students to research other female political and military leaders throughout history.

OBJECTIVE ③ INSTRUCT

The Origins of Chinese Culture

▶ **Key Ideas**
- The family is central to Chinese society.
- The Chinese communicate with gods through ancestor spirits and oracle bones.
- China's written language is not connected to its spoken language.
- Shang artisans make silk and excel at bronzework.

 WORLD ART AND CULTURES TRANSPARENCIES
AT5 Chinese bronze

 ELECTRONIC LIBRARY OF PRIMARY SOURCES
"Building a Town," from *Shih ching*

MORE ABOUT . . .
Ancestor Worship

The Chinese are one of many peoples who practice ancestor worship. Members of cultures that follow this practice believe that deceased relatives are no less a part of the family for being dead. Instead, the dead continue to influence matters of the living. Ancestor worship in China declined sharply after communists gained control of the country in 1949. Before this, burning incense at tabletop shrines in honor of an ancestor was common.

 SPOTLIGHT ON

Lady Hao's Tomb
Archaeologists have discovered several Shang royal tombs near Anyang. While most of these vast underground tombs had been robbed over the centuries, a significant one was unearthed intact—the tomb of Fu Hao.

Lady Hao was a wife of king Wu Ding, who ruled during the 1200s B.C. Her relatively small grave contained some 460 bronze artifacts, 750 jade objects, and more than 6,880 cowry shells. The other, far larger Shang royal tombs must have contained even greater wealth.

Writings found in other places reveal a remarkable figure in Lady Hao. On behalf of her husband, she led more than one military campaign, once with a force of 13,000 troops. She also took charge of rituals dedicated to the spirits of Shang ancestors, a duty reserved for the most distinguished members of the royal family.

---

clearing. The higher classes lived in timber-framed houses with walls of clay and straw. These houses lay inside the city walls. The peasants lived in hovels outside the city.

The Shang surrounded their cities with massive earthen walls for protection. The archaeological remains of one city include a wall of packed earth 118 feet wide at its base that encircled an area of 1.2 square miles. It likely took 10,000 men more than 12 years to build such a structure. Like the pyramids of Egypt, these walls demonstrate the Shang rulers' ability to raise and control large forces of workers.

Shang peoples needed walled cities because they were constantly waging war. The chariot, one of the major tools of war, was probably first introduced by contact with cultures from western Asia. The professional warriors, who made up the noble class, underwent lengthy training to learn the techniques of driving and shooting from horse-drawn chariots.

Social Classes Shang society was sharply divided between nobles and peasants. The Shang were governed by a ruling class of warrior-nobles headed by a king. These noble families owned the land. They governed the scattered villages within the Shang lands and sent tribute to the Shang ruler in exchange for local control.

Meanwhile, peasants tilled the soil for their overlords. The farmers had no plows, only wooden digging sticks, and hoes and sickles made of stone. (The Shang made magnificent bronze weapons and ceremonial vessels, but they believed bronze was too precious to be used for mere tools.) The soil was so rich, though, that it yielded two crops a year of millet, rice, and wheat.

The Origins of Chinese Culture

The culture that grew up in China had strong bonds that made for unity. From earliest times, the group seems to have been more important than the individual. Above all, people's lives were governed by their duties to two important authorities—their family and their king or emperor.

Family and Society The family was central to Chinese society. The most important virtue was respect for one's parents. The elder men in the family controlled the family's property and made important decisions. Women, on the other hand, were treated as inferiors. They were expected to obey their fathers, their husbands, and later, their own sons. When a girl was between 13 and 16 years old, her marriage was arranged, and she moved into the house of her husband. Only by bearing sons for her husband's family could she hope to improve her status.

A person's chief loyalty throughout life was to the family. Beyond this, people owed obedience and respect to the ruler of the Middle Kingdom, just as they did to the elders in their family.

Religious Beliefs In China, the family was closely linked to religion. The Chinese believed that the spirits of family ancestors had the power to bring good fortune or disaster to living members of the family. The Chinese did not regard these spirits as mighty gods. Rather, the spirits were more like troublesome or helpful neighbors who demanded attention and respect. Every family paid respect to the father's ancestors and made sacrifices in their honor.

Through the spirits of the ancestors, the Shang consulted the gods. The Shang worshiped a supreme god, Shang Di, as well as many lesser gods. Shang kings consulted the gods through the use of **oracle bones,**

THINK THROUGH HISTORY
A. Compare What did Shang cities have in common with those of Sumer?
A. Answer City walls for protection.

This Shang oracle bone was found in the city of Anyang.

48 Chapter 2

Task: Groups will research a technology developed in ancient China and present annotated collages describing past and present uses of the technology.

Purpose: To learn more about ancient Chinese culture and its relevance today.

Activity: Create five groups and assign each group one of these topics: writing, silk, coined money, cast iron, bronzework. Tell groups to use the chapter and other sources to research their topics. Each

group will need to do the following: write a description of how the ancient Chinese used the technology and how it is used today; make a collage of illustrations showing ancient and modern uses of the technology; write a short description of each image in the collage. Groups should present their work to the class.

 Building a Portfolio: Remind students to add their best work to their portfolio.

ALTERNATIVE ASSESSMENT BOOK
Standards for Evaluating a Cooperative Activity

Standards for Evaluation
Reports should . . .

- present clear examples and descriptions of the uses of each material or technology
- create a coherent and informative display
- show evidence of thorough research

Chinese Writing

The earliest writing systems in the world—including Chinese, Sumerian, and Egyptian—developed from pictographs, or simplified drawings of objects. The writing system used in China today is directly related to the pictographic writing found on Shang oracle bones. As you can see in the chart below, the ancient pictographs can still be recognized in many modern Chinese characters.

	ox	goat, sheep	tree	moon	earth	water	field	heaven	to pray
Ancient symbol	屮	羊	米	D	土	氵	田	呆	禮
Modern character	牛	羊	木	月	土	水	田	天	祝

animal bones and tortoise shells on which priests had scratched questions for the

animal bones and tortoise shells on which priests had scratched questions for the gods. After inscribing a question on the bone, a priest applied a hot poker to it, which caused it to crack. The priests then interpreted the cracks to see how the gods had answered.

Development of Writing The earliest evidence of Chinese writing comes from the oracle bones. In the Chinese method of writing, each character stands for an idea, not a sound. Recall that many of the Egyptian hieroglyphs stood for sounds in the spoken language. In contrast, there were practically no links between China's spoken language and its written language. One could read Chinese without being able to speak a word of it. (This seems less strange when you think of our own number system. Both a French person and an American can understand the written equation $2 + 2 = 4$. But an American may not understand the spoken statement "Deux et deux font quatre.")

The Chinese system of writing had one major advantage. People in all parts of China could learn the same system of writing, even if their spoken languages were very different. Thus, the Chinese written language helped unify a large and diverse land.

The disadvantage of the Chinese system was the enormous number of written characters to be memorized—a different one for each idea. A person needed to know over 1,000 characters to be barely literate. To be a true scholar, one needed to know at least 10,000 characters. For centuries, this severely limited the number of literate, educated Chinese. As a general rule, a noble's children learned to write, but a peasant's children did not.

Shang Technology and Artistry People who were skilled in special crafts made up a separate class in Chinese society. Like other commoners, this group lived outside the walls of cities such as Anyang. They manufactured weapons, jewelry, and religious items for the city's nobles.

Bronzeworking was the leading craft in which Shang artisans excelled. Beautiful bronze objects were used in religious rituals and were also symbols of royal power. Some of these objects were small and graceful, such as bronze bells. Others were massive caldrons, weighing almost a ton.

In earliest Shang times, the Chinese also learned how to make silk cloth by drawing the fine threads from a silkworm's cocoon and weaving them into a light, beautiful fabric. Nobles prided themselves on their finely embroidered silk shoes, which they regarded as a symbol of civilization.

This detail from the ritual vessel shown on page 25 reveals the artistry of Shang bronze workers.

Early River Valley Civilizations **49**

Zhou Bring New Ideas

Key Ideas
• The Zhou use the Mandate of Heaven to justify their overthrow of the Shang.
• Feudalism is established in China, which leads to an increase in local warfare.
• Coined money and iron are used during the Zhou Dynasty era.
• War and the collapse of traditional values bring an end to the Zhou Dynasty.

History from Visuals

Dynastic Cycle in China
Interpreting the Diagram
Explain to students that the diagram begins at the top of the circle, the noon position. Have students read the stages in the cycle.

Extension Activity Ask pairs of students to use the diagram to explain the decline of the Zhou Dynasty.

CRITICAL THINKING ACTIVITY
CLASS TIME: 10 MINUTES

Analyzing Effects
To help students understand the effects of Zhou technology, have them complete the chart below after they read the section titled "Improvements in Technology and Trade" on page 51.

Zhou Technology	Effects
built roads and canals between cities	
introduced coined money	
made iron tools	

Zhou Bring New Ideas

Around 1027 B.C., a people called the Zhou (joh) overthrew the Shang and established their own dynasty. Due to their prior contact with the Shang, the Zhou had adopted much of the Shang culture. Therefore, the change in dynasty did not bring a new culture. Nevertheless, Zhou rule brought new ideas to Chinese civilization.

To justify their conquest, the Zhou leaders declared that the final Shang king had been such a poor ruler that the gods had taken away the Shang's rule and given it to the Zhou. This justification developed over time into a broader view that royal authority came from heaven. A just ruler had divine approval, known as the **Mandate of Heaven.** A wicked or foolish king could lose the Mandate of Heaven and so lose the right to rule. The Duke of Shao, an aide of the Zhou leader who conquered the Shang, described the mandate:

A VOICE FROM THE PAST
Heaven, unpitying, has sent down ruin on Yin [another name for Shang]. Yin has lost the Mandate, and we Zhou have received it. I dare not say that our fortune would continue to prosper, even though I believe that heaven favors those who are sincere in their intentions. I dare not say, either that it would end in certain disaster. . . .
The Mandate of Heaven is not easy to gain. It will be lost when men fail to live up to the reverent and illustrious virtues of their forefathers.
DUKE OF SHAO, quoted in *The Chinese Heritage*

Vocabulary
mandate: a command or instruction from a higher authority.

Strong dynasty establishes peace and prosperity; it is considered to have Mandate of Heaven.

New dynasty gains power, restores peace and order, and claims to have Mandate of Heaven.

In time, dynasty declines and becomes corrupt; taxes are raised; power grows weaker.

Dynastic Cycle in China
Role of Mandate of Heaven

Dynasty is overthrown through rebellion and bloodshed; new dynasty emerges.

Disasters such as floods, famines, peasant revolts, and invasions occur.

Old dynasty is seen as having lost Mandate of Heaven; rebellion is justified.

The Mandate of Heaven became central to the Chinese view of government. Floods, riots, and other calamities might be signs that the ancestral spirits were displeased with a king's rule. In that case, the Mandate of Heaven might pass to another noble family. This was the Chinese explanation for rebellion, civil war, and the rise of a new dynasty.

Chinese history is marked by a succession of dynasties until dynastic rule was finally overthrown in the early 1900s. Historians describe the pattern of rise, decline, and replacement of dynasties as the **dynastic cycle.**

Control Through Feudalism The Zhou Dynasty controlled lands that stretched far beyond the Huang He in the north to the Yangtze in the south. In response to the challenge of governing this vast area, they gave control over different regions to members of the royal family and other trusted nobles. This established a system called feudalism. **Feudalism** is a political system in which nobles, or lords, are granted the use of lands that legally belong to the king. In return, the nobles owe loyalty and military service to the king and protection to the people who live on their estates. (Similar systems would arise centuries later in both Japan and Europe.)

At first, the local lords lived in small walled towns and had to submit to the superior strength and control of the Zhou rulers. Gradually, however, the lords grew stronger as the towns grew into cities and expanded into the surrounding territory. Peoples who had been hostile toward the lords gradually accepted their rule and adopted Zhou ways. As a result, the local lords became less dependent on the king. More and more, they fought among themselves and with neighboring peoples for wealth and territory.

THINK THROUGH HISTORY
C. Synthesizing
According to Chinese beliefs, what role did the Mandate of Heaven play in the dynastic cycle?
C. Answer The Mandate of Heaven helped explain the cycle of rise, decline, and replacement of dynasties: disaster and decline showed that the mandate was lost and justified rebellion; the ability to restore order showed a new rule had gained the mandate.

CONNECTIONS ACROSS THE CURRICULUM

American History *Manifest Destiny*
Throughout history, different groups have used the idea of destiny to explain and justify their actions. In the 1840s, thousands of settlers in the United States moved west, where land was plentiful and they could make a new start. A magazine editor described this westward movement as "the fulfillment of our manifest destiny to overspread the continent allotted by Providence for the free development of our yearly multiplying million."

People began to use the phrase "manifest destiny" to describe the belief that the destiny of Americans was to spread out toward the West and introduce the virtues of democracy to new areas. Manifest destiny was not beneficial to everyone in the United States. Native Americans already living in the West were forced to leave their traditional lands. Others died fighting to keep them. Ask students to compare the quote from the Duke of Shao with the quote from the American magazine editor. Do they express similar ideas? How so? How did these ideas relieve people of responsibility for their actions?

Improvements in Technology and Trade Although warfare was common throughout the Zhou Dynasty, the era also produced many innovations. As large cities grew, the Zhou built roads and canals to supply them. These in turn stimulated trade and agriculture. The Zhou also introduced coined money, which further improved trade. To run the daily operations of the cities, a new class of civil servants, or government administrative workers, emerged.

The major technological advancement was the use of iron. The Zhou developed blast furnaces that allowed them to produce cast iron. This skill would not be matched in Europe until the Middle Ages. The Zhou used iron to create weapons, especially dagger-axes and swords. They also used it for common agricultural tools such as sickles, knives, and spades. Since iron is stronger than bronze, iron tools made farm work easier and more productive. The ability to grow more food helped Zhou farmers support thriving cities.

These Chinese coins shaped like a hoe and a knife come from the Zhou period. Their shapes may reflect the practice of using tools such as hoes and knives for payment before coins existed.

A Period of Warring States The Zhou ruled from around 1027 to 256 B.C. For the first 300 years of this long period, the Zhou empire was generally peaceful and stable. Gradually, however, Zhou rule weakened. In 771 B.C., nomads from the north and west sacked the city of Hao, the Zhou capital. They murdered the Zhou monarch, but a few members of the royal family escaped eastward to the city of Luoyang (lwoh-YAHNG). Here in this new capital on the Huang He, the Zhou Dynasty pretended to rule for another 500 years.

In fact, the Zhou kings at Luoyang were almost powerless, and they could not control the noble families. Trained as warriors, the lords sought every opportunity to pick fights with neighboring lords. As their power grew, these warlords claimed to be kings in their own territory. As a result, the later years of the Zhou are often called "the time of the warring states."

Even the style of warfare changed. Under feudalism, nobles had fought according to an honorable code of conduct. With the decline of law and order, professional warriors and mercenaries set the rules of battle. Peasant foot soldiers, supported by cavalry, replaced chariots as the main force on the battlefield. New weapons came into use, such as the crossbow, which would not be introduced in Europe until the Middle Ages.

In this time of bloodshed, traditional values collapsed. At the very heart of Chinese civilization was a love of order, harmony, and respect for authority. Now there was chaos, arrogance, and defiance. How could China be saved? The dynastic cycle was about to bring a new start at a time when migrations and invasions were changing the lands of all the early civilizations.

Section 4 Assessment

1. TERMS & NAMES

Identify
- loess
- oracle bone
- Mandate of Heaven
- dynastic cycle
- feudalism

2. TAKING NOTES

Create a time line of the major developments in the early Chinese dynasties, using a form such as the one below.

Which event do you think was the most critical turning point? Why?

3. ANALYZING

The group was often more important than the individual in Chinese culture. In your judgment, what are the benefits and drawbacks of this belief?

THINK ABOUT
- family roles
- the characteristics of a ruler
- role of spirit gods

4. ANALYZING THEMES

Power and Authority Do you think that the Zhou Dynasty's downfall resulted because of their method of control? Why or why not?

THINK ABOUT
- feudalism
- the large division of rich and poor
- the vast controlled lands
- the noble-king relationship

Early River Valley Civilizations **51**

Chapter 2 Assessment

TERMS & NAMES

1. irrigation, p. 28
2. city-state, p. 29
3. polytheism, p. 29
4. empire, p. 31
5. mummification, p. 37
6. hieroglyphics, p. 38
7. subcontinent, p. 42
8. monsoon, p. 42
9. Mandate of Heaven, p. 50
10. feudalism, p. 50

REVIEW QUESTIONS

Answers will vary.

11. Region that stretches from the eastern end of the Mediterranean, through Mesopotamia, to the northern end of the Persian Gulf; so-called for its curved shape and fertile soil.

12. Unpredictable floods; small, defenseless region; limited natural resources.

13. To overcome environmental disadvantages, Sumerians needed to construct irrigation systems, build protective walls, and conduct trade. These projects required organization, cooperation, and leadership, which were the beginnings of organized government.

14. Egyptians believed that kings ruled eternally. Pyramids were built as tombs for the kings.

15. Without the Nile, Egyptian civilization would not have been as prosperous or may not even have existed at all.

16. That it was strong and centralized.

17. The people wore out the land; the Indus River changed course, leaving the land without the necessary nutrients that resulted during floods.

18. Mountain ranges and deserts cover most of China; the Huang He and Yangtze provide a fertile plain.

19. People in all parts of China could communicate using the same system of writing even if their spoken languages were different.

20. A dynasty rises and prospers. Eventually, it becomes corrupt and declines. Disasters occur, and the dynasty is seen as having lost divine approval. The dynasty is overthrown, and a new dynasty rises and prospers.

TERMS & NAMES

Briefly explain the importance of each of the following to early river valley civilizations, 3500–450 B.C.

1. irrigation
2. city-state
3. polytheism
4. empire
5. mummification
6. hieroglyphics
7. subcontinent
8. monsoon
9. Mandate of Heaven
10. feudalism

Interact *with* History

On page 26, you looked at the justice of Hammurabi's Code. Now that you have read about the development of four civilizations, think about how laws differ from place to place. How have they developed and changed over time? What similarities do you see between Hammurabi's Code and the laws you live under today? How are they different? Discuss your opinions with a small group.

REVIEW QUESTIONS

SECTION 1 (*pages 27–32*)
City-States in Mesopotamia

11. What is the Fertile Crescent and why is it called that?

12. Name three disadvantages of Sumer's natural environment.

13. What circumstances led to the beginning of organized government?

SECTION 2 (*pages 33–41*)
Pyramids on the Nile

14. Why did the Egyptians build pyramids?

15. Herodotus remarked that Egypt was the "gift of the Nile." What did he mean by this?

SECTION 3 (*pages 42–45*)
Planned Cities on the Indus

16. What does the uniformity of Indus Valley cities tell us about their government?

17. Give two reasons historians use to explain the downfall of Indus Valley cities.

SECTION 4 (*pages 46–51*)
River Dynasties in China

18. Why is it not surprising that China's early settlements developed where they did?

19. What was the great advantage of the Chinese written language?

20. Explain the dynastic cycle in China.

Visual Summary

Early River Valley Civilizations

	Environment	Power & Authority	Science & Technology
Sumer	• Flooding of Tigris and Euphrates unpredictable • No natural barriers • Limited natural resources for making tools or buildings	• Independent city-states, often warring • City-states governed first by priests, then by generals who became kings • City-states eventually united into first empires by conquerors	• Irrigation • Cuneiform • Bronze • Wheel, sail, plow
Egypt	• Flooding of the Nile predictable • Nile an easy transportation link between Egypt's villages • Deserts were natural barriers	• Kingdom with strong government organization • Theocracy, with pharaohs ruling as gods • Pharaohs built pyramids	• Hieroglyphics • Pyramids • Mathematics, geometry • Medicine
Indus Valley	• Indus flooding unpredictable • Monsoon winds • Mountains, deserts were natural barriers	• Strong centralized government • Planned cities • Social divisions not significant	• Writing (not yet deciphered) • Cities built on precise grid • Plumbing and sewage systems
China	• Huang He flooding unpredictable • Mountains, deserts natural barriers • Geographically isolated from other ancient civilizations	• Community and family more important than individual • Sharp divisions between nobles and peasants • Mandate of Heaven	• Writing • Silk • Coined money • Cast iron

52 Chapter 2

Interact *with* History

Possible Responses: Sumerian cities had their own codes of law. Hammurabi created a single code of law. Over time, laws have become more humane. Similarities—both reinforce the idea that a government has a responsibility for what happens in society. Differences—Hammurabi's Code set different punishments for rich and poor, men and women.

CRITICAL THINKING

1. RELIGIOUS BELIEFS

Create a Venn diagram like the one shown below to indicate differences and similarities in religious beliefs among these ancient civilizations.

2. PUBLIC WORKS

THEME POWER AND AUTHORITY Think about a massive public project that might take place today, such as building a new subway system or a large dam. In terms of government power and authority, how would this be similar to the building of the pyramids? How would it be different?

3. WOMEN IN ANCIENT SOCIETIES

Women were treated differently in the four civilizations discussed in this chapter. If you had been a woman during this time, in which civilization would you have preferred to live? Why?

4. ANALYZING PRIMARY SOURCES

The following is an excerpt from an ancient Egyptian hymn praising the Nile. Read the paragraph and answer the questions below it.

A VOICE FROM THE PAST

The Lord of Fishes, He Who Makes the marsh birds to Go Upstream. There are no birds which come down because of the hot winds. He who makes barley and brings emmer [a kind of wheat] into being, that he may make the temples festive. If he is sluggish, then nostrils are stopped up, and everybody is poor. If there be thus a cutting down in the food offerings of the gods, then a million men perish among mortals, covetousness is practiced, the entire land is in a fury, and great and small are on the execution-block. . . . When he rises, then the land is in jubilation, then every belly is in joy, every backbone takes on laughter, and every tooth is exposed.

"Hymn to the Nile," from *Ancient Near Eastern Texts*

- How does this quote show the importance of the Nile?
- What does the hymn show about ancient Egyptian culture?

CHAPTER ACTIVITIES

1. LIVING HISTORY: Unit Portfolio Project

THEME INTERACTION WITH ENVIRONMENT Your unit portfolio project focuses on showing how people in history have interacted with the environment (see page 3). For Chapter 2, you might use one of the following ideas to add to your portfolio.

- You are a news reporter reporting on the flood conditions in early Sumer. Ask classmates to role-play citizens before and after the invention of irrigation ditches. Tape-record your interviews.
- Write four poems, one for each civilization in the chapter. Include some reference to how each civilization interacted with the environment.
- Make a map of China showing how natural barriers helped to isolate Chinese civilization from other areas. Create your map on paper using an outline map, or make a salt map to show the features in three-dimensional relief.

2. CONNECT TO TODAY: Cooperative Learning

THEME SCIENCE AND TECHNOLOGY Indus Valley cities were laid out on a precise grid system. They were planned cities. Most cities without a grid system probably developed over a long period of time. Work with a team to create a street map of your hometown.

- Look at street maps of Washington, D.C. and Boston. Boston was not a planned city. Washington, D.C. was planned. How can you tell?

 Using the Internet, the library, or government resources, research the structure of your hometown, then draw it. Was it a planned city?

3. INTERPRETING A TIME LINE

Revisit the unit time line on pages 2–3 and study the segment for Chapter 2. Which of the events are examples of a well-organized government? Why?

FOCUS ON GEOGRAPHY

Look at the four ancient cities shown on the following climate map.

- Which cities are located in desert climates?
- Which city is not located in a dry climate? What is its climate region called?

Connect to History Identify which civilization each city belongs to. Which of these civilizations developed the latest?

☐	Tropical-wet
☐	Tropical-dry
☐	Semidesert
☐	Desert
☐	Mediterranean
☐	Humid subtropical
☐	Humid continental
■	Subarctic
☐	Mountain

Climate Regions of the Ancient World

Early River Valley Civilizations **53**

1. LIVING HISTORY

Standards for Evaluation

An effective interview should meet the following criteria:

- Shows an understanding of the farming challenges and the Sumerian way of life that existed before irrigation.
- Presents a clear explanation of how irrigation improved farming and changed life for Sumerians.
- Includes information about organized government.

Standards for Evaluation

Effective poems should meet the following criteria:

- Use creative language to express ideas about each civilization.
- Describe the relationship between each civilization and the environment.
- Show effort and imagination.

Standards for Evaluation

An effective map should meet the following criteria:

- Shows an accurate outline of China.
- Includes all important natural barriers, located accurately.
- Has clear labels on all natural barriers.

2. CONNECT TO TODAY

Standards for Evaluation

An effective street map should meet the following criteria:

- Clearly depicts the structure of the hometown.
- Accurately shows that the town is either planned or unplanned.

3. INTERPRETING A TIME LINE

Possible Responses: The building of the Great Pyramid, the rise of planned cities, and the creation of Hammurabi's code. All require planning, a variety of skilled workers, and supervision. Without an organized government to provide structure and a work plan, none of these projects would have been successful.

FOCUS ON GEOGRAPHY

1. Memphis, Ur, Mohenjo-Daro.
2. Anyang; Humid continental.

Connect to History Memphis—Egypt; Ur—Sumer; Mohenjo-Daro—Indus Valley; Anyang—China. China developed latest.

CRITICAL THINKING

1. RELIGIOUS BELIEFS

Possible Responses: Sumer—bleak concept of afterlife. Egypt—pharaohs were gods. China—ancestral spirits, oracle bones. Similarities: polytheism, belief in afterlife.

2. PUBLIC WORKS

Possible Responses: Similarities—require organization, funded by government, need engineering knowledge, employ skilled and unskilled laborers. Differences—project today would be paid for by government but contracted out to private companies; higher level of technology would make project faster and safer.

3. WOMEN IN ANCIENT SOCIETIES

Possible Responses: Egypt—women could propose marriage, seek divorce, and trade property. Sumer—women there could pursue many occupations, and own property.

4. ANALYZING PRIMARY SOURCES

Possible Responses: Shows importance by describing the negative effects that resulted if the Nile didn't rise. Egyptians' livelihoods were tied directly to the Nile; when the Nile was not favorable, people became more aggressive and lawless.

People and Ideas on the Move

	Key Ideas	**COPY MASTERS**	**ASSESSMENT**
SECTION 1 Indo-European Migrations *pp. 57–61*	*Migrations of Indo-Europeans into parts of Europe and South Asia introduce new ideas and languages and result in a blend of new and old cultures.*	*In-Depth Resources: Unit 1* • **Guided Reading,** p. 35 • **Primary Source:** from the *Rig Veda,* p. 42; from the *Bhagavad-Gita,* p. 43	*Section 1 Assessment,* p. 61 *Formal Assessment* • Section Quiz, p. 28 *Alternative Assessment Book* • Standards for Evaluating a Cooperative Activity
SECTION 2 Roots of Hinduism and Buddhism *pp. 62–66*	*Hinduism has no one founder but promotes a unified world view and a rigid caste system. Buddhism's founder, Siddhartha Gautama, preaches the way of moderation and rejects the Aryan caste system.*	*In-Depth Resources: Unit 1* • **Guided Reading,** p. 36 • **Literature:** from the *Ramayana,* p. 46; from *Siddhartha,* p. 47 • **History Makers:** Siddhartha Gautama, p. 49	*Section 2 Assessment,* p. 66 *Formal Assessment* • Section Quiz, p. 29 *Alternative Assessment Book* • Standards for Evaluating a Cooperative Activity
SECTION 3 Seafaring Traders Extend Boundaries *pp. 67–71*	*Ancient sea traders spread goods, culture, and innovative ideas in the Mediterranean and beyond. The Phoenicians are not only a great seafaring people but give the world the first written alphabet.*	*In-Depth Resources: Unit 1* • **Guided Reading,** p. 37 • **Skillbuilder Practice:** Forming Opinions, p. 39 • **Primary Source:** from Dolphin Fresco from Knossos, p. 44 • **History Makers:** Herodotus, p. 50	*Section 3 Assessment,* p. 71 *Formal Assessment* • Section Quiz, p. 30 *Alternative Assessment Book* • Standards for Evaluating a Cooperative Activity
SECTION 4 The Origins of Judaism *pp. 72–77*	*The religion of the ancient Hebrews is the world's first major monotheistic religion. The Hebrews establish covenants with God, who is over all people. Their ethical and moral systems, as set forth in the Torah and Ten Commandments, become a foundation for Christianity and Islam.*	*In-Depth Resources: Unit 1* • **Guided Reading,** p. 38 • **Geography Application:** Early Eastern Mediterranean Civilizations, p. 40 • **Primary Source:** The Ten Commandments, p. 45 • **Connections Across Time and Cultures:** Religions in the Ancient World, p. 51	*Section 4 Assessment,* p. 77 *Formal Assessment* • Section Quiz, p. 31 *Alternative Assessment Book* • Standards for Evaluating a Product or Performance
CHAPTER RESOURCES	**Chapter Overview** *Migrations and trade networks carry new ideas, languages, and cultures throughout the Mediterranean and as far east as South Asia. Three major world religions, Hinduism, Buddhism, and Judaism, emerge during this period.*	*Telescoping the Times* • Chapter Summary, pp. 9–12 *Planning for Block Schedules*	*Chapter Assessment,* pp. 78–79 *Chapter Activities,* p. 79 *Formal Assessment* • Chapter Test, forms A and B, pp. 32–37 *Test Generator* *Alternative Assessment Book*

2000 B.C.–259 B.C.

TECHNOLOGY

 Warm-Up Transparency 3

 Electronic Library of Primary Sources
- "Hymn 129," from the *Rig Veda*

 INTERNET RESOURCES
www.mlworldhistory.com

 Warm-Up Transparency 3

 Geography Transparencies
- GT3 Hindu India and Buddhist Sites

 World Art and Cultures Transparencies
- AT6 Indian terra cotta Mother Goddess

 Religions of the World
- Hinduism • Buddhism

 Electronic Library of Primary Sources
- from *The Life of Gotama the Buddha*

 Warm-Up Transparency 3

 World Art and Cultures Transparencies
- AT7 Palace of Minos at Knossos

 Electronic Library of Primary Sources
- "Hanno's Voyage"

 INTERNET RESOURCES
www.mlworldhistory.com

 Warm-Up Transparency 3

 Critical Thinking Transparencies
- CT3 Time Machine: Major Religions 2500 B.C.–A.D. 552
- CT39 Chapter 3 Visual Summary

 Religions of the World
- Judaism

 Electronic Library of Primary Sources
- from the Book of Genesis and the Book of Exodus in the King James Bible

 INTERNET RESOURCES
www.mlworldhistory.com

 Chapter Summaries on Audiocassette in English and Spanish

 INTERNET RESOURCES
www.mlworldhistory.com

Block Scheduling (90 MINUTES)

Day 1

Section 1, pp. 57–61

 COOPERATIVE ACTIVITY
Comparing Social Systems, p. 59 (Teacher's Edition)

Section 2, pp. 62–66

 COOPERATIVE ACTIVITY
Interviewing, p. 65 (Teacher's Edition)

Section Assessments,
pp. 61, 66

Day 2

Section 3, pp. 67–71

 COOPERATIVE ACTIVITY
Creating a Board Game, p. 69 (Teacher's Edition)

Section 4, pp. 72–77

Section Assessments, pp. 71, 77

Chapter Assessments, pp. 78–79

Yearly Pacing *Chapter 3 Total:* 2 days *Yearly Total:* 85 days

 Planning for Block Schedules

Customizing for Special Needs

Students Acquiring English

 Access for Students Acquiring English
- **Guided Reading** for Sections 1–4 (Spanish), pp. 33–36
- **Chapter Summary** (Spanish), pp. 30–32
- **Skillbuilder Practice** Forming Opinions (Spanish), p. 37
- **Geography Application** Early Eastern Mediterranean Civilizations, (Spanish), p. 38–39

 Chapter Summaries on Audiocassette in English and Spanish

 INTERNET RESOURCES
www.mlworldhistory.com
The Diverse Classroom.

Less Proficient Readers

 In-Depth Resources: Unit 1
- **Guided Reading** for Sections 1–4, pp. 00–00
- **Skillbuilder Practice** Forming Opinions, p. 37
- **Geography Application** Early Eastern Mediterranean Civilizations, p. 40

 Telescoping the Times
- Chapter Summary, pp. 9–12

Chapter Summaries on Audiocassette

Gifted and Talented Students

In-Depth Resources: Unit 1

Primary Sources:
- from the *Rig Veda*, p. 42
- from the *Bhagavad Gita*, p. 43
- from Dolphin Fresco from Knossos, p. 44
- The Ten Commandments, p. 45

History Makers:
- Siddhartha Gautama, p. 49
- Herodotus, p. 50

Connections to Literature READINGS FOR STUDENTS

In-Depth Resources: Unit 1
- from the *Ramayana*, p. 46
- from *Siddhartha*, by Hermann Hesse, p. 47

Enrichment Reading
- Llewelyn, Morgan
The Horse Goddess
Boston: Houghton, 1982

This historical novel set in the eighth century B.C., tells the story of the daughter of a Celtic chief who decides to flee her tribe.

- Reps, Paul and Nyogen Senzaki
Zen Flesh, Zen Bones
Boston: Shambhala, 1994

Entertaining Zen anecdotes and stories to live by.

 P E = Pupil's Edition   = Overhead Transparency   = Software   = Video

= Copy Master   = CD-ROM   = Audiocassette   = Internet

53B

People and Ideas on the Move, 3500 B.C.–259 B.C.

Accessing Prior Knowledge

- Ask students to read the captions to each picture and discuss what they already know about each topic.

Making Judgments

- Have students look at the picture and caption related to India. What influence do they think religion has in people's lives?

- Ask students to note where all the major cities are on the map. What does this tell them about the importance of waterways to ancient civilizations?

Geography Connection

Ask students to locate India and Asia Minor on the map.

- What geographic features do these two regions have in common? *Major rivers, mountains, sea coasts*

- Why would India be more vulnerable than Asia Minor to invaders from the north? *It has a major valley and large rivers; Asia Minor is very mountainous*

CHAPTER
3

People and Ideas on the Move, 3500 B.C.–259 B.C.

PREVIEWING THEMES

Interaction with Environment

Early peoples often migrated from their lands both to escape hostile circumstances and to find new homes that promised a better life. Many times they responded to changing climates that hindered their way of life. Once resettled, they had to deal with the environment of their new homeland.

Economics

Traders long ago went to sea to transport their goods to other parts of the world. Among the most expert of early trading peoples were the Phoenicians. They so dominated the Mediterranean that it was called their lake. Sea traders also traveled between India and Arabia, spreading ideas as well as merchandise.

Religious and Ethical Systems

Three major world religions practiced by millions today developed during this time. Hinduism and Buddhism originated in India, while Judaism developed in Southwest Asia. Each has deeply influenced the way that people look at their world and judge human behavior.

INTERNET CONNECTION

Visit us at **www.mlworldhistory.com** to learn more about people and ideas on the move.

THE ANCIENT WORLD, 1500 B.C.–259 B.C.

EUROPE

ATLANTIC OCEAN

Massilia

Rome

SPAIN

Sardinia

ITALY

Adriatic Sea

Aegean Sea

GREECE

Athens

Gades

Carthage

Sicily

Mediterranean Sea

Knossos
Crete

Ale

E

This wide-eyed face is actually a glass bead from a necklace produced in the powerful **Phoenician city-state of Carthage** around **400 B.C.** The Phoenicians were excellent glass workers. They made elaborate pieces that were traded in port towns around the Mediterranean.

Early Indo-European tribes
Hittite Empire
Phoenician colonies
Kingdom of Magadha

0   500 Miles
0   1,000 Kilometers

N

AFRICA

0° Prime Meridian

54

GEOGRAPHY THEMES

Place

Ask students to note the importance of seas, rivers, and mountains in determining the movement of peoples in ancient times. To locate the physical barriers that Indo-Europeans had to overcome as they spread throughout Europe and Southwest Asia, have students turn to page 977 in the Atlas. Ask them to name the major waterways that promoted maritime trade. *Possible answers might include the mountains of Afghanistan, the Mediterranean Sea, Red Sea, Indian Ocean, and Indus River.*

Movement

Tell students that this chapter is primarily about movement—of people, raw materials, trade goods, and ideas. Explain that in some cases the movements of people from one area to another took several generations. Whole families were born, lived, and died while they were on the move. Remind students that trade goods, along with cultural items, frequently changed hands several times before they reached their final destination.

ADDITIONAL RESOURCES

Books for the Teacher

- Castleden, Rodney. *Minoans: Life in Bronze Age Crete.* London and New York: Routledge, 1990.

- Jacobs, Louis. *The Jewish Religion: A Companion.* New York: Oxford UP, 1995.

- Kulke, Hermann and Dietmar Rothermund. *A History of India.* London and New York: Routledge, 1990.

- Macqueen, J. G. *The Hittites and Their Contemporaries in Asia Minor.* Boulder: Westview, 1975.

- Reat, N. Ross. *Buddhism: A History.* Fremont, CA: Asian Humanities Press, 1994.

Books for the Student

- Demi. *Buddha.* New York: Henry Holt, 1996. An account of Buddha's life and teachings.

- Edey, Maitland A. *The Sea Traders.* New York: Time-Life, 1974. Descriptions of the Mediterranean cultures.

- Odijk, Pamela. *The Phoenicians.* Needham Heights, MA: Silver Burdett, 1989.

- Wood, Angela. *Judaism.* New York: Thomson Learning, 1995.

Videos

- *India: The Empire of the Spirit.* Ambrose Video, 1992. 800-526-4663.

- *The Age of Iron: 2000 B.C.–A.D. 200.* Social Studies School Service, 1985. 800-421-4246.

Reverence for cows, particularly milk cows, stretches back to the earliest days of the **Hindu religion.** Hindu scriptures call the cow Devi, or goddess. They also associate cows with Aditi, the mother of the gods herself. Cows still enjoy a special status in Hindu religion. In **India** today, killing or harming cows is forbidden. The animals are also free to wander about in cities—like these cows sitting in the middle of a busy street.

In one of the most famous episodes in the Bible, the Queen of Sheba visits **Israel's King Solomon.** The Arabian queen had heard of Solomon's great wisdom and had come to test it with difficult questions. When Solomon answered them all, the queen exclaimed: ". . . I did not believe the reports until I had come and my own eyes had seen it; your wisdom and prosperity far surpass the report that I had heard." This fresco by the 15th-century Italian artist Piero della Francesca illustrates the queen's visit.

55

HISTORY THROUGH ART

15th-Century Fresco: *King Solomon and the Queen of Sheba*

Piero della Francesca

This fresco is one of four huge panels by Piero della Francesca depicting scenes from the Bible. A fresco is a painting made on fresh plaster, using paints mixed with water. First the artist sketches the picture on the wall. He then applies as much fresh plaster within the lines of the sketch as he can paint in one day.

The artist must work quickly before the plaster dries or the paint will flake off. The next day, any unpainted plaster is chipped away and a new surface applied. The four panels took della Francesca 12 years to finish.

Such works of art were more than just decoration. Because most people in the 1500s could not read, they learned their Bible stories from these paintings. To make the story of King Solomon and the queen seem more contemporary, della Francesca painted them in

the clothing and setting of Renaissance Europe.

Interpreting the Art If you were seeing this painting for the first time, what would it tell you about King Solomon? *Possible answers: He is obviously someone of great importance and wealth who is receiving homage or gifts from someone also of some importance.* What questions about the story of King Solomon does the painting raise?

Interact *with* History

Interact *with* History

This Interact with History feature motivates students by inviting them to put themselves in a key historical situation—an invasion of their land by a foreign enemy. As they think about dealing with an invader, students will analyze the issues, explore their options, and become decision makers.

Purpose

- to set the stage for studying the migrations and invasions of Indo-European people into Europe, Asia, and Africa
- to help students understand how the interaction of different peoples results in the spread of technology, ideas, and culture
- to help students see how the interaction of ancient peoples has helped to shape their own modern civilization

Teaching Strategy

Thinking Critically After students have thought about being in the situation described on this page, have them answer the key questions and give reasons for their answers.

EXAMINING *the* ISSUES

Following are suggestions for addressing each bulleted question.

1 What would make it difficult to live in peace with a conqueror? What would make it possible?

2 Have students recall other times in history when a conquered people had to carry on their traditions in secret. How would people live such a double life?

3 Ask students what they would take with them and where they might go.

Making Connections Ask students to discuss the positive and negative aspects of one people invading another. Where is the same process occurring today? *Africa, Balkans, some nations of the former Soviet Union.*

You are drawing water from your well when, without warning, a magnificent white horse appears on the horizon. You have heard stories about this horse. You know that, once a year, it is sent out by a foreign king to roam freely outside his land. The armed soldiers who are following the horse will claim all the land it travels through for their king.

You have three choices. You could stay and fight for your land. However, there are so many soldiers that it is unlikely that you and the other villagers would win. You can stay and accept the domination of the new ruler from the north. Or you can gather up your family and flee, as many others have done before you.

Will the invaders capture and enslave you? Or will they allow you to continue to live as you have?

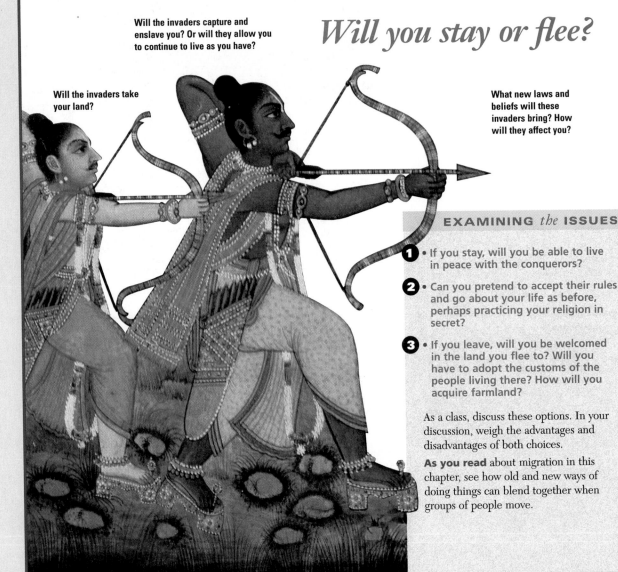

Will the invaders take your land?

Will you stay or flee?

What new laws and beliefs will these invaders bring? How will they affect you?

EXAMINING *the* ISSUES

1 • If you stay, will you be able to live in peace with the conquerors?

2 • Can you pretend to accept their rules and go about your life as before, perhaps practicing your religion in secret?

3 • If you leave, will you be welcomed in the land you flee to? Will you have to adopt the customs of the people living there? How will you acquire farmland?

As a class, discuss these options. In your discussion, weigh the advantages and disadvantages of both choices.

As you read about migration in this chapter, see how old and new ways of doing things can blend together when groups of people move.

Follow Up

A feature on the chapter assessment will ask students to reevaluate their responses to the situation presented on this page.

Indo-European Migrations

TERMS & NAMES
- Indo-Europeans
- steppes
- migration
- Hittites
- Anatolia
- Aryans
- *Vedas*
- Brahmin
- caste
- *Mahabharata*

MAIN IDEA

Indo-European peoples migrated into Europe, India, and Southwest Asia and interacted with peoples living there.

WHY IT MATTERS NOW

Half the people living today speak languages that stem from the original Indo-European languages.

SETTING THE STAGE In India and in Mesopotamia, civilizations first developed along lush river valleys. Even as large cities such as Mohenjo-Daro and Harappa declined, agriculture and small urban communities flourished. These wealthy river valleys attracted seminomadic tribes. These peoples may have left their own homelands because of politics or changes in the environment.

Indo-Europeans Migrate

Background
This steppe area included parts of present-day Romania, Moldova, Ukraine, southern Russia, and Kazakhstan.

The **Indo-Europeans** were a group of seminomadic peoples who came from the **steppes**—dry grasslands that stretched north of the Caucasus (KAW·kuh·suhs). The Caucasus are the mountains between the Black and Caspian seas. (See the map on pages 54–55.) These primarily pastoral people herded cattle, sheep, and goats. The Indo-Europeans also tamed horses and rode into battle in light, two-wheeled chariots. They lived in tribes that spoke forms of a language that we call Indo-European.

The Indo-European Language Family The languages of the Indo-Europeans were the ancestors of many of the modern languages of Europe, Southwest Asia, and South Asia. English, Spanish, Persian, and Hindi all trace their origins back to different forms of the original Indo-European language.

Vocabulary
Slavic-speakers: speakers of a language that developed into most of today's eastern European languages.

Historians can actually tell where different Indo-European tribes settled by the languages they spoke. Some Slavic-speakers moved north and west. Others, who spoke early Celtic, Germanic, and Italic languages, moved west through Europe. Still others, Greek- and Persian-speakers, went south. The Aryans (AIR·ee·uhnz), who spoke an early form of Sanskrit, penetrated the mountain passes of the Hindu Kush and entered India.

Notice the similarities of words within the Indo-European family of languages.

Language Family Resemblances

English	mother	father	daughter	new	six
Sanskrit	mātár	pitár	duhitá	návas	sát
Persian	muhdáhr	puhdáhr	dukhtáhr	now	shahsh
Spanish	madre	padre	hija	nuevo	seis
German	Mutter	Vater	Tochter	neu	sechs

An Unexplained Migration No one is quite sure why these people left their homelands in the steppes. The lands where their animals grazed may have dried up. Their human or animal population may have grown too large to feed. They may also have tried to escape from invaders, or from an outbreak of disease.

Whatever the reason, Indo-European nomads began to migrate outward in all directions between 1700 and 1200 B.C. These **migrations,** movements of a people from one region to another, did not happen all at once, but in waves over a long period of time.

People and Ideas on the Move **57**

SECTION 1 RESOURCES

PRINT RESOURCES

 IN-DEPTH RESOURCES: UNIT 1
Guided Reading, p. 35
Primary Sources: from the *Rig Veda*, p. 42; from the *Bhagavad-Gita*, p. 43
Literature: from the *Ramayana*, p. 46

ACCESS FOR STUDENTS ACQUIRING ENGLISH
Guided Reading (Spanish), p. 33

FORMAL ASSESSMENT
Section Quiz, p. 28

 ALTERNATIVE ASSESSMENT BOOK

TECHNOLOGY RESOURCES

 CD-ROM
Electronic Library of Primary Sources

 INTERNET www.mlworldhistory.com

Section 1 Overview

OBJECTIVES

(1) To describe the spread of Indo-Europeans and their language.

(2) To identify the Hittite empire and the effects of its technology on other societies.

(3) To summarize the Aryan invasion of India and the culture that arose as a result.

SKILLBUILDERS

- Interpreting charts, p. 57
- Interpreting maps: location, movement, p. 58
- Interpreting maps: location, human-environment interaction, p. 61

CRITICAL THINKING

- Analyzing effects, p. 59
- Making inferences, p. 60
- Forming opinions, p. 61
- Analyzing themes, p. 61

FOCUS

5-Minute Warm-Up

▶ *Perceiving Effects*
To help students understand the migrations of people and their impact on different cultures.

1. Study the map on p. 58. Which groups migrated into southern Europe?

2. What geographic barrier did the Indo-Aryans face when migrating to India?

 WARM-UP TRANSPARENCY 3

OBJECTIVE ① INSTRUCT

Indo-Europeans Migrate

▶ *Key Ideas*
- Indo-European nomads migrate in waves into Europe and Asia.
- Their language is the basis of many modern European and Asian languages.

 IN-DEPTH RESOURCES: UNIT 1
Guided Reading, p. 35

 ACCESS FOR STUDENTS ACQUIRING ENGLISH
Guided Reading (Spanish), p. 33

Indo-European Migrations, Starting about 1700 B.C.

Interpreting the Map Ask students to look carefully at the migration patterns of the Indo-Europeans. What geographic features might have prevented them from crossing paths with each other? How might this separation have contributed to the development of modern nations? *Mountains, seas, and rivers usually prevented groups from intermingling. Such isolation fostered the development of individual languages and customs. The areas where each group settled correspond roughly to boundaries of modern nations.*

Extension Activity Have students choose a group of Indo-Europeans not discussed at length in the text, such as the Celts or Slavs. Ask them to find the modern names of the countries they entered and to describe some of the influences they left behind.

SKILLBUILDER Answers
1. The Celts, who reached the British Isles
2. Possible Response: They moved south from their homeland to the Black Sea region.

OBJECTIVE 2 INSTRUCT

Hittites Blend Empire and Technology

Key Ideas
- The Hittites dominate Southwest Asia by 1650 B.C.
- They spread their own and others' ideas throughout Southwest Asia.
- Their superiority in war and their skill in iron smelting help them build an empire.

Indo-European Migrations, Starting about 1700 B.C.

The origins and migrations of the Indo-European peoples are controversial topics among scholars. This map presents a widely held view of where the Indo-Europeans came from and how they migrated. However, it is not the only view. In fact, there are many differing views.

Earliest Indo-European migrations
Later migrations

GEOGRAPHY SKILLBUILDER: Interpreting Maps
1. **Location** *Which Indo-European people reached the farthest west?*
2. **Movement** *Describe the movement of the Indo-Europeans in their earliest migrations.*

Hittites Blend Empire and Technology

By about 2000 B.C., one group of Indo-European speakers, the **Hittites,** occupied **Anatolia** (AN·uh·TOH·lee·ah), also called Asia Minor. Anatolia is a huge peninsula in modern-day Turkey that juts out into the Black and Mediterranean seas. Anatolia was a high, rocky plateau, rich in timber and agriculture. Nearby mountains held important mineral deposits. Separate Hittite city-states came together to form an empire there in about 1650 B.C. The city of Hattusas (hah·TOO·sahs) was its capital.

The Hittite empire went on to dominate Southwest Asia for 450 years. Hittites occupied Babylon, the chief city in the Tigris-Euphrates Valley, and struggled with Egypt for control of northern Syria. Neither the Hittites nor the Egyptians were able to get the upper hand. So, the two peoples ended their conflicts by signing an unusual peace treaty. In it, they each pledged to help the other fight off future invaders.

Hittites Adopt and Adapt The Hittites used their own Indo-European language with one another. However, for international use, they adopted Akkadian, the language of the Babylonians they had conquered. Akkadian was already widely spoken in Mesopotamia, and Babylonian culture was more advanced. The Hittites thus blended their own traditions with those of other, more advanced peoples. In the process, they spread many innovative ideas throughout Southwest Asia.

The Hittites borrowed ideas about literature, art, politics, and law from the Mesopotamian peoples they encountered. However, they always managed to give these ideas a distinctive twist. Their own legal code, for example, was similar to Hammurabi's Code but was more forgiving. Murderers were not automatically pun-

---

Less Proficient Readers: *Comparing and Contrasting* Pair a less proficient reader with a more able reader. Have them read the text on page 59 under the heading "Aryan Invaders Transform India." Then have them chart the similarities and differences between the two groups.

Their finished charts might look something like this:

	Aryans	Non-Aryans
Name:	"the nobles"	"dark"
Appearance:	tall, fair skinned	shorter, dark skinned
Language:	Indo-European, not written	non–Indo-European, written
Communities:	pastoral	urban
Gods:	Indra, Agni	Shiva, mother goddesses

ished by death. A convicted murderer could make up for the crime by giving the victim's family a slave or a child from his own family.

Chariots and Iron Bring Victory The Hittites excelled in the technology of war. They conquered an empire even against Egyptian opposition—largely through their superior chariots and their iron weapons. The Hittite war chariot was light and easy to maneuver even at high speeds. The chariot had two wheels and a wooden frame covered with leather and was pulled by two or sometimes four horses. On the battlefield, the Hittite chariot proved itself a superb fighting machine. It helped make the Hittites conquerors.

The Hittites used iron in their chariots, and they owed many of their military victories to the skill of their ironworkers. Ancient peoples had long known that iron was stronger than bronze. They also knew that it could hold a sharper edge. However, the process of purifying iron ore and working it into weapons and tools is complex. For centuries, prehistoric people used only the purified iron they obtained from meteorites. Around 1500 B.C., the Hittites were the first in Southwest Asia to smelt iron and harden it into weapons of war. The raw materials they needed—iron ore and wood to make charcoal—were easily available to them in the mountains of Anatolia. Knowledge of iron technology traveled widely with the Hittites—in both their trade and conquests.

Despite its military might, the powerful Hittite empire fell quite suddenly around the year 1190 B.C. As part of a great wave of invasions, tribes attacked from the north and burned the Hittite capital city. Hittite supremacy in Southwest Asia had ended.

Aryan Invaders Transform India

In about 1500 B.C., the Hittites were establishing themselves in Anatolia. At the same time, another Indo-European people, the **Aryans**, crossed over the northwest mountain passes into the Indus River Valley of India. Though they left almost no archaeological record, their sacred literature, the **Vedas** (VAY·duhz), left a fairly reliable picture of Aryan life. The *Vedas* are four collections of prayers, magical spells, and instructions for performing rituals. The most important of the collections is the *Rig Veda*. The *Rig Veda* contains 1028 hymns, all devoted to Aryan gods.

For many years, no written form of the *Vedas* existed. Instead, elders of one generation passed on this tradition orally to men of the next generation. If a prayer was uttered incorrectly, they believed terrible consequences might result. So accuracy was crucial.

A Caste System Develops The Aryans ("the nobles" in their language) called the people they found in India *dasas* ("dark"), referring to the color of their skin. (*Dasa* eventually became the Aryan word for slave.) The Aryans differed from the *dasas* in many ways. Aryans were taller, lighter in skin color, and spoke a different language. Unlike the earlier inhabitants of the Indus Valley, the Aryans had not developed a writing system. They were also a pastoral people and counted their wealth in cows. The *dasas*, on the other hand, were town dwellers who lived in communities protected by walls. The Aryans offered sacrifices to heroic nature gods, such as Indra, the thunder god, and Agni, the fire god. Archaeological evidence seems to show that the *dasas* worshiped life-giving principles, such as the "Great God" Shiva and various mother goddesses.

When they first arrived in India, Aryans were divided into three social classes: **Brahmins** (priests), warriors, and peasants or traders. The class that an Aryan belonged to determined his or her role in society. At first, the three classes mixed freely. Eventually, non-Aryan laborers or craftsmen (*shudras*) formed a fourth group.

Hittites sometimes owned small gold statues of their gods—probably intended to protect them from danger or bad fortune.

The Indian Caste System
Interpreting the Diagram
Discuss with students why a particular body part might have been associated with a particular occupation.

Extension Activity Ask students to discuss in small groups which modern occupations might be assigned to each of the four major castes. Which occupations would belong to untouchables? Have students share their choices with the class.

MORE ABOUT . . .
The Bhagavad-Gita

The dialogue between Arjuna and Krishna is one of the most famous parts of the *Mahabharata*. It has been published separately as the *Bhagavad-Gita* (the "Song of God"). One of the most revered books in India, it has also influenced many prominent leaders in the West.

 IN-DEPTH SOURCES: UNIT 1
Primary Source: from the *Bhagavad-Gita,* p. 42

MORE ABOUT . . .
The Mahabharata Wars

Historians and literature scholars have often wondered how many of the events described in the *Mahabharata* are true. In recent years archaeologists have begun to answer their questions as they find and excavate sites mentioned in the epic poem. Some of these sites have yielded fragments of gray pottery commonly associated with Aryan settlement.

 IN-DEPTH SOURCES: UNIT 1
Primary Source: from the *Rig Veda*, p. 43

 ELECTRONIC LIBRARY OF PRIMARY SOURCES:
"Hymn 129," from the *Rig Veda*

The Aryan Caste System

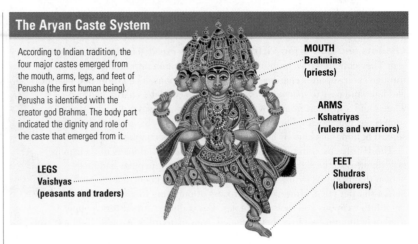

According to Indian tradition, the four major castes emerged from the mouth, arms, legs, and feet of Perusha (the first human being). Perusha is identified with the creator god Brahma. The body part indicated the dignity and role of the caste that emerged from it.

MOUTH
Brahmins (priests)

ARMS
Kshatriyas (rulers and warriors)

FEET
Shudras (laborers)

LEGS
Vaishyas (peasants and traders)

As the Aryans settled in India, they developed closer contacts with non-Aryans. To regulate those contacts, the Aryans made class restrictions more rigid. *Shudras* did work that Aryans did not want to do. V*arna,* or skin color, was a distinguishing feature of this system. So the four major groups came to be known as the *varnas.* Much later—in the fifteenth century A.D.—explorers from Portugal encountered this social system and called these groups **castes** (kasts).

As time went on, the four basic castes gradually grew more complex—with hundreds of subdivisions. People were born into their caste for life. Their caste membership determined the work they did, the man or woman they could marry, and the people with whom they could eat. Ritual purity—for example, habits of eating and washing that made a person physically and spiritually clean—became all-important. Those who were the most impure because of their work (butchers, gravediggers, collectors of trash) lived outside the caste structure. They were known as "untouchables," since even their touch endangered the ritual purity of others.

Aryan Kingdoms Arise Over the next few centuries, Aryans extended their settlements east, along the Ganges and Yamuna river valleys. (See map on page 61.) Progress was slow because of difficulties clearing the jungle for farming. This task grew easier when iron came into use in India about 1000 B.C.

When the Aryans first arrived in India, chiefs were elected by the entire tribe. Around 1000 B.C., however, minor kings who wanted to set up territorial kingdoms arose among the Aryans. They struggled with one another for land and power. And each claimed his authority as a right from the gods. Out of this strife emerged a major kingdom: Magadha. Under a series of ambitious kings, Magadha began expanding in the sixth century B.C. by taking over surrounding kingdoms. By the second century B.C., Magadha had expanded south to occupy almost all of the Indian subcontinent.

One of the great epics of India, the **Mahabharata** (muh·HAH·BAHR·ah·tuh), reflects the struggles that took place in India as the Aryans moved relentlessly south. The poem is the story of a great war between two sets of cousins, the Pandavas and the Kauravas. The *Mahabharata*'s 106,000 verses make it the longest single poem in the world. For several hundred years, it survived as an oral tradition.

CONNECT *to* TODAY

Untouchables Then and Now
In the sixth century B.C., ritual purity was so important to upper-caste Indians that untouchables had to ring a bell to warn that they were coming near. Even the shadow of an untouchable falling on upper-caste Hindus would contaminate them. They would have to bathe before worshiping or eating.

In the 20th century, the great Indian leader Mahatma Gandhi called the untouchables *harijans,* or "children of God." Through his efforts, caste distinctions were outlawed by the Indian constitution. Later, the 1955 Untouchability Act provided penalties for discrimination. However, 3,000-year-old traditions do not die easily. Most former untouchables in India today still suffer from extreme poverty and caste discrimination.

THINK THROUGH HISTORY
B. Making Inferences How were the more physical forms of work viewed by Aryans?
B. Possible Answer As impure and degrading.

CONNECTIONS ACROSS TIME AND PLACE

Tracing Modern Meanings
Remind students that the term "Aryan" was appropriated by Nazi Germany in the 1930s. Ask students why and how Hitler used the term. Some students might know that the Nazis used "Aryan" to refer to "racially pure" Germans and other Northern Europeans whom Hitler regarded as superior to other types of people. Ask students what other groups use the term today. Students might respond that neo-Nazi groups in Europe and North America also call themselves Aryans. Ask students how the Nazi idea of "racial purity" compares with the Aryan idea of "ritual purity"?

EXPLORING PRIMARY SOURCES

A Voice from the Past Ask students to paraphrase the quotation on page 61 from the epic poem the *Mahabharata.* Make sure students understand that Krishna and Arjuna believe that the "Self" or "Soul" is eternal and cannot be destroyed or killed. How might such an attitude comfort soldiers in warfare? How might it prolong bloodshed?

Elements of the *Mahabharata* indicate that a blending of cultures was taking place between Aryan and non-Aryan peoples. For example, Krishna, a semi-divine hero of the *Mahabharata,* is described as dark-faced. This suggests that he is non-Aryan.

One of the most famous incidents in all of Indian literature occurs when Krishna instructs one of the Pandavas, Arjuna (ahr·JUH·nuh), on the proper way to live one's life. Arjuna loses the will to fight when he sees his cousins lined up among the enemies he faces. He asks Krishna how we can find joy in killing our own kinsmen. Krishna answers that the eternal spirit (or Self) of every human being cannot kill or be killed. However, Arjuna must still do his duty and wage war:

A VOICE FROM THE PAST
He who thinks this Self [eternal spirit] to be a slayer, and he who thinks this Self to be slain, are both without discernment; the Soul slays not, neither is it slain. . . . But if you will not wage this lawful battle, then will you fail your own (caste) law and incur sin. . . . The people will name you with dishonor; and to a man of fame dishonor is worse than death.

KRISHNA, speaking in the *Mahabharata*

The violence and confusion of the time led many, like Krishna himself, to speculate about the place of the gods and human beings in the world. As a result of these speculations, religion in India gradually changed. New religions were born, which you will read about in Section 2.

Aryan Invasions of India, 1500–250 B.C.

Lines of Aryan penetrations
Consolidation of kingdoms
(PAKISTAN) Modern place name

(AFGHANISTAN) HINDU KUSH MTS.
Harappa
CHINA
(PAKISTAN)
Mohenjo-Daro
Indus R.
BAHAWALPUR
THAR DESERT
HIMALAYAS
SMALL STATES
GANGES PLAIN
Ganges R.
Yamuna R.
MAGADHA
(BANGLADESH)
Narmada R.
INDIA
Gulf of Khambhat
Arabian Sea
DECCAN PLATEAU
WESTERN GHATS
Tungabhadra R.
Cauvery R.
EASTERN GHATS
Bay of Bengal
Mouths of the Ganges
INDIAN OCEAN
(SRI LANKA)
0   250 Miles
0   500 Kilometers

GEOGRAPHY SKILLBUILDER:
Interpreting Maps
1. **Location** *What waterway served as the focal point for the Aryan kingdom of Magadha?*
2. **Human-Environment Interaction** *Why do you think the Aryans migrated to the east of the Western Ghats?*

History from Visuals

Aryan Invasions of India, 1500–250 B.C.
Interpreting the Map Ask students to study the map and explain why they think the invaders usually advanced down river valleys. *Possible answers: Travel would have been easier and faster on water or alongside rivers than overland; greater sources of food and water for armies.*

Extension Activity Aryan invaders initially consolidated their kingdoms in the northeast section of India. Ask for volunteers to investigate what made this region so attractive. Have them report to the class on their findings.

SKILLBUILDER Answers
1. The Ganges River
2. *Possible Response:* A less mountainous area would be easier to settle.

ASSESS & RETEACH

Section 1 Assessment
Have students write down the number(s) of the page(s) in the section on which they found the answer to each question.

Section Quiz

FORMAL ASSESSMENT
Section Quiz, p. 28

Reteaching Activity
CLASS TIME: 10 MINUTES

Ask students which of the Section Assessment questions they found most difficult. Conduct a class discussion to review the answers.

CLOSE ACTIVITY

CLASS TIME: 20 MINUTES

Making Judgments
Ask students to list the major achievements of the Indo-Europeans as discussed in the chapter. Have them rank the achievements in order of historical importance. Discuss with them the reasons for their choices.

Section ➊ Assessment

1. TERMS & NAMES
Identify
• Indo-Europeans
• steppes
• migration
• Hittites
• Anatolia
• Aryans
• *Vedas*
• Brahmin
• caste
• *Mahabharata*

2. TAKING NOTES
Re-create the web below on your own paper, and fill in the names of some modern languages that stem from Indo-European roots.

Indo-European

Why did so many languages originate from Indo-European roots?

3. FORMING OPINIONS
What important contributions did the Aryan invaders make to the culture and way of life in India?

THINK ABOUT
• roles in society
• religion
• literature

4. ANALYZING THEMES
Interaction with Environment For what environmental reasons might the Indo-Europeans have migrated?

THINK ABOUT
• weather
• occupational needs
• health

People and Ideas on the Move **61**

ANSWERS

1. TERMS & NAMES
Indo-Europeans, p. 57
steppes, p. 57
migration, p. 57
Hittites, p. 58
Anatolia, p. 58
Aryans, p. 59
Vedas, p. 59
Brahmin, p. 59

caste, p. 60
Mahabharata, p. 60

2. TAKING NOTES
Possible Responses: English, French, Spanish, Greek, Hindi, Persian, Russian, Swedish; the migrations of Indo-Europeans into Europe and Asia

3. FORMING OPINIONS
Possible Responses: **roles in society:** Aryan caste system ruled India for over 3,000 years. **religion:** Aryan deities of the *Vedas* entered the Hindu religion. **literature:** The *Vedas, Upanishads,* and *Mahabharata* are great literary works with Aryan subjects or themes.

4. ANALYZING THEMES
Possible Responses: **weather:** Grazing lands may have dried up. **occupational needs:** Their population may have grown too large to feed. **health:** They may have been escaping from diseases or invaders.

① To describe the origins, beliefs, and development of Hinduism.

② To identify the founder and practices of Jainism.

③ To explain the origin, beliefs, and practices of Buddhism.

④ To summarize the spread of Buddhism in later centuries.

CRITICAL THINKING
- Making inferences, pp. 63, 66
- Synthesizing, p. 64
- Comparing, p. 65

FOCUS
5-Minute Warm-Up

▶ **Identifying Main Ideas**
Have students answer these questions to understand Hindu and Buddhist traditions.

1. Read the History Makers on page 64. According to the passage, what would signs such as a long tongue and golden-tinged skin indicate about a child?

2. What did Siddhartha's mother know about him even before he was born?

 WARM-UP TRANSPARENCY 3

 OBJECTIVE ① INSTRUCT

Hinduism Develops Over Centuries

▶ **Key Ideas**
- Although Hinduism lacks a single founder, all Hindus share a common world-view and stress the interconnectedness of life.
- Indians develop the caste system to organize their society.
- Jainism stresses reverence for the soul in all life.

 IN-DEPTH RESOURCES: UNIT 1
Guided Reading, p. 36

ACCESS FOR STUDENTS ACQUIRING ENGLISH
Guided Reading (Spanish), p. 34

RELIGIONS OF THE WORLD
Hinduism

TERMS & NAMES
- reincarnation
- karma
- Jainism
- Siddhartha Gautama
- enlightenment
- nirvana

2 Roots of Hinduism and Buddhism

MAIN IDEA	WHY IT MATTERS NOW
The religious beliefs of the Vedic Age eventually developed into Hinduism and Buddhism.	Almost one-fifth of the world's people today practice one of these two religions.

SETTING THE STAGE At first, the Aryans and non-Aryans followed their own forms of religion. Then as the two groups intermingled, the gods and forms of their religions also tended to blend together. This blending resulted in the worship of thousands of gods. Different ways of living and different beliefs made life more complex for both groups. This complexity led some people to question the world and their place in it. They even questioned the enormous wealth and power held by the Brahmin priests. These priests officiated at elaborate state ceremonies and sacrifices. Out of this turmoil, new religious ideas arose that have continued to influence millions of people today.

Hinduism Develops Over Centuries

Hinduism is a collection of religious beliefs that developed slowly over a long period of time. Some aspects of the religion can be traced back to ancient times. In a Hindu marriage today, for example, the bride and groom marry in the presence of the sacred fire as they did centuries ago. Verses from the *Vedas* are recited daily by the faithful. Also, some non-Aryan gods known in Vedic times, such as Krishna of the *Mahabharata*, continue to be worshiped.

From time to time, scholars have tried to organize the many popular cults, gods, and traditions into one grand system of belief. However, Hinduism—unlike religions such as Buddhism, Christianity, or Islam—cannot be traced back to one founder with a single set of ideas.

Vishnu grew to become a major Hindu god after the age of the *Vedas*. He is seen here as the whole Universe in all its variety. He is blue, the color of infinity.

Origins and Beliefs Hindus share a common world-view. They see religion as a way of liberating the soul from the illusions, disappointments, and mistakes of everyday existence. Sometime between 750 and 550 B.C., Hindu teachers tried to interpret and explain the hidden meaning of the Vedic hymns. As they meditated on the *Vedas*, they asked: What is the nature of reality? What is morality? Is there eternal life? What is the soul? The teachers' comments were later written down and became known as the *Upanishads* (oo·PAHN·ih·shahdz).

The *Upanishads* are written as dialogues, or discussions, between a student and a teacher. In the course of the dialogues, the two explore how a person can achieve liberation from desires and suffering. This is described as *moksha* (MOHK·shah), a state of perfect understanding of all things. The teacher distinguishes between atman, the individual soul of a living being, and Brahman, the world soul that contains and

Background
Both the *Vedas* and the *Upanishads* are counted among Hinduism's sacred books.

PRINT RESOURCES

 IN-DEPTH RESOURCES: UNIT 1
Guided Reading, p. 36
   Literature: from *Siddhartha*, p. 47
   History Makers: Siddhartha Gautama, p. 49

ACCESS FOR STUDENTS ACQUIRING ENGLISH
Guided Reading (Spanish), p. 34

FORMAL ASSESSMENT
Section Quiz, p. 29

TECHNOLOGY RESOURCES

GEOGRAPHY TRANSPARENCIES
GT3 Hindu India and Buddhist Sites, 563–483 B.C.

WORLD ART AND CULTURES TRANSPARENCIES
AT6 Indian terra cotta Mother Goddess

 CD-ROM
Religions of the World: Hinduism, Buddhism
Electronic Library of Primary Sources

 INTERNET www.mlworldhistory.com

unites all atmans. The interconnectedness of all life is a basic concept in all Indian religions. Here is how one teacher explains the unifying spirit of Brahman:

A VOICE FROM THE PAST

Thou art woman, Thou art man, Thou art the lad and the maiden too. Thou art the old man tottering on his staff: Once born thou comest to be, thy face turned every way! A dark-blue moth art Thou, green [parrot] with red eyes. Pregnant with lightning—seasons, seas: Thyself beginningless, all things dost Thou pervade. From thee all worlds were born.

Svetasvatara Upanishad. IV. 3–4

When a person understands the relationship between atman and Brahman, that person achieves perfect understanding *(moksha)* and a release from life in this world. This understanding does not usually come in one lifetime. By the process of **reincarnation** (rebirth), an individual soul or spirit is born again and again until *moksha* is achieved. A soul's **karma**—good or bad deeds—follows from one reincarnation to another. Karma influences specific life circumstances, such as the caste one is born into, one's state of health, wealth or poverty, and so on.

Hinduism Changes and Develops Hinduism has gone through many changes over the last 2,500 years. The world soul, Brahman, was sometimes seen as having the personalities of three gods: Brahma, the creator; Vishnu, the protector; and Shiva, the destroyer. Vishnu also took on many forms or personalities, for example, as Krishna, the divine cowherder, and as Rama, the perfect king. Over the centuries, Brahma gradually faded into the background, while the many forms of a great Mother Goddess grew in importance.

Hindus today are free to choose the deity they worship or to choose none at all. Most, however, follow a family tradition that may go back centuries. They are also free to choose among three different paths for achieving *moksha*. They are the path of right thinking, the path of right action, or the path of religious devotion.

Hinduism and Society Hindu ideas about karma and reincarnation strengthened the caste system. If a person was born as an upper-caste male—a Brahmin, warrior, or merchant—his good fortune was said to come from good karma earned in a former life. However, a person who was born as a female, a laborer, or an untouchable might be getting the results of bad deeds in a former life. With some exceptions, only men of the top three varnas could hope to achieve *moksha* in their present life. The laws of karma worked with the same certainty as the world's other natural laws. Good karma brought good fortune and bad karma resulted in bad fortune.

Together, the beliefs of Hinduism and its caste structure dominated every aspect of a person's life. These beliefs determined what one could eat and how one ate it, personal cleanliness, the people one could associate with, how one dressed, and so on. Today, even in the most ordinary activities of daily life, Hindus turn to their religion for guidance.

New Religions Arise The same period of speculation reflected in the *Upanishads* also led to the rise of two other religions: Jainism (JY·nihz·uhm) and Buddhism. Mahavira, the founder of **Jainism,** was born about 599 B.C. and died in 527 B.C. Mahavira believed that everything in the universe has a soul and so should not be harmed. Jain monks carry the doctrine of nonviolence to its logical conclusion. They sweep ants off their path and wear gauze masks over their mouths to avoid breathing in an insect accidentally.

A Jain man wears a mask and carries a brush to prevent harm to small creatures.

63

THINK THROUGH HISTORY
A. Making Inferences How might the lack of a single founder result in Hinduism changing more over time than other religions?
A. Answer Not having a single founder means that no set of original beliefs will determine Hinduism's development. The religion can thus change more freely than religions with a founder.

Background
The doctrine of nonviolence *(ahimsa)* is important both to Hindus and Jains.

MORE ABOUT . . .
Brahma, Brahman, Brahmin
These three terms are often confused. **Brahma** refers to "the creator God," who appears in many origin myths. Although his image is found in most temples, he is no longer worshiped as a major god. **Brahman** refers to the "World Soul," often contrasted with atman, the individual soul. **Brahmin** is the name of one of the four major castes, or varnas. All Hindu priests are Brahmins.

MORE ABOUT . . .
Jains
Jains emphasize right acts more than right knowledge, believing that we can know only a part of the truth. Jains tell the now-famous story of the six blind men trying to describe an elephant. Each feels a different part of the elephant and reports the animal is like a snake (its trunk), a rope (its tail), or the trunk of a tree (its leg). Each knows only a fraction of the truth about what the elephant really looks like.

TEACHING OPTIONS

CUSTOMIZING FOR SPECIAL NEEDS

Gifted and Talented Students:
Writing Verse Ask students to rewrite the A Voice from the Past selection from the *Upanishad* in their own words.

Alternatively, some students may wish to write a verse of their own that expresses the unity of all life but uses other symbols to replace the old man, the moth, or the parrot of the *Upanishad*

selection. Remind students that to convey unity their writing should include men, women, plant and animal life, and some elements of nature. Ask them to write a paragraph or two on what they learned by doing this exercise.

WORLD ART AND CULTURES TRANSPARENCIES
AT6 Indian terra cotta Mother Goddess

CONNECTIONS ACROSS THE CURRICULUM

Literature Suggest to students that they read stories about some of the popular Hindu gods, such as Krishna or Rama. Stories of Krishna may be found in mythology collections or translations of the *Bhagavata Purana*. Stories of

Rama are included in the epic the *Ramayana* and in mythology anthologies. Have them report back to the class on how these stories illustrate some of the Hindu beliefs discussed in the text.

 IN-DEPTH RESOURCES: UNIT 1
Literature: from the *Ramayana*, p. 46

Teacher's Edition 63

In keeping with this nonviolence, followers of Jainism looked for occupations that would not harm any creature. So they have a tradition of working in trade and commerce.

Because of their business activities, Jains today make up one of the wealthiest communities in India. Jains have traditionally preached tolerance of all religions. As a result, they have made few efforts to convert followers of other faiths. Because of this tolerance, Jains have not sent out missionaries. So, almost all the nearly 5 million Jains in the world today live in India.

HISTORY MAKERS

Siddhartha Gautama
c. 563–483 B.C.

According to Buddhist tradition, signs predicted even before his birth that Siddhartha Gautama would be a great man. His mother Mahamaya had dreamt of a beautiful elephant that was bright as silver. When asked to interpret the dream, Brahmin priests declared that the child to be born would either be a great monarch or a Buddha (an enlightened one).

Tradition also relates that at Gautama's birth, he exhibited the signs of a child destined for greatness. There were 32 such signs, including golden-tinged skin, webbed fingers and toes, a knob on the top of his skull, a long tongue, a tuft of hair between his eyebrows, and a thousand-spoked wheel on each foot. Some images of the Buddha display these traits.

The Buddha Seeks Enlightenment

Buddhism developed out of the same period of religious questioning that shaped modern Hinduism and Jainism. The founder of Buddhism, **Siddhartha Gautama** (sihd·DAHR·tuh GOW·tuh·muh) was born into a noble family that lived in Kapilavastu, in the foothills of the Himalayas in Nepal. According to Buddhist legend, the baby exhibited the marks of a great man. A prophecy indicated that if the child stayed at home he was destined to become a world ruler. If the child left home, however, he would become a universal spiritual leader. To make sure the boy would be a great king, his father isolated him in his palace. Separated from the world, Siddhartha married and had a son.

Siddhartha's Quest Siddhartha never ceased thinking about the world that lay outside the palace, which he had never seen. When he was 29, he ventured outside the palace four times. First he saw an old man, next a sick man, then a corpse being carried to the cremation grounds, and finally a wandering holy man who seemed at peace with himself. Siddhartha understood these events to mean that every living thing experiences old age, sickness, and death and that only a religious life offers a refuge from this inevitable suffering. Siddhartha decided to spend his life searching for religious truth and an end to suffering. So, soon after learning of his son's birth, he left the palace.

Siddhartha wandered through the forests of India for six years seeking **enlightenment,** or wisdom. He tried many ways of reaching an enlightened state. He first debated with other religious seekers. Then he fasted, eating only six grains of rice a day. (It was said that his stomach became so empty that by poking a finger into it, he could touch his backbone.) Yet none of these methods brought him to the truth, and he continued to suffer. Finally, he sat in meditation under a large fig tree. After 49 days of meditation, he achieved an understanding of the cause of suffering in this world. From then on, he was known as the Buddha, meaning "the enlightened one."

Vocabulary
fasted: did not eat.

Origins and Beliefs The Buddha preached his first sermon to five companions who had accompanied him on his wanderings. That first sermon became a landmark in the history of the world's religions. In it, he laid out the four main ideas that he had understood in his enlightenment. He called those ideas the Four Noble Truths:

First Noble Truth	Everything in life is suffering and sorrow.
Second Noble Truth	The cause of all suffering is people's selfish desire for the temporary pleasures of this world.
Third Noble Truth	The way to end all suffering is to end all desires.
Fourth Noble Truth	The way to overcome such desires and attain enlightenment is to follow the Eightfold Path, which is called the Middle Way between desires and self-denial.

64 Chapter 3

The Eightfold Path was like a staircase. For the Buddha, those who were seeking enlightenment had to master one step at a time. Most often, this mastery would occur over many lifetimes. Here is how he described the Middle Way and its Eightfold Path:

A VOICE FROM THE PAST
What is the Middle Way? . . . It is the Noble Eightfold Path—Right Views, Right Resolve, Right Speech, Right Conduct, Right Livelihood, Right Effort, Right Mindfulness, and Right Concentration. This is the Middle Way.

The Buddha, from Samyutta Nikaya

By following the Eightfold Path, anyone could reach **nirvana,** the Buddha's word for release from selfishness and pain. The Buddha's teachings included many ideas from the Hindu tradition. However, they also differed sharply from that tradition.

As in Hinduism, the Buddha accepted the idea of reincarnation. He also accepted a cyclical, or repetitive, view of history, where the world is created and destroyed over and over again. However, the Buddha rejected the many gods of Hinduism. Instead, he taught a way of enlightenment. Like many of his time, the Buddha reacted against the privileges of the Brahmin priests, and thus he rejected the caste system. The final goals of both religions—*moksha* for Hindus and nirvana for Buddhists—are similar. Both involve a perfect state of understanding and a break from the chain of reincarnations.

The Religious Community The five disciples who heard the Buddha's first sermon were the first monks admitted to a *sangha*, or Buddhist religious order. At first, the *sangha* was a community of Buddhist monks and nuns. However, *sangha* eventually referred to the entire religious community. It included Buddhist laity (those who hadn't devoted their entire life to religion). The religious community, together with the Buddha and the *dharma* (Buddhist doctrine or law), make up the "Three Jewels" of Buddhism. Every day, Buddhists all over the world recognize the importance of the Three Jewels of their faith by declaring: "I take refuge in the Buddha. I take refuge in the law. I take refuge in the community."

Buddhism and Society Because of his rejection of the caste system, many of the Buddha's early followers included laborers and craftspeople. He also gained a large following in northeast India, where the Aryans had less influence. The Buddha reluctantly admitted women to religious orders. He feared, however, that women's presence would distract men from their religious duties.

Monks and nuns took vows (solemn promises) to live a life of poverty, to be nonviolent, and not to marry. They wandered throughout India spreading the Buddha's teachings. Missionaries carried only a begging bowl to receive daily charity offerings from people. During the rainy season, they retreated to caves high up in the hillsides. Gradually, these seasonal retreats became permanent monasteries—some for men, others for women. One monastery, Nalanda, developed into a great university that also attracted non-Buddhists.

The teachings of the Buddha were written down shortly after his death. Buddhist sacred literature also includes commentaries, rules about monastic life, manuals on how to meditate,

Buddhist tradition tells that just before he died, the Buddha lay peacefully on his right side between two trees. Reclining Buddhas, like this one in Laos, point to this calm acceptance of death as the ideal.

65

and legends about the Buddha's previous reincarnations (the *Jatakas*). This sacred literature was first written down in the first century B.C.

Buddhism in India During the centuries following the Buddha's death, missionaries were able to spread his faith over large parts of Asia. Buddhist missionaries went to Sri Lanka and Southeast Asia in the third century B.C. Buddhist ideas also traveled along Central Asian trade routes to China. However, Buddhism never gained a significant foothold in India, the country of its origin. Several theories exist about Buddhism's gradual disappearance in India. One theory states that Hinduism simply absorbed Buddhism. The two religions constantly influenced each other. Over time, the Buddha came to be identified by Hindus as one of the ten incarnations (reappearances on earth) of the god Vishnu. Hindus, thus, felt no need to convert to Buddhism. They believed it had already become a part of their own religion.

Nonetheless, despite the small number of Buddhists in India, the region has always been an important place of pilgrimages for Buddhists. Today, as they have for centuries, Buddhist pilgrims flock to visit spots associated with the Buddha's life. These sites include his birthplace at Kapilavastu, the fig tree near Gaya, and the site of his first sermon near Varanasi. Buddhists also visit the *stupas*, or sacred mounds, that are said to contain his relics. The pilgrims circle around the sacred object or sanctuary, moving in a clockwise direction. They also lie face down on the ground and leave flowers. These three actions—circling a shrine, lying face down as a sign of humility, and offering flowers—are important rituals in Buddhist worship.

Trade and the Spread of Buddhism As important as missionaries were to the spread of Buddhism, traders played an even more crucial role in this process. Along with their products, traders carried Buddhism beyond India to Sri Lanka. Buddhist religion was also brought southeast along trade routes to Burma, Thailand, and the island of Sumatra. Likewise, Buddhism followed the Central Asian trade routes, called the Silk Roads, all the way to China. From China, Buddhism spread to Korea—and from Korea to Japan. The movement of trade thus succeeded in making Buddhism the most widespread religion of East Asia. Throughout human history, trade has been a powerful force for the spread of ideas. Just as trade spread Buddhism in East Asia, it helped spread cultural influences in another major region of the world: the Mediterranean basin, as you will learn in Section 3.

CONNECT to TODAY

Buddhism in the West
Throughout the 20th century, large numbers of Asians have immigrated to live in the West, particularly in North America. Many of them naturally brought their Buddhist religion with them. Today, Buddhist temples have become a common feature of many large cities in the West.

Since the 1950s, many non-Asians who were dissatisfied with the religions of the West have turned to Buddhism for insight into life's meaning and for peace of mind. They have particularly responded to Zen Buddhism, which stresses everyone's ability to reach enlightenment during this lifetime. Today, Buddhism can claim 920,000 Asian and non-Asian believers in North America alone.

Vocabulary
pilgrimages: travels to holy places.

Section 2 Assessment

1. TERMS & NAMES
Identify
- reincarnation
- karma
- Jainism
- Siddhartha Gautama
- enlightenment
- nirvana

2. TAKING NOTES
Compare Hindu and Buddhist beliefs and practices using a Venn diagram like the one below.

Hinduism only — Both — Buddhism only

3. MAKING INFERENCES
How might the belief in reincarnation provide a form of social control?

THINK ABOUT
- karma
- the belief in the interrelatedness of all life
- caste

4. THEME ACTIVITY
Religious and Ethical Systems Create an illustrated information board showing the life of Siddhartha Gautama. Include family background, accomplishments, and a list of his religious and ethical beliefs.

66 Chapter 3

ANSWERS

1. TERMS & NAMES
reincarnation, p. 63
karma, p. 63
Jainism, p. 63
Siddhartha Gautama, p. 64
enlightenment, p. 64
nirvana, p. 65

2. TAKING NOTES
Hinduism: caste system, animal sacrifice
Both: reincarnation, cyclical view of history, belief in a state of enlightenment (Hindu *moksha*, Buddhist nirvana)
Buddhism: The Middle Way (Eightfold Path), Four Noble Truths

3. MAKING INFERENCES
Possible Responses: **karma:** Karma motivates people to obey society's laws. **belief in the interrelatedness of all life:** People would be reluctant to harm any life form. **caste:** Those born into a lower caste might work hard to achieve a higher caste in their next life.

4. THEME ACTIVITY
Standards for Evaluation
An effective bio board should . . .
- include family background
- show important aspects of the subject's personality, beliefs, and achievements
- be well organized and well written and presented

TERMS & NAMES
• Minoans
• Aegean Sea
• Knossos
• King Minos
• Phoenicians

3 Seafaring Traders Extend Boundaries

MAIN IDEA

Trading societies extended the development of civilizations beyond the Fertile Crescent region.

WHY IT MATTERS NOW

Traders spread knowledge of reading and writing, including an ancient form of the alphabet that we use today.

SETTING THE STAGE Buddhism spread to Southeast Asia and to East Asia partly through missionaries, but even more importantly through Buddhist traders. In the Mediterranean, the same process took place: traders in the region carried many new ideas from one society to another. They carried new ways of writing, of governing, and of worshiping their gods.

Minoans Trade Far and Wide

A powerful seafaring people, the **Minoans** (mih·NOH·uhnz) dominated trade in the eastern Mediterranean from about 2000 to 1400 B.C. They lived on Crete, a large island on the southern edge of the **Aegean Sea** (ee·JEE·uhn). The Minoans produced some of the finest painted pottery of the time. They traded that pottery, along with swords, figurines, and vessels of precious metals, over a large area.

Along with their goods, Minoans also exported their art and culture. These included a unique architectural style, burial customs, and religious ritual. Minoan culture had an enormous influence on Greece, for example. Trading turned Crete into a kind of "stepping stone" for cultural exchange throughout the Mediterranean world.

Unearthing a Brilliant Civilization Archaeologists in the 19th century excavated **Knossos,** the Minoan capital city. There, they

found the remains of an advanced and thriving culture. It must have been a peaceful one as well, since Minoan cities did not seem to need fortifications to protect them. The archaeologists named the civilization they found in Crete *Minoa* after **King Minos** (MY·nuhs). According to a legend, Minos was a king who kept a half-human,

half-bull monster, called the Minotaur (MIHN·uh·TAWR). He kept the monster locked inside a labyrinth, a complicated maze from which no one could escape.

The excavation of Knossos and its colorful painted walls produced a great deal of information about Minoans. The wall paintings, as well as the official seals and painted vases, show the Minoans as graceful, athletic people who loved nature and beautiful objects. They also enjoyed vigorous sports such as boxing, wrestling, and bull-leaping.

Many Minoan artworks depict women and their role in religious ceremonies. The art suggests that women held a higher rank than in most neighboring cultures. A great Mother Earth Goddess seems to have ruled over the other gods of Crete. Also, priestesses took charge of some shrines, aided by male assistants.

Daily Life

Bull Leapers of Knossos

The bronze statue above captures the death-defying jump of a Minoan bull leaper in mid-flight. Many works of Minoan art show young men performing incredible acrobatic leaps over the horns of angry bulls. In one case, the gymnast jumps over the bull's horns, makes a somersault off its back, and lands behind its tail.

In another gymnastic feat, some team members hang on to the horns of a bull, using their bodies to cushion its horns and to force its head low, while another team member jumps over its back.

What was the reason for this bull-leaping? Was it a sport? Just a "fun" activity? An initiation for young warriors? Or a religious ritual? Most likely it was all of those. It probably also expressed a deep link between Minoans and nature, symbolized by the bull.

Daily *Life*
Bull Leapers of Knossos
(See page 67.)

Bulls figure prominently in Minoan culture. Ask students why do they think the Minoans focused so much attention on this animal. *Some students might hypothesize that the Minoans may have associated the bull's strength, size, and vitality with the power of natural forces such as storms and earthquakes. Thus, they may have sought to control or communicate with these natural forces through their relationship with the bull.*

 IN-DEPTH RESOURCES: UNIT 1
Primary Source: from Dolphin Fresco from Knossos, p. 44

 WORLD ART AND CULTURES TRANSPARENCIES
AT7 Palace of Minos at Knossos

OBJECTIVE ② INSTRUCT

Phoenicians Spread Trade and Civilization

Key Ideas

• The Phoenicians create separate city-states along the Mediterranean.

• They are highly skilled sailors who venture beyond the Mediterranean Sea.

• Phoenicians establish rich trading routes throughout the region.

• They disperse ideas as well as goods, including their written alphabet.

 IN-DEPTH RESOURCES: UNIT 1
History Makers: Herodotus, p. 50

 ELECTRONIC LIBRARY OF PRIMARY SOURCES
"Hanno's Voyage"

The Minoans sacrificed bulls and other animals to their gods. In at least one case, a young man was sacrificed. Excavation of a mountain temple revealed the bones of a 17-year-old boy on an altar, along with the skeletons of three priests. The positions of the skeletons suggest that the priests carried out the human sacrifice just before the building collapsed.

Minoan Culture's Mysterious End The Minoan civilization finally ended about 1200 B.C. The reasons for its end are unclear. Could it have been the result of some natural disaster? Did the island become overpopulated? Or was it overrun by invaders?

The civilization had withstood previous disasters. In about 1700 B.C., a great disaster, perhaps an earthquake, destroyed most Minoan towns and cities. The Minoans rebuilt the cities with equal richness. Then again in 1470 B.C. a series of earthquakes rocked Crete. The quakes were followed by a violent volcanic eruption on the neighboring island of Thera. Imagine the frightening catastrophe: first the shaking of the earth, then the fiery volcanic blast, next a huge tidal wave on Crete's northern coast, and finally a dense rain of white volcanic ash.

The disaster of 1470 B.C. was a blow from which the Minoans did not recover. This time, the Minoans did not succeed in rebuilding their cities. Nonetheless, Minoan civilization did linger on for almost 300 years. After that, invaders from Greece may have taken advantage of their weakened condition to destroy them. Some Minoans fled to the mountains to escape the ruin of the kingdom. Crete's influence as a major sea power and cultural force was over.

Phoenicians Spread Trade and Civilization

About 1100 B.C., after Crete's decline, the most powerful traders along the Mediterranean were the **Phoenicians** (fih·NIHSH·uhnz). Phoenicia was mainly the area now known as Lebanon. Phoenicians never united into a country. Instead, they founded a number of wealthy city-states around the Mediterranean that sometimes competed with one another. (See the map on pages 54–55.) The first cities in Phoenicia, such as Byblos, Tyre (tyr), and Sidon (SYD·uhn), were important trading centers.

The Phoenicians were remarkable shipbuilders and seafarers. They were the first Mediterranean people to venture beyond the Strait of Gibraltar. Some scholars believe that the Phoenicians traded for tin with inhabitants of the southern coast of Britain. Some evidence exists for an even more remarkable feat—sailing around the continent of Africa by way of the Red Sea and back through the Strait of Gibraltar.

Phoenicians made vows to their cruel gods and goddesses, shown in statues like these from Byblos. The Phoenicians would sacrifice their first-born children and animals to please these deities.

THINK THROUGH HISTORY
B. Summarizing
What adjectives might describe Minoan civilization?
B. Answer seagoing, artistic, advanced, peaceful

Background
Lebanon is found on the eastern end of the Mediterranean Sea. The Straits of Gibraltar are on the western end.

TEACHING OPTION **BLOCK SCHEDULING** **COOPERATIVE ACTIVITY: Creating a Board Game of Ancient Civilizations** CLASS TIME 25 MINUTES

Task: Students create board games about the Minoan and Phoenician civilizations.

Purpose: To learn more about two significant ancient trading societies

Activity: Have students divide into two groups. One group will create a board game about the Minoans and the other group will do the same about the Phoenicians. The games should require knowledge about each civilization to score points or advance on the board. There should be penalties for not knowing the right answers (lose a turn or points, go back a number of squares). The two groups will show each other their games, receive comments and suggestions, and revise the games.

📁 *Building the Portfolio:* Students can write a brief description of their game for their portfolio.

Standards for Evaluation
The game should . . .

• show students' knowledge of Minoan or Phoenician civilization

• provide clear directions and rules for playing the game

• offer rewards and penalties for right and wrong answers, respectively

• be visually pleasing and well organized

Such a trip was not repeated again for 2,000 years. The Greek historian Herodotus (hih·RAHD·uh·tuhs) relates the feat.

A VOICE FROM THE PAST
The Phoenicians set out from the Red Sea and sailed the southern sea [the Indian Ocean]; whenever autumn came they would put in and sow the land, to whatever part of Libya [Africa] they might come, and there await the harvest; then, having gathered in the crop, they sailed on, so that after two years had passed, it was in the third that they rounded the Pillars of Heracles [Strait of Gibraltar] and came to Egypt. There they said (what some may believe, though I do not) that in sailing round Libya they had the sun on their right hand [in reverse position].

HERODOTUS, in *History*, Book IV (5th century B.C.).

Commercial Outposts Around the Mediterranean The Phoenicians' most important city-states in the eastern Mediterranean were Sidon and Tyre, both known for their production of purple dye; Berytus (now Beirut, in Lebanon); and Byblos, a trading center for papyrus. Phoenicians built colonies along the northern coast of Africa and the coasts of Sicily, Sardinia, and Spain. The colonies strung out like beads on a chain about 30 miles apart—about the distance a Phoenician ship could sail in a day. The greatest Phoenician colony was at Carthage (KAHR·thihj), in North Africa. Settlers from Tyre founded Carthage in about 725 B.C.

The Phoenicians traded goods they got from other lands—wine, weapons, precious metals, ivory, and slaves. They also were known as superb craftsmen who worked in wood, metal, glass, and ivory. Their famous purple dye was produced from the murex, a kind of snail that lived in the waters off Sidon and Tyre. One snail, when left to rot, produced just a drop or two of a liquid of a deep purple color. Some 60,000 snails were needed to produce one pound of dye.

Phoenicia's Great Legacy: The Alphabet As merchants, the Phoenicians needed a way of recording transactions clearly and quickly. So, the Phoenicians developed a writing system that used symbols to represent sounds. The Phoenician system was phonetic—that is, one sign was used for one sound. In fact, the word *alphabet* comes directly from the first two letters of the Phoenician alphabet: *aleph* and *beth*. As they traveled around the Mediterranean, the Phoenicians introduced this writing system to their trading partners. The Greeks, for example, adopted the Phoenician alphabet and changed the form of some of the letters.

Few examples of Phoenician writing exist. Most was on papyrus, which crumbled easily over time. However, the Phoenician contribution to the world was enormous. With a simplified alphabet, learning was now accessible to many more people.

Phoenician trade was upset when their eastern cities were captured by Assyrians in 842 B.C. However, these defeats encouraged exiles to set up city-states like Carthage to the west. The Phoenician homeland later came under the control of the Babylonians, and still later, of the Persian empire of King Cyrus I. Their conquerors recognized the Phoenicians' superb ability both as shipbuilders and as seamen. Nonetheless, one of their most lasting contributions remains the spread of the alphabet.

Background
Byblos was so famous for its papyrus that it gave the Greeks their word for book, *biblos*, from which the English word *Bible* comes.

Background
Though not the first, the Phoenician alphabet was one of the earliest. And because they were traders, the Phoenicians spread the idea of the alphabet far and wide.

Alphabets—Ancient and Modern

Phoenician	Greek	English
	A	A
	B	B
	Γ	C
	Δ	D
	E	E
		F
		G
	Z	
	H	H
	Θ	
	I	I
		J
	K	K
	Λ	L
	M	M
	N	N
	Ξ	
	O	O
	Π	P
		Q
	P	R
	Σ	S
	T	T
	Υ	U
	Φ	
		V
	X	W
		X
	Ψ	Y
	Ω	Z

SKILLBUILDER: Interpreting Charts
1. *Which letters show the most similarity across the three alphabets?*
2. *Why might one language have fewer letters in its alphabet than another?*

MORE ABOUT . . .
Byblos
Byblos, one of the oldest towns in the world to be inhabited continuously, exported papyrus (in Greek *byblos, byblinos*) to Greece. Over time, the Greek *byblos* came to mean "book." The Christian scriptures were originally written on papyrus. The Greek term *byblos* was used to refer to them. Eventually it evolved into the English word *bible*.

MORE ABOUT . . .
Dyers of Phoenicia
The name of the entire Phoenician civilization is derived from the purple dye it made so famous. The Greek poet Homer used the word *phoenix* to refer to a dark red or purplish-brown color. The Greeks applied the term to the people who developed a beautiful purple dye from snails. What the Phoenicians called themselves may never be known.

History from Visuals

Alphabets—Ancient and Modern

Interpreting the Chart Make sure students understand that although the Phoenicians left out some vowel sounds in their phonetic alphabet *(u, y)*, the vowels *a, e, i,* and *o* appear as sounds that can stand alone.

Extension Activity Have students write their names and a short message in English, using the Phoenician alphabet. Ask them to exchange messages with a classmate and decipher each other's work.

SKILLBUILDER Answers
1. Possible Responses: a, h, k, m, o, t
2. Possible Response: One language might have fewer sounds than another.

TEACHING OPTION / **BLOCK SCHEDULING** — **SKILLBUILDER MINI-LESSON: Forming and Supporting Opinions** — **CLASS TIME 20 MINUTES**

Explaining the Skill By referring to facts, examples, and historical parallels, students can form and support their opinions. For example, in forming an opinion about a civilization, students would use historical research, the people's own words and artifacts, and examples from other civilizations to support their views.

Applying the Skill: *Phoenician Civilization* Ask students what they believe was

the Phoenicians' greatest contribution: trade or a written alphabet? Have them write a brief statement, citing facts from the text and their own research to support their opinion. *Possible answers: By establishing so many trade routes, Phoenicians accelerated the exchange of ideas, culture and goods; they spread their own technology; they advanced the science of seamanship and navigation.*

By establishing a written alphabet, they created an accurate method of recording business transactions; helped foster Greek civilization; and enabled many countries to develop a written history, literature, and legal system.

 IN-DEPTH RESOURCES: UNIT 1
Skillbuilder Practice: Forming Opinions, p. 39

Teacher's Edition 69

Daily Life

The Tyrian purple dye ranged from a pale pink to a deep royal purple. The shade depended on the amount of murex secretions used, how long the dye was exposed to light, and whether secretions from nonmurex snails were added. One expert has calculated that one pound of the finest dye, requiring up to 60,000 snails to make, would cost $28,000 today!

MORE ABOUT . . .
Wearers of Royal Purple

In classical Rome, only the emperor was allowed to wear the deepest, richest color of Tyrian purple. The cost of the dye prohibited most people from buying it. Thus, the story that the barge of Antony and Cleopatra flaunted an entire purple sail revealed the impressive wealth and rank of the Egyptian queen.

MORE ABOUT . . .
Origins of Glassware

Scholars believe that the first glass containers were made in Egypt and Mesopotamia in about 1500 B.C. Glass was so difficult to make that glass objects were considered as valuable as jewels. The Phoenicians probably learned the craft from the Mesopotamians.

Phoenician Financial News

Dye Prices Go Up!

Murex, the snail from which the famous purple dye is made, is now an exclusive Phoenician monopoly.

Workers break the murex shell, then take out the shellfish and put it in large vats. When the snails have died and rotted, they excrete a yellow liquid. When exposed to the sun for long periods, the liquid turns purple. The small amount of dye extracted from huge numbers of snails means that only the richest Romans can afford to use the dye for their robes. Thus the dye has been named "royal purple."

Residents living near dye centers complain of the stench of rotting snails and the huge piles of empty shells left near the factories.

This bronze plaque from the gates in the city of Balawat shows sailors leaving Tyre on yet another profitable trading expedition.

Shipping News

As usual, Phoenician shipping fleets are exploring new territories. The latest trip has taken our vessels past the Rock of Gibraltar into the Atlantic Ocean. Consider the danger faced by our sailors as they row past the placid Mediterranean . . . into who-knows-what. These brave mariners have only the gods and their skill to rely on.

Home Construction
Carthage, Tyre, Sidon

Crowded conditions within these walled towns have led to the construction of two-story homes. Many are adding balconies onto the second story, so residents can look out over the city wall. Walls are still being constructed of brick or clay and covered with stucco. Some of the latest homes sport bathrooms, with tubs featuring a bath seat.

Glassmaking

The glass manufacturing and export business is growing by leaps and bounds. The sands of Lebanon are rich in silica and make the best glass in the Mediterranean area. Borrowing techniques from Palestine has resulted in the creation of window glass. Romans are extremely interested in this process and are also experimenting with glassblowing techniques. Less expensive glass is quickly replacing metal in Roman home decoration.

The horse and date palm have been chosen as official symbols on Carthaginian coins.

EUROPE
ATLANTIC OCEAN
ANATOLIA
AFRICA
ASIA
PACIFIC OCEAN
INDIAN OCEAN
Black Sea
Caspian Sea
Aral Sea
Mediterranean Sea
Nile R.
Red Sea
Arabian Sea
Bay of Bengal
Persian Gulf
Indus R.
Ganges R.
Huang He (Yellow)
Danube R.
Euphrates R.
Tigris R.
c of Cancer
Tropic of Cancer
40°N
20°N
20°W
60°E
100°E
120°E
140°E

0   1,000 Miles
0   2,000 Kilometers

GEOGRAPHY SKILLBUILDER: Interpreting Maps
1. **Movement** *What area of the ancient world had the greatest number of land routes?*
2. **Human-Environment Interaction** *What natural inland feature often served as a highway for trade?*

The Long Reach of Ancient Trade

Trading in ancient times also connected the Mediterranean Sea with other centers of world commerce, such as South and East Asia. Several land routes crossed Central Asia and connected to India through Afghanistan. Two sea routes began by crossing the Arabian Sea to ports on the Persian Gulf and the Red Sea. From there, traders either went overland to Egypt, Syria, and Mediterranean countries, or they continued to sail up the Red Sea. To cross the Arabian Sea, sailors learned to make use of the monsoon winds. These winds blow from the southwest during the hot months and from the northeast during the cool season.

To widen the variety of their exports, Indian traders used other monsoon winds to travel to Southeast Asia and Indonesia. Once there, they obtained spices and other products not native to India.

Though traveling was difficult in ancient times, trading networks like those of the Phoenicians assured the exchange of products and information. Along with their goods, traders carried ideas, religious beliefs, art, and ways of living. They helped with the process of cultural diffusion as well as with moving merchandise.

Phoenician traders by their travels made crucial contributions to world civilization. At nearly the same time, another eastern Mediterranean people, the Jews, were creating a religious tradition that has lasted for more than 3,000 years. This is discussed in Section 4.

Vocabulary
monsoon: a wind that affects climate by changing direction in certain seasons.

Section 3 Assessment

1. TERMS & NAMES
Identify
• Minoans
• Aegean Sea
• Knossos
• King Minos
• Phoenicians

2. TAKING NOTES
Below is a list of accomplishments. Copy the chart beneath the list on your paper. Then fill in the chart, identifying feats that were Minoan and those that were Phoenician.

• dominated trade (2000–1400 B.C.)
• set up numerous city-states
• developed an alphabet
• produced a famous purple dye
• jumped over bulls for fun
• produced fine painted pottery

Minoan	Phoenician

3. EVALUATING SOURCES
Go back to page 69. Read Herodotus's account of how the Phoenicians sailed around Africa. What words show Herodotus's doubt? Why do you think he expresses doubts?

THINK ABOUT
• the sources that reported the feat
• Herodotus as a historian
• the Phoenicians' seafaring skills
• the fact that the trip was not repeated for 2000 years

4. ANALYZING THEMES
Economics The Phoenicians founded wealthy city-states around the Mediterranean. These city-states often competed with one another. Do you think it would have made more sense for the city-states to cooperate or did competition make them stronger? Explain your reasons.

THINK ABOUT
• advantages of a unified country
• advantages of independence
• benefits of competition

People and Ideas on the Move **71**

ANSWERS

1. TERMS & NAMES
Minoans, p. 67
Aegean Sea, p. 67
Knossos, p. 67
King Minos, p. 67
Phoenicians, p. 68

2. TAKING NOTES
Minoans: first, fifth, sixth feats in the list
Phoenicians: second, third, fourth feats in the list

3. EVALUATING SOURCES
"What some may believe, though I do not." *Possible Responses:* Herodotus was a historian. He did not want to tarnish his reputation by reporting something unlikely. There was no evidence of a second trip, so Herodotus was rightly skeptical.

4. ANALYZING THEMES
Economics
Cooperation: Had Phoenicians united, they could have pooled their resources and been an even stronger and more profitable trading power. Competition: This keeps traders on their toes, so Phoenicians in all cities would have been better merchants.

Section 4 Overview

OBJECTIVES

1. To summarize the history and beliefs of the ancient Hebrews.

2. To describe Israel under Saul, David, and Solomon.

3. To describe Israel's destruction and the Hebrews' exile in Babylon.

SKILLBUILDERS

- Interpreting Maps: movement, location, p. 73

CRITICAL THINKING

- Contrasting, p. 74
- Summarizing, p. 75
- Drawing conclusions, pp. 76, 77
- Making inferences, p. 76
- Identifying problems, p. 76

FOCUS

5-Minute Warm-Up

▶ **Making Inferences**
Answering these questions will help students understand the importance of ancient Palestine to the Jewish faith.

1. Study the map on p. 73. What makes ancient Palestine the crossroads of this region?

2. Why might Jews and other people fight over this territory?

 WARM-UP TRANSPARENCY 3

OBJECTIVE ① INSTRUCT

The Search for a Promised Land

▶ **Key Ideas**
- The Hebrews regard ancient Palestine as the promised land.
- The Hebrews worship one God.
- The judges and prophets interpret God's laws to the Hebrews.

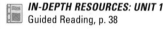 ***IN-DEPTH RESOURCES: UNIT 1***
Guided Reading, p. 38

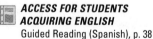 ***ACCESS FOR STUDENTS ACQUIRING ENGLISH***
Guided Reading (Spanish), p. 38

⊙ ***RELIGIONS OF THE WORLD***
Judaism

⊙ ***ELECTRONIC LIBRARY OF PRIMARY SOURCES:***
from the Book of Genesis in the King James Bible

TERMS & NAMES
- Palestine
- Canaan
- Torah
- Abraham
- monotheism
- covenant
- Moses
- Israel
- Judah
- tribute

MAIN IDEA	WHY IT MATTERS NOW
The Hebrews maintained monotheistic religious beliefs that were unique in the ancient world.	From this tradition, Judaism, the religion of the Jews, evolved. Judaism is one of the world's major religions.

SETTING THE STAGE The Phoenicians lived in a region at the eastern end of the Mediterranean Sea that was later called **Palestine**. The Phoenicians were not the only ancient people to live in Palestine. Nor were they the only Palestinian people to make a great contribution to world civilization. The area of Palestine called **Canaan** (KAY·nuhn) was the ancient home of the Hebrews, later called the Jews. Their history, legends, and moral laws are a major influence on Western culture, and they began a tradition also shared by Christianity and Islam.

Background
Many scholars use the name *Israelite,* instead of *Hebrew.*

The Search for a Promised Land

Ancient Palestine's location made it a cultural crossroads of the ancient world. By land, it connected Asia and Africa and two great empires, both eager to expand. To the east lay Assyria and Babylonia and to the west Egypt. Palestine's seaports opened onto the two most important waterways of that time: the Mediterranean, which connected to the Atlantic Ocean, and the Red Sea, which flowed into the Indian Ocean. The Hebrews settled in Canaan, the part of ancient Palestine that lay between the Jordan River and the Mediterranean Sea. In fact, Hebrews often used the word *Canaan* to refer to all of ancient Palestine. According to the Bible, Canaan was the land God had promised to the Hebrew people.

SPOTLIGHT ON

Philistines

The Philistines were another ancient people who settled in Canaan. The Greeks called the area where they lived "Palestine" after the Philistines. Much of what we know about the Philistines comes from their neighbors, the Hebrews, who disliked them and fought with them over control of the land.

The Philistines enjoyed definite military advantages over the Hebrews. They had a fleet of ships and swift chariots. More importantly, they knew how to forge iron into swords and shields. Over time, Hebrews learned the secret of smelting iron and were able to fight the Philistines on more even terms.

From Ur to Egypt Most of what we know about the early history of the Hebrews is contained in the first five books of the Hebrew Bible. Jews call these books the **Torah** (TAWR·uh) and consider them the most sacred writings in their tradition. Christians respect them as part of the Old Testament. As in other sacred literatures, the books of the Torah describe some events that actually happened. However, those books also contain stories told to teach important lessons.

In the Torah, God chose **Abraham** (AY·bruh·HAM) to be the "father," or first, of the Hebrew people. God's first words to Abraham expressed a promise of land and a pledge: "Go from your country and your kindred and your father's house to the land that I will show you. I will make of you a great nation, and I will bless you, and make your name great. . . ." (Genesis 12:1–2)

The Torah says that Abraham was a shepherd who lived in the city of Ur, in Mesopotamia. The Torah tells that God commanded him to move his people and their flocks to Canaan. This would have occurred around 2000 B.C. The story of how and why he moved to Canaan is told in the Book of Genesis. Abraham, his family, and their herds made their way from the lower Tigris and Euphrates region to Canaan. Then, possibly around 1650 B.C., the descendants of Abraham moved again—this time to Egypt.

Vocabulary
Bible: the name given to the sacred books of Judaism, as well as to those of Christianity.

Background
The Book of Genesis is the first book of the Bible. *Genesis* means "beginning."

The God of Abraham The Bible tells how Abraham and his family roamed for many years from Mesopotamia to Canaan to Egypt and back to Canaan. All the while, their

---

SECTION 4 RESOURCES

PRINT RESOURCES

 IN-DEPTH RESOURCES: UNIT 1
Guided Reading, p. 38
Geography Application: Early Civilizations, p. 40
Primary Source: The Ten Commandments, p. 45
Connections Across Time and Cultures; p. 51

ACCESS FOR STUDENTS ACQUIRING ENGLISH
Guided Reading (Spanish), p. 36
Geography Application: (Spanish), p. 38

 FORMAL ASSESSMENT
Section Quiz, p. 31

TECHNOLOGY RESOURCES

 CRITICAL THINKING TRANSPARENCIES
CT3 Time Machine: Major Religions 2500 B.C.–A.D. 552
CT39 Chapter 3 Visual Summary

⊙ **CD-ROM**
Religions of the World: Judaism
Electronic Library of Primary Sources

 INTERNET www.mlworldhistory.com

God, whose name was Yahweh, went with them. Gods worshiped by other people at that time were often local, associated with a specific place. Because the God of the Hebrews did not belong to any one place, the Hebrews could carry their worship of him wherever they went.

Unlike the other groups around them, who were polytheists, the Hebrews were monotheists. They prayed only to one God. **Monotheism** (MAHN·uh·thee·IHZ·uhm), a belief in a single god, comes from the Greek words *mono,* meaning "one" and *theism,* meaning "god-worship." The Hebrews had made a startling leap. They proclaimed Yahweh as the one and only God. In their eyes, Yahweh had power not only over the Hebrews, but over all peoples, everywhere. To the Hebrews, God was not a physical being, and no physical images were to be made of him.

The Hebrews asked Yahweh for protection from their enemies, just as other people prayed to their gods to defend them. According to the Bible, Yahweh looked after the Hebrews not so much because of ritual ceremonies and sacrifices, but because Abraham had promised to obey him. In return, Yahweh had promised to protect Abraham and his descendants. This mutual promise between God and the founder of the Hebrew people is called a **covenant** (KUHV·uh·nuhnt). This was the first of a series of covenants that Yahweh and the Hebrews would make together.

Background
In the Book of Exodus, God strikes down the first-born of the Egyptians, but he "passes over" the homes of the Hebrews. Passover celebrates this episode.

"Let My People Go." The Bible says the Hebrews migrated to Egypt because of a drought and threat of a famine. At first, the Hebrews were given places of honor in the Egyptian kingdom. Later, however, they were forced into slavery, their lives made "bitter with hard service, in mortar and brick, and in all kinds of work in the field." (Exodus 1:14)

The Hebrews fled Egypt—perhaps between 1300 and 1200 B.C. Jews call this event "the Exodus," and they remember it every year during the festival of Passover. The Torah says that the man who led the Hebrews out of slavery was named **Moses**. At Passover, it is told that at the time of Moses' birth, the Egyptian pharaoh felt threatened by the number of Hebrews in Egypt. He thus ordered all Hebrew male babies to be killed. Moses'

On Moses' return from Mount Sinai, he saw the Hebrews worshiping a golden calf and angrily broke the tablets of the Law. The 17th-century Italian painter Guido Reni depicts this dramatic moment.

GEOGRAPHY SKILLBUILDER:
Interpreting Maps
1. **Movement** Along what waterway did Abraham begin his wanderings away from his native city?
2. **Location** How did Canaan's location make it a true crossroads of the eastern Mediterranean?

Canaan, the Crossroads, 2000–600 B.C.

- Kingdom of Judah, 980 B.C.
- Kingdom of Israel, 980 B.C.
- Assyrian Empire, 650 B.C.
- Babylonian Empire, 600 B.C.
- Wanderings of Abraham
- Route of Hebrews out of Egypt

73

Jewish Festivals
Many Jewish festivals commemorate events in Hebrew history. Passover celebrates the Hebrews' safe exit from Egypt. According to the account in the Torah, God killed the first-born children in Egyptian families but "passed over" the Hebrew children. Shavuot commemorates Moses' receipt of the Torah on Mount Sinai. Observance of Sukkot reminds Jews of the huts Hebrews lived in during their wanderings in the wilderness.

ELECTRONIC LIBRARY OF PRIMARY SOURCES:
from the Book of Exodus in the King James Bible

History from Visuals

Canaan, the Crossroads, 2000–600 B.C.

Interpreting the Map Have students study the geographic features of Canaan and the surrounding areas. Ask them to list the reasons Canaan would be a prime target for outside invaders. *It occupies a strategic military and trade position between Africa and Asia; it has seaports, several cities that could serve as sources of supplies and revenue, and fertile land.*

Extension Activity Ask students to compare this map to a physical or climate map of the area in ancient times. On which parts of their journeys did the Hebrews encounter mountains or deserts?

SKILLBUILDER Answers
1. Euphrates River
2. It has a strategic position for trade between Africa and Asia; it has harbors for seaports; it has fertile land.

IN-DEPTH RESOURCES: UNIT 1
Geography Application: Early Eastern Mediterranean Civilizations, p. 40

CUSTOMIZING FOR SPECIAL NEEDS

Less Proficient Readers: *Analyzing Covenants* Pair less proficient readers with able readers. Ask them to read "The God of Abraham" on pages 72–73. Suggest they make a chart showing what God and the Hebrews promised each other

when they made a covenant. Tell students to keep their chart and add to it after they have read the section titled "A New Covenant" on page 74.

Students' charts might look like this:

	God	Hebrews
1st Covenant	To protect Abraham and his descendants.	To obey God.
2nd Covenant		

mother hid her baby in the reeds along the banks of the Nile. There, an Egyptian princess found and adopted him. Though raised in luxury, he did not forget his Hebrew birth. When God commanded him to lead the Jews out of Egypt, he obeyed. From that time on, Moses has been considered the greatest figure in Jewish history.

The Ten Commandments*

The first four commandments concerned the Hebrews' relationship with God:

- I am the Lord thy God. . . . Thou shalt have no other gods before me.
- Thou shalt not make unto thee any graven image. . . .
- Thou shalt not take the name of the Lord thy God in vain. . . .
- Remember the Sabbath day to keep it holy.

The last six commandments concerned the Hebrews' relationship with one another:

- Honor thy father and thy mother. . . .
- Thou shalt not kill.
- Thou shalt not commit adultery.
- Thou shalt not steal.
- Thou shalt not bear false witness against thy neighbor.
- Thou shalt not covet . . . anything that is thy neighbor's.

*Jews and Catholics word the commandments in ways slightly different from this version.

A New Covenant While the Hebrews were traveling across the Sinai (SY·ny) Peninsula, Moses climbed to the top of a mountain—Mount Sinai—to pray. The Bible says he spoke with God. When Moses came down from Mount Sinai, he brought down two stone tablets on which Yahweh had written ten laws, the Ten Commandments of the Bible.

These commandments and the other teachings that Moses delivered to his people became the basis for the civil and religious laws of Judaism. The Hebrews believed that these laws formed a new covenant between God and the Hebrew people. God promised to protect the Hebrews. They, in turn, promised to keep God's commandments. The covenant was based on the idea that God is just—and not arbitrary. In addition, the laws given to Moses required a high standard of moral conduct.

The Land and People of the Bible The Torah reports that the Hebrews wandered for 40 years in the Sinai Desert. Later books of the Bible tell about the history of the Hebrews after their wanderings. After the death of Moses, they returned to Canaan, where Abraham had lived. The Hebrews frequently fought with their neighbors over land. They were also making a change from a nomadic, tribal society to settled herders, farmers, and city dwellers. They were learning new technologies from neighboring peoples in ancient Palestine. These changes in their previously simple way of life made settling down a difficult experience for the Hebrews.

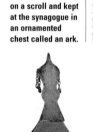

Tradition dictates that the Torah should be written on a scroll and kept at the synagogue in an ornamented chest called an ark.

The Hebrews Are Ruled by Judges When the Hebrews arrived in Canaan, they were loosely organized into twelve tribes. These tribes lived in separate territories and were self-governing. In times of emergency, the Bible reports that God would raise up judges. They would unite the tribes and provide judicial and military leadership during a crisis. What the judges had in common was charisma, a personal magnetism that attracted many followers to their cause. In the course of time, God chose a series of judges, one of the most prominent of whom was a woman, Deborah.

Hebrew Law Deborah's leadership was unusual for a Hebrew woman. The roles of men and women were quite separate in Hebrew society. This was generally the case among peoples of the region. Women could not officiate at religious ceremonies. In general, a Hebrew woman's most important duty was to raise her children and provide moral leadership for them.

The Ten Commandments were part of a code of laws delivered to Moses. The code included other rules regulating social and religious behavior. In some ways, this code resembled Hammurabi's Code with its attitude of "an eye for an eye and a tooth for a tooth." However, its strict justice was softened by expressions of God's mercy. The code was later interpreted by religious teachers called prophets. The prophets believed that they had been chosen as messengers to reveal God's will to his people. They constantly urged the Hebrews to stay true to their covenant with God.

The prophets taught that the Hebrews had a duty both to worship God and to live justly with one another. The goal was a moral life lived in accordance with God's laws. In the words of the prophet Micah, "He has told you, O mortal/ what is good;/ and what does the Lord require/of you/but to do justice, and to love/kindness,/ and to walk humbly with your/God?" This emphasis on right conduct and the worship of one God is called ethical monotheism—a Hebrew idea that has influenced human behavior for thousands of years through Judaism, Christianity, and Islam. From ethical monotheism, the three religions derive much of the moral force that characterizes them.

THINK THROUGH HISTORY
B. Summarizing
What does Hebrew law require of believers?
B. Answer To worship God and to treat other human beings fairly.

The Kingdom of Israel

Canaan—the land that the Hebrews believed had been promised them by God—combined largely harsh features such as arid desert, rocky wilderness, grassy hills, and the dry, hot valley of the Jordan River. Water was never plentiful; even the numerous limestone formations soaked up any excess rainfall. After first settling in the south-central area of ancient Palestine, the Hebrews expanded south and north.

Saul and David Establish a Kingdom The judges occasionally pulled together the widely scattered tribes for a united military effort. Nonetheless, Philistines continued to threaten the Hebrews' position in ancient Palestine. The Hebrews got along somewhat better with their Canaanite neighbors. After the exile, the only large tribe left was the tribe of Judah. As a result, Hebrews came to be called *Jews* and their religion, *Judaism*.

From about 1020 to 922 B.C., the Hebrews united under three able kings: Saul, David, and Solomon. The new kingdom was called **Israel** (IHZ·ree·uhl). For 100 years, Israel enjoyed its greatest period of power and independence.

Saul, the first of the three kings, was chosen largely because of his success in driving out the Philistines from the central hills of ancient Palestine. Saul is portrayed in the Bible as a tragic man, who was given to bouts of jealousy. After his death, he was succeeded by his son-in-law, David. King David, an extremely popular leader, united the tribes, established Jerusalem as the capital, and founded a dynasty.

Background
Solomon formed alliances by marrying the sisters or daughters of other kings. The Bible says that he had 700 wives, who turned him away from God. (I Kings 11:3–4)

Solomon Builds the Kingdom About the year 962 B.C., David was succeeded by his son Solomon, whose mother was Bathsheba. Solomon was the most powerful of the Hebrew kings. He built a trading empire with the help of his friend Hiram, the king of the Phoenician city of Tyre. Solomon also beautified the capital city of Jerusalem. The crowning achievement of his extensive building program in Jerusalem was a great temple, which he built to glorify God. The temple was also to be a permanent home for the Ark of the Covenant, which contained the tablets of Moses's law.

The temple that Solomon built was not large, but it gleamed like a precious gem. Bronze pillars stood at its entrance. The temple was stone on the outside, while its inner walls were made of cedar covered in gold. The main hall was richly decorated with brass and gold. Solomon also built a royal palace even more costly and more magnificent than the temple.

CONNECT to TODAY

The State of Israel
On May 14, 1948, Jews and many non-Jews around the world celebrated the birth of the modern state of Israel. Israel owes its existence in part to the idea of the Promised Land. Jewish tradition kept that idea alive for almost 18 centuries after Jewish rule had ended in Palestine. By the 1800s, persecution of Jews in Europe led many to believe that Jews should return to the land given to them by God—to Palestine.

In the late 1800s, a movement called *Zionism* called for "a (Jewish) home in Palestine secured by law." In 1947, after the horrors of Nazism, the United Nations answered that call. It established Israel as a Jewish homeland. Jews had regained their Promised Land.

MORE ABOUT . . .
Solomon's Architects
To design his temple and its furnishings, Solomon asked the help of his friend Hiram, king of Tyre. Hiram sent Phoenician designers and craftsmen to create the building. In gratitude, Solomon rewarded the Phoenicians with generous supplies of wheat and oil.

MORE ABOUT . . .
Solomon's Trade Network
Solomon's ambition was to create a large overland trade network. The Hebrew trade network was never fully developed, but Solomon's contacts in other countries proved useful when the Hebrews were dispersed after the fall of Jerusalem (see page 76).

CONNECT to TODAY
The State of Israel
Ask students to compare the geographic boundaries of the current state of Israel to the ancient kingdom. How much of the original kingdom have the Jews recovered? What economic, political, and military benefits does their territory offer them?

OBJECTIVE 2 INSTRUCT

The Kingdom of Israel

▶ **Key Ideas**
• Hebrews expand their territory by conquering their neighbors.
• Hebrews unite under Saul, David, and Solomon.
• King Solomon builds a trading empire, beautifies Jerusalem, and erects a great temple.
• After Solomon's death, the kingdom splits into Israel and Judah.

TEACHING OPTION **BLOCK SCHEDULING**
IDENTIFYING ANCIENT ROOTS OF MODERN CULTURE
CLASS TIME 20 MINUTES

Task: Students will draw on the content of Chapter 3 to identify how ancient cultures have helped to shape our modern Western world. They will list items that are still in use or have served as the basis for modern versions (for example, the Indo-European language gave rise to most modern European languages).

Materials Needed: Use the horizontal chart transparency and a grease pen or list the following

categories on the chalkboard: Law, Religious Beliefs, Technology, Language, Economics (trade, agriculture, manufacturing), Culture (arts, sports).

Activity: Under each category, ask the class to call out the ancient item (for example, the first written alphabet) that has a direct connection to modern life (for example, our modern alphabet) and the people who developed it (the Phoenicians).

Conclusion: Discuss with the class the connection between the achievements of ancient civilizations and the ways we talk, think, worship, conduct business, organize society, and play in our modern world.

CRITICAL THINKING TRANSPARENCIES
CT80 Charts (Horizontal)

Have students consider how Solomon's wisdom might be applied to contemporary family issues. Ask them to develop the plot of a short story they might write to illustrate their ideas. How do they think Solomon would have resolved the issue?

The Babylonian Captivity

Key Ideas

• After a long struggle, Israel falls to the Assyrians.

• Judah resists the Assyrians for about 116 years, then falls to the Babylonians.

• Survivors are sent into exile in Babylon for 50 years but return to rebuild the Temple.

ASSESS & RETEACH

Section 4 Assessment

Have pairs of students make flash cards of the section's terms and names to test their knowledge.

 FORMAL ASSESSMENT
Section Quiz, p. 31

Reteaching Activity

CLASS TIME: 15 MINUTES

Use the map of Canaan, the Crossroads, page 73, to help review the main ideas of the section.

 CRITICAL THINKING TRANSPARENCIES

CT3 Time Machine: Major Religions 2500 B.C.–A.D. 552

CT39 Chapter 3 Visual Summary

CLOSE ACTIVITY

CLASS TIME: 20 MINUTES

Creating a Time Line

Ask students to construct a time line of major events in Jewish history. Have them evaluate which of those events either resulted in a covenant with God or were motivated by a covenant. Help them understand how religious beliefs can help shape a people's history.

HISTORY MAKERS

King Solomon
962?–922? B.C.

Solomon's fame as a wise man became a legend. In the Bible, he prays to God for "an understanding mind," which God grants him.

Soon after, the story goes, two women and a baby boy were brought before him. Each woman claimed the baby was hers. After hearing their testimony, Solomon declared, "Divide the living boy in two; then give half to the one and half to the other." He then waited for the women's reactions.

One said: "Please, my lord, give her the living boy; certainly do not kill him!" However, the other woman accepted: "It shall be neither mine nor yours; divide it."

By his great wisdom, Solomon knew that the woman who would give up the child to save it was the real mother.

The Kingdom Divides Solomon's building projects required high taxes and badly strained the kingdom's finances. In addition, men were forced to spend one month out of every three working on the temple. The expense and forced labor caused much discontent. As a result, after Solomon's death, the Jews in the northern part of the kingdom—geographically distant from the south—revolted. By 922 B.C., the kingdom had divided in two—with Israel in the north and **Judah** (JOO-duh) in the south.

The next 200 years was a period of confusing ups and downs for the two kingdoms. Sometimes they fought each other; sometimes they joined together to fight common enemies. Each of the kingdoms had periods of prosperity, followed by low periods.

The Babylonian Captivity

Disaster finally struck as the independence of the two kingdoms was lost. In 738 B.C., both Israel and Judah began paying **tribute**—peace money paid by a weaker power to a stronger—to Assyria. By paying tribute, Israel and Judah hoped to assure that the mighty Assyrian empire would not attack. Then everything began to fall apart. The Assyrians began the siege of Samaria, the capital of Israel, in 725. By 722, the whole northern kingdom had fallen to the Assyrians.

The southern kingdom of Judah resisted for another 150 years before it too was destroyed. The destruction of Judah was to come at the hands of the Babylonians. After conquering Israel, the Assyrians rapidly lost power to a rising Babylonian empire. The Babylonian king Nebuchadnezzar (nehb-uh-kuhd-NEHZ-uhr) ran the Egyptians out of Syria and ancient Palestine, and he twice attacked Jerusalem. The city finally fell in 586 B.C. Solomon's Temple was destroyed in the Babylonian victory. Many of the survivors were exiled to Babylon. During their exile in Babylon, the Bible describes how the prophet Ezekiel urged his people to keep their religion alive in a foreign land.

Then about 50 years after the fall of Judah, another change of fortune occurred: in 539 B.C., the Persian king Cyrus the Great conquered Babylon. The next year, Cyrus allowed some 40,000 exiles to return to Jerusalem to rebuild the Temple. Many, however, were kept in Babylonia.

Work on the Second Temple was completed in 515 B.C. The walls of Jerusalem were rebuilt in 445 B.C. Soon, however, other empires would rise and fall in Southwest Asia. These new empires would take control both of ancient Palestine and the destiny of the Jewish people.

THINK THROUGH HISTORY
C. Drawing Conclusions How might geographical distance make the split of Israel and Judah more likely?
C. Possible Answers Poor communications in ancient times would have made it difficult for the king to enforce his laws in distant places. Geographical distance meant little contact between Israel and Judah; so they would have had different ways of thinking and living.

D. Possible Answer Their religion was more important to their lives than even the defense of their capital.
THINK THROUGH HISTORY
D. Making Inferences The Temple was rebuilt before the walls of Jerusalem. What does this fact indicate about the Jews after the Babylonian captivity?

Section 4 Assessment

1. TERMS & NAMES

Identify
• Palestine
• Canaan
• Torah
• Abraham
• monotheism
• covenant
• Moses
• Israel
• Judah
• tribute

2. TAKING NOTES

On your own paper, create a time line showing major Hebrew leaders. Then, below the time line, give one piece of information about each.

2000 B.C. |———————|———|

Abraham:
Father of Jewish people

3. IDENTIFYING PROBLEMS

What were the main problems faced by the Hebrews between 2000 B.C. and 700 B.C.?

THINK ABOUT
• the quest for a homeland
• other peoples
• hardships
• problems among Hebrews

4. THEME ACTIVITY

Interaction with Environment You are the leader of a Hebrew tribe. Write a short speech explaining to your people why Palestine is the best choice as a homeland.

ANSWERS

1. TERMS & NAMES
Palestine, p. 72
Canaan, p. 72
Torah, p. 72
Abraham, p. 72
monotheism, p. 73
covenant, p. 73
Moses, p. 73
Israel, p. 75

Judah, p. 76
tribute, p. 76

2. TAKING NOTES
2000 B.C., Abraham; 1300 B.C., Moses; 1200 B.C., Deborah; 1020–922 B.C., Saul, David, Solomon

3. IDENTIFYING PROBLEMS
Possible Responses: constantly moving from place to place; being forced into slavery in Egypt; fighting with neighbors over land; worshiping other gods; performing forced labor; paying high taxes; dividing the Hebrew kingdom in two

4. THEME ACTIVITY
Standards for Evaluation
The speech should. . .
• mention God had chosen this land for the Hebrews
• describe prior ties to the land
• explain Palestine's (Canaan's) strategic location
• discuss chances for raising families and building a nation

The Flood Story

The tale of a devastating flood appears among the legends of ancient peoples throughout the world. In some versions, the story of the flood serves to explain how the world came to be. In others, the flood is heaven's punishment for evil deeds committed by humans. At the right is a fifth-century A.D. view of Noah and his ark in the Hebrew flood story.

HEBREW LITERATURE
The Torah

When Yahweh saw how wickedly humans were acting, he was sorry that he had created them. Only one man, Noah, found favor in God's eyes.

And God said to Noah, "I have determined to make an end of all flesh, for the earth is filled with violence because of them. . . . Make yourself an ark of cypress wood; make rooms in the ark, and cover it inside and out with pitch. . . . And of every living thing, of all flesh, you shall bring two of every kind in the ark, to keep them alive with you; they shall be male and female. . . .

The rain fell on the earth forty days and forty nights. . . . At the end of the forty days Noah opened the window of the ark . . . and . . . sent out the dove from the ark; and the dove came back in the evening and there in its beak was a freshly plucked olive leaf; so Noah knew the waters had subsided from the earth. . . .

Then God said to Noah, "Go out of the ark, you and your wife, and your sons and your sons' wives with you. Bring out with you every living thing that is with you. . . . I establish my covenant with you, that . . . never again shall there be a flood to destroy the earth."

MESOPOTAMIAN MYTH
The Epic of Gilgamesh

In this legend, Utnapishtim, like Noah, escapes a worldwide flood by building an ark. The gods are unable to sleep because of the uproar caused by humans. To have peace, they agree to destroy the human race in a great flood. However, Ea, the god of wisdom, warns Utnapishtim of the coming catastrophe in a dream.

O man of Shurrupak, son of Ubara-Tutu; tear down your house and build a boat, abandon possessions and look for life. . . .

I loaded into (the boat) all that I had of gold and of living things, my family, my kin, the beasts of the field both wild and tame, and all the craftsmen. I sent them on board. . . .

For six days and six nights the winds blew, torrent and tempest and flood overwhelmed the world. . . . When the seventh day dawned the storm from the south subsided, the sea grew calm, the flood was stilled; I looked at the face of the world and there was silence, all mankind was turned to clay. . . . I opened a hatch and the light fell on my face. Then I bowed low, I sat down and I wept, the tears streamed down my face, for on every side was the waste of water.

A RETELLING OF AN INDIAN TALE
The Fish Incarnation of Vishnu

The Hindu god Vishnu is said to have reappeared on earth many times. In his first earthly incarnation, he took the form of Matsya, the fish, and saved mankind.

One day, as the sage Manu was praying at the river Ganges, a small fish asked for his protection. Manu put the fish in an earthen jar, but soon the fish was too big for the jar. So Manu put it into the river, but soon it outgrew the river. So Manu put the fish in the ocean. By now Manu began to suspect the divine nature of this fish.

The fish told Manu there would be a great deluge [flood]. He advised Manu to build a large boat and take seven Rishis (saints), the seeds of various kinds of plants and one of each type of animal. When the deluge came, the fish said, he would take the ark and its inhabitants to safety.

Sure enough, when the deluge occurred, the fish was there. Manu tied the boat to the horns of the fish, using the divine snake Vasuki as a rope. The fish then pulled the boat through the waters until it reached a mountain peak.

Connect *to* History

Drawing Conclusions List the similarities among the different versions. Why do you think that stories from such different geographical areas and time periods are so similar?

 SEE SKILLBUILDER HANDBOOK, PAGE 1006

Connect *to* Today

Researching Look in newspapers and magazines for accounts of people fleeing a great flood. Share what you find with the class.

 CD-ROM For another perspective on the Flood Story, see World History: Electronic Library of Primary Sources.

People and Ideas on the Move **77**

Multiple Stories of the Flood
As students read stories of the Great Flood from different traditions, have them consider reasons for the similarities and differences among these stories.
Ask them to bear in mind the following:

- All of the stories began within an oral tradition, which means that the biblical, Mesopotamian, and Hindu stories all have multiple versions. Some students may wish to compare different wordings of the story that appear in the Book of Genesis, Revised Standard Version (for example, 6:5–8 and 6:9–11, or 7:1–3 and 7:13–16).

- Though the stories are similar, some of their differences are striking. In the biblical version, for example, God promises never to send another flood to destroy humankind. In the Hindu tradition, the history of the world is believed to be cyclical. Another great flood could again sweep away most of humanity.

- In age, the Mesopotamian version precedes the Hebrew version. Because the Hindu myth was transmitted orally and written down only much later, it is difficult to date its origin.

IN-DEPTH RESOURCES: UNIT 1
Connections Across Time and Cultures: Religions in the Ancient World, p. 51

Connect *to* History

Drawing Conclusions

Students will note as similarities the flood itself, its use to cleanse the earth of a corrupt humanity, and the intervention by a god or hero to save a few virtuous people and most of the animals and plants. Students may conclude that the stories are similar because they may have been introduced by invaders, travelers, or traders and adopted by native peoples, and because such natural disasters as floods may be a common experience around the world.

Encourage students to discuss the reasons for and against the argument that the Middle Eastern and South Asian cultures may have borrowed the story from one another. How might ancient trade networks have helped spread such stories?

Connect *to* Today

Researching
In looking for artwork of the biblical flood, students can view European Christian art and also African and North American Indian versions, works clearly influenced by the stories of Christian missionaries. Students will find few pictures of the flood in the art of India, but will find the fish (Matsya) among the ten avatars (appearances on earth) of the god Vishnu.

TERMS & NAMES

1. Indo-Europeans, p. 57
2. caste, p. 60
3. reincarnation, p. 63
4. karma, p. 63
5. Siddhartha Gautama, p. 64
6. Minoans, p. 67
7. Phoenicians, p. 68
8. Torah, p. 72
9. monotheism, p. 73
10. Moses, p. 73

REVIEW QUESTIONS

Answers may vary for some questions.

11. war, disease, climatic change

12. chariot design, iron smelting

13. Aryans spoke a different language, were physically different, had no system of writing, and were a pastoral people.

14. In Hinduism, an individual soul passes from one incarnation to another until it achieves *moksha,* which is perfect understanding. A soul's karma is the sum of its good and bad deeds. Karma determines the reincarnations a soul will experience.

15. Buddhism rejected the caste system, so those in lower castes had more to gain from conversion to that religion. Those in higher castes would be less likely to give up their status.

16. goods such as pottery, swords, figurines; cultural influences like architecture, burial customs, religious rituals

17. a written alphabet

18. Ethical monotheism is a Hebrew idea that stresses right action and the worship of one God. Through Judaism, Christianity, and Islam, ethical monotheism has influenced human behavior for centuries.

19. resentment over taxes imposed to finance building projects; resentment over forced labor

20. Because early Judaism was monotheistic, their God was not as arbitrary as many gods of the time were and demanded high moral standards. Hebrews also believed that their God ruled over all peoples, not just over Hebrews.

Chapter 3 Assessment

TERMS & NAMES

Briefly explain the importance of each of the following in the years 3500 B.C. to 259 B.C.

1. Indo-Europeans
2. caste
3. reincarnation
4. karma
5. Siddhartha Gautama
6. Minoans
7. Phoenicians
8. Torah
9. monotheism
10. Moses

Interact *with* History

On page 56, you considered staying or fleeing from a foreign invader before you knew what some of the consequences of your decision might be. Now that you've read the chapter, reconsider your decision to stay or flee. Would you still make the same choice, or have you changed your mind? Discuss the consequences of your decision on your life.

REVIEW QUESTIONS

SECTION 1 *(pages 57–61)*
Indo-European Migrations

11. Name three reasons that historians give to explain why Indo-Europeans migrated.

12. What are two technologies that helped the Hittites build their empire?

13. How were the Aryans different from the non-Aryans *(dasas)* that they encountered when migrating to India?

SECTION 2 *(pages 62–66)*
Roots of Hinduism and Buddhism

14. In Hinduism, how are the ideas of karma, reincarnation, and *moksha* connected?

15. Why were lower castes more likely to convert to Buddhism?

SECTION 3 *(pages 67–71)*
Seafaring Traders Extend Boundaries

16. What did the Minoans export?

17. What is Phoenicia's greatest legacy to the world?

SECTION 4 *(pages 72–77)*
The Origins of Judaism

18. What is ethical monotheism and why is it important?

19. What caused the division of Solomon's kingdom?

20. Name two ways that early Judaism differed from other religions of the time.

Visual Summary

People and Ideas on the Move

	Hinduism	Buddhism	Judaism
Number of Gods	Many gods, all faces of Brahman	Originally, no gods	One God
Holy Books	*Vedas; Upanishads, Mahabharata,* and others	Books on the teachings and life of the Buddha	The Torah and other books of the Hebrew Bible
Moral Law	Karma	Eightfold Path	Ten Commandments
Leaders	Brahmins	Monks	Priests, judges, kings, prophets
Final Goal	*Moksha*	Enlightenment, Nirvana	A moral life through obedience to God's law

78 Chapter 3

Interact *with* History

Make sure students explore the consequences of their answers. If they choose to stay under the conqueror's rule, they should think about the changes in their lives that are likely to happen. If they choose to flee, how will they survive? After thinking through their choices, some students may decide on another course of action.

CRITICAL THINKING

1. EFFECTS OF MIGRATION

How important were the migrations of the Indo-European peoples? How lasting were the changes that they brought to their new homelands? Explain your conclusion.

2. WORLD RELIGIONS

THEME RELIGIOUS AND ETHICAL SYSTEMS Using a chart like the one below, fill in the information about the three world religions listed.

Religion	Founder	Approximate Time Originated	Area Originated
Hinduism			
Buddhism			
Judaism			

3. SOLOMON'S KINGDOM

How would you evaluate King Solomon's reign? Was he a good king? Support your opinion with evidence from the chapter.

4. ANALYZING PRIMARY SOURCES

The following passage tells how the Hebrews came to the prophet Samuel to ask him to appoint a king to rule over them. Read the paragraph and answer the questions below it.

> **THE BIBLE**
> Then all the elders of Israel gathered together and came to Samuel at Ramah and said to him, ". . . Appoint for us then a king to govern us, like other nations. . . ." Samuel prayed to the Lord, and the Lord said to Samuel, "Listen to the voice of the people in all that they say to you; for they have not rejected you, but they have rejected me from being king over them. Just as they have done to me from the day I brought them out of Egypt to this day forsaking me and serving other gods, so also they are doing to you."
>
> **I SAMUEL 8:4–8**

- How does the writer present the idea of choosing a king? What words give you that impression?
- According to this passage, who was Israel's real king?

CHAPTER ACTIVITIES

1. LIVING HISTORY: Unit Portfolio Project

THEME INTERACTION WITH ENVIRONMENT Your unit portfolio project focuses on showing how people in history have interacted with the environment. For Chapter 3, you might use one of the following ideas to add to your portfolio.

- You are an Indo-European scout. Draw a map showing your chief the route to the place where you want your people to migrate. Then, explain to the chief why you have chosen this place.
- Write a dialogue between King Minos and a Minoan sailor describing the dangers of seagoing trade routes. Be specific. Include possible ways to minimize these dangers.
- Write a myth telling about events that might have occurred as the Phoenicians sailed around Africa. The events can clearly be imaginary, but they should be based on the geography of the route that the Phoenicians reportedly took.

2. CONNECT TO TODAY: Cooperative Learning

THEME ECONOMICS Although the caste system was officially abolished by the Indian government in 1955, a castelike system based on occupations still exists in India today. Work with a team to research and create a bar graph. In the bar graph, compare the percentage of people in certain occupations in today's India with the percentage of the wealth they own. For example, 2% of the working population in today's India are government officials and white collar workers; they own, say, 25% of the country's wealth.

Use the Internet, magazines, or your library to research statistics about the topic. Look for statistics that answer such questions as: What percentage of working people in today's India belong to each major occupational group? What percentage of the country's wealth is owned by people in these occupational groups?

- Look for statistics. Figure out how to show those figures visually in a bar graph.
- Label the graph clearly.
- Compare the working population in India today with the ownership of wealth in the country.

FOCUS ON TIME LINES

Review the time line below. It shows the development of new ideas in the ancient world. Then make two charts.
- In the first chart, group the new ideas by category.
- In the second chart, list the new ideas by order of importance.

Connect to History
How could ironworking help Aryans to carry out their migrations in India? To conquer territory? To settle territory?

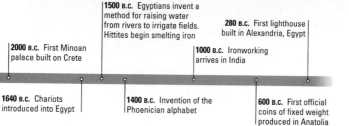

3000 B.C. Writing invented in Mesopotamia

2650 B.C. The "step" pyramid designed in Egypt

1640 B.C. Chariots introduced into Egypt

2000 B.C. First Minoan palace built on Crete

1500 B.C. Egyptians invent a method for raising water from rivers to irrigate fields. Hittites begin smelting iron

1400 B.C. Invention of the Phoenician alphabet

1000 B.C. Ironworking arrives in India

280 B.C. First lighthouse built in Alexandria, Egypt

600 B.C. First official coins of fixed weight produced in Anatolia

People and Ideas on the Move **79**

CHAPTER ACTIVITIES

1. LIVING HISTORY

Standards for Evaluation
Maps and explanations should meet the following criteria:

- Show the intended route, with all features clearly labeled.
- List reasons for choosing the location.

Standards for Evaluation
Dialogues should meet the following criteria:

- Use information from the text in referring to routes.
- Describe the specific dangers of seagoing trade routes and ways to minimize them.

Standards for Evaluation
Myths should meet the following criteria:

- Be based on the geography of Phoenicia and Africa.
- Include heroic characters, fantasy creatures, and a moral framework.

2. CONNECT TO TODAY

Cooperative Learning

Standards for Evaluation
Bar graphs should meet the following criteria:

- Present statistical information accurately.
- Be labeled clearly.
- Site resources used in research.

FOCUS ON TIME LINES

- *Time line by category:* **Communication and Business:** Mesopotamian writing, Phoenician alphabet, Anatolian coins; **Building:** Egyptian pyramid, Minoan palace, Egyptian lighthouse; **Transportation:** Egyptian chariots; **Farming and Industry:** Egyptian irrigation/Hittite iron smelting, Indian ironworking
- *Time line by order of importance:* Answers will vary but students should explain their choices.

Connect to History *Possible Responses:* Iron war vehicles and weapons could be used to travel and conquer territory. Iron tools would help in settlement.

CRITICAL THINKING

1. EFFECTS OF MIGRATION

Possible Responses: The migrations of the Indo-Europeans were very important and brought long-lasting changes. Indo-European languages are the basis for nearly half the languages spoken today. Other Indo-European groups developed iron smelting. Their religious beliefs evolved into Hinduism and Buddhism.

2. WORLD RELIGIONS

Hinduism: no central founder, developed over many centuries, India. Buddhism: Siddhartha Gautama, late 600s B.C., India. Judaism: Abraham, around 2000 B.C., Ur

3. SOLOMON'S KINGDOM

Possible Responses: Students who think Solomon was a good king might point to his wisdom, unification efforts, building projects, trading empire. Those who think the opposite might point to high taxes, forced labor, poverty.

4. ANALYZING PRIMARY SOURCES

Possible Responses: The writer does not approve of the Hebrews' demand for a king, as conveyed by such language as "rejected me," "forsaking me," and "serving other gods." As a people chosen by God, the Hebrews were not supposed to be like other nations and want ". . . a king to govern us." In the writer's view, God is the Israelites' real king.

PLANNING GUIDE
First Age of Empires

	Key Ideas	**COPY MASTERS**	**ASSESSMENT**
SECTION 1 **The Empires of Egypt and Nubia Collide** *pp. 83–87*	The New Kingdom forges a brilliant Egyptian Empire, which is eventually conquered and ruled by the Nubians of Kush. The Kushites later establish an Egyptian-style kingdom of their own farther south.	*In-Depth Resources: Unit 1* • **Guided Reading,** p. 52 • **Literature:** "Ozymandias," p. 63 • **History Makers:** Hatshepsut, p. 66	P E *Section 1 Assessment,* p. 87 *Formal Assessment* • Section Quiz, p. 40 *Alternative Assessment Book* • Standards for Evaluating a Cooperative Activity
SECTION 2 **Assyria Dominates the Fertile Crescent** *pp. 88–91*	The Assyrians absorb Egypt into a Mesopotamian Empire and perfect terror as a means of rule. The Chaldeans and Medes finally annihilate Assyria, only to be swallowed up by the growing Persian Empire.	*In-Depth Resources: Unit 1* • **Guided Reading,** p. 53 • **Geography Application:** Babylon, p. 57 • **Primary Source:** from *Assyrian Capture of Jerusalem,* p. 59 • **Literature:** "The Destruction of Sennacherib," p. 67 • **History Makers:** Sennacherib, p. 67 • **Connections Across Time and Cultures:** Empires of Southwest Asia, p. 68	P E *Section 2 Assessment,* p. 91 *Formal Assessment* • Section Quiz, p. 41 *Alternative Assessment Book* • Standards for Evaluating a Cooperative Activity
SECTION 3 **Persia Unites Many Lands** *pp. 92–96*	Persian kings forge a multicultural empire stretching from the Indus River to the Nile. Persia pioneers enlightened tolerance in government and supports the Zoroastrian religion.	*In-Depth Resources: Unit 1* • **Guided Reading,** p. 54 • **Primary Source:** "To the Fire" from the *Zend-Avesta,* p. 60 • **Literature:** "Babylon," p. 65	P E *Section 3 Assessment,* p. 96 *Formal Assessment* • Section Quiz, p. 42 *Alternative Assessment Book* • Standards for Evaluating a Cooperative Activity
SECTION 4 **An Empire Unifies China** *pp. 97–101*	Amid the social chaos of the crumbling Zhou Dynasty, Chinese philosophers develop three major schools of thought. Shi Huangdi unifies China in a brutal military campaign and builds the Great Wall.	*In-Depth Resources: Unit 1* • **Guided Reading,** p. 55 • **Skillbuilder Practice:** Recognizing Effects, p. 56 • **Primary Sources:** from *Intrigues of the Warring States,* p. 61; from the *Analects* by Confucius, p. 62	P E *Section 4 Assessment,* p. 101 *Formal Assessment* • Section Quiz, p. 43 *Alternative Assessment Book* • Standards for Evaluating a Cooperative Activity
CHAPTER RESOURCES	**Chapter Overview** A series of empires, each one bigger than the last, forges regional unity among the old heartlands of civilization from the Nile to the Iranian Plateau. Meanwhile, the Chinese Empire emerges as a cultural and political unit.	*Telescoping the Times* • Chapter Summary, pp. 13–15 *Planning for Block Schedules*	P E *Chapter Assessment,* pp. 102–103 *Chapter Activities,* p. 103 *Formal Assessment* • Chapter Test, forms A and B, pp. 44–49 *Test Generator* *Alternative Assessment Book*

1570 B.C.–200 B.C.

TECHNOLOGY

 Warm-Up Transparency 4

 Battles of the World
• Kadesh 1275 B.C.

 Electronic Library of Primary Sources
• "The Kushite Takeover"

 INTERNET RESOURCES
www.mlworldhistory.com

 Warm-Up Transparency 4

Electronic Library of Primary Sources
• "An Assyrian Palace"

INTERNET RESOURCES
www.mlworldhistory.com

 Warm-Up Transparency 4

 World Art and Cultures Transparencies
• AT8 Persian drinking horn

Critical Thinking Transparencies
• CT4 Political Decision-Making in the First Age of Empires

Electronic Library of Primary Sources
• "Customs of the Persians"

 Patterns of Interaction: Building Empires

 Warm-Up Transparency 4

Geography Transparencies
• GT4 Empires of the World, 1570-202 B.C.

 World Art and Cultures Transparencies
• AT9 Chinese terra cotta army figures

 Critical Thinking Transparencies
• CT40 Chapter 4 Visual Summary

 Religions of the World
• Confucianism

 Chapter Summaries on Audiocassette in English and Spanish

 INTERNET RESOURCES
www.mlworldhistory.com

 ## Block Scheduling (90 MINUTES)

Day 1
Section 1, pp. 83–87
 COOPERATIVE ACTIVITY
Investigating Nubian Cultures,
p. 84 (Teacher's Edition)

Section 2, pp. 88–91
 COOPERATIVE ACTIVITY
Advising a King,
p. 89 (Teacher's Edition)

Section Assessments,
pp. 87, 91

Day 2
Section 3, pp. 92–96
 COOPERATIVE ACTIVITY
Making a Persia Poster,
p. 93 (Teacher's Edition)

Section 4, pp. 97–101
 COOPERATIVE ACTIVITY
Debating Chinese Philosophies,
p. 99 (Teacher's Edition)

Section Assessments,
pp. 96, 101

Chapter Assessment,
pp. 102–103

Yearly Pacing **Chapter 4 Total:** 2 days **Yearly Total:** 85 days

 Planning for Block Schedules

Customizing for Special Needs

Students Acquiring English

 Access for Students Acquiring English
• **Guided Reading** for Sections 1–4 (Spanish), pp. 43–46
• **Chapter Summary** (Spanish), pp. 40–42
• **Skillbuilder Practice** Recognizing Effects (Spanish), p. 47
• **Geography Application** Babylon (Spanish), pp. 48

 Chapter Summaries on Audiocassette
in English and Spanish

 Patterns of Interaction Building Empires (Spanish)

 INTERNET RESOURCES
www.mlworldhistory.com
The Diverse Classroom.

Less Proficient Readers

In-Depth Resources: Unit 1
• **Guided Reading** for Sections 1–4, pp. 52–55
• **Skillbuilder Practice** Recognizing Effects, p. 56
• **Geography Application** Babylon, p. 57

Telescoping the Times
• Chapter Summary, pp. 13–15

Chapter Summaries on Audiocassette

Gifted and Talented Students

In-Depth Resources: Unit 1

Primary Sources:
• from *Assyrian Capture of Jerusalem,* p. 59
• "To the Fire" from the *Zend-Avesta,* p. 60
• from *Intrigues of the Warring States,* p. 61
• from the *Analects* by Confucius, p. 62

History Makers
• Hatshepsut, p. 66
• Sennacherib, p. 67

Connections to Literature READINGS FOR STUDENTS

In-Depth Resources: Unit 1
• Literature: "Ozymandias," p. 63; "The Destruction of Sennacherib," p. 64

Enrichment Reading
• **Hodges, Margaret**
The Avenger
New York: Scribner, 1982

Two boys fight side by side during the Persian Wars in 490 B.C.

• **Lyttle, Richard B.**
The Golden Path: The Lure of Gold Through History
New York: Atheneum, 1983

The power and beauty of gold through history.

First Age of Empires 1570 B.C.–200 B.C.

Accessing Prior Knowledge

• Ask students what they think an empire is. *Possible response: An extensive group of territories or peoples governed by one ruler.* Point out that although the United States is powerful, it is not an empire.

Analyzing Art and Culture

• Focus on the artworks featured on this page and discuss the differences in style. These reflect broad differences in the cultures that produced the works. As students read the chapter, they should look for other traces of these differences—for example, in religious ideas, styles of government, and attitudes toward conquered peoples.

GEOGRAPHY CONNECTION

Have students identify each of the four empires shown on the map.

• What major transportation route connected cities in the Persian Empire? in the Kushite Empire?

• What two regions of early river valley civilization did the Assyrian Empire control?

First Age of Empires, 1570 B.C.–200 B.C.

PREVIEWING THEMES

Interaction with Environment
In this first age of empires, different cultures engaged in monumental projects. These included the Royal Road in Persia, the Great Wall of China, fortified walled cities such as Nineveh, and extensive irrigation ditches and canals. The projects demonstrated these cultures' ability to adapt to and control the environment.

Empire Building
Throughout this period, people from Africa to China spread their influence across vast regions and built the world's earliest great empires.

Science & Technology
Advanced weaponry helped Assyria conquer its neighbors. A network of roads connected the far-flung Persian Empire. Other technology also played a key role in establishing and maintaining history's early empires.

INTERNET CONNECTION

Visit us at www.mlworldhistory.com to learn more about Egypt, Nubia, Assyria, Persia, and China.

ANCIENT EMPIRES, 650 B.C.–200 B.C.

Ashurbanipal, an Assyrian monarch who reigned from **668–627 B.C.,** fights a lion. The lion hunt was a royal sport of Assyrian kings. The king is portrayed as a mighty warrior, a conqueror of nature, even of the lion.

EUROPE

Black Sea

Royal Road

Caspian Sea

Sardis

Nineveh

Mediterranean Sea

Mesopotamia

Euphrates R.

Tigris R.

SYRIAN DESERT

Babylon

Susa

Persepolis

Memphis • Cairo

Persian Gulf

AFRICA

Niger R.

Nile River

Red Sea

ARABIAN PENINSULA

Napata

Ara S.

Meroë

The Nubian king **Taharqa,** who reigned from **690–664 B.C.,** celebrated with inscriptions and proclamations his military victories. He added inscriptions about sporting events, and even his mother's visit on his coronation. He also commissioned statues of himself, such as this one ordered for his temple.

80

GEOGRAPHY THEMES

Place

Have students note where the events of this chapter take place. They might compare a contemporary map with the one on this page to see what countries now occupy the areas in question. Have students focus on geographical features of these places, such as rivers, mountains, and proximity to various seas. Invite them to speculate on why the first empires emerged in these places and how geography may have influenced their destinies.

Region

Refer to the opening map again and point out that two distant areas are spotlighted: one in East Asia and one in a belt that runs from southwestern Asia to North Africa. Explain that each of these areas can be defined as a region. Within each region, the various states that emerged interacted and affected one another. Tell students to watch for broad themes that characterized historical developments in each region.

ADDITIONAL RESOURCES

Books for the Teacher

• David, A. Rosalie. *Discovering Ancient Egypt.* New York: Facts on File, 1994.

• Mackey, Sandra. *The Iranians: Persia, Islam, and the Soul of a Nation.* New York: Dutton, 1996. Iranian civilization from Cyrus the Great to the present.

Books for the Student

• Bianchi, Robert. *The Nubians: People of the Ancient Nile.* Brookfield: Millbrook, 1994.

• Freeman, Charles. *The Legacy of Ancient Egypt.* New York: Facts on File, 1997.

• Lazo, Caroline. *The Terra Cotta Army of Emperor Qin.* New York: New Discovery, 1993. The story of Shi Huangdi and the army of clay figures.

Videos

• *The Great Wall of China.* Ambrose Video, 1992. 800-526-4663.

• *Life Under the Pharaohs.* Coronet/MTI, 1989. 800-221-1274.

Software

• *Decisions, Decisions: Ancient Empires.* CD-ROM, Diskette. Tom Snyder Productions, 1996. 800-342-0236. Faced with an encroaching empire, what should a leader do?

• *Everyday Life in Ancient Egypt.* CD-ROM. Society for Visual Education, 1995. 800-829-1900.

• *The First Emperor of China.* CD-ROM. Social Studies School Service, 1993. 800-421-4246.

Shi Huangdi, the ruler of a kingdom in China, assumed the title of "First Emperor" in **221 B.C.** He attempted to unify China, defeat nomadic invaders, abolish the feudal system, and establish a new social order. So fierce was he that he was said to have "the heart of a tiger and a wolf."

Darius and Xerxes built the grand palace of the Persian kings at **Persepolis** in the fifth century B.C. This great building, a symbol of the majesty of the Persian Empire, was destroyed by Alexander the Great and his Greek army in their invasion of Persia in **331–330 B.C.**

Kush Empire
Assyrian Empire
Persian Empire
Qin Dynasty
Royal Road
Great Wall

0   500 Miles
0   1000 Kilometers

81

HISTORY THROUGH ART

Assyrian Sculpture

Assyrian artists excelled in carving low reliefs, sculptures in which the figures project slightly from a supporting background. The image of Ashurbanipal is part of a series of hunting scenes carved in relief on alabaster panels that adorned the king's palace in Nineveh. Such scenes served as potent visual propaganda, glorifying the king as the source of Assyrian might and the protector of cosmic order.

Interpreting the Art Invite students to compare this image with the Paleolithic painting shown at the bottom of page 13. How are the depictions of wild animals similar? How are they different? *Possible responses: Both images depict animals realistically (though the Assyrian image is more detailed) and give a sense of motion. The Assyrian image focuses on a highly tense moment in which a fierce animal*

attacking a hunter is dealt a fatal wound; the Paleolithic image shows various animals running freely and gracefully.

What attitude toward nature might each image be expressing? *The Assyrian image might suggest that nature is a threat to be conquered; the Paleolithic image, that nature is a force to be revered.*

Interact with History

This Interact with History feature motivates students by inviting them to put themselves in a key historical situation—that of a common person in a time of lawlessness and military rule. Imagining themselves as traveling merchants who face increasing dangers on the road, students will analyze the issues, explore their options, and become decision-makers.

Purpose

- to set the stage for studying the first empires

- to help students understand some of the forces that led to empire building

- to help students make connections with people and events they will study in this chapter

Teaching Strategy

Thinking Critically After students have imagined themselves in the situation described on this page, have them answer the key questions and give reasons for their decision.

EXAMINING the ISSUES

Following are suggestions for addressing each bulleted question.

1 Ask students if they have heard arguments urging government to "get tough on crime." What concerns might drive such arguments?

2 Ask students if they have heard criticisms of government power. What are the arguments?

3 What conditions would have to be present in a society for slavery to exist there?

4 How would students feel if our laws, taxes, and police power had been imposed on us by outside conquerors?

Making Connections Explain to students that in the days of the early city-states, many lands had no government rule. They were just open, lawless territories, dangerous to cross.

Interact with History

You are a merchant who travels great distances with your camel caravan in order to sell and trade goods. Your life has become increasingly difficult because bandits and thieves plague the roads. They ambush and rob unwary travelers, particularly merchants selling their wares. There is a new military power expanding its empire throughout the region of your travels that is suppressing the worst of the outlaw bands. At the same time that it is putting down lawlessness and disorder, however, the military empire is imposing harsh laws and heavy taxes on the regions that it conquers.

Empire—Good or Bad?

An armed cavalry escort protects a caravan from an armed raiding party. Mounted troops bring a new sense of order and safety to travelers and merchants.

A raiding party plans to attack a caravan. The caravan carries a fortune in exotic goods, including silks and spices from distant lands.

Merchant caravans, such as this one, cross the Fertile Crescent and travel the Silk Road from China. Such caravans are often raided by thieves.

EXAMINING the ISSUES

1 • Why might a merchant or other common person favor the establishment of a strong empire?

2 • Why might such a person oppose a strong empire?

3 • Why might a victorious army enslave a subject people?

4 • What advantages or abuses might a strong military power bring to a region?

In small groups, answer the questions, then report back to the class. In your discussion, remember what you've learned about military conquest and the behavior of such groups as the Sumerians, Egyptians, and Hittites.

As you read about the empires in this chapter, consider how the winners treat the people under their power and how the conquered people respond.

82 Chapter 4

Follow Up

A feature on the chapter assessment will ask students to reevaluate their responses to the situation presented on this page.

1 The Empires of Egypt and Nubia Collide

TERMS & NAMES
- Hyksos
- New Kingdom
- Hatshepsut
- Thutmose III
- Nubia
- Ramses II
- Kush
- Piankhi
- Meroë

MAIN IDEA

Two empires along the Nile, Egypt and Nubia, forged commercial, cultural, and political connections.

WHY IT MATTERS NOW

Neighboring civilizations participate in cultural exchange as well as conflict.

Section 1 Overview

OBJECTIVES

1. To identify key events in the history of Egypt's New Kingdom.
2. To explain why the Egyptian Empire declined.
3. To summarize the Kushite conquest of Egypt.
4. To describe the achievements of the Kushite kingdom of Meroë.

SKILLBUILDER

- Interpreting Maps: place, region, p. 85

CRITICAL THINKING

- Recognizing effects, p. 84
- Making inferences, p. 86
- Comparing, p. 86
- Recognizing bias, p. 87
- Analyzing themes, p. 87

SETTING THE STAGE During the Middle Kingdom (about 2080–1640 B.C.), trade with Mesopotamia and the Indus Valley enriched Egypt, located in northeastern Africa. Meanwhile, up the Nile River, less than 600 miles south of the Egyptian city of Thebes, a major kingdom had developed in the region of Nubia. For centuries, the Nubian kingdom of Kush traded with Egypt. The two kingdoms influenced each other.

The New Kingdom of Egypt

After the prosperity of the Middle Kingdom, Egypt descended into war and violence. This was caused by a succession of weak pharaohs and power struggles among rival nobles. The weakened country fell to invaders who swept across the Isthmus of Suez in chariots, a weapon of war unknown to the Egyptians. These invaders, nomads called **Hyksos** (HIHK·sohs), ruled Egypt from 1640 to 1570 B.C. The Hyksos invasion shook the Egyptians' confidence in the desert barriers that had protected their kingdom.

Around 1600 B.C., a series of warlike rulers began to restore Egypt's power. Among those who helped drive out the Hyksos was Queen Ahhotep (ah·HOH·tehp). The queen took over when her husband died in battle. The next pharaoh, Kamose (KAH·mohs), won a great victory over the hated Hyksos. His successors drove the Hyksos completely out of Egypt and pursued them across the Sinai Peninsula into Palestine.

After overthrowing the Hyksos rulers, the pharaohs of the **New Kingdom** (about 1570–1075 B.C.) sought to strengthen Egypt by building an empire. Egypt now entered its third period of glory in the New Kingdom. During this time it was wealthier and more powerful than ever before.

Egypt's Empire Builders in the New Kingdom Equipped with bronze weapons and two-wheeled chariots, the Egyptians became conquerors. The pharaohs of the Eighteenth Dynasty (1570–1365 B.C.) set up an army including archers, charioteers, and infantry, or foot soldiers. The symbols of royal power had always been the red crown and the white crown. Now the pharaohs added a new piece of royal headgear—the blue crown, a war crown shaped like a battle helmet.

Among the rulers of the New Kingdom, **Hatshepsut** (hat·SHEHP·soot), who boldly declared herself pharaoh around 1472 B.C., was unique. She took over because her stepson, the male heir to the throne, was a young child at the time. Unlike other New Kingdom rulers, Hatshepsut spent her reign encouraging trade rather than just waging war.

Vocabulary
dynasty: a series of rulers from a single family.

HISTORY MAKERS

Hatshepsut
reigned 1472–1458 B.C.

Hatshepsut was an excellent ruler of outstanding achievement who made Egypt more prosperous. As pharaoh, she sent traders down the Red Sea to bring back gold, ebony, baboons, and myrrh trees.

As male pharaohs had done, Hatshepsut planned a tomb for herself in the Valley of the Kings. Carved reliefs on the walls of the temple reveal the glories of her reign.

The inscription from Hatshepsut's obelisk (tall stone shaft) at Karnak trumpets her glory and her feelings about herself:

"I swear as Re loves me, as my father Amon favors me, as my nostrils are filled with satisfying life, as I wear the white crown, as I appear in the red crown, . . . as I rule this land like the son of Isis . . ."

First Age of Empires **83**

FOCUS
5-Minute Warm-Up

▶ *Making Inferences*
Have students answer these questions to explore the relationship between Egypt and Nubia.

1. Based on the image and caption on page 84, who—Egypt or Nubia—dominates whom?

2. Name one way that Egypt gained from contact with Nubia.

 WARM-UP TRANSPARENCY 4

OBJECTIVE 1 INSTRUCT

The New Kingdom of Egypt

▶ *Key Ideas*
- Warlike rulers drive Hyksos invaders out of Egypt and found a glittering New Kingdom.
- The new pharaohs build an empire to buffer their heartland from further invasions.
- The female pharaoh Hatshepsut strengthens Egypt through trade.
- Egyptian expansion is stemmed at the Battle of Kadesh.
- New Kingdom art and architecture peak under Ramses II.

IN-DEPTH RESOURCES: UNIT 1
Guided Reading, p. 52

ACCESS FOR STUDENTS ACQUIRING ENGLISH
Guided Reading (Spanish), p. 43

SECTION 1 RESOURCES

PRINT RESOURCES

 IN-DEPTH RESOURCES: UNIT 1
Guided Reading, p. 52
Literature: "Ozymandias," p. 63
History Makers: Hatshepsut, p. 66

 ACCESS FOR STUDENTS ACQUIRING ENGLISH
Guided Reading (Spanish), p. 43

FORMAL ASSESSMENT
Section Quiz, p. 40

 ALTERNATIVE ASSESSMENT BOOK

TECHNOLOGY RESOURCES

 CD-ROM
Battles of the World
Electronic Library of Primary Sources

INTERNET www.mlworldhistory.com

Hatshepsut's stepson, **Thutmose III** (thoot·MOH·suh), proved to be a much more warlike ruler. In fact, in his eagerness to ascend to the throne, Thutmose III may even have murdered his stepmother, Hatshepsut. Between the time he took power and his death around 1425 B.C., Thutmose III led a number of victorious invasions into Palestine and Syria. Under Thutmose's rule, Egyptian armies also pushed farther south into **Nubia,** a region of Africa that straddled the upper Nile River. From the Blue Nile, the southern boundary of Nubia, to the shores of the Mediterranean was a distance of approximately 1,000 miles. From Nubia, Egyptian soldiers returned carrying gold, cattle, ivory, and many captives whom they enslaved. The destinies of Egypt and Nubia would be connected for hundreds of years.

Egypt was now a mighty empire. It controlled lands around the Nile and far beyond. In addition, it drew boundless wealth from them. Contact with other cultures brought Egypt new ideas as well as material goods. Egypt had never before—nor has it since—commanded such power and wealth as during the reigns of the New Kingdom pharaohs.

The Egyptians and the Hittites By about 1400 B.C., Egyptian armies had crossed the Sinai Peninsula and conquered parts of Syria and Palestine. These conquests brought the Egyptians into conflict with the Hittites. The Hittites had moved into Asia Minor around 1900 B.C. and later expanded southward into Palestine.

After several battles, the Egyptian and Hittite armies met at the Battle of Kadesh around 1285 B.C. There the two armies fought each other to a standstill. The pharaoh, **Ramses II** (RAM·SEEZ), and a Hittite king later made a treaty that promised "peace and brotherhood between us forever." Their alliance lasted for the rest of the century.

An Age of Builders Like the Old Kingdom with its towering pyramids, rulers of the New Kingdom erected magnificent palaces, temples, and tombs. In search of security in the afterlife, they hid their splendid tombs beneath desert cliffs. In this way, they would not be plundered by grave robbers and looters. The site they chose was the remote Valley of the Kings near Thebes. Besides royal tombs, the pharaohs of this period also built great palaces and magnificent temples. Indeed, the word *pharaoh* means "great house" and comes from this time period. The word became a royal title.

Ramses II, whose reign extended from approximately 1290 to 1224 B.C., stood out among the great builders of the New Kingdom. He lived to the age of 99 and was the father of 150 children. At Karnak, he added to a monumental temple to Amon (AH·muhn), Egypt's chief god. Ramses also ordered a temple to be carved into the red sandstone cliffs above the Nile River at Abu Simbel (AH·boo SIHM·buhl). Egypt's last great pharaoh ordered these temples decorated with enormous statues of himself. The ears alone measured over three feet. Although these buildings are huge and impressive, they were not as skillfully built as those of the Old Kingdom.

The Empire Declines

The empire that Thutmose III had built and Ramses II had ruled came apart slowly after 1200 B.C. as other strong civilizations rose to challenge Egypt's power. Shortly after Ramses died, the entire eastern Mediterranean suffered a wave of invasions around 1200 B.C. These invasions destroyed many kingdoms.

Invasions by Land and Sea Both the Egyptian empire and the Hittite kingdom were attacked by "the People of the Sea." Scholars have not conclusively identified these invaders, although they may well have been the Philistines often mentioned

In this wall painting from an Egyptian tomb, Nubians bring tribute to the pharaoh.

---

in the Bible. Whoever they were, the People of the Sea caused great destruction.

From the east, the tribes of Palestine often rebelled against their Egyptian overlords. From the west, even the vast desert no longer stopped Libyans from raiding Egyptian villages.

Egypt's Empire Fades After these invasions, Egypt never recovered its previous power. Egypt broke apart into regional units. Isolated rural populations erected their own walled defenses. In Egypt's former empire numerous small kingdoms arose. Each was eager to protect its independence. As the empire faded to a distant memory, princes of these small kingdoms treated Egyptian officials with contempt.

Powerless at home and abroad, Egypt fell to its neighbors' invasions. Libyans crossed the desert to the Nile delta. There they established independent dynasties. From 950 to 730 B.C., Libyan pharaohs ruled Egypt and erected cities. Far from imposing their own culture, the Libyans embraced the Egyptian way of life. When the Nubians came north to seize power, they, too, would adopt the Egyptian religion, manners, and culture.

The Kushites Conquer the Nile Region

For centuries, Nubia, the area along the upper Nile River south of Egypt, had been a source of products and slaves for Egypt. Egypt's domination of Nubia and the Nubian kingdom of **Kush** lasted for about a thousand years, between 2000 B.C. and 1000 B.C. During this time, Egyptian armies raided and even occupied Kush for a brief period. But as Egypt fell into decline around 1000 B.C., Kush was emerging as a regional power. Nubia would now establish its own Kushite dynasty on the throne of Egypt.

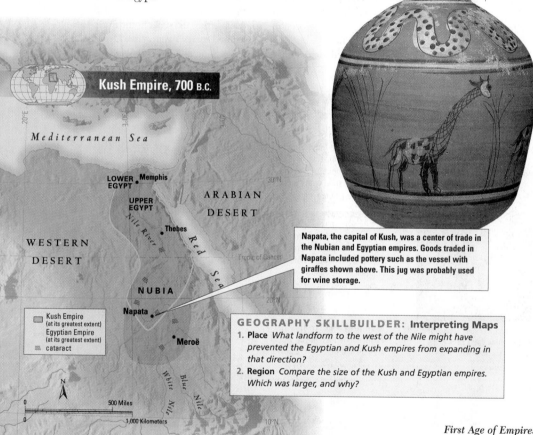

Kush Empire, 700 B.C.

Napata, the capital of Kush, was a center of trade in the Nubian and Egyptian empires. Goods traded in Napata included pottery such as the vessel with giraffes shown above. This jug was probably used for wine storage.

GEOGRAPHY SKILLBUILDER: Interpreting Maps
1. **Place** What landform to the west of the Nile might have prevented the Egyptian and Kush empires from expanding in that direction?
2. **Region** Compare the size of the Kush and Egyptian empires. Which was larger, and why?

First Age of Empires **85**

Teacher's Edition 85

Nubian Transportation

To get boats past the cataracts, Nubians constructed slipways along the river banks—troughlike roads filled with mud. Logs embedded every 18 inches or so in this slippery goo rotated easily, allowing the Nubians to drag their boats around the cataracts.

MORE ABOUT . . .
Nubian Clothing

Nubians added their own twist to the clothing styles of Egypt. They wore leather garments brightly decorated with beads sewn in diamond patterns. Sometimes they also wore leather caps decorated with animal figures cut out of mirrorlike mica. Nubian royalty wore caps decorated with cobras in front and headbands with two streamers hanging down behind. They also wore stacks of bracelets on their arms and up to ten rings on each hand.

The People of Nubia Nubia lay south of Egypt between the first cataract of the Nile and the division of the river into the Blue and White Niles. Despite several cataracts around which boats had to be carried, the lengthy Nile provided the best north-south trade route. Several Nubian kingdoms (including Kush) served as a trade corridor. They linked Egypt and the Mediterranean world to the north with the interior of Africa to the south and to the Red Sea. Along the river, goods and ideas flowed back and forth for centuries. The first Nubian kingdom, Kerma, arose shortly after 2000 B.C. Kerma's kings were buried in chambers larger than those in any Egyptian pyramid. Red-and-black Kerma pottery of great beauty fetched high prices from Egyptian nobles. Kerma prospered during Egypt's Hyksos period.

The Interaction of Egypt and Nubia With Egypt's revival during the New Kingdom, pharaohs forcefully imposed Egyptian rule on Nubia's next great kingdom, Kush. During a long period, Egypt ruled Kush. Egyptian governors, priests, soldiers, and artists strongly influenced the Nubians. Indeed, Kush's capital, Napata, became the center for the spread of Egyptian culture to Kush's other African trading partners.

Kushite princes went to Egypt. They learned the Egyptian language and worshiped Egyptian gods. They adopted the customs and clothing styles of the Egyptian upper class. When they returned home, the Kushite nobles brought back royal rituals and hieroglyphic writing. They built pyramids based on Egyptian models, but with steeper sides.

With Egypt's decline, beginning about 1100 B.C., Kush regained its independence. The Kushites viewed themselves as the guardians of Egyptian values. They sought to restore the Egyptian way of life. They tried to do this by conquering Egypt and ousting its Libyan rulers.

Piankhi Captures the Egyptian Throne In 751 B.C., a Kushite king named **Piankhi** led an army down the Nile and overthrew the Libyan dynasty that had ruled Egypt for over 200 years. He united the entire Nile Valley from the delta in the north to Napata in the south. Piankhi and his descendants became Egypt's Twenty-fifth Dynasty. After his victory, Piankhi erected a monument in his homeland of Kush. It tells the story of his military triumph, which he viewed as the restoration of Egypt's glory.

THINK THROUGH HISTORY
B. Making Inferences Why might the Kushites have viewed themselves as guardians of Egyptian values?
B. Possible Answer For centuries, Nubian nobles received their education in Egypt. When they returned home, they carried back Egyptian styles and ideas, which strongly influenced Nubian culture.

HISTORY THROUGH ART: Sculpture

The interaction of Egypt and Nubia can be seen in the art and sculpture of the two kingdoms. The portrait of the Egyptian pharaoh to the left is over a thousand years older than that of the Nubian king to the right.

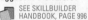
Connect to History

Comparing What similarities can you see between the two portraits? What qualities do they suggest in the rulers?

SEE SKILLBUILDER HANDBOOK, PAGE 996

Connect to Today

Planning a Portrait What are some elements that you would include in a portrait of a powerful person in today's society?

Granite sculpture of Amenemhat III of Egypt as a sphinx dates back to the Twelfth Dynasty, 1844–1797 B.C.

This granite sphinx of King Taharqa of Nubia comes from the Amon Temple at Kawa, 690–664 B.C.

Connect to History

Comparing
Both portraits show serene and regal rulers with strikingly similar expressions and crowns. Both rulers are depicted as being dignified and powerful.

Connect to Today

Planning a Portrait
Suggest that students browse through news magazines and compile photo portraits of powerful people.
• Have them note each person's field of endeavor. They may find that in the United States people can attain power through many fields besides politics—business, entertainment, news media, and so on.
• Ask students to jot down anything they think the powerful people have in common—clothing, attitude, expressions, possessions, and so on.

On the monument he had words inscribed that celebrated his victory. The inscription provided a catalog of the riches of the north, including those of Egypt and Syria:

A VOICE FROM THE PAST
Then the ships were laden with silver, gold, copper, clothing, and everything of the Northland, every product of Syria and all sweet woods of God's-Land. His Majesty sailed upstream [south], with glad heart, the shores on his either side were jubilating. West and east were jubilating in the presence of His Majesty.
PIANKHI, monument in Cairo Museum

However, Piankhi's dynasty proved short-lived. In 671 B.C., the Assyrians, a warlike people from Southwest Asia, conquered Egypt. The Kushites fought bravely, but they were forced to retreat south up the Nile by the Assyrians. There the Kushites would experience a golden age, despite their loss of Egypt.

The Golden Age of Meroë

After their defeat by the Assyrians, the Kushite royal family eventually moved south to **Meroë** (MEHR-oh-EE). Far enough away from Egypt to provide security, Meroë lay closer to the Red Sea than Napata did. It became active in the booming trade between Africa, Arabia, and India.

The Wealth of Kush It was here that Kush made use of rich natural resources to thrive independently of Egypt for several hundred years. Unlike Egyptian cities along the Nile, Meroë enjoyed significant rainfall. And, unlike Egypt, Meroë boasted abundant supplies of iron ore. Meroë became a major center for the manufacture of iron weapons and tools.

Background
The use of iron weapons favored people who could forge iron and paved the way for an age of empires.

In Meroë, ambitious merchants loaded iron bars, tools, and spearheads onto their donkeys. They then transported the goods to the Red Sea, where they exchanged these goods for jewelry, fine cotton cloth, silver lamps, and glass bottles. As the mineral wealth of the central Nile valley flowed out of Meroë, luxury goods from India and Arabia flowed in. The Kushite kings lived like pharaohs, ruling from palaces and spending the afterlife in splendid stone-faced pyramids. Unlike the Egyptian pharaohs, their succession was determined by the agreement of the leaders and nobles.

The Decline of Meroë After four centuries of prosperity, from about 250 B.C. to A.D. 150, Meroë began to decline. The rise of Aksum, a rival power located 400 miles southeast, contributed to Meroë's fall. With a seaport along the Red Sea, Aksum now dominated North African trade. Aksum defeated Meroë around A.D. 350.

Centuries earlier, around the time the Kushite pharaoh sat on Egypt's throne, a new empire had gathered in the north. Like Kush, Assyria would come to dominate Egypt.

This armlet dates from Meroë in the late first century B.C. It is made of gold with fused-glass inlays. On the hinge is a goddess wearing a vulture headdress and a double crown.

Section 1 Assessment

1. TERMS & NAMES
Identify
- Hyksos
- New Kingdom
- Hatshepsut
- Thutmose III
- Nubia
- Ramses II
- Kush
- Piankhi
- Meroë

2. TAKING NOTES
Create a time line showing important events in the history of Egypt and Kush.

1570 B.C. ————————— A.D. 350

Egyptian New Kingdom   Aksum defeats Meroë

Which empire was invaded more often? Why?

3. RECOGNIZING BIAS
Read the temple inscription written by Piankhi and quoted at the top of this page. Explain how an Egyptian might have written the inscription differently.

THINK ABOUT
- what bias Piankhi had
- how Egyptians benefited from Piankhi's invasion
- why Egyptians might have disagreed with Piankhi

4. ANALYZING THEMES
Empire Building How did Egypt and Nubia strengthen each other at various times in their histories?

THINK ABOUT
- the role of trade and the movement of goods
- the impact of military movements
- the influence of cultural developments

First Age of Empires **87**

ANSWERS

1. TERMS AND NAMES
Hyksos, p. 83
New Kingdom, p. 83
Hatshepsut, p. 83
Thutmose III, p. 84
Nubia, p. 84
Ramses II, p. 84
Kush, p. 85
Piankhi, p. 86
Meroë, p. 87

2. TAKING NOTES
Possible Responses:
1472 B.C. Hatshepsut makes herself pharaoh; 1285 B.C. Battle of Kadesh; 1290–1224 B.C. Ramses II rules; 1200 B.C. People of the Sea attack Egypt; 1100 B.C. Kush regains independence; 950–730 B.C. Libyans rule Egypt; 671 B.C. Kushites lose to Egypt to

Assyrians. Egypt was invaded more; internal power struggles weakened it.

3. RECOGNIZING BIAS
Possible Responses: An Egyptian might have praised the Kushites for restoring the Egyptian way of life or criticized them for ruling in place of Egyptians.

4. ANALYZING THEMES
Possible Responses: Under Thutmose III, Egyptians brought gold, cattle, ivory, and slaves from Nubia. Under Egyptian control, Nubian princes adopted much of Egyptian culture. When Nubians seized power over Egypt, they tried to restore the Egyptian way of life.

1. To analyze the impetus for, and sources of, Assyrian military strength.

2. To evaluate Assyrian rule and cultural achievements.

3. To trace the course of Assyrian decline.

SKILLBUILDER
• Interpreting maps: location, p. 90

CRITICAL THINKING
• Analyzing causes, p. 88
• Recognizing causes, p. 90
• Making inferences, p. 90
• Clarifying, p. 91
• Forming and supporting opinions, p. 91

FOCUS
5-Minute Warm-Up

▶ **Making Generalizations**
To help students understand Assyrian military power, have them answer these questions.

1. Study the picture and captions on page 89. What word best describes Assyrian warriors?

2. What weapons did the Assyrians use?

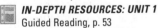 **WARM-UP TRANSPARENCY 4**

OBJECTIVE ❶ INSTRUCT

A Mighty Military Machine

▶ **Key Ideas**
• The Assyrians become a fierce military nation from fighting off constant invasions.

• Advanced technology and tactics give the Assyrians military superiority over all their contemporaries.

📖 *IN-DEPTH RESOURCES: UNIT 1*
Guided Reading, p. 53

Literature: "The Destruction of Sennacherib," p. 64

History Makers: Sennacherib, p. 67

📖 *ACCESS FOR STUDENTS ACQUIRING ENGLISH*
Guided Reading (Spanish), p. 44

TERMS & NAMES
• Assyria
• Sennacherib
• Nineveh
• Ashurbanipal
• Medes
• Chaldeans
• Nebuchadnezzar

2 Assyria Dominates the Fertile Crescent

MAIN IDEA	WHY IT MATTERS NOW
Assyria developed a military machine, conquered an empire, and established imperial administration.	Some leaders still use military force to extend their rule, stamp out opposition, and gain wealth and power.

SETTING THE STAGE For more than two centuries, the Assyrian army advanced across Southwest Asia. It overwhelmed foes with its military strength. After the Assyrians seized control of Egypt, the Assyrian king Esarhaddon proclaimed, "I tore up the root of Kush, and not one therein escaped to submit to me." The last Kushite pharaoh retreated to Napata, Kush's capital city.

A Mighty Military Machine

Beginning around 850 B.C., **Assyria** (uh·SEER·ee·uh) acquired a large empire. It accomplished this by means of a sophisticated military organization and state-of-the-art weaponry. For a time, this campaign of conquest made Assyria the greatest power in Southwest Asia.

The Rise of a Warrior People The Assyrians came from the northern part of Mesopotamia. Their flat, exposed farmland made them easy to attack. Invaders swept down from the nearby mountains. The Assyrians may have developed their warlike behavior in response to these invasions. Lacking natural barriers such as mountains or deserts, they repelled invaders by developing a strong army. Through constant warfare, Assyrian kings built an empire that stretched from east and north of the Tigris River all the way to central Egypt.

One of these Assyrian kings, **Sennacherib** (sih·NAK·uhr·ihb), bragged that he had sacked 89 cities and 820 villages, burned Babylon, and ordered most of its inhabitants killed. Centuries later, in the 1800s, the English poet George Gordon, Lord Byron, romanticized the Assyrians' bloody exploits in a poem:

> **A VOICE ABOUT THE PAST**
> The Assyrian came down like a wolf on the fold,
> And his cohorts were gleaming in purple and gold;
> And the sheen of their spears was like stars on the sea,
> When the blue wave rolls nightly on deep Galilee.
> **GEORGE GORDON, LORD BYRON,** "The Destruction of Sennacherib"

This detail of a sandstone relief shows an Assyrian soldier with a shield and iron-tipped spear.

Military Organization and Conquest Assyria was a society which glorified military strength. Its soldiers were well equipped for conquering an empire. Making use of the iron-working technology of the time, the soldiers covered themselves in stiff leather and metal armor. They wore copper or iron helmets, padded loincloths, and leather skirts layered with metal scales. Their weapons were iron swords and iron-pointed spears. Infantry, archers, and spear throwers protected themselves with huge shields.

Advance planning and technical skill allowed the Assyrians to lay siege to enemy cities. When deep water blocked their passage, engineers would bridge the rivers with pontoons, or floating structures used to support a bridge. Tying inflated animal skins

THINK THROUGH HISTORY
A. Analyzing Causes What caused the Assyrians to develop a strong army and large empire?
A. Possible Answer No natural barriers to invasion; needed strong army to repel invaders; constant warfare produced large empire.

Vocabulary
siege: a military blockade to force a city to surrender.

SECTION 2 RESOURCES

PRINT RESOURCES

📖 *IN-DEPTH RESOURCES: UNIT 1*
Guided Reading, p. 53
Geography Application: Babylon, p. 57
Primary Source: from *Assyrian Capture of Jerusalem*, p. 59
Literature: "The Destruction of Sennacherib," p. 64
History Makers: Sennacherib, p. 67

📖 *ACCESS FOR STUDENTS ACQUIRING ENGLISH*
Guided Reading (Spanish), p. 44
Geography Application: (Spanish), p. 48

FORMAL ASSESSMENT
Section Quiz, p. 41

📖 *ALTERNATIVE ASSESSMENT BOOK*

TECHNOLOGY RESOURCES

💿 **CD-ROM**
Electronic Library of Primary Sources

🌐 **INTERNET** www.mlworldhistory.com

Assyrian Military Power

Assyrian warriors were ferocious in combat. In this relief—sculpture that has figures standing out from a flat background—they are shown launching an assault on a fortified city. The Assyrian war machine included a variety of weapons and methods of attack.

❶ Ladders

While Assyrian archers launched waves of arrows against their opponents defending the city walls, Assyrian troops threw their ladders up against the walls and began their climb into the enemy's stronghold.

❷ Weapons

Troops were armed with the best weapons of the time, iron-tipped spears, as well as iron daggers and swords. They were also protected with armor and large shields.

❸ Tactics

The Assyrians were savage in their treatment of defeated opponents. Those who weren't slaughtered in the initial attack were often impaled or beheaded, while women and children were sometimes murdered or sold into slavery.

❹ Tunnels

The Assyrian army used sappers—soldiers who dug tunnels to sap, or undermine, the foundations of the enemy's walls so that they would fall.

together, they connected these pontoons to the shore with beams. Then they erected a raised dirt roadway at both ends. An armed guard protected the soldiers who installed a support structure of stones, brush, and clay.

Before attacking, the Assyrians dug beneath the city's walls to weaken them. Then, with disciplined organization, foot soldiers marched shoulder to shoulder. A trained cavalry, or troops riding horses, galloped into battle, following their generals, who rode in chariots. With courage and coordination, foot soldiers approached to within an arrow's shot of the city walls. At a signal from their commander, they stopped, strung their bows, and released a shower of arrows. Wave upon wave of arrows hissed over the walls of the besieged city. Meanwhile, another group of troops hammered the city's gates with massive, iron-tipped battering rams. When at last the city gates splintered, the Assyrians showed no mercy. They killed or enslaved their victims. Because soldiers received a bounty for severed heads, many of the defeated were beheaded.

One Assyrian king bragged of burning 3,000 captives to death. Another told how "all the chiefs who had revolted I flayed, with their skins I covered the pillar, some in the midst I walled up, others on stakes I impaled, still others I arranged around the pillar on stakes." To prevent later rebellions, the Assyrians forced groups of captives to leave their homelands. They were forced to settle far away as exiles in the empire's distant provinces and dependent states.

An Expanding Empire

Between 850 and 650 B.C., the kings of Assyria defeated Syria, Palestine, and Babylonia. Reaching beyond the Fertile Crescent, Assyrian rule extended into Egypt and Anatolia. With the conquest of Egypt, the Assyrian Empire had established itself in North Africa.

First Age of Empires **89**

Assyrian Empire, 650 B.C.

Interpreting the Map Point out the inset map that shows where in the world this empire is located. Have students use the scale to measure and compare distances on the main map–for example, from Nineveh to Babylon *(about 550 miles)* and from Nineveh to Memphis *(about 1,300 miles)*.

Extension Activity Ask students to calculate how much of the trip from Babylon through Nineveh to Memphis could have been done by water and how much by land. *Possible response: Nearly all 550 miles from Babylon to Nineveh up the Tigris, 650 overland from Nineveh to Sidon, 500 between Sidon and the Nile delta over the Mediterranean Sea, and 150 up the Nile to Memphis.*

SKILLBUILDER Answers

1. About 1,500 miles.
2. It extends along the Nile to Thebes, which had belonged to the Egyptian and then the Kushite Empires.

MORE ABOUT . . .
Ashurbanipal's Library

The first systematically collected and catalogued library in the ancient Middle East included letters, contracts, chronicles, and literary, scientific, and religious works. Many were Sumerian and Akkadian texts as ancient to Assyrians as Latin classics are to us.

OBJECTIVE 3 INSTRUCT

The Empire Crumbles

Key Ideas

- The Chaldeans and Medes join hands to smash Assyrian power.
- The Chaldeans rebuild Babylon into a wonder of the ancient world, featuring such marvels as the hanging gardens.

IN-DEPTH RESOURCES: UNIT 1
Geography Application: Babylon, p. 57

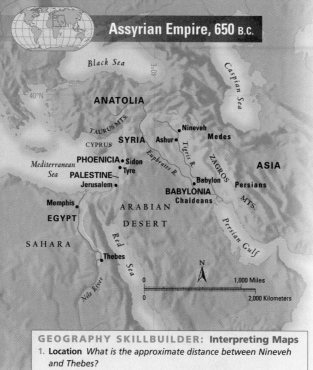

Assyrian Empire, 650 B.C.

GEOGRAPHY SKILLBUILDER: **Interpreting Maps**
1. **Location** *What is the approximate distance between Nineveh and Thebes?*
2. **Location** *What is the southernmost part of the Assyrian Empire and to what other empire did it previously belong?*

Assyrian Rule At its peak around 650 B.C., this empire included almost all of the old centers of civilization and power in Southwest Asia. With great efficiency, the Assyrians organized their conquered territories into an empire. Assyrian officials governed lands closest to Assyria as provinces and made them dependent territories. Assyrian kings influenced these dependent regions by choosing their rulers. Or, they supported kings who aligned themselves with Assyria. Assyrian armies protected the dependent territories from invasion by other enemies.

In addition, the military campaigns added new territory to the empire. This brought in taxes and tribute to the Assyrian treasury. These became an instrument of control. If a conquered people refused to pay, the Assyrians destroyed their cities and sent the people into exile. By these means the Assyrians developed an effective method of governing an extended empire.

Assyrian Culture Some of Assyria's most fearsome warriors earned a reputation as great builders. For example, the same King Sennacherib who had burned Babylon also established Assyria's capital at **Nineveh** (NIHN·uh·vuh) along the Tigris River. This great walled city, about three miles long and a mile wide, was famous as the largest city of its day. In the ruins of Nineveh and other Assyrian cities, archaeologists found finely carved sculptures. Two artistic subjects particularly fascinated the Assyrians: brutal military campaigns and the lion hunt.

In addition to the treasures of empire, Nineveh also held one of the ancient world's largest libraries. King **Ashurbanipal** (AH·shur·BAH·nuh·PAHL) prided himself on his ability to read in several languages: "The beautiful writings in Sumerian that are obscure, in Akkadian that are difficult to bear in mind, it was my joy to repeat." This kingly reader collected more than 25,000 clay tablets from throughout the Fertile Crescent. Some were dictionaries containing the same words in several languages. When archaeologists uncovered the library's remains in the mid-1800s, the dictionary tablets enabled scholars to better understand Mesopotamian writing.

The Empire Crumbles

Ashurbanipal proved to be one of the last of the mighty Assyrian kings. Assyrian power had spread itself too thin. Also, the cruelty displayed by the Assyrians had earned them many enemies. Shortly after Ashurbanipal's death, Nineveh fell.

Decline and Fall Just as Assyrians had destroyed so many cities, Assyria's enemies demolished Nineveh. In 612 B.C., a combined army of **Medes** (meedz), **Chaldeans** (kal·DEE·uhnz), and others rammed open the city's gates. Their armies burned and leveled Nineveh. The fire glazed the tablets in the library, which preserved them for archaeologists to study centuries later. So thoroughly did the armies destroy Nineveh that two centuries later only mounds remained.

B. Possible Answer
Efficient organization; military power; taxes; tribute; system of provinces made dependent territories.
THINK THROUGH HISTORY
B. Recognizing Causes What methods enabled the Assyrians to rule their empire effectively?

THINK THROUGH HISTORY
C. Making Inferences Why might the Assyrian warrior kings have had such a great interest in writing and reading?
C. Possible Answer
They may have envisioned the writing of their history as a way to impress future generations with their military achievements.

TEACHING OPTION BLOCK SCHEDULING

WRITING FOR OR AGAINST PEACE

CLASS TIME
20 MINUTES

Task: Students will write a letter arguing for or against maintaining peace with Assyria.

Materials Needed: Students will refer to information under the heading "An Expanding Empire," beginning on the previous page.

Activity: Ask students to imagine that they are citizens of a city-state whose ruler is considering whether to resist or to maintain peace with the mighty Assyrian Empire. Have each student choose the identity of a citizen, such as a merchant, scribe, teacher, weaver, official, priest, or soldier. Then have

students write a brief letter to the ruler, explaining why maintaining peace would or would not benefit them and their people.

Conclusion: Invite students to explain their position to the rest of the class.

Many people in the region rejoiced at Nineveh's destruction. The Hebrew prophet Nahum (NAY·huhm) gave voice to the feelings of many:

Rebirth of Babylon Under the Chaldeans After defeating the Assyrians, the Chaldeans made Babylon their capital. Around 600 B.C., Babylon became the center of a new empire, more than 1,000 years after Hammurabi had ruled there. A Chaldean king named **Nebuchadnezzar** (NEHB·uh·kuhd·NEHZ·uhr) restored Babylon. The most impressive part of his palace may have been the famous hanging gardens. Greek scholars later listed them as one of the Seven Wonders of the World. According to legend, one of Nebuchadnezzar's wives missed the flowering shrubs of her mountain homeland. To please her, the king had fragrant trees and mountain shrubs planted on terraces. They rose 75 feet above Babylon's flat, dry plain. Slaves watered the plants from hidden pumps.

Indeed, the entire city was a wonder. Its walls were so thick that, according to one report, a four-horse chariot could wheel around on top of them. To ensure that the world knew who ruled Babylon, even the bricks were inscribed, "I am Nebuchadnezzar, King of Babylon."

The highest building in Babylon was a great, seven-tiered ziggurat more than 300 feet high. It was visible for miles. At night, priests observed the stars from the top of this tower and others in the city. They kept detailed records of how the stars and planets seemed to change position in the night sky. The Chaldeans' observations formed the basis for both astronomy and astrology.

Nebuchadnezzar's empire fell shortly after his death. The Persians who next came to power adopted many Assyrian military, political, and artistic inventions. The Persians would use the organization the Assyrians had developed to stabilize the region.

Lions made of glazed bricks decorated walls along the broad road that passed the Ishtar Gate of Nebuchadnezzar in Babylon.

THINK THROUGH HISTORY
D. Clarifying What was Nahum's opinion about the collapse of the Assyrian Empire?
D. Possible Answer This cruel empire would have no mourners; it would be dispersed and no one would care.

Section ② Assessment

1. TERMS & NAMES
Identify
• Assyria
• Sennacherib
• Nineveh
• Ashurbanipal
• Medes
• Chaldeans
• Nebuchadnezzar

2. TAKING NOTES
Create a diagram showing the causes of the rise and of the decline of Assyrian power.

3. FORMING AND SUPPORTING OPINIONS
The Assyrians relied almost exclusively on military power in building, maintaining, and ruling their empire. Explain whether you think this was a good strategy.

THINK ABOUT
• the causes of Assyrian military power
• the stability of the empire
• the methods that empires use to become stronger

4. THEME ACTIVITY
Science and Technology
Work with a partner to draw a mural highlighting how developments in technology influenced the rise and decline of the Assyrian Empire.

First Age of Empires **91**

MORE ABOUT . . .
The Fall of Babylon
Babylon was protected by an 11-mile-long outer wall that Nebuchadnezzar had built to keep enemies from pressing "on the flank of Babylon." When the forces of the Persian king Cyrus laid siege to the city in 539 B.C., the Chaldean king Belshazzar had enough food stockpiled inside the outer wall to last for years, but Cyrus noticed that the Euphrates River ran under the wall. He had a canal dug from the river to some nearby marshes, draining enough water out to let his men wade under the great wall. Pro-Persian Babylonians then opened the inner gates for them.

ASSESS & RETEACH

Section 2 Assessment
Have students work through the assessment items in pairs. They can quiz each other on the terms and names, develop a written conclusion for the next two items, and create a sketch for the mural in item 4.

Section Quiz
FORMAL ASSESSMENT
Section quiz, p. 41

Reteaching Activity
CLASS TIME: 10 MINUTES
Have students look through the chapter and suggest names and events to help you fill out a time line on the chalkboard.

CLOSE ACTIVITY

CLASS TIME: 10 MINUTES

Predicting
Write the words *Successes* and *Failures* as column headings on the chalkboard. Then have students help you list successes and failures of the Assyrian Empire that they think the next empire builders, the Persians, would learn from.

ANSWERS

1. TERMS AND NAMES
Assyria, p. 88
Sennacherib, p. 88
Nineveh, p. 90
Ashurbanipal, p. 90
Medes, p. 90
Chaldeans, p. 90
Nebuchadnezzar, p. 91

2. TAKING NOTES
Possible Responses: Causes of increasing power:
1. Need to defend against attacks
2. Use of iron-working technology
3. Success at advanced planning
Causes of declining power:
1. Hatred by conquered people
2. Overextension
3. Unity among Assyria's foes

3. FORMING AND SUPPORTING OPINIONS
Some students might argue that empires often rely on military power. Others might point out that Assyrians relied on a technological advantage that other countries could soon copy and that their brutal methods made them unpopular rulers.

4. THEME ACTIVITY
Possible Responses: Murals may show Assyrians clad in metal armor, armed with iron swords and iron-pointed spears, holding shields, and using an iron-tipped battering ram.

OBJECTIVES

1. To explain the rise of the Persian Empire.

2. To describe the unique features of the Persian government and its official religion, Zoroastrianism.

SKILLBUILDER

- Interpreting Maps: region, p. 94

CRITICAL THINKING

- Summarizing, p. 93
- Recognizing effects, p. 95
- Comparing, pp. 95, 96
- Hypothesizing, p. 96
- Analyzing themes, p. 96

FOCUS
5-Minute Warm-Up

▶ *Evaluating*
Have students answer these questions to examine alternative approaches to ruling an empire.

1. Read the first paragraph under the heading "The Rise of Persia" on page 92. How did Persia's style of rule differ from Assyria's style?

2. Why might Persia's style be more effective?

 WARM-UP TRANSPARENCY 4

OBJECTIVE ① INSTRUCT

The Rise of Persia

▶ *Key Ideas*
- The Persians prosper from mineral wealth and trading opportunities in their Iranian homeland.
- Cyrus the Great forges a diverse empire based on visionary political tolerance.

 IN-DEPTH RESOURCES: UNIT 1
Guided Reading, p.54
Literature: "Babylon," p. 65

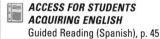 *ACCESS FOR STUDENTS ACQUIRING ENGLISH*
Guided Reading (Spanish), p. 45

 WORLD ART AND CULTURES TRANSPARENCIES
AT8 Persian drinking horn

 ELECTRONIC LIBRARY OF PRIMARY SOURCES
"Customs of the Persians"

---

3 Persia Unites Many Lands

TERMS & NAMES
- Cyrus
- Cambyses
- Darius
- satrap
- Royal Road
- Zoroaster

MAIN IDEA	WHY IT MATTERS NOW
The Persian Empire ruled with tolerance and wise government.	Tolerance and wise government are characteristics of the most successful methods of rule.

SETTING THE STAGE The Medes, along with the Chaldeans, helped to overthrow the Assyrian Empire in 612 B.C. The Medes marched to Nineveh from their homeland in the area of present-day northern Iran. Meanwhile, the Medes' close neighbor to the south, Persia, began to expand its horizons and territorial ambitions.

The Rise of Persia

The Assyrians employed military force to control a vast empire. In contrast, the Persians would base their empire on tolerance and diplomacy. They relied on a strong military to back up their policies. Ancient Persia included what is today Iran.

CONNECT *to* TODAY

The Natural Wealth of Iran
Iran has always had substantial mineral wealth and natural resources. These have attracted invaders throughout the ages. In the past, its rich deposits of iron, copper, and lapis lazuli attracted bands of invading nomads and warriors, including Assyrian raiders. Equally important, Iran's mineral wealth encouraged trade with the outside world.

Today, huge reserves of oil lie beneath the surface of Iran. Various foreign powers compete for these rich oil fields. The Iranian government awards contracts to companies to develop oil fields in Iran and the Persian Gulf. Iran's economy relies heavily on revenue from its oil reserves.

The Persian Homeland About 1000 B.C., Indo-Europeans first migrated from Central Europe and southern Russia to the mountains and plateaus east of the Fertile Crescent. This area extended from the Caspian Sea in the north to the Persian Gulf in the south. In addition to prosperous farmland, ancient Iran boasted a wealth of minerals. These included copper, lead, gold, silver, and gleaming blue lapis lazuli. A thriving trade put the settlers in contact with their neighbors to the east and the west.

At first, dozens of tiny kingdoms ruled in the region. The Medes and others joined forces to overthrow the Assyrian Empire in 612 B.C. Eventually two major powers emerged: the Medes and the Persians. A remarkable ruler would soon lead Persia to dominate not only the Medes but also a huge empire.

Cyrus the Great Founds an Empire The rest of the world paid little attention to the Persians until 550 B.C. That year, **Cyrus** (SY·ruhs), Persia's king, began his conquest of several neighboring kingdoms in Iran. A new power was rising in the region. Eventually, the Persians extended their rule from the Indus River in the east to Anatolia in the west. This empire spanned over two thousand miles.

Cyrus's soldiers wore leather pants and thick felt boots. Riding mountain ponies, they shot arrows from the short bows that their ancestors had used on the steppes of Russia. Their leader proved to be a military genius. He led his army from victory to victory between 550 and 539 B.C. Cyrus and his armies conquered the entire Fertile Crescent and most of Anatolia.

Even more than his military genius, though, Cyrus's most enduring legacy was his method of governing. His kindness toward conquered peoples revealed a wise and tolerant view of empire. For example, when Cyrus's army marched into a city, his generals enforced strict discipline against looting and burning. Unlike other conquerors, Cyrus believed in honoring local customs and religions. Instead of destroying the local temple, Cyrus would kneel there to pray.

Vocabulary
legacy: something handed down from the past.

PRINT RESOURCES

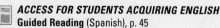 *IN-DEPTH RESOURCES: UNIT 1*
Guided Reading, p. 54
Primary Source: "To the Fire" from the *Zend-Avesta,* p. 60
Literature: "Babylon," p. 65

 ACCESS FOR STUDENTS ACQUIRING ENGLISH
Guided Reading (Spanish), p. 45

 FORMAL ASSESSMENT
Section Quiz, p. 42

 ALTERNATIVE ASSESSMENT BOOK

TECHNOLOGY RESOURCES

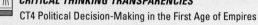 *WORLD ART AND CULTURES TRANSPARENCIES*
AT8 Persian drinking horn

 CRITICAL THINKING TRANSPARENCIES
CT4 Political Decision-Making in the First Age of Empires

CD-ROM
Electronic Library of Primary Sources

 VIDEO *Patterns of Interaction: Building Empires*

INTERNET www.mlworldhistory.com

Under Persian rule, subject peoples enjoyed remarkable freedom. Indeed, Babylon peacefully opened its gates for Cyrus in 539 B.C. Thankful for the bloodless victory, Cyrus offered prayers to Babylon's chief god, Marduk. According to Persian accounts, "all the inhabitants of Babylon . . . princes and governors included, bowed to Cyrus and kissed his feet, jubilant and with shining faces."

Cyrus also allowed the Jews, who had been deported from their homeland by the Babylonians, to return to Jerusalem in 538 B.C. Under Persian rule, the Jews rebuilt their city and temple. They also resumed their sacred rituals. Many portions of the Old Testament first appeared in written form during this period. The Jews were forever grateful to Cyrus, whom they considered one of God's anointed ones. The Hebrew prophet Ezra tells of Cyrus's kindness:

The tomb of Cyrus the Great still stands. It is notable for its simplicity when compared with other royal tombs of the ancient world.

> **THE BIBLE**
> This is the word of Cyrus king of Persia: The Lord the God of heaven has given me all the kingdoms of the earth, and he himself has charged me to build him a house at Jerusalem in Judah. To every man of his people now among you I say, God be with him, and let him go up to Jerusalem in Judah, and rebuild the house of the Lord the God of Israel, the God whose city is Jerusalem.
> **EZRA** 1:2–3.

THINK THROUGH HISTORY
A. Summarizing
What are some examples of Cyrus's tolerant method of governing?
A. Possible Answer
Kindness toward conquered peoples; looting and burning by troops forbidden; local customs and religions honored; subject peoples granted certain freedoms.

This stone relief of Darius on his throne shows him receiving his heir, the royal prince, Xerxes.

This wise and tolerant ruler was above all a warrior. Cyrus lost his life in battle, fighting nomadic invaders on the eastern border of his empire. According to the Greek historian Arrian, his simple, house-shaped tomb bore these poignant words: "O man, I am Cyrus the son of Cambyses. I established the Persian Empire and was king of Asia. Do not begrudge me my memorial."

Persian Rule and Religion

The task of organizing and unifying conquered territories fell to rulers who followed Cyrus. They succeeded by combining Persian control with local self-government.

Cambyses and Darius Cyrus died in 530 B.C. His son **Cambyses** (kam·BY·seez), named after Cyrus's father, extended the Persian Empire by conquering Egypt. However, the son neglected to follow his father's wise example. Cambyses publicly scorned the Egyptian religion. He ordered the images of Egyptian gods to be burned. After ruling for only eight years, Cambyses died. Immediately, widespread rebellions broke out across the empire. Persian control had seemed strong a decade earlier. It now seemed surprisingly fragile.

Cambyses's successor, **Darius** (duh·RY·uhs), a noble of the ruling dynasty, had begun his career as a member of the king's bodyguard. An elite group of Persian soldiers, the Ten Thousand Immortals, helped Darius seize the throne in 522–521 B.C. Darius spent the first three years of his reign putting down revolts. He spent the next few years establishing an unusually efficient and well-organized administration.

Soon the new king extended Persian conquests in the east. He led armies up into the mountains of present-day Afghanistan and down into the river valleys of India. The immense Persian Empire now embraced Egypt and Anatolia in the west, part of India in the east, and the Fertile Crescent in the center. This vast empire extended over 2,500 miles from east to west. Darius's only failure, and that of his son, was his inability to conquer Greece.

First Age of Empires **93**

CONNECT *to* TODAY
The Natural Wealth of Iran
Iran's oil has been as much a curse as a blessing. Since it was discovered, Russia, Turkey, Britain, Germany, the United States, and the Soviet Union have fought over Iranian oil on Iranian soil or interfered with Iranian affairs in other ways. Suggest that students track a few weeks' worth of news stories about Iran and its neighbors to see how oil resources affect these countries today.

MORE ABOUT . . .
The Accession of Darius
Mystery surrounds Darius's taking of the Persian throne. According to official Persian histories, an impostor seized the throne after Cambyses died. He claimed to be Cambyses' brother Bardiya, the legitimate heir to the throne. Darius realized the hoax, rushed home, and saved the Persian Empire by taking over. Greek historians said the impersonator was so good that he fooled Bardiya's own mother. Modern historians suspect the "fraud" actually was Bardiya.

OBJECTIVE 2 INSTRUCT

Persian Rule and Religion

Key Ideas
• Darius's conquests bring the Persian Empire to its greatest size.
• Darius sets up an efficient government, builds good roads, and introduces coins.
• The prophet Zoroaster preaches ideas that anticipate Christianity and Islam.
• The Persian Empire unites a patchwork of cultures through tolerance and inclusion.

CRITICAL THINKING TRANSPARENCIES
CT4 Political Decision-Making in the First Age of Empires

TEACHING OPTION | **BLOCK SCHEDULING** | **COOPERATIVE ACTIVITY: Making a Persia Poster** | **CLASS TIME 30 MINUTES**

Task: Students will create a poster promoting the virtues of the Persian Empire to potential visitors and investors.

Purpose: To focus students on various dimensions of the Persian Empire.

Activity: Divide the class into groups of three. Have students picture themselves working for some version of a Persian chamber of commerce and brainstorm types of information they might present in

a promotional poster for distribution throughout the ancient world—for example, accommodations, roads, portraits of the ruler, and history briefs. Each student should take responsibility for preparing material on several topics. Groups will present and explain their posters to the class.

Building a Portfolio: Students might keep copies of their individual contributions for their portfolios.

ALTERNATIVE ASSESSMENT BOOK
Standards for Evaluating a Cooperative Activity

Standards for Evaluation
Posters should . . .

• give a lively picture of Persian society
• contain accurate information
• cover a range of relevant topics
• look attractive

Teacher's Edition 93

Persian Empire, 500 B.C.

Interpreting the Map Point out the line that shows the borders of the Assyrian Empire and the shades of purple that mark the conquests of various Persian kings. Suggest that students use the scale to measure the distances between each of the four areas Darius conquered. *Approximate distances in miles: northeast Africa to southeast Europe—600; southeast Europe to Caucasus—750; Caucasus to Caspian-Aral region—250; Caspian-Aral region to northeast Africa—1,600.*

Extension Activity Have students compare this map with a contemporary one and figure out which modern countries lie partially or completely within the territories Darius ruled. *Libya, Egypt, Israel, Lebanon, Syria, Turkey, Greece, Macedonia, Bulgaria, Romania, Ukraine, Georgia, Armenia, Azerbaijan, Iraq, Kuwait, Iran, Uzbekistan, Turkmenistan, Afghanistan, Pakistan.*

SKILLBUILDER Answers
1. Egypt.
2. Western Egypt beyond the Nile River, southeastern edge of Macedonia, the Mediterranean and Black Seas to the Indus River.

MORE ABOUT . . .
Subjects of the Persian Empire
The Persian Empire gathered under one tent an enormous variety of peoples: urban sophisticates of Egypt and Babylon; seafaring traders of Lydia and Greece; rugged farmers and herders of Persia and Media; and uncivilized nomads of Scythia and Parthia. Many of these peoples spoke distinct languages, and none had a sense of national identity.

Persian Empire, 500 B.C.

Legend:
- Persian Empire under Cyrus
- Persian Empire under Cambyses
- Persian Empire under Darius
- Former Assyrian Empire
- The Royal Road

GEOGRAPHY SKILLBUILDER: Interpreting Maps
1. **Region** *What part of the ancient world did Cambyses add to the Persian Empire?*
2. **Region** *Compare the map of the Persian Empire with that of the Assyrian Empire. What areas did the Persians rule that the Assyrians did not?*

Provinces and Satraps Although a great warrior, Darius's greatest genius lay in administration. To govern his sprawling empire, the king divided it into 20 provinces. These provinces were roughly similar to the homelands of the many groups of people within the Persian Empire. Under Persian rule, the people of each province still practiced their own religion. They also spoke their own language and followed many of their own laws. This administrative policy of many groups—sometimes called "nationalities"—living by their own laws within one empire would be repeatedly practiced in Southwest Asia. This continued in the early 1900s in the Ottoman Empire.

Although tolerant of the many groups within his empire, Darius still ruled with absolute power. In each province of the Persian Empire, Darius installed a governor called a **satrap** (SAY·TRAP), who ruled locally. To ensure his satraps' loyalty, Darius sent out inspectors known as the "King's Eyes and Ears." They checked up on the administration of each province in every corner of the kingdom. Darius also appointed an army leader and a tax collector for each province.

Two other tools helped the Persian king hold his empire together. An excellent road system and the use of standard money helped unite the empire. The famous **Royal Road** of the Persian Empire ran from Susa in Persia to Sardis in Anatolia, a distance of 1,677 miles.

Darius borrowed his second idea, manufacturing metal coins, from the Lydians of Asia Minor. For the first time, coins of a standard value circulated throughout an extended empire. No longer did people have to weigh and measure odd pieces of gold or silver to pay for what they bought. Like the road system, the wider use of standardized coins promoted trade. Trade, in turn, helped to hold the empire together.

94 Chapter 4

Visual Learners Have students trace an outline of the map on this page and copy the Egyptian, Kushite, Assyrian, and Persian Empires onto it. Refer them to the maps on pages 85 and 90 for further information. They should use different colors to delineate the different empires. This activity may help reveal the pattern that empire building followed in this region: bigger and bigger, with each new empire swallowing and then expanding on the previous empire.

Gifted and Talented Students Two writers who give contemporary accounts of Persia around the time of Darius are the Greek historians Herodotus and Xenophon. Herodotus traveled widely, and his nine-book *History* gives a lively account of what he saw and heard. Xenophon passed through Persia as a soldier and wrote of his adventures in the *Anabasis*. Students may enjoy looking up one or both accounts and sharing anecdotes from them with the class.

The Royal Road

One of the ways in which societies build and maintain empires is by establishing systems of communication and transportation. The Royal Road built by the Persian Empire connected Susa in Persia to Sardis in Anatolia. Because of this road, royal commands could quickly reach most parts of the empire.

This four-horse chariot dates from the 6th–4th century B.C. It is the type of vehicle that would have traveled the Royal Road in the time of Darius. The studs on the wheels were designed to help prevent the chariot from slipping. The large wheels provided a smoother ride over rough ground.

Neither snow, nor rain, nor heat, nor gloom of night stays these couriers from the swift completion of their appointed rounds.
Greek historian Herodotus, writing in the 400s B.C. about the Persian messengers on the Royal Road.

A Ride Along the Royal Road

The Road
The road was 1,677 miles in length. There were 111 post or relay stations spaced about 15 miles apart along the road, similar to the American Pony Express system. Other roads branched off the main road to distant parts of the empire.

The Ride
Relay stations were equipped with fresh horses for the king's messengers. Royal messengers could cover the length of the Royal Road in seven days. Normal travel time along the road was longer. A caravan, for example, might take three months to travel the whole distance.

Patterns of Interaction
"There is nothing in the world which travels faster than these Persian couriers," Herodotus wrote about the messengers of the Royal Road. Strong road networks like the Royal Road enabled empires to expand and maintain control over people and places. Like the Persians, the Inca of South America created a road system thousands of miles long. These roads allowed the Inca to extend their rule over as many as 16 million people. Empires throughout history have shared characteristics such as efficient communication systems, effective leaders, and powerful armies.

A bronze figure of a Persian horseman.

  Building Empires: The Rise of the Persians and the Inca

Connect *to* History
Recognizing Effects How would the Royal Road enable the ruler to maintain power in the empire?

SEE SKILLBUILDER HANDBOOK, PAGE 995

Connect *to* Today
Comparing What systems of communication and transportation today might be compared to the Royal Road of the Persians?

First Age of Empires **95**

GlobalImpact
The Royal Road

To help students appreciate the Persian achievement, have them pick a place 1,700 miles from their present location—the approximate length of the Royal Road—and research how they would get there, what it would cost, how long it would take, and what services and amenities they would use.

Then have students subtract one element of modern travel at a time and imagine how each subtraction would change their journey.

Viewing the Video
Show *Building Empires: The Rise of the Persians and the Inca* to investigate the origin and expansion of empires in history.

- The first segment of the video examines the mighty Persian Empire, which controlled much of the ancient world from the 500s to the 300s B.C.

- The second segment introduces students to the Inca, who in the 1400s and 1500s built a "land of the four quarters" that rivaled the Roman Empire in size.

Using the *Teacher's Resource Book* as a guide, have students consider what impact empires have had on history; compare the empires explored in the video with other empires and with struggles for power and influence today; and enrich the lesson with primary-source and visual-literacy activities included in the resource book.

PATTERNS OF INTERACTION
Building Empires: The Rise of the Persians and the Inca
Videocassette: Tape 1

Connect *to* History
Recognizing Effects
Possible Response: The ruler could hear news from distant territories while it was still fresh and send messages back quickly. Otherwise, the ruler's reactions would always be out-of-date and local officials might move toward independence.

Connect *to* Today
Comparing
Recent breakthroughs in transportation and communication that compare to the Royal Road in importance might include (in reverse time order) the Internet, satellite communications, the interstate freeway system, nationwide telephone service, railroads, and the invention of the postage stamp (which occurred less than 200 years ago).

Persian Religion By the time of Darius's rule, about 2,500 years had passed since the first Sumerian city-states had been built. During those years, people of the Fertile Crescent had endured war, conquest, and famine. This gave rise to a basic question: Why should so much suffering and chaos exist in the world? A Persian prophet and religious reformer named **Zoroaster** (ZAWR·oh·AS·tuhr), who lived around 600 B.C., offered an answer.

This stone relief from the royal palace at Persepolis depicts the Persian god Ahura Mazda. The ancient Persians believed that this god embodied light and truth.

Zoroaster taught that two spiritual armies fight for possession of a person's soul. The god of truth and light, Ahura Mazda (ah·HUR·uh MAZ·duh), leads one army. The god of evil and darkness, Ahriman (AH·rih·muhn), leads the other. At the end of time, Zoroaster preached, all souls would be judged according to which side they had chosen. Followers of Ahura Mazda would be lifted into paradise. Followers of Ahriman would suffer forever in a fiery pit. A collection of books called the *Avesta* became the holy writings of the Zoroastrian religion. In Zoroaster's religion, people's own choices controlled their fate. At the final judgment, those who had chosen the side of goodness would not be doomed to a dismal underworld. Instead, they would ascend to paradise.

The Zoroastrian religion developed ideas about heaven, hell, and a final judgment that were similar to concepts in Judaism, Christianity, and Islam. The faith of Zoroaster spread eastward into India. There, it became the Parsi sect, the largest group of Zoroastrians in the world today. Zoroastrianism also was an important influence in the development of Manicheanism, a religious system that competed with early Christianity for believers. The cult of Mithra, a Zoroastrian god, spread westward to become a popular religion among the military legions in the Roman Empire.

The Persian Legacy Through their tolerance and good government, the Persians brought political order to Southwest Asia. They preserved ideas from earlier civilizations and found new ways to live and rule. Their respect for other cultures helped to preserve those cultures for the future. The powerful dynasty Cyrus established in Persia lasted 200 years and grew into a huge empire. Likewise in China, as you will learn in Section 4, great empires arose that dominated their regions.

Section ③ Assessment

1. TERMS & NAMES
Identify
- Cyrus
- Cambyses
- Darius
- satrap
- Royal Road
- Zoroaster

2. TAKING NOTES
Create a Venn diagram to show the similarities and differences between Cyrus and Darius.

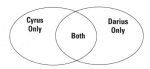

Which of the differences do you consider most important? Why?

3. HYPOTHESIZING
Why do you think Persians and other peoples were able to turn their thoughts to religion?

THINK ABOUT
- past history of peoples in the Fertile Crescent
- living conditions in the Persian Empire
- role of leaders in the Persian Empire

4. ANALYZING THEMES
Empire Building How did Darius's methods of administration give stability to his empire?

THINK ABOUT
- the structure of the empire
- policy of tolerance
- the role of the satrap

4 An Empire Unifies China

TERMS & NAMES
- Confucius
- filial piety
- bureaucracy
- Daoism
- Legalism
- *I Ching*
- yin and yang
- Qin dynasty
- Shi Huangdi
- autocracy

MAIN IDEA

The social disorder of the warring states contributed to Chinese philosophy and unification.

WHY IT MATTERS NOW

The people, events, and ideas that shaped China's early history continue to influence China's role in today's world.

SETTING THE STAGE The Zhou Dynasty, as you read in Chapter 2, endured for at least eight centuries, from approximately 1027 B.C. to 256 B.C. For the first 300 years of their long reign, the Zhou kings controlled a large empire, including both eastern and western lands. Local rulers represented the king, but he had the ultimate power. By the latter years of the Zhou Dynasty, the lords of dependent territories began to think of themselves as independent kings. Their bloody warfare led to the decline of the Zhou Dynasty.

Philosophy and the Social Order

China's ancient values of social order, harmony, and respect for authority were put aside toward the end of the Zhou Dynasty. To restore these values, Chinese scholars and philosophers developed different solutions.

Confucius Urges Harmony China's most influential scholar was **Confucius** (kuhn·FYOO·shuhs). Born in 551 B.C., Confucius lived at a time when the Zhou Dynasty was being torn apart by warring lords. He led a scholarly life, studying and teaching history, music, and moral character.

Confucius believed that social order, harmony, and good government could be restored in China if society was organized around five basic relationships. These were the relationships between: 1) ruler and subject, 2) father and son, 3) husband and wife, 4) older brother and younger brother, and 5) friend and friend. A code of proper conduct regulated each of these relationships. For example, rulers should practice kindness and virtuous living. In return, subjects should be loyal and law-abiding.

Three of Confucius's five relationships were based upon the family. Confucius stressed that children should practice what he called **filial piety,** or respect for their parents and elders:

A VOICE FROM THE PAST
In serving his parents, a filial son renders utmost respect to them at home; he supports them with joy; he gives them tender care in sickness; he grieves at their death; he sacrifices to them with solemnity . . .
CONFUCIUS, the *Analects*

Confucius was not content to be merely a great teacher. He wanted to reform Chinese society by showing a prince or duke how to govern wisely. Impressed by Confucius's wisdom, the duke of Lu appointed him Minister of Justice. According to legend, Confucius so overwhelmed people by his kindness and courtesy that almost overnight, crime vanished from Lu. When the duke's ways changed, however, Confucius felt compelled to resign.

This 18th-century painting shows Chinese students taking an examination on the Confucian classics. They wish to advance in the government. Written tests for civil servants in China go back to the Han Dynasty.

First Age of Empires **97**

Section 4 Overview

OBJECTIVES

1. To compare the Chinese ethical systems that arose in the late Zhou period.
2. To describe the impact of the Qin Dynasty on Chinese history.

SKILLBUILDERS
- Interpreting charts, p. 99
- Interpreting maps: region, human-environment interaction, p. 100

CRITICAL THINKING
- Summarizing, p. 99
- Recognizing effects, p. 100
- Hypothesizing, p. 101

FOCUS
5-Minute Warm-Up

▶ *Perceiving Effects*
Answering these questions will help students grasp the potential impact of Confucian ideas.

1. Read A Voice from the Past on page 97. According to Confucius, how should a son treat his parents?
2. Why might order and harmony within families contribute to order and harmony in society?

 WARM-UP TRANSPARENCY 4

OBJECTIVE ① INSTRUCT

Philosophy and the Social Order

▶ *Key Ideas*
- Confucius seeks to organize Chinese society around five basic social relationships.
- Confucian ideas lay the groundwork for a civil service staffed by gentleman scholars.
- Daoists seek accord with nature.
- Legalists urge strong, harsh rule and strict censorship.
- Ordinary Chinese consult folk wisdom in books like the *I Ching* and in ideas like yin and yang.

 IN-DEPTH RESOURCES: UNIT 1
Guided Reading, p. 55
Primary Source: from *Intrigues of the Warring States,* p. 61

ACCESS FOR STUDENTS ACQUIRING ENGLISH
Guided Reading (Spanish), p. 46

SECTION 4 RESOURCES

PRINT RESOURCES
IN-DEPTH RESOURCES: UNIT 1
Guided Reading, p. 55
Skillbuilder Practice: Recognizing Effects, p. 56
Primary Sources: from *Intrigues of the Warring States,* p. 61; from the *Analects* by Confucius, p. 62

ACCESS FOR STUDENTS ACQUIRING ENGLISH
Guided Reading (Spanish), p. 46
Skillbuilder Practice: (Spanish), p. 47

FORMAL ASSESSMENT
Section Quiz, p. 43

TECHNOLOGY RESOURCES
GEOGRAPHY TRANSPARENCIES
GT4 Empires of the World, 1570-202 B.C.

WORLD ART AND CULTURES TRANSPARENCIES
AT9 Chinese terra cotta army figures

CRITICAL THINKING TRANSPARENCIES
CT40 Chapter 4 Visual Summary

CD-ROM
Religions of the World

 INTERNET www.mlworldhistory.com

Scholars in Ancient China

Confucius was just one of a whole class of scholars, many of whom wandered from state to state in China during the late Zhou period, when China had broken down into warring states. Rulers wanted fresh ideas to help them keep order and justify their own authority. It became quite normal for them to support many scholars in the hope of finding one gem among the many polished pebbles.

In the fourth century B.C., King Xuan of Qi had about 1,000 philosophers living in his capital. They had no duties except to debate and discuss ideas.

HISTORY MAKERS
Confucius and Laozi

Chinese politicians often turned to Laozi for consolation and to Confucius for advice. Confucius said practical things like, "People must have sufficient to eat; there must be a sufficient army; and there must be confidence of the people in the ruler." Laozi offered far more mystical statements: "Exterminate the sage, discard the wise, and the people will benefit a hundred fold."

Ask students which philosopher they would rather have as a teacher. Why?

 IN-DEPTH RESOURCES: UNIT 1
Primary Source: from the *Analects* by Confucius, p. 62

Confucius spent the remainder of his life teaching. The only record of his ideas are the writings of his students. His students later collected his words in a book called the *Analects*. A disciple named Mencius (MEHN·shee·uhs) also spread Confucius's ideas. Both Confucius and Mencius taught that leaders should be virtuous.

Confucian Ideas About Government Confucius said that education could transform a humbly born person into a gentleman. In saying this, he laid the groundwork for the creation of a **bureaucracy,** a trained civil service, or those who run the government. According to Confucius, a gentleman had four virtues: "In his private conduct he was courteous, in serving his master he was punctilious [precise], in providing for the needs of the people he gave them even more than their due; in exacting service from the people, he was just." Education became critically important to career advancement in the bureaucracy.

Confucianism was never a religion, but it was an ethical system. It became the foundation for Chinese government and social order. In addition, the ideas of Confucius spread beyond China and influenced civilizations throughout East Asia.

Daoists Seek Harmony For Confucius, the social order of family and government was most important. For another Chinese thinker named Laozi, who may have lived during the sixth century B.C., only the natural order was important. His book *Dao De Ching (The Way of Virtue)* expressed Laozi's belief. He said that a universal force called the Dao (tow), meaning "the Way," guides all things.

If you seek order and harmony, said Laozi, go up into the hills, sit by a stream, and observe a drifting cloud or a soft breeze. Observe that nothing in nature strives for fame, power, or even wisdom. The cloud, the breeze, and the stream move without effort because they follow the Dao or way.

Of all the creatures of nature, according to Laozi, only humans fail to follow the Dao. They argue about questions of right and wrong, good manners and bad. According to Laozi, such arguments are pointless.

The philosophy of Laozi came to be known as **Daoism.** Its search for knowledge and understanding of nature led Daoism's followers to pursue scientific studies. Daoists made contributions to the sciences of alchemy, astronomy, and medicine.

Legalists Urge Harsh Rule In sharp contrast to the followers of Confucius was a group of practical political thinkers called the Legalists. They believed that a highly efficient and powerful government was the key to restoring order. They got their

HISTORY MAKERS

Confucius
551–479 B.C.

Born to a poor family, Confucius earned his living as a teacher. But he longed to put his principles into action by advising political leaders. Finally, at around age 50, Confucius won a post as minister in his home state.

According to legend, he set such a virtuous example that a purse lying in the middle of the street would lie untouched for days. As Confucius said, "If a ruler himself is upright, all will go well without orders. But if he himself is not upright, even though he gives orders, they will not be obeyed."

Driven from office by political intrigue, Confucius returned to teaching. He considered himself a failure because he had never held high office. Yet Confucius's ideas have molded Chinese thought for centuries.

Laozi
6th century B.C.

Legend has it that Laozi's mother carried him in her womb for 62 years and that he was born with white hair and wrinkled skin. Laozi's followers claimed that he was a contemporary of Confucius.

Unlike Confucius and the Legalists, however, Laozi believed that government should do as little as possible and leave the people alone:

Therefore in governing the people, the sage empties their minds but fills their bellies, weakens their wills but strengthens their bones. He always keeps them innocent of knowledge and free from desire, and ensures that the clever never dare to act.

Laozi thought that people could do little to influence the outcome of events. Daoism offered communion with nature as an alternative to political chaos.

Background
The *Analects* was compiled around 400 B.C. It became a fundamental part of traditional education in China. The word *analects* means "selections from a literary work."

Vocabulary
social order: having to do with relations between people.
natural order: having to do with relations between all living things.

Vocabulary
legend: a story handed down from earlier times, especially one believed to be historical.

CONNECTIONS ACROSS TIME AND PLACE

Confucius in the Modern World Confucianism remains influential in Korea and Vietnam and among overseas Chinese, but in mainland China the Communists have made strong efforts to stamp it out. The concept of a state run by a bureaucracy of scholars trained in ancient ideas has given way to that of a state run by a bureaucracy of party officials trained in communist ideology. Have students discuss whether Confucianism is more like a religion or more like a political "-ism"—such as communism.

 RELIGIONS OF THE WORLD
Confucianism

CONNECTIONS ACROSS THE CURRICULUM

Language Arts English translations of the *Analects* of Confucius, the *Dao De Ching,* and the *I Ching* are commonly available in the United States. Suggest that students use one of these books as the subject of their next book report. They should be able to find one or more of the books in a good public library.

Chinese Ethical Systems

Confucianism	Daoism	Legalism
• Social order, harmony, and good government should be based on family relationships. • Respect for parents and elders is important to a well-ordered society. • Education is important both to the welfare of the individual and to society.	• The natural order is more important than the social order. • A universal force guides all things. • Human beings should live simply and in harmony with nature.	• A highly efficient and powerful government is the key to social order. • Punishments are useful to maintain social order. • Thinkers and their ideas should be strictly controlled by the government.

SKILLBUILDER: Interpreting Charts
1. *Which of these three systems stress the importance of government and a well-ordered society?*
2. *Which system emphasizes the natural order over the social order?*
3. *Which of these systems seems to be most moderate and balanced? Explain.*

name from their belief that government should use the law to end civil disorder and restore harmony. Among the founders of **Legalism** were Hanfeizi and Li Si.

The Legalists taught that a ruler should provide rich rewards for people who carried out their duties well. Likewise, the disobedient should be harshly punished. In practice, the Legalists stressed punishment more than rewards. For example, anyone caught outside his own village without a travel permit should have his ears or nose chopped off, said the Legalists.

The Legalists believed in controlling ideas as well as actions. They suggested that a ruler burn all writings that might encourage people to think critically about government. After all, it was for the prince to govern and the people to obey. Eventually, Legalist ideas gained favor with a prince of a new dynasty that replaced the Zhou. That powerful ruler was soon to put an end to China's long period of disorder.

I Ching* and Yin and Yang** People with little interest in these philosophical debates consulted a book of oracles called ***I Ching (also spelled *Yi Jing*) to answer ethical or practical problems. Readers used the book by throwing a set of coins, interpreting the results, and then reading the appropriate oracle. The *I Ching (The Book of Changes)* helped people to lead a happy life by dispensing good advice and simple common sense.

Ancient thinkers developed the concept of **yin and yang,** two powers that together represented the natural rhythms of life. Yang represents the masculine qualities in the universe, yin the feminine. Both forces represent the rhythm of the universe and complement each other. Both the *I Ching* and yin and yang helped Chinese people understand how they fit into the world.

The Qin Dynasty

A short-lived dynasty replaced the Zhou Dynasty in the third century B.C. It emerged from the western state of Qin (chihn). The 13-year-old **Qin Dynasty** ruler who came to the throne in the third century B.C. employed Legalist ideas to subdue warring states and unify his country.

A New Emperor Takes Control After ruling for over 20 years, in 221 B.C., the Qin ruler assumed the name **Shi Huangdi** (shihr hwahng·dee), which means "First Emperor." The new emperor had

First Age of Empires **99**

THINK THROUGH HISTORY
A. Summarizing How did the Legalists think that a society could be made to run well?
A. Possible Answer Government should use law to end civil disorder and restore harmony; the obedient should be rewarded and the disobedient punished; ideas should be controlled by government.

SPOTLIGHT ON

Yin and Yang
The symbol of yin and yang is a circle divided into halves, as shown in the emblem above. The circle represents the harmony of yin (earth, female, passive) and yang (heaven, male, active). Yin is represented by the tiger and the color orange; yang is represented by the dragon and the color blue.

Ancient Chinese thinkers believed that pain is caused by an imbalance in the body between the forces of yin and yang. They believed that acupuncture helped to restore this balance by releasing blocked energy.

History from Visuals

Chinese Ethical Systems
Interpreting the Chart Remind students to read the chart by column to get an overview of each system and by row to grasp contrasts between systems. Having read the rows, do they think the systems are mutually exclusive, or could someone hold two or more views in the same row at the same time? Ask for examples.

Extension Activity Ask students which system the government and our society of the Untied States most closely follow.

SKILLBUILDER Answers
1. Confucianism and Legalism.
2. Daoism.
3. *Possible Response:* Confucianism; it avoids the extremes of Daoist emphasis on natural order over social and Legalist emphasis on punishment and control.

SPOTLIGHT ON
Yin and Yang

The concept of yin and yang expresses the view that duality is basic to the world. Have students chart the dualities stated in the text and add others from their experience, such as good/evil, day/night, or odd/even. Point out that computer software is written in a two-digit system: 0/1 (off/on).

OBJECTIVE ② INSTRUCT

The Qin Dynasty

Key Ideas
• Shi Huangdi, the first Qin emperor, uses military power to unite China and crush dissent.

• He creates a road network and standardizes currency, writing, weights and measures, and laws.

• He has the Great Wall built to fend off invaders from the north.

• The Chinese overthrow the Qin Dynasty almost immediately after Shi Huangdi's death.

TEACHING OPTION | BLOCK SCHEDULING

COOPERATIVE ACTIVITY: Debating Chinese Philosophies

CLASS TIME 30 MINUTES

Task: Students will debate which Chinese philosophy—Daoism, Confucianism, and Legalism—could best be used to solve problems in the modern world.

Purpose: To gain a deeper insight into Chinese philosophy and relate it to current social and political issues.

Activity: Divide the class into three groups and assign each group a school of Chinese philosophy. First, each group should conduct research to learn the basic ideas of its philosophy and the other philosophies. Based on the research, the group should prepare arguments showing how its philosophy is best able to help solve problems of the

modern world. Then have the class conduct a debate, with each group sending a spokesperson to the podium.

 ALTERNATIVE ASSESSMENT BOOK
Standards for Evaluating a Cooperative Activity

begun his reign by halting the internal battles that had sapped China's strength. Next he turned his attention to defeating invaders and crushing internal resistance to his rule. Shi Huangdi's armies attacked the invaders north of the Yellow River and south as far as what is now Vietnam. His victories doubled China's size. Shi Huangdi was determined to unify China.

The Qin emperor acted decisively to crush political opposition at home. To destroy the power of rival warlords, Shi Huangdi instituted a policy called "strengthening the trunk and weakening the branches." He commanded all the noble families to live at the capital city under his suspicious gaze. This edict, according to tradition, uprooted 120,000 noble families. Seizing their land, the emperor carved China into 36 administrative districts. He sent Qin officials to control them.

To silence criticism, the emperor and his prime minister, the Legalist philosopher Li Su, murdered hundreds of Confucian scholars. They also ordered "useless" books burned. These books were the works of Confucian thinkers and poets who disagreed with the Legalists. Practical books about medicine and farming were spared. Through measures such as these, Shi Huangdi established an **autocracy**—a government in which the ruler has unlimited power and uses it in an arbitrary manner.

A Program of Centralization Shi Huangdi's sweeping program of centralization included the building of a highway network of over 4,000 miles. He forced peasants to work on roads against their will. He also set uniform standards for Chinese writing, law, currency, and weights and measures, down to the length of cart axles. This last standard ensured that all vehicles could fit into the ruts of China's main roads.

Under Shi Huangdi's rule, irrigation projects increased farm production. Trade blossomed, thanks to the new road system. Trade pushed a new class—merchants—into prominence. Despite these social advances, harsh taxes and repressive government made the Qin regime unpopular. Shi Huangdi had unified China at the expense of human freedom.

THINK THROUGH HISTORY
B. Recognizing Effects What were the positive and negative effects of Shi Huangdi's rule?
B. Possible Answer He unified the empire and made changes that boosted trade, transportation, and communication. He was a cruel dictator who used slave labor, murdered people to stifle criticism, and burned books.

GEOGRAPHY SKILLBUILDER: Interpreting Maps
1. **Region** How far south did the Qin empire extend?
2. **Human-Environment Interaction** How does the wall's location reflect its function?

Great Wall of China Scholars hated Shi Huangdi for his book burning; poor people hated him for their forced labor in building a unified wall. Earlier, Zhou rulers had erected smaller walls to discourage attacks by northern nomads. Shi Huangdi determined to close the gaps and unify the wall 1,400 miles to the west. Now enemies would have to gallop halfway to Tibet to get around it.

The Great Wall of China arose on the backs of hundreds of thousands of peasants. The wall builders worked neither for wages nor for love of empire. They faced a terrible choice: work on the wall or die. Many of the laborers worked on the wall and died anyway, victims of the crushing labor or the winter winds. The Great Wall of China is so huge that it is one of the few human-made features on Earth visible from space.

The Fall of the Qin The Qin Dynasty proved short-lived. Though fully as cruel as his father, Shi Huangdi's son proved less able. Peasants rebelled just three

---

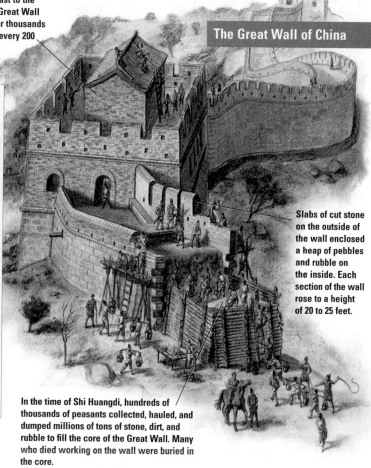

From the Yellow Sea in the east to the Gobi Desert in the west, the Great Wall twisted like a dragon's tail for thousands of miles. Watch towers rose every 200 to 300 yards along the wall.

The Great Wall of China

Although Shi Huangdi built the earliest unified wall, the wall as it exists today dates from the later Ming Dynasty (1368–1644).

Slabs of cut stone on the outside of the wall enclosed a heap of pebbles and rubble on the inside. Each section of the wall rose to a height of 20 to 25 feet.

In the time of Shi Huangdi, hundreds of thousands of peasants collected, hauled, and dumped millions of tons of stone, dirt, and rubble to fill the core of the Great Wall. Many who died working on the wall were buried in the core.

years after the second Qin emperor took office. One of their leaders, a peasant from the land of Han, marched his troops into the capital city. By 202 B.C., the harsh Qin Dynasty gave way to the Han Dynasty.

While the Chinese explored the best ways to govern, ancient Greece was experimenting with different forms of government, as you will read in Chapter 5.

Section 4 Assessment

1. TERMS & NAMES

Identify
- Confucius
- filial piety
- bureaucracy
- Daoism
- Legalism
- *I Ching*
- yin and yang
- Qin Dynasty
- Shi Huangdi
- autocracy

2. TAKING NOTES

Create a web like the one below, and indicate how the chaos of the warring states affected Chinese philosophy, politics, and the growth of cities.

Philosophy — Chaos of the warring states — Politics — Cities

3. HYPOTHESIZING

In 1776, the American Declaration of Independence declared that "all men are created equal." How would followers of the three philosophical traditions in China react to that statement?

THINK ABOUT
- their views on equality
- views on opposition to government

4. THEME ACTIVITY

Interaction with Environment Make a chart that compares and contrasts the monumental projects of the Persian Royal Road and the Great Wall of China. Include their purposes, how they changed the environment, and how they affected the peoples living there.

First Age of Empires **101**

ANSWERS

1. TERMS AND NAMES
Confucius, p. 97
filial piety, p. 97
bureaucracy, p. 98
Daoism, p. 98
Legalism, p. 99
I Ching, p. 99
yin and yang, p. 99
Qin Dynasty, p. 99
Shi Huangdi, p. 99
autocracy, p. 100

2. TAKING NOTES
Possible Responses:
Philosophy—Confucius, the Legalists, and Laozi offered solutions to the chaos. Politics—Shi Huangdi took harsh steps to impose unity and stability. Cities—People moved to them for protection.

3. HYPOTHESIZING
Possible Responses: Confucius would reject the statement because he tried to restore an unequal social order. Legalists might have objected for justifying opposition to government. Laozi might have agreed, believing that governments tend to enforce inequality.

4. THEME ACTIVITY
Possible Responses: Royal Road—built to improve communication and transportation, connected peoples and regions; Great Wall—built to prevent attacks by nomads, helped define borders, helped unify people, established barrier where no natural barrier had been.

MORE ABOUT . . .
The Great Wall

Some scholars believe China was in no great danger from northern invaders when the Great Wall was built. They suggest that instead the project was launched to keep potential troublemakers busy.

Shi Huangdi had raised huge armies to conquer China, and once the job was done, the armies remained. The emperor knew that without employment those troops might make trouble, and that concern may have led him to have them complete the Great Wall. The wall did eventually prove useful, preventing barbarian incursions until Genghis Khan punched his way through 14 centuries later.

ASSESS & RETEACH

Section 4 Assessment

Suggest that students work through the assessment items in small groups, recording written responses to compare with those of another group when they are done.

Section Quiz

FORMAL ASSESSMENT
Section Quiz, p. 43

Reteaching Activity

CLASS TIME: 10 MINUTES

Use the Guided Reading worksheet for section 4 to go over this material again.

IN-DEPTH RESOURCES: UNIT 1
Guided Reading, p. 55

CRITICAL THINKING TRANSPARENCIES
CT40 Chapter 4 Visual Summary

CLOSE ACTIVITY

CLASS TIME: 10 MINUTES

Evaluating Decisions
Remind students that many of Shi Huangdi's policies, though helpful in achieving social order for a time, ultimately provoked mass rebellion. Ask students to look at the decisions Shi Huangdi made. Then have each student evaluate one decision in terms of a possible Confucian or Daoist alternative. Would the alternative have been a better choice? Why or why not?

Teacher's Edition **101**

TERMS & NAMES

1. Ramses II, p. 84
2. Kush, p. 85
3. Assyria, p. 88
4. Ashurbanipal, p. 90
5. Cyrus, p. 92
6. Royal Road, p. 94
7. Zoroaster, p. 96
8. Confucius, p. 97
9. Daoism, p. 98
10. Shi Huangdi, p. 99

REVIEW QUESTIONS

11. Both rulers expanded their empires through conquest. Under Thutmose III, Egypt conquered Nubia. Under Piankhi, the Nubians conquered Egypt.

12. Each lost influence as other nearby civilizations developed and challenged their power. Palestinian tribes, Libyans, Kushites, the People of the Sea, and small kingdoms challenged Egyptian rule. The Assyrians challenged the Kushite rulers.

13. Assyrian soldiers entered battles well-equipped with iron or copper armor, helmets, shields, swords, and spears. They were well-organized, planning and executing sieges with discipline and ruthlessness.

14. They built great cities, such as Nineveh, accumulated an impressive library, and produced finely carved reliefs.

15. He honored local customs and religions, allowed subject peoples remarkable freedom, and allowed Jews to return to Jerusalem in 538 B.C. He combined imperial control with a high degree of local autonomy.

16. He divided the empire into 20 provinces, and he appointed a governor, inspectors, an army leader, and a tax collector for each province. The excellent road system and the use of coins of standard value helped hold the empire together.

17. Zoroaster taught that the spiritual armies of good and of evil fight for the possession of a person's soul and that all souls would be judged according to which side they had chosen.

18. The later Zhou kings ruled in name only. Warring lords held power and frequently fought with one another.

19. Confucius emphasized order and virtue. The Legalists believed that harsh rule was necessary to maintain order. Laozi thought that government should leave people alone.

TERMS & NAMES

Briefly explain the importance of each of the following to the first great age of empires.

1. Ramses II
2. Kush
3. Assyria
4. Ashurbanipal
5. Cyrus
6. Royal Road
7. Zoroaster
8. Confucius
9. Daoism
10. Shi Huangdi

Interact *with* History

On page 82, you thought about the advantages and disadvantages of empire before studying the rise of the first great empires. Now that you've read the chapter, rethink the advantages and disadvantages of empire. Do empires benefit conquered peoples? Do empires impose penalties on those they conquer? Which outweighs the other? Discuss your opinions with a small group.

Visual Summary

First Age of Empires

Egypt 1570–1075 B.C.
- Pharaohs set up a professional army.
- Pharaohs invaded surrounding territories in Africa and Southwest Asia.
- Egypt drew vast wealth from the lands it controlled around the Nile and far beyond.

Nubia 751 B.C.–A.D. 350
- Nubia and Egypt interacted and spread their culture to their trading partners.
- The kings of Nubia conquered Egypt, ousted Libyan rulers, and restored Egyptian way of life.
- Nubia made use of abundant natural resources to establish trade between Africa, Arabia, and India.

EMPIRE BUILDING

Assyria 850–612 B.C.
- Assyria developed a sophisticated military organization and state-of-the-art weaponry to conquer an empire.
- The empire engaged in brutal treatment of its conquered peoples.
- Kings used harsh taxes as well as military power to control conquered peoples.

Persia 550–330 B.C.
- Persian kings were tolerant in their treatment of peoples and cultures that made up their empire.
- Kings permitted a high degree of local self-government, so that conquered peoples enjoyed remarkable freedom.
- The empire was divided into 20 provinces, each ruled by a satrap (or governor).

China 221–202 B.C.
- Confucian and Legalist ideas laid the groundwork for a strong central government and a bureaucracy.
- Chinese emperors of the Qin Dynasty defeated invaders and crushed internal resistance.
- China crushed political opposition at home in a sweeping program of centralization.

REVIEW QUESTIONS

SECTION 1 *(pages 83–87)*
The Empires of Egypt and Nubia Collide

11. How were the reigns of Thutmose III and Piankhi alike?

12. Explain how the declines of the New Kingdom in Egypt and the Kushite empire in Meroë were similar.

SECTION 2 *(pages 88–91)*
Assyria Dominates the Fertile Crescent

13. Why was the Assyrian military so powerful?

14. What were the positive achievements of the Assyrian Empire?

SECTION 3 *(pages 92–96)*
Persia Unites Many Lands

15. Give two examples to show the enlightened view of empire held by Cyrus.

16. How was Darius able to rule such a large empire with absolute power?

17. Summarize the beliefs of Zoroaster.

SECTION 4 *(pages 97–101)*
An Empire Unifies China

18. Why are the later years of the Zhou Dynasty called "the time of the warring states"?

19. Summarize differences in how Confucius, the Legalists, and Laozi viewed government.

20. How did the Great Wall help to unify China?

20. The Great Wall helped to unify China by erecting a barrier against invading nomads from the north who threatened Chinese civilization and by enclosing Chinese territory.

Interact *with* History

Possible Responses: Advantages of empire include encouragement of trade and protection from enemies, bandits, local power struggles. Disadvantages include demand for heavy taxes, tribute, or military or public works service; eclipsing of local cultures by the conquerors' culture; concentration of power in the hands of one or a few people who do not have to answer to their subjects for their actions. This last disadvantage outweighs any advantages.

CRITICAL THINKING

1. IMPACT OF EMPIRES

THEME **EMPIRE BUILDING** With the creation of large empires, local leaders lost power. What was good and bad about this shift in power from local to empire rulers? Explain.

2. EVALUATING RULERS

Copy the table below and complete it by evaluating the military, economic, and political conditions in the empire under each leader. Then explain which leader you consider the most successful.

Leader	Military Strengths	Economic Growth	Political Stability
Thutmose III			
Sennacherib			
Cyrus			
Darius			
Shi Huangdi			

3. HISTORICAL CONTEXT

Compare the conditions that led to Zoroastrianism to the conditions that led to Confucianism. How were they similar?

4. ANALYZING PRIMARY SOURCES

The following quotation from Confucius reflects his beliefs about human nature and politics. Read the paragraph and answer the questions below it.

A VOICE FROM THE PAST

Guide the people with governmental measures and control or regulate them by the threat of punishment, and the people will try to keep out of jail, but will have no sense of honor or shame. Guide the people by virtue and control or regulate them by *li* [moral rules and customs], and the people will have a sense of honor and respect.

CONFUCIUS, the *Analects*

- How might Ramses II, Sennacherib, and Cyrus respond to this statement? Explain.
- Do you think the U. S. government should follow this advice?

CHAPTER ACTIVITIES

1. LIVING HISTORY: Unit Portfolio Project

THEME **INTERACTION WITH ENVIRONMENT** Your unit portfolio tracks the ways early peoples adjusted to their environments (see page 3). For Chapter 4, you might use one of the following ideas to add to your portfolio:

- Create a mural that shows how plains, rivers, roads, walls, and other elements of the natural and human environment influenced the developments of Egypt, Assyria, Persia, and China.
- Create a map highlighting how the climates and geographic features of Egypt, Assyria, Persia, and China are similar and different. Write a short analysis of how climate and geography affected these empires.
- Write a short story set in one of the empires described in this chapter. In your story, include descriptions of the environment and demonstrate how it influenced the lives of people.

2. CONNECT TO TODAY: Cooperative Learning

THEME **SCIENCE AND TECHNOLOGY** The Assyrians and the Chinese built their power on technological innovation. Today, countries continue to compete to develop improved military technology. Work with a team to find out how much the United States and one other country spend on their militaries today.

Using the Internet or magazines, research statistics about the topic. Look for statistics that answer such questions as: How much money does each country spend on its military? What percentage of the country's total government spending goes to the military? What is the total world spending for military?

- Present the statistics in a table, bar graph, or other visual.
- Consider whether the money is spent for current conflicts, for maintaining a peacetime military, for research and development, or for other uses. Note any patterns in military spending by region, by level of economic prosperity, or by any other trait. Write a summary of your findings.

3. INTERPRETING A TIME LINE

Revisit the unit time line on pages 2–3. Compare three events listed on the Chapter 4 time line. How were they similar?

FOCUS ON ART

The relief below comes from Ashurbanipal's palace at Nineveh. It depicts the king and queen at a garden party. The queen is sitting on a throne and the king is reclining on a couch. In the tree hangs the head (circled in yellow) of one of the defeated opponents of the Assyrian conqueror.

- What elements in the relief suggest that the monarchs are relaxing?
- What characteristics of the Assyrians does this relief seem to express?

Connect to History What details in the relief show causes of the Assyrian Empire's downfall?

CRITICAL THINKING

1. IMPACT OF EMPIRES

Possible Responses: The shift was good because local leaders often fought or were too weak to defend against invaders. The shift was bad because it reduced local control of communities and added another layer of government for people to support.

2. EVALUATING RULERS

Possible Responses: All leaders strengthened the military. Darius and Shi Huangdi promoted economic growth. Cyrus established stable rule, whereas Shi Huangdi's harsh policies created unrest. Darius was most successful—a great warrior, administrator, and promoter of trade.

3. HISTORICAL CONTEXT

Possible Responses: Prolonged conflict might have led people to seek spiritual solutions to suffering and disorder.

4. ANALYZING PRIMARY SOURCES

Possible Responses: Ramses II might agree with the emphasis on virtue and order. Sennacherib might agree that threats of punishment work effectively, but he might disagree about whether people will ever have a sense of honor and respect. Cyrus might agree, or he might argue that government should not try to impose a moral code.

New Directions in Government and Society
2000 B.C.–A.D. 700

Cicerone denuncia Catilina
(Cicero denouncing Catiline)

This fresco was painted by the Italian artist Cesare Maccari (1840–1919) in the 1880s.

The fresco is found on a wall of Maccari Hall (named for the painter) in the Italian Senate building, the Palazzo Madama, in Rome. It is one of several frescoes by Maccari showing scenes from the history of the Roman Senate and extolling the virtues of members of the Senate.

In this painting, Cicero (standing at the left), a member of the Senate and ancient Rome's greatest orator, denounces another senator, Catiline (seated at the right), in 63 B.C., for plotting to seize control of the government through armed insurrection. In a famous oration, Cicero rebukes Catiline, saying "How long will you abuse our patience, Catiline?" Reportedly, Catiline had also been involved in an earlier unsuccessful scheme.

To Maccari, Cicero represents eloquence. Honesty, courage, and respect for one's homeland are some of the other virtues the artist spotlights in his Senate frescoes.

The Roman Senate was a governing and advisory body that existed for more than a thousand years, both under the Roman Republic and the Empire. It was made up mainly of the members of wealthy families.

104

In this 19th century painting, *Cicerone denuncia Catilina*, by Cesare Maccari, the Roman senate watches as Cicero denounces Catiline for plotting to overthrow the government. The Romans, who valued the notion of law and order, lived under an early form of democracy.

105

This unit initially focuses on the great civilizations of Greece and Rome, which dominate the Mediterranean world for a thousand years. The Greeks and Romans set standards in the arts, philosophy, and government that profoundly affect the thought and institutions of later civilizations.

In shaping a new kind of society, Greece creates the idea of democracy, or government by the people. The Romans develop the republic, a form of government in which citizens have the right to choose their leaders.

Eventually, the Roman Republic is replaced by a mighty empire that extends its rule and its trade throughout Europe and into Africa and Asia. During the Roman Empire, in the first century A.D., the teachings of Jesus Christ give birth to Christianity.

Meanwhile, empires in both India and China establish powerful dynasties and develop strong, vibrant cultures. The Mauryan and Gupta empires temporarily unify India, and through trade, Indian culture spreads to much of Asia. China is unified under the Han dynasty, which rules for 400 years.

In East and West Africa, diverse cultures grow as people adapt to the varied environments of the continent. Trade and mass migrations to the south play an important role in the early history of Africa.

Human settlement comes to the Americas with the migration of peoples from Asia across a land bridge more than 10,000 years ago. The first civilizations in the Americas emerge in Mexico and Peru and strongly influence those that follow.

New Directions in Government and Society

Teaching Strategies

Comparing and Contrasting The Unit Time Line may serve as a springboard for comparing and contrasting empires and kingdoms that existed during roughly the same time period. Such comparisons can lead to class discussions concerning the reasons certain empires survive longer than others.

Students could draw on information contained in the pupil's edition to compare two empires by considering several categories of characteristics: environmental, political, technological, economic, military. These comparisons should help the class explain the relative longevity of empires.

Class Discussion Discussion could revolve around questions such as:

- What advantages does an empire with a strong central government have?
- What are the disadvantages of an empire's having no outlet to the sea?
- How does a strong economy help an empire to grow and remain powerful?

Theme: Power and Authority Students may address the central theme of this unit—Power and Authority—by examining what factors allowed one empire, kingdom, or dynasty to take over power from another in the same region.

New Directions in Government and Society

	2000 B.C.	1750 B.C.	1500 B.C.	1250 B.C.	1000 B.C.	75

CHAPTER 5 2000 B.C.–300 B.C.
Classical Greece

2000 B.C. Crete Minoan civilization thrives

1600 B.C. Greece Mycenaean kings dominate Greece

1450 B.C. Crete Mycenaeans invade Crete

1200 B.C. Anatolia Trojan War is fought

800 B.C. Greece City-states begin to rise

1400 B.C. Crete Minoan civilization disappears

1200 B.C. Greece Dorian Age begins

800 B.C. Greece Homer composes epics

CHAPTER 6 500 B.C.–A.D. 500
Ancient Rome and Early Christianity

◄ Roman painting from Pompeii

CHAPTER 7 300 B.C.–A.D. 550
India and China Establish Empires

CHAPTER 8 1500 B.C.–A.D. 500
African Civilizations

1000 B.C. East Africa Kingdom of Aksum arises

◄ African mask ►

CHAPTER 9 40,000 B.C.–A.D. 700
The Americas: A Separate World

1200 B.C. Mexico Olmec culture arises in southern Mexico

1000 B.C. Mexico Zapotec civilization arises

10,500 B.C. to 9500 B.C.

10,500 B.C. Chile Monte Verde shows evidence of human life

10,000 B.C. North America Ice Age ends and land bridge disappears

9,500 B.C. New Mexico Humans gather at Clovis site

900 B.C. South America Chavín civilization emerges

2000 B.C.	1750 B.C.	1500 B.C.	1250 B.C.	1000 B.C.	75

CONNECTIONS ACROSS THE CURRICULUM

Geography Being able to identify the locale of events is a significant aspect of historical understanding. You might encourage students to fill in the outline maps in *Geography Skills and Outline Maps* by using the time line for Unit 2 to determine where the events took place.

Regions At times, only the regions where events took place may be known. Even though some locales cannot be pinpointed, students may still gain important knowledge from labeling the areas where events occurred. Regions may also be colored in to aid in labeling.

Location When specific sites can be identified, students may research exact locations and insert labels for them on their maps.

Links in Time and Space If appropriate, students may also show connections between one development or one event and another. For example, the movements of migratory peoples or the establishment and expansion of an empire may be traced across both space and time. Combining the geography of the maps with the chronological element of the time line will help students form a fuller context for their understanding of history.

Time Line

| 750 B.C. | 500 B.C. | 250 B.C. | 1 B.C. A.D. 1 | A.D. 250 | A.D. 500 |

600 B.C. *Greece* Sparta develops strong military

594 B.C. *Greece* Solon reforms Athens

461 B.C. *Greece* Age of Pericles begins

338 B.C. *Macedonia* Philip conquers Greece

334 B.C. *Greece* Alexander begins to build empire

◄ 338 B.C. *Macedonia*

500 B.C. *Rome* Republic thrives

451 B.C. *Rome* Roman laws are carved on Twelve Tables

264 B.C. *Carthage* Punic Wars with Rome begin

146 B.C. *Rome* Rome destroys Carthage

44 B.C. *Rome* Julius Caesar is killed

27 B.C. *Rome* Octavian rules Roman Empire; *Pax Romana* begins

A.D. 29 *Jerusalem* Jesus is crucified

A.D. 285 *Rome* Empire divides into East and West

A.D. 330 *Constantinople* New capital of Roman Empire established

A.D. 476 *Rome* Western Roman Empire falls

▼ A.D. 100s *China*

321 B.C. *India* Chandragupta founds Mauryan Empire

269 B.C. *India* Asoka builds Mauryan Empire

202 B.C. *China* Liu Bang founds Han Dynasty

141 B.C. *China* Wudi rules Han Dynasty

A.D. 65 *China* First Buddhist monastery built

A.D. 105 *China* Chinese invent paper

A.D. 220 *China* Han Dynasty declines

A.D. 320 *India* Chandra Gupta I starts Gupta Empire

A.D. 500 *India* Mathematician calculates value of pi

500 B.C. *West Africa* Nok develop iron-making technology

250 B.C. *East Africa* Kingdom of Meroë at height

250 B.C. *West Africa* Djenné-Djeno established

A.D. 100s *Africa* Bantu speakers begin massive migrations throughout Africa

A.D. 100 *East Africa* Zoskales becomes first king of Aksum

A.D. 250 *West Africa* Djenné-Djeno reaches its height

A.D. 325 *East Africa* King Ezana converts to Christianity and expands Aksum

◄ 900 B.C. *South America*

500 B.C. *Mexico* Zapotec build Monte Albán

400 B.C. *Mexico* Olmec civilization begins to decline

200 B.C. *South America* Nazca culture arises

A.D. 100 *South America* Moche civilization emerges

| 50 B.C. | 500 B.C. | 250 B.C. | 1 B.C. A.D. 1 | A.D. 250 | A.D. 500 |

TIME LINE 107

Living History
Unit 2 Portfolio Project

THEME Power and Authority

Much of world history is the story of the ups and downs in the endless struggle for power. Your portfolio will compare and contrast the groups and individuals in this unit who grasp power and establish their authority. How do those people get the power, and how do they keep it? What systems of government do they establish? You can compare and contrast city-states, kingdoms, empires, even democracies.

Living History Project Choices
Each Chapter Assessment offers you choices of ways to track power and authority in that chapter. Activities include the following:

Chapter 5 epic poem, museum exhibit, talk show

Chapter 6 diagrams, persuasive argument, role-play

Chapter 7 bar chart, collage, editorial

Chapter 8 speech, dialogue, game

Chapter 9 historical fiction, time capsule, picture

Portfolio Project

Theme: Power and Authority The portfolio projects for Unit 2 involve an analysis of:

• the nature of power and authority
• the qualities of a good leader
• the balance of power in government
• the elements beyond political or military strength that reinforce or weaken the exercise of power

Student projects dealing with the theme of Power and Authority range from the creation of poems and graphic pieces to conducting television interviews. The variety of project types is intended to appeal to diverse learning styles; for example, linguistic learners.

Projects for Linguistic Learners
Students whose learning style is verbal will find project choices that suit their learning style. Students will be encouraged to work in such areas as:

• literature (epic poems and a historical short story)
• journalism (a newspaper editorial)
• the media (a television talk show)
• argument (persuasive writing)
• performance (role play)

Additional Skills Tasks may draw on other skills in addition to the verbal. For example, a role play or a television talk show may attract students with performance or video skills. Students gifted in those areas should be encouraged to attempt these projects. In group settings, such students may complement the skills of verbally oriented students and thus improve the final result.

The Western Civilization Videodisc

SECTION B: Greek and Hellenistic Civilizations, 200 B.C.—31 B.C.

Side One:
Frame 11883

SECTION C: Roman Civilization and the Origins of Christianity, 31 B.C.—A.D. 700

Side One:
Frame 14758

Universal Play
Button

See Master Guide, page 20 for Section B, page 39 for Section C.

CHAPTER 5

Classical Greece

	Key Ideas	**COPY MASTERS**	**ASSESSMENT**
SECTION 1 Cultures of the Mountains and the Sea pp. 111–114	The island cultures of Minoa and Crete develop in the Mediterranean, while Greek-speaking peoples, separated by mountainous terrain, establish individual city-states.	*In-Depth Resources: Unit 2* • **Guided Reading,** p. 1 • **Literature:** from *The Odyssey* by Homer, p. 14	PE *Section 1 Assessment,* p. 114 *Formal Assessment* • Section Quiz, p. 52 *Alternative Assessment Book* • Standards for Evaluating a Cooperative Activity
SECTION 2 Warring City-States pp. 115–119	Rival city-states develop distinct political systems. Athens takes its first steps toward democracy, and Sparta develops into a military state.	*In-Depth Resources: Unit 2* • **Guided Reading,** p. 2 • **Primary Source:** from *The History of Herodotus,* p. 9	PE *Section 2 Assessment,* p. 119 *Formal Assessment* • Section Quiz, p. 53 *Alternative Assessment Book* • Standards for Evaluating a Cooperative Activity
SECTION 3 Democracy and Greece's Golden Age pp. 120–127	Athens reaches a golden age in the arts, science, economics, and military power. War with Sparta and a plague bring an end to Athenian achievement.	*In-Depth Resources: Unit 2* • **Guided Reading,** p. 3 • **Skillbuilder Practice,** p. 6 • **Geography Application,** p. 7 • **Primary Sources:** *Plague in Athens,* p. 10; from *The Republic,* p. 11; from *Politics,* p. 13 • **History Makers:** Sophocles, p. 17 • **Connections Across Time and Cultures,** p. 19	PE *Section 3 Assessment,* p. 125 *Formal Assessment* • Section Quiz, p. 54 *Alternative Assessment Book* • Standards for Evaluating a Product or Performance
SECTION 4 Alexander—Empire Builder pp. 128–131	Alexander conquers Greece, Persia, and Egypt and extends his empire to the Indus River. He spreads Greek culture throughout the empire.	*In-Depth Resources: Unit 2* • **Guided Reading,** p. 4	PE *Section 4 Assessment,* p. 131 *Formal Assessment* • Section Quiz, p. 55 *Alternative Assessment Book* • Standards for Evaluating a Cooperative Activity
SECTION 5 The Spread of Hellenistic Culture pp. 132–135	Hellenistic culture, a blend of Greek and other cultures, flourishes throughout Greece, Egypt, and Asia. Its achievements have a lasting influence on Western civilization.	*In-Depth Resources: Unit 2* • **Guided Reading,** p. 5 • **History Makers:** Archimedes, p. 18	PE *Section 5 Assessment,* p. 135 *Formal Assessment* • Section Quiz, p. 56 *Alternative Assessment Book* • Standards for Evaluating a Cooperative Activity
CHAPTER RESOURCES	**Chapter Overview** The early Mediterranean cultures set standards in the arts, law, government, and sciences that are spread by Alexander the Great and eventually have a profound influence on the thought and institutions of Western nations.	*Telescoping the Times* • Chapter Summary, pp. 17–19 *Planning for Block Schedules*	PE *Chapter Assessment,* pp. 136–137 *Chapter Activities,* p. 137 *Formal Assessment* • Chapter Test, forms A and B, pp. 57–62 *Test Generator* *Alternative Assessment Book*

2000 B.C.–300 B.C.

TECHNOLOGY

 Warm-Up Transparency 5

 INTERNET RESOURCES
www.mlworldhistory.com

 Warm-Up Transparency 5

 Geography Transparencies
• GT5 Greek View of the World, 494 B.C.

 Electronic Library of Primary Sources
• "The Spartan Discipline for Youths"

 INTERNET RESOURCES
www.mlworldhistory.com

 Warm-Up Transparency 5

 World Art and Cultures Transparencies
• AT10 Greek vase painting

 Electronic Library of Primary Sources
• "The Athenians and the Spartans"

 INTERNET RESOURCES
www.mlworldhistory.com

 Warm-Up Transparency 5

 Battles of the World
• The Battle of Gaugamela

 Electronic Library of Primary Sources
• "Alexander Speaks to His Soldiers"

 INTERNET RESOURCES
www.mlworldhistory.com

 Warm-Up Transparency 5

 World Art and Cultures Transparencies
• AT11 Marble figures

 Critical Thinking Transparencies
• CT5 Elements of Greek Culture

 Electronic Library of Primary Sources
• from "Archimedes' Engines"

 Chapter Summaries on Audiocassette in English and Spanish

 INTERNET RESOURCES
www.mlworldhistory.com

Block Scheduling (90 MINUTES)

Day 1
Section 1, pp. 111–114

 COOPERATIVE ACTIVITY
Role-Playing Greek Myths, p. 113 (Teacher's Edition)

Section 2, pp. 115–119

 COOPERATIVE ACTIVITY
Researching Sparta and Athens, p. 116 (Teacher's Edition)

Section Assessments, pp. 114, 119

Day 2
Section 3, pp. 120–127

Section 4, pp. 128–131

 COOPERATIVE ACTIVITY
Researching the Life of Alexander the Great, p. 129 (Teacher's Edition)

Section Assessments, pp. 125, 131

Day 3
Section 5, pp. 132–135

 COOPERATIVE ACTIVITY
Multimedia Report on Hellenistic Culture, p. 134 (Teacher's Edition)

Section Assessment, p. 135

Chapter Assessment, pp. 136–137

> **Yearly Pacing** *Chapter 5 Total:* 3 days *Yearly Total:* 85 days

 Planning for Block Schedules

Customizing for Special Needs

Students Acquiring English

 Access for Students Acquiring English
• **Guided Reading** for Sections 1–5 (Spanish), pp. 53–57
• **Chapter Summary** (Spanish), pp. 50–52
• **Skillbuilder Practice** Analyzing Motives (Spanish), p. 58
• **Geography Application** The Peloponnesian War (Spanish), p. 59

 Chapter Summaries on Audiocassette in English and Spanish

 INTERNET RESOURCES
www.mlworldhistory.com
The Diverse Classroom.

Less Proficient Readers

 In-Depth Resources: Unit 2
• **Guided Reading** for Sections 1–5, pp. 1–5
• **Skillbuilder Practice** Analyzing Motives, p. 6
• **Geography Application** The Peloponnesian War, p. 7

 Telescoping the Times
• Chapter Summary, pp. 17–19

Chapter Summaries on Audiocassette

Gifted and Talented Students

 In-Depth Resources: Unit 2

Primary Sources:
• from *The History of Herodotus,* p. 9
• *Plague in Athens* by Thucydides, p. 10
• from *The Republic* by Plato, p. 11
• from *Politics* by Aristotle, p. 13

History Makers
• Sophocles, p. 17
• Archimedes, p. 18

Connections to Literature READINGS FOR STUDENTS

 In-Depth Resources: Unit 2
Literature: from *The Odyssey* by Homer, p. 14

Enrichment Reading
• **Wolf, Christa**
Cassandra
New York: Noonday, 1984

An exciting historical novel about the fall of Troy.

• **McDougal, Littell**
The Language of Literature, Grade 10
Sophocles, *Antigone,* p. 936

 = Pupil's Edition   = Overhead Transparency   = Software   = Video

= Copy Master   = CD-ROM   = Audiocassette   = Internet

107B

Classical Greece
2000 B.C.–300 B.C.

Making Predictions

Point out to students that on the map, Greece is small compared to Alexander's empire, yet the chapter is mainly devoted to Greece.

• What do they predict about Greece's influence in world history?

• Can they predict how Greek civilization spread so far?

Drawing Conclusions and Analyzing

• Have students read Socrates' quote and discuss what they think it means.

• Ask students to study the mosaic of Alexander on his horse. How does this image show his power?

Geography Connection

Ask students to study Macedonia and Greece on the map.

• What is the land formation of Greece called? *peninsula*

• Why might Macedonia want to add Greece to its territory? *access to much more of the sea, more cities, strategic position in the Mediterranean*

CHAPTER 5

Classical Greece,
2000 B.C.–300 B.C.

PREVIEWING THEMES

Power and Authority
In Egypt, Persia, and China, rulers had claimed their earthly power as a divine right. In the Greek city-state of Athens, a new form of government developed—democracy—in which citizens had the authority to exercise power.

Cultural Interaction
The Minoans of Crete had introduced Egyptian and Southwest Asian cultural ideas to Greek-speaking peoples. In turn, the conqueror Alexander the Great spread Greek culture throughout much of Asia. Greek and Asian cultures then blended to create Hellenistic culture.

Empire Building
Earlier conquerors, such as the Persians, had created empires that contained many diverse peoples. Alexander conquered the Persian Empire to create a vast new empire of his own.

INTERNET CONNECTION

Visit us at **www.mlworldhistory.com** to learn more about ancient Greece, Alexander, and related topics.

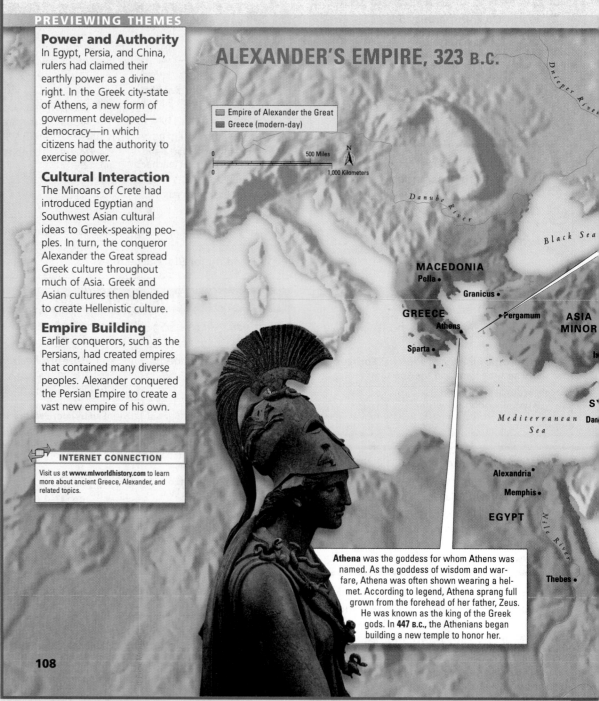

ALEXANDER'S EMPIRE, 323 B.C.

■ Empire of Alexander the Great
■ Greece (modern-day)

0   500 Miles
0   1,000 Kilometers

Dnieper River

Danube River

Black Sea

MACEDONIA
Pella •
Granicus •
GREECE
Athens •   • Pergamum   ASIA MINOR
Sparta •

Mediterranean Sea

Alexandria •
Memphis •

EGYPT   *Nile River*

Thebes •

Athena was the goddess for whom Athens was named. As the goddess of wisdom and warfare, Athena was often shown wearing a helmet. According to legend, Athena sprang full grown from the forehead of her father, Zeus. He was known as the king of the Greek gods. In **447 B.C.**, the Athenians began building a new temple to honor her.

108

GEOGRAPHY THEMES

Location

Ask students to note the location of Greece in relation to the Mediterranean Sea and to Europe, Asia Minor, and Africa. Point out that the Greek mainland is largely a peninsula. Based on Greece's location, ask them whether they think this is a place where sea trade is likely to develop. What types of geographic information would they need to answer this question? *Possible Responses: information on terrain and elevation, climate and weather, locations of coastal towns and navigable harbors, accessible forests to supply wood for shipbuilding*

Place

Tell students that in ancient Greece, geography played a key role in the way of life that developed in this region. Ask students to speculate on the various ways that being near the sea might influence where people settle, what economic activities they engage in, and what type of transportation they develop.

ADDITIONAL RESOURCES

Books for the Teacher

- Martin, Thomas R. *Ancient Greece: From Prehistoric to Hellenistic Times.* New Haven: Yale UP, 1996.

- Sacks, David. *Encyclopedia of the Ancient Greek World.* New York: Facts on File, 1994.

Books for the Student

- Adkins, Lesley and Roy A. *Handbook to Life in Ancient Greece.* New York: Facts on File, 1997. Three thousand years of Greek history and archaeology.

- Nardo, Don. *Age of Pericles.* Lucent, 1996. A description of Greece's golden age.

Videos

- *Athenian Democracy.* Britannica, 1993. 800–554–9862. Athens' brief experiment with democracy.

- *Greek Civilization.* Society for Visual Education, 1989. 800–829–1900. Elements of Greek culture that had the most impact on Western civilization.

- *Greek Thought/The Rise of Greek Civilization.* Crystal Productions, 1989. 800–255–8629. Democracy and philosophy.

Software

- *Ancient Greece.* CD-ROM. Educational Software Institute, 1994. 800–955–5570. Government, social rules, mythology, and daily life.

In **399 B.C.**, in Athens, the philosopher **Socrates** spoke to friends moments before his death. A jury found him guilty of not worshiping the gods and of teaching dangerous ideas to young people. His sentence was to drink a cup of poison. Socrates stated that he accepted his fate because "no evil can befall a good man either in life or death." Jacques Louis David painted this scene of Socrates' end in 1787.

This mosaic shows **Alexander the Great** leading the charge at the Battle of Issus in **333 B.C.** Alexander ordered this bold charge against troops that greatly outnumbered his army. Alexander's startled enemies panicked and fled.

Alexandria Eschate

Alexandria Areion

PERSIA

Babylon

Susa

Persepolis

ARABIA

Caspian Sea

Arabian Sea

HISTORY THROUGH ART

The Goddess Athena and The Death of Socrates

The statue of the goddess Athena and the painting by Jacques Louis David, *The Death of Socrates* (1787), are separated by more than 2,000 years. Yet both works of art reflect the classical principles of simplicity, order, and balance.

These ideals inspired the French painter Jacques Louis David, who painted in the neoclassical art style. As in *The Death of Socrates*, this style stresses simple backgrounds, strong contrasts of light and dark, powerfully developed human forms, and balanced compositions. The figure of Socrates, surrounded by his students, stands out in the light, his arm raised as he teaches for the last time.

During the French Revolution, David used the neoclassical style to portray Napoleon (*see Chapter 23, p. 571*).

Interpreting the Art What qualities of Socrates' do you think the painter wanted to show? *Possible Answers: Courage, wisdom, leadership, integrity* How does David show the feelings of Socrates' students? *His students are in shadow, their heads bowed in sorrow or turned toward Socrates to hear his last words.*

Interact with History

This Interact with History feature motivates students by inviting them to think of themselves as part of a key historical culture—the ancient Greek civilization. As they examine these images and quotations, students will analyze the culture's values and explore their own responses to the works.

Purpose

- to introduce students to some of the values and cultural achievements of ancient Greece
- to help students become aware of Greek influence on the modern world
- to help students connect with the people, ideas, and events they will study in the chapter

Teaching Strategy

Thinking Critically After students have considered themselves as part of Greek culture, have them answer the key questions and give reasons for their responses.

EXAMINING *the* ISSUES

Following are suggestions for addressing each bulleted question.

1 Have students examine the posture and attitude of the two figures and what they represent. In what way does the relief illustrate Pericles' words?

2 Ask students what qualities Greeks valued in their heroes and athletes.

3 Ask students to think about the roles that heroic stories and the quality of beauty might have played in Greek life and thoughts.

Making Connections Ask students to discuss what values are expressed by modern sculptures, paintings, architecture, and advertisements, especially those featuring famous events, athletes, or heroes.

Interact *with* History

What is the first thing that comes to mind when you think of ancient Greece? You can learn much about what a culture values from its works of art, literature, and from the statements of its leaders and philosophers. Look at these famous works of art from Greece and read the quotations.

What did the Greeks value?

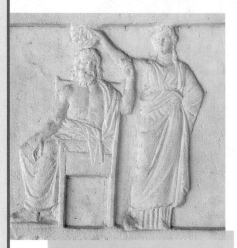

This stone relief panel of Democracy crowning Athens was placed in the marketplace, where citizens could see it daily.

"Our constitution is called a democracy because power is in the hands not of a minority but of the whole people."
Pericles, an Athenian statesman

"The river-god . . . Achelous took the form of a bull and attacked him fiercely . . . but Hercules . . . conquered him and broke off one of his horns."
**Edith Hamilton, in *Mythology*
(from Apollodorus)**

This Greek vase depicts the mythological hero Hercules, noted for his strength and courage, battling Achelous.

The Greeks often used sculptures of graceful maidens, called caryatids, as building support columns.

"For we are lovers of the beautiful, yet simple in our tastes. . . ."
Thucydides, a historian

EXAMINING *the* ISSUES

1 • What does the relief panel suggest about the role of democracy in Greek society?

2 • What special qualities do heroes and athletes possess?

3 • Why would the Greeks carve a statue of a lovely woman onto a building column or decorate their pottery with a heroic scene?

Break into small groups and talk about what common elements you see in these artworks. Also discuss what the quotes tell you about Greek culture and ideals. In what ways do you think Greek values still influence us today?

As you read about ancient Greece—its history, culture, and forms of government—note what roles these ideals played in Greek society.

110 Chapter 5

Follow-Up

A feature on the chapter assessment will ask students to reevaluate their responses to the images and quotes presented on this page.

① Cultures of the Mountains and the Sea

TERMS & NAMES
- Mycenaeans
- Trojan War
- Dorians
- Homer
- epics
- myths

MAIN IDEA

Physical geography caused separate groups of Greek-speaking peoples to develop isolated societies.

WHY IT MATTERS NOW

The seeds of much of Western cultural heritage were planted during this time period.

SETTING THE STAGE In ancient times, Greece was not a united country. It was a collection of separate lands where Greek-speaking people lived. By 2000 B.C., the Minoans lived on the large Greek island of Crete. The Minoans created an elegant civilization that had great power in the Mediterranean world. At the same time, Indo-European peoples migrated from the plains along the Black Sea and Anatolia. The Indo-Europeans settled in mainland Greece. Seaborne commercial networks spread ideas as well as resources throughout the eastern Mediterranean.

Geography Shapes Greek Life

Vocabulary
peninsula: a piece of land that extends into a body of water and is connected to the mainland

Ancient Greece consisted mainly of a mountainous peninsula jutting out into the Mediterranean Sea. It also included approximately 1,400 islands in the Aegean (ih·JEE·uhn) and Ionian (eye·OH·nee·uhn) seas. Lands on the western coast of Anatolia were also part of ancient Greece. (See the map on page 112.) The region's physical geography directly shaped Greek traditions and customs.

The Sea The sea shaped Greek civilization just as rivers shaped the ancient civilizations of Egypt, the Fertile Crescent, India, and China. In one sense, the Greeks did not live *on* a land but *around* a sea. Greeks rarely traveled more than 85 miles to reach the coastline. The Aegean Sea, the Ionian Sea, and the neighboring Black Sea were important transportation routes for the Greek people. These liquid highways linked most parts of Greece. As the Greeks became skilled sailors, sea travel also connected Greece with other societies. Sea travel and trade were also important because Greece itself was poor in natural resources. Greece lacked timber, precious metals, and usable farmland.

Nestled at the base of a mountain range, this coastal Greek city has a rugged shoreline.

A. Possible Answers The closeness of the sea promoted trade between city-states and surrounding societies. The mountains isolated the valleys. This fostered independence and made it more difficult to establish central control.

THINK THROUGH HISTORY
A. Analyzing Causes In what ways did Greece's location by the sea and its mountainous land affect the development of its society?

The Land Rugged mountains covered about three-fourths of ancient Greece. Mountains divided the land into a number of different regions. The mountain chains ran mainly from northwest to southeast along the Balkan peninsula. They significantly influenced Greek political life. Unlike the Egyptians or the Chinese, it was difficult to unite the ancient Greeks under a single government. Greece developed small, independent communities within each little valley and its surrounding mountains. Most Greeks gave their loyalty to these local communities.

In ancient times, the uneven terrain also made land transportation difficult. Early Greek roads were little more than dirt paths. For example, the city-state of Sparta was only about 60 miles from Olympia, the site of the Olympic Games. Yet it took Spartans almost seven days to travel that distance.

Much of the land itself was stony and only a small part of it— approximately 20 percent—was arable, or suitable for farming.

Greece, 600 B.C.

Interpreting the Map Help students understand that the inset map shows the variations in elevation on the segment labeled West/East on latitude line 38 degrees North. Ask students to describe aspects of Greece's geography that helped it establish a thriving sea trade. *Possible Answers: Easy access to sea; mountainous terrain making overland routes too long and hazardous; islands, inlets, and bays provide harbors; colonial outposts along coast provide trade, supplies*

Extension Activity Have students trace the most direct trade route from Athens to the Black Sea and to Corcyra in the Ionian Sea.

SKILLBUILDER Answers

1. Greeks conduct most of their trade by sea routes.

2. The rugged, mountainous topography would have made communication and overland trade difficult among settlements and encouraged independent development.

GEOGRAPHY SKILLBUILDER: Interpreting Maps
1. **Movement** *Based on the map, how did Greek traders conduct most of their trade?*
2. **Human-Environment Interaction** *How might the topography or surface features of Greece have affected communications among early Greek settlements?*

OBJECTIVE ② INSTRUCT

Mycenaean Civilization Develops

Key Ideas

• Mycenaeans develop a strong culture led by wealthy warrior-kings.

• They invade Crete and preserve and spread aspects of Minoan culture.

• Mycenaean kings defeat Troy and become the dominant power in the Aegean region.

Tiny but fertile valleys covered about one-fourth of Greece. The small streams that watered these valleys were not suitable for large-scale irrigation projects.

With so little fertile farmland or fresh water for irrigation, Greece was never able to support a large population. It is estimated that no more than a few million people lived in ancient Greece at any given time. Even this small population couldn't expect the land to support a life of luxury. As a result, the Greeks based their diet on basic staple crops such as grains, grapes, and olives. A desire for more living space, grassland for raising livestock, and adequate farmland may have been factors that motivated the Greeks to seek new sites for colonies.

The Climate Climate was the third important environmental influence on Greek civilization. Greece has a varied climate with temperatures averaging 48 degrees Fahrenheit in the winter and 80 degrees Fahrenheit in the summer. In ancient times, these moderate temperatures supported an outdoor life for many Greek citizens. Men spent much of their leisure time at outdoor public events. They met often to discuss public issues, exchange news, and take an active part in civic life.

Mycenaean Civilization Develops

As Chapter 3 explained, a large wave of Indo-Europeans migrated from the Eurasian steppes to Europe, India, and Southwest Asia. Some of these people who settled on the Greek mainland around 2000 B.C. were later known as **Mycenaeans.** The name came from their leading city, Mycenae (my·SEE·nee).

Mycenae was located on a steep, rocky ridge and surrounded by a protective wall up to 20 feet thick. The fortified city of Mycenae could withstand almost any attack. From

---

TEACHING OPTION | BLOCK SCHEDULING

CONNECTIONS ACROSS THE CURRICULUM

Art: *Treasures from Mycenaean Tombs*
Tell students that excavated Mycenaean royal tombs have yielded a wealth of astonishing artifacts from this era: solid gold funeral masks, gold crowns, gold cups, engraved rings and seals, weapons, and ornaments of all kinds. Color pictures of these artifacts can be found in books such as *Art History*

by Marilyn Stokstad (Harry N. Abrams, Publisher, 1995); *Minoan and Mycenaean Art* by Reynold Higgins (Oxford University Press, 1981); or the videocassette *Crete & Mycenae* (Museum Without Walls, Social Studies School Service, 1997, 1–800–421–4246). These artifacts reveal the sophistication and skill of Mycenaean craftworkers.

Have interested students work with the art teacher to make models of some of these artifacts, using papier-mâché, modeling clay, or other materials, and coloring them with acrylic or enamel paint. The models can be displayed in class. Ask the students to write a brief description of what they learned about Mycenaean culture by doing the artwork.

Mycenae, a warrior-king ruled the surrounding villages and farms. Similar Mycenaean palace-forts dotted the southern part of Greece. Influential and militaristic rulers controlled the Mycenaean communities in towns such as Tiryns and Athens. These kings dominated Greece from about 1600 to 1200 B.C.

Culture and Trade The nobles who lived within the fortresses enjoyed a life of surprising splendor. They feasted in great halls 35 feet wide and 50 feet long. During banquets, the firelight from a huge circular hearth glittered on a dazzling variety of gold pitchers and silver cups. When the royal Mycenaeans died, they were buried with their richest treasures. Warrior-kings won their enormous wealth by controlling local production and commercial trade. They also led their armies in search of plunder. However, few other Mycenaeans had the wealth of the warrior-kings. Wealthy kings of the Bronze Age (2000–1100 B.C.) wielded bronze weapons and drank from cups of gold. The common people used tools made from less expensive materials such as stone and wood. Most were farmers, but others worked as weavers, goat herders, or stonemasons.

The warrior-kings of Mycenae also invaded Crete. The Minoan civilization had flourished on Crete for 600 years. The civilization ended abruptly and mysteriously in 1400 B.C. The Mycenaean invasions prevented the Minoans from rebuilding. However, the Mycenaeans preserved elements of Minoan culture by making it part of their own lives.

From their contact with the Minoans, the Mycenaeans saw the value of seaborne trade. Mycenaean traders sailed to islands in the Aegean, coastal towns of Anatolia, and to cities in Syria, Egypt, Italy, and Crete. The Minoans influenced Mycenaean culture in other ways as well. The Mycenaeans adapted the Minoan writing system to the Greek language and decorated vases with Minoan designs. Their legacy survived in the form of legends. These legends later formed the core of Greek religious practice, art, politics, and literature. Western civilization has roots in these early Greek civilizations.

The Trojan War About 1200 B.C. the Mycenaean kings fought a ten-year war against Troy, an independent trading city located in Anatolia. According to legend, a Greek army besieged and destroyed Troy because a Trojan youth had kidnapped Helen, the beautiful wife of a Greek king.

For many years, historians thought that the legendary stories told of the **Trojan War** were totally fictional. Then around 1870, a German archaeologist, Heinrich Schliemann, began excavating a hill in northwestern Turkey. He found the remains of nine layers of city life, one of which may date from this time period. His discoveries suggest that the stories of the Trojan War may have been based on real cities, people, and events.

In 1988, another German historian, Manfred Korfmann, excavated an ancient maritime cemetery near the hill believed to be the site of ancient Troy. Although some scholars disagree, Korfmann believes the Trojan War was a struggle for control of a crucial waterway in the Aegean Sea. In any event, the attack on Troy was probably one of the last campaigns of the Mycenaeans.

Greek Culture Declines Under the Dorians

Not long after the Trojan War, Mycenaean civilization collapsed. Around 1200 B.C., sea raiders attacked and burned palace after palace. At Mycenae, a layer of ashes from a terrible fire covered the entire palace site. According to tradition, a new group of people, the **Dorians** (DAWR·ee·uhnz), moved into this war-torn countryside. The Dorians spoke a dialect of Greek and were distant relatives of the Bronze Age Greeks.

The Dorians were far less advanced than the Mycenaean Greeks. The centralized economy collapsed and trade eventually came to a standstill with their arrival. Most

Classical Greece **113**

Greek stories tell of their army's capture of the legendary city of Troy. Some scholars think that the hollow wooden horse of Western literature may actually have been a gigantic siege engine or battering ram.

important to historians, Greeks appear to have temporarily forgotten the art of writing during the Dorian Age. No written record exists from the 400-year period between 1150 and 750 B.C. Without written records, little is known about this period of decline.

Epics of Homer   Lacking writing, the Greeks of this time learned about the Trojan War through the spoken word. Their greatest storyteller, according to Greek tradition, was a blind man named **Homer.** Little is known of his personal life. Some historians believe Homer composed his **epics,** narrative poems celebrating heroic deeds, between 750 and 700 B.C. The Trojan War forms the backdrop for Homer's two great epic poems, *The Iliad* and *The Odyssey.*

The heroes of *The Iliad* are warriors: the fierce Greek, Achilles (uh·KIHL·eez), and the courageous and noble Hector of Troy. In the following dramatic excerpt, Hector's wife begs him not to fight Achilles:

> **A VOICE FROM THE PAST**
> "O Hector, your courage will be your destruction; and you have no pity on your little son or on me, who will soon be your widow. . . if I lose you, it would be better for me to die. . . ."
> Then tall Hector. . . answered, "Wife, I too have thought upon all this. But I would feel deep shame if like a coward I stayed away from battle. All my life I have learned to be brave and to fight always in the front ranks of the Trojans, winning glory for myself. . . ."
> **HOMER,** *The Iliad*

This is a marble sculpture of Polyphemus, a cyclops, or one-eyed monster, in Homer's *The Odyssey.*

Hector's response to his wife gives insight into the Greek heroic ideal of *aretē* (ar·uh·TAY), meaning virtue and excellence. A Greek could display this ideal on the battlefield, in combat, or in athletic contests.

Homer's other epic, *The Odyssey,* concerns the adventures of Odysseus (oh·DIH·see·uhs). Odysseus uses his wits and trickery to defeat the Trojans. Much of this epic is set after the war. It concerns his ten-year journey home and the strange and mysterious lands Odysseus visits along the way.

Greeks Create Myths   The Greeks developed a rich set of **myths,** or traditional stories, about their gods. Through these myths, the Greeks sought to understand the mysteries of nature and the power of human passions. Myths explained the changing of the seasons, for example.

Greeks attributed human qualities, such as love, hate, and jealousy, to their gods. The gods quarreled and competed with each other constantly. However, unlike humans, the gods lived forever. Zeus, the ruler of the gods, lived on Mount Olympus with his wife, Hera. Hera was often jealous of Zeus' relationships with other women. Athena, goddess of wisdom, was Zeus' daughter and his favorite child. The Greeks thought of Athena as the guardian of cities, especially of Athens, which was named in her honor. You will learn about Athens and other cities in Section 2.

Section ❶ Assessment

1. TERMS & NAMES

Identify
- Mycenaeans
- Trojan War
- Dorians
- Homer
- epics
- myths

2. TAKING NOTES

Re-create the graph below on your paper and fill in examples of how geography affected early Greek civilization.

Geographic Feature	Effects
sea	
land	
climate	

3. DRAWING CONCLUSIONS

Why did the lack of writing represent a setback to the development of Greek civilization?

THINK ABOUT
- Minoan and Mycenaean accomplishments
- uses of writing
- other forms of communication

4. ANALYZING THEMES

Cultural Interaction Why do you think that early Greek epics and myths are so well known and studied in today's society?

THINK ABOUT
- *aretē*
- Greek ideals compared to ideals in today's world
- early Greeks' purpose of storytelling

2 Warring City-States

TERMS & NAMES
- polis
- acropolis
- monarchy
- aristocracy
- oligarchy
- phalanx
- tyrant
- helot
- democracy
- Persian Wars

MAIN IDEA

The growth of city-states in Greece led to the development of several political systems, including democracy.

WHY IT MATTERS NOW

Many political systems in today's world mirror the varied forms of government that evolved in Greece.

SETTING THE STAGE After the sea peoples invaded mainland Greece around 1200 B.C., the Dorians moved into the area. Greek civilization experienced a period of decline during the Dorian period. After many centuries, Dorians and Mycenaeans alike identified less with the culture of their ancestors and more with their local city-state. By 750 B.C. the Greeks saw the rise of powerful city-states.

Rule and Order in Greek City-States

By 750 B.C., the city-state, or **polis,** was the fundamental political unit in ancient Greece. A polis was made up of a city and its surrounding countryside, which included numerous villages. Most city-states controlled between 50 and 500 square miles of territory. They were often home to fewer than 20,000 residents. At the agora (the public center), or on a fortified hilltop called an **acropolis** (uh·KRAHP·uh·lihs), male citizens gathered to conduct business.

Greek Political Structures There were many ways to rule a Greek polis. In some city-states, much like river-valley civilizations, kings or monarchs ruled in a government called a **monarchy.** In time, some city-states adopted an **aristocracy** (AR·uh·STAHK· ruh·see), a government ruled by a small group of noble, land-owning families. These very rich families often gained political power after working in a king's military cavalry.

Later, as trade expanded, a new class of wealthy merchants and artisans emerged in some cities. When these groups became dissatisfied with aristocratic rule, they sometimes took power or shared it with the nobility. They formed an **oligarchy,** a government ruled by a few powerful people. The idea of representative government also began to take root in many city-states. Regardless of its political structure, each polis enjoyed a close-knit community. Most Greeks looked down on all non-Greek foreigners, whom they considered barbarians.

A. Possible Answer
Individual citizens would tend to feel more confident and personally responsible for defending the city-state. They might demand a share in governing themselves.

THINK THROUGH HISTORY
A. Making Inferences How would the ability to own weapons change the outlook of ordinary citizens?

A New Kind of Army Emerges During the Dorian Age, only the rich could afford bronze spears, shields, breastplates, and chariots. Iron later replaced bronze in the manufacture of weapons. Harder than bronze, iron was more common and therefore cheaper. Soon, ordinary citizens could afford to arm and defend themselves.

The shift from bronze to iron weapons made possible a new kind of army composed of merchants, artisans, and small landowners. Citizens were expected to defend the polis. Foot soldiers, called hoplites, stood side by side, holding a spear in one hand and a shield in the other. This fearsome formation, or **phalanx** (FAY·lanks), was the most powerful fighting force in the ancient world.

Background
The term *hoplite* comes from the word *hoplon,* a shield that covered half of the soldier's body.

Tyrants Seize Power No ruler could ignore the power of the citizen-soldiers. In many city-states, unemployed farmers and debt-ridden artisans joined in revolt against the

Classical Greece **115**

Armed with spears, shields, and protective headgear, Greek foot soldiers marched into battle. Artists often re-created scenes like the one pictured above on Greek pottery.

Section 2 Overview

OBJECTIVES

1. To identify the different political systems that developed in the Greek city-states.

2. To describe the military government of Sparta.

3. To explain how Athenian and Spartan governments differed.

4. To summarize the battles and results of the Persian Wars.

SKILLBUILDER
- Interpreting charts, p. 117
- Interpreting maps: movement, location, p. 119

CRITICAL THINKING
- Making inferences, p. 115
- Contrasting, pp. 118, 119
- Recognizing effects, p. 119

FOCUS

5-Minute Warm-Up

▶ **Making Generalizations**
Have students answer these questions to explore different types of government.

1. Study the chart on p. 117. What form does the U.S. government most closely resemble?

2. What two things are the same in this form and the U.S. government?

📜 **WARM-UP TRANSPARENCY 5**

OBJECTIVE ① INSTRUCT

Rule and Order in Greek City-States

▶ **Key Ideas**
- The basic political unit in Greece is the polis, or city-state, which is run only by male citizens.
- Each city-state is ruled by a monarchy, aristocracy, or oligarchy.
- A new type of army emerges, made up of citizen-soldiers.

📖 **IN-DEPTH RESOURCES: UNIT 2**
Guided Reading, p. 2

📖 **ACCESS FOR STUDENTS ACQUIRING ENGLISH**
Guided Reading (Spanish), p. 54

SECTION 2 RESOURCES

PRINT RESOURCES

📖 **IN-DEPTH RESOURCES: UNIT 2**
Guided Reading, p. 2
Primary Source: from *The History of Herodotus,* p. 9
Connections Across Time and Cultures: Ideas of Government in Greece and China, p. 19

📖 **ACCESS FOR STUDENTS ACQUIRING ENGLISH**
Guided Reading (Spanish), p. 54

📖 **FORMAL ASSESSMENT**
Section Quiz, p. 53

📖 **ALTERNATIVE ASSESSMENT BOOK**

TECHNOLOGY RESOURCES

📜 **GEOGRAPHY TRANSPARENCIES**
GT5 Greek View of the World, 494 B.C.

💿 **CD-ROM**
Electronic Library of Primary Sources

🌐 **INTERNET** www.mlworldhistory.com

Teacher's Edition **115**

Sparta Builds a Military State

Key Ideas
- Sparta develops into a military state, extending its power by conquering the Messenians.
- An assembly, Council of Elders, and ephors govern Sparta. Only ruling families and working-class people are citizens.
- Education for Spartan boys centers on military training. Both boys and girls learn to put service to the state first.

ELECTRONIC LIBRARY OF PRIMARY SOURCES
"The Spartan Discipline for Youths"

SPOTLIGHT ON
Warrior-Women

Ask students why historians might have been skeptical about the existence of female Amazon warriors. How might the Kazakhstan evidence reshape our views on women's roles in ancient societies? *The evidence seems to suggest that in some ancient societies women may have had more active roles than was previously thought.*

MORE ABOUT . . .
Spartan Education

Military training and service totally dominated a Spartan man's life. At age 20, he was allowed to marry but still had to live in the barracks for another 10 years. After completing his military service, he remained on active reserve for another 30 years. Only after age 60 could a Spartan man retire from military service to live with his family.

---

nobles. Powerful individuals, called **tyrants,** gained control of the government by appealing to the poor and the discontented for support.

The rule of some city-states passed from one tyrant to the next as competing groups took power. Other cities, however, found new ways of governing. Among these city-states were two of the most powerful, Sparta and Athens.

Sparta Builds a Military State

Located in the southern part of Greece known as the Peloponnesus (PEHL·uh·puh·NEE·sus), Sparta was nearly cut off from the rest of Greece by the Gulf of Corinth. (See the map on page 112.) Unlike other city-states, Sparta built a military state.

SPOTLIGHT ON

Warrior-Women

Greek myths of an army of fierce warrior-women called Amazons have thrilled readers for centuries. Legend has it that the Amazons fought and governed, while their husbands cooked and cleaned. Skilled archers and swordswomen, Amazons were expected to kill before marrying.

For centuries historians dismissed tales of the Amazons as fantasy. In 1997, however, Russian and American archaeologists unearthed contrary evidence. In Pokrovka, Kazakhstan, they dug up 44 burial mounds. Inside they found the skeletons of women buried with swords and iron daggers.

Scientists think these ancient women may have inspired Greek legend. These finds have also cast new light on the roles of women in societies long ago.

Sparta Dominates Messenians While other city-states founded colonies abroad, Sparta conquered neighboring Messenia around 725 B.C. and took over the land. The Messenians became **helots** (HEHL·uhts), peasants forced to stay on the land they worked. Each year, the Spartans demanded half of the helots' yearly crop. Around 600 B.C., the Messenians, who outnumbered the Spartans eight to one, revolted. The Spartans just barely put down the revolt, and then dedicated themselves to the creation of a strong city-state.

Sparta's Government and Society Two groups governed Sparta. An assembly, composed of all free adult males, elected officials and voted on major issues. The second group was the Council of Elders. It proposed laws on which the assembly voted. Five elected officials called ephors carried out the laws the council passed. These men controlled education and prosecuted court cases. In addition, two kings ruled over Sparta's military.

Like its political structure, Sparta's population was diverse and consisted of several social groups. The first were citizens descended from the original inhabitants of the region. This group included the ruling families who owned the land. A second group, noncitizens but free, worked in commerce and industry. The helots, near the bottom of Spartan society, were a little higher than slaves. Some also served as household servants or worked for the citizen hoplite warriors.

Background
The kings of Sparta were not monarchs in the traditional sense but hereditary military leaders.

Spartan Education For men, daily life centered around military training. Training was rigorous. At the age of seven, boys left home and moved into army barracks. Wearing no shoes, they marched in light tunics during the day and slept on hard benches at night. Trainees gulped down meager meals of coarse black porridge. Such schooling produced tough soldiers.

Spartan girls also led hardy lives. Although they did not receive military training, they ran, wrestled, and played sports. Like the boys, they also learned to put service to Sparta above even love of family. As adults, women managed the family estates while their husbands served the polis. Although Spartan women did not have the right to vote, their roles in Spartan society surprised men from other Greek city-states. This was particularly true in Athens, where citizens expected women to remain out of sight and quietly raise children.

From around 600 until 371 B.C., the Spartans had the most powerful army in Greece, but they paid a high price for that position. All forms of individual expression were discouraged. As a result, Spartans did not value the arts and had practically no time for artistic expression. Spartans valued duty, strength, and discipline over individuality, beauty, and freedom.

Spartan women, such as the runner below, took part in athletic contests.

Task: Student groups will research daily life in either Sparta or Athens and present oral reports to the class comparing the two city-states.

Purpose: To compare and contrast the ways of life in these two city-states

Activity: Divide students into five groups. Assign one of the following topics to each group to compare and contrast Athens and Sparta: role of government in the lives of individuals, purpose of education for

boys and girls, responsibilities and privileges of citizens and noncitizens, roles of women in society, opportunities for artistic expression. After completing their research, each group can make either a contrast and comparison chart or write a report to present their findings to the class.

Building a Portfolio: Students should add their charts or reports to their portfolio, along with an explanation of the assignment.

ALTERNATIVE ASSESSMENT BOOK
Standards for Evaluating a Cooperative Activity

Standards for Evaluation
Oral reports or charts should . . .
- demonstrate students' understanding of their topics
- clearly convey the differences and similarities between Athens and Sparta
- show evidence of sound research

Athens Builds a Limited Democracy

Located on a rocky hill in eastern Greece, Athens lay to the north of Sparta. (See the map on page 112.) In outlook and values, Athens contrasted sharply with Sparta. An ambassador from the city-state of Corinth once compared the Spartans to the Athenians in a speech to the Spartan assembly. He told the Spartans that though they had the strongest army in Greece, they were too cautious. He also said that the Spartans lacked imagination and curiosity. Athenians, he said, were always eager to learn new ideas because they had been educated to think and act as free people.

Political Developments in Athens Like other city-states, Athens went through a power struggle between rich and poor. However, Athenians avoided civil war by making timely reforms. Athenian reformers tried to create **democracy,** rule by the people. In Athens, citizens participated directly in political decision making.

Not everyone in Athens had a part in this new form of political participation. Only free adult males counted as citizens. Women, slaves, and foreigners living in Athens were excluded from citizenship and had few rights. Slaves formed about one-third of the Athenian population. They worked in mines, farmed fields, and did housework.

In general, Athenian women focused their attention on child rearing, weaving cloth, preparing meals, and managing the household. In this excerpt, a Greek historian describes what a husband expected from his wife:

For Athenian women, life centered around home and the family.

> **A VOICE FROM THE PAST**
> You will need to stay indoors. . . . The greatest joy of all will be to prove yourself . . . a better helpmate to myself and to the children, a better guardian of our home, so will your honor increase. . . . [By being dutiful] you will enjoy your food, grow vigorous in health, and your complexion will in very truth be lovelier.
> **XENOPHON,** *Oeconomicus*

In addition to having no part in government, women had very little to do with the city's intellectual life.

Solon's Political and Economic Reforms Repeated clashes occurred between the aristocrats who governed Athens and the common people. A group of peasants foiled an attempt by an Athenian nobleman named Cylon (SI·luhn) to establish a tyranny. In return, they demanded a written code of laws. In 621 B.C., the Greek lawmaker Draco wrote the first legal code, dealing mainly with contracts and property ownership. Draco's code included such unfair practices as debt slavery, in which small farmers worked as slaves to repay their debts. As a result, conflicts between the aristocrats and the poor continued. To prevent civil war, in 594 B.C. the aristocrats chose a trusted statesman named Solon (SO·luhn) to head the government. Athenians gave him full power to reform the law.

Solon outlawed debt slavery. He allowed all citizens to participate and debate policies in the Athenian assembly. In another political move, Solon introduced the legal concept that any citizen could bring charges against wrongdoers. In addition, his economic reforms benefited many. For example, by encouraging the export of grapes and olives, Solon initiated a profitable overseas trade and demand for these products.

Although Solon initiated political and economic changes, he neglected land reforms. At the end of his rule, fighting erupted between wealthy landowners and the poor

Classical Greece **117**

Background
The legal code prepared by Draco was so harsh that the word *draconian* has become a synonym for "extreme cruelty or severity."

Forms of Government

Monarchy
- State ruled by a king
- Rule is hereditary
- Some rulers claim divine right
- Practiced in Mycenae (1450 B.C.)

Aristocracy
- State ruled by nobility
- Rule is hereditary and based on land ownership
- Social status and wealth support rulers' authority
- Practiced in Athens (594 B.C.)

Oligarchy
- State ruled by a small group of citizens
- Rule is based on wealth
- Ruling group controls military
- Practiced in Sparta (800–600 B.C.)

Direct Democracy
- State ruled by its citizens
- Rule is based on citizenship
- Majority rule decides vote
- Practiced in Athens (461 B.C.)

SKILLBUILDER:
Interpreting Charts
1. *Which forms of government feature rule based on wealth or property ownership?*
2. *In which form of government do citizens have the most power?*

The Persian Wars

Key Ideas

- In the first Persian War, the highly trained Greek armies defeat King Darius's forces.
- Ten years later the city-states are badly divided. Athens and Sparta rally to defeat Xerxes' army and navy.
- Victory over the Persians gives the Greeks renewed self-confidence and sets the stage for Athens' golden age.

CONNECT *to* TODAY

Modern Marathons

Since the 1970s, marathons, or long-distance endurance runs, have become a popular sport. Each year, tens of thousands of runners enter one of the many marathons held around the United States. Ask students whether participation in these races today reflects the same values that led the early Greeks to participate in athletic competitions. Why or why not?

MORE ABOUT . . .
Thermopylae

The Greek historian Herodotus in his *History of the Persian Wars* said this about the Spartans at Thermopylae: "Here they defended themselves to the last, such as still had swords using them and the others resisting with their hands and teeth; till the barbarians . . . had encircled them upon every side. . . . Thus nobly did the Spartans behave. . . ." The Spartans' sacrifice at Thermopylae rallied the divided Greeks to defeat the Persians.

IN-DEPTH RESOURCES: UNIT 2
Primary Source: from *The History of Herodotus*, p. 9

---

farmers. Around 546 B.C., a nobleman and military leader named Pisistratus (py·SIS·truh·tuhs) seized power and became one of Athens' first tyrants. Seeking power at the expense of the nobles, he provided funds to help peasants buy farm equipment. He financed this reform by a tax on agricultural production. Pisistratus also launched a massive building program that gave jobs to the poor and earned him their support.

Reforms of Cleisthenes Beginning in 508 B.C., the Athenian leader Cleisthenes (KLYS·thuh·NEEZ) introduced further reforms. He worked to make Athens a full democracy by reorganizing the assembly to break up the power of the nobility. He also increased the power of the assembly by allowing all citizens to submit laws for debate and passage. Cleisthenes then created the Council of Five Hundred. This body proposed laws and counseled the assembly. Council members were chosen by lot, or at random. While these reforms allowed Athenian citizens to participate in a limited democracy, only one-fifth of Athenian residents were actual citizens.

The Persian Wars

Danger of a helot revolt led to Sparta becoming a military state. Danger of revolution among poverty-stricken farmers led to Athens becoming a democracy. The greatest danger of all—invasion by Persian armies—moved Sparta and Athens alike to their greatest glory.

Battle at Marathon The **Persian Wars,** between Greece and the Persian Empire, began in Ionia on the coast of Anatolia. Greeks had long been settled there, but around 520 B.C., the Persians conquered the area. When Ionian Greeks revolted, Athens sent ships and soldiers to their aid. The Persian king Darius defeated the rebels and then vowed to destroy Athens in revenge.

In 490 B.C., a Persian fleet carried 25,000 men across the Aegean Sea and landed northeast of Athens on a plain called Marathon. There, 10,000 Athenians, neatly arranged in phalanxes, waited for them. Vastly outnumbered, the Greek soldiers charged. The Persians, who wore light armor and lacked training in this kind of land combat, were no match for the disciplined Greek phalanx. After several hours, the Persians fled the battlefield. The casualties reportedly numbered 6,400 Persians and only 192 Athenians.

Though the Athenians won the land battle, their city now stood defenseless. According to tradition, army leaders chose a young runner named Pheidippides (fy·DIP·uh·DEEZ) to race back to Athens. He brought news of the Persian defeat so that Athenians would not give up the city without a fight. Sprinting the distance from Marathon to Athens, Pheidippides delivered his message, collapsed, and died. The Greek army soon set off rapidly and were actually waiting in Athens when the Persian ships sailed into the harbor. The Persians quickly sailed away in retreat.

Thermopylae and Salamis Ten years later, in 480 B.C., Darius the Great was dead. His son and successor Xerxes (ZURK·seez) tried to crush Greece. Xerxes assembled an enormous invasion force of ships and men. By then, however, the Greeks were badly divided. Some city-states agreed to fight the Persians. Others thought it wiser to let Xerxes destroy Athens and return home. Some Greeks even fought on the Persian side. Consequently, Xerxes' army met no resistance as it marched down the eastern coast of Greece.

When Xerxes came to a narrow mountain pass at Thermopylae (thur·MAHP·uh·lee), 7,000 Greeks, including 300 Spartans, blocked his way. The Persian king underestimated their power. They fought for three days before a traitor told the Persians about

---

CONNECT *to* TODAY

Modern Marathons

Today, the word *marathon* refers to a foot race of 26 miles, 385 yards. One of the largest and best known is the Boston Marathon. The history of this grueling race dates back to the Persian Wars and Pheidippides' run from Marathon to Athens.

After running at top speed for approximately 25 miles, Pheidippides arrived in Athens. He gasped "Rejoice, we conquer," and instantly died. His heroic run inspired officials at the 1896 Olympic Games in Athens to add a 26-mile marathon to their competition.

In 1908, officials in London further lengthened the race. King Edward VII decided he wanted it to begin at Windsor Castle—385 yards from the city's Olympic Stadium. The photo below shows Lameck Aquita of Kenya, who won the 1997 Boston Marathon with a time of 2 hours, 10 minutes, 34 seconds.

---

118 Chapter 5

THINK THROUGH HISTORY
B. Contrasting How would you compare the ideals of Spartan and Athenian society?
B. Possible Answers Spartans valued physical and military strength and discipline. They did not care much for the arts and ideas. The Athenians valued their political freedom, family life, and using the mind.

---

a secret path around the cliffs. Fearing defeat, the Spartans held the pass while the other Greek forces retreated. The Spartans' valiant sacrifice—all were killed—made a great impression on all Greeks.

Meanwhile, in Athens, the citizens debated how best to defend the city. Themistocles, an Athenian statesman, convinced Athenians to evacuate the city and fight at sea. He positioned the Greek fleet in a narrow channel near the island of Salamis (SAL·uh·mihs), a few miles southwest of Athens. After setting fire to Athens, Xerxes sent his warships to block both ends of the channel. However, the channel was too narrow to permit the Persian fleet to maneuver well. Greek ships drove their battering rams straight into the wooden hulls, punching holes in the Persian warships. Xerxes watched in horror as more than one-third of his fleet sank. The Spartans defeated the rest of the Persian army at a third battle on the plain of Plataea (pluh·TEE·uh) in 479 B.C.

Consequences of the Persian Wars
With the Persian threat ended, all the Greek city-states felt a new sense of confidence and freedom. Athens, in particular, basked in the glory of the Persian defeat. After the war, Athens became the leader of an alliance of 140 city-states called the Delian (DEE·lee·uhn) League. The league drove the Persians from the territories surrounding Greece and ended the threat of future attacks. Soon thereafter, Athens began to use its powerful navy to control the other league members. The prestige of victory and the wealth of the empire set the stage for a dazzling burst of creativity in Athens. The city was entering its brief, golden age.

C. Possible Answers The Persian Wars united many Greek city-states under Athens. It left them determined to build up a defensive navy to prevent future attacks. Victory produced confidence and paved the way for a new burst of creativity.

THINK THROUGH HISTORY
C. Recognizing Effects How did the Persian Wars affect the Greek people, especially the Athenians?

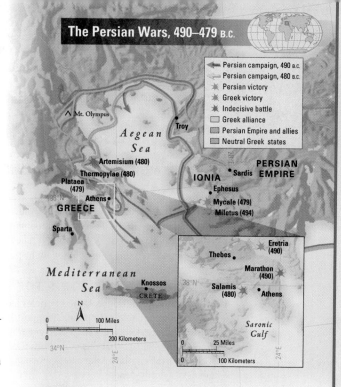

The Persian Wars, 490–479 B.C.

- ➡ Persian campaign, 490 B.C.
- ➡ Persian campaign, 480 B.C.
- ✴ Persian victory
- ✴ Greek victory
- ✴ Indecisive battle
- ☐ Greek alliance
- ☐ Persian Empire and allies
- ☐ Neutral Greek states

Mt. Olympus
Aegean Sea
Troy
Artemisium (480)
Thermopylae (480)
Plataea (479)
Athens
GREECE
Sparta
IONIA Sardis **PERSIAN EMPIRE**
Ephesus
Mycale (479)
Miletus (494)

Mediterranean Sea
Knossos
CRETE

Thebes Eretria (490)
Marathon (490)
Salamis (480) Athens
Saronic Gulf

0 100 Miles
0 200 Kilometers

0 25 Miles
0 100 Kilometers

GEOGRAPHY SKILLBUILDER: Interpreting Maps
1. **Movement** By what routes did the Persians choose to attack Greece? Explain why.
2. **Location** Where did most of the battles of the Persian Wars occur? How might their citizens be affected?

History from Visuals

The Persian Wars
Interpreting the Map Tell students to read the map key carefully to distinguish between the first and second Persian campaigns and to identify Persian and Greek victories and indecisive battles. Make sure students understand that the numbers in parentheses are dates of battles.

Extension Activity Ask students what advantages, judging by the map, might the Greeks have had in fighting the Persians. *Possible Response: familiarity with terrain, shorter supply lines than Persians, better training in land combat, better knowledge of coastal waters*

SKILLBUILDER Answers
1. In both campaigns, the Persians attack by land and sea. Their fleet could supply the army and fight the Greek navy, while the land forces could capture seaports and coastal towns.
2. In or near Greek city-states. The citizens were profoundly affected by the destruction of their homes, the loss of men to the fighting, and the change in political rule to run the war.

GEOGRAPHY TRANSPARENCIES
GT5 Greek View of the World, 494 B.C.

Section 2 Assessment

1. TERMS & NAMES
Identify
- polis
- acropolis
- monarchy
- aristocracy
- oligarchy
- phalanx
- tyrant
- helot
- democracy
- Persian Wars

2. TAKING NOTES
Create a time line of the major battles of the Persian Wars in Greece, using a chart such as the one below. For each battle, include the victor.

first battle — second battle — third battle — fourth battle

Pretend that you are a newspaper reporter in ancient Greece. Write appropriate headlines for each battle.

3. CONTRASTING
How was living in Athens different from living in Sparta?

THINK ABOUT
- roles of citizens
- type/form of government
- societal values

4. THEME ACTIVITY
Power and Authority Draw a cartoon or write a political monologue about democracy from an Athenian slave's point of view.

Classical Greece **119**

ASSESS & RETEACH

Section 2 Assessment
Have students work in small groups to help one another answer the questions.

Section Quiz
FORMAL ASSESSMENT
Section Quiz, p. 53

Reteaching Activity
CLASS TIME: 15 MINUTES
Use the chart and the map in Section 2 to help review the main ideas of this section.

CLOSE ACTIVITY

CLASS TIME: 15 MINUTES

Analyzing Cause and Effect
To help students understand how the outnumbered Greeks could defeat the Persians, ask them to create a web listing Greek developments in war, trade, and government that might have contributed to their victory. Ask them to discuss the effects of the victory on Greek culture.

ANSWERS

1. TERMS & NAMES
polis, p. 115
acropolis, p. 115
monarchy, p. 115
aristocracy, p. 115
oligarchy, p. 115
phalanx, p. 115
tyrant, p. 116
helot, p. 116
democracy, p. 117
Persian Wars, p. 118

2. TAKING NOTES
Battle at Marathon, Athenians; confrontation at Thermopylae, Persians; Salamis, Athenians; Plataea Plain, Spartans

3. CONTRASTING
Possible Responses: Athens had built a democracy, Sparta was ruled by kings and was a military state; for men, daily life in Athens was centered around the polis; in Sparta, daily life for men was centered around military training; Athenians valued beauty, individuality, and freedom of thought; Spartans valued duty, strength, and discipline.

4. THEME ACTIVITY
Standards for Evaluation
An effective cartoon or monologue should. . . .
- demonstrate knowledge of Athenian democracy
- make an effective statement from the slave's point of view

Teacher's Edition **119**

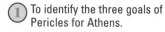
1. To identify the three goals of Pericles for Athens.

2. To describe Greek styles in sculpture and drama.

3. To explain the major conflicts in the Peloponnesian War.

4. To identify the contributions of Socrates, Plato, and Aristotle.

SKILLBUILDER

• Interpreting charts, p. 120

CRITICAL THINKING

• Distinguishing fact from opinion, p. 121
• Summarizing, p. 122
• Analyzing motives, p. 123
• Making inferences, p. 124
• Forming opinions, p. 125
• Analyzing themes, p. 125
• Compare/contrast, p. 127
• Analyzing issues, p. 127

FOCUS

5-Minute Warm-Up

▶ *Recognizing Effects*
To examine Athens' golden age, have students answer these questions:

1. Read "Setting the Stage" on p. 120. What happened during Athens' golden age?

2. Has the golden age had any lasting effects in the world?

 WARM-UP TRANSPARENCY 5

OBJECTIVE 1 INSTRUCT

Pericles' Three Goals for Athens

▶ *Key Ideas*
• Pericles helps create direct democracy, strengthens the navy, and beautifies Athens.

📖 *IN-DEPTH RESOURCES: UNIT 2*
Guided Reading, p. 3
Connections Across Time and Cultures: Ideas of Government in Greece and China, p. 19

📖 *ACCESS FOR STUDENTS ACQUIRING ENGLISH*
Guided Reading (Spanish), p. 55

---

3 Democracy and Greece's Golden Age

TERMS & NAMES
• direct democracy
• classical art
• tragedy
• comedy
• Peloponnesian War
• philosophers
• Socrates
• Plato
• Aristotle

MAIN IDEA
Democratic principles and classical culture flourished during Greece's golden age.

WHY IT MATTERS NOW
At its height, Greece set lasting standards in art, politics, literature, and philosophy that are still adhered to today.

SETTING THE STAGE During Athens' golden age, drama, sculpture, poetry, philosophy, architecture, and science all reached new heights. For 50 years (from 480 to 430 B.C.), Athens experienced a growth in intellectual and artistic learning. The artistic and literary legacies of this time continue to inspire and instruct people around the world.

Pericles' Three Goals for Athens

A wise and able statesman named Pericles led Athens during its golden age. Honest and fair, Pericles held onto popular support for 32 years. He was a skillful politician, an inspiring speaker, and a respected general. He so dominated the life of Athens from 461 to 429 B.C. that this period often is called the Age of Pericles. He had three goals: (1) to strengthen Athenian democracy, (2) to hold and strengthen the empire, and (3) to glorify Athens.

Stronger Democracy To strengthen democracy, Pericles increased the number of paid public officials. Earlier, only wealthier citizens could afford to hold public office because most positions were unpaid. Pericles increased the number of officials who were paid salaries. Now even the poorest could serve if elected or chosen by lot. Consequently, Athens had more citizens engaged in self-government than any other city-state. This reform made Athens one of the most democratic governments in history. However, political rights were still limited to those with citizenship status.

The introduction of **direct democracy**, a form of government in which citizens rule directly and not through representatives, was an important legacy of Periclean

Athenian and United States Democracy

Athenian Democracy	Both	U. S. Democracy
• Citizens: male; 18 years old; born of citizen parents	• Political power exercised by citizens	• Citizens: born in United States or completed citizenship process
• Laws voted on and proposed directly by assembly of all citizens	• Three branches of government	• Representatives elected to propose and vote on laws
• Leader chosen by lot	• Legislative branch passes laws	• Elected president
• Executive branch composed of a council of 500 men	• Executive branch carries out laws	• Executive branch made up of elected and appointed officials
• Juries varied in size	• Judicial branch conducts trials with paid jurors	• Juries composed of 12 jurors
• No attorneys; no appeals; one-day trials		• Defendants and plaintiffs have attorneys; long appeals process

SKILLBUILDER: Interpreting Charts
1. *What does this chart suggest to you about the origins of U. S. democracy?*
2. *What is the main difference between Athenian democracy and democracy in the United States?*

SECTION 3 RESOURCES

PRINT RESOURCES

📖 *IN-DEPTH RESOURCES: UNIT 2*
Guided Reading, p. 3
Skillbuilder Practice: Analyzing Motives, p. 6
Geography Application: The Peloponnesian War, p. 7
Primary Sources: *Plague in Athens*, p. 10; from *The Republic*, p. 11; from *Politics*, p. 13
History Makers: Sophocles, p. 17
Connections Across Time and Cultures: p. 19

📖 *ACCESS FOR STUDENTS ACQUIRING ENGLISH*
Guided Reading (Spanish), p. 55
Skillbuilder Practice: (Spanish), p. 58

Geography Application: (Spanish), p. 59

📖 *FORMAL ASSESSMENT*
Section Quiz, p. 54

TECHNOLOGY RESOURCES

 WORLD ART AND CULTURES TRANSPARENCIES
AT10 Greek vase painting

💿 **CD-ROM**
Electronic Library of Primary Sources

 INTERNET www.mlworldhistory.com

Athens. Few other city-states practiced this style of government. In Athens, male citizens who served in the assembly established all the important government policies that affected the polis. In a speech for the slain soldiers killed in the first year of the Peloponnesian War, Pericles expressed his great pride in Athenian democracy:

A VOICE FROM THE PAST
Our constitution is called a democracy because power is in the hands not of a minority but of the whole people. When it is a question of settling private disputes, everyone is equal before the law; when it is a question of putting one person before another in positions of public responsibility, what counts is not membership in a particular class, but the actual ability which the man possesses. No one, so long as he has it in him to be of service to the state, is kept in political obscurity because of poverty.

PERICLES, *Funeral Oration*

Athenian Empire Pericles tried to enlarge the wealth and power of Athens. He used the money from the Delian League's treasury to build Athens' 200-ship navy into the strongest in the Mediterranean. A strong navy was important because it helped Athens strengthen the safety of its empire. Athenian prosperity depended on gaining access to its surrounding waterways. It needed overseas trade to obtain supplies of grain and other raw materials.

Glorifying Athens Pericles also used money from the empire to beautify Athens. Without the Delian League's approval, he persuaded the Athenian assembly to vote huge sums of the league's money to buy gold, ivory, and marble. Still more money went to a small army of artisans who worked for 15 years (447–432 B.C.) to build one of architecture's noblest works—the Parthenon.

Greek Styles in Art

The Parthenon, a masterpiece of craftsmanship and design, was not novel in style. Rather, Greek artisans built the 23,000-square-foot building in the traditional style that had been used to create Greek temples for 200 years. In ancient times, this temple built to honor Athena contained examples of Greek art that set standards for future generations of artists around the world.

Greek Sculpture Within the Parthenon stood a giant statue of Athena, the goddess of wisdom and the protector of Athens. Pericles entrusted much of the work on the temple, including the statue of Athena, to the sculptor Phidias (FIDH·ee·uhs). The great statue of the goddess not only contained precious materials such as gold and ivory, it stood 38 feet tall!

Phidias and other sculptors during this golden age aimed to create figures that were graceful, strong, and perfectly formed. Their faces showed neither laughter nor anger, only serenity. Greek sculptors also tried to capture the grace of the idealized human body in motion. Their values of order, balance, and proportion became the standard of what is called **classical art.**

Classical works such as the Parthenon and the statue of Athena showcased the pride that Athenians had for their city. (See History Through Art, page 122.)

Greek Drama

The Greeks invented drama and built the first theaters in the west. Theatrical productions in Athens were both an expression of civic pride and a tribute to the gods.

HISTORY MAKERS

Pericles
494?–429 B.C.

Pericles came from a rich and high-ranking noble family. His aristocratic father had led the Athenian assembly and fought at the Battle of Salamis in the Persian Wars. His mother was the niece of Cleisthenes, an influential statesman.

Well known for his political achievements as a leader of Athens, some historians say Pericles the man was harder to know. One historian wrote,

[Pericles] no doubt, was a lonely man. Among the politicians, including his supporters, he had no friend. He avoided all social activity . . . [and] he only went out [of his home] for official business. . . .

(continued from page 121)

- The tragedies of Aeschylus, Sophocles, and Euripides focus on serious themes and a tragically flawed hero.
- Comedies, such as those by Aristophanes, often use slapstick humor and satire to criticize Athenian life.

 IN-DEPTH RESOURCES: UNIT 2
History Makers: Sophocles, p. 17

History Through Art

MORE ABOUT . . .
The Parthenon

Unlike some Greek temples, the Parthenon served only the goddess Athena. Built between 447 and 432 B.C., it measured 228 feet by 101 feet and gave impressive evidence of Athens' wealth and power. Sculptures on each side depicted Greek history and mythology. The building stood intact until A.D. 1687, when it was used to store a supply of gunpowder. When a Venetian general bombarded the temple, the powder exploded, destroying most of the building.

MORE ABOUT . . .
Masks for Greek Drama

In Greek drama the actors wore masks to indicate the nature of the characters they played or to show their emotions. The masks were also useful because men played women's roles, and the same actors often played more than one role. The large protruding lips of each mask served as a megaphone to amplify the actors' voices so the audience could hear them.

 WORLD ART AND CULTURES TRANSPARENCIES
AT10 Greek vase painting

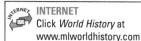 **INTERNET**
Click *World History* at
www.mlworldhistory.com

Architecture and Sculpture

The Parthenon, the most magnificent building on the Acropolis, shows the classical Greek ideals of balance and proportion in art. The Parthenon is so harmonious with its site, it appears to grow directly out of solid rock. Its architects knew geometrical principles and how to modify them to please the eye. Its 46 support columns lean slightly inward. Brightly painted sculptural friezes (decorative relief panels) and statues adorned the rectangular building.

Athena in the Parthenon
Greek statues depicted their gods in idealized human form. Inside the marble temple stood a huge statue of Athena, nearly 40 feet high. It portrayed the goddess in full battle armor, holding a six-foot high figure of victory. This is a copy of the original statue, which vanished during the fifth century A.D.

Theater at Delphi
Public theater performances during the fifth century B.C. were sponsored by the state. Hundreds of theaters were built, such as this one preserved at Delphi in central Greece. Notice how this theater is set directly into the natural setting of the hillside. The masks used by the actors in tragedies and comedies became favorite subjects in Greek art.

Connect *to* History

Summarizing What are the main things you associate with classical Greek art? Give examples from buildings and sculpture shown on this page.

SEE SKILLBUILDER HANDBOOK, PAGE 992

Connect *to* Today

Researching Look around your local community to find buildings and artworks that show Greek influences. Work in small groups to develop a guidebook to these treasures.

INTERNET CONNECTION

Visit us at www.mlworldhistory.com to learn more about Greek art.

Connect *to* History

Summarizing
Possible Answers:
Greek buildings show balance, order, and proportion in their design. The temple forms a unit with its site, the Acropolis. The human form is shown as idealized (statues) or stylized (masks). Emphasis was on beauty, serenity, and grace rather than on realistic and natural representations. Greek theater was used to educate and criticize Athenian life as well as to entertain the people.

Connect *to* Today

Researching
Have students take pictures or use their work from Connections Across Time and Place to create their guidebooks. Ask them to describe the architectural or artistic features that show Greek influence. What do they think the builders or artists wanted to convey to the public by using Greek styles? *For example, Greek architecture often is used to convey the values of order, stability, learning, and reason.*

Actors used colorful costumes, masks, and sets to dramatize stories about leadership, justice, and the duties owed to the gods. As part of their civic duty, wealthy citizens bore the cost for producing the plays. The Greeks wrote two kinds of drama—tragedy and comedy.

Tragedy A **tragedy** was a serious drama about common themes such as love, hate, war, or betrayal. These dramas featured a main character, or tragic hero. The hero usually was an important person and often gifted with extraordinary abilities. A tragic flaw—an error in judgment or personality defect—usually caused the hero's downfall. Often this flaw was hubris, or excessive pride.

In ancient times, Greece had three notable dramatists who wrote tragedies: Aeschylus (EHS·kuh·luhs), Sophocles (SAHF·uh·kleez), and Euripides (yoo·RIP·uh·DEEZ). Aeschylus wrote more than 80 plays, of which seven survive. His most famous work is the trilogy *The Oresteia* (ohr·es·STEE·uh), based on the family of Agamemnon, commander of the Greeks at Troy. Sophocles wrote about 100 plays, including the tragedies *Oedipus the King* and *Antigone*. Euripides, author of the play *Medea*, often featured sympathetic portrayals of women in his plays.

Comedy In contrast to Greek tragedies, a **comedy** contained scenes filled with slapstick situations and crude humor. Many Greek comedies were satires, or works that poked fun at a subject. Playwrights often made fun of customs, politics, respected people, or ideas of the time. Aristophanes (AR·ih·STAHF·uh·neez) wrote the first great comedies of the stage, including *The Birds* and *Lysistrata*. For example, *Lysistrata*, named for its female lead, portrayed the women of Athens forcing their husbands to end the Peloponnesian War. The fact that Athenians could listen to criticism of themselves showed the freedom and openness of public discussion that existed in democratic Athens.

Spartans and Athenians Go to War

Tensions between Athens and Sparta had been building for years. Hostilities became especially strong as Athens evolved from a limited city-state to a vast naval empire. Many people in both cities thought war was inevitable. Instead of trying to avoid conflict, leaders in both Athens and Sparta pressed for a war to begin, as both groups of leaders believed their own city had the advantage.

Peloponnesian War Sparta declared war against Athens in 431 B.C. When the **Peloponnesian War** between the two city-states began, Athens had the strongest sea power in Greece. Sparta had the advantage on land because the inland city could not easily be attacked by sea. Pericles' strategy was to avoid land battles with the superior Spartan army and wait for an opportunity to strike Sparta's allies from the sea.

Eventually the Spartans marched into Athenian territory. They swept over the countryside, burning the Athenians' local food supply. Pericles responded by bringing residents from the surrounding countryside inside the safety of Athens' city walls. The city was safe from hunger as long as ships could sail into port with food from Athenian colonies and other foreign states.

Sparta Gains the Edge However, two events spelled disaster for Athens. In the second year of the war, a frightful plague killed roughly one-third to two-thirds of Athens' population, including Pericles. In 415 B.C., Athens suffered a second disaster. The Athenian assembly sent a huge fleet carrying 27,000 soldiers to destroy the polis of

THINK THROUGH HISTORY
B. Analyzing Motives What might have been Pericles' goals in the Peloponnesian War?
B. Possible Answers To protect access to the liquid highway and the city's trade in grain and other raw materials; to rid Athens of its Spartan enemy; to continue to use Delian League funds; and to spread the empire by acquiring overseas colonies.

SPOTLIGHT ON

The Plague
An unidentified disease struck Athens during the height of the war. The disease caused a terrible plague in 430 B.C.

According to Thucydides (thoo·SID·ih·DEEZ), the plague's symptoms included high fever, inflamed eyes, sore throat, coughing, extreme thirst, vomiting, and red blisters on the skin. As the disease spread, some victims lost their eyes or their fingers or toes. Many thousands died.

The following excerpt is from Thucydides' account of the Peloponnesian Wars:

They became infected by nursing one another and died like sheep. . . . Bodies of dying men lay one upon another. . . . The temples . . . were full of corpses of those who had died in them.

Classical Greece **123**

 OBJECTIVE **4** INSTRUCT

Spartans and Athenians Go to War

> **Key Ideas**
> • Sparta and Athens begin the Peloponnesian War.
> • After years of war, Athens surrenders to Sparta.
> • Athens loses its empire, power, and wealth; and confidence in democratic rule declines.

 IN-DEPTH RESOURCES: UNIT 2
Geography Application: The Peloponnesian War, p. 7

ELECTRONIC LIBRARY OF PRIMARY SOURCES
"The Athenians and the Spartans"

CRITICAL THINKING ACTIVITY
CLASS TIME: 15 MINUTES

Recognizing Causes and Effects
Have students use a flow chart to list causes and effects in the Peloponnesian War.

Cause: Athens-Sparta rivalry Effect: War	→	Cause: Athens at first wins Effect:	→	Cause: Effect:

SPOTLIGHT ON
The Plague
Ironically, war and trade, two activities at which Athens excelled, may have brought the plague to the city-state. The disease spread from Ethiopia to Libya and Egypt, then attacked Athens. The plague spared the Spartan army, leading Athenians to wonder if they were being punished by the gods for their hubris.

 IN-DEPTH RESOURCES: UNIT 2
Primary Source: *Plague in Athens* by Thucydides, p. 10

Explaining the Skill: Analyzing motives means examining the reasons a person, group, or government took a particular action. These reasons often relate to the prior needs, plans, and goals of that person or group.

Applying the Skill: Tell students that Athens's motives for seeking war with Sparta may have been rooted in Pericles' three goals. Have them answer the following questions.

1. How could strengthening democracy have helped lead Athens into war? *Leaders could be swayed by popular opinion; civic pride could convince citizens Athens was invincible.*

2. How could war be used to expand or strengthen Athens' trade empire? *Athens would need supplies and secure lines of communication; her navy could conquer other ports and keep her enemies from trading with other cities.*

3. How might the war increase Athens' prestige? *A victory would make Athens the dominant military, economic, and cultural power in the region.*

 IN-DEPTH RESOURCES: UNIT 2
Skillbuilder Practice: Analyzing Motives, p. 6

Teacher's Edition **123**

Philosophers Search for Truth

Key Ideas
- Greek thinkers believe the universe and its laws can be studied and understood.
- Socrates questions the traditional Greek values and is condemned to death.
- In *The Republic,* Plato describes his ideal society—an oligarchy, not a democracy.
- Aristotle's rules of logic are the forerunners of the modern scientific method.
- The ideas of Socrates, Plato, and Aristotle shape European thought for centuries to come.

 IN-DEPTH RESOURCES: UNIT 2
Primary Sources: from *The Republic* by Plato, p. 11; from *Politics* by Aristotle, p. 13

CRITICAL THINKING ACTIVITY
CLASS TIME: 10 MINUTES

Analyzing Motives
Ask students to explain what Socrates meant by the statement "The unexamined life is not worth living." How might this statement help to explain both his interest in searching for the truth and his willingness to die for his beliefs?

Syracuse, one of Sparta's wealthiest allies. The expedition suffered an unmistakable defeat in 413 B.C. The Athenian historian Thucydides recalled: "They [the Athenians] were destroyed with a total destruction—their fleet, their army—there was nothing that was not destroyed, and few out of many returned home." Somehow, a terribly weakened Athens fended off Spartan attacks for another nine years. Finally, in 404 B.C., Athens and its allies surrendered.

War Brings Political Changes After 27 years of war, Athens had lost its empire, power, and wealth. In addition, general confidence in democratic government began to falter. One leader after another proved weak, corrupt, or traitorous. The assembly often changed its decisions and did not stick to a single political program.

Philosophers Search for Truth

In this time of questioning and uncertainty, several great thinkers appeared. They were determined to seek the truth, no matter where the search led them. The Greeks called such thinkers **philosophers,** meaning "lovers of wisdom." These Greek thinkers based their philosophy on the following two assumptions: (1) The universe (land, sky, and sea) is put together in an orderly way, and subject to absolute and unchanging laws, and (2) people can understand these laws through logic and reason.

One group of philosophers, the Sophists, questioned people's unexamined beliefs and ideas about justice, and other traditional values. One of the most famous Sophists was Protagoras, who took a position questioning the existence of the traditional Greek gods. He also argued that there was no universal standard of truth, saying "Man [the individual] is the measure of all things. . . ." These were radical and dangerous ideas to many of the citizens of Athens.

This Pompeiian mosaic from the first century A.D. pays tribute to the philosopher Plato (third from the left) as he teaches his followers.

Socrates One of the strongest critics of the Sophists was **Socrates** (SAHK·ruh·TEEZ). Unlike the Sophists, he believed that absolute standards did exist for truth and justice. However, he encouraged Greeks to go further and question themselves and their moral character. Historians believe that it was Socrates who once said, "The unexamined life is not worth living." Those who understood Socrates admired him deeply. The majority of citizens, however, could not understand this strange old man and his ideas.

In 399 B.C., when Socrates was about 70 years old, he was brought to trial for "corrupting the youth of Athens" and "neglecting the city's gods." In his own defense, Socrates said that his teachings were good for Athens because they forced people to think about their values and actions. The jury disagreed and condemned him to death. Later, he died after drinking a slow-acting poison.

Plato A student of Socrates, **Plato** (PLAY·toh), was approximately 28 years old when his teacher died. Later, Plato wrote down the conversations of Socrates "as a means of philosophical investigation." Sometime between 385 and 380 B.C., Plato wrote his most famous work, *The Republic.* In it, he set forth his vision of a perfectly governed society. It was not a democracy. In his ideal society, all citizens would fall naturally into three groups: farmers and artisans, warriors, and the ruling class. The person with the greatest

THINK THROUGH HISTORY
C. Making Inferences Why would philosophers start questioning traditional beliefs at this particular time in Athens' history?
C. Possible Answers Athens' defeat by its rival Sparta would have caused its citizens to have spiritual doubts. This might lead them to consider radical ideas and make them more willing to question traditional attitudes.

CUSTOMIZING FOR SPECIAL NEEDS

Gifted and Talented Students:
Corresponding with Greek Philosophers
Have students read a section of at least one primary source and one secondary source on either Socrates, Plato, or Aristotle (for example, Plato's discussion of the philosopher-king as ruler) or one of the historians Herodotus or Thucydides (for example,

Thucydides' analysis of the causes of the Peloponnesian War).

After reading the sources, have students write a letter to the person they have chosen in which they state two things they admire about this person, two things they understand or agree with in his writings,

and two things they do not understand or disagree with. After students have completed their letters, conduct a class discussion on the questions they have raised. Ask them what they think the philosophers' responses to their questions might have been.

HISTORY MAKERS

Socrates
469–399 B.C.

Socrates was one of the most powerful thinkers in history. He encouraged his students to examine their beliefs. Socrates asked them a series of leading questions to show that people hold many contradictory opinions. This method of teaching by a question-and-answer approach is known as the *Socratic method*. He devoted his life to gaining self-knowledge and once said, "There is only one good, knowledge; and one evil, ignorance."

Plato
427–347 B.C.

Born into a wealthy Athenian family, Plato had careers as a wrestler and a poet before he became a philosopher. He studied with Socrates. After his teacher died in 399 B.C., Plato left Greece and traveled to North Africa and Italy. He later returned to Athens and founded a school called The Academy in 387 B.C. The school lasted for approximately 900 years. It was Plato who once stated, "Philosophy begins in wonder."

Aristotle
384–322 B.C.

Aristotle, the son of a physician, was one of the brightest students at Plato's academy. He came there as a young man and stayed for 20 years until Plato's death. In 335 B.C., Aristotle opened his own school in Athens called the Lyceum. The school eventually rivaled the Academy. Aristotle once argued, "He who studies how things originated and came into being . . . will achieve the clearest view of them."

insight and intellect from the ruling class would be chosen philosopher-king. Plato's writings dominated philosophic thought in Europe for nearly 1,500 years. His only rivals in importance were Socrates and his own pupil, Aristotle (AR·ih·STAHT·uhl).

Aristotle The philosopher **Aristotle** questioned the nature of the world and of human belief, thought, and knowledge. Aristotle came close to summarizing all the knowledge up to his time. He invented a method for arguing according to rules of logic. He later applied his method to problems in the fields of psychology, physics, and biology. His work provides the basis of the scientific method used today.

One of Aristotle's most famous pupils was Alexander, son of King Philip of Macedonia. Around 343 B.C., Aristotle accepted the king's invitation to tutor the 13-year-old prince. Alexander's status as a student abruptly ended in 336 B.C., when he became the ruler of Macedonia. You will learn about Alexander the Great in Section 4.

Section ③ Assessment

1. TERMS & NAMES

Identify
- direct democracy
- classical art
- tragedy
- comedy
- Peloponnesian War
- philosophers
- Socrates
- Plato
- Aristotle

2. TAKING NOTES

Using a diagram like the one below, show Pericles' three goals for Athens, giving examples.

Pericles' Goals

Which goal had the greatest impact on the modern world?

3. FORMING AND SUPPORTING OPINIONS

Socrates believed in absolute standards for truth and justice. Sophists believed that standards of truth and justice are in the eye of the beholder. What is your opinion? Support your opinion with reasons and examples.

THINK ABOUT
- differences in values
- purpose of law
- circumstances

4. ANALYZING THEMES

Empire Building How does the concept of "hubris" from Greek tragedy apply to the Peloponnesian War?

THINK ABOUT
- Spartans' and Athenians' opinion of themselves
- why "hubris" is a tragic flaw
- why the war started

Classical Greece **125**

ANSWERS

1. TERMS & NAMES
direct democracy, p. 120
classical art, p. 121
tragedy, p. 123
comedy, p. 123
Peloponnesian War, p. 123
philosophers, p. 124
Socrates, p. 124
Plato, p. 124
Aristotle, p. 125

2. TAKING NOTES
strengthen Athens' democracy: increased number of paid public officials, increased citizen participation; *hold and strengthen empire:* built navy through Delian League's funds, protected overseas trade; *glorify Athens:* hired artists, built architectural projects and the Parthenon

3. FORMING AND SUPPORTING OPINIONS
Agree with the Sophists: many cultural differences exist in the world; only one set of rules for justice and truth would not work because people would rebel. Agree with Socrates: standards exist for what is right and wrong; governing people in this way is

more feasible because everyone knows what is expected.

4. ANALYZING THEMES
"Hubris" means the excessive pride that often leads to the downfall of a hero. Athens under Pericles was excessively proud of its sea power and seriously underestimated Sparta.

Sports Through Time

Throughout history, communities worldwide have valued athletes who possess great physical strength, agility, and balance. In ancient times, the Greeks believed that athletic competitions were a way to please the gods and honor dead heroes. One of Greece's many athletic festivals—the Olympic Games—continues today. Dedicated to the god Zeus, the Olympics began in 776 B.C. The Greeks even suspended wars between city-states so that athletes could compete. This love of sport lives on among different people and cultures throughout the world today.

Olympics in Greece

Every four years, some 40,000 Greeks crowded into the stadium built in Olympia to watch the competitions. The earliest games featured foot races of about 200 yards. Later, athletes also competed in wrestling, boxing, jumping, javelin-and discus-throwing events. Athletes were proud of their bodies and emphasized physical fitness. Myron's famous marble sculpture of a discus thrower is dated about 450 B.C. The sculpture survives in this Roman copy (left) of the Greek bronze.

Greece — Japan

Mexico

Nigeria

a closer look GREEK SPORTS

Victorious Olympians received a crown made of wild olive leaves.

Olympic chariot racing began in the seventh century B.C. Prizes went to the chariot's owner, not the driver.

126 Chapter 5

Sumo Wrestling in Japan

Sumo wrestling is a sport that is native to Japan. Originally sponsored by imperial families, it dates back to the eighth century. Sumo's popularity remains strong and today is considered the national sport of Japan. During a match, wrestlers wear loincloths and battle each other inside a 15-foot circle. Many of these athletes weigh more than 300 pounds. All use their size and strength to overpower an opponent.

Mayan Ball Courts in Mexico

This photograph of a site at Chichen Itza in Mexico shows a stone ring Mayans once used when playing an ancient game. During the seventh century, Mayan athletes played a ball game on walled I-shaped courts. Participants wore protective padding around their waist and on one knee. The object was to get a rubber ball through the stone ring without touching it with their hands. The ball court game had close ties to the Mayans' religious beliefs. While the exact rules are unknown, the losers were usually sacrificed to the gods.

Soccer in Nigeria

Soccer is one of the most popular sports in the world. Known as football in some countries, soccer developed in England during the 1800s. Few items are needed to play the game: a ball, an open field, and players who are willing to run. The Nigerian soccer player pictured above was a participant in the 1994 World Cup, an international soccer competition. The World Cup attracts all-star teams from around the world.

Crowds flocked to the hippodrome to watch horse races during the Olympic Games. This bronze statue shows a jockey riding bareback at one of these spectacular events.

> **Connect to History**
>
> **Compare/Contrast** Choose two of the sports or games illustrated on this page, such as modern soccer and the Mayan ball game. Then compare and contrast them.
>
> SEE SKILLBUILDER HANDBOOK, PAGE 996
>
> **Connect to Today**
>
> **Analyzing Issues** Consider the ancient Greek practice of interrupting conflicts to allow athletes to compete. Write a brief editorial (paragraph) discussing the role of sports and games as a way to promote world peace or reduce hostile behavior.

Classical Greece **127**

MORE ABOUT . . .
Sumo Wrestling

Sumo wrestling is one of Japan's most popular spectator sports. Only baseball has more fans. Most matches are short but intense, lasting less than a minute. Contestants are allowed to trip, slap, and push each other but cannot use their fists. Many top sumo wrestlers compete in six major tournaments a year. Each tournament lasts for 15 days with wrestlers facing different opponents each day. Many matches are carried live on nationwide television.

MORE ABOUT . . .
Mayan Ball Courts

All Mayan cities had ball courts. Scholars believe the ball games were reenactments of a Maya creation myth. In the myth, two Hero Twins defeat the gods of the underworld in a ball game. The gods kill them for daring to win, but the two victorious heroes return to life again.

Connect to History

Possible Responses: Students selecting the Mayan ball game and soccer might mention that in each game the players cannot touch the ball with their hands. Both the Olympics and the Mayan ball game were conducted to express or act out of the cultures' religious beliefs.

Connect to Today

Student responses should defend a position on the topic. Suggest they investigate international competitions, athletic exchange programs, and other sports efforts that promote goodwill (for example, Ted Turner's Goodwill Games). What effect have these events and programs had on international relations? On the athletes themselves?

Students might read sports biographies and autobiographies to find out what role sports has played in people's lives. Also, they might interview the school coach or local professional athletes to get their views on the topic.

OBJECTIVES

(1) To describe Philip's conquest of Greece.

(2) To explain how Alexander defeated the Persian Empire.

(3) To summarize Alexander's military conquests and their impact on future cultures.

SKILLBUILDER

• Interpreting maps: region, p. 130

CRITICAL THINKING

• Analyzing causes, p. 128
• Analyzing motives, p. 130
• Hypothesizing, p. 131

FOCUS

5-Minute Warm-Up

▶ **Clarifying**

To help students understand the achievements of Alexander, have them answer these questions.

1. Read History Makers on p. 129. Why is the horse unruly, and how does Alexander tame him?

2. What does Alexander's father believe about his son after the boy tames the horse?

🏛 **WARM-UP TRANSPARENCY 5**

OBJECTIVE ① INSTRUCT

Philip Builds Macedonia's Power

Key Ideas

• Philip II of Macedonia builds a powerful professional army and defeats his enemies.

• He conquers a divided Greece but is murdered before he can invade Persia.

• Alexander continues his father's empire building.

 IN-DEPTH RESOURCES: UNIT 2 Guided Reading, p. 4

 ACCESS FOR STUDENTS ACQUIRING ENGLISH Guided Reading (Spanish), p. 56

TERMS & NAMES
• Philip II
• Macedonia
• Demosthenes
• Alexander the Great
• Darius III

MAIN IDEA	WHY IT MATTERS NOW
Alexander the Great conquered Persia and Egypt and extended his empire to the Indus River in northwest India.	Alexander's empire extended across three continents that today consist of many nations and diverse cultures.

SETTING THE STAGE The Peloponnesian War severely weakened several Greek city-states. This caused a rapid decline in their military and economic power. To make matters worse, in the 50 years after Sparta defeated Athens in 404 B.C., the two city-states had continued to fight each other. In the nearby kingdom of Macedonia, King **Philip II** took note. Philip dreamed of first taking control of Greece. Then Philip planned to move against Persia and seize its vast wealth. Philip also hoped to avenge the Persian invasion of Greece in 480 B.C.

Philip Builds Macedonia's Power

MACEDONIA
Aegean Sea
Thebes
Athens

Just north of Greece, the kingdom of **Macedonia** had rough mountains and a cold climate. The Macedonians were a tough people who lived in mountain villages rather than city-states. The Macedonian language was related to Greek. Most Macedonian nobles thought of themselves as Greeks. The Greeks, however, looked down on the Macedonians as uncivilized foreigners who had no great philosophers, sculptors, or writers. They did, however, have an important resource in their shrewd and fearless kings.

Philip's Army In 359 B.C., Philip II became king of Macedonia. Though only 23 years old, he quickly proved to be a brilliant general and a ruthless politician. Philip transformed the rugged peasants under his command into a well-trained professional army. He organized his troops into phalanxes that were 16 men across and 16 deep. Philip used this heavy phalanx formation armed with 18-foot pikes to pave the way for cavalry strikes through enemy lines.

Once his phalanx had broken through, Philip used the fast-moving cavalry to crush his disorganized opponents. When he first used these tactics against northern opponents who had invaded Macedonia, Philip's powerful army proved unbeatable. Within a short time, he was preparing to invade Greece.

Conquest of Greece The Athenian orator **Demosthenes** (dee·MAHS·thuh·NEEZ) tried to warn the Greeks of the threat Philip and his army posed. He urged them to unite against him. However, the Greek cities could not agree on any single policy. Finally, in 338 B.C., Athens and Thebes—two Greek city-states—joined forces against Philip. By then it was too late. The Macedonians soundly defeated the Greeks at the battle of Chaeronea (KAIR·uh·NEE·uh). Philip's 18-year-old son Alexander led a successful cavalry charge that helped win the battle. The defeat at Chaeronea ended Greek freedom and independence. The city-states retained self-government in local affairs. However, Greece itself remained firmly under the control of a succession of foreign powers—the first of which was Philip's Macedonia.

Although Philip planned to invade Persia next, he never got the chance. At his daughter's wedding in 336 B.C., a former guardsman stabbed him to death. With the support of the army, Philip's son Alexander immediately proclaimed himself king of Macedonia.

This bust of King Philip II dates from the 4th century B.C. Under Philip's leadership, Macedonia became a major power in the Greek-speaking world.

A. Possible Answer It weakened Greece and left it vulnerable. Athens itself was defeated, and the other city-states could not agree on a united policy against the Macedonians.

THINK THROUGH HISTORY
A. Analyzing Causes How did the Peloponnesian War pave the way for Philip's conquest of Greece?

SECTION 4 RESOURCES

PRINT RESOURCES

 IN-DEPTH RESOURCES: UNIT 2 Guided Reading, p. 4

ACCESS FOR STUDENTS ACQUIRING ENGLISH Guided Reading (Spanish), p. 56

FORMAL ASSESSMENT Section Quiz, p. 55

ALTERNATIVE ASSESSMENT BOOK

TECHNOLOGY RESOURCES

 CD-ROM Battles of the World Electronic Library of Primary Sources

 INTERNET www.mlworldhistory.com

Because of his accomplishments over the next 13 years, he became known in history as **Alexander the Great.**

Alexander Defeats Persia

Although Alexander was only 20 years old when he became king in 336 B.C., he was well prepared to lead. Under Aristotle's teaching, Alexander had learned science, geography, and literature. Alexander especially enjoyed Homer's description of the heroic deeds performed by Achilles during the Trojan War. To inspire himself, he kept a copy of the *Iliad* under his pillow.

As a young boy, Alexander learned to ride a horse, use weapons, and command troops. Once he became king, Alexander promptly demonstrated that his military training had not been wasted. When Thebes, a city in central Greece, rebelled, he destroyed the city. About 6,000 people were killed. The survivors were sold into slavery. Frightened by his cruelty, the other Greek cities quickly gave up any idea of rebellion.

Invasion of Persia With Greece now secure, Alexander felt free to carry out Philip's plan to invade Persia. In 334 B.C., he led 35,000 soldiers across the Hellespont into Anatolia. Persian messengers raced along the Royal Road to spread the alarm about the invasion. Within a short time, a Persian army of about 40,000 men rushed to defend Persia. The two forces met at the Granicus River. Instead of waiting for the Persians to make the first move, Alexander ordered an elite cavalry unit to attack. Leading his troops into battle, Alexander smashed the Persian defenses.

Alexander's victory at Granicus alarmed the Persian king, **Darius III.** Vowing to crush the Macedonians, he raised a huge army of between 50,000–75,000 men to face the Macedonians near Issus. Realizing that he was outnumbered, Alexander surprised his enemies. He ordered his finest troops to break through a weak point in the Persian lines. The army then charged straight at Darius. To avoid capture, the frightened king fled, followed by his panicked army. This victory gave Alexander control over Anatolia.

Alexander's Ambitions Grow Shaken by his defeat, Darius tried to negotiate a peace settlement. He offered Alexander the western third of his empire. Alexander's advisers urged him to accept. However, the rapid collapse of Persian resistance fired Alexander's ambition. He rejected Darius's offer and confidently announced his plan to conquer the entire Persian Empire.

Then Alexander marched into Egypt, a Persian territory, in 332 B.C. The Egyptians welcomed Alexander as a liberator. During his stay, he visited the temple of the god Zeus-Ammon. Alexander was crowned pharaoh—a title that Ptolemy used later to begin the Ptolemic pharaoh line. Alexander also founded the city of Alexandria at the mouth of the Nile.

Conquering the Persian Empire After leaving Egypt, Alexander moved east into Mesopotamia to confront Darius. The desperate Persian king assembled an army of 250,000 men. The Persian chariots were armed with deadly scythes protruding from the wheel hubs. The two armies collided at Gaugamela (GAW·guh·MEE·luh), a small village near the ruins of ancient Nineveh. Alexander launched a massive phalanx attack followed by a cavalry charge. As the Persian lines crumbled, Darius again panicked and fled. Alexander's victory at Gaugamela ended Persia's power. The Macedonian army now marched unopposed into Persia's wealthiest provinces.

Background
The Hellespont is the ancient name for the Dardanelles, the narrow straits that separate Europe from Asia Minor.

Vocabulary
scythes: razor-sharp knives or blades.

HISTORY MAKERS

Alexander
356–323 B.C.

When Alexander was only eight or nine years old, he tamed a horse that none of his father's grooms could manage. Alexander had noticed that the horse, Bucephalus, acted wild because he was afraid of his shadow. By speaking to the horse gently and turning him to face the sun, Alexander was able to ride him. Seeing this, Philip told his son, "You'll have to find another kingdom; Macedonia isn't going to be big enough for you."

Alexander took his father's advice. Riding Bucephalus at the head of an army, he conquered a region from Greece to the Indus Valley. When the horse died in what is now Pakistan, Alexander named the city of Bucephala after it. Maybe he was tired of the name *Alexandria*. He'd already named at least a dozen cities after himself!

Interpreting the Map To follow Alexander's conquests, tell students to read across the map from left to right beginning in the northwest corner of the map at Troy. Point out that star-shaped symbols represent major battle sites. Have them trace the extent of Alexander's empire. Ask them to find three of the many cities Alexander named after himself.

Extension Activity Have students read more about battles shown on the map such as Granicus, Issus, and Gaugamela. Students might also compare this map with the present-day map of the area on page 973 of the atlas to see which cities still exist.

SKILLBUILDER Answers
1. Africa, Europe, Asia
2. Kingdoms of Lysimachus, Cassander, Antigonas, Ptolemy, Seleucus

---

OBJECTIVE ③ INSTRUCT

Alexander's Other Conquests

▶ **Key Ideas**
- Alexander extends his empire into Central Asia, hoping to reach the continent's end.
- His conquests end at the Indus Valley, and he dies preparing to wage another campaign.
- Antigonus, Ptolemy, and Seleucus divide Alexander's empire and rule as absolute monarchs.
- Alexander's conquests result in the blending of Greek and Persian cultures.

 ELECTRONIC LIBRARY OF PRIMARY SOURCES
"Alexander Speaks to His Soldiers"

Alexander and Darius (riding horses, near bottom) fight face to face in this Persian painting. The two rulers never battled this closely in real life.

Within a short time, Alexander's army occupied the capitals of Babylon, Susa, and Persepolis. These cities yielded a huge treasure, which Alexander distributed among his army. After a stay of several months, a fire broke out in Persepolis, Persia's royal capital. Some historians say Alexander left the city in ashes to signal the total destruction of the Persian Empire. The Greek historian Arrian wrote about Alexander's expeditions about 500 years later. Arrian explains that the fire was set in revenge for the Persian burning of Athens 150 years before. But others doubt that the fire was planned.

Alexander's Other Conquests

Alexander now reigned as the unchallenged ruler of southwest Asia. He was more interested in expanding his empire than in governing it. He left the ruined Persepolis to pursue Darius and conquer Persia's remote Asian provinces. Darius's trail led Alexander to a deserted spot south of the Caspian Sea. There he found Darius already dead, murdered by one of his provincial governors. Rather than return to Babylon, Alexander continued east. During the next three years, his army fought its way across the desert wastes and mountains of Central Asia. He pushed on, hoping to reach the farthest edge of the continent.

Alexander in India In 327 B.C., Alexander and his army reached and crossed into the Indus Valley. At the Hydaspes River, a powerful Indian army that included 200 elephants blocked their path. After winning a fierce battle, Alexander's soldiers marched some 200 miles farther, but their morale was low. They had been fighting for 11 years and had marched more than 11,000 miles. They had endured both scorching

B. Possible Answer
Alexander believed it was his destiny to conquer and rule men. The defeat of the Persians only fueled his dreams of further world conquest. It opened the way for Alexander's armies to continue to expand the empire into Asia.

THINK THROUGH HISTORY
B. Analyzing Motives Why did Alexander continue his conquests after Darius was dead?

Alexander and His Successors, 336–300 B.C.

Legend:
- Alexander's empire at its height, 323 B.C.
- Path of conquest
- ✳ Major battle

0 — 500 Miles
0 — 1,000 Kilometers

Map labels: KINGDOM OF LYSIMACHUS, Black Sea, PAPHLAGONIA, CAUCASUS MTS., Caspian Sea, KINGDOM OF CASSANDER, BITHYNIA, Dardanelles (Hellespont), Granicus (334), Troy, Ancyra, Sardis, Thebes, Aegean Sea, Athens, KINGDOM OF ANTIGONUS, Tarsus, TAURUS MTS., ARMENIA, MEDIA ATROPATENE, Alexandria Eschate, Maracanda, HINDU KUSH MTS., CRETE, CYPRUS, Issus (333), Gaugamela (331), Ecbatana, Bactra, Aornos (327), KINGDOM OF SELEUCUS, Taxila, Euphrates R., Tigris R., Mediterranean Sea, Damascus, Tyre, Babylon, Susa, ZAGROS MOUNTAINS, Indus R., Alexandria, Gaza, NABATAEA, Persian Gulf, Persepolis, Alexandria, DESERT OF GEDROSIA, Memphis, ARABIAN DESERT, MAURY EMPI, Ammonium, KINGDOM OF PTOLEMY, LIBYAN DESERT, Nile R., Tropic of Cancer

GEOGRAPHY SKILLBUILDER: Interpreting Maps
1. **Region** Onto which continents did Alexander's empire reach at its height?
2. **Region** Which kingdoms succeeded the empire of Alexander the Great after his death in 323 B.C.?

130

TEACHING OPTION

CONNECTIONS ACROSS THE CURRICULUM

Geography: Alexander's Empire Past and Present In 334 B.C. with an army of 35,000 foot soldiers and 5,000 cavalry, Alexander left Macedonia and waged a campaign of conquest lasting 11 years and covering over 11,000 miles. By the time he died, his empire stretched from Greece and Egypt to India. Have students name the bodies of water that border Alexander's empire. Then ask them to compare the map on page 130 with the current map in the atlas on page 973 and list the present-day nations in the area he conquered. *Egypt, Libya, Turkey, Greece, Bulgaria, Afghanistan, Syria, Iraq, Iran, Pakistan.* Finally, have students speculate about what problems Alexander or his successors would have had in managing this huge empire. *Possible Responses: Problems in communication, government, blending cultures, protecting borders, raising money, training and maintaining an army, succession of new leaders*

ALEXANDER'S EMPIRE

332 B.C.
Alexander entered Egypt and founded the city of Alexandria.

336 B.C.
Philip II was assassinated. Alexander became king of Macedonia at age 20.

334 B.C.
Alexander led 35,000 soldiers across the Hellespont or Dardanelles into Anatolia.

327 B.C.
Alexander's army reached the Indus Valley.

323 B.C.
Alexander caught fever and died at age 32. His generals began a power struggle.

MACEDONIA
PERSIA
EGYPT

323 B.C.
Ptolemy seized Egypt and became a pharaoh.

312 B.C.
Seleucus took Persian Empire.

306 B.C.
Antigonus I became king of Macedonia.

deserts and drenching monsoon rains. The exhausted soldiers yearned to go home. Bitterly disappointed, Alexander agreed to turn back.

On their homeward journey, Alexander and his troops crossed a brutally hot desert. Everyone was desperately thirsty. Some of the men collected water in a helmet—which they offered to their general. According to Arrian, Alexander saw an opportunity to inspire his discouraged men by sharing their hardship:

> **A VOICE FROM THE PAST**
> He received it [the water], and thanked those who had brought it; and . . . poured it out in the sight of all the troops; and at this . . . the whole army was so much heartened that you would have said that each and every man had drunk that water which Alexander thus poured out.
>
> **ARRIAN**, *Anabasis*

By the spring of 323 B.C., Alexander and his army had returned west to Babylon. Restless as always, Alexander announced plans to organize and unify his empire. He would construct new cities, roads, and harbors and conquer Arabia. However, Alexander never carried out his plans. One year after his return, he became seriously ill with a fever. Eleven days later, Alexander died—a month short of his 33rd birthday.

Alexander's Legacy As he lay dying, Alexander correctly predicted that his empire would go to the strongest general. His Macedonian generals fought among themselves until three ambitious generals won out. Antigonus (an·TIG·uh·nus) became king of Macedonia and took control of the Greek city-states. Ptolemy (TAHL·uh·mee) seized Egypt, took the title of pharaoh, and established a dynasty. Seleucus (sih·LOO·kuhs) took most of the old Persian Empire, which became known as the Seleucid empire. Ignoring the democratic traditions of the Greek polis, these rulers and their descendants governed with complete power over their subjects.

Alexander's conquests ended the era of independent Greek city-states. As he and his army marched through the Persian Empire, thousands of Greek artists, merchants, and officials followed. Alexander himself adopted Persian dress and customs and married a Persian woman. He included Persians and people from other lands in his army. As time passed, Greek settlers throughout the empire also adopted new ways. A vibrant new culture emerged from the blend of Greek, Egyptian, and Eastern customs.

Section 4 Assessment

1. TERMS & NAMES
Identify
- Philip II
- Macedonia
- Demosthenes
- Alexander the Great
- Darius III

2. TAKING NOTES
Using a diagram like the one below, label how far north, south, east, and west Alexander ruled.

north

west — **Alexander's Rule** — east

south

Which conquests do you think was the most significant? Why?

3. HYPOTHESIZING
If Alexander had lived, do you think he would have been as successful in ruling his empire as he was in building it?

THINK ABOUT
- skills needed for military leadership
- skills needed to govern an empire
- Alexander's demonstrated abilities

4. THEME ACTIVITY
Empire Building In small groups, create an illustrated time line of Alexander's conquests. Include at least five main events.

Classical Greece **131**

### Sidebar notes (left margin)

C. Possible Answers Yes—the empire might still have splintered without Alexander's personality to bind his followers together. No—Alexander might have had time to carry out his plans to consolidate and unify the empire.

THINK THROUGH HISTORY
C. Hypothesizing Was the power struggle that followed Alexander's death inevitable?

ANSWERS

1. TERMS & NAMES
Philip II, p. 128
Macedonia, p. 128
Demosthenes, p. 128
Alexander the Great, p. 129
Darius III, p. 129

2. TAKING NOTES
north: Macedonia; south: Egypt; west: Greece; east: India

Answers will vary. Each conquest brought the customs, ideas, and learning of the conquered people into the new culture that developed from this mixture.

3. HYPOTHESIZING
Students who support Alexander's ability to govern may point to his intelligence and ability to lead. Students who disagree may mention his inflexible attitude and that military skills are not the same as political skills.

4. THEME ACTIVITY
Standards for Evaluation
The illustrated time line should. . .
- show evidence of teamwork
- present events in accurate, chronological order
- be labeled clearly, neatly

MORE ABOUT . . .
Blending an Empire

As Alexander's empire grew, he sought to unite Macedonians and Persians. He adopted a Persian style of dress, married a Persian princess who was a daughter of King Darius III, and presided over a mass marriage of thousands of his soldiers to Persian women. He also brought Persian troops into his army and made the young Persian nobles part of his elite cavalry.

ASSESS & RETEACH

Section 4 Assessment
Have students work in small groups to answer the questions. Then put the chart in Question 2 on the board and complete it as a class.

Section Quiz

 FORMAL ASSESSMENT
Section Quiz, p. 55

Reteaching Activity
CLASS TIME: 15 MINUTES

Review the time line on page 131 to reteach the major events of Alexander's empire building.

CLOSE ACTIVITY

CLASS TIME: 20 MINUTES

Analyzing Causes
In 11 years, Alexander never lost a battle. Using the cause-and-effect graphic organizer transparency, ask the class to list the major battles described in the section. Then work with the class to analyze the reasons for each victory. How much did Alexander owe to his father's work? How strong or united were his opponents? What strategies did Alexander use in each fight?

 CRITICAL THINKING TRANSPARENCIES
CT75 Cause and Effect

TERMS & NAMES
• Hellenistic
• Alexandria
• Euclid
• Archimedes
• Colossus of Rhodes

5 The Spread of Hellenistic Culture

MAIN IDEA

Hellenistic culture, a blend of Greek and other influences, flourished throughout Greece, Egypt, and Asia.

WHY IT MATTERS NOW

Western civilization today continues to be influenced by diverse cultures.

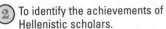

SETTING THE STAGE Alexander the Great's ambitions were cultural as well as military and political. He started new cities as outposts of Greek culture. These cities, from Egyptian Alexandria in the south to the Asian Alexandrias in the east, adopted many Greek patterns and customs. After Alexander's death, trade, a shared Greek culture, and the Greek language continued to link these cities together. But each region had its own traditional ways of life, religion, and government that no ruler could afford to overlook. Alexander's successors gradually began dynasties in each of these lands. They encouraged local traditions while transplanting Greek culture.

Hellenistic Culture in Alexandria

This is a 19th-century illustration of the great Lighthouse of Alexandria. A fire at the top of the over 400-foot building guided ships into the Egyptian harbor.

After Alexander's death, a vibrant new culture emerged. Greek (Hellenic) culture blended with Egyptian, Persian, and Indian influences. This blending became known as **Hellenistic** culture. Koine (koy·NAY), the popular spoken language used in Hellenistic cities such as Alexandria, was the direct result of cultural blending. The word *koine* came from the Greek word for common. The language was a dialect of Greek. This language enabled educated people and traders from diverse backgrounds to communicate in cities throughout the Hellenistic world.

Trade and Cultural Diversity Among the many cities of the Hellenistic world, the African city of **Alexandria** became the foremost center of commerce and Hellenistic civilization. Alexandria occupied a strategic site on the western edge of the Nile delta. Ships from all around the Mediterranean docked in its spacious harbor. Its warehouses bulged with wheat and other products from the Nile Valley. Alexandria's thriving commerce enabled it to grow and prosper. By the third century B.C., its diverse population exceeded half a million people. Greek officials, Jewish merchants, and Egyptian priests mingled in crowded marketplaces with visitors from the rest of Africa, Persia, and India. Alexandria became an international community, with a rich mixture of customs and traditions from Egypt and from the Aegean.

Alexandria's Greatest Attractions Both residents and visitors admired Alexandria's great beauty. Broad avenues lined with statues of Greek gods divided the city into blocks. Rulers built magnificent royal palaces overlooking the harbor. A much visited tomb contained Alexander's elaborate glass coffin. Soaring more than 400 feet over the harbor stood an enormous stone lighthouse called the Pharos. This lighthouse contained a polished bronze mirror that reflected the light from a blazing fire.

Alexandria's greatest attractions were its famous museum and library. The museum was a temple dedicated to the Muses, the Greek goddesses of arts and sciences. (The word *museum* comes from muse.) It contained art

THINK THROUGH HISTORY
A. Recognizing Causes Why was the culture of the Hellenistic period so different from that of classical Greece?
A. Possible Answer The blending of many cultures and the introduction of foreign ideas modified Greek cultural life. The culture's impact was wider than ever before, and it also became more diverse.

---

galleries, a zoo, botanical gardens, and even a dining hall. The museum was an institute of advanced study.

Teachers and students were only a short distance from the nearby Alexandrian Library. Its collection of half a million papyrus scrolls included many of the masterpieces of ancient literature. As the first true research library in the world, it helped promote the work of a gifted group of scholars. These scholars greatly respected the earlier works of classical literature and learning. They produced commentaries that explained these works.

Science and Technology

During the Hellenistic period, the center of scholarship gradually shifted away from Athens. Hellenistic scholars, particularly in Alexandria, succeeded brilliantly in preserving Greek and Egyptian learning in the sciences. Until the scientific advances of the 16th and 17th centuries, scholars in Alexandria provided most of the scientific knowledge available to the West.

Astronomy Alexandria's museum contained a small observatory in which astronomers could study the planets and stars. One astronomer, Aristarchus (AR·ih·STAHR·kuhs) of Samos, reached two significant scientific conclusions. In one conclusion, he estimated that the sun was at least 300 times larger than the earth. Although he greatly underestimated the sun's true size, Aristarchus disproved the widely held belief that the sun was smaller than Greece. In another conclusion, Aristarchus proposed that the earth and other planets revolve around the sun. Unfortunately for science, other astronomers refused to support Aristarchus' theories. By the second century A.D., Alexandria's last renowned astronomer, Ptolemy, incorrectly placed the earth at the center of the solar system. Astronomers accepted this view for the next 14 centuries.

Hipparchus invented the system of longitude and latitude used on maps and sky charts. Here he is shown marking the position of a star.

Greek Astronomy

The Earth

Eratosthenes' estimate of the circumference —24,662 miles

circumference

actual circumference—24,860 miles

The Sun

Earth

Aristarchus' estimate–300 times the size of earth

The sun is actually 1.3 million times the size of the earth

The Solar System

Ptolemy's view of the universe

Saturn
Jupiter
Mars
Sun
Venus
Mercury
Moon
Earth

SKILLBUILDER: Interpreting Charts
The foundations of modern scientific thought were laid during the Hellenistic period.
1. *Where were Greek astronomers' ideas most incorrect compared with modern concepts?*
2. *Which estimate is closest to modern measurements? How could the Hellenists be so accurate?*

While Hellenistic astronomers debated the earth's position in the solar system, a scholar named Eratosthenes (EHR·uh·TAHS·thuh·NEEZ) closely calculated the earth's true size. Eratosthenes was the director of the Alexandrian Library. He was also a highly regarded astronomer, poet, historian, and mathematician. He skillfully used geometry to compute the earth's circumference at 24,662 miles. Today, we compute the earth's circumference at 24,860 miles. His estimate was within 1 percent of our modern calculations.

Classical Greece **133**

OBJECTIVE 2 INSTRUCT

Science and Technology

▶ **Key Ideas**
• Hellenistic astronomers develop theories that shape European thought for centuries.
• Euclid develops the science of geometry, and Archimedes' laws serve as the basis for many mechanical inventions.

 IN-DEPTH RESOURCES: UNIT 2
History Makers: Archimedes, p.18

 ELECTRONIC LIBRARY OF PRIMARY SOURCES
from "Archimedes' Engines"

CRITICAL THINKING TRANSPARENCIES
CT5 Elements of Greek Culture Before and After Alexander

History from Visuals

Greek Astronomy

Interpreting the Chart Help students understand that Greek astronomers had very little objective knowledge about the universe on which to base their calculations and theories. Even so, they that knew that the earth was round, the sun was a star, and other planets orbited around a fixed point.

Extension Activity Why might astronomers have found it easier to accept Ptolemy's view of the solar system than Aristarchus's view? *The latter's view ran counter to common sense and contradicted the traditional view of the world at that time.*

SKILLBUILDER Answers
1. Ptolemy incorrectly placed the earth at the center of the solar system. Aristarchus overestimated the size of the earth.
2. The estimate of the earth's circumference. The Hellenists had some knowledge of geometry to help explain their observations.

TEACHING OPTIONS CONNECTIONS ACROSS TIME AND PLACE

CONNECTIONS ACROSS THE CURRICULUM

Ptolemy and Columbus In the second century A.D., the astronomer Ptolemy of Alexandria was well known for his mapping skills and his studies of astronomy. In western Europe in the 1400s, Ptolemy's map of the world circulated widely. It showed most of the world covered by land and greatly underestimated the distance between Spain and China. See Rand McNally's *Atlas of World Exploration* for a copy of the map. Discuss with students what Christopher Columbus thought he would encounter, based on Ptolemy's map, on his first voyage across the Atlantic. How does the map help explain why he and others thought that sailing west would be a faster, easier route to Asia?

Mathematics: *How Did They Do It?* In the third century B.C., the Greek astronomer Eratosthenes computed the earth's circumference without leaving his home in northern Africa. He observed that the shadows cast by objects at noon grew shorter and shorter the closer one got to the equator. Invite the geometry teacher, or an interested student, to demonstrate to the class how this observation enabled Eratosthenes to make his calculations. Ask the teacher or student to illustrate his or her explanation with a large beachball or other sphere so that students can visualize the problem and its solution.

GlobalImpact
Pythagorean Theorem

Long before Pythagoras, the Egyptians in 2000 B.C. discovered a "magic 3—4—5" triangle. When they wanted crop fields with true right angles, they knotted a length of rope into 12 equal sections. They stretched the rope around three stakes to form a triangle that had sides of 3, 4, and 5 units. The angle opposite the side with 5 units was always a right angle. Have students try this for themselves.

3   5
right angle
4

Philosophy and Art

Key Ideas
- Stoics seek to control desire and live in harmony with natural and divine laws.
- Epicureans seek to harmonize body and mind.
- Hellenistic sculptors reject classical ideals and create more realistic works.

WORLD ART AND CULTURES TRANSPARENCIES
AT11 Marble bas-relief of Aristokles of Athens and marble figure of Nike of Samothrace

---

GlobalImpact

Greece, A.D. 800

Pythagorean Theorem

Geometry students remember Pythagoras for his theorem on the triangle but its principles were known earlier. This formula states that the square of a right triangle's hypotenuse equals the sum of the squared lengths of the two remaining sides. Chinese mathematicians knew this theory perhaps as early as 1100 B.C. Egyptian surveyors put it to practical use even earlier.

However, the work of the school Pythagoras founded caught the interest of later mathematicians. Shown is Euclid's proof in Greek along with a Chinese and an Arabic translation. The Arabs who conquered much of Alexander's empire spread Greek mathematical learning to the West. The formula became known as the Pythagorean theorem throughout the world.

Arabic, A.D. 1250   **Chinese, A.D. 1607**

Mathematics and Physics Both Eratosthenes and Aristarchus used a geometry text compiled by **Euclid** (YOO·klihd). Euclid was a highly regarded mathematician who opened a school of geometry in Alexandria. His best-known book, the *Elements,* contained 465 carefully presented geometry propositions and proofs. Muslim and European universities used the *Elements* until well into the 1900s. It is sometimes said that only the Bible has been more widely used and studied. Euclid's work is still the basis for courses in geometry.

Another important Hellenistic scientist, **Archimedes** (AHR·kuh·MEE·deez) of Syracuse, studied at Alexandria. He accurately estimated the value of pi (π)—the ratio of the circumference of a circle to its diameter. He showed its value to be between $3\frac{10}{71}$ and $3\frac{1}{7}$. Archimedes also explained the law of the lever and invented the compound pulley to lift heavy objects. The writer Plutarch described how Archimedes demonstrated to an audience of curious onlookers how something heavy can be moved by a small force:

> ### A VOICE FROM THE PAST
> Archimedes took a . . . ship . . . which had just been dragged up on land with great labor and many men; in this he placed her usual complement of men and cargo, and then sitting at some distance, without any trouble, by gently pulling with his hand the end of a system of pulleys, he dragged it towards him with as smooth and even a motion as if it were passing over the sea.
> **PLUTARCH,** *Parallel Lives: Marcellus*

Gifted in both geometry and physics, Archimedes also put his genius to practical use. He invented the Archimedes screw, a device that raised water from the ground, and a catapult or missile-throwing machine. Building on the knowledge of Archimedes, Hellenistic scientists later built a force pump, pneumatic machines, and even a steam engine.

Philosophy and Art

Like earlier Greek philosophers, Hellenistic scholars believed that the universe followed rational principles. They felt that philosophy offered the best way to understand these principles. The teachings of Plato and Aristotle continued to be very influential in Hellenistic philosophy. In the third century B.C., however, new schools of philosophy were concerned with how people should live their lives. Two major philosophies developed during the Hellenistic period—Stoicism and Epicureanism.

Stoicism and Epicureanism A Greek philosopher named Zeno (335–263 B.C.) founded the school of philosophy called Stoicism (STOH·ih·SIHZ·uhm). Stoics believed in a divine power who controlled the universe. They proposed that people should live a virtuous life in harmony with natural law. Stoics also preached that vices such as human desires, power, and wealth were dangerous distractions that should be controlled. Stoicism explained nature and provided an ethical approach to life. The philosophy also promoted social unity and encouraged its followers to focus on things they could control. Its ethical doctrine appealed to people of many different races, cultures, and economic backgrounds.

Task: Student groups select a Hellenistic scientist, mathematician, physicist, or philosopher mentioned in the section and make a presentation explaining the person's work and how it is viewed today.

Purpose: To understand the achievements and influence of Hellenistic scientists and thinkers.

Activity: Divide students into seven groups. Have each group choose one of the following people to

write about: Aristarchus, Eratosthenes, Euclid, Ptolemy, Archimedes, Zeno, Epicurus. The group should also copy or create illustrations, diagrams, photos, or drawings for their talk.

Building a Portfolio: Students can include a description of their presentation.

ALTERNATIVE ASSESSMENT BOOK
Standards for Evaluating a Cooperative Activity

Standards for Evaluation
The presentations should. . .

- clearly identify the person's achievements, using illustrations where appropriate
- explain current views of these contributions.
- demonstrate students' understanding of Hellenistic culture

Epicurus (EHP·uh·KYUR·uhs) founded the school of thought called Epicureanism. He taught that the universe was composed of atoms and ruled by gods who had no interest in humans. Epicurus believed that the only real objects were those that the five senses perceived. He taught that the greatest good and the highest pleasure came from virtuous conduct and the absence of pain. Epicureans proposed that the main goal of humans was to achieve harmony of body and mind. Today, the word *epicurean* means one devoted to pursuing human pleasures. However, during his lifetime, Epicurus advocated moderation in all things.

Realism in Sculpture Like science, sculpture flourished during the Hellenistic age. Rulers, wealthy merchants, and cities all purchased statues to honor the gods, commemorate heroes, and portray ordinary people in everyday situations. The largest known Hellenistic statue was created on the island of Rhodes. Known as the **Colossus of Rhodes,** this bronze statue stood more than 100 feet high. The colossal statue could not have stood with its feet straddling the harbor entrance, as legend suggests.

One of the seven wonders of the ancient world, the Colossus of Rhodes was toppled by an earthquake about 225 B.C. Later, the bronze was sold for scrap. Another great Hellenistic statue was discovered by archaeologists in 1863, the famous Winged Victory of Samothrace. It commemorates a naval victory by the Greeks against foes who would have enslaved them.

Hellenistic sculpture moved away from the harmonic balance and idealized forms of the classical age. Sculptors created more realistic and emotional works. Instead of the serene face and perfect body of an idealized man or woman, Hellenistic sculptors created more natural works. They felt free to explore new subjects, carving ordinary people such as an old, wrinkled peasant woman.

By 150 B.C., the Hellenistic world was in decline. A new city, Rome, was growing and gaining strength. Through Rome, Greek-style drama, architecture, sculpture, religion, and philosophy were preserved and eventually became the core of Western civilization.

Winged Victory of Samothrace is one of the few surviving examples of Hellenistic art. The dramatic statue is now in the Louvre in Paris. It shows a winged figure standing on the bow of a ship. Notice how the deep relief makes the wind appear to ripple through her gown.

Section 5 Assessment

1. TERMS & NAMES

Identify
- Hellenistic
- Alexandria
- Euclid
- Archimedes
- Colossus of Rhodes

2. TAKING NOTES

Using a chart like the one below, list Hellenistic achievements in each of the following categories.

Category	Achievements
astronomy	
geometry	
philosophy	
art	

Select one category from the chart and make a poster highlighting Hellenistic achievements in that area.

3. SYNTHESIZING

Describe how the growth of Alexander's empire spread Greek culture.

THINK ABOUT
- public vs. private art
- realistic vs. ideal representations
- the decline of the polis

4. ANALYZING THEMES

Cultural Interaction The Hellenistic culture brought together Egyptian, Greek, Persian, and Indian influences. How is American culture a combination of different influences? Give examples of those influences.

THINK ABOUT
- American immigration
- geographic regions/influences
- your own cultural background

Classical Greece **135**

Chapter **5** Assessment

TERMS & NAMES

1. Trojan War, p. 113
2. Homer, p. 114
3. polis, p. 115
4. phalanx, p. 115
5. classical art, p. 121
6. Aristotle, p. 125
7. Macedonia, p. 128
8. Alexander the Great, p. 129
9. Hellenistic, p. 132
10. Archimedes, p. 134

REVIEW QUESTIONS

Answers may vary on some questions.

11. Greece depended on sea travel because its mountaneous terrain made overland travel difficult.

12. Myths helped to explain the mysteries of nature and of human behavior, taught cultural values, and provided entertainment

13. Sparta, Athens

14. Delian League formed; Athens became the dominant city-state; flourishing of creativity in Athens

15. Pericles sought to strengthen Athenian democracy; to hold and strengthen Athens' empire; and to glorify Athens

16. Socrates, Plato, Aristotle

17. Greece was not united and had not agreed upon one policy regarding Macedonia; Philip had a powerful army and brilliant tactics

18. It reached across three continents from Greece in the west to India in the east, Macedonia in the north, and Egypt in the south.

19. Greek, Persian, Egyptian, Indian

20. They believed that the greatest good and highest pleasure came from right conduct and moderation in all things; the goal of life was pleasure; withdrawing from the world into one's self was considered a worthy achievement.

TERMS & NAMES

Briefly explain the importance of each of the following to Classical Greece.

1. Trojan War
2. Homer
3. polis
4. phalanx
5. classical art
6. Aristotle
7. Macedonia
8. Alexander the Great
9. Hellenistic
10. Archimedes

Interact *with* History

On page 110, you drew certain conclusions about what qualities Greeks valued without knowing details about their history. Now that you have read the chapter, reexamine the artworks and reread the Greeks' words. Conduct a class debate about how the values and heritage of Greece have influenced modern society.

REVIEW QUESTIONS

SECTION 1 *(pages 111–114)*
Cultures of the Mountains and the Sea

11. Why was sea travel so important to early Greece?

12. Why did the Greeks develop myths?

SECTION 2 *(pages 115–119)*
Warring City-States

13. What were the two most powerful city-states in early Greece?

14. What were the consequences of the Persian Wars?

SECTION 3 *(pages 120–125)*
Democracy and Greece's Golden Age

15. What were Pericles' three goals for Athens?

16. Who were the three renowned philosophers of the golden age?

SECTION 4 *(pages 128–131)*
Alexander—Empire Builder

17. Why was Greece so easily conquered by Macedonia?

18. What was the full extent of Alexander's empire before his death?

SECTION 5 *(pages 132–135)*
The Spread of Hellenistic Culture

19. What four influences blended to form Hellenistic culture?

20. What did the Epicureans believe?

Visual Summary

The Legacy of Greece

Government
- Direct democracy; citizens rule by majority vote
- Written code of laws
- Citizens bring charges of wrongdoing; trial by jury
- Expansion of citizenship to all free adult males, except foreigners

Arts
- Drama and poetry
- Sculpture portraying ideals of beauty
- Painted pottery showing scenes of Greek life
- Classical architecture

Greek Civilization

Culture
- Greek language
- Mythology about gods and goddesses
- Olympic Games
- Philosophers search for truth

Science and Technology
- Disagreement whether sun or earth at center of universe
- Accurate estimate of circumference of earth
- Euclid's geometry textbook
- Development of lever, pulley, pump

136 Chapter 5

Interact *with* History

Students should note that Greek culture has influenced nearly every aspect of modern society including the areas of government, law, arts and sciences, education, architecture, philosophy, and sports. Students may debate whether these influences have proved too confining, with their emphasis on the ideal and rational, or whether they provide standards that are relevant today.

CRITICAL THINKING

1. POWERFUL MEN

There is a saying that "the measure of man is what he does with power." Would you consider Alexander the Great or Pericles a "better" man? Why?

2. CLASSICAL GREEK INFLUENCES

THEME CULTURAL INTERACTION Copy the web below on your paper. Fill in examples of how classical Greece has influenced the United States.

3. EMPIRE BUILDERS

THEME EMPIRE BUILDING Thinking back to Pericles and Alexander the Great, what qualifications or characteristics do you think are needed for a leader to build an empire? Why?

4. ANALYZING PRIMARY SOURCES

In the following selection from *Politics*, Aristotle presents his views on where the power of the state should reside. His conclusions reflect the idea that moderation is the best path to civic virtue. Read the paragraph and then answer the questions that follow.

> **A VOICE FROM THE PAST**
> Where ought the sovereign power of the state to reside? . . . The state aims to consist as far as possible of those who are alike and equal, a condition found chiefly among the middle section. . . . The middle class is also the steadiest element, the least eager for change. They neither covet, like the poor the possessions of others, nor do others covet theirs, as the poor covet those of the rich. . . . Tyranny often emerges from an over-enthusiastic democracy or from an oligarchy, but much more rarely from middle class constitutions . . .

- What is Aristotle arguing here?
- How closely does this model of an ideal state correspond to the reality of Athenian democracy?
- Do you agree with Aristotle? Support your opinion.

CHAPTER ACTIVITIES

1. LIVING HISTORY: Unit Portfolio Project

THEME POWER AND AUTHORITY Your unit portfolio project focuses on how people in history have gained power and authority. For Chapter 5, you might use one of the following ideas.

- Write an epic poem (about 2–3 pages) about a legendary battle or hero that you read about in Chapter 5. Use Homer's *The Iliad* or *The Odyssey* as a reference.
- Design a museum exhibit with the title POWER AND AUTHORITY IN CLASSICAL GREECE. Include a sketch of the exhibit layout and a one-page description of the exhibit.
- Create an imaginary television talk show about this topic: What makes a leader successful? Guests should include people mentioned in this chapter. Prepare a list of questions the host will ask. Videotape the show.

2. CONNECT TO TODAY: Cooperative Learning

THEME CULTURAL INTERACTION Like many other facets of classical Greek culture, the influence of classical Greek art and architecture spread throughout the world, including the United States.

Create a "Then and Now" board showing examples of art and architecture in the United States that were influenced by classical Greek styles.

 Using the Internet or the library, find examples from classical Greece and then compare them with contemporary buildings and art.

- Find examples from classical Greece. Sketch, photocopy, or otherwise render them on a poster board.
- Find buildings or other art that show evidence of a classical Greek influence. Photograph or render them on the poster board.
- Label the board clearly. Include at least four examples.

3. INTERPRETING A TIME LINE

Revisit the unit time line on page 106. Look at the Chapter 5 section of the time line. Can you find evidence of how geography or a natural phenomenon might have influenced an event? Explain your conclusion.

FOCUS ON GEOGRAPHY

Notice the present-day boundaries that appear on this map of Alexander's empire.

- What modern nations were once part of this empire?
- How did the physical characteristics of the empire block its unification and lead to the formation of separate nations?

Connect to History
Compare Greece's size to the area it once controlled. How did it influence such a large area?

CHAPTER ACTIVITIES

1. LIVING HISTORY

Standards for Evaluation
Epic poems should meet the following criteria:

- Use a character or battle from the text and depict events in the formal style of Homer.
- Present one episode, with a beginning, middle, and end.

Standards for Evaluation
Museum exhibit designs should meet the following criteria:

- Illustrate the main ideas in the text.
- Showcase several people, events, and artifacts.
- Provide a layout of the museum.
- Describe what the exhibit will include and what ideas it will communicate.

Standards for Evaluation
Talk show projects should meet the following criteria:

- Have a host and panel members who represent people in the chapter.
- Create an introduction for the talk show host.
- Provide questions on the subject "What Makes a Leader Successful?"

2. CONNECT TO TODAY COOPERATIVE LEARNING

Standards for Evaluation
"Then and Now" displays should meet the following criteria:

- Show evidence of sound research.
- Contain students' drawings or photographs of local buildings.
- Provide a brief written summary of the information.

3. INTERPRETING A TIME LINE

Possible Responses: Minoan civilization may have been destroyed by an earthquake; mountainous terrain of Greece helped give rise to isolated city-states; narrow channel at Salamis influenced the course of the second Persian War.

FOCUS ON GEOGRAPHY

- Students may name the nations labeled in boldface caps.
- The empire was divided by deserts, mountain ranges, rivers, and seas.

Connect to History Possible Response: Alexander the Great spread Greek culture along the route of his conquests.

CRITICAL THINKING

1. POWERFUL MEN
Possible Responses: Students should be able to support their choices. Pericles was a better man because he initiated programs for the common good, such as public art and architecture projects, theater; Alexander the Great was a better man because he was able to create a huge empire, spread Greek culture, and gain the loyalty of his men and many former enemies.

2. CLASSICAL GREEK INFLUENCES
Answers may vary The U.S. government, architectural styles, philosophic traditions, art styles, value of the individual, sports, literature

3. EMPIRE BUILDERS
Possible Responses: charisma: to gather people's support; ideas: to help change or create a better place than before; military strategy: to help in empire building; opportunism: to know when an opportunity shows itself and quickly take advantage

4. ANALYZING PRIMARY SOURCES
Aristotle argues that political power is safest when placed in the middle classes. This ideal was not fully realized in Athens. Whether students agree or not, they should provide evidence to support their arguments.

CHAPTER 6

Ancient Rome and Early Christianity

	Key Ideas	COPY MASTERS	ASSESSMENT
SECTION 1 The Romans Create a Republic pp. 141–145	*The early Romans establish a republic on the Italian peninsula, conquer all of Italy, and defeat Carthage in a series of wars. The Romans create an extensive trade network.*	**In-Depth Resources: Unit 2** • **Guided Reading,** p. 20	PE *Section 1 Assessment,* p. 145 *Formal Assessment* • Section Quiz, p. 65 *Alternative Assessment Book* • Standards for Evaluating a Cooperative Activity
SECTION 2 The Roman Empire Brings Change pp. 146–152	*Problems in the republic lead to civil war. The republic collapses, and Julius Caesar becomes dictator. After Caesar's assassination, Octavian emerges as Rome's first emperor.*	**In-Depth Resources: Unit 2** • **Guided Reading,** p. 21 • **Geography Application:** The Roads of the Roman Empire, p. 26 • **Primary Source:** from *The Gallic War* by Julius Caesar, p. 28 • **Literature:** from *Julius Caesar* by William Shakespeare, p. 32 • **History Makers:** Cleopatra, p. 35; Julius Caesar, p. 36	PE *Section 2 Assessment,* p. 152 *Formal Assessment* • Section Quiz, p. 66 *Alternative Assessment Book* • Standards for Evaluating a Cooperative Activity
SECTION 3 The Rise of Christianity pp. 153–157	*Christianity begins with the teachings of Jesus in Judea. The new religion spreads quickly throughout the empire.*	**In-Depth Resources: Unit 2** • **Guided Reading,** p. 22 • **Primary Source:** from Emperor Galerius' Edict of Toleration, p. 29	PE *Section 3 Assessment,* p. 156 *Formal Assessment* • Section Quiz, p. 67 *Alternative Assessment Book* • Standards for Evaluating a Cooperative Activity
SECTION 4 The Decline of the Roman Empire pp. 158–163	*The Roman Empire splits in two. Economic, military, and political decay and outside invaders bring down the Western Roman Empire, but the eastern half survives.*	**In-Depth Resources: Unit 2** • **Guided Reading,** p. 23 • **Primary Source:** Dinner with Attila the Hun, from *Historical Graeci Minores* by Prescus, p. 30 • **Skillbuilder Practice:** Summarizing, p. 25	PE *Section 4 Assessment,* p. 162 *Formal Assessment* • Section Quiz, p. 68 *Alternative Assessment Book* • Standards for Evaluating a Cooperative Activity
SECTION 5 Rome and the Roots of Western Civilization pp. 164–167	*Greco-Roman culture continues to influence the arts, science and technology, government, and legal systems of the Western world and other parts of the globe.*	**In-Depth Resources: Unit 2** • **Guided Reading,** p. 24 • **Primary Source:** Letter on the Eruption of Vesuvius by Pliny the Younger, p. 31 • **Connections Across Time and Cultures:** Hellenistic Culture and Roman Culture, p. 37 • **Science and Technology:** Roman Construction Technology, p. 38	PE *Section 5 Assessment,* p. 167 *Formal Assessment* • Section Quiz, p. 69 *Alternative Assessment Book* • Standards for Evaluating a Cooperative Activity
CHAPTER RESOURCES	**Chapter Overview** *Rome becomes the center of an empire, which aids in the spread of Christianity. Eventually the Western Empire falls, while the Eastern Empire remains. The Greco-Roman culture helps shape Western thought and culture for centuries.*	*Telescoping the Times* • Chapter Summary, pp. 21–23 *Planning for Block Schedules*	PE *Chapter Assessment,* pp. 168–169 *Chapter Activities,* p. 169 *Formal Assessment* • Chapter Test, forms A and B, pp. 70–75 *Test Generator* *Alternative Assessment Book*

TECHNOLOGY

 Warm-Up Transparency 6

 Electronic Library of Primary Sources
- "Hannibal Crosses the Alps"

 World Art and Cultures Transparencies
- AT12 The Forum

 INTERNET RESOURCES
www.mlworldhistory.com

 Warm-Up Transparency 6

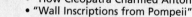 *Geography Transparencies*
- GT6 Expansion of the Roman Empire, 500 B.C.–A.D. 117

 Electronic Library of Primary Sources
- "How Cleopatra Charmed Antony"
- "Wall Inscriptions from Pompeii"

 Battles of the World
- The Battle of Alesia, 52 B.C.

 Warm-Up Transparency 6

 Electronic Library of Primary Sources
- from the Gospel According to Matthew in the King James Bible

 Religions of the World
- Christianity

 INTERNET RESOURCES
www.mlworldhistory.com

 Warm-Up Transparency 6

 Electronic Library of Primary Sources
- from *Agricola*
- from the *Satyricon*

 INTERNET RESOURCES
www.mlworldhistory.com

 Warm-Up Transparency 6

 World Art and Cultures Transparencies
- AT13 Roman Painting
- AT14 Trajan's Column

 Critical Thinking Transparencies
- CT6 Lasting Contributions of Roman Society
- CT42 Chapter 6 Visual Summary

 INTERNET RESOURCES
www.mlworldhistory.com

 Chapter Summaries on Audiocassette in English and Spanish

 INTERNET RESOURCES
www.mlworldhistory.com

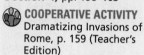 **Block Scheduling** (90 MINUTES)

Day 1
Section 1, pp. 141–145

 COOPERATIVE ACTIVITY
A Session of the Senate, p. 143 (Teacher's Edition)

Section 2, pp. 146–152

 COOPERATIVE ACTIVITY
A Debate About Historical Motives, p. 147 (Teacher's Edition)

Section Assessments, pp. 145, 152

Day 2
Section 3, pp. 153–157

COOPERATIVE ACTIVITY
Mapping Paul's Travels, p. 155 (Teacher's Edition)

Section 4, pp. 158–163

COOPERATIVE ACTIVITY
Dramatizing Invasions of Rome, p. 159 (Teacher's Edition)

Section Assessments, pp. 157, 162

Day 3
Section 5, pp. 164–167

COOPERATIVE ACTIVITY
Picture Essay on Roman Architecture, p. 165 (Teacher's Edition)

Section Assessment, p. 167

Chapter Assessment, pp. 168–169

Yearly Pacing *Chapter 6 Total:* 3 days *Yearly Total:* 85 days

 Planning for Block Schedules

Customizing for Special Needs

Students Acquiring English

 Access for Students Acquiring English
- **Guided Reading** for Sections 1–5 (Spanish), pp. 64–68
- **Chapter Summary** (Spanish), pp. 61–63
- **Skillbuilder Practice** Summarizing (Spanish), p. 69
- **Geography Application** The Roads of the Roman Empire (Spanish), p. 70–71

 Chapter Summaries on Audiocassette in English and Spanish

 INTERNET RESOURCES
www.mlworldhistory.com
The Diverse Classroom.

Less Proficient Readers

 In-Depth Resources: Unit 2
- **Guided Reading** for Sections 1–5, pp. 20–24
- **Skillbuilder Practice** Summarizing, p. 25
- **Geography Application** The Roads of the Roman Empire, p. 70

 Telescoping the Times
- Chapter Summary, pp. 21–23

 Chapter Summaries on Audiocassette

Gifted and Talented Students

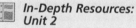 *In-Depth Resources: Unit 2*

Primary Sources:
- from *The Gallic War* by Julius Caesar, p. 28
- from Emperor Galerius's Edict of Toleration, p. 29
- Letter on the Eruption of Vesuvius by Pleny the Younger, p. 31

History Makers
- Cleopatra, p. 35
- Julius Caesar, p. 36

Connections to Literature READINGS FOR STUDENTS

 In-Depth Resources: Unit 2
Literature: from *Julius Caesar* by William Shakespeare, p. 32

Enrichment Reading
- **Graves, Robert**
  I, Claudius
  New York: Vintage, 1961

  This fascinating story of a Roman ruler is full of intrigue and murder.

McDougal Littell Literature Connections
- **William Shakespeare**
  Julius Caesar
  (with related readings)

  This great play concerns events surrounding the assassination of the Roman ruler Julius Caesar. Containing some of Shakespeare's greatest writing, the play raises important questions about loyalty and honor.

 PE = Pupil's Edition   = Overhead Transparency   = Software   = Video

 = Copy Master   = CD-ROM   = Audiocassette   = Internet

Ancient Rome and Early Christianity 500 B.C.–A.D. 500

Accessing Prior Knowledge and Making Predictions

• Ask students to list any Romans they can name (Julius Caesar, Marc Anthony) and discuss what they already know about them.

• Have students brainstorm a list of topics they predict will be covered in the chapter.

Making Inferences

• Ask students to locate Rome on the map on this page. Write the sentence "All roads lead to Rome" on the chalkboard. Ask students to discuss what this statement says both literally and figuratively about the place of Rome in the Roman world.

Geography Connection

Ask students to study the region around the Mediterranean Sea.

• Where are most of the major cities located in relation to bodies of water?

• What advantages would this location give to these cities?

CHAPTER 6 Ancient Rome and Early Christianity, 500 B.C.–A.D. 500

PREVIEWING THEMES

Power and Authority
The government of Rome began with kings, who were eventually displaced. Under the republic, government was based on laws and rule was by elected officials. Eventually, power was taken over by absolute rulers, called emperors, who exercised unlimited authority.

Empire Building
The Romans created a vast and powerful empire. At its height, it extended into three continents—Europe, Asia, and Africa. For several centuries, Rome brought Roman civilization and peace and prosperity to its empire. By the fifth century, internal weaknesses and outside invaders caused the empire to decline and eventually collapse.

Religious and Ethical Systems
Religion was important in the life of ancient Rome. Early Romans worshiped many gods, as had the Greeks. Jews in the Roman province of Judea were monotheistic, believing in only one god. From the home of the Jews arose another monotheistic religion, Christianity, based on the teachings of Jesus of Nazareth. Christianity grew and spread throughout Roman lands and beyond.

INTERNET CONNECTION

Visit us at www.mlworldhistory.com to learn more about ancient Rome and early Christianity.

138

THE ROMAN WORLD, 500 B.C.–A.D. 120

Settlements: Etruscan Italy, 500 B.C.
Settlements: Greek Italy, 500 B.C.
Roman Empire, 265 B.C.
Roman Empire, A.D. 120

375 Miles
750 Kilometers

N

North Sea
BRITAIN
Rhine River
GERMANY
EUROPE
GAUL
ATLANTIC OCEAN
Po River
Ravenna
Massilia
APPENNINES
Adriatic Sea
MACE
Tiber River
Rome
ITALY
Mediterranean Sea
Carthage
Syracuse
L

War elephants played an important role in many ancient battles, terrorizing and trampling the enemy. **Hannibal of Carthage** used them in his invasion of the Roman Empire in **218 B.C.** This vase from the period shows an elephant with its mahout, or driver. Archers shot at the enemy from the towerlike structure the elephant carried.

GEOGRAPHY THEMES

Location

Ask students to locate Rome on the map on these two pages. Have them point out other place names on the map that are familiar or still in use today, such as Greece, Paris, and Jerusalem.

Students can then list place names that are unfamiliar. Have them describe the territory called the "Roman World" in terms of the oceans and continents it touches.

Place

Using this map, ask students to describe the location of the city of Rome in relation to the Alps and to the Mediterranean Sea. Discuss the location of places students have studied, such as Egypt, in relation to Rome. Then ask students to brainstorm two or three ways geographical location affected the development of Rome.

ADDITIONAL RESOURCES

Books for the Teacher

• Ferrill, Arthur. *The Fall of the Roman Empire.* London: Thames and Hudson, Ltd., 1986. Excellent description of the Roman army.

• Kamm, Antony. *The Romans.* London and New York: Routledge and Kegan Paul, 1995. Overview of the Roman civilization.

• *Rome: Echoes of Imperial Glory.* Alexandria, VA: Time-Life, 1994.

Books for the Student

• Adkins, Lesley and Roy A. *Handbook to Life in Ancient Rome.* New York: Facts on File, 1994.

• Hardy, W.G. *The Greek and Roman World.* Cambridge, MA: Schenkman, 1970.

• Nardo, Don. *The Roman Empire.* San Diego: Lucent Books, 1994. Life of the Romans.

Videos

• *The Roman Empire and Its Civilization.* Society for Visual Education, 1985. 800-829-1900. Roman history and institutions.

• *Roman City.* PBS Video, 1994. 800-344-3337. Life in the frontier territory of Gaul.

• *Rome and Pompeii.* Cambridge Social Studies, 1993. 800-468-4227.

Software

• *Rome.* CD-ROM. Queue, 1994. 800-232-2224.

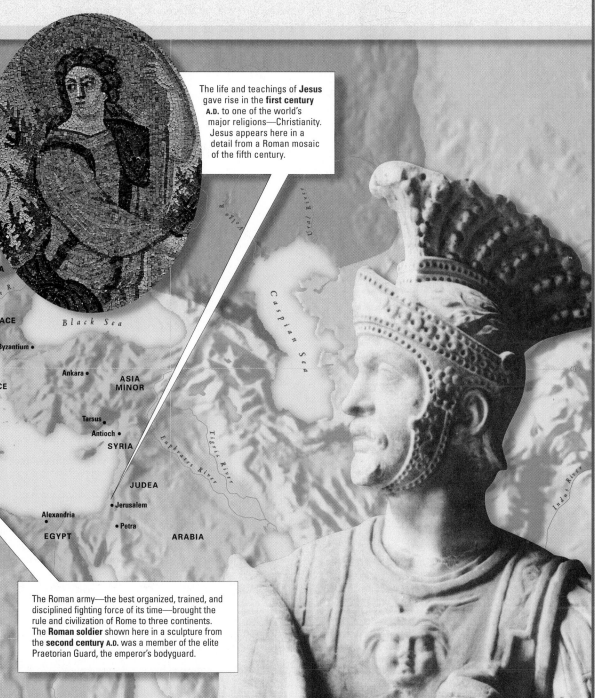

The life and teachings of **Jesus** gave rise in the **first century A.D.** to one of the world's major religions—Christianity. Jesus appears here in a detail from a Roman mosaic of the fifth century.

The Roman army—the best organized, trained, and disciplined fighting force of its time—brought the rule and civilization of Rome to three continents. The **Roman soldier** shown here in a sculpture from the **second century A.D.** was a member of the elite Praetorian Guard, the emperor's bodyguard.

HISTORY THROUGH ART

The Good Shepherd, Fifth-Century Mosaic

This beautiful mosaic from the fifth century A.D. was discovered in the mausoleum of a Roman nobleman, Galla Placidia, in Ravenna, Italy. Jesus is depicted here as the good shepherd (see page 154 for full view).

Mosaics are pictures made by setting small pieces (called tesserae) of colored glass, stone, ceramic, and even precious metals into mortar to decorate walls, floors, and ceilings. Mosaics become a permanent part of a building's structure. The Greeks were the first to use the technique, which was refined by the Romans and perfected by Christians and Muslims.

In *The Good Shepherd* mosaic, colored glass was used for the rich colors of the blue background and for Jesus' robe and cross. Candles lit in the mausoleum's interior would bring the colors vividly to life. Visitors to the vault might feel that they were in the presence of something more than just glass and stone.

Interpreting the Art Which stories told by Jesus does this mosaic represent? *Parable of good shepherd keeping flock safe, also of retrieving the lost sheep.* Why might someone prefer to have a mosaic rather than a painting in their home? *Possible answers: mosaics can be made part of the walls or flooring, have brighter colors, and are more permanent.*

This Interact with History feature motivates students by inviting them to put themselves in a key historical situation—the evaluation of a leader. As they think about deciding whether to support or oppose the leader, students will analyze the issues, explore their options, and become decision makers.

Purpose

- to set the stage for studying the Roman Empire and its legacy
- to help students understand the qualities of a good leader and the impact leaders can have
- to help students connect with the people and events they will study in this chapter

Teaching Strategy

Thinking Critically After students have reflected on this page, have them answer the key questions, giving reasons for their answers.

EXAMINING *the* ISSUES

Following are suggestions for addressing each bulleted question.

1 Ask students to list three adjectives that describe a good leader, and then compile a class list. Challenge students to reach a consensus on the top five qualities.

2 Which, if any, of the criticisms of the Roman leader apply to modern world leaders?

3 Have students compare leaders like President Lincoln and President Kennedy. What qualities did they share in common? How were they different?

Making Connections Ask students why a leader is important to a group or nation. What would happen if there were no leaders? Discuss with them the role of student leaders in their school.

Interact *with* History

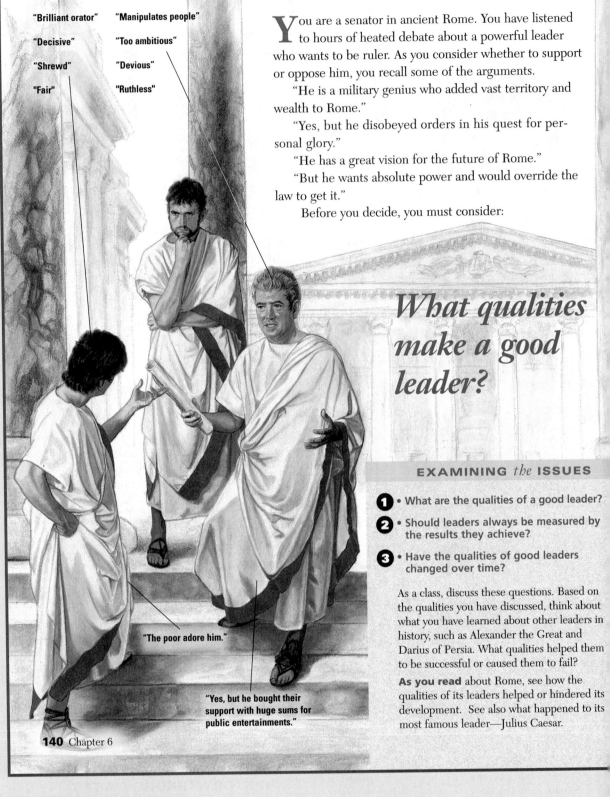

"Brilliant orator"   "Manipulates people"

"Decisive"   "Too ambitious"

"Shrewd"   "Devious"

"Fair"   "Ruthless"

"The poor adore him."

"Yes, but he bought their support with huge sums for public entertainments."

140 Chapter 6

You are a senator in ancient Rome. You have listened to hours of heated debate about a powerful leader who wants to be ruler. As you consider whether to support or oppose him, you recall some of the arguments.

"He is a military genius who added vast territory and wealth to Rome."

"Yes, but he disobeyed orders in his quest for personal glory."

"He has a great vision for the future of Rome."

"But he wants absolute power and would override the law to get it."

Before you decide, you must consider:

What qualities make a good leader?

EXAMINING *the* ISSUES

1 • What are the qualities of a good leader?

2 • Should leaders always be measured by the results they achieve?

3 • Have the qualities of good leaders changed over time?

As a class, discuss these questions. Based on the qualities you have discussed, think about what you have learned about other leaders in history, such as Alexander the Great and Darius of Persia. What qualities helped them to be successful or caused them to fail?

As you read about Rome, see how the qualities of its leaders helped or hindered its development. See also what happened to its most famous leader—Julius Caesar.

Follow Up

A feature on the chapter assessment will ask students to reevaluate their responses to the situation presented on this page.

① The Romans Create a Republic

TERMS & NAMES
- republic
- patrician
- plebeian
- tribune
- consul
- senate
- dictator
- legion
- Hannibal
- Scipio

MAIN IDEA

The early Romans established a republic, which grew powerful and spread its influence.

WHY IT MATTERS NOW

Some of the most fundamental values and institutions of Western civilization began in the Roman Republic.

SETTING THE STAGE While the great civilization of Greece was in decline, a new civilization to the west was developing and increasing its power. The city of Rome grew from a small village to a mighty empire. It adopted and preserved much of Greek art, philosophy, religion, and drama. And it created a lasting legacy of its own.

The Beginnings of Rome

According to Roman legend, the city was founded in 753 B.C. by Romulus and Remus, twin sons of the god Mars and a Latin princess. The twins were abandoned on the Tiber River as infants and raised by a she-wolf. They decided to build a city near the spot. In reality, Rome developed because of its strategic location and its fertile soil. Rome was built on seven rolling hills at a curve on the Tiber River, near the center of the Italian peninsula. It was midway between the Alps and Italy's southern tip. Rome also was near the midpoint of the Mediterranean Sea. The historian Livy wrote about the city's site:

> **A VOICE FROM THE PAST**
> Not without reason did gods and men choose this spot for the site of our city—the [salubrious] hills, the river to bring us produce from the inland regions and sea-borne commerce from abroad, the sea itself, near enough for convenience yet not so near as to bring danger from foreign fleets, our situation in the very heart of Italy—all these advantages make it of all places in the world the best for a city destined to grow great.
> **LIVY,** *The Early History of Rome*

The earliest settlers on the Italian peninsula arrived in prehistoric times. From about 1000 to 500 B.C., three groups inhabited the region and eventually battled for control. They were the Latins, the Greeks, and the Etruscans. The Latins were farmers and shepherds who wandered into Italy across the Alps around 1000 B.C. They settled on either side of the Tiber River in a region they called Latium. They built the original settlement at Rome, a cluster of wooden huts atop one of its seven hills, Palatine Hill. These settlers were the first Romans. (See the map on pages 138–139.)

Between 750 and 600 B.C., Greek settlers established about 50 colonies on the coasts of southern Italy and Sicily. The cities became prosperous and commercially active. They brought all of Italy, including Rome, into closer contact with Greek civilization. The Greeks also taught the Romans how to grow grapes and olives.

The Etruscans were native to northern Italy. They were skilled metalworkers and engineers. The Etruscans strongly influenced the development of Roman civilization. They had a system of writing, and the Romans adopted their alphabet. They also influenced Rome's architecture, especially the use of the arch.

Romans borrowed religious ideas from both the Greeks and the Etruscans. The Romans adopted Etruscan rituals that they believed helped them to win the favor of the gods. Roman gods even took on the personalities and legends of the Greek gods. Romans, however, gave their gods different names. Thus Zeus, the king of the Greek gods, became Jupiter in Rome, and Hera, the queen of the gods, became Juno.

Ancient Rome and Early Christianity **141**

THINK THROUGH HISTORY
A. Making Inferences Why was the geographical location of Rome an advantage?
A. Answer Rome's central location on Italian peninsula and its site at midpoint of Mediterranean good for trade.

Background
The name *Rome* is Etruscan in origin.

Section 1 Overview

OBJECTIVES

① To describe how geography influenced Rome's development.

② To explain the main institutions of the Roman Republic.

③ To describe how the Punic Wars helped increase Roman power.

SKILLBUILDER

- Interpreting charts, p. 143
- Interpreting maps: movement, region, p. 145

CRITICAL THINKING

- Making inferences, pp. 141, 142
- Recognizing effects, pp. 144, 145
- Forming opinions, p. 145
- Analyzing themes, p. 145

FOCUS
5-Minute Warm-Up

▶ **Making Judgments**
Answering these question will help students understand the rivalry between Rome and Carthage.

1. Read History Makers on p. 144. What goal did Hannibal's father give him for his life?

2. How did Hannibal fulfill his motto "conquer or die" at the end of his life?

　WARM-UP TRANSPARENCY 6

OBJECTIVE ① INSTRUCT

The Beginnings of Rome

▶ **Key Ideas**
- Rome is founded at a strategic location on the Italian peninsula.
- Latins, Greeks, and Etruscans settle Roman territory and intermix with one another.
- The Romans adopt religious, technical, and cultural ideas from the Greeks and Etruscans.

　IN-DEPTH RESOURCES: UNIT 1
　Guided Reading, p. 20

　ACCESS FOR STUDENTS ACQUIRING ENGLISH
　Guided Reading (Spanish), p 64

SECTION 1 RESOURCES

PRINT RESOURCES

　IN-DEPTH RESOURCES: UNIT 2
　Guided Reading, p. 20

　ACCESS FOR STUDENTS ACQUIRING ENGLISH
　Guided Reading (Spanish), p. 64

　FORMAL ASSESSMENT
　Section Quiz, p. 65

　ALTERNATIVE ASSESSMENT BOOK

TECHNOLOGY RESOURCES

　WORLD ART AND CULTURES TRANSPARENCIES
　AT12 The Forum

　CD-ROM
　Electronic Library of Primary Sources

　INTERNET www.mlworldhistory.com

The Early Republic

Around 600 B.C., an Etruscan became king. However, Rome was not controlled by the Etruscan cities. Under its Etruscan kings, Rome grew from a collection of hilltop villages to a city that covered nearly 500 square miles. Much of Rome was rich agricultural land. Various kings ordered the construction of Rome's first temples and public buildings. By royal order, the swampy valley below the Palatine Hill was drained, making a public meeting place. Later it became the Forum, the heart of Roman political life.

The last king of Rome was Tarquin the Proud. A harsh tyrant, he was driven from power in 509 B.C. Roman aristocrats, wealthy landowners who resented the Etruscan kings, overthrew him. The Romans declared they would never again be ruled by a king. They swore to put to death anyone who plotted to make himself king.

Having deposed the monarch, the Romans established a new government. They called it a republic, from the Latin phrase *res publica*, which means "public affairs." A **republic** is a form of government in which power rests with citizens who have the right to vote to select their leaders. In Rome, citizenship with voting rights was granted only to free-born male citizens.

Patricians and Plebeians In the early republic, different groups of Romans struggled for power. One group was the **patricians,** the aristocratic landowners who held most of the power. The other important group was the **plebeians,** the common farmers, artisans, and merchants who made up the majority of the population.

The patricians inherited their power and social status. They claimed that their ancestry gave them the authority to make laws for Rome and its people. The plebeians were citizens of Rome with the right to vote. They, however, were barred by law from holding most important government positions. In time, the Senate allowed them to form their own assembly and elect representatives called **tribunes.** Tribunes protected the rights of the plebeians from unfair acts of patrician officials. Eventually, plebeian pressure on the patricians gained them additional political power.

Twelve Tables An important victory for the plebeians was to force the creation of a written law code. With laws unwritten, patrician officials often interpreted the law to suit themselves. In 451 B.C., a group of ten officials began writing down Rome's laws. The laws were carved on twelve tablets, or tables, and hung in the Forum. They became the basis for later Roman law. The Twelve Tables established the idea that all free citizens, patricians and plebeians, had a right to the protection of the law.

Government Under the Republic In the first century B.C., Roman writers boasted that Rome had achieved a balanced government. What they meant was that their government had taken the best features of a monarchy (government by a king), an aristocracy (government by nobles), and a democracy (government by the people). In place of a king, Rome had two officials called **consuls.** Like kings, they commanded the army and directed the government. However, their power was limited. First, a consul's

Once the center of political power and intrigue, the Forum now lies in ruin in the center of modern Rome.

Comparing Republican Governments

	Rome	United States of America
Executive	Two consuls, elected by the assembly for one year—chief executives of the government and commanders-in-chief of the army.	A president, elected by the people for four years—chief executive of the government and commander-in-chief of the army.
Legislative	Senate of 300 members, chosen from aristocracy for life—controls foreign and financial policies, advises consuls.	Senate of 100 members, elected by the people for six-year terms—makes laws, advises president on foreign policy.
	Centuriate Assembly, all citizen-soldiers are members for life—selects consuls, makes laws.	House of Representatives of 435 members, elected by the people for two years—makes laws, originates revenue bills.
	Tribal Assembly, citizens grouped according to where they live are members for life—elects tribunes and makes laws.	
Judicial	Praetors, eight judges chosen for one year by Centuriate Assembly—two oversee civil and criminal courts (the others govern provinces).	Supreme Court, nine justices appointed for life by president—highest court, hears civil and criminal appeals cases.
Legal Code	Twelve Tables—a list of rules that were the basis of Roman legal system	U.S. Constitution—basic law of the United States
Citizenship	All adult male landowners	All native-born or naturalized persons

> **SKILLBUILDER: Interpreting Charts**
> 1. *What similarities do you see in the governments of the Roman Republic and the United States?*
> 2. *Which government seems more democratic? Why?*

Vocabulary
veto: comes from the Latin for "I forbid."

term was only one year long. The same person could not be elected consul again for ten years. Second, one consul could always overrule, or veto, the other's decisions.

The **senate** was the aristocratic branch of Rome's government. It had both legislative and administrative functions in the republic. By tradition, there were 300 members, chosen from the upper class of Roman society. Later, plebeians were allowed in the senate. Because membership was for life, the senate provided continuity. It also exercised enormous influence over both foreign and domestic policy.

The assemblies were the more democratic side of the government. All citizen-soldiers were members of the Centuriate Assembly. In the early days of the republic, this patrician-controlled assembly appointed the consuls and made laws. It had less power than the senate. An assembly organized by the plebeians, the Tribal Assembly, elected the tribunes and made laws for the common people. Later, it won the right to make laws for the republic.

In times of crisis, the republic could appoint a **dictator**—a leader who had absolute power to make laws and command the army. A dictator's power lasted for only six months. Dictators were chosen by the consuls and then elected by the senate.

The Roman Army All citizens who owned land were required to serve in the army. To secure certain public offices, ten years of military service were required. Roman soldiers were organized into large military units called legions. The Roman **legion** was made up of some 5,000 heavily armed foot soldiers (infantry). A

Vocabulary
legion: also means a multitude.

SPOTLIGHT ON

Roman Legions

The legions were the fighting force that spread Rome's power around the Mediterranean. Each legion had a nickname and a flag, called its eagle. Losing the eagle in battle was a disgrace.

Legions were self-sufficient and could live off the land. They did their own construction and even built roads and bridges.

Each soldier had armor, a helmet, a shield, a sword, and a dagger. He also carried tools for digging and stakes that became part of a wall around the camp. In addition, each soldier brought a cooking pot, clothing, and any other items he needed.

Ancient Rome and Early Christianity **143**

Rome Spreads Its Power

Key Ideas
• Rome conquers nearly all of Italy and begins to build its empire.
• Rome establishes a rich trading network but is challenged by Carthage, its main rival.
• In the Punic Wars, Rome defeats Carthage and dominates the Mediterranean.

HISTORY MAKERS
Hannibal

The Roman historian Livy tells of a conversation between Scipio and Hannibal, who met in Ephesus in 193 B.C. after Hannibal's defeat. Scipio asked the Carthage general to name the greatest military commanders of all time. Hannibal named Alexander, then Pyrrhus, and then himself. Scipio asked Hannibal how he would rank himself if he had beaten Scipio. Hannibal replied that then he would be first of all generals. Ask students if they think Hannibal was a great leader. Why or why not?

 ELECTRONIC LIBRARY OF PRIMARY SOURCES
"Hannibal Crosses the Alps"

---

group of soldiers on horseback (cavalry) supported each legion. Legions were divided into smaller groups of 80 men, each of which was called a century. In battle, the strength of the legion was its flexibility. Each century in a legion could act independently. The military organization and fighting skill of the Roman army were key factors in Rome's rise to greatness.

Rome Spreads Its Power

For hundreds of years after the founding of the republic, Rome sought to expand its territories through conquest and trade.

Rome Conquers Italy Roman power grew slowly but steadily as the legions battled for control of the Italian peninsula. By the fourth century B.C., Rome dominated central Italy. Then it suffered a major defeat. In 390 B.C., the Gauls, a Celtic people from the Po River Valley, north of the Apennines, sacked Rome. However, the Romans quickly recovered and rebuilt the city. They reestablished control by subduing one rival after another. They defeated the Etruscans to the north and the Greek city-states to the south. By 265 B.C., the Romans were masters of all Italy except the Po Valley.

Rome had different laws and treatment for different parts of its conquered territory. The neighboring Latins on the Tiber became full citizens of Rome. In territories farther from Rome, conquered peoples were given all the rights of Roman citizenship

HISTORY MAKERS

Hannibal
247–183 B.C.

When Hannibal was only a boy of nine, his father, Hamilcar Barca, a general in Carthage's army, made him swear that he would always hate Rome and seek to destroy it. Hannibal became a lifelong foe of Rome. His war cry was "conquer or die!"

After his defeat at the battle of Zama and Carthage's loss in the Second Punic War, Hannibal took refuge among Rome's enemies. He fought against Roman forces as an ally of the kings of Syria and Bithynia. When Roman agents came for him in Bithynia on the Black Sea in Anatolia in 183 B.C., he committed suicide rather than submit to Rome.

except the vote. All other conquered groups fell into a third category, allies of Rome. Rome did not interfere with its allies, as long as they sent troops to the Roman army and did not make treaties of friendship with any other state. The new citizens and allies became partners in Rome's growth. This lenient policy toward defeated enemies helped Rome to succeed in building a long-lasting empire. For the 250 years after 265 B.C., Roman power spread far beyond Italy.

Rome's Commercial Network Rome's location gave it easy access to the riches of the lands ringing the Mediterranean Sea. Roman merchants moved by land and sea. They traded Roman wine and olive oil for a variety of foods, raw materials, and manufactured goods from other lands. However, other large and powerful cities interfered with Roman access to the Mediterranean. The dominant city on the Mediterranean was Carthage, once a colony of Phoenicia. Carthage was located on a peninsula on the North African coast. Eventually Rome and Carthage fought bitterly for control of the Mediterranean.

War with Carthage In 264 B.C., Rome and Carthage went to war. This was the beginning of the long struggle known as the Punic Wars.

Between 264 and 146 B.C., Rome and Carthage fought three wars. The first, for control of Sicily and the western Mediterranean, lasted 23 years (264–241 B.C.). It ended in the defeat of Carthage. Rome took the rich, grain-growing island of Sicily as the chief prize of victory. It thus gained its first province, or administrative unit, overseas. An uneasy peace followed. The Second Punic War began in 218 B.C. The mastermind behind the war was a 29-year-old Carthaginian general named **Hannibal.** Hannibal was a brilliant military strategist who wanted to avenge Carthage's earlier defeat.

Hannibal assembled an army of 50,000 infantry, 9,000 cavalry, and 60 elephants with the intent of capturing Rome. To surprise the Romans, he led his army on a long trek from Spain across France and through the Alps. Although he had lost more than half his men and most of his elephants, Hannibal invaded northern Italy. For more than a decade, he marched his forces up and down the Italian peninsula at

C. Answer Since most conquered peoples were content with their treatment by Rome, the empire could concentrate on further expansion.
THINK THROUGH HISTORY
C. Recognizing Effects How did its treatment of conquered people affect Rome's expansion?

Vocabulary
Punic: comes from the Latin word for Phoenician.

Gifted and Talented Students:
Researching the Punic Wars
Have interested students research the Punic Wars in more detail. Students may present their final reports as different types of newspaper articles: editorials

for or against Roman destruction of Carthage; news stories about one or more important battles; or feature articles about the personalities involved in the struggle.

Economics: *Trade and Profit*
Review with students the basic economics of trade. Discuss the link between profit and individual enterprise. Then use these questions to explore how the desire for profit helped fuel the

commercial expansion of Rome: How did merchants hope to make a profit? *By selling goods for more than they paid for them.* How might merchants use their profits? *By starting a new venture or by lending money to other merchants.*

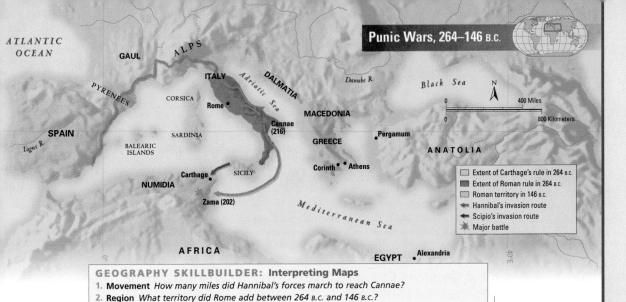

Punic Wars, 264–146 B.C.

ATLANTIC OCEAN

GAUL
ALPS
ITALY
PYRENEES
CORSICA
Rome
Adriatic Sea
DALMATIA
Danube R.
Black Sea
MACEDONIA
SPAIN
SARDINIA
BALEARIC ISLANDS
Tagus R.
Cannae (216)
GREECE
Pergamum
ANATOLIA
Corinth Athens
NUMIDIA
Carthage
SICILY
Zama (202)
Mediterranean Sea
AFRICA
EGYPT Alexandria

0 400 Miles
0 800 Kilometers
N

Extent of Carthage's rule in 264 B.C.
Extent of Roman rule in 264 B.C.
Roman territory in 146 B.C.
Hannibal's invasion route
Scipio's invasion route
Major battle

GEOGRAPHY SKILLBUILDER: Interpreting Maps
1. **Movement** How many miles did Hannibal's forces march to reach Cannae?
2. **Region** What territory did Rome add between 264 B.C. and 146 B.C.?

Vocabulary
pillaged: took goods by force in wartime.

will. His soldiers lived off the land. They seized crops and cattle and pillaged farmhouses. Hannibal won his greatest victory at Cannae, in 216 B.C. There his army inflicted enormous losses on the Romans. However, the Romans regrouped and with the aid of many allies stood firm. They prevented Hannibal from capturing Rome.

Finally the Romans found a daring military leader to match Hannibal's boldness. A general named **Scipio** (SIHP·ee·oh) devised a plan to attack Carthage. This strategy forced Hannibal to return to defend his native city. In 202 B.C., at Zama near Carthage, the Romans finally defeated Hannibal.

By the time of the Third Punic War (149–146 B.C.), Carthage was no longer a threat to Rome. Yet some Romans remembered the devastation Carthage had brought to Italy and were angered by its return to prosperity. An aged and influential senator named Cato ended all his speeches with the same message: "Carthage must be destroyed." In 149 B.C., Rome laid siege to Carthage. In 146 B.C., the city was set afire and its 50,000 inhabitants sold into slavery. Its territory was made the new province of Africa.

D. Answer
Eliminated major rival in area and gave Rome control of western half of the Mediterranean.

THINK THROUGH HISTORY
D. Recognizing Effects Why were the Punic Wars important?

Rome Controls the Mediterranean Rome's victories in the Punic Wars gave it domination over the western Mediterranean. The Romans went on to conquer the eastern half. Rome took control of Macedonia, Greece, and parts of Anatolia. By about 70 B.C., Rome's Mediterranean empire stretched from Anatolia on the east to Spain on the west.

Section 1 Assessment

1. TERMS & NAMES

Identify
- republic
- patrician
- plebeian
- tribune
- consul
- senate
- dictator
- legion
- Hannibal
- Scipio

2. TAKING NOTES

Using a time line like the one below, show the main events that mark the growth of Rome into a powerful republic.

509 B.C.—Romans overthrow Etruscan king

What was the most important event, and why do you think so?

3. FORMING OPINIONS

Do you think the Roman Republic owed its success more to its form of government or to its army? Why?

THINK ABOUT
- the structure of the republic
- how citizenship spread
- Rome's policies toward conquered peoples

4. ANALYZING THEMES

Power and Authority How did the office of dictator contribute to the balance and stability of the Roman Republic?

THINK ABOUT
- the role of the dictator
- the power of consuls
- the need for speedy decisions in a crisis

Ancient Rome and Early Christianity **145**

ANSWERS

1. TERMS & NAMES
republic, p. 142
patrician, p. 142
plebeian, p. 142
tribune, p. 142
consul, p. 142
senate, p. 143
dictator, p. 143
legion, p. 143
Hannibal, p. 144
Scipio, p. 145

2. TAKING NOTES
Possible Responses: 509 B.C.—republic established; 451 B.C.—Twelve Tables created; 265 B.C.—Italy conquered; 264–146 B.C.—Punic Wars fought; 70 B.C.—Rome controlled the Mediterranean. Answers will vary but students should explain their choices.

3. FORMING OPINIONS
Possible Responses: The army's conquests expanded the territory of Rome, which increased Rome's power and wealth. However, the republic that Rome established gave it a stability that allowed it to grow by absorbing conquered peoples or making them allies.

4. ANALYZING THEMES
Possible Response: A dictator could make the speedy decisions needed in a crisis, whereas the consuls could veto each other's decisions, and the senate and assembly might take too long to make critical decisions.

TERMS & NAMES
• civil war
• Julius Caesar
• triumvirate
• absolute ruler
• Augustus
• *Pax Romana*
• gladiator

2 The Roman Empire Brings Change

MAIN IDEA	WHY IT MATTERS NOW
The creation of the Roman Empire transformed Roman government, society, economy, and culture.	The Roman Empire has served throughout history as a model of political organization and control.

SETTING THE STAGE Rome grew rapidly, and growth brought political, economic, and social changes. Some leaders attempted reforms, but the republican government was unable to deal with the problems caused by these changes.

Expansion Creates Problems in the Republic

The Punic Wars and Rome's increasing wealth and expanding empire brought many problems. The most serious was the widening gap between rich and poor.

Rich landowners lived on huge estates called latifundia. Many of these estates had been created by occupying conquered lands and by taking farms left untended by soldiers serving in the army. Romans had made slaves of thousands of captured peoples during the wars. These slaves were made to work on the latifundia. By 100 B.C., slaves formed perhaps one-third of Rome's population.

Small farmers found it difficult to compete with the large estates run by slave labor. Some could not afford to repair the damage caused by Hannibal's invasion. They sold their lands to wealthy landowners. Many of these farmers, a large number of whom were returning soldiers, became homeless and jobless. Most stayed in the countryside and worked as seasonal migrant laborers. Some headed to Rome and other cities looking for work. The landless and unskilled in the cities found few jobs. They joined the ranks of the urban poor, a group that totaled about one-fourth of Roman society.

While wealthy Romans became corrupted by money and luxury, discontent arose among the slaves. Resentment also grew among the poor. Class tensions planted the seeds of the republic's collapse.

Cicero, Rome's greatest orator, was a strong defender of the republic. This marble bust is from the first century B.C.

The Republic Collapses

Two brothers, Tiberius and Gaius Gracchus (GRAK·us), attempted to help Rome's poor. As tribunes, they proposed reforms. The reforms included limiting the size of estates and giving land to the poor. Tiberius spoke eloquently about the plight of the landless former soldiers:

> **A VOICE FROM THE PAST**
> The savage beasts have their . . . dens . . . , but the men who bear arms and expose their lives for the safety of their country, enjoy . . . nothing more in it but the air and light . . . and wander from place to place with their wives and children.
> **TIBERIUS GRACCHUS** quoted in Plutarch, *The Lives of Noble Greeks and Romans*

The brothers were strongly opposed by senators who felt threatened by their ideas. Both met violent deaths—Tiberius in 133 B.C. and Gaius in 121 B.C. A period of **civil war,** or conflict between groups within the same country, followed their deaths.

THINK THROUGH HISTORY
A. Making Inferences What problems did increasing wealth bring to Rome?
A. Answer Problems included growing gap between rich and poor, more slavery, corruption, and growing numbers of homeless and jobless.

Changes in the character of the army had led to the rise of politically powerful military leaders. Generals began recruiting soldiers from the landless poor by promising them land. These soldiers fought for pay and owed allegiance only to their commander. They replaced the citizen-soldiers whose loyalty had been to the republic. It now was possible for a politician supported by his own troops to take over by force.

Two such generals were Gaius Marius and Lucius Cornelius Sulla. During 88–82 B.C., their supporters fought a bloody civil war. The war ended with Sulla being named dictator. Rivalries between generals continued to threaten the republic. Eventually an ambitious and daring leader, **Julius Caesar** (SEE·zuhr), emerged to bring order to Rome.

Julius Caesar Takes Control In 60 B.C., Julius Caesar joined forces with Crassus, a wealthy Roman, and Pompey, a popular general. With their help, Caesar was elected consul in 59 B.C. For the next ten years, these men dominated Rome as a **triumvirate,** a group of three rulers.

Caesar was a strong leader and a genius at military strategy. Abiding by tradition, he served only one year as consul. He then appointed himself governor of Gaul (now France). During 58–50 B.C., Caesar led his legions in a grueling but successful campaign to conquer all of Gaul. Because he shared fully in the hardships of war, he won his men's loyalty and devotion. Here he speaks of rallying his troops in battle:

> **A VOICE FROM THE PAST**
> I had no shield with me but I snatched one from a soldier in the rear ranks and went forward to the front line. Once there, I called to all the centurions by name and shouted encouragement to the rest of the men. . . . My arrival gave the troops fresh hope. . . .
> **JULIUS CAESAR,** *Commentaries*

The reports of Caesar's successes in Gaul made him very popular with the people of Rome. Pompey, who had become his political rival, feared Caesar's ambitions. In 50 B.C., the senate, at Pompey's urgings, ordered Caesar to disband his legions and return home.

Caesar's next move led to civil war. He defied the senate's order. On the night of January 10, 49 B.C., he took his army across the Rubicon River in Italy, the southern limit of the area he commanded. He marched his army swiftly toward Rome, and Pompey fled. Caesar's troops defeated Pompey's armies in Greece, Asia, Spain, and Egypt. In 46 B.C., Caesar returned to Rome, where he had the support of the army and the masses. That same year, the senate appointed him dictator; in 44 B.C., he was named dictator for life.

Caesar's Reforms Caesar governed as an **absolute ruler,** one who has total power. He made sweeping changes. He granted Roman citizenship to many people in the provinces. He expanded the senate, adding friends and supporters from Italy and the provinces. Caesar helped the poor by creating jobs, especially through the construction of new public buildings. He started colonies where the landless could own land and increased pay for soldiers.

Many nobles and senators were troubled by Caesar's growing power, success, and popularity. Some feared losing their influence. Others considered him a tyrant. A number of important senators, led by Marcus Brutus and Gaius Cassius, plotted his assassination. On March 15, 44 B.C., they stabbed him to death in the senate chamber.

Beginning of the Empire After Caesar's death, civil war broke out again and destroyed what was left of the Roman Republic. Three of Caesar's supporters banded

Background
All future Roman emperors would take the name "Caesar" as a title, and the word would be adopted in other languages: kaiser (German) and czar (Russian).

B. Possible Answer Caesar had total power, and there were no governmental means to remove him from office.

THINK THROUGH HISTORY
B. Analyzing Motives Why did Caesar's rivals feel they had to kill him?

HISTORY MAKERS

Julius Caesar
100–44 B.C.

In 44 B.C, on March 15 (known to Romans as the Ides of March), Caesar prepared to go to speak to the Senate, unaware that important senators plotted his death. According to legend, his wife, Calpurnia, begged him not to go. She said she had seen him in a dream dying in her arms of stab wounds. He earlier had been warned of danger by a soothsayer (fortune teller).

When Caesar arrived at the Senate chamber, he sat in his chair. Soon the plotters encircled him, took knives hidden in their togas, and stabbed him 23 times. They were led by Gaius Cassius and Caesar's friend Marcus Brutus. Caesar's last words were "Et tu, Brute?" ("You, too, Brutus?")

—sidebar column—

(continued from page 146)

dictator whose reforms and ambitions alarm the ruling class.

- Caesar's death signals the end of the republic, and Octavian becomes Rome's first emperor.

 IN-DEPTH RESOURCES: UNIT 2
History Makers: Cleopatra, p. 3
Primary Source: from *The Gallic War* by Julius Caesar, p. 28

 ELECTRONIC LIBRARY OF PRIMARY SOURCES
"How Cleopatra Charmed Antony"
"Wall Inscriptions from Pompeii"

 BATTLES OF THE WORLD
The Battle of Alesia, 52 B.C.

MORE ABOUT . . .
Marius and Sulla

As consul, Marius needed troops to put down a rebellion in North Africa. He promised recruits they would be given land in exchange for their service. However, the senate rejected Marius's promise. The soldiers were so angry that eventually civil war erupted. General Sulla was called to restore order. After this conflict, soldiers looked to their commanders, not to consuls or senators, to fulfill their needs.

HISTORY MAKERS
Julius Caesar

Caesar's most lasting reform was to set up a new calendar, called the Julian calendar. Based on a solar year instead of moon cycles, it had 365 days and added one extra day every fourth year. Ask students to find out why the seventh month, July, was named for Julius Caesar. *His birthday was in that month.*

 IN-DEPTH RESOURCES: UNIT 2
History Makers: Julius Caesar, p. 36

Ancient Rome and Early Christianity **147**

—bottom teaching band—

TEACHING OPTION | **BLOCK SCHEDULING** | **COOPERATIVE ACTIVITY: A Debate About Historical Motives** | **CLASS TIME 25 MINUTES**

Task: Students will research and debate a position on one of the following: "Resolved: Julius Caesar committed treason by crossing the Rubicon"; "Resolved: Assassins of Julius Caesar were motivated by a desire for power."

Purpose: To help students understand that motivations may be complex.

Activity: Divide students into four groups, assigning each group a topic and position. Each group will write an opening position statement and at least three arguments to support their positions. A representative from each group will debate the opposing side on their topic. Time each speaker. Have the class choose which side in each debate states and supports their position the best.

 Building a Portfolio: Students may wish to include their team's position statement and arguments in their portfolios.

ALTERNATIVE ASSESSMENT BOOK
Standards for Evaluating a Cooperative Activity

Standards for Evaluation
Debating teams should . . .

- make a clear position statement
- present three clear arguments
- use primary and secondary sources

Teacher's Edition **147**

together to crush the assassins. Caesar's 18-year-old grand-nephew and adopted son Octavian (ahk·TAY·vee·uhn) joined with an experienced general named Mark Antony and a powerful politician named Lepidus. In 43 B.C., they took control of Rome and ruled for ten years as the Second Triumvirate. Among those killed in the Triumvirate's purge of Caesar's enemies was Cicero, a defender of the republic in the senate.

The Second Triumvirate ended in jealousy and violence. Octavian forced Lepidus to retire. He and Mark Antony then became rivals. While leading troops against Rome's enemies in Anatolia, Mark Antony met Queen Cleopatra of Egypt. He fell in love with her and followed her to Egypt. Octavian accused Antony of plotting to rule Rome from Egypt, and another civil war erupted. Octavian defeated the combined forces of Antony and Cleopatra at the naval battle of Actium in 31 B.C. Later, Antony and Cleopatra committed suicide.

Octavian claimed he would restore the republic, and, in fact, did retain some of its forms and traditions. The senate, for example, continued to meet, and Octavian consulted it on important matters. However, Octavian became the unchallenged ruler of Rome. Eventually he accepted the title of **Augustus** (aw·GUHS·tuhs), or "exalted one." He also kept the title *imperator*, or "supreme military commander," a term from which *emperor* is derived. Rome was now an empire ruled by one man.

A Vast and Powerful Empire

Rome was at the peak of its power from the beginning of Augustus' rule in 27 B.C. to A.D. 180. For 207 years, peace reigned throughout the empire, except for some fighting with tribes along the borders. This period of peace and prosperity is known as the *Pax Romana*— "Roman peace."

During this time, the Roman Empire included more than 3 million square miles. Its population numbered between 60 and 80 million people. About 1 million people lived in the city of Rome itself.

An Economy Based on Agriculture and Trade Agriculture was the most important industry in the empire. All else depended on it. About 90 percent of the people were engaged in farming. Most Romans survived on the produce from their local area. Additional foodstuffs (when needed) and luxury items for the rich were obtained through trade. In Augustus' time, a silver coin called a denarius was in use throughout the empire. Having common coinage made trade between different parts of the empire much easier.

Rome had a vast trading network. Ships from the east traveled the Mediterranean protected by the Roman navy. Cities such as Corinth in Greece, Ephesus in Anatolia, and Antioch on the eastern coast of the Mediterranean grew wealthy. Rome also traded with China and India.

A complex network of roads linked the empire to such far-flung places as Persia and southern Russia. These roads were originally built by the Roman army for military purposes. The most important of the roads were the Silk Roads, named for the overland routes on which silk from China came through Asia to the Romans. Other luxury goods traveled along the same routes. Trade also brought Roman ways to the provinces and beyond.

Trade in the Roman Empire, A.D. 200

Roman Empire, A.D. 200

Trade Goods
- Grain
- Slaves
- Metals
- Olive oil
- Wine
- Silk
- Wild animals

0   500 Miles
0   1,000 Kilometers

GEOGRAPHY SKILLBUILDER: Interpreting Maps
1. **Movement** *From what three continents did trade goods come to Rome?*
2. **Location** *Which goods were supplied by all three areas?*

Managing a Huge Empire The borders of the Roman Empire measured some 10,000 miles. By the second century A.D., the empire reached from Spain to Mesopotamia, from North Africa to Britain. Included in its provinces were people of many languages, cultures, and customs.

The Roman army drew upon the men of the provinces as auxiliary, or support, forces. They were not citizens of Rome. But they learned Roman customs and became citizens when they were discharged from military service. In this way, the army also spread the Roman way of life to the provinces and Roman rights to non-Romans.

A Sound Government Augustus was Rome's ablest emperor. He stabilized the frontier, glorified Rome with splendid public buildings, and created a system of government that survived for centuries. He set up a civil service. That is, he paid workers to manage the affairs of government, such as the grain supply, tax collection, and the postal system. Although the senate still functioned, civil servants drawn from plebeians and even former slaves actually administered the empire.

After Augustus died in A.D. 14, the senate chose his adopted son Tiberius as his successor. During the *Pax Romana,* some of Rome's emperors were able and intelligent. Some were cruel. Two, Caligula and Nero, were either insane or unstable. Yet the system of government set up by Augustus proved to be stable. This was due mainly to the effectiveness of the civil service in carrying out day-to-day operations.

The Emperors and Succession Rome's peace and prosperity depended upon the orderly transfer of power. Because Rome had no written law for selecting a new emperor, a crisis or a civil war was always a possibility when an emperor died. The succession problem was temporarily solved by the leaders known as the Five Good Emperors. Beginning with Nerva in A.D. 96, each of them adopted as his heir a

Ancient Rome and Early Christianity **149**

THINK THROUGH HISTORY
C. Summarizing
Summarize how Roman culture spread to the provinces.

Vocabulary
civil service: persons employed in the civil administration of government

C. Answer The Romans brought customs and rights to the provinces through trade and through the use of men from the provinces as a part of the Roman army.

CONNECTIONS ACROSS TIME AND PLACE

Civil Service A government run by civil service employees is not a new idea. Although the Roman civil service is more well known in the West, China also established this system. The Sung Dynasty (A.D. 960-1279) took power away from aristocrats and gave it to the most qualified candidates.

In the United States, the civil service system began in the late 1800s. Up to that time, government jobs were handed out by the party in power. The assassination of President James Garfield by a frustrated office-seeker led to the creation of the Civil Service Commission to select candidates. Ask interested students to do a brief report on the U. S. civil service system— how many people are employed, what branches of government they serve, and how one becomes a civil servant.

Caligula

Bad Emperors		
Caligula	**Nero**	**Domitian**
• 37–41	• 54–68	• 81–96
• Mentally disturbed	• Good administrator but vicious	• Ruled dictatorially
• Assassinated after short, brutal reign	• Murdered many	• Feared treason everywhere and executed many
	• Persecuted Christians	• Assassinated
	• Committed suicide	

Nero

OBJECTIVE ④ INSTRUCT

Life in Imperial Rome
▶ **Key Ideas**
- Although men control family affairs, men and women are nearly social equals.
- Education is reserved for upper-class boys and not offered to girls or children of the poor.
- Slaves, widely used in Roman life, are regarded as property and have no legal rights.
- Rome adopts many Greek deities and creates a strong link between religion and government.
- To control the poor, Rome offers food and public spectacles.

 ELECTRONIC LIBRARY OF PRIMARY SOURCES
"Wall Inscriptions from Pompeii"

CRITICAL THINKING ACTIVITY
CLASS TIME: 10 MINUTES

Drawing Conclusions
Ask students to study the chart of "bad" and "good" Roman emperors. Discuss with the class the benefits and drawbacks of having one person rule an empire or nation. What are the advantages of a single ruler at the top? What are the risks?

Possible answers: *Advantages: decisions can be made more quickly, the ruler's ideas and programs can be carried out without opposition, the ruler can reform laws and social conditions, and he can appoint a good successor. Risks: An unjust or insane ruler can make arbitrary laws, persecute or execute people as he pleases, use the military and wealth of the nation for his own gain, and either fail to appoint a successor or appoint a bad one.*

---

respected leader who had the support of both the army and the people to be the next emperor. The reign of Marcus Aurelius, the last of the five, ended in A.D. 180. His death marked the beginning of the empire's decline and the end of the *Pax Romana*.

Life in Imperial Rome

Merchants, soldiers, slaves, foreigners, and philosophers all shared the crowded, noisy streets of Rome. However, most people in the Roman Empire did not live in the cities and towns. They lived in the countryside and worked on farms. For all Romans, life changed as Rome moved from republic to empire.

Men and Women Throughout its history, Rome emphasized the values of discipline, strength, and loyalty. A person with these qualities was said to have the important virtue of *gravitas*. The Romans were a practical people. They honored strength more than beauty, power more than grace, and usefulness more than elegance.

At the heart of Roman society was the family. By law and custom, the eldest man, known as the paterfamilias, or "father of the family," had power to rule the household. He controlled all property and had authority over all family members. He could disown newborn children, banish family members, or even sell them into slavery.

By the time of the empire's establishment, Roman women, both rich and poor, had become nearly the social equals of men. Upper-class women ran the household and were given authority and respect. They had more personal freedom than the women of Greece and than most women would have until the 19th century. Roman women could own property and testify in court. However, they could not vote. Officially they were expected to remain in the background. But they frequently attended the public baths (where most Romans went to bathe), plays, festivals, and games. Lower-class women could work at such jobs as spinners, weavers, shopkeepers, midwives, entertainers, and waitresses.

Children and Education Romans favored boy children over girls. Boys would become citizens with the right to vote and would carry on family traditions. Girls were not even given their own names. Daughters received the feminine form of the father's name, with "the elder" or "the younger" or a number added, such as Octavia II.

Few children went to school. Those who did were usually boys from noble or wealthy families. Their schooling continued until they officially became adults at 16. Girls from these families most

Vocabulary
gravitas: Latin for weightiness.

This Roman husband and wife from first-century Pompeii show their pride at being able to read and write. Their portrait includes writing implements and a scroll.

CUSTOMIZING FOR SPECIAL NEEDS

Students Acquiring English:
Vocabulary Activity Discuss with students the differences between each pair of words as used in the section to describe Roman values: strength/beauty; power/grace; usefulness/elegance. Have students work with those more proficient in English to think

of sentences that illustrate the different meanings of each pair. For example, students might write, *Plastic tableware has little* elegance *but its* usefulness *makes it popular.* Students might also draw pictures, for example, a picture of a wrestler to show power and of a dancer to show grace.

CONNECTIONS ACROSS TIME AND PLACE

The Transition of Power
Discuss with students why the orderly transition of power is important for a nation's stability and welfare. Tell students that in the United States, the Constitution stipulates that if something should happen to the president the order of succession is the vice

president, the Speaker of the House, the president pro tempore of the Senate, the secretary of state, and the secretary of the treasury. Ask them to find out the names of the current office holders. Who would be president if something should happen to the first three officials?

Good Emperors

Nerva	Trajan	Hadrian	Antoninus Pius	Marcus Aurelius
• 96–98	• 98–117	• 117–138	• 138–161	• 161–180
• Began custom of adopting heir	• Empire reached its greatest extent • Undertook vast building program • Enlarged social welfare	• Consolidated earlier conquests • Reorganized the bureaucracy	• Reign largely a period of peace and prosperity	• Brought empire to height of economic prosperity • Defeated invaders • Wrote philosophy

Trajan

THINK THROUGH HISTORY

D. Contrasting How did the lives of Roman girls differ from those of boys?

D. Answer Boys went to schools; most girls didn't; society favored boys; girls didn't get their own names; girls married early to older men.

often were educated at home and were prepared for marriage and motherhood. They were usually married at the age of 12 to 15, to much older husbands.

Poor children, whether they lived in the city or on a farm, had to work. They did not go to school and generally remained illiterate.

Slaves and Captivity Slavery was a significant part of Roman life. It was widespread and important to the economy. The Romans made more use of slaves than any previous civilization. Numbers of slaves may have reached as high as one-third of the population.

Most slaves were conquered peoples brought back by victorious Roman armies and included men, women, and children. Children born to slaves also became slaves. Slaves could be bought and sold. According to Roman law, slaves were the property of their owner. They could be punished, rewarded, set free, or put to death as their master saw fit. Slaves worked both in the city and on the farm. Many were treated cruelly and worked at hard labor all day long. Some—strong, healthy males—were forced to become **gladiators,** or professional fighters, who fought to the death in public contests. Other slaves, particularly those who worked in wealthy households, were better treated.

Occasionally, slaves would rebel. None of the slave revolts succeeded. More than a million slaves lost their lives attempting to gain their freedom.

Gods and Goddesses The earliest Romans worshipped powerful spirits or divine forces, called *numina,* that they thought resided in everything around them. Closely related to these spirits were the Lares (LAIR·eez), who were the guardian spirits of each family. After the Romans came into contact with Etruscans and Greeks, they began to think of these powerful spirits as having humanlike forms and individual personalities. They were given Roman names. Romans honored these powerful gods and goddesses through various rituals, hoping to gain favor and avoid misfortune.

In Rome, government and religion were linked. The deities were symbols of the state. Romans were expected to honor them not only in private rituals at shrines in their homes but also in public worship ceremonies conducted by priests in temples. Among the most important Roman gods and goddesses were Jupiter, father of the gods; Juno, his wife, who supposedly watched over women; and Minerva, goddess of wisdom and of the arts and crafts. During the empire, worship of the emperor also became part of the official religion of Rome.

By A.D. 100, many Romans had become interested in the religions of Asia. These religions had practices and beliefs that were more personal and emotional than the somber rituals connected with Rome's deities.

"Bread and Circuses"—Food and Entertainment By the time of the empire, wealth and social status had made huge differences in how people lived. Classes had little in common. The rich lived extravagantly. They spent large sums of money on homes, gardens, slaves, and luxuries. They gave banquets that lasted for many hours and included foods that were rare and costly, such as boiled ostrich and parrot-tongue pie.

Ancient Rome and Early Christianity **151**

Charioteers race their chariots in this ancient wall painting from Pompeii.

CONNECT to TODAY

Charioteers—Professional Athletes

Professional athletes are well-known personalities in the United States. In addition to the large salaries paid by their teams, athletes earn extra money endorsing products from athletic shoes to fast food. Some athletes even become actors; a few have become politicians.

Charioteers were popular athletes in ancient Rome. They were usually slaves or freed slaves. They raced for one of four "factions" (something like a modern team)—the whites, greens, reds, or blues. They competed for large cash prizes. When a charioteer won a big race, his portrait would appear on walls all over the city.

However, most people in Rome barely had the necessities of life. During the time of the empire, much of the city's population was unemployed. The government supported these people with daily rations of grain. In the shadow of Rome's great temples and public buildings, poor people crowded into rickety, sprawling tenements. Fire was a constant danger.

To distract and control the masses of Romans, the government provided free games, races, mock battles, and gladiator contests. By A.D. 250, there were 150 holidays a year. On these days of celebration, the Colosseum, a huge arena that could hold 50,000, would fill with the rich and the poor alike. The spectacles they watched combined bravery and cruelty, honor and violence. In the animal shows, wild creatures brought from distant lands, such as tigers, lions, and bears, fought to the death. In other contests, gladiators engaged in combat with animals or with each other, often until one of them was killed.

The *Pax Romana* had brought 200 years of peace and prosperity to Rome. During this time, a new religion called Christianity developed and began to spread throughout the empire.

Background
Many Roman cities had arenas similar to the Colosseum that were used for public entertainment.

Section 2 Assessment

1. TERMS & NAMES

Identify
- civil war
- Julius Caesar
- triumvirate
- absolute ruler
- Augustus
- *Pax Romana*
- gladiator

2. TAKING NOTES

Make a bulleted chart like the one below, showing how Rome changed during the *Pax Romana*.

Changes in Rome
•
•
•

Which changes do you consider negative? Why?

3. ANALYZING CAUSES

What role did Julius Caesar play in the decline of the republic and the rise of the empire?

THINK ABOUT
- the problems facing the republic
- how Caesar helped restore order
- Caesar's defiance of the senate
- Caesar's rule as dictator

4. THEME ACTIVITY

Empire Building Role-play a discussion in the Roman Forum, in which various members of society comment on conditions in the Roman Empire during the *Pax Romana*. Participants might include a senator, a civil servant, a slave, a merchant, and a landless and jobless former soldier. Working in small teams, one for each participant, focus on the changes that have come with the rise of the empire.

152 CHAPTER 6

3 The Rise of Christianity

TERMS & NAMES
- Jesus
- apostle
- Peter
- Paul
- Diaspora
- bishop
- pope
- Constantine
- heresy

MAIN IDEA

Christianity arose in Roman-occupied Judea and spread throughout the Roman Empire.

WHY IT MATTERS NOW

As the world's most widespread religion, Christianity guides the lives of millions today.

SETTING THE STAGE The worship of Roman gods was impersonal, practiced without a great deal of emotion. Priests used sacred rites to intercede on behalf of worshippers. A new religion called Christianity, born as a movement within Judaism, emphasized the personal relationship between God and people. It attracted many Romans.

Jews Come Under Roman Rule

Roman power spread to Judea, the home of the Jews, around 63 B.C. At first the Jewish kingdom remained independent, at least in name. Jewish kings ruled as representatives of Rome. Some Jews allied with the Romans and accepted their plans to "Romanize" Jerusalem. The ruler Herod, for example, was a Romanized Jew. His loyalties were divided between Rome and the Jewish people, but he ruled with an iron hand and angered many Jews. When he died, the Jews began a revolt against Roman influence that lasted for ten years. Rome finally took control of the Jewish kingdom and made it the province of Judea in A.D. 6.

In an attempt to restore order in Judea, the Romans gave control of religious matters and local affairs to the Jewish court called the Sanhedrin. Jews were divided into two major factions. One group, called the Zealots, wanted to rid their homeland of the Romans. Another group believed that the Messiah, or savior, was soon to appear. According to biblical tradition, God had promised that the Messiah would restore the kingdom of the Jews.

Vocabulary
Zealot: has come to mean a fanatically committed person.

The Life and Teachings of Jesus

Jesus was born in the town of Bethlehem in Judea. The date is uncertain but is thought to have been around 6 to 4 B.C. Jesus was both a Jew and a Roman subject. He was raised in the village of Nazareth in northern Palestine. Jesus was baptized by the prophet known as John the Baptist. As a young man, he took up the trade of carpentry.

Background
The original dating of the birth of Jesus made in the sixth century A.D. is now generally recognized as being four to six years in error.

The cross became the universal symbol of Christianity. This jewel-studded cross was made by a goldsmith centuries after the death of Jesus.

Jesus' Message At the age of 30 Jesus began his public ministry. For the next three years, he preached, taught, did good works, and reportedly performed miracles. His teachings contained many ideas from Jewish tradition, such as monotheism, or belief in only one god, and the principles of the Ten Commandments. Jesus emphasized God's personal relationship to each human being. He stressed the importance of people's love for God, their neighbors, their enemies, and even themselves. He also taught that God would end wickedness in the world and would establish an eternal kingdom after death for people who sincerely repented their sins.

Jesus gathered about himself twelve special disciples, or pupils. Historical records of the time mention very little about Jesus. The main source of information about Jesus' life and teachings are the Gospels, the first four books of the New Testament of the Bible. Some of the Gospels are thought to have been written by one or more of Jesus' disciples, who later came to be called **apostles**.

Vocabulary
Gospel: means good news.

Ancient Rome and Early Christianity **153**

Section 3 Overview

OBJECTIVES

① To explain how the Jews came under Roman rule.

② To summarize the life and teachings of Jesus.

③ To trace the spread of Christianity in the Roman Empire.

④ To analyze Christianity's appeal.

SKILLBUILDER
- Interpreting maps: location, region, p. 156

CRITICAL THINKING
- Hypothesizing, pp. 154, 157
- Recognizing effects, p. 155
- Making inferences, p. 156
- Analyzing motives, p. 157
- Analyzing themes, p. 157

FOCUS

5-Minute Warm-Up

▶ **Summarizing**
Have students answer these questions to examine the rise and influence of Christianity.

1. Study the map on p. 156. What major cities had become Christianized by A.D. 325?

2. Could a missionary reach all of these cities by sea?

  WARM-UP TRANSPARENCY 6

OBJECTIVE ① INSTRUCT

Jews Come Under Roman Rule

▶ **Key Ideas**
- Although some Jews rebel under Roman rule, others look for a Messiah to free them.

  IN-DEPTH RESOURCES: UNIT 2
  Guided Reading, p. 23

  ACCESS FOR STUDENTS ACQUIRING ENGLISH
  Guided Reading (Spanish), p. 66

OBJECTIVE ② INSTRUCT

The Life and Teachings of Jesus

▶ **Key Ideas**
- Jesus preaches a new testament; his apostles spread his teachings.

Teacher's Edition **153**

Christianity Spreads Through the Empire

(See page 155.)

▶ **Key Ideas**

- In spite of Roman opposition, Christianity slowly spreads throughout the empire.
- The apostle Paul helps make Christianity more universal.
- After the Zealot revolt, the Romans destroy Jerusalem and drive most Jews from Judea.
- Christianity, despite persecution, becomes a powerful new religion and spreads beyond the empire.

 RELIGIONS OF THE WORLD
Christianity

CRITICAL THINKING ACTIVITY

CLASS TIME: 10 MINUTES

Comparing

To help students recognize some of the similarities and differences between Christianity and Judaism, work with the class to complete the Venn diagram below, using phrases such as the following: belief in one God *shared*; belief that Jesus is the Messiah *Christian*; belief that Jews are the chosen people of God *Jewish*; acceptance of Gentiles and Jews alike *Christian*; adherence to Jewish law *Jewish*.

Belief in one God

Christians — Jews

Jesus is Messiah | Chosen people

Jesus is portrayed in this glass mosaic from the fifth century as "the good shepherd," tending his flock, watching over the faithful.

As Jesus preached from town to town, his fame grew. He attracted large crowds, and many people were touched by his message. Many believed him to be the long-awaited Messiah, the son of God. Because Jesus ignored wealth and status, his message had special appeal to the poor. "Blessed are the meek: for they shall inherit the earth," he said. His words, as related in the Gospels, are simple and direct:

> **THE BIBLE**
> Love your enemies, do good to those who hate you, bless those who curse you, and pray for those who mistreat you. If anyone hits you on the cheek, let him hit the other one too; if someone takes your coat, let him have your shirt as well. Give to everyone who asks you for something, and when someone takes what is yours, do not ask for it back. Do for others just what you want them to do for you.
> The Gospel of Luke, 6:27–31

Jesus' Death Jesus' growing popularity concerned both Roman and Jewish leaders. When Jesus visited Jerusalem about A.D. 29, enthusiastic crowds greeted him as the Messiah, or king. The chief priests of the Jews denied that Jesus was the Messiah. They said his teachings were blasphemy, or contempt for God. The Roman governor Pontius Pilate thought that Jesus, whom the Romans mockingly called "King of the Jews," challenged the authority of Rome. Pilate arrested Jesus and sentenced him to be crucified, or nailed to a large wooden cross to die.

After Jesus' death, his body was placed in a tomb. According to the Gospels, three days later his body was gone, and a living Jesus began appearing to his followers. Then one day it was said that he ascended into heaven. The apostles were more than ever convinced that Jesus was the Messiah. It was from this belief that Jesus came to be referred to as Jesus Christ. *Christos* is a Greek word meaning "messiah" or "savior." The name Christianity was derived from "Christ."

The followers of Jesus were strengthened by their conviction that he had triumphed over death. Led by **Peter,** the first apostle, they spread the teachings of Jesus throughout Palestine and Syria. The cross on which he had been crucified became a symbol for their beliefs.

154 Chapter 6

THINK THROUGH HISTORY
A. Hypothesizing
Why did the followers of Jesus think he was the Messiah?
A. Answer He reportedly worked miracles, did good works, preached the word of God, rose after death.

EXPLORING PRIMARY SOURCES: New Testament Parables

Tell students that Jesus often used everyday situations and told stories called parables to teach moral lessons. The parable of the prodigal son tells about a young man who leaves home and spends all his inheritance. After living in poverty, the young man returns to ask his father's forgiveness. He is welcomed home with open arms. Through the parable, Jesus taught that God's love could overcome sin.

Ask students to find examples of other parables: the two builders and the two foundations (Matthew 7:24-27); the sower and the soils (Matthew 13: 3-8); the good Samaritan (Luke 10:30-37). Have them summarize the parables and discuss Jesus' use of commonplace events to make his points.

 ELECTRONIC LIBRARY OF PRIMARY SOURCES
from the Gospel According to Matthew in the King James Bible

Christianity Spreads Through the Empire

Jesus' teachings did not contradict Jewish law, and his first followers were Jews. Soon, however, these followers began to create a new religion based on his messages. Despite political and religious opposition, the new religion of Christianity spread slowly but steadily throughout the Roman Empire.

Paul's Mission One man, the apostle **Paul,** had enormous influence on Christianity's development. Paul was a Jew whose Hebrew name was Saul. He had never met Jesus and at first was an enemy of Christianity. While traveling to Damascus in Syria, he reportedly had a vision of Christ. He then began using his Roman name, Paul, and spent the rest of his life spreading and interpreting Christ's teachings.

The *Pax Romana*, which made travel and the exchange of ideas fairly safe, provided the ideal conditions for Christianity to spread. The excellent Roman road system made passage by land easy, and common languages—Latin and Greek—allowed the message to be easily understood. Paul was able to travel freely from city to city around the eastern Mediterranean to preach. He wrote influential letters, called Epistles, to groups of believers. In his teaching, Paul stressed that Jesus was the son of God who died for people's sins. He also declared that Christianity should welcome all converts, Jew or Gentile (non-Jew). He said: "There is neither Jew nor Greek, there is neither slave nor free, there is neither male nor female; for you are all one in Christ Jesus." It was this universality that enabled Christianity to become more than just a local religion.

THINK THROUGH HISTORY
B. Recognizing Effects How did conditions in the Roman Empire contribute to the spread of Christianity?
B. Answer Travel was easy and safe because of peace in Empire.

Jewish Rebellion During the early years of Christianity, much Roman attention was focused on the land of Jesus' birth and on the Jews. In A.D. 66, a band of Zealots rebelled against Rome. In A.D. 70, the Romans stormed Jerusalem and destroyed the Temple complex. All that remained was a western portion of the wall, which today is the holiest Jewish shrine. The Jewish fortress near Masada held out until A.D. 73. About a half million Jews were killed in the course of this rebellion.

The Jews made another attempt to break free of the Romans in A.D. 132. Another half-million Jews died in three years of fighting. Although the Jewish religion survived, the Jewish political state ceased to exist for more than 1,800 years. Most Jews were driven from their homeland into exile. This dispersal of the Jews is called the **Diaspora.**

Persecution of the Christians Christians also posed a problem for Roman rulers because Christians refused to worship Roman gods. This refusal was seen as opposition to Roman rule. Some Roman rulers also used Christians as scapegoats for political and economic troubles. In A.D. 64, for example, when the emperor Nero was blamed for a disastrous fire in Rome, he said Christians were responsible and ordered them to be persecuted. Both the apostles Peter and Paul were put to death in Rome some time after A.D. 60.

Vocabulary
scapegoats: groups or individuals that innocently bear the blame for others

The emperors who followed Nero in the first century did not continue the persecutions. Later, however, as the *Pax Romana* began to crumble, the Romans exiled, imprisoned, or executed Christians for refusing to worship Roman gods. Thousands were crucified, burned, or killed by wild animals in the circus arenas. Other Christians and even some non-Christians regarded persecuted Christians as martyrs. Martyrs were people willing to sacrifice their lives for the sake of a belief or a cause.

Despite persecution, Christianity became a powerful religious force. By the late third century A.D., there were millions of Christians in the Roman Empire. Missionaries spread the faith throughout the empire and beyond.

Ancient Rome and Early Christianity **155**

GlobalImpact
The Jewish Diaspora

The movement of Jews into Europe and other parts of the world occurred slowly. Ask students to research some of the topics connected with that story, such as the leader Judas Maccabee, the siege of Masada, the development of Yiddish language, the Hebrew calendar, the building of synagogues, the Bar Kokhba Revolt. Direct students to references such as *A Historical Atlas of the Jewish People from the Times of the Patriarchs to the Present,* ed. by Eli Barnavi (Knopf, 1992) and *Pictorial History of the Jewish People* by Nathan Ausubel (Crown, 1984).

MORE ABOUT . . .
Persecution of Christians

According to the Roman historian Tacitus, Nero blamed the Christians of Rome for the fire that destroyed the slums. He killed the Christians in gruesome ways: they were covered with animal skins and then attacked by dogs or fastened to crosses and set on fire. The Christians' strength under such persecution inspired many onlookers to convert to Christianity.

GlobalImpact

The Jewish Diaspora

Centuries of Jewish exile followed the destruction of their Temple and the fall of Jerusalem in A.D. 70. This period is called the Diaspora, from the Greek word for "dispersal." Jews fled to many parts of the world. Some moved to Babylonia and the Arabian Desert. Others went to Syria, Egypt, and Spain.

Eventually, Jews spread into France, England, and the Rhineland, where they lived in small groups. In the 1100s, many European Jews were expelled from their homes. Some moved to Turkey, Palestine, and Syria. Others went to Poland and nearby neighboring areas.

The statelessness of the Jews did not end until the creation of Israel in 1948.

TEACHING OPTION | **BLOCK SCHEDULING**

COOPERATIVE ACTIVITY: Mapping Paul's Travels

CLASS TIME 20 MINUTES

Task: Students will research the life and travels of Paul and create three maps showing his three voyages.

Purpose: To learn about the mission of Paul and the cities he visited.

Activity: Paul made three separate voyages in his missionary work. Divide students into three groups and assign each group one of the three voyages to research. Each group will briefly describe the cities that Paul visited, summarize his missionary activities in each city during a particular voyage, and draw a map showing his route among the cities. Each group can present their findings to the class, beginning with the first voyage.

Building a Portfolio: Students who include a copy of the report and map in their portfolio should write a brief description of their contribution.

ALTERNATIVE ASSESSMENT BOOK
Standards for Evaluating a Cooperative Activity

Standards for Evaluation
Maps and presentations should . . .
• demonstrate students' knowledge of Paul's mission and voyages
• show clearly his travel routes
• describe the cities visited on each trip

Teacher's Edition **155**

Spread of Christianity in the Roman World to A.D. 500

Interpreting the Map Ask students to notice the similarities between the spread of Christianity and the boundaries of the Roman Empire. Then ask them to notice where Christianity developed first. *near the most populated areas* Have them study the geographic barriers to travel such as mountains, rivers, and oceans. Ask them to discuss why they think the spread of Christianity paralleled the boundaries of the empire so closely. *Missionaries used the roads and trade routes of the empire to travel to distance places.*

Extension Activity After they have studied the map, ask students to write one sentence that summarizes the information the map presents. *From 325 to 500, Christianity developed first in the major cities, then spread outward to reach every province of the Roman Empire.*

SKILLBUILDER Answers
1. Anatolia
2. Britain to the north, Egypt to the south, Spain to the west, and Armenia to the east.

Spread of Christianity in the Roman World to A.D. 500

Legend:
- Christian areas around 325
- Christian areas around 500
- Boundary of Roman Empire, 395

GEOGRAPHY SKILLBUILDER: Interpreting Maps
1. **Location** Where was Christianity most widespread in A.D. 325?
2. **Region** What was the extent (north to south, east to west) of Christianity's spread by A.D. 500?

OBJECTIVE ④ INSTRUCT

A World Religion

► **Key Ideas**
- Christianity grows because it appeals to common people, portrays a loving God, and promises eternal life after death.
- Christians establish a Church hierarchy and make Rome the official center of the Church.
- Emperor Constantine converts to Christianity and officially ends the persecution of Christians.
- Church leaders compile the New Testament, fight heresies, and define the Church's basic beliefs.

A World Religion

The widespread appeal of Christianity was the result of a variety of reasons. Christianity grew because it:

- embraced all people—men and women; slaves, the poor, and nobles.
- gave hope to the powerless.
- appealed to those who were repelled by the extravagances of imperial Rome.
- offered a personal relationship with a loving God.
- promised eternal life after death.

Early Christian Church Christians soon began to give their religion a structure, much as the Roman Empire had a hierarchy. At the local level, a priest led each small group of Christians. A **bishop,** who was also a priest, supervised several local churches. The apostle Peter had traveled to Rome from Jerusalem and became the first bishop there. According to tradition, Jesus referred to Peter as the "rock" on which the Christian Church would be built. As a result, all priests and bishops traced their authority to him.

Eventually, every major city had its own bishop. However, later bishops of Rome claimed to be the heirs of Peter. These bishops said that Peter was the first **pope,** the father or head of the Christian Church. They said that whoever was bishop of Rome was also the leader of the whole Church. Also, as Rome was the capital of the empire, it seemed the logical choice to be the center of the Church.

Constantine Accepts Christianity A critical moment in Christianity occurred in A.D. 312, when the Roman emperor **Constantine** was fighting three rivals for his title. He had marched to the Tiber River at Rome to battle his chief rival. On the day before the battle at Milvian Bridge, Constantine prayed for divine help. He reported that he then

THINK THROUGH HISTORY
C. Making Inferences Why were the citizens of the Roman Empire so receptive to a new religion at this time?

Vocabulary
hierarchy: a group of persons organized in order of ranks, with each level subject to the authority of the one above.

C. Answer It embraced all people, gave hope to powerless, appealed to those who were repelled by Roman extravagances, offered personal relationship with God, promised life after death.

CREATING AN ORGANIZATION CHART

Task: Students will use information in the text to create an organization chart of the early Christian Church

Purpose: To learn how early Christians organized their new religion

Materials Needed: Textbooks, paper, and pencils or pens

Activity: Have students work in small groups to construct an organization chart of the Church, based on the description in the text. Charts should show the pope at the top, supported by a row of bishops, who oversee the more numerous local priests, who minister to the people. Students should label each box clearly and list the basic function of each level in the hierarchy.

Conclusion: Discuss with students why the early Christians may have needed to organize their new religion and what advantages such an organization gives to its members. How does this system reflect the Roman influence of many early Christians? *The Church hierarchy is based on the Roman system of government.*

saw a cross of light in the heavens bearing the inscription, "In this sign, conquer." Constantine ordered artisans to put the Christian symbol on his soldier's shields. Constantine and his troops were victorious in battle. He gave credit for his success to the help of the Christian God.

In the next year, A.D. 313, Constantine announced an end to the persecution of Christians. In the Edict of Milan, he declared Christianity to be one of the religions approved by the emperor. The edict granted "both to the Christians and to all men freedom to follow the religion that they choose." Christianity continued to gain strength. In 380, the emperor Theodosius made it the empire's official religion.

Discord and Harmony As Christianity grew, disagreements about beliefs developed among its followers. Church leaders called any belief that appeared to contradict the basic teachings a **heresy.** Dispute over beliefs became intense. In an attempt to end conflicts, Church leaders sought to set a single, official standard of belief. These beliefs were compiled in the New Testament, which contained the four Gospels, the Epistles of Paul, and other documents. In A.D. 325, Constantine decided to end the disputes and the disorder they caused. He called Church leaders to Nicaea in Anatolia. There they wrote the Nicene Creed, which defined the basic beliefs of the Church.

The Fathers of the Church Also influential in defining Church teachings were several early writers and scholars who have been called the Fathers of the Church. One of the most important was Augustine, who became bishop of the city of Hippo in North Africa in 396. Augustine taught that while humans needed the grace of God to be saved, God was merciful and gave his grace freely.

One of Augustine's most famous books is *The City of God.* It was written after Rome was plundered in the fifth century. Augustine wrote that the fate of cities such as Rome was not important because the heavenly city, the city of God, could never be destroyed:

A VOICE FROM THE PAST
The one consists of those who live by human standards, the other of those who live according to God's will. . . . By two cities I mean two societies of human beings, one of which is predestined to reign with God for all eternity, the other is doomed to undergo eternal punishment with the Devil.
ST. AUGUSTINE, *The City of God*

Christianity increased in both power and wealth despite the empire's growing internal and external problems.

HISTORY MAKERS

Constantine
A.D. 285?–337

Constantine was a deeply religious man. He initially believed in the traditional Roman gods. He identified with the god Apollo, whom he claimed to have seen in a vision.

Sometime after his conversion to Christianity in A.D. 312, Constantine reportedly remarked that "God is the cause of the exploits I have performed." He maintained that he received revelations and instructions from God.

Although he legalized Christianity throughout the empire and took a leading role in the affairs of the Christian Church, Constantine was not formally baptized until he was on his deathbed in 337.

Section 3 Assessment

1. TERMS & NAMES

Identify
- Jesus
- apostle
- Peter
- Paul
- Diaspora
- bishop
- pope
- Constantine
- heresy

2. TAKING NOTES

Using a sequence graphic like the one below, show the five or six events that led to the spread of Christianity throughout the Roman Empire.

Rome takes over Jewish kingdom.

Which event do you think had the biggest impact? Explain.

3. HYPOTHESIZING

Do you think Christianity would have developed in the same way if it had arisen in an area outside the Roman Empire? Explain.

THINK ABOUT
- Jesus' growing popularity
- the effect of actions Rome took against Jesus and his followers
- the depth of belief of Jesus' followers
- the advantages of being part of a vast empire

4. ANALYZING THEMES

Religious and Ethical Systems Who do you think did more to spread Christianity—Paul or Constantine?

THINK ABOUT
- Paul's travels
- the opening of Christianity to the Gentiles
- Constantine's power as an emperor

Ancient Rome and Early Christianity **157**

ANSWERS

1. TERMS & NAMES
Jesus, p. 153
apostle, p. 153
Peter, p. 154
Paul, p. 155
Diaspora p. 155
bishop, p. 156
pope, p. 156
Constantine, p. 156
heresy, p. 157

2. TAKING NOTES
Possible Responses: Rome takes over Jewish kingdom; Jesus gathers many followers; Paul and other missionaries spread Jesus' message; Constantine issues Edict of Milan; Theodosius makes Christianity the empire's official religion.

3. HYPOTHESIZING
Some students might suggest that Christianity would have grown more slowly outside the empire. Others might say that it would have spread just as fast or faster without Roman persecutions. Students should support their hypotheses with facts.

4. ANALYZING THEMES
Possible Response: Some students might say Paul did more to spread Christianity because he carried it throughout the empire and welcomed Gentiles. Others might say that Constantine did more because he accepted Christianity and ended the persecution.

Section 4 Overview

OBJECTIVES

1. To summarize the decline of the Roman Empire.

2. To describe the reforms of Diocletian and Constantine.

3. To trace the fall of the Western Roman empire.

SKILLBUILDER

- Interpreting charts, p. 160
- Interpreting maps: movement, location, p. 161

CRITICAL THINKING

- Analyzing causes, p. 158
- Supporting opinions, p. 159
- Analyzing motives, p. 160
- Hypothesizing, p. 162
- Drawing conclusions, p. 162
- Comparing, p. 163

FOCUS

5-Minute Warm-Up

▶ **Making Inferences**
To help students understand the fall of the Roman Empire, ask them to answer these questions

1. Study the map on page 161. Which tribes of invaders reached Rome?

2. What can you infer about Rome's military strength?

 WARM-UP TRANSPARENCY 6

OBJECTIVE ① INSTRUCT

A Century of Crisis

▶ **Key Ideas**
- Rome suffers an economic decline.
- The Roman army cannot defend the empire.
- As people's loyalty and service to the empire decline, only the armies remain active in politics.

 IN-DEPTH RESOURCES: UNIT 2
Guided Reading, p. 24

 ACCESS FOR STUDENTS ACQUIRING ENGLISH
Guided Reading (Spanish), p. 69

 ELECTRONIC LIBRARY OF PRIMARY SOURCES
from *Agricola*

158 Chapter 6

TERMS & NAMES
- inflation
- mercenary
- Diocletian
- Constantinople
- Alaric
- Attila

MAIN IDEA
Internal problems and nomadic invasions spurred the division and decline of the Roman empire.

WHY IT MATTERS NOW
The decline and fall of great civilizations is a repeating pattern in world history.

SETTING THE STAGE In the third century A.D., Rome faced many problems. They came both from within the empire and from outside. Drastic economic, military, and political reforms would be needed to hold off collapse.

A Century of Crisis

Historians generally agree that the Roman Empire began its decline at the end of the reign of the last of the Five Good Emperors, Marcus Aurelius (A.D. 161–180). The rulers that followed in the next century had little or no idea of how to deal with the problems facing the empire. Most, like Aurelius' son Commodus, were brutal and incompetent. They left the empire greatly weakened.

Rome's Economy Declines During the *Pax Romana*, bustling trade flowed over routes patrolled by Roman legions and ships. Rome's treasuries were enriched by gold and silver taken from conquered territories. Most important of all, the empire's farms grew enough grain to feed the population of the cities. During the third century A.D., all three sources of prosperity evaporated.

Hostile tribes outside the boundaries of the empire and pirates on the Mediterranean Sea disrupted trade. Frequent wars were costly. The wealthy spent money on luxury goods from China, India, and Arabia. This spending drained the empire of gold and silver. Since the empire's expansion had come to an end, there were no new sources of precious metals.

This Roman road, still in use in Manchester, England, was part of a 53,000-mile network of paved roads that connected the far-flung empire.

Desperate to pay its mounting expenses, including the rising cost of defense, the government raised taxes. It also started minting coins that contained less and less silver. It hoped to create more money with the same amount of precious metal. However, the economy soon suffered from **inflation,** a drastic drop in the value of money coupled with a rise in prices.

Agriculture faced equally serious problems. Harvests in Italy and western Europe became increasingly meager because overworked soil had lost its fertility. Farmland was destroyed by warfare. The higher taxes imposed by the government caused many poor farmers to abandon their lands. The use of cheap slave labor had discouraged improvements in technology. Serious food shortages resulted for all these reasons. Eventually, disease spread and the population declined.

Rome Faces Military Upheaval The empire's economic crisis was worsened by its growing military troubles. Throughout the third century, Germanic tribes repeatedly overwhelmed the Roman legions guarding the northern frontiers. At the same time, Persia threatened Roman territory in Syria and Anatolia. (Romans

158 Chapter 6

THINK THROUGH HISTORY
A. Analyzing Causes What caused the weakening of the Roman economy?
A. Answer Inflation, meager harvests, disruption of trade.

SECTION 4 RESOURCES

PRINT RESOURCES

 IN-DEPTH RESOURCES: UNIT 2
Guided Reading, p. 23
Skillbuilder Practice: Summarizing, p. 25
Primary Source: "Dinner with Atilla the Hun," from *Historici Graeci Minores,* by Priscus, p. 30

ACCESS FOR STUDENTS ACQUIRING ENGLISH
Guided Reading (Spanish), p. 67
Skillbuilder Practice: (Spanish), p. 69

 FORMAL ASSESSMENT
Section Quiz, p. 68

 ALTERNATIVE ASSESSMENT BOOK

TECHNOLOGY RESOURCES

 CD-ROM
Electronic Library of Primary Sources

INTERNET www.mlworldhistory.com

called all invaders "barbarians," a term that they used to refer to non-Romans.) Rome's most humiliating defeat occurred in A.D. 260, when the Persians captured the emperor Valerian.

In the army, discipline and loyalty had collapsed. Soldiers gave their loyalty not to Rome but to their commanders, who fought among themselves for the throne. To defend against the increasing threats to the empire, the government began to recruit **mercenaries,** foreign soldiers who fought for money. While mercenaries would accept lower pay than Romans, they felt little sense of loyalty to the empire.

Roman Politics Decay Loyalty was in fact a key problem, perhaps the most serious of all. In the past, Romans cared so deeply about their republic that they willingly sacrificed their lives for it. Conditions in the later centuries of the empire caused citizens to lose their sense of patriotism. They became indifferent to the empire's fate.

Romans had once considered holding political office to be an honor. It was also an opportunity to gain wealth. By the 200s, however, local officials usually lost money because they were required to pay for the costly public circuses and baths out of their own pockets. Few people chose to serve the government under those conditions.

Only the armies remained actively interested in politics. In a 50-year period (A.D. 235–284), armies in the provinces and in Rome proclaimed 50 generals to be emperors of Rome. Of these "barracks emperors," 26 briefly won the approval of the Roman senate; 25 died violently.

Emperors Attempt Reform

Remarkably, the empire survived intact for another 200 years. Its life was prolonged by reforming emperors and by its division into two parts: eastern and western.

Diocletian Reforms the Empire In A.D. 284, **Diocletian,** a strong-willed army leader, became the new emperor. With amazing boldness, he restored order in the empire and increased its strength. To accomplish this, he governed as an absolute ruler and severely limited personal freedoms.

Diocletian doubled the size of the Roman armies, drafting prisoners of war and hiring German mercenaries. He attempted to control inflation by setting fixed prices for goods. He also ordered farmers to remain on their lands and other workers to stay in their jobs for life. To restore the prestige of the office of emperor, Diocletian claimed descent from the ancient Roman gods. He viewed Christianity as a threat and passed decrees to persecute the Christians.

Diocletian believed that the empire had grown too large and too complex for one ruler. In his most significant reform, he divided the empire into the Greek-speaking East (Greece, Anatolia, Syria, and Egypt) and the Latin-speaking West (Italy, Gaul, Britannia, and Spain). He took the eastern half for himself and appointed a co-ruler for the West, General Maximian. Each emperor also selected an assistant, who was to be his successor. While Diocletian shared authority, he kept overall control. His half of the empire, the East, included most of the empire's great cities and trade centers and was far wealthier than the West.

Diocletian's reforms slowed the decline of the empire. The borders became safe again, and the emperor's prestige was restored. Because of ill health, Diocletian took the extraordinary step of retiring in A.D. 305.

However, his plans for orderly succession failed. Civil war broke out immediately. By 311, four rivals were competing for power.

THINK THROUGH HISTORY
B. Supporting Opinions Do you think Diocletian was a good emperor?

B. Answer Agree— He secured Rome's boundaries, stabilized economy and rule, restored prestige of emperor. Disagree— limited personal freedoms, persecuted Christians, plans for orderly succession failed and civil war resulted.

HISTORY MAKERS

Diocletian
A.D. 245?–313

Diocletian, who may have been born the son of a slave in the province of Dalmatia, raised the office of emperor to a form of divine monarch. He declared himself to be a son of Jupiter, the father of the gods. He devised elaborate ceremonies to present himself in a godlike aura.

When he appeared in public, trumpets heralded his entrance. Anyone who approached the imperial presence had to kneel and kiss the hem of the his robe. He had his clothing and shoes decorated with precious gems. By his actions, Diocletian sought to restore the dignity of the emperor. He also hoped to give himself greater security by making assassination appear to be a crime against the gods.

Ancient Rome and Early Christianity **159**

Invaders Overrun the Western Empire

Key Ideas

• Internal and economic problems and invading tribes bring down the Western Roman Empire.

• Although Rome's power is gone, its cultural heritage endures.

MORE ABOUT . . .
Three Names for Byzantium

The city's name has changed over the centuries to reflect the nationalities of its rulers. According to legend, Byzantium was named by early Greek settlers for Byzas, their leader. Around A.D. 330 Emperor Constantine renamed the city Constantinople, capital of the Eastern Empire. Finally, in 1453, the city fell to the Turks, who called it Istanbul.

History from Visuals

Interpreting the Chart After students have studied the chart, have them choose one contributing factor from each column that they consider the most important to the fall of the Western Empire. Ask students to discuss the reasons for their choices.

Extension Activity Ask students to choose only one factor from the chart and write a short statement on how it contributed to the Western Roman Empire's decline.

SKILLBUILDER Answers

1. **Possible Responses:** a strong political organization, finding new sources of grain and precious metals, social reforms, a strong military.

2. Answers will vary, but students should be prepared to explain their choice.

Among them was an ambitious young commander named Constantine, the same Constantine who would later end the persecution of Christians.

Constantine Moves the Capital Constantine gained control of the western part of the empire in A.D. 312 and continued many of the social and economic policies of Diocletian. In 324 Constantine also secured control of the East, thus restoring the concept of a single ruler.

In A.D. 330, Constantine took a step that would have great consequence for the empire. He moved the capital from Rome to the Greek city of Byzantium (bih-ZAN-shee-uhm), in what is now Turkey. The new capital stood on the Bosporus Strait, strategically located for trade and defense purposes on a crossroads between West and East.

With Byzantium as its capital, the center of power in the empire shifted from Rome to the East. Soon the new capital was protected by massive walls and filled with imperial buildings modeled after those in Rome. The city was given a new name— **Constantinople** (KAHN-stan-tuhn-OH-puhl), city of Constantine. After Constantine's death, the empire would again be divided. The East would survive; the West would fall.

Invaders Overrun the Western Empire

The decline of the Western Roman Empire took place over many years. Its final collapse was the result of worsening internal problems, the separation of the Western Empire from the wealthier Eastern part, and outside invasions.

Since the days of Julius Caesar, Germanic peoples had gathered on the northern borders of the Empire. Some groups settled into a peaceful farming life. Eventually they adopted Roman ways, such as speaking Latin and becoming Christians. Other groups remained nomads. From A.D. 376 to 476, huge numbers of Germans poured

THINK THROUGH HISTORY
C. Analyzing Motives Why did Constantine choose the location of Byzantium for his new capital?
C. Answer It was strategically located for trade and defense.

Multiple Causes: Fall of the Western Roman Empire

Contributing Factors

Political	Social	Economic	Military
• Political office seen as burden, not reward	• Decline in interest in public affairs	• Poor harvests	• Threat from northern European tribes
• Military interference in politics	• Low confidence in empire	• Disruption of trade	• Low funds for defense
• Civil war and unrest	• Disloyalty, lack of patriotism, corruption	• No more war plunder	• Problems recruiting Roman citizens; recruiting of non-Romans
• Division of empire	• Contrast between rich and poor	• Gold and silver drain	• Decline of patriotism and loyalty among soldiers
• Moving of capital to Byzantium		• Inflation	
		• Crushing tax burden	
		• Widening gap between rich and poor and increasingly impoverished Western empire	

Immediate Causes

• Pressure from Huns	• Invasion by Germanic tribes and by Huns	• Sack of Rome	• Conquest by invaders

FALL OF ROMAN EMPIRE

SKILLBUILDER: Interpreting Charts
1. Could changes in any contributing factors have reversed the decline of the empire?
2. Which contributing factors—political, economic, or military—were the most significant in the fall of the Western Roman Empire?

160 Chapter 6

SKILLBUILDER MINI-LESSON: Summarizing

CLASS TIME 20 MINUTES

Explaining the Skill: To summarize means to restate a passage in *one's own words* to highlight only the main ideas and facts (key dates, statistics, measurements). Summarizing can help to clarify the meaning of the material and make it easier to remember. To summarize, first list the main ideas and facts of a passage, then restate them in one sentence or a brief paragraph.

Applying the Skill: Ask students to read the passage under the heading "Constantine Moves the Capital" and identify the main points as if they were preparing to write a summary of the passage. These points should include the following:

1. By 324, Constantine ruled both the Western and Eastern empires.

2. In 330, Constantine moved the capital from Rome to Byzantium, shifting the center of power.

3. Constantine fortified Byzantium and renamed it Constantinople.

4. The Western Empire fell after Constantine died, but the eastern half survived.

 IN-DEPTH RESOURCES: UNIT 2
Skillbuilder Practice: Summarizing, p. 25

Invasions into the Roman Empire, A.D. 350–500

Eastern Roman Empire
Western Roman Empire
Burgundians
Franks, Alemanni
Huns
Ostrogoths
Saxons, Angles, Jutes
Vandals
Visigoths

0   500 Miles
0   1,000 Kilometers

GEOGRAPHY SKILLBUILDER: Interpreting Maps
Movement *What group of invaders came the greatest distance?*
Location *What areas of the empire were not threatened by invasion?*

into Roman territory—Ostrogoths, Visigoths, Franks, Angles, Saxons, Burgundians, Alemanni, and Vandals. Gradually, they overwhelmed the structures of Roman society. Finally, they drove the last Roman emperor from the throne.

The Huns Move West The main reason for the Germanic invasions of the Empire was the movement into Europe of the Huns. The Huns were fierce Mongol nomads from central Asia. They began invading the frontier regions of the Rhine and Danube rivers around A.D. 370, destroying all in their path. The pressure from the Huns forced other groups to move as well—into the Roman Empire.

The following description from a fourth-century Roman historian shows how intensely the Huns were feared and scorned:

> **A VOICE FROM THE PAST**
> The nation of the Huns . . . surpasses all other barbarians in wildness of life. . . . And though [the Huns] do just bear the likeness of men (of a very ugly pattern), they are so little advanced in civilization that they . . . feed upon the . . . half-raw flesh of any sort of animal. . . . When attacked, . . . they fill the air with varied and discordant cries . . . they fight in no regular order of battle, but by being extremely swift and sudden in their movements, they disperse . . . spread havoc over vast plains, and . . . pillage the camp of their enemy almost before he has become aware of their approach.
>
> **AMMIANUS MARCELLINUS,** *The Chronicle of Events (Rerum gestarum libri)*

Background
Most of the Germanic invaders were Christians.

Germanic Invasions Germanic people near the Rhine River—Franks, Burgundians, and Vandals—fled the invading Huns and sought refuge in Roman lands. When the Rhine River froze during an especially cold winter in 406, Vandal warriors and their families swarmed across the ice. They met little resistance and kept moving through the Roman province of Gaul. The Western Empire was now so disorganized that it was unable to field an army to stop them.

By the early fifth century, the city of Rome itself was vulnerable to attack. More than 600 years had passed since a foreign army, that of Hannibal, had threatened

Ancient Rome and Early Christianity **161**

This skull from the period, still retaining its hair, shows a kind of topknot in the hair that some Germanic peoples fashioned to identify themselves.

Rome. Then in 408 Visigoths, led by their king, **Alaric** (AL·ur·ihk), marched across the Alps toward Rome. After putting the city under siege, hordes of Germans stormed Rome in 410 and plundered it for three days.

Attila the Hun Meanwhile, the Huns, who were indirectly responsible for the Germanic assault on the Empire, became a direct threat. In 444 they united for the first time under a powerful chieftain named **Attila** (AT·uhl·uh). With his 100,000 soldiers, Attila terrorized both halves of the empire. In the East, his armies attacked and plundered 70 cities. (They failed, however, to scale the high walls of Constantinople.)

The Huns then swept into the West. In A.D. 452, Attila's forces advanced against Rome, but they were weakened by famine and disease. As a result, Pope Leo I was able to negotiate their withdrawal. Although the Huns were no longer a threat to the empire after Attila's death in 453, the Germanic invasions continued. In 455 Vandals, under Gaiseric, sacked Rome, leaving it in chaos. Famine struck, and its population eventually dropped from about one million to 20,000.

Rome's Last Emperor The Roman emperor in the West had become practically powerless. Germanic tribes now fought one another for possession of the Western provinces. Spain belonged to the Visigoths, North Africa to the Vandals. Gaul was overrun by competing tribes—Franks, Burgundians, and Visigoths. Britannia was invaded by Angles and Saxons. Italy was falling victim to raids by the Ostrogoths.

The last Roman emperor was a 14-year-old boy named Romulus Augustulus. In 476 he was deposed by a German general named Odoacer (oh·doh·AY·sur) and sent into exile. After that, no emperor even pretended to rule Rome and its western provinces. Roman power in the western half of the Empire had disappeared.

The eastern half of the Empire, which came to be called the Byzantine Empire, not only survived but flourished. It preserved the great heritage of Greek and Roman culture for another 1,000 years. (See Chapter 11.) The Byzantine emperors ruled from Constantinople and saw themselves as heirs to the power of Augustus Caesar. The empire endured until 1453, when it fell to the Ottoman Turks.

Even though Rome's political power in the West ended, its cultural influence, through its ideas, customs, and institutions, continued to be deeply embedded in Western civilization.

Section 4 Assessment

1. TERMS & NAMES

Identify
- inflation
- mercenary
- Diocletian
- Constantinople
- Alaric
- Attila

2. TAKING NOTES

Identify the causes of each of the effects listed in the chart below.

Decline of the Roman Empire

Effects	Causes
Inflation	
Untrustworthy army	
Decreased citizen interest in government	

How did these problems open the empire to invading peoples?

3. DRAWING CONCLUSIONS

How do you think the splitting of the empire into two parts helped it survive for another 200 years?

THINK ABOUT
- the differences between the eastern and western halves of the empire
- the advantages of a smaller empire

4. THEME ACTIVITY

Empire Building Imagine you are a journalist in the Roman Empire. Write an editorial in which you comment—favorably or unfavorably—on Constantine's decision to move the capital of the empire. Present the facts of the move, but focus the editorial on the effects you think the move will have on Rome and its citizens.

ANSWERS

1. TERMS & NAMES
inflation, p. 158
mercenary, p. 159
Diocletian, p. 159
Constantinople, p. 160
Alaric, p. 162
Attila, p. 162

2. TAKING NOTES
Entries may include: **Inflation:** Gold and silver squandered; coins worth less. **Untrustworthy army:** Soldiers fought for money. **Decreased interest in government:** Citizens had little influence; officials burdened with debts. The empire couldn't maintain its defenses; army was weakened.

3. DRAWING CONCLUSIONS
Possible Response: The wealthier eastern half included most of the empire's great cities and trading centers. By creating a smaller area that was easier to defend, Constantine was able to preserve the empire for another 200 years.

4. THEME ACTIVITY
Standards for Evaluation
Editorials should . . .
- state the facts of the move
- clearly express the writer's opinion about this action
- cite reasons supporting the writer's opinion in terms of the effects of the move on Rome and its citizens

The Fall of the Roman Empire

Since the fifth century, historians and others have argued over the empire's fall. They have attributed it to a variety of causes, coming both from within and outside the empire. The following excerpts are examples of the differing opinions.

HISTORICAL COMMENTARY
Edward Gibbon

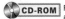

In the 1780s Gibbon published *The History of the Decline and Fall of the Roman Empire*. In this passage, Gibbon explains that a major cause of the collapse was that the empire was simply just too large.

The decline of Rome was the natural and inevitable effect of immoderate greatness. Prosperity ripened the principle of decay; the causes of destruction multiplied with the extent of conquest; and, as soon as time or accident had removed the artificial supports, the stupendous fabric yielded to the pressure of its own weight. The story of its ruin is simple and obvious; and instead of inquiring why the Roman Empire was destroyed, we should rather be surprised that it had subsisted so long.

EYEWITNESS ACCOUNT
St. Jerome

This early Church leader did not live to see the empire's end, but he vividly describes his feelings after a major event in Rome's decline—the attack and plunder of the city by Visigoths in 410. He said:

"It is the end of the world ... Words fail me. My sobs break in ... The city which took captive the whole world has itself been captured."

HISTORICAL COMMENTARY
Arther Ferrill

In his book *The Fall of the Roman Empire* (1986), Arther Ferrill argues that the fall of Rome was a military collapse.

In fact the Roman Empire of the West did fall. Not every aspect of the life of Roman subjects was changed by that, but the fall of Rome as a political entity was one of the major events of the history of Western man. It will simply not do to call that fall a myth or to ignore its historical significance merely by focusing on those aspects of Roman life that survived the fall in one form or another. At the opening of the fifth century a massive army, perhaps more than 200,000 strong, stood at the service of the Western emperor and his generals. The destruction of Roman military power in the fifth century was the obvious cause of the collapse of Roman government in the West.

HISTORICAL COMMENTARY
Finley Hooper

In this passage from his *Roman Realities* (1967), Hooper argues against the idea of a "fall."

The year was 476. For those who demand to know the date Rome fell, that is it. Others will realize that the fall of Rome was not an event but a process. Or, to put it another way, there was no fall at all—ancient Roman civilization simply became something else, which is called medieval. [It evolved into another civilization, the civilization of the Middle Ages.]

Connect *to* History

Comparing Compare the reasons given in these excerpts for the fall of Rome. Which seem the most valid to you? Why?

 SEE SKILLBUILDER HANDBOOK, PAGE 996

Connect *to* Today

Comparing In 1991, the Union of Soviet Socialist Republics collapsed after nearly 70 years of existence. Research that fall and discuss one way in which the Soviet Union's decline can be compared to the fall of Rome.

CD-ROM For more information about the fall of the Roman Empire, see the World History Electronic Library of Primary Sources.

Why the Fall of Rome Matters Now

As students discuss these excerpts on the fall of the Roman Empire, you might have them consider the broader picture: Why does the fall of the Roman Empire matter? Ask them to consider the following points.

The fall of the Roman Empire matters because it provides an example of how a long period of peace and prosperity can end in civil war, invasion by stronger forces, poverty, and famine for many people.

It also matters because the culture of the United States and Western European countries is based in many ways on the culture of Rome. We share many of the same problems that brought about the downfall of the Roman Empire, and our government reflects many ideals of the Roman Republic, which was supplanted by the empire.

Finally, it matters because the story of the Roman Empire provides us with clear examples of great leaders, good leaders, and poor leaders.

ELECTRONIC LIBRARY OF PRIMARY SOURCES
from the *Satyricon*

MORE ABOUT . . .
Edward Gibbon

Edward Gibbon, one of the world's most famous historians, first thought of writing about the Roman Empire while visiting the city of Rome in 1764. He published the first of nine volumes of The *Decline and Fall of the Roman Empire* in 1776. The final three volumes were published in 1788. Although some of Gibbon's theories about what caused the decline of Rome were later proved wrong, his work has served as a classic example of historical study. He also served as a member of the English Parliament's House of Commons for eight years, where he distinguished himself in an unusual way—by never speaking before the Commons!

Connect *to* History

Comparing
Possible Responses:
Gibbon attributes the fall to the empire's size and wealth, which led to decay. Ferrill emphasizes the decline of Rome's military power.

Hooper says that there was no fall, only a change. All three answers may be true—if one accepts multiple causes and the "fall" as a gradual process.

Connect *to* Today

Comparing Suggest to students that they use the *Reader's Guide to Periodical Literature* for 1991 and 1992 to find magazine articles about the collapse of the USSR. Then ask them to review the headings of the chart on page 160. Ask them

to look for political, social, economic, and military factors that contributed to the collapse of the USSR. Have them discuss one factor that was similar in the fall of Rome and the USSR.

OBJECTIVES

 To describe the legacy of the Greco-Roman civilization.

 To identify Roman achievements in the arts, sciences, and law.

CRITICAL THINKING

- Summarizing, p. 164
- Supporting opinions, p. 165
- Drawing conclusions, pp. 166, 167
- Comparing, p. 166
- Hypothesizing, p. 167
- Analyzing themes, p. 167

FOCUS

5-Minute Warm-Up

▶ **Drawing Conclusions**
Answering these questions will help students understand the legacy of Greco-Roman culture.

1. Read "Setting the Stage" on page 164. What two cultures helped Rome create a great civilization?

2. Now study the photo and caption on page 165. What conclusion can you draw about the influence of Roman art on Western artists?

 WARM-UP TRANSPARENCY 6

OBJECTIVE ❶ INSTRUCT

The Legacy of Greco-Roman Civilization

▶ **Key Ideas**
- The mixing of Greek, Hellenistic, and Roman culture produces Greco-Roman culture.
- Roman fine arts and literature follow Greek forms but express Roman virtues.

 IN-DEPTH RESOURCES: UNIT 2
Guided Reading, p. 24
Primary Source: Letter on the Eruption of Vesuvius by Pliny the Younger, p. 31
Connections Across Time and Cultures: Hellenistic Culture and Roman Culture, p. 37

 ACCESS FOR STUDENTS ACQUIRING ENGLISH
Guided Reading (Spanish), p. 68

TERMS & NAMES
- Greco-Roman culture
- Pompeii
- Virgil
- Tacitus
- aqueduct

5 Rome and the Roots of Western Civilization

MAIN IDEA	WHY IT MATTERS NOW
The Romans developed many ideas and institutions that became fundamental to Western civilization.	Evidence of Roman culture is found throughout Europe and North America and in Asia and Africa.

SETTING THE STAGE Romans borrowed and adapted cultural elements freely, especially from the Greek and Hellenistic cultures. Rome created a great civilization, whose art and architecture, language and literature, engineering, and law became its legacy to the world.

The Legacy of Greco-Roman Civilization

Under the Roman Empire, hundreds of territories were knitted into a single state. Each Roman province and city was governed in the same way. The Romans were proud of their ability to rule, but they acknowledged Greek leadership in the fields of art, architecture, literature, and philosophy.

By the second century B.C., Romans had conquered Greece and had come to greatly admire Greek culture. Educated Romans learned the Greek language. As Horace, a Roman poet said, "Greece, once overcome, overcame her wild conqueror." The mixing of elements of Greek, Hellenistic, and Roman culture produced a new culture, called **Greco-Roman culture.** This is also often called classical civilization.

Roman artists, philosophers, and writers did not merely copy their Greek and Hellenistic models. They adapted them for their own purposes and created a style of their own. Roman art and literature came to convey the Roman ideals of strength, permanence, solidity.

Roman Fine Arts Romans learned the art of sculpture from the Greeks. However, while the Greeks were known for the beauty and idealization of their sculpture, Roman sculptors created realistic portraits in stone. Much Roman art was practical in purpose, intended for public education.

The reign of Augustus was a period of great artistic achievement. At that time the Romans further developed a type of sculpture called bas-relief. In bas-relief, or low-relief, images project from a flat background. Roman sculptors used bas-relief to tell stories and to represent crowds of people, soldiers in battle, and landscapes. (See Trajan's Column on page 169.)

Roman artists were particularly skilled in creating mosaics. Mosaics were pictures or designs made by setting small pieces of stone, glass, or tile onto a surface. Most Roman villas, the country houses of the wealthy, had at least one colored mosaic.

THINK THROUGH HISTORY
A. Summarizing
What were the origins of Greco-Roman culture?
A. Answer an intermixing of Greek, Hellenistic, and Roman cultures

Gladiators and leopards fight to the death in this third-century mosaic.

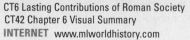

Romans also excelled at the art of painting. Most wealthy Romans had bright, large murals, called frescoes, painted directly on their walls. Few have survived. The best examples of Roman painting are found in the Roman town of **Pompeii,** and date from as early as the second century B.C. In A.D. 79, Mount Vesuvius erupted, covering Pompeii in a thick layer of ash and killing about 2,000. The ash acted to preserve many buildings and works of art.

Learning and Literature Romans borrowed much of their philosophy from the Greeks. Stoicism, the philosophy of the Greek teacher Zeno, was especially influential. Stoicism encouraged virtue, duty, moderation, and endurance. One of the most noted Stoics was the emperor Marcus Aurelius. His steadfastness is shown in his *Meditations:* "In the midst of it all, you must take your stand, good-temperedly and without disdain."

In literature, as in philosophy, the Romans found inspiration in the works of the Greeks. Writers used Roman themes and ideas while following Greek forms and models.

The poet **Virgil** spent ten years writing the most famous work of Latin literature, the *Aeneid* (ih·NEE·ihd), the epic of the legendary Aeneas. Virgil modeled the *Aeneid*, written in praise of Rome and Roman virtues, after the Greek epics of Homer. Here he speaks of government as being Rome's most important contribution to civilization:

The Roman influence can be seen in this neoclassic 19th-century sculpture of George Washington in toga and tunic.

A VOICE FROM THE PAST
. . . Romans, never forget that government is your medium! Be this your art:—to practice men in habit of peace, Generosity to the conquered, and firmness against aggressors.
VIRGIL, *Aeneid*

While Virgil's writing carries all the weight and seriousness of the Roman character, the poet Ovid wrote light, witty poetry for enjoyment. In the *Amores,* Ovid relates that he can only compose when he is in love: "When I was from Cupid's passions free, my Muse was mute and wrote no elegy."

The Romans also wrote excellent prose, especially history. Livy compiled a multivolume history of Rome from its origins to 9 B.C. He used legends freely, creating more of a national myth of Rome than a true history. **Tacitus** (TAS·ih·tuhs), another Roman historian, is notable among ancient historians because he presented the facts accurately. He also was concerned about the Romans' lack of morality. In his *Annals* and *Histories,* he wrote about the good and bad of imperial Rome.

Roman Achievements

The presence of Rome is still felt daily in the languages, the institutions, and the thought of the Western world.

Latin, the Language of Rome Latin remained the language of learning in the West long after the fall of Rome. It was the official language of the Roman Catholic Church into the 20th century.

Latin was adopted by different peoples and developed into French, Spanish, Portuguese, Italian, and Romanian. These languages are called Romance languages because of their common Roman heritage. Latin also influenced other languages. For example, more than half the words in English have a basis in Latin.

Architecture, Engineering, and Technology Visitors from all over the empire marveled at the architecture of Rome. The arch, the dome, and concrete were combined to build spectacular structures, such as the Colosseum.

Ancient Rome and Early Christianity **165**

During the Middle Ages, a series of earthquakes damaged the Colosseum. For several centuries, people used the huge building as a ready-made stone quarry. They carried away the broken marble, stone, and concrete to construct houses, churches, and public buildings. Part of ancient Rome literally helped build modern Italy.

MORE ABOUT . . .
The Games

The Roman crowds at the games always liked something new. For instance, a group of archers might be pitted against several panthers. Gladiators might have to fight with unmatched weapons, one with a sword, perhaps, and one with a trident. Hunters brought tigers, elephants, hippopotamuses, and rhinoceroses for the slaughter. So many wild animals were collected for the games that in certain provinces, some species were wiped out.

MORE ABOUT . . .
The Invention of Concrete

The Romans invented concrete, which is a mixture of sand, gravel, and water. It is an extraordinarily useful building material. Unlike stone or marble, concrete is lighter, easier to work with, and more versatile. The Romans poured or shaped it into many of the complex columns, arches, and forms found in their buildings. The diversity and beauty of these buildings, even as ruins, continue to amaze architects today.

 IN-DEPTH RESOURCES: UNIT 2
Science and Technology: Roman Construction Technology, p. 38

The Colosseum

The Colosseum was one of the greatest feats of Roman engineering and a model for the ages. The name comes from the Latin word *colossus*, meaning "gigantic." Its construction was started by the Emperor Vespasian and was completed by his sons, emperors Titus and Domitian. For centuries after its opening in A.D. 80, excited spectators, both rich and poor, cheered a variety of free, bloody spectacles presented for their entertainment. Gladiator fought gladiator to the death. Wild animals were hunted and slaughtered. Christians were devoured by lions. The poor sat in the higher seats, the rich and powerful closer to the action.

The Colosseum in Rome as it appears today.

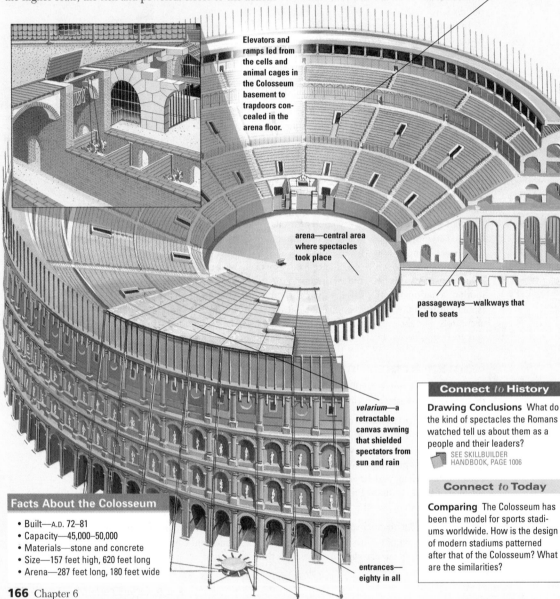

exits—giant staircases that allowed the building to be emptied in minutes

Elevators and ramps led from the cells and animal cages in the Colosseum basement to trapdoors concealed in the arena floor.

arena—central area where spectacles took place

passageways—walkways that led to seats

velarium—a retractable canvas awning that shielded spectators from sun and rain

entrances— eighty in all

Facts About the Colosseum

- Built—A.D. 72–81
- Capacity—45,000–50,000
- Materials—stone and concrete
- Size—157 feet high, 620 feet long
- Arena—287 feet long, 180 feet wide

166 Chapter 6

Connect *to* History

Drawing Conclusions What do the kind of spectacles the Romans watched tell us about them as a people and their leaders?

SEE SKILLBUILDER HANDBOOK, PAGE 1006

Connect *to* Today

Comparing The Colosseum has been the model for sports stadiums worldwide. How is the design of modern stadiums patterned after that of the Colosseum? What are the similarities?

Connect *to* History

Drawing Conclusions
Possible Responses: The Roman leaders tried to find ways to keep people distracted from their own problems so they wouldn't rebel or cause trouble for the government. The Roman crowds seemed to need more and more violent and unusual spectacles to satisfy them. They didn't seem to value human lives very highly, especially not those of slaves or foreigners.

Connect *to* Today

Comparing
Modern stadiums are also round or oval and many have roofs to protect crowds from the elements. All stadiums have several tiers of seats that allow thousands of people to look down on a level playing field. Passageways, stairs, and entrances placed around the stadium reduce congestion and direct the flow of human traffic to different levels of seating. These clever methods of presenting a spectacle and controlling a large crowd of spectators were used in building the Colosseum.

Arches also supported bridges and aqueducts. **Aqueducts** were designed by Roman engineers to bring water into cities and towns. When the water channel spanned a river or ravine, the aqueduct was lifted high up on arches.

Because Roman architectural forms were so practical, they have remained popular. Thomas Jefferson began a Roman revival in the United States in the 18th century. Many large public buildings, such as the U.S. Capitol and numerous state capitols, include Roman features.

Roman roads were also technological marvels. The army built a vast network of roads constructed of stone, concrete, and sand that connected Rome to all parts of the empire. Many lasted into the Middle Ages; some are still used.

Roman System of Law Rome's most lasting and widespread contribution was its law. Early Roman law dealt mostly with the rights of Roman citizens. As the empire grew, however, the Romans came to believe that laws should be fair and apply equally to all people, rich and poor. Slowly, judges began to recognize certain standards of justice. These standards were influenced largely by the teachings of Stoic philosophers and were based on common sense and practical ideas. Some of the most important principles of Roman law were:

water

This is a photo of a Roman aqueduct in modern Spain that has survived. The cross section shows how the water moved within the aqueduct.

- All persons had the right to equal treatment under the law.
- A person was considered innocent until proven guilty.
- The burden of proof rested with the accuser rather than the accused.
- A person should be punished only for actions, not thoughts.
- Any law that seemed unreasonable or grossly unfair could be set aside.

The principles of Roman law endured to form the basis of legal systems in many European countries and of places influenced by Europe, including the United States.

Rome's Enduring Influence By preserving and adding to Greek civilization, Rome strengthened the Western cultural tradition. The world would be a very different place had Rome not existed. Historian R. H. Barrow has stated that Rome never fell because it turned into something even greater—an idea—and achieved immortality.

Around the same time that Rome was developing its enduring culture, different but equally complex empires were growing in India and China, as you will see in Chapter 7.

C. Answer Language, law, and government different; perhaps Greek and Hellenistic culture lost.

THINK THROUGH HISTORY
C. Hypothesizing
How would the world be different if Rome had not existed?

Section 5 Assessment

1. TERMS & NAMES

Identify
- Greco-Roman culture
- Pompeii
- Virgil
- Tacitus
- aqueduct

2. TAKING NOTES

Using a chart like the one below, list the accomplishments of Roman culture.

Fine Arts	Literature	Engineering	Law

Choose one and write a few paragraphs on its importance.

3. DRAWING CONCLUSIONS

Which principle of law do you think has been Rome's greatest contribution to modern legal systems?

THINK ABOUT
- equality before the law
- innocent until proven guilty
- unfair laws could be set aside

4. ANALYZING THEMES

Power and Authority Why do you think the Greek philosophy of Stoicism was so appealing to Romans?

THINK ABOUT
- Stoic philosophy
- the Roman citizen-soldier
- Roman law

Ancient Rome and Early Christianity **167**

MORE ABOUT . . .
Roman Civil and Criminal Law
The body of Roman law began as civil law, or laws that chiefly dealt with the rights of individual citizens. When a person was murdered, for example, his or her relatives sought satisfaction from the courts under the provisions of civil law. The family of the murderer might have to pay a sum of money to the family of the murdered person. In criminal law, the government prosecutes and punishes criminals and either imprisons or executes them. The Romans did not develop criminal law until late in the empire's history.

ASSESS & RETEACH

Section 5 Assessment
Have students work individually to answer the questions, and then go over their answers with a partner.

Section Quiz
 FORMAL ASSESSMENT
Section Quiz, p. 69

Reteaching Activity
CLASS TIME: 10 MINUTES

Ask students to think about their own communities, and then have them eliminate items influenced by Roman civilization, including laws, buildings, art, literature, and sports. What would be left? Use the activity to discuss the importance of ancient Rome to their everyday lives.

CRITICAL THINKING TRANSPARENCIES
CT42 Chapter 6 Visual Summary

CLOSE ACTIVITY

CLASS TIME: 10 MINUTES

Reviewing Main Ideas
To help review the main ideas of this section, ask students to state what they consider to be the greatest achievement of the Romans. Then ask them to name an achievement that has directly touched their own lives. *literature, buildings, laws, fine arts, sports*

CRITICAL THINKING TRANSPARENCIES
CT6 Lasting Contributions of Roman Society

Teacher's Edition **167**

TERMS & NAMES

1. republic, p. 142
2. senate, p. 143
3. Hannibal, p. 144
4. Julius Caesar, p. 147
5. Augustus, p. 148
6. Jesus, p. 153
7. Paul, p. 155
8. Constantine, p. 156
9. inflation, p. 158
10. Virgil, p. 165

REVIEW QUESTIONS

Answers will vary.

11. consuls, senate, and assembly

12. Rome made close neighbors full citizens; those farther away became citizens but without the right to vote. Others became allies with a measure of independence.

13. Augustus became sole ruler of an empire. To manage Rome's affairs, he set up a civil service system.

14. Much of Rome's population was jobless. The government supported the poor with food and entertainment. Most poor people lived in crowded, rickety tenement buildings. Rich Romans lived extravagantly, spending huge sums on houses, gardens, slaves, and banquets.

15. Paul traveled widely, preaching the message of Jesus. He declared that Christianity should welcome anyone, Jew or non-Jew.

16. Nero saw Christians' refusal to worship him as an attack on the Roman state. Later emperors wanted to force Christians to worship Roman gods.

17. Diocletian divided the empire into eastern and western halves, each to be governed by its own emperor.

18. Over many years, Germanic and other invaders overran the western half, which had been weakened by internal problems.

19. Romans admired Greek art, architecture, literature, and philosophy, and merged them into their own culture.

20. European languages might sound different. Legal systems might not place as much emphasis on personal rights. The Christian Church and Western architecture, literature, and philosophy might have evolved differently.

Ancient Rome and Early Christianity

1000 B.C.

Early Rome
- 1000 B.C. Latins enter region
- 753 B.C. Rome founded

900 B.C.

800 B.C.

700 B.C.

600 B.C.

500 B.C.

Roman Republic
- 509 B.C. Republic created
- 451 B.C. Twelve Tables written
- 405–265 B.C. Italy conquered
- 264–146 B.C. Punic Wars fought
- 44 B.C. **Julius Caesar** assassinated

400 B.C.

300 B.C.

200 B.C.

Roman Empire
- 27 B.C. Empire and *Pax Romana* begin with reign of **Augustus**

100 B.C.
- A.D. 29 **Jesus** crucified
- A.D. 64 Christian persecution begins

0
- A.D. 79 Pompeii destroyed
- A.D. 180 *Pax Romana* ends
- A.D. 253 Germanic tribes enter frontier regions

A.D. 100
- A.D. 285 **Diocletian** divides empire into East and West
- A.D. 313 Christianity given recognition

A.D. 200
- A.D. 324 **Constantine** reunites empire

A.D. 300
- A.D. 370 Huns invade frontier
- A.D. 380 Christianity made official religion
- A.D. 395 Empire permanently split

A.D. 400
- A.D. 410 Visigoths attack Rome
- A.D. 455 Vandals sack Rome

A.D. 500
- A.D. 476 Last emperor deposed

TERMS & NAMES

Briefly explain the importance of each of the following to ancient Rome or to the rise of Christianity.

1. republic	6. Jesus
2. senate	7. Paul
3. Hannibal	8. Constantine
4. Julius Caesar	9. inflation
5. Augustus	10. Virgil

REVIEW QUESTIONS

SECTION 1 *(pages 141–145)*
The Romans Create a Republic

11. Name the three main parts of government under the Roman republic.

12. How did Rome treat different sections of its conquered territory?

SECTION 2 *(pages 146–152)*
The Roman Empire Brings Change

13. How did Augustus change Roman government?

14. How did Rome's population fare during the golden age of the *Pax Romana*?

SECTION 3 *(pages 153–157)*
The Rise of Christianity

15. How did the apostle Paul encourage the spread of Christianity?

16. Why did the Roman emperors persecute Christians?

SECTION 4 *(pages 158–162)*
The Decline of the Roman Empire

17. What was the most important reform that the Emperor Diocletian made?

18. How did the western Roman Empire fall?

SECTION 5 *(pages 164–167)*
Roman Culture and the Roots of Western Civilization

19. Why did so much of Roman culture have a Greek flavor?

20. How might Western civilization be different today without the cultural legacy of the Roman Empire?

Interact *with* History

On page 140, you considered the qualities that made a good leader before knowing what the Romans thought about leadership. Now that you have read the chapter, reevaluate your decision. What qualities were needed for Roman leaders to be effective? What qualities hindered their success? How would you rate the overall leadership of the Roman Empire? Discuss your opinions with a small group.

Interact *with* History

Possible Responses: Students may mention writing and speaking skills, political and administrative knowledge, and good judgment. Pride, extravagance, and arrogance hindered success. Overall quality of Roman leadership: students might point out weak or poor leaders who led to the downfall of the Roman Empire; on the other hand, Romans administered a vast empire for over 400 years, creating many of the institutions we use today.

CRITICAL THINKING

1. FROM REPUBLIC TO EMPIRE

On a large sheet of paper, create a Venn diagram like the one below. Use the diagram to compare the Roman Republic with the Roman Empire when both were at the peak of their power.

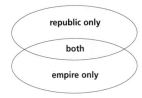

republic only

both

empire only

2. PERSECUTION OF CHRISTIANS

THEME **RELIGIOUS AND ETHICAL SYSTEMS** Many Christians sacrificed their lives rather than give up their beliefs during the periods of Roman persecution. What kind of person do you think became a martyr? Consider the personal characteristics of individuals who refused to renounce their faith even in the face of death.

3. DIOCLETIAN

What do you think of Diocletian's decision to divide the Roman Empire into two parts? Was it wise? Consider Diocletian's possible motives and the results of his actions.

4. ANALYZING PRIMARY SOURCES

The rule of Augustus began a long period of peace and prosperity that spread from Rome into the provinces. The following decree from the Roman province of Asia, which appeared in 9 B.C., suggests how the governing class felt about their first emperor.

> **A VOICE FROM THE PAST**
> Whereas the divine providence that guides our life has displayed its zeal and benevolence by ordaining for our life the most perfect good, bringing to us Augustus, whom it has filled with virtue for the benefit of mankind, employing him as a saviour for us and our descendants, him who has put an end to wars and adorned peace; . . . and the birthday of the god [Augustus] is the beginning of all the good tidings brought by him to the world.

- How did the officials of this province feel toward Augustus? What descriptive words and phrases support your conclusion?
- Do you think Augustus deserved this evaluation? Why or why not?

CHAPTER ACTIVITIES

1. LIVING HISTORY: Unit Portfolio Project

THEME **POWER AND AUTHORITY** Your unit portfolio project focuses on tracing the development and decline of power and authority (see page 107). For Chapter 6, you might use one of the following ideas to add to your portfolio.

- Draw two diagrams, side by side, to compare the balance of government achieved by the Roman Republic with the balance of power achieved by the Constitution of the United States.
- As an adviser to Octavian, write a persuasive argument convincing him to become the sole ruler of Rome but not to abolish the Senate.
- With another student, role-play the meeting of Pope Leo and Attila in A.D. 452, in which the pope persuades the Hun to withdraw his forces. Record the meeting on videotape or audiotape or as a written dialogue.

2. CONNECT TO TODAY: Cooperative Learning

THEME **EMPIRE BUILDING** The spread of the Roman Republic owed much to strategic alliances made with territories distant from Rome. The United States, too, has used alliances to bolster its strength in the world. Work with a team to prepare and present a short television documentary about the relationship between the United States and one of its allies today.

INTERNET Using the Internet or library resources, research information about the alliance. Devise a script that answers questions such as why the United States made the alliance, what special historical circumstances surrounded the alliance, and how the alliance has benefited both nations.

- Make comparisons with the Roman Republic. Do additional research on the republic's system of alliances if needed.
- Draw a conclusion about whether or not the United States used its alliances for building a kind of "empire" or for other reasons.

3. INTERPRETING A TIME LINE

Revisit the time line on pages 106–107. Did Christianity arise before, during, or after the *Pax Romana*? Explain your reasoning.

FOCUS ON **ART**

Trajan's Column in Rome is a monument that shows the Emperor Trajan's victories against Dacia (modern Romania) on a relief spiral 650 feet long. This detail depicts Roman soldiers defeating the Dacians.

- What kinds of equipment do the Roman soldiers have?

Connect to History Public monuments like Trajan's Column appeared all over the empire.

- Why do you think the Romans told their history with images on monuments rather than with words?
- What values are the Romans celebrating on monuments like Trajan's Column?

1. LIVING HISTORY: UNIT PORTFOLIO PROJECT

Standards for Evaluation
Diagrams should meet the following criteria:

- Show clearly the balance of power in each system.
- Include the hierarchy and succession of power.
- Show what power citizens have in each system.

Standards for Evaluation
Arguments should meet the following criteria:

- Mention Octavian's leadership qualities.
- Explain why he would be a better ruler than others.
- Explain the role of the Senate and why the Senate should not be abolished.

Standards for Evaluation
Dialogues should meet the following criteria:

- Clearly reflect the goals of the pope and Attila.
- Present the pope's arguments for asking Attila to withdraw.
- Present Attila's objections and the pope's replies that win the debate.

2. CONNECT TO TODAY: COOPERATIVE LEARNING

Standards for Evaluation
Documentaries should meet the following criteria:

- Identify the country chosen and explain the history of its alliance with the United States.
- Compare the U.S. alliance with that of Rome and its allies.
- Present strong evidence for the conclusion drawn.

3. INTERPRETING A TIME LINE

Christianity arose *during* the *Pax Romana*. Octavian (Caesar Augustus) was emperor at the time of Jesus' birth. Christianity spread throughout the empire during the next 300 years, which also coincided with the *Pax Romana*.

FOCUS ON **ART**

Possible Responses: The Romans are wearing helmets and body armor and are using shields and swords.

Connect to History Romans told their history in images because many Romans could not read and because pictures would be understood by people who spoke a language other than Latin. The Romans were celebrating martial and civic values: strength, courage, power, honor, discipline, conquest.

CRITICAL THINKING

1. FROM REPUBLIC TO EMPIRE
Republic only: balanced government, popular representation. Both: senate; strong military; expanding territory; rich landowners; landless poor. Empire only: powerful emperor; long-distance trade; Christianity.

2. PERSECUTION OF CHRISTIANS
Possible Response: Christians must have been courageous, faithful, and committed to die for their beliefs.

3. DIOCLETIAN
Some students may feel the decision was flawed because division weakened the empire. The Western Empire became more vulnerable to decay and invasion from outside. As proof, they might point to the eventual fall of the Western Empire. Others may argue that Diocletian's decision was justified. It allowed the Eastern Empire to continue after the Western Empire had fallen.

4. ANALYZING PRIMARY SOURCES
They thought Augustus was a hero. They said he was "filled with virtue," "a saviour," and even a "god." Most students would probably agree that Augustus deserved the officials' praise for ending the terrible civil wars and for bringing prosperity to the empire.

India and China Establish Empires

	Key Ideas	COPY MASTERS	ASSESSMENT

SECTION 1
First Empires of India
pp. 173–176

Key Ideas

Both the Mauryan and Gupta empires temporarily unify India. During part of the Mauryan Empire, government policies are based on Buddhist teachings of nonviolence and tolerance. Indian culture thrives during the Gupta Empire.

 In-Depth Resources: Unit 2
- **Guided Reading,** p. 39
- **Primary Source:** from *Arthasastra* by Kautlya, p. 45
- **Literature:** from the *Panchatantra* by Vishmusharmam, p. 49
- **History Makers:** Chandra Gupta II, p. 52

PE *Section 1 Assessment,* p. 176

Formal Assessment
- Section Quiz, p. 78

Alternative Assessment Book
- Standards for Evaluating a Product or Performance

SECTION 2
Trade Spreads Indian Religions and Culture
pp. 177–180

Changes in Buddhism and Hinduism make these religions more personal and appealing to the masses. India enters a highly productive period in art, literature, science, and mathematics. Through trade, Indian culture spreads to much of Asia.

 In-Depth Resources: Unit 2
- **Guided Reading,** p. 40
- **Primary Source:** from the *Puranas,* p. 46
- **Literature:** from *Shakuntala* by Kalidasa, p. 50

PE *Section 2 Assessment,* p. 180

Formal Assessment
- Section Quiz, p. 79

Alternative Assessment Book
- Standards for Evaluating a Cooperative Activity

SECTION 3
Han Emperors in China
pp. 181–187

The Han Dynasty unifies China and develops a highly structured, bureaucratic government, which lasts about 400 years. Advances in technology and culture are made, but laws favoring landowners create economic and political instability.

In-Depth Resources: Unit 2
- **Guided Reading,** p. 41
- **Skillbuilder Practice:** Formulating Historical Questions, p. 42
- **Geography Application:** The Great Wall of China, p. 43
- **Primary Source:** from *Lessons for Women* by Ban Zhao, p. 47
- **History Makers:** Wudi, p. 53
- **Connections Across Time and Cultures:** Governing an Empire, p. 54

PE *Section 3 Assessment,* p. 187

Formal Assessment
- Section Quiz, p. 80

Alternative Assessment Book
- Standards for Evaluating a Cooperative Activity

CHAPTER RESOURCES

Chapter Overview

Empires in both India and China establish powerful dynasties and develop strong, vibrant cultures. Invaders in India introduce new customs and knowledge to Indian society. In China, conquered peoples are made part of Chinese culture through marriage and education. Ruling styles and cultural advances vary in each empire.

 Telescoping the Times
- Chapter Summary, pp. 25–27

Planning for Block Schedules

PE *Chapter Assessment,* pp. 188–189

Chapter Activities, p. 189

Formal Assessment
- Chapter Test, forms A and B, pp. 81–86

Test Generator

Alternative Assessment Book

TECHNOLOGY

 Warm-Up Transparency 7

 Geography Transparencies
- GT7 India Under the Mauryan Dynasty, 250 B.C.

 Electronic Library of Primary Sources
- from the *Arthasastra*
- from the Code of Manu

 INTERNET RESOURCES
www.mlworldhistory.com

 Warm-Up Transparency 7

 World Art and Cultures Transparencies
- AT15 Buddhist cave painting

 Religions of the World
- Buddhism
- Hinduism

 Electronic Library of Primary Sources
from the *Ramayana*

 INTERNET RESOURCES
www.mlworldhistory.com

 Warm-Up Transparency 7

 World Art and Cultures Transparencies
- AT16 Chinese tomb rubbing

 Critical Thinking Transparencies
- CT7 The Technological Revolution in Han China

 Religions of the World
- Confucianism

 Patterns of Interaction: Trade Connects the World

 INTERNET RESOURCES
www.mlworldhistory.com

 Chapter Summaries on Audiocassette in English and Spanish

 INTERNET RESOURCES
www.mlworldhistory.com

Block Scheduling (90 MINUTES)

Day 1

Section 1, pp. 173–176

Section 2, pp. 177–180

 COOPERATIVE ACTIVITY
Researching Indian Arts, p. 178 (Teacher's Edition)

Section 3, pp. 181–187

 COOPERATIVE ACTIVITY
Comparing Bureaucracies, p. 183 (Teacher's Edition)

Section Assessments, pp. 176, 180, 187

Chapter Assessment, pp. 188–189

Yearly Pacing *Chapter 7 Total:* 1 day *Yearly Total:* 85 days

 Planning for Block Schedules

Customizing for Special Needs

Students Acquiring English

 Access for Students Acquiring English
- **Guided Reading** for Sections 1–3 (Spanish), pp. 75–77
- **Chapter Summary** (Spanish), pp. 72–74
- **Skillbuilder Practice** Formulating Historical Questions, (Spanish) p. 78
- **Geography Application** The Great Wall of China (Spanish), p. 79

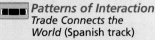 *Patterns of Interaction* Trade Connects the World (Spanish track)

 Chapter Summaries on Audiocassette in English and Spanish

 INTERNET RESOURCES
www.mlworldhistory.com
The Diverse Classroom

Less Proficient Readers

 In-Depth Resources: Unit 2
- **Guided Reading** for Sections 1–3, pp. 39–41
- **Skillbuilder Practice** Formulating Historical Questions, p. 42
- **Geography Application** The Great Wall of China, p. 43

 Telescoping the Times
- Chapter Summary, pp. 25–27

 Chapter Summaries on Audiocassette

Gifted and Talented Students

 In-Depth Resources: Unit 2

Primary Sources:
- from *Arthasastra* by Kautilya, p. 45
- from the *Puranas,* p. 46
- from *Lessons for Women* by Ban Zhao, p. 47

History Makers
- Chandra Gupta II, p. 52
- Wudi, p. 53

Connections to Literature READINGS FOR STUDENTS

In-Depth Resources: Unit 2
Literature: from the *Panchatantra* by Vishmusharmam, p. 49
from Shakuntala by Kalidasa, p. 50

Enrichment Reading
- Lee, Sherman
Far Eastern Art
New York: Abrams, 1994

This stunning book shows great Indian, Chinese, and Japanese art from the 5th century B.C. to the present.

- Mascaro, Juan, trans.
The Dhammapada
New York: Penguin, 1973

Buddhist tales of travel, adventure, and foolishness.

PE = Pupil's Edition	= Overhead Transparency	= Software	= Video
= Copy Master	= CD-ROM	= Audiocassette	= Internet

India and China Establish Empires 300 B.C.–A.D. 550

Accessing Prior Knowledge

• Ask students to read the captions accompanying the artifacts and discuss what they have learned so far about religious beliefs in these two regions.

Drawing Conclusions and Making Inferences

• After students read about silk making in China, ask them this question: What did the Chinese think would happen if other cultures learned how to make silk?

• After reading about the bronze money tree from Han China, ask students to infer the value placed on money and wealth by the Han Empire.

Geography Connection

Ask students to study the map of India and China in A.D. 200.

• Which region seems better situated for overseas trade, India or China? Why?

• Which cities in China could become important centers of overseas trade?

PREVIEWING THEMES

Power and Authority

Alexander the Great used military power to invade India. In China, rival kings fought for power after the Qin Dynasty ended. In both countries, generals seized power and used their authority to strengthen government.

Cultural Interaction

From the time of the Aryan nomads, Indian civilization was a product of interacting cultures. Starting in the 100s B.C., new invaders changed Indian culture. In China, the government pressured conquered peoples to adopt Chinese culture.

Religious and Ethical Systems

By 250 B.C., Hinduism and Buddhism were India's two main religions. Both changed over time to have more popular appeal. In China, government officials began to be educated in the ethical teachings of Confucius.

INTERNET CONNECTION

Visit us at **www.mlworldhistory.com** to learn more about India and China.

INDIA AND CHINA, A.D. 200

India, A.D. 200

By about A.D. 300, Shiva was one of the most popular Hindu gods in India. This statue shows Shiva dancing on the demon of ignorance. Shiva holds fire in one hand, symbolizing his power to destroy the universe so that he can re-create it. Although terrifying, he was often merciful to humans.

170

GEOGRAPHY THEMES

Region

Ask students to look closely at the maps here and at the physical geography map of Asia on page 977 in the Atlas. Direct them to note which geographic features are common to both India and China. *Possible answers: Mountains,* *deserts, plateaus, and rivers.* Then ask which geographic feature separates these regions. *Answer: Himalaya Mountains.* Discuss with students how geography might affect interaction between these two regions.

Movement

Explain that trade plays an important role in the growth of the cultures discussed in this chapter. Ask students to study the map showing the Silk Road on this page and the world map on page 972 in the Atlas. Then ask the following questions: Where to the west of China might the Silk Road be headed? Which regions along the way might have been trading partners with China? Encourage students to hypothesize how this route might have linked China with India. You might also ask students to describe the kinds of cultural information and knowledge that trading partners often exchange.

ADDITIONAL RESOURCES

Books for the Teacher

- Bentley, Jerry H. *Old World Encounters.* New York: Oxford UP, 1993. Cross-cultural encounters from the age of the Silk Road on.

- Wolpert, Stanley A. *India.* Berkeley: U of California P, 1991. Study of South Asian civilization.

- de Bary, William Theodore, comp. *Sources of Chinese Tradition.* New York: Columbia UP, 1960. Primary sources, with background information, from all periods of Chinese history.

Books for the Student

- Kanitkar, Helen, and Hemant Kanitkar. *Asoka and Indian Civilization.* San Diego: Greenhaven, 1980.

- Kranz, Rachel. *Across Asia by Land.* New York: Facts on File, 1991. History of the trade routes that tied East to West.

▬▬▬ Videos

- *China: A History.* Society for Visual Education, 1988. 800-829-1900. Effects of isolation on Chinese civilization.

- *The Silk Road.* Ambrose Video, 1990. 800-526-4663.

◉ Software

- *The Silk Road.* CD-ROM. Social Studies School Service, 1995, 800-421-4246. The Silk Road region in the past and present.

In **3 B.C.**, during the **Han** Dynasty, thousands of Chinese people ran along the roads, singing and dancing to worship a goddess called Queen Mother of the West. She is represented by a tiny figure on each branch of this bronze money tree, found in Sichuan. Perhaps through the goddess's magic, the branches of this tree grow the round coin with the square hole used in Han times.

Silk was such a valuable trade item that Chinese law made it a crime to let foreigners know the secret of silk making. According to legend, this **princess** smuggled silkworms out of **China** by hiding them in her crown. Actually, Nestorian Christian monks smuggled silkworms out in A.D. 555.

THE SILK ROADS

Yen (Beijing)

Luoyang
Chang'an (Xi'an)

Yellow Sea

Nanjing

CHINA

Panyu (Guangzhou)

South China Sea

PACIFIC OCEAN

171

■ Han Dynasty
■ Modern China
□ Modern India

0 — 250 Miles
0 — 500 Kilometers

N

HISTORY THROUGH ART

The Dancing Shiva

The statue of the Hindu god Shiva is an icon, or a figure with specific meanings associated with it. When Shiva is shown dancing, as he is here, he is called *Nataraja*, which means "Lord of Dance." Nataraja is a symbol of the rhythm of the universe. The objects the dancing Shiva holds and the gestures he makes symbolize specific powers he has and represent the five acts of creation that are part of Hindu philosophy.

The hourglass-shaped drum Shiva holds in his back right hand symbolizes creation. His front right hand is held in a pose that means "don't be afraid" and symbolizes protection. His front left arm is held across his chest to represent an elephant trunk, which symbolizes solace. The fire in Shiva's back left hand symbolizes destruction and the end of the universe. Shiva stands on the demon to rid the universe of ignorance.

Interpreting the Art What other religious figures are often depicted in statues? Do these statues show the figures in specific poses that have special meanings?

Interact with History

This Interact with History feature motivates students by inviting them to put themselves in a key historical situation: a weaver in an ancient Indian empire is asked to be a spy. As they imagine themselves having to decide between loyalty to friends and loyalty to self, students will weigh their options, visualize the situation, and become decision-makers.

Purpose

- to prepare students for studying the rise of empires in India and China
- to help students understand the control that was exerted by emperors
- to help students make connections with people and events they will study in this chapter

Teaching Strategy

Thinking Critically After students have imagined themselves in the situation described on this page, have them answer the key questions and give reasons for their decisions.

EXAMINING *the* ISSUES

Following are suggestions for addressing each bulleted question.

1 If you know someone has committed a crime and you don't tell anyone about it, are you helping the criminal?

2 How do you think you might feel if you knew that someone was spying on you? Would you be able to trust anyone?

3 Is it right for anyone to try to control others by spying?

Making Connections Ask students to discuss the way other emperors in Rome and Persia exercised power.

Follow Up

A feature on the chapter assessment will ask students to reevaluate their responses to the situation presented on this page.

Interact *with* History

You are a weaver working at your loom when a stranger enters your shop. You fear it is one of the emperor's inspectors, coming to check the quality of your cloth. The man eyes you sternly and then, in a whisper, asks if you will spy on other weavers in your neighborhood. If you take the job, you will be paid the equivalent of four years' earnings. But you would have to turn in one of your friends, whom you suspect is not paying enough sales tax to the government.

Would you be a spy?

This man sits by the window and writes down what he sees. He may be a spy for the emperor.

This person points toward something in the street. He comments on the scene to his friend.

This soldier's job is to check that everyone pays taxes. He seems to be suspicious of the man carrying bananas.

Two people duck behind this woman to gossip about their neighbors

EXAMINING *the* ISSUES

1 • Do citizens have the responsibility to turn in people who are committing crimes?

2 • What kinds of tensions might exist in a society where people spy on each other?

3 • Is it right for a government to control people by spying on them?

As a class, discuss these questions. In your discussion, review what you know about how other emperors exercised power in places such as Persia and Rome.

As you read about the emperors of India and China, notice how they try to control their subjects' lives.

172 Chapter 7

1 First Empires of India

TERMS & NAMES
- Mauryan Empire
- Asoka
- religious toleration
- Tamil
- Gupta Empire
- patriarchal
- matriarchal

MAIN IDEA

The Mauryas and the Guptas established Indian empires, but neither unified India permanently.

WHY IT MATTERS NOW

The diversity of peoples, cultures, beliefs, and languages in India continues to pose challenges to Indian unity today.

SETTING THE STAGE By 600 B.C., almost 1,000 years after the Aryan migrations, many small kingdoms were scattered throughout India. In 326 B.C., Alexander the Great brought the Indus Valley in the northwest under Greek control—but left the region almost immediately. Soon after, a great Indian military leader, Chandragupta Maurya (CHUHN·druh·GUP·tuh MAH·oor·yuh), seized power for himself.

Chandragupta Maurya Builds an Empire

Background
Chandragupta may have been a younger son of the Nanda king.

Chandragupta Maurya may have been born in the powerful kingdom of Magadha. Centered on the lower Ganges River, the kingdom had been ruled for centuries by the Nanda family. Chandragupta gathered an army, killed the Nanda king, and in about 321 B.C. claimed the throne. This began the **Mauryan Empire.**

Chandragupta Unifies North India Chandragupta moved northwest, seizing all the land from Magadha to the Indus. Around 305 B.C., Chandragupta began to battle Seleucus I, one of Alexander the Great's generals. Seleucus had inherited the eastern part of Alexander's empire. He wanted to reestablish Greek control over the Indus Valley. After several years of fighting, however, Chandragupta defeated Seleucus, who gave up some of his territory to Chandragupta. By 303 B.C., the Mauryan Empire stretched more than 2,000 miles, uniting north India politically for the first time. (See the map on page 175.)

THINK THROUGH HISTORY
A. Evaluating Decisions
Explain whether Chandragupta was wise to use heavy taxes to finance his army.
A. Possible Answers Yes, because he needed the army to defeat enemies. No, because he was hurting the economy.

To win his wars of conquest, Chandragupta raised a vast army: 600,000 soldiers on foot, 30,000 soldiers on horseback, and 9,000 elephants. To clothe, feed, and pay these troops, the government levied high taxes. For example, farmers had to pay up to one half the value of their crops to the king. The government heavily taxed income from trading, mining, and manufacturing.

Running the Empire Chandragupta relied on an adviser named Kautilya (kow·TIHL·yuh), who was a member of the priestly caste. Kautilya wrote a ruler's handbook called the *Arthasastra* (AHR·thuh·SHAHS·truh). This book teaches how to hold a vast empire together.

Following Kautilya's advice, Chandragupta created a highly bureaucratic government. He carefully chose his officials and had them closely supervised. Chandragupta divided the empire into four provinces, each headed by a royal prince. Each province was then divided into local districts, whose officials assessed taxes and enforced the law.

City Life and Country Life Eager to stay at peace with the Indian emperor, Seleucus sent an ambassador, Megasthenes (muh·GAS·thuh·neez), to Chandragupta's capital. In his diary, Megasthenes wrote glowing descriptions of Chandragupta's palace. The palace was filled

SPOTLIGHT ON

Kautilya's *Arthasastra*
The *Arthasastra* states,

> The welfare of the king does not lie in the fulfillment of what is dear to him; whatever is dear to the subjects constitutes his welfare.

Although this sounds noble, the *Arthasastra* is better known for proposing tough-minded policies. For example, the manual suggests that the king hire an army of spies to gather information about his subjects by posing as priests, students, beggars, or merchants. The *Arthasastra* also urges the king to make war against neighboring kingdoms that are weak.

Although Kautilya began the *Arthasastra,* other royal advisers added to it for centuries to come. The manual is often compared to a 16th-century European book on how to rule: *The Prince* by Machiavelli, which also offers hardheaded political advice.

India and China Establish Empires **173**

Section 1 Overview

OBJECTIVES

1. To describe the rise and fall of India's first unified kingdom.

2. To compare events in India's three regions after the fall of the Mauryan Empire.

3. To describe the rise of the Gupta Empire and daily life in India during this period.

SKILLBUILDER

- Interpreting maps: region, place, p. 175

CRITICAL THINKING

- Evaluating decisions, p. 173
- Making inferences, p. 174
- Clarifying, p.174
- Contrasting, p. 176
- Supporting opinions, p. 176

FOCUS
5-Minute Warm-Up

▶ **Evaluating**
Have students answer these questions to explore how an empire develops under different rulers.

1. Read the History Makers feature on page 174. What kind of leader was Chandragupta?

2. How was Asoka different from Chandragupta as an emperor?

 WARM-UP TRANSPARENCY 7

OBJECTIVE ❶ INSTRUCT

Chandragupta Maurya Builds an Empire

▶ **Key Ideas**
- Chandragupta Maurya unifies much of northern India through conquest.
- Chandragupta creates a bureaucratic government and exempts farmers from military service.

 IN-DEPTH RESOURCES: UNIT 2
Primary Source: from *Arthasastra* by Kautilya, p. 45

 ELECTRONIC LIBRARY OF PRIMARY SOURCES
from the *Arthasastra*

(continued on next page)

SECTION 1 RESOURCES

PRINT RESOURCES

IN-DEPTH RESOURCES: UNIT 2
Guided Reading, p. 39
Primary Source: from *Arthasastra* by Kautilya, p. 45
Literature: from the *Panchatantra* by Vishmusharmam, p. 49
History Makers: Chandra Gupta II, p. 52

ACCESS FOR STUDENTS ACQUIRING ENGLISH
Guided Reading (Spanish), p. 75

FORMAL ASSESSMENT
Section Quiz, p. 78

ALTERNATIVE ASSESSMENT BOOK

TECHNOLOGY RESOURCES

GEOGRAPHY TRANSPARENCIES
GT7 India Under the Mauryan Dynasty, 250 B.C.

CD-ROM
Electronic Library of Primary Sources

INTERNET www.mlworldhistory.com

Teacher's Edition **173**

(continued from page 173)
• Chandragupta's grandson, Asoka, rules by Buddhist principles and spreads this religion.

 IN-DEPTH RESOURCES: UNIT 2
Guided Reading, p. 39

ACCESS FOR STUDENTS ACQUIRING ENGLISH
Guided Reading (Spanish), p. 75

MORE ABOUT . . .
Asoka

Today Asoka is one of India's most celebrated leaders. Yet it wasn't until 1837, when Asoka's edicts were deciphered, that he became a well-known historical figure. The edicts reveal information about Asoka and his policies. In some edicts he shows a paternalistic or fatherly feeling toward his subjects. He refers to them as "my children."

HISTORY MAKERS
Chandragupta Maurya and Asoka

Religion played an important role in the lives of Chandragupta and his grandson. Ask students to compare the ruling styles and religious beliefs of these two men. Encourage interested students to research and compare Jainism and Buddhism and present their findings to the class.

OBJECTIVE **2** INSTRUCT

A Period of Turmoil

▶ Key Ideas
• After Asoka's death, the Andhra dynasty dominates central India for hundreds of years.
• Invaders pour into northern India. Some southern rulers break away from the empire. Three ancient kingdoms wage war.

⊙ **ELECTRONIC LIBRARY OF PRIMARY SOURCES**
from the Code of Manu

---

with gold-covered pillars, numerous fountains, and imposing thrones. His capital city featured beautiful parks and bustling markets.

Megasthenes also described the countryside and how farmers lived:

A VOICE FROM THE PAST

[Farmers] are exempted from military service and cultivate their lands undisturbed by fear. They do not go to cities, either on business or to take part in their tumults. It therefore frequently happens that at the same time, and in the same part of the country, men may be seen marshaled for battle and risking their lives against the enemy, while other men are ploughing or digging in perfect security under the protection of these soldiers.

MEGASTHENES, in *Geography* by Strabo

In 301 B.C., Chandragupta's son assumed the throne and ruled for 32 years. Then Chandragupta's grandson, **Asoka** (uh·SOH·kuh), brought the Mauryan Empire to its greatest heights.

Asoka Promotes Buddhism Asoka became king of the Mauryan Empire in 269 B.C. At first, he followed Kautilya's philosophy of waging war to expand his power. He led a long campaign against his neighbors to the southeast in the state of Kalinga. During this bloody war, 100,000 soldiers were slain and even more civilians perished.

Although victorious, Asoka felt sorrow over the slaughter at Kalinga. As a result, he studied Buddhism and decided to rule by Buddha's teaching of nonviolence and "peace to all beings." Throughout the empire, Asoka erected huge stone pillars inscribed with his new policies. Some edicts guaranteed that Asoka would treat his subjects fairly and humanely. Others preached nonviolence. Still others urged **religious toleration**—acceptance of people who held different beliefs—and acceptance of people of all cultural backgrounds.

Asoka had extensive roads built so that he could visit the far corners of India. He also improved conditions along these roads to make travel easier for his officials and to improve communication in the vast empire. For example, he had trees planted to provide shade. Every nine miles, he had wells dug and rest houses built. This allowed travelers to stop and refresh themselves. Asoka even ordered the creation of watering places for animals. Such actions demonstrated Asoka's concern for his subjects' well-being.

Noble as Asoka's policies of toleration and nonviolence were, they failed to hold the empire together once Asoka was gone. Soon after he died in 232 B.C., the empire began to break up.

 This carved set of three lions appeared on top of one of Asoka's pillars. This trio of lions is still used as a symbol of India.

HISTORY MAKERS

Chandragupta Maurya
?–298 B.C.

Chandragupta feared being assassinated—maybe because he had killed a king to get his throne. To avoid being poisoned, he made servants taste all his food. To avoid being murdered in bed, he slept in a different room every night. A guard of armed women surrounded him at all times and killed anyone who came inside their lines.

Although Chandragupta was a fierce warrior for most of his life, in 301 B.C., he voluntarily gave up his throne and converted to Jainism. Jainists taught nonviolence and respect for all life. With a group of monks, he traveled to southern India. There he followed the Jainist custom of fasting until he starved to death.

Asoka
?–232 B.C.

One of Asoka's edicts states,

If one hundredth part or one thousandth of those who died in Kalinga . . . should now suffer similar fate, [that] would be a matter of pain to His Majesty.

Even though Asoka wanted to be a loving, peaceful ruler, he still had to control a huge empire. To do so, he had to balance Kautilya's methods of keeping power and Buddha's urgings to be unselfish.

After converting to Buddhism, Asoka softened Chandragupta's harsher policies. Instead of spies, he employed officials to look out for his subjects' welfare. He kept his army but sought to rule humanely. In addition, Asoka sent missionaries to Southeast Asia to spread Buddhism.

A Period of Turmoil

Asoka's death left a power vacuum that was felt through the entire subcontinent. In northern and central India, regional kings challenged the imperial government. The kingdoms of central India, which had only been loosely held in the Mauryan Empire,

174 Chapter 7

THINK THROUGH HISTORY
B. Making Inferences Did Mauryan India place a high value on agriculture? What information in this quotation indicates that?
B. Possible Answer Yes. Farmers were exempt from military service so they could keep growing food.

Vocabulary
edicts: official, public announcements of policy.

THINK THROUGH HISTORY
C. Clarifying Which of Asoka's actions show the influence of Buddha's teaching of "peace to all beings"?
C. Possible Answer He urged acceptance of people of all beliefs and cultures; he practiced nonviolence; he promoted his subjects welfare by making travel easier.

TEACHING OPTIONS

CONNECTIONS ACROSS TIME AND PLACE

Nonviolence The Buddhist principle of nonviolence, which Asoka used to rule the Mauryan Empire, has been used by other great leaders to create political and social change. Mahatma Gandhi used nonviolent resistance to gain India's independence from Britain. Martin Luther King, Jr., used nonviolent resistance to gain civil rights for African Americans. Ask students to name forms of nonviolent resistance, such as sit-ins, marches, fasts, and strikes. Then ask students why they think nonviolence is a powerful tool for creating change.

EXPLORING PRIMARY SOURCES

A Voice from the Past The quote from Megasthenes may lead readers to believe that Mauryan Empire farmers received preferential treatment. However, farmers had to pay heavy taxes to support the army.

Megasthenes was a Greek ambassador in Chandragupta's empire. Ask students how Megasthenes's point of view shows bias, or one-sidedness. Then ask what might have motivated Megasthenes to use bias. *Possible answers: It makes farmers sound privileged. Motivation: ensure that India stayed at peace with Greece.*

regained their independence soon after the death of Asoka. The Andhra (AHN·druh) Dynasty arose and dominated the region for hundreds of years. Because of their central position, the Andhras profited from the extensive trade between north and south India and also built up trade with Rome, Sri Lanka, and Southeast Asia.

At the same time, northern India had to absorb a flood of new people fleeing political instability in other regions of Asia. For 500 years, wave after wave of Greeks, Persians, and Central Asians poured through the mountain passes into northern India. Without a doubt, these invaders disrupted Indian society. But they also introduced new languages and customs that added to the already rich blend of Indian culture.

Southern India also experienced turmoil. Some rulers in southern India broke away from the empire after Asoka's death. In addition, India's southern tip was home to three kingdoms that had never been conquered by the Mauryans. The people who lived in this region spoke the **Tamil** (TAM·uhl) language and are called the Tamil people. These three kingdoms often were at war with one another and with other states.

Background
When the Aryans entered India about 1500 B.C., they drove many of the pre-Aryans south to this region.

Indian Empires, 250 B.C.–A.D. 400

- Mauryan Empire, 250 B.C.
- Gupta Empire, A.D. 400
- Areas under Gupta influence
- Tamil kingdoms

HINDU KUSH MTS.
HIMALAYAS
CHINA
Indus R.
THAR DESERT
Mathura
Ayodhya
Ganges R.
Prayaga
Pataliputra
Brahmaputra R.
20°N
Narmada R.
Mouths of the Ganges
Arabian Sea
Godavari R.
WESTERN GHATS
EASTERN GHATS
Bay of Bengal
Cauvery R.
INDIAN OCEAN
N
0   500 Miles
0   1,000 Kilometers
80°E

GEOGRAPHY SKILLBUILDER: Interpreting Maps
1. **Region** *Compare the region occupied by the Gupta Empire to that occupied by the Mauryan Empire. Discuss size, location, and physical characteristics.*
2. **Place** *The two empires had one boundary—the northeast boundary—that was roughly the same. Explain why neither empire expanded further in this direction.*

The Gupta Empire

After 500 years of invasion and turmoil, a strong leader again arose in the northern state of Magadha. His name was Chandra Gupta (GUP·tuh), but he was no relation to India's first emperor, Chandragupta Maurya. India's second empire, the **Gupta Empire,** oversaw a great flowering of Indian civilization, especially Hindu culture.

Chandra Gupta Builds an Empire The first Gupta emperor came to power, not through battle, but by marrying the daughter of an old, influential royal family. After this useful marriage, Chandra Gupta I took the title of "Great King of Kings" in A.D. 320. His empire included Magadha and the area just to the north of it, with the central region of the Ganges River as a power base.

Chandra Gupta I's son, Samudra (suh·MU·druh) Gupta, became king in A.D. 335. Although he was a lover of poetry and music, Samudra also had a warlike side. He expanded the empire with 40 years of war and conquest. This gave him control over most of the lands immediately surrounding his father's empire.

Daily Life in India The Gupta era is the first period about which historians have much information concerning daily life in India. Most Indians lived in small villages, where life followed a stable rhythm that beat steadily on for centuries. Craftspeople and merchants clustered in specific districts. They had shops on the street level and lived in the rooms above.

India and China Establish Empires **175**

History from Visuals

Indian Empires, 250 B.C.–A.D. 400
Interpreting the Map Tell students to read the map key and use it to identify the territory of the two empires and the area under Gupta influence.

Extension Activity Have students compare this map with the map of modern Asia in the Atlas, page 976. Ask students how the boundaries of modern India compare with those of the Mauryan and Gupta Empires. Also ask them to name the present-day countries that exist in what was the territory of the Mauryan Empire. *Bangladesh, Bhutan, Nepal, Pakistan, Afghanistan.*

SKILLBUILDER Answers
1. Possible Response: The Mauryan Empire is larger; it extends farther to the northwest and south; it included Hindu Kush, and the Gupta Empire did not. Both empires included the Indus, Ganges, Narmada, and Godavari rivers.
2. The Himalayas lie beyond the northeast boundary and blocked expansion in that direction.

 GEOGRAPHY TRANSPARENCIES
GT7 India Under the Mauryan Dynasty, 250 B.C.

OBJECTIVE 3 INSTRUCT

The Gupta Empire

▶ *Key Ideas*
- The Gupta family unifies northern India into the Gupta Empire.
- Most Indians are farmers living in small villages. Families may be headed by men or women.
- The Gupta Empire makes advances in religion, science, culture, and trade.

IN-DEPTH RESOURCES: UNIT 2
History Makers: Chandra Gupta II, p. 52

CUSTOMIZING FOR SPECIAL NEEDS

Less Proficient Readers Some students may need extra help to understand the events that took place in India after the fall of the Mauryan Empire. Have these students work in pairs or small groups. Partners or group members should reread the passage titled "A Period of Turmoil" and then take turns pointing to a region on the map and explaining what happened there. Remind students to look back at the text if they can't remember information about a region.

CUSTOMIZING FOR SPECIAL NEEDS

Gifted and Talented Students Have students read the literature selection for this section in the Teacher's Resources. Before they read, explain that the story is a fable and ask students what they know about fables. Make sure students understand that a fable is a story that teaches a lesson. After they read, have students hold a group discussion to answer the questions at the end of the story and identify the lesson of the story.

 IN-DEPTH RESOURCES: UNIT 2
Literature: from the *Panchatantra* by Vishmusharmam, p. 49.

Empires of India
321 B.C.–A.D. 415

Interpreting the Time Line Tell students to read the time line and describe the events included in it. Then have students determine the length of the Mauryan and Gupta dynasties. *Events: When rulers assumed the throne and when the last ruler in each dynasty died. Mauryan dynasty—89 years; Gupta dynasty—95 years.*

Extension Activity Ask students to use the time line to make generalizations about the duration of each empire, and when periods of warring and great cultural achievement occurred. *Empires lasted less than 100 years; period of warring in the beginning, cultural achievements at the end.*

ASSESS & RETEACH

Section 1 Assessment
Have students work in pairs to answer the questions. Then have partners compare their answers with another pair.

Section Quiz

FORMAL ASSESSMENT
Section quiz, p. 78

Reteaching Activity
CLASS TIME: 15 MINUTES

Draw a time line on the board from 321 B.C. to A.D. 420 and have students fill in when the Mauryan and Gupta emperors came to power and what they accomplished. Also have students fill in events during the 500 years of turmoil.

CLOSE ACTIVITY

CLASS TIME: 30 MINUTES

Identifying Key Concepts
Distribute seven index cards to pairs of students and have them write one item from the Terms & Names list on each card. Then have partners mix the cards and put them facedown in a pile. Partners should take turns choosing a card and telling what they know about the term or name on it. Tell partners to review the section if they need help.

176 Chapter 7

Empires of India, 321 B.C.–A.D. 415

Mauryan Empire   Gupta Empire

320 B.C.   A.D. 420

321 B.C. Chandragupta kills the king and claims the throne.

301 B.C. Chandragupta's son assumes the throne.

269 B.C. Chandragupta's grandson Asoka becomes king. Height of the Mauryan Empire.

232 B.C. Asoka dies.

500 years of turmoil follow Asoka's death.

A.D. 320 Chandra Gupta I becomes king.

A.D. 335 Chandra Gupta's son Samudra becomes king.

A.D. 375 Chandra Gupta II becomes king. Gupta Empire reaches its height.

A.D. 415 Chandra Gupta II dies.

The majority of villagers, however, were farmers, who walked daily from their homes to the fields outlying the town. Most Indian families were **patriarchal,** headed by the eldest male. Parents, grandparents, uncles, aunts, and children all worked together to raise their crops. Because drought was common, farmers often had to irrigate their crops. There was a tax on water, and every month, people had to donate a day's worth of labor to maintain wells, irrigation ditches, reservoirs, and dams. As in Mauryan times, farmers owed a large part of their earnings to the king.

Southern India followed a different cultural pattern. Some Tamil groups were **matriarchal,** which meant that the mother, rather than the father, was head of the family. Property, and sometimes the throne, was passed through the female line. One famous Tamil ruler was the queen of the Pandyas, whom Megasthenes described as having an army of 500 elephants, 4,000 cavalry, and 13,000 infantry.

Height of the Gupta Empire While village life followed unchanging traditional patterns, the royal court of the third Gupta emperor was a place of excitement and growth. Many Indians consider this emperor, Chandra Gupta II, to be the prince of princes among the Guptas because of his heroic and gallant qualities.

Chandra Gupta II defeated the Shakas—an enemy kingdom to the west. He added their west coast territory to his empire. This allowed the Guptas to take part in the profitable trade between India and the Mediterranean world. Chandra Gupta II also strengthened his empire through peaceful means by negotiating diplomatic and marriage alliances. For example, he arranged for his daughter to marry a king who controlled the western Deccan (a plateau in south-central India).

Chandra Gupta II ruled for 40 years. Faxian, a Chinese Buddhist who traveled in India during Chandra Gupta II's reign, recorded that his subjects seemed generally happy. During the reign of the first three Guptas, India experienced a period of great achievement in art, literature, religious thought, science, and mathematics. These will be discussed in Section 2. After the death of Chandra Gupta II, another wave of invaders again threatened northern India. These fierce fighters, called the Hunas, were cousins to the Huns who were disrupting the Roman Empire at the same time. Over the next 100 years, the Gupta Empire broke into small separate kingdoms. Many of these were overrun by the Huns and other Central Asian nomads.

THINK THROUGH HISTORY
D. Contrasting
How were the family systems of north and south India different?
D. Answer In north India, men lead the family and inherit property. In some areas of the South, women do.

Section ① Assessment

1. TERMS & NAMES
Identify
- Mauryan Empire
- Asoka
- religious toleration
- Tamil
- Gupta Empire
- patriarchal
- matriarchal

2. TAKING NOTES
Create a Venn diagram comparing the Mauryan and Gupta empires.

Mauryan Empire Only   Both Empires   Gupta Empire Only

Which similarity do you consider most important? Explain.

3. SUPPORTING OPINIONS
Which of the Indian rulers described in this section would you rather live under? Explain your opinion.

THINK ABOUT
- whether the ruler maintained peace and order—and how
- what methods the ruler used to influence his subjects
- developments in art and culture during the ruler's reign

4. THEME ACTIVITY
Power and Authority With a partner, prepare an exhibit called "Symbols of Power." For three of the rulers described in this section, choose an object or image that symbolizes how that ruler exercised power. Write captions explaining why the symbols are appropriate.

176 Chapter 7

ANSWERS

1. TERMS & NAMES
Mauryan Empire, p. 173
Asoka, p. 174
religious toleration, p. 174
Tamil, p. 175
Gupta Empire, p. 175
patriarchal, p. 176
matriarchal, p. 176

2. TAKING NOTES
Possible Responses:
Mauryan—Chandragupta used spies, Asoka followed teachings of Buddha. Both—Unified through force, required high taxes, lasted for about 100 years. Gupta—Defeated the Shakas, period of great cultural achievements, invaded by Hunas.

3. SUPPORTING OPINIONS
Possible Responses:
Chandragupta Maurya, because he tried to control crime; Asoka, because he believed in nonviolence and promoted his subjects' welfare; Chandra Gupta II, because there was a cultural flowering during his reign.

4. THEME ACTIVITY
Standards for Evaluation
An exhibit should meet the following criteria:
- Symbols show something significant about the rulers' methods of exercising power.
- Captions explain why the symbols were chosen.

Trade Spreads Indian Religions and Culture

TERMS & NAMES
- Mahayana
- Theravada
- Brahma
- Vishnu
- Shiva
- Kalidasa
- Silk Roads

MAIN IDEA

Indian religions, culture, and science evolved and spread to other regions through trade.

WHY IT MATTERS NOW

The influence of Indian culture and religions is very evident throughout Southeast Asia today.

SETTING THE STAGE The 500 years between the Mauryan and Gupta empires was a time of upheaval. Invaders poured into India, bringing new ideas and customs. In response, Indians began to change their own culture.

Changes in Religious Thought

By 250 B.C., Hinduism and Buddhism were India's two main faiths. (See Chapter 3.) Hinduism is a complex polytheistic religion that blended Aryan and pre-Aryan beliefs. Buddhism teaches that desire causes suffering and that humans should overcome desire by following the Eightfold Path. Over the centuries, both religions had become increasingly removed from the people. Hinduism became dominated by priests, while the Buddhist ideal of self-denial was difficult to follow.

A More Popular Form of Buddhism The Buddha had stressed that each person could reach a state of peace called nirvana. Nirvana was achieved by rejecting the sensory world and embracing spiritual discipline. After the Buddha died, his followers developed many different interpretations of his teachings.

Although the Buddha had forbidden people to worship him, some began to teach that he was a god. Some Buddhists also began to believe that many people could become Buddhas. These potential Buddhas, called bodhisattvas (BOH·dih·SUHT·vuhs), could choose to give up nirvana and work to save humanity through good works and self-sacrifice. The new ideas changed Buddhism from a religion that emphasized individual discipline. It became a mass religion that offered salvation to all and allowed popular worship. By the first century A.D., Buddhists had divided over the new doctrines. Those who accepted them belonged to the **Mahayana** (MAH·huh·YAH·nuh) sect. Those who held to the Buddha's stricter, original teachings belonged to the **Theravada** (THEHR·uh·VAH·duh) sect. This is also called the Hinayana (HEE·nuh·YAH·nuh) sect, but *Theravada* is preferred.

These new trends in Buddhism inspired Indian art. For example, artists carved huge statues of the Buddha for people to worship. Wealthy Buddhist merchants who were eager to do good deeds paid for the construction of stupas—mounded stone structures built over holy relics. Buddhists walked the paths circling the stupas as a part of their meditation. Merchants also commissioned the carving of cave temples out of solid rock. Artists then adorned these temples with beautiful sculptures and paintings.

A Hindu Rebirth Like Buddhism, Hinduism had become remote from the people. By the time of the Mauryan Empire, Hinduism had developed a complex set of sacrifices that could be performed only by the priests. People who weren't priests had less and less direct connection with the religion.

Gradually, through exposure to other cultures and in response to the popularity of Buddhism, Hinduism changed. Although the religion continued to

THINK THROUGH HISTORY
A. Making Inferences Would the Buddha have approved of the new art? Explain.
A. Possible Answer No, because he had told people not to worship him.

This Buddha is carved in the Gandharan artistic style—a blend of Greco-Roman and Indian styles. For example, the flowing robes are similar to those seen on Roman imperial statues.

India and China Establish Empires **177**

SECTION 2 RESOURCES

PRINT RESOURCES

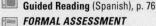 **IN-DEPTH RESOURCES: UNIT 2**
Guided Reading, p. 40
Primary Source: from the *Purarus*, p. 46
Literature: from *Shakuntala* by Kalidasa, p. 50

ACCESS FOR STUDENTS ACQUIRING ENGLISH
Guided Reading (Spanish), p. 76

FORMAL ASSESSMENT
Section Quiz, p. 79

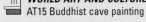 **ALTERNATIVE ASSESSMENT BOOK**

TECHNOLOGY RESOURCES

 WORLD ART AND CULTURES TRANSPARENCIES
AT15 Buddhist cave painting

 CD-ROM
Religions of the World
Electronic Library of Primary Sources

INTERNET www.mlworldhistory.com

Section 2 Overview

OBJECTIVES

(1) To explain why and how religion changed in India.

(2) To describe achievements in Indian literature, art, science, and mathematics.

(3) To summarize Indian trade activity and its effects on India and other Asian cultures.

SKILLBUILDER

- Interpreting maps: movement, p. 179

CRITICAL THINKING

- Making inferences, p. 177
- Drawing conclusions, p. 178
- Summarizing, p. 179
- Analyzing causes, p. 180
- Recognizing effects, p. 180
- Analyzing themes, p. 180

FOCUS
5-Minute Warm-Up

▶ **Interpreting**
To help students understand how cultures interact through trade, have them answer these questions.

1. Study the map and map key on page 179. Which trade products did the Gupta Empire produce?

2. What products did the empire need to get through trade?

WARM-UP TRANSPARENCY 7

OBJECTIVE (1) INSTRUCT

Changes in Religious Thought

▶ **Key Ideas**
- The focus of Buddhism changes from an individual discipline to a mass religion.

(continued on next page)

 RELIGIONS OF THE WORLD
Hinduism
Buddhism

 IN-DEPTH RESOURCES: UNIT 2
Primary Source: from the *Puranas*, p. 46

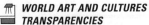 **WORLD ART AND CULTURES TRANSPARENCIES**
AT15 Buddhist cave painting

CONNECT *to* TODAY
Entertainment in India

The Indian movie industry is centered in Bombay, which is sometimes referred to as Bollywood. Popular Indian movies follow a certain formula. The themes reflect close family ties, struggles for justice, and loyalty to friends. Movies always have six to eight songs, colorful dances, brave heroes, and beautiful heroines. Discuss with students formulas used in popular American movies.

MORE ABOUT . . .
Kalidasa

Shakuntala became known in Europe through the 18th-century German writer Goethe. Kalidasa is often described as the Indian Shakespeare.

---

embrace hundreds of gods, a trend toward monotheism was growing. Many people began to believe that there was only one divine force in the universe. The various gods represented parts of that force. The three most important gods were **Brahma** (BRAH·muh), creator of the world; **Vishnu** (VIHSH·noo), preserver of the world; and **Shiva** (SHEE·vuh), destroyer of the world. Of the three, Vishnu and Shiva were by far the favorites. Many Indians began to devote themselves to these two gods. As Hinduism evolved to a more personal religion, its appeal to the masses grew.

Flowering of Indian Culture

Just as Hinduism and Buddhism underwent changes, so did Indian culture and learning. India entered a highly productive period in literature, art, science, and mathematics that continued until roughly A.D. 500.

Literature and the Performing Arts One of India's greatest writers, **Kalidasa** (KAHL·ee·DAHS·uh), may have been the court poet for Chandra Gupta II, who reigned from A.D. 375 to 415. Kalidasa's most famous play is *Shakuntala*. It tells the story of a beautiful girl who falls in love with and marries a middle-aged king. After Shakuntala and her husband are separated, they suffer tragically because of a curse that prevents the king from recognizing his wife when they meet again. Generations of Indians have continued to admire Kalidasa's plays because they are skillfully written and emotionally stirring.

Southern India also has a rich literary tradition. In the second century A.D., the city of Madurai in southern India became a site of writing academies. More than 2,000 Tamil poems from this period still exist. In the following excerpt from a third-century poem, a young man describes his sweetheart cooking him a meal:

> **A VOICE FROM THE PAST**
> There dwells my sweetheart, curving and lovely,
> languid of gaze, with big round earrings,
> and little rings on her tiny fingers.
>   She has cut the leaves of the garden plantain
> and split them in pieces down the stalk
> to serve as platters for the meal.
> Her eyes are filled with the smoke of cooking.
> Her brow, as fair as the crescent moon,
> is covered now with drops of sweat.
>   She wipes it away with the hem of her garment
> and stands in the kitchen, and thinks of me.
>
> **ANONYMOUS TAMIL POET,** quoted in *The Wonder That Was India*

In addition to literature, drama was very popular. In southern India, traveling acting troupes put on performances in cities across the region. Women as well as men took part in these shows that combined drama and dance. Many of the classical dance forms in India today are based on techniques explained in a book written between the first century B.C. and the first century A.D.

Astronomy, Mathematics, and Medicine The expansion of trade spurred the advance of science. Because sailors on trading ships used the stars to help them figure their position at sea, knowledge of astronomy increased. From Greek invaders, Indians adapted Western methods of keeping time. They began to use a calendar based on the cycles of the sun rather than the moon, adopted a seven-day week, and divided each day into hours.

During the Gupta Empire (A.D. 320 to about 500), knowledge of astronomy increased further. Almost 1,000 years before Columbus, Indian astronomers proved

---

CONNECT *to* TODAY

Entertainment in India
Today, drama remains hugely popular in India. India has the largest movie industry in the world. About twice as many full-length feature films are released yearly in India as in the United States.

India produces both popular and serious films. Indian popular films are often love stories that blend music, dance, drama, and action adventure. India's serious films have received worldwide critical praise. In 1992, the Indian director Satyajit Ray received a lifetime achievement Academy Award for making artistic films. His films brought Indian culture to a worldwide audience.

Source: *International Motion Picture Almanac,* 1997

THINK THROUGH HISTORY
B. Drawing Conclusions
Why did the changes in Buddhism and Hinduism make them more popular?
B. Possible Answer
Because they allowed people to hope for salvation and personally take part in worship

---

that the earth was round by observing a lunar eclipse. During the eclipse, the earth's shadow fell across the face of the moon. The astronomers noted that the earth's shadow was curved, indicating that the earth itself was round.

Indian mathematics was among the most advanced in the world. Modern numerals, the zero, and the decimal system, were invented in India. Around A.D. 500, an Indian named Aryabhata (AHR·yuh·BUHT·uh) calculated the value of pi (Π) to four decimal places. He also calculated the length of the solar year as 365.3586805 days. This figure is very close to modern calculations made with an atomic clock.

In medicine, two important medical guides were compiled. These works classified more than 1,000 diseases and described more than 500 medicinal plants. Hindu physicians knew how to perform surgery—including plastic surgery—and possibly gave inoculations.

The Spread of Indian Trade

In addition to knowledge, India has always been rich in precious resources. Spices, diamonds, sapphires, gold, pearls, and beautiful woods—including ebony, teak, and fragrant sandalwood—have always been valuable items of exchange. Trade between India and regions as distant as Africa and Sumeria began more than 4,000 years ago. Trade continued to expand even after the Mauryan Empire ended around 185 B.C.

Overland Trade, East and West The groups who invaded India after the end of Mauryan rule helped to expand India's trade to new regions. For example, Central Asian nomads brought Indians information about the caravan routes that crisscrossed central Asia.

These caravan routes were known as **Silk Roads** because traders used them to bring silk from China to Western Asia and on to Rome. Once Indians learned of the Silk Roads, they realized that they could make great profits by acting as middlemen.

Asian Trade Routes, A.D. 400

Trade route

Trade products produced
- Cloth
- Grains
- Ivory
- Metal
- Precious stones
- Silk
- Enslaved persons
- Spices
- Timber
- Tortoiseshell

GEOGRAPHY SKILLBUILDER: Interpreting Maps
1. **Movement** Since people usually trade for goods they do not make themselves, which products were most likely to travel from Gupta India to Arabia?
2. **Movement** How far did trade goods travel to get from Luoyang in China to Alexandria in Egypt?

179

Middlemen are go-betweens in business transactions. For example, Indian traders would buy goods from traders coming out of China and sell those goods to traders who were traveling to Rome. To aid their role as middlemen, Indians built trading stations at oases all along the Silk Roads.

Sea Trade, East and West Sea trade also increased. Traders used coastal routes around the rim of the Arabian Sea and up the Persian Gulf to bring goods from India to Rome. In addition, traders from southern India would sail to Southeast Asia to collect spices. They bought the spices back to India and sold them to merchants from Rome.

Archaeologists have found hoards of Roman gold coins in southern India. Records show that some Romans were upset about the amount of gold their countrymen spent on Indian luxuries. They believed that a state with a healthy economy must collect gold rather than spend it.

Rome wasn't India's only trading partner. India imported African ivory and gold and exported cotton cloth. Rice and wheat went to Arabia in exchange for dates and horses. After trade with Rome declined around the third century A.D., India's sea trade with China increased. The Chinese imported Indian cotton cloth, monkeys, parrots, and elephants and sent India silk.

Effects of Indian Trade Increased trade led to the rise of banking in India. Commerce was quite profitable. Bankers were willing to lend money to merchants and charge them interest on the loans. Interest rates varied, depending on how risky business was. During Mauryan times, the annual interest rate on loans used for overseas trade had been 240 percent! During the Gupta Empire, bankers no longer considered sea trade so dangerous, so they charged only 15 to 20 percent interest a year.

A number of Indian merchants went to live abroad and brought Indian culture with them. As a result, people throughout Asia picked up and adapted a variety of Indian traditions. For example, Indian culture affected styles in art, architecture, and dance throughout Southeast Asia. Indian influence was especially strong in Thailand, Cambodia, and on the Indonesian island of Java.

Traders also brought Indian religions to new regions. Hinduism spread to Nepal, a region northeast of India; to Sri Lanka, an island off southeastern India; and to Borneo, an island in Indonesia. Buddhism spread because of traveling Buddhist merchants and monks. In time, Buddhism even influenced China. You will learn about this in Section 3.

Vocabulary
oases: plural of oasis, which is a watering place in a desert.

GlobalImpact

The Spread of Buddhism

Buddhism became a missionary religion during Asoka's reign. From his capital city **(1)**, Asoka sent out Buddhist missionaries. After Indians began trading along the Silk Roads, Buddhist monks travelled these routes and converted people on the way.

Buddhist monks from India established their first monastery in China **(2)** in A.D. 65, and many Chinese became Buddhists. From China, Buddhism reached Korea in the fourth century and Japan in the sixth century.

Today, Buddhism is a major religion throughout East and Southeast Asia. The Theravada school is strong in Myanmar, Cambodia **(3)**, Sri Lanka **(4)**, and Thailand. The Mahayana school is strong in Japan and Korea.

THINK THROUGH HISTORY
D. Analyzing Causes Why would dangerous conditions make bankers charge higher interest on loans for trade?
D. Possible Answer Dangers cause shipments to be lost, so bankers charge high interest to pay for the losses.

Section 2 Assessment

1. TERMS & NAMES
Identify
- Mahayana
- Theravada
- Brahma
- Vishnu
- Shiva
- Kalidasa
- Silk Roads

2. TAKING NOTES
Create a diagram like the one shown. For each category, list one or more specific developments in Indian culture.

Indian Culture	
Religion	
Literature/Arts	
Science/Math	
Trade	

3. RECOGNIZING EFFECTS
What do you think was the most significant effect of the changes in Buddhism and Hinduism? Explain.

THINK ABOUT
- the effect on people who practiced the religion
- the effect on art and culture
- the effect on other countries

4. ANALYZING THEMES
Cultural Interaction Cite three of the cultures that interacted with India. Explain the result of each cultural interaction.

THINK ABOUT
- interaction because of trade
- the influence of art, science, religion

ANSWERS

1. TERMS & NAMES
Mahayana, p.177
Theravada, p. 177
Brahma, p. 178
Vishnu, p. 178
Shiva, p. 178
Kalidasa, p. 178
Silk Roads, p. 179

2. TAKING NOTES
Possible Responses:
Religion—Mahayana Buddhism, Hinduism became more personal. Literature/Arts—Buddhist sculptures, Kalidasa wrote *Shakuntala*. Science/Math—The decimal system, medical guides. Trade—Profited from Silk Roads trade; traded with Rome, Africa, Southeast Asia, Arabia, China.

3. RECOGNIZING EFFECTS
Possible Responses: More people were able to take part in popular worship; religion inspired art; both religions spread to many other countries.

4. ANALYZING THEMES
Possible Responses: Greeks–Indians learned western timekeeping; Central Asian nomads–taught Indians about Silk Roads trade; Southeast Asia–Indians spread Hinduism, Buddhism, and artistic styles.

Han Emperors in China

TERMS & NAMES
- Han Dynasty
- centralized government
- civil service
- monopoly
- assimilation

MAIN IDEA

The Han Dynasty expanded China's borders and developed a system of government that lasted for centuries.

WHY IT MATTERS NOW

The pattern of a strong central government has remained a permanent part of Chinese life.

Section 3 Overview

OBJECTIVES

1. To describe the rise and rule of the Han Dynasty.
2. To examine Han government structure.
3. To characterize Han technology, commerce, and culture.
4. To describe the period of political instability in the middle of the Han period.

SKILLBUILDERS

- Interpreting maps: place, location, p. 182
- Interpreting charts, p. 187

CRITICAL THINKING

- Making inferences, pp. 183, 184
- Hypothesizing, p. 185
- Recognizing effects, p. 187
- Identifying problems, p. 187

SETTING THE STAGE Under Shi Huangdi, the Qin Dynasty had unified China. Shi Huangdi conquered the rival kings who ruled small states throughout China and established a strong government. After Shi Huangdi died in 210 B.C., his son proved to be a weak, ineffective leader. China's government fell apart.

The Han Restore Unity to China

Rumblings of discontent during the Qin Dynasty grew to roars in the years after Shi Huangdi's death. The peasants—bitter over years of high taxes, harsh labor quotas, and a severe penal system—rebelled. The rival kings—eager to regain control of the regions they had held before Shi Huangdi—raised armies and fought over territory.

The Founding of the Han Dynasty During the civil war that followed, two powerful leaders emerged. Xiang Yu (shee·ANG yoo) was an aristocratic general who was willing to allow the warlords to keep their territories if they would acknowledge him as their feudal lord. Liu Bang (LEE·oo bahng) was one of Xiang Yu's generals.

Eventually, Liu Bang turned against Xiang Yu. The two fought their final battle in 202 B.C. Liu Bang won and declared himself the first emperor of the Han Dynasty. The **Han Dynasty,** which ruled China for more than 400 years, is divided into two periods. The Former Han ruled for about two centuries, until A.D. 9. After a brief period when the Han were out of power, the Later Han ruled for almost another two centuries. The Han Dynasty so influenced China that even today many Chinese call themselves "people of the Han."

Liu Bang's first goal was to destroy the rival kings' power. He followed Shi Huangdi's policy of establishing **centralized government,** in which a central authority controls the running of a state. Reporting to Liu Bang's central government were hundreds of local officials of provinces called commanderies.

To win popular support, Liu Bang departed from Shi Huangdi's strict legalism. He lowered taxes and softened harsh punishments. People throughout the empire appreciated the peace and stability that Liu Bang brought to China.

The Empress Lü When Liu Bang died in 195 B.C., his son became emperor—in name only. The real ruler was his mother, Empress Lü. Although Lü had not been Liu Bang's only wife, she had powerful friends at court who helped her seize power. The empress outlived her son and retained control of the throne by naming first one infant and then another as emperor. Because the infants were too young to rule, she remained in control. When Empress Lü died in 180 B.C., people who remained loyal to Liu Bang's

Background
In feudal societies, nobles receive land in exchange for service to a higher noble or king.

HISTORY MAKERS

Liu Bang
256–195 B.C.

Although Liu Bang was born a peasant, legend says that dragons attended his birth. According to Chinese belief, this meant he would rise to great power.

Liu Bang was a village official who turned rebel general after Shi Huangdi died. He wasn't a great military leader. According to one story, nomads once captured him and held him for ransom.

However, Liu Bang had other skills that made him a successful emperor. Wisely, he chose educated advisers. He strengthened the central government. With foreign powers, he knew when to negotiate and when to use force. He was such a strong leader that Chinese historians call him "Gaozu," which means exalted founder.

FOCUS

5-Minute Warm-Up

▶ **Making Generalizations** Answering these questions will help students understand the concept of centralized government.

1. Study the Chinese bureaucracy diagram on page 183. What are the highest and lowest positions in the Chinese bureaucracy?

2. Which positions within the Chinese bureaucracy might be similar to the president, vice president, and cabinet members in the U.S. government?

 WARM-UP TRANSPARENCY 7

OBJECTIVE ① INSTRUCT

The Han Restore Unity to China

▶ **Key Ideas**

- Liu Bang, the first Han emperor, establishes political and social stability.
- After Liu Bang dies, his wife seizes power from their son through a palace plot.
- Wudi continues Liu Bang's centralizing policies and expands the empire through war.

(continued on next page)

SECTION 3 RESOURCES

PRINT RESOURCES

IN-DEPTH RESOURCES: UNIT 2
Guided Reading, p. 41
Skillbuilder Practice: Formulating Historical Questions, p. 42
Geography Application: The Great Wall of China, p. 43
Primary Source: from *Lessons for Women* by Ban Zhao, p. 47
History Makers: Wudi, p. 53
Connections Across Time and Cultures: Governing an Empire, p. 54

ACCESS FOR STUDENTS ACQUIRING ENGLISH
Guided Reading, p. 77; **Skillbuilder Practice**, p. 78; **Geography Application**, p. 79

FORMAL ASSESSMENT
Section Quiz, p. 80

TECHNOLOGY RESOURCES

WORLD ART AND CULTURES TRANSPARENCIES
AT16 Chinese tomb rubbing

CRITICAL THINKING TRANSPARENCIES
CT7 The Technological Revolution in Han China

CD-ROM
Religions of the World

VIDEO *Patterns of Interaction: Trade Connects the World*

OBJECTIVE ❶ INSTRUCT

(continued from page 181)

 IN-DEPTH RESOURCES: UNIT 2
Guided Reading, p. 41

 ACCESS FOR STUDENTS ACQUIRING ENGLISH
Guided Reading (Spanish), p. 77

History from Visuals

Han Dynasty, 202 B.C.–A.D. 220

Interpreting the Map Have students read the map key and the maps. Then ask students to describe how the territory controlled by the Han Empire changed over time.

Extension Activity Tell students that the later Han moved their capital from Xi'an to Luoyang. Have students use the map to figure out what advantages the new capital had. *Possible Response: Its easterly location put a greater distance between the capital and invading nomads. Its location on a major river made shipping and trade easier.*

SKILLBUILDER Answers
1. 1.5 million square miles.
2. Along the northwest border, because it isn't protected by natural barriers and invaders often came from this direction.

*Global*Impact
Xiongnu and the Huns

Have students use the map of the Han Dynasty on page 182 to trace the movements of the Xiongnu.

MORE ABOUT . . .
Empress Lü

Empress Lü was ruthless in her pursuit of power and made many enemies in the court. However, once in power, she realized she would need supporters and so created moderate ruling policies. She lowered taxes and repealed some unpopular laws.

Han Dynasty, 202 B.C.–A.D. 220

Former Han, 200 B.C.

GEOGRAPHY SKILLBUILDER: Interpreting Maps
1. **Place** What was the approximate size, in square miles, of the Han empire at its greatest extent?
2. **Location** Along which border did the Chinese build the Great Wall? Why did they build it there and not in other places?

family, rather than to Lü's family, came back into power. They rid the palace of the old empress's relatives by executing them.

Such palace plots occurred often throughout the Han Dynasty. Traditionally, the emperor chose the favorite among his wives as the empress and appointed one of her sons as successor. Because of this, the palace women and their families competed fiercely for the emperor's notice. The families would make alliances with influential people in the court. The resulting power plays distracted the emperor and his officials so much that they sometimes could not govern efficiently.

*Global*Impact

Xiongnu and the Huns
Eventually, Wudi defeated the Xiongnu. After their defeat, the nomads moved deeper into Asia. This had long-range effects. As the Xiongnu pushed south and west, they displaced other nomadic peoples. Because of this, successive waves of central Asian invaders pushed into northwestern India.

In addition, some historians theorize that over the centuries, the Xiongnu wandered thousands of miles westward across central Asia into Europe. The fierce horse-riding Huns who invaded the Roman Empire may have been the distant grandsons of the Xiongnu.

The Martial Emperor When Liu Bang's great-grandson took the throne, he continued Liu Bang's centralizing policies. Wudi (woo·dee), who reigned from 141 to 87 B.C., held the throne longer than any other Han emperor. He is called the martial emperor because he adopted the policy of expanding the Chinese empire through war.

Wudi's first set of enemies were the Xiongnu (shee·UNG·noo), a nomadic people known for their fierceness as arrow-shooting warriors on horseback. The Xiongnu roamed the steppes to the north and west of China. They made raids into China's settled farmland and stole grain, farm animals, valuable items, and hostages. The early Han emperors tried to buy off the Xiongnu by sending them thousands of pounds of silk, rice, alcohol, and money. Usually, the Xiongnu just accepted these gifts and continued their raids.

Vocabulary
martial: warlike.

182 Chapter 7

Geography Activity: *The Great Wall of China* The wall that was once a deterrent to invaders is now an attraction for tourists. The course of the Great Wall is as long as from New York City to Omaha, Nebraska. Have pairs of students work together to complete the Geography Application located in the

Teacher's Resources. Go over the answers with the class after all students have completed the activity.

 IN-DEPTH RESOURCES: UNIT 2
Geography Application: *The Great Wall of China*, p. 43

Gifted and Talented Students:
Wudi Biography Distribute to students the biography of Wudi in the Teacher's Resources. Have students read the biography and then work in pairs to answer the questions. After all pairs have finished, have them discuss their answers as a group. Encourage

students to share what they learned about Wudi with the rest of the class.

 IN-DEPTH RESOURCES: UNIT 2
History Makers: *Wudi*, p. 53

When Wudi realized that the bribes were simply making the Xiongnu stronger, he sent more than 100,000 soldiers to fight them. To help defeat the Xiongnu, Wudi also made allies of their enemies:

A VOICE FROM THE PAST
The Xiongnu had defeated the king of the Yuezhi people and had made his skull into a drinking vessel. As a result the Yuezhi . . . bore a constant grudge against the Xiongnu, though as yet they had been unable to find anyone to join them in an attack on their enemy. . . . When the emperor [Wudi] heard this, he decided to try to send an envoy to establish relations with the Yuezhi.

SIMA QIAN, *Records of the Grand Historian*

After his army forced the nomads to retreat into Central Asia, Wudi attempted to make his northwest border safe by settling his troops on the Xiongnu's former pastures. Although this tactic succeeded for a time, nomadic raiders continued to cause problems during much of China's later history.

Wudi also colonized areas to the northeast, now known as Manchuria and Korea. He sent his armies south, where they conquered mountain tribes and set up Chinese colonies all the way into what is now Vietnam. By the end of Wudi's reign, the empire had expanded nearly to the bounds of present-day China.

A Highly Structured Government

Just as Han emperors tried to control the people they conquered, they exerted vast control over the Chinese themselves. Because the Chinese considered their emperor to be semidivine, they accepted his exercise of power. He was in charge of keeping order on a cosmic level. If the emperor did his job well, China had peace and prosperity. If he failed, the heavens showed their displeasure with earthquakes, floods, and famines. However, the emperor did not rule alone.

Structures of Han Government The Chinese emperor relied on a complex bureaucracy to help him rule. Running the bureaucracy and maintaining the imperial army were expensive. To raise money, the government levied taxes. Like the farmers in India, Chinese peasants owed part of their yearly crops to the government. Merchants also paid taxes.

Besides taxes, the peasants owed the government a month's worth of labor or military service every year. With this source of labor, the Han emperors built roads, canals, and irrigation ditches. The emperors also filled the ranks of China's vast armies and expanded the Great Wall that stretched across the northern frontier.

Confucianism, the Road to Success Wudi's government employed more than 130,000 people. The bureaucracy included 18 different ranks of **civil service** jobs—government jobs that civilians obtained by taking examinations. At times, Chinese emperors rewarded loyal followers with government posts. However, another way to fill government posts evolved under the Han. This method involved testing applicants' knowledge of Confucianism—the teachings of Confucius, who had lived 400 years before.

The early Han emperors had employed some Confucian scholars as court advisers, but it was Wudi who began actively to favor them. Confucius had taught that gentlemen should practice "reverence [respect], generosity, truthfulness, diligence [hard work], and kindness." Because these were exactly the qualities he wanted his government officials to have, Wudi set up a school where hopeful job applicants from all over China could come to study Confucius's works.

Background
According to the Mandate of Heaven, divine forces appointed Chinese emperors to rule—and would take away the throne if they governed badly.

A. Possible Answer Because people with these qualities would do what was best for the emperor and the people, rather than for themselves.

THINK THROUGH HISTORY
A. Making Inferences
Why would Wudi want his officials to have qualities such as diligence?

SPOTLIGHT ON

Chinese Bureaucracy
The Chinese bureaucracy reflected top-down rule. Each level of officials had authority over the officials below them. The emperor had authority over all.

India and China Establish Empires **183**

OBJECTIVE 2 INSTRUCT

A Highly Structured Government

▶ **Key Ideas**
- Han emperors use a bureaucracy to run the empire.
- Civil service job applicants are tested on their knowledge of Confucianism.

RELIGIONS OF THE WORLD
Confucianism

WORLD ART AND CULTURES TRANSPARENCIES
AT16 Chinese tomb rubbing

SPOTLIGHT ON
Chinese Bureaucracy

A German sociologist of the early 1900's named Max Weber made a list of the characteristics of a bureaucracy. These include having a leader who delegates authority to others and having a chain of command. Ask students if these characteristics seem to apply to Chinese bureaucracy. Also ask students to think of other organizations that use bureaucracies, such as corporations and schools.

TEACHING OPTION | **BLOCK SCHEDULING** | **COOPERATIVE ACTIVITY: Comparing Bureaucracies** | **CLASS TIME: 30 MINUTES**

Task: Groups will create diagrams of the government bureaucracies in the United States and in the Roman Empire (27 B.C.–A.D. 476) and compare these with the Chinese bureaucracy.

Purpose: To understand and compare the structure of government bureaucracies in world history.

Activity: Divide the class into groups of four. Two group members will create a diagram of the federal bureaucracy in the United States. The other two

group members will do the same for the Roman Empire. Each pair of group members will write a paragraph that compares its bureaucracy with the Chinese bureaucracy and draws conclusions about which positions in each bureaucracy are similar.

Building a Portfolio: Students should add their best work to their portfolio.

ALTERNATIVE ASSESSMENT BOOK
Standards for Evaluating a Cooperative Activity

Standards for Evaluation
Diagrams should . . .
- show how the bureaucracies are structured

Comparisons should . . .
- clearly explain similarities and differences between the bureaucracies
- show thoughtful analysis

Teacher's Edition **183**

Han Technology, Commerce, and Culture

▶ Key Ideas

- Advances in technology influence all aspects of Chinese life.
- Agriculture is thought to be the most important occupation, but commerce is very important too.
- Chinese culture is unified through assimilation and by recording China's history.
- Most women devote themselves to family, but some pursue other goals.

 CRITICAL THINKING TRANSPARENCIES
CT7 The Technological Revolution in Han China

 IN-DEPTH RESOURCES: UNIT 2
Primary Source: from *Lessons for Women* by Ban Zhao, p. 47

Viewing the Video

Show *Trade Connects the World: Silk Roads and the Pacific Rim* to explore how the exchange of goods and ideas has influenced cultures and economies around the world.

- The first segment of the video describes the hazards of traveling the Silk Roads—and the riches that inspired people to take the risk.
- The second segment examines the explosive economic growth of nations that are part of the trade region called the Pacific Rim.

Using the *Teacher's Resource Book* as a guide, ask students to consider how trade can connect distant countries; compare the effects of trade described in the video with the effects trade has on students' everyday lives; and enrich the lesson with primary-source and visual-literacy activities included in the resource book.

 PATTERNS OF INTERACTION
Trade Connects the World: Silk Roads and the Pacific Rim
Videocassette: Tape 1

After their studies, job applicants took formal examinations in history, law, literature, and Confucianism. In theory, anyone could take the exams. In practice, few peasants could afford to educate their sons. So only sons of wealthy landowners had a chance at a government career. In spite of this flaw, the civil service system begun by Wudi worked so efficiently that it continued in China until 1912.

Han Technology, Commerce, and Culture

The 400 years of Han rule saw not only improvements in education but also great advances in Chinese technology and culture. In addition, the centralized government began to exert more control over commerce and manufacturing.

Technology Revolutionizes Chinese Life Advances in technology influenced all aspects of Chinese life. Paper was invented in A.D. 105. Before that, books were usually written on silk. But paper was cheaper, so books became more readily available. This helped spread education in China. The invention of paper also affected Chinese government. Formerly, all government documents had been recorded on strips of wood. Paper was much more convenient to use for record-keeping, so Chinese bureaucracy expanded.

Other technological advances included a collar harness that made it possible for horses to pull heavy loads. The Chinese perfected a plow that was more efficient because it had two blades, improved iron tools, and invented the wheelbarrow. In addition, the Chinese began to use watermills to grind grain.

Agriculture Versus Commerce During the Han Dynasty, the population of China swelled to 60 million. Because there were so many people to feed, Confucian scholars and ordinary Chinese people considered agriculture the most important and

Vocabulary
commerce: the buying and selling of goods.

THINK THROUGH HISTORY
B. Making Inferences
Which of the inventions discussed here helped the task of feeding China's huge population?
B. Possible Answer
The collar harness, the plow, the iron tools, the wheel barrow, and the watermill.

Global Impact: Trade Networks

Silk Roads

Why would anyone struggle over mountains and across deserts to buy fabric? The ancients valued silk because it was strong, lightweight, and beautiful. Traders made fortunes carrying Chinese silk to the West. Because of this, the caravan trails that crossed Asia were called Silk Roads, even though many other valuable trade goods were also carried along these routes. The Silk Roads also encouraged cultural diffusion.

Camel Caravans

No trader traveled the whole Silk Road. Mediterranean merchants went part of the way, then traded with Central Asian nomads. The nomads went east until they met Chinese traders near India. Many traders traveled in camel caravans, as shown in this sculpture.

From this point, ships carried silk and spices to Rome. The Romans paid a pound of gold for a pound of Chinese silk!

184 Chapter 7

0 ——— 500 Miles
0 ——— 1,000 Kilometers

Task Students will watch a 10-minute video examining ancient and modern trade and then complete an activity from the *Teacher's Resource Book.*

Materials Needed: *Trade Connects the World: Silk Roads and the Pacific Rim* (videocassette), *Teacher's Resource Book.*

Activity: Before students watch the video, explain that it shows the hazards of ancient trade along the Silk Roads and the impact of present-day trade in the Pacific Rim. Briefly discuss with students how trade today might be different from trade along the Silk Roads. (Today, trade is less dangerous, airplanes and huge ships are used, more and bigger items are shipped today, governments regulate and sometimes restrict trade.)

Conclusion: After viewing the video, have students complete a related activity from the *Teacher's Resource Book,* which provides instructional support, visual-literacy activities, and primary-source activities.

honored occupation. An imperial edict, written in 167 B.C., stated this philosophy quite plainly:

A VOICE FROM THE PAST

Agriculture is the foundation of the world. No duty is greater. Now if [anyone] personally follows this pursuit diligently, he has yet [to pay] the impositions of the land tax and tax on produce. . . . Let there be abolished the land tax and the tax on produce levied upon the cultivated fields.

BAN GU and **BAN ZHAO** in *History of the Former Han Dynasty*

Although the same decree dismissed commerce as the least important occupation, manufacturing and commerce were actually very important to the Han empire. The government established monopolies on the mining of salt, the forging of iron, the minting of coins, and the brewing of alcohol. A **monopoly** occurs when a group has exclusive control over the production and distribution of certain goods.

For a time, the government also ran huge silk mills—competing with private silk weavers in making this luxurious cloth. As contact with people from other lands increased, the Chinese realized how valuable their silk was as an item of trade. Because of this, the techniques of silk production became a closely guarded state secret. Spurred by the worldwide demand for silk, Chinese commerce expanded along the Silk Roads to most of Asia and, through India, all the way to Rome.

Unifying Chinese Culture As the Han empire expanded its trade networks, the Chinese began to learn about the foods, animals, and fashions that were common in foreign lands. Similarly, the expansion of the Han empire through conquest brought people of many different cultures under Chinese rule. To unify the empire, the Chinese government encouraged **assimilation,** or the process of making these conquered peoples part of Chinese culture. To accomplish this, the government sent

MORE ABOUT . . .
Silk Production

Silk production originated in China in about 2700 B.C. According to legend, the secret of raising silkworms and obtaining silk from their cocoons was discovered by the empress of China in 2640 B.C. The Chinese domesticated the silkworm and the silkworm's main food source, the mulberry tree. To get silk thread, the worm is killed in the cocoon, and the cocoon is unwound in a single continuous thread more than 2,000 feet long. The science of silk production, called "sericulture," was kept secret in China for thousands of years. However, silk production eventually spread to Japan, India, and Persia. Although China lost its silk monopoly, it remains a major producer of raw silk today.

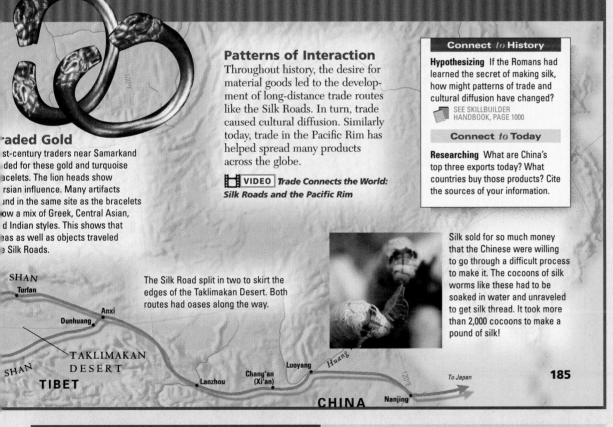

Patterns of Interaction

Throughout history, the desire for material goods led to the development of long-distance trade routes like the Silk Roads. In turn, trade caused cultural diffusion. Similarly, today, trade in the Pacific Rim has helped spread many products across the globe.

VIDEO *Trade Connects the World: Silk Roads and the Pacific Rim*

Connect *to* History

Hypothesizing If the Romans had learned the secret of making silk, how might patterns of trade and cultural diffusion have changed?

SEE SKILLBUILDER HANDBOOK, PAGE 1000

Connect *to* Today

Researching What are China's top three exports today? What countries buy those products? Cite the sources of your information.

...aded Gold

...st-century traders near Samarkand ...ded for these gold and turquoise ...acelets. The lion heads show ...rsian influence. Many artifacts ...und in the same site as the bracelets ...ow a mix of Greek, Central Asian, ...d Indian styles. This shows that ...eas as well as objects traveled ...e Silk Roads.

SHAN
Turfan
Anxi
Dunhuang
SHAN TAKLIMAKAN DESERT
TIBET
Lanzhou
Chang'an (Xi'an)
Luoyang
Huang
To Japan
CHINA
Nanjing

The Silk Road split in two to skirt the edges of the Taklimakan Desert. Both routes had oases along the way.

Silk sold for so much money that the Chinese were willing to go through a difficult process to make it. The cocoons of silk worms like these had to be soaked in water and unraveled to get silk thread. It took more than 2,000 cocoons to make a pound of silk!

185

Connect *to* History	Connect *to* Today
Hypothesizing **Possible Response:** There would have been less trade along the Silk Roads, because people from the West would not have had to get their silk from China. This would have lessened cultural diffusion.	*Researching* Students can use a current almanac or encyclopedia to answer the questions. *Possible answer: In 1994, China's top three exports were textiles, garments, and footwear, all of which may have been traded to Hong Kong, the United States, Japan, and Germany.*

Rebellion and Restoration

Key Ideas
- Landowners acquire land from farmers forced into debt by inheritance customs.
- Wang Mang overthrows the Han to restore economic and political order to China.
- The Han Dynasty is restored, and it operates for another 200 years.

IN-DEPTH RESOURCES: UNIT 2
Primary Source: from *Lessons for Women* by Ban Zhao, p. 47
Connections Across Time: Governing an Empire, p. 54

MORE ABOUT . . .
Sima Qian

Records of the Grand Historian was a monumental work, 130 chapters long. Scholars of later periods used it as a model for writing about subsequent dynasties. Sima Qian suffered a great deal to complete his book. For defending a general who had surrendered to the Xiongnu, Sima Qian was given the choice of castration or death. He chose castration because he wanted to finish writing China's history.

Chinese farmers to settle newly colonized areas. The government also encouraged them to intermarry with local peoples. Government officials set up schools to train local people in the Confucian philosophy and then appointed local scholars to government posts.

Several writers also helped to unify Chinese culture by recording China's history. Sima Qian (SU·MAH chee·YEHN), who lived from 145 to 85 B.C., is called the "Grand Historian" for his work in compiling a history of China from the ancient dynasties to Wudi. To write accurately, Sima Qian visited historical sites, interviewed eyewitnesses, researched official records, and examined artifacts. The resulting book is called *Records of the Grand Historian*.

Another famous Chinese book was the *History of the Former Han Dynasty*. Ban Biao (BAHN bee·OW), who lived from A.D. 3 to 54, started the project. After his death, his son Ban Gu (bahn goo) and later his daughter Ban Zhao (bahn jow) worked on it. Ban Zhao also wrote a guide called *Lessons for Women*.

Wives, Nuns, and Scholars Although Ban Zhao gained fame as a historian, most women during the Han Dynasty led quiet lives at home. Confucian teachings dictated that women were to devote themselves to their families. They were supposed to obey their parents in childhood and their husband and husband's parents after they married. To add to their family's honor, women were to be faithful, pure, and modest.

A few upper-class women broke out of this mold. As explained earlier, some empresses wielded great power. Daoist and later Buddhist nuns were able to gain an education and lead lives apart from their families. Women in aristocratic and landowning families also sometimes pursued education and culture.

Rebellion and Restoration

In spite of economic and cultural advances, the Han emperors faced grave problems. One of the main problems was an economic imbalance caused by customs that allowed the rich to gain more wealth at the expense of the poor.

The Rich Take Advantage of the Poor According to custom, a family's land was divided equally among all of the father's male heirs. Unless a farmer could afford to buy more land during his lifetime, each generation inherited smaller plots. With such small plots of land, farmers had a hard time raising enough food to sell or even to feed the family. Because of this, small farmers often went into debt and had to borrow money from large landowners, who charged very high interest rates. If the farmer couldn't pay back the debt, the landowner took possession of the farmer's land.

Large landowners were not required to pay taxes, so when their land holdings increased, the amount of land that was left for the government to tax decreased. With less money coming in, the government pressed harder to collect money from the small farmers. As a result, the gap between rich and poor increased.

Wang Mang Overthrows the Han During this time of economic change, political instability grew. At the palace, court advisers, palace servants, and rival influential families wove complex plots to influence the emperor's choice of who would succeed him as ruler. From about 32 B.C. until A.D. 9, one inexperienced emperor replaced another. Chaos reigned in the palace, and with peasant revolts, unrest spread across the land as well.

Finally, Wang Mang (wahng mahng), a Confucian scholar and member of the court, decided that a strong ruler was needed to restore order. For six years he had been acting as regent for the infant who had been crowned emperor. In A.D. 9, Wang Mang took the imperial title for himself and overthrew the Han, thus ending the first half of the Han Dynasty known as the Former Han.

This is the lid of a Chinese bronze vessel from Han times. The figures on top are women who are weaving cloth, perhaps silk.

Background
In China, the family name comes first and the personal name comes second. These historians belong to the Ban family.

Vocabulary
regent: a person who rules temporarily while a monarch is too young

---

Explaining the Skill: As students read about historical events, they should ask themselves questions about the events, such as what caused them and why they are important. Answering the questions they ask will help students better understand the events they read about.

Applying the Skill: Have students reread the passage titled, "The Rich Take Advantage of the Poor" on page 186. Then have them work in small groups to write questions about the situation using the words *who, what, when, why,* and *how.* Questions might include these: How was a family's land divided? Why were the plots of land so small? What effect did the size of the plots have on farmers? Who loaned

money to the farmers? When did landowners take possession of a farmer's land? What happened to the amount of taxable land? Group members should answer the questions orally.

IN-DEPTH RESOURCES: UNIT 2
Skillbuilder Practice: Formulating Historical Questions, p. 42

Two Great Empires: Han China and Rome

Han Dynasty—202 B.C. to A.D. 220	Roman Empire—27 B.C. to A.D. 476
• Empire replaced rival kingdoms	• Empire replaced republic
• Centralized, bureaucratic government	• Centralized, bureaucratic government
• Built roads and defensive walls	• Built roads and defensive walls
• Conquered many diverse peoples in regions bordering China	• Conquered many diverse peoples in regions of three continents
• At its height—area of 1,500,000 square miles and a population of 60,000,000	• At its height—area of 3,400,000 square miles and a population of 55,000,000
• Chinese became common written language throughout empire	• Latin did not replace other written languages in empire
• Ongoing conflict with nomads	• Ongoing conflict with nomads
• Empire fell apart; restored by Tang dynasty in 618	• Empire fell apart; never restored

Silk was the trade good that linked the Han and Roman Empires. Han artists often did beautiful paintings on silk, such as this one.

> **SKILLBUILDER: Interpreting Charts**
> 1. *How long did each empire last? During what years were they both in existence?*
> 2. *How were Han China and the Roman Empire similar? How were they different?*

Wang Mang tried to bring the country under control. He minted new money to relieve the treasury's shortage. He set up public granaries to help feed China's poor. He took away large landholdings from the rich and planned to redistribute the land to farmers who had lost their land. This plan angered powerful landholders. And Wang Mang's larger supply of money disrupted the economy because it allowed people to increase their spending, which encouraged merchants to raise prices.

Then, in A.D. 11, a great flood left thousands dead and millions homeless. The public granaries did not hold enough to feed the displaced, starving people. Huge peasant revolts rocked the land. The wealthy, opposed to Wang Mang's land policies, joined in the rebellion. The rebels assassinated Wang Mang in A.D. 23. Within two years, a member of the old imperial family took the throne and began the second period of Han rule—called the Later Han.

The Later Han Years With peace restored to China, the first decades of the Later Han Dynasty were quite prosperous. The government sent soldiers and merchants westward to regain control of posts along the Silk Roads. But this expansion couldn't make up for social, political, and economic weaknesses within the empire itself. Within a century, China suffered from the same economic imbalances, political intrigues, and social unrest that had toppled the Former Han. By 220, the Later Han Dynasty had disintegrated into three rival kingdoms.

THINK THROUGH HISTORY
C. Recognizing Effects How did Wang Mang's policies help cause his own downfall?
C. Possible Answer His land reform turned the wealthy against him, his economic policies caused problems, and his policies to help the poor were inadequate during the flood.

Section 3 Assessment

1. TERMS & NAMES

Identify
• Han Dynasty
• centralized government
• civil service
• monopoly
• assimilation

2. TAKING NOTES

Create a spider map like the one shown to record the methods that Han rulers used to centralize the government.

Centralized Government

Explain which method you think was most important and why.

3. IDENTIFYING PROBLEMS

What problem do you think was most responsible for weakening the Han Dynasty's power?

THINK ABOUT
• problems at court
• problems with non-Chinese peoples
• economic and social problems

4. THEME ACTIVITY

Religious and Ethical Systems Review the five qualities that Confucius said all gentlemen should practice (see page 183). Working with a small team, think of actions that government officials could take to demonstrate each of those qualities. Choose the best actions and illustrate them on a motivational poster that could hang in a government office.

India and China Establish Empires **187**

ANSWERS

1. TERMS & NAMES
Han Dynasty, p. 181
centralized government, p. 181
civil service, p. 183
monopoly, p. 185
assimilation, p. 185

2. TAKING NOTES
Possible Responses: Required local officials to report to central government; built up bureaucracy; created civil service, based on exams; established monopolies in many industries

3. IDENTIFYING PROBLEMS
Possible Responses: The method of choosing an heir, because it led to distracting plots and power plays; the nomads, because they forced China to levy taxes to maintain a large army; the distribution of wealth, because poor people kept losing land to the rich, which caused peasant uprisings

4. THEME ACTIVITY
Standards for Evaluation
A motivational poster should meet the following criteria:
• It suggests concrete actions for government officials.
• The actions exemplify the five Confucian qualities.

TERMS & NAMES

1. Mauryan Empire, p. 173
2. Asoka, p. 174
3. religious toleration, p. 174
4. Gupta Empire, p. 175
5. Kalidasa, p. 178
6. Silk Roads, p. 179
7. Han Dynasty, p. 181
8. centralized government, p. 181
9. civil service, p. 183
10. assimilation, p. 185

REVIEW QUESTIONS

11. They united north India into one political unit for the first time, constructed an extensive road system, and promoted policies of nonviolence and toleration.

12. Central India, under the Andhrans, profited from extensive trade. Immigrants to northern India brought new languages, traditions, and customs. Some southern rulers broke away from the empire.

13. The southern tip of India was home to Tamil speakers. Neither the Mauryans nor the Guptas conquered this region. Some Tamil groups were matriarchal.

14. As Buddhism became popular, statues of the Buddha and cave temples decorated with sculptures and paintings were created.

15. They proved that the earth was round, developed zero and the decimal system, found the value of pi to four decimal places, measured the solar year, compiled medical guides, and performed surgery.

16. Indians traded spices from Southeast Asia. Indian merchants in Southeast Asia influenced art, architecture, dance, and religion there.

17. Wudi held power longer than any other Han emperor, expanded the empire, drove back the Xiongnu, and set up a civil service system.

18. In theory, the system was open to anyone. However, few peasants could afford to educate their sons, so the wealthy maintained an advantage in competing for careers in government.

19. The government ran huge silk mills. Silk was a valuable trade item. Through trade, China learned about customs and ideas of other lands.

20. Large landowners were not required to pay taxes. As their land holdings increased, the amount of land the government could tax decreased. This led to economic instability.

Visual Summary

India and China Establish Empires

321 B.C.
300 B.C.

Mauryan Empire

Mauryan Empire

- 321 B.C.—**Chandragupta Maurya** seized throne and began Mauryan Empire

200 B.C.

- 269 B.C.—**Asoka** began rule; conquered Kalinga; regretted slaughter and converted to Buddhism; sent out missionaries

100 B.C.

- 232 B.C.—**Asoka** died; empire started to break apart

- 185 B.C.—Greeks invaded India, beginning five centuries of turmoil

1 B.C.
A.D. 1

Han Dynasty

Han Dynasty

- 202 B.C.—**Liu Bang** started Han Dynasty; strengthened central government

- 141 B.C.—**Wudi** began reign; conquered neighboring regions; started civil service

A.D. 100

- Chinese invented paper, collar harness, watermill

- A.D. 9—**Wang Mang** temporarily overthrew the Han

A.D. 200

- 1st century A.D.— Later Han rulers encouraged Silk Road trade with West

Gupta Empire

Gupta Empire

- Buddhism and Hinduism developed more popular forms

A.D. 300

- A.D. 320—**Chandra Gupta** began empire

- A.D. 375—**Chandra Gupta II** started reign; Indian art, literature, and dance flowered

A.D. 400

- A.D. 500—Indian astronomers realized earth was round; mathematician calculated value of pi and length of solar year

- Trade spread Indian culture, Hinduism, and Buddhism

A.D. 500

TERMS & NAMES

Briefly explain the importance of each of the following to the empires in India and China between 321 B.C. and A.D. 550.

1. Mauryan Empire
2. Asoka
3. religious toleration
4. Gupta Empire
5. Kalidasa
6. Silk Roads
7. Han Dynasty
8. centralized government
9. civil service
10. assimilation

REVIEW QUESTIONS

SECTION 1 (pages 173–176)
First Empires of India

11. List three significant accomplishments of the Mauryan rulers.

12. How did India change during the 500 years between the decline of the Mauryan Empire and the rise of the Gupta Empire?

13. How did the southern tip of India differ from the rest of India?

SECTION 2 (pages 177–180)
Trade Spreads Indian Religions and Culture

14. How did changes in Buddhism influence art in India?

15. Summarize the main advances in science and mathematics by Indians prior to A.D. 500.

16. Describe the economic and cultural links between India and Southeast Asia.

SECTION 3 (pages 181–187)
Han Emperors in China

17. Explain why Wudi was one of China's most significant rulers.

18. Under the Chinese civil service system, who could become government officials?

19. How did silk influence China's government, economy, and culture during the Han period?

20. How did economic problems lead to the decline of the Han?

Interact *with* History

On page 172, you looked at a situation in which a government hired people to spy on each other. Now that you have read the chapter, reevaluate your decision about being a spy. What do you think are the best methods for a government to use to control large numbers of people? Consider the methods used by Chandragupta, Asoka, and the Han emperors.

Interact *with* History

Possible Responses: Students who originally wanted to spy on their neighbors may now disagree with Kautilya's advice for rulers. Others may say that spying was a legitimate occupation in the early Mauryan Empire. Some students may feel that Asoka's policies of nonviolence and acceptance are the best methods for controlling large numbers of people.

CRITICAL THINKING

1. INFLUENCING GOVERNMENT

THEME RELIGIOUS AND ETHICAL SYSTEMS Contrast Buddhism's influence on India's government with Confucianism's influence on China's government. Contrast the teachings, the motive of the rulers who tried to implement those teachings, and how long the influence lasted.

2. COMPARING EMPIRES

Create a table such as the one below and fill in the information about each empire.

Empire	Period of Influence	Key Leaders	Significant Achievements
Mauryan			
Gupta			
Han			

3. EVALUATING SUCCESS

Was the Mauryan, Gupta, or Han empire most successful? Identify the standards you used to evaluate success and how each empire measured up to these standards.

4. ANALYZING PRIMARY SOURCES

The following quotation, from one of Asoka's edicts, describes Asoka's reaction after he conquered Kalinga. Read the quotation and answer the questions below it.

> **A VOICE FROM THE PAST**
> Kalinga was conquered by his Sacred and Gracious Majesty when he had been consecrated eight years. 150,000 persons were thence carried away captive, 100,000 were slain, and many times that number died. . . . Thus arose his Sacred Majesty's remorse for having conquered the Kalingas, because the conquest of a country previously unconquered involves the slaughter, death, and carrying away captive of the people.
>
> **ASOKA,** in *A History of Modern India*
> by Percival Spear

- Judging from this edict, what did the conquest of Kalinga cause Asoka to realize about the nature of war?
- Why would this realization have motivated him to investigate Buddhism? Support your answer with details from the text.
- If more rulers had shared Asoka's belief, how might world history have been different?

CHAPTER ACTIVITIES

1. LIVING HISTORY: Unit Portfolio Project

THEME POWER AND AUTHORITY Your unit portfolio project focuses on people who grab power and establish their authority (see page 107). For Chapter 7, you might use one of the following ideas to add to your portfolio.

- Draw a bar chart comparing how long five different rulers held power. In a paragraph below the bar chart, explain which three rulers you think were most significant and why. Is length of rule the main element in deciding how significant a ruler was?
- Create a collage of sketches and photocopies showing the methods of exercising power used by rulers of the Mauryan, Gupta, and Han empires.
- Write a newspaper editorial either praising or criticizing Asoka and his methods of governing. Use historical examples to show the wisdom or the foolishness of his actions.

2. CONNECT TO TODAY: Cooperative Learning

THEME CULTURAL INTERACTION Throughout its history, India has been strongly affected by the many cultural groups who migrated onto the subcontinent. Work with a team to research the different peoples living in India today and how they interact with one another.

INTERNET Using the Internet, reference books, or magazines, research information about the different peoples of India. Look for statistics and data that answer such questions as, How many different languages are spoken in India? How many different religions are practiced in India? Are any groups of people in India currently in conflict with each other?

As a team, create an encyclopedia article about the peoples of India today. Include graphs to show how India's population is distributed among various groups and text that describes those groups and how they interact today.

3. INTERPRETING A TIME LINE

Revisit the unit time line on pages 106-107. On the Chapter 7 time line, which events named reflect cultural achievements? Explain which of these events influenced India or China.

FOCUS ON ART

Look carefully at this 16-inch high, bronze sculpture from Han China.

- Would you describe this sculpture as realistic or not? Why?
- Do you think the scene depicted by the sculpture was typical of Han life? Why or why not?

Connect to History Think about the different classes that made up Han society. Which do you think is most likely the subject of this sculpture? Explain.

189

CHAPTER ACTIVITIES

1. LIVING HISTORY

Standards for Evaluation
A bar chart should meet the following criteria:

- Shows the length of rule of five different rulers.
- Presents data accurately.
- Is accompanied by a paragraph explaining why three of the rulers are most significant and whether length of rule corresponds to a ruler's significance.

Standards for Evaluation
A collage should meet the following criteria:

- Represents all three empires.
- Includes images that clearly convey each ruler's methods of exercising power.
- Presents information in a thoughtful manner.

Standards for Evaluation
A newspaper editorial should meet the following criteria:

- Clearly states the writer's opinion of Asoka and his methods of governing.
- Provides historical examples to support the writer's opinion.
- Shows an understanding of Asoka's actions as a ruler.

2. CONNECT TO TODAY

Possible Responses: About 180 different languages are spoken in India. There are 14 major languages and more than 700 dialects. India's major religions are Hinduism, Islam, Christianity, Sikhism, Buddhism, and Jainism. Various groups throughout India continue to experience conflicts with each other.

3. INTERPRETING A TIME LINE

The construction of the first Buddhist monastery and the invention of paper reflect cultural achievements in China. The calculation of pi reflects cultural achievements in India.

FOCUS ON ART

Possible Responses:
- Realistic—the sizes of the horse and people are proportional, and neither is portrayed in a distorted way.
- Yes—it may show a landowner or government official traveling around on business.

Connect to History *Possible Response:* A member of the upper classes, such as a scholar, bureaucrat, or wealthy landowner; poor farmers couldn't afford horse-drawn carts with shade umbrellas.

CRITICAL THINKING

1. INFLUENCING GOVERNMENT

Buddhism stressed nonviolence and acceptance of all people; Confucianism stressed hard work and truthfullness. Asoka used Buddhism to benefit all his subjects. Wudi used Confucianism to strengthen his centralized government. Buddhism's influence on Indian government ended with Asoka. Confucianism's influence on Chinese government lasted until the early 1900s.

2. COMPARING EMPIRES

Possible Responses: Mauryan: 321 – 232 B.C.; Chandragupta, Asoka; united north India for the first time. Gupta: A.D. 320 – 415; Chandra Gupta I, Chandra Gupta II; flowering of Indian culture. Han: 202 B.C.–A.D. 220; Liu Bang, Wudi; created centralized government and bureaucracy.

3. EVALUATING SUCCESS

Possible Responses: The Mauryan— policies of toleration and nonviolence. The

Gupta—flowering of Indian culture. The Han—strong government and the longest-lasting empire.

4. ANALYZING PRIMARY SOURCES

Possible Responses:
- War leads to the deaths of innocent people.
- Asoka felt remorse for these deaths and looked for a more peaceful way to rule.
- Less war and fewer empires.

African Civilizations

	Key Ideas	**COPY MASTERS**	**ASSESSMENT**
SECTION 1 Diverse Societies in Africa *pp. 193–198*	*Africa is a land of contrasting geography. Early Africans adapt to these varied environments, developing diverse cultures in West and East Africa unique to the particular area.*	*In-Depth Resources: Unit 2* • **Guided Reading,** p. 55 • **Skillbuilder Practice:** Identifying Problems, p. 58 • **Primary Source:** Nok Sculpture, p. 61 • **History Makers:** The Nok Culture, p. 68	*Section 1 Assessment,* p. 198 *Formal Assessment* • Section Quiz, p. 89 *Alternative Assessment Book* • Standards for Evaluating a Product or Performance
SECTION 2 The Kingdom of Aksum and East African Trade *pp. 199–202*	*The kingdom of Aksum in East Africa takes control of Red Sea trade routes and becomes an international trading center. Aksum adopts Christianity and creates a cosmopolitan culture but declines as a trading power when Islamic invaders seize control of Africa's east coast.*	*In-Depth Resources: Unit 2* • **Guided Reading,** p. 56 • **Primary Sources:** from *Natural History* by Pliny the Elder, p. 62; from *Periplus of the Erythrean Sea,* p. 63; from *A History of the Sudan,* p. 64 • **Literature:** from the *Kebra Negast,* p. 65 • **History Makers:** Ezana, p. 69	*Section 2 Assessment,* p. 202 *Formal Assessment* • Section Quiz, p. 90 *Alternative Assessment Book* • Standards for Evaluating a Cooperative Activity
SECTION 3 Patterns of Change: Migration *pp. 203–205*	*Mass movements of people are an important influence on world history. From 500 B.C. to A.D. 1500, migrations of Bantu-speaking peoples into the southern half of Africa create new cultures as they adapt their skills to the lands they occupy and intermix with other people.*	*In-Depth Resources: Unit 2* • **Guided Reading,** p. 57 • **Geography Application:** Desertification and Migration in Africa, p. 59 • **Connections Across Time and Cultures:** Migrations: Bantu and Indo-European, p. 70	*Section 3 Assessment,* p. 205 *Formal Assessment* • Section Quiz, p. 91 *Alternative Assessment Book* • Standards for Evaluating a Product or Performance
CHAPTER RESOURCES	**Chapter Overview** *Africans create diverse cultures as they adapt to the varied environments of the continent. Cities with advanced cultures and technologies become great trading centers in West and East Africa while the migrations of Bantu-speaking peoples into southern and eastern Africa create new and unique cultures.*	*Telescoping the Times* • Chapter Summary, pp. 29–31 *Planning for Block Schedules*	*Chapter Assessment,* pp. 206–207 *Chapter Activities,* p. 207 *Formal Assessment* • Chapter Test, forms A and B, pp. 92–97 *Test Generator* *Alternative Assessment Book*

1500 B.C.–A.D. 500

TECHNOLOGY

 Warm-Up Transparency 8

 Geography Transparencies
- GT5 Greek View of the World, 494 B.C.

 World Art and Cultures Transparencies
- AT17 Nok terra cotta sculpture

 Electronic Library of Primary Sources
"Tracking Father Elephant"

 INTERNET RESOURCES
www.mlworldhistory.com

 Warm-Up Transparency 8

 Geography Transparencies
- GT8 Empires of Ancient Africa, 900 B.C.–A.D. 700

 World Art and Cultures Transparencies
- AT18 Aksumite carved stone

 Critical Thinking Transparencies
- CT8 Facts and Opinions in the Kingdom of Aksum

 Electronic Library of Primary Sources
"The Aksumite Empire"

INTERNET RESOURCES
www.mlworldhistory.com

 Warm-Up Transparency 8

 Critical Thinking Transparencies
- CT44 Chapter 8 Visual Summary

 Electronic Library of Primary Sources
from "Hunters of Modern Africa"

 INTERNET RESOURCES
www.mlworldhistory.com

 Chapter Summaries on Audiocassette in English and Spanish

 INTERNET RESOURCES
www.mlworldhistory.com

 Block Scheduling (90 MINUTES)

Day 1	Day 2	
Section 1, pp. 193–198	**Section 2**, pp. 199–202	**Section 3**, pp. 203–205
Section Assessment, p. 198	**COOPERATIVE ACTIVITY** Investigating Ethiopian Art, p. 200 (Teacher's Edition)	**Section Assessments**, pp. 202, 205
		Chapter Assessment, pp. 206–207

Yearly Pacing *Chapter 8 Total:* 2 days *Yearly Total:* 85 days

 Planning for Block Schedules

Customizing for Special Needs

Students Acquiring English

 Access for Students Acquiring English
- **Guided Reading** for Sections 1–3 (Spanish), pp. 84–86
- **Chapter Summary** (Spanish), pp. 81–83
- **Skillbuilder Practice** Identifying Problems (Spanish), p. 87
- **Geography Application** Desertification and Migration in Africa (Spanish), pp. 88–89

 Chapter Summaries on Audiocassette in English and Spanish

INTERNET RESOURCES
www.mlworldhistory.com
The Diverse Classroom.

Less Proficient Readers

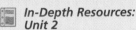 *In-Depth Resources: Unit 2*
- **Guided Reading** for Sections 1–3, pp. 55–57
- **Skillbuilder Practice** Identifying Problems, p. 58
- **Geography Application** Desertification and Migration in Africa, p. 59

Telescoping the Times
- Chapter Summary, pp. 29–31

 Chapter Summaries on Audiocassette

Gifted and Talented Students

 In-Depth Resources: Unit 2

Primary Sources:
- Nok sculpture, p. 61
- from *Natural History* by Pliny the Elder, p. 62
- from *Periplus of the Erythrean Sea*, p. 63
- from *A History of the Sudan*, p. 64

History Makers
- The Nok Culture, p. 68
- Ezana, p. 69

Connections to Literature READINGS FOR STUDENTS

 In-Depth Resources: Unit 2
- Literature: from the *Kebra Negast*, p. 65

Enrichment Reading

Courlander, Harold
A Treasury of African Folklore
New York: Marlowe, 1996
Appealing folktales from many African regions.

McDougal Littell
The Language of Literature, Grade 10

Stephen Vincent Benét, "By the Waters of Babylon," p. 713
Traditional, "Old Song," p. 982

 PE = Pupil's Edition   = Overhead Transparency   = Software   = Video

 = Copy Master = CD-ROM   = Audiocassette = Internet

African Civilizations, 1500 B.C.–A.D. 500

Accessing Prior Knowledge

- Ask students to read the captions accompanying the pictures of the Sahara and the Masai and to discuss what they know from Chapter 1 about adaptations early people made to survive in their environments.

Predicting and Making Inferences

- Have students read the caption about the kingdom of Aksum and note its position on the map. Then ask them to predict how Christianity spreads to Aksum.

- Ask students what Aksum's adoption of the Roman Empire's official religion implies about the kingdom's relationship with the empire.

Geography Connection

- Have students note Africa's location in relation to Europe and Asia. Ask students to identify the likeliest areas for cultural interaction between peoples of Africa and the other continents.

- Ask students why Aksum might have been more advantageous for the development of civilization than the Sahara or the plains of southern Kenya.

CHAPTER
8
African Civilizations, 1500 B.C.–A.D. 500

PREVIEWING THEMES

Interaction with Environment
To survive in the diverse, often harsh, environments of Africa, early peoples learned to adjust and adapt. Various cultures evolved as Africans developed ways of life suited to their particular geography and climate.

Power and Authority
All African societies developed means of providing their members with stability and order. These methods ranged from simple family ties to complex kingships.

Cultural Interaction
Migration—and the resulting mingling of peoples—is one of the major ways cultures spread and change. Mass migrations, such as those of the Bantu-speaking peoples, changed the face of the world and have had an ongoing influence on world culture.

> ▱ **INTERNET CONNECTION**
>
> Visit us at **www.mlworldhistory.com** to learn more about African civilizations.

AFRICA, A.D. 350

N

| 0 | 1000 Miles |
| 0 | 2000 Kilometers |

Vegetation Regions
- ▨ Mediterranean
- ▢ Desert
- ▨ Savanna
- ▨ Rain Forest

Tropic of Cancer

Although largely barren, the **Sahara** is a major source of an important trading commodity—salt. Africans extract it by adding water to hollows dug in the salty soil. As harvesters like this one pour water from the larger to the smaller holes, the salt becomes more concentrated. When the water finally evaporates, the harvesters collect the precious crystals.

ATLANTIC OCEAN

GEOGRAPHY THEMES

Place

Remind students that this chapter emphasizes the role of geography in shaping people's societies and cultures. Using the map on this page and on page 194, ask students what they notice about the environments of Africa. *They are diverse.* Have them speculate on how these varied environments would influence the development of societies in Africa.

Movement

Discuss with students the meaning of the word *migration*. (*Migration is the act of permanently changing one's residence from one region to another.*) Discuss the "push-pull" factors that have always compelled people to migrate. (*These factors include changes in climate or the availability of natural resources, economic pressure resulting from increasing population, and technological developments that can open new areas to settlement.*)

ADDITIONAL RESOURCES

Books for the Teacher

• Martin, Phyllis M., and Patrick O'Meara. *Africa.* Bloomington, Ind.: Indiana UP, 1986. An overview of Africa's history and culture.

• Matthiessen, Peter. *The Tree Where Man Was Born.* New York: Dutton, 1972. Observes the human and natural world of East Africa.

• Oliver, Roland Anthony. *The African Experience.* New York: HarperCollins, 1992. Overview of social and political developments, with emphasis on the prehistory of Africa.

Books for the Student

• Ajayi, J. F. Ade. *Historical Atlas of Africa.* New York: Cambridge UP, 1985. Maps, photos, drawings, and text describe African history.

Videos

• *Africa Before the Europeans: 100–1500.* Social Studies School Service, 1985. 800-421-4246.

• *The People of Origin.* Altschul Group, 1991. 800-323-9084. The San people of southern Africa.

• *Slima the Dhowmaker.* Coronet/ MTI, 1980. 800-321-3106. Slima's village in Tanzania has been making trading ships for 2,000 years.

Software

• *History and Culture of Africa.* CD-ROM. Queue, 1997. 800-232-2224. A tour of the African continent, revealing its diverse geography, peoples, and cultures.

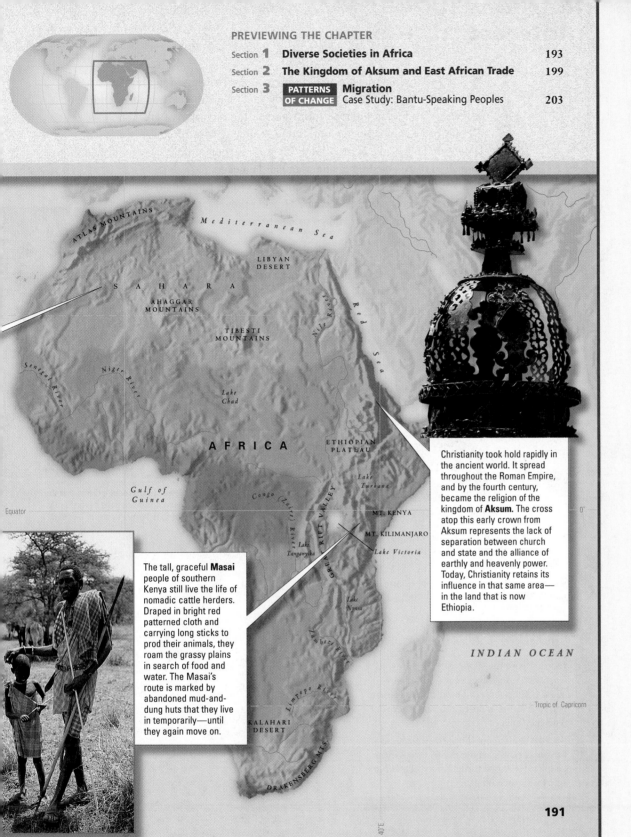

The tall, graceful **Masai** people of southern Kenya still live the life of nomadic cattle herders. Draped in bright red patterned cloth and carrying long sticks to prod their animals, they roam the grassy plains in search of food and water. The Masai's route is marked by abandoned mud-and-dung huts that they live in temporarily—until they again move on.

Christianity took hold rapidly in the ancient world. It spread throughout the Roman Empire, and by the fourth century, became the religion of the kingdom of **Aksum.** The cross atop this early crown from Aksum represents the lack of separation between church and state and the alliance of earthly and heavenly power. Today, Christianity retains its influence in that same area— in the land that is now Ethiopia.

191

HISTORY THROUGH ART

Ethiopia's Christian Art

The intricate crown shown above exemplifies the profound effect Christianity had on the art of Ethiopia. In general pattern and shape, the cross that tops the crown resembles many crosses used to this day in Ethiopian religious processions.

Christianity also influenced architectural forms, including churches literally carved out of the rocky

highlands south of Aksum by the Ethiopian king Lalibela (see the photo on page 365). It is said that before becoming king, he miraculously flew to Jerusalem. There Christ showed him the city and told him that when he ruled he was to build a second Jerusalem in Africa. King Lalibela tried to re-create the city in Ethiopia, situating 11 rock-hewn churches along a river named after the Jordan River in Palestine.

Interpreting the Art Read the fourth paragraph on page 35 of Chapter 2 and look at the crowns shown there. How does the symbolism of the Aksumite crown resemble and differ from that of the crown of Upper and Lower Egypt? *Like the Egyptian crown, the Aksumite crown expresses unity, but whereas the Egyptian crown expresses the union of two earthly kingdoms, the Aksumite crown expresses the union of an earthly kingdom with the kingdom of heaven.*

Interact *with* History

Purpose

- to set the stage for studying the Bantu migrations
- to help students understand some of the effects of migrations
- to help students make connections with people and events they will study in this chapter

Teaching Strategy

Thinking Critically After students have imagined themselves in the situation described on this page, have them answer the key questions and give reasons for their decision.

EXAMINING *the* ISSUES

Following are suggestions for addressing each bulleted question.

1 Ask students to explain how their school deals with the issue of language when newcomers who know little English arrive at their school.

2 Ask students to describe how their community has benefited from various immigrant groups. What local businesses have immigrants established or contributed to?

3 Ask students to list foods, holiday customs, and other aspects of community life that are influenced by immigrant groups.

Making Connections Invite students to discuss current trends in migration and how these trends might shape the future of their community.

Interact *with* History

You belong to a small band of hunter-gatherers living in southern Africa around 100 B.C. You eat edible roots and plants the women and children in your group find in the forest, and animals the men trap or kill. One evening as you are sitting around the fire listening to a storyteller, you see a large group of people approaching. They are carrying iron spears and driving animals and are chanting in an unfamiliar language.

Your first reaction to these newcomers is fear. But you are also curious. Who are they? What do they want? How do they live? As they draw closer, you go to meet them.

What effects will these newcomers have on the community?

Having traveled large distances, these people might have valuable survival skills to share.

Their spears could indicate that the newcomers are good hunters or that they are hostile invaders—or both.

The hunter-gatherer community is small and tightly knit. There is, however, room to expand to accommodate the newcomers.

EXAMINING *the* ISSUES

1 • What problems, such as language, food, and shelter, might people face in dealing with newcomers?

2 • How might both native people and newcomers benefit from their interaction?

3 • In what ways would such interactions change everyone involved?

Discuss these questions as a class. In your discussion, remember what you've learned about other peoples who dealt with foreigners, such as the Indo-European invaders of Asia and India.

As you read about the early African civilizations in this chapter, notice how African peoples developed varied lifestyles and interacted with each other.

192

Follow Up

A feature on the chapter assessment will ask students to reevaluate their responses to the situation presented on this page.

① Diverse Societies in Africa

TERMS & NAMES
- Sahara
- savanna
- Sahel
- desertification
- extended family
- clan
- animism
- griot
- Djenné-Djeno
- Nok

MAIN IDEA

African peoples developed diverse societies as they adapted to varied environments.

WHY IT MATTERS NOW

Differences among modern societies are also based on people's interactions with their environments.

SETTING THE STAGE "Geography is the mother of history. Nowhere in the world is this more powerfully illustrated than in Africa. The most [powerful] force in Africa's experience is Africa's environment—the combined elements of geophysical features, location, and climate. . . . Africa has been a continent of abundant life but speedy death. Partly because of this . . . Africa has been the first habitat of man but the last to become truly [livable]." That is how Ali A. Mazrui, African scholar and creator of the television series *The Africans,* summed up his homeland. In the continent's widely varied environments, Africans developed unique cultures and societies—including the great civilizations of Egypt, Carthage, and Kush.

A Land of Geographic Contrasts

Africa is the second largest continent in the world. It stretches 4,600 miles from east to west and 5,000 miles from north to south. With a total of 11.7 million square miles, it occupies about one-fifth of the earth's land surface. The elevation of the continent is like a plate turned upside down. Narrow coastlines (50 to 100 miles) lie on either side of a central plateau. Waterfalls and rapids often form as rivers drop down to the coast from the plateau, making navigation impossible to or from the coast. Africa's coastline has few harbors, ports, or inlets. Because of this, the coastline is actually shorter than that of Europe, a land one-third Africa's size.

Vocabulary
tropics: the area of the globe that lies between the Tropic of Capricorn and the Tropic of Cancer.

As the map on the next page shows, Africa straddles the equator, and most of the continent is in the tropics. But it includes a large range of the earth's environments—from steamy coastal plains to snow-capped mountain peaks. Some parts of Africa suffer from constant drought, while others receive over 400 inches of rain a year. Vegetation varies from sand dunes and rocky wastes to dense green rain forests.

Vocabulary
uninhabitable: unsuitable for human life.

From Deserts to Rain Forests Each African environment offers its own challenges to people and wildlife. Deserts make up about 40 percent of the continent. They are largely uninhabitable and also hamper people's movement to more welcoming climates. During the day, temperatures can reach 136°F, and any rain that falls evaporates quickly. The largest deserts are the **Sahara** in the north and the Kalahari (kahl·uh·HAHR·ee) in the south. Stretching from the Atlantic Ocean to the Red Sea, the Sahara covers an area roughly the size of the United States. Only a small part of the Sahara consists of sand dunes. The rest is mostly a flat, gray wasteland of scattered rocks and gravel.

Another very different—but also partly uninhabitable—African environment is the rain forest. This densely wooded region stretches across about half of the middle of Africa, and covers about 5 percent of the continent. The rain forest

SPOTLIGHT ON

Tsetse Fly

The deadliest creature lurking in the gloom of the rain forests is neither the Congo python nor the wild leopard. It is a small fly called the tsetse (TSHET·see). Tsetse flies carry a disease that is deadly to livestock and can cause fatal sleeping sickness in humans.

The tsetse fly has played a major role in African history. Its presence prevented Africans from using cattle, donkeys, and horses to farm near the rain forests. This destructive insect also prevented invaders—especially Europeans—from colonizing fly-infested territories.

(shown at 3 to 7 times life size)

African Civilizations **193**

SECTION 1 RESOURCES

PRINT RESOURCES

IN-DEPTH RESOURCES: UNIT 2
Guided Reading, p. 55
Skillbuilder Practice: Identifying Problems, p. 58
Primary Source: Nok sculpture, p. 61
History Makers: The Nok Culture, p. 68

ACCESS FOR STUDENTS ACQUIRING ENGLISH
Guided Reading (Spanish), p. 84
Skillbuilder Practice: (Spanish), p. 87

FORMAL ASSESSMENT
Section Quiz, p. 89

ALTERNATIVE ASSESSMENT BOOK

TECHNOLOGY RESOURCES

GEOGRAPHY TRANSPARENCIES
GT5, Greek View of the World, 494 B.C.

WORLD ART AND CULTURES TRANSPARENCIES
AT17 Nok terra cotta sculpture

CD-ROM
Electronic Library of Primary Sources

INTERNET www.mlworldhistory.com

Section 1 Overview

OBJECTIVES

① To identify the different geographic regions of Africa.

② To explain how early Africans adapted to their environments.

③ To summarize the achievements of early West African societies.

SKILLBUILDER

- Interpreting maps: location, region, p. 194

CRITICAL THINKING

- Making inferences, p. 195
- Drawing conclusions, p. 196
- Summarizing, p. 197
- Comparing, p. 198
- Analyzing causes, p. 198

FOCUS

5-Minute Warm-Up

▶ **Interpreting**
Have students answer these questions to explore the vegetation regions of Africa.

1. See the map on page 194. What fraction of Africa is rain forest?

2. Look at the maps on pages 194 and 207. Which looks larger—the United States or Africa's deserts?

🖫 **WARM-UP TRANSPARENCY 8**

OBJECTIVE ① INSTRUCT

A Land of Geographic Contrasts

▶ **Key Ideas**
- Deserts and rain forests in a third of Africa support few people.
- Fertile coastal regions in the north and south are densely populated by farmers and herders.
- Most Africans live on savannas, which cover two-fifths of Africa and support much agriculture.

🖫 **IN-DEPTH RESOURCES: UNIT 2**
Guided Reading, p. 55

🖫 **ACCESS FOR STUDENTS ACQUIRING ENGLISH**
Guided Reading (Spanish), p. 84

SPOTLIGHT On
Tsetse Fly
(see page 193)

Suggest that students research more about environmental diseases in Africa, such as malaria and river blindness. Where do these diseases occur? How have they affected the development of African societies?

History from Visuals

Vegetation Regions of Africa

Interpreting the Map As students examine the vegetation zones on the map, point out that Africa is divided by the equator. How might this fact affect climates in Africa? *Climates range from tropical near the equator to more temperate farther north and south.*

Extension Activity Tell students that the tropics lie between the Tropic of Cancer in the north latitudes and the Tropic of Capricorn in the south latitudes. Ask students to calculate about how many of Africa's 11.7 million square miles lie in the tropics. *About 7 million.*

SKILLBUILDER Answers
1. Each covers about 40 percent.
2. The zones more or less match up: rain forest with rain forest, savanna with savanna, desert with desert, and Mediterranean with Mediterranean.

MORE ABOUT . . .
Savanna Vegetation

Savanna vegetation has developed various "strategies" for survival. For example, Acacia trees have tough bark, which armors them against grass fires. Small leaves and deep roots help them endure droughts. In addition, the trees have thorns and harbor biting ants, which discourage animals from eating the leaves.

---

is hot and humid and receives enormous amounts of rain. Sometimes called "nature's greenhouse," it produces mahogany and teak trees up to 150 feet tall. Their leaves and branches form a dense canopy that keeps sunlight from reaching the forest floor. As a result, there are few small plants in the rain forest, despite the fact that movies often portray it as a vegetation-clogged jungle.

From Fertile Farmlands to Grassy Plains The northern coast and the southern tip of Africa, on the other hand, have welcoming climates and fertile soil. Summers are sunny, dry, and hot, while winters are mild. Rainfall is moderate. Because these coastal areas with Mediterranean vegetation are so fertile, they are densely populated with farmers and herders.

Vegetation Regions of Africa

Widely scattered acacia trees dot the flat, grassy plains of the savanna. Giraffes especially like the acacia leaves, which most other animals cannot reach.

The dense trees and lack of edible vegetation in the humid rain forest make it an unwelcome environment for most people.

Legend:
- Rain forest
- Savanna
- Desert
- Mediterranean

GEOGRAPHY SKILLBUILDER: Interpreting Maps
1. **Location** *About what percent of Africa is desert? savanna?*
2. **Region** *If you were to fold a map of Africa in half along the equator, what do you notice about the similar vegetation zones above and below the fold?*

194 Chapter 8

TEACHING OPTIONS

CONNECTIONS ACROSS THE CURRICULUM

Geography Early maps of distant lands or the world were largely the product of rumor, myth, or the map maker's fancy. This was especially true of European maps of Africa, whose interior was a mystery to Europeans till modern times. Not till Europeans began exploring Africa extensively in the 19th

century were map makers able to chart the interior accurately. To help students understand how inaccurate early maps could be, show them the map depicting the ancient Greek view of the world on the Chapter 5 geography transparency. Then have them compare that map with the one on this page. Ask them how the

Greek view of Africa resembles and differs from the current view. *It resembles the current view most in showing Africa's Mediterranean and Red Sea coasts and the Nile; it differs most in showing Africa's southern limits. What might explain the differences? The Greek map could only be as*

accurate as Greeks' knowledge of the world, which did not extend far from the coasts and river valleys they had made contact with.

 GEOGRAPHY TRANSPARENCIES
GT5, Greek View of the World, 494 B.C.

The largest number of people in Africa, however, live on the **savannas,** or grassy plains. Covered with tall grasses and dotted with acacia trees, the savannas cover over 40 percent of the continent. Dry seasons alternate with rainy seasons—often, two of each a year. The topsoil throughout Africa is thin, and heavy rains strip away minerals. In most years, however, the savannas support abundant agriculture. Major crops are grains such as sorghum and millet, rice, wheat, and maize (corn).

Africa's savanna is not just an endless plain, however. It includes mountainous highlands, swampy tropical stretches, and the land at the southern edge of the Sahara Desert, the **Sahel** (suh·HAYL). Sahel means "coastline" in Arabic, and the ancient north African people may have named it this because the Sahara seemed to them a vast ocean of sand. Each year, however, the desert takes over more and more of the Sahel. This steady process of drying of the soil is called **desertification.**

Early Humans Adapt to Their Environments

The first humans appeared in the Great Rift Valley, a deep gash in the earth's crust that runs through the floor of the Red Sea and across eastern Africa. People moved outward from this area in the world's first migration, adapting to the vastly different environments they encountered. They developed technologies that helped them survive in—and then alter—their surroundings. For example, first using pointed sticks as spears, they progressed to shaping spear points out of stone, and later, iron.

Nomadic Lifestyle Africa's earliest peoples were nomadic hunter-gatherers who roamed from place to place seeking sources of food. Today, some of the San of the Kalahari Desert and the BaMbuti (bah·uhm·BOO·tee) of the rain forests of Congo are still hunter-gatherers. The San, for example, travel in small bands of a few related families. The men hunt with spears and bows and arrows, and the women and children gather roots and berries. As shown in the Daily Life feature on page 196, they know and use the resources of their environment well.

Africans who lived in areas that supported a variety of animals eventually learned to domesticate and raise them for food. Called herders, or pastoralists, these people kept cattle, goats, or sheep. Like the hunter-gatherers, they were nomads, driving their animals to find water and good pastures for grazing during the dry season. Millions of modern Africans are pastoral herders as well. The Masai (mah·SEYE) of Tanzania and southern Kenya, for example, still measure their wealth by the size of their herds.

Transition to a Settled Lifestyle Most early Africans continued to hunt, although they eventually learned to grow their own food, rather than gathering what grew wild. Experts believe that agriculture probably began by 10,000 B.C. in Africa. Between 8000 and 4000 B.C., the Sahara received increased rainfall and turned into a savanna. But about 4000 B.C., the Sahara began to dry up again. To survive, many early farmers moved east into the Nile Valley and south into West Africa. Many settled on the savannas, which had the best agricultural land. Some peoples also learned to farm in the rain forest, where they planted root crops, such as yams, that needed little sun.

Agriculture drastically changed the way Africans lived on the savannas. Growing their own food enabled them to settle in one location, where they built permanent shelters. Settlements expanded because reliable food supplies meant longer, healthier lives and an increased birthrate. The increased food supply also freed some members of the community to practice activities other than farming. These activities included working metal, making pottery, or crafting jewelry.

African Civilizations **195**

THINK THROUGH HISTORY
A. Making Inferences Why might herders have remained nomadic?
A. Answer They had to keep moving to find food and water for their animals during the dry season.

CONNECT *to* TODAY

Nomads in Nairobi
In the drought of 1997, Masai herders traveled hundreds of miles in search of grass for their starving cattle. They drove their animals through plains and along modern highways onto land near the Kenyan capital, Nairobi. The cattle ate whatever grass they could find, including several acres surrounding the transmitters of the Kenya Broadcasting Corporation.

In a tense confrontation, company officials finally allowed the Masai to use the land for grazing—possibly because it saved them the cost of hiring people to cut the grass.

Nomad Nutritional News

Point out to students that the San people inhabit the harsh Kalahari Desert in southwestern Africa. Ask students to imagine living in such a harsh environment. What would daily life be like?

MORE ABOUT . . .
Nomad Nutrition

Like the San, the BaMbuti people of the Ituri Forest in Zaire are nomadic hunter-gatherers. Much of their diet consists of roots, nuts, fruits, and fungi they gather in the forest. Snails, termites, fish, and snakes provide nutritious animal protein. Honey is also an important part of the diet because it is considered a delicacy.

Although adept at hunting forest animals such as wild pigs, antelope, and monkeys, the BaMbuti smoke most of the meat and trade it to farming villages at the fringes of the forest for yams, corn, peanuts, and beans.

Because of their knowledge of forest plants, the BaMbuti are skilled in making medicines that they say can cure a variety of afflictions, including headaches, toothaches, and fevers.

Nomad Nutritional News

A Movable Feast

San women make a picnic of it when they take their children out to gather food for their families. The women carry sharp wooden digging sticks as well as net bags holding ostrich eggshells filled with water. Around her body, each woman fastens a two-compartment bag called a *kaross,* which carries more than 20 pounds of food—fruits, nuts, melons, roots, tubers, termites, caterpillars, and locusts. These foods satisfy about three-quarters of the San's daily caloric needs.

Making a Bee-Line

Once the rains begin to fall, San men and women know that they will soon get their fill of honey. During the short rainy season, the San note where the bees fly at sunset, when they return to their hives. A San who finds a good hive immediately smokes out the bees and removes the sticky, sweet treat. He doesn't bypass unripe hives, though. He marks them with a small heap of stones and returns later to retrieve the honey. Tampering with marked hives is a serious crime, one that the San may punish by death. So bee-ware.

Thirsty? Look for a three-pronged leaf and dig down about a foot. You'll find a juicy *bi* bulb like this one that you can mash and mix with chewed leaves for a refreshing drink.

Ate Too Much?
See a Shaman

Shamans, or healers, often beat drums and chant to create the right atmosphere for healing. To cure indigestion and other illnesses, they use sacred objects and medicine in a ceremony attended by the patient's family. Don't visit a shaman unless you're willing to believe in his or her powers, though. Your trust is the shaman's most important medicine.

The Gourmet Corner:

A One-Egg Omelet
One ostrich egg is the equivalent of two dozen hens' eggs, a handy fact to know if you're an omelet fan. A San cook shares her recipe: Take one ostrich egg. To save the shell for carrying water, tap a hole in the crown. With a twig, remove the membrane. To scramble the egg, twirl the stick in the hole. Pour the scrambled egg into a tortoise-shell pan and then into a hole lined with hot coals. Build the fire up around the hole to cook the top of your omelet. Dust the ash off the completed omelet, clean the bottom, and serve it to 15 or 20 friends.

An empty ostrich eggshell and the omelet in progress.

Connect *to* History

Drawing Conclusions How do the San use their extensive knowledge of their environment?

SEE SKILLBUILDER HANDBOOK PAGE 1006

Connect *to* Today

Researching Gather information about a modern nomadic culture, such as the Masai of southern Kenya and Tanzania, by using the library or Internet. In what ways is this culture similar to that of the San? How does it differ?

Connect *to* History

Drawing Conclusions
Possible Response: The San use their knowledge to make tools, to find and prepare drinks, and to find, gather, and prepare food.

Connect *to* Today

Researching
For information on the Masai, students might consult *Maasai Days* by Cheryl Bensen or *Maasai* by Tepilit Ole Saitoti or search for a web site on Kenya. Suggest that students make a chart like this one to compare the San and a nomadic culture.

	San	Masai
Sources of food and water		
Shelter		
Use of resources		
Community Life		

These increasingly large and complex settlements of people required more organization and regulation than smaller communities. Various types of governing bodies developed to fill this need. Some governments consisted of a village chief and/or a council of the leaders of individual family groups. As strong groups moved to extend their land and conquered weaker settlements, they centralized their power and their governments. Some of these societies eventually developed into great kingdoms.

Africans Share Common Characteristics No matter what environment they lived in and what style of life they adopted, the societies south of the Sahara—like all human cultures—shared common elements. One of these elements was the importance of the basic social unit, the family. Besides parents and children, this primary group often included grandparents, aunts, uncles, and cousins in an **extended family.** Ties often expanded to the **clan,** a group that shared common ancestors.

African peoples not only organized themselves into family groups. They also developed belief systems that helped them understand and organize information about their world. Nearly all of these local religions involved a belief in one creator, or god. They generally also included elements of **animism,** a religion in which spirits played an important role in regulating daily life. Animists believe that these spirits are present in animals, plants, and other natural forces, and also take the form of the souls of their dead ancestors.

Although all African societies had a language, most were not written down. History, literature, and culture were shared orally by specialized storytellers. In West Africa, for example, these storytellers, or **griots** (gree·OHZ), kept this history alive, passing it from parent to child:

> **A VOICE FROM THE PAST**
> I am a griot . . . master in the art of eloquence. . . . we are vessels of speech, we are the repositories [storehouses] which harbor secrets many centuries old. . . . without us the names of kings would vanish. . . . we are the memory of mankind; by the spoken word we bring to life the deeds . . . of kings for younger generations. . . . for the world is old, but the future springs from the past.
>
> **DJELI MAMADOU KOUYATE,** from *Sundiata, an Epic of Old Mali*

Early Societies in West Africa

To add to information provided by Africa's oral historians, archaeologists have continued to look for evidence of the history of Africa south of the Sahara. Recent discoveries in West Africa have proved how old and extensive that history is. Archaeologists believe that early peoples moved into this area from the north as desertification forced them to find better farmland. Discoveries in the areas of modern Mali and Nigeria reveal that West Africans developed advanced societies and cities long before outsiders came to the continent.

Djenné-Djeno Archaeologists uncovered the remains of one of these cities, **Djenné-Djeno**

(jeh·NAY jeh·NOH), or ancient Djenné, in 1977 on a tributary of the Niger River. In excavating a huge tell, or mound covering the remains of a series of civilizations, they discovered hundreds of thousands of artifacts. These objects included pottery, copper hair ornaments, clay toys, glass beads, stone bracelets, and iron knives. The oldest objects dated from 250 B.C., making Djenné-Djeno the oldest known city

The water that surrounded Djenné-Djeno provided food and also offered a transportation route, which made the city a bustling trade center.

197

in Africa south of the Sahara. The city was abandoned some time after A.D. 1400. About that time, another city, Djenné, arose about two miles away.

At its height, Djenné-Djeno had some 50,000 residents. They lived in round reed huts plastered with mud. Later, they built enclosed houses made of mud bricks. They fished in the Niger River, raised rice on its fertile floodplains, and herded cattle. By the third century B.C., they had discovered how to smelt iron. They exchanged their rice, fish, and pottery for copper, gold, and salt with other peoples who lived along the river. Djenné-Djeno was linked to other towns not only by the Niger, but also by overland camel routes. For that reason, it became a bustling trading center.

The Nok Culture Although Djenné-Djeno was its oldest town, West Africa's earliest known culture was that of the **Nok** (nahk) people. They lived in what is now Nigeria between 500 B.C. and A.D. 200. Their name came from the village where the first artifacts from their culture were discovered. Like the residents of Djenné-Djeno, the Nok were farmers. They were also the first West African people known to smelt iron. They used it to make tools for farming and weapons for hunting. These iron implements lasted longer than ones made of wood or stone, and vastly improved the lives of the Nok.

This terra cotta elephant head reveals both the artistry of its Nok creator and the fact that elephants played a role in that people's daily lives.

The Nok developed iron-making technology about 500 B.C., nearly 300 years before it arose in Djenné-Djeno. In fact, they may have brought the technology to Djenné-Djeno. The similarity of artifacts found in these two distant places suggests that the Nok may have settled in Djenné-Djeno at one time.

Nok artifacts have been found in an area stretching for 300 miles between the Niger and Benue rivers. Many are sculptures made of terra cotta, a reddish-brown clay. They often depict human or animal heads in great artistic detail, showing the Nok's skill. The features of some of the heads reveal more about history than just the skill of their creators, however. One of the heads, for example, shows a distinctive hairdo arranged in six buns, a style that is still worn by some people in Nigeria. This similarity suggests that the Nok may have been the direct ancestors of some modern Africans.

While the early inhabitants of West Africa were developing cities, cultures, and technologies that would write their name on the pages of history, East Africa was undergoing its own cultural evolution.

THINK THROUGH HISTORY
C. Comparing In what ways were the cultures of Djenné-Djeno and the Nok alike?
C. Answer Both peoples were farmers and ironmakers, and they created similar artifacts. The Nok may have settled in Djenné-Djeno at one time.

Section 1 Assessment

1. TERMS & NAMES
Identify
• Sahara
• savanna
• Sahel
• desertification
• extended family
• clan
• animism
• griot
• Djenné-Djeno
• Nok

2. TAKING NOTES
Use a flow chart like the one below to trace the main events that followed the development of agriculture on the African savannas.

[Development of agriculture]
→ [ ]
→ [ ]

Write a news headline for one of these developments.

3. ANALYZING CAUSES
How does adapting to different environments lead to the development of diverse cultures?

THINK ABOUT
• natural resources
• Nok accomplishments
• migrations of different groups of people

4. THEME ACTIVITY
Interaction with Environment Take an imaginary journey to one of the four African vegetation zones. Then write a short diary entry or letter describing what you see and experience. Explain your difficulties adapting to this environment and tell what you learn.

198 Chapter 8

---

2 The Kingdom of Aksum and East African Trade

TERMS & NAMES
- Aksum
- Adulis
- Ezana

MAIN IDEA

The kingdom of Aksum became an international trading power and adopted Christianity.

WHY IT MATTERS NOW

Ancient Aksum, which is now Ethiopia, is still a center of Eastern Christianity.

SETTING THE STAGE In the eighth century B.C., before the Nok were spreading their culture throughout West Africa, the kingdom of Kush in East Africa had become powerful enough to conquer Egypt. (See Chapter 4.) However, fierce Assyrians swept into Egypt during the next century and drove the Kushite pharaohs south. Kush nevertheless remained a powerful kingdom for over 1,000 years—until it was conquered by another even more powerful kingdom.

The Rise of the Kingdom of Aksum

The kingdom that arose was **Aksum** (AHK·soom). It was located south of Kush on a rugged plateau on the Red Sea, in what is now Eritrea and Ethiopia. A legend traces the founding of the kingdom of Aksum and the Ethiopian royal dynasty to the son of King Solomon of ancient Israel and the Queen of Sheba. That dynasty includes the 20th-century ruler Haile Selassie. In fact, the history of Aksum may have begun as early as 1000 B.C., when Arab peoples crossed the Red Sea into Africa. There they mingled with Kushite herders and farmers and passed along their written language, Ge'ez (GEE·ehz). They also shared their skills of working stone and building dams and aqueducts.

The first mention of Aksum was in a Greek guidebook written around A.D. 100, *Periplus of the Erythraean Sea*. It describes Zoskales (ZAHS·kuh·leez), thought to be the first king of Aksum. He was "a stickler about his possessions and always [greedy] for getting more, but in other respects a fine person and well versed in reading and writing Greek." Greece was not the only country to interact with Aksum, however. Under Zoskales and other rulers, Aksum began conquering people in other lands. The Aksumites seized areas along the Red Sea and the Blue Nile in Africa. They also crossed the Red Sea and took control of lands on the southwestern Arabian Peninsula.

Aksum Controls International Trade Aksum's location and expansion into surrounding areas

Aksum, A.D. 300–700

GEOGRAPHY SKILLBUILDER: Interpreting Maps
1. **Location** What nearby waterways enabled Aksum to become a major trading center?
2. **Movement** What continents or countries did Aksum's trade routes give it access to?

199

Section 2 Overview

OBJECTIVES

1. To explain how maritime trade led to Aksum's growth.
2. To give examples of the achievements of Aksum.
3. To explain the effects of the Muslim invasion of Aksum.

SKILLBUILDER
- Interpreting maps: location, movement, p. 199

CRITICAL THINKING
- Analyzing causes, pp. 201, 202
- Recognizing effects, p. 201
- Analyzing themes, p. 202

FOCUS

5-Minute Warm-Up

▶ **Interpreting**
To help students grasp the importance of Aksum's location, have them answer these questions.

1. Look at the map on page 199. What ports did Aksum control?
2. How many miles did traders have to travel to reach the Mediterranean from Adulis via the Red Sea and Memphis?

 WARM-UP TRANSPARENCY 8

OBJECTIVE 1 INSTRUCT

The Rise of the Kingdom of Aksum

▶ **Key Ideas**
- After Arab peoples mingle with Kushite farmers and herders, the kingdom of Aksum emerges.
- Aksum expands by conquest and controls maritime trade as far as the Indian Ocean.
- Aksum reaches its peak under the strong rule of Ezana.

IN-DEPTH RESOURCES: UNIT 2
Guided Reading, p. 56
Primary Sources: from *Natural History*, p. 62; from *Periplus*, p. 63; from *A History of the Sudan*, p. 64
Literature: from the *Kebra Negast*, p. 65

ACCESS FOR STUDENTS ACQUIRING ENGLISH
Guided Reading (Spanish), p. 85

ELECTRONIC LIBRARY OF PRIMARY SOURCES
"The Aksumite Empire"

SECTION 2 RESOURCES

PRINT RESOURCES

📖 **IN-DEPTH RESOURCES: UNIT 2**
Guided Reading, p. 56
Primary Sources: from *Natural History*, p. 62; from *Periplus,* p. 63; from *Sudan*, p. 64
Literature: from the *Kebra Negast,* p. 65
History Makers: Ezana, p. 69

📖 **ACCESS FOR STUDENTS ACQUIRING ENGLISH**
Guided Reading (Spanish), p. 85

📖 **FORMAL ASSESSMENT**
Section Quiz, p. 90

TECHNOLOGY RESOURCES

🎞 **GEOGRAPHY TRANSPARENCIES**
GT8 Empires of Ancient Africa, 900 B.C.–A.D. 700

🎞 **WORLD ART AND CULTURES TRANSPARENCIES**
AT18 Aksumite carved stone

🎞 **CRITICAL THINKING TRANSPARENCIES**
CT8 Facts and Opinions in the Kingdom of Aksum

💿 **CD-ROM**
Electronic Library of Primary Sources

🌐 **INTERNET** www.mlworldhistory.com

made it an important trading center. It was a hub for caravan routes to Egypt and Meroë, the capital of Kush. Its miles of coastline and ports on the Red Sea gave it influence over sea trade on the Mediterranean Sea and Indian Ocean as well. Traders from Egypt, Arabia, Persia, India, and the Roman Empire crowded Aksum's chief seaport, **Adulis** (AHD·uh·luhs), near present-day Massawa. As a result, Aksum soon became an international trading power.

Aksumite merchants traded necessities such as salt and luxuries such as rhinoceros horns, tortoise shells, ivory, emeralds, and gold. In return, they chose from items such as imported cloth, glass, olive oil, wine, brass, iron, and copper. Around A.D. 550, an Egyptian merchant named Cosmas described how Aksumite agents bargained for gold from the people in southern Ethiopia:

A VOICE FROM THE PAST
They take along with them to the mining district oxen, lumps of salt, and iron, and when they reach its neighborhood they . . . halt . . . and form an encampment, which they fence round with a great hedge of thorns. Within this they live, and having slaughtered the oxen, cut them in pieces and lay the pieces on top of the thorns along with the lumps of salt and the iron. Then come the natives bringing gold in nuggets like peas . . . and lay one or two or more of these upon what pleases them. . . . Then the owner of the meat approaches, and if he is satisfied he takes the gold away, and upon seeing this its owner comes and takes the flesh or the salt or the iron.

COSMAS, quoted in *Travellers in Ethiopia*

A Strong Ruler Expands the Kingdom The kingdom of Aksum reached its height between A.D. 325 and 360, when an exceptionally strong ruler, **Ezana** (AY·zah·nah), occupied the throne. Determined to establish and expand his authority, Ezana first conquered the part of the Arabian peninsula that is now Yemen. Then, in 330, Ezana turned his attention to Kush, which already had begun to decline. In 350, he conquered the Kushites and burned Meroë to the ground:

A VOICE FROM THE PAST
I carried war against [them] when they had rebelled. . . . I burnt their towns of stone and their towns of straw. At the same time, my men plundered [stole] their grain, their bronze, their iron and their copper, destroyed the idols in their homes, their stocks of corn and of cotton; and they threw themselves into the river. . . .

KING EZANA OF AKSUM, quoted in *Africa: Past and Present*

A Cosmopolitan Culture Develops

From the beginning, Aksumites had a diverse cultural heritage. This blend included traditions of the Arab peoples who crossed the Red Sea into Africa and those of the Kushite peoples they settled among. As the kingdom expanded and became a powerful trading center, it attracted people from all over the ancient world.

The port city of Adulis was particularly cosmopolitan. It included people from Aksum's widespread trading partners, such as Egypt, Arabia, Greece, Rome, Persia, India, and even Byzantium. In the babble of tongues heard in Aksum, Greek stood out as the international language of the time, much as English does in the world today.

The Spread of Christianity The Aksumites, like other ancient Africans, traditionally believed in one god. They called their god Mahrem and believed that their king was directly descended from him. They were also animists, however, and worshiped the spirits of nature and honored their dead ancestors. They offered sacrifices—often as many as a dozen oxen at a time—to those spirits, to Mahrem, and often, to the Greek god of war, Ares.

Vocabulary
cosmopolitan: including elements from many parts of the world.

THINK THROUGH HISTORY
A. Analyzing Causes What conditions led to Aksum's becoming a Christian Kingdom?

A. Answer Its status as a trade center where ideas were exchanged, and Ezana's conversion to Christianity.

Merchants exchanged more than raw materials and finished goods in Aksum. They shared ideas as well. One of these ideas was a new religion, Christianity. Based on the teachings of Jesus and a belief in one God—monotheism—Christianity began in Palestine about A.D. 30. It spread throughout the Roman Empire and then to Aksum. King Ezana's conversion and his devout practice of Christianity strengthened its hold in Aksum.

In A.D. 451, a dispute arose over the nature of Christ—whether he was solely divine, or both divine and human. This dispute led to a split between Egypt and Ethiopia on the one hand and the church of Constantinople and Rome on the other. The Egyptian and Ethiopian churches, which believed in the wholly divine nature of Christ, followed their separate paths. They became the Coptic Church of Egypt and the Ethiopian Orthodox Church. The influence of these churches has continued. The Ethiopian Orthodox Church today boasts a membership of more than 22 million people—over half the population of the country.

Aksumite Architecture The establishment of Christianity was just one lasting achievement of the Aksumites. They also developed a unique architecture. They used stone instead of mud bricks to construct vast royal palaces and public buildings. Like the Egyptians, the Aksumites used no mortar. Instead, they carved stones to fit together tightly. Aksum's kings also built huge stone pillars called stelae (STEE·lee). These presumably were meant to celebrate the kings' conquests and to demonstrate Aksum's greatness. Some are 60 feet tall and were among the largest structures in the ancient world. Ezana left a lasting reminder of Aksum's spiritual and structural achievements in his last stele. He dedicated this soaring stone to the Christian God, "the Lord of heaven, who in heaven and upon earth is mightier than everything that exists."

Language and Agriculture The inscription on Ezana's stele is written in Ge'ez, the language brought to Aksum by its early Arab inhabitants. Aside from Egypt and Meroë, Aksum was the only ancient African kingdom known to have developed a written language. It was also the first state south of the Sahara to mint its own coins. Made of bronze, silver, and gold, these coins were imprinted with the saying, "May the country be satisfied." Ezana apparently hoped that this inscription would make him popular with the people. Every time they used a coin, it would remind them that he had their interests at heart.

In addition to these cultural achievements, the Aksumites adapted creatively to their rugged, hilly environment. They created a new method of agriculture, terrace farming. This enabled them to greatly increase the productivity of their land. Terraces, or steplike ridges constructed on mountain slopes, helped the soil retain water and prevented its being washed downhill in heavy rains. The Aksumites dug canals to channel water from mountain streams into the fields. They also built dams and cisterns, or holding tanks, to store water.

THINK THROUGH HISTORY
B. Recognizing Effects How did Aksum's location and interaction with other regions affect its development?

B. Answer Its location on water and land trade routes gave it access to new ideas and products, markets for it own products, and the means of conquering and expanding its kingdom.

The Fall of Aksum

Aksum's cultural and technological achievements enabled it to last for 800 years. The kingdom finally declined, however, under invaders who practiced the religion called Islam (ihs·LAHM). Its founder was the prophet Muhammad, and by the time of his death in 632, his followers had conquered all of Arabia. This territory included Aksum's lands on the Arabian coast of the Red Sea. The Islamic invaders went on to conquer vast territories in the Mediterranean world, spreading their religion as they went. Because Aksum had protected

This towering stone pillar, or stele, was built to celebrate Aksum's achievements. Still standing today, its size and elaborate inscriptions make it an achievement in its own right.

Global Impact

A Road Paved with Gold: Aksum to Rome

The kingdom of Aksum had a tremendous impact on the ancient Mediterranean world. It particularly influenced one of the most important powers of the time, the Roman Empire. Roman ships came to Adulis weekly to trade with the Aksumites. Many Roman merchants lived in Adulis, and in the capital city, Aksum.

One of the chief commodities that linked the two powers was gold. The Aksumites had access to it from inland gold mines, and the Romans needed it to support the monetary system of their growing empire. Rome and Aksum were linked not only by gold, however. They also shared a spiritual link in their commitment to Christianity.

African Civilizations **201**

Global Impact
A Road Paved with Gold: Aksum to Rome

Because of Aksum's close economic and religious ties to the Roman and Byzantine Empires, it became subject to repeated urgings by the empires to help curb the growth of their rival, Sassanid Persia. But Aksum mostly kept out of this power game, perhaps because the Persian army was near and Aksum's allies were far.

Ask students how being on the outskirts of the Roman and Byzantine Empires affected Aksum's relations with the empires. *Aksum was close enough to the empires to benefit from their trade but far enough to resist being treated as a tool of imperial policy.*

MORE ABOUT . . .
Aksumite Coins

The first Aksumite coins bear an image of the king along with the pagan symbols of a disc and a crescent. An inscription attests to the king's divine descent from Mahrem. Beginning with Ezana, the disc and crescent are replaced by a cross, and inscriptions such as "By this cross [the king] will conquer" appear. At first, inscriptions were in Greek, the language of the eastern Mediterranean. But while Greek continued to be used on coins for world trade, Ge'ez came to be used on coins for local trade.

OBJECTIVE 3 INSTRUCT

The Fall of Aksum
Key Ideas
- Islamic invaders seize Aksum's territory on the Arabian coast.
- Further invasions on the African coast cut Aksum off from the sea and drive Aksumites inland.
- Aksum is geographically isolated and declines as a trading power.

TEACHING OPTION

CONNECTIONS ACROSS TIME AND PLACE

Ethiopia and Eritrea Isolated from its coastal territory, the kingdom of Aksum lived on to become the kingdom of Ethiopia. But over the centuries, divisions and feudal wars weakened the nation. Coastal areas were invaded by Ottoman Turks in the 16th century and later fell prey to the Egyptians. Italy seized the coast in 1885 and named it Eritrea. Parts of Eritrea were regained by Emperor Menelik II of Ethiopia in 1896 but were lost again when Italy invaded in 1935 and seized control of all Ethiopia. Following Italy's defeat in World War II, Eritrea once again became part of Ethiopia. But in 1961, Eritreans began a war for independence that raged for 30 years. Finally, in 1993, Ethiopia recognized Eritrea's independence. Eritrea, for its part, has allowed Ethiopia to use its ports. Ask students to find the two nations on a modern map. Then ask why, on the basis of the map, it might be important for Ethiopia to retain access to Eritrea's ports. *Without access to Eritrea's ports, much of Ethiopia would be cut off from the Red Sea and its trade routes.*

This 15th-century Ethiopian fan shows the Christian influence that began in Aksum and continues in the area today. It may have been used during the church service to keep flies from settling on the communion bread and wine.

Muhammad's family and followers during his rise to power, however, his followers initially did not invade Aksum's territories on the African coast of the Red Sea. Retaining control of that coastline enabled Aksum to remain a trading power.

Before long, though, the invaders seized footholds on the African coast as well. In 710 they destroyed Adulis. This conquest cut Aksum off from the major ports along both the Red Sea and the Mediterranean. As a result, the kingdom declined as an international trading power. But it was not only Aksum's political power that weakened. Its spiritual identity and environment were also endangered.

As the invaders spread Islam to the lands they conquered, Aksum became isolated from other Christian settlements. To escape the advancing wave of Islam, Aksum's rulers moved their capital over the mountains into what is now northern Ethiopia. There, depletion of the forests and soil erosion as well as Aksum's new geographic isolation led to its decline as a world power.

Although the kingdom of Aksum reached tremendous heights and left a lasting legacy in its religion, architecture, and agriculture, it lived out its lifespan within a fairly small area. Other cultures, both in Africa and around the world, have developed not by expanding locally, but by moving over great distances. As their living circumstances changed, they adapted to the other peoples and environments they encountered.

Section 2 Assessment

1. TERMS & NAMES

Identify
- Aksum
- Adulis
- Ezana

2. TAKING NOTES

Use a web like the one below to list the achievements of Aksum.

Aksum's achievements

Write a paragraph comparing Aksum's achievements with those of another empire, such as Egypt or Rome.

3. ANALYZING CAUSES

Why did the kingdom of Aksum decline?

THINK ABOUT
- the rise and spread of Islam
- Aksum's relocation
- changes in the environment

4. ANALYZING THEMES

Power and Authority Do you think that the kingdom of Aksum would have reached the same heights if Ezana had not become king? Explain your answer.

THINK ABOUT
- Ezana's accomplishments
- Aksum's importance as a trading center
- Ezana's conversion to Christianity
- the decline of Aksum

ANSWERS

1. TERMS & NAMES
Aksum, p. 199
Adulis, p. 200
Ezana, p. 200

2. TAKING NOTES
Possible Responses: Controlled international trade; spread Christianity; built stelae; developed terrace farming.
Paragraphs will vary, but should show knowledge of Aksum's and another empire's achievements.

3. ANALYZING CAUSES
Possible Responses: Aksum could not hold off the onslaught of Islam and became isolated religiously and geographically. Depletion of natural resources hastened its decline.

4. ANALYZING THEMES
Possible Responses: No—Ezana's conversion to Christia[nity] enabled him to unite the king[dom] and form close ties with Christ[ian] empires. Yes—Aksum's locati[on] gave it a unique chance to become a major trade center. Any competent leader could have developed its potential.

③ Migration

CASE STUDY: Bantu-Speaking Peoples

TERMS & NAMES
• Bantu-speaking peoples

MAIN IDEA	WHY IT MATTERS NOW
Throughout history, people have been driven to uproot themselves and explore their world.	Migration continues to shape the modern world.

SETTING THE STAGE Human history is a motion picture, a vibrating spectacle of movement, collision, settlement, and more movement. Human beings have always been driven to search for new opportunities. The desire to move on in search of a better life seems to be built into human nature.

Migrations Through History

Aside from the general human desire for change, migrations have many specific causes. Some of these are listed in the chart below.

PATTERNS OF CHANGE: Migration

Cause	Example	Effect
Environmental change	Shift in climate, depletion of natural resources, drought, earthquake	Redistribution of world's population, blending of cultures
Economic pressure	Increasing population, famine, unemployment	Shifts in population
Political and religious persecution	Slave trade, war, ethnic cleansing, repression	Dislocation and oppression of peoples, spread of ideas and religions
Technological development	Tools, agriculture, iron smelting, communications and transportation networks	Development of civilizations and empires

SKILLBUILDER: Interpreting Charts
1. *Which causes of migration have remained important throughout history? Explain.*
2. *Which cause do you think is most important in modern migrations? Why?*

As an important pattern in human culture, migrations have influenced world history from its outset. The first human beings began populating the globe as they were pushed to move on by environmental change, population growth, and technological advances, such as the smelting of iron. In the 15th century, the Ottomans' drive for power pushed them to move all over the ancient world to create a massive empire. Seventeenth-century European settlers were pulled to America by the hope of religious tolerance and improving their lives economically.

One way experts can trace the patterns of this movement of people through history is by studying the spread of languages. People bring their languages with them when they move to new places. And languages, like the people who speak them, are living things that evolve and change in regular ways. If two languages have similar words for a particular object or idea, for example, it is likely that the people who spoke them were in close contact at one time.

PATTERNS OF CHANGE 203

SECTION 3 RESOURCES

PRINT RESOURCES

IN-DEPTH RESOURCES: UNIT 2
Guided Reading, p. 57
Geography Application: Desertification and Migration in Africa, p. 59
Connections Across Time and Cultures: Migrations: Bantu and Indo-European, p. 70

ACCESS FOR STUDENTS ACQUIRING ENGLISH
Guided Reading (Spanish), p. 86
Geography Application: (Spanish), pp. 88–89

FORMAL ASSESSMENT
Section Quiz, p. 91

ALTERNATIVE ASSESSMENT BOOK

TECHNOLOGY RESOURCES

CRITICAL THINKING TRANSPARENCIES
CT44 Chapter 8 Visual Summary

CD-ROM
Electronic Library of Primary Sources

INTERNET www.mlworldhistory.com

Section 3 Overview

OBJECTIVES

① To summarize the causes and effects of human migration.

② To describe the Bantu migrations into the southern half of Africa.

SKILLBUILDERS

• Interpreting charts, p. 203
• Interpreting maps: human-environment interaction, movement, p. 205

CRITICAL THINKING

• Clarifying, p. 204
• Analyzing causes, p. 205
• Comparing and contrasting, p. 205

FOCUS
5-Minute Warm-Up

▶ *Interpreting*
Have students answer these questions to explore the Bantu migrations.

1. Compare the map on page 205 with the one on page 194. What vegetation regions did the Bantu-speaking peoples migrate through?

2. Why might people have avoided settling in the equatorial rain forest or the Namib Desert?

WARM-UP TRANSPARENCY 8

OBJECTIVE ① INSTRUCT

Migrations Through History

▶ *Key Ideas*
• Human migrations take place for a variety of reasons.
• Migrations have influenced world history and continue to affect the modern world.

IN-DEPTH RESOURCES: UNIT 2
Guided Reading, p. 57
Connections Across Time and Cultures: Migrations: Bantu and Indo-European, p. 70

ACCESS FOR STUDENTS ACQUIRING ENGLISH
Guided Reading (Spanish), p. 86

Teacher's Edition 203

Migration

(see page 203)

Interpreting the Chart Have students identify the main idea of the chart. *Causes and effects of human migration.* What is iron smelting an example of? *Technological development.* What is one cause of migration that can result in the blending of cultures? *Environmental change.*

Extension Activity How might environmental change and economic pressure combine to cause people to migrate? *Possible response: If the population in an area outgrows the natural resources available there, people might have to migrate in search of new resources.*

SKILLBUILDER Answers
The following are possible responses.

1. All have, possibly because people have remained basically the same.
2. Environmental change; people are depleting the earth's resources. Economic pressure; the gap between rich and poor is growing. Political and religious persecution; persecution is growing in many parts of the world. Technological development; modern irrigation, communications, and transportation systems enable people to live in previously forbidding regions.

OBJECTIVE ② INSTRUCT

Massive Migrations

► **Key Ideas**

- Bantu speakers belong to many different ethnic groups but share some cultural characteristics.
- Bantu-speaking farmers and herders from southeastern Nigeria migrate southward and settle throughout most of Africa south of Sahara.
- The intermingling of Bantu cultures with other cultures creates new cultures.

 ELECTRONIC LIBRARY OF PRIMARY SOURCES
from "Hunters of Modern Africa"

Massive Migrations

Language is one major element that unites or divides people. One group of African languages, the Niger-Congo, includes over 900 individual languages. A family of languages in this group developed from a single parent tongue, Proto-Bantu. The speakers of these related languages belong to many different ethnic groups, but often are referred to collectively as **Bantu-speaking peoples.** (The word *Bantu* itself means "the people.") These early Africans made one of the greatest migrations in history and populated the southern third of the continent. The Bantu-speaking people lived in the savanna south of the Sahara in the area that is now southeastern Nigeria. Starting in the first few centuries A.D. and continuing until recent times, a small number of Bantu speakers moved southward throughout Africa, spreading their language and culture.

This carved wood mask mingles human and animal features. It probably was used by Bantu speakers in a ceremony to communicate with natural or ancestral spirits.

Bantu Culture Bantu speakers were not one people, but a group of peoples who shared certain cultural characteristics. They were farmers and nomadic herders who developed and passed along the skill of ironworking. Many experts believe they were related to the Nok peoples.

Beginning at least 2,000 years ago or earlier, small groups of Bantu speakers began spreading south and east. They shared their skills with the people they met, adapted their methods to suit each new environment, and learned new ways. They followed the Congo River through the rain forests. There they farmed the riverbanks—the only place that received enough sunlight to support agriculture.

As they moved eastward into the savannas, they adapted their techniques for herding goats and sheep to raising cattle. Passing through what is now Kenya and Tanzania, they learned to cultivate new crops. One such crop was the banana, which came from Southeast Asia via Indonesian travelers. In this way, they were able to expand and vary their food supply. Within 1,500 years or so—a short time in the span of history—the Bantu speakers reached the southern tip of Africa.

Some of their farming methods quickly exhausted the land, however. The search for new, fertile soil kept the migrating people on the move. A 19th-century Scottish missionary and explorer, David Livingstone, described the farming methods of one group of Bantu speakers, which had probably changed little over time:

> **A VOICE FROM THE PAST**
> Food abounds, and very little labor is required for its cultivation. . . . When a garden becomes too poor for good crops . . . the owner removes a little farther into the forest, applies fire around the roots of the larger trees to kill them, cuts down the smaller, and a new, rich garden is ready for the seed.
>
> **DAVID LIVINGSTONE,** quoted in *History of World Societies*

Effects of the Migration Although it isn't possible to know exactly what caused the Bantu-speaking peoples to migrate, anthropologists have proposed a logical explanation. These experts suggest that once these peoples developed agriculture, they were able to produce more food than they could by hunting and gathering. As a result, the population in West Africa increased. Because this enlarged population required more food, the earliest Bantu speakers planted more land, and soon there wasn't enough land to go around. They couldn't go north in search of land, because the area was densely populated and the Sahara was slowly advancing toward them. The areas that

THINK THROUGH HISTORY
A. Clarifying How did the Bantu deal with the problems they encountered in their migrations?
A. Answer They adapted their old ways to new environments and learned new ways from the people they encountered.

Task: Students will complete a worksheet and answer other questions to explore possible links between rainfall patterns and the routes of Bantu migrations. They will then discuss other migrations.

Materials Needed: Use copies of the Geography Application worksheet for Chapter 8 and the textbook.

Activity: Have students study the worksheet and answer the questions. Then ask these questions:

204 Chapter 8

1. Compare the rainfall maps for 7000 B.C. to the present with the map on textbook page 194. Then look at the map on textbook page 205. Describe, in terms of vegetation and rainfall, the regions people did not migrate through or to. *Central equatorial region—rain forest where it rains heavily throughout the year; far southern interior, west and south coastal areas, parts of east coast—desert or savanna where little rain falls.*

2. Why might migrants have avoided these regions? *Probably avoided central rain forest because it lacked grazing areas and received too much rain and too little sunlight to grow most crop plants.*

Conclusion: Have students discuss what they know about other mass migrations.

 IN-DEPTH RESOURCES: UNIT 2
Geography Application: Desertification in Africa, p. 59

THINK THROUGH HISTORY
B. Analyzing Causes What circumstances might have caused the Bantu to migrate?
B. Answer
Development of agriculture, increased population, and resulting need for more fertile land.

once had been savanna were undergoing desertification. So the people moved southward.

Within only 1,500 years, the Bantu speakers had populated much of the southern half of Africa. The area was sparsely populated with peoples like the BaMbuti and the San. These Africans were not Bantu speakers and lived then, as they still do, by hunting and gathering.

Territorial wars often broke out as the Bantu speakers spread south into these peoples' lands. Fighting with iron-tipped spears, the newcomers easily drove off the BaMbuti and the San, who were armed only with stone weapons. Today, the BaMbuti are confined to a corner of the Congo Basin. The San live only around the Kalahari Desert in northwestern South Africa, Namibia, and Botswana.

The Bantu speakers also exchanged ideas and intermarried with the people they joined, however. This intermingling created new cultures with unique customs and traditions. Although the Bantu migrations produced a great diversity of cultures, they also left a unifying influence on the continent. As a result of these migrations, in Africa today there are at least 60 million people who speak one of the hundreds of Bantu languages.

Migration continues to shape the modern world as new factors make living conditions difficult. For example, political refugees leave or are forced out of countries for places that offer them safe haven. A worldwide process of urbanization also sets people in motion. It draws them from rural areas where there is little opportunity for advancement to cities such as Mexico City. In the next chapter, you will see how early Americans underwent a process of growth similar to that of early Africans.

Bantu Migrations, 500 B.C.–A.D. 1500

AFRICA

Lake Victoria
Lake Tanganyika
Lake Nyasa
Zambezi
NAMIB DESERT
KALAHARI DESERT
Limpopo R.
ATLANTIC OCEAN
Orange R.
INDIAN OCEAN
Tropic of Capricorn

Bantu migration routes

0   500 Miles
0   1,000 Kilometers

GEOGRAPHY SKILLBUILDER: Interpreting Maps
1. **Human-Environment Interaction** What geographic features did the Bantu speakers encounter in the course of their migrations?
2. **Movement** Compare this map with the one on page 194. Why didn't the Bantu speakers migrate northward?

Section 3 Assessment

1. TERMS & NAMES
Identify
• Bantu-speaking peoples

2. TAKING NOTES
In a chart like the one below, list three reasons why people migrate. Give an example of a migration that occurred for each reason.

Reason for migration	Example
1.	
2.	
3.	

3. COMPARING AND CONTRASTING
How might the migrating Bantu speakers and the peoples they encountered have reacted to each other?
THINK ABOUT
• Bantu culture
• territorial wars
• cultural adaptation

4. THEME ACTIVITY
Cultural Interaction With a classmate, act out an encounter between a native of southern Africa and a Bantu speaker who has just migrated into the area.

PATTERNS OF CHANGE 205

1. TERMS & NAMES
Bantu-speaking peoples, p. 204

2. TAKING NOTES
Possible Responses:
Environmental change—prehistoric people; population pressure—prehistoric people; economic pressure—European settlers; empire building—Ottomans; religious freedom—European settlers.

3. COMPARING AND CONTRASTING
Possible Responses: They might have been curious about each other, willing to share ideas; Bantu speakers might have been viewed as aggressors to defend against.

4. THEME ACTIVITY
Standards for Evaluation
Skits should
• show awareness of characteristics of the Bantu speakers and another African culture
• demonstrate knowledge of the results of cultural interaction
• depict a realistic encounter

History from Visuals

Bantu Migrations, 500 B.C.–A.D. 1500

Interpreting the Map Have students use the scale of miles to estimate the distance covered by the migration route from Lake Victoria to the Orange River. *About 2,000 miles.*

Extension Activity Ask students what they think the tapering of the arrows on the map signifies. *That fewer people reached the end of a route than began it; some of the people who set out on a migration settled or died along the way.*

SKILLBUILDER Answers
1. Lakes, rivers, mountains, plains, and deserts.
2. Because to the north lay the Sahara and the Sahel, which was undergoing desertification.

ASSESS & RETEACH

Section 3 Assessment
Have students respond to the items individually and then exchange papers to compare their responses.

Section Quiz
FORMAL ASSESSMENT Section Quiz, p. 91

Reteaching Activity
CLASS TIME: 5 MINUTES

Review item 2 in the section assessment by drawing the graphic organizer on the chalkboard.

CRITICAL THINKING TRANSPARENCIES
CT44 Chapter 8 Visual Summary

CLOSE ACTIVITY

CLASS TIME: 10 MINUTES

Recognizing Causes and Effects
On the chalkboard make a chart with column headings like those on page 203. Then have students help you fill it in with general causes of the Bantu migrations and specific examples and effects of each cause.

Chapter 8 Assessment

TERMS & NAMES

1. Sahara, p. 193
2. desertification, p. 195
3. extended family, p. 197
4. animism, p. 197
5. griot, p. 197
6. Djenné-Djeno, p. 197
7. Nok, p. 198
8. Aksum, p. 199
9. Ezana, p. 200
10. Bantu-speaking peoples, p. 204

REVIEW QUESTIONS

Answers will vary.

11. Welcoming—Mediterranean and savanna; not welcoming—rain forest, desert.

12. Increased rainfall turned the Sahara into a savanna suitable for farming.

13. Djenné-Djeno was linked to other towns by the Niger River and overland camel routes, providing easy access for traders.

14. Aksum was located along key trade routes between Asia, Africa, and Europe.

15. Ezana united his people under Christianity and expanded his kingdom through conquest and trade.

16. Aksum was isolated religiously and geographically by the invasion of Muslim peoples.

17. Languages grow and change and show evidence of contact between peoples and cultures.

18. The development of agriculture led to an increase in population and a need for more food. The land could not supply that food, partly because of desertification as the Sahara expanded southward. So Bantu speakers moved south, away from the Sahara and desertification.

19. Because the Bantu speakers were able to adapt well to different environments, had skills such as agriculture and ironworking they could teach to the peoples they settled among, and persisted in exploring as far south as they could go in Africa.

20. Environmental changes, technological developments, and economic and social pressures.

TERMS & NAMES

Briefly explain the importance of each of the following to African civilizations in the period from 1500 B.C. to A.D. 500.

1. Sahara
2. desertification
3. extended family
4. animism
5. griot
6. Djenné-Djeno
7. Nok
8. Aksum
9. Ezana
10. Bantu-speaking peoples

Interact with History

On page 192, you considered the effects newcomers would have on a community. Now that you've read the chapter and learned about people's interactions with their environments and with other cultures, how would you modify your answer? Discuss your ideas with a small group.

REVIEW QUESTIONS

SECTION 1 (pages 193–198)

Diverse Societies in Africa

11. Which two vegetation zones of Africa are welcoming to human habitation? Which two are not?

12. How did agriculture develop in Africa?

13. What circumstances enabled Djenné-Djeno to become a bustling trade center?

SECTION 2 (pages 199–202)

The Kingdom of Aksum and East African Trade

14. Why was Aksum able to control international trade?

15. In what ways did Ezana contribute to the rise of his kingdom?

16. Why did Aksum fall?

SECTION 3 (pages 203–205)

Patterns of Change: Migration

17. Why is language important in the study of migrations?

18. What caused the Bantu-speaking peoples to migrate?

19. Why were the migrations of Bantu speakers so extensive and successful?

20. Name three conditions that cause people to migrate.

Visual Summary

African Civilizations

Power and Authority

- Some cultures were governed by family clan leaders or village chiefs.
- Migratory peoples, such as the Bantu speakers, exerted their power by spreading their beliefs and influence to other cultures.
- Aksum became so large and strong that it centralized its power and became a great kingdom.

Interaction with Environment

- The Bantu-speaking peoples left environments that could not support them and migrated to more welcoming lands.
- The location of Djenné-Djeno on a tributary of the Niger enabled it to become a bustling center of trade.
- The Aksumites developed techniques such as terrace farming to harness their environment.

Cultural Interaction

- The Bantu-speaking peoples migrated throughout southern Africa, spreading their language and culture.
- Since Aksum was a major trading center, its people interacted constantly with cultures from throughout the ancient world.
- The Nok shared their ironworking and agricultural skills with other peoples they came in contact with, such as those of Djenné-Djeno.

Interact with History

Possible Responses: The arrival of newcomers who farmed would drastically change the way native hunter-gatherers lived. The newcomers could grow their own food, so they would settle in one place. As their settlements grew, the resources available to hunter-gatherers would shrink. Eventually the hunter-gatherers would have to adopt the newcomers' way of life, fight the newcomers to defend remaining hunting grounds, or try to survive on land too difficult to farm.

CRITICAL THINKING

1. GRIOTS—STILL GOING STRONG?

Reread the quote on page 197 by Djeli Mamadou Kouyate. Why does he consider his job as griot so important? Who or what takes the place of griots in the modern world?

2. MOVING ON AND MORE

Environmental change, technological development, economic pressure, and political and religious persecution give rise to migrations. These conditions also can affect each other, however. For example, technological developments such as industrialization can contribute to environmental change. Using a diagram like the one below, list examples of mutual effects of these conditions in the boxes.

3. REACTING TO MIGRATION

THEME CULTURAL INTERACTION People have different cultural characteristics and personal qualities. Which of these might determine how individuals react to and interact with migrating people who settle among them?

4. ANALYZING PRIMARY SOURCES

Pliny, a scholar and naturalist, lived in Rome during the first century A.D. The following paragraph expresses his thoughts about the peoples who lived in central Africa at that time. Read the quotation and answer the questions below it.

> **A VOICE FROM THE PAST**
> The Atlas tribe is primitive and subhuman. . . . When they observe the rising and setting sun they utter terrible curses against it, as the cause of disaster to themselves and their fields. Nor do they have dreams in their sleep like the rest of mankind. . . . The Blemmyae are reported as being without heads; their mouth and eyes are attached to their chest . . . . The Strapfeet are people with feet like thongs who naturally move by crawling.
> **PLINY THE ELDER,** *Natural History*

- What was Pliny's biased view of Africans?
- How might he have developed that view?
- What does his point of view suggest about how people should read history?

CHAPTER ACTIVITIES

1. LIVING HISTORY: Unit Portfolio Project

THEME POWER AND AUTHORITY Your unit portfolio project focuses on showing how people in history have exercised and been affected by power and authority (see page 107). For Chapter 8, you might use one of the following ideas to add to your portfolio.

- Write a speech in which Ezana expresses his belief in Christianity to Aksum's citizens.
- Present a dialogue in which two Aksumites discuss how the presence of foreigners and foreign products affects their daily lives.
- Design a game called "Power Play." Set the game in fourth-century Africa. Include situations that helped or hindered the rise of kingdoms, such as desertification, development of ironworking technology, and the spread of religions. Have players do whatever they have to do—migrate, trade, seize territories, or adjust and adapt—to gain power.

2. CONNECT TO TODAY: Cooperative Learning

THEME INTERACTION WITH ENVIRONMENT Modern Africans still face many of the same environmental issues that their ancestors dealt with. Drought, overuse of land, and desertification are problems that affect the present and will help determine the future.

Use the Internet or magazines to research the ways a current African ethnic group or country is struggling to survive in its environment. Then write a short report of your findings.

- Describe the group or country and its current problems and indicate how the people are trying to solve them.
- Draw comparisons with problems Africans faced in the past.

3. INTERPRETING A TIME LINE

Look back at the unit time line on pages 106–107. Which group or kingdom of peoples in Africa from 1500 B.C. to A.D. 500 do you think had the most lasting influence on the world? Explain your answer.

FOCUS ON GEOGRAPHY

Look at the size of Africa compared with that of several other major continents and countries.

- How does the size of the Sahara compare with that of the United States?
- How do you think the population of Africa compares with that of the countries shown?

Connect to History How does the map clarify the extent of the migrations of Bantu speakers?

Africa

United States

China

India

Europe

207

---

1. LIVING HISTORY

Standards for Evaluation
A speech should meet these criteria:

- Clearly reveals Ezana's beliefs as presented in the text.
- Gives examples of ways Christianity would benefit listeners personally and Aksum politically.

Standards for Evaluation
A dialogue should meet these criteria:

- Identifies each speaker by gender, occupation, and other details.
- Uses language that distinguishes one speaker from the other.
- Presents both good and bad effects the presence of foreigners has on the speakers' daily life.

Standards for Evaluation
A game should meet these criteria:

- Provides a structure for succeeding or losing at the end of play.
- Uses examples from the text as playing situations.
- Provides internal explanations of why one move is better than another.
- Contains stopping places that allow players to explain their choices for gaining power.

2. CONNECT TO TODAY

Standards for Evaluation
A report should meet these criteria:

- Shows understanding of environmental problems faced and ways people are dealing with them.
- Makes valid comparisons with environmental problems of the past.

3. INTERPRETING A TIME LINE

Possible Responses: The Bantu speakers, because they made one of the greatest migrations in history, spreading their languages and cultures throughout southern Africa; today about 60 million Africans speak a Bantu language. The Nok people, because they were the first West African people known to have developed iron-making technology, which vastly improved life for many Africans.

CRITICAL THINKING

1. GRIOTS—STILL GOING STRONG?

Possible Responses: Griots believe the future is rooted in the past; they pass on unwritten stories and secrets of history to keep their culture alive. Media such as magazines, television, and the World Wide Web transmit much of modern culture.

2. MOVING ON AND MORE

Possible Responses: Env. chg.→econ. press.—Irish potato famine; env. chg.→pol./rel. pers.—killing of bison and effect on Native Americans; tech. dev.→econ. press.—industrialization and exploitation of workers; econ. press.→pol./rel. pers.—African Americans' migration to cities; tech. dev.→ env. chg.—pollution due to industrialization.

3. REACTING TO MIGRATION

Possible Responses: How isolated and self-sufficient they have been, how protective of their land and open to new ways they are.

4. ANALYZING PRIMARY SOURCES

Possible Responses: Pliny thought Africans primitive or freakish. He probably received inaccurate information based on hearsay and took it at face value. Readers must remember that history is interpretive—written from a limited or biased perspective.

FOCUS ON GEOGRAPHY

Answer: The Sahara has about the same area as the United States. ***Answer:*** The population of Africa is much smaller.

Connect to History The map makes dramatically clear the vast distances the Bantu speakers covered.

PLANNING GUIDE

The Americas: A Separate World

	Key Ideas	COPY MASTERS	ASSESSMENT	
SECTION 1 Hunters and Farmers in the Americas *pp. 211–215*	*More than 10,000 years ago, humans migrate from Asia to the Americas across a land bridge. Originally hunters and gatherers, these groups develop farming methods and create settlements.*	**In-Depth Resources: Unit 2** • **Guided Reading,** p. 71 • **Geography Application:** The Mystery of Poverty Point, p. 75 • **Primary Source:** The Habitation of Monte Verde, p. 77 • **Science and Technology:** High Tech Dating Techniques, p. 87	P E **Section 1 Assessment,** p. 215 **Formal Assessment** • Section Quiz, p. 100 **Alternative Assessment Book** • Standards for Evaluating a Cooperative Activity	
SECTION 2 Early Mesoamerican Civilizations *pp. 216–220*	*The first civilization in the Americas, the Olmec, emerges in southeastern Mexico around 1200 B.C., followed by the Zapotec of the Oaxaca Valley. Both cultures influence later civilizations.*	**In-Depth Resources: Unit 2** • **Guided Reading,** p. 72 • **Primary Sources:** Zapotec urn, p. 78 • **Literature:** from *Mexico* by James A. Michener, p. 81 • **History Makers:** The Zapotec Culture, p. 84	P E **Section 2 Assessment,** p. 220 **Formal Assessment** • Section Quiz, p. 101 **Alternative Assessment Book** • Standards for Evaluating a Product or Performance	
SECTION 3 Early Civilizations of the Andes *pp. 221–223*	*Andean civilization arises in the river valleys along the Peruvian coast. Around 900 B.C. the Chavín culture emerges in the mountains, followed by the coastal Nazca and Moche civilizations.*	**In-Depth Resources: Unit 2** • **Guided Reading,** p. 73 • **Skillbuilder Practice:** Distinguishing Fact from Opinion, p. 74 • **Primary Source:** The Excavation of a Moche Tomb, p. 79 • **History Makers:** The Chavín Culture, p. 85 • **Connections Across Time and Cultures:** p. 86	P E **Section 3 Assessment,** p. 223 **Formal Assessment** • Section Quiz, p. 102 **Alternative Assessment Book** • Standards for Evaluating a Product or Performance	
CHAPTER RESOURCES	**Chapter Overview** *Human settlement of the Americas begins toward the end of the last Ice Age. The first civilizations emerge in Mexico and Peru. The Olmec, Zapotec, Chavín, Nazca, and Moche cultures strongly influence those that come after them.*	**Telescoping the Times** • Chapter Summary, pp. 33–35 **Planning for Block Schedules**	P E **Chapter Assessment,** pp. 224–225 **Chapter Activities,** p. 225 **Formal Assessment** • Chapter Test, forms A and B, pp. 103–108 **Test Generator** **Alternative Assessment Book**	

TECHNOLOGY

 Warm-Up Transparency 9

 Electronic Library of Primary Sources
- "Coming to America"
- from "The Olsen-Chubbuck Site: A Paleo-Indian Bison Kill"

 INTERNET RESOURCES
www.mlworldhistory.com

 Warm-Up Transparency 9

 Critical Thinking Transparencies
- CT9 Mother Cultures of Mesoamerican Civilization, 1200–200 B.C.

 World Art and Cultures Transparencies
- AT19 Zapotec jade mask

 Electronic Library of Primary Sources
- from "New Light on the Olmecs"

 INTERNET RESOURCES
www.mlworldhistory.com

 Warm-Up Transparency 9

 Geography Transparencies
- GT9 Chavín de Huánter, 900–200 B.C.

 Critical Thinking Transparencies
- CT45 Chapter 9 Visual Summary

 World Art and Cultures Transparencies
- AT20 Nazca Lines

 INTERNET RESOURCES
www.mlworldhistory.com

 Chapter Summaries on Audiocassette in English and Spanish

INTERNET RESOURCES
www.mlworldhistory.com

Block Scheduling (90 MINUTES)

Day 1
Section 1, pp. 211–215
Section 2, pp. 216–220

 COOPERATIVE ACTIVITY
Designing Storyboards,
p. 213 (Teacher's Edition)

Section Assessments,
pp. 215, 220

Day 2
Section 3, pp. 221–223
Section Assessment, p. 223
Chapter Assessment,
pp. 224–225

Yearly Pacing *Chapter 9 Total:* 2 days *Yearly Total:* 85 days

 Planning for Block Schedules

Customizing for Special Needs

Students Acquiring English

 Access for Students Acquiring English
- **Guided Reading** for Sections 1–3 (Spanish), pp. 93–95
- **Chapter Summary** (Spanish), pp. 90–92
- **Skillbuilder Practice** Distinguishing Fact from Opinion (Spanish), p. 96
- **Geography Application** The Mystery of Poverty Point (Spanish), p. 97

 Chapter Summaries on Audiocassette in English and Spanish

INTERNET RESOURCES
www.mlworldhistory.com
The Diverse Classroom.

Less Proficient Readers

 In-Depth Resources: Unit 2
- **Guided Reading** for Sections 1–3, pp. 71–73
- **Skillbuilder Practice** Distinguishing Fact from Opinion, p. 74
- **Geography Application** The Mystery of Poverty Point, p. 75

 Telescoping the Times
- Chapter Summary, pp. 33–35

 Chapter Summaries on Audiocassette

Gifted and Talented Students

In-Depth Resources: Unit 2

Primary Sources:
- The Habitation of Monte Verde, p. 77
- Zapotec urn, p. 78
- The Excavation of a Moche Tomb, p. 79

History Makers
- The Zapotec Culture, p. 84
- The Chavín Culture, p. 85

Connections to Literature READINGS FOR STUDENTS

 In-Depth Resources: Unit 2
Literature: from *Mexico* by James A. Michener, p. 81

Enrichment Reading
- **Eagle, Chokecherry Gall**
Beyond the Lodge of the Sun
Rockport, MA: Element, 1997
Adventure stories of the Iroquois and Chippewa.

- **Erdoes, Richard and Alfonso Ortiz**
American Indian Myths and Legends
New York: Pantheon, 1984
An anthropologist and a storyteller collaborate to present the vibrant folklore tradition of Native Americans.

 = Pupil's Edition   = Overhead Transparency   = Software   = Video

= Copy Master   = CD-ROM   = Audiocassette   = Internet

The Americas: A Separate World, 40,000 B.C.– A.D. 700

Accessing Prior Knowledge

• Ask students: Based on what you have learned from previous chapters, how might early peoples in the Americas have lived off the land before cities were established?

Making Predictions

Point out that these pages refer to three different cultures: Olmec, Moche, and Nazca. Ask students to predict what these cultures may have had in common.

Geography Connection

1. What are the major differences in geography between Central and South America? *Central America is much smaller, is mainly mountainous, and has two main peninsulas; South America has one major range of mountains, contains a large central basin, and has many major rivers.*

2. What common geographical features do the Olmec, Moche, and Nazca cultures share? *All are located near water, are either in or near mountains, and have major cities near or on the coast.*

CHAPTER 9

The Americas: A Separate World, 40,000 B.C.– A.D. 700

PREVIEWING THEMES

Power and Authority
In southern Mexico and later around modern-day Peru, the first civilizations in the Americas arose as people came together to create more powerful and structured societies.

Interaction with Environment
The Olmec in Mesoamerica took advantage of their fertile surroundings, while the groups in South America carved societies out of rough, mountainous terrain. The early American civilizations flourished only after controlling their environment.

Cultural Interaction
From their art to their technology, the early Mesoamerican and South American civilizations influenced the better-known empires that followed them.

◀▶ INTERNET CONNECTION

Visit us at **www.mlworldhistory.com** to learn more about early American cultures.

AMERICAN CIVILIZATIONS
1200 B.C.–A.D. 700

0   1000 Miles
0   2000 Kilometers
N

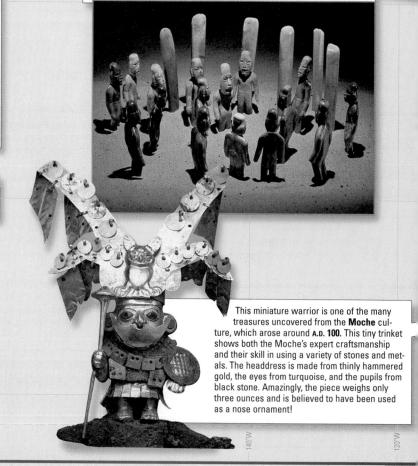

The Olmec, the Americas' oldest known civilization, emerged around **1200 B.C.** Among other things, they were master sculptors. Archaeologists found these seven-inch-high stone figures, arranged as shown here, buried beneath an Olmec ceremonial court.

Fiji

This miniature warrior is one of the many treasures uncovered from the **Moche** culture, which arose around **A.D. 100**. This tiny trinket shows both the Moche's expert craftsmanship and their skill in using a variety of stones and metals. The headdress is made from thinly hammered gold, the eyes from turquoise, and the pupils from black stone. Amazingly, the piece weighs only three ounces and is believed to have been used as a nose ornament!

208

GEOGRAPHY THEMES

Region

Point out to students that the land area on the map is referred to as the Americas. Have students note the continents that make up the Americas, and the oceans that surround them. Also have them use the map scale to get an idea of the distances that separate the various parts of the Americas. Ask students to think about what the land and peoples of the Americas might have in common that would distinguish them from the land and peoples in other parts of the world.

Movement

Tell students that in this chapter they will read about migrations of people and about some early cultures that influenced later cultures in the same areas. Ask students to think about how people and ideas might travel vast distances despite major geographic obstacles, such as mountains, deserts, and jungles.

 ELECTRONIC LIBRARY OF PRIMARY SOURCES
"Coming to America"

ADDITIONAL RESOURCES

Books for the Teacher

- Benson, Elizabeth P., and Beatriz de la Fuente. *Olmec Art of Ancient Mexico.* Washington, D.C.: National Gallery of Art, 1996.

- Bruhns, Karen Olsen. *Ancient South America.* New York: Cambridge UP, 1994.

Books for the Student

- Bunson, Stephen and Margaret. *Encyclopedia of Ancient Mesoamerica,* New York: Facts on File, 1996.

- McIntosh, Jane. *Archeology.* New York: Knopf, 1994. Techniques used by archaeologists and historians to unearth past civilizations.

Videos

- *Central America: The Burden of Time.* Social Studies School Service, 1991. 800-421-4246. The lessons we can learn from the Olmec civilization.

- *The First Nations.* Altschul Group, 1989. 800-323-9084. Ways of life in North America.

- *Loot: The Plundered Heritage.* Coronet/MTI, 1990. 800-221-1274. Artifacts of Latin America's great pre-Columbian civilizations.

Software

- *Exploring Ancient Cities.* CD-ROM. Teacher's Discovery, 1996. 800-543-4180. Roam the streets of ancient cities.

- *Introduction to Archaeology.* CD-ROM. Queue, 1995. 800-232-2224. Visit archaeological sites.

The Nazca culture, which emerged around **200 B.C.** in South America, is perhaps best known for its **Nazca Lines**—giant drawings of various creatures on top of the region's dry plains. This enhanced drawing of a waving human, which one scientist named Owl-man, is 105 feet long. One of the more outrageous explanations for the mysterious drawings is that they served as landing strips for extraterrestrial visitors!

209

HISTORY THROUGH ART

Nazca Lines

The Nazca Lines were first studied by historian Paul Kosok in the early 1940s. Since then German scientist Maria Reiche has devoted most of her life to analyzing and preserving the hundreds of animals, geometric designs, and radiating lines drawn by the ancient Nazca people on the arid, barren plains.

Because these huge designs can be seen only from the air, their purpose has puzzled scientists. They may be astronomical measurements or religious symbols. Some popular writers have claimed that they were landing sites for alien spacecraft or weaving patterns for giant textiles.

After nearly 60 years of intensive research, scholars still don't have many answers. Like the owl-man in the illustration, the Nazca Lines continue to tantalize and mystify those who view them.

Interpreting the Art Why do you think this illustration is called Owl-man? *because the face looks like an owl perched on a human body* Why were these patterns studied only in the past 60 years? *because they had to be seen from the air, and the development of the airplane made this possible*

Interact *with* History

Interact *with* History

This Interact with History feature motivates students by inviting them to put themselves in the position of a nomadic hunter. As students think about how they would trap the mastodon, they will analyze the issues, explore their options, and become decision makers.

Purpose
• to help students understand the importance of agriculture in the rise of civilization in the Americas
• to set the stage for studying the early cultures in Central and South America
• to enable students to connect with the people and events they will study in this chapter

Teaching Strategy
Thinking Critically After students have thought about the question asked on this page, have them answer the key questions and give reasons for their answers.

EXAMINING *the* ISSUES

Following are suggestions for addressing each bulleted question.

❶ Have students think about ways that primitive hunters might trap an animal much larger than themselves.

❷ Ask students what weapons a primitive hunting group might use to kill large animals.

Making Connections Discuss with students the risks and uncertainty of hunting a mastodon or other large game. If they were members of a pre-historic tribe, what other ways might they think of to obtain a steady supply of food?

Follow Up
A feature on the chapter assessment will ask students to reevaluate their responses to the situation presented on this page.

You live in ancient North America, where most people must hunt for their food. Along with several members of your group, you have been hunting the mastodon for days. The giant beast is a challenging but rewarding prey. While the animal stands more than 14 feet high and weighs more than a ton, it will provide much meat, as well as hides for clothing and shelter.

Suddenly in the clearing you spot the massive creature. Aside from spears, your only weapons are some crude tools and your superior intelligence.

How would you kill a mastodon?

As the group determines its strategy, its members seek protection behind boulders and loose rocks.

Your group carries several shovels for digging holes.

Should a hunter get too close, the mastodon might crush him under his large feet, or stab him with his sharp tusks.

EXAMINING *the* ISSUES

❶ • How might the group use the shovels to trap the mastodon?

❷ • Aside from spears and tools, what else could be used as a weapon against the animal?

As a class, discuss these questions. In your discussion, consider how this situation speaks to the difficulties of life in a hunter-gatherer society.

As you read about the growth of civilizations in the Americas, notice how the old hunting and gathering way of life dramatically changed with the development of agriculture.

210

1 Hunters and Farmers in the Americas

TERMS & NAMES
• Beringia
• Ice Age
• maize

MAIN IDEA

Although isolated, the first Americans developed in ways similar to the other earliest humans.

WHY IT MATTERS NOW

The Americas' first inhabitants developed the basis for American civilizations to come.

SETTING THE STAGE While civilizations were developing in Africa, Asia, and Europe, they were also emerging in the Americas. Human settlement in the Americas is relatively recent compared to that in other parts of the world. However, it followed a similar pattern. At first the ancient people of the Americas survived mainly by hunting. Over time, they developed farming methods that ensured a more reliable supply of food. This in turn led to the growth of the first civilizations in the Americas.

The Earliest Americans

The American continents include North and South America. They are connected and span two hemispheres, from the frigid Arctic Circle in the north to the icy waters around Antarctica in the south. Although this land mass narrows greatly around modern-day Panama, it stretches unbroken for more than 10,000 miles. This large and rugged land is isolated from the rest of the world by vast oceans. Yet, at one time, thousands of years ago, the Americas were connected by a land bridge to Asia. Most experts believe that the first people came to the Americas from Asia over this land bridge. The land bridge is known as **Beringia.**

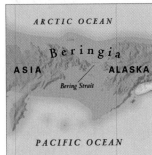

ARCTIC OCEAN

Beringia

ASIA   ALASKA

Bering Strait

PACIFIC OCEAN

Peopling the Americas The first Americans arrived sometime toward the end of the last **Ice Age,** which lasted from roughly 1.6 million to 10,000 B.C. During this period huge sheets of moving ice, called glaciers, spread southward from the Arctic Circle. They covered large portions of North America. The buildup of glaciers locked up huge amounts of the earth's water. It lowered sea levels and created a land corridor between Asia and Alaska across what is now the Bering Strait.

Herds of wild animals from Siberia, including the mastodon, migrated across the flat, treeless plains of the Beringia land bridge. Gradually, Siberian hunters followed these animals into North America. They most likely were unaware that they were entering a new continent. These migrants became the first Americans.

Thomas Canby, a writer for *National Geographic* magazine, spent a year with archaeologists as they searched for ancient burial sites throughout the Americas. From his experience, Canby envisioned the type of world that might have greeted the first Americans:

A VOICE ABOUT THE PAST
What a wild world it was! To see it properly, we must board a time machine and travel back into the Ice Age. The northern half of North America has vanished, buried beneath ice sheets two miles thick. Stretching south to Kentucky, they buckle the earth's crust with their weight. . . . Animals grow oversize. . . . Elephant-eating jaguars stand tall as lions, beavers grow as big as bears, South American sloths as tall as giraffes. With arctic cold pushing so far southward, walrus bask on Virginia beaches, and musk-oxen graze from Maryland to California.

THOMAS CANBY, "The Search for the First Americans"

The Americas: A Separate World **211**

Teacher's Edition **211**

No one knows for sure when the first Americans arrived. Some scholars contend that the migration across the land bridge began as early as 40,000 B.C. Others argue it occurred as late as 12,000 B.C. For years, many researchers have regarded the discovery of spearheads dating back to 9500 B.C. near Clovis, New Mexico, to be the earliest evidence of humankind in the Americas.

However, recent discoveries of possible pre-Clovis sites have challenged this theory. One such discovery was made at Monte Verde, Chile, near the southern tip of the Americas. Researchers there have found evidence of human life dating back to 10,500 B.C. Underneath this site—a sandy bank near a creek—archaeologists discovered pieces of animal hide and various tools. They also found a preserved chunk of mastodon meat and a child's single footprint. The evidence at Monte Verde suggests

Migration Routes, 40,000–10,000 B.C.

Spearheads similar to these were first discovered near Clovis, New Mexico, and later throughout North America. Many of these artifacts date back to around 9500 B.C.

Recent findings at Monte Verde, Chile, have provided evidence of human life in the Americas as early as 10,500 B.C.

Clovis, New Mexico 9,500 B.C.

Monte Verde, Chile 10,500 B.C.

□ Glacier ice, 12,000 B.C.
▨ Beringia
◀— Possible land migration routes
◀⇢ Possible water migration route
□ Fossil site

0 — 2,000 Miles
0 — 4,000 Kilometers

GEOGRAPHY SKILLBUILDER: Interpreting Maps
1. **Location** What two continents does the Beringia land bridge connect?
2. **Movement** From where do scholars believe the first Americans came? How did they come?

212 Chapter 9

---

that the first Americans arrived well before the Clovis era. To reach southern Chile at such an early date, experts believe, humans would have had to cross the land bridge at least 20,000 years ago.

They also could have come by boat. Most experts believe the earliest Americans traveled by foot across the land bridge. However, some scholars think they also may have paddled from Asia to the Pacific Coast in small boats.

Hunters and Gatherers Questions remain about how and when the first Americans arrived. What appears more certain—from the discovery of chiseled spearheads and charred bones at ancient sites—is that the earliest Americans lived as hunters. Perhaps their most challenging and rewarding prey was the mastodon. Weighing more than a ton, this animal provided meat, hide, and bones for making food, clothing, shelters, and tools.

Eventually, large animals like the mastodon became extinct. Hunters soon turned to smaller prey, such as deer and rabbits, for their survival. They also fished and gathered edible plants and fruits. Because they were hunters, the earliest Americans found it necessary to move regularly in search of food. Whenever they did settle in one place for a short time, prehistoric Americans lived in caves or temporary shelters in the open air.

With the end of the Ice Age, around 12,000 to 10,000 years ago, came the end of land travel across Beringia. As the great glaciers melted, sea levels rose. The ancient land bridge disappeared under the Bering Strait. By this time, however, humans inhabited most regions of the Americas. Wherever they roamed, from the grassy plains of the modern-day United States to the steamy tropical forests of Central America, the first Americans adapted to the variety of environments they inhabited. In doing so, they carved out unique ways of life.

Agriculture Prompts a New Way of Life

Gradually, the earliest Americans became more familiar with plant foods. They began to experiment with simple methods of farming. Their efforts at planting and harvesting eventually led to the birth of agriculture. This in turn dramatically changed their way of life.

The Development of Farming Around 7000 B.C., a revolution quietly began in what is now central Mexico. There, people began to rely more on wild edible plants, raising some of them from seeds. By 5000 B.C. many had begun to grow these preferred plants. They included squashes, gourds, beans, avocados, and chilies. By 3400 B.C., these early farmers grew **maize,** or corn. Maize soon became the most important crop. This highly nourishing crop flourished in the tropical climate of Mexico. There, a family of three could raise enough corn in four months to feed themselves for up to two years.

Gradually, people settled in permanent villages in the Tehuacan (TAY·wuh·KAHN) Valley, south of present-day Mexico City. There, they raised corn and other crops. Eventually the techniques of agriculture spread over most of North and South America. However, it is believed that people in some areas, such as Peru and eastern North America, may have discovered the secrets of cultivating local edible plants independently.

The Americas: A Separate World **213**

Researchers found the bones of these bison in a sand dune near Casper, Wyoming. These animals are believed to have been killed around 8000 B.C.

Both archaeologists and paleon-tologists are concerned with dig-ging up the remains of early life buried for thousands, even mil-lions, of years. Archaeologists look for human remains, particu-larly artifacts such as tools, household goods, and art objects. The study of animals and their bones is the work of paleontolo-gists. Both types of scientists use great care and planning in their work.

 IN-DEPTH RESOURCES: UNIT 2
Science and Technology: High Tech Dating Techniques, p. 87

MORE ABOUT . . .
La Brea

The La Brea tar pits are an ancient "pitch spring," a site where crude oil once flowed out of the ground. During prehistoric times, animals who became stuck in the tar would die and become fossilized. The site was discovered by Spanish explorer Gaspar de Portolá in 1769.

Archaeologist and paleontologists have found La Brea to be one of the world's richest sources of Ice Age fossils. Since excavation efforts first began in the early 1900s, scientists have recovered nearly a million skeletons of saber-toothed tigers, giant wolves, llamas, camels, horses, giant ground sloths, and other ancient animals that once roamed North and Central America. These find-ings showed scientists that ani-mals such as the horse and camel had evolved in both the Old and New Worlds.

Interested students might enjoy reading more about this topic. Suggested resources: National Geographic Index and *Trapped in Tar* by Caroline Arnold, New York: Clarion, 1987.

Digging Up the Past

It is mainly through the work of archaeologists and paleontologists that we know as much as we do about ancient America, as well as the other ancient lands of the world. Archaeology is the study of prehistoric human cultures. Paleontology is the study of ancient animals and plants. Both are sciences, requiring specialized skills and techniques. The men and women in both fields must show patience, precision, and a careful touch. Their job is to extract from the earth the fragile fossils and artifacts of the past.

Below is a dig at the La Brea tar pits, in what is now downtown Los Angeles. There, paleontologists found the remains of numerous prehistoric animals. They included saber-toothed tigers, mammoths, bison, and birds.

Using such tools as picks and brushes, workers clear away soil without damaging the animal remains.

Unearthed remains must be covered for protection from the sun and rain.

A digger uses a jackhammer-type instrument to loosen the extremely hard dried tar.

Diggers use a sieve to shake free tiny fossils that may be lodged in soil.

Tools of the Trade
The most commonly used tool on the site is a bricklayer's trowel (far left). Workers use the durable instrument for a variety of tasks, including digging and scraping. To recover fragile remains, diggers must use delicate, tiny tools, such as dental picks (left).

214

Where To Dig?
How do researchers know where to dig in the first place? One way is by using an instrument called a soil-resistivity meter. This device transmits electric currents into the soil and registers any abnormalities in the currents—usually caused by buried objects.

Connect *to* History
Analyzing Issues What things are paleontologists concerned with during a dig?
SEE SKILLBUILDER HANDBOOK, PAGE 1001

Connect *to* Today
Examining a Dig Read an account of a dig at a prehistoric site. Then write a brief report explaining what researchers found as well as some of the spe-cific methods they used.

Connect *to* History

Analyzing Issues
Possible Responses:
Extracting plant and animal fossils without harming them, protecting the fossils from weather and accidental damage, keeping the objects intact, making sure they don't overlook smaller fossils, and interpreting what the fossils have to tell us about plants and animals—and their role in human life—in the past.

Connect *to* Today

Examining a Dig
Tell students to search for articles using the Internet, INFOTRAC, or library periodicals indexes. They can ask their reference librarian for help with key search words. For their class reports, students should describe the location of the archaeo-logical dig, what scientists have found there, and the methods scientists used to remove and catalog items.

white and black maize

The Effects of Agriculture

Before Agriculture

- People hunted or gathered what they ate.
- Families continually moved in search of big game.
- Groups remained small due to the scarcity of reliable sources of food.
- Humans devoted much of their time to obtaining food.

After Agriculture

- People enjoyed a more reliable and steady source of food.
- Families settled down and formed larger communities.
- Humans concentrated on new skills: arts and crafts, architecture, social organization.
- Complex societies eventually arose.

 beans

avocados

potatoes

peppers

SKILLBUILDER: Interpreting Charts

1. How did the early Americans' way of life change after the development of agriculture?
2. How might the establishment of agriculture have helped humans to develop new skills and interests?

Over the next several centuries, farming methods became increasingly advanced. In central Mexico, for example, native farmers created small islands in swamps and shallow lakes by stacking layers of vegetation, dirt, and mud. They then planted crops on top of the island soil. The surrounding water provided continuous irrigation. These floating gardens, known as chinampas, were very productive, yielding up to three harvests a year.

Farming Brings Great Change "[The] . . . transition from a foraging to a farming way of life," noted American scientist Bruce Smith, "was a major turning point in the long evolutionary history of our species." Indeed, in the Americas as in other regions of the world, agriculture brought great and lasting change to peoples' way of life.

The cultivation of corn and other crops provided a more reliable and expanding food supply. This encouraged population growth and the establishment of large, settled communities. As the population grew, and as farming became more efficient and productive, more people turned their attention to nonagricultural pursuits. They developed specialized skills in arts and crafts, building trades, and other fields. Differences between social classes—between rich and poor, ruler and subject—began to emerge. With the development of agriculture, society became more complex and sophisticated. The stage was set for the rise of more advanced civilizations.

B. Possible Answer
Its effects were significant: it led to a more reliable and increased food supply, which in turn led to population growth, settled communities, and eventually the establishment of civilizations.

THINK THROUGH HISTORY
B. Making Inferences
Why might the development of agriculture be characterized by some as a turning point in human history?

Section 1 Assessment

1. TERMS & NAMES

Identify
- Beringia
- Ice Age
- maize

2. TAKING NOTES

The events listed in the following chart had important effects on the development of the Americas. Identify the main effects for each.

Cause	Effects
Beringia land bridge forms.	
Large animals become extinct.	
Early Americans experiment with farming.	
Crops provide a reliable food supply.	

3. FORMING OPINIONS

Why do you think early Americans, isolated from the rest of the world, developed in ways similar to other early humans?

THINK ABOUT
- similarities among all human beings
- availability of similar resources
- the development from hunting to farming

4. ANALYZING THEMES

Power and Authority What type of person might hold power in a hunter-gatherer society? in a settled, agricultural society?

THINK ABOUT
- qualities needed to succeed in a hunting society
- qualities most admired in a settled, farming society

The Americas: A Separate World **215**

ANSWERS

1. TERMS & NAMES
Beringia, p. 211
Ice Age, p. 211
maize, p. 213

2. TAKING NOTES
Possible Response: Beringia land bridge forms— Animals and hunters cross into North America. Large animals become extinct—Hunters turn to smaller prey and plants. Early Americans experiment with farming—Agriculture arises. Crops provide a reliable food supply—Population grows, and settled communities arise.

3. FORMING OPINIONS
Possible Response: Early humans used easily-available food sources first. These included wild animals that could be hunted. When hunters could no longer rely on big game, they developed other more complex ways of getting food, such as farming.

4. ANALYZING THEMES
Possible Response: Authority in a hunting society might be based on physical strength and courage; authority in a settled society might be based on strong administrative skills.

TERMS & NAMES
• Mesoamerica
• Olmec
• Zapotec
• Monte Albán

Section 2 Overview

OBJECTIVES

 To describe the achievements of Olmec civilization.

 To trace the rise and fall of the Zapotec.

 To explain the impact of early Mesoamerican cultures.

SKILLBUILDER

• Interpreting maps: movement, p. 217

CRITICAL THINKING

• Making inferences, p. 216
• Clarifying, p. 217
• Hypothesizing, p. 218
• Comparing, p. 219
• Analyzing issues, p. 219
• Drawing conclusions, p. 220
• Forming Opinions, p. 220

FOCUS

5-Minute Warm-Up

▶ **Making Inferences**
Have students answer the following questions to help them understand the Olmec civilization.

1. Study the map on page 217. What two cities served as Olmec centers of civilization?

2. Trace the possible trade routes of the Olmec civilization. How might they explain the fact that seashells were found in many Olmec cities?

WARM-UP TRANSPARENCY 9

OBJECTIVE ① INSTRUCT

Mesoamerica's Mother Culture

▶ **Key Ideas**
• Mesoamerica encompasses the ancient cultures of Mexico and Central America.
• The Olmec develop the first true civilization in the Americas.

 IN-DEPTH RESOURCES: UNIT 2
Guided Reading, p. 72

ACCESS FOR STUDENTS ACQUIRING ENGLISH
Guided Reading (Spanish), p. 94

---

2 Early Mesoamerican Civilizations

MAIN IDEA	WHY IT MATTERS NOW
The Olmec created the Americas' first civilization, which in turn influenced later civilizations in the region.	Later American civilizations relied on the technology and achievements of earlier cultures to move forward.

SETTING THE STAGE The story of developed civilizations in the Americas begins in a region archaeologists and historians refer to as **Mesoamerica.** This area stretches south from central Mexico to the northern reaches of modern-day Honduras. It was here, more than 3,000 years ago, that the first complex societies in the Americas arose.

Mesoamerica's Mother Culture

Mesoamerica's first known civilization builders were a people known as the **Olmec.** They began carving out a thriving society around 1200 B.C. in the humid jungles of southern Mexico. The Olmec influenced neighboring groups, as well as the later civilizations of the region. Thus, they often are called Mesoamerica's "mother culture."

The Rise of Olmec Civilization Around 1860, a worker clearing a field in the hot coastal plain of southeastern Mexico uncovered an extraordinary stone sculpture. It stood five feet tall and weighed an estimated eight tons. The sculpture was of an enormous head, wearing a headpiece that resembled a football helmet. The head was carved in a strikingly realistic style, with thick lips, a flat nose, and large oval eyes. (See History Through Art on page 219.) Archaeologists had never seen anything like it in the Americas.

This head, along with others that were discovered later, was a remnant of the Olmec civilization. The Olmec flourished from 1200 B.C. to 400 B.C. They lived along the Gulf Coast of Mexico, in the modern-day Mexican states of Veracruz and Tabasco.

On the surface, the Gulf Coast seemed an unlikely site for a high culture to take root. The region was hot and humid and covered with swamps and jungle. In some places, giant trees formed a thick cover that prevented most sunlight from reaching the ground. Up to 100 inches of rain fell every year. The rainfall swelled rivers and caused severe flooding.

However, the region also had certain advantages. There were abundant deposits of salt and tar, as well as fine clay used in making pottery. There was also wood and rubber from the rain forest. The hills to the north provided hard stone from which the Olmec could make tools and monuments. The rivers that laced the region provided a ready means of transport. Perhaps most important, the flood plains of these rivers provided fertile land for farming.

The Olmec used their abundant resources to build thriving communities. The oldest site, San Lorenzo, dates back to around 1150 B.C. Here, and at other sites, archaeologists uncovered important clues that offered a glimpse into the Olmec world.

Olmec Society At San Lorenzo archaeologists discovered earthen mounds, courtyards, and pyramids. Set among these earthworks were large stone monuments. They included columns, altars, and more colossal, sculpted heads, which may have represented particular Olmec rulers. These giant monuments weigh as much as 44 tons. Researchers are left to wonder how the Olmec moved them to various centers of

This Olmec figure represents either a wrestler or ball player. The Olmec played a game in which two opponents battled to place a ball in a goal. The loser often was sacrificed.

THINK THROUGH HISTORY
A. Making Inferences In what ways did the Olmec's environment help in the creation of its civilization?
A. Possible Answer The region supplied abundant natural resources, and the surrounding flood plains provided fertile farmland.

SECTION 2 RESOURCES

PRINT RESOURCES

IN-DEPTH RESOURCES: UNIT 2
Guided Reading, p. 72
Primary Source: Zapotec urn, p. 78
Literature: from *Mexico*, p. 81
History Makers: The Zapotec Culture, p. 78

ACCESS FOR STUDENTS ACQUIRING ENGLISH
Guided Reading (Spanish), p. 94

FORMAL ASSESSMENT
Section Quiz, p. 101

TECHNOLOGY RESOURCES

WORLD ART AND CULTURES TRANSPARENCIES
AT19 Zapotec jade mask

CRITICAL THINKING TRANSPARENCIES
CT9 Mother Cultures of Mesoamerican Civilization, 1200–200 B.C.

CD-ROM
Electronic Library of Primary Sources

INTERNET www.mlworldhistory.com

worship. Some scholars suspect that Olmec workers moved these sculptures over land on rolling logs to the river banks. From there, they rafted the monuments along numerous waterways to various sites.

The organization needed for such an undertaking is one reason scholars think San Lorenzo was home to a small ruling class of priests and nobles. These rulers may have commanded a much larger group of peasant farmers living in the surrounding country.

To the east of San Lorenzo, another significant Olmec site, La Venta, rose around 900 B.C. Here, researchers discovered a 100-foot-high mound of earth and clay. This structure may have served as the tomb of a great Olmec ruler. Known as the Great Pyramid, the mound also may have been the center of the Olmec religion. Based on other artifacts found at sites like La Venta, experts believe the Olmec prayed to a variety of nature gods.

Jaguar Worship Most of all they probably worshiped the jaguar spirit. Numerous Olmec sculptures and carvings depict a half-human, half-jaguar creature. Some scholars believe that the jaguar represented a powerful rain god. Others contend that there were several jaguar gods, representing such vital things as the earth, fertility, and maize. As anthropologist Peter Furst points out, the jaguar was central to Olmec religion:

> **A VOICE ABOUT THE PAST**
> You can almost call the Olmec the people of the jaguar. In tropical America, jaguars were the shamans [medicine men] of the animal world, the alter ego [other identity] of the shaman. They are the most powerful predators. That's why in Olmec art you get these combinations of jaguars and humans.
> **PETER FURST,** quoted in "New Light on the Olmec"

Trade and Commerce Archaeologists once believed that sites such as La Venta were ceremonial centers where important rituals were performed but few people lived. In recent years, however, experts have begun to revise that view. According to Mexican archaeologist Rebecca González, "La Venta was not just an empty ceremonial spot visited by Olmec priests and nobles, but a prosperous community of fishers, farmers, traders, and specialists, such as the artisans and the sculptors."

Indeed, the Olmec appear to have been a prosperous people who directed a large trading network throughout Mesoamerica. Olmec goods traveled as far as Mexico City to the north and Honduras to the south. In addition, raw materials—including iron ore and various stones—reached San Lorenzo from faraway regions. This trade network helped boost the Olmec economy and spread Olmec influence to other parts of Mesoamerica.

Olmec Civilization, 900 B.C.

Olmec homeland
Oaxaca Valley
Possible trade routes
Centers of Olmec civilization
Other Olmec sites
Limit of Mesoamerica

EASTERN SIERRA MADRE
Tropic of Cancer
Gulf of Mexico
YUCATAN PENINSULA
Bay of Campeche
San Lorenzo La Venta
Oaxaca Valley
N
0   250 Miles
0   500 Kilometers
PACIFIC OCEAN

GEOGRAPHY SKILLBUILDER: Interpreting Maps
1. **Movement** Judging from the map, what was one way in which the Olmec spread their influence?
2. **Movement** What difficulties might the Olmec have encountered in developing their trade routes?

CONNECT to TODAY

Jaguar Worship
Some descendants of the Olmec and other Mesoamerican peoples still practice jaguar worship. In the spring, villagers in Acatlan, Mexico, put on jaguar masks and draw blood in mock combat. They do this in the hope that the jaguar will shed its own blood, in the form of rain, to water the fields. In another ritual, shown here, a boy becomes a jaguar dancer to bring rain.

THINK THROUGH HISTORY
C. Hypothesizing
What things might lead to the disappearance of an entire civilization?
C. Possible Answer
An overwhelming enemy attack, disease, crop failure, drought.

Decline of the Olmec For reasons that are not fully understood, Olmec civilization eventually collapsed. Scholars believe San Lorenzo was destroyed around 900 B.C. La Venta may have fallen sometime around 400 B.C. Some experts speculate that outside invaders caused the destruction. Others believe the Olmec may have destroyed their own monuments upon the death of their rulers.

Because the Olmec apparently left no written records, scholars may never know the full truth. Nevertheless, Olmec artifacts continue to offer up tantalizing clues about this first known Mesoamerican civilization.

Zapotec Civilization Arises

By the time Olmec civilization had collapsed, another people—the **Zapotec**—were developing an advanced society to the southwest, in what is now the Mexican state of Oaxaca (wuh·HAH·kah). Though they showed traces of Olmec influence, the Zapotec built a unique civilization. This ancient group dominated Oaxaca for more than a thousand years.

Peoples of the Oaxaca Valley Oaxaca is a rugged region of mountains and valleys in southern Mexico. In the center of the state, three valleys meet to form a large open area known as the Oaxaca Valley. (See map on page 217.) Though much of Oaxaca is hot and dry, this valley has fertile soil, a mild climate, and enough rainfall to support agriculture. As a result, various peoples have made the Oaxaca Valley their home, including the ancient Zapotec.

For centuries the Zapotec lived in scattered villages throughout the valley. By 1000 B.C., however, one site—San José Mogote—was emerging as the main power in the region. At this site, the Zapotec constructed stone platforms. They also built temples and began work on monumental sculptures. By 500 B.C. they also had developed early forms of hieroglyphic writing and a calendar system.

MORE ABOUT . . .
Olmec Sites

The Olmec built their houses and temples out of wood and thatch, which decompose over time. For that reason, Olmec sites today mainly consist of large, earthen mounds and stone monuments, though experts can make out the outlines of temples and other buildings.

OBJECTIVE **2** INSTRUCT

Zapotec Civilization Arises

▶ **Key Ideas**
- Zapotec civilization emerges in the Oaxaca Valley of Mexico.
- The Zapotec develop a writing system and calendar and build an impressive city, Monte Albán.

 IN-DEPTH RESOURCES: UNIT 2
Literature: from *Mexico* by James A. Michener, p. 81

History Makers: The Zapotec Culture, p. 84

CRITICAL THINKING ACTIVITY
CLASS TIME: 15 MINUTES

Recognizing Causes and Effects
Ask students to create a tree diagram to show the various factors that contributed to the rise of Zapotec culture, culminating in the creation of Monte Albán. Possible chart:

HISTORY THROUGH ART: Sculpture

A Legacy of Sculpture

More than 2,000 years after the Olmec's collapse, the ancient society's sculpture remains its most lasting legacy. From the colossal stone heads to the tiny jade figures, these carvings reveal the Olmec's expert craftsmanship and commitment to detail. They also provide a glimpse of the values and beliefs of the Americas' oldest known civilization.

Giant Altars
The Olmec carved a number of impressive altars. Like the one pictured to the right, they often depicted a priest or shaman emerging from the structure. In numerous altars, the priest cradles a child. Some scholars believe that this may have signified the importance of the notion of dynasty—with the child representing the heir to the throne—in Olmec society.

218 Chapter 9

TEACHING OPTION | **BLOCK SCHEDULING**

COMPARING CULTURES

Task: Students will reinforce their learning about the Olmec and Zapotec cultures by creating trading cards featuring these groups and some of their major artifacts.

Materials Needed: Packs of 3x5 cards, colored pens or pencils, student textbooks, and copies of *National Geographic* articles "Gifts for the Jaguar

God," Sept 1956, pp. 367–375, and "New Light on the Olmecs," Nov 1993, p. 88(27); and an article from *School Arts*, April 1994, p. 31(4), "Not Aztec, Not Mayan, Zapotec Sculpture from Oaxaca."

Activity: Divide the class into small groups, assigning each group a particular part of the chapter section or one of the articles. On their cards each group will sketch two or three items related to their

assigned reading and put relevant facts and statistics on the back of each card.

Conclusion: Have each group share with the class what their cards show about Olmec or Zapotec civilizations. Ask each group to trade their cards with another group; make sure all students see all the cards. Collect the cards to use later as part of a chapter review.

THINK THROUGH HISTORY
D. Comparing
How does Monte Albán's population compare to the populations of today's major cities?

D. Possible Answer
It was much smaller; many of today's large cities have several million residents.

The Zapotec Flourish at Monte Albán Around 500 B.C., Zapotec civilization took a major leap forward. High atop a mountain at the center of the Oaxaca Valley, the Zapotec built the first real urban center in the Americas: **Monte Albán.** This city, with its commanding view of the entire valley, grew and prospered over the next several centuries. By 200 B.C., Monte Albán was home to around 15,000 people. The city eventually would reach a peak population of 25,000.

From A.D. 250 to A.D. 700, Monte Albán was truly impressive. At the heart of the city was a giant plaza paved with stones. Towering pyramids, temples, and palaces, all made out of stone, surrounded this plaza. There was even a building that may have acted as an observatory for gazing at the stars. Nearby was a series of stone carvings of corpses. Their thick lips and flat noses show a clear influence of Olmec style.

For more than a thousand years the Zapotec controlled the Oaxaca Valley and the surrounding region. Sometime after A.D. 600, however, the Zapotec began to decline. Some scholars believe they may have suffered a loss of trade or other economic difficulties. As with the Olmec, the fall of Zapotec civilization remains a puzzle.

The Early Mesoamericans' Legacy

Although both the Zapotec and Olmec civilizations eventually collapsed, each culture left its mark on the Mesoamerican civilizations that followed.

Vocabulary
motif: a repeated theme in a literary or artistic work.

The Olmec Leave Their Mark The Olmec contributed much to later Mesoamerican civilizations. They influenced the powerful Maya, who will be discussed in Chapter 16. Olmec art styles, especially the use of the jaguar motif, can be seen in the pottery and sculpture of later peoples in the region. In addition, future Mesoamerican societies copied the Olmec pattern of urban design. Like the Olmec, later civilizations built cities by combining pyramids, plazas, and monumental sculpture.

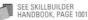

Jade Figures

With little technology at their disposal, the Olmec mastered the difficult art of carving jade. Jade is a hard and tough but highly colorful stone. "The tough material was mastered as though it were a plastic," one scholar said of the Olmec's work. As shown here, the Olmec often carved jaguar figures out of jade. The jaguar-god was a powerful deity in Olmec society.

Colossal Heads

Perhaps the most recognizable Olmec sculptures are the giant stone heads. Researchers have uncovered more than a dozen Olmec heads. The largest one stands 11 feet tall. Some scholars say that the heads represent idolized warriors or ball players. However, most experts believe they depict individual rulers.

Connect to History

Analyzing Issues What characteristics of Olmec society does each of these sculptures convey?

SEE SKILLBUILDER HANDBOOK, PAGE 1001

Connect to Today

Comparing Consider the better-known sculptures and monuments in your country. What do they say about your civilization?

The Americas: A Separate World **219**

MORE ABOUT . . .
Monte Albán

Monte Albán was later occupied by the Mixtec, another important culture of the Oaxaca region, who added to the city. Today Monte Albán draws many visitors, who marvel at the size and magnificence of its structures. Ask interested students to research the layout of the city and sketch the main city design, including main buildings. They can label each building and describe its function.

 IN-DEPTH RESOURCES: UNIT 2
Primary Source: Zapotec urn, p. 78

 WORLD ART AND CULTURES TRANSPARENCIES
AT9 Zapotec jade mask

OBJECTIVE 3 INSTRUCT

The Early Mesoamericans' Legacy

▶ **Key Ideas**
- The Olmec exert considerable influence on Mesoamerican cultures through their art, urban design, rituals, and social organization.
- The Zapotec legacy is their writing and calendar systems and their creation of Monte Albán.

CRITICAL THINKING ACTIVITY
CLASS TIME: 10 MINUTES

Summarizing
To help students summarize the Olmec and Zapotec legacies, have them fill out a chart like the one below.

Culture	Legacy
Olmec	art styles, urban design, ball games, elite rule
Zapotec	writing, calendar, city of Monte Albán

 CRITICAL THINKING TRANSPARENCIES
CT9 Mother Cultures of Mesoamerican Civilization, 1200–200 B.C.

Connect to History

Analyzing Issues
Possible Responses: The altar—Religious rituals and succession were important to the Olmec. The colossal head—The Olmec had great respect for their rulers. The jade jaguar—The Olmec showed particular reverence for the jaguar deity.

Connect to Today

Comparing
Possible Responses: The Statue of Liberty—The statue says that we are a people devoted to the ideas of freedom and liberty. Mount Rushmore —We honor important leaders.

Vietnam War Memorial and various monuments to the soldiers killed in the Civil War, World War I, World War II, and the Korean War—We have respect and reverence for those who died in the service of their country.

Daily *Life*

Working Hard for Water

Ask students to suppose that in a city of 25,000 people, each person needs 3 gallons of water per day. If water jars held 5 gallons each, how many jars of water would the city require every day?

25,000 x 3 = 75,000 ÷ 5 = 15,000

If two people were needed to carry four jars, how many workers would be needed each day?

15,000 ÷ 4 = 3750 x 2 = 7500

Point out that such a water-carrying system implies a strong central government able to organize its citizens.

ASSESS & RETEACH

Section 2 Assessment

Have pairs of students help each other answer the questions. Encourage them to act out their answer to question 4 in class, taking on the role of traders.

Section Quiz

FORMAL ASSESSMENT
Section Quiz, p. 101

Reteaching Activity

CLASS TIME: 20 MINUTES

Have students stand up around the edge of the room. Each student gives one fact about either the Olmec or Zapotec culture. Those who cannot give a fact without repeating one already given must sit down.

CLOSE ACTIVITY

CLASS TIME: 30 MINUTES

Recognizing Sequences

Ask students to construct a flow chart tracing the main events in the rise and fall of Olmec and Zapotec civilizations.

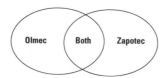

Daily *Life*

Working Hard For Water

Monte Albán's position upon a mountain top (depicted in this photograph of its ruins) added to its magnificence. But it also presented a daily problem for the city's residents: limited access to water.

Perched so high above the valley, Monte Albán had no natural waterways leading into the city. Scholars believe that city leaders may have organized citizens to carry drinking water up the mountain—as far as 1,500 feet—in jars.

The Olmec also left behind the notions of planned ceremonial centers, ritual ball games, and an elite ruling class. And while there is no clear evidence that the Olmec used a written language, their descendants or a related people carved out stone symbols that may have influenced later glyph writing.

Zapotec Contributions The Zapotec left behind their own legacy. It included a hieroglyphic language and a calendar system based on the movement of the sun. In addition, the Zapotec are noted as the Americas' first city builders. Monte Albán combined ceremonial grandeur with residential living space. This style influenced the development of future urban centers and became a hallmark of Mesoamerican civilizations.

As the Zapotec and Olmec flourished and then declined, civilizations were also taking shape in South America. Along the rough and mountainous terrain in what is now Peru, ancient peoples came together. There, they created more advanced and complex societies.

E. Possible Answers Olmec's sculpture and planned ceremonial centers; Zapotec's hieroglyphic language and calendar system.

THINK THROUGH HISTORY
E. Forming Opinions What do you consider to be the Olmec's and Zapotec's most important contributions to later cultures? Why?

Section 2 Assessment

1. TERMS & NAMES

Identify
- Mesoamerica
- Olmec
- Zapotec
- Monte Albán

2. TAKING NOTES

Compare the Olmec and Zapotec cultures by using a Venn diagram similar to the one below.

Olmec — Both — Zapotec

Design another way to show this same information.

3. DRAWING CONCLUSIONS

Why do you think the Olmec are called Mesoamerica's "mother culture"? Consider the Olmec's influence on later groups in the region.

THINK ABOUT
- architecture
- religion
- art

4. THEME ACTIVITY

Cultural Interaction As a trader from a small Mesoamerican village, you have just returned from your first visit to the Olmec site at La Venta. Write a description of what you might tell your family about the wondrous things you saw in and around the site. Prepare to present the description orally to the class.

ANSWERS

1. TERMS & NAMES
Mesoamerica, p. 216
Olmec, p. 216
Zapotec, p. 218
Monte Albán, p. 219

2. TAKING NOTES
Possible Responses: Olmec—ritual ball games, magnificent sculptures, jaguar worship.
Both—pyramids, giant plazas.
Zapotec—major urban center, hieroglyphic language, calendar.

3. DRAWING CONCLUSIONS
Possible Response: The Olmec developed numerous institutions and styles that many later peoples of the region incorporated. These included Olmec sculpture and architecture styles, as well as the notion of ceremonial centers, ritual ball games, and an elite ruling class.

4. THEME ACTIVITY
Standards for Evaluation
Students' descriptions should
- describe the buildings and objects they saw
- convey their emotional reactions
- express their opinions about the people who created the s

3 Early Civilizations of the Andes

MAIN IDEA	WHY IT MATTERS NOW
Around the harsh terrain of the Andes Mountains in South America, various groups created flourishing civilizations.	Like the early Andean civilizations, people today must adapt to their environment in order to survive.

SETTING THE STAGE While civilizations were emerging in Mesoamerica, advanced societies were also arising in South America. The early cultures of South America arose in difficult environs, namely the rugged terrain of the Andes Mountains. However, like the peoples of Mesoamerica, the early Andean cultures controlled their surroundings and created flourishing civilizations.

Societies Grow in the Andes Region

The Andes Mountains stretch some 4,000 miles down the western edge of South America, from Colombia in the north to Chile in the south. After the Himalayas in southern Asia, the Andes is the highest mountain range in the world. The Andes has a number of peaks over 20,000 feet in elevation. It was in the northern Andes region, in what is now Peru, that South America's first advanced civilizations emerged.

Early Settlements Along the Coast Peru was a difficult place to launch a civilization. The Andes are steep and rocky, with generally poor soil. Ice and snow cover the highest elevations year-round. Overland travel often is difficult. The climate is also severe: hot and dry during the day, and often freezing at night.

Between the mountains and the Pacific Ocean lies a narrow coastal plain. Most of this plain is harsh desert where rain seldom falls. In some places, however, rivers cross the desert on their path from the mountains to the sea. It was in these river valleys that the first settlements occurred.

Between 3600 and 2500 B.C. people began to establish temporary villages along the Pacific coast. These first inhabitants were hunter-gatherers who relied on seafood and small game for their survival. Eventually, around 3000 B.C., these people began to farm. By 1800 B.C., a number of thriving communities existed along the coast.

The Chavín Period The first influential civilization in South America arose not on the coast, however, but in the mountains. This culture, known as the **Chavín** (sha·VEEN), flourished from around 900 B.C. to 200 B.C. Archaeologists named the culture after a major ruin, Chavín de Huántar, in the northern highlands of Peru. This site is situated more than 10,000 feet above sea level. It features pyramids, plazas, and massive earthen mounds.

Chavín culture spread quickly across much of northern and central Peru. Archaeologists have found no evidence of political or economic organization within the culture. Thus, they conclude that the Chavín were primarily a religious civilization. According to this theory, Chavín de Huántar and other similar sites were important religious centers rather than outposts of a powerful empire. Nevertheless, the spread of Chavín art styles and religious images—as seen in stone carving, pottery, and textiles—demonstrates the powerful influence of this culture. Ancient Peruvians may have visited Chavín temples to pay their respects. They then carried ideas back to their communities. The Chavín are believed to

The Chavín's artistic styles influenced peoples throughout the Andes region. Here, a Chavín ceramic vessel depicts images of snarling cats.

The Americas: A Separate World **221**

Other Andean Civilizations Flourish

▶ **Key Ideas**
• In southern Peru, the Nazca create art works and irrigation systems.
• In northern Peru, the Moche create a thriving culture.

MORE ABOUT . . .
Nazca Lines

Show students the art transparency of another Nazca design. Explain that the spider, nearly 150 feet long, is one of the more preserved patterns on the Nazca plain.

 WORLD ART AND CULTURES TRANSPARENCIES
AT20: Nazca Lines

History from Visuals

Early Civilizations, 1200 B.C.–A.D. 700

Interpreting the Map Have students identify the color codes in the map key used to represent cultures. Which cultures emerged in the same region? *Chavín, Moche, Nazca*

Extension Activity Ask students to research one of the cultures on the map and report their findings to the class.

SKILLBUILDER Answers
1. The Andes Mountains.
2. They enjoyed a more hospitable environment of lush vegetation and fertile land.

 IN-DEPTH RESOURCES: UNIT 2
History Makers: The Chavín Culture, p. 85
Connections Across Time and Cultures: Patterns of Human Settlement, p. 86

 GEOGRAPHY TRANSPARENCIES
GT9 Chavín de Huánter, 900–200 B.C.

SPOTLIGHT ON

Headhunters

The striking images on their pottery indicate that the Nazca may have been headhunters. In numerous ceramic and textile designs, Nazca artisans depict the taking of human heads, probably from enemies in combat. Many ancient cultures believed the head to have special power as the seat of the soul. Taking and displaying the head of an enemy was considered a way of increasing the strength and well-being of a community.

Throughout history, headhunting has been practiced around the world, from New Zealand to the Balkan region in southeastern Europe. Scattered reports of head-hunting continued well into the mid-20th century.

have established certain patterns that helped unify Andean culture and lay the foundation for later civilizations in Peru. Thus, like the Olmec, the Chavín may have acted as a "mother culture."

Other Andean Civilizations Flourish

Around the time Chavín culture declined, other civilizations were emerging in Peru. First the Nazca and then the Moche (MO-chay) built advanced societies that flourished for centuries in the Andes region.

Nazca Achievements The **Nazca** culture flourished along the southern coast of Peru from around 200 B.C. to A.D. 600. This area is extremely dry. The Nazca developed extensive irrigation systems, including underground canals, that allowed them to farm the land. The Nazca are known for their beautiful textiles and pottery. Both feature images of animals and mythological beings.

They are even more famous, however, for an extraordinary but puzzling set of creations known as the Nazca Lines. On a large, rock-strewn plain, the Nazca made huge drawings by scraping away stones to reveal the lighter soil underneath. The drawings depict various plants and animals, including a monkey, birds, and other creatures. These drawings are so huge, however, that they can be seen only from the air. Scientists believe that the Nazca made these drawings for their gods.

Moche Culture Meanwhile, on the northern coast of Peru, another civilization was reaching great heights. This was the **Moche** culture, which lasted from about A.D. 100 to A.D. 700. The Moche took advantage of the rivers that flowed from the Andes Mountains. They built impressive irrigation systems to water their wide range of

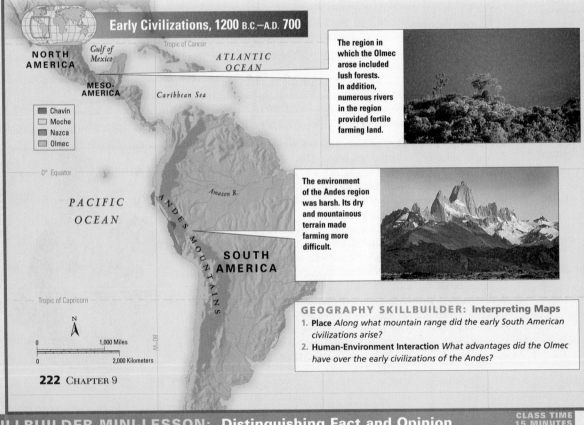

Early Civilizations, 1200 B.C.–A.D. 700

NORTH AMERICA
Gulf of Mexico
Tropic of Cancer
ATLANTIC OCEAN
MESO-AMERICA
Caribbean Sea

■ Chavín
□ Moche
■ Nazca
■ Olmec

0° Equator
Amazon R.
PACIFIC OCEAN
ANDES MOUNTAINS
SOUTH AMERICA

Tropic of Capricorn

N

0   1,000 Miles
0   2,000 Kilometers

222 CHAPTER 9

The region in which the Olmec arose included lush forests. In addition, numerous rivers in the region provided fertile farming land.

The environment of the Andes region was harsh. Its dry and mountainous terrain made farming more difficult.

GEOGRAPHY SKILLBUILDER: Interpreting Maps
1. **Place** Along what mountain range did the early South American civilizations arise?
2. **Human-Environment Interaction** What advantages did the Olmec have over the early civilizations of the Andes?

SKILLBUILDER MINI-LESSON: Distinguishing Fact and Opinion

CLASS TIME 15 MINUTES

Explaining the Skill: Facts are events, dates, and statistics or statements that can be checked for accuracy. Opinions are the judgments, beliefs, and feelings of the writer or speaker; these statements cannot be checked for accuracy.

Applying the Skill: Read the two paragraphs under "Nazca Achievements." To practice distinguishing fact from opinion, create a chart listing the facts in the section on one side and the opinions on the other.

Facts	Opinions
Nazca culture: 200 B.C. to A.D. 600 Nazca created extensive irrigation, textiles, pottery. They created huge drawings seen only from the air.	Nazca made drawings for their gods. The drawings have astronomical meanings.

 IN-DEPTH RESOURCES: UNIT 2
Skillbuilder Practice: Distinguishing Fact from Opinion, p. 74

Early Civilizations Around the World

The Americas

1200 B.C. Olmec civilization arises.

900 B.C. Chavín culture emerges.

500 B.C. Zapotec establish Monte Albán.

200 B.C. Nazca culture emerges.

A.D. 100 Moche culture arises.

1200 B.C. — 1000 B.C. — 500 B.C. — A.D. 1 — A.D. 120

Africa, Asia, and Europe

Around 1200 B.C. Egyptian Empire begins to decline.

480 B.C. Golden Age of Greece begins.

202 B.C. Han Dynasty begins in China.

Around A.D. 120 Roman Empire reaches its height.

crops, which included corn, beans, potatoes, squash, and peanuts. According to Peruvian archaeologist Walter Alva, the Moche enjoyed a variety of foods:

A VOICE ABOUT THE PAST

The Moche enjoyed a diet rich in protein and probably better balanced than that of many modern Peruvians. Fish from the nearby Pacific were eaten fresh or sun dried. They ate Muscovy ducks and guinea pigs. To drink, there was potent *chicha*, a cloudy beverage fermented from corn that had been ground and boiled. Deer, now rare, were abundant. . . . Crayfish in irrigation ditches supplemented seafood from the coast.

WALTER ALVA, "Richest Unlooted Tomb of a Moche Lord"

THINK THROUGH HISTORY
B. Analyzing Issues How were archaeologists able to gain so much information about the Moche without the help of a written language?
B. Possible Answer The Moche's elaborate pottery provided a great deal of information about their everyday life.

Moche tombs uncovered in the recent past have revealed a civilization with enormous wealth. Archaeologists have found beautiful jewelry crafted from gold, silver, and semiprecious stones. The Moche were also brilliant ceramic artists. They created pottery that depicted scenes from everyday life. Moche pots show doctors healing patients, women weaving cloth, and musicians playing instruments. They also show fierce soldiers armed with spears, leading enemy captives. Although the Moche never developed a written language, their pottery provides a wealth of detail about Moche life.

Nevertheless, many questions about the Moche remain. Experts still do not fully understand Moche religious beliefs. Nor do they know why the Moche fell. Like many early cultures of the Americas, the Moche remain something of a mystery.

Unlike the lands you will read about in the next chapter—which were unified by the spread of Islam—the Americas would remain a patchwork of separate civilizations until the early 16th century. Around that time the Europeans would begin to arrive and bring dramatic and lasting changes to the American continents.

Section 3 Assessment

1. TERMS & NAMES

Identify
• Chavín
• Nazca
• Moche

2. TAKING NOTES

Use a chart like the one below to record important details about the earliest Andean civilizations.

Culture	Time Span	Location	Achievements
Chavín			
Nazca			
Moche			

What achievements, if any, did all three cultures share?

3. HYPOTHESIZING

Would the Chavín culture have been more influential if it had arisen along the Peruvian coast? Why or why not?

THINK ABOUT
• the harsh environment of the Andes Mountain region
• the effect of environment on the spread of culture
• the nature of Chavín influence

4. ANALYZING THEMES

Interaction with Environment Describe how the Nazca and the Moche adapted to their environment in order to build flourishing societies.

The Americas: A Separate World **223**

ANSWERS

1. TERMS & NAMES
Chavín, p. 221
Nazca, p. 222
Moche, p. 222

2. TAKING NOTES
Possible Responses: Chavín—around 900 B.C.–200 B.C./northern and central Peruvian highlands/ important religious centers; influential art styles and religious images. Nazca—around 200 B.C.–A.D. 600/Peru's southern coast/ irrigation systems, textiles, pottery, Nazca Lines. Moche—A.D. 100–A.D. 700/ northern coast of Peru/irrigation systems, great wealth, elaborate pottery.

3. HYPOTHESIZING
Possible Responses: Yes. It might have been easier for the Chavín to spread their culture along the more hospitable coastal region. No. The fact that people made the difficult pilgrimage to the site indicates the culture's influence did not depend on location.

4. ANALYZING THEMES
Possible Response: To overcome their dry climate, the Nazca and Moche developed elaborate irrigation systems. This allowed them to farm the land.

Chapter 9 Assessment

TERMS & NAMES

1. Beringia, p. 211
2. Ice Age, p. 211
3. maize, p. 213
4. Mesoamerica, p. 216
5. Olmec, p. 216
6. Zapotec, p. 218
7. Monte Albán, p. 219
8. Chavín, p. 221
9. Nazca, p. 222
10. Moche, p. 222

REVIEW QUESTIONS

Answers will vary.

11. They found spearheads and charred bones at ancient sites.

12. It was highly nourishing and flourished in the tropical climate.

13. In a hunting society, people lived in small groups and had to continually move to obtain food; in an agricultural society, people grew their own food and thus could live in settled, large communities.

14. Along the Gulf Coast of Mexico, in the modern-day Mexican states of Veracruz and Tabasco.

15. The region had abundant resources for making pottery, tools, and monuments; and its rivers provided a means of transport and fertile land for farming.

16. Zapotec stone carvings resemble those of the Olmec. Zapotec sites, with their plazas, temples, and pyramids, show Olmec influences.

17. The city contained temples, palaces, and an observatory and housed thousands of residents.

18. Through their art styles and religious ideas.

19. Scholars believe they were created for the Nazca gods, although the lines' exact purposes remain unknown.

20. They created extensive irrigation systems.

TERMS & NAMES

Briefly explain the importance of each of the following to the early peoples and civilizations of the Americas.

1. Beringia
2. Ice Age
3. maize
4. Mesoamerica
5. Olmec
6. Zapotec
7. Monte Albán
8. Chavín
9. Nazca
10. Moche

Interact *with* History

On page 210 you examined ways to kill the mastodon and discussed the difficulties of living in a hunter-gatherer society. Now that you have read the chapter, discuss why the early Americans moved from a hunting to a farming existence. In what ways was food gathering easier in an agricultural society?

REVIEW QUESTIONS

SECTION 1 *(pages 211–215)*
Hunters and Farmers in the Americas

11. How do archaeologists know that the first Americans lived as hunters?

12. Why was corn such an important food crop to the people of Mexico and Central America?

13. What were the main differences between hunter-gatherer societies and those based primarily on agriculture?

SECTION 2 *(pages 216–220)*
Early Mesoamerican Civilizations

14. Where did the Olmec, the Americas' first known civilization, arise?

15. How did the Olmec's location contribute to the development of their civilization?

16. How did the Olmec influence the Zapotec civilization?

17. How do archaeologists know that the Zapotec city of Monte Albán was more than just a ceremonial center?

SECTION 3 *(pages 221–223)*
Early Civilizations of the Andes

18. In what ways did the Chavín influence other peoples of the Andes region?

19. What do scholars believe the Nazca Lines represented?

20. How were the Nazca and Moche able to develop productive farmland?

Visual Summary

The Americas: A Separate World

The Earliest Americans

- Hunted big game and later fished and gathered berries and plants
- Lived in small groups, as they had to move continually in search of food
- Eventually developed farming and settled down into large communities
- Developed various new skills, including arts and crafts, architecture, and social and political organization
- Gradually forged more complex societies

Early South American Societies

The Chavín
- Established powerful religious worship centers
- Created influential artistic styles

The Nazca and Moche
- Developed extensive irrigation systems for farming
- Crafted intricate ceramics and textiles and other decorative art

Early Mesoamerican Societies

The Olmec
- Designed and built pyramids, plazas, and monumental sculptures
- Developed ceremonial centers, ritual ball games, and a ruling class
- Directed a large trade network throughout Mesoamerica

The Zapotec
- Built a magnificent urban center at Monte Albán
- Developed early forms of hieroglyphic writing and a calendar system

224 Chapter 9

Interact *with* History

Have students consider that in a hunting society, (1) considerable energy and resources are expended in finding, hunting, killing, and preparing food and (2) people would rarely know where and how much food was available at any one time. In contrast, agricultural societies could (1) plan their food supplies and control which foods were grown, (2) farm in areas that people could access easily, and (3) expend more energy on preparing food and experimenting with new foods.

CRITICAL THINKING

1. STAGES TO CIVILIZATION

The early Americans' way of life developed through several stages, starting with hunting. Use a sequence graphic like the one below to show the stages of this development up to and including the time of the first civilizations.

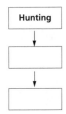

Hunting

2. CHALLENGING LOCATIONS

THEME INTERACTION WITH ENVIRONMENT What unique environmental challenges did the early Mesoamerican and South American peoples face as they built thriving civilizations?

3. EARLY WAYS OF LIFE

Would you rather have lived in a hunting society or a settled farming society? Explain your answer.

4. ANALYZING PRIMARY SOURCES

In his article "The Chavín Cult," historian Brian Fagan describes the mysterious shrine of Chavín de Huántar.

A VOICE ABOUT THE PAST
Its U-shaped temple opens east toward the nearby Mosna River and the rising sun. The sacred precinct faces away from the nearby prehistoric settlement, presenting a high, almost menacing, wall to the outside world. The entire effect is one of mystery and hidden power. . . . Worshippers entered the sacred precincts by a roundabout route, passing along the temple pyramid to the river, then up some low terraces that led into the heart of the shrine. Here they found themselves in a sacred landscape set against a backdrop of mountains. Ahead of them lay the hidden place where the axis of the world passed from the sky into the underworld, an oracle [a place for predicting the future] famous for miles around.

BRIAN FAGAN, quoted in *The Peru Reader*

- How might visitors have felt upon entering this shrine for the first time? Why?

- Do you think the mystery and majesty of this place helped spread the Chavín culture's influence? Explain.

CHAPTER ACTIVITIES

1. LIVING HISTORY: Unit Portfolio Project

THEME POWER AND AUTHORITY Your unit portfolio project focuses on the growth and use of power and authority in ancient history. (See page 107.) For Chapter 9 you might use one of the following ideas to add to your portfolio.

- Write a piece of historical fiction about an early American in which you describe how the first ruler gained power or how some people got rich.
- With a partner, design and prepare a time capsule that members of one of the first civilizations might have created to preserve the memory of their powerful and successful society.
- Speculate about why the Olmec or another civilization declined. Then draw a picture showing a key aspect of that decline. Include a caption.

2. CONNECT TO TODAY: Cooperative Learning

THEME CULTURAL INTERACTION One way that a culture's influence spread was by direct contact between people. Members of advanced civilizations, especially traders, carried their influential ideas with them as they traveled. Today, cultural influence is still spread in a similar way.

Work with a team to create and role-play two distinct meetings. In the first meeting, a trader from an ancient American civilization shares ideas and descriptions of his or her society with a farmer from a distant settlement. In the second meeting, an American salesperson from today shares similar information with a farmer in a distant land.

- Decide exactly what information you want the person from each of the dominant cultures to pass on.
- Establish a set of specific questions that the curious farmers will ask in order to draw out information about each culture.

3. INTERPRETING A TIME LINE

Revisit the time line on pages 106–107. Look above the Chapter 9 time line. Write about three other events that are happening in the world at this time.

FOCUS ON GEOGRAPHY

Notice the location of the early Mesoamerican and South American civilizations.

- How many miles apart by land do they appear to be?

- What geographic factors would have made interaction between the two regions difficult?

Connect to History
Based on the map, why do you think it took so many thousands of years to travel from the land bridge in upper North America to the southern tip of South America?

Early America, 1200 B.C.–A.D. 700

ATLANTIC OCEAN
Tropic of Cancer
Gulf of Mexico
MESOAMERICA
Caribbean Sea
Early Mesoamerican Civilizations
PACIFIC OCEAN
0°
SOUTH AMERICA
Early Andean Civilizations
ANDES MOUNTAINS
N
0   1,000 Miles
0   2,000 Kilometers
80°W
225

CHAPTER ACTIVITIES

1. LIVING HISTORY: UNIT PORTFOLIO PROJECT

Standards for Evaluation
Historical fiction pieces should meet the following criteria:

- Feature characters based on information in the text.
- Present situations that reveal how people gain political or financial power.
- Have a beginning, middle, and end.

Standards for Evaluation
Time capsule designs should meet the following criteria:

- Contain only those items important and available to early American civilizations.
- Reflect the values and beliefs of early Americans.
- Show students' knowledge of the time period.

Standards for Evaluation
Historical speculations should meet the following criteria:

- Show students' knowledge of environmental conditions of the time.
- Contain a drawing that illustrates one or more components of students' speculation.
- Provide a clear caption for the illustration.

2. CONNECT TO TODAY: COOPERATIVE LEARNING

Standards for Evaluation
Role-played meetings should meet the following criteria:

- Identify the two people involved in each meeting.
- Contain questions designed to elicit information about U.S. culture.
- Reveal the main beliefs and characteristics of each culture.

3. INTERPRETING A TIME LINE

Students should pick three topics, such as the items in Chapter 7—the Chinese invention of paper, the Buddhist monastery built, or the Indian calculation of *pi*—that can be researched easily.

FOCUS ON GEOGRAPHY

- The two areas of civilization are about 2500 miles apart.
- Distance and high mountain ranges would have made interaction between the two difficult.

Connect to History *Possible Response:*
The great distances involved, along with mountainous terrain, jungles, and major rivers, would have slowed the rate of migration.

CRITICAL THINKING

1. STAGES TO CIVILIZATION
Possible Responses: Hunting; fishing, gathering edible plants, hunting smaller animals; farming; creation of complex societies.

2. CHALLENGING LOCATIONS
Possible Responses: The Olmec faced jungle and heavy rainfall that often caused severe flooding; the Zapotec living in Monte Albán struggled to maintain an adequate water supply; the peoples of the Andes region faced a rugged, dry mountain climate.

3. EARLY WAYS OF LIFE
Possible Responses: Hunting society—It was more adventurous and exciting; there was a greater sense of freedom; life seemed less complicated; settlements were small and less crowded. Farming society—The food supply was more secure; you could settle down in one place and have time to pursue interests besides food gathering.

4. ANALYZING PRIMARY SOURCES
Possible Responses: Visitors would have been awestruck and possibly afraid because of the mysterious shrine and the sense that they were close to the world of spirits. Yes, the architectural and religious ideas portrayed by the mysterious site probably had a strong influence on other cultures.

UNIT 3

An Age of Exchange and Encounter

500–1500

The Siege of Jerusalem by the Crusaders

A 15th-century manuscript, probably French, from the collection of the British Library, fancifully depicts the siege of Jerusalem in 1099 during the First Crusade.

In the late 11th century, Muslim powers are dominating the Mediterranean region. Western Christians organize military expeditions to gain control of the Holy City of Jerusalem, and other places associated with the life of Jesus Christ, from the Muslims.

In July 1099, a Christian army of about 1,200 to 1,500 cavalry and 12,000 foot soldiers lays siege to Jerusalem. The city is being held by Egyptians of the Fatimid dynasty, who are Shi'ite Muslims.

On July 13–14, 1099, siege towers are brought to the walls. Soldiers armed with shields, swords, and bows and arrows scale the ladders. The walls are breached on July 15, and the Muslim governor surrenders the city to the Crusaders.

All Muslims and Jews in Jerusalem—men, women, and children—are killed in the slaughter that follows the surrender. According to an eyewitness: "Piles of heads, hands, and feet were to be seen in the streets of the city. . . . But these were small matters compared to what happened at the Temple of Solomon [where] men rode in blood up to their knees and bridle reins."

The Crusades are an example of the encounters between civilizations in this age when religious zeal, glory, trade expansion, and territorial gain motivate actions.

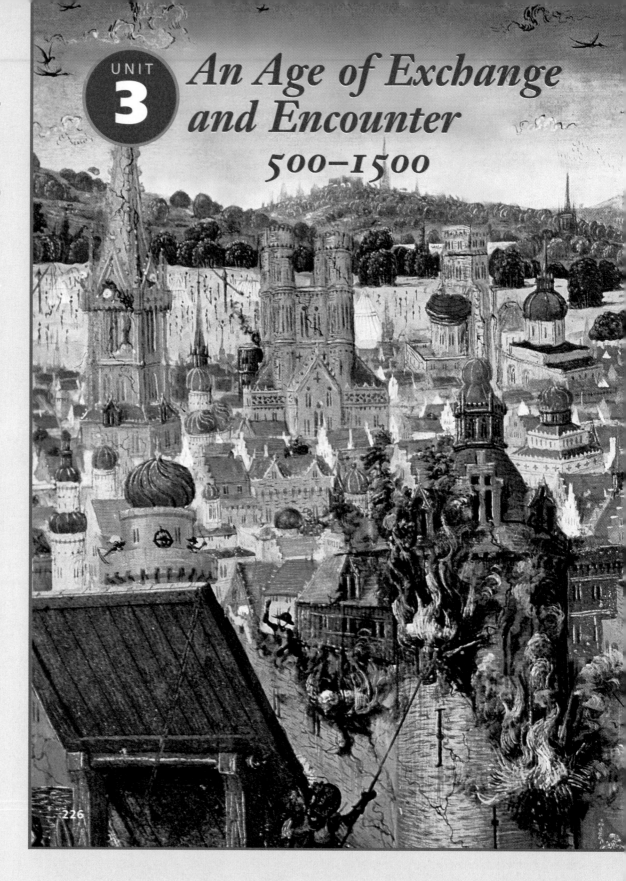

UNIT 3

An Age of Exchange and Encounter

500–1500

226

In this manuscript entitled *The Siege of Jerusalem by the Crusaders*, Christians battle Muslims for control of the holy city. Religion was just one of the issues over which empires fought as they tried to spread their influence.

Previewing the Unit

This unit describes a thousand-year period of exchange and encounter between civilizations in Europe, Asia, and Africa.

In southwestern Asia, the Prophet Muhammad founds the religion of Islam. Through conquest, Muslims spread the teachings of Islam across North Africa and into Europe.

Meanwhile, following the split of the Roman Empire in two, the Eastern Roman Empire prospers as the Byzantine Empire, while the Western Roman Empire falls. Byzantine culture influences Russia. The Christian Church divides into the Eastern Orthodox and Roman Catholic churches.

Nomadic Turks from central Asia move westward and adopt Islam. The Seljuks, as these Turks are called, conquer Persia and Anatolia and establish an empire. They, in turn, are subdued by other central Asian nomads, the Mongols. The Mongols overrun much of Asia—including China—and eastern Europe.

In western Europe, Charlemagne unites Germanic kingdoms into an empire. After his empire dissolves, people look to local leaders for protection from invaders, and the feudal system develops. The power of the Catholic Church increases and leads to the Crusades, attempts to wrest control of the holy lands of Christianity from Muslims. In this period, England and France become nations, and their rivalry results in the Hundred Years' War.

Africans organize themselves into different types of societies. Hunter-gatherer cultures and stateless societies predominate in the region south of the Sahara. Muslim states form in North Africa, and powerful empires and states develop in other parts of the continent. Some of these peoples grow rich trading with Asia.

An Age of Exchange and Encounter

Teaching Strategies

Cause and Effect Time lines provide an effective means for visually tracing a sequence of cause and effect. The time-line format allows students to make a strong graphic connection between or among events in such a way that the links stay fixed in their minds.

The links include the connection between

- the fall of one empire and the rise of another
- the invention of a weapon and a military victory
- the rise to power of a leader and the outbreak of war
- economic crisis and social unrest
- political chaos and economic crisis

Identifying a Sequence To practice the skill of identifying cause-effect sequences, students might work in groups. The group would start out by picking two time-line events as causes. Then, they will hunt for other events (either on the time line or in the unit chapters) that can logically be recognized as effects of either of these causes. For example, "**527 Constantinople** Justinian I becomes Byzantine emperor" could be linked to either "**528–533 Constantinople** The Justinian Code is created" or "**537 Constantinople** The Church of Hagia Sophia is completed." (In this case, both effects are drawn from a unit chapter.)

If the cause-effect connection is not clear to you or to some students, the group should be prepared to explain its reasons for the choice of certain events as effects.

An Age of Exchange and Encounter

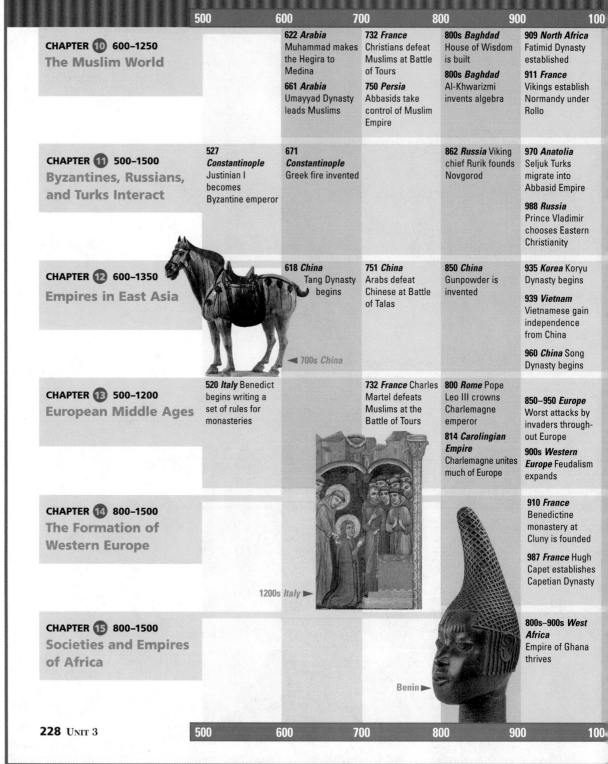

	500	600	700	800	900	100
CHAPTER 10 600–1250 The Muslim World		**622 Arabia** Muhammad makes the Hegira to Medina **661 Arabia** Umayyad Dynasty leads Muslims	**732 France** Christians defeat Muslims at Battle of Tours **750 Persia** Abbasids take control of Muslim Empire	**800s Baghdad** House of Wisdom is built **800s Baghdad** Al-Khwarizmi invents algebra	**909 North Africa** Fatimid Dynasty established **911 France** Vikings establish Normandy under Rollo	
CHAPTER 11 500–1500 Byzantines, Russians, and Turks Interact	**527 Constantinople** Justinian I becomes Byzantine emperor	**671 Constantinople** Greek fire invented		**862 Russia** Viking chief Rurik founds Novgorod	**970 Anatolia** Seljuk Turks migrate into Abbasid Empire **988 Russia** Prince Vladimir chooses Eastern Christianity	
CHAPTER 12 600–1350 Empires in East Asia		**618 China** Tang Dynasty begins	**751 China** Arabs defeat Chinese at Battle of Talas	**850 China** Gunpowder is invented	**935 Korea** Koryu Dynasty begins **939 Vietnam** Vietnamese gain independence from China **960 China** Song Dynasty begins	
CHAPTER 13 500–1200 European Middle Ages	**520 Italy** Benedict begins writing a set of rules for monasteries		**732 France** Charles Martel defeats Muslims at the Battle of Tours	**800 Rome** Pope Leo III crowns Charlemagne emperor **814 Carolingian Empire** Charlemagne unites much of Europe	**850–950 Europe** Worst attacks by invaders throughout Europe **900s Western Europe** Feudalism expands	
CHAPTER 14 800–1500 The Formation of Western Europe					**910 France** Benedictine monastery at Cluny is founded **987 France** Hugh Capet establishes Capetian Dynasty	
CHAPTER 15 800–1500 Societies and Empires of Africa					**800s–900s West Africa** Empire of Ghana thrives	

◀ 700s China

1200s Italy ▶

Benin ▶

228 UNIT 3

| | 500 | 600 | 700 | 800 | 900 | 100 |

CUSTOMIZING FOR SPECIAL NEEDS

Gifted and Talented Students You may ask interested students to choose an event on the time line that interests them (for instance, gun powder is invented or Joan of Arc is burned at the stake.) and do research on it. They may read a book or watch a historically accurate film about this event, or they may read several articles about it. Major historical happenings or periods are often the focus of Web sites on the Internet.

After students complete their research, ask them to prepare a report to deliver to the class. The report may take the form of an oral presentation (with visual aids and/or sound effects, if possible), a poster, or a drawing or painting illustrating some aspect of the event.

CONNECTIONS ACROSS THE CURRICULUM

Art Ask individual students to focus on one of the artworks in this Unit Time Line to learn more about it. Point out that all of the artworks also appear later in the unit and are accompanied there by explanatory captions.

Nonetheless, students should go beyond the material provided in the text to learn more about the period in which the work originated, the style of the work, the artist if he or she is known, and the meaning the artist is attempting to convey. They can then report their findings to the class.

Students may also want to look at other works by the same artist or works on a similar theme, in a similar style, or from the same period.

1000s *Africa, Asia, Europe* Abbasids, Fatimids, Umayyads rule Muslim Empire	**1100s** *Spain* Muslim Ibn Rushd writes philosophy			

◄ *1100s Baghdad*

| **1054** *Rome, Constantinople* Christian Church divides **1071** *Turkey* Seljuks defeat Byzantines | **1100s** *Turkey* Seljuk Empire declines **1100s** *Russia* Moscow founded | **1242** *Russia* Kiev falls to the Mongols | | **1453** *Turkey* Constantinople falls to the Turks **1480** *Russia* Ivan III refuses to pay Mongol tribute |

◄ *1000s Russia*

| **1020s** *China* Song Dynasty issues paper currency | **1127** *China* Dynasty of Southern Song flourishes **1192** *Japan* Kamakura Shogunate begins | **1209** *Mongolia* Genghis Khan begins Mongol conquests **1279** *China* Kublai Khan conquers Song Dynasty | **1330s** *Persia* Ilkhanate government falls apart **1368** *China* Chinese rebels overthrow Mongols | |

▼ *1400s France*

| **1075** *Holy Roman Empire* Henry IV clashes with Pope Gregory VII | **1122** *Holy Roman Empire* Concordat of Worms compromise reached **1152** *Holy Roman Empire* Frederick I becomes king | | | |

| **1095** *France* Pope Urban II issues call for First Crusade | **1187** *Palestine* Jerusalem falls to Muslims led by Saladin | **1204** *Byzantine Empire* Crusaders loot city of Constantinople **1215** *England* King John agrees to Magna Carta | **1337** *France* Hundred Years' War begins between England and France **1347** *Italy* Bubonic plague spreads to Europe | **1431** *France* Joan of Arc is burned at the stake **1453** *France* End of the Hundred Years' War |

| **1076** *Ghana* Muslim Almoravids conquer Ghana | **1148** *Morocco* Almohad Dynasty takes control of Muslim Morocco | **1235** *Mali* Sundiata founds Mali Empire | **1324** *Mali* Mansa Musa goes on a hajj **1352** *Mali* Muslim traveler Ibn Battuta visits Mali | **1420** *Southern Africa* Mutota begins Mutapa Empire **1450** *Great Zimbabwe* City of Great Zimbabwe is abandoned |

THEME | Religious and Ethical Systems

Your portfolio for Unit 3 will show how religious and ethical systems affect all aspects of the lives of people in this time period. The effects you track will be political, economic, social, and intellectual as well as spiritual. As the young religions grow, you will see the blending of cultures, power struggles between religions, and the blurring of the lines between politics and religion.

Living History Project Choices
Each Chapter Assessment offers you choices of ways to show the effects of religious and ethical systems in that chapter. Activities include the following:

Chapter 10 poster, talk show, letter

Chapter 11 documentary script, report, dialogue

Chapter 12 photo essay, mural, tour

Chapter 13 character sketch, poster, time line

Chapter 14 newscast, cartoon, speech

Chapter 15 interview, skit, diagram

Portfolio Project

Theme: Religious and Ethical Systems The portfolio projects for Unit 3 focus students' attention on:

- the influence of religious belief on decisions of government and daily life
- the effects of belief on architecture and other visual arts
- major religious figures and their ideas
- the role religion has played in the political and military spheres

Projects relating to the theme of religious and ethical systems range from a photo essay and "virtual" guided tour of a Buddhist temple to the script for a newscast describing the Crusaders' entry into Jerusalem.

Projects for Visual Learners
Religious material lends itself to visual depiction, and religions themselves have elaborate visual traditions. Visual learners will be able to choose from a variety of projects. Students will be encouraged to visually display their grasp of the theme of religious and ethical systems by working in areas such as:

- photography
- charts and posters
- murals
- television talk shows
- architecture
- time lines
- video

The Western Civilization Videodisc

SECTION D: The Foundations of Europe, 700–1200

Side One: Frame 17108

SECTION E: The Middle Ages in Full Blossom, 1200–1500

Side One: Frame 19988

Universal Play Button

See Master Guide, page 63 for Section D, page 88 for Section E.

PLANNING GUIDE
The Muslim World

	Key Ideas	**COPY MASTERS**	**ASSESSMENT**
SECTION 1 **The Rise of Islam** pp. 233–237	The Prophet Muhammad founds the religion of Islam and helps spread its ideas throughout the Arabian Peninsula, unifying the Arabs. Islam is a powerful influence on all aspects of its followers' lives.	*In-Depth Resources: Unit 3* • **Guided Reading,** p. 1 • **Skillbuilder Practice:** Making Inferences, p. 4 • **Primary Source,** from *The Qur'an,* p. 7 • **History Makers:** Muhammad, p. 14	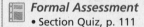 *Section 1 Assessment,* p. 237 *Formal Assessment* • Section Quiz, p. 111 *Alternative Assessment Book* • Standards for Evaluating a Cooperative Activity
SECTION 2 **The Spread of Islam** pp. 238–241	Through conquest, Muslims create an empire that stretches from Spain to India. Although the empire later splits among different groups, its people continue to speak Arabic and to maintain a lucrative Muslim trade network.	*In-Depth Resources: Unit 3* • **Guided Reading,** p. 2 • **Geography Application:** Rule and Taxation under the Umayyads, p. 5 • **Primary Source:** The Duties of the Caliph, p. 8	*Section 2 Assessment,* p. 241 *Formal Assessment* • Section Quiz, p. 112 *Alternative Assessment Book* • Standards for Evaluating a Cooperative Activity
SECTION 3 **Muslim Achievement** pp. 242–247	Muslim society, centered in cities, benefits from a mix of cultures and traditions. Learning flourishes in this environment, and Muslim scholars make important advances in the arts and sciences.	*In-Depth Resources: Unit 3* • **Guided Reading,** p. 3 • **Primary Sources:** *On Mental Discipline,* p. 9; from *The Life of Ibn Sina,* p. 10 • **Literature:** from *The Arabian Nights,* p. 11 • **History Makers:** Al-Razi (Rhazes), p. 15 • **Connections Across Time and Cultures:** Advancing Knowledge and Culture, p. 16	*Section 3 Assessment,* p. 247 *Formal Assessment* • Section Quiz, p. 113 *Alternative Assessment Book* • Standards for Evaluating a Cooperative Activity
CHAPTER RESOURCES	**Chapter Overview** Islam arises in Arabia and, through conquest, Muslims spread their empire and Muhammad's teachings to three continents. Despite a split in the empire, its trade increases and its people prosper. In cities a variety of cultures and traditions blend, and scholarship flourishes.	*Telescoping the Times* • Chapter Summary, pp. 37–39 *Planning for Block Schedules*	*Chapter Assessment,* pp. 248–249 *Chapter Activities,* p. 249 *Formal Assessment* • Chapter Test, forms A and B, pp. 114–119 *Test Generator* *Alternative Assessment Book*

TECHNOLOGY

 Warm-Up Transparency 10

 World Art and Cultures Transparencies
- AT21 Egyptian Qur'an

 Religions of the World
- Islam

 Electronic Library of Primary Sources
- from the Qur'an

 INTERNET RESOURCES
www.mlworldhistory.com

 Warm-Up Transparency 10

 Critical Thinking Transparencies
- CT10 The Spread of Islam

 Religions of the World
- Islam

 Electronic Library of Primary Sources
- "Pilgrimage to Mecca"

 INTERNET RESOURCES
www.mlworldhistory.com

 Warm-Up Transparency 10

 Geography Transparencies
- GT10 Baghdad During Its Golden Age, 765–950

 World Art and Cultures Transparencies
- AT22 Interior Dome in Great Mosque of Córdoba

 Critical Thinking Transparencies
- CT46 Chapter 10 Visual Summary

 Electronic Library of Primary Sources
- "Men and Women"

 INTERNET RESOURCES
www.mlworldhistory.com

 Chapter Summaries on Audiocassette in English and Spanish

 INTERNET RESOURCES
www.mlworldhistory.com

Block Scheduling (90 MINUTES)

Day 1
Section 1, pp. 233–237

 COOPERATIVE ACTIVITY
Presenting a Scene, p. 235 (Teacher's Edition)

Day 1 — Section 2
Section 2, pp. 238–241

 COOPERATIVE ACTIVITY
Producing a Newscast, p. 240 (Teacher's Edition)

Section Assessments, pp. 237, 241

Day 2
Section 3, pp. 242–247

 COOPERATIVE ACTIVITY
Creating a Brochure, p. 243 (Teacher's Edition)

Section Assessment, p. 247

Chapter Assessments, pp. 248–249

Yearly Pacing *Chapter 10 Total:* 2 days *Yearly Total:* 85 days

Planning for Block Schedules

Customizing for Special Needs

Students Acquiring English

 Access for Students Acquiring English
- **Guided Reading** for Sections 1–3 (Spanish), pp. 102–104
- **Chapter Summary** (Spanish), pp. 99–101
- **Skillbuilder Practice** Making Inferences (Spanish), p. 105
- **Geography Application** Rule and Taxation under the Umayyads (Spanish), p. 106

 Chapter Summaries on Audiocassette in English and Spanish

 INTERNET RESOURCES
www.mlworldhistory.com
The Diverse Classroom.

Less Proficient Readers

 In-Depth Resources: Unit 3
- **Guided Reading** for Sections 1–3, pp. 1–3
- **Skillbuilder Practice** Making Inferences, p. 4
- **Geography Application** Rule and Taxation under the Umayyads, p. 5

 Telescoping the Times
- Chapter Summary, pp. 37–39

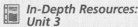 *Chapter Summaries on Audiocassette*

Gifted and Talented Students

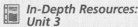 *In-Depth Resources: Unit 3*

Primary Sources:
- from *The Qur'an,* p. 7
- The Duties of the Calif, p. 8
- *On Mental Discipline,* p. 9
- from *The Life of Ibn Sina,* p. 10

History Makers:
- Muhammad, p. 14
- Al Razi (Rhazes), p. 15

Connections to Literature READINGS FOR STUDENTS

 In-Depth Resources: Unit 3
- **Literature:** from *The Arabian Nights,* p. 11

Enrichment Reading
- **Bayat, Mojeh and Mohammed Ali Jamnia** *Tales from the Land of the Sufis,* Boston: Shambhala, 1994

Best-loved Persian tales.

- **Maalouf, Amin** *The Crusades Through Arab Eyes* New York: Schocken, 1984.

First-hand account of the battles and bloodshed of the Crusades.

 = Pupil's Edition   = Overhead Transparency   = Software   = Video

 = Copy Master   = CD-ROM   = Audiocassette   = Internet

The Muslim World, 600–1250

Accessing Prior Knowledge

- Ask students to list on the chalkboard what they know about the Muslim world or about Islam.

Making Inferences

- Ask students to read the three captions related to the pictures on these pages and to suggest three different characteristics of Muslims during this time.

Geography Connection

- Have students find Arabia on the map and describe its location in terms of the lands and bodies of water that surround it.

- Ask students whether Europe seems close to or far from Arabia. Tell them that despite the distance, Muslim armies would one day threaten to overrun Europe.

CHAPTER
10

The Muslim World, 600–1250

PREVIEWING THEMES

Religious and Ethical Systems

Islam, a monotheistic religion, developed during the 600s. The teachings of Muhammad were embraced by Arab peoples, who spread the religion through Southwest Asia and parts of Africa and Europe.

Empire Building

As Muslims spread the religion of Islam, they captured new lands and the people of those lands came under Muslim rule. The leaders following Muhammad built a huge empire that by A.D. 750 stretched from the Atlantic Ocean to India. It included millions of people from diverse ethnic, language, and religious groups.

Cultural Interaction

Muslim tolerance of conquered peoples and the emphasis on learning blended the cultural traits of people under Muslim rule. The ideas of ancient Greeks and Indians combined with new ideas. This began a brilliant age of learning and cultural sharing that marked the Muslim world between 750 and 1250.

INTERNET CONNECTION

Visit us at **www.mlworldhistory.com** to learn more about the Muslim world.

MUSLIM WORLD, 1200

■ Byzantine Empire
□ Muslim World

EUROPE
Tours •
FRANCE
SPAIN
Córdoba •
Granada •
Tangier •
ATLANTIC OCEAN
Black Sea
Constantinople •
Mediterranean Sea
Damascus •
Baghdad •
Jerusalem •
Alexandria •
Cairo •
EGYPT
SAHARA DESERT
AFRICA
ARABIA
Medina •
Mecca •
Red Sea

A parade of musicians and Muslim horsemen carrying banners with religious inscriptions leads a celebration. Celebrations such as this often took place after the month of fasting called Ramadan. The illustration is from the **1100s** in a manuscript of the *Maqamat* by the poet al-Hariri.

230

GEOGRAPHY THEMES

Human/Environment Interaction

Tell students that knowing the geography of Arabia will help them understand Islam. Have them use the map on this page and a map of world climates to determine the climate of the region. Ask them to speculate on the characteristics of people who could survive and even thrive in such a place during the time this chapter covers. *Possible response: The people were resourceful and tough.* Tell students that the ideas and ways of the nomads of the Arabian Desert played a key role in the development of Islam and the rise of the Muslim Empire.

Movement

Tell students that Arabs moved out of their region into surrounding lands, spreading their religion as they went. Then ask students what they think might have happened when Muslim culture met another strong culture, such as that of Persia or Byzantium. *Possible responses: One culture prevailed; the cultures blended.*

ADDITIONAL RESOURCES

Books for the Teacher

• Cleary, Thomas. *The Essential Koran: The Heart of Islam.* San Francisco: Harper, 1993.

• Hourani, Albert. *A History of the Arab Peoples.* Cambridge: Belknap, 1991.

• Qadir, C. A. *Philosophy and Science in the Islamic World.* New York: Routledge, 1988.

Books for the Student

• Abderrahman, Ayoub, et al. *Umm El Madayan: An Islamic City Through the Ages.* Boston: Houghton, 1994. History of a fictional Islamic city in North Africa.

• Barlow, Christopher. *Islam.* London: Batsford, 1983. Balanced introduction to Islamic history.

• Beshore, George. *Science in Early Islamic Culture.* New York: Watts, 1988.

Videos

• *The Conquest of Spain.* Ambrose Video, 1995. 800-526-4663. Muslims conquer Spain and rule for seven centuries.

• *Foundations.* Ambrose Video, 1993. 800-526-4663. Muhammad, Mecca, and the split in Islam.

• *Islam and the Sciences.* Social Studies School Service, 1978. 800-421-4246.

Software

• *Religions of the World.* CD-ROM. Available from McDougal Littell.

Following a dream in which he spoke with Aristotle, Caliph al-Ma'mun ordered a **House of Wisdom** to be built in **Baghdad** in the early **800s.** It contained a library, an academy, and translation facilities for scientific and philosophical works, especially those from Greece, Byzantium, Persia, and India. There was an observatory nearby. Pictured here are scholars studying in a library in Baghdad.

This aerial view shows the holiest shrine of Islam, located in **Mecca.** Millions of pilgrims come to Mecca as part of their religious obligations. The cube located in the middle of the mosque is the Ka'aba. Muslims believe this house of worship was originally built by Abraham.

ASIA

INDIA

PACIFIC OCEAN

INDIAN OCEAN

Equator 0°

Tropic of Capricorn

40°N

HISTORY THROUGH ART

The Public Library of Hulwan

The library scene above is an early illustration in al-Hariri's *Maqamat,* an 11th-century collection of tales that is considered a masterpiece of literary style and learning. The scene shows an expert in a particular text teaching the text to his pupils.

In this activity, the teacher would dictate the text to his pupils, who would memorize it. (Many texts were rhymed to aid the memory.) Then the teacher would explain the text. The study was completed when a pupil could repeat back to the teacher both the text and the explanation. The teacher would then issue a license to teach the text.

The license included the names of all those who had transmitted the text, going back to the original author. The author of one text issued the following license: "I entrust my book to you with my writing from my hand to yours. I give you authorization for the poem and you may transmit it from me. It has been produced after being heard and read."

Interpreting the Art What does the preceding quotation—and the image—express about the process of transmitting knowledge in medieval Muslim culture? *Possible response: Knowledge was transmitted orally from person to person, linking authors, teachers, and pupils together through a sense of kinship, trust, and responsibility.*

Interact *with* History

This Interact with History feature motivates students by inviting them to put themselves in a key historical situation—the exchange of an idea between cultures. Imagining themselves as a medieval European learning about Arabic numerals from a Muslim, students will analyze the issues, explore their options, and become decision makers.

Purpose

• to set the stage for studying the development and spread of Muslim culture

• to help students understand some of the effects of intercultural exchange

• to help students make connections with people and events they will study in this chapter

Teaching Strategy

Thinking Critically After students have imagined themselves in the situation described on this page, have them answer the key questions and explain their decision.

EXAMINING *the* ISSUES

Here are suggestions for addressing each bulleted question.

1 Have one student multiply the Arabic numerals on the board and describe the process orally while another student does the same with the Roman numerals. Ask what happened with the Roman numerals.

2 Why would traders and others who use math daily prefer Arabic numerals to Roman?

3 What in language does a small set of characters make it possible to do? How do numerals in arithmetic work like characters in language?

4 How long does it take for basic ideas—like the best way to multiply numbers—to spread from one culture to another today?

Making Connections Have students discuss what the exchange of ideas between cultures has meant to the United States.

Interact *with* History

Around 825, an Arab mathematician, al-Khwarizmi of Baghdad, studied Indian math and wrote a book on using "Hindu" numerals. He suggested that not only mathematicians but also merchants should use the numerals.

You are an ambitious Italian merchant in the 1400s, visiting Muslim lands. You hear about these "Arabic" numerals that are widely used in transactions with Muslim traders. You wonder if they have any advantages for your business.

In the marketplace, you buy four necklaces at a cost of 23 dinars each. You ask the merchant to show you the calculation using Roman and then Arabic numerals. The problem is IV necklaces at XXIII dinars, or 4×23. You observe that computation with Arabic numerals is much easier and quicker.

Baker measures flour.

What makes an idea useful?

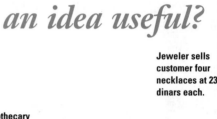

Jeweler sells customer four necklaces at 23 dinars each.

Apothecary weighs out medicinal products.

Butcher divides a carcass.

232 Chapter 10

EXAMINING *the* ISSUES

1 • Do the math problem using both sets of numerals. What is the advantage of using the Arabic numerals?

2 • Of what use would this system of numbers be to a businessperson?

3 • In what ways is the Arabic numeral system like a universal language?

4 • The mathematical idea of Arabic numbers spread to many cultures. In what ways do ideas move from one culture to another?

Discuss these questions with your classmates. In your discussion, consider what makes an idea useful and what kinds of ideas spread fastest. Think about ideas that have to do with business, as well as ideas in such areas as religion and science.

As you read about the spread of Islam and the development of Muslim culture in this chapter, notice in what ways ideas are accepted and spread.

Follow Up

A feature on the chapter assessment will ask students to reevaluate their responses to the situation presented on this page.

1 The Rise of Islam

TERMS & NAMES
- Allah
- Muhammad
- Islam
- Muslim
- Hijrah
- Qur'an
- mosque
- hajj
- Sunna
- shari'a

MAIN IDEA

Muhammad unified the Arab people both politically and through the religion of Islam.

WHY IT MATTERS NOW

As the world's fastest growing major religion, Islam has a strong impact on the lives of millions today.

SETTING THE STAGE The cultures of the Arabian Peninsula were in constant contact with each other for centuries. Southwest Asia (often referred to as the Middle East) was a bridge between Africa, Asia, and Europe, where goods were traded and new ideas were shared. One set of shared ideas would become a powerful force for change in the world—the religion of Islam.

Deserts, Towns, and Travelers

The Arabian Peninsula is a crossroads of three continents—Africa, Europe, and Asia. At its longest and widest points, the peninsula is about 1,200 miles from north to south and 1,300 miles from east to west. Only a tiny strip of fertile land in south Arabia and Oman and a few oases can support agriculture. The remainder of the land is desert, which in the past was inhabited by nomadic Arab herders.

Vocabulary
oases: places in the desert made fertile by the presence of water.

Desert and Town Life On this desert, the nomads, called Bedouins (BEHD·oo·ihnz), were organized into tribes and groups called clans. These clans provided security and support for a life made difficult by the extreme conditions of the desert. The tribesmen took pride in their ability to adapt to the desert conditions and to defend themselves against raids by other clans seeking water, grazing territory, livestock, or food supplies. Because of the desert nomads' fighting ability, they eventually became the core of armies who would build a huge empire in the 600s and 700s. The Bedouin ideals of courage and loyalty to family, along with their warrior skills, would become part of the Islamic way of life.

The areas with more fertile soil and the larger oases had enough water to support farming communities. By the early 600s, many Arabs had chosen to settle in an oasis or in a market town. A few generations earlier, the town dwellers had themselves been nomads. They, however, left the Bedouin life behind for life in settled areas. Larger towns near the western coast of Arabia became market towns for local, regional, and long-distance trade goods.

Crossroads of Trade and Ideas By the early 600s, trade routes connected Arabia to the major ocean and land trade routes. Trade routes through Arabia ran from the extreme south of the peninsula to the Byzantine and Sassanid empires to the north. Merchants from these two empires moved along the caravan routes, trading for goods from the Silk Roads of the east. They transported spices and incense from Yemen and other products to the west. They also carried information and ideas from the world outside Arabia. By the early 600s, cities such as Petra and Palmyra had

Petra, one of the early Arab trading cities, was literally a rock city. Buildings were carved out of the red sandstone cliffs. The name Petra means "rock" in Greek.

The Muslim World **233**

SECTION 1 RESOURCES

PRINT RESOURCES

IN-DEPTH RESOURCES: UNIT 3
Guided Reading, p. 1
Skillbuilder Practice: Making Inferences, p. 4
Primary Source: from *The Qur'an*, p. 7
History Makers: Muhammad, p. 14

ACCESS FOR STUDENTS ACQUIRING ENGLISH
Guided Reading (Spanish), p. 102
Skillbuilder Practice (Spanish), p. 105

FORMAL ASSESSMENT
Section Quiz, p. 111

ALTERNATIVE ASSESSMENT BOOK

TECHNOLOGY RESOURCES

WORLD ART AND CULTURES TRANSPARENCIES
AT21 Egyptian *Qur'an*

CD-ROM
Religions of the World
Electronic Library of Primary Sources

INTERNET www.mlworldhistory.com

Section 1 Overview

OBJECTIVES

1. To describe Arabia and its people in the period before the rise of Islam.

2. To explain how Muhammad became the Prophet and how he began to unify the Arabian Peninsula under Islam.

3. To identify the basic beliefs and practices of Islam.

SKILLBUILDER
- Interpreting maps: location, movement, p. 234

CRITICAL THINKING
- Summarizing, pp. 234, 235, 237
- Recognizing effects, p. 237

FOCUS
5-Minute Warm-Up

▶ *Interpreting*
Answering these questions will help students understand how the location of Arabia contributed to the spread of Islam.

1. Look at the map on page 234. Where is Arabia in relation to Europe, Africa, and the rest of Asia?

2. Why might Arabia's location make it a likely place for cultures to exchange ideas?

WARM-UP TRANSPARENCY 10

OBJECTIVE ① INSTRUCT

Deserts, Towns, and Travelers

▶ *Key Ideas*
- Arabia is a desert region connected by trade routes to the outside world.
- Nomadic herders called Bedouins live in the desert.
- Some Bedouins settle down as farmers on oases or as town dwellers.
- Mecca becomes an important trade and pilgrimage center.

IN-DEPTH RESOURCES: UNIT 3
Guided Reading, p. 1

ACCESS FOR STUDENTS ACQUIRING ENGLISH
Guided Reading (Spanish), p. 102

Teacher's Edition **233**

Trade Routes, A.D. 570

Interpreting the Map Have students describe the most direct route a trader might have taken from Muscat to Alexandria. *West by land to Mecca, then northwest on the Red Sea to its northern limit, then northwest across Egypt.*

Extension Activity Have students trace Arabia on a separate sheet of paper. Then have them find out what cities and kingdoms existed on Arabia's fringes around A.D. 570 and add these entities to their map. Students might consult sources such as Ismail and Lois al Faruqi's *Cultural Atlas of Islam.*

SKILLBUILDER Answers
1. It has access to land and sea transportation routes and links three continents.
2. Because Mecca was the hub for many trade routes, people with different ideas would meet there and take new ideas with them to other places.

OBJECTIVE 2 INSTRUCT

The Prophet Muhammad

Key Ideas
- Muhammad gains converts by teaching that Allah is the one and only God.
- Muhammad and his followers leave Mecca and establish a power base in Medina.
- Muhammad and his growing army of Bedouin followers subdue Mecca and go on to unify much of Arabia under Islam.

Trade Routes, A.D. 570

Land route
Sea route
Hijrah
Byzantine Empire
Sassanid Empire

GEOGRAPHY SKILLBUILDER: Interpreting Maps
1. **Location** Why is Arabia's location a good one for trade?
2. **Movement** Why was the location of Mecca ideal for the spread of ideas?

long been prosperous trading centers on the caravan routes.

The city of Mecca, in western Arabia, became an important stop on the trade route. During certain holy months, caravans stopped in Mecca. They brought religious pilgrims who came to worship at an ancient shrine in the city. Mecca housed a simple house of worship called the Ka'aba (KAH·buh). The Arabs associated this house of worship with Abraham, a believer in one God. Over the years, they had introduced the worship of many gods and spirits to the place. The Ka'aba contained over 360 idols brought here by many tribes. Many people traveled to this site as a pilgrimage.

The concept of belief in one God, called **Allah** (AL·luh) in Arabic, was no stranger to the Arabian Peninsula. A tradition of belief in one God had long been followed by a few people, known as *hanifs.* Many Christians and Jews lived in Arab lands and practiced monotheism. Into this mixed religious environment of Mecca, around A.D. 570, Muhammad was born.

THINK THROUGH HISTORY
A. Summarizing What religious traditions were in practice in the Arabian Peninsula?
A. Possible Answer Belief in one god and also belief in many gods and spirits.

The Prophet Muhammad

Muhammad (mu·HAM·id) was born into the clan of a powerful Meccan family. Orphaned at the age of six, the boy was raised by his grandfather and uncle. He received little schooling and began working in the caravan trade as a very young man. Muhammad became a trader and business manager for Khadijah (kah·DEE·juh), a wealthy businesswoman. When Muhammad was 25, he and Khadijah married. Theirs was both a good marriage and a good business partnership.

Revelations Muhammad took great interest in religion and often spent time alone in prayer and meditation. At about the age of 40, Muhammad's life was changed overnight when a voice called to him while he meditated in a cave outside Mecca. According to Muslim belief, the voice was that of the angel Gabriel, who told Muhammad that he was a messenger of God. "What shall I proclaim?" asked Muhammad. The voice answered:

THE QUR'AN
Proclaim! In the name of thy Lord and Cherisher, who created man out of a (mere) clot of congealed blood. Proclaim! And thy Lord is most bountiful. He who taught (the use of) the pen taught man that which he knew not.
Qur'an Surah 96:1–5

After much soul-searching, Muhammad came to believe that the Lord who spoke to him through Gabriel was Allah. Muhammad became convinced that he was indeed the last of the prophets. He taught that Allah was the one and only God and that all other gods must be abandoned. People who agreed to this basic principle of Islam were called Muslims. In Arabic, **Islam** (ihs·LAHM) means "submission to the will of Allah."

Background
Muhammad is often referred to as The Prophet.

TEACHING OPTION **BLOCK SCHEDULING**

SKILLBUILDER MINI-LESSON: Making Inferences

CLASS TIME 15 MINUTES

Explaining the Skill: Making inferences from various pieces of information means drawing conclusions based on facts, examples, and the source's use of language. For example, in an account of the Second Punic War, a writer may not come right out and explain why the war was fought. Therefore, readers must make inferences about the reasons. To make inferences, readers must use clues in the text

along with their personal experience, historical knowledge, and common sense.

Applying the Skill: To answer the Think Through History question on this page, students will first need to identify clues in the text and draw on their own common sense. Suggest that students study the paragraphs under "Crossroads of Trade and Ideas," beginning on page 233. Have them list facts and examples from the text from which they can

make an inference. *Sample: Arabia was linked by trade routes to other lands and cultures; merchants from these lands brought their own ideas and beliefs to Arabia; Mecca was an important stop on trade routes through Arabia; pilgrims from other lands came to worship their gods at a shrine in Mecca; Bedouins and Meccans worshiped many gods.*

 IN-DEPTH RESOURCES: UNIT 3
Skillbuilder Practice: Making Inferences, p. 4

Muslim (MOOZ·lim) means "one who has submitted." Muhammad's wife, Khadijah, and several close friends and relatives were his first followers.

By 613, Muhammad had begun to preach publicly in Mecca. At first, he had little success. Many Meccans believed his revolutionary ideas would lead to neglect of the traditional Arab gods. They feared that Mecca would lose its position as a pilgrimage center if people accepted Muhammad's monotheistic beliefs. Some of his followers were even beaten up or stoned in the streets.

The Hijrah Facing such hostility, Muhammad decided to leave Mecca. In 622, following a small band of supporters he sent ahead, Muhammad resettled in the town of Yathrib, over 200 miles to the north of Mecca. This migration became known as the **Hijrah** (hih·JEE·ruh). The Hijrah to Yathrib marked a turning point for Muhammad. He attracted many devoted followers. Later, Yathrib was renamed Medina, meaning "city of the Prophet."

In Medina, Muhammad displayed impressive leadership skills. He fashioned an agreement that joined his own people with the Arabs and Jews of Medina as a single community. These groups accepted Muhammad as a political leader. As a religious leader, he drew many more converts who found the message and the Messenger appealing. Finally, Muhammad also became a military leader in the hostilities between Mecca and Medina.

Returning to Mecca Many of the region's Bedouin tribes converted to Islam and joined Muhammad and his followers. During the years that the Muslims and the Meccans battled against each other, Mecca's power as a city declined. In 630, the Prophet and 10,000 of his followers marched to the outskirts of Mecca. Facing sure defeat, Mecca's leaders surrendered. The Prophet entered the city in triumph.

THINK THROUGH HISTORY
B. Summarizing
Identify four major events in the life of Muhammad.
B. Possible Answer
Revelations from God, first preaching, Hijrah, return to Mecca.

When he entered the city, Muhammad went to the Ka'aba and declared, "Truth has come and falsehood has vanished." Then he destroyed the idols in the Ka'aba and had the call to prayer made from the roof of the Ka'aba.

Most Meccans pledged their loyalty to Muhammad, and many converted to Islam. By doing so, they joined the *umma*, or Muslim religious community. Muhammad died two years later, at about the age of 62. However, he had taken great strides toward unifying the entire Arabian Peninsula under Islam.

SPOTLIGHT On

The Dome of the Rock

The Dome of the Rock, located in Jerusalem, is the earliest surviving Islamic monument. It was completed in 691. It is situated on Mount Moriah, the site of a Jewish temple destroyed by Romans in A.D. 70.

The rock on the site is the spot from which Muslims say Muhammad ascended to heaven to learn of Allah's will. With Allah's blessing, Muhammad returned to earth to bring God's message to all people. Jews identify the same rock as the site where Abraham was prepared to sacrifice his son Isaac.

The dome itself is wooden and about 60 feet in diameter. The supporting structure includes mosaic designs, columns, and many windows.

MORE ABOUT . . .
The Prophet Muhammad

From Medina, Muhammad ordered armed raids against Meccan caravans. These raids may have begun as a way for the migrants to support themselves economically. Revenge may also have been a factor. The Qur'an justified violence aimed at those who persecuted Muslims: "Permission is given to those who fight because they have suffered wrong . . . and those who have been expelled from their homes in defiance of right" (22:39–40).

📋 **IN-DEPTH RESOURCES: UNIT 3**
History Makers: Muhammad, p.14

SPOTLIGHT On
The Dome of the Rock

In September 1996, violence erupted near the Dome of the Rock after Israeli workers opened a tunnel that runs alongside the compound containing the Dome of the Rock and the Al-Aqsa Mosque. The tunnel connects the Western Wall—Judaism's holiest site—with the Via Dolorosa, where Jesus is said to have walked before his crucifixion.

Palestinians had opposed opening the tunnel because they felt it would violate the compound, which is the third holiest site for Muslims. When word of the opening spread, they rallied at the compound and clashed with Israeli forces. Israeli soldiers and Palestinian police fired at each other, killing 15 Israelis and 60 Palestinians.

Interested students might want to make a diagram showing the location of the Dome of the Rock, the Al-Aqsa Mosque, the Western Wall, and the tunnel.

TEACHING OPTION | **BLOCK SCHEDULING** | COOPERATIVE ACTIVITY: Presenting a Scene | **CLASS TIME 30 MINUTES**

Task: Students will write and present a scene from a play titled *Muhammad Returns,* set in Mecca in 630, in which people who witnessed Muhammad's confrontation with the leaders of Mecca after the leaders' surrender discuss what they saw and heard.

Purpose: To explore Muhammad's character and to analyze the friction between the Meccans and the Muslims from Medina.

Activity: Divide the class into groups of five. Each

group should discuss how best to portray Muhammad through the eyewitnesses, what kinds of issues might be brought up regarding the confrontation with the conquered Meccans, and what the Meccans' response might be. Have students turn their ideas into a script, with dialogue and stage directions. Then invite the groups to present their scenes to the class.

📁 **Building a Portfolio:** Students may make a copy of their group's script for their portfolio.

Standards for Evaluation
Scenes should . . .

• present the meeting in a dramatic fashion

• clearly portray Muhammad's character as a leader

• address the issues that faced the opposing groups

Beliefs and Practices of Islam

Key Ideas
- Muslims believe that there is only one God, Allah.
- All believers must carry out the Five Pillars of Islam.
- The Qur'an, the book said to contain Allah's revelations to Muhammad, is a basic source of authority for Muslims.
- Jews, Christians, and Muslims all share certain beliefs.

 RELIGIONS OF THE WORLD
Islam

MORE ABOUT . . .
Ramadan

According to Islamic tradition, Allah revealed the Qur'an to Muhammad in the month of Ramadan, the ninth month of the Muslim calendar. This calendar is based on the cycles of the moon. Months alternate between 29 and 30 days, from crescent moon to crescent moon. So Ramadan does not necessarily fall in the same season from one year to the next.

MORE ABOUT . . .
The Ulama

Some *ulama* have practiced their profession as individuals, and others have banded together in schools to interpret the Qur'an and other scriptures. Historically, the *ulama* did not parrot the beliefs of the political authorities; in fact, they took great pains to keep separate from the state. In the eyes of Muslims, this gave the *ulama* great moral authority and high social status.

Beliefs and Practices of Islam

The main teaching of Islam is that there is only one God, Allah. All other beliefs and practices follow from this teaching. Islam teaches that there is good and evil, and that each individual is responsible for the actions of his or her life. The holy book of the Muslims, the **Qur'an** (kuh·RAN), states, "And if any one earns sin, he earns it against his own soul" (Surah 4:111). Muslims believe that each person will stand before Allah on a final judgment day and enter either heaven or hell.

Artists decorating the Qur'an do it as a holy act. The design is geometric and often repeats to show the infinite quality of Allah. Muslims use abstract designs because they are not permitted to picture Muhammad or the angels.

The Five Pillars To be a Muslim, all believers have to carry out five duties. These duties demonstrate a Muslim's submission to the will of God. These duties are known as the Five Pillars of Islam.

- **Faith** To become a Muslim, a person has to testify to the following statement of faith: "There is no God but Allah, and Muhammad is the Messenger of Allah." This simple statement is heard again and again in Islamic rituals and in Muslim daily life.
- **Prayer** Five times a day, Muslims face toward Mecca to pray. They may assemble at a **mosque** (mahsk), an Islamic house of worship. Or they may pray wherever they find themselves. The duty of praying serves to bring Muslims closer to God.
- **Alms** Muhammad taught that all Muslims have a responsibility to support the less fortunate. Muslims meet that social responsibility by giving alms, or money for the poor, through a special religious tax.
- **Fasting** During the Islamic holy month of Ramadan, Muslims fast. They eat and drink nothing between dawn and sunset. A simple meal is eaten at the end of the day. The duty of fasting reminds Muslims that they have "greater needs than bread."
- **Pilgrimage** All Muslims perform the **hajj** (haj), or pilgrimage to Mecca, at least once in a lifetime. In the past, this involved a grueling journey across deserts, mountains, and seas. Today, many pilgrims arrive by airplane. During the pilgrimage events in Mecca, pilgrims wear identical garments so that all stand as equals before God.

A Way of Life Muslims do not separate their personal life from their religious life. Carrying out the Five Pillars of Islam ensures that Muslims live their religion while serving in their community. Along with the Five Pillars, there are other customs, morals, and laws for Islamic society that affect Muslims' daily lives. Believers are forbidden to eat pork or to drink wine or other intoxicating beverages. Friday afternoons are set aside for communal worship and prayer. Muslims who are able to do so gather at a mosque to worship. Unlike many other religions, Islam has no priests or central religious authority. Every Muslim is expected to worship God directly. Islam does, however, have a scholar class called the *ulama*, who are concerned with learning and law. The ulama includes religious teachers who study the words and deeds of Muhammad and apply them to everyday life.

Sources of Authority The original source of authority for Muslims is Allah. According to Islamic belief, Allah expressed his will through the Angel Gabriel, who

This tenth-century Turkish prayer rug has a traditional design. The design has an arch at one end. The arch must point to Mecca while the prayers are taking place.

Sacred Writings Like the Buddha and Jesus, Muhammad spoke, rather than wrote, his message. Following his death, however, Islam, like Buddhism and Christianity, became a religious culture founded on a body of sacred texts. Have students compare the ways the teachings of these three religions assumed written form.

Visual Learners Have students construct a chart, like the one below, to compare Islam, Christianity, and Judaism.

	Gods	Holy Books	Prophets
Islam			
Christianity			
Judaism			

revealed it to Muhammad as the Qur'an. While Muhammad lived, his followers listened to his prayers and teachings and memorized and recited the Revelations. Soon after the Prophet's death, it was suggested that the revelations of Muhammad be collected in a book. This book is the Qur'an.

The Qur'an is written in Arabic, and Muslims consider only the Arabic version to be the true word of God. Only Arabic can be used in worship. Wherever Muslims carried the Qur'an, Arabic became the language of worshipers and scholars. Thus, the Arabic language spread widely as Muslim control expanded into different lands.

Muslims believe that Muhammad's mission as a prophet was to receive the Qur'an and to demonstrate how to apply it in life. To them, the **Sunna** (SOON·uh), or Muhammad's example, is the best model for proper living. The guidance of the Qur'an and Sunna was assembled in a practical form to aid Muslims in applying the will of Allah to their daily lives. This body of law is known as **shari'a** (shah·REE·ah). This system of law regulates the family life, moral conduct, and business and community life of Muslims. It does not separate religious matters from criminal or civil matters, but brings all aspects of life together. Because shari'a applies to all who follow the teachings of the Prophet, it brings a sense of unity to all Muslims.

Links to Judaism and Christianity To Muslims, Allah is the same God that is worshiped in Christianity and Judaism. However, Muslims view Jesus as a prophet, not the Son of God. The Qur'an is regarded as the word of God as revealed to Muhammad, in the same way that Jews and Christians believe the Torah and the Gospels were revealed to Moses and the New Testament writers. Muslims believe that the Qur'an perfects the earlier revelations from God. To them, it is the final book, and Muhammad was the final prophet. All three religions believe in heaven and hell and a day of judgment. The Muslims trace their ancestry to Abraham, as do the Jews and Christians.

The bonds among the three monotheistic religions were reflected in the way the Muslims treated Christians and Jews. Both Christians and Jews were known as "people of the book," because each religion had a holy book with teachings similar to those of the Qur'an. Shari'a law required Muslim leaders to extend religious tolerance to Christians and Jews. A huge Muslim empire, as you will learn in Section 2, grew to include people of many different cultures and religions.

THINK THROUGH HISTORY
C. Summarizing
What are the sources of authority for Muslims?
C. Answer Allah, Qur'an, Sunna.

Background
Arab Muslims consider themselves descended from Abraham's son Ismail.

Daily Life

Muslim Prayer

Five times a day—dawn, noon, mid-afternoon, sunset, and evening—Muslims face toward Mecca to pray. Worshipers are called to prayer by a *muezzin*. The call to prayer sometimes is given from a *minaret* tower like those pictured above. In large cities, muezzins call worshipers to prayer using public address systems and even the radio.

Because they believe that standing before Allah places them on holy ground, Muslims perform a ritual cleansing before praying so that they will not contaminate the holy ground. They also remove their shoes.

Muslims may pray at a mosque, called a *masjid* in Arabic, meaning "place of kneeling to God." This term refers to the movements of prayer, which involve both the body and the mind in worship.

MORE ABOUT . . .
The Qur'an
The Qur'an, also spelled *Koran*, contains 114 chapters, or *surahs,* many of which are written in rhymed prose. Because Muslims believe that the Qur'an came directly from God in its Arabic form, they consider translations of it to be interpretations or paraphrases. Translations may help a reader understand the revelations, but they lack the authority of the Arabic original.

 IN-DEPTH RESOURCES: UNIT 3
Primary Sources: from *The Qur'an,* p. 7

 WORLD ART AND CULTURES TRANSPARENCIES
AT21 Egyptian Qur'an

 ELECTRONIC LIBRARY OF PRIMARY SOURCES
from the Qur'an

ASSESS & RETEACH

Section 1 Assessment
Have students work in groups of three to respond to the items. Have them define in their own words the terms in item 1.

Section Quiz
 FORMAL ASSESSMENT
Section Quiz, p. 111

Reteaching Activity
CLASS TIME: 15 MINUTES
Go over the key terms to help students understand the key people, ideas, and events in this section.

CLOSE ACTIVITY

CLASS TIME: 15 MINUTES

Comparing
Have students help you fill in a Venn diagram showing similarities and differences between the basic beliefs of Jews, Christians, and Muslims. The diagram might look like this:

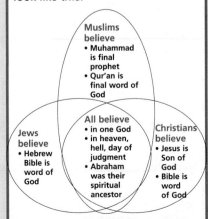

Section 1 Assessment

1. TERMS & NAMES

Identify
- Allah
- Muhammad
- Islam
- Muslim
- Hijrah
- Qur'an
- mosque
- hajj
- Sunna
- shari'a

2. TAKING NOTES

Create a diagram like the one shown below. Fill in at least three details for each category.

Islam		
Events in the Life of Muhammad	Beliefs of Islam	Sources of Authority

Based on your notes, write three paragraphs on Islam.

3. RECOGNIZING EFFECTS

Explain how the beliefs and practices of Islam created unity and strength among Muslims in the 600s.

THINK ABOUT
- why individuals felt they were part of a community
- what Muslims did to carry out the Five Pillars of Islam
- how Muslims viewed the relationship between religion and politics

4. THEME ACTIVITY

Religious and Ethical Systems With a small group, write a conversation that involves a supporter of Muhammad, a person who opposes Muhammad, and a pilgrim visiting Mecca who knows nothing about Muhammad. Place the conversation in a marketplace setting in Mecca. Read or perform your conversation for the class.

The Muslim World **237**

ANSWERS

1. TERMS AND NAMES
Allah, p. 234
Muhammad, p. 234
Islam, p. 234
Muslim, p. 235
Hijrah, p. 235
Qur'an, p. 236
mosque, p. 236
hajj, p. 236
Sunna, p. 237
shariah, p. 237

2. TAKING NOTES
Events in the Life of Muhammad: divine revelations; Hijrah to Medina; Mecca captured. **Beliefs of Islam:** one God, Allah; Five Pillars; rules for personal life; tolerance of Jews and Christians. **Sources of Authority:** Allah; Qur'an; Sunna.

3. RECOGNIZING EFFECTS
Possible Responses: Fasting and making a pilgrimage to Mecca gave Muslims common experiences. Facing Mecca to pray and giving alms reminded individuals of their membership in a community.

4. THEME ACTIVITY
Standards for Evaluation
The conversation should
- use dialogue that reflects historical conditions
- provide insight into the behavior of individuals
- capture and hold the interest of the audience

Teacher's Edition **237**

OBJECTIVES

 1 To describe how Muhammad's successors spread Islam.

 2 To list sources of conflict within the Umayyad Muslim state.

3 To explain how Muslim lands were split among rival groups.

SKILLBUILDER

- Interpreting maps: location, movement, p. 241

CRITICAL THINKING

- Recognizing causes, p. 239
- Summarizing, p. 240
- Recognizing effects, p. 241
- Hypothesizing, p. 241
- Analyzing themes, p. 241

FOCUS

5-Minute Warm-Up

▶ *Perceiving Causes*
Have students answer these questions to grasp how Muslims treated conquered people.

1. Read "Treatment of Conquered Peoples" on page 239. Why did many people conquered by Muslims convert to Islam?

2. Explain Muslims' treatment of Christians and Jews.

 WARM-UP TRANSPARENCY 10

OBJECTIVE **1** INSTRUCT

Muhammad's Successors Spread Islam

▶ *Key Ideas*
- Muhammad's early successors defend and expand Islam.
- Many conquered people choose to convert to Islam, though Muslims tolerate other religions.

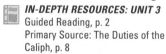 *IN-DEPTH RESOURCES: UNIT 3*
Guided Reading, p. 2
Primary Source: The Duties of the Caliph, p. 8

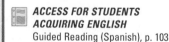 *ACCESS FOR STUDENTS ACQUIRING ENGLISH*
Guided Reading (Spanish), p. 103

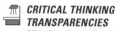 *CRITICAL THINKING TRANSPARENCIES*
CT10 The Spread of Islam

 ELECTRONIC LIBRARY OF PRIMARY SOURCES
"Pilgrimage to Mecca"

2 The Spread of Islam

TERMS & NAMES
- caliph
- Umayyads
- Shi'a
- Sunni
- Sufi
- Abbasids
- al-Andalus
- Fatimid

MAIN IDEA

In spite of internal conflicts, the Muslims created a huge empire that included lands on three continents.

WHY IT MATTERS NOW

Muslims' influence on three continents produced cultural blending that has continued into the modern world.

SETTING THE STAGE When Muhammad died in 632, the community faced a crisis. Muslims, inspired by the message of Allah, believed they had a duty to carry the word of God to the world. However, they lacked a clear way to choose a new leader. Eventually, the issue of leadership would divide the Muslim world.

Muhammad's Successors Spread Islam

Muhammad had not named a successor or instructed his followers how to choose one. Relying on ancient tribal custom, the Muslim community elected as their leader Abu-Bakr, a loyal friend of Muhammad and a man respected for his devotion to Islam. In 632, Abu-Bakr became the first **caliph** (KAY·lihf), a title that means "successor" or "deputy."

"Rightly Guided" Caliphs Abu-Bakr and the next three elected caliphs—Umar, Uthman, and Ali—all had known Muhammad and supported his mission. They used the Qur'an and Muhammad's actions as guides to leadership. For this, they are known as the "rightly guided" caliphs. Their rule was called a caliphate (KAY·lih·FAYT).

Abu-Bakr had promised the Muslim community he would uphold what Muhammad stood for. Shortly after the Prophet's death, some tribes on the Arabian Peninsula abandoned Islam. Others refused to pay taxes, and a few individuals even declared themselves prophets. For two years, Abu-Bakr used military force to reassert the authority of Muhammad's successors in the Muslim community. In that time, his troops gained experience and organized themselves into an effective mobile army.

By the time Abu-Bakr died in 634, the Muslim state controlled all of Arabia. Under Umar, the second caliph, swift and highly disciplined armies conquered Syria and lower Egypt, which were part of the Byzantine Empire. They also took parts of the Persian Empire. The next two caliphs, Uthman and Ali, continued to expand Muslim territory both eastward and westward. The "rightly guided" caliphs were able to gain the support of military and naval forces of the conquered lands. They used these forces to aid in further conquests. By 750, from the Atlantic Ocean to the Indus River, the Muslim Empire stretched 6,000 miles—about two times the distance across the continental United States. (See the map on page 241.)

Reasons for Success The four "rightly guided" caliphs made great progress in their quest to spread Islam. Muslims of the day saw the victories as a sign of Allah's support of Islam. Muslims drew energy and inspiration from their faith and were willing to struggle to extend and defend Islam. Historians have identified many reasons for the Muslims' military success in addition to the faith of the Muslim soldiers. The Muslim armies were well disciplined and expertly commanded. Their tactics enabled them to overwhelm forces unaccustomed to their style of warfare.

From 632 to 750, highly mobile troops mounted on camels were successful in conquering lands in the name of Allah.

SECTION 2 RESOURCES

PRINT RESOURCES

 IN-DEPTH RESOURCES: UNIT 3
Guided Reading, p. 2
Geography Application: Rule and Taxation under the Umayyads, p. 5
Primary Source: The Duties of the Caliph, p. 8

 ACCESS FOR STUDENTS ACQUIRING ENGLISH
Guided Reading (Spanish), p. 103
Geography Application (Spanish), p. 106

 FORMAL ASSESSMENT
Section Quiz, p. 112

 ALTERNATIVE ASSESSMENT BOOK

TECHNOLOGY RESOURCES

CRITICAL THINKING TRANSPARENCIES
CT10 The Spread of Islam

CD-ROM
Religions of the World
Electronic Library of Primary Sources

INTERNET www.mlworldhistory.com

The success of the Muslim armies was also due to weakness in the two empires north of Arabia. The Byzantine and Persian empires had been in conflict for a long period of time. By the time the Muslim army invaded their lands, they were exhausted militarily. Another reason for Muslim success was the persecution of Byzantine or Persian populations who did not support the official state religions, Christianity or Zoroastrianism. The persecuted people often welcomed the invaders, seeing them as liberators.

Treatment of Conquered Peoples Many conquered peoples chose to accept Islam. They were attracted by the appeal of the message of Islam, as well as by the economic benefit for Muslims of not having to pay a poll tax. Because the Qur'an forbade forced conversion, Muslims allowed conquered peoples to retain their own religion. Christians and Jews, as "people of the book," received special consideration. They paid a poll tax each year in exchange for exemption from military duties. They were also subject to various restrictions on their lives. The following account by an Arab army officer shows how he treated people in Persia:

> **A VOICE FROM THE PAST**
> In the name of God, the Merciful and the Compassionate. This is what Suwayd ibn Muqarrin gave to the inhabitants of Qumis and those who are dependent on them, concerning safe-conduct for themselves, their religions, and their property, on condition they pay the *jizya* [a poll tax] from the hand for every adult male, according to his capacity, that they show goodwill and do not deceive, that they guide [the Muslim traveler], and that they accommodate Muslims who make a halt with them for a day and a night with their average food. If they change this or make light of their obligations, the pact [*dhimma*] with them is void.
>
> **SUWAYD IBN MUQARRIN** quoted in *Islam: From the Prophet Muhammad to the Capture of Constantinople*

In practice, tolerance like this was extended to other groups as well. Though they were not allowed to spread their religion, Christians and Jews played important roles as officials, scholars, and bureaucrats in the Muslim state.

Internal Conflict Creates a Crisis

Despite spectacular gains on the battlefield, the Muslim community had difficulty maintaining a unified rule. The murder of Uthman in 656 triggered a civil war, with various groups struggling for power. Ali, as Muhammad's cousin and son-in-law, was the natural choice as a successor to Uthman. However, his right to rule was challenged by Muawiya, a governor of Syria. Then, in 661, Ali too was assassinated. The elective system of choosing a caliph died with him.

A family known as the **Umayyads** (oo·MYE·yadz) came to power. They set up a hereditary system of succession. The Umayyads also made another important change. The Muslim capital was moved to Damascus, a distant city in the recently conquered province of Syria. This location, away from Mecca, made controlling conquered territories easier. However, the Arab Muslims felt it was too far away from their lands. In addition, the Umayyads abandoned the simple life of previous caliphs and began to surround themselves with wealth and ceremony similar to that of non-Muslim rulers. These actions, along with the leadership issue, gave rise to a fundamental division in the Muslim community.

Ceremonial weapons such as this battle-ax were often decorated with fine artistic designs.

The Muslim World **239**

Muslims Control Areas of Three Continents

▶ Key Ideas

- The Abbasids take power in 750 and will rule for 500 years.
- An Umayyad prince sets up a Muslim dynasty in Spain.
- The Abbasids serve as the main religious authority but lose some political control over the vast empire to independent Muslim states.
- The Muslim trade network crisscrosses the empire and extends as far as China in the east and below the Sahara in the south.

---

*Global*Impact

Elephant Diplomacy

Harun al-Rashid's gift of the elephant hints at the lavishness of the Abbasid court. His vast palace, bustling with hundreds of officials and thousands of servants, and his sumptuous banquets dazzled foreign visitors. Harun was a great patron of the arts. It is said that he was so delighted by some verses he read that he rewarded the poet with more than 100,000 silver pieces.

The splendor of Harun and his court took romanticized form in the folk classic of Arabic literature, *The Thousand and One Nights.* In some of these tales, Harun wanders through nighttime Baghdad in disguise, seeking amusement.

Encourage interested students to read tales involving Harun. Each student might then summarize a tale for the class. Make sure the content and the language of the tale are appropriate for a classroom presentation.

Sunni–Shi'a Split In the interest of peace, the majority of Muslims accepted the Umayyads' rule. A minority did continue to resist, and around some of these groups an alternate view of the office of caliph developed. In this view, the caliph—the person most responsible for spreading Muhammad's message—needed to be a relative of the Prophet. This group was called **Shi'a,** meaning the "party" of Ali. Those who did not outwardly resist the rule of the Umayyads later became known as **Sunni,** meaning followers of Muhammad's example. Among those who did not actively resist Umayyad rule were many who believed that the Umayyads had become too concerned with worldly affairs and had lost touch with their religion.

Another group, the **Sufi** (SOO·fee), reacted to the luxurious life of the Umayyads by pursuing a life of poverty and devotion to a spiritual path. They tried to achieve direct personal contact with God through mystical means, such as meditation and chanting. In some ways they were similar to Christian and Buddhist monks. The Sufis played an important role in keeping Muslims focused on the Qur'an and tradition. Later, they became very active as missionaries in newly conquered lands. Another religious development was the growth of scholarship in various branches of Islamic learning and law. The study of the traditions of Muhammad, Arabic language, and the development of schools of shari'a established standards of Islamic conduct.

Vigorous religious and political opposition to the Umayyad caliphate led to its downfall. Rebel groups overthrew the Umayyads in the year 750. The most powerful of those groups, the **Abbasids** (AB·uh·SIHDZ), took control of the empire.

Muslims Control Areas of Three Continents

When the Abbasids came to power in 750, they ruthlessly murdered the remaining members of the Umayyad family. One prince named Abd al-Rahman escaped the slaughter and fled to Spain. There he set up an Umayyad dynasty. Spain had already been conquered and settled by Muslims from North Africa, who were known as Berbers. The Berbers were led by Tariq, a powerful military figure. So revered was Tariq that a famous rock peninsula was named for him. The name today reflects his presence: Jabal Tariq—Gibraltar. The Berber armies advanced north to within 100 miles of Paris before being halted at the Battle of Tours in 732. The Berbers then settled back into southern Spain, where they helped form an extraordinary Muslim state called **al-Andalus** (al·AN·duh·LUS).

*Global*Impact

Elephant Diplomacy

The Abbasids ruled a huge empire and were constantly searching for ways to hold it together and hold off outside attacks. The Abbasids viewed their relationship with the Kingdom of the Franks, ruled by Charlemagne, as essential to their ability to remain strong. They saw the Franks as possible allies against the Umayyads in al-Andalus (Spain).

To cement the relationship with Charlemagne, Caliph Harun al-Rashid sent an envoy with gifts to the court of Charlemagne. Among the gifts sent to the Frankish king was an elephant named Abu al-Abbas. It was the only elephant the caliph possessed.

The diplomatic trip was successful. Charlemagne marched against the Umayyad lands early in his reign.

Abbasids Consolidate Power The Abbasids' strength lay in the former Persian lands, including Iraq, Iran, and central Asia. To solidify power, in 762 they moved the capital of the empire to a newly created city, Baghdad, in southern Iraq. The location on key trade routes gave the caliph access to trade goods, gold, and information about parts of the empire in Asia, Africa, and Europe.

The Abbasids developed a strong bureaucracy to conduct the huge empire's affairs. A treasury kept track of the money flow. A chancery prepared letters and documents. A special department managed the business of the army. Diplomats from the empire were sent to courts in Europe (for example, Charlemagne's court), Africa, and Asia to conduct imperial business. To support this bureaucracy, the Abbasids taxed land, imports, and exports, and non-Muslims' wealth.

Rival Groups Divide Muslim Lands The Abbasid caliphate lasted from 750 to 1258. During that time, the Abbasids increased their authority by consulting religious leaders. But they failed to keep complete political control of the immense territory. Independent Muslim states sprang up, and local leaders dominated many smaller regions. The **Fatimid** (FAT·uh·MIHD) Dynasty, named after

---

B. Answer Sunni, Shi'a, Sufi. Sunni follow the Sunna and believe the Muslim leader should be capable of leading the community. Shi'a are followers of Ali and believe the leader should be a descendant of Muhammad. Sufi pursue a life of meditation and personal contact with God.

THINK THROUGH HISTORY
B. Summarizing What are three groups within Islam and how do they differ?

Background
The Spanish name for Arabs and Berbers was Moors, because they came from the old Roman province of Mauritania.

Task: Student groups will produce a newscast announcing the overthrow of the Umayyads and the takeover of the Muslim Empire by the Abbasids.

Purpose: To examine the fall of the Umayyads and the events surrounding the rise of the Abbasids.

Activity: Each group's researchers will find out how the Abbasids came to power and how they dealt

with the Umayyad family. News writers will prepare a script explaining the events. News readers will present the reports orally.

 Building a Portfolio: Students may want to add a copy of the script to their portfolio.

ALTERNATIVE ASSESSMENT BOOK
Standards for Evaluating a Cooperative Activity

Standards for Evaluation
Newscast scripts should . . .

- clearly explain the events being presented
- remain neutral in the presentation of facts
- follow a recognizable format for modern newscasts

Muhammad's daughter Fatima, began in North Africa and spread across the Red Sea to western Arabia and Syria. Although politically divided, the Abbasid Empire and the smaller powers remained unified in other ways. Religion, language, trade, and the economy tied the lands together.

Muslim Trade Network The two major sea-trading zones—those of the Mediterranean Sea and the Indian Ocean—linked the Muslim Empire into a world system of trade by sea. The land network connected the Silk Roads of China and India with Europe and Africa. Muslim merchants needed only a single language, Arabic, and a single currency, the Abbasid dinar, to travel from Córdoba to Baghdad and on to China.

To encourage the flow of trade, Muslim money changers set up banks in cities throughout the empire. Banks offered letters of credit, called *sakks*, to merchants. A merchant with a *sakk* from a bank in Baghdad could exchange it for cash at a bank in any other major city in the empire. In Europe, the word *sakk* was pronounced "check." Thus, the practice of using checks dates back to the Muslim Empire.

At one end of the Muslim Empire was the city of Córdoba in al-Andalus. In the tenth century, this city had a population of 500,000; Paris, in contrast, had 38,000. The city's mix of Muslims, Christians, and Jews created a cosmopolitan atmosphere that attracted poets and philosophers as well as scientists and doctors. Many non-Muslims adopted the Arabic language and Muslim customs. Córdoba became a dazzling center of Muslim culture, boasting 70 libraries, 700 mosques, and 27 free schools.

In Córdoba, Damascus, Cairo, and Baghdad, a cultural blending of people fueled a period of immense achievements in the arts and the sciences.

THINK THROUGH HISTORY
C. Recognizing Effects Why would a single language and a single currency be such an advantage to a trader?
C. Answer There would be no problem in changing money to a local currency and no need for interpreters, who might make mistakes.

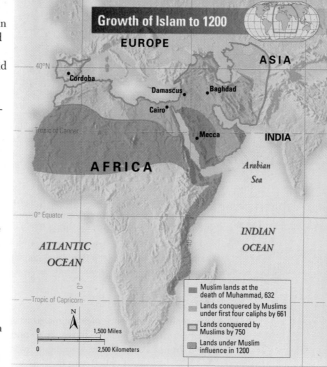

Growth of Islam to 1200

EUROPE
ASIA
40°N
Córdoba
Damascus • Baghdad
Cairo
Tropic of Cancer
Mecca
INDIA
AFRICA
Arabian Sea
0° Equator
ATLANTIC OCEAN
INDIAN OCEAN
Tropic of Capricorn

N
0   1,500 Miles
0   2,500 Kilometers

- Muslim lands at the death of Muhammad, 632
- Lands conquered by Muslims under first four caliphs by 661
- Lands conquered by Muslims by 750
- Lands under Muslim influence in 1200

GEOGRAPHY SKILLBUILDER: Interpreting Maps
1. **Location** To which continents did Islam spread by 1200?
2. **Movement** In which time period was the largest amount of land conquered?

The Muslim World **241**

Section 2 Assessment

1. TERMS & NAMES

Identify
- caliph
- Umayyads
- Shi'a
- Sunni
- Sufi
- Abbasids
- al-Andalus
- Fatimid

2. TAKING NOTES

Create a table like the one below. For each group of rulers, identify the period of their rule and at least two developments that affected the growth or strength of Islam during that period.

Rulers	Period of Rule	Developments in Islam
Rightly Guided Caliphs		
Umayyads		
Abbasids		

3. HYPOTHESIZING

How do you think Shi'a Muslims felt about the Abbasids taking power in 750?

THINK ABOUT
- how the Shi'a viewed the Umayyads
- where the Shi'a lived
- actions of Abbasids while in power

4. ANALYZING THEMES

Empire Building What evidence supports the conclusion that the Islamic empires were well-run?

THINK ABOUT
- relationships between Muslims and non-Muslims
- efforts to promote trade
- the role of the military

History from Visuals

Growth of Islam to 1200
Interpreting the Map Ask students to describe the location of the lands that came under Muslim influence between 750 and 1200. *Muslims influenced lands across a broad swath of territory in northern Africa south of the coastal regions, as well as a strip of land along Africa's east coast.*

Extension Activity Invite students to speculate about what form Muslim influence might have taken in Africa.

SKILLBUILDER Answers
1. Asia, Africa, Europe.
2. Under the first four caliphs by 661.

ASSESS & RETEACH

Section 2 Assessment
Distribute the questions among groups of students, have them present their answers orally, and then discuss the answers with the class.

Section Quiz
FORMAL ASSESSMENT
Section Quiz, p. 112

Reteaching Activity
CLASS TIME: 10 MINUTES

Ask students to form groups of three. Have each student find information related to one of the points to think about in item 4 of the section assessment. Students should then pool their information and answer the question.

CLOSE ACTIVITY

CLASS TIME: 10 MINUTES

Summarizing
On the chalkboard write two column headings: *Unifying* and *Divisive*. Then have students come to the board to list factors that helped hold the Muslim Empire together and factors that threatened to break it up. *Unifying factors might include religion, language, trade, and the economy; divisive factors might include the rise of independent Muslim states and dominance of smaller regions by local leaders.*

ANSWERS

1. TERMS AND NAMES
caliph, p. 238
Umayyads, p. 239
Shi'a, p. 240
Sunni, p. 240
Sufi, p. 240
Abbasids, p. 240
al-Andalus, p. 240
Fatimid, p. 240

2. TAKING NOTES
Rightly Guided Caliphs: 632–661; spread of Islam east and west, tolerance of Jews and Christians. Umayyads: 661–750; split between Sunni and Shi'a, development of Sufi movement. Abbasids: 750–1258; shift of capital to Baghdad, growth of Muslim trade network.

3. HYPOTHESIZING
Possible Responses: The Shi'a may have supported the Abbasids' takeover because they found the Umayyads too worldly and because both they and the Abbasids were based in Persia. The Shi'a may have opposed the Abbasids' worldly focus on trade and empire.

4. ANALYZING THEMES
Possible Responses: Muslims' tolerance of non-Muslims won non-Muslims' support. Well-trained, well-led Muslim armies suggest Muslim leaders ran military affairs well. Muslims' banks and single currency helped trade.

OBJECTIVES

 To describe Muslim society during the Abbasid caliphate.

To explain how Muslims worked to preserve scientific learning.

To give examples of Muslim advances in the sciences.

SKILLBUILDER
• Interpreting graphs, p. 242

CRITICAL THINKING
• Summarizing, p. 243
• Recognizing effects, pp. 243, 245
• Drawing conclusions, p. 247
• Clarifying, p. 247
• Comparing, p. 247
• Evaluating, p. 247

FOCUS

5-Minute Warm-Up

▶ **Predicting**
Answering these questions will help students understand the importance of learning in Muslim culture.

1. Read A Voice from the Past on page 243. What is Muhammad's attitude toward learning?

2. What effect do you predict this attitude would have on study and scholarship in the Muslim world?

 WARM-UP TRANSPARENCY 10

OBJECTIVE ① INSTRUCT

Muslim Society

▶ **Key Ideas**
• Muslim cities combine many cultural traditions.
• Muslim society has four social classes.
• Women have a limited but vital role in Muslim society.

IN-DEPTH RESOURCES: UNIT 3
Guided Reading, p. 3

ACCESS FOR STUDENTS ACQUIRING ENGLISH
Guided Reading (Spanish), p. 104

GEOGRAPHY TRANSPARENCIES
GT10 Baghdad During Its Golden Age, 765–950

ELECTRONIC LIBRARY OF PRIMARY SOURCES
"Men and Women"

TERMS & NAMES
• House of Wisdom
• calligraphy

3 Muslim Achievement

MAIN IDEA	WHY IT MATTERS NOW
Muslims combined and preserved the traditions of many peoples and also advanced learning in a variety of areas.	Many of the ideas developed during this time became the basis of today's scientific and academic disciplines.

SETTING THE STAGE The Abbasids governed during a prosperous age of Muslim history. Riches flowed into the empire from all over Europe, Asia, and Africa. Rulers could afford to build luxurious cities. They supported the scientists, mathematicians, and philosophers that those cities attracted. In the special atmosphere created by Islam, the scholars preserved existing knowledge and produced an enormous body of original learning.

Muslim Society

Over time, the influence of Muslims grew as the empire encompassed people from a variety of lands. Jobs in the bureaucracy and in the army were available to many different groups. At centers of learning in Syria, Persia, Spain, and Egypt, the halls echoed with the Arabic language, the language of the Qur'an. The many cultural traditions combined with the Arabic culture to create an international flavor. Muslim society had a sophistication matched at that time only by the Tang Empire of China. That cosmopolitan character was most evident in urban centers.

The Rise of Muslim Urban Centers Throughout the empire, market towns blossomed into cities. Migrants from the countryside and new converts came to cities looking for opportunities. Until the construction of Baghdad, Damascus was the leading city. Damascus was known for fine cloth called damask and for outstanding steel swords and armor. It was also the cultural center of Islamic learning. Other cities grew up around power centers, such as Córdoba, the Umayyad capital, and Cairo, the Fatimid capital. (See the map on page 241.) Urban centers, which symbolized the strength of the dynasty, grew to be impressive.

The Abbasid capital, Baghdad, impressed all who saw it. Caliph al-Mansur chose the site for his capital on the west bank of the Tigris River, in 762. Extensive planning went into the city's distinctive circular design, formed by three circular protective walls. The caliph's palace of marble and stone sat in the innermost circle, along with the grand mosque. Originally, the main streets between the middle wall and the palace were lined with shops. Later, the marketplace moved to a district outside the walls. Baghdad's population approached one million at its peak.

Four Social Classes Baghdad's population, made up of different cultures and social classes, was typical for a large Muslim city in the eighth and ninth centuries. Muslim society was made up of four classes. The upper class included those who were Muslims at birth. Converts to Islam were found in the second class. This class paid a higher tax than the upper class,

Urban Centers, A.D. 900

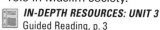

Population chart showing Baghdad (approx. 900,000), Constantinople (approx. 300,000), Córdoba (approx. 200,000), and Rome (approx. 35,000).

Source: Tertius Chandler and Gerald Fox, *3,000 Years of Urban Growth.*

SKILLBUILDER:
Interpreting Graphs
1. *How much larger in population was Baghdad than Córdoba?*
2. *How would the population of the largest city in your state compare to the population of Baghdad in A.D. 900?*

SECTION 3 RESOURCES

PRINT RESOURCES
IN-DEPTH RESOURCES: UNIT 3
Guided Reading, p. 3
Primary Sources: *On Discipline,* p. 9; from *Ibn Sina,* p. 10
Literature: from *The Arabian Nights,* p. 11
History Makers: Al-Razi (Rhazes), p. 15
Connections Across Time and Cultures, p. 16

ACCESS FOR STUDENTS ACQUIRING ENGLISH
Guided Reading (Spanish), p. 104

FORMAL ASSESSMENT
Section Quiz, p. 113

TECHNOLOGY RESOURCES
GEOGRAPHY TRANSPARENCIES
GT10 Baghdad During Its Golden Age, 765–950

WORLD ART AND CULTURES TRANSPARENCIES
AT22 Interior Dome in Great Mosque of Córdoba

CRITICAL THINKING TRANSPARENCIES
CT46 Chapter 10 Visual Summary

CD-ROM
Electronic Library of Primary Sources

INTERNET www.mlworldhistory.com

but lower than other classes of non-Muslim people. The third class consisted of the "protected people" and included Christians, Jews, and Zoroastrians. The lowest class was composed of slaves. Many slaves were prisoners of war, and all were non-Muslim. Slaves most frequently performed household work or fought in the military.

Role of Women The Qur'an states, "Men are the managers of the affairs of women," and "Righteous women are therefore obedient." However, the Qur'an also declares that men and women, as believers, are equal. The shari'a gave Muslim women specific legal rights concerning marriage, family, and property. Muslim women had more rights than European women of the same time period. The Qur'an provided for the care of widows and orphans, allowed divorce, and protected the woman's share of an inheritance.

Responsibilities of Muslim women varied with the income of their husbands. The wife of a poor man would often work in the fields with her husband. Wealthier women supervised the household and its servants. They had access to education, and among them were poets and scholars. Rich or poor, the woman was responsible for the raising of the children. In the early days of Islam, women could also participate in public life and gain an education.

Muslim Scholarship Extends Knowledge

Muslims had practical reasons for supporting the advancement of science. Rulers wanted qualified physicians treating their ills. The faithful throughout the empire relied on mathematicians and astronomers to calculate the times for prayer and the direction of Mecca. The energy that Muslims devoted to preserving and extending knowledge, however, went beyond practical concerns. Their attitude reflected a deep-seated curiosity about the world and a quest for truth that reached back as far as the Prophet. Muhammad himself believed strongly in the power of learning:

A VOICE FROM THE PAST
Acquire knowledge. It enableth its possessor to distinguish right from wrong; it lighteth the way to Heaven; it is our friend in the desert, our society in solitude, our companion when friendless; it guideth us to happiness; it sustaineth us in misery; it is an ornament amongst friends, and an armour against enemies.
MUHAMMAD, quoted in *The Sayings of Muhammad*

The Prophet's emphasis on study and scholarship led to strong support of places of learning by Muslim leaders. After the fall of Rome in A.D. 476, Europe entered a period of upheaval and chaos, an era in which scholarship suffered. The scientific knowledge gained up to that time might have been lost. Thanks to Muslim leaders and scholars, much of that knowledge was preserved and expanded. Both Umayyads and Abbasids encouraged scholars to collect and translate scientific and philosophical texts. In the early 800s, Caliph al-Ma'mun opened in Baghdad a combination library, academy, and translation center called the **House of Wisdom.** There, scholars of

The Muslim World **243**

In a miniature painting from Persia, women are shown having a picnic in a garden. Gardens were seen as earthly representations of paradise.

OBJECTIVE **3** INSTRUCT

Arts and Sciences Flourish in the Muslim World

▶ **Key Ideas**
- Muslim contributions to medicine, mathematics, and science advance learning.
- Muslims blend existing philosophical and artistic traditions with their own ideas and also create original works.

 IN-DEPTH RESOURCES: UNIT 3
Primary Sources: *On Mental Discipline*, p. 9; from *The Life of Ibn Sina*, p. 10
History Makers: Al-Razi (Rhazes), p. 15
Connections Across Time and Cultures: Advancing Knowledge and Culture, p. 16

 WORLD ART AND CULTURES TRANSPARENCIES
AT22 Interior Dome in Great Mosque of Córdoba

Global Impact
Medical Reference Books

Starting in the 1100s, scholars brought their translations of Arabic medical books back to Christian Europe. Much of the expertise exhibited in those books went far beyond the knowledge of the European medical community. Invite students to imagine that a scholar has brought back to Italy from Muslim Spain a translation of *The Canon of Medicine*. He has let an esteemed Italian physician examine this encyclopedia for a week. Have students write a dialogue that might have taken place between the scholar and the physician when the scholar came back to retrieve the encyclopedia.

---

different cultures and beliefs worked side by side translating texts from Greece, India, Persia, and elsewhere into Arabic.

Arts and Sciences Flourish in the Muslim World

Scholars at the House of Wisdom included researchers, editors, linguists, and technical advisers. These scholars developed standards and techniques for research that are a part of the basic methods of today's research. Some Muslim scholars incorporated Greek ideas into their own work in fresh new ways. Others created original work of the highest quality. In these ways, Muslims in the Abbasid lands, especially in Córdoba and Baghdad, set the stage for a later revival of European learning. Muslim contributions in the sciences were most recognizable in medicine, mathematics, and astronomy.

Global Impact

Medical Reference Books
When Europeans learned that Muslims had preserved important medical texts, they wanted to translate the texts into Latin. In the 11th century, scholars traveled to libraries in places such as Toledo, Spain, where they began translating —but only after they learned to read Arabic.

Through this process, European medical schools gained access to vital reference sources such as al-Razi's *Comprehensive Book* and Ibn Sina's *The Canon of Medicine*. Ibn Sina's five-volume encyclopedia guided doctors of Europe and Southwest Asia for six centuries. For nearly 500 years, al-Qasim's work, *The Method,* which contained original drawings of some 200 medical tools, was the foremost textbook on surgery in Europe.

Medical Advances A Persian scholar named al-Razi (Rhazes) was the greatest physician of the Muslim world and, more than likely, of world civilization between A.D. 500 and 1500. He wrote an encyclopedia called the *Comprehensive Book* that drew on knowledge from Greek, Syrian, Arabic, and Indian sources as well as on his own experience. Al-Razi also wrote a *Treatise on Smallpox and Measles*, which was translated into several languages. He believed patients would recover more quickly if they breathed cleaner air. To find that location, he hung shreds of meat all around Baghdad. He observed which shreds spoiled more slowly, perhaps because of cleaner air. Then he made a recommendation for the location of a hospital.

Math and Science Stretch Horizons Among the ideas that Muslim scholars introduced to modern math and science, two especially stand out. They are the reliance on scientific observation and experimentation, and the ability to find mathematical solutions to old problems. As for science, Muslims translated and studied Greek texts. But they did not follow the Greek method of solving problems. Aristotle, Pythagoras, and other Greek thinkers preferred logical reasoning over uncovering facts through observation. Muslim scientists preferred to solve problems by conducting experiments in laboratory settings.

Muslim scholars believed, as Aristotle did, that mathematics was the basis of all knowledge. Al-Khwarizmi, a mathematician born in Baghdad in the late 700s, studied Indian rather than Greek sources. He wrote a textbook in the 800s explaining "the art of bringing together unknowns to match a known quantity." He called this technique *al-jabr*—today called algebra.

Many of the advances in mathematics were related to the study of astronomy. The sciences of mathematics and optics, along with scientific observation, led to major advances in astronomy. Muslim observatories charted stars, comets, and planets. Ibn al-Haytham (Alhazen), a brilliant mathematician, produced a book called *Optics* that revolutionized ideas about vision. Through thoughtful experiments, Ibn al-Haytham showed that people see objects because rays pass from the objects to the eyes, not from the eyes to the objects as was commonly believed. His studies about optics were used in developing lenses for telescopes and microscopes.

Philosophy and Religion Blend Views In addition to scientific works, scholars at the House of Wisdom in Baghdad translated works of philosophers like Aristotle and Plato into Arabic. In the 1100s, Muslim philosopher Ibn Rushd (Averroës), who lived in Córdoba, tried in his writings to harmonize Aristotle's and Plato's views with those of Islam. Some Islamic religious thinkers attacked Ibn Rushd for using Greek philosophical methods to interpret the shari'a. However, Ibn Rushd

Background
Europeans changed Arabic names to ones they could pronounce. You will see the European names in parentheses.

Background
Ibn is a word used to mean "the son of."

TEACHING OPTIONS CONNECTIONS ACROSS THE CURRICULUM

Mathematics Ask students how al-Khwarizmi described his algebra technique. Write the answer on the chalkboard. *He called it "the art of bringing together unknowns to match a known quantity."* Discuss with students whether this description fits what they know about algebra. You might put the following simple algebraic equation on the chalkboard to aid discussion: $8 \times 5 - n = 31$. *(The unknown, n, equals 9.)*

CONNECTIONS ACROSS TIME AND PLACE

Al-Khwarizmi's Inspiration Al-Khwarizmi looked to Indian sources for mathematical inspiration. One of those sources might have been the work of Brahmagupta, an Indian mathematician born in A.D. 598. Like al-Khwarizmi, Brahmagupta was also a brilliant astronomer. In his book *The Opening of the Universe*, he wrote about eclipses, the phases of the moon, and the positions of the planets. In the same book, he described elements of mathematics, such as arithmetical progression, proofs of geometrical theorems, and the quadratic equation—a type of algebraic equation.

Astronomy

Muslim interest in astronomy developed from the need to fulfill three of the Five Pillars of Islam—fasting during Ramadan, performing the hajj, and praying toward Mecca.

A correct lunar calendar was needed to mark religious periods such as the month of Ramadan and the month of the hajj. Studying the skies helped fix the locations of cities so that worshipers could face toward Mecca as they prayed. To correctly calculate the locations, Muslim mathematicians developed trigonometry. Cartographers (mapmakers) illustrated the information.

The cartographer al-Idrisi prepared this map as part of a series of maps for a ruler of Sicily. The maps were done in the 1100s. The map below of the world looks upside down to modern eyes because North is at the bottom. The body of water at the right is the Mediterranean, and the Arabian Peninsula juts out into the Indian Ocean.

Before telescopes, observations of the skies were made with the naked eye. The device shown above is called an armillary sphere. By aligning the top rings with various stars, astronomers could calculate the time of day or year. This aided in setting the calendar correctly. Muslims had a number of observatories. The most famous one was located at Samarkand, which is in modern Uzbekistan.

The astrolabe was an early scientific instrument used by Muslims and others to measure the angles of the sun and the stars above the horizon. It was like a very simple computer. The device was a brass disk engraved with a star map and having a movable bar used for sighting the angle of the sun or stars. To find the location north or south of the equator, the user rotated the rings to the positions of the stars on any given night.

Connect to History

Recognizing Effects How did fulfilling religious duties lead Muslims to astronomy and a better understanding of the physical world?

 SEE SKILLBUILDER HANDBOOK, PAGE 995.

Connect to Today

Researching Muslim astronomers developed instruments to improve their observations of the sky. Today, there are telescopes both on earth and in space. Do some research to find out what new information is being discovered from the Hubble telescope in space.

The Muslim World **245**

Muslim Astronomy
Astrolabes, armillaries, and quadrants were the basic tools of the many astronomical observatories throughout the Muslim world. Muslim astronomers continually tried to improve the precision of these observational and computational instruments. As a result, measures of planetary motion improved, as did the tables used to map the stars. Astronomers using advanced instruments even roughly calculated the circumference and diameter of the earth.

MORE ABOUT . . .
Al-Idrisi
Besides making maps, al-Idrisi wrote one of the greatest works of medieval geography, *The Pleasure Excursion of One Who Is Eager to Traverse the Regions of the World*. In it he combined information from Arabic and Greek geographic works with information he gathered through firsthand observation. Al-Idrisi chose and dispatched expert draughtsmen to various countries to observe and record what they saw. He also drew on personal experience, having traveled in North Africa, western Europe, and Asia Minor.

Connect to History

Recognizing Effects
Possible Response: Muslims' religious duties included fasting during the month of Ramadan, performing the hajj (pilgrimage to Mecca), and praying five times a day while facing Mecca. Fulfilling these duties required knowledge of the physical world, which astronomers and mathematicians provided by determining the direction of Mecca and the months of the lunar calendar. (Each month began and ended with the first appearance of the crescent moon, which astronomers could calculate.)

Connect to Today

Researching
Students might want to use the Internet, newspapers, and magazines to research the Hubble Space Telescope, which was launched into Earth orbit in 1993, to find out what kinds of information it is transmitting back to astronomers.

In the *Muqaddimah,* Ibn Khaldun offered an original view of the rise and fall of dynasties. He described a process in which every dynasty would eventually be weakened— by oppression, excessive spending and waste, or poor leadership— and fall to a new dynasty. Ask students to cite examples of this kind of historical rise and fall. Then have them make up an aphorism, or brief saying, that incorporates Ibn Khaldun's view.

MORE ABOUT . . .
Rumi

The great Sufi poet Rumi wrote thousands of mystical poems in the Persian language. Rumi could be inspired to recite new verses almost anywhere—in the bath or on the road. Luckily, he had a faithful companion who would write them all down.

MORE ABOUT . . .
The Thousand and One Nights

This collection includes the well-known stories of Aladdin, Ali Baba, and Sindbad the Sailor. The premise of the collection is that a king who has killed his unfaithful wife determines to marry and kill a new wife every day. Scheherazade, the daughter of the king's vizier, has a plan to end this madness. She marries the king and then begins telling a story every evening. Hoping to hear the next day how each story turns out, the king delays Scheherazade's execution. Finally, he gives up his murderous ways altogether.

HISTORY MAKERS

Ibn Khaldun
1332–1406

Ibn Khaldun was literally a history maker. He produced a massive history of Muslim North Africa. However, Arnold Toynbee, a 20th-century historian, called Ibn Khaldun's Islamic history master-piece *Muqaddimah* (an introduction to history) "the greatest work of its kind that has ever yet been created by any mind in any time or place."

In his six-volume study of world civilization, Ibn Khaldun introduced the ideas of sociology, economics, politics, and education and showed how they combined to create historical and social change.

He also established principles for writing about history that required historians to examine critically all facts they presented.

This interior view of the Great Mosque of Córdoba shows a new architectural style. Two tiers of arches support the ceiling.

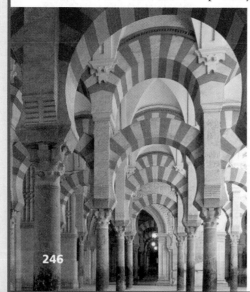

246

argued that Greek philosophy and Islam both had the same goal: to find the truth.

Moses Ben Maimon (Maimonides), a Jewish physician and philosopher, was born in Córdoba and lived in Egypt. Like Ibn Rushd, he faced strong opposition for his ideas, but he came to be recognized as the greatest Jewish philosopher. Writing during the same time as Ibn Rushd, Maimonides produced a book, *The Guide of the Perplexed,* that blended philosophy, religion, and science.

Muslim Literature Literature was a strong tradition in Arabia before Islam. Bedouin poets, reflecting the spirit of desert life, com-posed poems celebrating ideals such as bravery, love, generosity, and hospitality. Those themes continued to appear in poetry written after the rise of Islam.

The Qur'an, held sacred by Muslims, is the standard for all Arabic literature and poetry. Early Muslim poets sang the praises of the Prophet and of Islam and, later, of the caliphs and other patrons who supported them. During the age of the Abbasid caliphate, literary tastes expanded to include poems about nature and the pleasures of life and love.

The Sufis were especially known for their poetry that focused on mystical experiences with God. The following poem by the greatest of all Sufi poets, Rumi, describes an experience of sensing God:

> ### A VOICE FROM THE PAST
> As salt resolved in the ocean
> I was swallowed in God's sea,
> Past faith, past unbelieving,
> Past doubt, past certainty.
>
> Suddenly in my bosom
> A star shone clear and bright;
> All the suns of heaven
> Vanished in that star's light.
>
> **JALAL AL-DIN RUMI,** translated by A. J. Arberry, *Persian Poems*

Popular literature included *The Thousand and One Nights,* a collection of enter-taining stories that included fairy tales, parables, and legends. The core of the collec-tion has been linked to India and Persia, but peoples of the Muslim Empire added stories and arranged them, beginning around the 10th century.

Muslim Art and Architecture As they expanded, the Arabs entered regions that had rich artistic traditions. These traditions continued, with modifications inspired, and sometimes imposed, by Islam. For example, Islam forbade the depiction of living beings, based on the idea that only Allah can create life. Thus, picturing living beings was considered idolatry. With the drawing of such images prohibited, many artists turned to **calligraphy,** or the art of beautiful handwrit-ing. Others expressed themselves through the decorative arts, such as woodwork, glass, ceramics, and textiles.

It is in architecture that the greatest cultural blending of the Muslim world can be seen. To some extent, the location of a building reflected the culture of people of the area. For example, the Great Mosque of Damascus was built on the site of a Christian church. In many ways, the huge dome and vaulted ceiling of the mosque blends Byzantine architecture with Muslim ideas. In Syrian areas, the architecture includes features that were very Roman, including baths using Roman heating systems. In Córdoba, the Great Mosque incorporated multi-lobed interwoven arches in a style unknown before. The style

Background
"Aladdin" and "Ali Baba and the Forty Thieves" are popular tales from *The Thousand and One Nights.*

Task: Students will read a story from *The Thousand and One Nights.* Then pairs of students will outline a plot for a story modeled on the structure of the original.

Materials Needed: Use copies of "The Third Dervish's Tale" in the teacher resource materials.

Activity: Have students read the story. Then have pairs of students outline the plot elements of the

story and use the outline as a model for outlining the plot of their own story. This story might be set in modern times or in a fantasy world, but it should incorporate key structural elements of the original, such as a main character, a problem the character faces, and events centering on the problem.

Conclusion: Have each pair of students exchange its plot outline with another pair. Pairs

should discuss how the elements of their plots differ from or resemble the original. They might explain to each other why they incorporated certain elements from the original and changed or dropped others. Invite students to read their outlines to the class or to post them on a bulletin board.

 IN-DEPTH RESOURCES: UNIT 3
Literature: from *The Arabian Nights,* p. 11

HISTORY THROUGH ART: Calligraphy

This picture of a man praying is made up of the words of the Muslim declaration of faith.

Calligraphy, or ornamental writing, is important to Muslims because it is considered a way to reflect the glory of Allah. In pictorial calligraphy, pictures are formed using the letters of the alphabet. Prayers are written in the shape of a bird, plant, boat, or other object.

The bird's body is made up of words of a statement of faith.

Connect to History

Clarifying How would these images help Muslims practice their religion?

SEE SKILLBUILDER HANDBOOK, PAGE 992.

Connect to Today

Comparing With what kinds of art do other religions in the modern age express their religious ideas?

---

was based on principles used in earlier mosques. These blended styles appear in all the lands occupied by the Muslims.

The values of many cultures were recognized by the Muslims and combined with Islamic values. A 9th-century Muslim philosophical society showed that it recognized the empire's diverse nature when it described its "ideal man":

A VOICE FROM THE PAST

The ideal and morally perfect man should be of East Persian derivation, Arabic in faith, of Iraqi education, a Hebrew in astuteness, a disciple of Christ in conduct, as pious as a Greek monk, a Greek in the individual sciences, an Indian in the interpretation of all mysteries, but lastly and especially a Sufi in his whole spiritual life.

IKHWAN AS-SAFA, quoted in *The World of Islam*

C. Answer The very best parts of each culture can combine to produce an outstanding one.

THINK THROUGH HISTORY
C. Drawing Conclusions What is the advantage of blending various traditions within a culture?

The elements of Muslim life remained and blended with local culture wherever Islam spread. Though the unified Muslim state broke up, Muslim culture continued. Three Muslim empires, the Ottoman, the Safavid, and the Mughal, would emerge that would reflect the blended nature of the culture of this time. The knowledge developed and preserved by the Muslim scholars would be drawn upon by European scholars in the time known as the Renaissance, beginning in the 14th century.

Section 3 Assessment

1. TERMS & NAMES

Identify
• House of Wisdom
• calligraphy

2. TAKING NOTES

Create a web diagram like the one below, showing the key elements of Muslim culture. In each circle write 3 aspects of that element.

Which of these most strengthened the Abbasid rule? Explain.

3. EVALUATING

List what you consider to be the five most significant developments in scholarship and the arts during the reign of the Abbasids. Explain the standards you used to make your selections.

THINK ABOUT
• reasons for each development
• immediate and practical impact
• long-term significance

4. THEME ACTIVITY

Cultural Interaction Look at the Voice from the Past above. On a map, mark the location of each of the specific places identified. Link the points together. Shade in the area. About how large an area in miles is covered? What might be learned about cultural blending from this map?

The Muslim World **247**

ANSWERS

TERMS AND NAMES
House of Wisdom, p. 243
calligraphy, p. 246

TAKING NOTES
Possible Responses: **Urban Life:** cities like Baghdad and Córdoba; home to learning centers; linked to other cities by trade. **Society:** our classes; protection of

women's legal rights; tolerance of other religions and customs. **Arts and Literature:** no pictures of the Prophet; calligraphy as an art form; poetry highly valued. **Science and Math:** House of Wisdom; medical advances; growth of math and astronomy. The trade network probably strengthened the Abbasids most.

3. EVALUATING
Standards for Evaluation
Students should give reasons for each selection. They might list Ibn Sina's *The Canon of Medicine* for its impact on medicine in both Muslim and Christian worlds.

4. THEME ACTIVITY
Maps should use points, lines,

and area markings to convey information clearly. The area covered is about 3,000 miles east to west and 1,500 miles north to south.

Possible Response: The lands Muslims controlled or influenced included a variety of cultures from which Muslims could draw to enrich their own culture.

Chapter ⑩ Assessment

TERMS & NAMES

1. Islam, p. 234
2. Allah, p. 234
3. Hijrah, p. 235
4. hajj, p. 236
5. shariah, p. 237
6. caliph, p. 238
7. Shi'a, p. 240
8. Sufi, p. 240
9. House of Wisdom, p. 243
10. calligraphy, p. 246

REVIEW QUESTIONS

Answers will vary.

11. Arabia was mostly desert, with a few farming communities and larger towns on the west coast. Its location made it a crossroads of trade and ideas between Europe, Africa, and Asia.

12. They feared Mecca would lose its position as a pilgrimage center if people accepted his monotheistic beliefs.

13. They are faith, prayer, alms, fasting, and pilgrimage. They are duties every Muslim attempts to carry out to show submission to the will of God.

14. They believed that followers of all three religions worshiped the same God; held similar beliefs about heaven, hell, and a day of judgment; and were the descendants of Abraham. They treated Jews and Christians with toleration.

15. They drew upon the duty Muslims felt toward their faith, their armies were well trained and well led, and they won non-Muslims' support because they tolerated religious diversity.

16. The Shi'a believed that the caliph should be a relative of Muhammad and that the Umayyads had lost touch with their religion. The Sunni believed the leader only needed to demonstrate leadership of the community.

17. The Abbasids controlled key trade routes linking Asia, Africa, and Europe; they had a strong bureaucracy to run their empire; and Muslims set up banks in cities throughout the empire.

18. Cities were well-organized, growing, and culturally diverse and were the home of educational institutions. Society was divided into four classes, and women were legally protected.

19. Besides having practical reasons, such as improving health and helping people know when to pray, scholars inherited a deep-seated curiosity about the world from Muhammad. Unlike Greek scientists, Muslim scientists emphasized

---

TERMS & NAMES

Briefly explain the importance of each of the following to the people in the Muslim world between 600 and 1200.

1. Islam
2. Allah
3. Hijrah
4. hajj
5. shari'a
6. caliph
7. Shi'a
8. Sufi
9. House of Wisdom
10. calligraphy

Interact *with* History

In this chapter, you learned that ideas spread through trade, war and conquest, and through scholarly exchange. With a partner, make a list of at least five ways to spread an idea in today's world—ways that were not available to Muslims in A.D. 600–1250.

Visual Summary

The Muslim World

Empire Building

Four major Muslim dynasties build empires on parts of three continents.

- 661–750: Umayyad Dynasty
- 750–1258: Abbasid Dynasty
- 756–976: Umayyads of al-Andalus (Spain)
- 909–1171: Fatimid Dynasty (North Africa, Egypt, Western Arabia, and Syria)

Islam

Religion

- Muhammad receives revelations from Allah.
- The Five Pillars of Islam are Muslims' basic religious duties.
- The sources of authority—the Qur'an and the Sunna—guide daily life.
- Islam divides into several branches, including Sunni and Shi'a.

Achievements

Muslim scholars preserve, blend, and expand knowledge, especially in mathematics, astronomy, architecture, and medical science.

REVIEW QUESTIONS

SECTION 1 (pages 233–237)
The Rise of Islam

11. Describe the geographic setting in which Islam developed.
12. Why did many people in Mecca reject Muhammad's ideas at first?
13. List the Five Pillars of Islam and explain their significance.
14. How did early Muslims view and treat Jews and Christians?

SECTION 2 (pages 238–241)
The Spread of Islam

15. List three reasons why the "rightly guided" caliphs were so successful in spreading Islam.
16. Summarize the main reasons for the split between the Sunni and the Shi'a.
17. Why did trade flourish under the Abbasids?

SECTION 3 (pages 242–247)
Muslim Achievement

18. In what ways did urban life in Muslim lands reflect Muslim culture?
19. Explain why Muslim scholars were so productive, particularly in the areas of mathematics, science, and medicine.
20. How did the art and the architecture of the Muslims differ from that of other cultures you have studied?

---

conducting experiments in laboratory settings. They had access to information from many cultures.

20. It was inspired by Islam. Since Islam forbade the depiction of living beings, artists focused on abstract forms and calligraphy. Architecture reflected the culture of people in each area, and thus varied from place to place.

Interact *with* History

Possible Responses: Print media (modern books, magazines, newspapers), television, radio, Internet, audio or video recordings.

CRITICAL THINKING

1. ISLAM AND OTHER CULTURES

How did the development of Islam influence the blending of cultures in the region where Europe, Africa, and Asia come together? Consider ways that Islam encouraged or discouraged interaction among people of various cultures.

2. ISLAM'S EXPANSION

THEME EMPIRE BUILDING Create a time line listing the five most important events in the development and expansion of Islam between 570 and 1200. Explain the significance of each selection and why you left other important dates off the time line.

3. RELIGIOUS DUTIES

In what way did the religious duty of prayer affect the lives of Muslims everywhere?

4. ANALYZING PRIMARY SOURCES

Abd al-Latif, a legal and medical scholar who lived in Baghdad in the late 1100s and early 1200s, urged young people to become scholars. Among his suggestions is one urging people to learn history. Read the paragraph and answer the questions below it.

A VOICE FROM THE PAST
One should read histories, study biographies and the experiences of nations. By doing this, it will be as though, in his short life space, he lived contemporaneously with peoples of the past, was on intimate terms with them, and knew the good and the bad among them. . . . You should model your conduct on that of the early Muslims. Therefore, read the biography of the Prophet, study his deeds and concerns, follow in his footsteps, and try your utmost to imitate him.

ABD AL-LATIF, quoted in *A History of the Arab Peoples*

- Why does al-Latif advocate studying history?

- Why does he want people to study the life of Muhammad?

- Do you agree with him about the importance of studying history? Explain. What about studying about Muhammad? Or other significant leaders? Explain your answer.

CHAPTER ACTIVITIES

1. LIVING HISTORY: **Unit Portfolio Project**

THEME RELIGIOUS AND ETHICAL SYSTEMS Your unit portfolio project focuses on how religious and ethical systems affected all aspects of the lives of people at this time. For Chapter 10, you might use one of the following ideas to add to your portfolio:

- Create a poster showing the Five Pillars of Islam. Draw, trace, or photocopy images that demonstrate the responsibilities of believers. Add notes to clarify these responsibilities.

- With several other students, create a talk show with members representing various religions—a Hindu, a Buddhist, a Jew, a Christian, and a Muslim. Discuss the issue of leading an ethical or proper life based on one's religious beliefs. Present the talk show to the class or videotape it for presentation.

- Write a letter to Muhammad, describing for him what happened in the centuries immediately following his death and telling about his legacy today.

2. CONNECT TO TODAY: **Cooperative Learning**

THEME CULTURAL INTERACTION Between 600 and 1200, Islam provided a powerful force of unity, eventually linking lands from Spain to Iran. Islam became established in many lands. Work with a team to create maps and charts showing countries where Muslims live in our world.

 Using the Internet or almanacs, do research to find the countries in which Islam is practiced today.

- Using a world map, identify by colors the countries of the world where Muslims can be found as a part of the culture. Devise a color code that shows countries where Islam spread between 600 and 1200.

3. INTERPRETING A TIME LINE

Revisit the Unit time line on pages 228–229. In the events for Chapter 10, find the date for the establishment of the House of Wisdom. What event was occurring about the same time in Europe? Which other areas experienced contact with the Muslims?

FOCUS ON CHARTS

The Muslim culture spread to Europe and the Americas. Here are some countries in those regions with Muslim populations.

- Which nations have a population of Muslims that is similar to that of the United States in terms of percentage?

- Which nations have approximately the same population of Muslims in actual numbers?

Connect to History
- Why is the percentage figure for Spain surprising?

Source: *The Cambridge Illustrated History of the Islamic World*

Muslim Population, 1990s		
Country	Population	% of Total Population
Europe		
Albania	2,275,000	70.0
Bulgaria	1,200,000	13.0
France	3,500,000	6.1
Germany	1,700,000	2.1
Spain	300,000	0.8
United Kingdom	1,500,000	2.7
Americas		
Argentina	370,000	1.1
Brazil	500,000	0.3
Canada	350,000	1.3
Guyana	130,000	13.0
Surinam	150,000	30.0
USA	6,000,000	2.4

The Muslim World **249**

A Global View

A Global View

Teaching Strategies

World Religions: A Global View presents an overview of some of the world's major religions in a contemporary context, showing religion as an enduring and vital part of our modern world. For historical information related to each religion, see the Chapter Connection references throughout.

These pages may be usefully presented at the beginning of a course to give students a sense of the contemporary practice of the religions before they study the religions' historical development. Or the pages for each religion may be presented as the religion is introduced in the text. World Religions can also be presented as a contemporary overview after Islam, the last major faith to develop, is treated (Chapter 10).

To students who wonder why Confucianism is distinguished from the "five major religions," you might explain that because of its strong emphasis on ethical activity in this world, Confucianism is considered by some to be a philosophy rather than a religion.

The Study of Religions

Encourage students to examine each religion on its own terms and not to judge it by the standards of other religions. You might explain to students that this approach may involve trying to deal in a nonbiased fashion with concepts that run counter to their own beliefs.

You may wish to ask the class to go beyond the study of the five major religions presented here. You might divide the class into groups and assign each group another religious tradition to study. Groups could then present the results of their research to the class.

Religion is defined as an organized system of beliefs, ceremonies, practices, and worship that centers on one or more gods. As numerous chapters in this book explain, religion has had a significant impact on world history. Throughout the centuries, religion has guided the beliefs and actions of millions around the globe. It has brought people together. But it has also torn them apart.

Religion continues to be a dominant force throughout the world—affecting everything from what people wear to how they behave. There are thousands of religions in the world. The following pages concentrate on five major religions, as well as Confucianism. They examine some of the characteristics and rituals that make these religions similar as well as unique. They also present some of each religion's sects and denominations.

North America

2%
2%
11%
85%

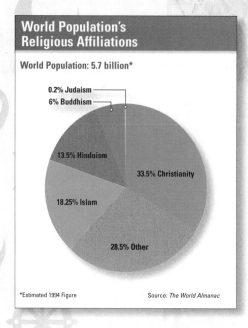

World Population's Religious Affiliations

World Population: 5.7 billion*

0.2% Judaism
6% Buddhism
13.5% Hinduism
33.5% Christianity
18.25% Islam
28.5% Other

*Estimated 1994 Figure   Source: *The World Almanac*

Latin America

11%
89%

Books Bowker, John. *World Religions: The Great Faiths Explored and Explained.* New York: DK Publishing, 1997. An amply illustrated overview of world religions, including ancient and native religions.

Clarke, Peter B., ed. *The World's Religions: Understanding the Living Faiths.* Pleasantville: Reader's Digest, 1993. Religions from historical and contemporary perspectives.

Osborne, Mary Pope. *One World, Many Religions: The Ways We Worship.* New York: Knopf, 1996. A discussion of seven major world religions, with bibliography.

Videos *Beliefs and Believers.* RMI Media Productions, 1992. Twenty-four one-hour videos dealing with myth, doctrine, ritual, and ethics in world religions.

Faith and Belief: Five Major World Religions. Knowledge Unlimited, 1992. Origins and beliefs of Hinduism, Buddhism, Judaism, Christianity, and Buddhism.

CD-ROM *Religions of the World.* Yorkshire International Thomson Multimedia, 1995. Worship, scriptures, artifacts, festivals, and sacred buildings of eight world religions. Over 1,000 graphics. Available from McDougal Littell.

Europe

2.5%
15.5%
82%

Commonwealth of Independent States (Former USSR)

15%
38%
19%
28%

Israel

2%
2%
11%
85%

China*

1%
2%
6%
91%

Southwest Asia

2%
2%
96%

Africa

10%
41%
49%

India

1%
2%
3%
11%
83%

Southeast Asia

6%
9%
15%
42%
28%

Religious Affiliation

- ■ **Christian**
- ■ **Muslim**
- ■ **Hindu**
- ■ **Buddhist**
- ■ **Jewish**
- ■ **Other**
- ■ **Officially Nonreligious***

*Communist China is officially atheist (disbelieving in the existence of God). Unofficially, the Chinese practice a number of belief systems, including Buddhism, Taoism, Confucianism, and a variety of folk religions.

World Religions **251**

Religious Affiliation

You may wish to stress to your students that the percentages presented here are based on estimates of the numbers of people affiliated with the religions. The percentages are derived from official census figures, which may contain some inaccuracies because of flawed sampling methods and the political agendas of the reporting countries. The figures do, however, give a reasonable picture of the religious beliefs of the world's people, based on the best data available.

Some interested students may wish to investigate possible inaccuracies in current population estimates. Information might be obtained through a local library, a local census bureau office, or population sites on the World Wide Web.

"Officially Nonreligious"

In certain countries, such as Communist China and the former Soviet Union, the governments are or have been officially antireligious. As a result, the official counting of religious and nonreligious citizens may be biased in favor of the nonreligious, in an effort to demonstrate popular support for the government policy.

In addition, social pressures against religious observance in such countries often lead people to hide their true beliefs. Thus, the category "Officially Nonreligious" must be regarded skeptically.

 RELIGIONS OF THE WORLD CD-ROM
Overview

Logical-Mathematical Learners
You might ask some students to convert the percentages for each religion to actual world population figures. (To do so, students must multiply 5.7 billion by the percentage for each religion.) *Answers: Christianity—1,909,500,000; Islam—1,040,250,000; Hinduism—769,500,000; Buddhism—342,000,000;* Judaism—11,400,000; Other—1,624,500,000

Ask students which of the two forms of the data is more meaningful to them and why. They might also discuss situations in which it is preferable to express data as percentages or as population numbers.

Mathematics You might ask students to create bargraphs showing the data presented in the pie charts, using the vertical axis to display percentages from 0% to 100% and the bars to represent each major religion, either in the world or in a specific region. These graphs may be plotted manually, on graph paper, or by means of one of the many available computer graphing programs.

When students have created their bar graphs, ask them to compare the pie charts and the bar graphs as means for displaying data. Have them describe what they think are the strong points of each format.

Buddhism

Sects

Buddhists are united in their respect for the Buddha and in their search for nirvana (enlightenment and liberation from suffering). But various groups understand the Buddha's message in somewhat different ways.

Theravada Buddhism is marked by an effort to stay as close as possible to the Buddha's recorded teachings. The Theravada ideal is the arhat, a saint who reaches nirvana alone. The arhat's pursuit of nirvana is carried out in a monastery, away from the world.

Mahayana Buddhism is more accepting of change and of the world. It considers reaching nirvana as an effort of all believers working together. The Mahayana ideal is the bodhisattva, who delays personal nirvana and returns to the world to help others attain nirvana.

Mantrayana Buddhism gets its name from mantras—phrases recited over and over in prayer or meditation. Elements of Mantrayana practices can be found in both Theravada and Mahayana traditions.

Worship

The most common form of Buddhist worship is meditation (deep thought or reflection) before sacred images of the Buddha. Believers may meditate before shrines in their homes or in temples. They may offer gifts of food, flowers, or candles out of respect for or worship of the Buddha. (Some Buddhists consider the Buddha a god, though he himself did not.) Both in temples and at home, worshipers burn incense and light candles before images of the Buddha. The light of the candles recalls the light of Buddha's wisdom.

Buddhism

Buddhism has been a dominant religious, cultural, and social force throughout Asia. Today, most Buddhists live in Sri Lanka, East and Southeast Asia, and Japan. Buddhism consists of several different sects. A religious sect is a group within a religion that distinguishes itself by one or more unique beliefs. Buddhists are united in their belief of the Buddha's teachings, known as the dharma.

Major Buddhist Sects

Theravada   Mahayana

Buddhism

Mantrayana

Chapter Connection
For a more in-depth examination of Buddhism, including a closer look at its origins and beliefs, see pages 64–66 of Chapter 3, and page 177 of Chapter 7.

Worship

Central to the Buddhist religion is its creator, Siddhartha Gautama, who became known as the Buddha, or "enlightened one." Statues of the Buddha, such as this one in Japan, appear in many forms and sizes throughout Asia. The Buddha preached that the key to happiness was detachment from all worldly goods and desires. This was achieved by following the Eightfold Path and the Middle Way, a life between earthly desires and extreme forms of self-denial.

ICONS, TEXTS & SYMBOLS

Wheel of the Law
The Buddha is said to have "set in motion the wheel of the dharma" during his first sermon. His teaching often is symbolized by a wheel.

The Spread of Buddhism Two countries, India and China, have been largely responsible for the missionary work that has converted millions of Asians to Buddhism. The adoption of Theravada or Mahayana Buddhism by Asian countries has largely depended on whether they were introduced to Buddhism by missionaries from India or from China. Theravada missionaries from India made numerous converts in Sri Lanka, Burma, Laos, Thailand, and Cambodia. Chinese Mahayanists carried their form of Buddhism to Korea, Japan, and Tibet.

Coming-of-Age Ceremonies In countries where Theravada Buddhism predominates, many boys and girls go through ceremonies in which they are recognized as adults. The ceremonies, intended for children between 8 and 12 years of age, temporarily initiate them as novice monks and nuns. Dressed as princes and princesses, like the Prince Gautama, the children walk in a procession to a monastery, along with musicians and guests. There, they remove their royal clothes and have their heads shaved—renouncing the world. Boys may stay with the monks for a day or for several years, depending on whether they want a monastic education.

Leadership

Those who dedicate their entire life to the teachings of the Buddha are known as Buddhist monks and nuns. In many Buddhist sects, monks are expected to lead a life of poverty, meditation, and study. Here, Buddhist monks in Thailand carry what are known as begging bowls. To learn humility, monks must beg for food and money. They are not allowed to speak to or notice their donors. Any communication with donors is believed to lessen the spirituality of the act.

Ritual

Women in Rangoon, Myanmar, sweep the ground so that monks can avoid stepping on and killing any insects. Many Buddhists believe in rebirth. Rebirth is the notion that human beings, after death, are reborn and continue to exist in one form or another. This also applies to animals, birds, fish, and insects. Buddhists believe that all living beings possess the potential for spiritual growth—and the possibility of rebirth as humans. Because of this, Buddhists take special care not to kill any living being.

The Three Cardinal Faults
This image depicts what Buddhists consider the three cardinal faults of humanity: greed (the pig); hatred (the snake); and delusion (the rooster).

Sacred Writings
This palm leaf is part of an 11th-century text called the *Perfection of Wisdom Sutra*, which contains some 8,000 verses. The text, written in Sanskrit, relates the life and teachings of the Buddha.

Leadership

There are significant religious and social differences in the leadership styles of Theravada and Mahayana Buddhism.

Theravada Buddhists try to follow the Buddha's own ideas on what an ideal society should be like. In his view, the king, the monks, and the laity (ordinary people) had important responsibilities to one another. For example, monks guided the spiritual development of the community. Laypeople, in return, had to provide support to the monks in the form of money and food.

Mahayana Buddhists tend to downplay Buddhism as a social force and concentrate more on its spiritual features. As a result, Mahayana clergy play a more limited political and social role than do Theravada monks.

Ritual

One of the most important symbols in Buddhist ritual and art is the lotus flower, which has acquired deep religious meaning over the centuries. The lotus flower takes root in mud but blossoms on the surface of tranquil water. Through the lotus, Buddhists are reminded that the spiritual life of a believer can blossom in enlightenment even though it is rooted in the impurity of the world and the heart.

References to the lotus occur in early Buddhist scriptures. As a result of the long tradition about the lotus, worshipers often offer lotus flowers at shrines and temples. Festival days, such as the Buddha's birthday (the day of the first full moon in May) provide special occasions for offering the lotus.

 RELIGIONS OF THE WORLD CD-ROM
Buddhism

CONNECTIONS ACROSS THE CURRICULUM

Zen Buddhism and the Arts Zen is a form of Mahayana Buddhism that developed in Japan around the 12th century. Zen is characterized by the directness of its teaching. It favors direct experience gained through rigorous sitting meditation (zazen) over philosophical speculation about the Buddha's message. Through this meditation, it is thought, a person can achieve sudden insight into reality, called satori, and ultimately nirvana. Zen teachers often use seemingly nonsensical questions, called koans.

Koans are intended to short-circuit the thinking process and bring students to satori. One famous koan is "What is the sound of one hand clapping?"

In the arts, Zen is most famous for its haiku poems and sand gardens. Haiku are short 17-syllable poems that are intended to capture the pure impression of a moment, unfiltered by thought. For example, this is how the 17th-century poet Matsuo Basho described a sensitive encounter with summer and the brevity of

life: "So soon to die, / and no sign of it is showing— / locust cry."

In a Zen sand garden, oddly shaped stones covered with moss are surrounded by sand raked in straight lines and curves. Such a garden shows the purity and simplicity in the heart of a true practitioner of Zen. Students may wish to bring in pictures of Zen sand gardens and show them to the class.

Teacher's Edition 253

Christianity

Sects

There are many more Protestant groups than could have been mentioned on this page. Others include Congregationalist churches, the United Church of Christ, the Mennonites, the Quakers, the Seventh Day Adventists, the Christian Scientists, and the Jehovah's Witnesses. Each of the more than 250 Christian denominations has its own teachings, history, and organization.

Some Christians look sadly on the divisions in their religion, since such divisions contradict Jesus' wish "that they [Jesus' followers] may all be one." More recently, there has been a tendency to accept diversity—for example, in organizations such as the National Council of Churches.

Some students may wish to study and discuss with the rest of the class a Christian tradition of interest or importance to them.

Ritual

The Christian calendar contains important days (sometimes called feast days or holy days) that give a religious dimension to the year and recall important events in Christian history. In many traditions, the most important of these days are Christmas, Easter, and Pentecost (marking the descent of the Holy Spirit to inspire Jesus' closest followers, called the Apostles). Many Christians also observe religious seasons. For example, Advent and Lent are seasons of reflection and self-denial.

You may wish to ask students to pick an important day or season of the Christian calendar, study its rituals, and discuss them with the rest of the class. Photos or videos can enhance the discussion.

Christianity

Christianity is the largest religion in the world, with about 1.9 billion followers. It is based on the life and teachings of Jesus Christ. Most Christians are members of one of three major groups: Roman Catholic, Protestant, or Eastern Orthodox. Christianity teaches the existence of only one God. All Christians regard Jesus as the son of God. They believe that Jesus entered the world and died to save humanity from sin. Christians believe that they reach salvation by following the teachings of Jesus Christ.

Major Christian Sects

Eastern Orthodox   Roman Catholic

Christianity

AME   Protestant   Baptist

Lutheran   Methodist

Episcopal   Pentecostal

Mormon   Church of God

Presbyterian

*There are 30 Protestant denominations of over 400,000 members in each in the United States alone.

Chapter Connection
For more about Christianity, see pages 153–57 of Chapter 6. To learn about the Protestant and Catholic Reformations, see sections 3 and 4 of Chapter 17.

Ritual

Each year, hundreds of thousands of Christians from all over the world visit the Basilica of Guadalupe in northern Mexico City. The church is considered the holiest in Mexico. It is near the site where the Virgin Mary, the mother of Jesus Christ, is said to have appeared twice in 1531. Out of deep respect for Mary, some pilgrims approach the holy cathedral on their knees.

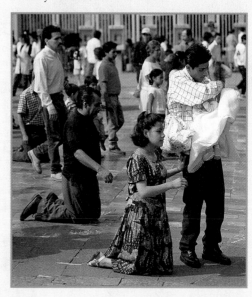

ICONS, TEXTS & SYMBOLS

The Cross
The cross, a symbol of the crucifixion of Jesus Christ, represents Jesus' love for humanity in dying for its sins.

TEACHING OPTIONS   **CUSTOMIZING FOR SPECIAL NEEDS**   **EXPLORING PRIMARY SOURCES**

Gifted and Talented Students: Comparing Water is essential to the Christian rite of baptism. It symbolizes the washing away of the sin that every human being is born with (Original Sin) and a birth into a new life.

Ask students to do research about the role of water in the ceremonies of a non-Christian religion, such as Hinduism. Have them explain the function of water in that religion and compare it with water's role in Christian ceremonies, especially baptism. Students may go beyond world religions to other traditions (Native American, Polynesian, Australian Aborigine, Maori, Inuit, African, etc.).

And Jesus came and said to them, "All authority in heaven and on earth has been given to me. Go therefore and make disciples of all nations, . . . teaching them to obey everything that I have commanded you. And remember, I am with you always, to the end of the age." (Matthew 28:18–20)

These words of Jesus appear at the end of the Gospel of Matthew. The writer recorded them as Jesus' final advice to his followers. Ask students what effect these words may have had on the spread of Christianity as a world religion.

Worship

Christians worship in many different ways. Pictured here is a Protestant worship service in the United States. Most Protestant services share several basic features. The service includes praying, singing, reading from the Bible, and a sermon by a minister. The laity, or church members who are not ministers, participate extensively in the service. Some services include baptism and communion.

Leadership

In some Christian churches, the person who performs services in the local church is known as a priest. Shown here is a priest of the Ethiopian Christian Church holding a picture of the Virgin Mary with her infant, Jesus. These priests, like those in other Christian sects, perform such duties as presiding over the liturgy, as well as over marriages and funerals. Rules of behavior for priests differ throughout the Christian world. For example, priests with the Ethiopian Church may marry, while Roman Catholic priests may not.

The Bible

The Bible is the most sacred book of the Christian religion. It is divided into two major parts. The Old Testament focuses on Jewish history and religion. The New Testament describes the teachings of Jesus Christ.

A Cross of Palms

Palm Sunday marks the beginning of Holy Week in the Christian calendar. On this day, palms are distributed in remembrance of the palms laid before Jesus' feet as he entered Jerusalem days before his death.

World Religions **255**

Worship

Perhaps the most important rite of worship in Christianity is Holy Communion. This is a commemoration of Jesus' actions and words during his Last Supper with his disciples, when he identified bread and wine with his body and blood.

Christian denominations differ in their ideas about the meaning of communion. In Eastern Orthodoxy, Roman Catholicism, and some Protestant denominations, the communion service is viewed as an actual reenactment of Christ's sacrifice of his life for the human race. The bread and wine are considered to be in some sense Christ's actual body and blood.

Many Protestants, however, look upon communion as a remembrance of Christ's death rather than a reenactment of it. These Protestants differ in their beliefs about the nature of the bread and wine.

Leadership

In most Christian churches, a group of clergy looks after the spiritual welfare of believers. They preside at worship services, baptize people, perform marriages, and preside at funerals.

Leaders of local Orthodox, Roman Catholic, and Episcopalian churches are called priests. These priests are granted special authority to administer the Christian sacraments.

In many Protestant groups, leaders of local churches are called ministers. A minister's calling and education give him or her the right to preside at worship. Nonetheless, Protestants tend to stress the equality of Christians, so the differences in the roles of the clergy and the people are less important than in other Christian groups. In fact, some Protestants—like the Quakers—have no ministers.

 RELIGIONS OF THE WORLD CD-ROM
Christianity

CONNECTIONS ACROSS TIME AND PLACE

Spread of Christianity Around the World Over the centuries, Christians have converted people throughout the world. Motivation for Christians' missionary work came from Jesus himself, who asked his followers to carry the faith to the whole world.

The first missionary efforts are recorded in the Acts of the Apostles and the letters of Saint Paul. Early missionaries spread throughout the Roman Empire. As Germanic peoples moved into the Empire,

Christians made efforts to convert them. Later, Byzantine missionaries worked in Eastern Europe among Slavic peoples. During the Middle Ages in the West, work continued among Vikings and Arabs.

The 16th century brought Catholics and Protestants to Africa, Asia, and the Americas. Besides religion, missionaries also brought education and Western ways of living. They also provided health care and some relief from poverty.

Students may wish to choose periods of history and study the work of prominent Christian missionaries, such as Saint Paul, Saints Cyril and Methodius, Albert Schweitzer, and Mother Teresa. They could examine the missionaries' methods and how those methods affected non-Christians. Students may discuss whether they agree or disagree with the missionaries' approaches.

Hinduism

Sects

Followers of Shaktism worship the supreme goddess of Hinduism, Shakti ("energy" or "force"). She may take on merciful aspects—such as Lakshmi, the partner of Vishnu—or destructive forms, such as Kali the Destroyer.

Hindus who follow Vaishnavism pay special devotion to Vishnu, the preserver.

Followers of Shaivism are devoted to the worship of Shiva, the destroyer. They seek to rid their souls of earthly bonds to attain "the nature of Shiva."

Reform Hinduism arose in the 19th century as a response to contact with Islam and the West. Reformers advocated strict monotheism, denounced statues and the caste system, and supported rights for women and Western forms of education.

Ritual

Hindus worship in both temples and at home—as individuals and families, not as congregations. A temple normally contains a principal shrine dedicated to an important god or goddess.

A temple usually also contains numerous other shrines, each devoted to a particular god. Individuals devoted to particular divinities perform their worship at those gods' altars. Hindus do not feel that they are worshiping the images of the gods; they believe that the gods themselves inhabit the images. Temples are also the scene of annual festivals celebrating high-points in the lives of the gods.

At home, worship takes place around a family shrine, called a *puja*. The shrine is dedicated to a god or goddess that is part of the family tradition.

Hinduism

Hinduism, the world's oldest religion, is the major religion of India. It also has followers in Indonesia, as well as in parts of Africa, Europe, and the Western Hemisphere. Hinduism is a collection of religious beliefs that developed over thousands of years. Hindus worship several gods, which represent different forms of Brahman. Brahman is the most divine spirit in the Hindu religion. Hinduism, like Buddhism, stresses that persons reach true enlightenment and happiness only after they free themselves from their earthly desires. Followers of Hinduism achieve this goal through worship, the attainment of knowledge, and a lifetime of virtuous acts.

Major Hindu Sects

Shaktism

Reform Hinduism

Hinduism

Vaishnavites

Shaivites

Chapter Connection
For a closer look at the origins and beliefs of Hinduism, see pages 62–63 of Chapter 3, and pages 177–78 of Chapter 7.

Ritual
Each year, thousands of Hindus make a pilgrimage to India's Ganges River. The Ganges is considered a sacred site in the Hindu religion. Most Hindus come to bathe in the water, an act they believe will cleanse and purify them. The sick and disabled come in the belief that the holy water might cure their ailments. After most Hindus die, they are cremated. Some then have their ashes cast into the Ganges. According to traditional belief, this assures them an entry into Paradise.

ICONS, TEXTS & SYMBOLS

The Sacred Om
The sound *OM*, or *AUM*, represented here, is the most sacred syllable for Hindus. It often is used in prayers.

Om For many centuries, Hindus everywhere have revered the syllable *Om* as the most sacred of mantras. *Om* actually consists of three sounds (ah-oo-m). The sounds represent several groups of three that have special importance for Hindus. First of all, they represent the dimensions of earth, air, and heaven.

Next, they refer to the three most important Hindu gods: Brahma, Vishnu, and Shiva. Finally, the sounds symbolize the three collections of the Vedas: Rig, Sama, and Yajur.

Om is used in meditation, at the beginning and end of prayers, and at the beginning of sacred texts.

Linguistic Learners Over the centuries, Hinduism has coexisted comfortably with religions as diverse as Buddhism, Jainism, Islam, and Christianity. This fact points to an idea that is clearly expressed in Hindu tradition: that other religions are different paths to the same God.

Ramakrishna, a 19th-century Hindu

saint, stated, "God has made different religions to suit different aspirations, times, and countries. All doctrines are only so many paths; but a path is by no means God Himself." Hindu thinkers have taught that when the heart and mind are truly enlightened, an understanding of religions' essential unity will follow.

Leadership

Gurus, or spiritual teachers, like the one shown here, play a major role in spreading Hindu beliefs. These holy men are believed to have had the gods' words revealed to them. They interpret and provide insight into the religion. Gurus also travel to villages throughout the country and teach the ways of Hinduism to those villagers who cannot read.

Celebration

Each spring, Hindus in India celebrate the festival of Holi. This festival is a tribute to Shiva, one of the leading gods of Hinduism. Shiva is considered to be beyond good and evil. Hindus call him the Destroyer because he occasionally destroys the world in order to recreate it. The Holi festival honors Shiva with loud and colorful parades in some parts of India. In one of the more dramatic rituals, shown here, a throng gathers in a sacred temple in the village of Nandgaon. There, they are showered with colored powder and dyed water.

The Vedas

The Vedas are the oldest Hindu scriptures—and are older than the sacred writings of any other major religion. They contain prayers and hymns, as well as works of philosophy.

Brahma

This statue represents Brahma, creator of the universe. Brahma, Vishnu, and Shiva are the three main gods of Hinduism. Vishnu is the preserver of the universe, while Shiva is its destroyer.

Leadership

Spiritual leadership in the Hindu community is the responsibility of the Brahmin class. Because of good works performed in previous lives, Brahmins have earned a karma that entitles them to be born in the highest social class, or caste.

Brahmins take on the roles of priests, philosophers, artists, and teachers in Hindu society. They are responsible for performing sacrifices in temples and for the care of the shrines of the gods. Some of the priestly sacrifices can be traced back 3,000 years.

So much is expected of Hinduism's spiritual leaders that a Brahmin who has committed a crime receives a far more severe punishment than a Shudra (a member of the lowest caste) who has committed the same crime.

Celebration

Another joyous Hindu festival is Diwali, which marks the beginning of the Hindu new year. When it gets dark, believers light many small lamps. The lights serve to frighten away demons and welcome back the god Rama, who, tradition says, was driven out of his kingdom.

A celebration focused more on the family is the ceremony of the sacred thread. It is a coming-of-age ceremony for boys in the three highest of the four castes. Sometimes, it is celebrated the day before a boy marries. The boy's father drapes a sacred thread over his son's left shoulder and under his right arm. From that moment on, the boy will wear the thread as a symbol that he is "twice born," having been born first into the world and then into the religious life.

 RELIGIONS OF THE WORLD CD-ROM
Hinduism

257

CUSTOMIZING FOR SPECIAL NEEDS

***Gifted and Talented Students:** Pilgrimages*
Pilgrimages are journeys to places that are considered to possess special spiritual power owing to their connection with gods, saints, or events of religious importance. By visiting these holy places, believers are thought to become more holy themselves.

During the more than 3,000 years of their religion's existence, the Hindus of India have set apart between

58,000 and 64,000 sites in their country as *tirthas,* or places of pilgrimage.

After the building of railroads in India, Hindus began taking 10-week "all-India pilgrimages." These take pilgrims to holy sites in the north, in the south, and on the eastern and western coasts of the country.

Interested students may wish to compare the traditions of pilgrimage in Hinduism and another

religion (e.g., Buddhism, Christianity, Islam, or Judaism). In a report to the rest of the class, they could compare the two religions' ideas about who must or should go on pilgrimage, as well as the locations and histories of the religions' places of pilgrimage and the religious rituals associated with those places. Visuals of the places and the rituals might aid the discussion.

Islam

Sects

The split between Sunni and Shi'a Muslims arose from a dispute over who should succeed Muhammad as political leader of the Muslim community. Two theories emerged as to who should lead Muslims. The Sunni sect believed that any religious leader who had demonstrated a deep understanding of Muslim tradition had earned the right to leadership. In contrast, the Shi'a sect believed that only those directly related to the Prophet through Ali, Muhammad's cousin, could legitimately rule. Today, the Shi'a tradition is concentrated mainly in Iran, while Sunni Islam predominates in the rest of the Islamic world.

Celebration

The end of Ramadan fasting is celebrated by a major Islamic holiday called Eid al-Fitr. The celebration begins with a worship service that may be held in a mosque or a public place designed to hold a large number of people.

Later, the site of the celebration switches to the home. There, many festive foods that were not eaten during Ramadan, including sweets, are shared with family members and friends. The celebration may continue for three days or longer in Muslim countries. To help those less fortunate, many Muslims contribute money that allows the poor to share in the joy of the season.

The other great Islamic religious holiday, called Eid al-Adha, takes place in the last month of the Islamic calendar. Eid al-Adha commemorates the faithfulness of the prophet Abraham, who was willing to sacrifice his own son to obey God's command.

Islam

Islam is a religion based on the teachings of the prophet Muhammad. Followers of Islam, known as Muslims, live throughout the world. They are concentrated from southwest to central Asia and parts of Africa. Islam also has many followers in Southeast Asia. Islam teaches the existence of only one God, called *Allah* in the Arabic language. Muslims believe in all prophets of Judaism and Christianity. They show their devotion by performing lifelong acts of worship known as the Five Pillars of Islam. These include faith, prayer, almsgiving (charity), fasting, and pilgrimage. Islam affects nearly every aspect of Muslims' lives.

Major Islamic Sects

Sunni

Islam

Shi'a

Chapter Connection

For a closer look at Islam, including the rise and spread of Islam, and significant Muslim achievements, see Chapter 10.

Celebration

During the sacred month known as Ramadan, Muslims fast, or abstain from food and drink, from dawn to sunset. They do this as a sign of obedience, humility, and self-control. The fasting traditionally ends with eating a few dates and milk or water, followed by the sunset prayer. These foods accompany the other dishes that families, such as the one shown here, eat each night during the month.

The most important night of Ramadan is called the Night of Power (Laylat al-Qadr). This is believed to be the night the angel Gabriel, the messenger of God, first spoke to Muhammad.

ICONS, TEXTS & SYMBOLS

Crescent Moon
The crescent moon has become a familiar symbol for Islam. It may be related to the new moon that begins each month in the Islamic lunar calendar, which orders religious life for Muslims.

Linguistic Learners Islam has no ordained clergy. Instead, scholars and spiritual leaders emerge after they have shown evidence of superior learning or judgment. Islamic scholars may specialize in one or several areas of religious knowledge and practice. An *alim* pursues in-depth studies of the Qur'an and the

recorded sayings of Muhammad, called *hadith*. A *faqih* decides cases and makes judgments based on guidance from the Qur'an and other Islamic traditions. A *hafiz* memorizes the Qur'un, while a *qari* specializes in chanting texts from Islam's sacred book.

You might ask some linguistic learners to organize these names and functions in a chart and explain them to the class.

Science: *The Muslim Calendar*
Unlike the solar calendar used in the West, the Muslim calendar is lunar—that is, based on the phases of the moon. The lunar year is about 11 days shorter than the solar year. As a result, Muslim dates "jump backward" 11 days each year with respect to the dates of the Gregorian calendar used in the

West, so that during a period of 32.5 solar years, a Muslim date moves through all four seasons.

Students may wish to discuss what would happen if American holidays moved through the seasons. How might celebrations of a holiday like the Fourth of July be different in different seasons?

Worship

At least once in their lifetime, all Muslims who are physically and financially able, go on hajj, or pilgrimage, to the holy city of Mecca in Saudi Arabia. There, pilgrims perform several rites, or acts of worship. One rite, shown here, is walking seven times around the Ka'aba—the house of worship that Muslims face in prayer.

The climax of the hajj is the day when millions of believers stand at a place named Arafat. There, they ask forgiveness of God on the same spot where Muhammad gave a farewell sermon.

Ritual

Five times a day Muslims throughout the world face Mecca and pray to Allah. This prayer ritual, known as Salat, occurs at dawn, noon, late afternoon, sunset, and evening. Muslims recite these prayers at work, or school, or wherever they happen to be. Pictured here are Muslims praying at an intersection in Alexandria, Egypt.

Prayer Rug
Muslims often pray by kneeling on a rug. The design of the rug includes a pointed or arch-shaped pattern. The rug must be placed so that the arch points toward Mecca.

The Qur'an
The Qur'an, the sacred book of Muslims, consists of verses grouped into 114 chapters, or surahs. The book is the spiritual guide on matters of faith and practice for all Muslims. In addition, it contains teachings that guide Muslim daily life.

World Religions **259**

Worship

The basic ceremony of formal Islamic worship is called the *salah*. In areas that have a large enough Muslim population, the *salah* takes place in a mosque. Instead of containing chairs or pews, the worship space in a mosque is a large, often carpeted area that faces toward the Ka'aba in Mecca.

Muslim men and boys are required to participate in congregational worship on Friday at noon. Because of household duties, women and girls are exempt from this responsibility. At the beginning of a formal worship service, Muslims raise their hands up to their ears and declare "Allahu Akbar" ("God is greatest").

At each stage of the ceremony, worshipers stand, bow, and touch their foreheads to the ground twice. Verses from the Qur'an are read and prayers are said in Arabic. During the service, the congregation is led by an imam. The imam is not a priest but a worship leader chosen by the congregation.

Ritual

Muslims may eat all foods except those specifically forbidden (*haram*) by the Qur'an. Foods that are *haram* include pork, blood, and the meat of animals found dead, animals of prey, and animals slaughtered in the name of any god but Allah. When slaughtering meat, a Muslim butcher pronounces the name of Allah. This tradition arose to recognize God's generosity and his work as the Creator, and meat so blessed is said to be *halal*. Since both Jews and Christians worship the same God as Muslims, Islamic law allows Muslims to eat meat slaughtered by Jews or Christians.

 RELIGIONS OF THE WORLD CD-ROM
Islam

TEACHING OPTION

CONNECTIONS ACROSS TIME AND PLACE

The Other Scriptures of Islam Muslims regard the Qur'an—the final revelation from God to the Prophet Muhammad—as the last in a centuries-long series of revelations beginning with God's message to Abraham, founder of the Jewish people. As a result, Muslims accept certain scriptures revealed to Jewish and Christian prophets as inspired by God. The scriptures, other than the Qur'an, that Muslims accept as Allah's words are
• *Suhuf* ("Scrolls"), revealed to Abraham

• *Tawrah* ("Torah"), given to Moses
• *Zabur* ("Psalms"), received by David
• *Injeel* ("Gospel"), revealed to Jesus

Accepting these previous scriptures is an essential part of Islamic faith. For Muslims, the scriptures show how God gradually revealed religious truth to humans when they were ready to receive it. Muslims' acceptance of these scriptures also demonstrates their belief that Islam is the fulfillment of the religious tradition of Jews and Christians.

As a result, Muslims consider Jews and Christians "people of the Book," because they, like Muslims, received scriptures revealed by God. You might wish to ask students how this sense of kinship with Jews and Christians might help to explain the policy of religious tolerance practiced by Muslim rulers during their almost-800-year presence in Spain.

Teacher's Edition **259**

Judaism

Sects

In the 19th century, Jews divided into three groups. The divisions were based on how closely believers followed the traditions recorded in the Torah and in commentaries on the Torah (the Talmud).

In Orthodox Judaism, believers follow traditional dietary (kosher) laws. During worship, Orthodox Jews pray in Hebrew—with men and women sitting apart. Orthodox men always cover their heads out of respect for God. Married women cover their heads with hats, scarves, or wigs.

Reform Judaism arose from efforts to adapt Judaism to life in the West. Reform Jews tend to select elements of tradition for observance and have changed some traditional practices—for example, allowing women to serve as rabbis.

Conservative Judaism represents an attempt to strike a balance between Orthodox and Reform Judaism. Conservatives balance tradition with the needs of the modern world.

Celebration

The Jewish year is marked by a series of holy days that remind Jews of their beliefs, history, and traditions.

Rosh Hashanah is a one- or two-day festival that marks the beginning of the new year in the Jewish calendar. Passover, or Pesach, lasts for seven or eight days and recalls the departure of the Jews from Egypt, where they had been enslaved.

Students may wish to read about and discuss other holy days or periods in the Jewish calendar—for example, Yom Kippur, Hanukkah, and Succoth.

Judaism

Judaism is the religion of the more than 13 million Jews throughout the world. Judaism was the first major religion to teach the existence of only one god. The basic laws and teachings of Judaism come from the Torah, the first five books of the Hebrew Bible. Judaism teaches that a person serves God by studying the Torah and living by its teachings.

Major Jewish Sects

Reform   Orthodox

Judaism

Conservative

Chapter Connection

For an historical examination of Judaism, as well as the development of the Kingdom of Israel, see pages 72–76 of Chapter 3.

Celebration

Jews celebrate a number of holidays that honor their history as well as their God. Pictured here are Jews celebrating the holiday of Purim. Purim is a festival honoring the survival of the Jews who, in the fifth century B.C., were marked for death by their Persian rulers.

The story—found in the Book of Esther in the Hebrew Bible—describes how Esther, the Jewish queen of Persia, convinced the Persian king to spare her people. Jews celebrate Purim by sending food and gifts to friends, neighbors, and the poor. In addition, they dress in costumes and hold carnivals and dances.

ICONS, TEXTS & SYMBOLS

The Star of David

The Star of David, also called the Shield of David, is the universal symbol of Judaism. The emblem refers to King David, who ruled the kingdom of Israel from about 1000–962 B.C.

TEACHING OPTIONS	MULTIPLE LEARNING STYLES	CRITICAL THINKING

Visual Learners Jewish art tends to be nonrepresentational. The law against "graven images" (statues) in the Book of Exodus (20) has discouraged the depiction of people and animals in religious art. Nevertheless, a number of European artworks depict events in Jewish history.

You could ask visually-oriented students to display artworks depicting various biblical events and to read to the class the corresponding passages in the Bible. Incidents of possible interest include the creation of the world, the sacrifice of Isaac, the finding of Moses in the bulrushes, the parting of the Red Sea, and David's battle with Goliath.

Contrasting The coming-of-age ceremonies in Judaism have parallels in other religious traditions. You might ask students to contrast the sacred-thread ceremony in Hinduism, the coming-of-age ceremonies in Buddhism, and the rite of confirmation in Christianity with Jewish traditions.

Books on world religions will provide students with material.

You might ask students to discuss what aspects of religious experience and of growing up are emphasized in each of the traditions. Ask them to point out similarities and differences among them.

Ritual

Some Jews follow strict dietary laws based on passages from the Hebrew Bible. These laws have established what is kosher, or acceptable, for Jews to eat. Kosher laws forbid the eating of animals considered unclean. These animals include pigs and shellfish.

The preparation of food is a significant part of kosher law. Animals must be killed in a certain way—a single cut across the neck made with a knife absent of nicks. This is intended to kill the animal as quickly and painlessly as possible. Before the meat is cooked, it must be drained of its blood.

There are additional kosher laws that determine everything from the preparation of food to what foods may not be eaten together. Shown here, a rabbi inspects a kitchen in the United States to ensure that it follows kosher guidelines.

Worship

Several women worship at the Western Wall—a place of prayer and pilgrimage held sacred to the Jewish people. The ancient structure formed the western wall of the courtyard of the Second Temple of Jerusalem. The Romans destroyed the temple in A.D. 70. The wall, which dates back to the second century B.C., measures about 160 feet long and about 60 feet high. Located in Jerusalem, it is also known as the Wailing Wall. This term was coined by European travelers who witnessed some Jews loudly mourning the destruction of the temple.

Yarmulke
Out of respect for God, Jewish men are not supposed to leave their head uncovered. Therefore, many Orthodox and Conservative Jews wear a skullcap known as a yarmulke, or kippah.

The Torah Scroll
During a synagogue service, the Torah scroll is lifted, while the congregation declares: "This is the Law which Moses set before the children of Israel."

Ritual

Significant events in the life of a Jew are marked by ritual.

One of the most important ceremonies in the life of a Jewish boy is that of his coming of age. At the age of 13, a boy accepts the full responsibilities of an adult in his religion and community. He becomes a bar mitzvah ("son of the commandments") by going through a bar mitzvah service in a synagogue. During the ceremony, he reads aloud from the Torah.

A girl can have a bat mitzvah ("daughter of the commandments") ceremony at the age of 12 or 13. The ritual recognizes her as a Jewish woman.

Some students may wish to study more deeply the traditions of coming of age and marriage in the Jewish faith. If possible, they should attend one or both of these services and discuss their experience with the class.

Worship

Jewish houses of worship are called synagogues (often *temples* in the Reform and Conservative traditions). A synagogue is usually built so that the congregation faces toward Jerusalem during worship. An ark, or cabinet, at the front of the synagogue contains the scroll of the Torah, the most sacred books of the Hebrew Bible. A lamp called the eternal light hangs before the ark, symbolizing the eternal presence of God.

A rabbi ("teacher") reads prayers and passages of the Bible during the service. He or she also delivers the sermon. During worship, the rabbi is assisted by a cantor (or musical leader) who chants prayers.

Playing recordings of Jewish sacred music might help students appreciate the Eastern origins and atmosphere of Jewish worship.

 RELIGIONS OF THE WORLD CD-ROM
Judaism

TEACHING OPTION | **CONNECTIONS ACROSS THE CURRICULUM**

Science, the Arts, Ideas In the 19th and 20th centuries, the magnitude of Jewish scientists', artists', and thinkers' influence on thought and creative expression in the Western world far exceeded the magnitude of the Jewish population. Karl Marx, Sigmund Freud, and Albert Einstein are just three examples of Jewish thinkers who permanently changed the course of thought in the West and the world.

Karl Marx created the theory of communism. Marx's ideas motivated others to rethink economic relations in the capitalist societies of Western Europe. Sigmund Freud founded the technique of psychoanalysis. His theory of the unconscious revealed a dimension of the mind that most people had never suspected. The theory of relativity formulated by the physicist Albert Einstein overturned the Newtonian view of the

universe that had dominated scientific thought in the West since the 1600s.

You might ask students to study and discuss in class great Jewish figures in the sciences and arts. A general history of the Jewish people should highlight such creative geniuses as Marc Chagall (painting), Milton Friedman (economics), Leonard Bernstein (music), and Saul Bellow (literature).

Confucianism

Golden Rule

Several religious thinkers and philosophers have formulated rules of conduct similar to Confucius' Golden Rule. The most famous is Jesus' statement in the Gospel of Matthew: "In everything, do to others what you would have them do to you."

The rule may be framed positively (Jesus' "Do to others . . .") or negatively (Confucius' "Do not do unto others . . ."). The moral content of the rule, however, remains essentially the same. It urges us to see other people as similar to ourselves—a moral breakthrough in the ancient world.

Some students may wish to discuss the implications of the positive and negative versions of the Golden Rule—for example, with regard to performing or avoiding actions and to seeing actions from one's own or another person's point of view.

Celebration

In celebrating Confucius' birthday, followers of the philosopher are also rejoicing in his 1,500 years of influence in Asia. Confucius was born about 551 B.C. in northeastern China. By the age of 3, he had lost his father; but his impoverished mother instilled a love of learning in him, and he eventually became a successful teacher.

One way Confucius tried to spread his ethical views in China was by holding government office. China's leaders, however, found his honesty and frankness to be impractical, even dangerous.

Despite his political setbacks, Confucius' reputation as a man of conscience and thought attracted many followers. Since then, his thoughts have influenced millions.

Confucianism

A look at the world's major religions would not be complete without an examination of Confucianism. With no clergy, or gods to worship, Confucianism is not considered a religion in the traditional sense. However, this ancient philosophy guides the actions and beliefs of millions of Chinese and other peoples of the East. Thus, it often is viewed as a major religion.

Confucianism is a way of life based on the teachings of the Chinese scholar Confucius. It stresses social and civic responsibility. It also provides people with an ethical system to follow. Over the centuries, however, Confucianism has greatly influenced people's spiritual beliefs as well. While East Asians declare themselves to follow any one of a number of religions, many also claim to be Confucian.

"Do not do unto others what you would not want others to do unto you."

CONFUCIUS'S GOLDEN RULE

Chapter Connection
For a closer look at the life and teachings of Confucius, see pages 97–99 of Chapter 4.

Celebration
While scholars remain uncertain of Confucius's date of birth, people throughout East Asia celebrate it on September 28. In Taiwan, it is an official holiday, known as Teachers' Day (shown above). Aside from honoring Confucius, the holiday pays tribute to teachers, who play a significant role in Confucianism. Confucius himself was a teacher, and he believed that education was an important part of a fulfilled life. In Confucianism, teachers are highly regarded, and their authority is just below that of a father.

ICONS, TEXTS & SYMBOLS

The Yin–Yang
The yin–yang symbol represents opposite forces in the world working together. It symbolizes the social order and harmony that Confucianism stresses.

Tzu-kung [a disciple] asked about the true gentleman. The Master [Confucius] said, "He does not preach what he practices till he has practiced what he preaches. . . . A gentleman can see a question from all sides without bias. . . . A gentleman takes as much trouble to discover what is right as lesser men take to discover what will pay."

These words of Confucius were recorded by his students in the *Analects*. To Confucius, the gentleman is the fully developed human being. The gentleman has important moral qualities. What moral qualities are emphasized in this passage? How does Confucius' view of the gentleman differ from modern notions?

Visual Learners Much traditional Chinese painting reflects Confucius' ideals of harmony and serenity, both in human interaction and in nature. In fact, Chinese landscape painting excels at showing human beings as elements of a serene world pattern. Such ideals are not exclusive to Confucianism in China. Buddhism and Taoism are also strong religious traditions in China, and they also stress the calm order of the universe. Show students World Art and Cultures Transparencies AT25 (Court Ladies Preparing Newly Woven Silk) and AT60 (Sorting of Cocoons) to illustrate this point. You might also ask students to look in art books for illustrations of Chinese paintings that depict the tranquil world idealized by Chinese religion.

Ritual

A key aspect of Confucianism is respect for family members and elders. This helped promote the religious practice throughout East Asia of honoring ancestors. In homes such as the one in China shown here, residents build shrines to honor their deceased relatives. The family offers prayers and food at the shrine. Family members then eat the meal—believing the ancestors have already tasted it. The Chinese believe showing respect for ancestors will ensure continued cooperation and aid from their deceased relatives.

Worship

Confucius is said to have preached more about social order than religious matters. In spite of this, the Chinese scholar has come to be viewed by many as a god. By the sixth century A.D., every district in China had a temple dedicated to Confucius. Since then, millions of people have come to revere him as a spiritual leader. Here, children in Taiwan take part in a ceremony honoring Confucius.

The Analects
The earliest and most authentic record of Confucius's ideas was recorded by his students. Around 400 B.C., they compiled Confucius's words in a book called the *Analects*.

World Religions **263**

Ritual

Confucius' ethics emphasized earthly rather than heavenly matters. Nevertheless, Confucius approved of the rituals of traditional Chinese religion. These included sacrifices to the gods and to ancestors as well as ceremonies for foretelling the future.

While he did not express precise teachings about the supernatural, Confucius did believe in a heavenly force for good. He taught that the first requirement for living a fully human life was respect for the will of heaven. He is quoted as having said, "Heaven appointed me to teach my doctrines." A phrase often quoted from his writings is "He who offends the gods has no one to pray to."

Worship

Respect for Confucius has not been limited to Asians. Jesuit missionaries who arrived in China in the late 1500s came to believe that many of Confucius' teachings were really Christian. Some missionaries even wrestled with the question of whether Chinese converts to Christianity could continue to participate in Confucian ancestor worship. The missionaries admired Confucius so much that they translated his writings into Latin. By the early 1600s, Confucius was a widely read writer in the West.

Some Jesuits compared Confucius to Aristotle (whom they called the Philosopher) by calling him the Philosopher of the Chinese. His high moral standards and humanistic view of the world reminded them of the ideas of the Greek philosopher and the humanistic ideals of the Renaissance. By the early 18th century, however, the pope had put an end to the Jesuits' attempts to link Confucianism with Christianity.

 **RELIGIONS OF THE WORLD
CD-ROM**
Confucianism

CONNECTIONS ACROSS TIME AND PLACE

The Chinese Examination System The teachings of Confucius inspired one of the major features of Chinese government: the examinations for civil servants. Written tests for government posts go back to the Han Dynasty (202 B.C.–A.D. 220). They reflected the Confucian respect for learning as a path to wisdom. Under the Tang Dynasty (618–907), the exams demanded a detailed knowledge of the literature of Confucianism, including the works believed to have been written by Confucius himself.

Passing the examinations became essential for social mobility. By long study, a poor man could move up to become rich and powerful. As a result, many who failed the examinations continued to take them even into old age. Despite its theoretical fairness, however, the system favored the children of the rich, who had the money and leisure to prepare for the exams.

In a concern for objectivity, the tests tended to emphasize dry fact over creativity. By the 19th century, a whole series of exams awaited those who wanted to rise in the civil service. The so-called final exam, given every three years, allowed only about 100 of several thousand candidates to pass. The hundred who succeeded would rise to the top of the imperial bureaucracy.

Teacher's Edition **263**

A Comparison Teaching Strategies

World Religions: A Comparison provides a useful summary of information concerning the five world religions and Confucianism presented in the *World Religions* feature of the Pupil's Edition. It provides in an accessible format essential information that can be supplemented by information in the textbook, by further reading, or by your knowledge or that of your students.

You might encourage the class to expand its understanding of the beliefs and values of each faith by further study. Stress that the digest of beliefs and values presented in the comparison chart is just a starting point and that each belief system can be the subject of in-depth research and study. The results of this study could provide valuable material for discussions and reports.

One important source for religious teachings is the holy book(s) of each faith. These books are listed in the chart, and they represent each religion's deepest expression of its teachings. Interested students may wish to read selections from these books.

You could ask the students what the texts seem to be saying about the religion(s) they have chosen to study. Some students may not be sure about what the texts are saying. This uncertainty can lead to a useful discussion about how students can better understand what they have read.

Stress that all these texts are to be treated with respect and that truly appreciating them may involve going beyond the views and opinions of our own culture. Drawing attention to culturally biased opinions expressed in class may help students understand this sometimes difficult concept.

A Comparison

	Buddhism	Christianity	Hinduism	Islam	Judaism	Confucianism
Followers Worldwide*	338 million	1.9 billion	764 million	1 billion	13.4 million	Not available
Name of Deity	The Buddha did not teach a personal deity.	God	Three main Gods: Brahma, Vishnu, Shiva	God (Allah)	God (Yahweh)	Confucius (viewed by many as a god)
Founder	The Buddha	Jesus Christ	No one founder	Muhammad	Abraham	Confucius
Holy Book	No one book—sacred texts, including the *Perfection of Wisdom Sutra*	Bible	No one book—sacred texts, including the Vedas, the Puranas	Qur'an	Hebrew Bible, including the Torah	the *Analects*, the Five Classics
Leadership	Buddhist monks and nuns	Clergy (priests/ ministers)	Guru, Holy Man, Brahmin priest	No clergy	Rabbis	No Clergy
Basic Beliefs	•Persons achieve complete peace and happiness, known as nirvana, by eliminating their attachment to worldly things. •Nirvana is reached by following the Noble Eightfold Path: Right views; Right aspirations; Right speech; Right conduct; Right livelihood; Right endeavor; Right mindfulness; Right meditation.	•There is only one God, who watches over and cares for his people. •Jesus Christ was the son of God. He died to save humanity from sin. His death and resurrection made eternal life possible for others.	•The soul never dies, but is continually reborn. •Persons achieve happiness and enlightenment after they free themselves from their earthly desires. •Freedom from earthly desires comes from a lifetime of worship, knowledge, and virtuous acts.	•Persons achieve salvation by following the Five Pillars of Islam and living a just life. These pillars are: faith; almsgiving, or charity to the poor; fasting, which Muslims perform during Ramadan; pilgrimage (to Mecca); and prayer.	•There is only one God, who watches over and cares for his people. •God loves and protects his people, but also holds people accountable for their sins and shortcomings. •Persons serve God by studying the Torah and living by its teachings.	•Social order, harmony, and good government should be based on strong family relationships. •Respect for parents and elders is important to a well-ordered society. •Education is important both to the welfare of the individual and to society.

*estimated 1994 figures

Assessment

REVIEW QUESTIONS

Buddhism

1. According to the Buddha, how does one achieve happiness and fulfillment?

Christianity

2. Why is Jesus Christ central to the Christian religion?

Hinduism

3. Explain the importance of the Ganges River in Hinduism.

Islam

4. What is the most important night of Ramadan? Why?

Judaism

5. Why do Jews consider the Western Wall to be sacred?

Confucianism

6. How has Confucianism's emphasis on familial respect affected religious worship in East Asia?

ANALYZING PRIMARY SOURCES

In her book, *A History of God*, Karen Armstrong explains why religion is such a powerful force in people's lives:

> ### A VOICE FROM THE PAST
> . . . Human beings are spiritual animals. Indeed, there is a case for arguing that *Homo sapiens* is also *Homo religiosus*. Men and women started to worship gods as soon as they became recognizably human; they created religions at the same time they created works of art. . . . These early faiths expressed the wonder and mystery that seem always to have been an essential component of the human experience of this beautiful yet terrifying world. Like art, religion has been an attempt to find meaning and value in life, despite the suffering that flesh is heir to.

- Based on information from the previous pages, how might religion give life meaning and value?
- Do you agree or disagree with Armstrong? Explain.

CRITICAL THINKING

1. COMPARING AND CONTRASTING

Using information from the text and chart, choose two religions and identify their similarities and differences in a Venn diagram like the one below.

2. COMMON THREADS

The previous pages reveal items and activities that play an important role in more than one religion. Determine what some are and explain how each is significant to different religions.

ACTIVITIES

1. LIVING HISTORY: Unit Portfolio Project

THEME **RELIGIOUS AND ETHICAL SYSTEMS** Your unit portfolio project focuses on religious and ethical systems around the world (see page 229). You may want to include one of the following activities in your portfolio.

- Imagine you are a newspaper reporter who has been granted entrance to a Buddhist monastery. Write a brief article describing what you think a day in the life of a Buddhist monk might be like.
- Write a persuasive speech in order to convince someone that Confucianism can be considered a religion.
- Write a dialogue between two people in which each explains the workings of one of the major religions to the other.

2. CONNECT TO TODAY: Cooperative Learning

As the previous pages explained, the world's major religions contain various sects. Sects are smaller groups within a religion. These groups hold one or more unique beliefs, which make them slightly different from other followers.

Working in small groups, find out what makes the major sects of a particular religion different. As a group, report your findings to the class.

 Use the Internet and other sources to research the unique beliefs and practices of the major sects of a religion.

- Each group member should be responsible for one sect. He or she should write a brief report detailing the beliefs and practices that make that sect unique.
- The group should then present its findings to the class by having each group member read aloud his or her report.

Byzantines, Russians, and Turks

	Key Ideas	**COPY MASTERS**	**ASSESSMENT**
SECTION 1 **Byzantium Becomes the New Rome** *pp. 269–273*	*The Byzantine Empire, or new Rome, develops in the eastern provinces of the Roman Empire. The emperor of the new Rome builds up eastern culture. The Church splits into the Eastern Orthodox and Roman Catholic churches.*	*In-Depth Resources: Unit 3* • **Guided Reading,** p. 18 • **Primary Sources:** from *Secret History* by Procopius, p. 24; *The Hagia Sophia,* p. 25 • **Literature:** from *The Belt of Gold* by Cecelia Holland, p. 28 • **History Makers:** Theodora, p. 31 • **Connections Across Time and Cultures:** Ancient Rome and the New Rome, p. 33	P E *Section 1 Assessment,* p. 273 *Formal Assessment* • Section Quiz, p. 122 *Alternative Assessment Book* • Standards for Evaluating a Cooperative Activity
SECTION 2 **Russians Adapt Byzantine Culture** *pp. 274–278*	*Russian culture develops from a blending of Slavic and Viking peoples. Through trade, Greek Byzantine culture influences Russian culture. Before the Mongol invasions, Kiev is the center of Russian culture. Eventually, Moscow becomes the dominant cultural center.*	*In-Depth Resources: Unit 3* • **Guided Reading,** p. 19 • **Skillbuilder Practice:** Formulating Historical Questions, p. 21 • **Geography Application:** Growth of Early Russia, p. 22 • **Primary Source:** from *Russian Primary Chronicle,* p. 26 • **History Makers:** Ivan III, p. 32	P E *Section 2 Assessment,* p. 278 *Formal Assessment* • Section Quiz, p. 123 *Alternative Assessment Book* • Standards for Evaluating a Cooperative Activity
SECTION 3 **Turkish Empires Rise in Anatolia** *pp. 279–281*	*Nomadic Turks known as Seljuks capture Baghdad from the Persians. The Turks and Persians form a strong bond because of the Turks' support of Persian culture. A lack of leadership, the Crusades, and Mongol invasions bring an end to the Seljuk Empire.*	*In-Depth Resources: Unit 3* • **Guided Reading,** p. 20 • **Primary Source:** Pope Urban II's Call for a Crusade, p. 27	P E *Section 3 Assessment,* p. 281 *Formal Assessment* • Section Quiz, p. 124 *Alternative Assessment Book* • Standards for Evaluating a Product or Performance
CHAPTER RESOURCES	**Chapter Overview** *The Roman Empire splits in two and the Byzantine Empire develops in the East. Through trade, Byzantine ideas influence the culture and religion of Russia. Turks adopt Islam and set up an empire in Persia and the eastern flank of Byzantium. Christians and Muslims battle during the Crusades. Mongol invaders bring down the Turks.*	*Telescoping the Times* • Chapter Summary, pp. 41–43 *Planning for Block Schedules*	P E *Chapter Assessment,* pp. 282–283 *Chapter Activities,* p. 283 *Formal Assessment* • Chapter Test, forms A and B, pp. 125–130 *Test Generator* *Alternative Assessment Book*

Interact, 500–1500

TECHNOLOGY

 Warm-Up Transparency 11

 Geography Transparencies
- GT11 The Byzantine Empire Under Justinian, 527–565

 World Art and Cultures Transparencies
- AT23 Theodora and Her Court

 Religions of the World
- Christianity

Electronic Library of Primary Sources
- "The Character of Justinian and Theodora," from *Secret History*

 Warm-Up Transparency 11

 Electronic Library of Primary Sources
- The Court of the Great Khan

INTERNET RESOURCES
www.mlworldhistory.com

 Warm-Up Transparency 11

World Art and Cultures Transparencies
- AT24 Turkish painting on silk

Critical Thinking Transparencies
- CT11 Comparing Seven Empires
- CT47 Chapter 11 Visual Summary

 Electronic Library of Primary Sources
from "The Merits of Turks"

 INTERNET RESOURCES
www.mlworldhistory.com

 Chapter Summaries on Audiocassette in English and Spanish

 INTERNET RESOURCES
www.mlworldhistory.com

Block Scheduling (90 MINUTES)

Day 1

Section 1, pp. 269–273

 COOPERATIVE ACTIVITY
A Travel Brochure for Istanbul, p. 270 (Teacher's Edition)

Section 2, pp. 274–278

 COOPERATIVE ACTIVITY
Eyewitness History, p. 275 (Teacher's Edition)

Section 3, pp. 279–281

Section Assessments, pp. 273, 278, 281

Chapter Assessment, pp. 282–283

Yearly Pacing *Chapter 11 Total:* 1 day *Yearly Total:* 85 days

 Planning for Block Schedules

Customizing for Special Needs

Students Acquiring English

 Access for Students Acquiring English
- **Guided Reading** for Sections 1–3 (Spanish), pp. 111–113
- **Chapter Summary** (Spanish), pp. 108–110
- **Skillbuilder Practice** Formulating Historical Questions (Spanish), p. 114
- **Geography Application** Growth of Early Russia (Spanish), p. 115

 Chapter Summaries on Audiocassette in English and Spanish

INTERNET RESOURCES
www.mlworldhistory.com
The Diverse Classroom

Less Proficient Readers

 In-Depth Resources: Unit 3
- **Guided Reading** for Sections 1–3, pp. 18–20
- **Skillbuilder Practice** Formulating Historical Questions, p. 21
- **Geography Application** Growth of Early Russia, p. 22

 Telescoping the Times
- Chapter Summary, pp. 41–43

 Chapter Summaries on Audiocassette

Gifted and Talented Students

In-Depth Resources: Unit 3

Primary Sources:
- from *Secret History* by Procopius, p. 24
- *The Hagia Sophia*, p. 25
- from *Russian Primary Chronicle*, p. 26
- Pope Urban II's Call for a Crusade, p. 27

History Makers
- Theodora, p. 31
- Ivan III, p. 32

Connections to Literature READINGS FOR STUDENTS

 In-Depth Resources: Unit 3
- Literature: from *The Belt of Gold* by Cecelia Holland, p. 28

Enrichment Reading

Norwick, John J.
Byzantium, The Early Centuries
New York: Knopf, 1996

An exciting narrative of the first five centuries of the Byzantine Empire.

Schwartz, Susan

Shards of Desire
New York: Doherty, 1996

A fantasized adventure of the Byzantine Empire.

 = Pupil's Edition   = Overhead Transparency   = Software   = Video

 = Copy Master   = CD-ROM   = Audiocassette   = Internet

265B

Byzantines, Russians, and Turks Interact, 500–1500

Predicting

- Ask students to read the captions accompanying each picture and predict whether the conflicts in this chapter will be religious, cultural, or both. What evidence can students show for their prediction?

Recognizing Sequences and Making Inferences

- After reading about the Byzantines and Turks, ask students to cite in chronological order three events in the development of Christianity and Islam.

- After reading about Yaroslav's daughter, ask students how a marriage between a prince and princess from two different empires might strengthen the political relationship between those empires.

Geography Connection

Ask students to study the three empires on the map.

- Which empire seems more isolated from other regions? Why?

- What route might the Russians have taken to get from Kiev to Constantinople?

PREVIEWING THEMES

Religious and Ethical Systems

Two world religions, Islam and Christianity, repeatedly met head-to-head as Arabs and Turks battled Byzantines and Crusaders. Both Islam and Christianity, meanwhile, attracted masses of converts. At the same time, disputes over doctrine split each religion into competing branches.

Cultural Interaction

Byzantine influence inspired the growth of a unique Russian culture. The Turks meanwhile adopted Islam. They also sponsored a rebirth of Persian culture and created a dynamic cultural blend.

Empire Building

The Byzantines, Slavs, Arabs, Turks, and Mongols waged bloody wars to expand their territories. However, each empire also brought together people of diverse traditions. In this way, they promoted the exchange of goods and ideas.

INTERNET CONNECTION

Visit us at **www.mlworldhistory.com** to learn more about the Byzantines, Slavs, and Turks between 500 and 1500.

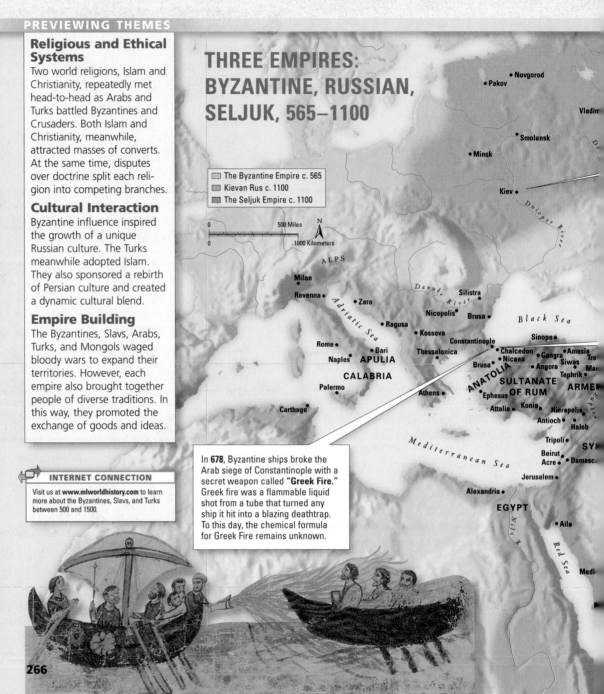

THREE EMPIRES: BYZANTINE, RUSSIAN, SELJUK, 565–1100

- The Byzantine Empire c. 565
- Kievan Rus c. 1100
- The Seljuk Empire c. 1100

In **678**, Byzantine ships broke the Arab siege of Constantinople with a secret weapon called **"Greek Fire."** Greek fire was a flammable liquid shot from a tube that turned any ship it hit into a blazing deathtrap. To this day, the chemical formula for Greek Fire remains unknown.

266

GEOGRAPHY THEMES

Movement

Explain that invasions are important to the development of the cultures discussed in this chapter. Discuss with students why one culture might want to invade another culture and how invasions can blend two cultures. Then ask these questions: Based on the map and map key, which empire do you think will invade and conquer Byzantium? Why might a culture want to invade Russia from the north? *Possible Responses: the Seljuk Empire; to get to Byzantium*

Location

Tell students that the Byzantine Empire is important because it influenced other cultures discussed in this chapter. Explain that as the Byzantine empire developed, other civilizations tried to take advantage of, or take over, the trade and wealth in this region. Ask students to locate the Byzantine Empire on the map and describe the advantages of its location. Then ask if the other cultures on the map have the same advantages.

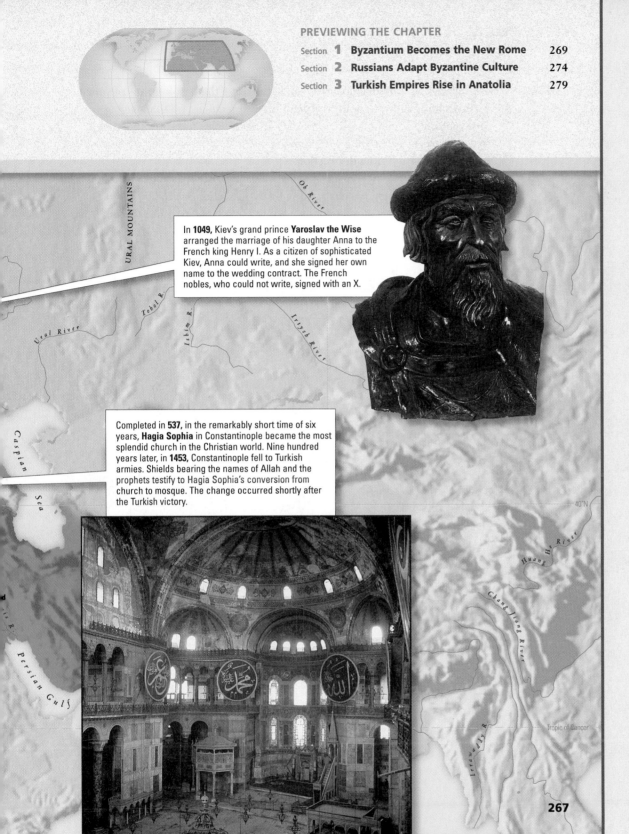

In **1049,** Kiev's grand prince **Yaroslav the Wise** arranged the marriage of his daughter Anna to the French king Henry I. As a citizen of sophisticated Kiev, Anna could write, and she signed her own name to the wedding contract. The French nobles, who could not write, signed with an X.

Completed in **537,** in the remarkably short time of six years, **Hagia Sophia** in Constantinople became the most splendid church in the Christian world. Nine hundred years later, in **1453,** Constantinople fell to Turkish armies. Shields bearing the names of Allah and the prophets testify to Hagia Sophia's conversion from church to mosque. The change occurred shortly after the Turkish victory.

267

ADDITIONAL RESOURCES

Books for the Teacher

• Fennell, John L. I. *A History of the Russian Church to 1448.* White Plains: Longman, 1995.

• Mitchell, Stephen. *Anatolia: Land, Men, and Gods in Asia Minor.* New York: Oxford UP, 1993. Christianity in Anatolia during Byzantine times.

• Roberts, J. M. *The Penguin History of the World.* New York: Penguin, 1987. Information on Turks, Seljuks, and Abbasids.

Books for the Student

• Corrick, James A. *The Byzantine Empire.* San Diego: Lucent Books, 1997. An overview of the empire.

• Sherrard, Philip. *Byzantium.* New York: Time-Life Books, 1966. History and culture.

• Stewart, Desmond. *Early Islam.* New York: Time-Life Books, 1967.

Videos

• *Early Russia.* Social Studies School Service. 800-421-4246. Outlines the merging of indigenous cultures, Byzantine influences, and Western ideas.

💿 Software

• *Treasures of Russia: Intro to Russian Art.* CD-ROM. Educational Software Institute. 800-955-5570. Includes overview of Russian historical, spiritual, and cultural heritage.

HISTORY THROUGH ART

The Hagia Sophia

The Hagia Sophia was built as a monument to Christianity and a testament to the supremacy of Byzantine culture. Today, the Hagia Sophia represents a blend of eastern and western architectural styles and the influence of two religions.

The oblong shape, massive columns, and spacious interior are borrowed from Roman public buildings.

The domes, which became standard features of orthodox churches, and vaulted arches recall Near Eastern architectural styles. In Byzantine times, the walls were covered with expensive colored marble and the vaults and domes were decorated with beautiful mosaics and paintings of Christian saints. In 1453, Sultan Mehmet converted the church into a mosque. The mosaics were plastered over and shields bearing the names of Islamic prophets were hung on the walls. Four minarets, high towers from which Muslims are called to prayer, were added over the years. After the Hagia Sophia became a museum in 1935, the Byzantine mosaics were uncovered.

Interpreting the Art Two religions used the Hagia Sophia as a place of worship. What does this say about the way the building made people feel?

Interact *with* History

Interact *with* History

This Interact with History feature motivates students by inviting them to put themselves in a key historical situation—a diplomat in the Byzantine Empire. As they imagine themselves having to decide between using force and using diplomacy to end a conflict, students will analyze issues, explore their options, and become decision makers.

Purpose

• to prepare students for studying the empires discussed in this chapter

• to help students understand some of the decisions faced by empire rulers

• to help students make connections with the people and events they will study in this chapter

Teaching Strategy

Thinking Critically After students have imagined themselves in the situation described on this page, have them answer the key questions and give reasons for their decisions.

EXAMINING *the* ISSUES

Following are suggestions for addressing each bulleted item.

1 How could diplomacy save lives and money?

2 What diplomatic strategies are available to you? Can diplomacy show strength and power?

3 Should going to war be a first choice or a last resort? At what point should one empire declare war on another?

Making Connections Ask students to discuss the role of diplomacy in the Persian empire (Chapter 4). What was the Persians' attitude toward diplomacy and war?

Follow Up

A feature on the chapter assessment will ask students to reevaluate their responses to the situation presented on this page.

You are a Byzantine diplomat working to serve the best interests of your emperor and your empire. Byzantium is threatened by a rampaging army moving from the north down to Constantinople. You know that diplomacy, or clever negotiating with foreign powers, has been important in preserving Byzantium from destruction.

Your mission is to convince the invading chief to stop advancing on the city. Will you threaten the chief with military retaliation, try to buy him off, or arrange a marriage between him and a Byzantine noblewoman to form an alliance?

How will you save the empire?

If shrewdness and good sense fail, a display of Byzantine military forces might scare the enemy away.

As the Byzantine ambassador, you may be proposing to pay yearly tribute to the invading chief if he will just leave the empire alone.

You may also be offering the chief a lavish, all-expense-paid trip to Constantinople. Such visits could impress potential invaders with Byzantine hospitality, wealth, and (above all) power.

EXAMINING *the* ISSUES

As you weigh your options, consider

1 • the advantages of diplomacy over war

2 • new diplomatic strategies to stop the coming attack

3 • circumstances that might convince you to recommend war

Which option(s) will you choose? Explain your choice(s).

As you read this chapter, think about how empires keep themselves alive over long periods of time.

268 Chapter 11

1 Byzantium Becomes the New Rome

TERMS & NAMES
- Justinian Code
- Hagia Sophia
- patriarch
- icon
- iconoclast
- excommunication
- schism
- Cyrillic alphabet

MAIN IDEA

Constantinople ruled an eastern empire that survived for over a thousand years.

WHY IT MATTERS NOW

Byzantine culture deeply influenced Orthodox Christianity, a major branch of modern Christianity.

SETTING THE STAGE The western Roman Empire crumbled in the 5th century as it was overrun by invading Germanic tribes. (See Chapter 6.) The threat to the empire, however, was already apparent in the 4th century. Emperor Constantine rebuilt the old port city of Byzantium on the Bosporus strait for two reasons. In Byzantium, he could respond to the danger of the Germanic tribes. He could also be close to his rich eastern provinces. He renamed the city Constantinople and in the year 330, he made it the capital of the empire.

A New Rome in a New Setting

Constantine planned Constantinople as the new capital of the empire—the New Rome. As a result of his decision, the empire's center of power moved eastward. The eastern provinces then began to develop independently of the declining West. An eastern empire would gradually come into being.

Justinian: A New Line of Caesars Because of the difficulties of communication between the eastern and troubled western parts of the empire, they were officially divided in two in 395. Despite this separation, Constantine's successors in the East continued to see themselves as Roman emperors. In 527, a high-ranking Byzantine nobleman named Justinian succeeded his uncle to the throne of the eastern empire.

In his official writings, court historian Procopius (pruh·KOH·pee·uhs) described Justinian as a serious, even-tempered ruler who worked from dawn to midnight. But in *The Secret History* (a book of gossip published after Justinian's death), Procopius portrays Justinian as "deceitful, devious, false, hypocritical, two-faced, cruel, skilled in dissembling his thought, never moved to tears by either joy or pain . . . a liar always."

Whatever his true character, the new emperor quickly decided to make good on his claim to be the head of the whole Roman Empire—of both eastern and western parts. In 533, he sent his best general Belisarius (behl·uh·SAIR·ee·uhs) to recover North Africa from the Vandals. Belisarius got the job done in a few months. Two years later, Belisarius attacked Rome and took it from the Ostrogoths. But the city was repeatedly attacked by other Germanic tribes. In the next 16 years, Rome changed hands six times. After numerous campaigns, Justinian's armies won nearly all of Italy and parts of Spain. Justinian now ruled almost all the territory that Rome had ever ruled. He could honestly call himself a new Caesar.

The Absolute Power of the Emperors Like the last of the old Caesars, the Byzantine emperors ruled with absolute power. They headed not just the state but the Church as well. They appointed and dismissed bishops at will. The politics, however, were brutal, not spiritual. Emperors lived under constant risk of assassination. Of the 88 Byzantine emperors, 29 died violently, and 13 abandoned the throne to live in monasteries.

Byzantines, Russians, and Turks Interact **269**

THINK THROUGH HISTORY

A. Drawing Conclusions How could a historian like Procopius give two such different accounts of the same person? Which do you believe?

A. Possible Answers Procopius may have been biased in both cases: to please the emperor with the favorable account; to express his dislike of the emperor with the unfavorable one. There may be some truth in both descriptions.

Both sides of this gold medallion display Emperor Justinian as a military commander. But the coin really celebrates a victory by General Belisarius. The emperor often feared that the general's popularity would outshine his own.

Section 1 Overview

OBJECTIVES

1. To describe Byzantine politics and the rise of Emperor Justinian.
2. To describe Justinian's achievements, and life in Constantinople.
3. To characterize Byzantine education.
4. To identify the causes of the Byzantine Empire's collapse.
5. To explain why the Eastern and Western churches created two traditions.

SKILLBUILDER
- Interpreting charts, p. 273

CRITICAL THINKING
- Drawing conclusions, p. 269
- Analyzing motives, pp. 270, 273
- Recognizing effects, p. 273
- Analyzing themes, p. 273

FOCUS

5-Minute Warm-Up

▶ **Identifying Main Ideas**
Have students answer these questions to explore the ways culture can influence religion.

1. Read the Connect to Today feature on page 272. On what points do the churches agree?
2. On what points do the churches differ?

📖 *WARM-UP TRANSPARENCY 11*

OBJECTIVE 1 INSTRUCT

A New Rome in a New Setting

▶ **Key Ideas**
- As emperor of Byzantium, Justinian recovers most of the territory that Rome ruled.
- Byzantine emperors exercise absolute power as heads of church and state.

📖 *IN-DEPTH RESOURCES: UNIT 3*
Guided Reading, p. 18
Connections Across Time and Cultures: Ancient Rome and the New Rome, p. 33

📖 *ACCESS FOR STUDENTS ACQUIRING ENGLISH*
Guided Reading (Spanish), p.111

SECTION 1 RESOURCES

PRINT RESOURCES

📖 *IN-DEPTH RESOURCES: UNIT 3*
Guided Reading, p. 18
Primary Sources: *Secret History*, p. 24; *The Hagia Sophia*, p. 25
Literature: from *The Belt of Gold* by Cecelia Holland, p. 28
History Makers: Theodora, p. 31
Connections Across Time and Cultures, p. 33

📖 *ACCESS FOR STUDENTS ACQUIRING ENGLISH*
Guided Reading (Spanish), p. 111

📖 *FORMAL ASSESSMENT*
Section Quiz, p. 122

TECHNOLOGY RESOURCES

📐 *GEOGRAPHY TRANSPARENCIES*
GT11 The Byzantine Empire Under Justinian, 527–565

📐 *WORLD ART AND CULTURES TRANSPARENCIES*
AT23 Theodora and her Court

💿 **CD-ROM**
Religions of the World
Electronic Library of Primary Sources

🌐 **INTERNET** www.mlworldhistory.com

Building the New Rome

Key Ideas
- Justinian's legal scholars create a uniform code of laws based on Roman laws.
- Justinian builds, repairs, and beautifies buildings in Constantinople.
- Constantinople bustles with commerce and culture.

 IN-DEPTH RESOURCES: UNIT 3
Primary Source: *The Hagia Sophia*, p. 25
Literature: from *The Belt of Gold* by *Cecelia* Holland, p. 28

MORE ABOUT . . .
Justinian's Palace

Justinian's palace featured gilded trees with clockwork birds, gilded mechanical roaring lions, and a huge throne rigged to rise suddenly high into the air. All this glitter and magic was used to intimidate foreign rulers and make them feel fortunate for any diplomatic gestures the "grand" Byzantines made toward them.

History from Visuals

Constantinople, A.D. 550

Interpreting the Map Have students read the map and then make lists to categorize the various elements shown in the map. For example, students should make lists of the city's forums, walls, gates, and churches.

Extension Activity Suggest students read the articles on the Byzantine Empire in the December 1983 issue of *National Geographic*. Ask volunteers to share what they learn from the articles with the rest of the class.

 GEOGRAPHY TRANSPARENCIES
GT11 The Byzantine Empire Under Justinian, 527–565

Building the New Rome

A separate government and difficult communications with the West gave the Byzantine Empire its own character—different from that of the western empire. The citizens thought of themselves as sharing in the Roman tradition, but few spoke Latin anymore. Most Byzantines spoke Greek. They also belonged to the eastern branch of the Christian Church.

To regulate a complex society, Justinian set up a panel of ten legal experts. Between 528 and 533, they combed through 400 years of Roman law and legal opinions. Some of those laws had become outdated. Some repeated or even contradicted other laws. The panel's task was to create a single, uniform code for Justinian's New Rome.

The result of the panel's work was a body of civil law known as the **Justinian Code**. After its completion, the code consisted of four works.

1. The *Code* contained nearly 5,000 Roman laws, which the experts still considered useful for the Byzantine Empire.
2. The *Digest* quoted and summarized the opinions of Rome's greatest legal thinkers about the laws. This massive work ran to a total of 50 volumes.
3. The *Institutes* was a textbook that told law students how to use the laws.
4. The *Novellae* (New Laws) presented legislation passed after 534.

The Justinian Code decided legal questions that regulated whole areas of Byzantine life. Marriage, slavery, property, inheritance, women's rights, and crimes were just some of those areas. Although Justinian himself died in 565, his code served the Byzantine Empire for 900 years.

Creating the Imperial Capital While his scholars were creating the legal code, Justinian launched into the most ambitious public building program ever seen in the Roman world. He rebuilt the crumbling fortifications of Constantinople. The city's coasts were ringed by a 14-mile stone wall. The city was also protected on its only land approach by a deep moat and three walls. The innermost of these was 25 feet thick and had towers 70 feet tall. Justinian saw to it that these massive fortifications were repaired.

Church building was the emperor's greatest passion. His beautiful churches also helped him show the close connection between church and state in his empire. The crowning glory of his reign was **Hagia Sophia** (HAY·ee·uh soh·FEE·uh), which means "Holy Wisdom" in Greek. A church of the same name had been destroyed in riots that swept Constantinople in 532. When Justinian rebuilt Hagia Sophia, he resolved to make it the most splendid church in the Christian world. Down through the centuries, rich mosaics glittered in the light of a thousand lamps and candles. In fact, more than 400 years after Justinian built his cathedral, the beauty of Hagia Sophia helped convince visiting Russian nobles that their country should adopt Byzantine Christianity.

As part of his building program, Justinian enlarged his palace into a vast complex. He also built baths, aqueducts, law courts, schools, and hospitals. By the time the emperor was finished with his projects, the city teemed with an excitement unmatched anywhere in the eastern and western empires.

Constantinople, A.D. 550

[Map: Constantinople, A.D. 550 — showing Gate of Charisius, Church of St. Salvator in Chora, Moat, Wall of Theodosius, River Lycus, Cistern, Aqueduct, Church of the Apostles, Golden Horn, Harbor of Phosphorion, Wall of Constantine, Forum of the Ox, Forum of Theodosius, Mese, Forum of Constantine, Hagia Sophia, Augusteum, Forum of Arcadius, Hippodrome, Great Palace, Harbor of Theodosius, Harbor of Julian, Golden Gate, Sea Wall, Sea of Marmara, Balkan Peninsula, Black Sea, Anatolia. Scale: 0 .5 Mile / 0 1 Kilometer]

Background
Ethnically, the empire was extremely diverse. Copts, Syrians, Thracians, Armenians, Germans, Huns, and many other groups made up its population.

Vocabulary
code: a general system of laws, from the Latin *codex*, meaning "book."

THINK THROUGH HISTORY
B. Analyzing Motives Why do you think governments so often build magnificent buildings like Hagia Sophia?
B. Possible Answer Possibly to impress or intimidate those they govern; to impress foreign powers.

| TEACHING OPTION | BLOCK SCHEDULING | COOPERATIVE ACTIVITY: A Travel Brochure for Istanbul | CLASS TIME 30 MINUTES |

Task: Groups will create and present travel brochures for Istanbul (formerly Constantinople).

Purpose: To learn about Constantinople today.

Activity: Brainstorm with the class a list of tourist activities (going to museums and historic sites, shopping, taking tours, eating in restaurants, enjoying local entertainment, using maps). Then have groups of students use travel guides to research and create travel brochures for Istanbul. Brochures should include descriptions of a few museums, historical sites, and tours, and information about restaurants, hotels, shopping areas and entertainment venues. Encourage groups to include maps and illustrations in their brochures. Then have groups present them to the class.

 Building a Portfolio: If brochures are among their best work, students should add them to their portfolio.

ALTERNATIVE ASSESSMENT BOOK
Standards for Evaluating a Cooperative Activity

Standards for Evaluation
Brochures should . . .

- clearly describe sites and attractions in Istanbul
- show evidence of research
- be thoughtfully laid out

The emperor often presided over wild chariot races at the Hippodrome, as this fourth-century ivory carving shows. When he dropped a white handkerchief, the races began.

Constantinople's Hectic Pace The main street running through Constantinople was the Mese (MEHS-ee) or "Middle Way." It ran from the imperial complex through a series of public squares and then in two branches to the outer walls. Merchant stalls lined the main street and filled the side streets. A stone roof sheltered the crowds shopping in this giant open-air market. Products from the most distant corners of Asia, Africa, and Europe passed through these stalls. Shoppers could buy tin from England, wine from France, cork from Spain, and ivory and gold from Africa. Fur, honey, and timber came from Russia, spices from India, and silk from China. Everywhere food stands filled the air with the smell of their delicacies, while acrobats and street musicians performed.

Meanwhile, citizens could enjoy free entertainment at the Hippodrome, which offered wild chariot races and circus acts. The Hippodrome (from Greek words meaning "horse" and "racecourse") held 60,000 spectators. Fans of the different teams formed rowdy gangs named for the colors worn by their heroes.

In 532, two such factions, the Blues and the Greens, sparked citywide riots called the Nika Rebellion (because the mob cried "*Nika!*" or "Victory!"). Both sides were angry at the government. They felt the city prefect (mayor) had been too severe in putting down a previous riot of Hippodrome fans. Even though Justinian dismissed the prefect, the mobs were not satisfied. They packed the Hippodrome and proclaimed a new emperor. Belisarius, however, broke in with his troops and slaughtered about 30,000 rebels.

Much credit for saving the day must go to Justinian's wife, Theodora. As her husband's steely adviser, Theodora had immense power. During the Nika Rebellion, when Justinian considered fleeing the city, Theodora rallied him with a fiery speech:

A VOICE FROM THE PAST
My opinion is that now is a poor time for flight, even though it bring safety. For any man who has seen the light of day will also die, but one who has been an emperor cannot endure to be a fugitive. If now you wish to go, Emperor, nothing prevents you. There is the sea, there are the steps to the boats. But take care that after you are safe, you do not find that you would gladly exchange that safety for death.

THEODORA, quoted by Procopius in *History of the Wars*

Byzantium Preserves Learning

Byzantine families valued education and sent their children to monastic or public schools or hired private tutors. Basic courses focused on Greek and Latin grammar, philosophy, and rhetoric. The classics of Greek and Roman literature served as textbooks. Students memorized Homer. They learned geometry from Euclid, history from Herodotus, and medicine from Galen. The modern world owes Byzantine scholars a huge debt for preserving many of the great works of Greece and Rome.

HISTORY MAKERS

**Empress Theodora
500–548**

The most powerful woman in Byzantine history rose from deep poverty. Theodora's father was a bear-keeper. Early in life, Theodora herself was an actress, a despised profession in Byzantium. But she caught Justinian's eye, and in 525, they married.

As empress, Theodora became a power in her own right. She met with foreign envoys, wrote to foreign leaders, passed laws, and built churches. During a political crisis, Theodora even confiscated the property of the general Belisarius. After she died in 548, Justinian was so depressed that he passed no major laws for the rest of his reign—a sign of Theodora's political influence.

Byzantines, Russians, and Turks Interact **271**

The Empire Confronts Its Enemies

▶ *Key Ideas*
- Illness destroys a huge percentage of Byzantium's population.
- Centuries of foreign attacks reduce the Byzantine empire.

CRITICAL THINKING ACTIVITY

Making a Causes Chart
To help students understand and remember the many causes of the fall of Byzantium, have them use a cluster web like the one below. Explain that the web may have as many branches as necessary. *Possible branches: street riots, palace intrigues, disease, the rise of Islam, the Crusades.*

Why Byzantium Fell

The Church Divides

▶ *Key Ideas*
- Differences between the Eastern and Western churches divide Christianity into two separate traditions.
- Missionaries convert many Slavs to Eastern Orthodox Christianity.

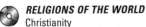 *RELIGIONS OF THE WORLD*
Christianity

The Empire Confronts Its Enemies

Constantinople remained rich and powerful for centuries. After Justinian's death in 565, however, the empire suffered countless setbacks. There were street riots, religious quarrels, palace intrigues, and foreign dangers. Each time the empire moved to the edge of collapse, it found some way to revive—only to face another crisis.

The Mysterious Plague of Justinian The first crisis actually began before Justinian's death. It was a disease that resembled what we now know as the bubonic plague. This horrifying illness hit Constantinople in the later years of Justinian's reign. The plague probably arrived from India on ships infested with rats. In 542, at its peak, it is estimated that 10,000 people were dying every day. The illness broke out every 8 to 12 years until around 700, when it finally faded out. By that time, it had destroyed a huge percentage of the Byzantine population. The smaller population left the empire exposed to its enemies.

Attacks from East and West Byzantium's enemies pressed in on all sides. Lombards overran Justinian's conquests in the west. Avars, Slavs, and Bulgars made frequent raids on the northern borders. The powerful Sassanid Persians attacked relentlessly in the east. The Persians and Avars struck against Constantinople itself in 626. With the rise of Islam, Arab armies attacked the city in 674 and once again in 717. Russians attempted invasions of the city three times between 860 and 1043. In the 11th century, the Turks took over the Muslim world and fought their way slowly into Anatolia. The Crusades brought armies of knights from Western Europe who pillaged Constantinople in 1204 on their way to fight the Turks.

As their first line of defense, the Byzantines used bribes, diplomacy, and political marriages to prop up their shaky empire. These strategies, however, were not enough. So, in the 7th century, Emperor Heraclius reorganized the empire along military lines. Provinces became *themes*, or military districts. Each theme was run by a general who reported directly to the emperor.

In spite of these measures, the Byzantine Empire slowly shrank under the impact of foreign attacks. By 1350, it was reduced to the tip of Anatolia and a strip of the Balkans. Yet thanks to its walls, its fleet, and its strategic location, the city held out for another 100 years. Finally, Constantinople fell to the Ottoman Turks in 1453.

Background
Except during Justinian's reign, the Byzantine Empire was relatively small for most of its 1,000-year history. The empire generally included most of Anatolia, Greece, and some of present-day Bulgaria and the former Yugoslavia.

CONNECT *to* TODAY

The Orthodox and Roman Catholic Churches Today
Today, the Orthodox Church has about 218 million members worldwide. Roman Catholics number about 968 million. In 1965, the two churches met to discuss their differences and explore the possibilities of reunion.

Statements issued in the late 1980s outlined areas of agreement. Both churches believe that Jesus established seven sacraments, or ceremonies, for Christian worship. Of these sacraments, they consider Holy Communion the most important.

They also agree on the need for priests in the Church. However, as in the 11th century, they still disagree on the role of the pope, on the issue of divorce, and on whether priests may marry.

The Church Divides

During those many centuries, the Eastern Church in Constantinople continued to flourish. At the same time, however, distance and lack of contact slowly caused the doctrines and rituals of Western and Eastern Christianity to diverge. The Church would eventually split into the Eastern Orthodox and Roman Catholic churches.

A Split Between Rome and Constantinople Eastern Christianity built its heritage on the works of early church fathers. One was Saint Basil, who, around 357, wrote rules for the life of monks. Another key figure was Saint John Chrysostom (KRIHS·uhs·tuhm). As bishop of Constantinople from 398 to 404, Chrysostom was the **patriarch** (PAY·tree·AHRK), or leading bishop of the East. But even the patriarch bowed to the emperor.

A controversy that tested the emperor's authority over religious matters broke out in the 8th century. In 730, Emperor Leo III banned the use of **icons,** religious images used by eastern Christians to aid their devotions. The emperor thought the use of icons amounted to idol worship. The army supported the emperor's view, and enthusiastic **iconoclasts** (eye·KAHN·uh·KLASTS), or "icon-breakers," broke into churches to destroy images. But the people rioted,

Background
Today, *iconoclast* means "someone who overthrows respected ideas and traditions."

Religious Schisms Early Christianity was not the only religion to have experienced a schism. In the 600s, Islam split into the Sunni and Shi'a branches. Protestants broke away from the Catholic Church in the 1500s. Buddhism divided into the Mahayana and Theraveda schools by the first century A.D. Encourage pairs of students to choose one of these religious splits and use an encyclopedia to find the reasons behind it. Ask partners to share their information with the class.

Biology and Health The bubonic plague, malaria, and typhus have profoundly affected history. Have students conduct research to learn about major outbreaks of these diseases, how the diseases can be controlled, and what is being done today to keep people safe from such diseases. *Possible answers: The plague—spread by fleas from rats, killed 25% of the* European population in the mid-1300s, prevented by killing rats and by good hygiene. Typhus—spread by lice, killed 3 million during the Russian Revolution, can be cured with antibiotics and prevented by using good hygiene and insecticides; Malaria—spread by mosquitoes, kills 1-2 million per year today, can be controlled with swamp drainage and insecticides.

The 11th Century: Differences Between Two Christian Traditions

Roman Catholic	Eastern Orthodox
• Services are conducted in Latin.	• Services are conducted in Greek or local languages.
• The pope has authority over all other bishops.	• The patriarch and other bishops head the church as a group.
• The pope claims authority over all kings and emperors.	• The emperor claims authority over the patriarch and other bishops of the empire.
• Priests may not marry.	• Priests may be married.
• Divorce is not permitted.	• Divorce is allowed under certain conditions.

SKILLBUILDER: Interpreting Charts
1. *Which church seemed to allow for greater diversity among its members? Why?*
2. *Who would have more political power: the pope or the patriarch?*

A reliquary is a decorated container that holds the remains of holy persons, called saints. This tin reliquary, produced in the 12th century, contains pieces of the bones of Saints Cyril and Methodius.

and the clergy rebelled. In the West, the pope became involved in this eastern dispute and supported the use of icons. One pope even ordered the **excommunication** of a Byzantine emperor—that is, he declared that the emperor was an outcast from the Church. In 843, more than a hundred years after the controversy began, an order from an empress named Theodora restored icons to Eastern churches.

Differences between the Eastern and Western churches, however, continued to grow. (See the chart above.) In 1054, matters came to a head when the pope and the patriarch excommunicated each other in a dispute over religious doctrine. After this **schism** (SIHZ·uhm), or split, Christianity was permanently divided between the Roman Catholic Church in the West and the Orthodox Church in the East.

Byzantine Missionaries Convert the Slavs As West and East grew apart, the two traditions of Christianity competed for souls. Missionaries from the Orthodox Church, for example, took their form of Christianity north to the Slavs. Two of the most successful eastern missionaries, Saint Methodius and Saint Cyril (SEER·uhl), worked among the Slavs in the 9th century. Cyril and Methodius invented an alphabet for the Slavic languages. With an alphabet, Slavs would be able to read the Bible in their own tongues. Many Slavic languages, including Russian, are now written in what is called the **Cyrillic** (suh·RIHL·ihk) **alphabet**.

The Orthodox missionaries opened up highways for Byzantine influence in Slavic lands. As these missionaries were carrying out their work among the Slavs, an important new Slavic nation was forming.

Section 1 Assessment

1. TERMS & NAMES
Identify
• Justinian Code
• Hagia Sophia
• patriarch
• icon
• iconoclast
• excommunication
• schism
• Cyrillic alphabet

2. TAKING NOTES
Using a cluster like the one below, show Justinian's accomplishments as emperor of the New Rome.

Justinian

In your opinion, was Justinian a great leader? Explain.

3. ANALYZING MOTIVES
Why do you think Justinian decided in the late 520s that it was the right time to reform Roman law?

THINK ABOUT
• the situation of the empire
• the role of laws in societies
• the state of Roman laws before reform

4. ANALYZING THEMES
Religious and Ethical Systems Do you think the differences between the Eastern and Western churches could have been reconciled before the Church split? Why? Working in small teams, brainstorm several reasons why the Church separated. For each reason, list two or three ways in which the problems might have been resolved.

Byzantines, Russians, and Turks Interact **273**

ANSWERS

1. TERMS & NAMES
Justinian Code, p. 270
Hagia Sophia, p. 270
patriarch, p. 272
icon, p. 272
iconoclast, p. 272
excommunication, p. 273
schism, p. 273
Cyrillic alphabet, p. 273

2. TAKING NOTES
Possible Responses: Conquered most of Italy and parts of Spain; established Justinian Code; rebuilt Constantinople's fortifications; rebuilt the Hagia Sophia; enlarged his palace; built aqueducts, courts, schools, hospitals; encouraged trade, education.

3. ANALYZING MOTIVES
Possible Responses: The Byzantine Empire had a separate government and character from that of the West. It needed its own organized system of laws to regulate life in this new era. Roman law was disorganized and contradictory and so needed reform.

4. ANALYZING THEMES
Possible Responses: Yes—Both sides could have united over the icon issue. No—Differences in beliefs about divorce and marriage for priests might have been too deep for compromise.

---

(1) To summarize the Slavic, Greek, and Viking roots of Russia and Russian culture.

(2) To describe the rise and fall of the principality of Kiev.

(3) To explain how the Mongol invasions united Russia and empowered Moscow.

SKILLBUILDER

• Interpreting maps: human-environment interactions pp. 275, 278

CRITICAL THINKING

• Making inferences, p. 274
• Analyzing motives, pp. 275, 277
• Contrasting, p. 276
• Analyzing, p. 276
• Recognizing effects, p. 278
• Analyzing themes, p. 278

FOCUS

5-Minute Warm-Up

▶ *Making Inferences*
Answering these questions will help students understand how Russian culture developed.

1. Study the map on page 275. Toward what empire to the south might the Vikings be headed?

2. Which territory are they invading along the way?

WARM-UP TRANSPARENCY 11

OBJECTIVE ① INSTRUCT

Both Slavic and Greek

Key Ideas

• The first unified Russian territory develops north of the Black Sea.

• Vikings dominate Slavic villagers and found the principality of Kiev.

• The Slavs absorb Greek Byzantine ideas through trade with Constantinople.

IN-DEPTH RESOURCES: UNIT 3
Geography Application: Growth of Early Russia, p. 22
Primary Source: from *Russian Primary Chronicle*, p. 26

(continued on next page)

---

2 Russians Adapt Byzantine Culture

TERMS & NAMES
• Slavs
• boyars
• Olga
• Vladimir
• Yaroslav the Wise
• Alexander Nevsky
• czar

MAIN IDEA	WHY IT MATTERS NOW
Russia grew out of a blending of Slavic and Byzantine cultures with Eastern Orthodox traditions.	The early history of Russia separated it from the West, causing mutual misunderstandings that still exist today.

SETTING THE STAGE At the beginning of the 9th century, the Byzantines regarded the forests north of the Black Sea as a wilderness. In their minds, those forests were inhabited only by "barbarians," who sometimes made trouble along their borders. They would soon consider these Slavic peoples as fellow Byzantine Christians.

Background
Like the Greeks, the Byzantines labeled anyone who did not speak Greek as a "barbarian."

Both Slavic and Greek

Midway through the 9th century, the **Slavs**—the people from the forests north of the Black Sea—began trading with Constantinople. As they traded, they began absorbing Greek Byzantine ideas. Russian culture grew out of this blending of Slavic and Greek traditions.

The Land of Russia's Birth Russia's first unified territory originated west of the Ural Mountains in the region that runs from the Black Sea to the Baltic. Hilly grasslands are found in the extreme south of that area. The north, however, is densely forested, flat, and swampy. Slow-moving, interconnecting rivers allow boat travel across these plains in almost any direction. Three great rivers, the Dnieper (NEE·puhr), the Don, and the Volga, run from the heart of the forests to the Black Sea or the Caspian Sea.

In the early days of the Byzantine Empire, these forests were inhabited by tribes of Slavic farmers and traders. They spoke similar languages but had no political unity. Sometime in the 800s, small bands of adventurers came down among them from the north. These Varangians, or Rus as they were also called, were most likely Vikings. Eventually, the Vikings built forts along the rivers and settled among the Slavs.

Slavs and Vikings Russian legends say the Slavs invited the Viking chief Rurik to be their king. So in 862, he founded Novgorod (NAHV·guh·rahd), Russia's first important city. That account is given in *The Primary Chronicle*, a history of Russia written by monks

THINK THROUGH HISTORY
A. Making Inferences Why might a territory with plains and rivers be difficult to defend against invaders?
A. Answer Plains would offer few natural obstacles to invaders. Rivers could actually help invaders to move into the territory.

Many rivers in Russia are full of rocks and dangerous rapids. Vikings like the ones in this woodcut would lift up their boats and carry them past those dangers. Even so, many Vikings died in Russian rivers.

SECTION 2 RESOURCES

PRINT RESOURCES

IN-DEPTH RESOURCES: UNIT 3
Guided Reading, p. 19
Skillbuilder Practice: Formulating Historical Questions, p. 21
Geography Application: Growth of Early Russia, p. 22
Primary Source: from *Russian Primary Chronicle,* p. 26
History Makers: Ivan III, p. 32

ACCESS FOR STUDENTS ACQUIRING ENGLISH
Guided Reading (Spanish), p. 112

Skillbuilder Practice: (Spanish), p. 114
Geography Application: (Spanish), p. 115

FORMAL ASSESSMENT
Section Quiz, p. 123

TECHNOLOGY RESOURCES

CD-ROM
Electronic Library of Primary Sources
INTERNET www.mlworldhistory.com

in the early 1100s. Around 880, a nobleman from Novgorod named Oleg moved south to Kiev (KEE·ehf), a city on the Dnieper River. From Kiev, the Vikings could sail by river and sea to Constantinople. There they could trade for the products from distant lands.

The merchandise they brought to Constantinople included timber, fur, wax, honey, and their Slavic subjects whom they sold as slaves. In fact, the word *slave* originates from *Slav.*

Kiev grew into a principality, a small state ruled by a prince. As it did, the Viking nobles intermarried with their Slavic subjects. They also adopted Slavic culture. The society remained strictly divided between peasant masses and the nobles, or **boyars.** Gradually, however, the line between Slavs and Vikings vanished.

Kiev Becomes Orthodox In 957, a member of the Kievan nobility paid a visit to Constantinople and publicly converted to Christianity. Her name was Princess **Olga.** From 945 to 955, she governed Kiev until her son was old enough to rule. Her son resisted Christianity. However, soon after Olga's grandson **Vladimir** (VLAD·uh·meer) came to the throne about 980, he considered conversion to Christianity. *The Primary Chronicle* reports that Vladimir sent out teams to observe the major religions of the times. Three of the teams returned with lukewarm accounts of Islam, Judaism, and Western Christianity. But the team from Byzantium told quite a different story:

A VOICE FROM THE PAST
. . . the Greeks led us to the buildings where they worship their God, and we knew not whether we were in heaven or on earth. For on earth there is no such splendor or such beauty, and we are at a loss how to describe it. We only know that God dwells there among men and . . . we cannot forget that beauty.
from *The Primary Chronicle*

This report convinced Vladimir to convert to Byzantine Christianity and to make all his subjects convert, too. In 989, a baptism of all the citizens of Kiev was held in the Dnieper River. Kiev, already linked to Byzantium by trade, now looked to Constantinople for religious guidance. Vladimir imported teachers to instruct the people in the new faith. All the beliefs and traditions of Orthodox Christianity flourished in Kiev. Vladimir appreciated the Byzantine idea of the emperor as supreme ruler of the church. So the close link between Church and state took root in Russia as well.

Kiev's Power and Decline

Thanks to its Byzantine ties, Kiev grew from a cluster of crude wooden forts to the glittering capital of prosperous and educated people. The rise of Kiev marks the appearance of Russia's first important unified territory.

Byzantines, Russians, and Turks Interact **275**

Background
Vikings could dominate the Slavs partly because of superior weaponry. They used two-edged swords and battle axes.

B. Answer
Uniformity in religion might make people easier to govern; one important source of dissent would be eliminated. Vladimir may have wanted to extend his power even over his subject's deepest beliefs.
THINK THROUGH HISTORY
B. Analyzing Motives Why do you think Vladimir thought it was important that all his subjects become Christian?

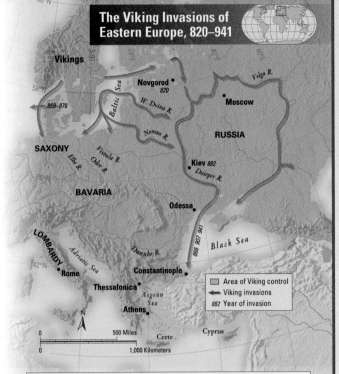

The Viking Invasions of Eastern Europe, 820–941

Area of Viking control
Viking invasions
882 Year of invasion

0 500 Miles
0 1,000 Kilometers

GEOGRAPHY SKILLBUILDER: Interpreting Maps
1. **Human-Environment Interaction** *Which geographical feature of Russia did Vikings use to further their invasions?*
2. **Human-Environment Interaction** *Besides east, what is the other basic direction taken by Vikings in their Eastern European invasions? Why do you think they chose to attack in that direction?*

OBJECTIVE 1 INSTRUCT

(continued from page 274)

- Vladimir of Kiev converts to Orthodox Christianity and forces his subjects to follow suit.

  IN-DEPTH RESOURCES: UNIT 3
  Guided Reading, p. 19

  ACCESS FOR STUDENTS ACQUIRING ENGLISH
  Guided Reading (Spanish), p. 112

History from Visuals

The Viking Invasions of Eastern Europe, 820–941
Interpreting the Map Ask students to approximate the latitude of Kiev. *About 50°N.* Have them use the map of North America on page 980 of the Atlas to approximate the latitude of their own location and compare this with Kiev's.

Extension Activity Using the world map on pages 972–973 of the Atlas, have students compare the sea route and river route from Scandinavia to Constantinople. Discuss with them the pros and cons of each route.

SKILLBUILDER Answers
1. Russian rivers.
2. Possible answers: South. The climate farther south was less harsh than in Scandinavia. Because of the better climate, there would be rich farms, cattle, and food to plunder.

OBJECTIVE 2 INSTRUCT

Kiev's Power and Decline

▶ *Key Ideas*
- Under Yaroslav, Kiev becomes a commercial and cultural center.
- A new system of succession and the disruption of trade lead to the decline of Kiev.

  IN-DEPTH RESOURCES: UNIT 3
  History Makers: Ivan III, p. 32

TEACHING OPTION | **BLOCK SCHEDULING** | **COOPERATIVE ACTIVITY: Eye Witness History** | **CLASS TIME 30 MINUTES**

Task: Groups will develop and present to the class eyewitness accounts from citizens of early Russia.

Purpose: To help students understand the various cultures that influenced the development of Russia

Activity: Tell small groups of students to research and prepare eyewitness accounts of a farmer, a trader, or a noble from the Slavic, Byzantine Greek, or Viking culture. Each account should explain who the

individual is, what role he or she played in the development of Russian culture, and something about daily life. Groups can use their textbooks and the library to find more information. Remind students to use a first-person narrator in their accounts. Groups should choose one member to role-play their character for the class. Encourage students to use simple props or costumes.

ALTERNATIVE ASSESSMENT BOOK
Standards for Evaluating a Cooperative Activity

Standards for Evaluation
Eyewitness accounts should . . .

- show evidence of research and planning
- clearly dramatize the role of the culture in Russian history
- reflect an understanding of the cultures

Teacher's Edition 275

MORE ABOUT . . .
Power Struggles in Kiev

Yaroslav himself had to fight his brothers for the throne. Vladimir had 10 sons by different women. For 21 years the brothers struggled for power. Only two brothers, Boris and Gleb, refused to take up arms against their siblings. Following the teachings of Jesus, the two refused to fight evil with evil. They were quickly assassinated. Later they were canonized and revered by Russians.

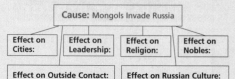

OBJECTIVE ③ INSTRUCT

Mongol Invasions Favor the Rise of Moscow

▶ **Key Ideas**

• Mongols destroy Kiev and set up an empire that lasts for 200 years.

• Mongols allow religious and cultural freedom in exchange for high taxes and obedience.

• Mongol rule helps Moscow rise and unites Russia.

• Ivan III makes the final break with the Mongols by refusing to pay their tribute.

CRITICAL THINKING ACTIVITY

CLASS TIME: 15 MINUTES

Making an Effects Chart

To help students understand the effects of the Mongol invasion on Russia, have them complete a chart like the one below.

Cause: Mongols Invade Russia

| Effect on Cities: | Effect on Leadership: | Effect on Religion: | Effect on Nobles: |

Effect on Outside Contact: | **Effect on Russian Culture:**

Kievan Russia Vladimir led the way in establishing Kiev's power. He expanded his state west into Poland and north almost to the Baltic Sea. He also fought off troublesome nomads from the steppes to the south.

In 1019, Vladimir's son **Yaroslav the Wise** came to the throne and led Kiev to even greater glory. Like the rulers of Byzantium, Yaroslav skillfully married off his daughters and sisters to the kings and princes of Western Europe. Those marriages helped him to forge important trading alliances. At the same time, he created a legal code tailored to Kiev's commercial culture. Many of its rules dealt with crimes against property. For example, Yaroslav's code called for a fine of three *grivnas* for cutting off a person's finger, but 12 *grivnas* for plowing over a property line. Yaroslav also built the first library in Kiev. Under his rule, Christianity prospered. By the 12th century, Kiev could even boast of having 400 churches. However, the wooden churches proved to be as temporary as Kiev's glory.

Power Struggles Bring on Kiev's Decline The decline of the Kievan state started with the death of Yaroslav in 1054. Yaroslav had made a crucial error. Yaroslav divided his realm among his sons—instead of following the custom of passing on the throne to the eldest son. His sons tore the state apart fighting for the choicest territories. And because this system of dividing among sons continued, each generation saw new struggles. The Crusades added to Kiev's troubles by disrupting trade. Then, just when it seemed that things could not get worse, they got far worse.

Mongol Invasions Favor the Rise of Moscow

In the middle 1200s, a ferocious group of horsemen from central Asia slashed their way into Russia. These nomads were the Mongols. (See Chapter 12.) They had exploded onto the world scene at the beginning of the 1200s under Genghis Khan (JEHNG·gihs KAHN), one of the most feared warriors of all time.

Mongols may have been forced to move out by economic or military pressures. They may have been lured by the wealth of cities to the west. Whatever their reasons for leaving, Mongols rode their swift horses across the steppes of Asia and on into

Background
Under Yaroslav's system, younger brothers were supposed to move up to better properties as their elders died. However, the brothers didn't always die in the right order!

HISTORY THROUGH ART: **Fine Art**

Madonna with Child and Angels (about 1463), Fra Filippo Lippi (Italy)

Christian religious art in the West strives to show the holy in realistic situations. Eastern Orthodox icons depict a spiritual world that is far removed from what some consider the "real" world. In Western art, the divine seems near and familiar. In the East, the divine looks far from our human level, but like windows, icons can help believers glimpse heaven.

Connect *to* History

Contrast What are the differences between the styles of these two paintings? Consider the mother, the child, and the background.

SEE SKILLBUILDER HANDBOOK, PAGE 1009

Connect *to* Today

Analyzing Go to a house of worship near you. See if and how the spiritual is portrayed there.

The Mother of God of Vladimir (12th century), icon commissioned by the grand duke of Kiev

---

Connect *to* History

Contrasting
Possible responses: Fra Filippo Lippi's painting features a landscape with perspective in the background. The face of Lippi's Madonna is of normal proportions. Her pose suggests maternal tenderness. The infant is childlike. The icon painting has a flat background covered with a stylized pattern. The Madonna's body and face are elongated. Her head is tilted in a stylized, unnatural way. The infant looks like a small adult.

Connect *to* Today

Analyzing
Suggest one or two students call local churches to find out the best time to visit. They can share their findings with the rest of the class. Students may also want to look in a newspaper or magazine to locate nearby museums that have collections of early Christian art.

Europe. Their savage killing and burning won them a reputation for ruthless brutality. When Genghis Khan died in 1227, his successors continued the conquering that he had begun. At its fullest extent, the Mongol Empire stretched from the Yellow Sea to the Baltic Sea and from the Himalayas to northern Russia.

In 1240, the Mongols attacked and demolished Kiev. They rode under the leadership of Batu Khan, Genghis's grandson. So many inhabitants were slaughtered, a Russian historian reported, that "no eye remained to weep." A Roman Catholic bishop traveling through Kiev five years later wrote, "When we passed through that land, we found lying in the field countless heads and bones of dead people." After the fall of Kiev, Mongols ruled all of southern Russia. For over 200 years, the Mongol Empire in Russia held power. The empire's official name was the "Khanate of the Golden Horde": *Khanate,* from the Mongol word for "kingdom"; *Golden,* because gold was the royal color of the Mongols; *Horde,* from the Mongol word for "camp."

Mongol Rule in Russia Under Mongol rule, the Russians could follow all their usual customs, as long as they made no sign of rebellion. As fierce as they were, the Mongols tolerated all the religions in their realms. The Church acted as a mediator between the people and the Mongols. It also pacified the oppressors by praying for them. Church leaders found a religious meaning in the Mongol occupation of the country. They explained it as a punishment for the people's sins. Icons gained importance at this time, and Russians used the images to help escape their painful political realities.

The Mongols demanded just two things from Russians: slavish obedience and massive amounts of tribute. The Mongols themselves made sure Russians remained obedient. However, they made local nobles collect the tribute. As long as the money was delivered, the nobles could keep their titles. Novgorod's prince and military hero **Alexander Nevsky,** for example, advised his fellow princes to cooperate with the Mongols. The Russian nobles crushed revolts against the Mongols and collected oppressive taxes for the foreign rulers. At his death, Nevsky willed the principality of Moscow to his son Daniel. Daniel founded a line of princes there that in 200 years would rise to great prominence.

Mongol rule isolated the Russians more than ever from their neighbors in Western Europe, cutting them off from many new ideas and inventions. However, during this period, forces were at work that would eventually lead to Russia's liberation and to the rise of a new center of power: Moscow.

Mongol Rule Serves Moscow's Interests In some ways, the Mongols actually helped to unite Russia. Kievan Russia had been a collection of small independent principalities. Mongol rulers looked upon Russia as their unified empire, and all Russian principalities had to pay tribute to the Mongol Khan.

The rise of Moscow also began under the Mongols. The city was first founded in the 1100s. By 1156, it was a crude village protected by a log wall. Nonetheless, Moscow was located near three rivers: the Volga, Dnieper, and Don. From that strategic position, a prince of Moscow who could gain control of the three rivers could eventually control nearly all of European Russia.

That opportunity for expansion would not arise until the 14th century. In the late 1320s, Moscow's Prince Ivan I had earned the gratitude of the Mongols by helping to crush a Russian revolt against Mongol rule. For his services, the Mongols appointed Ivan I as tax collector of all the Slavic lands they had conquered. They also gave him the title of "Great Prince." Ivan had now become without any

HISTORY MAKERS

Alexander Nevsky
1220?–1263

Alexander of Novgorod was about 20 when he carved his name on Russian history. In 1240, the Swedes attacked the principality of Novgorod to stop its expansion. Alexander soundly defeated the invading Swedes at the Neva River. Grateful Russians called him Nevsky ("of the Neva") in honor of his victory.

In 1242, his fame grew even greater. In that year, the Teutonic Knights, a brotherhood of Germanic warriors, invaded the Baltics and Russia to convert them to Catholicism. Alexander cut the German armies to pieces on a frozen channel between two lakes—his famous "Battle on the Ice." For this victory and for his long protection of the Russian church, Alexander was declared a saint of the Russian Orthodox Church in 1547.

The Khanate of the Golden Horde, 1294

Interpreting the Map Tell students to locate the Khanate of the Golden Horde and the Russian Principalities on the map. Then ask what reasons the Mongols might have had for relocating the capital of the Golden Horde. *Possible answers: First capital was too far away from major centers of population; Mongols could not control the empire from such a distance.*

Extension Activity Have pairs of students use an encyclopedia to find three present-day countries that were once part of the Mongol Empire. *Possible answers: China, Korea, Mongolia, Iran, Turkey, Armenia, Burma, Vietnam, Cambodia, Laos, Thailand, India, Pakistan, Russia*

SKILLBUILDER Answers
1. Over 2,800 miles.
2. Possible Answer: Other Mongols.

ASSESS & RETEACH

Section 2 Assessment
Have students work in small groups to answer the questions. Then ask volunteers to share their answers with the class.

Section Quiz
 FORMAL ASSESSMENT
Section quiz, p. 123

Reteaching Activity
CLASS TIME: 20 MINUTES

Have pairs of students work together to write sentences that use items from the Terms & Names list. Challenge partners to use more than one term or name in a single sentence.

CLOSE ACTIVITY

CLASS TIME: 30 MINUTES

Making an Effects Chart
Write the following terms on the board as column heads: Slav, Greek Byzantine, Viking, Mongol. Then have students copy the chart and work in small groups to fill in the columns with information about how each culture affected the development of Russia and Russian culture. When all groups are finished, discuss their answers as a class.

The Khanate of the Golden Horde, 1294

[Map]

GEOGRAPHY SKILLBUILDER: Interpreting Maps
1. About how many miles did the Khanate of the Golden Horde stretch from east to west?
2. What people controlled most of the kingdoms surrounding Mongol Russia?

Map labels: Kiev (1240), Moscow, Vladimir (1238), RUSSIAN PRINCIPALITIES, Sarai (new), Black Sea, Sarai (old) (1242), Constantinople, KHANATE OF THE GOLDEN HORDE, Seljuk Turks, Aral Sea, Syr Darya, Lake Balkhash, CHAGATAI KHANATE, Tabriz, Maragheh, CAUCASUS MOUNTAINS, Caspian Sea, Jerusalem, Baghdad (1258), ILKHANATE (PERSIA), HIMALAYAS, DELHI SULTANATE, URAL MOUNTAINS, Ob R., Irtysh R., Don R., Volga, Dnieper R., Euphrates R., Tigris R., Indus R.

Legend: Khanate of the Golden Horde at its greatest extent; Capital; (1258) Year of Mongol conquest; 0 500 Miles; 0 1,000 Kilometers

---

doubt the most powerful of all Russian princes. He also became the wealthiest and was known as "Ivan Moneybags."

Ivan was also able to convince the Patriarch of Kiev, the leading bishop of Eastern Europe, to move to Moscow. The move enhanced the city's prestige and gave Moscow's princes a powerful ally: the Church. Ivan I and his successors used numerous strategies to enlarge their territory: land purchases, wars, trickery, shrewd marriages. From generation to generation, they schemed to gain control over the small states around Moscow.

Vocabulary
enhanced: improved

An Empire Emerges The Russian state would become a genuine empire during the long, 43-year reign of Ivan III (1462–1505). This prince was only a boy of 13 when Constantinople fell to the Turkish Empire in 1453. In 1472, Ivan III managed to marry the niece of the last Byzantine emperor. He then began calling himself **czar** (zahr), the Russian version of Caesar. (The title became official only during the reign of Ivan IV.) By calling himself czar, however, Ivan III openly claimed to make Russia the "Third Rome."

Background
Rome itself was first; Constantinople was the Second Rome; the third was Russia, according to Ivan.

In 1480, Ivan made the final break with the Mongols. He refused to pay their tribute. Following his refusal, Russian and Mongol armies faced each other on either side of the Ugra River, about 150 miles southwest of Moscow. However, neither side wanted to fight. So, after a time, both armies turned around and marched home. Russians have traditionally considered this bloodless standoff as marking Russia's liberation from Mongol rule. After that liberation, the czars could openly pursue an empire.

The Mongols were not the only conquering people to emerge from central Asia. As you will learn in Section 3, Turks would begin establishing an empire in Southwest Asia. In one form or another, their empire would last from the 11th century to the 20th century.

Section 2 Assessment

1. TERMS & NAMES
Identify
- Slavs
- boyars
- Olga
- Vladimir
- Yaroslav the Wise
- Alexander Nevsky
- czar

2. TAKING NOTES
Make a chart like the one below to show the effects of Mongol rule in Russia.

Nobles	Church	People	Moscow Princes

3. RECOGNIZING EFFECTS
How did Vladimir's conversion to Christianity affect the citizens, society, and government of Kiev?

THINK ABOUT
- the laws he passed
- the customs he encouraged
- the policies he followed

4. ANALYZING THEMES
Empire Building The Mongols were fierce conquerors, and their rule cut Russia off from the rest of the world. Even so, their policies helped to pull Russia together as a territory. How? Give reasons and examples from the text to support your opinion.

THINK ABOUT
- Mongol policies in Russia
- the Church's attitude toward the Mongols
- the role and power of the nobility

ANSWERS

1. TERMS & NAMES
Slavs, p. 274
boyars, p. 275
Olga, p. 275
Vladimir, p. 275
Yaroslav the Wise, p. 276
Alexander Nevsky, p. 277
czar, p. 278

2. TAKING NOTES
Possible Responses: Nobles—collected tribute; put down revolts. Church—tolerated by Mongols; acted as link between Mongols and Russians. People—paid high taxes; developed a devotion to icons. Moscow Princes—became tax collectors for Mongols; gained control of small states around Moscow.

3. RECOGNIZING EFFECTS
Possible Responses: Vladimir's subjects were required to convert to Christianity. Byzantine teachers taught religion to the Kievans. The prince became head of the Church in Kiev.

4. ANALYZING THEMES
Possible Responses:
Independent principalities were unified. Russian religion and culture were preserved. The Church sanctioned Mongol rule, thus giving its approval to the new unified territory. The nobility retained some authority.

Turkish Empires Rise in Anatolia

MAIN IDEA

Turkish people converted to Islam and founded new empires that would renew Muslim civilization.

WHY IT MATTERS NOW

In the 20th century, the collapse of the Turkish empire left ethnic and religious hostilities that still affect the world.

SETTING THE STAGE To the east of Constantinople and south of Russia, the powerful Muslim empire of the Abbasids had ruled since the 8th century. (See Chapter 10.) By the late 10th century, however, their empire seemed ripe for conquest.

The Turks March from Central Asia

As early as 1300 B.C., Chinese records mention a people called the *Durko* living west of their borders. The *Durko* may well have been the Turks. For centuries, these nomads rode their horses over the vast plains. They herded goats and sheep, lived in tents, and used two-humped camels to carry their goods. The Islamic world first met them as raiders and traders along their northeastern frontiers. In the 10th century, the Turks began converting to Islam and slowly migrating into the Abbasid Empire.

From Slaves to Masters When the Abbasids first noticed the military skills of the Turks, they began buying Turkish children to raise as slaves, train as soldiers, and employ as bodyguards. The Abbasids came to prize the slaves for their skill and loyalty. On this subject, one author wrote: "One obedient slave is better than 300 sons; for the latter desire their father's death, the former [desires] long life for his master." Over time, Turkish military slaves, or **mamelukes,** became a powerful force in the Abbasid Empire. The mameluke forces soon became stronger than their Abbasid caliph masters in Baghdad.

This foreign influence could not have come at a worse time for the Abbasids. For 200 years, their empire had been losing significant stretches of territory. Spain broke away in 756, six years after the Abbasids came to power. After setting up their capital in Baghdad, the Abbasids saw other parts of their empire break away: Morocco in 788 and Tunisia in 800. In 809, some regions of Persia were lost. Then, in 868, the Abbasids lost control of Egypt.

Finally, in 945, Persian armies moved into Baghdad and put an end to the caliph's political power. Even though the caliph continued as the religious leader of Islam, he gave up all political power to the new Persian ruler.

The Rise of the Seljuks At this time of weakness and division, large numbers of Turks migrated into the Abbasid Empire around 970. One of the first of these migrating Turkish groups was known as the **Seljuks** (SEHL-jooks), after the family that led them. By the year 1000, the Seljuks had converted to the Sunni branch of Islam. Despite their conversion, however, they continued to make war on other Muslims. In 1055, they attacked and captured Baghdad from the Persians.

Twenty years later, the Seljuk sultans marched on the Byzantine Empire. At the Battle of Manzikert in 1071, the Turks crushed the Byzantines. Within ten years, the Seljuks occupied most of Anatolia, the eastern flank of Byzantium. This brought the

A mameluke horseman aims his bow at the enemy in this drawing from around the year 1300.

A. Answer Slaves would be loyal because their position depended on their masters' position.

THINK THROUGH HISTORY
A. Recognizing Motives How would giving slaves position and power assure their loyalty?

Vocabulary
caliph: an Islamic religious and political leader.

Background
For a discussion of the split between Sunni and Shi'ite Muslims, see Chapter 10, page 240.

OBJECTIVES

1. To describe the rise of the Seljuk Turks and their impact on Persian culture.

2. To explain how internal problems and foreign attack ended Seljuk power.

CRITICAL THINKING
- Recognizing motives, p. 279
- Contrasting, p. 280
- Analyzing issues, p. 281

FOCUS
5-Minute Warm-Up

▶ *Drawing Conclusions*
To understand how Turkish rulers helped renew Muslim civilization, have students answer these questions.

1. Read the History Makers feature on page 280. What are two ways that Malik Shah showed support for the Muslim religion?

2. What facts indicate that Malik Shah did not have the full support of his family?

WARM-UP TRANSPARENCY 11

OBJECTIVE ① INSTRUCT

The Turks March from Central Asia

▶ *Key Ideas*
- The Turks enter the Abbasid empire as military slaves and gradually gain power.
- Migrating Turks called Seljuks capture Baghdad and occupy Anatolia and eastern Byzantium.
- Seljuk rulers promote and support Persian culture.

IN-DEPTH RESOURCES: UNIT 3
Guided Reading, p. 20

ACCESS FOR STUDENTS ACQUIRING ENGLISH
Guided Reading (Spanish), p.113

ELECTRONIC LIBRARY OF PRIMARY SOURCES
from "The Merits of Turks"

SECTION 3 RESOURCES

PRINT RESOURCES

IN-DEPTH RESOURCES: UNIT 3
Guided Reading, p. 20
Primary Source: Pope Urban II's Call for a Crusade, p. 27

ACCESS FOR STUDENTS ACQUIRING ENGLISH
Guided Reading (Spanish), p. 113

FORMAL ASSESSMENT
Section Quiz, p. 124

ALTERNATIVE ASSESSMENT BOOK

TECHNOLOGY RESOURCES

WORLD ART AND CULTURES TRANSPARENCIES
AT24 Turkish painting on silk

CRITICAL THINKING TRANSPARENCIES
CT11 Comparing Seven Empires
CT47 Chapter 11 Visual Summary

CD-ROM
Electronic Library of Primary Sources

 INTERNET www.mlworldhistory.com

HISTORY MAKERS

Malik Shah
1055–1092

Malik Shah, the third and greatest Seljuk sultan, was a conqueror like the sultans before him. However, he is remembered today for his love of art, science, and literature. Among his achievements, he built the great mosque Masjid-i-Jame (shown above) in Isfahan. Malik also established religious tolerance throughout his empire.

He patronized intellectuals and artists like Omar Khayyam (OH·mahr ky·YAHM), who is most famous today for the *Rubaiyat* (ROO·bee·AHT). The *Rubaiyat* is a collection of poems describing the poet's love of life's pleasures. Omar also created a more accurate calendar for Malik.

Malik Shah was also capable of great cruelty. When his brother Takash revolted against him, Malik punished Takash by blinding him. Malik Shah died suddenly at the age of 37, possibly poisoned by his wife.

Turks closer to Constantinople than the Arabs or Persians had ever come. This near conquest of the New Rome also inspired the name of the Seljuk sultanate of Rum (from "Rome"). Rum survived in Anatolia after the rest of the Seljuk Empire had crumbled.

The Turks Secure Persian Support Seljuk rulers wisely courted the support of their newly conquered Persian subjects. In fact, the founder of the Seljuk Dynasty, Toghril Beg, chose the Persian city of Isfahan (IHS·fuh·HAHN) as the capital of his kingdom. This favorable treatment made the Persians loyal supporters of the Seljuks, and the Turks often appointed them as government officials. The brilliant Nizam al-Mulk, for example, was a Persian who served as the **vizier,** or prime minister, of the most famous of Seljuk sultans, **Malik Shah.**

The bond between Turks and Persians also grew strong because of Turkish admiration of Persian learning. The nomadic Seljuks had arrived in Southwest Asia basically illiterate. They were unfamiliar with the traditions of Islam, which they had just adopted. As a result, they looked to their Persian subjects for both cultural and religious guidance. The Turks adopted Persian as the language of culture and adopted features of the Persian way of life that they so admired. Seljuk rulers were called *shahs*, from the Persian word for a king. They also promoted Persian writers like the mystical Islamic poet Jalaludin Rumi, whose poetry is widely read today. Rumi often wrote of his desire to achieve a personal experience of God. In this poem, he expresses that desire in passionate terms:

> **A VOICE FROM THE PAST**
> Burning with longing-fire
> Wanting to sleep with my head on your doorsill,
> My living is composed only of this trying to be in your presence.
> **JALALUDIN RUMI,** quoted in *Unseen Rain*

Seljuk shahs like the great Malik Shah took pride in supporting Persian artists and architects. Malik beautified the city of Isfahan, for example, by building many splendid mosques.

The Turks' political and cultural preference for the Persians caused the almost complete disappearance of the Arabic language from Persia. Only religious scholars studying the Qur'an used Arabic. As a result of their policy, the Seljuks won strong support from Persians, who were proud of their long heritage. Like other conquering peoples throughout history, the Seljuk Turks found that they had much to learn from those whom they had defeated.

Turks saw control of cities as the key to victory. This drawing from an early 13th-century manuscript illustrates a siege of a city that took place two centuries earlier. Notice the two soldiers being catapulted over the wall.

280

---

280   Chapter 11

Seljuks Confront Crusaders and Mongols

Malik Shah ruled as the last of the strong Seljuk leaders. After his unexpected death in 1092, no capable shah appeared to replace him. So, the Seljuk Empire quickly disintegrated into a loose collection of minor kingdoms. Just at that point, the West launched a counterattack against the Turks. This series of military campaigns is called the Crusades.

The Seljuks and the Crusaders Pope Urban II launched the First Crusade in 1095. He called for Christians to drive the Turks out of Anatolia and recover Jerusalem. Armies from Western Europe soon poured through Constantinople and proceeded on to Palestine. In 1099, the Crusaders captured Jerusalem and massacred its Jewish and Muslim inhabitants. They established a Latin Christian kingdom that lasted about a century.

Eventually, a fragment of the former Seljuk Empire gathered enough strength to fight back. Under their famous Kurdish captain Saladin, the Muslims recovered Jerusalem in 1187. Eventually, Saladin and his Western opponent King Richard I of England signed a truce. Their agreement gave Jerusalem to the Muslims but granted Western pilgrims access to Christian holy places.

The popes called for further Crusades. But each new one was weaker than the last. The Western threat to the Turks was fading. However, just as the menace of the Crusades was subsiding, the Muslim world suffered another devastating shock. This time it came from the east.

Seljuks Face the Mongols The new threat to Turkish power was the Mongol army of conquest and destruction led by Genghis Khan. Early in the 1200s, Genghis Khan had forged his Mongol tribes into a unified force and conquered China.

In the course of their rampage west, the Mongol armies leveled any cities that dared to resist them. They slaughtered whole populations. In 1258, when Genghis's grandson Hulagu finally took Baghdad, he had tens of thousands of people killed. He burned down the caliph's palace. Mongol belief warned against the spilling of sacred blood. So Hulagu executed the last Abbasid caliph by having him wrapped in a carpet and trampled to death by horses.

With untold brutality, Genghis Khan and his successors shaped the biggest land empire in history. (See Chapter 12 for more about the Mongol Empire.) The warrior Mongols, however, knew little about administering their territory. As a result, their vast empire crumbled in just a few generations. And out of the rubble of the Mongol Empire rose another group of Turks—the Ottomans. They would build an empire that lasted into the 20th century. You will learn about more about the Ottoman Empire in Chapter 18.

Background
For a full discussion of the Crusades, see Chapter 14, page 343.

Background
Christian holy places included sites believed to be connected with Jesus' life, death, and resurrection.

Section 3 Assessment

1. TERMS & NAMES
Identify
- mamelukes
- Seljuks
- vizier
- Malik Shah

2. TAKING NOTES
Create a time line like the one below to show the events in the last 200 years of the Abassid Empire.

756
Spain
breaks
away

3. ANALYZING ISSUES
In what ways would it be accurate to say that the Persians actually won over their Turkish conquerors?

THINK ABOUT
- religion
- culture
- political influence

4. THEME ACTIVITY

Empire Building Between Abbasid and Mongol rule, Baghdad was occupied and governed by four different powers. In a chart like the one below, summarize important events and features of those occupations.

Occupiers	Events/Features
Abbasids	
Persians	
Seljuks	
Mongols	

Byzantines, Russians, and Turks Interact **281**

ANSWERS

1. TERMS & NAMES
mamelukes, p. 279
Seljuks, p. 279
vizier, p. 280
Malik Shah, p. 280

2. TAKING NOTES
788, Morocco breaks away; 800, Tunisia breaks away; 809, parts of Persia are lost; 868, Abbasids lose control of Egypt; 945, Baghdad falls to Persians.

3. ANALYZING ISSUES
Possible Responses: The Turks looked to the Persians for religious and cultural guidance. The Turks adopted the language and customs of the Persians. Persians held powerful offices in the Turkish government.

4. THEME ACTIVITY
Possible Responses:
Abbasids—Made Baghdad their capital; mamelukes gained power over Abbasid caliphs. Persians—Captured Baghdad in 945; caliph lost political power to the sultan. Seljuks—Captured Baghdad in 1055; supported Persian culture. Mongols—Occupied Baghdad in 1258; burned down the caliph's palace and executed the last caliph.

TERMS & NAMES

1. Justinian Code, p. 270
2. Hagia Sophia, p. 270
3. Patriarch, p. 272
4. icon, p. 272
5. Slavs, p. 274
6. boyars, p. 275
7. Vladimir, p. 275
8. Alexander Nevsky, p. 277
9. Seljuks, p. 279
10. Malik Shah, p. 280

REVIEW QUESTIONS

11. **Possible Responses:** Constantine created a new eastern capital so he could respond to the danger of Germanic tribes and be close to his rich eastern provinces.

12. The Code—5,000 Roman laws; The Digest—summaries of legal opinions; The Institutes—instructions on the use of the laws; The Novellae (New Laws)—laws passed after 534.

13. **Possible Responses:** Beautiful churches and public buildings; the crowded marketplace along the Mese with products from many lands; street performers; the chariot races and circus acts at the Hippodrome; rowdy gangs.

14. Lombards attacked in the west; Avars, Slavs, and Bulgars in the north; Sassanid Persians in the east; Persians, Avars, Arabs, Russians, Crusaders invaded Constantinople; Turks invaded Anatolia

15. *The Primary Chronicle* says that Rurik was a Viking chief who was invited by the Slavs to be their king. It also says that Rurik founded Novgorod in 862.

16. The Vikings sailed by river and sea to Constantinople. They traded timber, fur, wax, honey, and slaves for products found in Constantinople.

17. Vladimir sent out teams of representatives to study the major religions of the times. The team that sudied Eastern Christianity was very enthusiastic about what it saw. This persuaded Vladimir to convert to the Eastern faith.

18. (a) It was located near three rivers, helping to make it a center for transportation and trade; (b) the Patriarch's relocation to Moscow brought prestige to the city and allied Moscow princes with the Church; (c) Ivan's wealth, power, and shrewdness helped him gain control of smaller states around Moscow.

19. Abbasids bought Turkish children to raise as slaves and train as soldiers

---

TERMS & NAMES

Briefly explain the importance of each of the following to the Byzantines, Russians, and Turks between 500 and 1500.

1. Justinian Code
2. Hagia Sophia
3. patriarch
4. icon
5. Slavs
6. boyars
7. Vladimir
8. Alexander Nevsky
9. Seljuks
10. Malik Shah

Interact *with* History

On page 268, you considered diplomatic ways of saving the Byzantine Empire from an invading army. Which non-military approach did you choose and why? Now that you've read about the Byzantine Empire, do you think that you chose the right strategy? Discuss your present ideas on handling the invader with the class.

REVIEW QUESTIONS

SECTION 1 *(pages 269–273)*
Byzantium Becomes the New Rome

11. Why did Constantine decide to create a new eastern capital for the Roman Empire?
12. Name and describe the contents of the four parts of the Justinian Code.
13. What were some important features of life in Constantinople?
14. Which peoples attacked the Byzantine Empire? What part of the empire did they invade?

SECTION 2 *(pages 274–278)*
Russians Adapt Byzantine Culture

15. What does *The Primary Chronicle* say about Rurik and the origin of Novgorod?
16. Describe the trade that developed between the Vikings and Constantinople.
17. According to *The Primary Chronicle*, how did Vladimir choose Byzantine Christianity?
18. How did each of the following contribute to the growth and prestige of Moscow: (a) its geography; (b) the Patriarch of Kiev; (c) Ivan I?

SECTION 3 *(pages 279–281)*
Turkish Empires Rise in Anatolia

19. Explain how Turkish children could move from slaves to masters.
20. List five ways the Turks showed respect for their Persian subjects.

Visual Summary

Byzantines, Russians, and Turks

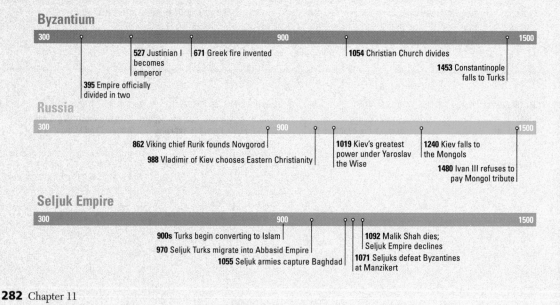

Byzantium

300 — 900 — 1500

527 Justinian I becomes emperor
671 Greek fire invented
1054 Christian Church divides
1453 Constantinople falls to Turks
395 Empire officially divided in two

Russia

300 — 900 — 1500

862 Viking chief Rurik founds Novgorod
988 Vladimir of Kiev chooses Eastern Christianity
1019 Kiev's greatest power under Yaroslav the Wise
1240 Kiev falls to the Mongols
1480 Ivan III refuses to pay Mongol tribute

Seljuk Empire

300 — 900 — 1500

900s Turks begin converting to Islam
970 Seljuk Turks migrate into Abbasid Empire
1055 Seljuk armies capture Baghdad
1092 Malik Shah dies; Seljuk Empire declines
1071 Seljuks defeat Byzantines at Manzikert

282 Chapter 11

---

and bodyguards. Eventually the slaves became a powerful force that would topple caliphs in Baghdad.

20. They chose the Persian city of Isfahan as the capital; appointed Persians to government posts; adopted Persian language and customs; supported Persian writers and artists; used Persian architectural styles.

Interact *with* History

Possible Responses: After reading about the decline of the Byzantine Empire, students may now say that military action is more effective than diplomacy. Others may decide that displaying military forces at the same time they are offering a diplomatic solution would impress upon invaders the consequences of refusing diplomacy.

CRITICAL THINKING

1. THE JUSTINIAN CODE

THEME EMPIRE BUILDING What were Justinian's goals in creating his law code? List several reasons why a leader might want to codify (organize) the laws. Explain the influence that the Justinian Code had in the Byzantine Empire.

2. LIVING UNDER THE MONGOLS

What advantages might Alexander Nevsky see in cooperating with the Mongols? What disadvantages can you see? Would you support such a policy? Why or why not?

3. THE VIKINGS, TURKS, AND MONGOLS

The Vikings, Turks, and Mongols moved into foreign lands. Where did they come from? Where did they settle? How did they interact with the native population? Recreate the chart below. Answer the questions above to fill in the chart. Show how these groups were similar or different.

	Where from?	Where settled?	Interactions with people
Vikings			
Turks			
Mongols			

4. ANALYZING PRIMARY SOURCES

The following is an account of Batu Khan's attack on the city of Riazan, in western Russia. *The Tale of the Destruction of Riazan* is found in church histories written during the 16th and 17th centuries. Partly fiction and partly fact, historians believe the description of the attack is generally accurate.

A VOICE FROM THE PAST
On the dawn of the sixth day the pagan warriors began to storm the city, some with firebrands [torches of burning wood], some with battering rams, and others with countless scaling ladders for ascending the walls of the city. . . . And the Tatars [Mongols] cut down many people, including women and children. Still others were drowned in the river. And they killed without exception all monks and priests. And they burned this holy city with all its beauty and wealth. . . . And churches of God were destroyed, and much blood was spilled on the holy altars. And not one man remained alive in the city. All were dead. . . . And this happened for our sins.

from ZENKOVSKY, Medieval Russia's Epics, Chronicles, and Tales

• How does the historian portray the Mongol invaders?

• According to the writer, why were the people of Riazan defeated by the Mongols?

• How does a historian's belief system influence the interpretation of history?

CHAPTER ACTIVITIES

1. LIVING HISTORY: Unit Portfolio Project

THEME RELIGIOUS AND ETHICAL SYSTEMS Your portfolio project shows how religions affected people's lives. For this chapter, you might choose to use one of the following ideas for your portfolio.

• Find a photograph of a holy place connected with the Byzantine, Russian, or Turkish empires. Write a two-minute documentary script explaining the meaning or importance of the religious site that you are focusing on. Record your documentary on audio- or videocassette and present it to the class.

• Meet in a team as Vladimir's delegates did to research different faiths. Each of you will investigate a different religious or ethical system. Combine the group's findings into a chart. Then write a personal report explaining which of these faiths best represents you and why.

• Write a dialogue between two advisers of an Abbasid caliph. One adviser gives reasons for training the mamelukes as soldiers to defend the empire. The other tries to convince the caliph that this policy is dangerous.

2. CONNECT TO TODAY Cooperative Learning

THEME CULTURAL INTERACTION When the Turks settled among the Persians, they took on Persian ways. When two peoples make contact, they tend to adopt aspects of each other's way of life. Today, contact among nations and peoples is occurring more frequently than at any other time in history.

Working in small groups, use the Internet, magazines, newspapers, or the library to find examples of how two peoples today have influenced each other. The group could focus on language, food, clothing, music, social customs, religion, system of government. The group should present the results of its research on an illustrated bulletin board with captions.

3. INTERPRETING A TIME LINE

Look at the time lines on page 282. How many years did the Byzantine Empire last? How long did Mongol rule last in Russia? How long did it take the Seljuk Empire to decline after the Seljuks took Baghdad?

FOCUS ON CHARTS

Study this chart of empires, their dates, territories, and populations.

• Which of the empires below lasted the longest time? the shortest?

• Which empire had the greatest territory and population?

Connect to History Is there any connection between how big an empire is or the number of people it rules and how long it lasts?

Seven Empires

	Dates	Greatest Territory*	Greatest Population**
Egyptian	2780 B.C.–1075 B.C.	0.4	4.5
Persian	550 B.C.–330 B.C.	2.0	14.0
Roman	27 B.C.–A.D. 476	3.4	54.8
Byzantine	A.D. 395–A.D.1453	1.4	30.0
Mali	A.D. 1200–A.D. 1400	0.9	3.0
Mongol	A.D. 1206–A.D. 1380	11.7	125.0
Aztec	A.D. 1325–A.D. 1521	0.2	6.0

*Estimated in millions of square miles
**Estimated in millions of people

---

1. LIVING HISTORY

Standards for Evaluation
A documentary script should meet the following criteria:

• Identifies the holy place and its culture.
• Clearly explains the place's meaning.
• Discusses the importance of the holy place in history.

Standards for Evaluation
A chart should meet the following criteria:

• Clearly displays information about each religion.
• Includes basic information, such as the religious practices and the important ideas of the faith.
• Is accompanied by a paragraph from each group member explaining why he or she is best represented by one of the faiths.

Standards for Evaluation
A dialogue should meet the following criteria:

• Clearly presents each advisor's point of view.
• Contains speeches focused on the advantages and drawbacks of training mamelukes to be soldiers.
• Shows an understanding of the historical reasons for and effects of training mamelukes.

2. CONNECT TO TODAY:

Standards for Evaluation
A bulletin board display should meet the following criteria:

• Shows evidence of research
• Presents clear examples of how two peoples have influenced each other.
• Includes appropriate pictures and captions.

3. INTERPRETING A TIME LINE

The Byzantine Empire lasted for 1,058 years. Mongol rule in Russia lasted for 238 years. Thirty-seven years after the Seljuks took Baghdad, the Seljuk Empire began to decline.

FOCUS ON CHARTS

Answers: The Egyptian empire lasted the longest time, while the Mongol empire lasted the shortest time. The Mongol empire had the greatest territory and population.

Connect to History *Possible Answer:* There appears to be no connection. The Mongol empire ruled the most land and people but lasted the shortest time. Yet the Aztec empire, with many fewer people and much less land, lasted only twenty years longer.

CRITICAL THINKING

1. THE JUSTINIAN CODE

Possible Responses: Justinian wanted a uniform law code he could use to regulate a complex society. A leader might codify laws to make them clear, consistent, and just. The Justinian Code regulated areas such as marriage, property, and crimes.

2. LIVING UNDER THE MONGOLS

Possible Responses: Advantages—Russians could avoid bloodshed; nobles could retain their authority. Disadvantages—payment of heavy tribute; loss of freedom. Students should explain their answers.

3. THE VIKINGS, TURKS, AND MONGOLS

Possible Answers: Vikings—came from north of the Baltic Sea; settled north of Black Sea; were leaders of the Slavs. Turks—may have been nomads living west of China; settled in Persia; made war on other Muslims, captured Baghdad. Mongols—came from central Asia; conquered and settled in Russia and the Seljuk Empire; ruled over conquered areas.

4. ANALYZING PRIMARY SOURCES

Possible Responses: Bloody and brutal invaders; the people were being punished for their sins; historians understand events according to their own values and beliefs.

PLANNING GUIDE
Empires in East Asia

	Key Ideas	COPY MASTERS	ASSESSMENT
SECTION 1 **Two Great Dynasties in China** *pp. 287–293*	*During the Tang and Sung Dynasties, China becomes the richest, most powerful, and most advanced country in the world. Its trading routes extend throughout Asia.*	**In-Depth Resources: Unit 3** • **Guided Reading,** p. 34 • **History Makers:** Wu Zhao, p. 49 • **Connections Across Time and Cultures:** Two Golden Ages: Greece and China, p. 51	[PE] *Section 1 Assessment,* p. 291 *Formal Assessment* • Section Quiz, p. 133 *Alternative Assessment Book* • Standards for Evaluating a Product or Performance
SECTION 2 **The Mongol Conquests** *pp. 294–298*	*The Mongols, a nomadic people from the Central Asian steppes, succeed in conquering most of Asia and eastern Europe. They establish the largest empire the world has ever seen and briefly rule China.*	**In-Depth Resources: Unit 3** • **Guided Reading,** p. 35 • **Primary Source:** from *The Secret History of the Mongols,* p. 42	[PE] *Section 2 Assessment,* p. 298 *Formal Assessment* • Section Quiz, p. 134 *Alternative Assessment Book* • Standards for Evaluating a Cooperative Activity
SECTION 3 **Empire of the Great Khan** *pp. 299–302*	*Mongol rule opens China to foreign visitors and to extensive trade both internally and abroad. Marco Polo's visit to China introduces the country and its many inventions to Europe.*	**In-Depth Resources: Unit 3** • **Guided Reading,** p. 36 • **Primary Source:** Marco Polo at the Mongol Court, p. 43 • **History Makers:** Kublai Khan, p. 50	[PE] *Section 3 Assessment,* p. 302 *Formal Assessment* • Section Quiz, p. 135 *Alternative Assessment Book* • Standards for Evaluating a Cooperative Activity
SECTION 4 **Feudal Powers in Japan** *pp. 303–307*	*Japanese civilization is shaped by Chinese influence, the clan system, and a feudal system. Rival war lords eventually set an emperor over all of Japan.*	**In-Depth Resources: Unit 3** • **Guided Reading,** p. 37 • **Skillbuilder Practice:** Making Inferences, p. 39 • **Geography Application:** p. 40 • **Primary Sources:** from *The Diary of Lady Murasaki,* p. 44; A Samurai Instructs His Son, p. 45 • **Literature:** from *The Tale of Genji,* p. 46; *from The Pillow Book,* p. 47,	[PE] *Section 4 Assessment,* p. 307 *Formal Assessment* • Section Quiz, p. 136 *Alternative Assessment Book* • Standards for Evaluating a Product or Performance
SECTION 5 **Kingdoms of Southeast Asia and Korea** *pp. 308–311*	*India and China heavily influence Vietnam, Cambodia, Korea, and other Southeast Asian cultures. These kingdoms struggle to remain independent.*	**In-Depth Resources: Unit 3** • **Guided Reading,** p. 38	[PE] *Section 5 Assessment,* p. 311 *Formal Assessment* • Section Quiz, p. 137 *Alternative Assessment Book* • Standards for Evaluating a Cooperative Activity
CHAPTER RESOURCES	**Chapter Overview** *China, the most advanced country in the world, is conquered by the Mongols, who overrun most of Asia and eastern Europe. They rule briefly before losing their empire. China and India influence the cultures of Japan, Korea, and many Southeast Asian kingdoms.*	*Telescoping the Times* • Chapter Summary, pp. 45–47 *Planning for Block Schedules*	[PE] *Chapter Assessment,* pp. 312–313 *Chapter Activities,* p. 313 *Formal Assessment* • Chapter Test, forms A and B, pp. 138–143 *Test Generator* *Alternative Assessment Book*

TECHNOLOGY

 Warm-Up Transparency 12

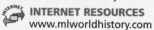 *Geography Transparencies*
- GT12 China in Early Dynasties

World Art and Cultures Transparencies
- AT25 Chinese tapestry

Electronic Library of Primary Sources
from *Ten-Thousand-Word Memorial*

INTERNET RESOURCES
www.mlworldhistory.com

 Warm-Up Transparency 12

Electronic Library of Primary Sources
- from *The History of the World Conquerer*

INTERNET RESOURCES
www.mlworldhistory.com

 Warm-Up Transparency 12

Battles of the World
- The Battle of Kyushu

Electronic Library of Primary Sources
- "The Tartars," from *Travels of Marco Polo*

INTERNET RESOURCES
www.mlworldhistory.com

 Warm-Up Transparency 12

World Art and Cultures Transparencies
- AT26 Descent of Amida

Critical Thinking Transparencies
- CT12 Japanese Cultural Borrowings from China

Electronic Library of Primary Sources
"The Manners and Customs of Early Japan"

INTERNET RESOURCES
www.mlworldhistory.com

 Warm-Up Transparency 12

World Art and Cultures Transparencies
- AT27 Cambodian Sculpture

Critical Thinking Transparencies
- CT48 Chapter 12 Visual Summary

Electronic Library of Primary Sources
from *Reminiscences in Retirement*

 Chapter Summaries on Audiocassette in English and Spanish

INTERNET RESOURCES
www.mlworldhistory.com

 Block Scheduling (90 MINUTES)

Day 1
Section 1, pp. 287–293

 COOPERATIVE ACTIVITY
Create a Display,
p. 289 (Teacher's Edition)

Section 2, pp. 294–298

COOPERATIVE ACTIVITY
Debating Ways of Life,
p. 295 (Teacher's Edition)

Section Assessments,
pp. 291, 298

Day 2
Section 3, pp. 299–302

 COOPERATIVE ACTIVITY
Letters to the Editor,
p. 301 (Teacher's Edition)

Section 4, pp. 303–307

Section 5, pp. 308–311

COOPERATIVE ACTIVITY
Tracing Cultural
Influences, p. 309
(Teacher's Edition)

Section Assessments,
pp. 302, 307, 311

Chapter Assessment,
pp. 312–313

Yearly Pacing *Chapter 12 Total:* 2 days **Yearly Total:** 85 days

 Planning for Block Schedules

Customizing for Special Needs

Students Acquiring English

 Access for Students Acquiring English
- **Guided Reading** for Sections 1–5 (Spanish), pp. 120–124
- **Chapter Summary** (Spanish), pp. 117–119
- **Skillbuilder Practice** Making Inferences (Spanish), p. 125
- **Geography Application** The Ainu People (Spanish), p. 126

 Chapter Summaries on Audiocassette in English and Spanish

 INTERNET RESOURCES
www.mlworldhistory.com
The Diverse Classroom.

Less Proficient Readers

 In-Depth Resources: Unit 3
- **Guided Reading** for Sections 1–5, pp. 34–38
- **Skillbuilder Practice** Making Inferences, p. 39
- **Geography Application** The Ainu People, p. 40

 Telescoping the Times
- Chapter Summary, pp. 45–47

 Chapter Summaries on Audiocassette

Gifted and Talented Students

In-Depth Resources: Unit 3

Primary Sources:
from *The Secret History of the Mongols,* p. 42

Marco Polo at the Mongol Court, p. 43

from *The Diary of Lady Murasaki,* p. 44

A Samurai Instructs His Son, p. 45

History Makers
Wu Zhao, p. 49

Kublai Khan, p. 50

Connections to Literature READINGS FOR STUDENTS

 In-Depth Resources: Unit 3
Literature: from *The Tale of Genji* by Lady Murasaki, p. 46;
from *The Pillow Books* by Sei Shonagon, p. 47.

Enrichment Reading

Bowring, Richard
The Diary of Lady Murasaki
New York: Penguin, 1996

Portraits of the difficult aristocrats and spineless courtiers of the 11th century Herin Court of Japan.

Yourcenar, Marguerite
"The Last Love of Prince Genji" *from Oriental Tales.*
New York: Noonday, 1990.

A modern tale of the 11th century Japanese court.

 = Pupil's Edition   = Overhead Transparency   = Software   = Video

 = Copy Master   = CD-ROM   = Audiocassette   = Internet

CHAPTER 12

Empires in East Asia, 600–1350

Empires in East Asia, 600-1350

Accessing Prior Knowledge

- Ask students what was happening in Europe and in the Americas during this period.

- Have students discuss what they already know about China, Japan, and Korea.

Analyzing

Have students look at these two pages before beginning their study of East Asia.

- What do the three pictures suggest about the history of China, Korea, and Japan during 600-1350?

- How would the Silk Roads have helped to spread Chinese civilization to the West?

Geography Connection

Ask students to study the areas covered by the Tang and Song dynasties.

- By what two ways could foreign traders reach both dynasties? *Silk Roads and sea routes*

- By 1126, how had the Song Dynasty changed? *The dynasty ruled all of southern China.*

PREVIEWING THEMES

Religious and Ethical Systems

Buddhism, which had reached China from India, spread from China to Korea and Japan. In Japan, Buddhism mixed with the traditional religion, Shinto. Both Hindu and Buddhist missionaries from India spread their religions across Southeast Asia.

Empire Building

The Tang Dynasty built China into the most powerful and advanced empire in the world in the 700s and 800s. In the 1200s, China fell under the control of another group of empire builders, the Mongols. For a century, the Mongols controlled most of Eurasia in the largest unified land empire in history.

Cultural Interaction

Two trends dominated this period of history. First, Chinese culture spread to the rest of East Asia, influencing Korea, Japan, and mainland Southeast Asia. Second, the rise of the Mongols and their great conquests led to interaction between nomadic and settled peoples across all of Asia.

INTERNET CONNECTION

Visit us at **www.mlworldhistory.com** to learn more about East Asian history.

TANG AND SONG CHINA, 600–1279

Caspian Sea

Aral Sea

☐ Tang Dynasty at furthest extent
■ Song Dynasty to 1126
▨ Song Dynasty after 1126
⌁ Grand Canal
⌁ Great Wall, 814

Battle of Talas (751)

0   1,000 Miles
0   2,000 Kilometers

N

Indus River

HIMALAYA

THAR DESERT

INDIA

Led by Genghis Khan, the fearsome **Mongol cavalry** swept out of Mongolia in **1209** and began a bloody conquest of Asia. By 1260, Genghis's successors controlled a vast empire extending from Korea to Kiev.

284

GEOGRAPHY THEMES

Location

Tell students that the location of kingdoms on the Asian mainland and in the Southeast Asian islands played a major role in determining how cultures of those kingdoms developed. The Mongols easily swept eastward into China but were stopped by the Himalaya Mountains and by the seas from traveling further south and east. However, the seas did not deter India and China from reaching Southeast Asia and from significantly influencing the cultures of many island kingdoms. Have students look ahead at the map on page 308 to see the locations of these islands.

Movement

Tell students that in this chapter they will read about the movement of peoples and ideas between East and West. The Mongols swept over Europe and Asia, marking the first time a pastoral people dominated such a large area of settled societies. China's cultural influence spread to neighboring kingdoms such as Korea, Japan, and Vietnam. Foreigners who visited China returned with many new ideas and inventions. Buddhism spread throughout East Asia.

ADDITIONAL RESOURCES

Books for the Teacher

• Cotterell, Arthur. *East Asia: From Chinese Predominance to the Rise of the Pacific Rim.* New York: Oxford UP, 1994.

• Murowchick, Robert, general ed. *China: Ancient Culture, Modern Land.* Norman, OK: U Oklahoma Press, 1994. The evolution of Chinese culture and history.

Books for the Student

• Cotterell, Arthur. *Ancient China.* New York: Knopf, 1994. The art of war, life in the fields, food and drink, medicine, and other aspects of imperial China.

• Lewis, Brenda Ralph. *Growing Up in Samurai Japan.* London: Batsford, 1981.

Videos

• *China in Transition: 581–1279.* Social Studies School Service, 1985. 800-421-4246.

• *Genghis Khan.* Teacher's Discovery, 1995. 800-543-4180.

• *The Mongol Onslaught.* Social Studies School Service, 1985. 800-421-4246.

Software

• *History and Culture of China.* CD-ROM. Queue, 1997. 800-232-2224. Includes discussion of dynastic rule and geographical isolation.

The man sitting behind the desk is a **Chinese scholar-official** in charge of a local district. In the **600s**, the rulers of the Tang Dynasty revived and expanded the civil service system begun by the Han emperors.

This **Japanese temple guardian** dates from the **1200s**. Such statues once stood outside Buddhist and Shinto temples to protect them from evil.

285

HISTORY THROUGH ART

Mongol Warrior

In the late 1100s and early 1200s, the Mongols swept across Central Asia and eastern Europe with the speed and ferocity of a firestorm. With their horses at full gallop, as shown in this painting, warriors were able to shoot to the side, front, and back. Timing the release of the arrow to come between the paces of their horses, these warriors were deadly accurate while making themselves a difficult target to hit.

The painting also shows the typical weapons and gear that every Mongol warrior carried into battle. The saddle, which helped protect the horse, was made with stirrups, an invention of the steppes. The stirrups allowed the rider to stand and shoot while guiding his horse with his knees. The quiver could hold up to 60 arrows, some armor-piercing. The painting does not show the armor typically worn by the Mongol warriors.

Interpreting the Art What does the painting show about the rider's skill as a warrior? *He is shooting behind him and guiding his horse without holding the reins.* The rider's quiver, which could hold about 60 arrows, is nearly empty—what does this tell you? *The rider has been shooting at many enemies or at a lot of game on a hunt.*

Interact *with* History

This Interact with History feature motivates students by inviting them to put themselves in a key historical situation—deciding which new invention they will bring back from an exotic society. As they think about which invention to choose, students will analyze the issues, explore their options, and become decision makers.

Purpose

- to introduce students to the history of China, Japan, and Korea
- to help students understand the impact of East Asian countries on Western development
- to help students connect with the people and events they will study in this chapter

Teaching Strategy

Thinking Critically After students have thought about the situation described on this page, have them answer the key questions and give reasons for their decision.

EXAMINING *the* ISSUES

Following are suggestions for addressing each bulleted question.

1 Ask students what the other society would need to know in order to use the new item.

2 Will any of these items prolong life or make it more enjoyable? If so, how?

3 Which of these items will people in another society consider most valuable?

4 Are any of these items capable of harming a society? If so, how?

Making Connections Ask students to name some inventions from the past 50 years that have affected how people live, work, travel, or play. Have them speculate on future inventions and how they might change people's lives.

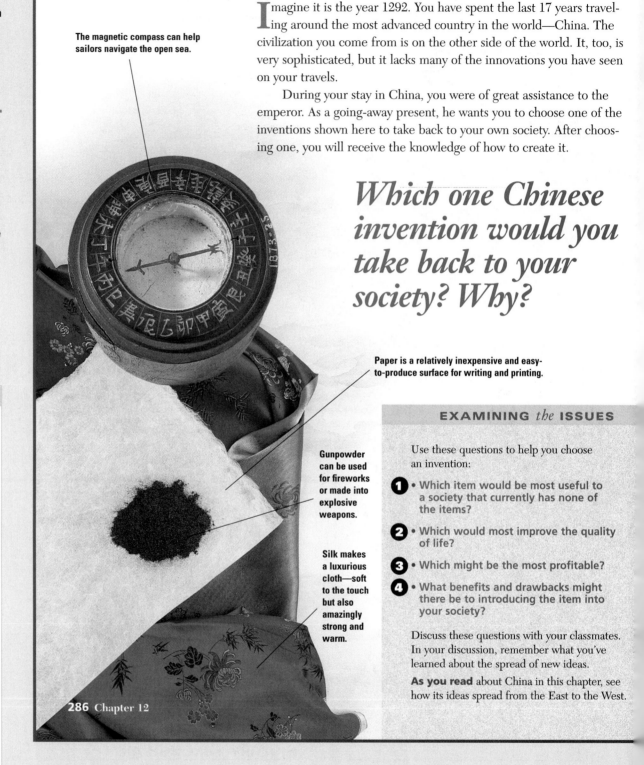

The magnetic compass can help sailors navigate the open sea.

Paper is a relatively inexpensive and easy-to-produce surface for writing and printing.

Gunpowder can be used for fireworks or made into explosive weapons.

Silk makes a luxurious cloth—soft to the touch but also amazingly strong and warm.

286 Chapter 12

Imagine it is the year 1292. You have spent the last 17 years traveling around the most advanced country in the world—China. The civilization you come from is on the other side of the world. It, too, is very sophisticated, but it lacks many of the innovations you have seen on your travels.

During your stay in China, you were of great assistance to the emperor. As a going-away present, he wants you to choose one of the inventions shown here to take back to your own society. After choosing one, you will receive the knowledge of how to create it.

Which one Chinese invention would you take back to your society? Why?

EXAMINING *the* ISSUES

Use these questions to help you choose an invention:

1 • Which item would be most useful to a society that currently has none of the items?

2 • Which would most improve the quality of life?

3 • Which might be the most profitable?

4 • What benefits and drawbacks might there be to introducing the item into your society?

Discuss these questions with your classmates. In your discussion, remember what you've learned about the spread of new ideas.

As you read about China in this chapter, see how its ideas spread from the East to the West.

Follow-Up

A feature on the chapter assessment will ask students to reevaluate their responses to the situation presented on this page.

Two Great Dynasties in China

MAIN IDEA

During the Tang and Song dynasties, China experienced an era of prosperity and technological innovation.

WHY IT MATTERS NOW

Chinese inventions from this period, such as printing, gunpowder, and the compass, changed history.

Section 1 Overview

OBJECTIVES

1. To identify the main rulers of the Tang Dynasty and the extent of their empire.

2. To describe the causes and effects of the Song family's flight south.

3. To summarize the achievements of the Tang and Song empires.

4. To describe changes in Chinese society.

SKILLBUILDER
- Interpreting charts, p. 289

CRITICAL THINKING
- Synthesizing, p. 287
- Recognizing effects, pp. 288, 291
- Analyzing causes, p. 290
- Making inferences, pp. 291, 293

SETTING THE STAGE After the Han Dynasty collapsed in A.D. 220, nomadic peoples from the northern steppe and Tibet conquered much of northern China. For 350 years, no emperor was strong enough to hold China together. More than 30 local dynasties rose and fell. By 589, an emperor named Sui Wendi had united northern and southern China once again. He restored a strong central government. Under the next two dynasties, the Tang and the Song, China experienced a golden age. It became the richest, most powerful, and most advanced country in the world.

The Tang Dynasty Expands China

Sui Wendi declared himself the first emperor of the Sui (sway) Dynasty. The dynasty lasted through only two emperors from 589 to 618. The Sui emperors' greatest accomplishment was the completion of the Grand Canal. This waterway connected the Huang He (Yellow River) and the Yangtze River. The canal provided a vital route for trade between the northern cities and the southern rice-producing region of the Yangtze delta.

To dig the 1,000-mile waterway, tens of thousands of peasant men and women toiled five years. Perhaps as many as half of the workers died on the job. Thousands more toiled and died to rebuild the Great Wall. The endless labor on state projects turned the people against the Sui Dynasty. Overworked and overtaxed, they finally revolted. In 618, a member of the imperial court strangled the second Sui emperor.

THINK THROUGH HISTORY
A. Synthesizing
What Sui accomplishments helped the Tang Dynasty become powerful?
A. Answer United China, restored central government, built Grand Canal, rebuilt Great Wall.

Tang Rulers Create a Powerful Empire While short-lived, the Sui Dynasty built a strong foundation for the great achievements of the next dynasty, the Tang (tahng). The Tang Dynasty ruled for nearly 300 years (618–907). The Tang emperor who began these achievements was **Tang Taizong,** whose brilliant reign lasted from 627 to 649.

Under the Tang rulers, the empire expanded. Taizong's armies reconquered the northern and western lands that China had lost since the decline of the Han Dynasty. By 668, China had extended its influence over Korea as well. The ruler during the campaign in Korea was the empress **Wu Zhao** (woo jow). From about 660 on, she held the real power while weak emperors sat on the throne. Finally, in 690, Empress Wu assumed the title of emperor for herself—the only woman ever to do so in China.

Tang rulers further strengthened the central government of China. They expanded the network of roads and canals begun by the Sui. This helped to pull the empire together. However, Tang Taizong also remembered the Sui emperors' mistake of overtaxing peasants. Therefore, he lowered taxes and took some lands from the wealthy to give to peasants. He and his successors also promoted foreign trade and improvements in agriculture. Tang China prospered.

Horses symbolized the power of the Tang Dynasty. Tang artists were famous for their glazed pottery horses such as this one, which was created in the early 700s.

Empires in East Asia **287**

FOCUS

5-Minute Warm-Up

▶ *Evaluating*
To help students understand China's history, have them answer these questions.

1. Read the chart of inventions on page 289. Which item could be made only in China?

2. Which of these items were you surprised to learn had been invented by the Chinese?

 WARM-UP TRANSPARENCY 12

OBJECTIVE ❶ INSTRUCT

The Tang Dynasty Expands China

▶ *Key Ideas*
- The Sui emperors build a foundation for the Tang Dynasty.
- The Tang create a powerful empire, improve trade and agriculture, and restore China's civil service bureaucracy.

(continued on next page)

 GEOGRAPHY TRANSPARENCIES
GT12 China in Sui, Tang, and Song Dynasties, 589–1279

SECTION 1 RESOURCES

PRINT RESOURCES

IN-DEPTH RESOURCES: UNIT 3
Guided Reading, p. 34
History Makers: Wu Zhao, p. 49
Connections Across Time and Cultures: Two Golden Ages: Greece and China, p. 51

ACCESS FOR STUDENTS ACQUIRING ENGLISH
Guided Reading (Spanish), p. 120

FORMAL ASSESSMENT
Section Quiz, p. 133

TECHNOLOGY RESOURCES

GEOGRAPHY TRANSPARENCIES
GT12 China in Sui, Tang, and Song Dynasties, 589–1279

WORLD ART AND CULTURES TRANSPARENCIES
AT25 Chinese tapestry

CD-ROM
Electronic Library of Primary Sources

INTERNET www.mlworldhistory.com

OBJECTIVE ① INSTRUCT

(continued from page 287)
- Tang Dynasty weakens, and rebels take over the capital.

 IN-DEPTH RESOURCES: UNIT 3
Guided Reading, p. 34

 ACCESS FOR STUDENTS ACQUIRING ENGLISH
Guided Reading (Spanish), p. 120

HISTORYMAKERS
Tang Taizong
Wu Zhao

Have students construct a Venn diagram showing which accomplishments and characteristics the two rulers had in common and which were unique to one or the other.

 IN-DEPTH RESOURCES: UNIT 3
History Makers: Wu Zhao, p. 49

MORE ABOUT . . .
Civil Service Exams

Competition for civil service positions was fierce. To ensure that exams were graded fairly, examiners assigned numbers to the tests and removed the applicants' names. Further, all exams were copied by scribes before they were graded so no one would recognize an applicant's handwriting.

 ELECTRONIC LIBRARY OF PRIMARY SOURCES
from *Ten-Thousand-Word Memorial*

OBJECTIVE ② INSTRUCT

The Song Dynasty Restores China

▶ **Key Ideas**
- Song Taizu reunites China, creating the Song Dynasty.
- The Song cannot stop the Jurchen from conquering northern China.
- The Song flee south and build a grand new capital.

 IN-DEPTH RESOURCES: UNIT 3
Connections Across Time and Cultures: Two Golden Ages: Greece and China, p. 51

HISTORYMAKERS

Tang Taizong
600–649

The man who restored the Middle Kingdom to its glory was a distinguished general named Li Shimin. He seized the imperial throne in 626 after killing off his brothers as rivals and forcing his father, the first Tang emperor, to step aside. As emperor, Li Shimin took the title Taizong, meaning "Great Ancestor."

Taizong's military campaigns extended China's borders north to Manchuria, south to Vietnam, and west to the Aral Sea. China's power and influence reached much farther. At home, aided by his gifted advisers, Taizong reformed the government organization and law code. These became models for all of East Asia.

Wu Zhao
625–705

At the age of 13, the beautiful Wu Zhao arrived at the court of Tang Taizong to become one of the emperor's secondary wives. After Taizong's death, she became a favored wife of his son and successor. Wu Zhao soon rose above rival wives and became the emperor's chief wife, or empress.

For many years, Empress Wu virtually ruled China on behalf of the sickly emperor. After his death, two of their sons briefly held the throne. Frustrated by their lack of ability, she took the throne herself at the age of 65. She was 80 when she finally lost power.

A strong leader, Wu Zhao continued the work begun by Taizong to build and expand China.

Scholar-Officials To manage their large empire, the Tang rulers needed to restore China's vast bureaucracy. The civil service examination system begun by the Han Dynasty had fallen into disorder. The Tang rulers revived and expanded the system to recruit good officials. They opened schools around the country to train young scholars in Confucianism, poetry, and other subjects covered in the exams. The few who passed the tough exams became part of an elite group of scholar-officials.

In theory, the exams were open to all men, even commoners. However, only the wealthy could afford the necessary years of education. Also, men with political connections could obtain high positions without taking the exams.

Despite these flaws, the system created a remarkably intelligent and capable governing class in China. Before the Tang Dynasty, a few noble families dominated the country. As the examination system grew in importance, talent and education became more important than noble birth in winning power. As a result, many moderately wealthy families shared in China's government.

The Tang Lose Power By the mid-700s, the Tang Dynasty was weakening. To pay for military expansion, Tang rulers reimposed crushing taxes. These brought hardship to the people but still failed to meet the rising costs of government. In times of famine, peasants fled their villages and roved the countryside in bandit gangs.

Moreover, the Tang could not control the vast empire they had built. In 751, Arab armies soundly defeated the Chinese on China's western frontier at the Battle of Talas. (See the map on pages 284–285.) Central Asia passed out of Chinese control and into foreign hands. After this time, border attacks and internal rebellions steadily chipped away at the power of the imperial government. Finally, in 907, Chinese rebels sacked and burned the Tang capital at Chang'an and murdered the last Tang emperor, a child.

The Song Dynasty Restores China

After the end of the Tang Dynasty, rival warlords divided China into separate kingdoms. In 960, an able general reunited China and proclaimed himself Song Taizu, the first Song (sung) emperor. The Song Dynasty, like the Tang, lasted about three centuries (960–1279). Although the Song ruled a smaller empire than either the Han or the Tang, China remained stable, powerful, and prosperous.

Song armies never regained the western lands lost after 751. Nor did they regain northern lands that had been lost to nomadic tribes during the Tang decline. For a time, Song emperors tried to buy peace with their northern enemies. They paid hefty annual

288 Chapter 12

B. Possible Answer
Created intelligent and capable governing class, reduced power of noble families, raised prestige of education, spread power across wider group.
THINK THROUGH HISTORY
B. Recognizing Effects What resulted from the revival of the civil service system?

Background
Recall the Mandate of Heaven (page 50), a concept the Chinese held to explain the decline and fall of dynasties.

Less Proficient Readers
Creating a Diagram Pair less proficient readers with more able ones and have them read the section of text on this page titled "The Tang Lose Power." Then ask students to diagram the multiple causes that led to the downfall of the Tang Dynasty. Students' diagrams might look like this:

tributes of silver, silk, and tea. This policy, however, ultimately failed to stop their threat. In the early 1100s, a Manchurian people called the Jurchen conquered northern China and established the Jin empire. The Jurchen forced the Song to retreat south across the Huang He. After 1126, the Song emperors ruled only southern China.

The Song ruling family fled south. They established a grand new capital at Hangzhou, a coastal city south of the Yangtze. Despite its military troubles, the dynasty of the Southern Song (1127–1279) saw rapid economic growth. The south had become the economic heartland of China. Merchants in southern cities grew rich from trade with Chinese in the north, nomads of Central Asia, and people of western Asia and Europe.

An Era of Prosperity and Innovation

The period of the Tang and Song dynasties was one of intense growth. China grew in population, trade, wealth, new ideas, and artistic achievements. In the span of three or four centuries, China's population nearly doubled, soaring to 100 million. By the Song era, China had at least ten cities with a population of 1 million each. China was the most populous country in the world. It was also the most advanced.

Science and Technology Artisans and scholars made important technological advances during the Tang and Song eras. Among the most important inventions were movable type and gunpowder. With **movable type,** a printer could arrange blocks of individual characters in a frame to make up a page for printing. Previously, printers had carved the words of a whole page into one large block. The development of gunpowder led to the creation of explosive weapons such as bombs, grenades, small rockets, and cannons. Other important inventions of this period include porcelain, the mechanical clock, paper money, and the use of the magnetic compass for sailing.

Inventions of Tang and Song China

	Date	Description	Impact
Porcelain	Late 700s	Bone-hard, white ceramic made of a special clay and a mineral found only in China	Became a valuable export—so associated with Chinese culture that it is now called "china"; technology remained a Chinese secret for centuries
Mechanical clock	700s	Clock in which machinery (driven by running water) regulated the movements	Early Chinese clocks short-lived; idea for mechanical clock carried by traders to medieval Europe
Printing	Block printing: 700s Movable type: 1040	Block printing: one block on which a whole page is cut; movable type: individual characters arranged in frames, used over and over	Printing technology spread to Korea and Japan; movable type also developed later in Europe
Gunpowder	800s	Explosive powder made from mixture of saltpeter, sulfur, and charcoal	First used for fireworks, then weapons; technology spread west within 300 years
Paper money	1020s	Paper currency issued by Song government to replace cumbersome strings of metal cash used by merchants	Contributed to development of large-scale commercial economy in China
Magnetic compass (for navigation)	1100s	Floating magnetized needle that always points north-south; device had existed in China for centuries before it was adapted by sailors for use at sea	Helped China become a sea power; technology quickly spread west

SKILLBUILDER: Interpreting Charts
1. Which inventions eventually affected warfare and exploration?
2. Which of these inventions do you think had the greatest impact on history? Why?

Empires in East Asia **289**

MORE ABOUT . . .
Tribute Paid
The amount of tribute the Song paid the Jurchen depended on who was stronger. An 1141 treaty set the annual tribute at 500,000 units of silver and silk. When the Jurchen failed to conquer the Song in 1165, the tribute dropped to 100,000 units. When the Song later failed to conquer the Jurchen, the Jurchen fined them 3 million units and raised the tribute to 600,000 units.

OBJECTIVE 3 INSTRUCT

An Era of Prosperity and Innovation

► *Key Ideas*
- The Tang and Song dynasties create a golden age in China.
- Advances in science, technology, and agriculture increase China's wealth and population.
- China becomes a great sea power.
- Chinese writers and painters achieve new heights of beauty and expression.

History from Visuals

Inventions of Tang and Song China
Interpreting the Diagram
Within how many years did all of these inventions arise? *400* Which inventions contributed most to China's economic success? *paper money and magnetic compass*

Extension Activity Have students create a double time line of inventions—one Chinese and one European—to show the influence of China. Students can use encyclopedias to find inventions for the European time line.

SKILLBUILDER Answers
1. Gunpowder, magnetic compass.
2. Answers will vary, but students should be able to give reasons for their choice.

TEACHING OPTION **BLOCK SCHEDULING** **COOPERATIVE ACTIVITY: Create a Display** **CLASS TIME 20 MINUTES**

Task: Students will research one invention listed in the chart and create a display and written report.

Purpose: To learn about China's achievements during the Tang and Song dynasties and the impact of China's inventions on Western development.

Activity: Students should work in groups of four or five. Have each group research one of the six

inventions, focusing on how the invention came about, how it worked, what it was made of, and how Westerners adapted it. Ask each group to create a display illustrating the invention and to write a brief report on its history and development.

Building a Portfolio: Students adding a report to their portfolio should attach a statement explaining their contribution to the report.

 ALTERNATIVE ASSESSMENT BOOK Standards for Evaluating a Cooperative Activity

Standards for Evaluation
Displays and reports should . . .

- graphically illustrate the invention
- show its current form and uses
- explain the history and use of the item

Agriculture The rapid growth of China resulted from advances in farming. Farmers especially improved the cultivation of rice. In about the year 1000, China imported from Vietnam a new variety of fast-ripening rice. This allowed the farmers to harvest two rice crops each year rather than one. To make sure that farmers knew about the improved variety, Chinese officials distributed seedlings throughout the country. The agricultural improvements enabled China's farmers to produce more food. This was necessary to feed the rapidly expanding population in the cities.

Trade and Foreign Contacts Under the Tang and Song emperors, foreign trade flourished. Tang imperial armies guarded the great Silk Roads, which linked China to the West. Eventually, however, China lost control over these routes during the long Tang decline. After this time, Chinese merchants relied increasingly on ocean trade. Chinese advances in sailing technology, including use of the magnetic compass, made it possible for sea trade to expand. During the Song period, China developed into the greatest sea power in the world.

Up and down China's long coastline, the largest port cities in the world bustled with international trade. Merchant ships carried trade goods to Korea and Japan. They sailed across the Indian Ocean to India, the Persian Gulf, and even the coast of Africa. Chinese merchants established trading colonies around Southeast Asia. Many foreign traders, mostly Arabs, resided in Chinese cities. Through trade and travel, Chinese culture spread throughout East Asia. One major cultural export was Buddhism. This religion spread from China to Japan, Korea, and Vietnam.

The exchange of goods and ideas was two-way. During Tang times, tea first arrived in China from Southeast Asia. The Chinese became avid tea drinkers as well as tea producers. New ideas in mathematics and astronomy developed from contact with India. Foreign religions, including Islam and some Eastern sects of Christianity, also spread to China and won followers there.

A Golden Age of Art The prosperity of the Tang and Song dynasties nourished an age of artistic brilliance. The spread of wealth, education, and urban culture stimulated a high level of artistic creativity. Scholar-officials, for example, were expected to write poetry and to own at least one fine painting.

The Tang period produced great poetry. Two of its most celebrated poets were Li Bo, who wrote about life's pleasures, and Du Fu, who praised orderliness and Confucian virtues. Du Fu also wrote critically about war and the hardships of soldiers. Once he himself was captured by rebels and taken to Chang'an, the capital city. He had sent his family to the village of Fuzhou for safety. Here he describes their separation.

A VOICE FROM THE PAST
The same moon is above Fuzhou tonight; From the open window she will be watching it alone, The poor children are too little To be able to remember Chang'an. Her perfumed hair will be dampened by the dew, The air may be too chilly on her delicate arms. When can we both lean by the wind-blown curtains And see the tears dry on each other's face?

DU FU, "Moonlight Night"

Chinese painting reached new heights of beauty and expression during the Song Dynasty. Painting of this era shows the influence of the Daoist love of nature. Artists emphasized the beauty of natural landscapes—lofty mountains, rippling brooks—and objects such as a single branch or flower. The artists did not use brightly colored paints. Black ink was their favorite paint. Said one Song artist, "Black is ten colors."

Song artist Ju Ran painted this masterpiece, *Buddhist Monastery in Stream and Mountain Landscape,* in the late tenth century.

Changes in Chinese Society

China's prosperity produced many social changes during the Tang and Song periods. Chinese society became increasingly mobile. People moved to the cities in increasing numbers. The Chinese also experienced greater social mobility than ever before. The growing cities offered many opportunities for managers, professionals, and skilled workers. However, the most important avenue for social advancement was the civil service system.

Levels of Society During Tang and Song times the power of the old aristocratic families faded. A new, much larger upper class emerged, made up of scholar-officials and their families. Such a class of powerful, well-to-do people is called the **gentry.** The gentry attained their status through education and civil service positions, rather than through land ownership. However, many scholar-officials also became wealthy enough to own land.

Below the gentry was an urban middle class. It included merchants, shopkeepers, skilled artisans, minor officials, and others. At the bottom of urban society were laborers, soldiers, and servants. In the countryside lived the largest class by far, the peasants. They toiled for wealthy landowners as they had for centuries.

The Status of Women Women had always been subservient to men in Chinese society. Their status further declined during the Tang and Song periods. This was especially true among the upper classes in cities. There a woman's work was deemed less important to the family's prosperity and status. Changing attitudes affected peasant families less, however. Peasant women worked in the fields and helped produce their family's food and income.

One sign of the changing status of women was the custom of binding the feet of upper-class girls. The practice of foot binding began during this period and continued into the 20th century. When a girl was very young, her feet were bound tightly with cloth, which eventually broke the arch and curled all but the big toe under. This produced what was admiringly called a "lily-foot." Women with bound feet were crippled for life. To others in society, such a woman reflected the wealth and prestige of her husband, who could afford such a beautiful but impractical wife.

The social, economic, and technological transformations of the Tang and Song period permanently shaped Chinese civilization. They endured even as the Middle Kingdom fell to a group of nomadic outsiders, the Mongols, whom you will learn about in Section 2.

Daily *Life*

A Scholar's Fingernails
Many scholar-officials eventually adopted the fashion of growing their fingernails long. A two-inch fingernail showed clearly that the owner did no manual labor. However, long nails did not prevent the scholar from following the pursuits of the gentry, such as writing poetry, painting, or practicing calligraphy. The photograph above is of a Chinese doctor in the late 19th century.

OBJECTIVE ④ INSTRUCT

Changes in Chinese Society

▶ *Key Ideas*
- Chinese society becomes increasingly mobile, with more rural people moving to cities.
- The society is composed of the gentry, urban middle and lower classes, and peasants.
- The status of women declines.

Daily *Life*
A Scholar's Fingernails

How do men and women today provide clues about their status or role in society? Have students explain their answers, giving details.

ASSESS & RETEACH

Section 1 Assessment
Have students individually draft answers to the questions, then trade papers with a partner for peer evaluation. Students should then finalize their answers.

📋 *FORMAL ASSESSMENT*
Section Quiz, p. 133

Reteaching Activity
CLASS TIME: 15 MINUTES

Go over the answers to those questions that students found most difficult.

CLOSE ACTIVITY

CLASS TIME: 30 MINUTES

Clarifying
Divide the class into two teams. Direct each team to review the material in this section. Have the teams stand on opposite sides of the room, and ask them questions about the Tang and Song dynasties. For each wrong answer, a team member sits down. The team with the most students still standing at the end wins.

Section ① Assessment

1. TERMS & NAMES

Identify
- Tang Taizong
- Wu Zhao
- movable type
- gentry

2. TAKING NOTES

Create a Venn diagram showing the similarities and differences between the Tang and Song dynasties.

Tang only

Both

Song only

3. RECOGNIZING EFFECTS

What impact did improvements in transportation have on Tang and Song China?

THINK ABOUT
- ways transportation was improved
- how these improvements were made
- relationships among regions in China
- trade with other countries

4. ANALYZING THEMES

Empire Building What actions taken by the Sui, Tang, and Song emperors strengthened China's empire? What actions weakened it?

THINK ABOUT
- military gains and losses
- changes to the government
- improvements in transportation and trade
- cultural changes

Empires in East Asia **291**

ANSWERS

developed into great sea power, created paper money and movable type. Both: prospered through trade, improved agriculture, created great art and literature.

3. RECOGNIZING EFFECTS
Possible Responses: Expanded roads and canals linked regions of China and spurred trade.

Advances in sailing technology expanded sea trade and cultural exchange with other nations.

4. ANALYZING THEMES
Possible Responses:
Strengthened: Built Grand Canal (Sui); guarded Silk Roads, improved roads, promoted trade, restored civil service (Tang);

improved agriculture, expanded sea trade, issued paper money (Song). Weakened: imposed high taxes, lost control of empire (Tang); lost northern China (Song).

SOMETHING IN COMMON

OBJECTIVES

(1) To identify differences and similarities in healing arts across cultures.

(2) To point out the impact of technology on the healing arts.

FOCUS

▶ Ask students if they have heard of any folk remedies for common illnesses. Examples might be "Chicken soup helps cure a cold" and "Feed a cold and starve a fever."

• Do you think any of these remedies actually work? How do you know? (For example, researchers have found that steam from chicken soup helps clear nasal passages.)

• How do you think these ideas are passed from one generation to another?

MORE ABOUT . . .
Chinese Acupuncture

Acupuncture is not only used to treat illness and minor injuries, it is also used as an anesthetic during surgery. Once the needles are inserted at specific points in the patient's body, they block all pain. Patients can be fully awake during an operation. Western scientists are not sure how acupuncture achieves this effect. They speculate that the needles stimulate the brain to produce natural pain killers, called endorphins, or that they prevent pain messages from reaching the central nervous system. Whatever the explanation, acupuncture works as a highly effective anesthetic.

Healing Arts

Since illness is a part of living, every society has developed ways to treat health problems. For thousands of years, Chinese doctors have used acupuncture to relieve pain and cure diseases. During the Song Dynasty, the Chinese carefully studied human anatomy and created charts and models of the body. These improved the practice of acupuncture.

Acupuncture developed from traditional Chinese beliefs about the forces of nature. Likewise, in other cultures, the healing arts have been shaped by the cultures' beliefs about nature. Think about this connection as you read about the practices described here.

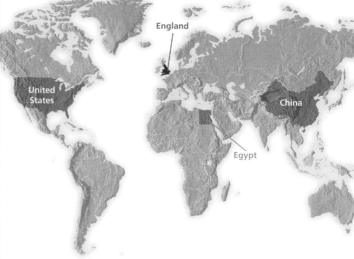

Chinese Acupuncture

Acupuncture is based on the belief that an energy force known as *qi* (chee) flows through the body and keeps people alive. According to this idea, *qi* flows along channels called meridians. Pain or illness arises when the *qi* does not flow properly. The treatment is to insert slender needles in the body at specific points (such as the ear) along the meridians, depending on the problem. This adjusts the flow of *qi* and restores health.

a closer look CHINESE MEDICINE

Qigong (chee-GONG) is a traditional Chinese healing art. It combines movement with deep breathing and meditation. These exercises are designed to maintain health by keeping the *qi* in proper balance.

Science Botany pharmacognosists, scientists who study medicinal plants, have estimated that in the United States, one fourth of all medications come from plants. In some societies, this number might be one half to two thirds. Two well-known examples are aspirin, derived from willow bark, and the heart medicine digitalis, derived from the foxglove plant. Interested students may wish to research such medicinal plants as aloe, privet, goldenseal, camphor, and witch hazel.

Alternative Medicines Interest in alternative medicines such as herbal treatments and vitamin/mineral supplements has increased in this country. In response, some observers have called for greater control of these products by the Food and Drug Administration. Others say the government is trying to reduce access to the products. Have interested students investigate the controversy and report back to the class, stating clearly what each side believes and what is at stake for U.S. consumers.

A Physician, Ancient Egypt

Health care in ancient Egypt was remarkably complex. The Egyptians believed that gods and demons influenced health. Therefore, a doctor's treatment often called for certain spells, chants, or prayers. At the same time, doctors had a great deal of practical knowledge about symptoms and useful treatments and medicines. The Egyptians passed down their medical knowledge by recording it on scrolls and tablets. This stone tablet from about 2600 B.C. shows a portrait of Hesy-Re, one of the earliest known physicians.

Stone Age Surgery, England

Archaeologists have discovered many Stone Age skulls, such as this one found in England, with portions deliberately removed. This procedure, called trepanning (trih·PAN·ihng), may have been performed to allow demons to escape the head. In some cases, it probably helped relieve painful pressure on the skull resulting from injury or disease. Remarkably, scientists can see evidence in the trepanned skulls that many patients survived for a long time after their operation.

Modern Surgery, U.S.A.

The scientific approach of Western medicine reflects the modern belief that technology can improve people's lives. Brain surgery, as shown below, has been transformed by high-tech equipment, specialized training, pain-killing drugs, and other advances. Today's scientific medicine has made some diseases less threatening and increased the human life span.

The tradition of Chinese herbal medicine dates back thousands of years. This modern pharmacy in Singapore dispenses Chinese medicines. Pharmacists may stock 1,500 herbs for use as remedies. Medicines can also include bark, twigs, and animal or insect parts.

Connect to History

Making Inferences Look again at the healing arts of the four cultures described on these pages. How are each culture's beliefs about nature reflected in the culture's health practices?

 SEE SKILLBUILDER HANDBOOK, PAGE 1005

Connect to Today

Interviewing Conduct a brief interview with someone who practices a non-Western or "alternative" type of medicine. Find out if this type of medicine has changed over time and, if so, how. Share what you learn with your classmates.

INTERNET CONNECTION

Visit us at **www.mlworldhistory.com** to learn more about the healing arts.

Empires in East Asia **293**

Section 2 Overview

OBJECTIVES

1. To describe the geography of the steppe and the lifestyles of nomadic and settled peoples.

2. To explain the Khans' success in conquering most of Asia and parts of Europe.

3. To summarize the extent of the Mongol Empire and its divisions.

SKILLBUILDER

- Interpreting maps: region, location, p. 298

CRITICAL THINKING

- Identifying problems, pp. 294, 297
- Making Inferences, pp. 295, 298
- Summarizing, p. 296

FOCUS

5-Minute Warm-Up

▶ **Interpreting Maps**
Answering these questions will help students understand the extent of the Mongol Empire.

1. Study the map on page 298. Between which longitudes does the empire lie?

2. What major bodies of water do the empire's borders touch?

 WARM-UP TRANSPARENCY 12

OBJECTIVE 1 INSTRUCT

Nomads of the Asian Steppe

▶ **Key Ideas**
- The Eurasian steppe is a vast grassland serving as a trade route and as a pasture for nomads.
- Steppe nomads are pastoralists who move in seasonal patterns and live in clans.
- Steppe nomads trade with settled communities but also raid them periodically.

📖 *IN-DEPTH RESOURCES: UNIT 3*
Guided Reading, p. 35

📖 *ACCESS FOR STUDENTS ACQUIRING ENGLISH*
Guided Reading (Spanish), p. 121

---

2 The Mongol Conquests

TERMS & NAMES
- pastoralist
- clan
- Genghis Khan

MAIN IDEA	WHY IT MATTERS NOW
The Mongols, a nomadic people from the steppe, conquered settled societies across much of Asia.	The Mongols built the largest unified land empire in world history.

SETTING THE STAGE While the Chinese grew prosperous during the Song Dynasty, a great people far to the north were also gaining strength. The Mongols of the Asian steppe lived their lives on the move. They prided themselves on their skill on horseback, their discipline, their ruthlessness, and their courage in battle. They also wanted the wealth and glory that would come with conquering mighty empires. Conflict between these nomadic people and settled peoples across Eurasia was about to explode into violence. The Mongol conquests would forever transform Asia and Europe.

Nomads of the Asian Steppe

Across the landmass of Eurasia—from Manchuria to Hungary—stretches a vast belt of dry grassland called the steppe. The significance of the steppe to neighboring civilizations was twofold. First, it served as a land trade route connecting the East and the West. Second, it was home to nomadic peoples who frequently swept into the cities to plunder, loot, and conquer.

Geography of the Steppe There are two main expanses of the Eurasian steppe. The western steppe spans from Central Asia to eastern Europe. It was the original home of many of the ancient invaders you have read about, including the Hittites and the Aryans. The eastern steppe, covering the area of present-day Mongolia, was the first home of the Huns, the Turks, and the Mongols.

Very little rain falls on the steppe, but the dry, wind-swept plain supports short, hardy grasses. Temperature changes can be extreme. The temperature in Mongolia, for example, ranges from –57°F in winter to 96°F in the summer.

Rainfall is somewhat more plentiful and the climate milder in the western steppe than in the east. For this reason, movements of people have historically tended to be toward the west and the south.

The boundaries of the steppe were constantly shifting and were often less geographical than political. One way of defining where the steppe ended was to say where cultivated fields began. The Chinese, for example, were constantly trying to push back the line in order to extend the area under their cultivation.

The Nomadic Way of Life

Nomadic peoples were **pastoralists**—that is, they herded

THINK THROUGH HISTORY
A. Identifying Problems What conditions on the steppe might have discouraged agriculture?
A. Possible Answer Lack of rainfall, windy conditions, temperature extremes.

The Steppe

SIBERIA
EUROPE
Moscow
Kiev
WESTERN STEPPE
Aral Sea
Constantinople
Caspian Sea
Tashkent
Samarkand
Kashgar
INDIA
ASIA
Karakorum
GOBI DESERT
EASTERN STEPPE
Beijing
CHINA
Kaifeng

0 1,000 Miles
0 2,000 Kilometers

GEOGRAPHY SKILLBUILDER: Interpreting Maps
1. **Region** About how far does the western steppe extend from west to east?
2. **Location** About how far is Beijing from the edge of the eastern steppe?

SECTION 2 RESOURCES

PRINT RESOURCES

📖 *IN-DEPTH RESOURCES: UNIT 3*
Guided Reading, p. 35
Primary Source: from *The Secret History of the Mongols*, p. 42

📖 *ACCESS FOR STUDENTS ACQUIRING ENGLISH*
Guided Reading (Spanish), p. 121

📖 *FORMAL ASSESSMENT*
Section Quiz, p. 134

📖 *ALTERNATIVE ASSESSMENT BOOK*

TECHNOLOGY RESOURCES

💿 **CD-ROM**
Electronic Library of Primary Sources

🌐 **INTERNET** www.mlworldhistory.com

Many people on the Mongolian steppe still follow the nomadic way of life. This photograph shows modern Mongolians outside their yurt.

domesticated animals. They were constantly on the move, searching for good pasture to feed their herds. Nomads did not wander. Rather, they followed a familiar seasonal pattern and returned on a regular basis to the same campsites. Keeping claim to land that was not permanently occupied was difficult. Battles frequently arose among nomadic groups over grassland and water rights.

Asian nomads practically lived on horseback as they followed their huge herds over the steppe. They depended on their animals for food, clothing, and housing. Their diet consisted of meat and mare's milk. They wore clothing made of skins and wool, and they lived in portable felt tents called yurts.

Steppe nomads traveled together in kinship groups called **clans.** The members of each clan claimed to be descended from a common ancestor. Clans required good leaders to make decisions about when to leave one pasture for another and to devise military strategies. Different clans sometimes came together when they needed a large force to attack a common enemy or raid their settled neighbors.

Steppe Nomads and Settled Societies The differing ways of life of nomadic and settled peoples resulted in constant interaction between them. Often, they engaged in peaceful trade. The nomads exchanged horses, for example, for basic items they lacked, such as grain, metal, cloth, and tea. Nomads were accustomed to scarcity and hardship. They prided themselves on their toughness. However, they were sometimes tempted by the rich land and relative wealth of townspeople and took what they wanted by force. As a result, settled peoples lived in constant danger of raids.

Time and again in history, nomadic peoples rode out of the steppe to invade border towns and villages. When a state or empire was strong and organized, it could protect its frontier. The Chinese, for example, built and rebuilt the Great Wall in an attempt to keep out nomadic invaders. If the state or empire became divided and weak, this provided an opportunity for nomads to increase their attacks and gain more plunder. They might even take over a region and settle there.

Occasionally, a powerful group, such as the Mongols under Genghis Khan, was able to conquer a whole empire and become its rulers. Over generations, these nomadic rulers often became part of the civilization they conquered.

The Rise of the Mongols

For centuries, the Mongol people had roamed the eastern steppe in loosely organized clans. It took a military and political genius to unite the Mongols into a force with a single purpose—conquest.

Genghis Khan Unites the Mongols Around 1200, a Mongol khan, or clan leader, named Temujin sought to unify the clans under his leadership. Across the Mongolian steppe, he defeated his rivals one by one, showing no mercy. In 1206, Temujin accepted the title **Genghis Khan,** or "universal ruler" of the Mongol clans.

Over the next 21 years, Genghis led the Mongols in conquering much of Asia. His first goal was China. After invading the northern Jin empire in 1215, however, his attention turned to the Islamic region west of Mongolia. Angered by the murder of Mongol traders and an

THINK THROUGH HISTORY
B. Making Inferences How might a strong, organized empire defend its frontier?
B. Possible Answers Building defensive walls, maintaining border armies, maintaining internal control over frontier regions, keeping loyalty of army and civil servants.

HISTORY MAKERS

Genghis Khan
1162?–1227

Temujin, according to legend, was born with a blood clot in his fist. In his lifetime, his hands were often covered with the blood of others.

When he was about nine, his father was poisoned by the Tatars, a rival people. For a time, he and his family lived in extreme poverty, abandoned by their clan. When in manhood he fought and defeated the Tatars, he slaughtered every male taller than a cart axle. The survivors—the females and only the youngest male children—were brought up as his followers.

While driven by revenge, Genghis also loved conquest. He once remarked to his personal historian:

Man's greatest good fortune is to chase and defeat his enemy, seize his total possessions, leave his married women weeping and wailing, [and] ride his [horse]. . . .

Empires in East Asia **295**

History from Visuals

(See map on page 294.)
The Steppe

SKILLBUILDER Answers
1. about 4,000 miles from west to east
2. around 200 miles

OBJECTIVE 2 INSTRUCT

The Rise of the Mongols

▶ **Key Ideas**
- Mongol clans unite under the leadership of Genghis Khan and conquer Central Asia.
- Genghis Khan, a brilliant organizer and strategist, uses new weapons, technology, and terror to overwhelm his enemies.

ELECTRONIC LIBRARY OF PRIMARY SOURCES
from *The History of the World Conqueror*

HISTORY MAKERS
Genghis Khan

A political and military genius, Temujin was proclaimed Genghis Khan by an assembly of Mongol chieftains after he became ruler of Mongolia.

Although known more for his military conquests, Genghis Khan also promoted literacy among his people and established the Yasa, the first Mongol code of laws. He appointed army officers on the basis of achievement, not family connections, making them loyal to him alone.

Gifted and talented students may want to read the primary source on Genghis Khan.

IN-DEPTH RESOURCES: UNIT 3
Primary Source: from *The Secret History of the Mongols,* p. 42

COOPERATIVE ACTIVITY: Debating Ways of Life

Task: Students will debate the relative merits of the nomadic versus the settled way of life.

Purpose: To help students empathize with other people and understand the differences between nomads and settled people.

Activity: Divide the class into two groups, one

representing nomads and the other settled peoples, both farmers and townspeople. Have each group research the lifestyle and culture of their assigned people as they were in 1200–1350. Each group should select a coordinator, timekeepers, researchers, and debaters to present their side.

Then have students debate which is the better way of life. They should address issues such as freedom, security, social behavior, material goods, culture, and relationship to nature.

ALTERNATIVE ASSESSMENT BOOK
Standards for Evaluating a Cooperative Activity

A Mighty Fighting Force

Interpreting the Diagram Ask students to study the diagram and to name at least three things that made the Mongol army self-sufficient. *Possible Answer: Soldiers had their families with them, carried their own food supply, and took their livestock and homes with them.*

Extension Activity Ask interested students to research the yurt, or Mongol dwelling, which is still in use today. Have them report to the class on how this strong, mobile dwelling is made and what advantages it would give to an army on the move.

MORE ABOUT . . .
Mongol Battle Tactics

On the battlefield, men from the same clan were not allowed to fight side by side. Allegiance to the commander outweighed all clan loyalties. Commanders used signal flags to communicate with distant units. A huge pair of kettle-drums, eight to ten feet across and mounted on camels, gave the signal for a battle to begin.

MORE ABOUT . . .
Horse's Blood

Mongol warriors relied on their horses and took good care of them. Drawing small amounts of blood from a horse did not harm the animal. A similar practice is still carried out by other pastoral peoples today. The Nuer, Masai, and other cattle herders of Africa cut the veins of their cattle and collect the blood to drink.

---

ambassador at the hands of the Muslims, Genghis launched a campaign of terror across Central Asia. "In retribution for every hair on their heads it seemed that a hundred thousand heads rolled in the dust," wrote a court historian of Genghis's revenge. The Mongols destroyed one city after another—Utrar, Samarkand, Bukhara—and slaughtered many inhabitants. By 1221, Central Asia was under Mongol control.

Genghis the Conqueror Several characteristics lay behind Genghis Khan's stunning success as a conqueror. First, he was a brilliant organizer. He assembled his Mongol warriors into a mighty fighting force (see below). Following the model of the Chinese military, Genghis grouped his warriors in armies of 10,000. These in turn were organized into 1,000-man brigades, 100-man companies, and 10-man platoons. He put his most battle-proven and loyal men in command of these units.

Second, Genghis was a gifted strategist. He used various tricks to confuse his enemy. Sometimes, a small Mongol cavalry unit would attack, then pretend to gallop away in flight. The enemy usually gave chase. Then the rest of the Mongol army would appear suddenly and slaughter the exhausted enemy forces. Another strategy was to make the enemy believe that the Mongol army was bigger than it actually was. This was done by dressing prisoners or lifelike dummies as Mongol warriors. Genghis also used spies brilliantly to find out enemy weaknesses.

Third, Genghis adopted new weapons and technologies used by his enemies. For example, he put captured Chinese engineers to work building catapults and creating gunpowder charges. He then used the weapons to conquer other Chinese cities.

Finally, Genghis Khan used cruelty as a weapon. He believed in terrifying his enemies into surrender. If a city refused to open its gates to him, he might kill the entire population when he finally captured the place. The terror the Mongols inspired spread ahead of their armies, which led many towns to surrender without a fight. As one Arab historian wrote, "In the countries that have not yet been overrun by them, everyone spends the night afraid that they may appear there too."

C. Answer Assembled a well-organized army, dressed prisoners or dummies as warriors, adopted new technology, used terror as a weapon.

THINK THROUGH HISTORY
C. Summarizing What were some of the tactics Genghis Khan used in war?

Below his armor, each cavalry warrior wore silk underwear. When warriors were wounded by an arrow, often the arrowhead did not pierce the strong silk. The warriors could use the silk to help pull the arrow cleanly out of a wound.

A Mighty Fighting Force

Mongol soldiers were superb horsemen, having spent all their lives in the saddle. Annual game roundups gave young men the chance to practice skills they would use in battle and gave their leaders the opportunity to spot promising warriors.

When on the move, each soldier was accompanied by three extra horses. By changing mounts, soldiers could stay in the saddle for up to ten days and nights at a time. When charging towards a target, they covered as much as 120 miles a day. If food was scarce, a Mongol soldier might make a small gash in the neck of one of his horses and sustain himself by drinking the blood.

A key to Mongol horsemanship was the stirrup, which was invented on the steppe in the second century B.C. Stirrups enabled a mounted warrior to stand, turn, and shoot arrows behind him.

The cavalry warrior's weapons included leather armor, a lance, a dagger, a bow and arrows, and his stout, sturdy horse.

296 Chapter 12

CUSTOMIZING FOR SPECIAL NEEDS

Less Proficient Readers
Identifying Main Ideas Pair less proficient readers with more able readers and have them read the section on this page titled "Genghis the Conquerer." Ask the partners to discuss the text and then make a web diagram or a chart listing the main ideas and supporting details. A chart might look like this:

Genghis Khan's Tactics	
Main Idea	**Supporting Details**
Organizer	Organized his army into units
Strategist	Used tricks to confuse his enemy
Adopted new techniques	Built catapults; created gunpowder charges
Used cruelty as a weapon	Killed the whole population of cities so that other cities would surrender quickly

The Mongol Empire

Genghis Khan died in 1227—not from violence, but from illness. His successors, however, continued to expand his empire. In less than 50 years, the Mongols conquered territory from China to Poland. In so doing, they created the largest unified land empire in history. (See the map on page 298.)

The Khanates Following the death of Genghis Khan, his son Ogadai became the Great Khan. The Great Khan headed the whole Mongol Empire. Under his leadership, Mongol armies commanded by Genghis's other sons and grandsons drove armies south, east and west out of Inner Asia. They completed their conquest of northern China and invaded Korea. They leveled the Russian city of Kiev and reached the banks of the Adriatic Sea. The cities of Venice and Vienna were within their grasp. No one knows how far west into Europe the Mongols might have penetrated. But Ogadai died in 1241. The commanders were called back to their capital to elect his successor. The westward campaign ended.

By 1260, the Mongol Empire was divided into four large khanates, each of them ruled by a descendant of Genghis. These four were the Khanate of the Great Khan (Mongolia and China), the Khanate of Chagatai (Central Asia), the Ilkhanate (Persia), and the Khanate of the Golden Horde (Russia). Kublai Khan, a grandson of Genghis Khan, named himself the Great Khan in 1260.

The Mongols as Rulers Many of the areas invaded by the Mongols never recovered. The populations of some cities were wiped out. Even worse, the Mongols destroyed ancient irrigation systems in areas such as the Tigris and Euphrates valleys. Thus the land could no longer support resettlement. One Persian assessed the destruction:

> **A VOICE FROM THE PAST**
> There can be no doubt that even if for a thousand years to come no evil befalls the country, yet will it not be possible to completely repair the damage, and bring back the land to the state in which it was formerly.
> **HAMD-ALLAH MUSTAWFI**, *The Geographical Part of the Nuzhat al-Qulub*

Over time, some Mongol rulers adopted aspects of the culture of the people they ruled. The Ilkhans and the Golden Horde became Muslims. The Great Khans made use of Chinese institutions. The growing cultural differences among the khanates contributed to the eventual splitting up of the empire.

The Mongol Peace From the mid-1200s to the mid-1300s, the Mongols imposed stability and law and order across much of Eurasia. This period is sometimes called the Mongol Peace. The Mongols guaranteed safe passage of trade caravans, travelers, and missionaries from one end of the empire to another. Trade between Europe and Asia had

Mongol women took primary responsibility for the needs of the camp, milked the livestock, and treated the wounded. Some also fought as warriors.

The khan and other leaders had great mobile yurts pulled by teams of oxen.

A Mongol army was like a moving city. The cavalry of 10,000 was accompanied by an even greater number of family members, and by tens of thousands of horses and livestock.

Empires in East Asia **297**

OBJECTIVE ③ INSTRUCT

The Mongol Empire

▶ *Key Ideas*
- The Mongol conquests create the largest land empire yet known.
- Over time, the empire is divided into four khanates.
- After conquering an area, the Mongols often adopt many aspects of the local culture.
- The period of Mongol peace encourages trade and cultural exchange between Europe and Asia.

MORE ABOUT . . .
The Bubonic Plague
(See page 298.)

Historians can only speculate that Mongols were responsible for transmitting bubonic plague to Europe. If they actually did spread the plague, then the Mongols unwittingly killed far more people through infection than through warfare.

TEACHING OPTIONS | CONNECTIONS ACROSS TIME AND PLACE | EXPLORING PRIMARY SOURCES

Terrorist Tactics With students, compare the terrorist tactics used by the Mongols with those used by anti-government and rebel groups today. Point out that in both cases the purpose is psychological. The Mongols wanted to convince the enemy that resistance was useless. Present-day terrorist groups are often small, weak organizations that want people to think they are powerful. Although almost 800 years separate the two groups, they are alike in that civilians suffer the most from their attacks.

A Voice From the Past Tell students to use what they know about ancient Mesopotamia to calculate the loss of the irrigation systems to the Persians (see Chapter 2, section 1, pp. 27–28). About how old were the irrigation systems when the Mongols destroyed them? *(3,000–4,000 years)* Ask students to write a brief statement describing the loss to the Persians in terms of being able to grow crops and sustain cities.

Teacher's Edition   297

The Mongol Empire, 1294

— Border of Mongol Empire
⇒ Campaigns of Genghis Khan
⇒ Campaigns of his successors
⋯ Route of Marco Polo
ᶰᶰ Great Wall

GEOGRAPHY SKILLBUILDER: Interpreting Maps
1. **Region** *What khanate controlled Russia? Persia? Korea?*
2. **Region** *What parts of Asia did the Mongols fail to control?*

Messengers carried medallions like the one above as passports, so they could travel safely across the Mongol Empire.

never been more active. Ideas and inventions traveled along with the trade goods. Many Chinese innovations, such as gunpowder, reached Europe during this period.

Other things spread along with the goods and the ideas. Some historians speculate that the epidemic of bubonic plague that devastated Europe during the 1300s was first spread by the Mongols. (See Chapter 14.) The disease might have spread along trade routes or have been passed to others by infected Mongol troops.

For a brief period of history, the nomadic Mongols were the lords of city-based civilizations across Asia, including China. As you will read in Section 3, China continued to thrive under Mongol rule.

Section 2 Assessment

1. TERMS & NAMES
Identify
• pastoralist
• clan
• Genghis Khan

2. TAKING NOTES
Using a chart like the one below, list the series of events leading to the creation of the Mongol Empire.

> Genghis Khan unites Mongols.

Write a news report describing the most important event you listed.

3. MAKING INFERENCES
What characteristics of Mongol culture do you think contributed to their military success? Explain your response.

THINK ABOUT
• how the nomadic way of life shaped Mongol culture
• the personality and leadership qualities of Genghis Khan
• Mongol weapons and tactics

4. THEME ACTIVITY
Cultural Interaction Draw a diagram showing the interaction between various cultures and the Mongols who conquered them. Consider influence on economic development, military tactics, and religious beliefs.

ANSWERS

1. TERMS & NAMES
pastoralist, p. 294
clan, p. 295
Genghis Khan, p. 295

2. TAKING NOTES
Possible Responses: Genghis Khan conquers Central Asia; his son Ogadai becomes Great

Khan; Mongols spread conquest south, east, and west; Ogadai dies and westward campaign ends; Mongol Empire controls much of Eurasia.

3. MAKING INFERENCES
Possible Responses: Nomadic groups fought among themselves,

which geared them for warfare; mobile way of life was well suited for war; large supply caravans gave armies mobility and flexibility; riding skills, stirrups made cavalry powerful; contact with other cultures brought new weapons and tactics.

4. THEME ACTIVITY
Diagrams may show that Mongols got catapults and gu[npowder] from the Chinese; the Ilkhans and Golden Horde co[n]verted to Islam; Mongol attac[ks] destroyed cities; and the Mongol Peace promoted trad[e]

3 Empire of the Great Khan

TERMS & NAMES
- Kublai Khan
- Marco Polo

MAIN IDEA

Kublai Khan ruled China and encouraged foreign trade, but the Yuan Dynasty was beset by problems.

WHY IT MATTERS NOW

The influence of Chinese ideas on Western civilization began with the Mongols' encouragement of trade.

SETTING THE STAGE Kublai Khan, the grandson of Genghis Khan, assumed the title Great Khan in 1260. In theory, the Great Khan ruled the entire Mongol Empire. In reality, the empire had split into four khanates. Other descendants of Genghis ruled Central Asia, Persia, and Russia as semi-independent states. The Great Khan focused instead on extending the power and range of his own khanate, which already included Mongolia, Korea, Tibet, and northern China. To begin, Kublai had to fulfill the goal of his grandfather to conquer all of China.

Kublai Khan Conquers China

It took three generations of Mongol leaders to complete the conquest of China begun by Genghis Khan. In 1234, Genghis's son Ogadai conquered northern China. This opened southern China to direct attack. Chinese soldiers in the south held off the Mongols for 40 years, but the armies of Kublai Khan finally overwhelmed them in 1279.

Throughout China's long history, the Chinese feared and fought off invasions of northern nomads. China sometimes lost territory to nomadic groups, but no foreigner had ever ruled the whole country. The first to do so was Kublai Khan.

Beginning a New Dynasty As China's new emperor, **Kublai Khan** founded a new dynasty called the Yuan (yoo•AHN) Dynasty. It lasted less than a century, until 1368, when it was overthrown. However, the Yuan era was an important period in Chinese history for several reasons. First, Kublai Khan united China for the first time in 300 years. For this he is considered one of China's great emperors. Second, the control imposed by the Mongols across all of Asia opened China to greater foreign contacts and trade. Finally, Kublai and his successors tolerated Chinese culture and made few changes to the system of government.

Unlike his Mongol ancestors, Kublai spent almost his entire life in China. Far from the Mongolian steppe, he did not share his ancestors' hatred of civilization. On the contrary, he rather enjoyed living in the luxurious manner of a Chinese emperor. He maintained a beautiful summer palace at Shangdu, on the border between Mongolia and China. He also built a new square-walled capital at the site of modern Beijing. The size of Kublai's palace in Beijing greatly impressed the European traveler Marco Polo, who called it "the largest that was ever seen."

This helmet was worn by a Mongol officer.

Background
Shangdu is the origin of the English word Xanadu, *which means an idyllic, beautiful place.*

A VOICE FROM THE PAST
The hall is so vast and so wide that a meal might well be served there for more than 6,000 men. . . . The whole building is at once so immense and so well constructed that no man in the world . . . could imagine any improvement in design or execution.

MARCO POLO, *The Travels of Marco Polo*

Empires in East Asia **299**

Teacher's Edition **299**

This detail from a 13th-century Japanese scroll depicts Japanese warriors fighting off a Mongol warship.

Kublai built this palace to enhance his prestige, but his new capital meant something more. Previously, the Great Khans had ruled their empire from Mongolia. Moving the capital from Mongolia to China was a sign that Kublai intended to make his mark as emperor of China.

Failure to Conquer Japan After conquering China, Kublai Khan tried to extend his rule to Japan. In 1274 and again in 1281, the Great Khan sent huge fleets against Japan. The Mongols forced Koreans to build, sail, and provide provisions for the boats, a costly task that almost ruined Korea. Both times the Japanese turned back the Mongol fleets.

The second fleet carried 150,000 Mongol, Chinese, and Korean warriors—the largest seaborne invasion force in history until World War II. After 53 days, Japanese warriors had fought the invaders to a standstill. Then, on the following day, the sky darkened and a typhoon swept furiously across the Sea of Japan. Mongol ships were upended, swamped, and dashed to bits against the rocky shore, despite their sailors' attempts to escape onto the open sea. Many Mongols drowned and the Japanese quickly slew many others. For centuries afterward, the Japanese spoke reverently of the *kamikaze*, or "divine wind," that had saved Japan.

HISTORY MAKERS

**Kublai Khan
1215–1294**

As ruler of both China and the Mongol Empire, Kublai Khan straddled two worlds. He built luxurious palaces, dressed as a Chinese emperor, and supported the work of Chinese artists. However, he remained a Mongol warrior at heart.

The Great Khan is said to have planted a plot of grass from the steppe in the gardens at Beijing to remind himself of his home. He also loved to hunt and enclosed a large hunting ground at his palace at Shangdu.

Kublai also preserved the customs of his nomadic ancestors. Every August 28, he performed the Mongol ritual of the scattering of mare's milk to honor his ancestors and ensure a year of good luck. The rite involved calling out the name of Genghis Khan and scattering over the ground the milk that came from a special herd of white horses.

Mongol Rule in China

Early in Kublai Khan's reign, one of his Chinese advisers told him, "I have heard that one can conquer the empire on horseback, but one cannot govern it on horseback." This advice illustrates the problems faced by Kublai Khan in ruling China. Mongol ways would not work in a sophisticated civilization like China's. Besides, the number of Mongols in China was few compared to the huge native population. Kublai would need to make use of Chinese institutions and non-Mongol officials to help him rule successfully.

The Mongols and the Chinese The Mongol rulers had little in common with their Chinese subjects. Because of their differences, the Mongols kept their separate identity. Mongols lived apart from the Chinese and obeyed different laws. They even kept the Chinese out of high government offices, although they retained as many Chinese officials as possible to serve on the local level. The Mongol rulers gave most of the highest government posts to Mongols and to foreigners. Foreigners included Muslims from western Asia and Christians such as Marco Polo of Venice. The Mongols believed that foreigners were more trustworthy than the Chinese since the foreigners had no local loyalties.

300 Chapter 12

Background
Since the decline of the Tang Dynasty after 900, robbers and warring peoples had nearly shut down the caravan routes across Central Asia.

Despite his differences with the Chinese, Kublai Khan was an able leader. He restored the Grand Canal, which had been built during the Sui Dynasty, and extended it 135 miles north to Beijing. Along its banks a paved highway ran for 1,100 miles, from Hangzhou to Beijing. These routes ensured the north of a steady supply of grain and other goods from the southern heartland.

Encouragement of Foreign Trade Kublai Khan also encouraged foreign trade. The Mongol Peace made the caravan routes across Central Asia safe for trade and travel. Kublai Khan established post roads, or mail routes, that linked China to India and Persia and greatly improved trade. He invited foreign merchants to visit China. Most of them were Muslims from India, Central Asia, and Persia. Many European travelers, including Christian missionaries, also reached China.

Over the Silk Roads and other routes, traders transported Chinese silk and porcelain, which continued to be desired in Europe and western Asia. Other Chinese products and inventions that went west included printing, gunpowder, the compass, paper currency, and playing cards.

Marco Polo at the Mongol Court The most famous European to visit China in these years was a young Venetian trader, **Marco Polo.** With his father and uncle, he traveled by caravan on the Silk Roads, arriving at Kublai Khan's court around 1275. Marco had learned several Asian languages in his travels, and Kublai Khan sent him to various Chinese cities on government missions. Polo served the Great Khan well for 17 years. In 1292, two years before Kublai died, the Polos left China and made the long journey back to Venice. They traveled by sea around Southeast Asia and India.

THINK THROUGH HISTORY
B. Analyzing Motives Why do you think Kublai Khan employed Marco Polo?
B. Possible Answers He preferred to use foreigners in important posts, since he trusted them more; Polo knew several languages and was an experienced traveler.

Later, during a war against Venice's rival city, Genoa, Marco Polo was captured and imprisoned. In prison he had time to tell the full story of his travels and adventures. To his awed listeners, he spoke of China's fabulous cities, its fantastic wealth, and the strange things he had seen there. He mentioned the burning of "black stones" (coal) in Chinese homes. (Coal as a fuel was little known in Europe.) He also recorded the practical workings of the khan's government and aspects of Chinese life. Here is his description of trade in Beijing.

A VOICE FROM THE PAST
More precious and costly wares are imported into Khanbalik [Beijing] than into any other city in the world. . . . All the treasures that come from India—precious stones, pearls, and other rarities—are brought here. So too are the choicest and costliest products of Cathay [China] itself and every other province. . . . Every day more than 1,000 cart loads of silk enter the city; for much cloth of gold and silk is woven here.
MARCO POLO, *The Travels of Marco Polo*

A fellow prisoner gathered Polo's stories into a book. It was an instant success in Europe, but most readers did not believe a word of it. They thought Polo's account was a marvelous collection of tall tales. It was clear to Marco Polo, however, that the civilization he had visited was the greatest in the world.

The End of Mongol Rule

During the last years of Kublai Khan's reign, cracks began to form under the surface of Mongol rule. In an attempt to further expand his empire, he sent several expeditions into Southeast Asia. His armies and navies suffered many humiliating defeats at a huge expense of lives and equipment. Heavy spending on fruitless wars, on public

HISTORY MAKERS

Marco Polo
1254?–1324
The man who described Kublai Khan to Europeans left behind very little information about himself. He was 17 when he set out from Venice with his father and uncle, who were on their second visit to Kublai's court. According to Marco, Kublai recognized his "merit and worth" and sent him on special missions around the empire. His impressions of China became the basis of his book, but he described few actual events about his life.

Since his book first appeared, people have debated whether or not Marco Polo actually saw all that he claimed to have seen. He is not mentioned in Chinese accounts of this time. His tales also fail to mention such common features of China as tea, acupuncture, or foot binding.

On his deathbed, Polo was asked if his travel stories were true. He replied that he had told barely half of what he had seen.

Empires in East Asia **301**

MORE ABOUT . . .
The Postal Route
Kublai Khan's postal route was maintained by some 10,000 postal houses, which linked all parts of the kingdom. Each postal house was located about 25 miles from the next. Supplies and fresh horses for the couriers were kept at each house. Letters and other communications could move rapidly from one end of the empire to the other. Interested students can compare this system with the U.S. pony express.

HISTORYMAKERS
Marco Polo

After Marco's mother died when he was young, the future explorer was raised by an aunt and uncle to be a merchant. He learned how to use foreign money, handle cargo, and evaluate products. He also proved to have a gift for languages.

Discuss with students what characteristics Marco must have had to accomplish what he did. Have them write a want ad for someone to replace him in the Chinese court. What qualifications would they list?

 ELECTRONIC LIBRARY OF PRIMARY SOURCES
"The Tartars," from *Travels of Marco Polo*

OBJECTIVE 3 INSTRUCT

The End of Mongol Rule

▶ *Key Ideas*
• Fruitless wars, taxation, and overspending set the stage for Mongol decline.
• After the death of Kublai Khan, Chinese rebels finally overthrow the Mongols.
• Although the Mongol rulers are gone, they have influenced cultures from Europe to Asia.

TEACHING OPTION   BLOCK SCHEDULING   **COOPERATIVE ACTIVITY: Letters to the Editor**   CLASS TIME 30 MINUTES

Task: Students will write letters to the editor of a newspaper commenting on Marco Polo's writings and travels.

Purpose: To develop an appreciation for Marco Polo's achievements and their impact on Europe.

Activity: Tell students to visualize themselves living in Italy when Marco Polo's travels are first becoming known. Have them write letters to the editor of a newspaper expressing their opinions about Marco, praising his work, doubting his stories, or commenting on how his tales affect citizens of his day. Tell students to back up their opinions with specific details from the chapter, the primary source, or their own reading.

📁 *Building a Portfolio:* Students adding a letter to their portfolio should attach an explanation of the assignment.

ALTERNATIVE ASSESSMENT BOOK
Standards for Evaluating a Cooperative Activity

Standards for Evaluation
Letters should . . .

• demonstrate correct letter form
• clearly state the writer's opinion
• provide details to support that opinion

Teacher's Edition **301**

Dynasties of China, 500–1400

- **850** Gunpowder invented
- **1215** Genghis Khan invades northern China
- **1275** Marco Polo reaches China
- Sui
- Tang
- Song
- Southern Song
- Yuan
- 500 A.D.
- 800 A.D.
- WARFARE AND REVOLT
- 1100 A.D.
- 1400 A.D.
- **627** Tang Taizong becomes emperor
- **690** Empress Wu Zhao assumes throne
- **751** Chinese lose Battle of Talas
- **1024** Government issues paper money
- **1040** Movable type invented
- **1126** Song Dynasty retreats to south
- **1260** Kublai becomes Great Khan

works, and on the luxuries of the Yuan court burdened the treasury and created resentment among the overtaxed Chinese. This presented problems that Kublai's less able successors could not resolve.

Yuan Dynasty Overthrown Kublai Khan died in 1294. He was nearly 80. Mongol rule weakened after his death. Although the Yuan Dynasty remained in power for another 74 years, family members struggled among themselves over who would rule. In one 8-year period, four different khans took the throne.

Rebellions broke out in many parts of China in the 1300s. The Chinese had long resented their Mongol rulers, and the Mongol humiliation of the Chinese only increased under Kublai Khan's successors. The rebellions were also fueled by years of famine, flood, and disease, along with growing economic problems and official corruption. In 1368, Chinese rebels finally overthrew the Mongols and seized power. The rebel leader founded a new dynasty—the Ming—which you will read about in Chapter 19.

Some Mongols remained in China during the Ming Dynasty and were valued for their skill as cavalrymen. Many others, however, returned to their homelands on the Mongolian steppe.

Decline of the Mongol Empire By the end of the Yuan Dynasty in China, the entire Mongol Empire had disintegrated. The government of the Ilkhanate in Persia fell apart in the 1330s. The Chagatai khans ruled Central Asia until the 1370s. Only the Golden Horde in Russia stayed in power. The Golden Horde ruled Russia for 250 years. As discussed in Chapter 11, Ivan III finally asserted Russia's independence from the Mongols in 1480.

The rise and fall of Mongol rule affected civilizations from eastern Europe to China. Despite the efforts of Kublai Khan, Mongol domination never extended to Japan. However, several centuries earlier, the Japanese had embraced the influence of an outside culture—that of China—as its civilization developed. This development is described in Section 4.

THINK THROUGH HISTORY
C. Analyzing Causes What factors contributed to the decline and fall of the Yuan Dynasty?
C. Possible Answer Military defeats, costly wars, heavy government spending and taxes, ineffective rulers, resentment of foreign rule by Chinese, natural disaster, economic problems, corruption, rebellion.

Section 3 Assessment

1. TERMS & NAMES
Identify
- Kublai Khan
- Marco Polo

2. TAKING NOTES
Create a web diagram showing the impact of Kublai Khan on East Asia.

Kublai Khan

Choose an event from your diagram and explain how it affected China. Did the event make China stronger or weaker?

3. EVALUATING DECISIONS
Judging from the events of the Yuan Dynasty, do you think the Mongol policies toward the Chinese were effective?

THINK ABOUT
- the accomplishments of Kublai Khan as emperor of China
- the Mongols' policies towards the Chinese
- the military campaigns of Kublai Khan
- the fate of the Yuan Dynasty

4. ANALYZING THEMES
Cultural Interaction What evidence is there that the Chinese way of life influenced the Mongol conquerors?

THINK ABOUT
- the seat of Kublai Khan's empire
- Kublai's actions as emperor of China

ANSWERS

1. TERMS & NAMES
Kublai Khan, p. 299
Marco Polo, p. 301

2. TAKING NOTES
Possible Responses: conquered China, improved communication within China and across Asia, failed to conquer Japan, reunited China, established a Mongol dynasty (Yuan), extended foreign trade, fought unsuccessful wars in Southeast Asia.

3. EVALUATING DECISIONS
Possible Responses: No—the policies only made the Chinese resent the Mongols and eventually rebel; granting the Chinese more power and freedom might have led them to accept Mongol rule. Yes—the Chinese resented foreign rule, and strong policies kept them at bay; only weakened leadership allowed the dynasty to be overthrown.

4. ANALYZING THEMES
Possible Responses: Kublai Khan spent years in China and adopted many of its ways; he built luxurious palaces and dressed as a Chinese emperor; he moved the capital from Mongolia to Beijing; he kept Chinese government institutions in place.

Feudal Powers in Japan

MAIN IDEA

Japanese civilization was shaped by cultural borrowing from China and the rise of feudalism and military rulers.

WHY IT MATTERS NOW

An openness to adapting innovations from other cultures is still a hallmark of Japanese society.

SETTING THE STAGE Japan lies east of China, in the direction of the sunrise. In fact, the name *Japan* comes from the Chinese words *ri ben*, which mean "origin of the sun." From ancient times, Japan had borrowed ideas, institutions, and culture from the Chinese people. Japan's genius was its ability to take in new ideas and make them uniquely its own.

The Growth of Japanese Civilization

Japan's island location shaped the growth of its civilization. About 120 miles of water separate Japan from its closest neighbor, Korea, and 500 miles separate Japan from China. In their early history, the Japanese were close enough to feel the civilizing effect of China. Yet they were far enough away to be reasonably safe from invasion.

The Geography of Japan About 4,000 islands make up the Japanese archipelago (AHR·kuh·PEHL·uh·GOH), or island group, that extends in an arc about 1,200 miles long. If Japan were superimposed over eastern North America, the islands would extend from Montreal, Canada, to Tallahassee, Florida. Most Japanese people have always lived on the four largest islands: Hokkaido (hah·KY·doh), Honshu (HAHN·shoo), Shikoku (shih·KOH·koo), and Kyushu (kee·OO·shoo).

Japan's geography has both advantages and disadvantages. Southern Japan enjoys a mild climate with plenty of rainfall. The country is so mountainous, however, that only 15 percent of the land is suitable for farming. Natural resources such as coal, oil, and iron are in short supply. During the late summer and early fall, strong tropical storms called typhoons occur. Earthquakes and tidal waves are also threats.

Vocabulary
typhoons: tropical cyclones that occur in the western Pacific or Indian oceans. (Cyclones in the Atlantic and Caribbean are called hurricanes.)

Early Japan The first historic mention of Japan comes from Chinese writings of about A.D. 300. Japan at this time was not a united country. Instead, hundreds of clans controlled their own territories.

Each clan worshiped its own nature gods and goddesses. In different parts of Japan, people honored thousands of local deities. Their varied customs and beliefs eventually combined to form Japan's earliest religion. In later times, this religion was called **Shinto** (SHIHN·toh), meaning "way of the gods."

Shinto had no complex rituals or philosophy. Instead, it was based on respect for the forces of

Japan to 1300

KOREA
CHINA
Yellow Sea
Sea of Japan
JAPAN
Hokkaido
Honshu
Heian (Kyoto)
Nara
Mt. Fuji
Edo (Tokyo)
Kamakura
Shikoku
Kyushu
PACIFIC OCEAN

GEOGRAPHY SKILLBUILDER:
Interpreting Maps
1. **Location** How far is the southern end of Japan from Korea? from China?
2. **Location** On what island did Japan's major cities develop?

SECTION 4 RESOURCES

PRINT RESOURCES

IN-DEPTH RESOURCES: UNIT 3
Guided Reading, p. 37
Skillbuilder Practice: Making Inferences, p. 39
Geography Application: The Ainu People, p. 40
Primary Sources, pp. 44, 45
Literature, pp. 46, 47
ACCESS FOR STUDENTS ACQUIRING ENGLISH
Guided Reading (Spanish), p. 123
Skillbuilder Practice (Spanish), p. 125
Geography Application (Spanish), p. 126

FORMAL ASSESSMENT
Section Quiz, p. 136

TECHNOLOGY RESOURCES

WORLD ART AND CULTURES TRANSPARENCIES
AT26 Descent of Amida

CRITICAL THINKING TRANSPARENCIES
CT12 Japanese Cultural Borrowings From China

CD-ROM
Electronic Library of Primary Sources

INTERNET www.mlworldhistory.com

Section 4 Overview

OBJECTIVES

1. To describe Japan's location and early history.
2. To summarize China's influence on Japan.
3. To describe the highly refined life of the Heian court.
4. To summarize the feudal period in Japan.

SKILLBUILDER
- Interpreting maps: location, p. 303

CRITICAL THINKING
- Synthesizing, p. 304
- Making inferences, pp. 305, 306
- Drawing conclusions, p. 307

FOCUS
5-Minute Warm-Up

▶ **Making Inferences**
Answering these questions will help students understand the early history of Japan.

- Look at the map on page 303. Describe the geography of Japan's major island.
- Which of its neighbors would you expect to have the most influence on Japan? Why?

WARM-UP TRANSPARENCY 12

OBJECTIVE ① INSTRUCT

The Growth of Japanese Civilization

Key Ideas
- Japan's location provides protection but allows Chinese cultural influence.
- Early Japan is populated by hundreds of competing clans.
- The Yamatos establish a line of emperors, but clans are the power behind the throne.

IN-DEPTH RESOURCES: UNIT 3
Guided Reading, p. 37

ACCESS FOR STUDENTS ACQUIRING ENGLISH
Guided Reading (Spanish), p. 123

(See map on page 303.)
Japan to 1300

SKILLBUILDER Answers
1. About 250 miles from Korea; about 200 miles from China
2. Honsu.

IN-DEPTH RESOURCES: UNIT 3
Geography Application: The Ainu People, p. 40

ELECTRONIC LIBRARY OF PRIMARY SOURCES
"The Manners and Customs of Early Japan"

CONNECT *to* TODAY
The Rising Sun

Ask students what they think might have happened in 1945–46 to discredit Japanese emperors' claims to divinity? *Japan had lost World War II and was occupied by U.S. forces.*

OBJECTIVE ② INSTRUCT

The Japanese Adapt Chinese Ideas

Key Ideas
- Chinese culture begins to reach Japan by way of Korea.
- Japan accepts Buddhism, adapting some Shinto beliefs to the new religion.
- Japan adopts many Chinese customs and ideas but retains rule by noble families.

WORLD ART AND CULTURES TRANSPARENCIES
AT26 Descent of Amida

CRITICAL THINKING TRANSPARENCIES
CT12 Japanese Cultural Borrowings From China

---

nature and on the worship of ancestors. Shinto worshipers believed in *kami*, divine spirits that dwelled in nature. Any unusual or especially beautiful tree, rock, waterfall, or mountain was considered the home of a *kami*.

The Yamato Emperors By the fifth century, the Yamato clan had established itself as the leading clan. The Yamato claimed to be descended from the sun goddess Amaterasu. By the seventh century, the Yamato chiefs called themselves the emperors of Japan. The early emperors did not control the entire country, or even much of it, but the Japanese gradually accepted the idea of an emperor.

Although many of the Yamato rulers lacked real power, the dynasty was never overthrown. When rival clans fought for power, the winning clan claimed control of the emperor and then ruled in the emperor's name. Japan had an emperor who reigned as a figurehead and a power behind the throne who actually ruled. This dual structure became an enduring characteristic of Japanese government.

The Japanese Adapt Chinese Ideas

About the year 500, the Japanese began to have more contact with mainland Asia. They were soon influenced by Chinese ideas and customs, which they first learned about from Korean travelers. During the sixth century, many Koreans migrated to Japan, bringing Chinese influences with them.

Buddhism in Japan One of the most important influences brought by Korean travelers was Buddhism. In the mid-700s, the Japanese imperial court officially accepted Buddhism in Japan. By the eighth or ninth century, Buddhist ideas and worship had spread through Japanese society. Buddhism was more complex than Shintoism. Its teachings, as well as the beauty and mystery of its ceremonies and art, impressed many Japanese. The Japanese, however, did not give up their Shinto beliefs. Some Buddhist rituals became Shinto rituals, and some Shinto gods and goddesses were worshipped in Buddhist temples.

Cultural Borrowing from China Interest in Buddhist ideas at the Japanese court soon grew into an enthusiasm for all things Chinese. The most influential convert to Buddhism was Prince Shotoku (shoh·toh·ku), who served as regent for his aunt, the empress Suiko. In 607, Prince Shotoku sent the first of three missions to Tang China. His people studied Chinese civilization firsthand. Some 600 scholars, painters, musicians, and monks traveled on each mission. Over the next 200 years, while the Tang Dynasty was at its height, the Japanese sent many such groups to learn about Chinese ways.

The Japanese adopted the Chinese system of writing, which first reached Japan through the Koreans. Japanese artists painted landscapes in the Chinese manner. The Japanese even followed Chinese styles in the simple arts of everyday living, such as cooking, gardening, drinking tea, and hairdressing.

For a time, Japan even modeled its government on China's. Prince Shotoku planned a strong central government like that of the Tang rulers. Shotoku also tried to introduce China's examination system. However, this attempt failed. In Japan, noble birth remained the key to winning a powerful position. Unlike China, Japan continued to be a country where a few great families held power.

The Japanese adapted Chinese ways to suit their own needs. While they learned much, they still retained their own traditions. Eventually, the Japanese imperial court decided it had learned enough from Tang China. In the late ninth century, it ended formal missions to the Tang empire, which had fallen into decline. Although Chinese cultural influence would remain strong in Japan, Japan's own culture was about to bloom.

Vocabulary
regent: one who rules on behalf of another.

THINK THROUGH HISTORY
A. Synthesizing
How did Chinese culture spread to Japan?
A. Answer Via Korean travelers and direct contact with the Tang court.

Rule During U.S. Occupation
Japan did not experience foreign rule until 1945 when the United States began a seven-year occupation following World War II. The United States sought to disband Japan's military and establish a democracy. The Americans ruled in a traditionally Japanese way, as the power behind the throne. Changes were more lasting because they were introduced and administered by Japanese officials. Have interested students research the effect of the U.S. occupation on the way the Japanese viewed the emperor.

A Voice from the Past Have students think of an incident in their own lives that parallels the event described in the last paragraph of the excerpt from *The Pillow Book,* on page 305. The incident might have occurred in their home, a classroom, the principal's office, or the locker room. Have students write a paragraph describing the incident and how they felt about it, using the excerpt from *The Pillow Book* as their model.

Life in the Heian Period

In 794, the imperial court moved its capital from Nara to Heian (HAY·ahn), the modern Kyoto (kee·OH·toh). Many of Japan's noble families also moved to Heian. Among the upper class in Heian, a highly refined court society arose. This era in Japanese history, from 794 to 1185, is called the Heian period.

Vocabulary
etiquette: the code governing correct behavior and appearance.

Gentlemen and ladies of the court filled their days with elaborate ritual and artistic pursuits. Rules dictated every aspect of court life—the length of swords, the color of official robes, forms of address, even the number of skirts a woman wore. Etiquette was also extremely important. Loud laughter or mismatched clothing, for instance, caused deep embarrassment. Noble women wore their hair down to their ankles, blackened their teeth with cosmetics, and dyed their clothing to match the seasons. Everyone at court was expected to write poetry and to paint. Japanese aristocrats looked down on the common people, who could not share in court refinement.

The best accounts of Heian society come from the diaries, essays, and novels written by the women of the court. Two of the finest writers of the period were Lady Murasaki Shikibu and Sei Shonagon. Lady Murasaki's 11th-century masterpiece, *The Tale of Genji,* is an account of the life of a prince in the imperial court. This long prose narrative, full of detail and emotion, is considered the world's first novel. Sei Shonagon wrote vivid sketches of court life in her diary, called *The Pillow Book.* Here she lists some things that gave her pleasure:

One maid combs her lady's hair while another reads to her in this print depicting a scene from *The Tale of Genji.*

A VOICE FROM THE PAST

I greatly enjoy [conversing with] someone who is pleased with himself and who has a self-confident look, especially if he is a man. It is amusing to observe him as he alertly waits for my next repartee; but it is also interesting if he tries to put me off my guard by adopting an air of calm indifference as if there were not a thought in his head.

I realize that it is very sinful of me, but I cannot help being pleased when someone I dislike has a bad experience.

Entering the Empress's room and finding that ladies-in-waiting are crowded around her in a tight group, I go next to a pillar which is some distance from where she is sitting. What a delight it is when Her Majesty summons me to her side so that all the others have to make way!

SEI SHONAGON, *The Pillow Book*

THINK THROUGH HISTORY
B. Making Inferences
Based on the excerpt from Shonagon's book, what personality characteristics does the writer admire?
B. Possible Answer
Intelligence, wit, composure, spite, competitiveness.

Feudalism Erodes Imperial Authority

During the Heian period, Japan's central government was relatively strong. However, this strength was soon to be challenged by great landowners and clan chiefs who acted more and more as independent local rulers.

Decline of Central Power For most of the Heian period, the rich Fujiwara family held the real power in Japan. Members of this family held many influential posts. By about the middle of the 11th century, however, the power of the central government and the Fujiwaras began to slip. Court families grew more interested in luxury and artistic pursuits than in governing.

Empires in East Asia **305**

OBJECTIVE ③ INSTRUCT

Life in the Heian Period

▶ *Key Ideas*
- A highly refined court society arises in the Heian period.
- Elaborate rituals and codes of behavior govern all aspects of court life.
- Both men and women are expected to pursue the arts of painting and poetry.

📖 *IN-DEPTH RESOURCES: UNIT 3*
Primary Sources: from *The Diary of Lady Murasaki,* p. 44
Literature: from *The Tale of Genji* by Lady Murasaki Shikibu, p. 46; from *The Pillow Book* by Sei Shonagon, p. 47

MORE ABOUT . . .
Heian Court Dress

Court women wore up to 12 silk dresses, one on top of another, each of a different color. The display of colors when the wind blew or when a woman entered a carriage was noted and commented upon by others in the court. The number of skirts worn, their colors, and their order were dictated by both social status and aesthetic norms.

OBJECTIVE ④ INSTRUCT

Feudalism Erodes Imperial Authority

▶ *Key Ideas*
- As the power of the central government declines, Japan becomes a feudal society.
- Clan wars give rise to the samurai, warriors who follow a strict code of honor.
- Shoguns and their samurai rule Japan, although rival lords still battle each other.

| TEACHING OPTION | BLOCK SCHEDULING | SKILLBUILDER MINI-LESSON: Making Inferences | CLASS TIME 20 MINUTES |

Explaining the Skill: Making inferences means drawing conclusions based on clues in the text (facts, examples, author's language) and on personal experiences, historical knowledge, and common sense. For example, we can use clues in the text of the excerpt from *The Pillow Book* to infer that Sei Shonagon is a member of the imperial court.

Applying the Skill: Read A Voice from the Past on this page. What values can you infer the writer holds? Create a chart like the one to the right to help you make inferences.

📖 *IN-DEPTH RESOURCES: UNIT 3*
Skillbuilder Practice: Making Inferences, p. 39

Clues in the Text	Personal Knowledge	Inference
Enjoys matching wits in conversation		
Feels bad and good when an enemy falls		
Enjoys being singled out by royalty		
Likes to make a grand entrance		

Daily *Life*

Japan, 1185

Study of the samurai, Japan's eminent warrior class for over 1,000 years, tells a great deal about Japan's history and values. Bushido—the moral code of the samurai—became, in many ways, the moral code of the Japanese people.

Discuss with students these examples of the samurai life and code.

- A samurai's foremost allegiance was to his feudal lord, taking precedence over his duties to his family.

- The samurai understood the meaning of "death before dishonor" and preferred suicide to capture by an enemy.

- Over time, samurai changed their tactics and their arms. For example, in their first skirmish with the Mongols, they expected to fight man-to-man, but the Mongols advanced in columns and rows. In subsequent battles with the Mongols, the samurai advanced in groups.

- Samurai women—wives and daughters—were expected to observe the same strict code as the men. Some women were highly skilled in combat arts and fought on the battlefield.

- The samurai were also adept at nonmilitary arts, particularly in later centuries. They practiced arts such as poetry, calligraphy, and the tea ceremony.

Samurai Warrior News

Latest Uniforms

A samurai's armor consists of leather shin guards and thigh guards, billowing knickers, a kimono, metal-cased shoulder guards, a chest protector, an iron collar, a cotton skullcap, an iron facemask, and a visored helmet with leather horns.

This suit of armor is made of steel, wood, bronze, deerskin, and bear pelts.

Don't Leave Home Without It

A proper samurai would rather die than part with his sword. No wonder. Extraordinary craftsmanship goes into each weapon. Swordsmiths prepare themselves by undergoing purification rites.

Then they work dressed all in white. To give the blade superior strength, the swordsmith uses clay to protect the broad back of the sword from the hammering, heating, and cooling that produces the razor-sharp edge. For beauty, swordsmiths add inlaid hilt guards, scabbard ornaments, and handgrips made of sharkskin.

Lady Tomoe Gozen, a famous female warrior of the 1180s, enters bravely into battle.

The Zen Way

The Zen school of Buddhism is becoming popular among the samurai class. The Zen emphasis on spirituality through self-discipline and meditation appeals to this group of warriors.

Samurai vs. Knights

A class of elite warriors similar to the samurai is forming in Europe. Here is how the two groups compare.

Japanese Samurai	European Knights
• Live by code of honor called Bushido, which values bravery and loyalty to their lord above all else. Will commit ritual suicide rather than face defeat or dishonor.	• Live by code of honor called chivalry, which values bravery and loyalty to heavenly God, earthly lord, and chosen lady. Code also demands that knights show humility.
• Fight for lord in exchange for an allowance.	• Fight for lord in exchange for land.
• Expect women to live up to same values of honor and courage.	• Regard women as weak creatures to be idolized and defended.
• Enter into battle with iron and leather armor, swords, and bows and arrows.	• Enter into battle with chain mail or plate armor, broadsword, and lance.

Connect *to* **History**

Making Inferences What qualities did samurai most prize?

SEE SKILLBUILDER HANDBOOK PAGE 1005

Connect *to* **Today**

Research Find out what happened to the samurai in Japan's later history. How long did this warrior class last? Did it change in any way?

Making Inferences From the information presented in the Daily Life feature, students can infer that the samurai valued such qualities as loyalty, bravery, honor, skill in martial and other arts, discipline, courage, intelligence, and strength. Students may enjoy reading the primary source for this section.

IN-DEPTH RESOURCES: **UNIT 3**
Primary Source: "A Samurai Instructs His Son," p. 45

Research The samurai lost their status when Japan officially abolished feudalism in 1871. However, the Bushido code continued to influence Japanese life through World War II. Students can research the history of the samurai in books such as *Samurai* by Harry Cook (New York: Sterling, 1993); *The Samurai* by Stephen Turnbull (New York: Macmillan, 1977); *A Samurai Castle* by Fiona Macdonald (New York: Bedrick, 1995).

Large landowners living away from the capital set up private armies. The countryside became lawless and dangerous. Armed soldiers on horseback preyed on farmers and travelers, and pirates took control of the seas. For safety, farmers and small landowners traded parts of their land to strong warlords in exchange for protection. With more land, the lords gained more power. This marked the beginning of a feudal system of localized rule like that of ancient China and medieval Europe.

Samurai Warriors Since wars between rival lords were commonplace, each lord surrounded himself with a bodyguard of loyal warriors called **samurai** (SAM·uh·RY). (*Samurai* means "one who serves.") Samurai lived according to a demanding code of behavior. In later centuries, this code was called **Bushido** (BUSH·ih·DOH), or "the way of the warrior." A samurai was expected to show reckless courage, reverence for the gods, fairness, and generosity toward those weaker than himself. Dying an honorable death was judged more important than living a long life.

The Kamakura Shogunate During the late 1100s, Japan's two most powerful clans fought for power. After almost 30 years of war, the Minamoto family emerged victorious. In 1192, the emperor gave a Minamoto leader named Yoritomo the title of **shogun,** meaning "supreme general of the emperor's army." In effect, the shogun had the powers of a military dictator. Officials, judges, taxes, armies, roads—all were under his authority.

Following tradition, the emperor still reigned from Kyoto. (Kyoto was rebuilt on the ruins of Heian, which had been destroyed in war.) However, the real center of power was at the shogun's military headquarters at Kamakura (KAHM·uh·KUR·uh). The 1200s are known in Japanese history as the Kamakura shogunate. The pattern of government in which shoguns ruled through puppet emperors lasted in Japan until 1868.

Under the early shoguns, the local lords still held great power. A lord who loyally served the shogun received almost a free hand in ruling his own province. At the same time, the shoguns strengthened their own control by assigning a military governor to each province. These governors, called daimyo (DY·mee·OH), or "great lords," were responsible for maintaining peace and order. Over time, the daimyo came to exercise great power, as you will see in Chapter 19.

The Kamakura shoguns were strong enough to turn back the two naval invasions sent by the great Mongol ruler Kublai Khan in 1274 and 1281. However, the Japanese victory over the Mongols drained the shoguns' treasury. Loyal samurai were bitter when the government failed to pay them. The Kamakura shoguns lost prestige and power. Samurai attached themselves more closely to their local lords, who soon fought one another as fiercely as they had fought the Mongols.

Although feudal Japan no longer courted contact with China, it would continue to absorb Chinese ideas and shape them into the Japanese way. As you will read in Section 5, China's culture also influenced Korea and certain kingdoms of Southeast Asia.

THINK THROUGH HISTORY
C. Drawing Conclusions
What advantages were there to preserving the imperial dynasty, even if it lacked real power?
C. Answer The dynasty helped to unify the country, to preserve a figure of central authority, and to create sense of order and tradition.

Section 4 Assessment

1. TERMS & NAMES

Identify
- Shinto
- samurai
- Bushido
- shogun

2. TAKING NOTES

Create a time line showing the main periods and events in Japanese history between the years 300 and 1300.

What event would you consider the most important turning point in Japan's early history? Why?

3. DRAWING CONCLUSIONS

Was the rise of the shogun beneficial for Japan overall? Explain.

THINK ABOUT
- problems developing in feudal Japan
- powers of the shogun
- achievements under the Kamakura shoguns

4. THEME ACTIVITY

Religious and Ethical Systems Work with a small group to create a short play, set in the 600s, about a Japanese family's decision to adopt Buddhism. Consider what changes occurring in Japanese society might make individuals more receptive to beliefs that came from China. Indicate how the family blends Buddhism with its traditional Shinto beliefs.

Empires in East Asia **307**

MORE ABOUT . . .
Japanese Shoguns
The title "shogun" is an abbreviation of *sei-i tai shogun,* meaning "barbarian-quelling generalissimo." There were three main shogunates in Japanese history: Kamakura, Ashikaga, and Tokugawa. In 1867, the last shogun, Yoshinobu Tokugawa, was forced to turn over administration of civil and military affairs to the emperor, ending nearly 700 years of shogun rule.

ASSESS & RETEACH

Section 4 Assessment
Have students work in pairs to answer each question and then share their answers with another pair of students.

📖 **FORMAL ASSESSMENT BOOK** Section Quiz, p. 136

Reteaching Activity
CLASS TIME: 20 MINUTES

Work with the class to create a cause-and-effect flow chart of the events in Section 4. Review the main ideas of the section as you complete the chart.

CLOSE ACTIVITY

CLASS TIME: 30 MINUTES

Making Judgments
Divide the class into four groups. Assign each group one of the four headings in the section. Ask each group to list the major events in Japanese history described in their section and to evaluate the positive and negative effects of these events on Japan's development.

OBJECTIVES

1 To describe the kingdoms of Southeast Asia and the influence of India and China.

2 To summarize early Korean history.

SKILLBUILDERS

• Interpreting maps: location, movement, p. 308

CRITICAL THINKING

• Making inferences, p. 309
• Comparing, p. 311
• Recognizing effects, p. 311

FOCUS
5-Minute Warm-Up

Making Predictions
Have students answer these questions to help them understand the history of Southeast Asia and Korea.

• Study the map on page 308. Name the four smaller kingdoms (other than Japan) that make up East Asia.

• Which kingdoms would you expect to be influenced by China the most? Why?

 WARM-UP TRANSPARENCY 12

OBJECTIVE **1** INSTRUCT

Kingdoms of Southeast Asia

Key Ideas
• Southeast Asia, culturally and politically diverse, controls seaways vital to trade.

• Trade brings Indian and Chinese cultures to the area.

• The Khmer rule the mainland; Srivijayas control the islands.

• Vietnam, though influenced by China, remains independent.

 IN-DEPTH RESOURCES: UNIT 3
Guided Reading, p. 38

 ACCESS FOR STUDENTS ACQUIRING ENGLISH
Guided Reading (Spanish), p. 124

---

5 Kingdoms of Southeast Asia and Korea

TERMS & NAMES
• Khmer Empire
• Angkor Wat
• Koryu Dynasty

MAIN IDEA	WHY IT MATTERS NOW
Several smaller kingdoms prospered in East and Southeast Asia, a region culturally influenced by China and India.	Chinese cultural influences still affect East and Southeast Asia today.

SETTING THE STAGE To the south of China lies the region called Southeast Asia. It includes the modern countries of Myanmar (Burma), Laos, Cambodia, Vietnam, Malaysia, Indonesia, Thailand, Singapore, Brunei, and the Philippines. Thousands of miles from this region, to China's northeast, lies the Korean peninsula. This peninsula is currently divided between North Korea and South Korea. In the shadow of powerful China, many small but prosperous kingdoms rose and fell in Southeast Asia and Korea.

Kingdoms of Southeast Asia

In Southeast Asia's river valleys and deltas and on its islands, many kingdoms had centuries of glory and left monuments of lasting beauty.

Geography of Southeast Asia Southeast Asia lies between the Indian and Pacific oceans and stretches from Asia almost to Australia. It consists of two main parts: (1) the mainland peninsula, which borders China to the north and India to the west, and (2) the islands, the largest of which include Sumatra, Borneo, and Java. All of Southeast Asia lies within the warm, humid tropics. Monsoon winds bring the region long annual rains.

Southeast Asia has never been united, either politically or culturally. Seas and straits separate the islands. On the mainland, five great rivers flow from the north and cut valleys to the sea. Between the valleys rise hills and mountains, making travel and communication difficult. Over time, many different peoples settled the region, so it was home to a great variety of languages and cultures.

Throughout Southeast Asia's history, the key to political power often has been control of trade routes and harbors. Powerful local lords

Background
The mainland peninsula of Southeast Asia is called Indochina.

East Asia, 900–1200

Map showing East Asia with labels: ASIA, GOBI DESERT, TAKLAMAKAN DESERT, KOREA, Sea of Japan, Heian (Kyoto), Edo (Tokyo), Nara, Kamakura, JAPAN, Yellow Sea, Huang He, CHINA (SONG), Hangzhou, TIBET, HIMALAYAS, Ganges R., Yangtze R., INDIA, VIETNAM, Mekong R., Tropic of Cancer, PACIFIC OCEAN, Philippine Islands, Bay of Bengal, KHMER, Angkor Wat, South China Sea, Malay Peninsula, INDIAN OCEAN, Malacca, Strait of Malacca, Sumatra, SRIVIJAYA, Borneo, Celebes, Spice Islands, Palembang, Equator 0°, Sunda Strait, Borobudur, Java. Scale: 500 Miles / 1,000 Kilometers. Legend: — Trade route. 40° N, 120° E.

GEOGRAPHY SKILLBUILDER:
Interpreting Maps
1. **Location** Where is the Strait of Malacca and why was it important to trade?
2. **Movement** Name one way Chinese culture might have spread around Southeast Asia.

---

charged merchants high fees to use their ports, pass through their waterways, or protect their ships from piracy. The lords could do this because Southeast Asia lies on the most direct sea route between the Indian Ocean and the South China Sea. Two important waterways connect the two seas: the Strait of Malacca, between the Malay Peninsula and Sumatra, and the Sunda Strait, between Sumatra and Java.

Influence of India and China Indian merchant boats sailing the monsoon winds began arriving in Southeast Asia by the first century A.D. In the period that followed, Hindu and Buddhist missionaries spread their faiths. Across the region, kingdoms arose that followed these religions and were modeled on Indian political ideas. Gradually, Indian influence shaped many aspects of the region's culture. The people of Southeast Asia adopted many Hindu practices. Southeast Asian poets wrote long, elegant poems in India's ancient language of Sanskrit. Many early Indian influences on Southeast Asian culture are evident today in its religions, languages, and art forms.

Chinese ideas and culture spread southward in the region through migration and trade. At different times, the Chinese also exerted political influence over parts of mainland Southeast Asia, either through direct rule or by demanding tributes from local rulers.

The Khmer Empire The **Khmer** (kmair) **Empire,** in what is now Cambodia, was for centuries the main power on the Southeast Asian mainland. An early Khmer kingdom, called Funan, dominated much of the sea trade between India and China. By around 800, the Khmer had expanded their state into an empire at the expense of neighboring kingdoms. They reached their peak of power around 1200.

Improved rice cultivation helped the Khmer become prosperous. The Khmer built elaborate irrigation systems and waterways. These advances made it possible to grow three or four crops of rice a year in an area that had previously produced only one.

At their capital, Angkor, Khmer rulers built extensive city-and-temple complexes. One of these, called **Angkor Wat,** is among the world's greatest architectural achievements. The complex, which covers nearly a square mile, was built as a symbolic mountain dedicated to the Hindu god Vishnu. The Khmer also used it as an observatory.

Island Trading Kingdoms While the Khmer Empire expanded on the mainland, a dynasty called Sailendra ruled an agricultural kingdom on the island of Java. The Sailendra kings left behind another of the world's great architectural monuments, the Buddhist temple at Borobudur. The temple was built around 800. Like Angkor Wat, it reflects strong Indian influence. The massive complex has nine terraced levels like a stepped pyramid.

The Sailendra Dynasty eventually fell under the domination of the powerful island empire of Srivijaya. At its height from the 7th to the 13th centuries, Srivijaya ruled the Strait of Malacca and other waters around the islands of Sumatra, Borneo, and Java. It grew wealthy by taxing the trade that passed

Built in the 1100s, Angkor Wat is the world's largest religious structure. The vine-covered sculpture (inset) is the image of an ancient Khmer ruler.

Empires in East Asia **309**

Korean Dynasties

▶ **Key Ideas**

• Although Korea develops its own culture, it is greatly influenced by China.

• The Han dynasty conquers Korea but is forced out when Koreans unite under Silla rule.

• The wealthy Koryu Dynasty, battered by Mongols and internal rebellions, eventually falls.

• The Koryu period is noted for its pottery, literature, and scholarship.

 ELECTRONIC LIBRARY OF PRIMARY SOURCES
from *Reminiscences in Retirement*

MORE ABOUT . . .
The Period of Silla Rule

For nearly three centuries, the Silla Kingdom enjoyed peace and prosperity unequaled in most parts of the world. In this period, Korean arts, religion, commerce, and education developed rapidly. The capital city of Silla, which is now Kyongju City, housed nearly 1 million people. By the ninth century, it had become the fourth largest city in the known world.

During the Silla period, China and Korea enjoyed strong political ties. Korean paper, called *hanji*, was highly prized by Chinese artists and scholars. Korea adopted Buddhism and Confucian political ideas from China.

---

through its waters. The Srivijayas established their capital, Palembang, on Sumatra. Palembang became a great center of Buddhist learning, where Chinese monks could study instead of traveling to India.

Vietnam The people of Southeast Asia least influenced by India were the Vietnamese. Located in the coastal region just south of China, Vietnam fell under Chinese domination. Around 100 B.C., during the mighty Han Dynasty, China took northern Vietnam.

This Vietnamese print depicts Trung Trac and Trung Nhi, two heroines in Vietnam's history. These sisters led a revolt against the Chinese occupation in A.D. 39.

The Vietnamese remained under Chinese control for 1,000 years. When China's Tang Dynasty grew weaker in the early 900s, Vietnam broke away. It became an independent kingdom in 939.

The Vietnamese absorbed many Chinese cultural influences, including Buddhism. However, they also preserved a strong spirit of independence and kept their own cultural identity. Vietnamese women, for example, traditionally had more freedom and influence than their Chinese counterparts.

Rulers of the Ly Dynasty (1009–1225) established their capital at Hanoi, on the Red River delta. They slowly expanded Vietnam by conquering neighboring peoples to the south. The Mongols tried to conquer Vietnam and captured Hanoi three times (in 1257, 1285, and 1287), but each time the Vietnamese forced them to withdraw.

Korean Dynasties

According to a Korean legend, the first Korean state was founded by the hero Tan'gun, whose father was a god and whose mother was a bear. Another legend relates that it was founded by a royal descendant of the Chinese Shang Dynasty. These legends reflect two sides to the development of Korean culture. On one side, the Koreans were a distinct people who developed their own native traditions. On the other side, their culture was shaped by Chinese influences since early dynastic times. However, like the Japanese, the Koreans adapted borrowed culture to fit their own needs and maintained a distinct way of life.

Geography of Korea Korea is located on a peninsula that juts out of the Asian mainland toward Japan. Its area is about the same size as the state of Utah. Korea's climate is hot in the summer and very cold in the winter. Like Japan, Korea is a mountainous land, and only a limited portion of the peninsula can be farmed. A mountainous barrier lies between Korea and its northern neighbor, Manchuria. Because of the mountains and the seas, Korea developed somewhat in isolation from its neighbors.

Early History In early Korea, as in early Japan, different clans or tribes controlled different parts of the country. In 108 B.C., the Han empire conquered much of Korea and established a military government there. Through the Chinese, Koreans learned about such ideas as centralized government, Confucianism, Buddhism, and writing.

During the period of Han rule, the various Korean tribes began to gather together into federations. Eventually, these federations developed into three rival kingdoms. In the mid-600s, one of these kingdoms, the Silla, defeated the other kingdoms and chased out the Chinese. The Silla gained control over the whole Korean peninsula.

Under Silla rule, the Koreans built Buddhist monasteries and produced elegant stone and bronze sculptures. They also developed a writing system suitable for writing Korean phonetically though still using Chinese characters.

310 Chapter 12

Visual Learners: Studying Southeast Asian Sculpture
Students can learn a great deal about the history and culture of Southeast Asia by looking at photographs of relief sculpture at Angkor Wat and Borobudur. Resources include books on Asian art and guidebooks for Cambodia and Indonesia. Ask students to look for scenes of city life and evidence of maritime trade. Some students may wish to make sketches from the photographs to share with the rest of the class.

Protecting Angkor Wat The temple complex at Angkor suffered from neglect during the Vietnam War and Cambodian civil unrest. The structures are threatened by water damage, thick jungle growth, and thieves who pry sculptures loose to sell abroad. The temple complex has been on UNESCO's World Heritage Danger List since 1992. Cambodian leaders now hope the tourist industry will provide funds needed to preserve the site.

The Koryu Dynasty By the tenth century, Silla rule had weakened. Around 935, a rebel officer named Wang Kon gained control of the country and became king. He named his new dynasty Koryu. The name is an abbreviation of Koguryo (one of the three kingdoms), and is the origin of the modern name Korea. The **Koryu Dynasty** lasted four and a half centuries, from 935 to 1392.

The Koryu Dynasty modeled its central government after China's. It established a Confucian civil service examination system and a university to train male scholars. However, this system did not provide the social mobility for Koreans that it did for many Chinese. Koryu society was sharply divided between a landed aristocracy and the rest of the population, including the military, commoners, and slaves. Despite the examination system, the sons of nobles received the best positions, and these positions became hereditary. Wealthy nobles built their land holdings into huge estates, which left the other groups to scrape by with little.

These problems spurred a series of rebellions in the 1100s. Although the Koryu Dynasty managed to remain in power, it soon faced a larger threat. In 1231, the Mongols swept into Korea. They demanded a crushing tribute from the Koryu rulers. The tribute included 20,000 horses, clothing for 1 million soldiers, and many children and artisans, who were to be taken away as slaves.

The harsh period of Mongol occupation lasted until the 1350s, when the Mongol empire collapsed. Mounting oppression and taxation of the people by Korea's wealthy landlords eventually led to a new round of revolts. In 1392, a group of scholar-officials and military leaders overthrew the Koryu Dynasty and instituted land reforms. They established a new dynasty, called the Choson (or Yi) Dynasty, which would rule for 518 years.

Koryu Culture The Koryu period produced great achievements in Korean culture. Inspired by Song porcelain artists, Korean artists produced the much-admired celadon pottery, famous for its milky green glaze. (Knowledge of the secret formula for celadon disappeared during the Mongol occupation.) Writers and scholars produced fine poetry and wrote the first national history of Korea.

Korean artisans produced one of the great treasures of the Buddhist world. Over a period of 60 years, Korean printers carved thousands of large wooden blocks for printing the entire canon of Buddhist scriptures. This set of blocks was destroyed by the Mongols, but the disaster sparked a national effort to re-create them. The more than 81,000 blocks in the new set remain in Korea today.

THINK THROUGH HISTORY
B. Comparing How did the Koryu government compare with the early imperial government of Japan (page 304)?
B. Possible Answer Both were modeled after the Tang government, with a civil service system. The Koryu civil service system did not provide much mobility; a few nobles held the most power and the best positions.

CONNECT to TODAY

Two Koreas
From the Koryu period until the end of World War II, Korea was united culturally and politically. In 1945, Japanese forces in North Korea surrendered to the Soviets. Those in South Korea surrendered to the U.S. military. This arbitrary division of Korea continues today.

Many Koreans look forward to a day when Korea is reunited. Some experts believe that such an event is on the horizon. By the 1990s, communist North Korea was on the brink of economic disaster. The economy of the south, on the other hand, continued to expand. Such differences will make the process of reunification difficult if and when it does occur.

Section ⑤ Assessment

1. TERMS & NAMES
Identify
• Khmer Empire
• Angkor Wat
• Koryu Dynasty

2. TAKING NOTES
List five important kingdoms or dynasties covered in this section, and at least two major accomplishments of each.

Kingdom or Dynasty	Accomplishment

3. RECOGNIZING EFFECTS
Give examples to show how geography influenced the history and culture of Southeast Asia and of Korea.

THINK ABOUT
• the climate
• location relative to other countries
• natural features of water and land

4. THEME ACTIVITY
Religious and Ethical Systems Create a map showing how Hinduism and Buddhism entered Southeast Asia from China and India.

Empires in East Asia **311**

Chapter 12 Assessment

TERMS & NAMES

1. Tang Taizong, p. 287
2. Wu Zhao, p. 287
3. pastoralist, p. 294
4. Genghis Khan, p. 295
5. Kublai Khan, p. 299
6. Marco Polo, p. 301
7. Shinto, p. 303
8. samurai, p. 307
9. Angkor Wat, p. 309
10. Koryu Dynasty, p. 311

REVIEW QUESTIONS

11. It created a remarkable and intelligent governing class in China, called the gentry, that was open to anyone with the talent and opportunity for learning.

12. Introduction of a new strain of rice increased productivity, which allowed the growth of cities that became centers of scientific and cultural advancement.

13. Nomads raided towns in order to steal things they lacked, while settled peoples wanted to expand onto land used by nomads.

14. The Mongols established the largest land empire in history and promoted trade throughout Eurasia.

15. He tolerated Chinese culture and supported Chinese artists. He used Chinese institutions but gave the high government posts to Mongols and foreigners, allowing the Chinese to serve only locally.

16. Restoration of the Grand Canal, the construction of roads, and growth in trade helped the economy improve.

17. Japan enthusiastically adopted many elements of Chinese culture, including Buddhism, Chinese writing, and styles of Chinese art. Japan tried, but failed, to imitate China's examination system.

18. The power of the central government declined as aristocratic families fought one another and as peasants began paying taxes to local lords rather than to the central government.

19. Some, such as the Khmer, prospered through rice production. Others, such as Srivijaya, prospered through trade.

20. The Koryu Dynasty set up a civil service examination system, started a university, and produced celadon pottery.

TERMS & NAMES

Briefly explain the importance of each of the following to East Asia between 600 and 1350.

1. Tang Taizong
2. Wu Zhao
3. pastoralist
4. Genghis Khan
5. Kublai Khan
6. Marco Polo
7. Shinto
8. samurai
9. Angkor Wat
10. Koryu Dynasty

Interact with History

Through the activity on page 286, you looked at the importance of Chinese inventions on world history. (After reading the chapter, you may have recognized that this imaginary situation was inspired by the travels of Marco Polo.) Now that you've read the chapter, consider the impact of Chinese inventions and how they spread. Would you now choose a different invention? Is there any other invention you would choose instead of those on page 286? Discuss these questions with a small group.

REVIEW QUESTIONS

SECTION 1 *(pages 287–291)*
Two Great Dynasties in China

11. Why was the reform of the civil service under the Tang so significant?

12. How did changes in agriculture support other developments during the Song dynasty?

SECTION 2 *(pages 294–298)*
The Mongol Conquests

13. Why were nomads and settled peoples often in conflict?

14. What were the most important accomplishments of the Mongol Empire?

SECTION 3 *(pages 299–302)*
Empire of the Great Khan

15. Explain how Kublai Khan treated his Chinese subjects.

16. How did China's economy improve during the Yuan Dynasty?

SECTION 4 *(pages 303–307)*
Feudal Powers in Japan

17. Describe the impact of Chinese culture on Japan in the 600s and 700s.

18. Explain how feudalism developed in Japan beginning in the 1200s.

SECTION 5 *(pages 308–311)*
Kingdoms of Southeast Asia and Korea

19. Describe the two sources of prosperity for Southeast Asian empires, and give examples of empires that prospered each way.

20. What were the major accomplishments of the Koryu Dynasty?

Visual Summary

Empires in East Asia

Japan

- Distinct geography and culture
- Shinto religion
- Heian period
- Feudal system

Interaction with China
- Buddhism
- Writing system
- Civil service

Mongols

- Nomadic way of life
- Clan-based leadership

Interaction with China
- Mongols' conquest of China
- Spread of Chinese ideas through Mongol Empire across Eurasia

China

- Revival of civil service system
- Strengthening of central government
- Golden age of culture, science, and technology

Southeast Asia

Interaction with China
- Vietnam: Buddhism, civil service
- Other areas: spread of ideas through migration and trade

- Location on trade routes between China and India
- Indian cultural influence: political ideas and religions

Korea

Interaction with China
- Buddhism
- Writing system
- Civil service
- Printing
- Porcelain

- Distinct geography and culture
- Divided society controlled by wealthy landowners

312 Chapter 12

Interact with History

In this chapter, students have had a chance to see the impact of inventions on various cultures. Ask them to discuss what they know about the impact of the inventions they chose. Do they think another invention, such as a writing system, would have more far-reaching effects? Discuss with them, perhaps using a concept web, the multiple effects one invention might have on a culture.

CRITICAL THINKING

1. HYPOTHESIZING

THEME **EMPIRE BUILDING** How might history have been different if the Mongols had conquered all or most of Europe? Discuss the possible immediate and long-term consequences for Europe and the rest of the Mongol Empire.

2. DEVELOPMENTS AND CHANGE

For each of the following developments, create a diagram like the one shown and identify two results from it: (a) construction of the Grand Canal, (b) stirrups, and (c) the compass.

3. RISE AND FALL OF DYNASTIES

This chapter describes the rise and fall of three Chinese dynasties. What recurring patterns occur in the decline of these dynasties? What advice might you give a Chinese emperor, based on those patterns?

4. ANALYZING PRIMARY SOURCES

The following is part of a message sent by Kublai Khan to Japan's imperial court in 1266, as recorded by a Chinese historian. Read the passage and answer the questions below it.

A VOICE FROM THE PAST
The Emperor of the Great Mongols addresses the King of Japan as follows: . . . I am sending you my envoys bearing my personal message. It is my hope that the communication between our two countries be opened and maintained and that our mutual friendship be established. A sage regards the whole world as one family; how can different countries be considered one family if there is not friendly communication between them? Is force really necessary to establish friendly relations? I hope that you will give this matter your most careful attention.

SUNG LIEN, quoted in *The Essence of Chinese Civilization*

- What is Kublai Khan asking of the Japanese?
- Based on what you have read about the Mongols and Japan, what do you think Kublai's real goal was?

CHAPTER ACTIVITIES

1. LIVING HISTORY: Unit Portfolio Project

THEME **RELIGIOUS AND ETHICAL SYSTEMS** Your unit portfolio project focuses on how belief systems have affected people's lives (see page 229). For Chapter 12, you might use one of the following ideas to add to your portfolio:

- Prepare a photo essay on one of the massive temple complexes of Southeast Asia, such as Angkor Wat or Borobudur. In the essay, show how the design of the complex reflected the religious influences on the region.
- Create a mural portraying the essential beliefs of Shintoism.
- Give a "virtual" guided tour of a traditional Buddhist temple in Korea, Japan, or Vietnam. Using slides or overhead images, show how the architecture relates to Buddhist practices and the country's culture.

2. CONNECT TO TODAY: Cooperative Learning

THEME **CULTURAL INTERACTION** For 100 years, the Mongols were the lords of settled societies across Eurasia. Today, modern civilization threatens to extinguish the nomadic way of life. Traditionally nomadic groups such as the Kurds, whose homeland includes parts of Turkey, Iraq, and Iran, have faced many challenges and changes. Work with a team to prepare a report on the challenges faced by the Kurds or another traditionally nomadic people today.

Using the Internet, magazines, or reference books, research the history of the Kurds or another group and their way of life today.

- How have modern political boundaries and population growth in their region affected their way of life?
- What is their political status in the countries in which they live? Are they treated the same as others? How has their status affected their way of life?

3. INTERPRETING A TIME LINE

Revisit the unit time line on pages 228–229, and study the segment for Chapter 12. Which events from East Asia had the greatest impact on developments outside of this region? Explain your response.

FOCUS ON **GEOGRAPHY**

Study the maps of China's population distribution in the Tang and Song dynasties.

- During the Tang Dynasty, which areas of China were most densely populated?
- Overall, how had China's population changed by the Song Dynasty?

Connect to History What political and economic developments in China were related to this population change?

Source: John King Fairbank, *China: A New History*

Empires in East Asia **313**

CHAPTER ACTIVITIES

1. LIVING HISTORY

Standards for Evaluation
Photo essays should meet the following criteria:

- Show how the design reflected the various religious influences on the region.
- Include labels and captions for all main parts of the temple complex.

Standards for Evaluation
Murals should meet the following criteria:

- Reveal students' understanding of the main elements in Shintoism.
- Clearly depict the main beliefs and practices of the Shinto religion.

Standards for Evaluation
Virtual tours should meet the following criteria:

- Show the relationship of the architecture to Buddhist practices and the country's culture.
- Clearly describe the design and structure of the temple.

2. CONNECT TO TODAY: COOPERATIVE LEARNING

Standards for Evaluation
Reports should meet the following criteria:

- Describe the Kurds' way of life.
- Show how modern political boundaries and population pressures affect their way of life.
- Describe their political status and their current treatment.

3. INTERPRETING A TIME LINE

Possible Response: Chinese inventions probably had the greatest impact outside Asia because of their influence on European history.

FOCUS ON **GEOGRAPHY**

- East and north.
- The population spread throughout China.

Connect to History *Possible Responses:* Politically, the Tang and Song dynasties established a stable form of government, reviving the civil service. Trade flourished and the country prospered, which led to an increase in population in those areas under Tang and Song rule. Economically, the introduction of a new strain of rice made several crops per year possible in the south. A system of roads and canals made transporting food to the north and east easier, which also helped to increase the population.

CRITICAL THINKING

1. HYPOTHESIZING
Immediate consequences: destruction of cities and government; great loss of life; one or more European khanates; brief period of Mongol rule. *Long-term consequences:* expanded trade; faster spread of Asian culture and diseases; greater political and cultural unity.

2. DEVELOPMENTS AND CHANGE

Possible Responses: (a) improved trade between northern cities and rice regions; rebellion against Sui. (b) increased warriors' skill in battle; made Mongol cavalry a fearsome fighting unit; (c) enabled sea trade to expand; contributed to China's prosperity.

3. RISE AND FALL OF DYNASTIES
Recurring patterns: growing unrest, peasant rebellions; military pressure from outside invaders. Advice: treat peasants well, keep trade flourishing, defend borders.

4. ANALYZING PRIMARY SOURCES
Khan wanted to open diplomatic relations. Answers should reflect Kublai's thirst for conquest and later attempts to invade Japan; students might note the veiled threat in the message.

Teacher's Edition **313**

PLANNING GUIDE
European Middle Ages

	Key Ideas	**COPY MASTERS**	**ASSESSMENT**
SECTION 1 **Germanic Kingdoms Unite Under Charlemagne** *pp. 317–321*	*Invasions cause the fall of the Roman Empire, which is replaced by small kingdoms. The leader of the Frankish kingdom converts to Christianity. This religion spreads through western Europe as the Frankish kingdom expands. Charlemagne builds the Frankish kingdom into an empire.*	*In-Depth Resources: Unit 3* • **Guided Reading,** p. 52 • **History Makers:** Charlemagne, p. 66	P E *Section 1 Assessment,* p. 321 *Formal Assessment* • Section Quiz, p. 146 *Alternative Assessment Book* • Standards for Evaluating a Cooperative Activity
SECTION 2 **Feudalism in Europe** *pp. 322–326*	*New invasions create chaos in western Europe. People look to local leaders, rather than to a central ruler, for protection. The system of feudalism develops, in which protection is provided in exchange for land or labor. Social classes become well defined under this system.*	*In-Depth Resources: Unit 3* • **Guided Reading,** p. 53 • **Primary Source:** The Duties of Lords and Vassals, p. 59 • **Literature:** from *Piers Plowman,* p. 63 • **History Makers:** Leif Ericson, p. 67	P E *Section 2 Assessment,* p. 326 *Formal Assessment* • Section Quiz, p. 147 *Alternative Assessment Book* • Standards for Evaluating a Cooperative Activity
SECTION 3 **The Age of Chivalry** *pp. 327–331*	*Feudal lords create private armies of knights, who live by a complex set of ideals that guide behavior. Warfare is brutal, but poems idealize the life of a knight. In literature and songs, women are glorified as objects of romantic love. In reality most women are powerless.*	*In-Depth Resources: Unit 3* • **Guided Reading,** p. 54 • **Skillbuilder Practice:** Comparing, p. 56 • **Primary Source:** from *The Art of Courtly Love,* p. 60 • **Literature:** from *The Song of Roland,* p. 65 • **Connections Across Time and Cultures:** Roles of Women, p. 68 • **Science & Technology:** Medieval Technology in Hand Weapons, p. 69	P E *Section 3 Assessment,* p. 331 *Formal Assessment* • Section Quiz, p. 148 *Alternative Assessment Book* • Standards for Evaluating a Product or Performance Activity
SECTION 4 **The Church Wields Power** *pp. 332–335*	*German kings' attempts to revive Charlemagne's empire and his alliance with the Church by invading Italy fail. The Church resents the power German kings have to appoint church officials.*	*In-Depth Resources: Unit 3* • **Guided Reading,** p. 55 • **Geography Application:** Feudal Europe's Religious Influences, p. 57 • **Primary Sources:** Letters of Gregory VII and Henry IV, p. 61	P E *Section 4 Assessment,* p. 335 *Formal Assessment* • Section Quiz, p. 149 *Alternative Assessment Book* • Standards for Evaluating a Cooperative Activity
CHAPTER RESOURCES	**Chapter Overview** *After Charlemagne's empire dissolves, people look to local leaders for protection from invaders. Feudalism and knighthood develop as a result of this need for protection. Later kings fail to revive Charlemagne's empire. They struggle with the Church for power.*	*Telescoping the Times* • Chapter Summary, pp. 49–51 *Planning for Block Schedules*	P E *Chapter Assessment,* pp. 336–337 *Chapter Activities,* p. 337 *Formal Assessment* • Chapter Test, forms A and B, pp. 150–155 *Test Generator* *Alternative Assessment Book*

500–1200

TECHNOLOGY

 Warm-Up Transparency 13

 Geography Transparencies
- GT13 The Empire of Charlemagne, 814

 World Art and Cultures Transparencies
- AT28 Sarcophagus of Charlemagne

 Electronic Library of Primary Sources
- from *Life of Charlemagne*

 INTERNET RESOURCES
www.mlworldhistory.com

 Warm-Up Transparency 13

 World Art and Cultures Transparencies
- AT29 Viking Ship

 Critical Thinking Transparencies
- CT13 Development of Feudalism

 Electronic Library of Primary Sources
- from the Assizes of Romania

 INTERNET RESOURCES
www.mlworldhistory.com

 Warm-Up Transparency 13

 Electronic Library of Primary Sources
- from "The Art of Courtly Love"

 Patterns of Interaction Arming for War

 INTERNET RESOURCES
www.mlworldhistory.com

 Warm-Up Transparency 13

 Critical Thinking Transparencies
- CT49 Chapter 13 Visual Summary

 Electronic Library of Primary Sources
- from the Investiture Controversy

 INTERNET RESOURCES
www.mlworldhistory.com

 Chapter Summaries on Audiocassette in English and Spanish

 INTERNET RESOURCES
www.mlworldhistory.com

Block Scheduling (90 MINUTES)

Day 1
Section 1, pp. 317–321
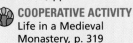 **COOPERATIVE ACTIVITY**
Life in a Medieval Monastery, p. 319 (Teacher's Edition)

Section 2, pp. 322–326
 COOPERATIVE ACTIVITY
Life in a Feudal Society, p. 324 (Teacher's Edition)

Section Assessments, pp. 321, 326

Day 2
Section 3, pp. 327–331
Section Assessment, p. 331

Day 3
Section 4, pp. 332–335
 COOPERATIVE ACTIVITY
Researching Henry IV and Pope Gregory VII, p. 334 (Teacher's Edition)

Section Assessment, p. 335

Chapter Assessment, pp. 336–337

Yearly Pacing **Chapter 13 Total:** 3 days **Yearly Total:** 85 days

 Planning for Block Schedules

Customizing for Special Needs

Students Acquiring English

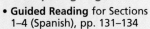 *Access for Students Acquiring English*
- **Guided Reading** for Sections 1–4 (Spanish), pp. 131–134
- **Chapter Summary** (Spanish), pp. 128–130
- **Skillbuilder Practice** Comparing (Spanish), p. 135
- **Geography Application** Feudal Europe's Religious Influences (Spanish), p. 136

 Patterns of Interaction:
Arming for War (Spanish Track)

 Chapter Summaries on Audiocassette in English and Spanish

 INTERNET RESOURCES
www.mlworldhistory.com
The Diverse Classroom.

Less Proficient Readers

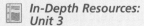 *In-Depth Resources: Unit 3*
- **Guided Reading** for Sections 1–4, pp. 52–55
- **Skillbuilder Practice** Comparing, p. 56
- **Geography Application** Feudal Europe's Religious Influences, p. 57

 Telescoping the Times
- Chapter Summary, pp. 49–51

 Chapter Summaries on Audiocassette

Gifted and Talented Students

 In-Depth Resources: Unit 3
Primary Sources:
- The Duties of Lords and Vassals, p. 59
- from *The Art of Courtly Love*, p. 60
- Letters of Gregory VII and Henry IV, p. 61

History Makers
- Charlemagne, p. 66
- Leif Ericson, p. 67

Connections to Literature READINGS FOR STUDENTS

 In-Depth Resources: Unit 3
Literature: from *Piers Plowman*, p. 63; from *The Song of Roland*, p. 65

Enrichment Reading
- Bradley, M. Zimmer
  The Mists of Avalon
  New York: Knoft, 1983
  A popular and thrilling tale of the chivalric age.

McDougal Littell
The Language of Literature, Grade 10

Sir Thomas Mallory, from *Le Morte d'Arthur*, p. 904
John Steinbeck, from *The Acts of King Arthur*, p. 923
Adrienne Rich, "The Knight," p. 932

 = Pupil's Edition   = Overhead Transparency   = Software   = Video

= Copy Master   = CD-ROM   = Audiocassette   = Internet

European Middle Ages, 500–1200

Accessing Prior Knowledge

- Ask students to read the captions accompanying each picture. Then ask students to share what they know about knights and chivalry.

Making Inferences and Drawing Conclusions

- After reading about Charlemagne, ask students what the cross and the sword he carries might symbolize.

- After reading about Gregory the Great, ask students to draw conclusions about what the duties and role of a pope might have been.

Geography Connection

Ask students to study the map of western Europe.

- Which territory dominates this region?

- Which present-day countries in Europe are named on this map?

CHAPTER 13

European Middle Ages, 500–1200

PREVIEWING THEMES

Religious and Ethical Systems

During the Middle Ages, the Church was a unifying force. It shaped people's beliefs and guided their conduct. Most Europeans at this time shared a common bond of faith. Their religious beliefs affected their daily lives.

Empire Building

In western Europe, the Roman Empire fell apart into many small kingdoms. During the Middle Ages, two powerful leaders—Charlemagne and Otto the Great—tried to revive the idea of empire. They both allied with the Church.

Power and Authority

Weak rulers and the decline of central authority led to a feudal system of relationships. Under this system, local lords with large estates assumed power. The Church too played a growing role in government affairs. This led to power struggles between political leaders and popes.

INTERNET CONNECTION

Visit us at **www.mlworldhistory.com** to learn more about the European Middle Ages and related topics.

EUROPE ABOUT 1140

0 200 Miles
0 400 Kilometers

SCOTLAND
IRELAND
Dublin
North Sea
KINGDOM OF ENGLAND
London
ATLANTIC OCEAN
Aachen
Cologne
Tri
Wor
Paris
Seine
Loire
KINGDOM OF FRANCE
Lyon

During the Middle Ages, legends of gallant knights rescuing damsels in distress from fire-breathing dragons became popular subjects of stories and paintings. One example is *St. George and the Dragon* by Paolo Uccello, shown here. Fabulous tales of the warrior **St. George** date back to the 500s. Representing the heroic ideals of knighthood, St. George is the patron saint of **England.**

314

GEOGRAPHY THEMES

Region

Ask students to identify the date of this map of Europe (about 1140). Then ask them to compare this map with the map of Charlemagne's empire on page 321. Between 814 and 1140, did this region expand or decrease in size? Which area was part of Charlemagne's empire but not part of the Holy Roman Empire? Ask students to speculate on why the boundaries within western Europe changed over time.

Location

Ask students to locate the Papal States on the map. How might the Holy Roman Empire have provided protection to the Papal States? Explain that the Church became very strong in Europe. Holy Roman emperors and popes had many struggles over who should have power to make certain decisions. How might the location of the Papal States have made these power struggles more likely? Do you think these struggles would have occurred if the Papal States were far away from the Holy Roman Empire?

ADDITIONAL RESOURCES

Books for the Teacher

- McKitterick, Rosamond, ed. *The New Cambridge Medieval History,* Vol. 2. New York: Cambridge UP, 1995. Early medieval Europe, c. 700–c. 900

- Prestwich, Michael. *Armies and Warfare in the Middle Ages.* New Haven: Yale UP, 1996.

- Kelly, Amy. *Eleanor of Aquitaine and the Four Kings.* Cambridge: Harvard UP, 1979. Biography.

- Tierney, Brian and Sidney Painter. *Western Europe in the Middle Ages, 300–1475.* New York: Knopf, 1983.

Books for the Student

- Gies, Frances and Joseph Gies. *Life in a Medieval Village.* New York: HarperCollins, 1991.

- Jordan, William Chester, ed. *The Middle Ages: An Encyclopedia for Students.* 4 vols. New York: Scribner's, 1996.

Videos

- *The Dark Ages: Europe After the Fall of Rome.* Society for Visual Education, 1995. 800-829-1900. Includes reenactments.

- *Life in a Medieval Town.* Britannica, 1992. 800-554-9862.

Software

- *Middle Ages.* CD-ROM. Society for Visual Education, 1993. 800-829-1900. Feudalism, the rise of the middle class, the Crusades, daily life.

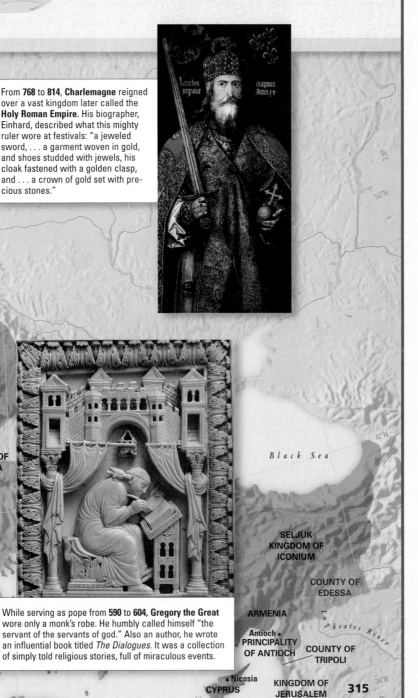

From **768** to **814**, **Charlemagne** reigned over a vast kingdom later called the **Holy Roman Empire.** His biographer, Einhard, described what this mighty ruler wore at festivals: "a jeweled sword, . . . a garment woven in gold, and shoes studded with jewels, his cloak fastened with a golden clasp, and . . . a crown of gold set with precious stones."

While serving as pope from **590** to **604**, **Gregory the Great** wore only a monk's robe. He humbly called himself "the servant of the servants of god." Also an author, he wrote an influential book titled *The Dialogues.* It was a collection of simply told religious stories, full of miraculous events.

315

HISTORY THROUGH ART

St. George and the Dragon
Paolo Uccello

Paolo Uccello was just one of many painters to depict the myth of St. George and the Dragon. According to well-known legend, George was a warrior-saint who rescued the daughter of a king. In the legend, he uses his magic sword to slay the dragon that was her captor. Historians believe the mythical character of St. George is based on a third-century Christian martyr from Palestine who rescued a king's daughter in exchange for a promise that the king's subjects would be baptized. St. George was tortured and killed on April 23, 303 for his religious beliefs. He was made patron saint of England in 1350. An annual feast on April 23 celebrates his legend.

In Uccello's painting, the hands of the princess are bound and she is tied to the dragon. Stormy skies and the dark gaping mouth of the cave create a menacing atmosphere. The painting seems to be set in the dragon's evil world. The knight on his white horse stands out as the opposite of all the darkness and evil. He has broken into this dark world to save the princess.

Interpreting the Art How does Uccello create depth in this painting? What do you think the swirling clouds represent?

Interact *with* History

This Interact with History feature motivates students by inviting them to put themselves in a key historical situation—that of a peasant living and working on a feudal estate. As they imagine themselves confronting the realities and limitations of this situation, students will analyze issues, explore their options, and become decision makers.

Purpose

- to prepare students for studying feudalism in western Europe
- to help students understand the rigid structure of feudal society
- to help students connect with the people and events in this chapter

Teaching Strategy

Thinking Critically After students have imagined themselves in the situation described on this page, have them answer the key questions and give reasons for their decisions.

EXAMINING *the* ISSUES

Following are suggestions for addressing each bulleted item.

1 What are the things you know will be provided? Do you think you would experience many changes in your life as a peasant?

2 Do you think you would grow to fear the outside world or marvel at what it might contain? Why?

3 How are you restricted from doing things? What are some choices that are not available to you? Who has more control over your life, you or your lord?

4 If you did not stay on the estate, where would you go?

Making Connections Ask students to discuss what having freedom means and how important it is to them today.

Follow Up

A feature on the chapter assessment will ask students to reevaluate their responses to the situation presented on this page.

You are living in the countryside of western Europe during the 1100s. Like about 90 percent of the population, you are a peasant working the land. Your family's hut is located in a small village on your lord's estate. The lord provides your basic needs, including housing, food, and protection.

Opportunities to leave the estate are rare. Within your lifetime, you will probably travel no more than 25 miles from your home.

What is good and bad about the small world of a peasant's life?

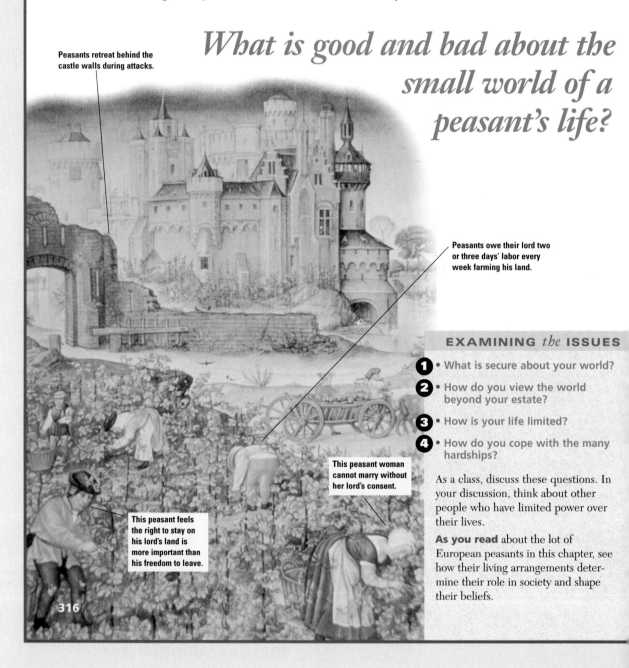

Peasants retreat behind the castle walls during attacks.

Peasants owe their lord two or three days' labor every week farming his land.

This peasant woman cannot marry without her lord's consent.

This peasant feels the right to stay on his lord's land is more important than his freedom to leave.

EXAMINING *the* ISSUES

1 • What is secure about your world?

2 • How do you view the world beyond your estate?

3 • How is your life limited?

4 • How do you cope with the many hardships?

As a class, discuss these questions. In your discussion, think about other people who have limited power over their lives.

As you read about the lot of European peasants in this chapter, see how their living arrangements determine their role in society and shape their beliefs.

1 Germanic Kingdoms Unite Under Charlemagne

TERMS & NAMES
- Middle Ages
- Franks
- monastery
- secular
- Carolingian Dynasty
- Charlemagne

MAIN IDEA

Many Germanic kingdoms that succeeded the Roman Empire were reunited under Charlemagne's empire.

WHY IT MATTERS NOW

Charlemagne spread Christian civilization through northern Europe, where it had a permanent impact.

SETTING THE STAGE The gradual decline of the Roman Empire ushered in an era of European history called the **Middle Ages,** or the medieval period. It spanned from around 500 to 1500. During these centuries, new institutions slowly emerged to replace those of the fallen Roman Empire. Unified civilizations flourished in China and Southwest Asia. Medieval Europe, though, remained fragmented.

Invasions Trigger Changes in Western Europe

By the end of the fifth century, invaders from many different Germanic groups overran the western half of the Roman Empire. Repeated invasions and constant warfare sparked new trends. A series of changes altered government, economy, and culture:

- **Disruption of Trade** Merchants faced invasions from both land and sea. Their businesses collapsed. The breakdown of trade destroyed Europe's cities as economic centers. Money became scarce.

- **Downfall of Cities** With the fall of the Roman Empire, cities were abandoned as centers of administration.

- **Population Shifts** As Roman centers of trade and government collapsed, nobles retreated to the rural areas. Roman cities were left without strong leadership. Other city dwellers also fled to the countryside, where they grew their own food. The population of western Europe became mostly rural.

THINK THROUGH HISTORY
A. Recognizing Effects How did the fall of the Roman Empire lead to disorder in western Europe?
A. Answer Strong government vanished, economic life was in turmoil, cities were abandoned, and learning declined.

The Decline of Learning The Germanic invaders who stormed Rome could not read or write. Among Roman subjects themselves, the level of learning sank sharply as more and more families left for rural areas. Few people except priests and other church officials were literate.

Knowledge of Greek, long important in Roman culture, was almost lost. Few people could read Greek works of literature, science, and philosophy. The Germanic tribes, though, had a rich oral tradition of songs and legends. However, they had no written language.

Vocabulary
dialects: various ways words from the same language are pronounced or used in different regions.

Loss of a Common Language As German-speaking peoples mixed with the Roman population, Latin began to change. It was no longer understood from region to region. Different dialects developed as new words and phrases became part of everyday speech. By the 800s, French, Spanish, and other Roman-based languages had evolved from Latin. The development of various languages mirrored the continued breakup of a once unified empire.

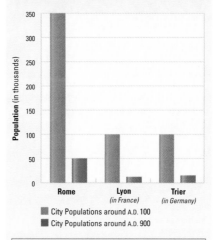

Population of Three Roman Cities

Rome — Lyon (in France) — Trier (in Germany)

Population (in thousands): 0, 50, 100, 150, 200, 250, 300, 350

■ City Populations around A.D. 100
■ City Populations around A.D. 900

SKILLBUILDER:
Interpreting Graphs
1. How much did Rome's population decrease from around A.D. 100 to 900?
2. What does the bar graph suggest about trends that occurred after the fall of the Roman Empire?

European Middle Ages **317**

SECTION 1 RESOURCES

PRINT RESOURCES

 IN-DEPTH RESOURCES: UNIT 3
Guided Reading, p. 52
History Makers: Charlemagne, p. 66

 ACCESS FOR STUDENTS ACQUIRING ENGLISH
Guided Reading (Spanish), p. 131

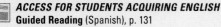 **FORMAL ASSESSMENT**
Section Quiz, p. 146

 ALTERNATIVE ASSESSMENT BOOK

TECHNOLOGY RESOURCES

 GEOGRAPHY TRANSPARENCIES
GT13 The Empire of Charlemagne, 814

 WORLD ART AND CULTURES TRANSPARENCIES
AT28 Sarcophagus of Charlemagne

 CD-ROM
Electronic Library of Primary Sources

 INTERNET www.mlworldhistory.com

Section 1 Overview

OBJECTIVES

1. To identify the effects of Germanic invasions on the western Roman Empire.

2. To explain Germanic ideas about government and describe the first Frankish king.

3. To show how Christianity spread among Germanic peoples.

4. To summarize events leading to the rise of the Frankish kingdom.

5. To describe the rise and fall of Charlemagne's empire.

SKILLBUILDERS
- Interpreting graphs, p. 317
- Interpreting maps: region, p. 321

CRITICAL THINKING
- Recognizing effects, p. 317
- Making inferences, p. 319
- Evaluating, p. 321
- Synthesizing, p. 321
- Analyzing themes, p. 321

FOCUS
5-Minute Warm-Up

▶ *Interpreting Maps*
To examine the development of Charlemagne's empire, have students answer these questions.

1. Study the map on page 321. How did Charlemagne's conquests change his empire?

2. Which city lies just outside Charlemagne's empire?

 WARM-UP TRANSPARENCY 13

OBJECTIVE ① INSTRUCT

Invasions Trigger Changes in Western Europe

▶ *Key Ideas*
- Germanic invasions lead to disorder in western Europe.
- Learning declines in western Europe as a result of invasions.
- New languages develop as Germanic speakers mix with the Roman population.

 IN-DEPTH RESOURCES: UNIT 3
Guided Reading, p. 52

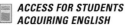 **ACCESS FOR STUDENTS ACQUIRING ENGLISH**
Guided Reading (Spanish), p. 131

Population of Three Roman Cities

(See page 317.)

Interpreting the Graph Have students read the graph and think about presenting the information in it using numbers only. Why is the bar graph more effective?

Extension Activity Have pairs of students make a bar graph using the populations of three modern European cities. Current population statistics can be found in an almanac or encyclopedia.

SKILLBUILDER Answers
(See page 317.)
1. By about 300,000 people.
2. Decline in city populations, movement of people away from cities.

OBJECTIVE 2 INSTRUCT

Germanic Kingdoms Emerge

▶ **Key Ideas**
• Germanic kingdoms replace Roman provinces and orderly government declines.
• Clovis, a Frankish leader, creates a united kingdom and spreads Christianity.

OBJECTIVE 3 INSTRUCT

Germanic Peoples Adopt Christianity

▶ **Key Ideas**
• Christianity spreads in Europe through politics and missionaries.
• Monasteries in western Europe become centers of learning.
• Under Pope Gregory I, the Church becomes a political as well as a spiritual power.

Germanic Kingdoms Emerge

In the years of upheaval between 400 and 600, small Germanic kingdoms replaced Roman provinces. The borders of those kingdoms changed constantly with the fortunes of war. The Church was an institution that survived the fall of the Roman Empire. During this time of political chaos, the Church provided order and security.

The Concept of Government Changes Along with shifting boundaries, the entire concept of government changed. Loyalty to public government and written law had unified Roman society. Family ties and personal loyalty, rather than citizenship in a public state, bound Germanic society together. Unlike the Romans, Germanic peoples lived in small communities. These were governed by unwritten rules and traditions.

Every Germanic chief led a band of warriors who had pledged their loyalty to him. In peacetime, these followers lived in their lord's hall. He gave them food, weapons, and treasure. In battle, warriors fought to the death at their lord's side. They considered it a disgrace to outlive him.

Germanic warriors willingly died for a leader they respected. Yet they felt no obligation to obey a king they didn't even know. Nor would they obey an official sent to collect taxes or administer justice in the name of an emperor they had never met. The Germanic stress on personal ties made it impossible to establish orderly government for large territories.

In the Roman province of Gaul, a Germanic people called the **Franks** held power. Their leader, Clovis (KLOH-vihs), would eventually bring Christianity to this region.

The Franks Under Clovis Clovis's wife, Clothilde, urged him to convert to her faith. She believed in a traditional form of Christianity. In 496 Clovis led his warriors into

This ivory carving shows Clovis's conversion to Christianity in 496. A bishop baptizes him as his wife, Clothilde, looks on.

battle against another Germanic army. Fearing defeat, Clovis appealed to the Christian God. "For I have called on my gods," he prayed, "but I find they are far from my aid . . . Now I call on Thee. I long to believe in Thee. Only, please deliver me from my enemies." The tide of the battle shifted and the Franks triumphed. Afterward, Clovis and 3,000 of his warriors asked a bishop to baptize them.

The Church in Rome welcomed Clovis's conversion and supported his military campaigns against other Germanic peoples. By 511, Clovis had united the Franks into one kingdom. The strategic alliance between Clovis's Frankish kingdom and the Church marked the beginning of a special partnership between two powerful forces.

Germanic Peoples Adopt Christianity

Politics played a key role in spreading Christianity. By 600, the Church, with the help of Frankish rulers, had converted many Germanic peoples. These new converts had settled in Rome's former lands.

Missionaries also succeeded in spreading Christianity. These religious travelers often risked their lives to advance their beliefs. During the fourth and fifth centuries, they worked among the Germanic and Celtic groups that bordered the Roman Empire. In southern Europe, the fear of coastal attacks by Muslims also spurred many people to become Christians.

Monasteries and Convents To adapt to rural conditions, the Church built religious communities called **monasteries.** There Christian men called monks gave up all their

---

Students Acquiring English: Previewing Vocabulary Pair students acquiring English with proficient readers to preview the vocabulary for this section. Have partners take turns reading aloud the items in the list of terms and names. Then have them look up the items in the glossary, beginning on page 1015. The glossary is also printed in Spanish, beginning on page 1031. You may wish to use this strategy with other sections in this chapter.

Less Proficient Readers:
Formulating Historical Questions Review this skill with students, using the Skillbuilder Handbook, page 999. After students have read the first page of this chapter, brainstorm with them a list of questions about the events in the text, such as When did Germanic invaders overrun western Europe? and How did they change the government? Have students work in pairs to answer these questions and apply this strategy to other parts of the chapter.

 IN-DEPTH RESOURCES: UNIT 3 Skillbuilder Practice: Formulating Historical Questions, p. 21

private possessions. Monks became servants of God. Nuns, women who also followed this religious way of life, lived in convents.

Around 520, Benedict, an Italian monk, began writing a book describing a strict yet practical set of rules for monasteries. Benedict's sister, Scholastica (skuh·LAS·tik·uh), headed a convent. There she adapted the same rules for women. These guidelines became a model for many other religious communities in western Europe. Monks and nuns devoted their lives to prayer and good works.

Monasteries also became Europe's best-educated communities. Monks opened schools, maintained libraries, and copied books. In 731, Venerable Bede, an English monk, wrote a history of England. Scholars still consider it the best historical work of the early Middle Ages. In the 600s and 700s, monks made beautiful copies of religious writings, decorated with ornate letters and brilliant pictures. The monks' illuminated manuscripts preserved at least part of Rome's intellectual heritage.

THINK THROUGH HISTORY
B. Making Inferences What valuable role did monasteries play during this time of chaos?
B. Possible Answers Represented an orderly, religious way of life; kept learning alive.

Gregory I Expands Papal Power In 590, Gregory I, also called Gregory the Great, became pope. As head of the Church in Rome, Gregory broadened the authority of the papacy, or pope's office, beyond its spiritual role. Under Gregory, the papacy also became a **secular,** or worldly, power involved in politics. The pope's palace was the center of Roman government. Gregory used Church revenues to raise armies, repair roads, and help the poor. He also negotiated peace treaties with invaders such as the Lombards. Gregory had begun to act as the mayor of Rome. Yet his influence extended beyond the city's boundaries.

According to Gregory, the entire region from Italy to England, from Spain to western Germany, fell under his responsibility. Gregory strengthened the vision of Christendom. It was a spiritual kingdom that fanned out from Rome to the most distant churches. This idea of a churchly kingdom, ruled by a pope, would become a central theme of the Middle Ages. Meanwhile, secular rulers set their sights on expanding their own political kingdoms.

A European Empire Evolves

After the Roman Empire dissolved, small kingdoms sprang up all over Europe. For example, England splintered into seven tiny kingdoms. Some of them were no larger than the state of Connecticut. The Franks controlled the largest and strongest of Europe's kingdoms in an area that was formerly the Roman province of Gaul. The Franks' first Christian king, Clovis, laid down the foundations for this kingdom.

By the time Clovis died in 511, he had extended his rule over most of what is now France. Clovis greatly strengthened the Merovingian (MEHR·uh·VIHN·jee·uhn) Dynasty, which was named after his legendary ancestor.

Clovis's Descendants By 700, an official known as the *major domo,* or mayor of the palace, had become the most powerful person in the kingdom. Officially, the mayor of the palace had charge of the royal household and estates. Unofficially, he commanded armies and made policy. In effect, the mayor of the palace ruled the kingdom.

In 719, a mayor of the palace named Charles Martel (Charles the Hammer) held more power than the king. Charles Martel extended the Franks' reign to the north, south, and east. He also defeated a Muslim raiding party from Spain at the Battle of Tours in 732. The outcome of this battle held great significance for Christian Europeans. If the Muslims had won, western Europe might have become a part of

Benedict
480?–543

At 15, Benedict left school and hiked up to the Sabine Hills, where he lived in a cave as a hermit. After learning about Benedict's deep religious conviction, a group of other monks persuaded Benedict to lead their monastery. Benedict declared:

We must prepare our hearts and bodies for combat under holy obedience to the divine commandments. . . . We are therefore going to establish a school in which one may learn the service of the Lord.

In his book describing the rules for monastic life, Benedict emphasized a balance between work and study. Such guidelines turned monasteries into centers of order, stability, and learning.

Benedict's Rule provides guidance on every aspect of life, from how much monks should eat to what kind of bed they should sleep on. The Rule says that no monk should be overtaken by indigestion after a meal because this would mean he had overindulged. Why might people want such structure in their lives? Is it possible to find such structure outside a monastery?

OBJECTIVE 4 INSTRUCT

A European Empire Evolves

▶ **Key Ideas**
• Charles Martel expands Frankish rule through conquest.
• Pepin, Martel's son, becomes king and forms an alliance between Frankish kings and the pope.
• Charlemagne, Pepin's son, inherits a strengthened kingdom.

 IN-DEPTH RESOURCES: UNIT 3
History Maker: Charlemagne, p. 66

CRITICAL THINKING ACTIVITY
CLASS TIME: 15 MINUTES

Analyzing Sequence
Suggest students connect events in this section using a chart like the one below.

Martel becomes powerful official
↓
Martel expands kingdom
↓
Martel passes on power to his son
↓
↓
↓

Task: Students groups will research and write reports on life in a medieval monastery. Groups will present their reports to the class.

Purpose: To learn more about the Middle Ages.

Activity: Brainstorm with students a list of questions about life in medieval monasteries, such as What did monks eat? What happened if they broke a rule? What did their clothes look like? Have groups choose three of these questions and make up two

more questions to answer in their reports. Group members should share the tasks of researching, organizing information, writing, and creating illustrations. Groups should present to the class one or two of the questions from their reports and the answers.

 Building a Portfolio: If reports are among their best work, students should add them to their portfolio.

ALTERNATIVE ASSESSMENT BOOK
Standards for Evaluating a Cooperative Activity

Standards for Evaluation
Reports should . . .

• clearly answer students' questions
• be thoughtfully organized
• show evidence of research and group effort

MORE ABOUT . . .
Charlemagne's Palace

Charlemagne built a magnificent palace to rival that of the Byzantine emperor, Justinian. Imported Italian marble decorated a reception hall. Gold and silver lamps lighted the palace chapel, and gold mosaics adorned the chapel's dome. Charlemagne studied maps inlaid into gold and silver tables. Because he loved to swim, Charlemagne built a marble pool that could hold 100 people and was filled with water from a hot spring.

 WORLD ART AND CULTURES TRANSPARENCIES
AT28 Sarcophagus of Charlemagne

OBJECTIVE 5 INSTRUCT

Charlemagne Takes Center Stage

Key Ideas
- Charlemagne's conquests reunite western Europe into an empire and spread Christianity.
- Charlemagne establishes a centralized government.
- Charlemagne supports learning and culture.
- Charlemagne's heirs divide his empire and central authority breaks down.

 ELECTRONIC LIBRARY OF PRIMARY SOURCES
from *Life of Charlemagne*

CRITICAL THINKING ACTIVITY
CLASS TIME: 15 MINUTES

Recognizing Causes and Effects
To help students understand Charlemagne's achievements, have them complete a chart like the one below.

Charlemagne's Actions	Effect of Actions
conquered new lands	
	Charlemagne crowned emperor
limited power of nobles	

Frankish Rule

730	740	760	780	800

732 Charles Martel defeats the Muslims at the Battle of Tours.

751 Pepin the Short becomes the first king ever anointed by the pope.

771 Charlemagne becomes the sole king of the Franks and continues his conquest of Europe.

the Muslim Empire. Charles Martel's victory at the Battle of Tours halted the Muslim invasion. This conquest made him a Christian hero.

At his death, Charles Martel passed on his power to his son, Pepin the Short. Pepin wanted to become king. He shrewdly cooperated with the pope. On behalf of the Church, Pepin agreed to fight the Lombards. They were invading central Italy and threatening Rome. In exchange, the pope anointed Pepin "king by the grace of God." Thus began the reign of Frankish rulers called the **Carolingian** (KAR·uh·LIHN·juhn) **Dynasty.** It lasted from 751 to 987.

Charlemagne Extends Frankish Rule Pepin the Short died in 768. He left a greatly strengthened Frankish kingdom to his two sons, Carloman and Charles. After Carloman's death in 771, Charles, known as **Charlemagne** (SHAHR·luh·MAYN), or Charles the Great, quickly seized control of the entire kingdom.

Charlemagne was an imposing figure. He stood six feet four inches tall. His admiring secretary, a monk named Einhard, described Charlemagne's achievements:

> **A VOICE FROM THE PAST**
> [Charlemagne] was the most potent prince with the greatest skill and success in different countries during the forty-seven years of his reign. Great and powerful as was the realm of Franks, Karl [Charlemagne] received from his father Pippin, he nevertheless so splendidly enlarged it . . . that he almost doubled it.
>
> **EINHARD,** from *Life of Charlemagne*

Charlemagne Takes Center Stage

Charlemagne built an empire greater than any known since ancient Rome. Each summer Charlemagne led his armies against the enemies that surrounded his kingdom. He fought the Muslims in Spain and tribes from other Germanic kingdoms. Charlemagne conquered new lands to both the south and the east. Through these conquests, Charlemagne spread Christianity. He reunited western Europe for the first time since the Roman Empire. By 800, the Carolingian empire exceeded the Byzantine Empire. It included two-thirds of Italy, all of present-day France, a small part of Spain, and all of German Saxony. Charlemagne had become the most powerful king in western Europe.

In 800, Charlemagne traveled to Rome to crush an unruly mob that had attacked the pope. In gratitude, Pope Leo III crowned him emperor. The coronation was historic. A pope had claimed the political right to confer the title "Roman Emperor" on a European king. This event signaled the joining of Germanic power, the Church, and the heritage of the Roman Empire.

Charlemagne's Government Charlemagne strengthened his royal power by limiting the authority of the nobles. To govern his empire, Charlemagne sent out royal agents. They made sure that the powerful landholders, called counts, governed their counties justly. Charlemagne also regularly visited every part of his kingdom. He

Background
After his successful military campaign in Italy, Pepin gave the conquered territory around Rome to the pope. This gift of land was called the Papal States.

TEACHING OPTIONS

CONNECTIONS ACROSS TIME AND PLACE

Handwriting You make a handwritten copy of a book page. You give this copy to a friend, who makes another handwritten copy from it. Unfortunately, your handwriting is difficult to read and your friend puts errors in her copy. This is what happened in Charlemagne's time as monks translated and copied classical

works in Latin. The development of a more legible script changed this. The improved handwriting style led to the accurate preservation of many Latin texts. How might this clearer handwriting affect us today? *Possible Answers: Because the improved handwriting style led to more accurate translations, historians studying them today get a more accurate picture of the past.*

EXPLORING PRIMARY SOURCES

A Voice from the Past Einhard was not only Charlemagne's biographer but also his trusted friend and adviser for 23 years. The *Life of Charlemagne* expresses Einhard's gratitude for Charlemagne's support and friendship. Is Einhard's biography an accurate source of information about Charlemagne? How

might friendship have influenced the way Einhard wrote about Charlemagne? *Possible Answers: No, Einhard was predisposed to favor Charlemagne. Einhard probably wrote only complimentary information about Charlemagne.*

843 Treaty of Verdun divides
Charlemagne's empire among
his three grandsons.

820   840

813 Louis the Pious inherits the throne from
Charlemagne.

Charlemagne's Empire, 768–843

- Frankish Kingdom before Charlemagne, 768
- Areas conquered by Charlemagne, 814
- Division by Treaty of Verdun, 843

ENGLAND

North Sea

Aachen

Paris

EAST FRANKISH KINGDOM (Louis the German)

SLAVIC STATES

Elbe R.

Danube R.

ATLANTIC OCEAN

Tours

WEST FRANKISH KINGDOM (Charles the Bald)

CENTRAL KINGDOM (Lothair)

Pavia

Corsica

PAPAL STATES

Rome

SPAIN

Mediterranean Sea

0   250 Miles
0   500 Kilometers

N

GEOGRAPHY SKILLBUILDER:
Interpreting Maps
1. **Region** By 814, what was the extent of Charlemagne's empire (north to south, east to west)?
2. **Region** Based on the map, why did the Treaty of Verdun signal the decline of Charlemagne's empire?

judged cases, settled disputes, and rewarded faithful followers. He also kept a close watch on the management of his huge estates. They were the source of Carolingian wealth and power.

Cultural Revival One of Charlemagne's greatest accomplishments was his encouragement of learning. Charlemagne surrounded himself with English, German, Italian, and Spanish scholars. For his many sons and daughters and other children at the court, Charlemagne opened a palace school. He ordered monasteries to open schools that trained future monks and priests. Monasteries expanded their libraries. Monks labored to make handwritten copies of Latin books.

THINK THROUGH HISTORY
C. Evaluating What were Charlemagne's most notable achievements?
C. Answer Reuniting western Europe for the first time since the Roman Empire, spreading Christianity, encouraging learning, governing effectively.

Charlemagne's Heirs Are Weak Rulers A year before Charlemagne died in 814, he crowned his only surviving son, Louis the Pious, as emperor. Louis was a devoutly religious man. He might have fared better as a monk. Louis proved an ineffective ruler.

Louis left three sons: Lothair (loh·THAIR), Charles the Bald, and Louis the German. Louis's sons fought one another for the empire. The civil war ended in 843 when the brothers signed the Treaty of Verdun. This pact divided Charlemagne's empire into three kingdoms. After the treaty, Carolingian kings lost power. As central authority broke down, the lack of strong rulers led to a new system of governing and landholding.

Section 1 Assessment

1. TERMS & NAMES
Identify
- Middle Ages
- Franks
- monastery
- secular
- Carolingian Dynasty
- Charlemagne

2. TAKING NOTES
Create a chart like the one below to summarize how each person listed helped spread Christianity.

	Method of Spreading Christianity
Clovis	
Benedict	
Gregory I	
Charles Martel	
Charlemagne	

Which of these people do you think was the most influential in spreading Christianity? Why?

3. SYNTHESIZING
After the fall of the Roman Empire, learning declined. How was this trend offset during the early Middle Ages?
THINK ABOUT
- the establishment of monasteries
- Charlemagne's accomplishments

4. ANALYZING THEMES
Empire Building Why do you think Charlemagne succeeded in building such a vast empire?
THINK ABOUT
- Charlemagne's personality
- his military leadership
- his religious beliefs
- his relationship with the Church

ANSWERS

1. TERMS & NAMES
Middle Ages, p. 317
Franks, p. 318
monastery, p. 318
secular, p. 319
Carolingian Dynasty, p. 320
Charlemagne, p. 320

2. TAKING NOTES
Possible Responses: Clovis—converted himself and his army. Benedict—wrote rule book for monasteries. Gregory I—extended papal power; blended church and government power. Charles Martel—defeated Muslims at Battle of Tours. Charlemagne—spread

Christianity through conquests; was crowned emperor by pope.

3. SYNTHESIZING
Possible Responses: Monks opened schools, maintained libraries, copied books, and wrote scholarly works. Charlemagne opened a palace school and supported learning.

4. ANALYZING THEMES
Possible Responses:
Charlemagne had a commanding presence, strong Christian faith, and exceptional military skills. The empire he inherited was already strong. Military conquest and the spread of Christianity further strengthened it.

History from Visuals

Charlemagne's Empire, 768–843
Interpreting the Map In which year was Charlemagne's empire the largest? How did the Treaty of Verdun change the empire?
Answers: largest—814; treaty divided empire into three sections

Extension Activity Compare this map with the map of modern Europe in the Atlas, page 978. What present-day nations were part of Charlemagne's empire?
Answers: France, Italy, Belgium, Germany, Switzerland, Spain, Austria, Slovenia, Croatia, the Netherlands

SKILLBUILDER Answers
1. North Sea to Mediterranean Sea (north to south); Elbe and Danube rivers to Atlantic Ocean (east to west).
2. The vast region unified under one ruler was split among three rulers.

 GEOGRAPHY TRANSPARENCIES
GT13 The Empire of Charlemagne, 814

ASSESS & RETEACH

Section 1 Assessment
Have pairs of students work together to answer the questions and note the pages where the answers can be found.

Section Quiz
FORMAL ASSESSMENT
Section Quiz, p. 146

Reteaching Activity
CLASS TIME: 15 MINUTES

Use the Guided Reading Worksheet for Section 1 to review the key ideas of this section.

 IN-DEPTH RESOURCES: UNIT 3
Guided Reading, p. 52

CLOSE ACTIVITY

CLASS TIME: 25 MINUTES

Role-Playing
Divide the class into six groups and assign each group one of the following figures: Clovis, Benedict, Gregory I, Charles Martel, Pepin, and Charlemagne. Have groups go through the section to make a list of facts about the figure. Then have group members take turns standing up in front of the class and sharing a fact by role-playing the figure.

Section 2 Overview

OBJECTIVES

 To explain the effects of new invasions on western Europe.

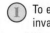 To summarize the structure and effects of feudalism.

To explain the role of the manor system in the feudal economy.

SKILLBUILDER

• Interpreting maps: location, movement, p. 323

CRITICAL THINKING

• Recognizing effects, p. 323
• Summarizing, p. 324
• Contrasting, p. 325
• Comparing, p. 325
• Analyzing causes, p. 325
• Making inferences, p. 326
• Evaluating, p. 326

FOCUS

5-Minute Warm-Up

▶ *Interpreting Diagrams*

Answering these questions will help students understand the structure of feudal society.

1. Look at the illustration on page 324. What are the titles of the figures?

2. Who are the most powerful and least powerful figures?

 WARM-UP TRANSPARENCY 13

OBJECTIVE 1 INSTRUCT

New Invasions Trouble Western Europe

▶ *Key Ideas*

• Vikings are skillful seafarers and vicious invaders.

• Invasions weaken central governments. People turn to local leaders for protection.

 IN-DEPTH RESOURCES: UNIT 3
Guided Reading, p. 53
History Makers: Leif Ericson, p. 67

 ACCESS FOR STUDENTS ACQUIRING ENGLISH
Guided Reading (Spanish), p. 132

 WORLD ART AND CULTURES TRANSPARENCIES
AT29 Viking ship

TERMS & NAMES
• lord
• fief
• vassal
• knight
• serf
• manor
• tithe

MAIN IDEA	WHY IT MATTERS NOW
Europeans developed feudalism, a political and military system of protective alliances and relationships.	The rights and duties of feudal relationships helped shape today's forms of representative government.

SETTING THE STAGE After the Treaty of Verdun, Charlemagne's three feuding grandsons broke up the kingdom even further. Part of this territory also became a battleground as new waves of invaders attacked Europe. The political turmoil and constant warfare led to the rise of feudalism—a military and political system based on land ownership and personal loyalty.

New Invasions Trouble Western Europe

Between 800 and 1000, invasions completely destroyed the Carolingian Empire. Muslim invaders from the south seized Sicily and raided Italy. They sacked Rome in 846. Magyar invaders struck from the east. Like the earlier Huns and Avars, the Magyar warriors terrorized Germany and Italy. And from the north sailed the most dreaded attackers of all—the Vikings.

Vikings: Raiders, Traders, and Explorers The Vikings set sail from a wintry, wooded region called Scandinavia (SKAN·duh·NAY·vee·uh). The Vikings, a Germanic people, were also called Northmen or Norsemen. They worshiped warlike gods. The Vikings took pride in nicknames like Eric Bloodaxe and Thorfinn Skullsplitter.

The Vikings carried out their raids with terrifying speed. Clutching swords and heavy wooden shields, these helmeted warriors beached their ships. They struck and then quickly shoved out to sea again. By the time local troops arrived, the Vikings were gone.

Viking warships were awesome. The largest of these long ships held 300 warriors. They took turns rowing the ship's 72 oars. The prow of each ship swept grandly upward, often ending with the carved head of a sea monster. A ship might weigh 20 tons when fully loaded. Yet it could sail in a mere three feet of water. Rowing up shallow creeks, the Vikings looted inland villages and monasteries.

The Vikings were not only warriors but also traders, farmers, and outstanding explorers. Vikings ventured far beyond western Europe. They journeyed down rivers into the heart of Russia, to Constantinople, and even across the icy waters of the North Atlantic. A Viking explorer named Leif (leef) Ericson most likely reached North America around 1000, almost 500 years before Columbus.

About the same time Ericson reached the Americas, the Viking terror in Europe faded away. As Vikings gradually accepted Christianity, they stopped raiding monasteries. Also, a warming trend in Europe's climate made farming easier in Scandinavia. As agricultural settlements in Iceland and Greenland prospered, fewer Scandinavians adopted the seafaring life of Viking warriors.

Background
The Vikings in Russia, called Varangians, settled down to become traders and nation builders. Their earlier invasions of Russia led to the establishment of the first Russian state, in the mid-800s. (See Chapter 11.)

This curled oak prow is a model of a magnificent Viking ship found in Oseberg, Norway. Up to 30 Vikings rowed such ships, which were over 70 feet long.

322

SECTION 2 RESOURCES

PRINT RESOURCES

 IN-DEPTH RESOURCES: UNIT 3
Guided Reading, p. 53
Primary Source: The Duties of Lords and Vassals, p. 59
Literature: from *Piers Plowman*, p. 63
History Makers: Leif Ericson, p. 67

 ACCESS FOR STUDENTS ACQUIRING ENGLISH
Guided Reading (Spanish), p. 132

 FORMAL ASSESSMENT
Section Quiz, p. 147

TECHNOLOGY RESOURCES

 WORLD ART AND CULTURES TRANSPARENCIES
AT29 Viking Ship

 CRITICAL THINKING TRANSPARENCIES
CT13 Development of Feudalism

 CD-ROM
Electronic Library of Primary Sources

INTERNET www.mlworldhistory.com

Map Legend:
- Viking invasion routes
- Magyar invasion routes
- Muslim invasion routes
- Viking areas
- Magyar areas
- Muslim areas

To Iceland
North Sea
SCANDINAVIA
Baltic Sea
IRELAND
ENGLAND
London
Paris
Aachen
Tours
RHINELAND
BURGUNDY
FRANCE
ALPS
Rhône R.
Rhine R.
Danube R.
PYRENEES
Genoa
Pisa
Corsica
Rome
Sardinia
Sicily
Mediterranean Sea
Crete
ATLANTIC OCEAN
CALIPHATE OF CÓRDOBA
W. Dvina R.
Volga R.
Dnieper R.
RUSSIA
Kiev
Volga R.
Caspian Sea
Black Sea
Constantinople
BYZANTINE EMPIRE
CARPATHIAN MTS.

0 500 Miles
0 1,000 Kilometers

GEOGRAPHY SKILLBUILDER: Interpreting Maps
1. **Location** What lands did the Vikings raid?
2. **Movement** Why were the Viking, Magyar, and Muslim invasions so threatening to Europe?

Magyars and Muslims As the Viking invasions declined, Europe became the target of new assaults. The Magyars, a group of nomadic people, attacked from the east. They were superb horseback riders. The Magyars swept across the plains of the Danube River and invaded western Europe in the late 800s. The Magyars did not settle conquered land. Instead, they captured people to sell as slaves. They attacked isolated villages and monasteries. The Magyars overran northern Italy and reached as far west as the Rhineland and Burgundy.

The Muslims struck from the south. From there, they controlled the Mediterranean Sea, and disrupted trade. In the 600s and 700s, the Muslims tried to conquer and settle in Europe. By the 800s and 900s, their goal was also plunder. The Muslims were excellent sailors. They attacked settlements on the Atlantic and Mediterranean coasts and as far inland as Switzerland.

The invasions of Vikings, Magyars, and Muslims caused widespread disorder and suffering. Most western Europeans were living in constant danger. Central authority proved powerless. They no longer looked to a central ruler for security. Instead, many turned to local rulers with their own armies. Leaders who could fight the invaders attracted followers and gained political strength.

Feudalism Structures Society

In 911, two former enemies faced each other in a peace ceremony. Rollo was the head of a Viking army. He had been plundering the rich Seine (sayn) River valley for years. Charles the Simple was the king of France but held little power. Charles granted the Viking leader a huge piece of French territory. It became known as Northmen's land, or Normandy. In return, Rollo placed his hands between the king's hands and swore a pledge of loyalty.

European Middle Ages **323**

THINK THROUGH HISTORY
A. Recognizing Effects What was the impact of Viking, Magyar, and Muslim invasions on medieval Europe?
A. Answer Left villages and monasteries in ruins; weakened authority of central rulers; spurred people to rely on local leaders for protection

MORE ABOUT . . .
A Vassal's Oath to His Lord

A vassal swore an oath to be faithful and to serve his lord against all others. However, a lord did not have complete power over his vassal. Charlemagne ruled that if a lord tried to kill a vassal, take his land, steal his wife or daughter, fail to defend him, or make him a serf, the vassal was no longer obliged to serve the lord.

ELECTRONIC LIBRARY OF PRIMARY SOURCES
from the Assizes of Romania

MORE ABOUT . . .
Feudalism

In feudal Europe, nobody truly owned land. The king was a vassal to God. The King's fief, it was believed, was a gift from God for being a wise ruler. Nobles were vassals to the king, who gave them land in exchange for services. Nobles then granted smaller fiefs to lesser nobles. Tenants, or free peasants, held very small pieces of land from minor lords in exchange for services or rent. The structure of feudal society is well expressed in this phrase: "No man without a master; no land without a lord."

A New Social Order The worst years of the invaders' attacks roughly spanned from 850 to 950. During this time, rulers and warriors like Charles and Rollo made similar agreements in many parts of Europe. The system of governing and landholding called feudalism had emerged in Europe. A similar feudal system existed in China under the Zhou Dynasty that ruled from around the 11th century B.C. until 256 B.C. Feudalism in Japan began in A.D. 1192 and ended in the 19th century.

The feudal system was based on mutual obligations. In exchange for military protection and other services, a **lord**, or landowner, granted land called a **fief.** The person receiving a fief was called a **vassal.** Charles the Simple, the lord, and Rollo, the vassal, showed how this two-sided bargain worked. Feudalism depended on the control of land.

The Feudal Pyramid To visualize the structure of feudal society, think of a pyramid. At the peak reigned the king. Next came the most powerful vassals—wealthy landowners such as nobles and bishops. Serving beneath these vassals were knights. **Knights** were mounted warriors who pledged to defend their lords' lands in exchange for fiefs. At the base of the pyramid were landless peasants who toiled in the fields.

MTHINK THROUGH HISTORY
B. Summarizing What are the key characteristics of feudalism?
B. Answer System of government based on landholding; alliances based on loyalty, military service, and land grants

Peasants

Peasants

Knights

Knights

Church Official

Noble

King

In practice, the feudal system did not work so simply. Relationships between various lords and their vassals were never clear-cut. The same noble might be a vassal to several different lords. The feudal pyramid often became a complex tangle of conflicting loyalties. Both lords and vassals tried to use these relationships to their own advantage.

Social Classes Are Well Defined In the feudal system, status determined a person's prestige and power. Medieval writers classified people into three groups: those who fought (nobles and knights), those who prayed (men and women of the Church), and those who worked (the peasants). Social class was usually inherited.

In Europe during the Middle Ages, the vast majority of people were peasants. Most peasants were serfs. **Serfs** were people who could not lawfully leave the place where they were born. Though bound to the land, serfs were not slaves. Their lords could not sell or buy them. The wealth of the feudal lords came from the labor of peasants.

Vocabulary
status: social ranking.

TEACHING OPTION | **BLOCK SCHEDULING**
COOPERATIVE ACTIVITY: Life in a Feudal Society
CLASS TIME 30 MINUTES

Task: Partners will research the life of a medieval character and write and present interviews.

Purpose: To learn more about feudal society.

Activity: Partners should choose a character who is a noble, clergy member, or peasant, such as a young knight, scribe, monk, nun, peasant, or a lord's son or daughter. Partners should research the every-day life of their character, including what he or she does for a living and the privileges and limitations of his or her class. Next, partners should write four interview questions to ask the character about his or her life and the answers to the questions. Partners will present this information by role-playing an interviewer and the character.

 Building a Portfolio: Remind students to add their strongest work to their portfolio.

ALTERNATIVE ASSESSMENT BOOK Standards for Evaluating a Cooperative Activity

Standards for Evaluation
Interviews should . . .

• show evidence of extensive research
• present accurate information
• include supporting details

March: Two Workmen in a Garden by Simon Bening (about 1515)

This medieval painting shows a noble and two workmen who live on a manor. During the Middle Ages, "fashion police" made sure that people dressed according to their social class. Peasants could not lawfully wear the clothes of a noble.

Connect *to* History

Contrasting How does the clothing of the three people in the painting reflect their status and responsibilities in medieval society?

SEE SKILLBUILDER HANDBOOK, PAGE 1009

Connect *to* Today

Comparing How would you visually show that today's styles, especially among teenagers, blur the distinctions among various social classes?

Manors: The Economic Side of Feudalism

The **manor** was the lord's estate. During the Middle Ages, the manor system was the basic economic arrangement. The manor system rested on a set of rights and obligations between a lord and his serfs. The lord provided the serfs with housing, strips of farmland, and protection from bandits. In return, serfs tended the lord's lands, cared for his animals, and performed other tasks to maintain the estate. Peasant women shared in the farmwork with their husbands. All peasants, whether free or serf, owed the lord certain duties. These included at least a few days' labor each week and a certain portion of their grain.

A Self-Contained World Peasants rarely traveled more than 25 miles from their own manor. By standing in the center of a plowed field, they could see their entire world at a glance. A manor usually covered only a few square miles of land. It typically consisted of the lord's manor house, a church, and workshops. Generally, 15 to 30 families lived in the village on a manor. Fields, pastures, and forests surrounded the village. Sometimes a stream wound through the manor. Streams and ponds provided fish, which served as an important source of food.

The manor was largely a self-sufficient community. The serfs and peasants raised or produced nearly everything that they and their lord needed for daily life—crops, fuel, cloth, leather goods, and lumber. The only outside purchases were salt, iron, and a few unusual objects such as millstones. These huge stones were used to grind flour.

The Harshness of Manor Life For the privilege of living on the lord's land, peasants paid a high price. They paid a tax on all grain ground in the lord's mill. Any attempt to dodge taxes by baking bread elsewhere was treated as a crime. Peasants also paid a tax on marriage. Weddings could take place only with the lord's consent. After all these payments to the lord, peasant families owed the village priest a **tithe**, or church tax. A tithe represented one-tenth of their income.

Background
Farming was the chief economic activity during the Middle Ages.

THINK THROUGH HISTORY
C. Analyzing Causes How might the decline of trade during the early Middle Ages have contributed to the self-sufficiency of the manor system?
C. Answer The limited amount of outside goods available led to communities that produced everything they needed.

European Middle Ages **325**

OBJECTIVE ③ INSTRUCT

Manors: The Economic Side of Feudalism

▶ *Key Ideas*
• A lord gives serfs land, shelter, and protection in exchange for work.
• On a manor, peasants produce almost everything needed for daily life.
• Peasants pay high taxes and live a harsh life under the manor system.

MORE ABOUT . . .
Peasant Life

Peasants owned very little outright. Usually a family had a few animals—pigs, hens, or a cow—and some owned tools such as a hoe, an axe, a spade, or a barrel. Wealthier peasants owned more household items. Peasants usually shared their cottages with their farm animals, for the animals' safety. A small fire used for cooking and warmth was kept burning in the center of the cottage. There was no chimney and the smoke left the cottage through a hole in the roof.

Connect *to* History

Contrasting
Suggest that students make a chart like the one here to contrast the people in the painting. *Possible Answer:* The lord of the manor, the nobleman on the left, wears a fur-collared cloak, probably signaling his wealth and his authority over the two peasants on the right. Dressed for hard labor, they both wear simple caps and loose-fitting tunics.

	Nobleman	Peasants
Clothing		
Status		
Responsibilities		

Connect *to* Today

Comparing
Some students might clip ads for blue jeans and name-brand athletic shoes—clothing characteristic of many teenagers regardless of class.

A Medieval Manor

Interpreting the Diagram Ask students how they can tell that the manor house and the church are the most important buildings. *Answer: They are the largest buildings.*

Extension Activity Have pairs of students use an encyclopedia to find out why the manor had a spring and a fall planting and why one field was left fallow. *Answers: A spring and fall planting meant food was available all year. A field was left fallow to recover its soil nutrients.*

 IN-DEPTH RESOURCES: UNIT 3
Literature: *Piers Plowman*, p. 63

ASSESS & RETEACH

Section 2 Assessment

Have students work on the questions individually, then compare their answers with those of a partner.

Section Quiz

 FORMAL ASSESSMENT
Section Quiz, p. 147

Reteaching Activity

CLASS TIME: 20 MINUTES

Have small groups review the section using the map, diagrams, and illustration. Group members should take turns using what they learned in the section to explain to each other what each image is and what it reveals about the causes, effects, or structure of feudalism.

CLOSE ACTIVITY

CLASS TIME: 25 MINUTES

Role-Playing Terms and Names

Have students work in groups to role-play the items in the list of terms and names. Group members should take turns choosing an item from the list and giving clues to its meaning, such as "I live on Lord Randall's estate and I help care for his horses. Who am I?" The other group members should try to guess the answer. Groups should role-play every item in the list.

A Medieval Manor

This diagram shows the arrangement of a typical medieval manor. These self-contained communities dotted the countryside throughout western Europe. Manors included farmland usually ranging in size from 900 to 3,000 acres.

Fallow Field
Spring Planting Field
Forest
Fall Planting Field
Serfs' Cottages
Pond
Lord's Manor House
Meadow
Church
Blacksmith
Oven
Well
Mill
Orchard

Serfs lived in crowded cottages with only one or two rooms. They warmed their dirt-floor houses by bringing pigs inside. At night the family huddled on a pile of straw that often crawled with insects. Peasants' simple diet consisted mainly of vegetables, coarse brown bread, grain, cheese, and soup.

Piers Plowman, written by William Langland in 1362, reveals the hard life of English peasants:

D. Possible Answers Hunger, poverty, underfed children

THINK THROUGH HISTORY
D. Making Inferences What does this excerpt suggest about the problems peasant families faced?

> **A VOICE FROM THE PAST**
> What by spinning they save, they spend it in house-hire,
> Both in milk and in meal to make a mess of porridge,
> To cheer up their children who chafe for their food,
> And they themselves suffer surely much hunger
> And woe in the winter, with waking at nights
> And rising to rock an oft restless cradle
>
> **WILLIAM LANGLAND,** *Piers Plowman*

Despite the hardships they endured, serfs accepted their lot in life as part of the Church's teachings. They, like most Christians during medieval times, believed that God determined a person's place in society.

Section 2 Assessment

1. TERMS & NAMES

Identify
- lord
- fief
- vassal
- knight
- serf
- manor
- tithe

2. TAKING NOTES

Create a cause-and-effect chart like the one below. Show the reasons why feudalism developed and its consequences.

Causes

↓

Rise of Feudalism

↓

Effects

3. EVALUATING

What benefits do you think a medieval manor provided to the serfs who lived there? What were the drawbacks?

THINK ABOUT
- the duties and rights of serfs
- serfs' living conditions
- the diagram of the medieval manor on this page

4. THEME ACTIVITY

Power and Authority Work with a partner to draw up a contract between a lord and a vassal, such as a knight, or between the lord of a manor and a serf. Include the responsibilities, obligations, and rights of each party. Refer to information mentioned in the text.

ANSWERS

1. TERMS & NAMES
lord, p. 324
fief, p. 324
vassal, p. 324
knight, p. 324
serf, p. 324
manor, p. 325
tithe, p. 325

2. TAKING NOTES
Possible Responses: Causes—Magyar, Muslim, and Viking invasions; decline of centralized government. Effects—increased emphasis on warfare and the control of land; well-defined social classes.

3. EVALUATING
Possible Responses: Benefits—fulfilled basic needs for food, shelter, and protection; provided security and a sense of belonging to a community. Drawbacks—limited freedom; backbreaking labor; no awareness of the outside world; poor living conditions.

4. THEME ACTIVITY
Standards for Evaluation
An effective contract should meet the following criteria:
- Demonstrates knowledge of the feudal system.
- Spells out the rights and obligations of each party.
- Contains accurate informatio

TERMS & NAMES
• chivalry
• tournament
• troubadour

MAIN IDEA

The code of chivalry for knights glorified combat and romantic love.

WHY IT MATTERS NOW

Chivalry has shaped modern ideas of romance in Western cultures.

SETTING THE STAGE During the Middle Ages, nobles constantly fought one another. Their feuding kept Europe in a fragmented state for centuries. Through warfare, feudal lords defended their estates, seized new territories, and increased their wealth. Lords and their armies lived in a violent society that prized combat skills. By the 1100s, a code of behavior arose. High ideals guided warriors' actions and glorified their roles.

Warriors on Horseback

Background
The Muslims who invaded Spain in the 700s and established a civilization there were called Moors.

Mounted soldiers became valuable in combat during the reign of Charlemagne's grandfather, Charles Martel, in the 700s. Charles Martel had observed that the Muslim cavalry often turned the tide of battles. As a result, he organized Frankish troops of armored horsemen, or knights.

Saddles and Stirrups The leather saddle was developed on the Asian steppes around 200 B.C. Stirrups were developed in India around the same time. Both changed the technology of warfare in Europe during the 700s. The saddle kept a warrior firmly seated on a moving horse. Stirrups allowed him to stand up while riding and to maneuver heavier weapons. Without stirrups to brace him, a charging warrior was likely to topple off his own horse.

Frankish knights, galloping full tilt, could knock over enemy foot soldiers and riders on horseback. Gradually, mounted knights became the most important part of an army. The horses they owned were status symbols. Warhorses played a key military role.

The Warrior's Role in Feudal Society By the 11th century, western Europe was a battleground of warring nobles vying for power. To defend their territories, feudal lords raised private armies. In exchange for military service, feudal lords used their most abundant resource—land. They rewarded knights, their most skilled warriors, with fiefs from their sprawling estates. Wealth from these fiefs allowed knights to devote their lives to war. Knights could afford to pay for costly weapons, armor, and warhorses.

As the lord's vassal, a knight's main obligation was to serve in battle. From each of his knights, a lord typically demanded about 40 days of mounted combat each year. Knights' pastimes also often revolved around training for war. Wrestling and hunting helped knights gain strength and practice the skills they would need on the battlefield.

These two-inch high iron spikes, called caltrops, were strewn over a battlefield or in front of a castle. They could maim galloping warhorses or enemy foot soldiers.

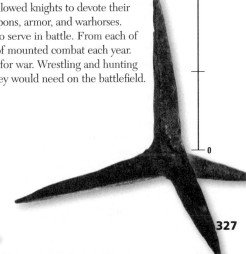

— 2 inches

— 0

327

CRITICAL THINKING
• Comparing, p. 328
• Making inferences, pp. 329, 330
• Summarizing, p. 331
• Forming opinions, p. 331
• Analyzing themes, p. 331

OBJECTIVES

① To describe the technology of warfare and the warrior's role in feudal society.

② To explain the standards and training of a knight, and the brutality he faced.

③ To describe the way chivalry, knighthood, and women are portrayed in medieval literature.

④ To summarize the roles and status of medieval women.

FOCUS
5-Minute Warm-Up

▶ **Interpreting Diagrams**
Have students answer these questions to explore the concept of chivalry.

1. Study the diagram on page 328. What are three skills a boy learned before he became a knight?

2. What did boys do to learn these skills?

🗑 **WARM-UP TRANSPARENCY 13**

OBJECTIVE ① INSTRUCT

Warriors on Horseback

▶ **Key Ideas**
• Leather saddles and stirrups help mounted warriors win battles.
• Private armies of knights fight for nobles in exchange for land.

📰 **IN-DEPTH RESOURCES: UNIT 3**
Guided Reading, p. 54

📰 **ACCESS FOR STUDENTS ACQUIRING ENGLISH**
Guided Reading (Spanish), p. 133

SECTION 3 RESOURCES

PRINT RESOURCES

📰 **IN-DEPTH RESOURCES: UNIT 3**
Guided Reading, p. 54
Skillbuilder Practice: Comparing, p. 56
Primary Source: from *The Art of Courtly Love*, p. 60
Literature: from *The Song of Roland*, p. 65
Connections Across Time and Cultures: Roles of Women, p. 68

📰 **ACCESS FOR STUDENTS ACQUIRING ENGLISH**
Guided Reading (Spanish), p. 133
Skillbuilder Practice: (Spanish), p. 135

📰 **FORMAL ASSESSMENT**
Section Quiz, p. 148

TECHNOLOGY RESOURCES

💿 **CD-ROM**
Electronic Library of Primary Sources

📼 **VIDEO** *Patterns of Interaction: Arming for War*

🌐 **INTERNET** www.mlworldhistory.com

Interpreting the Diagram Ask students to describe the duties of a knight-in-training. Then ask how the training changed as the boy grew older.

Extension Activity Have students make a list of the typical duties and responsibilities of a present-day youth at ages 7, 14, and 21. Was the life of a knight-in-training harder or easier than a young person's life today?

MORE ABOUT . . .
Tournaments

Early tournaments were nothing more than deadly brawls in which knights formed teams and attacked one another. One such tournament that included 3,000 knights took place in 1180 in Lagny-sur-Marne in France. By the end of the day, scores lay dead or wounded.

OBJECTIVE **2** INSTRUCT

Knighthood and Chivalry

Key Ideas
- Knights must maintain standards of character and behavior or be punished.
- Young nobles in training to be knights take part in mock battles called tournaments.
- Medieval warfare is bloody and brutal.

MORE ABOUT . . .
Medieval Weaponry

The *Arming for War* video includes extensive information on the longbow and other weapons of the medieval period.

 PATTERNS OF INTERACTION
Arming for War: Modern and Medieval Weapons
Videocassette: Tape 4

Education of a Knight

PAGE The education of a young noble began early. At age 7, his parents sent him off to the castle of another lord. As a page, he waited on his hosts and learned courtly manners. He played chess to learn war strategies. To develop fighting skills, the page practiced sword fighting.

 KNIGHT At around age 21, a squire became a full-fledged knight. An English squire might have heard his lord say these words during the knighting ceremony: "In the name of God, Saint Michael, and Saint George, I dub thee knight. Be valiant."

SQUIRE At around age 14, the page was raised to the rank of squire. A squire acted as a servant to a knight. The squire took care of the knight's armor, weapons, and warhorse. The squire also escorted the knight to battles.

Knighthood and Chivalry

Early in the Middle Ages, knights were expected to display courage in battle and loyalty to their lord. By the 1100s, the code of **chivalry** (SHIHV·uhl·ree), a complex set of ideals, demanded that a knight fight bravely in defense of three masters. He devoted himself to his earthly feudal lord, his heavenly Lord, and his chosen lady. The chivalrous knight also protected the weak and the poor. The ideal knight was loyal, brave, and courteous. Most knights, though, failed to meet these high standards. They treated the lower classes brutally.

A cowardly knight who disregarded the code of chivalry faced public shame. First, his armor was stripped off, and his shield was cracked. Next, his spurs were cut off, and his sword was broken over his head. People then threw the knight into a coffin and dragged him to church. There a priest would chant a mock funeral service.

War Games for Glory Sons of nobles began training for knighthood at an early age and learned the code of chivalry. After being dubbed a knight, most young men traveled with companions for a year or two. The young knights gained experience fighting in local wars. Some knights took part in mock battles called **tournaments**. Tournaments combined recreation with combat training. Two armies of knights charged each other. Trumpets blared, and lords and ladies cheered. Like real battles, tournaments were fierce and bloody competitions. Winners could usually demand large ransoms from defeated knights.

Brutal Reality of Warfare The small-scale violence of tournaments did not match the bloodshed of actual battles, especially those fought at castles. By the 1100s, stone castles were encircled by massive walls and guard towers. These castles dominated much of the countryside in western Europe. The castle was the home of the lord and lady, their family, knights and other men-at-arms, and servants. It also was a fortress, designed for defense.

A castle under siege was a gory sight. Attacking armies used a wide range of strategies and weapons to force castle residents to surrender. Defenders of a castle poured boiling water, hot oil, or molten lead on enemy soldiers. Expert archers were stationed on the roof of the castle. Armed with crossbows, they fired deadly bolts that could pierce full armor.

328 Chapter 13

Background
The word *chivalry* comes from the French words *cheval* (horse) and *chevalier* (horse-riding knight).

A. Possible Answers Contests of athletic skill; large, cheering audiences; financial profit for the winners
THINK THROUGH HISTORY
A. Comparing How do medieval tournaments resemble modern sports competitions?

Vocabulary
siege: a military blockade staged by enemy armies trying to capture a fortress.

TEACHING OPTION | **BLOCK SCHEDULING** | **WRITING APPLICATION ACTIVITY** | **CLASS TIME 20 MINUTES**

Task: Students will work in small groups to write a modern code of chivalry based on contemporary standards of behavior.

Materials Needed: Writing materials; student textbooks.

Activity: Remind students that the medieval code of chivalry demanded that knights do certain things, such as fight bravely, serve their lords, and protect the weak and poor, in order to be considered chivalrous. Have groups create a modern code of chivalry that shows what people today must do to be considered loyal, brave, and courteous. Modern codes will consist of a list of three ideals of behavior,

for example, be kind to all people, protect the defenseless, respect the elderly. Explain that modern codes will apply to men and women.

Conclusion: Invite group members to share their codes of chivalry with the class. Then discuss as a class whether and how people should be punished for ignoring the code.

Castles and Siege Weapons

Attacking armies carefully planned how to capture a castle. Engineers would inspect the castle walls for weak points in the stone. Then enemy soldiers would try to ram the walls, causing them to collapse. At the battle site, attackers often constructed the heavy and clumsy weapons shown here.

Siege Tower
- had a platform on top that lowered like a drawbridge
- could support weapons and soldiers

Mantlet
- shielded soldiers

Battering Ram
- made of heavy timber with a sharp metal tip
- swung like a pendulum to crack castle walls or to knock down drawbridge

Trebuchet
- worked like a giant slingshot
- propelled objects up to a distance of 980 feet

Tortoise
- moved slowly on wheels
- sheltered soldiers from falling arrows

Mangonel
- flung huge rocks that crashed into castle walls
- propelled objects up to a distance of 1,300 feet

An Array of High-Flying Missiles

Using the **trebuchet**, enemy soldiers launched a wide variety of missiles over the castle walls:

- pots of burning lime
- boulders
- severed human heads
- captured soldiers
- diseased cows
- dead horses

Connect to History

Making Inferences How do these siege weapons show that their designers knew the architecture of a castle well?

SEE SKILLBUILDER HANDBOOK, PAGE 1005

Connect to Today

Researching Modern technology has made warfare far less personal than it was during the Middle Ages. Find examples of recent weapons. Describe how they affect the way war is conducted.

European Middle Ages **329**

Medieval castles were designed in response to the weaponry they had to withstand. Wooden castles were easily destroyed by the burning missiles slung by siege weapons. They began to be replaced by fortified stone castles in the middle of the 12th century. As siege weapons became more powerful, castle walls were built higher and thicker—exposed walls could be as thick as 33 feet. Rectangular towers were rounded off to deflect missiles. As protection against battering rams, castle doors were reinforced with one or more iron grilles and sometimes by a second door. Some castles had double walls.

IN-DEPTH RESOURCES: UNIT 3
Science and Technology: Medieval Technology in Hand Weapons, p. 69

MORE ABOUT . . .
The Trebuchet

This weapon was invented in China and came to western Europe through Byzantium. In its early form, the force that propelled the missile was created by men pulling on ropes attached to one end of a beam. In the latter part of the 12th century, Europeans replaced the men and ropes with a huge counterweight, which gave the weapon more power and accuracy.

Connect to History

Making Inferences
Possible Answers: Siege towers were built so that soldiers could climb high castle walls. Mangonels and trebuchets could hurl heavy objects that would break down castle walls or fly over them. Battering rams were made to crack castle walls and break down drawbridges.

Connect to Today

Researching
Students can use an encyclopedia or a magazine index such as the *Reader's Guide to Periodical Literature* to learn about modern weapons that are controlled from remote areas, such as guided missiles.

The Literature of Chivalry

▶ **Key Ideas**
- Epic poems idealize chivalry and knighthood.
- Popular songs and poems about a knight's undying love present artificial images of women.

 IN-DEPTH RESOURCES: UNIT 3
Primary Source: from *The Art of Courtly Love*, p. 60

 ELECTRONIC LIBRARY OF PRIMARY SOURCES
from "The Art of Courtly Love"

MORE ABOUT . . .
Roland

Count Roland did accompany Charlemagne on a military campaign in Spain in 778. Roland and the rest of Charlemagne's rear guard were ambushed and killed by Basque soldiers. (The Basque were a people living in Spain.) Here the facts end and the legend begins. In the poem, the small rear guard is transformed into 20,000 knights, and the Basque attackers turn into 100,000 Muslim warriors.

 IN-DEPTH RESOURCES: UNIT 3
Literature: from *The Song of Roland*, p. 65

CONNECT *to* TODAY
Modern Love Songs

Many of the ballads written in the Middle Ages told stories of knights who had been scorned by the women they loved. Ask students to recite lyrics to their favorite songs about love. Is love tragic, sad, or happy in these songs? What words show this? Do modern love songs idealize romance and present false images of men and women?

The Literature of Chivalry

In the 1100s, the themes of medieval literature downplayed the brutality of knighthood and feudal warfare. Many stories idealized castle life. They glorified knighthood and chivalry, tournaments and real battles. Songs and poems about a knight's undying love for a lady were also popular.

Epic Poetry Feudal lords and their ladies enjoyed listening to epic poems. These poems recounted a hero's deeds and adventures. Many epics retold stories about legendary heroes of the early Middle Ages, such as King Arthur and Charlemagne.

The Song of Roland is one of the earliest and most famous medieval epic poems. It praises a band of French soldiers who perished in battle during Charlemagne's reign. The poem transforms the event into a struggle. A few brave French knights led by Roland battle an overwhelming army of Muslims from Spain. Roland's friend, Turpin the Archbishop, stands as a shining example of medieval ideals. Turpin represents courage, faith, and chivalry:

> **A VOICE FROM THE PAST**
> And now there comes the Archbishop.
> He spurs his horse, goes up into a mountain,
> summons the French; and he preached them a sermon:
> "Barons, my lords, [Charlemagne] left us in this place.
> We know our duty: to die like good men for our King.
> Fight to defend the holy Christian faith."
> from *The Song of Roland*

Medieval musicians often played a harp or a lute, like the one shown here, to accompany recitals of poems celebrating warrior-heroes.

Love Poems and Songs Under the code of chivalry, a knight's duty to his lady became as important as his duty to his lord. In many medieval poems, the hero's difficulties resulted from a conflict between those two obligations.

Troubadours were poet-musicians at the castles and courts of Europe. They composed short verses and songs about the joys and sorrows of romantic love. Sometimes troubadours sang their own verses in the castles of their lady. They also sent roving minstrels to carry their songs to courts.

A troubadour might sing about love's disappointments: "My loving heart, my faithfulness, myself, my world she deigns to take/ Then leave me bare and comfortless to longing thoughts that ever wake."

Other songs told of lovesick knights who adored ladies they would probably never win: "Love of a far-off land/For you my heart is aching/And I can find no relief." The code of chivalry promoted a false image of knights. In turn, these love songs created an artificial image of women. In the troubadour's eyes, noblewomen were always beautiful and pure.

The most celebrated woman of the age was Eleanor of Aquitaine (1122–1204). Troubadours flocked to her court in the French duchy of Aquitaine. Later, as queen of England, Eleanor was the mother of Richard the Lion-Hearted and King John. Richard himself composed romantic songs and poems. Eleanor's daughter, Marie of Champagne, turned love into a subject of study like logic or law. She presided at a famed Court of Love. Troubled lovers came there to air their grievances.

CONNECT *to* TODAY

Modern Love Songs

Many love songs played on the radio or cable TV share similarities with the love songs of troubadours from the 1100s and 1200s. Modern lyrics echo themes featured in troubadours' songs—happiness and heartbreaks, devoted lovers and unfaithful lovers, trust and jealousy.

The titles of modern love songs reflect the legacy of medieval troubadours' songs. Here are some examples:

- "Heartbreaker"
- "True Love"
- "Your Cheatin' Heart"
- "Power of Love"
- "Can't Help Falling in Love"

THINK THROUGH HISTORY
B. Making Inferences How was the code of chivalry like the idea of romantic love?
B. Possible Answer Both presented distorted, unrealistic images of men and women.

Explaining the Skill: Comparing several sets of historical ideas or beliefs can help students understand the culture the ideas came from.

Applying the Skill: Make two columns on the board labeled "Chivalry" and "Romantic Love." Ask students to name as many ideas associated with chivalry and romantic love as they can find on this page. Add these to the chart on the board. Here are

some examples: Chivalry—knights are always faithful and brave; they are always heroes who have great adventures. Romantic Love—full of joys and sorrows; knights adore ladies from afar; ladies are always beautiful and pure. After the chart is complete, ask students to look for similarities in the two sets of ideas. Here are some similarities: both concerned with knights, important to behave in a certain way,

promote a false image of men and women. Then ask students to give examples of how chivalry and romantic love affect the way women and men are portrayed in the modern world. Students might mention advertisements and romance novels.

IN-DEPTH RESOURCES: UNIT 3
Skillbuilder Practice: Comparing, p. 56

The Shifting Role of Women

The Church viewed women as inferior to men. In contrast, the idea of romantic love placed noblewomen on a pedestal where they could be worshipped. A true knight pledged to protect all women. He also might love, serve, and adore a particular lady, preferably from afar.

Yet as feudalism developed across western Europe, women's status actually declined. Their roles became increasingly limited to the home and convent.

For the vast majority of women life remained unchanged for centuries. During the Middle Ages, most women were still poor and powerless. Their roles were confined to performing endless labor, bearing children, and taking care of their families.

Women in Power Under the feudal system, a noblewoman could inherit an estate from her husband. Upon her lord's request, she could also send his knights to war. When her husband was off fighting, the lady of a medieval castle might act as military commander and a warrior. Noblewomen often played a key role in defending castles. They hurled rocks and fired arrows at attackers. Some women even dressed in armor, mounted warhorses, and mobilized a cavalry of knights.

However, unlike knights, women were not eligible to receive land as reward in exchange for military service. Women also held less property. Lords passed down their fiefs to their sons, not their daughters.

Women's Falling Status As the Middle Ages progressed, noblewomen wielded less real power than they had in earlier years. Eleanor of Aquitaine was a notable exception. As queen of England, she ruled at times for her husband, Henry II, and later for her sons, Richard and John. Few other women had such authority.

The Church played a part in medieval women's declining fortunes. The Church tried to regain control of religious appointments and organizations. It reclaimed convents and monasteries that noblewomen had founded or supported. As you will read in Section 4, the influence of the Church was far-reaching.

ammabus quiete pfrm sempiterna. p eundem

MS Bruxelles, B.R. 9961–62, fol. 91v. Copyright Bibliotheque Royale Albert Ier, Brussels, Belgium.

Knights were not the only warriors glorified in medieval paintings. These noblewomen show their courage and combat skills in defending a castle against enemies.

THINK THROUGH HISTORY
C. Summarizing
What privileges did noblewomen have in medieval society?
C. Answer Respect and admiration, power to inherit her husband's estate, and, with his consent, send his knights to war.

Section ③ Assessment

1. TERMS & NAMES
Identify
• chivalry
• tournament
• troubadour

2. TAKING NOTES
Using a web diagram like the one below, show ideas associated with chivalry.

Which have remnants in today's society? Explain.

3. FORMING OPINIONS
Do you think the idea of romantic love helped or hindered women? Why?

THINK ABOUT
• pros and cons of placing women on a "pedestal"
• the Church's view of women
• the lyrics of love songs quoted in the text

4. ANALYZING THEMES
Religious and Ethical Systems What positive effects might the code of chivalry have had on feudal society?

THINK ABOUT
• the ideals of chivalry
• the education of a knight
• the importance of religious faith
• the violence and constant warfare during the Middle Ages

European Middle Ages **331**

OBJECTIVE ④ INSTRUCT

The Shifting Role of Women

► **Key Ideas**
• Most medieval women are poor and powerless. They labor endlessly.
• Although noblewomen control some matters, they begin to lose real power.

IN-DEPTH RESOURCES: UNIT 3
Connections Across Time and Cultures: Roles of Women, p. 68

ASSESS & RETEACH

Section 3 Assessment
Ask students to work in small groups to answer the questions. Then discuss as a class responses to question 3.

Section Quiz
FORMAL ASSESSMENT
Section Quiz, p. 148

Reteaching Activity
CLASS TIME: 25 MINUTES

Divide the class into four groups and assign each group one of the four main parts of the section. Have each group summarize the main ideas in their part. Then have groups present this information to the class.

CLOSE ACTIVITY

CLASS TIME: 25 MINUTES

Writing Help-Wanted Ads
Have students work in pairs to create medieval help-wanted ads written from the point of view of someone who needs the services of a knight. As an example, write on the board "WANTED: Courageous knight to help defend my castle." Students should list the requirements, duties, and benefits of the job. Invite students to share their ads with the class.

Section 4 Overview

OBJECTIVES

1. To describe the Church's structure, influence, and power.

2. To explain the relationship between the Church and the German Empire.

3. To list events in the power struggle between the popes and German emperors.

4. To summarize the conflict between the Church and Frederick I.

5. To explain why the feudal states of Germany did not unify during the Middle Ages.

SKILLBUILDER

• Interpreting maps: region, location, p. 334

CRITICAL THINKING

• Analyzing motives, p. 333
• Making inferences, p. 334
• Analyzing causes, p. 335
• Evaluating decisions, p. 335
• Analyzing themes, p. 335

FOCUS

5-Minute Warm-Up

▶ **Making Generalizations**
Have students answer these questions to explore how the Church influenced people's lives.

1. Read the Daily Life feature on page 333. What beliefs did people have about witches?

2. What are two superstitions the Church frowned on?

 WARM-UP TRANSPARENCY 13

OBJECTIVE ① INSTRUCT

The Scope of Church Authority

Key Ideas
• Church structure is made up of different ranks of religious officials.

• Shared religious beliefs are a unifying force in a society defined by class structure.

(continued on next page)

TERMS & NAMES
• clergy
• sacrament
• canon law
• Holy Roman Empire
• lay investiture

4 The Church Wields Power

MAIN IDEA	WHY IT MATTERS NOW
Church leaders and political leaders competed for power and authority.	Today many religious leaders still voice their opinions on political issues.

SETTING THE STAGE Amid the weak central governments in feudal Europe, the Church emerged as a powerful institution. It shaped the lives of people from all social classes. As the Church expanded its political role, strong rulers began to question the pope's authority. Dramatic power struggles unfolded in the Holy Roman Empire—the scene of mounting tensions between popes and emperors.

The Scope of Church Authority

In crowning Charlemagne emperor in 800, the Church sought to influence both spiritual and political matters. Three hundred years earlier, Pope Gelasius I recognized the conflicts that could arise between the two great forces—the Church and the state. He wrote, "There are two powers by which this world is chiefly ruled: the sacred authority of the priesthood and the authority of kings."

Gelasius suggested an analogy to solve such conflicts. God had created two symbolic swords. One sword was religious. The other was political. The pope held a spiritual sword. The emperor wielded a political one. Gelasius thought that the pope should bow to the emperor in political matters. In turn, the emperor should bow to the pope in religious matters. If each ruler kept the authority in his own realm, Gelasius suggested, the two leaders could share power in harmony.

In reality, though, the Church and state disagreed on the boundaries of either realm. Clashes erupted throughout the Middle Ages. The Church and various European governments competed for power.

This jeweled tiara, which a pope would wear in a procession, reflects the wealth, power, and authority of his office.

Church Structure Somewhat like the system of feudalism, the Church established its own organization. The distribution of power was based on status. Church structure consisted of different ranks of **clergy,** or religious officials. The pope headed the Church in Rome. All clergy, including bishops and priests, fell under his authority. Bishops supervised priests, the lowest ranking members of the clergy. Bishops also settled disputes over Church teachings and religious practices. For most people, local priests served as the main contact with the Church.

Religion as a Unifying Force Feudalism and the manor system created divisions among people. Shared beliefs in the teachings of the Church bonded people together. During an era of constant warfare and political turmoil, the Church was a stable force. The Church provided Christians with a sense of security and a religious community to which they might belong. The Middle Ages in Europe were aptly named the Age of Faith. Religion at this time occupied center stage.

Medieval Christians' everyday lives were often harsh. Still, they could all follow the same path to salvation—everlasting life in heaven. Priests and other religious officials administered the **sacraments,** or important religious ceremonies. These rites paved the

Background
The clergy was also part of the feudal system. In the early Middle Ages, some bishops, like other vassals, owed military service to their lord and fought courageously in battles.

332 Chapter 13

SECTION 4 RESOURCES

PRINT RESOURCES

IN-DEPTH RESOURCES: UNIT 3
Guided Reading, p. 55
Geography Application: Feudal Europe's Religious Influences, p. 57
Primary Source: Letters of Gregory VII and Henry IV, p. 61
ACCESS FOR STUDENTS ACQUIRING ENGLISH
Guided Reading (Spanish), p. 134
Geography Application: (Spanish), p. 136
FORMAL ASSESSMENT
Section Quiz, p. 149

ALTERNATIVE ASSESSMENT BOOK

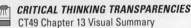 TECHNOLOGY RESOURCES

CRITICAL THINKING TRANSPARENCIES
CT49 Chapter 13 Visual Summary

 CD-ROM
Electronic Library of Primary Sources

 INTERNET www.mlworldhistory.com

THINK THROUGH HISTORY
A. Analyzing Motives Why did medieval peasants support the Church?
A. Answer The Church offered unity, security, hope, a social life, and order in an unstable world.

way for achieving salvation. For example, through the sacrament of baptism, people became part of the Christian community. Through confirmation, baptized people of their own will publicly acknowledged their membership in the Church.

At the local level, the village church was a unifying force in the daily lives of most people. It served as a religious and social center. People worshiped together at the church. They also met and talked with other villagers. Religious holidays, especially Christmas and Easter, were occasions for social gatherings and festive celebrations.

Church Justice The scope of the Church's authority was both religious and political. The Church provided a unifying set of spiritual beliefs and rituals. The Church also created a system of justice to guide people's conduct. All medieval Christians, kings and peasants alike, were subject to **canon law,** or the law of the Church, in matters such as marriage and religious practices. The Church also established courts to try people accused of violating canon law. Two of the harshest punishments that offenders faced were excommunication and interdict.

Popes used the threat of excommunication—banishment from the Church—to wield power over political rulers. For example, a disobedient king's quarrel with a pope might result in excommunication. This meant the king would be denied salvation. Excommunication also freed all the king's vassals from their duties to him. If an excommunicated king continued to disobey the pope, the pope, in turn, could use an even more frightening weapon—the interdict. Under an interdict, many sacraments and religious services could not be performed in the king's lands. As Christians, the king's subjects believed that without such sacraments they might be doomed to eternal suffering in hell. In the 11th century, excommunication and the possible threat of an interdict would force a German emperor to submit to the pope's commands.

The Church and the Holy Roman Empire

Background
The Holy Roman Empire was located in the region of present-day Germany.

After the death of Charlemagne, the **Holy Roman Empire** was the strongest kingdom that arose from the ruins of his empire. When Pope Leo III crowned Charlemagne emperor in 800, he unknowingly set the stage for future conflicts between popes and emperors.

Otto I Allies with the Church The most effective ruler of medieval Germany was Otto I. He was known as Otto the Great. Otto, crowned king in 936, consciously copied the policies of his boyhood hero, Charlemagne. Like Charlemagne, Otto formed a close alliance with the Church. To limit the nobles' strength, Otto sought help from the clergy. He built up his power base by gaining the support of the bishops and abbots, the heads of monasteries. Otto dominated the Church in Germany. He also used his power to defeat unruly German princes.

Following in Charlemagne's footsteps, Otto also invaded Italy on the pope's behalf. In 962, the pope rewarded Otto by crowning him emperor.

Signs of Future Conflicts The German-Italian empire Otto created was first called the Roman Empire of the German Nation. It later became known as the Holy Roman Empire. The Holy Roman Empire remained the strongest state in Europe until about 1100. However, Otto's attempt to revive Charlemagne's empire caused trouble for future German leaders. Italian nobles resented German rule. Popes too came to fear the political power that the German emperors held over Italy.

European Middle Ages **333**

Daily Life

An Age of Superstition

Along with their devout Christian faith, many people during the Middle Ages also clung to superstitious beliefs. Medieval people expected the dead to reappear as ghosts. A friendly goblin might do a person a good deed, but an evil witch might cause great harm. Medieval people thought an evil witch had the power to exchange a healthy child for a sickly one.

The medieval Church frowned upon superstitions such as these:
- Preparing a table with three knives to please good fairies
- Making a vow by a tree, a pond, or any place but a church
- Believing that a person could change into the shape of a wolf
- Believing that the croak of a raven or meeting a priest would bring a person good or bad luck

---

OBJECTIVE 1 INSTRUCT

(continued from page 332)
- Everyone, including kings, follows the Church's system of justice.

 IN-DEPTH RESOURCES: UNIT 3
Guided Reading, p. 55

ACCESS FOR STUDENTS ACQUIRING ENGLISH
Guided Reading (Spanish), p. 134

Daily Life
An Age of Superstition

People who are superstitious believe that one action can cause or prevent another action. For example, some people believe that by carrying a rabbit's foot, they can prevent incidents of bad luck. Ask students to give examples of other superstitions they know about.

OBJECTIVE 2 INSTRUCT

The Church and the Holy Roman Empire

▶ *Key Ideas*
- King Otto I of Germany forms an alliance with the Church and invades Italy.
- Italian nobles resent German rule, and popes fear Germany's rising power.

MORE ABOUT . . .
Otto the Great

Soon after his coronation, Otto I demonstrated how much control his empire had over the pope. He declared that the emperor would have to approve new candidates for pope before they could be officially inducted. When Pope John XII began negotiating with Otto's enemies, Otto had him deposed and a new pope selected. For the next century, popes were often chosen by the emperors.

| TEACHING OPTION | BLOCK SCHEDULING | **GEOGRAPHY APPLICATION ACTIVITY** | CLASS TIME 30 MINUTES |

Task: Students will read about the influence of Christianity in feudal Europe and then use a map to answer questions about what they read.

Materials Needed: Copies of the Geography Application worksheet for Chapter 13.

Activity: Discuss with students what they have learned in this chapter about how Christianity grew in Europe. (Students might mention the rise of Christianity

under Clovis and the spread of Christianity under Charlemagne.) Then review with students the differences between the Roman Catholic and the Eastern Orthodox churches (Chapter 11, page 273, chart). Next, distribute the Geography Application worksheet. Have students work independently to answer the questions. Students can check their answers with a partner.

Conclusion: Ask volunteers to share their answers. Then encourage interested students to create a time line using the events they read about in this activity.

 IN-DEPTH RESOURCES: UNIT 3
Geography Application: Feudal Europe's Religious Influences, p. 57

Holy Roman Emperor Clashes with the Pope

Key Ideas
- The pope and the emperor struggle over who should appoint clergy.
- The Church and the empire reach a compromise, but central authority in Germany declines.

 ELECTRONIC LIBRARY OF PRIMARY SOURCES
from the Investiture Controversy

CRITICAL THINKING ACTIVITY
CLASS TIME: 20 MINUTES

Recognizing Causes and Effects
To help students connect events in this section, have them make a chart like the one below. Tell students to include at least six events in their charts.

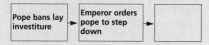

Pope bans lay investiture → Emperor orders pope to step down →

History from Visuals

The Holy Roman Empire, 1100
Interpreting the Map Have students compare this map with the map on page 321. How is the Holy Roman Empire different from Charlemagne's empire?

Extension Activity The 18th-century French philosopher Voltaire once wrote that the Holy Roman Empire ". . . is neither holy, nor Roman, nor an Empire." What might Voltaire have meant by this?

SKILLBUILDER Answers
1. The Holy Roman Empire is made up of 12 separate states. This fragmentation would pose problems for a ruler trying to unify the empire.
2. The boundaries of the Papal States fall within the southern portion of the Holy Roman Empire.

Holy Roman Emperor Clashes with the Pope

The Church began to resent the control that kings, such as Otto, exercised over clergy and their offices. The focus of this resentment was **lay investiture**—a ceremony in which kings and nobles appointed church officials. Whoever controlled lay investiture wielded the real power in naming bishops. They were powerful clergy whom kings sought to control. Church reformers felt that bishops should not be under the power of any king. In 1075, Pope Gregory VII banned lay investiture.

The furious young German emperor, Henry IV, immediately called a meeting of the German bishops he had appointed. With their approval, the emperor sent a vicious letter to Gregory VII. Henry called Gregory "not pope, but false monk" and ordered him to step down from the papacy. Gregory fired back and excommunicated Henry. Afterward, German bishops and princes sided with the pope. Determined to save his throne, Henry tried to win the pope's forgiveness.

Showdown at Canossa In January 1077, Henry journeyed over the snowy Alps to the Italian town of Canossa (kuh·NAHS·uh). He approached the castle where Pope Gregory was a guest. Gregory later described the scene:

A VOICE FROM THE PAST
There, having laid aside all the belongings of royalty, wretchedly, with bare feet and clad in wool, he [Henry IV] continued for three days to stand before the gate of the castle. Nor did he desist from imploring with many tears the aid and consolation of the apostolic mercy until he had moved all of those who were present there. . . .
POPE GREGORY, cited in *Basic Documents in Medieval History*

The Pope was obligated to forgive any sinner who begged so humbly. Still, Gregory kept Henry waiting in the snow for three days before ending his excommunication.

The meeting in Canossa was one of the most dramatic confrontations of the Middle Ages. Yet it actually solved nothing. A triumphant Henry rushed home to punish the nobles who had rebelled against him. The pope had gained an even greater victory by humiliating the proudest ruler in Europe. The key question of lay investiture remained undecided.

Concordat of Worms Gregory's and Henry's successors continued to fight over lay investiture until 1122. That year, representatives of the Church and the emperor met in the German city of Worms (wurms). There they reached a compromise known as the Concordat of Worms. By its terms, the Church alone could grant a bishop his ring and staff, symbols of Church office. Yet the emperor had the veto power to prevent the appointment of a bishop.

During Henry's struggle, German princes regained much of the power they had lost under Otto the Great. A later German ruler, Frederick I, would resume the battle to build up royal authority.

The Holy Roman Empire, 1100

Friesland
Saxony
POLAND
Aachen
Lorraine
Franconia
Worms
Bohemia
FRANCE
Swabia
Bavaria
KINGDOM OF HUNGARY
Burgundy
Carinthia
Lombardy
Po R.
Papal States
Tuscany
Adriatic Sea
Rome
Spoleto
50°N

Rhine R.
Elbe R.
Danube R.
Rhône R.

The Holy Roman Empire
Papal States

N

0   250 Miles
0   500 Kilometers

Mediterranean Sea

334 Chapter 13

GEOGRAPHY SKILLBUILDER: Interpreting Maps
1. **Region** How many states make up the Holy Roman Empire? What does this suggest about ruling it as an empire?
2. **Location** How does the location of the Papal States make them an easy target for frequent invasions by Germanic rulers?

THINK THROUGH HISTORY
B. Making Inferences Why was Henry's journey to Canossa a political maneuver?
B. Possible Answer Confident that the pope would forgive him, Henry could then reclaim his throne and punish the rebellious nobles who betrayed him.

COOPERATIVE ACTIVITY: Researching Henry IV and Pope Gregory VII
CLASS TIME 25 MINUTES

Task: Groups will research the lay investiture conflict between Henry IV and Pope Gregory VII and present letters expressing each man's opinion.

Purpose: To learn more about the conflict between the Holy Roman Empire and the Church.

Activity: Divide the class into groups of four. In each group, pairs of students will research the

conflict between Henry IV and Pope Gregory VII, and one pair will write a letter from one man's point of view expressing his opinion about lay investiture. The other pair should write a letter in response from the other man's point of view. Volunteers from each group will read their letters to the class.

📁 **Building a Portfolio:** Students might add their letters to their portfolio.

IN-DEPTH RESOURCES: UNIT 3
Primary Source: from *Letters of Gregory VII and Henry IV*, p. 61

Standards for Evaluation
Letters should . . .
- show evidence of research
- clearly show each man's point of view
- relate to each other

Renewed Church Conflicts Under Frederick I

Vocabulary
Barbarossa: "red beard" in Italian.

By 1152, the seven German princes who elected the German king realized that Germany needed a strong ruler to keep the peace. The princes chose Frederick I. His red beard earned him the nickname "Barbarossa."

Frederick I was the first ruler to call his lands the Holy Roman Empire. However, this region was actually a patchwork of feudal territories. His forceful personality and military skills enabled him to dominate the German princes. Yet whenever he left the country, disorder returned.

Following Otto the Great's example, Frederick did not focus on building royal power in Germany. Instead, he repeatedly invaded the rich cities of Italy. Frederick's brutal tactics spurred Italian merchants to unite against him. Like Henry IV, Frederick angered the pope, who joined the merchants. Together, Frederick's enemies formed an alliance called the Lombard League.

In 1176, the foot soldiers of the Lombard League faced Frederick's army of mounted knights at the Battle of Legnano (lay·NYAHN·oh). In an astonishing victory, these foot soldiers used crossbows to defeat feudal knights for the first time in history.

In 1177, Frederick made peace with the pope and returned to Germany. Frederick's military defeat, though, had undermined his authority with the German princes. Their power continued to grow in spite of Frederick's efforts. After he drowned in 1190, Frederick's empire dissolved into an array of fragmented feudal states.

This stained-glass portrait of Frederick I projects an image of imperial power. Yet like Henry IV, Frederick's clashes with the pope eroded the emperor's authority.

C. Possible Answer German kings' continued attempts to revive Charlemagne's empire and his alliance with the Church sparked wars with Italian cites and clashes with the pope.

THINK THROUGH HISTORY
C. Analyzing Causes What long-lasting political trend kept German states separate during the Middle Ages?

German States Remain Separate

By getting involved in Italian politics, German kings after Frederick continued their attempts to revive Charlemagne's empire and his alliance with the Church. This policy led to wars with Italian cities and to further clashes with the pope. These conflicts were among several reasons why the feudal states of Germany did not unify during the Middle Ages.

The system of German princes electing the king weakened royal authority. German rulers controlled fewer royal lands to use as a base of power than French and English kings, who were establishing strong central authority. These kings made changes in the legal system that would lay the foundation for modern unified nation-states.

As you will read in Chapter 14, feudalism in France and England spurred the rise of powerful leaders. They would create strong and enduring nations. Gradually, orderly government would replace the fighting and frequent warfare that characterized feudal societies, such as Germany.

Section 4 Assessment

1. TERMS & NAMES
Identify
• clergy
• sacrament
• canon law
• Holy Roman Empire
• lay investiture

2. TAKING NOTES
Create a time line like the one below for the Holy Roman Empire. Write the significance of each date shown.

For which events did the Church and rulers engage in a power struggle? Why?

3. EVALUATING DECISIONS
Do you think the Concordat of Worms was a fair compromise for both the emperor and the Church? Why or why not?

THINK ABOUT
• the Church's authority in spiritual matters
• the emperor's political power
• the problems that remained unresolved

4. THEME ACTIVITY
Power and Authority Work with a partner to play the roles of Henry IV and Pope Gregory VII. Based on your role-play, write a dialogue about their meeting at Canossa.

European Middle Ages **335**

ANSWERS

1. TERMS & NAMES
clergy, p. 332
sacrament, p. 332
canon law, p. 333
Holy Roman Empire, p. 333
lay investiture, p. 334

2. TAKING NOTES
936—Otto I crowned king
962—Otto I crowned emperor
1077—Henry IV's journey to Canossa (power struggle)
1122—Concordat of Worms (power struggle)
1190—Frederick I's empire breaks up into feudal states

3. EVALUATING DECISIONS
Possible Answers: Yes—It gave the Church the right to appoint bishops. No—The emperor still had ultimate control over the appointment of bishops.

4. ANALYZING THEMES
Standards for Evaluation
An effective dialogue should meet the following criteria:
• Clearly identifies each person.
• Includes historical details presented in the text.
• Shows a clear understanding of the historical events.

OBJECTIVE 4 INSTRUCT

Renewed Church Conflicts Under Frederick I

▶ *Key Ideas*
• King Frederick I of Germany angers the Church by invading the rich cities of Italy.
• Italian merchants backed by the Church defeat Frederick in battle. Central power dissolves again.

OBJECTIVE 5 INSTRUCT

German States Remain Separate

▶ *Key Idea*
• Power struggles with the Church and within the empire keep feudal states fragmented.

ASSESS & RETEACH

Section 4 Assessment
Have students work independently to answer the questions and then form small groups to check and discuss their answers.

Section Quiz
FORMAL ASSESSMENT
Section Quiz, p. 149

Reteaching Activity
CLASS TIME: 30 MINUTES

Have pairs of students create a time line using all the dates in this section. Time lines should include descriptions of important events that happened on or between specific dates. Then discuss with students when and how German emperors angered the pope and how this affected centralized power in the empire.

 CRITICAL THINKING TRANSPARENCIES
CT49 Chapter 13 Visual Summary

CLOSE ACTIVITY

CLASS TIME: 40 MINUTES

Writing and Answering Questions
Have pairs of students write a question for each of the five main parts of this section. Questions should ask something specific about the content of each part. Have pairs exchange their work and answer each other's questions. Finally, discuss questions and answers as a class.

TERMS & NAMES

1. monastery, p. 318
2. Charlemagne, p. 320
3. vassal, p. 324
4. serf, p. 324
5. manor, p. 325
6. chivalry, p. 328
7. troubadour, p. 330
8. clergy, p. 332
9. Holy Roman Empire, p. 333
10. lay investiture, p. 334

REVIEW QUESTIONS

Answers may vary on some questions.

11. Made the Church a secular power; used Church money to raise armies, repair roads, help poor; negotiated peace treaties.

12. Halted the Muslim invasion of western Europe; made Charles Martel a Christian hero.

13. This event signaled the joining of Germanic power, the Church, and the heritage of the Roman Empire.

14. Vikings, Magyars and Muslims.

15. A lord granted land to a vassal in exchange for military protection and other services.

16. A lord provided his serfs with housing, farmland, and protection. Serfs paid their lords with farmwork, a portion of their crops, and various taxes.

17. At age 7, a boy learned courtly manners, war strategies, and fighting skills. At age 14, he became the servant of a knight. At age 21, he became a full-fledged knight.

18. A troubadour's songs told about the joys and sorrows of romantic love, lovesick knights, and beautiful and pure noble-women.

19. God created two symbolic swords—one religious, one political. The pope held the spiritual sword. The emperor held the political. Gelasius thought that the pope should bow to the emperor in political matters and the emperor should bow to the pope in spiritual matters. If each kept to the authority in his own realm, the two leaders could share power in harmony.

Chapter 13 Assessment

TERMS & NAMES
Briefly explain the importance of each of the following during the Middle Ages from 500 to 1200.

1. monastery
2. Charlemagne
3. vassal
4. serf
5. manor
6. chivalry
7. troubadour
8. clergy
9. Holy Roman Empire
10. lay investiture

Interact *with* History

On page 316, you imagined what the world was like from the viewpoint of a peasant living on a medieval manor. Now that you've read the chapter, reconstruct a more accurate picture. What was a peasant's daily life like? Why did peasants cling to their religious beliefs and the teachings of the Church? Discuss your ideas in a small group.

REVIEW QUESTIONS

SECTION 1 (*pages 317–321*)
Germanic Kingdoms Unite Under Charlemagne

11. How did Gregory I increase the political power of the pope?
12. What was the outcome of the Battle of Tours?
13. What was the significance of the pope's declaring Charlemagne emperor?

SECTION 2 (*pages 322–326*)
Feudalism in Europe

14. Which invading peoples caused turmoil in Europe during the 800s?
15. What exchange took place between lords and vassals under the feudal system?
16. What duties did a lord of a manor and his serfs owe one another?

SECTION 3 (*pages 327–331*)
The Age of Chivalry

17. Briefly describe the stages of becoming a knight.
18. What were common subjects of troubadours' songs during the Middle Ages?

SECTION 4 (*pages 332–335*)
The Church Wields Power

19. What was Gelasius's two-swords theory?
20. Describe the conflict between Pope Gregory VII and Henry IV and its outcome.

Visual Summary

European Middle Ages

Feudalism
- Form of government based on landholding
- Alliances between lords and vassals
- Oaths of loyalty in exchange for land and military service
- Ranking of power and authority

POLITICAL SYSTEM

Chivalry
- Displays of courage and valor in combat
- Devotion to a feudal lord and heavenly lord
- Respect toward women

CODE OF BEHAVIOR

MEDIEVAL SOCIETY

ECONOMIC SYSTEM

Manors
- Lord's estate
- Set of rights and obligations between serfs and lords
- Self-sufficient community producing a variety of goods

BELIEF SYSTEM

The Church
- Unifying force of Christian faith
- Power over people's everyday lives
- Involvement in political affairs

20. Pope Gregory VII banned lay investiture because he didn't think kings and nobles should appoint church officials. Henry IV became angry and ordered Gregory to step down as pope. Gregory excommunicated Henry. Henry begged for the pope's forgiveness and received it. The question of lay investiture remained undecided.

Interact *with* History

Possible Responses: A peasant's daily life was extremely hard. It began and ended in a dirty, crowded cottage, and included lots of hard work, many restrictions, and few joys. A peasant spent his life in debt to his lord and had little hope of becoming independent or gaining much wealth. Church teachings helped peasants accept their lot in life. The Church also provided security, community, and a social center.

CRITICAL THINKING

1. THE ROLE OF THE CHURCH
In what ways did the Church act as a system of government during the Middle Ages?

2. CHARLEMAGNE AND HIS LEGACY
THEME EMPIRE BUILDING Copy the three overlapping circles below to show how Otto I and Frederick I tried to imitate Charlemagne's approach to empire building.

Charlemagne's Empire

Otto I's Roman Empire of the German Nation

All

Frederick I's Holy Roman Empire

3. THE POWER OF LANDOWNERS
Why do you think the ownership of land became an increasing source of power for feudal lords?

4. ANALYZING PRIMARY SOURCES
In *The Canterbury Tales,* the English poet Geoffrey Chaucer tells a series of stories about characters from the Middle Ages. Read the following passage about a knight. Then answer the questions below it.

> **A VOICE FROM THE PAST**
> There was a *knight,* a most distinguished man,
> Who from the day on which he first began
> To ride abroad had followed chivalry,
> Truth, honor, generous, and courtesy.
> He had done nobly in sovereign's war
> And ridden in battle, no man more,
> As well as Christian in heathen places
> And ever honored for his noble graces.

- How does Chaucer characterize the knight?
- What qualities of knighthood do you think are missing from Chaucer's description? Use information from the text to support your answer.

CHAPTER ACTIVITIES

1. LIVING HISTORY: Unit Portfolio Projects
THEME RELIGIOUS AND ETHICAL SYSTEMS Your unit portfolio project focuses on showing the influence of the Church during the Middle Ages. For Chapter 13, you might use one of the following ideas to add to your portfolio.

- Write a character sketch of a religious or historical figure described in this chapter.
- Create a poster titled "The Age of Faith" focusing on the role that the Church played in the daily lives of Europeans.
- Create a time line tracing the most important power plays between religious and political leaders during the Middle Ages. Refer to the text for ideas.

2. CONNECT TO TODAY: Cooperative Learning
THEME POWER AND AUTHORITY Through warfare, knights helped feudal lords defend their estates, seize new territories, and gain more power. In mock battles called tournaments, knights developed their combat skills. Work with a team to design a video war game that imitates a medieval tournament between knights. Describe your ideas in a proposal that you might send to a video game company.

INTERNET Use the Internet or books to find out more about medieval tournaments. Think about video games that are based on combat experiences. You might adapt some of the rules to your game. Use these questions to help you brainstorm ideas.

- What are the rules of the game?
- What is the system of keeping score of wins and losses?
- How should captured prisoners be treated?
- Which weapons should be used and which should be banned?

3. INTERPRETING A TIME LINE
Revisit the unit time line for Chapter 13 on pages 228–229. Which two important events in other parts of the world roughly coincide with the expansion of feudalism in western Europe? Give reasons to support your choices.

FOCUS ON ART

Chess was a popular game during the Middle Ages. The chess pieces portray important people from medieval society. Work with someone in class who plays chess to answer these questions:

- What element of medieval society do you think each chess piece represents?

- How do these chess pieces reflect the power of various members of medieval society?

Connect to History
Why do you think that learning to play chess was an important part of a knight's education?

337

CHAPTER ACTIVITIES

1. LIVING HISTORY

Standards for Evaluation
An effective character sketch should meet the following criteria:

- Thoroughly describes the figure and why he or she was important.
- Includes details and specific information about the figure.
- Displays an understanding of the figure's role in history.

Standards for Evaluation
An effective poster should meet the following criteria:

- Makes connections between the Church and war, politics, education, and social classes.
- Shows an understanding of the role of the Church in the Middle Ages.
- Displays information in a thoughtful and clear manner.

Standards for Evaluation
An effective time line should meet the following criteria:

- Presents information about Otto I, Henry IV, Pope Gregory VII, and Frederick I.
- Includes in chronological order descriptions of the events of the power plays.
- Shows an understanding of the conflicts between the religious and political leaders.

2. CONNECT TO TODAY

Standards for Evaluation
An effective video game proposal should meet the following criteria:

- Clearly states the purpose and rules of the game.
- Includes information about how to play and how to score.
- Reflects an understanding of how medieval tournaments were conducted.

3. INTERPRETING A TIME LINE

Have students study the events in the column between 900 and 1000 on the time line. After choosing two events, ask students to share their choices.

FOCUS ON ART

Possible Responses: (from left to right) pawn/peasant; rook/castle; horse/knight; bishop; queen; king. The height of each piece reflects the hierarchy of power in medieval society. Crowns, crosses, and the horse show the power each figure had in medieval society. The pawn is bareheaded and short. This reflects the low status of peasants.

Possible Response: Playing chess taught knights how to plan a battle by learning to anticipate and counter an opponent's moves.

CRITICAL THINKING

1. THE ROLE OF THE CHURCH
Possible Responses: The Church provided order and unity, established laws and a system of justice, had its own organization in which the distribution of power was based on status, exercised political power.

2. CHARLEMAGNE AND HIS LEGACY
Possible Responses: Charlemagne—crowned emperor; formed alliance with Church; encouraged learning. Otto—crowned emperor; formed alliance with Church. Frederick—called his lands Holy Roman Empire. All—invaded Italy; limited nobles' power.

3. THE POWER OF LANDOWNERS
Possible Responses: After the fall of the Roman Empire, invasions in Europe led to the migration of people to rural areas. As agriculture became more important, land ownership became a source of power. Under the feudal system, local lords with large estates held the most power.

4. ANALYZING PRIMARY SOURCES
Possible Responses: Chaucer characterizes the knight as honorable, generous, courteous, brave, and religious. Qualities missing from this description include devoted (to his lord and his lady), loyal, protective, brutal, and fierce.

The Formation of Western Europe

	COPY MASTERS	ASSESSMENT

Key Ideas

SECTION 1
Church Reform and the Crusades
pp. 341–347

A spiritual revival leads to Church reform, new religious orders, and the building of Gothic cathedrals. The Crusades, though unsuccessful, strengthen European monarchies and increase trade with the Middle East.

In-Depth Resources: Unit 3
- **Guided Reading,** p. 70
- **Geography Application:** The Reconquista, p. 75
- **Primary Source:** *Massacre at Acre,* p. 77

 Section 1 Assessment, p. 346

Formal Assessment
- Section Quiz, p. 158

Alternative Assessment Book
- Standards for Evaluating a Cooperative Activity

SECTION 2
Trade, Towns, and Financial Revolution
pp. 348–351

New farming methods and a growing food supply lead to expansion of trade and finance and the growth of towns. Interest in learning is revived as universities are established and ancient works are rediscovered.

In-Depth Resources: Unit 3
- **Guided Reading,** p. 71
- **Literature:** from *The Canterbury Tales* by Geoffrey Chaucer, p. 81

 Section 2 Assessment, p. 351

 Formal Assessment
- Section Quiz, p. 159

 Alternative Assessment Book
- Standards for Evaluating a Product or Performance

SECTION 3
England and France Develop
pp. 352–355

England, united under the Normans, and France, united by the Capetain dynasty, take the first steps toward representative government. King John is forced to sign the Magna Carta, and Philip IV includes commoners in the council.

In-Depth Resources: Unit 3
- **Guided Reading,** p. 72
- **Primary Source:** from the Magna Carta, p. 78
- **History Makers:** William the Conqueror, p. 84
- **Connections Across Time and Cultures:** New Beginnings for Democracy, p. 86

 Section 3 Assessment, p. 355

 Formal Assessment
- Section Quiz, p. 160

Alternative Assessment Book
- Standards for Evaluating a Cooperative Activity

SECTION 4
A Century of Turmoil
pp. 356–361

Church teachings are challenged, and the papacy loses prestige. The bubonic plague kills nearly one third of Europe's population, and the Hundred Years' War brings an end to the Middle Ages.

In-Depth Resources: Unit 3
- **Guided Reading,** p. 73
- **Skillbuilder Practice:** Recognizing Effects, p. 74
- **Primary Sources:** Plague in Sienna, p. 79; Joan of Arc's Trial, p. 80
- **History Makers:** Joan of Arc, p. 85

 Section 4 Assessment, p. 361

Formal Assessment
- Section Quiz, p. 161

Alternative Assessment Book
- Standards for Evaluating a Cooperative Activity

CHAPTER RESOURCES

Chapter Overview

The Church is revitalized but its Crusades fail to capture Jerusalem. Rising prosperity and trade create thriving towns. France and England develop more representative government. Bubonic plague and the Hundred Years' War bring an end to the Middle Ages.

Telescoping the Times
- Chapter Summary, pp. 53–55

Planning for Block Schedules

 Chapter Assessment, pp. 362–363

Chapter Activities, p. 363

 Formal Assessment
- Chapter Test, forms A and B, pp. 162–167

■ *Test Generator*

Alternative Assessment Book

800–1500

TECHNOLOGY

 Warm-Up Transparency 14

 World Art and Cultures Transparencies
- AT30 *Notre Dame*
- AT31 *Entry of the Crusaders into Constantinople, 12 April 1204*

 Religions of the World
- Christianity

 Electronic Library of Primary Sources
"The Knight in Battle"

 INTERNET RESOURCES
www.mlworldhistory.com

 Warm-Up Transparency 14

 Geography Transparencies
- GT14 *Trade and Manufacturing in Medieval Europe, 1000–1300*

 Electronic Library of Primary Sources
- from "A Description of the Most Noble City of London"
- from *The Divine Comedy*

 INTERNET RESOURCES
www.mlworldhistory.com

 Warm-Up Transparency 14

 Electronic Library of Primary Sources
- from *Calendar of Coroner's Rolls*

 INTERNET RESOURCES
www.mlworldhistory.com

 Warm-Up Transparency 14

 Critical Thinking Transparencies
- CT14 *Rise of the Middle Class*

 Battles of the World
- The Battle of Agincourt

 Electronic Library of Primary Sources
- from "The Battle of Agincourt"

 Patterns of Interaction:
- The Spread of Epidemic Disease

 Chapter Summaries on Audiocassette in English and Spanish

 INTERNET RESOURCES
www.mlworldhistory.com

Block Scheduling (90 MINUTES)

Day 1
Section 1, pp. 341–347

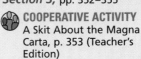 **COOPERATIVE ACTIVITY**
Book Reports on the Crusades, p. 344 (Teacher's Edition)

Section 2, pp. 348–351

Section Assessments,
pp. 346, 351

Day 2
Section 3, pp. 352–355

COOPERATIVE ACTIVITY
A Skit About the Magna Carta, p. 353 (Teacher's Edition)

Section 4, pp. 356–361

COOPERATIVE ACTIVITY
Research Warfare in the Middle Ages, p. 360 (Teacher's Edition)

Section Assessments,
pp. 355, 361

Yearly Pacing *Chapter 14 Total:* 2 days *Yearly Total:* 85 days

 Planning for Block Schedules

Customizing for Special Needs

Students Acquiring English

 Access for Students Acquiring English
- **Guided Reading** for Sections 1–4 (Spanish), pp. 141–144
- **Chapter Summary** (Spanish), pp. 138–140
- **Skillbuilder Practice** Recognizing Effects (Spanish), p. 145
- **Geography Application** The Reconquista (Spanish), p. 146

 Patterns of Interaction:
The Spread of Epidemic Diseases (Spanish)

 Chapter Summaries on Audiocassette in English and Spanish

 INTERNET RESOURCES
www.mlworldhistory.com
The Diverse Classroom.

Less Proficient Readers

 In-Depth Resources: Unit 3
- **Guided Reading** for Sections 1–4, pp. 70–73
- **Skillbuilder Practice** Recognizing Effects, p. 74
- **Geography Application** The Reconquista, p. 75

 Telescoping the Times
- **Chapter Summary,** pp. 53–55

 Chapter Summaries on Audiocassette

Gifted and Talented Students

 In-Depth Resources: Unit 3

Primary Sources:
- *Massacre at Acre,* p. 77
- from the Magna Carta, p. 78
- *Plague in Siena,* p. 79
- *Joan of Arc's Trial,* p. 80

History Makers
- William the Conqueror, p. 84
- Joan of Arc, p. 85

Connections to Literature READINGS FOR STUDENTS

 In-Depth Resources: Unit 3
- from *The Canterbury Tales* by Geoffrey Chaucer, p. 81

Enrichment Reading
- **Lofts, Norah** *Madselin* New York: Doubleday, 1983

A love story set during the Norman invasions of England in 1066.

McDougal Littel Literature Connections

- **Chaucer, Geoffrey** *The Canterbury Tales* (with related readings)

Filled with wit and humor, this classic work provides a rich portrait of medieval life.

 P E = Pupil's Edition   = Overhead Transparency   = Software   = Video

= Copy Master   = CD-ROM   = Audiocassette   = Internet

The Formation of Western Europe, 800–1500

Accessing Prior Knowledge

This chapter covers the Crusades to Jerusalem, the bubonic plague, medieval cathedrals, and Joan of Arc.

• Ask students to discuss what they know about these subjects. List on the chalkboard some of the facts they give.

• What more would they like to know? Have them write one or two questions they would like to have answered.

Making Inferences

Point out that even though the chapter is about western Europe, parts of Southwest Asia and North Africa are also shown on the map.

• What inferences can students make about the influence of these areas on the development of western Europe?

Geography Connection

Ask students to study the map on these two pages.

• What modern nations existed in some form in the late 14th century? *Ireland, England, Scotland, France, Portugal, Norway, Sweden, Denmark, Poland, Hungary, Bulgaria, and Crete*

The Formation of Western Europe, 800–1500

PREVIEWING THEMES

Religious and Ethical Systems
The Christian beliefs of the Middle Ages inspired the building of great cathedrals and helped shape the origins of European states. They also inspired the Crusades and guided the development of universities.

Economics
Medieval Europeans developed new methods of trade and new systems of finance and commerce. In response to population growth and territorial expansion, towns developed and learning revived.

Cultural Interaction
Although destructive in many ways, the Crusades resulted in a great deal of cultural exchange. The Christian world of medieval Europe learned and adopted much from the Muslim world and vice versa.

INTERNET CONNECTION

Visit us at **www.mlworldhistory.com** to learn more about medieval Europe, the Crusades, the medieval Muslim world, and related topics.

WESTERN EUROPE IN THE LATE 14th CENTURY

NORWAY

SWEDEN

SCOTLAND

North Sea

DENMARK

Bal
Se

IRELAND

ENGLAND

TEU
KNI

London •

• Tournai

POL

HOLY
ROMAN
EMPIRE

Paris •

ATLANTIC
OCEAN

• Orléans

FRANCE

HUN

*Bay of
Biscay*

AQUITAINE

• Genoa

VENICE
Adriatic Sea

SE
PF

NAVARRE

CORSICA
(Genoa)

PAPAL
STATES

• Rome

PORTUGAL

CASTILE

ARAGON

SARDINIA
(Aragon)

KINGDOM
OF
NAPLES

PRINCIP
OF ALB

KINGDOM
OF
SICILY

The **Bubonic Plague** swept through Europe beginning in 1347. Here victims of the Bubonic Plague are shown being placed in coffins before their burial at Tournai in **1349**.

338

20 W

GEOGRAPHY THEMES

Movement

Ask students to identify the Mediterranean Sea on the map. Point out that this sea provides easy access between Europe and Southwest Asia and North Africa. Ask students how western Europe might be affected by movement between Europe and Southwest Asia.

Possible Responses: Trade goods and ideas from those regions could influence the people of western Europe.

Location

Have students find Constantinople on the map. Tell them that this city was the capital of the Byzantine Empire. How did Constantinople's location help make

it one of the wealthiest and most influential cities of the Middle Ages? *Possible Responses: It is a center of trade between Eastern Europe and lands bordering the Mediterranean.*

Place

Tell students that the Crusaders captured a narrow strip of land running

from Jerusalem to an area northeast of Antioch. Ask students to examine the map and give reasons why they think the Crusader kingdoms were primarily near the Mediterranean. *Possible Responses: Much of the inland area was desert; Crusaders needed to be close to their supply lines along the Mediterranean.*

ADDITIONAL RESOURCES

Books for the Teacher

- Cantor, Norman F. *The Civilization of the Middle Ages.* New York: Harper, 1993.
- Leyser, Henrietta. *Medieval Women.* New York: St. Martin's, 1995. A social history of women in England, A.D. 450–1500.
- Tuchman, Barbara W. *A Distant Mirror.* New York: Knopf, 1978. Description of the tumultuous 1300s.

Books for the Student

- Giblin, James Cross. *When Plague Strikes.* New York: Harper, 1996. Vivid history of the bubonic plague.
- Jones, Terry, and Alan Ereira. *Crusades.* New York: Facts on File, 1995. Balanced account of the Crusades.
- Macaulay, David. *Cathedral: The Story of Its Construction.* Boston: Houghton, 1973.

▬▬▬ *Videos*

- *The Black Death.* Ambrose Video, 1995. 800–526–4663.
- *The Crusades.* Society for Visual Education, 1989. 800–829–1900.
- *Cathedral: The Story of Its Construction.* Unicorn Projects, Inc., PBS.

💿 *Software*

- *Life in Feudal Europe.* CD-ROM. Teacher's Discovery, 1996. 800–543–4180. Explore a 14th-century castle.
- *Middle Ages.* CD-ROM. Queue, 1994. 800–232–2224. Insight into daily life and the Crusades.

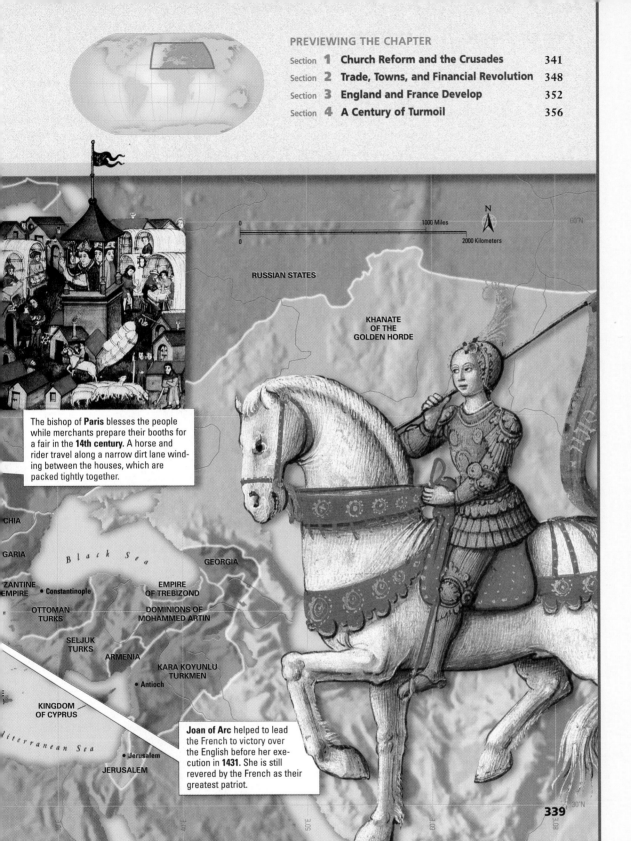

The bishop of **Paris** blesses the people while merchants prepare their booths for a fair in the **14th century.** A horse and rider travel along a narrow dirt lane winding between the houses, which are packed tightly together.

Joan of Arc helped to lead the French to victory over the English before her execution in **1431.** She is still revered by the French as their greatest patriot.

339

HISTORY THROUGH ART

Blessing the Lendit (June) Fair at St. Denis

In medieval times, artists communicated stories and events through elaborate pictures. In the center of this picture, the bishop blesses the opening of the famous St. Denis fair, held in Paris, France. The blessing of commerce was an important part of this festival.

Around the tower, several inns with their signposts (a swan, a fleur-de-lis, and other symbols) are open for business. On the right-hand side of the picture, three people are eating at one of the inns. On the left-hand side, a scribe and merchant wait patiently in their booths for customers. At the bottom of the illustration, a shepherd leads his flock into the marketplace.

Interpreting the Art How many different activities in the fair can you see? The artist has made different people in the picture different sizes. What can you infer from this about the people's relative importance? *The most important people, clergy, are the largest; merchants, less important, are smaller; and laborers, least important, are the smallest.*

Interact with History

The Interact with History feature motivates students by having them think about joining a Crusade to free Jerusalem. As they consider whether to go, they will analyze the issues, explore their options, and become decision makers.

Purpose

- to set the stage for studying western European history
- to help students understand the various influences that helped shape western Europe
- to enable students to connect with the people and events they will study in this chapter

Teaching Strategy

Thinking Critically Ask students whether they have ever joined a cause or group that had noble ideals. What activities were they involved in, and what happened to the group?

EXAMINING *the* ISSUES

Following are suggestions for addressing each bulleted question.

1 There were few facilities for travelers, few medical services, little public sanitation, and many people who took advantage of Crusaders.

2 Explain that many people went on the Crusades out of fervor for God and that Crusaders ransacked the wealthiest cities of the old Roman Empire.

3 Students may respond that they would be safe from danger and might feel good about caring for others; a disadvantage might be missing a chance for adventure, service, and wealth.

4 Students might present arguments about service to God and country, and the hope of financial gain.

Making Connections Ask students why people would risk everything to join a Crusade and fight in a faraway place.

Interact *with* History

You are a squire in training to be a knight in France. The knight you serve has decided to join a Crusade to capture the city of Jerusalem from the Muslims. The knight has given you the choice of accompanying him on his expedition to the Holy Land (the biblical region of Palestine) or staying home to look after his family and manor. You would also look after your parents, who do not wish you to go. You are torn between the desire for adventure and possible riches that you might find on the Crusade, and fear of the hazards that await you on such a dangerous journey. On an earlier Crusade, the knight and his friends plundered towns and manors. They acquired jewels and precious objects. But some were also imprisoned, held for ransom, robbed, and murdered.

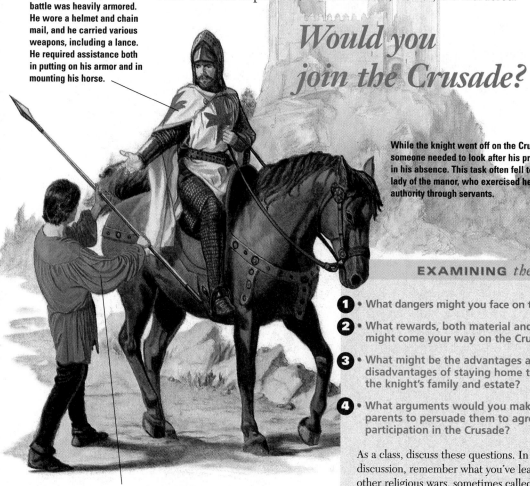

The knight as he went into battle was heavily armored. He wore a helmet and chain mail, and he carried various weapons, including a lance. He required assistance both in putting on his armor and in mounting his horse.

Would you join the Crusade?

While the knight went off on the Crusade, someone needed to look after his property in his absence. This task often fell to the lady of the manor, who exercised her authority through servants.

A squire acted as a personal servant to the knight. A squire rode at his master's side in battle, in which he took an active part. One of his responsibilities in battle was to take charge of the prisoners.

EXAMINING *the* ISSUES

1 • What dangers might you face on the Crusade?

2 • What rewards, both material and personal, might come your way on the Crusade?

3 • What might be the advantages and disadvantages of staying home to defend the knight's family and estate?

4 • What arguments would you make to your parents to persuade them to agree to your participation in the Crusade?

As a class, discuss these questions. In your discussion, remember what you've learned about other religious wars, sometimes called holy wars or crusades.

As you read about the Crusades in this chapter, see how events turned out for the Crusaders, especially the participants in the Children's Crusade.

Follow Up

A feature on the chapter assessment will ask students to reevaluate their responses to the situation presented on this page.

1 Church Reform and the Crusades

MAIN IDEA

The Catholic Church underwent reform and launched Crusades (religious wars) against Muslims and others.

WHY IT MATTERS NOW

The Crusades resulted in trade and exploration between Christians and Muslims but left a legacy of distrust.

TERMS & NAMES
- simony
- St. Francis of Assisi
- Gothic
- Urban II
- Crusade
- Saladin
- Richard the Lion-Hearted
- Reconquista
- Inquisition

SETTING THE STAGE Between A.D. 500 and A.D. 1000, Vikings attacked and looted Church monasteries. They destroyed many of these centers of learning. At that time, the Church suffered severe problems. Some priests could barely read their prayers. Some popes were men of questionable morals. Many bishops and abbots cared more about their positions as feudal lords than about their duties as spiritual leaders. However, over the next 300 years the Church and medieval life changed dramatically.

Monastic Revival and Church Reform

Beginning in the 1000s, a spiritual revival spread across Europe. This revival was led by the monasteries. The reformers wanted to return to the basic principles of the Christian religion. New religious orders were founded. Influenced by the piety of the new monasteries, the popes began to reform the Church. They restored and expanded its power and authority. A new age of religious feeling was born—the Age of Faith.

> **Vocabulary**
> piety: religious devotion and reverence for God.

Problems in the Church Many problems troubled the Church at that time, but reformers were most distressed by three. First, many village priests married and had families. Such marriages were against Church rulings. Second, positions in the Church were sold by bishops, a practice called **simony** (SY·muh·nee). Third, the practice of lay investiture put kings in control of church bishops. Church reformers believed bishops should be appointed by the Church alone.

Reform Begins at Cluny Reforms began quietly in 910 with the founding of a Benedictine monastery at Cluny (KLOO·nee) in France. The monks there strictly followed the Benedictine rule. Soon Cluny's reputation for virtue inspired the founding of similar monasteries throughout western Europe. By the year 1000, there were 300 houses under Cluny's leadership. In 1098, another order was founded, the Cistercian (sih·STUR·shuhn) monks. The Cistercian life of hardship won many followers, helping to bring about further reforms.

> **Vocabulary**
> papacy: the position or office of the pope.

The reform movement, begun at Cluny, influenced the papacy. Pope Leo IX, who took office in 1049, enforced Church laws against simony and the marriage of priests. Pope Gregory VII was elected pope in 1073. He had spent time at Cluny and was determined to purify the Church. Gregory extended the reforms begun by Leo.

Reform and Church Organization The popes who followed Leo and Gregory reorganized the Church to continue the policy of reform. In the 1100s and 1200s the Church was restructured to resemble a kingdom, with the pope at its head. The pope's group of advisers was called the papal Curia. The Curia also acted as a court. It developed canon law (the law of the Church) on matters such as marriage, divorce, and inheritance. The Curia also decided cases based on these laws. Diplomats for the pope traveled through Europe dealing with bishops and kings. This extended the power of the pope.

This scene of monastic life comes from a Book of Hours, a book of prayers for private use that followed the hours of the day.

The Formation of Western Europe **341**

SECTION 1 RESOURCES

PRINT RESOURCES

 IN-DEPTH RESOURCES: UNIT 3
Guided Reading, p. 70
Geography Application: The Reconquista, p. 75
Primary Source: *Massacre at Acre*, p. 77

ACCESS FOR STUDENTS ACQUIRING ENGLISH
Guided Reading (Spanish), p. 141
Geography Application: The Reconquista, p. 146

FORMAL ASSESSMENT
Section Quiz, p. 158

TECHNOLOGY RESOURCES

WORLD ART AND CULTURES TRANSPARENCIES
AT30 Notre Dame
AT31 *Entry of the Crusaders into Constantinople*

CD-ROM
Religions of the World
Electronic Library of Primary Sources

INTERNET www.mlworldhistory.com

Section 1 Overview

OBJECTIVES

1. To describe the spiritual revival and the Church reforms that began in the 1000s.

2. To describe the Gothic cathedrals of the 1100s.

3. To summarize the causes and outcomes of the early Crusades.

4. To describe the later Crusades and their consequences.

SKILLBUILDER
- Interpreting maps: place, movement, region, p. 344

CRITICAL THINKING
- Making inferences, p. 342
- Drawing conclusions, p. 343
- Summarizing, p. 345
- Recognizing effects, p. 346
- Forming and supporting opinions, p. 346
- Comparing, p. 347

FOCUS
5-Minute Warm-Up

▶ **Recognizing Sequences**
Answering the following questions will help students understand the sequence of Crusades.

1. Study the map on page 344. The Second Crusade started from which three points?

2. Which Crusade(s) actually reached Jerusalem?

WARM-UP TRANSPARENCY 14

OBJECTIVE 1 INSTRUCT

Monastic Revival and Church Reform

▶ **Key Ideas**
- The Church is weakened by clergy marriages, simony, and secular control by kings.
- Church reform and reorganization extend papal authority in Europe.
- New religious orders revitalize the church.

IN-DEPTH RESOURCES: UNIT 3
Guided Reading, p. 70

ACCESS FOR STUDENTS ACQUIRING ENGLISH
Guided Reading (Spanish), p. 141

Teacher's Edition **341**

MORE ABOUT . . .
Hildegard of Bingen

MORE ABOUT . . .
Hildegard of Bingen

MORE ABOUT . . .
Hildegard of Bingen

Hildegard of Bingen, the well-educated daughter of an aristocratic family, is one of the more famous women of medieval times. Sent by her family to live in a convent, she produced a voluminous body of writings, including a record of her mystical experiences and works on science and medicine.

She also carried on an extensive correspondence with many prominent people of the time. One recent writer has commented that she was like "the Dear Abby of the twelfth century to whom everyone came or wrote for advice or comfort."

 RELIGIONS OF THE WORLD
Christianity

OBJECTIVE ❷ INSTRUCT

Cathedrals—Cities of God

▶ *Key Ideas*
- Gothic architecture begins to replace the heavier Romanesque style.
- Gothic cathedrals are built across Europe and embellished with rich decorative arts.

 WORLD ART AND CULTURES TRANSPARENCIES
AT30 Notre Dame

MORE ABOUT . . .
Cathedral Building

Building the cathedrals of Europe represented an enormous undertaking for the towns. The cathedral of Amiens, France, for example, covered 208,000 square feet, enough to hold the entire population of Amiens. Ask interested students to find out the size and capacity of some of the larger sports stadiums in the United States to compare them with these cathedrals.

The Church collected taxes in the form of tithes. These consumed one-tenth the yearly income from every Christian family. The Church performed social services such as caring for the sick and the poor. Most hospitals in medieval Europe were operated by the Church. By the early 1200s, popes had achieved remarkable success in their reforms. The practice of simony and the marriage of clergy both declined dramatically. The popes established their authority throughout Europe.

Preaching Friars In the early 1200s, wandering friars traveled from place to place preaching and spreading the Church's ideas. Like monks, friars took vows of chastity, poverty, and obedience. Unlike monks, friars did not live apart from the world in monasteries. Instead, they preached to the poor throughout Europe's towns and cities. Friars owned nothing and lived by begging.

The Dominicans, one of the earliest orders of friars, were founded by Dominic, a Spanish priest. Because Dominic emphasized the importance of study, many Dominicans were scholars. Another order of friars, the Franciscans, was founded by the Italian **St. Francis of Assisi** (uh·SEE·zee). The son of a rich merchant, Francis gave up his wealth and turned to preaching when he was about 20 years old. He placed much less importance on scholarship than did Dominic. Francis treated all creatures as if they were his spiritual brothers and sisters.

Religious Orders for Women Women as well as men participated in the spiritual revival. Women joined the Dominicans. In 1212, the Franciscan order for women, known as the Poor Clares, was founded by Clare and her friend Francis of Assisi. In Germany, Hildegard of Bingen, a mystic and musician, founded a Benedictine convent in 1147. Unlike the men, women were not allowed to travel from place to place as preachers. However, they too lived in poverty and worked to help the poor and sick.

Cathedrals—Cities of God

Although the friars chose to live in poverty, evidence of the Church's wealth could be seen everywhere in the Middle Ages. This was especially true in the cathedrals that were built in Europe around this time.

A New Style of Church Architecture Between about 800 and 1100, churches were built in the Romanesque (ROH·muh·NEHSK) style. The churches had round arches and a heavy roof held up by thick walls and pillars. The thick walls had tiny windows that let in little light.

In the early 1100s, a new style of architecture, known as **Gothic,** evolved. The term *Gothic* comes from a Germanic tribe named the Goths. It describes the particular church architecture that spread throughout medieval Europe. Unlike the heavy, gloomy Romanesque buildings, Gothic cathedrals thrust upward as if reaching toward heaven. Light streamed in through huge stained-glass windows. Soon Gothic cathedrals were built in many towns of France. In Paris, the vaulted ceiling of the Cathedral of Notre Dame (NOH·truh DAHM) eventually rose to over 100 feet. Then Chartres, Reims, Amiens, and Beauvais built even higher cathedrals.

In all, nearly 500 Gothic churches were built between 1170 and 1270. Other arts of the medieval world clustered around the Gothic cathedral—sculpture, woodcarvings, and the stained-glass windows. The cathedral represented the City of God. As such, it was decorated with all the richness that people on earth could offer.

In this 13th-century painting, St. Clare (kneeling) is received by St. Francis (standing, with halo).

342 Chapter 14

Background
Because of his love of nature, St. Francis was named the patron saint of ecology in 1979 by Pope John Paul II.

THINK THROUGH HISTORY
A. Making Inferences Why might women have preferred life in a religious order to secular life in the Middle Ages?
A. Possible Answer Women had very little freedom during this period. A life in the convent might have enabled them to pursue their own intellectual and artistic interests, which could have been difficult if not impossible for them to do in a secular life.

CONNECTIONS ACROSS THE CURRICULUM

Art: *Decorating the Cathedrals* Gothic cathedrals contained elaborate decorative arts—stained glass, wood carvings, statuary, and gold leaf. Ask students to research one or more of the arts used in cathedrals.

Have them prepare a display showing an example of the artwork (photocopied or hand copied) with an attached page or two explaining how the artwork was created.

CONNECTIONS ACROSS TIME AND PLACE

Washington National Cathedral Although the magnificent Gothic cathedrals of Europe were built over 700 years ago, Gothic cathedral building did not die out. In the United States, the Washington National Cathedral, begun during the first decade

of this century, was finally dedicated in 1990. Ask students to research the Washington National Cathedral and prepare a visual report that includes pictures and/or drawings of the cathedral with a brief description of the cathedral's layout and furnishings.

HISTORY THROUGH ART: Church Architecture

① pointed, ribbed vaults

③ tall spires

② flying buttresses

The cathedral of Chartres (shahrt) is a masterpiece of Gothic architecture. In addition to its stained-glass windows, the cathedral has hundreds of sculptures. The stone carvings that frame every door illustrate Bible stories. The cathedral has two bell towers.

Chartres Cathedral has some of the most beautiful stained-glass windows of any Gothic cathedral in Europe. The windows illustrate stories from the Bible. As illiterate peasants walked past the 176 windows, they could view those stories. This window depicts the parable of the Good Samaritan.

The master builders in France, where the Gothic style originated, developed certain techniques of structural engineering. These were key to Gothic architecture: ① pointed, ribbed vaults that supported the roof's weight and framed huge stained-glass windows, ② flying buttresses that both supported the walls from the outside and acted as wind braces, and ③ pointed arches and tall spires that seemed to be pointing to heaven.

Connect to History

Drawing Conclusions Gothic architecture was designed to achieve more height and light. What elements in the style of Gothic architecture might affect the sense of height and light inside?

 SEE SKILLBUILDER HANDBOOK, PAGE 1006

Connect to Today

Taking a Tour Take a walk past the churches in your neighborhood. Notice the stained-glass windows. Do they tell a story? What figures or events do they illustrate?

The Crusades

The Age of Faith also inspired wars of conquest. In 1093, the Byzantine emperor Alexius Comnenus sent an appeal to Robert, Count of Flanders. That letter was also read by Pope **Urban II.** The emperor asked for help against the Muslim Turks. They were threatening to conquer his capital, Constantinople:

A VOICE FROM THE PAST

Come then, with all your people and give battle with all your strength, so that all this treasure shall not fall into the hands of the Turks. . . . Therefore act while there is still time lest the kingdom of the Christians shall vanish from your sight and, what is more important, the Holy Sepulchre [the tomb where Jesus was buried] shall vanish. And in your coming you will find your reward in heaven, and if you do not come, God will condemn you.

EMPEROR ALEXIUS COMNENUS, quoted in *The Dream and the Tomb*

Vocabulary
Holy Land: Palestine; the area where Jesus had lived and preached.

Shortly after this appeal, Pope Urban II issued a call for what he termed a "holy war," a **Crusade,** to gain control of the Holy Land. Over the next 200 years a number of such

The Formation of Western Europe **343**

History from Visuals

The Crusades, 1096–1204

Interpreting the Map Have students identify the colors associated with the Muslim lands, the Christian lands, and the lands captured and held by the Crusaders. Through which cities did most of the crusading armies pass?

Extension Activity Have students carefully study the map and then discuss why they think that Italian merchants, in particular, profited heavily from the Crusades.

SKILLBUILDER Answers
1. Seljuk Turks
2. The Fourth Crusade; Constantinople
3. Spain and Portugal

MORE ABOUT . . .
The Crusaders

The Crusaders came from all walks of life and included laborers, farm boys, priests, archbishops, knights, foot soldiers, and kings. They were inspired by a deep faith and a yearning to see the holy places where Christ had walked.

They called themselves the "pilgrims of Christ." Over the time of the Crusades, hundreds of thousands journeyed to the Holy Land. About one fourth of the Crusaders died along the way, and another fourth died in the wars.

Those who survived often suffered terribly to defend the small strip of land they called the Kingdom of Jerusalem. Many spent half their lives in Muslim prisons before being ransomed or released. They returned to Europe as old men in frail health.

The Crusades, 1096–1204

Christian lands
Muslim lands
Kingdoms established by the Crusaders
First Crusade, 1096–1099
Second Crusade, 1147–1149
Third Crusade, 1189–1191
Fourth Crusade, 1202–1204

GEOGRAPHY SKILLBUILDER: Interpreting Maps
1. **Place** What Muslim power ruled lands close to the Christian city of Constantinople?
2. **Movement** Which Crusade did not make it to Jerusalem? Where did this Crusade end?
3. **Region** Where in Europe were Muslim and Christian lands adjacent to one another?

Crusades were launched. The goal of these military expeditions was to recover Jerusalem and the Holy Land from the Muslim Turks.

Causes of the Crusading Spirit The Crusades had both economic goals and religious motives. Pope Urban's call brought a tremendous outpouring of religious feeling and support for the Crusade. This support came from great lords and humble peasants alike. In 1096, between 50,000 and 60,000 knights became Crusaders. With red crosses sewn on tunics worn over their armor and the battle cry of "God wills it!" on their lips, the Crusaders marched eastward. Few would return from the journey.

Kings and the Church saw the Crusades as an opportunity to get rid of quarrelsome knights who fought each other. These knights threatened the peace of the kingdoms, as well as Church property. Others who participated were younger sons who, unlike their oldest brother, did not stand to inherit their father's property. They were looking for land and a position in society. Knights and commoners alike were fired by religious zeal. According to Pope Urban II, if the knights died on Crusade, they were assured of a place in heaven.

In later Crusades, merchants profited by making cash loans to finance the Crusade. They also leased their ships for a hefty fee to transport armies over the Mediterranean Sea. In addition, the merchants of Pisa, Genoa, and Venice hoped to win control of key trade routes to India, Southeast Asia, and China from Muslim traders.

The First and Second Crusades By early 1097, three armies of knights and people of all classes had gathered outside Constantinople. Most of the Crusaders were French. But Germans, Englishmen, Scots, Italians, and Spaniards came as well.

The Crusaders were ill-prepared for their holy war in this First Crusade. They knew nothing of the geography, climate, or culture of the Holy Land. They had no grand strategy to capture Jerusalem. The nobles argued among themselves and couldn't agree

344 Chapter 14

TEACHING OPTION — **BLOCK SCHEDULING**

COOPERATIVE ACTIVITY: Book Reports on the Crusades

CLASS TIME 20 MINUTES

Task: Students will work in groups to read books on the Crusades and present an oral report in class.

Purpose: To help students understand the motives of Crusaders and the hardships they faced.

Activity: Divide students into groups of three or four. Each group will select a book on the Crusades

from one of the following categories: historical fiction, art books, histories, and biographies of principal leaders. Each group will present an oral report on the book, illustrating their talk whenever possible with maps and photocopies or hand-drawn pictures.

For historical fiction, students should focus on such topics as a brief biography of the writer (if possible),

the historical setting and background for the story, a summary of the plot, the author's presentation of medieval life, the levels of society represented, and what the student reader learned about medieval life and times from the book.

 ALTERNATIVE ASSESSMENT BOOK
Standards for Evaluating a Cooperative Activity

on a leader. Also, they had not set up adequate supply lines. Finally, however, an army of 12,000 (less than one-fourth the original army) approached Jerusalem. The Crusaders besieged the city for a month. On July 15, 1099, they captured the city.

All in all, the Crusaders had won a narrow strip of land. It stretched about 400 miles from Edessa in the north to Jerusalem in the south. Four feudal Crusader states were carved out of this territory, each ruled by a European noble.

The Crusaders' states were extremely vulnerable to Muslim counterattack. In 1144, Edessa was reconquered by the Turks. The Second Crusade was organized to recapture the city. But its armies straggled home in defeat. In 1187, Europeans were shocked to learn Jerusalem itself had fallen to the Muslim leader **Saladin** (SAL·uh·dihn).

THINK THROUGH HISTORY
4. Summarizing
What, if anything, had the Crusaders gained by the end of the Second Crusade?
4. Possible Answer
The Crusader armies gained nothing and went home in defeat.

The Third and Fourth Crusades

The Third Crusade to recapture Jerusalem was led by three of Europe's most powerful monarchs. These were the French king Philip Augustus, the German emperor Frederick I (Barbarossa), and the English king **Richard the Lion-Hearted.** Barbarossa drowned on the journey, and Philip Augustus argued with Richard and went home. Richard was left to regain the Holy Land from Saladin.

Both Richard and Saladin were ruthless fighters who respected each other. After many battles, the two agreed to a truce in 1192. Jerusalem remained under Muslim control. In return, Saladin promised that unarmed Christian pilgrims could freely visit the city's holy places.

In 1198, the powerful Pope Innocent III appealed for still another Crusade to capture Jerusalem. The knights who took part in this Fourth Crusade became entangled in Italian and Byzantine politics. They ended up looting the city of Constantinople in 1204, ending the Fourth Crusade. There was a breach (a split) between the Church in the east, whose capital was Constantinople, and the Church in the west, whose capital was Rome. This breach, caused in part by the Crusaders' actions, became permanent.

Background
In the looting of Constantinople, Crusaders stole the relics from the great cathedral. They loaded the jewel-studded communion table onto a Venetian ship. The ship sank, and its priceless cargo was never recovered.

HISTORY MAKERS

Saladin
1138–1193

Saladin was the most famous Muslim leader of the 1100s. His own people considered him a most devout man. Even the Christians regarded him as honest and brave.

He wished to chase the Crusaders back into their own territories. He said:

I think that when God grants me victory over the rest of Palestine, I shall divide my territories, make a will stating my wishes, then set sail on this sea for their far-off lands and pursue the Franks there, so as to free the earth from anyone who does not believe in Allah, or die in the attempt.

Richard the Lion-Hearted
1157–1199

Richard was noted for his good looks, charm, courage, grace—and ruthlessness. When he heard that Jerusalem had fallen to the Muslims, he was inspired with religious zeal. He joined the Crusade, leaving others to rule England in his place.

Richard mounted a siege on the city of Acre. Saladin's army was in the hills overlooking the city, but it was not strong enough to defeat the Crusaders. When finally the city fell, Richard had the Muslim survivors— some 3,000 men, women, and children—slaughtered. The Muslim army watched helplessly from the hills.

The Crusading Spirit Dwindles

In the 1200s, Crusades became increasingly common and unsuccessful. The religious spirit of the First Crusade faded, replaced by a search for personal gain.

The Later Crusades In several later Crusades, armies marched not to the Holy Land but to North Africa. The French king who led the last two Crusades, Louis IX, won wide respect in Europe. He was later declared a saint. None of these attempts conquered much land, however.

The Formation of Western Europe **345**

MORE ABOUT . . .
The Capture of Jerusalem
As the Crusader army approached Jerusalem, the city's governor prepared for a long siege. He poisoned the wells surrounding the city and ordered all the sheep and goats to be brought inside the city walls.

When the Crusaders arrived, they found no water or food available. They besieged the city for over a month in brutal heat, hot winds, and choking dust. Ask students what might have made the Crusaders endure such hardship.

HISTORY MAKERS
Saladin

Saladin could be chivalrous even to his enemies. When he learned that Richard the Lion-Hearted was ill, he sent his own physician and a gift of snow and peaches.

Richard the Lion-Hearted

Richard earned such a reputation for fierceness among the Muslims that for centuries naughty Muslim children were told, "Be quiet, or England will come after you."

Ask students to read about these two men and report to the class. Gifted and talented students can read the primary source.

 IN-DEPTH RESOURCES: UNIT 4
Primary Source: *Massacre at Acre*, p. 77

OBJECTIVE 4 INSTRUCT

The Crusading Spirit Dwindles

▶ *Key Ideas*
• Later Crusades end in failure.
• Spain drives out the Muslims and is united as a Christian country.
• The Crusades weaken the papacy, strengthen European kings, and increase trade with the Middle East.

TEACHING OPTIONS   **CUSTOMIZING FOR SPECIAL NEEDS**   **MULTIPLE LEARNING STYLES**

Gifted and Talented Students:
Women and the Crusades Large numbers of women participated in or contributed to the Crusades. Although little is known about the efforts of common women, chroniclers mention a few aristocratic women, such as Eleanor of Aquitaine, who accompanied their husbands on the long march.

Many aristocratic women who stayed home had to manage their husbands' estates and business affairs. Other women often ran inns and shops in towns where armies passed on their way to the Holy Land. Ask students to research and prepare a report on the role that Eleanor of Aquitaine played in the Crusades.

Visual Learners: Video of the Crusades Have a group of visual learners view the video *The Crusades: Saints and Sinners* [26 mins. Social Studies School Service, (800) 421-4246]. This video is a vivid recreation of the First Crusade, filmed partly on location.

The story explores the complex motivations of Crusaders and examines the ironies of conducting a "holy war." Have students write down three or four things they learned from the video, and what they liked or didn't like about how it portrayed the life and times of that era.

The Children's Crusade took place in 1212. Thousands of children set out for the Holy Land. They were armed only with the belief that God would give them Jerusalem. On their march south to the Mediterranean, many died from cold and starvation. One group even turned back. The rest drowned at sea or were sold into slavery.

A Spanish Crusade In Spain, Muslims (called Moors) had controlled most of the country until the 1100s. The **Reconquista** (ray·kawn·KEES·tuh) was a long effort to drive the Muslims out of Spain. By the late 1400s, the Muslims held only the tiny kingdom of Granada. In 1492, Granada fell to the Christian army of Ferdinand and Isabella, the Spanish monarchs.

Spain had a large Jewish population. Many achieved high positions in finance, government, and medicine. Many Jews (and Muslims) converted to Christianity during the late 1400s. To unify their country under Christianity and to consolidate their power, Isabella and Ferdinand made use of the **Inquisition.** This was a tribunal held by the Church to suppress heresy. Heretics were people whose religious beliefs differed from the teachings of the Church. The inquisitors suspected Jewish and Muslim converts of heresy. A person who was suspected of heresy might be questioned for weeks and even tortured. Once suspects confessed, they were often burned at the stake. Eventually, in 1492, the monarchs expelled all practicing Jews and Muslims from Spain.

The Effects of the Crusades The failure of later Crusades lessened the power of the pope. The Crusades weakened the feudal nobility. Thousands of knights lost their lives and fortunes.

On the positive side, the Crusades played a part in stimulating trade between Europe and Southwest Asia. The goods imported from Southwest Asia included spices, fruits, and cloth.

For Muslims, the Crusades also had both good and bad effects. The intolerance and prejudice displayed by Christians in the Holy Land left behind a legacy of bitterness and hatred. This legacy continues to the present. For Christians and Jews who remained in the region after the fall of the Crusader states, relations with their Muslim masters worsened. However, European merchants who lived and traded in the Crusader states were encouraged to continue their trading after the collapse of the states. This trade with the West benefited both Christians and Muslims.

The Crusades grew from the forces of religious fervor, feudalism, and chivalry as they came together with explosive energy. This same energy could be seen in the growth of trade, towns, and universities in medieval Europe.

The Crusades

Causes

- Muslims control Palestine (the Holy Land) and threaten Constantinople.
- Byzantine emperor calls for help.
- Pope wants to reclaim Palestine and reunite Christendom.
- Pope appeals to Christian knights.
- Knights feel religious zeal and want land, riches, and adventure.
- Italian cities desire commercial power.

Effects

- Byzantine Empire is weakened.
- Pope's power declines.
- Power of feudal nobles weakens.
- Kings become stronger.
- Religious intolerance grows.
- Italian cities expand trade and grow rich.
- Muslims increasingly distrust Christians.
- Trade grows between Europe and the Middle East.
- European technology improves as Crusaders learn from Muslims.

THINK THROUGH HISTORY
C. Recognizing Effects What were the effects of the Reconquista?
C. Possible Answers Most of Spain reconquered from Muslims; Muslims and Jews expelled from Spain; country unified under Christianity.

Section ① Assessment

1. TERMS & NAMES
Identify
- simony
- St. Francis of Assisi
- Gothic
- Urban II
- Crusade
- Saladin
- Richard the Lion-Hearted
- Reconquista
- Inquisition

2. TAKING NOTES
Using a time line like the one below, show four or five key events that summarize the Age of Faith.

900 1000 1100 1200 1300 1400 1500

Write a paragraph describing one event in detail.

3. FORMING AND SUPPORTING OPINIONS
Which of the Church's problems—marriage of priests, simony, lay investiture—do you think was most harmful to the Church? Why?

THINK ABOUT
- the effects of each problem
- the reforms that corrected each problem

4. THEME ACTIVITY
Cultural Interaction With a partner, develop a scene from a play in which Richard the Lion-Hearted, in 1192, meets Saladin for the first time and the two warriors work out a truce. Include stage directions, but focus mainly on what the men say to each other. Be prepared to present the scene as a dialogue.

346 Chapter 14

The Crusades

In the Crusades, both Christians and Muslims believed that God was on their side. They both felt justified in using violence to win or to keep the Holy Land. The following excerpts show their belief in God's approval for their deeds. The quotation from Norman Cantor explains where this attitude has led.

SPEECH
Pope Urban II

In 1095, Pope Urban II gave one of the most influential speeches of history when he issued a plea that resulted in the First Crusade. The pope assured his listeners that God was on their side.

Let the holy sepulcher of our Lord and Saviour, which is possessed by the unclean nations, especially arouse you. . . . This royal city [Jerusalem], situated at the center of the earth, is now held captive by the enemies of Christ and is subjected, by those who do not know God, to the worship of the heathen. Accordingly, undertake this journey eagerly for the remission of your sins, with the assurance of the reward of imperishable glory in the kingdom of heaven.

LETTER
Saladin

The German emperor Frederick I (Barbarossa) wrote the Muslim leader Saladin a letter threatening him if Saladin should attack Jerusalem. The following is an excerpt of Saladin's reply, written after he had recaptured Jerusalem.

Whenever your armies are assembled . . . we will meet you in the power of God. We will not be satisfied with the land on the seacoast, but we will cross over with God's good pleasure and take from you all your lands in the strength of the Lord. . . . And when the Lord, by His power, shall have given us victory over you, nothing will remain for us to do but freely to take your lands by His power and with His good pleasure. . . . By the virtue and power of God we have taken possession of Jerusalem and its territories; and of the three cities that still remain in the hands of the Christians . . . we shall occupy them also.

HISTORICAL ACCOUNT
William of Tyre

William of Tyre was a Christian bishop who drew upon eyewitness accounts of the capture of Jerusalem by the Crusaders in writing his account.

It was impossible to look upon the vast numbers of the slain without horror; everywhere lay fragments of human bodies, and the very ground was covered with the blood of the slain. It was not alone the spectacle of headless bodies and mutilated limbs strewn in all directions that roused horror in all who looked upon them. Still more dreadful was it to gaze upon the victors themselves, dripping with blood from head to foot, an ominous sight which brought terror to all who met them. It is reported that within the Temple enclosure alone about ten thousand infidels perished, in addition to those who lay slain everywhere throughout the city in the streets and squares, the number of whom was estimated as no less.

HISTORIAN'S COMMENTARY
Norman Cantor

Historian Norman Cantor explains the lasting legacy of the Crusades—even today when nation fights nation, each sincerely believes that God is on its side.

The most important legacy of the crusading movement was the sanctification [making holy] of violence in pursuit of [ideas]. This was not a new concept, but it took on new force when the pope and the flower of Christian chivalry acted it out in holy wars. The underlying concept outlived its religious origin, . . . and the state gradually replaced the Church as a holy cause.

Connect *to* History

Comparing Use specific phrases or passages from Urban's speech and from Saladin's letter to show how their attitudes are similar.

SEE SKILLBUILDER HANDBOOK, PAGE 996

Connect *to* Today

Researching Find accounts in newspapers or magazines of how some groups today feel morally justified in using violence. Share your accounts with the class.

CD-ROM For another perspective on the Crusades, see **World History: Electronic Library of Primary Sources,**

The Formation of Western Europe **347**

---

different **Perspectives**

Why the Crusades Matter Now
As students discuss these perspectives on the Christian and Muslim attitudes toward the Crusades, you might have them consider the bigger picture: why do the Crusades matter now?

• On a positive note, the Crusades opened up Europe to ancient Greek and Roman thought and discoveries, paving the way for the Renaissance.

• Trade between Europe and the Middle East enhanced the European economy and created the forerunners of modern banking and financial institutions.

• Art and literature benefited from the rediscovery of Greek and Roman artworks and aesthetic ideals.

• On the negative side, the persecution by Christians of non-Christians left a lasting bitterness that some might argue still exists in the region today.

• The idea that violence is justifiable, and even honorable, when used for a "higher cause" was later taken up by Europe's monarchs. Defense of the state became the "higher cause" that justified the use of violence. That idea remains with us today.

Connect *to* History

Comparing Both men believe that God is on their side, and both claim Jerusalem. Have students create a chart like the one below and fill in the spaces with appropriate quotes.

Belief in God's Approval	Claim on Jerusalem
Urban	
Saladin	

Connect *to* Today

Researching Have students work in small groups to think of people today who believe they are justified in using violence. You might suggest such groups as the Irish Republican Army in Northern Ireland; various ultra-conservative groups in Palestine or Lebanon (Islamic Jihad, Hamas, or Hezbollah); the Sikhs in India; or revolutionary groups in Peru or Mexico. Have students research one of these groups and report on it in class.

1. To describe medieval advances in agriculture.

2. To identify reasons for the expansion of trade and finance in the Middle Ages.

3. To describe how the growth of trade encouraged the growth of medieval towns.

4. To explain the new interest in learning in the Middle Ages.

CRITICAL THINKING

- Recognizing effects, pp. 348, 349
- Summarizing, p. 350
- Supporting opinions, p. 351
- Analyzing causes, p. 351
- Analyzing themes, p. 351

FOCUS

5-Minute Warm-Up

▶ **Making Generalizations**
To help students understand the influence of medieval times on modern life, have them answer these questions.

1. Read Daily Life on page 349. List people in your class or in the news who have one of the names mentioned.

2. What family relationship is implied in names like Williamson, Anderson, Carlson?

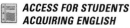
WARM-UP TRANSPARENCY 14

OBJECTIVE 1 INSTRUCT

A Growing Food Supply

▶ **Key Ideas**
- Medieval farmers develop various methods to increase food production.

IN-DEPTH RESOURCES: UNIT 3
Guided Reading, p. 71

ACCESS FOR STUDENTS ACQUIRING ENGLISH
Guided Reading (Spanish), p. 142

---

2 Trade, Towns, and Financial Revolution

TERMS & NAMES
- three-field system
- guild
- burgher
- vernacular
- Dante Alighieri
- Geoffrey Chaucer
- Thomas Aquinas
- scholastics

MAIN IDEA	WHY IT MATTERS NOW
European cities challenged the feudal system as agriculture, trade, finance, and universities developed.	The various changes in the Middle Ages laid the foundations for modern Europe.

SETTING THE STAGE While Church reform, cathedral building, and the Crusades were taking place, other important changes were occurring in medieval society. Between 1000 and 1300, agriculture, trade, and finance made remarkable progress. Towns and cities grew. This was in part due to the growing population and territorial expansion of western Europe. The creativity unleashed during this age also sparked the growth of learning and the birth of an institution new to Europe—the university.

A Growing Food Supply

Europe's great revival would have been impossible without better ways of farming. Expanding civilization requires an increased food supply. Farming was helped by a warmer climate that lasted from about 800 to 1200. Farmers began to cultivate lands in regions once too cold to grow crops. They also developed new methods to take advantage of more available land.

Using Horsepower For hundreds of years, peasants depended on oxen to pull their plows. Oxen lived on the poorest straw and stubble. They were easy to keep, but they moved very slowly. Horses needed better food, but a team of horses could plow twice as much land in a day as a team of oxen.

Before they could use horses, however, people needed a new type of harness. Harnesses of the early Middle Ages went around the horse's neck. They nearly strangled the animal when it pulled. Sometime before 900, farmers in Europe began using a new technology. This was a harness that fitted across the horse's chest, taking pressure off its neck and windpipe. As a result, horses gradually replaced oxen for plowing and for pulling wagons.

The Three-Field System At the same time, villagers began to organize their land differently. Under the old, two-field system, peasants divided the village's land into two great fields. They planted one field with crops and left the other to lie fallow, or unplanted to avoid exhausting the soil, for a year. So if a village had 600 acres, each year farmers used 300 acres for raising food, leaving the other 300 acres fallow.

Around 800, some villages began to organize their land into three fields. With the same 600 acres, they used 200 acres for a winter crop of wheat or rye. In spring, they planted another 200 acres with oats, barley, peas, or beans. The remaining 200 acres lay fallow. Under this new, **three-field system,** farmers could grow crops on two-thirds of their land each year, not just on half of it. As a result, food production increased. Villagers had more to eat. The food was also better for them, because peas, beans, and lentils are good sources of vegetable protein. The result was an increase in population. People could raise larger families. Well-fed people could better resist disease and live longer. With horses, a farmer plowed more land in a day. This meant that teams cleared forests for new fields. All over Europe, axes rang as the great forests began to fall.

A variety of farm chores is shown in this 14th-century agricultural almanac.

A. Possible Answers Food production increased, people had more to eat, population increased.

THINK THROUGH HISTORY
A. Recognizing Effects What were the main consequences of the three-field system?

SECTION 2 RESOURCES

PRINT RESOURCES

IN-DEPTH RESOURCES: UNIT 3
Guided Reading, p. 71
Literature: from *The Canterbury Tales* by Geoffrey Chaucer, p. 81

ACCESS FOR STUDENTS ACQUIRING ENGLISH
Guided Reading (Spanish), p. 142

FORMAL ASSESSMENT
Section Quiz, p. 159

ALTERNATIVE ASSESSMENT BOOK

TECHNOLOGY RESOURCES

GEOGRAPHY TRANSPARENCIES
GT14 Trade and Manufacturing in Medieval Europe, 1000–1300

CD-ROM
Electronic Library of Primary Sources

INTERNET www.mlworldhistory.com

Trade and Finance Expand

Just as agriculture was expanding, so were trade and finance. This was in part a response to population growth. By the 1000s, artisans and craftsmen were manufacturing goods by hand for local and long-distance trade. Trade routes spread across Europe from Flanders to Italy. Italian merchant ships traveled the Mediterranean to ports in Byzantium such as Constantinople. They also traveled to Muslim ports along the North African coast. Trade routes were opened to Asia, in part by the Crusades.

Background
Great fairs were held several times a year, usually during religious festivals, when many people would be in town. People could visit the stalls set up by merchants from all parts of Europe.

Fairs and Trade Most trade took place in towns. Peasants from nearby manors traveled to town on fair days, hauling items to trade. Cloth was the most common trade item. Other items included bacon, salt, honey, cheese, wine, leather, dyes, knives, and ropes. Such local fairs met all the needs of daily life for a small community. No longer was everything produced on a self-sufficient manor.

The Guilds Great fairs were made possible by the guilds, which controlled the crafts and trade. A **guild** was an association of people who worked at the same occupation. It was similar to a union today. In medieval towns, guilds controlled all wages and prices in their craft. Each guild usually met in its own guild hall. The first guilds were formed by merchants who controlled all the trade in their town.

As towns grew, skilled artisans—such as wheelwrights, glassmakers, winemakers, tailors, and druggists—began craft guilds. Guilds enforced standards of quality. Bakers, for example, were required to sell loaves of bread of a standard size and weight and at a fair price.

Only masters of the trade could be guild members. Becoming a master wasn't easy. First a child was apprenticed for five to nine years to a master to learn the trade. Then the apprentice became a journeyman and could go to work for wages. As the final step, a journeyman made an item—whether it was a shoe, a barrel, or a sword—that qualified as a "master piece." Journeymen whose product met guild standards were welcomed into the guild as masters.

Background
In most crafts, both husbands and wives worked at the family trade. In some guilds, especially for cloth-making, women formed the majority.

A Financial Revolution This medieval world of fairs and guilds created a need for large amounts of cash. Before a merchant could make a profit selling his goods at a fair, he first had to purchase goods from distant places. Usually, this meant he had to borrow money, but the Church forbade Christians from lending money at interest, a sin called usury. Where, then, did merchants go for a loan?

THINK THROUGH HISTORY
B. Recognizing Effects How did the exclusion of Jews from many aspects of life in medieval Europe affect their ways of earning a living?
B. Possible Answer With few other avenues open to them, and with Church rules against Christians' engaging in moneylending, many Jews undertook finance.

Many of Europe's Jews lived in the growing towns and were moneylenders. Moneylending was one of the few ways of making a living allowed them. In this largely Christian world, Jews were kept on the fringes of society. Guilds excluded them. They had to live in segregated parts of towns called ghettos. Because Jews were forbidden to hold land, they had never become part of the feudal system. Over time, the Church relaxed its rule on usury. Banking became an important business, especially in Italy.

Urban Splendor Reborn

All over Europe, trade blossomed, and better farming methods caused a spurt of population growth. Scholars estimate that between 1000 and 1150, the population of western Europe rose from around 30 million to about 42 million. Towns grew and flourished. Compared to great cities like Constantinople, European towns were primitive and tiny. Europe's largest city, Paris, probably had no more than 60,000 people by the year 1200. A typical town in medieval Europe had only about 1,500 to 2,500 people. Nevertheless, these small communities became a powerful force for change.

The Formation of Western Europe **349**

Daily *Life*

Surnames

Many people can trace their last names, or surnames, back to a medieval occupation. For example, a man who made thatched roofs for cottages became Thatcher.

The name Smith refers to a man who "smites," or works, metal. There is also Brownsmith, one who works copper; Goldsmith, one who works gold; and Silversmith, one who works silver.

Someone who made things out of wood might be surnamed Carpenter. Someone who made or repaired wooden barrels might be called Cooper.

Place names also became surnames, such as Holland and Welsh (a person from Wales). Sometimes, a person new to the area simply received the surname Newman. Surnames can also derive from family relationships, as does Williamson.

OBJECTIVE 2 INSTRUCT

Trade and Finance Expand

▶ **Key Ideas**
- Medieval trade routes expand, and trade fairs become regular events.
- Guilds train artisans and control the production and quality of crafts.
- The Church relaxes its rules against moneylending, and banking becomes an important function.

Daily *Life*
Surnames

Ask students to choose a common western European surname (or their own surname) to research. They might select a common surname, such as Smith or Anderson, from the telephone book. Students can write a brief report on what they find out about their name and post their paper on the bulletin board for others in the class to read.

OBJECTIVE 3 INSTRUCT

Urban Splendor Reborn

▶ **Key Ideas**
- With the increase in trade, medieval towns flourish, despite their unsanitary conditions.
- A growing middle class of townspeople gain their freedom from feudal structures.

💿 **ELECTRONIC LIBRARY OF PRIMARY SOURCES**
from "A Description of the Most Noble City of London"

TEACHING OPTION | **BLOCK SCHEDULING** | **GEOGRAPHY TRANSPARENCY ACTIVITY** | **CLASS TIME 20 MINUTES**

Task: To help students understand the role of trade in the growth of countries in the Middle Ages.

Materials Needed: Geography Transparency G14; student notebooks and pens or pencils

Activity: Students will view the transparency and answer these questions: Why was Venice ideally situated for trade? *It was centrally located for both overland and sea routes from three continents.* What

natural resources on the British Isles helped promote manufacturing there? *lead, iron, tin* What items could Europeans buy in Egypt? *horses, slaves, indigo, silk* What cities would be good sources for textiles? *London, York, Nuremberg, Milan, Brussels, Cologne, Bruges, Amsterdam*

Conclusion: Discuss with students how each region had something the others needed, and that no

one region had everything. How would these facts both encourage trade and offer the potential for conflict between nations or trading partners?

🏛 **GEOGRAPHY TRANSPARENCIES**
G14 Trade and Manufacturing in Medieval Europe, 1000–1300

Teacher's Edition **349**

The Revival of Learning

▶ *Key Ideas*
- As universities develop, scholars begin writing in the common language.
- Ancient Greek and Roman works, translated from Arabic, help shape European thought.
- Thomas Aquinas's ideas about religion and human nature strongly influence western Europe.

 ELECTRONIC LIBRARY OF PRIMARY SOURCES
from *The Divine Comedy*

MORE ABOUT . . .
Medieval Universities

Because the medieval university had no buildings, classes met in rented rooms or in the choir section of a church. Lucky students sat on a bench. Most squatted on the straw-covered floor as they tried to memorize the master's lecture. With writing materials scarce, all student exams were oral. Books were handwritten, and a single book might cost the equivalent of $600 or $700. Often the only textbook for a course belonged to the teacher, who read it aloud and offered his own comments.

Trade and Towns Grow Together By the later Middle Ages, trade was the very lifeblood of the new towns, which sprang up at ports, at crossroads, on hilltops, and along rivers. All over Europe, as trade grew, towns swelled with people. The excitement and bustle of towns drew many people. They were no longer content with their old feudal existence. Even though they were legally bound to their lord's manor, many serfs ran away. As people left life on the manor for life in towns, they challenged the traditional ways of feudal society in which everyone had his place. They did not return to the manor, and towns grew rapidly.

Most medieval towns developed haphazardly. Streets were narrow, filled with horses, pigs, oxen, and their refuse. With no sewers, most people dumped household waste, both animal and human, into the street in front of the house. Most people never bathed, and their houses lacked fresh air, light, and clean water. Because houses were built of wood with thatched roofs, they were a constant fire hazard. All in all, there were many drawbacks to living in a medieval town. Nonetheless, many people chose to move to such towns to pursue the economic and social opportunities they offered.

Towns and the Social Order So many serfs had left the manors by the 1100s that according to custom, a serf could now become free by living within a town for a year and a day. As the saying went, "Town air makes you free." Many of these runaway serfs, now free people, made better lives for themselves in towns.

The merchants and craftsmen of medieval towns did not fit into the traditional medieval social order of noble, clergy, and peasant. At first, towns came under the authority of feudal lords, who used their authority to levy fees, taxes, and rents. As trade expanded, the **burghers,** or town dwellers, resented this interference in their trade and commerce. They organized themselves and demanded privileges. These included freedom from certain kinds of tolls or the right to govern the town. At times they fought against their landlords and won these rights by force.

This drawing of the bishop of Paris blessing the people at a fair dates from the 14th century. The scene shows town dwellers going about their business, including merchants in their fair booths.

THINK THROUGH HISTORY
C. Summarizing
What were the advantages of town life for many former serfs?
C. Possible Answer
Economic and social opportunities.

The Revival of Learning

Growing trade and growing cities brought a new interest in learning. At the center of the growth of learning stood a new European institution—the university. Athens, Alexandria, Rome, and Constantinople had all been centers of learning, but never before had the world seen the university as it arose in western Europe.

Scholars and Writers The word *university* originally designated a group of scholars meeting wherever they could. People, not buildings, made up the medieval university. Universities arose at Paris and at Bologna, Italy, by the end of the 1100s. Others followed at the English town of Oxford and at Salerno, Italy. Most students were the sons of burghers or well-to-do artisans. For most students, the goal was a job in government or the Church. Earning a bachelor's degree in theology might take 5 to 7 years in school; becoming a master of theology took at least 12 years of study.

At a time when serious scholars and writers were writing in Latin, a few remarkable poets began using a lively **vernacular,** or the everyday language of their homeland. Some of these writers wrote masterpieces that are still read today. **Dante Alighieri** wrote *The Divine Comedy* (1321) in Italian. **Geoffrey Chaucer** wrote *The Canterbury Tales* (about 1387–1400) in English. Christine de Pisan wrote *The City of Ladies* (1405) in French. Since most people couldn't read or understand Latin, these writers brought literature to

---

EXPLORING PRIMARY SOURCES

A Voice from the Past Geoffrey Chaucer used a pilgrimage to Canterbury as the frame for his collection of stories, *The Canterbury Tales.* In his General Prologue to the tales, Chaucer describes the pilgrims, who represented all classes of English society of the 1300s. For example, the plowman, the parson, and the knight represent the workers, clergy, and aristocracy. The physician, the merchant, and others represent the middle class.

At the beginning of each tale, Chaucer gives a detailed description of the teller's life and appearance, which provides more insight into the medieval world. The stories cover a wide variety of subjects and offer different viewpoints on life in the Middle Ages.

Have students read the General Prologue and choose one of the characters to investigate further. Students should also read the prologue to their chosen character's tale. Ask them to write a brief description of the character, explaining what aspect of life in the Middle Ages he or she represents. Students might also enjoy reading the literature selection on Chaucer.

 IN-DEPTH RESOURCES: UNIT 3
Literature: from *The Canterbury Tales* by Geoffrey Chaucer, p. 81

Vocabulary
pilgrimage: a journey to a sacred place or shrine.

many people. For example, Chaucer's *Canterbury Tales* describes a pilgrimage to the shrine of St. Thomas à Becket. It was read aloud at gatherings:

> **A VOICE FROM THE PAST**
> It happened in that season that one day
> In Southwark, at *The Tabard*, as I lay
> Ready to go on pilgrimage and start
> For Canterbury, most devout at heart,
> At night there came into that hostelry
> Some nine and twenty in a company
> Of sundry folk happening then to fall
> In fellowship, and they were pilgrims all
> That towards Canterbury meant to ride.
>
> **GEOFFREY CHAUCER,** the Prologue to *The Canterbury Tales*, translated by Nevill Coghill

The Muslim Connection The revival of learning sparked European interest in the works of ancient scholars. At the same time, the growth of trade was accelerated by the Crusades. This brought Europeans into contact with Muslims and Byzantines. These people had preserved in their libraries the writings of the old Greek philosophers. In the 1100s, Christian scholars from Europe began visiting Muslim libraries in Spain. Few Western scholars knew Greek. Jewish scholars translated Arabic versions of works by Aristotle and other Greek writers into Latin. All at once, Europeans acquired a huge new body of knowledge. This included science, philosophy, law, mathematics, and other fields. In addition, the Crusaders learned from, and brought back to Europe, superior Muslim technology in ships, navigation, and weapons.

Aquinas and Medieval Philosophy Christian scholars were excited by the Greek writings. Could a Christian scholar use Aristotle's logical approach to truth and still keep faith with the Bible?

In the mid-1200s, the scholar **Thomas Aquinas** (uh·KWY·nuhs) argued that the most basic religious truths could be proved by logical argument. Between 1267 and 1273, Aquinas wrote the *Summa Theologica*. Aquinas's great work, influenced by Aristotle, combined ancient Greek thought with the Christian thought of his time. Aquinas and his fellow scholars who met at the great universities were known as schoolmen, or **scholastics**. The scholastics used their knowledge of Aristotle to debate many issues of their time. Their teachings on law and government influenced the thinking of western Europeans, particularly the English and French. Accordingly, they began to develop democratic institutions and traditions.

D. Possible Answer Aristotle's work influenced Arab thinkers such as Avicenna and Averroes, both of whom wrote commentaries on Aristotle, as well as the scholars at universities in medieval Europe.

THINK THROUGH HISTORY
D. Supporting Opinions Why do you suppose that Aristotle was called "the master of those who know" and "the philosopher" in medieval times?

SPOTLIGHT ON

Arab Scholars

A number of Islamic scholars had a great influence on European thought. The woodcut from 1584 above shows Ibn Sina, known in the West as Avicenna. He was a Persian philosopher, astronomer, poet, and physician. A book of his that greatly affected Western thought was *The Cure,* an interpretation of the philosophy of Aristotle. This work, translated into Latin, influenced the scholastics.

Another scholar was Ibn Rushd, known in the West as Averroes, who lived in Córdoba, Spain. He achieved fame for his commentaries on the works of Aristotle. These works were translated from Arabic into Latin and were used in universities throughout Christian Europe in the 1200s. Ibn Rushd's work greatly influenced Western thinkers.

Section 2 Assessment

1. TERMS & NAMES

Identify
- three-field system
- guild
- burgher
- vernacular
- Dante Alighieri
- Geoffrey Chaucer
- Thomas Aquinas
- scholastics

2. TAKING NOTES

Using a web diagram like the one below, show how medieval society changed between 1000 and 1300.

Changes in Medieval Society

3. ANALYZING CAUSES

What was the effect of towns on the feudal system?

THINK ABOUT
- where the new townsfolk came from
- the saying "Town air makes you free"
- the changes experienced by townspeople

4. ANALYZING THEMES

Economics How did guilds improve the quality of goods and business practices?

THINK ABOUT
- who enforced standards of quality
- who could become guild members

The Formation of Western Europe **351**

ANSWERS

1. TERMS & NAMES
three-field system, p. 348
guild, p. 349
burgher, p. 350
vernacular, p. 350
Dante Alighieri, p. 350
Geoffrey Chaucer, p. 350
Thomas Aquinas, p. 351
scholastics, p. 351

2. TAKING NOTES
Possible Responses:
Agriculture improves; population increases; towns grow; trade expands; universities arise.

3. ANALYZING CAUSES
Possible Response: Towns undermined the feudal system by offering former serfs and new town dwellers economic and social opportunities. These burghers worked together to secure their freedom from lords.

4. ANALYZING THEMES
Possible Response: Guilds set standards for quality, weights, measures, and prices for their goods, such as a loaf of bread. An individual had to master a craft before becoming a guild member.

TERMS & NAMES
• William the Conqueror
• Henry II
• Eleanor of Aquitaine
• Magna Carta
• parliament
• Philip II
• Louis IX

Section 3 Overview

OBJECTIVES

(1) To describe the various invaders who contributed to English culture.

(2) To explain how England's government took the first steps toward democracy.

(3) To describe the contributions of France's Capetian rulers.

SKILLBUILDER
• Interpreting charts, p. 355

CRITICAL THINKING
• Summarizing, pp. 353, 355
• Clarifying, p. 354
• Contrasting, p. 355

FOCUS
5-Minute Warm-Up

▶ **Making Inferences**
To help students understand something about English history, have them answer the following questions.

1. Read Connect to Today on page 353. What was Robin Hood's main goal as an outlaw?

2. What can you infer about the nature of King John from this text?

 WARM-UP TRANSPARENCY 14

OBJECTIVE ① INSTRUCT

England Absorbs Waves of Invaders

▶ **Key Ideas**
• For centuries, England is invaded by Germanic tribes, who are united by King Canute.
• The Battle of Hastings marks the beginning of Norman rule in England.

▣ **IN-DEPTH RESOURCES: UNIT 3**
Guided Reading, p. 72
History Makers: William the Conqueror, p. 84

▣ **ACCESS FOR STUDENTS ACQUIRING ENGLISH**
Guided Reading (Spanish), p. 143

3 England and France Develop

MAIN IDEA	WHY IT MATTERS NOW
As the kingdoms of England and France began to develop into nations, certain democratic traditions evolved.	Modern concepts of jury trials, common law, and legal rights developed during this period.

SETTING THE STAGE By the early 800s, small Anglo-Saxon kingdoms covered the former Roman province of Britain. In Europe, the decline of the Carolingian Empire in the 900s left a patchwork of feudal states controlled by local lords. Gradually, the rise of the burghers, the growth of towns and villages, and the breakup of the feudal system were leading to changes in government and the development of nations.

England Absorbs Waves of Invaders

For centuries, invaders from various regions in Europe landed on English shores. Many of them stayed, bringing their own ways and changing English culture.

William the Conqueror, from a 13th-century English history book.

Early Invasions In the 800s, Britain was battered by fierce raids of Danish Vikings. These invaders were so feared that a special prayer was said in churches: "God, deliver us from the fury of the Northmen." Only Alfred the Great, king from 871 to 899, managed to turn back the Viking invaders. Gradually he and his successors united the kingdom under one rule, calling it England—"land of the Angles." The Angles were one of the Germanic tribes that had invaded Britain.

In 1016, the Danish king Canute (kuh·NOOT) conquered England, molding Anglo-Saxons and Vikings into one people. In 1042, King Edward the Confessor, a descendant of the Anglo-Saxon Alfred the Great, took the throne. Edward died in January 1066 without an heir. A great struggle for the throne erupted, and that led to one last invasion.

The Norman Conquest The invader was William, duke of Normandy, who became known as **William the Conqueror.** Normandy is a region in the north of France that had been conquered by the Vikings. The Normans were descended from the Vikings, but they were French in language and in culture. As King Edward's cousin, William claimed the English crown and invaded England with a Norman army. William was ambitious, tough, and an imposing figure. An anonymous monk of the time described him:

A VOICE FROM THE PAST
[William was] great in body and strong, tall in stature but not ungainly. He was also temperate in eating and drinking. . . . In speech he was fluent and persuasive, being skilled at all times in making clear his will. If his voice was harsh, what he said was always suited to the occasion. . . .
ANONYMOUS MONK OF CAEN

William's rival was Harold Godwinson, the Anglo-Saxon who claimed the throne. And he was equally ambitious. On October 14, 1066, Normans and Saxons fought the battle that changed the course of English history—the Battle of Hastings. After Harold was killed by an arrow in his eye, the Normans won a decisive victory.

SECTION 3 RESOURCES

PRINT RESOURCES

 IN-DEPTH RESOURCES: UNIT 3
Guided Reading, p. 72
Primary Source: from the Magna Carta, p. 78
History Makers: William the Conqueror, p. 84
Connections Across Time and Cultures: New Beginnings for Democracy, p. 86

ACCESS FOR STUDENTS ACQUIRING ENGLISH
Guided Reading (Spanish), p. 143

FORMAL ASSESSMENT
 Section Quiz, p. 160

ALTERNATIVE ASSESSMENT BOOK

TECHNOLOGY RESOURCES

 CD-ROM
Electronic Library of Primary Sources

 INTERNET www.mlworldhistory.com

After his victory, William declared all England his personal property. The English lords who supported Harold lost their lands. William then granted fiefs to about 200 Norman lords who swore oaths of loyalty to him personally. In this way he laid the foundation for centralized government.

England's Evolving Government

William the Conqueror's descendants owned land both in Normandy and in England. The English King **Henry II** added to these holdings by marrying **Eleanor of Aquitaine.** She brought with her more lands from France. Over the next centuries English kings tried to achieve two goals. First, they wanted to hold and add on to their French lands. Second, they wanted to strengthen their own power over the nobles and the Church.

Monarchs, Nobles, and the Common Law Eleanor of Aquitaine was one of the most remarkable women in history. She was wife to two kings and mother to two kings. She married Louis VII of France when the Second Crusade began. In 1147, she accompanied him to the Holy Land. Shortly afterward their marriage was annulled. Eleanor then married Henry Plantagenet, who was to become Henry II of England. Their marriage produced four sons. Two became English kings—Richard the Lion-Hearted and John. The marriage also brought Henry a large territory in France called Aquitaine. He added Aquitaine to the lands in Normandy he had already inherited from William the Conqueror. Because Henry held lands in France, he was a vassal to the French king. But he was also a king in his own right.

Henry ruled England from 1154 to 1189. He strengthened the royal courts of justice by sending royal judges to every part of England at least once a year. They collected taxes, settled lawsuits, and punished crimes. Henry also introduced the use of the jury in English courts. A jury in medieval England was a group of loyal people—usually 12 neighbors of the accused—who answered a royal judge's questions about the facts of a case. Jury trials became a popular means of settling disputes. Only the king's courts were allowed to conduct them.

Over the centuries, case by case, the rulings of England's royal judges formed a unified body of law that became known as common law. Today these principles of English common law are the basis for law in many English-speaking countries, including the United States.

The Magna Carta Henry was succeeded first by his son Richard the Lion-Hearted, hero of the Third Crusade. When Richard died, his younger brother John took the throne. John ruled from 1199 to 1216. He failed as a military leader, earning the nickname John Softsword. John lost Normandy and all his lands in northern France to the French. This loss forced a confrontation with his own nobles.

Some of John's problems stemmed from his own character. He was mean to his subjects and tried to squeeze money out of them. John raised taxes to an all-time high to finance his wars. His nobles revolted. On June 15, 1215, they forced John to agree to the most celebrated document in English history, the **Magna Carta** (Great Charter). This document, drawn up by English nobles and reluctantly approved by King John, guaranteed certain basic political rights. The nobles wanted to safeguard their own feudal rights and limit the king's powers. In later years, however, English people of all classes argued that certain clauses in the Magna Carta applied to every citizen. Guaranteed rights included no taxation without representation, a jury trial, and the protection of the law. The Magna Carta guaranteed what are now considered basic legal rights both in England and in the United States.

CONNECT *to* TODAY

Robin Hood in the Movies
During the time of King Richard and King John, Robin Hood was said to live in Sherwood Forest with his band of merry men. According to the stories about him, he was an outlaw who robbed from the rich and gave to the poor. He attempted to remedy some of the injustices committed under King John.

There have been many film versions of the story of Robin Hood. Douglas Fairbanks starred in a silent *Robin Hood* (1922). Errol Flynn (above right) starred in *The Adventures of Robin Hood* (1938), a version celebrated for its rousing action. Disney released an animated *Robin Hood* in 1973. Kevin Costner starred in the popular *Robin Hood: Prince of Thieves* (1991).

Capetian Dynasty Rules France

Key Ideas

- The Capetian kings of France expand their territory and influence.
- King Philip II regains land from England, triples the land under his control, and establishes a central government.
- Louis IX strengthens the monarchy and the central government of France.
- Philip IV includes the Third Estate in the meeting of the Estates General, which helps increase royal power.

 ELECTRONIC LIBRARY OF PRIMARY SOURCES
from Calendar of Coroner's Rolls

CRITICAL THINKING ACTIVITY
CLASS TIME: 15 MINUTES

Drawing Conclusions
Ask students to look at the map of France in their Atlas on page 978. Have them put themselves in the Capetians' position. Why would they want to control Paris? How would control of Paris help them increase their power?

MORE ABOUT . . .
Philip II

Philip II harbored bitter feelings against the kings of England. During the last years of England's Henry II, Philip goaded Henry's sons into rebelling against their father. After the Crusades, Henry's successor, Richard the Lion-Hearted, was killed in a war against Philip. The French king finally received satisfaction after defeating Richard's successor, King John. The victory gave him control of most of England's land in France.

The Model Parliament Another important step toward democratic government resulted from Edward I's struggles to hang onto his last remaining French lands. In 1295, Edward needed to raise taxes for a war against the French. Edward summoned two burgesses (citizens of wealth and property) from every borough and two knights from every county to serve as a **parliament,** or legislative group. In November 1295, knights, burgesses, bishops, and lords met together at Westminster in London. This is now called the Model Parliament because its new makeup (commoners, or non-nobles, as well as lords) served as a model for later kings.

Over the next century, from 1300 to 1400, the king called the knights and burgesses whenever a new tax was needed. In Parliament, these two groups gradually formed an assembly of their own called the House of Commons. Nobles and bishops met separately as the House of Lords. Under Edward I, Parliament was in part a royal tool that weakened the great lords. As time went by, however, Parliament became strong. Like the Magna Carta, it provided a check on royal power.

Capetian Dynasty Rules France

The kings of France, like those of England, looked for ways of increasing their power. After the breakup of Charlemagne's empire, French counts and dukes ruled their lands independently under the feudal system. By the year 1000, France was divided into about 30 feudal territories. In 987, the last member of the Carolingian family—Louis the Sluggard—died. Hugh Capet (kuh·PAY), an undistinguished duke from the middle of France, succeeded him. The Capet family ruled only a small territory, but at its heart stood Paris. Hugh Capet began the Capetian dynasty of French kings that ruled France from 987 to 1328.

France Becomes a Separate Kingdom Hugh Capet, his son, and his grandson all were weak rulers, but time and geography favored the Capetians. Their territory, though small, sat astride important trade routes in northern France. For 200 years, Capetian kings tightened their grip on this strategic area. The power of the king gradually spread outward from Paris. Eventually, the growth of royal power would unite France.

Philip II Expands His Power One of the most powerful Capetians was **Philip II,** called Philip Augustus, who ruled from 1180 to 1223. As a child, Philip had watched his father lose land to King Henry II of England. When Philip became king at the age of 15, he set out to weaken the power of the English kings in France. Philip was crafty, unprincipled, and willing to do whatever was necessary to achieve his goals.

The coronation of Philip II in the cathedral of Reims.

Philip had little success against Henry II or Henry's son, Richard the Lion-Hearted. However, when King John seized the English throne, it was another matter. Philip earned the name Augustus (from the Latin word meaning "majestic"), probably because he greatly increased the territory of France. He seized Normandy from King John in 1204 and within two years had gained other territory. By the end of Philip's reign, he had tripled the lands under his direct control. For the first time, a French king had become more powerful than any of his vassals.

Philip Augustus not only wanted more land, he also wanted a stronger central government. He established royal officials called bailiffs. They were sent from Paris to every district in the kingdom to preside over the king's courts and collect the king's taxes.

Vocabulary
borough: a self-governing town.

THINK THROUGH HISTORY
B. Clarifying What was the Model Parliament and why did it come to be considered a model?
B. Possible Answer An assembly of citizens and knights from all over England called together by Edward I as a legislative group to raise taxes. It served as a model to later kings who wished to call together a representative assembly.

TEACHING OPTIONS **CONNECTIONS ACROSS TIME AND PLACE**

The English Parliament The Parliament of Great Britain is still composed of the House of Commons and the House of Lords, just as it was during the Middle Ages. However, the monarchy today no longer exercises real power. Ask students to research the structure of modern-day British government and prepare an organization chart, showing the components of the government. Have students include captions explaining the function of each component of government.

CONNECTIONS ACROSS THE CURRICULUM

Art: *Images of Medieval Monarchs* The picture of Philip II shown on this page is just one of many illustrations, statues, and carvings of medieval kings and queens. Encourage students to make a booklet of images of medieval monarchs mentioned in this chapter. Students may photocopy or trace the portraits from books and fill in the colors if they desire. Make sure students write a caption for each image, giving birth and death dates and listing two or three significant facts or achievements for each person.

The Development of England and France

England	France
• William the Conqueror, duke of Normandy, invades England in 1066.	• Hugh Capet establishes Capetian Dynasty in 987, which rules until 1328.
• Henry II (ruled 1154–1189) introduces use of the jury in English courts.	• Philip II (ruled 1180–1223) increases the territory of France.
• Under pressure from his nobles, King John agrees to Magna Carta in 1215.	• Louis IX (ruled 1226–1270) strengthens France's central government.
• Edward I calls Model Parliament in 1295.	• Philip IV (ruled 1285–1314) adds Third Estate to Estates-General.

SKILLBUILDER: Interpreting Charts
1. Which French duke conquered England?
2. Which English king and French king contributed to the growth of a representative assembly?

C. Answer The First Estate was made up of Church leaders; the Second Estate was made up of the great lords; the Third Estate was made up of commoners.

THINK THROUGH HISTORY
C. Summarizing What three estates made up the Estates-General?

Philip II's Heirs France's central government was made even stronger during the reign of Philip's grandson, **Louis IX,** who ruled from 1226 to 1270. Unlike his grandfather, Louis was pious and saintly. He was known as the ideal king. After his death, he was made a saint by the Catholic Church. Louis created a French appeals court, which could overturn the decisions of local courts. These royal courts of France strengthened the monarchy while weakening feudal ties.

In 1302, Philip IV, who ruled France from 1285 to 1314, was involved in a quarrel with the pope. The pope refused to allow priests to pay taxes to the king. Philip disputed the right of the pope to control Church affairs in his kingdom. As in England, the French king usually called a meeting of his lords and bishops when he needed support for his policies. To win wider support against the pope, Philip IV decided to include commoners in the meeting.

In France, the Church leaders were known as the First Estate, and the great lords as the Second Estate. The commoners that Philip invited to participate in the council became known as the Third Estate. The whole meeting was called the Estates-General.

Like the English Parliament in its early years, the Estates-General helped to increase royal power against the nobility. Unlike Parliament, however, the Estates-General never became an independent force that limited the king's power. However, centuries later, the Third Estate would be the key to overthrowing the French monarchy. Now, in the 14th century, there was much turmoil. This included religious disputes, plague, and war. This disorder threatened the fragile achievements of England and France in beginning to establish a democratic tradition.

Section 3 Assessment

1. TERMS & NAMES
Identify
- William the Conqueror
- Henry II
- Eleanor of Aquitaine
- Magna Carta
- parliament
- Philip II
- Louis IX

2. TAKING NOTES
Using a graphic, name each major step toward a democratic government and describe why it was important. Add steps as needed.

(Step)
(Description)

Which of the steps are similar to U.S. practices? Explain.

3. CONTRASTING
Contrast the way in which England and France began developing as nations.

THINK ABOUT
- the character of William, duke of Normandy, versus the character of Hugh Capet
- the rise of the Normans to power in England
- the rise of the Capetians to power in France

4. THEME ACTIVITY
Power and Authority
Imagine that you are an adviser to the king. Write him a letter in which you argue for or against including commoners in the Parliament or Estates-General. Tell the king the advantages and disadvantages of including commoners in the group.

The Formation of Western Europe **355**

ANSWERS

1. TERMS & NAMES
William the Conqueror, p. 352
Henry II, p. 353
Eleanor of Aquitaine, p. 353
Magna Carta, p. 353
parliament, p. 354
Philip II, p. 354
Louis IX, p. 355

2. TAKING NOTES
Possible Responses: Centralized government—policies of English and French kings applied to all; Courts—led to a unified body of law in England and an appeals court in France; Magna Carta— guaranteed basic rights; Parliament/Estates General—

included commoners/middle class in making laws.

3. CONTRASTING
Possible Response: William led an invasion of England in 1066 and granted fiefs to 200 Norman lords. Although Hugh Capet was a weak ruler, Capetians gradually consolidated their power.

4. THEME ACTIVITY
Standards for evaluation: Letters should . . .
- clearly state arguments for or against including commoners.
- list advantages or disadvantages of commoners' participation

History from Visuals

The Development of England and France

Interpreting the Chart Have students notice what span of time this chart covers. Which French and English kings were contemporaries? *Henry II and Philip II; King John and Philip II; Edward I and Philip IV*

Extension Activity Ask students to read more about one of the kings and to write a brief report giving some interesting anecdotes about the monarch.

SKILLBUILDER Answers
1. William the Conqueror
2. Edward I and Philip IV

ASSESS & RETEACH

Section 3 Assessment
Have students work in small groups to discuss the questions and review one another's responses.

FORMAL ASSESSMENT
Section Quiz, p. 160

Reteaching Activity
CLASS TIME: 15 MINUTES

If students have not already constructed the diagram for question 2, have them do so. Then discuss the charts in class, making sure students understand the significance of each step.

CLOSE ACTIVITY

CLASS TIME: 35 MINUTES

Role-Playing
Assign pairs of students either the name of someone mentioned in the section or an object or institution, such as the Magna Carta or the Estates General. Each pair must write a statement of 25 words or less, describing who they are and why they are important to French and English history. Have students read their statements aloud and let the rest of the class guess who or what they are.

Teacher's Edition **355**

OBJECTIVES

1. To identify the problems faced by the Church during the 1300s and early 1400s.

2. To describe the bubonic plague and its effects on Europe.

3. To describe the Hundred Years' War and its impact.

SKILLBUILDER

- Interpreting charts, p. 359

CRITICAL THINKING

- Contrasting, p. 357
- Hypothesizing, p. 358
- Comparing, p. 358
- Recognizing effects, pp. 359, 361
- Identifying problems, p. 361
- Analyzing themes, p. 361

FOCUS

5-Minute Warm-Up

▶ **Interpreting Maps**
Answering the following questions will help students understand the effects of the bubonic plague.

1. Study the map on page 359. How many states would still be populated if the plague struck?

2. How would such a disaster affect trade between the eastern and western parts of the country?

 WARM-UP TRANSPARENCY 14

OBJECTIVE ① INSTRUCT

A Church Divided

▶ **Key Ideas**
- Philip IV sets the rule of kings above papal rule.
- The papacy's move from Rome to Avignon, France, eventually leads to Great Schism.
- Scholars who criticize Church excesses are dealt with harshly.

IN-DEPTH RESOURCES: UNIT 3
Guided Reading, p. 73

ACCESS FOR STUDENTS ACQUIRING ENGLISH
Guided Reading (Spanish), p. 144

TERMS & NAMES
- Avignon
- Great Schism
- John Wycliffe
- Jan Hus
- bubonic plague
- Hundred Years' War
- Joan of Arc

4 A Century of Turmoil

MAIN IDEA	WHY IT MATTERS NOW
During the 1300s, Europe was torn apart by religious strife, the bubonic plague, and the Hundred Years' War.	Events of the 1300s led to a change in attitudes toward religion and the state, a change reflected in modern attitudes.

SETTING THE STAGE At the turn of the century between the 1200s and 1300s, church and state seemed in good shape, but trouble was brewing. The Church seemed to be thriving. Ideals of fuller political representation seemed to be developing in France and England. However, the 1300s were filled with disasters, both natural and manmade. By the end of the century, the medieval way of life was beginning to disappear.

A Church Divided

At the beginning of the 1300s, the papacy seemed in some ways still strong. Soon, however, both pope and Church were in desperate trouble.

Pope and King Collide The pope in 1300 was an able but stubborn Italian. Pope Boniface VIII attempted to enforce papal authority on kings as previous popes had. When King Philip IV of France asserted his authority over French bishops, Boniface responded with a papal bull (an official document issued by the pope). It stated, "We declare, state, and define that subjection to the Roman Pontiff is absolutely necessary for the salvation of every human creature." In short, kings must always obey popes. Philip merely sneered at this bull. In fact one of Philip's ministers is said to have remarked that "my master's sword is made of steel, the pope's is made of [words]." Instead of obeying the pope, in September 1303 Philip had him held prisoner. The king planned to bring him to France for trial. The pope was rescued, but the elderly Boniface died a month later. Never again would a pope be able to force monarchs to obey him.

Boniface VIII served as pope from 1294 to 1303. This woodcut of Boniface was done in Venice in 1592.

Vocabulary
Pontiff: the pope.

Avignon and the Great Schism While Philip IV failed to keep Pope Boniface captive, in 1305 he persuaded the College of Cardinals to choose a French archbishop as the new pope. Clement V, the selected pope, shortly moved from Rome to the city of **Avignon** (av·vee·NYAWN) in France. Popes would live there for the next 67 years.

The move to Avignon badly weakened the Church. When reformers finally tried to move the papacy back to Rome, however, the result was even worse. In 1378, Pope Gregory XI died while visiting Rome. The College of Cardinals then met in Rome to choose a successor. As they deliberated, they could hear a mob outside screaming, "A Roman, a Roman, we want a Roman for pope, or at least an Italian!" Finally, the cardinals announced to the crowd that an Italian had been chosen: Pope Urban VI. Many cardinals regretted their choice almost immediately. Urban VI's passion for reform and his arrogant personality caused French cardinals to elect another pope a few months later. They chose Robert of Geneva, who spoke French. He took the name Clement VII.

Background
People outside France concluded that the Avignon popes were pawns of the French kings. They believed that the Church was held captive in Avignon just as, centuries before, the Jews had been held captive in Babylon. This period in Church history came to be called the Babylonian Captivity.

SECTION 4 RESOURCES

PRINT RESOURCES

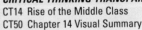 **IN-DEPTH RESOURCES: UNIT 3**
Guided Reading, p. 73
Skillbuilder Practice: Recognizing Effects, p. 74
Primary Source: Plague in Siena, p. 79; Joan of Arc's Trial, p. 80
History Makers: Joan of Arc, p. 85

ACCESS FOR STUDENTS ACQUIRING ENGLISH
Guided Reading (Spanish), p. 144
Skillbuilder Practice: (Spanish), p. 145

FORMAL ASSESSMENT
Section Quiz, p. 161

TECHNOLOGY RESOURCES

 CRITICAL THINKING TRANSPARENCIES
CT14 Rise of the Middle Class
CT50 Chapter 14 Visual Summary

CD-ROM
Battles of the World
Electronic Library of Primary Sources

 VIDEO *Patterns of Interaction:* The Spread of Epidemic Disease

INTERNET www.mlworldhistory.com

Now there were two popes. Each declared the other to be a false pope, excommunicating his rival. The French pope lived in Avignon, while the Italian pope lived in Rome. This began the split in the Church known as the **Great Schism** (SIHZ-uhm), or division.

The Council of Constance had as its major task to end the Great Schism by choosing a new pope. In 1414, when the Council of Constance began its meetings, there were a total of three popes: the Avignon pope, the Roman pope, and a third pope elected by an earlier council at Pisa. With the help of the Holy Roman Emperor, the council forced all three popes to resign. In 1417, the council chose a new pope, Martin V, ending the Great Schism.

A Scholarly Challenge to Church Authority The papacy was further challenged in the late 1300s and early 1400s by two professors. One was an Englishman named **John Wycliffe** (WIHK-lihf). He preached that Jesus Christ, not the pope, was the true head of the Church. He was much offended by the worldliness and wealth many clergy displayed. The pope himself, as Wycliffe noted, lived in shameful luxury, serving dinner on gold and silver plates to guests dressed in costly furs. Wycliffe believed that the clergy should own no land or wealth.

Wycliffe also taught that the Bible alone—not the pope—was the final authority for Christian life. He helped spread this idea by inspiring an English translation of the New Testament of the Bible, which at the time was available only in French or Latin. Wycliffe's radical ideas were discussed widely throughout England. Influenced by Wycliffe's writings, **Jan Hus,** a professor in Bohemia (now part of the Czech Republic), taught that the authority of the Bible was higher than that of the pope. Hus was excommunicated in 1412. In 1414, the German emperor Sigismund arranged the Council of Constance. He urged Hus to attend and even gave him safe conduct. When Hus arrived at the meeting, however, he was seized and tried as a heretic, then burned at the stake in 1415.

This scene from a 15th-century book shows Jan Hus being burned at the stake in 1415.

The Bubonic Plague Strikes

Artists of the 1300s depicted death as the Grim Reaper, a skeleton on horseback whose scythe cut people down. The image is appropriate—approximately one-third of the population of Europe died of the deadly disease known as the **bubonic plague.**

Origins and Symptoms of the Plague The plague began in Asia. Traveling the trade lanes, it infected most of Asia and the Muslim world. Inevitably it reached Europe. In 1347, a fleet of Genoese merchant ships arrived in Sicily carrying a dread cargo. This was the disease that became known as the Black Death. It got the name because of the purplish or blackish spots it produced on the skin. The disease swept through Italy. From there it followed trade routes to France, Germany, England, and other parts of Europe.

Unlike catastrophes that pull communities together, this epidemic was so terrifying that it ripped apart the very fabric of society. Giovanni Boccaccio, an Italian writer of the time, described its effect:

A VOICE FROM THE PAST
This scourge had implanted so great a terror in the hearts of men and women that brothers abandoned brothers, uncles their nephews, sisters their brothers, and in many cases wives deserted their husbands. But even worse, . . . fathers and mothers refused to nurse and assist their own children.

GIOVANNI BOCCACCIO, *The Decameron*

The Formation of Western Europe **357**

THINK THROUGH HISTORY
A. Contrasting
What was the true source of religious authority, according to the different beliefs of the time?
A. Possible Answer
There was confusion and disagreement about where true religious authority resided. Some thought it resided with the pope, others with a Church council, and still others with the Bible alone.

MORE ABOUT . . .
Urban VI

Urban VI offended many cardinals by threatening to excommunicate them. When he was told that by law he had to warn a cardinal three times before he could excommunicate the person, the pope answered, "I can do anything, if it be my will and judgment." Many scholars believe that Urban's offensive and irrational behavior was a sign of mental illness.

OBJECTIVE 2 INSTRUCT

The Bubonic Plague Strikes

▶ *Key Ideas*
• The bubonic plague begins in Asia and sweeps across Europe, killing nearly one-fourth of the population.
• Every few years, the plague further reduces population and disrupts society.
• Lack of workers breaks down the manorial system.
• Many people become disillusioned with the Church, pessimistic about the future, or preoccupied with pleasure.

IN-DEPTH RESOURCES: UNIT 3
Primary Source: Plague in Siena, p. 79

MORE ABOUT . . .
Superstitions About the Plague

In an age that still believed that the planets influenced human affairs, doctors at the University of Paris claimed that the plague was caused by the unfavorable alignment of certain planets. Others believed that the plague was carried by "poisonous vapors," released by disastrous earthquakes in Asia, that had drifted over Europe.

TEACHING OPTIONS

CONNECTIONS ACROSS THE CURRICULUM

Biology: The Bubonic Bacteria
The bacteria that cause bubonic plague, *Yersinia pestis,* infect victims through a complex process—they live in the bellies of the fleas that live on rats and other rodents. The fleas bite humans, passing the bacteria on.

In a more serious form of plague, the pneumonic plague, the bacteria can be airborne, passing from victim to victim through coughing or sneezing. In the deadliest form, septicemic plague, the bacteria attack the victim's bloodstream. Ask students to research these varieties of plague, all of which were present during the bubonic plague years, and give a brief description of how each affects its victims.

EXPLORING PRIMARY SOURCES

A Voice from the Past Giovanni Boccaccio wrote his most famous work, *The Decameron,* which is quoted on this page, between about 1349 and 1353. The book is composed of 100 stories told by ten characters—three young men and seven young women—who flee to the country to escape the bubonic plague raging in Florence.

In the Introduction to *The Decameron,* Boccaccio writes his eyewitness account of how the plague affected Florence. Ask students to read the Introduction to *The Decameron,* keeping a reading journal with their responses to Boccaccio's descriptions. Students can share their journals in class.

Teacher's Edition 357

Epidemic Disease

The victims of this terrible plague developed a raging fever together with black swellings on their neck and joints. The death rate was appalling. Victims were often buried in mass graves, and whole villages emptied as people died or fled in fear. Gifted and talented students might want to read the primary source on this topic.

IN-DEPTH RESOURCES: UNIT 3
Primary Source: from Plague in Siena, p. 79

MORE ABOUT . . .
The Plague and the Flagellants
Many people believed the plague was God's punishment for the sins of humankind. A group known as the Flagellants arose, their purpose being to atone for their own and others' sins. Bands of Flagellants traveled from town to town, beating themselves with whips studded with iron tips, often ripping the flesh from their bare backs.

Viewing the Video
Show *The Spread of Epidemic Disease: Bubonic Plague and Smallpox* to demonstrate how interaction between peoples can spread catastrophic disease—a pattern repeated in history.

• The first segment of the video explores the origins and effects of bubonic plague in Europe in the 1400s.

• The second segment investigates the impact of smallpox on the Americas, starting in the early 1500s.

Using the Teacher's Resource Book as a guide, discuss the historical impact of epidemic diseases; compare the outbreaks explored in the video with recent epidemics; and enrich the lesson with primary-source and visual-literacy activities included in the resource book.

PATTERNS OF INTERACTION
The Spread of Epidemic Disease: Bubonic Plague and Smallpox
Videocassette: Tape 2

The Bubonic Plague

The bubonic plague, or Black Death, was a killer disease that swept repeatedly through many areas of the world. It wiped out two-thirds of the population in some areas of China, destroyed populations of Muslim towns in Southwest Asia, and then decimated a third of the European population.

We see death coming into our midst like black smoke...
—Welsh poet Ieuan Gethin in 1349

Detail of *The Plague* by Micco Spadaro, mid-1600s

The Plague in the 14th Century

Death Toll, 1300s		KEY ☠ = 4 million
Western Europe	☠☠☠☠☠	20–25 million
Southwest Asia	☠	4 million
China	☠☠☠☠☠☠☠☠☠	35 million

Route of the Plague

The horse-riding Mongols likely carried infected fleas and rats in their food supplies as they swooped into China.

In 1345–46, a Mongol army besieged Kaffa, on the Black Sea. A year later, Italian merchants who lived there fled back to Italy, unknowingly bringing the plague with them.

The disease came with merchants along the trade routes of Asia to all parts of southern Asia, southwest Asia, and eventually Africa.

Black rats carried fleas from one area to another—fleas that were infested with a bacillus called *Yersinia pestis*. In those days, people did not bathe—and almost all had fleas and lice. In addition, medieval people threw their garbage and sewage into the streets. These unsanitary streets became breeding grounds for more rats. The fleas carried by rats leapt from person to person, thus spreading the bubonic plague with incredible speed.

Symptoms
• Painful swellings called buboes (BOO·bohz) in the lymph nodes, particularly those in the armpits and groin
• Sometimes purplish or blackish spots on the skin
• Extremely high fever, chills, delirium, and in most cases, death

Patterns of Interaction
The bubonic plague was just one of the several lethal diseases that have swept from one society to another throughout history. Such diseases as smallpox and influenza have wiped out huge numbers of people, sometimes—as with the Aztecs—virtually destroying civilizations. The spread of disease has been a physical and very tragic result of cultures' interacting with one another across place and time.

VIDEO *The Spread of Epidemic Disease: Bubonic Plague and Smallpox*

358 Chapter 14

Connect to History
Hypothesizing Had people known the cause of the bubonic plague, what might they have done to slow its spread?
SEE SKILLBUILDER HANDBOOK, PAGE 1000

Connect to Today
Comparing What diseases of today might be compared to the bubonic plague? Why?

Connect to History
Hypothesizing
Possible Answers: They might have bathed, fumigated their homes and clothing, killed rats and fleas, used better methods of sanitation, quarantined victims, prevented people from leaving towns and spreading the disease, and burned all contaminated items.

Connect to Today
Comparing
Possible Answers: Tell students to think of diseases they have read or heard about in the news, such as the Ebola virus. They can also research the topic on the Internet or INFOTRAC.

Tell them that other potentially deadly diseases include influenza, drug-resistant tuberculosis (which is highly contagious), and malaria (which is spread by mosquitoes). Recent strains of these diseases are returning as major health threats. Because people are traveling from one continent to another in unprecedented numbers, new diseases can spread rapidly.

Frightened people looked around for a scapegoat. They found one in the Jews, who were blamed for bringing on the plague by poisoning the wells. All over Europe, Jews were driven from their homes or, worse, massacred.

The bubonic plague took about four years to reach almost every corner of Europe. In any given community, approximately three-quarters of those who caught the disease died. Before the bubonic plague ran its course, it killed almost 25 million Europeans and many more millions in Asia and North Africa.

Effects of the Plague The plague returned every few years, though it never struck as severely as in the first outbreak. However, the periodic attacks further reduced the population.

The economic effects of the plague were enormous. Town populations fell. Trade declined. Prices rose. Fewer people meant that workers were scarce everywhere. Farmland was abandoned or used to pasture sheep, which required less labor. Serfs had often been unpaid or poorly paid for their labor. They left the manor in search of better wages. The old manorial system began to crumble. Nobles fiercely resisted peasant demands for higher wages, causing peasant revolts in England, France, Italy, and Belgium.

The Church suffered a loss of prestige when its prayers and penances failed to stop the onslaught of the bubonic plague. In addition, many clergy deserted their flocks or charged high fees to perform services for the dying.

Many people who saw how abruptly life could end became pessimistic about life itself, fearing the future. As one poet of the time wrote, "Happy is he who has no children." Art and literature of the time reflect an unusual awareness of death. On the other hand, many people became occupied with pleasure and self-indulgence. They displayed the attitude of "Eat, drink, and be merry, for tomorrow you may die."

The bubonic plague and its aftermath disrupted medieval society, hastening changes that were already in the making. The society of the Middle Ages was collapsing. The century of war between England and France was that society's final death struggle.

THINK THROUGH HISTORY
B. Recognizing Effects What were some of the effects of the plague?
B. Possible Answers Population declined; workers scarce; farmland abandoned; serfs sought higher wages; manor system crumbled; nobles resisted demands for higher wages; Church lost prestige; pessimism increased.

The Hundred Years' War

When the last Capetian king died without a successor, England's Edward III claimed the right to the French throne as grandson of Philip IV. The war that Edward III launched for that throne continued on and off from 1337 to 1453. It became known as the **Hundred Years' War** and added to the century's miseries. The war was a seesaw affair, fought on French soil. Victory passed back and forth between the two countries. Finally, between 1421 and 1453, the French rallied and drove the English out of France entirely, except for the port city of Calais.

The Battle of Crécy While the French eventually won the war, the English won three important battles in France. The first and most spectacular was the Battle of Crécy (KREHS·ee). Some of the combatants were still operating under medieval ideals of chivalry. They were anxious to perform noble deeds in war. They looked with contempt on the common foot soldiers and archers who fought alongside them. However, in the Battle of Crécy, it was the English archers who won the day.

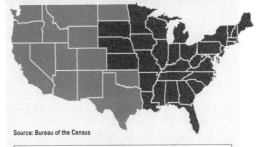

If the Plague Struck America Today

The bubonic plague reportedly wiped out about one-third of Europe's population in the 1300s. In the United States today, a one-third death toll would equal nearly 79 million people, or the number living in the states represented by the color ▨ .

Source: Bureau of the Census

SKILLBUILDER: Interpreting Charts
1. *How many states on the chart would have lost their entire population to the plague?*
2. *How might the chart help explain why many Europeans thought the world was ending?*

History from Visuals

If the Plague Struck America Today

Interpreting the Chart Have students identify what each color represents. Point out that the colored area represents the equivalent of 33% of the population. Mention that a plague would not be confined only to those states colored on the chart.

Extension Activity Have students stand up and count off by threes. Ask all the "one's" to sit down. Explain to the class that had the plague struck their school, the "fallen" students would represent the number killed by the disease in their class.

SKILLBUILDER Answers
1. 14
2. Possible Response: With such a large proportion of one's country falling to the plague, it would be easy to believe the world was ending.

OBJECTIVE ③ INSTRUCT

The Hundred Years' War

▶ *Key Ideas*
• The Hundred Years' War pits France against England in a struggle for land.
• The English longbow is used to defeat the French and spells the end of chivalrous warfare.
• Joan of Arc leads France to victory but is captured and executed by the English.
• The Hundred Years' War gives rise to nationalism, empowers the French king and the English Parliament, and marks the end of the Middle Ages.

CRITICAL THINKING TRANSPARENCIES
CT14 Rise of the Middle Class

The Formation of Western Europe **359**

Explaining the Skill: Historians want to know not only why something happened in the past but also what effect it had on subsequent events to help them see how events are related.

Applying the Skill: Have students look over their responses to the Think Through History question on this page. Ask them to diagram their answers in a cause-and-effect flow chart:

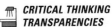

Cause: bubonic plague → Effect: reduced population → Effect: farmland abandoned

Effect: serfs sought higher wages → Effect: manor system crumbled

Effect: Church lost prestige → Effect: pessimism rose

IN-DEPTH RESOURCES: UNIT 3
Skillbuilder Practice: Recognizing Effects, p. 74

SPOTLIGHT On
The Longbow

For a description of a typical English longbowman, have students read about the knight's yeoman in the General Prologue to *The Canterbury Tales*.

MORE ABOUT . . .
The Battle of Agincourt

On the morning of the battle, the English archers hammered long pointed stakes at an angle into the ground, forming a barrier that could penetrate the chest of a charging warhorse.

When the French armies charged, the English archers let fly a cloud of arrows that reached nearly 100 feet high, then plummeted down on the armor-clad French. As the arrows reached their mark, there was a loud banging and clanking of arrows off the steel armor and screams from frightened and wounded horses.

ELECTRONIC LIBRARY OF PRIMARY SOURCES
from "The Battle of Agincourt"

BATTLES OF THE WORLD
The Battle of Agincourt

Important Events in the Middle Ages

| 987 Capetian Dynasty begins in France | 1096 First Crusade begins | 1189 Third Crusade begins | 1273 Thomas Aquinas completes *Summa Theologica* | 1302 First meeting of Estates-General | 1378 The Great Schism begins | 1492 Muslims and Jews driven out of Spain Columbus lands in America |

THE HUNDRED YEARS' WAR

| 1066 Norman conquest of England | 1147 Second Crusade begins | 1215 Magna Carta signed | 1295 Model Parliament meets | 1347 Bubonic plague devastates Europe | 1429 Joan of Arc leads the French army that lifts the siege of Orléans |

English and French forces met near the town of Crécy on August 26, 1346. English men-at-arms and their longbowmen were outnumbered by a French army three times its size, including armored knights and a force of archers with crossbows. Mounted on warhorses and protected by heavy armor, French knights believed themselves invincible and attacked.

Meanwhile, English longbowmen let fly thousands of arrows at the oncoming French. The crossbowmen, out of range and peppered with English arrows, retreated in panic. A French noble, seeing the crossbowmen fleeing, shouted, "Slay these rascals who get in our way!" The knights trampled their own archers in an effort to cut a path through them. English longbowmen sent volley after volley of deadly arrows. They unhorsed knights who then lay helplessly on the ground in their heavy armor. Then, using long knives, the English foot soldiers attacked, slaughtering the French. At the end of the day, more than a third of the French force lay dead. Among them were some of the most honored in chivalry. The longbow, not chivalry, had won the day.

Background
The English archers aimed for the horses' unprotected rumps. Wounded horses fell, causing chaos.

SPOTLIGHT On

The Longbow

The bow and arrow reached one of its peaks from the 1200s through the early 1400s with the longbow. The string of the "short bow" was drawn back to the chest. The longbow was as tall as a man, or taller, and the string was pulled back to the archer's ear. A six-foot-tall man might have a bow seven feet tall.

English archers usually carried a case with extra bowstrings and a sheaf of 24 arrows with them into battle. The arrows were balanced in flight by feathers. The arrows were dangerous at a range of 300 yards. They were absolutely fatal within 100 yards. Writers of the time say that the sound of several thousand arrows whistling through the air was terrifying.

Poitiers and Agincourt The English repeated their victory ten years later at the Battle of Poitiers (pwah·TYAY). Near the town of Poitiers, France, the French believed they had caught the English at a disadvantage. When the overconfident knights charged on foot, English longbowmen greeted them with volleys of arrows so thick that the air grew dark. French knights were helpless. The French king John and his son Philip were captured and held for ransom.

The third English victory, the Battle of Agincourt (AJ·ihn·KAWRT), took place in 1415. Again the English army was outnumbered, with their 6,000 troops against a French force of 20,000 to 30,000. Led by King Henry V, English archers again won a victory over the heavily armored French knights. The success of the longbow in these battles spelled doom for chivalric warfare. The mounted, heavily armored medieval knight was soon to become extinct.

Joan of Arc Five years after Agincourt, the French and English signed a treaty stating that Henry V would inherit the French crown at the death of the French king Charles VI. The French had lost hope. Then, in 1429, a teenage French peasant girl named **Joan of Arc** felt moved by God to rescue France from its English conquerors. She believed that heavenly voices spoke to her. They told her to drive the English out of France and give the French crown to France's true king, Charles VI's son.

Joan convinced Charles that she was sincere. On May 7, 1429, Joan led the French army into battle against an English fort that blocked the roads to Orléans. The English had been besieging the city for over six months. Without help, the city's

360 Chapter 14

Task: Students will research and create a pictorial display of the weapons and battle gear used during the Hundred Years' War.

Purpose: To understand how warfare was conducted during the Hundred Years' War.

Activity: Groups of students will research weapons and battle gear used during the Hundred Years' War. They will then draw or photocopy pictures and write captions for each item, describing

how it was used and what role it played in changing warfare. Suggested sources: *Armor* by Charlotte Yue (Boston: Houghton Mifflin, 1994); *An Historical Guide to Arms and Armor* (New York: Facts on File, 1991); *Knights in Shining Armor* by Gail Gibbons (Boston: Little Brown, 1995).

 Building a Portfolio: Students who wish to add a copy of their display should attach a statement describing their contribution to the work.

ALTERNATIVE ASSESSMENT BOOK
Standards for Evaluating a Cooperative Activity

Standards for Evaluation
Pictorial displays should . . .

- show a variety of medieval weapons used in the Hundred Years' War
- include captions that describe the weapons, how they were used, and how they changed warfare

defenders could not hold out much longer. The English forts had to be taken in order to lift the siege. It was a hard-fought battle for both sides, and the French finally retreated in despair. But suddenly, Joan and a few soldiers charged back toward the fort. The entire French army stormed after her. The siege of Orléans was broken. Joan of Arc guided the French onto the path of victory.

After that victory, Joan persuaded Charles to go with her to Reims. There he was crowned king on July 17, 1429. Joan helped turn the tide for France. In 1430, she was captured in battle by the Burgundians, England's allies. They turned her over to the English. The English, in turn, handed her over to Church authorities to stand trial. Although the French king Charles VII owed his crown to Joan, he did nothing to rescue her. Condemned as a witch and a heretic because of her claim to hear voices, Joan was tied to a stake and burned to death on May 30, 1431.

The Impact of the Hundred Years' War The long, exhausting war finally ended in 1453, with the English left with only the French port of Calais. For France, the war—despite its terrible costs in lives, property, and money—ultimately raised the power and prestige of the French monarch. Nonetheless, it took a long time for some regions in France to recover.

The war gave birth in both countries to a feeling of nationalism. No longer did people think of the king as simply a feudal lord, but as a national leader fighting for the glory of the country.

Following the Hundred Years' War, the English suffered a period of internal turmoil known as the War of the Roses, in which two noble houses fought for the throne. Nevertheless, this war was responsible for strengthening the English Parliament. Edward III's constant need for money to finance the war led him to call Parliament as many as 27 times, asking for new taxes. Gradually, Parliament's "power of the purse" became firmly established, sowing another seed of democracy.

The end of the Hundred Years' War in 1453 is considered by some historians as the end of the Middle Ages. The twin pillars of the medieval world—intense religious devotion and the code of chivalry—both crumbled. The Age of Faith died a slow death. This death was caused by the Great Schism, the scandalous display of wealth by the Church, and the discrediting of the Church during the bubonic plague. The Age of Chivalry died on the battlefields of Crécy, Poitiers, and Agincourt.

HISTORY MAKERS

JOAN OF ARC
1412?–1431

When Joan was just 13 she began to have visions and hear what she believed were voices of the saints urging her to help Charles VII drive the English from France. When helping to lift the English siege of Orléans, she said:

You, men of England, who have no right in the kingdom of France, the King of Heaven sends the order through me, Joan the Maid, to return to your own country.

In 1430, she was turned over to a Church court for trial. Because of her claim to hear voices, Joan was tried for witchcraft and heresy. In truth, her trial was more political than religious. The English were embarrassed that a teenage girl had defeated them.

HISTORY MAKERS
Joan of Arc

Although illiterate, Joan displayed remarkable powers, which some believe included clairvoyance—that is, the ability to know future or distant events without using one's normal five senses. Ask students to read more about Joan of Arc and report to the class how she demonstrated her unusual powers. Gifted and talented students might wish to read the primary source for this section.

IN-DEPTH RESOURCES: UNIT 3
Primary source: Joan of Arc's Trial, p. 80
History Makers: Joan of Arc, p. 85

ASSESS & RETEACH

Section 4 Assessment
Divide the questions among groups of students, and have them present their answers orally.

FORMAL ASSESSMENT
Section Quiz, p. 161

Reteaching Activity
CLASS TIME: 20 MINUTES

Ask students to list ways that European history might have been different if the Church had not split, the bubonic plague had been stopped at Venice, and England had won the Hundred Years' War.

CRITICAL THINKING TRANSPARENCIES
CT50 Chapter 14 Visual Summary

CLOSE ACTIVITY

CLASS TIME: 30 MINUTES

Recognizing Causes and Effects
On a blank sheet of paper, have students write down the main causes and effects from question 2, putting each one on a separate line. Then have students cut or tear the lines apart. Working in small groups, they will shuffle the strips of paper, then reassemble them in the correct order. Discuss the major changes in medieval society after the Hundred Years' War.

Section 4 Assessment

1. TERMS & NAMES

Identify
- Avignon
- Great Schism
- John Wycliffe
- Jan Hus
- bubonic plague
- Hundred Years' War
- Joan of Arc

2. TAKING NOTES

Using a chart like the one below, identify the main cause and the long-term effect of the three events.

	Main Cause	Long-Term Effect
Split in Church		
Bubonic plague		
Hundred Years' War		

Which event had some positive economic effects? Explain.

3. IDENTIFYING PROBLEMS

What problems did survivors face after the bubonic plague swept through their town?

THINK ABOUT
- the number of dead
- the social, political, and economic chaos

4. ANALYZING THEMES

Religious and Ethical Systems Do you think John Wycliffe and Jan Hus posed a real threat to the Church? Why or why not?

THINK ABOUT
- the two men's ideas
- the condition of the Church at the time

The Formation of Western Europe **361**

Teacher's Edition **361**

TERMS & NAMES

1. Crusade, p. 343
2. Reconquista, p. 346
3. Inquisition, p. 346
4. three-field system, p. 348
5. scholastics, p. 351
6. Magna Carta, p. 353
7. parliament, p. 354
8. Great Schism, p. 357
9. bubonic plague, p. 357
10. Hundred Years' War, p. 359

REVIEW QUESTIONS

11. By marrying, village priests went against Church rulings. By selling Church positions (simony), bishops seemed to be using their power to gain wealth at the expense of the Church. By appointing bishops, kings gained undue influence over the Church.

12. The main goal was to gain control of the Holy Land.

13. In the short term, productivity increased; in the longer term, population increased (leading to the growth of towns and related effects).

14. Towns drew serfs away from the manor; the new middle class challenged feudal authority.

15. Before the Church relaxed its rules on usury, Jews served as moneylenders, allowing merchants to finance purchases. After the crusades, Christian trade with Muslims contributed to Europe's financial revolution.

16. He claimed all of England as his personal property. Then he granted fiefs to about 200 loyal Norman lords, assuring central control of England.

17. King John raised taxes to an all-time high to pay for wars in which he lost enormous amounts of territory. His nobles revolted and forced him to grant them basic political rights as listed in the Magna Carta.

18. Wycliffe believed that Jesus Christ, not the pope, was head of the Church; he was offended by the worldliness and wealth of the clergy; the Bible was the final authority for Christian life.

19. The Church lost prestige when its prayers and penances failed to stop the plague and when priests abandoned their duties out of fear. People began looking for ways to establish an individual relationship with God.

20. Knights proved to be no match for longbowmen, whose arrow barrages won several victories during the war.

Chapter ⑭ Assessment

TERMS & NAMES

Briefly explain the importance of each of the following to western Europe during the medieval period.

1. Crusade
2. Reconquista
3. Inquisition
4. three-field system
5. scholastics
6. Magna Carta
7. parliament
8. Great Schism
9. bubonic plague
10. Hundred Years' War

Interact *with* History

On page 340, you thought about whether or not you would join a Crusade before completely understanding what the Crusades were and what sort of advantages and sacrifices they entailed. Now that you've read the chapter, reexamine whether or not you would join a Crusade. What might a Crusader bring home from his travels? What problems might a Crusader encounter on his adventures? Discuss your opinions with a small group.

REVIEW QUESTIONS

SECTION 1 *(pages 341–346)*
Church Reform and the Crusades

11. What were the three main abuses that most distressed Church reformers? Explain the problem with each.

12. What was the main goal of the Crusades?

SECTION 2 *(pages 348–351)*
Trade, Towns, and Financial Revolution

13. Name a short-term and a longer-term effect of the switch to the three-field system.

14. How did the growth of towns hurt the feudal system?

15. What role did Jews and Muslims play in Christian Europe's financial revolution?

SECTION 3 *(pages 352–355)*
England and France Develop

16. How did William the Conqueror extend his rule over all of England after the Battle of Hastings?

17. What circumstances led King John to accept the Magna Carta?

SECTION 4 *(pages 356–361)*
A Century of Turmoil

18. Summarize the main ideas of John Wycliffe.

19. Why did the bubonic plague cause people to turn away from the Church?

20. How did the Hundred Years' War end European armies' reliance on mounted knights?

Visual Summary

The Church
The great Gothic cathedrals that soared heavenward were symbols of the Church's power. Yet this power did not go unchallenged. For decades, kings and popes engaged in power struggles.

Crusades
Although the First Crusade captured Jerusalem, later Crusades accomplished little.

Farming
Better farming methods—such as the three-field system and the use of horses—made it possible for farmers to grow more food. This brought a population increase in the Middle Ages.

The Bubonic Plague
The bubonic plague killed millions and weakened the manorial economy.

EUROPE IN THE MIDDLE AGES

Trade and Towns
As people moved from farms into towns, trade expanded, and guilds formed for both merchants and artisans.

Learning
Europe's first universities developed in the Middle Ages. Interest in learning grew in part as a result of the rediscovery of ancient Greek writings.

Government
England and France developed strong central governments in which arose the first stirrings of democracy in medieval Europe. This can be seen in Parliament and the Estates-General.

Hundred Years' War
The Hundred Years' War further weakened feudal power. The longbow doomed armored knights.

362 Chapter 14

Interact *with* History

Students should mention that many Crusaders brought home items from the Middle East such as silks, gold, and spices. But they also brought back some of the learning in mathematics, astronomy, philosophy, and art that the Muslims had preserved from the Greek and Roman eras. Crusaders encountered such problems as desert climate, diseases, lack of food, hostile populations, robbers, and unscrupulous merchants and traders.

CRITICAL THINKING

1. EDUCATION AFTER THE CRUSADES

THEME **CULTURAL INTERACTION** How might life have been different for Europeans if Muslims had not shared their knowledge and skills?

2. THE GREAT SCHISM

Using a problem-solution outline like the one below, summarize the Great Schism. Describe the problem, identify at least two attempted solutions, and note how the Church finally solved the problem.

```
        Great Schism
  ┌─────────────────────┐
  │ Description:         │
  └─────────────────────┘
       │           │
       ▼           ▼
 ┌──────────┐ ┌──────────┐
 │Solution 1│ │Solution 2│
 └──────────┘ └──────────┘
       │           │
       └─────┬─────┘
             ▼
      ┌────────────┐
      │ Resolution │
      └────────────┘
```

3. JOAN OF ARC AND THE 15TH CENTURY

How does Joan of Arc's story reflect the violence and pessimism of the early 1400s?

4. ANALYZING PRIMARY SOURCES

In 1295, Edward I of England sent letters such as the following to sheriffs throughout the land, announcing a meeting of Parliament. Read the letter and answer the questions below it.

A VOICE FROM THE PAST

The king to the sheriff of Northampton, greeting. Whereas we wish to have a conference and discussion with the earls, barons, and other nobles of our realm concerning the provision of remedies for the dangers that in these days threaten the same kingdom . . . we command and firmly enjoin you that without delay you cause two knights, of the more discreet and more capable of labor, to be elected from the aforesaid county, and two citizens from each city of the aforesaid county, and two burgesses from each borough, and that you have them come to us . . . to do whatever in the aforesaid matters may be ordained by common counsel.

- Why is the king calling a meeting of Parliament?
- Who will represent the cities and boroughs, and how will they be chosen?

CHAPTER ACTIVITIES

1. LIVING HISTORY: Unit Portfolio Project

THEME **RELIGIOUS AND ETHICAL SYSTEMS** Your unit portfolio project focuses on how religion affected life during the Middle Ages (see page 229). For Chapter 14, you might add one of the following ideas to your portfolio.

- Prepare the script for a newscast announcing the capture of Jerusalem by Crusaders and its impact on Christians and Muslims.
- Draw a cartoon about the clash between King Philip IV and Pope Boniface VIII. Try to show the conflict between religious and secular leaders.
- Write a speech that John Wycliffe might have given expressing his radical ideas about the Church.

2. CONNECT TO TODAY: Cooperative Learning

THEME **ECONOMICS** The bubonic plague and the Hundred Years' War both had a major impact on the economy of medieval Europe. The plague, for example, meant that populations fell, trade declined, prices rose, farmland was abandoned, and workers were scarce and demanded higher wages. Even today, disease, natural catastrophes, and war can have a great impact on an economy. Work with a team to research and present to the class the effect of war, disease, or natural catastrophe on the economy of a country.

INTERNET Use the Internet, magazines, or books to research the topic. You might choose a war such as the U.S. Civil War, World War II, or the Vietnam War. You might choose a disease such as heart disease or cancer. You might choose a natural disaster such as a hurricane or flood.

- As part of your presentation, make a graph that shows statistical information about the impact of the event you have chosen on the economy.
- Compare your team's event with those of other teams to determine their relative economic impacts.

3. INTERPRETING A TIME LINE

Revisit the unit time line on pages 228–229. Which events during the medieval period in Europe were triggered by a struggle for individual power?

FOCUS ON **ART**

The painting below shows Richard the Lion-Hearted (left) unhorsing Saladin during the Third Crusade. In fact the two men never met in personal combat. Notice the way the two leaders are depicted.

- What elements suggest that Richard is the hero of this painting?
- What elements suggest that Saladin is the villain?

Connect to History What evidence of the artist's bias is there in this painting about the confrontation between Islam and Christianity?

CHAPTER ACTIVITIES

1. LIVING HISTORY

Standards for Evaluation
Newscast scripts should meet the following criteria:

- Answer the *who, what, where, when, why,* and *how* questions.
- Create "person in the street" responses to the main events.
- Suggest appropriate graphics to include with the report.

Standards for Evaluation
Cartoons should meet the following criteria:

- Identify the characters and conflict clearly.
- Express a definite point of view.
- Communicate humor or other strong feeling.
- Use cartoon elements—simple drawings, balloon dialogue—to communicate the ideas.

Standards for Evaluation
Speeches should meet the following criteria:

- Are written from the first-person point of view.
- Contain convincing arguments about the value of Wycliffe's ideas.
- Anticipate criticism of the speaker's ideas and answer it.

2. CONNECT TO TODAY: COOPERATIVE LEARNING

Standards for Evaluation
Team reports should meet the following criteria:

- Present specific data about the event and its results.
- Use graphic elements to organize information.
- Include summary material that compares one team's event with that of another team.

3. INTERPRETING A TIME LINE

Possible Responses: The First Crusade; the Norman Conquest; the Magna Carta; the Hundred Years' War.

FOCUS ON **ART**

- Richard is shown unhorsing Saladin and is given a more heroic appearance.
- Saladin is being unseated by Richard; his color is odd and he has a malevolent expression on his face.

Connect to History *Possible Response:* The artist shows Richard defeating Saladin in a combat that never took place; he also portrays Saladin as a villain.

CRITICAL THINKING

1. EDUCATION AFTER THE CRUSADES
Possible Responses: Without trade with Muslims, the financial revolution wouldn't have occurred; without the knowledge preserved from the ancient Greeks, advancements in science, mathematics, and other fields might not have occurred so early.

2. THE GREAT SCHISM
Possible Responses: Description—The College of Cardinals chose an Italian in Rome as the new pope. French cardinals chose their own pope in France. Solution 1—Each pope declared the other to be false and excommunicated him. Solution 2—The Council of Constance selected a pope. Resolution—The council and Holy Roman Emperor forced all three popes to resign. In 1417, they chose a new pope.

3. JOAN OF ARC
Possible Response: Despite her heroic acts, Joan was accused of being a witch and a heretic and was executed.

4. ANALYZING PRIMARY SOURCES
Possible Responses: To discuss threats to the kingdom. Two citizens from each city and two burgesses from each borough are to be elected to attend.

Societies and Empires of Africa

	Key Ideas	COPY MASTERS	ASSESSMENT

SECTION 1
North and Central African Societies

pp. 367–370

South of the Sahara, African peoples form hunting-gathering societies and stateless societies. In North Africa groups of Muslim reformers form two successive Muslim states, the Almoravid and Almohad empires.

 In-Depth Resources: Unit 3
• **Guided Reading,** p. 87
• **Primary Source:** *What to Wear to Mecca,* p. 93

PE *Section 1 Assessment,* p. 370

Formal Assessment
• Section Quiz, p. 170

Alternative Assessment Book
• Standards for Evaluating a Cooperative Activity

SECTION 2
West African Empires and Civilizations

pp. 371–377

In West Africa three empires—Ghana, Mali, and Songhai—thrive by controlling the trade of gold and salt. Muslim merchants and teachers bring Islam to West Africa. Other major states develop there, including the Hausa city-states, the Yoruba kingdoms of Ife and Oyo, and Benin.

 In-Depth Resources: Unit 3
• **Guided Reading,** p. 88
• **Geographical Application:** Ibn Battuta Travels to Mali, p. 91
• **Primary Sources:** Benin bronze sculpture, p. 94; The Making of Benin Bronzes, p. 95
• **Literature:** from *Sundiata: An Epic of Old Mali,* p. 97
• **History Makers:** Ibn Battuta, p. 100
• **Connections Across Time and Cultures:** Trade Routes in Asia and West Africa, p. 102

PE *Section 2 Assessment,* p. 377

Formal Assessment
• Section Quiz, p. 171

Alternative Assessment Book
• Standards for Evaluating a Cooperative Activity

SECTION 3
Eastern City-States and Southern Empires

pp. 378–381

Cities on Africa's east coast thrive on trade with Asia, using Swahili as a trade language. Muslim traders bring Islam to East Africa. The Shona states Great Zimbabwe and Mutapa in southern Africa control the gold trade from the interior to the east coast.

In-Depth Resources: Unit 3
• **Guided Reading,** p. 89
• **Skillbuilder Practice:** Analyzing Causes, p. 90
• **Primary Sources:** from *The Book of Roger* by Al-Idvisi, p. 96
• **History Makers:** Mutota, p. 101

PE *Section 3 Assessment,* p. 381

Formal Assessment
• Section Quiz, p. 172

Alternative Assessment Book
• Standards for Evaluating a Product or Performance

CHAPTER RESOURCES

Chapter Overview

Africans develop different types of societies, including hunting-gathering and stateless societies south of the Sahara and in Muslim states in North Africa. Other African peoples form powerful empires and states in West, East, and southern Africa, growing rich through trade with Muslim merchants, who spread Islam.

 Telescoping the Times
• Chapter Summary, pp. 57–59

Planning for Block Schedules

PE *Chapter Assessment,* pp. 382–383

Chapter Activities, p. 383

Formal Assessment
• Chapter Test, forms A and B, pp. 173–178

Test Generator

Alternative Assessment Book

TECHNOLOGY

 Warm-Up Transparency 15

 Electronic Library of Primary Sources
• "How To Get Rich Quickly"

 INTERNET RESOURCES
www.mlworldhistory.com

 Warm-Up Transparency 15

 Geography Transparencies
• GT15 The Growth of Mali and Songhai, 1200–1591

 World Art and Cultures Transparencies
• AT32 Ghana terra cotta sculpture
• AT33 Benin bronze

 INTERNET RESOURCES
www.mlworldhistory.com

 Warm-Up Transparency 15

 Critical Thinking Transparencies
• CT15 African Trading Societies, 800–1500
• CT51 Chapter 15 Visual Summary

 Electronic Library of Primary Sources
• "Mogadishu in 1331"

 INTERNET RESOURCES
www.mlworldhistory.com

 Chapter Summaries on Audiocassette in English and Spanish

 INTERNET RESOURCES
www.mlworldhistory.com

Block Scheduling (90 MINUTES)

Day 1
Section 1, pp. 367–370

 COOPERATIVE ACTIVITY
Researching African Societies, p. 368 (Teacher's Edition)

Day 2
Section 3, pp. 378–381

Section Assessment, p. 381

Chapter Assessment, pp. 382–383

Section 2, pp. 371–377

COOPERATIVE ACTIVITY
Presenting West African Arts, p. 375 (Teacher's Edition)

Section Assessments, pp. 370, 377

Yearly Pacing *Chapter 15 Total:* 2 days *Yearly Total:* 85 days

 Planning for Block Schedules

Customizing for Special Needs

Students Acquiring English

 Access for Students Acquiring English
• **Guided Reading** for Sections 1–3 (Spanish), pp. 151–153
• **Chapter Summary** (Spanish), pp. 148–150
• **Skillbuilder Practice** Analyzing Causes (Spanish), p. 154
• **Geography Application** Ibn Battuta Travels to Mali (Spanish), pp. 155–166

 Chapter Summaries on Audiocassette in English and Spanish

 INTERNET RESOURCES
www.mlworldhistory.com
The Diverse Classroom.

Less Proficient Readers

 In-Depth Resources: Unit 3
• **Guided Reading** for Sections 1–3, pp. 87–89
• **Skillbuilder Practice** Analyzing Causes, p. 90
• **Geography Application** Ibn Battuta Travels to Mali, p. 91

 Telescoping the Times
• Chapter Summary, pp. 57–59

 Chapter Summaries on Audiocassette

Gifted and Talented Students

 In-Depth Resources: Unit 3
Primary Sources:
• *What to Wear to Mecca*, p. 93
• Benin bronze sculpture, p. 94
• The Making of Benin Bronzes, p. 95
• from *The Book of Roger* by Al-Idrisi, p. 96

History Makers
• Ibn Battuta, p. 100
• Mutota, p. 101

Connections to Literature READINGS FOR STUDENTS

 In-Depth Resources: Unit 3
Literature: from *Sundiata: An Epic of Old Mali*, p. 97

Enrichment Reading
• **Abrahams, Roger D., ed.**
African Folktales
New York: Pantheon, 1983.
A collection of 100 memorable tales.

• **Taylor, Stephen**
Shaka's Children
New York: Harper, 1995
An exciting story of the Zulu world's intrigues and battles.

 = Pupil's Edition   = Overhead Transparency   = Software   = Video

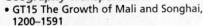 = Copy Master   = CD-ROM   = Audiocassette   = Internet

Societies and Empires of Africa, 800–1500

Predicting

- Have students look at the image of the illustrated map and read the accompanying caption. Ask students to predict how Africa's wealth influences interactions between Africans and Europeans.

Making Inferences

- Have students reread the same caption. What do they think was one major source of wealth for the West African empires?

- Ask students to look at the Yoruba artwork and read the caption. What does the mother's treatment of the wooden twin suggest about family ties in Yoruba society?

Geography Connection

- Have students identify each empire on the inset map. Which one was the largest? How far did it extend inland from the west coast?

- Have students find the Aksumite port of Adulis on the main map. Ask them to recall which regions of Asia it traded with. Then have them find the ports along Africa's Indian Ocean coast and tell them that these cities too would thrive on trade with Asia.

CHAPTER 15

Societies and Empires of Africa, 800–1500

PREVIEWING THEMES

Religious and Ethical Systems

Beginning about 640, Islam spread into North Africa. Two groups of Muslim reformers—the Almoravids and the Almohads—built North African empires. Merchants and traders spread Islam into both West and East Africa, where it influenced rulers.

Interaction with Environment

In parts of Africa, hunter-gatherers used up an area's food supply and then moved on. In some Saharan villages, workers built houses of salt, the only available resource. The location of gold deposits determined where trade routes—and empires—were located.

Economics

Extensive trade networks developed in Africa because different regions had items—such as gold and salt—that other regions wanted. African city-states and empires that were able to control and tax such trade became wealthy and powerful.

INTERNET CONNECTION

Visit us at www.mlworldhistory.com to learn more about African civilizations, trade, and related topics.

364

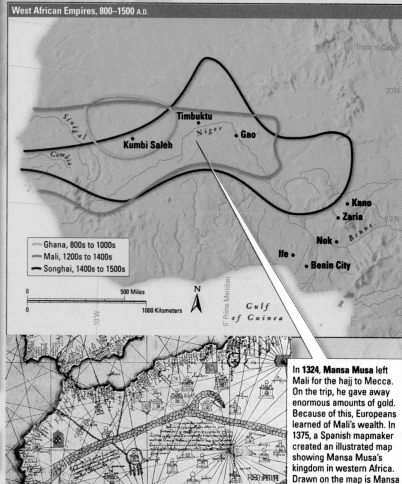

AFRICA, 800–1500

West African Empires, 800–1500 A.D.

Tropic of Cancer

20°N

Senegal
Gambia
Niger
Benue

Timbuktu
Gao
Kumbi Saleh
Kano
Zaria
Nok
Ife
Benin City

10°N

— Ghana, 800s to 1000s
— Mali, 1200s to 1400s
— Songhai, 1400s to 1500s

0   500 Miles
0   1000 Kilometers

N

0° Prime Meridian
10°W
20°W

Gulf of Guinea

In **1324, Mansa Musa** left Mali for the hajj to Mecca. On the trip, he gave away enormous amounts of gold. Because of this, Europeans learned of Mali's wealth. In 1375, a Spanish mapmaker created an illustrated map showing Mansa Musa's kingdom in western Africa. Drawn on the map is Mansa Musa holding a gold nugget.

GEOGRAPHY THEMES

Movement

Ask students to note the distance between Fez and Timbuktu on the main map. Have them identify the major landform that separates the two cities and identify the city that was likely to have greater contact with the Mediterranean world. Ask students to speculate on the obstacles to commerce between Fez and Timbuktu.

Place

Tell students that in this chapter natural resources and location will play key roles in the ways of life that develop. Have students turn to pages 193–194 to review what they have learned about Africa's climates and vegetation regions. Then have students identify cities or towns from the map on page 365 that occupy each of the vegetation regions. Ask students to write a few sentences describing what the landforms, soil, climate, and resources of each site might be. Students might also predict whether each site would be heavily or lightly populated, given its geography.

ADDITIONAL RESOURCES

Books for the Teacher

• Davidson, Basil. *Africa in History.* New York: Macmillan, 1991.

• Freeman-Grenville, G. S. *The New Atlas of African History.* New York: Simon, 1991.

• Turnbull, Colin. *The Forest People.* New York: Simon, 1961. Describes the culture of the Mbuti.

Books for the Student

• Liptak, Karen. *Endangered Peoples.* Watts, 1993. Describes the struggles of the San and Mbuti peoples.

• McKissack, Patricia and Fredrick. *The Royal Kingdoms of Ghana, Mali, and Songhay.* New York: Holt, 1994.

Videos

• *Africa: History Denied.* Knowledge Unlimited, 1995. 800-356-2303. Explores the civilization centered at Great Zimbabwe.

• *Caravans of Gold/Kings and Cities.* Knowledge Unlimited, 1996. 800-356-2303. Traces the routes of the African gold trade.

• *The Roots of African Civilization.* Society for Visual Education, 1996. 800-829-1900. Covers cultures and societies of precolonial West Africa.

Software

• *History and Culture of Africa.* CD-ROM. Queue, 1997. 800-232-2224. Covers Africa's empires and art, early contacts with Europeans.

The **Yoruba people** of **West Africa** consider twins lucky. When one twin dies as an infant, they create a wooden twin image, which the mother treats as a living child on special occasions. For example, she will offer it food, wash it, and make it clothes. This wooden twin image wears a beaded jacket that has a twin on each shoulder.

In the **13th century, King Lalibela** of Ethiopia claimed to have a dream in which Christ appeared to him. Awed by this, Lalibela decided to build a city of 11 churches carved out of solid rock. The church of St. George is shaped like a cross. According to legend, angels helped the stonemasons in their work.

HISTORY THROUGH ART

Twin Figure with Jacket

In Yoruba culture, twins are special beings who can bring good fortune to those who honor them properly and misfortune to those who neglect or offend them. If a twin dies, a figure like the one above immediately takes its place. The mother then tends it as though it were the living child. The child's soul takes refuge in the figure and thus provokes no misfortune.

The elaborate beaded jacket on this figure suggests that the dead twin was born into a royal family. It is a miniature version of the vest worn by priests of Shango, the Yoruba god of thunder and lightning who is also considered the father of twins. The figures on the shoulders of the jacket are mounted horsemen. Those on the front are birds, symbolizing the powers of "our mothers," older women said to be able to turn themselves into harmful birds at night.

In many Yoruba families a twin figure is passed from one generation to the next. Each helps preserve the memory of a particular family member and serves as a reference point to events in family and local history.

Interpreting the Art How might studying twin figures in their place of origin and questioning the families "related" to them be helpful to historians?

Interact *with* History

This Interact with History feature motivates students by inviting them to put themselves in a key historical situation—the interaction between traders from medieval North Africa and Timbuktu. As students imagine themselves meeting with traders from Timbuktu, they will analyze the issues, explore their options, and become decision-makers.

Purpose

- to set the stage for studying societies and empires of Africa
- to help students explore the role of trade in the rise of African city-states and empires
- to help students make connections with people and events they will study in this chapter

Teaching Strategy

Thinking Critically After students have imagined themselves in the situation described on this page, have them answer the key questions and give reasons for their decision.

EXAMINING *the* ISSUES

Here are suggestions for addressing each bulleted question.

1 Have students name trade items that are highly valued in their society. What makes these items valuable?

2 Ask students to consider how oil might be valued in a society without cars or electricity. Why might oil be more valuable in an industrial society than in a hunting-gathering society?

3 Have students name items that might have been much more valuable to Africans in the 1100s than they are to people now. Have students explain their responses.

Making Connections Have students consider ways modern governments control trade, such as taxing exports and imports.

Interact *with* History

You are a trader who has traveled from a North African seaport south across the Sahara. You have arrived at the great trading center of Timbuktu. Among your trade items are manufactured goods and salt. In Timbuktu, you will meet with traders from the gold-mining regions to the south. You want to receive as much gold as possible for your trade items. The traders from the south want to receive as much salt and as many manufactured goods as they can in exchange for their gold. Together you must come to an agreement about what various trade items are worth.

What makes trade items valuable?

To survive the trip across the Sahara, traders stopped at oases for water. However, it was 500 miles to Timbuktu from the nearest oasis! The journey was very hard.

The camel was the only animal that could go without water long enough to cross the Sahara.

This cloth was shipped across the Mediterranean Sea to North Africa. Then it began the long journey to Timbuktu.

Workers in the Sahara endured hardship to mine this salt. In a hot climate, salt helps the human body to retain water. Salt was scarce in the gold-mining region.

The king often demanded these gold nuggets as taxes. The bag contained gold dust, which the trader used as money.

These beautiful cowrie shells came all the way from East Africa. They were used as money.

EXAMINING *the* ISSUES

1 • Does an item have to be a luxury to be extremely valuable?

2 • How do scarcity, usefulness, and transportation cost affect an item's value?

3 • Do all items have the same value to all people?

As you discuss these questions in class, think about what you have learned about other trading peoples, such as the Phoenicians and the Europeans.

As you read about trade in the various regions of Africa, notice what steps rulers took to control trade moving through their territory.

Follow Up

A feature on the chapter assessment will ask students to reevaluate their responses to the situation presented on this page.

North and Central African Societies

TERMS & NAMES
- lineage
- stateless societies
- patrilineal
- matrilineal
- Maghrib
- Almoravids
- Almohads

MAIN IDEA

North and central Africa developed hunting-gathering societies, stateless societies, and Muslim states.

WHY IT MATTERS NOW

Modern African nations often must find ways to include these various peoples and traditions in one society.

SETTING THE STAGE Throughout history, different groups of Africans have found different ways to organize themselves to meet their political, economic, and social needs. In the varied regions of Africa, climate and topography, or landforms, influenced how each community developed. Some people built desert empires united by religion. Others near the coast created political systems based on extended family ties. Still others lived in the rain forest and formed close-knit family groups to support themselves by hunting and gathering. Section 1 examines these three types of African societies. In addition, many African groups developed kingdoms and city-states—which are discussed in Sections 2 and 3.

Hunting-Gathering Societies

Hunting-gathering societies—the oldest form of social organization in the world—began in Africa. Hunting-gathering societies still exist in Africa today, though they form an extremely small percentage of the population. Scattered throughout Africa, these groups speak their own languages and often use distinctive hunting techniques. However, they all rely on hunting and gathering for survival. By studying these groups, scholars learn clues about how hunter-gatherers may have lived in the past. However, no hunter-gatherers today live precisely as prehistoric peoples did.

Forest Dwellers The Efe (AY·fay) are just one of several hunting-gathering societies in Africa. They make their home in the Ituri Forest in the Democratic Republic of Congo (formerly Zaire). Like their ancestors, the modern-day Efe live in small groups of no more than 50 members, all of whom are related. Each family occupies its own grass-and-brush shelter within a camp, but their homes are rarely permanent. Their search for food causes them to be somewhat nomadic. As a result, the Efe collect few possessions and move to new camps as they use up the resources in the surrounding area.

In the Efe society, women are the gatherers. They walk through the forest searching for roots, yams, mushrooms, and wild seeds. Efe men and older boys do all the hunting. Sometimes they gather in groups to hunt small antelope called duikers. At other times, hunters go solo and use poison-tipped arrows to kill mammals such as monkeys. On some occasions, Efe men collect wild honey, a prized delicacy of the forest. Unlike prehistoric hunter-gatherers, the Efe add to their diet by trading honey, wild game, and other forest products for crops grown by farmers in nearby villages.

Social Structure A respected older male, such as a father, uncle, or father-in-law, typically serves as group leader.

A. Possible Answer A larger group would use up an area's resources too quickly and have to move more often.

THINK THROUGH HISTORY
A. Drawing Conclusions Considering the way the Efe live, why might they need to limit their groups to 50 members or less?

CONNECT to TODAY

Hunter-Gatherers

The girl shown below is a member of the Efe people. Today the Efe and other hunter-gatherers live in tropical rain forests in several African nations. However, they make up less than 1 percent of the population of Africa.

Hunter-gatherers also exist on other continents. The Inuit of North America have traditionally fished and hunted. Today, some use modern equipment such as rifles and snowmobiles. However, many have abandoned hunting to look for wage-paying work.

Modern society has disrupted the hunting-gathering culture of the Aborigines of Australia. They suffer high rates of poverty, disease, and unemployment. Today, Aborigines make up less than 2 percent of Australia's population.

SECTION 1 RESOURCES

PRINT RESOURCES

IN-DEPTH RESOURCES: UNIT 3
Guided Reading, p. 87
Primary Source: *What to Wear to Mecca*, p. 93

ACCESS FOR STUDENTS ACQUIRING ENGLISH
Guided Reading (Spanish), p. 151

FORMAL ASSESSMENT
Section Quiz, p. 170

ALTERNATIVE ASSESSMENT BOOK

TECHNOLOGY RESOURCES

CD-ROM
Electronic Library of Primary Sources

INTERNET www.mlworldhistory.com

Section 1 Overview

OBJECTIVES

1. To explain how hunting and gathering societies are organized.
2. To describe how a stateless society is governed.
3. To summarize the ways Islamic law governs Muslim states.

SKILLBUILDER
- Interpreting maps: location, region, p. 368

CRITICAL THINKING
- Drawing conclusions, p. 367
- Making inferences, p. 369
- Recognizing effects, p. 370
- Comparing, p. 370

FOCUS

5-Minute Warm-Up

Making Generalizations
To examine types of African societies, have students answer these questions.

1. Look at the map on page 368. Which type of society occupied the smallest regions?

2. Based on the charts with the map, how do the ways of governing in stateless societies and Muslim states differ?

WARM-UP TRANSPARENCY 15

OBJECTIVE 1 INSTRUCT

Hunting-Gathering Societies

Key Ideas
- Hunting-gathering societies like the Efe of central Africa gather wild foods to survive.
- The Efe use informal, mutually agreed-upon rules for sharing food and belongings.

IN-DEPTH RESOURCES: UNIT 3
Guided Reading, p. 87

ACCESS FOR STUDENTS ACQUIRING ENGLISH
Guided Reading (Spanish), p. 151

CONNECT to TODAY
Hunter-Gatherers

Efforts to integrate forest-dwelling hunter-gatherers into life outside

(continued on next page)

(continued from page 367)

the forest have often backfired. Some Efe were resettled in plantation villages where they were supposed to lead a more settled life, growing their own food. But the food upset their diet, and many suffered sunstroke after being exposed to sunlight much stronger than they were used to in the forest. Have students research current threats to the way of life of groups living in the Ituri Forest.

History from Visuals

Selected African Societies, 800–1500

Interpreting the Map and Charts Have students use the map key to identify which types of societies existed south of the Sahara. *Hunter-gatherer and stateless* When did the Almoravid Empire exist? *11th century*

Extension Activity Have students use the map "Vegetation Regions of Africa" on page 194 to identify the vegetation regions each type of society inhabited. Why might the vegetation regions the San lived in have led them to be hunter-gatherers? *They lived in or near deserts, which were too dry to support much agriculture.*

SKILLBUILDER Answers
1. North and northwest Africa
2. They constantly had to move to new areas in search of food.

OBJECTIVE ② INSTRUCT

Stateless Societies

▸ **Key Ideas**
- The structure of many African societies is based on extended families called lineages.
- In stateless societies, such as the Igbo, lineages share power.

(continued on next page)

Although members of the group listen to and value this man's opinion, he does not give orders or act as chief. Each family within the band makes its own decisions and is free to come and go. Group members settle arguments through long discussions. If conflicts cannot be settled by talking, a group member may decide to move to a different hunting band. Daily life for the Efe is not governed by formal, written laws. However, they do have logical guidelines that determine how members share food and possessions.

Stateless Societies

As in other parts of the world, family organization is central to African society. In many African societies, families are organized in groups called lineages. The members of a **lineage** (LIHN·ee·ihj) believe they are descendants of a common ancestor. Besides its living members, a lineage includes past generations (spirits of ancestors) and future generations (children not yet born). Within a lineage, members feel strong loyalties to one another.

South of the Sahara, many African groups developed systems of governing based on lineages. In some African societies, lineage groups took the place of rulers. These societies, known as **stateless societies,** did not have a centralized system of power. Instead, authority in a stateless society was balanced among lineages of equal power so that no one family had too much control. Most often, members of a stateless society worked through their differences to cooperate and share power. The Igbo (IHG·boh) people—also called Ibo—of southern Nigeria lived in a stateless society as early as the ninth century. (Although the Igbo lived in West Africa, their political structure was similar to stateless societies found in central Africa.) If a dispute arose within an Igbo village, respected elders from

When a respected elder of the Tiv dies his skull and thigh bone are made into an *imborirungu,* shown here. The living elders use the *imborirungu* to try to communicate with the dead leader's soul.

Stateless Societies

Stateless societies did not have centralized power. Instead, power was balanced among lineage groups, usually within villages.

- The **Tiv,** in what is today Nigeria, had no formal government.
- The **Igbo** of southern Nigeria resolved disputes by having elders from different lineages meet.
- The **Nuer** of the southern Sudan organized over 250,000 people without an official ruler.

Muslim States

In North Africa, two groups of Muslim reformers founded empires.

- In the 11th century, the **Almoravid** Dynasty controlled Mauritania, Morocco, and part of Spain.
- Beginning in the mid-1100s, the **Almohad** Dynasty controlled Morocco, much of the Maghrib, and part of Spain.

Selected African Societies, 800–1500

Hunter-Gatherers

The seminomadic hunter-gatherers lived by gathering wild foods and hunting animals. When they exhausted an area's resources, they moved on.

- The **Efe** lived in the Ituri Forest of what is now the Democratic Republic of Congo. They were hunter-gatherers who traded with farming villages.
- The **San** (also called the **Bushmen**) lived in most of southern Africa and part of East Africa.

Oran
Fez • Tlemcen
Marrakech •
ALMORAVID EMPIRE
ALMOHAD EMPIRE
Mediterranean Sea
ASIA
SAHARA
Tropic of Cancer
Niger R.
AFRICA
Tiv
Igbo
Nuer
Efe Mbuti
ATLANTIC OCEAN
Pygmies
Luba
L. Victoria
Congo
San
INDIAN OCEAN
Tropic of Capricorn

0   1,500 Miles
0   3,000 Kilometers

- ☐ 0–500 feet
- ☐ 500–2,000 feet
- ☐ Over 2,000 feet
- — Stateless society
- — Muslim state
- — Hunter-gatherers

GEOGRAPHY SKILLBUILDER: Interpreting Maps
1. **Location** Where were the Muslim states located?
2. **Region** Why would hunter-gatherers be spread across such a large region?

368

TEACHING OPTION | **BLOCK SCHEDULING** | **COOPERATIVE ACTIVITY: Researching African Societies** | **CLASS TIME 30 MINUTES**

Task: Student groups will research the economic, political, and social life of a hunter-gatherer or stateless society in modern Africa and present an oral report on their findings.

Purpose: To recognize the diversity of African ethnic groups.

Activity: Divide students into five groups. Have each group learn more about one of these societies: Tiv, Igbo, Nuer, Efe (Mbuti), or San. Group members should divide the task of providing information on (1) the region the society inhabits, including its physical features; (2) major sources of livelihood or dominant occupations; (3) the system used for making decisions; (4) the way the society traces lineage (matrilineally or patrilineally); (5) religious

beliefs and practices; (6) roles of women and men according to life stage. After completing their research, each group should make an oral report telling what they have learned about the society they researched. A useful resource for this activity is *From Afar to Zulu* by Haskins and Biondi.

ALTERNATIVE ASSESSMENT BOOK
Standards for Evaluating a Cooperative Activity

Background
British colonizers mis-
spelled "Igbo" as
"Ibo." That is why
there are two
spellings.

different lineages settled the problem. While this political structure served the Igbo well for many centuries, Igbos later encountered challenges from European colonizers who expected one single leader to rule over the whole society. (See Chapter 27.)

Tracing Family Descent In African societies, the way a society traces lineage decides inheritance rights and what groups individuals belong to. Members of a **patrilineal** society trace their ancestors through their fathers. Inheritance passes from father to son. When a son marries, then he, his wife, and their children remain part of his father's extended family.

In a **matrilineal** society, children trace their ancestors through their mothers. Young men from a matrilineal culture inherit land and wealth from their mother's family. Although group memberships and inheritance rights in a matrilineal society are based on descent from women, men usually hold the positions of authority.

Background
In matrilineal soci-
eties that are also
kingdoms, the king's
heir is his sister's son,
not his own son.

Age-Set System In many African societies, young people form close ties to individuals outside their lineage through the age-set system. An age set consists of young people within a region who are born during a certain time period. Each age set passes together through clearly identified life stages, such as warrior or elder. Ceremonies mark the passage to each new stage.

Men and women have different life stages, and each stage has its own duties and importance. Responsibilities can include working on community building projects, herding cattle, or assisting in the raising of children. Societies like the Igbo use the age-set system to teach discipline, community service, and leadership skills to their young.

THINK THROUGH HISTORY
**B. Making
Inferences** What
advantages might an
age-set system have
for a society?
B. Possible Answers
people belong to a
group of their peers;
there is recognition of
important milestones;
there are clear expec-
tations for different
stages of life; every
age group has impor-
tance.

Muslim States

While stateless societies developed south of the Sahara, Islam played a vital role in the political history of North Africa. After Muhammad's death in 632, Muslims swept across the northwest part of the continent. They converted many by conquest and others peacefully. By 670, Muslims ruled Egypt and had entered the **Maghrib,** the part of North Africa that is today the Mediterranean coast of Morocco, Tunisia, and Algeria.

As Islam spread, some African rulers converted to Islam. These African Muslim rulers then based their government upon Islamic law. Muslims believe that God's law is a higher authority than any human law. Therefore, Muslim rulers often relied on religious scholars as government advisers.

Islamic Law In Islam, following the law is a religious obligation. Muslims do not separate their personal life from their religious life, and Islamic law regulates almost all areas of human life. Because of this, Islamic law helped to bring order to Muslim states. It provided the state with a set of values that shaped a common identity.

In addition to unifying individual states, law helped to unify the Muslim world. Even though various Muslim states might have ethnic or cultural differences, they lived under a common law. Islamic law has been such a significant force in African history that some states—especially in North Africa—are still politically and socially influenced by it today.

Among those who converted to Islam were the Berbers. Fiercely independent desert dwellers, the Berbers were the original inhabitants of North Africa. Until their conquest by the Muslim Arabs in the 600s, some of these nomadic African people were Christians and Jews. While they accepted Islam as their faith, many maintained their Berber identities and loyalties. Two Berber groups, the Almoravids and the Almohads, founded empires that united the Maghrib under Muslim rule.

Almoravid Reformers In the 11th century, Muslim reformers founded the Almoravid (AL·muh·RAHV·uhd) Dynasty. Its members came from a Berber group liv-

Societies and Empires of Africa **369**

Daily Life

Negotiating Conflict

In a stateless society, the power to negotiate conflicts shifts from generation to generation as circumstances demand.

Look at the diagram of two lineages above. If **d** is in conflict with **f**, then **c** will side with his brother **d** and **e** will side with his brother **f**. Therefore, the parents— **1** and **2**—will meet to negotiate.

If **f** is in conflict with **g**, both entire lineages will take sides in the dispute. Therefore, the members of the oldest surviving generation—**A** and **B**—must meet to negotiate.

(continued from page 368)

- Lineage, traced through fathers (patrilineal) or mothers (matrilineal), decides inheritance rights and group membership.
- In many societies, people are grouped by age as well as lineage, and each life stage has its own responsibilities.

MORE ABOUT . . .
Matrilineal Societies

A matrilineal society is not the same as a matriarchy, a society ruled by women. In matrilineal societies, positions of authority are still held by men, usually by either brothers or uncles (mothers' brothers). The Ashanti and Akan peoples of Ghana and the Bemba of Zaire are matrilineal societies.

Daily Life
Negotiating Conflict

Have students compare the way conflicts are settled in a stateless society with the ways they are settled in families and between unrelated individuals in U.S. society. Do students think that negotiating conflict through kinship systems would work at the community, state, or national level in U.S. society? Why or why not?

OBJECTIVE 3 INSTRUCT

Muslim States

▶ *Key Ideas*
- The spread of Islam leads to the founding of Muslim states in North Africa.
- Islamic law helps to order and unify Muslim North Africa.
- Two of the first Muslim states in North Africa are the Almoravid and Almohad empires.

IN-DEPTH RESOURCES: UNIT 3
Primary Source: *What to Wear to Mecca,* p. 93

**TEACHING
OPTION**

CONNECTIONS ACROSS TIME AND PLACE

Islamic Law and Social Change The Qur'an and Muhammad's sayings and practices set basic, unchangeable standards of conduct. Over time, however, Muslim religious leaders had to face issues or behaviors that divine revelation had not addressed. Their efforts yielded the *shari'a,* a legal system that was to govern most aspects of people's lives in the Muslim world for centuries.

In this system, a jurist would solve a legal problem by

first consulting the Qur'an and the *hadith*, a record of Muhammad's divinely inspired sayings and practices. If these sources did not address the problem specifically, the jurist reached an opinion using principles applied to closely parallel problems that had been addressed by divine revelation. If the opinion was unanimously agreed to by other scholars, it became an infallible expression of God's will.

In the 900s, when scholars reached agreement on all

existing opinions, the shari'a became a rigid, static body of laws. But since the 1800s, jurists have sought to adapt the shari'a to meet changing conditions of Muslim society. In African Muslim states, the *shari'a* is now confined to family law, where it has been adapted to meet present needs.

Have interested students compare how the shari'a influences everyday life in modern Morocco and Saudi Arabia.

SPOTLIGHT ON

Marrakech

Located in west central Morocco, Marrakech was once the capital of both the Almoravid and the Almohad dynasties. During the height of its prosperity in the 1400s, the city's location on the edge of the Sahara made it an important trade center. It was filled with bustling markets like the present-day wool market shown above.

Marrakech also became an important Islamic religious center. It attracted scholars and thinkers from throughout the Islamic world. Today, with a population of over 600,000, Marrakech is Morocco's third largest city and once again a hub of trade. As in the past, Marrakech is famous for its fine leather work and carpets.

---

ing in the western Sahara in what is today Mauritania. The movement began after a devout Berber Muslim made a hajj, or pilgrimage, to Mecca. On his journey home, he convinced a Muslim scholar from Morocco named Abd Allah Ibn Yasin to return with him to teach his people about Islam. Ibn Yasin's teachings soon attracted followers, and he founded a strict religious brotherhood, known as the **Almoravids.** According to one theory about the name's origin, the group lived in a *ribat*, or fortified monastery. They were therefore called the "people of the *ribat*"—al-Murabitun, which eventually became "Almoravid."

In the 1050s, Ibn Yasin led the Almoravids in an effort to spread Islam through conquest. Although Ibn Yasin died in battle in 1059, the Almoravids went on to take Morocco and found Marrakech. It became their capital. They overran the West African empire of Ghana by 1076. The Almoravids also captured parts of southern Spain, where they were called Moors.

Almohads Take Over In the mid-1100s, the **Almohads** (AL·moh·HADZ), another group of Berber Muslim reformers, wrested power from the Almoravids. The Almohads began as a militant religious movement in the Atlas Mountains of Morocco. (In Arabic, the Almohads are known as *al-Muwahhidun*, meaning "those who affirm the unity of God.")

The Almohads followed the teachings of Ibn Tumart. After a pilgrimage to Mecca, Ibn Tumart denounced the later Almoravid rulers for moving away from the traditional practice of Islam. He urged his followers to strictly obey the teachings of the Qur'an and Islamic law. The Almohads, led by Abd al-Mumin, fought to oust the Almoravids and remain true to traditional Islamic beliefs.

By 1148 the Almohads controlled most of Morocco and ended Almoravid rule. The new Muslim reformers kept Marrakech as their capital. By the end of the 12th century, they had conquered much of southern Spain. In Africa, their territory stretched from Marrakech to Tripoli and Tunis on the Mediterranean. The Almohad Dynasty gradually declined and broke up into individual Muslim dynasties. While the Almohad Dynasty lasted just over 100 years, it united the Maghrib under one rule for the first time.

Stronger empires were about to emerge to the south of the Almohad Empire. Societies in West Africa—discussed in Section 2— created magnificent empires that boasted tremendous economic and political power and strong links to international trade routes.

Section 1 Assessment

1. TERMS & NAMES
Identify
- lineage
- stateless societies
- patrilineal
- matrilineal
- Maghrib
- Almoravids
- Almohads

2. TAKING NOTES
Using a web diagram like the one below, list characteristics of stateless societies.

stateless societies

How might these characteristics have helped stateless societies to endure for many centuries?

3. COMPARING
In what ways are hunting-gathering societies and stateless societies similar?

THINK ABOUT
- family structures
- social structures
- methods of handling conflict

4. THEME ACTIVITY
Religious and Ethical Systems Working with a partner, prepare a time line showing the impact of Islam on North Africa. Include significant events for the period described in this section.

370 Chapter 15

ANSWERS

2 West African Empires and Civilizations

TERMS & NAMES
- Ghana
- Mali
- Sundiata
- Mansa Musa
- Ibn Battuta
- Songhai
- Hausa
- Yoruba
- Benin

MAIN IDEA

West Africa contained several powerful empires and states, including Ghana, Mali, and Songhai.

WHY IT MATTERS NOW

These empires demonstrate the richness of African culture before European colonization.

SETTING THE STAGE While the Almohads and Almoravids were building empires in North Africa, three powerful empires flourished in West Africa. These ancient African empires arose in the Sahel—the savanna region just south of the Sahara. They grew strong through the controlling of trade.

Ghana: Land of Gold

By A.D. 200, trade across the Sahara had existed for centuries. However, this trade remained infrequent and irregular because of the harsh desert conditions. Most pack animals—oxen, donkeys, and horses—could not travel very far in the hot, dry Sahara without rest or water. Then in the third century A.D., Berber nomads began using camels. The camel could plod steadily over much longer distances, covering as much as 60 miles in a day. In addition, it could travel up to ten days without water, twice as long as most pack animals. With the camel, nomads blazed new routes across the desert and trade increased.

The trade routes crossed the savanna through the region farmed by the Soninke (soh·NIHN·keh) people. The Soninke people called their ruler *ghana*, or war chief. Muslim traders began to use the word to refer to the Soninke region. By the 700s, Soninke rulers of the kingdom of **Ghana** were growing rich from taxing the goods that traders carried through their territory.

Gold-Salt Trade The two most important trade items were gold and salt. Gold came from a forest region south of the savanna between the Niger (NY·juhr) and Senegal (SEHN·ih·GAWL) rivers. Miners dug gold from shafts as deep as 100 feet or sifted it from fast-moving streams. Some sources estimate that until about 1350, at least two-thirds of the world's supply of gold came from West Africa. Although rich in gold, West Africa's savanna and forests lacked salt, a material essential to human life. The Sahara contained deposits of salt. In fact, in the Saharan village of Taghaza, workers built their houses from salt blocks because it was the only material available.

Arab and Berber traders crossed the desert with camel caravans loaded down with salt. They also carried cloth, weapons, and manufactured goods from ports on the Mediterranean. After a long journey, they reached the market towns of the savanna. Meanwhile, African traders brought gold north from the forest regions.

Merchants met in trading cities, where they exchanged goods under the watchful eye of the king's tax collector. In addition to taxing trade, royal officials made sure that all traders weighed goods fairly and did business according to law. Royal guards also provided protection from bandits.

Empire of Ghana In his royal palace, the king stored gold nuggets and slabs of salt (collected as taxes). Only the king had the right to own gold nuggets, although gold dust freely circulated in the marketplace. By this means, the king limited the supply of gold and kept its price from falling. Ghana's African ruler acted as a religious leader,

Miners in a forest region of West Africa dug up gold nuggets like this. The king of Ghana passed a law that all nuggets should be given to him.

Background
Salt helps the human body retain water in hot weather. It also preserves food so that it does not spoil so quickly.

THINK THROUGH HISTORY
A. Recognizing Effects What were positive and negative effects of the king's control of trade?
A. Answer Positive—weighed goods fairly, did business according to law, kept price of gold up; Negative—taxed traders for goods.

Societies and Empires of Africa **371**

Section 2 Overview

OBJECTIVES

1. To explain how the gold-salt trade led to the rise of Ghana.

2. To describe how Sundiata and Mansa Musa advanced Mali.

3. To summarize how the Songhai Empire developed and declined.

4. To identify Benin and the Hausa and Yoruba city-states.

SKILLBUILDER
- Interpreting maps: region, human-environment interaction, p. 372

CRITICAL THINKING
- Recognizing effects, p. 371
- Analyzing causes, pp. 373, 375
- Making inferences, p. 374
- Drawing conclusions, pp. 376, 377
- Comparing, p. 376
- Analyzing Themes, p. 376

FOCUS
5-Minute Warm-Up

▶ *Interpreting*
To help students see the impact of trade on West African empires, have them answer the questions.

1. Study the inset map on page 372. What did traders from Timbuktu and Fez offer?

2. Which empire controlled the most trade routes?

📜 *WARM-UP TRANSPARENCY 15*

OBJECTIVE ① INSTRUCT

Ghana: Land of Gold

▶ *Key Ideas*
- The main trans-Saharan trade items are gold and salt.
- Muslim merchants spread Islam to West Africa.
- The Almoravids conquer Ghana, disrupting the gold-salt trade.

📖 *IN-DEPTH RESOURCES: UNIT 3*
Guided Reading, p. 88
Connections Across Time and Cultures: Trade Routes in Asia and West Africa, p. 102

📖 *ACCESS FOR STUDENTS ACQUIRING ENGLISH*
Guided Reading (Spanish), p. 152

SECTION 2 RESOURCES

PRINT RESOURCES
📖 *IN-DEPTH RESOURCES: UNIT 3*
Guided Reading, p. 88
Geography Application: Ibn Battuta Travels to Mali, p. 91
Primary Sources, pp. 94, 95
Literature: from *Sundiata: An Epic of Old Mali,* p. 97
History Makers: Ibn Battuta, p. 100
Connections Across Time and Cultures, p. 102
📖 *ACCESS FOR STUDENTS ACQUIRING ENGLISH*
Guided Reading (Spanish), p. 152
Geography Application (Spanish), p. 155

📄 *FORMAL ASSESSMENT*
Section Quiz, p. 171

TECHNOLOGY RESOURCES
📽 *GEOGRAPHY TRANSPARENCIES*
GT15 The Growth of Mali and Sounghai, 1200–1591
📽 *WORLD ART AND CULTURES TRANSPARENCIES*
AT32 Ghana sculpture; AT33 Benin bronze
🌐 **INTERNET** www.mlworldhistory.com

West African Empires, 800–1500

Interpreting the Map Have students name the cities shown on the inset map that served as the southernmost and northernmost points on the gold-salt trade route. *Southernmost—Timbuktu; northernmost—Fez* Have students find this same route on the main map. Then have them use the map key to identify the empires.

Extension Activity Have students discuss why the value and price of salt would rise as each trader sold it to the next. *The price would rise to increase each trader's margin of profit.*

SKILLBUILDER Answers

1. Ghana was smallest and Songhai largest; Songhai encompassed most of Ghana and Mali and stretched farther east and north.
2. The environment contributed salt but caused a problem because it lacked water.

MORE ABOUT . . .
Ancient and Modern Ghana

The modern nation of Ghana was named in honor of the ancient empire, but there is no direct relation between the two. The Ghana Empire lay several hundred miles northwest of modern Ghana in what is now southeastern Mauritania and western Mali. During the empire's height, the capital city of Kumbi Saleh and the city of Audagost were probably the largest cities in West Africa. Each may have had more than 15,000 people.

 WORLD ART AND CULTURES TRANSPARENCIES
AT32 Ghana terra cotta sculpture

West African Empires, 800–1500

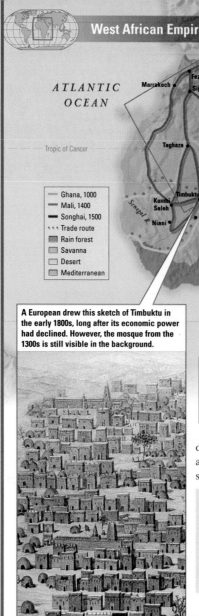

At Fez, the traders buy goods brought across the Mediterranean.

They load up with water at Sijilmasa. It will take 25 days to reach Taghaza.

At Taghaza, they take on salt and more water.

They trade the salt and other goods for gold at Timbuktu. They also load up on water and food for the return journey.

Map Key:
- Ghana, 1000
- Mali, 1400
- Songhai, 1500
- Trade route
- Rain forest
- Savanna
- Desert
- Mediterranean

A European drew this sketch of Timbuktu in the early 1800s, long after its economic power had declined. However, the mosque from the 1300s is still visible in the background.

GEOGRAPHY SKILLBUILDER: Interpreting Maps
1. **Region** *Compare the regions occupied by the Ghana, Mali, and Songhai empires in terms of size and location.*
2. **Human-Environment Interaction** *How did the environment both contribute resources to and cause problems for traders?*

---

chief judge, and military commander. He headed a large bureaucracy and could call up a huge army. In 1067, a Muslim geographer and scholar named al-Bakri wrote a description of Ghana's royal court:

A VOICE FROM THE PAST
The king adorns himself . . . wearing necklaces and bracelets. . . . The court of appeal is held in a domed pavilion around which stand ten horses with gold embroidered trappings. Behind the king stand ten pages holding shields and swords decorated with gold, and on his right are the sons of the subordinate [lower] kings of his country, all wearing splendid garments and with their hair mixed with gold.

AL-BAKRI, quoted in *Africa in the Days of Exploration*

By the year 800, Ghana had become an empire. Because Ghana's king controlled trade and commanded a large army, he could demand taxes and gifts from the chiefs of surrounding lands. As long as the chiefs made their payments, the king left them in peace to rule their own people.

Islamic Influences While Islam spread through North Africa by conquest, south of the Sahara, Islam spread through trade. Muslim merchants and teachers settled in the states south of the Sahara and introduced their faith there.

Eventually, Ghana's rulers converted to Islam. By the 11th century, Muslim advisers were helping the king run his kingdom. While Ghana's African rulers and many members of the court accepted Islam, many people in the empire clung to their animistic beliefs and practices. Much of the population never converted. Those who did kept many of their former beliefs, which they observed along with Islam. Among the upper class, Islam's growth encouraged the spread of literacy. To study the Qur'an, converts to Islam had to learn to read and write Arabic.

Background
Al-Bakri claimed that Ghana's army was 200,000 strong. Some modern scholars believe that figure was exaggerated.

Background
Animism is the belief that spirits—residing in animals, plants, and natural forces—play an important role in regulating daily life.

Science The source of all salt is brine, or salty water from seas or salt lakes. Salt deposits that now lie underground were formed by the evaporation of seawater millions of years ago. Salt is necessary to good health. Human blood contains salt, and human cells must have salt to work properly. In a hot, dry region like the Sahel, salt is especially important to human health.

Since ancient times, salt has been valued as both a preservative and a flavoring. Ask students to research current uses for salt in manufacturing or to report to the class on major sources of salt today and modern methods of extracting it.

Timbuktu Today Timbuktu is a city in the West African nation of Mali. Although small caravans still carry salt to the city in the winter, the gold that made trans-Saharan trade flourish vanished long ago. Since the 1600s Timbuktu's population has declined. Three great mosques built during the Songhai Empire remain, but they are endangered by the Sahara's encroaching sands. The United Nations has put these mosques on its World Heritage List of endangered sites.

Interested students might visit the Internet site for UNESCO's World Heritage List to learn more about what international organizations are doing to preserve such African cultural treasures.

In 1076 the Muslim Almoravids of North Africa completed their conquest of Ghana. Although the Almoravids eventually withdrew from Ghana, the war had badly disrupted the gold-salt trade. Ghana never regained its power.

Empire of Mali

By 1235 the kingdom of **Mali** had emerged. Its founders were Mande-speaking people, who lived south of Ghana. Like Ghana's, Mali's wealth was built on gold. As Ghana remained weak, people who had been under its control began to act independently. In addition, miners found new gold deposits farther east. This caused the most important trade routes to shift eastward, which made a new group of people—the people of Mali—wealthy. It also allowed them to seize power.

Sundiata Conquers an Empire Mali's first great leader, **Sundiata** (sun·JAHT·ah), came to power by crushing a cruel, unpopular leader. Then, in the words of a Mande oral tradition, "the world knew no other master but Sundiata." Sundiata became Mali's *mansa*, or emperor. Through a series of military victories, he took over the kingdom of Ghana and the trading cities of Kumbi and Walata. A period of peace and prosperity followed.

Sundiata proved to be as great a leader in peace as he had been in war. He put able administrators in charge of Mali's finances, defense,

HISTORY MAKERS

Sundiata
?–1255

Sundiata came from the kingdom of Kangaba near the present-day Mali-Guinea border. According to oral tradition, he was one of 12 royal brothers who were heirs to the throne of Kangaba.

When Sumanguru, ruler of a neighboring state, overran Kangaba in the early 1200s, he wanted to eliminate rivals, so he murdered all of Sundiata's brothers. He spared Sundiata, who was sickly and seemed unlikely to survive. However, as Sundiata grew up, he gained strength and became a popular leader of many warriors. In 1235, Sundiata's army defeated Sumanguru and his troops.

Although a Muslim, Sundiata also performed traditional African religious ceremonies as emperor. This helped him unify his empire.

Mansa Musa
?–1332

The strongest of Sundiata's successors, Mansa Musa was a devout Muslim. On his hajj, Mansa Musa stopped in Cairo, Egypt. Five hundred slaves, each carrying a staff of gold, arrived first. They were followed by 80 camels, each carrying 300 pounds of gold dust. Hundreds of other camels brought supplies. Thousands of servants and officials completed the procession.

An Egyptian official wrote:

This man Mansa Musa spread upon Cairo the flood of his generosity: there was no person, officer of the court, or holder of any office of the Sultanate who did not receive a sum of gold from him.

Mansa Musa gave away so much gold that the value of this precious metal declined in Egypt for 12 years.

and foreign affairs. From his new capital at Niani, he promoted agriculture and reestablished the gold-salt trade. Niani became an important center of commerce and trade. People began to call Sundiata's empire Mali, meaning "where the king lives."

Mansa Musa Expands Mali Sundiata died in 1255. Influenced by Arab traders, some of Mali's next rulers became Muslims. These African Muslim rulers built mosques, attended public prayers, and supported the preaching of Muslim holy men. The most famous of them was **Mansa Musa** (MAHN·sah moo·SAH), who may have been Sundiata's grandnephew.

Like Sundiata, Mansa Musa was a skilled military leader who exercised royal control over the gold-salt trade and put down every rebellion. His 100,000-man army kept order and protected Mali from attack. Under Mansa Musa, the empire expanded to roughly twice the size of the empire of Ghana. To govern his far-reaching empire, he divided it into provinces and appointed governors, who ruled fairly and efficiently.

A devout Muslim, Mansa Musa went on a hajj to Mecca from 1324 to 1325. When he returned, Mansa Musa ordered the building of new mosques at the trading cities of Timbuktu (TIHM·buhk·TOO) and Gao. Timbuktu became one of the most important cities of the empire. It attracted Muslim judges, doctors, religious leaders, and scholars from far and wide to its mosques and universities.

This is a Spanish mapmaker's idea of how Mansa Musa looked.

Societies and Empires of Africa **373**

Empire of Songhai

▶ **Key Ideas**
- Songhai gains control of trans-Saharan trade routes.
- Sunni Ali expands the Songhai Empire by military conquest.
- The Songhai Empire thrives under the skilled administration of Askia Muhammad.
- Songhai falls to a Moroccan army, ending the period of West African empires.

🏛 *GEOGRAPHY TRANSPARENCIES*
The Growth of Mali and Songhai, 1200–1591

Daily *Life*

Islam in West Africa

Have students research differences in the treatment of women in Muslim societies today. They might contrast the roles of women in Saudi Arabia or Iran with the roles of Muslim women in such largely Muslim nations in Africa as Mali, Niger, or Senegal.

MORE ABOUT . . .
Askia Muhammad

Like Mansa Musa, Askia Muhammad made a pilgrimage to Mecca. On his return, he revived Timbuktu as a center of Muslim learning. A Moroccan traveler who used the name Leo Africanus described Askia Muhammad's Timbuktu this way: "Here there are many doctors, judges, priests and other learned men that are well maintained at the king's cost. Various manuscripts and written books are brought here . . . and sold for more money than any other merchandise."

Travels of Ibn Battuta In 1352, one of Mansa Musa's successors prepared to receive a traveler and historian named **Ibn Battuta** (IHB·uhn ba·TOO·tah). A native of Tangier in North Africa, Ibn Battuta had traveled for 27 years, visiting most of the countries in the Islamic world.

After leaving the royal palace, Ibn Battuta visited Timbuktu and other cities in Mali. He found he could travel without fear of crime. As a devout Muslim, he praised the people for their study of the Qur'an, but criticized them for not strictly practicing Islam's moral code. However, Mali's justice system also impressed him:

> **A VOICE FROM THE PAST**
> They are seldom unjust, and have a greater abhorrence of injustice than any other people. Their sultan shows no mercy to anyone who is guilty of the least act of it. There is complete security in their country. Neither traveler nor inhabitant in it has anything to fear from robbers.
>
> **IBN BATTUTA**, quoted in *Africa in the Days of Exploration*

Ibn Battuta left Mali in 1353. Within 50 years, the once-powerful empire began to weaken. Most of Mansa Musa's successors lacked his ability to govern well. In addition, the gold trade that was one basis of Mali's wealth again shifted eastward as new goldfields were developed.

Empire of Songhai

As Mali declined in the 1400s, people who had been under its control began to break away. Among them were the **Songhai** (SAWNG·HY) to the east. They built up an army, extended their territory to the large bend in the Niger River near Gao, and gained control of the all-important trade routes. Gao was the capital of their empire.

Sunni Ali, a Conquering Hero The Songhai had two extraordinary rulers. One was Sunni Ali, who built a vast empire by military conquest. Sunni Ali's rule began in 1464 and lasted almost 30 years.

Sunni Ali built a professional army that had a riverboat fleet of war canoes and a mobile fighting force on horseback. He forged the Songhai empire through his skill as a military commander and his aggressive leadership. In 1468, Sunni Ali achieved his first major military triumph. He captured the city of Timbuktu, which had been an important part of Mali's empire.

Five years later, he took Djenné, also a trade city that had a university. To take Djenné, Sunni Ali besieged the city for seven years before it fell in 1473. Sunni Ali sealed the takeover of Djenné by marrying its queen.

Askia Muhammad Governs Well After Sunni Ali's death in 1492, his son succeeded him as ruler. Almost at once, he faced a major revolt by Muslims who were angry that he did not practice their religion faithfully. The leader of the revolt was a devout Muslim named Askia Muhammad. He drove Sunni Ali's son from power and replaced him.

Daily *Life*

Islam in West Africa

South of the Sahara, many converts to Islam also kept their African beliefs. They found ways to include their traditional rituals and customs into their new religion.

The status of women in West African societies demonstrates how local custom altered Muslim practice. In many 15th-century Muslim societies, women seldom left their homes. When they did, they veiled their faces. Muslim women in West Africa, however, did not wear veils. They also mingled freely with men in public—which shocked visiting Muslim religious leaders.

Cultural blending also affected architecture. West Africans used local techniques to build the mosque at Kawara, shown below. They sculpted it beautifully from mud.

THINK THROUGH HISTORY
C. Making Inferences Why might the people who had been conquered by Mali want to break away?
C. Possible Answers Because they resented being controlled by Mali; because they wanted to take over trade for themselves.

MULTIPLE LEARNING STYLES

TEACHING OPTION

Gifted and Talented Students
Oral Reading Around his 60th birthday, Ibn Battuta dictated his memoirs to Ibn Juzayy, who made a book of them. The book gained fame for its unique account of West and East Africa in the 14th century. The Africa scholar Basil Davidson thinks it "one of the best travel books ever made" and calls Ibn Battuta "a wonderful teller of tales whose cast of characters has sting and savour that bring him to life even after six hundred years."

Have students find copies of Ibn Battuta's account of Mali. Ask them to choose excerpts from his travelogue to read aloud to the class. One student might also present a brief biographical sketch of Ibn Battuta. Before reading to the class, each student should list on the board any words he or she thinks listeners may not know and then explain these words to the class.

As a follow-up activity, students might enjoy making an audiotape of their favorite passages interspersed with West African music. Review the readings that students choose to ensure that the content and language are appropriate for a classroom presentation.

During his 35-year rule, Askia Muhammad proved to be an excellent administrator. He set up an efficient tax system and chose able officials. Adding to the centralized government created by Sunni Ali, he appointed officials to serve as ministers of the treasury, army, navy, and agriculture. Under his rule, the well-governed empire thrived.

Despite its wealth and learning, the Songhai Empire lacked modern weapons. In 1591, a Moroccan fighting force of several thousand men equipped with gunpowder and cannons crossed the Sahara and invaded Songhai. The Moroccan troops quickly defeated the Songhai warriors, who were armed only with swords and spears. The collapse of the Songhai Empire ended a 1,000-year period in which powerful kingdoms and empires ruled the central region of West Africa.

Other Peoples of West Africa

While empires rose and fell in some parts of West Africa, in other areas city-states developed. As in Ghana, Mali, and Songhai, Muslim traditions influenced some of these city-states. Other city-states held to their traditional African beliefs.

Hausa City-States Compete The **Hausa** (HOW·suh) were a group of people named after the language they spoke. The city-states of the Hausa people first emerged between the years 1000 and 1200 in the savanna area east of Mali and Songhai in what is today northern Nigeria. Songhai briefly ruled the Hausa city-states, but they soon regained their independence. In such city-states as Kano, Katsina, and Zazzau (later Zaria), local rulers built walled cities for their capitals. These cities had populations of 50,000 or more. From their capitals, Hausa rulers governed the farming villages outside the city walls.

Each ruler depended on the crops of the farmers and on a thriving trade in salt, grain, and cotton cloth made by urban weavers. Because they were located on trade routes that linked other West African states with the Mediterranean, Kano and Katsina became major trading states. They profited greatly from supplying the needs of caravans. Kano was noted for its woven and dyed cloth and for its leather goods.

Zazzau, the southernmost state, conducted a vigorous trade in enslaved persons. Zazzau's traders raided an area south of the city and sold their captives to traders in other Hausa states. These traders sold them to other North or West African societies in exchange for horses, harnesses, and guns. The Hausa kept some enslaved workers to build and repair city walls and grow food for the cities.

All the Hausa city-states had similar forms of government. Rulers held great power over their subjects, but ministers and other officials acted to check this power. For protection from outside enemies and from each other, each city-state raised an army of mounted horsemen. Although rulers often schemed and fought to gain control over their neighbors, none succeeded for long. The constant fighting among city-states prevented any one of them from building a Hausa empire.

Yoruba Kings and Artists Like the Hausa, the **Yoruba** (YAWR·uh·buh) people all spoke a common language. Originally the Yoruba-speaking people belonged to a number of small city-states in the forests on the southern edge of the savanna in what is today Benin and southwestern Nigeria. In these communities most people farmed. Over time, some of these smaller communities joined together under strong leaders. This led to the formation of several localized Yoruba kingdoms.

Considered divine, Yoruba kings served as the most important religious and political leaders in their kingdoms. All Yoruba chiefs traced their descent from the first ruler of Ife (EE·fay). According to legend,

SPOTLIGHT ON

Queen Amina's Reign

In the 1500s, the Hausa city-state of Zazzau (later called Zaria) was governed by Queen Amina. She was remembered as the "headdress among the turbans." Her rule was distinguished for its military conquests.

The *Kano Chronicle,* a history of the city-state of Kano, records:

At this time Zaria, under Queen Amina, conquered all the towns as far as Kawararafa and Nupe. Every town paid tribute to her. . . . Her conquests extended over 34 years.

Queen Amina's commitment to her Muslim faith also led her to encourage Muslim scholars, judges, and religious leaders from religious centers at Kano and Timbuktu to come to Zazzau.

This modern Hausa village in Nigeria has many traditionally constructed mud buildings.

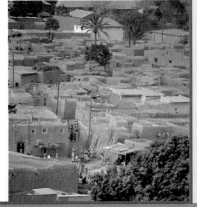

History Through Art

Benin Sculpture Much of the art of Benin was commissioned by Benin's wealthy kings to decorate the palace or honor important people such as chiefs and priests. This court art took many forms, including heads, figurines, and masks in bronze, wood, or terra cotta. Some sculptured heads held a large carved ivory tusk, a symbol of the path to the world of the ancestors.

 IN-DEPTH RESOURCES: UNIT 3
Primary Sources: Benin bronze sculpture, p. 94; The Making of Benin Bronzes, p. 95

 WORLD ART AND CULTURES TRANSPARENCIES
AT33 Benin bronze

MORE ABOUT . . .
Benin Portrait Heads

Benin portrait heads were meant to show not what a person looked like but what the person's status was. Hairstyles or decorations could indicate social standing.

MORE ABOUT . . .
Benin Plaques

Benin's sculptors made many fine heads and fixtures for the palaces of the king, but Benin artists were equally famous for bronze plaques nailed to courtyard pillars. The plaques recorded major events in the history of the kingdom, its ruler, and his court. Images of animals, warriors, and noblemen were commonly used. Some plaques included portraits of the early Portuguese explorers who visited Benin in the 1500s.

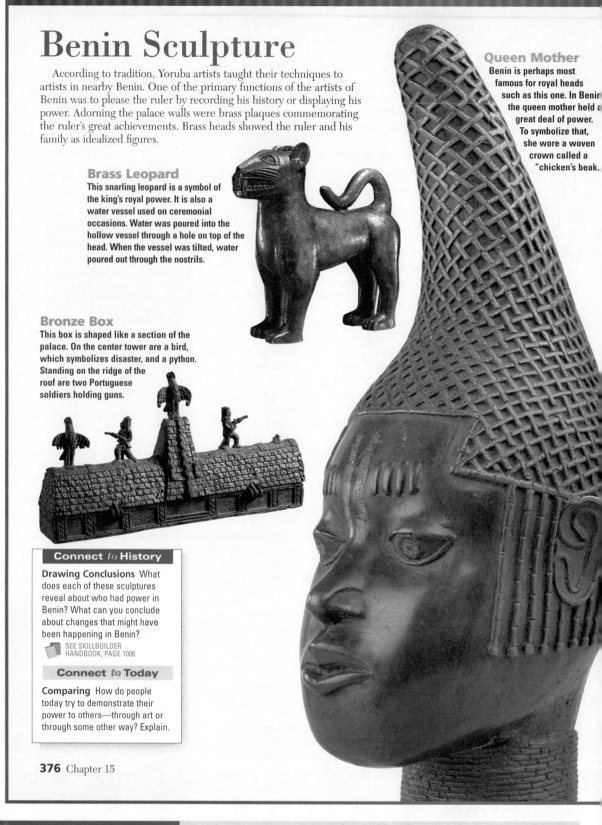

Benin Sculpture

According to tradition, Yoruba artists taught their techniques to artists in nearby Benin. One of the primary functions of the artists of Benin was to please the ruler by recording his history or displaying his power. Adorning the palace walls were brass plaques commemorating the ruler's great achievements. Brass heads showed the ruler and his family as idealized figures.

Brass Leopard
This snarling leopard is a symbol of the king's royal power. It is also a water vessel used on ceremonial occasions. Water was poured into the hollow vessel through a hole on top of the head. When the vessel was tilted, water poured out through the nostrils.

Bronze Box
This box is shaped like a section of the palace. On the center tower are a bird, which symbolizes disaster, and a python. Standing on the ridge of the roof are two Portuguese soldiers holding guns.

Queen Mother
Benin is perhaps most famous for royal heads such as this one. In Benin the queen mother held a great deal of power. To symbolize that, she wore a woven crown called a "chicken's beak."

Connect *to* History

Drawing Conclusions What does each of these sculptures reveal about who had power in Benin? What can you conclude about changes that might have been happening in Benin?

SEE SKILLBUILDER HANDBOOK, PAGE 1006

Connect *to* Today

Comparing How do people today try to demonstrate their power to others—through art or through some other way? Explain.

Connect *to* History

Drawing Conclusions
Possible Response: The brass leopard and the statue of the queen mother are both symbols of the power of the king. The leopard was probably a particularly powerful animal in Benin tradition. Great as the queen mother's power was, it derived from the power of her son as ruler, so her place in society reflected the greater authority of the king. The bronze box suggests the growing threat of the Portuguese to Benin. The symbolism of disaster through the bird and the gun-wielding Portuguese atop the palace suggest that the power of the king is declining.

Connect *to* Today

Comparing
Have students make a Venn diagram comparing the symbols of power used in Benin with those used by the president of the United States. The diagram might look like this:

Ruler of Benin
- palace
- servants
- clothing
- crown

Both
- military
- guard
- title

President
- White House
- Secret Service
- Air Force One
- limousine

the creator sent this first ruler down to earth at Ife, where he founded the first Yoruba state. His many sons became the heads of other Yoruba kingdoms. All Yoruba chiefs regarded the king of Ife as their highest spiritual authority. To demonstrate his power, each king surrounded himself with a large royal court and soldier-bodyguards. However, a secret society of religious and political leaders limited the king's rule by reviewing the decisions he made.

Ife and Oyo were the two largest Yoruba kingdoms. Ife, developed by 1100, was the most powerful Yoruba kingdom until the late 1600s, when Oyo became more prosperous. As large urban centers, both Ife and Oyo had high walls surrounding them. With fertile soil and ample rainfall, most rural farms in the surrounding areas produced surplus food, which was sent to the cities. This enabled city dwellers to become traders and craftspeople.

The Ife produced gifted artists who carved in wood and ivory. They produced terra cotta sculptures and cast in bronze, brass, and copper. Some scholars believe that the rulers supported artists, who may have lived at court. Many clay and metal casts portray Ife rulers in an idealistic way.

Kingdom of Benin To the south and west of Ife, near the delta of the Niger River, lay the kingdom of **Benin** (buh·NIHN). Like the Yoruba people of Ife and Oyo, its people made their homes in the forest. The first kings of Benin date from the 1300s. Like the Yoruba kings, the oba, or ruler, of Benin based his right to rule on claims of descent from the first king of Ife.

In the 1400s, the oba named Ewuare made Benin into a major West African state. He did so by building a powerful army. He used it to control an area that by 1500 stretched from the Niger River delta in the east to what is today Lagos, Nigeria. Ewuare also strengthened Benin City by building walls around it. Inside the city, broad streets were lined by neat rows of houses.

The huge palace contained many courtyards and works of art. Artists working for the oba created magnificent brass heads of the royal family and copper figurines. Brass plaques on the walls and columns of the royal palace of the oba showed legends, historical scenes, and the great deeds of the oba and his nobles. According to tradition, Benin artists learned their craft from an Ife artist brought to Benin by the oba to teach them.

In the 1480s, Portuguese trading ships began to sail into Benin's port at Gwatto. The Portuguese traded with Benin merchants for pepper, leopard skins, ivory, and enslaved persons. This began several centuries of European interference in Africa—during which they enslaved Africans and seized African territory for colonies. Meanwhile, East Africans—discussed in Section 3—prospered from trade and developed thriving cities and empires.

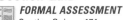

Although carved sometime within the last two centuries, this mother and child is done in a traditional Yoruba style.

Vocabulary
terra cotta: a reddish-brown clay, hard ceramic.

Section ❷ Assessment

1. TERMS & NAMES
Identify
• Ghana
• Mali
• Sundiata
• Mansa Musa
• Ibn Battuta
• Songhai
• Hausa
• Yoruba
• Benin

2. TAKING NOTES
Compare the Mali Empire and the Songhai Empire using a Venn diagram like the one below.

Mali

both

Songhai

3. DRAWING CONCLUSIONS
Which of the two—the Yoruba people or the people of Benin—had more influence on the other? Explain.

THINK ABOUT
• when the kingdoms flourished
• political traditions of each
• artistic traditions of each

4. ANALYZING THEMES
Economics What do you think was the most effective method Ghana used to regulate its economy? Explain.

THINK ABOUT
• trade routes
• ownership of gold
• taxes

Societies and Empires of Africa **377**

Teacher's Edition 377

Section 3
Overview

OBJECTIVES

1 To describe the role of east-coast trading cities in the economy of East Africa.

2 To explain how Islam influenced East African peoples.

3 To identify Great Zimbabwe and Mutapa as Shona states that rose in southern Africa.

SKILLBUILDERS
- Interpreting charts, p. 378
- Interpreting maps: movement, human-environment interaction, p. 379

CRITICAL THINKING
- Analyzing causes, p. 379
- Summarizing, p. 379
- Drawing conclusions, p. 380
- Making inferences, p. 381
- Comparing, p. 381

FOCUS
5-Minute Warm-Up

▶ **Perceiving Causes and Effects**

Have students answer these questions to explore cultural interaction in East Africa.

1. Read Global Impact on page 378. What were two results of contact between Bantu speakers and Arabs?

2. What are the origin and meaning of the word *Swahili*?

 WARM-UP TRANSPARENCY 15

OBJECTIVE 1 INSTRUCT

East Coast Trade Cities

▶ **Key Ideas**
- East African seaports rise through trade with Asia.
- Swahili is the trade language.
- Kilwa's southerly location and control of Sofala make it rich.
- The Portuguese take over southeastern African trade.

 IN-DEPTH RESOURCES: UNIT 3
Guided Reading, p. 89
Primary Source: from *The Book of Roger* by Al-Idrisi, p. 96

 ACCESS FOR STUDENTS ACQUIRING ENGLISH
Guided Reading (Spanish), p. 153

---

3 Eastern City-States and Southern Empires

MAIN IDEA	WHY IT MATTERS NOW
From 1000 to 1500, East African city-states and southern African empires gained wealth and power through trade.	The country of Zimbabwe and cities such as Mogadishu and Mombasa have their roots in this time period.

SETTING THE STAGE As early as the third century, the kingdom of Aksum had taken part in an extensive trade network. From its Red Sea port, Aksum traded with Arabia, Persia, India, and Rome. In the 600s, Muslim forces gained control of Arabia, the Red Sea, and North Africa. The Muslims cut off the Aksumites from their port. The Aksumites moved their capital south from Aksum to Roha (later called Lalibela) shortly before 1100. In the meantime, other cities on the east coast were thriving on Indian Ocean trade.

*Global*Impact

Swahili

Over the centuries, contacts between two peoples—Bantu speakers and Arabs—led to the creation of a new people and a new language. Many Arab traders married African women. In time, people of mixed Arab and African ancestry came to be called Swahili. The word comes from an Arabic term meaning "people of the coast" and refers to the East African coast.

Although Swahili peoples do not share a single culture, they do speak a common language. Swahili is a Bantu language with many words borrowed from Arabic. Today, Swahili is spoken by about 30 million people—about half of all people who speak a Bantu language. In Tanzania and Kenya, Swahili is the official language.

East Coast Trade Cities

By 1100, waves of Bantu-speaking people had migrated across central Africa to the east coast. There they established farming and fishing villages. At the same time, traders took advantage of the monsoons to make their way across the Indian Ocean to East Africa. Slowly, the existing coastal villages grew into bustling seaports, built on trade between East African merchants and traders from Arabia, Persia, and India. As trade increased, many Muslim Arab and Persian traders settled in these port cities. Arabic blended with the Bantu language to create the **Swahili** (swah·HEE·lee) language.

Persian traders moved south from the Horn of Africa—a triangular peninsula near Arabia. They brought Asian manufactured goods to Africa and African raw materials to Asia. In the coastal markets, Arab traders sold porcelain bowls from China and jewels and cotton cloth from India. They bought African ivory, gold, tortoiseshell, ambergris, leopard skins, and rhinoceros horns to carry to Arabia.

By 1300, more than 35 trading cities dotted the coast from Mogadishu in the north to Kilwa and Sofala in the south. Like the empires of West Africa, these seaports grew wealthy by controlling all incoming and outgoing trade. Some cities also manufactured trade goods for export. For example, weavers in Mogadishu and Sofala made cloth. Workers in Mombasa and Malindi made iron tools.

Background
More Bantu-speaking people moved south than east. Eventually, they settled much of southern Africa.

Vocabulary
ambergris: a grayish-white substance from the intestines of sperm whales, used to make perfume.

In some parts of Africa, cowrie shells were used for currency. The cowrie is a sea snail that lives in the Indian Ocean. Its shell is beautifully colored.

378

Trade Goods		
Raw Materials	**Point of Origin**	**Products Made**
• leopard skins	• savanna region	• saddles
• tortoiseshell	• shells of hawksbill sea turtles	• combs
• gold	• mines in southern Africa	• coins, jewelry
• ivory	• tusks from elephants in savanna region	• carved chess pieces and sword hilts

SKILLBUILDER: Interpreting Charts
1. *Which raw materials came from the savanna region?*
2. *Rank the raw materials in order of value, and explain your decision.*

SECTION 3 RESOURCES

PRINT RESOURCES

 IN-DEPTH RESOURCES: UNIT 3
Guided Reading, p. 89
Skillbuilder Practice: Analyzing Causes, p. 90
Primary Source: from *The Book of Roger* by Al-Idrisi, p. 96
History Makers: Mutota, p. 101

 ACCESS FOR STUDENTS ACQUIRING ENGLISH
Guided Reading (Spanish), p. 153
Skillbuilder Practice (Spanish), p. 154

 FORMAL ASSESSMENT
Section Quiz, p. 172

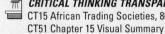 **ALTERNATIVE ASSESSMENT BOOK**

TECHNOLOGY RESOURCES

CRITICAL THINKING TRANSPARENCIES
CT15 African Trading Societies, 800–1500
CT51 Chapter 15 Visual Summary

CD-ROM
Electronic Library of Primary Sources

INTERNET www.mlworldhistory.com

The City-State of Kilwa In 1331, Ibn Battuta visited Kilwa. He called it one of the most beautiful cities in the world. He admired the luxurious way that its Muslim rulers and merchants lived. The richest families lived in fine houses of coral and stone. They slept in beds inlaid with ivory and their meals were served on Chinese porcelain. Wealthy Muslim women wore silk robes and gold and silver bracelets.

Kilwa grew rich because it was as far south on the coast as a ship from India could sail in one monsoon season. Therefore, trade goods from southerly regions had to funnel into Kilwa, so Asian merchants could buy them.

In addition, in the late 1200s Kilwa had seized the port of Sofala, which was a trading center for gold mined inland. By controlling Sofala, Kilwa was able to control the overseas trade of gold from southern Africa. This made Kilwa the wealthiest, most powerful coastal city-state.

THINK THROUGH HISTORY
A. Analyzing Causes What were the two main reasons Kilwa became so wealthy?
A. Answer Its favorable location caused trade to funnel into the city; It controlled Sofala and its gold trade.

Portuguese Conquest In 1488, the first Portuguese ships rounded the southern tip of Africa and sailed north, looking for a sea route to India. They wanted to gain profits from the Asian trade in spices, perfumes, and silks. When the Portuguese saw the wealth of the East African city-states, they decided to conquer those cities and take over the trade themselves.

Using their heavy ships' guns, the Portuguese took Sofala, Kilwa, and Mombasa. They burned parts of Kilwa and built forts on the sites of Kilwa and Mombasa. The Portuguese remained a presence on the East African coast for the next two centuries.

Islamic Influences

As in West Africa, Muslim traders introduced Islam to the East African coast, and the growth of commerce caused it to spread. Even the smallest towns had a mosque for the faithful. A Muslim sultan, or ruler, governed most cities. In addition, most government officials and wealthy merchants were Muslims.

B. Answer The Qadi judged religious cases; the wazirs and amirs judged nonreligious cases; the Sultan (or Shaikh) judged cases that were specially referred to him.

Islamic Law In 1331, Ibn Battuta visited the East African city of Mogadishu. He described how Muslim religious leaders and government officials decided legal matters:

> **A VOICE FROM THE PAST**
> The Shaikh [sultan] takes his place in his hall of audience and sends for the Qadi [judge]. He takes his place on the Shaikh's left and then the lawyers come in and the chief of them sit in front of the Shaikh. . . . Then food is brought and . . . those who are in the audience chamber eat in the presence of the Shaikh. . . . After this the Shaikh retires to his private apartments and the Qadi, the wazirs [government ministers] . . . and . . . chief amirs [military commanders] sit to hear causes and complaints. Questions of religious law are decided by the Qadi, other cases are judged by the . . . wazirs and amirs. If a case requires the views of the [Shaikh], it is put in writing for him. He sends back an immediate reply.
> **IBN BATTUTA**, *Travels of Ibn Battuta*

THINK THROUGH HISTORY
B. Summarizing Name the four types of people who decided legal matters and what type of cases they judged.

Societies and Empires of Africa **379**

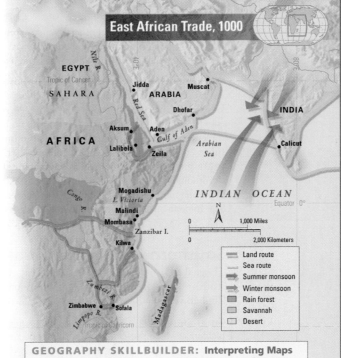

East African Trade, 1000

EGYPT
Tropic of Cancer
SAHARA
Jidda
ARABIA
Muscat
Dhofar
Aksum
Aden
Gulf of Aden
INDIA
AFRICA
Lalibela
Zeila
Arabian Sea
Calicut
Congo R.
Mogadishu
L. Victoria
Malindi
INDIAN OCEAN
Equator 0°
Mombasa
Zanzibar I.
Kilwa
0   1,000 Miles
0   2,000 Kilometers

Land route
Sea route
Summer monsoon
Winter monsoon
Rain forest
Savannah
Desert

Zambezi R.
Zimbabwe
Sofala
Limpopo R.
Tropic of Capricorn
Madagascar

GEOGRAPHY SKILLBUILDER: Interpreting Maps
1. **Movement** How far did a trader have to travel to make a round trip from Calicut in India to Kilwa in Africa and back again?
2. **Human-Environment Interaction** Which monsoon would a trader rely on to sail from India to Africa?

History from Visuals

(see page 378)

Trade Goods

Interpreting the Chart Have students use the chart to find out what products were made from ivory. *Chess pieces and sword hilts.* Where did east-coast traders get gold? *Southern Africa*

Extension Activity Have students find out what raw materials are exported from African nations south of the Sahara today.

SKILLBUILDER Answers
1. Leopard skins and ivory
2. Possible response: Gold, ivory, leopard skins, tortoiseshell; gold is rarest, ivory is harder to get than leopard skins, tortoiseshells are easiest to get.

History from Visuals

East African Trade, 1000

Interpreting the Map Have students use the map key to identify the directions of the summer and winter monsoons.

Extension Activity Have students discuss why there were more overland trade routes south of the equator than north. *Possible responses: The south had more highly valued goods; the region was easier to cross.*

SKILLBUILDER Answers
1. About 6,000 miles
2. The winter monsoon

OBJECTIVE 2 INSTRUCT

Islamic Influences

▶ **Key Ideas**
• Muslim traders spread Islam to East Africa, where rulers, officials, and native traders adopt it.
• Muslim traders begin exporting slaves from East Africa to Asia.

ELECTRONIC LIBRARY OF PRIMARY SOURCES
"Mogadishu in 1331"

TEACHING OPTION   **BLOCK SCHEDULING**

SKILLBUILDER MINI-LESSON: Analyzing Causes

CLASS TIME 10 MINUTES

Explaining the Skill: History often involves more than a simple string of causes and effects, with one event following another. For example, a cause can have more than one effect, and an effect can have more than one cause or be the cause of something else.

Applying the Skill: *Kilwa's Wealth* To help students answer the Think Through History

question on this page, have them read the paragraphs entitled "The City-State of Kilwa." Then have them chart the causes and effects that explain Kilwa's rise to wealth. At right is one example:

IN-DEPTH RESOURCES: UNIT 3
Skillbuilder Practice: Analyzing Causes, p. 90

cause Kilwa was the southernmost port Indian traders could reach and return from in one monsoon season.

cause Kilwa seized Sofala, a trading center for gold mined inland.

cause/effect Trade goods from southern Africa had to funnel through Kilwa so Asian traders could buy them.

cause/effect Kilwa controlled overseas trade of gold from southern Africa.

effect Kilwa grew wealthy.

379

Most rulers, government officials, and merchants were Muslim. However, the vast majority of people along the East African coast held on to their traditional religious beliefs. This was also true of the people who lived in inland villages.

Enslavement of Africans Along with luxury goods, Arab Muslim traders exported enslaved persons from the East African coast. Traders sent Africans acquired through kidnapping and raids to markets in Arabia, Persia, and Iraq. The wealthy in these countries often bought enslaved persons to do burdensome domestic tasks. Muslim traders shipped enslaved Africans across the Indian Ocean to India, where Indian rulers employed them as soldiers. Enslaved Africans also worked on docks and ships at Muslim-controlled ports and as household servants in China.

Although traders had been enslaving East Africans and selling them overseas since about the ninth century, the numbers remained small—perhaps about 1,000 a year. The trade in enslaved persons did not increase dramatically until the 1700s. At that time, Europeans started to buy captured Africans for their colonial plantations.

Southern Africa and Great Zimbabwe

The gold and ivory that helped the coastal city-states grow rich came from the interior of southern Africa. In southeastern Africa the Shona people established a city called **Great Zimbabwe** (zihm·BAHB·way), which grew into an empire built on the gold trade.

Great Zimbabwe By 1000, the Shona people had claimed the fertile, well-watered plateau between the Zambezi and Limpopo rivers in modern Zimbabwe. The area was well suited to farming and cattle raising. Its location also had economic advantages. Great Zimbabwe stood near an important trade route linking the inland gold-fields with the coastal trading city of Sofala. Sometime after 1000, Great Zimbabwe gained control of these trade routes. From the 1200s through the 1400s, it became the capital of a thriving state. Its leaders taxed the traders who traveled these routes. They also demanded payments from less powerful chiefs. The city of Great Zimbabwe was the economic, political, and religious center of its empire.

By 1450, the city of Great Zimbabwe was abandoned. No one knows for sure why it happened. According to one theory, cattle grazing had worn out the grasslands. In addition, farming had worn out the soil, and people had used up the salt and timber. The area could no longer support a large population.

Ruins of Zimbabwe Almost everything that is known about Great Zimbabwe comes from its impressive 60 acres of ruins. Portuguese explorers knew about the site in the

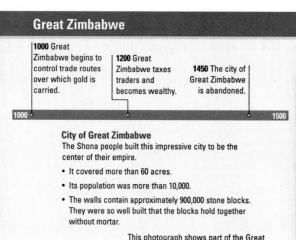

Great Zimbabwe

1000 Great Zimbabwe begins to control trade routes over which gold is carried.

1200 Great Zimbabwe taxes traders and becomes wealthy.

1450 The city of Great Zimbabwe is abandoned.

1000 ●————————————————————● 1500

City of Great Zimbabwe
The Shona people built this impressive city to be the center of their empire.

• It covered more than 60 acres.
• Its population was more than 10,000.
• The walls contain approximately 900,000 stone blocks. They were so well built that the blocks hold together without mortar.

This photograph shows part of the Great Enclosure and the cone-shaped tower. ➤

This picture of a person standing next to the tower shows how very high both the tower and the enclosing walls are.

1500s. Karl Mauch, a German explorer, was one of the first Europeans to physically rediscover the remains of these stone dwellings in 1871.

The word *zimbabwe* comes from a Shona phrase meaning "stone enclosure." The ruins consist of two complexes of stone buildings that once housed the royal palace of Great Zimbabwe's rulers. The Great Enclosure is a massive curving wall up to 36 feet high and 15 feet thick. Because there was no way for soldiers to climb to the top of the walls, archaeologists theorize that they were not used primarily as defenses. The massive walls were probably built to impress visitors with the strength of Zimbabwe and its ruler. Inside the walls stands a cone-shaped tower. Among the ruins were found tall figures of birds, carved from soapstone. Archaeologists believe the construction of Great Zimbabwe may have taken 400 years.

Mutapa Empire According to Shona oral tradition, a man named Mutota left Great Zimbabwe about 1420 to find a new source of salt. Traveling north, he settled in a valley with fertile soil, good rainfall, and ample wood. There he founded a new state to replace Great Zimbabwe. As the state grew, its leader Mutota used his army to dominate the northern Shona people living in the area. He forced them to make payments to him.

These conquered people called Mutota and his successors *mwene mutapa,* meaning conqueror or "master pillager." The Portuguese who arrived on the East African coast in the early 1500s believed *mwene mutapa* to be a title of respect for the ruler. The term is also the origin of the name of the **Mutapa** Empire. By the time of Mutota's death, the Mutapa Empire had conquered all of what is now Zimbabwe except the eastern portion. By 1480 Mutota's son Matope claimed control of the area along the Zambezi River to the Indian Ocean coast.

The Mutapa Empire was able to mine gold deposited in nearby rivers and streams. In addition, Mutapa rulers forced people in conquered areas to mine gold for them. The rulers sent gold to the coastal city-states in exchange for luxuries. Even before the death of Matope, the southern part of his empire broke away. However, the Mutapa Dynasty continued to remain in control of the smaller empire.

In the 1500s, the Portuguese tried to conquer the empire. When they failed to do so, they resorted to interfering in Mutapa politics. They helped to depose one ruler and put one they could control on the throne. This was a forerunner of increasing European interference in Africa in centuries to come.

D. Possible Answer
To get control of the gold trade.

THINK THROUGH HISTORY
D. Making Inferences Why do you think the Portuguese wanted to conquer the Mutapa Empire?

This is a Portuguese portrait of one of the kings of the Mutapa Empire.

Section ③ Assessment

1. TERMS & NAMES

Identify
- Swahili
- Great Zimbabwe
- Mutapa

2. TAKING NOTES

Use a chart like the one below to explain one example of cultural interaction brought about by trade on the coast of East Africa.

cultural group	cultural group

→ ↓ ←

resulting interaction

Do you think this interaction had a positive or negative effect? Explain.

3. COMPARING

Compare the Portuguese who arrived in East Africa with the rulers of the Mutapa Empire.

THINK ABOUT
- how they treated other groups of people
- what motivated their actions

4. THEME ACTIVITY

Interaction with Environment Create a chart, sketch, or collage that demonstrates how the people of Great Zimbabwe interacted with their environment, both positively and negatively, over time.

Societies and Empires of Africa **381**

ANSWERS

1. TERMS & NAMES
Swahili, p. 378
Great Zimbabwe, p. 380
Mutapa, p. 381

2. TAKING NOTES
Possible Responses: Bantu speakers, Arabs—create Swahili; positive. Muslim traders, East Africans—bring Islam to East Africa; positive. Portuguese, Mutapa Empire—Portuguese interfere in Mutapa politics, influence ruler; negative.

3. COMPARING
Possible Responses: Both were conquerors; both were interested in dominating trade and acquiring wealth; both tried to force other groups to do what they wanted.

4. THEME ACTIVITY
Standards for Evaluation
An effective chart, sketch, or collage should . . .
- clearly show how people of Great Zimbabwe used their environment
- clearly show good and bad effects on the environment.

Chapter 15 Assessment

TERMS & NAMES

1. lineage, p. 368
2. stateless societies, p. 368
3. patrilineal, p. 369
4. matrilineal, p. 369
5. Ghana, p. 371
6. Mali, p. 373
7. Ibn Battuta, p. 374
8. Songhai, p. 374
9. Swahili, p. 378
10. Great Zimbabwe, p. 380

REVIEW QUESTIONS

11. Older male serves as group leader, offering opinions, but every family makes its own decisions; members resolve arguments through long discussions.

12. Society is organized by groups of individuals who are roughly the same age; these groups go through life stages together and have clearly defined responsibilities for each stage.

13. Both were begun by Muslim reformers.

14. It regulated and taxed the gold-salt trade.

15. By conquest, through trade

16. It was based on both agriculture and trade; trade goods included salt, grain, cotton cloth, leather goods, enslaved persons, harnesses, guns.

17. The mixing of Arabic-speaking and Bantu-speaking peoples eventually created a third language, Swahili.

18. To control the gold trade

19. Rulers, government officials, and wealthy merchants—especially on the coast.

20. Great Zimbabwe came first. A man named Mutota left the area, traveled north, and founded the Mutapa Empire, which eventually included most of Zimbabwe.

TERMS & NAMES

Briefly explain the importance of each of the following to the societies and empires of Africa from 800 to 1500.

1. lineage
2. stateless societies
3. patrilineal
4. matrilineal
5. Ghana
6. Mali
7. Ibn Battuta
8. Songhai
9. Swahili
10. Great Zimbabwe

Interact *with* History

On page 366, you looked at a situation in which traders exchanged gold for salt. Now that you've read the chapter, reevaluate what makes trade items valuable. How did environmental conditions affect what items had value in Africa? Did government policies have any effect on value? Consider what you learned about trading states in both West and East Africa.

REVIEW QUESTIONS

SECTION 1 *(pages 367–370)*
North and Central African Societies

11. How is a dispute settled in Efe society?
12. What is an age-set system?
13. How were the beginnings of the Almoravid and Almohad empires similar?

SECTION 2 *(pages 371–377)*
West African Empires and Civilizations

14. What accounted for Ghana's financial success?
15. Name two ways Islam spread through Africa.
16. Describe the economy of the Hausa city-states.

SECTION 3 *(pages 378–381)*
Eastern City-States and Southern Empires

17. How did the Swahili language evolve?
18. Why was it important for Kilwa to control Sofala?
19. Who was most affected by the introduction of Islam to East Africa?
20. What was the relationship of Great Zimbabwe to the Mutapa Empire?

Visual Summary

Societies and Empires of Africa

	Organization & Time Periods	Significant Facts
Igbo people	• Existed as a stateless society from **9th through 19th centuries**	• Elders resolved conflicts
Almoravids	• Muslim state from **mid-1000s to mid-1100s**	• Founded city of Marrakech
Almohads	• Muslim state from **mid-1100s to mid-1200s**	• Unified the Maghrib under one authority for first time in history
Ghana	• West African empire from **700s to 1076**	• Grew wealthy and powerful by controlling gold-salt trade
Mali	• West African empire from **1235 to 1400s**	• Mansa Musa's hajj made Mali's wealth famous
Songhai	• West African empire that flourished in the **1400s and 1500s**	• Conquered Mali and gained control of trade routes
Benin	• West African trading kingdom strong in **1400s and 1500s**	• Famous for bronze and brass works of art
Kilwa	• East African city-state flourished from **1200s to 1400s**	• Grew wealthy from trade
Great Zimbabwe	• Capital of trade-based empire from **1200s until about 1450**	• City abandoned, perhaps because natural resources were used up
Mutapa Empire	• Founded **about 1420** by man from Great Zimbabwe	• Remained independent in spite of Portuguese attempts to conquer

382 Chapter 15

Interact *with* History

Possible Responses: West Africa had much gold but lacked salt, which was plentiful in the Sahara, and was also in need of the variety of manufactured goods produced around the Mediterranean. These factors heightened the value of salt and manufactured goods in West Africa. The Mediterranean region lacked a natural supply of gold, heightening the value of gold there.

East Africa had access to abundant raw materials that Asians lacked, such as gold and ivory, giving these items great value to Asians. Asians, in turn, had manufactured goods that East Africa lacked, giving those items great value in East Africa.

Taxation, control of trade routes, and limits on amounts of raw materials that could be traded helped African rulers regulate the value of trade goods.

CRITICAL THINKING

1. ADAPTING TO THE DESERT

THEME INTERACTION WITH ENVIRONMENT How did people adapt to the harsh conditions of the Sahara? Discuss both traders who crossed the Sahara and people who lived in the Saharan village of Taghaza.

2. AFRICAN LEADERS, 800–1500

Create a chart like the one below. For each leader, list what group of people he led and one of his significant achievements.

Leader	Group	Significant achievement
Ibn Yasin		
Ibn Tumart		
Mansa Musa		
Askia Muhammad		
Ewuare		
Mutota		

3. TRADE NETWORKS

Do you think that Africa in the year 1300 was connected to most of the world through trade, or was it relatively isolated from the rest of the world? Support your answer with evidence from the chapter.

4. ANALYZING PRIMARY SOURCES

The following quotation comes from a description of Timbuktu, written by Leo Africanus, a Muslim traveler. Read the paragraph and then answer the questions below it.

> **A VOICE FROM THE PAST**
> The rich king of Timbuktu hath many plates and scepters of gold, some whereof weigh 1,300 pounds: and he keeps a magnificent and well-furnished court. When he travelleth any whither he rideth upon a camel which is led by some of his noblemen; and so he doth likewise when he goeth forth to warfare, and all his soldiers ride upon horses. Whoever will speak unto this king must first fall down before his feet, and then taking up earth must first sprinkle it upon his own head and shoulders.
>
> **LEO AFRICANUS**, *A Geographical History of Africa*

- Do you think Leo Africanus was impressed by the ruler of Timbuktu or not? Explain your opinion.
- How did the king of Timbuktu demonstrate his royal status?

CHAPTER ACTIVITIES

1. LIVING HISTORY: Unit Portfolio Project

THEME RELIGIOUS AND ETHICAL SYSTEMS Your unit portfolio project focuses on the growth and influence of religious and ethical systems. For Chapter 15, you might use one of the following ideas to add to your portfolio:

- Write an interview with one Muslim ruler from this chapter. Discuss how Islam influenced his political decisions.
- With a small group, put on a skit enacting the story of how the creator caused the first Yoruba state to be established.
- Create a diagram showing which levels of East African society converted to Islam and which retained African beliefs.

2. CONNECT TO TODAY: Cooperative Learning

THEME ECONOMICS In this chapter, you read about how trade affected the economies of East African city-states. Today, much of eastern Africa still relies heavily on trade.

Work with a team to create a map that shows what goods present-day East African nations trade and who their trading partners are.

 Using the Internet or your library, research East African trade today.

- Find information on exports and imports, quantities shipped, where the goods are going, and how they are being transported.
- Look for examples of trade maps in this textbook, in historical atlases, and on the Internet.
- Create your own map showing East African trade today.

3. INTERPRETING A TIME LINE

Revisit the unit time line on pages 228–229. Use the Chapter 15 time line to find out when Great Zimbabwe was abandoned. Then use the other chapter time lines to name another event that was happening about the same time.

FOCUS ON **GEOGRAPHY**

Look at this map of western Africa in 1997. The map shows where some of the ethnic groups that you studied in this chapter live today. The groups are labeled in red.

- Which is the most widespread ethnic group? In what nations does that group live?
- Which groups live in modern Nigeria?

Connect to History
Compare this map to the map on page 368. Which groups are on both maps? Do they live in the same regions that they used to inhabit?

Western Africa, 1997

CHAPTER ACTIVITIES

1. LIVING HISTORY

Standards for Evaluation
An interview should meet the following criteria:

- Asks questions that reflect an understanding of the basic ideas of Islam and knowledge of the ruler's decisions.
- Gives responses that reflect views the ruler is likely to have held.

Standards for Evaluation
A skit should meet the following criteria:

- Accurately tells the legend describing the founding of Ife.
- Dramatizes the story so it is clear to the audience.

Standards for Evaluation
A diagram should meet the following criteria:

- Shows different levels of East African society.
- Identifies which levels were likely to hold which beliefs.
- Presents the information in a clear, visually interesting way.

2. CONNECT TO TODAY

Standards for Evaluation
A map should meet the following criteria:

- Contains accurate trade information.
- Effectively uses other trade maps as models.
- Uses map elements that clearly identify goods, quantities shipped, destinations, and modes of transport.

3. INTERPRETING A TIME LINE

Great Zimbabwe was abandoned about 1450.

Possible Response: About the same time, Constantinople fell to the Turks and the Hundred Years' War ended in France (1453).

FOCUS ON **GEOGRAPHY**

Answer: Berbers; Mauritania, Morocco, Algeria, Tunisia, Libya.
Answer: Hausa, Yoruba, Tiv, Igbo.

Connect to History Tiv, Igbo; yes.

CRITICAL THINKING

1. ADAPTING TO THE DESERT
Possible Responses: Traders learned to use the camel, which could travel long distances without water. Villagers in Taghaza built their homes from the salt available there.

2. AFRICAN LEADERS
Possible Responses: **Ibn Yasin**—Berbers/Almoravids, began Almoravid movement; **Ibn Tumart**—Berbers/Almohads, began Almohad movement; **Mansa Musa**—Mali, built mosques; **Askia Muhammad**—Songhai, built up centralized government; **Ewuare**—Benin, made Benin key West African state; **Mutota**—Mutapa Empire, conquered Shona people, founded new state

3. TRADE NETWORKS
Possible Responses: It was connected to most of the world. Before 1350, West Africa supplied much of the world's gold. It imported manufactured goods from the Mediterranean. Aksum traded with Egypt, Arabia, Persia, India, Rome. East Africans traded with Persia, Arabia, India, China.

4. ANALYZING PRIMARY SOURCES
Possible Responses: Yes, he was impressed because he records details that show the king's power. The king shows his status by displaying gold and requiring his subjects to abase themselves before him.

**Marine Painting
Ludolf Backhuysen
(1631–1708)**

Ludolf Backhuysen (also spelled Bakhuyzen) was a Dutch artist renowned for depicting the drama and movement of ships, whether in the harbor or on the high seas. In his time, he was the most popular marine painter in the Netherlands.

The Dutch ships shown here are the types of vessels used by many Europeans in exploration and trade in the late 17th century. The painting captures the perils to mariner and ship alike of long journeys over unfriendly seas to distant lands.

These voyages of exploration were made possible by advancements in ship design and navigational instruments. Sturdier ships and more accurate maps allowed sea captains and their crews to venture far from the sight of land toward previously uncharted territory.

The motives behind this era of worldwide exploration by the Europeans were many. A longing for riches was the principal motive. The wish to spread Christianity was another. The desire for adventure and the hope of fame also were powerful reasons. The Age of Exploration is often summed up as a mission for "glory, God, and gold."

By the end of this period, Portugal, Spain, the Netherlands, Britain, and France had spread European civilization to almost all areas of the globe.

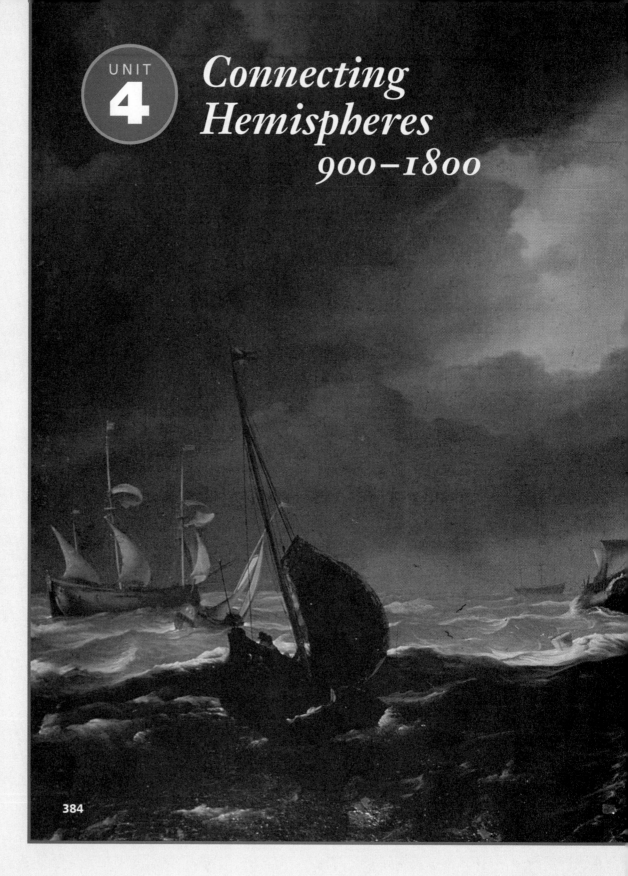

UNIT
4

Connecting Hemispheres
900–1800

384

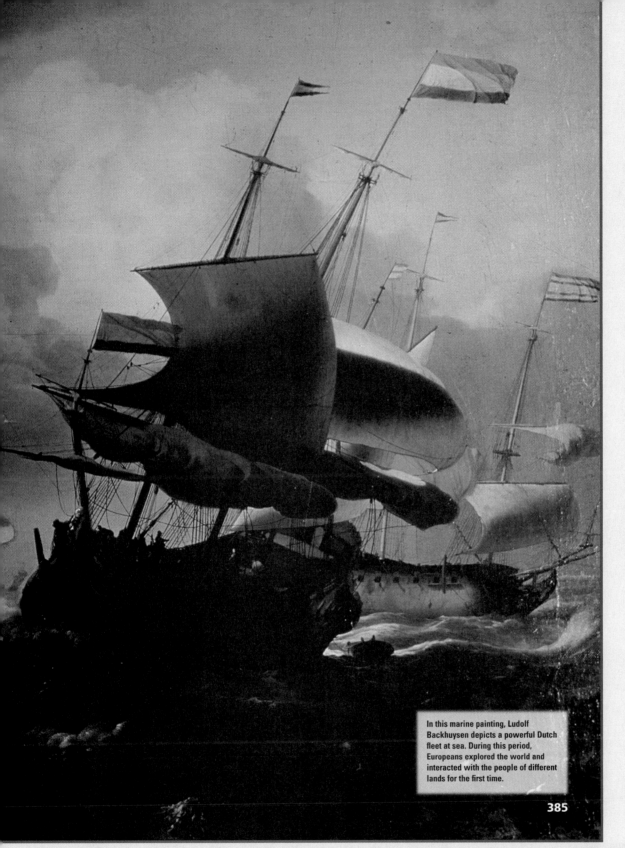

In this marine painting, Ludolf Backhuysen depicts a powerful Dutch fleet at sea. During this period, Europeans explored the world and interacted with the people of different lands for the first time.

385

This unit covers the developments in the eastern and western hemispheres that result in connections through exploration and trade beginning in the late 1400s.

In the Americas, many diverse civilizations, including the Mayan, Aztec, and Incan, flourish prior to the arrival of the Europeans. These complex societies have common patterns of trade, religion, and social structure.

Europe is transformed from 1300 to 1650 by two powerful intellectual movements, the Renaissance and the Reformation. The Renaissance produces an outpouring of artistic creativity and a scientific revolution. The Reformation splits Christianity into Protestant and Catholic divisions.

In the area stretching from the Balkans to India, three potent Islamic empires emerge between the 1300s and the 1500s. The Ottomans of Turkey, the Safavids of Persia, and the Mughals of India thrive but eventually fall to both internal and external pressures.

The intellectual curiosity that produced the Renaissance and the new technology that resulted from the scientific revolution help lead Europeans to embark on voyages to explore the world.

The desire for profit and the hope of spreading Christianity send Europeans to the Far East. Goods and ideas are exchanged with the peoples of Asia. However, the Chinese and the Japanese eventually restrict European influence, preferring self-sufficiency.

The European exploration and colonization of the Americas begins with the voyages of Columbus. Interactions between Americans and Europeans leads to a global exchange of foods, animals, and ideas; the enrichment of Europe; and the devastation of Native American cultures.

Connecting Hemispheres

Teaching Strategies

Summarizing The ability to condense the pattern of events for a time period or a civilization is an important skill for students to employ as they work with the Unit Time Lines. Summarizing allows students to move from the level of individual events to that of the patterns at work in world history.

Cultural Interaction and Exploration
You might ask students to examine the period between 1500 and 1600 to summarize patterns of contact among different civilizations. You might ask the class to group cultural interactions according to whether they occurred:

- within a continent (the Incan Empire reaches its height, Babur founds the Mughal Empire), or
- between continents (African slaves exported to the Americas, the Portuguese reach China, the circumnavigation of the globe by Magellan's crew, the conquest of the Aztecs and the Incas)

Cultural contact might also be summarized from the point of view of whether it was essentially peaceful or hostile in its intent. In fact, during the 1500s, a good deal of cultural interaction took place as a result of a desire to overcome another government or people, or to change others' religious beliefs.

The class might also discuss cultural interactions today and how the process may differ from that of the 1500s. The existence of the mass media and of modern transportation could be highlighted as important means of cultural interaction today.

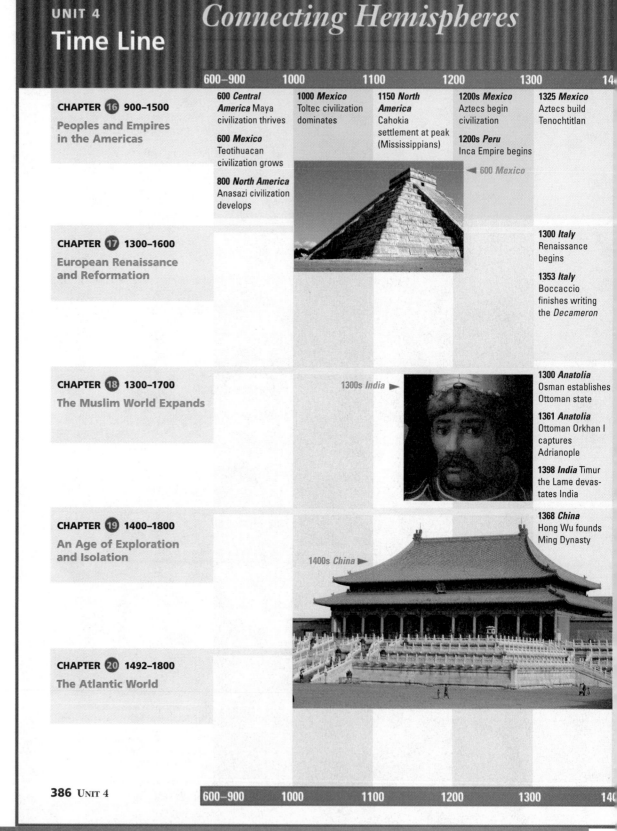

	600–900	1000	1100	1200	1300	14
CHAPTER **16** 900–1500 **Peoples and Empires in the Americas**	**600** *Central America* Maya civilization thrives **600** *Mexico* Teotihuacan civilization grows **800** *North America* Anasazi civilization develops	**1000** *Mexico* Toltec civilization dominates	**1150** *North America* Cahokia settlement at peak (Mississippians)	**1200s** *Mexico* Aztecs begin civilization **1200s** *Peru* Inca Empire begins ◀ **600** *Mexico*	**1325** *Mexico* Aztecs build Tenochtitlan	
CHAPTER **17** 1300–1600 **European Renaissance and Reformation**					**1300** *Italy* Renaissance begins **1353** *Italy* Boccaccio finishes writing the *Decameron*	
CHAPTER **18** 1300–1700 **The Muslim World Expands**		1300s *India* ▶			**1300** *Anatolia* Osman establishes Ottoman state **1361** *Anatolia* Ottoman Orkhan I captures Adrianople **1398** *India* Timur the Lame devastates India	
CHAPTER **19** 1400–1800 **An Age of Exploration and Isolation**		1400s *China* ▶			**1368** *China* Hong Wu founds Ming Dynasty	
CHAPTER **20** 1492–1800 **The Atlantic World**						

600–900	1000	1100	1200	1300	14

CONNECTIONS ACROSS THE CURRICULUM

Geography You may want to use the *Geography Transparencies* (in full color) and the Geography Applications copymasters in the *In-Depth Resources* book to help students understand the physical settings of developments on the unit time line.

Geography Transparencies Map transparencies in Unit 4 depict developments such as "The Expansion of the Inca Empire, 1230–1525" or events such as "The Fall of Constantinople, 1453" (Chapter 18). The latter map details how the Turkish army found a small open gate in the walls of Constantinople and poured in to take the city.

You might show the map transparencies to the class as the Unit Time Line is discussed. (Teacher material accompanying the transparencies provides background and questions with answers.) You could also provide the map in advance to students who wish to present it as part of an oral report.

Geography Applications
Discussion of the Unit Time Line may also provide an opportunity for students to work with the Geography Applications. Copymasters such as "Mayan Irrigation Techniques" (Chapter 16) or "Trade in Renaissance Europe" (Chapter 17) feature introductory text, followed by a map and one page of questions.

1500s England

▼ 1675 *North America*

1438 *Peru*
Pachacuti becomes ruler of Incas

1500s *Peru*
Inca Empire at height

1502 *Mexico*
Montezuma becomes Aztec ruler

1455 *Germany*
Gutenberg Bible produced on printing press

1497 *Italy*
Leonardo da Vinci paints *The Last Supper*

1508 *Italy*
Michelangelo begins painting Sistine Chapel

1517 *Germany*
Martin Luther begins Reformation

1534 *England*
Henry VIII breaks from Church

1601 *England*
William Shakespeare writes *Hamlet*

1603 *England*
Queen Elizabeth I dies, ending Tudor rule

1453 *Europe*
Ottomans conquer Constantinople

1498 *Portugal*
Vasco da Gama sails to India

1501 *Persia*
Safavid Isma'il conquers Persia

1526 *India*
Babur founds Mughal Empire

1529 *Anatolia*
Suleiman the Magnificent rules Ottoman Empire

1631 *India* Shah Jahan builds Taj Mahal

1658 *India*
Aurangzeb rules Mughal Empire

1419 *Portugal*
Prince Henry starts navigation school

1433 *China* Last voyage of Zheng He

1494 *Spain and Portugal* Treaty of Tordesillas splits "New World"

1514 *China*
First Portuguese ships reach China

1522 *Spain*
Magellan's crew sails around world

1603 *Japan*
Tokugawa regime begins

1636 *China*
Manchus conquer Korea

1644 *China*
Manchus found Qing Dynasty

1721 *Japan*
Edo (Tokyo) becomes world's largest city

1793 *China*
British seek trade concessions with Chinese

1492 *Americas*
Columbus sails to Hispaniola

1502 *Africa*
First slaves exported for work in the Americas

1521 *Mexico*
Cortés conquers Aztecs

1533 *Peru* Pizarro conquers Inca

1607 *North America* English settle Jamestown

1608 *Canada*
Champlain founds Quebec

1675 *North America* Colonists and Indians clash in King Philip's War

1739 *North America*
South Carolina slaves lead Stono Rebellion

1754 *North America*
French and Indian War begins

387

Living History
Unit 4 Portfolio Project

THEME Cultural Interaction

Your portfolio for Unit 4 will trace the ways cultures interact with one another and show the results of those influences. Types of interaction include conquest, trade, migration, and heritage. Results include the sharing of technology, religious concepts, political ideas, goods, crops, foods, diseases, and knowledge of all kinds.

Living History Project Choices
Each Chapter Assessment offers you choices of ways to show the cultural interaction in that chapter. Activities include the following:

Chapter 16 dialogue, poster, article

Chapter 17 magazine, letter, role-play, painting, interview

Chapter 18 letter, political cartoon, inscription

Chapter 19 letter, reply, editorial

Chapter 20 description, collage, debate

Portfolio Project

Theme: Cultural Interaction The portfolio projects for Unit 4 ask students to consider the complex process of cultural interaction. The focus for the projects will be cultural exchanges as they occurred between 900 and 1800 on the continents of Europe, Asia, and the Americas. Some of the crucial aspects of this question that are dealt with in the projects include:

• the relationship between conquering and conquered peoples

• changes in daily life brought about by trade contacts among peoples

• the colonial experience from the point of view of colonizers and colonized

• the exchange of religious ideas between and among peoples

• the transfer of artistic influences from one people to another

Students Acquiring English
Students acquiring English (SAE) may have a unique perspective to offer on the implications of cultural interaction. Limitations of language may be overcome by assigning projects that call on students' art skills or that require a relatively controlled level of language.

Each chapter of this unit features at least one activity that offers students acquiring English the opportunity to display their understanding of cultural interaction.

You might encourage students acquiring English to discuss, to write about, or to depict in art their own experiences of cultural interaction.

The Western Civilization Videodisc

SECTION F: The Italian Renaissance, 1300–1550

 Side One: Frame 22568

SECTION G: The Reformation, 1517–1600

Side One: Frame 25328

Universal Play Button

See Master Guide, page 112 for Section F, page 141 for Section G.

People and Empires in the Americas

	Key Ideas	COPY MASTERS	ASSESSMENT
SECTION 1 Diverse Societies of North America *pp. 391–394*	*The dwellings and characteristics of Native American cultures, such as the Pueblos and Mound Builders, reflect their different environments. Common patterns of trade, religion, and social structure link diverse Native American peoples.*	*In-Depth Resources: Unit 4* • **Guided Reading**, p. 1 • **Primary Sources:** Hopewell Artifact, p. 8; from the Iroquois Constitution, p. 9	PE *Section 1 Assessment*, p. 394 *Formal Assessment* • Section Quiz, p. 181 *Alternative Assessment Book* • Standards for Evaluating a Cooperative Activity
SECTION 2 Mayan Kings and Cities *pp. 395–399*	*Mayan civilization flourishes in Mesoamerica during the first millennium A.D. Mayan cities and farms, religious practices, and achievements reflect a highly advanced culture. By the 900s, however, the Maya are in decline.*	*In-Depth Resources: Unit 4* • **Guided Reading**, p. 2 • **Skillbuilder Practice:** Drawing Conclusions, p. 5 • **Geography Application:** Mayan Irrigation Techniques, p. 6 • **Primary Source:** from *Popul Vuh*, p. 10 • **Connections across Time and Cultures:** Age of Pyramids in Ancient Egypt and Mesoamerica, p. 17	PE *Section 2 Assessment*, p. 399 *Formal Assessment* • Section Quiz, p. 182 *Alternative Assessment Book* • Standards for Evaluating a Cooperative Activity
SECTION 3 The Aztecs Control Central Mexico *pp. 400–406*	*In the Valley of Mexico, the Aztecs emerge in the 1200s, building on the foundations of earlier cultures. They conquer neighboring states to create the largest empire in Mesoamerica. By the 1500s, the empire begins to unravel.*	*In-Depth Resources: Unit 4* • **Guided Reading**, p. 3 • **Literature:** from *Quetzalcoatl*, p. 12 • **History Makers:** Montezuma II, p. 15	PE *Section 3 Assessment*, p. 406 *Formal Assessment* • Section Quiz, p. 183 *Alternative Assessment Book* • Standards for Evaluating a Cooperative Activity
SECTION 4 The Inca Create a Mountain Empire *pp. 407–411*	*In the Peruvian Andes, the Inca in the 1400s establish the largest empire in the Americas. They create a highly controlled economy and an official religion. In the early 1500s, civil war weakens the empire.*	*In-Depth Resources: Unit 4* • **Guided Reading**, p. 4 • **Primary Source:** The Discovery of Machu Picchu, p. 11 • **History Makers:** Pachacuti, p. 16	PE *Section 4 Assessment*, p. 411 *Formal Assessment* • Section Quiz, p. 184 *Alternative Assessment Book* • Standards for Evaluating a Product or Performance
CHAPTER RESOURCES	**Chapter Overview** *In the Americas, Native American, Mayan, Aztec, and Inca civilizations develop prior to the arrival of the Europeans. These civilizations, reflecting their geographic diversity, all develop sophisticated social, political, and economic institutions.*	*Telescoping the Times* • Chapter Summary, pp. 61–63 *Planning for Block Schedules*	PE *Chapter Assessment*, pp. 412–413 *Chapter Activities*, p. 413 *Formal Assessment* • Chapter Test, forms A and B, pp. 185–190 *Test Generator* *Alternative Assessment Book*

TECHNOLOGY

 Warm-Up Transparency 16

World Art and Cultures Transparencies
• AT34 Anasazi Mural

Electronic Library of Primary Sources
• "The Anasazi"—Riddles in the Ruins

INTERNET RESOURCES
www.mlworldhistory.com

 Warm-Up Transparency 16

Electronic Library of Primary Sources
• from "Exploring Maya Copán"

INTERNET RESOURCES
www.mlworldhistory.com

 Warm-Up Transparency 16

World Art and Cultures Transparencies
• AT35 Aztec Necklace and Earrings

Electronic Library of Primary Sources
• "Human Sacrifice Among the Aztecs"

INTERNET RESOURCES
www.mlworldhistory.com

 Warm-Up Transparency 16

Geography Transparencies
• GT16 The Expansion of the Inca Empire, 1230–1535

Critical Thinking Transparencies
• CT16 Mesoamerican Empires Before Columbus

 Patterns of Interaction: Building Empires

Electronic Library of Primary Sources:
• from Royal Commentaries of the Incas

 Chapter Summaries on Audiocassette in English and Spanish

INTERNET RESOURCES
www.mlworldhistory.com

Block Scheduling (90 MINUTES)

| **Day 1**
Section 1, pp. 391–394

 COOPERATIVE ACTIVITY
Describing a Culture Area, p. 393 (Teacher's Edition)

Section 2, pp. 395–399

 COOPERATIVE ACTIVITY
Comparing Civilizations, p. 398 (Teacher's Edition) | *Section Assessments,*
pp. 394, 399
Day 2
Section 3, pp. 400–406

 COOPERATIVE ACTIVITY
The Aztec World, p. 403 (Teacher's Edition)

Section 4, pp. 407–411 | *Section Assessments,*
pp. 406, 411

Chapter Assessment,
pp. 412–413 |

Yearly Pacing Chapter 16 Total: 2 days Yearly Total: 85 days

 Planning for Block Schedules

Customizing for Special Needs

Students Acquiring English

 Access for Students Acquiring English
- **Guided Reading** for Sections 1–4 (Spanish), pp. 160–163
- **Chapter Summary** (Spanish), pp. 157–159
- **Skillbuilder Practice:** Drawing Conclusions (Spanish), p. 164
- **Geography Application** Mayan Irrigation Techniques (Spanish), p. 165

 Chapter Summaries on Audiocassette in English and Spanish

 Patterns of Interaction: *Building Empires* (Spanish track)

INTERNET RESOURCES
www.mlworldhistory.com
The Diverse Classroom.

Less Proficient Readers

 In-Depth Resources: Unit 4
- **Guided Reading** for Sections 1–4, pp. 1–4
- **Skillbuilder Practice:** Drawing Conclusions, p. 5
- **Geography Application** Mayan Irrigation Techniques, p. 6

 Telescoping the Times
- Chapter Summary, pp. 61–63

 Chapter Summaries on Audiocassette

Gifted and Talented Students

 In-Depth Resources: Unit 4
Primary Sources
- Hopewell Artifact, p. 8
- from the Iroquois Constitution, p. 9
- from *Popul Vuh*, p. 10
- The Discovery of Machu Picchu, p. 11

History Makers
- Montezuma II, p. 15
- Pachacuti, p. 16

Connections to Literature READINGS FOR STUDENTS

 In-Depth Resources: Unit 4
Literature: from *Quetzalcoatl*, p. 12

Enrichment Reading
- **Jennings, Gary**
  Aztec
  New York: Tome, 1980
  A popular story that follows the rise of a memorable character from his lowly station to warrior.

- **Bierhorst, John, ed.**
  The Hungry Woman: Myths and Legends of the Aztecs
  New York: Morrow, 1984
  An exciting collection of myths and legends from Aztec culture.

 PE = Pupil's Edition   = Overhead Transparency   = Software   = Video

= Copy Master   = CD-ROM   = Audiocassette   = Internet

387B

People and Empires in the Americas, 900–1500

Accessing Prior Knowledge

- Ask students what they can recall about cultures such as the Inca and the Aztec. Also, what do they remember about the Meso-american cultures they encountered in Chapter 9?

- Tell them to look over the unit time line on pp. 386–387. What was going on in other parts of the world during the period covered by Chapter 16?

Making Predictions

Ask students to predict, based on the images and captions, how important religion might be to each culture represented. What clues helped them to make their predictions?

Geography Connection

Have students study the map and answer the following questions.

- Which cultures flourished at about the same time? *Aztec, Inca, Mimbres*

- In what ways would the climates of these cultural areas be different? In what ways might the climates be similar?

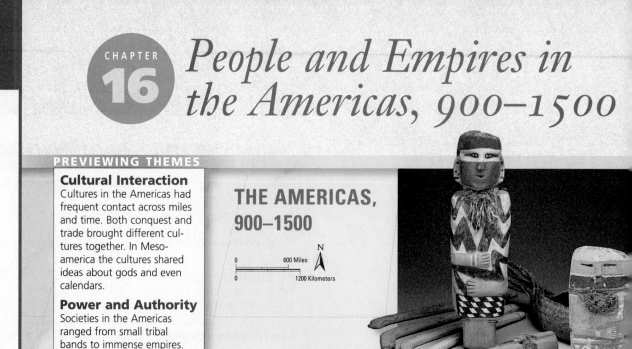

CHAPTER
16

People and Empires in the Americas, 900–1500

PREVIEWING THEMES

Cultural Interaction
Cultures in the Americas had frequent contact across miles and time. Both conquest and trade brought different cultures together. In Meso-america the cultures shared ideas about gods and even calendars.

Power and Authority
Societies in the Americas ranged from small tribal bands to immense empires. Some empires were ruled by priest-kings, and others by warrior-kings. In Peru, a wel-fare state took care of all the people within the empire.

Religious and Ethical Systems
In the Americas, religion was a powerful force. Many soci-eties combined religious and state rule. To please the gods, people built huge temples and other struc-tures. They built empires and captured slaves in the name of the gods. Much of their art was focused on the gods and the need to please them.

THE AMERICAS, 900–1500

N

0   600 Miles

0   1200 Kilometers

These ritual figures from the **Mimbres culture** about **1350** were found in a basket in a remote loca-tion in New Mexico. Their exact meaning is unknown. Since the other objects with them seem to be about hunting, they were prob-ably intended as an offering.

This Eagle Knight shows how important warriors were to the **Aztec** society. It was found in the Eagle Knight House near the Great Temple of **Tenochtitlan**. The fierce-looking knight belonged to the Aztec nobility and dedicated himself to the service of the god Sol. The Aztecs ruled a large empire between **1200 and 1521**.

INTERNET CONNECTION

Visit us at **www.mlworldhistory.com** to learn more about people of the Americas.

388

GEOGRAPHY THEMES

Location

Have students note the location of the various cultures listed on the map. Then have them look at the Atlas maps on pages 980, 982. In what modern countries were these ancient cultures located? *Anasazi, Hohokam, Adena, Hopewell, Mississippian—United States; Aztec—* Mexico; Maya—Mexico, Guatemala, El Salvador, Belize, Honduras; Inca— Ecuador, Peru, Bolivia, Chile, Argentina Invite students to speculate about how residents of these modern countries might still be influenced by the ancient cultures that once thrived there.

Place

Have students use the map to identify landforms and other geographic fea-tures that might have affected life in the various culture areas. Ask what influ-ence geography might have had on those cultures. For example, how would a culture like the Inca have reflected some of the conditions of life in the highland Andes?

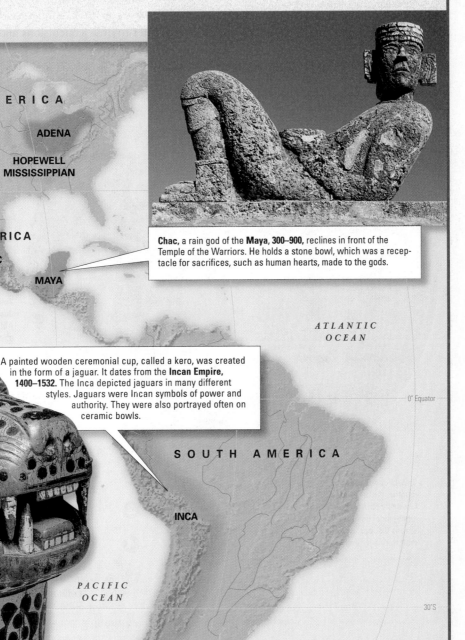

NORTH AMERICA

ANASAZI
and
HOHOKAM

ADENA

HOPEWELL
MISSISSIPPIAN

MESOAMERICA

AZTEC

MAYA

ATLANTIC
OCEAN

0° Equator

SOUTH AMERICA

INCA

PACIFIC
OCEAN

30°S

389

Chac, a rain god of the **Maya, 300–900,** reclines in front of the Temple of the Warriors. He holds a stone bowl, which was a receptacle for sacrifices, such as human hearts, made to the gods.

A painted wooden ceremonial cup, called a kero, was created in the form of a jaguar. It dates from the **Incan Empire, 1400–1532.** The Inca depicted jaguars in many different styles. Jaguars were Incan symbols of power and authority. They were also portrayed often on ceramic bowls.

ADDITIONAL RESOURCES

Books for the Teacher

• Kopper, Philip. *The Smithsonian Book of North American Indians.* Washington, DC: Smithsonian Books, 1986. Pre-Columbian cultures in North America

Books for the Student

• Hakim, Joy. *The First Americans.* New York: Oxford UP, 1993. History of North American tribes up to first European contact

• Marrin, Albert. *Inca and Spaniard: Pizarro and the Conquest of Peru.* New York: Atheneum, 1989.

• Cameron, Ian. *Kingdom of the Sun God: A History of the Andes and Their People.* New York: Facts on File, 1990.

Videos

• *The Anasazi: Builders of America's First Cities.* Society for Visual Education, 1996. 800-829-1900. Introduction to the cliff-dwelling culture

• *The Americas Before the Europeans.* Social Studies School Service, 1985. 800-421-4246. Why the Maya, Aztec, and Inca fell to the Spanish

Software

• *Exploring the Lost Maya.* CD-ROM. Queue, 1996. 800-232-2224.

• *The Amazon Trail.* CD-ROM or diskette. The Learning Company, 1996. 800-685-6322. Journey down the Amazon River in search of the ancient Inca.

HISTORY THROUGH ART

The Human Form in Ancient American Art

One of the most striking differences between Greco-Roman art and art in the ancient Americas is the portrayal of the human form. For example, the ancient Greeks idealized the human body in their art and sculpture. In the Americas, however, the human form was simply a general shape on which to place headdresses, masks, jewelry, or certain attributes of animals or deities. These adornments were rendered with meticulous detail. In the Eagle Knight, for instance, the figure's humanity is far less important than the symbols of the eagle that surround his head, arms, and knees. The artist is not celebrating human nature but the power of the eagle to bestow its spirit and special qualities on the human.

These costumes and adornments were used to teach people religious concepts and traditions, because most early American cultures had no written scripture. Instead, symbols showed people the many aspects of their complex, spirit-filled world.

Interpreting the Art What qualities or attributes do you think the artists of the Eagle Knight and rain god wanted to convey? *Possible Answers: Eagle Knight: strength, fierceness, speed; Rain god: abundance, power, permanence*

Interact *with* History

The Interact with History feature motivates students by having them think about the purpose of the mask pictured here. As they study the image, they will analyze its aspects, explore different opinions, and make decisions about different cultures.

Purpose

- to set the stage for studying early North and South American native cultures
- to help students understand the different world-views of native peoples
- to enable students to connect with the people and events they will encounter in this chapter

Teaching Strategy

Thinking Critically Ask students to think of times when they wore masks. What was the occasion? Whom did they choose to be, and why? How did they feel while wearing the mask?

EXAMINING *the* ISSUES

Following are suggestions for addressing each bulleted question.

1 Ask students to think about where in North America red cedar trees, killer whales, ravens and salmon exist together. What is the environment like in that region?

2 Have students think about the roles killer whales, ravens, and salmon might have played in this culture.

3 Ask students what functions masks served in early cultures.

4 Ask students what are some of the ways scientists and historians learn about early cultures.

Making Connections What have students learned about masks in earlier chapters? Ask them to think about the ways masks are used in modern culture. How do these uses compare with the uses in early cultures?

Interact *with* History

As a historian studying a culture with no written language, you are forced to study the artifacts of that culture. In many ways you are like a detective. You look at the evidence and clues to draw conclusions about the culture. Imagine you have found the mask shown on this page. Study the clues and see how much you can learn about the Bella Coola.

These images are of ravens and a killer whale found in the Pacific Ocean.

What does this mask reveal about the society?

This mask, used by the Bella Coola during a ceremony, tells the legend of Ahlquntam II, the chief god in the land of creation.

Carved of red cedar and painted, the mask was moved by strings and mechanical devices across the rear house wall during a ceremony.

Legend says Ahlquntam II used the sun as a canoe to cross the sky. He wore a cloak lined with salmon.

EXAMINING *the* ISSUES

1 • What do the materials and images used reveal about the environment in which the Bella Coola lived?

2 • What do the images or figures tell you about what was important in the culture?

3 • Why might it be important to know by whom or when the mask might have been worn?

4 • How else might you find out information about this culture?

Discuss these questions with your classmates. Think about the kinds of information you have learned about other cultures that did not have a written language. You may recall ways historians learned about the very earliest cultures.

As you read this chapter, examine the masks made by different peoples of the Americas. Think about what those masks reveal about the various cultures.

Follow Up

A feature on the chapter assessment will ask students to reevaluate their responses to the questions presented on this page.

Diverse Societies of North America

TERMS & NAMES
- potlatch
- Anasazi
- pueblos
- Mississippian
- Iroquois
- totems

MAIN IDEA

Complex North American societies were linked to each other through culture and economics.

WHY IT MATTERS NOW

Traditions and ideas from these cultures became part of the cultures of North America.

SETTING THE STAGE Between 40,000 and 12,000 years ago, hunter-gatherers migrated across the Bering Strait land bridge from Asia and began to populate the Americas. Migrating southward, those first Americans reached the southern tip of South America by somewhere between 12,000 and 7000 B.C. At the same time, they spread out across North America. Over the centuries, early North American peoples adapted to their environment, creating a diverse set of cultures.

Complex Societies Build and Trade

In some ways, the early cultures north of the Rio Grande River were less developed than those of South America and Mesoamerica. The North American groups created no great empires. They left few ruins as spectacular as those of ancient Mexico or Peru. Nevertheless, the first peoples of North America did create complex societies. These societies were able to conduct long-distance trade and construct magnificent buildings.

Northwest Coast—Cultures of Abundance The Pacific Northwest—from Oregon to Alaska—was rich in resources and supported a sizable population. To the Kwakiutl, Nootka, and Haida peoples, the most important resource was the sea. They hunted whales in canoes. Some canoes were large enough to carry at least 15 people. In addition to the many resources of the sea, the coastal forest provided plentiful food. In this abundant environment, the Northwest Coast tribes developed societies in which differences in wealth created social classes. Families displayed their rank and prosperity in an elaborate ceremony called the **potlatch** (PAHT·LACH). In this ceremony, they gave food, drink, and gifts to the community.

Cliff Palace, located at Mesa Verde, Colorado, was an Anasazi pueblo. It had 200 rooms.

Pueblo People Construct Complex Buildings The dry, desert lands of the Southwest were a much harsher environment than the temperate Pacific coast. However, as early as 3000 B.C. the peoples of the Southwest were beginning to farm the land. Among the most successful of these early farmers were the Hohokam (huh·HOH·kuhm) of central Arizona. They used irrigation to produce harvests of corn, beans, and squash. Their use of pottery rather than baskets, and certain religious rituals, showed contact with Mesoamerican peoples to the south.

Background
Around 300 B.C. Mesoamerican people migrated into the valleys of Arizona.

The Hohokam were also influenced by a people to the north: the **Anasazi** (AH·nuh·SAH·zee). They lived where the present-day states of Utah, Arizona, Colorado, and New Mexico meet. The Anasazi built impressive cliff dwellings, such as the ones at Mesa Verde, Colorado. These houses were built in shallow caves in the sheer walls of deep canyons. By the A.D. 900s, the Anasazi were living in **pueblos** (PWEHB·lohs), villages of large, apartment-style compounds made of stone and sun-baked clay.

People and Empires in the Americas **391**

North American Culture Areas about 1400

Interpreting the Map Have students examine the map and find the group(s) that once lived where students live now.

Extension Activity Have pairs of students question each other about the location of specific tribes, based on the following model: *In which culture area were the Cree found? Subarctic*

SKILLBUILDER Answers
1. Great Plains
2. Eastern Woodlands and Northwest Coast

MORE ABOUT . . .
Kivas

Kivas had both religious and political significance as the center of clan and village activities. Almost entirely underground, the circular kivas were entered by a ladder descending through the ceiling. Kiva walls were traditionally decorated with colorful murals that depicted sacred subjects or scenes of everyday life.

 WORLD ART AND CULTURES TRANSPARENCIES
AT34 Anazasi Mural

 ELECTRONIC LIBRARY OF PRIMARY SOURCES
"The Anasazi"

 IN-DEPTH RESOURCES: UNIT 4
Primary source: Hopewell Artifact, p. 8

North American Culture Areas about 1400

Inuit
Kutchin
Inuit
Inuit
Hudson Bay
Inuit
Tlingit
Beaver
Cree
Bella Coola
Blackfoot
Ojibwa
Kwakiutl
Nez Percé
Mandan
Algonquin
Huron
PACIFIC OCEAN
Crow
Lakota
Iroquois
Coo
Shoshone
Cheyenne
Miami
Delaware
40°N
Pomo
Arapaho
Shawnee
Osage
Hopi
Apache
Cherokee
Navajo
Pueblo
Papago
Comanche
Natchez
Gulf of Mexico
Caribbean Sea
ATLANTIC OCEAN

0   1,000 Miles
0   2,000 Kilometers
Tropic of Cancer

Native American Cultures
- Arctic
- Subarctic
- Northwest Coast
- Plateau
- Great Basin
- California
- Southwest
- Great Plains
- Eastern Woodlands
- Southeast
- Mesoamerica
- **Osage** Tribe name

GEOGRAPHY SKILLBUILDER: Interpreting Maps
1. **Region** Which culture group had the largest number of tribes?
2. **Human-Environment Interaction** In which culture areas would movement of trade goods be made easier by river and lake connections?

One of the largest pueblos, begun around A.D. 900, was Pueblo Bonito, a Spanish name meaning "beautiful village." Its construction required a high degree of social organization and inventiveness. Like other people of the Americas, the Anasazi did not have horses, mules, or the wheel. Instead, they relied on human labor to quarry sandstone from the canyon walls and move it to the site. Skilled builders then used a mudlike mortar to construct walls up to five stories high. Windows were small to keep out the burning sun. When completed, Pueblo Bonito probably housed about 1,000 people and contained more than 600 rooms. In addition, a number of underground ceremonial chambers called kivas (KEE-vuhs) were used for a variety of religious practices.

Many Anasazi pueblos were abandoned around 1200. Their descendants, the Pueblo peoples, continued many Anasazi customs. Pueblo groups like the Hopi and Zuni used kivas for religious ceremonies. They also created beautiful pottery and woven blankets. They traded these, along with corn and other farm products, with Plains Indians to the east, who supplied bison meat and hides. These nomadic Plains tribes eventually became known by such names as the Comanche, Kiowa, and Apache.

This Anasazi pitcher dates from A.D. 1100. The black and white spirals form a traditional design.

Mound Builders Forge Ties with Eastern Peoples Beyond the Great Plains, in the wooded lands east of the Mississippi River, other ancient peoples—the Mound Builders—were creating their own unique traditions. Beginning around 800 B.C., two cultures, known as Adena and Hopewell, built large burial mounds and filled them with finely crafted copper and stone objects. Some mounds, such as Ohio's Great Serpent Mound, had the shape of animals when seen from above.

Background
Tribes in the Plains are classified into groups based on one of six basic language families.

392 Chapter 16

CUSTOMIZING FOR SPECIAL NEEDS

Access for Students Acquiring English: *Word Origins* Tell students that as a result of the early Spanish settlement of the American Southwest, many Spanish words have been added to the English language. For example, the Spanish word *pueblo*, meaning "village" or "people," was used to describe some Southwest tribes. The Pueblo region was first ruled by Spain and then by Mexico.

Ask students if they can think of other Spanish words that have entered the English language. Make a list of these words on the board. *Examples: patio, rodeo, plaza, mesa, sombrero, siesta*

CONNECTIONS ACROSS TIME AND PLACE

Pueblos Many Pueblo peoples today still live in traditional villages that dot the desert landscape of northern New Mexico and Arizona. Well-known pueblos include Acoma, Taos, and Zuñi. Although Pueblo peoples have adopted some modern ways, they maintain many of their ancient customs, including religious rituals. Many groups also continue to produce traditional craft goods of great beauty, such as pottery and rugs. Encourage interested students to find out more about modern Pueblo life and report back to the class.

The last Mound Builder culture, the **Mississippian,** lasted from A.D. 800 until the arrival of Europeans in the 1500s. These people built giant earthen pyramids such as the one at Cahokia (kuh·HOH·kee·uh), Illinois. They created thriving villages based on farming and trade. Between 1000 and 1200, as many as 10,000 people lived at Cahokia, the leading site of Mississippian culture. Cahokia was led by priest-rulers, who regulated farming activities. The priest-rulers may have been influenced by the cultures of Mesoamerica. The heart of the community was a 100-foot-high, flat-topped pyramid, which was crowned by a wooden temple.

These Mississippian lands were located in a crossroads region between east and west. They enjoyed easy transportation on the Mississippi and Ohio rivers. They came into contact with many other peoples, including those of the Eastern Woodlands.

Woodlands Tribes Build Alliances The eastern tribes had much in common with the Mississippian peoples, including a similar environment. Despite the similar environment, woodlands groups developed a variety of cultures. They spoke distinct languages belonging to language families such as Algonquian, Iroquoian, and Muskogean. The woodlands peoples often clashed with each other over land. In some areas, tribes formed political alliances to ensure protection of tribal lands. The best example of a political alliance was the **Iroquois** (IHR·uh·KWOY), a group of tribes speaking related languages living in the eastern Great Lakes region. In the late 1500s, five of these tribes in upper New York—the Mohawk, Oneida, Onondaga, Cayuga, and Seneca—formed the Iroquois League. According to legend, Chief Hiawatha created this league. His goal was to promote joint defense and cooperation among the tribes. The confederacy lasted for almost 200 years.

THINK THROUGH HISTORY
A. Drawing Conclusions Of what value would a political alliance be to an individual tribe?
A. Answer It would provide protection from enemies.

Cultural Connections

The Iroquois alliance was a notable example of a political link between early North American peoples. For the most part, however, the connections between native North Americans were economic and cultural. They traded, had similar religious beliefs, and shared social patterns.

Trading Networks Tie Tribes Together Trade was a major factor linking the peoples of North America. Trade centers and traveling merchants were found throughout North America. Along the Columbia River in Oregon, the Chinook people established a lively marketplace that brought together trade goods from all over the West. The Mississippians were also active traders. Their trade network stretched from the Rocky Mountains to the Atlantic coast and from the Great Lakes to the Gulf of Mexico. Sometimes goods traveled hundreds or even thousands of miles from their original source. This was especially true of exotic items such as colored feathers or copper jewelry.

Religion Shapes Views of Life Another practice early Americans shared was religion. Nearly all native North Americans believed that the world around them was filled with nature spirits. Most Native Americans recognized a number of sacred spirits. Some groups held up one supreme being, or Great Spirit, above all others. North American peoples believed that the spirits gave them rituals and customs to guide them in their lives and to satisfy their basic needs. If people practiced these rituals, they would live in peace and harmony.

Native American religious beliefs also included great respect for the land as the source of life. Native Americans used the land but tried to alter it as little as possible. The land was sacred, not something that could be bought and sold. Later, when

Background
The belief that natural objects have a spirit is called animism.

People and Empires in the Americas **393**

SPOTLIGHT ON

Cahokia Monk's Mound
In 1809, in southern Illinois, a group of French monks founded a monastery on top of an unusual mound. The mound was about 100 feet high and consisted of four terraces that covered about 15 acres.

Four years later, the monks abandoned the site. Later explorations would show that their settlement had been in the middle of one of the greatest pre-Columbian Native American cities.

The large mound eventually became known as Monk's Mound. It was located inside a stockade that enclosed about 40 acres of land. To an observer standing in the enclosure on the first day of spring, the sun would appear to rise directly over the mound itself.

SPOTLIGHT ON
Cahokia Monk's Mound

In its day, Cahokia was the largest settlement north of Mexico. It was named for a subtribe of the Illini—the Cahokia—who lived in the area at the time the site was discovered. Located a few miles west of present-day Collinsville, Illinois, the settlement covered nearly six square miles and contained some 120 mounds. Have students use the Internet or other sources to find out more about Cahokia or other mound-builder sites.

OBJECTIVE 2 INSTRUCT

Cultural Connections

▶ **Key Ideas**
• Trade networks link Native American peoples across North America.
• Native Americans worship diverse spirits and show great reverence for the land.
• The family is the basis for tribal social organization.

CRITICAL THINKING ACTIVITY
CLASS TIME: 10 MINUTES

Categorizing
Draw the web below on the board. Ask students to fill in the web by listing some of the shared beliefs of Native American peoples.

TEACHING OPTION | **BLOCK SCHEDULING**

COOPERATIVE ACTIVITY: Describing a Culture Area

CLASS TIME 25 MINUTES

Task: Students will make a chart describing a Native American culture area.

Purpose: To find out more about Native American cultures.

Activity: Have small groups of students research one of the Native American culture areas covered in the section—Northwest, Southwest, Mound Builders, Woodlands—or another grouping listed on the map

on page 392. Ask students to prepare a chart that includes information such as environmental conditions; geography; types of food, clothing and shelter; crafts; religious practices; organization; and other important cultural features. Encourage students to use maps, diagrams, and pictures with their charts.

📁 **Building a Portfolio:** Have students write a brief description of the chart and their contribution to it.

📖 *ALTERNATIVE ASSESSMENT BOOK*
Standards for Evaluating a Cooperative Activity

Standards for Evaluation
Charts should . . .

• present specific details on a culture area
• have all information clearly labeled
• be well organized and designed

Teacher's Edition **393**

394 Chapter 16

Europeans arrived in North America, the issue of ownership of land became a problem. A Native American expressed his view of this dilemma:

A VOICE FROM THE PAST
Some of our chiefs make the claim that the land belongs to us. It is not what the Great Spirit told me. He told me that the land belongs to Him, that no people own the land, and that I was not to forget to tell this to the white people.

KANNEKUK, Kickapoo prophet, quoted in *Through Indian Eyes*

Harmony with nature was an important part of Native American life, and so was harmony in relationships with people.

Shared Social Patterns The family was the basis for social organization for Native Americans. Generally, the family unit was the extended family, including parents, children, grandparents, and other close relatives. Some tribes further organized families into clans: groups of families descended from a common ancestor. In some tribes, clan members lived together in large houses or groups of houses.

Common among American Indian clans was the use of **totems** (TOH·tuhmz). The term refers to a natural object that an individual, clan, or group identifies itself with. The totem was used as a symbol of the unity of a group or clan. It also helped define certain behaviors and the social relationships of a group. The term comes from an Ojibwa Indian language spoken in the Great Lakes area, but refers to a cultural practice found throughout the Americas. For example, Northwestern peoples displayed totem symbols on masks, boats, and huge poles set in front of their houses. Others used totem symbols in rituals or dances associated with important group events such as marriages, the naming of children, or the planting or harvesting of crops.

There were hundreds of different patterns of North American Indian life. Some societies were small and dealt with life in a limited region of the vast North American continent. Other groups were much larger, and were linked by trade and culture to other groups in North America and Mesoamerica. As you will learn in Section 2, peoples in Mesoamerica and South America also lived in societies that varied from simple to complex. Three of these cultures—the Maya, the Aztec, and the Inca—would develop sophisticated ways of life like those of highly developed cultures in other parts of the globe.

Totem poles marked important events such as the naming of a chief.

THINK THROUGH HISTORY
B. Making Inferences What artificial symbols are used by nations or organizations in a way similar to totems?
B. Possible Answers Flags, mascots, religious signs

Section ❶ Assessment

1. TERMS & NAMES
Identify
- potlatch
- Anasazi
- pueblos
- Mississippian
- Iroquois
- totems

2. TAKING NOTES
Draw a Venn diagram like the one below. Compare and contrast Native Americans of the Northwest Coast and the Southwest.

Northwest Coast

Both

Southwest

How did environment affect the development of these cultures?

3. COMPARING
In what ways did the peoples of North America share similar cultural patterns?

THINK ABOUT
- how the people viewed the environment
- the role of family in their lives
- religion

4. ANALYZING THEMES
Cultural Interaction What evidence is there that societies in North America interacted with each other?

THINK ABOUT
- how goods were obtained
- ways to defend against enemies
- what kinds of evidence historians find and consider valid

394 Chapter 16

ANSWERS

1. TERMS & NAMES
potlatch, p. 391
Anasazi, p. 391
pueblos, p. 391
Mississippian, p. 393
Iroquois, p. 393
totems, p. 394

2. TAKING NOTES
Possible Responses: Differ-
ences, *Northwest Coast:* gathered food and hunted, fished; differences in wealth created social classes; had potlatches. *Differences, Southwest:* irrigated desert lands; used pottery; built cliff dwellings, pueblos, kivas; *Similarities:* believed in nature spirits; believed in Great Spirit; believed land was for everyone; sought harmony with nature; felt family was the basic unit.

3. COMPARING
Possible Responses: Most of the native people shared a love of the earth, valued the family unit, believed in the Great Spirit, and used totems.

4. ANALYZING THEMES
Possible Responses: Cultural groups throughout North America traded for goods they needed. Groups established alliances such as the Iroquois League for defense. Artifacts, ruins, and stories offer evidence of such interaction.

2 Mayan Kings and Cities

TERMS & NAMES
• Tikal
• glyph
• codex
• *Popol Vuh*

MAIN IDEA

The Maya developed a highly complex civilization based on city-states controlled by dynasties of kings.

WHY IT MATTERS NOW

Descendants of the Maya still occupy the same territory.

SETTING THE STAGE In the early centuries A.D., most North American peoples were beginning to develop complex societies. Further south, the peoples of Mexico and Central America were entering into the full flower of civilization. A prime example of this cultural flowering was the Maya, who built an extraordinary civilization in the heart of Mesoamerica.

Maya Create Urban Kingdoms

The homeland of the Maya stretched from southern Mexico into northern Central America. This area includes a highland region and a lowland region. The lowlands lie to the north. They include the dry scrub forest of the Yucatan (YOO·kuh·TAN) Peninsula and the dense, steamy jungles of southeastern Mexico and northern Guatemala. The highlands are further south—a range of cool, cloud-wreathed mountains that stretch from southern Mexico to El Salvador.

While the Olmec were building their civilization along the Gulf Coast in the period from 1200 B.C. to 400 B.C., the Maya were also evolving. They took on Olmec influences, blending these with local customs. By A.D. 250, Mayan culture had burst forth in a flourishing civilization.

Urban Centers The period from A.D. 250 to 900 is known as the Classic Period of Mayan civilization. During this time, the Maya built spectacular cities such as **Tikal** (tee·KAHL), a major center in northern Guatemala. Other important sites included Copan, Palenque, Uxmal, and Chichen Itza. Each of these was an independent city-state, ruled by a god-king and serving as a center for religious ceremonies and trade.

Mayan cities featured giant pyramids, temples, palaces, and elaborate stone carvings dedicated to the gods and to important rulers. Tens of thousands of people lived in residential areas surrounding the city center, which bustled with activity.

Mesoamerican Civilizations 200 B.C.–A.D. 1521

- Teotihuacan Civilization, 200 B.C.–A.D. 700
- Toltec Heartland, A.D. 900–1100
- Aztec Civilization, A.D. 1200–1521
- Mayan Civilization, A.D. 250–900

Tropic of Cancer

Gulf of Mexico

Lake Texcoco
Tula
Teotihuacan
Tenochtitlan
20°N
Uxmal
Chichen Itza
Yucatan Peninsula
Palenque
Tikal
Piedras Negras
Copan

0 — 250 Miles
0 — 500 Kilometers

N

PACIFIC OCEAN

GEOGRAPHY SKILLBUILDER: Interpreting Maps
The map shows about 1,700 years of occupation of Mesoamerica. During this time cultures influenced each other through trade and the conquering of lands.
1. **Region** Which civilization occupied the Yucatan Peninsula?
2. **Region** What other civilization areas were eventually incorporated into the Aztec area?

Section 2 Overview

OBJECTIVES

① To describe key features of Mayan kingdoms.

② To explain Mayan beliefs and achievements.

③ To identify reasons for the decline of the Maya.

SKILLBUILDER

• Interpreting maps: region, p. 395
• Interpreting charts, p. 399

CRITICAL THINKING

• Drawing conclusions, pp. 396, 397, 399
• Analyzing motives, p. 397
• Making inferences, p. 398

FOCUS

5-Minute Warm-Up

▶ *Evaluating*
Answering the following questions will help students understand Mayan culture.

1. Read the History Through Art on p. 397. What did the tower openings on "The Snail" show?

2. El Castillo was built on top of what older structure?

 WARM-UP TRANSPARENCY 16

OBJECTIVE ① INSTRUCT

Maya Create Urban Kingdoms

▶ *Key Ideas*

• The Mayan civilization stretches from what is now southern Mexico to El Salvador.

• Mayan cities are supported by trade and agriculture.

• In Mayan society, nobles rank highest, followed by merchants, artisans, and peasants.

IN-DEPTH RESOURCES: UNIT 4
Guided Reading, p. 2

ACCESS FOR STUDENTS ACQUIRING ENGLISH
Guided Reading (Spanish), p. 161

SECTION 2 RESOURCES

PRINT RESOURCES

IN-DEPTH RESOURCES: UNIT 4
Guided Reading, p. 2
Skillbuilder Practice: Drawing Conclusions, p. 5
Geography Application: Mayan Irrigation Techniques, p. 6
Primary Source: from *Popul Vuh*, p. 10
Connections Across Time and Cultures: Age of Pyramids in Ancient Egypt and Mesoamerica, p. 17

ACCESS FOR STUDENTS ACQUIRING ENGLISH
Guided Reading (Spanish), p. 161
Skillbuilder Practice (Spanish), p. 164

Geography Application (Spanish), p. 165

FORMAL ASSESSMENT
Section Quiz, p. 182

ALTERNATIVE ASSESSMENT BOOK

TECHNOLOGY RESOURCES

CD-ROM
Electronic Library of Primary Sources

INTERNET www.mlworldhistory.com

Interpreting the Map Have students look at the map and identify the symbols and colors used to convey information. Which color is used to represent the Maya? *green* Point out that students will learn in Section 3 about the other cultures shown on the map.

Extension Activity Have students use the Atlas, page 980, to identify the modern countries in which the following sites are located: Copán, Tikal, and Uxmal. *Honduras, Guatemala, and Mexico*

SKILLBUILDER Answers
1. Maya
2. Teotihuacan and Toltec

MORE ABOUT . . .
The Mayan Ball Game
In the ball game, which had its origins in Olmec culture, players wearing heavy pads tried to hit a hard rubber ball through stone rings set high above the ground. They could use any part of their body except their hands or feet. Teams scored by getting the ball through the ring or by making certain plays. The leader of the losing team was often sacrificed to the gods.

OBJECTIVE ② INSTRUCT

Religion Shapes Mayan Life

▶ **Key Ideas**
- Mayans worship many gods and create elaborate rituals.
- Mayan calendars, math, and astronomy support their religious practices.
- Their written language is preserved in stone carvings and a few remaining books.

396 Chapter 16

Archaeologists have identified at least 50 major Mayan sites, all with monumental architecture. For example, Pyramid IV at Tikal stretched 212 feet into the jungle sky. In fact, the Tikal pyramids were the tallest structures in the Americas until 1903, when the Flatiron Building was built in New York City. In addition to temples and pyramids, each Mayan city featured a ball court. In this stone-sided playing field, the Maya played a game that had religious and political significance. The Maya believed the playing of this game would maintain the cycles of the sun and moon and bring life-giving rains.

Agriculture and Trade Support Cities Although the Mayan city-states were independent of each other, they were linked through alliances and trade. Cities exchanged the products of their local environment such as salt, flint, feathers, shells, and honey. Also traded were craft goods like cotton textiles and jade ornaments. While the Maya did not have a uniform currency, cacao (chocolate) beans sometimes served as one.

As in the rest of Mesoamerica, agriculture—particularly the growing of maize, beans, and squash—provided the basis for Mayan life. For years, experts assumed that the Maya practiced slash-and-burn agriculture. This method involves farmers clearing the land by burning existing vegetation and planting crops in the ashes. Evidence now shows, however, that the Maya also developed more sophisticated methods, including planting on raised beds above swamps and on hillside terraces. These methods allowed Mayan farmers to produce large amounts of food to be traded in the cities.

Kingdoms Built on Dynasties Successful farming methods led to the accumulation of wealth and the development of social classes. The noble class, which included priests and the leading warriors, occupied the top rung of Mayan society. Below them came merchants and those with specialized knowledge, such as master artisans. Finally, at the bottom, came the peasant majority.

The Mayan king sat at the top of this class structure. He was regarded as a holy figure and his position was hereditary. When he died, he passed the throne on to his eldest son. Other sons of the ruler might expect to join the priesthood.

This is the death mask of a seventh-century ruler of Palenque, a Mayan city-state. The mask is a mosaic of jade with eyes of shell and obsidian.

Religion Shapes Mayan Life

Religion influenced most aspects of Mayan life. The Maya believed in many gods, who inhabited 13 layers of the sky and the 9 layers of the underworld. There were gods of corn, of death, of rain, and of war. Gods could be good or evil, and sometimes both. Gods also were associated with the four directions and with different colors: white for north, black for west, yellow for south, red for east, and green in the center. The Maya believed that each day was a living god whose behavior could be predicted with the help of an intricate system of calendars.

Religious Practices The Maya worshiped their gods in various ways. They prayed and made offerings of food, flowers, and incense. They also pierced their bodies with sharp needles and offered their blood, believing that this would nourish the gods. Sometimes the Maya even carried out human sacrifice, usually of captured enemies. At Chichen Itza (chee·CHEHN ee·TSAH), in the Yucatan, they threw captives into a deep sinkhole lake, called a *cenote* (say·NO·tay), along with gold, jade, and other offerings. The Maya believed that human sacrifice pleased the gods and kept the world in balance. Nevertheless, the Maya's use of sacrifice never reached the extremes of some other Mesoamerican peoples.

Math Develops to Support Religion Mayan religious beliefs also led to the development of the calendar, mathematics, and astronomy. Mayans believed that time was

396 Chapter 16

THINK THROUGH HISTORY
A. Drawing Conclusions What does the ability to construct complex buildings reveal about a society?

Background
Only the wealthy consumed chocolate as a drink. It was flavored with honey and vanilla.

A. Answer Workers had to be available for more than raising food and had to be highly organized and skilled in construction of larger buildings.

SKILLBUILDER MINI-LESSON: Drawing Conclusions

CLASS TIME 20 MINUTES

Explaining the Skill: Drawing conclusions means analyzing the implications of what you have read and forming an opinion about its meaning or consequences. To draw conclusions, look closely at the facts, then decide what those facts mean.

Applying the Skill: Look over your responses to Think Through History on this page. Summarize the facts and your conclusions in a diagram.

Facts	
Many temples and pyramids built	Building carried out in many cities at the same time
Buildings constructed with great precision and accuracy	Tallest and largest structures in Americas for centuries

Conclusions

Conclusions
People had to have free time to devote to building projects, and Mayan government had to organize them. The Mayans were not only great engineers and builders but had a sophisticated and well-organized society.

IN-DEPTH RESOURCES: UNIT 4
SKILLBUILDER PRACTICE: Drawing Conclusions, p. 5

Chichen Itza

Mayan cities feature very large structures that seem to be designed for ceremonial or religious purposes. Inscriptions on the buildings, the buildings' contents, chambers, and even the locations of the buildings reveal important information about the culture. Chichen Itza, a Mayan city located on the Yucatan Peninsula in Mexico, has huge buildings to honor rulers, warriors, and gods.

This carved stone throne takes the form of a snarling jaguar, painted red, with eyes and spots of jade and fangs of shell. It represents the jaguar god of the underworld. It sits inside a chamber of a four-sided pyramid. The chambers are parts of a pyramid that occupied the same site at an earlier time. El Castillo, the pyramid below, was constructed over it.

El Caracol—"The Snail"
Resembling a modern observatory, El Caracol shows the Mayans' knowledge of astronomy. Window-like openings in the tower align with the sunset during both spring and autumn equinoxes. The Maya studied the movements of the sun, moon, and stars because these movements related to the activities of the gods.

El Castillo—"The Castle"
This temple, also called the Pyramid of Kukulcan, sat at the top of four spectacular stairways. It was dedicated to the worship of Kukulcan, the feathered serpent god. The stairs to the temple were constructed so that at certain times of the day it looked as if a writhing serpent was crawling up them.

Connect *to* History

Analyzing Motives In what ways do the huge buildings at Chichen Itza show how the Mayan people felt about their gods?

 SEE SKILLBUILDER HANDBOOK, PAGE 994

Connect *to* Today

Drawing Conclusions What conclusions might someone make about U.S. culture from viewing the heads of the presidents at Mount Rushmore?

397

Connect *to* History

Analyzing Motives
Possible Response: The size and grandeur of the buildings shows the awe, and perhaps fear, the Maya felt for their gods and the importance of religion in their lives. The Mayan belief that each day was a living god meant they would need a way to communicate with that god to ensure a favorable outcome to each day. The size and complexity of the Mayan buildings implies that the entire society was organized around religious rituals. Students can compare the Maya to the Egyptians, who constructed whole cities devoted to religious worship.

Connect *to* Today

Drawing Conclusions
Possible Answer: Observers might conclude that the office of the president was one of great power and prestige and that these presidents in particular were esteemed for their achievements.

Discuss with students that societies build monuments to reflect their most important values. The presidents at Mount Rushmore represent the values of freedom, leadership, courage, compassion, and statesmanship.

SPOTLIGHT ON

Calendar Glyph

The glyph shown above is the date "9 Zotz" on the 365-day calendar. The symbol stands for the name of the month. The number is represented by the bar, which equals 5, and dots, which together equal 4.

Pictured above is a group of Mayan hieroglyphs from Temple 18 at Palenque. They are undecoded. Like Egyptian hieroglyphics, the glyphs can be grouped into two categories: those that are word signs and those that are syllables. The way the glyphs are translated involves deciding if the sign sets are word pictures or syllables.

Many of the glyphs on stone monuments are records of kings and the history of their rule. Other glyphs provide information on the Mayan gods and religious activities.

---

a burden carried on the back of a god. At the end of a day, month, or year, one god would lay the burden down and another would pick it up. A day would be lucky or unlucky, depending on the nature of the god. Thus it was very important to have an accurate calendar to know which god was in charge of the day.

The Maya developed a 260-day religious calendar, which consisted of twenty 13-day months. A second 365-day solar calendar consisted of eighteen 20-day months, with a separate period of five days at the end. The two calendars were linked together like meshed gears so that any given day could be identified in both cycles. The calendar helped identify the best time to plant crops, attack enemies, or crown new rulers.

The Maya based their calendar on careful observation of the planets, sun, and moon. Highly skilled Mayan astronomers and mathematicians calculated the solar year at 365.2420 days. (Only .0002 of a day too short!) The Mayan astronomers were able to attain such great precision by using a math system that included the concept of zero. The Maya used a shell symbol for zero, dots for the numbers 1 to 4, and a bar for 5. The Mayan number system was a base 20 system. They used the numerical system primarily for calendar and astronomical work, not to count people or objects.

Written Language Preserves History The Maya also developed the most advanced writing system in the ancient Americas. Mayan writing consisted of about 800 hieroglyphic symbols, or **glyphs** (glihfs). Some of these glyphs stand for whole words, while others represent syllables. The Maya used their writing system to record important historical events, carving their glyphs in stone or recording them in a bark-paper book known as a **codex** (KOH·DEHKS). Only three of these ancient books have survived.

Other original books telling of Mayan history and customs do exist, however. These were written down by Mayan peoples after the arrival of the Spanish. The most famous of these books, the **Popol Vuh** (POH·pohl VOO), recounts the Highland Maya's version of the story of creation. "Before the world was created, Calm and Silence were the great kings that ruled," reads the first sentence in the book. "Nothing existed, there was nothing."

> **A VOICE FROM THE PAST**
> Then let the emptiness fill! they said. Let the water weave its way downward so the earth can show its face! Let the light break on the ridges, let the sky fill up with the yellow light of dawn! Let our glory be a man walking on a path through the trees! "Earth!" the Creators called. They called only once, and it was there, from a mist, from a cloud of dust, the mountains appeared instantly.
>
> From the *Popol Vuh*

Mysterious Mayan Decline

The remarkable history of the Maya ended in mystery. In the late 800s, the Maya suddenly abandoned many of their cities. Some Mayan sites in the Yucatan, such as Chichen Itza and Uxmal, continued to thrive for several more centuries. Invaders

---

from the north, the Toltec, moved into the lands occupied by the Maya. These warlike peoples from central Mexico changed the culture. The high civilization of Mayan cities like Tikal and Copan disappeared.

No one knows exactly why this happened, though experts offer several overlapping theories. By the 700s, warfare had broken out among the various Mayan city-states. This violence caused some Maya to flee their cities and take refuge in the jungle. Increased warfare disrupted trade and produced economic hardship. In addition, population growth and over-farming may have caused ecological damage, causing food shortages, famine, and disease. All these circumstances probably contributed to the fall of Mayan civilization. By the time the Spanish arrived in the early 1500s, the Maya were divided into small, weak city-states that gave little hint of their former glory.

As the Mayan civilization faded, other peoples of Mesoamerica were growing in strength and sophistication. Like the Maya, these peoples would trace some of their ancestry to the Olmec. Eventually, these people would dominate the Valley of Mexico and lands beyond it, as you will learn in Section 3.

THINK THROUGH HISTORY
C. Evaluating Which of the causes for the fall of the Maya do you think was most important? Explain.
C. Possible answer Invaders from the north

Vocabulary
theocracy: combined state and religious rule

A trio of modern Mayan women sell textiles at the marketplace. The traditional designs on their clothing and the textiles have been used on Mayan fabrics for hundreds of years.

Maya

Traits of Civilization	Strength Leading to Power	Weakness Leading to Decline
Religious beliefs and theocracy	United culture / Loyalty to the king	Many physical and human resources funneled into religious activities
Independent city-states	Wealthy and prosperous culture	Frequent warfare occurs between kingdoms
Intensive agriculture	Production of more food feeds a larger population	Soil depletion and population growth creates need for more land

SKILLBUILDER: Interpreting Charts
1. Which trait aids in building a sense of loyalty to the ruler?
2. How can intensive agriculture be both a strength and a weakness?

Section 2 Assessment

1. TERMS & NAMES

Identify
- Tikal
- glyph
- codex
- *Popol Vuh*

2. TAKING NOTES

Draw a diagram like the one below and fill in details that support the main idea in the center. You may want to review the characteristics of a civilization found in Chapter 1.

The Maya developed a highly complex civilization in Mesoamerica.

| Supporting detail | Supporting detail | Supporting detail |

3. DRAWING CONCLUSIONS

How important do you think the development of advanced mathematics was in the creation of the Mayan calendar?

THINK ABOUT
- how records are kept over long periods of time
- the need for numbers larger than 20
- the need for precision

4. THEME ACTIVITY

Religious and Ethical Systems Imagine that you are a reporter visiting Mayan city-states. Write a one-page article that describes various aspects of the Mayan religion.

People and Empires in the Americas **399**

ANSWERS

1. TERMS & NAMES
Tikal, p. 395
glyph, p. 398
codex, p. 398
Popol Vuh, p. 398

2. TAKING NOTES
Possible Responses: The Maya built spectacular city-states ruled by dynasties of god-kings; created huge architectural sites; developed sophisticated farming methods; created a complex religious system; developed advanced mathematics, astronomy, and writing systems.

3. DRAWING CONCLUSIONS
Advanced mathematics was critical to the development of the Mayan calendar. The Maya needed a system of mathematics to record celestial movements over the years, to handle large numbers, and to calculate the solar and lunar year with great precision.

4. THEME ACTIVITY
Standards for Evaluation
The news articles should . . .
- describe how the Maya organized their society around religion
- explain how the Maya worshiped
- show how religion affected Mayan science and technology

OBJECTIVES

① To describe two early cultures of the Valley of Mexico: Teotihuacan and the Toltecs.

② To explain the rise of the Aztecs and their society.

③ To characterize the main features of Aztec religion.

④ To identify factors that led to the decline of the Aztecs.

SKILLBUILDER
• Interpreting charts, p. 406

CRITICAL THINKING
• Making inferences, p. 401, 406
• Comparing, p. 402
• Clarifying, p. 403
• Contrasting, p. 405
• Recognizing effects, p. 406

FOCUS
5-Minute Warm-Up

▶ **Identifying Main Ideas**
To help students understand Aztec culture, have them answer the following questions.

1. Read Connect to Today on page 402. What did the Mexico City workers uncover?

2. Why haven't more sites been excavated?

 WARM-UP TRANSPARENCY 16

OBJECTIVE ① INSTRUCT

The Valley of Mexico

▶ **Key Ideas**
• The Valley of Mexico provides a fertile home for several powerful cultures.
• Teotihuacan becomes a major city and trade center.
• The Toltecs rise to power and introduce the legend of Quetzalcoatl.

 IN-DEPTH RESOURCES: UNIT 4
Guided Reading, p. 3

ACCESS FOR STUDENTS ACQUIRING ENGLISH
Guided Reading (Spanish), p. 162

3 The Aztecs Control Central Mexico

MAIN IDEA	WHY IT MATTERS NOW
Through alliances and conquest, the Aztecs created a powerful empire in Mexico.	This time period saw the origins of one of the 20th century's most populous cities, Mexico City.

SETTING THE STAGE While the Maya were developing their civilization to the south, other high cultures were evolving in central Mexico. Some of the most important developments took place in and around the Valley of Mexico. This valley, where modern Mexico City is located, eventually became the site of the greatest empire of Mesoamerica, the Aztec. The Aztecs were preceded by two other important civilizations who traced their ancestry to the Olmec and Zapotec.

The Valley of Mexico

The Valley of Mexico, a mountain basin 7,000 feet above sea level, served as the home base of several powerful cultures. The valley had several large, shallow lakes at its center, accessible resources, and fertile soil. These advantages attracted the people of Teotihuacan (TAY-oh-TEE-wah-KAHN) and the Toltecs. They settled in the valley and developed advanced civilizations that controlled much of the area. (See the map on page 395.)

Teotihuacan: An Early City-State The first major civilization of central Mexico was Teotihuacan, a city-state whose ruins lie just outside Mexico City. In the first century A.D., villagers at this site began to plan and construct a monumental city, even larger than Monte Albán, in Oaxaca.

At its peak in the sixth century, Teotihuacan had as many as 125,000 people, making it one of the largest cities in the world at the time. In the heart of the city was the giant Pyramid of the Sun. This 200-foot-tall pyramid was larger at its base than Egypt's Great Pyramid. The city also included numerous apartment compounds and artisan workshops.

Teotihuacan became the center of a thriving trade network that extended far into Central America. The city's most valuable trade item was **obsidian** (ahb-SIHD-ee-uhn),

Below is the Street of the Dead at Teotihuacan. Along the sides of the mile and a half long street are pyramid platforms that were originally topped with temples. The Pyramid of the Sun is visible in the distance.

Background
The Olmec civilization was located further south in Mexico and was the first major civilization in all of Mexico.

400

PRINT RESOURCES

 IN-DEPTH RESOURCES: UNIT 4
Guided Reading, p. 3
Literature: from *Quetzalcoatl*, p. 12
History Makers: Montezuma II, p. 15

 ACCESS FOR STUDENTS ACQUIRING ENGLISH
Guided Reading (Spanish), p. 162

 FORMAL ASSESSMENT
Section Quiz, p. 183

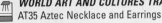 **ALTERNATIVE ASSESSMENT BOOK**

TECHNOLOGY RESOURCES

 WORLD ART AND CULTURES TRANSPARENCIES
AT35 Aztec Necklace and Earrings

 CD-ROM
Electronic Library of Primary Sources

 INTERNET www.mlworldhistory.com

a hard, glassy green or black rock found in the Valley of Mexico and used to make razor sharp weapons. There is no evidence that Teotihuacan conquered its neighbors or tried to create an empire. However, evidence of art styles and religious beliefs from Teotihuacan have been found throughout Mesoamerica.

After centuries of growth, the city abruptly declined. By 750 it was virtually abandoned. The vast ruins astonished later settlers in the area, who named the site Teotihuacan, meaning "City of the Gods."

Toltecs Take Over After the fall of Teotihuacan, no single culture dominated central Mexico for decades. Then, around 900, a new people from the southwest, the Toltecs, rose to power. For the next three centuries, the Toltecs ruled over the heart of Mexico from their capital at Tula, just north of Mexico City. Like other Mesoamericans, they built pyramids and temples. They also carved tall pillars in the shape of armed warriors.

In fact, the Toltecs were an extremely warlike people whose empire was based on conquest. They worshiped a fierce war god who demanded blood and human sacrifice from his followers. According to legend, an early Toltec king, Topiltzin, tried to replace this war god with a god of peace. That god was named **Quetzalcoatl** (keht·SAHL·koh·AHT·uhl), the Feathered Serpent. Magically, Topiltzin and Quetzalcoatl merged, becoming a single god-king and ruling in peace. Followers of the war god rebelled, however, overthrowing Quetzalcoatl and returning the Toltecs to their warlike ways. Through trade and conquest, Toltec power spread as far as the Yucatan, where it influenced late-Mayan culture. By the early 1200s, however, the Toltec reign had ended.

The Quetzalcoatl legend lived on, though, taking on the power of myth. According to legend, after his exile from Tula, the god traveled east, crossing the sea on a raft of snakes. It was said that he would return one day, bringing a new reign of light and peace. That myth would come back to haunt the greatest empire of Mexico, the Aztecs.

Aztecs Build an Empire

The Aztecs arrived in the Valley of Mexico around A.D. 1200. It was home to a number of small city-states that had survived the collapse of Toltec rule. The Aztecs, who were then called the Mexica, were a poor, nomadic people from the harsh deserts of northern Mexico. Fierce and ambitious, they soon adapted to local ways, finding work as soldiers-for-hire to local rulers.

According to an Aztec legend, the Aztecs' sun god, Huitzilopochtli (wee·tsee·loh·POHCH·tlee), told them to found a city of their own. He said to look for a place where an eagle perched on a cactus, holding a snake in its mouth. Part of the legend is captured in these words:

> **A VOICE FROM THE PAST**
> The place where the eagle screams,
> where he spreads his wings;
> the place where he feeds,
> where the fish jump,
> where the serpents
> coil up and hiss!
> This shall be Mexico Tenochtitlan
> and many things shall happen!
>
> *Cronica Mexicayotl*

THINK THROUGH HISTORY
A. Making Inferences Why would the followers of the war god rebel against the king?
A. Answer They did not wish to worship a peaceful god or perhaps feared the wrath of the war god if they did not worship him.

Background
The eagle on a cactus with the snake appears on the national flag of Mexico.

SPOTLIGHT ON

Quetzalcoatl: Feathered Serpent God
The story of Quetzalcoatl is found throughout Mesoamerican culture. This god, as seen above, was a combination of a snake and the brightly colored quetzal bird. He had his origins in Teotihuacan, where he represented the earth and rain.

He was later adopted by the Toltecs, who saw him as the god of the morning and evening star, Venus, and as a bringer of culture. The Maya also worshiped Quetzalcoatl, as did the Aztecs. They saw him as a god of learning and a symbol of death and rebirth.

The quetzal bird that represents the god is found throughout the forests of Central and South America. Its three-foot-long emerald green tail feathers were highly valued by the Maya and the Aztecs, who traded to obtain them.

Today, the quetzal bird appears on the coat of arms of the country of Guatemala. Also, the currency of that country is called the quetzal.

People and Empires in the Americas **401**

SPOTLIGHT ON
Quetzalcoatl: Feathered Serpent God
Ask pairs of students to find out more about Quetzalcoatl and to bring images of the deity to class. Have students discuss the images and compare and contrast the way the deity was portrayed in different cultures. You might also show students a picture of a quetzal bird. Invite gifted students to read the literature selection.

IN-DEPTH RESOURCES: UNIT 4
Literature: from *Quetzalcoatl*, p. 12

OBJECTIVE 2 INSTRUCT

Aztecs Build an Empire

▶ **Key Ideas**
• The Aztecs settle in the Valley of Mexico and found the city of Tenochtitlan.
• The Aztecs form the Triple Alliance and build an empire through conquest.
• The emperor and nobles, whose wealth is based on tribute, rule Aztec society.
• Tenochtitlan, the Aztecs' island capital, becomes an impressive urban center.

MORE ABOUT . . .
The Aztecs and Mexico
The Aztec name is derived from Aztlán ("White Land"), which was their mythical place of origin in the north. The Aztecs' earlier name for themselves, Mexica, gave rise to the country name Mexico.

TEACHING OPTION | **BLOCK SCHEDULING** | **ART APPLICATION ACTIVITY** | **CLASS TIME 25 MINUTES**

Task: Students will work in groups to make an Aztec mask or jewelry design.

Materials Needed: Colored construction paper, scissors, glue, drawing paper and colored pencils, colored pictures of Aztec art.

Activity: Show students the art transparency for this section and give them books or magazine articles showing Aztec art. Divide interested students into small groups. They can make an Aztec mask or design a piece of jewelry in the Aztec style. Ask them to think about the purpose of their mask or jewelry and what animals, spirits, and images the Aztecs used in their designs. Suggested sources: *Treasures of the Great Temple,* by Eduardo Matos, La Jolla, CA: Alti Publications, 1990; *Aztec Art,* by Esther Pasztory, New York: H.M. Abrams, 1983; *Art of the Aztecs and Its Origins,* by Henri Stierling, New York: Rizzoli, 1982.

Conclusion: Have each group present their mask or design to the class and explain why they used the colors and images they did. Have them discuss what they learned about Aztec art and images from this experience.

WORLD ART AND CULTURES TRANSPARENCIES
A35 Aztec Necklace and Earrings

Teacher's Edition **401**

MORE ABOUT . . .
The Aztec Empire

By the early 1500s, the Aztecs were trying to extend their control over the territories they had conquered. To do so, they arranged marriages between Aztec nobles and the noble families of subject states. They also kept garrisons of soldiers in the provinces. These soldiers received land grants and acted as colonists, thereby bringing Aztec culture to far-flung regions of the empire.

To give students a more detailed look at the Aztec civilization, you might wish to show the videocassette *Aztecs* (30 min.) from the *Indians of North America* series (Social Studies School Service, 800-421-4246).

CONNECT *to* TODAY
Aztec Ruins Unearthed

Point out that building projects in Mexico City, and especially construction of the city's subway system, have unearthed many ancient ruins and relics. Have students find out more about modern Mexico City and its ancient ruins. Suggest they search the Internet, INFOTRAC, and other online sources for information.

INTERNET
Click *World History* at www.mlworldhistory.com

They found such a place on a small island in Lake Texcoco, at the center of the valley. There, in 1325, they founded their city, which they named Tenochtitlan (teh·NOCH·tee·TLAHN).

Aztecs Grow Stronger Over the years, the Aztecs gradually increased in strength and number. In 1428, they joined with two other city-states—Texcoco and Tlacopan—to form the **Triple Alliance.** This alliance became the leading power in the Valley of Mexico and soon gained control over neighboring regions. By the early 1500s, they controlled a vast Mesoamerican empire, which stretched from central Mexico to the Atlantic and Pacific coasts and south into Oaxaca. This empire was divided into 38 provinces. It had an estimated population of between 5 and 15 million people.

The Aztec state based its power on military conquest and the tribute it gained from conquered people. The Aztecs exercised loose control over much of their empire. They often let local rulers govern their own regions. The Aztecs did demand tribute, however, in the form of gold, maize, cacao beans, cotton, jade, and other products. If local rulers failed to pay tribute, or otherwise defied the Aztecs, the Aztec warriors would respond brutally. They would destroy villages and capture or slaughter the inhabitants.

Nobles Rule Aztec Society At the height of the Aztec Empire, military leaders held great power in Aztec society. Along with government officials and priests, these military leaders made up the noble class. Many nobles owned vast estates, which they ruled over like lords, living a life of great wealth and luxury.

The other two broad classes in Aztec society were the commoners and the slaves. Commoners included merchants, artisans, soldiers, and farmers who owned their own land. The merchants were a special type of elite. They often traveled widely, acting as spies for the emperor and gaining great wealth for themselves. The lowest class, the slaves, were captives who did many different jobs.

The emperor sat at the top of the Aztec social pyramid. Although he sometimes consulted with top generals or officials, his power was absolute. He lived in royal splendor in a magnificent palace, surrounded by servants and his wives. Visitors had to treat him like a god. They entered his presence in bare feet and cast their eyes down so as not to look at him.

Trade Brings Wealth The Aztecs controlled an extensive trade network, which brought many products from faraway regions to the capital at Tenochtitlan. The economic heart of the city was the huge market of Tlatelolco (TLAH·tehl·AWL·koh). According to Hernando Cortés, the Spanish conqueror of Mexico, this market was larger than any in Spain:

> **A VOICE FROM THE PAST**
> Day after day 60,000 people congregate here to buy and sell. Every imaginable kind of merchandise is available from all parts of the Empire, foodstuffs and dress, . . . gold, silver, copper, . . . precious stones, leather, bone, mussels, coral, cotton, feathers. . . . Everything is sold by the piece or by measurement, never by weight. In the main market there is a law court in which there are always ten or twelve judges performing their office and taking decisions on all marketing controversies.
>
> **HERNANDO CORTÉS,** *Letters of Information*

Much of the agricultural produce sold at the market was grown on *chinampas,* farm plots built on the marshy fringes of the lake. These plots, which spread out from Tenochtitlan in all directions, were extremely productive. They provided the food needed for a huge urban population.

CONNECT *to* TODAY

Aztec Ruins Unearthed
On February 21, 1978, electric company workers broke through a thick layer of concrete on a street in Mexico City. Underneath the street was an enormous piece of carved rock. It was the statue of the Aztec moon goddess. The location of the accidental find proved to be the Great Temple of Tenochtitlan, the most sacred Aztec shrine.

The world's largest city, Mexico City, is built on the ruins of Tenochtitlan. Although the lake that surrounded the Aztec capital is gone, many of the ruins of Aztec civilization remain. Most of these ruins lie buried beneath city streets, but a few major sites such as the Great Temple have been excavated and rebuilt.

TEACHING OPTIONS

EXPLORING PRIMARY SOURCES

A Voice from the Past Tell students that a number of Spaniards—including Cortés, Bernal Díaz, and various priests—wrote chronicles that provide valuable details about Aztec life. Although many of these writers praised Aztec achievements, particularly the sophistication of Tenochtitlan, the Spanish destroyed most of the city and built their new capital on top of the Aztec ruins.

Have students read portions of other chronicles by Europeans and discuss the writers' knowledge and opinions about the native populations.

CONNECTIONS ACROSS THE CURRICULUM

Economics: Barter System
Although the Aztecs sometimes used cacao beans as a form of currency, most transactions were accomplished through the barter system. Have students consider the difficulties of running a huge urban market like Tlatelolco without the convenience of a standard medium of exchange.

Ask groups of students to make lists of Aztec trade goods and to speculate on their worth relative to other items. Encourage groups to discuss their ideas and come up with a master barter list.

Tenochtitlan: A Planned City By the early 1500s, Tenochtitlan had become an extraordinary urban center. With an estimated population of 200,000 people, it was larger than London or any other European capital of the time. Tenochtitlan remained on its original island site. To connect the island to the mainland, Aztec engineers built three raised roads called causeways over the water and marshland. Other cities ringed the lake, creating a dense concentration of people in the Valley of Mexico. One of Cortés's soldiers, Bernal Díaz, was amazed to find a bustling urban civilization in the heart of Mexico:

A VOICE FROM THE PAST
When we saw all those cities and villages built in the water, and other great towns on dry land, and that straight and level causeway leading to Mexico, we were astounded. These great towns and cues [pyramids] and buildings rising from the water, all made of stone, seemed like an enchanted vision. . . . Indeed, some of our soldiers asked whether it was not all a dream.
BERNAL DÍAZ, *The Conquest of New Spain*

In Tenochtitlan, palaces, temples, markets, and residential districts were connected by streets and avenues. Canals divided the city, allowing canoes to bring people and cargo directly into the city center. Aqueducts funneled fresh water in from the mainland.

At the center of the city was a huge, walled complex, filled with palaces, temples, and government buildings. The main structure in this complex was the Great Temple. It was a giant pyramid with twin temples at the top, the Aztec religious center.

Background
The twin temples were dedicated to the sun god and the rain god.

Religion, the Center of Aztec Life

Religion played a major role in Aztec society. In Tenochtitlan there were hundreds of temples and religious structures dedicated to the gods. The Aztecs adopted many of their gods and religious beliefs from other Mesoamerican peoples, particularly the Toltecs.

Aztec religious practice centered on elaborate public ceremonies designed to communicate with the gods and win their favor. At these ceremonies, priests made offerings to the gods and presented ritual dramas, songs, and dances featuring masked performers. The Aztec ceremonial calendar was full of religious festivals, which varied according to the god being honored.

Sacrifices for the Sun God The most important rituals involved the sun god, Huitzilopochtli. According to Aztec belief, Huitzilopochtli made the sun rise every day, but only when he was nourished by human blood. Without regular offerings of blood, the sun would fall from the sky and all life would perish. For that reason, Aztec priests carried out human sacrifice on a massive scale. Thousands of victims, usually prisoners of war, were led to the altar atop the Great Temple, where priests carved out their hearts using obsidian knives.

To fulfill this sacred duty, the priests required a steady supply of war captives. This in turn pushed the Aztec military to carry out new conquests. The battle tactics of Aztec warriors were designed to provide live prisoners of war for the sacrifices.

C. Answer They were needed for sacrifice to the gods.
THINK THROUGH HISTORY
C. Clarifying Why were so many war captives taken?

Men on a flying wheel and dancers entertain warriors on a festival day. Sacrificial offerings are carried to the top of the pyramid. The picture is a detail from a fresco at the National Palace in Mexico, painted by Diego Rivera in 1950.

403

OBJECTIVE ❸ INSTRUCT

Religion, the Center of Aztec Life

▶ **Key Ideas**
- Aztec religion centers on the worship of many gods through elaborate public ceremonies.
- Human sacrifice is essential in Aztec religion to renew the sun each day.
- The need for sacrificial victims compels the Aztecs to conquer more lands and capture more prisoners.

 ELECTRONIC LIBRARY OF PRIMARY SOURCES
"Human Sacrifice Among the Aztecs"

CRITICAL THINKING ACTIVITY
CLASS TIME: 15 MINUTES

Summarizing
Have students summarize the link between Aztec religion and Aztec military conquest by completing the following flow chart.

worship of sun god requires human blood
↓
human sacrifice performed on a large scale
↓
conquest required to capture more sacrificial victims

Measuring Time

Personal experiences and changes in the environment force all humans to sense time. How that passage of time is measured is a cultural characteristic that reflects the needs of the society. For example, if the society needs to know when a yearly flood will take place, the measuring of time will provide an answer. The need to get many people to work together at an identical time requires a different measurement of time. Cultures have devised a variety of ways to measure time to meet their needs. As you compare and contrast the methods of measuring time on these pages, think about what needs each of these timepieces helps meet.

In 1884, nations around the world agreed to set standard time zones. They begin at the Prime Meridian. There are 24 standard zones that cover the earth's surface at intervals of 60 minutes.

Aztec Sun Stone at Tenochtitlan

Religious activities in the 14th century surrounding both the day and the year required a method of identifying the time period and the god who controlled it. Originally located in the main ceremonial plaza of Tenochtitlan, the Aztec calendar stone measures 13 feet in diameter and weighs 24 tons. In the center is the sun god Tonatiuh. He is surrounded by symbols of movement and the four worlds preceding the time of the Aztecs: Tiger, Water, Wind, and Rain of Fire. In the ring just outside these panels, 20 segments represent the 20 days that make up each of the 18 months of the Mesoamerican year. The year was composed of 360 days plus 5 extra days that were considered to be unlucky.

 AZTEC CALENDARS

The Aztec gods pictured here were closely associated with the calendar and the passage of time. Since gods ruled specific periods of time, it was important to know which gods controlled the day. During the time they ruled, offerings were made to them.

404 Chapter 16

Sundial

The need to know which part of the day to pray or assemble created a need for a timepiece with more exactness. The earliest known sundial dates from about the eighth century B.C. The style pictured above was used by the astronomer Ptolemy in Alexandria in A.D. 125–141.

A sundial tells time by measuring the angles of a shadow cast by the sun. A flat triangular piece of metal is set in the center of the dial. The shadow it casts on the dial tells the time. The dial face is divided into hours, and sometimes half and quarter hours. Many sundials have faces numbered from 5 A.M. to 7 P.M. in Roman numerals.

Chinese Mechanical Clock

Built in A.D. 1090, during the Song Dynasty, this clock's movements were driven by water flowing into buckets on a waterwheel inside the clock tower. As each bucket filled, a lever tilted, the wheel turned, and a new bucket was filled. Every 15 minutes, bells and gongs rang. To chime the hours, revolving figures appeared at the clock windows. For accuracy, the mechanical movement was coordinated with the celestial globe at the top of the tower.

Wristwatch

Wristwatches became popular during World War I when soldiers and pilots needed both convenience and precision in measuring time. This modern navigator style chronograph shows the time, acts as a stop watch, and can calculate miles per hour.

The Aztecs, like the Maya, used two calendars to calculate time—a 260-day religious calendar and a 365-day solar one. They meshed as if they were a pair of wheels. Once every 52 years both cycles started on the same day.

Connect _to_ History

Contrasting For which need for measuring time were the majority of the clocks/calendars invented?

 SEE SKILLBUILDER HANDBOOK, PAGE 992

Connect _to_ Today

Reporting Find out the reasons for the origin of daylight-savings time. Also try to find out what impact daylight-savings time has on the use of electricity in the United States. Write a brief report on your findings.

 INTERNET CONNECTION

Visit us at **www.mlworldhistory.com** to learn more about time measurement through history.

People and Empires in the Americas **405**

Masks such as this were sometimes placed on the head of a dead person. The mosaic pattern dates from the Teotihuacan era and was repeated in Aztec masks. The mosaic pieces are jade, coral, and shell on an obsidian base.

Problems in the Aztec Empire

Eventually, the Aztecs' need for an ever-expanding empire created problems for them. In 1502 a new ruler, **Montezuma II** (MAHN·tih·ZOO·muh), was crowned emperor. Under Montezuma, the Aztec empire began to weaken. For nearly a century, the Aztecs had been demanding tribute and sacrificial victims from the provinces under their control. Now, with the population of Tenochtitlan growing ever greater, the emperor called for even more tribute and sacrifice. A number of provinces rose up against Aztec oppression. This began a period of unrest and rebellion, which the military had to put down.

Montezuma tried to reduce pressure on the provinces caused by great demands for tribute payment. He froze and reduced the number of government officials. But resentment continued to grow. Then, as domestic problems simmered, another threat appeared: the arrival of the Spanish. To many Aztecs, the strangers from across the sea brought to mind the old legend regarding the return of Quetzalcoatl.

Further south in the high mountain valleys of the Andes, another empire was developing, one that would transcend the Aztec empire in land area, power, and wealth. The Inca, too, worshiped the sun and had large armies, but the society they built was much different from that of the Aztecs, as you will see in Section 4.

THINK THROUGH HISTORY
D. Making Inferences Why would freezing the number of government officials reduce the need for tribute money?
D. Answer They would not need to be paid.

Aztec		
Traits of Civilization	**Strength Leading to Power**	**Weakness Leading to Decline**
Religious beliefs and theocracy	United culture Loyalty to the king	Many physical and human resources funneled into religious activities
Powerful army	Adds land, power, and prisoners for religious sacrifice	Need for prisoners changes warfare style to less deadly and less aggressive
Empire of tribute states	Provides wealth and power and prisoners for religious sacrifice	Tribute states are rebellious and need to be controlled

SKILLBUILDER: Interpreting Charts
1. *How was the tribute system both a strength and a weakness?*
2. *How are the army and religious beliefs linked in the Aztec Empire?*

Section 3 Assessment

1. TERMS & NAMES
Identify
• obsidian
• Quetzalcoatl
• Triple Alliance
• Montezuma II

2. TAKING NOTES
Draw a chain of events diagram like the one below and fill in the main events that led to the establishment and growth of the Aztec Empire.

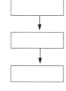

3. RECOGNIZING EFFECTS
How did the Aztec need for victims for sacrifice lead to problems controlling the empire?

THINK ABOUT
• reactions of the conquered peoples
• changes in army tactics

4. THEME ACTIVITY
Power and Authority With a small group of students, write a short play in which Montezuma discusses with his advisers how to gain control of rebellious provinces of the Aztec Empire. Be sure one adviser wants to keep peace at all costs.

406 Chapter 16

ANSWERS

1. TERMS & NAMES
obsidian, p. 400
Quetzalcoatl, p. 401
Triple Alliance, p. 402
Montezuma II, p. 406

2. TAKING NOTES
Possible Responses:
Arrive in Valley of Mexico
Build Tenochtitlan
Form the Triple Alliance
Conquer many lands

3. RECOGNIZING EFFECTS
Possible Responses: Demands for victims for sacrifice aroused the hatred of the conquered peoples. The goal of the army was to capture their enemies, not kill them. After a time, a number of provinces rebelled against Aztec rule.

4. THEME ACTIVITY
Standards for Evaluation
Dialogues should . . .
• reflect historical conditions
• provide insight into character
• provide reasonable options controlling the provinces

4 The Inca Create a Mountain Empire

TERMS & NAMES
• Pachacuti
• ayllu
• mita
• quipu

MAIN IDEA

The Inca built a vast empire supported by taxes, governed by a bureaucracy, and linked by extensive road systems.

WHY IT MATTERS NOW

The Inca system of government was similar to some socialist governments in the 20th century.

SETTING THE STAGE While the Aztecs were ruling in Mexico, another people—the Inca—were creating an equally powerful state in South America. From their capital in southern Peru, the Inca spread outward in all directions. They brought various Andean peoples under their control and built the largest empire ever seen in the Americas.

The Inca Come to Power

Like the Aztecs, the Inca built their empire on cultural foundations thousands of years old. Ancient civilizations such as Chavín, Moche, and Nazca had already established a tradition of high culture in Peru. They were followed by the Huari and Tiahuanaco cultures of southern Peru and Bolivia. The Chimu, an impressive civilization of the 1300s based in the northern coastal region once controlled by the Moche, came next. The Inca would create an even more powerful state, however, extending their rule over the entire Andean region.

Incan Beginnings The word *Inca* was originally the name of the ruling family of a group of people living in a high plateau of the Andes. After wandering the highlands for years, the Inca finally settled on fertile lands in the Valley of Cuzco. By the 1200s, the Inca had established their own small kingdom in the valley.

During this early period, the Inca developed traditions and beliefs that helped launch and unify their empire. One of these traditions was the belief that the Incan ruler was descended from the sun god, Inti, who would bring prosperity and greatness to the Incan state. Only men from one of 11 noble lineages believed to be descendants of the sun god could be selected as the Incan leader. These 11 families were called *orejones*, "Big Ears," because of the large plugs they wore in their earlobes.

Another tradition was the custom of worshiping dead rulers, who were preserved as sacred mummies. The mummies were brought to all important events and housed in special chambers. These royal mummies and their descendants retained rights to all the wealth and property accumulated during the king's lifetime. Succeeding rulers had to acquire their own wealth, which led them to conquer new territories.

Pachacuti Builds an Empire At first the Incan kingdom grew slowly. In 1438, however, a powerful and ambitious ruler, **Pachacuti** (PAH·chah·KOO·tee), took the throne. Under his leadership, the Inca expanded quickly, conquering all of Peru and then moving into neighboring lands. By 1500 the Inca ruled an empire that stretched 2,500 miles along the western coast of South America, from Ecuador in the north to Chile and Argentina in the south. The Inca called this

This gold mask is covered with cinnabar, a red ore. The eyes are formed of tree resin. The ear spools are marks of nobility. The mask is from the Siccan culture, which was conquered by the Chimu.

HISTORY MAKERS

Pachacuti

As the second son of the Inca ruler Viracocha, Pachacuti was not in line to succeed his father. In the early 1400s, however, Cuzco was attacked by the enemy state of Chanca. Viracocha and his first son, Urcon, fled the city. However, Pachacuti stood his ground and defeated the enemy. He then seized the throne from his brother to become the new king.

Pachacuti, whose name meant "World Transformer" (or in some translations "Earthshaker"), ruled for 33 years, until 1471, creating the largest empire in the Americas.

Pachacuti has been compared to Philip II of Macedonia. His son, Topa Yupanqui, who further enlarged the empire, has been compared to Alexander the Great.

SECTION 4 RESOURCES

PRINT RESOURCES

IN-DEPTH RESOURCES: UNIT 4
Guided Reading, p. 4
Primary Source: The Discovery of Machu Picchu, p. 11
History Maker: Pachacuti, p. 16

ACCESS FOR STUDENTS ACQUIRING ENGLISH
Guided Reading (Spanish), p. 163

FORMAL ASSESSMENT
Section Quiz, p. 184

ALTERNATIVE ASSESSMENT BOOK

TECHNOLOGY RESOURCES

GEOGRAPHY TRANSPARENCIES
GT16 The Expansion of the Inca Empire, 1230–1535

CRITICAL THINKING TRANSPARENCIES
CT16 Mesoamerican Empires Before Columbus

VIDEO Patterns of Interaction: *Building Empires*

CD-ROM
Electronic Library of Primary Sources

INTERNET www.mlworldhistory.com

Section 4 Overview

OBJECTIVES

(1) To describe the Inca rise to power.

(2) To explain how the Incan government functioned.

(3) To list the basic features of Incan religion.

(4) To describe discord in the Incan Empire.

SKILLBUILDERS

• Interpreting maps: place, human-environment interaction, p. 408
• Interpreting charts, p. 411

CRITICAL THINKING

• Forming and supporting an opinion, p. 408
• Recognizing effects, p. 409
• Analyzing motives, p. 411

FOCUS

5-Minute Warm-Up

▶ *Making Inferences*
Answering the following questions will help students understand the Incan Empire.

1. Study the map on p. 408. About how many miles long is the Incan Empire?

2. What feature shown on the map would help Incan rulers communicate with all parts of the empire?

WARM-UP TRANSPARENCY 16

OBJECTIVE (1) INSTRUCT

The Inca Come to Power

▶ *Key Ideas*
• The Inca settle the valley of Cuzco, establishing an 11-family royal lineage.

• They believe the Incan ruler is descended from the sun god and that past rulers should be worshipped.

• The Inca conquer a vast territory, using military power and wise diplomacy.

IN-DEPTH RESOURCES: UNIT 4
Guided Reading, p. 4

ACCESS FOR STUDENTS ACQUIRING ENGLISH
Guided Reading (Spanish), p. 163

History from Visuals

South American Cultures 100–1535

Interpreting the Map The South American cultures are all in a narrow strip along the Andes Mountains and the valleys. What advantages might this give the Inca Empire? *Agricultural conditions and cultures would tend to be similar.*

Extension Activity Have students look at the Atlas map of South America on page 982. Then ask them to list which modern countries include portions of the old Incan Empire. *Ecuador, Peru, Bolivia, Chile, Argentina*

SKILLBUILDER Answers
1. Moche and Chimu
2. Long distances and mountainous terrain make communication and transportation difficult.

OBJECTIVE 2 INSTRUCT

Inca Government Creates Unity

Key Ideas
- The Inca create a central bureaucracy to rule their empire.
- They build cities and roads to unify the empire, and create a state-run economy.
- The Inca develop calendars and accounting methods but not a written language.

South American Cultures, 100–1535

PACIFIC OCEAN

ANDES MTS.

ANDES MOUNTAINS

Chan Chan

Machu Picchu
Cuzco

Lake Titicaca

Amazon R.

Equator

Tropic of Capricorn

Moche, 100–700
Chimu, 1000–1470
Inca, 1438–1535
Inca roads

0   500 Miles
0   1,000 Kilometers

GEOGRAPHY SKILLBUILDER: Interpreting Maps
1. **Place** The lands of which earlier South American cultures were included in the Incan Empire?
2. **Human-Environment Interaction** Look at the shape and terrain of the Incan Empire. What problems related to geography might occur in controlling the land?

empire Tihuantinsuya, or "Land of the Four Quarters." It included about 80 provinces and perhaps as many as 16 million people.

Pachacuti and his successors accomplished this feat of conquest through a combination of diplomacy and military force. The Inca had a powerful military but used force only when necessary. The Inca were clever diplomats. Before attacking, they typically offered enemy states an honorable surrender. They would allow them to keep their own customs and rulers in exchange for loyalty to the Incan state. Because of this kind treatment, many states gave up without resisting.

Once an area was defeated, the Inca would make every effort to gain the loyalty of the newly conquered people. According to a 16th-century Spanish observer:

A VOICE FROM THE PAST
The Inca always had the mastery, but when the enemies were vanquished, they were not destroyed; on the contrary, orders were given to release the captives and restore the spoils, and allow them to retain their estates. For the Inca desired to show them that they should not be so mad as to revolt against his royal person and reject his friendship; rather they should wish to be his friends, as were those in other provinces.

PEDRO DE CIEZA DE LEÓN, *Chronicle of Peru*

Incan Government Creates Unity

The Inca were also extraordinary organizers and administrators. To control the huge empire, the rulers divided their territory and its people into manageable units, governed by a central bureaucracy. The Inca created an efficient economic system to support the empire and an extensive road system to tie it together. They also imposed a single official language, Quechua (KEHCH·wuh), and founded schools to teach Incan ways. Certain social groups were identified by officially dictated patterns on clothing. All of these actions were calculated to unify the variety of people controlled by the Inca.

Incan Cities Show Government Presence To exercise control over their empire, the Inca built many cities in conquered areas. The architecture of government buildings was the same all over the empire, making the presence of the government apparent. As in Rome, all roads led to the capital, Cuzco. The heart of the Incan Empire, Cuzco was a splendid city of temples, plazas, and palaces. "Cuzco was grand and stately," wrote Cieza de León. "It had fine streets, . . . and the houses were built of solid stones, beautifully joined." Like the Romans, the Inca were masterful engineers and stonemasons. Though they had no iron tools and did not use the wheel, Incan builders carved and transported huge blocks of stone, fitting them together perfectly without mortar. Many Incan walls still stand in Cuzco, undisturbed by the region's frequent earthquakes.

Incan Government Organizes Communities The Incan system of government was based on age-old patterns of community cooperation. Small groups of people known as **ayllu** (EYE·loo) worked together for the common good, building irrigation

408 Chapter 16

THINK THROUGH HISTORY
A. Forming and Supporting an Opinion Of all the methods used to create unity, which do you think would be most successful? Why?
A. Possible Answer Probably the strongest answer is language. It allowed easy communication throughout the empire.

---

canals and agricultural terraces on steep hillsides. The ayllu also stored food and other supplies to distribute during hard times.

The Inca took this principle of community organization and welfare and applied it to their empire. They incorporated the ayllu structure into a governing system based on the decimal system. They divided families into groups of 10, 100, 1,000, and 10,000. Each group was led by a chief. He was part of a chain of command. That chain stretched from the community and regional levels all the way to Cuzco, where the Incan ruler and his council of state held court. In general, local administration was left in the hands of local rulers, and villages were allowed to continue their traditional ways. If a community resisted Incan control, however, the Inca might relocate the whole group to a different territory. The resisters would be placed under the control of rulers appointed by the high rulers.

The main demand the Incan state placed on its subjects was for tribute, mainly in the form of labor. The labor tribute was known as **mita** (MEE·tuh). It required all able-bodied citizens to work for the state a certain number of days every year. Mita workers might labor on state farmlands, produce craft goods for state warehouses, or help build public works, such as roads, palaces, or irrigation canals.

Roads Link the Empire The most spectacular public works project was the Incan road system. A marvel of engineering, this road system symbolized the power of the Incan state. The 14,000-mile-long network of roads and bridges spanned the empire, traversing rugged mountains and harsh deserts. The roads ranged from paved stone to simple paths. Along the roads, the Inca built guest houses to provide shelter for weary travelers. A system of runners, known as *chasquis* (SHAH·skeys), traveled these roads as a kind of postal service, carrying messages from one end of the empire to the other. The road system also allowed the easy movement of troops to bring control to zones where trouble might be brewing.

State Controls the Economy Incan power was also evident in economic life. The Incan state controlled most economic activity, regulating the production and distribution of goods. Land was organized into upper and lower geographical units, each producing goods the other could not. The units were linked together to create a total economy. Unlike the Maya and the Aztec, the Inca allowed little private commerce or trade.

Historians have compared the Incan system to a type of socialism or a modern welfare state. Citizens were expected to work for the state and were cared for in return. For example, the aged and disabled were often supported by the state. The state also held public feasts, distributing food and maize beer as a reward for citizens' labor.

Land ownership was divided in three ways: state lands, religious lands, and community lands. Farmers worked on all three types of land. Expanding on irrigation systems developed by earlier people, the Inca created a massive water management system that stored water for the dry season. They even straightened an entire river channel to better provide water for agriculture.

With a terracing system they produced crops such as maize and quinoa, a grain native to the Andes. The Inca developed a method for freeze-drying potatoes. They then stored the freeze-dried potatoes, called *chuño*, in huge warehouses for times of shortages of food. The *chuño* could be kept indefinitely.

Government Keeps Records Despite the sophistication of many aspects of Incan life, the Inca never developed a writing system. History and literature were

People and Empires in the Americas **409**

A miniature silver llama illustrates how important the llama was in Incan society. It helped transport goods and food in the mountains, provided wool and meat, and was offered to the gods as a sacrifice.

INK THROUGH HISTORY

3. Recognizing Effects How would relocating troublesome people help government control of an area?

3. Answer Reduce the ability of the troublemakers to gather followers.

Background The irrigation systems were originally built by the Moche, Chimu, and Tiwankans.

SPOTLIGHT ON

Incan Relay Messengers

Communication in the Incan Empire was the task of runner-messengers called *chasquis*. The system worked like a modern relay race. A runner would "hand off" a memorized message or package to another runner waiting at a way station. That runner would sprint to the next station along the road.

The stations were placed about every mile or so along the main roads, which covered about 3,100 miles. In this way, a message could travel 140 miles a day. The distance from Cuzco to the coast could be covered in just three days. A century later, the same journey took the Spanish 12 days on horseback!

The *chasquis* who traveled the Inca roads served in 15-day shifts. This job was a part of their mita labor tax.

SPOTLIGHT ON
Inca Relay Messengers

Ask students to calculate how long it would take *chasquis* to cover the following routes, assuming a speed of 140 miles a day:
(a) Cuzco to Quito, 1500 miles;
(b) Quito to Santiago, Chile, 3000 miles. *(a) 11 days; (b) 21 days*

MORE ABOUT . . .
Incan Roads

The Incan road system had two main arteries, one running through the mountains and the other along the coast, with spur roads connecting them. Typically, these roads were built of stone and lined with trees, and had a channel of drinking water running alongside. They spanned chasms on suspension bridges made of woven vines.

MORE ABOUT . . .
The Incan Empire

The Building Empires video includes a detailed look at Incan history, government, and engineering.

PATTERNS OF INTERACTION
Building Empires: The Rise of the Persians and the Inca
Videocassette: Tape 1

CRITICAL THINKING TRANSPARENCIES
CT16 Mesoamerican Empires Before Columbus

| TEACHING OPTION | BLOCK SCHEDULING | GEOGRAPHY APPLICATION ACTIVITY | CLASS TIME 30 MINUTES |

Task: To help students understand the expansion and consolidation of the Incan Empire

Materials Needed: Geography Transparency G16; history textbook; student notebooks and pens/pencils

Activity: Have students view the transparency, making sure they understand that each colored section represents an addition to the Incan Empire.

Ask them to copy in their notebooks the dates listed in the legend. Referring to their textbooks, students will list three or four main facts about Inca history at each time period.

Conclusion: Discuss with students the importance of leadership, military power, administration, and communication in building and maintaining the empire. Ask them to compare this empire with those

of Alexander the Great and the Mongols. In what ways were they similar and in what ways did they differ?

GEOGRAPHY TRANSPARENCIES
G16 The Expansion of the Inca Empire, 1230–1535

Teacher's Edition **409**

The Temple of the Sun

Cuzco's Temple of the Sun, or Coricancha, was mostly destroyed by the Spaniards, though a portion remains in a church built on the site. At one point, according to a Spanish conquistador, 700 gold plates, looking "like boards from a chest," were stripped from the walls. When melted down, each plate produced more than four pounds of pure gold. The total value was about $22 million in today's currency.

OBJECTIVE 3 INSTRUCT

Religion Supports the State

▶ **Key Ideas**
- Incan religion reinforces the power of the state.
- The Inca worship nature spirits, especially the sun god, Inti.
- Young men and women are drafted for lifetime service to the state church.

CRITICAL THINKING ACTIVITY
CLASS TIME: 15 MINUTES

Comparing
Ask students to fill out the chart below with information comparing the Incan religion with that of the Aztecs in Section 3.

Inca	Aztecs
creator god and sun god	sun god
animal sacrifices	human sacrifices
elaborate calendar	elaborate calendar

One and one-half miles up a mountain, Machu Picchu could only be reached by a log bridge across a deep canyon. Although the details of its origin and its abandonment are unclear, some historians believe that it was a religious or ceremonial city.

memorized as part of an oral tradition. For numerical information, the Inca created an accounting device known as the **quipu** (see "Spotlight" on page 18), a set of knotted strings that could be used to record data. The knots and their position on the cord indicated numbers. Additionally, the colors of the cords indicated categories of information important to the government. For example, red strings were used to count warriors.

The Inca also developed an elaborate calendar system with two types of calendars, one for night and one for day. They were used primarily for religious purposes. Like the calendars of the Maya and the Aztec, the two calendars provided information about the gods who, the Inca believed, ruled the day and time. Like the Maya, Incan mathematicians and astronomers used complicated methods to create calendars necessary for the proper worship of the gods.

Religion Supports the State

As in ancient Mexico, religion was important to the Inca and helped reinforce the power of the state. The Inca worshiped fewer gods than the Aztecs. The Inca focused on key nature spirits such as the moon, the stars, and thunder. In the balance of

nature, the Inca saw patterns for the way humans should relate to each other and to the earth. Chief of the Incan gods was a creator god called Viracocha. Next in importance was the sun god, Inti. Because the Incan ruler was considered a descendant of Inti, sun worship amounted to worship of the king.

Background
Notice the similarity to the Egyptian ideas about the sun and the ruler.

Incan priests led the sun-worship services, assisted by young women known as *mamakuna,* or "virgins of the sun." These women, all unmarried, were drafted by the Inca for a lifetime of religious service. The young women were trained in religious activities, as teachers, spinners, weavers, and beer makers. Young men, known as *yamacuna,* also served as full-time workers for the state and in religious activities. Sacrifice of llamas and exchange of goods were a part of the religious activities. The goods were distributed by the priest to the people as gifts from the gods.

The Temple of the Sun in Cuzco was the most sacred of all Incan shrines. It was heavily decorated in gold, a metal the Inca referred to as "sweat of the sun." According to Garcilaso de la Vega, the son of an Inca princess, the temple even had a garden crafted entirely from precious metals.

A VOICE FROM THE PAST
Here could be seen all sorts of plants, flowers, trees, animals, both small and large, wild and tame, tiny crawling creatures such as snakes, lizards, and snails, as well as butterflies and birds of every size. . . . All of these valuable works were made by the goldsmiths attached to the Temple, from the tribute of gold and silver that arrived every year from all the provinces of the Empire.

GARCILASO DE LA VEGA, *The Incas*

| EXPLORING PRIMARY SOURCES | CONNECTIONS ACROSS TIME AND PLACE |

A Voice from the Past
Garcilaso de la Vega was born in Peru in 1539, during the final days of the Inca, to an Inca princess and a Spanish conquistador. As a young man, he studied Incan history and customs. At age 21, he left Peru for Spain, never to return. Later in life, he recorded his stories and observations in a famous book, *Royal Commentaries of the Incas.* Suggest that students read portions of the book and discuss it in class.

 ELECTRONIC LIBRARY OF PRIMARY SOURCES
from *Royal Commentaries of the Incas*

Ancient Cities
Tell students that modern Cuzco is built on Incan foundations and still contains many remnants of Incan architecture. Ask students to research the remnants of Incan civilization in Cuzco. Then have them think of other cities in the world— such as Athens, Rome, or Cairo—that still have remnants of their ancient past. Ask students to consider how and why cities sometimes preserve these old remains.

Students might enjoy reading the primary source for this section, which describes the discovery of an ancient Incan site.

 IN-DEPTH RESOURCES: UNIT 4
Primary Source: The Discovery of Machu Picchu, p. 11

In addition to producing beautiful gold and silver articles, Incan artisans even covered walls in Cuzco with shining sheets of gold.

Cuzco was the administrative and ceremonial capital of the Incan Empire. It included a sun temple and storage areas. Other Incan cities also had monumental architecture and seemed to have multiple purposes. For example, Machu Picchu, discovered by Hiram Bingham in 1912, was isolated and mysterious. Like Cuzco, Machu Picchu also had a sun temple, public buildings, a water system, and a central plaza. Some sources suggest it was an estate of Pachacuti. Others believe it was a retreat for Inca rulers or the elite. Its true function has not been determined.

Discord in the Empire

Vocabulary
litter: a chair that is carried by bearers

In the early 1500s, the Inca empire was at the height of its glory. King Huayna Capac toured the empire in a royal litter, covered with gold and surrounded by attendants. Trouble was on the way, however. Stopping in Quito, Ecuador, the king opened a gift box. Out flew butterflies and moths, considered an evil omen. About 1525, while still in Quito, Huayna Capac died of disease. Soon after his death, civil war broke out between Huayna Capac's sons, Atahualpa (ah·tah·WAHL·pah) and Huascar (WAHS·kahr), who both claimed the throne. Atahualpa won, but the war tore the empire apart. As you will learn in Chapter 20, within a few years, the Spanish arrived. Taking advantage of Incan weakness, they would soon divide and conquer the empire.

Inca

Traits of Civilization	Strength Leading to Power	Weakness Leading to Decline
Religious beliefs and theocracy	United culture Loyalty to the emperor	Many physical and human resources funneled into religious activities
Major road systems	Connected entire empire and aided control	Enemy could also use roads to move troops
Type of welfare state with huge bureaucracy	Care for entire population during good and bad times	People unable to care for themselves with the elimination of the welfare state

SKILLBUILDER: Interpreting Charts
1. *In your opinion, which of the three traits leading to power was the most valuable? Briefly discuss your reasons.*
2. *Which trait did you find repeated in the Maya and Aztec Empires?*

Section 4 Assessment

1. TERMS & NAMES

Identify
• Pachacuti
• ayllu
• mita
• quipu

2. TAKING NOTES

Draw a diagram like the one below and fill in the methods the Inca used to achieve the idea in the center.

The Inca built a vast empire, which was largely unified under their control.

Which of these methods for unification were acceptable to the conquered people? Explain.

3. ANALYZING MOTIVES

Why do you think the Inca used the ayllu system as the basis for governing the people of the empire?

THINK ABOUT
• ways to control a large empire
• the ease of using a system that already existed

4. THEME ACTIVITY

Power and Authority Choose a partner to debate the value of the welfare state of the Inca. One partner should support the welfare state and the other should be against it. Focus the debate on the advantages and disadvantages of the Incan welfare state.

People and Empires in the Americas **411**

Teacher's Edition **411**

TERMS & NAMES

1. pueblos, p. 391
2. Mississippian, p. 393
3. Iroquois, p. 393
4. Tikal, p. 395
5. glyph, p. 398
6. Quetzalcoatl p. 401
7. Triple Alliance, p. 402
8. Montezuma II, p. 406
9. Pachacuti, p. 407
10. mita, p. 409

REVIEW QUESTIONS

Answers will vary.

11. They were diverse because they developed in different environments.

12. Native Americans in North America had in common trade, religious beliefs, and social patterns (importance of family).

13. Religion influenced most aspects of Mayan life. Gods were associated with death, war, weather, directions, and color, among many other things. Mayans believed each day was a god. They had many ways to worship gods. Religious beliefs led Mayans to the development of calendars, mathematics, and astronomy.

14. The Maya developed a solar calendar, a system of mathematics that included the concept of zero, and the most advanced writing system in the ancient Americas.

15. The Aztecs built their empire by forming the Triple Alliance and controlled it by demanding tribute and responding harshly to defiance.

16. Trade brought great wealth to the Aztec Empire and helped to spread Aztec culture.

17. The Aztecs believed that the sun god Huitzilopochtli made the sun rise every day, as long as he was nourished by human blood. Without it, the sun would fall from the sky and all life would perish.

18. Dead Inca rulers and their descendants retained rights to all wealth and property accumulated during the ruler's lifetime. Succeeding rulers had to acquire their own wealth, which led them to conquer new territories.

19. The Incan government imposed a single official language, founded schools to teach Incan ways, created structured communities, required tribute in the form of labor, regulated the production and distribution of goods, and cared for the aged and disabled.

Visual Summary

People and Empires in the Americas

North America
600–1600

- Government by a variety of small tribes to very complex societies
- Similar religious beliefs in the Great Spirit
- Economy influenced by the environment
- Trade links to other groups

Mesoamerica: Maya
250–900

- Government by city-state kings
- Religion plays a major role in society and rule
- Trade links between city-states and other Mesoamerican groups
- Math and astronomy develop to support religious beliefs
- Pyramid builders
- Written language using hieroglyphs

Mesoamerica: Aztec
1200–1521

- Government by warrior-kings
- Religion plays a major role in society and rule
- Trade links between tribute states and other Mesoamerican groups
- Human sacrifice practiced for religious offerings
- Pyramid builders
- Pictorial written language

South America: Inca
1400–1532

- Government by theocracy—sun-god king
- Religion plays a major role in society and rule
- Social welfare state cares for all people
- Extensive road system links the country together

412 Chapter 16

20. The Incan ruler was considered a descendant of Inti, the sun god and one of the most important gods. Thus, worship of Inti amounted to worship of the king.

TERMS & NAMES

Briefly explain the importance of each of the following to the development of Native American cultures in North America, Mesoamerica, or South America.

1. pueblos
2. Mississippian
3. Iroquois
4. Tikal
5. glyph
6. Quetzalcoatl
7. Triple Alliance
8. Montezuma II
9. Pachacuti
10. mita

REVIEW QUESTIONS

SECTION 1 (pages 391–394)
Diverse Societies of North America

11. Why were Native American societies in North America so diverse?

12. What were the three things that most Native Americans in North America had in common?

SECTION 2 (pages 395–399)
Mayan Kings and Cities

13. What role did religion play in Mayan life?

14. What were three major achievements of the Mayan civilization?

SECTION 3 (pages 400–406)
The Aztecs Control Central Mexico

15. How did the Aztecs build and control their empire?

16. What role did trade play in the Aztec Empire?

17. Why did the Aztecs sacrifice human beings to their gods?

SECTION 4 (pages 407–411)
The Inca Create a Mountain Empire

18. How did the Inca custom of worshiping dead rulers affect the conquest of new territories?

19. List three ways in which the Inca government involved itself in people's lives.

20. How did Inca religion reinforce the power of the state?

Interact *with* History

From the mask clues and detective thinking, you should have determined that the Bella Coola society was a salmon fishing society that lived in forests by the Pacific Ocean. They probably used the mask in a ceremony about the chief god bringing fish to the people. Using the guide questions on the Interact page, look back in the chapter at the masks in each section to see what you can determine about other cultures.

Interact *with* History

CRITICAL THINKING

1. NATIVE AMERICAN RELIGIOUS BELIEFS

THEME RELIGIOUS AND ETHICAL SYSTEMS Compare the religious beliefs of the Maya, the Aztecs, and the Inca. How were they similar? How were they different?

2. CONTROLLING THE VALLEY OF MEXICO

From the beginning of the first century A.D., the Valley of Mexico was controlled by three major cultural groups. Find two dates for each culture and place them on the time line below. Write a brief description of the importance of each date.

3. INCAN GOVERNMENT AND SOCIETY

What can you infer about the values of the Inca from the fact that the government provided care for citizens who were aged or unable to care for themselves?

4. ANALYZING PRIMARY SOURCES

The following quotation is an Iroquois prayer to the Great Spirit and to other spirits in nature. Read the prayer and answer the questions below it.

> **A VOICE FROM THE PAST**
> We return thanks to our mother, the earth, which sustains us. We return thanks to the rivers and streams, which supply us with water. . . . We return thanks to the corn, and to her sisters, the beans and squashes, which give us life. . . . We return thanks to the sun, that he has looked upon the earth with a beneficent eye. . . . We return thanks to the Great Spirit . . . who directs all things for the good of his children.
> Quoted in *In the Trail of the Wind*

- How did the Iroquois feel about nature?
- What role did the Great Spirit play for the Iroquois?

CHAPTER ACTIVITIES

1. LIVING HISTORY: Unit Portfolio Project

THEME CULTURAL INTERACTION Your unit portfolio project focuses on showing cultural interaction through conquest, trade, migration, and heritage (see page 387). For Chapter 16, you might use one of the following ideas to add to your portfolio:

- Imagine you are a Chinook trader from the Northwest Coast heading for an intertribal marketplace on the Columbia River. Do research on the trade items of peoples of the Northwest and those of the interior plains. Write a dialogue between you as a Chinook trader and one or more traders from other areas discussing the goods you will trade.

- The Toltec culture influenced the religious ideas of both the Aztec and the Maya. Do research on the Toltec, Maya, and Aztec gods. Then make a poster that illustrates how some of the Toltec gods were portrayed in the Maya and Aztec cultures.

- INTERNET Aztec cultural ruins have been excavated in Mexico City. Using the Internet, magazines, and books, research how the Plaza of the Three Cultures and the Great Temple have preserved the cultures of the people of Mexico. Then write a one-page news article that describes these places and shows the heritage of the Mexican people.

2. CONNECT TO TODAY: Cooperative Learning

THEME POWER AND AUTHORITY The Iroquois League, or Confederacy, originally formed over 400 years ago, in 1570, is still in operation today. Work with a team to prepare a six-page advertising brochure that discusses the founding of the confederacy, its history through the years, and how it is functioning today. Use the Internet, magazines, and books such as *White Roots of Peace: The Iroquois Book of Life* to research the topic.

3. INTERPRETING A TIME LINE

Revisit the unit time line on pages 386–387. Find the dates for Chapter 16. Look at the dates for other cultures in this unit. Which empires were in power in other parts of the world at about the same time as the Aztecs and the Inca?

FOCUS ON GEOGRAPHY

This Spanish map (1519?) is a bird's-eye view of the island city of Tenochtitlan. Notice the roadway connections to the mainland and the canals that connected parts of the city.

- How many direct links to the mainland are there?
- What appears to be in the center of the city?

Connect to History Why was this location selected for a city?

People and Empires in the Americas **413**

CHAPTER ACTIVITIES

1. LIVING HISTORY: UNIT PORTFOLIO PROJECT

Standards for Evaluation
Dialogues should meet the following criteria:

- Show the results of sound research.
- Reflect the variety of goods offered by traders.
- Depict the culture of each trader.

Standards for Evaluation
Posters should meet the following criteria:

- Show the major Toltec gods adapted by the Maya and Aztecs.
- Include labels describing similarities and differences among the gods.

Standards for Evaluation
News articles should meet the following criteria:

- Explain the historical meaning of the Plaza of the Three Cultures and the Great Temple.
- Use journalism's five W's and one H to organize the data.
- Describe the importance of these cultural sites to Mexican culture today.

2. CONNECT TO TODAY: COOPERATIVE LEARNING

Standards for Evaluation
Brochures should meet the following criteria:

- Describe the origin of the Iroquois Confederacy and its role in tribal history.
- Explain its function and relevance in today's world.
- Use graphics to illustrate the copy.

3. INTERPRETING A TIME LINE

The Ottomans and Safavids had empires at the same time as did the Maya, Aztecs, and Inca.

FOCUS ON GEOGRAPHY

- four
- a huge temple

Connect to History Legend says the sun god told the Aztecs to find a location where they would see an eagle perched on a cactus and grasping a snake in its beak. This location is where they saw the bird of prey and where they built their city.

CRITICAL THINKING

1. NATIVE AMERICAN RELIGIOUS BELIEFS

Similarities: Believed deities ruled over every object and aspect of life; regarded rulers as divine; used prayer, ritual, and ceremony to communicate with deities; believed their societies should be organized around religion. *Differences:* Maya and Aztecs believed human sacrifices were necessary; Inca believed in fewer gods, major god was the sun.

2. CONTROLLING THE VALLEY OF MEXICO

Possible Response: (1) Teotihuacan—First century A.D., build a huge city-state; 750, abandon the site. (2) Toltec—900, rise to power, build pyramids, temples; 1200, decline in power. (3) Aztecs—1200, arrive in the Valley of Mexico; 1325, found Tenochtitlan; 1428, form Triple Alliance, 1502, Montezuma II comes to power

3. INCAN GOVERNMENT AND SOCIETY

The Inca valued their people at all stages of life and believed it was the state's responsibility to care for them.

4. ANALYZING PRIMARY SOURCES

The Iroquois felt grateful to nature; The Great Spirit ruled over all for the good of all his children.

	Key Ideas	COPY MASTERS	ASSESSMENT
SECTION 1 Italy: Birthplace of the Renaissance pp. 417–422	*The Renaissance, a period of intellectual and artistic creativity, flourishes in Italy, beginning about 1300. Versatile artists transform painting, sculpture, and literature.*	*In-Depth Resources: Unit 4* • **Guided Reading,** p. 18 • **Primary Sources:** from *The Courtier,* p. 25; from *The Prince,* p. 26 • **Literature:** from *The Agony and the Ecstasy,* p. 29 • **History Makers:** Niccolò Machiavelli, p. 32 • **Connections Across Time and Cultures:** p. 34	P E *Section 1 Assessment,* p. 422 *Formal Assessment* • Section Quiz, p. 193 *Alternative Assessment Book* • Standards for Evaluating a Cooperative Activity
SECTION 2 The Northern Renaissance pp. 423–427	*In the 1400s, Renaissance ideas spread to northern Europe, where German and Flemish masters create distinctive works of art. The books of northern Renaissance writers and philosophers become widely available because of the invention of the printing press.*	*In-Depth Resources: Unit 4* • **Guided Reading,** p. 19 • **Geography Application:** Trade in Renaissance Europe, p. 23	P E *Section 2 Assessment,* p. 427 *Formal Assessment* • Section Quiz, p. 194 *Alternative Assessment Book* • Standards for Evaluating a Cooperative Activity
SECTION 3 Luther Starts the Reformation pp. 428–432	*Martin Luther, a German monk, challenges the authority of the Catholic Church and triggers the Reformation—a movement for religious reform. The Reformation spreads to England when King Henry VIII breaks ties with the Catholic Church.*	*In-Depth Resources: Unit 4* • **Guided Reading,** p. 20 • **Skillbuilder Practice:** Synthesizing, p. 22 • **Primary Sources:** A Conference with Elizabeth I, p. 27; Report on the English Reformation, p. 28 • **History Makers:** Elizabeth I, p. 33	P E *Section 3 Assessment,* p. 432 *Formal Assessment* • Section Quiz, p. 195 *Alternative Assessment Book* • Standards for Evaluating a Cooperative Activity
SECTION 4 The Reformation Continues pp. 433–437	*John Calvin develops a system of Protestant theology that gains popularity among other European reformers. To stem the spread of Protestantism, the Catholic Church initiates its own reforms.*	*In-Depth Resources: Unit 4* • **Guided Reading,** p. 21	P E *Section 4 Assessment,* p. 436 *Formal Assessment* • Section Quiz, p. 196 *Alternative Assessment Book* • Standards for Evaluating a Cooperative Activity
CHAPTER RESOURCES	**Chapter Overview** *Two great European movements—the Renaissance and the Reformation—usher in dramatic cultural and social changes. The Renaissance marked the flowering of artistic creativity, while the Reformation led to new Christian beliefs.*	*Telescoping the Times* • Chapter Summary, pp. 65–67 *Planning for Block Schedules*	P E Chapter Assessment, pp. 438–439 **Chapter Activities,** p. 439 *Formal Assessment* • Chapter Test, forms A and B, pp. 197–202 **Test Generator** *Alternative Assessment Book*

TECHNOLOGY

 Warm-Up Transparency 17

 World Art and Cultures Transparencies
- AT36 Leonardo da Vinci's *The Last Supper*
- AT37 *Mona Lisa*

 Electronic Library of Primary Sources
- "The Art of Painting" from *Notebooks*

 INTERNET RESOURCES
www.mlworldhistory.com

 Warm-Up Transparency 17

 World Art and Cultures Transparencies
- AT38 Van Eyck's *Wedding Portrait*

 INTERNET RESOURCES
www.mlworldhistory.com

 Warm-Up Transparency 17

 Electronic Library of Primary Sources
- from the Ninety-Five Theses

 Religions of the World
- Christianity

 INTERNET RESOURCES
www.mlworldhistory.com

 Warm-Up Transparency 17

 Geography Transparencies
- GT17 Reformation: Lutheranism and Calvinism, 1500–1600

 Critical Thinking Transparencies
- CT17 Protestant and Catholic Reformations
- CT53 Chapter 17 Visual Summary

 Electronic Library of Primary Sources
- "The St. Bartholomew's Day Massacre"
- "Luther: Giant of His Time and Ours"

 Religions of the World
- Christianity

Chapter Summaries on Audiocassette in English and Spanish

INTERNET RESOURCES
www.mlworldhistory.com

 ## Block Scheduling (90 MINUTES)

Day 1
Section 1, pp. 417–422

 COOPERATIVE ACTIVITY
Creating Trading Cards, p. 419 (Teacher's Edition)

Section 2, pp. 423–427

 COOPERATIVE ACTIVITY
Planning a Utopian Community, p. 425

Section Assessments, pp. 422, 427

Day 2
Section 3, pp. 428–432

COOPERATIVE ACTIVITY
Reporting on the Wives of Henry VIII, p. 431 (Teacher's Edition)

Section 4, pp. 433–437

COOPERATIVE ACTIVITY
Neighborhood Survey of Religious Groups, p. 434 (Teacher's Edition)

Section Assessments, pp. 432, 436

Chapter Assessment, pp. 438–439

Yearly Pacing *Chapter 17 Total:* 2 days *Yearly Total:* 85 days

Planning for Block Schedules

Customizing for Special Needs

Students Acquiring English

 Access for Students Acquiring English
- **Guided Reading,** for Sections 1–4 (Spanish), pp. 170–173
- **Chapter Summary:** (Spanish), pp. 167–169
- **Skillbuilder Practice:** Synthesizing (Spanish), p. 174
- **Geography Application:** Trade in Renaissance Europe (Spanish), p. 175

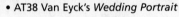 **Chapter Summaries on Audiocassette** in English and Spanish

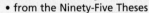 **INTERNET RESOURCES**
www.mlworldhistory.com
The Diverse Classroom.

Less Proficient Readers

 In-Depth Resources: Unit 4
- **Guided Reading,** for Sections 1–4, pp. 18–21
- **Skillbuilder Practice:** Synthesizing, p. 22
- **Geography Application:** Trade in Renaissance Europe, p. 23

 Telescoping the Times
- Chapter Summary, pp. 65–67

Chapter Summaries on Audiocassette

Gifted and Talented Students

 In-Depth Resources: Unit 4

Primary Sources
- from *The Courtier*, p. 25
- from *The Prince*, p. 26
- A Conference with Elizabeth, p. 27
- Report on the English Reformation, p. 28

History Makers
- Niccolò Machiavelli, p. 32
- Elizabeth I, p. 33

Connections to Literature READINGS FOR STUDENTS

 In-Depth Resources: Unit 4
Literature: from *The Agony and the Ecstasy,* p. 29

Enrichment Reading
- **Penman, Sharon Kay**
The Sunne in Splendour
New York: Penguin, 1984

A richly detailed story about Richard III involving fifteenth-century battle scenes, political intrigues, and family conflicts.

McDougal Littell
Literature Connections

- **Shakespeare, William**
The Tragedy of Romeo and Juliet
(with related readings)

Shakespeare's great Renaissance drama of love, conflict, and tragedy.

 P E = Pupil's Edition   = Overhead Transparency   = Software   = Video

= Copy Master   = CD-ROM = Audiocassette = Internet

European Renaissance and Reformation, 1300–1600

Accessing Prior Knowledge

- Ask students to read the captions accompanying each picture and to discuss what they already know about the people and situations.

Predicting and Making Inferences

- After students read about Anne Boleyn and the circumstances surrounding her marriage to King Henry VIII, ask them what they think might happen to her if she does not give birth to a male heir to the English throne.

- Ask students how they think Raphael felt about the culture of ancient Greece, based on the people he features in his painting.

Geography Connection

Ask students to note the distance between England and the Papal States.

- What geographic features isolate England from most of Europe?

- How might isolation and distance contribute to England's break with the Catholic Church in Rome?

CHAPTER 17

European Renaissance and Reformation, 1300–1600

PREVIEWING THEMES

Cultural Interaction

Most medieval European art expressed either the values of Christianity or the code of chivalry. During the Renaissance, scholars and artists developed new cultural and artistic ideas based on the rediscovery of the literature of classical Greece and Rome.

Religious and Ethical Systems

For centuries, religious leaders had sought to reform the Catholic Church. They wanted to make it live up to its ideals. In the 1500s, Martin Luther began a reform movement called the Reformation. This led to the founding of Protestant churches.

Revolution

European scholars gained access to classical documents that they thought had been lost after the fall of Rome. This revolutionized their thinking. New ideas and values swept Europe. The invention of the printing press aided the spread of these revolutionary ideas. The printing press also spread ideas that called for a revolutionary rejection of the pope's authority.

INTERNET CONNECTION

Visit us at **www.mlworldhistory.com** to learn more about Renaissance artists, the Reformation, and related topics.

EUROPE, 1500

ATLANTIC OCEAN

IRE

By **1527**, King Henry VIII of England was sure that his queen was too old to bear a son. **Anne Boleyn** caught his eye. Anne was pretty and young enough to have children. When the pope refused to end Henry's first marriage, Henry started his own church. An English archbishop ended Henry's marriage and Anne became Henry's second wife.

414

GEOGRAPHY THEMES

Location

Have the students note the boundaries of the Holy Roman Empire and the Papal States. Then have them turn to page 978 in the Atlas to examine modern European nations that now fall within these borders. Ask them to name five European countries that eventually arose from this vast region. *Italy, Germany, the Netherlands, Switzerland, Austria.* Have students speculate why the territory comprising the Holy Roman Empire eventually was carved up into smaller nations.

Human-Environment Interaction

Tell students that the map shows cities, falling within and around the area of the Papal States, that became thriving centers of trade. Ask students to speculate what role geography might have played in the economic development of these cities. *Many of the cities are located near or on a coastline, making them easily accessible to overseas trade.* Ask students to discuss why cities that are centers of trade are more likely to be exposed to new cultural ideas. Have them cite examples from historical periods they have previously studied.

ADDITIONAL RESOURCES

Books for the Teacher

- Aston, Margaret, ed. *The Panorama of the Renaissance.* New York: Abrams, 1996.

- Ozment, Steven E. *Protestants: The Birth of a Revolution.* New York: Doubleday, 1992. Shows the significance of becoming a Protestant during the Reformation.

Books for the Student

- Pierre, Michel. *The Renaissance.* Morristown: Silver Burdett, 1987.

- Romei, Francesca. *Leonardo da Vinci.* New York: Bedrick Books, 1995. Portrays the life of the artist, inventor, and scientist.

Videos

- *Printing Transforms Knowledge.* Society for Visual Education, 1986. 800-829-1900. Presents the impact of the printing press on education and the Reformation.

- *Exploring the Renaissance.* Knowledge Unlimited, 1994. 800-356-2303. Describes the revival in art, letters, and learning.

- *Martin Luther: Beginning of the Reformation.* Britannica, 1993. 800-554-9862.

- *Henry VIII.* Teacher's Discovery, 1996. 800-543-4180. Provides a lively look at the English king.

Software

- *Renaissance and Reformation.* CD-ROM. Queue, 1994. 800-232-2224. Presents the revival of classical learning and art, and the revolt against the Church.

In **1401**, the wool manufacturers of **Florence** decided to pay for new doors for the baptistery of the cathedral. They held a contest to choose the artist. The designs of **Lorenzo Ghiberti** won. Ghiberti labored on the bronze doors more than 20 years. Each door was divided into panels, showing Biblical scenes. This panel shows the Old Testament story of Jacob and Esau.

Raphael's painting *School of Athens* was finished in **1508** in Rome. It shows the influence of Greek thought on the Renaissance. Under the center arch stand Plato and Aristotle. To their left, Socrates argues with several young men. Pythagoras draws a lesson on a slate and Ptolemy holds a globe. Other people in the crowd are Renaissance artists and philosophers.

415

HISTORY THROUGH ART

Gates of Paradise

Lorenzo Ghiberti

The city of Florence entered its golden age through Lorenzo Ghiberti's set of gleaming bronze doors. Each Biblical scene, such as the story of Jacob and Esau, creates the illusion of a grand theatrical stage. The background trees and buildings seem like props that stand far behind the people in the foreground. Yet the metal used for the sculpture is just about four inches deep. Ghiberti's use of perspective, realism, and detail is typical of Renaissance artists.

During the Renaissance, questions of religion were very much on the minds of Europeans. Italian artists created thousands of pictures of the Madonna, saints, and other Biblical figures. However, their portrayal of religious subjects differed from medieval artists. Ghiberti, for example, reveals the character of religious figures and shows the parts they play.

Ghiberti included two self-portraits in the doors. Perhaps this suggests how Ghiberti embodies such Renaissance values as pride in achievement, individuality, and creativity. Ghiberti's new doors were so magnificent that the artist Michelangelo later likened them to the gates of paradise.

Interpreting the Art: Why does Ghiberti's panel of Jacob and Esau seem so dramatic and lifelike?

Interact *with* History

This Interact with History feature motivates students by inviting them to role-play a historian who is examining a Renaissance work of art. As students look at Jan van Eyck's painting, they will gain first-hand experience in using a painting as a primary source.

Purpose

• to set the stage for studying the Renaissance

• to help students understand how some artists document history through their creative works

• to help students make connections with other paintings they will study in this chapter

Teaching Strategy

Thinking Critically After students have imagined themselves in the situation described on this page, have them answer the key question and support their responses.

EXAMINING *the* ISSUES

Following are suggestions for addressing each bulleted question.

1 Students may mention the role of religion and politics, views of men and women, and kinds of social relationships and customs.

2 Students may mention that people's clothing, their surroundings, and their poses can reveal personality traits and status.

3 Have students brainstorm a list of adjectives they would use to describe an object of beauty. Are these qualities mirrored in art forms?

Making Connections Ask students to discuss examples of modern art that reflect the values of today's society.

Follow Up

A feature on the chapter assessment will ask students to reevaluate their responses to the situation presented on this page.

Interact *with* History

You are a historian looking at primary sources from the Renaissance. One of them is this painting by Jan van Eyck.

Chancellor Rolin, a powerful government official in Burgundy (later part of France), asked the artist to paint this portrait. You are analyzing it to discover Rolin's values and how he wanted to be viewed by others. You can also use the art to learn about the times.

What do we learn from art?

1 Van Eyck used a recently rediscovered technique called perspective, which makes distant objects look smaller than close ones. He also used oil paints, a new invention.

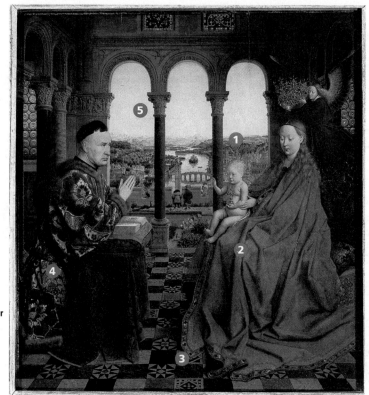

5 Renaissance artists were influenced by classical art. The columns and arches show classical influence.

4 Renaissance artists portrayed the importance of individuals. Chancellor Rolin is kneeling to show respect, but he wears a fur-trimmed robe that shows his high status.

2 This painting shows the infant Jesus and his mother Mary in 15th century Europe. By portraying biblical characters in their own time, Renaissance artists showed the importance of religion in their lives.

3 Van Eyck included many details simply for the sake of beauty. These include the fancy design on the floor, the folds of Mary's cloak, and the scenery outside the arches.

EXAMINING *the* ISSUES

1 • What does art tell us about the values and beliefs of the society that produced it?

2 • What does art show about how people of that society viewed themselves?

3 • How does art reflect a society's standards of beauty?

As a class, discuss these questions. In your discussion, review what you know about art in other places such as Egypt, India, China, and Benin.

As you read about the Renaissance, notice what the art of that time reveals about European society.

① Italy: Birthplace of the Renaissance

TERMS & NAMES
- **Renaissance**
- **humanism**
- **secular**
- **patron**
- **perspective**
- **vernacular**

MAIN IDEA

The European Renaissance, a rebirth of learning and the arts, began in Italy in the 1300s.

WHY IT MATTERS NOW

Renaissance ideas about classical studies, art, and literature still influence modern thought.

SETTING THE STAGE During the late Middle Ages, Europeans suffered from both war and plague. Those who survived wanted to enjoy life. As a result, they questioned the Church, which taught Christians to endure suffering to get a heavenly reward. They also questioned the structures of medieval society, which blocked social advancement. Educated people gradually began to reject medieval values and look to the classical past for ideas.

Italy's Advantages

The years 1300 to 1600 saw an explosion of creativity in Europe. Historians call this period the **Renaissance** (REHN·ih·SAHNS). The term means rebirth—in this case a rebirth of art and learning. The Renaissance began in northern Italy around 1300 and later spread north. One reason northern Europe lagged behind is that France and England were locked in the Hundred Years' War. Italy also had three advantages that fostered the Renaissance: thriving cities, a wealthy merchant class, and the classical heritage of Greece and Rome.

Urban Centers Overseas trade, spurred by the Crusades, had led to the growth of large city-states in northern Italy. The region also had many sizable towns. Thus, northern Italy was urban while the rest of Europe was still mostly rural. Since cities are often places where people exchange new ideas, they were an ideal breeding ground for an intellectual revolution.

The bubonic plague struck these cities hard, killing up to 60 percent of the population. This brought economic changes. Because there were fewer laborers, survivors could demand higher wages. In addition, the reduced population shrank opportunities for business expansion. Wealthy merchants began to pursue other interests, such as art.

Merchants and the Medici Milan, Florence, and other Italian city-states ran their own affairs. Each collected taxes and had its own army. Because city-states were relatively small, a high percentage of citizens could be intensely involved in political life. Merchants were the wealthiest, most powerful class, and they dominated politics. Unlike nobles, merchants did not inherit social rank. Success in business depended mostly on their own wits. As a result, many successful merchants believed they deserved power and wealth because of their individual merit. Individual achievement was to become an important Renaissance theme.

Florence came under the rule of one powerful family, the Medici (MEHD·ih·chee). They had made a fortune in trade and banking. Cosimo de' Medici was the wealthiest European of his time. In 1434, he won control of Florence's government. He did not seek political office for himself, but instead influenced members of the ruling council by giving them loans. For 30 years, he was virtually dictator of Florence.

Background
Florence lost up to 55,000 out of a population of 85,000.

A. Possible Answers
Because if he were elected, he might lose his office; by staying behind the scenes, he could try to influence whoever held office.

THINK THROUGH HISTORY
A. Making Inferences Why do you suppose Cosimo de' Medici preferred to rule from behind the scenes rather than openly?

SPOTLIGHT ON

Other Renaissances

A Renaissance can be a rebirth of the arts and learning at any time in history. For example, the Tang (618–907) and Song (960–1279) dynasties in China oversaw a period of great artistic and technological advances.

Like the Italian Renaissance, the achievements of the Tang and the Song had roots in an earlier time—the Han Dynasty (202 B.C. to A.D. 220). After the Han collapsed, China experienced turmoil.

When order was restored, Chinese culture flourished. The Chinese invented gunpowder and printing. The most famous Chinese poets of all time wrote literary masterpieces. Breakthroughs were made in architecture, painting, and pottery. In many ways, the Tang and Song period was a true Renaissance.

European Renaissance and Reformation **417**

Section 1 Overview

OBJECTIVES

① To explain the conditions in Italy that gave rise to the Renaissance.

② To identify the values and ideas prized during the Renaissance.

③ To describe the artistic breakthrough and achievements of Renaissance artists.

④ To summarize influential literary works and techniques of key Renaissance writers.

CRITICAL THINKING
- Making inferences, p. 417
- Analyzing causes, p. 418
- Synthesizing, p. 419
- Clarifying, p. 420
- Supporting opinions, p. 422
- Analyzing themes, p. 422

FOCUS
5-Minute Warm-Up

▶ **Analyzing a Painting**
Have students answer these questions to explore the techniques of Renaissance art.

1. Read Perspective in Paintings on page 419, and study the diagram and painting. What optical illusion does the artist Raphael create in his painting?

2. Why does the use of perspective make the painting seem realistic?

 WARM-UP TRANSPARENCY 17

OBJECTIVE ① INSTRUCT

Italy's Advantages

▶ **Key Ideas**
- The Renaissance begins in northern Italy's urban centers around 1300.
- Italian merchants and bankers, such as the Medicis, support the arts.
- Renaissance scholars revive the study of Greek and Roman cultures.

📖 *IN-DEPTH RESOURCES: UNIT 4*
Guided Reading, p. 18

📖 *ACCESS FOR STUDENTS ACQUIRING ENGLISH*
Guided Reading (Spanish), p. 170

SECTION 1 RESOURCES

PRINT RESOURCES

📖 *IN-DEPTH RESOURCES: UNIT 4*
Guided Reading, p. 18
Primary Sources: *The Courtier*, p. 25; *The Prince*, p. 26
History Makers: Niccolò Machiavelli, p. 32
Literature: from *The Agony and the Ecstasy*, p. 29
Connections Across Time and Cultures, p. 34

📖 *ACCESS FOR STUDENTS ACQUIRING ENGLISH*
Guided Reading (Spanish), p. 170

📖 *FORMAL ASSESSMENT*
Section Quiz, p. 193

TECHNOLOGY RESOURCES

🖨 *WORLD ART AND CULTURES TRANSPARENCIES*
AT36 Leonardo da Vinci's *The Last Supper*
AT37 *Mona Lisa*

💿 **CD-ROM**
Electronic Library of Primary Sources

🔗 **INTERNET** www.mlworldhistory.com

(See page 417.)

In the 1920s, Harlem, a neighborhood of New York City, became the center of a literary and artistic movement called the Harlem Renaissance. During this period, African-American creativity flowered. Writers, painters, and musicians created works of art celebrating African-American culture. Some of the best-known artists of the Harlem Renaissance were Langston Hughes, Zora Neale Hurston, Paul Robeson, Duke Ellington, and Bessie Smith.

 IN-DEPTH RESOURCES: UNIT 4
Connections Across Time and Cultures: Flowerings of Creativity and Knowledge, p.34

HISTORYMAKERS
Medici Family

Ask students to use an encyclopedia to find out more about the Medicis. Interesting family members include Giuliano, Catherine, Marie, and Piero.

OBJECTIVE ② INSTRUCT

Classical and Worldly Values

Key Ideas
- Humanists focus on human potential and achievements.
- The basic spirit of the Renaissance is secular.
- Popes and merchants become patrons of the arts.
- The ideal Renaissance individual excels in many fields.
- Upper-class Renaissance women are well-educated but lack power.

 IN-DEPTH RESOURCES: UNIT 4
Primary Source: from *The Courtier*, p. 25

HISTORYMAKERS

Medici Family

Giant banks with branches in many cities are nothing new. The Medici bank had branch offices not only throughout Italy but also in the major cities of Europe.

A rival family grew so jealous of the Medici that they plotted to kill Lorenzo (see bust below) and his brother Giuliano. As the Medici attended Mass, assassins murdered Giuliano at the altar. Drawing his sword, Lorenzo escaped to a small room and held off his attackers until help arrived. Then he had the killers brutally, publicly executed.

More positively, Lorenzo was a generous patron of the arts who collected many rare manuscripts. Eventually the Medici family made their library available to the public.

Cosimo de' Medici died in 1464, but his family retained control of Florence. His grandson, Lorenzo de' Medici, came into power in 1469. He became known as Lorenzo the Magnificent. Like his grandfather, Lorenzo ruled as a dictator yet kept up the appearance of having an elected government. Although the Medici did not foster true republican government, they aided the Renaissance by supporting the arts.

Classical Heritage Renaissance scholars looked down on the art and literature of the Middle Ages and wanted to return to the learning of the Greeks and Romans. One reason the Renaissance began in Italy is that artists and scholars drew inspiration from the ruins of Rome that surrounded them.

In the 1300s, scholars studied ancient Latin manuscripts, which had been preserved in monasteries. Then, when Constantinople fell to the Ottoman Turks in 1453, Byzantine scholars fled to Rome with ancient Greek manuscripts—which Italian scholars had assumed were lost forever.

Classical and Worldly Values

As scholars studied these Greek works, they became increasingly influenced by classical ideas. These ideas helped them to develop a new outlook on life, which had several characteristics.

Classics Lead to Humanism The study of classical texts led to **humanism,** which focused on human potential and achievements. Instead of trying to make classical texts agree with Christian teaching as medieval scholars had, humanists studied them to understand ancient Greek values. Humanists influenced artists and architects to carry on classical traditions. In addition, humanists popularized the study of subjects common to classical education, such as history, literature, and philosophy. These subjects are called the humanities.

Enjoyment of Worldly Pleasures In the Middle Ages, some religious people had proved their piety by wearing rough clothing and eating the plainest foods. However, humanists suggested that a person might enjoy life without offending God. In Renaissance Italy, the wealthy openly enjoyed material luxuries, fine music, and tasty foods.

Most people remained devout Catholics. However, the basic spirit of Renaissance society was **secular**—worldly and concerned with the here and now. Even church leaders became more worldly. They lived in beautiful mansions, threw lavish banquets, and wore expensive clothes.

Patrons of the Arts In addition to seeking pleasure, Renaissance popes beautified Rome by spending huge amounts of money for art. They became **patrons** of the arts by financially supporting artists. Renaissance merchants also were patrons of the arts. Wealthy families such as the Medici generously supported artists. By having their portraits painted or by donating public art to the city, the wealthy demonstrated their own importance.

The Renaissance Man Renaissance writers first introduced the idea that some people were artistic geniuses. Though genius was rare, all educated people were expected to create art. In fact, the ideal individual strove to master almost every area of study. A man who excelled in many fields was praised as a "universal man." Later ages called such people "Renaissance men."

A book called *The Courtier* (1528) by Baldassare Castiglione (KAHS·teel·YOH·nay) taught how to become such a person. A young man, said Castiglione, should be

THINK THROUGH HISTORY
B. Analyzing Causes What were the three advantages that caused the Renaissance to start in Italy?
B. Answer Italy had many cities, where people could exchange ideas; the cities were run by merchants, who supported the arts; Italian scholars and artists had access to classical art and literature.

Background
The words *humanist* and *humanities* come from the Latin word *humanitas*, which referred to the literary culture that every educated person should know.

TEACHING OPTION

CONNECTIONS ACROSS TIME AND PLACE

Government Support of the Arts
President Franklin Roosevelt radically changed the relationship between the U.S. government and the arts by forming the Works Progress Administration (WPA) during the New Deal. Between 1935 and 1938, the WPA became the largest public arts program in the world. At one point, it employed over 40,000 people. Artists created posters, painted murals

on public buildings, and designed stage sets and props for plays. The WPA also hired actors, dancers, musicians, and writers. In 1943, the federal arts program ended.

In 1965, Congress created the National Endowment for the Arts (NEA). Its goal was to fund art projects around the United States. The NEA's budget grew from $16 million in 1970 to $180 million in 1979.

Congress maintained a strong level of funding throughout the 1980s.

Since 1989, government support of the arts has fallen under attack because NEA funds have helped to support controversial artists. In 1997, the National Endowment for the Arts was budgeted for $99.5 million. Discuss with students why governments fund the arts. Do students think arts funding is an appropriate use of taxpayers' money?

charming, witty, and well educated in the classics. He should dance, sing, play music, and write poetry. In addition, he should be a skilled rider, wrestler, and swordsman. Above all, he should have self-control:

This is a 19th-century engraving of the Renaissance writer Baldassare Castiglione.

The Renaissance Woman According to *The Courtier*, upper-class women also should know the classics and be charming. Yet they were not expected to seek fame. They were expected to inspire art but rarely to create it. Upper-class Renaissance women were far better educated than the women of the Middle Ages. However, most Renaissance women had less influence than medieval women had.

A few women, such as Isabella d'Este, did exercise power. Born into the ruling family of the city-state of Ferrara, she married the ruler of another city-state, Mantua. She brought many Renaissance artists to her court and acquired an art collection that was famous throughout Europe. She was also skilled in politics. When her husband was taken captive in war, she defended Mantua and won his release.

Renaissance Revolutionizes Art

Supported by patrons like Isabella d'Este, dozens of talented artists worked in northern Italy. As the Renaissance advanced, artistic styles changed. Medieval artists used religious subjects and tried to convey a spiritual ideal. Renaissance artists also often portrayed religious subjects, but they used a realistic style copied from classical models. Greek and Roman subjects also became popular.

Following the new emphasis on individuals, painters began to paint prominent citizens. These realistic portraits revealed what was distinctive about each person. In addition, artists such as the sculptor and painter Michelangelo (MY·kuhl·AN·juh·LOH) glorified the human body. (See page 420.)

New Techniques Donatello (DAHN·uh·TEHL·oh) made sculpture more realistic by carving natural postures and expressions that reveal personality. He revived a classical form by carving the statue *David*. It was the first European sculpture of a large, free-standing nude since ancient times. Renaissance artists, such as the painter Masaccio (muh·SAH·chee·oh), also rediscovered the technique of **perspective,** which indicates three dimensions.

Perspective in Paintings

Perspective is a technique that creates the appearance of three dimensions. Classical artists used perspective, but medieval artists abandoned the technique. In the 1400s, Italian artists rediscovered perspective. Since then, it has remained an important part of Western art.

horizon   vanishing point

Perspective is based on an optical illusion. As parallel lines stretch away from a viewer, they seem to draw together—until they meet at a spot on the horizon called the vanishing point.

Marriage of the Virgin (1504), Raphael

C. Possible Answer Because merchants were proud of their individual achievements, they wanted their portraits to show them as distinctive individuals.

THINK THROUGH HISTORY
C. Synthesizing Merchants believed in their own individual merit. How did this belief affect artistic styles?

OBJECTIVE ③ INSTRUCT

Renaissance Revolutionizes Art

▶ *Key Ideas*
• Many Renaissance artists develop new techniques, such as perspective.
• Leonardo da Vinci typifies the true Renaissance man.
• Raphael creates realistic masterpieces.
• A few Italian women gain recognition as painters.

History from Visuals

Perspective in Paintings
Interpreting the Diagram Point out to students that the location of the vanishing point in Raphael's painting is the opened door of the church. Explain that some Renaissance artists used grids and devices with peepholes to help calculate perspective.

Extension Activity Have students draw a picture that lacks perspective.

Task: Groups of students will make trading cards of Italian Renaissance painters.

Purpose: To broaden understanding of Renaissance artists.

Activity: Divide students into small groups. Have group members research the Italian Renaissance artists they wish to represent in their set of trading cards. Examples of Renaissance artists not discussed in the text include Brunelleschi, Luca della Robbia,

Fra Angelico, and Botticelli. Using index cards, students can draw the artists on one side and write biographical information, interesting facts, and titles of famous works on the other side.

📁 **Building a Portfolio:** Students who wish to add the trading cards to their portfolios should highlight their own contributions.

📋 **ALTERNATIVE ASSESSMENT BOOK**
Standards for Evaluating a Cooperative Activity

Standards for Evaluation
Trading cards should . . .

• contain accurate and detailed information about the artist
• show evidence of thorough research
• list the artists' most notable works

History Through Art

Renaissance Art
Renaissance artists and architects saw nature as the standard for balance and proportion. They imitated these qualities to add realism to their own work. Renaissance artists re-created lifelike depictions of people. Renaissance architects tried to make all parts of a building appear perfectly balanced in size and shape. Michelango displayed remarkable versatility as both an artist and architect.

MORE ABOUT . . .
The Sistine Chapel

To paint the ceiling of the Sistine Chapel, Michelangelo lay stretched on his back atop a high scaffold. The paint dripped into his eyes. During the day, he endured the heat of the sun beating upon the roof of the chapel. At night, he worked by candlelight. "I have been here a thousand years," Michelangelo wrote to his father. "I am more exhausted than any man ever was."

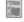 **IN-DEPTH RESOURCES: UNIT 4**
Literature: from *The Agony and the Ecstasy* by Irving Stone, p. 29

MORE ABOUT . . .
David

Michelangelo considered himself a sculptor above all. He ranked sculpture as "the first of the arts." In this art form, he said, "each act, each limb, each bone is given life, and lo, man's body is raised breathing, alive, in wax or clay or stone." Michelangelo's *David* embodies these lofty qualities.

Michelangelo–Renaissance Artist

Like Leonardo da Vinci, Michelangelo Buonarroti was a true Renaissance man. He excelled at almost every area of study. Michelangelo was a painter, a sculptor, an architect, and a poet.

Michelangelo is most famous for the way he portrayed the human body in painting and sculpture. Influenced by classical art, he created figures that are forceful and show heroic grandeur and power. By doing this, he explored the Renaissance theme of human potential.

St. Peter's Basilica
As an architect, he designed this dome to top St. Peter's Basilica [Church] in Rome. Michelangelo began working on the church in 1546. It still wasn't finished when he died in 1564. Another architect had to finish the dome.

Sistine Chapel
From 1508 to 1512, Michelangelo painted the ceiling of the Sistine Chapel in Rome. This detail shows the Biblical prophet Joel. Many of the panels show classical influences, such as the two youths who stand behind Joel instead of angels. Like many Renaissance artists, Michelangelo blended Christian and Greek ideals.

David
Influenced by classical statues, Michelangelo sculpted *David* from 1501 to 1504. Michelangelo portrayed the Biblical hero in the moments just before battle. His posture is graceful, yet his figure also displays strength. The statue, which is 18 feet tall, towers over the viewer. This conveys a sense of power.

420 Chapter 17

Connect *to* History

Clarifying How does the work of Michelangelo show that he was influenced by Renaissance values? Explain.

 SEE SKILLBUILDER HANDBOOK, PAGE 992

Connect *to* Today

Researching Look through books on 20th century art to find artists who work in more than one medium, such as painting and sculpture. Share your findings with the class.

Connect *to* History
Clarifying
Possible Response:
Michelangelo's artwork glorifies the human body and reflects classical influence. He was a Renaissance man who excelled in many fields.

Connect *to* Today
Researching
Possible Responses: Other examples of versatile artists include Pablo Picasso, Marcel Duchamp, and Andy Warhol. Students should support their findings with illustrations of the artist's works.

Leonardo, Renaissance Man

Leonardo da Vinci (LAY·uh·NAHR·doh duh·VIHN·chee) was a painter, sculptor, inventor, and scientist. A true "Renaissance man," he was deeply interested in how things worked. He studied how a muscle moves or how veins are arranged in a leaf. He filled his notebooks with observations and sketches of new inventions, and he incorporated his findings in his art.

Among his many masterpieces, Leonardo painted one of the best-known portraits in the world, the Mona Lisa. The woman in the portrait seems so real that many writers have tried to explain the thoughts behind her slight smile. Leonardo also produced a famous religious painting, *The Last Supper.* It shows the personalities of Jesus' disciples through facial expressions.

Raphael Advances Realism

Raphael (RAF·ee·uhl) was younger than Michelangelo and Leonardo. He learned from studying their works. One of Raphael's favorite subjects was the Madonna and child. Raphael often portrayed their expressions as gentle and calm.

In his greatest achievement, Raphael filled the walls of Pope Julius II's library with several paint-ings. One of these, *School of Athens* (page 414), conveys the classical influence of the Renaissance. It shows classical and Renaissance figures together. Listening to Greek philosophers are Raphael and Michelangelo, among others.

Women Painters Although Renaissance society generally restricted women's roles, a few Italian women became painters. Sofonisba Anguissola (ahng·GWEES·soh·lah) was the first woman artist to gain an international reputation. She is known for portraits of her sisters and of prominent people such as King Phillip II of Spain. Artemisia Gentileschi (JAYN·tee·LEHS·kee) trained with her painter father and helped with his work. In her own paintings, Gentileschi painted pictures of strong, heroic women.

Renaissance Writers Change Literature

Renaissance writers produced works that not only reflected their time, but also used techniques that writers rely on today. Some followed the example of the medieval writer Dante. He wrote in the **vernacular,** his native language, instead of classical Latin. Dante's native language was Italian. In addition, Renaissance writers wrote either for self-expression or to portray the individuality of their subjects. In these ways, writers of the Renaissance began trends that modern writers still follow.

Leonardo da Vinci
1452–1519

Leonardo da Vinci's notebooks—and life—are mysterious in many ways. Some 3,500 pages closely covered with writings and drawings survive, but these may be only one-fourth of what Leonardo produced.

His writing is clear and easy to read—but only if you look at it in a mirror. He wrote backwards in "mirror-writing." No one knows why he took the time to do this.

Leonardo planned scholarly works that he never wrote, and he planned great feats of engineering that were never built. Only 17 of his paintings survive, and several of those were unfinished. The drawing above is the only self-portrait known to exist. And yet the work that Leonardo did produce is so amazing that his reputation as one of the world's geniuses is secure.

Raphael
1483–1520

One of the artists influenced by Leonardo, Raphael began his career early. His father, Giovanni Santi, was a painter, and Raphael learned the basics of his art in his father's studio. At a young age, Raphael went to study with a painter named Perugino. He stayed there about ten years and then went to Florence.

In 1508, Raphael was asked by Pope Julius II to work for him in Rome. Raphael created a series of magnificent frescoes, paintings done on wet plaster, for the pope's private rooms in the Vatican.

Raphael, unlike many of his fellow artists, was easy to like. When he died on his 37th birthday after a short illness, many Romans—including the pope and his court—were stricken with grief and went into mourning.

Vocabulary
Madonna: a term for Mary, the mother of Jesus; it comes from a former Italian title for women, meaning "my lady."

Background
During most of the Middle Ages, educated Europeans wrote everything in Latin.

Find Leonardo da Vinci's painting *The Virgin of the Rocks* and Raphael's painting *Madonna of the Goldfinch* in an art book and show them to the class. Guide students to note the following similarities between these two works of art. The figures in both paintings are roughly arranged in a triangle, with the Madonna's head placed at the peak. The Madonna in each painting is portrayed as a loving, kind-hearted mother. Ask students to draw other parallels between the paintings.

WORLD ART AND CULTURES TRANSPARENCIES
AT36 Leonardo da Vinci's *The Last Supper*
AT37 *Mona Lisa*

ELECTRONIC LIBRARY OF PRIMARY SOURCES
"The Art of Painting" from *Notebooks*

OBJECTIVE 3 INSTRUCT

Renaissance Writers Change Literature

▶ **Key Ideas**
- Petrarch, an early humanist, writes outstanding poetry.
- Boccaccio writes stories exposing the follies of human nature.
- Machiavelli writes *The Prince,* a political guidebook for rulers.
- Women Renaissance writers tend to focus on personal subjects.

CONNECTIONS ACROSS THE CURRICULUM

Technology Leonardo da Vinci caught a glimpse of marvelous machines of the future. His notebooks contain mechanical drawings and descriptions for an astonishing range of inventions. Da Vinci designed an alarm clock with a tilting lever that could awaken the sleeper. He wrote in his notebook that the alarm clock was intended for "those who watch jealously over their use of time."

Here are some other examples:
- parachute
- armored tank
- flying machine
- diving suit
- submarine
- power loom
- machine gun
- construction crane

Have interested students research one of Leonardo da Vinci's inventions and find illustrations and descriptions of some of his drawings. Ask students to compare Leonardo's plan for an invention with its modern-day counterpart.

422 Chapter 17

Petrarch and Boccaccio Francesco Petrarch (PEE·trahrk) was one of the earliest and most influential humanists. He was also a great poet. Petrarch wrote both in Italian and in Latin. In Italian, he wrote sonnets—14-line poems. They were about a mysterious woman named Laura, who was his ideal. (Little is known of Laura except that she died of the plague in 1348.) In classical Latin, he wrote letters to his many important friends.

The Italian writer Boccaccio (boh·KAH·chee·oh) is best known for the *Decameron*, a series of realistic, sometimes off-color stories. The stories are supposedly told by a group of worldly young people waiting in a villa to avoid the plague sweeping through Florence. The humor of the *Decameron* is cutting. Boccaccio presents the follies of his characters—and all humans—with some sarcasm.

Machiavelli Advises Rulers *The Prince* (1513), by Niccolò Machiavelli (MAK·ee·uh·VEHL·ee), also examines the imperfect conduct of human beings. He does so in the form of a political guidebook. In *The Prince,* Machiavelli examines how a ruler can gain power and keep it in spite of his enemies. In answering this question, he began with the idea that most people are selfish, fickle, and corrupt.

To succeed in such a wicked world, Machiavelli said, a prince must be strong as a lion and shrewd as a fox. He might have to trick his enemies and even his own people for the good of the state. In *The Prince,* Machiavelli was not concerned with what was morally right, but with what was politically effective:

> **A VOICE FROM THE PAST**
> Everyone admits how praiseworthy it is in a prince to keep faith, and to live with integrity and not with craft. Nevertheless our experience has been that those princes who have done great things have held good faith of little account, and have known how to circumvent the intellect of men by craft, and in the end have overcome those who have relied on their word.
>
> **NICCOLÒ MACHIAVELLI**, *The Prince*

Niccolò Machiavelli, shown here with his hand on a book, was much more than just a cynical political thinker. He was also a patriot, a poet, and a historian.

Women Writers The women writers who gained fame in the Renaissance usually wrote about personal subjects, not politics. Yet, some of them had great influence. Vittoria Colonna exchanged sonnets with Michelangelo and helped Castiglione publish *The Courtier.* Her own poems are often very personal. For example, when her husband was away at war, she wrote to him, "Your uncertain enterprises do not hurt you; / but we who wait, mournfully grieving, / are wounded by doubt and fear."

Toward the end of the 15th century, Renaissance ideas began to spread north from Italy to countries such as France, Germany, and England. Northern artists and thinkers would adapt the Renaissance ideals in their own ways.

Section 1 Assessment

1. TERMS & NAMES
Identify
- Renaissance
- humanism
- secular
- patron
- perspective
- vernacular

2. TAKING NOTES
Using a big-idea outline like the one below, record the main ideas from the section about the Italian Renaissance.

Renaissance
I. Italy's advantages
  A.
  B.
  C.
II. Classical and worldly values

3. SUPPORTING OPINIONS
Name three people from this section whom you regard as a "Renaissance man" or a "Renaissance woman." Explain your choices.

THINK ABOUT
- the idea of the "universal man"
- Castiglione's description of such a person
- which people from this section seem to match that description

4. ANALYZING THEMES
Revolution How did the Renaissance revolutionize European art and thought?

THINK ABOUT
- changes in ideas since medieval times
- changes in artistic techniques
- changes in artistic subjects

422 Chapter 17

---

2 The Northern Renaissance

TERMS & NAMES
- Utopia
- printing press
- Gutenberg Bible

MAIN IDEA

In the 1400s, northern Europeans began to adapt the ideas of the Renaissance.

WHY IT MATTERS NOW

Renaissance ideas such as the importance of the individual are a strong part of modern thought.

Background
Flanders was a region in northern Europe. It included part of France and part of the Netherlands. The people of Flanders are the Flemish.

SETTING THE STAGE The work of such artists as Leonardo da Vinci, Michelangelo, and Raphael showed the Renaissance spirit. All three artists demonstrated an interest in classical culture, a curiosity about the world, and a belief in human potential. These ideas impressed scholars and students who visited Italy. Merchants also carried these ideas when they traveled out of Italy. By the late 1400s, Renaissance ideas had spread to northern Europe—especially England, France, Germany, and Flanders.

The Northern Renaissance Begins

By 1450 the population of northern Europe, which had been shattered by the bubonic plague, was beginning to recover. In addition, the destructive Hundred Years' War between France and England ended in 1453. Many cities grew rapidly. Urban merchants became wealthy enough to sponsor artists. This happened first in Flanders, which was rich from long-distance trade and the cloth industry. Then it happened in other countries.

As Section 1 explained, Italy was divided into city-states. In contrast, England and France were unified under strong monarchs. These rulers often sponsored the arts. For example, Francis I of France purchased Renaissance paintings. He also invited Leonardo da Vinci to retire in France, and hired Italian artists and architects to rebuild his castle at Fontainebleau (FAHN·tihn·BLOH). When completed, Fontainebleau became a showcase of the French Renaissance. Because of monarchs like Francis, royal courts played a major role in introducing Renaissance styles to northern Europe.

As Renaissance ideas spread out of Italy, they mingled with northern traditions. As a result, the northern Renaissance developed its own character. Many humanists there were more interested in religious ideas than in the secular themes popular in Italy. The Renaissance ideal of human dignity inspired some northern humanists to develop plans for social reform based on Christian values.

Albrecht Dürer painted *Adoration of the Trinity* after returning from studying in Italy.

Artistic Ideas Spread

A. Answer By making Italian artists flee north

THINK THROUGH HISTORY
A. Analyzing Causes How did the war in Italy spread the Renaissance?

In 1494, a French king claimed the throne of Naples in southern Italy and launched an invasion through northern Italy. As the war dragged on, many Italian artists and writers left for a safer life in northern Europe. With them, they brought the styles and techniques of the Renaissance. In addition, artists who studied in Italy also carried Renaissance ideas north.

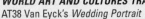

SECTION 2 RESOURCES

PRINT RESOURCES

IN-DEPTH RESOURCES: UNIT 4
Guided Reading, p. 19
Geography Application: Trade in Renaissance Europe, p. 23

ACCESS FOR STUDENTS ACQUIRING ENGLISH
Guided Reading, (Spanish), p. 171
Geography Application: (Spanish), p. 175

FORMAL ASSESSMENT
Section Quiz, p. 194

ALTERNATIVE ASSESSMENT BOOK

TECHNOLOGY RESOURCES

WORLD ART AND CULTURES TRANSPARENCIES
AT38 Van Eyck's *Wedding Portrait*

INTERNET www.mlworldhistory.com

Section 2 Overview

OBJECTIVES

1. To explain the origins and characteristics of the Northern Renaissance.
2. To trace the impact of the Renaissance on German and Flemish painters.
3. To profile key Northern Renaissance writers.
4. To explain how printing spread Renaissance ideas.

CRITICAL THINKING

- Analyzing causes, p. 423
- Contrasting, p. 424
- Making inferences, p. 425
- Summarizing, p. 426
- Recognizing effects, p. 427

FOCUS

5-Minute Warm-Up

▶ *Recognizing Effects*
Answering these questions will help students understand the enduring impact of Northern Renaissance writers.

1. Read the Connect to Today on page 426. Give examples of William Shakespeare's popularity among worldwide audiences today.

2. Name two Shakespearean plays that were recently made into Hollywood movies.

WARM-UP TRANSPARENCY 17

OBJECTIVE 1 INSTRUCT

The Northern Renaissance Begins

▶ *Key Ideas*
- England and France are unified under strong monarchs who often sponsor the arts.
- Renaissance ideas spreading from Italy mingle with northern European traditions.
- The Northern Renaissance develops distinctive features.

IN-DEPTH RESOURCES: UNIT 4
Guided Reading, p. 19

ACCESS FOR STUDENTS ACQUIRING ENGLISH
Guided Reading (Spanish), p. 171

Artistic Ideas Spread

▶ **Key Ideas**

• Artists studying in Italy bring Renaissance ideas to northern Europe.

• The realism of Dürer's paintings and engravings inspire other German artists.

• Flanders becomes the artistic center of northern Europe.

• Flemish painters Van Eyck and Bruegel focus on realistic details.

 IN-DEPTH RESOURCES: UNIT 4
Geography Application: Trade in Renaissance Europe, p. 23

MORE ABOUT . . .
Albert Dürer

Dürer also wrote books on geometry and artistic theory. He was the first person to publish scientific literature in German.

Daily *Life*
Flemish Peasant Life

Ask students to find a colored photograph of a modern wedding reception from a magazine or another source. Have them work in groups to compare the photograph with Bruegel's painting. Ask students to note how Bruegel directs the viewer's eye through the picture with color and action.

 WORLD ART AND CULTURES TRANSPARENCIES
AT38 Van Eyck's *Wedding Portrait*

German Painters Perhaps the most famous person to do this was the German artist Albrecht Dürer (DYUR·uhr). The son of a goldsmith, Dürer decided to become a painter. After serving an apprenticeship, he traveled to Italy to study in 1494.

After returning to Germany, Dürer produced woodcuts and engravings that became influential. Many of his prints portray religious subjects such as the one on page 423. Others portray classical myths. He also painted realistic landscapes and a self-portrait in which he portrayed himself as a Renaissance man. The popularity of Dürer's work helped to spread Renaissance styles. His work inspired other German artists.

Dürer's emphasis upon realism influenced the work of another German artist, Hans Holbein (HOHL·byn) the Younger. Holbein specialized in painting portraits that are almost photographic in detail. He enjoyed great success in England, where he painted portraits of King Henry VIII and other members of the royal family.

Flemish Painters As in Italy, wealthy merchant families in Flanders were attracted to the Renaissance emphasis on individualism and worldly pleasures. Their patronage helped to make Flanders the artistic center of northern Europe.

As in Italy, the Renaissance in Flanders was marked by an interest in realism. The first great Flemish Renaissance painter was Jan van Eyck (yahn van YK). Van Eyck lived from sometime in the late 1300s to 1441 and worked at the height of the Italian Renaissance.

Oil-based paints had recently been developed. Van Eyck used them to develop techniques that painters still use. Because oil paint does not dry quickly, it can be blended more easily than other paints. By applying layer upon layer of paint, van Eyck was able to create a variety of subtle colors in clothing and jewels. Oil painting became popular and spread to Italy.

Daily *Life*

Flemish Peasant Life
The Flemish painter Pieter Bruegel often portrayed peasants. Many of his paintings provide information about peasant life in the 1500s.

Peasant Wedding (1568), shown below, portrays a wedding feast in a rough but clean barn. The bride sits under the paper crown hanging on a piece of green cloth. Two young men who may be her brothers are pouring drinks and passing out plates.

Who, then, is the groom? Possibly the man sitting across the table from the bride and leaning back on a three-legged stool.

Children and at least one dog have come to the party. The couple to the right of the bride and the man on the far right with a sword are dressed more elegantly than the other guests. They may be wealthy townsfolk related to the groom.

B. Answer It spread from the North to Italy, instead of moving from Italy to the North.

THINK THROUGH HISTORY
B. Contrasting
How was the development and spread of oil painting different from many other Renaissance developments?

Literature The American poet William Carlos Williams (1883–1963) found the paintings of Bruegel (also spelled *Brueghel*) a source of inspiration for his own work. Williams received, posthumously, the 1963 Pulitzer Prize in poetry for *Pictures from Brueghel, and Other Poems*. In this book, Williams wrote a series of poems—"word pictures"—that captured the images and mood of several of Bruegel's paintings.

Find the following paintings in art history books or the Internet.

• *The Wedding Dance in the Open Air*
• *Kermess*
• *Haymaking*
• *The Harvesters*
• *The Parable of the Blind*
• *The Fall of Icarus*
• *Children's Games*

Bring reproductions of these paintings to class, and have students read aloud the corresponding poems by Williams. Challenge students to write their own poems based on Bruegel's paintings.

In addition to new techniques, van Eyck's paintings display unusually realistic details and reveal the personality of their subjects. His work influenced later artists in northern Europe.

Flemish painting reached its peak after 1550 with the work of Pieter Bruegel (BROY-guhl) the Elder. Like van Eyck, Bruegel was interested in realistic details and individual people. He captured scenes from everyday peasant life such as weddings, dances, harvests, and the changing seasons. Bruegel also produced paintings that illustrated proverbs or taught a moral. Some of his paintings protested harsh Spanish rule over his country.

In all his work, Bruegel's rich colors, vivid details, and balanced use of space give a sense of life and feeling. He was also very skillful in portraying large numbers of people. Not only did Bruegel produce a large number of paintings, he inspired two sons and three grandsons to also became painters.

Northern Writers Try to Reform Society

Just as Italian art influenced northern European painters, so did Renaissance ideas influence the writers and philosophers of northern Europe. These writers adopted the ideal of humanism. However, some gave it a more religious slant. Because of this, some northern humanists are also called Christian humanists.

Christian Humanists The best known of the Christian humanists were Desiderius Erasmus (DEHZ·ih·DEER·ee·uhs ih·RAZ·muhs) of Holland and Thomas More of England. The two were close friends.

Born in Rotterdam, Erasmus received honors from princes, kings, and cardinals for his brilliant writings. In 1509, while he was a guest in More's house, Erasmus wrote his most famous work, *The Praise of Folly*. This book poked fun at greedy merchants, heartsick lovers, quarrelsome scholars, and pompous priests. Although some of Erasmus's most stinging barbs were aimed at the clergy, his work is strongly Christian. Erasmus believed in a Christianity of the heart, not one of ceremonies or rules. He thought that in order to improve society, all people should study the Bible.

Also concerned with society's flaws, Thomas More tried to show a better model. In 1516, he wrote the book *Utopia* about an imaginary land inhabited by a peace-loving people. In Greek, **Utopia** means "no place," but in English it has come to mean an ideal place because of More's book. In Utopia, greed, corruption, war, and crime had been weeded out. Because the Utopians weren't greedy, they had little use for money:

> Gold and silver, of which money is made, are so treated . . . that no one values them more highly than their true nature deserves. Who does not see that they are far inferior to iron in usefulness since without iron mortals cannot live any more than without fire and water?
>
> **THOMAS MORE**, *Utopia*

The French humanist François Rabelais (RAB·eh·LAY) provided a contrast to Erasmus and More in several ways. They wrote in Latin, while Rabelais wrote his comic adventure *Gargantua and Pantagruel* in vernacular French. More secular than either Erasmus or More, Rabelais believed that human beings were basically good. They should live by their instincts rather than religious rules. As he told of the wild adventures of the giants Gargantua and Pantagruel, he poked fun at his society. Rabelais's humor was uproarious and earthy, although he made many serious points about the nature of humanity, education, and government.

William Shakespeare William Shakespeare wrote in Renaissance England. Many people regard him as the greatest playwright of all time. Shakespeare was born in

The Christian humanist Thomas More wrote about a nearly perfect society called Utopia. He did this to show his own society how to improve.

THINK THROUGH HISTORY
C. Making Inferences What point do you think More was making about his own society?
C. Possible Answers That they were too greedy or that they loved money too much.

OBJECTIVE 3 INSTRUCT

Northern Writers Try to Reform Society

Key Ideas
- Renaissance ideas influence northern European writers and philosophers.
- Christian humanist writers express their social and religious concerns.
- William Shakespeare's brilliant plays dramatize human nature.
- The Renaissance in England is also called the Elizabethan Age, named after Queen Elizabeth I.

CRITICAL THINKING ACTIVITY
CLASS TIME: 15 MINUTES

Summarizing
As students read, have them complete the chart below with details about the writers discussed in this section.

Writer	Nationality	Famous Work
Shakespeare	English	*Hamlet*

MORE ABOUT . . .
Utopia

The idea of a perfect society predates the publication of *Utopia* in 1516. Greek thinkers such as Plato and Plutarch described their own versions of such ideal places.

TEACHING OPTION | BLOCK SCHEDULING | **COOPERATIVE ACTIVITY: Planning a Utopian Community** | CLASS TIME 30 MINUTES

Task: Students will meet in small groups to design a utopian community. Groups will present oral reports, including visual aids, that describe their plans.

Purpose: To apply the ideas of Thomas More's *Utopia* to planning a community.

Activity: Have student groups address the following questions to help them plan their "perfect" communities: Are the community's values or beliefs similar to More's vision of a utopian society? What laws or guidelines should be established that might promote a spirit of harmony? How will the community survive financially? What are families like?

📁 **Building a Portfolio:** Students might wish to place a written version of their plans in their portfolios.

📋 **ALTERNATIVE ASSESSMENT BOOK**
Standards for Evaluating a Cooperative Activity

Standards for Evaluation
Plans for a utopian community should . . .

- address key aspects of communities, such as laws, economics, values, and social organization
- provide specific details
- include clear, informative visual aids

CONNECT *to* TODAY

William Shakespeare

Shakespeare's plays were very popular in London in the 1600s. They are popular today as well, but they appear in many places besides London. Shakespearean festivals are regularly held in such places as Stratford-upon-Avon, England; Stratford, Ontario, Canada; and Austin, Texas.

Even though he has been dead for almost 400 years, Shakespeare is one of Hollywood's favorite writers. In the 1990s, two film versions of *Hamlet* hit the theaters, as did a version of *Romeo and Juliet*. The poster below is from the 1990 version of *Hamlet*, starring Mel Gibson and Glenn Close.

1564 in Stratford-upon-Avon, a small town about 90 miles northwest of London. By 1592 he was living in London and writing poems and plays.

His works display a masterful command of the English language and a deep understanding of human beings. He revealed the souls of men and women through scenes of dramatic conflict. His most famous plays include the tragedies *Macbeth, King Lear, Hamlet, Romeo and Juliet,* and the comedy *A Midsummer Night's Dream.* Many of these plays frankly examine human flaws. However, Shakespeare also had one of his characters deliver a speech that expresses the Renaissance's high view of human nature:

A VOICE FROM THE PAST

What a piece of work is a man, how noble in reason, how infinite in faculties, in form and moving, how express and admirable in action, how like an angel in apprehension [understanding], how like a god! the beauty of the world; the paragon of animals.

WILLIAM SHAKESPEARE, *Hamlet*

Like many Renaissance writers, Shakespeare revered the classics and drew on them for inspiration and plots. One of his great tragedies, for example, tells the story of the assassination of Julius Caesar—the Roman general and statesman.

The Elizabethan Age The Renaissance in England is also called the Elizabethan Age, for Queen Elizabeth I. She reigned from 1558 to 1603. Elizabeth was well-educated and knew French, Italian, Latin, and Greek. In addition to running a kingdom (see page 432), she also wrote poetry. As queen, she patronized artists and writers. Poet Edmund Spenser dedicated his long poem *The Faerie Queene* (1590) to her with these words: "To the most high, mighty, and magnificent Empress, renowned for piety, virtue, and all gracious government, Elizabeth."

Printing Spreads Renaissance Ideas

One thing that helped spread Renaissance ideas throughout Europe was a new invention that adapted Chinese technology. The Chinese had invented block printing, in which a printer carved a word or letter on a wooden block, inked the block, and then used it to print on paper. Around 1045, Bi Sheng invented movable type, or a separate piece of type for each character in the language. However, since the Chinese writing system contained thousands of different characters, most Chinese printers found movable type impractical.

Gutenberg Invents the Printing Press During the 13th century, block-printed items reached Europe from China. European printers began to use block printing to create whole pages to bind into books. However, this process was too slow to satisfy the Renaissance demand for knowledge and books. Johann Gutenberg, a craftsman from Mainz, Germany, reinvented movable type around 1440. The method was practical for Europeans because their languages have a very small number of letters in their alphabets.

Gutenberg then invented the **printing press.** The printing press is a machine that presses paper against a tray full of inked movable type. Using this invention, Gutenberg printed a complete Bible, the **Gutenberg Bible,** in about 1455. It was the first full-size book printed with movable type.

History of Book Making

- 2700 B.C., Egyptians write books on papyrus scrolls.
- 1000 B.C., Chinese make books by writing on strips of bamboo.
- A.D. 300, Romans write on sheets of parchment (treated animal skin). These are sewn together into books.
- 800, Irish monks hand-write and hand-illustrate *The Book of Kells*.
- About 1455, Gutenberg prints the first complete book on a printing press—similar to the one shown at left.

Only 46 copies of the Gutenberg Bible still exist in the world. Because of this, each copy is considered priceless. A part of a page is shown above.

Printing Spreads Learning The printing press had a revolutionary impact on European society. It enabled a printer to produce hundreds of copies, all exactly alike, of a single work. For the first time, books were cheap enough that many people could buy them. Printing spread quickly to other cities in Europe. By 1500, presses in about 250 cities had printed between 9 and 10 million books.

New ideas spread more quickly than ever before. At first printers produced many religious works. Soon they began to provide books on other subjects such as travel guides and medical manuals. The availability of books encouraged people to learn to read and so caused a rise in literacy.

Writing in vernacular languages also increased because even people who could not afford a classical education could now buy books. Printers produced the Bible in the vernacular, which allowed more people to read it. People began to interpret the Bible for themselves and to become more critical of priests and their behavior. This eventually led to demands for religious reform.

The End of the Renaissance In both Italy and northern Europe, the Renaissance had stirred a burst of creative activity. Artists in both regions studied classical culture, praised individual achievement, and produced works using new techniques. During the 1600s, new ideas and artistic styles appeared. Nonetheless, Renaissance ideals continued to influence European thought. For example, the Renaissance belief in the dignity of the individual played a key role in the gradual rise of democratic ideas.

THINK THROUGH HISTORY
E. Recognizing Effects What were the major effects of the invention of the printing press?
E. Answers Books became affordable; books were published on many subjects; new ideas spread; writing in vernacular languages increased; people formed their own opinions about religion.

Section 2 Assessment

1. TERMS & NAMES
Identify
- Utopia
- printing press
- Gutenberg Bible

2. TAKING NOTES
On a time line like the one below, show important events in the Northern Renaissance.

Which of the events do you think was most important? Explain.

3. RECOGNIZING EFFECTS
Choose one Northern Renaissance figure. Explain how he or she was influenced by Renaissance ideas.

THINK ABOUT
- the influence of humanism
- the use of new techniques
- the concept of the Renaissance man or woman

4. THEME ACTIVITY
Cultural Interaction Working in a small team, reproduce a map of Europe in 1500. On the map, use arrows, pictures, and captions to show the spread of Renaissance ideas and developments. Include not only the spread of ideas north from Italy, but also innovations that spread southward from northern Europe.

European Renaissance and Reformation **427**

ANSWERS

TERMS & NAMES
• indulgence
• Reformation
• Lutheran
• Protestant
• Peace of Augsburg
• annul
• Anglican

Section 3 Overview

OBJECTIVES

1. To analyze historical forces and religious issues that sparked the Reformation.

2. To trace Martin Luther's role in the religious movement to reform the Catholic Church.

3. To analyze the impact of Luther's religious revolt.

4. To explain the spread of the Protestant faith to England during King Henry VIII's reign.

CRITICAL THINKING

• Analyzing causes, p.428
• Synthesizing, p. 429
• Drawing conclusions, p. 430
• Analyzing motives, p. 430
• Recognizing effects, p. 432
• Supporting opinions, p. 432
• Analyzing themes, p. 432

FOCUS

5-Minute Warm-Up

▶ **Perceiving Causes and Effects**

Answering these questions will help students analyze the events related to Henry VIII's reign.

1. Read the time line on page 431. How many times did Henry VIII marry?

2. How are the events shown for 1527 and 1529 connected?

 WARM-UP TRANSPARENCY 17

OBJECTIVE ① INSTRUCT

Causes of the Reformation

▶ **Key Ideas**

• The spread of Renaissance ideas and claims of corruption among the clergy undermine the Catholic Church's authority.

• In the 1300s and 1400s, John Wycliffe and John Huss criticize church practices.

• In the late 1400s, Savonarola calls for church reform.

📋 **IN-DEPTH RESOURCES: UNIT 4**
Guided Reading, p. 20

📋 **ACCESS FOR STUDENTS ACQUIRING ENGLISH**
Guided Reading (Spanish), p. 172

③ Luther Starts the Reformation

MAIN IDEA	WHY IT MATTERS NOW
Martin Luther's protest over abuses in the Catholic Church led to the founding of Protestant churches.	Nearly one-fourth of the Christians in today's world are Protestants.

SETTING THE STAGE By the tenth century, the church in Rome had come to dominate religious life in northern and western Europe. However, the Roman Catholic Church had not won universal approval. Over the centuries, rulers, scholars, and members of the clergy criticized church practices. Even though church leaders made several important reforms during the Middle Ages, the problems lingered.

Causes of the Reformation

By 1500, additional forces weakened the Church. The Renaissance emphasis on the secular and the individual challenged Church authority. The printing press spread these secular ideas. In addition, rulers resented the popes' attempts to control them. In Germany—divided into many competing states—it was difficult for the pope or the emperor to impose central authority. Finally, northern merchants resented paying church taxes to Rome. Spurred by political and social forces, a new movement for religious reform began in Germany. It then swept much of Europe.

Problems in the Catholic Church Critics of the Church claimed that its leaders were corrupt. The popes who ruled during the Renaissance patronized the arts, spent extravagantly on personal pleasure, and fought wars. Pope Pius II admitted, "If the truth be confessed, the luxury and pomp of our courts is too great." Another pope, Alexander VI, publicly admitted that he had several children. These popes were too busy pursuing worldly affairs to have much time for spiritual duties.

The lower clergy had problems as well. Many priests and monks were so poorly educated that they could scarcely read, let alone teach people. Others broke their priestly vows by marrying, or by gambling or drinking to excess.

As this portrait shows, the friar Girolamo Savonarola was a serious-minded man. Disapproving of the worldly values of his time, he urged the people of Florence to give up their luxuries.

Early Calls for Reform Influenced by reformers, people had come to expect higher standards of conduct from priests and church leaders. In the late 1300s and early 1400s, John Wycliffe of England and Jan Hus of Bohemia had advocated church reform. They denied that the pope had the right to worldly power. They also taught that the Bible had more authority than Church leaders. In the 1500s, Christian humanists like Desiderius Erasmus and Thomas More added their voices to the chorus of criticism.

In the 1490s, an Italian friar named Girolamo Savonarola (jih·RAHL·uh·MOH SAV·uh·nuh·ROH·luh) came to Florence. He preached fiery sermons calling for reform. In 1497, the people of Florence responded to Savonarola by burning their worldly possessions, such as gambling equipment, in a giant bonfire. Only a year later, the Florentines turned against Savonarola, and he was executed for heresy.

THINK THROUGH HISTORY
A. Analyzing Causes How did political, social, and economic forces weaken the Church?
A. Answers Political—Rulers resented the popes' attempts to control them and Germany was not unified; Social—Printing press spread Renaissance ideas that challenged Church authority; Economic—Merchants resented paying Church taxes.

SECTION 3 RESOURCES

PRINT RESOURCES

📋 ***IN-DEPTH RESOURCES: UNIT 4***
Guided Reading, p. 20
Skillbuilder Practice: Synthesizing, p. 22
Primary Sources: A Conference with Elizabeth I, p. 27; Report on the English Reformation, p. 28
History Makers: Elizabeth I, p. 33

📋 ***ACCESS FOR STUDENTS ACQUIRING ENGLISH***
Guided Reading (Spanish), p. 172
Skillbuilder Practice: (Spanish), p. 174

📋 ***FORMAL ASSESSMENT***
Section Quiz, p. 195

📋 ***ALTERNATIVE ASSESSMENT BOOK***

TECHNOLOGY RESOURCES

💿 **CD-ROM**
Electronic Library of Primary Sources

🌐 **INTERNET** www.mlworldhistory.com

Luther Challenges the Church

Although some reformers died for their beliefs, their calls for change lived on. In addition, many Europeans were reading religious works for themselves and forming their own opinions about the Church. The atmosphere in Europe was ripe for reform by the early 1500s.

Martin Luther The son of a miner, Martin Luther became a monk in 1505. From 1512 until his death he taught scripture at the University of Wittenberg in the German state of Saxony. All he wanted was to be a good Christian, not to lead a religious revolution.

In 1517 Luther decided to take a public stand against the actions of a friar named Johann Tetzel. Tetzel was raising money to rebuild St. Peter's Cathedral in Rome. He did this by selling indulgences. An **indulgence** was a pardon. It released a sinner from performing the penalty—such as saying certain prayers—that a priest imposed for sins. Indulgences were not supposed to affect God's right to judge. Unfortunately, Tetzel gave people the impression that by buying indulgences, they could buy their way into heaven.

The 95 Theses Luther was troubled by Tetzel's tactics. He wrote 95 Theses, or formal statements, attacking the "pardon-merchants." On October 31, 1517, he posted his theses on the door of the castle church in Wittenberg and invited other scholars to debate him. Someone copied Luther's words and took them to a printer. Quickly, Luther's name became known all over Germany. His actions began the **Reformation,** a movement for religious reform. It led to the founding of Christian churches that did not accept the pope's authority.

Soon Luther went far beyond criticizing indulgences. He wanted a full reform of the Church. His teachings rested on three main ideas:

- People could win salvation only by faith in God's gift of forgiveness. The Church taught that faith and "good works" were needed for salvation.
- All Church teachings should be clearly based on the words of the Bible. The pope and church traditions were false authorities.
- All people with faith were equal. Therefore, people did not need priests to interpret the Bible for them.

HISTORY MAKERS

Martin Luther
1483–1546

Martin Luther was sometimes unhappy as a child. Like many parents of that time, his father and mother were very strict. Luther later told stories of their beating him.

In one way, fear led Luther to become a monk. His father wanted him to go to law school, but at the age of 21, Luther was caught in a terrible thunderstorm. Lightning struck close to him. Convinced he would die, he cried out, "Saint Anne, help me! I will become a monk."

Even as a monk, Luther felt sinful, lost, and rejected by God. He confessed his sins regularly, fasted, and did penance. However, by studying the Bible, Luther came to the conclusion that faith alone was the key to salvation. Only then did he experience peace.

The Response to Luther

Luther himself was astonished at how rapidly his ideas spread and attracted followers. Many rulers and merchants had been unhappy with the Church for political and economic reasons. They saw Luther's protests as an excuse to throw off Church control.

The Pope's Threat Initially, the Church officials in Rome viewed Luther simply as a rebellious monk who needed to be punished by his superiors. However, as Luther's ideas became increasingly radical, the pope realized that the monk was a serious threat. In one angry reply to Church criticism, Luther actually suggested that Christians drive the pope from the Church by force.

In 1520, Pope Leo X issued a decree threatening Luther with excommunication unless he took back his statements. Luther did not take back a word. Instead, his students at Wittenberg gathered around a bonfire and cheered as he threw the pope's decree into the flames. Leo excommunicated Luther.

The Emperor's Opposition A devout Catholic, the Holy Roman emperor also opposed Luther's teaching. Although only 20 years old, Emperor Charles V controlled

European Renaissance and Reformation **429**

The Peasants' Revolt

German peasants had revolted several times in the 1400s before Luther's teachings incited them to rebel. Crops failed in 1523 and 1524, and peasants complained of new fees imposed by their lords. Luther's words, taken out of context, justified their uprisings: "A Christian man is the most free lord of all and subject to none."

SPOTLIGHT On
Witch Hunts

The witchcraft mania, which had a long-standing history in Europe, eventually made its way to the New England colonies. Ask students to research the Salem witchcraft trials of 1692.

CRITICAL THINKING ACTIVITY
CLASS TIME: 10 MINUTES

Analyzing Events
Have students create a tree diagram like the one below and list at least three of Luther's ideas or views that gained popularity.

Luther's Popular Ideas

Personal interpretation of the Bible	Religious freedom for Christians	Independence from the Catholic Church

---

a vast empire, including Germany. He summoned Luther to the town of Worms in 1521 to stand trial. German princes and bishops crowded into the hall to witness the testimony. Told to recant, or take back his statements, Luther refused.

A VOICE FROM THE PAST
I am bound by the Scriptures I have quoted and my conscience is captive to the Word of God. I cannot and I will not retract anything, since it is neither safe nor right to go against conscience. I cannot do otherwise, here I stand, may God help me. Amen.

LUTHER, quoted in *The Protestant Reformation* by Lewis W. Spitz

A month after Luther made that speech, Charles issued an imperial order, the Edict of Worms. It declared Luther an outlaw and a heretic. According to this edict, no one in the empire was to give Luther food or shelter. All his books were to be burned. However, the ruler of the state where Luther lived disobeyed the emperor. For almost a year after the trial, Prince Frederick the Wise of Saxony sheltered Luther in one of his castles. While there, Luther translated the New Testament into German.

Luther returned to Wittenberg in 1522. There he discovered that many of his ideas were already being put into practice. Priests dressed in ordinary clothes and called themselves ministers. They led services in German instead of in Latin. Some ministers had married, because Luther taught that the clergy should be free to wed. Instead of continuing to seek reforms in the Catholic Church, Luther and his followers had become a separate religious group, called **Lutherans.**

The Peasants' Revolt Some people began to apply Luther's revolutionary ideas to society. In 1524, German peasants, excited by reformers' talk of Christian freedom, demanded an end to serfdom. Bands of angry peasants went about the countryside raiding monasteries, pillaging, and burning.

The revolt horrified Luther. He wrote a pamphlet urging the German princes to show the peasants no mercy. With brutal thoroughness, the princes' armies crushed the revolt. They massacred as many as 100,000 people. Feeling betrayed by Luther, many peasants rejected his religious leadership. However, through writings and lectures, Luther remained influential until the end of his life.

SPOTLIGHT On
Witch Hunts

Soon after the Reformation began, the number of people executed for being witches rose dramatically. From 1561 to 1670 in Germany, 3,229 people accused of witchcraft were burned at the stake, as the engraving above shows. Between 1559 and 1736 in England, almost 1,000 witches were put to death. Eighty percent of the people accused of witchcraft were women.

Some historians think that people felt so frightened by the ongoing religious conflicts they blamed them on witches. Other historians believe that religious reformers stirred up negative feelings about women that had long been part of Western culture. All agree that those executed for witchcraft were innocent victims.

Germany at War In contrast to the bitter peasants, many northern German princes supported Lutheranism. While some princes genuinely shared Luther's beliefs, others liked Luther's ideas for selfish reasons. They saw his teachings as a good excuse to seize Church property and to assert their independence from Charles V.

In 1529, German princes who remained loyal to the pope agreed to join forces against Luther's ideas. Princes who supported Luther signed a protest against that agreement. These protesting princes came to be known as Protestants. Eventually, the term **Protestant** was applied to Christians who belonged to non-Catholic churches.

Still determined that his subjects remain Catholic, Holy Roman Emperor Charles V went to war against the Protestant princes of Germany. Even though he defeated them in 1547, he failed to force them back into the Catholic Church.

Weary of fighting, Charles ordered all German princes, both Protestant and Catholic, to assemble in the city of Augsburg. At that meeting, the princes agreed that the religion of each German state was to be decided by its ruler. This famous religious settlement, signed in 1555, was known as the **Peace of Augsburg.**

THINK THROUGH HISTORY
C. Drawing Conclusions Why would Luther and his followers want the Bible and sermons to be in German?
C. Possible Answer If people were to interpret the Bible for themselves, they had to know what it said—and most people did not know Latin.

THINK THROUGH HISTORY
D. Analyzing Motives Explain the different motives that German princes had for becoming Lutheran.
D. Possible Answers Religious—because they agreed with Luther; economic—to gain property by seizing lands owned by the Catholic church; political—to gain more independence from their Catholic emperor

---

Music Martin Luther was very interested in music. In fact, he wrote many hymns still sung today, including the famous Protestant hymn "A Mighty Fortress Is Our God." In the countries where Lutheranism flourished, a great tradition of church music developed.

Bring recordings of some of this music

to class. For example, you may wish to have students listen to works by Johann Sebastian Bach, who wrote most of his compositions for the church. Other Reformation composers include Buxtehude, Pachelbel, and Böhm.

As you play musical selections to the class, ask students how they think the music expresses the mood of this era.

Less Proficient Readers To help students understand the impact of Luther's beliefs, have them complete the chart like the one below.

Person or Group	Action or Outcome	Explanation
Pope Leo X	Excommunication (1520)	Banished Luther from the Catholic Church
Charles V	Edict of Worms (1521)	Declared Luther an outlaw and heretic
Northern German princes	Peace of Augsburg (1555)	Allowed German princes to decide the religion that would be followed in their lands.

England Becomes Protestant

The Catholic Church soon faced another great challenge to its authority. Unlike Luther, the man who broke England's ties to the Roman Catholic Church did so for political and personal, not religious, reasons.

Henry VIII Wants a Son When Henry became king of England, he was a devout Catholic. Political needs soon tested his religious loyalty. He needed a male heir. Henry's father had become king after a long civil war. Henry feared that a similar war would start if he died without a son as his heir. He and his wife, Catherine of Aragon, had one living child—a daughter, Mary—but no woman had ever successfully claimed the English throne.

By 1527, Henry was convinced that the 42-year-old Catherine would have no more children. He wanted to divorce her and take a younger queen. Church law did not allow divorce. However, the pope could **annul**, or set aside, Henry's marriage if he could find proof that it had never been legal in the first place. Excuses were frequently found to annul royal marriages if they produced no heirs. In 1527, King Henry asked the pope to annul his marriage, but the pope turned him down. The pope did not want to offend Catherine's powerful nephew, the Holy Roman Emperor Charles V.

Background
The pope had taken the losing side in a war against Emperor Charles V, who was now holding him pris-oner. The pope did not dare annul Henry's marriage to Charles's aunt.

The Reformation Parliament Henry solved his marriage problem himself. In 1529, he called Parliament into session and asked it to pass a set of laws that ended the pope's power in England. This Parliament is known as the Reformation Parliament.

In 1533, Henry secretly married Anne Boleyn (BUL·ihn), who was in her twenties. Parliament legalized Henry's divorce from Catherine. In 1534, Henry's break with the pope was made complete when Parliament voted to approve the Act of Supremacy. This act made the English king, not the pope, the official head of England's Church.

Consequences of Henry's Changes Soon after making himself supreme head of the Church of England, Henry closed all English monasteries. He seized their wealth and lands. The monasteries had owned perhaps 20 percent of the land in England, so this act vastly increased royal power and enriched Henry's treasury.

Henry did not get the male heir he sought immediately. After Anne Boleyn gave birth to a girl, she fell out of Henry's favor. Eventually, he ordered her imprisoned in the Tower of London and later beheaded in 1536. Before his death, Henry married four more times. His third wife gave him a son named Edward.

HISTORY MAKERS

Henry VIII
1491–1547

When Henry became king in 1509, he was young, strong, handsome, and intelligent. He loved sports, literature, music, and food. He also loved his Roman Catholic faith.

In 1521, he wrote a pamphlet attacking Martin Luther and his teachings. Impressed by Henry's loyalty, the pope gave him a special title, "Defender of the Faith."

Even Henry's religious actions were driven by political ambition. One of his motives for defending Catholicism was to keep up with his fellow European monarchs. Earlier popes had granted Spanish monarchs the title "Catholic Sovereigns" and French monarchs the title "Most Christian." Although Henry was proud of his papal honor, eventually his political needs drove him to break with the Church.

Henry VIII's Family Causes Religious Turmoil

1509 Henry VIII becomes king.

1516 Daughter Mary is born.

1527 Henry asks the pope to end his first marriage; the pope refuses.

1529 Henry breaks with pope; begins Protestant Anglican church.

1533 Henry marries Anne Boleyn; daughter Elizabeth is born.

1537 Henry's third wife has son, Edward. She dies from complications.

1540-1542 Henry divorces fourth wife and beheads fifth wife.

1536 Anne Boleyn is beheaded.

1547 Henry dies; his sixth wife outlives him; Edward VI begins six-year rule; Protestants are strong.

1553 Catholic Mary I begins rule and kills Protestants.

1558 Elizabeth I begins rule; she restores Protestant church.

1500 — 1560

European Renaissance and Reformation **431**

OBJECTIVE 4 INSTRUCT

England Becomes Protestant

▶ *Key Ideas*
- The pope refuses to annul King Henry VIII's marriage.
- Henry resolves the marriage problem by asking Parliament to end the pope's power in England.
- Parliament passes an act making the English king, not the pope, the head of the Church of England.
- Clashes over religious reform heighten when Henry's heirs take the throne.
- Henry's daughter Elizabeth I returns England to Protestantism during her reign.

HISTORY MAKERS
Henry VIII

At the time of Henry's break with Rome, most English people were devout Catholics. There was a small minority of dissenters—people who wanted to reform the church. However, Henry was care-ful to change nothing about the way people worshiped, which explains why there was not greater outcry about his actions.

History from Visuals

Henry VIII's Family Causes Religious Turmoil

Interpreting the Time Line
Ask students to notice how many years are represented on the time line. *60.* How many rulers of England are shown on the time line? *4.* How many years did Mary reign as queen? *5.*

Extension Ask students to create a diagram of a family tree, based on the time line, that shows Henry VIII's six wives and his children.

TEACHING OPTION **BLOCK SCHEDULING** **COOPERATIVE ACTIVITY: Reporting on the Wives of Henry VIII** **CLASS TIME 30 MINUTES**

Task: Groups of students will create front pages of newspaper issues reporting on activities of different wives of Henry VIII.

Purpose: To learn more about the lives of Henry's six wives and to learn more daily life at court.

Activity: Divide the class into six groups and assign each group one of Henry's six wives. Students should choose an interesting date to highlight—for example, the wedding day, a childbirth announcement,

and the wife's execution or death. Students should then research the event. The front page may include news stories, interviews, and human-interest features. Different students in the group might serve as researchers, writers, editors, and layout designers.

📁 **Building a Portfolio:** Remind students to choose their strongest work for their portfolio.

📄 **ALTERNATE ASSESSMENT BOOK**
Standards for Evaluating a Cooperative Activity

Standards for Evaluation
Front pages should . . .

- contain attention-getting headlines
- present well-organized, engaging stories and features based on research
- show evidence of careful planning

Teacher's Edition **431**

HISTORY MAKERS
Elizabeth I

Ask students to make a list of Elizabeth's strengths as a ruler. Answers might include courage, intelligence, convictions.

 IN-DEPTH RESOURCES: UNIT 4
Primary Source: A Conference with Elizabeth I, p. 27
History Maker: Elizabeth I, p. 33

ASSESS & RETEACH

Section 3 Assessment
Have pairs of students take turns quizzing each other on the questions.

Section Quiz
 FORMAL ASSESSMENT
Section Quiz, p. 195

Reteaching Activity
CLASS TIME: 10 MINUTES

Use the Guided Reading Worksheet for Section 3 to review the main ideas of the section.

 IN-DEPTH RESOURCES: UNIT 4
Guided Reading, p. 20

CLOSE ACTIVITY

CLASS TIME: 20 MINUTES

Comparing
Have students create a Venn diagram, like the one below, comparing the English and German protests against the Catholic Church. In drawing comparisons, students should include both the motives for the protests and the outcomes

German protests / English protests

 IN-DEPTH RESOURCES: UNIT 4
Primary Source: Report on the English Reformation, p. 28

After Henry's death in 1547, each of his three children eventually ruled. This created religious turmoil. Edward VI became king at age nine and ruled only six years. During his reign, the Protestants gained power. Edward's half-sister Mary ruled next. She was a Catholic who returned the English Church to the rule of the pope. Mary had many Protestants killed. England's next ruler was Anne Boleyn's daughter, Elizabeth.

Elizabeth Restores Protestantism Inheriting the throne in 1558, Elizabeth I returned her kingdom to Protestantism. In 1559, Parliament followed Elizabeth's request and set up a national church much like the one under Henry VIII. This was to be the only legal church in England. People were required to attend its services or pay a fine. Parliament declared that Elizabeth was head of the Church of England, or **Anglican** Church.

Elizabeth decided to establish a state church that moderate Catholics and moderate Protestants might both accept. As a concession to Protestants, priests in the Church of England were allowed to marry. They could deliver sermons in English, not Latin. As a concession to Catholics, the Church of England kept some of the trappings of the Catholic service such as rich robes and golden crucifixes. Under Elizabeth, the Book of Common Prayer was revised to be somewhat more acceptable to Catholics.

The Spanish Armada While Elizabeth was able to restore religious peace to her country, she soon faced the threat of invasion from the king of Catholic Spain. Philip II planned to attack England for several reasons. One reason was that Elizabeth had supported Protestant subjects who rebelled against him. In 1588, Philip assembled an invasion force of 130 ships, 8,000 sailors, and 19,000 soldiers. This force—known as the Spanish Armada—reached the southwest coast of England on July 29. However, bad weather and the English fleet defeated the Spanish completely.

Although Elizabeth's reign was triumphant, she had some difficulties. Money was one problem. In the late 1500s, the English began to think about building an American empire as a new source of income. (See Chapter 19.) While colonies strengthened England economically, they did not enrich the queen directly. The queen's constant need for money would carry over into the next reign and lead to bitter conflict between the monarch and Parliament. In the meantime, other countries experienced bloody religious conflicts.

HISTORY MAKERS

Elizabeth I
1533–1603

Elizabeth I was the third of Henry VIII's children to rule England. Like her father, Elizabeth had a fierce temper and a robust nature. Athletic as a girl, she showed amazing energy and strength into her sixties.

When the Spanish Armada threatened England, Elizabeth rode into the camp of soldiers preparing to defend their country. For this occasion, she wore her brightest red wig adorned with two white plumes that were easy for all to see above the soldier's long pikes.

From her horse, Elizabeth gave encouragement to her soldiers:

I know I have the body of a weak and feeble woman, but I have the heart and stomach of a king, and a king of England, too, and I think foul scorn [of] . . . any prince of Europe [who] should dare invade the borders of my realm.

THINK THROUGH HISTORY
E. Recognizing Effects How did Henry VIII and his three children cause religious turmoil in England?
E. Answer Under their rule, England switched back and forth from Catholic to Protestant to Catholic to Protestant again. Many people were persecuted and martyred, by both Henry and Mary.

Section 3 Assessment

1. TERMS & NAMES
Identify
- indulgence
- Reformation
- Lutheran
- Protestant
- Peace of Augsburg
- annul
- Anglican

2. TAKING NOTES
Using a cause-and-effect graphic like the one below, show the main cause and several effects of Luther's action in posting the 95 Theses.

```
                    ┌──────────┐
                    │  effect  │
                    └──────────┘
┌───────┐   ┌──────────┐   ┌──────────┐
│ cause │ → │  Luther  │   │  effect  │
└───────┘   │ posts the│   └──────────┘
            │95 Theses.│
            └──────────┘   ┌──────────┐
                    │  effect  │
                    └──────────┘
```

Which effect do you think had the most permanent impact? Explain.

3. SUPPORTING OPINIONS
Who do you think had a better reason to break with the Church, Luther or Henry VIII? Support your answer with details from the text.

THINK ABOUT
- why Luther criticized the Church
- what Henry asked the pope to do for him
- the Church's response to Luther
- the pope's response to Henry

4. ANALYZING THEMES
Revolution Which of Luther's ideas do you think might have motivated the peasants to revolt in 1524? Explain.

THINK ABOUT
- Luther's criticisms of the Church
- what change the peasants demanded
- the actions the peasants took

ANSWERS

1. TERMS AND NAMES
indulgence, p. 429
Reformation, p. 429
Lutheran, p. 430
Protestant, p. 430
Peace of Augsburg, p. 430
annul, p. 431
Anglican, p. 432

2. TAKING NOTES
Possible Responses: Cause: Tetzel sells indulgences under false pretenses. Effects: Luther protests; pope excommunicates Luther; Luther declared a heretic; Lutheran church begins; German peasants revolt; Charles V goes to war against Protestant princes of Germany. Impact: Lutheran church—led to permanent break between Catholics and Protestants.

3. DRAWING CONCLUSIONS
Possible Responses: Luther's reasons—legitimate complaints about indulgences and other Church problems; excommunication. Henry's reasons—his annulments denied; pope's po[li]cal maneuvers.

4. ANALYZING THEMES
Possible Responses: The equality of all Christians spur[red] peasants to demand an end t[o] serfdom. Peasants disrespec[ted] Church authority by raiding th[e] monasteries.

4 The Reformation Continues

TERMS & NAMES
- predestination
- Calvinism
- theocracy
- Presbyterian
- Anabaptist
- Catholic Reformation
- Jesuits
- Council of Trent

MAIN IDEA

John Calvin and other Reformation leaders began new Protestant churches. The Catholic Church also made reforms.

WHY IT MATTERS NOW

Many Protestant churches began during this period, and many Catholic schools are the result of Catholic reforms.

SETTING THE STAGE Under the leadership of Elizabeth I, the Church of England remained similar to the Catholic Church in many of its doctrines and ceremonies. Meanwhile, other forms of Protestantism were developing elsewhere in Europe.

Calvin Begins Another Protestant Church

In 1521, the year Luther stood trial at Worms, John Calvin was a 12-year-old boy. Born in France, Calvin grew up to have as much influence on Protestants as Luther did. Calvin would give order to the new faith that Luther had begun.

Calvin and His Teachings In 1536, Calvin published a book called *Institutes of the Christian Religion.* This work expressed Calvin's ideas about God, salvation, and human nature. It also created a system of Protestant theology.

Calvin taught that men and women are sinful by nature. Taking Luther's idea that humans cannot earn salvation, Calvin went on to say that God chooses a very few people to save. Calvin called these few the "elect." He believed that God has known since the beginning of time who will be saved. This doctrine is called **predestination.** The religion based on Calvin's teachings is called **Calvinism.**

Calvin Runs Geneva Calvin believed that the ideal government was a **theocracy,** a government controlled by religious leaders. In 1541, Protestants in Geneva, Switzerland, asked Calvin to lead their city. When Calvin arrived there in the 1540s, Geneva was a self-governing city of about 20,000 people.

Calvin and his followers ran the city according to strict rules. Everyone attended religion class. No one wore bright clothing or played card games. Authorities would imprison, excommunicate, or banish those who broke such rules. Anyone who preached different doctrines might be burned at the stake. Yet, to many Protestants, Calvin's Geneva was a model city of highly moral citizens.

Calvinism Spreads One of the admiring visitors to Geneva was a preacher from Scotland named John Knox. When he returned home in 1559, Knox put Calvin's ideas to work in Scottish towns. Each community church was governed by a small group of laymen called elders or presbyters (PREHZ·buh·tuhrs). Followers of Knox became known as **Presbyterians.** In the 1560s, Protestant nobles led by Knox succeeded in making Calvinism Scotland's official religion. They also deposed their Catholic queen in favor of her infant son.

Elsewhere, Swiss, Dutch, and French reformers adopted the Calvinist form of church organization. One reason Calvin is considered so influential is that many Protestant churches today

Background
The deposed queen was Mary, Queen of Scots—Elizabeth I's cousin and heir. Many English Catholics wanted Mary to rule. Eventually, Elizabeth had Mary executed for taking part in plots against her.

HISTORY MAKERS

John Calvin
1509–1564

Unlike Luther, Calvin wrote little about his personal life. A quiet boy, he grew up to study law and philosophy at the University of Paris. Early in the 1530s, he came under the influence of French followers of Luther. When King Francis I ordered these Protestants arrested, Calvin fled. Eventually, he made his way to Geneva, Switzerland.

Calvin and his followers rigidly regulated morality in Geneva. Perhaps because of this, Calvinism is often described as strict and grim. However, Calvin taught that people should enjoy God's gifts. He wrote that it was not

> anywhere forbidden to laugh, or to enjoy food, or to add new possessions to old . . . or to be delighted with musical harmonies, or to drink wine.

European Renaissance and Reformation **433**

Section 4 Overview

OBJECTIVES

1. To explain John Calvin's Protestant teachings and their spread throughout northern and western Europe.

2. To describe the beliefs of other reformers and the roles of women in the Reformation.

3. To trace the reforms within the Catholic Church.

SKILLBUILDER

- Interpreting maps: region, location, p. 434

CRITICAL THINKING

- Analyzing causes, p. 434
- Making inferences, p. 435
- Evaluating decisions, p. 436

FOCUS

5-Minute Warm-Up

▶ *Interpreting Maps*
Answering the following questions will help students understand the impact of the Protestant and Catholic faiths on Europe.

1. Study the map on page 434. Where was the Protestant religion stronger, in northern Europe or southern Europe?

2. Were the German States primarily Catholic or Protestant?

🏛 *WARM-UP TRANSPARENCY 17*

OBJECTIVE ① INSTRUCT

Calvin Begins Another Protestant Church

▶ *Key Ideas*
- John Calvin creates a system of Protestant theology.
- Calvin runs the city of Geneva as a theocracy.
- Scottish, Swiss, Dutch, and French reformers adopt a Calvinist form of church organization.

📋 *IN-DEPTH RESOURCES: UNIT 4*
Guided Reading, p. 21

📋 *ACCESS FOR STUDENTS ACQUIRING ENGLISH*
Guided Reading (Spanish), p. 173

SECTION 4 RESOURCES

PRINT RESOURCES

📋 *IN-DEPTH RESOURCES: UNIT 4*
Guided Reading, p. 21

📋 *ACCESS FOR STUDENTS ACQUIRING ENGLISH*
Guided Reading (Spanish), p. 173

📋 *FORMAL ASSESSMENT*
Section Quiz, p. 196

📋 *ALTERNATIVE ASSESSMENT HANDBOOK*

TECHNOLOGY RESOURCES

🏛 *GEOGRAPHY TRANSPARENCIES*
GT17 Reformation: Lutheranism and Calvinism, 1500–1600

🏛 *CRITICAL THINKING TRANSPARENCIES*
CT17 Protestant and Catholic Reformation
CT53 Chapter 17 Visual Summary

💿 **CD-ROM**
Electronic Library of Primary Sources

🌐 **INTERNET** www.mlworldhistory.com

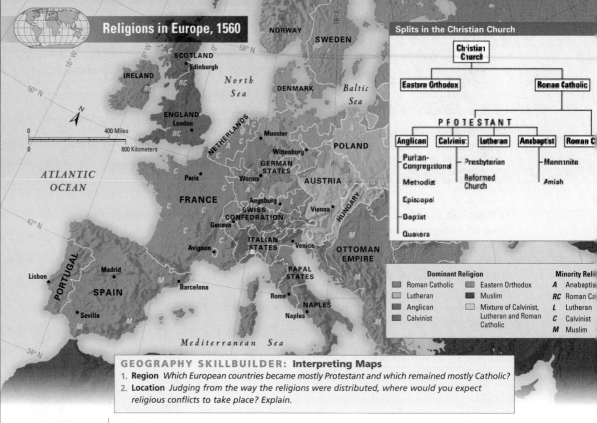

Religions in Europe, 1560

Splits in the Christian Church

GEOGRAPHY SKILLBUILDER: Interpreting Maps
1. **Region** *Which European countries became mostly Protestant and which remained mostly Catholic?*
2. **Location** *Judging from the way the religions were distributed, where would you expect religious conflicts to take place? Explain.*

trace their roots to Calvin. Over the years, however, many of them have softened Calvin's strict teachings.

In France, Calvin's followers were called Huguenots. Hatred between Catholics and Huguenots frequently led to violence. The worst outbreak of fury occurred in Paris on August 24, 1572—the Catholic feast of St. Bartholomew's Day. At dawn, Catholic mobs began hunting for Protestants and brutally murdering them. The massacres spread to other cities and lasted six months. Thousands, perhaps up to 12,000, Huguenots were killed.

Other Reformers

Protestants taught that the Bible is the source of all truth about religion and that all people should read it to discover those truths. As Christians began to interpret the Bible for themselves, new Protestant groups formed over differences in belief.

Although Catholic, Marguerite of Navarre held unorthodox, mystical personal beliefs. She supported the call for reform in the Church.

The Anabaptists One such group baptized only those persons who were old enough to decide to be Christian. They said that people who had been baptized as children should be rebaptized as adults. These believers were called **Anabaptists** from the Greek for "baptize again." Anabaptists also taught that church and state should be separate, and they refused to fight in wars. They shared their possessions. Viewing Anabaptists as radicals who threatened society, both Catholics and Protestants persecuted them. Yet, the Anabaptists survived and became the forerunners of the Mennonites and the Amish. Their teaching influenced the later Quakers and Baptists, who split from the Anglican church.

Women of the Reformation Many women played prominent roles in the Reformation, especially from 1519 to 1580. For example, Marguerite of Navarre, the sister of King Francis I, protected John Calvin from being

434 Chapter 17

executed for his beliefs while he lived in France. Other noblewomen played similar roles in protecting reformers.

Several wives of reformers also achieved fame. Katherina Zell, married to prominent reformer Matthew Zell of Strasbourg, once scolded a minister for speaking harshly of another. The minister responded by saying that she had "disturbed the peace." Katherina Zell answered his criticism sharply:

A VOICE FROM THE PAST
Do you call this disturbing the peace that instead of spending my time in frivolous amusements I have visited the plague infested and carried out the dead? I have visited those in prison and under sentence of death. Often for three days and three nights I have neither eaten nor slept. I have never mounted the pulpit, but I have done more than any minister in visiting those in misery.

KATHERINA ZELL, quoted in *Women of the Reformation*

Luther's wife Katherina von Bora played a more typical, behind-the-scenes role. However, her young life was unusual. Sent to a convent at about age 10, Katherina had taken the vows of a nun by 16. Inspired by Luther's teaching, she escaped from her convent. Some stories claim she escaped by hiding in an empty barrel that had contained smoked herring.

After marrying Luther, Katherina had six children. She managed the family finances, fed all who visited their house, and supported her husband's work. She submitted respectfully to Luther but also argued with him about woman's equal role in marriage. Their well-run household became a model for others to follow.

As Protestant religions became more firmly established, their organization became more formal. Male religious leaders narrowly limited women's activities to the home and discouraged them from being leaders.

The Catholic Reformation

While Protestant churches won many followers, millions remained true to Catholicism. Helping Catholics to remain loyal was a movement within the Catholic Church to reform itself. This movement is now known as the **Catholic Reformation.** One great Catholic reformer was Ignatius (ihg·NAY·shuhs) of Loyola.

Ignatius of Loyola Ignatius grew up in his father's castle in Loyola, Spain. The great turning point in his life came in 1521 when he was injured in a war. During his recovery, Ignatius thought about his past sins and about the life of Jesus. His daily devotions, he believed, cleansed his soul. In 1522, he began writing a book called *Spiritual Exercises* that laid out a day-by-day plan of meditation, prayer, and study. Ignatius compared spiritual and physical exercise:

A VOICE FROM THE PAST
Just as walking, traveling, and running are bodily exercises, preparing the soul to remove ill-ordered affections, and after their removal seeking and finding the will of God with respect to the ordering of one's own life and the salvation of one's soul, are Spiritual Exercises.

IGNATIUS OF LOYOLA, *Spiritual Exercises*

For the next 18 years, Ignatius gathered followers. In 1540, the pope made Ignatius's followers a religious order called the Society of Jesus. Members of the order were commonly called **Jesuits** (JEHZH·u·ihts).

The Jesuits concentrated on three activities. First, they founded superb schools throughout Europe. Jesuit teachers were rigorously trained in both classical studies and theology. The Jesuits' second mission was to convert non-Christians to Catholicism, so they sent out missionaries. Their third goal was to stop Protestantism from

 Global Impact

Jesuit Missionaries
The work of Jesuit missionaries has had a lasting impact around the globe. By the time Ignatius died in 1556, about a thousand Jesuits were working in Europe, Africa, Asia, and the Americas. Two of the most famous Jesuit missionaries of the 1500s were Francis Xavier, who worked in India, and Matteo Ricci, who worked in China.

One reason the Jesuits had such a permanent impact is that they founded schools, colleges, and universities throughout the world. For example, the Jesuits today run about 45 high schools and 28 colleges and universities in the United States. Two of these are Boston College and Marquette University.

European Renaissance and Reformation **435**

In Catholic countries, the Inquisition stepped up its activities, threatening Protestants and heretics with imprisonment or death. Even the most faithful believers might be reported by their enemies to the Inquisition. Ignatius of Loyola himself was brought before the Inquisition several times. However, he was always found innocent.

ASSESS & RETEACH

Section 4 Assessment

Assign pairs of students to answer the questions and find supporting information in the text.

Section Quiz

FORMAL ASSESSMENT
Section Quiz, p. 196

Reteaching Activity

CLASS TIME: 10 MINUTES

Use the chart that appears with the map on page 434 to review the classification of various religious groups belonging to the Christian Church.

CRITICAL THINKING TRANSPARENCIES
CT53 Chapter 17 Visual Summary

CLOSE ACTIVITY

CLASS TIME: 15 MINUTES

Arranging Events in Sequential Order

Have students create a flow chart of major steps that popes took to reform the Catholic Church from 1534 to 1559.

436 Chapter 17

This Italian painting of the Council of Trent shows the large number of church leaders who met to discuss Catholic reforms.

spreading. The zeal of the Jesuits overcame the drift toward Protestantism in Poland and southern Germany.

Reforming Popes Two popes of the 1500s took the lead in reforming the Catholic Church. Paul III, who was pope from 1534 to 1549, took four important steps toward reform. First, he directed a council of cardinals to investigate indulgence selling and other abuses within the Church. Second, he approved the Jesuit order. Third, he used the Inquisition to seek out and punish heresy in papal territory. Fourth, and most important, he decided to call a great council of Church leaders to meet in Trent, in northern Italy. In the years between 1545 and 1563, at the **Council of Trent,** Catholic bishops and cardinals agreed on several doctrines:

- The church's interpretation of the Bible was final. Any Christian who substituted his or her own interpretation was a heretic.
- Christians need faith and good works for salvation. They were not saved by faith alone, as Luther argued.
- The Bible and Church tradition were equally powerful authorities for guiding Christian life.
- Indulgences were valid expressions of faith. (But the false selling of indulgences was banned.)

Another reforming pope, Paul IV, vigorously carried out the council's decrees. In 1559, he had officials draw up a list of books considered dangerous to the Catholic faith. This list was known as the Index of Forbidden Books. Catholic bishops throughout Europe were ordered to gather up the offensive books (including Protestant Bibles) and burn them in bonfires. In Venice alone, 10,000 books were burned in one day.

Legacy of the Reformation The Reformation had enduring effects. Protestant churches flourished, despite religious wars and persecutions. Because of the Reformation, religion no longer united Europe. As the Church's power declined, individual monarchs and states gained power. This paved the way for modern nation-states. In addition, the reformers' successful revolt against Church authority laid the groundwork for a rejection of Christian belief that occurred in Western culture in later centuries. Therefore, through its political and social effects, the Reformation helped to set the stage for the modern world.

Background
This Inquisition was called the Roman Inquisition. It generally was more moderate than the Spanish Inquisition described in Chapter 14.

Section 4 Assessment

1. TERMS & NAMES

Identify
- predestination
- Calvinism
- theocracy
- Presbyterian
- Anabaptist
- Catholic Reformation
- Jesuits
- Council of Trent

2. TAKING NOTES

Using a chart like the one below, compare the ideas of the reformers who came after Luther.

Reformers	Ideas
John Calvin	
Anabaptists	
Catholic Reformers	

3. EVALUATING DECISIONS

Which of the steps taken by Popes Paul III and Paul IV to reform the Catholic Church do you think were wise? Which were unwise? Explain.

THINK ABOUT
- the goals of the reforming popes
- whether the steps clearly addressed those goals
- possible effects of each step

4. THEME ACTIVITY

Religious and Ethical Systems In a group of three, hold a debate on whether Calvin was right to establish such a strict theocracy in Geneva. Debate such points as whether church leaders should be political rulers and whether government should try to control personal morality. One team member should support Calvin's policy, one should oppose it, and one should act as moderator.

436 Chapter 17

ANSWERS

1. TERMS AND NAMES
predestination, p. 433
Calvinism, p. 433
theocracy, p. 433
Presbyterian, p. 433
Anabaptist, p. 434
Catholic Reformation, p. 435
Jesuits, p. 435
Council of Trent, p. 436

2. TAKING NOTES
Possible Responses: John Calvin—People are sinful by nature; ideal government is a theocracy. Anabaptists—Only adults baptized; church and state separate. Catholic Reformers—Church interpretation of Bible is final; need faith and good works to be saved.

3. EVALUATING DECISIONS
Possible Responses: Wise—Calling the council of cardinals and the Council of Trent helped clarify the Catholic position on controversial issues; approving the Jesuits helped combat Protestantism and spread Catholicism. Unwise—Using the Inquisition may have made mar-

tyrs out of Protestants; creati the Index of Forbidden Books blocked the spread of new id

4. THEME ACTIVITY
Debates should present the id and actions of Calvin accurat explore the positive and nega impacts of Calvin's theocracy and contain well-reasoned arguments.

different PERSPECTIVES

The Reformation

Martin Luther's criticisms of the Catholic church grew sharper over time. Some Catholics, in turn, responded with personal attacks on Luther. In recent times, historians have focused less on the theological and personal issues connected with the Reformation. Instead, many modern scholars analyze political, social, and economic conditions that contributed to the Reformation.

LETTER
Martin Luther

 Although Luther began by criticizing the practice of selling indulgences, he soon began to attack the whole system of church government. In 1520, he sent the pope the following criticism of the Church leaders who served under him in Rome.

The Roman Church has become the most licentious [sinful] den of thieves. . . . They err who ascribe to thee the right of interpreting Scripture, for under cover of thy name they seek to set up their own wickedness in the Church, and, alas, through them Satan has already made much headway under thy predecessors. In short, believe none who exalt thee, believe those who humble thee.

ENGRAVING
Anonymous

In the early 1500s, an anonymous Catholic author published an engraving attacking Luther's "game of heresy." The following lines are part of a poem that appeared on the engraving.

I have in my simple way foreseen
What Luther's teaching promises
to bring:
Great rebellion and bloodletting,
Much hatred and strife.
The fear of God will vanish forever,
Together with the whole of Scripture,
And authority will everywhere
be despised.

HISTORIAN'S COMMENTARY
Steven Ozment

In 1992, historian Steven Ozment published *Protestants: The Birth of a Revolution*. Here he comments on some of the political aspects of the Reformation.

Beginning as a protest against arbitrary, self-aggrandizing, hierarchical authority in the person of the pope, the Reformation came to be closely identified in the minds of contemporaries with what we today might call states' rights or local control. To many townspeople and villagers, Luther seemed a godsend for their struggle to remain politically free and independent; they embraced his Reformation as a conserving political force, even though they knew it threatened to undo traditional religious beliefs and practices.

HISTORIAN'S COMMENTARY
G. R. Elton

In *Reformation Europe*, published in 1963, G. R. Elton notes the role of geography and trade in the spread of Reformation ideas.

Could the Reformation have spread so far and so fast if it had started anywhere but in Germany? At any rate, the fact that it had its beginnings in the middle of Europe made possible a very rapid radiation in all directions; the whole circle of countries surrounding the Empire came one after the other under its influence. Germany's position at the center of European trade also helped greatly. German merchants carried not only goods but Lutheran ideas and books to Venice and France; the north German Hanse [a trade league] transported the Reformation to the Scandinavian countries, parceled up with bales of cloth and cargoes of grain; trading links with Germany did much to encourage the growth of Lutheranism in the eastern lands.

Connect *to* History

Analyzing Causes How did politics and economics help spread the Reformation?

Comparing Compare Luther's attitude toward Church leaders with the Catholic attitudes toward him.

SEE SKILLBUILDER HANDBOOK, PAGES 995 and 996

Connect *to* Today

Comparing How do religious leaders spread their ideas today?

 CD-ROM For another perspective on the Reformation, see the World History: Electronic Library of Primary Sources.

European Renaissance and Reformation **437**

different **Perspectives**

Why the Reformation Matters Now

As students discuss these perspectives on the Reformation, have them make a list evaluating the impact of the Reformation on modern life. Ask students to organize their list in a chart with the following headings: *Political Life, Economic Life, Family Life, Towns and Villages, Religious Tolerance.*

MORE ABOUT . . .
Protestants versus Catholics

The attacks on Protestants by Catholics and Catholics by Protestants were harsh, abusive, and cruel. Even such respected leaders as Martin Luther and Thomas More wrote books that criticize and insult one another.

ELECTRONIC LIBRARY OF PRIMARY SOURCES
• "The St. Bartholomew's Day Massacre"
• "Luther: Giant of His Time and Ours"

MORE ABOUT . . .
Attacks on Luther

Henry VIII of England also had unkind words for Martin Luther: "What serpent so venomous as he who calls the pope's authority tyrannous?" Though Henry himself later rejected the pope's authority, he never changed his opinion of Luther.

Connect *to* History

Analyzing Causes
Possible Responses: Political motives helped spread the Reformation; many towns and villages turned Protestant in order to remain independent. Germany's strategic location at the center of European trade contributed to the spread of the Reformation. This economic advantage provided other benefits. Besides goods, German merchants carried Protestant ideas to Italy, France, Scandinavia and other places.

Comparing
Possible Responses: Luther and the anonymous Catholic writer accuse each other of wickedness, hurl insults, and attack each other's religious doctrines.

Connect *to* Today

Comparing
Possible Responses: Students might mention books, magazines, revivals, television, and the Internet. Students also might note that Christian missionaries still work in countries around the world.

Teacher's Edition **437**

Chapter 17 Assessment

TERMS & NAMES

1. Renaissance, p. 417
2. humanism, p. 418
3. secular, p. 418
4. printing press, p. 426
5. indulgence, p. 429
6. Reformation, p. 429
7. Protestant, p. 430
8. Peace of Augsburg, p. 430
9. Catholic Reformation, p. 435
10. Council of Trent, p. 436

REVIEW QUESTIONS

Answers will vary.

11. Merchants' belief in individual merit would become a recurring theme in the Renaissance; merchants also were patrons of the arts.

12. Artists chose secular and classical subjects (as well as Christian subjects), painted prominent individuals, glorified the human body, and used new artistic techniques and a more realistic style.

13. Northern European rulers purchased Renaissance paintings and hired Italian artists and architects to work on important projects.

14. Dürer's prints portray both religious and classical subjects. He painted realistic landscapes and a self-portrait.

15. Humanists set out to improve society by writing works that criticized society or described the perfect society.

16. On a church door Luther posted his *95 Theses* criticizing the selling of indulgences.

17. The Holy Roman Emperor wanted to force the Protestant German princes to rejoin the Catholic church.

18. In 1534, Henry VIII assumed control of the English Church with Parliament's approval. After Mary I tried to restore Catholicism, Elizabeth I persuaded Parliament to set up the Anglican church.

19. Calvin taught that humans were sinful by nature, that God chooses a very few people to save, that God has known since the beginning of time who those few were, and that theocracy was the best government.

20. Jesuits founded schools throughout Europe, converted non-Christians to Catholicism, and helped stop the spread of Protestantism.

TERMS & NAMES

Briefly explain the importance of each of the following to European history from 1300 to 1600.

1. Renaissance
2. humanism
3. secular
4. printing press
5. indulgence
6. Reformation
7. Protestant
8. Peace of Augsburg
9. Catholic Reformation
10. Council of Trent

Interact *with* History

On page 416, you looked at a painting and discussed what you learned about Renaissance society from that painting. Now choose one other piece of art from the chapter. Explain what you learn about Renaissance or Reformation society from that piece of art.

REVIEW QUESTIONS

SECTION 1 *(pages 417–422)*
Italy: Birthplace of the Renaissance

11. How did the merchant class in northern Italy influence the Renaissance?

12. How did art change during the Renaissance?

SECTION 2 *(pages 423–427)*
The Northern Renaissance

13. How did northern European rulers encourage the spread of Renaissance ideas?

14. How does Albrecht Dürer's work reflect Renaissance ideas?

15. What did Christian humanists set out to do, and what method did they use?

SECTION 3 *(pages 428–432)*
Luther Starts the Reformation

16. What act by Martin Luther set off the Reformation?

17. Why did the Holy Roman Emperor go to war against Protestant German princes?

18. How did England establish a state church apart from the Catholic Church?

SECTION 4 *(pages 433–436)*
The Reformation Continues

19. What were the main teachings of John Calvin?

20. What role did the Jesuits play in the Catholic Reformation?

Visual Summary

European Renaissance and Reformation

Effect in Renaissance	Social Change	Effect in Reformation
• Art celebrates individual and personal expression.	• Growing emphasis on individual	• Individuals interpret Bible for themselves.
• Merchants sponsor artists and pay to beautify city.	• Growing prosperity of merchants	• German merchants resent flow of money to Church in Rome.
• Rulers sponsor artists and philosophers.	• Decline of feudalism and growing power of princes and kings	• Rulers defy pope and become Protestant.
• Political, social, and artistic theories spread.	• Printing press and spread of learning	• Luther's 95 Theses spread; Bible printed in vernacular languages, so more people have access.

Interact *with* History

Possible Responses: Students may cite some of these features: more concern for human rather than spiritual matters; emphasis on ordinary people in everyday situations; pride in individuality and creativity; admiration for classical culture; interest in realism; enjoyment of wordly pleasures; uniqueness of each individual, including Biblical figures.

CRITICAL THINKING

1. POWER OF THE WRITTEN WORD

THEME REVOLUTION Beginning in the 1300s, Europeans overturned many of the structures and ideas of the Middle Ages. How did the printing press contribute to this revolution? Explain.

2. REFORMING THE REFORMER

Choose one of the Protestant groups who came after Luther, such as Calvinists or Anabaptists. Do you think they thought Luther went too far in reforming Catholic Church practices or not far enough? Explain your answer by citing differences in their beliefs.

3. RENAISSANCE AND REFORMATION TODAY

Go back through the chapter and take note of Renaissance and Reformation developments that still influence modern life. Record your findings on a chart like the one shown.

Legacy of the Renaissance and Reformation in Modern Life	
Artistic	Political
Religious	Social

4. ANALYZING PRIMARY SOURCES

In the following excerpt from *The Prince,* Niccolò Machiavelli discusses what a ruler should do to win a good reputation among his subjects. Read the paragraph and answer the questions below it.

A VOICE FROM THE PAST
A prince must also show himself a lover of merit [excellence], give preferment [promotion] to the able, and honour those who excel in every art. Moreover he must encourage his citizens to follow their callings [professions] quietly, whether in commerce, or agriculture, or any other trade that men follow. . . . [The prince] should offer rewards to whoever does these things, and to whoever seeks in any way to improve his city or state.

- How was Machiavelli's description of a prince's duties influenced by Renaissance values?

- Do you agree with Machiavelli that a prince should do these things? Explain the effect you think such behavior would have on the prince's subjects.

CHAPTER ACTIVITIES

1. LIVING HISTORY: Unit Portfolio Project

THEME CULTURAL INTERACTION Your unit portfolio project focuses on the spread of ideas among cultures (see page 387). For Chapter 17, you might use one of the following ideas to add to your portfolio.

- Design the cover and prepare the table of contents for a 15th-century magazine devoted to Europe's classical heritage. The table of contents should include article titles and a brief summary of each article.

- As Francis I, write a letter to Leonardo da Vinci asking him to retire in France. Explain why you want Italian artists to come to your country.

- With a partner, role-play the reunion of two art students in 1500. One has returned from Italy; the other studied in Flanders. They should compare their techniques and views about art. Audiotape the role-play.

2. CONNECT TO TODAY: Cooperative Learning

THEME RELIGIOUS AND ETHICAL SYSTEMS During the late 20th century, both Protestants and Catholics made delayed responses to the Reformation. In the 1960s, the Catholic Church held a council called Vatican II to promote additional reforms. In 1997, several U.S. Protestant denominations signed a document agreeing to form closer ties with one another.

Work with a team to create a poster that explains one of these developments and how it is a response to the Reformation.

INTERNET Use the Internet, news magazines, encyclopedias, or books to research the topic. Look for specific information about what was decided during Vatican II or in the Protestant agreement.

- In your group, decide what are the most important points about Vatican II or the Protestant agreement. Discuss how these points either carry on or undo the work of the Reformation.

- Display your information on a poster. You may convey the information in either a written or an illustrated form, as long as it is clear and accurate.

3. INTERPRETING A TIME LINE

Revisit the Unit Time Line on pages 386–387. On the Chapter 17 time line, identify important writers of the period. Did they write before or after the invention of the printing press?

FOCUS ON ART

Look carefully at this drawing of a machine from the notebooks of Leonardo da Vinci. Notice the blade that curves around the center shaft and the round mechanism at the bottom of the shaft.

- What might happen if the shaft started to turn?
- What do you think Leonardo was trying to invent when he drew this machine?
- What modern machine does this drawing remind you of?

Connect to History A ruler paid Leonardo for some of his ideas for machines. How might a ruler use a machine like the one shown here?

European Renaissance and Reformation **439**

CHAPTER ACTIVITIES

1. LIVING HISTORY: UNIT PORTFOLIO PROJECT

Standards for Evaluation
A magazine format should meet the following criteria:

- Uses an effective visual on the cover.
- Describes how classical ideas influenced European ideas in both article titles and summaries.

A letter should meet the following criteria:

- Is written in the voice of Francis I.
- Uses persuasive language to lure da Vinci to France.
- Explains Francis I's goals in inviting Renaissance artists to his court.

A role-play should meet the following criteria:

- Demonstrates knowledge of how to write dialogue.
- Reveals a knowledge of artistic trends in both Italy and northern Europe in 1500.

2. CONNECT TO TODAY: COOPERATIVE LEARNING

Standards for Evaluation
A poster should meet the following criteria:

- Explains or illustrates specific points of either Vatican II or the Protestant agreement of 1997.
- Shows either that Vatican II carries on the work of the Reformation or that the Protestant agreement seeks to undo some of the divisions dating from the Reformation.

3. INTERPRETING A TIME LINE

Possible Response: Boccaccio wrote before the printing press was invented; Shakespeare wrote after its invention.

FOCUS ON ART

Possible Answers: If the shaft turned, the blade would begin to revolve. This might have been an early flying machine or propeller. It looks a little like a helicopter. A ruler could use this machine to attack his enemies from the air during war or to spy on them.

CRITICAL THINKING

1. POWER OF THE WRITTEN WORD

Possible Responses: The availability of books helped spread Renaissance philosophical, political, and social beliefs. These publications undermined medieval values and society.

2. REFORMING THE REFORMER

Possible Responses: The Calvinist view of predestination more extreme than Luther's doctrine of grace. The Anabaptists' ideas about adult baptism, separation of church and state, and pacifism were also more radical.

3. RENAISSANCE AND REFORMATION TODAY

Possible Responses: Artistic—use of perspective, oil painting, and realism; literature in vernacular languages. Political—Machiavelli's views on governing; loss of Church power. Religious—Protestant denominations; Bible in vernacular languages; Jesuit schools. Social—individualism; secular values.

4. ANALYZING PRIMARY SOURCES

Possible Responses: Suggests that a prince should be a patron of the arts. Agree—Encourages hard work, and patriotism. Disagree—interfering in people's private lives.

	Key Ideas	**COPY MASTERS**	**ASSESSMENT**
SECTION 1 The Ottomans Build a Vast Empire pp. 443–447	Turkish religious warriors along the Byzantine frontier capture Constantinople and build an enduring empire. Their realm combines elements from many cultures and religions and eventually stretches from the Balkans to North Africa and Persia.	**In-Depth Resources: Unit 4** • **Guided Reading,** p. 35 • **Skillbuilder Practice:** Following Chronological Order, p. 38 • **Primary Source:** Suleiman the Magnificent, p. 41 • **Literature:** from The Bride of Suleiman, p. 45 • **History Makers:** Suleiman, p. 48	**Section 1 Assessment,** p. 447 **Formal Assessment** • Section Quiz, p. 205 **Alternative Assessment Book** • Standards for Evaluating a Cooperative Activity
SECTION 2 Patterns of Change: Cultural Blending pp. 448–450	Interactions among diverse people in the Islamic world give rise to a new cultural mix. The Safavids draw on Shi'i religious ideology, ancient Persian traditions, and Ottoman political ideas to forge a new Persian culture.	**In-Depth Resources: Unit 4** • **Guided Reading,** p. 36	**Section 2 Assessment,** p. 450 **Formal Assessment** • Section Quiz, p. 206 **Alternative Assessment Book** • Standards for Evaluating a Cooperative Activity
SECTION 3 The Mughals Establish an Empire in India pp. 451–457	The Mughals, Sunni Muslim Turks from Central Asia, conquer India and bring together Turks, Persians, and Indians in a vast empire.	**In-Depth Resources: Unit 4** • **Guided Reading,** p. 37 • **Geography Application:** Europe Discovers the Riches of India, p. 39 • **Primary Sources:** Akbar, p. 43; Jahangir's Birthday, p. 44 • **History Makers:** Shah Jahan, p. 49 • **Connections Across Time and Cultures:** How To Treat the Conquered, p. 50	**Section 3 Assessment,** p. 457 **Formal Assessment** • Section Quiz, p. 207 **Alternative Assessment Book** • Standards for Evaluating a Cooperative Activity
CHAPTER RESOURCES	**Chapter Overview** Between the 14th and the 16th centuries, three powerful Islamic empires emerge between India and the Balkans. The Ottomans of Turkey, the Safavids of Persia, and the Mughals of India successfully deal with ethnic, cultural, and religious diversity, but eventually fall prey to internal corruption and external pressure.	**Telescoping the Times** • Chapter Summary, pp. 69–71 **Planning for Block Schedules**	**Chapter Assessment,** pp. 458–459 **Chapter Activities,** p. 459 **Formal Assessment** • Chapter Test, forms A and B, pp. 208–213 **Test Generator** **Alternative Assessment Book**

1300–1700

TECHNOLOGY

 Warm-Up Transparency 18

 Geography Transparencies
- GT18 The Fall of Constantinople, 1453

 World Art and Cultures Transparencies
- AT39 Ottoman miniature painting

 Electronic Library of Primary Sources
"Descriptions of the Turks and the Christians"
"The Fall of Constantinople"

INTERNET RESOURCES
www.mlworldhistory.com

 Warm-Up Transparency 18

 Electronic Library of Primary Resources
"Report on Persia, Persians, and 'Abbas I"

INTERNET RESOURCES
www.mlworldhistory.com

 Warm-Up Transparency 18

 Critical Thinking Transparencies
- CT18 Muslim Empires in Anatolia and India
- CT54 Chapter 18 Visual Summary

 World Art and Cultures Transparencies
- AT22 Great Mosque of Córdova
- AT30 Notre Dame Cathedral
- AT40 Mughal miniature painting

INTERNET RESOURCES
www.mlworldhistory.com

 Chapter Summaries on Audiocassette in English and Spanish

INTERNET RESOURCES
www.mlworldhistory.com

Block Scheduling (90 MINUTES)

Day 1
Section 1, pp. 443–447

 COOPERATIVE ACTIVITY
Reporting on the Fall of Constantinople,
p. 444 (Teacher's Edition)

Day 2
Section 3, pp. 451–457

 COOPERATIVE ACTIVITY
Debating the Decline of the Mughal Empire,
p. 455 (Teacher's Edition)

Section 2, pp. 448–450

 COOPERATIVE ACTIVITY
Writing Historical Dialogues, p. 449
(Teacher's Edition)

Section Assessments,
pp. 447, 450

Section Assessment,
p. 457

Chapter Assessment,
pp. 458–459

Yearly Pacing *Chapter 18 Total:* 2 days   *Yearly Total:* 85 days

 Planning for Block Schedules

Customizing for Special Needs

Students Acquiring English

 Access for Students Acquiring English
- **Guided Reading** for Sections 1–3 (Spanish), pp. 180–182
- **Chapter Summary** (Spanish), pp. 177–179
- **Skillbuilder Practice:** Following Chronological Order (Spanish), p. 183
- **Geography Application:** Europe Discovers the Riches of India (Spanish), p. 184

 Chapter Summaries on Audiocassette in English and Spanish

INTERNET RESOURCES
www.mlworldhistory.com
The Diverse Classroom.

Less Proficient Readers

 In-Depth Resources: Unit 4
- **Guided Reading** for Sections 1–3, pp. 35–37
- **Skillbuilder Practice** Following Chronological Order, p. 38

 Telescoping the Times
- Chapter Summary, pp. 69–71

 Chapter Summaries on Audiocassette

Gifted and Talented Students

 In-Depth Resources: Unit 4

Primary Sources
- Suleiman the Magnificent, p. 41
- Akbar, p. 43
- Jahangir's Birthday, p. 44

History Makers
- Suleiman, p. 48
- Shah Jahan, p. 49

Connections to Literature READINGS FOR STUDENTS

 In-Depth Resources: Unit 4
Literature: from *The Bride of Suleiman*, p. 45

Enrichment Reading

 Beck, Brenda
Folktales of India
Chicago: U of Chicago P, 1987
Colorful stories of origins, families, and difficult choices.

Bon, Ottaviano
The Sultan's Seraglio
London: Sagi, 1966
An intimate portrait of life in the Ottoman Court in Istanbul from 1604–1607.

 = Pupil's Edition   = Overhead Transparency   = Software   = Video

= Copy Master   = CD-ROM   = Audiocassette   = Internet

439B

The Muslim World Expands, 1300–1700

Accessing Prior Knowledge

• Ask students to read the captions accompanying each picture and to discuss what they already know about the people, the cultures, and the situations.

Predicting and Making Inferences

• After students look at Shah Jahan's picture and read about him, ask them to predict how his habits may have contributed to the fall of the Mughal Empire.

• Ask students what they can infer about the Ottomans from the painting of the attack on Constantinople.

Geography Connection

Ask students to note the borders of the three Islamic empires shown on the map.

• What geographic feature might have prevented the Mughal Empire from expanding farther east?

• What geographic features gave each empire access to trade routes?

CHAPTER
18

The Muslim World Expands, 1300–1700

PREVIEWING THEMES

Cultural Interaction
As powerful societies moved to expand their empires, Turkish, Mongol, Persian, and Arab ways of life came face to face. The result was a flowering of Islamic culture, which peaked in the 16th century.

Empire Building
Many conquerors emerged in the Muslim world between the 12th and 16th centuries. From their conquests arose three of the great empires of history—the Ottomans in Turkey, the Safavids in Iran, and the Mughals in India.

Power and Authority
The rulers of all three great Muslim empires of this era based their authority on the Islamic religion. Advanced technology and effective artillery supported this authority on the battlefield.

INTERNET CONNECTION

Visit us at **www.mlworldhistory.com** to learn more about the Ottoman, the Safavid, and the Mughal empires.

EMPIRE BUILDERS, 1700

Danube River

EUROPE

Dnepr River

Black Sea

Adrianople •

• Constantinople (Istanbul)

Algiers •

• Tunis

Mediterranean Sea

Damascus

• Cairo

Nile River

AFR

Constantinople was one of the most influential cities of the 15th-century world and seemed invulnerable. Its legend lasted far into the next century when Italian Jacopo Palma Giovane recreated the clamor and chaos of its fall to the **Ottomans** in his painting *The First Attack on Constantinople by the Turks in 1453*. This 51-day Ottoman siege by 125 ships, 100,000 men, and cannons that launched half-ton boulders turned the city into a Muslim outpost.

440

GEOGRAPHY THEMES

Location

Have students note where each of the three empires covered in this chapter is located in relation to the others and to Europe, Asia, and Africa. Which empire had the most direct access to Europe? *Ottoman.* Which empire had the most direct access to Africa? *Ottoman.*

Which empire was most hemmed in by its neighbors? *Safavid.* Have them discuss how location may have affected the policies of each of the individual empires. How might geographical location have influenced the interactions among the three empires?

Region

Remind students that a region is an area that can be considered a unit because it exhibits common geographic, social, or political features. Despite the fact that this area was divided among three distinct empires at the beginning of the 18th century, it also

had general regional characteristics. Have students examine the map, the Previewing Themes box, and the captions, and suggest features that might make these three empires a region. *Religion, similar geography, lack of natural barriers.*

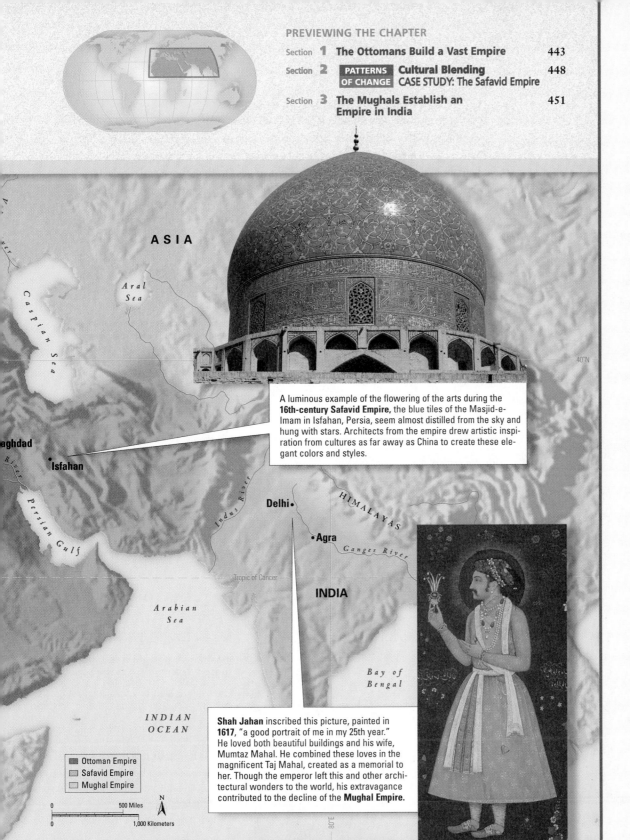

ASIA

*Aral
Sea*

Caspian Sea

aghdad

•Isfahan

Persian Gulf

Delhi•

HIMALAYAS

•Agra

Indus River

Ganges River

Tropic of Cancer

INDIA

*Arabian
Sea*

*Bay of
Bengal*

**INDIAN
OCEAN**

■ Ottoman Empire
□ Safavid Empire
□ Mughal Empire

N

0   500 Miles
0   1,000 Kilometers

A luminous example of the flowering of the arts during the **16th-century Safavid Empire,** the blue tiles of the Masjid-e-Imam in Isfahan, Persia, seem almost distilled from the sky and hung with stars. Architects from the empire drew artistic inspiration from cultures as far away as China to create these elegant colors and styles.

Shah Jahan inscribed this picture, painted in **1617,** "a good portrait of me in my 25th year." He loved both beautiful buildings and his wife, Mumtaz Mahal. He combined these loves in the magnificent Taj Mahal, created as a memorial to her. Though the emperor left this and other architectural wonders to the world, his extravagance contributed to the decline of the **Mughal Empire.**

ADDITIONAL RESOURCES

Books for the Teacher

• Mansel, Philip. *Constantinople: City of the World's Desire, 1453-1924.* New York: St. Martin's, 1996.

• Wheatcroft, Andrew. *The Ottomans.* New York: Viking Penguin, 1994. Government, politics, and social customs in the Ottoman Empire.

• Richards, J. F. *The Mughal Empire.* New York: Cambridge UP, 1993. Political and economic history under the Mughals.

Books for the Student

• Irving, Clive. *Crossroads of Civilization: 3,000 Years of Persian History.* New York: Barnes & Noble, 1980. Dramatic history of Persia, 559 B.C.–A.D. 1941.

• Wigner, Annabel. *Elizabeth and Akbar: Portraits of Power.* New York: Dufour, 1987.

▬▬ Videos

• *Ancient and Modern: The Fall and Rise of the Middle East.* Britannica, 1984. 800-554-9862. Probes the factors that retarded Ottoman growth.

• *The Ottoman Empire: 1280-1683.* Social Studies School Service, 1985. 800-421- 4246. Profiles the Ottoman sultans and depicts their vast empire.

• *Suleyman the Magnificent.* Lucerne Media, 1990. 800-341-2293. Dramatizes the achievements of the Ottoman sultan.

HISTORY THROUGH ART

The First Attack on Constantinople by the Turks in 1453

Jacopo Palma Giovane

Jacopo Palma Giovane (1544–1628) was a leading artist in Venice in the early 17th century. He was an assistant to the renowned Renaissance painter Titian and completed that artist's Pietá, one of the greatest works of Italian art, after Titian's death.

Palma Giovane was known primarily for his depiction of historical subjects. In this portrayal of the siege of Constantinople by Turkish Muslims under the Ottoman ruler Mehmet II, he captures all the emotion and drama of the five-week conflict. The overall darkness of the painting conveys the confusion and desperation of a battle fought through a long night. The flaming reds of the Turks' tunics and weapons and the face of the soldier in the foreground seem to

be illuminated by the imminent Turkish victory.

Interpreting the Art Do you think this painting offers a realistic or an idealized view of the siege of Constantinople? What details or overall characteristics of the painting make you think so?

Interact *with* History

This Interact with History feature motivates students by inviting them to put themselves in the position of a 15th-century Ottoman sultan. Students will analyze the issues the conquerors of people with diverse customs faced, explore various options for dealing with the conquered people, and become decision makers.

Purpose

- to help students understand some of the issues that faced empire builders
- to provide an introduction to the concept of cultural blending
- to set the stage for the study of the growth of three Muslim empires

Teaching Strategy

Thinking Critically After students have imagined themselves in the situation described on this page, have them answer the key question and give reasons for their decisions.

EXAMINING *the* ISSUES

Following are suggestions for addressing each bulleted question.

1 Have students consider what it might feel like to be taken captive and forced to adopt a different way of life. How might they resist or show their dissatisfaction?

2 Have students think about how the United States has tried to integrate its own conquered people—Native Americans—into the society. How successful have these efforts been?

3 Ask students to brainstorm ways in which people of many customs and religions in the United States have learned to coexist. What similar strategies might the Ottomans have developed?

Making Connections Ask students to discuss the responsibilities of a conqueror to the people he conquers.

Interact *with* History

You are a 15th-century Ottoman sultan, the ruler of a growing empire. To increase your power and control over the area, you go to war against your neighbors. With a well-trained army and modern weapons, you conquer most of them easily. They do not share your religion and way of life, however, and if you allow them too much freedom, they might rebel. On the other hand, enslaving them and keeping them under strict control might sap your empire's resources.

How will you treat the people you conquer?

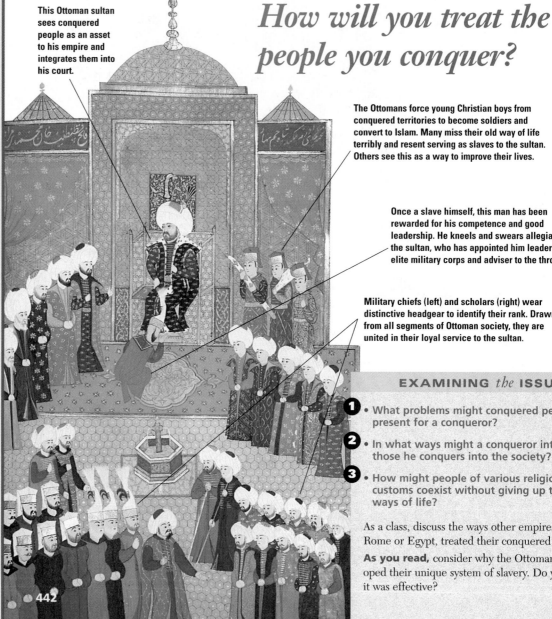

This Ottoman sultan sees conquered people as an asset to his empire and integrates them into his court.

The Ottomans force young Christian boys from conquered territories to become soldiers and convert to Islam. Many miss their old way of life terribly and resent serving as slaves to the sultan. Others see this as a way to improve their lives.

Once a slave himself, this man has been rewarded for his competence and good leadership. He kneels and swears allegiance to the sultan, who has appointed him leader of the elite military corps and adviser to the throne.

Military chiefs (left) and scholars (right) wear distinctive headgear to identify their rank. Drawn from all segments of Ottoman society, they are united in their loyal service to the sultan.

442

EXAMINING *the* ISSUES

1 • What problems might conquered people present for a conqueror?

2 • In what ways might a conqueror integrate those he conquers into the society?

3 • How might people of various religions and customs coexist without giving up their ways of life?

As a class, discuss the ways other empires, such as Rome or Egypt, treated their conquered peoples.

As you read, consider why the Ottomans developed their unique system of slavery. Do you think it was effective?

Follow Up

A feature on the chapter assessment will ask students to reevaluate their responses to the situation presented on this page.

The Ottomans Build a Vast Empire

TERMS & NAMES
- ghazi
- Osman
- Timur the Lame
- Mehmet II
- Suleiman the Lawgiver
- janissary
- *devshirme*

MAIN IDEA

The Ottomans established a Muslim empire that combined many cultures and lasted for more than 600 years.

WHY IT MATTERS NOW

Many modern societies—from Algeria to the Balkan countries—had their origins under Ottoman rule.

SETTING THE STAGE In 1300, the Byzantine Empire had begun to shrink, and the Mongols had destroyed the Turkish Seljuk sultanate, or kingdom, of Rum. Anatolia was inhabited mostly by the descendants of nomadic Turks. They were a militaristic people who had a long history of invading other countries. They were loyal to their own groups and were not united by a strong central power.

Turks Settle in Christian Byzantium

Many Anatolian Turks saw themselves as **ghazis** (GAH·zees), or warriors for Islam. The ghazis were similar to the Christian knights in Europe during the Middle Ages. However, they formed military societies under the leadership of an emir and followed a strict Islamic code of conduct. They raided the territories of the "infidels," or people who didn't believe in Islam. These "infidels" lived on the frontiers of the Byzantine Empire.

Vocabulary
emir: a prince or chief (derived from the Arabic *'amir,* meaning "commander").

Osman Establishes a State The most successful ghazi was **Osman.** People in the West called him Othman, however, and named his followers Ottomans. Osman built a small state in Anatolia between 1300 and 1326. His successors expanded it by buying land, forming alliances with other emirs, and conquering everyone they could.

The Ottomans' military success was largely based on the use of gunpowder. They replaced their archers on horseback with musket-carrying foot soldiers. They also were among the first people to use cannons as offensive weapons. Even heavily walled cities fell to an all-out attack by the Turks.

The second Ottoman leader, Orkhan I, felt strong enough to declare himself sultan, meaning "overlord" or "one with power." And in 1361, the Ottomans captured Adrianople (ay·dree·uh·NOH·puhl), the second most important city in the Byzantine Empire. A new Turkish Empire was on the rise.

The Ottomans acted kindly toward the people they conquered, however. They ruled through local officials appointed by the sultan and often improved the lives of the peasants. Most Muslims were required to serve in Turkish armies but did not have to pay a personal tax to the state. Non-Muslims did not have to serve in the army but had to pay the tax.

Timur the Lame Rebels Most of the conquered peoples seem to have adjusted to this somewhat lenient rule. The rise of the Ottoman Empire was briefly interrupted in the early 1400s, though, by a rebellious warrior and conqueror from Samarkand in central Asia. He was called Timur-i-Lang, or **Timur the Lame,** in his homeland. Europeans called him Tamerlane. Timur claimed to be descended

HISTORY MAKERS

Osman
1258–1326?

Osman I was just one of many ghazi princes who operated along the Byzantine frontier until 1301. At that time he gained sudden fame by defeating a 2,000-man Byzantine army with a much smaller force. This victory drew people eager for adventure, and enabled Osman to undertake larger conquests.

Osman's greatest success came in the last year of his life. That year his forces conquered the city of Bursa in northwest Turkey. Osman himself was too old and weak to lead the battle. Therefore, his son, Orkhan, commanded the troops. When Osman died, he probably had no idea that this conquest marked the birth of one of history's largest and longest-lived empires.

SECTION 1 RESOURCES

PRINT RESOURCES
IN-DEPTH RESOURCES: UNIT 4
Guided Reading, p. 35
Skillbuilder Practice: Following Chronological Order, p. 38
Primary Source: Suleiman the Magnificent, p. 41
Literature: from *The Bride of Suleiman,* p. 45
History Makers: Suleiman, p. 48

ACCESS FOR STUDENTS ACQUIRING ENGLISH
Guided Reading (Spanish), p. 180
Skillbuilder Practice, (Spanish), p. 183

FORMAL ASSESSMENT
Section Quiz, p. 205

TECHNOLOGY RESOURCES
GEOGRAPHY TRANSPARENCIES
GT18 The Fall of Constantinople, 1453

WORLD ART AND CULTURES TRANSPARENCIES
AT39 Ottoman miniature painting

CD-ROM
Electronic Library of Primary Sources

INTERNET www.mlworldhistory.com

Section 1 Overview

OBJECTIVES

1. To describe the origins of the Ottoman Empire.

2. To trace the expansion of Ottoman power under Mehmet II and Selim the Grim.

3. To identify the cultural and political achievements of Suleiman the Lawgiver.

4. To summarize the causes of the slow decline of the Ottoman Empire.

SKILLBUILDERS
- Interpreting maps: region, movement, p. 445
- Interpreting charts, p. 446

CRITICAL THINKING
- Recognizing effects, p. 444
- Analyzing motives, p. 444
- Making inferences, p. 446
- Summarizing, p. 447
- Evaluating decisions, p. 447
- Analyzing themes, p. 447

FOCUS
5-Minute Warm-Up

Interpreting Maps
To help students gain an appreciation of the extent of the Ottoman Empire, have them answer the following questions.

1. Look at the map on p. 445. What continents did the Ottoman Empire include?

2. What bodies of water might have facilitated the expansion of the empire?

WARM-UP TRANSPARENCY 18

OBJECTIVE 1 INSTRUCT

Turks Settle in Christian Byzantium

Key Ideas
- Bands of Muslim warriors called ghazis carve out a state in Byzantine Anatolia.
- Timur the Lame crushes the Ottomans and slows the growth of the empire.

IN-DEPTH RESOURCES: UNIT 4
Guided Reading, p. 35

ACCESS FOR STUDENTS ACQUIRING ENGLISH
Guided Reading (Spanish), p. 180

Osman and his followers adopted the white cap of the ghazis and wore it to set themselves apart from ordinary people. This head-gear was later incorporated into the outfits of the Ottoman janissary corps. Why do you think the Ottomans retained this symbol of their ghazi roots?

OBJECTIVE **2** INSTRUCT

Powerful Sultans Spur Dramatic Expansion

▶ **Key Ideas**
- Led by Mehmet II, the Ottomans take Constantinople and end the Byzantine Empire.
- Selim the Grim expands the Ottoman Empire into North Africa.

 ELECTRONIC LIBRARY OF PRIMARY SOURCES
"Descriptions of the Turks and the Christians"

CRITICAL THINKING ACTIVITY
CLASS TIME: 10 MINUTES

Hypothesizing
Ask students to consider whether the Ottomans would have been able to build an empire if they had not taken Constantinople. Students might list reasons for both possible answers in a two-column chart before deciding.

Could Build an Empire	Could Not Build an Empire

---

from the Mongol conqueror, Genghis Khan. Although historians doubt the truth of this claim, Timur was certainly as ferocious as Genghis Khan. He was also physically impressive. Tall and with a large head, he had a dark, rosy complexion. This was set off by white hair, which he had had since he was a child.

Timur conquered both Russia and Persia. He also burned the powerful city of Baghdad in present-day Iraq to the ground. In 1398, he swept through northern India, leaving destruction and decaying corpses in his wake. He butchered the inhabitants of Delhi and made a pyramid of their skulls. Moving back west into Anatolia, he crushed the Ottoman forces at the Battle of Ankara in 1402. This defeat halted the expansion of their empire. Timur then took their sultan back to Samarkand in an iron cage. The sultan died in captivity. Timur himself died three years later on his way to conquer China. His body was returned to Samarkand, where he was buried in a magnificent tomb. That tomb remains a glorious sight today.

Timur the Lame's steely strength blazes from his eyes in this painting by an unknown 14th-century Italian artist.

Powerful Sultans Spur Dramatic Expansion

As soon as Timur moved out of Anatolia on the way to China, war broke out among the four sons of the Ottoman sultan. Mehmet I defeated his brothers and took the throne. His son, Murad II, restored the Ottoman military to its former power. Murad defeated the Venetians, invaded Hungary, and overcame an army of Italian crusaders in the Balkans. He was the first of four powerful sultans who kept the Ottoman Empire expanding through 1566.

Mehmet II Conquers Constantinople Murad's son **Mehmet II,** or Mehmet the Conqueror, achieved the most dramatic feat in Ottoman history. By the time Mehmet took power in 1451, the ancient city of Constantinople had shrunk from a population of a million to a mere 50,000. Although it controlled no territory outside its walls, it still dominated the Bosporus Strait. Controlling this waterway meant that it could choke off traffic between the Ottomans' territories in Asia and in the Balkans.

Mehmet II decided to face this situation head-on. "Give me Constantinople!" he thundered, shortly after taking power at age 21. He spent two years building a force of 125 ships and 100,000 foot soldiers. Then, in April 1453, he launched his attack. The Byzantine emperor in Constantinople sent desperate appeals to the Christian West, but only 700 volunteers from Italy responded.

Mehmet's forces began firing on the city walls with mighty cannons. One of these was a 26-foot gun that fired 1,200-pound boulders. Constantinople's 7,000 defenders could barely man all the walls. A chain across the Golden Horn between the Bosporus Strait and the Sea of Marmara kept the Turkish fleet out of the city's harbor. But beginning on the night of April 21, Mehmet's army advanced. They dragged 70 ships over a hill on greased runners from the Bosporus to the harbor. Constantinople was thus under attack from two sides. The city held out for five weeks, but the Turks finally found a break in the wall and gained entry to the city. The Muslim historian Oruc reported:

> **A VOICE FROM THE PAST**
> The ghazis, entering by force on every side, found a way in through the breaches in the fortress made by the guns. . . . Mounting on the tower they destroyed the infidels who were inside and entered the city. They looted and plundered. They seized their money and possessions and made their sons and daughters slaves. . . . They plundered for three days, and after three days plunder was forbidden.
>
> **ORUC,** quoted in *The Muslim Discovery of Europe*

THINK THROUGH HISTORY
A. Recognizing Effects What were Timur the Lame's accomplishments?
A. Answer He brought Russia, Persia, and India under his control and stopped the expansion of the Ottoman Empire.

THINK THROUGH HISTORY
B. Analyzing Motives Why was taking Constantinople so important to Mehmet II?
B. Answer It controlled many waterways that kept the Ottoman Empire divided.

Background
Conquerors did not usually limit the plundering of the cities they captured. Mehmet stopped the sacking of Constantinople after three days to protect the treasures he had won.

TEACHING OPTION | BLOCK SCHEDULING | **COOPERATIVE ACTIVITY: Reporting on the Fall of Constantinople** | CLASS TIME 30 MINUTES

Task: Students will prepare a newscast documenting the fall of Constantinople.

Purpose: To experience the drama and significance of this historical event.

Activity: Working as a class, students will plan and present a multifaceted newscast, including segments such as a summary of the week's events, reports of up-to-the-minute developments, debates between Turkish and Byzantine officials, human-interest stories, on-the-scene interviews, and editorial commentaries.

Small groups of students should each choose a segment of the newscast to work on. One group should take responsibility for organizing the individual segments into a finished newscast.

 ALTERNATIVE ASSESSMENT BOOK
Standards for Evaluating a Cooperative Activity

 GEOGRAPHY TRANSPARENCIES:
GT18 The Fall of Constantinople, 1453

 ELECTRONIC LIBRARY OF PRIMARY SOURCES
"The Fall of Constantinople"

Mehmet then proceeded to the Hagia Sophia on the Bosporus. This was the most important church in the Eastern Christian world. Reportedly, he found a soldier hacking at the marble floors. The church now belonged to the Muslim sultan. Therefore, Mehmet insisted that it be treated with respect. He had the soldier put to death. He then declared the Hagia Sophia a mosque. Muslim prayers were held there the first Friday the Ottomans occupied the city.

Mehmet the Conqueror, as he was now called, proved to be an able ruler as well as a magnificent warrior. He opened Constantinople to new citizens of many religions and backgrounds. Jews, Christians, and Muslims, Turks and non-Turks all flowed in. They helped rebuild the city that was now called Istanbul.

Background
Between the reigns of Mehmet II and Selim the Grim, Bayazid II oversaw the internal development and economic growth of the Ottoman Empire.

Selim the Grim Takes Islam's Holy Cities The next important sultan came to power in 1512. He did so by overthrowing his father and murdering his brothers. To protect his position, he also executed his nephews and all but one of his sons. It is small wonder that he is known as Selim the Grim. For all his brutality, Selim was an effective sultan and a great general. In 1514, he defeated the Safavids (suh·FAH·vihdz) of Persia at the Battle of Chaldiran. Then he swept south through Syria and Palestine and into North Africa. At the same time that Cortez was toppling the Aztec Empire in the Americas, Selim captured Mecca and Medina, the holiest cities of Islam. Finally he took Cairo, the intellectual center of the Muslim world. This conquest ended the Egyptian Mameluke Dynasty. The once-great civilization of Egypt had become just another province in the growing Ottoman Empire.

Suleiman the Lawgiver

Mehmet the Conqueror and Selim the Grim had achieved impressive military successes. However, the Ottoman Empire didn't reach its peak size and grandeur until the reign of Selim's son, Suleiman I (SOO·lay·mahn). Suleiman came to the throne in

Ottoman Empire, 1451–1566

Legend:
- Ottoman Empire, 1451
- Acquisitions to 1481
- Acquisitions to 1521
- Acquisitions to 1566
- ★ Battles

AUSTRIA · Vienna 1529 · HUNGARY · Mohács 1526 · Belgrade · Danube R. · CRIMEA · Black Sea · CAUCASUS · Caspian Sea · ITALY · Rome · Adriatic Sea · BALKANS · GOLDEN HORN · Bosporus · Istanbul (Constantinople) · Chaldiran 1514 · Madrid · SPAIN · Naples · Taranto · GREECE · Lepanto 1571 · Athens · Tehran · Algiers · Tunis · Palermo · ALGERIA · TUNISIA · Mediterranean Sea · Crete · Cyprus · SYRIA · Damascus · PERSIA · Baghdad · AFRICA · PALESTINE · Jerusalem · MESOPOTAMIA · Tripoli · TRIPOLI · Cairo · EGYPT · ARABIA · SAHARA DESERT · Nile R. · Red Sea · Persian Gulf · Medina · Tropic of Cancer

0 500 Miles
0 1,000 Kilometers

GEOGRAPHY SKILLBUILDER: Interpreting Maps
1. **Region** By what year did the Ottoman Empire reach its farthest westward extent?
2. **Movement** What landforms might have prevented the Ottomans from expanding farther east?

445

MORE ABOUT . . .
Selim the Grim

Like many tyrants of his age, Selim was fond of literature and the arts and wrote poetry in three languages. But his troops knew him as *Yafuz*—"the Inflexible." He went through subordinate officers called viziers at such a clip that the phrase, "May you become the Sultan's vizier" came to be understood as a curse.

OBJECTIVE ③ INSTRUCT

Suleiman the Lawgiver

Key Ideas
- Suleiman's conquests expand the empire to its greatest size.
- An efficient social structure incorporates Christian slaves in a policy known as *devshirme*.
- Ottoman achievements under Suleiman include liberal laws and architectural masterpieces.

History from Visuals

Ottoman Empire, 1451–1566

Interpreting the Map Point out that the box at the upper left explains the colors that show the size of the Ottoman Empire during a particular period of time. Which color shows the conquests of Selim the Grim (1512–1520)? *Orange.*

Extension Activity Have students turn to the map on pages 266–267 and compare the size of the Byzantine Empire in 565 with that of the Ottoman Empire in 1566. Why were the territories included in these empires so similar? Possible Answer: *Both empires were centered at Constantinople and faced similar geographic and political barriers.*

SKILLBUILDER Answers
1. 1521
2. Caucasus Mountains

TEACHING OPTION · **BLOCK SCHEDULING** · **SKILLBUILDER MINI-LESSON: Following Chronological Order** · **CLASS TIME 15 MINUTES**

Explaining the Skill Understanding the relationships between events—causes and effects, problems and solutions—depends on knowing how the events relate in time. Using dates provided in the text and clue words about time, such as *Then he swept south . . .* and *At the same time that Cortez . . .* found on this page, students can place events they read about in correct chronological order.

Applying the Skill Ask students to make a time line of events in the development of the Ottoman Empire from Osman's capture of Bursa through Selim the Grim's defeat of the Safavids at the Battle of Chaldiran.

1326
Osman captures Bursa

1514
Selim defeats Safavids at Chaldiran

IN-DEPTH RESOURCES: UNIT 4
Skillbuilder Practice: Following Chronological Order, p. 38

1520 and ruled for 46 years. His own people called him **Suleiman the Lawgiver.** He was known in the West, though, as Suleiman the Magnificent. This title was a tribute to the splendor of his court and to his cultural achievements.

The Empire Reaches Its Limits Suleiman was above all a military leader. He conquered the important city of Belgrade in 1521. The next year, Turkish forces captured the island of Rhodes in the Mediterranean. With that conquest, the Ottomans dominated the whole eastern Mediterranean.

Applying their immense naval power, the Ottomans captured Tripoli. They then continued conquering peoples along the North African coastline. Finally, they reached the Moroccan border. Although the Ottomans occupied only the coastal cities of Africa, they managed to control trade routes to the interior of the continent.

In 1525, Suleiman advanced into Hungary and Austria, throwing central Europe into a panic. Suleiman's armies then pushed to the outskirts of Vienna, Austria. But there the Ottoman expansion ended. When the 1529 siege of Vienna failed, Suleiman devoted himself to domestic affairs for two years. He then moved his forces east to deal with border uprisings with Safavid Persia. Reigning from Istanbul, Suleiman had waged war with central Europeans, North Africans, and central Asians. He had become the most powerful monarch on earth. Only Charles V, head of the Hapsburg Empire in Europe, came close to rivaling his power.

Highly Structured Social Organization Suleiman's massive Ottoman Empire required an efficient government structure and social organization. The empire was a complex military state. The Ottoman family—a dynasty that ruled for 600 years—held the power. Surrounding the family was the palace bureaucracy. It was staffed by the sultan's 20,000 personal slaves.

Among the sultan's slaves were the **janissaries.** This elite force of 30,000 was drawn from the peoples of conquered Christian territories as part of a policy called **devshirme** (dehv·SHEER·meh). Under the *devshirme* system, the sultan's army took boys from their families, educated them, converted them to Islam, and trained them as soldiers. Their superb discipline made them the heart of the Ottoman war machine. In fact, Christian families sometimes bribed officials to take their children into the janissary corps, because the brightest ones could rise to high government posts. The Ottomans also took non-Muslim girls from their families to become slaves to the wealthy.

In accordance with Islamic law, the Ottomans granted freedom of worship to other religious communities—particularly to Christians and Jews. They treated these communities as *millets*, or nations. They allowed each to follow its own religious laws and

Suleiman the Lawgiver's magnificent turban marked him as an influential man. But it was his outstanding contributions to Ottoman territory and culture that made his mark in history.

THINK THROUGH HISTORY
C. Making Inferences What were the advantages and disadvantages of the *devshirme* system to the recruited slaves?
C. Possible Answers Advantages—Education; chance to rise to high positions. Disadvantages—Loss of freedom, forced to adopt new religion, language, and lifestyle and to become soldiers.

Organization of Ottoman Government

Sultan
Supreme military and political ruler

Imperial Council (Divan)
Advisers drawn from *devshirme*

Social / Military Administration
Local administrators/military
Landowners/tax collectors

Religious / Judicial Administration
Heads of individual religious *millets*
Muslim   Jewish   Christian

SKILLBUILDER: Interpreting Charts
1. *What was the relationship between the heads of the religious* millets *and the military leaders?*
2. *How does this organization show the incorporation of conquered peoples?*

practices. The head of the *millets* reported to the sultan and his staff. This patchwork system kept conflict among people of the various religions to a minimum. But it may have sowed the seeds of modern ethnic conflicts in the area.

Cultural Achievements Binding the Ottoman Empire together in a workable social structure was surely Suleiman's crowning achievement. Suleiman was required to follow Islamic law, which covered most social matters. He did, however, simplify the system of taxation and reduce the government bureaucracy. These two changes bettered the daily life of almost every citizen. These reforms helped earn him the title of Lawgiver.

Suleiman had broad interests, which contributed to the cultural achievements of the empire. Even amid his many military campaigns, he found time to study poetry, history, geography, astronomy, mathematics, and architecture. He employed one of the world's finest architects, Sinan, who was probably from Albania. Sinan's masterpiece, the Mosque of Suleiman, is an immense complex topped with domes and half domes. It includes four schools, a college, a library, a bath, and a hospital.

Art and literature also flourished under Suleiman's rule. Both painters and poets looked to Persia and Arabia for models. The works that they produced used these foreign influences to express original Ottoman ideas in the Turkish style.

Despite Suleiman's magnificent social and cultural achievements and his splendid city of Istanbul, though, the Ottoman Empire was losing ground. Its decline had already begun.

Suleiman's artistic nature was reflected in everything he did, including his signature (above).

THINK THROUGH HISTORY
D. Summarizing
What were the major cultural achievements of Suleiman's reign?
D. Answer Legal reforms, architecture, art, literature.

The Empire Declines Slowly

Suleiman himself set the stage for this decline. Perhaps fearing for his position, he killed his ablest son and drove another into exile. His third son, the incompetent Selim II, inherited the throne. In 1571, Spain and Italy destroyed Selim's Turkish fleet at the Battle of Lepanto. This was a rare defeat for the Ottomans' superior sea power.

At the same time, corruption was eating away at the government. As each sultan grew older, his possible heirs began jockeying for power. It became customary for each new sultan to have his brothers strangled with the silk string of a bow. The sultan would then keep his sons prisoner in the harem, cutting them off from education or contact with the world. This practice produced a long line of weak, ignorant sultans who eventually brought ruin on the empire.

The great Ottoman Empire crumbled slowly. It continued to influence the world into the early 20th century. It was finally dissolved with the creation of the nation of Turkey after World War I. But throughout its long life, other Muslim empires were on the rise.

 Section 1 Assessment

1. TERMS & NAMES

Identify
- ghazi
- Osman
- Timur the Lame
- Mehmet II
- Suleiman the Lawgiver
- janissary
- devshirme

2. TAKING NOTES

Using a chart like the one below, list the main rulers of the Ottoman Empire and their chief accomplishments.

Ottoman Ruler	Major Accomplishment

Rank these leaders in order of their impact on the Ottoman Empire.

3. EVALUATING DECISIONS

Do you think that the Ottomans were wise in staffing their military and government with slaves? Why or why not?

THINK ABOUT
- the loyalty of slaves to the sultan
- the training slaves received
- others who might have served in the government

4. ANALYZING THEMES

Empire Building Do you think that Suleiman's religious tolerance helped or hurt the Ottoman Empire? Explain.

THINK ABOUT
- Suleiman's treatment of non-Muslims
- the effect on the individual religious groups
- the long-term effect on the empire as a whole

The Muslim World Expands **447**

A N S W E R S

1. TERMS & NAMES
ghazi, p. 443
Osman, p. 443
Timur the Lame, p. 443
Mehmet II, p. 444
Suleiman the Lawgiver, p. 446
janissary, p. 446
devshirme, p. 446

2. TAKING NOTES
Possible Responses: Osman—establishes Ottoman state; Murad II—expands empire; Mehmet II—conquers Constantinople; Selim the Grim—defeats Safavids and captures Islamic holy cities; Suleiman I— unifies and expands empire; Selim II—loses Battle of Lepanto.

Students may cite Suleiman I as having the greatest impact.

3. EVALUATING DECISIONS
Possible Responses: Yes— Slaves received excellent education and training and had the chance to rise to high positions; they were loyal to the sultan. No—Slaves were forcibly taken

from their homes and would be alert for opportunities to rebel or escape from the palace.

4. ANALYZING THEMES
Possible Responses: Helped— kept people of various religions happy; Hurt—did not encourage people to think of themselves as part of one Ottoman nation.

Teacher's Edition **447**

To explain how cultural blending results in new cultures.

 To summarize the rise and fall of the Safivids.

SKILLBUILDERS
- Interpreting charts, p. 448
- Interpreting maps: movement, location, p. 450

CRITICAL THINKING
- Summarizing, p. 448
- Making inferences, p. 449
- Comparing, p. 450
- Analyzing motives, p. 450

FOCUS

5-Minute Warm-Up

▶ *Interpreting Charts*
To introduce students to the concept of cultural blending, have them answer these questions.

1. Look at the chart on page 448. What activities cause cultures to interact?

2. What generalizations can you draw about where and when cultural blending takes place?

 WARM-UP TRANSPARENCY 18

OBJECTIVE ① INSTRUCT

Patterns of Cultural Blending

▶ *Key Ideas*
- Cultures interact as migration, trade, war, and spread of religions bring peoples into contact.
- Cultural blending is an important ongoing pattern in world history.

 IN-DEPTH RESOURCES: UNIT 4
Guided Reading, p. 36

 ACCESS FOR STUDENTS ACQUIRING ENGLISH
Guided Reading (Spanish), p. 181

 ELECTRONIC LIBRARY OF PRIMARY SOURCES
"Report on Persia, Persians, and 'Abbas I'"

---

❷ Cultural Blending

PATTERNS OF CHANGE CASE STUDY: The Safavid Empire

MAIN IDEA	WHY IT MATTERS NOW
Many world cultures incorporate influences from various peoples and traditions.	Modern Iran, which plays a key role in global politics, is descended from the culturally diverse Safavid Empire.

SETTING THE STAGE The Ottoman Empire provides a striking example of how inter-action among peoples can produce a blending of cultures. This mixture often combines the best of contributing cultures in new and exciting ways.

Patterns of Cultural Blending

As the 17th-century British poet John Donne observed, "No man is an island." But no group of people, or culture, is an island, either. Throughout history, peoples have mingled and interacted, giving rise to new cultural blends.

Causes of Cultural Blending Cultural blending usually occurs in places where two or more cultures interact. This interaction most often is prompted by one or a combination of the following four activities: migration, trade, conquest, and pursuit of religious converts or religious freedom. Societies that are able to benefit from cultural blending are open to new ways and willing to adapt and change.

The blending that contributed to the culture of the Ottomans, for example, depended on all of these activities except migration. Surrounded by the peoples of Christian Byzantium, the Turks were motivated to win both territory for their empire and converts to their Muslim religion. Suleiman's interest in learning and culture prompted him to bring the best foreign artists and scholars to his court.

Cultural Blending Through History Similar patterns of blending have occurred throughout the world and across the ages. A few examples are shown below.

A. Answer
Migration, trade, conquest, pursuit of religious converts or religious freedom.
THINK THROUGH HISTORY
A. Summarizing
What four activities often contribute to cultural blending?

PATTERNS OF CHANGE: Cultural Blending

Location	Interacting Cultures	Reason for Interaction	Some Results of Interaction
India—1000 B.C.	Aryan and Dravidian Indian	Migration	Vedic culture, forerunner of Hinduism
East Africa—A.D. 700	Arab, African, Indian, Islamic, Christian	Trade, religious converts	New trade language, Swahili
Russia—A.D. 1000	Christian and Slavic	Religious converts	Eastern Christianity, Russian identity
Mexico—A.D. 1500	Spanish and Aztec Indian	Conquest	Mestizo culture, Mexican Catholicism
United States—A.D. 1900	European, Asian, Caribbean	Migration, religious freedom	Cultural diversity

SKILLBUILDER: Interpreting Charts
1. *What aspects of culture, such as language and religion, did these cultural blendings affect?*
2. *What evidence of cultural blending do you see in the United States today?*

SECTION 2 RESOURCES

PRINT RESOURCES

 IN-DEPTH RESOURCES: UNIT 4
Guided Reading, p. 36

 ACCESS FOR STUDENTS ACQUIRING ENGLISH
Guided Reading (Spanish), p. 181

 FORMAL ASSESSMENT
Section Quiz, p. 206

 ALTERNATIVE ASSESSMENT BOOK

TECHNOLOGY RESOURCES

 CD-ROM
Electronic Library of Primary Sources

 INTERNET www.mlworldhistory.com

The Safavids Build a Shi'i Empire

Conquest and ongoing cultural interaction also fueled the development of another empire—the **Safavids.** Originally, the Safavids were members of an Islamic religious brotherhood. They were named after their founder, Safi al-Din, who died in 1334. Although the Safavids were of Iranian origin, they claimed that they were descended from the prophet Muhammad. In the 15th century, the Safavids aligned themselves with the Shi'i branch of Islam.

The Shi'i Safavids were persecuted on religious grounds by the Ottoman Sunni Muslims. This treatment was a departure from the Sunni's traditional religious tolerance. The Safavids were also squeezed geographically between the Ottomans and Uzbek tribespeople. (See the map on page 450.) To protect themselves from these potential enemies, the Safavids concentrated on building a powerful army.

Isma'il Conquers Persia The Safavid military became a force to reckon with. They wore unique red headgear with 12 folds, and so became known as the "redheads." In 1499, the leader of the redheads was a 14-year-old named **Isma'il** (is·MAH·eel). Despite his youth, he was a brilliant warrior. Within two years, he had seized most of what is now Iran. To celebrate his achievement, he took the ancient Persian title of shah, or king. He also established Shi'i Islam as the state religion:

A VOICE FROM THE PAST

[Isma'il] is loved and revered by his people as a god, and especially by his soldiers, many of whom enter into battle without armour, expecting their master . . . to watch over them in the fight. . . . The name of God is forgotten throughout Persia and only that of Isma'il is remembered.

A 16TH-CENTURY VENETIAN TRAVELER, quoted in *Encyclopedia of Islam*

Despite the reverence of his people, however, Isma'il became a religious tyrant. Any citizen who did not convert to Shi'ism was put to death. Isma'il destroyed the Sunni population of Baghdad in his confrontation with the Ottomans. Their leader, Selim the Grim, later ordered the execution of all Shi'a in the Ottoman empire. As many as 40,000 died. Their final faceoff was at the Battle of Chaldiran in 1514. But the confrontation between the cultures did not end then. In fact, it still continues today.

Isma'il's son Tahmasp took up the struggle. He expanded the Safavid Empire up to the Caucasus Mountains northeast of Turkey and brought Christians under Safavid rule. In adding this territory to the empire, Tahmasp laid the groundwork for the golden age of the Safavids.

Cultural Blending During the Reign of Shah Abbas This golden age came under **Shah Abbas,** or Abbas the Great. He took the throne in 1587. During his reign, he helped create a Safavid culture that drew from the best of the Ottoman, Persian, and Arab worlds.

Shah Abbas reformed both military and civilian aspects of life. He limited the power of the military redheads. He then created two new armies that would be loyal to him alone. One of these was an army of Persians. The other was a force like the Ottoman janissaries, which Abbas recruited from the Christian north. He equipped both of these armies with modern artillery. Abbas also reformed his government. He punished corruption severely and promoted only officials who proved their competence and loyalty.

Shah Abbas established relations with Europe. As a result, industry and art flourished. He also brought Chinese artisans to the

THINK THROUGH HISTORY
B. Making Inferences Which of Isma'il's traits do you think made him such a successful conqueror?
B. Possible Answers His expertise as a warrior; his singleminded devotion to Shi'i Islam; his ruthlessness.

Safavid Empire, 1683

RUSSIA

Aral Sea

CAUCASUS MTS.

Caspian Sea

Trabzon

Tabriz

Tehran

Herat

Mosul

Baghdad

Isfahan

ARABIA

Basra

PERSIA

Shiraz

Hormuz

Euphrates R.

Tigris R.

Persian Gulf

UZBEKS

Amu Darya

N

500 Miles

1,000 Kilometers

- Ottoman Empire
- Safavid Empire
- Mughal Empire

GEOGRAPHY SKILLBUILDER:
Interpreting Maps
1. **Movement** *What waterways might have enabled the Safavids to interact with other cultures?*
2. **Location** *Why might the Safavids not have expanded further?*

Safavid Empire. This collaboration gave rise to gorgeous artwork. These decorations beautified the many mosques, palaces, and marketplaces of Abbas's rebuilt capital city of **Isfahan.**

The most important result of Western influence on the Safavids, however, may have been the demand for Persian carpets. This demand helped change carpet weaving from a local craft to a national industry.

The Dynasty Declines Quickly Shah Abbas unfortunately made the same mistake the Ottoman monarch Suleiman made. He killed or blinded his ablest sons. Abbas was succeeded by his incompetent grandson, Safi. This pampered young prince led the Safavids down the same road to decline that the Ottomans had taken, only more quickly.

By 1722, tribal armies from Afghanistan were taking over the eastern portions of the Safavid realm. Ottoman forces were attacking from the west. Some historians claim that these attacks marked the downfall of the Safavids.

In 1736, however, a ruler from a Sunni family—Nadir Shah Afshar—took command. He conquered all the way to India and created a new Persian empire. But Nadir Shah was a cruel man as well as an inspired military leader. One of his own troops assassinated him. With Nadir Shah's death in 1747, his empire also fell apart.

The Safavid Legacy Although the Safavid Empire died out as a political power, the culture that it produced endured. In this culture, the worldly and artistic features of Persian civilization mingled with the religious elements of Shi'ism. The Safavids also borrowed many ways from their enemies, the Ottomans. They based their government on the Ottoman model, welcomed foreigners into their empire, and created a slave army similar to the janissaries.

At the same time that the Safavids flourished, cultural blending and conquest led to the growth of a new empire in India, as you will learn in Section 3.

Section 2 Assessment

1. TERMS & NAMES
Identify
- Safavid
- Isma'il
- Shah Abbas
- Isfahan

2. TAKING NOTES
Using a cause-and-effect diagram like the one below, indicate the events that enabled the Safavids to build a powerful empire.

Events → Effect

Powerful Safavid Empire

3. ANALYZING MOTIVES
Within a century after the Safavids adopted Shi'i Islam, their leader, Isma'il, became a religious tyrant. Why might he have become so intolerant?

THINK ABOUT
- the persecution of Safavids by Ottoman Sunni Muslims
- the role of religion in Safavid life
- the geographic location of the Safavid Empire

4. THEME ACTIVITY
Cultural Interaction Write a letter from Shah Abbas to a Chinese artist persuading him to come teach and work in the Safavid Empire. In the letter, explain why the Safavids are interested in Chinese art and how they treat people from other cultures.

450 CHAPTER 18

---

3 The Mughals Establish an Empire in India

TERMS & NAMES
- Mughal
- Babur
- Akbar
- Jahangir
- Nur Jahan
- Sikh
- Shah Jahan
- Taj Mahal
- Aurangzeb

MAIN IDEA

The Mughal Empire brought Turks, Persians, and Indians together in a vast empire.

WHY IT MATTERS NOW

The legacy of great art and deep social division left by the Mughal Empire still influences southern Asia.

SETTING THE STAGE In the late 15th century, India included lush lands studded with cities and temples. The Hindu lower classes labored in the service of their Muslim or Hindu masters. At the same time, nomadic warriors roamed the highlands to the northwest, eager for battle.

Early History of the Mughal Empire

The people who invaded India called themselves **Mughals,** which means "Mongols." The land they invaded had been through a long period of turmoil. The Gupta Empire crumbled in the 600s. First, Arabs invaded. Then, warlike Muslim tribes from central Asia carved northwestern India into many small kingdoms. Those kingdoms were ruled by leaders called Rajputs, or "sons of kings."

Ongoing Conflicts The 8th century began with a long, bloody clash between Hindus and Muslims in this fragmented land. For almost 300 years, though, the Hindus held off the Arab Muslims. They were able to advance only as far as the Indus River valley. Starting around the year 1000, however, well-trained Turkish armies swept into India. Led by Sultan Mahmud (muh·MOOD) of Ghazni, they devastated Indian cities and temples in 17 brutal campaigns. These attacks left the region weakened and vulnerable to other conquerors. Delhi eventually became the capital of a loose empire of Turkish warlords called the Delhi Sultanate. These sultans treated the Hindus as conquered people.

Between the 13th and 16th centuries, 33 different sultans ruled this divided territory from its seat in Delhi. In 1398, Timur the Lame destroyed Delhi so completely that, according to one witness, "for two whole months, not a bird moved in

Growth of the Mughal Empire, 1526–1707

- Mughal Empire, 1526—Babur
- Added by 1605—Akbar
- Added by 1707—Aurangzeb

KASHMIR, PUNJAB, Kabul, Lahore, HIMALAYAS, Brahmaputra R., Indus R., Delhi, Agra, Ganges R., Patna, Benares, BENGAL, Dacca, Tropic of Cancer, Calcutta, Arabian Sea, Surat, Bombay, DECCAN PLATEAU, Bay of Bengal, Madras, Calicut, Pondicherry, Cochin, CEYLON

GEOGRAPHY SKILLBUILDER:
Interpreting Maps
1. **Movement** During which time period was the most territory added to the Mughal Empire?
2. **Location** What landform might have prevented the empire from expanding farther east?

451

SECTION 3 RESOURCES

PRINT RESOURCES

IN-DEPTH RESOURCES: UNIT 4
Guided Reading, p. 37
Geography Application: Europe Discovers India, p. 39
Primary Sources: Akbar, p. 43; Jahangir's Birthday, p. 44
History Makers: Shah Jahan, p. 49
Connections Across Time and Cultures, p. 50

ACCESS FOR STUDENTS ACQUIRING ENGLISH
Guided Reading (Spanish), p. 182
Geography Application (Spanish), p. 184

FORMAL ASSESSMENT
Section Quiz, p. 207

TECHNOLOGY RESOURCES

WORLD ART AND CULTURES TRANSPARENCIES
AT40 Mughal miniature painting

CRITICAL THINKING TRANSPARENCIES
CT18 Muslim Empires in Anatolia and India
CT54 Chapter 18 Visual Summary

INTERNET www.mlworldhistory.com

Section 3 Overview

OBJECTIVES

1 To describe the rise of the Mughal empire.

2 To analyze the policies and achievements of Akbar.

3 To list the triumphs and failures of Akbar's successors.

SKILLBUILDER

- Interpreting maps: movement, location, p. 451

CRITICAL THINKING

- Comparing, p. 452
- Analyzing causes, p. 454
- Making inferences, pp. 455, 456
- Recognizing effects, p. 457
- Comparing and contrasting, p. 457
- Analyzing themes, p. 457

FOCUS

5-Minute Warm-Up

▶ **Drawing Conclusions**
To spark students' interest in the Mughal Empire, have them answer these questions.

1. Look at the Daily Life feature on page 456. Name one gift the king rejected.

2. What evidence does this feature give about the wealth of the Mughal Empire?

📖 **WARM-UP TRANSPARENCY 18**

OBJECTIVE 1 INSTRUCT

Early History of the Mughal Empire

▶ **Key Ideas**
- Centuries of bitter conflict mark Hindu-Muslim relations in India.
- Babur conquers India and founds the Mughal empire

📋 **IN-DEPTH RESOURCES: UNIT 4**
Guided Reading, p. 37

📋 **ACCESS FOR STUDENTS ACQUIRING ENGLISH**
Guided Reading (Spanish), p. 182

📖 **CRITICAL THINKING TRANSPARENCIES**
CT18 Muslim Empires in Anatolia and India

(See page 451.)

Interpreting the Map Have students locate the Indus River, which was as far as the Arab conquests penetrated into India.

Extension Activity Ask students to identify the geographic and political features that may have limited the size of the Mughal Empire. *The Himalayas, the Bay of Bengal, and the Arabian Sea to the north, east, and southwest, and the Safavid Empire to the west.*

SKILLBUILDER Answers
1. To 1605 under Akbar
2. The Himalayas

OBJECTIVE 2 INSTRUCT

The Golden Age of Akbar

▶ **Key Ideas**
• Akbar's liberal policies promote religious and social harmony.
• Architecture, the arts, and literature flower under Akbar's reign.

📘 **IN-DEPTH RESOURCES: UNIT 4**
Connections Across Time and Cultures: How To Treat the Conquered, p. 50

HISTORY MAKERS
Akbar

Ever sensitive to public opinion, Akbar made a point of standing at an open window of his palace every morning so that his people could see him and feel a connection with their emperor.

📘 **IN-DEPTH RESOURCES: UNIT 4**
Primary Source: Akbar, p. 43

---

the city." Delhi eventually was rebuilt. But it was not until the 16th century that a leader arose who would unify the empire.

Babur Founds an Empire In 1494, an 11-year-old boy named **Babur** inherited a kingdom in the area that is now Uzbekistan and Tajikistan. It was only a tiny kingdom, and his elders soon took it away and drove him south. But the boy built up an army. In the years that followed, he swept down into India and laid the groundwork for the vast Mughal Empire.

Babur was a strong, sensitive leader. According to legend, he could leap a wall holding a man under each arm. But he also wrote poetry and loved art and gardens. He was a brilliant general as well. In 1526, for example, Babur led 12,000 troops to victory against an army of 100,000 commanded by a sultan of Delhi. Perhaps it was his sensitivity to his soldiers that made him such an effective leader:

> **A VOICE FROM THE PAST**
> Some in the army were very anxious and full of fear. Nothing recommends anxiety and fear. . . . Why? Because what God has fixed in eternity cannot be changed. But . . . it was no reproach to be afraid and anxious. . . . Why? Because those thus anxious and afraid were there with a two or three months' journey between them and their homes; our affair was with a foreign tribe and people; none knew their tongue, nor did they know ours.
> **BABUR,** *The Babur-Nama (Memoirs of Babur)*

A year later, Babur also defeated a massive Rajput army. After Babur's death, his incompetent son, Humayun, lost most of the territory Babur had gained. Babur's 13-year-old grandson took over the throne after Humayun's death.

Background
One of the secrets of Babur's success is that he lashed cannons together to fire massive volleys against troops mounted on elephants.

The Golden Age of Akbar

HISTORY MAKERS

Akbar
1542–1605

Akbar was brilliant and curious, especially about religion. He even invented a religion of his own—the "Divine Faith"—which combined elements of Hinduism, Jainism, Christianity, and Sufism. The religion attracted few followers, however, and offended Muslims so much that they attempted a brief revolt against Akbar in 1581. When he died, so did the "Divine Faith."

Surprisingly, despite his wisdom and his achievements, Akbar could not read. He hired others to read to him from his library of 24,000 books.

Babur's grandson was called **Akbar,** which means "Great One." Akbar certainly lived up to his name by ruling India with wisdom and tolerance from 1556 to 1605.

A Liberal Ruler Akbar was a Muslim, and he firmly defended religious freedom. He proved his tolerance by marrying, among others, two Hindus, a Christian, and a Muslim. He allowed his wives to practice their religious rituals in the palace. He proved his tolerance again by abolishing both the tax on Hindu pilgrims and the hated *jizya*, or tax on non-Muslims. He even appointed a Spanish Jesuit to tutor his second son. Akbar was a genius at cultural blending.

Akbar governed through a bureaucracy of officials. Natives and foreigners, Hindus and Muslims, could all rise to high office. This approach contributed to the quality of his government. Akbar's chief finance minister, Todar Mal, for example, created a clever—and effective—taxation policy. He calculated the tax as a percent of the value of the peasants' crops, similar to the present-day U.S. graduated income tax. Because this tax was fair and affordable, the number of peasants who paid it increased. This payment brought in much needed money for the empire.

Akbar's land policies had more mixed results. He gave generous land grants to his bureaucrats. After they died, however, he reclaimed the lands and distributed them as he saw fit. On the positive side, this policy prevented the growth of feudal aristocracies. On the other hand, it did not encourage dedication and hard work by the Mughal officials. Their children would not inherit the land or benefit from their parents' work. So the officials apparently saw no point in devoting themselves to their property.

THINK THROUGH HISTORY
A. Comparing In what ways were Akbar's attitudes toward religion similar to those of Suleiman the Lawgiver?
A. Answer They were both extremely tolerant—Akbar in both his personal life and government policies, and Suleiman through the *millet* system.

EXPLORING PRIMARY SOURCES

A Voice from the Past Though the troops of his opponent, Sultan Ibrahim, outnumbered Babur's by almost ten to one, Babur believed that the reason for their defeat was that they were demoralized and underpaid. He wrote about the sultan, "Ibrahim could [not] . . . share out his treasure. How should he content his braves when he was ruled by avarice and had a craving insatiable to pile coin on coin? He . . . provided nothing for his military operations . . . ." Discuss with students how this quotation helps explain Babur's victory and reinforces the effectiveness of his humane leadership.

CONNECTIONS ACROSS THE CURRICULUM

Economics Discuss how tax policies might affect the economic well-being of an empire or a nation. Make sure that students understand that governments must balance their need to gain revenue with the need to avoid undue tax burdens on their people. Point out that the relationship between taxes and economic health has always been the subject of considerable debate in the United States. How are the issues in the United States the same or different from those in Akbar's India? What are the advantages and disadvantages of the graduated income tax to governments and to their people?

A Military Conqueror For all his humanity, however, Akbar recognized military power as the root of his strength. He believed in war for its own sake. "A monarch should ever be intent on conquest," he said, "otherwise his neighbors rise in arms against him." Like the Safavids and the Ottomans, Akbar equipped his armies with heavy artillery. Cannons enabled him to crack into walled cities and extend his rule into much of the Deccan plateau. In a brilliant move, he appointed some Rajputs as officers. In this way he turned potential enemies into allies. This combination of military power and political wisdom enabled Akbar to unify a land of at least 100 million people—more than all of Europe put together.

A Flowering of Culture As Akbar extended the Mughal Empire, he welcomed influences from the many cultures it included. This cultural mingling affected art, education, politics, and the language as well. Persian was the language of Akbar's court and of high culture. The common people, however, spoke Hindi, a mixture of Persian and a local language. Hindi remains one of the most widely spoken languages in India today. Out of the Mughal armies, where soldiers of many backgrounds rubbed shoulders, came yet another new language. This language was Urdu, which means "from the soldier's camp." A blend of Arabic, Persian, and Hindi, Urdu is today the official language of Pakistan.

The arts flourished at the Mughal court, especially in the form of book illustrations. These small, highly detailed and colorful paintings were called miniatures. They were brought to a peak of perfection in the Safavid Empire. Babur's son, Humayun, brought two masters of this art to his court to teach it to the Mughals. Some of the most famous Mughal miniatures adorned the *Akbarnamah* ("Book of Akbar"), the story of the great emperor's campaigns and deeds. Indian art drew from Western traditions as well. After Akbar's time, for example, portraits of the Mughal emperors showed them wearing halos like Western saints.

Literature and Architecture Hindu literature also enjoyed a revival in Akbar's time. Akbar established a large library. The poet Tulsi Das, for example, was a contemporary of Akbar's. He retold the epic love story of Rama and Sita from the 4th-century B.C. Indian poem *Ramayana* (rah·MAH·yuh·nuh) in Hindi. This retelling, the *Ramcaritmanas*, is now even more popular than the original.

Akbar devoted himself to architecture, too. The style developed under his reign is still known as Akbar period architecture. Its massive, but graceful, structures are decorated with intricate stonework that depicts Hindu themes. The capital city of Fatehpur Sikri is one of the most important examples of this type of architecture. Akbar had this red-sandstone city built to thank a holy man who had predicted the birth of his first son. It included a great mosque, many palaces and other houses, as well as official and religious buildings. This magnificent city was abandoned after only 15 years because its water supply ran out. Ironically, the son whose birth it honored eventually rebelled against his father. He may even have plotted to cause his father's death.

Akbar's Successors

With Akbar's death in 1605, the Mughal court changed to deal with the changing times. The next three emperors were powerful men, and each left his mark on the Mughal Empire.

Headgear had symbolic importance in the society of Hindus in India. An important person's turban might include 50 yards of cloth wound around and held together with a jeweled pin such as this one.

The Muslim World Expands **453**

Background
In Hindu myth, Rama was the perfect king, one of the personalities of the protector god, Vishnu.

CONNECT *to* TODAY
Women Rulers

South Asia gave the world not only two women prime ministers, but also its first woman premier. She was Sirimavo Bandaranaike of Sri Lanka, an island off the southern tip of India. Bandaranaike was elected in 1960 and again (by a landslide) in 1970, ruling a total of 11 years. Ask students to speculate why women have been able to gain political power so often in this cultural region.

MORE ABOUT . . .
Nur Jahan

Legends surround Nur Jahan's life, perhaps reflecting her charismatic power. She was born, it is said, while her parents were in flight from Persia. They abandoned the child under a tree, but a cobra protected her, shading her from the hot sun with its hood until her remorseful parents returned. Nur Jahan married a Persian refugee in India, but he was hacked to bits in a quarrel with the governor of Bengal. Nur Jahan was then called to serve at court, where she caught the emperor's eye. Four years later, at the age of 34, she was married to him.

MORE ABOUT . . .
Mumtaz Mahal

According to tales, it was love at first sight between Prince Khurram, who later became Shah Jahan, and Mumtaz Mahal. On seeing her, he reportedly said, "Oh, that I were a glove upon that hand." After her marriage, Mumtaz Mahal traveled everywhere with her husband, even on military campaigns. She gave birth to four of his sons, including the next emperor, Aurangzeb, on the battlefield.

CONNECT *to* TODAY
Women Rulers

Since World War II, India has seen the rise of several powerful women. Unlike Nur Jahan, however, they achieved power on their own—not through their husbands.

Indira Gandhi headed the Congress-I Party and dominated Indian politics for almost 30 years. She was elected prime minister in 1966 and again in 1980. Gandhi was assassinated in 1984 by Sikh terrorists.

In neighboring Pakistan, Benazir Bhutto (shown below), took charge of the Pakistan People's Party after her father was executed by his political enemies. She won election as her country's prime minister in 1988—the first woman to run a modern Muslim state. Pakistan's president unseated her, but she was reelected in 1993. In 1996, however, the president again ousted her from office. The supreme court ruled that her government was corrupt. Ironically, that was partially because her husband had made corrupt business deals.

Jahangir and Nur Jahan Akbar's son called himself **Jahangir** (juh·hahn·GEER)—"Grasper of the World." And he certainly did hold India in a powerful grasp. It was not his own hand in the iron glove, though, since Jahangir was an extremely weak ruler. For most of his reign, he left the affairs of state to his wife.

Jahangir's wife was the Persian princess **Nur Jahan.** She was a remarkably talented women with a variety of interests. Tiger hunting was among her favorite pastimes, and she rode horses with legendary skill. She composed poetry whenever the mood struck her. She also designed clothes that still influence Indian fashions. Above all, she was a brilliant politician who perfectly understood the use of power. As the real ruler of India from 1611 to 1622, she installed her father as prime minister in the Mughal court. She saw Jahangir's son Khusrau as her ticket to future power. But when Khusrau rebelled against his father, Nur Jahan ousted him. She then shifted her favor to another son, the future emperor, Shah Jahan.

This rejection of Khusrau affected more than the political future of the empire. It was also the basis of a long and bitter religious conflict. Both Nur Jahan and Jahangir rejected Akbar's religious tolerance and tried to promote only Islam in the Mughal state. When Khusrau rebelled against his father, he turned to the **Sikhs.** This was a nonviolent religious group whose doctrines blended Buddhism, Hinduism, and Sufism (Islamic mysticism). Their leader, Guru Arjun, sheltered Khusrau and defended him. In response, the Mughal rulers had Arjun arrested and tortured to death. The Sikhs thus became the target of the Mughals' particular hatred.

Shah Jahan Like his grandfather, **Shah Jahan** was a cultured man. He could not tolerate competition, however, and secured his throne by assassinating all his possible rivals. But he did have a great passion for two things: beautiful buildings and his wife Mumtaz Mahal (moom·TAHZ mah·HAHL). Nur Jahan had arranged this marriage between Jahangir's son and her niece for political reasons. Shah Jahan, however, fell genuinely in love with his Persian princess.

In 1631, Mumtaz Mahal died at age 38 giving birth to her 14th child. "Empire has no sweetness," the heartbroken Shah Jahan lamented, "life has no relish for me now." To enshrine his wife's memory, he ordered that a tomb be built "as beautiful as she was beautiful." Fine white marble and fabulous jewels were gathered from many parts of Asia. Some 20,000 workers labored for 22 years to build the famous tomb now known as the **Taj Mahal.** This memorial has been called one of the most beautiful buildings in the world. Its towering marble dome and slender towers look like lace and seem to change color as the sun moves across the sky. The inside of the building is as magnificent as the exterior. It is a glittering garden of thousands of carved marble flowers inlaid with tiny precious stones.

Shah Jahan also built the Red Fort at Delhi and completed the Peacock Throne, a priceless seat of gold encrusted with diamonds, rubies, emeralds, and pearls. The throne has a canopy that displays the figure of a peacock lined with blue sapphires. This magnificent throne was lost to the conqueror Nadir Shah in 1739.

The People Suffer But while Shah Jahan was building lovely things, his country was suffering. A Dutch merchant who was in India during a famine at that time reported that ". . . men abandoned towns and villages and wandered helplessly . . . eyes sunk deep in head, lips pale and covered with slime, the skin hard, the bones showing through. . . ." Farmers needed tools, roads, and ways of irrigating their crops and dealing with India's harsh environment. What they got instead were taxes and more taxes to support the building of monuments, their rulers' extravagant living, and war.

THINK THROUGH HISTORY
B. Analyzing Causes How did the Mughals' dislike of the Sikhs develop?
B. Answer They sheltered and defended Jahangir's son, who had rebelled against his father.

Background
Shortly after Shah Jahan spent huge sums of money on the Taj Mahal, King Louis XIV began building his elaborate palace at Versailles. Both rulers heavily taxed their people to pay for their extravagance.

454 Chapter 18

TEACHING OPTION **BLOCK SCHEDULING**

ART APPLICATION ACTIVITY

CLASS TIME 20 MINUTES

Task: Students will examine photographs of various buildings throughout the world.

Materials Needed: The feature about Versailles on page 521 and the image and information about Angkor Wat on page 309 of this text. Art transparencies A22, A30, and A47 also provide images of world-famous architecture. Also see the book *Great Architecture of the World* edited by John Julius.

454 Chapter 18

Activity: Have students choose a selection of buildings from a variety of times and places. Ask them to note their overall impression of each building and to identify the particular characteristics that contribute to that impression.

Conclusion: Ask students to write descriptive or expository paragraphs or poems capturing their responses to the buildings. Suggest that they

consider the similar impulses that motivated people to construct such monuments as well as the different forms the buildings took. Have students share their writing orally with the class.

 WORLD ART AND CULTURES TRANSPARENCIES
AT22, Great Mosque of Córdova; AT30, Notre Dame Cathedral; AT47, St. Basil's Cathedral

THINK THROUGH HISTORY
C. Making Inferences Do you think Shah Jahan's policies helped or harmed the Mughal Empire?

C. Possible Answer Helped—Left lasting legacy of architecture. Harmed—Did not improve the hard lives of his people.

All was not well in the royal court either. When Shah Jahan became ill in 1657, his four sons scrambled for the throne. The third son, **Aurangzeb** (AWR·uhng·zehb), moved first and most decisively. In a bitter civil war, he executed his older brother, who was his most serious rival. Then he arrested his father and put him in prison. When Shah Jahan died several years later, a mirror was found in his room, angled so that he could gaze from his cell at the reflection of the Taj Mahal. Aurangzeb, however, had his eyes on the empire.

Aurangzeb Aurangzeb ruled from 1658 to 1707. He was a master at military strategy and an aggressive empire builder. Although he expanded the Mughal holdings to their greatest size, the power of the empire weakened during his reign.

This loss of power was due largely to Aurangzeb's oppression of the people. He rigidly enforced Islamic laws, outlawing drinking, gambling, and other vices. He also appointed censors to police his subjects' morals and make sure they prayed at the appointed times. He also tried to erase all the gains Hindus had made under Akbar. For example, he brought back the hated tax on non-Muslims and dismissed Hindus from high positions in his government. He banned the construction of new temples and had Hindu monuments destroyed. Not surprisingly, these actions outraged the Hindus.

The Hindu Rajputs, whom Akbar had converted from potential enemies to allies, rebelled. Aurangzeb defeated them repeatedly, but never completely. In the southwest, militant Hindus called Marathas founded their own breakaway state. Aurangzeb captured their leader, but the Marathas turned to guerrilla warfare. Aurangzeb could never conquer them. Meanwhile, the Sikhs had transformed themselves into a militant brotherhood. They began to build a state in the Punjab, an area in northwest India.

Set in a formal garden and mirrored in a reflecting pool, the Taj Mahal draws tourists to Agra, southeast of New Delhi in India. It remains a monument to both love and the Mughal Empire.

The Muslim World Expands **455**

India, 1620
Mughal Society News

These news items present actual events and customs of the Mughal court as reported by various observers. One of these observers, Thomas Roe of the British East India Trading company, spent three years trying to negotiate a treaty with Jahangir, but finally went home with only a few minor trade agreements. One of his difficulties apparently was the uninspired gifts his English sponsors provided him to woo the emperor. Such gifts earned the monarch's forceful "thumbs down."

Have interested students do independent research into the Mughal court. Good sources include Waldemar Hansen's *The Peacock Throne* and Bamber Gascoigne's *The Great Moghuls*. Suggest that they collect interesting details and produce their own edition of *Mughal Society News* to share with the class.

Mughal Society News

Diet News

A person who does a good deed for the Mughal emperor may be rewarded with his weight in rupees (a unit of money). In fact, both the emperor's flute player and his astrologer recently received this generous prize. Sources said that the stout astrologer pocketed 200 rupees more than the musician.

The Doctor Is In

When a woman of the Mughal court gets sick, she must not be seen by a male doctor. The doctor first wraps his head in a cashmere shawl, which serves as a blindfold. He follows a servant into the women's quarters, where the patient lies hidden behind a curtain. If she needs to have a wound treated, the patient sticks her arm or leg out through the curtain. The doctor then examines the patient from his side of the curtain.

Woman of the Week

Naming Nur Jahan, the monarch's favorite queen "Woman of the Week" is a king-size understatement. Woman of the century is more like it. But people in the know go even further and call her "Light of the World"—and for good reason. In addition to being the true power behind Jahangir's throne, she excels in the arts, business, and sports.

Nur Jahan's bold, original designs for cloth, dresses with long trains, and even carpets dominate India's fashion scene. From her harem, Nur Jahan runs a bustling trade in indigo and cloth. She's also an accomplished huntress, and last week killed four tigers.

Nur Jahan is the power behind the throne and even designs the royal wardrobe.

The Shopping Corner

If you're trying to impress the emperor, bring him a unique gift. This is how he voted on recent offerings:

Thumbs Up
- walnut-sized ruby
- portraits of English royal family
- unusual fish

Thumbs Down
- faded velvet
- mirror with loose frame
- map showing a compressed view of India

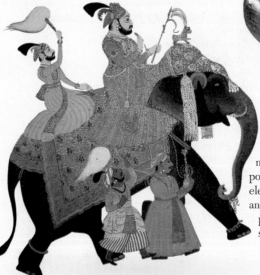

Moving Day

Relocating the Mughal royal court requires as much effort as moving a small city. Simply transporting the royal tents requires 100 elephants, 500 camels, 400 carts, and 100 human bearers. When the procession stops for the night, it spans a length of 20 miles.

Connect *to* **History**

Making Inferences What can you conclude about the lives of women in the Mughal court?

SEE SKILLBUILDER
HANDBOOK, PAGE 1005

Connect *to* **Today**

Women's Studies Using information from the "Connect to Today" feature on page 454 and the library or the Internet, research the public role of women in several Muslim cultures today. How has the role of women changed since Mughal times?

Connect *to* **History**

Possible Answer:
Women generally were protected from the outside world. They and their families apparently accumulated many possessions, since moving was such a major undertaking. One woman, Nur Jahan, was extraordinarily powerful, but this was probably due to her unique talents and position as queen.

Connect *to* **Today**

Women's Studies
Women's roles differ greatly in the Islamic world. In Turkey, for example, women enjoy almost full participation in public life. In Saudi Arabia, they are prohibited by law even from driving cars. In Afghanistan, the Taliban have virtually erased women from public life and stripped them of all rights. In some countries, such as Egypt and Algeria, for example, conservatives are struggling to erase the gains women have made.

Aurangzeb had to levy oppressive taxes to pay for the wars against these increasing numbers of enemies. He had done away with all taxes not authorized by Islamic law, so he doubled the taxes on Hindu merchants. This increased tax burden deepened the Hindus' bitterness and led to further rebellion. As a result, Aurangzeb needed to raise more money to increase his army. The more territory he conquered, the more desperate his situation became.

The Empire's Decline and Decay

By the end of Aurangzeb's reign, he had drained the empire of its resources. Most of his subjects felt little or no loyalty to him. According to a Dutch observer, "The condition of the common people in India is very miserable. . . . Their huts are low, built generally of mud . . . their bedding is scanty and thin . . . of little use when the weather is bitterly cold. . . . The nobles live in indescribable luxury and extravagance, caring only to indulge themselves whilst they can in every kind of pleasure." Over two million people died in a famine while Aurangzeb was away waging war.

As the power of the central state weakened, the power of local lords grew. After Aurangzeb's death, his sons fought a war of succession. Bahadur, who won the war, was over 60 when he gained the throne. This exhausted emperor did not last long. In fact, three emperors reigned in the 12 years after Aurengzeb died. By the end of this period, the Mughal emperor was nothing but a wealthy figurehead. He ruled not a united empire but a patchwork of independent states.

As the Mughal Empire was rising and falling and creating its cultural legacy, Western traders were slowly building their own power. The Portuguese were the first Europeans to reach India. In fact, they arrived just before Babur did. But they were ousted by the Dutch, who, in turn, gave way to the French and the English. The great Mughal emperors did not feel threatened by the European traders. Shah Jahan let the English build a fortified trading post at Madras. In 1661, Aurangzeb casually handed them the port of Bombay. Aurangzeb had no idea that he had given India's next conquerors their first foothold in a future empire.

THINK THROUGH HISTORY
D. Recognizing Effects How did Aurangzeb's personal qualities and political policies affect the Mughal Empire?
D. Answer He depleted the empire's resources and began the weakening of central power that led to its ruin.

Perhaps to offset their excessive spending, the Mughal rulers were weighed once a year. They donated their weight in gold and silver to the people. Here, Jahangir weighs Prince Khurran.

MORE ABOUT . . .
Europeans in India
Indian cloth was the great prize sought by European traders, who had only coarse linen and wool. Several types of cotton fabric are actually named for Indian cities— madras for Madras and calico for Calicut.

IN-DEPTH RESOURCES: UNIT 4
Geography Application: Europe Discovers the Riches of India, p. 39

OBJECTIVE **4** INSTRUCT

The Empire's Decline and Decay

▶ **Key Ideas**
• The Mughal Empire breaks apart after Aurangzeb's death.
• The region attracts European empire builders.

ASSESS & RETEACH

Section 3 Assessment
Have pairs of students work on question 4.

Section Quiz
FORMAL ASSESSMENT
Section Quiz, p. 207

Reteaching Activity
CLASS TIME: 10 MINUTES
Have students compare their time lines in question 2 and make a combined class time line.

CRITICAL THINKING TRANSPARENCIES
CT54 Chapter 18 Visual Summary

CLOSE ACTIVITY

CLASS TIME: 15 MINUTES

Comparing and Contrasting
Have students, as a class, create a Venn diagram in which they list the similarities and differences of the Ottoman, the Safavid, and the Mughal empires.

Section **3** Assessment

1. TERMS & NAMES

Identify
• Mughal
• Babur
• Akbar
• Jahangir
• Nur Jahan
• Sikh
• Shah Jahan
• Taj Mahal
• Aurangzeb

2. TAKING NOTES

Using a time line like the one below, indicate the effects each leader had on the Mughal Empire. Write positive effects above the line and negative effects below.

Effects on Mughal Empire

+

| Babur | Akbar | Jahangir/ Nur Jahan | Shah Jahan | Aurangzeb |

–

3. COMPARING AND CONTRASTING

In what ways was the golden age of Akbar similar to and different from the flowering of the Safavid Empire under Shah Abbas and of the Ottoman Empire under Suleiman I?

THINK ABOUT
• the rulers' cultural and military achievements
• their tolerance of other cultures
• their successors

4. ANALYZING THEMES

Power and Authority Do you think Shah Jahan made good use of his power and authority? Why or why not?

THINK ABOUT
• how Shah Jahan came to power
• the beautiful buildings he built
• conditions in India during his reign

The Muslim World Expands **457**

ANSWERS

1. TERMS & NAMES
Mughal, p. 451
Babur, p. 452
Akbar, p. 452
Jahangir, p. 454
Nur Jahan, p. 454
Sikh, p. 454
Shah Jahan, p. 454
Taj Mahal, p. 454
Aurangzeb, p. 455

2. TAKING NOTES
Possible Responses: Pos.— Babur expanded the empire; Akbar left a better government and a flowering of culture; Neg.—Jahangir and Nur Jahan sparked religious conflict with the Sikhs; Shah Jahan made life difficult for Hindus; Aurangzeb waged costly wars.

3. COMPARING AND CONTRASTING
Possible Responses: Similar— Governmental reform, cultural blending and flowering, military leadership; **Different**—Akbar didn't murder his sons.

4. ANALYZING THEMES
Possible Responses: Yes—Shah Jahan kept the empire together and built magnificent buildings that reflected the empire's glory; No—He turned his back on his suffering people while constructing beautiful buildings, living extravagantly, and pursuing war.

Teacher's Edition **457**

TERMS & NAMES

1. Timur the Lame, p. 443
2. Mehmet II, p. 444
3. Suleiman the Lawgiver, p. 446
4. *devshirme,* p. 446
5. Isma'il, p. 449
6. Shah Abbas, p. 449
7. Babur, p. 452
8. Akbar, p. 452
9. Nur Jahan, p. 454
10. Aurangzeb, p. 455

REVIEW QUESTIONS

Answers will vary.

11. They used modern technology—muskets and cannons—to achieve military success and treated the conquered peoples humanely.

12. He opened Constantinople to Jews, Christians, and non-Turks.

13. Mecca and Medina were the holiest cities of Islam, and Cairo was its intellectual center. Capturing them gave the Ottomans almost total control of the Muslim world.

14. Male slaves could hold high posts in the government and join the janissaries; female slaves served the wealthy Ottoman families.

15. Positive—his military prowess and brilliance as a warrior; Negative—his religious intolerance in imposing Shi'ism as the state religion.

16. An army recruited from conquered people, like the janissaries; use of modern artillery; government reforms with rewards based on merit; support for the arts and learning.

17. The Safavids blended the literate, urban features of Persian civilization with the mystical elements of Shi'ism; they engaged in trade and cultural exchange with nations as far away as China.

18. The Mughals had to overcome Turkish warlords of the Delhi Sultanate and other warlike tribes from Central Asia led by Rajputs.

19. He married two Hindus, a Christian, and a Muslim; abolished taxes on non-Muslims; appointed a Spanish Jesuit to tutor his son; and allowed people of all faiths to compete for high office.

20. Nur Jahan and Jahangir persecuted Sikhs; Shah Jahan mistreated Hindus; Aurangzeb reversed Akbar's tolerant policies and levied oppressive taxes on Hindus.

Chapter ⑱ Assessment

TERMS & NAMES

Briefly explain the importance of each of the following to the Ottoman, Safavid, or Mughal empires.

1. Timur the Lame
2. Mehmet II
3. Suleiman the Lawgiver
4. *devshirme*
5. Isma'il
6. Shah Abbas
7. Babur
8. Akbar
9. Nur Jahan
10. Aurangzeb

Interact *with* History

On page 442, you considered how you might treat the people you conquered. Now that you have learned more about three Muslim empires, in what ways do you think you would change your policies? In what ways would you follow and differ from the Ottomans' example? Discuss your thoughts with a small group of classmates.

REVIEW QUESTIONS

SECTION 1 *(pages 443–447)*
The Ottomans Build a Vast Empire

11. Why were the Ottomans such successful conquerors?

12. How did Mehmet the Conqueror show his tolerance of other cultures?

13. Why was Selim the Grim's capture of Mecca, Medina, and Cairo so significant?

14. What role did slaves play in Ottoman society?

SECTION 2 *(pages 448–450)*
Cultural Blending
Case Study: The Safavid Empire

15. According to the 16th-century Voice from the Past on page 449, "The name of God is forgotten throughout Persia and only that of Isma'il is remembered." What deeds—both positive and negative—contributed to Isma'il's fame?

16. What ideas did Shah Abbas borrow from his enemies, the Ottomans?

17. In what other ways did the Safavids interweave foreign ideas into their culture?

SECTION 3 *(pages 451–457)*
The Mughals Establish an Empire in India

18. What opposition did the Mughals face when they invaded India?

19. In what ways did Akbar defend religious freedom during his reign?

20. How did Akbar's successors promote religious conflict in the empire?

Visual Summary

The Muslim World Expands

Ottoman Empire

1200		1400			1600		1800

- **1280–1326** Reign of Osman I
- **1361** Ottomans capture Adrianople
- **1451–1481** Reign of Mehmet II
- **1453** Turks take Constantinople
- **1520–1566** Reign of Suleiman I
- **1571** Defeat at Battle of Lepanto begins decline of Ottoman Empire

Safavid Empire

1200		1400			1600		1800

- **1501** Isma'il seizes Persia and declares himself shah
- **1508** Isma'il conquers Baghdad
- **1587–1629** Reign of Shah Abbas
- **1722** Afghans and Ottomans seize Safavid lands

  Safavid Empire collapses

Mughal Empire

1200		1400			1600		1800

- **1494** Babur begins his rise to power
- **1526** Babur seizes Delhi
- **1556–1605** Reign of Akbar
- **1628–1658** Reign of Shah Jahan
- **1658–1707** Reign of Aurangzeb
- **1719** Mughal Empire declines

Interact *with* History

Possible Responses: Students might try to emulate the Ottomans' military success, tolerance, and cultural achievements. They will probably want to avoid the Ottoman rulers' violent elimination of competition for the throne and their practice of producing weak, uneducated successors.

CRITICAL THINKING

1. CONSTANTINOPLE'S LAST STAND

Why do you think that so few European countries helped defend Constantinople from the Ottomans? In considering your answer, review what you learned about the results of the Crusades in the Holy Roman Empire in Chapter 14.

2. GROWTH OF AN EMPIRE

THEME EMPIRE BUILDING Conquest of new territories certainly contributed to the growth of the Muslim empires you read about. How might it have also hindered this growth?

3. MUSLIM MIRROR ON THE WALL

Using a Venn diagram like the one below, compare the personal traits and policies of Suleiman I and Akbar.

4. ANALYZING PRIMARY SOURCES

The Greek historian Kritovoulos was appointed a governor in the court of Mehmet II after his conquest of Constantinople. In the following quotation, Kritovoulos gives his view of Mehmet's actions. Read the paragraph and answer the questions below it.

> **A VOICE FROM THE PAST**
> When the Sultan [Mehmet] had captured the City of Constantinople, almost his very first care was to have the City repopulated. He also undertook the further care and repairs of it. He sent an order in the form of an imperial command to every part of his realm, that as many inhabitants as possible be transferred to the City, not only Christians but also his own people and many of the Hebrews.
> **KRITOVOULOS,** *History of Mehmet the Conqueror*

- Does the tone of this statement indicate that Kritovoulos thought Mehmet dealt fairly with Constantinople? Why or why not?
- Why do you think Mehmet wanted to open the city to Christians and Hebrews as well as Muslims? Support your answer with information from the chapter.

CHAPTER ACTIVITIES

1. LIVING HISTORY: Unit Portfolio Project

THEME CULTURAL INTERACTION Your unit portfolio project focuses on the cultural interaction that resulted from the expansion of the Muslim world (see page 387). For Chapter 18 you might use one of the following ideas to add to your portfolio.

- Expand your ideas for the Interact with History activity on the previous page into a speech to your people. Explain your policies and ask for your people's support.
- Draw a political cartoon showing that the Safavids borrowed ideas from their enemies, the Ottomans.
- Write an inscription for Akbar's tombstone, focusing on his religious tolerance and on the mix of cultures in his government bureaucracy.

2. CONNECT TO TODAY: Cooperative Learning

THEME POWER AND AUTHORITY The Muslim empires you have studied based their rule on the Islamic religion. Islam remains an important social and political force in modern Turkey, Iran, India, and Pakistan.

Work with a team to find out the status of Muslims in one of these countries today. Then collaborate with the other teams to create a summary chart of these modern Muslim countries.

Using the Internet or other reference sources, determine the status of Muslims in your team's country.

- What role do Muslims play in the government?
- Do the country's leaders promote religious tolerance? Explain.
- What is the overall economic status of Muslims?

3. INTERPRETING A TIME LINE

Look at the time lines on the facing page. Which empire lasted longest? Which was the shortest lived?

FOCUS ON GRAPHS

Compare the territory and population of the following seven empires at their height.

- Which four empires had about the same territory?
- Which of those empires had the fewest people per square mile?

Connect to History
Why might the Safavid Empire have remained so relatively small?

The Muslim World Expands **459**

CHAPTER ACTIVITIES

1. LIVING HISTORY

Standards for Evaluation
A speech should meet the following criteria:

- Clearly states a general position and specific policies.
- Is brief and to the point.
- Elicits listener enthusiasm and support.

Standards for Evaluation
A political cartoon should meet the following criteria:

- Communicates a clear idea about the Safavids.
- Includes specific characters or images that represent the Safavids and the Ottomans.
- Uses well-chosen words, if necessary, to support the message.

Standards for Evaluation
A tombstone inscription should meet the following criteria:

- Reflects an understanding of Akbar's life and achievements.
- Uses strong, descriptive language.
- Follows standard epitaph style.

2. CONNECT TO TODAY

Standards for Evaluation
A chart should meet the following criteria:

- Presents the political, religious, and economic status of Muslims in the countries chosen.
- Organizes information in a clear, easy-to-follow graphic display.
- Includes verbal summaries as needed.

3. INTERPRETING A TIME LINE

Ottoman; Safavid

FOCUS ON GRAPHS

- Ottoman, Safavid, Mughal, Mali
- Kingdom of Mali

Connect to History *Possible Response:* It was squeezed between the Ottoman and Mughal empires and was unable to expand either its territory or its population.

CRITICAL THINKING

1. CONSTANTINOPLE'S LAST STAND

Possible Responses: The failure of Christianity to overcome the Muslims during the Crusades was a bitter memory. In addition, the Ottomans had a powerful army.

2. GROWTH OF AN EMPIRE

Possible Responses: Overaggressive empire building, such as during Aurangzeb's reign led to overspending, rebellion, and the decline of the empire. Adding territory without tolerance for the conquered people could also be destructive.

3. MUSLIM MIRROR ON THE WALL

Possible Responses: Suleiman I—simplified tax system, Akbar—gave land grants to bureaucrats, created effective tax policy. Both—strong military leader; reformed bureaucracy; practiced religious tolerance; supported the arts, learning, and other cultures.

4. ANALYZING PRIMARY SOURCES

Possible Responses: The repeated use of the word *care* implies that he thought Mehmet was dealing very fairly and humanely with Constantinople and its people; Mehmet was tolerant of other religions and wished to take advantage of the skills of the local people.

An Age of Exploration and Isolation

	Key Ideas	COPY MASTERS	ASSESSMENT

SECTION 1
Europeans Explore the East
pp. 463–468

The desire for profit and the hope of spreading Christianity motivate European exploration, and new technology makes it possible. The Portuguese dominate exploration until other Europeans, especially the Dutch, establish their own trading empires.

 In-Depth Resources: Unit 4
- **Guided Reading,** p. 51
- **Primary Sources:** Exploration of Cape Verde, p. 57; The Treaty of Tordesillas, p. 58
- **History Makers:** Vasco da Gama, p. 64
- **Science and Technology:** A Revolution in Cartography, p. 67

PE **Section 1 Assessment,** p. 468

Formal Assessment
- Section Quiz, p. 216

Alternative Assessment Book
- Standards for Evaluating a Cooperative Activity

SECTION 2
China Rejects European Outreach
pp. 469–473

After a series of successful voyages of exploration, China withdraws into isolation. Both the Ming and the Qing dynasties limit foreign trade and follow a policy of self-sufficiency.

 In-Depth Resources: Unit 4
- **Guided Reading,** p. 52
- **Skillbuilder Practice:** Interpreting Graphs, p. 54
- **Geography Application:** The Voyages of Zheng He, p. 55
- **Primary Source:** from *The Journals of Matteo Ricci,* p. 59
- **Literature:** from *The Dream of the Red Chamber,* p. 61

PE **Section 2 Assessment,** p. 473

Formal Assessment
- Section Quiz, p. 217

Alternative Assessment Book
- Standards for Evaluating a Cooperative Activity

SECTION 3
Japan Limits Western Contacts
pp. 474–477

After a period of severe disorder, the Tokugawa Shogunate unifies Japan. In the two centuries of peace and prosperity that follow, the Japanese close their country to foreign ideas by banning Christianity and severely restricting foreign trade.

 In-Depth Resources: Unit 4
- **Guided Reading,** p. 53
- **Literature:** Haiku, p. 63
- **History Makers:** Tokugawa Ieyasu, p. 65
- **Connections Across Time and Cultures:** Breakdown of Feudal Societies, p. 66

PE **Section 3 Assessment,** p. 477

Formal Assessment
- Section Quiz, p. 218

Alternative Assessment Book
- Standards for Evaluating a Product or Performance

CHAPTER RESOURCES

Chapter Overview

Seeking spices and converts, European nations lead successful voyages of exploration to the East. China and Japan both limit foreign contact after a brief period of acceptance.

Telescoping the Times
- Chapter Summary, pp. 73–75

Planning for Block Schedules

PE **Chapter Assessment,** pp. 478–479

Chapter Activities, p. 479

Formal Assessment
- Chapter Test, forms A and B, pp. 219–224

 Test Generator

Alternative Assessment Book

1400–1800

 Warm-Up Transparency 19

 World Art and Cultures Transparencies
- AT41 Portuguese Tower of Belém

 INTERNET RESOURCES
www.mlworldhistory.com

 Warm-Up Transparency 19

 Electronic Library of Primary Sources
- Letter to King George III

 INTERNET RESOURCES
www.mlworldhistory.com

 Warm-Up Transparency 19

 Geography Transparencies
- GT19 Tokugawa Ieyasu Unites Japan, 1603

 World Art and Cultures Transparencies
- AT42 Japanese screen painting

 Critical Thinking Transparencies
- CT19 The Impact of Exploration on East Asia
- CT55 Chapter 19 Visual Summary

 Electronic Library of Primary Sources
- from *The Life and Letters of St. Francis Xavier*
- from the Act of Seclusion

 INTERNET RESOURCES
www.mlworldhistory.com

 Chapter Summaries on Audiocassette in English and Spanish

 INTERNET RESOURCES
www.mlworldhistory.com

Block Scheduling (90 MINUTES)

Day 1	Day 2	
Section 1, pp. 463–468	*Section 2,* pp. 469–473	*Section 3,* pp. 474–477
COOPERATIVE ACTIVITY Writing a Progress Report, p. 466 (Teacher's Edition)	**COOPERATIVE ACTIVITY** Panel Discussion, p. 470 (Teacher's Edition)	*Section Assessments,* pp. 473, 477
Section Assessment, p. 468		*Chapter Assessment,* pp. 478–479

Yearly Pacing *Chapter 19 Total:* 2 days *Yearly Total:* 85 days

 Planning for Block Schedules

Customizing for Special Needs

Students Acquiring English

 Access for Students Acquiring English
- **Guided Reading** for Sections 1–3 (Spanish), pp. 189–191
- **Chapter Summary** (Spanish), pp. 186–188
- **Skillbuilder Practice** Interpreting Graphs (Spanish) p. 192
- **Geography Application** The Voyages of Zheng He (Spanish), p. 193

 Chapter Summaries on Audiocassette in English and Spanish

 INTERNET RESOURCES
www.mlworldhistory.com
The Diverse Classroom.

Less Proficient Readers

 In-Depth Resources: Unit 4
- **Guided Reading** for Sections 1–3, pp. 51–53
- **Skillbuilder Practice** Interpreting Graphs, p. 54
- **Geography Application** The Voyages of Zheng He, p. 55

 Telescoping the Times
- Chapter Summary, pp. 73–75

 Chapter Summaries on Audiocassette

Gifted and Talented Students

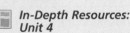 *In-Depth Resources: Unit 4*
Primary Sources:
- Exploration of Cape Verde, p. 57
- The Treaty of Tordesillas, p. 58
- from *The Journals of Matteo Ricci,* p. 59

History Makers
- Vasco da Gama, p. 64
- Tokugawa Ieyasu, p. 65

Connections to Literature READINGS FOR STUDENTS

 In-Depth Resources: Unit 4
Literature: from *The Dream of the Red Chamber,* p. 61

Enrichment Reading

Spence, Jonathan D.
The Question of Hu
New York: Vintage, 1989

A suspenseful narrative of the 1722 travels of a Chinese Catholic and a Jesuit missionary to France.

Wood, Francis
Did Marco Polo Go to China?
New York: Westview, 1996

A readable presentation of the passionate debate concerning the authenticity of Marco Polo's travels.

An Age of Exploration and Isolation, 1400–1800

Accessing Prior Knowledge

- Ask students to look at the pictures, read each related caption, and discuss what they know about previous interaction between the West and the East.

Predicting and Making Inferences

- After reading about Europeans' improving their navigational techniques, what can students predict about how these skills might be used?

- Ask students what they might infer about the possible response of the Japanese to Europeans, from looking at the print of the samurai warrior.

Geography Connection

Ask students to study the maps of Europe and Asia on these two pages.

- Which were the five major European countries that became involved in trade with the East? *Portugal, Spain, France, the Netherlands, England.*

- What geographic feature may have been a cause of Japan's isolation? *It was an island.*

CHAPTER 19

An Age of Exploration and Isolation, 1400–1800

PREVIEWING THEMES

Cultural Interaction
European exploration of Asia resulted in a meeting of different cultures. While this cultural interaction spurred the exchange of many goods and ideas, the people of Asia also resisted European influence.

Economics
The desire for wealth was a driving force behind European exploration of the East. Europeans sought control over the trade of popular goods from Asian countries; European merchants and sailors took to the seas in search of these lands.

Science & Technology
Europeans were able to explore faraway lands only after they improved their sailing technology. Innovations in shipbuilding and navigational techniques allowed Europeans to expand far beyond their borders.

INTERNET CONNECTION
Visit us at www.mlworldhistory.com to learn more about this age of exploration and isolation.

EUROPE AND ASIA, AROUND 1500

Norwegian Sea

North Sea

Baltic Sea

Moscow

ENGLAND
London Amsterdam
NETHERLANDS Paris
FRANCE
EUROPE

OTTOMAN EMPIRE

SPAIN
Rome

Lisbon
PORTUGAL

Tripoli

Mediterranean Sea

By the **early 1400s, Europeans** were improving their navigational techniques in an effort to explore the lands beyond their shores. Here, for example, a French mapmaker uses an instrument to determine his position on the globe.

GEOGRAPHY THEMES

Location

Have students locate on the map Europe, Africa, South Asia (India), and East Asia (China and Japan). (Refer to the Atlas map on pages 972–973 to show students that the only water route to the east took ships around the tip of southern Africa.) Then have them use the distance scale to roughly estimate sailing distances from the port of Lisbon to the coasts of India, China, and Japan. *About 14,500 miles; 19,000; 19,500.* Make a chart of those distances on the chalkboard. You might also ask students to roughly estimate the distance if the journey to India could have been made overland. *About 6,000 miles.*

Movement

From the caption related to Japan, students should conclude that European explorers and traders were able to sail to Japan during this time period. First, ask students whether they think it was possible that a ship could sail from Europe to East Asia without making any stops. *Possible Response: No—the distance was too great; ships had to stop to find food and water for their crews.* Then, ask students how the lands between Europe and Japan might have been affected by European exploration and trade. Have them reread the first theme, cultural interaction, to help answer this question.

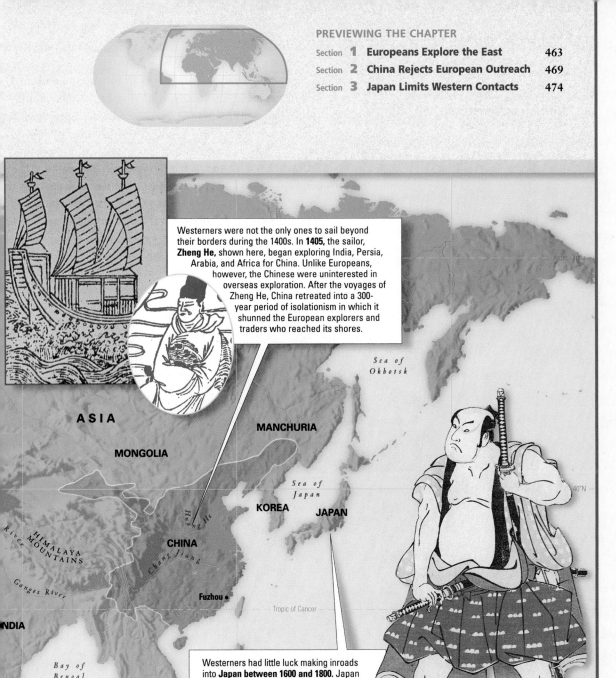

Westerners were not the only ones to sail beyond their borders during the 1400s. In **1405**, the sailor, **Zheng He,** shown here, began exploring India, Persia, Arabia, and Africa for China. Unlike Europeans, however, the Chinese were uninterested in overseas exploration. After the voyages of Zheng He, China retreated into a 300-year period of isolationism in which it shunned the European explorers and traders who reached its shores.

Westerners had little luck making inroads into **Japan between 1600 and 1800.** Japan had a strong military tradition, reflected in this 18th century print of a samurai warrior. In addition, Japan's unified culture made it difficult for European traders to establish themselves there. Like the Chinese, the Japanese eventually closed their borders to outsiders and began a long period of isolationism.

Holy Roman Empire
Ming Empire (1368–1644)

0 500 Miles
0 1,000 Kilometers

N

461

ADDITIONAL RESOURCES

Books for the Teacher

- Berry, Mary Elizabeth. *The Culture of Civil War in Kyoto.* Berkeley: U of California P, 1994.

- Boorstin, Daniel J. *The Discoverers.* New York: Random, 1983. European explorers.

- Levathes, Louise. *When China Ruled the Seas: The Treasure Fleet of the Dragon Throne, 1405–1433.* New York: Simon, 1994.

Books for the Student

- Hale, John R. *Age of Exploration.* Alexandria, Virginia: Time-Life Books, 1974.

- Reid, Struan. *Exploration by Sea.* New York: New Discovery Books, 1994. European trade empires.

▬▬▬ Videos

- *Asia: 1600–1800.* Social Studies School Service, 1985. Asians respond to Western intrusions.

- *Forbidden City: The Great Within.* Cambridge Social Studies, 1995. 800-468-4227.

- *The Golden Age of Exploration.* Knowledge Unlimited, 1997. 800-356-2303.

◉ Software

- *Exploration.* CD-ROM. Queue, 1997. 800-232-2224. Describes the voyages of the Portuguese, Columbus, and other explorers.

- *Stowaway!* CD-ROM. Social Studies School Service, 1994. 800-421-4246. Explore an 18th-century British warship.

HISTORY THROUGH ART

Woodblock Print

The image of a samurai warrior is an 18th-century Japanese woodblock print. Woodblock print is the type of Japanese art best known to the Western world. It is the most famous art of the Tokugawa period (1603 to 1868). Because woodblock prints were inexpensively produced, they were popular among the common people. They depicted contemporary manners and customs, scenes of everyday

life, beautiful women, kabuki actors, and rural landscapes. Woodblock prints are a valuable source of information about the lifestyle and social trends of the period. At first the prints were done in black and white. Later they were executed in brilliantly vibrant colors. Woodblock prints were a collaborative effort. An artist drew the design. A carver pasted the design on a block of wood and did the carving. A printer

made the prints, and a publisher distributed them.

This print dramatically captures the samurai wearing the traditional short silk kimono and baggy trousers and carrying both the samurai's long and short sword.

Interpreting the Art Does this print seem effective in depicting the self-confidence and tenacity of a samurai warrior? In what ways?

Interact *with* History

This Interact with History feature motivates students by asking them to choose whether to go on a voyage of exploration. As they imagine themselves making this decision, students will consider the benefits and hazards of taking this journey and become decision makers.

Purpose

- to set the stage for European exploration of the East
- to help students understand some of the reasons for exploration
- to help students make connections with the various people and events that they will study in this chapter

Teaching Strategy

Thinking Critically After students have imagined themselves in the situation described on this page, have them answer the key questions and give reasons for their decision.

EXAMINING *the* ISSUES

Following are suggestions for addressing each bulleted question.

1 Ask students whether they think modern-day space voyages to Mars or other planets will prove beneficial. *Answers might point to the possible discovery of valuable minerals or of knowledge that would lead to advances on Earth.*

2 Ask students whether they would participate in such voyages. *Answers might hinge on whether or not students believed in the value of the voyages, were adventuresome, or wanted to contribute to the advancement of science.*

Making Connections Encourage students to discuss interactions between people of different cultures in other time periods about which they have read.

Interact *with* History

Claiming new lands could bring glory and prestige to your country.

It is a gray and windy morning in 1430. You are standing on a dock in the European country of Portugal staring out at the dark and mysterious Atlantic Ocean. You, like most people at the time, have no idea what lies beyond the horizon. Now you may find out. You have been asked to go on a voyage of exploration.

You've heard all the terrifying stories of sea monsters and shipwrecks. You've heard the warnings that the currents along parts of western Africa are "so terrible that no ship having once passed . . . will ever be able to return." You also have heard that possible financial gain awaits those who help explore and claim new lands. Now, as the captain calls for you to come aboard, you must decide.

Would you go?

The large hold of your ship could carry back gold, jewels, and other valuable items found in distant lands.

Raging waves could destroy your ship and leave you at the mercy of the sea.

EXAMINING *the* ISSUES

1 • What possible rewards might come from exploring the seas for new lands?

2 • What are the risks involved in embarking on a voyage into the unknown?

Discuss these questions with your classmates. In your discussion, recall what you have learned about the lands beyond Europe and what they have to offer.

As you read about the age of exploration and isolation, see what goals prompted Europeans to explore and to what extent they achieved these goals.

462 Chapter 19

Follow Up

A feature on the chapter assessment will ask students to reevaluate their responses to the situation presented on this page. Remind students that their opinions may change as they learn more about the European voyages of exploration.

Europeans Explore the East

TERMS & NAMES
- **Bartolomeu Dias**
- **Prince Henry**
- **Vasco da Gama**
- **Treaty of Tordesillas**
- **Dutch East India Company**

MAIN IDEA	WHY IT MATTERS NOW
Driven by the desire for wealth and Christian converts, Europeans began an age of exploration.	European exploration was an important step toward the global interaction that characterizes the world today.

SETTING THE STAGE By the early 1400s, Europeans were ready to venture beyond their borders. As Chapter 17 explained, the Renaissance encouraged, among other things, a new spirit of adventure and curiosity. This spirit of adventure—along with several other important factors—prompted Europeans to explore the world around them. This chapter and the next one describe how these explorations began a long process that would bring together the peoples of many different lands and permanently change the world.

Many Factors Encourage Exploration

Europeans had not been completely isolated from the rest of the world before the 1400s. Beginning around 1100, European crusaders battled Muslims for control of the Holy Lands in Southwest Asia. In 1275, the Italian trader Marco Polo reached the court of Kublai Khan in China. For the most part, however, Europeans had neither the interest nor the ability to explore foreign lands. That changed by the early 1400s. The desire to grow rich and to spread Christianity, coupled with advances in sailing technology, spurred an age of European exploration.

Europeans Seek Greater Wealth The desire for new sources of wealth was the main reason for European exploration. Through overseas exploration, merchants and traders hoped ultimately to benefit from what had become a profitable business in Europe: the trade of spices and other luxury goods from Asia. The people of Europe had been introduced to these items during the Crusades, the wars fought between Christians and Muslims from 1096 to 1270 (see Chapter 14). After the Crusades ended, Europeans continued to demand such spices as nutmeg, ginger, cinnamon, and pepper—all of which added flavor to the bland foods of Europe. Because demand for these goods was greater than the supply, merchants could charge high prices and thus make great profits.

The Muslims and Italians controlled the trade of goods from East to West. Muslims sold Asian goods to Italian merchants, who controlled trade across the land routes of the Mediterranean region. The Italian merchants resold the items at increased prices to merchants throughout Europe. Other European traders did not like this arrangement. Paying such high prices to the Italians severely cut into their own profits. By the 1400s, European merchants—as well as the new monarchs of England, Spain, Portugal, and France—sought to bypass the Italian merchants. This meant finding a sea route directly to Asia.

The Spread of Christianity The desire to spread Christianity also fueled European exploration. Aside from leaving Europeans with a taste for spices, the Crusades left feelings of hostility between Christians and Muslims. European nations believed that they had a sacred duty not only to continue fighting

An Age of Exploration and Isolation **463**

A. Possible Answer The Italians controlled the trade and charged them high prices for the trade goods.
THINK THROUGH HISTORY
A. Analyzing Issues Why did many European merchants dislike the way goods were traded from East to West?

This globe depicts the Europeans' view of the world around 1492. Europe and Africa, shown here, were the lands Europeans had explored most by that time.

Section 1 Overview

OBJECTIVES

1. To identify the factors that led to European exploration.

2. To describe how Portugal established a sea route to Asia.

3. To identify which nations set up trading empires in the East and where those nations dominated.

SKILLBUILDER

- Interpreting maps: place, region, p. 467

CRITICAL THINKING

- Analyzing issues, pp. 463, 466, 468
- Summarizing, p. 464
- Analyzing motives, p. 465
- Recognizing effects, pp. 467, 468
- Making inferences, p. 468
- Analyzing themes, p. 468

FOCUS

5-Minute Warm-Up

▶ **Interpreting Maps**
Answering the following questions will help students understand the impact of European exploration in the East.

1. Study the map on p. 467. Which European country sent out the first voyages of exploration to the East?

2. What European countries had established trading posts in the East by 1700?

🏛 *WARM-UP TRANSPARENCY 19*

OBJECTIVE ① INSTRUCT

Many Factors Encourage Exploration

▶ **Key Ideas**
- Profit is the main motive for European exploration in the 1400s.
- Europeans also hope to spread Christianity to other lands.
- Technological advances make long-distance voyages possible.

📖 *IN-DEPTH RESOURCES: UNIT 4* Guided Reading, p. 51

📖 *ACCESS FOR STUDENTS ACQUIRING ENGLISH* Guided Reading (Spanish), p. 189

SECTION 1 RESOURCES

PRINT RESOURCES

📖 *IN-DEPTH RESOURCES: UNIT 4*
Guided Reading, p. 51
Primary Source: Exploration of Cape Verde, p. 57; The Treaty of Tordesillas, p. 58
History Makers: Vasco da Gama, p. 64
Science and Technology: A Revolution in Cartography, p. 67

📖 *ACCESS FOR STUDENTS ACQUIRING ENGLISH*
Guided Reading (Spanish), p. 189

📖 *FORMAL ASSESSMENT*
Section Quiz, p. 216

📖 *ALTERNATIVE ASSESSMENT BOOK*

TECHNOLOGY RESOURCES

🏛 *WORLD ART AND CULTURES TRANSPARENCIES*
AT41 Portuguese Tower of Belém

🌐 **INTERNET** www.mlworldhistory.com

Portugal Leads the Way

Key Ideas
- Prince Henry pushes for voyages of exploration.
- Portuguese sailors establish a direct sea route to Asia.
- Columbus's voyage west across the Atlantic intensifies the rivalry between Spain and Portugal.

 IN-DEPTH RESOURCES: UNIT 4
Primary Source: Exploration of Cape Verde, p. 57

WORLD ART AND CULTURES TRANSPARENCIES
AT41 Portuguese Tower of Belém

CRITICAL THINKING ACTIVITY
CLASS TIME: 15 MINUTES

Analyzing Causes
Have students use a graphic organizer to show the causes of European exploration. *Desire for profit; hope to spread Christianity; technological advances.*

Ask students which of these causes might have prompted wealthy individuals to finance voyages of exploration.

HISTORYMAKERS
Prince Henry

Briefly discuss Henry's personal characteristics and his devotion to his work. Then ask students to imagine that the king has invited Henry to travel to the Portuguese capital to attend a party celebrating the return of a ship from Africa. Have them write Henry's response either accepting the invitation or declining to go.

Muslims, but also to convert non-Christians throughout the world.

Europeans hoped to obtain popular goods directly from the peoples of Asia. They also hoped to Christianize them. **Bartolomeu Dias,** an early Portuguese explorer, explained his motives: "to serve God and His Majesty, to give light to those who were in darkness and to grow rich as all men desire to do."

Technological Advances While "God, glory, and gold" were the primary motives for exploration, advances in technology made the voyages of discovery possible. During the 1200s, it would have been nearly impossible for a European sea captain to cross 3,000 miles of ocean and return again. The main problem was that European ships could not sail against the wind. In the 1400s, shipbuilders designed a new vessel—the caravel. The caravel was sturdier than earlier vessels. In addition, its triangular sails allowed it to sail effectively against the wind.

Europeans also improved their navigational techniques. To better determine their location on the sea, sailors used the astrolabe, which the Muslims had perfected. The astrolabe was a brass circle with carefully adjusted rings marked off in degrees. Using the rings to sight the stars, a sea captain could tell how far north or south of the equator he was. Explorers were also able to more accurately track their direction by using a magnetic compass invented by the Chinese.

THINK THROUGH HISTORY
B. Summarizing
How does the phrase, "God, glory, and gold" summarize the Europeans' motives for exploration?
B. Possible Answer
European explorers wanted to spread Christianity, bring fame and prestige to themselves and their country, and enrich themselves.

HISTORY MAKERS

Prince Henry
1394–1460

For his role in promoting Portuguese exploration, Prince Henry is often called Henry the Navigator. Historians paint Henry as a quiet and extremely driven man. So consumed was he by the quest to find new lands, that he reportedly shunned female companionship.

Throughout his life, Henry supposedly showed little emotion. It was said that no one ever saw him lose his temper. When angry with someone, Henry allegedly just waved them from his presence, uttering, "I commend you to God, may you be fortunate." While some considered him to be cold and distant, others insisted that the prince had a sensitive side. One writer claimed that upon learning of the death of a friend, Henry wept nonstop for several days.

Portugal Leads the Way

The leader in developing and applying these sailing innovations was Portugal. Located on the Atlantic Ocean at the southwest corner of Europe, Portugal first established trading outposts along the west coast of Africa. Eventually, Portuguese explorers pushed farther east into the Indian Ocean.

The Portuguese Explore Africa Portugal took the lead in overseas exploration in part due to strong government support. The nation's most enthusiastic supporter of exploration was **Prince Henry,** the son of Portugal's king. Henry's dreams of overseas exploration began in 1415 when he helped conquer the Muslim city of Ceuta in North Africa. There, he had his first glimpse of the dazzling wealth that lay beyond Europe. Throughout Ceuta, the Portuguese invaders found exotic stores filled with pepper, cinnamon, cloves, and other spices. In addition, they encountered large supplies of gold, silver, and jewels.

Henry returned to Portugal determined to reach the source of these treasures in the East. The prince also wished to spread the Christian faith. In 1419, Henry founded a navigation school on the southwestern coast of Portugal. Map makers, instrument makers, shipbuilders, scientists, and sea captains gathered there to perfect their trade.

Within several years, Portuguese ships began creeping down the western coast of Africa. By the time Henry died in 1460, the Portuguese had established a series of trading posts along the shores of Africa. There, they traded with Africans for such profitable items as gold and ivory. Eventually, they traded for African captives to be used as slaves. Having established their presence along Africa's western coast, Portuguese explorers plotted their next daring move. They would find a sea route to Asia.

Portuguese Sailors Reach Asia The Portuguese believed that to reach Asia by sea, they would have to sail around the southern tip of Africa. In 1488, Portuguese captain Bartolomeu Dias ventured

---

The Caravel Ask students how they would have gone about designing a ship for the special needs of the long-distance explorer. The ship had to be large enough to carry cargo but agile enough to sail against the wind. The caravel's designers combined the features of two existing ships that offered those qualities. One was a kind of dhow called a *caravos,* a lateen-rigged vessel capable of hauling cargo of the size that explorers would need. Arabs had been sailing this type of dhow along the coasts of Egypt and Tunis since ancient times. The other model ship, known as a *caravela,* plied the waters of a river in northern Portugal. Designers liked this vessel's superb maneuverability.

Linguistic Learners Tell students that in 1471, Portuguese explorers arrived at a region later known as the Gold Coast, or modern Ghana. Soon they controlled the West African trade in gold—one-tenth of the world's production. The riches of West Africa would help bankroll Portugal's exploration of the East. Invite students to theorize about how the first Portuguese, arriving at the Gold Coast, discovered that the region held such riches. Have them create and present a dialogue between a Portuguese sea captain and an African leader in which the European attempts to find out if there is gold in the area and then tries to establish a trading relationship.

The Tools of Exploration

Out on the open seas, winds easily blew ships off course. With only the sun, moon, and stars to guide them, few sailors willingly ventured beyond the sight of land. In order to travel to distant parts of the world, European inventors and sailors experimented with new tools for navigation and new designs for sailing ships.

The triangular sails allowed the caravel to sail effectively against the wind. With these sails the ship could tack (sail on a zigzag course) more directly into the wind than could a square-rigged ship.

The improved rudder allowed the caravel to turn more easily.

The large cargo area was capable of carrying the numerous supplies needed for long voyages.

This 16th century Italian compass (with its lid beside it) is typical of those taken by navigators on the great voyages of exploration. The compass was invented by the Chinese.

Here, a naval officer uses a sextant, which replaced the astrolabe in measuring the height of the stars above the horizon.

Connect *to* History

Analyzing Motives Why did inventors and sailors develop better tools for navigation?

 SEE SKILLBUILDER HANDBOOK, PAGE 994

Connect *to* Today

Modern Sailing Investigate what types of navigational or other tools modern sailors use. Choose one tool and write a brief explanation of what it does. Be prepared to present your report to the class.

An Age of Exploration and Isolation **465**

Besides their sailing technology, Europeans developed another valuable aid to the expansion of trade—the shipboard cannon. Designers overcame great technical problems to be able to mount these powerful weapons all around a sailing ship's perimeter. Bristling with cannons, European warships defeated Muslim fleets in the Indian Ocean and controlled trade routes from Africa to the East Indies.

📖 ***IN-DEPTH RESOURCES: UNIT 4***
Science and Technology: A Revolution in Cartography, p. 67

MORE ABOUT . . .
The Sextant

The sextant incorporated a telescope, mirrors, and an arc of a circle calibrated in degrees. With this device, a mariner could read the angle of elevation above the horizon of the moon, the sun, or another star. With this information, the exact time of day, and published tables, the ship's latitude could be determined.

MORE ABOUT . . .
The Compass

The Italian compass shown here has a *T,* which stands for "north wind" but represents the direction north. The association of wind with direction is ancient. Before the invention of the magnetic compass, sailors throughout the world used familiar local winds to determine direction. (They also took note of where the sun rose and set.) Even after the compass came into use, the link between the wind and direction remained strong—and not just among Italian sailors. For example, Spanish mariners called compass directions *los vientos* ("the winds"). Portuguese sailors called their compass card, printed with the various compass directions, a *rosa dos ventos,* or "wind rose."

Connect *to* History

Analyzing Motives
Possible Responses: They might have been motivated by the basic need to improve the ability to navigate ships or by the desire to bring glory and wealth to their country; they might simply have delighted in the innovative and demanding task of improving navigational tools.

Connect *to* Today

Modern Sailing
You may wish to suggest to students the following strategies for investigating modern navigational tools and preparing a report on their findings:

• Check library resources and the Internet to locate information on modern maritime navigation.

• Obtain a visual of the navigational tool they select to be used with the explanatory paragraph.

Daily *Life*

A Rough Trip

Ask students to find out more about life aboard a ship in the age of exploration and to imagine they are on such a voyage. How long did a trip from Portugal to the southern tip of Africa take? *Six months.*

MORE ABOUT . . .
Vasco da Gama

In July 1497, da Gama sailed from Lisbon with four vessels and 170 men. Ten months later, after an unparalleled feat of navigation, they arrived in Calicut. Da Gama announced that he came seeking "Christians and spices." He found spices but no Christians. Instead, he and the explorers who later followed his route found many states, none Christian, and an ancient seagoing commerce run mainly by Muslims.

 IN-DEPTH RESOURCES: UNIT 4
History Maker: Vasco da Gama, p. 64
Primary Source: The Treaty of Tordesillas, p. 58

OBJECTIVE ❸ INSTRUCT

Trading Empires in the Indian Ocean

Key Ideas
- Portugal builds a trading empire that reaches the East Indies.
- Other nations compete with Portugal for Indian Ocean trade.
- The Dutch East India Company becomes dominant in the region.

Daily *Life*

A Rough Trip

Life aboard a ship during the age of exploration was no pleasure cruise. With no refrigeration system, foods such as fruits, vegetables, and meats quickly rotted. For nourishment, sailors often had to rely on a rock-hard, bland-tasting biscuit, known as hardtack.

In addition, swift and brutal punishment often awaited those who broke the ship's rules. The most common punishment was with the "cat-o'-nine-tails," a whip made of nine knotted cords (shown here). The sailor was tied down and repeatedly struck on his bare back.

---

farther down the coast of Africa until he reached the tip. As he arrived, a huge storm rose and battered his fleet for days. When the storm ended, Dias realized his ships had been blown around the tip to the other side of the continent. Dias explored the southeast coast of Africa and then considered sailing to India. However, his crew was exhausted and food supplies were low. As a result, the captain returned home.

With the southern tip of Africa finally rounded, the Portuguese continued pushing east. In 1498, the Portuguese explorer **Vasco da Gama** reached the port of Calicut, on the southwestern coast of India. Da Gama and his crew were amazed by the spices, as well as the rare silks and precious gems, that filled Calicut's shops. The Portuguese sailors filled their ships with such spices as pepper and cinnamon and returned to Portugal in 1499. The Portuguese gave da Gama a hero's welcome. His remarkable voyage of 27,000 miles had given Portugal a direct sea route to India.

Spanish Claims Before da Gama's historic voyage, as the Portuguese established trading posts along the west coast of Africa, Spain watched with increasing envy. The Spanish monarchs also desired a direct sea route to the treasures of Asia.

In 1492, an Italian sea captain, Christopher Columbus, convinced Spain to finance what was at that time a bold plan: finding a route to Asia by sailing west across the Atlantic Ocean. In October of that year, Columbus reached the shores of an island in the Caribbean. Columbus's voyage would open the way for European colonization of the American continents—a process that would forever change the world. The immediate impact of Columbus's voyage, however, was to increase tensions between Spain and Portugal.

Columbus thought that he had indeed reached Asia. Believing him to be right, Portugal suspected that Columbus had claimed for Spain lands that Portuguese sailors might have reached first. The rivalry between Spain and Portugal grew more tense. In 1493, Pope Alexander VI stepped in to keep peace between the two nations. He suggested an imaginary dividing line, drawn north to south, through the Atlantic Ocean. All lands to the west of the line, known as the Line of Demarcation, would be Spain's. All lands to the east of the line would belong to Portugal.

Portugal complained that the line gave too much to Spain. So it was moved farther west to include parts of modern-day Brazil for the Portuguese. In 1494, Spain and Portugal signed the **Treaty of Tordesillas,** in which they agreed to honor the line. The era of exploration and colonization was about to begin in earnest.

Trading Empires in the Indian Ocean

With da Gama's voyage, Europeans had finally opened direct sea trade with Asia. They also opened an era of violent conflict in the East. European nations scrambled to establish profitable trading outposts along the shores of South and Southeast Asia. And all the while they battled the region's inhabitants, as well as each other.

Portugal's Trading Empire In the years following da Gama's voyage, Portugal built a bustling trading empire throughout the Indian Ocean. As they moved into the region, they took control of the spice trade from Muslim merchants. In 1509, Portugal extended its control over the area when it defeated a Muslim fleet off the coast of India.

The following year, the Portuguese captured Goa, a port city on India's west coast. They made it the capital of their trading empire. They then sailed farther east to Indonesia, also known as the East Indies. In 1511, a Portuguese fleet attacked the city of Malacca on the west coast of the Malay peninsula. In capturing the town, the

---

Background
Dias named Africa's southern tip the Cape of Storms. However, Portugal's ruler was so pleased with the explorer's journey, that he renamed it the Cape of Good Hope.

THINK THROUGH HISTORY
C. Analyzing Issues
How did the Treaty of Tordesillas ease tensions between Spain and Portugal?
C. Possible Answer
It appeased both nations by granting them their own territories to colonize.

Background
Indonesia is the fourth most populous country in the world. It consists of some 13,670 islands, but only about 7,000 are inhabited.

Task: Groups of students will choose one of the European trading empires and write an official government report detailing how their mission has progressed from the start to around the year 1700.

Purpose: To examine in depth the successes and failures of each trading empire.

Activity: Each group will choose or be assigned one of the trading empires—Portugal, Spain, England,

France, or the Netherlands. They will research their empire's quest for profits from the Indian Ocean trade—how it got started, problems it encountered, outposts established, and status at the time of the report, around 1700. They will address their report to their ruler or ruling body.

📁 **Building a Portfolio:** Students who wish to add this report to their portfolios should note their specific contributions.

 ALTERNATIVE ASSESSMENT BOOK
Standards for Evaluating a Cooperative Activity

Standards for Evaluation
Reports should . . .
- clearly detail the history of one European country's Indian Ocean trade
- include failures as well as successes
- show evidence of research using a variety of sources

Portuguese seized control of the Strait of Malacca. Seizing this waterway gave them control of the Moluccas. These were islands so rich in spices that they became known as the Spice Islands.

In convincing his crew to attack Malacca, Portuguese sea captain Afonso de Albuquerque stressed his country's intense desire to crush the Muslim-Italian domination over Asian trade:

A VOICE FROM THE PAST

. . . If we deprive them [Muslims] of this their ancient market there, there does not remain for them a single port in the whole of these parts, where they can carry on their trade in these things. . . . I hold it as very certain that if we take this trade of Malacca away out of their hands, Cairo and Mecca are entirely ruined, and to Venice will no spiceries . . . [be] . . . conveyed except that which her merchants go and buy in Portugal.

AFONSO DE ALBUQUERQUE, from *The Commentaries of the Great Afonso Dalbuquerque*

D. Possible Answer
It brought down the prices of many Asian goods, so more Europeans could afford them.
THINK THROUGH HISTORY
D. Recognizing Effects How did the European domination of the Indian Ocean trade eventually impact Europeans back home?

Portugal did indeed break the old trade network from the East—much to the delight of European consumers. Portuguese merchants brought back goods from Asia at about a fifth of what they cost when purchased through the Arabs and Italians. As a result, more Europeans could afford these items.

In time, Portugal's success in Asia attracted the attention of other European nations. As early as 1521, a Spanish expedition led by Ferdinand Magellan arrived in the Philippines. Spain claimed the islands and began settling them in 1565. By the early 1600s, the rest of Europe had begun descending upon Asia. They were looking to establish their own trade empires in the East.

Other Nations Drive Out the Portuguese Beginning around 1600, the English and Dutch began to challenge Portugal's dominance over the Indian Ocean trade. The Dutch Republic is also known as the Netherlands. It is a small country situated along

Europeans in the East, 1700

European territories: Dutch, English, French, Portuguese, Spanish
European trading posts: Dutch, English, French, Portuguese, Spanish
Dias's route, Aug. 1487– Feb.1488
da Gama's route, July 1497–May 1498

GEOGRAPHY SKILLBUILDER: Interpreting Maps
1. **Place** Which Asian country had the most European trade outposts by 1700?
2. **Region** Where was the Dutch influence the greatest?

467

MORE ABOUT . . .
Afonso de Albuquerque

Afonso de Albuquerque was more than just a sea captain. He gained fame as "the Portuguese Mars" (Mars was the Roman god of war) for his leadership of the armed fleets that took Goa and the Strait of Malacca. Albuquerque also served his king as the viceroy of India, governing the Portuguese holdings there for six years. He died at sea off Goa in 1515, while returning to Portugal after the new king had replaced him and ordered him home.

History from Visuals

Europeans in the East, 1700

Interpreting the Map Have students go to the key to determine da Gama's route. Then have them follow the route from Lisbon in Portugal, along the coasts of Africa, to Calicut in India. Then, have them use the distance scale to determine the distance traveled to reach Calicut. *Answer: About 15,000 miles.*

Extension Activity Invite students to speculate about why so many European nations established trading posts in India. *Possible Responses: India had spices and other goods for trade; India was a good central location from which to pursue the Indian Ocean trade.*

SKILLBUILDER Answers
1. India.
2. The East Indies.

TEACHING OPTIONS

MULTIPLE LEARNING STYLES

Logical-Mathematical Learners Remind students that as a result of Portugal's success in establishing a trading empire in the East, the cost to consumers of Asian goods fell to about a fifth of their former price. Have students make a chart listing a variety of fairly expensive consumer goods available today and showing both the retail price and one-fifth of the retail price. (They might find prices for such goods in newspaper advertisements or department store fliers.) Invite students to discuss what they think the effects might be today of such a radical drop in prices.

CONNECTIONS ACROSS THE CURRICULUM

Economics Invite students to speculate about the economy of the East Indies before the appearance of Europeans. Tell them that in the 1500s, some 90 percent of Southeast Asians (including the people of the East Indies) made a living from agriculture. Most of them raised rice for local markets, but many had turned to commercial crops such as spices or sugar, which could be traded for manufactured goods, silk, and other luxuries. For Southeast Asia, this era was a golden age. Long-distance trade, even before the Europeans arrived, had increased wealth and introduced new products, cultures, and ideas.

Teacher's Edition 467

the North Sea in northwestern Europe. Since the early 1500s, Spain had ruled this area. In 1581, the people of the region declared their independence from Spain and established the Dutch Republic.

In a short time, the Netherlands became a leading sea power. By 1600, the Dutch owned the largest fleet of ships in the world—20,000 vessels. Together, the English and Dutch broke Portuguese control of the Asian region. The two nations then battled one another for dominance of the area. Each nation had formed an East India Company to establish and direct trade throughout Asia. These companies had the power to mint money, make treaties, and even raise their own armies. The **Dutch East India Company** was richer and more powerful than England's company. As a result, the Dutch eventually drove out the English and established their dominance over the region.

European Trade Outposts In 1619, the Dutch established their trading headquarters at Batavia on the island of Java. From there they expanded west to conquer several nearby islands. In addition, the Dutch seized both the port of Malacca and the valuable Spice Islands from Portugal. Throughout the 1600s, the Netherlands increased its control over the Indian Ocean trade. With so many goods from the East traveling to the Netherlands, the nation's capital, Amsterdam, became a leading commercial center. By 1700, the Dutch ruled much of Indonesia and had trading posts in numerous Asian countries. They also controlled the Cape of Good Hope on the southern tip of Africa.

By this time, however, Britain and France had gained a foothold in the region. Having failed to gain control of the larger area, the English East India Company focused much of its energy on establishing outposts in India. There, the English built up a successful business trading fine cloth on the European market. In 1664, France also entered the Asia trade with its own East India Company. The company struggled at first, as it faced continual attacks by the Dutch. The French company finally established an outpost in India in the 1720s. However, it never showed a strong profit.

As the Europeans battled for a share of the profitable Indian Ocean trade, their influence in inland Southeast Asia remained relatively limited. European traders did gain control of numerous port cities throughout the region. However, their influence rarely spread beyond the ports into the countries' interiors. From 1500 to about 1800—when Europeans began to conquer much of the region—the peoples of Asia remained largely unaffected by European contact. As the next two sections explain, European traders who sailed farther east to seek riches in China and Japan had even less success in spreading Western culture.

Section 1 Assessment

1. TERMS & NAMES
Identify
- Bartolomeu Dias
- Prince Henry
- Vasco da Gama
- Treaty of Tordesillas
- Dutch East India Company

2. TAKING NOTES
Trace the establishment of Portugal's trading empire in the Indian Ocean by supplying the significant event for each date shown on the time line below.

| 1419 | | 1498 |
| 1488 | 1511 |

Write the lead paragraph for a news story about one of the time line events.

3. MAKING INFERENCES
What did the Treaty of Tordesillas reveal about Europeans' attitudes toward non-European lands and peoples?

THINK ABOUT
- the dispute between the Portuguese and Spanish
- how the treaty settled the dispute

4. ANALYZING THEMES
Science and Technology In what ways did Europeans owe some of their sailing technology to other peoples of the world?

THINK ABOUT
- the astrolabe
- the compass

2 China Rejects European Outreach

TERMS & NAMES
- Ming Dynasty
- Hongwu
- Yonglo
- Zheng He
- Manchus
- Qing Dynasty
- Kangxi

MAIN IDEA	WHY IT MATTERS NOW
Advances under the Ming and Qing dynasties left China self-contained and uninterested in European contact.	China's independence from the West continues today, even as it forges new economic ties with the outside world.

SETTING THE STAGE Europeans made healthy profits in the Indian Ocean trade. Looking for additional sources of wealth, they sought a trading relationship with China. By the time westerners arrived in the 1500s, China had driven out its Mongol rulers and had united under the Ming Dynasty.

The Ming Dynasty

By the time the first Portuguese ships dropped anchor off the Chinese coast in 1514, China had become the dominant power in the region under the rule of the **Ming Dynasty** (1368–1644). In recognition of China's power, vassal states from Korea to Southeast Asia paid their Ming overlords regular tribute, a payment by one nation to another to acknowledge its submission. China expected the Europeans to do the same. The Ming rulers would not allow outsiders from distant lands to threaten the peace and prosperity they had brought to China following the end of Mongol rule.

The Rise of the Ming **Hongwu,** the son of a peasant, commanded the rebel army that drove the Mongols out of China in 1368. That same year he became the first emperor of the Ming Dynasty. Hongwu continued to rule from the former Yuan capital of Nanjing in the south. He began reforms designed to restore agricultural lands devastated by war, erase all traces of the Mongol past, and promote China's power and prosperity. Hongwu's agricultural reforms increased rice production and improved irrigation. He also encouraged the introduction of fish farming and the growing of commercial crops, such as cotton and sugar cane.

The first Ming emperor used respected traditions and institutions to bring stability to China. For example, he encouraged a return to Confucian moral standards. He improved imperial administration by restoring the merit-based civil service examination system. Later in his rule, however, when problems began to develop, Hongwu became a ruthless tyrant. Suspecting plots against his rule everywhere, he conducted purges in which many thousands of government officials were killed.

Hongwu's death in 1398 led to a power struggle. His son **Yonglo** (yung·lu) emerged victorious from this struggle. Yonglo continued many of his father's policies, although he moved the royal court to Beijing. In addition, Yonglo had a far-ranging curiosity about the outside world. In 1405—before Europeans began to sail beyond their borders—he launched the first of seven voyages of exploration. All were led by a Chinese Muslim admiral named **Zheng He** (jung huh).

The Voyages of Zheng He Zheng He's expeditions were remarkable for their magnitude. Everything about them was large—distances traveled, size of the fleet, and measurements of the ships themselves. The earliest voyages were to Southeast Asia and India. Later expeditions roamed as far as Arabia and eastern Africa.

Vocabulary
vassal states: countries that recognize the overlordship, or domination, of another country.

Background
Confucianism stressed social order, harmony, and good government through education, strong family relationships, and respect for elders.

Vocabulary
purges: ways of ridding a nation, or political party, of people considered undesirable.

This blue and white porcelain vase, with its finely detailed pattern, is from the Ming Dynasty. Ming porcelain is considered to be one of the culture's most famous achievements.

An Age of Exploration and Isolation **469**

Section 2 Overview

OBJECTIVES

1. To identify the successes of the early Ming emperors.
2. To describe China and Korea under the Qing dynasty.
3. To describe daily life in Ming and Qing China.

SKILLBUILDER
- Interpreting graphs, p. 472

CRITICAL THINKING
- Making inferences, pp. 470, 472
- Summarizing, p. 471
- Recognizing effects, p. 473
- Making decisions, p. 473

FOCUS

5-Minute Warm-Up

▶ **Making Inferences**
To help students understand something about Chinese history, have them answer the following questions.

1. Read the Spotlight On the Forbidden City on p. 470. Why was the palace complex called the Forbidden City?

2. What can you infer about the nature of China and of the emperor from this feature?

WARM-UP TRANSPARENCY 19

OBJECTIVE ① INSTRUCT

The Ming Dynasty

▶ **Key Ideas**
- The early Ming emperors stabilize China and help it prosper.
- The voyages of Zheng He showcase China's power and expand its tribute system.
- China officially limits trade with foreign merchants.
- Europeans help increase Chinese manufacturing and commerce and introduce Christianity.

SECTION 2 RESOURCES

Hypothesizing
Ask students how history might have been different if the Chinese had continued to launch voyages like those of Zheng He for another hundred years. *Lead students to see that China's powerful fleet might well have clashed with European fleets seeking Indian Ocean trade.*

MORE ABOUT . . .
China's Trade Policies

Limits on trade did not begin with the arrival of Europeans. China had long restricted the access of Japan, Indonesia, and other neighboring lands, assigning specific ports through which they could trade. As a result, merchants turned to smuggling in order to meet the great demand for Chinese silks, porcelains, and other precious goods. Smuggling had a further effect—it encouraged the emergence of numerous Chinese and Japanese pirates, who preyed on the merchants' boats and made off with their illicit cargoes.

SPOTLIGHT*On*
The Forbidden City

The palace complex contained living quarters, libraries, galleries, and audience halls for tribute ceremonies. Beautiful gardens of pines, cypresses, and rare flowers adorned the grounds. Ask students whether they would have enjoyed living in a place like this. Be sure that they weigh the pleasures of palace life against the limits of walled-in isolation.

Yonglo hoped to impress the world with the power and splendor of Ming China and also hoped to expand China's tribute system. Zheng He's voyages accomplished these goals. From about 40 to 300 ships sailed in each expedition. Among them were fighting ships, storage vessels, and huge "treasure" ships up to 440 feet long. The fleet's crews numbered over 27,000 on some voyages. They included sailors, soldiers, carpenters, interpreters, accountants, doctors, and religious leaders. Like some huge floating city, the fleet sailed from port to port along the Indian Ocean.

Everywhere Zheng He went, he distributed gifts, such as gold, silver, silk, and scented oils, to show Chinese superiority. As a result, more than 16 countries sent tribute to the Ming court. Many envoys traveled to China. Still, Chinese scholar-officials complained that these voyages wasted valuable resources. After the seventh voyage ended in 1433, there were no more. China withdrew into its self-sufficient isolation.

Ming Relations with Foreign Countries China's official trade policies in the 1500s reflected its isolation. To keep the influence of outsiders to a minimum, only the government was to conduct foreign trade, through three coastal ports. In reality, trade flourished up and down the coast. Profit-minded Chinese merchants smuggled cargoes of silk, porcelain, and other valuable goods out of the country into the eager hands of European merchants. Usually, Europeans paid for their purchases with silver—much of it from mines in the Americas.

Demand for Chinese goods had a ripple effect on the economy. Industries such as silk making and ceramics grew rapidly. Manufacturing and commerce increased. However, China did not become highly industrialized for two main reasons. First, the whole idea of commerce offended China's Confucian beliefs. Merchants, it was said, made their money "supporting foreigners and robbery." Second, Chinese economic policies traditionally favored agriculture. Taxes on agriculture stayed low. Taxes on manufacturing and trade skyrocketed.

Accompanying European traders into China were Christian missionaries. The missionaries brought Christianity as well as a variety of European inventions, including the clock and the prism. The first missionary to have an impact was an Italian Jesuit, Matteo Ricci. He gained special favor at the Ming court through his intelligence and his ability to speak and write Chinese. However, many educated Chinese opposed Christianity.

SPOTLIGHT*On*

The Forbidden City
A stunning monument to China's isolationism was an extravagant palace complex at the capital city, Beijing. It was built by emperor Yonglo between 1404 and 1420. The palace was known as the Forbidden City because all commoners and foreigners were forbidden to enter without special permission. Inside the complex's 35-foot-tall red walls, the emperors of China conducted the business of state and lived in luxury and isolation.
Only the emperor, his family, and his court lived in the palace—which contained 9,000 rooms. Maintaining such a splendid palace city was expensive. For example, every day some 6,000 cooks made meals for 10,000 to 15,000 people. In 1949, the palace complex was converted into a museum and opened to the public.

Vocabulary
envoys: government representatives sent to a foreign country.

THINK THROUGH HISTORY
A. Making Inferences What do you think the people of other countries thought about China when they were visited on one of Zheng He's voyages?
A. Possible Answer That China must be very powerful to send so many ships, men, and goods on such a voyage and, therefore, they should pay tribute.

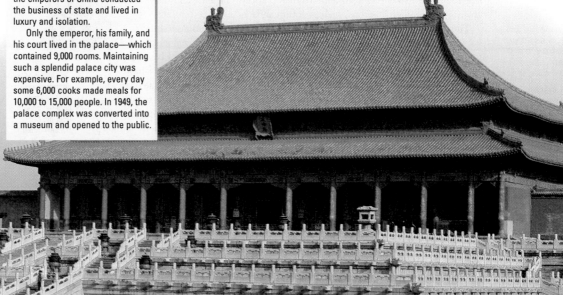

COOPERATIVE ACTIVITY: Panel Discussion

CLASS TIME 30 MINUTES

Task: Students will take on the roles of Chinese officials and merchants and European traders and will discuss their concerns related to China's foreign trade.

Purpose: To examine issues surrounding China's trading relationship with foreign countries.

Activity: Have students brainstorm to create a list of issues associated with the China trade. Each group will then look at each problem from the perspective

of a Chinese government official, a Chinese merchant, or a European trader and prepare a set of discussion points. One member of each group will join the panel to discuss the issues. Students not on the panel should take notes on the points made by other groups.

Building a Portfolio: Students might wish to add their group's discussion points to their portfolios, along with a list of the main points presented by the other groups.

ALTERNATIVE ASSESSMENT BOOK
Standards for Evaluating a Cooperative Activity

Standards for Evaluation
Discussion points should . . .

• clearly state issues related to China's foreign trade
• reflect one particular point of view
• be presented appropriately during the panel discussion

The first missionary to have an impact was an Italian Jesuit, Matteo Ricci. He gained special favor at the Ming court through his intelligence and his ability to speak and write Chinese. However, many educated Chinese opposed Christianity.

The Qing Dynasty

By 1600, the Ming had ruled for more than 200 years, and the dynasty was weakening. Its problems grew—ineffective rulers, corrupt officials, and a government out of money. Higher taxes and bad harvests pushed millions of peasants toward starvation. Civil strife and rebellion followed.

Beyond the northeast end of the Great Wall lay Manchuria. In 1644, the **Manchus** (MAN·chooz), the people of that region, invaded China. The Ming could not repel the invasion, and the dynasty collapsed. The Manchus took over Beijing, and the Manchu leader became China's new emperor. As the Mongols had done, the Manchus took a Chinese name for their dynasty, the **Qing** (chihng) **Dynasty.** They would rule China for more than 260 years and bring Taiwan, Chinese Central Asia, Mongolia, and Tibet into China.

China Under the Qing Dynasty Many Chinese resisted rule by the non-Chinese Manchus. Rebellions flared up periodically for decades. The Manchus forced Chinese men to wear their hair in a pigtail as a sign of submission to their rule. The Manchus, however, slowly earned the people's respect. They upheld China's traditional Confucian beliefs and social structures. They made the country's frontiers safe and restored China's prosperity. Two powerful Manchu rulers contributed greatly to the acceptance of the new dynasty.

The first, **Kangxi** (kahng·shee), became emperor in 1661 and ruled for some 60 years. Kangxi reduced government expenses and lowered taxes. A scholar and patron of the arts, Kangxi gained the support of Chinese intellectuals by offering them government positions. He also enjoyed the company of the Jesuits at court. They informed him of the latest developments in science, medicine, and mathematics in Europe.

Under Kangxi's grandson Qian-long (chyahn·lung), who ruled from 1736 to 1795, China reached its greatest size and prosperity. An industrious emperor like his grandfather, Qian-long often rose at dawn to work on the problems of the empire. Those problems included armed nomads on its borders, Christian missionaries, and European merchants.

Manchus Continue a Policy of Isolation To the Chinese, their country—the Middle Kingdom—had been the cultural center of the universe for two thousand years. If foreign states wished to trade with China, they would have to follow Chinese rules. These included trading only at special ports and paying tribute.

The Dutch, masters of the Indian Ocean trade by the time of Qian-long, accepted these restrictions. Their diplomats paid tribute to China's emperor through gifts and by performing the required "kowtow" ritual. This ritual involved their kneeling in front of the emperor and touching their heads to the ground nine times. As a result, the Chinese accepted the Dutch as trading partners. The Dutch returned home with traditional porcelains and silk, as well as China's highly prized new trade item—tea. By 1800, tea would make up 80 percent of shipments to Europe.

An Age of Exploration and Isolation **471**

HISTORY MAKERS

Kangxi
1654–1722

The emperor Kangxi had too much curiosity to remain isolated in the Forbidden City. To calm the Chinese in areas devastated by the Manchu conquest, Kangxi set out on a series of "tours."

On tours I learned about the common people's grievances by talking with them. . . . I asked peasants about their officials, looked at their houses, and discussed their crops.

In 1696, with Mongols threatening the northern border, Kangxi exhibited the kind of leadership unheard of in later Ming times. Instead of waiting in the palace for news from the front, he personally led 80,000 troops to victory over the Mongols.

Have students list some characteristics traditionally ascribed to hermits, such as being gruff, quiet, misunderstood, self-sufficient, and antisocial. Discuss how these characteristics might apply to a "hermit kingdom."

OBJECTIVE ❸ INSTRUCT

Daily Life in Ming and Qing China

Key Ideas
- China remains largely a country of farmers.
- Women have important family responsibilities but suffer by being treated as socially inferior.
- The Chinese enjoy traditional cultural pursuits.

📖 **IN-DEPTH RESOURCES: UNIT 4**
Literature: from *The Dream of the Red Chamber*, p. 61

History from Visuals

The Growth of Early Modern China

Interpreting Graphs What two fifty-year periods had the slowest rate of growth? *From 1650 to 1700 and from 1850 to 1900 (as indicated by the most gradual slope in the line).*

Extension Activity Ask students how the peace and prosperity of the 1600s and 1700s contributed to the population boom. *Possible Response: Fewer deaths occurred from warfare and starvation.*

SKILLBUILDER Answers
1. By about 250 percent.
2. A larger population means a growth in towns, where people live close together and exchange ideas and customs.

---

on one knee. Qian-long denied Britain's request. As Qian-long made clear in a letter to the British king, China was self-sufficient:

A VOICE FROM THE PAST
. . . There is nothing we lack, as your principal envoy and others have themselves observed. We have never set much store on strange or ingenious objects, nor do we need any more of your country's manufactures.
QIAN-LONG, from a letter to King George III of Great Britain

In the 1800s, the British, Dutch, and others would attempt to chip away at China's trade restrictions until the empire itself began to crack, as Chapter 28 will describe.

In the 17th and 18th centuries, Korea's strict isolation from the outside world caused it to be described as "the hermit kingdom." In the 1990s, this description can still be applied to communist North Korea. Closed to outsiders, North Korea has very little contact with other nations, even South Korea. China is still its only real ally.

Korea Under the Manchus In 1636, even before they came to power in China, the Manchus conquered nearby Korea and made it a vassal state. As a member of the Chinese tribute system, Korea had long existed in China's shadow. Koreans organized their government according to Confucian principles. They adopted China's technology, its culture, and especially its policy of isolation.

When the Manchus established the Qing Dynasty, Korea's political relationship with China did not change. If anything, it grew stronger. Under the Manchus, Korea was China's "little brother." Below the surface, however, Korea did change. The Manchu invasion, combined with a Japanese attack in the 1590s, provoked strong feelings of nationalism in the Korean people. This sentiment was most evident in their art. Instead of traditional Chinese subjects, many artists chose to explore popular Korean themes. Painters, for example, depicted Korean wrestling matches. They painted Korean peasants tending their fields and landscapes of the Korean countryside.

Daily Life in Ming and Qing China

The Chinese devotion to agriculture began to pay off during the late Ming and early Qing dynasties. Greater rice production, along with the general peace and prosperity of the 1600s and 1700s, ushered in a better life for most Chinese. During this period, the population also doubled. It reached more than 300 million in 1800.

The Growth of Early Modern China

A Population Boom

This detail from Zhang Zeduan's painting, *Going Up-River at the Qing Ming Festival*, reflects the growth of urban life under the Ming and Qing.

SKILLBUILDER: Interpreting Graphs
1. By roughly what percentage did China's population increase between 1650 and 1900?
2. How might the growth of population, towns, and culture be related?

THINK THROUGH HISTORY
C. Making Inferences Why do you think the kowtow ritual was so important to the Chinese emperor?
C. Possible Answer It reaffirmed for him the Chinese belief that their culture was vastly superior to others.

SKILLBUILDER MINI-LESSON: Interpreting Graphs

CLASS TIME 20 MINUTES

Explaining the Skill Graphs offer illustrations of statistics and often make numerical information and relationships easier to grasp. Visual features such as color and size as well as labels and measurements on a graph all help clarify the information presented. Point out to students that the information in the graph is reinforced or supplemented by the inclusion of pictorial material.

Applying the Skill: *The Growth of Early Modern China* Have students study the line graph on this page, noting how the lines and dots are used to communicate information. Then ask,
1. What was the increase in population between 1650 and 1900? *More than 300 million.*
2. During what 100-year period did the greatest growth occur? What was the increase in that period? *1750–1850; about 200 million.*

3. About what year did the growth spurt begin to taper off? *Around 1850.*
4. What does the painting of an urban scene tell about China during this period? *Possible Answer: The cities were growing in population and becoming more crowded.*

 IN-DEPTH RESOURCES: UNIT 4
Skillbuilder Practice: Interpreting Graphs, p. 54

Family and the Role of Women Most Chinese families farmed the land. They farmed in much the same way as their ancestors had for thousands of years. During the Qing Dynasty, irrigation and the use of fertilizer increased. Farmers began to grow new crops. These crops, such as corn and sweet potatoes, had been brought by the Europeans from the Americas. With increased food production, nutrition and diet improved. Such changes encouraged families to expand, and a population explosion followed.

These expanded Chinese families favored sons over daughters. Only a son was allowed to carry on vital religious rituals. A son would raise his own family under his parents' roof, assuring aging parents of help with the farming. Because of this, females were not valued, and many female infants were killed as a result. Men dominated the household and their wives, but women did have some significant responsibilities. Besides working in the fields, they supervised the children's education and managed the family's finances. Although most women were forced to remain secluded in their homes, some found outside jobs as midwives or textile workers, for example.

Still, women generally suffered as a result of their inferior status in Chinese society. One glaring example was the continuation of the traditional practice of foot-binding. One-half to two-thirds of all Chinese women in this period may have undergone this painful procedure, which left them barely able to walk. The practice continued into the 20th century.

Cultural Developments The culture of early modern China was based mainly on traditional forms. It was a conservative reaction to changes in Chinese life. These changes included the Manchu conquest, the coming of the Europeans, and the population growth. The great masterpiece of traditional Chinese fiction was written during this period. *Dream of the Red Chamber* by Cao Zhan examines upper-class Manchu society in the 1700s. It has been praised for the sensitive portrayal of its female characters.

Most artists of the time painted in traditional styles, which valued technique over creativity. In pottery, technical skill as well as experimentation led to the production of high-quality ceramics, including porcelain.

Drama was a popular entertainment, especially in rural China, where literacy rates were low. Plays that presented Chinese history and portrayed cultural heroes served two purposes. They entertained people, and they also helped unify Chinese society by creating a kind of national culture.

While China was attempting to preserve its traditions and its isolation, another civilization that developed in relative seclusion—the Japanese—was in conflict. As you will learn in Section 3, it faced problems caused both by internal power struggles and by the arrival of foreigners.

Under the Ming and Qing, the arts, including painting, flourished. This detail, from one of two paintings entitled *Occupations of the Court Ladies*, shows society's privileged women relaxing.

Vocabulary
midwives: women who are trained to assist expectant mothers in childbirth.

D. Possible Answer Produced little creativity but provided sense of stability in time of change and helped to unify Chinese society.
THINK THROUGH HISTORY
D. Recognizing Effects What were the consequences of the emphasis on tradition in the culture of early modern China?

Section 2 Assessment

1. TERMS & NAMES

Identify
• Ming Dynasty
• Hongwu
• Yonglo
• Zheng He
• Manchus
• Qing Dynasty
• Kangxi

2. TAKING NOTES

Complete a chart like the one below, listing five relevant facts about each emperor.

Emperor	Relevant Facts
Hongwu	
Yonglo	
Kangxi	
Qian-long	

Choose one emperor and write a one-paragraph biography using the information listed in the chart and text.

3. MAKING DECISIONS

When Qian-long expected Lord George Macartney to kowtow, what do you think Macartney should have done? Why?

THINK ABOUT
• cultural differences
• effect on trading
• the kowtow ritual
• political correctness

4. THEME ACTIVITY

Cultural Interaction Work in small groups to draw, paint, or sketch a mural of a Zheng He expedition. Include the figures, objects, maps, and symbols necessary to convey relevant information from the text. Use the pictures and maps in this chapter for additional ideas. Present the mural to your class.

ASSESS & RETEACH

Section 2 Assessment
Have students work individually on the questions. Then have them share with the class the charts they drew for question 2.

Section Quiz
FORMAL ASSESSMENT BOOK
Section quiz, p. 217

Reteaching Activity
CLASS TIME: 15 MINUTES

Use the Guided Reading Worksheet for Section 2 to review the key ideas of this section.

IN-DEPTH RESOURCES: UNIT 4
Guided Reading, p. 52

CLOSE ACTIVITY

CLASS TIME: 20 MINUTES

Role-Playing
Have interested students reenact the meeting of Lord George Macartney and Emperor Qian-long in 1793. Other students may then ask them about their actions and what each culture had expected of the other in such an interaction.

ANSWERS

1. TERMS & NAMES
Ming Dynasty, p. 469
Hongwu, p. 469
Yonglo, p. 469
Zheng He, p. 469
Manchus, p. 471
Qing Dynasty, p. 471
Kangxi, p. 471

2. TAKING NOTES
Possible Responses: Hongwu— defeated Mongols; ruled 1368–1398; first Ming emperor; encouraged agriculture, Confucian standards, administrative reforms; became brutal. Yonglo—1398, assumed throne; moved capital to Beijing; built Forbidden City; sponsored first Zheng He voyage; increased number of tributaries. Kangxi—ruled 1661–1722; first Manchu emperor; lowered taxes; defeated Mongols; patronized arts. Qian-long—ruled 1736–1795 at China's greatest size and prosperity; hard-working; dealt with border unrest and European missionaries and traders.

3. MAKING DECISIONS
Possible Responses: Kowtow to gain trade; bow to compromise; stand to show equality; refuse to see him to show disfavor.

4. THEME ACTIVITY
Cultural Interaction
Possible Responses: Murals may include maps; drawings of ships, crew, Zheng He, dignitaries paying tribute.

Teacher's Edition **473**

3 Japan Limits Western Contacts

TERMS & NAMES
- daimyo
- Oda Nobunaga
- Toyotomi Hideyoshi
- Tokugawa Shogunate
- kabuki
- haiku

MAIN IDEA
The Tokugawa regime unified Japan and began a 200-year period of isolation, autocracy, and economic growth.

WHY IT MATTERS NOW
Even now, Japan continues to limit and control dealings with foreigners, especially in the area of trade.

SETTING THE STAGE In the 1300s, the unity that had been achieved in Japan in the previous century broke down. Shoguns, or military leaders, in the north and south fought for power. Although these two rival courts came back together at the end of the century, a series of politically weak shoguns let control of the country slip from their grasp.

Strong Leaders Take Control

In 1467, civil war shattered Japan's feudal system. The country collapsed into chaos. Centralized rule ended. Power drained away from the shogun to territorial lords in hundreds of separate domains.

This samurai armor consists of leather and iron plates. It was made in 1714 for the Lord of Akita, a region in northwest Japan.

Local Lords Rule A violent era of disorder followed. This time in Japanese history, which lasted from 1467 to 1568, is known as the *Sengoku*, or "Warring States," period. Powerful samurai seized control of old feudal estates. They offered peasants and others protection in return for their loyalty. These warrior-chieftains, called **daimyo** (DYE·mee·OH), became lords in a new kind of Japanese feudalism. Under this system, security came from this group of powerful warlords. The emperor at Kyoto became a figurehead.

The new Japanese feudalism resembled European feudalism in many ways. The daimyo built fortified castles and created small armies of samurai on horses. Later they added foot soldiers with muskets (guns) to their ranks. Rival daimyo often fought each other for territory. This led to endless disorder throughout the land.

New Leaders Restore Order A number of ambitious daimyo hoped to gather enough power to take control of the entire country. One of them, the brutal and ambitious **Oda Nobunaga** (oh·dah noh·boo·nah·gah), defeated his rivals and seized the imperial capital Kyoto in 1568.

Following his own motto, "Rule the empire by force," Nobunaga sought to eliminate his remaining enemies. These included rival daimyo as well as wealthy Buddhist monasteries aligned with them. In 1575, Nobunaga's 3,000 musketeers crushed an enemy force of samurai cavalry. This was the first time firearms had been used effectively in battle in Japan. However, Nobunaga was not able to unify Japan. He committed seppuku, the ritual suicide of a samurai, in 1582, when one of his own generals turned on him.

Nobunaga's best general, **Toyotomi Hideyoshi** (toh·you·toh·mee hee·deh·yoh·shee), continued his fallen leader's mission. Hideyoshi set out to destroy the daimyos that remained hostile. By 1590, by combining brute force with shrewd political alliances, he controlled most of the country. Hideyoshi did not stop with Japan. With the idea of eventually conquering China, he invaded Korea in 1592 and began a long campaign against the Koreans and their Ming Chinese allies. When Hideyoshi died in 1598, his troops withdrew from Korea.

474 Chapter 19

Vocabulary
domains: the lands belonging to a single lord.

Vocabulary
figurehead: a person holding a position of seeming leadership but having no real power.

Vocabulary
musketeers: soldiers armed with muskets.

Tokugawa Shogunate Unites Japan

One of Hideyoshi's strongest daimyo allies, Tokugawa Ieyasu (toh·koo·gah·wah ee·yeh·yah·soo), completed the unification of Japan. In 1600, Ieyasu defeated his rivals at the Battle of Sekigahara. His victory earned him the loyalty of daimyo throughout Japan. Three years later, Ieyasu became the sole ruler, or shogun. He then moved Japan's capital to his power base at Edo, a small fishing village that would later become the city of Tokyo.

Japan was unified, but the daimyo still governed at the local level. To keep them from rebelling, Ieyasu required that they spend every other year in the capital. Even when they returned to their lands, they had to leave their families behind as hostages in Edo. Through this "alternate attendance policy" and other restrictions, Ieyasu tamed the daimyo. This was a major step toward restoring central-ized government to Japan. As a result, the rule of law overcame the rule of the sword.

Ieyasu founded the **Tokugawa Shogunate,** which would continue until 1867. On his deathbed in 1616, Ieyasu advised his son and successor, Hidetada, "Take care of the people. Strive to be virtuous. Never neglect to protect the country." Most of the Tokugawa shoguns followed that advice, and their rule brought a welcome stability to Japan.

Tokugawa Society and Culture

Japan enjoyed more than two centuries of stability, prosperity, and isolation under the Tokugawa shoguns. The farming community produced more food, and the population rose. Still, the vast majority of peasants, weighed down by heavy taxes, led lives filled with misery. The people who prospered in Tokugawa society were the merchant class and the rich. However, everyone, rich and poor alike, benefited from a flowering of Japanese culture during this era.

Social History In Japan, as in China, Confucian values influenced ideas about society. According to Confucius, the ideal society depended on agriculture, not urban commerce. Farmers, not merchants, made ideal citizens. In the real world of Tokugawa Japan, however, peasant farmers bore the main tax burden and faced more difficulties than any other class. Many of them abandoned farm life and headed for the expanding towns and cities. There they mixed with samurai, artisans, and merchants—the other main classes of Tokugawa society.

By the mid-1700s, Japan began to shift from a rural to an urban society. Edo had grown by that time from a small town in 1600 to perhaps the largest city in the world. Its population was more than one million. The rise of large commercial centers increased employment opportunities for women. Women found jobs in entertainment, textile manufacturing, and publishing. Still, the typical Japanese woman led a sheltered and restricted life as a peasant wife. She worked in the fields, managed the household, cared for the children, and obeyed her husband without question.

Culture Under the Tokugawa Shogunate Traditional culture continued to thrive. Samurai attended ceremonial noh dramas based on tragic themes. They read tales of

Japanese Society

Emperor
Held highest rank in society but had no political power

Daimyo
Large landowners

Shogun
Actual ruler

Samurai **Warriors**
Loyal to daimyo and shogun

Peasants
Four-fifths of the population

Artisans
Craftspeople such as artists and blacksmiths

Merchants
Low status but gradually gained influence

An Age of Exploration and Isolation **475**

ancient warriors and their courage in battle. In their homes, they hung paintings that showed scenes from classical literature.

Such traditional entertainment faced competition in the cities from new styles of drama, art, and literature. Townspeople attended **kabuki** theater. These were dramas in which actors in elaborate costumes, using music, dance, and mime, performed skits about modern urban life. The paintings they enjoyed were often woodblock prints showing sophisticated city life.

Townspeople read popular stories about self-made merchants or the hardships of life. This new type of urban fiction was created by the novelist Saikaku. The people also read **haiku** (HI·koo), poetry which does not express ideas, but presents images. For example, Matsuo Basho, the greatest of all the Japanese haiku poets, wrote just before his death in 1694:

A VOICE FROM THE PAST
On a journey, ailing—
My dreams roam about
Over a withered moor.

MATSUO BASHO, from *Matsuo Basho*

Tabi ni yande
Yume wa Kareno o
Kakemeguru

MATSUO BASHO, in Japanese

Kabuki theater makes use of extravagant costumes, mask-like makeup, and exaggerated postures and gestures. This contemporary photo shows a dancer costumed as a lion.

Contact Between Europe and Japan

Europeans began coming to Japan in the 16th century, during a time of severe disorder. At first, the Japanese were curious about these newcomers. They welcomed the traders and missionaries, who introduced fascinating new technologies and ideas. Within a century, the aggressive Europeans had worn out their welcome.

Portuguese Sailors and Technology Reach Japan The Japanese first encountered Europeans in 1543, when shipwrecked Portuguese sailors washed up on the shores of southern Japan. Portuguese merchants soon followed. They hoped to involve themselves in Japan's trade with China and Southeast Asia. The Portuguese brought clocks, eyeglasses, tobacco, firearms, and other unfamiliar items from Europe. Japanese merchants, eager to expand their markets, were happy to receive the newcomers and their goods.

The daimyo, too, welcomed the strangers. They were particularly interested in the Portuguese muskets and cannons. One warlord listened intently to a Japanese observer's description of a musket:

SPOTLIGHT ON

Introduction of Firearms
Europeans introduced firearms to Japan in the mid-1500s, when every daimyo sought an advantage over his rivals. Imagine the warlords' surprise when they first saw a lead pellet explode from a musket! Then imagine their eagerness to own firearms when they realized the musket's killing power.

Japanese gunsmiths set to work copying the European musket. Some 30 years later, they had mastered the technology. However, soldiers still had trouble firing the gun, and daimyos didn't know how to use their musketeers effectively. Nobunaga's victory in 1575 proved that those problems could be solved and led to daimyos arming their troops with muskets.

A VOICE FROM THE PAST
In their hands they carried something two or three feet long, straight on the outside with a passage inside, and made of a heavy substance. . . . This thing with one blow can smash a mountain of silver and a wall of iron. If one sought to do mischief in another man's domain and he was touched by it, he would lose his life instantly.

ANONYMOUS JAPANESE WRITER, quoted in *Sources of Japanese Tradition* (1958)

Firearms forever changed the time-honored tradition of the Japanese warrior, whose principal weapon had been the sword. Many samurai, who retained the sword as their principal weapon, would lose their lives to musket fire in future combat. The cannon also had a huge impact on Japan. Daimyo had to build fortified castles to withstand the destructive force of cannonballs. The castles attracted merchants, artisans, and others to surrounding lands. Many of these lands grew into the towns and cities of modern Japan.

Christian Missionaries in Japan In 1549, Christian missionaries began arriving in Japan. The Japanese accepted the missionaries in part because they associated them with the muskets and other

---

European goods that they wanted. The religious orders of Jesuits, Franciscans, and Dominicans came to convert the Japanese. Francis Xavier, a Jesuit, led the first mission to Japan and baptized about a hundred converts. Missionaries converted about 300,000 Japanese to Christianity by the year 1600.

The success of the missionaries upset Tokugawa Ieyasu. He found aspects of the Christian invasion troublesome. Missionaries, actively seeking converts, scorned traditional Japanese beliefs and sometimes involved themselves in local politics. At first, Ieyasu did not take any action. He feared driving off the Portuguese, English, Spanish, and Dutch traders who spurred Japan's economy. By 1612, however, the shogun had come to fear religious uprisings more. He banned Christianity and focused on ridding his country of all Christians.

Repression of Christianity continued off and on for the next two decades. In 1637, the issue came to a head. An uprising in southern Japan of some 30,000 peasants, led by dissatisfied samurai, shook the Tokugawa regime. Because so many of the rebels were Christian, the shogun decided that Christianity was at the root of the rebellion. After that, the shoguns ruthlessly persecuted Christians. All Japanese were forced to demonstrate faithfulness to some branch of Buddhism. These policies eventually eliminated Christianity in Japan.

The Closed Country Policy The persecution of Christians was part of an attempt to control foreign ideas. When Europeans first arrived, no central authority existed to contain them. The strong leaders who later took power did not like the introduction of European ideas and ways, but they valued European trade. As time passed, the Tokugawa shoguns realized that they could safely exclude both the missionaries and the merchants. By 1639, they had sealed Japan's borders and instituted a "closed country policy."

One port, Nagasaki, remained open to foreign traders. However, only Dutch and Chinese merchants were allowed into the port. Since the Tokugawa shoguns controlled Nagasaki, they now had a monopoly on foreign trade, which continued to be profitable.

For more than 200 years, Japan remained basically closed to Europeans. Japan would continue to develop as a self-sufficient country, free from European attempts to colonize or to establish their presence.

The Europeans had met with much resistance in their efforts to open the East to trade. Expansion to the West in the Americas, as you will learn in Chapter 20, would prove much more successful.

THINK THROUGH HISTORY
C. Comparing How was the treatment of Europeans different in Japan and China? How was it similar?
C. Possible Answers The Japanese were more receptive at first to European contact than the Chinese were; however, both countries eventually rebuffed European influences and entered an age of isolation.

SPOTLIGHT ON

Zen Buddhism

The form of Buddhism that had the greatest impact on Japanese culture was Zen Buddhism. It especially influenced the samurai.

Zen Buddhists sought spiritual enlightenment through meditation. Strict discipline of mind and body was the Zen path to wisdom. Zen monks would sit rigidly for hours. If they showed signs of losing concentration, a Zen master might shout at them or hit them with a stick.

Some masters helped disciples free themselves from ordinary ways of thinking by asking them riddles, such as "When both hands are clapped, they make a sound. What is the sound of one hand clapping?"

Section 3 Assessment

1. TERMS & NAMES

Identify
- daimyo
- Oda Nobunaga
- Toyotomi Hideyoshi
- Tokugawa Shogunate
- kabuki
- haiku

2. TAKING NOTES

Japan was unified by a succession of daimyos. Using a chart like the one below, show the accomplishments of each.

Daimyo	Accomplishments
Nobunaga	
Hideyoshi	
Ieyasu	

3. FORMING AN OPINION

Do you think Japan's closed country policy effectively kept Western ideas and customs out of Japan?

THINK ABOUT
- the attitude toward European presence
- reaction to past restrictions on Christianity and trade
- the role of Nagasaki

4. THEME ACTIVITY

Cultural Interaction Reread about the role of women in China on page 473 and about the role of women in Japan on page 475. What are the similarities and the differences between the two? Create a Venn diagram to compare and contrast them.

An Age of Exploration and Isolation **477**

ANSWERS

MORE ABOUT . . .
Francis Xavier

Francis Xavier epitomized the missionary spirit of the Jesuits. Through selfless devotion, he helped establish Christianity in India, Malacca, and the Spice Islands. His strong beliefs and aura of goodness attracted many converts. In 1549, he sought a new challenge among the more culturally advanced Japanese, whom he called "the best people yet discovered." He then extended his mission to China, which he recognized as the most influential culture in the East. China, however, was closed to Europeans, and he died in 1552, waiting to enter the country.

 ELECTRONIC LIBRARY OF PRIMARY SOURCES
from *The Life and Letters of St. Francis Xavier*

SPOTLIGHT ON
Zen Buddhism

Tell students that characteristics of an enlightened master of Zen Buddhism included serenity, fearlessness, and spontaneity. Ask students how these characteristics might be reflected in Japanese culture, for example, in the arts, in sports, or in garden design.

ASSESS & RETEACH

Section 3 Assessment
Have a student volunteer lead a class discussion of question 3.

Section Quiz
 FORMAL ASSESSMENT BOOK
Section Quiz, p. 218

Reteaching Activity
CLASS TIME: 20 MINUTES

Have students create a time line of major events in Japan from 1400 to 1800.

 CRITICAL THINKING TRANSPARENCIES
CT55 Chapter 19 Visual Summary

CLOSE ACTIVITY

CLASS TIME: 30 MINUTES

Creating a Haiku
Suggest that students, working independently or in small groups, compose a haiku referring to some person or incident in the section. Then read the poems to the class.

 IN-DEPTH RESOURCES: UNIT 4
Literature: Haiku, p. 63

Teacher's Edition 477

Chapter 19 Assessment

TERMS & NAMES

1. Bartolomeu Dias, p. 464
2. Vasco da Gama, p. 466
3. Treaty of Tordesillas, p. 466
4. Dutch East India Company, p. 468
5. Ming Dynasty, p. 469
6. Manchus, p. 471
7. Qing Dynasty, p. 471
8. Oda Nobunaga, p. 474
9. Toyotomi Hideyoshi, p. 474
10. Tokugawa Shogunate, p. 475

REVIEW QUESTIONS

11. Desire for new sources of wealth; desire to spread Christianity; technological advancements in sailing and navigation.

12. He encouraged exploration by establishing a navigation school for sailors to perfect their trade.

13. Dias showed that the southern tip of Africa could be circumnavigated; da Gama established a sea route from Europe to India.

14. The Dutch owned the largest fleet of ships in the world, and the Dutch East India Company was more powerful and better financed than other nations' trading companies.

15. Idea of commerce offended China's Confucian beliefs; economic policy gave priority to agriculture.

16. The clock and the prism.

17. Ineffective rulers, corrupt officials, government out of money, high taxes, bad harvests.

18. It was an era of disorder when powerful warrior-chieftains, called daimyo, seized control of old feudal estates and set up new type of feudalism and often fought each other for territory.

19. Confucian ideal—Japan was an agricultural society and the farmer was the ideal citizen. In reality—farmers were overburdened and over-taxed and often moved to the city for a better life.

20. Kabuki plays, popular stories, haiku, and woodblock prints.

TERMS & NAMES

Briefly explain the importance of the following to European exploration and the growth of China and Japan.

1. Bartolomeu Dias
2. Vasco da Gama
3. Treaty of Tordesillas
4. Dutch East India Company
5. Ming Dynasty
6. Manchus
7. Qing Dynasty
8. Oda Nobunaga
9. Toyotomi Hideyoshi
10. Tokugawa Shogunate

Interact *with* History

On page 462, you decided whether or not to go on a voyage of exploration. Now that you have read the chapter, reevaluate your decision. If you decided to go, did what you read reaffirm your decision? Why or why not? If you chose not to go, explain what your feelings are now. Discuss your answers within a small group.

REVIEW QUESTIONS

SECTION 1 (pages 463–468)
Europeans Explore the East

11. What factors helped spur European exploration?

12. What role did Portugal's Prince Henry play in overseas exploration?

13. What was the significance of Bartolomeu Dias's voyage? Vasco da Gama's?

14. Why were the Dutch so successful in establishing a trading empire in the Indian Ocean?

SECTION 2 (pages 469–473)
China Rejects European Outreach

15. Why didn't China undergo widespread industrialization?

16. Name two technological advancements the missionaries brought to China.

17. List five reasons why the Ming Dynasty fell to civil disorder.

SECTION 3 (pages 474–477)
Japan Limits Western Contacts

18. Why was the period between 1467 and 1568 called the Age of the Warring States?

19. What was the difference between the Confucian ideal of society and the real society of Japan?

20. Briefly describe the new drama, literature, and art found in Japanese cities.

Visual Summary

An Age of Exploration and Isolation

EXPLORATION

- In 1405, Zheng He of China launches voyages of exploration to southeast Asia, India, Arabia, and eastern Africa.

- Beginning in the early 1500s, the Portuguese establish trading outposts throughout Asia and gain control of the spice trade.

- The Dutch drive out the Portuguese by the early 1600s and establish their own trading empire in the East.

- Europeans sail farther east to China and Japan in search of more trade; both nations ultimately reject European advances.

ISOLATION

- China abandons its voyages of exploration in 1433.

- Beginning in the 1500s, the Chinese severely restrict trade with foreigners.

- Japan outlaws Christianity in 1612 and drives out Christian missionaries.

- Beginning in the mid 1600s, the Japanese institute a "closed country policy" and remain isolated from Europe for 200 years.

478 Chapter 19

Interact *with* History

Possible Responses: Students who originally wanted to go may now say that the rewards weren't great enough to go through all the hardships and give up that much time from their lives. Others may say that the opportunity to bring glory and prestige to their country and make some financial gain was worth the sacrifice.

CRITICAL THINKING

1. SAILING INNOVATIONS

THEME SCIENCE AND TECHNOLOGY Of all the technological advances that helped prompt European exploration, which do you think was the the most important? Why?

2. EMPERORS OF THE FORBIDDEN CITY

How might an emperor's attitude toward living in the Forbidden City affect his leadership? Consider how he might view his country, its people, and the outside world. Also think about the role of leaders and the values you think they should hold.

3. MISSIONARIES IN JAPAN

In a time line like the one below, trace the developments which led to Japan's expulsion of Christianity.

4. ANALYZING PRIMARY SOURCES

Emperor Kangxi invited Christian missionaries to his court, where they shared ideas about science, religion, government, and trade. In the following personal account, Kangxi reflects on what he has learned from the Europeans.

A VOICE FROM THE PAST

But I was careful not to refer to these Westerners as "Great Officials," and corrected Governor Liu Yin-shu when he referred to the Jesuits Regis and Fridelli . . . as if they were honored imperial commissioners. For even though some of the Western methods are different from our own, and may even be an improvement, there is little about them that is new. The principles of mathematics all derive from the Book of Changes, and the Western methods are Chinese in origin: this algebra—"A-erh-chu-pa-erh"—springs from an Eastern word. And though it was indeed the Westerners who showed us something our ancient calendar experts did not know— namely how to calculate the angles of the northern pole—this but shows the truth of what Chu Hsi arrived at through his investigation of things: the earth is like the yolk within an egg.

KANGXI, quoted in *Emperor of China: Self-portrait of K'ang-hsi*

- What do you think is Kangxi's attitude toward Westerners?
- Do you think Kangxi is a true scholar?

CHAPTER ACTIVITIES

1. LIVING HISTORY: Unit Portfolio Project

THEME CULTURAL INTERACTION Your Unit Portfolio project focuses on the ways in which different cultures interact (see page 387). For Chapter 19, you might use one of the following ideas to add to your portfolio.

- Imagine you are the Jesuit missionary, Matteo Ricci. Write a letter home describing your impressions of Chinese rule and culture.
- Draft a reply for King George III to the letter written by China's emperor, Qian-long, on page 472. Convince the emperor to open China by explaining the benefits of economic and cultural interaction.
- Imagine you are a Malaccan newspaper editor. Write an editorial about the arrival of Europeans, as well as their motives for being there.

2. CONNECT TO TODAY: Cooperative Learning

THEME ECONOMICS The primary force behind overseas exploration was economic, as Europeans sailed beyond their borders in search of new sources of wealth. Today the West retains strong economic ties with Asia. In recent years, maintaining those ties with China has been a hotly debated topic in the United States.

Work with a small team and prepare to debate another team over the issue of U.S. trade with China.

INTERNET Using the Internet, magazines, and other library sources, research the issues involved in the debate over U.S. trade with China.

- After being assigned one or the other position on the issue, work together to gather information that supports your side's position.
- In front of the class, debate a group that has taken the opposite position.

3. INTERPRETING A TIME LINE

Reexamine the unit time line on pages 386–387. Convert the Chapter 19 time line into a cartoon strip that conveys the same information.

FOCUS ON GEOGRAPHY

This map, produced by the German cartographer Henricus Martellus in about 1490, is believed to be the first world map to incorporate the discoveries made by Bartolomeu Dias.

- Where is Europe on the map?
- What is the continent in the lower left corner of the map?

Connect to History Obtain a modern-day world map and compare it with this one. How do you rate Martellus's assumptions of how the world to the east of Africa looked?

	Key Ideas	**COPY MASTERS**	**ASSESSMENT**
SECTION 1 Spanish Conquests in the Americas *pp. 483–488*	Columbus lands in the Caribbean Islands, and Spain and Portugal begin the colonization of the Americas. The Spanish destroy the Aztec and Inca empires.	*In-Depth Resources: Unit 4* • **Guided Reading,** p. 68 • **Primary Sources:** from *The Journal of Christopher Columbus,* p. 75; from *The Broken Spears,* p. 77 • **Literature:** from *The Feathered Serpent,* p. 79 • **History Makers:** Magellan, p. 82; Cortés, p. 83	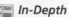 *Section 1 Assessment,* p. 488 **Formal Assessment** • Section Quiz, p. 227 **Alternative Assessment Book** • Standards for Evaluating a Cooperative Activity
SECTION 2 Competing Claims in North America *pp. 490–494*	European nations lay claim to large parts of North America, but England drives out the French and Dutch and creates thirteen colonies.	*In-Depth Resources: Unit 4* • **Guided Reading,** p. 69 • **Skillbuilder Practice:** Contrasting, p. 72	*Section 2 Assessment,* p. 494 **Formal Assessment** • Section Quiz, p. 228 **Alternative Assessment Book** • Standards for Evaluating a Cooperative Activity
SECTION 3 The Atlantic Slave Trade *pp. 495–499*	The slave trade decimates African social and family life, and millions of slaves are brought to the Americas to work in mines and on plantations.	*In-Depth Resources: Unit 4* • **Guided Reading,** p. 70 • **Primary Source:** from *The Life of Olaudah Equiano,* p. 78	*Section 3 Assessment,* p. 499 **Formal Assessment** • Section Quiz, p. 229 **Alternative Assessment Book** • Standards for Evaluating a Cooperative Activity
SECTION 4 The Columbian Exchange and Global Trade *pp. 500–503*	The colonization of the Americas leads to a global exchange of food, plants, animals, and diseases that enriches the European diet and economy and further shatters the native civilizations of the New World.	*In-Depth Resources: Unit 4* • **Guided Reading,** p. 71 • **Geography Application:** The Potato Impacts the World, p. 73 • **Connections Across Time and Cultures:** Impact of the Columbian Exchange, p. 84	*Section 4 Assessment,* p. 503 **Formal Assessment** • Section Quiz, p. 230 **Alternative Assessment Book** • Standards for Evaluating a Product or Performance
CHAPTER RESOURCES	**Chapter Overview** The European exploration and colonization of the Americas lead to an economic and cultural revolution in Europe and the devastation of Native American cultures in the New World.	*Telescoping the Times* • Chapter Summary, pp. 77–80 *Planning for Block Schedules*	*Chapter Assessment,* pp. 504–505 *Chapter Activities,* p. 505 **Formal Assessment** • Chapter Test, forms A and B, pp. 231–236 **Test Generator** **Alternative Assessment Book**

TECHNOLOGY

 Warm-Up Transparency 20

 World Art and Cultures Transparencies
- AT43 *Meeting of Cortés and Montezuma*

 Electronic Library of Primary Sources
- "On the Destruction of the Indies"
- from *Letter to King Charles V of Spain*

 Patterns of Interaction:
The Spread of Epidemic Disease

 INTERNET RESOURCES
www.mlworldhistory.com

 Warm-Up Transparency 20

 Electronic Library of Primary Sources
- "The French Lose Quebec"

 INTERNET RESOURCES
www.mlworldhistory.com

 Warm-Up Transparency 20

 World Art and Cultures Transparencies
- AT44 Meynell's *Slaves Below the Deck of the Albanez*

 Critical Thinking Transparencies
- CT20 The Atlantic Slave Trade, 1451–1870

 Electronic Library of Primary Sources
- Letter to the King of Portugal

 INTERNET RESOURCES
www.mlworldhistory.com

 Warm-Up Transparency 20

 Geography Transparencies
- GT20 Spain's Colonies Provide Wealth, 1600–1790

 Critical Thinking Transparencies
- CT56 Chapter 20 Visual Summary

 Electronic Library of Primary Sources
- "Concerning the Dearness of All Things and the Remedy Thereof"

 Patterns of Interaction
The Geography of Food

 Chapter Summaries on Audiocassette in English and Spanish

 INTERNET RESOURCES
www.mlworldhistory.com

 Block Scheduling (90 MINUTES)

Day 1
Section 1, pp. 483–488

 COOPERATIVE ACTIVITY
Displaying Explorers' Sailing Ships, p. 484 (Teacher's Edition)

Day 2
Section 2, pp. 490–494

 COOPERATIVE ACTIVITY
Planning a Journey, p. 493 (Teacher's Edition)

Section Assessments, pp. 488, 494

Section 3, pp. 495–499

COOPERATIVE ACTIVITY
Writing a Report, p. 496 (Teacher's Edition)

Section 4, pp. 500–503
Section Assessments, pp. 499, 503

Chapter Assessment, pp. 504–505

Yearly Pacing **Chapter 20 Total:** 2 days **Yearly Total:** 85 days

Planning for Block Schedules

Customizing for Special Needs

Students Acquiring English

 Access for Students Acquiring English
- **Guided Reading,** for Sections 1–4 (Spanish), pp. 198–201
- **Chapter Summary:** (Spanish), pp. 195–197
- **Skillbuilder Practice:** Contrasting (Spanish), p. 202
- **Geography Application:** The Potato Impacts the World (Spanish), p. 203

 Patterns of Interaction: Geography of Food (Spanish track)

Chapter Summaries on Audiocassette in English and Spanish

 INTERNET RESOURCES
www.mlworldhistory.com
The Diverse Classroom.

Less Proficient Readers

 In-Depth Resources: Unit 4
- **Guided Reading,** for Sections 1–4, pp. 68–71
- **Skillbuilder Practice:** Contrasting, p. 72
- **Geography Application:** The Potato Impacts the World, p. 73

Telescoping the Times
- Chapter Summary, pp. 77–80

Chapter Summaries on Audiocassette

Gifted and Talented Students

 In-Depth Resources: Unit 4

Primary Sources:
- from *The Journal of Christopher Columbus*, p. 75
- from *The Broken Spears*, p. 77
- from *The Life of Olaudah Equiano*, p. 78

History Makers:
- Magellan, p. 82
- Cortés, p. 83

Connections to Literature READINGS FOR STUDENTS

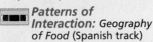 *In-Depth Resources: Unit 4*
Literature: from *The Feathered Serpent*, p. 79

Enrichment Reading

- **Cliff, Michelle**
Free Enterprise
New York: Plume, 1994

A gripping story about the slave trade.

- **Pate, Alexs**
The Amistad
New York: Penguin, 1997

The exciting tale of a slave revolt. This story was the basis of a major motion picture directed by Steven Spielberg.

 = Pupil's Edition   = Overhead Transparency   = Software   = Video

 = Copy Master   = CD-ROM   = Audiocassette   = Internet

The Atlantic World, 1492–1800

Accessing Prior Knowledge

• Ask students what they know about Columbus. Discuss with them any other early voyages to the Americas they might have heard of. Then ask them if they know about recent controversies over the impact of Columbus's voyage to the Americas.

Making Judgments

• Have students read each of the captions and then decide which of the three themes listed to the right (cultural interaction, economics, or empire building) seems to be the dominant theme expressed by each image and the caption that explains it.

Geography Connection

Ask students to look at the map on these two pages.

• What two main worlds were connected by the voyage of Columbus? *the Eastern and Western hemispheres, or Europe and Africa in the east and North and South America in the west*

CHAPTER 20

The Atlantic World, 1492–1800

PREVIEWING THEMES

Cultural Interaction
The voyages of Columbus prompted a worldwide exchange of everything from religious and political ideas to new foods and plants. In addition, they paved the way for the creation of new multicultural societies in the Americas.

Economics
The vast wealth to be had from colonizing the Americas sealed the fate of millions of Native Americans and Africans. Europeans forced them to toil in gold and silver mines, as well as on huge tobacco and sugar plantations.

Empire Building
Over the span of several centuries, Europeans conquered the Americas' native inhabitants. As a result, they built powerful American empires.

INTERNET CONNECTION

Visit us at www.mlworldhistory.com to learn more about American colonization.

The Italian sea captain **Christopher Columbus** reached the Americas in **1492**. This engraving, by Theodore de Bry, a 16th-century Flemish engraver, shows gift-bearing Indians welcoming Columbus. Shortly after exchanging greetings, Columbus claimed the natives' Caribbean island for Spain.

THE WESTERN WORLD AROUND 1500

Oct. 12, 1492 Columbus lands on San Salvador Island

Gulf of Mexico

Caribbean Sea

NORTH AMERICA

AZTEC EMPIRE

PACIFIC OCEAN

INCA EMPIRE

SOUTH AMERICA

In **1533**, the Spanish, led by **Francisco Pizarro**, conquered the mighty Inca Empire in Peru. This illustration by a Native American, Felipe Guamán Poma de Ayala, depicts the Indians' view of the conquering Spaniards.

480

GEOGRAPHY THEMES

Movement

Have students note and identify the four continents pictured on these pages. *North America, South America, Europe, and Africa.* Tell them that the movement of people—in large numbers and small—across vast areas of the globe has occurred throughout human history. Ask them which way the movement is going on these pages, and which forms of travel this movement would have taken. *From east to west; on the Atlantic Ocean and Caribbean Sea and on the lands of North and South America; forms of travel: ships, horses, by foot*

Human/Environment Interaction

Remind students that the presence of large numbers of people in a place causes major changes to the environment. Some of these changes have a positive impact and some have a negative impact. An example of a positive impact would be an increased food supply. An example of a negative impact might be pollution. Have them note the kind of natural environment the European explorers found when they came to the Americas and what kinds of changes they made to this environment.

ADDITIONAL RESOURCES

Books for the Teacher

- Dor-Ner, Zvi. *Columbus and the Age of Discovery.* New York: Morrow, 1991.

- Lewis, Bernard. *Cultures in Conflict.* New York: Oxford UP, 1995.

- Marks, Richard Lee. *Cortés: The Great Adventurer and the Fate of Aztec Mexico.* New York: Knopf, 1993.

- Sale, Kirkpatrick. *The Conquest of Paradise: Christopher Columbus and the Columbian Legacy.* New York: Knopf, 1990.

Books for the Student

- Baquedano, Elizabeth. *Aztec, Inca, & Maya.* New York: Knopf, 1993.

- Jones, Constance. *Africa, 1500-1900.* New York: Facts on File, 1993.

- Meltzer, Milton. *Columbus and the World Around Him.* New York: Watts, 1990.

- Platt, Richard. *Pirate.* New York: Knopf, 1994.

Videos

- *Christopher Columbus: His Voyages and His Legacy.* Britannica, 1990. 800-554-9862.

- *Slavery in the Americas and the Triangular Trade.* Britannica, 1992. 800-554-9862.

Software

- *Explorers of the New World.* CD-ROM. Teacher's Discovery, 1995. 800-543-4180.

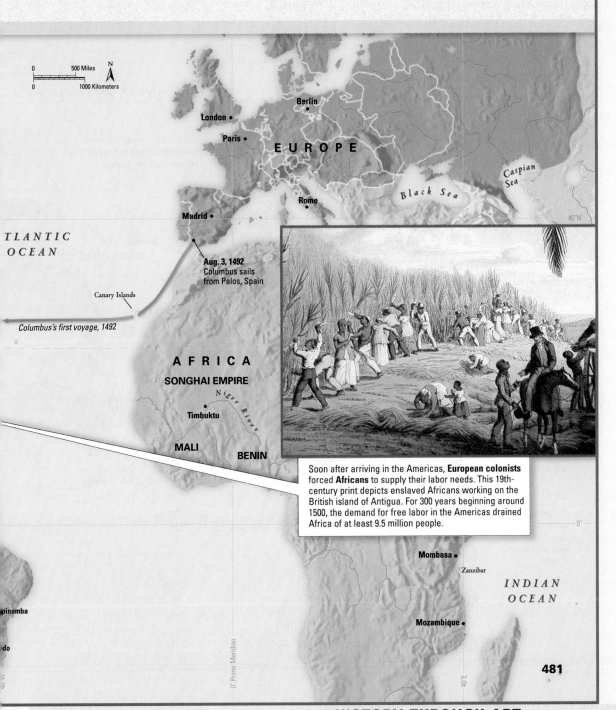

Soon after arriving in the Americas, **European colonists** forced **Africans** to supply their labor needs. This 19th-century print depicts enslaved Africans working on the British island of Antigua. For 300 years beginning around 1500, the demand for free labor in the Americas drained Africa of at least 9.5 million people.

481

HISTORY THROUGH ART

Pictures of the Conquest of Mexico

Felipe Guamán Poma de Ayala

Felipe Guamán Poma de Ayala was a native wise man of Peru. He painted scenes depicting the conquest of his native land by the Spanish in the 16th century. A codex, or manuscript volume, entitled *Nueva Cronica y Buen Gobierno,* was compiled by Poma de Ayala and completed in 1613. In many of the

illustrations in this work the horse plays a key role. The use of the horse helped the Spanish conquerors to cover great distances in a short period of time. Horses also enabled the Spanish to defeat native armies even though the invaders were outnumbered.

Other native artists also depicted the Spanish conquests of the Americas and the role of the horse in these expeditions. For example, Tlaxcalan artists

depicted Spanish soldiers on horseback in the highlands of Guatemala. Diego Duran's history of the conquest of Mexico also shows the horse playing a prominent role.

Interpreting the Art What does the Spanish soldier seem to stand for? Is this art likely to be a piece of propaganda? Why or why not?

Interact with History

This Interact with History feature motivates students by inviting them to choose between fighting on the side of the Aztecs or the Spanish. As they imagine themselves choosing sides, students will analyze the issues, explore their options, and become decision-makers.

Purpose
- to set the stage for the Spanish conquest of the Americas
- to help students understand some of the reasons for exploration and conquest
- to help students make connections with the people and events they will study in this chapter

Teaching Strategy
Thinking Critically After students have imagined themselves in the situation described on this page, have them answer the key questions and give reasons for their decisions.

EXAMINING *the* ISSUES

Following are suggestions for addressing each bulleted question.

1 Have students recall making a decision about joining a club or school group about which they knew little.

2 Ask students whether they would rather join a group of people like themselves, or one whose members are different.

3 Have students consider being in a position in which they are asked to take a side during an unpleasant conflict. What would they gain by choosing sides? By remaining neutral?

Making Connections Ask students to discuss the issue of choosing sides in situations involving conquest, such as the Roman, Assyrian, and Persian empires.

Interact *with* History

The year is 1520. You are a Native American living in central Mexico, and you are suddenly faced with a decision that may change your life forever. A group of white invaders, known as the Spanish, are engaged in fierce battle with the nearby Aztecs. You and many others have long hated the powerful Aztecs, who rule the land with a harsh and cruel hand. However, you are frightened of these newcomers who ride on large beasts and fire loud weapons.

Many of your friends are joining different sides of the fight. You can choose not to fight at all. However, if you do decide to fight, you must choose a side.

Which side would you choose?

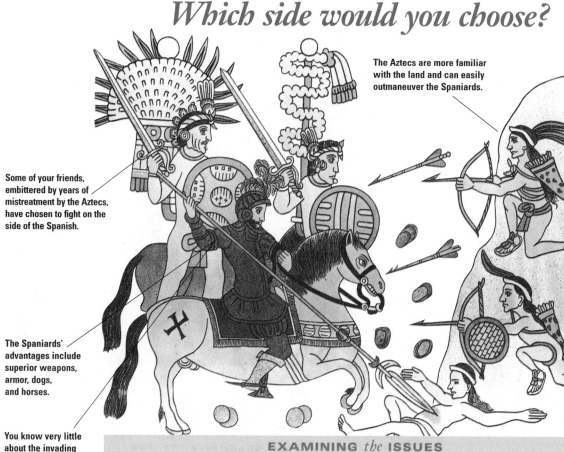

The Aztecs are more familiar with the land and can easily outmaneuver the Spaniards.

Some of your friends, embittered by years of mistreatment by the Aztecs, have chosen to fight on the side of the Spanish.

The Spaniards' advantages include superior weapons, armor, dogs, and horses.

You know very little about the invading Spanish and what they have in mind for you.

EXAMINING *the* ISSUES

1 • What risks are involved in supporting the invaders, whom you know almost nothing about?

2 • Does the fact that the Aztecs share a similar culture and heritage with you make a difference in your decision?

3 • What are the advantages and disadvantages of not fighting at all?

Discuss these questions with your classmates. In your discussion, examine whether invading armies throughout history have made life better or worse for people in the areas they conquer.

As you read about colonization in the Americas, see what course many natives took and learn the outcome of the battle between the Aztecs and Spanish.

482 Chapter 20

Follow Up
A feature on the chapter assessment will ask students to reevaluate their responses to the situation presented on this page.

1 Spanish Conquests in the Americas

TERMS & NAMES
- Christopher Columbus
- colony
- Hernando Cortés
- conquistadors
- Montezuma II
- Francisco Pizarro
- mestizo
- *encomienda*

MAIN IDEA

The voyages of Columbus prompted the Spanish to carve out the first European colonies in the Americas.

WHY IT MATTERS NOW

Throughout the Americas, Spanish culture, language, and descendants are the legacy of this period.

SETTING THE STAGE As you read in the previous chapter, competition for wealth in the East among European nations was fierce. This competition prompted sea captain **Christopher Columbus** to make a daring voyage for Spain in 1492. Instead of sailing east, Columbus sailed west across the Atlantic in search of an alternate trade route to Asia and its riches. Columbus never reached Asia. Instead he stepped onto an island in the Caribbean. That event set in motion a process that would bring together the peoples of Europe, Africa, and the Americas. And the world would change forever.

Columbus's Voyage Paves the Way

No one paid much attention as the *Niña, Pinta,* and *Santa María* slid out of a Spanish port around dawn on August 3, 1492. In a matter of months, however, Columbus's fleet would make history. It would reach the shores of what was to Europeans an astonishing new world.

First Encounters In the early hours of October 12, 1492, the long-awaited cry came. A lookout aboard the *Pinta* caught sight of a shoreline in the distance. *"Tierra! Tierra!"* he shouted. "Land! Land!" By dawn, Columbus and his crew were ashore. Thinking he had successfully reached the East Indies, Columbus called the surprised inhabitants who greeted him, *los indios.* The term translated into "Indian," a word mistakenly applied to all the native peoples of the Americas. In his memoirs, Columbus recounted his first meeting with the native peoples:

A VOICE FROM THE PAST
I presented them with some red caps, and strings of glass beads to wear upon the neck, and many other trifles of small value, wherewith they were much delighted, and became wonderfully attached to us. Afterwards they came swimming to the boats where we were, bringing parrots, balls of cotton thread, javelins, and many other things which they exchanged for the articles we gave them . . . in fact they accepted anything and gave what they had with the utmost good will.

CHRISTOPHER COLUMBUS, *Journal of Columbus*

This portrait of Christopher Columbus was painted by the Spanish artist Pedro Berruguete, who lived at the same time. It is believed to be the most accurate depiction of the Italian sea captain.

Columbus, however, had miscalculated where he was. He had not reached the East Indies. Scholars believe he landed instead on an island in the Bahamas in the Caribbean Sea. The natives there were not Indians, but a group who called themselves the Taino. Nonetheless, Columbus claimed the island for Spain. He named it San Salvador, or "Holy Savior."

Columbus, like other explorers, was interested in gold. Finding none on San Salvador, he explored other islands throughout the Caribbean, staking his claim to each one. "It was my wish to bypass no island without taking possession," he wrote.

In early 1493, Columbus returned to Spain. The reports he relayed about his journey delighted the Spanish monarchs. Spain's rulers, who had funded his first voyage, agreed

The Atlantic World **483**

THINK THROUGH HISTORY
A. Clarifying
Why did Columbus refer to Native Americans as Indians?
A. Possible Answer Because he thought he had reached the East Indies.

SECTION 1 RESOURCES

PRINT RESOURCES

IN-DEPTH RESOURCES: UNIT 4
Guided Reading, p. 68
Primary Sources: from *The Journal of Christopher Columbus,* p. 75; from *The Broken Spears,* p. 77
Literature: from *The Feathered Serpent,* p. 79
History Makers: Magellan, p. 82; Cortés, p. 83

ACCESS FOR STUDENTS ACQUIRING ENGLISH
Guided Reading (Spanish), p. 198

FORMAL ASSESSMENT
Section Quiz, p. 227

TECHNOLOGY RESOURCES

WORLD ART AND CULTURES TRANSPARENCIES
AT43 *Meeting of Cortés and Montezuma*

CD-ROM
Electronic Library of Primary Sources

VIDEO *Patterns of Interaction: The Spread of Epidemic Disease*

INTERNET www.mlworldhistory.com

Section 1 Overview

OBJECTIVES

1. To describe the Spanish conquest of the Americas beginning with Columbus.

2. To describe the conquest of the Aztec and Inca by the Spanish.

3. To identify the effects of Spanish colonization on the Americas.

SKILLBUILDERS
- Interpreting maps: movement, region, p. 484
- Interpreting graphs, p. 486

CRITICAL THINKING
- Clarifying, p. 483
- Making inferences, p. 485
- Analyzing issues, p. 486
- Contrasting, pp. 487, 489
- Analyzing causes, p. 488
- Recognizing bias, p. 488

FOCUS
5-Minute Warm-Up

▶ **Interpreting Maps**
To help students understand the European exploration of the Americas, have them answer these questions.

1. Look at the map on page 484. Who besides the Spanish made voyages to South America?

2. Which country explored the coast of California?

WARM-UP TRANSPARENCY 20

OBJECTIVE ① INSTRUCT

Columbus's Voyage Paves the Way

▶ **Key Ideas**
- Columbus lands on San Salvador and claims it for Spain.
- Explorer Pedro Cabral claims Brazil for Portugal.
- Portuguese explorer Ferdinand Magellan leads a crew that is the first to circumnavigate the globe.

IN-DEPTH RESOURCES: UNIT 4
Guided Reading, p. 68

ACCESS FOR STUDENTS ACQUIRING ENGLISH
Guided Reading (Spanish), p. 198

European Exploration of the Americas, 1492–1682

Interpreting the Map Have students trace with a finger the route of one explorer at a time.

Extension Activity Have students speculate on why the English and French explorers stayed much farther north than the Spanish. *Students may suggest that since the Spanish had already laid claim to parts of South America and the islands, the other countries wanted to claim their own lands as far away as possible.*

SKILLBUILDER Answers

1. Four
2. The Spanish and Portuguese explored South and Central America; the French, Dutch, and English explored North America.

MORE ABOUT . . .
What Columbus Found

In the West Indies, Columbus and his crew discovered a new way to get a good night's sleep. The native people slept in hanging beds called *hamacas*. The crew made and strung their own *hammocks* on board ship, above the wet deck and the rats.

 IN-DEPTH RESOURCES: UNIT 4
Primary Source: from *The Journal of Christopher Columbus*, p. 75

MORE ABOUT . . .
Magellan

Although Balboa was the first European to see the Pacific Ocean, Magellan named it. After sailing through the stormy Atlantic, Magellan rounded the tip of South America and sailed into a quiet sea, which he named *Pacific*, meaning "peaceful."

 IN-DEPTH RESOURCES: UNIT 4
History Makers: Magellan, p. 82

European Exploration of the Americas, 1492–1682

Explorers' Routes
- ← Spanish
- ← Portuguese
- ← French
- ← English
- ← Dutch

GEOGRAPHY SKILLBUILDER: Interpreting Maps

1. **Movement** How many different voyages did Columbus make to the Americas?
2. **Region** Which general region did the Spanish and Portuguese explore? Where did the English, Dutch, and French explore?

to finance three more trips. Columbus embarked on his second voyage to the Americas in September of 1493. He journeyed no longer as an explorer, but as an empire builder. He commanded a fleet of some 17 ships and several hundred armed soldiers. He also brought 1,000 settlers. The Spanish intended to transform the islands of the Caribbean into **colonies,** or lands that are controlled by another nation.

Columbus and his followers began a process of colonization that would reach nearly every corner of the Americas. Over the next two centuries, other European explorers began sailing across the Atlantic in search of unclaimed lands.

Other Explorers Take to the Seas In 1500, Portuguese explorer Pedro Álvares Cabral reached the shores of modern-day Brazil and claimed the land for his country. A year later, Amerigo Vespucci (vehs·POO·chee), an Italian in the service of Portugal, also traveled along the eastern coast of South America. Upon his return to Europe, he claimed that the newly discovered land was not part of Asia, but a "new" world. In 1507, a German mapmaker named the new continent America in honor of Vespucci. Eventually, America become the name for both continents in the Western Hemisphere.

In 1519, Portuguese explorer Ferdinand Magellan led the boldest exploration yet. Several years earlier, Spanish explorer Vasco Núñez de Balboa had marched through modern-day Panama and had become the first European to gaze upon the Pacific Ocean. Soon after, Magellan convinced the king of Spain to fund his voyage into the newly discovered ocean.

With about 230 men and five ships, Magellan sailed around the southern end of South America and into the mysterious waters of the Pacific. The fleet sailed for months without seeing land. Food supplies soon ran out. "We were eating biscuits

---

TEACHING OPTION · **BLOCK SCHEDULING** · COOPERATIVE ACTIVITY: **Displaying Explorers' Sailing Ships** · CLASS TIME 30 MINUTES

Task: Students will research sailing ships of the Spanish era of exploration, as well as life on board such ships, and create a classroom display.

Purpose: To learn about ship design of 500 years ago and what life was like aboard these ships.

Activity: Small groups will read and research to find out about the ships; draw pictures or make

mockups of the ships; and read about the sailing conditions of the time. Help students design a space in the classroom for the mockups or graphics of these ships, as well as the information to accompany them. Re-creations of the *Niña* and the *Pinta* are now on display in Corpus Christi, Texas.

 Building a Portfolio: If this report is among their best work, students should add it to their portfolios.

ALTERNATIVE ASSESSMENT BOOK
Standards for Evaluating a Cooperative Activity

Standards for Evaluation
The display should . . .

- present clear graphic examples.
- provide detailed written descriptions.
- show evidence of research using a variety of sources.

that were no longer biscuits but crumbs full of weevils [beetles]," one crew member wrote. "We also often ate sawdust."

After exploring the island of Guam, Magellan and his crew eventually reached the Philippines. Unfortunately, Magellan became involved in a local war there and was killed. His crew, greatly reduced by disease and starvation, continued sailing west toward home. Out of Magellan's original crew, only 18 men and one ship arrived back in Spain in 1522—nearly three years after they had left. They were the first persons to circumnavigate, or sail around, the world.

Spain Builds an American Empire

In 1519, as Magellan embarked on his historic voyage, a Spaniard named **Hernando Cortés** landed on the shores of Mexico. After colonizing several Caribbean islands, the Spanish had turned their attention to the American mainland. Cortés marched inward, looking to claim new lands for Spain. Cortés and the many other Spanish explorers who followed him were known as **conquistadors** (conquerors). Lured by rumors of vast lands filled with gold and silver, conquistadors carved out colonies in regions that would become Mexico, South America, and the United States. The Spanish were the first European settlers in the Americas. As a result of their colonization, the Spanish greatly enriched their empire and left a mark on the cultures of North and South America that exists today.

Cortés Conquers the Aztecs

Soon after landing in Mexico, Cortés learned of the vast and wealthy Aztec Empire in the region's interior. (See Chapter 16.) After marching for weeks through difficult mountain passes, Cortés and his force of roughly 600 men finally reached the magnificent Aztec capital of Tenochtitlan (teh·NAWCH·tee·TLAHN). The Aztec emperor, **Montezuma II,** was convinced at first that Cortés was an armor-clad god. He agreed to give the Spanish explorer a share of the empire's existing gold supply. The conquistador was not satisfied. Cortés, who admitted that he and his comrades had a "disease of the heart that only gold can cure," forced the Aztecs to mine more gold and silver. In the spring of 1520, the Aztecs rebelled against the Spanish intruders and drove out Cortés's forces.

The Spaniards, however, struck back. Despite being greatly outnumbered, Cortés and his men conquered the Aztecs in 1521. Several factors played a key role in the

HISTORY MAKERS

Hernando Cortés
1485–1547

To look at Hernando Cortés, it may have been difficult to guess he was a daring conquistador. According to one description, Cortés stood only about five feet, four inches tall and had a "deep chest, no belly to speak of, and was bow-legged. He was fairly thin."

But what Spain's first conquistador may have lacked in physical strength, he more than made up for in determination, courage, and ruthlessness. Upon arriving in Mexico, for example, Cortés reportedly burned his ships to keep his men from turning back. The Aztecs also experienced Cortés's toughness when they refused to surrender after months of fierce fighting. In response, Cortés ordered that the Aztec capital, Tenochtitlan, be destroyed.

Montezuma II
1480?–1520

While Cortés was a feared leader, Montezuma was a much beloved ruler who showed particular talent as an orator. "When he spoke," commented one historian, "he drew the sympathy of others by his subtle phrases and seduced them by his profound reasoning."

His words, however, would ultimately fail him. During a speech in which he tried to convince his subjects to make peace with the Spanish, the crowd denounced him as a traitor. "What is that which is being said by that scoundrel of a Montezuma . . ." shouted Montezuma's own cousin, Cuauhtémoc. ". . . We must give him the punishment which we give to a wicked man." And with that, the crowd stoned to death the Aztec ruler.

Native Population of Central Mexico

Interpreting the Graph Help students read the graph by explaining the horizontal axis, which shows the periods of time (20 years per entry). Then have them examine the vertical axis, which shows the population in millions.

Extension Activity Ask students why the population loss might have started out very high and then slowed somewhat over time. *Possible response: The largest number of native Americans died of European diseases, which they caught as soon as they encountered the Spanish. Over time they would have developed some immunity to disease.*

SKILLBUILDER Answers

1. 96 percent

2. It made it much easier for the Spanish, for the natives' dwindling population meant that they could offer little resistance.

MORE ABOUT . . .
Smallpox

The video *The Spread of Epidemic Disease* discusses how smallpox arrived in the Americas and what effects it had there.

PATTERNS OF INTERACTION
The Spread of Epidemic Disease: Bubonic Plague and Smallpox
Videocassette: Tape 2

Native Population of Central Mexico

Source: *The Population of Latin America*

SKILLBUILDER:
Interpreting Graphs

1. By what percentage did the native population decrease between 1519 and 1605?

2. How did the sharp decline in the native population—due greatly to disease—affect the Spaniards' attempts to conquer the region?

---

stunning victory. First, the Spanish had the advantage of superior weaponry. Aztec arrows were no match for the Spaniards' muskets and cannons.

Second, Cortés was able to enlist the help of various native groups. With the aid of a native woman translator named Malinche, Cortés learned that some natives resented the Aztecs. They hated their harsh practices, including human sacrifice. Through Malinche, Cortés convinced these natives to fight on his side.

Finally, and most important, the natives could do little to stop the invisible warrior that marched alongside the Spaniards—disease. Measles, mumps, smallpox, and typhus were just some of the diseases Europeans had brought with them to the Americas. Native Americans had never been exposed to these diseases. Thus, they had developed no natural immunity to them. As a result, they died by the hundreds of thousands. By the time Cortés launched his counterattack, the Aztec population had been greatly reduced by smallpox and measles. In time, European disease would truly devastate the natives of central Mexico.

Pizarro Subdues the Inca In 1532, another conquistador, **Francisco Pizarro,** marched an even smaller force into South America. He conquered the mighty Inca Empire. (See Chapter 16.) Pizarro and his army of about 200 met the Inca ruler, Atahualpa (Ah·tuh·WAHL·puh), near the city of Cajamarca. Atahualpa, who commanded a force of about 30,000, brought several thousand mostly unarmed men for the meeting. The Spaniards crushed the Inca force and kidnapped Atahualpa.

Atahualpa offered to fill a room once with gold and twice with silver in exchange for his release. However, after receiving the ransom, the Spanish strangled the Inca king. Demoralized by their leader's death, the remaining Inca force retreated from Cajamarca. Pizarro then marched on the Inca capital, Cuzco. He captured it without a struggle.

As Cortés and Pizarro conquered the once mighty civilizations of the Americas, fellow conquistadors defeated other native peoples. Spanish explorers also conquered the Maya in Yucatan and Guatemala. By the middle of the 16th century, Spain had created a wide-reaching American empire. It included New Spain (Mexico and parts of Guatemala), as well as other lands in Central and South America and the Caribbean.

Spain's Pattern of Conquest In building their new American empire, the Spaniards drew from techniques used during the *reconquista* of Spain. When conquering the Muslims, the Spanish lived among them and imposed upon them their Spanish culture. The Spanish settlers to the Americas, known as *peninsulares*, were mostly men. As a result, marriage between Spanish settlers and native women was common. These marriages created a large **mestizo**—or mixed Spanish and Native American—population. Their descendants live today in Mexico, other Latin American countries, and the United States.

Although the Spanish conquerors lived among and intermarried with the native people, they also oppressed them. In their effort to exploit the land for its precious resources, the Spanish forced Native Americans to labor within a system known as **encomienda.** Under this system, natives farmed, ranched, or mined for Spanish landlords. These landlords had received the rights to the natives' labor from Spanish authorities. The holders of *encomiendas* promised the Spanish rulers that they would act fairly and respect the workers. However, many abused the natives and worked many laborers to death, especially inside dangerous mines. The Spanish employed the same system in the Caribbean.

Background
The Aztecs practice of human sacrifice was based on the belief that if they did not feed human blood to the sun, it would fail to rise.

THINK THROUGH HISTORY
C. Analyzing Issues
What factors enabled the Spanish to defeat the Aztecs?
C. Possible Answer
Superior weaponry, help from other natives, and the spread of European diseases.

Background
Beginning around 1100, the *reconquista* was a centuries-long effort to drive the Muslims out of Spain.

Students Acquiring English: *Spanish and English Vocabulary* Use the Spanish words in the lesson as a springboard to consider the many English words that come from Spanish. Beginning with the words *mestizo* and *encomienda*, have students use a Spanish-English dictionary to find the meaning of each and then write each on a word chart like the one shown to the right. Then

suggest they consider words that are identified with the American southwest—*corral, mesa, lariat, mustang, canyon, arroyo, machete, junta, tortilla, patio, fiesta, stampede, burro, adobe, padre, plaza, frijole,* and others. Have them look up each word in an etymological dictionary to see if the original Spanish word is the same or different from the form today, and what the word originally meant. Have

them also enter this information on the chart. Ask students to identify the kinds of words that came into English from Spanish.

English Word/Def.	Spanish Word	Meaning
mustang: half-wild horse	mestengo	untamed

The Portuguese in Brazil One area of South America that remained outside of Spanish control was Brazil. In 1500, Cabral claimed the land for Portugal. During the 1530s, colonists began settling Brazil's coastal region. Finding little gold or silver, the settlers began growing sugar. Clearing out huge swaths of forest land, the Portuguese built giant sugar plantations. The demand for sugar in Europe was great, and the colony soon enriched Portugal. In time, the colonists pushed further west into Brazil. They settled even more land for the production of sugar.

Along the way, the Portuguese—like the Spanish—conquered Native Americans and inflicted thousands of them with disease. Also like the Spanish, the Portuguese enslaved a great number of the land's original inhabitants.

Spain Expands Its Influence

Spain's American colonies helped make it the richest, most powerful nation in the world during much of the 16th century. Ships filled with treasures from the Americas continually sailed into Spanish harbors. This newfound wealth helped usher in a golden age of art and culture in Spain. (See Chapter 21.)

Throughout the 16th century, Spain also increased its military might. To protect its treasure-filled ships, Spain built a powerful navy. The Spanish also strengthened their other military forces, creating a skillful and determined army. For a century and a half, Spain's army never lost a battle. Meanwhile, Spain enlarged its American empire by settling in parts of what is now the United States.

Conquistadors Push North Dreams of new conquests prompted Spain to back a series of expeditions into the southwestern United States. The Spanish actually had settled in parts of the United States before they even dreamed of building an empire on the American mainland. In 1513, Spanish explorer Juan Ponce de León wandered through modern-day Florida and claimed it for Spain.

By 1540, after building an empire that stretched from Mexico to Peru, the Spanish once again looked to the land that is now the United States. That year, Francisco Vásquez de Coronado led an expedition throughout much of present-day Arizona, New Mexico, Texas, Oklahoma, and Kansas. He was searching for another wealthy empire to conquer. Coronado found little gold amidst the dry deserts of the Southwest. As a result, the Spanish monarchy assigned mostly priests to explore and colonize the future United States.

In this 19th-century illustration, Coronado leads his army back to Mexico after failing to find wealth in the southwest United States. During his return, Coronado fell from his horse and had to travel part of the way on a stretcher.

Catholic priests had accompanied conquistadors from the very beginning of American colonization. The conquistadors had come in search of wealth. The priests who accompanied them had come in search of converts. In the winter of 1609–1610, Pedro de Peralta, governor of Spain's northern holdings—called New Mexico—led settlers to a tributary on the upper Rio Grande. Together they built a capital called Santa Fe, or "Holy Faith." In the next two decades, a string of Christian missions arose among the Pueblo, the native inhabitants of the region. Scattered missions, forts, and small ranches dotted the lands of New Mexico. These became the headquarters for advancing the Catholic religion.

Opposition to Spanish Rule Spanish priests worked to spread Christianity in the Americas. They also pushed for better treatment of Native Americans. Priests spoke out against the cruel treatment of natives. In particular, they criticized the harsh

The Atlantic World **487**

ASSESS & RETEACH

Section 1 Assessment

Have students work in pairs, with one asking the questions and the other answering them.

Section Quiz

 FORMAL ASSESSMENT
Section Quiz, p. 227

Reteaching Activity

CLASS TIME: 10 MINUTES

Use the Guided Reading worksheet for Section 1 to review the main ideas of the section.

 IN-DEPTH RESOURCES: UNIT 4
Guided Reading, p. 68

CLOSE ACTIVITY

CLASS TIME: 10 MINUTES

Role-Playing

Have interested students play the roles of Cortés, Montezuma, Pizarro, and Atahualpa. Other students will then interview them about their goals, ambitions, views of conquest, reactions to cultural interaction, and other issues.

---

pattern of labor that emerged under the *encomienda* system. "There is nothing more detestable or cruel," Dominican monk Bartolomé de Las Casas wrote, "than the tyranny which the Spaniards use toward the Indians for the getting of pearl [riches]."

Largely in response to the writings of Las Casas and others, the Spanish government abolished the *encomienda* system in 1542. To meet the colonies' desperate need for labor, Las Casas suggested the use of Africans. "The labor of one . . . [African] . . . [is] more valuable than that of four Indians," Las Casas declared. The priest later changed his view and denounced African slavery. However, many others promoted it. The Spanish, as well as the other nations that colonized the Americas, would soon enslave Africans to meet their growing labor needs.

Native Resistance Opposition to the Spanish method of colonization came not only from Spanish priests, but from the natives themselves. Resistance to Spain's attempt at domination began shortly after the Spanish arrived in the Caribbean. In November of 1493, Columbus encountered resistance in his attempt to conquer the present-day island of St. Croix. Before finally surrendering, the inhabitants defended themselves by firing poison arrows. Efforts to control the Taino on Hispaniola were even more difficult. After several rebellions, the Taino submitted to Columbus for several years. They revolted yet again in 1495.

As late as the end of the 17th century, natives in New Mexico fought against Spanish rule. While there were no silver mines to work in the region, the natives there still felt the weight of Spanish force. In converting the natives to Christianity, Spanish priests and soldiers often burned their sacred objects and prohibited many native rituals. The Spanish also forced natives to work for them and sometimes abused them physically. Native Americans who practiced their own religion were beaten.

In 1680, Popé, a Pueblo ruler, led a well-organized uprising against the Spanish. The rebellion involved some 17,000 warriors from villages all over New Mexico. The native fighters drove the Spanish back into New Spain. For the next 12 years—until the Spanish regained control of the area—the southwest region of the future United States once again belonged to its original inhabitants. By this time, however, the rulers of Spain had far greater concerns. Nearly 80 years before Popé ran the Spanish out of New Mexico, the other nations of Europe had begun to establish their own colonies in the Americas.

This European drawing of the 1600s depicts Indians taking revenge on a Spanish colonist—by pouring gold down his throat.

THINK THROUGH HISTORY
E. Analyzing Causes
Why did the natives of New Mexico revolt against Spanish settlers?
E. Possible Answer
Spanish attempts to destroy their culture and repressive measures, including beatings.

Section 1 Assessment

1. TERMS & NAMES

Identify
• Christopher Columbus
• colony
• Hernando Cortés
• conquistadors
• Montezuma II
• Francisco Pizarro
• mestizo
• *encomienda*

2. TAKING NOTES

Using a diagram like the one below, trace the major events in the establishment of Spain's empire in the Americas beginning with Columbus's arrival.

Columbus arrives in Americas

3. RECOGNIZING BIAS

Reread "A Voice from the Past" on page 483. How might Columbus's view of the Taino Indians have led the Spanish to think they could take advantage of and impose their will on the natives?

THINK ABOUT
• the Taino's desire for Spanish items even of "small value"
• the Taino's willingness to give whatever they had to the Spanish
• the Taino's appearance as a peaceful people

4. THEME ACTIVITY

Empire Building Working in small groups, debate the merits of Spain's colonization of the Americas. Have one half of the group take the position of conquistadors, and the other take the position of Native Americans.

THINK ABOUT
• how colonization of the Americas affected Spain
• what effect colonization had on the Native Americans

ANSWERS

1. TERMS & NAMES

Christopher Columbus, p. 483
colony, p. 484
Hernando Cortés, p.485
conquistadors, p. 485
Montezuma II, p. 485
Francisco Pizarro, p. 486
mestizo, p. 486
encomienda, p. 486

2. TAKING NOTES

Possible Steps: Columbus arrives in the Americas; Cortés defeats the Aztecs; Pizarro conquers the Inca; conquistadors colonize the southwest United States.

3. RECOGNIZING BIAS

Possible Answers: The Spanish may have taken the Taino's generosity and naïvete about the worth of material goods as an invitation to take whatever they wanted; the Spanish also may have assumed that the natives' gentleness meant they could be subdued.

4. THEME ACTIVITY

Possible Responses:
Conquistadors: colonization good—increased Spain's wea and power; introduced native Christianity; spread Spanish c ture. Native Americans: colonization bad—brought diseas and warfare; led to enslaveme suppressed native culture.

The Legacy of Columbus

In the years and centuries since his historic journeys, people still debate the legacy of Christopher Columbus's voyages. Some argue they were the heroic first steps in the creation of great and democratic societies. Others claim they were the beginnings of an era of widespread cruelty and bloodshed.

HISTORIAN'S COMMENTARY
Samuel Eliot Morison

Morison, a strong supporter of Columbus, laments that the sea captain died without realizing the true greatness of his deeds.

One only wishes that the Admiral might have been afforded the sense of fulfillment that would have come from foreseeing all that flowed from his discoveries; that would have turned all the sorrows of his last years to joy. The whole history of the Americas stems from the Four Voyages of Columbus; and as the Greek city-states looked back to the deathless gods as their founders, so today a score of independent nations and dominions unite in homage to Christopher, the stout-hearted son of Genoa, who carried Christian civilization across the Ocean Sea.

ESSAY
Alphonse Lamartine

Lamartine, a French writer and politician, praises Columbus for bringing the virtues of civil society to the Americas.

All of the characteristics of a truly great man are united in Columbus. Genius, labor, patience, obscurity of origin, overcome by energy of will; mild but persisting firmness . . . fearlessness of death in civil strife; confidence in the destiny—not of an individual but of the human race. . . . He was worthy to represent the ancient world before that unknown continent on which he was the first to set foot, and carry to these men of a new race all the virtues, without any of the vices, of the elder hemisphere. So great was his influence on the destiny of the earth, that none more than he ever deserved the name of Civilizer.

EYEWITNESS ACCOUNT
Bartolomé de Las Casas

Las Casas was an early Spanish missionary who watched fellow Spaniards unleash attack dogs on Native Americans. He predicted that Columbus's legacy would be one of disaster for America's original inhabitants.

. . . Their other frightening weapon after the horses: twenty hunting greyhounds. They were unleashed and fell on the Indians at the cry of *Tómalo!* ["Get them!"] Within an hour they had preyed on one hundred of them. As the Indians were used to going completely naked, it is easy to imagine what the fierce greyhounds did, urged to bite naked bodies and skin much more delicate than that of the wild boars they were used to. . . . This tactic, begun here and invented by the devil, spread throughout these Indies and will end when there is no more land nor people to subjugate and destroy in this part of the world.

ESSAY
Suzan Shown Harjo

Harjo, a Native American, disputes the so-called benefits that resulted from Columbus's voyages and the European colonization of the Americas that followed.

"We will be asked to buy into the thinking that . . . genocide and ecocide are offset by the benefits of horses, cut-glass beads, pickup trucks, and microwave ovens."

Connect *to* History

Contrasting What opposing ideas are presented on this page?

 SEE SKILLBUILDER HANDBOOK, PAGE 996

Connect *to* Today

Supporting an Opinion
Find several opinions about Columbus in 1992—the 500th anniversary of his discovery of America. Choose the opinion you agree with most and write a brief paper explaining why.

CD-ROM For another perspective on the legacy of Columbus, see World History: Electronic Library of Primary Sources.

*different*Perspectives

Why the Legacy of Columbus Matters Now
The same kinds of attitudes that led to the destruction of the pre-Columbian Native American cultures are still present in many areas of American society today. Sports teams use Native American names for their teams and Native American images for their team logos. Many companies use Native American images in marketing their goods. Native Americans point out that they are not mascots, but persons, and that the same people who do fake Indian dances and yell war whoops at a major league baseball game would never think of performing actions that would insult people who are African American, Jewish, or female.

Have the class do some research on the kinds of issues Native Americans are talking about in today's world. Suggestions include how Native Americans are portrayed in the media (especially the use of names and logos in the sports arena), land rights, pollution of Native American reservations, Native American sovereignty, and so forth. If there is a Native American center in your community, ask a spokesperson to come to the school to speak to students. If not, find such an organization in a city nearby and have students write, call, or use the Internet to contact the organization and find out in which areas of interest to Native Americans they are working.

 ELECTRONIC LIBRARY OF PRIMARY SOURCES
"On the Destruction of the Indies"

Connect *to* History

Contrasting
Possible Responses:
The first idea is that Columbus civilized the Americas by bringing Western virtues to these lands, virtues that eventually would help create great new societies; the second, opposing idea is that Columbus opened the way to a cruel colonization that devastated nearly an entire population.

Connect *to* Today

Supporting an Opinion
You might suggest to students that they use the *Reader's Guide to Periodical Literature* to locate articles from 1992 on the 500th anniversary of Columbus's discovery of America. Students should be able, by scanning the titles of the articles, to pick out several different opinions. They might also check newspaper files on microfilm in the library for relevant articles from 1992.

OBJECTIVES

1. To identify the French, English, and Dutch colonial activities in North America.

2. To summarize competing claims in North America.

3. To describe the Native American response to the land claims made by European nations.

SKILLBUILDER

- Interpreting maps: region, place, p. 493

CRITICAL THINKING

- Summarizing, p. 491
- Contrasting, pp. 491, 492
- Analyzing issues, p. 493
- Identifying problems, p. 494
- Making inferences, p. 494
- Analyzing themes, p. 494

FOCUS

5-Minute Warm-Up

▶ **Summarizing**

To understand the sufferings endured by the English colonists at Jamestown, have students answer these questions.

1. Read "A Voice from the Past" on page 491. What seems to be killing the colonists?

2. What are the prospects of the colonists at this point?

 WARM-UP TRANSPARENCY 20

OBJECTIVE ➊ INSTRUCT

European Nations Settle North America

▶ **Key Ideas**

- The French colonize the St. Lawrence and Mississippi river valleys and begin the fur trade.

- The English settle at Jamestown and seek religious freedom in Massachusetts.

- The Dutch encourage a diverse population in New Netherland.

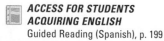 **IN-DEPTH RESOURCES: UNIT 4**
Guided Reading, p. 69

 ACCESS FOR STUDENTS ACQUIRING ENGLISH
Guided Reading (Spanish), p. 199

---

2 Competing Claims in North America

TERMS & NAMES
- New France
- Jamestown
- Pilgrims
- Puritans
- New Netherland
- French and Indian War
- Metacom

MAIN IDEA	WHY IT MATTERS NOW
Several European nations fought for control of North America, and England eventually emerged victorious.	The English settlers in North America left a legacy of law and government that guides the United States today.

SETTING THE STAGE Spain's successful colonization efforts in the Americas did not go unnoticed. Other European nations soon became interested in obtaining their own valuable colonies across the Atlantic. The Treaty of Tordesillas had divided the newly discovered lands between Spain and Portugal. However, other European countries ignored the treaty. They set out to build their own empires in the Americas.

European Nations Settle North America

Magellan's voyage showed that ships could reach Asia by way of the Pacific Ocean. Spain claimed the route around the southern tip of South America. Other European countries hoped to find an easier and more direct route to the Pacific. If it existed, a northwest route through North America to Asia would become a highly profitable trade route. Not finding the route, the French, English, and Dutch instead established colonies in North America.

CONNECT to TODAY

Cajun Culture

French culture still thrives in Louisiana due in large part to the influence of people known as Cajuns. Cajuns are the descendants of French colonists who in 1604 settled the region known as Acadia in eastern Canada. Battles with the British led thousands of Acadians to move to French settlements in Louisiana, where their legacy lives on.

Today, more than 1 million Louisianans speak French. In addition, Cajun food, such as a spicy, thick soup called gumbo, is popular not only in the Bayou region but also throughout the United States. Also popular around the nation are the fast-paced sounds of Cajun zydeco music.

Explorers Establish New France Just as Columbus had before them, the early French explorers sailed west with dreams of reaching the East Indies. One such explorer was Giovanni da Verrazzano (VEHR·uh·ZAHN·noh), an Italian in the service of France. In 1524, he sailed to North America in search of a possible sea route to the Pacific. While he did not find the route, Verrazzano did discover what is today New York Harbor. Ten years later, the Frenchman Jacques Cartier (kahr·TYAY) reached a gulf off the eastern coast of Canada that led to a broad river. Cartier named the river the St. Lawrence. He followed it inward until he reached a large island dominated by a hill. He named the island Mont Royal, which later became known as Montreal. In 1608, another French explorer, Samuel de Champlain, sailed up the St. Lawrence. He laid claim to a region he called Quebec. The settlement grew. It eventually became the base of France's colonial empire in North America, known as **New France.**

After establishing Quebec, the French penetrated the heart of the North American continent. In 1673, French priest Jacques Marquette and trader Louis Joliet explored the Great Lakes and the upper Mississippi River. Nearly 10 years later, Sieur de La Salle explored the lower Mississippi. He claimed the entire river valley for France. He named it Louisiana in honor of the French king, Louis XIV. By the early 1700s, New France covered much of what is now the midwest United States and eastern Canada. (See the map on page 493.)

A Trading Empire France's North American empire was immense. But it was sparsely populated. By 1760, the European population of New France had grown to only about 65,000. A large number of French colonists had no desire to build towns or raise families. These settlers included Catholic priests who sought to convert

---

PRINT RESOURCES

 IN-DEPTH RESOURCES: UNIT 4
Guided Reading, p. 69
Skillbuilder Practice: Contrasting, p. 72

 ACCESS FOR STUDENTS ACQUIRING ENGLISH
Guided Reading (Spanish), p. 199
Skillbuilder Practice: (Spanish), p. 202

 FORMAL ASSESSMENT
Section Quiz, p. 228

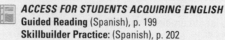 **ALTERNATIVE ASSESSMENT BOOK**

TECHNOLOGY RESOURCES

CD-ROM
Electronic Library of Primary Sources

INTERNET www.mlworldhistory.com

Native Americans. They also included young, single men engaged in what had become New France's main economic activity: fur trade.

By the late 1500s, one of the hottest fashion trends in Europe was hats made of beaver skin. Beavers were almost extinct in Europe but plentiful in North America. This led to a thriving trade in furs. Unlike the English, the French were less interested in occupying territories than they were in making money off the land.

The English Settle at Jamestown The explorations of the Spanish and French fired the imagination of the English. In 1606, a company of London investors obtained from King James a charter to found a colony in North America. In 1607, the company's three ships—and more than 100 settlers—pushed out of an English harbor. Four months later, the North American shore rose along the horizon. After reaching the coast of Virginia, the vessels slipped into a broad coastal river. They sailed inland until they reached a small peninsula. There, the colonists climbed off their ships and claimed the land as theirs. They named the settlement **Jamestown** in honor of their king.

The colony's start was disastrous. The settlers were more interested in finding gold than planting crops. They soon fell victim to their harsh surroundings. During the first few years, seven out of every ten people died of hunger, disease, or fighting with the Native Americans. After several months in this hostile environment, one settler described the terrible situation:

A VOICE FROM THE PAST
Thus we lived for the space of five months in this miserable distress . . . our men night and day groaning in every corner of the fort, most pitiful to hear. If there were any conscience in men, it would make their hearts to bleed to hear the pitiful murmuring and outcries of our sick men for relief, every night and day for the space of six weeks: some departing out of the World, many times three or four in a night; in the morning their bodies trailed out of their cabins like dogs, to be buried.

A JAMESTOWN COLONIST, quoted in *A New World*

Despite their nightmarish start, the colonists eventually gained a foothold in their new land. Jamestown became England's first permanent settlement in North America. The colony's outlook improved greatly after farmers there discovered tobacco. High demand in England for tobacco turned it into a profitable cash crop, or a crop grown primarily for sale. The colony, however, continued to struggle financially. Jamestown's investors finally let King James take over the colony. As a royal colony, Jamestown slowly grew and prospered.

Puritans Create a "New England" In 1620, as the colonists at Jamestown were struggling to survive, a group known as **Pilgrims** founded a second English colony, Plymouth, in Massachusetts. Persecuted for their religious beliefs in England, these colonists sought religious freedom. Eight years later, a group known as **Puritans** also sought religious freedom from England's Anglican Church. They established a larger colony at nearby Massachusetts Bay.

The Puritans wanted to build a model community that would set an example for other Christians to follow. Although the colony experienced early difficulties, it gradually took hold. This was due in large part to the numerous families in the colony, unlike the mostly single, male population in Jamestown. Family life created a sense of order among the settlers. It also ensured that the population would reproduce itself.

The Dutch Found New Netherland Following the English and French into North America were the Dutch. The Dutch had established the Dutch East India Company in 1602 to compete for trade in the Indian Ocean. Several years later, they turned

The Atlantic World **491**

THINK THROUGH HISTORY
A. Summarizing
Why were France's North American holdings so sparsely populated?
A. Possible Answer
Because most of the settlers were priests or fur trappers who had no desire to build towns or start families.

Background
Puritans took their name from their desire to "purify" the English church.

THINK THROUGH HISTORY
B. Contrasting
In what ways did the colonies at Jamestown and Massachusetts Bay differ?
B. Possible Answer
Jamestown: economic motivation; early suffering; mostly male. Massachusetts Bay: religious motivation; stable; numerous families

The first English colonists arrive at Jamestown in 1607, as depicted in this 19th-century engraving.

CONNECT *to* TODAY
Cajun Culture
(see page 490)

Zydeco is a blend of white Cajun and black Creole music, creating a mix of country, jazz, and rhythm and blues. Zydeco is usually played faster than Cajun and emphasizes the beat while simplifying the melody. Have a few students find a CD of some Cajun music in their school or community library and bring it to class to play.

MORE ABOUT . . .
The Fur Trade
From the 1600s to the 1800s, the beaver was hunted until the species was almost extinct. In the late 1600s, 1 beaver pelt could buy a cooking kettle or a pound of tobacco, and 12 pelts could buy a rifle. Both Canada and the United States have now passed laws regulating the hunting season for beavers.

MORE ABOUT . . .
Jamestown
Captain John Smith, one of the original Jamestown colonists, wrote about the lust for gold among the settlers: "No talke, no hope, no worke, but dig gold, wash gold, refine gold, load gold." This was unfortunate, for the colonists found no gold in Virginia.

TEACHING OPTIONS

MULTIPLE LEARNING STYLES

Linguistic Learners Have students imagine they are Jamestown colonists living through the first dreadful winter in America. Have them write letters to their families back in England telling of the hardships, illnesses, deaths, and so forth. If the student's character is dying, have the colonist write his or her last words to his or her family. Or, they might write to relatives in England, requesting supplies. If they choose to write for supplies, have them give specific details about what they miss most from England and what specific items would be the most useful.

EXPLORING PRIMARY SOURCES

A Voice from the Past King James had given the Jamestown colonists specific instructions on where to settle. He told them to settle on a navigable river and to stay on an island, 100 miles from the sea and in a place without a lot of woods. He also said, "Neither must you plant in a low and moist place, because it will prove unhealthy." In fact, the colonists settled in a location that was very low and moist, full of trees, and infested with mosquitoes carrying malaria. The excerpt quoted above in "A Voice from the Past" illustrates some of the consequences of the colonists' choice of location.

Teacher's Edition **491**

When the English took over New Netherland, the English language quickly outpaced Dutch. Today, however, there are many familiar words borrowed from Dutch in the English language, including *cooky, boss, crib,* and *spook.*

OBJECTIVE ② INSTRUCT

The Fight for North America

Key Ideas

- The English drive the Dutch from New Netherland and rename the colony New York.
- The Seven Years' War in Europe spills over into conflicts between French and English colonists in North America.
- The English defeat the French and rule eastern North America.

SPOTLIGHT ON
Pirates

Blackbeard was finally trapped by a British navy crew in 1718 in an inlet of Okracoke Island, off North Carolina. It is said of Blackbeard's last battle that he fought with a pistol in one hand and a cutlass in the other, before dying with more than 25 wounds in his body. Ask students to find more information about Blackbeard's last battle and bring copies of the accounts they find to class. Volunteers might read their accounts to the class.

---

their attention to the Americas. In 1609, Henry Hudson, an Englishman in the service of the Netherlands, sailed west. He was searching for a northwest sea route to Asia. Hudson did not find a route. He did, however, explore three waterways near present-day New York that were later named for him—the Hudson River, Hudson Bay, and Hudson Strait.

The Dutch claimed the region along these waterways. They established a fur trade with the Iroquois Indians. They also built trading posts along the Hudson River at Fort Orange (now Albany) and on Manhattan Island, at the mouth of the river. Dutch merchants quickly formed the Dutch West India Company. In 1621, the Dutch government granted the company permission to colonize the region and expand the thriving fur trade. The Dutch holdings in North America became known as **New Netherland.**

Although the Dutch company profited from its fur trade, it was slow to attract Dutch colonists. To encourage settlers to come and stay, the colony opened its doors to a variety of peoples. Gradually, more Dutch, as well as Germans, French, Scandinavians, and other Europeans settled the area. The colony's population was so ethnically diverse that one visitor called it a great "confusion of tongues." The Dutch reputation for religious tolerance also drew people of many faiths, including Protestants, Catholics, Muslims, and Jews.

Colonizing the Caribbean During the 1600s, the nations of Europe also colonized the Caribbean. The French seized control of several Caribbean islands, including present-day Haiti, Guadeloupe, and Martinique. The English settled Barbados and Jamaica. In 1634, the Dutch captured what are now the Netherlands Antilles and Aruba from Spain.

On these islands, the Europeans built huge tobacco and sugar plantations. These products, although profitable, demanded a large and steady supply of free labor. Enslaved Africans eventually would supply this labor.

The Fight for North America

SPOTLIGHT ON

Pirates

The battle for colonial supremacy occurred not only on land, but also on the sea. Acting on behalf of their government, privately owned armed ships, known as privateers, attacked merchant ships of enemy nations and sank or robbed them.

Also patrolling the high seas were pirates. Unlike privateers, pirates were not licensed by any country. They attacked ships for their gold and did not care what nation the vessels represented. Pirates were ruthless men who did not hesitate to kill for treasure.

One of the most well-known pirates was Edward B. Teach, whose prominent beard earned him the nickname Blackbeard (above). According to one account, Blackbeard attempted to frighten his victims by sticking "lighted matches under his hat, which appeared on both sides of his face and eyes, naturally fierce and wild. . . ."

As they expanded their settlements in North America, the nations of France, England, and the Netherlands battled each other for colonial supremacy. After years of skirmishes and war, the English gained control of much of the continent.

The English Oust the Dutch To the English, New Netherland had become a "Dutch wedge" separating its northern and southern colonies. In 1664, the English king, Charles II, granted his brother, the Duke of York, permission to drive out the Dutch. When the duke's fleet arrived at New Netherland, the Dutch surrendered without firing a shot. The Duke of York claimed the colony for England and renamed it New York.

With the Dutch gone, the English continued to colonize the Atlantic coast of North America. By 1750, about 1.3 million English settlers lived in 13 colonies stretching from New Hampshire to Georgia.

England Battles France The English soon became hungry for more land to suit their growing colonial population. So they pushed further west into the continent. By doing so, however, they collided with France's North American holdings. France and England, long-time enemies, had brought their dislike for one another with them to North America. As their colonies expanded, they began to interfere with each other. It seemed that a major conflict was on the horizon.

That conflict began in 1754. That year a dispute over land claims in the Ohio Valley led to a war between the British and French on the North American continent. The conflict became known as

THINK THROUGH HISTORY
C. Contrasting
How were the Dutch and French colonies different from the English colonies in North America?
C. Possible Answer
The English colonies were more populated while the Dutch and French colonies were established mainly for commercial reasons. New England was begun for religious reasons.

Background
In 1707, England united with Scotland to become the United Kingdom of Great Britain.

SKILLBUILDER MINI-LESSON: Contrasting

CLASS TIME 15 MINUTES

Explaining the Skill Finding the differences between ideas, institutions, behaviors, or events helps students understand historical events more clearly. Often, one concept is easier to grasp if its features can be contrasted with similar features of something else. For example, understanding the rules of rugby might be made easier by contrasting them with the rules of soccer or football.

Applying the Skill: *Think Through History Question* To answer the Think Through History question on this page, students will first need to review pages 490–492. Have them take note of the green subheads on these pages. Then ask the following questions.

1. What sort of empire was France's North American territory? *a trading empire*

2. Who founded New England, and what was their main reason for settling there? *Puritans; religious freedom*

3. Which colony had the most diversity of people and languages? Who founded it? *New Netherland; the Dutch*

 IN-DEPTH RESOURCES: UNIT 4
Skillbuilder Practice: Contrasting, p. 72

Europeans in N. America, 1754

UNCLAIMED

Hudson Bay

NEW-FOUNDLAND

Lake Winnipeg

Quebec

ACADIA

Great Salt L.

Boston

New York

ATLANTIC OCEAN

Santa Fe

St. Augustine

FLORIDA

New Orleans

Gulf of Mexico

HAITI

CUBA

JAMAICA

Santo Domingo

Mexico City

Caribbean Sea

500 Miles

1,000 Kilometers

Disputed
English
French
Spanish

Holdings after 1763

UNCLAIMED

Hudson Bay

Lake Winnipeg

Quebec

ST-PIERRE AND MIQUELON

Great Salt L.

Boston

New York

ORIGINAL 13 COLONIES

ATLANTIC OCEAN

Charleston

Tropic of Cancer

Gulf of Mexico

HAITI

CUBA

JAMAICA

Mexico City

Caribbean Sea

0   500 Miles

0   1,000 Kilometers

English
French
Russian
Spanish

GEOGRAPHY SKILLBUILDER: Interpreting Maps
1. **Region** Which nation claimed the largest area of the present-day United States in 1754?
2. **Place** How did Britain's North American empire change after 1763?

the **French and Indian War.** The war became part of a larger conflict known as the Seven Years' War. Britain and France—along with their European allies—also battled for territorial and colonial supremacy in Europe and the West Indies.

In North America, the British colonists, with the help of the British Army, defeated the French in 1763. The French surrendered most of their colonial holdings on the continent. As a result of the French and Indian War, the British seized control of nearly the entire eastern half of North America.

Native American Reaction

As in Mexico and South America, the arrival of Europeans in the present-day United States had a great impact on Native Americans. European colonization brought mostly disaster for the lands' original inhabitants, as many fell to disease and warfare.

A Strained Relationship French and Dutch settlers developed a mostly cooperative relationship with the Native Americans. This was due mainly to the mutual benefits of the fur trade. Native Americans did most of the trapping and then traded the furs to the French for such items as guns, hatchets, mirrors, and beads. The Dutch also cooperated with Native Americans in an effort to establish a fur-trading enterprise.

The groups, however, did not live together in complete harmony. Dutch settlers engaged in fighting with various Native American groups over land claims and trading rights. In 1643, for example, the Dutch and Wappinger tribe fought a bloody battle in which hundreds died. For the most part, however, the French and Dutch colonists lived together peacefully with their North American hosts.

The same could not be said of the English. Early relations between English settlers and Native Americans were cooperative. However, they quickly worsened—mostly over

The Atlantic World **493**

Comparing and Contrasting

Ask students why they think the Dutch and French at first had better relationships with Native Americans than did the English. Have them put their ideas in a chart like the one here.

Nation	Relationship with Native Americans	Reason
Dutch		
French		
English		

ASSESS & RETEACH

Section 2 Assessment

Have students list the pages in the section on which answers to each question can be found.

Section Quiz

 FORMAL ASSESSMENT
Section Quiz, p. 228

Reteaching Activity
CLASS TIME: 15 MINUTES

Review the students' charts for the Taking Notes activity in the section assessment. The reasons they have listed for establishment of the settlement should form the persuasive letter they write.

CLOSE ACTIVITY

CLASS TIME: 15 MINUTES

Summarizing the Section

Have students make a chart that lists the English, French, and Dutch colonies in North America, their locations, the reasons for the settlements, and the valuable products and crops of the colonies.

King Philip's War was one of the bloodiest battles fought between English colonists and Native Americans. About 600 colonists and 3,000 Indians were killed during the fighting.

the issues of land and religion. Unlike the French and Dutch, the English sought to populate their colonies in North America. This meant pushing the natives off their land. The English colonists seized more and more land for their swelling population—and to grow more tobacco. As a result, tensions between the two groups rose.

Misunderstandings over religion also heightened tensions. The English settlers, particularly the Puritans, considered Native Americans heathens—people without a faith. Over time, many Puritans viewed Native Americans as agents of the devil and as a threat to their godly society. For their part, Native Americans developed a similarly hard view toward the white invaders.

Settlers and Native Americans Battle The hostility between the English settlers and Native Americans led to warfare. As early as 1622, the Powhatan tribe attacked colonial villages around Jamestown and killed about 350 settlers. The colonists eventually struck back and massacred hundreds of Powhatan.

One of the bloodiest battles colonists and Native Americans waged was known as King Philip's War. It began in 1675 when the Native American ruler **Metacom** (also known as King Philip) led an attack on 52 colonial villages throughout Massachusetts. In the months that followed, both sides massacred hundreds of victims. After a year of fierce fighting, the colonists defeated the natives. Throughout the 17th century, many more smaller skirmishes erupted throughout North America. While the Native Americans fought fiercely, they were no match for the colonists' rifles and cannons.

Natives Fall to Disease More destructive than the Europeans' weapons were their diseases. Like the Spanish in Central and South America, the Europeans who settled North America brought with them several diseases. And just as had happened in Mexico and Peru, the diseases devastated the native population in North America.

In 1616, for example, an epidemic of smallpox ravaged Native Americans living along the New England coast. The population of one tribe, the Massachusett, dropped from 24,000 to 750 by 1631. Thousands of other natives throughout the region also perished. "They died on heapes, as they lay in their houses," observed one eyewitness. From South Carolina to Missouri, nearly whole tribes fell to smallpox, measles, and other diseases.

Throughout the Americas, the loss of native life due to disease was incredible. One of the effects of this loss was a severe shortage of labor in the colonies. In order to meet their growing labor needs, European colonists from South America to North America soon turned to another group: Africans, whom they would enslave by the millions.

E. Identifying Problems Why did the issues of land and religion cause such strife between the Native Americans and English settlers?
E. Possible Answer The settlers continually wanted more land for their growing population as well as their crops; they also viewed the natives as godless devils.

Background
To celebrate their victory over Metacom, the Puritans cut off his head and displayed it at Plymouth for many years.

Section 2 Assessment

1. TERMS & NAMES
Identify
• New France
• Jamestown
• Pilgrims
• Puritans
• New Netherland
• French and Indian War
• Metacom

2. TAKING NOTES
Copy this chart and fill in the location of each settlement and the main reasons for its establishment.

Name of Settlement	General Location	Reasons for Establishment
New France		
New Netherland		
Massachusetts Bay		

Write a letter convincing someone to settle in one of the settlements.

3. MAKING INFERENCES
What may have been one reason the English eventually beat the French in North America?
THINK ABOUT
• how England's colonies differed from those of the French
• English and French colonial populations on the eve of the French and Indian War

4. ANALYZING THEMES
Cultural Interaction
Imagine that you have been asked to settle a dispute between a group of English colonists and Native Americans. Summarize each side's grievances and offer possible solutions.

494 Chapter 20

ANSWERS

1. TERMS & NAMES
New France, p. 490
Jamestown, p. 491
Pilgrims, p.491
Puritans, p. 491
New Netherland, p. 492
French and Indian War, p. 493
Metacom, p. 494

2. TAKING NOTES
New France: eastern Canada and much of midwest United States/Christian missionary and fur trading post; New Netherland: upper east coast of United States/ fur trading post; Massachusetts Bay: upper east coast of United States/religious refuge

3. MAKING INFERENCES
Possible Response: The English, unlike the French and Dutch, populated their colonies in North America, so that by the eve of the French and Indian War, England's colonial population was more than 1 million, while France's was only 65,000.

4. ANALYZING THEMES
Possible Responses: Colonis[t] grievances—need more land growing population and farmi[ng] Native Americans are heathe[n] Native Americans' grievance[s]- colonists are pushing them o[ff] their land. Possible solutions— share the land by establishing boundary lines.

The Atlantic Slave Trade

MAIN IDEA

To meet their growing labor needs, Europeans enslaved millions of Africans in forced labor in the Americas.

WHY IT MATTERS NOW

Descendants of enslaved Africans represent a significant part of the Americas' population today.

SETTING THE STAGE Sugar plantations and tobacco farms required a large supply of workers to make them profitable for their owners. European owners had planned to use Native Americans as a source of cheap labor. But millions of Native Americans died from disease and warfare. Therefore, the Europeans in Brazil, the Caribbean, and the southern colonies of North America soon turned to Africa for workers.

The Evolution of African Slavery

Beginning around 1500, European colonists began enslaving Africans in the Americas in order to meet their great demand for large numbers of people to work as cheap labor.

Slavery in Africa As it had in other parts of the world, slavery had existed in Africa for many years. In most regions, however, it was a relatively minor institution. The spread of Islam into Africa during the seventh century, however, ushered in an increase in slavery and the slave trade. African rulers justified enslavement with the Muslim belief that non-Muslim prisoners of war could be bought and sold as slaves. As a result, between 650 and 1600, black as well as white Muslims transported as many as 4.8 million Africans—mostly prisoners of war and criminals—to the Muslim lands of Southwest Asia. Once there, these enslaved Africans worked primarily as domestic servants.

In most African and Muslim societies, slaves had some legal rights and opportunity for social mobility. In the Muslim world, slaves even occupied positions of influence and power. Some served as generals in the army. Others bought large estates and even owned slaves of their own. In African societies, slaves could escape their bondage in numerous ways, including marrying into the family they served. Furthermore, slavery in Africa was not hereditary. Thus the sons and daughters of slaves were considered free.

The Desire for Africans The first Europeans to explore Africa were the Portuguese during the 1400s. Initially, Portuguese traders were more interested in trading for gold than for captured Africans. That changed, however, with the colonization of the Americas. At first, European colonists in the Americas forced Native Americans to work their profitable mines and plantations. As natives began dying by the millions from disease, Europeans became desperate for new workers.

To resupply their labor force, colonists in the Americas soon looked to Africa. Europeans saw several advantages in using Africans. First, many Africans had been exposed to various European diseases and had built up some immunity to them. Second, many Africans had experience in farming and thus could be taught large-scale plantation work. Third, Africans—strangers to the Americas—had little knowledge of

The Atlantic World **495**

A. Possible Answer
In Muslim society, slaves had legal rights and opportunities for social mobility; in Africa, slaves could escape their bondage in numerous ways, and slavery was not hereditary.

THINK THROUGH HISTORY
A. Summarizing
What were some characteristics of Muslim and African slavery?

SPOTLIGHT ON

Slavery

The enslavement of human beings by others is believed to be as old as civilization itself. Slavery probably began with the development of farming about 10,000 years ago. Farming gave people the need to force prisoners of war to work for them.

Slavery has existed in numerous societies around the world. People were enslaved in civilizations from Egypt to China to India, as well as among Indians in America, and in Greece and Rome.

Race was not always a factor in slavery. Often, slaves were captured prisoners of war, or people of a different nationality or religion. In ancient Rome, for example, both owners and slaves were white.

However, the slavery that developed in the Americas was based largely on race. Europeans viewed black people as naturally inferior. Because of this, slavery in the Americas was hereditary—children of slaves were also slaves.

MORE ABOUT . . .
Slavery on Barbados

Plantation owners on Barbados determined that it was more profitable to buy new slaves to replace those who died from disease and overwork than to institute measures to provide for a more humane life for slaves. This attitude extended even to slave women of childbearing age. Children were seen as an economic drain because of the time it took for them to mature and become useful as workers.

MORE ABOUT . . .
King Affonso

King Affonso was originally just looking for trading partners. He asked Portugal to send people to the Congo who specialized in construction, farming, and trading. But the Portuguese were more interested in developing the slave trade than in aiding the Congo. They invaded the area in 1665 and killed Affonso in the course of defeating his troops.

 ELECTRONIC LIBRARY OF PRIMARY SOURCES
Letter to the King of Portugal

---

the land and had no familiar tribes in which to hide. As a result, they were less likely to try to escape.

In time, the buying and selling of Africans for work in the Americas—known as the **Atlantic slave trade**—became a massive enterprise. Between 1500 and 1600, nearly 300,000 Africans were transported to the Americas. During the next century, that number climbed to almost 1.5 million. By the time the Atlantic slave trade ended around 1870, Europeans had imported about 9.5 million Africans to the Americas.

Spain and Portugal Lead the Way The Spanish took an early lead in importing Africans to the Americas. As early as 1511, a small number of Africans were working in the copper mines on Hispaniola. In time, Spain moved on from the Caribbean and began to colonize the American mainland. As a result, the Spanish imported and enslaved thousands more Africans. By 1650, nearly 300,000 Africans labored throughout Spanish America on plantations and in gold and silver mines.

By this time, however, the Portuguese had surpassed the Spanish in the importation of Africans to the Americas. During the 1600s, Brazil dominated the European sugar market. As the colony's sugar industry grew, so too did European colonists' demand for slaves. During the 17th century, more than 40 percent of all Africans brought to the Americas went to Brazil. By the time the slave trade ended, Brazil had received more than 3.6 million Africans. That was nearly 10 times the number of Africans who would arrive in North America.

The development of sugar, shown here in its cane form, helped spur the growth of slavery in the Americas.

Slavery Spreads Throughout the Americas As the other European nations established colonies in the Americas, their demand for cheap labor grew. Thus, they also began to import and enslave large numbers of Africans. A majority of these slaves labored on sugar, tobacco, and coffee plantations in the Dutch, French, and English colonies in the Caribbean.

As England's presence in the Americas grew, it came to dominate the Atlantic slave trade. From 1690 until the nation abolished the slave trade in 1807, England was the leading carrier of enslaved Africans. By the time the slave trade ended, the English had transported nearly 1.7 million Africans to their colonies in the West Indies.

A much smaller number of enslaved Africans eventually arrived in what is now the United States. In all, nearly 400,000 Africans were imported to Britain's North American colonies. Once in North America, however, the slave population steadily grew. By 1830, roughly 2 million slaves toiled in the United States.

African Cooperation and Resistance Many African rulers and merchants played a willing role in the Atlantic slave trade. Those African leaders who had been selling Africans as slaves to Muslims and other African rulers saw little difference in selling them to Westerners. Most European traders, rather than travel inland, waited in ports along the western and eastern coasts of Africa. African merchants, with the help of local rulers, captured Africans to be enslaved. They then delivered them to the Europeans in exchange for gold, guns, and other goods.

As the slave trade grew, some African rulers voiced their opposition to the practice. One such ruler was King Nzinga Mbemba of Congo in west-central Africa. Mbemba, also known as Affonso, had originally participated in the slave trade. However, he soon realized its devastating effect on African societies. In 1526, he wrote a letter to the king of Portugal in which he protested the taking of Africans for enslavement:

> **A VOICE FROM THE PAST**
> And we cannot reckon how great the damage is, since . . . merchants are taking every day our natives, sons of the land and the sons of our noblemen and vassals and our relatives, because the thieves and men of bad conscience grab them . . . they grab them and get them to be sold; and so great, Sir, is the corruption . . . that our country is being completely depopulated, and Your Highness should not agree with this nor accept it. . . . *it is our will that in these Kingdoms there should not be any trade of slaves nor outlet for them.*
>
> **KING AFFONSO,** quoted in *African Civilization Revisited*

Background
The total number of Africans taken from Africa during the Atlantic slave trade is thought to be even higher. Scholars believe that many Africans perished during the voyage to the Americas. Thus, they were unaccounted for.

B. Possible Answer
Slaves had built up immunity to many diseases, they were experienced in farming and were in an alien environment which made them less likely to escape.

Background
By 1690, the slave population on the British island of Barbados was 60,000—three times that of the white population.

Task: To write a report for King Affonso of Congo to support his letter to the king of Portugal.

Purpose: To learn about the slave trade.

Activity: Have students brainstorm arguments against the slave trade. Then divide the class into groups of four. Have each group choose a different argument and write a paragraph developing that one

argument. Have the groups combine their paragraphs into one report that will be sent to the king.

📁 **Building a Portfolio** If students feel this report is among their best work, they should add it to their portfolios. They should specify which paragraph in the report is theirs.

ALTERNATIVE ASSESSMENT BOOK
Standards for Evaluating a Cooperative Activity

Standards for Evaluation
Reports should . . .

• clearly describe the negative impact of the slave trade on African societies.

• show evidence of research using a variety of sources.

• express clear positions and support them with facts and examples.

THINK THROUGH HISTORY

C. Analyzing Issues
Why did many African rulers participate in the Atlantic slave trade?
C. Possible Answer
It was profitable, and they saw little difference between trading African slaves to Muslims and other Africans and Westerners.

Despite Affonso's plea, the slave trade continued and steadily grew. Lured by its profits, many African rulers continued to participate. As for African merchants, they simply developed new trade routes to avoid rulers who refused to cooperate.

A Forced Journey

After being captured, African men and women were shipped to the Americas as part of a profitable trade network. Along the way, millions of captured Africans endured a dehumanizing voyage across the Atlantic. Many died on the way.

The Triangular Trade Africans transported to the Americas were part of a transatlantic trading network known as the **triangular trade.** Over one trade route, Europeans transported manufactured goods to the west coast of Africa. There, traders exchanged these goods for captured Africans. The Africans were then transported across the Atlantic Ocean and sold in the West Indies. Merchants then bought sugar, coffee, and tobacco in the West Indies and sailed back to Europe to sell these products.

On another triangular route, merchants carried rum and other goods from the New England colonies to Africa. There they exchanged their merchandise for Africans. The traders then transported the Africans to the West Indies and sold them for sugar and molasses. They then sold these goods to rum producers in New England.

Various other transatlantic routes existed. In fact, the "triangular" trade encompassed a network of trade routes crisscrossing the Northern and Southern colonies, the West Indies, England, Europe, and Africa. The network carried a variety of traded goods. These included furs, fruit, tar, and tobacco, as well as millions of African people.

The Middle Passage The voyage that brought captured Africans to the West Indies and later to North and South America was known as the **middle passage.** It was so named because it was considered the middle leg of the transatlantic trade triangle.

Triangle Trade System, 1451–1870

Africans Enslaved in the Americas, 1451–1870

Total Number Imported: 9.5 Million*

- 40% Caribbean Islands (Dutch, French, British)
- 4% British North America
- 2% Europe, Asia
- 16% Spanish America and Spanish Caribbean
- 38% Portuguese Brazil

* Estimated Source: *The Atlantic Slave Trade: A Census*

GEOGRAPHY SKILLBUILDER: Interpreting Maps
1. **Movement** What items were transported to Africa and traded for captured Africans?
2. **Region** According to the graph, what region of the Americas imported the most Africans? Which imported the second most?

The Atlantic World **497**

OBJECTIVE ② INSTRUCT

A Forced Journey

▶ **Key Ideas**
- African slaves become part of a triangular trade involving Europe, Africa, and the Americas.
- Millions of slaves endure the middle passage across the Atlantic.
- Over one fifth of African passengers die during the middle passage, some by suicide.

CRITICAL THINKING TRANSPARENCIES
CT20 The Atlantic Slave Trade, 1451–1870

History from Visuals

Triangle Trade System, 1451–1870

Interpreting the Map Have students read both the map and the circle graph and compare and contrast the different kinds of information to be found in each. For example, the map shows the routes and products and human cargo of the triangular trade, while the graph gives the percentages of the slave population taken to each area of the world.

Extension Activity Have students point to the route on the map of the middle passage. They might point to a number of spots, because the middle passage was the voyage across the ocean. The route was different, depending on where enslaved Africans were sent.

SKILLBUILDER Answers
1. Tobacco, rum, manufactured goods, guns
2. The Caribbean was first, Brazil was second.

TEACHING OPTION BLOCK SCHEDULING **INTERPRETING ART** CLASS TIME 20 MINUTES

Task Students will look at an art transparency to examine the horrors of life aboard a slave ship. They should note the close quarters of the enslaved Africans as well as other discomforts of the voyage.

Materials Needed Use copies of Art Transparency AT44, *Slaves Below the Deck of the Albanez.* You might also use the drawing of the interior of a slave ship on page 498.

Activity Mention to students that the British had outlawed the slave trade in 1807. A British patrol captured the slave ship *Albanez* in 1846. A British naval officer painted the scene on the slave ship; it shows conditions that were found on many such ships. Have the class help you make a list of the horrible conditions aboard a slave ship.

Conclusion Ask students which conditions aboard a slave ship they would have found the most intolerable. What would they have done in those circumstances? How might they have attempted to improve conditions?

WORLD ART AND CULTURES TRANSPARENCIES
AT44, *Slaves Below the Deck of the Albanez*

This design of a British slave ship offers a glimpse of what life was like for enslaved Africans during their trip to the Americas.

MORE ABOUT . . .
The Middle Passage

The captain of a slave ship was either a "tight packer" or a "loose packer," referring to the number of slaves he would jam into the ship's hold. Tight packers would arrange people in spoon style, lying on top of one another. The more slaves a captain could pack in, the more money he made.

IN-DEPTH RESOURCES: UNIT 4
Primary Source: from *The Life of Olaudah Equiano*, p. 78

OBJECTIVE ③ INSTRUCT

Slavery in the Americas

Key Ideas
- Upon reaching the Americas, Africans are sold for work in mines or on plantations.
- Slaves resist slavery through sabotage, uprisings, escape, and preserving their cultural heritage.

MORE ABOUT . . .
Slave Resistance

In addition to other forms of resistance, slaves also found ways to supplement their meager food rations. Some took their masters' pigs, buried the pigs' hides, and then pretended they were eating possum, which was available to slaveowners and slaves alike. Others stole chickens and scattered the feathers to make it look as though a fox had been in the hen house. When slaves raided the potato fields, they released pigs into the fields and blamed the destruction on them.

Sickening cruelty characterized this journey. In the bustling ports along the African coasts, European traders packed Africans into the dark holds of large ships. On board a slave ship, Africans fell victim to whippings and beatings from merchants, as well as diseases that swept through the vessel. The smell of blood, sweat, and excrement filled the hold. African captives often lived in their own vomit and waste. One African, Olaudah Equiano, recalled the inhumane conditions on his trip from West Africa to the West Indies at age 11 in 1756:

A VOICE FROM THE PAST

I was soon put down under the decks, and there I received such a salutation [greeting] in my nostrils as I never experienced in my life; so that, with the loathsomeness of the stench, and crying together, I became so sick and low that I was not able to eat . . . but soon, to my grief, two of the white men offered me eatables; and on my refusing to eat, one of them held me fast by the hands, and laid me across . . . the windlass, and tied my feet, while the other flogged me severely.

OLAUDAH EQUIANO, quoted in *Eyewitness: The Negro in American History*

Olaudah Equiano

Background
After working for some time in the West Indies, Equiano was freed. He eventually went to England, where he crusaded against slavery.

Numerous Africans died aboard the slave ships from disease or from cruel treatment by merchants. Many others committed suicide by plunging into the ocean rather than be enslaved. Scholars estimate that roughly 20 percent of the Africans aboard each slave ship perished during the brutal trip to the Americas.

Slavery in the Americas

Africans who survived their ocean voyage entered a difficult life of bondage in the Americas. Forced to work in a strange land, enslaved Africans coped in a variety of ways. Many embraced their African culture, while others rebelled against their enslavers.

A Harsh Life Upon arriving in the Americas, captured Africans usually were auctioned off to the highest bidder. A British minister who visited a slave market in Brazil commented on the process: "When a customer comes in, they [the slaves] are turned before him; such as he wishes are handled by the purchaser in different parts, exactly as I have seen butchers feeling a calf."

After being sold, slaves worked in mines or fields or as domestic servants. Whatever their task, slaves lived a grueling existence. Many lived on little food in small, dreary huts. They worked long days and often suffered whippings and beatings. In much of the Americas, slavery was a lifelong condition, as well as a hereditary one. This meant that the sons and daughters of slaves were born into a lifetime of bondage.

Resistance and Rebellion To cope with the horrors of slavery, Africans developed a way of life based strongly on their cultural heritage. They kept alive such things as their musical traditions as well as the stories of their ancestors.

Enslaved Africans also found ways to resist their bondage. They made themselves less productive by breaking hoes, uprooting plants, and working slowly. This resistance hurt their owners' profit. Although they were unfamiliar with the land, thousands of slaves also ran away.

Some slaves pushed their resistance to open revolt. As early as 1522, about 20 slaves on Hispaniola attacked and killed several Spanish colonists. Larger revolts

---

A Voice from the Past Olaudah Equiano told his story in his autobiography, *The Interesting Narrative of the Life of Olaudah Equiano*, which was published in 1789 and soon became a bestseller. It is the first of a genre of world literature written by African slaves, former slaves, or postslavery African Americans who have described their struggles for freedom. Other examples of this kind of literature

include the autobiographical writings of the black abolitionist Frederick Douglass, the African American educator Booker T. Washington, and modern activists Malcolm X and Dr. Martin Luther King, Jr.

Equiano wrote his story for several reasons. Many white people tried to defend slavery by saying that black people were well suited for heavy work. They

said slaves were well treated and that since they could not read and write, they did not need to be free. Equiano wanted to show these arguments for the lies that they were. He had learned to read and write, and he wanted to show whites that they were wrong and to provide a model for other black people. Have students get a copy of Equiano's book from the library and read aloud selected sections in class.

occurred throughout Spanish settlements during the 16th century. In Colombia, for example, enslaved Africans destroyed the town of Santa Marta in 1530.

Occasional uprisings also occurred throughout Brazil, the West Indies, and North America. In 1739, a group of slaves in South Carolina led an uprising known as the Stono Rebellion. They killed several colonists and then engaged the local militia in battle. Many slaves died during the fighting. Those who were captured were executed. Despite the ultimate failure of slave revolts, uprisings continued into the 1800s.

Consequences of the Atlantic Slave Trade

The Atlantic slave trade had a profound impact on both Africa and the Americas. In Africa, numerous cultures lost generations of their fittest members—their young and able—to European traders and plantation owners. In addition, countless African families were torn apart. Many of them were never reunited. The slave trade devastated African societies in another way: by introducing guns into the continent. More effective than spears, guns were in great demand by African rulers seeking to conquer new territory. Firearms, which African chiefs and kings traded for potential slaves, helped spread war and conflict throughout Africa.

While they were unwilling participants in the growth of the colonies, African slaves contributed greatly to the economic and cultural development of the Americas. Their greatest contribution was their labor. Without their back-breaking work, colonies such as those on Haiti and Barbados may not have survived. In addition to their muscle, enslaved Africans also brought their expertise, especially in agriculture. Africans from the Upper Guinea region in West Africa, for example, brought their rice-growing techniques to South Carolina. There, they helped make that colony a profitable rice producer. Africans also brought with them their culture. Aspects of their culture—including art, music, and food—continue to influence American societies.

The influx of so many Africans to the Americas also has left its mark on the very population itself. From the United States to Brazil, many of the nations of the Western Hemisphere today have substantial African-American populations. Furthermore, many Latin American countries—where intermarriage between slaves and colonists was much more common than in North America—have sizable mixed-race populations.

As the next section explains, Africans were not the only cargo transported across the Atlantic during the colonization of the Americas. The settlement of the Americas brought many different items from Europe, Asia, and Africa to North and South America. It also introduced items from the Americas to the rest of the world.

THINK THROUGH HISTORY
D. Summarizing In what ways did enslaved Africans resist their bondage?
D. Possible Answer They cut down on their work productivity, they ran away, and they sometimes rebelled.

E. Possible Answer Their labor and techniques helped build many societies; many aspects of their culture still influence the American way of life; they have influenced the racial makeup of the Americas.

THINK THROUGH HISTORY
E. Recognizing Effects What are some of the contributions that Africans have made to the Americas?

CONNECT to TODAY

Gullah
One legacy of African slaves lives in the quick-paced words of Gullah. Gullah is a combination of English and colonial speech and the languages from several West African societies. Nearly 6,000 African words have been identified in Gullah. The American descendants of slaves still speak Gullah on the Sea Islands of South Carolina and Georgia and on the mainland nearby.

Gullah speakers live in relatively isolated communities. Over the years they have contributed words to the language spoken in the United States. The words include goober (peanut), juke (as in jukebox), and voodoo (witchcraft).

Section 3 Assessment

1. TERMS & NAMES
Identify
• Atlantic slave trade
• triangular trade
• middle passage

2. TAKING NOTES
Using a diagram like the one below, list the ways in which the Atlantic slave trade affected both Africa and the Americas.

Consequences of the Slave Trade	
In Africa	**In the Americas**
1.	1.
2.	2.
3.	3.

3. CONTRASTING
How was slavery in the Americas different from slavery in Africa and Muslim lands?
THINK ABOUT
• the length of bondage
• the children of slaves
• opportunities for slaves within each society
• racial basis

4. THEME ACTIVITY
Cultural Interaction
Reread the excerpt from King Affonso's letter on page 496. Imagine you are an African ruler. Write your own letter to a European leader in which you try to convince him or her to stop participating in the slave trade. Include in your letter the various aspects of slavery and the slave trade you learned about in this section.

The Atlantic World **499**

Section 4 Overview

OBJECTIVES

 To explain the Columbian Exchange.

② To identify aspects of the Commercial Revolution.

CRITICAL THINKING

- Making inferences, pp. 500, 502, 503
- Forming opinions, p. 501
- Summarizing, p. 503
- Analyzing themes, p. 503

FOCUS

5-Minute Warm-Up

▶ **Interpreting Maps**
Have students answer these questions to help them understand the Columbian Exchange.

1. Look at the map on page 501. What animal traveled from the Americas to Europe?

2. What insect was taken to the Americas?

 WARM-UP TRANSPARENCY 20

OBJECTIVE ① INSTRUCT

The Columbian Exchange

▶ **Key Idea**
- Colonization of the Americas sets up a global exchange.

📋 **IN-DEPTH RESOURCES: UNIT 4**
Guided Reading, p. 71

📋 **ACCESS FOR STUDENTS ACQUIRING ENGLISH**
Guided Reading (Spanish), p. 201

OBJECTIVE ② INSTRUCT

A Commercial Revolution

▶ **Key Ideas**
- Colonial trade promotes an economic revolution in Europe.
- Joint-stock companies invest in overseas colonies.
- Mercantilism demands a favorable balance of trade.
- The Commercial Revolution promotes city growth and gives rise to a middle class.

---

4 The Columbian Exchange and Global Trade

TERMS & NAMES
- Columbian Exchange
- Commercial Revolution
- capitalism
- joint-stock company
- mercantilism
- favorable balance of trade

MAIN IDEA	WHY IT MATTERS NOW
The colonization of the Americas introduced new and different items into the Eastern and Western hemispheres.	This global exchange of goods permanently changed Europe, Asia, Africa, and the Americas.

SETTING THE STAGE The colonization of the Americas dramatically changed the world. It prompted both voluntary and forced migration of millions of people. It also led to the establishment of new and powerful societies. European settlement of the Americas also changed the world in less noticeable but equally important ways. It led to the exchange of new items that greatly affected the lives of people throughout the world.

The Columbian Exchange

The global transfer of foods, plants, and animals during the colonization of the Americas was known as the **Columbian Exchange**. Ships from the Americas brought back a wide array of items that Europeans, Asians, and Africans had never before seen. They included such plants as tomatoes, squash, pineapples, tobacco, and cacao beans (for chocolate).

Perhaps the most important items to travel from the Americas to the rest of the world were corn and potatoes. Corn and potatoes were inexpensive to grow and highly nutritious. Over time, both crops became an important and steady part of diets throughout the world. These foods helped people live healthier and longer lives. Thus they played a significant role in boosting the world's population. The planting of the first white potato in Ireland and the first sweet potato in China probably changed more lives than the deeds of 100 kings.

In this Spanish illustration, a medicine man tends to an Aztec with smallpox.

Traffic across the Atlantic did not flow in just one direction, however. Europeans introduced various livestock animals into the Americas. These included horses, cattle, and pigs. Foods from Africa (including some that originated in Asia) migrated west in European ships. They included bananas, black-eyed peas, and yams.

Some aspects of the Columbian Exchange had a tragic impact on many Native Americans. Disease was just as much a part of the Columbian Exchange as goods and food. The diseases Europeans brought with them, which included smallpox and measles, led to the death of millions of Native Americans.

A Commercial Revolution

The establishment of colonial empires in the Americas influenced the nations of Europe in still other ways. New wealth from the Americas was coupled with a dramatic growth in overseas trade. These together prompted a wave of new business and trade practices in Europe during the 16th and 17th centuries. These practices—many of which served as the root of today's financial dealings—dramatically changed the economic atmosphere of Europe. Together they became known as the **Commercial Revolution.**

**THINK THROUGH HISTORY
A. Making Inferences**
Why is the Columbian Exchange considered a significant event?
A. Possible Answer It greatly improved diets and lifestyles in Europe and Asia and helped prompt an increase in the world's population; it also led to the death of millions of Native Americans by way of disease.

SECTION 4 RESOURCES

PRINT RESOURCES

📋 **IN-DEPTH RESOURCES: UNIT 4**
Guided Reading, p. 71
Geography Application: The Potato Impacts the World, p. 73
Connections Across Time and Cultures: Impact of the Columbian Exchange, p. 84

📋 **ACCESS FOR STUDENTS ACQUIRING ENGLISH**
Guided Reading (Spanish), p. 201
Geography Application (Spanish), p. 203

📋 **FORMAL ASSESSMENT**
Section Quiz, p. 230

TECHNOLOGY RESOURCES

🎞 **GEOGRAPHY TRANSPARENCIES**
GT20 Spain's Colonies Provide Wealth, 1600–1790

🎞 **CRITICAL THINKING TRANSPARENCIES**
CT56 Chapter 20 Visual Summary

💿 **CD-ROM**
Electronic Library of Primary Sources

📼 **VIDEO** Patterns of Interaction: The Geography of Food

🌐 **INTERNET** www.mlworldhistory.com

GlobalImpact: Food Exchange

The culinary life we owe Columbus is a progressive dinner in which the whole human race takes part but no one need leave home to sample all the courses.

Raymond Sokolov

Frightening Foods

Several foods from the Americas that we now take for granted at first amazed and terrified Europeans.

Early on, people thought the tomato was harmful to eat. "If I should eat this fruit," explained one Italian man, "it would be injurious and harmful to me." One German official warned that the tomato "should not be taken internally."

In 1619, officials in Burgundy, France, banned the potato, explaining that "too frequent use of them caused the leprosy." In 1774, starving peasants in Prussia refused to eat the spud.

The Columbian Exchange

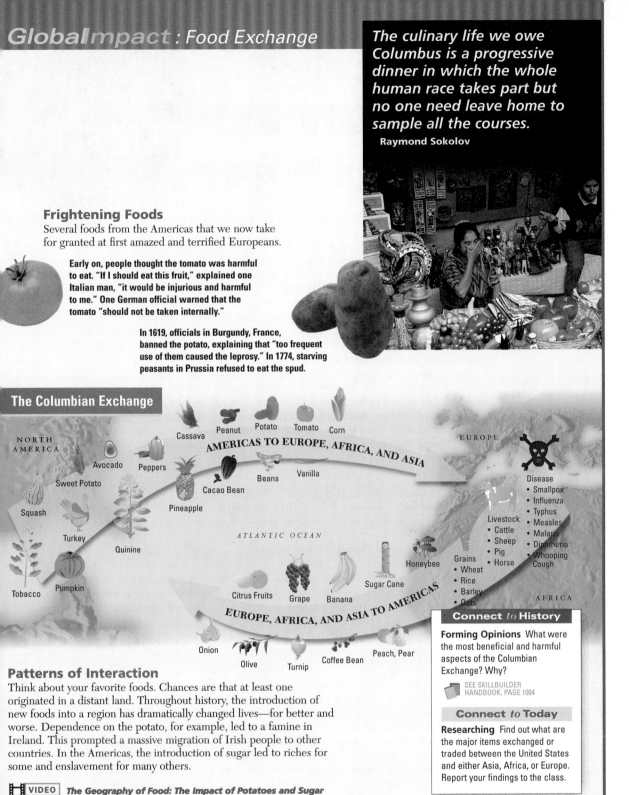

AMERICAS TO EUROPE, AFRICA, AND ASIA

NORTH AMERICA

EUROPE

Cassava · Peanut · Potato · Tomato · Corn
Avocado · Peppers
Sweet Potato · Beans · Vanilla
Squash · Cacao Bean
Pineapple
Turkey · Quinine
Tobacco · Pumpkin

ATLANTIC OCEAN

Disease
• Smallpox
• Influenza
• Typhus
• Measles
• Malaria
• Diphtheria
• Whooping Cough

Livestock
• Cattle
• Sheep
• Pig
• Horse

Grains
• Wheat
• Rice
• Barley
• Oats

Honeybee
Sugar Cane
Citrus Fruits · Grape · Banana

AFRICA

EUROPE, AFRICA, AND ASIA TO AMERICAS

Onion · Olive · Turnip · Coffee Bean · Peach, Pear

Patterns of Interaction

Think about your favorite foods. Chances are that at least one originated in a distant land. Throughout history, the introduction of new foods into a region has dramatically changed lives—for better and worse. Dependence on the potato, for example, led to a famine in Ireland. This prompted a massive migration of Irish people to other countries. In the Americas, the introduction of sugar led to riches for some and enslavement for many others.

 VIDEO *The Geography of Food: The Impact of Potatoes and Sugar*

Connect *to* History

Forming Opinions What were the most beneficial and harmful aspects of the Columbian Exchange? Why?

SEE SKILLBUILDER HANDBOOK, PAGE 1004

Connect *to* Today

Researching Find out what are the major items exchanged or traded between the United States and either Asia, Africa, or Europe. Report your findings to the class.

GlobalImpact

Food Exchange

Today in the United States, food crops that were cultivated by Native Americans make up about one third of the annual harvest; corn accounts for 15 percent of that amount. The following six crops each have yearly sales totaling more than 1 billion dollars: corn, cotton, tobacco, potatoes, tomatoes, peanuts. Have students create a class cookbook of their favorite meals that contain one or more of the five food items in this group.

Viewing the Video

Show *The Geography of Food: The Impact of Potatoes and Sugar* to examine how people have brought foods from one part of the globe to another, with positive and negative effects.

- The first segment of the video investigates how the potato, a South American food, affected the diet and nutrition of many Europeans—including Prussian royalty and Irish peasants.
- The second segment looks at sugar, an Asian crop that made its way to Europe and the Americas. Sugar made many rich, led to the enslavement of millions, and transformed a region of the world.

Using the Teacher's Resource Book as a guide, have students consider how food exchanges can connect distant countries; discuss how foods from other places affect students' everyday lives; and enrich the lesson with primary-source and visual-literacy activities included in the resource book.

PATTERNS OF INTERACTION
The Geography of Food: The Impact of Potatoes and Sugar
Videocassette: Tape 2

IN-DEPTH RESOURCES: UNIT 4
Geography Application: The Potato Impacts the World, p. 73

Connections Across Time and Cultures: Impact of the Columbian Exchange, p. 84

Connect History

Forming Opinions
Possible Responses:
Beneficial–the introduction of corn and potatoes into Europe, because they improved diets and helped people live longer; harmful—diseases from Europe, because they killed millions of Native Americans.

Connect *to* Today

Researching
Suggest that students use various resources to find the information required about trade between the United States and Asia, Africa, or Europe. For example, students might consult magazines (by means of the *Readers' Guide to Periodical Literature*), newspapers, current encyclopedias (in book, CD-ROM, and on-line form), almanacs (such as *Information Please*), the *Statistical Abstract of the United States,* as well as the Internet.

Three Worlds Meet, 1492–1700

Interpreting the Time Line
Help students to understand the time line by showing them that it uses three colors, each of which stands for a different group: orange for Europeans, blue for Africans, and purple for Americans. Point out that each event is keyed to a particular color and group.

Extension Activity Ask students to make a list of additional events from the chapter they might add to the time line for each of the three colors (groups).

MORE ABOUT . . .
Spanish Gold

Spain may have been too rich for its own good. Other nations and individuals began to attack Spanish ships and holdings to get some of the gold for themselves and to keep Spain from getting too powerful. In Spain, meanwhile, the lust for gold blinded many people to the need for skilled work, farming, manufacturing, and trade.

 ELECTRONIC LIBRARY OF PRIMARY SOURCES
"Concerning the Dearness of All Things and the Remedy Therefor"

 GEOGRAPHY TRANSPARENCIES
GT20 Spain's Colonies Provide Wealth, 1600–1790

Three Worlds Meet, 1492–1700

1492
Columbus embarks on a voyage that will bring together the worlds of Europe, Africa, and the Americas.

1521
The Aztec Empire in Mexico is conquered by Hernando Cortés.

Europeans
Africans
Americans

1492   1510   1530

1511
Africans begin working as slaves in the Americas.

1533
The Inca Empire in South America falls to Francisco Pizarro.

The Rise of Capitalism One aspect of the European Commercial Revolution was the growth of **capitalism.** Capitalism is an economic system based on private ownership and the investment of wealth for profit. No longer were governments the sole owners of great wealth. Due to overseas colonization and trade, numerous merchants had obtained great wealth. These merchants continued to invest their money in trade and overseas exploration. Profits from these investments enabled merchants and traders to reinvest even more money in other enterprises. As a result, businesses across Europe grew and flourished.

The increase in economic activity in Europe led to an overall increase in many nations' money supply. This in turn brought on inflation, or the steady rise in the price of goods. Inflation occurs when people have more money to spend and thus demand more goods and services. Because the supply of goods is less than the demand requires, the goods become both scarce and more valuable. Prices, then, rise. At this time in Europe, the costs of many goods rose. Spain, for example, endured a crushing bout of inflation during the 1600s, as boatloads of gold and silver from the Americas greatly increased the nation's money supply.

Joint-Stock Companies Another business venture developed during this period was the **joint-stock company.** The joint-stock company worked much like the modern-day corporation. It involved a number of people pooling their wealth for a common purpose.

In Europe during the 1500s and 1600s, that common purpose was American colonization. It took large amounts of money to establish overseas colonies. Moreover, while profits may have been great, so were risks. Many ships, for instance, never completed the long and dangerous ocean voyage. Because joint-stock companies involved numerous investors, the individual members paid only a fraction of the total colonization cost. If the colony failed, investors lost only their small share. If the colony thrived, the investors shared in the profits. It was a joint-stock company that was responsible for establishing Jamestown, England's first North American colony.

The Growth of Mercantilism During this time, the nations of Europe adopted a new economic policy known as **mercantilism.** The theory of mercantilism held that a country's power depended mainly on its wealth. It was wealth, after all, that allowed nations to build strong navies and purchase vital goods. As a result, the goal of every nation became the attainment of as much wealth as possible.

According to the theory of mercantilism, a nation could increase its wealth and power in two ways. First, it could obtain as much gold and silver as possible. Second, it could establish a **favorable balance of trade,** in which it sold more goods than it bought. A nation's ultimate goal under mercantilism was to become self-sufficient, not

Vocabulary
invest: to spend time, money, or effort for future advantage or benefit.

THINK THROUGH HISTORY
B. Making Inferences Why would a joint-stock company be popular with investors in overseas colonies?
B. Possible Answer Because they paid only a fraction of the total colonization cost.

CUSTOMIZING FOR SPECIAL NEEDS

Less Proficient Readers: *Vocabulary Activity* Pair a less proficient reader with a more proficient reader and ask them to help each other learn the key terms in this section. One strategy they might use to remember a term's meaning is to "interview" the term, playing the part of journalists investigating the who, what, where, when, how, and why of a situation.

An example interview question is, "Who are you?" For *capitalism*, the answer might be, "I am an economic system based on private ownership and the investment of wealth for profit." For the *joint-stock company*, students might ask, "What do you want?" The answer might be, "I want to pool the wealth of a number of different people for a common purpose, such as colonization of the Americas."

Have students apply this strategy to other key terms in the section: *Columbian Exchange; Commercial Revolution; mercantilism;* and *favorable balance of trade*.

1607
Colonists found Jamestown, first permanent English settlement in North America.

1628
Puritans establish the Massachusetts Bay Colony in North America.

1700
The number of enslaved Africans imported to the Americas reaches almost 1.5 million. It will climb to nearly 6 million by the end of the century.

| 1610 | 1630 | 1670 | 1690 |

1650
The number of Africans toiling in Spanish America reaches 300,000.

1675
Native Americans battle colonists in King Philip's War.

dependent on other countries for goods. An English author of the time wrote about the new economic idea of mercantilism:

A VOICE FROM THE PAST
Although a Kingdom may be enriched by gifts received, or by purchases taken from some other Nations. . . . these are things uncertain and of small consideration when they happen. The ordinary means therefore to increase our wealth and treasure is by Foreign Trade, wherein we must ever observe this rule: to sell more to strangers yearly than we consume of theirs in value.
THOMAS MUN, quoted in *World Civilizations*

THINK THROUGH HISTORY
C. Summarizing
What role did colonies play in the policy of mercantilism?
C. Possible Answer They provided gold and silver, as well as raw materials, and were a market for the home country to sell its goods.

Mercantilism went hand in hand with colonization, for colonies played a vital role in this new economic practice. Aside from providing silver and gold, colonies provided raw materials that could not be found in the home country, such as wood or furs. In addition to playing the role of supplier, the colonies under mercantilism also provided a market. The home country could sell its goods to their colonies.

Changes in European Society The economic changes that swept through much of Europe during the age of American colonization also led to changes in European society. The Commercial Revolution spurred the growth of towns and the rise of the merchant class. Merchants—because they controlled great wealth—rose in status.

The changes in European society, however, only went so far. While towns and cities grew in size, much of Europe's population continued to live in rural areas. And although merchants and traders enjoyed a period of social mobility, a majority of Europeans remained poor. More than anything else, the Commercial Revolution increased the wealth of European nations. Also, as Chapter 21 will describe, the new economic practices helped to expand the power of European rulers.

Section 4 Assessment

1. TERMS & NAMES
Identify
• Columbian Exchange
• Commercial Revolution
• capitalism
• joint-stock company
• mercantilism
• favorable balance of trade

2. TAKING NOTES
For each Columbian Exchange item or aspect below, write where it originated and explain its significance.

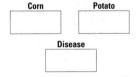

Corn		Potato

	Disease	

Write an explanation of one of the items to someone who has never encountered it.

3. MAKING INFERENCES
Why were colonies considered so important to the nations of Europe?

THINK ABOUT
• the philosophy of mercantilism
• the notion of a favorable balance of trade

4. ANALYZING THEMES
Economics Do you think the economic changes in Europe during the era of American colonization qualify as a revolution? Why or why not?

THINK ABOUT
• the legacy of the new business and trade practices
• how the economic changes affected European society as a whole

The Atlantic World **503**

ANSWERS

1. TERMS & NAMES
Columbian Exchange, p. 500
Commercial Revolution, p. 500
capitalism, p. 502
joint-stock company, p. 502
mercantilism, p. 502
favorable balance of trade, p. 502

2. TAKING NOTES
Corn: the Americas; nutritious basis of many diets
Potato: the Americas; became staple throughout the world
Disease: Europe; killed millions of Native Americans

3. MAKING INFERENCES
Possible Responses: The mercantilistic philosophy of Europe drove nations to acquire colonies to obtain wealth. Colonies provided precious metals, raw materials, and markets for European goods, allowing European nations to establish a favorable balance of trade with their colonies.

4. ANALYZING THEMES
Possible Responses: Yes—many of the new practices, including capitalism and joint-stock companies, served as the root of today's economy. No—Europe's population remained mostly rural, and many Europeans remained poor.

TERMS & NAMES

1. conquistadors, p. 485
2. Montezuma II, p. 485
3. *encomienda*, p. 486
4. Jamestown, p. 491
5. French and Indian War, p. 493
6. Atlantic slave trade, p. 496
7. triangular trade, p. 497
8. Columbian Exchange, p. 500
9. Commercial Revolution, p. 500
10. mercantilism, p. 502

REVIEW QUESTIONS

Answers may vary.

11. To seek an alternative trade route to Asia.

12. To enrich Spain, to colonize the land, and to convert Native Americans to Christianity.

13. Because the Spanish abused the natives and tried to destroy their culture.

14. Sugar and tobacco.

15. The English took control of nearly the entire eastern half of the United States.

16. Slaves were experienced at farming, they had built up some immunity to disease, they were unfamiliar with the land and could not blend in with the white population, so were less likely to escape.

17. Slaves were crammed into the dark bottom of the boat, where they lived among their own waste and suffered from disease, beatings, and poor food.

18. African slaves resisted by preserving their cultural heritage, sabotaging work efforts, running away, and forming armed rebellions.

19. Corn and potatoes were inexpensive and nutritious and thus improved diets throughout Europe and Asia.

20. Mercantilism held that a country's true power was measured by its wealth, which came by obtaining as much gold and silver as possible and by establishing a favorable balance of trade.

Chapter 20 Assessment

TERMS & NAMES

Briefly explain the importance of each of the following in the European colonization of the Americas.

1. conquistadors
2. Montezuma II
3. *encomienda*
4. Jamestown
5. French and Indian War
6. Atlantic slave trade
7. triangular trade
8. Columbian Exchange
9. Commercial Revolution
10. mercantilism

Interact *with* History

On page 482 you examined the choices some Native Americans faced during the invasion by Spanish conquistadors. Now that you have read the chapter, rethink the choice you made. If you chose to side with the Spaniards, would you now change your mind? Why or why not? If you decided to fight with the Aztecs, what are your feelings now? Discuss your opinions with a small group.

REVIEW QUESTIONS

SECTION 1 *(pages 483–488)*
Spanish Conquests in the Americas

11. Why did Columbus set sail on the Atlantic?

12. List three goals of the Spanish in the Americas.

13. Why did Popé lead a rebellion against the Spanish?

SECTION 2 *(pages 490–494)*
Competing Claims in North America

14. What did the Europeans mostly grow in their Caribbean colonies?

15. What was the result of the French and Indian War?

SECTION 3 *(pages 495–499)*
The Atlantic Slave Trade

16. What factors led European colonists to use Africans to resupply their labor force?

17. Describe the conditions on board a slave ship.

18. Name several ways in which enslaved Africans resisted their position in the Americas.

SECTION 4 *(pages 500–503)*
The Columbian Exchange and Global Trade

19. Why was the introduction of corn and potatoes to Europe and Asia so significant?

20. Explain the economic policy of mercantilism.

Visual Summary

The Atlantic World

GLOBAL INTERACTION

Europeans

- Beginning around 1500, the Spanish and Portuguese colonize Central and South America and establish prosperous overseas empires.
- Throughout the 1600s and 1700s, the English, French, and Dutch battle for control of North America, with the English emerging victorious.
- Over time, Europeans take control of nearly all of the Americas and create new societies.

Africans

- Beginning around 1500, millions of Africans are taken from their homeland and forced to labor as slaves for Europeans in the Americas.
- Numerous Africans perish during the brutal ocean voyage to the Americas, known as the middle passage.
- Africans eventually become an important part of the Americas, as they populate the various regions and lend aspects of their culture to American societies.

Native Americans

- Between 1520 and 1533, the once mighty Aztec and Inca empires fall to the invading Spanish.
- Throughout the Americas, the native population is devastated by European conquests and diseases.
- In Central and South America, many Spanish settlers and Native Americans intermarry, creating a large mestizo population that thrives today.

504 Chapter 20

Interact *with* History

Possible Responses: Students who originally chose to side with the Spaniards may now say that the Spaniards were cruel and unjust in their treatment of Native Americans. Others may say their decision to fight for the Aztecs was unwise, because they were defeated by the Spanish.

CRITICAL THINKING

1. THE TOOLS OF CONQUEST

THEME EMPIRE BUILDING   In conquering much of the Americas, Europeans were aided by several things. What were they? Which do you consider to be the most important? Why?

2. EXPLORERS OF THE WEST

Copy the chart below on your paper. For each explorer named, write which nation sponsored him and the regions he explored.

Explorer	Nation	Regions
Pedro Álvares Cabral		
Ferdinand Magellan		
Francisco Vásquez de Coronado		
Jacques Cartier		
Samuel de Champlain		
Henry Hudson		

3. A HISTORIC VOYAGE

It has been said that Columbus's voyage began a process that changed the world forever. Explain the meaning of this statement. In your explanation, consider all the peoples and places American colonization impacted and what effects it had on them.

4. ANALYZING PRIMARY SOURCES

In 1630, a Puritan minister, John Cotton, delivered a sermon to fellow Puritans as they embarked on their journey to America. In it, Cotton tried to reassure the future colonists that they could legitimately claim a new land.

A VOICE FROM THE PAST

Where there is a vacant place, there is liberty for . . . [Christians] . . . to come and inhabit, though they neither buy it nor ask their leaves. . . . Indeed, no nation is to drive out another without special commission from Heaven . . . unless the natives do unjustly wrong them, and will not recompense the wrongs done in a peaceable fort [way]. And then they may right themselves by lawful war and subdue the country unto themselves.

JOHN COTTON, quoted in *The Annals of America*

- What do you think Native Americans might have said about Cotton's statement that America was a "vacant place"?

- How might the last part of Cotton's statement have helped the Puritans to justify taking land from the Native Americans?

- How is this passage an example of a biased statement?

CHAPTER ACTIVITIES

1. LIVING HISTORY: Unit Portfolio Project

THEME CULTURAL INTERACTION   Your unit portfolio project focuses on showing how different cultures have interacted in history. (See page 387.) For Chapter 20, you might use one of the following ideas to add to your portfolio:

- Draw a political cartoon that contrasts the Europeans' and Native Americans' view of American colonization.

- Write a newspaper editorial explaining how Africans helped create the societies that grew in the Americas.

- Imagine you are a Native American entering an English colony for the first time. Write a journal entry describing your encounter with the culture.

2. CONNECT TO TODAY: Cooperative Learning

THEME ECONOMICS   The Columbian Exchange marked the beginning of worldwide trade. The plants, foods, and animals that traveled across hemispheres during the Columbian Exchange are now just some of the many foods and items that are traded around the globe today.

Work with a team to chart the global trade of a chosen food or item.

INTERNET   Using the Internet, magazines, or books, track the movement of the item from its country of origin to its various destinations around the world.

- Determine how much of the item the various countries import. Compare the cost of the item in these countries.

- Compare your team's item with those of the other teams to determine which is the most popular.

3. INTERPRETING A TIME LINE

Revisit the time line on pages 386–387. Examine the Chapter 20 time line. Which two events do you think had the most lasting effects on the Americas? Explain why.

FOCUS ON ART

This Aztec drawing depicts natives attacking several Spaniards, who after killing Indian nobles, took refuge in a nearby palace.

- How does the image depict the clash of cultures in the Americas?

- What is the drawing's point of view regarding the Aztec warriors? The Spanish?

Connect to History Of the factors that enabled the Spanish to defeat the Aztecs, which one is visible in this drawing?

The Atlantic World **505**

UNIT 5

Absolutism to Revolution

1500-1900

***Detail of** From Porfirio's Dictatorship to the Revolution, by David Alfáro Siqueiros*

This dramatic section from a mural by Mexican artist David Alfáro Siqueiros shows the power and determination of a people united to fight for a political cause. Mexico, like many countries from the 1700s to 1900s, suffered through a series of revolutions in its transformation from a monarchy to a democracy.

The revolution depicted in this mural was an uprising of peasants, farmers, and military and political leaders in 1910 against President Porfirio Díaz. Although Díaz had tried to improve Mexico's economy, he had ruthlessly suppressed all opposition. Under his rule, foreign investors and a few Mexican elite became wealthy, while the peasants and other workers sank deeper into poverty. The revolt, led by Francisco Madero, ousted Díaz, who went into exile in France.

David Alfáro Siqueiros (1898–1974) used the history of Mexico as inspiration for his vivid murals. After his experiences fighting in the Spanish Civil War in the 1930s, Siqueiros identified with the poor and powerless in his own country. His murals often satirize the lifestyles of the wealthy classes while portraying revolutionaries as strong and fearless. The mural *From Porfirio's Dictatorship to the Revolution* can be seen today in the National Museum of History in Mexico City.

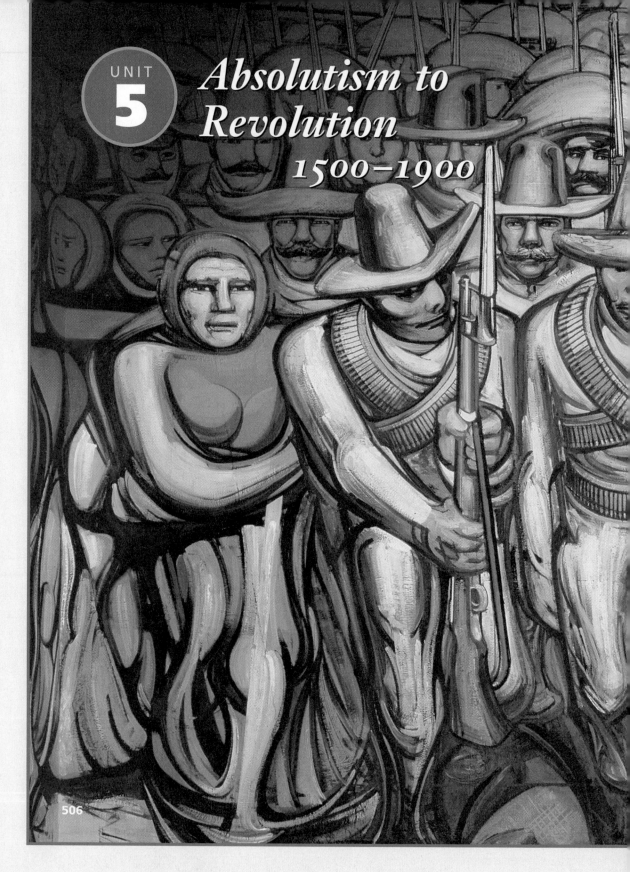

UNIT 5 *Absolutism to Revolution*
1500–1900

506

This scene is from a mural entitled *From Porfirio's Dictatorship to the Revolution*, by the Mexican artist David Alfaro Siqueiros. During this time, revolution swept the globe as people from Europe to Latin America overthrew old institutions.

507

This unit covers the struggles of people in Europe and the New World to build their own nations and to create new forms of government that more clearly reflect the will of the governed.

From 1500 to 1800 marks the era of absolute monarchs in Europe. Although in some countries monarchs have vast power and wealth, toward the end of the 1500s, the force of constitutional law is already limiting royal power in such nations as England and the Netherlands.

The Enlightenment ushers in a new era of discovery and inquiry. Philosophers believe that human reason can create a more humane and just government, religion, and society. These ideas influence the American Revolution and the resulting creation of a democratic federal government.

Revolution sweeps through France, overthrowing the monarchy. Instead of creating a democracy, however, France embraces Napoleon, who attempts to conquer most of Europe. After his downfall, Europe enjoys a brief period of peace and stability.

The forces of nationalism spur Germany, Italy, and several Latin American nations to forge their own political identities in the 1800s. Although Latin American nations throw off colonial rule, they struggle to build stable governments and to ensure prosperity for their people.

Absolutism to Revolution

Teaching Strategies

Synthesizing One way to help students synthesize the material in Unit 5 is to present the *Patterns of Interaction* video *Struggling Toward Democracy: Revolutions in Latin America and South Africa* as you begin the unit. In each unit, one 12-minute video focuses on a major theme of one of the unit chapters. In Unit 5, the video focuses on Chapter 24, which also develops the unit theme: Revolution.

Synthesizing Through Video The videos for each unit seek to synthesize the elements of a historical pattern, underscoring those elements that hold true over time—at times, over thousands of years. The Unit 5 video shows how ideas can spark revolutions. The case studies that illustrate the power of ideas are the democratic revolutions in 19th-century Venezuela and 20th-century South Africa. You might also point out the revolutionary thinkers in the Unit Time Line (Montesquieu, Voltaire, Diderot) and recall their impact on the revolutions in Europe and Latin America.

Patterns of Interaction The *Patterns of Interaction Resource Book* provides you with an overview of each video, pre-viewing classroom activities (including vocabulary previews) and post-viewing activities that include text and visual primary sources and map activities.

	1500	1550	1600	1650	170
CHAPTER 21 1500–1800 **Absolute Monarchs in Europe**	**1520–1566** *Ottoman Empire* Suleiman I reigns as sultan **1533** *Russia* Ivan the Terrible assumes throne at age three	**1581** *Russia* Czar Ivan the Terrible kills his son and heir **1588** *England* English navy defeats Spanish Armada	**1611** *England* First King James Bible is printed **1618** *Bohemia* Thirty Years' War begins **1643** *France* Louis XIV begins 72-year reign **1649** *England* Oliver Cromwell and Puritans execute English king	**1661** *France* Louis XIV begins 40-year building of palace at Versailles **1689** *England* William of Orange becomes king	
CHAPTER 22 1550–1789 **Enlightenment and Revolution**	**1543** *Poland* Copernicus presents heliocentric theory **1590** *Holland* Zacharias Janssen develops microscope	**1572** *Denmark* Tycho Brahe discovers nova in space	**1609** *Italy* Galileo uses telescope to study moon **1633** *Italy* Inquisition condemns Galileo	**1660** *Britain* Navigation Acts restrict trade in American colonies **1687** *Britain* Newton presents the law of gravity	
	▲ 1500s				
CHAPTER 23 1789–1815 **The French Revolution and Napoleon**			1700s *France* ▶		
CHAPTER 24 1789–1900 **Nationalist Revolutions Sweep the West**					

1500	1550	1600	1650	170

CONNECTIONS ACROSS THE CURRICULUM

Literature Literature dealing with history offers the advantage of evoking the sights, sounds, thoughts, and personalities associated with historical events. Such literature possesses an immediacy that ordinary historical narrative usually cannot create. You may wish to focus on certain events or

personalities in the Unit Time Line by asking students to read the selections in the *In-Depth Resources* books that accompany the program.

Literary selections for Unit 5 cover the following topics:
• **Chapter 21** The court of Louis XIV
• **Chapter 22** Galileo's trial for heresy

• **Chapter 23** Robespierre's Reign of Terror
• **Chapter 24** Toussaint L'Ouverture and the Haitian revolution.

See **In-Depth Resources: Unit 5** Students might read the Unit 5 literary selections outside of class for a later in-class discussion or for written analysis. Since the selections are

relatively short, the class might read the texts aloud in class. (The text for Chapter 22 is taken from the play *The Recantation of Galileo Galilei* by Eric Bentley and might be rehearsed and presented by students to the rest of the class.) A discussion of historical setting and character could then follow.

1703 *Russia*
Peter the Great orders
St. Petersburg to be
built

1740 *Austria*
Maria Theresa inherits
throne

1756 *Prussia*
Frederick the Great
starts Seven Years'
War

◄ *1700s Prussia*

1740 *Britain*
Samuel Richardson
publishes novel *Pamela*

1748 *France*
Montesquieu publishes
Spirit of the Laws

1759 *France*
Voltaire writes *Candide*

1751 *France* Diderot
begins publishing
Encyclopedia

1762 *Russia*
Catherine the Great
becomes empress

1776 *America* Colonies
declare independence
from Britain

1788 *United States*
Constitution ratified

1789 *France*
French Revolution
begins

1793 *France*
King Louis XVI
executed by guillotine

1793-1794 *France*
Robespierre conducts
Reign of Terror

1804 *France* Napoleon
becomes emperor

1805-1812 *France*
Napoleon conquers
most countries in
Europe

1815 *France* Napoleon
defeated at Waterloo

1815 *Austria* Congress
of Vienna restores old
European boundaries

1804 *Haiti* gains
independence
from France

1821 *Mexico* declares
independence

1830 *Greece* wins full
independence

1848 *Europe* Revolutions
sweep Europe

1861 *Russia*
Alexander II frees
the serfs

1870 *Italy*
Italy is unified

1871 *Germany* Franco-
Prussian War ends;
Germany is unified

◄ *1800s Greece*

Living History
Unit 5 Portfolio Project

THEME Revolution

Your portfolio for Unit 5 will compare and contrast the different kinds of revolutions that take place during this time period. While some groups overthrow governments, others overthrow long-held ideas about science, economy, religion, and even art. You can compare and contrast the causes of these revolutions, how they occur, and their results.

Living History Project Choices
Each Chapter Assessment offers you choices of ways to show the revolutionary changes that take place in that chapter. Activities include the following:

Chapter 21 poster, editorial, HistoryMaker

Chapter 22 magazine cover, news report, song lyrics

Chapter 23 interviews, cartoons, dialogue

Chapter 24 newspaper report, speech, how-to book

Portfolio Project

Theme: Revolution The portfolio projects for Unit 5 stress the theme of reform and radical political and social changes that overturned established orders in Europe between 1600 and 1900. The transformations that students will be asked to focus on include:

- the English Civil War and the Glorious Revolution in Great Britain
- Peter the Great's efforts at westernizing Russia
- the American and French Revolutions and
- the revolutions in Europe and Latin America during the 19th century

Students will be asked to show their understanding of underlying social and political causes, the ideals, and the outcomes of these upheavals. And they may choose among oral, written, and spoken formats to do so.

Projects for Interpersonal Learners
Certain students learn best when working in groups, where they can share ideas and insights. These interpersonal learners tend to organize, communicate, and socialize well. To accommodate the learning styles of such students, many of the projects suggested in the units can be turned into group activities.

Of course, certain project suggestions are already intended for groups. For example, in Unit 5, the interview projects in Chapters 23 and 24 will be performed by more than one student.

Nonetheless, you might decide to designate the projects for an entire unit as group projects. Creating posters, song lyrics, newspaper editorials, History Maker biographies, or magazine covers need not be individual tasks.

The Western Civilization Videodisc

SECTION H: The Beginnings of the
Nation–State, 1600–1715

Side One:
Frame 28153

SECTION I: The Enlightenment, French
Revolution, and Napoleon, 1715–1815

Side One:
Frame 30803

Universal Play
Button

See Master Guide, page 166 for Section H,
page 189 for Section I.

	Key Ideas	COPY MASTERS	ASSESSMENT
SECTION 1 **Spain's Empire and European Absolutism** *pp. 513–517*	In the 1500s, Philip II of Spain becomes the strongest ruler in Europe, helping establish absolute monarchy. But in time Spain weakens, and the Netherlands breaks away from Spanish rule.	**In-Depth Resources: Unit 5** • **Guided Reading,** p. 1	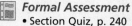 *Section 1 Assessment,* p. 517 *Formal Assessment* • Section Quiz, p. 239 *Alternative Assessment Book* • Standards for Evaluating a Cooperative Activity
SECTION 2 **France's Ultimate Monarch** *pp. 518–525*	Religious wars plague France in the 1500s. With the rise of Louis XIV, France becomes Europe's most powerful nation. Louis's rule extends French power and prestige, but he leads the country into crippling wars.	**In-Depth Resources: Unit 5** • **Guided Reading,** p. 2 • **Primary Source:** Louis XIV's Advice to His Son, p. 9 • **Literature:** from *The Cat and the King,* p. 13	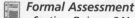 *Section 2 Assessment,* p. 523 *Formal Assessment* • Section Quiz, p. 240 *Alternative Assessment Book* • Standards for Evaluating a Cooperative Activity
SECTION 3 **Central European Monarchs Clash** *pp. 526–530*	Central Europe also becomes the scene of devastating wars. The most destructive conflict, the Thirty Years' War, severely weakens the Holy Roman Empire. Afterward, Austria and Prussia struggle for power.	**In-Depth Resources: Unit 5** • **Guided Reading,** p. 3 • **Geography Application:** Old Empires and New Powers, p. 7 • **History Makers:** Maria Theresa, p. 16	*Section 3 Assessment,* p. 530 *Formal Assessment* • Section Quiz, p. 241 *Alternative Assessment Book* • Standards for Evaluating a Cooperative Activity
SECTION 4 **Russian Czars Increase Power** *pp. 531–535*	Russian rulers begin to dominate the nobility in the 16th and 17th centuries. Under Peter the Great, Russia opens up to the West and becomes a key European power.	**In-Depth Resources: Unit 5** • **Guided Reading,** p. 4 • **Skillbuilder Practice:** Evaluating Decisions, p. 6 • **Primary Source:** Peter the Great's Reforms, p. 10	*Section 4 Assessment,* p. 535 *Formal Assessment* • Section Quiz, p. 242 *Alternative Assessment Book* • Standards for Evaluating a Cooperative Activity
SECTION 5 **Parliament Limits the English Monarchy** *pp. 536–539*	English kings battle Parliament for power in the 1600s, leading to civil war. Parliament wins, and a Puritan government is formed. The monarchy is later restored, but its power is limited by law.	**In-Depth Resources: Unit 5** • **Guided Reading,** p. 5 • **Primary Sources:** from *Diary of Samuel Pepys,* p. 11; from the English Bill of Rights, p. 12 • **History Makers:** Wm. of Orange, p. 17 • **Connections Across Time and Cultures,** p. 18	*Section 5 Assessment,* p. 539 *Formal Assessment* • Section Quiz, p. 243 *Alternative Assessment Book* • Standards for Evaluating a Cooperative Activity
CHAPTER RESOURCES	**Chapter Overview** From 1500 to 1800, absolute monarchs rule in Europe. In countries such as Spain and France, rulers wield great power and build major monuments to their rule. In countries such as England and the Netherlands, constitutional law limits royal power.	**Telescoping the Times** • Chapter Summary, pp. 81–83 **Planning for Block Schedules**	*Chapter Assessment,* pp. 540–541 *Chapter Activities,* p. 541 *Formal Assessment* • Chapter Test, forms A and B, pp. 244–249 **Test Generator** *Alternative Assessment Book*

TECHNOLOGY

  Warm-Up Transparency 21

 Geography Transparencies
- GT21 Hapsburg Europe, 1560

World Art and Cultures Transparencies
- AT45 St. George Civic Guard Company

Electronic Library of Primary Sources
- "Defeat of the Spanish Armada"

INTERNET RESOURCES
www.mlworldhistory.com

Warm-Up Transparency 21

Electronic Library of Primary Sources
- "Two Views of Versailles"

INTERNET RESOURCES
www.mlworldhistory.com

Warm-Up Transparency 21

Critical Thinking Transparencies
- CT74 Compare and Contrast

Electronic Library of Primary Sources
- from *Essay on Forms of Government*

INTERNET RESOURCES
www.mlworldhistory.com

Warm-Up Transparency 21

World Art and Cultures Transparencies
- AT46 *Peter I the Great*
- AT47 Saint Basil's Cathedral

Critical Thinking Transparencies
- CT21 The Age of Absolute Monarchs

Electronic Library of Primary Sources
- from *Letters of Peter the Great*

Warm-Up Transparency 21

Critical Thinking Transparencies
- CT57 Chapter 21 Visual Summary

Electronic Library of Primary Sources
- "The Restoration of Charles II"

INTERNET RESOURCES
www.mlworldhistory.com

Chapter Summaries on Audiocassette in English and Spanish

INTERNET RESOURCES
www.mlworldhistory.com

Block Scheduling (90 MINUTES)

Day 1
Section 1, pp. 513–517

COOPERATIVE ACTIVITY
Promoting a Country, p. 515 (Teacher's Edition)

Section 2, pp. 518–525

COOPERATIVE ACTIVITY
Designing Palace Displays, p. 521 (Teacher's Edition)

Section Assessments,
pp. 517, 523

Day 2
Section 3, pp. 526–530

COOPERATIVE ACTIVITY
Reporting on the War, p. 527 (Teacher's Edition)

Section 4, pp. 531–535

COOPERATIVE ACTIVITY
Reporting on Modernization, p. 533 (Teacher's Edition)

Section Assessments,
pp. 530, 535

Day 3
Section 5, pp. 536–539

COOPERATIVE ACTIVITY
Making a Pamphlet, p. 537 (Teacher's Edition)

Section Assessment, p. 539

Chapter Assessment,
pp. 540–541

Yearly Pacing *Chapter 21 Total:* 3 days *Yearly Total:* 85 days

Planning for Block Schedules

Customizing for Special Needs

Students Acquiring English

Access for Students Acquiring English
- **Guided Reading** for Sections 1–5 (Spanish), pp. 208–212
- **Chapter Summary** (Spanish), pp. 205–207
- **Skillbuilder Practice** Evaluating Decisions (Spanish), p. 213
- **Geography Application** Old Empires and New Powers (Spanish), p. 214

Chapter Summaries on Audiocassette in English and Spanish

INTERNET RESOURCES
www.mlworldhistory.com
The Diverse Classroom.

Less Proficient Readers

In-Depth Resources: Unit 5
- **Guided Reading** for Sections 1–5, pp. 1–5
- **Skillbuilder Practice** Evaluating Decisions, p. 6
- **Geography Application** Old Empires and New Powers, p. 7

Telescoping the Times
- Chapter Summary, pp. 81–83

Chapter Summaries on Audiocassette

Gifted and Talented Students

In-Depth Resources: Unit 5

Primary Sources:
- Louis XIV's Advice to His Son, p. 9
- Peter the Great's Reforms, p. 10
- from *Diary of Samuel Pepys*, p. 11
- from the English Bill of Rights, p. 12

History Makers
- Maria Theresa, p. 16
- William of Orange, p. 17

Connections to Literature READINGS FOR STUDENTS

In-Depth Resources: Unit 5
Literature: from *The Cat and the King*, p. 13

Enrichment Reading
- Babel, Isaac
"The King," *Collected Stories*
New York: Penguin, 1994

Gangsters, helpless police, and regular raids enliven this story of Moldavanka aristocrats at a wedding ceremony in Odessa.

- Sutcliff, Rosemary
Bonnie Dundee
New York: Dutton, 1984

In this story a rebellious teenager rejects his family's beliefs in 17th century Scotland and sides with the king's cavalry.

PE = Pupil's Edition		= Overhead Transparency		= Software		= Video	
= Copy Master		= CD-ROM		= Audiocassette		= Internet	

Absolute Monarchs in Europe, 1500–1800

Predicting and Making Inferences

- How do students think government in England might change after Cromwell's rule?

- Have students look at the pictures and captions and consider what they reveal about European life at the time.

Interpreting Maps

- Ask students to look at the map and identify the major European powers of the time. (Point out that this chapter covers events in Europe over a period of several centuries.)

- Which major powers occupy land in the Holy Roman Empire?

- Which countries do Bourbon rulers control?

Geography Connection

Have students compare this map with the map of modern Europe on page 978 in the Atlas.

- Which countries now occupy the lands once controlled by the Hapsburgs?

- What challenges might governing an ethnically diverse population pose for a ruler?

CHAPTER 21
Absolute Monarchs in Europe, 1500–1800

PREVIEWING THEMES

Power and Authority
Because of the Reformation and the Age of Exploration, Europe experienced religious, economic, and political turmoil. To deal with these crises, European rulers increased their power. They claimed God gave them the authority to do so.

Revolution
When the Spanish king tried to wipe out Protestantism, the Spanish Netherlands revolted. When English kings tried to increase their power at the expense of Parliament, they lost their thrones. England had two revolutions—one bloody and one bloodless.

Economics
When Spain imported tons of silver from the Americas, it experienced severe inflation. Spain spent much money to buy goods from the Spanish Netherlands, which had a thriving commercial empire. France used the practice of mercantilism to improve its economy.

INTERNET CONNECTION
Visit us at **www.mlworldhistory.com** to learn more about European monarchs.

EUROPE, 1650

Oliver Cromwell overthrew the English king in **1649** and set up a republican government. However, he eventually seized as much power as any monarch. He waged war, doubled the late king's budget, and regulated the economy. He also banned newspapers, hired spies to keep track of his enemies, and executed his opponents.

SCOTLAND
IRELAND
North Sea
ENGLAND
UNITE
NETHERL
Amsterdam •
Utrecht •
London •
• Paris
• Nantes
FRANCE
Bay of Biscay
SWITZER
SAV
M
G
TUS
CO
Ge
PORTUGAL
Lisbon •
• Madrid
SPAIN
MINORCA
Gr. Br.
SAR
Au
• Gibraltar
Mediterranean Sea

☐ French Bourbon lands
☐ Spanish Bourbon lands
☐ Austrian Hapsburg lands
☐ Prussian lands
☐ British Stuart lands
☐ Russian lands
— Boundary of Holy Roman Empire

0   100 Miles
0   200 Kilometers

510

GEOGRAPHY THEMES

Region

Tell students that the idea of region is important to the events covered in this chapter. Ask them what major powers occupy the region of Europe. *France, England, Austria, Spain, the Holy Roman Empire, and Prussia.* Why might this region become a center of conflict between powers with territorial ambitions? *Because no single power dominates it.* Why might Peter the Great's desire to establish a major seaport at St. Petersburg cause Sweden concern? *Possible response: Because it might help Russia compete with Sweden for economic and military dominance of the Baltic region.*

Location

Ask students to locate Russia on this map. Point out that this country is not part of western Europe and that it is separated from Europe by a great distance. Discuss with students the possible benefits and drawbacks of Russia's location in relation to western Europe.

How might Russia's location affect its development? *Possible responses: Benefits—Russia might be less likely to go to war with or be invaded by western European countries. Drawbacks—Russia might be less able to exchange goods and ideas with western European countries. Distance could slow Russia's development.*

In **1703**, **Peter the Great** ordered the city of **St. Petersburg** to be built upon a swamp. Instead of sinking into the mud, St. Petersburg quickly grew into one of the most beautiful cities in Europe. The palace below was built by a later Russian monarch, Catherine the Great.

The Spanish painter **Diego Velázquez** painted this portrait of his enslaved servant, Juan de Pareja, in **1650**. Velázquez taught Pareja to be a painter and granted him his freedom, also in **1650**. The painting is notable for the human dignity it gives to its subject.

ADDITIONAL RESOURCES

Books for the Teacher

- Duffy, James P. *Czars: Russia's Rulers for More Than One Thousand Years.* New York: Facts on File, 1995.

- Wolf, John B. *Louis XIV.* New York: Norton, 1968.

Books for the Student

- Miller, John. *Bourbon and Stuart: Kings and Kingship in France and England in the Seventeenth Century.* New York: Watts, 1987.

- Swisher, Clarice. *The Glorious Revolution.* San Diego: Lucent, 1995. English Parliament gains supremacy over the monarchy.

- Taylor, Laurence. *The Seventeenth Century.* Morristown: Silver Burdett, 1984. Daily life in Europe through illustrations.

▄▄▄ Videos

- *Europe: State and Power— 1453–1700.* Social Studies School Service, 1985. 800-421-4246.

- *The Rise of National Monarchies: 15th to 16th Centuries.* Cambridge Social Studies, 1991. 800-468-4227.

- *The Spanish Armada.* Ambrose Video, 1997. 800-526-4663.

◉ Software

- *The Baroque.* CD-ROM. Society for Visual Education, 1994. 800-829-1900.

- *Thirty Years' War.* Educational Software Institute, 1995. 800-955-5570.

HISTORY THROUGH ART

Juan de Pareja

Diego Velázquez

When *Juan de Pareja* was displayed beside works of other great artists of Velázquez's day, it struck the artists that "everything else seemed like painting but this alone like truth."

In contrast to the smooth, unified finish that typified paintings of the period, the surface of Velázquez's portrait shows variations that produce convincing optical effects. In depicting Pareja's costume, for example, Velázquez played warm tones off cool tones by varying the thickness of the gray paint applied over the medium-light-brown ground. To suggest that the bodice and cloak consist of a coarser material than the sleeve, he applied brushstrokes more close-ly together and gently rubbed the surface, thereby reflecting more light. The result of such techniques is to heighten the sense of Pareja's presence.

Interpreting the Art Compare this portrait with Hyacinthe Rigaud's portrait of Louis XIV on page 524. How might Velázquez have depicted the king differently?

This Interact with History feature motivates students by inviting them to put themselves in a key historical situation—an absolute monarch's demonstration of power. As students imagine themselves designing their own palace, they will analyze the issues, explore their options, and become decision-makers.

Purpose

- to set the stage for studying the era of absolute monarchy in Europe
- to help students understand how monarchs in Europe held and exercised power during this era
- to help students make connection with people and events they will study in this chapter

Teaching Strategy

Thinking Critically After students have imagined themselves in the situation described on this page, have them answer the key questions and give reasons for their decision.

EXAMINING *the* ISSUES

Here are suggestions for addressing each bulleted question.

1 In considering this question, student monarchs should weigh the threat to their rule against the need to convince others of their power. Which concern takes priority?

2 Ask students to think about what qualities in a ruler might impress people and ensure their loyalty and support.

3 Have students recall buildings or other structures that impressed them, and ask them to consider the reasons for their reaction.

Making Connections Have students consider ways that rulers in other periods they have studied used palaces and other large-scale building projects to project a sense of their power.

Interact *with* History

Y̲ou are the monarch of a European nation. After a long struggle—during which your life was in danger—you have come into power. Now that you have the throne, you want to make sure that no one ever threatens you again. In addition, you want everyone to believe that you are the greatest ruler in all of Europe. You decide to build a palace that will impress both your subjects and visitors to your kingdom.

How will you design your palace?

The workers in this painting are building a 2,000-room palace for Louis XIV of France. The royal court will live there.

Instead of defensive walls and moats, elegant gardens and lawns will surround the palace. This is to impress visitors, especially rival monarchs and statesmen.

In the foreground, workers move champagne-colored stones for the palace walls. The king chose these stones for their beauty.

The Building of Versailles, Adam François van der Meulen, 1632-1690, The Royal Collection © Her Majesty Queen Elizabeth II

EXAMINING *the* ISSUES

1 • What will be your palace's main function: as a fortress, the seat of government, housing for the court, or a place to entertain visitors?

2 • What qualities do you want people to associate with your rule: military strength, wealth, political power, cultural brilliance?

3 • How can a palace demonstrate the qualities that you have decided are important? What features should the palace have?

As a class, discuss these questions. You may want to refer back to other royal building projects that you have studied. Some examples are the hanging gardens in Babylon, the castles in feudal Europe, and Great Zimbabwe in Africa.

As you read about absolute monarchs in Europe, notice their building projects. Especially note the projects of Philip II of Spain, Louis XIV of France, and Peter the Great of Russia.

512 Chapter 21

Follow Up

A feature on the chapter assessment will ask students to reevaluate their responses to the situation presented on this page.

1 Spain's Empire and European Absolutism

TERMS & NAMES
- Philip II
- absolute monarch
- divine right

MAIN IDEA

During a time of religious and economic instability, Philip II ruled Spain with a strong hand.

WHY IT MATTERS NOW

When faced with crises, many heads of government take on additional economic or political powers.

SETTING THE STAGE From 1520 to 1566, Suleiman I exercised great power as sultan of the Ottoman Empire. A European monarch of the same period—Charles V—came close to matching Suleiman's power. As the Hapsburg king, Charles inherited Spain, Spain's American colonies, parts of Italy, and lands in Austria and the Netherlands. As the elected Holy Roman emperor, he ruled much of Germany. It was the first time since Charlemagne that a European ruler controlled so much territory.

Spain's Powerful Empire

A devout Catholic, Charles not only fought Muslims but also opposed Lutherans. In 1555, he unwillingly agreed to the Peace of Augsburg. It allowed German princes to choose the religion for their territory. The following year, Charles V divided his immense empire and retired to a monastery. To his brother Ferdinand, he left Austria and the Holy Roman Empire. His son, **Philip II,** inherited Spain, the Spanish Netherlands, and the American colonies.

Philip II's Empire Philip was shy, serious, and—like his father—deeply religious. However, he could be aggressive for the sake of his empire. In 1580, the king of Portugal died without an heir. Because Philip was the king's nephew, he seized the Portuguese kingdom. Counting Portuguese strongholds in Africa, India, and the East Indies, he now had an empire that circled the globe.

Philip's empire provided him with incredible wealth. By 1600, American mines had supplied Spain with an estimated 339,000 pounds of gold. Between 1550 and 1650, roughly 16,000 tons of silver bullion were unloaded from Spanish galleons. The king of Spain claimed between a fourth and a fifth of every shipload of treasure as his royal share. With this wealth, Spain was able to support a large standing army of 50,000 soldiers.

Defender of Catholicism When Philip took power, Europe was experiencing religious wars, caused by the Reformation. However, religious conflict was not new to Spain. The Reconquista—the campaign to drive Muslims from Spain—had been completed only 64 years before. In addition, Philip's great-grandparents Isabella and Ferdinand had used the Inquisition to investigate suspected heretics.

Philip saw himself as part of this tradition. He believed it was his duty to defend Catholicism against the Muslims of the Ottoman Empire and the Protestants of Europe. In 1571 the pope called on all Catholic princes to take up arms against the mounting power of the Ottoman Empire. Philip responded like a true crusader. Two hundred and fifty Spanish and Venetian ships defeated a large Ottoman fleet in

Vocabulary
bullion: gold or silver in the form of solid bars.

HISTORY MAKERS

Philip II of Spain
1527–1598

The most powerful ruler in Europe, Philip was also the hardest working. He demanded reports, reports, and more reports from his advisers. Then, in his tiny office, he would agonize over decisions. Often he could not bring himself to choose one policy over another. Then the government of Spain would grind to a halt.

Yet Philip would not allow anyone to help him. When his father was still emperor, he told Philip not to trust his advisers completely. Perhaps Philip followed his father's advice too closely. Deeply suspicious, he trusted no one for long. As his own court historian wrote, "His smile and his dagger were very close."

Absolute Monarchs in Europe **513**

Section 1 Overview

OBJECTIVES

1. To describe Spanish power under Philip II.
2. To explain weaknesses in the Spanish Empire.
3. To describe the birth of the Netherlands.
4. To explain the origins of absolute monarchy.

CRITICAL THINKING
- Making inferences, p. 514
- Identifying problems, p. 515
- Drawing conclusions, p. 517

FOCUS

5-Minute Warm-Up

▶ *Perceiving Causes*

To help students understand absolute rule, have them answer these questions.

1. Read History Makers on page 513. Name two qualities of Philip II that hindered him from ruling effectively.
2. Why might the government have stopped functioning when Philip could not make a decision?

   WARM-UP TRANSPARENCY 21

OBJECTIVE 1 INSTRUCT

Spain's Powerful Empire

▶ *Key Ideas*
- In 1556 Philip II becomes king of Spain, the wealthiest, most powerful nation in Europe.
- Philip defends Roman Catholicism against Protestantism and Islam.
- Spanish riches help stimulate a golden age in the arts.

   IN-DEPTH RESOURCES: UNIT 5
   Guided Reading, p. 1

   ACCESS FOR STUDENTS ACQUIRING ENGLISH
   Guided Reading (Spanish), p. 208

   GEOGRAPHY TRANSPARENCIES
   GT21 Hapsburg Europe, 1560

SECTION 1 RESOURCES

PRINT RESOURCES

IN-DEPTH RESOURCES: UNIT 5
Guided Reading, p. 1

ACCESS FOR STUDENTS ACQUIRING ENGLISH
Guided Reading (Spanish), p. 208

FORMAL ASSESSMENT
Section Quiz, p. 239

ALTERNATIVE ASSESSMENT BOOK

TECHNOLOGY RESOURCES

GEOGRAPHY TRANSPARENCIES
GT21 Hapsburg Europe, 1560

WORLD ART AND CULTURES TRANSPARENCIES
AT45 Banquet of the Officers of St. George Civic Guard Company

CD-ROM
Electronic Library of Primary Sources

INTERNET www.mlworldhistory.com

SPOTLIGHT On
The Defeat of the Spanish Armada

The Spanish Navy reigned supreme on the Atlantic until 1588. That year, the Spanish Armada—the naval fleet assembled to invade England—went down to defeat.

After a series of raids on his treasure ships, King Philip II of Spain dispatched about 130 ships. They carried 19,000 soldiers to the English Channel in the summer of 1588. England, however, was ready. English warships outmaneuvered the Spanish vessels and bombarded the Armada with their heavier long-range cannons. (See picture above.) Stormy weather further damaged the Armada.

The defeat of the Armada was a significant event. It dealt a crippling blow to Spain's dominance on the high seas. It also opened the way for the rest of Europe to venture into the Americas.

a fierce battle near Lepanto. In 1588, Philip launched the Spanish Armada in an attempt to punish Protestant England. However, his fleet was defeated.

Although this setback weakened Spain seriously, its wealth gave it the appearance of strength for a while longer. Philip's gray granite palace, the Escorial, had massive walls and huge gates that demonstrated his power. The Escorial also reflected Philip's faith. Within its walls stood a monastery as well as a palace.

Golden Age of Spanish Art Spain's great wealth did more than support navies and build palaces. It also allowed monarchs and nobles to become patrons of artists. During the 16th and 17th centuries, Spain experienced a golden age in the arts. The works of two great painters show both the faith and the pride of Spain during this period.

Born in Crete, El Greco (GREHK·oh) spent much of his adult life in Spain. His real name was Domenikos Theotokopoulos, but Spaniards called him El Greco, meaning "the Greek." El Greco's art often puzzled the people of his time. He chose brilliant, sometimes clashing colors, distorted the human figure, and expressed emotion symbolically in his paintings. Although unusual, El Greco's techniques showed the deep Catholic faith of Spain. He painted saints and martyrs as huge, long-limbed figures that have a supernatural air.

The paintings of Diego Velázquez (vuh·LAHS·kehs), on the other hand, showed the pride of Spain's monarchy. Velázquez, who painted 50 years after El Greco, was the court painter to Philip IV of Spain. He is best known for his portraits of the royal family and scenes of court life. Like El Greco, he was noted for using rich colors. (See his painting of Juan de Pareja on page 511.)

Don Quixote The publication of *Don Quixote de la Mancha* in 1605 is often called the birth of the modern European novel. In this book, Miguel de Cervantes (suhr·VAN·teez) wrote about a poor Spanish nobleman. This nobleman went a little crazy after reading too many books about heroic knights. Hoping to "right every manner of wrong," Don Quixote rode forth in a rusty suit of armor, mounted on a feeble nag. At one point he mistook some windmills for giants:

> He rushed with [his horse's] utmost speed upon the first windmill he could come at, and, running his lance into the sail, the wind whirled about with such swiftness, that the rapidity of such motion presently broke the lance into shivers, and hurled away both knight and horse along with it, till down he fell, rolling a good way off into the field.
>
> **MIGUEL DE CERVANTES**, *Don Quixote de la Mancha*

Some critics believe that Cervantes was mocking chivalry, the knightly code of the Middle Ages. Others maintain that the book is about an idealistic person who longs for the romantic past because he is frustrated with his materialistic world.

Problems Weaken the Spanish Empire

Certainly, the age in which Cervantes wrote was a materialistic one. The gold and silver coming from the Americas made Spain temporarily wealthy. However, such treasure helped to cause long-term economic problems.

Inflation and Taxes One of these problems was severe inflation, which had two causes. First, Spain's population had been growing. As more people demanded food and other goods, merchants were able to raise prices. Second, as silver bullion flooded the market, its value dropped. It took increased amounts of silver to buy things.

Spain's economic decline also had other causes. When Spain expelled the Jews and Moors (Muslims) around 1500, it lost many valuable artisans and businesspeople. In addition, Spain's nobles did not have to pay taxes. The tax burden fell on the lower classes. That burden prevented them from accumulating enough wealth to start their own businesses. Therefore, Spain never developed a middle class.

Making Spain's Enemies Rich Guilds that had emerged in the Middle Ages still dominated business in Spain. Such guilds used old-fashioned methods. This made Spanish cloth and manufactured goods more expensive than those made elsewhere. As a result, Spaniards bought much of what they needed from France, England, and the Netherlands. Spain's great wealth flowed into the pockets of foreigners, who were mostly Spain's enemies.

To finance their wars, Spanish kings borrowed money from German and Italian bankers. When shiploads of silver came in, the money was sent abroad to repay debts. The economy was so feeble that Philip had to declare the Spanish state bankrupt three times.

The Dutch Revolt In the Spanish Netherlands, Philip had to maintain an army to keep his subjects under control. The Dutch had little in common with their Spanish rulers. While Spain was Catholic, the Netherlands had many Calvinist congregations. Also, Spain had a sluggish economy, while the Dutch were involved in trade and had a prosperous middle class.

Philip raised taxes in the Netherlands and took steps to crush Protestantism. In response, in 1566, angry Protestant mobs swept through Catholic churches. They destroyed religious paintings and statues. Philip then sent an army under the Spanish duke of Alva to punish them. On a single day in 1568, the duke executed 1,500 Protestants and suspected rebels.

In the struggle against the Spanish, William of Orange emerged as a great leader. William's motives for fighting the Spaniards were political, not religious. He wanted to free the Netherlands from Spain. At first, William lost battle after battle. Then, in 1574, when the Spaniards had the city of Leiden under seige, the Dutch took a desperate step. Their lands were called the Low Countries, because much of the land was actually below sea level. Only great dikes kept the seawater from flooding over the fields. The Dutch opened the floodgates, flooding the land with water. The floods drove the Spanish troops from their camp outside Leiden.

Finally, in 1579, the seven northern provinces of the Netherlands, which were largely Protestant, united and declared their independence from Spain. They became the United Provinces of the Netherlands. The ten southern provinces (present-day Belgium) were Catholic and remained under Spanish control.

The Independent Dutch Prosper

The United Provinces of the Netherlands was different from other European states of the time. For one thing, religious toleration was practiced there. In addition, the United Provinces was not a kingdom but a republic. Each province had an elected governor, whose power depended on the support of merchants and landholders.

Absolute Monarchs in Europe **515**

THINK THROUGH HISTORY
B. Identifying Problems Explain why Spain's economy did not really benefit from the gold and silver from the Americas.
B. Possible Answer It caused inflation; it also did not go to buy Spanish goods but was used to buy foreign goods or to pay off foreign loans.

Background William was a prince of the House of Orange, a dynasty that originated in Orange, France.

Global Impact

Tulip Mania

Tulips came to Europe from Turkey around 1550. People went wild over the flowers' delicate beauty and exotic colors and began to buy rare varieties.

The supply of tulips could not meet the demand, and prices began to rise. One man even traded his mansion for three bulbs! Soon people were spending all their savings on bulbs and taking out loans to buy more.

Tulip mania reached a peak between 1633 and 1637. Then people began to doubt whether prices could continue to rise. In fact, tulip prices sank rapidly. Many Dutch families lost property and were left with bulbs that were nearly worthless.

Even so, tulips remained popular in the Netherlands—which is one of the world's biggest exporters of tulip bulbs today.

Global Impact

Tulip Mania

During the tulip craze, some bulbs sold for the equivalent of hundreds of dollars each. Speculation was so rampant that bulbs might be sold and resold several times without ever leaving the ground. Ask students if they think such a speculative mania could ever occur again. Then have them explain their views.

OBJECTIVE 3 INSTRUCT

The Independent Dutch Prosper

▶ *Key Ideas*
• Religious toleration is practiced in the Dutch republic.
• Dutch traders make the Netherlands a center of European trade and banking.
• Dutch art flourishes in a climate of prosperity.

WORLD ART AND CULTURES TRANSPARENCIES
AT45 Banquet of the Officers of St. George Civic Guard Company

TEACHING OPTION | **BLOCK SCHEDULING** | **COOPERATIVE ACTIVITY: Promoting a Country** | **CLASS TIME 30 MINUTES**

Task: Students will create an annotated poster promoting Spain or the Netherlands in the 1600s.

Purpose: To synthesize and convey information on two important countries in the 17th century.

Activity: Groups of students research life in Spain or the Netherlands in the 1600s. Then each makes an annotated poster on the attractions of life in that country. Topics might include economic life, politics, arts and culture, geography and resources, and

social trends. Students should combine text and visuals in an interesting way. Each group then presents its poster to the class with a short talk.

 Building a Portfolio: Have students include a description of the product in their portfolio, along with an explanation of their role in its preparation.

ALTERNATIVE ASSESSMENT BOOK Standards for Evaluating a Cooperative Activity

Standards for Evaluation
Posters should . . .

• be informative, lively, and accurate
• present a realistic picture of life in Spain or the Netherlands during the 1600s through words and visuals
• be designed and executed carefully

Teacher's Edition **515**

Jan Vermeer

Vermeer's work was barely recognized during his life, and he struggled with financial difficulties. A number of his paintings were given to local bakers and grocers in exchange for food. Some of the food, such as loaves of bread and jugs of milk, made its way into his paintings.

Absolutism in Europe

Key Ideas

• Absolute monarchs try to ensure that all power stays in their hands.

• They believe that God gives them the right to rule.

• Both the centralization of state authority and crises in Europe fuel the growth of absolute rule.

CRITICAL THINKING ACTIVITY
CLASS TIME: 10 MINUTES

Synthesizing

On the chalkboard write the heading *Reasons for Absolutism* and circle it. Then invite students to help you make a cluster diagram showing major reasons for the rise of absolute monarchs. The diagram might look like this:

This painting by Rembrandt is called *The Syndics.* A syndic was a city official. Such art shows that city leaders and the middle class played a major role in Dutch society.

Dutch Trading Empire The stability of the government allowed the Dutch people to concentrate on economic growth. The merchants of Amsterdam bought surplus grain in Poland and crammed it into their warehouses. When they heard about poor harvests in southern Europe, they shipped the grain south while prices were highest. Western Europe was also short of timber, a fact that Dutch merchants were quick to use for their benefit. They shipped Scandinavian lumber to Spain, France, Italy, and England, all in ships owned by Dutch capitalists. The Dutch had the largest fleet of ships in the world—perhaps 4,800 ships in 1636. Gradually, the Dutch replaced the Italians as the bankers of Europe. One reason for this is that the trade routes of the Atlantic became more important than those of the Mediterranean.

Dutch Art During the 1600s, the Netherlands became what Florence had been during the 1400s. It boasted not only the best banks but also many of the best artists in Europe. As in Florence, wealthy merchants sponsored many of these artists.

The greatest Dutch artist of the period was Rembrandt van Rijn (REHM·BRANT vahn RYN). Rembrandt painted portraits of wealthy middle-class merchants. He also produced group portraits. In *The Syndics* (shown above), he portrayed a group of city officials. Rembrandt showed the individuality of each man by capturing his distinctive facial expression and posture. Rembrandt also used sharp contrasts of light and shadow to draw attention to his focus.

Another artist fascinated with the effects of light was Jan Vermeer (YAHN vuhr·MEER). Like many other Dutch artists, he chose domestic, indoor settings for his portraits. He often painted women doing such familiar activities as pouring milk from a jug or reading a letter. Unlike Rembrandt, who was famous in his time, Vermeer did not become widely admired until the late 19th century. The work of both Rembrandt and Vermeer reveals how important merchants, civic leaders, and the middle class in general were in 17th-century Netherlands.

Absolutism in Europe

Even though Philip II lost his Dutch possessions, he was a forceful ruler in many ways. He tried to control every aspect of his empire's affairs. During the next few centuries, many European monarchs would also claim the authority to rule without limits.

Background
The large fleet helped the Dutch East India Company to dominate the Asian spice trade and the Indian Ocean trade. This added to Dutch prosperity.

CONNECTIONS ACROSS THE CURRICULUM

Economics Unlike the Netherlands in the 16th and 17th centuries, Spain never developed much of a middle class. Encourage students to investigate why. They might consider these obstacles: (1) the expulsion of Jews and Moors, (2) the government's failure to invest in productive ventures, (3) high government spending and taxation, (4) the Spanish public's generally negative attitude toward moneymaking, (5) limited opportunities for advancement outside the nobility and the church, and (6) severe inflation. Have students compare these factors with those that helped the Dutch middle class flourish.

MULTIPLE LEARNING STYLES

Visual Learners Invite interested students to find paintings by Dutch or Spanish artists of the 16th and 17th centuries, including Ribera, Zurbarán, and Velázquez of Spain and Honthorst, Hals, Rembrandt, Vermeer, Kalf, and Ruisdael of the independent Netherlands. Ask students to bring examples to class and to discuss how similarities and differences in the cultures of the two countries are expressed in the artworks. Encourage students to read about the artists and their cultures to inform their analysis.

The Theory of Absolutism These rulers wanted to be **absolute monarchs,** kings or queens who believed that all power within their state's boundaries rested in their hands. Their goal was to control every aspect of society. Absolute monarchs believed in **divine right,** the idea that God created the monarchy and that the monarch acted as God's representative on earth. An absolute monarch answered only to God, not to his or her subjects.

These ideas were not new to the 16th century. Absolute rulers from ancient times included Darius in Persia, Shi Huangdi in China, and the Roman Caesars. After the decline of the Roman Empire, however, European monarchs had been weak. The feudal nobility, the Church, and other rulers had limited the power that any one monarch could wield.

Growing Power of Europe's Monarchs As Europe emerged from the Middle Ages, monarchs grew increasingly powerful. The decline of feudalism, the rise of cities, and the growth of national kingdoms all helped to centralize authority. In addition, the growing middle class usually backed monarchs, because they promised a peaceful, supportive climate for business. Monarchs used the wealth of colonies to pay for their ambitions. Church authority also broke down during the late Middle Ages and the Reformation. That opened the way for monarchs to assume even greater control. In 1576, Jean Bodin, an influential French writer, defined absolute rule:

> The first characteristic of the sovereign prince is the power to make general and special laws, but—and this qualification is important—without the consent of superiors, equals, or inferiors. If the prince requires the consent of superiors, then he is a subject himself; if that of equals, he shares his authority with others; if that of his subjects, senate or people, he is not sovereign.
>
> **JEAN BODIN,** *Six Books on the State*

Crises Lead to Absolutism The 17th century was a period of great upheaval in Europe. Religious and territorial conflicts between states led to almost continuous warfare. This caused governments to build huge armies and to levy even heavier taxes on an already suffering population. These pressures in turn would bring on widespread unrest. Sometimes peasants revolted. In response to these crises, monarchs tried to impose order by increasing their own power. As absolute rulers, they regulated everything from religious worship to social gatherings. To seem more powerful, they increased the size of their courts. They created new government bureaucracies to control their countries' economic life. Their goal was to free themselves from the limitations imposed by the nobility and by representative bodies such as Parliament. Only with such freedom could they rule absolutely, as did the most famous monarch of his time, Louis XIV of France.

Section ❶ Assessment

1. TERMS & NAMES

Identify
- Philip II
- absolute monarch
- divine right

2. TAKING NOTES

On a chart like the one shown, list the conditions that allowed European monarchs to gain power. Then list the ways they exercised their increased power.

3. DRAWING CONCLUSIONS

What does the art described in this section reveal about the cultures of Spain and the Netherlands?

THINK ABOUT
- what the art of Velázquez and El Greco reveals about Spain
- what the art of Rembrandt and Vermeer reveals about the Netherlands

4. THEME ACTIVITY

Economics With a partner, create an illustrated poster contrasting the economies of Spain and the Netherlands around 1600. Compare such characteristics as

- sources of wealth
- existence of a middle class
- trends such as inflation or high taxes
- who controlled financial services

Absolute Monarchs in Europe **517**

2 France's Ultimate Monarch

TERMS & NAMES
• Edict of Nantes
• Cardinal Richelieu
• skepticism
• Louis XIV
• intendant
• Jean Baptiste Colbert
• War of the Spanish Succession

MAIN IDEA	WHY IT MATTERS NOW
After a century of war and riots, France was ruled by Louis XIV, the most powerful monarch of his time.	Louis used his power to build a great palace and sponsor art that is part of France's cultural legacy.

SETTING THE STAGE In 1559, King Henry II of France died, leaving four young sons. Three of them ruled, one after the other, but all proved incompetent. The real power behind the throne during this period was their mother, Catherine de Médicis. Catherine tried to preserve royal authority, but growing conflicts between Catholics and Huguenots—French Protestants—rocked the country.

Religious Wars Create a Crisis

Between 1562 and 1598, Huguenots and Catholics fought eight religious wars. Chaos spread through France. For example, in 1572 the St. Bartholomew's Day Massacre in Paris sparked a six-week, nationwide slaughter of Huguenots.

Henry of Navarre The massacre occurred when many Huguenot nobles were in Paris. They were attending the marriage of Catherine's daughter to a Huguenot prince, Henry of Navarre. Most of these nobles died, but Henry survived. Descended from the popular medieval king Louis IX, Henry was robust, athletic, and handsome. In 1589, when both Catherine and her last son died, Prince Henry inherited the throne. He became Henry IV, the first king of the Bourbon dynasty in France. As king, he showed himself to be decisive, fearless in battle, and a clever politician.

Many Catholics, including the people of Paris, opposed Henry. For the sake of his war-weary country, Henry chose to give up Protestantism and become a Catholic. Explaining his conversion, Henry declared, "Paris is well worth a Mass."

In 1598, Henry took another step toward healing France's wounds. He declared that the Huguenots could live in peace in France and set up their own houses of worship in some cities. This declaration of religious toleration was called the **Edict of Nantes.**

Background
Catherine was descended from the Renaissance de' Medici family. She spelled her name the French way.

Background
The Bourbon dynasty took its name from a French town.

Phillipe de Champaigne painted many portraits of the powerful Cardinal Richelieu. This triple portrait shows his front view and two profiles.

Aided by an adviser who enacted wise financial policies, Henry devoted his reign to rebuilding France and its prosperity. He restored the French monarchy to a strong position. After a generation of war, most French people welcomed peace. Some people, however, hated Henry for his religious compromises. In 1610, a fanatic leaped into the royal carriage and stabbed Henry to death.

Louis XIII and Cardinal Richelieu
After Henry IV's death, his son Louis XIII reigned. Louis was a weak king, but in 1624 he appointed a strong minister who made up for all of Louis's weaknesses.

Cardinal Richelieu (RIHSH·uh·LOO) became, in effect, the ruler of France. For

THINK THROUGH HISTORY
A. Recognizing Effects What were the effects of Henry's conversion to Catholicism and of the Edict of Nantes?
A. Possible Answers They restored peace to France by ending religious wars, but they prompted a fanatic to assassinate Henry.

B. Possible
Answers By taking
away their fortifica-
tions, he lessened the
chance they could
defy the king's orders;
by increasing middle-
class officials, he
made the king more
independent of noble
influence.

THINK THROUGH HISTORY
B. Making
Inferences How did
Richelieu's actions
toward Huguenots
and the nobility
strengthen the
monarchy?

several years, he had been a hard-working leader of the Catholic church in France. Although he tried sincerely to lead according to moral principles, he was also ambitious and enjoyed exercising authority. As Louis XIII's minister, he was able to pursue his ambitions in the political arena.

This lean-faced, hawk-nosed cardinal took two steps to increase the power of the Bourbon monarchy. First, he moved against Huguenots. He believed that Protestantism often served as an excuse for political conspiracies against the Catholic king. Although Richelieu did not end the Huguenots' right to worship, he forbade Protestant cities from having walls. He did not want them to be able to defy the king and then withdraw behind strong defenses.

Second, he sought to weaken the nobles' power. Richelieu ordered nobles to take down their fortified castles. He increased the power of government agents who came from the middle class. This action ended the need for the king to use noble officials.

Richelieu also wanted to make France the strongest state in Europe. The greatest obstacle to this, he believed, was the Hapsburg rulers whose lands surrounded France. Hapsburgs ruled Spain, Austria, the Netherlands, and parts of Germany. To limit Hapsburg power, Richelieu involved France in the Thirty Years' War.

Background
Skepticism goes back
to the Greek philoso-
phers who lived as
early as the 200s B.C.
Like the French skep-
tics, Greek skeptics
argued against
strongly held beliefs.

Writers Express Skepticism As France regained political power, a new French intellectual movement developed. French thinkers had witnessed the religious wars with horror. What they saw turned them toward **skepticism,** the idea that nothing can ever be known for certain. These thinkers expressed an attitude of doubt toward churches that claimed to have the only correct set of doctrines. To doubt old ideas, skeptics thought, was the first step toward finding truth.

Michel de Montaigne lived during the worst years of the French religious wars. After the death of a dear friend, Montaigne retired to his library and thought deeply about life's meaning. To communicate his ideas, Montaigne developed a new form of literature, the essay. An essay is a brief work that expresses a person's thoughts and opinions.

In one essay, Montaigne pointed out that whenever a new belief arose, it replaced an old belief that people once accepted as truth. In the same way, he went on, the new belief would also probably be replaced by some different idea in the future. For these reasons, Montaigne believed that humans could never have absolute knowledge of what is true. To remind himself of this, he had the beams of his study painted with the sentence "All that is certain is that nothing is certain."

Another French writer of the time, René Descartes, was a brilliant thinker. In his *Meditations of First Philosophy,* Descartes examined the skeptical argument that one could never be certain of anything. Descartes used his observations and his reason to answer such arguments. In doing so, he created a philosophy that influenced modern thinkers and helped to develop the scientific method. Because of this, he became an important figure in the Enlightenment. (See Chapter 22.)

Louis XIV Rules Absolutely

The efforts of Henry IV and Richelieu to strengthen the French monarchy paved the way for the most powerful ruler in French history—**Louis XIV.** In Louis's view, he and the state were one and the same. He reportedly boasted, *"L'état, c'est moi,"* meaning "I am the state." Although Louis XIV became the strongest king of his time, when he began his reign he was only a five-year-old boy.

Louis, the Boy King When Louis became king in 1643, the true ruler of France was Richelieu's successor, Cardinal Mazarin (MAZ·uh·RAN). Mazarin's greatest triumph

Absolute Monarchs in Europe **519**

SPOTLIGHT ON

The Three Musketeers
The uneasy relationship between Louis XIII and Cardinal Richelieu provides the background for a lively work of historical fiction—*The Three Musketeers.*

It was written by Alexandre Dumas *père* (the father) in 1844. The novel is based on actual events involving the intrigues at Louis XIII's royal court. The main characters, the musketeers, are members of Louis's guard. They often become involved in sword fights, using weapons like the one shown below. From this novel comes the famous slogan "All for one and one for all." Hollywood has produced at least six film versions of this classic, a sign of its lasting popularity.

SPOTLIGHT ON
The Three Musketeers
Suggest that students view film versions of *The Three Musketeers* on video. Then have a class discussion about how French history is portrayed in the films.

MORE ABOUT . . .
The Bourbons
The Bourbons are one of the most famous ruling dynasties of Europe. Beginning with Henry IV, a number of French kings came from this family. Bourbons also held royal titles in Spain, Sicily, and other parts of Europe. The current king of Spain, Juan Carlos, is a Bourbon.

MORE ABOUT . . .
Limits on Nobles
Cardinal Richelieu also tried to curb the power of the nobility by banning luxurious clothing and prohibiting sword fights, a favorite recreation of noble lords. Neither measure succeeded.

OBJECTIVE ② INSTRUCT

Louis XIV Rules Absolutely

▶ *Key Ideas*
• Cardinal Mazarin rules France during Louis XIV's childhood.
• Mazarin raises taxes and strengthens the central government, despite nobility-led riots.
• After Mazarin's death, Louis rules independently, becoming the most powerful king in the history of France.
• Louis's finance minister, Jean Baptiste Colbert, tries to make France economically self-sufficient.

IN-DEPTH RESOURCES: UNIT 5
Primary Source: Louis XIV's Advice to His Son, p. 9

TEACHING OPTIONS

CONNECTIONS ACROSS THE CURRICULUM

Literature French literature during the period covered here is marked by two sometimes-conflicting tendencies: freedom of thought and obedience to requirements of clear, sober expression. Both Montaigne in his *Essays* and Descartes in his *Discourse on Method* exemplified freedom by adopting a skeptical outlook, but whereas

Montaigne let his imagination and style roam, Descartes sought to bring order and clarity to his thought and style.

Suggest that students read from and discuss these works or the works of other French writers of the period, such as Pascal, Corneille, Molière, Racine, La Fontaine, and Madame de Sévigné.

CUSTOMIZING FOR SPECIAL NEEDS

Less Proficient Readers To help less proficient readers understand Richelieu's policies, pair them with a more proficient reader. Have each pair reread the paragraphs under "Louis XIII and Cardinal Richelieu" silently. The less proficient reader should then identify the important ideas and explain

why they are important. The more proficient reader must agree or disagree and explain why. Each student should then write a summary of the reading, read their summaries to each other, and come up with a new summary on which they both agree.

HISTORY MAKERS

**Louis XIV
1638–1715**

Although Louis XIV stood only 5 feet 5 inches tall, his erect and dignified posture made him appear much taller. (It also helped that he wore high-heeled shoes.)

Louis had very strong likes and dislikes. He hated cities and loved to travel through France's countryside. The people who traveled with him were at his mercy, however, for he allowed no stopping except for his own comfort.

Louis liked to be informed of every detail in his government. He explained to his son the secrets of his success:

> Two things without doubt were absolutely necessary: very hard work on my part, and a wise choice of persons capable of seconding it.

It is small wonder that the vain Louis XIV liked to be called the Sun King. He believed that, as with the sun, all power radiated from him.

---

came in 1648, with the ending of the Thirty Years' War. The peace treaty made France the most powerful country in Europe.

Many people in France, particularly the nobles, hated Mazarin because he increased taxes and strengthened the central government. From 1648 to 1653, violent anti-Mazarin riots tore France apart. At times, the nobles who led the riots threatened the young king's life. Even after the violence was over, Louis never forgot his fear or his anger at the nobility. He determined to become so strong that they could never threaten him again.

In the end, the rebellion failed for three reasons. Its leaders distrusted one another even more than they distrusted Mazarin. In addition, the government used violent repression. Finally, peasants and townspeople grew weary of disorder and fighting. For many years afterward, the people of France accepted the oppressive laws of an absolute king. They were convinced that the alternative—rebellion—was even worse.

Louis Takes Control When Cardinal Mazarin died in 1661, the 23-year-old Louis took control of the government himself. A courtier remembered coming into the king's apartments that morning with the chancellor and hearing Louis announce, "The scene has changed. In the government of my realm . . . I shall have other principles than those of the late cardinal. You know my wishes, gentlemen; it now remains for you to execute them."

Louis weakened the power of the nobles by excluding them from his councils. In contrast, he increased the power of the government agents called **intendants,** who collected taxes and administered justice. To keep power under central control, he made sure that local officials communicated regularly with him.

Economic Growth Louis devoted himself to helping France attain economic, political, and cultural brilliance. No one assisted him more in achieving these goals than his minister of finance, **Jean Baptiste Colbert** (kawl·BEHR). Colbert believed in the theory of mercantilism. To prevent wealth from leaving the country, Colbert tried to make France self-sufficient. He wanted it to be able to manufacture everything it needed instead of relying on imports.

To expand manufacturing, Colbert gave government funds and tax benefits to French companies. To protect France's industries, he placed a high tariff on goods from other countries. Colbert also recognized the importance of colonies, which provided raw materials and a market for manufactured goods. The French government encouraged people to migrate to France's colony in Canada. There the fur trade added to French commerce.

After Colbert's death, Louis announced a policy that slowed France's economic progress. In 1685 he cancelled the Edict of Nantes, which protected the religious freedom of Huguenots. In response, thousands of Huguenot artisans and business people fled the country. Louis's policy thus robbed France of many skilled workers.

Louis's Grand Style

In his personal finances, Louis spent a fortune to surround himself with luxury. For example, each meal was a feast. An observer claimed that the king once devoured four plates of soup, a whole pheasant, a partridge in garlic sauce, two slices of ham, a salad, a plate of pastries, fruit, and hard-boiled eggs in a single sitting! Nearly 500 cooks, waiters, and other servants worked to satisfy his tastes.

Louis Controls the Nobility Every morning, the chief valet woke Louis at 7:30. Outside the curtains of Louis's canopy bed stood at least 100 of the most privileged nobles at court. They were waiting to help the great king dress. Only four would be allowed the honor of handing Louis his slippers or holding his sleeves for him.

Meanwhile, outside the bedchamber, lesser nobles waited in the palace halls and hoped Louis would notice them. A kingly nod, a glance of approval, a kind word—these marks of royal attention determined whether a noble succeeded or failed. A duke recorded how Louis turned against nobles who did not come to court to flatter him:

> He looked to the right and to the left, not only upon rising but upon going to bed, at his meals, in passing through his apartments, or his gardens. . . . He marked well all absentees from the Court, found out the reason of their absence, and never lost an opportunity of acting toward them as the occasion might seem to justify. . . . When their names were in any way mentioned, "I do not know them," the King would reply haughtily.
>
> **DUKE OF SAINT-SIMON**, *Memoirs of Louis XIV and the Regency*

Having the nobles at the palace increased royal authority in two ways. It made the nobility totally dependent on Louis. It also took them from their homes, thereby giving more power to the intendants. Louis required hundreds of nobles to live with him at the splendid palace he built at Versailles, 11 miles southwest of Paris.

The Splendor of Versailles Everything about the Versailles palace was immense. It faced a huge royal courtyard dominated by a statue of Louis XIV. The palace itself stretched for a distance of about 500 yards.

D. Possible Answer
He wanted to control the nobles' lives (and thwart their ability to plot against him), so he made them live at court, where he could watch them.

THINK THROUGH HISTORY
D. Making Inferences How did Louis's treatment of the nobles reflect his belief in his absolute authority?

The Palace at Versailles

- cost—an estimated $2 billion in 1994 dollars
- 36,000 laborers and 6,000 horses worked on the palace

- two wings—each 150 yards long
- main building—about 500 yards long
- about 2,000 rooms

This photograph shows the gardens of Versailles as they appear today. Versailles was built with
- 15,000 acres of gardens, lawns, and woods
- 1,400 fountains

It took so much water to run all the fountains at the same time that it was only done on special occasions. On other days, when the king walked in the garden, servants would turn on fountains just before he reached them. To conserve water, the servants would turn them off after he walked away.

MORE ABOUT . . .
Building the Palace
Why Louis XIV chose Versailles as the site for a large-scale palace remains a mystery. Already there stood a small, unfashionable hunting lodge built by his father on a sandy, shifting hill. Louis insisted, over his architects' objections, on leaving the lodge and building around it. As the project grew, the hill itself had to be enlarged. Supplying water was also a problem.

But as one biographer put it, "Versailles was the love of [Louis's] life." Whenever he was away from it, he required daily reports on the progress of the building. He continued to add to and improve the palace until he died, and he probably never saw it completely free of scaffolding.

MORE ABOUT . . .
Versailles as Showplace
As the fame of Versailles grew, princes all over Europe began to demand a Versailles of their own. Colbert took advantage of this fashion to increase French exports. He encouraged the establishment of factories to produce luxury items that once came from other countries. The finest of these items, which surpassed anything made outside France, went to Versailles and were shown to foreign visitors. By 1683, Colbert had raised France's national revenue to four times that of England and nearly ten times that of the Venetian Republic.

TEACHING OPTION | **BLOCK SCHEDULING** | **COOPERATIVE ACTIVITY: Designing Palace Displays** | **CLASS TIME 30 MINUTES**

Task: Students will design a display on a major European palace of the period 1500–1800.

Purpose: To convey a sense of royal life and priorities during the age of absolute monarchs.

Activity: Have groups of students do research and create a display on a major European palace built during the years 1500–1800. Possibilities include Versailles, the Escorial, Nymphenburg, Sans Souci, Blenheim Palace, and the Winter Palace. Displays should include text describing the buildings and grounds, along with visuals such as photos, drawings, and models. Have each group present its display and explain its palace's features.

Building a Portfolio: Students may add to their portfolio a copy of their palace description, along with a list of items included in the display.

ALTERNATIVE ASSESSMENT BOOK
Standards for Evaluating a Cooperative Activity

Standards for Evaluation
Displays should . . .

- provide a comprehensive view of the subject
- combine both textual and visual information
- show care and thought in their organization and presentation

Teacher's Edition 521

Molière's comedies ridicule human folly, poking fun at misers, hypocrites, and snobs. Targets of his barbed humor sometimes took offense. His greatest play, *Tartuffe,* so angered some Parisians that they called for him to be burned at the stake. Louis XIV protected him, however, and supported his work.

OBJECTIVE ④ INSTRUCT

Louis Fights Disastrous Wars

Key Ideas
- Louis XIV builds up a huge army and wages war to expand French territory and influence.
- Other European nations join forces to equal French power.
- France gains but eventually weakens from constant war.

CRITICAL THINKING ACTIVITY
CLASS TIME: 10 MINUTES

Summarizing
Help students recall facts about Louis's wars by filling in a chart like the one below.

Wars	Results
Spanish Netherlands	France gained 12 towns
Dutch Netherlands	France gained several towns and the Franche-Comté region
Spanish Succession	Louis's grandson allowed to remain king of Spain; France lost N. American territories

The painting below shows the Siege of Namur, which took place during Louis XIV's war with the League of Augsburg.

In fact, the palace was so long that food from the kitchens was often cold by the time servants reached Louis's chambers.

Because of its great size, Versailles was like a small royal city. Its rich decoration and furnishings clearly showed Louis's wealth and power to everyone who came to the palace. The elaborate ceremonies there impressed the king's subjects and aroused the admiration and envy of all other European monarchs.

Patronage of the Arts Versailles was a center of the arts during Louis's reign. Louis made opera and ballet more popular. He even danced the title role in the ballet *The Sun King*. One of his favorite writers was Molière (mohl-YAIR), who wrote some of the funniest plays in French literature. Molière's comedies include *Tartuffe*, which mocks religious hypocrisy. *The Would-be Gentleman* mocks the newly rich, and *The Imaginary Invalid* mocks hypochondriacs.

Not since Augustus of Rome had there been a monarch who aided the arts as much as Louis. Under Louis, the chief purpose of art was no longer to glorify God, as it had been in the Middle Ages. Nor was its purpose to glorify human potential, as it had been in the Renaissance. Now the purpose of art was to glorify the king and promote values that supported Louis's absolute rule.

Louis Fights Disastrous Wars

Under Louis, France was the most powerful country in Europe. In 1660, France had about 20 million people. This was four times as many as England and 10 times as many as the Dutch republic. The French army, numbering 100,000 in peacetime and 400,000 in wartime, was far ahead of other states' armies in size, training, and weaponry.

Attempts to Expand France's Boundaries In 1667, just six years after Mazarin's death, Louis invaded the Spanish Netherlands. Through this campaign, he gained 12 towns. Encouraged by his success, he personally led an army into the Dutch Netherlands in 1672. The Dutch saved their country by opening the dikes and flooding the countryside. This was the same tactic they had used in their revolt against Spain a century earlier. The war ended in 1678 with the Treaty of Nijmegen. France gained several towns and a region called Franche-Comté.

Louis decided to fight additional wars, but his luck had run out. By the end of the 1680s, a European-wide alliance had formed to stop France. By joining together, weaker countries could match France's strength. This defensive strategy was meant to achieve a balance of power, in which no single country or group of countries could dominate others.

In 1689, the Dutch prince William of Orange became the king of England. He joined the League of Augsburg, which consisted of the Hapsburg emperor, the kings of Sweden and Spain, and the leaders of several smaller European states. Joined together, these countries equaled France's strength.

Background
Louis adopted the title *Sun King* for himself. He decorated Versailles with suns and statues of Apollo, the Greek god of the sun.

THINK THROUGH HISTORY
E. Recognizing Effects How did Louis's wars against weaker countries backfire?
E. Possible Answer He motivated his enemies to band together and thereby become strong enough to rival France.

TEACHING OPTIONS

CONNECTIONS ACROSS TIME AND PLACE

Balance of Power In international relations, the matching of power against power is called balance of power. This policy has figured importantly in world politics since the days of absolute monarchs. Until the 20th century, the political world consisted of several separate balance-of-power systems, including the European, American, Chinese, and Indian. Beginning with alliances formed in World War I, most nations became integrated into a single balance-of-power system. Invite students to find out how the quest for a balance of power has played out over the years. Have them draw parallels between old and new alliances.

MULTIPLE LEARNING STYLES

Interpersonal Learners Ask students to hold a mock press conference between reporters and two kings: Louis XIV and William of Orange. Have two students play the kings' roles, and have the rest act as reporter-interviewers. Questions should concern the European wars of the late 1600s and the reasons for those wars. The kings should faithfully represent views that would correspond to royal and national interests at the time. If desired, students can switch roles at various points in the press conference.

France at this time had been weakened by a series of poor harvests. That, added to the constant warfare, brought great suffering to the French people. So, too, did new taxes, which Louis imposed to finance his wars.

War of the Spanish Succession Tired of hardship, the French people longed for peace. What they got was another war. In 1700, the childless king of Spain, Charles II, died after promising his throne to Louis XIV's 17-year-old grandson, Philip of Anjou. The two greatest powers in Europe, enemies for so long, were now both ruled by Bourbons.

Other countries felt threatened by this increase in the Bourbon dynasty's power. In 1701, England, Austria, the Dutch republic, Portugal, and several German and Italian states joined together against France and Spain. The long struggle that followed is known as the **War of the Spanish Succession.**

The costly war dragged on until 1713. The Treaty of Utrecht was signed in that year. Under its terms, Louis's grandson was allowed to remain king of Spain so long as the thrones of France and Spain were not united.

The big winner in the war was Great Britain. From Spain, Britain took Gibraltar, a fortress that controlled the entrance to the Mediterranean. Spain also granted a British company an *asiento*—permission to send enslaved Africans to Spain's American colonies. This increased Britain's involvement in trading enslaved Africans. In addition, France gave Britain the North American territories of Nova Scotia and Newfoundland, and abandoned claims to the Hudson Bay region. The Austrian Hapsburgs took the Spanish Netherlands and other Spanish lands in Italy. Prussia and Savoy were recognized as kingdoms.

Louis's Death and Legacy Louis's last years were more sad than glorious. Realizing that his wars had ruined France, he regretted the suffering he had brought to his people. He died in bed in 1715. News of his death prompted rejoicing throughout France. The people had had enough of the Sun King.

Louis left a mixed legacy to his country. France was certainly a power to be reckoned with in Europe. But the staggering debts and resentment over the royal abuse of power would plague Louis XIV's heirs. Eventually, this resentment led to revolution. In the meantime, Louis's enemies in Prussia and Austria had been experimenting with their own forms of absolute monarchy, as you will learn in Section 3.

Background
Louis XIV lived so long that he outlived his son and two grandsons. His great-grandson succeeded him as Louis XV.

Debt of the Royal Family, 1643–1715

Livres (in millions)

A livre is equal to approximately $10.50 in 1992 U.S. dollars.
Source: *Early Modern France 1560-1715*

SKILLBUILDER: Interpreting Charts
1. *How many times greater was the royal debt in 1715 than in 1643?*
2. *What was the royal debt of 1715 equal to in 1992 dollars?*

Section **2** Assessment

1. TERMS & NAMES

Identify
- Edict of Nantes
- Cardinal Richelieu
- skepticism
- Louis XIV
- intendant
- Jean Baptiste Colbert
- War of the Spanish Succession

2. TAKING NOTES

On a time line like the one shown, list the major events of Louis XIV's reign.

```
 |----+----+----+----|
1643              1715
```

Identify which events on your time line strengthened the French monarchy and which weakened it.

3. SUPPORTING OPINIONS

Many historians think of Louis XIV as the perfect example of an absolute monarch. Do you agree? Explain why or why not.

THINK ABOUT
- the description of an absolute monarch at the end of Section 1
- the ways in which Louis XIV fits that description
- any ways in which Louis XIV does not fit the description

4. ANALYZING THEMES

Economics How did the policies of Colbert and Louis XIV affect the French economy? Explain both positive and negative effects.

THINK ABOUT
- Colbert's attempts to make France self-sufficient
- what happened when Louis cancelled the Edict of Nantes
- the cost of Versailles and wars

Absolute Monarchs in Europe **523**

ANSWERS

1. TERMS & NAMES
Edict of Nantes, p. 518
Cardinal Richelieu, p. 518
skepticism, p. 519
Louis XIV, p. 519
intendant, p. 520
Jean Baptiste Colbert, p. 520
War of the Spanish Succession, p. 523

2. TAKING NOTES
Possible Responses: 1643 L. becomes king; 1648–1653 Riots disrupt F.; 1661 L. starts rule; 1667 L. invades Sp. Neth.; 1672 L. invades D. Neth.; 1685 L. voids Edict of Nantes; 1701–1713 L. fights War of Sp. Suc.; 1715 L. dies. Strengthen—1661, 1667, 1672; weaken—1648–1653, 1685, 1701–1713, 1715.

3. SUPPORTING OPINIONS
Possible Responses: Yes—regulated worship by voiding Edict of Nantes, weakened nobility by using intendants and making nobles live at court, built palace to show power, used mercantilist policies to control economy.

4. ANALYZING THEMES
Possible Responses: C.'s mercantilism helped economy by building up and protecting French industries. L. helped economy by using C.'s policies but hurt it by voiding Edict of Nantes, which drove out Huguenots, and by taxing and spending to fund building and wars.

Power Clothes

Traditionally, rulers have used clothing to show their status as monarchs. Past rulers frequently wore symbols that only rulers were allowed to wear. In addition, they often chose clothing that indicated wealth or military strength. For example, in one portrait Louis XIV of France wears the uniform of a Roman general to show his military might. As you study the following pictures, notice whether the rulers conveyed power through royal symbols, wealth, or military strength.

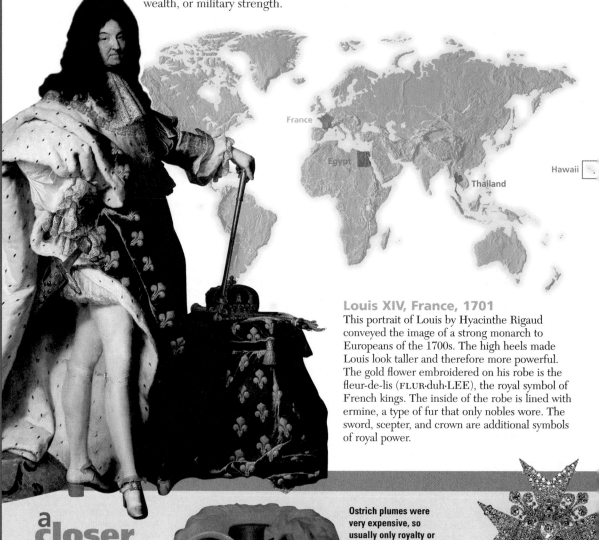

France

Egypt

Thailand

Hawaii

Louis XIV, France, 1701

This portrait of Louis by Hyacinthe Rigaud conveyed the image of a strong monarch to Europeans of the 1700s. The high heels made Louis look taller and therefore more powerful. The gold flower embroidered on his robe is the fleur-de-lis (FLUR·duh·LEE), the royal symbol of French kings. The inside of the robe is lined with ermine, a type of fur that only nobles wore. The sword, scepter, and crown are additional symbols of royal power.

a **closer look** LOUIS XIV

Ostrich plumes were very expensive, so usually only royalty or the nobility wore them. This plumed hat belonged to Louis.

CUSTOMIZING FOR SPECIAL NEEDS

Gifted and Talented Students Fashion became a major symbol of wealth and power in Europe in the 16th century. During the centuries of absolute monarchs, European capitals became centers of fashion extravagance. In part, this was the result of colonial expansion, which led to the importation of new and luxurious fabrics and dyes, as well as the acquisition of gold and silver to pay for them. Increasingly, merchants and other middle-class Europeans found that they were able to afford fine clothing.

At the same time, noble families tried to maintain their distinction from other social classes by restricting others from dressing luxuriously. Suggest that interested students research clothing styles worn by European nobles during the age of absolute monarchs. Have them report to the class on fashion trends of the 16th through 19th centuries and where and why those styles were popular.

Queen Hatshepsut, Egypt, 1490 B.C.

Although a woman, Hatshepsut ruled as pharaoh. This red granite statue shows her wearing two symbols of royal power—the false beard and the headdress with the asp (snake), both worn only by pharaohs.

High Chief Boki and his wife, Liliha; Hawaii, about 1824

In Hawaii, only male chiefs of high rank could wear feather garments, such as the cloak and helmets shown here. The red and yellow feathers came from birds native to the islands. Each cloak required about a half million feathers.

King Bhumibol Adulyadej, Thailand, 1990

Just as Louis XIV liked to dress as a Roman general, many modern rulers portray themselves as military leaders. Here King Bhumibol Adulyadej prays while wearing a white military uniform and rows of medals.

This is a copy of a diamond cross that Louis XIV had. The stones in the middle are set in the design of a dove. The dove's beak is a ruby.

This bust shows the elaborate wigs that French monarchs and nobles wore.

Connect to History

Clarifying Which of the rulers on this page wear clothing that displays wealth? military power? symbols that only rulers were allowed to wear?

 SEE SKILLBUILDER HANDBOOK, PAGE 992.

Connect to Today

Clarifying In today's world, many books and articles tell businesspeople how to dress to convey a sense of power. Find at least one of these books or articles and read to discover the main points of advice. List the main points and share them with the class.

Absolute Monarchs in Europe **525**

OBJECTIVES

1. To describe the Thirty Years' War.

2. To explain the growth of central European kingdoms.

3. To identify conflicts between Prussia and Austria.

SKILLBUILDER

- Interpreting maps: place, region, p. 527

CRITICAL THINKING

- Analyzing motives, p. 526
- Drawing conclusions, p. 527
- Contrasting, p. 528
- Clarifying, p. 529
- Making inferences, p. 530
- Recognizing effects, p. 530

FOCUS

5-Minute Warm-Up

▶ **Making Inferences**
Have students answer these questions to examine the relative merits of two absolute rulers in central Europe.

1. Read History Makers on page 529. Describe one domestic policy of each ruler.

2. What character trait of each ruler might have motivated each policy?

 WARM-UP TRANSPARENCY 21

OBJECTIVE ① INSTRUCT

The Thirty Years' War

▶ **Key Ideas**
- In 1618, Protestant and Catholic states in Germany go to war.
- The Thirty Years' War causes great destruction.
- The Peace of Westphalia ends the war in 1648, with major effects on central European states and their allies.

 IN-DEPTH RESOURCES: UNIT 5
Guided Reading, p. 3

 ACCESS FOR STUDENTS ACQUIRING ENGLISH
Guided Reading (Spanish), p. 210

3 Central European Monarchs Clash

MAIN IDEA	WHY IT MATTERS NOW
After a period of turmoil, absolute monarchs ruled Austria and the Germanic state of Prussia.	Prussia built a strong military tradition in Germany that contributed in part to world wars in the 20th century.

SETTING THE STAGE For a brief while, it appeared that the German rulers had settled their religious differences through the Peace of Augsburg (1555). They had agreed that the faith of each prince would determine the religion of his subjects. Churches in Germany could be either Lutheran or Catholic, but not Calvinist.

The Thirty Years' War

The peace was short-lived—soon to be replaced by a long war. After the Peace of Augsburg, the Catholic and Lutheran princes of Germany watched each other suspiciously. Each religion tried to gain followers. In addition, both sides felt threatened by Calvinism, which was spreading in Germany and gaining many followers. As tension mounted, the Lutherans joined together in the Protestant Union in 1608. The following year, the Catholic princes formed the Catholic League. Now, only a spark would set off a war.

Bohemian Protestants Revolt That spark came in 1618. The future Holy Roman emperor, Ferdinand II, was head of the Hapsburg family. As such, he ruled the Czech kingdom of Bohemia. The Protestants in Bohemia did not trust Ferdinand, who was a foreigner and a Catholic. When he closed some Protestant churches, the Protestants revolted. Ferdinand sent an army into Bohemia to crush the revolt. Several German Protestant princes took this chance to challenge their Catholic emperor.

Thus began the **Thirty Years' War**—a conflict over religion, over territory, and for power among European ruling families. Historians think of it as having two main phases: the phase of Hapsburg triumphs and the phase of Hapsburg defeats.

This engraving shows the siege of the German city of Magdeburg in 1631. The city was destroyed during the Thirty Years' War.

Hapsburg Triumphs The Thirty Years' War lasted from 1618 to 1648. During the first 12 years, Hapsburg armies from Austria and Spain crushed the troops hired by the Protestant princes. They succeeded in putting down the Czech uprising. They also defeated the German Protestants who had supported the Czechs.

Ferdinand II paid his army of 125,000 men by allowing them to plunder, or rob, German villages. This huge army destroyed everything in

A. Possible Answer
To punish Protestants who aided the Czech uprising.

THINK THROUGH HISTORY
A. Analyzing Motives Why did Ferdinand attack northern Germany?

SECTION 3 RESOURCES

PRINT RESOURCES

 IN-DEPTH RESOURCES: UNIT 5
Guided Reading, p. 3
Geography Application: Old Empires and New Powers, p. 7
History Makers: Maria Theresa, p. 16

 ACCESS FOR STUDENTS ACQUIRING ENGLISH
Guided Reading (Spanish), p. 210
Geography Application (Spanish), p. 214

FORMAL ASSESSMENT
Section Quiz, p. 241

ALTERNATIVE ASSESSMENT BOOK

TECHNOLOGY RESOURCES

CD-ROM
Electronic Library of Primary Sources

 INTERNET www.mlworldhistory.com

its path. The mayor of Magdeburg in northern Germany described the horrible
destruction of his city:

A VOICE FROM THE PAST
In this frenzied rage, the great and splendid city that had stood like a fair princess in the
land was now . . . given over to the flames, and thousands of innocent men, women,
and children, in the midst of a horrible din of heartrending shrieks and cries, were tortured and put to death in so cruel and shameful a manner that no words would suffice
to describe it nor no tears to bewail it.

OTTO VON GUERICKE, quoted in *Readings in European History*

Hapsburg Defeats The Protestant Gustavus Adolphus of Sweden and his disciplined
army of 13,000 shifted the tide of war in 1630. They drove the Hapsburg armies out of
northern Germany. However, Gustavus Adolphus was killed in battle in 1632.

Cardinal Richelieu and Cardinal Mazarin of France dominated the remaining years
of the war. Although Catholic, these two cardinals feared the Hapsburgs more than
the Protestants. They did not want other European rulers to have as much power as
the French king. Therefore, in 1635, Richelieu sent French troops to join the German
and Swedish Protestants in their struggle against the Hapsburg armies.

Peace of Westphalia The war did great damage to Germany. Its population dropped
from 20 million to about 16 million. Both trade and agriculture were disrupted, and
Germany's economy was ruined. Germany had a long, difficult recovery from this devastation. That is a major reason that it did not become a unified state until the 1800s.

The Peace of Westphalia (1648) ended the war and had important consequences.
First, it weakened the Hapsburg states of Spain and Austria. Second, it strengthened
France by awarding it German territory. Third, it made German princes independent of
the Holy Roman emperor. Fourth, it ended religious wars in Europe. Fifth, it introduced
a new method of peace negotiation. In that method, still used today, all participants meet
to settle the problems of a war and decide the terms of peace.

Europe After the Thirty Years' War, 1648

Population Losses During the War

GEOGRAPHY SKILLBUILDER: Interpreting Maps
1. **Place** Name at least five modern European countries that existed at the end of the Thirty Years' War.
2. **Region** Refer to the inset map. Which regions lost the most population in the Thirty Years' War?

The Hapsburgs, a royal German family, were one of the chief ruling dynasties of Europe from the 16th century to the 20th. Hapsburgs ruled Austria continuously from 1282 to 1918. They also ruled Hungary, Bohemia, Spain, and other lands. The Holy Roman Empire was under Hapsburg control from the mid-1400s until its disintegration in 1806.

OBJECTIVE ② INSTRUCT

Central Europe Differs from the West

Key Ideas
- The formation of states in central Europe occurs more slowly than in western Europe.
- Central European nobles hold down serfs and block the development of strong kings.
- The Holy Roman Empire loses strength after the Thirty Years' War, but Austria remains a powerful force in central Europe.

CRITICAL THINKING ACTIVITY
CLASS TIME: 10 MINUTES

Perceiving Causes and Effects
Have students fill in a chart like the one below, listing actions and effects that helped central European nobles maintain power.

Nobles' Power
Action: kept control over serfs
Effect: increased wealth
Action:
Effect:

Beginning of Modern States The treaty thus abandoned the idea of a Catholic empire that would rule most of Europe. It recognized Europe as a group of independent states that could negotiate for themselves. Each independent state was seen as essentially equal to the others. This marked the beginning of the modern state system and was the most important result of the Thirty Years' War.

Central Europe Differs from the West

The formation of strong states occurred more slowly in central Europe. The major powers of this region were the kingdom of Poland, the Holy Roman Empire, and the Ottoman Empire. None of them was well-organized in the mid-1600s.

Economic Contrasts One reason for this is that the economy of central Europe developed differently from that of western Europe. During the late Middle Ages, serfs in western Europe slowly won freedom and moved to towns. There, they joined middle-class townspeople, who gained economic power because of the commercial revolution and the development of capitalism. In turn, western European monarchs taxed the towns. They used the tax money to raise armies and reduce the influence of the nobility.

By contrast, the landowning aristocracy in central Europe passed laws restricting the ability of serfs to gain freedom and move to cities. These nobles wanted to keep the serfs on the land, where they could produce large harvests. The nobles could then sell the surplus crops to western European cities at great profit. To increase productivity, the aristocracy increased their control over their serfs. By 1700, Polish landowners could demand that their serfs work as much as six days a week. This left the serfs only one day a week to grow their own food.

Several Weak Empires The landowning nobles in central Europe not only held down the serfs but also blocked the development of strong kings. For example, the Polish nobility elected the Polish king and sharply limited his power. They allowed the king little income, no law courts, and no standing army.

The two empires of central Europe were also weak. Although Suleiman the Magnificent had conquered Hungary and threatened Vienna in 1529, the Ottoman Empire could not take its European conquest any farther. From then on the Ottoman Empire declined from its peak of power.

In addition, the Holy Roman Empire was seriously weakened by the Thirty Years' War. No longer able to command the obedience of the German states, the Holy Roman Empire had no real power. These old, weakened empires and kingdoms left a power vacuum in central Europe. In the late 1600s, two German-speaking families decided to try to fill this vacuum by becoming absolute rulers themselves.

This is the imperial crest of the Hapsburgs. It shows a double-headed eagle with a crown.

Austria Grows Stronger One of these families was the Hapsburgs of Austria. Even after the terrible losses in the Thirty Years' War, Austria remained the most powerful and important state within the Holy Roman Empire. The Austrian Hapsburgs took several steps to become absolute monarchs. First, during the Thirty Years' War, they reconquered Bohemia. The Hapsburgs wiped out Protestantism there and created a new Czech nobility that pledged loyalty to them. Second, after the war, the Hapsburg ruler centralized the government and created a standing army. Third, by 1699, the Hapsburgs had retaken Hungary from the Ottomans.

In 1711, Charles VI became the Hapsburg ruler. Charles's empire was a difficult one to rule. Within its borders lived a diverse assortment of people—Czechs, Hungarians, Italians, Croatians, and Germans. Only the fact that one Hapsburg ruler wore the Austrian, Hungarian, and Bohemian crowns kept the empire together.

Background
Western Europe included such countries as England, France, and the Netherlands.

THINK THROUGH HISTORY
C. Contrasting How did the economies of central and western Europe differ?
C. Answer Western Europe developed capitalism and towns, while central Europe remained more feudal.

Background
Bohemia was a kingdom. The Czechs were the people who lived there.

528 Chapter 21

TEACHING OPTION | **BLOCK SCHEDULING**

GEOGRAPHY APPLICATION ACTIVITY

CLASS TIME 20 MINUTES

Task: Students will list what they know about central Europe after the Thirty Years' War, determine what else they want to know, then complete a worksheet and note what they learned.

Materials Needed: Use the textbook and the Geography Application worksheet for Chapter 21.

Activity: On the board, write the following subject

headings: *Declining Powers* (Poland, Ottoman Empire, Holy Roman Empire) and *Rising Powers* (Austria, Prussia). Have students help you list under the headings what they know, based on textbook pages 528–529, about the situation in central Europe. Then have groups of students list questions they have about these subjects. Next they should study and complete the worksheet, also noting answers they

find to their own questions.

Conclusion: Under the headings on the board, have students help you list what they learned from the worksheet. Discuss questions still unanswered.

 IN-DEPTH RESOURCES: UNIT 5
Geography Application: Old Empires and New Powers, p. 7

Hapsburg ruler wore the Austrian, Hungarian, and Bohemian crowns kept the empire together.

Maria Theresa Inherits the Austrian Throne How could the Hapsburgs make sure that they continued to rule all those lands? Charles VI spent his entire reign working out an answer to this problem. By endless arm-twisting, he persuaded other leaders of Europe to sign an agreement that declared they would recognize Charles's eldest daughter as the heir to all his Hapsburg territories. That heir was a young woman named **Maria Theresa.** In theory, this agreement guaranteed Maria Theresa a peaceful reign. Instead, she faced years of war. Her main enemy was Prussia, a new state to the north of Austria.

Prussia and Austria Clash

Like Austria, Prussia rose to power in the late 1600s. Like the Hapsburgs of Austria, Prussia's ruling family, the Hohenzollerns, also had ambitions. Those ambitions threatened to upset central Europe's delicate balance of power.

Background
An elector was any of the German princes who helped elect the Holy Roman emperor.

The Rise of Prussia and Frederick the Great The Hohenzollerns built up their state from a number of small holdings—beginning with the German states of Brandenburg and Prussia. In 1640, a 20-year-old Hohenzollern named Frederick William inherited the title of elector of Brandenburg. After seeing the destruction of the Thirty Years' War, Frederick William, later known as the Great Elector, decided that having a strong army was the only way to ensure safety.

To protect their lands, the Great Elector and his descendants moved toward absolute monarchy. They created a standing army—the best in Europe. They built it to a force of 80,000 men. To pay for the army, they introduced permanent taxation. Beginning with the Great Elector's son, they called themselves kings. They also weakened the representative assemblies of their territories.

THINK THROUGH HISTORY
D. Clarifying
What steps did the Prussian monarchs take to become absolute monarchs?
D. Answer They created a standing army, limited the power of the nobles, and made military conquests.

Prussia's landowning nobility, the Junkers (YUNG-kuhrz), resisted the king's growing power. However, in the early 1700s, King Frederick William I bought their cooperation. He gave the Junkers the exclusive right to be officers in his army. Prussia became a rigidly controlled, military society.

Frederick William worried that his son, Frederick, was not military enough to rule. The prince loved music, philosophy, and poetry. In 1730, when he and a friend tried to run away, they were caught. To

HISTORY MAKERS

Maria Theresa
1717–1780

An able ruler, Maria Theresa also devoted herself to her family. Unlike many monarchs, she married for love. She gave birth to 16 children, 10 of whom reached adulthood.

Maria Theresa continued to advise her children even after they were grown. Perhaps her most famous child was Marie Antoinette, wife of Louis XVI of France. Maria Theresa often scolded Marie for spending too much money and making the French people angry.

As empress, Maria Theresa decreased the power of the nobility. Very religious, she cared more for the peasants' well-being than most rulers. She limited the amount of labor that nobles could force peasants to do. She argued: "The peasantry must be able to sustain itself."

Frederick the Great
1712–1786

Although they reigned during the same time, Frederick the Great and Maria Theresa were very different. Where Maria was religious, Frederick was practical and atheistic. Maria Theresa had a happy home life; Frederick married a woman whom he never cared for and neglected. Maria Theresa had a huge family; Frederick died without a son to succeed him.

An aggressor in foreign affairs, Frederick once wrote that "the fundamental role of governments is the principle of extending their territories." With regard to domestic affairs, he encouraged religious toleration and legal reform. Frederick earned the title "the Great" by achieving his goals for Prussia, in both domestic and foreign affairs.

Absolute Monarchs in Europe **529**

OBJECTIVE ③ INSTRUCT

Prussia and Austria Clash

▶ **Key Ideas**
• Under Hohenzollern rule, Prussia challenges Austrian power in central Europe.
• Prussian rulers Frederick William and Frederick the Great forge a military state that limits the power of the nobles.
• In the 1700s, Prussia battles Austria in wars that involve other European powers and produce mixed results.

⊙ **ELECTRONIC LIBRARY OF PRIMARY SOURCES**
from *Essay on Forms of Government*

HISTORY MAKERS
Maria Theresa and Frederick the Great

Maria Theresa was a highly religious, conservative ruler. Nevertheless, she promoted reforms that helped unify the Hapsburg domains. Ask students to find out more about this ruler, once called "the most human" of the Hapsburgs. They might want to consult Edward Crankshaw's biography *Maria Theresa.*

Considered one of history's great military leaders, Frederick the Great also earned a reputation as an enlightened monarch, supporting education, religious tolerance, and the rule of law. Encourage students to research and discuss Frederick's life and accomplishments. They might find useful information in *Frederick the Great* by Nancy Mitford.

📑 ***IN-DEPTH RESOURCES: UNIT 5***
History Makers: Maria Theresa, p. 16

TEACHING OPTION

CONNECTIONS ACROSS THE CURRICULUM

Art, Music, and Literature The chief artistic style in central Europe after the Thirty Years' War is known as the baroque. Baroque artists tried to capture the sense of drama and immediacy evoked by the massive political and cultural upheavals of the time.

Baroque art originated in Italy in the late 1500s as an expression of the Counter Reformation. The Roman Catholic Church, to counter the spread of Protestantism, encouraged artists to create works that would inspire renewed devotion in its followers by appealing directly to their senses and emotions. Church ceilings were painted with convincing views of saints and angels rising through limitless space, as if to open heaven to the eyes of the congregation.

By the mid-1600s the baroque had become the dominant style at royal courts throughout Europe. It met the demand of absolute monarchs for art and architecture whose monumental scale and sensuous richness would overwhelm people and symbolize the grandeur and power of the centralized state.

Invite students to find out more about baroque art, music, and literature and to bring examples to class.

CONNECT *to* TODAY
Quebec Separatists

Have students find out more about French culture in Quebec and the issues involved in the separatist movement. Ask students to make a list of these issues and discuss their implications for Canada.

MORE ABOUT . . .
Silesia

Silesia has long been a pawn in central European conflicts. Originally a Polish province, it passed to Bohemia, then to Austria, then to Prussia. Germany occupied the region during World War II. Later, Silesia was returned to Poland.

ASSESS & RETEACH

Section 3 Assessment

Ask pairs of students to share their responses to items 3 and 4 and to revise their answers based on any new insights or information.

Section Quiz

 FORMAL ASSESSMENT
Section Quiz, p. 241

Reteaching Activity

CLASS TIME: 10 MINUTES

Use the Compare and Contrast graphic organizer transparency to go over the answers to item 2 in the assessment.

 CRITICAL THINKING TRANSPARENCIES
CT74 Compare and Contrast

CLOSE ACTIVITY

CLASS TIME: 20 MINUTES

Perceiving Causes and Effects

Have groups of three students create a cause-effect chart on key developments in central Europe in the 17th and 18th centuries. The chart should have three main column headings: *Thirty Years' War, Weak Powers,* and *Rise of Prussia and Austria.* Each group member should chart causes and effects related to a different heading. Students might then display and discuss their charts.

CONNECT *to* TODAY

Quebec Separatists

In North America, the Seven Years' War was called the French and Indian War. As a result of this war, the British took over France's American colonies. Today Canada has a large French-speaking population, many of whom believe that they should be independent from Canada. A demonstration for independence is shown above.

In 1995, Quebec voters narrowly rejected a vote for independence. Before the vote was taken, Jacques Parizeau, then Quebec's premier and leader of the secessionist movement, said, "We, the people of Quebec, through our National Assembly, proclaim: Quebec is a sovereign [independent] country." Although the vote did not make Parizeau's declaration come true, separation continues to be an important issue in Quebec.

punish Frederick, the king ordered him to witness his friend's beheading. Despite such bitter memories, Frederick II, known as **Frederick the Great,** followed his father's military policies when he came to power. However, he also softened some of his father's laws, because he believed that a ruler should be like a father to his people:

A VOICE FROM THE PAST

A prince . . . is only the first servant of the state, who is obliged to act with probity [honesty] and prudence. . . . As the sovereign is properly the head of a family of citizens, the father of his people, he ought on all occasions to be the last refuge of the unfortunate.

FREDERICK II, *Essay on Forms of Government*

War of the Austrian Succession In 1740, Maria Theresa succeeded her father, just five months after Frederick II became king of Prussia. Frederick wanted the Austrian land of Silesia, which bordered Prussia. Silesia produced iron ore, textiles, and food products. Frederick assumed that because Maria Theresa was a woman, she would not be forceful enough to defend her lands. In 1740, he sent his army to occupy Silesia, beginning the War of the Austrian Succession.

Even though Maria Theresa had recently given birth, she journeyed to Hungary. There she held her infant in her arms as she asked the Hungarian nobles for aid. Even though the nobles resented their Hapsburg rulers, they pledged to give Maria Theresa an army. Great Britain also joined Austria to fight its longtime enemy France, which was Prussia's ally. Although Maria Theresa did stop Prussia's aggression, she lost Silesia at the Treaty of Aix-la-Chapelle in 1748.

The Seven Years' War Maria Theresa decided that the French kings were no longer Austria's chief enemies. She made an alliance with them. The result was a diplomatic revolution. When Frederick heard of her actions, he signed a treaty with Britain—Austria's former ally. Now, Austria, France, Russia, and others were allied against Britain and Prussia. Not only had Austria and Prussia switched allies, but for the first time Russia was playing a role in European affairs.

In 1756, Frederick attacked Saxony, an Austrian ally. Soon every great European power was involved in the war. Fought in Europe, India, and North America, the war lasted until 1763. It was called the **Seven Years' War.** The war did not change the territorial situation in Europe.

It was a different story on other continents. Both France and Britain had colonies in North America and the West Indies. Both were competing economically in India. The

THINK THROUGH HISTORY
E. Making Inferences Why would iron ore, agriculture, and textiles be helpful acquisitions for Frederick the Great?
E. Possible Answer Frederick needed to feed and clothe his troops and supply them with weapons. Also, by gaining these resources through conquest, he freed more of his own citizens to be in the army.

Section ③ Assessment

1. TERMS & NAMES

Identify
- Thirty Years' War
- Maria Theresa
- Frederick the Great
- Seven Years' War

2. TAKING NOTES

On a chart like the one shown, compare Maria Theresa and Frederick the Great.

Points of Comparison	Maria Theresa	Frederick the Great
years of reign		
foreign policy		
success in war		
their policies as monarchs		

3. RECOGNIZING EFFECTS

Name several ways that the Peace of Westphalia laid the foundations of modern Europe.

THINK ABOUT
- religious effects
- diplomatic effects
- political effects

4. THEME ACTIVITY

Power and Authority Write an outline for a lecture on "How to Increase Royal Power and Become an Absolute Monarch." In your outline, jot down examples that support your main points. The examples should be of Hapsburg and Hohenzollern actions that increased the power of those ruling families.

ANSWERS

1. TERMS & NAMES

Thirty Years' War, p. 526
Maria Theresa, p. 529
Frederick the Great, p. 529
Seven Years' War, p. 530

2. TAKING NOTES

Possible Responses: **Years of reign:** M. T.—1740–1780; F.—1740–1786. **Foreign policy:** M. T. allied with former enemy France; F. allied with Austria's former ally Britain. **Success in war:** M. T. lost Silesia in War of Aus. Suc. and did not regain it in 7 Years' War; F. gained Silesia in War of Aus. Suc. and neither gained nor lost in 7 Years' War. **Steps to become absolute monarchs:** M. T. imposed limits on nobility; F. followed his father's military policies.

3. RECOGNIZING EFFECTS

Possible Responses: Ended religious wars, allowing Europe to split into Catholic and Protestant areas; weakened Holy Roman Empire; recognized Europe as collection of independent states; began modern way of negotiating.

4. THEME ACTIVITY

Standards for Evaluation
An outline should
- be organized logically
- support key points with examples
- draw examples from Hapsbu or Hohenzollern history

4 Russian Czars Increase Power

TERMS & NAMES
- Ivan the Terrible
- boyars
- Peter the Great
- westernization

MAIN IDEA

Peter the Great made many changes in Russia to try to make it more like western Europe.

WHY IT MATTERS NOW

Many Russians today debate whether to model themselves on the West or to focus on traditional Russian culture.

SETTING THE STAGE Ivan III of Moscow, who ruled Russia from 1462 to 1505, accomplished several things. First, he conquered much of the territory around Moscow. Second, he liberated Russia from the Mongols. Third, he began to centralize the Russian government. This laid the foundation for the absolute monarchy that would come later.

From Ivan to the Romanovs

Ivan III was succeeded by his son, Vasily, who ruled for 28 years. Vasily continued his father's work of adding territory to the growing Russian state. He also increased the power of the central government, a trend that would continue under his son, Ivan IV.

The First Czar Ivan IV, called **Ivan the Terrible,** came to the throne in 1533 when he was only three years old. His young life was disrupted by struggles for power among Russia's landowning nobles, known as **boyars.** The boyars fought to control young Ivan. When he was 16, Ivan seized power and had himself crowned czar. This title meant "caesar," and Ivan was the first Russian ruler to use it officially. He also married the beautiful Anastasia, related to an old boyar family, the Romanovs.

The years from 1547 to 1560 are often called Ivan's "good period." He won great victories, added lands to Russia, gave Russia a code of laws, and ruled justly.

Rule by Terror Ivan's "bad period" began in 1560 after Anastasia died. Accusing the boyars of poisoning his wife, Ivan turned against them. He organized his own police force, whose chief duty was to hunt down and murder people Ivan considered traitors. The members of this police force dressed in black and rode black horses.

Using these secret police, Ivan executed many boyars, their families, and the peasants who worked their lands. Thousands of people died. Ivan seized the boyars' estates and gave them to a new class of nobles, who had to remain loyal to him or lose their land. One noble, Prince Kurbsky, described the suffering Ivan caused him:

Background
Prince Kurbsky was an adviser to Ivan and also won many battles for him. When Ivan turned against him, Kurbsky fled to Lithuania.

A VOICE FROM THE PAST
In front of your army have I marched—and marched again; and no dishonor have I brought upon you, but only brilliant victories. . . . But to you, O czar, was all this as naught; rather do you show us your intolerable wrath and bitterest hatred, and furthermore, burning stoves [a means of torture].
PRINCE ANDREW KURBSKY, letter to Czar Ivan IV

This portrait of Ivan IV is painted in the style of Russian icons. Perhaps this style was chosen to encourage deep respect for Ivan—who believed in his divine right to rule.

Absolute Monarchs in Europe **531**

SECTION 4 RESOURCES

PRINT RESOURCES

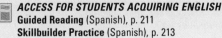
IN-DEPTH RESOURCES: UNIT 5
Guided Reading, p. 4
Skillbuilder Practice: Evaluating Decisions, p. 6
Primary Source: Peter the Great's Reforms, p. 10

ACCESS FOR STUDENTS ACQUIRING ENGLISH
Guided Reading (Spanish), p. 211
Skillbuilder Practice (Spanish), p. 213

FORMAL ASSESSMENT
Section Quiz, p. 242

TECHNOLOGY RESOURCES

WORLD ART AND CULTURES TRANSPARENCIES
AT46 *Peter I the Great*
AT47 *Saint Basil's Cathedral*

CRITICAL THINKING TRANSPARENCIES
CT21 *The Age of Absolute Monarchs, 1500–1800*

CD-ROM
Electronic Library of Primary Sources

INTERNET www.mlworldhistory.com

Section 4 Overview

OBJECTIVES

(1) To explain how Ivan III and later Russian rulers began to build a stronger Russian state.

(2) To characterize differences between Russia and western Europe and the emerging role of Peter the Great.

(3) To describe Peter's reforms and their impact on Russia.

SKILLBUILDER
- Interpreting maps: location, region, p. 533

CRITICAL THINKING
- Recognizing effects, p. 532
- Summarizing, p. 532
- Recognizing bias, p. 533
- Synthesizing, pp. 534, 535
- Supporting opinions, p. 535
- Analyzing themes, p. 535

FOCUS
5-Minute Warm-Up

▶ *Evaluating*
To understand how the foundation was laid for the absolute monarchy, in Russia, have students answer these questions.

1. Read Setting the Stage on page 531. What were three key accomplishments of Ivan III?

2. Which of these accomplishments was most essential to developing an absolute monarchy?

WARM-UP TRANSPARENCY 21

OBJECTIVE (1) INSTRUCT

From Ivan to the Romanovs

▶ *Key Ideas*
- A series of Russian czars, including Ivan the Terrible, tries to strengthen the Russian state and reduce the power of the boyars, or nobles.
- After an initial "good" period, Ivan creates a ruthless police state and persecutes all who oppose him.

(continued on next page)

Teacher's Edition **531**

(continued from page 531)

- Russia enters the Time of Troubles after Ivan's death, but Romanov rulers restore order.

 IN-DEPTH RESOURCES: UNIT 5
Guided Reading, p. 4

 ACCESS FOR STUDENTS ACQUIRING ENGLISH
Guided Reading (Spanish), p. 211

 WORLD ART AND CULTURES TRANSPARENCIES
AT47 Saint Basil's Cathedral

OBJECTIVE ② INSTRUCT

Peter the Great Takes the Throne

▶ **Key Ideas**
- In 1696 Peter the Great becomes sole ruler of Russia.
- Russia is still a land of nobles and serfs, isolated and backward.
- Peter visits western Europe to study its customs and technology.

HISTORYMAKERS
Peter the Great

Peter avoided the pomp and splendor of earlier czars. He also had a tremendous temper. He was known to beat his officials with a stick. Have students find out how Peter's oldest son died. *He was sentenced to death for opposing Peter's reforms, but he died in prison before the execution.*

 WORLD ART AND CULTURES TRANSPARENCIES
AT46 Peter I the Great Interrogating the Czarevich at Peterhof

 ELECTRONIC LIBRARY OF PRIMARY SOURCES
from Letters of Peter the Great and His Son Alexis

Eventually, Ivan committed an act that was both a personal tragedy and a national disaster. In 1581, during a violent quarrel, he killed his oldest son and heir. When Ivan died three years later, only his weak second son was left to rule.

Rise of the Romanovs Ivan's son proved to be physically and mentally incapable of ruling. After he died without an heir, Russia experienced a period of turmoil known as the Time of Troubles. Boyars struggled for power, and heirs of czars died under mysterious conditions. Several imposters tried to claim the throne.

Finally, in 1613, representatives from many Russian cities met to choose the next czar. Their choice was Michael Romanov, grandnephew of Ivan the Terrible's wife Anastasia. Thus began the Romanov dynasty, which ruled Russia for 300 years (1613–1917).

Peter the Great Takes the Throne

Over time, the Romanovs restored order to Russia. They strengthened government by passing a law code and putting down a revolt. This paved the way for the absolute rule of Czar Peter I. At first, Peter shared the throne with a feeble-minded half-brother. However, in 1696, Peter became sole ruler of Russia. He is known to history as **Peter the Great,** because he was one of Russia's greatest reformers. He also continued the trend of increasing the czar's power.

HISTORY MAKERS

Peter the Great
1672–1725

Peter the Great had the mind of a genius, the body of a giant, and the ferocious temper of a bear. One could not help but look up to Peter, who stood about 6 feet 8 inches tall. He was so strong that he was known to take a heavy silver plate and roll it up as if it were a piece of paper.

Peter had a good, if crude, sense of humor and loved to make practical jokes. But heaven help the person who crossed his path. If someone annoyed him, he would take his massive fist and knock the offender unconscious. If he were angrier, he would have the person's nostrils torn out with iron pincers.

Although Peter saw himself as a father to his people, he was cruel to his own family. When his oldest son opposed him, he had him imprisoned and killed.

Russia's Differences from Europe When Peter I came to power, Russia was still a land of boyars and serfs. Serfdom in Russia lasted much longer than it did in western Europe. Serfdom continued in Russia into the mid-1800s. When a Russian landowner sold a piece of land, he sold the serfs with it. Landowners could give serfs away as presents or to pay debts. It was also against the law for serfs to run away from their owners.

Most boyars knew little of western Europe. In the Middle Ages, Russia had looked to Constantinople, not to Rome, for leadership. Then Mongol rule had cut Russia off from the Renaissance and the Age of Exploration. Geographic barriers also isolated Russia. Its only seaport, Archangel, was choked with ice much of the year. The few travelers who reached Moscow were usually Dutch or German, and they had to stay in a separate part of the city.

Religious differences widened the gap between western Europe and Russia. The Russians had adopted the Eastern Orthodox branch of Christianity. Western Europeans were mostly Catholics or Protestants, and the Russians viewed them as heretics and avoided them.

Peter Visits the West In the 1680s, people in the German quarter of Moscow were accustomed to seeing the young Peter striding through their neighborhood on his long legs. (Peter was more than six and a half feet tall.) He was fascinated by the modern tools and machines in the foreigners' shops. Above all, he had a passion for ships and the sea. The young czar believed that Russia's future depended on having a warm-water port. Only then could Russia compete with the more modern states of western Europe.

Peter was 24 years old when he became sole ruler of Russia. In 1697, just one year later, he embarked on the "Grand Embassy," a long visit to western Europe. Peter's goal was to learn about European customs and industrial techniques. With him were 200 servants and 55 boyars. Never before had a czar traveled among Western "heretics."

On his journey, Peter insisted on keeping his identity a secret. He went to the Netherlands in the plain clothes of an ordinary worker

THINK THROUGH HISTORY
A. Recognizing Effects What were the long-term effects of Ivan's murder of his oldest son?
A. Answer First Russia was ruled by a weak czar, then it experienced turmoil as several struggled to gain power, and finally the Romanov dynasty was established.

THINK THROUGH HISTORY
B. Summarizing Restate the main reasons that Russia was culturally different from western Europe.
B. Answers It had a feudal rather than a commercial economy; it had been influenced by Constantinople and the Mongols; it followed a different form of Christianity.

TEACHING OPTION | **BLOCK SCHEDULING** | **SKILLBUILDER MINI-LESSON: Evaluating Decisions** | **CLASS TIME 15 MINUTES**

Explaining the Skill Historians evaluate decisions of the past partly by looking at the short-term and long-term consequences of those decisions. Students might evaluate their own decisions similarly. They might at first be glad they took an after-school job because of the extra spending money it brings. But that decision might not seem as good after their grades slip because they have less time to study.

Applying the Skill: *Evaluating Peter's Decision to Westernize Russia* Have students read about Peter's steps to westernize Russia on pages 533 and 535. Then ask these questions:
1. What were some key short-term effects of the decision to westernize Russia? *Possible responses: The Russian army was trained in western tactics; and St. Petersburg was built.*
2. What were some key long-term effects? *Possible response: Russia could compete militarily and*

commercially with western Europe.
3. Was the decision to westernize a good one? Why or why not? *Possible responses: Yes, because it helped make Russia a great European power; no, because westernizing the military required imposing heavy taxes, and building St. Petersburg cost many lives.*

 IN-DEPTH RESOURCES: UNIT 5
Skillbuilder Practice: Evaluating Decisions, p. 6

and labored as a ship's carpenter for four months. However, a Russian giant in a Dutch seaport attracted attention. Word of his identity soon spread. Yet if a fellow worker addressed him as "Your Majesty" or "Sire," he would not answer. After all, he was just plain "Carpenter Peter." Peter also visited England and Austria before returning home.

Peter Rules Absolutely

Inspired by his trip to the West, Peter resolved that Russia would compete with Europe on both military and commercial terms. Peter's goal of **westernization,** of using western Europe as a model for change, was not an end in itself. Peter saw it as a way to make Russia stronger.

Peter's Reforms Although Peter believed Russia needed to change, he knew that many of his people disagreed. As he said to one official, "For you know yourself that, though a thing be good and necessary, our people will not do it unless forced to." To force change upon his state, Peter increased his powers as an absolute ruler.

Peter brought the Russian Orthodox church under state control. He abolished the office of patriarch, head of the church. He set up a group called the Holy Synod to run the church—under his direction.

Like Ivan the Terrible, Peter reduced the power of the great landowners. He recruited able men from lower-ranking families. He then promoted them to positions of authority and rewarded them with grants of land. Because these men owed everything to the czar, they were loyal to him alone.

To modernize his army, Peter hired European officers, who drilled his soldiers in European tactics with European weapons. Being a soldier became a lifetime job. By the time of Peter's death, the Russian army numbered 200,000 men. To pay for this huge army, Peter imposed heavy taxes.

THINK THROUGH HISTORY
C. Recognizing Bias Judging from this remark, what was Peter's view of his people?
C. Possible Answers That they were backward and stubborn; that they were wrong and he was right.

CONNECT *to* TODAY

Russia: East vs. West
Peter's reforms sparked the beginning of a debate in Russia that continues today—whether to westernize or to focus on Russian culture. The breakup of the Soviet Union in 1991 has led to developments in both directions.

Many ethnic groups have established individual republics or are striving to do so. On the other hand, Russia and other former Soviet countries are experimenting with democracy and a market economy. These are distinctly Western traditions.

Because Russia straddles two continents—Asia and Europe—the tension between East and West will probably be an enduring part of its culture.

OBJECTIVE ③ INSTRUCT

Peter Rules Absolutely

▶ **Key Ideas**
• Peter decides to westernize Russia so it can compete with western Europe.
• He places religion under state control, limits nobles' power, and modernizes the army.
• He gains territory on the Baltic Sea and builds the warm-water seaport St. Petersburg to gain easier access to the West.

📑 **IN-DEPTH RESOURCES: UNIT 5**
Primary Source: Peter the Great's Reforms, p. 10

🗂 **CRITICAL THINKING TRANSPARENCIES**
CT21 The Age of Absolute Monarchs, 1500–1800

CONNECT *to* TODAY
Russia: East vs. West

Have students find out about nationalist sentiments in Russia since the fall of communism. What issues are involved? Which way does Russia seem to be going: toward the West or back to its traditions?

History from Visuals

The Expansion of Russia, 1500–1800

Interpreting the Map Point out that the colored areas on the map correspond to periods of Russian expansion identified in the key. By what year had Russia gained land on the Arctic Ocean? *1505.* To what major body of water did Ivan IV, who ruled from 1533 to 1584, gain access? *Caspian Sea.*

(continued on next page)

The Expansion of Russia, 1500–1800

Key:
- 1462
- Acquisitions to 1505
- Acquisitions to 1584
- Acquisitions to 1682
- Acquisitions to 1725
- Acquisitions to 1796

Labels on map: ARCTIC OCEAN, FINLAND, SWEDEN, St. Petersburg, Novgorod, Moscow, Warsaw, Kiev, POLAND, AUSTRIA, Azov, Constantinople, OTTOMAN EMPIRE, Black Sea, Caspian Sea, Mediterranean Sea, RUSSIA, Ob R., Yenisei R., Lena R., Volga R., Ural R., Dnieper R., Dniester R., Tomsk, Irkutsk, Nerchinsk, Amur R., MONGOLIA, MANCHURIA, Yakutsk, Okhotsk, Sea of Okhotsk, PACIFIC OCEAN

0 1,000 Miles
0 2,000 Kilometers

GEOGRAPHY SKILLBUILDER: Interpreting Maps
1. **Location** Locate the territories that Peter added to Russia during his reign, from 1682 to 1725. What bodies of water did Russia gain access to because of these acquisitions?
2. **Region** Who added a larger amount of territory to Russia—Ivan III, who ruled from 1462 to 1505, or Peter the Great?

TEACHING OPTION | **BLOCK SCHEDULING** | **COOPERATIVE ACTIVITY: Reporting on Modernization** | **CLASS TIME 30 MINUTES**

Task: Students will research other countries that have struggled with issues of modernization and give an oral report on their findings.

Purpose: To become more aware of the tensions and difficulties involved in modern nation building.

Activity: Begin by asking students what, based on their reading about Peter the Great, they think modernization means. *Students might say that it means adopting the latest technique, technology, or style or simply bringing society up to date.* Point out that modernization generally involves moving away from traditional values toward impersonal, practical ones, such as gathering scientific knowledge and applying it to technology so that goods and services can be produced more efficiently.

Have groups of students give an oral report on one of these modernizing countries: Japan during the Meiji period, Turkey under Atatürk, or Iran under Reza Shah Pahlavi. Students should describe how modernization affected the country's political system, economy, customs and social structure, environment, and arts.

 ALTERNATIVE ASSESSMENT BOOK
Standards for Evaluating a Cooperative Activity

Teacher's Edition 533

Extension Activity Ask students to name the five settlements on the map that were established in the territory Peter gained east of the Ob River. *Tomsk, Irkutsk, Nerchinsk, Yakutsk, Okhotsk.* Have students find out how Russians won and settled this region.

SKILLBUILDER Answers
1. Baltic Sea; Sea of Okhotsk, Pacific Ocean
2. Peter the Great

Daily *Life*
Russia, 1700

Peter introduced Western dress, customs, and usages to Russia often by force and against strong opposition. Yet by the end of his reign, members of the civil service, military, aristocracy, and to some extent even the middle class were clean-shaven and wore Western dress. Other Western innovations also won wide acceptance with time.

MORE ABOUT . . .
Personal Appearance

The shaving of beards came to symbolize Peter's reign. He actually shaved some boyars and officials himself. Traditionalists objected to shaving because they thought it impaired the image of God in men and made men look like cats, dogs, or monkeys. Peter also prohibited Russians from wearing the traditional long coat. In some cases, he cut the bottoms off nobles' coats.

MORE ABOUT . . .
Moscow

When Peter transferred the capital from Moscow to St. Petersburg, Moscow suffered not only a loss of status but also a "brain drain." Nobles were forced to move to St. Petersburg, and many merchants and artisans also moved. Population growth and new building slowed for a time, but later in Peter's reign, the city began to recover. Peter himself spurred new economic growth in Moscow by setting up new industries—such as a textile mill for making sailcloth—which encouraged private entrepreneurs to follow suit.

Daily *Life:* Russia, 1700

New Russian News

Your Money or Your Beard

About a year ago, as part of his attempt to westernize Russia, Peter the Great decided that the Russian custom of wearing beards showed too much Mongol influence. Our modernizing czar offered most men a hard choice: shave their beards, or plunk down money to keep their whiskers. Those who paid the beard tax received a token (shown below) to prove that they had the right to have hairy faces.

Peter's beard tax ranged from a sixth of a kopeck for a peasant to one hundred rubles a year for a wealthy merchant. The rich had to pay 60,000 times as much as the poor!

Now that the policy has been in effect for a year, the results are in. Most peasants and merchants and all priests and monks chose to pay rather than shave. All soldiers, officers, and court officials are clean-shaven for a good reason: Peter didn't give them a choice.

Winter Happenings: Moscow

It takes more than sub-zero temperatures to keep hardy Russians home. While some people brave the frigid air to sell their wares or to shop, others find delight at the fair.

Yesterday's outdoor market featured the rock-hard frozen carcasses of cows, sheep, pigs, and chickens piled into pyramidlike heaps. On hand-pulled sleds, shoppers carted home their purchases of meat, butter, eggs, and fish.

This winter scene shows bustling activity in Ivan the Great Square in Moscow.

Clowns, magicians, jugglers, and musicians entertained at the outdoor fair. For the athletic, there was an ice-skating rink, as well as a 35-foot ice hill to delight sledders. Dizzy visitors swung back and forth in boats suspended from a wooden frame.

Happy New Year!

Forward-looking Russians are celebrating the new year with festivities in January—instead of waiting until September, as their grandparents would have done. Just last month, Peter the Great decreed that Russia would adopt the calendar used by western Europe. He ushered in the calendar change with a fireworks display and a week of public feasting.

Build It Today, Move in Tomorrow

Need a new house or a replacement part for your current dwelling? Check out the carpenter's market at the end of any major street. There you'll find logs cut in a variety of lengths and widths and marked for easy assembly. In addition, ready-made beams, roof shingles, and door and window frames are also offered for sale.

With a little help from your friends, you can move into your new house in almost no time at all. Some tips for keeping that new house cozy in the winter:

- Buy windows with double glass.
- Keep ceilings low.
- Stuff the spaces between the logs with moss.
- Make a steep roof so that snow will slide off.

534 Chapter 21

Connect *to* History

Synthesizing How have Russians adapted to their cold climate? Discuss transportation, housing, and activities.

SEE SKILLBUILDER
HANDBOOK, PAGE 1007

Connect *to* Today

Researching At the library, research the records of the winter Olympics for the last 20 years to learn what events Russians (or Soviets) participated in and how many they won. What winter sports do modern Russians like and excel at?

Connect *to* History

Synthesizing
Possible Response: They have used sleds, built houses that withstand the cold and snow, and engaged in ice skating and other sports appropriate to cold-weather conditions.

Connect *to* Today

Researching
For records on the winter Olympics, suggest that students consult the sports section of a world almanac or the latest edition of *The Information*

Please Sports Almanac, which is available in both book and on-line formats.

Westernizing Russia As part of his attempts to westernize Russia, Peter

- introduced potatoes, which became a staple of the Russian diet
- started Russia's first newspaper and edited its first issue himself
- raised women's status by having them attend social gatherings
- ordered the nobles to give up their traditional clothes for Western fashions

Peter also believed education was a key to Russia's progress. In his journal, Peter (referring to himself as "the Czar") described his efforts to advance learning:

A VOICE FROM THE PAST

A school of marine [navigation] was opened, and schools for the other arts and sciences began to be introduced gradually. . . . At the same time the Czar permitted his subjects to leave the country in order to study the sciences in foreign lands. This was forbidden in former times under pain of death, but now not only was permission given for it but many were forced to undertake it.

CZAR PETER I, quoted in *Peter the Great*, edited by L. Jay Oliva

A New Capital To promote education and growth, Peter wanted a seaport that would make it easier to travel to the West. Therefore, Peter fought Sweden to gain a piece of the Baltic coast. After 21 long years of war, Russia finally won the "window on the sea" that Peter wanted.

Actually, Peter had secured that window many years before Sweden officially surrendered it. In 1703 he began building a new city on Swedish lands occupied by Russian troops. Although the swampy site was unhealthful, it seemed ideal to Peter. Ships could sail down the Neva River into the Baltic Sea and on to western Europe. Peter called the city St. Petersburg, after his patron saint.

 This 1753 painting shows a view of St. Petersburg from the water. The ships indicate that it did become a booming port, as Peter had wanted.

To build a city on a desolate swamp was no easy matter. Every summer, the army forced thousands of luckless serfs to leave home and work at St. Petersburg. An estimated 25,000 to 100,000 people died from the terrible working conditions and widespread diseases. When St. Petersburg was finished, Peter ordered many Russian nobles to leave the comforts of Moscow and settle in his new capital.

For better or for worse, Peter the Great had tried to reform the culture and government of Russia. To an amazing extent he had succeeded. By the time of his death in 1725, Russia was a power to be reckoned with in Europe. Meanwhile, another great European power, England, had been developing a form of government that limited the power of absolute monarchs, as you will see in Section 5.

D. Possible Answer He ordered peasants to work there, and he ordered nobles to move there.

THINK THROUGH HISTORY
D. Synthesizing Which of Peter's actions in the building of St. Petersburg demonstrate his power as an absolute monarch?

Section 4 Assessment

1. TERMS & NAMES
Identify
- Ivan the Terrible
- boyars
- Peter the Great
- westernization

2. TAKING NOTES
On a cluster diagram like the one shown, list the important events of Peter the Great's reign.

Peter the Great

3. SUPPORTING OPINIONS
Do you think Ivan the Terrible or Peter the Great was more of an absolute monarch? Explain the standards by which you made your decision.

THINK ABOUT
- ways that each increased the power of the Russian czar
- long term effects of each one's rule

4. ANALYZING THEMES
Power and Authority Which of Peter the Great's actions reveal that he saw himself as the highest authority in Russia? Explain.

THINK ABOUT
- steps he took to reduce the authority of others
- actions that overturned traditional sources of authority in Russia

Absolute Monarchs in Europe **535**

MORE ABOUT . . .
St. Petersburg

St. Petersburg was the first planned city in Russia. Peter insisted that the streets be broad, straight, paved with stone, and lined with houses built flush with the streets to form a continuous façade that would impress on-lookers. Houses were required to conform to standard patterns—one for each social class—drawn up by official architects. By Peter's death, more than 1,000 experts from western Europe, including architects, sculptors, painters, and gardeners —along with con-scripted Russian peasants and Swedish prisoners of war—had made St. Petersburg one of the wonders of Europe.

ASSESS & RETEACH

Section 4 Assessment
Suggest that students jot down important points that they want to include in each response before they write their final responses.

Section Quiz
FORMAL ASSESSMENT
Section Quiz, p. 242

Reteaching Activity
CLASS TIME: 10 MINUTES

Have pairs of students work together to answer item 3. Each partner should address a different point to think about. Then partners should pool their information to write a final answer.

CLOSE ACTIVITY

CLASS TIME: 15 MINUTES

Summarizing
Ask students to identify the reforms Peter the Great made to westernize Russia. List the reforms on the board. Then call on students to explain each reform and its significance.

ANSWERS

1. TERMS & NAMES
Ivan the Terrible, p. 531
boyars, p. 531
Peter the Great, p. 532
westernization, p. 533

2. TAKING NOTES
Possible Responses: Visited western Europe; took control of church; reduced power of landowners; modernized army; tried to westernize Russia; fought Sweden for Baltic land; had St. Petersburg built

3. SUPPORTING OPINIONS
Possible Responses: **Ivan**—Took title *czar*, which means "caesar"; expanded Russia; gave law code; organized his own police force; persecuted boyars; created new class of nobles. Aimed to increase and protect his own power more than to improve Russia. **Peter**—Took control of church; reduced power of landowners; strengthened army; imposed heavy taxes; forced nobles to move to St. Petersburg. Made reforms whether people wanted them or not.

4. ANALYZING THEMES
Possible Responses: Showed he saw himself above church by taking control of it; showed he saw himself above nobility by weakening it and forcing it to westernize; showed he saw himself above tradition by forcing Western customs on Russia.

Teacher's Edition **535**

1. To identify conflicts between English rulers and Parliament.

2. To explain the causes and results of the English Civil War.

3. To describe the Restoration and Glorious Revolution.

4. To explain political changes under William and Mary.

SKILLBUILDER

- Interpreting maps: movement, place, p. 537

CRITICAL THINKING

- Making inferences, p. 537
- Comparing, p. 537
- Contrasting, p. 539
- Evaluating decisions, p. 539

FOCUS

5-Minute Warm-Up

▶ **Predicting**

To examine the conflict between English rulers and Parliament, have students answer these questions.

1. Read Setting the Stage on page 536. What power of the English Parliament helped keep English rulers from becoming absolute monarchs?

2. How might Parliament have used its financial power to stop an English ruler from seizing absolute power?

 WARM-UP TRANSPARENCY 21

OBJECTIVE 1 INSTRUCT

Monarchs Clash with Parliament

▶ **Key Ideas**

- English kings clash with Parliament over money and power.
- Charles I dissolves Parliament when it opposes him.

IN-DEPTH RESOURCES: UNIT 5
Guided Reading, p. 5
Connections Across Time and Cultures: The Absolute Power of Rulers, p. 18

ACCESS FOR STUDENTS ACQUIRING ENGLISH
Guided Reading (Spanish), p. 212

TERMS & NAMES
- Charles I
- English Civil War
- Oliver Cromwell
- Restoration
- habeas corpus
- Glorious Revolution
- constitutional monarchy
- cabinet

5 Parliament Limits the English Monarchy

MAIN IDEA	WHY IT MATTERS NOW
Absolute rulers in England were overthrown, and Parliament gained power.	Many of the government reforms of this period contributed to the democratic tradition of the United States.

SETTING THE STAGE During her reign, Queen Elizabeth I of England had frequent conflicts with Parliament. Many of the arguments were over money, because the treasury did not have enough funds to pay the queen's expenses. By the time Elizabeth died in 1603, she left a huge debt for her successor to deal with. Parliament's financial power was one obstacle to English rulers' becoming absolute monarchs.

Monarchs Clash with Parliament

Elizabeth had no child, and her nearest relative was her cousin, James Stuart. Already king of Scotland, James Stuart became King James I of England in 1603. Although England and Scotland were not united until 1707, they now shared a ruler.

Background
James was the son of Mary, Queen of Scots—whom Elizabeth had executed for plotting against her.

James's Problems James inherited the unsettled issues of Elizabeth's reign. The key question was how much power Parliament would have in governing. James believed he had absolute authority to rule. He said in a speech, "Kings are justly called gods, for that they exercise a manner or resemblance of divine power upon earth."

Elizabeth had also believed in her divine right to rule, but she was more tactful than James. She flattered Parliament to get her way. James thought it was beneath him to try to win Parliament's favor. His worst struggles with Parliament were over money. Parliament was reluctant to pay for James's expensive court and foreign wars.

In addition, James offended the Puritan members of Parliament. Because James was a Calvinist, the Puritans hoped he would enact reforms to purify the English church of Catholic practices. However, James resented being told what to do. Except for agreeing to a new translation of the Bible, he refused to make Puritan reforms.

Charles I Fights Parliament In 1625, James died. **Charles I,** his son, took the throne. Charles always needed money—in part because he was at war with both Spain and France. Several times when Parliament refused to give him funds, he dissolved it.

By 1628, Charles was forced to call Parliament again. This time it refused to grant him any money until he signed a document that is known as the Petition of Right. In this petition, the king agreed to four points:

- He would not imprison subjects without due cause.
- He would not levy taxes without Parliament's consent.
- He would not house soldiers in private homes.
- He would not impose martial law in peacetime.

After agreeing to the petition, Charles ignored it. Even so, the petition was important. It set forth the idea that the law was higher

SPOTLIGHT ON

King James Bible

James I was very interested in religion and scholarship. It bothered him that although there were many English translations of the Bible, none was as well-written as he wanted. Therefore, he sponsored a committee of Bible scholars to create a new, royally approved translation.

The new version of the Bible was first printed in 1611. The King James Bible is noted for the elegance and power of its language. It is still read by millions of English-speaking Protestants throughout the world.

SECTION 5 RESOURCES

PRINT RESOURCES

IN-DEPTH RESOURCES: UNIT 5
Guided Reading, p. 5
Primary Source: from *Diary of Samuel Pepys,* p. 11; from the English Bill of Rights, p. 12
History Makers: William of Orange, p. 17
Connections Across Time and Cultures: The Absolute Power of Rulers, p. 18

ACCESS FOR STUDENTS ACQUIRING ENGLISH
Guided Reading (Spanish), p. 212

FORMAL ASSESSMENT
Section Quiz, p. 243

TECHNOLOGY RESOURCES

 CRITICAL THINKING TRANSPARENCIES
CT57 Chapter 21 Visual Summary

 CD-ROM
Electronic Library of Primary Sources

 INTERNET www.mlworldhistory.com

THINK THROUGH HISTORY
A. Making Inferences Explain how the Petition of Right contradicted the idea of absolute monarchy.

A. Possible Answer An absolute sovereign was supposed to be above everyone; the Petition of Right said that the law and Parliament could limit the power of the English monarch.

than the king. This contradicted theories of absolute monarchy. In 1629, Charles dissolved Parliament and refused to call it back into session. To get money, he imposed all kinds of fees and fines on the English people. His popularity decreased year by year.

English Civil War

Charles offended Puritans by upholding church ritual and a formal prayer book. In addition, in 1637, Charles tried to force the Presbyterian Scots to accept a version of the Anglican prayer book. He wanted both his kingdoms to follow one religion. The Scots rebelled, assembled a huge army, and threatened to invade England. To meet this danger, Charles needed money—money he could get only by calling Parliament into session. This gave Parliament a chance to oppose him.

War Topples a King During the autumn of 1641, Parliament passed laws to limit royal power. Furious, Charles tried to arrest Parliament's leaders in January 1642, but they escaped. Equally furious, a mob of Londoners raged outside the palace. Charles fled London and raised an army in the north of England, where people were loyal to him.

From 1642 to 1649, supporters and opponents of King Charles fought the **English Civil War.** Those who remained loyal to Charles were called Royalists or Cavaliers. On the other side were Puritan supporters of Parliament. Because these men wore their hair short over their ears, Cavaliers mockingly called them Roundheads.

At first neither side could gain a lasting advantage. However, by 1644 the Puritans found a general who could win—**Oliver Cromwell.** In 1646, Cromwell's New Model Army defeated the Cavaliers. By the following year, the Puritans held the king prisoner.

In 1649, Cromwell and the Puritans brought Charles to trial for treason. They found him guilty and sentenced him to death. The execution of Charles was revolutionary. Kings had often been overthrown, killed in battle, or put to death in secret. Never before had a reigning monarch faced a public trial and execution.

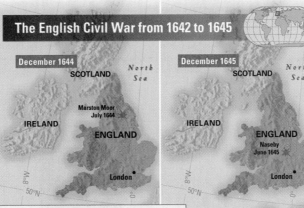

The English Civil War from 1642 to 1645

GEOGRAPHY SKILLBUILDER: Interpreting Maps
1. **Movement** Explain which side gained and which side lost territory during each year from 1643 to 1645.
2. **Place** Which side maintained control of the capital city of London? Why would this be important?

Areas controlled by Puritans
Areas controlled by Royalists
Battle

Cromwell's Rule Cromwell now held the reins of power. In 1649, he abolished the monarchy and the House of Lords. He established a commonwealth—a republican form of government. In 1653, Cromwell sent the remaining members of Parliament home. Cromwell's associate John Lambert drafted a constitution, the first written constitution of any modern European state. However, Cromwell eventually tore up the document and ruled as a military dictator.

B. Possible Answer He abolished the legislative body, which might interfere with him, and he set himself above the law.

Absolute Monarchs in Europe **537**

SPOTLIGHT**ON**
King James Bible
(see page 536)

The notion of translating the whole Bible into English belongs to the 14th-century Oxford theologian John Wycliffe. He believed that the Bible, rather than the pope and the church, was the authority for faith and morals. Therefore, the Bible's words had to be accessible to everyone. Invite students to trace the history of Bible translation in English up to the King James Bible.

OBJECTIVE 2 INSTRUCT

English Civil War

Key Ideas
• Charles I recalls Parliament, but the two sides soon clash.
• Supporters and opponents of Charles I fight a civil war.
• The Puritans, led by Oliver Cromwell, win the civil war.
• Charles I is executed, and Cromwell rules as a dictator.

History from Visuals

The English Civil War from 1642 to 1645

Interpreting the Maps Point out the colors showing the areas controlled by each side. Which part of England did the Puritans control during all four years? *the southeast part*

Extension Activity Have groups of students create a time line of key events in the civil war from 1646 through 1649.

SKILLBUILDER Answers
1. 1643—Royalists gained; 1644, 1645—Puritans gained.
2. The Puritans; this was important because London was the nation's capital and chief economic center.

TEACHING OPTION   BLOCK SCHEDULING   COOPERATIVE ACTIVITY: **Making a Political Pamphlet**   CLASS TIME 30 MINUTES

Task: Students will produce political pamphlets promoting the Royalist or Puritan cause.

Purpose: To promote an understanding of the issues in the English Civil War.

Activity: Have groups of students write and design a folded pamphlet that could be used to persuade others to join one of the sides in the English Civil War. Tell students that the pamphlet should lay out the arguments for war and the justness of the

Royalist or Puritan cause. Encourage students to include drawings or other graphic elements in their pamphlet.

Building a Portfolio: Students who choose to add their pamphlet to their portfolio should attach a note explaining their contribution to the project.

ALTERNATIVE ASSESSMENT BOOK Standards for Evaluating a Cooperative Activity

Standards for Evaluation
Pamphlets should . . .

• express a Royalist or Puritan point of view
• use persuasive language
• accurately portray historical circumstances

Teacher's Edition **537**

Restoration and Revolution

▶ **Key Ideas**
- After Cromwell's death, disillusionment with Puritan rule leads to the restoration of the monarchy under Charles II.
- James II takes the throne next but is deposed for his pro-Catholic bias and contempt for Parliament.
- William and Mary take power in the Glorious Revolution.

 ELECTRONIC LIBRARY OF PRIMARY SOURCES
"The Restoration of Charles II"

SPOTLIGHT ON
The London Fire

The Great Fire, which lasted four days and damaged four-fifths of the city, was the second disaster to strike London in two years. In the period 1664–1665 an outbreak of the plague had killed 75,000 Londoners. "Essentially," observes one scholar, " the plague was a disease of the badly housed poor." Indeed, it had always thrived in the filthy, rickety, and overcrowded inner city. The only cure for it was to raze the entire area. This the fire effectively did, making it possible for London to be redesigned along more open and orderly lines. After the fire the city was rebuilt mainly with brick, rather than timbered, structures.

Invite students to read more about historic London and to bring pictures of the city to class. They might begin by reading the larger excerpt of Samuel Pepys's account in the Teacher's Resources. They might also consult John Russell's *London,* an acclaimed pictorial history of the city.

 IN-DEPTH RESOURCES: UNIT 5
Primary Source: from *Diary of Samuel Pepys,* p. 11

Cromwell almost immediately had to put down a rebellion in Ireland. Henry VIII and his children had brought that country under English rule. In 1649 Cromwell landed on Irish shores with an army and crushed the uprising. The lands and homes of the Irish were taken from them and given to English soldiers. Fighting, plague, and famine killed an estimated 616,000 Irish.

Puritan Morality In England, Cromwell and the Puritans sought to reform society. They made laws that promoted Puritan morality and abolished activities they found sinful, such as going to the theater. In a speech, Cromwell explained his reasons for this:

> **A VOICE FROM THE PAST**
> I did hint to you my thoughts about the reformation of manners; and those abuses that are in this nation through disorder . . . should be much in your hearts. . . . I am confident our liberty and prosperity depends upon—reformation. To make it a shame to see men to be bold in sin and profaneness—and God will bless you. You will be a blessing to the nation.
> **OLIVER CROMWELL,** speech of September 17, 1656

Although a strict Puritan, Cromwell favored religious toleration for all Christians except Catholics. He even welcomed back Jews, who had been expelled from England in 1290.

Restoration and Revolution

Oliver Cromwell ruled until his death in 1658. Shortly afterward, the government he had established collapsed, and a new Parliament was selected. The English people were sick of military rule. In 1659, Parliament voted to ask the older son of Charles I to rule England.

Charles II Reigns When Prince Charles entered London in 1660, crowds shouted joyfully and bells rang. On this note of celebration, the reign of Charles II began. Because he restored the monarchy, the period of his rule is called the **Restoration.**

Charles also restored the theater, sporting events, and dancing, which the Puritans had banned. Theater, especially comedy, and the other arts flourished during the Restoration. For the first time, women appeared on the English stage to play female roles.

During Charles II's reign, Parliament passed an important guarantee of freedom, **habeas corpus.** This 1679 law gave every prisoner the right to obtain a writ or document ordering that the prisoner be brought before a judge. The judge would decide whether the prisoner should be tried or set free. Because of the Habeas Corpus Act, a monarch could not put someone in jail simply for opposing the ruler. Also, prisoners could not be held indefinitely without trials.

In addition, Parliament debated who should inherit Charles's throne. Because Charles had no legitimate child, his heir was his brother James, who was Catholic. A group called the Whigs opposed James, and a group called the Tories supported him. These two groups were the ancestors of England's first political parties.

Background
Habeas corpus comes from Latin words meaning "to have the body."

SPOTLIGHT ON

The London Fire

A disastrous fire broke out in London on September 2, 1666. It began in the house of the king's baker, near London Bridge. The flames, stirred by a strong east wind, leaped from building to building. People desperately tried to escape. The Thames River was crawling with boats filled with survivors and their belongings.

Samuel Pepys, a public official, wrote an eyewitness account of the fire in his diary:

> It made me weep to see it. The churches, houses, and all on fire and flaming at once; and a horrid noise the flames made, and the cracking of houses at their ruin.

In the end, the fire destroyed St. Paul's Cathedral, 87 parish churches, and around 13,000 houses. It was the worst fire in London's history.

TEACHING OPTIONS

CONNECTIONS ACROSS THE CURRICULUM

Literature The 17th-century English author John Milton wrote what are considered some of the greatest poems in the language, including *Paradise Lost.* But from 1641 to 1660 he focused on writing prose works in defense of religious and civil liberties. In "Areopagitica" Milton wrote what is now regarded as the classic statement against censorship. He also argued that power rests always with the people, who delegate it to a ruler but may, if it is abused, take it back and depose or even execute the tyrant. Have students find examples of Milton's poetry or prose to read and discuss in class.

CONNECTIONS ACROSS TIME AND PLACE

Irish Troubles Point out to students that present-day conflicts between Protestants and Catholics in Northern Ireland stem from events of the 1600s. England promoted Protestant emigration to Ireland, particularly to the north, and Irish Catholics steadily lost power and influence. The decisive blow to Catholics came in 1690, when the English army of King William of Orange defeated Irish forces loyal to the deposed Catholic king of England, James II. Today, a group known as the Orange Order, named after William, continues to uphold the Protestant domination of Northern Ireland.

James II and the Glorious Revolution In 1685, Charles II died, and James II became king. James soon offended his subjects by flaunting his Catholicism. Violating English law, he appointed several Catholics to high office. When Parliament protested, James dissolved it. In 1688, James's second wife gave birth to a son. English Protestants became terrified at the prospect of a line of Catholic kings.

James had an older daughter, Mary, who was Protestant. She was also the wife of William of Orange, a prince of the Netherlands. Seven members of Parliament invited William and Mary to overthrow James for the sake of Protestantism. When William led his army to London in 1688, James fled to France. This bloodless overthrow of King James II is called the **Glorious Revolution.**

THINK THROUGH HISTORY
C. Contrasting How was the overthrow of James II different from the overthrow of Charles I?
C. Possible Answers It was basically peaceful; there was no execution of the king; the monarchy was not abolished.

Political Changes

At their coronation, William and Mary vowed "to govern the people of this kingdom of England . . . according to the statutes in Parliament agreed on and the laws and customs of the same." By doing so, William and Mary recognized Parliament as their partner in governing. England had become not an absolute monarchy but a **constitutional monarchy,** where laws limited the ruler's power.

Bill of Rights To make clear the limits of royal power, Parliament drafted a Bill of Rights in 1689. This document listed many things that a ruler could not do:

- No suspending of Parliament's laws
- No levying of taxes without a specific grant from Parliament
- No interfering with freedom of speech in Parliament
- No penalty for a citizen who petitions the king about grievances

William and Mary officially consented to these and other limits on their royal power.

Cabinet System Develops After 1688, no British monarch could rule without consent of Parliament. At the same time, Parliament could not rule without the consent of the monarch. If the two disagreed, government came to a standstill.

During the 1700s, this potential problem was remedied by the development of a group of government ministers called the **cabinet**. These ministers acted in the ruler's name but in reality represented the major party of Parliament. Therefore, they became the link between the monarch and the majority in Parliament.

Over time, the cabinet became the center of power and policymaking. Under the cabinet system, the leader of the majority party in Parliament heads the cabinet and is called the prime minister. This system of English government continues today.

Background
Although the power of Parliament increased, England was still not democratic. Parliament represented the upper classes, not the majority of the English people.

CONNECT to TODAY
U.S. Democracy
The United States adopted many of the government reforms and institutions that the English developed during this period. These include the following:

- the right to obtain habeas corpus—a document that prevents authorities from holding a person in jail without being charged
- a Bill of Rights, guaranteeing such rights as freedom of speech and freedom of worship
- a strong legislature and strong executive, which act as checks on each other
- a cabinet, made up of heads of executive departments, such as the Department of State
- two dominant political parties

Section 5 Assessment

1. TERMS & NAMES
Identify
- Charles I
- English Civil War
- Oliver Cromwell
- Restoration
- habeas corpus
- Glorious Revolution
- constitutional monarchy
- cabinet

2. TAKING NOTES
On a chart like the one shown, list the causes of each monarch's conflicts with Parliament.

Monarch	Conflicts with Parliament
James I	
Charles I	
James II	

What patterns do you see in the causes of these conflicts?

3. EVALUATING DECISIONS
In your opinion, which decisions of Charles I made his conflict with Parliament worse? Explain.

THINK ABOUT
- decisions that lost him the support of Parliament
- decisions that lost him the support of his people

4. THEME ACTIVITY
Revolution Using a dictionary, encyclopedia, or your textbook for reference, write a definition of revolution. Then write a paragraph explaining how the English Civil War and the Glorious Revolution are examples of revolution.

Absolute Monarchs in Europe **539**

ANSWERS

1. TERMS & NAMES
Charles I, p. 536
English Civil War, p. 537
Oliver Cromwell, p. 537
Restoration, p. 538
habeas corpus, p. 538
Glorious Revolution, p. 539
constitutional monarchy, p. 539
cabinet, p. 539

2. TAKING NOTES
Possible Responses: **James I**—Believed in divine right to rule; wanted large funds to pay for court and wars; did not make Puritan reforms. **Charles I**—Wanted funds to finance wars; tried to force all subjects to be Anglican; resisted Parliament's attempts to restrict his power.

James II—Offended Protestants by flaunting his Catholicism; named Catholics to high office.

3. EVALUATING DECISIONS
Possible Responses: Alienated Parliament by dissolving it, ignoring Petition of Right, and trying to arrest Parliamentary leaders; alienated his subjects by imposing fines and fees on them and trying to force them all to be Anglican, thus encouraging them to support Parliament's struggle against him.

4. THEME ACTIVITY
Responses should
- clearly define revolution and explain how the examples fit the definition.

OBJECTIVE INSTRUCT

Political Changes
▶ **Key Ideas**
- William and Mary agree to govern with Parliament in a constitutional monarchy.
- Parliament drafts a Bill of Rights, limiting royal power.
- The cabinet, set up as a link between Parliament and the monarchy, becomes the center of power.

IN-DEPTH RESOURCES: UNIT 5
History Makers: William of Orange, p. 17
Primary Source: from the English Bill of Rights, p. 12

CONNECT to TODAY
U.S. Democracy
Have students find out how the U.S. and British governments differ in their legislative and executive branches.

ASSESS & RETEACH

Section 5 Assessment
Have pairs of students help each other with key terms by making word cards with definitions on the back. Students can take turns quizzing each other.

Section Quiz
FORMAL ASSESSMENT
Section Quiz, p. 243

Reteaching Activity
CLASS TIME: 10 MINUTES

Have pairs of students list statements summarizing the Royalist and Parliamentary positions, with each partner taking a different side. Partners should then present their positions to each other.

CRITICAL THINKING TRANSPARENCIES
CT57 Chapter 21 Visual Summary

CLOSE ACTIVITY

CLASS TIME: 15 MINUTES

Recognizing Sequences
Have small groups of students create time lines that show the main events covered in the section. Invite students to display their time lines and discuss how events in England in the 1600s led to the growth of constitutional rule.

Teacher's Edition **539**

Chapter **21** Assessment

TERMS & NAMES

1. absolute monarch, p. 517
2. divine right, p. 517
3. Louis XIV, p. 519
4. War of the Spanish Succession, p. 523
5. Thirty Years' War, p. 526
6. Seven Years' War, p. 530
7. Peter the Great, p. 532
8. English Civil War, p. 537
9. Glorious Revolution, p. 539
10. constitutional monarchy, p. 539

REVIEW QUESTIONS

11. He fought the Muslim Ottoman Empire, he sent the Spanish Armada to punish Protestant England; he tried to destroy Protestantism in the Netherlands.

12. A prince should not share power because if he has to get the consent of someone else, he becomes that person's subject, not ruler.

13. He relied on non-noble intendants (government agents), and he forced nobles to live at Versailles, where they were dependent on him.

14. He ran up huge debts; he fought unpopular wars and imposed taxes to finance them.

15. It weakened Spain and Austria, it strengthened France, it made German princes independent of the Holy Roman emperor, it ended religious wars in Europe, it introduced a new method of negotiating peace, and it began the modern state system, in which all states are independent and equal.

16. They were battling over territory.

17. Russian serfdom was firmly implanted; people knew little of ideas from the Renaissance and Age of Exploration; Russians had adopted Eastern Orthodox Christianity.

18. Westernization to enable Russia to compete militarily and commercially with western Europe.

19. Cavaliers (Royalists) and Roundheads (Puritans) fought from 1642 to 1649, provoked by conflicts between the king and Parliament over religion, money, and the extent of the king's power. The Roundheads won and beheaded Charles I.

20. Parliament often refused to grant monarchs funds; it forced Charles I to sign the Petition of Right; Parliament leaders invited William and Mary to rule, but only as the partners of Parliament; Parliament drafted a Bill of Rights.

Visual Summary

Absolute Monarchs in Europe

Long-Term Causes

- decline of feudalism
- rise of cities and growth of middle class
- growth of national kingdoms
- loss of Church authority

Immediate Causes

- religious and territorial conflicts
- buildup of armies
- need for increased taxes
- revolts by peasants or nobles

European Monarchs Claim Divine Right to Rule Absolutely

Immediate Effects

- regulation of religion and society
- larger courts
- huge building projects
- new government bureaucracies
- loss of power by nobility and legislatures

Long-Term Effects

- revolution in France
- western European influence on Russia
- English political reforms that influence U.S. democracy

TERMS & NAMES

Briefly explain the importance of each of the following during the age of absolute monarchs in Europe.

1. absolute monarch
2. divine right
3. Louis XIV
4. War of the Spanish Succession
5. Thirty Years' War
6. Seven Years' War
7. Peter the Great
8. English Civil War
9. Glorious Revolution
10. constitutional monarchy

REVIEW QUESTIONS

SECTION 1 *(pages 513–517)*
Spain's Empire and European Absolutism

11. Name three actions that demonstrate that Philip II of Spain saw himself as a defender of Catholicism.

12. According to French writer Jean Bodin, should a prince share power with anyone else? Explain why or why not.

SECTION 2 *(pages 518–525)*
France's Ultimate Monarch

13. Name two ways that Louis XIV controlled the French nobility.

14. In what ways did Louis XIV cause suffering to the French people?

SECTION 3 *(pages 526–530)*
Central European Monarchs Clash

15. What were six results of the Peace of Westphalia?

16. What was the reason that Maria Theresa and Frederick the Great fought two wars against each other?

SECTION 4 *(pages 531–535)*
Russia Czars Increase Power

17. List three differences between Russia and western Europe.

18. What were Peter the Great's goals for Russia?

SECTION 5 *(pages 536–539)*
Parliament Limits the English Monarchy

19. Describe the causes, participants, and outcome of the English Civil War.

20. List at least three ways that Parliament tried to limit the power of the English monarchy.

Interact *with* History

On page 512, you made decisions about what type of palace you would build if you were a monarch. Now that you have read the chapter, would you say that your palace was more like the one built by Philip II of Spain or that built by Louis XIV of France? Explain.

Interact *with* History

Standards for Evaluation
A response should meet these criteria:
- Shows knowledge of they key features of the Escorial and Versailles.
- Explains how the features of one palace more closely reflect the qualities the student wanted to demonstrate.

CRITICAL THINKING

1. IMPROVING THE ECONOMY

THEME **ECONOMICS** Of all the monarchs that you studied in this chapter, which one do you think helped his or her country's economy the most? Explain your answer by citing evidence from the chapter.

2. MONARCHS RULE ABSOLUTELY

Create a chart like the one shown. In the left-hand column of your chart, list actions that absolute monarchs often took to increase their power. Then for each action, name at least one monarch who actually did that. Use at least five different monarchs in your chart as examples.

Actions of absolute monarchs	Example of a monarch who did this

3. LAND GRABBERS

Many of the monarchs that you studied in this chapter tried to increase their countries' territory. Why might an absolute monarch want to gain territory? Explain what benefits these monarchs hoped to gain.

4. ANALYZING PRIMARY SOURCES

After the Glorious Revolution of 1688, Parliament passed the Bill of Rights in 1689. The following is an excerpt from that document. Read it and then answer the questions that follow.

A VOICE FROM THE PAST

That the pretended power of suspending [canceling] of laws or the execution [carrying out] of laws by regal authority without consent of Parliament is illegal; . . .

That it is the right of the subjects to petition [make requests of] the king, and all commitments [imprisonments] and prosecutions for such petitioning are illegal;

That the raising or keeping a standing army within the kingdom in time of peace, unless it be with consent of Parliament, is against the law; . . .

That election of members of Parliament ought to be free [not restricted].

Bill of Rights

- In what ways did Parliament limit the power of the monarch?
- How did the Parliament try to protect itself?

CHAPTER ACTIVITIES

1. LIVING HISTORY: Unit Portfolio Project

THEME **REVOLUTION** Your unit portfolio project focuses on showing the causes and results of various revolutions (see page 509). For Chapter 21, you might use one of the following ideas to add to your portfolio.

- Peter the Great tried to revolutionize Russian culture and society. Create an educational poster that Peter could have used to explain one practice he wanted his people to give up and what he wanted them to replace it with.
- Write an editorial stating whether you think the English Civil War or the Glorious Revolution was more revolutionary. To support your opinion, examine both short-term and long-term effects.
- Write a HistoryMaker, like the ones you've read throughout this textbook, focusing on Oliver Cromwell as a leader of a revolution.

2. CONNECT TO TODAY: Cooperative Learning

THEME **POWER AND AUTHORITY** One of the ideas that came out of this time period is that Parliament should prevent the English monarch from exercising too much power. In the United States, the legislative body also limits the power of the head of government. At the same time, in the United States the head of government—or chief executive—also limits the power of the legislature. Create a diagram that shows how these two branches of government limit each other's power.

- Use the Internet, the library, or other sources to research the various branches of the U.S. national government.
- Identify the legislative and executive branches of government and the powers of each. Especially note how each branch acts to limit the power of the other.
- Display this information on a diagram. Some of the diagrams in this textbook might provide ideas for how to use visual elements such as arrows to demonstrate relationships.

3. INTERPRETING A TIME LINE

Revisit the unit time line on pages 508–509. Use the Chapter 21 time line to find out when Louis XIV began his reign. What happened in England shortly after Louis took the throne? How might that have affected his views on monarchy?

FOCUS ON GEOGRAPHY

On the map, notice which modern European nations are still ruled by royal monarchs.

- Of the countries that you studied in this chapter, which have monarchs today?

Connect to History
- Which of those countries was a republic during the period of this chapter?
- Did the countries whose rulers exercised the most power retain the monarchy? Explain.

Modern European Monarchs

0   500 Miles
0   1,000 Kilometers

Nations with monarchs today

NORWAY
SWEDEN
UNITED KINGDOM
DENMARK
NETHERLANDS
BELGIUM
LUXEMBOURG
LIECHTENSTEIN
MONACO
SPAIN   ANDORRA
ATLANTIC OCEAN

CHAPTER ACTIVITIES

1. LIVING HISTORY

Standards for Evaluation
A poster should meet these criteria:

- Clearly explains both the old practice and the new practice.
- Accurately represents one of Peter's westernizing policies.
- Communicates visually and verbally.

Standards for Evaluation
An editorial should meet these criteria:

- Takes a clear position on the issue.
- Supports that position with historical evidence.
- Is organized logically.

Standards for Evaluation
A History Maker should meet these criteria:

- Accurately conveys biographical information.
- Focuses on Cromwell's leadership.
- Is written in a lively style.

2. CONNECT TO TODAY

Standards for Evaluation
A diagram should meet these criteria:

- Explains the powers of the executive and legislative branches and the ways each branch limits the other's power.
- Communicates visually and verbally.
- Is neat, colorful, and interesting to look at.

3. INTERPRETING A TIME LINE

Possible Response: Louis XIV began his reign in 1643. Six years later, the English king was executed. This may have motivated Louis to increase his own power.

FOCUS ON GEOGRAPHY

- Britain, Spain, and the Netherlands

CONNECT TO HISTORY The Netherlands was a republic during the period of this chapter; England was very briefly a republic after the Civil War.

Possible Response: In some countries where the monarch exercised almost absolute power, such as France and Russia, the monarchy no longer exists. In other countries ruled by absolute monarchs, such as Spain and England, the monarchy still exists.

CRITICAL THINKING

1. IMPROVING THE ECONOMY

Possible Responses: Peter I—Tried to modernize industry; promoted education; built St. Petersburg, aiding trade with the West. Frederick II—Won Silesia, which yielded iron ore, textiles, and food products.

2. MONARCHS RULE ABSOLUTELY

Possible Responses: Controlled religious life—Philip II, Louis XIV, Peter I; controlled society—Ivan IV, Louis XIV, Frederick II, Peter I; controlled economy—Louis XIV, Peter I; reduced power of nobles—Louis XIV, Maria Theresa, Ivan IV, Peter I.

3. LAND GRABBERS

Possible Responses: Gaining territory might expand rulers' power, provide resources rulers could use to bolster their army or their country's economy, or enable rulers to award land to nobles to gain loyalty.

4. ANALYZING PRIMARY SOURCES

Possible Responses: Parliament limited rulers' power by forbidding them from canceling or executing laws or keeping a standing army without Parliament's consent and by guaranteeing subjects' right to petition them without risking penalty. Parliament protected itself by declaring that its elections should be unrestricted.

Enlightenment and Revolution

	Key Ideas	COPY MASTERS	ASSESSMENT

SECTION 1
The Scientific Revolution
pp. 545–550

The Scientific Revolution begins as scientists replace old ideas with new theories. New approaches to science include using observation and experiments to develop theories. In astronomy, scientists challenge the earth-centered model of the universe.

 In-Depth Resources: Unit 5
- **Guided Reading,** p. 19
- **Skillbuilder Practice:** Clariflying, p. 23
- **Geography Application:** Three Theories of the Solar System, p. 24
- **Primary Source:** from *Starry Messenger,* p. 26
- **Literature:** from *The Recantation of Galileo Galilei,* p. 31
- **History Makers:** Copernicus, p. 34

[P][E] *Section 1 Assessment,* p. 550

Formal Assessment
- Section Quiz, p. 252

Alternative Assessment Book
- Standards for Evaluating a Cooperative Activity

SECTION 2
The Enlightenment in Europe
pp. 551–557

Enlightenment philosophers admire scientists' use of reason to understand the natural world. These philosophers promote the use of reason to understand government, religion, education, and economics. They advocate government reform and social improvement.

 In-Depth Resources: Unit 5
- **Guided Reading,** p. 20
- **Primary Sources:** from *The Social Contract,* p. 27; from *Two Treatises on Government,* p. 28; from *A Vindication of the Rights of Woman,* p. 29
- **History Makers:** Baron de Montesquieu, p. 35

[P][E] *Section 2 Assessment,* p. 556

Formal Assessment
- Section Quiz, p. 253

Alternative Assessment Book
- Standards for Evaluating a Cooperative Activity

SECTION 3
The Spread of Enlightenment Ideas
pp. 558–562

Enlightenment ideas circulate in pamphlets and formal discussions. The new ideals of order and reason are reflected in the arts and music. European monarchs make limited reforms based on Enlightenment ideas.

In-Depth Resources: Unit 5
- **Guided Reading,** p. 21
- **Connections Across Time and Cultures:** The Search for Truth and Reason, p. 36

[P][E] *Section 3 Assessment,* p. 562

Formal Assessment
- Section Quiz, p. 254

Alternative Assessment Book
- Standards for Evaluating a Cooperative Activity

SECTION 4
American Revolution: The Birth of a Republic
pp. 563–567

Colonists resist the laws and taxes imposed by the British. Colonial leaders use Enlightenment ideas to justify independence from Britain, and, after winning the Revolution, create a federal government.

In-Depth Resources: Unit 5
- **Guided Reading,** p. 22
- **Primary Source:** from The Declaration of Independence, p. 30

[P][E] *Section 4 Assessment,* p. 567

Formal Assessment
- Section Quiz, p. 255

Alternative Assessment Book
- Standards for Evaluating a Cooperative Activity

CHAPTER RESOURCES

Chapter Overview

In Europe, scientists question old ideas and use reason to make discoveries about the natural world. Philosophers support the use of reason to reform government, religion, and society. Enlightenment ideas are used to create a federal government in the newly created United States.

 Telescoping the Times
- Chapter Summary, pp. 85–87

Planning for Block Schedules

[P][E] *Chapter Assessment,* pp. 568–569

Chapter Activities, p. 569

Formal Assessment
- Chapter Test, forms A and B, pp. 256–261

💾 *Test Generator*

Alternative Assessment Book

TECHNOLOGY

 Warm-Up Transparency 22

 Geography Transparencies
- GT22 Maps of the World, 1492–1761

 World Art and Cultures Transparencies
- AT48 Vermeer's *The Astronomer*

 Electronic Library of Primary Sources
- "Of Studies"

 INTERNET RESOURCES
www.mlworldhistory.com

 Warm-Up Transparency 22

Electronic Library of Primary Sources
- from *The Persian Letters*
- from *Gulliver's Travels*

 INTERNET RESOURCES
www.mlworldhistory.com

 Warm-Up Transparency 22

 World Art and Cultures Transparencies
- AT49 Goya's *The Pottery Vendor* (cartoon for a tapestry)

Critical Thinking Transparencies
- CT22 The Spread of Enlightenment Ideas

Electronic Library of Primary Sources
- Letter to Catherine the Great

INTERNET RESOURCES
www.mlworldhistory.com

 Warm-Up Transparency 22

 Critical Thinking Transparencies
- CT58 Chapter 22 Visual Summary

 Electronic Library of Primary Sources
- Conflicting Accounts of the Battles at Lexington and Concord

 INTERNET RESOURCES
www.mlworldhistory.com

 Chapter Summaries on Audiocassette in English and Spanish

 INTERNET RESOURCES
www.mlworldhistory.com

Block Scheduling (90 MINUTES)

Day 1
Section 1, pp. 545–550
COOPERATIVE ACTIVITY Technology Interviews, p. 548 (Teacher's Edition)
Section Assessment, p. 550

Day 2
Section 2, pp. 551–557

COOPERATIVE ACTIVITY Enlightenment Philosophers, p. 553 (Teacher's Edition)
Section 3, pp. 558–562
COOPERATIVE ACTIVITY Researching Enlightenment Arts, p. 561 (Teacher's Edition)
Section Assessments, pp. 556, 562

Day 3
Section 4, pp. 563–567
COOPERATIVE ACTIVITY Reporting on the Enlightenment, p. 566 (Teacher's Edition)
Section Assessment, p. 567
Chapter Assessment, pp. 568–569

Yearly Pacing *Chapter 22 Total:* 3 days *Yearly Total:* 85 days
Planning for Block Schedules

Customizing for Special Needs

Students Acquiring English
Access for Students Acquiring English
- **Guided Reading** for Sections 1–4 (Spanish), pp. 219–222
- **Chapter Summary** (Spanish), pp. 216–218
- **Skillbuilder Practice** Clarifying (Spanish), p. 223
- **Geography Application** Three Theories of the Solar System (Spanish), pp. 224–225
Chapter Summaries on Audiocassette in English and Spanish
INTERNET RESOURCES www.mlworldhistory.com *The Diverse Classroom.*

Less Proficient Readers
In-Depth Resources: Unit 5
- **Guided Reading** for Sections 1–4, pp. 19–22
- **Skillbuilder Practice** Clarifying, p. 23
- **Geography Application** Three Theories of the Solar System, p. 24
Telescoping the Times
- Chapter Summary, pp. 85–87
Chapter Summaries on Audiocassette

Gifted and Talented Students
In-Depth Resources: Unit 5
Primary Sources:
- from *Starry Messenger*, p. 26
- from *The Social Contract*, p. 27
- from *Two Treatises on Government*, p. 28
- from *A Vindication of the Rights of Woman*, p. 29
- from The Declaration of Independence, p. 30
History Makers
- Copernicus, p. 34
- Baron de Montesquieu, p. 35

Connections to Literature READINGS FOR STUDENTS

In-Depth Resources: Unit 5
Literature: from *The Recantation of Galileo Galilei*, p. 31

Enrichment Reading
- **Fast, Howard** *Citizen Tom Paine* New York: Duell, 1943
In this historical novel, the hot temper, feisty character, and extensive travels of Tom Paine are brought to life.

McDougal Littell Literature Connections
- **Miller, Arthur** *The Crucible* (with related readings)
Injustice and hysteria take center stage in this historical drama about witchcraft accusations in Puritan New England.

PE = Pupil's Edition   = Overhead Transparency   = Software   = Video
= Copy Master   = CD-ROM   = Audiocassette   = Internet

Enlightenment and Revolution, 1550–1789

Introducing the Chapter

Accessing Prior Knowledge

- Ask students to read the captions that accompany the pictures and discuss what they already know about the people and the situations.

Making Inferences and Drawing Conclusions

- After reading about Catherine the Great and about Rembrandt's painting, ask students to infer whether life in Europe was changing or staying the same during the Enlightenment. How can students tell?

- After reading about Patrick Henry, ask students to draw conclusions about the changes Henry is demanding.

Geography Connection

Ask students to study the maps and to use the map key to answer the questions.

- In which cities and countries were the centers of Enlightenment located?

- On which two continents are the centers of Enlightenment located?

CHAPTER
22 Enlightenment and Revolution, 1550–1789

Revolution

Between the 16th and 18th centuries, a series of revolutions helped usher in the modern era in Western history. First was a revolution in understanding, called the Scientific Revolution. Second was a revolution of ideas, called the Enlightenment. Third was a revolution in action—the American Revolution.

Science and Technology

The Scientific Revolution began when some astronomers questioned the old understanding of how the universe operates—one that was deeply tied to people's religious beliefs. By shattering this view, the astronomers opened a new universe of scientific discovery.

Power and Authority

Like their counterparts in science, the political thinkers of the Enlightenment challenged established ideas about power and authority. A ruler does not own authority by divine right, the thinkers said. Rather, a ruler receives authority by the consent of the people. Such ideas led to the political upheaval of the American Revolution.

> **INTERNET CONNECTION**
>
> Visit us at **www.mlworldhistory.com** to learn more about the Scientific Revolution, the Enlightenment, and the American Revolution.

542

CENTERS OF ENLIGHTENMENT, 1750

✦ Enlightenment centers

0   300 Miles
0   600 Kilometers

Eastern North America

Boston

Philadelphia

Williamsburg

40°N

70°W

30°N

0   250 Miles
0   500 Kilometers

In **1775**, the brilliant orator **Patrick Henry** delivered his now famous speech to the Second Virginia Convention. In this speech he declared, "Give me liberty, or give me death!" In this 19th-century painting by artist Peter Rothermel, Henry speaks before the Virginia House of Burgesses. He repeatedly spoke against British laws that restricted the colonists' rights.

SPAIN

ATLANTIC OCEAN

34°N

24°W

26°N

16°W

GEOGRAPHY THEMES

Location

Ask students to note the centers of Enlightenment in Europe. Then ask how students can tell that most of the Enlightenment ideas came from western Europe and not from Russia or Poland? *Most of the centers are in this area.* Next, have students use the scale to calculate the distance between Geneva and Milan, *(about 200 miles);* Paris and Warsaw, *(about 1050 miles);* and London and Austria, *(about 775 miles)*. Point out that most of the centers of Enlightenment are close together in western Europe. Ask students how this might have affected the spread of ideas.

Movement

Ask students to look at the map of eastern North America. Remind students that in the 18th century, this region was the site of the British colonies. How can students tell from the map that the colonies were influenced by Europe?

How might Enlightenment ideas have spread to North America? Ask students to predict whether these ideas will strengthen or weaken ties between Europe and the colonies. Tell students to check their predictions as they read this chapter.

In **1762**, a former German princess succeeded her husband, Czar Peter III, and became Empress Catherine II of Russia. The brilliant empress ruled Russia for 34 years, vastly expanded Russian territory, and tried to create reforms. For her accomplishments, she is known to history as **Catherine the Great.**

The Guild of Surgeons-Anatomists of Amsterdam asked Rembrandt van Rijn to paint *Anatomy Lesson of Dr. Tulp* in **1632**. The corpse was that of a criminal. By the mid-1500s, European doctors had begun to dissect bodies for the first time to directly observe human anatomy. This contributed to a revolution in medical knowledge.

ADDITIONAL RESOURCES

Books for the Teacher

- Almond, Mark. *Revolution: 500 Years of Struggle for Change.* New York: De Agostini, 1996. Account of 27 revolutions and movements.

- Durant, Will, and Ariel Durant. *The Age of Reason Begins.* New York: Simon, 1965. History of Enlightenment from 1558 to 1648.

- Shapin, Steven. *The Scientific Revolution.* Chicago: U of Chicago P, 1996.

Books for the Student

- Christianson, Gale E. *Isaac Newton and the Scientific Revolution.* New York: Oxford UP, 1996.

- Wilson, Ellen Judy, and Peter Hanns Reill. *Encyclopedia of the Enlightenment.* New York: Facts on File, 1996.

Videos

- *The Age of Enlightenment.* Cambridge Social Studies, 1991. 800-468-4227.

- *The Age of Reason: Europe After the Renaissance.* Knowledge Unlimited, 1995. 800-356-2303.

- *Galileo and the Universe.* BFA Educational, 1972. 800-221-1274.

Software

- *The Scientific Revolution.* CD-ROM. Society for Visual Education, 1994. 800-829-1900.

HISTORY THROUGH ART

Anatomy Lesson of Dr. Tulp

Rembrandt van Rijn

At age 26, Rembrandt was hired to paint a group portrait of the annual anatomy demonstration performed by the chief surgeon of Amsterdam for the city's guild of surgeons. The painting made Rembrandt the most popular portraitist in Amsterdam.

Until this time, group portraits usually focused on the heads of the subjects, which were arranged in a row. The *Anatomy Lesson* departs from this style in several ways. The heads of the surgeons form a pyramid, not a line. Rembrandt's use of light places emphasis on the anatomy lesson and not on the surgeons. Each surgeon's face bears a different expression. Rembrandt seems to have caught a moment in time, much as a photographer does.

The subject of Rembrandt's painting reflects the changes in science that were sweeping through western Europe at the time. Instead of relying on ancient ideas to understand the natural world, scientists were observing, performing experiments, and using their own reason to figure things out.

Interpreting the Art What are the surgeons trying to learn from Dr. Tulp? Where do the individual surgeons and the doctor seem to be looking? How has Rembrandt caught a moment in time?

Interact *with* History

This Interact with History feature motivates students by inviting them to put themselves in the place of a key historical figure—Galileo Galilei. As they imagine themselves having to choose between death and denying ideas they know are right, students will analyze the issues, explore their options, and become decision makers.

Purpose

• to prepare students for studying the Scientific Revolution and the Enlightenment

• to help students understand the intellectual climate in which the Scientific Revolution began

• to help students connect with the events and historical figures they will study in this chapter

EXAMINING *the* ISSUES

Following are suggestions for addressing each bulleted question.

1 Do students think this idea would have disappeared if Galileo had been killed? Who else had this idea?

2 Students may mention nuclear weapons as an example of dangerous knowledge. Does modern scientific knowledge seem mostly harmful or helpful?

3 Have students think of countries or periods in history when people have been persecuted for their beliefs.

Follow Up

A feature on the chapter assessment will ask students to reevaluate their responses to the situation presented on this page.

It is the year 1633, and the Italian scientist Galileo Galilei faces a life-or-death dilemma. The Roman Inquisition, a court of the Catholic Church, has condemned him for holding an idea—that the earth revolves around the sun. The court has asked Galileo to publicly deny this idea. If he agrees, the court will show leniency. If he refuses, Galileo will likely face torture or a painful death.

The idea that the earth revolves around the sun had been put forth almost a century before by the Polish astronomer Copernicus. Galileo is firmly convinced that Copernicus was right. Galileo has been looking through a telescope at the planets and stars. What he has seen with his own eyes is proof enough of Copernicus's theory.

The church has denounced Copernicus's theory as dangerous to the faith. The idea that the earth is the center of the universe is part of church teachings. Church leaders have warned Galileo to stop defending the new theory. But Galileo has written a book that explains why Copernicus's ideas make sense. Now he is on trial.

Put yourself in the place of Galileo as he weighs the choice the Inquisition has given him.

Galileo tries to defend himself before the Inquisition. The court, however, demands that he recant.

Would you deny an idea you know to be true?

EXAMINING *the* ISSUES

1 • By silencing Galileo, the church wanted to suppress an idea. Do you think this was an effective strategy? Can an idea have a life of its own?

2 • Are there any cases in which an idea is too dangerous to be openly discussed or taught?

3 • Galileo faced persecution for teaching new ideas. Could this happen today?

Meet in small groups and discuss these questions. As you share ideas, recall other times in history when people expressed ideas that were different from accepted ones.

As you read this chapter, watch for the effects revolutionary ideas have on others.

544 Chapter 22

1 The Scientific Revolution

TERMS & NAMES
- Scientific Revolution
- Nicolaus Copernicus
- heliocentric theory
- Johannes Kepler
- Galileo Galilei
- scientific method
- Francis Bacon
- René Descartes
- Isaac Newton

MAIN IDEA

In the mid-1500s, scientists began to question accepted beliefs and make new theories based on experimentation.

WHY IT MATTERS NOW

Scientists' questioning led to the development of the scientific method still in use today.

SETTING THE STAGE The Renaissance inspired a spirit of curiosity in many fields. Scholars began to question ideas that had been accepted for hundreds of years. During the Reformation, religious leaders challenged accepted ways of thinking about God and salvation. While the Reformation was taking place, another revolution in European thought was also occurring. It challenged how people viewed their place in the universe.

The Roots of Modern Science

Before 1500, scholars generally decided what was true or false by referring to an ancient Greek or Roman author or to the Bible. Whatever Aristotle said about the material world was true unless the Bible said otherwise. Few European scholars questioned the scientific ideas of the ancient thinkers or the church by carefully observing nature for themselves.

The Medieval View During the Middle Ages, most scholars believed that the earth was an unmoving object located at the center of the universe. According to that belief, the moon, the sun, and the planets all moved in perfectly circular paths around the earth. Beyond the planets lay a sphere of fixed stars, with heaven still farther beyond. Common sense seemed to support this view. After all, the sun appeared to be moving around the earth as it rose in the morning and set in the evening.

This earth-centered view of the universe, called the geocentric theory, was supported by more than just common sense. The idea came from Aristotle, the Greek philosopher of the fourth century B.C. The Greek astronomer Ptolemy expanded the theory in the second century A.D. In addition, Christianity taught that God had deliberately placed earth at the center of the universe. Earth was thus a special place on which the great drama of life took place.

A New Way of Thinking Beginning in the mid-1500s, a few scholars published works that challenged the ideas of the ancient thinkers and the church. As these scholars replaced old assumptions with new theories, they launched a change in European thought that historians call the Scientific Revolution. The **Scientific Revolution** was a new way of thinking about the natural world. That way was based upon careful observation and a willingness to question accepted beliefs.

A combination of discoveries and circumstances led to the Scientific Revolution and helped spread its impact. By the late Middle Ages, European scholars had translated many works by Muslim scholars. These scholars had compiled a storehouse of ancient and current scientific knowledge. Based on this knowledge, medieval universities added scientific courses in astronomy, physics, and mathematics.

During the Renaissance, scholars uncovered many classical manuscripts. They found that the ancient authorities often did not agree with each other. Moreover,

THINK THROUGH HISTORY
A. Analyzing Issues Why did most people believe the geocentric theory?
A. Answer It was supported by common sense, the learned authority of Aristotle and Ptolemy, and church teachings.

This drawing from an astrology text of 1531 shows the signs of the zodiac moving around the earth. It is based on Ptolemy's system, with the earth at the center.

Section 1 Overview

OBJECTIVES

1. To list circumstances that led to the Scientific Revolution.
2. To summarize the development of the heliocentric theory and explain why it led to conflict.
3. To describe the scientific method and show how Bacon and Descartes advanced this approach.
4. To explain Newton's law of gravity.
5. To describe the importance of the scientific method in different fields.

CRITICAL THINKING
- Analyzing issues, p. 545
- Clarifying, pp. 546, 549
- Recognizing effects, p. 546
- Contrasting, p. 548
- Drawing conclusions, p. 550

FOCUS
5-Minute Warm-Up

▶ **Identifying Key Concepts**
To examine Enlightenment ideas, have students answer these questions.

1. Study the Changing Idea chart on page 548. What were the old methods used to understand the physical world?

2. What new methods replaced the old methods?

📜 **WARM-UP TRANSPARENCY 22**

OBJECTIVE ① INSTRUCT

The Roots of Modern Science

▶ **Key Ideas**
- Medieval scholars have a geocentric view of the universe.
- Exploration and new discoveries challenge old ways of thinking about the world and lead to the Scientific Revolution.

📄 **IN-DEPTH RESOURCES: UNIT 5**
Guided Reading, p. 19

📄 **ACCESS FOR STUDENTS ACQUIRING ENGLISH**
Guided Reading (Spanish), 219

(continued on next page)

OBJECTIVE **2** INSTRUCT

A Revolutionary Model of the Universe

▶ **Key Ideas**
- Scientists develop the heliocentric theory through observation and mathematics.
- Galileo's observations and his laws of motion support the heliocentric theory.
- Galileo's ideas conflict with religious teaching and authority, and lead to his arrest.

IN-DEPTH RESOURCES: UNIT 5
Geography Application: Three Theories of the Solar System, p. 24

History Makers: Copernicus, p. 34

WORLD ART AND CULTURES TRANSPARENCIES
AT48 Vermeer's *The Astronomer*

CRITICAL THINKING ACTIVITY
CLASS TIME: 15 MINUTES

Sequence
To help students understand the development of the heliocentric theory, have them create a flow chart like the one below. After each scientist's name, students should write his contribution to the theory.

Copernicus
↓
Tycho Brahe
↓
Johannes Kepler
↓
Galileo

European explorers traveled to Africa, Asia, and the Americas. Such lands were inhabited by peoples and animals previously unknown in Europe. These discoveries opened Europeans to the possibility that there were new truths to be found. The invention of the printing press during this period helped spread challenging ideas—both old and new—more widely among Europe's thinkers.

The age of European exploration also fueled a great deal of scientific research, especially in astronomy and mathematics. Navigators needed better instruments and geographic measurements, for example, to determine their location in the open sea. As scientists began to look more closely at the world around them, they made observations that did not match the ancient beliefs. They found they had reached the limit of the classical world's knowledge. Yet, they still needed to know more.

A Revolutionary Model of the Universe

The first major challenge to accepted scientific thinking came in the field of astronomy. The Scientific Revolution started when a small group of scholars began to question the geocentric theory.

This model shows how Copernicus saw the planets revolving around the sun—in perfect circles.

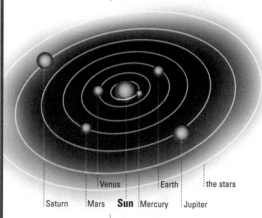

Saturn   Mars   **Sun**   Mercury   Jupiter
Venus   Earth   the stars

The Heliocentric Theory Although backed by authority and common sense, the geocentric theory did not accurately explain the movements of the sun, moon, and planets. This problem troubled a Polish cleric and astronomer named **Nicolaus Copernicus** (koh·PUR·nuh·kuhs). In the early 1500s, Copernicus became interested in an old Greek idea that the sun stood at the center of the universe. After studying planetary movements for more than 25 years, Copernicus reasoned that indeed, the stars, the earth, and the other planets revolved around the sun.

Copernicus's **heliocentric,** or sun-centered, **theory** still did not completely explain why the planets orbited the way they did. He also knew that most scholars and clergy would reject his theory because it contradicted their religious views. Fearing ridicule or persecution, Copernicus did not publish his findings until 1543, the last year of his life. He received a copy of his book, *On the Revolutions of the Heavenly Bodies,* on his deathbed.

While revolutionary, Copernicus's book caused little stir at first. Over the next century and a half, other scientists built on the foundations he had laid. A Danish astronomer, Tycho Brahe (TEE·koh brah), carefully recorded the movements of the planets for many years. Brahe produced mountains of accurate data based on his observations. However, it was left to his followers to make mathematical sense of them.

After Brahe's death in 1601, his assistant, a brilliant mathematician named **Johannes Kepler,** continued his work. After studying Brahe's data, Kepler concluded that certain mathematical laws govern planetary motion. One of these laws showed that the planets revolve around the sun in elliptical orbits instead of circles, as was previously thought. Kepler's laws showed that Copernicus's basic ideas were true. They demonstrated mathematically that the planets revolve around the sun.

Galileo's Discoveries In 1581, a 17-year-old Italian student named **Galileo Galilei** sat in a cathedral closely watching a chandelier swing on its chain. Aristotle had said that a pendulum swings at a slower rhythm as it approaches its resting place. Using his beating pulse, Galileo carefully timed the chandelier's swings. Aristotle's idea was wrong. Instead, each swing of the pendulum took exactly the same amount of time. Galileo had discovered the law of the pendulum.

THINK THROUGH HISTORY
B. Clarifying How did Copernicus arrive at the heliocentric theory?

THINK THROUGH HISTORY
C. Recognizing Effects How did Kepler's findings support the heliocentric theory?

546 Chapter 22

TEACHING OPTION   **BLOCK SCHEDULING**   **SKILLBUILDER MINI-LESSON: Clarifying**   CLASS TIME 30 MINUTES

Explaining the Skill: To clarify concepts in their reading material, students should define unfamiliar terms in the material and restate the content in their own words. This process can help reinforce students' understanding of the concepts.

Applying the Skill: To understand how the heliocentric model developed, students will need to

understand some key terms. Ask students to use a dictionary and the Glossary on page 1015 to define the following terms: *geocentric theory, heliocentric theory, revolved, orbited, elliptical orbit.*

Next, have students reread the passage titled "The Heliocentric Theory" on page 546. Then have students work in pairs to write questions about the main ideas of the passage. One possible question might be "How did the heliocentric theory develop?"

Suggest students use the Think Through History questions in the margin, as well as their own questions, and write their own answers to them. Partners should answer the questions in their own words and use their answers to write a summary of the passage. Encourage students to read their summaries aloud.

 IN-DEPTH RESOURCES: UNIT 5
Skillbuilder Practice: Clarifying , p. 23

In another study, Galileo found that a falling object accelerates at a fixed and predictable rate. Galileo also tested Aristotle's theory that heavy objects fall faster than lighter ones. According to legend, he dropped stones of different weights from the Leaning Tower of Pisa. He then calculated how fast each fell. Contrary to Aristotle's assumption, the objects fell at the same speed.

Later, Galileo learned that a Dutch lens maker had built an instrument that could enlarge far-off objects. Without seeing this device, Galileo successfully built his own telescope. After making some improvements, Galileo used his telescope to study the heavens in 1609.

Then in 1610, he published a series of newsletters called *Starry Messenger*, which described his astonishing observations. Galileo announced that Jupiter had four moons and that the sun had dark spots. He also noted that the earth's moon had a rough, uneven surface. His description of the moon's surface shattered Aristotle's theory that the moon and stars were made of a pure, perfect substance. Galileo's observations, as well as his laws of motion, also clearly supported the theories of Copernicus.

Conflict with the Church Galileo's findings frightened both Catholic and Protestant leaders because they went against church teaching and authority. If people believed the church could be wrong about this, they could question other church teachings as well.

In 1616, the Catholic Church warned Galileo not to defend the ideas of Copernicus. Although Galileo remained publicly silent, he continued his studies. Then, in 1632, he published *Dialogue Concerning the Two Chief World Systems.* This book presented the ideas of both Copernicus and Ptolemy, but it clearly showed that Galileo supported the Copernican theory. The pope angrily summoned Galileo to Rome to stand trial before the Inquisition.

Galileo stood before the court in 1633. Under the threat of torture, he knelt before the cardinals and read aloud a signed confession. In it, he agreed that the ideas of Copernicus were false.

> With sincere heart and unpretended faith I abjure, curse, and detest the aforesaid errors and heresies [of Copernicus] and also every other error . . . contrary to the Holy Church, and I swear that in the future I will never again say or assert . . . anything that might cause a similar suspicion toward me.
>
> **GALILEO GALILEI,** quoted in *The Discoverers*

Galileo was never again a free man. He lived under house arrest and died in 1642 at his villa near Florence. However, his books and ideas still spread all over Europe.

The Scientific Method

The revolution in scientific thinking that Copernicus, Kepler, and Galileo began eventually developed into a new approach to science called the scientific method. The **scientific method** is a logical procedure for gathering and testing ideas. It begins with a problem or question arising from an observation. Scientists next form a hypothesis, or unproved assumption. The hypothesis is then tested in an experiment or on the basis of data. In the final step, scientists analyze and interpret their data to reach a new conclusion. That conclusion either confirms or disproves the hypothesis.

The scientific method did not develop overnight. The work of two important thinkers of the 1600s, Francis Bacon and René Descartes, helped to advance the new approach.

Francis Bacon, an English politician and writer, had a passionate interest in science. He believed that by better understanding the world, scientists would generate practical knowledge that would improve people's lives. In his writings, Bacon attacked medieval

Galileo used this telescope to observe the moon. He saw that the moon's surface is rough, not smooth as others

CONNECT to TODAY

The Vatican Clears Galileo

In 1992, Pope John Paul II officially acknowledged that Galileo was correct in asserting that the earth revolves around the sun. His pronouncement came after a 13-year study of Galileo's case by a Vatican science panel.

The panel concluded that church leaders were clearly wrong to condemn Galileo but that they had acted in good faith. They were working within the knowledge of their time, the panel said. Therefore, they could not see how Galileo's discoveries could go along with their interpretation of the Bible.

Enlightenment and Revolution **547**

Major Steps in the Scientific Revolution

Interpreting the Chart Have students read the time line. Then ask students how they can tell that the scientific revolution was spreading by the 1600s. *Answer: Important scientific events are more frequent after 1600.*

Extension Activity Tell students to connect early events on the time line with later scientific developments. For example, the invention of the microscope in 1590 probably led to the observation of bacteria in 1674.

Newton Explains the Law of Gravity

▸ **Key Ideas**
- Newton's law of gravity explains how the same physical laws govern motion on the earth and in the heavens.

MORE ABOUT . . .
Newton's Law of Gravity

What does an apple have to do with gravity? According to George Stukeley, Newton's biographer and close friend, Newton was sitting in the shade of an apple tree when an apple fell nearby. Newton was in a thoughtful mood and began to wonder why apples always fall to the ground. Why don't they fall sideways or up? Newton reasoned that the earth must have a power that draws objects to it. This was the beginning of the law of gravity.

Major Steps in the Scientific Revolution

1572 Brahe discovers nova, or bright new star, which contradicts Aristotle's idea that universe is unchanging.

1609 Kepler publishes first two laws of planetary motion.

1610 Galileo publishes *Starry Messenger.*

1520   1570   1620

1543 Copernicus publishes heliocentric theory.
Vesalius publishes human anatomy textbook.

1590 Janssen invents microscope.

1620 Bacon's book *Novum Organum (New Instrument)* encourages experimental method.

This microscope dates from the 17th century.

Nicolaus Copernicus began the Scientific Revolution with his heliocentric theory.

scholars for relying too heavily on the conclusions of Aristotle and other ancient thinkers. He also criticized the way in which both Aristotle and medieval scholars arrived at their conclusions. They had reasoned from abstract theories. Instead, he urged scientists to experiment. Scientists, he wrote, should observe the world and gather information about it first. Then they should draw conclusions from that information. This approach is called empiricism, or the experimental method.

In France, **René Descartes** (day·KAHRT) also took a keen interest in science. He developed analytical geometry, which linked algebra and geometry. This provided an important new tool for scientific research.

Like Bacon, Descartes believed that scientists needed to reject old assumptions and teachings. As a mathematician, however, his approach to gaining knowledge differed from Bacon's. Rather than using experimentation, Descartes relied on mathematics and logic. He believed that everything should be doubted until proved by reason. The only thing he knew for certain was that he existed—because, as he wrote, "I think, therefore I am." From this starting point, he followed a train of strict reasoning to arrive at other basic truths.

Modern scientific methods are based on the ideas of Bacon and Descartes. Scientists have shown that observation and experimentation, together with general laws that can be expressed mathematically, can lead people to a better understanding of the natural world.

THINK THROUGH HISTORY
D. Contrasting How did Descartes's approach to science differ from Bacon's?
D. Answer
Descartes emphasized mathematical reasoning; Bacon, experimentation.

Changing Idea: Scientific Method

Old Science
Scholars generally relied on ancient authorities, church teachings, common sense and reasoning to explain the physical world.

New Science
In time, scholars began to use observation, experimentation, and scientific reasoning to gather knowledge and draw conclusions about the physical world.

Newton Explains the Law of Gravity

By the mid-1600s, the accomplishments of Copernicus, Kepler, and Galileo had shattered the old views of astronomy and physics. Later, the great English scientist **Isaac Newton** helped to bring together their breakthroughs under a single theory of motion.

Newton studied mathematics and physics at Cambridge University. By the time he was 24, Newton was certain that all physical objects were affected equally by the same forces. Kepler had worked out laws for a planet's motion around the sun. Galileo had studied the motion of pendulums. Newton's great discovery was that the same force ruled the motions of the planets, the pendulum, and all matter on earth and in space.

548 Chapter 22

Task: Partners will conduct interviews to find out how people of different generations have reacted to technological developments. Partners will present the results of their interviews.

Purpose: To learn how people feel about new ideas.

Activity: Tell partners to interview three people from three different generations to find out how they reacted to technological developments such as space travel, television, computers, and other recent developments. Partners should make a list of interview questions that ask people to recall an important development, how they learned about it, how they and others reacted to it, and how the new development affected their lives. Suggest students interview parents, grandparents, other relatives, neighbors, and friends. Have partners take notes during the interviews and use the notes as a basis for presenting the results of their interviews. Remind partners to include in their presentations background information about each interview subject, such as age, occupation, and whether the person is a friend or relative.

 ALTERNATIVE ASSESSMENT BOOK
Standards for Evaluating a Cooperative Activity

1628 Harvey reveals how human heart functions.

1637 Descartes's book *Discourse on Method* sets forth his scientific method of reasoning from the basis of doubt.

1662 Boyle discovers mathematical relationship between the pressure and volume of gases, known as Boyle's law.

1674 Leeuwenhoek observes bacteria through microscope.

1714 Fahrenheit invents mercury thermometer.

1620 — 1670 — 1720

1633 Galileo faces Inquisition for support of Copernicus's theory.

1643 Torricelli invents barometer.

1660 England establishes Royal Society to support scientific study.

1666 France establishes Academy of Sciences.

1687 Newton publishes law of gravity.

OBJECTIVE **5** INSTRUCT

The Scientific Revolution Spreads

▶ **Key Ideas**
- New tools and instruments help scientists make precise observations.
- The study of human anatomy leads to a greater understanding of the body and disease.
- The use of the scientific method in chemistry leads to a better understanding of matter.

THINK THROUGH HISTORY
E. Clarifying Why was the law of gravitation important?
E. Answer It explained motion both on the earth and in the heavens and helped prove that the same physical laws govern both.

He disproved the idea of Aristotle that one set of physical laws governed earth and another set governed the rest of the universe.

The key idea that linked motion in the heavens with motion on the earth was the law of universal gravitation. According to this law, every object in the universe attracts every other object. The degree of attraction depends on the mass of the objects and the distance between them.

In 1687, Newton published his ideas in a work called *Mathematical Principles of Natural Philosophy*—one of the most important scientific books ever written. The universe he described was like a giant clock. Its parts all worked together perfectly in ways that could be expressed mathematically. Newton believed that God was the creator of this orderly universe, the clockmaker who had set everything in motion.

Isaac Newton's law of gravity explained how the same physical laws governed motion both on the earth and in the heavens.

The Scientific Revolution Spreads

After astronomers explored the secrets of the universe, other scientists began to study the secrets of nature on earth. Careful observation and the use of the scientific method eventually became important in many different fields.

Scientific Instruments Scientists developed new tools and instruments to make the precise observations that the scientific method demanded. The first microscope was invented by a Dutch maker of eyeglasses, Zacharias Janssen (YAHN·suhn), in 1590. In the 1670s, a Dutch drapery merchant and amateur scientist named Anton van Leeuwenhoek (LAY·vuhn·HUK) used a microscope to observe bacteria swimming in tooth scrapings. He also saw red blood cells for the first time. His examination of grubs, maggots, and other such organisms showed that they did not come to life spontaneously, as was previously thought. Rather, they were immature insects.

In 1643, one of Galileo's students, Evangelista Torricelli (TAWR·uh·CHEHL·ee), developed the first mercury barometer, a tool for measuring atmospheric pressure and predicting weather. In 1714, the Dutch physicist Gabriel Fahrenheit (FAR·uhn·HYT) made the first thermometer to use mercury in glass. Fahrenheit's thermometer showed water freezing at 32°. A Swedish astronomer, Anders Celsius (SEHL·see·uhs), created another scale for the mercury thermometer in 1742. Celsius's scale showed freezing at 0°.

Medicine and the Human Body During the Middle Ages, European doctors had accepted as fact the writings of an ancient Greek physician named Galen. However, Galen had never dissected the body of a human being. Instead, he had studied the anatomy of pigs and other animals. Galen assumed that human anatomy was much the same. Galen's assumptions were proved wrong by Andreas Vesalius, a Flemish physician. Vesalius dissected human corpses (despite disapproval of this practice) and published his observations. His book, *On the Fabric of the Human Body* (1543), was filled with detailed drawings of human organs, bones, and muscle.

Enlightenment and Revolution **549**

MORE ABOUT . . .
Scientific Expeditions

In 1768, the English navigator and mapmaker James Cook set out on the first of three voyages to explore and chart the South Pacific. Cook's voyages were scientific expeditions. They were sponsored by the Royal Society of London, a group founded in the mid-1600s to encourage the growth of scientific knowledge. Astronomers, artists, and a botanist went with Cook to gather information about distant parts of the world. Captain Cook became the first European to chart the east coast of Australia and the islands of Tahiti, New Zealand, and Hawaii.

TEACHING OPTIONS | CUSTOMIZING FOR SPECIAL NEEDS | CUSTOMIZING FOR SPECIAL NEEDS

Less Proficient Readers:
Summarizing To help students understand the developments made possible by the Scientific Revolution, have them work in pairs to complete a chart describing the new ideas and discoveries that were happening in different areas of science. Tell partners to use a chart like the one here and write three items in each column.

Scientific Ideas and Discoveries		
Scientific Instruments	Biology and Medicine	Chemistry

Students Acquiring English:
Science Words Students acquiring English may have difficulty reading the passage titled "The Scientific Revolution Spreads" because of the specialized vocabulary it contains. To help these students, first review how to use the pronunciation guides. Then have students reread the subsection titled "Scientific Instruments," listing any words that are difficult to understand. Pair students with proficient readers to look up these words in a dictionary. Then have students go back to the text and make sure they understand it before repeating this process with the next subsection.

Teacher's Edition **549**

Daily *Life*

Smallpox Inoculations

In the 1600s and 1700s, few words raised as much dread as *smallpox.* This contagious disease killed many infants and young children and left others horribly scarred.

In the early 1700s, an English writer named Lady Mary Wortley Montagu observed women in Turkey deliberately inoculating their young children against smallpox. They did this by breaking the skin and applying some liquid taken from the sore of a victim.

Children who were inoculated caught smallpox, but they had a good chance of getting only a mild case. This protected them from ever having the disease again.

Lady Montagu bravely had her son inoculated. She brought the procedure back to Britain, and from there it spread all over Europe.

An English doctor named William Harvey continued Vesalius's work in anatomy. In 1628, he published *On the Motion of the Heart and Blood in Animals,* which showed that the heart acted as a pump to circulate blood throughout the body. He also described the function of blood vessels.

In the late 1700s, British physician Edward Jenner introduced a vaccine to prevent smallpox. Inoculation using live smallpox germs had been practiced in Asia for centuries. While beneficial, this technique was also dangerous. Jenner discovered that inoculation with germs from a cattle disease called cowpox gave permanent protection from smallpox for humans. Because cowpox was a much milder disease, the risks for this form of inoculation were much lower. Jenner used cowpox to produce the world's first vaccination.

Vocabulary
inoculation: injecting a germ into a person's body so as to create an immunity to the disease.

Discoveries in Chemistry Robert Boyle pioneered the use of the scientific method in chemistry. He is considered the founder of modern chemistry. In a book called *The Sceptical Chymist* (1661), Boyle challenged Aristotle's idea that the physical world consisted of four elements—earth, air, fire, and water. Instead, Boyle proposed that matter was made up of smaller primary particles that joined together in different ways. Boyle's most famous contribution to chemistry is Boyle's law. This law explains how the volume, temperature, and pressure of gas affect each other.

Another chemist, Joseph Priestley, separated one pure gas from air in 1774. He noticed how good he felt after breathing this special air and watched how alert two mice were while breathing it. Wrote Priestley, "Who can tell but that, in time, this pure air may become a fashionable article of luxury? Hitherto only two mice and I have had the privilege of breathing it." Meanwhile, in France, Antoine Lavoisier (lah·vwah·ZYAY) was performing similar experiments. In 1779, Lavoisier named the newly discovered gas oxygen.

Other scholars and philosophers applied a scientific approach to other areas of life. Believing themselves to be orderly, rational, and industrious, they thought of themselves as enlightened. They would become the leaders of a new intellectual and social movement called the Enlightenment.

Section ❶ Assessment

1. TERMS & NAMES

Identify
• Scientific Revolution
• Nicolaus Copernicus
• heliocentric theory
• Johannes Kepler
• Galileo Galilei
• scientific method
• Francis Bacon
• René Descartes
• Isaac Newton

2. TAKING NOTES

Use a web diagram such as the one below to show the events and circumstances that led to the Scientific Revolution.

Causes of the Scientific Revolution

3. DRAWING CONCLUSIONS

"If I have seen farther than others," said Newton, "it is because I have stood on the shoulders of giants." Who were the giants to whom Newton was referring? Could this be said of any scientific accomplishment? Explain.

4. THEME ACTIVITY

Science & Technology Working in groups of three or four, create a Scientific Revolution Discovery Board. Use these categories: Astronomy, Science, Medicine, Chemistry, Biology. Include important people, ideas, accomplishments.

550 Chapter 22

ANSWERS

TERMS & NAMES
• Scientific Revolution, p. 545
• Nicolaus Copernicus, p. 546
• heliocentric theory, p. 546
• Johannes Kepler, p. 546
• Galileo Galilei, p. 546
• scientific method, p. 547
• Francis Bacon, p. 547
• René Descartes, p. 548
• Isaac Newton, p. 548

2. TAKING NOTES
Possible Responses:
Renaissance discovery of new classical manuscripts leads scholars to question accepted knowledge; exploration broadens European horizons; printing press spreads ideas; discoveries of Copernicus and other scientists challenge accepted thinking.

3. DRAWING CONCLUSIONS
Possible Responses: Giants were Copernicus, Kepler, and Galileo. Yes, scientific discoveries give scientists a clearer understanding of how the world works. New discoveries lead to further questions for investigation and more discoveries.

4. THEME ACTIVITY
Standards for Evaluation
An effective Scientific Revolut[ion] Discovery Board should meet the following criteria:
• Introduces a range of people[,] ideas, and accomplishments[.]
• Is thoughtfully organized.
• Shows evidence of teamwor[k]

The Enlightenment in Europe

TERMS & NAMES
- Enlightenment
- social contract
- John Locke
- natural rights
- philosophe
- Voltaire
- Montesquieu
- separation of powers
- Jean Jacques Rousseau
- Mary Wollstonecraft

MAIN IDEA

A revolution in intellectual activity changed Europeans' view of government and society.

WHY IT MATTERS NOW

Freedoms and some forms of government in many countries today are a result of Enlightenment thinking.

SETTING THE STAGE The influence of the Scientific Revolution soon spread beyond the world of science. Philosophers admired Newton because he had used reason to explain the laws governing nature. People began to look for laws governing human behavior as well. They hoped to apply reason and the scientific method to all aspects of society—government, religion, economics, and education. In this way, the ideas of the Scientific Revolution paved the way for a new movement called the **Enlightenment,** or the Age of Reason. This movement reached its height in the mid-1700s.

Two Views on Government

The Enlightenment started from some key ideas put forth by two English political thinkers of the 1600s, Thomas Hobbes and John Locke. Both men experienced the political turmoil of England early in that century. However, they came to very different conclusions about government and human nature.

Hobbes's Social Contract Thomas Hobbes expressed his views in a work called *Leviathan* (1651). The horrors of the English Civil War convinced him that all humans were naturally selfish and wicked. Without governments to keep order, Hobbes said, there would be "war of every man against every man." In this state of nature, as Hobbes called it, life would be "solitary, poor, nasty, brutish, and short."

Hobbes argued that to escape such a bleak life, people gave up their rights to a strong ruler. In exchange, they gained law and order. Hobbes called this agreement, by which people created government, the **social contract.** Because people acted in their own self-interest, Hobbes said, the ruler needed total power to keep citizens under control. The best government was one that had the awesome power of a leviathan (sea monster). In Hobbes's view, such a government was an absolute monarchy, which could impose order and demand obedience.

Locke's Natural Rights The philosopher **John Locke** held a different, more positive, view of human nature. He believed that people could learn from experience and improve themselves. As reasonable beings, they had the natural ability to govern their own affairs and to look after the welfare of society. Locke criticized absolute monarchy and favored the idea of self-government.

According to Locke, all people are born free and equal, with three **natural rights**—life, liberty, and property. The purpose of government, said Locke, is to protect these rights. If a government fails to do so, citizens have a right to overthrow it. Locke

This engraving depicts the beheading of Charles I. Hobbes developed his political ideas out of the violent events in England in the early 1600s.

Enlightenment and Revolution **551**

A. Possible Answer People enter into a social contract with a strong ruler to gain safety and security.

B. Possible Answer Hobbes believed that humans were naturally selfish and wicked; Locke's view was more positive—humans were reasonable, could learn and grow, and had natural rights.

THINK THROUGH HISTORY
A. Clarifying According to Hobbes, why would people want to live under the rule of an absolute monarch?

THINK THROUGH HISTORY
B. Contrasting How does Locke's view of human nature differ from that of Hobbes?

SECTION 2 RESOURCES

PRINT RESOURCES

IN-DEPTH RESOURCES: UNIT 5
Guided Reading, p. 20
Primary Source: from *The Social Contract,* p. 27; from *Two Treatises on Government,* p. 28; from *A Vindication of the Rights of Women,* p. 29
History Makers: Baron de Montesquieu, p. 35

ACCESS FOR STUDENTS ACQUIRING ENGLISH
Guided Reading (Spanish), p. 220

FORMAL ASSESSMENT
Section Quiz, p. 253

ALTERNATIVE ASSESSMENT BOOK

TECHNOLOGY RESOURCES
CD-ROM
Electronic Library of Primary Sources
INTERNET www.mworldhistory.com

Section 2 Overview

OBJECTIVES

1. To explain Hobbes's and Locke's views on government.
2. To list important Enlightenment philosophers and concepts.
3. To describe women's contributions to the Enlightenment.
4. To explain the impact of the Enlightenment on Western civilization.

SKILLBUILDER
- Interpreting charts, p. 554

CRITICAL THINKING
- Clarifying, pp. 551, 554, 557
- Contrasting, p. 551
- Comparing, p. 552
- Analyzing issues, p. 553
- Summarizing, p. 554
- Drawing conclusions, p. 555
- Synthesizing, p. 556
- Analyzing themes, p. 556

FOCUS

5-Minute Warm-Up

▶ *Drawing Conclusions*
To understand Enlightenment ideas about government, have students answer these questions.

1. Study the Changing Idea chart on page 552. According to the old idea, where does a monarch's power come from?

2. According to the new idea, where should a government's power come from?

WARM-UP TRANSPARENCY 22

OBJECTIVE ① INSTRUCT

Two Views on Government

▶ *Key Ideas*
- Hobbes believes that people need a strong government to keep order.
- Locke believes that people have a natural ability to govern themselves.

(continued on next page)

(continued from page 551)

- Locke's ideas about government are the foundation of modern democracy.

IN-DEPTH RESOURCES: UNIT 5
Guided Reading, p. 20
Primary Source: from *Two Treatises on Government*, p. 28

ACCESS FOR STUDENTS ACQUIRING ENGLISH
Guided Reading (Spanish), p. 220

 OBJECTIVE ② INSTRUCT

The Philosophes Advocate Reason

▶ **Key Ideas**
- The five important philosophical concepts are reason, nature, happiness, progress, and liberty.
- Voltaire fights intolerance through his writing.
- Montesquieu believes a government's power should be divided into different branches.
- Rousseau believes governments should be formed through the agreement of free individuals.
- Beccaria's ideas about the justice system promote criminal justice.

ELECTRONIC LIBRARY OF PRIMARY SOURCES
from *The Persian Letters*

HISTORY MAKERS
Voltaire

Voltaire is credited with having made the following famous statement: "I disapprove of what you say, but I will defend to the death your right to say it." What does this statement indicate about Voltaire's views on free speech? How is it similar to beliefs about free speech in the United States?

Changing Idea: The Right to Govern

Old Idea
A monarch's rule is justified by divine right.

New Idea
A government's power comes from the consent of the governed.

published his ideas in 1690, two years after the Glorious Revolution. His book, *Two Treatises on Government*, served to justify the overthrow of James II.

Locke's theory had a deep influence on modern political thinking. His statement that a government's power comes from the consent of the people is the foundation of modern democracy. The ideas of government by popular consent and the right to rebel against unjust rulers helped inspire struggles for liberty in Europe and the Americas.

The Philosophes Advocate Reason

The Enlightenment reached its height in France in the mid-1700s. Paris became the meeting place for people who wanted to discuss politics and ideas. The social critics of this period in France were known as **philosophes** (FIHL·uh·SAHFS), the French word for philosophers. The philosophes believed that people could apply reason to all aspects of life—just as Isaac Newton had applied reason to science. Five important concepts formed the core of their philosophy:

1. **Reason** Enlightened thinkers believed truth could be discovered through reason or logical thinking. Reason, they said, was the absence of intolerance, bigotry, or prejudice in one's thinking.

2. **Nature** The philosophes referred to nature frequently. To them, what was natural was also good and reasonable. They believed that there were natural laws of economics and politics just as there were natural laws of motion.

3. **Happiness** A person who lived by nature's laws would find happiness, the philosophes said. They were impatient with the medieval notion that people should accept misery in this world to find joy in the hereafter. The philosophes wanted well-being on earth, and they believed it was possible.

4. **Progress** The philosophes were the first Europeans to believe in progress for society. Now that people used a scientific approach, they believed, society and humankind could be perfected.

5. **Liberty** The philosophes envied the liberties that the English people had won in their Glorious Revolution and Bill of Rights. In France, there were many restrictions on speech, religion, trade, and personal travel. Through reason, the philosophes believed, society could be set free.

Voltaire Combats Intolerance Probably the most brilliant and influential of the philosophes was François Marie Arouet. Using the pen name **Voltaire,** he published more than 70 books of political essays, philosophy, history, fiction, and drama.

Voltaire often used satire against his opponents. He made frequent targets of the clergy, the aristocracy, and the government. His sharp tongue made him enemies at the French court, and twice he was sent to prison. After his second jail term, Voltaire was exiled to England for two years. There, Voltaire came to admire the English government much more than his own. After he returned to Paris,

HISTORY MAKERS

Voltaire
1694–1778

Voltaire corresponded with several European monarchs and nobles. Among them was the Prussian king Frederick II. At the king's invitation, Voltaire spent three years at Frederick's palace. At first, the two men seemed like ideal companions. Both were witty. Both cared nothing for appearances and dressed in shabby, rumpled clothes. Each friend paid the other elegant compliments.

Before long, however, the king and the philosophe got on each other's nerves. Voltaire disliked editing Frederick's mediocre poetry. Frederick suspected Voltaire of some shady business dealings. Eventually, Voltaire tried to sneak away, but Prussian soldiers captured him and made him spend the night in jail.

After returning to France, Voltaire described the Prussian king as "a nasty monkey, perfidious friend, [and] wretched poet." Frederick returned the abuse, calling Voltaire a "miser, dirty rogue, [and] coward."

C. Possible Answer Nature good and reasonable, betterment and progress possible, believed in human liberty.

THINK THROUGH HISTORY
C. Comparing How were the philosophes' views similar to Locke's?

Vocabulary
satire: irony, sarcasm, or wit used to attack folly, vice, or stupidity.

Kinesthetic Learners: Role-Playing Students who process knowledge best through hands-on activities may benefit from using role-play to understand the philosophes' concepts. Have students work in groups of five. Each group member should choose one of the five philosophical concepts described on page 552. After group members have reviewed the concepts, have them discuss and describe them by role-playing philosophes. Encourage the philosophes to ask each other questions about the concepts. Suggest groups perform their discussions for the class.

Gifted and Talented Students: Montesquieu Biography After students have read the information about Montesquieu on page 553, distribute the biography of Montesquieu from the Teacher's Resources. Have students read the biography and then work in pairs to answer the questions. After all pairs have finished, have them discuss their answers as a group. Suggest students also discuss the new information they learned about Montesquieu from the biography. Then ask volunteers to present the questions and their answers to the rest of the class.

IN-DEPTH RESOURCES: UNIT 5
History Makers: *Baron de Montesquieu*, p. 35

much of his work mocked the laws and customs of France. He even dared to raise doubts about the Christian religion. The French king and France's Catholic bishops were outraged. In 1734, fearing another unpleasant jail term, Voltaire fled Paris.

Although he made powerful enemies, Voltaire never stopped fighting for tolerance, reason, freedom of religious belief, and freedom of speech. He used his quill pen as if it were a deadly weapon in a thinker's war against humanity's worst enemies—intolerance, prejudice, and superstition. Such attitudes were, he said, *l'infâme*—infamous or evil things. He often ended his letters with a fighting slogan, *"Écrasez l'infâme!"* (ay·crah·ZAY lahn·FAM). The phrase meant "Crush the evil thing!"

Montesquieu and the Separation of Powers Another influential French writer, the Baron de **Montesquieu** (MAHN·tuh·SKYOO), devoted himself to the study of political liberty. An aristocrat and lawyer, Montesquieu studied the history of ancient Rome. He concluded that Rome's collapse was directly related to its loss of political liberties.

Like Voltaire, Montesquieu believed that Britain was the best-governed country of his own day. Here was a government, he thought, in which power was balanced among three groups of officials. The British king and his ministers held executive power. They carried out the laws of the state. The members of Parliament held legislative, or lawmaking, power. The judges of the English courts held judicial power. They interpreted the laws to see how each applied to a specific case. Montesquieu called this division of power among different branches **separation of powers.**

Montesquieu oversimplified the British system (it did not actually separate powers this way). His idea, however, became a part of his most famous book, *On the Spirit of Laws (1748)*. In his book, Montesquieu proposed that separation of powers would keep any individual or group from gaining total control of the government. "Power," he wrote, "should be a check to power." Each branch of government would serve as a check on the other two. This idea later would be called "checks and balances."

Montesquieu's book was admired by political leaders in the British colonies of North America. His ideas about separation of powers and checks and balances became the basis for the United States Constitution.

> "Power should be a check to power."
> Baron de Montesquieu

Changing Idea: Government Powers

Old Idea	New Idea
Monarch rules with absolute authority.	Separation of government powers among executive, legislative, and judicial branches.

Rousseau: Champion of Freedom A third great philosophe, **Jean Jacques Rousseau** (roo·SOH), was passionately committed to individual freedom. The son of a poor Swiss watchmaker, Rousseau worked as an engraver, music teacher, tutor, and secretary. Eventually, Rousseau made his way to Paris and won recognition as a writer of essays. There he met and befriended other philosophes, although he felt out of place in the circles of Paris high society in which they traveled.

A strange, brilliant, and controversial figure, Rousseau strongly disagreed with other Enlightenment thinkers on many matters. Most philosophes believed that reason, science, and art would improve life for all people. Rousseau, however, argued that civilization corrupted people's natural goodness. "Man is born free, and everywhere he is in chains," he wrote. In the earliest times, according to Rousseau, people had lived as free and equal individuals in a primitive "state of nature." As people became civilized, however, the strongest among them forced everyone else to obey unjust laws. Thus, freedom and equality were destroyed.

> "Man is born free, and everywhere he is in chains."
> Jean Jacques Rousseau

Enlightenment and Revolution **553**

THINK THROUGH HISTORY
D. Analyzing Issues What advantages did Montesquieu see in the separation of powers?
D. Answer It would keep any individual or group from gaining total power; each branch would check the power of the other two.

MORE ABOUT . . .
Voltaire's Early Years

Voltaire, born in Paris, was the son of a lawyer. He received an excellent education but chose not to follow his father into law. Instead, he ended his schooling at age 16 and devoted himself to literary pursuits. He joined a group of irreverent young aristocrats and began to write witty political verses. As a young man, Voltaire got himself into a certain amount of trouble with his writing, but he also managed to meet like-minded people. Through acquaintances with philosophers, artists, and thinkers, and also through his own desire to learn and understand the world, Voltaire became a great thinker.

MORE ABOUT . . .
Jean Jacques Rousseau

All through his life, Rousseau was plagued by feelings of guilt, depression, and inferiority. His attempts to form friendships often failed, and he spent his life as an outsider in society. These difficulties may have been the result of a very unhappy childhood. Rousseau's mother died giving birth to him. His father made him feel guilty for this and was either warm and affectionate or very cold and rejecting toward his son. When Rousseau was ten years old, his father abandoned him. As an adult, Rousseau realized he was more comfortable opposing society that trying to fit into it.

TEACHING OPTION | **BLOCK SCHEDULING** | **COOPERATIVE ACTIVITY: Enlightenment Philosophers** | **CLASS TIME 45 MINUTES**

Task: Groups will write reports about Enlightenment philosophers.

Purpose: To understand the ideas of the Enlightenment philosophers.

Activity: Divide the class into five groups and assign each group one of the following philosophers: Hobbes, Locke, Voltaire, Montesquieu, Rousseau. Group members should work together to research and write reports about their philosopher. Each group's report should explain who the man was, his ideas about government, and how he agreed or disagreed with the ideas of one of the other philosophers. Each group should choose one member to present its report to the class.

📁 **Building a Portfolio:** Remind students to place their best work in their portfolios.

📑 **ALTERNATIVE ASSESSMENT BOOK** Standards for Evaluating a Cooperative Activity

Standards for Evaluation
Reports should . . .

• clearly state the philosophers' ideas
• show evidence of research and group effort
• explain how the philosophers agreed and disagreed

Teacher's Edition **553**

Rousseau believed that the only good government was one that was freely formed by the people and guided by the "general will" of society—a direct democracy. Under such a government, people agree to give up some of their freedom in favor of the common good. In 1762, he explained his political philosophy in a book called *The Social Contract.*

A VOICE FROM THE PAST
The heart of the idea of the social contract may be stated simply: Each of us places his person and authority under the supreme direction of the general will, and the group receives each individual as an indivisible part of the whole. . . .
 In order that the social contract may not be a mere empty formula, everyone must understand that any individual who refuses to obey the general will must be forced by his fellows to do so. This is a way of saying that it may be necessary to force a man to be free; freedom in this case being obedience to the will of all.
JEAN JACQUES ROUSSEAU, *The Social Contract*

Rousseau's view of the social contract differed greatly from that of Hobbes. For Hobbes, the social contract was an agreement between a society and its government. For Rousseau, it was an agreement among free individuals to create a society and a government.

Like Locke, Rousseau argued that legitimate government came from the consent of the governed. However, Rousseau believed in a much broader democracy than Locke had stood for. He argued that all people were equal and that titles of nobility should be abolished. Rousseau's ideas inspired many of the leaders of the French Revolution who overthrew the monarchy in 1789.

Beccaria Promotes Criminal Justice An Italian philosophe named Cesare Bonesana Beccaria (BAYK·uh·REE·ah) turned his thoughts to the justice system. He believed that laws existed to preserve social order, not to avenge crimes. In his celebrated book *On Crimes and Punishments* (1764), Beccaria railed against common abuses of justice. They included torturing of witnesses and suspects, irregular proceedings in trials, and punishments that were arbitrary or cruel. He argued that a person accused of a crime should receive a speedy trial, and that torture should never be used. Moreover, he said, the degree of punishment should be based on the seriousness of the crime. He also believed that capital punishment should be abolished.

Major Ideas of the Enlightenment

Idea	Thinker	Impact
Natural rights—life, liberty, property	Locke	Fundamental to U.S. Declaration of Independence
Separation of powers	Montesquieu	France, United States, Latin American nations use separation of powers in new constitutions
Freedom of thought and expression	Voltaire	Guaranteed in U.S. Bill of Rights and French Declaration of the Rights of Man and Citizen; European monarchs reduce or eliminate censorship
Abolishment of torture	Beccaria	Guaranteed in U.S. Bill of Rights; torture outlawed or reduced in nations of Europe and the Americas
Religious freedom	Voltaire	Guaranteed in U.S. Bill of Rights and French Declaration of the Rights of Man and Citizen; European monarchs reduce persecution
Women's equality	Wollstonecraft	Women's rights groups form in Europe and North America

SKILLBUILDER: Interpreting Charts
1. *What important documents reflect the influence of Enlightenment ideas?*
2. *In your opinion, which are the two most important Enlightenment ideas? Support your answer with reasons.*

Beccaria based his ideas about justice on the principle that governments should seek the greatest good for the greatest number of people. His ideas influenced criminal law reformers in Europe and North America.

Women and the Enlightenment

The philosophes challenged many assumptions about government and society. But they often took a traditional view toward women. Rousseau, for example, developed many progressive ideas about education. However, he believed that a girl's education should mainly teach her how to be a helpful wife and mother. Other male social critics scolded women for reading novels because they thought it encouraged idleness and wickedness. Still, some male writers argued for more education for women and for women's equality in marriage.

Women writers also tried to improve the status of women. In 1694, the English writer Mary Astell published *A Serious Proposal to the Ladies*. Her book addressed the lack of educational opportunities for women. In later writings, she used Enlightenment arguments about government to criticize the unequal relationship between men and women in marriage. She wrote, "If absolute sovereignty be not necessary in a state, how comes it to be so in a family? . . . If all men are born free, how is it that all women are born slaves?"

During the 1700s, other women picked up these themes. Among the most persuasive was **Mary Wollstonecraft,** who published an essay called *A Vindication of the Rights of Woman* in 1792. In the essay, she disagreed with Rousseau that women's education should be secondary to men's. Rather, she argued that women, like men, need education to become virtuous and useful. Even if they are to be mothers, education will make them better mothers. Wollstonecraft also believed that women not only should be able to be nurses but also should be able to become doctors. She also argued for women's right to participate in politics.

Women made important contributions to the Enlightenment in other ways. In Paris and other European cities, wealthy women helped spread Enlightenment ideas through social gatherings called salons. (The importance of salons is discussed later in this chapter.)

One woman fortunate enough to receive education in the sciences was Emilie du Châtelet (shah·tlay). Du Châtelet was an aristocrat trained as a mathematician and physicist. By translating Newton's work from Latin into French, she helped stimulate interest in science in France.

Impact of the Enlightenment

Over a span of a few decades, Enlightenment writers challenged long-held ideas about society. They examined such principles as the divine right of monarchs, the union of church and state, and unequal social classes. They held these beliefs up to the light of reason and found them unreasonable.

The philosophes mainly lived in the world of ideas. They formed and popularized new theories. Although they encouraged European monarchs to make reforms, they were not active revolutionaries. However, their theories eventually inspired the American and French revolutions and other revolutionary movements in the 1800s. Enlightenment thinking produced three other long-term effects that helped shape Western civilization.

HISTORY MAKERS

Mary Wollstonecraft
1759–1797

In *A Vindication of the Rights of Woman*, Mary Wollstonecraft argued that women deserved the same rights as men. "Let women share the rights and she will emulate [imitate] the virtues of men; for she must grow more perfect when emancipated," she wrote. The key to gaining equality and freedom, she argued, was better education.

Wollstonecraft herself received little formal education. She and her two sisters taught themselves by studying books at home. With her sisters, she briefly ran a school. These experiences shaped her thoughts about education.

After joining a London publisher, Wollstonecraft met many leading radicals of the day. One of them was her future husband, the writer Richard Godwin. She died at age 38, after giving birth to their daughter, Mary. This child, whose married name was Mary Wollstonecraft Shelley, went on to write the classic novel *Frankenstein*.

Enlightenment and Revolution **555**

Daily Life
Attitudes Toward Children

Before the mid-1700s, people commonly believed that children were naturally sinful. Parents raised their children with a harsh hand and treated them like miniature adults.

During the Enlightenment, such attitudes changed. People believed children should be better educated and could be allowed to mature into adulthood. Parents lessened the use of corporal punishment and increased play time.

By 1780, there was a new market for rocking horses, jigsaw puzzles, and baby clothes. In Britain, the first Mother Goose book of nursery rhymes appeared. Books like *The Newtonian System of the Universe Digested for Young Minds* by Tom Telescope appeared in print. Children even began to get discount tickets to museums and curiosity shows.

Belief in Progress The first effect was a belief in progress. Pioneers such as Galileo and Newton had discovered the key for unlocking the mysteries of nature in the 1500s and 1600s. With the door thus opened, the growth of scientific knowledge seemed to quicken in the 1700s. Scientists made key new discoveries in chemistry, physics, biology, and mechanics. The successes of the Scientific Revolution gave people the confidence that human reason could solve social problems. Philosophes and reformers urged an end to the practice of slavery. They also argued for more social equality and improvements in education. Through reason, a better society was possible.

A More Secular Outlook A second outcome was the rise of a more secular, or worldly, outlook. During the Enlightenment, people began to openly question their religious beliefs and the teachings of the church. Before the Scientific Revolution, people accepted the mysteries of the universe as the mysteries of God. One by one, scientists discovered that these mysteries could be explained mathematically. Newton himself was a deeply religious man, and he sought to reveal God's majesty through his work. However, his findings caused some people to change the way they thought about God.

Voltaire and other critics attacked some of the beliefs and practices of organized Christianity. They wanted to rid religious faith of superstition and fear and promote tolerance of all religions.

Importance of the Individual Faith in science and in progress produced a third outcome—the rise of individualism. As people began to turn away from the church and royalty for guidance, they looked to themselves instead.

The philosophes encouraged people to use their own ability to reason in order to judge what is right or wrong. They also emphasized the importance of the individual in society. Government, they argued, was formed by individuals to promote their welfare. The British thinker Adam Smith extended the emphasis on the individual to economic thinking. He believed that individuals acting in their own self-interest created economic progress. Smith's theory is discussed in detail in Chapter 25.

During the Enlightenment, reason took center stage. The greatest minds of Europe followed each other's work with interest and often met to discuss their ideas. Some of the kings and queens of Europe were also very interested. As you will learn in Section 3, they sought to apply some of the philosophes' ideas to create progress in their countries.

Section 2 Assessment

1. TERMS & NAMES

Identify
- Enlightenment
- social contract
- John Locke
- natural rights
- philosophe
- Voltaire
- Montesquieu
- separation of powers
- Jean Jacques Rousseau
- Mary Wollstonecraft

2. TAKING NOTES

In a chart like the one below, list the important ideas of Hobbes, Locke, Voltaire, Montesquieu, Rousseau, Beccaria, and Wollstonecraft.

Thinker	Key Idea

Choose one of these thinkers and write a paragraph on how his or her ideas are influential today.

3. SYNTHESIZING

For each of the statements below, identify who said it and explain what it means. Then say how each viewpoint reflects Enlightenment ideas.

- "Power should be a check to power."
- "Man is born free, and everywhere he is in chains."
- "Let women share the rights and she will emulate the virtues of men."

4. ANALYZING THEMES

Power and Authority

Compare the views of Hobbes, Locke, and Rousseau on government. How do their differing ideas reflect their understanding of human behavior?

THINK ABOUT
- how each philosopher viewed the "state of nature"
- what each considered the source of a government's authority

---

ANSWERS

TERMS & NAMES
- Enlightenment, p. 551
- social contract, p. 551
- John Locke, p. 551
- natural rights, p. 551
- philosophe, p. 552
- Voltaire, p. 552
- Montesquieu, p. 553
- separation of powers, p. 553
- Jean Jacques Rousseau, p. 553
- Mary Wollstonecraft, p. 555

2. TAKING NOTES
Possible Responses: Hobbes—social contract; Locke—consent of the governed; Voltaire—tolerance; Montesquieu—separation of powers; Rousseau—government by general will; Beccaria—abolition of torture; Wollstonecraft—access to education for women.

3. FORMING OPINIONS
Possible Responses: "Power"—Montesquieu; each branch of government should limit power of other branches; "Man"—Rousseau; civilization corrupted the state of nature; "Let women"—Wollstonecraft; give women equal rights and they will display men's goodness.

4. ANALYZING THEMES
Possible Responses: Hobbes—humans are naturally selfish a[nd] wicked; governments keep ord[er] Locke—humans naturally able [to] govern themselves; favored se[lf?-] government. Rousseau—peop[le] are naturally good; society cor[r-]upts them; power comes from the general will.

European Values

Writers and artists of the Enlightenment often used satire to comment on European values. Using wit and humor, they ridiculed ideas and customs for the purpose of improving society. Satire allowed artists to explore human faults and failings in a way that is powerful but not preachy. In the two literary excerpts and the drawing below, notice how the writer or artist makes his point.

LITERATURE
Voltaire

Voltaire wrote *Candide* (1759) to attack a philosophy called Optimism, which held that all is right with the world. The hero of the story, a young man named Candide, encounters the most awful disasters and human evils as he travels far and wide. In this passage, Candide has met a slave in Surinam, a Dutch colony in South America. The slave explains why he is missing a leg and a hand.

"When we're working at the sugar mill and catch our finger in the grinding-wheel, they cut off our hand. When we try to run away, they cut off a leg. I have been in both of these situations. This is the price you pay for the sugar you eat in Europe. . . .

"The Dutch fetishes [i.e., missionaries] who converted me [to Christianity] tell me every Sunday that we are all the sons of Adam, Whites and Blacks alike. I'm no genealogist, but if these preachers are right, we are all cousins born of first cousins. Well, you will grant me that you can't treat a relative much worse than this."

LITERATURE

Jonathan Swift

The narrator of *Gulliver's Travels* (1726), an English doctor named Lemuel Gulliver, takes four disastrous voyages that leave him stranded in strange lands. In the following passage, Gulliver tries to win points with the king of Brobdingnag—a land of giants—by offering to show him how to make guns and cannons. The reaction of the king, who is above such things, shows how Swift felt about the inhuman side of the human race.

[I told the king that] a proper quantity of this powder [gunpowder] rammed into a hollow tube of brass or iron . . . would drive a ball of iron or lead with such violence and speed, as nothing was able to sustain its force. That, the largest balls thus discharged, would not only destroy whole ranks of an army at once; but batter the strongest walls to the ground; sink down ships with a thousand men in each, to the bottom of the sea; and when linked together by a chain, would cut through masts and rigging; divide hundreds of bodies in the middle, and lay all waste before them. . . .

The king was struck with horror at the description I had given of those terrible engines. . . . He was amazed how so impotent and grovelling an insect as I (these were his expressions) could entertain such inhuman ideas, and in so familiar a manner as to appear wholly unmoved at all the scenes of blood and desolation, which I had painted as the common effects of those destructive machines; whereof, he said, some evil genius, enemy to mankind, must have been the first contriver [inventor].

ENGRAVING
Francisco Goya

The Spanish artist Francisco Goya issued a series of 80 engravings called *Los Caprichos* (*Caprices*) in 1797. In them, he criticized a range of "human errors and evils" and also satirized Spanish politics and society. In the image shown here, titled "Out Hunting for Teeth," Goya attacks superstition. He wrote this caption for the image:

The teeth of a man who has been hung are indispensable for casting a spell. Without this ingredient, nothing succeeds. A pity that people believe such nonsense.

Connect *to* **History**

Clarifying Write a statement that summarizes the main point each writer and artist is making. What techniques do they use to reinforce their messages?

 SEE SKILLBUILDER HANDBOOK, PAGE 992

Connect *to* **Today**

Writing Both Voltaire and Swift used a fictional travel narrative as a type of satire. Imagine you are an alien visitor to your school or community. Write a letter or a narrative that describes how the people you see think and behave.

CD-ROM For another perspective on the Enlightenment, see World History: Electronic Library of Primary Sources.

Enlightenment and Revolution **557**

different **Perspectives**

Satire
Satire is a style of writing or visual expression that uses humor to ridicule the practices of a society or institution. Many Enlightenment writers, such as Voltaire and Jonathan Swift, used satire to show readers the foolishness of certain ideas or conditions. Instead of openly criticizing society or government, these writers expressed their opinions through the words and actions of story characters. For example, in Voltaire's *Candide,* the optimistic title character continues to believe that all is for the best even though he is confronted with endless examples of evil and stupidity in the world. Voltaire's point is that Optimism lacks reason and anyone who follows the philosophy of the Optimists is also lacking in reason.

 ELECTRONIC LIBRARY OF PRIMARY SOURCES
from *Gulliver's Travels*

Connect *to* **History**

Clarifying
Possible Responses: Voltaire's main point is that Christian missionaries are hypocritical in their treatment of slaves. He shows this by contrasting the brutality of slavery with the missionaries' empty words about all men being sons of Adam. Swift uses humor to assert his belief that war and the instruments of war are inhuman and that people have become immune to the horrors of war. Goya creates an image more repulsive than humorous to show that he believes superstition is ridiculous and pathetic. All three men use humor and exaggeration to make their points.

Connect *to* **Today**

Writing
To help students get started, brainstorm a list of everyday situations that an alien visitor might think are strange. These could include going to a noisy cafeteria to eat lunch, responding to school bells, and playing sports in gym. Encourage students to use humor and exaggeration in their letters and narratives.

① To explain how Enlightenment ideas spread throughout Europe.

② To describe changes in art, music, and literature during the Enlightenment.

③ To show how Enlightenment ideas reformed monarchies in Prussia, Austria, and Russia.

CRITICAL THINKING

- Making inferences, p. 559
- Contrasting, p. 559
- Analyzing issues, p. 560
- Analyzing motives, p. 561
- Synthesizing, p. 562
- Drawing conclusions, p. 562

FOCUS

5-Minute Warm-Up

▶ **Identifying Key Concepts**
To help students understand how the Enlightenment changed monarchies, have them answer these questions.

1. Study the Changing Idea chart on page 561. Which ruler expected citizens to serve the monarch?

2. What were the new ideas about monarchs?

 WARM-UP TRANSPARENCY 22

OBJECTIVE ① INSTRUCT

A World of Ideas

▶ **Key Ideas**

- Philosophers, writers, artists, scientists, and others gather regularly to discuss new ideas.
- Diderot creates an encyclopedia containing current ideas about science, art, and government.
- Enlightenment ideas spread to intellectuals and the middle class throughout Europe.

IN-DEPTH RESOURCES: UNIT 5
Guided Reading, p. 21

ACCESS FOR STUDENTS ACQUIRING ENGLISH
Guided Reading (Spanish), p. 221

CRITICAL THINKING TRANSPARENCIES
CT22 The Spread of Enlightenment Ideas

TERMS & NAMES
- salon
- baroque
- neoclassical
- enlightened despot
- Catherine the Great

3 The Spread of Enlightenment Ideas

MAIN IDEA
Enlightenment ideas spread through the Western world and profoundly influenced the arts and government.

WHY IT MATTERS NOW
An "enlightened" problem-solving approach to government and society prevails in modern civilization today.

SETTING THE STAGE The philosophes' views often got them in trouble. In France it was illegal to criticize either the Catholic Church or the government. Many philosophes landed in jail or were exiled. Voltaire, for example, experienced both punishments. Nevertheless, Enlightenment ideas spread throughout Europe.

A World of Ideas

In the 1700s, Paris was the cultural and intellectual capital of Europe. Young people from around Europe—and also from the Americas—came to study, philosophize, and enjoy fine culture. The brightest minds of the age gathered there. From their circles radiated the ideas of the Enlightenment.

The Paris Salons The buzz of Enlightenment ideas was most intense in the mansions of several wealthy women of Paris. There, in their large drawing rooms, these hostesses held regular social gatherings called **salons.** At these events, philosophers, writers, artists, scientists, and other great intellects met to discuss ideas and enjoy artistic performances.

The most influential of the salon hostesses in Voltaire's time was Marie-Thérèse Geoffrin (zhuh·frehn). Self-educated and from the well-to-do middle class, Madame Geoffrin was friends with both philosophes and heads of state. She corresponded with the king of Sweden and Catherine the Great of Russia.

Diderot's *Encyclopedia* Madame Geoffrin also helped finance the project of a leading philosophe named Denis Diderot (DEE·duh·ROH). Diderot imagined a large set of books to which all the leading scholars of Europe would contribute articles and essays. This *Encyclopedia,* as he called it, would bring together all the most current and enlightened thinking about science, technology, art, government, and more. Diderot began publishing the first volumes in 1751.

This painting by Anicet Charles Lemonnier shows a salon in the home of Madame Geoffrin (inset, and seated third from right). The guests are listening to an actor reading aloud from a new play.

558

The Enlightenment views expressed in the articles soon angered both the French government and the Catholic Church. Their censors banned the work. They said it undermined royal authority, encouraged a spirit of revolt, and fostered "moral corruption, irreligion, and unbelief." Fearing arrest, some leading philosophes withdrew from the project and urged Diderot to quit. Diderot pressed on, however, and finally won permission to continue publishing the *Encyclopedia.* New volumes came out regularly under his editorship until 1772.

New Ideas Circulate The salons and the *Encyclopedia* helped spread Enlightenment ideas to educated people all over Europe. The enlightened thinkers of Europe considered themselves part of an intellectual community. They shared their ideas through books, personal letters, visits back and forth, and magazine articles. As one writer of the day described the flurry of communication, "Never have new ideas had such rapid circulation at such long distance."

Enlightenment ideas also eventually reached middle-class people through newspapers, pamphlets, and even political songs. Enlightenment ideas about government and equality attracted the attention of a growing literate middle class. This group had money but limited status and political power. With their money, middle-class people could afford to buy many books and support the work of artists. Through its purchasing power, this group had growing influence over European culture in the 1700s.

This detail of *Seated Woman with Book,* by French artist Jean-Baptiste Chardin, shows a middle-class woman whose interests include reading. In the 1700s, the middle class had more leisure time for such pursuits.

Art and Literature in the Age of Reason

The Enlightenment ideals of order and reason were reflected in the arts—music, literature, painting, and architecture. European art of the 1600s and early 1700s had been dominated by the style called **baroque**—a grand, ornate style. Monarchs had built elaborate palaces such as Versailles (see page 521). Musicians like the German composer Johann Sebastian Bach and the English composer George Frederick Handel had written dramatic organ and choral music. Artists had created paintings rich in color, detail, and ornate imagery.

Under the influence of the Enlightenment, styles began to change. The arts began to reflect the new emphasis on order and balance. Artists and architects worked in a simple and elegant style that borrowed ideas and themes from classical Greece and Rome. The style of the late 1700s is therefore called **neoclassical** ("new classical"). In music, the style of this period is called classical.

Classical Music Three composers in Vienna, Austria, rank among the greatest figures of the classical period in music. They were Franz Joseph Haydn, Wolfgang Amadeus Mozart, and Ludwig van Beethoven.

Haydn was particularly important in developing new musical forms, such as the sonata and symphony. Mozart was a gifted child who began composing music at the age of five and gave concerts throughout Europe as a youth. At 12, he wrote his first opera. Mozart's great operas—*The Marriage of Figaro, Don Giovanni,* and *The Magic Flute*—set a new standard for elegance and originality. Although he lived only to age 35, he wrote more than 600 musical works.

Beethoven showed enormous range in his work. He wrote beautiful piano music, string quartets, and stirring symphonies. Beethoven's earlier works were in the same classical style as Mozart's. However, his later compositions began new trends, which carried music into the Age of Romanticism.

Popularity of the Novel Writers in the 18th century also developed new styles and forms of literature. A number of European authors began writing novels—lengthy works of prose fiction. These books were popular with a wide middle-class audience,

Enlightenment and Revolution **559**

History Through Art

William Hogarth

Hogarth was one of the first artists to use painting as a form of political commentary. He admired the English satirical writers who were his contemporaries, and he attempted to bring satire into the visual arts. His paintings made fun of contemporary customs and manners and, like a novel, seem to include plot, characters, and layers of details. As he said, "I have endeavored to treat my subjects as a dramatic writer; my picture is my stage, and men and women my players." Hogarth liked to create series of paintings that followed the actions of one or more characters. Typically, these characters are shown encountering different evils of society. Hogarth's paintings were very popular with the English middle class.

MORE ABOUT . . .
English Painters

Before Hogarth, England had great architects but no great painters. Most painters in England had come over from the European continent. Hogarth's efforts to establish English artists included founding an academy for painters and organizing the first public exhibition of paintings by contemporary English painters.

🏛 **WORLD ART AND CULTURES TRANSPARENCIES**

AT49 Goya's *The Pottery Vendor* (cartoon for a tapestry)

Art in the Age of Enlightenment

The Enlightenment influenced many European painters of the middle and late 1700s. Increasingly, artists looked for inspiration in the material world—in nature and human nature. Some artists showed an Enlightenment interest in science and social issues in their work. Others emphasized a new sensitivity toward individuals.

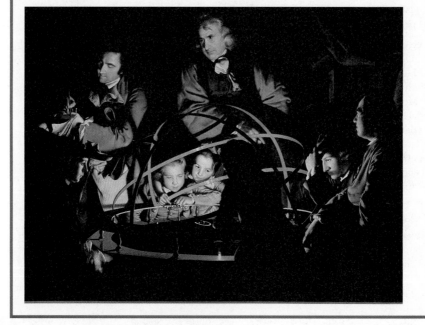

The Individual

The French painter Elisabeth-Louise Vigée-Le Brun was one of the most celebrated portrait artists of the late 1700s. She was the favorite painter of Queen Marie Antoinette of France. Her portraits bring out the personalities of her subjects. Her own energy, success, and independence also reflected the Enlightenment spirit. These qualities shine through this detail of a self-portrait with her daughter.

The Promise of Science

The English artist Joseph Wright of Derby was fascinated by science and its impact on people's lives. The painting below, *Philosopher Giving a Lecture on the Orrery*, shows children and adults gazing into a miniature planetarium. The way Wright uses light in this picture makes a point about how science can educate and enlighten people.

Politics and Society

The English artist William Hogarth often used satire in his paintings. In the painting above, *Canvassing for Votes—The Election*, he comments on political corruption. While the candidate flirts with the ladies on the balcony, his supporters offer a man money for his vote. Hogarth's detailed, realistic style and moralistic topics were meant—like the popular novels of his day—to appeal to a wide middle-class audience.

Connect *to* **History**

Analyzing Issues Imagine you are a philosophe who moonlights as an art critic. For each of these paintings, write a brief statement about how it reflects Enlightenment ideas.

📖 SEE SKILLBUILDER HANDBOOK, PAGE 1001

Connect *to* **Today**

Updating a Picture Choose one of the paintings on this page and think about how you might change it to depict politics, science, or people today. You might describe the modern version in words or using a sketch or other kind of artwork.

Connect *to* **History**

Analyzing Issues
Possible Responses:
Vigée-Le Brun's portrait is simple, not ornate. It shows the mother and child in a natural embrace. By emphasizing the individuality of her subjects, Vigée-Le Brun pays tribute to their humanity.

Hogarth uses satire to point out the corrupt nature of politics. He makes fun of politicians by portraying them as dishonest. Joseph Wright highlights the achievements of science and the human ability to reason in his painting.

Connect *to* **Today**

Updating a Picture
To help students get started, discuss the following questions: What are some recent technological developments and how do people view them—with amazement, fear, boredom, or excitement? What other roles in

society do women who are mothers have today? Are politics today corrupt? You might suggest students look at images in contemporary magazines to get more ideas.

who liked the entertaining stories written in everyday language. Writers—including many women—turned out a flood of popular novels in the 1700s.

English novelists such as Samuel Richardson and Henry Fielding developed many of the features of the modern novel. Their works had carefully crafted plots, used suspense and climax, and explored their characters' thoughts and feelings. Richardson's *Pamela* is often considered the first true English novel. It told the story of a young servant girl who refused the advances of her master. In Fielding's comic masterpiece *Tom Jones,* the hero of the book is an orphan who has been kicked out of his adopted home. He travels all over England and overcomes numerous obstacles to win the hand of his lady.

A third popular English novelist was Daniel Defoe, author of the adventure *Robinson Crusoe.* Crusoe is a sailor stranded on a tropical island. Through his wits and the help of a native he calls Friday, Crusoe learns how to survive on the island and is eventually rescued.

Enlightenment and Monarchy

From the salons, artists' studios, and concert halls of Europe, the Enlightenment spirit also swept through Europe's royal courts. Many philosophes, including Voltaire, believed that the best form of government was a monarchy in which the ruler respected the people's rights. The philosophes tried to convince monarchs to rule justly. Some monarchs embraced the new ideas and made reforms that reflected the Enlightenment spirit. They became known as **enlightened despots.** *Despot* means absolute ruler.

THINK THROUGH HISTORY
C. Analyzing Motives Why did the enlightened despots undertake reforms?
C. Possible Answers Intrigued by Enlightenment ideas, convinced by philosophes, wanted to make their countries stronger and own rule more effective.

The enlightened despots supported the philosophes' ideas. But they also had no intention of giving up any power. The changes they made were motivated by two desires: they wanted to make their countries stronger and their own rule more effective. The foremost of Europe's enlightened despots were Frederick II of Prussia, Holy Roman Emperor Joseph II of Austria, and Catherine the Great of Russia.

Frederick the Great Frederick II, the king of Prussia from 1740 to 1786, once wrote to Voltaire: "I must enlighten my people, cultivate their manners and morals, and make them as happy as human beings can be, or as happy as the means at my disposal permit." Frederick indeed committed himself to reforming Prussia. He granted many religious freedoms, reduced censorship, and improved education. He also reformed the justice system and abolished the use of torture. However, Frederick's changes only went so far. For example, he believed that serfdom was wrong, but he did nothing to end it. This was because he needed the support of wealthy landowners. As a result, he never challenged the power of the Junkers or tried to change the existing social order.

Perhaps Frederick's most important contribution was his attitude toward being king. He called himself "the first servant of the state." From the beginning of his reign, he made it clear that his goal was to serve and strengthen his country. This attitude was clearly one that appealed to the philosophes.

Changing Idea: Relationship Between Ruler and State

Old Idea
The state and its citizens exist to serve the monarch—as Louis XIV reportedly said, "I am the state."

New Idea
The monarch exists to serve the state and support citizens' welfare—as Frederick the Great said, a ruler is only "the first servant of the state."

Joseph II The most radical royal reformer was Joseph II of Austria. The son and successor of Maria Theresa, Joseph II ruled Austria from 1780 to 1790. He introduced legal reforms and freedom of the press. He also supported freedom of worship—even for Protestants, Orthodox Christians, and Jews. In his most radical reform, Joseph abolished serfdom and ordered that peasants be paid for their labor with cash. Not

Enlightenment and Revolution **561**

Enlightenment and Monarchy

▶ **Key Ideas**
• Frederick II of Prussia announces that his goal is to serve and strengthen his country.
• In Austria, Joseph II's radical reforms include freedom of worship and the end of serfdom.
• Catherine II of Russia makes limited reforms, which she later revokes.
• Catherine vastly enlarges the Russian Empire and wins a warm-weather port for her country.

CRITICAL THINKING ACTIVITY
CLASS TIME: 20 MINUTES

Comparing and Contrasting
Ask students which enlightened despot made the most sincere effort to reform his or her country. Then ask which one made the least effort. Remind students to use facts from the text to support their opinions.

MORE ABOUT . . .
Joseph II

In 1765, Joseph was appointed co-regent by his mother, Maria Theresa. He had very little power and could do almost nothing without his mother's approval. While in this position, he created a list of radical reforms, including mandatory military service for young nobles, religious toleration, an end to government spying on private affairs, limiting the power of nobles, and using the army for public works projects. Almost all of Joseph's proposed reforms conflicted with his mother's more conservative style. It was not until her death in 1780 that Joseph could implement his reforms.

TEACHING OPTION | BLOCK SCHEDULING
COOPERATIVE ACTIVITY: Researching Enlightenment Arts
CLASS TIME 40 MINUTES

Task: Student groups will develop oral reports about architecture and the arts during the Enlightenment.

Purpose: To help students recognize the Enlightenment's impact on culture.

Activity: Divide the class into five groups and assign each group one of the following topics:

painting and sculpture, architecture, music, literature, drama. Groups should conduct research to learn how their art form changed during the Enlightenment and who were the most important figures associated with it. (Students can begin their research using their textbooks and then move on to general and topical encyclopedias and other books.) Each group will develop and present an oral report that includes

examples of the art form. These can include pictures, books, audio recordings, videos, and other items. The literature and drama groups may wish to read aloud a short excerpt from a novel or a play.

 ALTERNATIVE ASSESSMENT BOOK
Standards for Evaluating a Cooperative Activity

Catherine the Great wrote letters to Voltaire and claimed to rule by enlightened principles. Voltaire, in turn, flattered Catherine, calling her "the star of the north," "benefactress of Europe," and "first person in the universe." Ask students if they believe Voltaire would truly have approved of Catherine's ruling style. With which of her decisions and actions might he have disagreed? What might have been his motivation for praising her?

 ELECTRONIC LIBRARY OF PRIMARY SOURCES
Letter to Catherine the Great

ASSESS & RETEACH

Section 3 Assessment
After students have answered the questions independently, have them compare their work with a partner.

Section Quiz
FORMAL ASSESSMENT BOOK
Section Quiz, p. 254

Reteaching Activity
CLASS TIME: 25 MINUTES

On the board, make a chart using the following three column heads: Ideas, Art and Literature, Enlightenment and Monarchy. Have students take turns adding information about each topic to the chart. Tell students to refer to their textbooks if they need help.

CLOSE ACTIVITY

CLASS TIME: 45 MINUTES

Creating Flash cards
Distribute ten index cards to small groups of students. Have group members choose ten important figures from the section and work together to make flash cards for the figures. Each flash card should include the name of the figure, a drawing of the figure or something associated with the figure, and, on the back, facts about the figure. After group members have finished, have them use the cards to quiz each other.

HISTORY MAKERS

Catherine the Great
1729–1796

Catherine was the daughter of a minor German prince. At age 15, she was summoned to the distant Russian court at St. Petersburg. She was to marry the Grand Duke Peter, heir to the Russian throne.

The marriage between Catherine and Peter was a disaster. Peter was mentally unstable. His chief pleasure was playing with toy soldiers. More than once he tormented his own dogs.

Catherine soon saw that Peter's weakness gave her a chance to seize power. She made important friends among Russia's army officers, and she became known as the most intelligent and best-informed person at court. In 1762, only months after her husband became czar as Peter III, Catherine had him arrested and confined. Soon afterward, Peter conveniently died, probably by murder.

surprisingly, the nobles firmly resisted this change. Like many of Joseph's reforms, it was undone after his death.

Catherine the Great The ruler most admired by the philosophes was Catherine II, known as **Catherine the Great.** She ruled Russia from 1762 to 1796. The well-educated empress read the works of philosophes, and she exchanged many letters with Voltaire. She ruled with absolute authority, but she also took steps to modernize and reform Russia.

In 1767, Catherine formed a commission to review Russia's laws. She presented it with a brilliant proposal for reforms based on the ideas of Montesquieu and Beccaria. Among other changes, she recommended allowing religious toleration and abolishing torture and capital punishment. Her commission, however, accomplished none of these lofty goals.

Catherine eventually put in place limited reforms, but she did little to improve the life of the Russian peasants. Her thinking about enlightened ideas changed after a massive uprising of serfs in 1773. With great brutality, Catherine's army crushed the rebellion. Catherine had previously favored an end to serfdom. However, the revolt convinced her that she needed the nobles' support to keep her throne. Therefore, she gave the nobles absolute power over the serfs. As a result, Russian serfs lost their last traces of freedom.

Catherine Expands Russia Peter the Great had fought for years to win a port on the Baltic Sea. Likewise, Catherine sought access to the Black Sea. In two wars with the Ottoman Turks, her armies finally won control of the northern shore of the Black Sea. Russia also gained the right to send ships through Ottoman-controlled straits leading from the Black Sea to the Mediterranean Sea.

Catherine also expanded her empire westward into Poland. In Poland, the king was relatively weak, and independent nobles held the most power. The three neighboring powers—Russia, Prussia, and Austria— each tried to assert their influence over the country. In 1772, these land-hungry neighbors each took a piece of Poland in what is called the First Partition of Poland. In further partitions in 1793 and 1795, they grabbed up the rest of Poland's territory. With these partitions, Poland disappeared from the map of Europe. It did not reappear as an independent country until after World War I.

By the end of her remarkable reign, Catherine had vastly enlarged the Russian empire. Meanwhile, as Russia was becoming an international power, another great power, Britain, faced a challenge in its 13 American colonies. Inspired by Enlightenment ideas, colonial leaders decided to cast off British rule and found an independent republic.

D. Possible Answer
It accurately describes two sides of her rule—she tried to make reforms, but she also ruled with absolute authority; it's not very accurate, since she was ultimately more despotic than enlightened.

THINK THROUGH HISTORY
D. Synthesizing
How accurately does the term *enlightened despot* describe Catherine the Great? Explain.

Section 3 Assessment

1. TERMS & NAMES
Identify
- salon
- baroque
- neoclassical
- enlightened despot
- Catherine the Great

2. TAKING NOTES
Copy the concept web shown below and add to it examples that illustrate the concepts.

Write two generalizations about the spread of Enlightenment ideas.

3. DRAWING CONCLUSIONS
What advantages do you think salons had over earlier forms of communication in spreading new ideas? Justify your response with specific references to the text.

THINK ABOUT
- who hosted the salons and where they were held
- who was invited to the salons
- church and state influence on publishing and education

4. THEME ACTIVITY
Power and Authority
Imagine you are a public relations consultant for Frederick the Great, Joseph II, or Catherine the Great. The monarch you represent wants to be named "Most Enlightened Despot of the 1700s." Write a press release or design a poster or flyer that presents reasons why your client should be given this honor.

ANSWERS

TERMS & NAMES
- salon, p. 558
- baroque, p. 559
- neoclassical, p. 559
- enlightened despot, p. 561
- Catherine the Great, p. 562

2. TAKING NOTES
Possible Responses: Circulation of Ideas—salons, *Encyclopedia*, books, letters, magazines, pamphlets; Art and Literature—neoclassical art, classical music, novel; Monarchy—enlightened despots, Frederick the Great, Joseph II, Catherine the Great.

3. DRAWING CONCLUSIONS
Possible Responses: Salons were hosted by wealthy middle-class women, who had an interest in educating themselves; many great artists and thinkers gathered to share ideas; salons were held in private homes, so guests could speak freely without the threat of jail or exile.

4. THEME ACTIVITY
An effective press release or poster should . . .
- show an understanding of the monarch's reforms and their effects
- include details and specific information
- use persuasive language

4 American Revolution: The Birth of a Republic

TERMS & NAMES
- Declaration of Independence
- Thomas Jefferson
- checks and balances
- federal system
- Bill of Rights

MAIN IDEA

Enlightenment ideas helped spur the American colonies to create a new nation.

WHY IT MATTERS NOW

The revolution created a republic, the United States of America, that became a model for many nations of the world.

Section 4 Overview

OBJECTIVES

(1) To describe the American colonies in the late 1700s.

(2) To list events that led to the American Revolution.

(3) To explain the Enlightenment's influence on American government.

SKILLBUILDERS

- Interpreting maps: region, human-environment interaction, p. 565
- Interpreting charts, p. 566

CRITICAL THINKING

- Recognizing effects, p. 563
- Analyzing causes, p. 564
- Comparing, p. 564
- Making inferences, p. 566
- Analyzing issues, p. 567
- Analyzing themes, p. 567

SETTING THE STAGE Philosophes such as Voltaire considered England's government the most progressive in Europe. England's ruler was no despot, not even an enlightened one. His power had been limited by law. The Glorious Revolution of 1688 had given England a constitutional monarchy. However, while the English monarch's power was being limited at home, the power of the English nation was spreading overseas.

Britain and Its American Colonies

When George III became king of Great Britain in 1760, his Atlantic coastal colonies were growing by leaps and bounds. Their combined population went from about 250,000 in 1700 to 2,150,000 in 1770, an eightfold increase. Economically, the colonies thrived on trade with the nations of Europe.

Along with increasing population and prosperity, a new sense of identity was growing in the colonists' minds. By the mid-1700s, colonists had been living in America for nearly 150 years. Each of the 13 colonies had its own government, and people were used to a great degree of independence. Colonists saw themselves less as British and more as Virginians or Pennsylvanians. However, they were still British subjects and were expected to obey British law.

In the 1660s, Parliament had passed trade laws called the Navigation Acts. These laws prevented colonists from selling their most valuable products to any country except Britain. In addition, colonists had to pay high taxes on imported French and Dutch goods. However, colonists found ways to get around these laws. Some merchants smuggled in goods to avoid paying British taxes. Smugglers could sneak in and out of the many small harbors all along the lengthy Atlantic coastline. British customs agents found it difficult to enforce the Navigation Acts.

For many years, Britain felt no need to tighten its hold on the colonies. Despite the smuggling, Britain's mercantilist policies had made colonial trade very profitable. Britain bought American raw materials for low prices and sold manufactured goods to the colonists. And despite British trade restrictions, colonial merchants also thrived. However, after the French and Indian War ended in 1763, Britain toughened its trade laws. These changes sparked growing anger in the colonies.

THINK THROUGH HISTORY
A. Recognizing Effects How did some colonists respond to the Navigation Acts?
A. Answer Smuggling.

Background
The French and Indian War was the part of the Seven Years' War fought in North America.

Many educated colonists were influenced by Enlightenment thought. This French snuff box pictures (left to right) Voltaire, Rousseau, and colonial statesman Benjamin Franklin.

Americans Win Independence

In 1760, when George III took the throne, most Americans had no thoughts of either revolution or independence. They still thought of themselves as loyal subjects of the British king. Yet by 1776, many Americans were willing to risk their lives to break free of Britain.

During the French and Indian War, Great Britain had run up a huge debt in the war against France. Because American colonists benefited from Britain's victory, Britain expected the colonists to help pay the costs of the war. In 1765, Parliament passed the Stamp Act. According

Enlightenment and Revolution **563**

FOCUS
5-Minute Warm-Up

▶ **Making Inferences**
To help students understand how Enlightenment ideas influenced American colonists, have them answer these questions.

1. Study the History Makers feature on page 564. What is one way Thomas Jefferson contributed to American independence?

2. Name two Enlightenment ideas that Jefferson supported.

📖 **WARM-UP TRANSPARENCY 22**

OBJECTIVE (1) INSTRUCT

Britain and Its American Colonies

▶ **Key Idea**
- British tax and trade laws regulate the colonists' import and export of goods.

 IN-DEPTH RESOURCES: UNIT 5
Guided Reading, p. 22

 ACCESS FOR STUDENTS ACQUIRING ENGLISH
Guided Reading (Spanish), p. 222

SECTION 4 RESOURCES

PRINT RESOURCES

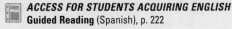 **IN-DEPTH RESOURCES: UNIT 5**
Guided Reading, p. 22
Primary Source: from the Declaration of Independence, p. 30

ACCESS FOR STUDENTS ACQUIRING ENGLISH
Guided Reading (Spanish), p. 222

FORMAL ASSESSMENT
Section Quiz, p. 255

 ALTERNATIVE ASSESSMENT BOOK

TECHNOLOGY RESOURCES

 CRITICAL THINKING TRANSPARENCIES
CT58 Chapter 22 Visual Summary

💿 **CD-ROM**
Electronic Library of Primary Sources

🌐 **INTERNET** www.mlworldhistory.com

(See page 563.)

Americans Win Independence

▶ **Key Ideas**

- England angers the colonists by expecting them to pay the costs of the French and Indian War.
- Colonists protest England's harsh taxes and begin to organize for war.
- Colonial leaders use Enlightenment ideas to justify independence and to write the Declaration of Independence.
- Americans are victorious because they were motivated to fight, among other reasons.

 ELECTRONIC LIBRARY OF PRIMARY SOURCES
Conflicting Accounts of the Battles at Lexington and Concord

HISTORYMAKERS
Thomas Jefferson

In his lifetime, Jefferson held many different government positions, including governor, congressman, minister to France, secretary of state, vice-president, and president. In retirement, he pursued his interests in music, architecture, and scientific experiments. He also studied religion, philosophy, law, and education. How do Jefferson's ideas, interests, and career reflect the spirit of the Enlightenment? Encourage students to use the list of important Enlightenment concepts on page 552 to think about and answer this question.

---

to this law, colonists had to pay a tax to have an official stamp put on wills, deeds, newspapers, and other printed material.

American colonists were outraged. They had never paid taxes directly to the British government before. Colonial lawyers argued that the stamp tax violated colonists' natural rights. In Britain, citizens consented to taxes through their representatives in Parliament. Because the colonists had no such representatives, Parliament could not tax them. The colonists demonstrated their defiance of this tax with angry protests and a boycott of British manufactured goods. The boycott proved so effective that Parliament gave up and repealed the Stamp Act in 1766.

Growing Hostility Leads to War Over the next decade, further events steadily led to war. Some colonial leaders, such as Boston's Samuel Adams, favored independence from Britain. They encouraged conflict with British authorities. At the same time, George III and his ministers made enemies of many moderate colonists by their harsh stands. In 1773, to protest an import tax on tea, Adams organized a raid against three British ships in Boston Harbor. The raiders dumped 342 chests of tea into the water. George III, infuriated by the "Boston Tea Party," as it was called, ordered the British navy to close the port of Boston. British troops occupied the city.

In September 1774, representatives from every colony except Georgia gathered in Philadelphia to form the First Continental Congress. This group protested the treatment of Boston. When the king paid little attention to their complaints, all 13 colonies decided to form the Second Continental Congress to debate their next move.

On April 19, 1775, British soldiers and American militiamen exchanged gunfire on the village green in Lexington, Massachusetts. The fighting spread to nearby Concord. When news of the fighting reached the Second Continental Congress, its members voted to raise an army under the command of a Virginian named George Washington. The American Revolution had begun.

Enlightenment Ideas Influence American Colonists Although a war had begun, the American colonists still debated their attachment to Great Britain. Many colonists wanted to remain part of Britain. A growing number, however, favored independence. They heard the persuasive arguments of colonial leaders such as Patrick Henry, John Adams, and Benjamin Franklin. These leaders used Enlightenment ideas to justify independence. The colonists had asked for the same political rights as people in Britain, they said, but the king had stubbornly refused. Therefore, the colonists were justified in rebelling against a tyrant who had broken the social contract.

In July 1776, the Second Continental Congress issued the **Declaration of Independence.** This document, written by **Thomas Jefferson,** was firmly based on the ideas of John Locke and the Enlightenment. The Declaration reflected these ideas in its eloquent argument for natural rights.

HISTORYMAKERS

Thomas Jefferson
1743–1826
The author of the Declaration of Independence, Thomas Jefferson of Virginia was a true figure of the Enlightenment. As a writer and statesman, he supported free speech, religious freedom, and other civil liberties. At the same time, he was also a slave owner.

Outside of politics, Jefferson was accomplished in many fields, including law, science, agriculture, and languages. He invented many practical devices, including an improved type of plow. One of the great architects of early America, he designed his magnificent home, Monticello. He also designed the Virginia state capitol building in Richmond and many buildings for the University of Virginia.

Of all his many achievements, Jefferson wanted to be most remembered for three: author of the Declaration of Independence, author of the Statute of Virginia for Religious Freedom, and founder of the University of Virginia.

> **A VOICE FROM THE PAST**
> We hold these Truths to be self-evident, that all Men are created equal, that they are endowed by their Creator with certain unalienable Rights, that among these are Life, Liberty, and the Pursuit of Happiness; that to secure these Rights, Governments are instituted among Men, deriving their just Powers from the Consent of the Governed.
> Declaration of Independence

Since Locke had asserted that people had the right to rebel against an unjust ruler, the Declaration of Independence included a long list

Vocabulary
boycott: refusal to buy goods produced in a certain place or by a certain group.

B. Answer Britain passed the act to help pay the costs of the war.

C. Possible Answer Jefferson wrote "Life, Liberty, and the Pursuit of Happiness"; Locke explained the natural rights as life, liberty, and property.
THINK THROUGH HISTORY
C. Comparing How do Jefferson's "unalienable rights" compare with the natural rights expressed by Locke?

TEACHING OPTIONS	CUSTOMIZING FOR SPECIAL NEEDS	EXPLORING PRIMARY SOURCES

Less Proficient Readers:
Paired Reading Have partners read the first part of the passage titled "Americans Win Independence," beginning on page 563. After both have finished, one partner should retell what was read while the other partner listens. Neither partner should look at the text.

The partner who is listening should not interrupt the retelling. After the retelling, the partner who was listening should correct any ideas that were not summarized correctly and add any important information that was left out. Partners can alternate the retelling and listening roles as they read this and other passages.

A Voice from the Past Read aloud the excerpt from the Declaration of Independence. Then work with students to paraphrase it. *We believe the following ideas are true and do not need to be proven: all people are created equal, they are given by God certain rights that can never be taken away, and among these rights are the right to life, to freedom, and to seek* happiness; to protect these rights, governments are established among people; these governments get their lawful power from the people they govern. Is the Declaration of Independence a social contract?

 IN-DEPTH RESOURCES: UNIT 5
Primary Source: from *The Declaration of Independence*, p. 30

of George III's abuses. The document ended by breaking the ties between the colonies and Britain. The colonies, the Declaration said, "are absolved from all allegiance to the British crown."

Success for the Colonists When war was first declared, the odds seemed heavily weighted against the Americans. Washington's ragtag, poorly trained army faced the well-trained forces of the most powerful country in the world. In the end, however, the Americans won their war for independence.

Several reasons explain their success. First, the Americans' motivation for fighting was much stronger than that of the British, since their army was defending their homeland. Second, the overconfident British generals made several mistakes. Third, time itself was on the side of the Americans. The British could win battle after battle, as they did, and still lose the war. Fighting an overseas war, 3,000 miles from London, was terribly expensive. After a few years, tax-weary British citizens clamored for peace.

Finally, the Americans did not fight alone. Louis XVI of France had little sympathy for the ideals of the American Revolution, but he was eager to weaken France's rival, Britain. French entry into the war in 1778 was decisive. In 1781, combined forces of about 9,500 Americans and 7,800 French trapped a British army commanded by Lord Cornwallis near Yorktown, Virginia. Unable to escape, Cornwallis surrendered. The Americans were victorious.

North America, 1783

British territory
French territory
Russian territory
Spanish territory
Claimed by U.S. and Great Britain
Claimed by U.S. and Spain

GEOGRAPHY SKILLBUILDER: Interpreting Maps
1. **Region** What feature formed the western border of the United States?
2. **Human-Environment Interaction** What European countries had claims on the North American continent in 1783?

Changing Idea: Colonial Attachment to Britain

Old Idea
American colonists considered themselves as subjects of the British king.

New Idea
After a long train of perceived abuses by the king, the colonists asserted their right to declare independence.

Americans Create a Republic

Shortly after declaring their independence, the 13 individual states recognized the need for a national government. As victory became certain, in 1781 all 13 states ratified a constitution. This plan of government was known as the Articles of Confederation. The Articles established the United States as a republic—a government in which citizens rule through elected representatives.

The Articles Create a Weak National Government To protect their authority, the 13 states created a loose confederation in which they held most of the power. Thus, the Articles of Confederation deliberately created a weak national government.

Enlightenment and Revolution **565**

History from Visuals

North America, 1783
Interpreting the Map Have students use the map key to identify which European country claimed the largest area of land on the map and which claimed the smallest. *Answers: Largest—Spain, Smallest—France*

Extension Activity Assign pairs of students one of the territories on the map. Tell partners to use an encyclopedia to learn more about this territory in 1783. Have partners share what they learned with the class.

SKILLBUILDER Answers
1. Mississippi River.
2. Spain, Russia, England.

CRITICAL THINKING ACTIVITY
CLASS TIME: 15 MINUTES

Analyzing Causes
To help students understand the events that led to the American Revolution, have them complete a chart like the one below.

Cause: Colonists protest the Stamp Act.
↓
Cause:
↓
Cause:
↓
Effect: The American Revolution begins.

OBJECTIVE 3 INSTRUCT

Americans Create a Republic

Key Ideas
• To protect their authority, the 13 states create a weak national government, which fails.
• Constitutional Convention delegates create a new system of government based on Enlightenment ideas.
• The new government system is made up of three branches.

(continued on next page)

TEACHING OPTION **BLOCK SCHEDULING** **MAKING NEW LAWS** **CLASS TIME 20 MINUTES**

Task: Students will work in small groups to write a list of American laws concerning taxes, trade, and government.

Materials Needed: Textbooks, writing instruments, paper.

Activity: Ask students to name some of the British laws and actions that angered the colonists.

Students might mention that the British imposed unfair taxes, restricted trade, and did not provide representation of the colonies in Parliament. Discuss with students how laws created by colonial leaders might have been different from British laws. Next, have groups of students write a list of three or four laws that the newly independent Americans might have written. These laws should concern taxes,

trade, and government. To help students get started, write this law on the board: "Americans may sell goods at the market price to all countries."

Conclusion: Ask groups to share their laws and explain their reasoning. Invite volunteers to write their laws on the board.

(continued from page 565)

• The Bill of Rights is created to further protect the rights of individual citizens.

MORE ABOUT . . .
The Colonies

Enlightenment ideas spread through the colonies in books and pamphlets. Literacy rates in the colonies were high among white males. While only one-third of males in England could read, in some colonies, over 50 percent of the males could read. Literacy rates in New England were particularly high because the Puritans who settled there advocated public education so that everyone, women included, could read the Bible.

History from Visuals

U.S. Constitution: An Enlightenment Document

Interpreting the Chart Explain that the purpose of the chart is to show where the ideas of Enlightenment thinkers are found in the Constitution. Point out the boldfaced names and bulleted phrases and tell students that these elements will help them read the chart. Next, ask students this question: From whose idea stems the freedom of speech and religion? *Voltaire's idea.*

Extension Activity Divide the class into five groups and assign each group a row from the chart. Have groups make a poster that uses words and images to display the Enlightenment idea and the way it is reflected in the Constitution. Display posters.

SKILLBUILDER Answers
1. Montesquieu's
2. Free speech, religious toleration, rights of accused, no torture

---

There were no executive or judicial branches. Instead, the Articles established only one body of government, the Congress. Each state, regardless of size, had one vote in Congress. Congress could declare war, enter into treaties, and coin money. It had no power, however, to collect taxes or regulate trade. Passing new laws was difficult because laws needed the approval of 9 of the 13 states.

These limits on the national government soon produced many problems. Although the new national government needed money in order to operate, it could only request contributions from the states. Angry Revolutionary War veterans bitterly complained that Congress still owed them back pay. Meanwhile, several states issued their own money. Some states even put tariffs on goods from neighboring states.

The nation's growing financial problems sparked a violent protest in Massachusetts. Debt-ridden farmers, led by a war veteran named Daniel Shays, demanded that the state lower taxes and issue paper money so that they could repay their debts. When the state refused, the rebels attacked several courthouses. Massachusetts authorities quickly crushed Shays's Rebellion.

A New Constitution Concerned leaders such as George Washington and James Madison believed that Shays's Rebellion underscored the need for a strong national government. In February 1787, Congress approved a Constitutional Convention to revise the Articles of Confederation. The Constitutional Convention held its first session on May 25, 1787. The 55 delegates were experienced statesmen who were familiar with the political theories of Locke, Montesquieu, and Rousseau.

Although the delegates shared basic ideas on government, they sometimes disagreed on how to put them into practice. For almost four months the delegates argued over important questions. Who should be represented in Congress? How many votes should each state have? The delegates' deliberations produced not only compromises but also new approaches to governing. Using the political ideas of the Enlightenment, the delegates created a new system of government.

The Federal System Like Montesquieu, the delegates distrusted a powerful central government controlled by one person or group. They therefore established three separate branches—legislative, executive, and judicial. This provided a built-in system of **checks**

THINK THROUGH HISTORY
D. Making Inferences What was the fundamental cause of the nation's problems under the Articles of Confederation?
D. Answer Weak federal government.

U.S. Constitution: An Enlightenment Document

Enlightenment Idea	U.S. Constitution
Locke A government's power comes from the consent of the people	• Preamble begins "We the people of the United States" to establish legitimacy. • Creates representative government • Limits government powers
Montesquieu Separation of powers	• Federal system of government • Powers divided among three branches • System of checks and balances
Rousseau Direct democracy	• Public election of president and Congress
Voltaire Free speech, religious toleration	• Bill of Rights provides for freedom of speech and religion.
Beccaria Accused have rights, no torture	• Bill of Rights protects rights of accused and prohibits cruel and unusual punishment.

SKILLBUILDER: Interpreting Charts
1. *From whose idea stems the system of checks and balances?*
2. *Which of the Enlightenment ideas are reflected in the Bill of Rights?*

TEACHING OPTION **BLOCK SCHEDULING** **COOPERATIVE ACTIVITY: Reporting on the Enlightenment** **CLASS TIME 45 MINUTES**

Task: Student pairs will find an article that reflects Enlightenment ideas and develop oral reports that explain how the article and ideas are connected.

Purpose: To recognize the influence of Enlightenment ideas today.

Activity: Brainstorm with students a list of Enlightenment thinkers' ideas. These should include separation of powers, elections and direct democracy,

freedom of speech and religion, protection of the accused, prohibition of torture, importance of reason and scientific inquiry, and a government's power comes from the consent of the governed.

Have partners look in local, regional, or national newspapers and magazines to find an article that reflects one or more of these ideas. For example, partners might use an article about a political election to show the idea of direct democracy and

the power of government coming from the governed. Have partners cut out or copy their article.

Each pair should prepare and present an oral report that describes what the article is about, tells which Enlightenment ideas and thinkers the article reflects, and explains how it does this.

 ALTERNATIVE ASSESSMENT BOOK
Standards for Evaluating a Cooperative Activity

and balances, with each branch checking the actions of the other two. For example, the president received the power to veto legislation passed by Congress. However, the Congress could override a presidential veto with the approval of two-thirds of its members.

Although the Constitution created a strong central government, it did not eliminate local governments. Instead, the Constitution set up a **federal system** in which power was divided between national and state governments.

The delegates agreed with Locke and Rousseau that governments draw their authority from the consent of the governed. The Constitution's preamble sums up this principle:

A VOICE FROM THE PAST
We the People of the United States, in order to form a more perfect Union, establish Justice, insure domestic Tranquillity, provide for the common defense, promote the general Welfare, and secure the Blessings of Liberty to ourselves and our Posterity, do ordain and establish this Constitution for the United States of America.
CONSTITUTION OF THE UNITED STATES OF AMERICA

E. Possible Answer
Federalists believed the Constitution reflected balance between federal and state powers; Antifederalists thought federal government too powerful, wanted Bill of Rights to protect individual freedoms.
THINK THROUGH HISTORY
E. Analyzing Issues
Explain the controversy over ratifying the Constitution. What did each side believe?

The Bill of Rights The delegates signed the new Constitution on September 17, 1787. In order to become law, however, the Constitution required approval by conventions in at least 9 of the 13 states. These conventions were marked by sharp debate. Supporters of the Constitution, called the Federalists, argued that the new government would provide a better balance between national and state powers. Their opponents, the Antifederalists, feared that the Constitution gave the central government too much power. They also wanted a bill of rights to protect the rights of individual citizens.

In order to gain support, the Federalists promised to add a bill of rights to the Constitution. This promise cleared the way for approval. Congress formally added to the Constitution the ten amendments known as the **Bill of Rights.** These amendments protected such basic rights as freedom of speech, press, assembly, and religion. Many of these rights had been advocated by Voltaire, Rousseau, and Locke.

The Constitution and Bill of Rights marked a turning point in people's ideas about government. Both documents put Enlightenment ideas into practice. They expressed an optimistic view that reason and reform could prevail and that progress was inevitable. Such optimism swept across the Atlantic. However, the monarchies and the privileged classes didn't give up power and position easily. As Chapter 23 explains, the struggle to attain the principles of the Enlightenment continued in France.

Global**Impact**

The French Revolution
The American Revolution inspired the growing number of French people who were seeking reform in their own country. They saw the new government of the United States as a step toward realizing the ideals of the Enlightenment. They hoped the next step would be reform in France.

The Declaration of Independence was widely circulated and admired in France. French officers like the Marquis de Lafayette, who fought for American independence, returned to France with stories of the war. Such personal accounts intrigued many a reader.

When the French bishop Charles-Maurice de Talleyrand wrote about this time period years later, he would say, "We talked of nothing but America."

Section ④ Assessment

1. TERMS & NAMES
Identify
• Declaration of Independence
• Thomas Jefferson
• checks and balances
• federal system
• Bill of Rights

2. TAKING NOTES
Create a chart like the one below. On the left, list problems faced by the Americans as colonists and in shaping their republic. On the right, record their actions and decisions to solve those problems.

Problem	Solution

Which of the solutions that you recorded represented a compromise?

3. ANALYZING ISSUES
How does the opening statement from the Declaration of Independence (page 564) reflect enlightened thinking?

4. ANALYZING THEMES
Revolution Do you think the American Revolution would have happened if there had not been an Age of Enlightenment? Explain.

THINK ABOUT
• John Locke's impact on government
• other British colonies
• Enlightenment ideas

Enlightenment and Revolution **567**

Global**Impact**
The French Revolution
In 1789, a French writer made this comment about the newly formed United States: "This vast continent which the seas surround will soon change Europe and the universe." What does this writer believe about the United States? What kind of change might the writer be talking about? Would kings and commoners have viewed this change in the same way? Explain.

ASSESS & RETEACH

Section 4 Assessment
Have pairs of students quiz each other on the list of terms and names. Then have them work together to answer the questions.

Section Quiz
FORMAL ASSESSMENT
Section Quiz, p. 255

Reteaching Activity
CLASS TIME: 30 MINUTES

Work with students to use the small and large heads in this section to make up questions about the section contents. For example, you can make up the following question from the first head in the section: "What was the relationship between Britain and its American Colonies?" List the questions on the board and have students copy them. Then have pairs of students work together to answer the questions. Go over students' answers.

CRITICAL THINKING TRANSPARENCIES
CT58 Chapter 22 Visual Summary

CLOSE ACTIVITY

CLASS TIME: 20 MINUTES

Making a Comic Strip
Have small groups of students work together to create a simple comic strip depicting one of the events in this section. Comic strips should be one to three cells and include dialogue or captions to explain what is happening in the pictures. Subjects for comic strips include American hostility toward the British, the drafting of important documents, and congressional debates about government. Encourage groups to share their work.

ANSWERS

1. TERMS & NAMES
• Declaration of Independence, p. 564
• Thomas Jefferson, p. 564
• checks and balances, pp. 566–567
• federal system, p. 567
• Bill of Rights, p. 567

2. TAKING NOTES
Possible Responses: Navigation Acts/smuggling; Stamp Act/boycott; import tax on tea/Boston Tea Party; weaknesses of Articles of Confederation/Constitutional Convention; distrust of central government/federal system.

3. ANALYZING ISSUES
Possible Response: It reflects the supremacy of reason, and shows a belief in human progress. It also includes the ideas that humans have natural rights, and that a government gets its power from the consent of the governed.

4. ANALYZING THEMES
Possible Responses: No; during Enlightenment, the average person started to question his or her happiness, which led to questioning authority. Yes; the people who came to America were self-reliant and individualistic; they were more open to change and revolution.

TERMS & NAMES

1. heliocentric theory, p. 546
2. Galileo Galilei, p. 546
3. Isaac Newton, p. 548
4. social contract, p. 551
5. natural rights, p. 551
6. separation of powers, p. 553
7. salon, p. 558
8. enlightened despot, p. 561
9. Declaration of Independence, p. 564
10. federal system, p. 567

REVIEW QUESTIONS

Answers may vary on some questions.

11. Center; earth revolved around the sun; Copernicus's theory.

12. (1) Identify a problem based on an observation, (2) form a hypothesis, (3) test the hypothesis, (4) analyze and interpret the results to reach a conclusion.

13. Telescope, to enlarge distant objects; microscope, to enlarge minute objects; thermometer, to measure temperature; barometer, to measure atmospheric pressure.

14. Hobbes thought that all people were naturally selfish and that governments were created to protect people from their own selfishness. He believed that an absolute monarchy was best. Locke thought that people had the natural ability to reason, govern their own affairs, and look after society. He believed that governments should be formed to protect these natural rights. Locke promoted self-government.

15. Loss of political liberties led to the fall of Rome; Montesquieu admired the separation of power.

16. Science offered new explanations of mysteries of nature; more people questioned religious teaching and authority.

17. The arts reflected order and balance; artists and architects borrowed ideas from classical Rome and Greece; the novel developed.

18. Greater religious toleration, reduced censorship, reduced torture, various other reforms; many reforms were limited or temporary, and all the enlightened despots failed to improve life of peasants.

19. There were no executive or judicial branches; Congress had no power to collect taxes or regulate trade; new laws were difficult to pass because nine of the 13 states needed to approve them.

TERMS & NAMES

Briefly explain the importance of each of the following to the Scientific Revolution, the Enlightenment, or the American Revolution (1550–1789).

1. heliocentric theory
2. Galileo Galilei
3. Isaac Newton
4. social contract
5. natural rights
6. separation of powers
7. salon
8. enlightened despot
9. Declaration of Independence
10. federal system

Interact *with* History

On page 544, you put yourself in the dilemma of Galileo. As you have read, Galileo did recant, but the idea he supported eventually became widely accepted. Think about the decisions of both Galileo and the church. Did the choices they made advance their goals? Discuss your opinions with a small group.

REVIEW QUESTIONS

SECTION 1 *(pages 545–550)*
The Scientific Revolution

11. According to Ptolemy, what was earth's position in the universe? How did Copernicus's view differ? Which did Kepler's observations support?

12. What are four steps in the scientific method?

13. List four new instruments that came into use during the Scientific Revolution. Identify the purpose of each one.

SECTION 2 *(pages 551–556)*
The Enlightenment in Europe

14. How did the ideas of Hobbes and Locke differ?

15. What did Montesquieu believe led to the fall of Rome? What did he admire about the government of Britain?

16. How did the Enlightenment lead to a more secular outlook?

SECTION 3 *(pages 558–562)*
The Spread of Enlightenment Ideas

17. Name three developments in the arts during the Enlightenment.

18. What sorts of reforms did the enlightened despots make? In what respects did their reforms fail?

SECTION 4 *(pages 563–567)*
American Revolution: The Birth of a Republic

19. Why did the Articles of Confederation result in a weak national government?

20. How did the writers of the U.S. Constitution put into practice the idea of separation of powers? A system of checks and balances?

Visual Summary

Enlightenment and Revolution, 1550–1789

Scientific Revolution

- Heliocentric theory challenges geocentric theory.
- Mathematics and observation support heliocentric theory.
- Scientific method develops.
- Scientists make discoveries in many fields.

A new way of thinking about the world develops—based on observation and a willingness to question assumptions.

Enlightenment

- People try to apply the scientific approach to all aspects of society.
- Political scientists propose new ideas about government.
- Philosophes advocate the use of reason to discover truths.
- Philosophes address social issues through reason.

Enlightenment writers challenge many accepted ideas about government and society.

Spread of Enlightenment Ideas

- Enlightenment ideas appeal to thinkers and artists across Europe.
- Salons help spread Enlightenment thinking.
- Ideas spread to literate middle class.
- Enlightened despots attempt reforms.

Enlightenment ideas sweep through European society and also to colonial America.

American Revolution

- Enlightenment ideas influence colonists.
- Britain taxes colonies after French and Indian War.
- Colonists denounce taxation without representation.
- War begins in Lexington and Concord.

Colonists declare independence, defeat Britain, and establish republic.

---

20. Separation of powers: created three separate branches of government—executive, legislative, and judicial; checks and balances: gave each of the three branches some control over the others.

Interact *with* History

Possible Responses: Students who originally refused to publicly deny the ideas about the universe may now say that Galileo's ideas would have had followers whether he lived or died. They may also believe that Galileo was right to recant his ideas instead of dying for them because the ideas were already circulating widely. Nothing Galileo did could have changed this. Others may say that Galileo should have stood up for what he believed in, regardless of the consequences.

CRITICAL THINKING

1. ROLE OF TECHNOLOGY

What role did new technology play in the Scientific Revolution?

2. THE U.S. CONSTITUTION

THEME POWER AND AUTHORITY What was the source of the Constitution's authority? How did this reflect Enlightenment ideas?

3. REVOLUTIONARY IDEAS

Create a two-column table like the one below. In the left column, list important new ideas that arose during the Scientific Revolution and Enlightenment. In the right column, briefly explain why the idea was revolutionary.

New Idea	Why Revolutionary

4. ANALYZING PRIMARY SOURCES

One of Voltaire's most passionate causes was religious toleration. The following excerpt comes from his *Treatise on Toleration* (1763). Voltaire wrote the essay in response to the case of a French Protestant who was falsely accused of murdering his Catholic son. The man was tortured and executed by French authorities. Read the passage and answer the questions that follow.

A VOICE FROM THE PAST
No great . . . eloquence is needed to prove that Christians should tolerate one another. I go even further and declare that we must look upon all men as our brothers. . . . Are we not all the children of one father and creatures of the same God? . . .

This little globe, nothing more than a point, rolls in space like so many other globes; we are lost in this immensity. Man, some five feet tall, is surely a very small part of the universe. One of these imperceptible [virtually invisible] beings says to some of his neighbors in Arabia or Africa: "Listen to me, for the God of all these worlds has enlightened me: there are nine hundred million little ants like us on earth, but only my anthill is beloved of God; he will hold all others in horror through all eternity; only mine will be blessed, the others will be eternally wretched."

- Summarize the main point conveyed in this passage. How does Voltaire illustrate his point?
- Do you think Voltaire is directing his message to one religion in particular or to all organized religions? Explain your response.

CHAPTER ACTIVITIES

1. LIVING HISTORY: Unit Portfolio Project

THEME REVOLUTION Your unit portfolio project focuses on showing the similarities and differences among revolutions (see page 509). For Chapter 22, you might use one of the following ideas to add to your portfolio:

- Design the cover for a special magazine issue that spotlights the most revolutionary thinker of the Scientific Revolution or Enlightenment. Indicate the focus of the articles that might appear inside the magazine by writing the table of contents page.
- Present a live or taped news report covering a major event of the American Revolution or early republic.
- Write song lyrics for a Revolutionary War ballad or march that explain why the Americans are fighting for independence.

2. CONNECT TO TODAY: Cooperative Learning

THEME SCIENCE AND TECHNOLOGY The Scientific Revolution produced ideas that profoundly changed how people viewed the natural world. In today's world, scientific discoveries have become commonplace. Yet often they are as revolutionary as those of the 16th century.

Work with a team to create a visual presentation highlighting a recent breakthrough in science or medicine. Focus on how the new knowledge changed what scientists previously thought about the topic.

INTERNET Use the Internet or magazines to research the topic. Look for information that will help you to understand the nature of the discovery and to explain why it is significant.

- Write two brief sentences that summarize the difference in scientific understanding before and after the breakthrough. For an example of such a summary, look at the box on page 548.
- Use text, charts, and other illustrations to explain the discovery's impact.

3. INTERPRETING A TIME LINE

Revisit the unit time line on pages 508–509. What events in Chapters 23 and 24 were probably influenced by the Enlightenment? Why?

FOCUS ON FINE ART

The Spanish artist Francisco Goya produced this engraving, titled *The Sleep of Reason Produces Monsters,* in 1797. Here is his caption: "Imagination abandoned by reason produces impossible monsters; united with her, she is the mother of the arts and the source of their wonders."
- What do you think the monsters represent?
- What is the artist saying will happen when a person lets his or her reason go to sleep?

Connect to History How does the engraving reflect the ideas of Enlightenment thinkers?

Enlightenment and Revolution **569**

PLANNING GUIDE
The French Revolution and Napoleon

	Key Ideas	COPY MASTERS	ASSESSMENT
SECTION 1 **Revolution Threatens the French King** *pp. 573–576*	*Members of the Third Estate demand a more representative government. The fall of the Bastille and the king's removal from Versailles signal the beginning of the French Revolution.*	**In-Depth Resources: Unit 5** • **Guided Reading,** p. 37 • **Literature:** from *A Tale of Two Cities,* p. 49 • **History Makers:** Marie Antoinette, p. 52	PE *Section 1 Assessment,* p. 576 **Formal Assessment** • Section Quiz, p. 264 **Alternative Assessment Book** • Standards for Evaluating a Product or Performance
SECTION 2 **Revolution Brings Reform and Terror** *pp. 577–583*	*The Legislative Assembly faces war and internal divisions. The king is executed, and Robespierre inaugurates the Reign of Terror. A third constitution puts power in the hands of the upper middle class.*	**In-Depth Resources: Unit 5** • **Guided Reading,** p. 38 • **Geography Application,** p. 43 • **Primary Sources,** pp. 45, 46, 47 • **History Makers:** Robespierre, p. 53 • **Across Time and Cultures,** p. 54 • **Science and Technology,** p. 55	PE *Section 2 Assessment,* p. 583 **Formal Assessment** • Section Quiz, p. 265 **Alternative Assessment Book** • Standards for Evaluating a Cooperative Activity
SECTION 3 **Napoleon Forges an Empire** *pp. 584–588*	*A brilliant general, Napoleon Bonaparte, becomes emperor of France and assumes broad powers. Through military victories, he establishes mastery over most of Europe.*	**In-Depth Resources: Unit 5** • **Guided Reading,** p. 39 • **Primary Source:** Napoleon's Proclamation at Austerlitz, p. 48	PE *Section 3 Assessment,* p. 588 **Formal Assessment** • Section Quiz, p. 266 **Alternative Assessment Book** • Standards for Evaluating a Cooperative Activity
SECTION 4 **Napoleon's Empire Collapses** *pp. 589–592*	*Napoleon makes political and military mistakes as he tries to increase his power. He is defeated, returns, is defeated again, and finishes his life in exile.*	**In-Depth Resources: Unit 5** • **Guided Reading,** p. 40 • **Skillbuilder Practice:** Interpreting Maps, p. 42	PE *Section 4 Assessment,* p. 592 **Formal Assessment** • Section Quiz, p. 267 **Alternative Assessment Book** • Standards for Evaluating a Product or Performance
SECTION 5 **The Congress of Vienna Convenes** *pp. 593–597*	*Following the plan of Metternich, the Congress of Vienna reestablishes stability in Europe after the defeat of Napoleon.*	**In-Depth Resources: Unit 5** • **Guided Reading,** p. 41	PE *Section 5 Assessment,* p. 596 **Formal Assessment** • Section Quiz, p. 268 **Alternative Assessment Book** • Standards for Evaluating a Cooperative Activity
CHAPTER RESOURCES	## Chapter Overview *Revolution leads to the overthrow and execution of the French king. After a period of instability, Napoleon takes control of France and of most of Europe. Napoleon's thirst for power leads to his downfall, and European leaders craft a lasting peace.*	*Telescoping the Times* • Chapter Summary, pp. 89–91 *Planning for Block Schedules*	PE *Chapter Assessment,* pp. 598–599 *Chapter Activities,* p. 599 **Formal Assessment** • Chapter Test, forms A and B, pp. 269–274 **Test Generator** **Alternative Assessment Book**

1789–1815

TECHNOLOGY

 Warm-Up Transparency 23

 Geography Transparencies
- G23 Early Sites of the French Revolution, 1789

 World Art and Cultures Transparencies
- AT50 *Portrait of Marie Antoinette*

 Electronic Library of Primary Sources
- from *Memoirs of Élisabeth Vigée-Lebrun*

INTERNET RESOURCES
www.mlworldhistory.com

 Warm-Up Transparency 23

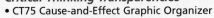 *Critical Thinking Transparencies*
- CT75 Cause-and-Effect Graphic Organizer

 Electronic Library of Primary Sources
- from "Execution by Guillotine"

INTERNET RESOURCES
www.mlworldhistory.com

 Warm-Up Transparency 23

 World Art and Cultures Transparencies
- AT51 *Napoleon Crossing the St. Bernard Pass*

 Electronic Library of Primary Sources
- from *The Letters of Napoleon I*

 Battles of the World
- The Battle of Austerlitz

INTERNET RESOURCES
www.mlworldhistory.com

 Warm-Up Transparency 23

 Electronic Library of Primary Sources
- "The Battle of Waterloo: The Finale"

INTERNET RESOURCES
www.mlworldhistory.com

 Warm-Up Transparency 23

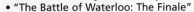 *Critical Thinking Transparencies*
- CT23 The French Revolution

 Electronic Library of Primary Sources
- from *Memoirs of Metternich*
- from "Frenchmen, Is This What You Want?"

INTERNET RESOURCES
www.mlworldhistory.com

 Chapter Summaries on Audiocassette in English and Spanish

 INTERNET RESOURCES
www.mlworldhistory.com

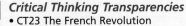

Block Scheduling (90 MINUTES)

Day 1
Section 1, pp. 573–576

Section 2, pp. 577–583

 COOPERATIVE ACTIVITY
Debating an Issue, p. 578 (Teacher's Edition)

Section Assessments, pp. 576, 583

Day 2
Section 3, pp. 584–588

COOPERATIVE ACTIVITY
Researching Napoleon and Nelson, p. 587 (Teacher's Edition)

Section 4, pp. 589–592

Section Assessments, pp. 588, 592

Day 3
Section 5, pp. 593–597

COOPERATIVE ACTIVITY
Investigating World Peace Organizations, p. 595 (Teacher's Edition)

Section Assessment, p. 596

Chapter Assessment, pp. 598–599

Yearly Pacing *Chapter 23 Total:* 3 days *Yearly Total:* 85 days

Planning for Block Schedules

Customizing for Special Needs

Students Acquiring English

 Access for Students Acquiring English
- **Guided Reading** for Sections 1–5 (Spanish), pp. 229–233
- **Chapter Summary** (Spanish), pp. 226–228
- **Skillbuilder Practice** Interpreting Maps (Spanish), p. 234
- **Geography Application** The French Revolution Under Siege (Spanish), p. 235

 Chapter Summaries on Audiocassette in English and Spanish

 INTERNET RESOURCES
www.mlworldhistory.com
The Diverse Classroom.

Less Proficient Readers

 In-Depth Resources: Unit 5
- **Guided Reading** for Sections 1–5, pp. 37–41
- **Skillbuilder Practice** Interpreting Maps, p. 42
- **Geography Application** The French Revolution Under Siege, p. 43

 Telescoping the Times
- Chapter Summary, pp. 89–91

 Chapter Summaries on Audiocassette

Gifted and Talented Students

 In-Depth Resources: Unit 5

Primary Sources
- from *A Declaration of the Rights of Man and of the Citizen, 1789,* p. 45
- "La Marseillaise," p. 46
- *from* The Execution of Louis XVI, p. 47
- Napoleon's Proclamation at Austerlitz, 1805, p. 48

History Makers
- Marie Antoinette, p. 52
- Maximilien Robespierre, p. 53

Connections to Literature READINGS FOR STUDENTS

 In-Depth Resources: Unit 5
Literature: from *A Tale of Two Cities* by Charles Dickens, p. 48

Enrichment Reading
- Sherwood, Frances
  Vindication
  New York: Penguin, 1994

  Mary Wollstonecraft, author of *A Vindication of the Rights of Woman,* is portrayed vividly in this fictionalized treatment of her life and times.

McDougal Littell
Literature Connections
- Dickens, Charles
  A Tale of Two Cities
  (with related readings)

  A classic tale of the French Revolution, with themes of love and self-sacrifice, heroes and quests.

 = Pupil's Edition   = Overhead Transparency   = Software   = Video

= Copy Master   = CD-ROM   = Audiocassette   = Internet

The French Revolution and Napoleon, 1789–1815

Accessing Prior Knowledge

- Ask students to read the captions accompanying each picture and to discuss what they already know about the people and the situations.

Predicting and Making Inferences

- After reading about Marie Antoinette's taste for fine clothes, ask students what they predict will happen to her.
- Ask students what they can tell about Napoleon's character from the painting of him astride his white horse.

Geography Connection

Ask students to study the border area of France and Spain.

- What is the geography of this area like?
- Could the geography protect Spain from its more powerful neighbor?

CHAPTER
23
The French Revolution and Napoleon, 1789–1815

PREVIEWING THEMES

Power and Authority
With absolute rulers dominating Europe, Enlightenment thinkers began questioning why so few held so much power. The French Revolution was an attempt to put power in the hands of the many. Power changed hands several times in this short period of history.

Revolution
The success of the American Revolution inspired the French, some of whom even participated in it. The French people were deeply affected by the colonists' overthrow of the British and, in turn, revolted against their own repressive rulers.

Economics
The gap between the rich and the poor widened when France's economy weakened. Hungry peasants and city dwellers were outraged by what they felt was unjust treatment. The economy of France became a major cause of the Revolution.

INTERNET CONNECTION

Visit us at **www.mlworldhistory.com** to learn more about the French Revolution, Napoleon, and related topics.

EUROPE, 1789

At Versailles, **Queen Marie Antoinette** spent so much money on clothes that in **1785** her enemies falsely accused her of buying a necklace with 647 diamonds. The rumor increased her unpopularity.

— Holy Roman Empire

ATLANTIC OCEAN

0   200 Miles
0   400 Kilometers

In Paris, a mob stormed the **Bastille,** the fortress looming in the background, and seized the weapons stored there. This **1789** event ignited the French Revolution.

SPAIN

⊙ Madrid

• Cádiz
• Gibraltar

570

GEOGRAPHY THEMES

Location

Ask students to note the political boundaries in Europe just before the French Revolution. Then have them turn to page 978 in the Atlas to examine Europe today. Ask them to name three European countries that did not exist in 1789. *Possibilities include Belgium,* *Greece, Germany, Italy, Czech Republic, Slovakia, Bosnia-Herzegovina, Croatia, and Albania.* Have students speculate about reasons for political changes in Europe over time.

Place

Tell students that geography played a key role in the political and military events discussed in this chapter. Ask them to examine this map and the one on page 979, to note the mountains between France and Italy, and to speculate about the difficulties involved in moving an army across the Alps. Explain that Napoleon's ability to conduct military campaigns despite physical barriers was one source of his success as a general. You might also ask students why Napoleon may have ridden a mule.

ADDITIONAL RESOURCES

Books for the Teacher

• Jones, R. Ben. *Napoleon: Man and Myth.* New York: Holmes, 1978.

• Kennedy, Emmet. *A Cultural History of the French Revolution.* New Haven: Yale UP, 1989.

• Schama, Simon. *Citizens: A Chronicle of the French Revolution.* New York: Knopf, 1989.

Books for the Student

• Robiquet, Jean. *Daily Life in the French Revolution.* Trans. James Kirkup. New York: Macmillan, 1965.

• Shenkman, Richard. *Legends, Lies, and Cherished Myths of World History.* New York: Harper, 1993.

Videos

• *The French Revolution.* Social Studies School Service, 800-421-4246.

• *Marie Antoinette: The Tragic Queen.* Arts and Entertainment, 1996.

• *Napoleon Bonaparte.* Films for the Humanities, 1988.

• *A Tale of Two Cities.* Social Studies School Service, 800-421-4246. British production (1958) starring Dirk Bogarde. With curriculum unit.

Software

• *French Revolution.* CD-ROM. Educational Software Institute, 800-955-5570.

• *Napoleonic Era.* CD-ROM. Educational Software Institute, 800-955-5570. Napoleon from different points of view.

After an alliance of nations defeated the French emperor Napoleon, the **Congress of Vienna** met in **1815** to decide who would rule in Europe. Aristocrats at the congress celebrated the victory with balls and banquets.

Napoleon led a French army into Italy and defeated France's enemy, Austria, in **1796**. This detail of *Napoleon Crossing the St. Bernard Pass* by Jacques Louis David presents a heroic Napoleon astride a magnificent stallion. Actually, Napoleon crossed the Alps on a mule, not a horse.

HISTORY THROUGH ART

Napoleon Crossing the St. Bernard Pass

Jacques-Louis David

The detail from *Napoleon Crossing the St. Bernard Pass* shows a young Napoleon on his way to military glory in Italy in 1796-1797. In the painting, Napoleon faces out from the foreground with the soaring Alps in the background.

The painter, Jacques-Louis David, was the most famous French artist of his time. He won fame for his huge paintings on classical themes, and he became a leading figure of Neoclassicism, a revival of classical forms stressing order and simplicity of style.

An ardent supporter of the Revolution and of Robespierre, David became a Deputy and voted for the execution of Louis XVI.

After the execution of Robespierre, David was arrested and spent time in prison. Later he became attached to Napoleon and painted a series of pictures glorifying the exploits of the Emperor.

Interpreting the Art In what ways does this painting glorify Napoleon? Do you consider this a piece of propaganda? Why or why not?

Interact *with* History

This Interact with History feature motivates students by inviting them to put themselves in a key historical situation—the French Revolution. As they imagine themselves confronted with an angry mob, students will analyze the issues, explore their options, and become decision makers.

Purpose

- to set the stage for studying the French Revolution
- to help students understand some of the forces that can fuel a revolution
- to help students make connections with the people and events they will study in this chapter

Teaching Strategy

Thinking Critically After students have imagined themselves in the situation described on this page, have them answer the key question and give reasons for their decision.

EXAMINING *the* ISSUES

Following are suggestions for addressing each bulleted question.

1 Have students describe riots they know about or have seen. What motivated people to riot?

2 Students may mention racial tensions, poverty, or a sense of being treated unfairly as causes of violence.

3 Have students brainstorm what problems a group of laborers and farmers (peasants) bent on revolution might face.

Making Connections Ask students to discuss the role of ordinary people in the American Revolution and in the English Civil War.

Follow Up

A feature on the chapter assessment will ask students to reevaluate their responses to the situation presented on this page.

Interact *with* History

The mob waves the severed heads of palace guards on poles.

City people shout demands for bread and equality.

Angry peasants carry shovels, rakes, and any other weapons they can find.

Some women carry branches that symbolize the liberty tree.

You are returning home from a bakery that is out of bread—again. You have no food to take to your starving children. You are desperate.

Suddenly you turn a corner and come upon the king's palace. King Louis and his wife are living there in luxury while your children and most of your fellow citizens are starving. You see a mob surrounding the palace, demanding food and relief from heavy taxes. They have turned violent.

Would you join the mob?

EXAMINING *the* ISSUES

1 • How could such a situation develop in one of the most advanced countries in the world?

2 • What could make people angry enough to behead others and then carry their heads on poles?

3 • How successful could a revolution of peasants be?

Discuss these questions with your classmates. In your discussion, remember what you've learned about other revolutionary conflicts, such as the American Revolution and the English Civil War.

As you read about the French Revolution in this chapter, see how events turn out for the peasants.

1 Revolution Threatens the French King

TERMS & NAMES
- Old Regime
- estate
- Louis XVI
- Marie Antoinette
- Estates-General
- National Assembly
- Tennis Court Oath
- Great Fear

MAIN IDEA

Economic and social inequalities in the Old Regime helped cause the French Revolution.

WHY IT MATTERS NOW

Throughout history, economic and social inequalities have at times led peoples to revolt against their governments.

SETTING THE STAGE In the 1700s, France was considered the most advanced country of Europe. It was the center of the Enlightenment. It had a large population and a prosperous foreign trade. France's culture was widely praised and emulated by the rest of the world. However, the appearance of success was deceiving. There was great unrest in France, caused by high prices, high taxes, and disturbing questions raised by the Enlightenment ideas of Rousseau and Voltaire.

The Old Regime

In the 1770s, the system of feudalism left over from the Middle Ages—called the **Old Regime**—remained in place. The people of France were still divided into three large social classes, or **estates.**

The Privileged Estates Two of the estates had privileges, including access to high offices and exemptions from paying taxes, that were not granted to the members of the third.

The Roman Catholic Church, whose clergy formed the First Estate, owned 10 percent of the land in France. It provided education and relief services to the poor and contributed about 2 percent of its income to the government.

The Second Estate was made up of rich nobles, much of whose wealth was in land. Although they made up only 2 percent of the population, the nobles owned 20 percent of the land and paid almost no taxes. The majority of the clergy and the nobility scorned Enlightenment ideas as radical notions that threatened their status and power as privileged persons.

This medallion bears the image of King Louis XVI of France.

The Third Estate About 98 percent of the people belonged to the Third Estate. The three groups that made up this estate differed greatly in their economic conditions.

Vocabulary
bourgeoisie: the middle class. (The term derives from the walled cities, or *bourgs,* in which the middle class began to develop in the 1200s.)

The first group—the bourgeoisie (BUR·zhwah·ZEE)—were merchants and artisans. They were well-educated and believed strongly in the Enlightenment ideals of liberty and equality. Although some of the bourgeoisie were as rich as nobles, they paid high taxes and lacked privileges like the other members of the Third Estate. Many felt that their wealth entitled them to a greater degree of social status and political power.

The workers of France's cities—cooks, servants, and others—formed the second group within the Third Estate, a group poorer than the bourgeoisie. Paid low wages and frequently out of work, they often went hungry. If the cost of bread rose, mobs of these workers might attack carts of grain and bread to steal what they needed.

Peasants formed the largest group within the Third Estate—more than 80 percent of France's 26 million people. Peasants paid about half their income in dues to nobles, tithes to the church, and taxes to the king's agents. They even paid taxes on such basic staples as salt. Peasants joined the urban poor in resenting the clergy and the nobles for their privileges and special treatment. The heavily taxed and discontented Third Estate was eager for change.

The French Revolution and Napoleon **573**

Section 1 Overview

OBJECTIVES

(1) To identify the three estates of the Old Regime.

(2) To summarize factors that led up to the French Revolution.

(3) To describe the creation of the National Assembly and the storming of the Bastille.

(4) To explain the importance of the Great Fear and the women's march on Versailles.

SKILLBUILDER

- Interpreting charts and political cartoons, p. 574

CRITICAL THINKING

- Analyzing motives, p. 575
- Recognizing effects, p. 576
- Forming opinions, p. 576
- Analyzing themes, p. 576

FOCUS

5-Minute Warm-Up

▶ **Perceiving Causes**

To help students understand revolution, have them answer these questions.

1. Look at the two paintings on page 575. What is the most striking difference between the two women?

2. How do poor people sometimes feel about wealthy people?

 WARM-UP TRANSPARENCY 23

OBJECTIVE (1) INSTRUCT

The Old Regime

▶ **Key Ideas**

- The clergy of the Roman Catholic Church form the First Estate.
- The Second Estate consists of rich nobles, who own 20 percent of the land and pay no taxes.
- The other 98 percent of the people make up the Third Estate. They are heavily taxed and discontented.

IN-DEPTH RESOURCES: UNIT 5
Guided Reading, p. 37

ACCESS FOR STUDENTS ACQUIRING ENGLISH
Guided Reading (Spanish), p. 229

SECTION 1 RESOURCES

PRINT RESOURCES

IN-DEPTH RESOURCES: UNIT 5
Guided Reading, p. 37
Literature: from *A Tale of Two Cities,* p. 49
History Makers: Marie Antoinette, p. 52

ACCESS FOR STUDENTS ACQUIRING ENGLISH
Guided Reading (Spanish), p. 229

FORMAL ASSESSMENT
Section Quiz, p. 264

ALTERNATIVE ASSESSMENT BOOK

TECHNOLOGY RESOURCES

GEOGRAPHY TRANSPARENCIES
GT23 Early Sites of the French Revolution, 1789

WORLD ART AND CULTURES TRANSPARENCIES
AT50 *Portrait of Marie Antoinette with Her Children*

CD-ROM
Electronic Library of Primary Sources

INTERNET www.mlworldhistory.com

Teacher's Edition **573**

The Three Estates

■ **First Estate**
- made up of clergy of Roman Catholic Church
- scorned Enlightenment ideas

■ **Second Estate**
- made up of rich nobles
- held highest offices in government
- disagreed about Enlightenment ideas

■ **Third Estate**
- included bourgeoisie, urban lower class, and peasant farmers
- had no power to influence government
- embraced Enlightenment ideas

Population of France, 1787

98% (Third Estate)

less than 1% (First Estate)

2% (Second Estate)

Percent of Income Paid in Taxes

2% (First Estate)	
0% (Second Estate)	
	50% (Third Estate)

0% 20% 40% 60% 80% 100%

SKILLBUILDER: Interpreting Charts and Political Cartoons
The Third Estate intensely resented the wealthy First and Second Estates.
1. *How do the chart and the graphs help explain the political cartoon?*
2. *Why might the First and Second Estates be opposed to change?*

The Forces of Change

In addition to the growing resentment of the lower classes, other factors were contributing to the revolutionary mood in France.

Enlightenment Ideas New views about power and authority in government were spreading among the Third Estate. The people began questioning long-standing notions about the structure of society and using words like *equality, liberty,* and *democracy.* The success of the American Revolution inspired them, and they discussed the radical ideas of Rousseau and Voltaire. Many shared the beliefs of the Comte d'Antraigues, a friend of Rousseau's:

> **A VOICE FROM THE PAST**
> The Third Estate is the People and the People is the foundation of the State; it is in fact the State itself; the other orders are merely political categories while by the *immutable laws of nature* the People is everything. Everything should be subordinated to it. . . . It is in the People that all national power resides and for the People that all states exist.
>
> **COMTE D'ANTRAIGUES,** quoted in *Citizens: A Chronicle of the French Revolution*

Economic Woes France's once prosperous economy was failing. The population was expanding rapidly, as were trade and production. However, the heavy burden of taxes made it impossible to conduct business profitably within France. The cost of living rose for everyone. In addition, bad weather in the 1780s caused widespread crop failures, resulting in a severe shortage of grain. The price of bread doubled in 1789, and many people faced starvation.

During this period, France's government sank deeply into debt. Extravagant spending by the king and queen was part of the problem. **Louis XVI,** who became king in 1774, inherited part of the debt from his predecessors. He also borrowed heavily in order to help the American revolutionaries in their war against Great Britain—France's chief rival—thereby nearly doubling the government's debt. When bankers, in 1786, refused to lend the government any more money, Louis faced serious problems.

A Weak Leader Strong leadership might have prevented the coming crisis, but Louis XVI was indecisive and allowed matters to drift. He paid little attention to his government advisers, preferring to spend his time hunting or tinkering with locks rather than attending to the details of governing.

Background
The ideas of Rousseau and Voltaire are also reflected in the United States Constitution.

574 Chapter 23

Louis had married his wife, **Marie Antoinette,** when he was 15 and she was 14. Because Marie was a member of the royal family of Austria, France's long-time enemy, she became unpopular as soon as she set foot in France. As queen, Marie spent so much money on gowns, jewels, and gifts that she became known as Madame Deficit.

Rather than cutting expenses and increasing taxes, Louis put off dealing with the emergency until France faced bankruptcy. Then, when he tried to tax aristocrats, the Second Estate forced him to call a meeting of the **Estates-General**—an assembly of representatives from all three estates—to get approval for the tax reform. He had the meeting—the first in 175 years—on May 5, 1789, at Versailles.

Revolution Dawns

The clergy and the nobles had dominated the Estates-General throughout the Middle Ages and expected to do so in the 1789 meeting. Under the assembly's medieval rules, each estate's delegates met in a separate hall to vote, and each estate had one vote. The two privileged estates could always outvote the Third Estate.

The National Assembly The Third Estate delegates, mostly members of the bourgeoisie whose views had been shaped by the Enlightenment, were eager to make changes in the government. They insisted that all three estates meet together and that each delegate have a vote. This would give the advantage to the Third Estate, which had as many delegates as the other two estates combined.

Siding with the nobles, the king ordered the Estates-General to follow the medieval rules. The delegates of the Third Estate, however, became more and more determined to wield power. A leading spokesperson for their viewpoint was a clergyman sympathetic to their cause, the Abbé Sieyès (AB·AY syay·YEHS), who argued, "What is the Third Estate? Everything. What has it been up to now in the political order? Nothing. What does it demand? To become something herein." In a dramatic speech, he suggested that the Third Estate delegates name themselves the **National Assembly** and pass laws and reforms in the name of the French people.

HISTORY MAKERS

Marie Antoinette
1755–1793

Marie Antoinette was a pretty, lighthearted, charming woman. However, she was unpopular with the French because of her spending and her involvement in controversial court affairs. She referred to Louis as "the poor man" and sometimes set the clock forward an hour to be rid of his presence.

Marie refused to wear the tight-fitting clothing styles of the day and introduced a loose cotton dress for women. The elderly, who viewed the dress as an undergarment, thought that Marie's clothing was scandalous. The French silk industry was equally angry.

In constant need of entertainment, Marie often spent her time playing cards. One year she lost the equivalent of $1.5 million by gambling in card games.

HISTORY THROUGH ART: Fine Art

A Woman of the Revolution [La maraîchère] (1795), Jacques Louis David

The gap between rich and poor in 18th-century France is clear in these portraits. David, painter of the Revolution, depicted a common woman (*left*) whose appearance displays none of the luxury of the French court (*right*).

Connect *to* History

Comparing What details of the women's expressions and clothing most clearly show the contrasts in lives?

SEE SKILLBUILDER HANDBOOK, PAGE 996.

Connect *to* Today

Contrasting How would you visually convey the gap between rich and poor in your country?

Marie Antoinette, Jacques Gautier d'Agoty

The French Revolution and Napoleon **575**

After a long night of excited debate, the delegates of the Third Estate agreed to Sieyès's idea by an overwhelming majority. On June 17, 1789, they voted to establish the National Assembly, in effect proclaiming the end of absolute monarchy and the beginning of representative government. This vote was the first deliberate act of revolution.

Three days later, the Third Estate delegates found themselves locked out of their meeting room. They broke down a door to an indoor tennis court, pledging to stay until they had drawn up a new constitution. Their pledge was called the **Tennis Court Oath.**

Storming the Bastille In response, Louis tried to make peace with the Third Estate by yielding to the National Assembly's demands. He ordered the nobles and the clergy to join the Third Estate in the National Assembly. At the same time, sensing trouble, the king stationed his mercenary army of Swiss guards in Paris, since he no longer trusted the loyalty of the French soldiers.

In Paris, rumors flew that foreign troops were coming to massacre French citizens. People gathered weapons in order to defend Paris against the king's foreign troops. On July 14, a mob tried to get gunpowder from the Bastille, a Paris prison. The angry crowd overwhelmed the king's soldiers, and the Bastille fell into the control of the citizens. The fall of the Bastille became a great symbolic act of revolution to the French people. Ever since, July 14 has been a French national holiday, similar to the U.S. Fourth of July.

Vocabulary
mercenary army: a group of soldiers who will work for any country or employer that will pay them.

Daily *Life*

The Women's March
When the women of Paris marched 12 miles in the rain to the luxurious palace at Versailles, they were infuriated. They deeply resented the extravagances of Louis and Marie Antoinette at a time when their own children were starving.

After forcing the king and queen out of the palace, the women followed Louis's family and entourage of almost 60,000 persons to Paris—another 12-mile march.

During their return, they sang that they were bringing "the baker, the baker's wife, and the baker's lad" to Paris. (They expected the "baker" to provide bread to alleviate the terrible hunger in the city.) Revolutionary leaders would later honor the women as heroes of the Revolution.

A Great Fear Sweeps France

Before long, rebellion spread from Paris into the countryside. From one village to the next, wild rumors circulated that the nobles were hiring outlaws to terrorize the peasants.

A wave of senseless panic called the **Great Fear** rolled through France. When the peasants met no enemy bandits, they became outlaws themselves. Waving pitchforks and torches, they broke into nobles' manor houses, tore up the old legal papers that bound them to pay feudal dues, and in some cases burned the manor houses as well.

In October 1789, approximately 6,000 Parisian women rioted over the rising price of bread. Their anger quickly turned against the king and queen. Seizing knives and axes, the women and a great many men marched on Versailles. They broke into the palace and killed two guards. The women demanded that Louis and Marie Antoinette come to Paris. Finally, the king agreed to take his wife and children to Paris.

Three hours later the king, his family, and servants left Versailles, never again to see their magnificent palace. Their exit signaled the change of power and radical reforms about to overtake France.

THINK THROUGH HISTORY
B. Recognizing Effects How did the women's march mark a turning point in the relationship between the king and the people?
B. Possible Answer The king had to bow to the will of the people.

Section ① Assessment

1. TERMS & NAMES
Identify
• Old Regime
• estate
• Louis XVI
• Marie Antoinette
• Estates-General
• National Assembly
• Tennis Court Oath
• Great Fear

2. TAKING NOTES
Use a web diagram like the one below to show the causes of the French Revolution.

( ) ( )

Causes of Revolution

( )

3. FORMING OPINIONS
Do you think that changes in the French government were inevitable?

THINK ABOUT
• the leadership of Louis XVI
• the French national debt
• Enlightenment ideas
• other world revolutions

4. ANALYZING THEMES
Economics How were the economic conditions in France similar to or different from those in England and the American colonies before their revolutions?

THINK ABOUT
• France's three estates
• the role of taxation
• France's national debt
• conditions in England before the Civil War
• conditions in the colonies before the American Revolution

2 Revolution Brings Reform and Terror

TERMS & NAMES
- Declaration of the Rights of Man
- Legislative Assembly
- émigrés
- sans-culottes
- guillotine
- Maximilien Robespierre
- Committee of Public Safety
- Reign of Terror

MAIN IDEA

The revolutionary government of France made reforms but also used terror and violence to retain power.

WHY IT MATTERS NOW

Some governments that lack the support of a majority of their people still use terrorism to control their citizens.

SETTING THE STAGE Peasants were not the only members of French society to feel the Great Fear; nobles and clergymen were equally afraid. Throughout France, bands of angry peasants struck out against members of the upper classes. In the summer of 1789, a few months before the women's march to Versailles, some nobles and clergymen in the National Assembly responded to the uprisings in an emotional late-night meeting.

The Assembly Reforms France

Throughout the night of August 4, 1789, noblemen made grand speeches, declaring their love of liberty and equality. Although motivated more by fear than by idealism, they joined other members of the National Assembly in sweeping away the feudal privileges of the First Estate and the Second Estate, thus making commoners and peasants equal to the nobles and the clergy. By morning, the Old Regime was dead.

The Rights of Man Three weeks later, on August 27, the National Assembly adopted a statement of revolutionary ideals called "A Declaration of the Rights of Man and of the Citizen," commonly known as the **Declaration of the Rights of Man.** Reflecting the influence of Enlightenment ideas and of the Declaration of Independence, the document stated that "men are born and remain free and equal in rights" and that "the aim of all political association is the preservation of the natural . . . rights of man. These rights are liberty, property, security, and resistance to oppression." Other articles of the famous document guaranteed citizens equal justice, freedom of speech, and freedom of religion. As the French people embraced the principles of the declaration, the expression "Liberty, Equality, Fraternity" became the slogan of the Revolution.

However, the Declaration of the Rights of Man did not apply to women. When Olympe de Gouges (aw·LAMP duh GOOZH) wrote a declaration of the rights of women, not only were her ideas rejected, but she eventually lost her head as an enemy of the Revolution.

A State-Controlled Church During 1790, many of the National Assembly's reforms focused on the relationship between church and state. The assembly took over church lands and declared that church officials and priests were to be elected by property owners and paid as state officials. Thus, the Catholic Church lost both its lands and its political independence. The reasons for the assembly's actions were economic. The delegates hesitated to further tax the bourgeoisie, who were strong supporters of the Revolution. However, the delegates were willing to sell church lands to help pay off France's large debt.

The French Revolution and Napoleon **577**

THINK THROUGH HISTORY
A. Synthesizing
How did the slogan "Liberty, Equality, Fraternity" sum up the goals of the Revolution?
A. Possible Answer
It conveyed the desire for freedom from old class structures, equal rights for all citizens, and unity among the French people.

HISTORY MAKERS

Olympe de Gouges
1748–1793

Olympe de Gouges was a playwright and journalist whose feminist writings reached a large audience. In 1791 this strong supporter of democracy demanded the same rights for French women that French men were demanding for themselves. In her "Declaration of the Rights of Woman and the Female Citizen," she challenged the oppression of male authority and the notion of male-female inequality:

Male and female citizens, being equal in the eyes of the law, must be equally admitted to all honors, positions, and public employment according to their capacity and without other distinctions besides those of their virtues and talents.

Section 2 Overview

OBJECTIVES

1. To explain the provisions of the Declaration of the Rights of Man.

2. To summarize the positions of the three factions that tried to govern France.

3. To explain how the war with Austria and the execution of the king affected the Revolution.

4. To describe the events of the Reign of Terror.

5. To explain what happened after the Terror came to an end.

SKILLBUILDER
- Interpreting charts, p. 578

CRITICAL THINKING
- Synthesizing, pp. 577, 581
- Identifying problems, p. 578
- Recognizing causes, pp. 580, 583
- Summarizing, p. 582

FOCUS
5-Minute Warm-Up

▶ **Recognizing Facts and Details**
To understand one means of controlling people, have students answer these questions.

1. Read about the guillotine on page 581. How did condemned persons die?

2. Why were some spectators displeased with the guillotine?

 WARM-UP TRANSPARENCY 23

OBJECTIVE ① INSTRUCT

The Assembly Reforms France

▶ **Key Ideas**
- The National Assembly sweeps away the privileges of the nobility and the clergy.

- The state takes control of the Catholic Church, alarming devout peasants.

- Louis XVI is caught as he tries to flee from France.

IN-DEPTH RESOURCES: UNIT 5
Guided Reading, p. 38
Primary Source: from A Declaration of the Rights of Man and of the Citizen, 1789, p. 45

ACCESS FOR STUDENTS ACQUIRING ENGLISH
Guided Reading (Spanish), p. 230

SECTION 2 RESOURCES

PRINT RESOURCES

IN-DEPTH RESOURCES: UNIT 5
Guided Reading, p. 38
Geography Application: The Revolution Under Siege, p. 43
Primary Source: from Declaration, p. 45; "La Marseillaise," p. 46; from The Execution of Louis XVI, p. 47
History Makers: Maximilien Robespierre, p. 53
Connections Across Time and Cultures, p. 54
Science and Technology, p. 55

ACCESS FOR STUDENTS ACQUIRING ENGLISH
Guided Reading (Spanish), p. 230
Geography Application: (Spanish), p. 235

FORMAL ASSESSMENT
Section Quiz, p. 265

TECHNOLOGY RESOURCES

CRITICAL THINKING TRANSPARENCIES
CT75 Cause-and-Effect Graphic Organizer

CD-ROM
Electronic Library of Primary Sources

INTERNET www.mlworldhistory.com

Conflicting Goals Cause Divisions

Key Ideas

- A new constitution ends the absolute monarchy.
- The Legislative Assembly is given the power to create laws.
- Old problems remain, and the government splits into three factions.

The assembly's actions alarmed millions of devout French peasants, who rallied to the support of their parish priests. Many French peasants, like their priests, were conservative Catholics. Although the assembly's move to make the church a part of the state was in accord with Enlightenment philosophy, it offended such Catholics, who believed that the pope should rule over a church independent of the state.

These changes in the church drove a wedge between the peasants and the bourgeoisie. From this time on, the peasants often opposed further revolutionary changes.

Louis Tries to Escape As the National Assembly restructured the relationship between church and state, Louis XVI pondered his fate as a monarch. Some of the king's advisers warned Louis that he and his family were in danger. Many supporters of the monarchy thought France unsafe and left the country. Then, in June 1791, Louis and his family tried to escape from France to the Austrian Netherlands. As they neared the French border, however, a postmaster recognized the king from his portrait on some paper money. The royal family was returned to Paris under guard. By his attempted escape, Louis XVI had increased the influence of his radical enemies and sealed his own doom.

Conflicting Goals Cause Divisions

For two years, the National Assembly argued over a new constitution for France. By 1791, the delegates had made significant changes in France's government and society.

A Limited Monarchy The National Assembly created a limited constitutional monarchy. The new constitution stripped the king of much of his authority and gave the Legislative Assembly the power to create French law. Although the king and his ministers would still hold the executive power to enforce laws, France's assemblymen would be the lawmakers in the country.

In September 1791, the National Assembly completed its new constitution, which Louis reluctantly approved, and then handed over its power to a new assembly—the **Legislative Assembly.** This assembly had the power to create laws and to approve or prevent any war the king declared on other nations.

Factions Split France Despite the new government, old problems, such as food shortages and government debt, remained. Angry cries for more liberty, more equality, and more bread soon caused the Revolution's leaders to turn against one another. The Legislative Assembly split into three general groups, each of which sat in a different part of the meeting hall. (The three divisions are summarized below.)

THINK THROUGH HISTORY
B. Identifying Problems What problems were not solved by the new government?
B. Answer Food shortages and government debt

The Legislative Assembly

Radicals	Moderates	Conservatives
• sat on the left side of the hall; were called left-wing and said to be on the left • opposed the king and the idea of a monarchy • wanted sweeping changes in government and proposed that common people have full power in a republic	• sat in the center of the hall and were called centrists • wanted some changes in government, but not as many as the radicals	• sat on the right side of the hall; were called right-wing and said to be on the right • upheld the idea of a limited monarchy • wanted few changes in government

SKILLBUILDER: Interpreting Charts

1. *What do the divisions in the Legislative Assembly say about the differences in French society?*
2. *What similarities and differences do you see between the political factions in the Legislative Assembly and those in the U.S. government today?*

Although these groups disagreed, there were groups in France that were far more extreme. **Émigrés** (EHM·ih·GRAYZ)—nobles and others who had fled France during the peasant uprisings—were on the extreme right. They hoped to undo the Revolution and restore the Old Regime.

On the extreme left, the most radical group was the **sans-culottes** (SANZ kyoo·LAHTS), "those without knee breeches." Unlike the upper classes, who wore fancy knee-length pants, sans-culottes wore regular trousers. They were Parisian wage-earners and small shopkeepers who wanted a greater voice in government, lower food prices, and an end to food shortages. Although they did not have a role in the assembly, they soon discovered other ways to exert their power as a group, especially by influencing one of the political clubs that developed later.

War and Extreme Measures

In 1792, the French were faced not only with reforms at home but also with a disastrous foreign war. Monarchs and nobles in many European countries feared the changes that were taking place in France. They worried that peasant revolts similar to the ones in France could break out in their own countries.

War with Austria French radicals hoped to spread their revolution to all the peoples of Europe. When Austria and Prussia proposed that France put Louis back on the throne, the Legislative Assembly responded by declaring war on Austria in April 1792. Prussia later joined Austria in the war against the French. By going to war with France, the European leaders believed, they would be helping Louis XVI to regain his position as an absolute monarch, as well as preserving their own positions as monarchs.

The war began badly for the poorly equipped French forces. By the summer of 1792, enemy armies were advancing toward Paris. On July 25, the Prussian commander threatened to destroy Paris if the revolutionaries harmed any member of the royal family. This rash statement infuriated the Parisians. On August 10, about 20,000 men and women invaded the Tuileries, the royal palace where Louis and his family were staying. The king's Swiss guard of 900 men fought desperately to defend Louis. The mob brutally massacred them and imprisoned Louis, Marie Antoinette, and their children in a stone tower. A witness in the palace recalled the scene:

In June 1792, rioters invaded the Tuileries—Louis's palace in Paris. They shouted at Louis and waved swords in his face for hours before being persuaded to leave peacefully.

A VOICE FROM THE PAST

I ran from place to place, and finding the apartments and staircases already strewed with dead bodies, I . . . ran away to the Dauphin's garden gate where some Marseillais [citizen soldiers from Marseille], who had just butchered several of the Swiss, were stripping them. One of them came up to me with a bloody sword in his hand, saying, "Hello, citizen! Without arms! Here, take this and help us to kill." But luckily . . . I managed to make my escape. Some of the Swiss who were persued took refuge in an adjoining stable. I concealed myself in the same place. They were soon cut to pieces close to me. . . .

UNNAMED ROYAL SERVANT, quoted in *The Days of the French Revolution*

France's war with Austria and Prussia also affected daily life in Paris. During the summer of 1792, Parisians learned that French troops were failing to hold back the approaching Prussian forces. Just as bands of volunteer soldiers were preparing to leave Paris and reinforce the French soldiers in the field, they heard rumors that the royalists imprisoned in Paris would seize control of the city in their absence. Angry

The French Revolution and Napoleon **579**

OBJECTIVE **3** INSTRUCT

War and Extreme Measures

▶ *Key Ideas*

• Fearing the loss of their own positions, European monarchs support Louis XVI, and France declares war on Austria.

• Louis XVI is imprisoned after a Parisian mob invades the royal palace.

• The "September massacres," in which Parisian mobs murder prisoners, lead the Legislative Assembly to depose the king and set aside the Constitution of 1791.

• In summer of 1792, mobs are the real rulers of the country.

• A new legislature votes to execute the king.

• Many French citizens become soldiers as Austrian forces press toward Paris.

CRITICAL THINKING ACTIVITY

CLASS TIME: 15 MINUTES

Making a Flowchart
To help students find connections between events in this section, have them make a simple flow chart like the one below.

TEACHING OPTION

CUSTOMIZING FOR SPECIAL NEEDS

CLASS TIME 20 MINUTES

Less Proficient Readers

Vocabulary Activity Pair a less proficient reader with a more proficient reader and ask them to help each other learn the key terms in this section. One strategy they might use to remember a term's meaning is to "interview" the term, playing the part of journalists investigating the who, what, where, when, how, and why of a situation.

An example interview question is "Who are you?" For the term émigrés on this page, the answer might be "I am a French aristocrat. I left France when the peasants on my estate set fire to my house. I wish that the king would put those upstarts in their place!" For sans-culottes, students might ask, "What do you want?" The answer might be "I work hard, but there

is still not enough bread. My son can't find work. The aristocrats live well while we starve. I want an end to royalty and enough bread to live."

Students can apply this strategy to learning any key term.

Teacher's Edition   579

THINK THROUGH HISTORY
C. Recognizing Causes What did the September massacres show about the mood of the people?
C. Possible Answer The people were impatient and fearful. They were willing to act violently.

Louis XVI was one of the first persons to be executed with the newly invented guillotine. He faced death with dignity, saying:

"I am innocent and shall die without fear. I would that my death might bring happiness to the French, and ward off the dangers which I foresee."

The execution of the king was a victory for the radicals in Paris, but it horrified European monarchs and made their opposition to the French Revolution stronger than ever.

📋 *IN-DEPTH RESOURCES: UNIT 5*
Primary Source: from The Execution of Louis XVI, p. 47

MORE ABOUT . . .
France's Citizen Army

In the face of national danger, the French people united in a heroic defense of the nation. A spirited marching song written during the French Revolution by a captain named Claude-Joseph Rouget de Lisle helped inspire the volunteer troops. It became La Marseillaise, the French National anthem.

Allons, enfants de la Patrie,
Le jour de gloire est arrivé!
Contre nous de la tyrannie
L'étendard sanglant est levé!
L'étendard sanglant est levé.
Entendez-vous, dans les campagnes,
Mugir ces féroces soldats?
Ils viennent jusque dans nos bras
Égorger nos fils, nos campagnes.
Aux armes, citoyens!

Let us go, our fatherland's children,
The day of glory has arrived.
The bloody flag of tyranny is raised against us. The bloody flag is raised.
Do you hear the fierce soldiers roar in our fields?
They rush right into our arms.
To slit our sons' and comrades' throats.
To arms, citizens!

📋 *IN-DEPTH RESOURCES: UNIT 5*
Primary Source: La Marseillaise, p. 46

---

citizens responded by taking the law into their own hands. For several days in early September, Parisians raided the prisons and murdered over 1,000 prisoners. Many royalists, nobles, and clergymen fell victim to the angry mobs in these so-called September massacres.

Faced with the threat of the Parisian radicals, the members of the Legislative Assembly gave up the idea of a limited monarchy. They set aside the Constitution of 1791, declared the king deposed, and dissolved their assembly, calling for the election of a new legislature.

The new governing body, elected in September, called itself the National Convention. Just as the new government took office, France had a stroke of luck. A French army won a battle against the Austrians and Prussians. For the moment, France was out of danger from abroad.

In this engraving, titled *Execution of Louis XVI*, a revolutionary presents Louis's head to the crowd after the king's execution in Paris.

Radicals Execute the King During the frenzied summer of 1792, the leaders of the mobs on the streets had more real power than any government assembly. Although the mobs were made up of the poor, their leaders came from the bourgeoisie.

Both men and women of the middle class joined political clubs. The most radical club in 1792 was the Jacobin (JAK·uh·bihn) Club, where violent speech-making was the order of the day. The Jacobins wanted to remove the king and establish a republic.

One of the prominent radical leaders was Jean Paul Marat (mah·RAH). During the Revolution, he edited a radical newspaper. His fiery editorials called for "five or six hundred heads cut off" to rid France of the enemies of the Revolution. Georges Danton (zhawrzh dahn·TAWN), a revolutionary leader who was devoted to the rights of Paris's poor people, joined the club as a talented speaker.

The National Convention, meeting in Paris on September 21, quickly abolished the monarchy and declared France a republic. Adult male citizens were granted the right to vote and hold office. Despite the important part they had already played in the Revolution, women were not given the right to vote. The delegates reduced Louis XVI's role from that of a king to that of a common citizen and prisoner. Then, guided by radical Jacobins, they tried Louis for treason and found him guilty. By a very close vote, they sentenced him to death.

On January 21, 1793, the ex-king walked with calm dignity up the steps of the scaffold to be beheaded by a machine called the **guillotine** (GIHL·uh·TEEN). Thousands died by the guillotine during the French Revolution.

France's Citizen Army The new republic's first problem was the continuing war with Austria and Prussia. Early in 1793, Great Britain, Holland, and Spain joined Prussia and Austria in an alliance known as the First Coalition. Forced to contend with so many enemies, France suffered a string of defeats.

The Jacobin leaders took extreme steps to meet the new danger. In February 1793, the National Convention decreed a draft into the army of 300,000 French citizens between the ages of 18 and 40. By 1794, the army had grown to 800,000 and included women.

GEOGRAPHY APPLICATION ACTIVITY

Task Students will examine a map to explore how much threat the French Revolution was under from external and internal enemies. They should note the central location of Paris, the fact of enemies on all sides, and the scattered internal enemies.

Materials Needed Use copies of the Geography Application worksheet for Chapter 23 or make a transparency of the map from that worksheet.

Activity Have the class help you make a list of the enemies of the Revolution. Then trace on the worksheet the locations of those enemies. If you are using a transparency, have individual students point out various locations. Have pairs of students collaborate to answer the questions from the worksheet.

Conclusion Ask students to comment on how seriously Paris was in danger at this time. What do they think might have happened if Paris had fallen? Why do they think the Reign of Terror happened in France at about this time?

 IN-DEPTH RESOURCES: UNIT 5
Geography Application: The French Revolution Under Siege, p. 43

The Guillotine

If you think the guillotine was a cruel form of capital punishment, think again. Dr. Joseph Ignace Guillotin proposed a machine that satisfied many needs—it was efficient, humane, and democratic. A physician and member of the National Assembly, Guillotin claimed that those executed with the device "wouldn't even feel the slightest pain."

Prior to the guillotine's introduction in 1792, many French criminals had suffered through horrible punishments in public places. Although public punishments continued to attract large crowds, not all spectators were pleased with the new machine. Some witnesses felt that death by the guillotine occurred much too quickly to be enjoyed by an audience.

Some doctors believed that a victim's head retained its hearing and eyesight for up to 15 minutes after the blade's deadly blow. All remains were eventually gathered and buried in simple graves.

Once the executioner cranked the blade to the top, a mechanism released it. The sharp weighted blade fell, severing the victim's head from his or her body.

Earlier Forms of Punishment

Criminals in 17th- and 18th-century France sometimes faced one or more of the following fatal penalties:

- Burning
- Strangulation
- Being broken on a wheel
- Hanging
- Dismemberment
- Beheading
- Being pulled apart by horses

Woman knitters, or *tricoteuses*, were regular spectators at executions and knitted stockings for soldiers as they sat near the base of the scaffold.

Beheading by Class

More than 2,100 people were executed during the last 132 days of the Reign of Terror. The pie graph below displays the breakdown of beheadings by class.

- ■ First Estate
- ■ Second Estate
- ■ Third Estate

Before each execution, bound victims traveled from the prison to the scaffold in horse-drawn carts during a 1½ hour procession through city streets.

Connect *to* History

Synthesizing In what ways was the guillotine an efficient means of execution?

SEE SKILLBUILDER HANDBOOK, PAGE 1007.

Connect *to* Today

Comparing France continued to use the guillotine until the late 1970s. Compare this instrument of capital punishment with the ones used in the United States today, and present your findings in an oral report. Speculate on what the goals of capital punishment are and whether they have been achieved—in the French Revolution or in today's world.

 INTERNET CONNECTION

Visit us at **www.mlworldhistory.com** to learn more about the French Revolution and Napoleon.

Although prerevolutionary France is often depicted as backward and strangled by the aristocracy and the church, many historians feel that this picture is wrong. They point to the springing up of new enterprises involving mechanization. Textile dyeing, silk production, sugar refining, textile manufacturing, and mining were all being revolutionized by increasingly sophisticated industrial technology.

IN-DEPTH RESOURCES: UNIT 5
Science and Technology: Science Helps Create the Metric System, p.55

MORE ABOUT . . .
The Guillotine

One reason for the development of the guillotine was the desire to apply capital punishment equally to all social classes. The guillotine, it was felt, would give even common prisoners the kind of dignified execution previously reserved for the upper classes.

ELECTRONIC LIBRARY OF PRIMARY SOURCES
from "Execution by Guillotine"

INTERNET
Click *World History* at www.mlworldhistory.com

Connect *to* History

Analyzing
Possible Answer: The guillotine was fast, allowing many executions in a short time. Elaborate rituals, complicated machinery, and lengthy waits for the victims to die were not involved.

Connect *to* Today

Comparing
Between 1987 and 1997 executions in the United States were carried out by hanging, electrocution, lethal injection, and firing squad. Students may speculate that the goals of capital punishment are to deter criminal behavior and to remove extreme criminals from society. Public executions during the French Revolution helped keep restless armed mobs from attacking the government. Executions were a way to show the Parisian mobs that the state was working for their benefit.

The Terror Grips France

▶ **Key Ideas**

• Maximilien Robespierre gains control of the revolutionary government.

• Robespierre and his supporters try to wipe out every trace of the French nobility.

• Robespierre institutes the Reign of Terror, a time of thousands of arbitrary executions.

MORE ABOUT . . .
Robespierre

Robespierre believed passionately that only persons of absolute virtue should be political leaders. He believed in freedom for Jews and slaves, in the abolition of the death penalty, and in absolute loyalty to the state. Convinced that true patriots should devote themselves wholeheartedly to an existence of unselfish work and moral regularity, he had no private life. It is ironic that this believer in virtue should have presided over one of the most brutal periods in French history.

 IN-DEPTH RESOURCES: UNIT 5
History Makers: Maximilien Robespierre, p. 53

On this late-18th-century French inkwell, the liberty cap worn by revolutionaries crushes a clergyman of the Old Regime.

The Terror Grips France

Foreign armies were not the only enemies of the French republic. The Jacobins had thousands of enemies within France itself—peasants who were horrified by the beheading of the king, priests who would not accept government control, and rival leaders who were stirring up rebellion in the provinces. How to contain and control these enemies became a central issue.

Robespierre Assumes Control As dozens of leaders struggled for power, **Maximilien Robespierre** (ROHBZ·peer) slowly gathered control into his own hands. Robespierre and his supporters set out to build a "republic of virtue." They tried to wipe out every trace of France's past monarchy and nobility. Many families named Leroy ("king"), for instance, changed their names to something less political. No household item was too small to escape the influence of Robespierre—even the kings, queens, and jacks in decks of cards were changed to figures that represented revolutionary ideals.

Firm believers in reason, the radicals changed the calendar to be more scientific. They divided the year into 12 months of 30 days and renamed each month. The new calendar had no Sundays because the radicals considered religion old-fashioned and dangerous. They even closed all churches in Paris, and towns all over France soon did the same.

In the summer of 1793, Robespierre became the leader of the **Committee of Public Safety.** As head of the committee, he decided who should be considered enemies of the republic. The committee often had people tried in the morning and guillotined the same afternoon. From July 1793 to July 1794, Robespierre governed France nearly as a dictator, and the period of his rule became known as the **Reign of Terror.** In his speeches, Robespierre justified the Reign of Terror, explaining that it enabled French citizens to remain true to the ideals of the Revolution. In this speech excerpt, Robespierre makes a connection between virtue and terror:

> **A VOICE FROM THE PAST**
> The first maxim of our politics ought to be to lead the people by means of reason and the enemies of the people by terror. If the basis of popular government in time of peace is virtue, the basis of popular government in time of revolution is both virtue and terror: virtue without which terror is murderous, terror without which virtue is powerless. Terror is nothing else than swift, severe, indomitable justice; it flows, then, from virtue.
> **MAXIMILIEN ROBESPIERRE,** quoted in *Problems of Western Civilization: The Challenge of History*

The most famous victim of the Terror was the widowed queen, Marie Antoinette. Calm and dignified, she rode in the death cart past jeering crowds. On the scaffold, she accidentally stepped on her executioner's foot. "Monsieur," she apologized, "I beg your pardon. I did not do it on purpose." Those were her last words.

The "enemies of the republic" who troubled Robespierre the most were fellow revolutionaries who challenged his leadership. In October 1793, revolutionary courts pronounced death sentences on many of the leaders who had first helped set up the republic. Their only crime was that they were less radical than Robespierre.

By the beginning of 1794, even Georges Danton found himself in danger. (Marat had already been stabbed to death by a young woman.) Danton's friends in the

THINK THROUGH HISTORY
D. Summarizing
How did Robespierre justify his use of terror?
D. Possible Answer
By saying that terror was the same thing as justice

582 Chapter 23

CUSTOMIZING FOR SPECIAL NEEDS

Gifted and Talented Students
Drawing Conclusions Ask students to read the biography of Robespierre in the Teacher's Resource materials and to answer the questions that accompany it. Then have them do some additional research to explore the possible discrepancy between Robespierre's

belief in virtue and freedom from tyranny and his involvement in the arbitrary judgments and hasty executions of the Reign of Terror. Ask them to draw a conclusion about Robespierre's actions.

CONNECTIONS ACROSS TIME AND PLACE

State Opposition to Religion
The closing of churches and elimination of Sundays from the calendar during the French Revolution demonstrate the strength of the radicals' opposition to religion. A similar situation occurred in Russia in 1917, when the Bolsheviks, led by Lenin, gained power. Basing his

ideas on the Communist Manifesto of Karl Marx, Lenin banned religion and closed the churches. In both France and Russia, people began to practice religion again when the antireligious governments fell.

National Convention, afraid to defend him, joined in condemning him to death. On the scaffold, he told the executioner, "Don't forget to show my head to the people. It's well worth seeing."

Besides leading political figures, thousands of unknown people were sent to death on the flimsiest of charges. A revolutionary court sentenced an 18-year-old youth to die by the guillotine for sawing down a tree that had been planted as a symbol of liberty. A tavern keeper was executed because he sold sour wine "to the defenders of the country."

During the Terror, approximately 3,000 people were executed in Paris. Some historians believe that as many as 40,000 were killed all together. About 85 percent were peasants or members of the urban poor or middle class—common people for whose benefit the Revolution had supposedly been carried out.

End of the Terror

By July 1794, the members of the National Convention knew that none of them were safe from Robespierre. To save themselves, they turned on him. A group of conspirators demanded his arrest, shouting, "Down with the tyrant!" The next day the Revolution's last powerful leader went to the guillotine. The Reign of Terror, the radical phase of the French Revolution, ended when Maximilien Robespierre lost his head on July 28, 1794.

French public opinion shifted dramatically to the right after Robespierre's death. People of all classes had grown weary of the Terror. They were also tired of the skyrocketing prices of bread, salt, and other necessities of life after the Terror.

In 1795, moderate leaders in the National Convention drafted a new plan of government. The third since 1789, the new constitution placed power firmly in the hands of the upper middle class and called for a two-house legislature and an executive body of five men, known as the Directory. The five directors were moderates, not revolutionary idealists. Some of them freely enriched themselves at the public's expense. Despite their corruption, however, they gave their troubled country a period of order.

The Directory also found the right general to command France's armies. This supremely talented young man was named Napoleon Bonaparte.

Vocabulary
conspirators: people involved in a secret plot.

Section 2 Assessment

1. TERMS & NAMES
Identify
• Declaration of the Rights of Man
• Legislative Assembly
• émigrés
• sans-culottes
• guillotine
• Maximilien Robespierre
• Committee of Public Safety
• Reign of Terror

2. TAKING NOTES
Recreate the cause-and-effect graphic below on your paper. Fill in the main events that occurred after the creation of the Constitution of 1791.

Assembly creates a constitution.

3. RECOGNIZING CAUSES
After the French rejected the king's absolute control, they struggled to create a more democratic government. However, in 1793, Robespierre became a dictator. What caused this to happen?

THINK ABOUT
• the political climate prior to Robespierre's rule
• the need for a leader
• Robespierre's personality

4. THEME ACTIVITY
Revolution Create a revolutionaries' "Wall of Fame." Working in small teams, write short biographies of revolutionary figures mentioned in this section (including pictures if possible). Then add biographies of other revolutionary figures—from England and the Americas—mentioned in the unit.

The French Revolution and Napoleon **583**

OBJECTIVES

(1) To explain how Napoleon Bonaparte came to power in France.

(2) To summarize the steps Napoleon took to restore order to France.

(3) To describe the extent and weaknesses of Napoleon's empire.

SKILLBUILDERS

- Interpreting charts, p. 585
- Interpreting maps: region, location, p. 588

CRITICAL THINKING

- Analyzing causes, p. 585
- Analyzing motives, p. 586
- Recognizing effects, p. 587
- Evaluating, p. 587
- Forming an opinion, p. 588
- Analyzing themes, p. 588

FOCUS

5-Minute Warm-Up

▶ *Summarizing*

Have students answer these questions to explore the influence of a hero on society.

1. Read History Makers on page 584. How did Napoleon reward his troops?

2. How did they feel about him?

▣ *WARM-UP TRANSPARENCY 23*

OBJECTIVE (1) INSTRUCT

Napoleon Grasps the Power

▶ *Key Ideas*

- Napoleon wins key battles to save the French republic.
- Napoleon seizes political control from the Directory.
- Napoleon's successes in battle and diplomacy lead to peace in Europe.

▣ *IN-DEPTH RESOURCES: UNIT 5*
Guided Reading, p. 39

▣ *ACCESS FOR STUDENTS ACQUIRING ENGLISH*
Guided Reading (Spanish), p. 231

---

(3) # Napoleon Forges an Empire

TERMS & NAMES
- Napoleon Bonaparte
- coup d'état
- plebiscite
- lycée
- concordat
- Napoleonic Code
- Battle of Trafalgar

MAIN IDEA	WHY IT MATTERS NOW
A military genius, Napoleon Bonaparte, seized power in France and made himself emperor.	In times of political turmoil, military dictators often seize control of nations, as in Haiti in 1991.

SETTING THE STAGE Napoleon was a short man (five feet three inches tall) who cast a long shadow over the history of modern times. He would come to be recognized as one of the world's greatest military geniuses, along with Alexander the Great of Macedonia, Hannibal of Carthage, and Julius Caesar of Rome. In only four years (1795–1799), Napoleon rose from relative obscurity to become master of France.

Napoleon Grasps the Power

Napoleon Bonaparte was born in 1769 on the Mediterranean island of Corsica. When he was nine years old, his parents sent him to a military school in northern France. In 1785, at the age of 16, he finished school and became a lieutenant in the artillery. When the Revolution broke out, Napoleon joined the army of the new government.

Hero of the Hour In October 1795, fate handed the young officer a chance for glory. When royalist rebels marched on the National Convention, a government official told Napoleon to defend the delegates. Napoleon and his gunners greeted the thousands of royalists with a cannonade. Within minutes, the attackers fled in panic and confusion. Napoleon Bonaparte became the hero of the hour and was hailed throughout Paris as the savior of the French republic.

In 1796, the Directory appointed Napoleon to lead a French army against the forces of Austria and the Kingdom of Sardinia. Crossing the Alps, the young general swept into Italy and won a series of remarkable victories, which crushed the Austrian troops' threat to France. Next, in an attempt to protect French trade interests and to disrupt British trade with India, Napoleon led an expedition to Egypt. Unfortunately, his luck did not hold. His army was pinned down in Egypt, and his naval forces were defeated by the British admiral Horatio Nelson. However, he managed to keep the reports of his defeat out of the press, so that by 1799 the words "the general" could mean only one man to the French—Napoleon.

Coup d'État By 1799, the Directory had lost control of the political situation and the confidence of the French people. Only the directors' control of the army kept them in power. Upon Napoleon's return from Egypt, the Abbé Sieyès urged him to seize political power. Napoleon and Josephine, his lovely socialite wife, set a plan in motion. Napoleon met with influential persons to discuss his role in the Directory, while Josephine used her connections with the wealthy directors to influence their decisions. The action began on November 9, 1799, when Napoleon was put in charge of the military. It ended the next day when his troops drove out the members of one chamber of the

Vocabulary
cannonade: a bombardment with heavy artillery fire.

HISTORY MAKERS

Napoleon Bonaparte
1769–1821

Napoleon Bonaparte had a magnetism that attracted the admiration of his men. His speeches were designed to inspire his troops to valorous feats. In one speech, he told soldiers, "If the victory is for a moment uncertain, you shall see your Emperor place himself on the front line."

Bonaparte was generous in his rewards to the troops. Many received the Legion of Honor—a medal for bravery. Sometimes Napoleon would take the medal from his own chest to present it to a soldier. (He kept a few spares in his pocket for these occasions.) A cavalry commander, Auguste de Colbert, wrote, "He awakened in my soul the desire for glory."

584 Chapter 23

SECTION 3 RESOURCES

PRINT RESOURCES

▣ *IN-DEPTH RESOURCES: UNIT 5*
Guided Reading, p. 39
Primary Source: Napoleon's Proclamation at Austerlitz, 1805, p. 48

▣ *ACCESS FOR STUDENTS ACQUIRING ENGLISH*
Guided Reading (Spanish), p. 231

▣ *FORMAL ASSESSMENT*
Section Quiz, p. 266

▣ *ALTERNATIVE ASSESSMENT BOOK*

TECHNOLOGY RESOURCES

▣ *WORLD ART AND CULTURES TRANSPARENCIES*
AT51 *Napoleon Crossing the St. Bernard Pass*

⊙ **CD-ROM** *Electronic Library of Primary Sources*
Battles of the World: The Battle of Austerlitz

↗ **INTERNET** www.mlworldhistory.com

THINK THROUGH HISTORY
A. Analyzing Causes For what reasons was Napoleon able to become a dictator?
A. Possible Answer General political chaos created a need for a strong leader, and Napoleon had control of the army.

national legislature. The legislature voted to dissolve the Directory. In its place, the legislature established a group of three consuls, one of whom was Napoleon. Napoleon quickly assumed dictatorial powers as the first consul of the French republic. A sudden seizure of power like Napoleon's is known as a coup—from the French phrase **coup d'état** (KOO day·TAH), or "blow of state."

At the time of Napoleon's coup, France was still at war. In 1799, British diplomats assembled the Second Coalition of anti-French powers—Britain, Austria, and Russia—with the goal of driving Napoleon from power. Once again, Napoleon rode from Paris at the head of his troops. Eventually, as a result of war and diplomacy, all three nations signed peace agreements with France. By 1802, Europe was at peace for the first time in ten years. Napoleon was free to focus his energies on restoring order in France.

Napoleon Rules France

At first, Napoleon pretended to be the constitutionally chosen leader of a free republic. In 1800, a **plebiscite** (PLEHB·ih·SYT), or vote of the people, was held to approve a new constitution, the fourth in eight years. Desperate for strong leadership, the people voted overwhelmingly in favor of the constitution, which gave all real power to Napoleon as first consul.

Restoring Order at Home Under Napoleon, France would have order and stability. He did not try to return the nation to the days of Louis XVI; instead, he kept many of the changes that had come with the Revolution. He supported laws that would both strengthen the central government and achieve some of the goals of the Revolution, such as a stable economy and more equality in taxation.

The first order of business was to get the economy on a solid footing. Napoleon set up an efficient tax-collection system and established a national bank. In addition to assuring the government a steady supply of tax money, these actions promoted sound financial management and better control of the economy.

Napoleon also needed to reduce government corruption and improve the delivery of government services. He dismissed corrupt officials and, in order to provide his government with trained officials, set up **lycées,** or government-run public schools. The students at the lycées included children of ordinary citizens as well as children of

Napoleon Brings Order After the Revolution

	The Economy	Government & Society	Religion
Goals of the Revolution	• Equal taxation • Lower inflation	• Less government corruption • Equal opportunity in government	• Less powerful Catholic Church • Religious tolerance
Napoleon's Actions	• Set up fairer tax code • Set up national bank • Stabilized currency • Gave state loans to businesses	• Appointed officials by merit • Fired corrupt officials • Created lycées • Created code of laws	• Recognized Catholicism as "faith of Frenchmen" • Signed concordat with pope • Retained seized church lands
Results	• Equal taxation • Stable economy	• Honest, competent officials • Equal opportunity in government • Public education	• Religious tolerance • Government control of church lands • Government recognition of church influence

SKILLBUILDER: Interpreting Charts
Napoleon's changes brought France closer to achieving the Revolution's goals.
1. Which goals of the Revolution did Napoleon achieve?
2. If you had been a member of the bourgeoisie in Napoleon's France, would you have been satisfied with the results of Napoleon's actions? Why or why not?

The French Revolution and Napoleon **585**

OBJECTIVE 2 INSTRUCT

Napoleon Rules France

▶ *Key Ideas*
• Napoleon gains power; voters approve a fourth constitution.
• Napoleon gives France order and stability.
• The Napoleonic Code establishes a uniform set of laws for France.
• Napoleon crowns himself as emperor of France.

CRITICAL THINKING ACTIVITY
CLASS TIME: 15 MINUTES

Perceiving Cause and Effect Relationships
To help students understand Napoleon's accomplishments, have them make two-column charts in which they list his actions and the benefits of the actions.

Action	Benefit

History from Visuals

Napoleon Brings Order After the Revolution

Interpreting the Chart Show students how to read the chart in multiple ways: read each column to compare Napoleon's actions with the goals of the Revolution, and read each row to get a full overview.

Extension Activity Ask students to think of topics for additional columns they might add to the chart. *Possible Responses: education, land reform, aristocracy*

SKILLBUILDER Answers
1. He provided equal taxation, equal opportunity in government, honest officials, religious tolerance, and state control of church lands
2. Probable answer is *yes*, because the country became stable. Some students may answer *no*, because the bourgeoisie received no special privileges.

TEACHING OPTION

CONNECTIONS ACROSS THE CURRICULUM

Economics Much of France's stability under Napoleon came from economic reforms. Discuss with students the practical meanings of these economic terms used in describing Napoleon's policies: *national bank, low inflation,* and *stable currency.*

A *national bank* system allows a central government to regulate banking activities. It eliminates problems that arise when private banks operate independently,

perhaps even issuing their own currencies. When a country has a national bank, people feel more secure about their bank deposits, so that their confidence in the government increases.

Inflation is a general rise in the level of prices. Increases in the prices of food, clothing, and housing are caused by decreases in the value of money. During extreme inflation, for example, a loaf of bread

might cost hundreds of dollars. Low inflation can lead to prosperity and political stability.

A *stabilized currency* results from a national banking system, low inflation, and other factors. Currency that does not change in value quickly and that is backed by a central government contributes to national stability and peace.

Napoleon Creates an Empire

▶ **Key Ideas**
- Napoleon tries to expand his empire in the Americas but fails in Saint Domingue.
- The United States buys the Louisiana Territory from Napoleon.
- Napoleon conquers much of Europe, but his navy is defeated in the Battle of Trafalgar.

 ELECTRONIC LIBRARY OF PRIMARY SOURCES
from *The Letters of Napoleon I*

MORE ABOUT . . .
Napoleon Bonaparte

Napoleon is popularly supposed to have wanted to rule the world to compensate for being short. Historians disagree about his height, however. After his autopsy, his height was reported as five feet two inches, but that figure was based on an old French system of measure. In modern terms, he may have been a little over five feet six inches tall.

 IN-DEPTH RESOURCES: UNIT 5
Primary Source: Napoleon's Proclamation at Austerlitz, 1805, p. 48

 WORLD ART AND CULTURES TRANSPARENCIES
AT51 *Napoleon Crossing the St. Bernard Pass*

 Battles of the World
The Battle of Austerlitz

the wealthy. The trained candidates could then be appointed to public office on the basis of merit rather than family connections.

Both the clergy and the peasants wanted to restore the position of the church in France. Napoleon signed a **concordat** (agreement) with Pope Pius VII, spelling out a new relationship between church and state. The government recognized the influence of the church but rejected church control in national affairs. Specifically the French government would appoint bishops, but the bishops would appoint parish priests. The concordat gained Napoleon the support of the organized church as well as the majority of the French people.

Napoleon thought that his greatest work was his comprehensive system of laws, known as the **Napoleonic Code.** Although the code gave the country a uniform set of laws and eliminated many injustices, it actually limited liberty and promoted order and authority over individual rights. The code took away some rights that women had won during the Revolution, such as the right to sell their property. Freedom of speech and of the press, also established during the Revolution, were restricted rather than expanded. The new laws also restored slavery in the French colonies of the Caribbean, which the revolutionary government had abolished.

The emperor Napoleon appears almost godlike in this 1806 portrait by Jean Auguste Dominique Ingres, entitled *Napoleon on His Imperial Throne.*

Napoleon Crowned as Emperor In 1804, Napoleon decided to make himself emperor, and the French voters supported him. On December 2, 1804, dressed in a splendid robe of purple velvet, Napoleon walked down the long aisle of Notre Dame Cathedral in Paris. The pope waited for him with a glittering crown. As thousands watched, the new emperor took the crown from the pope and placed it on his own head. With this arrogant gesture, Napoleon signaled that he was more powerful than the church, which had traditionally crowned the rulers of France.

Napoleon Creates an Empire

Napoleon was not content simply to be master of France. He wanted to control the rest of Europe and to reassert French power in the New World. He envisioned his western empire to include Louisiana, Florida, French Guiana, and the French West Indies. He knew that the key to this area was the sugar-producing French colony of Saint Domingue on the island of Hispaniola.

New World Territories In 1789, when the ideas of the Revolution had reached the planters in Saint Domingue, they had demanded that the National Assembly give them the same privileges as the people of France. Eventually, the slaves in the colony had demanded their freedom. A civil war had erupted, and slaves under the leadership of Toussaint L'Ouverture had seized control of the productive colony. In 1801, Napoleon decided to regain French control of the war-torn island and restore its productive sugar industry. Although he sent 23,000 soldiers to accomplish the task, the former slaves proved to be difficult to defeat, and thousands of soldiers died of yellow fever.

When the expedition to Saint Domingue was unsuccessful and the U.S. government showed interest in buying the port of New Orleans, Napoleon recognized an opportunity to make some money and cut his losses in the Americas. He offered to sell all of the Louisiana Territory to the United States, and in 1803 President

THINK THROUGH HISTORY
B. Analyzing Motives Why would Napoleon crown himself?
B. Possible Answer To show that he was not under the control of anyone

586 Chapter 23

CONNECTIONS ACROSS TIME AND PLACE

Disease and History The French expedition to Saint Domingue was unsuccessful largely because so many soldiers died of yellow fever. This was not the only time that disease affected Napoleon's armies. The campaign in Russia, Napoleon's first major defeat, was severely handicapped by an outbreak of typhus fever that at one point affected over 80,000 of Napoleon's men.

Diseases have long had a powerful effect on the course of history. One historian has argued that a severe type of malaria played a role in the fall of Rome because it caused the birthrate to fall steeply and produced chronic weakness and ill health—a general slackness of spirit. Hundreds of years later, smallpox decimated the Native American population

of Mexico and aided the Spanish conquest. In the early 20th century, the control of yellow fever made the construction of the Panama Canal possible. Interested students may wish to investigate other instances of the impact of disease on history.

THINK THROUGH HISTORY
C. Recognizing
Effects What effects
did Napoleon intend
the sale of Louisiana
to have on France?
on the United States?
on Britain?
C. Answer Napoleon
hoped to obtain the
money he needed to
continue his conquest
of Europe and to
increase the power of
the United States in
order to punish
Britain.

Jefferson's administration agreed to purchase the land for $15 million. Napoleon was delighted. He saw a twofold benefit to the sale: he would gain money to finance operations in Europe, and he would further punish his British enemies. He exulted, "The sale assures forever the power of the United States, and I have given England a rival who, sooner or later, will humble her pride."

Conquering Europe Napoleon abandoned his imperial ambitions in the New World and turned his attention to Europe. He had already annexed the Austrian Netherlands and parts of Italy to France and set up a puppet government in Switzerland. Now he looked to expand his influence further. Fearful of his ambitions, Britain persuaded Russia, Austria, and Sweden to join in a third coalition against France.

Napoleon met this challenge with his usual boldness. He rallied the troops and rode out to defeat the Third Coalition, exclaiming, "My army is formidable. . . . Once we had an Army of the Rhine, an Army of Italy, an Army of Holland; there has never been a French Army—but now it exists, and we shall soon see it in action." In a series of brilliant battles, Napoleon crushed the opposition. (See the map on page 588.) The commanders of the enemy armies could never predict his next move and took heavy losses. After the Battle of Austerlitz, Napoleon issued a proclamation expressing his pride in his troops:

> **A VOICE FROM THE PAST**
> Soldiers! I am pleased with you. On the day of Austerlitz, you justified everything that I was expecting of your intrepidity. . . . In less than four hours, an army of 100,000 men, commanded by the emperors of Russia and Austria, was cut up and dispersed. . . . 120 pieces of artillery, 20 generals, and more than 30,000 men taken prisoner—such are the results of this day which will forever be famous. . . . My nation will be overjoyed to see you again. And it will be enough for you to say, "I was at Austerlitz," to hear the reply: "There is a brave man!"
>
> **NAPOLEON,** quoted in *Napoleon* by André Castelot

THINK THROUGH HISTORY
D. Evaluating By
1805, how successful
had Napoleon been
in his efforts to build
an empire?
D. Possible Answer
Napoleon controlled
most of Europe except
Britain.

Eventually, the rulers of Austria, Prussia, and Russia all signed peace treaties with Napoleon, whose proud and patriotic army had enabled him to build the largest European empire since the Romans'. The only major enemy left undefeated was Britain, whose power lay in its navy. In 1805, Napoleon tried to remove the threat of that navy.

The Battle of Trafalgar In his war against the Third Coalition, Napoleon lost only one major battle, the **Battle of Trafalgar** (truh·FAL·guhr)—but that naval defeat was more important than all of Napoleon's victories on land. The battle took place in 1805 off the southern coast of Spain. The commander of the British fleet, Horatio Nelson—the admiral who had defeated Napoleon's fleet near Egypt in 1798—outmaneuvered the larger French-Spanish fleet, showing as much brilliance in warfare at sea as Napoleon had in warfare on land. (See map inset on page 588.) During the furious battle, Nelson was mortally wounded by a French sharpshooter. As he lay dying aboard his flagship, Nelson heard the welcome news of British victory. "Now I am satisfied," murmured the admiral. "Thank God, I have done my duty."

The destruction of the French fleet had two major results. First, it assured the supremacy of the British navy for the next hundred years. Second, it forced Napoleon to give up his plans of invading Britain. He had to look for another way to control his powerful enemy across the English Channel. Eventually, Napoleon's extravagant efforts to crush Britain would lead to his own undoing.

The French Empire During the first decade of the 1800s, Napoleon's victories had given him mastery over most of Europe. By 1812, the only major European countries free from Napoleon's control were Britain, the Ottoman Empire, Portugal, and Sweden.

As the map on page 588 shows, Napoleon controlled numerous supposedly independent lands in addition to those that were formally part of the French Empire. These included

Highly motivated British sailors under Admiral Nelson formed two squadrons and attacked the line of French ships, splitting them into smaller groups (see map on page 588). Nelson's sailors were better trained and more accurate shots than the sailors in the French fleet. In the end, the French commander was captured, and 19 or 20 French ships (of a total of 33) were surrendered to the British. Although Nelson was killed, no British ships were lost.

Nelson is commemorated with a huge statue in Trafalgar Square in the heart of London. The 17-foot-high statute stands atop a column that is 185 feet high.

| TEACHING OPTION | BLOCK SCHEDULING | COOPERATIVE ACTIVITY: Researching Napoleon and Nelson | CLASS TIME 30 MINUTES |

Task: Student groups will research the careers of Napoleon Bonaparte and Horatio Nelson and present to the class reports comparing the two men.

Purpose: To learn more about these two leaders.

Activity: Divide the class into groups of four. In each group, pairs of students should each research the life of one of the two men, paying special attention to the way each man interacted with his troops and to the specific military strategies that made each so successful. The pairs should then compare and contrast the two men so that in reports to the class, they can focus on the men's similarities and differences.

Building a Portfolio If the report is among their best work, students should add it to their portfolio.

ALTERNATIVE ASSESSMENT BOOK Standards for Evaluating a Cooperative Activity

Standards for Evaluation
Reports should . . .

• clearly convey the characteristics of Nelson and Napoleon
• compare the qualities of the two men
• show evidence of thorough research

French Empire and Battles, 1805–1812

Interpreting the Map Tell students to read the map key carefully to help them identify the territory of the French Empire and the nations controlled by Napoleon.

Extension Activity Have students read more about the tactics employed by the British in the Battle of Trafalgar.

SKILLBUILDER Answers
1. From the North Sea in the north to central Italy in the south, from Illyria in the east to the Atlantic Ocean in the west
2. Near the Strait of Gibraltar. Nelson divided the French fleet, enabling his forces to attack smaller groups of ships.

ASSESS & RETEACH

Section 3 Assessment
Have pairs of students take turns quizzing each other on the questions. Then have them start a time line of Napoleon's career.

Section Quiz

 FORMAL ASSESSMENT
Section Quiz, p. 266

Reteaching Activity
CLASS TIME: 15 MINUTES

Go over the key terms to help students understand the events in this section.

CLOSE ACTIVITY

CLASS TIME: 20 MINUTES

Analyzing Events
Using the map on page 588 in the text, write the names of countries in Europe on 3x5 file cards. Students draw a card and then arrange themselves in the front of the room as one of the countries at the height of Napoleon's empire. Students representing adjacent countries should stand next to each other and should face other countries appropriately. Each student will talk about who they are, where they are, and how they responded to Napoleon as their conqueror or ally.

French Empire and Battles, 1805–1813

French Empire
Controlled by Napoleon
Major battle

The Battle of Trafalgar, Oct. 21, 1805

British fleet
French and Spanish fleet
British thrust

By dividing Villeneuve's formation, Admiral Nelson captured nearly two-thirds of the enemy fleet.

GEOGRAPHY SKILLBUILDER: Interpreting Maps
1. **Region** What was the extent (north to south, east to west) of Napoleon's empire in 1812?
2. **Location** Where was the Battle of Trafalgar fought? What tactic did Nelson use, and why was it successful?

Spain, the Grand Duchy of Warsaw, and a number of German kingdoms in central Europe. The rulers of these countries were Napoleon's puppets; some, in fact, were his brothers and in-laws. Furthermore, the powerful countries of Russia, Prussia, and Austria were loosely attached to Napoleon's empire through alliances. Not totally under Napoleon's control, they were easily manipulated by threats of military action.

Ironically, Napoleon's power and military threats actually made the conquered peoples more conscious of their loyalty to their own nations. The French empire was huge but unstable. Napoleon was able to maintain it at its greatest extent for only five years (1807–1812). Then it quickly fell to pieces. Its sudden collapse was caused in part by Napoleon himself.

Section 3 Assessment

1. TERMS & NAMES
Identify
• Napoleon Bonaparte
• coup d'état
• plebiscite
• lycée
• concordat
• Napoleonic Code
• Battle of Trafalgar

2. TAKING NOTES
Create a time line showing events leading to the crowning of Napoleon as emperor of France.

Which of these events did Napoleon cause?

3. FORMING AN OPINION
There is an old question: "Do the times make the man, or does the man make the times?" In your opinion, was Napoleon the creator of or the creation of his times?

THINK ABOUT
• the government after the Terror
• Napoleon's defense of France
• Napoleon's popularity

4. ANALYZING THEMES
Power and Authority To keep his empire together, Napoleon had to deal with forces both inside and outside the French Empire. In your judgment, which area was more crucial to control?

THINK ABOUT
• the length of the period of civil unrest in France
• the power and activities of the other European nations

588 Chapter 23

ANSWERS

1. TERMS & NAMES
Napoleon Bonaparte, p. 584
coup d'état, p.585
plebiscite, p. 585
lycée, p. 585
concordat, p. 586
Napoleonic Code, p. 586
Battle of Trafalgar, p. 587

2. TAKING NOTES
1795—Napoleon defeats royalist rebels; 1796 to 1799—Napoleon wins many victories; 1799—Napoleon seizes power from the Directory; 1800—New constitution gives Napoleon all real power.

3. FORMING AN OPINION
Possible Responses: Some students will say that Napoleon became powerful because of his military abilities and the political chaos after the Terror. Others may think that Napoleon's strong personality would have dominated no matter the circumstances.

4. ANALYZING THEMES
Possible Responses: Some s[...] dents will argue that internal unrest was most important, because division and chaos a[...] home would have made milita[...] success impossible. Others m[...] say that victory against exter[...] enemies would have led to union within France.

4 Napoleon's Empire Collapses

TERMS & NAMES
• blockade
• Continental System
• guerrilla
• Peninsular War
• scorched-earth policy
• Waterloo
• Hundred Days

MAIN IDEA

Napoleon's conquests aroused nationalistic feelings across Europe and contributed to his downfall.

WHY IT MATTERS NOW

In the 1990s, nationalistic feelings contributed to the breakup of nations such as Yugoslavia.

SETTING THE STAGE Napoleon worried that his vast empire would fall apart unless he had an heir whose right to succeed him was undisputed, so he decided that he needed a son. Consequently, he divorced Josephine, who had failed to bear him a child, and formed an alliance with the Austrian royal family by marrying Marie Louise, the grand-niece of Marie Antoinette. In 1811, Marie Louise gave birth to a son, Napoleon II, whom his father named king of Rome.

Napoleon's Three Costly Mistakes

Napoleon's own personality proved to be the greatest danger to the future of his empire. "I love power," he once said, "as a musician loves his violin." It was the drive for power that had raised Napoleon to great heights, and the same love of power led to his doom. In his efforts to extend the French Empire and crush Britain, Napoleon made three disastrous misjudgments.

The Continental System In November 1806, Napoleon signed a decree ordering a **blockade**—a forcible closing of ports—to prevent all trade and communication between Great Britain and other European nations. Napoleon called this policy the **Continental System** because it was supposed to make continental Europe more self-sufficient. It was also intended to destroy Britain's commercial and industrial economy.

"Little Johnny Bull"—Great Britain—waves a sword at Napoleon as the emperor straddles the globe.

Background
England's navy had been the strongest in Europe ever since its defeat of the Spanish Armada in 1588.

Unfortunately for Napoleon, his blockade was not nearly tight enough. Aided by the British, smugglers managed to bring cargo from Britain into Europe. At times, Napoleon's allies disregarded his order—in fact, Napoleon's own brother Louis, whom Napoleon had made king of Holland, defied the policy. For these reasons, the blockade weakened British trade but did not destroy it.

In addition, Britain responded with its own blockade. The British navy stopped neutral ships bound for the continent and forced them to sail to a British port to be searched and taxed. Because the British had a stronger navy, they were better able than the French to make their blockade work.

American ships were among those stopped by the British navy. Angered, the U.S. Congress declared war on Britain in 1812. The War of 1812 ended in a draw, however, and was only a minor inconvenience to Britain in its struggle with Napoleon.

In effect, the Continental System hurt Napoleon more than it hurt his enemies. It weakened the economies of France and the other lands under Napoleon's control more than it damaged Britain.

The Peninsular War In 1808, Napoleon made a second costly mistake. Because Portugal was ignoring the Continental System, he sent an army through Spain to invade Portugal. When Spanish towns rioted in protest, Napoleon deposed the Spanish king and put his brother Joseph on the throne. This move outraged the Spanish people and enflamed their nationalistic feelings, since they remained fiercely loyal to their former monarch.

The French Revolution and Napoleon **589**

Section 4 Overview

OBJECTIVES

(1) To explain Napoleon's tactical and political mistakes.

(2) To summarize Napoleon's defeat, comeback, and final downfall.

SKILLBUILDER
• Interpreting maps and graphs, p. 591

CRITICAL THINKING
• Recognizing effects, p. 590
• Analyzing motives, p. 592

FOCUS
5-Minute Warm-Up

▶ *Interpreting a Political Cartoon*

To help students understand Napoleon's power, have them answer these questions.

1. What words describe Napoleon in the cartoon on page 589?

2. What words describe Britain in the cartoon?

 WARM-UP TRANSPARENCY 23

OBJECTIVE ① INSTRUCT

Napoleon's Three Costly Mistakes

▶ *Key Ideas*

• In a policy known as the Continental System, Napoleon unsuccessfully attempts to cut off trade between Great Britain and other European nations.

• The Peninsular War in Spain inflames Spanish nationalism and weakens France.

• The French invasion of Russia fails, with terrible loss of life.

 IN-DEPTH RESOURCES: UNIT 5
Guided Reading, p. 40

ACCESS FOR STUDENTS ACQUIRING ENGLISH
Guided Reading (Spanish), p. 232

SECTION 4 RESOURCES

PRINT RESOURCES

 IN-DEPTH RESOURCES: UNIT 5
Guided Reading, p. 40
Skillbuilder Practice: Interpreting Maps, p. 42

ACCESS FOR STUDENTS ACQUIRING ENGLISH
Guided Reading (Spanish), p. 232
Skillbuilder Practice (Spanish), p. 234

 FORMAL ASSESSMENT
Section Quiz, p. 267

 ALTERNATIVE ASSESSMENT BOOK

TECHNOLOGY RESOURCES

🖸 **CD-ROM**
Electronic Library of Primary Sources

🌐 **INTERNET** www.mlworldhistory.com

In addition, Spain was a devoutly Catholic nation with a long history of persecuting those who deviated from the faith. Because the French Revolution had weakened the Catholic Church in France, many Spanish Catholics feared that their French conquerors would undermine the church in Spain. In fact, the French did attack church power by outlawing the Spanish Inquisition, which was still prosecuting people accused of heresy.

For five years (1808–1813), bands of Spanish peasant fighters, known as **guerrillas,** struck at French armies in Spain. The guerrillas were not an army that Napoleon could defeat in open battle; they were ordinary people who ambushed French troops and then fled into hiding. The British added to the French troubles in Spain by sending troops to aid the rebels. Napoleon lost about 300,000 men during this **Peninsular War** (so called because Spain lies on the Iberian Peninsula). These losses weakened the French Empire.

In Spain and elsewhere, nationalism, or loyalty to one's own country, was becoming a powerful weapon against Napoleon. People who had at first welcomed the French as their liberators now felt abused by a foreign conqueror. Like the Spanish guerrillas, Germans and Italians and other conquered peoples turned against the French.

The Invasion of Russia In 1812, Napoleon's thirst for power led to his most disastrous mistake of all. Even though Alexander I had become Napoleon's ally, the Russian czar refused to stop selling grain to Britain. In addition, the French and Russian rulers suspected each other of having competing designs on Poland. Because of this breakdown in their alliance, Napoleon decided to invade Russia.

In June 1812, Napoleon and his Grand Army marched into Russia. Many of his troops were not French. They had been drafted from all over Europe, and they felt little loyalty to Napoleon.

As Napoleon's army entered Russia, Alexander pulled back his troops, refusing to be lured into an unequal battle. As the Russians retreated toward Moscow, they practiced a **scorched-earth policy,** burning grain fields and slaughtering livestock so as to leave nothing that the enemy could eat. Desperate soldiers deserted the French army to search for scraps of food.

On September 7, 1812, the two armies finally clashed in the Battle of Borodino. During the morning, the advantage swung back and forth between the Russians and the French. After several more hours of indecisive fighting, the Russians retreated—giving Napoleon a narrow victory that allowed him to take Moscow.

When Napoleon finally entered Moscow on September 14, he soon found it in flames. Rather than surrender Russia's "holy city" to the French, Alexander had set fire to it. Napoleon stayed in the ruined city for five weeks, expecting the czar to make a peace offer, but no offer ever came. By then, it was the middle of October, too late to advance farther and perhaps too late even to retreat.

Grimly, Napoleon ordered his starving army to turn back. As the snows began to fall in early November, Russian raiders mercilessly attacked Napoleon's ragged, retreating army. One French sergeant recorded, "Many of the survivors were walking barefoot, using pieces of wood as canes, but their feet were frozen so hard that the sound they made on the road was like that of wooden clogs."

As the soldiers staggered through the snow, many dropped in their tracks from wounds, exhaustion, hunger, and cold. The temperature fell to about 30 degrees below zero, so cold that birds fell dead from the sky. Finally, in the middle of December, the last survivors straggled out of Russia. Of his Grand Army, Napoleon had only 10,000 soldiers who were left fit to fight.

Napoleon's Russian Campaign, 1812

Advancing troops
Retreating troops
= 10,000 soldiers
= 10,000 lost troops

June 1812 Napoleon and his troops march across the Neman River and into Russia.
422,000

Napoleon sends troops to Polotsk to protect his left flank.
50,000

Reduced by desertion, disease, starvation, and capture, an army of 175,000 arrives in Smolensk. Another 30,000 die there.
175,000

Sept. 7, 1812 Napoleon's army fights the Battle of Borodino and suffers 30,000 casualties.
130,000

Sept. 14, 1812 Napoleon enters Moscow to find it in ashes, torched by the czar. He waits, hoping to induce the czar to surrender.

Oct. 18, 1812 Frustrated and starving, having waited too long for the czar, the 100,000 survivors of the Grand Army begin their hellish retreat through the cruel Russian winter.

November 1812 The army returns to Smolensk and finds famine. The remaining 24,000 march on, abandoning their wounded.
37,000

Dec. 6, 1812 Troops march for the Neman River. Only 10,000 make it out of Russia.
28,000

The 30,000 in Polotsk join the 20,000 survivors. Thousands drown while trying to cross the Berezina River.
50,000

RUSSIA

Western Dvina River · Polotsk · Glubokoye · Vitebsk · Smolensk · Vyazma · Borodino · Moscow R. · Moscow · Maloyaroslavets · Oka R.

Kovno · Vilna · Neman River · Molodechno · Borisov · Minsk · Dnieper R. · Berezina River

0 — 100 Miles
0 — 200 Kilometers

N

Source: Chart by Charles Joseph Minard, 1861

SSIA · ND DUCHY OF WARSAW

SKILLBUILDER: Interpreting Maps and Graphs
1. *How many troops did Napoleon start the Russian campaign with? How many survived?*
2. *Review the graph on the right. Why was Napoleon's decision to stay in Moscow until mid-October a tactical blunder?*

Retreat from Russia, 1812

Temperature (Degrees Fahrenheit): 35, 25, 15, 5, −5, −15, −25, −35

Moscow, Oct. 18 · Nov. 9 · Smolensk, Nov. 14 · Borisov, Nov. 28 · Dec. 1 · Molodechno, Dec. 6

Napoleon's Downfall

Napoleon's enemies were quick to take advantage of his weakness. Britain, Russia, Prussia, and Sweden joined forces against him in the Fourth Coalition. Napoleon had hoped that his marriage to Marie Louise would keep at least Austria on his side, but Austria also joined the coalition. All of the main powers of Europe were now at war with France.

The Coalition Defeats Napoleon In only a few months, Napoleon managed to raise another army. He faced his enemies outside the German city of Leipzig (LYP-sihg) in October 1813. At this crucial point, Napoleon's army no longer consisted of trained veterans. In the Battle of Leipzig, the allies cut his inexperienced army to pieces.

Napoleon's empire crumbled quickly. By January 1814, armies of Austrians, Russians, and Prussians were pushing steadily toward Paris. In March, the Russian czar and the Prussian king led their troops in a triumphant parade through the French capital. Napoleon wanted to fight on, but his generals refused.

In April 1814, the defeated emperor gave up his throne and accepted the terms of surrender drawn up by Alexander I. The victors gave Napoleon a small pension and exiled, or banished, him to Elba, a tiny island off the Italian coast. Although the allies expected no further trouble from Napoleon, they were wrong. Napoleon was a man of action who, at age 45, would find it difficult to retire.

Background
Royalists had called Louis XVI's son Louis XVII after his father was guillotined.

A Comeback Fails As Napoleon arrived on Elba, a Bourbon king arrived in Paris to rule France—Louis XVIII, brother of the guillotined king. (Louis XVI's son and heir had died in prison in 1795.) However, the new king quickly became unpopular among

The French Revolution and Napoleon **591**

This portrait by Paul Delaroche, entitled *Napoleon I After His Abdication*, shows Napoleon's depression after he abdicated his throne.

his subjects—especially the peasants, who suspected him of wanting to undo the Revolution's land reforms.

The news that the French king was in trouble was all the incentive Napoleon needed to try to regain power. He escaped from Elba and, on March 1, 1815, landed in France. In a proclamation, he urged the French to rally to his cause. "Victory will march at full speed," he said. "You will be the liberators of your country." Thousands of French people welcomed Napoleon back. The ranks of his army swelled with volunteers as it approached Paris. Within days, Napoleon was again emperor of France. Louis XVIII fled to the border.

In response, the European allies quickly marshaled their armies. The British army, led by the Duke of Wellington, prepared for battle near the village of **Waterloo** in Belgium. On June 18, 1815, Napoleon attacked. The British army defended its ground all day. Late in the afternoon, the Prussian army arrived. Together, the British and the Prussian forces attacked the French. Two days later, Napoleon's exhausted troops gave way, and the British and Prussian forces chased them from the field.

This defeat ended Napoleon's last bid for power, called the **Hundred Days.** Taking no chances this time, the British shipped Napoleon to St. Helena, a remote island in the South Atlantic. There, he lived in lonely exile for six years, writing his memoirs. He died in 1821 of a stomach ailment, perhaps cancer. Shortly before his death, he attempted to justify all he had done during his life:

> ### A VOICE FROM THE PAST
> Such work as mine is not done twice in a century. . . . I have saved the Revolution as it lay dying. I have cleansed it of its crimes, and have held it up to the people shining with fame. I have inspired France and Europe with new ideas that will never be forgotten.
> **NAPOLEON,** quoted in *Napoleon at St. Helena*

Without doubt, Napoleon was a military genius and a brilliant administrator. Yet all his victories must be measured against the millions of lives that were lost in his wars. Of his many achievements, only his law code and some of his reforms in France's government proved lasting—and they were not won on the battlefield. A later French statesman and writer, Alexis de Tocqueville, summed up Napoleon's character by saying, "He was as great as a man can be without virtue." Napoleon's defeat opened the door for the freed European countries to establish a new order.

Background
Napoleon was emperor for 10 years; he was exiled to Elba for 1 year; he ruled again for 100 days; then he was exiled to St. Helena for 6 years.

Section 4 Assessment

1. TERMS & NAMES
Identify
- blockade
- Continental System
- guerrilla
- Peninsular War
- scorched-earth policy
- Waterloo
- Hundred Days

2. TAKING NOTES
Create a two-column chart like the one below, listing Napoleon's three disastrous mistakes and the effects that each one had on his empire.

Napoleon's Mistakes	Effect on Empire

Which mistake was most serious? Why?

3. ANALYZING MOTIVES
What were the main reasons people in other European countries resisted Napoleon?

THINK ABOUT
- why some of his own allies refused to abide by the Continental System
- why the Spanish fought a guerrilla war for several years
- why the Russians destroyed their own crops and cities

4. THEME ACTIVITY
Power and Authority Using information from Sections 3 and 4, create a chart, sketch, or drawing to show what positive and negative effects Napoleon's rule had on France. Then judge Napoleon's use of power, showing your judgment in a visual way. Be prepared to defend your opinion.

ANSWERS

1. TERMS & NAMES
blockade, p. 589
Continental System, p. 589
guerrilla, p. 590
Peninsular War, p. 590
scorched-earth policy, p. 590
Waterloo, p. 592
Hundred Days, p. 592

2. TAKING NOTES
Possible Responses: Mistakes—Continental System, Peninsular War, Russian invasion. Effects—weakening of France, great loss of life and prestige, loss of much of army

3. ANALYZING MOTIVES
Possible Responses: Nationalistic feelings caused resistance to French control; invaded countries did not support Napoleon's drive for power; Russians did not want French rulers.

4. THEME ACTIVITY
Possible Responses: Positive effects might be the Napoleon Code, stable economy, fairer t ation, and religious tolerance. Negative effects might be the economic disruptions caused continual warfare, great loss life, and resistance fueled by nationalism.

The Congress of Vienna Convenes

TERMS & NAMES
- Congress of Vienna
- Klemens von Metternich
- balance of power
- legitimacy
- Holy Alliance
- Concert of Europe

MAIN IDEA

After exiling Napoleon, European leaders at the Congress of Vienna tried to restore order and reestablish peace.

WHY IT MATTERS NOW

International bodies such as the United Nations play an active role in trying to maintain world peace and stability today.

SETTING THE STAGE European heads of government were looking to establish long-lasting peace and stability on the continent after the defeat of Napoleon. They had a goal of a new European order—one of collective security and stability for the entire continent. A series of meetings in Vienna, known as the **Congress of Vienna,** were called to set up policies to achieve this goal. Originally, the Congress of Vienna was scheduled to last for four weeks. Instead, it went on for eight months.

Metternich Restores Stability

Most of the decisions made in Vienna during the winter of 1814–1815 were made in secret among representatives of the five "great powers." The rulers of three of these countries—King Frederick William III of Prussia, Czar Alexander I of Russia, and Emperor Francis I of Austria—were themselves in Vienna. Britain and France were represented by their foreign ministers. However, none of these men were as influential as the foreign minister of Austria, Prince **Klemens von Metternich** (MEHT·uhr·nihk).

Metternich distrusted the democratic ideals of the French Revolution. Like most other European aristocrats, he maintained that Napoleon's expansionist dictatorship had been a natural outcome of experiments with democracy. Metternich wanted to keep things as they were and remarked, "The first and greatest concern for the immense majority of every nation is the stability of laws—never their change."

Metternich had three goals at the Congress of Vienna. First, he wanted to prevent future French aggression by surrounding France with strong countries. Second, he wanted to restore a **balance of power,** so that no country would be a threat to others. Third, he wanted to restore Europe's royal families to the thrones they had held before Napoleon's conquests.

The Containment of France The congress made the weaker countries around France stronger:

- The former Austrian Netherlands and Dutch Republic were united to form the Kingdom of the Netherlands.
- A group of 39 German states were loosely joined as the newly created German Confederation, dominated by Austria.
- Switzerland was recognized as an independent nation.
- The Kingdom of Sardinia in Italy was strengthened by the addition of Genoa.

These changes allowed the countries of Europe to contain France and prevent it from overpowering weaker nations. (See the map on page 596.)

The French Revolution and Napoleon **593**

THINK THROUGH HISTORY
A. Analyzing Motives Why would aristocrats be against democracy?
A. Possible Answer They would lose power under a democratic government.

HISTORY MAKERS

Klemens von Metternich 1773–1859

Klemens von Metternich was a tall, handsome man whose charm worked equally well on his fellow diplomats and on the elegant ladies of Vienna. He spoke five languages fluently and thought of himself as a European, not as a citizen of any single country. "Europe has for a long time held for me the significance of a fatherland," he once said.

Early in his career, Metternich linked himself to the Hapsburgs, the rulers of Austria. In 1809, he became Austria's foreign minister, and he held that office for the next 39 years. Because of his immense influence on European politics, these years are often called the Age of Metternich.

Section 5 Overview

OBJECTIVES

(1) To explain the importance of the decisions made at the Congress of Vienna.

(2) To show how the ideas of the French Revolution continued to influence people throughout Europe.

SKILLBUILDER
- Interpreting maps: region, p. 596

CRITICAL THINKING
- Analyzing motives, p. 593
- Identifying effects, p. 595
- Summarizing, p. 596
- Evaluating, p. 596
- Analyzing themes, p. 596

FOCUS

5-Minute Warm-Up

▶ *Identifying Main Ideas*
To explore the work of peace organizations, have students answer these questions.

1. Read Connect to Today on page 595. What is the purpose of the United Nations?

2. What did the major powers agree to do after World War II?

WARM-UP TRANSPARENCY 23

OBJECTIVE ① INSTRUCT

Metternich Restores Stability

▶ *Key Ideas*
- Metternich influences European rulers to restore stability to Europe.
- France is kept intact, and a balance of power is established in Europe.
- Under the principle of legitimacy, rulers deposed by Napoleon are restored to power.
- The Congress of Vienna makes fair settlements and produces a lasting peace.

IN-DEPTH RESOURCES: UNIT 5
Guided Reading, p. 41

ACCESS FOR STUDENTS ACQUIRING ENGLISH
Guided Reading (Spanish), p. 233

SECTION 5 RESOURCES

PRINT RESOURCES

IN-DEPTH RESOURCES: UNIT 5
Guided Reading, p. 41

ACCESS FOR STUDENTS ACQUIRING ENGLISH
Guided Reading (Spanish), p. 233

FORMAL ASSESSMENT
Section Quiz, p. 268

ALTERNATIVE ASSESSMENT BOOK

TECHNOLOGY RESOURCES

CRITICAL THINKING TRANSPARENCIES
CT23 The French Revolution to the Congress of Vienna
CT59 Chapter 23 Visual Summary

CD-ROM
Electronic Library of Primary Sources

INTERNET www.mlworldhistory.com

At the Congress of Vienna, Metternich helped craft a fair and lasting peace by advocating moderation and cooperation among the countries of Europe. With regard to internal political policies, however, Metternich was much less flexible. He led a 30-year crusade to stamp out liberal and revolutionary ideas.

In a set of decrees issued in 1819, Metternich required German states to root out subversive ideas in their universities and newspapers. He established a permanent committee, with spies and informers, to punish any liberal or radical organizations. In general, Metternich advocated the ruthless suppression of any ideas promoting liberty and equality.

 ELECTRONIC LIBRARY OF PRIMARY SOURCES
from *Memoirs of Prince Klemens von Metternich*

 CRITICAL THINKING TRANSPARENCIES
CT23 The French Revolution to the Congress of Vienna

During the Congress of Vienna, diplomats exchanged secrets and made deals during the endless rounds of parties. Much of the congress's work was accomplished by means of such "diplomacy through entertainment."

Balance of Power Although the leaders of Europe wanted to weaken France, they did not want to go too far. If they severely punished France, they might encourage the French to take revenge. If they broke up France, then another country might become so strong that it would threaten them all. Thus, the victorious powers were surprisingly easy on the defeated nation. Although the French were required to give up all the territories Napoleon had taken, France remained intact, with roughly the same boundaries it had had in 1790. France also kept some of its overseas possessions, its army, and an independent government. As a result, France remained a major but diminished European power, and no country in Europe could easily overpower another.

Legitimacy The great powers affirmed the principle of **legitimacy**—agreeing that as many as possible of the rulers whom Napoleon had driven from their thrones should be restored to power. In France, the brother of Louis XVI returned to power as King Louis XVIII. He wisely adopted a constitution and ruled as a constitutional monarch. The congress also restored the Bourbon rulers of Spain and the Kingdom of the Two Sicilies. Hapsburg princes came back to rule several states in northern Italy. Many (though not all) of the former rulers of the German states of central Europe also regained their thrones. The participants in the Congress of Vienna believed that the return of the former monarchs would stabilize political relations among the nations.

Background
Most rulers in Europe at this time gained legitimacy by inheriting a throne.

The Congress of Vienna was a political triumph in many ways. Because its settlements were fair enough for no country to be left bearing a grudge, it did not sow the seeds of future wars. In that sense, it was more successful than many other peace meetings in history. For the first time, the nations of an entire continent were cooperating to control political affairs. On June 13, 1815, four days after the signing of the document that ended the congress, an observer wrote down his impressions:

> **A VOICE FROM THE PAST**
> It is contended that, on the whole, the Congress in its eight months of meetings has performed a tremendous task and never has a congress achieved more meaningful or grander results. . . . The majority of people now are saying: "The minister of foreign affairs [Metternich] has reaped honor from his work, from the conception and execution of the idea of the Congress of Vienna, and from the meeting of the sovereigns in consequence thereof."
> **CONFIDENTIAL AGENT,** quoted in *The Congress of Vienna: An Eyewitness Account*

How lasting was the peace? None of the five great powers waged war on one another until 1853, in the Crimean War. By agreeing to come to one another's aid in case of threats to peace, the European nations had temporarily assured that there would be a balance of power on the continent and that no nation would be able to expand at the expense of others. The Congress of Vienna had created a time of peace in Europe.

594 Chapter 23

Political Power Sharing The Congress of Vienna has not been the only meeting in which powerful nations have determined the political fate of vast regions of the world. In 1945, the leaders of the United States (President Franklin D. Roosevelt), Great Britain (Prime Minister Winston Churchill), and the Soviet Union (Premier Joseph Stalin) met at Yalta to make far-reaching decisions about the fate of Germany and Eastern Europe following World War II. In another instance, Great Britain, France, Germany, and Portugal carved out individual territories in colonial Africa at a meeting in Berlin in 1884.

Logical-Mathematical Learners Students who reason in abstract and logical ways may want to devise a game or conceptual model to investigate the ways in which a balance of power among nations works. Students might set up various hypothetical situations, then try to predict the outcomes of changes in the balance of power. For example, if one country begins to increase its troop strength, how might its neighbors react? How does balance of power in the Middle East work today?

Political Changes Beyond Vienna

Background
Conservatives wanted the political situation to return to what it had been before the French Revolution.

The Congress of Vienna was a victory for conservatives. Kings and princes were restored in country after country, in keeping with Metternich's goals. Nevertheless, there were important differences from one country to another. Louis XVIII's decision to rule France as a constitutional monarch meant that both Britain and France now had constitutional monarchies. Generally speaking, however, the governments in eastern Europe were more conservative than these. The rulers of Russia, Prussia, and Austria were absolute monarchs.

Conservative Europe The rulers of Europe were very jittery about the legacy of the French Revolution, especially the threatening revolutionary ideals of liberty, equality, and fraternity. Late in 1815, Czar Alexander, Emperor Francis I of Austria, and King Frederick William III of Prussia entered a league called the **Holy Alliance.** That agreement loosely bound them together. Finally, a series of alliances devised by Metternich, called the **Concert of Europe,** assured that nations would help one another if any revolutions broke out.

Across Europe, conservatives held firm control of the governments, but they could not contain the ideas that had emerged during the French Revolution. France after 1815 was deeply divided politically. Conservatives were happy with the monarchy of Louis XVIII and were determined to make it last. Liberals wanted the king to share more power with the Chamber of Deputies and to grant the middle class the right to vote. Many people in the lower class remained committed to the ideals of liberty, equality, and fraternity even though women and many poor men could not vote. In other countries as well, like Austria, Prussia, and the small German states, there was an explosive mixture of ideas and factions that would contribute directly to revolutions in 1830 and again in 1848.

Despite their efforts to undo the French Revolution, the leaders at the Congress of Vienna could not turn back the clock. The Revolution had given Europe its first experiment in democratic government. Although the experiment had failed, it had set new political ideas in motion. The major political divisions of the early 1800s had their roots in the French Revolution.

THINK THROUGH HISTORY
B. Identifying Effects What seeds of democracy had been sown by the French Revolution?
B. Possible Answers Sharing of power, social equality, freedom of speech and religion, fair taxation, voting rights

Revolution in Latin America The actions of the Congress of Vienna had consequences beyond Europe. When the congress restored Ferdinand VII to the Spanish throne, the reasons for the Spanish colonial revolts against Napoleon's puppet king, Joseph Bonaparte, should have disappeared. However, clashes among conservatives, liberals, and radicals erupted quickly.

In the colonies, the royalist *peninsulares* wanted to restore their power and control over the land, and the liberal Creoles saw their chance to retain and expand the powers they had seized. Revolts against the king broke out in many parts of Spanish America, with only Mexico remaining loyal to Ferdinand. In 1820, a liberalist revolt in Spain prompted the Spanish king to tighten control over both Spain and its American colonies. This action angered the Mexicans, who rose in revolt and successfully threw off Spain's control. A liberalist revolt in Portugal at about the same time created an opportunity for Brazilians to declare independence as well.

Long-Term Legacy The Congress of Vienna left a legacy that would influence world politics for the next 100 years. The continent-wide efforts to establish and maintain a balance of power diminished the size and the power of France, while the power of Britain and Prussia increased. Nationalism began to grow in Italy, Germany, Greece, and other areas that the congress had put under foreign control. Eventually, the nationalistic feelings would explode into revolutions, and new nations would be

CONNECT *to* TODAY

Congress of Vienna— United Nations

The work of the Congress of Vienna and the Concert of Europe was intended to keep the world safe from war. The modern equivalent is the United Nations, an international organization established in 1945 and continuing today, whose purpose is to promote world peace.

Like the Congress of Vienna, the United Nations was formed by major powers after a war (World War II). They agreed to cooperate to reduce tensions and bring greater harmony to international relations. Although not always successful, both the Concert of Europe and the United Nations used diplomacy to keep peace.

The French Revolution and Napoleon **595**

OBJECTIVE ② INSTRUCT

Political Changes Beyond Vienna

▶ **Key Ideas**
- The situation in Europe after the Congress of Vienna represents a victory for conservatives.
- A series of alliances, called the Concert of Europe, allows nations to help one another in case of internal revolutions.
- Latin American colonies revolt against Spanish rule.
- Nationalism grows, and democratic ideas begin to take hold in European nations.

CONNECT *to* TODAY
Congress of Vienna—United Nations

Ask students to check national newspapers for one week and to clip all articles referring to the United Nations. Have students share the articles and make a list of current UN activities.

TEACHING OPTION | **BLOCK SCHEDULING** | **COOPERATIVE ACTIVITY:** Investigating World Peace Organizations | **CLASS TIME 30 MINUTES**

Task: Pairs of students will choose peace organizations—such as the Congress of Vienna, the United Nations, NATO, and Amnesty International—to research. Then each pair will meet with another pair to exchange information and to develop a comparison of the organizations they chose.

Purpose: To learn more about historical efforts to establish peacekeeping organizations in the world.

Activity: Ask each pair of students to choose an organization dedicated to peace among nations and to research the activities and successes of the organization. Students should pay close attention to the purpose of the organization and to the ways in which the organization makes decisions. After the pair exchanges information with another pair of students, the four students should make a chart

comparing the two organizations and presenting conclusions about the positive and negative aspects of each.

 ALTERNATIVE ASSESSMENT BOOK
Standards for Evaluating a Cooperative Activity

The French Empire, 1810

Europe, 1817

French Empire
Countries controlled by Napoleon
Countries allied with Napoleon
Countries at war with Napoleon

Small German states
Boundary of the German Confederation

GEOGRAPHY SKILLBUILDER: Interpreting Maps
1. **Region** *What parts of Napoleon's French Empire did France lose as a result of the Congress of Vienna agreements?*
2. **Region** *In what sense did the territorial changes of 1815 reflect a restoration of order and balance?*

formed. European colonies also responded to the power shift. Spanish colonies took advantage of the events in Europe to declare their independence and break away from their European rulers.

On the other hand, ideas about the basis of power and authority had changed permanently as a result of the French Revolution. Old ideas about who should control governments were discarded. More and more, the principles of democracy were seen as the best way for equity and justice to prevail for all people. Europeans challenged old economic patterns of taxation and property ownership and began to adopt more equal treatment for all. The French Revolution changed the "business as usual" attitude that had dominated Europe for centuries. A new era had begun.

C. Answer Colonies wanted independence, and ideas about power and authority changed forever.
THINK THROUGH HISTORY
C. Summarizing How did the French Revolution affect not only Europe but also other areas of the world?

Section 5 Assessment

1. TERMS & NAMES
Identify
• Congress of Vienna
• Klemens von Metternich
• balance of power
• legitimacy
• Holy Alliance
• Concert of Europe

2. TAKING NOTES
Think about the ways in which the three main goals of Metternich's plan at the Congress of Vienna solved a political problem. Fill in the chart below.

Metternich's Plan	
Problem	Solution

What was the overall effect of Metternich's plan on France?

3. EVALUATING
From France's point of view, were the decisions made at the Congress of Vienna fair?

THINK ABOUT
• Metternich's three goals
• France's loss of territory
• the fears of the rest of Europe

4. ANALYZING THEMES
Power and Authority Why do you think liberals and conservatives differed over who should have power?

THINK ABOUT
• Old Regime privileges
• attitudes toward change
• Enlightenment ideas

596 Chapter 23

The French Revolution

Even today, historians have a wide variety of opinions about what caused the French Revolution and whether it was a good thing. The following excerpts, dating from the 1790s to 1859, show a variety of opinions about the Revolution.

SPEECH
Maximilien Robespierre

On February 5, 1794, the revolutionary leader Robespierre delivered a speech justifying the Revolution.

What is the goal for which we strive? A peaceful enjoyment of liberty and equality, the rule of that eternal justice whose laws are engraved, not upon marble or stone, but in the hearts of all men.

We wish an order of things where all low and cruel passions are enchained by the laws, all beneficent and generous feelings aroused; . . . where the citizen is subject to the magistrate, the magistrate to the people, the people to justice; where the nation safeguards the welfare of each individual, and each individual proudly enjoys the prosperity and glory of his fatherland.

LETTER
Thomas Paine

In 1790, Paine—a strong supporter of the American Revolution—defended the French Revolution against its critics.

It is no longer the paltry cause of kings or of this or of that individual, that calls France and her armies into action. It is the great cause of all. It is the establishment of a new era, that shall blot despotism from the earth, and fix, on the lasting principles of peace and citizenship, the great Republic of Man.

The scene that now opens itself to France extends far beyond the boundaries of her own dominions. Every nation is becoming her ally, and every court has become her enemy. It is now the cause of all nations, against the cause of all courts.

LITERATURE
Charles Dickens

In 1859, the English writer Dickens wrote *A Tale of Two Cities*, a novel about the French Revolution for which he did much research. In the following scene, Charles Darnay—an aristocrat who gave up his title because he hated the injustices done to the people—has returned to France and been put on trial.

His judges sat upon the bench in feathered hats; but the rough red cap and tricolored cockade was the headdress otherwise prevailing. Looking at the jury and the turbulent audience, he might have thought that the usual order of things was reversed, and that the felons were trying the honest men. The lowest, cruelest, and worst populace of a city, never without its quantity of low, cruel, and bad, were the directing spirits of the scene. . . .

Charles Evrémonde, called Darnay, was accused by the public prosecutor as an emigrant, whose life was forfeit to the Republic, under the decree which banished all emigrants on pain of Death. It was nothing that the decree bore date since his return to France. There he was, and there was the decree; he had been taken in France, and his head was demanded.

"Take off his head!" cried the audience. "An enemy to the Republic!"

ESSAY
Edmund Burke

A British statesman, Burke was one of the earliest and most severe critics of the French Revolution. In October 1793, he expressed this opinion.

"The Jacobin Revolution is carried on by men of no rank, of no consideration, of wild, savage minds, full of levity, arrogance, and presumption, without morals."

Connect *to* History

Summarizing In your own words, summarize the attitude toward the French Revolution expressed in each of these excerpts.

 SEE SKILLBUILDER HANDBOOK, PAGE 992.

Connect *to* Today

Research Find a modern view of the French Revolution and bring it to class. It may be a historian's analysis or an artistic portrayal, such as a novel or film.

 CD-ROM For another perspective on the French Revolution, see World History Electronic Library of Primary Sources.

Why the French Revolution Matters Now

As students discuss these perspectives on the French Revolution, you might have them consider the broader picture: why does the Revolution matter?

The French Revolution matters because it left a lasting political legacy that has affected people all around the world. The political legacy includes the following beliefs, some of which are contradictory:

• Political revolution can remake society for the better.
• Nationalism is a positive force for change.
• People should have civil liberties and equality before the law.
• Social position and wealth should depend on individual achievement, not inherited status.
• Democratic ideals and activism lead to war, class conflict, and savage dictatorship.
• The old ways were better because government was firm, society was orderly, and common people were respectful of authority.

The power of these beliefs has led to revolutions around the world. In the 1990s, conflicts in Bosnia, Zaire, Chechnya, and Palestine were fueled by several of them.

ELECTRONIC LIBRARY OF PRIMARY SOURCES
from "Frenchmen, Is This What You Want?"

Connect *to* History

Analyzing
Possible Responses:
Robespierre—The Revolution is justified because it will lead to a benevolent and just government under which individuals will enjoy peace and prosperity. Dickens—The Revolution gave power to the lowest and cruelest members of the populace, leading to rampant injustice and mob rule. Burke—The men of the Revolution are unprincipled savages. Paine—The great cause of eliminating despotism justifies revolution.

Connect *to* Today

Research
Students may wish to use one of the following:
• One of the film versions of *A Tale of Two Cities*
• The music from *Les Misérables*, a musical version of Victor Hugo's book about social conflicts in France after Napoleon's death
• *Guillotine, Its Legend and Lore* by Daniel Gerould. New York: Blast, 1990
• "The Great Revolution," *National Geographic Magazine*, July 1989

TERMS & NAMES

1. estate, p. 573
2. Great Fear, p. 576
3. Declaration of the Rights of Man, p. 577
4. guillotine, p. 580
5. Maximilien Robespierre, p. 582
6. coup d'état, p. 585
7. Napoleonic Code, p. 586
8. Continental System, p. 589
9. Waterloo, p. 592
10. Congress of Vienna, p. 593

REVIEW QUESTIONS

Answers will vary.

11. They were heavily taxed and had no political voice, no access to political office, and not enough to eat.

12. The Bastille symbolized the repression of the Old Regime.

13. Equal justice, freedom of speech, freedom of religion

14. It was an effort to wipe out those who wanted a return to the old ways. Members of Robespierre's government turned against him, and with his death, the Terror ended.

15. Napoleon established a code of laws, set up a fairer tax code, stabilized the economy, fired corrupt officials, gave equal opportunity in government, set up public schools, and reduced the power of the church while supporting religious tolerance.

16. He conquered much of Europe and put his relatives in charge of several nations.

17. Scorched-earth policy and the weather

18. In 1814, Napoleon's army had been weakened by losses in Russia and Spain, and enemy forces were too numerous. In 1815, the allies again had greater numbers of troops.

19. To prevent French aggression, to restore a balance of power in Europe, and to restore royal families to thrones held before Napoleon's conquests

20. The balance of power worked; mutual-aid agreements among nations helped ensure stability.

Visual Summary

The French Revolution and Napoleon

Long-Term Causes
- Enlightenment ideas—liberty and equality
- Example furnished by the American Revolution
- Social and economic injustices of the Old Regime

Immediate Causes
- Economic crisis—famine and government debt
- Weak leadership
- Discontent of the Third Estate

Revolution
- Fall of the Bastille
- National Assembly
- Declaration of the Rights of Man and a new constitution

Immediate Effects
- End of the Old Regime
- Execution of monarchs
- War with the First Coalition
- Reign of Terror
- Rise of Napoleon

Long-Term Effects
- Conservative reaction
- Decline in French power
- Spread of Enlightenment ideas
- Growth of nationalism
- Rise of international organizations (Congress of Vienna)
- Revolutions in Latin America

TERMS & NAMES

Briefly explain the importance of each of the following during the French Revolution or the rise and fall of Napoleon's rule.

1. estate
2. Great Fear
3. Declaration of the Rights of Man
4. guillotine
5. Maximilien Robespierre
6. coup d'état
7. Napoleonic Code
8. Continental System
9. Waterloo
10. Congress of Vienna

REVIEW QUESTIONS

SECTION 1 *(pages 573–576)*
Revolution Threatens the French King

11. Why were the members of the Third Estate dissatisfied with their way of life under the Old Regime?

12. Why was the fall of the Bastille important to the French people?

SECTION 2 *(pages 577–583)*
Revolution Brings Reform and Terror

13. Name three political reforms that resulted from the French Revolution.

14. What was the Reign of Terror, and how did it end?

SECTION 3 *(pages 584–588)*
Napoleon Forges an Empire

15. Summarize Napoleon's reforms in France.

16. What steps did Napoleon take to create an empire in Europe?

SECTION 4 *(pages 589–592)*
Napoleon's Empire Collapses

17. What factors led to Napoleon's defeat in Russia?

18. Summarize the reasons that the European allies were able to defeat Napoleon in 1814 and again in 1815.

SECTION 5 *(pages 593–597)*
The Congress of Vienna Convenes

19. What were Metternich's three goals at the Congress of Vienna?

20. How did the Congress of Vienna assure peace in Europe for the next 38 years?

Interact *with* History

On page 572, you looked at a French mob's actions before completely knowing why they occurred. Now that you've read the chapter, reevaluate your decision about joining the mob. Were the mob's actions justified? effective? Would you have advised different actions? Discuss your opinions with a small group.

Interact *with* History

Possible Responses: Students who originally wanted to join the mob may now say that the mob's actions led to terror and many unjust executions and that the peasants did not really benefit from their revolutionary actions. Others may say that the actions of the peasants were essential to starting and maintaining the momentum of the Revolution.

CRITICAL THINKING

1. CONGRESS OF VIENNA

THEME POWER AND AUTHORITY How did the Congress of Vienna affect power and authority in European countries after Napoleon's defeat? Consider both who held power in the countries and the power of the countries themselves.

2. NAPOLEON'S CAREER

Below is a chart of dates and events in Napoleon's career. Copy the chart on your paper. For each event, draw an arrow up or down to show whether Napoleon gained or lost power because of it.

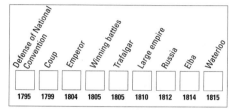

Defense of National Convention	Coup	Emperor	Winning battles	Trafalgar	Large empire	Russia	Elba	Waterloo
1795	1799	1804	1805	1805	1810	1812	1814	1815

3. EFFECTS OF REVOLUTION

There is a saying: "Revolutions devour their own children." What evidence from this chapter supports that statement? Why might revolutions generally be dangerous to their participants?

4. ANALYZING PRIMARY SOURCES

The following quotation from the South American liberator Simón Bolívar shows what he thought would happen if Napoleon came to the New World after his defeat at Waterloo. Read the paragraph and answer the questions below it.

> **A VOICE FROM THE PAST**
> If South America is struck by the thunderbolt of Bonaparte's arrival, misfortune will ever be ours if our country accords him a friendly reception. His thirst for conquest is insatiable [cannot be satisfied]; he has mowed down the flower of European youth . . . in order to carry out his ambitious projects. The same designs will bring him to the New World.

- What was Bolívar's judgment of Napoleon? What words convey it to you?

- Do you agree with Bolívar, or do you think Napoleon had less selfish motives for his actions? Support your opinion with details from the text.

CHAPTER ACTIVITIES

1. LIVING HISTORY: Unit Portfolio Project

THEME REVOLUTION Your unit portfolio project focuses on showing the similarities and differences among revolutions (see page 509). For Chapter 23, you might use one of the following ideas to add to your portfolio:

- Ask classmates to role-play French people from different estates as you interview them about their feelings toward the Revolution. Tape-record your interviews and add a commentary to create an "objective" newscast.

- Draw cartoons that compare and contrast a member of France's Third Estate with an American colonist.

- Write a dialogue between King George III of England and King Louis XVI of France, in which they discuss their problems with rebelling subjects.

2. CONNECT TO TODAY: Cooperative Learning

THEME ECONOMICS One major cause of the French Revolution was the extreme contrast between the lives of the few rich and the many poor in France. Some people feel that the gap between the rich and poor in the United States today is similar.

Work with a team to create a graph showing the distribution of wealth in the United States today.

Use the Internet or magazines to research the topic. Look for statistics that answer such questions as, What percentages of the population own various proportions of the country's wealth? What percentage of individuals live at or below the poverty line? How much is the wealthiest person in the United States worth?

- Look for parallel statistics. Figure out how to present them visually. You may use any type of graphic as long as it is labeled clearly.

- Make comparisons between the distribution of wealth in France before the Revolution and the distribution of wealth in the United States today.

3. INTERPRETING A TIME LINE

Revisit the unit time line on pages 508–509. Which three events entered for the period 1780–1815 do you think were most significant? Why?

FOCUS ON GEOGRAPHY

Notice the locations of Britain and France in this map.

- How far away from France is Britain?

- What geographical barrier protected Britain from becoming part of Napoleon's empire?

Connect to History What would Napoleon have needed to do to overcome that geographical barrier? Did he? What happened?

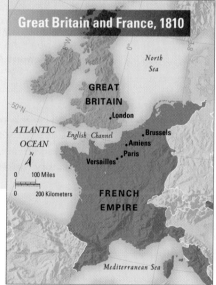

Great Britain and France, 1810

North Sea

GREAT BRITAIN

London

ATLANTIC OCEAN

English Channel

Brussels

Amiens

Paris

Versailles

FRENCH EMPIRE

0 100 Miles

0 200 Kilometers

Mediterranean Sea

	Key Ideas	COPY MASTERS	ASSESSMENT
SECTION 1 Latin American Peoples Win Independence *pp. 603–608*	*A slave revolt in Haiti leads to independence from French rule. Freedom from colonial rule is achieved throughout Latin America, but independence does not bring unity and prosperity as some liberators had hoped.*	*In-Depth Resources: Unit 5* • **Guided Reading,** p. 56 • **Skillbuilder Practice:** Hypothesizing, p. 60 • **Primary Source:** from Proclamation of 1813, p. 63 • **Literature:** from *All Souls' Rising,* p. 67 • **History Makers:** Simón Bolívar, p. 70	PE *Section 1 Assessment,* p. 608 *Formal Assessment* • Section Quiz, p. 277 *Alternative Assessment Book* • Standards for Evaluating a Product or Performance
SECTION 2 Revolutions Disrupt Europe *pp. 609–612*	*The forces of nationalism bring revolutions in Europe. With the exception of Greece, most revolutions fail, and by mid-century most of Europe returns to authoritarian rule.*	*In-Depth Resources: Unit 5* • **Guided Reading,** p. 57 • **Primary Source:** Letter to Thomas Moore, p. 64	PE *Section 2 Assessment,* p. 612 *Formal Assessment* • Section Quiz, p. 278 *Alternative Assessment Book* • Standards for Evaluating a Cooperative Activity
SECTION 3 Patterns of Change Nationalism Case Studies: Italy and Germany *pp. 613–618*	*The idea of nationalism eventually causes the breakup of the Austrian, Russian, and Ottoman empires. Italy is united through the efforts of Mazzini, Garibaldi, and Cavour. Prussian prime minister Otto von Bismarck succeeds in uniting and strengthening Germany.*	*In-Depth Resources: Unit 5* • **Guided Reading,** p. 58 • **Geography Application:** Languages Fuel Nationalism, p. 61 • **Primary Sources:** Proclamation of 1860, p. 65; Nationalist Speech by Otto von Bismarck, p. 66 • **Connections Across Time and Cultures:** Bonds that Create a Nation-State, p. 72	PE *Section 3 Assessment,* p. 618 *Formal Assessment* • Section Quiz, p. 279 *Alternative Assessment Book* • Standards for Evaluating a Cooperative Activity
SECTION 4 Revolutions in the Arts *pp. 619–623*	*During the first half of the 1800s, the Romantic movement in art, literature, and music arises in reaction to the rationalism of the Enlightenment. By mid-century, writers and artists shift to Realism in response to the harsh realities of the Industrial Age.*	*In-Depth Resources: Unit 5* • **Guided Reading,** p. 59 • **History Makers:** Beethoven, p. 71	PE *Section 4 Assessment,* p. 623 *Formal Assessment* • Section Quiz, p. 280 *Alternative Assessment Book* • Standards for Evaluating a Cooperative Activity
CHAPTER RESOURCES	**Chapter Overview** *During the first half of the century, Romantic idealism and nationalism spark revolutions in Latin America and Europe. Latin Americans succeed in throwing off colonial rule. However, revolutions throughout Europe fail to achieve their goals.*	*Telescoping the Times* • Chapter Summary, pp. 93–95 *Planning for Block Schedules*	PE *Chapter Assessment,* pp. 624–625 *Chapter Activities,* p. 625 *Formal Assessment* • Chapter Test, forms A and B, pp. 281–286 Test Generator *Alternative Assessment Book*

TECHNOLOGY

Warm-Up Transparency 24

World Art and Cultures Transparencies
• AT52 *Father Miguel Hidalgo Crowns Mexico and Breaks Chains Binding Her to Spain*

Electronic Library of Primary Sources
• from *Address to the Second National Congress of Venezuela, 1819*

Patterns of Interaction:
Struggling Toward Democracy

INTERNET RESOURCES
www.mlworldhistory.com

Warm-Up Transparency 24

INTERNET RESOURCES
www.mlworldhistory.com

Warm-Up Transparency 24

Geography Transparencies
• GT24 *Ethnic Groups of Austria-Hungary, 1867*

Critical Thinking Transparencies
• CT24 *The Unification of Germany and Italy*

Electronic Library of Primary Sources
• from *"Duties of Country"*

INTERNET RESOURCES
www.mlworldhistory.com

Warm-Up Transparency 24

World Art and Cultures Transparencies
• AT53 *Couturiere*

Critical Thinking Transparencies
• CT60 *Chapter 24 Visual Summary*

Electronic Library of Primary Sources
• *"Kubla Khan"*
• from *Frankenstein*

INTERNET RESOURCES
www.mlworldhistory.com

Chapter Summaries on Audiocassette in English and Spanish

INTERNET RESOURCES
www.mlworldhistory.com

Block Scheduling (90 MINUTES)

Day 1
Section 1, pp. 603–608

Section 2, pp. 609–612

 COOPERATIVE ACTIVITY
Creating Political Cartoons,
p. 611 (Teacher's Edition)

Section Assessments,
pp. 608, 612

Day 2
Section 3, pp. 613–618

 COOPERATIVE ACTIVITY
Interviewing Garibaldi,
p. 616 (Teacher's Edition)

Section 4, pp. 619–623

COOPERATIVE ACTIVITY
Presenting a Romantic Composer, p. 621 (Teacher's Edition)

Section Assessments,
pp. 618, 623

Chapter Assessment,
pp. 624–625

Yearly Pacing *Chapter 24 Total:* 2 days *Yearly Total:* 85 days

Planning for Block Schedules

Customizing for Special Needs

Students Acquiring English

Access for Students Acquiring English
• **Guided Reading** for Sections 1–4 (Spanish), pp. 240–243
• **Chapter Summary** (Spanish), pp. 237–239
• **Skillbuilder Practice** Hypothesizing (Spanish), p. 244
• **Geography Application** Languages Fuel Nationalism (Spanish), p. 245

Chapter Summaries on Audiocassette in English and Spanish

Patterns of Interaction Struggling Toward Democracy (Spanish track)

INTERNET RESOURCES www.mlworldhistory.com *The Diverse Classroom.*

Less Proficient Readers

In-Depth Resources: Unit 5
• **Guided Reading** for Sections 1–4, pp. 56–59
• **Skillbuilder Practice** Hypothesizing, p. 60
• **Geography Application** Languages Fuel Nationalism, p. 61

Telescoping the Times
• Chapter Summary, pp. 93–95

Chapter Summaries on Audiocassette

Gifted and Talented Students

In-Depth Resources: Unit 5
Primary Sources
• from Proclamation of 1813, p. 63
• Letter to Thomas Moore, p. 64
• Proclamation of 1860, p. 65
• Nationalist Speech by Otto von Bismarck, p. 66

History Makers
• Simón Bolívar, p. 70
• Beethoven, p. 71

Connections to Literature READINGS FOR STUDENTS

In-Depth Resources: Unit 5
• Literature: from *All Souls Rising*, p. 67

Enrichment Reading

• **Emil, Ludwig**
Bolívar: The Life of an Idealist
New York: Alliance, 1942

A lively story of Bolívar's childhood and later successes, this book features swords, battles, and cheering mobs.

• **McDougal Littell**
The Language of Literature, Grade 10
Guy de Maupassant, "Two Friends," p. 567

= Pupil's Edition	= Overhead Transparency	= Software	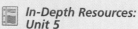 = Video
= Copy Master	= CD-ROM	= Audiocassette	= Internet

Nationalist Revolutions Sweep the West, 1789–1900

Accessing Prior Knowledge

- Ask students to look at the picture of the Arc de Triomphe and read the caption that accompanies it. What other monuments and symbols of military conquest and victory have they seen or read about in earlier chapters?

Making Judgments

- Have students read each of the captions and then decide which of the three themes listed to the left (revolution, power and authority, cultural interaction) seems to be the dominant theme expressed by the image and the caption that explains it.

Geography Connection

Ask students to look at the map on page 601.

- Why might the location of France have made governments throughout Europe apprehensive after the French Revolution of 1789? *France has a fairly central location and shares borders with a number of countries that might have feared revolution.*

CHAPTER 24
Nationalist Revolutions Sweep the West 1789–1900

PREVIEWING THEMES

Revolution
The 19th century was a time of revolutions around the Western world, as people under foreign rule established their own nation-states. The 1800s were also a time of revolutionary changes in literature, music, and art.

Power and Authority
In country after country, governments controlled by aristocrats came crashing down. In their place, revolutionaries set up republics and nation-states. With mixed success at first, members of the middle class increased their influence in government.

Cultural Interaction
The ideas of nationalism and democracy swept out over Europe from France, finally reaching across the Atlantic to the Americas. Likewise, the ideas of the Romantic movement and later the Realist movement revolutionized art, music, and literature.

INTERNET CONNECTION
Visit us at **www.mlworldhistory.com** to learn more about nationalism, romanticism, realism, and related topics.

600

REGIONS OF NATIONALIST REVOLUTIONS 1789–1900

Central and South America

In 1810, **Padre Miguel Hidalgo** issued his *Grito de Dolores* (Cry of Dolores). In it, he called for the poor of **Mexico** to revolt against Spanish rule. In this 20th-century mural by Mexican artist Juan O'Gorman, Mexicans of *all* classes revolt—which was not the case. O'Gorman also slips in his own politics: He inserts a communist symbol (the sickle) next to the religious banner.

0   1,000 Miles
0   2,000 Kilometers

GEOGRAPHY THEMES

Region
Remind students that regions have certain characteristics in common. Ask students why Havana, Port au Prince, and Santo Domingo might be considered as part of the same region. *They are all located in the Caribbean.* Ask students to identify other regions shown on the map on these two pages and to name a common characteristic of each. *Students might identify North America, Central America, South America, and Europe.* Ask students to identify the region in which they live. Then have them list characteristics of the region, including topography, climate, and so forth.

Movement
In this chapter students will study revolutions in Mexico, Central America, South America, and the Caribbean. Ask students to recall what they learned about European conquests in these regions in Chapter 20. Have them discuss how European revolutionary ideas might have arrived in these regions. Have them discuss the Spanish conquest of the Americas in terms of the movement of people and ideas across the ocean. Have them summarize the Spanish colonization of North, Central, and South America.

ADDITIONAL RESOURCES

Books for the Teacher

- Friedrich, Otto. *Blood and Iron: From Bismarck to Hitler, the Von Moltke Family's Impact on German History.* New York: HarperCollins, 1995.

- Tenenbaum, Barbara A., ed. *Encyclopedia of Latin American History and Culture.* New York: Scribner's, 1996.

Books for the Student

- Stefoff, Rebecca. *Independence and Revolution in Mexico, 1810–1940.* New York: Facts on File, 1993.

- Vinke, Herman. *Giuseppe Garibaldi.* New York: Chelsea House, 1987.

Videos

- *The Age of Revolutions: 1776–1848.* Social Studies School Service, 1985. 800–421–4246.

- *Bismarck: Germany from Blood and Iron.* Social Studies School Service, 1976. 800–421–4246.

- *Simón Bolivar.* Society for Visual Education, 1994. 800–829–1900.

Software

- *The 1848 Revolutions.* CD-ROM. Educational Software Institute, 1995. 800–955–5570.

- *Nineteenth-Century Nationalism.* CD-ROM. Society for Visual Education, 1994. 800–829–1900.

- *Romanticism.* CD-ROM. Society for Visual Education, 1994. 800–829–1900.

In **November 1860**, colorful Italian revolutionary **Giuseppe Garibaldi** met on a bridge in **Naples** with **Victor Emmanuel**, the king of Piedmont-Sardinia. To assure Italy's unity, Garibaldi made a grand gesture. During the Naples meeting, he handed over his southern conquests to Victor Emmanuel. By Garibaldi's generous act, north and south were joined. The Kingdom of Italy was born. This 19th-century fresco recalls the event.

In 1806, **Napoleon** began construction of the **Arc de Triomphe** in **Paris.** It was not completed until 1836—15 years after the emperor died. The heroic sculptures celebrate the victories of Napoleon's armies. Even today, the Arc de Triomphe is the largest triumphal arch in the world. It is also one of the symbols of France's capital city.

601

HISTORY THROUGH ART

20th-Century Mural

Juan O'Gorman

Juan O'Gorman (1905–1982) was an architect as well as a painter. The detail from the mural on page 600 shows Miguel Hidalgo, a priest, leading Mexicans in a rebellion against Spanish rule. The painter's father, Cecil Crawford O'Gorman, was also a well-known artist. Juan O'Gorman graduated from the school of architecture at the National University of Mexico in

Mexico City in 1927. He began designing houses in the International Style of the architect Le Corbusier. For a time he was head of the Department of Building Construction for Mexico City. He was also a professor of architecture at the National Polytechnic Institute.

Some of O'Gorman's major art works included mosaic designs on public buildings, murals, and frescoes. Some of his most important public murals were done at the Mexico City airport. The murals, which were

anti-Fascist and anti-Church, were destroyed in 1939 during a rightward turn of the Mexican government. This mural does not display an anti-clerical bias. Indeed, a priest (Miguel Hidalgo) is shown in a heroic pose in the forefront leading the people in revolt.

Interpreting the Art Have students explain why Hidalgo seems to be the hero in this mural. How does the artist make him look heroic?

Interact *with* History

This Interact with History feature motivates students by inviting them to put themselves in the position of an artist who is designing a national symbol. As they imagine themselves choosing a design, students will analyze the issues, explore their options, and become decision makers.

Purpose

- to set the stage for studying the spread of revolutions through the West during the 19th century
- to help students understand some of the causes and effects of revolution
- to help students make connections with the people and events they will study in this chapter

Teaching Strategy

Thinking Critically After students have imagined themselves in the situation described on this page, have them answer the key question and give reasons for their decision.

EXAMINING *the* ISSUES

Following are suggestions for addressing each bulleted question.

1 Ask students to think of some of the symbols that represent our country. What ideals do these symbols represent?

2 Point out that symbols can be borrowed from other cultures. For example, the eagle was a symbol of ancient Rome.

3 Ask students what elements of the American flag represent its past.

4 Ask students to look at the words on a dollar bill and on a quarter. How do they represent our ideals?

Making Connections Ask students to discuss the role of ordinary people in the American and French revolutions.

You are an artist in a nation that has just freed itself from foreign rule. The new government is asking you to design a symbol that will show what your country stands for. It's up to you to design the symbol that best suits the spirit of your people. Will your symbol be peaceful or war-like, dignified or joyful? Or will it be a combination of these and other qualities?

UNITED STATES
The olive branch and arrows symbolize a desire for peace but a readiness for war. The Latin phrase *E pluribus unum* means "Out of many, one," expressing unity in diversity.

AUSTRIA
The hammer and sickle symbolize agriculture and industry. The broken chains celebrate Austria's liberation from Germany at the end of World War II.

Your country is free. What kind of national symbol will you design?

PERU
The country's wealth is shown by the vicuña (with its silky fur), the quinine tree (which helps to cure malaria), and a horn of plenty.

BOTSWANA
Industry and livestock are connected by water, the key to the country's prosperity. *Pula* in the Setswana language means "rain," "water," "wealth."

URUGUAY
The shield features symbols of justice, strength, freedom, and prosperity.

EXAMINING *the* ISSUES

1 • What values and goals of your new country do you want to show?

2 • What symbol will you use?

3 • Will your symbol represent your country's past or future? Its land? Its goals?

4 • Will your design have words that also express values?

As a class, discuss these questions. During the discussion, think of the role played by symbols in expressing a country's view of itself and the world.

As you read about the rise of new nations in Latin America and Europe, think of how artists encourage national pride.

Follow Up

A feature on the chapter assessment will ask students to reevaluate their responses to the situation presented on this page.

1 Latin American Peoples Win Independence

TERMS & NAMES
- *peninsulares*
- creoles
- mulattos
- Simón Bolívar
- José de San Martín
- Miguel Hidalgo
- José Morelos

MAIN IDEA

Spurred by discontent and Enlightenment ideas, peoples in Latin America fought colonial rule.

WHY IT MATTERS NOW

Sixteen of today's Latin American nations gained their independence at this time.

SETTING THE STAGE By the late 1700s, the Americas, already troubled by Enlightenment ideas, were electrified by the news of the French Revolution. The French ideals of liberty, equality, and fraternity inspired many Latin Americans to rise up against their French, Spanish, and Portuguese masters.

Revolution in Haiti

The French colony called Saint Domingue was the first Latin American territory to free itself from European rule. Saint Domingue, now known as Haiti, occupied the western third of the island of Hispaniola in the Caribbean Sea.

Background
About 35,000 Europeans stood at the top of the social ladder in Haiti in the late 1700s. They were mainly French.

HISPANIOLA
HAITI
Caribbean Sea

Nearly 500,000 enslaved Africans—the vast majority of Saint Domingue's population—lived at the bottom of the social system. Most slaves worked on plantations, and they outnumbered their masters dramatically. White masters thus used brutal methods to terrorize slaves and keep them powerless.

The Fight for Freedom The slaves soon showed that, in fact, they were not powerless. In August 1791, an African priest named Boukman raised a call for revolution. Within a few days, 100,000 slaves rose in revolt. A leader soon emerged, Toussaint L'Ouverture (too·SAN loo·vair·TOOR), an ex-slave. Toussaint was untrained in the military and in diplomacy. Even so, he rose to become a skilled general and diplomat. It is said that he got the name L'Ouverture ("opening" in French) because he was so skilled at finding openings in the enemy lines. By 1801, Toussaint had moved into Spanish Santo Domingo (the eastern two-thirds of Hispaniola). He took control of the territory and freed the slaves.

In January 1802, 16,000 French troops landed in Saint Domingue to depose Toussaint. In May, Toussaint agreed to halt the revolution if the French would end slavery. Despite the agreement, the French soon accused him of planning another uprising. They seized him and sent him to a prison in the French Alps. In that cold mountain jail, he died 10 months later, in April 1803.

Haiti's Independence Toussaint's general, Jean-Jacques Dessalines (zhahn·ZHAHK day·sah·LEEN), took up the fight for freedom where Toussaint had left off. On January 1, 1804, General Dessalines declared the colony an independent country. It was the first black colony to free itself from European control. He called the country Haiti, which meant "mountainous land" in the language of the native Arawak inhabitants of the island.

Background
By 1600, almost the entire Arawak population had disappeared because of European conquest, warfare, disease, or slavery.

This statue, called *The Unknown Maroon of Saint Domingue,* stands in front of Haiti's National Palace. *Maroon* was a name for runaway slaves. Using a shell as a trumpet, the maroon is sounding the call to freedom.

SECTION 1 RESOURCES

PRINT RESOURCES

IN-DEPTH RESOURCES: UNIT 5
Guided Reading, p. 56
Skillbuilder Practice: Hypothesizing, p. 60
Primary Source: from Proclamation of 1813, p. 63
Literature: from *All Souls' Rising,* p. 67
History Makers: Simón Bolívar, p. 70

ACCESS FOR STUDENTS ACQUIRING ENGLISH
Guided Reading (Spanish), p. 240
Skillbuilder Practice (Spanish), p. 244

FORMAL ASSESSMENT
Section Quiz, p. 277

TECHNOLOGY RESOURCES

WORLD ART AND CULTURES TRANSPARENCIES
AT52 Father Miguel Hidalgo

CD-ROM
Electronic Library of Primary Sources

VIDEO *Patterns of Interaction: Struggling Toward Democracy*

INTERNET www.mlworldhistory.com

Section 1 Overview

OBJECTIVES

1. To describe how Haiti achieved independence.
2. To identify influences in Latin America's independence struggle.
3. To describe how Bolívar and San Martín ended Spanish rule.
4. To explain the role that Native Americans and mestizos played in achieving independence.
5. To show how Brazil's liberation differed from other countries'.
6. To show the negative effects of independence.

SKILLBUILDERS
- Interpreting charts, p. 604
- Interpreting maps: region, p. 608

CRITICAL THINKING
- Recognizing effects, p. 604
- Summarizing, p. 605
- Making inferences, pp. 606, 607
- Comparing, p. 606
- Forming and supporting opinions, p. 608
- Analyzing themes, p. 608

FOCUS

5-Minute Warm-Up

▶ **Interpreting Maps**
To help students understand the changes in Latin America, have them answer these questions.

1. Look at the map on page 608. On which coast did most of the battles take place?
2. Which countries retained colonies in Latin America, and where were they located?

🏛 *WARM-UP TRANSPARENCY 24*

OBJECTIVE 1 INSTRUCT

Revolution in Haiti

▶ **Key Idea**
- Haiti becomes the first black colony to gain independence.

IN-DEPTH RESOURCES: UNIT 5
Guided Reading, p. 56

ACCESS FOR STUDENTS ACQUIRING ENGLISH
Guided Reading (Spanish), p. 240

Teacher's Edition 603

Latin America Sweeps to Freedom

▶ Key Ideas

- Society in Latin America is based on class, with a small number of peninsulares holding most of the power, while large numbers of Native Americans are the most oppressed.
- The well-educated creole class leads the fight for independence in Latin America.
- Napoleon puts his brother on the Spanish throne, sparking rebellion in Latin America.

History from Visuals

The Divisions in Spanish Colonial Society in 1789

Interpreting the Chart Point out to students that the category "Europeans" in the chart is made up of two groups: peninsulares and creoles.

Extension Activity Ask students to add up the numbers on the chart to arrive at the total population of Spanish colonial society. *13,945,000* Have them identify the number of peninsulares in colonial society *15,000* and then discuss how such a comparatively small number of people could exercise power over so many.

SKILLBUILDER Answers
1. Indians and Europeans, or Indians and Creoles.
2. Peninsulares were an extremely small portion of the population (0.1%) but held all the real power in the colonies.

Latin America Sweeps to Freedom

Latin American colonial society was sharply divided into classes based on birth. At the top of Spanish American society were the **peninsulares** (peh·neen·soo·LAH·rehs), men who had been born in Spain. Only peninsulares could hold high office in Spanish colonial government. In this way, Spain kept the loyalty of its colonial leaders. **Creoles**, Spaniards born in Latin America, ranked after the *peninsulares*. Creoles could not hold high-level political office. But they could rise as officers in Spanish colonial armies. Together these two minority groups controlled wealth and power in the Spanish colonies.

Below the *peninsulares* and creoles came the mestizos (persons of mixed European and Indian ancestry) Next were the **mulattos** (persons of mixed European and African ancestry) and Africans. At the bottom of the social ladder stood Indians. Unlike enslaved Africans, Indians were of little economic value to the Spaniards. As a result, they were more severely oppressed than any other group.

This 18th-century painting shows a lower-class mestizo family in Mexico. Like many of the poor, this is a family of vendors. They are setting up their stand for market day.

Creoles Spearhead Independence Even though they could not hold high public office, creoles were the least oppressed of those born in Latin America. They were also the best educated. In fact, many wealthy young creoles traveled to Europe for their education. In Europe, they read about and adopted Enlightenment ideas. When they returned to Latin America, they brought ideas of revolution with them.

The Divisions in Spanish Colonial Society in 1789

Mestizos (7.3%) 1,030,000
Mulattos (7.6%) 1,070,000
EUROPEANS { Peninsulares (0.1%) 15,000
Creoles (22.8%) 3,070,000
Indians (55.8%) 7,860,000
Africans (6.4%) 900,000

SKILLBUILDER:
Interpreting Charts
1. Which two groups made up the vast majority of the population in Spanish America?
2. Looking at the chart, what was one possible reason that creoles felt resentful of the privileges of the peninsulares?

Creoles not only held revolutionary ideas. They also felt that Spain had inflicted serious injustices on them. A creole aristocrat wrote this complaint to the king of Spain:

A VOICE FROM THE PAST

[T]he Viceroys here and their retainers . . . mock, humiliate and oppress us. . . . The more distinguished the unhappy Americans are, the more they suffer. . . . Their honor and reputations are attacked, insulting them by depriving them of any honorific office of consequence.

MARQUÉS DE SAN JORGE, quoted in *Americas: The Changing Face of Latin America and the Caribbean*

Spanish royal officials suppressed actions and ideas that might fuel creole discontent. For example, Colombian patriot Antonio Nariño published a translation of the French *Declaration of the Rights of Man*. He was quickly sentenced to exile in Africa.

Background
The *peninsulares* got their name because they came from the Iberian Peninsula, where Spain is located.

THINK THROUGH HISTORY
A. Recognizing Effects How might creole officers serving in colonial armies become a threat to Spanish rule?
A. Possible Answer Since they received training in war, creoles might use it against the Spanish in a revolution.

Background
Of the 170 Spanish viceroys (colonial governors) between 1492 and 1810, 166 were *peninsulares;* only four were creoles.

Gifted and Talented Students
Toussaint L'Ouverture was an extraordinary historical figure and revolutionary leader. The grandson of an African king, born a slave in Saint Domingue, he was a complex and mysterious man. Ask students to read a biography of Toussaint and then write a brief report on him, focusing on his leadership of the revolution. As an alternative to a biography, you might have students read the Literature selection for this section from *All Souls' Rising* by Madison Smartt Bell, a novel about Toussaint L'Ouverture and the revolution in Haiti.

IN-DEPTH RESOURCES: UNIT 5
Literature: from *All Souls' Rising*, p. 67

Logical-Mathematical Learners To help students visualize the social classes of colonial Latin America, ask them to complete a Venn diagram like the one to the right and then use the figures from the chart on this page to indicate on the diagram the percentage of population each group represents.

Native American 55.8
Mestizo 7.3
European/ Creoles/Peninsulares 22.9
Mulatto 7.6
African 6.4

THINK THROUGH HISTORY
B. Summarizing
What factors caused the revolutions in Spanish America?
B. Possible Answer
Creole discontent over the privileges of the peninsulares; Enlightenment ideas from Europe; the Napoleonic Wars; Ferdinand VII deposed from the Spanish throne.

Events in Europe Trigger Latin American Revolutions Napoleon's conquest of Spain in 1808 finally triggered revolts in the Spanish colonies. After he had removed Spain's King Ferdinand VII, Napoleon made his brother Joseph king of Spain. Many creoles might have supported a Spanish king. However, they felt no loyalty to a king imposed by the French. Creoles argued that when the real king was removed, power shifted to the people.

In 1810, rebellion broke out in several parts of Latin America. In 1814, with the defeat of Napoleon, King Ferdinand VII returned to Spain. But the creoles had already begun their drive for independence. And they would continue until victory.

The *Libertadores* End Spanish Rule

The South American wars of independence produced two brilliant generals. Their leadership largely achieved victory for the rebels. One was **Simón Bolívar** (see·MAWN boh·LEE·vahr), a wealthy Venezuelan creole. Called *Libertador* (Liberator), Bolívar was at the same time romantic and practical, a writer and a fighter.

The other great liberator was **José de San Martín** (hoh·SAY day san mahr·TEEN). Unlike the dashing Bolívar, San Martín was a simple, modest man. But he too displayed great courage in battle. Though born in Argentina, he spent much of his youth in Spain as a career military officer. San Martín believed in strict military discipline. However, he also showed concern for the well-being of his troops.

Bolívar's Route to Victory Simón Bolívar's native Venezuela declared its independence from Spain in 1811. But the struggle for independence had only begun. Bolívar's volunteer army of revolutionaries suffered numerous defeats. Twice he had to go into exile. A turning point came in August 1819. Bolívar led over 2,000 soldiers on a daring march through the Andes into what is now Colombia. (See the 1830 map on page 608.) Coming from this direction, Bolívar took the Spanish army in Bogotá completely by surprise. There he won a decisive victory.

By 1821, Bolívar had won Venezuela's independence. He then marched south into Ecuador. In Ecuador, Bolívar would finally meet with José de San Martín. Together they would decide the future of the Latin American revolutionary movement.

San Martín Triumphs and Withdraws San Martín's Argentina had declared its independence in 1816. However, Spanish forces in nearby Chile and Peru still posed a threat. In 1817, San Martín led his army on a grueling march across the Andes to Chile. He was joined there by forces led by Bernardo O'Higgins, son of a former viceroy of Peru. With O'Higgins's help, San Martín finally freed Chile.

Next, in 1821 San Martín took his army north by sea to Lima, Peru. His plan was to drive out the remaining Spanish forces there. However, he needed a much larger force to accomplish this. This was the problem that faced both San Martín and Bolívar as they met at Guayaquil, Ecuador, in 1822.

No one knows how the two men reached an agreement. But San Martín left his army for Bolívar to command. Soon after, San Martín sailed for Europe. He died, almost forgotten, on French soil in 1850.

With unified revolutionary forces, Bolívar's army went on to defeat the Spanish at the Battle of Ayacucho (Peru) on December 9, 1824. In this last major battle of the war for independence, the Spanish colonies in Latin America won their freedom.

Educated in Spain from the age of six, José de San Martín returned to Latin America as a man in his early 30s. Fighting for 10 years, he became the liberator of Argentina, Chile, and Peru.

MORE ABOUT . . .
Classes in Colonial Latin America
Some mestizos and mulattos owned or rented small farms, or operated their own businesses. Most Africans worked as slaves on large plantations, although some free Africans lived in many Latin American towns. Lowest ranking of all were the millions of Native Americans. Legally free, they were usually treated no better than slaves.

OBJECTIVE 3 INSTRUCT

The *Libertadores* End Spanish Rule

▶ *Key Ideas*
- Simón Bolívar wins independence for Venezuela.
- José de San Martín defeats Spanish forces in Chile and then turns his army over to Bolívar.
- Bolívar defeats the Spanish in Peru, winning freedom for the Spanish colonies in America.

 IN-DEPTH RESOURCES: UNIT 5
Primary Source: from Proclamation of 1813, p. 63
History Makers: Simón Bolívar, p. 70

ELECTRONIC LIBRARY OF PRIMARY SOURCES
from Address to the Second National Congress of Venezuela, 1819

TEACHING OPTION | **BLOCK SCHEDULING** | **SKILLBUILDER MINI-LESSON: Hypothesizing** | **CLASS TIME 15 MINUTES**

Explaining the Skill Historians develop hypotheses, or possible explanations, about events to better understand why the events happened, what the consequences were or might be, and why the events are significant. Then they test their hypotheses against historical evidence to check their validity.

Applying the Skill: San Martín and Bolívar Ask students to speculate about what happened at the meeting in Guayaquil and why San Martín turned over his army to Bolívar. *Some historians think that San Martín left in anger after a quarrel with Bolívar. Others think San Martín deliberately stepped aside in favor of Bolívar so that the independence movement could unite behind a single leader.* You might have students look back at page 601 of the chapter opener and reread the caption that describes Garibaldi's action in turning over his conquests to Victor Emmanuel to explore similarities and differences between the actions of Garibaldi and San Martín.

 IN-DEPTH RESOURCES: UNIT 5
Skillbuilder Practice: Hypothesizing, p. 60

Bolívar was an inspiration to later revolutionaries throughout Latin America. For example, he inspired the Cubans who rose up against Spain in their struggle for independence in 1895, as well as a later revolution in Cuba led by Fidel Castro. Even rebellions as recent as the 20th century were, in part, inspired by the example of Simón Bolívar. Often these revolutions were influenced by a variety of sources, including Marxist doctrine as well as Bolívar's example.

Viewing the Video

Show *Struggling Toward Democracy: Revolutions in Latin America and South Africa* to examine how oppressed peoples in different times and places have fought for self-rule.

- The first segment of the video investigates the South American independence movement championed by "the Liberator," Simón Bolívar.

- The second segment chronicles a more recent struggle for equality: South Africa's anti-apartheid movement, led by Nelson Mandela.

Using the Teacher's Resource Book as a guide, discuss the meaning of the word "democracy"; compare the revolutions described in the video with recent struggles for democracy; and enrich the lesson with primary-source and visual-literacy activities included in the resource book.

PATTERNS OF INTERACTION
Struggling Toward Democracy: Revolutions in Latin America and South Africa
Videocassette: Tape 3

Ideas and Revolution

Revolutions are as much a matter of ideas as they are of weapons. And Simón Bolívar, the hero of Latin American independence, was both a thinker and a fighter. Through his education, readings, travels, and friendships, Bolívar was able to combine Enlightenment political ideas, ideas from Greece and Rome, and his own original thinking. The result was a system of democratic ideas that would help spark revolutions throughout Latin America.

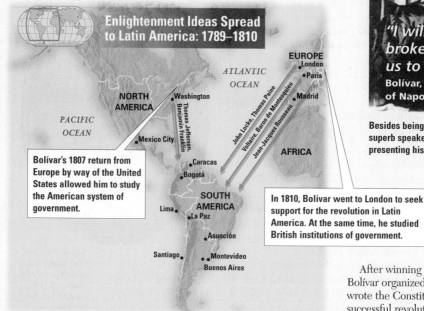

Enlightenment Ideas Spread to Latin America: 1789–1810

Bolívar's 1807 return from Europe by way of the United States allowed him to study the American system of government.

In 1810, Bolívar went to London to seek support for the revolution in Latin America. At the same time, he studied British institutions of government.

By 1800, the writings of Enlightenment authors were widely read throughout the Spanish American colonies.

"I will not rest until I have broken the chains that bind us to the will of Spain."
Bolívar, after watching the crowning of Napoleon

Besides being a military leader, Bolívar was also a superb speaker and statesman. He is shown here presenting his plans for a new government.

After winning independence in 1819, Simón Bolívar organized the Republic of Venezuela and wrote the Constitution of Bolivia. Like many successful revolutionaries, Simón Bolívar became disillusioned with Latin America's chaos after independence. Before his death in 1830, he commented bitterly: "Those who worked for South American independence have plowed the sea."

Bolívar admired Napoleon. But later, he was disappointed by Napoleon's betrayal of democracy.

606 Chapter 24

Patterns of Interaction

The Latin American independence movement is just one example of how the Enlightenment spread democratic ideals throughout the world. In countries facing oppressive conditions, a leader frequently emerges to establish a popular government. Even today, as can be seen in South Africa, democratic ideals inspire people to struggle for political independence and to overthrow oppressive governments.

 VIDEO *Struggling Toward Democracy: Revolutions in Latin America and South Africa*

Connect *to* History

Making Inferences How is Enlightenment thought reflected in Bolívar's ideas on Latin American independence and government?

SEE SKILLBUILDER HANDBOOK, PAGE 1005

Connect *to* Today

Comparing What recent events in today's world could be compared to Simón Bolívar's movement for Latin American independence?

Connect *to* History

Making Inferences
Possible Answer: The thinkers of the Enlightenment undermined the institutions of monarchy and a titled aristocracy by advocating ideals of equality, democracy, and individual rights. Bolívar, as the heir of these thinkers, translated their ideas into practice by fighting for political independence and democracy in Latin America.

Connect *to* Today

Comparing
Possible Answer: Some students might mention the independence achieved by the former republics of the Soviet Union when it dissolved in 1991, as well as the autonomy gained by former Soviet satellites in Eastern Europe. Other students might cite groups around the world, such as the Basques in Spain, that are fighting for greater autonomy.

Mexico Ends Spanish Rule

In most Latin American countries, creoles led the revolutionary movements. In Mexico, ethnic and racial groups mixed more freely. There Indians and mestizos played the leading role.

A Cry for Freedom In 1810, Padre **Miguel Hidalgo** (mee·GEHL ee·THAHL·goh), a priest in the small village of Dolores, took the first step toward independence. Hidalgo was a poor but well-educated man. He firmly believed in Enlightenment ideals. On September 16, 1810, he rang the bells of his village church. When the peasants gathered in the church, he issued a call for rebellion against the Spanish. Today, that call is known as the *grito de Dolores* (the cry of Dolores).

The very next day, Hidalgo's Indian and mestizo followers began a march toward Mexico City. This unruly army soon numbered 60,000 men. The Spanish army and creoles were alarmed by this uprising of the lower classes. In reaction, they joined forces against Hidalgo's army. Hidalgo was defeated in 1811. The rebels then rallied around another strong leader, Padre **José María Morelos** (moh·RAY·lohs). Morelos led the revolution for four years. However, in 1815, he was defeated by a creole officer, Agustín de Iturbide (ah·goos·TEEN day ee·toor·BEE·day).

Mexico's Independence Events in Mexico took yet another turn in 1820 when a revolution in Spain put a liberal group in power there. Mexico's creoles feared the loss of their privileges. So they united in support of Mexico's independence from Spain. Ironically, Agustín de Iturbide—the man who had defeated Padre Morelos—made peace with the last rebel leader. He proclaimed independence in 1821.

Before the Mexican revolution, Central America had been governed from Mexico. In 1821, several Central American states declared their independence from Spain and thus from Mexico as well. Iturbide, however, refused to recognize those declarations.

Iturbide (who had declared himself emperor) was finally overthrown in 1823. Central America then pulled together. The region declared its absolute independence from Mexico. It took the name the United Provinces of Central America.

Brazil's Royal Liberator

With no violent upheavals or bloody atrocities, Brazil's quest for independence was unique in this period of Latin American history. In fact, a member of the Portuguese royal family actually played a key role in freeing Brazil from Portugal.

The Portuguese Royal Family in Brazil In 1807, Napoleon's armies swarmed across the Pyrenees mountains to invade both Spain and Portugal. Napoleon's aim was to close the ports of these countries to British shipping. As French troops approached Lisbon, the Portuguese capital, Prince John (later King John VI) and the royal family boarded ships to escape capture. They also took their court and royal treasury with them. The royal family then sailed to Portugal's largest colony, Brazil. For 14 years, Brazil was the center of the Portuguese empire. During that time, Brazilians had developed a sense of their own uniqueness. Many of them could not imagine their country becoming a colony again. However, after Napoleon's defeat in 1815, the Portuguese government wanted exactly that.

By 1822, creoles demanded Brazil's independence from Portugal. Eight thousand Brazilians signed a petition asking Dom Pedro, King John's son, to rule. He agreed.

Margin notes (left column)

Background
Soon after his *grito*, Father Hidalgo declared an end to slavery and called for other sweeping social and economic reforms.

C. Possible Answers The royal family might spend more money there, since Brazil was now their home. They might take more interest in their Brazilian subjects and improve education, health, roads, etc., to improve the quality of life.

THINK THROUGH HISTORY
C. Making Inferences How do you think the royal family's living in Brazil might have helped Portugal's largest colony?

HISTORY MAKERS

**Padre José Morelos
1765–1815**

Born into poverty, José Morelos did not begin to study for the priesthood until he was 25. In his parish work, he mainly served poor Indians and mestizos. In 1811, he joined Padre Hidalgo, along with his parishioners. After Hidalgo's death, the skillful Morelos took command of the peasant army.

By 1813, his army controlled all of southern Mexico except for the largest cities. Morelos then called a Mexican congress to set up a democratic government. The supporters of Spain, however, finally caught up with the congress. As the rebels fled, Morelos stayed behind to fight. The Spanish finally captured and shot Morelos in 1815. Napoleon knew of this priest-revolutionary and said: "Give me three generals like him and I can conquer the world."

History from Visuals

Latin America, 1800
Latin America, 1830

Interpreting the Maps Point out to students that the best way to understand the differences between the two maps is to look at the different elements contained in each map key.

Extension Activity Have students compare the map of 1830 with the map in their Atlas on page 982 in order to see what countries have remained the same and what political boundaries and names have changed since 1830.

SKILLBUILDER Answers
1. Spain and Portugal
2. Mexico, United Provinces of Central America, Gran Colombia, Bolivia, Peru, Chile, Paraguay, Uruguay, United Provinces of La Plata

---

OBJECTIVE 6 INSTRUCT

Independence Brings Disunity

Key Idea
• Destruction caused by the wars for independence leaves Latin America poor and disunited.

ASSESS & RETEACH

Section 1 Assessment
Have students work in pairs to answer the questions.

Section Quiz
📋 FORMAL ASSESSMENT
Section Quiz, p. 277

Reteaching Activity
CLASS TIME: 10 MINUTES

Use the Guided Reading worksheet for Section 1 to review the main ideas of the section.

📋 IN-DEPTH RESOURCES: UNIT 5
Guided Reading, p. 56

CLOSE ACTIVITY

CLASS TIME: 15 MINUTES

Creating a Time Line
On the board, draw a time line with a beginning date of 1791 and an ending date of 1841. Ask the class to add important dates from this section.

Latin America, 1800

Latin America, 1830

Map 1800 key:
- British colonies
- Dutch colonies
- French colonies
- Portuguese colonies
- Spanish colonies

Map 1830 key:
- European colonies
- San Martín
- Bolívar
- Major battle
- (Sp) Spanish
- (Br) British

GEOGRAPHY SKILLBUILDER: Interpreting Maps
1. **Region** What two European countries held the largest colonial empires in Latin America in 1800?
2. **Region** Comparing the two maps, which independent countries had emerged by 1830 from Spanish territory in the Americas?

On September 7, 1822, he officially declared Brazil's independence. Brazil had won its independence through a bloodless revolution.

Independence Brings Disunity

Throughout Latin America, independence actually brought an increase in poverty. The wars had disrupted trade and devastated cities and countryside. After all the destruction, the dream of a united Latin America quickly fell apart. In South America, Bolívar's united Gran Colombia divided into Colombia, Ecuador, and Venezuela in early 1830. And by 1841, the United Provinces of Central America had split into the republics of El Salvador, Nicaragua, Costa Rica, Guatemala, and Honduras.

Meanwhile, the ideas of the French Revolution and the aftermath of the Napoleonic Wars were causing upheaval in Europe, as you will learn in Section 2.

Section 1 Assessment

1. TERMS & NAMES

Identify
• peninsulares
• creoles
• mulattos
• Simón Bolívar
• José de San Martín
• Miguel Hidalgo
• José Morelos

2. TAKING NOTES

Using a chart like the one below, compare independence movements in Latin America.

Where?	Who rebelled?	Why?	What happened?
Haiti			
Spanish South America			
Mexico			
Brazil			

3. FORMING AND SUPPORTING OPINIONS

Think about the background of many creole revolutionaries. What do you think might have been their tendencies as government leaders: toward democracy or authoritarianism? Explain your answer.

THINK ABOUT
• their education
• their professions
• their economic interests

4. ANALYZING THEMES

Power and Authority
Consider the following statement: "Through its policies, Spain gave up its right to rule in South America." Do you agree or disagree? Explain. Did Spain ever have the right to rule?

THINK ABOUT
• Spanish colonial society
• why independence movements arose
• who gained the power that Spain lost

608 Chapter 24

ANSWERS

1. TERMS & NAMES
peninsulares, p. 604
creoles, p. 604
mulattos, p. 604
Simón Bolívar, p. 605
José de San Martín, p. 605
Miguel Hidalgo, p. 607
José Morelos, p. 607

2. TAKING NOTES
Possible Responses: Haiti—slaves; freedom; independence. Spanish South America—creoles; freedom; independence. Mexico—Native Americans and mestizos/creoles; slavery; independence. Brazil—creoles and royal family; end colonial rule; independence.

3. FORMING AND SUPPORTING OPINIONS
Possible Responses:
Democracy—With their education, skills, and economic interests, creoles might become democratic leaders.

Authoritarianism—As military officers, creoles might use weapons instead of elections resolve political disputes.

4. ANALYZING THEMES
Possible Responses: Agree—Spain oppressed people in La America, so Spain deserved t lose its colonies. Disagree—Spain ruled its colonies by accepted European standard

Revolutions Disrupt Europe

TERMS & NAMES
- conservatives
- liberals
- radicals
- nationalism
- nation-state
- the Balkans
- Louis-Napoleon
- Alexander II

MAIN IDEA

Liberal and nationalist uprisings challenged the old conservative order of Europe.

WHY IT MATTERS NOW

The system of nation-states established in Europe during this period continues today.

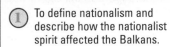

Section 2 Overview

OBJECTIVES

1. To define nationalism and describe how the nationalist spirit affected the Balkans.

2. To describe how revolutions and reforms affected Europe, especially France and Russia.

CRITICAL THINKING
- Summarizing, p. 611
- Analyzing issues, p. 612
- Drawing conclusions, p. 612

SETTING THE STAGE As revolutions shook the colonies in Latin America, Europe was also undergoing dramatic changes. Under the leadership of Austrian Prince Metternich, the Congress of Vienna tried to restore the old monarchies and territorial divisions that had existed before the French Revolution. On an international level, this attempt to turn back history succeeded. For the next century, Europeans seldom turned to war to solve their differences. Within these countries, however, the effort failed. Revolutions erupted across Europe between 1815 and 1848.

Nationalism Changes Europe

In the first half of the 1800s, three forces struggled for supremacy in European societies. **Conservatives**—usually wealthy property owners and nobility—argued for protecting the traditional monarchies of Europe. In certain cases, as in France, conservatives approved of constitutional monarchies. **Liberals**—mostly middle-class business leaders and merchants—wanted to give more power to elected parliaments, but only to parliaments in which the educated and the landowners could vote. **Radicals** favored drastic change to extend democracy to the people as a whole. They believed that governments should practice the ideals of the French Revolution. This was still a radical idea, even 30 years after the Revolution.

The Idea of the Nation-State As conservatives, liberals, and radicals debated issues of government, a new movement called nationalism was emerging. This movement would blur the lines that separated these political theories. **Nationalism** is the belief that one's greatest loyalty should not be to a king or an empire but to a nation of people who share a common culture and history. When the nation also had its own independent government, it became a **nation-state.**

Background
In 1815, only France, England, and Spain could be called nation-states. Ethnic unrest would soon change that.

Modern nationalism and the nation-state grew out of the French Revolution. Revolutionary leaders stressed the equality of all French people. The idea of equality fostered a sense of national pride in the French. That pride, in turn, helped French citizens' armies win stunning victories for the Revolution.

Background
Serbs revolted against the Ottomans in 1804 and 1815, winning self-rule within the Ottoman Empire in 1829. Full independence for Serbia came in 1878.

Nationalism Sparks Revolts in the Balkans The first people to win self-rule during this period were the Greeks. For centuries, Greece had been part of the Ottoman Empire. The Ottomans controlled most of **the Balkans.** That region includes all or part of present-day Greece, Albania, Bulgaria, Romania, and Turkey, and the former Yugoslavia. Greeks, however, had kept alive the memory of their ancient history and culture. Spurred on by the nationalist spirit, Greeks demanded that their

Carved on Napoleon's Arc de Triomphe, a fierce goddess of war leads French revolutionary volunteers into battle.

FOCUS

5-Minute Warm-Up

▶ *Clarifying*

To help students better understand the impact of emancipation, have them answer these questions.

1. Look at the Spotlight on Emancipation on p. 612. Who is pictured in the photograph accompanying the feature?

2. Did emancipation free the serfs from working the land?

WARM-UP TRANSPARENCY 24

OBJECTIVE ① INSTRUCT

Nationalism Changes Europe

▶ *Key Ideas*
- Conservatives, liberals, and radicals struggle for power in European nations.
- Nationalism and the idea of a nation-state begin to emerge.
- In the Balkans, the spirit of nationalism sparks a revolt against the Ottoman Empire, which results in full independence for Greece.

IN-DEPTH RESOURCES: UNIT 5
Guided Reading, p. 57
Primary Source: Letter to Thomas Moore, p. 64

ACCESS FOR STUDENTS ACQUIRING ENGLISH
Guided Reading (Spanish), p. 241

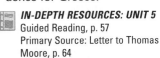

SECTION 2 RESOURCES

PRINT RESOURCES

IN-DEPTH RESOURCES: UNIT 5
Guided Reading, p. 57
Primary Source: Letter to Thomas Moore, p. 64

ACCESS FOR STUDENTS ACQUIRING ENGLISH
Guided Reading (Spanish), p. 241

FORMAL ASSESSMENT
Section Quiz, p. 278

ALTERNATIVE ASSESSMENT BOOK

TECHNOLOGY RESOURCES

INTERNET www.mlworldhistory.com

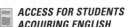

CONNECT *to* TODAY

Greeks and Turks on Cyprus

Ask students to consult either the *Reader's Guide to Periodical Literature* or the Internet to find recent information about the political situation on Cyprus.

The Tide of Reform in Western Europe

▶ *Key Ideas*

• In the 1830s and again in 1848, revolutions sweep Europe.

• In 1848 France establishes a republic, but within four years Louis-Napoleon becomes emperor.

• The weakness of Russia's industrial system is exposed by its defeat in the Crimean War.

• In 1861, the liberal Czar Alexander II frees the serfs, but his successor tightens czarist control.

CRITICAL THINKING ACTIVITY
CLASS TIME: 15 MINUTES

Summarizing

To help students understand the reforms and revolutions that occurred during the first half of the 1800s, have them complete a chart like the one below.

Revolutions/Reforms		
Nation	Date	Outcome
Belgium	1830	Independence from Dutch control
Italy		
Poland		

This 1839 lithograph shows Greeks in blue coats battling Ottoman Turks during the war for Greek independence.

country take its place among the nation-states of Europe. Because of this movement, a major Greek revolt broke out against the Ottoman Turks in 1821.

The most powerful governments opposed revolution in all its forms. However, the cause of Greek independence was popular with people around the world. Russians, for example, felt a connection to Greek Orthodox Christians, who were ruled by the Muslim Ottomans. Educated Europeans and Americans loved and respected ancient Greek culture, which they spent years studying in school. In his poetry, British romantic poet Lord Byron compared modern Greek nationalists to the ancient Spartans:

CONNECT *to* TODAY

Greeks and Turks on Cyprus

The hostility between Greeks and Turks continues to this day—with the island nation of Cyprus as its focal point. In 1974, Turkish troops invaded this island off the coast of Turkey with its majority Greek population. The Turks justified their invasion by saying that they were defending the rights of the minority of Turkish Cypriots. They captured the northern third of the island and declared the region an independent state.

The United Nations later established a "green line" on Cyprus—separating the Turkish north and the Greek south. However, the arrangement satisfies no one today. The Greek Cypriot government accuses the Turks of illegally seizing its territory. The Turks, in turn, maintain that they have the right to defend Turkish Cypriots from harm. The situation currently remains deadlocked.

> **A VOICE FROM THE PAST**
> The sword, the banner, and the field,
> Glory and Greece, around us see!
> The Spartan, borne upon his shield,
> Was not more free.
>
> **LORD BYRON,** from the poem "On this day I complete my thirty-sixth year"

In 1823, Byron made a large personal gift of £4,000 to the Greek fleet. After that, he went to Greece. There, he volunteered as a soldier for the Greek cause. He soon commanded a group of Greek soldiers. Unfortunately, he would not live to see the victory of the cause he fought for. In February of 1824, a cold Greek rain drenched the poet. Soon afterward, he caught a fever. He died from his illness in April.

Lord Byron wears the uniform of a Greek freedom fighter.

Eventually, with growing popular sympathy for Greece, the powerful nations of Europe took the side of the Greeks. In 1827, a combined British, French, and Russian fleet destroyed the Ottoman fleet at the Battle of Navarino. By 1830, Britain, France, and Russia signed a treaty recognizing the full independence of Greece.

The Tide of Reform in Western Europe

By the 1830s, the return to the old order—carefully arranged at the Congress of Vienna—was breaking down. Liberals and nationalists throughout Europe were openly revolting against conservative governments. In most cases, the liberal middle class—teachers, lawyers, and businesspeople—led the struggle for constitutional government and the formation of nation-states.

Waves of Failed Revolutions Revolutionary zeal swept across Europe. Nationalist riots broke out against Dutch rule in the Belgian city of Brussels. In November 1830, Belgians finally declared their independence from Dutch control. In Italy, nationalists

---

EXPLORING PRIMARY SOURCES

A Voice From the Past: Byron's career was a strange mixture of idealism and cynicism. Some of his poems portray a type of character who came to be known as the Byronic hero—idealistic, moody, proud, and defiant. Other poems by Byron are wonderfully funny and satirical. His letters show the same mix of idealism and satirical humor. You might read to students the primary source for this section, Byron's Letter to Thomas Moore, which he addressed to his friend from Greece. Ask students to write a sentence or two in which they describe Byron's mood in his letter as he faces military life.

 IN-DEPTH RESOURCES: UNIT 5 Primary Source: Byron's Letter to Thomas Moore, p. 64

CUSTOMIZING FOR SPECIAL NEEDS

Less Proficient Readers:
Analyzing Poetry Help students understand the passage from the poem by Lord Byron by explaining that the first line refers to a field of battle, with soldiers wielding their swords and carrying their banners, just as the ancient Greek warriors did. You may direct them to the painting shown on this page depicting a battle between Greeks and Turks. Explain that in ancient Sparta, a warrior who had fallen in battle was carried home on his shield. Then pair up a less proficient reader with a more proficient reader and have them address any other obstacles that the poem might present to comprehension.

worked to unite the many separate states on the Italian peninsula. Some were independent. Others were ruled by Austria, others by the pope. Eventually, Prime Minister Metternich sent Austrian troops to restore order in Italy. The Poles living under the rule of Russia staged a revolt in Warsaw late in 1830. Russian armies took an entire year to crush the Polish uprising. By the mid-1830s, it seemed as if the old order had reestablished itself. But with the political instability of the period, that impression did not last long.

In 1848, ethnic uprisings erupted throughout Europe. In Budapest, nationalist leader Louis Kossuth called for a parliament and self-government for Hungary. In Prague, Czech liberals demanded Bohemian independence. An unruly mob in Vienna itself clashed with police. That forced Metternich to resign and set off liberal uprisings throughout the German states.

But European politics continued to seesaw. Many of these liberal gains were lost to conservatives within a year. In one country after another, the revolutionaries failed to unite themselves or their nation. And conservatives regained their nerve and their power. By 1849, Europe had practically returned to the conservatism that had controlled governments before 1848.

Reform and Revolution in France Radicals participated in many of the 1848 revolts. Only in France, however, was the radical demand for democratic government the main goal of revolution. In 1830, France's King Charles X tried to stage a return to absolute monarchy. The attempt sparked riots that forced Charles to flee to Great Britain. He was replaced by Louis-Philippe, who had long supported liberal reforms in France. One French noble looked down on Louis. The aristocrat thought the king had "the manners of a citizen and the plainness of dress and demeanor very suitable to an American president, but unbecoming a descendant of Louis XIV [the Sun King]."

However, in 1848, after a lengthy reign of almost 18 years, Louis-Philippe fell from popular favor. Once again, a Paris mob overturned a monarchy and established a republic. Alphonse de Lamartine (lah·mahr·TEEN), one of France's leading poets, led the temporary government. After the victory of the Revolution of 1848, Lamartine proclaimed: "We are making together the most sublime of poems."

Far from being inspiring, the new republican government began to fall apart almost immediately. The radicals soon split into factions. One side, led by Lamartine, wanted only political reform. The other, led by Louis Blanc, also wanted social and economic reform. The differences set off bloody battles in Parisian streets. The violence turned French citizens away from the radicals. As a result, a moderate constitution was drawn up later in 1848. It called for a parliament and a strong president to be elected by the people.

This color engraving of the time shows Parisian revolutionaries fighting and dying behind the barricades in the Revolution of 1848.

France Accepts a Strong Ruler In December 1848, Louis-Napoleon Bonaparte, the nephew of Napoleon Bonaparte, won the presidential election. Four years later, **Louis-Napoleon** took the title of Emperor Napoleon III, which a large majority of French voters surprisingly accepted. The French were weary of instability and welcomed a strong ruler who would bring peace to France.

As France's emperor, Louis-Napoleon built railroads, encouraged industrialization, and promoted an ambitious program of public works. Gradually, because of Louis-Napoleon's policies, unemployment decreased in France, and the country experienced real prosperity.

A. Possible Answer
Absolute monarchy (Charles X) to liberal monarchy (Louis-Philippe) to radical republic (1848 revolution) to constitutional government (Louis-Napoleon Bonaparte) to monarchy (Emperor Napoleon III).

THINK THROUGH HISTORY
A. Summarizing
How would you outline the political swings occurring in France between 1830 and 1852?

SPOTLIGHT ON

Emancipation

On March 3, 1861, Czar Alexander II issued the Edict of Emancipation, freeing 20 million serfs with the stroke of a pen. Alexander, in fact, signed his edict one day before Abraham Lincoln became president of the United States. Less than two years later, President Lincoln issued the Emancipation Proclamation, freeing slaves in the United States. Lincoln's proclamation, like Alexander's edict, was issued on his authority alone.

Nonetheless, emancipation did not entirely fulfill the hopes of Russian serfs or former slaves in the United States. The peasant communities, like the one pictured above, still bound many Russian serfs to the land, while others earned poor livings as laborers in the cities. And Lincoln did not free all slaves—only those living under the Confederacy.

SPOTLIGHT ON

Emancipation

Ask students to read about Alexander's and Lincoln's motives for their proclamations of emancipation. What did each hope to achieve by emancipation?

MORE ABOUT . . .
The Crimean War

It was during the Crimean War that Florence Nightingale first gained fame and the Red Cross gained prominence. The war also inspired the British poet Alfred Lord Tennyson to write the poem "The Charge of the Light Brigade," romanticizing British bravery during a battle of that war.

ASSESS & RETEACH

Section 2 Assessment
Have students work individually to answer the questions. Then have them check their answers with a partner.

Section Quiz
 FORMAL ASSESSMENT
Section Quiz, p. 278

Reteaching Activity
CLASS TIME: 10 MINUTES

To help students remember the major uprisings in Europe in the first half of the 1800s, review the charts they have made for item 2 in the section assessment.

CLOSE ACTIVITY

CLASS TIME: 15 MINUTES

Comparing
Most of the revolutions that swept Europe during the first part of the century were led by the liberal middle class. Only in France were the revolutions led by radicals. Ask pairs of students to write a paragraph comparing the goals of the revolutions of 1830 and 1848 in France with the goals of revolutions elsewhere in Europe.

612 Chapter 24

Reform in Russia Unlike France, Russia in the 1800s had yet to make its leap into the modern industrialized world. Under Russia's feudal system, serfs were bound to the nobles whose land they worked. And nobles enjoyed almost unlimited power over them. By the 1820s, many Russians believed that serfdom must end. In their eyes, the system was morally wrong. It also prevented the empire from advancing economically. The czars, however, were reluctant to free the serfs. Freeing them would anger the landowners, whose support the czars needed.

Defeat Brings Change Eventually, Russia's lack of development became obvious to Russians and to the whole world. In 1853, Czar Nicholas I threatened to take over part of the Ottoman Empire in the Crimean War. However, Russia's industries and transportation system failed to provide adequate supplies for the country's troops. As a result, in 1856, Russia lost the war against the combined forces of France, Great Britain, Sardinia, and the Ottoman Empire. This was a humiliating defeat for the czar.

After the war, Nicholas's son, **Alexander II**, decided to move Russia toward modernization and social change. Through his reforms, Alexander and his advisers believed that Russia would compete with western Europe for world power.

Reform and Reaction The first and boldest of Alexander's reforms was a decree freeing the serfs in 1861. The abolition of serfdom, however, went only halfway. Peasant communities—rather than individual peasants—received about half the farmland in the country. Nobles kept the other half. The government paid the nobles for their land. Each peasant community, on the other hand, had 49 years to pay the government for the land it had received. So, while the serfs were legally free, the debt still tied them to the land.

Political and social reforms ground to a halt when terrorists assassinated Alexander II in 1881. His successor, Alexander III, tightened czarist control on the country. Alexander III and his ministers, however, encouraged industrial development to expand Russia's power. A major force behind Russia's drive toward industrial expansion was nationalism. Nationalism also stirred other ethnic groups. During the 1800s, such groups were uniting into nations and building industries to survive among other nation-states.

Background
In December 1825, when Nicholas became czar, a group of army officers (the "Decembrists") demanded liberal reforms. Nicholas crushed the Decembrists and then ruled with an iron fist.

B. Possible Answer The czars needed to reform Russia to bring its power up to the level of Western European powers. Nonetheless, czarist power rested on authoritarianism, as well as on the support of landowners who wanted to keep the feudal system.

THINK THROUGH HISTORY
B. Analyzing Issues Why were czars torn between social and economic reforms in their country?

Section 2 Assessment

1. TERMS & NAMES

Identify
- conservatives
- liberals
- radicals
- nationalism
- nation-state
- the Balkans
- Louis-Napoleon
- Alexander II

2. TAKING NOTES

Using a chart like the one below, list the major uprisings that challenged the old order of Europe in the first half of the 1800s. Group them under the year they occurred.

What ideal sparked most of these revolts? Explain.

3. DRAWING CONCLUSIONS

Why do you think some liberals might disapprove of the way Louis-Napoleon ruled France after the uprisings of 1848?

THINK ABOUT
- who the liberals were and what they believed in
- conditions in France in 1848
- Louis-Napoleon's actions and policies

4. THEME ACTIVITY

Cultural Interaction Imagine that you are a conservative, liberal, or radical in 1848. You have just heard that revolts have broken out in Europe. Write a letter to a friend, stating your political position and expressing your feelings about the uprisings. Then, express your thoughts about the future of Europe.

A N S W E R S

1. TERMS & NAMES
conservatives, p. 609
liberals, p. 609
radicals, p. 609
nationalism, p. 609
nation-state, p. 609
the Balkans, p. 609
Louis-Napoleon, p. 611
Alexander II, p. 612

2. TAKING NOTES
Possible Responses: 1821—Greece rebels against Ottoman Turks. 1830—Belgians declare independence from the Dutch; Italians try to unite; Poles rebel against Russia; French throw out Charles X. 1848—Hungarians call for self-government; Czechs demand independence for

Bohemia; liberals revolt in the German states; French demand democratic government.

Nationalism—People wanted to establish their own nation-states.

3. DRAWING CONCLUSIONS
Possible Responses: Liberals wanted to give power to parliaments, but Louis-Napoleon

declared himself sole ruler.

4. THEME ACTIVITY
Writers may express enthusiasm, caution, disgust, other emotion, depending on their political position. They should also make predictions about Europe's future.

TERMS & NAMES
- Camillo di Cavour
- Giuseppe Garibaldi
- Red Shirts
- Otto von Bismarck
- realpolitik
- kaiser

MAIN IDEA

The force of nationalism contributed to the formation of two new nations and a new political order in Europe.

WHY IT MATTERS NOW

Nationalism is the basis of world politics today and has often caused conflicts and wars.

SETTING THE STAGE Nationalism was the most powerful ideal of the 1800s. Its influence stretched throughout Europe. Nationalism shaped countries. It also upset the balance of power set up at the Congress of Vienna in 1815, and affected the lives of millions.

The Ideal of Nationalism

Nationalism during the 1800s fueled efforts to build nation-states. Nationalists were not loyal to kings, but to their *people*—to those who shared common bonds. These bonds might include a common history, culture, world-view, or language. Nationalists believed that people of a single "nationality," or ancestry, should unite under a single government. People would then identify with their government to create a united nation-state.

Romantic nationalists preached that a nation, like a person, has the right to independence. Independence would allow a nation's identity to develop.

As nationalists saw it, a number of links bound a people together as a nation. Some—though not all—had to exist before a nation-state would evolve and survive. The chart below summarizes those nationalist links.

Background

Nationalists often spoke of a "national character." Thus, they saw the French as "civilized"; the Germans as "scientific"; the English as "practical."

PATTERNS OF CHANGE: Nationalism

Bonds That Create a Nation-State	
Nationality	• A belief in a common ethnic ancestry—a belief that may or may not be true
Language	• Different dialects (forms) of one language; one dialect chosen as the "national language"
Culture	• A shared way of life (food, dress, behavior, ideals)
History	• A common past; common experiences
Religion	• A religion shared by all or most of the people
Territory	• A certain territory that belongs to the ethnic group; its "land"
Nation-State	• Defends the nation's territory and its way of life • Represents the nation to the rest of the world • Embodies the people and its ideals

SKILLBUILDER: Interpreting Charts
1. *Besides food, dress, behavior, and ideals, what are two other elements that could fall under the category of "culture"?*
2. *Which factors listed in the upper part of the chart are absolutely necessary to form a nation-state?*

PATTERNS OF CHANGE **613**

Section 3 Overview

OBJECTIVES

1. To identify the links that bind people into a nation-state.
2. To explain how nationalism weakened empires.
3. To summarize how Cavour unified Italy.
4. To describe how Prussia led the unification of Germany.
5. To explain the shift in the balance of power among nations.

SKILLBUILDER
- Interpreting charts, p. 613
- Interpreting maps: region, p. 615
- Interpreting maps: location, region, p. 617

CRITICAL THINKING
- Making inferences, p. 614
- Analyzing causes, p. 616
- Drawing conclusions, p. 617
- Analyzing issues, p. 618
- Analyzing themes, p. 618

FOCUS

5-Minute Warm-Up

▶ *Summarizing*
Have students answer the following questions to understand the concept of nationalism.

1. Read the first paragraph under "The Ideal of Nationalism" on p. 613. What are some of the common bonds that unite people into a nation?

2. How did nationalists believe that people who share a common bond should be united?

 WARM-UP TRANSPARENCY 24

OBJECTIVE ① INSTRUCT

The Ideal of Nationalism

▶ *Key Idea*
- Nationalists believe in uniting people who share a common history and culture.

 IN-DEPTH RESOURCES: UNIT 5
Guided Reading, p. 58

 ACCESS FOR STUDENTS ACQUIRING ENGLISH
Guided Reading (Spanish), p. 242

Teacher's Edition   613

SECTION 3 RESOURCES

PRINT RESOURCES

 IN-DEPTH RESOURCES: UNIT 5
Guided Reading, p. 58
Geography Application: Languages Fuel Nationalism, p. 61
Primary Sources: Proclamation of 1860, p. 65; Nationalist speech by Otto von Bismarck, p. 66
Connections Across Time and Cultures, p. 72
ACCESS FOR STUDENTS ACQUIRING ENGLISH
Guided Reading (Spanish), p. 242
Geography Application (Spanish), p. 245

FORMAL ASSESSMENT
Section Quiz, p. 279

TECHNOLOGY RESOURCES

GEOGRAPHY TRANSPARENCIES
GT24 Ethnic Groups of Austria-Hungary, 1867

CRITICAL THINKING TRANSPARENCIES
CT24 The Unification of Germany and Italy

CD-ROM
Electronic Library of Primary Sources

 INTERNET www.mlworldhistory.com

Interpreting the Chart Point out that two elements are represented in the chart: bonds that create a nation-state and the functions of a nation-state.

Extension Activity Ask students to explain how each of these bonds is represented in the United States.

SKILLBUILDER Answers

1. Art and architecture; literature; holidays; ways of working; sports and games.
2. *Possible Responses:* Language, history and territory.

OBJECTIVE **2** INSTRUCT

Nationalism Shakes Aging Empires

▶ **Key Ideas**

- The Austro-Hungarian Empire is weakened by various nationalist groups and finally dismantled at the end of World War I.
- The Russian czar's attempts to unify diverse cultures fail, and the empire finally collapses with the Bolshevik Revolution.
- Despite efforts at reform, the Ottoman Empire collapses at the end of World War I.

 IN-DEPTH RESOURCES: UNIT 5
Geography Application: Languages Fuel Nationalism, p. 61
Connections Across Time and Cultures: Bonds that Create a Nation-State, p. 72

 GEOGRAPHY TRANSPARENCIES
GT24 Ethnic Groups of Austria-Hungary, 1867

Nationalism Shakes Aging Empires

Three aging empires—the Austro-Hungarian Empire of the Hapsburgs, the Russian Empire of the Romanovs, and the Ottoman Empire of the Turks—were a jumble of ethnic groups. After all, territory and peoples had for centuries been pawns in a political chess game for these empires. Land and ethnic groups moved back and forth, depending on victories or defeats in war and on royal marriages. When nationalism emerged in the 19th century, ethnic unrest threatened and eventually toppled these empires.

A Force for Disunity or Unity? Nationalist movements were capable of tearing apart long-established empires. They could also create new, unified nation-states. Those who wanted to restore the old order from before the French Revolution saw nationalism as a force for disunity. The kingdoms and empires of the old order often ruled over a variety of ethnic groups. Conservatives of the old order reasoned that if each ethnic group wanted its own state, empires would split and crumble.

Gradually, however, rulers began to see that nationalism could also unify masses of people. The rulers of Europe had seen how the nationalist spirit inspired French citizen armies to conquer the armies of other European powers. Authoritarian rulers soon began to use nationalist feelings for their own purposes. They built nation-states in areas where they remained firmly in control. Nationalism worked as a force for disunity, shaking centuries-old empires. But it also worked as a force for unity. It gave rise to the nation-state that is basic to our world today.

The Breakup of the Austro-Hungarian Empire The Austro-Hungarian Empire brought together Hungarians, Germans, Czechs, Slovaks, Croats, Poles, Serbs, and Italians. In 1866, Prussia defeated Austria in the Austro-Prussian War. With its victory, Prussia gained control of the new North German Federation. Then, pressured by the Hungarians, Emperor Francis Joseph of Austria split his empire in half, declaring Austria and Hungary independent states—with himself as ruler of both.

Nevertheless, nationalist disputes continued to plague the empire for more than 40 years. Finally, after World War I, Austria-Hungary crumbled into separate nation-states.

In 1903, Ottoman troops moved against rebellious subjects in Salonika, Greece. A drawing of the period illustrates the event.

614 PATTERNS OF CHANGE

The Russian Empire Crumbles Nationalism also helped break up the 400-year-old empire of the czars in Russia. In addition to the Russians themselves, the czar ruled over 22 million Ukrainians, 8 million Poles, and smaller numbers of Lithuanians, Latvians, Estonians, Finns, Jews, Romanians, Georgians, Armenians, and Turks. Each group had its own culture.

The ruling Romanov dynasty of Russia was determined to maintain iron control over this diversity. However, their severe policy of Russification—imposing Russian culture on all the ethnic groups in the empire—strengthened nationalist feelings. The rise in nationalism then helped to disunify Russia. The weakened czarist empire finally could not withstand the double shock of World War I and the communist revolution. The last Romanov czar gave up his power in 1917.

The Ottoman Empire Weakens The Ottomans controlled Greeks, Slavs, Arabs, Bulgarians, and Armenians, in addition to the ruling Turks. In 1856, under pressure from the British and the French, the Ottomans issued reforms to grant equal citizenship to all the people under their rule. That measure, however, angered conservative Turks, who wanted no change in the situation, and caused tensions in the empire. For example, in response to nationalism in Armenia, the Ottomans carried out massacres and deportations of Armenians in 1894 to 1896 and in 1915. Like Austria-Hungary, the Ottoman Empire broke apart soon after World War I.

Background
In 1867, the Czechs demanded self-rule in the empire, like the Austrians and Hungarians. Ethnic groups in Hungary demanded their own states.

THINK THROUGH HISTORY
A. Making Inferences Why would a policy like Russification tend to produce results that are the opposite of those intended?
A. Possible Answer Trying to force a culture or language on a group of people will probably create resentment. As a reaction, the group will probably take even greater pride in its own language and culture.

TEACHING OPTIONS

CONNECTIONS ACROSS TIME AND PLACE

Nationalism and Disunity
Today nationalism continues to be a force for disunity. After the Soviet Union collapsed in 1991, forces of nationalism, contained by the Soviet government, once again appeared. Countries and regions demanded independent governments. Some countries, such as

Czechoslovakia, separated peacefully into two independent states. In other countries or regions once part of the Soviet Union, nationalism caused violent upheavals. Ask students to read about the former Yugoslavia or about Chechnya and write a brief report explaining how nationalism is a force in these areas.

CONNECTIONS ACROSS THE CURRICULUM

Biology The Hapsburg royal family, who ruled the Austro-Hungarian Empire until its fall in 1918, was one of the oldest and most famous royal families of Europe. The Hapsburgs increased their power and influence through judicious marriages to members of other royal houses. Have students research the

Hapsburg royal family and write a brief report describing the genetic effects of Hapsburg intermarriages, especially the famous Hapsburg chin. The report should also give some background on genetic theory to explain how physical traits can be magnified in intermarriage.

Cavour Unites Italy

While nationalism destroyed empires, it also built nations. Italy was one of the countries to form from the territory of crumbling empires. After the Congress of Vienna in 1815, Austria ruled the Italian provinces of Venetia and Lombardy in the north, and several small states. In the south, the Spanish Bourbon family ruled the Kingdom of the Two Sicilies.

Nevertheless, between 1815 and 1848, increasing numbers of Italians were no longer content to live under foreign rulers. Amid growing discontent, two leaders appeared—one was idealistic, the other practical. They had different personalities and pursued different goals. But each contributed to the unification of Italy.

The Movement for Unity Begins

In 1832, an idealistic 26-year-old Italian named Giuseppe Mazzini (maht·TSEE·nee) organized a nationalist group called Young Italy. No one older than 40 was allowed to join.

During the violent year of 1848, revolts broke out in eight states on the Italian peninsula. Mazzini briefly headed a republican government at Rome. He believed that nation-states were the best hope for social justice, democracy, and peace in Europe. However, the 1848 rebellions failed in Italy as they did elsewhere in Europe. The former rulers of the Italian states drove Mazzini and other nationalist leaders into exile.

Sardinia Leads Italian Unification

After 1848, Italian nationalists looked to the Kingdom of Piedmont-Sardinia for leadership. Piedmont-Sardinia was the largest and most powerful of the Italian states. The kingdom had also adopted a liberal constitution in 1848. So, to the Italian middle classes, unification under Piedmont-Sardinia seemed a sensible alternative to Mazzini's democratic idealism.

In 1852, Sardinia's King Victor Emmanuel II named Count **Camillo di Cavour** (kuh·VOOR) as his prime minister. Cavour was a wealthy, middle-aged aristocrat, who worked tirelessly to expand Piedmont-Sardinia's power. With careful diplomacy and well-chosen alliances, he achieved that expansion. Almost as a coincidence, he also achieved the unification of Italy. Mazzini distrusted Cavour. He believed correctly that Cavour wanted to strengthen Sardinia's power, not to unite Italy.

At first, Cavour's major goal was to get control of northern Italy for Sardinia. He carefully went about achieving this territorial goal through diplomacy and cunning. Cavour realized that the greatest roadblock to annexing northern Italy was Austria. To help him expel the Austrians from the north, Cavour found an ally in France. In 1858, the French emperor Napoleon III agreed to help drive Austria out of the northern provinces of Lombardy and Venetia. Cavour soon after provoked a war with Austria. A combined French-Sardinian army won two quick victories against Austria. Sardinia succeeded in taking over all of northern Italy, except Venetia, from the Austrians.

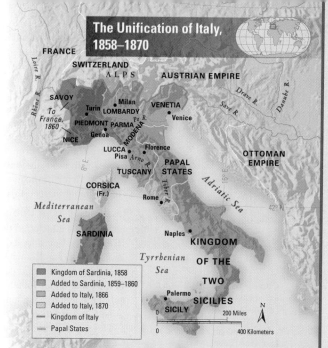

The Unification of Italy, 1858–1870

Kingdom of Sardinia, 1858
Added to Sardinia, 1859–1860
Added to Italy, 1866
Added to Italy, 1870
Kingdom of Italy
Papal States

0   200 Miles
0   400 Kilometers

GEOGRAPHY SKILLBUILDER:
Interpreting Maps

1. **Region** *During what time period was the greatest amount of territory unified in Italy?*
2. **Region** *What territory did the Italians actually lose during their process of unification?*

Cavour Unites Italy

▶ **Key Ideas**

- Mazzini attempts to unite Italy and free it from foreign rulers.
- Sardinia's prime minister, Cavour, wins most of northern Italy from the Austrians.
- Cavour arranges to unite Italy under the Sardinian king.
- Following unification, Italy suffers severe political and economic problems.

ELECTRONIC LIBRARY OF PRIMARY SOURCES
from "Duties of Country"

CRITICAL THINKING ACTIVITY
CLASS TIME: 15 MINUTES

Evaluating Decisions
Ask students to consider the differences between northern and southern Italy. Would it have been better to create two separate nations? Have them make up a chart in which they list the advantages and disadvantages of two separate nations.

History from Visuals

The Unification of Italy, 1858–1870

Interpreting the Map Have students identify which areas were added to the Kingdom of Sardinia and which areas were added to Italy later.

Extension Activity Ask students to read about one or more regions of Italy shown on this map—such as Lombardy and Tuscany—and write a report of two paragraphs describing its major cities, agricultural produce, brief history, and any other distinguishing characteristics.

SKILLBUILDER Answers
1. 1859–1860.
2. The provinces of Savoy and Nice.

Less Proficient Readers
Making a Summary To help students understand the three aging empires and their collapse, ask them to fill out a chart like the one to the right. You might then discuss which of the groups in each empire established its own independent state.

Empire	Culture Groups	When Collapsed
Austro-Hungarian	Hungarians, Germans, Czechs, Slovaks, Croats, Poles . . .	End of World War I
Russian		
Ottoman		

Gifted and Talented Students
Researching Mazzini Giuseppe Mazzini was a dreamer and visionary who believed that the formation of nation-states across Europe would bring peace and justice. Mazzini wrote about his vision. Have students:

- Locate some of Mazzini's writings. (You might suggest students consult one of

the following: Bolton King's *The Life of Mazzini*, Gwilym O. Griffith's *Mazzini: Prophet of Modern Europe,* or E. E. Y. Hales's *Mazzini and the Secret Societies.*)

- Choose one or more passages from Mazzini's writings.
- Read the passages aloud for the class.

For his contribution as a fighter for independence in Italy and in Latin America, Garibaldi was given the title "Hero of Two Worlds." Ask students to read about Garibaldi's campaigns in Latin America.

IN-DEPTH RESOURCES: UNIT 5
Primary Source: Proclamation of 1860, p. 65

MORE ABOUT . . .
Vatican City

Since 1929, Vatican City has been an independent country, the smallest in the world. It is about the size of a city park, with a population of about 1,000, and is contained entirely within the city of Rome. The pope is its absolute ruler. Like any country, it has its own mail and telephone systems. It has a diplomatic corps—its ambassadors are known as legates. Although it has no army or navy, it does have the Swiss Guard, a military unit whose job is to protect the pope and his residence.

OBJECTIVE 4 INSTRUCT

The Rise of Prussia

Key Ideas

- King William I of Prussia appoints Bismarck as prime minister.
- Bismarck goes to war to win two provinces from Denmark.
- The Prussians defeat the Austrians and gain control of a North German Confederation.
- Prussia defeats France, making Prussia the dominant force in Europe.

CRITICAL THINKING TRANSPARENCIES
CT24 The Unification of Germany and Italy

Cavour Looks South As Cavour was uniting the north of Italy, he began to consider the possibility of controlling the south. He secretly started helping nationalist rebels in southern Italy. In May 1860, a small army of Italian nationalists led by a bold and romantic soldier, **Giuseppe Garibaldi** (GAR-uh-BAWL-dee), captured Sicily. In battle, Garibaldi always wore a bright red shirt, as did his followers. As a result, they became known as the **Red Shirts.**

From Sicily, Garibaldi crossed to the Italian mainland and marched north. Volunteers flocked to his banner. In an election, voters gave Garibaldi permission to unite the southern areas he conquered with the Kingdom of Piedmont-Sardinia. Cavour arranged for King Victor Emmanuel II to meet Garibaldi in Naples. "The Red One" willingly agreed to step aside and let the Sardinian king rule.

Challenges After Unification In 1866, the Austrian province of Venetia, which included the city of Venice, became part of Italy. In 1870, Italian forces took over the last part of a territory known as the Papal States. The Roman Catholic popes had governed the territory as both its spiritual and earthly rulers. With this victory, the city of Rome came under Italian control. Soon after, Rome became the capital of the united Kingdom of Italy. The pope, however, would continue to govern a section of Rome known as Vatican City.

Despite unification, Italy suffered from many unsolved problems. Centuries of separation had bred fierce rivalries among the different Italian provinces. The greatest tension arose between the industrialized north and the agricultural south. The people of these two regions had very different ways of life, and they scarcely understood each other's versions of the Italian language. In the Italian parliament, disorganized parties with vague policies constantly squabbled. As a result, prime ministers and cabinets changed frequently.

In addition to its political instability, Italy also faced severe economic problems. Bloody peasant revolts broke out in the south. At the same time, strikes and riots troubled the northern cities. Meanwhile, the Italian government could not deal with the country's economic problems. As a result, Italy entered the 20th century as a poor country.

HISTORYMAKERS

**Giuseppe Garibaldi
1807–1882**

Giuseppe Garibaldi might have been a character out of a romantic novel. Fisherman, trader, naval commander, guerrilla fighter, poet, rancher, teacher, idealistic revolutionary in Europe and South America— Garibaldi captured the imagination of Europe. The red shirts of his soldiers helped spread his fame, but they started out simply as the cheapest way to clothe his soldiers.

The independence of Italy was Garibaldi's great dream. The French writer Alexandre Dumas wrote of him: "Once mention the word independence, or that of Italy, and he becomes a volcano in eruption."

Garibaldi's bravery attracted the attention of U.S. President Abraham Lincoln. In 1861, Lincoln offered him a command in the Civil War. Garibaldi declined for two reasons: he felt Lincoln did not condemn slavery strongly enough, and he told Lincoln that he wanted to command the entire Union Army!

**THINK THROUGH HISTORY
B. Analyzing Causes** Besides their old rivalries, what is another reason why the Italian provinces might have a hard time cooperating?
B. Possible Answers The provinces had no experience in working together. In fact, some had been independent and were used to acting alone.

CASE STUDY: Germany

The Rise of Prussia

Like Italy, Germany also achieved national unity in the mid-1800s. Since 1815, 39 German states had formed a loose grouping called the German Confederation. The two largest states, the Austro-Hungarian Empire and Prussia, dominated the confederation.

Prussia enjoyed several advantages that would eventually help it forge a strong German state. First of all, unlike the Austro-Hungarian Empire, Prussia had a mainly German population. As a result, nationalism actually unified Prussia, while ethnic groups in Austria-Hungary tore it apart. Moreover, Prussia's army was by far the most powerful in central Europe. Finally, Prussia industrialized more quickly than other German states.

Prussia Leads German Unification Like many other European powers, Prussia experienced the disorder of the revolutions of 1848. In that year, Berlin rioters forced the frightened and unstable Prussian king, Frederick William IV, to call a constitutional convention. The convention then drew up a liberal constitution for the kingdom.

In 1861, Wilhelm I succeeded Frederick William to the throne. The strong-minded Wilhelm first moved to reform the army and double the already powerful Prussian

---

Task: Groups of two to three students will research the life of Giuseppe Garibaldi and present an interview with Garibaldi.

Purpose: To explore the character of Garibaldi and learn more about his contribution to Italian unification.

Activity: Students will work together to read more about the life of Garibaldi and choose several interesting incidents from his life and campaigns in Italy. Students will make notes for an interview with Garibaldi, in which one or two students take the role of interviewer and another takes the role of Garibaldi. The interview will focus on one or two incidents in

his life. The interview will elicit not only a narrative of the incidents, but Garibaldi's ideas and feelings about his role as fighter for Italian unification. Students will present the interview for the class.

 ALTERNATIVE ASSESSMENT BOOK
Standards for Evaluating a Cooperative Activity

military. However, his liberal parliament refused him the money for his reforms.

Wilhelm saw the parliament's refusal as a major challenge to his authority. He was supported in his view by the Junkers (YUNG-kuhrz), members of Prussia's wealthy landowning class. The Junkers were strongly conservative and opposed liberal ideas. For that reason, Wilhelm drew all his ministers and army officers from the Junker class. In 1862, to help solve his problem with parliament, Wilhelm chose a conservative Junker named **Otto von Bismarck** as his prime minister. Bismarck was a master of what came to be known as **realpolitik**. This German term means "the politics of reality." The word described tough power politics with no room for idealism. With realpolitik as his style, Bismarck would become one of the commanding figures of German history.

Unable to persuade parliament to grant Wilhelm's desires, Bismarck took a dramatic step. With the king's approval, he declared that he would rule without the consent of parliament and without a legal budget. Those actions were in direct violation of the constitution. In his first speech as prime minister, he defiantly told members of the Prussian parliament, "The great questions of the day will not be settled by speeches or by majority decisions—that was the great mistake of 1848 and 1849—but by blood and iron."

Germany Expands Though he was devoted to country and king, Bismarck was also ambitious. One contemporary described him as a man "who is striving after supreme power, including military power." By working to expand Prussia, he could satisfy both his patriotism and his desire for power. In 1864, Bismarck took the first step toward molding an empire. He formed an alliance between Prussia and Austria. They then went to war against Denmark to win two border provinces, Schleswig and Holstein.

A quick victory increased national pride among Prussians. It also won new respect from other Germans and lent support for Prussia as head of a unified Germany. After the victory, Prussia governed Schleswig, while Austria controlled Holstein. Bismarck suspected that this arrangement would soon lead to friction between the two powers. And such tensions would suit his plans perfectly.

Bismarck Eliminates Austria To disable his powerful rival, Bismarck purposely stirred up border conflicts with Austria over Schleswig and Holstein. The tensions provoked Austria into declaring war on Prussia in 1866. This conflict became known as the Seven Weeks' War. As the name suggests, the war was over quickly. The Prussians used their superior training and equipment to win a smashing victory. They humiliated Austria. The Austrians lost the region of Venetia, which was given to Italy. They also had to accept Prussian annexation of yet more German territory.

With its victory in the Seven Weeks' War, Prussia took control of northern Germany. For the first time, the eastern and western parts of the Prussian kingdom were joined. In 1867, the remaining states of the north joined a North German Confederation, which Prussia dominated completely.

PATTERNS OF CHANGE 617

The Unification of Germany, 1865 – 1871

North Sea
DENMARK
SCHLESWIG
HOLSTEIN
Baltic Sea
Memel
Neman R.
NETHERLANDS
OLDENBURG
Hamburg
MECKLENBURG
EAST PRUSSIA
HANOVER
WEST PRUSSIA
RUSSIAN EMPIRE
WESTPHALIA
BRANDENBURG
Berlin
Vistula R.
Warsaw
BELGIUM
Rhine R.
Elbe R.
Oder R.
HESSE
Frankfurt
SAXONY
Ems
Sedan
LUX.
FRANCE
LORRAINE
ALSACE
WÜRTTEMBURG
BAVARIA
HOHENZOLLERN
Munich
Prague
BOHEMIA
AUSTRIAN EMPIRE
Vienna
SILESIA
Danube R.
SWITZERLAND
ITALY

Legend:
- Prussia, 1865
- Annexed by Prussia, 1866
- Joined Prussia in North German Confederation, 1867
- South German States (joined Prussia to form German Empire, 1871)
- Conquered from France, 1871
- German Empire, 1871

0 — 200 Miles
0 — 400 Kilometers

GEOGRAPHY SKILLBUILDER: Interpreting Maps
1. **Location** What was unusual about the territory of Prussia as it existed in 1865?
2. **Regions** After 1865, what year saw the biggest expansion of Prussian territory?

HISTORYMAKERS
Otto von Bismarck

Bismarck grew up on a country estate and spent several years there as an adult. In his later years, Bismarck often spoke of the time he spent on his estate, living the life of a country gentleman, as one of the happiest and most peaceful of his life and wondered why he had left such a pleasant life for the uncertainties of politics. Ask students to read more about the life of Bismarck and report some interesting personal anecdotes about him.

ASSESS & RETEACH

Section 3 Assessment
Have students work in small groups to discuss the questions and review one another's responses.

Section Quiz
 FORMAL ASSESSMENT
Section Quiz, p. 279

Reteaching Activity
CLASS TIME: 10 MINUTES

To help students understand the development of nation-states in Europe, have them review the events they have listed on the time line. Then have them choose one event and write one paragraph explaining its importance.

CLOSE ACTIVITY

CLASS TIME: 10 MINUTES

Forming and Supporting Opinions
Cavour and Bismarck both used cunning and deceit, and deliberately provoked war, in order to unite a people of common background and culture under a single government. Ask students to write several paragraphs explaining whether or not they believe these two men were justified in their actions. Have volunteers read their paragraphs to the class.

HISTORYMAKERS

Otto von Bismarck
1815–1898

Germans have still not decided how to judge Otto von Bismarck. To some Germans, he was the greatest and noblest of Germany's statesmen. They say he almost single-handedly unified the nation and raised it to greatness. To others, he was a devious politician who abused his powers and led Germany into dictatorship.

Bismarck's complex personality has also fascinated historians. By 1895, 650 books had already been written about his life. His speeches, letters, and his memoirs do not help to simplify him. They show him to be both cunning and deeply religious. At one moment, he could declare "It is the destiny of the weak to be devoured by the strong." At another moment he could claim "We Germans shall never wage aggressive war, ambitious war, a war of conquest."

The Franco-Prussian War By 1867, a few southern German states remained independent of Prussia. The majority of southern Germans were Catholics. So, many in the region resisted domination by a Protestant Prussia. However, Bismarck felt he could win the support of southerners if they faced a threat from outside. He reasoned that a war with France would rally the south.

Bismarck was an expert at manufacturing "incidents" to gain his ends. And he was successful with France. He published an altered version of a diplomatic telegram he had received. The telegram gave a false description of a meeting between Wilhelm I and the French ambassador. In the description, Wilhelm seemed to insult the French. Reacting to the insult, France declared war on Prussia on July 19, 1870.

At once, the Prussian army poured into northern France. In September 1870, the Prussian army surrounded the main French force at Sedan. Among the 80,000 French prisoners taken was Napoleon III himself—a beaten and broken man. Only Paris held out against the Germans. For four months, Parisians withstood a German siege. Finally, hunger forced them to surrender.

The Franco-Prussian War was the final stage in German unification. Now the nationalistic fever also seized people in southern Germany. They finally accepted Prussian leadership.

On January 18, 1871, at the captured French palace of Versailles, King Wilhelm I of Prussia was crowned **kaiser** (KY-zuhr), or emperor. Germans called their empire the Second Reich. (The Holy Roman Empire was the first.) Bismarck had achieved Prussian dominance over Germany and Europe "by blood and iron," as he had set out to do.

The Balance of Power Shifts

The 1815 Congress of Vienna established five Great Powers in Europe—Britain, France, Austria, Prussia, and Russia. The wars of the mid-1800s greatly strengthened one of the Great Powers, as Prussia became Germany. In 1815, the Great Powers were nearly equal in strength. By 1871, however, Britain and Germany were clearly the most powerful—both militarily and economically. Austria, Russia, and Italy lagged far behind. France struggled along somewhere in the middle. The European balance of power had broken down. This shift also found expression in the art of the period. In fact, during that century, artists, composers, and writers pointed to paths that European society should follow.

Background
Food became so scarce during the siege of Paris that people ate sawdust, leather, and rats. Parisians even slaughtered animals in the zoo for food.

Section ❸ Assessment

1. TERMS & NAMES
Identify
• Camillo di Cavour
• Giuseppe Garibaldi
• Red Shirts
• Otto von Bismarck
• realpolitik
• kaiser

2. TAKING NOTES
On your own paper, make a time line like the one below. On it, show the development of independent nation-states in Europe.

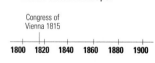
Congress of
Vienna 1815

1800 1820 1840 1860 1880 1900

3. ANALYZING ISSUES
Look at the quotation from Bismarck's "blood and iron" speech (page 617). How would you say his approach to settling political issues differed from the approach of liberals?

THINK ABOUT
• the goals of liberals
• the meaning of the phrase "blood and iron"
• Bismarck's goals and how he attained them

4. ANALYZING THEMES
Revolution How might Cavour and Garibaldi have criticized each other as contributors to Italian unity?

THINK ABOUT
• the personalities of the two men
• methods used by Cavour and Garibaldi to win Italian unity

ANSWERS

1. TERMS & NAMES
Camillo di Cavour, p. 615
Giuseppe Garibaldi, p. 616
Red Shirts, p. 616
Otto von Bismarck, p. 617
realpolitik, p. 617
kaiser, p. 618

2. TAKING NOTES
Possible Responses: Greece

wins independence from Ottomans, 1830; revolts throughout Europe, 1848; Victor Emmanuel II declared king of Italy, 1861; Seven Weeks' War between Prussia and Austria, 1866; Franco-Prussian War, 1870; William I crowned kaiser of new German Empire, 1871.

3. ANALYZING ISSUES
Possible Answers: Liberals wanted government by elected parliaments—issues would be settled by majority decisions. Bismarck preferred to settle issues by "blood and iron"—the blood of soldiers and the iron of weapons (or military equipment).

4. ANALYZING THEMES
Possible Answers: Cavour have criticized Garibaldi for being an impractical idealist was unable to lead a unified country. Garibaldi might have criticized Cavour for being a cold-hearted opportunist wh was more interested in powe than in a unified Italy.

MAIN IDEA

Artistic and intellectual movements both reflected and fueled changes in Europe during the 1800s.

WHY IT MATTERS NOW

Romanticism and realism continue to dominate the novels, dramas, and films produced today.

SETTING THE STAGE European countries passed through severe political troubles during the 1800s. At the same time, two separate artistic and intellectual movements divided the century in half. Thinkers and artists focused on ideas of freedom, the rights of individuals, and an idealistic view of history during the first half of the century. After the great revolutions of 1848, political focus shifted to men who practiced realpolitik. Similarly, intellectuals and artists expressed a "realistic" view of the world. In their view of the world, the rich pursued their selfish interests while ordinary people struggled and suffered.

The Romantic Movement

At the beginning of the 19th century, the Enlightenment idea of reason gradually gave way to another major movement: romanticism. **Romanticism** was a movement in art and ideas. It showed deep interest both in nature and in the thoughts and feelings of the individual. In many ways, romantic thinkers and writers reacted against the ideals of the Enlightenment. Romantics rejected the rigidly ordered world of the middle-class. They turned from reason to emotion, from society to nature. Nationalism also fired the romantic imagination. For example, a fighter for freedom in Greece, Lord Byron, also ranked as one of the leading romantic poets of the time.

The Ideas of Romanticism Emotion, sometimes wild emotion, was a key element of romanticism. Nevertheless, romanticism went beyond feelings. Romantics expressed a wide range of ideas and attitudes. In general, romantic thinkers and artists

- emphasized inner feelings, emotions, imagination
- focused on the mysterious and the supernatural; also, on the odd, exotic, and grotesque or horrifying
- loved the beauties of untamed nature
- idealized the past as a simpler and nobler time
- glorified heroes and heroic actions
- cherished folk traditions, music, and stories
- valued the common people and the individual
- promoted radical change and democracy

Not all romantics gave the same emphasis to these features. The brothers Jakob and Wilhelm Grimm, for example, concentrated on history and the sense of national pride it fostered. During the first half of the 19th century, they collected German fairy tales. They also created a dictionary and grammar of the German language. Both the tales and the dictionary of the Grimm brothers celebrated the spirit of

A. Possible Answer Romantics idealized the past as a simpler nobler time; glorified heroes and their actions; cherished folk traditions, music, and stories.

THINK THROUGH HISTORY
A. Analyzing Causes Which ideas of romanticism would encourage nationalism?

Background
The Grimm brothers also collected tales from other countries: England, Scotland, Ireland, Spain, the Netherlands, Scandinavia, and Serbia.

Though created in the early 20th century, this watercolor of British artist Arthur Rackham is full of romantic fantasy. It illustrates the tale "The Old Woman in the Wood" by Jakob and Wilhelm Grimm.

Nationalist Revolutions Sweep the West **619**

SECTION 4 RESOURCES

PRINT RESOURCES

📖 *IN-DEPTH RESOURCES: UNIT 5*
Guided Reading, p. 59
History Makers: Beethoven, p. 71

📖 *ACCESS FOR STUDENTS ACQUIRING ENGLISH*
Guided Reading (Spanish), p. 243

📖 *FORMAL ASSESSMENT*
Section Quiz, p. 280

📖 *ALTERNATIVE ASSESSMENT BOOK*

TECHNOLOGY RESOURCES

🖥 *WORLD ART AND CULTURES TRANSPARENCIES*
AT53 *Couturiere*

🖥 *CRITICAL THINKING TRANSPARENCIES*
CT60 Chapter 24 Visual Summary

💿 **CD-ROM**
Electronic Library of Primary Sources

🌐 **INTERNET** www.mlworldhistory.com

Section 4 Overview

OBJECTIVES

1️⃣ To define romanticism and give examples of romantic literature and music.

2️⃣ To explain the shift to realism and give examples of realistic art and literature.

CRITICAL THINKING
- Analyzing causes, pp. 619, 623
- Summarizing, p. 620
- Synthesizing, p. 622
- Comparing, p. 622
- Analyzing causes, p. 623

FOCUS
5-Minute Warm-Up

▶ *Clarifying*
Have students answer these questions to help them understand something about a great romantic composer.

1. Read the History Makers on Beethoven on p. 621. What handicaps did Beethoven fight against?

2. How did Beethoven's handicaps affect his work?

🏛 *WARM-UP TRANSPARENCY 24*

OBJECTIVE 1️⃣ INSTRUCT

The Romantic Movement

▶ *Key Ideas*
- Romanticism includes a number of key elements.
- Some romantic writers emphasize emotion, love of nature, history, and individualism, while others focus on the mysterious, the exotic, and the horrifying.
- Romantic composers, the greatest of whom is Beethoven, flourish in the 19th century.

📖 *IN-DEPTH RESOURCES: UNIT 5*
Guided Reading, p. 59

📖 *ACCESS FOR STUDENTS ACQUIRING ENGLISH*
Guided Reading (Spanish), p. 243

620 Chapter 24

SPOTLIGHT ON
Frankenstein

Suggest that students read excerpts from the novel *Frankenstein* and then discuss how it is different from and similar to movies they have seen or ideas they have about the monster.

 ELECTRONIC LIBRARY OF PRIMARY SOURCES
from *Frankenstein*

MORE ABOUT . . .
Romantic Literature

In the United States, Nathaniel Hawthorne (who wrote *The Scarlet Letter*), Herman Melville (who wrote *Moby Dick*), and the short-story writer Edgar Allan Poe were influenced in different ways by romanticism. Poe was a master of Gothic horror and wrote tales of mystery and madness.

MORE ABOUT . . .
Coleridge and Wordsworth

The poets Samuel Taylor Coleridge and William Wordsworth were close friends for many years and influenced each other's work. In 1798 they worked together on a collection of poems, *Lyrical Ballads,* an early example of English romantic poetry. The two men, along with the poet Robert Southey, were known as the Lake Poets because they lived in the Lake District of England.

While Coleridge is most famous for his poetry, his literary criticism was also an important influence on the Romantic Movement.

In William Wordsworth's preface to *Lyrical Ballads,* he wrote that poems should be written in language that was "really used by men," and that poetry should describe "situations from common life."

 ELECTRONIC LIBRARY OF PRIMARY SOURCES
"Kubla Khan"

---

being German. And they celebrated the German spirit long before Germans had united into a single country.

Other writers and artists focused on strong individuals. They glorified real or mythical rebels and leaders, such as Napoleon or the legendary King Arthur. Still others celebrated the beauty and mystery of unspoiled nature. For example, one of France's leading romantic novelists, Amandine Aurore Dupin (better known as George Sand), lovingly described the French countryside and country life. British writer Emily Brontë set her powerful romantic novel, *Wuthering Heights,* in the windswept moors of northern England. The British poet William Blake believed he could "see a World in a Grain of Sand/And a Heaven in a Wild Flower." In painting, English romantic artist Joseph Turner captured the raging of the sea. Another English artist, John Constable, celebrated the peaceful English countryside. Whatever their particular emphasis, romantic writers and artists affected all the arts.

Romanticism in Literature Germany produced one of the earliest and greatest romantic writers. In 1774, Johann Wolfgang von Goethe (YO·hahn VUHLF·gahng fuhn GER·tuh) published *The Sorrows of Young Werther.* Goethe's novel told of a sensitive young man whose hopeless love for a virtuous married woman drives him to suicide.

Victor Hugo led the French romantics. Hugo's huge output of poems, plays, and novels expressed romanticism's revolutionary spirit. His works also reflect the romantic fascination with history and support for the individual. His novels *Les Misérables* and *The Hunchback of Notre Dame* both show the struggles of individuals against a hostile society.

The British romantic poets William Wordsworth and Samuel Taylor Coleridge both honored nature as the source of truth and beauty. To Wordsworth, nature was richly alive. Coleridge, on the other hand, put the accent on horror and the supernatural in his poem "The Rime of the Ancient Mariner." Later English romantic poets, such as Byron, Shelley, and Keats, wrote poems celebrating rebellious heroes, passionate love, and the mystery and beauty of nature. Like many romantics, many of these British poets lived stormy lives and died young. Byron, for example, died at the age of 36, while Shelley died at 29.

The Gothic Novel The Gothic horror story was a form that became hugely popular. These novels often took place in medieval Gothic castles. They were also filled with fearful, violent, sometimes supernatural events. Mary Shelley, wife of the poet Percy Shelley, wrote one of the earliest and most successful Gothic horror novels, *Frankenstein.* The novel told the story of a monster created from the body parts of dead human beings. The following passage shows Mary Shelley's romantic imagination at work. She describes how the idea for the monster took shape. After an evening telling ghost stories with her husband and Lord Byron, the following vision appeared to her:

SPOTLIGHT ON
Frankenstein

In *Frankenstein,* a rational scientist, Dr. Frankenstein, oversteps the limits of humanity by creating life itself. Since his goal is unnatural, he succeeds only in creating a physical monster who cannot live with humans because of his ugliness.

In addition to Gothic horror, the novel embodies a number of major romantic themes. Mary Shelley warns of the danger of humans meddling with nature. Also, despite his horrible appearance, the creature is sensitive and gentle. Like many romantics of Shelley's day, the creature feels lost in an unsympathetic and alien world. Finally, his solitude drives him to madness.

The story of Frankenstein, originally published in 1818, still enjoys an enormous readership. The book has inspired many films—some serious, such as *Frankenstein* with actor Boris Karloff, and some satirical, such as producer Mel Brooks's *Young Frankenstein.*

A VOICE FROM THE PAST
Night waned upon this talk, and even the witching hour had gone by, before we retired to rest. When I placed my head on my pillow, I did not sleep, nor could I be said to think. My imagination, unbidden, possessed and guided me. . . . I saw—with shut eyes, but acute mental vision—I saw the pale student of [unholy] arts kneeling beside the thing he had put together. I saw the hideous phantasm of a man stretched out, and then, on the working of some powerful engine, show signs of life, and stir with an uneasy, half-vital motion.

MARY SHELLEY, Introduction to *Frankenstein*

Background
Dupin used the pen name George Sand because she knew that critics would not take a woman writer seriously.

Background
Victor Hugo championed the cause of freedom in France. When Napoleon III overthrew the Second Republic, Hugo left France in protest.

B. Possible Answers Beauty, mystery, terror, heroism, passion, love, tragedy, isolation.
THINK THROUGH HISTORY
B. Summarizing What are some of the feelings that are key to romantic literature and art?

TEACHING OPTIONS	
EXPLORING PRIMARY SOURCES	**CONNECTIONS ACROSS THE CURRICULUM**

A Voice From the Past Mary Shelley (1787–1851) was the daughter of famous parents—the radical English philosopher William Godwin and the free-thinking feminist Mary Wollstonecraft. Mary Godwin was just 16 when she met and ran away with the romantic poet Percy Bysshe Shelley. *Frankenstein* was first published in 1818 and was a great success. In an introduction written in 1831 for a new edition of the novel, Mary explains the circumstances during which she conceived the idea for the novel. Ask students to read the author's introduction, as well as the Preface, which she claims was written primarily by her husband.

Literature Many of the short lyric poems of romantic poets such as Wordsworth, Coleridge, Keats, Byron, and Shelley are suitable for presentation and discussion in class. Ask students to work in pairs to research several poems by romantic poets that demonstrate various characteristics of romantic poetry, such as the mysterious or exotic, the supernatural or horrifying, the joys of nature, and so on. Have them give dramatic readings of the poems and explain how the poems represent elements of romanticism.

Background
To express powerful emotions, romantic composers increased the size of symphony orchestras. They added large numbers of wind, brass, and percussion instruments.

Romantic Composers Emphasize Emotion Emotion dominated the music produced by romantic composers. Romantic composers moved away from the tightly controlled, formal compositions of the Enlightenment period. Instead, they celebrated heroism and villainy, tragedy and joy, with a new power of expression.

One of romanticism's first composers rose to become its greatest: Ludwig van Beethoven (LOOD·vihg vahn BAY·toh·vuhn). In his early years, Beethoven wrote the classical music of the Enlightenment. But in later years, he turned to romantic compositions. His Ninth Symphony soars, celebrating freedom, dignity, and triumph.

While they never matched Beethoven's greatness, later romantic composers also appealed to the hearts and souls of their listeners. Robert Schumann's compositions sparkle with merriment. Like many romantic composers, Felix Mendelssohn drew on literature, such as Shakespeare's *A Midsummer Night's Dream*, as the inspiration for his music. Polish composer and concert pianist Frederic Chopin (SHOH·pan) was popular both with other musicians and with the public. Chopin's compositions, such as his first and second piano concertos, contain melodies that are still familiar today.

Romanticism made music a popular art form. As music became part of middle-class life, musicians and composers became popular heroes of romanticism. Composer and pianist Franz Liszt (lihst), for example, achieved earnings and popularity equal to that of today's rock stars.

The Shift to Realism

By the middle of the 19th century, rapid industrialization had a deep effect on everyday life in Europe. And this change began to make the dreams of the romantics seem pointless. In literature and the visual arts, **realism** tried to show life as it is, not as it should be. Realist painting reflected the increasing political importance of the working class in the 1850s. The growing class of industrial workers lived grim lives in dirty, crowded cities. Along with paintings, novels proved especially suited to describing workers' suffering. The interest in science and the scientific method during this period encouraged this "realistic" approach to art and literature. Science operated through objective observation and the reporting of facts. That new invention, the camera, also recorded objective and precise images. In the same way, realist authors observed and reported as precisely and objectively as they could.

Writers Study Society Realism in literature flourished in France with writers such as Honoré de Balzac and Emile Zola. Balzac wrote a massive series of almost one hundred novels entitled *The Human Comedy*. These stories detail the lives of over 2,000 people from all levels of French society following the Revolution. They also describe in detail the brutal struggle for wealth and power among France's business class. Zola's explosive novels scandalized France at the end of the 1800s. He exposed the miseries of French workers in small shops, factories, and coal mines. His revelations shocked readers. His work spurred reforms of labor laws and working conditions in France.

The famous English realist novelist, Charles Dickens, created unforgettable characters and scenes. Many were humorous, but others showed the despair of London's

**Ludwig van Beethoven
1770–1827**

A genius of European music, Beethoven suffered the most tragic disability a composer can endure. At the age of 30, he began to go deaf. His deafness grew worse for 19 years. By 1819, it was total.

At first, Beethoven's handicap barely affected his career. His composing and concerts went on as before. By 1802, however, he knew that his hearing would only worsen. He suffered then from bouts of depression. The depressions would bring him to the brink of suicide. Nonetheless, he would rebound:

. . . It seemed unthinkable for me to leave the world forever before I had produced all that I felt called upon to produce. . . .

After 1819, Beethoven's friends had to write their questions to him in notebooks. He continued to compose, however, and left many "sketchbooks" of musical ideas he would never hear.

HISTORYMAKERS
Ludwig van Beethoven

As the son of an alcoholic father, Beethoven had a difficult childhood. As an adult, he was irritable, odd, and hard to get along with. Ask students to read more about the personal life of Beethoven and relate some interesting anecdotes to the class.

 IN-DEPTH RESOURCES: UNIT 5
History Makers: Beethoven, p. 71

MORE ABOUT . . .
Romanticism

Romanticism was a movement based on emotional sensitivity and expression. The romantics' emotionalism often led to what many people considered scandalous behavior. The poet Percy Shelley ran away with Mary Godwin while he was still married to another woman. (They were later married after Shelley's wife died.) The poet Lord Byron, the writer Goethe, and the composer Liszt all had numerous love affairs. Despite Liszt's popularity, England's Queen Victoria and Prince Albert refused to attend his concert in London because of his scandalous reputation.

OBJECTIVE ② INSTRUCT

The Shift to Realism

▶ *Key Ideas*
- With industrialization and a new interest in the scientific method, a realistic approach to art and literature emerges.
- Photography, first invented by Daguerre, becomes the art of the new industrial age.
- French and English realistic writers expose the misery of the working poor.

TEACHING OPTION | **BLOCK SCHEDULING** | **COOPERATIVE ACTIVITY: Presenting a Romantic Composer** | **CLASS TIME 20 MINUTES**

Task: Students will research one of the romantic composers and give a presentation about his work.

Purpose: To learn more about romanticism in music.

Activity: Groups of students will research a romantic composer and prepare a brief biographical report. Students will also obtain recordings of some of the composer's works and research some background on the musical pieces. The groups will

then give a presentation that includes playing one or two selections from the composer's work in class. The presentation will also include a biographical sketch, along with a picture of the composer, and an explanation of how the music reflects romantic ideas.

 Building a Portfolio: If students choose to include this work in their portfolio, have them include a note indicating the part they played in the presentation.

ALTERNATIVE ASSESSMENT BOOK
Standards for Evaluating a Cooperative Activity

Standards for Evaluation
Presentations should . . .
- include a concise biographical sketch
- include appropriate musical selections
- show how the music embodies romanticism

Teacher's Edition **621**

History Through Art

Artistic Movements

Romanticism included a wide variety of artistic styles. Some artists focused almost entirely on painting historical scenes. Others focused on landscape paintings with broad panoramas. In France, a small group of painters known as the Barbizon School (named for the village of Barbizon in the French forest of Fountainebleau) concentrated on painting small sections of a landscape—a field, a meadow, even a single tree.

 WORLD ART AND CULTURES TRANSPARENCIES
AT53 *Couturiere*

MORE ABOUT . . .
Realism

Many of Courbet's great realist paintings portray rural society as he had seen it in his birthplace of Ornans in provincial France. Courbet tried to show the people and events of rural society realistically, rather than sentimentally or satirically. He showed peasants as possessing an inherent dignity and worth, and this offended conservative elements in French society.

MORE ABOUT . . .
Impressionism

The term *impressionism* was coined in 1874 when Claude Monet exhibited a painting entitled *Impression: Sunrise*. A hostile art critic, unused to the unfinished, sketchy look of this new style of art, dismissed the entire art show as "impressionist." The term, which came to be applied to a whole group of artists, was intended as an insulting, derogatory name, but it soon became an expression of admiration.

Artistic Movements

In the 19th century, as always, artistic movements reflected the social conditions of the time. During the first half of the century, common people began to fight for political power. During that same period, romanticism was the dominant artistic style. By mid-century, political realism had taken over. At the same time, art began to celebrate working, sweating, everyday people. But the romantic ideal did not die. By the end of the century, a new movement called impressionism portrayed the life of middle-class people as a beautiful dream.

Realism

Realist artists reacted against the dreams of the romantics. These artists believed that their art should portray people as they really were, not as they should be. *The Winnowers*, by Gustave Courbet, the most famous realist, shows the world of everyday work. The winnowers are removing hulls from newly harvested grain. Courbet does not romanticize the work. He records it.

Romanticism

Romantic landscape artists idealized nature. Some emphasized the harmony between humans and nature. Others showed nature's power and mystery, as in this painting, *Moonrise Over the Sea*, by German artist Caspar David Friedrich. Still other romantic artists focused on heroes and scenes from history, legend, or literature.

Impressionism

Impressionists aimed at capturing their immediate "impression" of a brief moment. They used bright colors and loose brushwork to catch the fleeting light that sparkles and shimmers. As a result, *Poppies at Argenteuil* by Claude Monet shows less attention to exact "realistic" detail than does *The Winnowers*. It also does not express the sense of serene mystery of *Moonrise Over the Sea*.

Connect *to* History

Synthesizing Artists choose specific elements for their paintings to create the world they want to show. Compare the settings, use of color and light, sharpness of line, and atmosphere of these paintings.

 SEE SKILLBUILDER HANDBOOK, PAGE 1007

Connect *to* Today

Comparing Look for examples of modern art in books and magazines. Show examples of paintings where artists still use techniques that could be called romantic or realist or impressionist.

Connect *to* History	Connect *to* Today
Synthesizing Suggest that students make a chart like the one here to compare the three paintings.	**Comparing** Students will show examples of modern art that reflect techniques and points of view that are recognizably similar to those of romantic, realist, and impressionist artists of the 19th century.

	Moonrise Over the Sea	The Winnowers	Poppies at Argenteuil
setting			
color and light			
sharpness of line			
atmosphere			

working poor. In this passage, Dickens describes the gloom of working-class life:

A VOICE FROM THE PAST
It was a Sunday evening in London, gloomy, close, and stale. . . . Melancholy streets, in a penitential garb of soot, steeped the souls of the people who were condemned to look at them out of windows, in dire despondency. . . . No pictures, no unfamiliar animals, no rare plants or flowers. . . . Nothing for the spent toiler to do, but to compare the monotony of his seventh day with the monotony of his six days, think what a weary life he led, and make the best of it.

CHARLES DICKENS, *Little Dorrit*

Photographers Capture the Passing Moment As realist painters and writers detailed the lives of actual people, photographers could record an instant in time with scientific precision. The first practical photographs were called daguerreotypes (duh·GEHR·uh·TYPS). They were named after their French inventor, Louis Daguerre. Daguerre was an artist who created scenery for theaters. To improve the realism of his scenery, Daguerre developed his photographic invention. The images produced in his daguerrotypes were startlingly real and won him worldwide fame.

Daguerrotype prints were made on metal. However, the British inventor William Talbot invented a light-sensitive paper that he used to produce photographic negatives. The advantage of paper was that many prints could be made from one negative. The Talbot process also allowed photos to be reproduced in books and newspapers. Mass distribution gained a wide audience for the realism of photography. With its scientific, mechanical, and mass-produced features, photography was the art of the new industrial age.

"Ships at Low Tide," an early photograph taken in 1844 by William Talbot.

Impressionists React Against Realism Beginning in the 1860s, a group of painters in Paris reacted against the realistic style. Instead of showing life "as it really is," they tried giving their impression of a subject or a moment in time. For this reason, this style of art came to be known as impressionism. Fascinated by light, impressionist artists used pure, shimmering colors to capture a moment seen at a glance.

Artists like Edouard Manet (mah·NAY), Claude Monet (moh·NAY), Edgar Degas (duh·GAH), and Pierre-Auguste Renoir (ruhn·WHAR) also found new subjects for their art. Unlike the realists, impressionists showed a more positive view of the new urban society in Western Europe. Instead of abused workers, they showed shop clerks and dock workers enjoying themselves in dance halls and cafés. They painted performers in the theater and circuses. And they glorified the delights of the life of the rising middle class.

Section 4 Assessment

1. TERMS & NAMES
Identify
• romanticism
• realism
• impressionism

2. TAKING NOTES
Using a chart like the one below, contrast romanticism, realism, and impressionism. For each movement, provide a brief description, the social conditions that each reflects, and representative artists.

Movement	Description	Social Conditions	Artists
Romanticism			
Realism			
Impressionism			

3. ANALYZING CAUSES
How might a realist novel bring about changes in society? Describe the steps by which this might happen.
THINK ABOUT
• the conditions described in realist novels
• who reads realist novels
• how political change takes place

4. THEME ACTIVITY
Revolution Listen to a symphony or concerto by Beethoven. Imagine that you are a music critic who has previously heard only formal classical compositions. Write a review of Beethoven's piece. Make the theme of your review the revolutionary quality of Beethoven's music—which you may admire or dislike.

Nationalist Revolutions Sweep the West **623**

Chapter 24 Assessment

TERMS & NAMES
1. creoles, p. 604
2. Simón Bolívar, p. 605
3. conservatives, p. 609
4. liberals, p. 609
5. nationalism, p. 6
6. Camillo di Ca
7. Otto von B
8. realpoli
9. roman
10. rea

Teacher's Edition **623**

TERMS & NAMES

Briefly explain the importance of each of the following to the revolutions in Latin America or Europe.

1. creoles
2. Simón Bolívar
3. conservatives
4. liberals
5. nationalism
6. Camillo di Cavour
7. Otto von Bismarck
8. realpolitik
9. romanticism
10. realism

Interact _with_ History

On page 602, you were asked to create a symbol for your newly independent country. Show your symbol to the class. Explain the elements of your design and what they are intended to express. With your classmates' comments in mind, what might you change in your design?

REVIEW QUESTIONS

SECTION 1 *(pages 603–608)*

Latin American Peoples Win Independence

11. What caused the creoles in South America to rebel against Spain?

12. What role did Agustín de Iturbide play in the independence of Mexico and of the countries of Central America?

13. Who was Dom Pedro, and what role did he play in Brazil's move to independence?

SECTION 2 *(pages 609–612)*

Revolutions Disrupt Europe

14. Why did so many people in Europe and North America support the revolution of Greek nationalists against the Ottoman Empire?

15. How successful were the revolts of 1848? Explain.

SECTION 3 *(pages 613–618)*

Nationalism

Case Studies: Italy and Germany

16. How did nationalism in the 1800s work as a force both for disunity and for unity?

17. What approaches did Camillo di Cavour use to try to acquire more territory for Piedmont-Sardinia?

18. What strategy did Otto von Bismarck use to try to make Prussia the leader of a united Germany?

SECTION 4 *(pages 619–623)*

Revolutions in the Arts

19. Name two ideas or attitudes of the romantic movement that reflected the ideals of nationalism.

20. What new conditions caused a change in the arts from romanticism to realism?

REVIEW QUESTIONS

Answers will vary.

11. They resented that the peninsulares held nearly all high government offices. Their loyalty to Spain evaporated when Napoleon set his brother on the Spanish throne.

12. Iturbide began by opposing the Mexican revolution but wound up as the leader who proclaimed Mexico's independence. He tried to keep control of Central America, but when he fell from power after two years, Central America declared its independence from Mexico.

13. Dom Pedro, the ruler of Brazil, was the son of the king of Portugal; in 1822, he officially declared Brazil's independence from Portugal.

14. Both Europeans and Americans respected ancient Greek culture and so felt a sympathy for the Greeks of their own time. Russians felt a kinship with Greek Orthodox Christians.

15. Not very successful, because by 1849, Europe had practically returned to its pre-1848 status.

16. Disunity—It broke up centuries-old empires into nation-states; Unity—It inspired people with the same history, culture, and language to form nation-states.

17. He used careful diplomacy and well-chosen alliances, as well as cunning.

18. He provoked Austria and France into separate wars, reasoning that the two wars would unite the German people behind Prussia.

19. The Romantic Movement emphasized heroic actions, promoted radical change, favored democracy, was concerned with common people. Many nationalists shared these ideals.

20. Workers in the Industrial Age often lived grim lives in dirty, crowded cities.

Visual Summary

Nationalist Revolutions Sweep the West

Politics — **Milestones of the 1800s** — **Arts**

Politics	Year	Arts
1804 Haiti gains independence from France	1800	**1804** Beethoven completes his First Symphony
	1810	**1812** The Brothers Grimm publish a collection of fairy tales
1814 The Congress of Vienna begins		
1821 Bolívar wins Venezuela's independence from Spain	1820	**1818** Mary Shelley's *Frankenstein* is published
1824 Bolívar completes the liberation of Latin America		**1824** Lord Byron dies in Greece; Beethoven completes the Ninth Symphony—his last
1830 Greece wins full independence; revolts break out in France, Belgium, and Poland	1830	
		1831 Victor Hugo publishes *The Hunchback of Notre Dame*
	1840	**1836** Charles Dickens becomes an overnight success with his novel *Pickwick Papers*
1848 Revolutions sweep Europe	1850	**1839** Louis Daguerre reveals his photographic process
		1849 Gustave Courbet's early paintings receive public recognition
1861 Alexander II frees the serfs in Russia	1860	**1867** Claude Monet begins painting in the impressionist style
1870 Italy is unified	1870	
1871 The Franco-Prussian War ends; Germany is unified		
	1880	

Interact _with_ History

Possible Responses: Students may now revise their symbols to reflect the comments they hear from the class. For example, students might suggest a different animal to represent the fictional country or offer advice on colors or symbols. Ask students to display their new designs in the classroom.

CRITICAL THINKING

1. GARIBALDI'S CHOICE

THEME **POWER AND AUTHORITY** Giuseppe Garibaldi stepped aside to let Victor Emmanuel II rule areas that Garibaldi had conquered in southern Italy. Why do you think he made that choice?

2. NATIONALISM

Using a chart like the one below, describe the nationalist movement in each of the following countries and the results of those movements.

Country	Nationalism and its Results
Mexico	
Greece	
Italy	
Germany	

3. THE MEANS TO VICTORY

In the 1800s, revolutionaries often fought with inferior weapons and scarce supplies. How do you think nationalism might help revolutionaries overcome the disadvantages of old weapons and poor supplies to win a war for national independence? Explain.

4. ANALYZING PRIMARY SOURCES

In a speech to the German parliament in 1888, Otto von Bismarck called for further expansion of the army. In the following quote from that speech, "the Iron Chancellor" explains why Germany must always be prepared for war.

A VOICE FROM THE PAST
When I say that we must strive continually to be ready for all emergencies, I advance the proposition that, on account of our geographical position, we must make greater efforts than other powers would be obliged to make in view of the same ends. We lie in the middle of Europe. We have at least three fronts on which we can be attacked. France has only an eastern boundary; Russia only its western, exposed to assault. . . . So we are spurred forward on both sides to endeavors which perhaps we would not make otherwise.
OTTO VON BISMARCK, speech to the German parliament on February 6, 1888.

- According to Bismarck, what key factor makes Germany a potential target for invasion? Why?
- Do you think Bismarck might have been overstating the threat to Germany? Explain.

CHAPTER ACTIVITIES

1. LIVING HISTORY: Unit Portfolio Project

THEME **REVOLUTION** Your unit portfolio project focuses on showing the similarities and differences among revolutions (see page 509). For Chapter 24, you might use one of the following ideas to add to your portfolio.

- Ask classmates to role-play bystanders present at Padre Hidalgo's *grito de Dolores*. Ask them to express their feelings about what they have witnessed. Audiotape their comments and use them to write a newspaper report about Mexicans' reactions to the event.
- Write a speech that might have been delivered to a rally somewhere in Europe. Urge the country's leaders to help the Greeks in their struggle for independence from the Ottoman Empire.
- Create a "How-to Booklet for Nationalists," based on the strategies used either by Cavour or by Bismarck.

2. CONNECT TO TODAY: Research Project

THEME **CULTURAL INTERACTION** Romanticism and realism in the arts reflected social and political conditions. In various forms, these two artistic movements still exist today. Create a chart comparing romantic and realistic aspects of modern films.

Use the Internet, newspapers, magazines, or your own personal experience to search for romantic and realistic portrayals of social and political conditions in movies today.

- For your chart, make two lists—one for examples of modern films that are romantic and one for films that are realistic. Include still shots from movies that support your findings.
- In your search, consider movies from at least three countries.

3. INTERPRETING A TIME LINE

Revisit the unit time line on pages 508–509. If you were shown only the period from 1820 to 1848, what fate would you predict for Europe's old order? Why?

FOCUS ON **POLITICAL CARTOONS**

The 19th-century French cartoonist Charles Philipon was testing a law to see how far away an artist could get from the true features of Louis-Philippe before being condemned to prison and a fine. Since the French word *poire* ("pear") also means "fool,"

- how does the cartoonist show King Louis-Philippe developing as a monarch?
- what do you think was the legal fate of the cartoonist?

Connect to History What right was Charles Philipon standing up for by drawing his cartoon and testing the law?

LES POIRES,

Vendues pour payer les 6,000 fr. d'amende du journal le *Charivari*.

(CHEZ AUBERT, GALERIE VÉRO-DODAT.)

CRITICAL THINKING

Canton, China, about 1800

In this painting, the artist has included a wealth of detail that captures the era of Western expansion into Asia and Africa. On the left side of the painting, the flags of five European nations and the United States fly over the Canton harbor. The white, neoclassical architecture of the foreign warehouses and offices stands in stark contrast to the houses and river boats of the Chinese.

Canton (now called Guangzhou) was founded on the Pearl River sometime between 1111 and 771 B.C. The area's mild climate and abundant rainfall made it a major agricultural region. Canton was divided into sections by a series of high walls, parts of which can be seen in this painting. They were demolished in the 1920s. The painting also shows several types of Chinese sampans and junks— river boats that serve as homes and floating businesses to many Chinese families.

As a major trading center, Canton was a prime target for foreigners seeking to open China to Western trade. In the mid 1800s, British and French forces defeated Chinese forces in two Opium Wars. As part of the peace settlement, the city had to open its gates to Western businesses and trade. In response, Chinese patriots in Canton formed secret societies whose goal was to purge China of all foreign influence.

Industrialism and the Race for Empire
1700-1914

626

The flags of numerous nations fly along the harbor in Canton, China, in this scene painted by an unknown Chinese artist. By the late 1800s, the nations of Europe had built far-reaching empires that included much of Africa and parts of Asia.

627

Previewing the Unit

This unit describes the effects of the Industrial Revolution on Western nations and the nations' race to divide Asia and Africa among themselves. Colonial rule brings more hardships than benefits to native peoples, who eventually rebel against Western rulers.

During the 1800s, Britain, the United States, and some European countries undergo great changes as a result of the Industrial Revolution. The widening gap between rich and poor prompts a series of social and political reforms.

Nations in Western Europe and North America, along with Australia and New Zealand, adopt democratic institutions, but some of these nations also suppress their native populations. Changes in the arts and sciences transform people's daily lives and create a mass culture.

With their superior technology and weapons, Western nations compete to acquire territory in Africa, Asia, and the South Pacific. The colonies are rich in natural resources and markets for Western goods. Native resistance movements rebel against colonial rule.

Countries around the world must adapt to contact with Western nations. China falls under foreign domination, but Japan and Korea respond by modernizing their countries. Although Latin American nations free themselves from colonialism, they remain economically and politically unstable.

Industrialism and the Race for Empire

Teaching Strategies

Formulating Historical Questions
You may wish to encourage students to formulate questions concerning the events, patterns, and personalities featured in the Unit Time Lines. Such questions would deal with the causes of events, the reasons that made them so important, or the motivations for the actions of certain historical figures.

Using Historical Questioning
You might encourage students to develop questions to help them determine the factors that underlie events and personalities. For example, with a statement such as "**1893 Vietnam** France takes over Indochina," students might ask questions such as:

- How did the French go about taking control of Vietnam?
- Why did the French want territory in Southeast Asia?
- What were the reactions of the Vietnamese to attempts at a takeover?
- What were the long-term effects of French control on Vietnam and the Vietnamese?
- How did French control in Vietnam affect other European and Asian countries?

The results of this questioning process not only will bring students to a fuller understanding of the French take-over in Vietnam but also will help them to develop an essential skill for historical inquiry.

Industrialism and the Race for Empire

	1800	1815	1830	1845	186

CHAPTER 25 1700–1900
The Industrial Revolution

1700–1815

1701 **Britain** Jethro Tull invents seed drill	1793 **U.S.** Eli Whitney invents cotton gin
1733 **Britain** John Kay invents flying shuttle	1807 **U.S.** Robert Fulton launches steamboat, the *Clermont*
1764 **Britain** James Hargreaves invents spinning jenny	
1776 **Britain** Adam Smith publishes *The Wealth of Nations*	1811 **Britain** Luddites attack factories
	1813 **U.S.** Lowell textile factories open

1830 Britain Rail line between Liverpool and Manchester opened

1848 Germany Marx and Engels publish *The Communist Manifesto*

1850 Britain Population of city of Manchester reaches 300,000

CHAPTER 26 1815–1914
An Age of Democracy and Progress

1800s *United States* ▶

1832 Britain First Reform Bill passes

1837 Britain Victoria becomes queen

1838 Britain Chartist movement presents demands on People's Charter

1840 New Zealand Maoris sign treaty to accept British rule

1845 Ireland Great potato famine begins

1847 Mexico U.S. wins Mexican-American War

1848 U.S. Woman suffragists hold Seneca Falls Convention

1859 Britain Charles Darwin presents theory of evolution

CHAPTER 27 1850–1914
The Age of Imperialism

1800s *India* ▶

1853 Ottoman Empire Crimean War with Russia breaks out

1857 India Sepoy Mutiny

CHAPTER 28 1800–1914
Transformations Around the Globe

1823 U.S. President Monroe issues Monroe Doctrine

1833 Mexico Santa Anna becomes president

1839 China China and Britain fight first Opium War

1840s Mexico Benito Juárez begins liberal reform movement

1848 U.S. Treaty of Guadalupe Hidalgo adds California and other southwestern states to U.S.

1853 China Taiping rebels capture Nanjing and declare it new capital

1854 Japan Treaty of Kanagawa gives U.S. access to two ports

1800	1815	1830	1845	1860

MULTIPLE LEARNING STYLES

Kinesthetic Learners You may point out to students that many of the elements featured in the Unit 6 time line concern science and technology. Those two factors actually played a major role in the empire building occurring around the world during the 19th and early 20th centuries.

Have students create their own time lines that focus on the progress of science and technology. Stress to students that they need not follow the format of the Unit Time Lines. Show them other formats in their textbook or other books.

CONNECTIONS ACROSS TIME AND PLACE

Women in the 19th Century
You might ask interested students to do research and write a play scene dramatizing an event in the life of a woman or group of women appearing in the Unit 6 time line (Queen Victoria, woman suffragists, Empress Cixi). The scene should show an understanding of

the women's characters and of the importance of the event in their lives.

If you judge that the rest of the class might benefit from a scene (for example, if it provides insights into the woman and her life), you might ask if some students wish to present a reading of the scene in class.

1863 *France* Martin brothers develop open-hearth steel furnace

1866 *Sweden* Alfred Nobel invents dynamite

1875 *Britain* Labor unions win right to strike

1886 *U.S.* Forerunner of AFL labor union forms

1896 *U.S.* Henry Ford builds his first automobile

1800s *Germany* ▶

1860s *France* Louis Pasteur develops process of pasteurization

1865 *U.S.* Civil War ends

1867 *Canada* Dominion of Canada is formed

1871 *France* Paris Commune takes control of Paris

1875 *France* Third Republic begins

1879 *U.S.* Thomas Edison invents light bulb

1894 *France* Captain Alfred Dreyfus found guilty of espionage

1901 *Britain* Queen Victoria dies

1903 *Britain* Emmeline Pankhurst forms Women's Social and Political Union

1908 *U.S.* Henry Ford introduces the Model T

1869 *Egypt* Suez Canal completed

1871 *Congo* Stanley finds Dr. Livingstone in central Africa

1884-85 *Germany* Berlin Conference divides Africa among European nations

1885 *India* Formation of the Indian National Congress

1889 *Ethiopia* Menelik II leads Ethiopia

1893 *Vietnam* France takes over Indochina

1898 *Hawaii* U.S. annexes Hawaii

1898 *Philippines* U.S. acquires Philippine Islands

1902 *South Africa* Boer War ends

1905 *East Africa* Maji Maji rebellion

1907 *Persia* Russia and Britain divide Persia into spheres of influence

1908 *Persia* Oil discovered

1861 *China* Empress Cixi begins reign

1867 *Japan* Meiji era begins a period of modernization

1867 *Mexico* Juárez reelected president after France defeated

1868 *Cuba* Ten-year struggle for independence from Spain begins

1876 *Mexico* Porfirio Díaz comes to power

1894 *Korea* Sino-Japanese War begins

1898 *Cuba* Spanish-American War begins

1900 *China* Boxer Rebellion protests foreign influence in China

1904 *Manchuria* Russo-Japanese War for possession of Manchuria

1910 *Korea* Japan annexes Korea

1910 *Mexico* Mexican Revolution begins

1912 *China* Qing Dynasty falls; Sun Yixian elected president

1914 *Panama* Panama Canal opens

Living History
Unit 6 Portfolio Project

THEME Empire Building

Your portfolio for Unit 6 will follow the growth of nations as they build empires and dominate other cultures. You will record not only the effects on the empire-building nations, but also the effects of their colonizing on the lands and peoples whom they take over.

Living History Project Choices
Each Chapter Assessment offers you choices of ways to show the building of empires in that chapter. Activities include the following:

Chapter 25 debate, letter, poster

Chapter 26 handbill, editorial, political cartoon

Chapter 27 script, diary, display

Chapter 28 debate, advertisement, action figure

◀ 1800s *Japan*

Time Line **629**

Portfolio Projects

Empire Building Portfolio projects suggested for Unit 6 deal with the military, economic, social, and political aspects of empire building—from the point of view of both the colonizers and the colonized. Some features of the aspects of empire building covered in the projects include:

- the role of industrialization in enabling a nation to expand its territory and power
- the treatment of colonized peoples
- human rights in colonized territories
- how some nations try to deal with increasing foreign influence
- the problems caused by foreign economic competition from a powerful industrialized nation
- the vestiges of colonialist influence today.

Projects for Linguistic Learners
Portfolio projects for Unit 6 offer numerous possibilities for those students who learn best through verbal media (either oral or written). Those who excel in the spoken word may wish to participate in such debates as the one in Chapter 27 about the U.S. colonization of the Philippines.

Students who best display their knowledge in written form may decide to write a letter to the editor about the influx of cheap foreign products in an unindustrialized country or compose an editorial for a 19th-century New Zealand newspaper concerning Maori land rights.

The Western Civilization Videodisc

SECTION J: Industrial, Political and Social Revolutions, 1815–1850

Side One: Frame 33458

SECTION K: Colonialism, Nationalism and Militarism, 1850–1914

Side One: Frame 36067

Universal Play Button

See Master Guide, page 217 for Section J, page 240 for Section K.

Teacher's Edition **629**

PLANNING GUIDE
The Industrial Revolution

	Key Ideas	COPY MASTERS	ASSESSMENT
SECTION 1 The Beginnings of Industrialization *pp. 633–637*	In Britain, changes in agriculture lay the foundations for the Industrial Revolution. Other factors—including ample resources, an expanding economy, and political stability—provide the conditions for the rapid growth of industry.	*In-Depth Resources: Unit 6* • **Guided Reading,** p. 1 • **Primary Source:** from "The Opening of the Liverpool to Manchester Railway," p. 8 • **History Makers:** James Watt, p. 15	P E *Section 1 Assessment,* p. 637 *Formal Assessment* • Section Quiz, p. 289 *Alternative Assessment Book* • Standards for Evaluating a Product or Performance
SECTION 2 Patterns of Change: Industrialization Case Study: Manchester *pp. 638–642*	Industrialization transforms British society: cities grow, work patterns change, and a middle class emerges. The city of Manchester becomes a notable example of the benefits and drawbacks of the new industrial age.	*In-Depth Resources: Unit 6* • **Guided Reading,** p. 2 • **Geography Application:** British Population Moves to the Cities, p. 6 • **Primary Source:** Testimony on Child Labor in Britain, p. 9 • **Literature:** from *Mary Barton,* p. 12	P E *Section 2 Assessment,* p. 642 *Formal Assessment* • Section Quiz, p. 290 *Alternative Assessment Book* • Standards for Evaluating a Cooperative Activity
SECTION 3 Industrialization Spreads *pp. 643–646*	Industrial technologies travel from Britain to America, causing an industrial boom in the United States. Industrialization also spreads to continental Europe and contributes to the rise of imperialism.	*In-Depth Resources: Unit 6* • **Guided Reading,** p. 3 • **Primary Source:** "Life in a New England Factory," from *Voice of Industry,* p. 10	P E *Section 3 Assessment,* p. 646 *Formal Assessment* • Section Quiz, p. 291 *Alternative Assessment Book* • Standards for Evaluating a Cooperative Activity
SECTION 4 An Age of Reform *pp. 647–653*	Industrialization provokes positive and negative reactions in society. Some philosophers extol the virtues of free market capitalism, while others promote socialism, unionization, and a variety of reform movements designed to blunt the harsh effects of industrialism.	*In-Depth Resources: Unit 6* • **Guided Reading,** p. 4 • **Skillbuilder Practice:** Developing Historical Perspective, p. 5 • **Primary Source:** from *The Wealth of Nations,* p. 11 • **History Makers:** Saint-Simon, p. 16 • **Connections Across Time and Cultures:** Enlightenment Ideals in an Industrial Age, p. 17	P E *Section 4 Assessment,* p. 652 *Formal Assessment* • Section Quiz, p. 292 *Alternative Assessment Book* • Standards for Evaluating a Cooperative Activity
CHAPTER RESOURCES	**Chapter Overview** During the 1800s, Britain, the United States, and some European countries undergo a rapid process of industrialization. The Industrial Revolution creates great wealth but also great social and economic inequality, prompting a backlash of reform.	*Telescoping the Times* • Chapter Summary, pp. 97–99 *Planning for Block Schedules*	P E *Chapter Assessment,* pp. 654–655 *Chapter Activities,* p. 655 *Formal Assessment* • Chapter Test, forms A and B, pp. 293–298 ■ *Test Generator* *Alternative Assessment Book*

TECHNOLOGY

  Warm-Up Transparency 25

 Patterns of Interaction:
Technology Transforms an Age

INTERNET RESOURCES
www.mlworldhistory.com

    Warm-Up Transparency 25

 Geography Transparencies
• G25 The Industrial Revolution in Great Britain, 1850

World Art and Cultures Transparencies
• AT54 *Arkwright's Cotton Mill at Comford, Derbyshire, England*

Electronic Library of Primary Sources
• from "Child Labor in the Mines"
• "The Sentencing of the Luddites"

  Warm-Up Transparency 25

World Art and Cultures Transparencies
• AT55 Monet's *Saint Lazare Train Station, the Normandy Train*

Electronic Library of Primary Sources
• from *A New England Girlhood*

INTERNET RESOURCES
www.mlworldhistory.com

  Warm-Up Transparency 25

Critical Thinking Transparencies
• CT61 Chapter 25 Visual Summary
• CT25 Industrialists and Reformers

Electronic Library of Primary Sources
• from *The Communist Manifesto*
• from "How I Served My Apprenticeship"

INTERNET RESOURCES
www.mlworldhistory.com

     Chapter Summaries on Audiocassette in English and Spanish

  INTERNET RESOURCES
www.mlworldhistory.com

 ### Block Scheduling (90 MINUTES)

Day 1
Section 1, pp. 633–637
Section Assessment, p. 637

Day 2
Section 2, pp. 638–642

 COOPERATIVE ACTIVITY
Debating the Effects of Industrialization, p. 640 (Teacher's Edition)

Section Assessment, p. 642

Day 3
Section 3, pp. 643–646

 COOPERATIVE ACTIVITY
Planning an Industrial Fair, p. 645 (Teacher's Edition)

Section 4, pp. 647–652

 COOPERATIVE ACTIVITY
Playing an Identity Game, p. 651 (Teacher's Edition)

Section Assessments, pp. 646, 652

Chapter Assessment, pp. 654–655

Yearly Pacing *Chapter 25 Total:* 3 days *Yearly Total:* 85 days

Planning for Block Schedules

Customizing for Special Needs

Students Acquiring English

 Access for Students Acquiring English
• **Guided Reading** for Sections 1–4 (Spanish), pp. 250–253
• **Chapter Summary** (Spanish), pp. 247–249
• **Skillbuilder Practice** (Spanish), p. 254
• **Geography Application** (Spanish), p. 255

 Chapter Summaries on Audiocassette in English and Spanish

 Patterns of Interaction:
Technology Transforms An Age (Spanish track)

INTERNET RESOURCES
www.mlworldhistory.com
The Diverse Classroom.

Less Proficient Readers

 In-Depth Resources: Unit 6
• **Guided Reading** for Sections 1–4, pp. 1–4
• **Skillbuilder Practice** Developing Historical Perspective, p. 5
• **Geography Application** British Population Moves to the Cities, p. 6

 Telescoping the Times
• Chapter Summary, pp. 97–99

 Chapter Summaries on Audiocassette

Gifted and Talented Students

 In-Depth Resources: Unit 6

Primary Sources:
• from "The Opening of the Liverpool to Manchester Railway," p. 8
• Testimony on Child Labor in Britain, p. 9
• "Life in a New England Factory," from *Voice of Industry,* p. 10
• from *The Wealth of Nations,* p. 11

History Makers
• James Watt, p. 15
• Saint-Simon, p. 16

Connections to Literature READINGS FOR STUDENTS

 In-Depth Resources: Unit 6
Literature: from *Mary Barton,* p. 12

Enrichment Reading

• **Forrest, Anthony**
The Pandora Secret
New York: Hill, 1982

In 1804, inventor Robert Fulton leaves France to continue his work on a "plunging" boat for the British Admiralty. This exciting story of the first submarine is rich in period detail.

• **Moore, Ruth Nulton**
In Search of Liberty
Scottdale, PA: Herald, 1983

This memorable story traces the path of a Liberty penny through 200 years of American history.

PE = Pupil's Edition   = Overhead Transparency   = Software   = Video
= Copy Master   = CD-ROM   = Audiocassette   = Internet

The Industrial Revolution, 1700–1900

Accessing Prior Knowledge

• Ask students what they know about railroads. Ask them if any of their family members have ever worked in a factory.

Making Inferences and Predicting

• After students have surveyed the captions and pictures on these two pages, ask them what they think working conditions were like for people at this time.

• After students have looked at the pictures and captions on page 631, ask them to predict what workers might do in response to difficult working conditions.

Geography Connection

Ask students to look at the map of the United States on page 630.

• In what region of the United States were there no railroads? *The West.*

• In what direction were the railroads likely to expand? *Westward.*

CHAPTER
25
The Industrial Revolution, 1700–1900

PREVIEWING THEMES

Science & Technology
From the spinning jenny to the locomotive train, there was an explosion of inventions and technological advances. These improvements paved the way for the Industrial Revolution.

Empire Building
The global power balance shifted after the Industrial Revolution. This shift occurred because industrialized nations dominated the rest of the world.

Economics
The Industrial Revolution transformed economic systems. In part, this was because nations dramatically changed the way they produced and distributed goods.

⇦ **INTERNET CONNECTION**

Visit us at **www.mlworldhistory.com** to learn more about the Industrial Revolution.

EUROPE AND
THE U.S. IN THE 1800s

— U.S. Railroads 1840

0 _____ 1,000 Miles
0 _____ 2,000 Kilometers

Hudson Bay

CANADA

• New York
St Louis • Washington, D.C.

UNITED STATES
OF AMERICA

• New Orleans

Gulf of Mexico

PACIFIC OCEAN

Caribbean Sea

Locomotives began to crisscross the eastern **United States** in the **1840s.** At that time, train tracks started to connect some American cities. Railroads enabled raw materials and finished goods to move back and forth between mines, factories, cities, and ports.

630

GEOGRAPHY THEMES

Movement

Ask students to reread the captions on the map to identify examples of the movement of goods and ideas during the Industrial Revolution. One means of transporting goods is shown—the locomotive. Other means of transportation were developed during the 19th century, often making use of steam engines. Ask students to speculate about how the development of new means of transportation might have expedited movement of people and products during the 1800s. Further, you might ask students to speculate about the effect this increased efficiency might have had on the pace of life in the 19th century.

Human/Environment Interaction

Point out to students that industrialization brought about changes in the way people interacted with their environment. Have students discuss what some of those changes were and how the environment and human life were affected as a result. Mention that industrialization consumed large quantities of resources that had to be extracted from the earth, extended transportation networks (such as shipping routes and railroads), and produced pollution. Many of these changes harmed the environment and eventually became problems for human life as well.

ADDITIONAL RESOURCES

Books for the Teacher

• Burchell, Samuel C. *Age of Progress.* New York: Time-Life, 1966.

• Stearns, Peter N., and John H. Hinshaw. *The ABC-CLIO World History Companion to the Industrial Revolution.* Santa Barbara, Calif.: ABC-CLIO, 1996.

Books for the Student

• Addy, John. *Coal and Iron Community in the Industrial Revolution.* White Plains, N.Y.: Longman, 1978.

• Bland, Celia. *The Mechanical Age: The Industrial Revolution in England.* New York: Facts on File, 1995.

• Macaulay, David. *Mill.* Boston: Houghton, 1983.

• Tann, Jennifer. *Children at Work.* London: Batsford, 1981. Child labor in Great Britain, late 1700s to 1900.

▭ Videos

• *Coal, Blood, and Iron.* Coronet/ MTI, 1991. 800-321-3106. Coal sets the Industrial Revolution ablaze.

• *The Luddites.* Social Studies School Service, 1992. 800-421-4246. Violent resistance to new technology.

◉ Software

• *The Industrial Revolution.* CD-ROM. Society for Visual Education, 1994. 800-829-1900.

As industrialization swept across the countries of Western Europe in the **19th century,** workers began to organize. They did so in order to defend their interests against those of the factory owners. Here workers in **Germany** meet before a strike in order to plan their strategy.

British workers are shown here laboring in terrible smoke and heat. They are "drawing the retorts"—that is, releasing heat from the furnaces. The place shown is the Great Gas Light Establishment in Brick Lane in **London** in the early **1800s.**

HISTORY THROUGH ART

Great Gas Light Establishment, Brick Lane, London

This scene shows British workers laboring in difficult conditions to produce coke oven gas, or coal gas, which was made by roasting coal. As the coal turned into coke, various gases were released. Coke oven gas was used for illumination in England. The condi-

tions shown in this picture bring to mind the English poet William Blake's description of England's "dark satanic mills," or factories, in his poem *Milton* (1809).

Blake's was one of many critical voices raised in England in the late 18th and early 19th centuries against the dire consequences of the Industrial Revolution. Blake and William Wordsworth, among other writers of the time, worried about the impact of

industrialization on the English landscape, rural villages, and the lives of workers in factories.

Interpreting the Art What other scenes or images does this painting suggest? Does this illustration suggest an inferno? Might this scene be a proletarian version of the scenes of hell that are frequently depicted in Western art?

Interact *with* History

This Interact with History feature motivates students by inviting them to speculate about what they would do to change their situation in a dangerous factory setting. As they imagine themselves confronting these conditions, students will analyze the issues, explore their options, and become decision makers.

Purpose

• to set the stage for studying the Industrial Revolution

• to help students understand some of the causes and effects of the Industrial Revolution

• to help students make connections with the people and events they will study in this chapter

Teaching Strategy

Thinking Critically After students have imagined themselves in the situation described on this page, have them answer the key question and give reasons for their decision.

EXAMINING *the* ISSUES

Following are suggestions for addressing each bulleted question.

1 Ask students if they have ever had a job and, if so, what it was about the job that they liked least.

2 Have students speculate about the reasons for the conditions described here and how they might be changed.

3 Have students brainstorm solutions to the problem of getting out of a bad situation.

Making Connections Ask students to summarize the characteristics of revolution that they have learned about from their study of the American and French revolutions. Tell them to think about the ways in which the Industrial Revolution is similar to and different from those earlier revolutions.

Y ou are a 15-year-old living in England where the Industrial Revolution has spurred the growth of thousands of factories. Cheap labor is in great demand. Like millions of other teenagers, you do not go to school. Instead you work in a factory six days a week, 14 hours a day. The small pay you receive is needed to help support your family. You trudge to work before dawn every day and work until after sundown. The dangerous machines injure your fellow workers. Minding the machines is exhausting, dirty, and dangerous. Inside the factory the air is foul, and it is so dark it is hard to see.

What would you do to change your situation?

Children had to work around dangerous machinery in which a small hand could easily be caught and injured.

Adult overseers sometimes whipped exhausted children in order to keep them awake during their long, 14-hour days.

Children were expected to carry heavy loads as part of their job in the factory.

632

EXAMINING *the* ISSUES

1 • What factory conditions concern you the most?

2 • Would you attempt to change conditions in the factory?

3 • Would you join a union, go to school, or run away?

In small groups, discuss these questions; then share your conclusions with your class. In your discussions, think about how children live in pre-industrial and industrial societies all over the world.

As you read about the changes caused by industrialization, note how reform movements eventually improve conditions for all laborers, including children.

Follow Up

A feature on the chapter assessment will ask students to reevaluate their responses to the situation presented on this page.

1 The Beginnings of Industrialization

TERMS & NAMES
- Industrial Revolution
- enclosure
- crop rotation
- industrialization
- factors of production
- factory
- entrepreneur

MAIN IDEA	WHY IT MATTERS NOW
The Industrial Revolution started in England and soon spread elsewhere.	The changes that began in Britain paved the way for modern industrial societies.

SETTING THE STAGE In the United States, France, and Latin America, political revolutions brought in new governments. A different type of revolution now transformed the way people did work. The **Industrial Revolution** refers to the greatly increased output of machine-made goods that began in England during the 18th century. Before the Industrial Revolution, people wove textiles by hand. Beginning in the middle 1700s, machines did this and other jobs as well. The Industrial Revolution started in England and soon spread to Continental Europe and North America.

The Industrial Revolution Begins

By 1700, small farms covered England's landscape. Wealthy landowners, however, bought up much of the land that village farmers had once worked. Beginning in the early 1700s, large landowners dramatically improved farming methods. These agricultural changes amounted to an agricultural revolution. They eventually paved the way for the Industrial Revolution.

The Agricultural Revolution After buying up the land of village farmers, wealthy landowners enclosed their land with fences or hedges. The increase in their landholdings enabled them to cultivate larger fields, using new seeding and harvesting methods. Within these larger fields, called **enclosures,** landowners experimented to discover more productive farming methods to boost crop yields. The enclosure movement had two important results. First, landowners experimented with new agricultural methods. Second, large landowners forced small farmers to become tenant farmers or to give up farming and move to the cities.

Jethro Tull was one of the first of these scientific farmers. He saw that the usual way of sowing seed by scattering it across the ground was wasteful. Many of the seeds failed to take root. He solved this problem with an invention called the seed drill in about 1701. The seed drill allowed farmers to sow seeds in well-spaced rows at specific depths. A larger share of the seed germinated, boosting crop yields.

Crop Rotation The process of **crop rotation** proved to be one of the best developments of the scientific farmers. The process improved upon older methods of crop rotation, such as the medieval three-field system. One year, for example, a farmer might plant a field with wheat, which exhausted soil nutrients. The next year he planted a root crop, such as turnips, to restore nutrients. This might be followed in turn by barley, then clover.

Livestock breeders improved their methods, too. In the 1700s, for example, Robert Bakewell increased his mutton output by allowing only his best sheep to breed. Other farmers followed Bakewell's lead. Between 1700 and 1786 the average weight for lambs climbed from 18 to 50 pounds.

A. Possible Answer Enclosure resulted in experiments with new agricultural methods, and it caused many small farmers to move to the cities. Crop rotation produced increased yields.

THINK THROUGH HISTORY
A. Recognizing Effects What were some of the effects of enclosure and crop rotation?

Agricultural Revolution

Jethro Tull's Seed Drill

The seed drill enabled farmers to plant methodically. They abandoned the wasteful broadcast method of scattering handfuls of seed across the fields.

The Industrial Revolution **633**

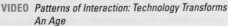

Section 1 Overview

OBJECTIVES

1. To explain the beginnings of industrialization in Britain.
2. To describe key inventions that furthered the Industrial Revolution.

SKILLBUILDER
- Interpreting graphs, p. 636

CRITICAL THINKING
- Recognizing effects, pp. 633, 634
- Making inferences, pp. 634, 637
- Synthesizing, pp. 635, 637
- Hypothesizing, p. 635
- Summarizing, p. 636

FOCUS
5-Minute Warm-Up

▶ *Clarifying*
To help students understand the range of inventions in this period, have them answer the following questions.

1. Read "Spotlight on Inventions in America" on page 637. Of the four bulleted inventions mentioned in the feature, which represented revolutions in communications?

2. Which of the four represented a revolution in agriculture? Which a revolution in manufacturing?

 WARM-UP TRANSPARENCY 25

OBJECTIVE 1 INSTRUCT

The Industrial Revolution Begins

▶ *Key Ideas*
- Improvements in farming methods in the 1700s boost crop yields and lead to enclosed lands.
- Many small farmers lose their land, move to the city, and become urban workers.
- Britain possesses ideal conditions for the growth of industry.

 IN-DEPTH RESOURCES: UNIT 6
Guided Reading, p. 1

 ACCESS FOR STUDENTS ACQUIRING ENGLISH
Guided Reading (Spanish), p. 250

Teacher's Edition **633**

These improvements in farming that began in the early 1700s made up an agricultural revolution. As food supplies increased and living conditions improved, England's population mushroomed. An increasing population boosted the demand for food and goods. As farmers lost their land to large enclosed farms, many became factory workers.

Britain's Advantages Why did the Industrial Revolution begin in England? In addition to a large population of workers, the small island country had extensive natural resources. And **industrialization**—the process of developing machine production of goods—required such resources. These natural resources included 1) water power and coal to fuel the new machines; 2) iron ore to construct machines, tools, and buildings; 3) rivers for inland transportation; 4) harbors from which its merchant ships set sail.

Economic Strength and Political Stability In addition to its natural resources, Britain had an expanding economy to support industrialization. Businesspeople invested in the manufacture of new inventions. Britain's highly developed banking system also contributed to the country's industrialization. People were encouraged by the availability of bank loans to invest in new machinery and expand their operations. Growing overseas trade, economic prosperity, and a climate of progress contributed to the increased demand for goods.

Britain's political stability gave the country a tremendous advantage over its neighbors. Though Britain took part in many wars during the 1700s, none of these struggles occurred on British soil. Furthermore, their military and political successes gave the British a positive attitude. Parliament also passed laws that protected business and helped expansion. Other countries had some of these advantages. However, Britain had all the **factors of production.** These were the resources needed to produce goods and services that the Industrial Revolution required. They included land, labor, and capital (or wealth).

*Global*Impact : *Revolutions in Technology*

Technology in the Textile Industry

The Industrial Revolution that began in Britain was spurred by a revolution in technology. This is most obvious in the textile industry where inventions in the late 1700s transformed the manufacture of cloth. These developments, in turn, had an impact on the rest of the world. For example, England's cotton came from plantations in the American South, where cotton production skyrocketed from 1790 to 1810 in response to demand from the textile mills of England.

John Kay's flying shuttle speedily carried threads of yarn back and forth when the weaver pulled a handle. The flying shuttle greatly increased the productivity of weavers.

James Hargreaves's spinning jenny dramatically increased the output of spinners. It helped them to keep pace with the weavers.

634 Chapter 25

Inventions Spur Technological Advances

In an explosion of creativity, inventions now revolutionized industry. Britain's textile industry clothed the world in wool, linen, and cotton. This industry was the first to be transformed. Cloth merchants boosted their profits by speeding up the process by which spinners and weavers made cloth.

Major Inventions in the Textile Industry By 1800, several major inventions had modernized the cotton industry. One invention led to another. In 1733, a machinist named John Kay made a shuttle that sped back and forth on wheels. This flying shuttle, a boat-shaped piece of wood to which yarn was attached, doubled the work a weaver could do in a day.

Because spinners could not keep up with these speedy weavers, a cash prize attracted contestants to produce a better spinning machine. Around 1764, a textile worker named James Hargreaves invented a spinning wheel he named after his daughter. Hargreaves's spinning jenny allowed one spinner to work eight threads at a time.

At first, textile workers operated the flying shuttle and the spinning jenny by hand. Richard Arkwright invented the water frame in 1769. The machine used the water-power from rapid streams to drive spinning wheels.

In 1779, Samuel Crompton combined features of the spinning jenny and the water frame to produce the spinning mule. The spinning mule made thread that was stronger, finer, and more consistent than earlier spinning machines. Run by water-power, Edmund Cartwright's power loom sped up weaving after its invention in 1787.

The water frame, the spinning mule, and the power loom were bulky and expensive machines. They took the work of spinning and weaving out of the house. Wealthy textile merchants set up the machines in large buildings called **factories.** At first,

Background
The spinning mule was so named because, just as a mule is the off-spring of a horse and donkey, this machine was the offspring of two inventions.

All work, even cotton spinning, is noble; work is alone noble.
—Scottish writer Thomas Carlyle in 1843

The first factories were built to house spinning and weaving machines in the textile industry and to keep the processes secret. Such factories were built close to rivers and streams, which provided a source of energy.

Patterns of Interaction

Inventions in the textile industry started in Britain and brought about the Industrial Revolution. This revolution soon spread to other countries in Europe and the United States. The process of industrialization is still spreading around the world, especially in Third World countries. A similar technological revolution is occurring in today's world of electronics. The telephone, television, and (more recently) the computer and the Internet are transforming the spread of information around the world.

VIDEO *Technology Transforms An Age: The Industrial and Electronic Revolutions*

The Industrial Revolution **635**

Connect to History

Synthesizing Technological innovation and industrialization took place in the textile industry during the Industrial Revolution. How might these forces have provided a model for other industries?

 SEE SKILLBUILDER HANDBOOK, PAGE 1007

Connect to Today

Hypothesizing How might the textile industry be affected by new technology, including the computer?

OBJECTIVE ② INSTRUCT

Inventions Spur Technological Advances

▶ *Key Ideas*
• Key inventions revolutionize industry during the 1700s and 1800s.
• The textile industry is the first to benefit, with the invention of machines to produce cotton cloth.
• Transportation expands with the invention of the steam engine and the construction of canals, roads, and railroads.

📖 *IN-DEPTH RESOURCES: UNIT 6*
History Maker: James Watt, p. 15
Primary Source: from "The Opening of the Liverpool to Manchester Railway," p. 8

CRITICAL THINKING ACTIVITY
CLASS TIME: 15 MINUTES

Summarizing
Have students make a chart like the one below and list major inventions or improvements in each category.

Textiles	Transport
Flying shuttle	Steam engine

Connect to History		**Connect to Today**	
Synthesizing **Possible Answer:** Many of the techniques of production and processes of standardization were applicable to other industries as the Industrial Revolution developed. This	can be seen, for example, in the improvements in transportation, in which the steam engine was adapted to a number of different methods of transportation, including boats and railroads.	*Hypothesizing* Computer technology will probably streamline the textile industry and reduce the number of jobs for unskilled workers. Students	may wish to do some research to find out about the latest techniques and technologies used in the textile industry, much of which is now automated.

THINK THROUGH HISTORY
D. Summarizing
What were the major inventions in the textile industry?
D. Possible Answer
Flying shuttle; spinning jenny; water frame; spinning mule; factory.

the new factories needed waterpower, so they were built near sources of water such as rivers and streams:

A VOICE FROM THE PAST

. . . A great number of streams . . . furnish water-power adequate to turn many hundred mills: they afford the element of water, indispensable for scouring, bleaching, printing, dyeing, and other processes of manufacture: and when collected in their larger channels, or employed to feed canals, they supply a superior inland navigation, so important for the transit of raw materials and merchandise.

EDWARD BAINS, *The History of Cotton Manufacture in Great Britain* (1835)

British Cotton Consumption

New inventions led to a big increase in the production and consumption of textiles, including cotton. The consumption of cotton rose dramatically in Britain during the 1800s. The following chart shows the increase in cotton consumption as measured in thousands of metric tons for each decade of the century.

Source: *Historical Statistics of the United States*

SKILLBUILDER: Interpreting Graphs
1. *In what decade did the steepest increase in cotton consumption in Britain take place?*
2. *In what two decades did the consumption of cotton level off or slightly decrease?*

England's cotton came from plantations in the American South in the 1790s. Removing seeds from the raw cotton by hand was hard work. In 1793, an American inventor named Eli Whitney invented a machine to speed the chore. His cotton gin multiplied the amount of cotton that could be cleaned. American cotton production skyrocketed from 1.5 million pounds in 1790 to 85 million pounds in 1810.

Improvements in Transportation Progress in the textile industry spurred other industrial improvements. The first such development, the steam engine, stemmed from the search for a cheap, convenient source of power. The earliest steam engine was used in mining as early as 1705. But this early model gobbled great quantities of fuel, making it expensive to run.

James Watt, a mathematical instrument maker at the University of Glasgow in Scotland, thought about the problem for two years. In 1765, Watt figured out a way to make the steam engine work faster and more efficiently while burning less fuel. In 1774, Watt joined with a businessman named Matthew Boulton. This **entrepreneur** (AHN·truh·pruh·NUR)—a person who organizes, manages, and takes on the risks of a business—paid Watt a salary and encouraged him to build better engines.

Water Transportation Steam could also be used to propel boats. An American inventor named Robert Fulton ordered a steam engine from Boulton and Watt. After its first successful trip in 1807, Fulton's steamboat, the *Clermont*, ferried passengers up and down New York's Hudson River.

In England, water transportation improved with the creation of a network of canals, or human-made waterways. By the mid-1800s, 4,250 miles of inland channels slashed the cost of transporting raw materials.

Road Transportation British roads improved, too, thanks largely to the efforts of John McAdam, a Scottish engineer. Working in the early 1800s, McAdam equipped roadbeds with a layer of large stones for drainage. On top, he placed a carefully smoothed layer of crushed rock. Even in rainy weather heavy wagons could travel over the new "macadam" roads without sinking in mud.

Private investors formed companies that built roads and then operated them for profit. People called the new roads turnpikes because travelers had to stop at tollgates (turnstiles or turnpikes) to pay a toll before traveling farther.

The Railway Age Begins Steam-driven machinery propelled English factories in the late 1700s. A steam engine on wheels—the railroad locomotive—drove English industry after 1820.

636 Chapter 25

In 1804, an English engineer named Richard Trevithick won a bet of several thousand dollars. He did this by hauling ten tons of iron over nearly ten miles of track in a steam-driven locomotive. Other British engineers soon built improved versions of Trevithick's locomotive. One of these early railroad engineers was George Stephenson. He had gained a solid reputation by building some 20 engines for mine operators in northern England. In 1821, Stephenson began work on the world's first railroad line. It was to run 27 miles from the Yorkshire coalfields to the port of Stockton on the North Sea. In 1825, the railroad opened. It used four locomotives that Stephenson had designed and built.

The Liverpool-Manchester Railroad News of this success quickly spread throughout Britain. The entrepreneurs of northern England wanted a railroad line to connect the port of Liverpool with the inland city of Manchester. The track was laid. In 1829 trials were held to choose the best locomotive for use on the new line. Five engines entered the competition. None could compare with the *Rocket*, designed by Stephenson and his son. Smoke poured from its tall smokestack and its two pistons pumped to and fro as they drove the front wheels. The *Rocket* hauled a 13-ton load at an unheard-of speed—more than 24 miles per hour. The Liverpool-Manchester Railway opened officially in 1830. It was an immediate success.

Railroads Revolutionize Life in Britain
First, railroads spurred industrial growth by giving manufacturers a cheap way to transport materials and finished products. Second, the railroad boom created hundreds of thousands of new jobs for both railroad workers and miners. These miners provided iron for the tracks and coal for the steam engines. Third, the railroads boosted England's agricultural and fishing industries, which could transport their products to distant cities. Finally, by making travel easier, railroads encouraged country people to take distant city jobs. Also, railroads lured city dwellers to resorts in the countryside. Like a locomotive racing across the country, the Industrial Revolution brought rapid and unsettling changes to people's lives.

E. Possible Answer Canals cut the cost of transporting materials; improved roads fostered the movement of heavy wagons; railroads linked manufacturing cities with raw materials.
THINK THROUGH HISTORY
E. Synthesizing How did improvements in transportation promote industrialization in Britain?

SPOTLIGHT ON
Inventions in America
Have students research one of the inventions listed here. Then have them explain basic facts about the invention and its inventor's life.

ASSESS & RETEACH

Section 1 Assessment
Have students work individually to answer the questions. Then invite students to read the letters they wrote for item 4 in class.

Section Quiz
FORMAL ASSESSMENT
Section Quiz, p. 289

Reteaching Activity
CLASS TIME: 10 MINUTES

Use the Guided Reading worksheet for Section 1 to review the main ideas of the section.

IN-DEPTH RESOURCES: UNIT 6
Guided Reading, p. 1

CLOSE ACTIVITY

CLASS TIME: 10 MINUTES

Making a Cause-Effect Diagram
Have students create a diagram or chart that shows the causes and effects of the agricultural revolution and Industrial Revolution. Then have students compare their charts.

	Causes	Effects
Agricultural Revolution		
Industrial Revolution		

Section 1 Assessment

1. TERMS & NAMES
Identify
• Industrial Revolution
• enclosure
• crop rotation
• industrialization
• factors of production
• factory
• entrepreneur

2. TAKING NOTES
Create a two-column chart like the one below that lists four natural resources needed for industrialization and how each is used.

Natural Resource	Use
1. coal	
2.	
3.	
4.	

3. MAKING INFERENCES
What effect did entrepreneurs have upon the Industrial Revolution?

THINK ABOUT
• new technological developments
• business opportunities
• increase in prosperity

4. THEME ACTIVITY

Science and Technology
Write a letter as a British government official during the Industrial Revolution. Write to a government official in a non-industrial nation about how the railroad has changed Britain.

The Industrial Revolution **637**

ANSWERS

1. TERMS & NAMES
Industrial Revolution, p. 633
enclosure, p. 633
crop rotation, p. 633
industrialization, p. 634
factors of production, p. 634
factory, p. 635
entrepreneur, p. 636

2. TAKING NOTES
Coal—fuel new machines; iron ore—construct new machines, tools, buildings; rivers—inland transportation; good harbors—docking stations for merchant ships.

3. MAKING INFERENCES
Possible Responses:
Entrepreneurs helped to promote the Industrial Revolution, because they were willing to risk their capital by investing it in new inventions and enterprises.

4. THEME ACTIVITY
Standards for Evaluation
An effective letter should . . .
• introduce several changes in British society
• be written in a thoughtful, coherent, and engaging manner
• give a clear sense of place and time

② Industrialization

PATTERNS OF CHANGE CASE STUDY: Manchester

MAIN IDEA	**WHY IT MATTERS NOW**
The factory system changed the way people lived and worked, introducing a variety of problems.	The difficult process of industrialization is being repeated in many less-developed countries today.

SETTING THE STAGE The Industrial Revolution eventually led to a better quality of life for most people. Yet the change to machine production also caused immense human suffering. In Britain, the Industrial Revolution proved to be a mixed blessing.

Industrialization Changes Ways of Life

The pace of industrialization quickened in Britain. By the 1800s more people could afford to heat their homes with coal from Wales and to dine on Scottish beef. They wore better clothing, too, woven on power looms in England's industrial cities. These cities soon swelled with workers. However, other people suffered from industrialization.

Growth of Industrial Cities For centuries, most Europeans had lived in rural areas. After 1800, the balance shifted toward cities. The growth of the factory system—manufacturing goods in a central location—brought waves of jobseekers to cities and towns. Between 1800 and 1850, the number of European cities boasting more than 100,000 inhabitants rose from 22 to 47. Most of Europe's urban areas at least doubled in population. This period was one of **urbanization**—city building and the movement of people to cities. Some cities, such as Glasgow and Berlin, tripled or even quadrupled in size.

Factories developed in clusters because entrepreneurs built them near sources of energy. Major new industrial centers sprang up between the coal-rich area of southern Wales and the Clyde River valley in Scotland. The biggest of these centers developed in England.

Britain's capital, London, was the country's most important city. Containing twice as many people as its closest rival (Paris), London became Europe's largest city. It had a population of about 1 million people by 1800. During the 1800s London's population exploded, providing a vast labor pool and market for new industry.

Newer cities challenged London's industrial leadership. Birmingham and Sheffield became iron-smelting centers. Leeds and Manchester dominated textile manufacturing. Along with the port of Liverpool, Manchester formed the center of Britain's bustling cotton industry. During the 1800s, Manchester experienced rapid growth. In 1760, the population of this market town was around 45,000. By 1850, it had swelled to 300,000 people.

As cities grew all over Europe, people crowded into tenements and row houses such as these in London.

Living Conditions No plans, no sanitary codes, and no building codes controlled the growth of England's cities. They lacked adequate housing, education, and police protection for the people who poured in from the countryside seeking jobs. Most of the unpaved streets had no drains and collected heaps of garbage. Workers lived in dark, dirty shelters, whole families crowding into one bedroom.

Not surprisingly, sickness was widespread. Cholera epidemics regularly swept through the slums of Great Britain's industrial cities. In 1842, a British government study showed an average life span to be 17 years for working-class people in one large city, compared with 38 years in a nearby rural area.

Elizabeth Gaskell's *Mary Barton* (1848) is a work of fiction. Nonetheless, its realistic description of the dank cellar dwelling place of one family in a Manchester slum presents a startlingly accurate portrayal of urban life at the time:

A VOICE FROM THE PAST
You went down one step even from the foul area into the cellar in which a family of human beings lived. It was very dark inside. The window-panes many of them were broken and stuffed with rags . . . . the smell was so fetid [foul] as almost to knock the two men down . . . . they began to penetrate the thick darkness of the place, and to see three or four little children rolling on the damp, nay wet brick floor, through which the stagnant, filthy moisture of the street oozed up. . . .

ELIZABETH GASKELL, *Mary Barton*

Elizabeth Gaskell (1810–1865) was a British writer whose novels such as *Mary Barton* (1848) and *North and South* (1855) show a sympathy for the working class. *Cranford* (1853) deals with the life of a peaceful English village.

Working Conditions Factory owners wanted to keep their machines running for as many hours a day as possible. As a result, the average worker spent 14 hours a day at the job, 6 days a week. Instead of changing with the seasons, the work was the same week after week, year after year. Workers had to keep up with the machines.

Industry also posed new dangers in work. Factories were seldom well-lit or clean. Machines injured workers in countless ways. A boiler might explode or a drive belt might catch the worker's arm. And there was no government program to provide aid in case of injury. The most dangerous conditions of all were found in the coal mines. Frequent accidents, damp conditions, and the constant breathing of coal dust made the average miner's life span ten years shorter than that of other workers.

Class Tensions Not everyone in the new cities lived miserably. Well-to-do merchants and factory owners built fancy homes in the suburbs. In addition, a new class began to emerge.

Though poverty gripped Britain's working classes, the Industrial Revolution created enormous amounts of money in the country. Most of this wealth lined the pockets of factory owners, shippers, and merchants. These wealthy people made up a growing **middle class**—a social class of skilled workers, professionals, businesspeople, and wealthy farmers.

The new middle class transformed the social structure of Great Britain. In the past, landowners and aristocrats occupied the top position in British society. With most of the wealth, they wielded the power. Now some factory owners, merchants, and investment bankers grew wealthier than the landowners and aristocrats.

Yet important social distinctions divided the two wealthy classes. Landowners looked down on those who had made their fortunes in the "vulgar" business world. Not until late in the 1800s were rich entrepreneurs considered the social equals of the lords of the countryside.

Gradually, a larger middle class—neither rich nor poor—emerged. This group included an upper middle class of government employees, doctors, lawyers, and managers of factories, mines, and shops. A lower middle class consisted of factory overseers and such skilled workers as toolmakers, mechanical drafters, and printers. These people enjoyed a comfortable standard of living.

During the years 1800 to 1850, however, poor workers saw little improvement in their own living and working conditions. Frustrated workers watched their livelihoods disappear as machines replaced them. In response, they smashed the machines they thought were putting them out of work. One group of such workers was called the Luddites. They were named after Ned Ludd. Ludd, probably a mythical English

THINK THROUGH HISTORY
A. Drawing Conclusions What was the impact of living and working conditions on workers?
A. Possible Answer Health was undermined; work was dangerous and could result in injuries.

B. Possible Answer An upper class made up of landowners and aristrocrats; an upper middle class made up of managers, merchants, government employees, doctors, lawyers; a lower middle class of factory overseers and skilled workers; working class.
THINK THROUGH HISTORY
B. Summarizing Describe the social classes in Britain.

MORE ABOUT . . .
Urban Growth

In the 1700s, Britain was primarily a rural country. By 1851, however, more of the British people lived in cities than in the countryside. In 1901, the ratio of urban to rural population was 3 to 1. The population of London at that time was 4.5 million.

IN-DEPTH RESOURCES: UNIT 6
Geography Application: British Population Moves to the Cities, p. 6

GEOGRAPHY TRANSPARENCIES
GT25 The Industrial Revolution in Great Britain, 1850

WORLD ART AND CULTURES TRANSPARENCIES
AT54 *Arkwright's Cotton Mill at Comford, Derbyshire, England*

MORE ABOUT . . .
Cholera

Polluted water was a major problem in British cities in the 1800s. In London, most drinking water came straight from the Thames River, which was filthy with sewage and industrial waste. In 1849, a cholera epidemic killed 400 Londoners a day.

Literature Elizabeth Gaskell's *Mary Barton* was an example of a literary style known as realism, which came into fashion during the 1800s. You might want to give students a copy of the literature selection from *Mary Barton*, which can be found in the Teacher's Resources for this chapter. Ask students to find works by Gaskell, Charles Dickens, William Makepeace Thackeray, or other realist writers of the time. Invite them to discuss the works and read passages in class.

IN-DEPTH RESOURCES: UNIT 6
Literature: from *Mary Barton*, p. 12

Visual Learners: *Creating a Political Cartoon* Suggest that students create a political cartoon that highlights a condition or problem associated with the Industrial Revolution in Great Britain. Some problems they might choose to illustrate include the pollution of the air, the hierarchy of social classes, the dangerous conditions in the factories, and the crowded conditions in tenements. Cartoons should combine drawings and text. Remind students that political cartoons convey a message in humorous and thought-provoking ways.

Luddites

The Luddites were angry not only about losing their jobs but also about the life changes forced on them by industrialization. Instead of working at home alongside their families, textile workers now had to labor under dehumanizing factory conditions. The term *Luddites* is still sometimes used to refer to people opposed to modern technology.

 ELECTRONIC LIBRARY OF PRIMARY SOURCES
"The Sentencing of the Luddites"

History from Visuals

Patterns of Change: Industrialization

Interpreting the Chart Have students read the headings on the chart. Point out that the left column lists general areas or categories affected by industrialization and the right column provides specific examples. Ask students to try to come up with other categories that might be added to the chart. *Possible Responses: Rural areas, families, careers and occupations.*

Extension Activity Have students add one other specific example to each category on the chart, based on their reading of the text. *Possible Response: Size of Cities—New cities challenging London for influence.*

SKILLBUILDER Answers
1. The workers suffered the most; the middle class benefited the most.
2. Advantages: Industrialization made a new middle class prosperous; it created jobs and wealth, as well as better housing and healthier diets.
   Disadvantages: It contributed to harsh living and working conditions; it exploited workers.

---

laborer, was said to have destroyed weaving machinery around 1779. The Luddites attacked whole factories in northern England beginning in 1811, destroying labor-saving machinery. Outside the factories, mob disorder took the form of riots, mainly because of the poor living and working conditions of the workers.

Positive Effects of the Industrial Revolution Despite the problems that followed industrialization, the Industrial Revolution eventually had a number of positive effects. It created jobs for workers. It contributed to the wealth of the nation. It fostered technological progress and invention. It greatly increased the production of goods and raised the standard of living. Perhaps most important, it provided the hope of improvement in people's lives.

The Industrial Revolution produced a number of other benefits as well. These included healthier diets; better housing; and cheaper, mass-produced clothing. Because the Industrial Revolution created a demand for engineers as well as clerical and professional workers, it expanded educational opportunities.

The middle and upper classes prospered immediately from the Industrial Revolution. For the workers it took longer, but their lives gradually improved during the 1800s. Labor eventually won higher wages, shorter hours, and better working conditions.

PATTERNS OF CHANGE: Industrialization

Effects of Industrialization	
Size of Cities	• Growth of factories, bringing job seekers to cities • Urban areas doubling, tripling, or quadrupling in size • Factories developing near sources of energy • Many new industrial cities specializing in certain industries
Living Conditions	• No sanitary codes or building controls • Lack of adequate housing, education, and police protection • Lack of running water and indoor plumbing • Frequent epidemics sweeping through slums • Eventually, better housing, healthier diets, and cheaper clothing
Working Conditions	• Industrialization creating new jobs for workers • Workers trying to keep pace with machines • Factories dirty and unsanitary • Workers running dangerous machines for long hours in unsafe conditions • Harsh and severe factory discipline • Eventually, higher wages, shorter hours, and better working conditions
Emerging Social Classes	• Growing middle class of factory owners, shippers, and merchants • Upper class of landowners and aristocrats resentful of rich middle class • Lower middle class of factory overseers and skilled workers • Workers overworked and underpaid • In general, a rising standard of living, with some groups excluded

SKILLBUILDER: Interpreting Charts
1. *Which social class benefited most and which suffered most from industrialization?*
2. *What were some of the advantages and disadvantages of industrialization?*

The long-term effects of the Industrial Revolution are still evident. Most people today in the industrialized countries can afford consumer goods that would have been considered luxuries fifty or a hundred years ago. Further, their living and working conditions are much improved over those of workers in the 19th century.

As the Industrial Revolution in Manchester demonstrated, economic success can unleash a variety of problems. Even today, the economic pressures of industrialization frequently lead to the overuse of natural resources and the abuse of the environment. The profits derived from industrialization, however, permit thoughtful governments to invest in urban improvements.

640 CHAPTER 25

TEACHING OPTION | **BLOCK SCHEDULING** | **COOPERATIVE ACTIVITY: Debating the Effects of Industrialization** | **CLASS TIME 30 MINUTES**

Task: Students will prepare position statements and debate the merits of the Industrial Revolution.

Purpose: To consider the economic, social, political, and environmental effects of industrialization.

Activity: Divide students into groups and assign each group a position in favor of or opposed to industrialization. Have groups research their position and gather evidence that supports it. Have students prepare position statements . Have opposing groups debate.

📁 **Building a Portfolio:** Students may add their position statements to their portfolio, along with an explanation of the assignment.

📖 **ALTERNATIVE ASSESSMENT BOOK**
Standards for Evaluating a Cooperative Activity

Standards for Evaluation
Position statements should . . .

• clearly state the issue being debated
• take a distinct position supported by facts and examples
• address opposing viewpoints directly and reasonably

The Mills of Manchester

Manchester's unique advantages made it a leading example of the new industrial city. This northern English town had ready access to water power. It also had available labor from the nearby countryside and an outlet to the sea at Liverpool.

"From this filthy sewer pure gold flows," wrote Alexis de Tocqueville (ah·lehk·SEE duh TOHK·vihl), the French writer, after he visited Manchester in 1835. Indeed, the industrial giant showed the best and worst of the Industrial Revolution. Manchester's rapid, unplanned growth made it a filthy sewer for the poor people who worked there. But gold certainly flowed toward the mill owners and the new middle class. Eventually, although not immediately, the working class saw their standard of living rise as well.

Manchester's businesspeople took pride in mastering each detail of the manufacturing process, working many hours and risking their own money. For their efforts, they pocketed high profits and erected gracious homes on the outskirts of town.

To provide the mill owners with their high profits, workers labored under terrible conditions. Children as young as six joined their parents in the factories. There, for six days a week, they toiled from 6 A.M. to 7 or 8 P.M., with only a half an hour for lunch and an hour for dinner. To keep the children awake, mill supervisors beat them. Tiny hands repaired broken threads in Manchester's spinning machines, replaced thread in the bobbins, or swept up cotton fluff. The dangerous machinery injured many children. The fluff filled their lungs and made them cough.

Until the first Factory Act passed in 1819, the British government exerted little control over child labor in Manchester and other factory cities. The act restricted working age and hours. For years after the act passed, young children still did heavy, dangerous work in Manchester's factories.

Putting so much industry into one place polluted the natural environment. The coal that powered factories and warmed houses blackened the air. Textile dyes and

C. Possible Answer
Factory owners profited by being able to pay children low wages; families also benefited from the wages children earned.

THINK THROUGH HISTORY
C. Drawing Conclusions Whose interests did child labor serve?

An English engraving of 1876 shows a bird's-eye view of the city of Manchester during the Industrial Revolution.

Manchester's Growth

Population:
- 1801: 93,400
- 1831: 232,800
- 1871: 476,000

SKILLBUILDER: Interpreting Graphs
1. How many people did the city of Manchester gain between 1801 and 1831? How many did it gain between 1831 and 1871?
2. What does the engraving show were the effects of such rapid growth?

641

OBJECTIVE 2 INSTRUCT

The Mills of Manchester

▶ **Key Ideas**
- Manchester becomes an example of the new industrial city.
- Textile factories produce great wealth for mill owners.
- Workers and the environment suffer the effects of industrialization.

History from Visuals

Manchester's Growth

Interpreting the Graph Ask students how many years the graph covers. *70 years.* Ask students how much the population grew during this period. *By 382,600.*

Extension Activity Ask students to estimate the size of Manchester in 1911 if it continued to grow at the same rate it did between 1831 and 1871. *About twice as large, or 950,000.*

SKILLBUILDER Answers
1. 1801–1831, 139,400; 1831–1871, 243,200.
2. There were negative effects on the environment, such as polluted air and water. Sanitation was a problem, as was decent housing.

TEACHING OPTION

CONNECTIONS ACROSS TIME AND PLACE

Pollution Have students research the problem of environmental pollution during the Industrial Revolution and today. Have them discuss the issue, considering questions such as the following: Is pollution better or worse now? What new pollution dangers exist now that did not exist in the 1800s? During this discussion, have students fill in information on a chart like the one here.

Pollution: Then & Now	
Then	Now
Coal smoke	Car exhaust
Dyes & sewage in water	Chemicals in water

The Day of a Child Laborer, William Cooper

William Cooper began working in a textile factory at the age of ten. He had a sister who worked upstairs in the same factory. In 1832, Cooper was called to testify before a parliamentary committee about the conditions among child laborers in the textile industry. The following sketch of his day is based upon his testimony.

5 A.M.—The workday began. Cooper and his sister rose as early as 4:00 or 4:30 in the morning in order to get to the factory for the start of their workday at 5:00. Children usually grabbed their breakfast on the run.

11 P.M.—Cooper's sister worked another two hours even though she had to be back at work at 5:00 the next morning.

12 noon—The children were given a 40-minute break for lunch. This was the only break they received during the whole course of the day.

3 P.M.—The children often became drowsy during the afternoon or evening hours. In order to keep them awake, adult overseers sometimes whipped the children.

6 P.M.—There was no break allowed for an evening meal. Children ate on the run. From 12:40 until 9:00 at night, the children worked without a break.

9 P.M.—William Cooper's day ended after an exhausting 16-hour shift at work.

CONNECT to TODAY

Child Labor

To save on labor costs in the 1990s, many corporations have moved their manufacturing operations overseas to poor countries. In sweatshops in these developing countries, young children work long hours under wretched conditions. They are unprotected by child labor laws. For mere pennies per hour, children sort vegetables, stitch soccer balls, or assemble expensive basketball shoes.

In the United States each year $178 billion worth of clothing is sold. Some studies estimate more than half of that clothing is manufactured in sweatshops where children work. Like the children who toiled in Manchester's factories in the 1800s, children labor to help support their families.

other wastes poisoned Manchester's Irwell River. The following description of the river was written by an eyewitness observer in 1862:

A VOICE FROM THE PAST
Steam boilers discharge into it their seething contents, and drains and sewers their fetid impurities; till at length it rolls on—here between tall dingy walls, there under precipices of red sandstone—considerably less a river than a flood of liquid manure.

HUGH MILLER, "Old Red Sandstone"

Manchester produced consumer goods and created wealth on a grand scale. Yet this unplanned industrial city also stood as a reminder of industrialization's dark side. In the 1800s, the industrialization that began in Great Britain spread to the United States and to continental Europe, as you will learn in Section 3.

Section 2 Assessment

1. TERMS & NAMES
Identify
- urbanization
- middle class

2. TAKING NOTES
Create a pyramid like the one below listing the social classes in industrial England. List the types of laborers and professionals included in each group.

```
        1.
    Upper Class
        2.
 Upper Middle Class
        3.
 Lower Middle Class
        4.
   Working Class
```

3. ANALYZING ISSUES
How did industrialization contribute to city growth?

THINK ABOUT
- growth of industry
- creation of jobs
- the economic advantages of centralization

4. ANALYZING THEMES
Economics How might a factory owner have justified the harsh conditions in his factory?

THINK ABOUT
- class distinctions
- the spread of factories
- financial gains

ANSWERS

1. TERMS & NAMES
urbanization, p. 638

middle class, p. 639

2. TAKING NOTES
1. Upper class: landowners, aristocrats; 2. Upper middle class: factory owners, merchants, government employees, doctors, lawyers, managers; 3. Lower middle class: factory overseers, skilled workers; 4. Working class: workers in factories, mines.

3. ANALYZING ISSUES
Possible Response:
Industrialization promoted the growth of cities because the factory system led to manufacturing goods in a central location, and this, in turn, created jobs and economic opportunity.

4. ANALYZING THEMES
Possible Responses: The fact[?] owner might have believed th[at?] without jobs many of his work[ers?] would starve; that hard work i[s?] better than no work; all factor[ies?] had the same conditions, so h[is?] were no worse; that if he wer[e?] making money, that was all th[at?] mattered.

3 Industrialization Spreads

MAIN IDEA

The industrialization that began in Great Britain spread to other parts of the world.

WHY IT MATTERS NOW

The Industrial Revolution set the stage for the growth of modern cities.

SETTING THE STAGE Britain's favorable location, geography, financial systems, political stability, and natural resources sparked its industrialization. British power-driven machinery began to mass-produce textiles and other goods at the end of the 1700s. Paying low wages to many workers, British merchants built the world's first factories. When these factories prospered, wealthy business leaders invented more labor-saving machines. They also built more factories, and eventually industrialized the country. The Industrial Revolution that began in Britain soon spread to other countries. They had similar conditions that made them ripe for industrialization.

Industrial Development in the United States

The United States possessed the same resources that allowed Britain to mechanize its industries and develop large-scale factories. America also had rushing rivers, rich deposits of coal and iron ore, and a supply of immigrant laborers. During the War of 1812, Britain blockaded the United States in an attempt to keep it from engaging in international trade. This blockade forced the young country to use its own resources to develop independent industries. Those industries would manufacture the goods the United States could no longer import.

Background
The War of 1812 began over British interference with America's merchant ships. It ended in a draw between Britain and the United States.

Industrialization in the United States As in Britain, industrialization in the United States began in the textile industry. Eager to keep the secrets of industrialization to itself, Britain had forbidden engineers, mechanics, and toolmakers to leave the country. In 1789, however, a young British mill worker named Samuel Slater emigrated to the United States. There Slater built a spinning machine from memory and a partial design. The following year, Moses Brown opened the first factory in the United States to house Slater's machines in Pawtucket, Rhode Island. But the Pawtucket factory mass-produced only one part of finished cloth, the thread.

In 1813, Francis Cabot Lowell and four other investors revolutionized the American textile industry. They mechanized every stage in the manufacture of cloth. Their weaving factory in Waltham, Massachusetts, earned the partners enough money to fund a larger operation in another Massachusetts town. When Francis Lowell died, the remaining partners named the town after him. By the late 1820s, Lowell, Massachusetts, had become a booming manufacturing center and a model for other such towns.

Thousands of workers, mostly young single women, flocked from their rural homes to work as mill girls in factory towns like Lowell. To ensure proper behavior, the young women were watched closely inside and outside the factory. The mill girls toiled over 12 hours a day, six days a week, for

These Massachusetts women of the mid-19th century are shown holding shuttles that were used during weaving.

Section 3 Overview

OBJECTIVES

1 To describe industrial growth in the United States.

2 To explain the spread of industry in Europe.

3 To identify the effects of industrialization on the rest of the world.

SKILLBUILDER

• Interpreting maps: region, movement, p. 644

CRITICAL THINKING

• Forming and supporting opinions, p. 644
• Analyzing causes, p. 645
• Clarifying, p. 646
• Recognizing bias, p. 646

FOCUS
5-Minute Warm-Up

▶ *Interpreting Maps*
Answering the following questions will help students understand the role of the railroads in the growth of the United States.

1. Look at the map on page 644. What was the total mileage of railroad track in 1840?

2. What was the total mileage in 1890?

WARM-UP TRANSPARENCY 25

OBJECTIVE 1 INSTRUCT

Industrial Development in the United States

▶ *Key Ideas*
• Like Britain, the United States offers conditions favorable to the growth of industry.

• British machinery spawns an American textile industry.

• American industry expands rapidly in the late 1800s, fueled by the growth of railroads.

IN-DEPTH RESOURCES: UNIT 6
Guided Reading, p. 3
Primary Source: "Life in a New England Factory," from *Voice of Industry*, p. 10

ACCESS FOR STUDENTS ACQUIRING ENGLISH
Guided Reading (Spanish), p. 252

SECTION 3 RESOURCES

PRINT RESOURCES

IN-DEPTH RESOURCES: UNIT 6
Guided Reading, p. 3
Primary Source: "Life in a New England Factory," p. 10

ACCESS FOR STUDENTS ACQUIRING ENGLISH
Guided Reading (Spanish), p. 252

FORMAL ASSESSMENT
Section Quiz, p. 291

ALTERNATIVE ASSESSMENT BOOK

TECHNOLOGY RESOURCES

WORLD ART AND CULTURES TRANSPARENCIES
AT55 Monet's *Saint Lazare Train Station, the Normandy Train*

CD-ROM
Electronic Library of Primary Sources

INTERNET www.mlworldhistory.com

decent wages. For some young women, the mill job meant a welcome alternative to becoming a servant, often the only other job open to them:

A VOICE FROM THE PAST
Country girls were naturally independent, and the feeling that at this new work the few hours they had of everyday leisure were entirely their own was a satisfaction to them. They preferred it to going out as "hired help." It was like a young man's pleasure in entering upon business for himself. Girls had never tried that experiment before, and they liked it.

LUCY LARCOM, *A New England Girlhood*

Textiles led the way, but clothing manufacture and shoemaking also underwent mechanization. Especially in the Northeast, skilled workers and farmers had formerly worked at home. Now they labored in factories in towns and cities such as Waltham, Lowell, and Lawrence, Massachusetts.

Later Expansion of U.S. Industry There was a great deal of industrial growth in the Northeast in the early 1800s. Nonetheless, the United States remained primarily an agricultural nation until the Civil War ended in 1865. During the last third of the 1800s, however, the country experienced a technological boom. As in Britain, a number of causes contributed to this boom. These included a wealth of natural resources, among them oil, coal, and iron; a burst of inventions, such as the electric light bulb and the telephone; and a swelling urban population that consumed the new manufactured goods.

Also as in Britain, railroads played a major role in America's industrialization. Cities like Chicago and Minneapolis expanded rapidly during the late 1800s. This was due to their location along the nation's expanding railroad lines. Chicago's stockyards and Minneapolis's grain industries prospered by selling their products to the rest of the country.

Indeed, the railroads themselves proved to be a profitable business. By the end of the 1800s, a limited number of large, powerful companies controlled over two-thirds of the nation's railroad tracks. Businesses of all kinds began to merge as the railroads had. Smaller companies joined together to form a larger one.

Building large businesses like railroads required a great deal of money. To raise the money, entrepreneurs sold shares of stock. People who bought stock became

Vocabulary
stock: a share in certain rights of ownership of a business.

The Growth of the United States

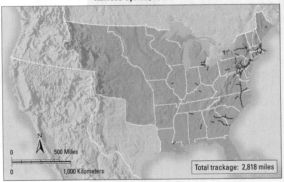
Railroad System, 1840
Total trackage: 2,818 miles

Railroad System, 1890
Total trackage: 208,152 miles

SKILLBUILDER: Interpreting Maps
1. **Region** In what part of the country were the first railroads built? By 1890, what other part of the country was densely covered by railroad tracks?
2. **Movement** In what direction did the railroads help people move across the country?

part-owners of these businesses called corporations. A **corporation** is a business owned by stockholders who share in its profits but are not personally responsible for its debts. In the late 1800s large corporations such as Standard Oil (founded by John D. Rockefeller) and the Carnegie Steel Company (founded by Andrew Carnegie) sprang up. They sought to control every aspect of their own industries in order to make big profits.

Big business—the giants that controlled entire industries—also made big profits by cutting the cost of producing goods. While workers earned small wages for long hours at hard labor, stockholders earned high profits and corporate leaders made fortunes.

Industrialization Reaches Continental Europe

European businesses yearned to adopt the "British miracle," the result of Britain's profitable new methods of manufacturing goods. Yet the troubles sparked by the French Revolution and the Napoleonic wars had halted trade, interrupted communication, and caused inflation in some parts of the continent. European countries were absorbed in the French Revolution and the Napoleonic wars between 1789 and 1815. They watched the gap widen between themselves and Britain. Nonetheless, industrialization eventually reached continental Europe.

Beginnings in Belgium Belgium led Europe in adopting Britain's new technology. Belgium had rich deposits of iron and coal as well as fine waterways for transportation.

Samuel Slater had smuggled to the United States the design of a spinning machine. Like him, British skilled workers played a key role in carrying industrialization to Belgium. A Lancashire carpenter named William Cockerill made his way to Belgium in 1799. He carried secret plans for building spinning machinery. Cockerill's son John eventually built an enormous industrial enterprise in eastern Belgium. It produced machinery, steam engines, and railway locomotives. Carrying the latest British advances, more British workers came to work with Cockerill. Several then founded their own companies in Europe.

German workers labor in a steel mill in this 1875 painting by Adolph von Menzel.

Germany Industrializes Germany was a politically divided empire. Economic isolation and scattered resources hampered countrywide industrialization in the early 1800s. Instead, pockets of industrialization appeared, as in the coal-rich Ruhr Valley of west-central Germany. Beginning around 1835, Germany began to copy the British model. Germany imported British equipment and engineers. German manufacturers also sent their children to England to learn industrial management.

Most important, Germany built railroads that linked its growing manufacturing cities, such as Frankfurt, with the Ruhr Valley's coal and iron deposits. In 1858, a German economist wrote, "Railroads and machine shops, coal mines and iron foundries, spinneries and rolling mills seem to spring up out of the ground, and smokestacks sprout from the earth like mushrooms."

Germany's economic strength spurred its ability to develop as a military power. By the late 19th century, Germany had become both an industrial and a military giant.

Expansion Throughout Europe In the rest of Europe, as in Germany, industrialization during the early 1800s proceeded by region rather than by country. Even in countries where agriculture dominated, pockets of industrialization arose. For example, Bohemia developed its spinning industry. Spain's Catalonia processed more cotton than Belgium. Northern Italy mechanized its textile production, specializing in silk spinning. Serf labor ran factories in regions around Moscow and St. Petersburg.

In France, continual industrial growth occurred only after 1850, when the central government constructed railroads. These railroads created a thriving national market for new French products.

The Industrial Revolution **645**

THINK THROUGH HISTORY
B. Analyzing Causes What factors slowed industrialization in Germany?
B. Answer Germany was politically divided, economically isolated, and its resources were scattered.

OBJECTIVE 2 INSTRUCT

Industrialization Reaches Continental Europe

▶ **Key Ideas**
• At first, war and unrest in Europe delay the growth of industry.
• Belgium is the first country in Europe to industrialize, followed by Germany.
• Other parts of Europe begin to develop industry in the mid-1800s, though progress is slow in some areas.

CRITICAL THINKING ACTIVITY
CLASS TIME: 15 MINUTES

Making a Web
Have students fill out a web like the one below with factors that impeded the growth of industry in continental Europe.

French Revolution and wars — political disunity in Germany — Obstacles to Industrial Growth — social structure — geographic problems

---

TEACHING OPTION | **BLOCK SCHEDULING** | **COOPERATIVE ACTIVITY: Planning an Industrial Fair** | **CLASS TIME 30 MINUTES**

Task: Students will plan an industrial fair that compares the products of today with those on display at London's Great Exhibition of 1851.

Purpose: To compare and contrast industrial technologies of the 1800s with those of the present.

Activity: Tell students that London hosted the Great Exhibition in 1851 to showcase industry throughout the world. Have students research this exhibition. Then ask groups to plan another exhibition that places modern products and technologies alongside those of the 1800s. Have them write a description of the exhibits.

📁 *Building a Portfolio:* Students may wish to add a description of their contribution to this project, along with a summary, to their portfolio.

📖 **ALTERNATIVE ASSESSMENT BOOK**
Standards for Evaluating a Cooperative Activity

Standards for Evaluation
Summaries should . . .

• explain why the group's featured technologies or products were chosen
• make connections between the Industrial Revolution and the industries of today

Teacher's Edition **645**

Worldwide Impact of Industrialization

Key Ideas
- The Industrial Revolution widens the gap between more-developed and less-developed nations.
- Industrialized countries exploit overseas colonies for resources and markets.
- Over time, standards of living rise in the industrial nations.

Global*Impact*
Industrialism Spreads to Egypt

Egypt was one of the few countries outside Europe and the United States to attempt industrialization in the 1800s. Others included Japan and Mexico, both in the late 1800s. Have students research these three cases and report on how they compared.

ASSESS & RETEACH

Section 3 Assessment
Have pairs of students work on the questions and share their answers with another pair of students.

Section Quiz

FORMAL ASSESSMENT
Section Quiz, p. 291

Reteaching Activity
CLASS TIME: 15 MINUTES

To help students understand the effects of industrialization, review the diagrams they have made for item 2 in the section assessment.

CLOSE ACTIVITY

CLASS TIME: 15 MINUTES

Writing an Editorial
Have students imagine that they are newspaper editors in the late 1800s. Ask them to write an editorial explaining the connection between industrialization and imperialism and to express an opinion on the issue. Tell them to support their view with evidence.

For a variety of reasons, many European countries did not industrialize. In some nations, the social structure delayed the adoption of new methods of production. The accidents of geography held back others. In Austria-Hungary and Spain, transportation posed great obstacles. Austria-Hungary's mountains defeated railroad builders. Spain lacked both good roads and waterways for canals.

Worldwide Impact of Industrialization

The Industrial Revolution shifted the world balance of power. It promoted competition between industrialized nations and increased poverty in less developed nations.

Global*Impact*

Industrialism Spreads to Egypt

When an Ottoman officer named Muhammad Ali (1769–1849) took power in Egypt, the new ruler sought to propel his country into the industrialized world. Muhammad Ali reformed Egypt's government and improved communications. He also established cotton mills, a glass factory, and a sugar refinery.

To earn the money required to purchase European goods and services, Muhammad Ali also advanced the development of commercial agriculture. During his rule, landlords forced peasants to become tenant farmers and grow cash crops for European markets. The modernizing and industrializing of Egypt were often done at the expense of the peasants.

Rise of Global Inequality Industrialization widened the gap between industrialized and non-industrialized countries, even while it strengthened their economic ties. To keep factories running and workers fed, industrialized countries required a steady supply of raw materials from less developed lands. In turn, industrialized countries viewed poor countries as markets for their manufactured products. A large inequality developed between the industrialized West and the rest of the world.

Britain led in exploiting its overseas colonies for resources and markets. Soon other European countries, the United States, Russia, and Japan followed Britain's lead, seizing colonies for their economic resources. Imperialism, the policy of extending one country's rule over many other lands, gave even more power and wealth to these already wealthy nations. Imperialism was born out of the cycle of industrialization, the development of new markets around the world, and the need for resources to supply the factories of Europe. (See Chapter 27.)

Transformation of Society Between 1700 and 1900, revolutions in agriculture, production, transportation, and communication changed the lives of people in Western Europe and the United States. Industrialization gave Europe tremendous economic power. Much of Europe was gaining the capability to produce many goods faster and more cheaply. In contrast, the economies of Asia and Africa were still based on agriculture and small workshops.

The industrialization that took place in the 1700s and 1800s revolutionized every aspect of society, from daily life to life expectancy. Despite the hardships early urban workers suffered, population, health, and wealth eventually rose dramatically in all industrialized countries. The development of a middle class created great opportunities for education and democratic participation. Greater democratic participation, in turn, fueled a powerful movement for social reform.

THINK THROUGH HISTORY
C. Clarifying Why did imperialism grow out of industrialization
C. Possible Answer Industrialized countries depended on less-developed lands for raw materials and as markets for manufactured goods. They seized colonies for their resources and markets.

Section 3 Assessment

1. TERMS & NAMES
Identify
- corporation

2. TAKING NOTES
Using a web diagram like the one below, show the effects of industrialization on the world.

3. RECOGNIZING BIAS
Go back to the quote from Lucy Larcom on page 644. Do you think her feelings about working in the mill are typical? Why or why not?

THINK ABOUT
- her experiences in a mill
- her possible bias

4. THEME ACTIVITY
Empire Building Draw a political cartoon that could have been used by the British government. It should show their sense of their own superiority over non-industrialized nations that they planned to colonize.

ANSWERS

1. TERMS & NAMES
corporation, p. 645

2. TAKING NOTES
Strengthened economic ties between countries; widened gap between industrialized and non-industrialized countries; promoted colonization

3. RECOGNIZING BIAS
Students who answer yes will note that she seems to be

speaking as a young woman from New England who chose to work in the mill and was pleased with the experience. Students who answer no may point out that since she recorded her thoughts and experiences in a memoir or journal, she may have been more independent than most young women.

4. THEME ACTIVITY
Standards for Evaluation
An effective cartoon should meet the following criteria:
- shows a British point of view
- demonstrates knowledge of industrialization
- includes a variety of detail that enriches the cartoon

TERMS & NAMES
- laissez faire
- Adam Smith
- capitalism
- utilitarianism
- socialism
- Karl Marx
- communism
- union
- collective bargaining
- strike

MAIN IDEA	WHY IT MATTERS NOW
The Industrial Revolution led to economic, social, and political reforms.	Many modern social welfare programs developed during this period.

SETTING THE STAGE In industrialized countries in the 1800s, many business leaders believed that progress opened a gap between rich and poor. These leaders cautioned governments to stay out of business and economic affairs. Reformers, however, felt that governments should play an active role in bettering conditions for the poor.

The Philosophers of Industrialization

The term **laissez faire** (LEHS·ay·FAIR) refers to the economic policy of letting owners of industry and business set working conditions without interference. That policy favors a free market unregulated by the government. The term comes from a French phrase that means "let do," and by extension, "let people do as they please."

Laissez-faire Economics Laissez faire stemmed from French economic philosophers of the 18th-century Enlightenment. They criticized the idea that nations grow wealthy by placing heavy tariffs on foreign goods. In fact, they argued, government regulations only interfered with the production of wealth. These philosophers believed that if the government allowed free trade—the flow of commerce in the world market without government regulation—the economy would prosper.

Adam Smith, a professor at the University of Glasgow, Scotland, defended the idea of a free economy, or free markets, in his 1776 book *The Wealth of Nations.* According to Smith, economic liberty guaranteed economic progress. Smith claimed that government need not interfere in the economy.

The Ideas of Malthus and Ricardo Economists Thomas Malthus and David Ricardo supported Smith's basic ideas. Like Smith, they believed that natural laws governed economic life. Their important ideas were the foundation of laissez-faire capitalism. **Capitalism** is an economic system in which money is invested in business ventures with the goal of making a profit. These ideas helped bring about the Industrial Revolution.

In *An Essay on the Principle of Population,* written in 1798, Thomas Malthus argued that population tended to increase more rapidly than the food supply. Without wars and epidemics to kill off the extra people, most were destined to be poor and miserable. The predictions of Malthus seemed to be coming true in the 1840s.

David Ricardo, a wealthy stockbroker, took Malthus's theory one step further in his book, *Principles of Political Economy and Taxation* (1817). Like Malthus, Ricardo believed that a permanent underclass would always be poor. In a market system, if there are many workers and abundant resources, then labor and resources are cheap. If there

Background
Ricardo stated the "iron law of wages." He argued that because of population growth wages would be just high enough to keep workers from starving.

HISTORY MAKERS

Adam Smith
1723–1790

In his book *The Wealth of Nations,* Smith argued that if individuals freely followed their own self-interest, the world would be an orderly and progressive place. After all, sellers made money by producing things that other people wanted to buy. Buyers spent money for the things they wanted most. In such a marketplace, Smith thought, social harmony would result without any government direction, "as if by an invisible hand." Smith's ideas were central to the development of capitalism.

Smith applied an invisible hand of his own. When the economist died, people discovered that he had secretly donated large chunks of his income to charities.

The Industrial Revolution **647**

SECTION 4 RESOURCES

PRINT RESOURCES

IN-DEPTH RESOURCES: UNIT 6
Guided Reading, p. 4
Skillbuilder Practice: Developing Historical Perspective, p. 5
Primary Source: from *The Wealth of Nations,* p. 11
History Makers: Saint-Simon, p. 16
Connections Across Time and Cultures: Enlightenment Ideals in an Industrial Age, p. 17

ACCESS FOR STUDENTS ACQUIRING ENGLISH
Guided Reading (Spanish), p. 253
Skillbuilder Practice (Spanish), p. 254

FORMAL ASSESSMENT
Section Quiz, p. 292

TECHNOLOGY RESOURCES

CRITICAL THINKING TRANSPARENCIES
CT25 Industrialists and Reformers
CT61 Chapter 25 Visual Summary

CD-ROM
Electronic Library of Primary Sources

INTERNET www.mlworldhistory.com

Section 4 Overview

OBJECTIVES

1. To identify ideas and thinkers that supported industrialization.
2. To explain the origins and main concepts of socialism.
3. To examine unionization and legislative reform.
4. To describe other reform movements of the 1800s.

SKILLBUILDER
- Interpreting charts, p. 650

CRITICAL THINKING
- Making inferences, pp. 648, 652
- Clarifying, p. 648
- Summarizing, pp. 649, 651
- Identifying problems, p. 652
- Analyzing themes, p. 652
- Contrasting, p. 653

FOCUS
5-Minute Warm-Up

▶ *Making Inferences*
To help students understand the origins of capitalism, have them answer the following questions.

1. Read the History Maker on Adam Smith on page 647. What was Smith's attitude toward government intervention in business?

2. Does Smith's economic theory assume an optimistic or pessimistic view of human nature?

WARM-UP TRANSPARENCY 25

OBJECTIVE 1 INSTRUCT

The Philosophers of Industrialization

▶ *Key Ideas*
- Laissez-faire thinkers support a free market and oppose government regulation.
- Economists Adam Smith, Thomas Malthus, and David Ricardo argue that natural law governs economic life.

IN-DEPTH RESOURCES: UNIT 6
Guided Reading, p. 4

ACCESS FOR STUDENTS ACQUIRING ENGLISH
Guided Reading (Spanish), p. 253

HISTORYMAKERS

Adam Smith

(See page 647)

Smith opposed government interference in business on principle, including efforts to help business. For example, he opposed the mercantilist policy of supporting industry through tariffs and other restrictions on competition. Ask students how trying to help business might be as harmful as trying to restrict it.

IN-DEPTH RESOURCES: UNIT 6
Primary Source: from *The Wealth of Nations*, p. 11
Connections Across Time and Cultures: Enlightenment Ideals in an Industrial Age, p. 17

OBJECTIVE ② INSTRUCT

Rise of Socialism

▶ Key Ideas

- Some thinkers oppose laissez-faire policies and favor government efforts to improve people's lives.

- Utilitarian thinkers Jeremy Bentham and John Stuart Mill argue that government should promote the general welfare.

- Socialists and Marxists propose state controls to achieve social and economic equality.

IN-DEPTH RESOURCES: UNIT 6
History Maker: Saint-Simon, p. 16

---

are few workers and scarce resources, then they are expensive. Ricardo believed that wages would be forced down as population increased.

Laissez-faire thinkers such as Smith, Malthus, and Ricardo opposed government efforts to help poor workers. They thought that creating minimum wage laws and better working conditions would upset the free market system, lower profits, and undermine the production of wealth in society.

Rise of Socialism

In contrast to laissez-faire philosophy, which advised governments to leave business alone, other theorists believed that governments should intervene. These thinkers believed that wealthy people or the government must take action to improve people's lives. The French writer Alexis de Tocqueville gave a warning:

> **A VOICE FROM THE PAST**
> Consider what is happening among the working classes. . . . Do you not see spreading among them, little by little, opinions and ideas that aim not to overturn such and such a ministry, or such laws, or such a government, but society itself, to shake it to the foundations upon which it now rests?
> **ALEXIS DE TOCQUEVILLE, 1848 speech**

Jeremy Bentham's skeleton, dressed in Bentham's clothes and topped off by a wax head, is preserved in a wooden cabinet at University College, London.

Utilitarianism Modifying the ideas of Adam Smith, an English philosopher named Jeremy Bentham introduced the philosophy of **utilitarianism.** Bentham wrote his most influential works in the late 1700s. He argued that people should judge ideas, institutions, and actions on the basis of their utility, or usefulness. He argued that the government should try to promote the greatest good for the greatest number of people. A government policy was only useful if it promoted this goal. Bentham argued that in general the individual should be free to pursue his or her own advantage without interference from the state.

John Stuart Mill, a philosopher and economist, led the utilitarian movement in the 1800s. Mill came to question unregulated capitalism. He believed it was wrong that workers should lead deprived lives that sometimes bordered on starvation. Mill wished to help ordinary working people with policies that would lead to a more equal division of profits. He also favored a cooperative system of agriculture and women's rights, including the right to vote. Mill called for the government to do away with great differences in wealth. Utilitarians also pushed for reforms in the legal and prison systems and in education.

Utopian Ideas Other reformers took an even more active approach. Shocked by the misery and poverty of the working class, a British factory owner named Robert Owen improved working conditions for his employees. Near his cotton mill in New Lanark, Scotland, Owen built houses, which he rented at low rates. He prohibited children under ten from working in the mills and provided free schooling.

Then, in 1824, he traveled to the United States. He founded a cooperative community in New Harmony, Indiana, in 1825. He intended this community to be a utopia, or perfect living place. New Harmony only lasted three years. However, it inspired the founding of other communities.

Socialism and Marxism French reformers such as Charles Fourier (FUR·ee·AY), Saint-Simon (san see·MOHN), and others sought to offset the effects of industrialization with a new kind of economic system called socialism. In **socialism,** the factors of production are owned by the public and operate for the welfare of all. Socialism grew out of an optimistic view of human nature, a belief in progress, and a concern for social justice.

648 Chapter 25

THINK THROUGH HISTORY
A. Making Inferences Economics came to be called the "dismal [gloomy] science," in part because of the ideas of Malthus and Ricardo. Why might their ideas have earned this phrase?
A. Possible Answer Malthus's ideas about overpopulation, wars, and epidemics, and Ricardo's "iron law of wages" were pessimistic concepts.

THINK THROUGH HISTORY
B. Clarifying How did Mill want to change the economic system?
B. Possible Answer He wanted to equalize the distribution of wealth and give the poor a break; he favored a cooperative system of agriculture.

Background
The word *utopia* comes from the name for an imaginary island in a book of the same name written by Sir Thomas More. It means "no place" in Greek. More's *Utopia* (1516) is a political essay that discusses life under an ideal government.

TEACHING OPTIONS | **CONNECTIONS ACROSS TIME AND PLACE**

Socialism Have students do research to find out about countries that have adopted socialist or Marxist forms of government since these ideas first appeared in the 1800s. You might direct students to the democratic socialist countries of Scandinavia or to such communist or formerly communist countries as Russia, China, Vietnam, and the nations of eastern Europe. Have students choose one of these countries and report to the class on the way socialism was implemented and what happened as a result. Ask students if any countries in the world today still practice socialism.

CUSTOMIZING FOR SPECIAL NEEDS

Gifted and Talented Students: Utopian Communities Invite students to find out more about utopian communities, either in Britain or the United States. Have students report to the class on a particular community or group of communities and the principles that inspired them. For example, they might examine New Harmony, Indiana, or Brook Farm, near Boston. Encourage students to show pictures or a diagram of the community, if possible. Have students explain what happened to the community, and why.

Socialists argued that the government should actively plan the economy rather than depending on free-market capitalism to do the job. They argued that government control of factories, mines, railroads, and other key industries would abolish poverty and promote equality. Public ownership, they believed, would help the workers, who were at the mercy of greedy employers.

The Communist Manifesto The writings of a German journalist named **Karl Marx** introduced the world to a radical type of socialism called Marxism. Marx and Friedrich Engels, a German whose father owned a textile mill in Manchester, outlined their ideas in a 23-page pamphlet called *The Communist Manifesto*. In their manifesto, Marx and Engels argued that human societies have always been divided into warring classes. In their own time, these were the middle-class "haves" or employers, called the bourgeoisie (BUR·zhwah·ZEE), and the "have-nots" or workers, called the proletariat (PROH·lih·TAIR·ee·iht). While the wealthy controlled the means of producing goods, the poor performed backbreaking labor under terrible conditions. This situation resulted in conflict:

A VOICE FROM THE PAST
Freeman and slave, patrician and plebeian, lord and serf, guild-master and journeyman, in a word, oppressor and oppressed, stood in constant opposition to one another, carried on an uninterrupted, now hidden, now open fight, a fight that each time ended, either in a revolutionary reconstitution of society at large, or in the common ruin of the contending classes.

KARL MARX AND FRIEDRICH ENGELS, *The Communist Manifesto* (1848)

According to Marx and Engels, the Industrial Revolution had enriched the wealthy and impoverished the poor. The two writers predicted that the workers would overthrow the owners: "The proletarians have nothing to lose but their chains. They have a world to win. Workingmen of all countries, unite."

The Future According to Marx Marx believed that the capitalist system, which produced the Industrial Revolution, would eventually destroy itself in the following way. Factories would drive small artisans out of business, leaving a small number of manufacturers to control all the wealth. The large proletariat would revolt, seize the factories and mills from the capitalists, and produce what society needed. Workers, sharing in the profits, would bring about economic equality for all people. The workers would control the government in a "dictatorship of the proletariat." After a period of cooperative living and education, the state or government would wither away as a classless society developed.

Marx called this final phase pure communism. Marx described **communism** as a form of complete socialism in which the means of production—all land, mines, factories, railroads, and businesses—would be owned by the people. Private property would in effect cease to exist. All goods and services would be shared equally.

Published in 1848, *The Communist Manifesto* produced few short-term results. Though widespread revolts shook Europe during 1848 and 1849, Europe's leaders eventually put down the uprisings. Only after the turn of the century did the fiery Marxist pamphlet produce explosive results. In the 1900s, Marxism inspired revolutionaries such as Russia's Lenin, China's Mao Zedong, Vietnam's Ho Chi Minh, and Cuba's Fidel Castro. These revolutionary leaders adapted Marx's beliefs and arguments to their own specific situations and needs.

In their pamphlet, Marx and Engels condemned the inequalities of early industrial economies. Yet several of Marx's and Engels's predictions have since proved wrong.

HISTORY MAKERS

**Karl Marx
1818–1883**

Karl Marx studied philosophy at the University of Berlin before he turned to journalism and economics. In 1849, Marx joined the flood of radicals who fled continental Europe for England. He had declared in *The Communist Manifesto* that "the working men have no country."

Marx's theories of socialism and the inevitable revolt of the working class made him very little money. He earned a meager living as a journalist. His wealthy coauthor and fellow German, Friedrich Engels, gave Marx financial aid.

THINK THROUGH HISTORY
C. Summarizing
What were the ideas of Marx and Engels concerning relations between the owners and the working class?
C. Possible Answer
Marx and Engels believed the working class and the owners were natural enemies.

HISTORY MAKERS
Karl Marx

Though a revolutionary, Marx disliked crowds and avoided demonstrations. He was said to be arrogant in debate and uncomfortable before mass audiences. He remained poor almost on principle, yet accepted the financial support of his friend Friedrich Engels. Suggest to students that they read more about Marx and discuss his life in class.

 ELECTRONIC LIBRARY OF PRIMARY SOURCES
from *The Communist Manifesto*

MORE ABOUT . . .
Revolutionary Upheaval

The most successful workers' revolt of the 1800s occurred in Paris in 1871. Calling for an end to unfair wages and working conditions, workers seized Paris and set up a people's government, called the Paris Commune. Although Marx supported this revolt, the workers were not communist-inspired. The Commune lasted just two months, then was crushed by French troops.

The Industrial Revolution **649**

Explaining the Skill Using historical perspective means evaluating a time in history based on the conditions that existed then instead of judging by what we know now. For example, given Marxism's record of totalitarianism and economic failure in the 20th century, some students might initially wonder why people believed that the theories of Karl Marx could improve their lives. However, knowing about the difficult conditions experienced by many workers during the Industrial Revolution can help students realize Marxism's appeal at the time.

Applying the Skill: *A Voice from the Past*
Ask students to reread "A Voice from the Past," then ask them the following questions:

1. What was the relationship between different social classes, according to Marx and Engels?

2. What was the end result of their relationship?

3. Do the terms *oppressor* and *oppressed* seem to adequately define all social relationships today?

IN-DEPTH RESOURCES: UNIT 6
Skillbuilder Practice: Developing Historical Perspective, p. 5

Capitalism vs. Marxism

Interpreting the Chart Have students read the title and headings and explain what the chart compares. *Ideas of capitalism and Marxism.* Point out that the chart is a list of ideas that do not necessarily match up from one column to the other.

Extension Activity Ask students how capitalism and Marxism differ in their idea of progress. *In capitalism, progress occurs when people pursue their self-interest. In Marxism, it occurs when the state is destroyed and a classless society emerges.*

SKILLBUILDER Answers

1. Intense class struggle; workers exploited by employers; labor of workers creates profit.

2. Answers will vary. Students might mention the breakup of the Soviet Union and economic reform in China as signs of the decline of Marxist ideas. Capitalist societies, on the other hand, seem to be prospering.

OBJECTIVE 3 INSTRUCT

Unionization and Legislative Reform

Key Ideas

- Workers organize unions to raise wages and improve conditions.
- Unions eventually become established and legal.
- Reform laws are passed in Britain and the United States to limit child labor and set work hours.

🏛 **CRITICAL THINKING TRANSPARENCIES**
CT25 Industrialists and Reformers

Capitalism vs. Marxism

Capitalist Ideas	Marxist Ideas
• Progress results when individuals follow their own self-interest.	• All great movements in history are the result of an economic class struggle.
• Businesses follow their own self-interest when they compete with one another for the consumer's money.	• The "haves" take advantage of the "have-nots."
• Each producer tries to provide goods and services that are better and less expensive than those of competitors.	• The Industrial Revolution intensified the class struggle.
• Consumers compete with one another to purchase the best goods at the lowest prices.	• Workers are exploited by employers.
• Market economy aims to produce the best products and the lowest prices.	• The labor of workers creates profit for employers.
• Government should not interfere in the economy.	• The capitalist system will eventually destroy itself. The state will wither away as a classless society develops.

Adam Smith   Karl Marx

SKILLBUILDER: Interpreting Charts

1. *Which ideas of Marxism seem to be a direct reaction to the Industrial Revolution?*
2. *Which system of ideas seems dominant in the world today? Support your opinion.*

They believed that economic forces alone dominated society. Time has shown, however, that religion, nationalism, ethnic loyalties, and a desire for democratic reforms may be as strong influences on history as economic forces. In addition, the gap between the rich and poor within the industrialized countries failed to widen in the way that Marx and Engels predicted, mostly because of the following types of reform.

Unionization and Legislative Reform

Factory workers faced long hours, dirty and dangerous working conditions, and the threat of being laid off. By the 1800s, working people became more active in politics. To press for reforms, workers joined together in voluntary associations called **unions.**

The Union Movement A union spoke for all the workers in a particular trade. Unions engaged in **collective bargaining**—negotiations between workers and their employers. They bargained for better working conditions and higher pay. If factory owners refused these demands, union members could **strike,** or refuse to work.

Skilled workers led the way in forming unions because their special skills gave them extra bargaining power. Management would have trouble replacing such skilled workers as carpenters, printers, and spinners. Thus the earliest unions helped the lower middle class more than they helped the poorest workers.

The union movement underwent slow, painful growth in both Great Britain and the United States. For years, the British government denied workers the right to form unions. The government saw unions as a threat to social order and stability. Indeed, the Combination Acts of 1799 and 1800 outlawed unions and strikes. Bravely ignoring the threat of jail or job loss, factory workers joined unions anyway. Parliament finally repealed the Combination Acts in 1824. After 1825, the British government unhappily tolerated unions.

British unions had shared goals of raising wages and improving working conditions. By 1875, British trade unions had won the right to strike and picket peacefully. They had also built up a membership of about 1 million people.

In the United States, skilled workers had belonged to unions since the early 1800s. In 1886, several unions joined together to form the organization that would become the

---

Linguistic Learners: *Internet Research* Invite students to use the Internet to research issues of labor organizing or legislative reform in the late 1800s. Students might find out about a particular union or labor struggle. A fruitful subject of investigation might be the Homestead steel strike of 1892, in

which Andrew Carnegie and Henry Clay Frick used Pinkerton guards to end a strike. Have students share the results of their research in a short report or class discussion.

INTERNET
Click on *World History* at www.mlworldhistory.com

Students Acquiring English
Vocabulary Study Pair less fluent English speakers with more fluent speakers and have them work with the key terms for this section. Encourage students to quiz each other on the meaning of the terms. More fluent students might also explain the meaning of terms based on word parts. For

example, *utilitarianism, socialism,* and *communism* all combine root words with the suffix *-ism.* In this context, *-ism* is added to designate a doctrine, theory, or system of principles related to the root word. Thus, *socialism* means "the belief that the wealth of a country should be shared equally among all its citizens."

American Federation of Labor (AFL). A series of successful strikes won AFL members higher wages and shorter hours.

Reform Laws In both Great Britain and the United States, new laws reformed some of the worst abuses of industrialization. In 1832, for example, Parliament set up a committee to investigate child labor. As a result of this committee's findings, Parliament passed the Factory Act of 1833. The new law made it illegal to hire children under 9 years old. Children from the ages of 9 to 12 could not work more than 8 hours a day. Young people from 13 to 17 could not work more than 12 hours. In 1842 the Mines Act prevented women and children from working underground.

This print shows an attack on the workhouse, a prison in which limited sentences at manual labor are served. The attack took place in Stockport, England, during demonstrations by workers in the 1830s. The workers are shown distributing bread from the workhouse.

In 1847, the Parliament passed a bill that helped working women as well as their children. The Ten Hours Act of 1847 limited the workday to ten hours for women and children who worked in factories.

Reformers in the United States also passed legislation to protect child workers. In 1904, a group of progressive reformers organized the National Child Labor Committee to end child labor. Arguing that child labor lowered wages for all workers, labor union members joined the reformers. Together these groups pressured national and state politicians to ban child labor and set maximum working hours. The Supreme Court in 1919 had objected to a federal child labor law. However, it did allow individual states to legally limit the working hours of women and, later, of men.

THINK THROUGH HISTORY
D. Summarizing
What were some of the important reform bills passed in Britain during this period?
D. Possible Answer
Factory Act of 1833; Mines Act of 1842; Ten Hours Act of 1847.

Other Reform Movements

Almost from the beginning, reform movements sprang up in response to the negative impact of industrialization. These reforms included improving the workplace and extending the right to vote to working-class men. The same impulse toward reform, along with the ideals of the French Revolution, also helped to end slavery and promote new rights for women and children.

Abolition of Slavery William Wilberforce, a highly religious man, was a member of Parliament who led the fight for abolition—the end of the slave trade and slavery in the British Empire. Parliament passed a bill to end the slave trade in the British West Indies in 1807. After he retired from Parliament in 1825, Wilberforce continued his fight to free the slaves. Britain finally abolished slavery in its empire in 1833.

THINK THROUGH HISTORY
E. Summarizing
What were some of the motives of British abolitionists?
E. Possible Answer
Religious beliefs; economic self-interest of competing workers; economic self-interest of those interested in hiring cheap labor rather than using slave labor.

British antislavery activists had mixed motives. Some were morally against slavery, such as the abolitionist William Wilberforce. Others viewed slave labor as an economic threat. Furthermore, a new class of industrialists developed who supported cheap labor rather than slave labor. They soon gained power in Parliament.

In the United States the movement to fulfill the promise of the Declaration of Independence by ending slavery grew in the early 1800s. The enslavement of African people finally ended in the United States when the Union won the Civil War in 1865.

With the end of the U.S. Civil War, enslavement persisted in the Americas only in Puerto Rico, Cuba, and Brazil. In Puerto Rico, slavery was ended in 1873. Spain finally abolished slavery in its Cuban colony in 1886. Not until 1888 did Brazil's huge enslaved population win freedom.

The Industrial Revolution **651**

OBJECTIVE 4 INSTRUCT

Other Reform Movements

▶ **Key Ideas**
- Industrialization spurs the growth of various reform movements.
- The abolition movement helps to end slavery by the late 1800s.
- Women fight for their rights, while education and prison reform make strides.

CRITICAL THINKING ACTIVITY
CLASS TIME: 10 MINUTES

Making Connections
Have students explain connections between industrialization and reform movements by filling in the chart below.

Reform	Link to Industrialization
Abolition	
Women's rights	
Education	

TEACHING OPTION | **BLOCK SCHEDULING** | **COOPERATIVE ACTIVITY: Playing an Identity Game** | **CLASS TIME 15 MINUTES**

Task: Students will play a guessing game—something like the television show *What's My Line?*—in which they try to guess the identity of other students posing as historical figures.

Purpose: To reinforce and further students' knowledge of key thinkers from the early Industrial Age.

Activity: Tell students that they are going to play a guessing game in which they try to identify important thinkers from the 1800s. Have pairs of students choose one of the people discussed in this section (such as Smith, Malthus, Ricardo, Bentham, Marx, and so forth) and do further research on that person's life and ideas. Then have them write a sentence or two describing the person but don't give away his or her identity in any obvious way. To play the game, students should say their sentences to the class. The class can then ask up to five questions to try to determine the identity of the person being portrayed.

 ALTERNATIVE ASSESSMENT BOOK
Standards for Evaluating a Cooperative Activity

Teacher's Edition **651**

652 Chapter 25

HISTORY MAKERS

Jane Addams
1860–1935

After graduating from college, Jane Addams wondered what to do with her life.

> I gradually became convinced that it would be a good thing to rent a house in a part of the city where many primitive and actual needs are found, in which young women who had been given over too exclusively to study, might . . . learn of life from life itself.

Addams and her friend Ellen Starr set up Hull House in a working-class district in Chicago. Eventually the facilities included a nursery, a gym, a kitchen, and a boarding house for working women. Hull House not only served the immigrant population of the neighborhood, it also trained social workers.

Women Fight for Change The Industrial Revolution proved a mixed blessing for women. On the one hand, factory work offered higher wages than work done at home. Women spinners in Manchester, for example, earned much more money than women who stayed home to spin cotton thread. On the other hand, women factory workers usually made only one-third as much money as men.

Women led reform movements to address this and other pressing social issues. During the mid-1800s, for example, women formed unions in the trades where they dominated. In Britain, some women served as safety inspectors in factories where other women worked. In the United States, college-educated women like Jane Addams ran settlement houses. These community centers served the poor residents of slum neighborhoods.

In both the United States and Britain, women who had rallied for the abolition of slavery began to wonder why their own rights should be denied on the basis of gender. The movement for women's rights began in the United States as early as 1848. Women activists around the world joined to found the International Council for Women in 1888. Delegates and observers from 27 countries attended the council's 1899 meeting.

Reforms Spread to Many Areas of Life In the United States and Western Europe, reformers tried to correct the problems troubling the newly industrialized nations. Public education and prison reform ranked high on the reformers' lists.

One of the most prominent U.S. reformers, Horace Mann of Massachusetts, favored free public education for all children. Mann, who spent his own childhood working at hard labor, warned, "If we do not prepare children to become good citizens . . . if we do not enrich their minds with knowledge, then our republic must go down to destruction." By the 1850s many states were starting to establish a system of public schools. In Western Europe, free public schooling became available in the late 1800s.

In 1831, French writer Alexis de Tocqueville had contrasted the brutal conditions in American prisons to the "extended liberty" of American society. Reformers took on the challenge of prison reform, emphasizing the goal of restoring prisoners to useful lives.

During the 1800s, democracy grew in the industrialized countries even as foreign expansion increased. The industrialized western democracies faced new challenges both at home and abroad. You will learn about these challenges in Chapter 26.

Section ④ Assessment

1. TERMS & NAMES
Identify
- laissez faire
- Adam Smith
- capitalism
- utilitarianism
- socialism
- Karl Marx
- communism
- union
- collective bargaining
- strike

2. TAKING NOTES
Compare capitalism with Marxism using a Venn diagram such as the one below.

Write a paragraph comparing and contrasting capitalism and Marxism.

3. IDENTIFYING PROBLEMS
What were the main problems faced by the unions during the 1800s? How did the unions overcome these problems?

THINK ABOUT
- government restrictions
- labor reforms
- skilled workers vs. unskilled workers

4. ANALYZING THEMES
Economics According to Marx and Engels, economic forces alone dominate society. How important do you think such forces are? Support your opinion using evidence from this and previous chapters.

THINK ABOUT
- other forces, like ethnic loyalties, desire for democracy
- causes of the Industrial Revolution
- the class structure

652 Chapter 25

ANSWERS

Industrialization

Industrialization eventually lifted the standard of living for many people in Europe and North America in the 1800s. Yet the process also brought suffering to countless workers who crowded into filthy cities to toil for starvation wages. The following excerpts reveal a variety of perspectives on this major historical event.

TESTIMONY
Ellison Jack

An 11-year-old girl who worked in the mines testified before a Parliamentary commission on child labor in 1842.

I have been working below three years on my father's account; he takes me down at two in the morning, and I come up at one and two next afternoon. I go to bed at six at night to be ready for work next morning. . . . I have to bear my burthen [burden] up four traps, or ladders, before I get to the main road which leads to the pit bottom. My task is four or five tubs. . . . I fill five tubs in twenty journeys.

I have had the strap [beating] when I did not do my bidding. Am very glad when my task is wrought, as it sore fatigues.

LETTER

Mary Paul

Mary Paul worked in a textile factory in Lowell, Massachusetts. In an 1846 letter to her father in New Hampshire, the 16-year-old expressed her satisfaction with her situation at Lowell.

I am at work in a spinning room tending four sides of warp which is one girl's work. The overseer tells me that he never had a girl get along better than I do. . . . I have a very good boarding place, have enough to eat. . . . The girls are all kind and obliging. . . . I think that the factory is the best place for me and if any girl wants employment, I advise them to come to Lowell.

BOOK
Andrew Carnegie

In his autobiography, published in 1920, the multimillionaire industrialist views with optimism the growth of American industry.

America is soon to change from being the dearest steel manufacturing country to the cheapest. Already the shipyards of Belfast are our customers. This is but the beginning. Under present conditions America can produce steel as cheaply as any other land, notwithstanding its higher-priced labor. There is no other labor so cheap as the dearest in the mechanical field, provided it is free, contented, zealous, and reaping reward as it renders service. And here America leads.

One great advantage which America will have in competing in the markets of the world is that her manufacturers will have the best home market. Upon this they can depend for a return upon capital, and the surplus product can be exported with advantage, even when the prices received for it do no more than cover actual cost, provided the exports be charged with their proportion of all expenses. The nation that has the best home market, especially if products are standardized, as ours are, can soon outsell the foreign producer.

BOOK
Friedrich Engels

Friedrich Engels, who managed a textile factory in Manchester, England, spent his nights wandering the city's slums.

Nobody troubles about the poor as they struggle helplessly in the whirlpool of modern industrial life. The working man may be lucky enough to find employment, if by his labor he can enrich some member of the middle classes. But his wages are so low that they hardly keep body and soul together. If he cannot find work, he can steal, unless he is afraid of the police; or he can go hungry and then the police will see to it that he will die of hunger in such a way as not to disturb the equanimity of the middle classes.

Connect *to* History

Contrasting Contrast two different points of view on the Industrial Revolution. Why do you think the viewpoints differ?

 SEE SKILLBUILDER HANDBOOK, PAGE 996

Connect *to* Today

Researching Find a modern view of industrialization in an editorial cartoon, a poem, an excerpt from a novel, or a photograph. Bring it to class and explain its point of view.

 CD-ROM For another perspective on the Industrial Revolution, see World History: Electronic Library of Primary Sources.

The Industrial Revolution **653**

---

different **Perspectives**

Industrialization: Before and After

As students discuss these perspectives, have them consider how life is different today as a result of the Industrial Revolution.

A list of effects might include some of the following points:

- The world has become more interconnected through the development of rapid transport and systems of communications, allowing a global exchange of people, information, and goods.
- Mass-produced goods—clothes, computers, cars, paper clips—have helped raise standards of living, but many traditional craft skills have been lost.
- Many people enjoy good diets, which may include exotic foods from around the world, but others still suffer hunger, in part because food production geared for mass markets may ignore local needs.
- Cities have developed to an extraordinary degree and offer great advantages, but they are often overcrowded, polluted, and dangerous.
- Many people enjoy good jobs at good pay, but others still work at menial labor or suffer stress or physical harm from poor work conditions.

ELECTRONIC LIBRARY OF PRIMARY SOURCES
from "How I Served My Apprenticeship" by Andrew Carnegie

Connect *to* History

Contrasting
Possible Response: The views of Ellison Jack and Mary Paul differ because their work conditions differed. Jack labored under miserable conditions, while Paul seemed to have had her basic needs met. Working in a mill represented a positive alternative to a less interesting life.

Connect *to* Today

Researching
Students might find a photograph of wage laborers in a factory along the United States-Mexico border or an article about the benefits enjoyed by high-tech workers in the computer industry. Perspectives on industrialization might vary from highly positive to highly negative.

Chapter 25 Assessment

TERMS & NAMES

1. Industrial Revolution, p. 633
2. enclosure, p. 633
3. factory, p. 635
4. urbanization, p. 638
5. middle class, p. 639
6. corporation, p. 645
7. laissez faire, p. 647
8. socialism, p. 648
9. Karl Marx, p. 649
10. collective bargaining, p. 650

REVIEW QUESTIONS

Answers will vary.

11. Water power and coal; iron ore; rivers; good harbors

12. Forced small farmers to give up farming; caused forced migration to cities; some farmers became tenant farmers

13. Possible Responses: steam engine, locomotive, factory, spinning jenny, flying shuttle. Student descriptions of impact will vary.

14. No sanitary codes; lack of adequate housing, education, police protection, running water, indoor plumbing; frequent epidemics

15. Some participants in Industrial Revolution became wealthier than landowners and threatened their power; spurred even more class divisions, resulting in upper class, upper middle class, lower middle class, working class.

16. Dyes and wastes poisoned the river; coal polluted the air.

17. Political turmoil caused by the French Revolution slowed trade, interrupted communication, and caused inflation.

18. Industrialized countries needed more natural resources from less developed countries for factories; industrialized countries also needed to develop new markets around the world; these needs fostered inequality.

19. Bourgeoisie ("haves," employers), proletariat ("have-nots," workers)

20. *Possible responses:* formed unions, served as safety inspectors, rallied for abolition of slavery, founded the International Council for Women

TERMS & NAMES

Briefly explain the importance of each of the following to industrialization.

1. Industrial Revolution
2. enclosure
3. factory
4. urbanization
5. middle class
6. corporation
7. laissez faire
8. socialism
9. Karl Marx
10. collective bargaining

Interact *with* History

On page 632, you looked at working conditions in an English factory in the 19th century before reading about the Industrial Revolution. Now that you've read the chapter, rethink your decision about what you would do to change your situation. What factory working conditions would you like to see change? What benefits might a union bring? What disadvantages might result if workers organize? Discuss your opinions with a small group.

REVIEW QUESTIONS

SECTION 1 (pages 633–637)
The Beginnings of Industrialization

11. What were the four natural resources needed for British industrialization?

12. How did the enclosure movement change agriculture in England?

13. Name two inventions that were created during the Industrial Revolution. Describe their impact.

SECTION 2 (pages 638–642)
Patterns of Change: Industrialization

14. Describe the living conditions in Britain during industrialization.

15. How did the new middle class transform the social structure of Great Britain during industrialization?

16. How did industrialization affect Manchester's natural environment?

SECTION 3 (pages 643–646)
Industrialization Spreads

17. Why were other European countries slower to industrialize than Britain?

18. What helps to explain the rise of global inequality during the Industrial Revolution?

SECTION 4 (pages 647–652)
An Age of Reforms

19. What were the two warring classes that Marx and Engels outlined in *The Communist Manifesto*?

20. Name two ways women fought for change during the Industrial Revolution.

Visual Summary

The Industrial Revolution

Economic Effects

- New inventions and development of factories
- Rapidly growing industry in the 1800s
- Increased production and higher demand for raw materials
- Growth of worldwide trade
- Population explosion and a large labor force
- Exploitation of mineral resources
- Highly developed banking and investment system
- Advances in transportation, agriculture, and communication

Social Effects

- Long hours worked by children in factories
- Increase in population of cities
- Poor city planning
- Loss of family stability
- Expansion of middle class
- Harsh conditions for laborers
- Workers' progress vs. laissez-faire economic attitudes
- Improved standard of living
- Creation of new jobs
- Encouragement of technological progress

Political Effects

- Child labor laws to end abuses
- Reformers urging equal distribution of wealth
- Trade unions
- Social reform movements, such as utilitarianism, utopianism, socialism, and Marxism
- Reform bills in Parliament

Interact *with* History

Possible Responses: Students may mention changing conditions such as poor lighting and bad air in the factories. Others might mention the bargaining power that a union could bring to bear upon the fight to improve working conditions. Still others may say that if workers organized, then individual productivity might decline.

CRITICAL THINKING

1. INDUSTRIAL REVOLUTION BRINGS CHANGE

How significant were the changes the Industrial Revolution brought to the world? How enduring were they? Explain your conclusion. Think about economic, social, and political changes.

2. TECHNOLOGICAL ADVANCES

THEME SCIENCE & TECHNOLOGY Create a chart like the one below that lists some of the major technological advances and their effects on industrial society.

Technological Advance	Effect(s)

3. MILITARY POWER

How did the Industrial Revolution help to increase Germany's military power?

4. ANALYZING PRIMARY SOURCES

The following quotation comes from Charles Dickens's *Hard Times,* first published in book form in 1854. In *Hard Times,* as well as in several of his other novels, Dickens exposes such evils of industrialization as child labor, polluted cities, and corrupt factory owners. The following excerpt begins the chapter "No Way Out." Read the paragraph and answer the questions that follow.

A VOICE FROM THE PAST
The Fairy Palaces burst into illumination before pale morning showed the monstrous serpents of smoke trailing themselves over Coketown. A clattering of clogs upon the pavement, a rapid ringing of bells, and all the melancholy mad elephants, polished and oiled up for the day's monotony, were at their heavy exercise again.

- What is Dickens's opinion of the factory town? What words give you that impression?

- Why do you think Dickens called the chapter "No Way Out"?

CHAPTER ACTIVITIES

1. LIVING HISTORY: Unit Portfolio Project

THEME EMPIRE BUILDING Your unit portfolio project focuses on how different nations built empires (see page 629). For Chapter 25, you might use one of the following ideas to add to your portfolio:

- Would a non-industrialized or an industrialized nation more likely be an empire builder in the 19th and 20th centuries? Stage a debate to discuss this question. Videotape the session.

- You are an artisan in a non-industrialized nation threatened by a flood of cheap European goods into your marketplace. Write a letter to the editor of a local paper describing your situation, with any suggestions for improvement.

- Work with a partner to create British posters advertising their manufactured goods in overseas, less-developed markets.

2. CONNECT TO TODAY: Cooperative Learning

THEME ECONOMICS You read about harsh child labor practices during the Industrial Revolution. Today, child labor still exists in many developing nations, with many of the same unsanitary, unsafe, and grueling conditions. Work with a team to find out what the various child labor situations are in different places.

 Using the Internet or your library, research organizations that are fighting child labor.

- Write a letter, or in some other manner voice your concern and support to these organizations.

3. INTERPRETING A TIME LINE

Revisit the unit time line on pages 628–629. Look at events for Chapter 25. Write two more entries that could be added to the time line from Chapter 25. Support your answer with evidence from the text.

FOCUS ON GRAPHS

The graph to the right shows population growth in four European cities from 1700 to 1900, that is, before and after the Industrial Revolution.

- Which city had the smallest population in 1700? How many people had it gained by 1900?

- Which city gained the most people in this period? How many people did it gain between 1700 and 1900?

Connect to History
Why did cities grow so rapidly in this period? What lured people to the cities?

The Growth of Cities, 1700-1900

Birmingham: 10,000 (1700), 1.2 Million (1900)
Berlin: 60,000 (1700), 2.4 Million (1900)
Paris: 500,000 (1700), 3.3 Million (1900)
Vienna: 110,000 (1700), 1.6 Million (1900)

0   400 Miles
0   800 Kilometers

CHAPTER ACTIVITIES

1. LIVING HISTORY

Standards for Evaluation
A debate should meet the following criteria:

- Uses information from the text.
- Presents facts about the main activities of both industrialized and non-industrialized nations.
- Contains two clear points of view, with examples.
- Is delivered clearly and articulately for listeners and for taping purposes.

Standards for Evaluation
A letter should meet the following criteria:

- Clearly identifies the problems posed by the flood of European goods.
- Describes the letter writer's own situation.
- Makes suggestions for improving the situation.

Standards for Evaluation
A poster should meet the following criteria:

- Clearly identifies one or more manufactured goods.
- Presents the advantages of British manufactured goods.
- Describes why less-developed markets should buy British goods.

2. CONNECT TO TODAY

Standards for Evaluation
A letter or other response should meet the following criteria:

- Contains clearly researched factual data about child labor.
- Presents information about groups that are fighting such abuses.
- Includes the point of view of the writer or protester.
- Suggests original ways to improve the situation.

3. INTERPRETING A TIME LINE

Student answers should provide clear reasons and support for choosing two more entries to add to the time line.

FOCUS ON GRAPHS

- Birmingham; 1,190,000.
- Paris; 2,800,000.

Connect to History *Possible Response:* People flocked to the cities in search of jobs, which they found in the factories spawned by the Industrial Revolution.

CRITICAL THINKING

1. INDUSTRIAL REVOLUTION BRINGS CHANGE
Possible Responses: New social classes emerged; new political philosophies erupted from the Industrial Revolution; the gap widened between industrialized nations and non-industrialized nations; new inventions like the railroad changed the way people transported goods and traveled; many of the changes are present in today's society.

2. TECHNOLOGICAL ADVANCES
Possible Responses: Kay's flying shuttle—helped speed up weaving; Arkwright's water frame—enabled more efficient weaving, created need for factories; cotton gin—sped up cleaning cotton; steam engine—provided power for factories.

3. MILITARY POWER
Possible Responses: Germany's factories increased the production of war material; massive economic strength fueled Germany's growing military might.

4. ANALYZING PRIMARY SOURCES
Possible Responses: Dickens despises factory towns; "monstrous serpents of smoke," "melancholy mad," and "monotony" create impression. Title refers to workers' feelings about their jobs.

An Age of Democracy and Progress

	Key Ideas	**COPY MASTERS**	**ASSESSMENT**
SECTION 1 Democratic Reform and Activism pp. 659–663	*After considerable struggle, Great Britain evolves into a constitutional monarchy, while in France the Third Republic emerges as a parliamentary democracy. Women in both nations fail to obtain the right to vote.*	*In-Depth Resources: Unit 6* • **Guided Reading,** p. 18 • **Primary Source:** from *Five Years of My Life, 1894–1899*, p. 25 • **History Makers:** Emmeline Pankhurst, p. 34	P E *Section 1 Assessment,* p. 663 *Formal Assessment* • Section Quiz, p. 301 *Alternative Assessment Book* • Standards for Evaluating a Cooperative Activity
SECTION 2 Self-Rule for British Colonies pp. 664–668	*The British colonies of Canada, Australia, and New Zealand become democratic states within the British empire. In Ireland the struggle for home rule fails. Ireland splits into an independent country and a British province.*	*In-Depth Resources: Unit 6* • **Guided Reading,** p. 19 • **Geography Application:** The British Settle Australia and New Zealand, p. 23 • **Primary Source:** Irish Petition to Emigrate, p. 26 • **Literature:** "Easter 1916," p. 29	P E *Section 2 Assessment,* p. 668 *Formal Assessment* • Section Quiz, p. 302 *Alternative Assessment Book* • Standards for Evaluating a Product or Performance
SECTION 3 Expansion and Crisis in the United States pp. 669–672	*The United States expands to the Pacific Ocean. The Civil War ends slavery, preserves the Union, and speeds the industrial development of the North. After the war, the country experiences an unprecedented economic boom.*	*In-Depth Resources: Unit 6* • **Guided Reading,** p. 20 • **Primary Source:** Railroad Poster, p. 27	P E *Section 3 Assessment,* p. 672 *Formal Assessment* • Section Quiz, p. 303 *Alternative Assessment Book* • Standards for Evaluating a Cooperative Activity
SECTION 4 Nineteenth Century Progress pp. 673–679	*Key inventions, new theories in physics and biology, and medical advances transform daily life for many people. New technologies and growing democratic institutions create a mass culture in the United States.*	*In-Depth Resources: Unit 6* • **Guided Reading,** p. 21 • **Skillbuilder Practice:** Analyzing Issues, p. 22 • **Primary Source:** Orville Wright's Diary, p. 28 • **Literature:** from *The Origin*, p. 31 • **History Makers:** Marie and Pierre Curie, p. 35 • **Connections Across Time and Cultures:** Breakthroughs in Science and Technology, p. 36	P E *Section 4 Assessment,* p. 679 *Formal Assessment* • Section Quiz, p. 304 *Alternative Assessment Book* • Standards for Evaluating a Product or Performance
CHAPTER RESOURCES	**Chapter Overview** *Democratic institutions evolve in western Europe, North America, Australia, and New Zealand, although native people are suppressed. Industrialization and democracy spur revolutionary changes in the arts and sciences, transforming people's daily lives.*	*Telescoping the Times* • Chapter Summary, pp. 101–103 *Planning for Block Schedules*	P E *Chapter Assessment,* pp. 680–681 *Chapter Activities,* p. 681 *Formal Assessment* • Chapter Test, forms A and B, pp. 305–310 **■** *Test Generator* *Alternative Assessment Book*

1815–1914

TECHNOLOGY

 Warm-Up Transparency 26

 World Art and Cultures Transparencies
- AT56 *The Lady of Shalott*

 Electronic Library of Primary Sources
- from *Prisons and Prisoners*

INTERNET RESOURCES
www.mlworldhistory.com

Warm-Up Transparency 26

Geography Transparencies
- GT26 Canada: Growth of the Dominion, 1867–Present

World Art and Cultures Transparencies
- AT57 Maori pigment container

Electronic Library of Primary Sources
- "The Irish Potato Famine"

Patterns of Interaction:
The Geography of Food

INTERNET RESOURCES
www.mlworldhistory.com

Warm-Up Transparency 26

Electronic Library of Primary Sources
- from *A Message to Congress on Indian Policy*

INTERNET RESOURCES
www.mlworldhistory.com

Warm-Up Transparency 26

Critical Thinking Transparencies
- CT26 Movers and Shakers, 1815–1914
- CT62 Chapter 26 Visual Summary

Electronic Library of Primary Sources
- from *Journal of the Voyage of HMS* Beagle

INTERNET RESOURCES
www.mlworldhistory.com

 Chapter Summaries on Audiocassette in English and Spanish

 INTERNET RESOURCES
www.mlworldhistory.com

Block Scheduling (90 MINUTES)

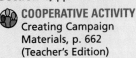

Day 1
Section 1, pp. 659–663

 COOPERATIVE ACTIVITY
Creating Campaign Materials, p. 662 (Teacher's Edition)

Section 2, pp. 664–668

Section Assessments,
pp. 663, 668

Day 2
Section 3, pp. 669–672

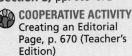 **COOPERATIVE ACTIVITY**
Creating an Editorial Page, p. 670 (Teacher's Edition)

Section 4, pp. 673–679

Section Assessments,
pp. 672, 679

Chapter Assessment,
pp. 680–681

Yearly Pacing *Chapter 26 Total:* 2 days *Yearly Total:* 85 days

Planning for Block Schedules

Customizing for Special Needs

Students Acquiring English

Access for Students Acquiring English
- **Guided Reading** for Sections 1–4 (Spanish), pp. 260–263
- **Chapter Summary** (Spanish), pp. 257–259
- **Skillbuilder Practice** Analyzing Issues (Spanish), p. 264
- **Geography Application** The British Settle Australia and New Zealand (Spanish), p. 265

 • **Patterns of Interaction** *The Geography of Food* (Spanish track)

 Chapter Summaries on Audiocassette in English and Spanish

Less Proficient Readers

In-Depth Resources: Unit 6
- **Guided Reading** for Sections 1–4, pp. 18–21
- **Skillbuilder Practice** Analyzing Issues, p. 22
- **Geography Application** The British Settle Australia and New Zealand, p. 23

 Telescoping the Times
- Chapter Summary, pp. 101–103

 Chapter Summaries on Audiocassette

INTERNET RESOURCES
www.mlworldhistory.com
The Diverse Classroom.

Gifted and Talented Students

 In-Depth Resources: Unit 6

Primary Sources
- from *Five Years of My Life, 1894–1899*, p. 25
- Irish Petition to Emigrate, p. 26
- Railroad Poster, p. 27
- Orville Wright's Diary, p. 28

History Makers
- Emmeline Pankhurst, p. 34
- Marie and Pierre Curie, p. 35

Connections to Literature READINGS FOR STUDENTS

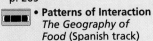 *In-Depth Resources: Unit 6*
Literature: "Easter, 1916," p. 29; from *The Origin*, p. 31

- **McDougal Littell**
The Language of Literature, Grade 10
R. K. Narayan, "Like the Sun," p. 608
Rabindranath Tagore, "The Cabulwallah," p. 622
Isaac Bashevis Singer, "The Son from America," p. 761
Linda Pastan, "Grudnow," p. 768

Santha Rama Rau, "By Any Other Name," p. 772

McDougal Littell
Literature Connections
- **Austin, Jane**
Pride and Prejudice
(with related readings)

This gentle and witty satire of courtship and marriage in 18th-century England is one of Jane Austin's best-loved novels.

 = Pupil's Edition   = Overhead Transparency   = Software   = Video

 = Copy Master   = CD-ROM   = Audiocassette = Internet

An Age of Democracy and Progress, 1815–1914

Accessing Prior Knowledge

Have students look over these two pages.

- Ask them to name two or three facts they already know about each topic portrayed in the images.

Making Predictions

Point out to students that each picture represents a process of momentous change.

- What is likely to happen as European immigrants encounter native cultures in Australia?

- As people become wealthier through industrial progress, how might this influence Western European democracies?

Geography Connection

Ask students to notice how few countries are democratic at this time and how far-flung the democracies are.

- What problems might Great Britain have in keeping control of its overseas colonies?

- Would the United States have similar problems in governing its western territories?

CHAPTER 26 — An Age of Democracy and Progress, 1815–1914

PREVIEWING THEMES

Empire Building
During the 1800s, Great Britain gradually allowed three of its colonies—Canada, Australia, and New Zealand—greater self-rule. At the same time, Britain maintained tight control over Ireland.

Economics
In western Europe and the United States, a growing middle class both demanded and benefited from democratic reforms. During the 1800s, U.S. economic growth and territorial expansion made the nation one of the leading industrial countries of the world.

Science and Technology
Breakthroughs in science and technology transformed daily life during the 19th century. From the electric light bulb to the automobile, emerging products speeded up the pace of life, shrank distances, and expanded the hours available for work or play.

INTERNET CONNECTION

Visit us at www.mlworldhistory.com to learn more about Western democracies in the 19th century.

WESTERN DEMOCRACIES, 1900

CANADA

UNITED STATES OF AMERICA

PACIFIC OCEAN

ATLANTIC OCEA

Kansas Pioneers, by George Melville Stone, depicts Americans making the westward journey across the **Great Plains** by Conestoga wagon. The Great Plains became part of the United States with the Louisiana Purchase of **1803**. During the 1800s, thousands of Americans migrated west.

NEW ZEALAND

◄— Australia 1,300 miles

GEOGRAPHY THEMES

Movement

In this chapter, three major migrations are discussed: the movement of British convicts and citizens to Australia; the movement of white, African American, and Asian settlers across the western United States; and the immigration of thousands of Irish to the United States.

As students read the chapter, encourage them to think about the following: Over what period of time did each migration occur? What effects did these migrations have on each country?

Ask students if any of these movements affected their own families in the past or the families of anyone they know.

Human-Environment Interaction

As Europeans moved to new and "undeveloped" lands, they greatly changed the environment. Point out to students that in the countries where they settled, Europeans used the land in vastly different ways than did most native peoples. They mined, cleared forest land, dammed or diverted waterways, and altered the shape of the landscape to meet their needs for manufacturing, farming, and building cities.

Encourage students to find photographs or paintings of what their area looked like before and after settlers came to the region.

IRELAND

GREAT BRITAIN

FRANCE

Tropic of Cancer

INDIAN OCEAN

Equator 0°

Tropic of Capricorn

AUSTRALIA

0   400 Miles
0   800 Kilometers

N

657   40°S

0° Prime Meridian

In Paris, the 984-foot-tall **Eiffel Tower** opened in **1889**. Bridge engineer Gustave Eiffel designed the tower to mark the hundredth anniversary of the French Revolution. It also served as a fitting monument to the age of industrial progress. The Eiffel Tower was the world's tallest structure until 1930.

This engraving shows British convicts being ferried to a prison ship in an English port. Beginning in **1788**, the British government sent many such convicts to its penal colony in **Australia**. Australia received British prisoners until the mid-1800s.

ADDITIONAL RESOURCES

Books for the Teacher

• Meltzer, Milton, ed. *Voices from the Civil War.* New York: Crowell, 1989. A documentary history of the war.

• Schroeder, Paul W. *The Transformation of European Politics, 1763–1848.* New York: Oxford UP, 1994.

Books for the Student

• Chamberlin, E. R. *The Nineteenth Century.* Morristown, NJ: Silver Burdett, 1984. Everyday life in Europe in the 1800s.

• Drabble, Margaret. *For Queen and Country: Britain in the Victorian Age.* New York: Seabury, 1978. The lives of ordinary British citizens.

Videos

• *The Glory of Europe—1900: Hey Day Fever.* Ambrose Video, 1977. 800-526-4663. Europe as the most dominant force in the world.

• *The Mechanical Paradise.* Ambrose Video, 1980. 800-526-4663. Engineers and inventors: 1870–1914.

Software

• *Impressionism and Its Sources.* CD-ROM. Queue. 800-232-2224.

• *The Victorian Era.* CD-ROM. Society for Visual Education, 1994. 800-829-1900. The growth of British industry, social and parliamentary reform, and women's changing role.

HISTORY THROUGH ART

Kansas Pioneers and British Convicts Bound for Australia

The United States and Australia were both settled by immigrants, but people left their homeland for widely different reasons. Immigrants to the U.S. wanted a better life. In contrast, British immigrants to Australia were shipped half way around the world by a government glad to get rid of them.

The composition of the two pictures reflects the different conditions of these immigrant groups. The Kansas pioneers stride confidently toward their new home. The two men in the foreground dominate even the oxen and covered wagon behind them. In contrast, the prison ship completely dwarfs the human cargo being ferried to meet it. This is undoubtedly how many prisoners felt on first viewing the ship.

Interpreting the Art What is the mood of each picture? *Kansas pioneers—optimistic, light; British convicts—dark, brooding, somber.* How does each artist view the people in these pictures? *Possible answers: Kansas pioneers—the pioneers all seem strong, unafraid, willing to encounter the unknown. No one is leading or driving them. British convicts—they are anonymous, huddled together, and completely under someone else's control.*

Interact *with* History

Interact *with* History

You live in a glorious age. Trains and telegraphs are not even 50 years old—and so much remains to be discovered! You're something of a tinkerer yourself. Maybe you can perfect a gas-powered engine and invent the car. Or maybe you can invent a device to use electricity to light up a room! But wait—if people could move five times faster, would they *really* be happier? What are the dangers of playing with strange new forces such as electricity and X-rays? Considering all the possible consequences . . .

What would you invent?

Automobiles provide a new level of mobility and freedom. The cost of early cars has meant that few can afford them. What will happen if the price comes down?

1906 Ford 6 Cylinder Touring Car
Price $2,500

6 cylinders—40 h. p. 4 to 50 miles per hour on high gear. *Perfected* magneto ignition—mechanical oiler, 114 inch wheel base, luxurious body for 5 passengers, weight 2000 pounds.

1906 Ford Runabout, as advanced as our touring car in design and even more surprising in price—will be fully illustrated and described in our next advertisement.

Both these Cars on exhibition at the New York Automobile Show.

Ford Motor Company
Detroit, Mich.

The invention of the electric light can turn night into day. What will people do with the extra daylight hours?

24172 Magneto Bell Telephone. Loudest talking, clearest tone and best constructed magneto phone on the market. As no batteries are required with this phone, the current being generated by means of a powerful generator in the telephone box, a large part of the expense of maintenance is eliminated. Suitable for use for exchange or private lines of any length. This instrument cannot be excelled in general excellence nor in appearance. The boxes being of highly polished hardwood, and metal parts of nickel, plated or oxidized. Full directions for putting up the phone and constructing lines accompany each instrument. Prices quoted below are for phone complete and do not include any materials for line construction. Weight, each phone, 15 lbs. Price, per phone...............$18.00 Price, per pair, complete for two stations ..... 35.00 For quotations of wire, insulators, etc., see No. 24211

With telephones, people can speak directly to one another from within their own homes. Will they ever get used to the wires running from their homes and along their roads?

EXAMINING *the* ISSUES

1 • What were the drawbacks of living in a time before telephones, cars, electric lights, radios, and so on?

2 • What might have been better about life before the "progress" of the 19th century—and for whom?

3 • How might inventions affect social life: the closeness of families, the gap between rich and poor, the power of different social groups?

Break into groups and have each group choose one truly beneficial invention of the past two centuries. Debate one another's choices and see if you can find some costs, as well as benefits, of each invention.

As you read this chapter, consider how invention and democracy were intertwined in the 19th century. How did each promote the other? Think about the Industrial Revolution and its consequences. Also consider more recent inventions, such as compact disc players and the Internet.

1 Democratic Reform and Activism

TERMS & NAMES
- suffrage
- Chartist movement
- Queen Victoria
- Third Republic
- Dreyfus affair
- anti-Semitism
- Zionism

MAIN IDEA

Spurred by the demands of ordinary people, Great Britain and France underwent democratic reforms.

WHY IT MATTERS NOW

During this period, Britain and France were transformed into the democracies they are today.

SETTING THE STAGE Urbanization and industrialization brought sweeping changes to Western nations. People looking for solutions to the problems created by these developments began to demand reforms. They wanted to improve conditions for workers and the poor. Many people also began to call for political reforms. They demanded that ordinary people be given a greater voice in government.

Britain Adopts Democratic Reforms

As Chapter 21 explained, Britain became a constitutional monarchy in the late 1600s. And it remains so today. Under this system of government, the monarch serves as the head of state, but Parliament holds the real power. The British Parliament consists of a House of Lords and a House of Commons. Members of the House of Lords either inherit their seats or are appointed. Members of the House of Commons are elected by the British people.

In the early 1800s, the British government was not a true democracy. Only about 6 percent of the population had the right to elect the members of the House of Commons. Voting was limited to men who owned a substantial amount of land. Women could not vote at all. As a result, the upper classes ran the government.

During the 1800s, however, democracy gradually expanded in Great Britain. The ideas of liberalism that were popular in France and other countries spread among Britain's growing middle and working classes. These groups demanded a greater share of the power held by the aristocratic landowners. Yet unlike the French, the British achieved reforms without the bitter bloodshed of revolution.

The Reform Bill of 1832 The first group to demand a greater voice in politics was the wealthy middle class—factory owners, bankers, merchants. Beginning in 1830, protests took place around England in favor of a bill in Parliament that would extend **suffrage,** or the right to vote. The Revolution of 1830 in France frightened parliamentary leaders. They feared that revolutionary violence would spread to Britain. Thus, Parliament passed the Reform Bill of 1832. This law eased the property requirements so that well-to-do men in the middle class could vote.

The Reform Bill also modernized the districts for electing members of Parliament. Many of the old districts were areas owned by aristocrats and actually contained few people. In contrast, cities such as Manchester and Sheffield had no representatives in Parliament. The Reform Bill eliminated the so-called "rotten boroughs," or empty districts, and gave the thriving new industrial cities more representation.

Workers Demand Suffrage Although the Reform Bill increased the number of British voters, only about one in five men were now eligible to

The House of Commons 1833 by Sir George Hayter shows this assembly a year after the important Reform Bill.

A. Possible Answers
Gave vote to middle class, gave representation to cities, reduced power base of aristocracy by eliminating "rotten boroughs," created momentum to reform.

THINK THROUGH HISTORY
A. Clarifying How did the Reform Bill increase democracy in Great Britain?

SECTION 1 RESOURCES

PRINT RESOURCES

 IN-DEPTH RESOURCES: UNIT 6
Guided Reading, p. 18
Primary Source: from *Five Years of My Life, 1894–1899*, p. 25
History Makers: Emmeline Pankhurst, p. 34

 ACCESS FOR STUDENTS ACQUIRING ENGLISH
Guided Reading (Spanish), p. 260

FORMAL ASSESSMENT
Section Quiz, p. 301

ALTERNATIVE ASSESSMENT BOOK

TECHNOLOGY RESOURCES

 WORLD ART AND CULTURES TRANSPARENCIES
AT56 *The Lady of Shalott*

CD-ROM
Electronic Library of Primary Sources

INTERNET www.mlworldhistory.com

Section 1 Overview

OBJECTIVES

1. To describe the evolution of British democracy.

2. To explain the origins and goals of the women's suffrage movement.

3. To trace the development of democratic institutions in France.

SKILLBUILDER
- Interpreting charts, p. 660

CRITICAL THINKING
- Clarifying, pp. 659, 662
- Making inferences, p. 660
- Synthesizing, p. 661
- Analyzing Issues, p. 663

FOCUS
5-Minute Warm-Up

▶ *Making Generalizations*
Answering the following questions will help students to understand social roles in the Victorian Age.

1. Read "Victorian Manners" on page 661. What must a gentleman never do?

2. If a young lady decides to take a walk and to visit a gentleman, what must she do?

 WARM-UP TRANSPARENCY 26

OBJECTIVE 1 INSTRUCT

Britain Adopts Democratic Reforms

▶ *Key Ideas*
- Parliament extends voting rights to the British middle class.
- Further reform bills extend voting rights to most adult male citizens.
- During Queen Victoria's reign, the monarchy becomes largely ceremonial.

 IN-DEPTH RESOURCES: UNIT 6
Guided Reading, p. 18

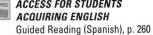 *ACCESS FOR STUDENTS ACQUIRING ENGLISH*
Guided Reading (Spanish), p. 260

Growth of Voting in Britain

Interpreting the Chart Point out that each circle contains more information than the previous one because each reform bill added new groups to the voters' rolls. Which group was added in 1832? *middle-class men.* In 1867? *working-class men* In 1884? *rural men.*

Extension Activity Ask students how a bill to raise working-class wages might have fared in Parliament— based on who was allowed to vote— if the bill had been introduced in 1832, 1867, and 1918. *It would have been defeated in 1832, may have gotten more votes in 1867, and had a chance of passing in 1918.*

SKILLBUILDER Answers
1. 7 percent
2. 21 percent

HISTORYMAKERS
Queen Victoria

The image of Victoria as a sour-faced conservative comes mainly from her later years. As a young queen she was lively and even frivolous. Ask students to compare Queen Victoria to Elizabeth I and Elizabeth II, other important English queens.

OBJECTIVE 2 INSTRUCT

Women Demand the Vote

▶ **Key Ideas**
- Activist women agitate for the right to vote.
- Gradually women use more drastic political tactics to obtain their goals.

💿 **ELECTRONIC LIBRARY OF PRIMARY SOURCES**
from *Prisons and Prisoners*

Growth of Voting in Britain

Before 1832
- 5%
- 95%

Percentage of population over age 20
- ■ had right to vote
- gained right to vote
- could not vote

1832
- 2%
- 5%
- 93%

Reform Bill granted vote to middle-class men.

1867, 1884
- 7%
- 21%
- 72%

Reforms granted vote to working-class men in 1867 and to rural men in 1884.

1918
- 26%
- 28%
- 46%

Reforms granted vote to women over 30.

Source: R.L. Leonard, *Elections in Britain*

> **SKILLBUILDER: Interpreting Charts**
> 1. *What percentage of the adults in Britain could vote in 1832?*
> 2. *By how much did the percentage of voters increase after the reforms of 1867 and 1884?*

The modern Parliament building was completed in 1867.

vote. The passage of the bill, however, encouraged reformers. Among the workers and other groups who still could not vote, a popular movement arose to press for more rights. It was called the **Chartist movement** because the group first presented its demands to Parliament on a petition called The People's Charter of 1838.

The People's Charter called for suffrage for all men and annual Parliamentary elections. It also proposed to reform Parliament in other ways. In Britain at the time, eligible men voted openly by voice. Since their vote was not secret, they could feel pressure to vote in a certain way. Moreover, members of Parliament had to own land and received no salary, so they needed to be independently wealthy. The Chartists wanted to make Parliament more responsive to the interests of the lower classes. To achieve this, they demanded a secret ballot, an end to the property requirements for serving in Parliament, and pay for members of Parliament.

Parliament rejected the Chartists' demands. However, their protests convinced many people that workers had sound complaints. Over the years, workers continued to press for political reform, and Parliament eventually responded. It gave the vote to working-class men in 1867 and to male rural workers in 1884. After 1884, therefore, most adult males in Britain had the right to vote. By the early 1900s, all the demands of the Chartists, except for annual elections, became law.

The Victorian Age The figure who presided over all this historic change was **Queen Victoria.** Victoria came to the throne in 1837 at the age of 18. She was queen for 64 years, one of the longest reigns in history. During the Victorian Age, the British empire reached the height of its wealth and power. Victoria was popular with her subjects, and she performed her duties wisely and capably. However, she was forced to accept a new, virtually powerless role for the British monarchy.

The kings who preceded Victoria in the 1700s and 1800s had exercised great influence over Parliament. The spread of democracy in the 1800s shifted political power almost completely to Parliament, and especially to the elected House of Commons. Now the government was completely run by the prime minister and the cabinet. Thus, ever since Queen Victoria, British monarchs have been mainly symbolic rulers with no political power.

Women Demand the Vote

By 1890, several industrial countries had universal male suffrage (the right of all men to vote). No country, however, allowed women to vote. As more men gained suffrage, more women demanded the same.

HISTORYMAKERS

Queen Victoria 1819–1901

Three years after her coronation, Queen Victoria fell in love with her cousin Albert, a German prince. She proposed to him and they were married in 1840. Together they had nine children. The strait-laced Prince Albert established a tone of polite propriety at court, and the royal couple presented a picture of loving family life that became a British ideal.

After Albert died in 1861, the Queen wore black silk for the rest of her life in mourning. She once said of Albert, "Without him everything loses its interest."

660 Chapter 26

B. Possible Answers Allowed people to vote their conscience, made voters less subject to intimidation, reduced power of bribery.
THINK THROUGH HISTORY
B. Making Inferences Why do you think the Chartists demanded a secret ballot rather than public voting?

C. Possible Answers Resisting change might have led to overthrow of monarchy, so accepting change helped preserve the British monarchy; wanted to avoid violence or revolution; calls for reform gained momentum and reform may have seemed inevitable.
THINK THROUGH HISTORY
C. Making Inferences Why might Queen Victoria have accepted a powerless new role for the British monarchy? Think about other monarchies in Europe in the 1800s.

TEACHING OPTIONS	CONNECTIONS ACROSS THE CURRICULUM

Mathematics Different types of graphs have different uses. Discuss what a pie chart reveals especially well—that is, changes in portions of a whole. The pie charts show clearly which groups increased over time and by how much.

Then encourage students to translate the information in the three pie charts into a single line graph that shows the growth of the total voting population in England—from the 7 percent of 1832, to the 28 percent of 1867, 1884, to the 74 percent of 1918. Explain to students that a line graph is particularly good for showing the direction of trends (up or down) over time.

CUSTOMIZING FOR SPECIAL NEEDS

Less Proficient Readers To help students gain a clear overview of the expansion of suffrage, have them create a time line showing when universal male suffrage was achieved in the United States, Australia, France, Britain, and New Zealand and when women gained the right to vote in each country. Have them obtain what information they can from the text and use encyclopedias to supply dates for this chart as needed.

	Brit	Aus	NZ	US	France
M	1884	1851	1853	1870	1848
F	1918	1902	1893	1920	1945

Victorian Ladies' News

Mind Your Tea and Cakes

Taking afternoon tea at about 5:00 P.M. has become as English as London fog, but tea drinkers should be careful to buy supplies only from reputable sources. Some so-called tea merchants add coloring to convert blackthorn leaves into something that looks like tea. In London, several factories dye recycled tea leaves for dishonest merchants to sell as new tea.

Be careful, too, about those cakes you serve with your tea. To get the brightest colors to decorate cakes, some dishonest bakers use dangerous chemicals: copper and zinc to get gold and silver; iron for blue and lead for red; and even arsenic for green.

Cholera Comes from Bad Water

London: This fall, Dr. John Snow published a revised edition of his 1849 pamphlet entitled "On the Mode of Communication of Cholera." In his pamphlet, Dr. Snow uses case examples to show that contaminated drinking water caused the cholera epidemics that killed thousands of poor Londoners in 1831–1832, 1848–1849, and 1854. Dr. Snow's critics scorn his theory, maintaining that cholera spreads from the air that surrounds rubbish heaps.

CHOLERA.

THE
DUDLEY BOARD OF HEALTH,
HEREBY GIVE NOTICE, THAT IN CONSEQUENCE OF THE
Church-yards at Dudley
Being so full, no one who has died of the
CHOLERA will be permitted to be buried
after *SUNDAY* next, (To-morrow) in either
of the Burial Grounds of *St. Thomas's*, or
St. Edmund's, in this Town.

All Persons who die from CHOLERA, must for the future
be buried in the Church-yard at Netherton.
BOARD of HEALTH, DUDLEY.
September 1st, 1832.

Riding the Rails

If you want to travel quickly and cheaply, you can't beat the new and improved British railways. Regular trains will speed you to your destination at 20 miles an hour; on express routes, you'll whiz along at nearly 40. Here are some tips for happier traveling:

- Bring your own candles if you intend to read at night.
- Prepare to rent a metal foot warmer if you're taking a winter journey.
- Bring your own food or prepare to brave the crowds at station restaurants.
- For long journeys, tote a chamber pot in a basket.

London's Paddington Station bustles with passengers in this painting.

Victorian Manners

The proper gentleman

- lets a lady walk or ride along the wall
- never speaks to a lady unless she speaks to him first
- precedes a lady walking upstairs and follows one walking downstairs
- takes the backward-facing seat in a carriage and gets out first to help a lady dismount
- never smokes in a lady's presence

The proper lady

- never walks alone or never walks unchaperoned if she is unmarried and under 30
- does not go alone to make a social call on a man
- never wears pearls or diamonds in the morning
- never dances more than three dances with the same partner

Connect *to* History

Synthesizing List examples from this page to demonstrate that popular culture in Victorian England admired both tradition and change.

SEE SKILLBUILDER HANDBOOK, PAGE 1007

Connect *to* Today

Researching Using the library or Internet, research some aspect of American culture that shows an example of either tradition or dramatic change. As possible subjects, consider transportation, communications, entertainment, or fashion.

An Age of Democracy and Progress **661**

Connect *to* History

Synthesizing
Examples of devotion to tradition: exacting rules regarding proper behavior for gentlemen and ladies, and rituals relating to tea. Indications of a fascination with innovation include new ideas about disease (Dr. Snow's theory of how cholera spreads) and a celebration of new technologies (high-speed trains).

Connect *to* Today

Researching
Examples of American fascination with change: constant outpouring of newer versions of software and hardware; celebration of artists who "break boundaries" and baffle the public. Reflections of American devotion to tradition: movie genres such as musicals; constant resurgence of "retro" styles in music and fashion; "golden oldies" radio stations; the recycling of American myths such as Superman; honoring of religious traditions and values.

Organization and Resistance During the 1800s, women in both Great Britain and the United States worked to gain the right to vote. In the United States, women such as Lucretia Mott and Elizabeth Cady Stanton organized a campaign for women's rights as early as 1848. From a convention in Seneca Falls, New York, they issued a declaration of women's rights modeled on the Declaration of Independence. "We hold these truths to be self-evident," the declaration stated, "that all men and women are created equal."

> ### A VOICE FROM THE PAST
> The history of mankind is a history of repeated injuries and usurpations on the part of man toward woman, having in direct object the establishment of an absolute tyranny over her. To prove this, let facts be submitted to a candid world.
> He has never permitted her to exercise her inalienable right to the elective franchise.
> He has compelled her to submit to laws in the formation of which she has no voice.
> **THE SENECA FALLS CONVENTION,** "Declaration of Sentiments"

British women, too, organized reform societies and protested unfair laws and customs. As women became more vocal, however, resistance to their demands grew. Many people, both men and women, thought that women's suffrage was too radical a break with tradition. Some claimed that women lacked the ability to take part in politics.

Militant Protests After decades of peaceful efforts to win the right to vote, some women took more drastic steps. In Britain, Emmeline Pankhurst formed the Women's Social and Political Union (WSPU) in 1903. The WSPU became the most militant organization for women's rights. Besides peaceful demonstrations and parades, its members heckled government speakers, cut telegraph wires, and committed arson. Their goal was to draw attention to the cause of women's suffrage.

Emmeline Pankhurst, her daughters Christabel and Sylvia, and other WSPU members were arrested and imprisoned many times. When they were jailed, the Pankhursts led hunger strikes to keep their cause in the public eye. British officials force-fed Sylvia and other activists to keep them alive. One WSPU member, Emily Davison, did give her life for the women's movement. As a protest, she threw herself in front of the king's horse at the English Derby.

Though the women's suffrage movement commanded wide attention between 1880 and 1914, its successes were gradual. Women did not win the right to vote in national elections in Great Britain and the United States until after World War I.

*Global*Impact
The Women's Movement

By the 1880s, women were working internationally to win more rights. In 1888, women activists from the United States, Canada, and Europe met in Washington, D.C., for the International Council of Women. In 1893, delegates and observers from 27 countries attended a large congress of women in Chicago. They came from lands as far apart as New Zealand, Argentina, Iceland, Persia, and China.

The first countries to grant women's suffrage were New Zealand (1893) and Australia (1902). Only in two European countries—Finland (1906, then part of the Russian Empire) and Norway (1913)—did women gain voting rights before World War I. In the United States, the territory of Wyoming allowed women to vote in 1869. Several other Western states followed suit.

Democracy in France

While Great Britain moved toward true democracy in the late 1800s, democracy finally took permanent hold in France. However, France's road to democracy was rocky.

The Third Republic In the aftermath of the Franco-Prussian War, France went through a series of crises. After being released by Prussia, Napoleon III spent his last years in exile in Britain. France's National Assembly met to decide on a new government.

Meanwhile, in March 1871, a radical government called the Paris Commune took control of Paris. In May, troops loyal to the National Assembly marched into the city. Parisian workers threw up barricades in the streets and fought the army block by block. After a week of fighting, the army stamped out the Communards, as supporters of the Commune were called. About 20,000 Parisians were massacred, and much of the city burned.

Not until 1875 could the National Assembly agree on a new government. Eventually, the members voted to set up a republic. In the words of a leading French politician, it

---

was "the system of government that divides us least." The **Third Republic,** as this new system was called, lasted over 60 years. However, France remained bitterly divided. A dozen political parties competed for power. Between 1871 and 1914, France averaged a change of government every ten months.

The Dreyfus Affair During the 1880s and 1890s, the unsteady Third Republic was threatened by monarchists, aristocrats, clergy, and army leaders. These groups wanted to return France to a monarchy or to have military rule. A controversy known as the **Dreyfus affair** became a battleground for these opposing forces. Widespread feelings of **anti-Semitism,** or prejudice against Jews, also played a role in this scandal.

In 1894, Captain Alfred Dreyfus, one of the few Jewish officers in the French army, was accused of selling military secrets to Germany. A court found him guilty, based on false evidence, and sentenced him to life in prison. In a few years, new evidence showed that Dreyfus had been framed by other army officers.

Public opinion was sharply divided over the scandal. Many army leaders, nationalists, leaders in the clergy, and anti-Jewish groups refused to let the case be reopened. They feared sudden action would cast doubt on the honor of the army. Dreyfus's defenders insisted that justice was more important and that he should be freed. In 1898, the writer Émile Zola published an open letter titled *J'accuse!* (I Accuse) in a popular French newspaper. In the letter, Zola denounced the army for covering up a scandal. Zola was given a year in prison for his views, but his letter gave strength to Dreyfus's cause. Eventually, the French government officially declared his innocence.

The Rise of Zionism The Dreyfus case showed the strength of anti-Semitism in France and other parts of Western Europe. However, persecution of Jews was even more severe in Eastern Europe. Russian officials, for example, permitted and even encouraged pogroms (puh·GRAHMS)—organized campaigns of violence against Jewish communities. From the late 1880s on, thousands of Jews fled Eastern Europe. Many headed for the United States.

For many Jews, the long history of exile and persecution convinced them that they should work for a separate homeland in Palestine. In the 1890s, a movement known as **Zionism** developed to pursue this goal. Its leader was Theodor Herzl (HEHRT·suhl), a writer in Vienna. It took many years, however, before the state of Israel was established, making the dream a reality.

E. Possible Answer Dreyfus, a Jewish army officer, was framed for spying. Army refused to reopen case; its stand was supported by nationalists, clergy, anti-Jewish groups. Others wanted to clear Dreyfus's name and expose the abuse of power by the military.

THINK THROUGH HISTORY
E. Analyzing Issues Explain the controversy over the Dreyfus affair.

Background
Zion is another name for Israel, the Jewish homeland.

Section 1 Assessment

1. TERMS & NAMES
Identify
- suffrage
- Chartist movement
- Queen Victoria
- Third Republic
- Dreyfus affair
- anti-Semitism
- Zionism

2. TAKING NOTES
List and evaluate five significant events from this section, using a table like the one shown. Next to each event, put a "+" if it expanded democracy, a "−" if it negatively affected democracy, and a "0" if it had a mixed impact.

Event	Evaluation

3. ANALYZING ISSUES
Look again at the excerpt from the Seneca Falls "Declaration of Sentiments" on page 662. Why do you think the members of the Seneca Falls Convention chose to model their demands on the Declaration of Independence? (It may be helpful to locate the similar section in a copy of the Declaration of Independence and compare the two passages.)

4. THEME ACTIVITY
Economics Among the Chartists' demands was pay for members of Parliament. Often when a U.S. legislature raises the pay for its own members, it creates controversy. Imagine such a raise is being considered. Write a "letter to the editor" that supports or criticizes the raise. Be sure to refer to the historical reasons for giving pay to legislators.

An Age of Democracy and Progress **663**

ANSWERS

1. TERMS & NAMES
suffrage, p. 659
Chartist movement, p. 660
Queen Victoria, p. 660
Third Republic, p. 663
Dreyfus affair, p. 663
anti-Semitism, p. 663
Zionism, p. 663

2. TAKING NOTES
Possible Answers: Tables might include Reform Bill of 1832, Chartist movement, expansion of male suffrage in Britain in 1867, Seneca Falls declaration, Paris Commune, Third Republic, Dreyfus affair.

3. ANALYZING ISSUES
Possible Responses: To show that their demands for rights were as legitimate as the colonists' demands for rights from Great Britain; to emphasize the injustice of womens' unequal status by comparing the tyranny of men to that of King George.

4. THEME ACTIVITY
Possible Responses: Letters to the editor should refer to the Chartists' demands for pay, have a logical organization, and present a well-reasoned argument.

To describe how Canada achieved self-rule.

 To explain how Australia and New Zealand became Western democracies.

 To describe the British domination of Ireland.

SKILLBUILDER

• Interpreting maps: place, region, p. 666
• Interpreting graphs, p. 667

CRITICAL THINKING

• Clarifying, p. 664
• Recognizing effects, p. 665
• Contrasting, p. 666
• Evaluating decisions, p. 668
• Comparing, p. 668
• Analyzing themes, p. 668

FOCUS

5-Minute Warm-Up

▶ **Key Ideas**

Help students understand the settlement of Australia and New Zealand by having them answer the following questions.

• Study the map on page 666. Which part of Australia most resembles Great Britain?

• Why would the settlers initially have avoided the northern and central parts of Australia?

 WARM-UP TRANSPARENCY 26

OBJECTIVE ① INSTRUCT

Canada Struggles for Self-Rule

▶ **Key Ideas**

• Conflict between French and English settlers leads to a partition of Canada.

• The Dominion of Canada is formed, and Canada expands to the Pacific.

 IN-DEPTH RESOURCES: UNIT 6
Guided Reading, p. 19

 ACCESS FOR STUDENTS ACQUIRING ENGLISH
Guided Reading (Spanish), p. 261

---

2 # Self-Rule for British Colonies

TERMS & NAMES
• dominion
• Maori
• Aborigine
• penal colony
• home rule

MAIN IDEA

Britain allowed self-rule in Canada, Australia, and New Zealand but delayed independence for Ireland.

WHY IT MATTERS NOW

Canada, Australia, and New Zealand are strong democracies today, while Ireland is divided and troubled.

SETTING THE STAGE By 1800, Great Britain had colonies around the world. These included small outposts in Africa and Asia. In these areas, the British managed trade with the local peoples, but they had little influence over the population at large. In the colonies of Canada, Australia, and New Zealand, on the other hand, European colonists had overrun and replaced the native populations. As Britain industrialized and prospered in the 1800s, so did these colonies. Like the United States, which had already broken away from British rule, some of these colonies were becoming strong enough to stand on their own.

Canada Struggles for Self-Rule

Canada was originally home to many Native American peoples, including the Algonquin, Huron, Cree, Blackfoot, and Inuit. The first European country to colonize Canada was France. Great Britain took possession of the country in 1763, following the French and Indian War. The thousands of French who remained there lived mostly in the lower St. Lawrence Valley. Many English-speaking colonists arrived in Canada after it came under British rule. Some came from Great Britain, and others were Americans who had stayed loyal to Britain after the American Revolution. They settled separately from the French—mostly along the Atlantic seaboard and north of the Great Lakes.

The earliest French colonists had included many fur trappers and missionaries. They tended to live among the Native Americans rather than displace them. Some French intermarried with Native Americans. As more French and British settlers arrived, they took over much of eastern and southern Canada. Native groups in the north and west, however, remained largely undisturbed until later in the 1800s.

French and English Canada Religious and cultural differences between the mostly Roman Catholic French and the mainly Protestant English-speaking colonists caused conflict in Canada. Both groups also pressed Britain for a greater voice in governing their own affairs. In 1791 the British Parliament tried to resolve both issues by creating two new Canadian provinces. Upper Canada (now Ontario) had an English-speaking majority. Lower Canada (now Quebec) had a French-speaking majority. Each province had its own elected assembly with limited powers.

The Durham Report The division of Upper and Lower Canada eased colonial tensions only temporarily. In both colonies, the royal governor and a small group of wealthy British held most of the power. During the early 1800s, the people in both colonies, led by middle-class professionals, began to demand political and economic reforms. In Lower Canada, these demands were also fueled by French resentment toward British rule. In the late 1830s, rebellions broke out in both

 SPOTLIGHT ON

Canadian Mounties
One of the most recognized symbols of Canada, the Royal Canadian Mounted Police, began its existence in the 1870s to patrol Canada's western frontier. One of its first tasks was to drive out whiskey smugglers from the United States.

The Mounties' main purpose was to prevent bloodshed as white settlers moved into traditional Native American lands in the west. Although it was meant to be a temporary force, the Mounties became Canada's national police force.

THINK THROUGH HISTORY
A. Clarifying Why did Britain create Upper Canada and Lower Canada? Who lived in each colony?
A. Answer Created to resolve conflicts between French and English and give each group greater voice in own affairs; Upper Canada mainly English-speaking; Lower Canada mainly French

---

SECTION 2 RESOURCES

PRINT RESOURCES

IN-DEPTH RESOURCES: UNIT 6
Guided Reading, p. 19
Geography Application: The British Settle Australia and New Zealand, p. 23
Primary Source: Irish Petition to Emigrate, p. 26
Literature: "Easter 1916," p. 29
ACCESS FOR STUDENTS ACQUIRING ENGLISH
Guided Reading (Spanish), p. 261
Geography Application: (Spanish), p. 265
FORMAL ASSESSMENT
Section Quiz, p. 302

TECHNOLOGY RESOURCES

GEOGRAPHY TRANSPARENCIES
GT26 Canada: Growth of the Dominion, 1867–Present
WORLD ART AND CULTURES TRANSPARENCIES
AT57 Maori pigment container
CD-ROM
Electronic Library of Primary Sources
VIDEO Patterns of Interaction: The Geography of Food
INTERNET www.mlworldhistory.com

Upper and Lower Canada. The British Parliament remembered the events that had led to the American Revolution. So, it sent a reform-minded statesman, Lord Durham, to investigate Canadians' demands for self-rule.

Durham's report, issued in 1839, urged two major reforms. First, Upper and Lower Canada should be reunited as the Province of Canada, and British immigration should be encouraged. In this way, Durham said, the French would slowly become part of the dominant English culture. Second, colonists in the provinces of Canada should be allowed to govern themselves in domestic matters. Parliament should regulate only in matters of foreign policy. Within ten years, both proposals had been carried out.

The Dominion of Canada By the mid-1800s, many Canadians believed that Canada needed a central government. A central government would be better able to protect the interests of Canadians against the United States, whose territory now extended from the Atlantic to the Pacific oceans. In 1867, Nova Scotia and New Brunswick joined with the Province of Canada to form the Dominion of Canada. As a **dominion,** Canada was self-governing in domestic affairs but remained part of the British Empire.

Canada's Westward Expansion Canada's first prime minister, John MacDonald, quickly expanded Canada westward by purchasing lands and persuading frontier territories to join the Canadian union. Canada stretched to the Pacific Ocean by 1871. MacDonald also began the construction of a transcontinental railroad to unite distant parts of the dominion. It was completed in 1885.

The dominion government also took other steps to strengthen Canada. It encouraged foreign investment to develop Canada's rich supply of natural resources. It also encouraged immigration to provide a labor force for Canada's farms and factories.

Australia and New Zealand

The British sea captain James Cook claimed New Zealand in 1769 and Australia in 1770 for Great Britain. Both lands were already inhabited. On New Zealand, Cook was greeted by the **Maoris,** a Polynesian people who had settled on New Zealand's two main islands around A.D. 800. Maori culture was based on farming, hunting, and fishing. Although the Maoris had driven away Dutch explorers in the 1640s, they made peace with Cook. As British colonization began, however, they stood ready to defend their land.

When Cook reached Australia, he considered the land uninhabited. In fact, Australia was sparsely populated by **Aborigines,** as Europeans later called the native peoples. These nomadic peoples fished, hunted, and gathered food. As they did not practice warfare among themselves, they at first raised little resistance to the flood of British immigrants who settled their country.

Britain's Penal Colony Britain began colonizing Australia in 1788—not with ordinary settlers, but with convicted criminals. The prisons in England were severely overcrowded. To solve this problem, the British government established a penal colony in Australia. A **penal colony** is a place where convicts were sent to serve their sentences as an alternative to prison. Many European nations used penal colonies as a way to prevent overcrowding of their prisons. After their release, the freed convicts could buy land and settle as free men and women.

THINK THROUGH HISTORY
B. Recognizing Effects How do you think Durham's recommendations affected French-speaking

B. Possible Answer Lost French-speaking province, subjected to greater political and cultural influence of English-speaking majority, became smaller minority; at the same time, all Canadians, including French, gained greater self-rule from Britain

CONNECT *to* TODAY

The Nunavut Territory

While Canada expanded westward in the 1870s, it also gained vast lands in the Arctic north. Most of the inhabitants of this sparsely populated region were Inuit. This native people had developed a way of life in the harsh Arctic climate over a period of thousands of years.

During the 20th century, the northern region became important to Canada for its rich natural resources and as a location for military bases. At the same time, the Inuit wanted more control over the resources of their native lands and a greater voice in their own affairs.

In the early 1990s, the Inuit and the Canadian government agreed to create a new self-governing territory called Nunavut in 1999. The name is an Inuit word meaning "Our Land." Nunavut includes the eastern two-thirds of the Northwest Territories—an area of land one-fifth the size of Canada.

CONNECT *to* TODAY
The Nunavut Territory

Although the snow house, or igloo, is the most familiar symbol of Inuit life, only Canadian Inuit built permanent winter snow houses. Two people could construct one of these ingenious dwellings out of snow blocks within one to three hours. Students might want to read about how snow houses are built and, in snow climates, try building one themselves.

🎞 *GEOGRAPHY TRANSPARENCIES*
GT26 Canada: Growth of the Dominion, 1867–Present

OBJECTIVE ② INSTRUCT

Australia and New Zealand

Key Ideas
- Captain Cook claims New Zealand and Australia.
- Britain uses Australia as a penal colony. Ex-convicts and free settlers develop a sheep-herding economy.
- Britain annexes New Zealand and defeats the rebellious Maori.
- Australia and New Zealand become democratic dominions of the British Empire.

🎞 *WORLD ART AND CULTURES TRANSPARENCIES*
AT57 Maori pigment container

CRITICAL THINKING ACTIVITY
CLASS TIME: 15 MINUTES

Analyzing Motives
Ask students to create a web chart to list reasons why the people of Canada, Australia, and New Zealand might want to remain within the British Empire.

Visual Learners Tell students that often the relationship between the "mother" country and her "children," or colonies, can be difficult, as our own history with England shows. Suggest that students draw political cartoons to express the relationship between Great Britain and its four colonies—Canada, New Zealand, Australia, and Ireland—as described in this section.

To help students get started, you might suggest that they represent Britain as a parent and the other countries as children—or in the case of Ireland a stepchild perhaps. Or have students brainstorm ideas for a few minutes before they begin their cartoons.

Gifted and Talented Students Encourage students to research the art, customs, and current situation of Aborigines and Maoris in Australia and New Zealand. Students might search for articles in periodicals such as *National Geographic* or find books on the history and culture of these two groups.

Students may be specially interested in the Aboriginal idea of the "Dream Time,"

Aboriginal dot art, and Maori woodwork. Ask them to try to see the world from an Aboriginal or Maori point of view. Students can prepare a brief multimedia report for the class.

🎞 *WORLD ART AND CULTURES TRANSPARENCIES*
AT57 Maori pigment container

MORE ABOUT . . .
Crime in Britain

In 1828, an estimated one out of every 822 residents of London was a professional criminal. Punishments were harsh to make up for the shortage of police officers (London had only 15). Over 160 offenses were punishable by death and many others by "transportation"—the shipping of criminals overseas. One criminal, for example, was sentenced to seven years in Australia for stealing two shoe buckles.

MORE ABOUT . . .
Settlement of Australia

Every convict who got discharged in Australia for good behavior received 30 acres of land—50 acres if he was married—plus 10 more acres for each child he had. Descendants of some early convicts thus ended up as major landowners.

History from Visuals

Australia and New Zealand to 1850

Interpreting the Map Ask students what the different colors on this map represent. *climate zones* In which climates zones did the Europeans mainly settle? *Mediterranean and woodlands*

Extension Activity Have students compare these maps to modern ones to see if the population patterns continued as shown here: Which is the most sparsely populated part of modern Australia? *The central desert area*

SKILLBUILDER Answers
1. Sydney, 1788
2. Australia: coastal regions of the northeast, northwest, southeast, and southwest; New Zealand: North Island

 IN-DEPTH RESOURCES: UNIT 6
Geography Application: The British Settle Australia and New Zealand, p. 23

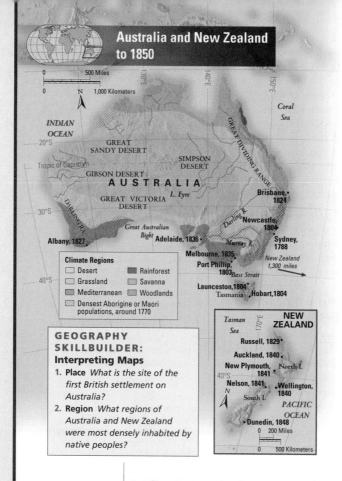

Australia and New Zealand to 1850

0 500 Miles
0 1,000 Kilometers

Climate Regions
- Desert
- Grassland
- Mediterranean
- Rainforest
- Savanna
- Woodlands
- Densest Aborigine or Maori populations, around 1770

GEOGRAPHY SKILLBUILDER:
Interpreting Maps
1. **Place** What is the site of the first British settlement on Australia?
2. **Region** What regions of Australia and New Zealand were most densely inhabited by native peoples?

NEW ZEALAND
Russell, 1829
Auckland, 1840
New Plymouth, 1841 North I.
Nelson, 1841 Wellington, 1840
South I. PACIFIC OCEAN
Dunedin, 1848
0 200 Miles
0 500 Kilometers

Free Settlers Arrive In time, the former convicts in both Australia and New Zealand were joined by other British settlers who came of their own free will. In the early 1800s, an Australian settler named John MacArthur experimented with breeds of sheep until he found one that produced high quality wool and thrived in the country's warm dry weather. Although sheep are not native to Australia, the raising and export of wool became its biggest business. Australians say that their country "rode to prosperity on the back of a sheep."

To encourage immigration, the government offered settlers cheap land. It used the money from land sales to lure laborers from Britain by paying the costs of the long voyage. The population grew steadily in the early 1800s and then skyrocketed after a gold rush in 1851.

The scattered settlements on Australia's east coast grew into separate colonies. Meanwhile, a few pioneers pushed westward across the vast dry interior and established outposts in western Australia. In the 1860s, settlers finally pressured the British to stop sending convicts to Australia.

Settling New Zealand European settlement of New Zealand grew more slowly. This was because the British did not claim ownership of New Zealand, as it did Australia. Rather, it recognized the land rights of the Maoris. Among the first British settlers in New Zealand were convicts who had escaped from Australia. In 1814, missionary groups began arriving from Australia seeking to convert the Maoris to Christianity.

The arrival of more foreigners stirred conflicts between the Maoris and the European settlers over land. Responding to the settlers' pleas, the British decided to annex New Zealand in 1838 and appointed a governor to negotiate with the Maoris. In a treaty signed in 1840, the Maoris accepted British rule in exchange for recognition of their land rights. Britain quickly established colonies around New Zealand. Many colonists successfully turned to producing wool and other agricultural products for export.

Self-Government Like many Canadians, the colonists of Australia and New Zealand wanted to rule themselves yet remain in the British Empire. During the 1850s, the colonies in both Australia and New Zealand became self-governing and created parliamentary forms of government. In 1901, the Australian colonies were united under a federal constitution as the Commonwealth of Australia. During the early 1900s, both Australia and New Zealand became dominions.

The people of Australia and New Zealand pioneered a number of political reforms. For example, the secret ballot, sometimes called the Australian ballot, was first used in Australia in the 1850s. In 1893, New Zealand became the first nation in the world to give full voting rights to women. These rights were granted only to white women of European descent.

THINK THROUGH HISTORY
C. Contrasting How did the colonial settlement of Australia and New Zealand differ?
C. Possible Answer Australia's colonization began first, as a penal colony; British considered Australia uninhabited and claimed ownership, whereas it recognized land rights of Marois; British encouraged settlement of Australia with land offers.

TEACHING OPTIONS | **CONNECTIONS ACROSS TIME AND PLACE**

Australian Development The Industrial Revolution in England displaced many rural and city people. Without work, many of these people were forced to steal for a living. One of England's responses to the rising crime rate and swollen prison population was to establish a penal colony in Australia.

England was not the only country to ameliorate overcrowded prison conditions at home by establishing penal colonies overseas. France, for example, transported many of its prisoners to New Caledonia and French Guiana. Tsarist Russia initiated the practice of sending prisoners to its colonies in Siberia. Have interested students compare Britain's penal colonies with those of France and Russia.

CONNECTIONS ACROSS THE CURRICULUM

Music Most Native American tribes use some forms of drums, rattles, sticks, and flutes in their music. Australian Aborigines use the didgeridoo, a hollowed out cylinder of wood blown like a trumpet, and the bull-roarer, a piece of wood or thick hide notched with holes and whirled around on the end of a long string. Students can see

and hear these instruments in the series *Music Around the World,* Sets 1 and 2 from Social Studies School Service (800)-421-4246. Or they may be able to find recordings of Native American and Aboriginal music at a local music store. Encourage students to research how these instruments are made and used.

Status of Native Peoples Native peoples and other non-Europeans were generally excluded from democracy and prosperity. As in the Americas, diseases brought by the Europeans killed a great number of both Aborigines and Maoris. As Australian settlement grew, the colonists displaced or killed many Aborigines. Sheep ranchers in particular took possession of vast tracts of land for grazing. Both the loss of open land and the spread of diseases contributed to the destruction of the Aborigines' way of life.

In New Zealand, tensions between settlers and Maoris continued to grow after it became a British colony. Between 1845 and 1872, the colonial government fought the Maoris in a series of wars. Reduced by disease and outgunned by British weapons, the Maoris were finally driven into a remote part of the country.

This photo from the early 20th century shows a Maori man with traditional dress and face markings.

The Irish Fight for Home Rule

English expansion into Ireland had begun in the 1100s, when the pope granted control of Ireland to the English king. English knights invaded Ireland, and many settled there to form a new aristocracy. The Irish, who had their own ancestry, culture, and language, bitterly resented the English presence.

This resentment grew stronger after English King Henry VIII tried to tighten England's hold on Ireland. In hopes of planting a pro-English population in Ireland, Henry VIII and some later English leaders (including Elizabeth I and Oliver Cromwell) encouraged English and Scottish subjects to move there. Large numbers did, mostly to the north. Religious differences between the native Irish, who were Catholic, and these Protestant settlers caused conflicts.

Laws imposed in the 1500s and 1600s limited the rights of Catholics. For example, Catholics could no longer hold public office. They had to pay taxes to support the Church of Ireland, which was Protestant. In addition, English was made Ireland's official language.

Many Irish hated British rule. However, the British government was determined to preserve its control over Ireland. It formally joined Ireland to Britain in 1801. Though a setback for Irish nationalism, this move did give Ireland representation in the British Parliament. One brilliant Irish leader, Daniel O'Connell, persuaded Parliament to pass the Catholic Emancipation Act in 1829. This law restored many rights to Catholics.

Background
The act that joined Ireland to Britain created the United Kingdom of Great Britain and Ireland. The 1707 Act of Union had created Great Britain out of England, Scotland, and Wales.

Background
Before the famine, the average Irish adult ate an estimated 9 to 14 pounds of potatoes a day.

The Great Famine In the 1840s, Ireland experienced one of the worst famines of modern history. For many years, Irish peasants had depended on potatoes as virtually their sole source of food. From 1845 to 1848, a plant fungus ruined nearly all of Ireland's potato crop. Out of a population of 8 million, about a million people died from starvation and disease over the next few years. A traveler described what he saw on a journey through Ireland in 1847:

A VOICE FROM THE PAST
We entered a cabin. Stretched in one dark corner, scarcely visible, from the smoke and rags that covered them, were three children huddled together, lying there *because they were too weak to rise*, pale and ghastly, their little limbs—on removing a portion of the filthy covering—perfectly emaciated, eyes sunk, voice gone, and evidently in the last stage of actual starvation.

WILLIAM BENNETT, quoted in *The Peoples of Ireland*

The Great Famine, 1845–1851

Fate of the Irish during the famine

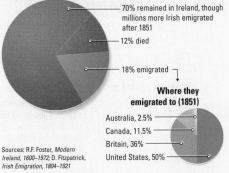

- 70% remained in Ireland, though millions more Irish emigrated after 1851
- 12% died
- 18% emigrated

Where they emigrated to (1851)

- Australia, 2.5%
- Canada, 11.5%
- Britain, 36%
- United States, 50%

Sources: R.F. Foster, *Modern Ireland, 1600–1972;* D. Fitzpatrick, *Irish Emigration, 1804–1921*

SKILLBUILDER: Interpreting Graphs
1. What percentage of Ireland's population died during the great famine?
2. Which country received the most Irish emigrants?

An Age of Democracy and Progress **667**

OBJECTIVE **3** INSTRUCT

The Irish Fight for Home Rule

▶ **Key Ideas**
- Irish Catholics struggle against British rule and Protestants.
- The great famine spurs Irish emigration.
- Ireland divides into a southern state and a northern province.

 ELECTRONIC LIBRARY OF PRIMARY SOURCES
"The Irish Potato Famine"

 IN-DEPTH RESOURCES: UNIT 6
Primary Source: Irish Petition to Emigrate, p. 26

MORE ABOUT . . .
The Great Famine

The *Geography of Food* video investigates why Irish peasants came to depend so heavily on potatoes and how the Great Famine affected Irish history and world history.

PATTERNS OF INTERACTION
The Geography of Food: The Impact of Potatoes and Sugar
Videocassette: Tape 2

History from Visuals

The Great Famine, 1845–1851
Interpreting the Graphs Have students study both pie graphs. Ask them how the smaller pie graph is related to the larger one. *The smaller graph represents the 18 percent of the population who emigrated and gives a breakdown of where they went.*

Extension Activity Ask students to calculate the number of Irish who emigrated and the number who went to each country, based on a population of 8 million people. *18% = 1.44 million; Aus = 36,000; Can = 165,500; Brit = 518,400; U.S. = 720,000*

SKILLBUILDER Answers
1. 12 percent
2. United States

TEACHING OPTION **BLOCK SCHEDULING**   ANALYZING CAUSES AND EFFECTS   **CLASS TIME 20 MINUTES**

Task Students will view the video on the Irish potato famine and analyze the causes and effects of the famine.

Materials Needed The video *The Geography of Food: The Impact of Potatoes and Sugar;* copies of the Cause and Effect graphic organizer.

Activity Have students view the video, taking notes as they can. Then ask students to work in small groups to create a cause and effect chart showing the contributing factors that led to the famine and the effects of the famine on Irish and U.S. history.

Conclusion: Discuss with students how a single disaster such as the potato famine can have multiple

causes, both human and natural, and multiple effects. How would Irish history have been different if the famine had been dealt with at the outset? What would have been the effect on Irish immigration to the United States?

CRITICAL THINKING TRANSPARENCIES
CT75 Cause and Effect

Teacher's Edition   667

"Troubles" in Northern Ireland

The best known militant group in Northern Ireland is the Irish Republican Army (IRA). Their roots go back to another underground army, The Irish Volunteers, and to the Fenians—a group founded in the wake of the potato famine to drive the British out of Ireland by force. In a sense, the potato famine still reverberates in Ireland and Great Britain.

 IN-DEPTH RESOURCES: UNIT 6
Literature: "Easter 1916," p. 29

ASSESS & RETEACH

Section 2 Assessment
Have students work through the assessment questions in small groups. Remind them to check the chapter opener to help them respond to the question related to themes.

Section Quiz
 FORMAL ASSESSMENT
Section Quiz, p. 302

Reteaching Activity
CLASS TIME: 15 MINUTES

Have students create a chart listing the Inuit, Aborigines, and Maori. Ask them to fill in the chart by listing the native country, one or two distinguishing characteristics, and the current situation of each group.

CLOSE ACTIVITY

CLASS TIME: 20 MINUTES

Identifying Problems and Solutions
Divide the class into three groups, each representing Canada, Australia, and Ireland. Have each group describe their problems in obtaining self-rule, the solutions they proposed, and the results.

During the famine years, about a million-and-a-half people fled from Ireland. Most went to the United States; others went to Britain, Canada, and Australia. At home, in Ireland, the British government enforced the demands of the English landowners that the Irish peasants pay their rent. Many Irish lost their land and fell hopelessly in debt, while large landowners profited from higher food prices. This situation fueled even greater Irish resentment toward their British overlords.

Demands for Home Rule During the second half of the 1800s, opposition to British rule over Ireland took two forms. Some people wanted Ireland to be completely independent. A greater number of Irish preferred **home rule**—local control over internal matters only. The British refused, however, to consider home rule for many decades.

One reason for Britain's opposition to home rule was concern for Ireland's Protestants. Protestants made up a small minority of the population. Most lived in the northern part of Ireland, known as Ulster. Irish Protestants feared being a minority in a country dominated by Catholics. Finally, in 1914, Parliament enacted a home rule bill for southern Ireland. Just one month before the plan was to take effect, World War I broke out in Europe. The issue of Irish independence was put on hold.

Rebellion and Division Frustrated over the delay in independence, a small group of Irish nationalists rebelled in Dublin in Easter week, 1916. British troops quickly put down the Easter Rising and executed its leaders. Their fate, however, aroused wider popular support for the nationalist movement.

After World War I ended, the Irish nationalists won a major victory in the elections for the British Parliament. To protest delays in home rule, the nationalist members decided not to attend Parliament. Instead, they formed an underground Irish government and led a series of violent attacks against British officials in Ireland. The attacks sparked war between the nationalists and the British government.

In 1921, Britain tried to end the violence by dividing Ireland and granting home rule to southern Ireland. Ulster, or Northern Ireland, remained a part of Great Britain. The south became a dominion called the Irish Free State. However, many Irish nationalists, led by Eamon De Valera, continued to seek total independence from Britain. In 1949, the Irish Free State declared itself the independent Republic of Ireland.

CONNECT *to* TODAY

"Troubles" in Northern Ireland

When Northern Ireland decided to stay united with Great Britain, many Catholics there refused to accept the partition, or division. Catholics also resented that the Protestant majority controlled Northern Ireland's government and economy.

In the late 1960s, Catholic groups began to demonstrate for more civil rights. Their protests touched off violent rioting and fighting between Catholics and Protestants. Militant groups on both sides engaged in terrorism. This violent period, called the "troubles," continued into the 1990s.

In 1994, militant groups on both sides agreed to a cease-fire and began face-to-face talks. Since then, terrorist attacks have still occurred, but uneasy negotiations continue.

This poster urg[es]
Protestant Nor[thern]
Ireland to reje[ct]
rule. The milita[ry]
foreshadows th[e]
continuing poli[tical]
troubles in Nor[thern]
Ireland today.

D. Possible
Answers *Yes*—
allowed the maj[ority]
in each part to h[ave]
its way; *No*—it
led to continuing [vio-]
lence and bloods[hed.]

THINK THROUGH HIS[TORY]

D. Evaluating Decisions Was
Britain's policy in [divid-]
ing Ireland succes[sful?]
Why or why not?

Section ② Assessment

1. TERMS & NAMES	2. TAKING NOTES	3. COMPARING	4. ANALYZING THEMES
Identify • dominion • Maori • Aborigine • penal colony • home rule	Using a chart like the one below, compare progress toward self-rule by recording significant political events in Canada, Australia, New Zealand, and Ireland during the period.	How was Great Britain's policy towards Canada beginning in the late 1700s similar to its policy towards Ireland in the 1900s? **THINK ABOUT** • the creation of Upper and Lower Canada • the division of Ireland into Northern Ireland and the Irish Free State	**Empire Building** At variou[s] times, England encouraged emigration to each of the colonies covered in this sectio[n]. What effects did this policy ha[ve] on these areas? **THINK ABOUT** • cultural divisions in Canada • native peoples in Canada, Australia, and New Zealand • political divisions in Ireland

Country	Political Events
Canada	
Australia	
New Zealand	
Ireland	

668 Chapter 26

ANSWERS

1. TERMS & NAMES
dominion, p. 665
Maori, p. 665
Aborigine, p. 665
penal colony, p. 665
home rule, p. 668

2. TAKING NOTES
Possible Responses: (Canada)
Given responsibility for own

affairs, mid-1800s; dominion status, 1867. (Australia) Self-governing, set up legislature, 1850s; male suffrage, secret ballot, 1850s; dominion, early 1900s. (New Zealand) Self-governing, set up legislature, 1850s; women gain suffrage, 1893; dominion, early 1900s. (Ireland) Joins Britain, gains rep-

resentation in Parliament, 1801; home rule bill passes, but does not take effect, 1914; southern Ireland becomes dominion, 1921, and becomes independent, 1949.

3. COMPARING
Possible Responses: In both, Britain created political divisions to resolve conflicts.

4. ANALYZING THEMES
Possible Responses: In Cana[da,] Australia, and New Zealand, t[he] British displaced the native po[p]ulations (in Canada, conflicts with French caused creation [of] Upper and Lower Canada); reli[-] gious differences became poli[ti-] cal division between northern and southern Ireland.

3 Expansion and Crisis in the United States

TERMS & NAMES
- manifest destiny
- Abraham Lincoln
- secede
- U.S. Civil War
- Emancipation Proclamation
- segregation

MAIN IDEA

The United States expanded across North America and fought a bloody civil war.

WHY IT MATTERS NOW

The 20th-century movements to ensure civil rights for African Americans and Hispanics are a legacy of this period.

SETTING THE STAGE The United States had won its independence from Britain in 1783. At the end of the Revolutionary War, the Mississippi River marked the western boundary of the new republic. As the original United States filled with settlers, land-hungry newcomers pushed beyond the Mississippi, looking for opportunity. The government helped them by acquiring new territory for settlement.

Americans Move Westward

Piece by piece, the United States added new territory. In 1803, President Thomas Jefferson bought the Louisiana Territory from France. The Louisiana Purchase nearly doubled the size of the new republic and extended its boundary to the Rocky Mountains. In 1819, Spain gave up Florida to the United States. In 1846, a treaty with Great Britain gave the United States part of the Oregon Territory. In the north, the nation now stretched from the Atlantic Ocean to the Pacific Ocean.

War with Mexico Meanwhile, the United States had entered a war with Mexico over Texas. When Mexico had gained its independence from Spain in 1821, it included the lands west of the Louisiana Purchase—from Texas to California. Many American settlers moved into these areas, with Mexico's acceptance. Some settlers were unhappy with Mexico's rule.

The largest number of American settlers were in the Mexican territory of Texas. In 1836, Texans revolted against Mexican rule. For nine-and-a-half years, Texas was an independent country. Then, in 1845, the United States annexed Texas. Mexico responded angrily to what it believed was an act of aggression.

Between May 1846 and September 1847, war flared between the two countries. In bitter fighting, U.S. troops captured Mexico City and forced Mexico to surrender. As part of the settlement of the Mexican-American War, Mexico ceded, or gave up possession of, territory to the United States. The Mexican Cession included California and a huge amount of territory in the Southwest. A few years later, in 1853, the Gadsden Purchase from Mexico brought the lower continental United States to its present boundaries.

U.S. Expansion, 1783–1853

- U.S. in 1783
- Louisiana Purchase, 1803
- Florida Cession, 1819
- By treaty with Great Britain, 1818 and 1842
- Texas Annexation, 1845
- Oregon, 1846
- Mexican Cession, 1848
- Gadsden Purchase, 1853

GEOGRAPHY SKILLBUILDER: Interpreting Maps
1. **Movement** What was the first territory to be added to the United States after 1783?
2. **Region** What present-day states were part of the Mexican Cession?

An Age of Democracy and Progress **669**

Section 3 Overview

OBJECTIVES

1. To trace U. S. expansion to the Pacific.
2. To describe the effect of the Civil War on the United States.
3. To explain the economic expansion after the Civil War.

SKILLBUILDER

- Interpreting maps: movement, region, page 669
- Interpreting maps: place, human-environment interaction, p. 671

CRITICAL THINKING

- Contrasting, p. 670
- Analyzing issues, p. 671
- Recognizing effects, p. 672
- Distinguishing fact from opinion, p. 672
- Analyzing themes, p. 672

FOCUS

5-Minute Warm-Up

▶ **Making Inferences**
By answering the following questions, students will better understand the motive for U.S. westward expansion.

- Read the first paragraph under "Manifest Destiny" on page 670. What was manifest destiny?
- How did government leaders use the concept?

WARM-UP TRANSPARENCY 26

OBJECTIVE 1 INSTRUCT

Americans Move Westward

▶ **Key Ideas**
- The United States acquires more territory from Mexico.
- Manifest destiny justifies westward expansion.

IN-DEPTH RESOURCES: UNIT 6
Guided Reading, p. 20

ACCESS FOR STUDENTS ACQUIRING ENGLISH
Guided Reading (Spanish), p. 262

SECTION 3 RESOURCES

PRINT RESOURCES

IN-DEPTH RESOURCES: UNIT 6
Guided Reading, p. 20
Primary Source: Railroad Poster, p. 27

ACCESS FOR STUDENTS ACQUIRING ENGLISH
Guided Reading (Spanish), p. 262

FORMAL ASSESSMENT
Section Quiz, p. 303

ALTERNATIVE ASSESSMENT BOOK

TECHNOLOGY RESOURCES

CD-ROM
Electronic Library of Primary Sources

INTERNET www.mlworldhistory.com

U.S. Expansion, 1783–1853
(See page 669.)

Interpreting the Map Ask students what each color represents. *a U.S. land acquisition* By how much did the U.S. grow during this period? *tripled in size*

Extension Activity Ask students whether any obvious cultural differences survive among the regions shown here. *Blue and purple areas show distinct Hispanic influences.*

SKILLBUILDER Answers
1. Louisiana Territory
2. California, Nevada, Utah, parts of Arizona, New Mexico, Colorado, and Wyoming

---

MORE ABOUT . . .
Manifest Destiny

It was newspaper editor John L. O'Sullivan who wrote that the United States had a "manifest destiny to overspread . . . the continent which Providence has given us for the development of the great experiment of liberty and . . . self-government entrusted to us."

 ELECTRONIC LIBRARY OF PRIMARY SOURCES
from A Message to Congress on Indian Policy

OBJECTIVE ② INSTRUCT

Civil War Tests Democracy

Key Ideas
- A civil war pits industrial North against agricultural South.
- The Emancipation Proclamation bans slavery in Confederate states.
- After the Civil War, Southern state laws limit freedom and opportunity for African Americans.

Manifest Destiny Many Americans eagerly supported their country's westward expansion. These people believed in **manifest destiny**—the idea that the United States had the right and duty to rule North America from the Atlantic Ocean to the Pacific Ocean. Government leaders used manifest destiny as a way of justifying any action that helped white settlers occupy new land. This included evicting Native Americans from their tribal lands.

The Indian Removal Act of 1830 made such actions official policy. This law enabled the federal government to force Native Americans living in the East to move to the West. Georgia's Cherokee tribe challenged the law before the Supreme Court. The Court, however, ruled the suit was invalid. Like many other Native American tribes, the Cherokees had to move. They traveled 800 miles to Oklahoma, mostly on foot, on a journey later called the Trail of Tears. About a quarter of the Cherokees died on the trip. A survivor recalled how the journey began:

> **A VOICE FROM THE PAST**
> The day was bright and beautiful, but a gloomy thoughtfulness was depicted in the lineaments of every face. . . . At this very moment a low sound of distant thunder fell on my ear . . . and sent forth a murmur, I almost thought a voice of divine indignation for the wrong of my poor and unhappy countrymen, driven by brutal power from all they loved and cherished in the land of their fathers.
> **WILLIAM SHOREY COODEY**, quoted in *The Trail of Tears*

When the Cherokees reached their destination, they ended up on land far inferior to that which they had been forced to leave. Nor did the trail end there. As whites moved west during the second half of the 19th century, the government continued to push Native Americans off their land to make room for the new settlers. Eventually, the government demanded that Native Americans abandon most of their lands and move to reservations.

Civil War Tests Democracy
America's westward expansion raised questions about what laws and customs should be followed in the West. Ever since the nation's early days, the northern and southern parts of the United States had followed different ways of life. Each section wanted to extend its own way of life to the new territories and states in the West.

North and South The North had a diversified economy with both farms and industry. For both its factories and farms, the North depended on free workers. The South's economy, on the other hand, was based on just a few cash crops, mainly cotton. Southern planters relied on slave labor.

The economic differences between the two regions led to a conflict over slavery. Many Northerners considered slavery morally wrong. They wanted to outlaw slavery in the new western states. Some wanted to abolish slavery altogether. Most white Southerners believed slavery was necessary for their economy. They wanted laws to protect slavery in the West so that they could continue to raise cotton on the fertile soil there.

The disagreement over slavery fueled a debate about the rights of the individual states against those of the federal government. Southern politicians argued that the states had freely joined the Union, and so they could freely leave. Most Northerners felt that the Constitution of the United States had established the Union once and for all—it could not be broken.

Civil War Breaks Out Conflict between the North and South reached a climax in 1860, when **Abraham Lincoln** was elected President. Southerners fiercely opposed Lincoln, who had promised to stop the spread of slavery. One by one, Southern states began to **secede,** or withdraw, from the Union. These states came together as the Confederate States of America.

670 Chapter 26

Vocabulary
manifest: clearly apparent or obvious.

THINK THROUGH HISTORY
A. Contrasting
What were the main economic differences between the Northern and Southern states?
A. Answer North had diversified economy with farms and industry, depended on free workers; South's economy relied on few cash crops and slave labor.

Task Students will create a newspaper editorial page focusing on manifest destiny.

Purpose To examine a key doctrine in American history from various perspectives.

Activity Groups of students will create part of an editorial page on manifest destiny. Students will write editorials or letters to the editor from various points

of view—Native Americans, Mexicans, Canadians, recent European immigrants, and so on. Each group will support or attack the doctrine.

📁 **Building a Portfolio** Students may want to include their part of the editorial page in their portfolios.

📄 **ALTERNATIVE ASSESSMENT BOOK**
Standards for Evaluating a Cooperative Activity

Standards for Evaluation
Letters or essays should . . .

- identify each writer and cultural or ethnic group
- present a strong argument for or against manifest destiny, with supporting details
- use historically appropriate examples

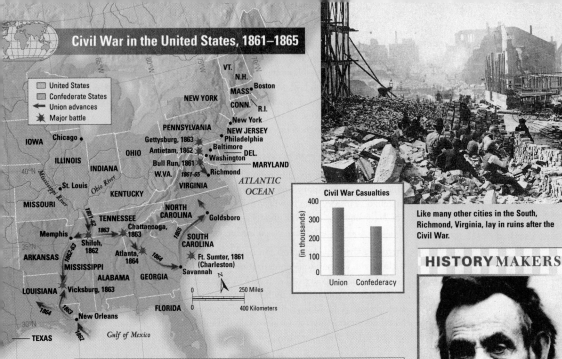

Civil War in the United States, 1861–1865

Legend:
- United States
- Confederate States
- → Union advances
- ✴ Major battle

Map locations include: IOWA, Chicago, ILLINOIS, INDIANA, OHIO, St. Louis, MISSOURI, KENTUCKY, TENNESSEE, Memphis, Shiloh 1862, ARKANSAS, MISSISSIPPI, Vicksburg 1863, LOUISIANA, ALABAMA, GEORGIA, Atlanta 1864, New Orleans, TEXAS, Gulf of Mexico, Chattanooga 1863, NORTH CAROLINA, SOUTH CAROLINA, Goldsboro, Savannah, FLORIDA, Ft. Sumter 1861 (Charleston), VT., N.H., MASS., Boston, NEW YORK, CONN., R.I., PENNSYLVANIA, NEW JERSEY, New York, Philadelphia, Baltimore, DEL., Washington, MARYLAND, Gettysburg 1863, Antietam 1862, Bull Run 1861, W.VA. 1861–65, Richmond, VIRGINIA, ATLANTIC OCEAN

Scale: 0 — 250 Miles, 0 — 400 Kilometers

Civil War Casualties (in thousands): bar chart showing Union (about 370) and Confederacy (about 260), scale 0, 100, 200, 300, 400.

Like many other cities in the South, Richmond, Virginia, lay in ruins after the Civil War.

GEOGRAPHY SKILLBUILDER: Interpreting Maps
1. **Place** Where and when was the northernmost battle fought in the war?
2. **Human-Environment Interaction** Which side do you think suffered the most devastation? Why?

On April 12, 1861, Confederate forces fired on Fort Sumter, a federal fort in Charleston, South Carolina. Lincoln ordered the army to bring the rebel states back into the Union. The **U.S. Civil War** had begun. Four years of fighting followed, most of it in the South. Although the South had superior military leadership, the North had a larger population, better transportation, greater resources, and more factories to turn out weapons and supplies. These advantages proved too much for the South to overcome. In April 1865, the South surrendered. The United States had survived the toughest test of its democracy.

Abolition of Slavery From the beginning of the war, Lincoln declared that it was being fought to save the Union and not to end slavery. Lincoln eventually decided that ending slavery would help to save the Union. Early in 1863, he issued the **Emancipation Proclamation,** declaring that all slaves in the Confederate states were free.

At first, the proclamation freed no slaves, because the Confederate states did not accept it as law. As Union armies advanced into the South, however, they freed slaves in the lands they conquered. The Emancipation Proclamation also showed people in Europe that the war was being fought against slavery. The proclamation made many Europeans, especially the British, less sympathetic to the South. They did not send the money and supplies that the South had hoped they would.

In the aftermath of the war, the U.S. Congress passed the Thirteenth Amendment to the Constitution, which forever abolished slavery in all parts of the United States. Soon after, the Fourteenth and Fifteenth Amendments extended the rights of citizenship to all Americans, black or white, and guaranteed former slaves the right to vote.

THINK THROUGH HISTORY
B. Analyzing Issues
Did the Emancipation Proclamation reflect a change in Lincoln's main goal for the war?
B. Answer No, he believed that ending slavery would help him achieve his primary goal—preserving the Union.

HISTORY MAKERS

Abraham Lincoln
1809–1865

Lincoln passionately believed in preserving the Union. His upbringing might help explain why. The son of rural, illiterate parents, he educated himself. After working as rail splitter, boatman, storekeeper, and surveyor, he taught himself to be a lawyer. This led to careers in law and politics—and eventually to the White House.

In Europe, people were more or less fixed in the level of society into which they had been born. Yet the United States had been founded on the belief that all men were created equal. Therefore, Lincoln was free to achieve whatever he could. Small wonder that he fought to preserve the democracy he described as the "last best hope of earth."

An Age of Democracy and Progress **671**

Postwar Economic Expansion

▶ **Key Ideas**
• After the Civil War, an economic boom is fueled by immigration, railroads, and the opening of the West.

 IN-DEPTH RESOURCES: UNIT 6
Primary Source: Railroad Poster, p. 27

---

*Global*Impact
Settling the West

About 40,000 Chinese workers helped build the transcontinental railroad. These workers achieved astounding feats, such as digging tunnels through solid rock. After the railroad was finished, many Chinese settled in San Francisco in what came to be known as Chinatown.

ASSESS & RETEACH

Section 3 Assessment
Have students write their response to each question then share their papers in small groups.

Section Quiz
 FORMAL ASSESSMENT
Section Quiz, p. 303

Reteaching Activity
CLASS TIME: 15 MINUTES

Ask students to create a time line of the events in this section and discuss how each event relates to U.S. history.

CLOSE ACTIVITY

CLASS TIME:

Hypothesizing
Ask students to suppose they are preparing a miniseries on U.S. history titled: *Before the Civil War, The Civil War,* and *After the Civil War.* Have students write a brief, informative, and dramatic blurb giving background information for each of the three parts.

Reconstruction From 1865 to 1877, Union troops occupied the South and enforced the constitutional protections. This period is called Reconstruction. After federal troops left the South, white Southerners passed laws that limited African Americans' rights and made it difficult for them to vote. Such laws also encouraged **segregation,** or separation, of blacks and whites in the South. African Americans continued to face discrimination in Northern states as well. Decades passed before African Americans made significant progress towards equality with other citizens.

Postwar Economic Expansion

While the South struggled to rebuild its shattered economy, the United States as a whole experienced a period of industrial expansion unmatched in history. The need for mass production and distribution of goods during the Civil War greatly speeded America's industrialization. By 1914, the United States was a leading industrial power in the world.

Immigration Industrialization could not have occurred so rapidly without the tremendous contribution of immigrants. During the 1870s, immigrants arrived at a rate of nearly 2,000 a day. By 1914, more than 20 million people had moved to the United States from Europe and Asia. Many settled in the growing industrial cities of the Northeast and Midwest. Others staked their claims in the open spaces of the West, lured by government offers of free land.

The Railroads As settlers moved west, so did the nation's rail system. In 1862, Congress had authorized money to build a transcontinental railroad. For seven years, Chinese and Irish immigrants, Mexican Americans, African Americans, and others did the backbreaking labor. They dug tunnels, built bridges, and hammered down the heavy steel tracks and wooden ties. When the transcontinental railroad was completed in 1869, railroads linked California with the Midwest and Eastern United States.

By 1900, nearly 200,000 miles of track spiderwebbed the nation. This massive system linked farm to city and boosted trade and industry. For one thing, the railroads bought huge quantities of steel. Also, trains brought materials such as coal and iron ore to factories and moved the finished goods quickly to market. They carried corn, wheat, and cattle from the Great Plains to processing plants in St. Louis, Chicago, and Minneapolis. These developments helped to make the United States a world leader in the great explosion of technological progress that marked the late nineteenth century.

---

*Global*Impact
Settling the West

The settling of the American West affected people in many parts of the world. Most of those drawn to the "Wild West" were American-born. However, many Europeans and Asians also arrived in search of work and land.

U.S. railroad companies, who owned much land in the West, sent agents to Europe to recruit people to buy and settle their land. Facing wars, overpopulation, and economic problems, many Europeans jumped at the offer. German and Scandinavian farmers, for example, settled widely in the upper Midwest.

The railroads also hired many immigrants as laborers—including thousands of Chinese. The Chinese sought opportunity in the United States for many of the same reasons Europeans did. Desperate families scraped together money to send one son to America. Once they arrived, however, the Chinese faced not only backbreaking labor but much discrimination.

Foreign Settlers in the West*, 1900
Top Five Countries of Origin
(in thousands)

*States and territories west of the Mississippi River
Source: U.S. Census Bureau

C. Possible Answer
Drew people to West, including many immigrants; by carrying raw materials to factories and finished goods to market, it boosted agriculture and industry; helped steel industry

THINK THROUGH HISTORY
C. Recognizing Effects How did railroads affect the growth of the United States?

Section **3** Assessment

1. TERMS & NAMES
Identify
• manifest destiny
• Abraham Lincoln
• secede
• U.S Civil War
• Emancipation Proclamation
• segregation

2. TAKING NOTES
Following the example below, create a time line showing the major events of the United States in the 19th century.

```
           [event     ]        [event    ]
           [two       ]        [four     ]
  [event  ]        [event   ]
  [one    ]        [three   ]
```

Indicate which events contributed to U.S. expansion and which events involved a war or other crisis. Label your time line "Expansion and Crisis in the United States."

3. DISTINGUISHING FACT FROM OPINION

Reread the quotation from William Shorey Coodey on page 670. What facts are conveyed in his statement? What opinions—judgment, beliefs, or feelings—does he express about the Trail of Tears? How does he use his description of events to help justify his opinions?

4. ANALYZING THEMES

Economics Imagine that circumstances had forced the North to surrender to the South in the Civil War. Therefore, two countries shared the region now occupied by the United States. What economic effects might this have had on the North? the South? the region as a whole?

THINK ABOUT
• the issue of slavery
• the impact of the Civil War
• postwar economic expansion of the United States

ANSWERS

1. TERMS & NAMES
manifest destiny, p. 670
Abraham Lincoln, p. 670
secede, p. 670
U.S Civil War, p. 671
Emancipation Proclamation, p. 671
segregation, p. 672

2. TAKING NOTES
1803 Louisiana Purchase; 1819

Florida Cession; 1838 Trail of Tears; 1836 Texas independence; 1845 Texas Annexation; 1846–47 Mexican-American War; 1848 Mexican Cession; 1853 Gadsden Purchase; 1861–65 Civil War; 1863 Emancipation Proclamation; 1865–77 Reconstruction; 1869 Transcontinental railroad completed

3. DISTINGUISHING FACT FROM OPINION
Possible Response: Facts: elements of weather, people present, eviction taking place. Opinions: description of thunder as "divine indignation" at the wrong done to "my poor and unhappy countrymen" and at the "brutal power" of the whites.

4. ANALYZING THEMES
Possible Response: If the Nor had surrendered, it probably wouldn't have developed as much industrially, slowing set ment of the West. The South would have remained agricultural, and the economy of the country as a whole probably would not have grown as fast

4 Nineteenth-Century Progress

TERMS & NAMES
• assembly line
• mass culture
• Charles Darwin
• theory of evolution
• radioactivity
• psychology

MAIN IDEA

Breakthroughs in science and technology transformed daily life and entertainment.

WHY IT MATTERS NOW

Electric lights, telephones, cars, and many other conveniences of modern life were invented during this period.

SETTING THE STAGE The Industrial Revolution happened because of inventions like the spinning jenny and the steam engine. In turn, the demands of growing industries spurred even greater advances in technology. By the late 1800s, advances in both industry and technology were occurring faster than ever before. In industrialized countries, economic growth produced many social changes. At the same time, a surge of scientific discovery pushed the frontiers of knowledge forward.

Inventions Change Ways of Life

In the early 1800s, coal and steam drove the machines of industry. By the late 1800s, new kinds of energy were coming into use. One was gasoline, which powered a new type of engine called an internal combustion engine. Small, light, and efficient, this engine would eventually make the automobile possible. Another kind of energy was the mysterious force called electricity. In the 1870s, the electric generator was developed, which produced a current that could power machines. This invention made it possible to bring the magic of electricity into daily life.

Edison the Inventor If electricity seemed like magic to people in the 19th century, Thomas Edison was perhaps the century's greatest magician. Over his career, Edison patented more than 1,000 inventions, including the light bulb and the phonograph.

Early in his career, Edison started a research laboratory in Menlo Park, New Jersey. Most of his important inventions were developed there, with help from the researchers he employed. Indeed, the idea of a laboratory for industrial research and development may have been Edison's most important invention.

Bell and Marconi Revolutionize Communication Other inventors helped harness electricity to transmit sounds over great distances. Alexander Graham Bell was a teacher of deaf students who invented the telephone in his spare time. He displayed his device at the Philadelphia Exposition of 1876. The emperor of Brazil used it to speak to his aide in another room. When he heard the reply he exclaimed, "My word! It speaks Portuguese!"

The Italian inventor Guglielmo Marconi used theoretical discoveries about electromagnetic waves to create the first radio in 1895. This device was important because it sent messages (using Morse Code) through the air, without the use of wires. Primitive radios soon became standard equipment for ships at sea. Not until later could radios transmit human voices.

Ford Sparks the Automobile Industry In the 1880s, German inventors used a gasoline engine to power a vehicle—the automobile.

An Age of Inventions

Light Bulb
Edison and his team invented the first practical electric light bulb in 1879. Within a few years, Edison had perfected a longer-lasting bulb and begun installing electric lighting in New York City.

Telephone
Alexander Graham Bell demonstrated the first telephone in 1876. It quickly became an essential of modern life. By 1900, there were nearly 2 million telephones in the United States. By 1912, there were 8.7 million.

An Age of Democracy and Progress **673**

Section 4 Overview

OBJECTIVES

1. To describe inventions of the late 19th century and their impact on daily life.

2. To explain the rise of mass culture.

3. To list 19th century advances in medicine and science.

4. To describe the emergence of the social sciences.

CRITICAL THINKING

• Making inferences, p. 674
• Recognizing effects, p. 675
• Analyzing causes, pp. 674, 677
• Clarifying, pp. 678, 679
• Comparing and contrasting, p. 679

FOCUS

5-Minute Warm-Up

▶ **Recognizing Effects**
Answering the following questions will help students understand the impact of 19th-century inventions.

1. Read "An Age of Inventions" on pages 673 and 674. Between 1910 and 1912, how many more people acquired telephones?

2. What invention enabled companies to make products more efficiently?

WARM-UP TRANSPARENCY 26

OBJECTIVE 1 INSTRUCT

Inventions Change Ways of Life

▶ **Key Ideas**
• Inventions in electronics, communication technology, manufacturing methods, and aircraft usher in a new industrial age.

IN-DEPTH RESOURCES: UNIT 6
Guided Reading, p. 21

Primary Source: Orville Wright's Diary, p. 28

ACCESS FOR STUDENTS ACQUIRING ENGLISH
Guided Reading (Spanish), p. 263

SECTION 4 RESOURCES

PRINT RESOURCES

IN-DEPTH RESOURCES: UNIT 6
Guided Reading, p. 21
Skillbuilder Practice: Analyzing Issues, p. 22
Primary Source: Orville Wright's Diary, p. 28
Literature: from *The Origin*, p. 31
History Makers: Marie and Pierre Curie, p. 35
Connections Across Time and Cultures, p. 36

ACCESS FOR STUDENTS ACQUIRING ENGLISH
Guided Reading (Spanish), p. 263
Skillbuilder Practice: (Spanish), p. 264

FORMAL ASSESSMENT
Section Quiz, p. 304

TECHNOLOGY RESOURCES

CRITICAL THINKING TRANSPARENCIES
CT26 Movers and Shakers, 1815–1914
CT62 Chapter 26 Visual Summary

CD-ROM
Electronic Library of Primary Sources

INTERNET www.mlworldhistory.com

An Age of Inventions

Automobile Assembly Line
Ford's major innovation was to improve efficiency in his factory. By introducing the assembly line, he reduced the time it took to build a car from 12.5 to 1.5 worker-hours.

Airplane
Through trial and error, the Wright brothers designed wings that provided lift and balance in flight. Their design is based on principles that are still used in every aircraft.

Automobile technology developed quickly, but since early cars were built by hand, they were expensive to buy and repair.

An American mechanic named Henry Ford decided to make cars that were affordable for most people. "The way to make automobiles is to make them all alike," he said, "just as one pin is like another when it comes from the pin factory." To build his cars alike, Ford used standardized, interchangeable parts. He also built them on an **assembly line**—a line of workers who each put a single piece on unfinished cars as they passed on a moving belt.

Assembly line workers could put together an entire Model T Ford in less than two hours. When Ford introduced this plain, black, reliable car in 1908, it sold for $850. As his production costs fell, Ford lowered the price. Eventually it dropped to less than $300—well within the reach of the middle class. Other factories adopted Ford's ideas. By 1914, more than 600,000 cars were traveling around on the world's roads.

The Wright Brothers Fly Two bicycle mechanics from Dayton, Ohio, named Wilbur and Orville Wright solved the age-old riddle of flight. On December 17, 1903, they flew a gasoline-powered flying machine at Kitty Hawk, North Carolina. The longest flight that day lasted only 59 seconds, but it was enough to begin a whole new industry—aircraft.

The Rise of Mass Culture

In earlier periods, art, music, and most theater had been largely the concern of the wealthy. This group had the money, leisure time, and education to enjoy high culture. It was not until about 1900 that people could speak of **mass culture**—the appeal of art, writing, music, and other forms of entertainment to a much larger audience.

French artist Henri de Toulouse-Lautrec designed this bicycle poster in 1896.

Changes Produce Mass Culture There were several causes for the rise of mass culture around the turn of the century. First, the spread of public education increased literacy in both Europe and North America. This, in turn, provided a mass market for books, newspapers, and magazines. Improvements in communications made it possible to meet the broad demand for information and entertainment. For example, new high-speed presses duplicated thousands of pages in a few hours. They made publications cheaper and easier to produce. The invention of the phonograph and records brought music directly into people's homes.

Working folks now had more time for leisure pursuits. By 1900, most industrial countries had limited the working day to ten hours. Most people worked Monday through Friday and a half-day on Saturday. This five-and-a-half day work week created the "weekend," a special time for relaxation. More leisure time in evenings and on weekends allowed workers to take part in activities that their grandparents never had time to enjoy.

Music Halls and Vaudeville A popular leisure activity was a trip to the local music hall. On a typical evening, a music hall might offer a dozen or more different acts. It might feature singers, dancers, comedians, jugglers, magicians, acrobats, and even trained parakeets. In the United States, musical variety shows were called vaudeville.

674 Chapter 26

Vaudeville acts traveled from town to town, appearing at theaters with names such as the Gaiety, the Grand, and the Orpheum.

Movies Are Born During the 1880s, several inventors worked at trying to record and project moving images. One successful design came from France. Another came from Thomas Edison's laboratory. The earliest motion pictures caused a sensation only because of their novelty. They were black and white, lasted less than a minute, and had no plot. One of Edison's first films, for example, showed nothing but a man sneezing.

By the early 1900s, filmmakers were producing the first feature films (see Something in Common, page 676). Movies quickly became big business. By 1910, five million Americans attended some 10,000 theaters each day to watch silent movies. The European movie industry experienced similar growth.

Sports Entertain Millions With new time at their disposal, ordinary people began to enjoy all kinds of sports and outdoor activities. For every person who played sports, even more enjoyed watching them. Spectator sports now became entertainment for many. In the United States, football and baseball soared in popularity. In Europe, the first professional soccer clubs formed and drew big crowds—120,000 fans turned out to watch a 1913 match in England. Favorite English sports such as cricket spread to the British colonies of Australia, India, and South Africa.

As a result of the growing interest in sports, the international Olympic Games began in 1896. They revived the ancient Greek tradition of holding an athletic competition among countries every four years. Fittingly, the first modern Olympics took place in Athens.

Fans pack a stadium to watch an English soccer championship in 1911.

New Ideas in Medicine and Science

Earlier centuries had established the scientific method as a road to knowledge. Now this method brought powerful new insights into nature as well as many practical results.

The Germ Theory of Disease An important breakthrough in the history of medicine was the germ theory of disease. It was developed by French chemist Louis Pasteur in the mid-1800s. While examining the fermentation process of alcohol, Pasteur discovered that it was caused by microscopic organisms he called bacteria. He also learned that heat killed bacteria. This led him to develop the process of *pasteurization* to kill germs in liquids such as milk. Soon, it became clear to Pasteur and others that bacteria also caused diseases.

A British surgeon named Joseph Lister read about Pasteur's work. He thought germs might explain why half of all surgical patients died of infections. In 1865, he ordered that his surgical wards be kept spotlessly clean. He insisted that wounds be washed in antiseptics, or germ-killing liquids. As a result, 85 percent of Lister's patients survived. Soon, other hospitals began to follow Lister's standards of cleanliness.

Public officials, too, began to understand that cleanliness helped prevent the spread of disease. Cities built plumbing and sewer systems and took other steps to improve public health. Meanwhile, medical researchers developed vaccines or cures for such deadly diseases as typhus, typhoid fever, diphtheria, and yellow fever. These advances helped people live longer, healthier lives.

An Age of Democracy and Progress **675**

C. Possible Answer Created better understanding of how infectious disease spreads, led to pasteurization, improved survival rates for surgery, led to installation of city sanitation, led to development of vaccines or cures for some deadly infectious diseases.

THINK THROUGH HISTORY
C. Recognizing Effects What impact did the germ theory of disease have on public health?

Mass Entertainment

In 1903, an American filmmaker named Edwin S. Porter presented the first feature film, *The Great Train Robbery.* Audiences packed theaters on both sides of the Atlantic to see it. Movies soon became one of the most popular forms of mass entertainment around the world. Today, billions of people still flock to movie theaters, despite newer forms of entertainment such as television and videos. One reason that going to the movies remains popular is the pleasure of shared experience—seeing a movie, a play, a circus, or sporting event as part of a large audience.

American Movies

Edwin S. Porter's *The Great Train Robbery* did something no other motion picture had done—it told a story! The silent, 12-minute action film portrayed a sensational robbery (shown in these stills) and the capture of bandits by a sheriff's posse. Films such as *The Great Train Robbery* launched a new art form. Movies made possible a new kind of visual storytelling, whose realistic images were a hit with a mass audience.

a **closer look** MOVIE STARS

676 Chapter 26

"Little Mary" Pickford, as she was affectionately known, is best remembered for portraying sweet, innocent roles.

Francis X. Bushman was a popular leading man. He is shown here in *Ben Hur* (1926).

Russian Circus

The Russian circus began when an English showman sent a troupe of stunt horse riders to Empress Catherine the Great in the 1790s. Russia has been famous for the popularity and quality of its circuses ever since. Most Russian circuses, like this one with animal trainer Vyacheslav Zolkin, feature trained bears. Russian circuses usually use a single ring so that audiences can sit close to the performers.

Chinese Opera

The performing arts have a long history in China. Characters in Chinese drama, such as this troupe from the Beijing Opera, wear elaborate silk costumes and stylized facial makeup or masks. The character of the actors is expressed in part through the symbolic use of color. This scene is from *The Story of the White Snake,* a tragic love story about a white snake that is transformed into a human being and marries a young man.

Camel Races in India

Seasonal festivals provide entertainment in rural areas throughout the world. Thousands of people from all over India, as well as foreign tourists, flock to the town of Pushkar in November for its annual fair. Although the main business is camel trading, the Pushkar fair is enlivened with dramas, food stalls, magic shows—and the races. Shown here is a camel rider racing at these annual festivities. These races are as eagerly anticipated as the Kentucky Derby is in the United States.

Theda Bara, the silent screen's "vamp," became an overnight sensation after her first starring role in 1915.

Connect *to* History

Analyzing Causes How does each type of entertainment reflect its country's culture?

SEE SKILLBUILDER HANDBOOK, PAGE 995

Connect *to* Today

Making a Chart List at least three other forms of entertainment that you enjoy during your leisure. Combine them in a class chart. Identify which ones are individual experiences and which are pop culture events.

INTERNET CONNECTION

Visit us at **www.mlworldhistory.com** to learn more about popular entertainment.

An Age of Democracy and Progress **677**

Connect *to* History

Analyzing Causes
Possible Responses: Bears acts are probably popular in the Russian circus because Russia has many species of bears; the Chinese opera features rich, elaborate spectacle, a style that evolved in the wealthy, highly sophisticated Chinese imperial courts; camels have long been the most practical form of transportation in northwestern Indian provinces such as Rajastan, which is mostly desert. It stands to reason that camel races would become popular there.

Connect *to* Today
Possible forms of entertainment include listening to live or recorded music, playing video or computer games, watching or playing baseball, basketball, or other sports, watching television, or shopping or browsing in the mall. Pop culture events would be those shared by others, such as a rock concert. Individual events would be those one can perform alone or with only a few others, such as a pick-up game of basketball.

HISTORY MAKERS

Charles Darwin
1809–1882
The key event in Charles Darwin's life was his five-year journey as a naturalist aboard the *H.M.S. Beagle.* The ship was on an expedition to survey the western and southern coast of South America and some Pacific islands. Darwin kept notebooks of the plants and animals he saw in various environments. After he came home, he used the data in these notebooks to develop his theory of evolution.

This photograph shows Marie Curie in her laboratory.

Darwin's Theory of Evolution No scientific idea of modern times aroused more controversy than the work of English biologist **Charles Darwin.** The cause of the controversy was Darwin's answer to the question that faced biologists: How can we explain the tremendous variety of plants and animals on earth? A widely accepted answer in the 1800s was the idea of special creation. According to this view, every kind of plant and animal had been created by God at the beginning of the world and had remained the same since then.

Darwin challenged the idea of special creation. Based on his research, he developed a theory that all forms of life, including human beings, evolved from earlier living forms that had existed millions of years ago.

In 1859, Darwin published his thinking in a book titled *The Origin of Species by Means of Natural Selection.* According to the idea of natural selection, populations tend to grow faster than the food supply and so must compete for food. The members of a species that survive are those that are fittest, or best adapted to their environment. These surviving members of a species produce offspring that share their advantages. Gradually, over many generations, the species may change. In this way, new species evolve. Darwin's idea of change through natural selection came to be called the **theory of evolution.**

The Origin of Species caused great excitement among scientists. At the same time, Darwin's ideas roused a storm of debate outside the scientific community. Many people believed that the idea of evolution directly contradicted the account of creation in the Bible. Even today, well over 100 years after *The Origin of Species* was first published, Darwin's ideas are controversial.

Mendel and Genetics Although Darwin said that living things passed on their variations from one generation to the next, he did not know how they did so. In the 1850s and 1860s, an Austrian monk named Gregor Mendel discovered that there is a pattern to the way that certain traits are inherited. Although his work was not widely known until 1900, Mendel's work began the science of genetics. Later, biologists discovered genes, the units of living matter that carry traits from parents to offspring.

Advances in Chemistry and Physics In 1803, the British chemist John Dalton theorized that all matter is made of tiny particles called atoms. Dalton showed that elements contain only one kind of atom, which has a specific weight. Compounds, on the other hand, contain more than one kind of atom.

In 1869, Dmitri Mendeleev (MEHN·duh·LAY·uhf), a Russian chemist, organized a chart on which all the known elements were arranged in order of weight, from lightest to heaviest. He left gaps where he predicted that new elements would be discovered. Later, his predictions proved correct. Mendeleev's chart, called the Periodic Table, is still used by scientists today.

A husband and wife team working in Paris discovered two of the missing elements. Marie and Pierre Curie found that a mineral called pitchblende released a powerful form of energy. In 1898, Marie Curie gave this energy the name **radioactivity.** The Curies discovered two new elements that they named radium and polonium. Both were highly radioactive. In 1903, the Curies shared the Nobel Prize for physics for their work on radioactivity. In 1911, Marie won the Nobel Prize for chemistry for the discovery of radium and polonium.

Physicists around 1900 tried to unravel the secrets of the atom. Earlier scientists believed that the atom was the smallest particle that existed. A British physicist named Ernest Rutherford suggested that atoms were made up of yet smaller particles. Each atom, he said, had a nucleus surrounded by one or more particles called electrons. Soon other physicists such as Max Planck, Neils Bohr, and Albert Einstein were studying the structure and energy of atoms. Their discoveries, discussed in Chapter 31, were fully as revolutionary as Newton's or Darwin's ideas.

The Social Sciences

The scientific theories of the 1800s prompted scholars to study human society and behavior in a scientific way. Interest in these fields grew enormously during that century, as global expeditions produced a flood of new discoveries about ancient civilizations and world cultures. This interest led to the development of modern social sciences such as archaeology, anthropology, and sociology.

An important new social science was **psychology,** the study of the human mind and behavior. The Russian biologist Ivan Pavlov broke new ground in psychology with a famous experiment in the early 1900s. Ordinarily, a dog's mouth waters at the smell of food. Pavlov began ringing a bell each time he gave food to a dog. Eventually, the dog learned to associate the bell with food. Each time the bell rang, the dog salivated, even if no food was present.

Pavlov concluded that an animal's reflexes could be changed, or conditioned, through training. He also applied these findings to humans. He believed that human actions were often unconscious reactions to experiences and could be changed by training.

Another pioneer in psychology, the Austrian doctor Sigmund Freud, also believed that the unconscious mind drives how people think and act. In Freud's view, unconscious forces such as suppressed memories, desires, and impulses help shape behavior. He created a type of therapy called psychoanalysis to help people deal with the psychological conflicts created by these forces.

As Chapter 31 explains, Freud's theories became very influential. However, his idea that the mind was beyond conscious control also shocked many people. The ideas of Freud and Pavlov challenged the fundamental idea of the Enlightenment—that reason was supreme. The new ideas about psychology began to shake the 19th-century faith that humans could perfect themselves and society through reason.

E. Possible Answer Because it explored how a part of the mind that people were not aware of—the unconscious—influences people's thoughts and behavior.

THINK THROUGH HISTORY
E. Clarifying Why was the work of Pavlov and Freud groundbreaking?

SPOTLIGHT ON
Social Darwinism

Charles Darwin was a biologist, but a number of 19th-century thinkers tried to apply his ideas about plants and animals to economics and politics. The leader in this movement was Herbert Spencer, an English philosopher.

Free economic competition, Spencer argued, was natural selection in action. The best companies make profits, while inefficient ones go bankrupt. Spencer applied the same rules to individuals. Those who were fittest for survival enjoyed wealth and success, while the poor remained poor because they were unfit. This idea became known as Social Darwinism.

Some Social Darwinists expanded these ideas into racist thinking. They claimed that certain groups of people were "fitter"—brighter, stronger, and more advanced—than others. These "superior races," they said, were intended by nature to dominate "lesser peoples." Many Europeans used such arguments to justify the spread of imperialism, which is described in Chapter 27.

Section ④ Assessment

1. TERMS & NAMES
Identify
• assembly line
• mass culture
• Charles Darwin
• theory of evolution
• radioactivity
• psychology

2. TAKING NOTES
Using a web diagram like the one below, connect the inventors, scientists, and thinkers with the invention, discovery, or new idea for which they were responsible.

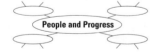
People and Progress

Which breakthrough do you think helped people the most? Why?

3. COMPARING AND CONTRASTING
How is the mass culture that rose at the end of the 19th century similar to mass culture today? How is it different? Explain your response.

THINK ABOUT
• the role of technology
• increase in leisure time
• new forms of entertainment

4. THEME ACTIVITY
Science and Technology
Choose one of the inventions, discoveries, or new ideas that occurred in this period and plan a museum exhibit of that breakthrough. Decide how to display the invention or discovery. Write a description of it, who was responsible for it, and how it has affected peoples' lives.

An Age of Democracy and Progress **679**

ANSWERS

1. TERMS & NAMES
assembly line, p. 674
mass culture, p. 674
Charles Darwin, p. 678
theory of evolution, p. 678
radioactivity, p. 678
psychology, p. 679

2. TAKING NOTES
Possible Response: Thomas Edison, Alexander Graham Bell, Guglielmo Marconi, Henry Ford, Wilbur and Orville Wright, Edwin Porter, Louis Pasteur, Joseph Lister, Charles Darwin, Gregor Mendel, John Dalton, Dmitri Mendeleev, Marie and Pierre Curie, Ernest Rutherford, Ivan Pavlov, Sigmund Freud. Answers should be supported.

3. COMPARING AND CONTRASTING
Possible Response: Similarities: new technology and leisure still shape mass culture; forms of mass entertainment such as movies still are popular. Differences: newer technology such as the Internet has transformed how people share culture; mass culture has become big business and is more global.

4. THEME ACTIVITY
Museum exhibits should contain photos or illustrations of the inventions, include labels describing the important parts of the inventions, and describe their impact on people's lives.

OBJECTIVE ④ INSTRUCT
The Social Sciences
▶ **Key Idea**
• Global cultural interactions stimulate the creation of new social sciences, such as psychology.

SPOTLIGHT ON
Social Darwinism

Spencer argued against governments helping the sick and infirm so that "natural selection" might eliminate these people and make society stronger. Ask students to debate this view.

ASSESS & RETEACH
Section 4 Assessment
After students have responded to the first three questions independently, engage the whole class in a discussion of question 4.

Section Quiz
FORMAL ASSESSMENT
Section Quiz, p. 304

Reteaching Activity
CLASS TIME: 20 MINUTES
Have students look over the Visual Summary on page 680. Ask them to rank the inventions in the order they consider the most important to modern life. Have them explain their choices.

CRITICAL THINKING TRANSPARENCIES
CT62 Chapter 26 Visual Summary

CLOSE ACTIVITY
CLASS TIME: 25 MINUTES
Creating a Poster
Suggest that students, working independently or in small groups, make or plan posters for a Turn-of-the-Century World Exposition celebrating 50 years (1860-1910) of achievement and progress. What items would they include on the poster, and why?

Teacher's Edition **679**

TERMS & NAMES

1. suffrage, p. 659
2. anti-Semitism, p. 663
3. dominion, p. 665
4. penal colony, p. 665
5. home rule, p. 668
6. manifest destiny, p. 670
7. Emancipation Proclamation, p. 671
8. segregation, p. 672
9. assembly line, p. 674
10. theory of evolution, p. 678

REVIEW QUESTIONS

Answers will vary.

11. Reform Bill of 1832, expansion of suffrage in 1867 and 1884, secret ballot, pay members of Parliament and an end to property requirement for serving in Parliament.

12. Its members carried out peaceful demonstrations and parades, heckled government speakers, cut telegraph wires, and committed arson.

13. Cultural and religious differences between English- and French-speaking Canadians.

14. It was not open to ordinary settlers but was used instead as a penal colony.

15. Britain was concerned about the Protestants in Northern Ireland, a small minority who wanted British protection.

16. Louisiana Purchase (from France), Florida Cession (from Spain), Texas Annexation, treaties with Britain, Mexican Cession, Gadsden Purchase (from Mexico).

17. Economic differences: North had a diversified economy with both farms and industry; South depended on a few cash crops, mainly cotton. Slavery issue: Southerners depended on slavery to protect their economy, while Northerners considered slavery morally wrong.

18. The members of a species that are best adapted to their environment will survive. Many people believed that evolution directly contradicted the account of creation in the Bible.

19. (a) genetics (b) showed that each element contains only one kind of atom (c) Periodic Table of elements (d) discovered radioactivity and two new elements (e) suggested atoms were made

---

Visual Summary

Democracy   Progress

1815

1825

1832 First Reform Bill in Britain

1835

1845

1848 Seneca Falls Convention

1850s Mendel experiments with genetics

1855

1859 Darwin's *Origin of Species*

1861 Outbreak of U.S. Civil War

1863 Emancipation Proclamation

1860s Medical advances of Pasteur and Lister

1865

1867 Suffrage extended to working-class men in Britain

Dominion of Canada formed

1869 Transcontinental railroad completed in United States

Mendeleev's Periodic Table of Elements

1871 Paris Commune

1875

1875 Third Republic in France

1876 Bell patents telephone

1879 Edison develops light bulb

1880s Internal combustion engine perfected

1884 Suffrage extended to male rural workers in Britain

1885

1893 Women gain voting rights in New Zealand

1895 Marconi invents radio

1896 First modern Olympic Games

1896 Henri Becquerel discovers radioactivity

1895

1894 Dreyfus affair begins

1896 Zionist movement founded

1903 First airplane flight by Wright brothers

1903 WSPU founded

1905

The Great Train Robbery released

1908 Ford introduces Model T

1915

up of smaller elements

20. After conditioning a dog's reflexes, Pavlov concluded that human actions were not always determined consciously. Freud worked to understand how suppressed memories, desires, and impulses help shape behavior and created psychoanalysis to help people deal with psychological problems.

TERMS & NAMES

Briefly explain the importance of each of the following to the reforms, crises, or advances of Western nations from 1815 to 1914.

1. suffrage
2. anti-Semitism
3. dominion
4. penal colony
5. home rule
6. manifest destiny
7. Emancipation Proclamation
8. segregation
9. assembly line
10. theory of evolution

REVIEW QUESTIONS

SECTION 1 *(pages 659–663)*
Democratic Reform and Activism

11. What political reforms had the effect of expanding democracy for men in Britain?

12. How did the Women's Social and Political Union call attention to its cause?

SECTION 2 *(pages 664–668)*
Self-Rule for British Colonies

13. What cultural conflict caused problems for Canada?

14. How did Australia's early history differ from that of other British colonies?

15. Why did the British government pass a home rule bill for southern Ireland only?

SECTION 3 *(pages 669–672)*
Expansion and Crisis in the United States

16. In what different ways did the United States gain territory in the 1800s?

17. How did the North and South differ economically? Why was the issue of slavery so divisive?

SECTION 4 *(pages 673–679)*
Nineteenth-Century Progress

18. What was Darwin's principle of natural selection? Why did many people oppose his theory of evolution?

19. What contributions did each of the following scientists make?
(a) Mendel (b) Dalton (c) Mendeleev (d) Marie Curie (e) Rutherford

20. How did Pavlov and Freud contribute to the study of psychology?

1906 Ford 6 Cylinder Touring Car

Price $2,500

6 cylinders—40 h. p. 4 to 50 miles per hour on high gear. *Perfected* magneto ignition—mechanical oiler, 114 inch wheel base, luxurious body for 5 passengers, weight 2000 pounds.

1906 Ford Runabout, as advanced as our touring car in design and even more surprising in price—will be fully illustrated and described in our next advertisement.

Both these Cars on exhibition at the New York Automobile Show.

Ford Motor Company
Detroit, Mich.

Interact *with* History

On page 658, you considered the benefits and drawbacks of technological progress. Now consider the inventions you read about in this chapter. Write a paragraph explaining which you think was most significant. State the reasons for your choice. Consider

- Which affected the most people?
- Which changed daily life the most?
- Which changed industry the most?
- Which produced the greatest benefit with the fewest drawbacks?

Share your paragraph with the class.

Interact *with* History

Possible Responses: Students should be able to explain why they believe their invention had the greatest impact on people, how it changed daily life and industry, and what its benefits and drawbacks were. Be sure they consider carefully the trade-offs between benefits and costs. Remind students that many inventions have had benefits and drawbacks that were not known at the time the item was developed.

CRITICAL THINKING

1. ASSEMBLY LINE WORK

THEME ECONOMICS Using the quotation from Henry Ford on page 674, explain how his attitude on making goods might have differed from those of a traditional craftsperson. From a worker's point of view, what would be the advantages and disadvantages of an assembly line?

2. AN ERA OF CHANGE

Create a web diagram of the major political, economic, social and cultural, and scientific and technological changes of the 1800s and early 1900s.

3. SOCIAL DARWINISM

Charles Darwin did not fully agree with the Social Darwinists. How do natural selection and economic competition differ?

4. ANALYZING PRIMARY SOURCES

On January 11, 1898, Major Esterhazy, the army officer who had actually committed the crimes of which Alfred Dreyfus was accused, was judged innocent by a court martial, or military court. Two days later, Émile Zola published an open letter about the Dreyfus affair. Part of that letter appears below.

A VOICE FROM THE PAST

It is only now that the Affair is beginning, because only now are men assuming clear positions: on the one hand, the guilty, who do not wish justice to be done; on the other, the followers of justice, who will give their lives so that justice may triumph.

I accuse the War Office of having carried on in the press an abominable campaign in order to screen their mistake and mislead the public.

I accuse the first Court Martial of having violated the law by condemning an accused man on the basis of a secret document and I accuse the second Court Martial of having, in obedience to orders, screened that illegal act by knowingly acquitting a guilty man.

As to the men I accuse, I do not know them. I have never seen them, I have no resentment or hatred toward them. I have but one passion—that of light.

- Of what crimes did Zola accuse the French War Office and the Courts Martial?
- What did Zola claim to be his motive for making these accusations?

CHAPTER ACTIVITIES

1. LIVING HISTORY: Unit Portfolio Project

THEME EMPIRE BUILDING Your unit portfolio project focuses on the effects of empire building on all the lands and peoples involved (see page 629). For Chapter 26 you might use one of the following ideas to add to your portfolio.

- Design and produce a handbill that might have been distributed by English-speaking Canadians demanding a representative government.
- Write an editorial that might have appeared in a newspaper in 19th-century New Zealand. In the editorial, address the issue of British settlers' taking land from the Maori, and the Maori response.
- Draw a political cartoon that reflects how Britain treated Ireland during the Great Famine.

2. CONNECT TO TODAY: Cooperative Learning

THEME SCIENCE AND TECHNOLOGY Breakthroughs in science, technology, and medicine transformed daily life in the 1800s. Many of those inventions and discoveries still affect us today. Work with a partner to make a collage of 19th-century breakthroughs as they are reflected in modern life.

- Begin by noting all the inventions and discoveries presented in the chapter. Then brainstorm ways that they might be represented visually.
- In magazines or newspapers, look for the pictures you need. If you cannot find a particular picture, try drawing it.
- Determine a creative way to identify the pictures and link them with the 19th-century breakthroughs.

3. INTERPRETING A TIME LINE

Revisit the time line on pages 628–629, and study the segment for Chapter 26. Which event do you think was the most significant? Why?

FOCUS ON **POLITICAL CARTOONS**

This 1852 English cartoon titled "A Court for King Cholera" depicts a poor section of the city. Notice the children playing with a dead rat and the woman picking through the rubbish heap. At the time, some health experts believed that the epidemic disease cholera spread from the air around rubbish heaps.

- What does the artist say about the unhealthy living conditions of the poor?
- Do you think the artist is sympathetic to the urban poor? Why or why not?

Connect to History What changes took place in the 19th century that helped eliminate the spread of diseases like cholera in Western cities?

An Age of Democracy and Progress **681**

CHAPTER ACTIVITIES

1. LIVING HISTORY: UNIT PORTFOLIO PROJECT

Standards for Evaluation
Handbills should meet the following criteria:

- Present a strong point of view.
- Contain a slogan to catch people's attention.
- Give specific data about the problem.
- Tell how to join the struggle.

Standards for Evaluation
Editorials should meet the following criteria:

- Express a strong point of view supported by facts.
- Present the Maori side of the issue.
- Recommend a course of action.

Standards for Evaluation
Political cartoons should meet the following criteria:

- Show a definite point of view
- Illustrate one aspect of Britain's treatment of Ireland.

2. CONNECT TO TODAY: COOPERATIVE LEARNING

Standards for Evaluation
Collages should meet the following criteria:

- Present a range of inventions and discoveries.
- Include labels or other descriptions.
- Show the value of the inventions.

3. INTERPRETING A TIME LINE

Students should give reasons for their choices and be able to discuss the significance of the event they choose.

FOCUS ON **POLITICAL CARTOONS**

- The artist shows how crowded and unsanitary conditions were
- Sympathetic: artist has compassion for people living in such conditions; Unsympathetic: artist shows that people create such conditions themselves

Connect to History Germ theory of disease; discovery by Dr. John Snow that cholera spread by contaminated drinking water; building of urban plumbing and sewage systems

---

CRITICAL THINKING

1. ASSEMBLY LINE WORK

Possible Responses: Ford: pride in efficiency vs. pride in work. Advantages: steady job, efficient use of time/energy, specialization. Disadvantages: repetition, impersonality.

2. AN ERA OF CHANGE

Possible Responses: Political: British democratic reforms, British monarchy, suffrage campaigns, Third Republic, self-rule for Canada, Australia, and New Zealand, U.S. territorial expansion, secession, and civil war. *Economic:* abolition of slavery in U.S., postwar expansion, transcontinental railroad, assembly line. *Social/Cultural:* colonization of Australia/New Zealand, Zionism, manifest destiny, settlement of the U.S. West, U.S. immigration, mass culture, Social Darwinism. *Sci/Tech:* light bulb, phonograph, telephone, radio, internal combustion engine, airplane, motion pictures, germ theory, pasteurization, theory of evolution, genetics, atomic theory.

3. SOCIAL DARWINISM

Possible Responses: Nature of adaptation, element of luck in entrepreneurship, inherited wealth.

4. ANALYZING PRIMARY SOURCES

- War Office: lied to public about case; Courts Martial: condemned innocent man; acquitted guilty man.
- His passion for "light," or truth and justice

	Key Ideas	COPY MASTERS	ASSESSMENT
SECTION 1 **Imperialists Divide Africa** pp. 685–689	*Western European nations race to divide Africa among themselves. They draw territorial boundaries without regard to Africans' ethnic, linguistic, and cultural divisions.*	**In-Depth Resources: Unit 6** • **Guided Reading,** p. 37 • **Geography Application:** David Livingstone Explores Southern Africa, p. 43 • **Primary Source:** British Contract with an African King, p. 45 • **Literature:** "The Burial," p. 49	PE *Section 1 Assessment,* p. 689 *Formal Assessment* • Section Quiz, p. 313 *Alternative Assessment Book* • Standards for Evaluating a Cooperative Activity
SECTION 2 **Imperialism Case Study: Nigeria** pp. 690–696	*Europeans use colonies, protectorates, spheres of influence, economic imperialism, and different patterns of management to control African colonies. African resistance movements emerge in response.*	**In-Depth Resources: Unit 6** • **Guided Reading,** p. 38 • **Primary Source:** Letter from Menelik II, p. 46 • **Literature:** from *Things Fall Apart,* p. 50 • **History Makers:** Menelik II, p. 52 • **Connections Across Time and Cultures:** Two Periods of Colonization and Imperialism, p. 54	PE *Section 2 Assessment,* p. 695 *Formal Assessment* • Section Quiz, p. 314 *Alternative Assessment Book* • Standards for Evaluating a Cooperative Activity
SECTION 3 **Muslim Lands Fall to Imperialist Demands** pp. 697–700	*After the death of Suleiman I, European nations divide the Ottoman Empire. A combined British-French-Ottoman force defeats the Russians in the Crimean War, and the British seize the Suez Canal.*	**In-Depth Resources: Unit 6** • **Guided Reading,** p. 39	PE *Section 3 Assessment,* p. 700 *Formal Assessment* • Section Quiz, p. 315 *Alternative Assessment Book* • Standards for Evaluating a Cooperative Activity
SECTION 4 **British Imperialism in India** pp. 701–705	*Britain gradually attains control over India, establishing the Raj. British rule gives rise to nationalist feelings and to resistance movements.*	**In-Depth Resources: Unit 6** • **Guided Reading,** p. 40 • **Skillbuilder Practice:** Analyzing Assumptions and Biases, p. 42 • **Primary Source:** Letter Opposing the English, p. 47	PE *Section 4 Assessment,* p. 705 *Formal Assessment* • Section Quiz, p. 316 *Alternative Assessment Book* • Standards for Evaluating a Cooperative Activity
SECTION 5 **Western Powers Rule Southeast Asia** pp. 706–709	*Western imperialists, including the United States, claim lands in the South Pacific, Southeast Asia, and Hawaiian Islands. Only Siam remains independent.*	**In-Depth Resources: Unit 6** • **Guided Reading,** p. 41 • **Primary Source:** In Favor of Imperialism, p. 48 • **History Makers:** Mongkut, p. 53	PE *Section 5 Assessment,* p. 709 *Formal Assessment* • Section Quiz, p. 317 *Alternative Assessment Book* • Standards for Evaluating a Cooperative Activity
CHAPTER RESOURCES	**Chapter Overview** *Western imperialists, with superior arms and technology, establish colonies in Asia and Africa. The Europeans export finished goods to the colonies and import raw materials and cash crops. Colonial rule provokes native resistance movements.*	**Telescoping the Times** • Chapter Summary, pp. 105–107 **Planning for Block Schedules**	PE Chapter Assessment, pp. 710–711 Chapter Activities, p. 711 *Formal Assessment* • Chapter Test, forms A and B, pp. 318–323 **Test Generator** *Alternative Assessment Book*

1850–1914

TECHNOLOGY

 Warm-Up Transparency 27

 Electronic Library of Primary Sources
- "The Boer War: The Suffering of the Civilian Population"
- "Stanley finds Livingstone"
- "Private Company Rule in the Congo"

INTERNET RESOURCES
www.mlworldhistory.com

 Warm-Up Transparency 27

 Electronic Library of Primary Sources
- from "Africa at the Center"

INTERNET RESOURCES
www.mlworldhistory.com

 Warm-Up Transparency 27

World Art and Cultures Transparencies
- AT58 *Reception at the Court of Sultan Selim III*

INTERNET RESOURCES
www.mlworldhistory.com

 Warm-Up Transparency 27

Geography Transparencies
- GT27 *India Under British Rule, 1805–1886*

World Art and Cultures Transparencies
- AT59 *Raja Ram Singh in Procession*

 Electronic Library of Primary Sources
- "The Rise of the Color Bar"

INTERNET RESOURCES
www.mlworldhistory.com

Warm-Up Transparency 27

Critical Thinking Transparencies
- CT27 *Comparing Imperialist Styles*
- CT63 *Chapter 27 Visual Summary*

 Electronic Library of Primary Sources
- from *Hawaii's Story by Hawaii's Queen*

INTERNET RESOURCES
www.mlworldhistory.com

 Chapter Summaries on Audiocassette in English and Spanish

 INTERNET RESOURCES
www.mlworldhistory.com

Block Scheduling (90 MINUTES)

Day 1
Section 1, pp. 685-689

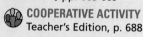 **COOPERATIVE ACTIVITY**
Teacher's Edition, p. 688

Section 2, pp. 690–696

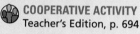 **COOPERATIVE ACTIVITY**
Teacher's Edition, p. 694

Section Assessments,
pp. 689, 695

Day 2
Section 3, pp. 697–700

 COOPERATIVE ACTIVITY
Teacher's Edition, p. 698

Section 4, pp. 701–705

 COOPERATIVE ACTIVITY
Teacher's Edition, p. 702

Section Assessments,
pp. 700, 705

Day 3
Section 5, pp. 706–709

 COOPERATIVE ACTIVITY
Teacher's Edition, p. 708

Section Assessment, p. 709

Chapter Assessment,
pp. 710–711

Yearly Pacing *Chapter 27 Total:* 3 days *Yearly Total:* 85 days

Planning for Block Schedules

Customizing for Special Needs

Students Acquiring English

 Access for Students Acquiring English
- **Guided Reading** for Sections 1–5 (Spanish), pp. 270–274
- **Chapter Summary** (Spanish), pp. 267–269
- **Skillbuilder Practice** Analyzing Assumptions and Biases (Spanish), p. 275
- **Geography Application** David Livingstone Explores Southern Africa (Spanish), p. 276

 Chapter Summaries on Audiocassette in English and Spanish

INTERNET RESOURCES
www.mlworldhistory.com
The Diverse Classroom

Less Proficient Readers

 In-Depth Resources: Unit 6
- **Guided Reading** for Sections 1–5, pp. 37–41
- **Skillbuilder Practice** Analyzing Assumptions and Biases, p. 42
- **Geography Application** David Livingstone Explores Southern Africa, p. 43

 Telescoping the Times
- Chapter Summary, pp. 105–107

Chapter Summaries on Audiocassette

Gifted and Talented Students

In-Depth Resources: Unit 6

Primary Sources:
- British Contract with an African King, p. 45
- Letter from Menelik II, p. 46
- Letter Opposing the British, p. 47
- In Favor of Imperialism, p. 48

History Makers
- Menelik II, p. 52
- Mongkut, p. 53

Connections to Literature READINGS FOR STUDENTS

 In-Depth Resources: Unit 6
Literature: "The Burial," p. 49; from *Things Fall Apart,* p. 50

- **McDougal Littell** *Language of Literature,* Grade 10
Doris Lessing, "No Witchcraft for Sale," p. 744

McDougal Littell *Literature Connections*

- Achebe, Chinua *Things Fall Apart* (with related readings)

In this classic story, the traditional ways of an Ibo village in Nigeria are challenged by new European ways.

 = Pupil's Edition   = Overhead Transparency   = Software   = Video

 = Copy Master   = CD-ROM   = Audiocassette   = Internet

The Age of Imperialism, 1850–1914

Making Predictions

Ask students to study the map on these two pages. Then ask them the following question.

• What predictions can you make about why European nations would want to acquire territory in Africa, Asia, and Australia? *Possible responses: wealth, prestige, Christian missionary work, manifest destiny, exporting unwanted population*

Making Inferences

Have students compare the size of the European countries with the size of the territories they acquired. What can students infer about the political organization and the military strength of the peoples in the occupied territories? *Most of the areas were probably politically chaotic or weak*

Geography Connection

• What nation held the most territory on all four continents (including North America)? *Great Britain*

• Africa was divided up among how many European nations? *Seven—Great Britain, France, Belgium, Germany, Italy, Portugal, and Spain*

CHAPTER 27 The Age of Imperialism, 1850–1914

PREVIEWING THEMES

Empire Building
The Industrial Revolution gave European nations the necessary technology to dominate other peoples. During the 1800s, the European powers competed with one another to claim parts of Africa, Southeast Asia, India, and the Pacific. Toward the end of the century, the United States established its own overseas colonies in the Pacific.

Economics
The imperialists regarded their colonies as captive markets as well as sources of raw materials and trade goods. The colonizers demanded production of cash crops at the expense of the peasants' own subsistence agriculture. In tropical areas, plantation agriculture increased the need for laborers and spurred immigration.

Power and Authority
Colonizers were divided on the best method of rule. Britain and the United States ruled indirectly, using local leaders and institutions where possible. The French and others ruled the colonies directly from a central authority. Often the two methods were blended.

INTERNET CONNECTION
Visit us at **http://www.mlworldhistory.com** to learn more about imperialism.

EUROPEAN COLONIES, 1850–1914

Territory Controlled By:
- Belgium
- France
- German Empire
- Great Britain
- Italy
- The Netherlands
- Portugal
- Russian Empire
- Spain
- United States
- Independent States

0   500 Miles
0   1,000 Kilometers

ATLANTIC OCEAN

This sculptured brass weight was used by the **Asante** people of Africa. The elaborate nature of the weight may indicate that trade was especially important to the Asante. The British traded with the Asante on the west coast of **Africa**, also known as the Gold Coast.

682

GEOGRAPHY THEMES

Place
A major attraction of the colonies for the imperialist powers was not only their wealth of natural resources but their strategic location in terms of controlling both land and waterway trading routes. Ask students to study the map on pages 682 and 683 and the map key indicating which European nations controlled which lands. Ask students what strategic advantages each colony gave its European ruler. Which country appears to dominate much of the seafaring routes? Have students predict how England, smallest of the European nations, came to control so much colonial territory. Remind students of the importance of naval power in this era and the need to control vital waterways.

Movement
Advances in naval technology made possible relatively quick trips between the homeland and the colonies. Europeans could dispatch colonial administrators and armies to these lands and bring back mineral and agricultural wealth. Have students trace with their fingers the possible routes taken by imperialists to African, Southwest Asian, and Southeast Asian colonies. Remind students that along with the imperialist forces came Western technologies, languages, religions, and customs.

Queen Victoria of **England** ruled during most of the Age of Imperialism. During her reign, the saying, "The sun never sets on the British Empire" was true of the colonial holdings of Britain.

Ethiopian ruler **Menelik II** defeated the Italians at the Battle of Adowa in **1896**. The Ethiopians' defeat of the Italians was one of the few successful resistances to the European imperialists.

PACIFIC
OCEAN

INDIAN
OCEAN

683

ADDITIONAL RESOURCES

Books for the Teacher

- Copland, Ian. *The Burden of Empire.* Melbourne, Australia: Oxford UP, 1990. Study of imperialism and colonialism.

- Wesseling, H. L. *Divide and Rule: The Partition of Africa, 1880-1914.* New York: Praeger, 1996.

Books for the Student

- Bayly, C. A. *Indian Society and the Making of the British Empire.* New York: Cambridge UP, 1988. Examines the British East India Company's rise in the period of Mughal decline.

- Rowell, Trevor. *The Scramble for Africa.* London: Batsford, 1987.

Videos

- *The Bible and the Gun/The Magnificent African Cake.* Knowledge Unlimited, 1984. 800-356-2303. Explores the effect of missionaries, slave trade, and imperialism.

- *The Lure of Empire: America Debates Imperialism.* Coronet/ MTI, 1974. 800-321-3106. Examines American annexation of the Philippines.

- *Zulus at War.* Ambrose Video, 1995. 800-526-4663. Depicts battles between Zulus and the British.

Software

- *Imperialism.* CD-ROM. Crystal Productions, 1994. 800-255-8629. Provides case studies, including the British in India and multiple powers in Africa.

HISTORY THROUGH ART

Ashanti Brass Weight

The brass weight shown on page 682 was made by the Ashanti (also spelled Asante) people. These weights were generally used to measure quantities of minerals, such as gold. Like many African peoples, the Ashanti used highly stylized forms and abstract designs in their art (see the Ashanti textile patterns on page 692).

The Ashanti lived on the west coast of Africa in an area so mineral rich that the Europeans dubbed it the Gold Coast. At the time the Europeans came, the Ashanti were among the most highly organized peoples in Africa. The British referred to them as a "nation" because of their bureaucratic government system.

Interpreting the Art What physical characteristics did the artist give the human figure in this picture?

Possible answers: "Corn row" hairstyle, face that looks like a combination of human and animal (perhaps leopard or lion) features, stylized body, an object in either hand. The figure dominates the animal being ridden. What does this suggest about the importance of the person? *Because the object was used for measurement, the person could represent a local authority or someone with authority in commercial matters.*

Interact *with* History

This Interact with History feature motivates students by asking them to evaluate the potential impact of imperialism. As they consider the question posed, they will analyze the issues, explore their options, and evaluate the impact of Western culture on Africa, Australia, and Asia.

Purpose

- to introduce students to the study of European colonization of foreign lands.
- to help students understand the benefits and problems of imperialism.
- to help students connect to the people and events they will encounter in this chapter.

Teaching Strategy

Thinking Critically Ask students what they remember from past chapters about what happens when a more technologically advanced people encounters a less developed people.

EXAMINING *the* ISSUES

Following are suggestions for answering each bulleted question.

1 Under what conditions might advanced technology be helpful? harmful?

2 Ask students how they would feel if someone from another land tried to force an alien culture on them.

3 Have students consider the rights of the original inhabitants and of those whose technology is used to develop the resources.

4 What does "too much power" mean? Is *any* power over others acceptable? Why or why not?

Making Connections Ask students if they were ever playing a game or working on a project that was taken over by someone else. How did they feel? What could they do if the person were older or stronger?

Interact *with* History

The 19th-century Europeans have access to steam engines and medical advances. They have the technical know-how to develop the resources of the land they control. They want to develop these resources to make themselves great profits. Many believe that they also have both the right and the responsibility to develop the lands and cultures of less advanced areas of the world.

You wonder about the Europeans' thinking. What rights and responsibilities do they really have? How much should they try to change other peoples and other cultures?

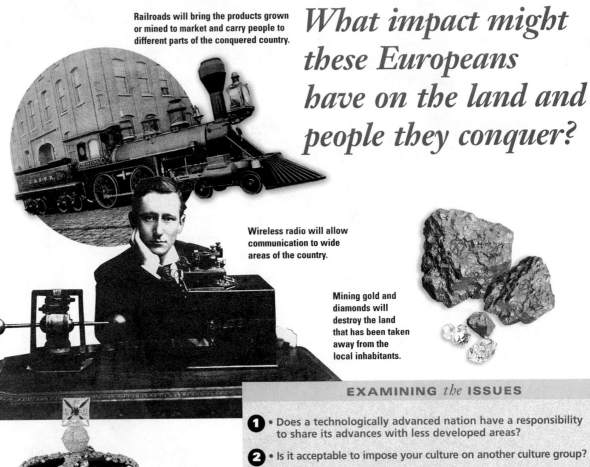

Railroads will bring the products grown or mined to market and carry people to different parts of the conquered country.

What impact might these Europeans have on the land and people they conquer?

Wireless radio will allow communication to wide areas of the country.

Mining gold and diamonds will destroy the land that has been taken away from the local inhabitants.

Local rule might be eliminated or replaced with rule by European monarchs and their representatives.

EXAMINING *the* ISSUES

1 • Does a technologically advanced nation have a responsibility to share its advances with less developed areas?

2 • Is it acceptable to impose your culture on another culture group?

3 • Who should benefit from the resources of a place?

4 • Is there such a thing as having too much power over others?

Discuss these questions with your classmates. In your discussion, remember what you have already learned about conquests and cultural changes.

As you read about imperialists in this chapter, look for their effects on both the colonizers and the colonized.

Follow-Up

A feature on the chapter assessment will ask students to reevaluate their responses to the question posed on this page.

1 Imperialists Divide Africa

TERMS & NAMES
- imperialism
- racism
- Social Darwinism
- Berlin Conference 1884–85
- Shaka
- Boer
- Great Trek
- Boer War

MAIN IDEA

Ignoring the claims of African ethnic groups, kingdoms, and city-states, Europeans established colonial claims.

WHY IT MATTERS NOW

African nations continue to feel the effects of the colonial presence of 100 years ago.

SETTING THE STAGE Industrialization stirred ambitions in many European nations. They wanted more resources to fuel their industrial production. They competed for new markets for their goods. They looked to Africa and Asia as sources of the raw materials and as markets for cloth, plows, guns, and other industrial products.

Africa Before Imperialism

In the mid-1800s, on the eve of the European domination of Africa, African peoples were divided into hundreds of ethnic and linguistic groups. Most continued to follow traditional beliefs, while others converted to Islam or Christianity. These groups spoke more than 1,000 different languages. Politically, they ranged from large empires that united many ethnic groups to independent villages. The largest empire in West Africa at its peak had a population of about 10 million people.

Although Europeans had established contacts with Africans as early as the 1450s, they actually controlled very little land. Powerful African armies were able to keep the Europeans out of most of Africa for 400 years. As late as 1880, Europeans controlled only 10 percent of the continent's land, mainly on the coast.

Furthermore, European travel into the interior on a large-scale basis was virtually impossible. Europeans could not navigate African rivers that had so many rapids and cataracts and drastically changing flows. Until the introduction of steam-powered riverboats, Europeans would not be able to conduct major expeditions into the interior of Africa.

Finally, large networks of Africans conducted trade. These trade networks kept Europeans from controlling the sources of trade items such as gold and ivory. These trade networks were specialized. The Chokwe, for example, devoted themselves to collecting ivory and beeswax in the Angola highlands. Others such as the Yao carried their goods to merchants on the coast.

THINK THROUGH HISTORY
A. Analyzing Causes Why did the Europeans control such a small portion of Africa in the 1800s?
A. Answer African armies and traders kept them out and the rivers were impassable, making it difficult to get inland.

This highly valued ivory mask is one of four taken from the King of Benin in 1897. It was worn with several others on the belt of a ceremonial costume of the king.

Nations Compete for Overseas Empires

Those Europeans who did penetrate the interior of Africa tended to be explorers, missionaries, or humanitarians who opposed the slave trade. Europeans and Americans learned about Africa through travel books and newspapers. These publications competed for readers by hiring reporters to search the globe for stories of adventure, mystery, or excitement.

The Congo Sparks Interest In the late 1860s, David Livingstone, a minister from Scotland, traveled with a group of Africans deep into central Africa. They were searching for the source of the Nile. When several years passed with no word from him or his party, many people feared he was dead. An American newspaper hired reporter Henry Stanley to find Livingstone. In 1871, he found Dr. Livingstone on the shores of Lake Tanganyika. Stanley's account of the meeting made headlines around the world.

The Age of Imperialism **685**

SECTION 1 RESOURCES

PRINT RESOURCES

 IN-DEPTH RESOURCES: UNIT 6
Guided Reading, p. 37
Geography Application: David Livingstone Explores Southern Africa, p. 43
Primary Source: British Contract with an African King, p. 45
Literature: "The Burial," p. 49

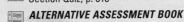 **ACCESS FOR STUDENTS ACQUIRING ENGLISH**
Guided Reading (Spanish), p. 270
Geography Application (Spanish), p. 276

 FORMAL ASSESSMENT
Section Quiz, p. 313

 ALTERNATIVE ASSESSMENT BOOK

TECHNOLOGY RESOURCES

 CD-ROM
Electronic Library of Primary Sources

INTERNET www.mlworldhistory.com

Section 1 Overview

OBJECTIVES

1 To describe Africa before European domination.

2 To summarize the motives of European colonizers.

3 To identify factors allowing the Europeans to control Africa.

4 To identify the three groups that clashed in South Africa.

SKILLBUILDERS
- Interpreting charts, p. 687
- Interpreting maps: region, p. 688

CRITICAL THINKING
- Analyzing causes, p. 685
- Making inferences, pp. 686, 689
- Analyzing issues, p. 687
- Recognizing effects, p. 688
- Contrasting, p. 689

FOCUS

5-Minute Warm-Up

▶ **Interpreting Maps**
Answering the following questions will help students understand the division of Africa.

- Look at the map on page 688. Which country holds the most territory in North Africa?

- What two strategic waterways are held by Spain and Britain?

 WARM-UP TRANSPARENCY 27

OBJECTIVE 1 INSTRUCT

Africa Before Imperialism

▶ **Key Ideas**
- Many ethnic groups but few Europeans rule in Africa.

 IN-DEPTH RESOURCES: UNIT 6
Guided Reading, p. 37

 ACCESS FOR STUDENTS ACQUIRING ENGLISH
Guided Reading (Spanish), p. 270

OBJECTIVE 2 INSTRUCT

Nations Compete for Overseas Empires

▶ **Key Ideas**
- Europeans learn about Africa from explorers.

(continued on next page)

OBJECTIVE 2 INSTRUCT

(continued from page 685)

- Henry Stanley claims the Congo River Valley for Belgium.
- Greed, nationalism, racism, and philanthropy motivate European colonialism.
- Superior arms, the steam engine, medicines, and African rivalries help Europeans dominate Africa.

 ELECTRONIC LIBRARY OF PRIMARY SOURCES
"The Boer War: The Suffering of the Civilian Population"
"Stanley Finds Livingstone"
"Private Company Rule in the Congo"

MORE ABOUT . . .
Collecting Wild Rubber

Rubber production under Belgium rule was one of the worst exploitations of Africans in the history of African colonialism. Armed soldiers drove people into the forest to collect wild rubber. Those who refused were killed, and their left hands taken as trophies to show the commissioner. The hands were then counted to determine that the soldiers had not wasted cartridges. European outrage over this practice forced the Belgians to stop.

MORE ABOUT . . .
Cecil Rhodes

Cecil Rhodes first went to South Africa as a young man to improve his health. He built an immense fortune in the diamond fields of southern Africa. He gave a portion of this fortune in his will to Oxford and Cambridge universities to establish scholarships for promising English-speaking students throughout the world. President Clinton studied at Oxford as a Rhodes scholar.

"Dr. Livingstone, I presume?" was the greeting of American reporter Henry Stanley in their famous meeting in 1871 at Lake Tanganyika. This picture is from a drawing based on Dr. Livingstone's own material.

In 1879, Stanley returned to Africa, and in 1882 he signed treaties with local chiefs of the Congo River valley. The treaties gave King Leopold II of Belgium personal control of these lands.

Leopold claimed that his primary motive in establishing the colony was to abolish the slave trade. However, he licensed companies that brutally exploited Africans, by forcing them to collect sap from rubber plants. The time required to do this interfered with the care of their own food crops. So severe were the forced labor, excessive taxation, and abuses of the native Congolese that humanitarians from around the world demanded changes. In 1908, the Belgian government took over the colony. The Belgian Congo, as the colony later became known, was 80 times larger than Belgium. Leopold's seizure of the Congo alarmed France. Earlier, in 1882, the French had approved a treaty that gave France the north bank of the Congo River. Soon Britain, Germany, Italy, Portugal, and Spain were also claiming parts of Africa.

Motives Driving Imperialism Economic, political, and social forces accelerated the drive to take over land in all parts of the globe. The takeover of a country or territory by a stronger nation with the intent of dominating the political, economic, and social life of the people of that nation is called **imperialism.** The Industrial Revolution provided European countries with a need to add lands to their control. As European nations industrialized, they searched for new markets and raw materials to improve their economies.

The race for colonies grew out of a strong sense of national pride as well as from economic competition. Europeans viewed an empire as a measure of national greatness. "All great nations in the fullness of their strength have desired to set their mark upon barbarian lands," wrote the German historian Heinrich von Treitschke, "and those who fail to participate in this great rivalry will play a pitiable role in time to come." As the competition for colonies intensified, each country was determined to plant its flag on as much of the world as possible.

Because of their advanced technology, many Europeans basically believed that they were better than other peoples. This belief was **racism,** the idea that one race is superior to others. The attitude was a reflection of a social theory of the time, called **Social Darwinism.** In this theory, Charles Darwin's ideas about evolution and "survival of the fittest" were applied to social change. Those who were fittest for survival enjoyed wealth and success and were considered superior to others. According to the theory, non-Europeans were considered to be on a lower scale of cultural and physical development because they did not have the technology that Europeans had. Europeans believed that they had the right and the duty to bring the results of their progress to other countries. Cecil Rhodes, a successful businessman and one of the major supporters of British expansion, clearly stated this position:

> **A VOICE FROM THE PAST**
> I contend that we [Britons] are the first race in the world, and the more of the world we inhabit, the better it is for the human race. . . . It is our duty to seize every opportunity of acquiring more territory and we should keep this one idea steadily before our eyes that more territory simply means more of the Anglo-Saxon race, more of the best, the most human, most honourable race the world possesses.
> **CECIL RHODES,** *Confession of Faith* 1877

B. Possible Answer British superiority to all other groups.

THINK THROUGH HISTORY
B. Making Inferences What attitude about the British does Rhodes's statement display?

CONNECTIONS ACROSS TIME AND PLACE

Civil Wars Point out that many current conflicts among African nations have their roots in the colonial era. In the 1800s and early 1900s, the European imperialists drew national boundaries with little thought about how they might affect native people. Natural enemies were forced together, and cultural families were split. After the colonial era ended following World War II, many emerging African nations fought prolonged, painful civil wars, as ethnic groups sought to regain their traditional lands or force enemies out. Interested students can read about such struggles in Nigeria, the Sudan, the former Belgian Congo, and Angola.

EXPLORING PRIMARY SOURCES

A Voice from the Past Ask students to identify phrases in the excerpt that suggest Cecil Rhodes held racist as well as nationalistic views. What did he mean by the statement "Britons are the first race in the world" and "the best, the most human, most honourable race the world possesses"? *Most students will recognize that he meant "first" as the primary, or most* significant, race. He also thought the Britons were superior to all other colonizers.

Have interested students read more about the life of this colorful Englishman. Tell them that Rhodes's life is a prime example of the positive and negative aspects of European imperialism.

The push for expansion also came from missionaries who worked to Christianize the peoples of Asia, Africa, and the Pacific Islands. Many missionaries believed that European rule was the best way to end evil practices such as the slave trade. They also wanted to "civilize," that is, to "westernize," the peoples of the foreign land.

Forces Enabling Imperialism External and internal forces contributed to the Europeans' conquest of Africa. The overwhelming advantage was the Europeans' technological superiority. The Maxim gun, invented in 1889, was the world's first automatic machine gun. European countries quickly acquired the Maxim, while the resisting Africans were forced to rely on outdated weapons.

European countries also had the means to control their empire. The invention of the steam engine allowed Europeans to easily travel upstream to establish bases of control deep in the African continent. Railroads, cables, and steamers allowed close communications within a colony and between the colony and its controlling nation. All these made control easier.

Even with superior arms and steam engines to transport them, Europeans might still have stayed confined to the coast. Europeans were highly susceptible to malaria. One discovery changed that—the drug quinine. Regular doses of quinine protected Europeans from attacks of this disease caused by mosquitoes.

Internal factors also made the European sweep through Africa easier. Africans' huge variety of languages and cultures discouraged unity among them. Wars fought between ethnic groups over land, water, and trade rights also prevented a unified stand. Europeans soon learned to play rival groups against each other. Finally, Africans fought at a tremendous disadvantage because they did not have the weapons and technology the Europeans had.

THINK THROUGH HISTORY
C. Analyzing Issues
Which external factor was most likely to have caused the downfall of African cultures?
C. Answer Answers will vary. Probably the strongest was the Maxim gun.

Europeans Enter Africa

European Motives
- Nationalism
- Economic competition
- European racism
- Missionary impulse

External Forces
- Maxim gun
- Railroads and steamships
- Cure for malaria

Internal Forces
- Variety of cultures and languages
- Low level of technology
- Ethnic strife

SKILLBUILDER:
Interpreting Charts
1. Which two of the internal forces were connected with each other? Explain.
2. Which of the European motives do you believe was the most powerful? Explain.

African Lands Become European Colonies

The scramble for African territory began in earnest about 1880. At that time, the French began to expand from the West African coast toward western Sudan. The discoveries of diamonds in 1867 and gold in 1886 in South Africa increased European interest in colonizing the land. No European power wanted to be left out of the race.

Berlin Conference Divides Africa The competition was so fierce that European countries feared war among themselves. To prevent fighting, 14 European nations met at the **Berlin Conference** in **1884–85** to lay down rules for the division of Africa. They agreed that any European country could claim land in Africa by notifying other nations of their claims and showing they could control the area. The European nations

The Age of Imperialism **687**

History from Visuals

Imperialism in Africa, 1913

Interpreting the Map Which imperial powers that claimed African land in 1878 had lost their colonies by 1914? Who took over these colonies? *Land held by the Ottoman Empire was acquired by France, Italy, and Britain. Boer colonies were absorbed into the Union of South Africa (modern-day South Africa), dominated by the British.*

Extension Activity Ask students to list the lands each nation claimed. Who had the most African lands? *France and Britain* Which country had the fewest? *Belgium* What was the largest European landholding in Africa? *French West Africa and Algeria*

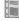 **IN-DEPTH RESOURCES: UNIT 6**
Primary Source: British Contract with an African King, p. 45
Literature: "The Burial," p. 49

SKILLBUILDER Answers
1. About 10%; about 96%
2. France and Britain; 35.6%; 32.3%

Political Divisions in Africa, 1913

- Independent states (3.4%)
- Italian (5.2%)
- Portuguese (6.8%)
- Belgian (7.9%)
- French (35.6%)
- German (7.9%)
- Spanish (.06%)
- British (32.3%)

Legend:
- Belgian
- Britain
- French
- German
- Italian
- Portuguese
- Spanish
- Independent states
- Boer
- Ottoman

GEOGRAPHY SKILLBUILDER: Interpreting Maps and Charts
1. **Region** About what percentage of Africa was colonized by Europeans in 1878? How much by 1913?
2. **Region** According to the map of 1913, which two imperial powers held the most land? According to the chart, what percentage of land in Africa was held by the two powers?

divided the rest of the continent with little thought to how African ethnic or linguistic groups were distributed. No African ruler attended these meetings, yet the conference sealed Africa's fate. By 1914, only Liberia and Ethiopia remained free from European control.

Demand for Product Shapes Colonies When European countries began colonizing, many believed that Africans would soon be buying European goods in great quantities. They were wrong; European goods were not bought. However, European businesses still needed raw materials from Africa. Businesses eventually developed cash-crop plantations to grow peanuts, palm oil, cocoa, and rubber. These products displaced the food crops grown by farmers to feed their families.

The major source of great wealth in Africa proved to be the continent's rich mineral resources. The Belgian Congo contained untold wealth in copper and tin. Even these riches seemed small compared to the gold and diamonds in South Africa.

THINK THROUGH HISTORY
D. Recognizing Effects What sort of problems might result from combining or splitting groups of people?
D. Answer Some might fight each other and some might fight to get back with those they were separated from.

688 Chapter 27

TEACHING OPTION | **BLOCK SCHEDULING** | **COOPERATIVE ACTIVITY: Dramatizing South African History** | **CLASS TIME 30-35 MINUTES**

Task: Students will research, write, and perform brief 5- to 10-minute skits dramatizing a central episode in the history of South Africa.

Purpose: To help students understand history from different points of view.

Activity: Students work in three groups: Zulus, Boers, and British. Each group writes and performs a

short skit that dramatizes an episode central to the history of the group they represent. Examples might include a war council among the Zulu whether to fight the British, a day on the Boers' Great Trek, or the discovery of gold in South Africa.

 Building a Portfolio Students may want to include a copy of the script in their portfolios.

ALTERNATIVE ASSESSMENT BOOK
Standards for Evaluating a Cooperative Activity

Standards for Evaluation
The script and presentation should . . .

- show careful research of the incident
- demonstrate knowledge of each group
- accurately present historical information

Three Groups Clash over South Africa

The history of South Africa is a history of Africans, Dutch, and British clashing over land and resources. Although the African lands seemed empty to the Europeans, there were huge areas claimed by various ethnic groups. The local control of these lands, especially in the east, had been in dispute for about 100 years.

Zulu Expansion From the late 1700s to the late 1800s, a series of local wars shook southern Africa. Around 1816, a Zulu chief, **Shaka,** used highly disciplined warriors and good military organization to create a large centralized state. Shaka's successors, however, were unable to keep the kingdom intact against the superior arms of the British invaders. The Zulu land became a part of British-controlled land in 1887.

Boers and British Settle in the Cape The Dutch first came to the Cape of Good Hope in 1652 to establish a way station for their ships sailing between the Dutch East Indies and home. Dutch settlers known as **Boers** (Dutch for "farmers") gradually took over native Africans' land and established large farms. When the British took over the Cape Colony in the 1800s, the two groups of settlers clashed over British policy regarding land and slaves.

In the 1830s, to escape the British, several thousand Boers began to move north. This movement has become known as the **Great Trek.** The Boers soon found themselves fighting fiercely with Zulu and other African groups whose land they were taking.

The Boer War Diamonds and gold were discovered in southern Africa in the 1860s and 1880s. Suddenly, "outsiders" from all parts of the world rushed in to make their fortunes. The Boers tried to keep the outsiders from gaining political rights. An attempt to start a rebellion against the Boers failed. The Boers blamed the British. In 1899, the Boers took up arms against the British.

In many ways the **Boer War** between the British and the Boers was the first modern "total" war. The Boers launched commando raids and used guerrilla tactics against the British. The British countered by burning Boer farms and imprisoning women and children in disease-ridden concentration camps. Britain won the war. In 1902, the Boer republics were joined into a self-governing Union of South Africa, controlled by the British.

The establishing of colonies signaled a change in the way of life of the Africans. The Europeans made efforts to change the political, social, and economic lives of the peoples they conquered. You will learn about these changes in Section 2.

D. Answer It was between two European nations not between Europeans and Africans.

**THINK THROUGH HISTORY
E. Contrasting** How was the struggle for land in the Boer War different from other takeovers in Africa?

Global Impact

Americans in the Boer War

Americans as well as nationals from other countries volunteered to fight in the Boer War (1899–1902). Although they joined both sides, most fought for the Boers. They believed the Boers were fighting for freedom against British tyrants.

One group of 46 Irish Americans from Chicago and Massachusetts caused an international scandal when they deserted their Red Cross unit and took up arms for the Boers.

Some Irish who fought for the Boers became leaders in the Irish rebellion when they returned home. John MacBride, a leader of a Boer unit that included many Irish Americans, later took part in the 1916 Easter Rising in Dublin. He was executed by the British.

Section ① Assessment

1. TERMS & NAMES

Identify
- imperialism
- racism
- Social Darwinism
- Berlin Conference 1884–85
- Shaka
- Boer
- Great Trek
- Boer War

2. TAKING NOTES

Copy the spider map below and fill in the four motives that caused the growth of imperialism during the late 1800s.

Imperialism

How did Europeans use Social Darwinism to justify empire-building?

3. MAKING INFERENCES

What can you infer about the Europeans' attitude toward Africans from the Berlin Conference?

THINK ABOUT
- who attended the conference
- the outcome of the conference

4. THEME ACTIVITY

Empire Building Create a time line that includes events that occurred in South Africa between 1800 and 1914. What motives caused most of these events?

The Age of Imperialism **689**

---

1. To explain different forms of colonial control.

2. To explain the patterns of imperialist management.

3. To describe British rule in Nigeria.

4. To summarize African resistance movements.

5. To debate effects of colonialism.

SKILLBUILDERS

- Interpreting charts, pp. 690, 691
- Interpreting maps: region, movement, p. 693
- Interpreting maps: region, p. 694

CRITICAL THINKING

- Comparing, pp. 691, 692
- Contrasting, p. 692
- Summarizing, p. 693
- Analyzing motives, p. 693
- Clarifying, p. 694
- Analyzing causes, p. 694
- Recognizing effects, p. 695
- Forming opinions, p. 695

FOCUS

5-Minute Warm-Up

► **Identifying Main Ideas**
To help students learn about European control of Africa, have them answer these questions.

- Read "Setting the Stage" on page 690. What did the Europeans ignore as they divided Africa?

- What was the Europeans' main goal in dominating Africa?

 WARM-UP TRANSPARENCY 27

OBJECTIVE 1 INSTRUCT

Colonial Control Takes Many Forms

► **Key Ideas**
- Europeans use four methods to control their colonies.

IN-DEPTH RESOURCES: UNIT 6
Guided Reading, p. 38

ACCESS TO STUDENTS ACQUIRING ENGLISH
Guided Reading (Spanish), p. 271

---

2 Imperialism

CASE STUDY: Nigeria

PATTERNS OF CHANGE

MAIN IDEA	WHY IT MATTERS NOW
Europeans embarked on a new phase of empire-building that affected both Africa and the rest of the world.	Many former colonies have political problems that are the result of colonial rule.

SETTING THE STAGE The Berlin Conference of 1884–85 was a Europeans' conference, and the Boer War was a Europeans' war. Europeans argued and fought among themselves over the lands of Africa. In carving up Africa, the European countries paid little or no attention to historical political divisions such as kingdoms or caliphates, or to ethnic and language groupings. Uppermost in the minds of the Europeans was the ability to control the land, its people, and their resources.

Colonial Control Takes Many Forms

The imperialism of the 18th and 19th centuries was conducted differently than the empire-building of the 15th and 16th centuries. In the earlier period, imperial powers often did not penetrate far into the conquered areas in Asia and Africa. Nor did they always have a substantial influence on the lives of the people. During this new period of imperialism, the Europeans demanded more influence over the economic, political, and social lives of the people. They were determined to shape the economies of the lands to benefit European economies. They also wanted the people to adopt European customs.

Forms of Colonial Control Each European nation had certain policies and goals for establishing colonies. To establish control of an area, Europeans used different techniques. Over time, four forms of colonial control emerged: colony, protectorate, sphere of influence, and economic imperialism. In practice, gaining control of an area might involve the use of several of these forms.

PATTERNS OF CHANGE: Imperialism

Forms of Imperialism	Characteristics	Example
Colony	A country or a region governed internally by a foreign power	Somaliland in East Africa was a French colony.
Protectorate	A country or territory with its own internal government but under the control of an outside power	Britain established a protectorate over the Niger River delta.
Sphere of Influence	An area in which an outside power claims exclusive investment or trading privileges	Liberia was under the sphere of influence of the United States.
Economic Imperialism	Independent but less developed nations controlled by private business interests rather than by other governments	The Dole Fruit company controlled pineapple trade in Hawaii.

SKILLBUILDER: Interpreting Charts
1. *Which two forms are guided by interests in business or trade?*
2. *What is the difference between a protectorate and a colony?*

SECTION 2 RESOURCES

PRINT RESOURCES

IN-DEPTH RESOURCES: UNIT 6
Guided Reading, p. 38
Primary Source: Letter from Menelik II, p. 46
Literature: from *Things Fall Apart*, p. 50
History Makers: Menelik II, p. 52
Connections Across Time and Cultures: Two Periods of Colonization and Imperialism, p. 54

ACCESS FOR STUDENTS ACQUIRING ENGLISH
Guided Reading (Spanish), p. 271

FORMAL ASSESSMENT
Section Quiz, p. 314

ALTERNATIVE ASSESSMENT BOOK

TECHNOLOGY RESOURCES

CD-ROM
Electronic Library of Primary Sources

INTERNET www.mlworldhistory.com

Patterns of Imperialist Management

In addition to the external form of control preferred by the colonizing country, European rulers also needed to develop methods of day-to-day management of the colony. Two basic methods of internal management emerged. Britain and other nations such as the United States in its Pacific Island colonies preferred indirect control. France and most other European nations wielded a more direct control. Later, when colonies gained independence, the management method used had an influence on the type of government chosen in the new nation.

Indirect Control Indirect control relied on existing political rulers. In some areas, the British asked a local ruler to accept British authority to rule. These local officials handled much of the daily management of the colony. In addition, each colony had a legislative council that included colonial officials as well as local merchants and professionals nominated by the colonial governor.

The assumption was that the councils would train local leaders in the British method of government and that a time would come when the local population would govern itself. This happened earlier in the British colonies of South Africa and Canada. In the 1890s, the United States began to colonize. It chose the indirect method of control for its colonies.

Direct Control The French and other European powers preferred a more direct control of their colonies. They viewed the Africans as children unable to handle the complex business of running a country. Based on this attitude, the Europeans developed a policy called **paternalism.** Using that policy, Europeans governed people in a fatherly way by providing for their needs but not giving them rights. To accomplish this, the Europeans brought in their own bureaucrats and did not train local people in European methods of governing.

The French also supported a policy of **assimilation.** That policy was based on the idea that in time, the local populations would become absorbed into French culture. To aid in the transition, all local schools, courts, and businesses were patterned after French institutions. In practice, the French abandoned the ideal of assimilation for all but a few places and settled for a policy of "association." They recognized African institutions and culture but regarded them as inferior to French culture. Other European nations used this style of rule but made changes to suit their European culture.

THINK THROUGH HISTORY
A. Comparing How was the policy of paternalism like Social Darwinism?
A. Possible Answer Both saw Europeans as better able to run a colony than the local population.

Management Methods

Indirect Control	Direct Control
• Local government officials were used	• Foreign officials brought in to rule
• Limited self-rule	• No self-rule
• Goal: to develop future leaders	• Goal: assimilation
• Government institutions are based on European styles but may have local rules	• Government institutions are based only on European styles
Examples • British colonies such as Nigeria, India, Burma • U.S. colonies on Pacific Islands	Examples • French colonies such as Somaliland, Vietnam • German colonies such as Tanganyika • Portuguese colonies such as Angola

SKILLBUILDER: Interpreting Charts
1. *In which management method are the people less empowered to rule themselves? Explain.*
2. *In what ways are the two management methods different?*

History from Visuals

Patterns of Change: Imperialism
(See page 690.)

Interpreting the Chart Which forms of control would not be used at the same time? *Colony/protectorate*

Extension Activity Have students make a chart with one column for the form of control and one for examples of each form. As they read the chapter, have them fill in other examples.

SKILLBUILDER Answers
1. Sphere of influence, economic imperialism
2. In a protectorate, the country maintains its own internal government, whereas a colony is governed by an outside power.

OBJECTIVE ② INSTRUCT

Patterns of Imperialist Management

▶ **Key Ideas**
• Britain and the United States use indirect control, while the French follow a policy of association.

History from Visuals

Management Methods
Interpreting the Chart Have students make a Venn diagram comparing British and French management methods.

Extension Activity Ask students to predict in writing which of these methods would best allow a colony to become self-governing. Why? Have them save their predictions until they read Chapter 35.

SKILLBUILDER Answers
1. Direct control: Foreign officials are the rulers; people have no direct rule.
2. Who was chosen to rule; goals of the methods; styles of government

---

TEACHING OPTIONS

CONNECTIONS ACROSS TIME AND PLACE

French Africa In the 1950s, when more blacks from French-African territories began to test their rights as French citizens, France rethought its policy of assimilation. Already, French franchise was limited to overseas residents who met strict educational and property qualifications. In 1958, General Charles de Gaulle gave the

African territories a choice: either accept the status of autonomous states within a French community or take immediate and total independence from France. Only Guinea chose independence. Have interested students research the history of Guinea to see how the nation has fared as an independent country.

EXPLORING PRIMARY SOURCES

African Kings and Europeans Give students the primary sources for sections 1 and 2. These sources show different responses to European contacts. In the letter, Menelik II is forging alliances against the Europeans. The British contract shows how little some Africans understood about what they were signing. Help students identify

the major issues in each document, what each person wants, and what is at stake for each party.

 IN-DEPTH RESOURCES: UNIT 6
Primary Sources: British Contract with an African King, and Letter from Menelik II, pp. 45, 46

Teacher's Edition 691

History Through Art

Textiles

In Africa, as in some other parts of the world with long-established traditions, garments provide a great deal of information about the person who wears them. For example, only the Ashanti king is allowed to wear certain silk kente patterns. On days when people come before him with disputes or petitions, he may choose to wear a particular pattern, such as the "Liar's Cloth," to convey a subtle message to those pleading their case that they should be truthful.

MORE ABOUT . . .
Uses of Textiles

• Men's and women's roles in society can be indicated by the parts they play in the manufacture of textiles. For example, women spin, weave, stamp, dye, and embroider many cloths. However, kente cloth is woven only by men.

• Making and selling textiles is one way women can gain some economic independence, which makes a difference in the social freedom women are allowed in their society.

• Political statements are often made by the wearers of certain adinkra prints or tie-dyed patterns. Sometimes the name or the picture of a leader is included.

African Weaving

When Europeans began colonizing Africa, they found a variety of cultures, many with distinctive textiles. Just as the colonizers learned to identify peoples from the textiles they wore, so historians also learn from these fabrics. For example, the materials used in the fabrics reveal clues about the environment of the weavers. The designs and patterns often used traditional symbols or myths of the culture. When and how the fabrics were used also provide information about the culture's celebrations and social roles. Many of these fabrics, such as the ones below, continue to be produced in modern times.

Adinkra Cloth
Gyaman people of the Ivory Coast produced this hand-printed and embroidered cloth. Stamp patterns were made from a gourd and dipped in a dye made of bark paste. The cloth was stamped with symbols. The name of each symbol represented a proverb, an event, or a human, animal, or plant. The symbol shown (rams' horns) is a sign of strength and humility.

Kuba Cloth
Made by Kuba people of Congo, this cloth was made of raffia, a palm-leaf fiber. The cloth design was based on traditional geometric styles. The cloth was worn at ceremonial events, was used as currency, and may have been offered for part of a dowry.

A modern-day Ivory Coast chief wears kente cloth. *Kente* is a general term for silk cloth. Only royalty are allowed to wear kente cloth.

Kente Cloth
This cloth was produced by the Asante people of Ghana. The word *kente* is not used by the Asante. It comes from a Fante (another society) word for basket. The Asante called the cloth *asasia*. Asasia production was a monopoly of the king of the Asante.

Connect *to* **History**

Contrasting Each of these textiles reflects a specific group. Identify characteristics that make the textiles different from each other.

SEE SKILLBUILDER HANDBOOK, PAGE 996

Connect *to* **Today**

Comparing To show their roots, some African Americans wear clothing with a kente cloth pattern. What other ethnic groups have specific clothing that connects them to their roots?

Connect *to* **History**

Contrasting Suggest to students that they consider what the cloth is made from, how it is made, and how it is decorated. The kente cloth is made from silk yarn, the adinkra from cotton, and the kuba cloth from raffia. The kente is woven in strips, which requires a completely different loom than the wider adinkra or the kuba cloth. The kente design emerges in the weaving and in the way the strips are sewn together. The adinkra pattern is stamped on the cloth, and the edges are embroidered. The kuba cloth starts out as a one-color cloth, which is then embroidered, and the edges of the embroidery are cut to create a pile or velvet effect.

Connect *to* **Today**

Comparing Most ethnic groups have some type of clothing or pattern that connects them to their roots. Students might mention Scottish or Irish tartans that identify the ancestral clans of these groups. The tartans are traditionally worn as kilts. Although many East Indians and Pakistanis now wear Western dress for everyday use, they wear saris or other traditional costumes for weddings and festivals. Many Native Americans wear patterns to identify their clans or family groups. Special headdresses, such as an Islamic woman's head covering or a male Sikh's turban, are related to religious affiliation as well as to place of origin.

A British Colony

A close look at Britain's rule of Nigeria illustrates the forms of imperialism used by European powers to gain control of an area, and also shows management methods used to continue the control of the economic and political life of the area.

In 1807, Britain outlawed the slave trade. The British freed some slaves on the West African coast, who then helped the British in overtaking other groups. To get a group's land, the British swayed that group's enemies to help fight them. The winning African groups might then bow to British control.

Later, the Royal Niger Company gained control of the palm-oil trade along the Niger River. In 1884–85, the Berlin Conference gave Britain a protectorate in lands along the Niger River. In 1914, the British claimed the entire area of Nigeria as a colony. But in this new age of imperialism, it was necessary to not only claim the territory but also to govern the people living there.

Nigeria is one of the most culturally diverse areas in Africa. About 250 different ethnic groups lived there. The three largest groups were the Hausa-Fulani in the north, the Yoruba in the southwest, and the Igbo in the southeast. The groups in the area claimed by Britain were different from each other in many ways including language, culture, and religion. The Hausa-Fulani people of the north were Muslim and were accustomed to a strong central government. The Igbo and Yoruba peoples relied on local chiefs or governing councils for control. The Hausa-Fulani and Yoruba were traditional enemies.

Britain did not have enough troops to govern such a wide and complex area. So it turned to indirect rule of the land. The British relied on local administrations and chiefs to keep order, avoid rebellion, and collect taxes.

Ruling indirectly through local officials functioned well in northern Nigeria. There the traditional government was most like the British style of government. The process did not work as well in eastern or southwestern Nigeria, where the chiefdoms and councils had trouble with British indirect rule. One reason was that the British appointed chiefs where there had been no chiefs before. Then the British restricted their powers. This left the chiefs with little real status and led to problems governing the area.

African Resistance

Across Africa, European attempts to colonize the lands were met with resistance. The contest between African states and European powers was never equal due to the Europeans' superior arms. Sometimes African societies tried to form alliances with

THINK THROUGH HISTORY
B. Summarizing Which forms of imperialistic control did Britain use in Nigeria?
B. Answer Protectorate, colony, and economic imperialism (Royal Niger Company)

THINK THROUGH HISTORY
C. Analyzing Motives Why was using local governments to control a colony a logical solution for the British?
C. Possible Answers Britain did not have enough troops to directly control the land. Also it might have reduced hostility by the local groups by having local government.

Nigeria, 1914

Hausa-Fulani
Igbo
Yoruba
— British-imposed border

FRENCH WEST AFRICA

0   250 Miles
0   500 Kilometers

Niger R.

Lake Chad

1851, British annex Lagos

NIGERIA

Benue R.

After 1884–85 Berlin Conference, Britain declares a protectorate over Niger Delta

Lagos

The Royal Niger Company controls the palm-oil trade

Niger R.

CAMEROONS

Gulf of Guinea

GEOGRAPHY SKILLBUILDER: Interpreting Maps
1. **Region** *How many major culture regions are found within the colony of Nigeria? What sort of problems might result from combining or splitting groups of people?*
2. **Movement** *Why might the British want to be able to control the Niger River?*

PATTERNS OF CHANGE 693

Resistance Movements in Africa, 1881–1914

Interpreting the Map Which resistance movements shown are the earliest? *Arabi Pasha, Mahdist State*

Extension Activity Ask students to arrange the resistance movements along a time line. Have them notice that many movements overlap in time. Ask them what might be the reasons for this fact. *Possible Answers: One movement could inspire others; trade routes among territories could spread word of resistance.*

SKILLBUILDER Answers
1. Anglo-Egyptian Sudan
2. Only the northwest corner of Africa; all other areas had resistance movements.

MORE ABOUT . . .
African Resistance
The arbitrary division of African territories was only part of the reason Africans resisted European domination. A more fundamental reason was the completely alien nature of Western civilization, with its emphasis on science and technology. The Herero, a group in western South Africa, observed, "The European is devoted to dead metals . . . we get our joy out of living creatures." The Europeans also bewildered Africans by settling land they claimed had no previous owners and by renaming lakes and rivers that had had African names for centuries.

---

the Europeans. They hoped the agreement would allow them to remain independent. In some cases the Europeans did help defeat the rivals, but they then turned on their African allies. Other times Africans resisted the Europeans with whatever forces they could raise. With the single exception of Ethiopia, all these attempts at resistance ultimately failed. Edward Morel, a British journalist who lived for a time in the Congo, made an observation about the Africans' fate:

A VOICE FROM THE PAST
Nor is violent physical opposition to abuse and injustice henceforth possible for the African in any part of Africa. His chances of effective resistance have been steadily dwindling with the increasing perfectibility in the killing power of modern armament.
Thus the African is really helpless against the material gods of the white man, as embodied in the trinity of imperialism, capitalistic exploitation, and militarism.
EDWARD MOREL, *The Black Man's Burden*

Unsuccessful Movements The unsuccessful resistance attempts included active resistance and religious movements. Algeria's almost 50-year resistance to French rule was one outstanding example of active resistance. In West Africa, Samori Touré led resistance against the French for 16 years.

Africans in German East Africa put their faith in a spiritual defense. African villagers resisted the Germans' insistence that they plant cotton, a cash crop for export, rather than attend to their own food crops. In 1905, the belief suddenly arose that a magic water *(maji-maji)* sprinkled on their bodies would turn the Germans' bullets into water. The uprising became known as the Maji Maji rebellion. When resistance fighters armed with spears and protected by the magic water attacked a German machine-gun post, they were mowed down by the thousands. Officially, Germans recorded 26,000 resisters dead. But almost twice that number perished in the famine that followed.

THINK THROUGH HISTORY
D. Clarifying What does Morel believe is the fate of Africa?
D. Answer Africans are unable to resist the power of white men.

Resistance Movements in Africa, 1881–1914

Algerian Berbers and Arabs 1830–1884
TUNISIA
Mediterranean Sea
Arabi Pasha 1881–1882
ALGERIA
LIBYA
EGYPT
Tropic of Cancer
Mande 1884–1898
Rabih 1897–1900
ANGLO-EGYPTIAN SUDAN
Mahdist State 1881–1898
FRENCH WEST AFRICA
L. Chad
Khartoum
BRITISH SOMALILAND
Daboya
Fashoda
Menelik II 1893–1896
GOLD COAST
ETHIOPIA
ITALIAN SOMALILAND
CAMEROONS
0° Equator
Asante 1900
UGANDA
BRITISH EAST AFRICA
INDIAN OCEAN
ATLANTIC OCEAN
BELGIAN CONGO
GERMAN EAST AFRICA
Maji Maji 1905–1906
N
Mashona 1896
0   1,000 Miles
0   2,000 Kilometers
ANGOLA
MADAGASCAR
Tropic of Capricorn
GERMAN SOUTHWEST AFRICA
SOUTHERN RHODESIA
Menalamba 1898–1904
Area of resistance
Herero and Hottentot 1904–1906
SOUTH AFRICA
Ndebele, 1896
ZULULAND

GEOGRAPHY SKILLBUILDER: Interpreting Maps
1. **Region** Which region had the largest area affected by resistance?
2. **Region** Was any region unaffected by resistance movements?

Ethiopia: A Successful Resistance
Ethiopia was the only African nation to successfully resist the Europeans. Its victory was due to one man—**Menelik II.** He became emperor of Ethiopia in 1889. He successfully played Italians, French, and British against each other, all of whom were striving to bring Ethiopia into their spheres of influence. In the meantime he built up a large arsenal of modern weapons purchased from France and Russia. About to sign a treaty with Italy, Menelik discovered differences between the wording of the treaty in Amharic—the Ethiopian language—and in Italian. Menelik believed he was giving up a tiny portion of Ethiopia. However, the Italians claimed all of Ethiopia as a protectorate. Meanwhile, Italian forces were advancing into northern Ethiopia. Menelik declared war. In 1896, in one of the greatest battles in the history of Africa—the Battle of Adowa—Ethiopian forces successfully defeated the Italians and maintained their nation's independence.

THINK THROUGH HISTORY
E. Analyzing Causes Why would the French and Russians sell arms to Ethiopia?
E. Possible Answer To prevent Britain from taking over Ethiopia.

Task: Students will research African resistance movements and create a classroom display.

Purpose: To help students understand that resistance to European occupation was widespread.

Activity: Students work in small groups to research a different resistance movement mentioned on the map or in the text. Students should report on

leaders, important battles, weapons, casualties, effect on the country, and any eyewitness accounts. Each group will prepare part of a classroom display, which might include graphs, charts, diagrams, time lines, illustrations, explanatory captions, and quotations.

 Building a Portfolio: Students adding this report to their portfolios should attach an explanation of the assignment.

ALTERNATIVE ASSESSMENT BOOK
Standards for Evaluating a Cooperative Activity

Standards for Evaluation
The visual presentation should . . .
• make good use of visual aids and organizers
• show evidence of careful and accurate research
• show students' knowledge of the topic

Impact of Colonial Rule

European colonial rule forever altered Africans' lives. For the most part, the effects were negative, but in some cases the Europeans brought benefits.

On the positive side, colonialism reduced local warfare. Now, under the control of the European military, raids between rival tribes were reduced. Humanitarian efforts in some colonies improved sanitation and brought hospitals and schools. As a result, life spans increased and literacy rates improved. Also positive was the economic expansion. African products came to be valued on the international market. To aid the economic growth, African colonies gained railroads, dams, and telephone and telegraph lines. But for the most part, these only benefited European business interests, not Africans' lives.

On the negative side, Africans lost control of their land and their independence. Many died of new diseases such as smallpox. They also lost thousands of their people in resisting the Europeans. Famines resulted from the change to cash crops in place of subsistence agriculture.

Africans also suffered from a breakdown of their traditional cultures. Traditional authority figures were replaced. Homes and property were transferred with little regard to their importance to the people. Men were forced to leave villages to find ways to support themselves and their families. They had to work in mines, on European-owned farms, or on government projects such as railroad building. Contempt for the traditional culture and admiration of European life undermined stable societies and caused identity problems for Africans.

The most troublesome political legacy from the colonial period was the dividing of the African continent. Long-term rival chiefdoms were sometimes united, while at other times, kinship groups were split between colonies. The artificial boundaries that combined or unnaturally divided groups created problems that plagued African colonies during European occupation. These boundaries continue to create problems for the nations that evolved from the former colonies.

The patterns of behavior of imperialist powers were similar, no matter where their colonies were located. Dealing with local traditions and peoples continued to cause problems in other areas of the world dominated by Europeans. Resistance to the European imperialists also continued, as you will see in Section 3.

Margin notes (left)

F. Possible Answer
The European military would not be there to prevent rival groups from attacking each other.

THINK THROUGH HISTORY
F. Recognizing Effects Why might the problems caused by artificial boundaries continue after the Europeans left?

HISTORY MAKERS

Samori Touré
about 1830–1900

Samori Touré is a hero of the Mandinka people. His empire is often compared to the great Mali Empire of the 1300s.

Touré was a nationalist who built a powerful Mandinkan kingdom by conquering neighboring states. His kingdom became the third largest empire in West Africa.

For 16 years, Touré opposed the French imperialists in West Africa. The well-armed Mandinkas were France's greatest foe in West Africa, and the two armies clashed several times. The Mandinkan Empire was finally brought down, not in battle, but by a famine.

Sekou Touré, the first president of the nation of Guinea in 1958, claimed to be the grandson of Samori Touré.

Section 2 Assessment

1. TERMS & NAMES

Identify
- paternalism
- assimilation
- Menelik II

2. TAKING NOTES

Re-create the chart below on your paper. Fill in the information on how Europeans controlled and managed other areas of the world.

European Imperialism	
Forms of Control	
Management Methods	

3. FORMING OPINIONS

Do you think Europeans could have conquered Africa if the Industrial Revolution had never occurred? Explain your answer.

THINK ABOUT
- the limited role of Europeans in Africa until the late 1800s
- what inventions changed Europeans' ability to enter Africa

4. THEME ACTIVITY

Power and Authority With a small group of students, divide into two teams, one representing the Europeans and one representing the Africans. Debate the following statement: "The negative effects of imperialism outweighed its positive results."

PATTERNS OF CHANGE **695**

ANSWERS

1. TERMS & NAMES
paternalism, p. 691
assimilation, p. 691
Menelik II, p. 694

2. TAKING NOTES
Possible Responses: Forms of Control—colony, protectorate, sphere of influence, economic imperialism; Management Methods—direct control, indirect control

3. FORMING OPINIONS
Possible Response: Inventions from the Industrial Revolution enabled Europeans to conquer Africa. They reached the interior using steamboats and railroads. Telegraphs and telephones gave them rapid communications. New weapons and quinine to treat malaria enabled European armies to defeat all other armies.

4. THEME ACTIVITY
Standards for Evaluation
Arguments should meet the following criteria:
- State the positive or negative effects of colonialism
- Use reasons and specific examples
- Summarize the argument in a closing statement

Right column (Teacher's Edition)

OBJECTIVE 4 INSTRUCT

Impact of Colonial Rule

▶ **Key Ideas**
- Colonialism has both positive and negative effects on African lands and peoples.
- Artificial boundaries plague Africa for years to come.

IN-DEPTH RESOURCES: UNIT 6
Connections Across Time and Cultures: Two Periods of Colonization and Imperialism, p. 54

HISTORY MAKERS
Samori Touré

Ask students what factors enabled the Mandinka to resist the French.

ASSESS & RETEACH

Section 2 Assessment
Have students work in pairs to answer the questions and then share their answers with another pair of students.

FORMAL ASSESSMENT BOOK
Section Quiz, p. 314

Reteaching Activity
CLASS TIME: 20 MINUTES

Hand out copies of the cause-and-effect graphic organizer. Divide students into three groups and have each group fill out a chart for Objectives 3, 4, or 5. Discuss their responses.

CRITICAL THINKING TRANSPARENCIES
CT75 Cause and Effect

CLOSE ACTIVITY

CLASS TIME: 25 MINUTES

Solving Problems
Have students role-play French, British, or U.S. colonial leaders and African leaders, such as Menelik II. Interview students, asking them to discuss what problems colonial rule has brought them and what solutions they have found. Ask them to explain the pros and cons of their solutions.

Views of Imperialism

The views of those who wielded power in overseas colonies usually clashed directly with those who spoke on behalf of the colonized. Speakers on both sides expressed themselves in emotionally intense language. The views represented a wide range of political opinions and moral beliefs, such as the following:

• Pro: Europeans, because they believe themselves to be a superior race, are morally obligated to teach their way of life to the less fortunate.

• Con: Europeans fail to see what wisdom other ancient cultures can teach them.

• Pro: Europeans achieve great status in their world of nations by the influence they exert over others.

• Con: The brutality with which Europeans rule contradicts their claim to be a "superior" culture.

• Pro: Europeans help less advanced societies by providing education and technology.

• Con: Europeans destroy other societies by breaking up families and weakening ancient traditions.

Discuss these opposing views with students. Help them to understand that each side truly believed in its own point of view.

ELECTRONIC LIBRARY OF PRIMARY SOURCES
from "Africa at the Center"

---

different PERSPECTIVES

Views of Imperialism

European imperialism extended to the continents beyond Africa. As imperialism spread, the colonizer and the colonized viewed the experience of imperialism in very different ways. Some Europeans were outspoken about the superiority they felt toward the peoples they conquered. Others thought imperialism was very wrong. Even the conquered had mixed feelings about their encounter with the Europeans.

ESSAY
J. A. Hobson

A journalist and essayist, Hobson was an outspoken critic of imperialism. His 1902 book, *Imperialism*, made a great impression on his fellow Britons.

For Europe to rule Asia by force for purposes of gain, and to justify that rule by the pretence that she is civilizing Asia and raising her to a higher level of spiritual life, will be adjudged by history, perhaps, to be the crowning wrong and folly of Imperialism. What Asia has to give, her priceless stores of wisdom garnered from her experience of ages, we refuse to take; the much or little which we could give we spoil by the brutal manner of our giving. This is what Imperialism has done, and is doing, for Asia.

POLITICAL CARTOON
Devilfish in Egyptian Waters
Notice that Egypt is not yet one of the areas controlled by the British.

THE DEVILFISH IN EGYPTIAN WATERS.

SPEECH
Jules Ferry

In a speech before the French National Assembly on July 28,1883, Jules Ferry summarized reasons for supporting French imperialism.

Nations are great in our times only by means of the activities which they develop; it is not simply 'by the peaceful shining forth of institutions . . .' that they are great at this hour. . . . Something else is needed for France: . . . that she must also be a great country exercising all of her rightful influence over the destiny of Europe, that she ought to propagate this influence throughout the world and carry everywhere that she can her language, her customs, her flag, her arms, and her genius.

SPEECH
Dadabhai Naoroji

Dadabhai Naoroji was the first Indian elected to the British Parliament. He was also a part of the founding of the Indian National Congress. In 1871, he delivered a speech answering a question about the impact of Great Britain on India. In the speech he listed positives and negatives about the rule of the British. The conclusion of the speech is printed below.

To sum up the whole, the British rule has been—morally, a great blessing; politically peace and order on one hand, blunders on the other, materially, impoverishment. . . . The natives call the British system "Sakar ki Churi," the knife of sugar. That is to say there is no oppression, it is all smooth and sweet, but it is the knife, notwithstanding. I mention this that you should know these feelings. Our great misfortune is that you do not know our wants. When you will know our real wishes, I have not the least doubt that you would do justice. The genius and spirit of the British people is fair play and justice.

Connect *to* History

Analyzing Effects For each excerpt, list the positive and negative effects of imperialism mentioned by the speaker.

SEE SKILLBUILDER HANDBOOK, PAGE 995.

Connect *to* Today

Research List the countries controlled by England as shown in the political cartoon. Research to find out what year each of them became independent. Make a chart showing the countries in order by the year they were freed from colonial status. Next to each one also write its current name.

CD-ROM For another perspective on imperialism, see *World History: Electronic Library of Primary Sources.*

Connect *to* History

Analyzing Effects
Possible Responses
Hobson: Positive—higher level of spiritual life; Negative—loss of wisdom from Asia, the brutal treatment of the Asian people

Naoroji: Positive—moral values, peace and order;

Negative—impoverishment, ignorance of Indian needs

Ferry: Positive—sharing of European (French) language, customs, arms, and genius with less developed countries

Connect *to* Today

Research To compile the chart, students might look up information in the *Statesman's Yearbook,* the almanac, or an encyclopedia. Ask students to indicate whenever the modern names of African countries represent a word or phrase in

the native language or the name of an ethnic group. Also, interested students might want to enlarge the chart to include other information, such as each country's population, ethnic mix, and chief imports and exports.

3 Muslim Lands Fall to Imperialist Demands

TERMS & NAMES
- geopolitics
- Crimean War
- Suez Canal

MAIN IDEA

European nations expanded their empires by seizing territories from Muslim states.

WHY IT MATTERS NOW

Political events in this vital resource area are still influenced by actions from the imperialistic period.

SETTING THE STAGE The European powers who carved up Africa among themselves also looked elsewhere to see what other lands they could control. The Muslim lands that rimmed the Mediterranean had largely been claimed as a result of Arab and Ottoman conquests. Now the Muslim power in those areas was weakening. Europeans competed with each other to gain control of this strategically important area.

Ottoman Empire Loses Power

The Ottoman Empire at its peak stretched from Hungary in the north, through Greece, around the Black Sea, south through Syria, and across Egypt all the way west to the borders of Morocco. But during the empire's last 300 years, it steadily declined in power. The declining empire had difficulties trying to fit into the modern world. However, the Ottomans made attempts to change before they finally were unable to hold back the European imperialist powers.

Reforms Fail When Suleiman I, the last great Ottoman sultan, died in 1566, he was followed by a succession of weak sultans. The ruling party broke up into a number of quarreling, often corrupt factions. Along with weakening power came other problems. Corruption and theft had caused financial losses. Coinage was devalued, causing inflation. Unemployed ex-soldiers and students caused trouble. Once a leader in scientific, mechanical, and administrative achievements, the Ottoman Empire fell further and further behind Europe.

When Selim III came into power in 1789, he attempted to modernize the army. The older janissary corps resisted his efforts. Selim III was overthrown and reform movements were temporarily abandoned. Meanwhile, nationalist feelings began to stir among the Ottoman's subject peoples. In 1830, Greece gained its independence, and Serbia gained self-rule. The Ottomans' weakness was becoming apparent to European powers, who were expanding their territories. They began to look for ways to take the lands away from the Ottomans.

Ottoman Empire, 1699–1914

(to Austria 1699, 1878) AUSTRIA · (to Russia 1783) RUSSIA · FRANCE · HUNGARY · ROMANIA · CRIMEA · (to Russia 1803, 1829) · ITALY · SERBIA · BULGARIA · Black Sea · ALBANIA · Istanbul · SPAIN · BALKANS (independent 1817, 1913) · GREECE · ANATOLIA · Caspian Sea · AZERBAIJAN (independent 1730) · ALGERIA (to France 1830) · TUNISIA (to France 1881) · Mediterranean Sea · Cyprus (to Britain 1878) · PERSIA · MOROCCO (to France 1912) · TRIPOLI (to Italy 1912) · EGYPT (partially independent 1841) · ARABIA · Persian Gulf · Red Sea · Tropic of Cancer · Mecca

- Ottoman Empire at its greatest extent in 1699
- Ottoman Empire in 1914
- Territory becomes part of

0 1,000 Miles
0 2,000 Kilometers

GEOGRAPHY SKILLBUILDER: Interpreting Maps
1. **Region** Approximately how much of the Ottoman Empire was lost by 1914?
2. **Region** How many European nations claimed parts of the Ottoman Empire? Which areas became independent?

The Age of Imperialism **697**

SECTION 3 RESOURCES

PRINT RESOURCES

 IN-DEPTH RESOURCES: UNIT 6
Guided Reading, p. 39

ACCESS FOR STUDENTS ACQUIRING ENGLISH
Guided Reading (Spanish), p. 272

FORMAL ASSESSMENT
Section Quiz, p. 315

ALTERNATIVE ASSESSMENT BOOK

TECHNOLOGY RESOURCES

 WORLD ART AND CULTURES TRANSPARENCIES
AT58 *Reception at the Court of Sultan Selim III*

INTERNET www.mlworldhistory.com

Section 3 Overview

OBJECTIVES

1. To summarize the decline of the Ottoman Empire.

2. To describe the Crimean War and the division of the Ottoman Empire.

SKILLBUILDERS
- Interpreting maps: region, p. 697
- Interpreting graphs and maps: place, location, p. 699

CRITICAL THINKING
- Analyzing causes, p. 698
- Recognizing effects, p. 699
- Clarifying, p. 700
- Comparing/contrasting, p. 700
- Analyzing themes, p. 700

FOCUS

5-Minute Warm-Up

▶ **Recognizing Effects**
Answering the following questions will help students understand the decline of the Ottoman Empire.

1. Study the map on page 697. At its height, what were the furthest boundaries of the Ottoman Empire to the east, west, north, and south?

2. By 1914, what were the only major cities still within the empire?

 WARM-UP TRANSPARENCY 27

OBJECTIVE 1 INSTRUCT

Ottoman Empire Loses Power

▶ **Key Ideas**
- The great Suleiman I is succeeded by a series of weak rulers.
- Selim III's reforms give rise to nationalist feelings.
- Europeans seize the opportunity to divide the empire.

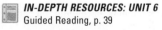 **IN-DEPTH RESOURCES: UNIT 6**
Guided Reading, p. 39

ACCESS FOR STUDENTS ACQUIRING ENGLISH
Guided Reading (Spanish), p. 272

History from Visuals

Ottoman Empire, 1699-1914
(See page 697)

Interpreting the Map Which countries acquired land from the Ottomans? *Austria, Russia, France, Italy, Britain, independent Azerbaijan, and partially independent Egypt*

Extension Activity Ask students to compare this map with the map on page 688. Have them list which parts of the African Ottoman Empire were taken by which European nations. *Egypt/Suez = Britain; Libya = Italy; Algeria, Tunisia = France*

SKILLBUILDER Answers
1. About two-thirds
2. Five European nations; Azerbaijan, Egypt, Balkans

OBJECTIVE 2 INSTRUCT

Europeans Grab Territory

▶ **Key Ideas**
- The Ottomans control access to the Atlantic and Mediterranean sea trade.
- The Ottomans, British, and French defeat the Russians in the Crimean War.
- Egypt loses control of the Suez Canal to Britain.
- Although Persia attempts to modernize, Russia and Britain take control.

 WORLD ART AND CULTURES TRANSPARENCIES
AT58 *Reception at the Court of Sultan Selim III*

MORE ABOUT . . .
Florence Nightingale

Although born into a wealthy British family, Florence Nightingale rejected marriage and a carefree

(continued on next page)

This 1897 lithograph shows the British forces at the Battle of Balaklava in the Crimean War. This battle was the inspiration for a famous poem by Alfred, Lord Tennyson, "The Charge of the Light Brigade."

Europeans Grab Territory

Geopolitics—an interest in or taking of land for its strategic location or products—played an important role in the fate of the Ottoman Empire. World powers were attracted to its strategic location. The Ottomans controlled access to the Mediterranean and the Atlantic sea trade. Merchants in landlocked countries that lay beyond the Black Sea had to go through Ottoman lands. Russia, for example, desperately wanted passage for its grain exports across the Black Sea and into the Mediterranean Sea. This desire strongly influenced Russia's relations with the Ottoman Empire. Russia attempted to win Ottoman favor, formed alliances with Ottoman enemies, and finally waged war against the Ottomans. Discovery of oil in Persia and the Arabian Peninsula around 1900 focused even more attention on the area.

Russia and the Crimean War Each generation of Russian czars launched a war on the Ottomans to try to gain land on the Black Sea. In 1853, war broke out between the Russians and the Ottomans. The war was called the **Crimean War,** after a peninsula in the Black Sea where most of the war was fought. Britain and France wanted to prevent the Russians from gaining control of additional Ottoman lands. So they entered the war on the side of the Ottoman Empire. The combined forces of the Ottomans, Britain, and France defeated Russia. The Crimean War was the first war in which women, led by Florence Nightingale, established their position as army nurses. It was also the first war to be covered by newspaper correspondents.

The Crimean War revealed the Ottoman Empire's military weakness. Despite the help of Britain and France, the Ottoman Empire continued to lose lands. The Russians came to the aid of Slavic people in the Balkans who rebelled against the Ottomans. The Ottomans lost control of Romania, Montenegro, Cyprus, Bosnia, Herzegovina, and an area that became Bulgaria. The Ottomans lost land in Africa, too. By the beginning of World War I, the Ottoman Empire was reduced to a small portion of its former size.

Observing the slow decline of the Ottoman Empire, some Muslim leaders decided that their countries would either have to adjust to the modern world or be consumed by it. Egypt and Persia both initiated political and social reforms, in part to block European domination of their lands.

Egypt Tries Reform Modernization came to Egypt as a result of the interest in the area created by the French Revolution. Egypt's strategic location at the head of the Red Sea appeared valuable to France and Britain. After Napoleon failed to win Egypt, a new leader emerged: Muhammad Ali. The Ottomans sent him to govern

A. Answer If the Ottoman Empire could not keep the Europeans out, they worried they would not be able to keep the Europeans out of their lands either.

THINK THROUGH HISTORY
A. Analyzing Causes Why would the decline of the Ottoman Empire make other Muslim countries try to change?

TEACHING OPTION ◢ **BLOCK SCHEDULING**   **COOPERATIVE ACTIVITY: Debating Issues**   **CLASS TIME 30 MINUTES**

Task: Students will debate the statement: "All countries should have equal access to strategic waterways such as the Suez Canal."

Purpose: To help students understand the history of the Suez Canal from different points of view.

Activity: Students form two groups to debate this question. They should research the history of the

Suez Canal, paying particular attention to the issues of nations' access in the late 1850s to vital waterways, the strategic importance of the canal, the relationships of the nations who use the canal, and the rights of the nation that must oversee and maintain the canal. Each group should designate members as researchers, presenters, coaches, time keepers, and producers of graphic aids. The class can decide which team presents the best case.

 Building a Portfolio: Students may want to write a brief description of this assignment to add to their portfolios.

📃 **ALTERNATIVE ASSESSMENT BOOK**
Standards for Evaluating a Cooperative Activity

Egypt, but he soon broke away from Ottoman control. In 1841, he fought a series of battles in which he gained control of Syria and Arabia. Through the combined efforts of European powers, he and his heirs were recognized as hereditary rulers of Egypt.

Muhammad Ali began a series of reforms in the military and in the economy. He personally directed a shift of Egyptian agriculture to a plantation cash crop—cotton. This brought Egypt into the international marketplace, but at a cost to the peasants. They lost the use of lands they traditionally farmed. They were forced to grow cash crops in place of food crops.

Muhammad Ali's efforts to modernize Egypt were continued by his grandson, Isma'il. Isma'il supported the construction of the **Suez Canal.** The canal was a man-made waterway that cut through the Isthmus of Suez. It connected the Red Sea to the Mediterranean. It was built mainly with French money and Egyptian labor. The Suez Canal was opened in 1869 with a huge international celebration. However, Isma'il's modernization efforts, such as irrigation projects and communication networks, were enormously expensive. Egypt soon found that it could not pay its European bankers even the interest on its $450 million debt. The British insisted on overseeing financial control of the canal, and in 1882 the British occupied Egypt.

British control of the Suez Canal remained an important part of British imperial policy. The canal was viewed as the "Lifeline of the Empire" because it allowed the British quicker access to its colonies in Asia and Africa. A British imperialist, Joseph Chamberlain, presented a speech to Parliament. In it he supported the continued control of the canal:

A VOICE FROM THE PAST
I approve of the continued occupation of Egypt; and for the same reasons I have urged upon this Government, . . . the necessity for using every legitimate opportunity to extend our influence and control in that great African continent which is now being opened up to civilization and to commerce. . . .

JOSEPH CHAMBERLAIN, in a speech, January 22, 1894

Persia Pressured to Change Elsewhere in southwest Asia, Russia and Britain competed to exploit Persia commercially and to bring that country under their own spheres of influence. Russia was especially interested in gaining access to the Persian Gulf and the Indian Ocean. Twice Persia gave up territories to Russia after military defeats in 1813 and 1828. Britain was interested in using Afghanistan as a buffer between India and Russia.

THINK THROUGH HISTORY
B. Recognizing Effects What two effects did raising cotton have on Egyptian agriculture?
B. Answer Brought Egyptians into the international market, reduced production of food crops.

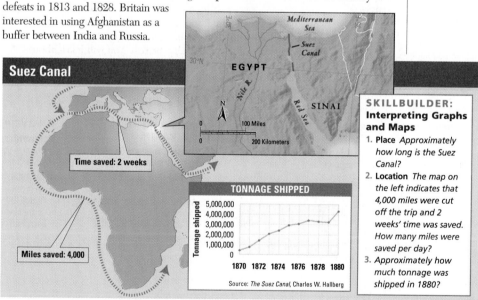

Suez Canal

Time saved: 2 weeks

Miles saved: 4,000

EGYPT

SINAI

Mediterranean Sea

Suez Canal

Nile R.

Red Sea

0   100 Miles

0   200 Kilometers

TONNAGE SHIPPED

Tonnage shipped: 5,000,000 / 4,000,000 / 3,000,000 / 2,000,000 / 1,000,000 / 0

1870 1872 1874 1876 1878 1880

Source: *The Suez Canal,* Charles W. Hallberg

SKILLBUILDER:
Interpreting Graphs and Maps

1. **Place** Approximately how long is the Suez Canal?
2. **Location** The map on the left indicates that 4,000 miles were cut off the trip and 2 weeks' time was saved. How many miles were saved per day?
3. Approximately how much tonnage was shipped in 1880?

The Age of Imperialism **699**

MORE ABOUT . . .
Florence Nightingale
(continued from page 698)

life to tend to the sick and suffering. She was superintendent of a women's hospital in London when the secretary of war asked her to take charge of nursing British wounded in the Crimean War. She saved many lives on the battlefield.

MORE ABOUT . . .
Muhammad Ali

Muhammad Ali's main goal was to turn Egypt into one vast plantation to benefit his family. He changed the tax system to divert benefits from former rulers and for a time held a monopoly over agricultural trade. As a result, his family became extremely wealthy and accumulated large landholdings.

History from Visuals

Suez Canal

Interpreting the Graph and Maps Once a ship is through the canal, how many more miles must it travel to get to the main body of the Red Sea? *About another 200 miles* What was the increase in tonnage shipped between 1872 and 1876? *About 1.5 million tons (1.5 to 3.0 million)*

Extension Activity Have students consult an encyclopedia or almanac to determine current traffic through the Suez Canal.

SKILLBUILDER Answers
1. About 100 miles
2. About 286 miles per day
3. About 4.2 million tons

TEACHING OPTION

CUSTOMIZING FOR SPECIAL NEEDS

CLASS TIME 30 MINUTES

Less Proficient Readers Pair less proficient readers with more able readers and ask them to read the text titled "Europeans Grab Territory" on pages 698–700. Then have the more proficient reader help the less able reader create a chart listing the motives of the Russians, British, and Persians and the actions each group took. Their completed chart might look like the one on the right.

	Motives	Actions
Russia	Wanted access to Persian Gulf and Indian Ocean	Took territories from Persia by force
Britain	Wanted Afghanistan as a barrier between Russia and India	Took Afghanistan by force
Persia	Wanted to raise capital to develop resources	Sold concessions to Europeans

ASSESS & RETEACH

Section 3 Assessment

Have students list the pages in the section where answers to the questions can be found.

 FORMAL ASSESSMENT BOOK
Section Quiz, p. 315

Reteaching Activity
CLASS TIME: 20 MINUTES

Have students reread A Voice from the Past on pages 699 and 700. Ask students to list each speaker's nationality, the tone of each quote, and the values that each speaker expresses. Discuss with them how these quotes clearly show the momentous changes occurring at that time in history.

CLOSE ACTIVITY

CLASS TIME: 25 MINUTES

Recognizing Causes and Effects

Ask different student groups to represent the Ottoman Empire, Egypt, Persia, France, and England. Have the Asian groups explain the cause-and-effect cycle that resulted in their occupation by European powers. Ask the European groups to explain their reasons for seizing control of these lands.

In 1857, Persia resisted British demands but was forced to give up all claims to Afghanistan. Britain's interest in Persia increased greatly after the discovery of oil there in 1908.

Persia lacked the capital to develop its own resources. To raise money and to gain economic prestige, the Persian ruler began granting concessions to Western businesses. Businesses bought the right to operate in a certain area or develop a certain product. For example, a British corporation, the Anglo-Persian Oil Company, began to develop Persia's rich oil fields in the early 1900s.

Tension arose between the often corrupt rulers, who wanted to sell concessions to Europeans, and the people. The people were often backed by religious leaders who feared change or disliked Western influence in their nation. In 1891, Nasir al-Din attempted to sell the rights to export and distribute Persian tobacco to a British company. This action outraged Sayyid Jamal al-Din al-Afghani, a modernist leader, who helped set up a tobacco boycott by the heavy-smoking Persians. In the following quote, he expresses his contempt for the Persian ruler:

Background
Britain needed oil for its ships, which now ran on oil rather than coal. Thus, they needed greater supplies of petroleum.

A VOICE FROM THE PAST
. . . He has sold to the foes of our Faith the greater part of the Persian lands and the profits derived from them, for example . . . tobacco, with the chief centers of its cultivation, the lands on which it is grown and the warehouses, carriers, and sellers, wherever these are found. . . .
In short, this criminal has offered the provinces of Persia to auction among the Powers, and is selling the realms of Islam and the abodes of Muhammad and his household to foreigners.

SAYYID JAMAL AL-DIN AL-AFGHANI, in a letter to Hasan Shirazi, April 1891

The tobacco boycott worked. Riots broke out and the ruler was compelled to cancel the concession. As unrest continued in Persia, the government was unable to control the situation. In 1906, a group of revolutionaries forced the ruler to establish a constitution. In 1907, Russia and Britain took over the country and divided it into spheres of influence.

In the Muslim lands, the European imperialists gained control by using economic imperialism and creating spheres of influence. Although some governments made attempts at modernization, in most cases it was too little too late. In other areas of the globe, imperialists provided the modernization. India, for example, became a colony that experienced massive change as a result of the occupation of the imperialist British. You will learn about India in Section 4.

THINK THROUGH HISTORY
C. Clarifying Why did al-Afghani condemn the actions of the Persian ruler?
C. Possible Answer He sold out the land and the profits from them to foreigners.

Section ❸ Assessment

1. TERMS & NAMES

Identify
• geopolitics
• Crimean War
• Suez Canal

2. TAKING NOTES

Re-create the diagram below and fill in at least three details that support the main idea.

Muslim states failed to keep European imperialists out of their lands.

Detail	Detail	Detail

What imperialistic forms of control did the Europeans use to govern these lands?

3. COMPARING AND CONTRASTING

How were the reactions of African and Muslim rulers to imperialism similar? How were they different?

THINK ABOUT
• African and Muslim patterns of resistance
• African and Muslim efforts toward modernization

4. ANALYZING THEMES

Economics Why did European imperialist powers want to take over Ottoman Empire lands?

THINK ABOUT
• the location of the Ottoman Empire
• its special resources
• European ambitions

ANSWERS

1. TERMS & NAMES
geopolitics, p. 698
Crimean War, p. 698
Suez Canal, p. 699

2. TAKING NOTES
Possible Responses: Ottoman Empire tries to reform but fails; Egyptian leaders cannot complete modernization; Persia falls to economic imperialism. The Europeans used economic imperialism and spheres of influence to govern these lands.

3. COMPARING AND CONTRASTING
Possible Responses: Both African and Muslim rulers resisted Europeans. Muslims tried to modernize to resist Western imperialism, while many Africans simply signed away their lands. Menelik II was the only African ruler to remain independent.

4. ANALYZING THEMES
The Ottoman Empire ruled much of North Africa, the Middle East, and Eastern Europe. It controlled key overland trade routes and sea trade on the Mediterranean and on the Atlantic Ocean and Black Sea. It also contained many important natural resources, such as oil. European nations wanted control trade and to obtain greater wealth.

4 British Imperialism in India

TERMS & NAMES
- sepoy
- "jewel in the crown"
- Sepoy Mutiny
- Raj

MAIN IDEA

As the Mughal Empire declined, Britain seized Indian territory until it controlled almost the whole subcontinent.

WHY IT MATTERS NOW

India, the second most populated nation in the world, has its political roots in this colony.

SETTING THE STAGE British economic interest in India began in the 1600s, when the British East India Company set up trading posts at Bombay, Madras, and Calcutta. At first, India's ruling Mughal Dynasty kept European traders under control. By 1707, however, the Mughal Empire was collapsing. Dozens of small states, each headed by a ruler or maharajah, broke away from Mughal control.

British Expand Control Over India

The East India Company quickly took advantage of the growing weakness of the Mughals. In 1757, Robert Clive led company troops in a decisive victory over Indian forces at the Battle of Plassey. From that time on, the East India Company was the leading power in India. The area controlled by the company grew over time. Eventually, it governed directly or indirectly an area that included modern Bangladesh, most of southern India, and nearly all the territory along the Ganges River in the north.

East India Company Dominates Officially, the British government regulated the East India Company's efforts both in London and in India. Until the beginning of the 19th century, the company ruled India with little interference from the British government. The company even had its own army, led by British officers and staffed by **sepoys,** or Indian soldiers. The governor of Bombay, Mountstuart Elphinstone, referred to the sepoy army as "a delicate and dangerous machine, which a little mismanagement may easily turn against us."

"Jewel in the Crown" Produces Trade Products At first, India was treasured by the British more for its potential than its actual profit. The Industrial Revolution had turned Britain into the world's workshop, and India was a major supplier of raw materials for that workshop. Its 300 million people were also a large potential market for British-made goods. It is not surprising, then, that the British considered India the brightest **"jewel in the crown"** — the most valuable of all of Britain's colonies.

The British set up restrictions that prevented the Indian economy from operating on its own. British policies called for India to produce raw materials for British manufacturing and to buy British finished goods. In addition,

Tea from the Lipton plantation in Darjeeling is loaded onto an elephant for transport to Calcutta.

The Age of Imperialism **701**

Section 4 Overview

OBJECTIVES

1. To summarize the British takeover of India.
2. To identify positive and negative features of British colonialism in India.
3. To describe early nationalist movements in India.

SKILLBUILDERS
- Interpreting maps: region, location, p. 702

CRITICAL THINKING
- Summarizing, p. 702
- Recognizing effects, pp. 703, 704
- Analyzing motives, p. 705
- Analyzing, p. 705
- Analyzing themes, p. 705

FOCUS
5-Minute Warm-Up

▶ *Identifying Main Ideas*
To help students understand nationalism in India, have them answer these questions.

- Read History Makers on page 705. After seeing his sister-in-law killed, what decision did Ram Mohun Roy make?
- How did his decision affect the Indian nationalist movements?

📖 *WARM-UP TRANSPARENCY 27*

OBJECTIVE ① INSTRUCT

British Expand Control Over India

▶ *Key Ideas*
- The East India Company seizes control of most of India.
- Britain considers India its primary colony.
- India benefits and suffers under British colonial rule.

📖 *IN-DEPTH RESOURCES: UNIT 6*
Guided Reading, p. 40

📖 *ACCESS FOR STUDENTS ACQUIRING ENGLISH*
Guided Reading (Spanish), p. 273

SECTION 4 RESOURCES

PRINT RESOURCES

📖 *IN-DEPTH RESOURCES: UNIT 6*
Guided Reading, p. 40
Skillbuilder Practice: Analyzing Assumptions, p. 42
Primary Source: Letter Opposing the English, p. 47

📖 *ACCESS FOR STUDENTS ACQUIRING ENGLISH*
Guided Reading (Spanish), p. 273
Skillbuilder Practice, (Spanish), p. 275

📖 *FORMAL ASSESSMENT*
Section Quiz, p. 316

TECHNOLOGY RESOURCES

🎞 *GEOGRAPHY TRANSPARENCIES*
GT27 India Under British Rule, 1805–1886

🎞 *WORLD ART AND CULTURES TRANSPARENCIES*
AT59 *Raja Ram Singh in Procession*

🎞 *CRITICAL THINKING TRANSPARENCIES*
CT27 Comparing Imperialist Styles, 1850–1900

💿 **CD-ROM**
Electronic Library of Primary Sources

🌐 **INTERNET** www.mlworldhistory.com

Western-held Territories in Asia, 1910

Interpreting the Map Which of the Indian exports listed on the map is the largest amount? The most valuable? *largest—oil seeds; most valuable—cotton*

Extension Activity Based on information provided by the map, ask students to list what features made India the "jewel in the crown" for Great Britain. Have them consider not only resources but also India's strategic location between the Far East, Western Asia, Africa, and the Pacific Islands. What problems might Great Britain have faced trying to trade in the Far East if it had not held India?

SKILLBUILDER Answers
1. Britain
2. India has access to trade with Southeast Asia, East Asia, and Africa.

MORE ABOUT . . .
British Economic Impact on Indian Classes

British economic policies affected Indian classes unequally, although they were supposed to improve the lot of poor farmers. In fact, the only classes to benefit from British rule were the zamindars, or landowners, who leased land to tenant farmers, and the entrepreneurs of Calcutta, who served as agents and bankers to the British. The farmers themselves, called cultivators, remained as poor as ever throughout the period of British rule.

Western-held Territories in Asia, 1910

India's Exports

- jute—765,000 tons in 1909
- wheat—1.3 million tons in 1914
- oilseeds—1.5 million tons in 1913
- tea—192 million pounds in 1900
- cotton—valued at 410 million rupees* in 1913
- hides and skins—valued at 160 million rupees in 1913

*A rupee is the Indian currency.

GEOGRAPHY SKILLBUILDER: Interpreting Maps
1. **Region** Which nation in 1900 held the most land in colonies?
2. **Location** How is the location of India a great advantage for trade?

Indian competition with British finished goods was prohibited. For example, India's own handloom textile industry was almost put out of business by imported British textiles. Cheap cloth and ready-made clothes from England flooded the Indian market and drove out local producers.

India became economically valuable only after the British established a railroad network. Railroads transported raw products from the interior to the ports and manufactured goods back again. The majority of the raw materials were agricultural products produced on plantations. Plantation crops included tea, indigo, coffee, cotton, and jute. Another crop was opium. The British shipped opium to China and exchanged it for tea, which they then sold in England.

Trading these crops was closely tied to international events. For example, the Crimean War in the 1850s cut off the supply of Russian jute to Scottish jute mills. This boosted the export of raw jute from Bengal, a province in India. Likewise, cotton production in India increased when the Civil War in the United States cut off supplies of cotton for British textile mills.

Impact of Colonialism India both benefited from and was oppressed by British colonialism. On the positive side, the laying of the world's third largest railroad network was a major British achievement. When completed, the railroads enabled India to develop a modern economy and brought unity to the connected regions. Along with the railroads, a modern road network, telephone and telegraph lines, dams, bridges, and irrigation canals enabled India to modernize. Sanitation and public health improved. Schools and colleges were founded, and literacy increased. Also, British troops cleared central India of bandits and put an end to local warfare among competing local rulers.

Vocabulary
jute: a fiber used for sacks and cord.

THINK THROUGH HISTORY
A. Summarizing On which continents are Indian goods being traded?
A. Answer Asia and Europe.

702 Chapter 27

TEACHING OPTION | **BLOCK SCHEDULING** | **COOPERATIVE ACTIVITY: Researching the Indian Handloom Industry** | **CLASS TIME 20 MINUTES**

Task: Students will research and write a report on the Indian handloom industry.

Purpose: To help students understand the impact of foreign rule on India.

Activity: Students work in small groups, each group researching a separate topic of the Indian handloom industry: its history, types of textiles

produced, fame in Europe, words added to English (such as *calico* or *chintz*), effect of British competition, return to the handloom as a political statement, comparison with African textiles, and the handloom industry in India today. Each group should write a brief report on its topic, using graphic aids.

Building a Portfolio: Students adding this report to their portfolios should explain the assignment.

 ALTERNATIVE ASSESSMENT BOOK
Standards for Evaluating a Cooperative Activity

Standards for Evaluation
Reports should . . .

- show information from various sources
- make effective use of visual aids
- demonstrate students' knowledge of the subject

On the negative side, the British held much of the political and economic power. The British restricted Indian-owned industries such as cotton textiles. The emphasis on cash crops resulted in a loss of self-sufficiency for many villagers. The conversion to cash crops reduced food production, causing famines in the late 1800s. The British officially adopted a hands-off policy regarding Indian religious and social customs. Even so, the increased presence of missionaries and the outspoken racist attitude of most British officials threatened Indian traditional life.

Indians Rebel

By 1850, the British controlled most of the Indian subcontinent. However, there were many pockets of discontent. Many Indians believed that in addition to controlling their land the British were trying to convert them to Christianity. The Indian people also resented the constant racism that the British expressed toward them.

Sepoy Rebellion As economic problems increased for Indians, so did their feelings of resentment and nationalism. In 1857, gossip spread among the sepoys, the Indian soldiers, that the cartridges of their new Enfield rifles were sealed with beef and pork fat. To use the cartridges, soldiers had to bite off the seal. Both Hindus, who consider the cow sacred, and Muslims, who do not eat pork, were outraged by the news.

A garrison commander was shocked when 85 of the 90 sepoys refused to accept the cartridges. The British handled the crisis badly. The soldiers who had disobeyed were jailed. The next day, on May 10, 1857, the sepoys rebelled. They marched to Delhi, where they were joined by Indian soldiers stationed there. They captured the city of Delhi. From Delhi, the rebellion spread to northern and central India.

Some historians have called this outbreak the **Sepoy Mutiny.** The uprising spread over much of northern India. Fierce fighting took place. Both British and sepoys tried to slaughter each other's armies. The East India Company took more than a year to regain control of the country. The British government sent troops to help them.

The Indians could not unite against the British due to weak leadership and serious splits between Hindus and Muslims. Hindus did not want the Muslim Mughal Empire restored. Indeed, many Hindus preferred British rule to Muslim rule. Most

Daily *Life*

British Army
Social class determined the way of life for the British Army in India. Upper-class men served as officers. Lower-class British served at lesser rank and did not advance past the rank of sergeant. Only men with the rank of sergeant and above were allowed to bring their wives to India.

Each English officer's wife attempted to re-create England in the home setting. Like a general, she directed an army of 20 to 30 servants.

Officers and enlisted men spent much of each day involved in sports such as cricket, polo, and rugby. Athletics were encouraged to keep the men from "drink and idleness." The upper-class officers also spent time socializing at fancy-dress dances, concerts, and after-polo events.

Indian Servants
Caste determined Indian occupations. Jobs were strictly divided by caste. Castes were divided into four broad categories called varna. Indian civil servants were of the third varna. House and personal servants were of the fourth varna.

Even within the varna, jobs were strictly regulated, which is why such large servant staffs were required. For example, in the picture above, although both were of the same varna, the person washing the man's feet was of a different caste than the person doing the fanning.

The social life of the servants centered around religious festivals and ceremonies marking important life passages. These included a child's first haircut, religious initiation, engagement, marriage, or childbirth.

The Age of Imperialism **703**

B. Possible Answer
Yes, he predicted problems with sepoy armies if they were not handled correctly. The mutiny was proof of this.

THINK THROUGH HISTORY
B. Recognizing Effects Look back at Elphinstone's comment on page 701. Did the Sepoy Mutiny prove him correct? Explain your answer.

OBJECTIVE 2 INSTRUCT

Indians Rebel

▶ *Key Ideas*
• Indians object to the racist attitudes of the British rulers.
• The Sepoy Mutiny turns into widespread rebellion.
• The British government takes direct control of India.

📖 *IN-DEPTH RESOURCES: UNIT 6*
Primary Source: Letter Opposing the English, p. 47

💿 *ELECTRONIC LIBRARY OF PRIMARY SOURCES*
"The Rise of the Color Bar"

Daily *Life*
British Army and Indian Servants

Ask students how the daily lives of British army officers differed from the lives of their Indian servants. How were they the same? *Students may point to the British dominance and their enjoyment of greater leisure time. Some students might note that both groups socialized only with their "own kind."*

MORE ABOUT . . .
The Sepoy Mutiny

Hindu and Muslim soldiers jumped to the conclusion that sealing the cartridges with animal fat was a deliberate move by the British to force them to convert to Christianity.

They reasoned that the religious pollution from touching the fat would be so damaging that they would be expelled from their religious groups. With nowhere else to go, the soldiers would have to convert to Christianity. Although the manufacturers of the cartridges sought to correct this mistaken idea, the Indians' distrust of the British deepened.

TEACHING OPTIONS

CONNECTIONS ACROSS THE CURRICULUM

Literature To find out more about the lives of the British and Indians under the Raj, students might wish to read stories and novels about this period in history. For a sympathetic British point of view, they can read the fiction of Rudyard Kipling. For stories from the Indian perspective, they can read Prem Chand (*The Gift of a Cow,* Bloomington, IN: Indiana UP, 1968) or the work of

Rabindranath Tagore (*The Crescent Moon,* New York: Macmillan, 1922). For a picture of Indian village life little changed from life under the Raj, they can read books by R.K. Narayan (*The Grandmother's Tale and Other Stories,* New York: Viking, 1994; *A Tiger for Malgudi,* New York: Viking, 1983).

MULTIPLE LEARNING STYLES

Visual Learners The new art of photography was popular during the time of British rule in India. Refer students to collections of photographs of British India by both European and Indian photographers (such as *The Last Empire: Photography in British India 1855-1911.* Millerton, NY: Aperture, 1976; *Princely India* by Raja Deen Dayal, New York: Knopf, 1980; and *Through Indian*

Eyes by Judith Mara Gutman, New York: Oxford UP, 1982). Ask students to analyze the photographs for information about the social attitudes of the British and the Indians. Each student should write a few paragraphs on a photograph of his or her choice taken in India between 1850 and 1914.

Teacher's Edition **703**

This English engraving shows the British troops defending the Royal Residency at Lucknow against a sepoy attack on July 30, 1857.

of the princes and maharajahs who had made alliances with the East India Company did not take part in the rebellion. The Sikhs, a religious group that had been hostile to the Mughals, also remained loyal to the British. Indeed, from then on, the bearded and turbaned Sikhs became the mainstay of Britain's army in India.

Turning Point The mutiny marked a turning point in Indian history. As a result of the mutiny, in 1858, the British government took direct command of India. The part of India that was under direct British rule was called the Raj. The term **Raj** referred to British rule over India from 1757 until 1947. India was divided into 11 provinces and some 250 districts. Sometimes a handful of officials were the only British among the million or so people in a district. A cabinet minister in London directed policy, and a British governor-general in India carried out the government's orders. After 1877, this official held the title of viceroy. To reward the many princes who had remained loyal to Britain, the British promised to respect all treaties the East India Company had made with them. They also promised that the Indian states that were still free would remain independent. Unofficially, however, Britain won greater and greater control of those states.

The Sepoy Mutiny fueled the racist attitudes of the English. The English attitude is illustrated in the following quote by Lord Kitchener, British commander in chief of the army in India:

> **A VOICE FROM THE PAST**
> It is this consciousness of the inherent superiority of the European which has won for us India. However well educated and clever a native may be, and however brave he may prove himself, I believe that no rank we can bestow on him would cause him to be considered an equal of the British officer.
>
> **LORD KITCHENER,** quoted in K. M. Panikkar, *Asia and Western Dominance*

The mutiny increased distrust between the British and the Indians. A political pamphlet suggested that both Hindus and Muslims "are being ruined under the tyranny and oppression of the . . . treacherous English."

704 Chapter 27

C. Possible Answers More of India was under British control; greater distrust between Indians and the British.

THINK THROUGH HISTORY
C. Recognizing Effects In what ways did the Sepoy Mutiny change the political climate of India?

Indian Nationalist Movements Begin

In the early 1800s, some Indians began demanding more modernization and a greater role in governing themselves. Ram Mohun Roy, a modern-thinking, well-educated Indian, began a campaign to move India away from traditional practices and ideas. Sometimes called the "Father of Modern India," Ram Mohun Roy called for an end to widow suicide, which he believed was a murderous act. He saw child marriages and the rigid caste separation as parts of religious life that needed to be changed to bring India into a more modern frame of mind. He believed that if the practices were not changed, India would continue to be controlled by outsiders. Roy's writings inspired other Indian reformers to call for adoption of Western ways. Roy also founded a social reform movement that worked for change in India.

Besides modernization and westernization, nationalist feelings started to surface in India. Indians resented a system that made them second-class citizens in their own country. Even Indians with a European education faced discrimination. They were barred from top posts in the Indian Civil Service. Those who managed to get middle-level jobs were paid less than Europeans. A British engineer on the East India Railway, for example, made nearly 20 times as much money as an Indian engineer.

A spirit of Indian nationalism led to the founding of two nationalist groups, the Indian National Congress in 1885 and the Muslim League in 1906. At first, such groups concentrated on specific concerns for Indians. Gradually their demands broadened. By the early 1900s, they were calling for self-government.

The nationalists were further inflamed in 1905 by the partition of Bengal. The province, which had a population of 85 million, was too large for administrative purposes. So the British divided it into a Hindu section and a Muslim section. Acts of terrorism broke out. The province was on the edge of open rebellion. In 1911, yielding to the pressure, the British took back the order and divided the province in a different way.

Conflict over the control of India continued to develop between the Indians and the British in the following years. Elsewhere in Southeast Asia, the same struggles for control of land took place between local groups and the major European powers that dominated them. You will learn about them in Section 5.

HISTORY MAKERS

Ram Mohun Roy
1772–1833

An extremely bright student, Ram Mohun Roy learned Persian, Sanskrit, and Arabic as a child. He spent many hours studying the religions of the world to understand people. He also studied the social and political ideas of the American and French revolutions.

Roy watched his sister-in-law burned alive on the funeral pyre of her husband. After that, he resolved to end practices that rooted India to the past. He challenged traditional Hindu culture and called for modernization of Hindu society.

The Hindu reform society he organized, Brahmo Samaj, shaped the thinking of the 19th-century Indian reformers. The society was the forerunner of the Indian nationalist movements.

Section 4 Assessment

1. TERMS & NAMES
Identify
• sepoy
• "jewel in the crown"
• Sepoy Mutiny
• Raj

2. TAKING NOTES
Re-create on your paper the cause-and-effect diagram below and fill in the effects of the three causes listed.

Cause	Effect
1. Decline of the Mughal Empire	
2. Colonial policies	
3. Sepoy Mutiny	

Which of the effects you listed later became causes?

3. ANALYZING
How did imperialism contribute to unity and the growth of nationalism in India?

THINK ABOUT
• the benefits of imperialism
• the negative effects of imperialism

4. ANALYZING THEMES
Empire Building How did economic imperialism lead to India's becoming a British colony?

THINK ABOUT
• the role of the British East India Company
• the Sepoy Mutiny

---

1. To summarize the acquisition of European colonies in Southeast Asia.

2. To describe how Siam remained independent.

3. To summarize U.S. acquisition of the Philippines and Hawaii.

CRITICAL THINKING

• Comparing, p. 706
• Analyzing motives, p. 707
• Recognizing effects, p. 707
• Drawing conclusions, p. 709

FOCUS

5-Minute Warm-Up

▶ **Making Inferences**
By answering these questions, students will understand more about the development of Southeast Asia.

1. Study the picture on page 706. What U.S. city does Singapore remind you of?

2. What influences from European rule does the picture show?

WARM-UP TRANSPARENCY 27

OBJECTIVE 1 INSTRUCT

Western Rivalries for Pacific Rim Lands

▶ **Key Ideas**

• European powers race to claim a part of Southeast Asia for themselves.

• The Dutch East India Company, which controls Indonesia, creates a rigid social hierarchy.

• The British encourage large-scale immigration of the Chinese to Malaysia.

• The French try to impose their culture on their colonies.

IN-DEPTH RESOURCES: UNIT 6
Guided Reading, p. 41

ACCESS FOR STUDENTS ACQUIRING ENGLISH
Guided Reading (Spanish), p. 274

---

5 Western Powers Rule Southeast Asia

TERMS & NAMES
• Pacific Rim
• King Mongkut
• Emilio Aguinald
• annexation
• Queen Liliuokalani

MAIN IDEA
Demand for Asian products drove Western imperialists to seek possession of Southeast Asian lands.

WHY IT MATTERS NOW
Southeast Asian independence struggles in the 20th century have their roots in this period of imperialism.

SETTING THE STAGE Just as the European powers rushed to divide Africa, they also competed to carve up the lands of Southeast Asia. These lands form part of the **Pacific Rim,** the countries that border the Pacific Ocean. Western nations desired the Pacific Rim lands for their strategic location along the sea route to China. Westerners also recognized the value of the Pacific colonies as sources of tropical agriculture, minerals, and oil.

Western Rivalries for Pacific Rim Lands

Early in the 19th century, the Dutch East India Company established control over most of the 3,000-mile-long chain of Indonesian islands. As the European powers began to appreciate the value of the area, they challenged each other for their own parts of the prize. The British established a major trading port at Singapore. The French took over Indochina on the Southeast Asian mainland. The Germans claimed New Guinea and the Marshall and Solomon islands.

Plantation Products Spur Competition The lands of Southeast Asia were perfect for plantation agriculture. The major focus was on sugar cane, coffee, cocoa, rubber, coconuts, bananas, and pineapple. As these products became more important in the world trade markets, European powers raced each other to claim lands.

Dutch Expand Control The Dutch East India Company, chartered in 1602, actively sought lands in Southeast Asia. It seized Melaka from the Portuguese and fought the British and Javanese for control of Java. The discovery of oil and tin on the islands and the desire for more rubber plantations prompted the Dutch to gradually expand their control over Sumatra, Borneo, Celebes, the Moluccas, and Bali. Finally the company ruled the whole island chain of Indonesia, then called the Dutch East Indies.

Management of plantations and trade brought a large Dutch population to the islands. In contrast to the British, who lived temporarily in India but retired in Britain, the Dutch thought of Indonesia as their home. They created a rigid social class system. The Dutch were on top, wealthy and educated Indonesians came next, and plantation workers resided at the bottom. The Dutch also forced farmers to plant one-fifth of their land in specified export crops.

British Take the Malayan Peninsula To compete with the Dutch, the British sought a trading base that would

A. Answer Both were trading companies that practiced economic imperialism

THINK THROUGH HISTORY
A. Comparing How was the Dutch East India Company like the British East India Company?

Traditional-style boats anchor in modern Singapore harbor. High-rise buildings of the 20th century mark Singapore as a major city. Today Singapore is a successful trading nation on the Pacific Rim.

SECTION 5 RESOURCES

PRINT RESOURCES

IN-DEPTH RESOURCES: UNIT 6
Guided Reading, p. 41
Primary Source: In Favor of Imperialism, p. 48
History Makers: Mongkut, p. 53

ACCESS FOR STUDENTS ACQUIRING ENGLISH
Guided Reading (Spanish), p. 274

FORMAL ASSESSMENT
Section Quiz, p. 317

ALTERNATIVE ASSESSMENT BOOK

TECHNOLOGY RESOURCES

CRITICAL THINKING TRANSPARENCIES
CT27 Comparing Imperialist Styles 1850–1900
CT63 Chapter 27 Visual Summary

CD-ROM
Electronic Library of Primary Sources

INTERNET www.mlworldhistory.com

serve as a stop for its ships that traveled the India-China sea routes. They found the ideal location—a large, sheltered harbor—on Singapore, an island just off the tip of the Malay Peninsula. The opening of the Suez Canal and the increased demand for tin and rubber combined to make Singapore one of the world's busiest ports.

Britain also gained colonies in Malaysia and in Burma (modern Myanmar). Malaysia had large deposits of tin and became the world's leading rubber exporter. Upper Burma provided teak, while central Burma exported oil. Needing workers to mine the tin and tap the rubber trees, Britain encouraged Chinese to immigrate to Malaysia. Chinese flocked to the area, and some of them became highly successful in business. As a result of such immigration, the Malays soon became a minority in their own country. Conflict between the resident Chinese and the native Malays remains unresolved today.

THINK THROUGH HISTORY
B. Analyzing Motives Why do you think so many Chinese would move to Malaysia?
B. Possible Answer They were probably in search of jobs due to overcrowding, famine, or political unrest.

French Control Indochina The French had been active in Southeast Asia since the turn of the century. They even helped the Nguyen (nuh·WIN) dynasty rise to power in Vietnam. In the 1840s, during the rule of an anti-Christian Vietnamese emperor, seven French missionaries were killed. Church leaders and capitalists who wanted a larger share of the overseas market demanded military intervention. Emperor Napoleon III ordered the French army to invade southern Vietnam. Later, the French added Laos, Cambodia, and northern Vietnam to the territory. The combined states would eventually be called French Indochina. In 1867, a governor of a Vietnamese state told how overpowering the French were:

A VOICE FROM THE PAST
Now, the French are come, with their powerful weapons of war to cause dissension among us. We are weak against them; our commanders and our soldiers have been vanquished. Each battle adds to our misery. . . . The French have immense warships, filled with soldiers and armed with huge cannons. No one can resist them. They go where they want, the strongest ramparts fall before them.
PHAN THANH GIAN, in a letter to his administrators

The French colonists tried to impose their culture on the Indochinese. Using direct colonial management, the French themselves filled all important positions in the government bureaucracy. They did not encourage local industry. Rice became a major export crop. Four times as much land was devoted to rice production. However, the peasants' consumption of rice decreased because rice was shipped out of the region. Anger over this reduction set the stage for Vietnamese resistance against the French.

C. Possible Answer Economies grew, education and health improved, areas unified but lost local leaders, migration resulted in cultural change.

THINK THROUGH HISTORY
C. Recognizing Effects What changes took place in Southeast Asia as a result of colonial control?

Colonial Impact In Southeast Asia, colonization brought mixed results. Economies grew based on cash crops or goods such as tin and rubber that could be sold on the world market. Roads, harbors, and rail systems linked areas and improved communication and transportation. These improvements were more for the benefit of European business than the local population. However, education, health, and sanitation did improve. Political changes included unification of areas at the cost of weaker local leaders and governments.

Unlike other colonial areas, millions of people from other areas of Asia and the world migrated to work on plantations and in the mines in Southeast Asia. This migration changed the cultural and racial makeup of the area. Southeast Asia became a melting pot of Hindus, Muslims, Christians, and Buddhists. The resulting cultural changes often led to racial and religious clashes that are still seen today.

The Age of Imperialism **707**

Global Impact

Migrating Rubber Plants
The rubber tree is native to the South American tropics. South American Indians first realized its potential and used the sap to make balls and "waterproof" shoes.

At first rubber sap was only a curiosity in Europe. Then American, Scottish, and British inventors discovered ways of processing it. In 1876, an English botanist collected seeds from wild trees in the Amazon rainforest and planted them in Kew Gardens in London. Later, young trees grown from those seeds were taken to Ceylon and the Malay Peninsula to start rubber plantations there.

The invention of automobiles created a huge demand for rubber. Rubber plantations soon mushroomed in Southeast Asia, Africa, and Central and South America.

Global Impact
Migrating Rubber Plants

What advantages might plantation rubber have over wild rubber? *Students' answers might include uniformity of the product, a greater area where it is grown, easier to harvest and market.*

MORE ABOUT . . .
Phan Thanh Gian

When Phan Thanh Gian saw the power of the French warships and cannons, he knew his nation was hopelessly outmatched. He told his countrymen: "It would be as senseless for you to wish to defeat your enemies by force of arms as for a young fawn to attack a tiger." To avoid further bloodshed, he ordered the madarins and war commanders to surrender without fighting.

Grief-stricken at delivering his country into French hands, Phan committed suicide. He left behind a letter to his district administrators and to the emperor, explaining why he took his own life.

TEACHING OPTIONS
CONNECTIONS ACROSS THE CURRICULUM

Science: Southeast Asian Crops Have students research why Southeast Asian lands are suitable for plantation economy. Students should describe the soil, climate, growing seasons, and agricultural traditions of the area. They can find information in books on Southeast Asia and on world farming methods.

They might prepare a booklet of plants most suitable for cash crops. The booklet could include illustrations of the plants, their places of origin, climate and soil conditions required, and product uses in the world market.

CONNECTIONS ACROSS THE CURRICULUM

Mathematics: Population Percentages Have students research the percentage of Chinese and Indians in Singapore and Malaysia, according to the latest census information they can find. Ask them to create a graph illustrating the percentage of total population each group represents. Students will find up-to-date information in the *Statesman's Yearbook* and the *Britannica Book of the Year.* Have students who are good in math help those who are less proficient. Caution students that when comparing countries, they should try to get statistics from the same census year for each country.

Teacher's Edition **707**

OBJECTIVE ② INSTRUCT

Siam Maintains Independence

► Key Ideas
- Siam remains independent by becoming a neutral zone between France and Britain.
- Siam escapes the effects of colonization by modernizing itself.

 IN-DEPTH RESOURCES: UNIT 6
History Makers: Mongkut, p. 53

OBJECTIVE ③ INSTRUCT

U.S. Acquires Pacific Islands

► Key Ideas
- Americans disagree about colonizing other countries, but economic interests spur U.S. imperialism.
- The United States defeats Spain and Filipino nationalists to acquire the Philippine Islands but promises early self-rule.
- U.S. businesses promote cash crops over food crops in the Philippines and Hawaii.
- U.S. companies overthrow the Hawaiian queen and establish a republic, which is annexed to the United States.

 ELECTRONIC LIBRARY OF PRIMARY SOURCES
from *Hawaii's Story by Hawaii's Queen*

 CRITICAL THINKING TRANSPARENCIES
CT27 Comparing Imperialist Styles, 1850–1900

Siam Maintains Independence

While its neighbors on all sides fell under the control of imperialists, Siam (present-day Thailand) maintained its independence throughout the colonial period. Siam lay between British-controlled Burma and French Indochina. (See map on page 702.) France and Britain both aimed to prevent the other from gaining control of Siam. Knowing this, Siamese kings skillfully promoted Siam as a neutral zone between the two powers.

Siam modernized itself under the guidance of **King Mongkut** and his son Chulalongkorn. In a royal proclamation, King Chulalongkorn showed his understanding of the importance of progress:

> ### A VOICE FROM THE PAST
> As the times and the course of things in our country have changed, it is essential to promote the advancement of all our academic and technical knowledge and to prevent it from succumbing [giving in] to competition from the outside. In order to achieve this, it is imperative to make haste in education so that knowledge and ability will increase.
> **KING CHULALONGKORN,** "Royal Proclamation in Education"

To accomplish the changes, Siam started schools, reformed the legal system, and reorganized the government. The government built its own railroads and telegraph systems and ended slavery. Because the changes came from their own government, the Siamese people escaped the social turmoil, racist treatment, and economic exploitation that occurred in other countries controlled by foreigners.

U.S. Acquires Pacific Islands

Because they fought for their independence from Britain, most Americans disliked the idea of colonizing other nations. However, two groups of Americans were outspoken in their support of imperialism. One group of ambitious empire-builders felt the United States should fulfill its destiny as a world power, colonizing like the Europeans. The other group, business interests, welcomed the opening of new markets and trade possibilities. Beginning in 1898, the United States began to acquire territory and to establish trading posts in the Pacific.

The Philippines Change Hands The United States acquired the Philippine Islands, Puerto Rico, and Guam as a result of the Spanish-American War in 1898. Gaining the Philippines touched off a debate in the United States over imperialism. President McKinley's views swayed many to his side. He told a group of Methodist ministers that he had concluded "that there was nothing left for us to do but to take them all [the Philippine Islands], and to educate Filipinos, and uplift and Christianize them."

Filipino nationalists who had already been fighting with the Spanish were not happy to trade one colonizer for another. **Emilio Aguinaldo** (eh·MEE·lyoh AH·gee·NAHL·doh), leader of the Filipino nationalists, claimed that the United States had promised immediate independence after the Spanish-American War ended. The nationalists declared independence and the establishment of the Philippine Republic.

The United States immediately plunged into a fierce struggle with the Filipino nationalists and defeated them in 1902. The United States promised the Philippine people that it would prepare them for self-rule. To achieve this goal, the United States provided many benefits to the islands. It built roads, railroads, and hospitals, and set up school systems. However, American businesses exploited the Philippines

Background
Siam was named Thailand in 1939.

The progressive Siamese King Mongkut ruled from 1851 to 1868. During his reign he modernized his land and prevented the British and French from taking over.

Vocabulary
Filipino: an inhabitant of the Philippine Islands

COOPERATIVE ACTIVITY: Creating a News Report

CLASS TIME 25 MINUTES

Task: Students will research, write, and perform a news report on the overthrow of Queen Liliuokalani.

Purpose: To help students empathize with people of another time and place.

Activity: Students work in three groups to research the confrontation between the queen and the committee of U.S. businessmen. Each group will

write and perform a brief news report of one of the following: (1) the queen's refusal to renew the treaty, (2) the overthrow and imprisonment of the queen, or (3) the swearing in of Dole. Students should select two anchorpeople, reporters on the scene, and the principal characters from their groups.

Building a Portfolio: Students adding scripts to their portfolios should explain the assignment.

ALTERNATIVE ASSESSMENT BOOK
Standards for Evaluating a Cooperative Activity

Standards for Evaluation
News reports should . . .
- clearly present the facts of the story
- reflect the opinions and attitudes of both sides
- present information in a lively, dramatic manner

economically. As with other Southeast Asian areas, businessmen encouraged growing cash crops such as sugar at the expense of basic food crops.

Hawaii Becomes a Republic U.S. interest in Hawaii began around the 1790s when Hawaii was a port on the way to China and East India. Beginning about the 1820s, sugar trade began to change the Hawaiian economy. Americans established sugar-cane plantations and became so successful that they imported laborers from China, Japan, and Portugal. By the mid-19th century, American sugar plantations accounted for 75 percent of Hawaii's wealth. At the same time, American sugar planters also gained great political power in Hawaii.

Then in 1890, the McKinley Tariff Act passed by the U.S. government set off a crisis in the islands. The act eliminated the tariffs on all sugar entering the United States. Now, sugar from Hawaii was no longer cheaper than sugar produced elsewhere. That change cut into the sugar producers' profits. Some U.S. business leaders pushed for **annexation** of Hawaii, or the adding of the territory to the United States. Making Hawaii a part of the United States meant that Hawaiian sugar could be sold for greater profits because American producers got an extra two cents a pound from the U.S. government.

About the same time, the new Hawaiian ruler, **Queen Liliuokalani** (luh·LEE·uh·oh·kuh·LAH·nee), took the throne. In 1893, she called for a new constitution that would increase her power. It would also restore the political power of Hawaiians at the expense of wealthy planters. To prevent this from happening, a group of American businessmen hatched a plot to overthrow the Hawaiian monarchy. In 1893, Queen Liliuokalani was removed from power.

Background
President McKinley, who had strong imperialist feelings, came to office in 1897 and encouraged annexation of Hawaii.

In 1894, Sanford B. Dole, a wealthy plantation owner, was named president of the new Republic of Hawaii. The president of the new republic asked the United States to annex it. Acting on the findings of a commission sent to the islands, President Cleveland refused. However, about five years later, in 1898, the Republic of Hawaii was annexed by the United States.

The period of imperialism was a time of great power and domination of others by mostly European powers. As the 19th century closed, the lands of the world were all claimed. The European powers now faced each other with competing claims. Their battles with each other would become the focus of the 20th century.

HISTORY MAKERS

**Queen Liliuokalani
1838–1917**

Liliuokalani was Hawaii's only queen and the last monarch of Hawaii. At the death of her younger brother, she became next in line for the throne. In 1891, she took that throne after the death of her older brother.

Liliuokalani bitterly regretted her brother's loss of power to American planters. She worked to regain power for the Hawaiian monarchy. As queen she refused to renew a treaty signed by her brother that would have given commercial privileges to foreign businessmen. It was a decision that would cost her the crown.

In 1895, she was forced to give up power. However, she continued to oppose the annexation of Hawaii by the United States as a part of the Oni pa'a (Stand Firm) movement.

Section 5 Assessment

1. TERMS & NAMES

Identify
- Pacific Rim
- King Mongkut
- Emilio Aguinaldo
- annexation
- Queen Liliuokalani

2. TAKING NOTES

Re-create on your paper the spider map below. In each circle, identify a Western power and the areas it controlled.

Western powers in Southeast Asia

3. DRAWING CONCLUSIONS

How did the reforms of the Siamese kings maintain Siam's independence?

THINK ABOUT
- what was happening to Siam's neighbors
- the results of the changes

4. THEME ACTIVITY

Empire Building Compose a series of letters to the editor expressing different views on the overthrow of the Hawaiian queen. Include both the Hawaiian and American views on this event.

HISTORY MAKERS
Queen Liliuokalani

The queen received a modern education and toured the Western world before taking the throne. A talented musician, she is best known for her song "Aloha Oe," the national song of farewell in Hawaii. She worked diligently to preserve Hawaiian culture.

ASSESS & RETEACH

Section 5 Assessment

Have students list the pages in the section on which the answers to the questions can be found.

 FORMAL ASSESSMENT BOOK
Section Quiz, p. 317

Reteaching Activity

CLASS TIME: 20 MINUTES

Hand out copies of the primary source for this section. Ask volunteers to read sections of the speech. List what the speaker wanted the United States to do. Then have students identify which of these goals the country accomplished, as described in this section.

 IN-DEPTH RESOURCES: UNIT 6
Primary Source: In Favor of Imperialism, p. 48

CRITICAL THINKING TRANSPARENCIES
CT63 Chapter 27 Visual Summary

CLOSE ACTIVITY

CLASS TIME: 25 MINUTES

Categorizing

Work with the class to complete a chart that lists the countries of Southeast Asia studied, the Western nation(s) that controlled each one, the country's chief products, and the positive and negative results of colonization.

ANSWERS

1. TERMS & NAMES

Pacific Rim, p. 706

King Mongkut, p. 708

Emilio Aguinaldo, p. 708

annexation, p. 709

Queen Liliuokalani, p. 709

2. TAKING NOTES

Dutch-Indonesia; British-Malayan Peninsula; French-Indochina; United States-Hawaii/Philippines

3. DRAWING CONCLUSIONS

Possible Responses: Siam's neighbors were dominated or taken over by European nations. Siam was able to stay independent because it modernized and could compete with Europeans. There was little social turmoil in Siam, and the king was able to stay in power and resist European demands.

4. THEME ACTIVITY

Standards for Evaluation:
The letters should meet the following criteria:
- Reflect accurate information about the topic.
- Present at least two viewpoints with supporting details.
- Be free from errors in spelling and grammar.

Chapter 27 Assessment

TERMS & NAMES

1. imperialism, p. 686
2. racism, p. 686
3. Berlin Conference 1884–1885, p. 687
4. paternalism, p. 691
5. Menelik II, 694
6. geopolitics, 698
7. Suez Canal, p. 699
8. "jewel in the crown," p. 701
9. Raj, p. 704
10. Queen Liliuokalani, p. 709

REVIEW QUESTIONS

Answers will vary.

11. The four motives were nationalism, economic competition, racism, and missionary impulse.

12. During the Boer War, many Africans lost their lives, had their crops destroyed, and their lands burned. The survivors were placed under European rule.

13. The most common forms of imperial rule were colonies, protectorates, spheres of influence, and economic imperialism.

14. Ethiopia resisted European rule largely because of the leadership of Emperor Menelik II. He played the Italians, the French, and the British against each other; bought a large arsenal of modern weapons from France and Russia; discovered flaws in a treaty with the Italians; and defeated the Italian troops.

15. The location of the lands made them attractive for trading purposes, as did the resources found on the lands.

16. The Muslim leaders tried reforms, modernization, and resistance; none of these methods worked.

17. The British used India as a market for manufactured goods, which drove native industries out of business. The British also diverted land to grow cash crops instead of food crops. India's natural resources, instead of being used to develop native industries, were exported to Great Britain.

18. The Sepoy Mutiny began when the sepoys heard a rumor that their new cartridges were sealed with beef and pork fat. The soldiers had to bite off the seal to use the cartridge. This offended both the Muslims, who did not eat pork, and the Hindus, who considered the cow sacred. The Sepoys viewed this incident as a British attempt to force their religion and culture on the Indians.

TERMS & NAMES

Briefly explain the importance of each of the following to the imperialism of 1850–1914.

1. imperialism
2. racism
3. Berlin Conference 1884–1885
4. paternalism
5. Menelik II
6. geopolitics
7. Suez Canal
8. "jewel in the crown"
9. Raj
10. Queen Liliuokalani

Interact *with* History

Make a chart showing the advantages and disadvantages to a local person living in a place that became a European colony. Next make a similar chart for a European living in a foreign place. How do they compare? Discuss with members of your class a way to decide whether the advantages outweigh the disadvantages for each group.

REVIEW QUESTIONS

SECTION 1 *(pages 685–689)*
Imperialists Divide Africa

11. What motives caused the nations of Europe to engage in imperialist activities?

12. What effect did the Boer War have on Africans?

SECTION 2 *(pages 690–695)*
Patterns of Change: Imperialism
Case Study: Nigeria

13. What are the forms of imperial rule?

14. How did Ethiopia resist European rule so successfully?

SECTION 3 *(pages 697–700)*
Muslim Lands Fall to Imperialist Demands

15. Why did the European nations have an interest in controlling the Muslim lands?

16. What methods did the Muslim leaders use to try to prevent European imperialism?

SECTION 4 *(pages 701–705)*
British Imperialism in India

17. How was the economy of India transformed by the British?

18. What caused the Sepoy Mutiny?

SECTION 5 *(pages 706–709)*
Western Powers Rule Southeast Asia

19. How did Siam manage to remain independent when others countries in the area were colonized?

20. Describe the attitudes held by Americans about colonizing other lands.

Visual Summary

The New Imperialism, 1850–1914

CAUSES

Nationalism
To gain power, European nations compete for colonies and trade.

Economic Competition
Demand for raw materials and new markets spurs a search for colonies.

Missionary Spirit
Europeans believe they must spread their Christian teachings to the world.

IMPERIALISM
Europeans exerted influence over the economic, political, and social lives of people they colonized.

EFFECTS

Colonization
Europeans control land and people in areas of Africa, Asia, and Latin America.

Colonial Economics
Europeans control trade in the colonies and set up dependent cash-crop economies.

Christianization
Christianity is spread to Africa, India, and Asia.

710 Chapter 27

19. The King of Siam played Britain and France against each other to make Siam a buffer zone between them. He and his descendants made great efforts to modernize Siam.

20. Some Americans wanted to join the Europeans in imperialist activities. Others thought imperialism violated the ideals of democracy.

Interact *with* History

Possible Responses: *Local person: Advantages:* Modern technology, education, medical care, and unified control of area. *Disadvantages:* Racism, economic imperialism, loss of freedom and control of land and culture. *European: Advantages:* New opportunities for wealth, travel, advancement. *Disadvantages:* Distance from family, strange climate and people, new diseases, potentially hostile population

CRITICAL THINKING

1. SUEZ CANAL

THEME ECONOMICS Why did the British view the Suez Canal as the lifeline of their empire?

2. RESISTANCE TO IMPERIALISM

Re-create on your paper the diagram below. For each geographic area, tell how the local people resisted the demands of the Europeans.

Africa	Muslim Lands	India	Southeast Asia

3. ECONOMIC EFFECTS OF IMPERIALISM ON COLONIES

How did imperialism alter the economic life of the lands Europeans colonized?

4. ANALYZING PRIMARY SOURCES

The following quotation is from Kwaku Dua III, king of the Asante people. He was being pressured by the British government to allow his kingdom to become a protectorate of Britain. Read the quotation and answer the questions below it.

> **A VOICE FROM THE PAST**
> The suggestion that Ashanti [Asante] in its present state should come and enjoy the protection of Her Majesty the Queen and Empress of India, I may say this is a matter of serious consideration, and which I am happy to say we have arrived at the conclusion, that my kingdom of Ashanti will never commit itself to any such conclusion, that Ashanti must remain independent as of old, at the same time to remain friendly with all white men. I do not write this with a boastful spirit, but in the clear sense of its meaning. Ashanti is an independent kingdom.
>
> **KWAKU DUA III** to Frederic M. Hodgson, December 27, 1889

- Briefly, what is Kwaku Dua III's answer to the queen?
- Why do you think Kwaku Dua III responded that he wanted to remain friendly to white men?
- What aspects of the response would lead you to believe that Kwaku Dua III did not feel inferior to the Queen of England?

CHAPTER ACTIVITIES

1. LIVING HISTORY: Unit Portfolio Project

THEME EMPIRE BUILDING Your unit portfolio project focuses on empire-building in lands around the globe by Western powers during the late 1800s and early 1900s (see page 629). For Chapter 27, you might use one of the following ideas to add to your portfolio:

- Imagine that it is 1899 and you are hosting a debate on the United States' takeover of the Philippine Islands. Your guests will be William McKinley and Emilio Aguinaldo. Prepare a script that includes at least five questions you will ask each of them and their possible responses.
- Write a series of diary entries or a poem from the point of view of a person in a land colonized by Europeans. Write a brief opening describing where you live and from what country the colonizers have come.

INTERNET Using the Internet, magazines, and books, collect at least four articles or illustrations with references to remaining imperialist influence in the countries discussed in this chapter. For example, you might find a Manila street with an American name or a picture of a French store in Hanoi. Mount the materials on a page and write a paragraph at the bottom that explains the imperialist connection.

2. CONNECT TO TODAY: Cooperative Learning

THEME POWER AND AUTHORITY Problems that continue to plague Africa today often have their roots in imperialism. Divide into small groups and choose one of the following countries: Somalia, Republic of South Africa, Angola, Democratic Republic of Congo (Zaire), Nigeria, and Chad. Research the country's history from colonialism to the present. Prepare a report on the history of the colony, including how imperialism has continued to affect life there.

3. INTERPRETING A TIME LINE

Revisit the unit time line on pages 628–629. Look at the Chapter 27 section. Name two events that occurred in Europe between 1850 and 1914 that demonstrated the growth of nationalism, which was one of the forces driving imperialism.

FOCUS ON GEOGRAPHY

Where the Sun Never Set
"The sun never sets on the British Empire" was a saying about the British Empire at the peak of its power.

- From the map below, what does this saying mean?
- Which British colony is also a continent?

Connect to History
Explain how such a small nation as Britain could gain such a large empire.

The Age of Imperialism **711**

CRITICAL THINKING

1. SUEZ CANAL
Without the Suez Canal, the British would have had to travel around the west coast of Africa to reach many of their colonies.

2. RESISTANCE TO IMPERIALISM
Africa—armed resistance all over the continent; Muslim Lands—attempts at modernization and reform; India—armed rebellion and formation of nationalist parties; Southeast Asia—armed resistance in some areas, modernization in others

3. ECONOMIC EFFECTS OF IMPERIALISM ON COLONIES
Production patterns of the colonies changed from subsistence crops to cash crops that would sell on the world market. Colonies had to buy European finished goods, which reduced production of local goods. Transportation and communication systems benefited Europeans, not the colonials.

4. ANALYZING PRIMARY SOURCES
- He refused her offer.
- He probably knew he could not completely resist the British and was trying to be diplomatic.
- He addressed the queen as an equal and stressed his country's independence.

CHAPTER ACTIVITIES

1. LIVING HISTORY

Standards for Evaluation
Scripts should meet these criteria:

- Present questions that require President McKinley to justify his actions.
- Present questions that allow Emilio Aguinaldo to discuss international law and human rights issues.
- Show responses that plausibly represent the stand of each man.

Standards for Evaluation
Diary entries or poems should meet the following criteria:

- Identify the person writing and his or her country.
- Present details about the effects of colonialism.
- Express strong feelings about colonialism and its effects.

Standards for Evaluation
Graphic examples and written paragraphs should meet the following criteria:

- Present clear images of remaining colonial influences.
- Clearly explain the imperialist connection between the past and present.

2. CONNECT TO TODAY: COOPERATIVE LEARNING

Standards for Evaluation
Reports should meet the following criteria:

- Accurately describe colonial and post-colonial conditions.
- Show the long-term effects of colonialism on the country.

3. INTERPRETING A TIME LINE

The Crimean War occurred because Russia wanted to gain lands from the Ottoman Empire. The Berlin Conference 1884–1885 reflected the intense rivalry for overseas colonies that nationalism inspired.

FOCUS ON GEOGRAPHY

- Because Britain had colonies around the world, the sun would always be shining on one of the colonies as the earth revolved.
- Australia

Connect to History: *Possible response:* Britain possessed a superior navy, a private imperialist arm in the British East India Company, the latest technology, and an unshakable belief that it was destined to spread British culture throughout the world.

CHAPTER 28

Transformations Around the Globe

	Key Ideas	COPY MASTERS	ASSESSMENT

SECTION 1
China Responds to Pressure from the West
pp. 715–719

China clings to its ancient traditions and self-sufficiency, but eventually succumbs to both external pressure from Western powers and internal population and governmental pressures.

 In-Depth Resources: Unit 6
- **Guided Reading,** p. 55
- **Geography Application:** The Opium Wars, p. 60.
- **Primary Source:** from Letter to Queen Victoria, p. 62
- **History Makers:** Cixi, p. 69

 Section 1 Assessment, p. 719
Formal Assessment
- Section Quiz, p. 326

Alternative Assessment Book
- Standards for Evaluating a Cooperative Activity

SECTION 2
Japan Modernizes
pp. 720–723

Japan also faces pressures from Western nations, but, unlike China, it begins to modernize rapidly. It also emulates the Western imperialistic model and annexes Korea.

In-Depth Resources: Unit 6
- **Guided Reading,** p. 56
- **Primary Source:** from *The Autobiography of Yukichi Fukuzawa,* p. 63

Section 2 Assessment, p. 723
Formal Assessment
- Section Quiz, p. 327

Alternative Assessment Book
- Standards for Evaluating a Cooperative Activity

SECTION 3
U.S. Economic Imperialism in Latin America
pp. 724–728

With its colonial legacy and political instability, Latin America remains economically underdeveloped after independence. In the late 1800s, the United States begins to exert great economic and political influence in Latin America.

In-Depth Resources: Unit 6
- **Guided Reading,** p. 57
- **Primary Source:** Building the Panama Canal, p. 64
- **Connections Across Time and Cultures:** Responses to Western Pressure, p. 71
- **Science and Technology:** Technology Revolutionizes Communications, p. 72

Section 3 Assessment, p. 727
Formal Assessment
- Section Quiz, p. 328

Alternative Assessment Book
- Standards for Evaluating a Product or Performance

SECTION 4
The Mexican Revolution
pp. 729–733

After territorial struggles with the United States, Mexico fights to achieve independence from France. It remains politically unstable, however, under the rule of military dictators. In the early 1900s, economic and political inequality incite the Mexican people to rebel.

In-Depth Resources: Unit 6
- **Guided Reading,** p. 58
- **Skillbuilder Practice:** Identifying Problems, p. 59
- **Primary Source:** from The Plan of Ayala, p. 65
- **Literature:** from *Tom Mix and Pancho Villa,* p. 66
- **History Makers:** Porfirio Díaz, p. 70

Section 4 Assessment, p. 733
Formal Assessment
- Section Quiz, p. 329

Alternative Assessment Book
- Standards for Evaluating a Cooperative Activity

CHAPTER RESOURCES

Chapter Overview

Countries in East Asia and Latin America respond to Western imperialism in different ways. China and Japan try to modernize. Latin America becomes dependent on exports and foreign investments. Mexico fights for independence and political stability.

 Telescoping the Times
- Chapter Summary, pp. 109–111

Planning for Block Schedules

Chapter Assessment, pp. 734–735
Chapter Activities, p. 735

Formal Assessment
- Chapter Test, forms A and B, pp. 330–335

 Test Generator

Alternative Assessment Book

TECHNOLOGY

Warm-Up Transparency 28

World Art and Cultures Transparencies
- AT60 Sorting of Cocoons (Chinese book illustration)

Electronic Library of Primary Sources
- from *Two Years in the Forbidden City*

INTERNET RESOURCES
www.mlworldhistory.com

Warm-Up Transparency 28

Geography Transparencies
- GT28 Japanese Imperialism, 1875–1910

World Art and Cultures Transparencies
- AT61 *Japanese Girl in Western Dress*

Electronic Library of Primary Sources
- from *Fifty Years of New Japan*

INTERNET RESOURCES
www.mlworldhistory.com

Warm-Up Transparency 28

Critical Thinking Transparencies
- CT28 Patterns of Resistance, 1830–1914

Electronic Library of Primary Sources
- from *The Rough Riders*

INTERNET RESOURCES
www.mlworldhistory.com

Warm-Up Transparency 28

Critical Thinking Transparencies
- CT64 Chapter 28 Visual Summary

World Art and Cultures Transparencies
- AT62 *Distribution of the Land*

Electronic Library of Primary Sources
- "Alamo Massacre"

INTERNET RESOURCES
www.mlworldhistory.com

Chapter Summaries on Audiocassette in English and Spanish

INTERNET RESOURCES
www.mlworldhistory.com

Block Scheduling (90 MINUTES)

Day 1

Section 1, pp. 715–719

 COOPERATIVE ACTIVITY
Debating Reform, p. 718 (Teacher's Edition)

Section 2, pp. 720–723

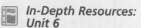 **COOPERATIVE ACTIVITY**
Creating an Itinerary, p. 722 (Teacher's Edition)

Section Assessments, pp. 719, 723

Day 2

Section 3, pp. 724–728

Section 4, pp. 729–733

 COOPERATIVE ACTIVITY
Making a Mural, p. 732 (Teacher's Edition)

Section Assessments, pp. 727, 733

Chapter Assessment, pp. 734–735

Yearly Pacing *Chapter 28 Total:* 2 days *Yearly Total:* 85 days

Planning for Block Schedules

Customizing for Special Needs

Students Acquiring English

Access for Students Acquiring English
- **Guided Reading** for Sections 1–4 (Spanish), pp. 281–284
- **Chapter Summary** (Spanish), pp. 278–280
- **Skillbuilder Practice** Identifying Problems (Spanish), p. 285
- **Geography Application** The Opium Wars (Spanish), p. 286

 Chapter Summaries on Audiocassette in English and Spanish

INTERNET RESOURCES
www.mlworldhistory.com
The Diverse Classroom.

Less Proficient Readers

In-Depth Resources: Unit 6
- **Guided Reading** for Sections 1–4, pp. 55–58
- **Skillbuilder Practice** Identifying Problems, p. 59
- **Geography Application** The Opium Wars, p. 60

Telescoping the Times
- Chapter Summary, pp. 109–111

 Chapter Summaries on Audiocassette

Gifted and Talented Students

In-Depth Resources: Unit 6

Primary Sources
- from Letter to Queen Victoria, p. 62
- from *The Autobiography of Yukichi Fukuzawa*, p. 63
- Building the Panama Canal, p. 64
- from The Plan of Ayala, p. 65

History Makers
- Cixi, p. 69
- Porfirio Díaz, p. 70

Connections to Literature READINGS FOR STUDENTS

In-Depth Resources: Unit 6
Literature: from *Tom Mix and Pancho Villa*, p. 66

Enrichment Reading
- Paterson, Katherine
Rebels of the Heavenly Kingdom
New York: Lodestar Books, 1983

In this story a Chinese peasant boy is kidnapped by bandits during the Taiping Rebellion.

McDougal Littell
Literature Connections

- Azuela, Mariano
The Underdogs
(with related readings)

Set during the aftermath of the Mexican Revolution in 1910, this is the story of Demetrio Macias, who has a ranch near the chaos and corruption of the revolutionary struggle.

 = Pupil's Edition   = Overhead Transparency   = Software   = Video

 = Copy Master   = CD-ROM = Audiocassette = Internet

Transformations Around the Globe, 1800–1914

Predicting

• From reading the section titles and looking at the images and captions, what kinds of global transformations do students expect to learn about in the chapter?

Accessing Prior Knowledge

• Ask students to recall what they have already learned about the history of China's and Japan's relationships with the outside world.

• What can students say about Latin American countries' struggles for independence from colonial rule?

Geography Connection

Have students study the map.

• Which countries are highlighted?

• Which two countries might find themselves in conflict over Korea?

CHAPTER 28 — Transformations Around the Globe, 1800–1914

PREVIEWING THEMES

Empire Building
During the 19th and early 20th centuries, many Western nations sought influence over other countries. Great Britain, additional European countries, and the United States tried to dominate various nations both politically and economically.

Cultural Interaction
Imperialism brought new religions, philosophies, and technological innovations to East Asia and Latin America. Chinese, Japanese, and Latin American people resisted some Western ideas and adapted others.

Revolution
As the world took the first steps toward becoming a global community, political and social unrest were common. Both China and Japan struggled to deal with foreign influence and modernize their governments. Mexicans staged a revolution that brought political and economic reforms.

INTERNET CONNECTION

Visit us at **www.mlworldhistory.com** to learn more about worldwide changes during the 19th and early 20th centuries.

A WORLD IN TURMOIL, 1850–1914

Rebel Mexican girls called *soldaderas* armed themselves with rifles and bullets to fight in their country's civil war in the early **1900s**. *Soldaderas* such as this one followed the troops of revolutionary leader Victoriano Huerta.

Map labels: Hudson Bay, CANADA, UNITED STATES OF AMERICA, Gulf of Mexico, MEXICO, BRITISH HONDURAS, GUATEMALA, EL SALVADOR, HONDURAS, COSTA RICA, PANAMA, DOMINICAN REPUBLIC, HAITI, PUERTO RICO, CUBA, JAMAICA, NICARAGUA, Caribbean Sea, VENEZUELA, COLOMBIA, FRENCH GUIANA, DUTCH GUIANA, BRITISH GUIANA, ECUADOR, BRAZIL, PERU, BOLIVIA, PACIFIC OCEAN, PARAGUAY, Tropic of Capricorn, CHILE, URUGUAY, ARGENTINA, ATLANTIC OCEAN

0 1,000 Miles
0 2,000 Kilometers

712

GEOGRAPHY THEMES

Region

Ask students to locate China, Mongolia, Manchuria, Korea, and Japan on the map. Point out that this region—the Far East—had maintained very little contact with the West before the 1800s. Ask students why this might have been so. *distance and differences in cultures*

Then have students locate Mexico, Central America, and South America. Ask them to suggest why this region is often called Latin America. *The first European colonists spoke either Spanish or Portuguese—languages that are closely related to Latin.* Encourage students to discuss similarities and differences between the Far East and Latin America.

Human/Environment Interaction

Ask students to use this map and the map on page 725 to identify some of the main resources of China, Japan, Mexico, and Latin America. Encourage them to consider geographic resources, such as good ports, navigable rivers, and oceans.

Tell students that political instability led to violent conflict in many of the countries they will study in this chapter. Ask what effects war might have had on the land and its resources. Have them discuss how these changes might have affected the economies of these countries.

ADDITIONAL RESOURCES

Books for the Teacher

• Spence, Jonathan D. *The Search for Modern China.* New York: Norton, 1990.

• Burns, E. Bradford. *Latin America: A Concise Interpretive History.* Englewood Cliffs, N.J.: Prentice, 1994.

Books for the Student

• Blumberg, Rhoda. *Commodore Perry in the Land of the Shogun.* New York: Lothrop, 1985. The United States pressures Japan to open its markets.

• Brown, Charles H. *Agents of Manifest Destiny: The Lives and Times of the Filibusters.* Chapel Hill: U North Carolina P, 1980. Expanding U.S. interests in Latin America.

Videos

• *The Battle of Tsushima—1905 A.D.* Ambrose Video, 1995. 800-526-4663. Japanese victory over Russia changes the balance of power in Asia.

• *China: The Mandate of Heaven.* Social Studies School Service, 1991. 800-421-4246. Chinese civilization—core values and cross-cultural influences.

• *Pancho Villa.* Society for Visual Education, 1994. 800-829-1900.

Software

• *History and Culture of Mexico.* CD-ROM. Queue, 1997. 800-232-2224.

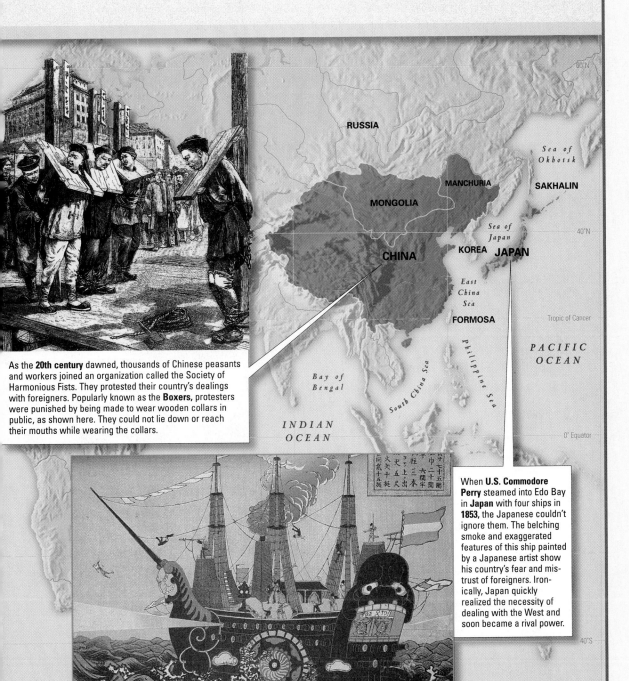

As the **20th century** dawned, thousands of Chinese peasants and workers joined an organization called the Society of Harmonious Fists. They protested their country's dealings with foreigners. Popularly known as the **Boxers**, protesters were punished by being made to wear wooden collars in public, as shown here. They could not lie down or reach their mouths while wearing the collars.

When **U.S. Commodore Perry** steamed into Edo Bay in **Japan** with four ships in **1853**, the Japanese couldn't ignore them. The belching smoke and exaggerated features of this ship painted by a Japanese artist show his country's fear and mistrust of foreigners. Ironically, Japan quickly realized the necessity of dealing with the West and soon became a rival power.

HISTORY THROUGH ART

Caricature

Caricature is a way of representing something in words or pictures in which its distinctive features are exaggerated. For this reason, caricatures are generally humorous or even grotesque. They are often used to comment on political and social situations.

This painting by a 19th-century Japanese artist from Tokyo is a caricature of a foreign trading ship. It humorously reflects the national negative attitudes toward and fear of foreigners—especially Westerners. This "black ship," as the Japanese called these foreign vessels, is made to look like a menacing monster, with its dark smoke and glaring eyes. Oddly, the artist gave the ship several Japanese touches as well, such as the pedestal lamp and the deckhouse shaped like a pagoda.

Accounts brought back from Japanese travelers who visited the West eventually helped give the people a more realistic view of the foreigners and whetted Japanese curiosity about the outside world.

Interpreting the Art In what ways do you think caricature is an effective way of presenting ideas? In what ways might it be misleading or biased?

Interact *with* History

This Interact with History feature motivates students by inviting them to put themselves in the position of a member of the Chinese local government in the 19th century. Students will analyze the pros and cons of trading with foreign nations and become decision makers.

Purpose

- to set the stage for studying China's dealings with the West
- to help students understand the issues that emerging nations face
- to clarify the reasons that nations become imperialistic

Teaching Strategy

Thinking Critically After students have imagined themselves in the situation described on this page, have them answer the key question and give reasons for their decision.

EXAMINING *the* ISSUES

Following are suggestions for addressing each bulleted question.

1 Encourage students to name imported items that are available in the United States today, such as Japanese electronics. Ask them to think about the benefits and drawbacks of these items to the United States.

2 Invite pairs of students to role-play a situation in which one has an item the other wants. Have them negotiate a trade that is mutually satisfactory.

3 Have students use what they've learned in earlier chapters to describe negative and positive interactions between countries.

Making Connections Have students revisit the Interact with History on page 286 to consider the West's interest in Chinese products.

Life is good for you as a member of the local government in 19th-century China, but it could be even better. People from the West are eager to trade with your country. China, however, produces all that its people need, and government officials discourage contact with foreigners. Many foreign products, such as ceramics, are inferior to Chinese goods. The foreigners, however, do offer items that can improve your life, including rifles, cameras, and small sticks called matches that can be scraped against a rock to start a fire. You are curious about these inventions. But you wonder why the foreigners are so eager to trade with China and what they hope to gain.

Would you trade with the foreigners?

Foreign traders make sure they get full value for their goods. They also may seek to gain political or economic influence in China, however.

Chinese laborers carry cartons of tea to trade for foreign goods such as ceramics and silk.

Merchants keep accurate records of all transactions.

EXAMINING *the* ISSUES

1 • How might foreign products affect the quality of life in China both positively and negatively?

2 • What demands might foreigners make on countries they trade with?

3 • Why might people seek out or resist foreign influence?

As a class, discuss these questions. Recall what happened in other parts of the world when different cultures came into contact for the first time.

As you read this chapter, compare the decisions various governments made about foreign trade and the reasons for those decisions.

714

Follow Up

A feature on the chapter assessment will ask students to reevaluate their responses to the situation presented on this page.

China Responds to Pressure from the West

TERMS & NAMES
- Opium War
- extraterritorial rights
- Taiping Rebellion
- sphere of influence
- Open Door Policy
- Boxer Rebellion

MAIN IDEA

Western economic pressure forced China to open to foreign trade and influence.

WHY IT MATTERS NOW

China has become an increasingly important member of the global community.

SETTING THE STAGE In the late 18th century, China had more people than any other empire in the world. Under the Manchus of the Qing Dynasty, the empire was stable and secure. The people lived by traditions that were thousands of years old.

China Resists Foreign Influence

Out of pride in their ancient culture, the Chinese looked down on all foreigners. In 1793, however, the Qing emperor agreed to receive an ambassador from England. The Englishman brought gifts of the West's most advanced technology—clocks, globes, musical instruments, and even a hot-air balloon. The emperor was not impressed. In a letter to England's King George III, he stated that the Chinese already had everything they needed. They were not interested in the "strange objects" and gadgets that the West was offering them.

China Remains Self-Sufficient The basis of Qing China's wealth was its healthy agricultural economy. During the 11th century, China had acquired a quick-growing strain of rice from Southeast Asia. By the time of the Qing Dynasty, the rice was being grown throughout the southern part of the country. Around the same time—the 17th and 18th centuries—Spanish and Portuguese traders brought maize, sweet potatoes, and peanuts from the Americas. These crops helped China increase the productivity of its land and more effectively feed its 300 million people. Better nutrition, in turn, led to a population boom.

China also had extensive mining and manufacturing industries. Rich salt, tin, silver, and iron mines produced great quantities of ore. The mines provided work for tens of thousands of people. The Chinese also produced beautiful silks, high-quality cottons, and fine porcelain. The Chinese people were essentially self-sufficient.

This 18th-century painted fan depicts Guangzhou in southern China as a cosmopolitan port, flying the flags of its many foreign traders. The rest of China, however, remained firmly isolated until the mid-19th century.

715

Section 1 Overview

OBJECTIVES

1. To explain China's resistance to foreigners in the 1800s.
2. To describe the peasant rebellions that shook China.
3. To summarize the effects of China's struggle with reform.
4. To outline the growth of nationalism in China.

SKILLBUILDER

- Interpreting maps: human-environment interaction, location, p. 718

CRITICAL THINKING

- Analyzing issues, p. 716
- Recognizing effects, p. 717
- Making inferences, p. 718
- Analyzing causes, p. 719

FOCUS

5-Minute Warm-Up

▶ *Interpreting Maps*
To help students understand the importance of China to foreign nations, have them answer the following questions.

1. Look at the map on page 718. Which nations had colonies in China between 1850 and 1911?
2. In what parts of China were the foreign spheres of influence and the colonies located?

WARM-UP TRANSPARENCY 28

OBJECTIVE 1 INSTRUCT

China Resists Foreign Influence

▶ *Key Ideas*
- In the early 1800s, China has little interest in trading with Western nations.
- The British import large amounts of tea from China and smuggle opium into the country.
- War breaks out when the British refuse to stop trading opium.

IN-DEPTH RESOURCES: UNIT 6
Guided Reading, p. 55

ACCESS FOR STUDENTS ACQUIRING ENGLISH
Guided Reading (Spanish), p. 281

The Tea-Opium Connection Because of their self-sufficiency, the Chinese had little interest in trading with the West. For decades, the only place they would allow foreigners to do business was at the southern port of Guangzhou (gwahng-joh). And the balance of trade at Guangzhou was clearly in China's favor. This means that China earned much more for its exports than it spent on imports. The British imported millions of pounds of tea from China every year and exported goods worth much less. They made up for the difference in silver. This imbalance drained Britain's silver supply.

European merchants were determined to find a product the Chinese would buy in large quantities. Eventually they found one—opium. Opium is a habit-forming narcotic made from the poppy plant. Chinese doctors had been using it to relieve pain for hundreds of years. In the late 18th century, however, British merchants smuggled opium into China for nonmedical use. It took a few decades for opium smoking to catch on, but by 1835, as many as 12 million Chinese people were addicted to the drug.

War Breaks Out This growing supply of opium caused great social, moral, and monetary problems for the country. The Qing emperor was angry. In 1839, one of the emperor's highest advisers wrote a letter to England's Queen Victoria about the problem:

> **A VOICE FROM THE PAST**
> By what right do they [British merchants] . . . use the poisonous drug [opium] to injure the Chinese people? . . . I have heard that the smoking of opium is very strictly forbidden by your country; that is because the harm caused by opium is clearly understood. Since it is not permitted to do harm to your own country, then even less should you let it be passed on to the harm of other countries.
> **LIN ZEXU,** quoted in *China's Response to the West*

The pleas went unanswered, and Britain refused to stop trading opium. The result was an open clash between the British and the Chinese—the **Opium War** of 1839. The battles took place mostly at sea. China's outdated ships were no match for Britain's steam-powered gunboats and sophisticated cannons. As a result, the Chinese suffered a humiliating defeat. In 1842, they signed a peace treaty, the Treaty of Nanjing.

This treaty gave Britain the island of Hong Kong. After signing another treaty in 1844, U.S. and other foreign citizens also gained **extraterritorial rights.** These rights provided exemption from Chinese law at four Chinese ports besides Guangzhou. Many Chinese greatly resented these privileges and the foreigners among them. And a bustling trade in opium continued.

Internal Problems Increase

Foreigners were not the greatest of China's problems in the mid-19th century, however. Its own population provided an overwhelming challenge. That population had grown to 430 million by 1850—a 30-percent gain in only 60 years. Yet food production had barely increased. As a result, hunger was widespread, even in good years. In the frequent bad years, the Huang He (Yellow River) broke through its dikes and flooded vast farming areas. Millions starved.

The Chinese government itself was riddled with corruption and could do little to ease its people's suffering. Dikes that might have held back the river had fallen into disrepair. Public granaries were empty. Talented people who were unable or unwilling to bribe state examiners often were denied government jobs. The people became discouraged, and opium addiction rose steadily. As their problems mounted, the Chinese actively began to rebel against the Qing Dynasty.

The Taiping Rebellion The rebellion that was to become China's largest was led by Hong Xiuquan (hung shee·oo·choo·ahn). The Treaty of Nanjing had granted Christian missionaries increased privileges in China. The missionaries greatly influenced this sensitive young man. Hong had mystical visions and wanted to save the world, beginning with China. He dreamed of a "Heavenly Kingdom of Great Peace." In this kingdom, all Chinese people would share China's vast wealth and no one would live in poverty. Hong's revolt was called the **Taiping Rebellion,** from the Chinese expression *taiping,* meaning "great peace."

Beginning in the late 1840s, Hong organized an army made up mainly of peasants—both men and women—from southern China. By 1853, 1 million people had joined his rebel forces. That year, Hong captured the city of Nanjing and declared it his capital. The Taiping government controlled large areas of southeastern China.

Over the next ten years, however, the Qing regained control of the country. Imperial troops, local militias, and British and French forces all fought against the Taiping. By 1864, they crushed the 14-year rebellion. But China paid a terrible price. Huge, hungry armies had destroyed fertile farmland in their search for food. At least 20 million—and possibly twice that many—people died.

China Wrestles with Reform

The Taiping Rebellion and other smaller uprisings put tremendous internal pressure on the Chinese government. And, despite the Treaty of Nanjing, external pressure from foreign powers was increasing. At the Qing court, stormy debates raged about how best to deal with these pressures. Some government leaders called for reforms patterned on Western ways. Others insisted on honoring Chinese traditions. The Chinese Empire was conservative overall, though. Clinging to traditional ways and resisting change started at the top.

The Dowager Empress Cixi Resists Change During the last half of the 19th century, there was only one person at the top in the Qing imperial palace. The Dowager Empress Cixi (tsoo·shee) ruled China, with only one brief gap, from 1861 until 1908.

Although she was committed to traditional values, the Dowager Empress did support certain reforms. In the 1860s, for example, she backed the self-strengthening movement. That program aimed to update China's educational system, diplomatic service,

THINK THROUGH HISTORY
B. Recognizing Effects What were the results of the Taiping Rebellion?
B. Possible Answer Little change in the status of the people and massive death and destruction.

Background
The Dowager Empress Cixi first served as ruler for two emperors who took the throne as children. When she gained the throne herself she was known as "dowager," or endowed empress.

HISTORY MAKERS

Hong Xiuquan
1814–1864

Hong Xiuquan came from a rural family. As a young man, he tried to move up in Chinese society by seeking a government post. However, he kept failing the civil service exam. In his early twenties, Hong had a dream that ordered him to fight evil. From then on, he worked to overthrow the "evil" Qing dynasty and the same Qing system that he had tried so hard to enter. To destroy evil, Hong and his rebel followers destroyed Qing artworks and outlawed such Qing symbols as the pigtail.

Hong slowly developed his own personal vision of Christianity. That vision led him to forbid opium, tobacco, alcohol, and gambling. Under Hong, men and women were treated as equals. Women, for example, could fight for Hong's cause just as men could. However, men and women were divided into separate divisions, and even husbands and wives were not allowed contact.

After winning Nanjing, Hong withdrew into his mystical visions. After years of bloody feuding among his lieutenants, Hong's Taiping government fell. After that defeat, thousands of his followers burned themselves to death rather than surrender to the emperor.

Transformations Around the Globe **717**

Foreign Influence in China, 1850–1911

Interpreting the Map Ask students which nations had both colonies and spheres of influence in China. *Britain, France, and Japan*

Extension Activity The United States did not have a colony or a sphere of influence in China during this period. Have students research the history of U.S. dealings with China.

SKILLBUILDER Answers
1. Britain, France, Germany, Japan, Russia
2. Britain; the Yangtze River

OBJECTIVE 4 INSTRUCT

Chinese Nationalism Grows

▶ **Key Ideas**
• Dowager Empress Cixi and others prevent changes to China's traditional government.
• Chinese frustration with the government and foreigner privilege erupt into the Boxer Rebellion.
• After the defeat of the Boxers, the Qing Dynasty begins to work toward reform.

 IN-DEPTH RESOURCES: UNIT 6
History Makers: Cixi, p. 69

 ELECTRONIC LIBRARY OF PRIMARY SOURCES
from *Two Years in the Forbidden City*

MORE ABOUT . . .
The Boxer Rebellion

Many women fought in the Boxer Rebellion in their own companies. Young single women from ages 12 to 18 were known as the Red Lanterns. Married women belonged to the Blue or the Black Lanterns. Widows fought in the Green Lanterns. Boxer women who did not fight formed a group called the Cooking-Pan Lanterns to help feed others.

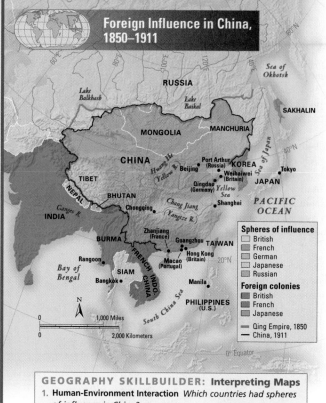

Foreign Influence in China, 1850–1911

GEOGRAPHY SKILLBUILDER: Interpreting Maps
1. **Human-Environment Interaction** Which countries had spheres of influence in China?
2. **Location** What foreign power shown on the map had access to inland China? What geographic feature made this possible?

---

and military. Under this program, China set up arsenals to manufacture steam-powered gunboats, rifles, and ammunition. By 1875, these ammunition supply and storage facilities were among the largest in the world.

The self-strengthening movement had mixed results, however. The ability to produce its own warships and ammunition was undoubtedly good for China's morale. But the Chinese hired foreigners to run many of its arsenals. These outsiders often didn't feel comfortable working with Chinese resources. So they imported both raw materials and factory machinery from abroad. This practice contributed to both an imbalance in trade for China and a lack of quality control. In addition, the movement lacked support from the Chinese people as a whole.

Other Nations Step In China's weak military technology and its economic and political problems were not a secret from the rest of the world. Throughout the late 19th century, many foreign nations took advantage of this weakness and attacked China. Treaty negotiations after each conflict gave the West increasing control over China's economy. As shown in the map, many of Europe's main political powers and Japan gained a strong foothold in China. This foothold, or **sphere of influence,** was a region in which the foreign nation controlled trade and investment.

The United States was a long-time trading partner with China. Americans worried that other nations would soon divide China into formal colonies and shut out American traders. To prevent this occurrence, in 1899 the United States declared the **Open Door Policy.** This policy proposed that China's "doors" be open to merchants of all nations. Britain and the other European nations agreed. The policy thus protected both American trading rights in China and China's freedom from colonization. But the country was still at the mercy of foreign powers.

Chinese Nationalism Grows

Humiliated by their loss of power, many Chinese pressed for strong reforms. Among them was China's young emperor, Guangxu (gwahng·shoo). In June 1898, Guangxu's aunt, the Dowager Empress Cixi, was relaxing at the summer palace. Assuming that he had her support, Guangxu introduced measures to modernize China. These measures called for overhauling China's educational system, strengthening the economy, modernizing the military, and streamlining the government. Guangxu asked progressive, creative advisers to help carry out his programs.

Most Qing officials saw these innovations as threats to their power. They reacted with alarm. In September 1899, they called the Dowager Empress back to the imperial court. Guangxu realized too late that he had misjudged her. Striking with the same speed as her nephew, the Dowager Empress Cixi placed him under arrest at the

THINK THROUGH HISTORY
C. Making Inferences What importance did spheres of influence have for China and for the nations involved?
C. Answer They weakened China's control over its economy and gave foreign nations the ability to exploit Chinese resources.

TEACHING OPTION ⬛ **BLOCK SCHEDULING**

COOPERATIVE ACTIVITY: Debating Reform

CLASS TIME 30 MINUTES

Task: Student groups will research the conflict between the Dowager Empress Cixi and Guangxu and then conduct a debate on reform in China.

Purpose: To help students understand China's struggle for reform.

Activity: Divide the class into groups of four. Within each group, two students should research the

reforms Guangxu made and why these reforms were necessary. The other pair should research the Dowager Empress Cixi's reaction to Guangxu's reforms and why she felt as she did. Groups can use their textbooks and library materials for their research.

After group members have finished their research, have them stage a debate between Guangxu and the empress. Two at a time, group members should take

turns role playing the figures and debating the need for reform. Remind students to be specific in their arguments and rebuttals. Encourage volunteers to conduct the debate for the class.

Finally, discuss with students what they learned about reform in China from their research.

 ALTERNATIVE ASSESSMENT BOOK
Standards for Evaluating a Cooperative Activity

palace. She then took back her own power. She reversed his reforms and executed a number of the movement's leaders. Guangxu's Hundred Days of Reform ended without a single long-term change. The Chinese people's frustration with their situation did change, however. It grew.

The Boxer Rebellion This widespread frustration finally erupted. Poor peasants and workers particularly resented the special privileges granted to foreigners. They also resented Chinese Christians, who were protected by foreign missionaries. To demonstrate their discontent, they formed a secret organization called the Society of Harmonious Fists. They soon came to be known as the Boxers. Their campaign against the Dowager Empress's rule and foreigner privilege was called the **Boxer Rebellion.**

In the spring of 1900, the Boxers descended on Beijing. Shouting "Death to the foreign devils," the Boxers surrounded the European section of the city. They kept it under siege for several months. The Dowager Empress expressed support for the Boxers but did not back her words with military aid. In August, a multinational force of 20,000 troops marched toward Beijing. Soldiers from Britain, France, Germany, Austria, Italy, Russia, Japan, and the United States quickly defeated the Boxers.

Despite the failure of the Boxer Rebellion, a strong sense of nationalism had emerged in China. The Chinese people realized that their country must resist more foreign intervention. Most important, however, the government must become responsive to their needs.

The Beginnings of Reform At this point, even the Qing court realized that China needed to make profound changes to survive. In 1905, the Dowager Empress sent a select group of Chinese officials on a world tour to study the operation of different governments. The group traveled to Japan, the United States, Britain, France, Germany, Russia, and Italy. On its return in the spring of 1906, the officials recommended that China restructure its government. They based their suggestions on the constitutional monarchy of Japan. The empress accepted this recommendation and began making reforms. Although she convened a national assembly within a year, change was slow. In 1908, the court announced that it would establish a full constitutional government by 1917.

Unfortunately, however, the turmoil in China did not end with these progressive steps. Unrest would continue for the next four decades as the Chinese faced internal and external threats. But as wholeheartedly as China had struggled to remain isolated from the outside world, its neighbor Japan responded to Western influence in a much different way.

Boxer rebels like this one drawn by a 20th-century artist were driven by a fierce hatred of foreigners. They used their fists, swords, and guns in an unsuccessful attempt to oust the "foreign devils" from China.

Section 1 Assessment

1. TERMS & NAMES
Identify
• Opium War
• extraterritorial rights
• Taiping Rebellion
• sphere of influence
• Open Door Policy
• Boxer Rebellion

2. TAKING NOTES
In a flow chart like the one below, list the major events in China's dealings with foreign nations between 1830 and 1900. Include both policies and actual confrontations.

1830   1839   1900
        Opium
        War

3. RECOGNIZING EFFECTS
Do you think the opium trade was finally more harmful or beneficial to China? Explain.

THINK ABOUT
• the effects of the Opium War
• other Chinese responses to foreign influence
• the aftermath of the Boxer Rebellion

4. THEME ACTIVITY
Cultural Interaction Under the long rule of the Dowager Empress Cixi, China fiercely resisted foreign influence. As a class or in a small group, role-play a debate among the Dowager Empress's advisers. Some should argue for continued isolation, and others for openness to foreign influence and trade.

Transformations Around the Globe **719**

Section 2 Overview

OBJECTIVES

① To describe why Japan ended its isolation and how it began modernizing.

② To trace the growth of Japanese imperialism in wars with China and Russia and in its policies toward Korea.

SKILLBUILDERS
- Interpreting charts, p. 721
- Interpreting political cartoons, p. 723

CRITICAL THINKING
- Recognizing effects, p. 721
- Making inferences, p. 722
- Clarifying, p. 723
- Forming an opinion, p. 723
- Analyzing themes, p. 723

FOCUS
5-Minute Warm-Up

▶ **Interpreting Charts**
To help students compare China's and Japan's responses to Western influence, have them answer these questions.

1. Look at the Venn diagram on page 721. Which country borrows Western ideas and ways?

2. Which country remains committed to traditional values?

 WARM-UP TRANSPARENCY 28

OBJECTIVE ① INSTRUCT

Japan Ends Its Isolation

Key Ideas
- Japan opens its ports to trade in 1854.
- The Japanese modernize quickly.

 IN-DEPTH RESOURCES: UNIT 6
Guided Reading, p. 56

ACCESS FOR STUDENTS ACQUIRING ENGLISH
Guided Reading (Spanish), p. 282

---

② Japan Modernizes

MAIN IDEA
Japan followed the model of Western powers by industrializing and expanding its foreign influence.

WHY IT MATTERS NOW
Japan's continued development of its own way of life has made it a leading world power.

SETTING THE STAGE In the early 17th century, Japan had shut itself off from almost all contact with other nations. Under the rule of the Tokugawa shoguns, the society was tightly ordered. The shogun parceled out land to the lords. The peasants worked for and lived under the protection of their lord and his samurai. This rigid system kept Japan free of civil war. Peace and relative prosperity reigned for two centuries.

Japan Ends Its Isolation

The Japanese had almost no contact with the industrialized world during this time of isolation. They continued, however, to trade with China and with Dutch traders from Indonesia. They also had diplomatic contact with Korea. However, trade was growing in importance, both inside and outside Japan.

Facing the Demand for Foreign Trade In the early 19th century, Westerners began trying to convince the Japanese to open their ports to trade. British, French, Russian, and American officials occasionally anchored off the Japanese coast. Like China, however, Japan repeatedly refused to receive them. Then, in 1853, U.S. Commodore Matthew Perry took four ships into what is now Tokyo Harbor. The Japanese were astounded by these massive black wooden ships that were powered by steam. They were also shocked by the cannons and rifles. These weapons could have wiped out hundreds of the fiercest samurai in a matter of seconds. The Tokugawa shogun realized he had no choice but to receive the letter Perry had brought from U.S. President Millard Fillmore:

A VOICE FROM THE PAST
It seems to be wise from time to time to make new laws. . . . If your Imperial Majesty were so far to change the ancient laws as to allow a free trade between the two countries [the U.S. and Japan], it would be extremely beneficial to both. . . . Our steamships, in crossing the great ocean, burn a great deal of coal, and it is not convenient to bring it all the way from America. We wish that our steamships and other vessels should be allowed to stop in Japan and supply themselves with coal, provisions, and water. They will pay for them, in money, or anything else your Imperial Majesty's subjects may prefer.
MILLARD FILLMORE, quoted in *Millard Fillmore Papers*

Polite as President Fillmore's letter was, Perry delivered it with a threat. He would come back with a larger fleet in a year to receive Japan's reply. That reply was the **Treaty of Kanagawa,** which was signed in 1854. Under the terms of the treaty, Japan opened two ports at which American ships could take on supplies. The treaty

Daily *Life*

Japanese Women
Japan not only restricted its citizens' contact with the outside world but it also severely confined its own women. The supreme duty of a woman was to honor the men in her life. Her restrictive dress and footwear helped ensure that she did not stray far from her place in the home.

As a child, she was expected to be obedient to her father, and as a wife, to her husband. Even as a widow, she was expected to submit to her son or sons.

In Japan today, increasing numbers of women work outside the home, most of them as "office ladies" or "OLs." These secretarial workers have no opportunity to advance, and are arguably no better off than their grandmothers were.

The number of women managers is increasing today, however, and Japanese women are becoming more vocal about playing an active role in their society.

SECTION 2 RESOURCES

PRINT RESOURCES

 IN-DEPTH RESOURCES: UNIT 6
Guided Reading, p. 56
Primary Source: from *The Autobiography of Yukichi Fukuzawa,* p. 63

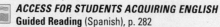 **ACCESS FOR STUDENTS ACQUIRING ENGLISH**
Guided Reading (Spanish), p. 282

 FORMAL ASSESSMENT
Section Quiz, p. 327

ALTERNATIVE ASSESSMENT BOOK

TECHNOLOGY RESOURCES

 GEOGRAPHY TRANSPARENCIES
GT28 Japanese Imperialism, 1875–1910

 WORLD ART AND CULTURES TRANSPARENCIES
AT61 *Japanese Girl in Western Dress*

 CD-ROM
Electronic Library of Primary Sources

 INTERNET www.mlworldhistory.com

also allowed the United States to set up an embassy in Japan. Once the United States had a foot in Japan's door, other Western powers soon followed. By 1860, Japan, like China, had granted foreigners permission to trade at treaty ports. It had also extended extraterritorial rights to many foreign nations.

Reform and Modernization Under the Meiji Reign The Japanese, however, were angry that the shogun had given in to the foreigners' demands. They feared that he was losing control over the country. The people rallied around Japan's young emperor, Mutsuhito (moot·soo·HEE·toh), who appealed to Japan's strong sense of pride and nationalism. In 1867, the Tokugawa shogun stepped down. He thus ended the military dictatorships that had lasted since the 12th century. Mutsuhito established a new government. He chose the name *Meiji* for his reign, which means "enlightened rule." Only 15 when he took over, Mutsuhito reigned for 45 years. This period of Japanese history—from 1867 to 1912—is called the **Meiji era.**

As part of this new enlightenment, the Meiji emperor realized that the best way to oppose Western imperialism was to adopt new ways. The feudal lords, for example, realized that private ownership of land prevented the entire country from benefiting from it. In one of the first acts of the Meiji era, they gave their land to the emperor.

Another way the Meiji government attempted to modernize Japan was by sending its statesmen to Europe and North America to study foreign ways. The Japanese chose what they believed to be the best Western civilization had to offer and adapted it to their own country. They admired Germany's strong centralized government, for example. And they used its constitution as a model for their own. As in Germany, a small group of men held political power in Japan. They were determined to build a mighty nation.

The Japanese also admired the discipline of the German army and the skill of the British navy. They attempted to imitate these European powers as they modernized their military. Japan adopted the American system of universal public education and required that all Japanese children attend school. Their teachers often included foreign experts. Students could go abroad to study as well.

China and Japan Confront the West

The Dowager Empress Cixi
(1862–1908)

China
- Remains committed to traditional values
- Loses numerous territorial conflicts
- Grants other nations spheres of influence within China
- Finally accepts necessity for reform

Both
- Have well-established traditional values
- Initially resist change
- Oppose Western imperialism

Japan
- Considers modernization to be necessary
- Borrows and adapts Western ways
- Strengthens its economic and military power
- Becomes an empire builder

The Meiji Emperor Mutsuhito
(1867–1912)

SKILLBUILDER: Interpreting Charts
1. *According to this Venn diagram, in what ways did China and Japan deal differently with Western influence?*
2. *What similar responses did each country share despite the different paths they followed?*

Transformations Around the Globe **721**

The emperor also energetically supported following the Western path of industrialization. By the early 20th century, the Japanese economy had become as modern as any in the world. The country built its first railroad line in 1872. The track connected Tokyo, the nation's capital, with the port of Yokohama, 20 miles to the south. By 1914, Japan had more than 7,000 miles of rails. Coal production grew from half a million tons in 1875 to more than 21 million tons in 1913. Meanwhile, large, state-supported companies built thousands of factories. Traditional Japanese industries, such as tea processing and silk production, expanded to give the country unique products to trade. Developing modern industries, such as shipbuilding and weapons production, made Japan competitive with the West.

Japanese Imperialism Grows

Japan's race to modernize paid off. By 1890, the country had several dozen warships and 500,000 well-trained, well-armed soldiers. It had become the strongest military power in Asia.

Japan had gained military, political, and economic strength. It then sought to eliminate the extraterritorial rights of foreigners. The Japanese foreign minister assured foreigners that they could rely on fair treatment in Japan. This was because its constitution and legal codes were similar to those of European nations, he explained. His reasoning was convincing, and in 1894, Britain and the other foreign powers abolished the extraterritorial rights of their citizens living in Japan. Japan's feeling of strength and equality with the Western nations rose.

As Japan's sense of power grew, the nation also became more imperialistic. Like many European nations, Japan saw empire building as a way of protecting its security and meeting economic needs. As in Europe, national pride also played a large part in this policy. The Japanese were determined to show the world that they were a powerful nation.

Japan Attacks China The Japanese first turned their sights to their Asian neighbors. Japan's neighbor, Korea, is not far from southern Japan (see the map on page 718). In 1876, Japan forced Korea to open three ports to Japanese trade. But China also considered Korea to be important as both a trading partner and a military outpost. Recognizing their similar interests in Korea, Japan and China signed a hands-off agreement. In 1885, both countries pledged that they would not send their armies into Korea.

In June 1894, however, China broke that agreement. Rebellions had broken out against Korea's king. He asked China for military help in putting them down. Chinese troops marched into Korea. Japan protested and sent its troops to Korea to fight the Chinese. The Sino-Japanese War had begun. Within a few months, Japan had driven the Chinese out of Korea, had destroyed the Chinese navy, and had begun taking over Manchuria. In 1895, China and Japan signed a peace treaty. This treaty gave Japan its first colonies—Taiwan and the Pescadores Islands.

Russo-Japanese War Most Western nations had expected China to win the showdown with Japan fairly easily. The Japanese victory surprised them. It also changed the world's balance of power. Russia and Japan emerged as the major powers—and enemies—in East Asia.

Russia and Japan soon went to war over Manchuria. This was a region north of Korea that was under Chinese rule. In 1903, Japan offered to recognize Russia's rights in Manchuria if the Russians would agree to stay out of Korea. But the Russians refused. So, in February 1904, Japan launched a surprise attack. It struck at the

*Global*Impact

Changing Image of the East
The Japanese victory over the Russians in 1905 exploded a strong Western myth. Many Westerners believed that white people were a superior race. The overwhelming success of European colonialism and imperialism in the Americas, Africa, and Asia had reinforced this belief. But the Japanese had shown Europeans that people of other races were their equals in modern warfare.

Unfortunately, Japan's military victory led to a different form of Western racism. Influenced by the ideas of Germany's emperor Wilhelm II, the West imagined the Japanese uniting with the Chinese and conquering Europe. The resulting racist Western fear of what it called the "yellow peril" influenced world politics for many decades.

Russian navy, which was anchored off the coast of Manchuria. In the resulting **Russo-Japanese War,** Japan drove Russian troops out of Korea. Japan won brutal land battles and captured most of Russia's Pacific fleet. It also destroyed Russia's Baltic fleet, which had sailed all the way around Africa to participate in the war.

In 1905, Japan and Russia began peace negotiations. U.S. president Theodore Roosevelt helped draft the treaty, which the two nations signed on a ship off Portsmouth, New Hampshire. This agreement, the Treaty of Portsmouth, gave Japan the captured territories. It also forced Russia to withdraw from Manchuria and to stay out of Korea.

Korea Under Japanese Occupation After defeating Russia, Japan attacked Korea with a vengeance. In 1905, it made Korea a protectorate. Japan sent in "advisers," who grabbed more and more power from the Korean government. The Korean king was unable to rally international support for his regime. In 1907, he gave up control of the country. Within two years the Korean Imperial Army was disbanded. In 1910, Japan officially imposed **annexation** in Korea, or brought that country under Japan's control.

The Japanese were harsh rulers. For the next 35 years, they forbade public protest. They shut down Korean newspapers and took over Korean schools. There they replaced the study of Korean language and history with that of Japan. They took land away from Korean farmers and gave it to Japanese settlers. They encouraged Japanese businessmen to start industries in Korea, but forbade Koreans from going into business in their own country. Resentment of the Japanese led to nonviolent protests and to a growing Korean nationalist movement. The Japanese did modernize Korean factories and transportation and communications systems, however. Despite this technological progress, Japan's repressive rule in Korea was an example of imperialism at its worst.

The rest of the world clearly saw the brutal results of Japan's imperialism in Korea. Nevertheless, the United States and other European countries moved ahead with their own imperialistic aims, as you will learn in Section 3.

Vocabulary
protectorate: a country under the partial control and protection of another nation.

THINK THROUGH HISTORY
C. Clarifying How did Japan treat the Koreans after it annexed the country?
C. Answer Harshly and brutally.

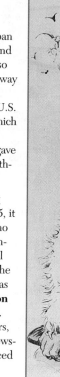

L'HOMME DU JOUR : LE MIKADO

ENCORE UN QUI VEND LA PEAU DE L'OURS
Dessin de Léandre.

SKILLBUILDER:
Interpreting Political Cartoons
1. *In this cartoon of the Russo-Japanese War, which animal represents Russia and which represents Japan?*
2. *Whom do you think the Japanese and the Russians are crushing?*

Section ② Assessment

1. TERMS & NAMES

Identify
• Treaty of Kanagawa
• Meiji era
• Russo-Japanese War
• annexation

2. TAKING NOTES

In a chart like the one below, list the steps that Japan took toward modernization and the events that contributed to its growth as an imperialistic power.

Modernization	Imperialism

Do you think that Japan could have become an imperialistic power if it had not modernized? Why or why not?

3. FORMING AN OPINION

In your view, was Japan's aggressive imperialism justified? Support your answer with examples from the text.

THINK ABOUT
• reasons for Japan's early isolation
• what Japan could gain from imperialism
• Japan's treatment of conquered peoples

4. ANALYZING THEMES

Empire Building What influences do you think were most important in provoking Japan to build its empire?

THINK ABOUT
• Japan's size and geographical features
• Japan's relations with China and Russia
• the interest of countries such as Britain and the United States in Japan

Transformations Around the Globe **723**

ANSWERS

1. TERMS & NAMES
Treaty of Kanagawa, p. 720
Meiji era, p. 721
Russo-Japanese War, p. 723
annexation, p. 723

2. TAKING NOTES
Possible Responses: Modernization—claimed feudal lands for government; studied Western ways; industrialized. Imperialism—abolished extraterritorial rights; forced Korean ports to open; fought Sino-Japanese and Russo-Japanese wars; annexed Korea.

3. FORMING AN OPINION
Possible Responses: Justified—Japan had to expand to compete in the global economy. Not justified—Japan didn't have to rule Korea as harshly as it did.

4. ANALYZING THEMES
Possible Responses: Because Japan is a small island, it was vulnerable to invaders. Having huge empire builders as neighbors forced Japan to expand in self-defense. The Japanese feared they might lose control of their country to the Western powers that traded at its ports.

History from Visuals

Political Cartoon

Interpreting the Cartoon Ask students to identify the two animals shown in the cartoon. Then have the class brainstorm adjectives that describe both these animals' temperaments and their activities. Write these adjectives on the board and refer to the list as students answer the Skillbuilder questions.

Extension Activity Suggest that interested students draw a cartoon that depicts the relationship between Japan and Korea during this era. Post students' cartoons on a bulletin board or have students present them to the class and discuss why they chose to portray these countries the way they did.

SKILLBUILDER Answers
1. Bear—Russia; hawk—Japan.
2. Possibly Manchuria.

ASSESS & RETEACH

Section 2 Assessment
Have students work in small groups to answer questions 3 and 4. Let the groups discuss their answers with the rest of the class.

Section Quiz
 FORMAL ASSESSMENT
Section Quiz, p. 327

Reteaching Activity
CLASS TIME: 10 MINUTES

Ask students to make a diagram, such as a flow chart, to summarize the events described in this section. Have students include dates for each event.

CLOSE ACTIVITY

CLASS TIME: 20 MINUTES

Drawing Conclusions
After students have completed question 2, divide the class into two groups: those who think Japan could have become an imperialist power without modernizing and those who think that modernization was essential. Let students confer for about ten minutes, gather the strongest evidence from their charts, and conduct a brief debate.

1. To explain how Latin America's colonial legacy and political instability shaped its history after independence.

2. To document how foreign powers influenced the growth of Latin American economies.

3. To describe U.S. intervention in Latin America.

SKILLBUILDER

• Interpreting maps: region, human-environment interaction, p. 725

CRITICAL THINKING

• Identifying problems, pp. 725, 728
• Analyzing motives, p. 726
• Making inferences, p. 727
• Forming opinions, p. 727
• Evaluating decisions, p. 728

FOCUS
5-Minute Warm-Up

▶ **Interpreting Maps**
To help students understand the reasons for U.S. imperialism in Latin America, have them answer these questions.

1. Look at the map on page 725. What countries were included in Latin America in 1830?

2. What Latin American natural resources might the United States want?

▥ *WARM-UP TRANSPARENCY 28*

OBJECTIVE ① INSTRUCT

Latin America After Independence

Key Ideas
• After independence, most Latin Americans remain poverty-stricken.

• Political power in Latin America is restricted to a few wealthy people, who support military dictators called caudillos.

▤ *IN-DEPTH RESOURCES: UNIT 6*
Guided Reading, p. 57

▤ *ACCESS FOR STUDENTS ACQUIRING ENGLISH*
Guided Reading (Spanish), p. 283

TERMS & NAMES
• caudillo
• Monroe Doctrine
• José Martí
• Spanish-American War
• Panama Canal
• Roosevelt Corollary

③ U.S. Economic Imperialism in Latin America

MAIN IDEA	WHY IT MATTERS NOW
The United States put increasing economic and political pressure on Latin America during the 19th century.	This policy set the stage for 20th-century relations between Latin America and the United States.

SETTING THE STAGE Latin America's long struggle to gain independence from colonial domination between the late 18th and the mid-19th centuries left the new nations in shambles. Weeds choked off farm fields. Cities and towns collapsed. The new nations faced a struggle for recovery as difficult as their struggle for independence had been.

Latin America After Independence

Political independence meant little for most citizens of the new Latin American nations. The majority remained poor, illiterate laborers caught up in a cycle of poverty.

Colonial Legacy During colonial times, most Latin Americans worked for large landowners. The employers paid their workers with vouchers that could be used only at their own supply stores. Since wages were low and prices were high, workers went into debt. Their debt accumulated and passed from one generation to the next. These "free" workers were almost like slaves in a system known as peonage.

The landowners, on the other hand, only got wealthier after independence. Many new Latin American governments took over the lands owned by native peoples and by the Catholic Church. They then put those lands up for sale. Wealthy landowners were the only people able to afford to buy them, and they snapped them up. But as one Argentinean newspaper reported, "Their greed for land does not equal their ability to use it intelligently." The unequal distribution of land and its poor use combined to prevent social and economic development in Latin America.

The land—and its rich resources—was and is Latin America's major asset. The peasants worked all of their lives in the fields and remained poor and propertyless, as many still are today.

Political Instability Political instability also was a widespread problem in 19th-century Latin America. Many Latin American army leaders had gained fame and power during their long struggle for independence. They often continued to assert their power. They controlled the new nations as dictators, or **caudillos.** By 1830, nearly all the countries of Latin America were ruled by caudillos. One typical caudillo was Juan Vicente Gómez. He was a ruthless man who ruled Venezuela for nearly 30 years after seizing power in 1908. "All Venezuela is my cattle ranch," he once boasted.

There were some exceptions, however. Reform-minded presidents, such as Argentina's Domingo Sarmiento, made strong commitments to improving education. During Sarmiento's presidency, between 1868 and 1874, the number of students in Argentina doubled. But such reformers usually didn't stay in office long. Eventually a caudillo would return to power, forcing the reformer out at the point of a bayonet or gun.

The caudillos found little opposition. The upper classes usually supported them because they opposed giving power to the lower classes. In addition, Latin Americans had gained little experience with democracy under European colonial rule. So the dictatorship of a caudillo did not seem unusual to them. But even when caudillos

---

SECTION 3 RESOURCES

PRINT RESOURCES

▤ *IN-DEPTH RESOURCES: UNIT 6*
Guided Reading, p. 57
Primary Source: Building the Panama Canal, p. 64
Connections Across Time and Cultures: Responses to Western Pressure, p. 71
Science and Technology: Technology Revolutionizes Communications, p. 72

▤ *ACCESS FOR STUDENTS ACQUIRING ENGLISH*
Guided Reading (Spanish), p. 283

FORMAL ASSESSMENT
▤ Section Quiz, p. 328
▤ *ALTERNATIVE ASSESSMENT BOOK*

TECHNOLOGY RESOURCES

▥ *CRITICAL THINKING TRANSPARENCIES*
CT28 Patterns of Resistance, 1830–1914

💿 **CD-ROM**
Electronic Library of Primary Sources

🖥 **INTERNET** www.mlworldhistory.com

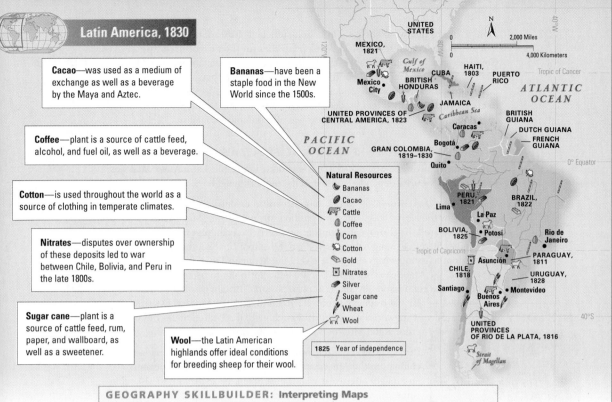

Latin America, 1830

Cacao—was used as a medium of exchange as well as a beverage by the Maya and Aztec.

Bananas—have been a staple food in the New World since the 1500s.

Coffee—plant is a source of cattle feed, alcohol, and fuel oil, as well as a beverage.

Cotton—is used throughout the world as a source of clothing in temperate climates.

Nitrates—disputes over ownership of these deposits led to war between Chile, Bolivia, and Peru in the late 1800s.

Sugar cane—plant is a source of cattle feed, rum, paper, and wallboard, as well as a sweetener.

Wool—the Latin American highlands offer ideal conditions for breeding sheep for their wool.

Natural Resources
- Bananas
- Cacao
- Cattle
- Coffee
- Corn
- Cotton
- Gold
- Nitrates
- Silver
- Sugar cane
- Wheat
- Wool

1825 Year of independence

GEOGRAPHY SKILLBUILDER: Interpreting Maps
1. **Region** Which Latin American countries remained under colonial rule in 1830?
2. **Human-Environment Interaction** Which country had the most different types of natural resources?

THINK THROUGH HISTORY
A. Identifying Problems What difficulties did lower-class Latin Americans continue to face after independence?

A. Possible Answer Poverty, lack of voice in government, lack of education.

weren't in power, most Latin Americans still lacked a voice in the government. Voting rights—and so, political power—were restricted to the relatively few members of the upper and middle classes who owned property or could read.

Economies Grow Under Foreign Influence

When colonial rule ended in Latin America in the early 1800s, the new nations were no longer restricted to trading with colonial powers. Britain and, later, the United States became Latin America's main trading partners.

Old Products and New Markets No matter with whom the new Latin American nations were trading, their economies continued to depend on exports. As during the colonial era, each country concentrated on one or two products. With advances in technology, however, Latin America's exports grew. The development of the steamship and the building of railroads in the 19th century, for example, greatly increased Latin American trade. Toward the end of the century, the invention of refrigeration helped increase Latin America's exports. The sale of beef, fruits and vegetables, and other perishable goods soared.

But foreign nations benefited far more from the increased trade than Latin America did. In exchange for their exports, Latin Americans imported European and North American manufactured goods. They therefore had little reason to develop their own manufacturing industries. And as long as Latin America remained unindustrialized, it could not play a leading role on the world stage.

Outside Investment and Interference Furthermore, Latin American countries used little of their export income to build roads, schools, or hospitals. Nor did they

Transformations Around the Globe **725**

MORE ABOUT . . .
Caudillos
(See page 724.)

Caudillos ruled Latin America with a combination of bribery, patronage, and force. Although the constitutions of many Latin American nations were patterned after the U.S. Constitution, the documents were seldom upheld. As one of Latin America's greatest liberators, Simón Bolívar, put it, "Treaties are scraps of paper; constitutions, printed matter; elections, battles; freedom, anarchy; and life, a torment."

History from Visuals

Latin America, 1830
Interpreting the Map
Encourage students to study the map key and identify the resources and products associated with each country. Suggest that interested students research the resources not included in the call-out boxes and report their findings to the class.

Extension Activity Ask students to use the map to make a time line of Latin American independence to share with the class. Point out that in some parts of Latin America, the struggle for independence went on for decades. Discuss how this long struggle for independence might have affected the development of Latin American economies.

SKILLBUILDER Answers
1. British Honduras; Jamaica; Cuba; Puerto Rico; French, Dutch, and British Guiana
2. Mexico

OBJECTIVE **2** INSTRUCT

Economies Grow Under Foreign Influence

▶ *Key Ideas*
- Latin America focuses on trade.
- Latin American countries' reliance on exports keeps them in debt.

TEACHING OPTION
CONNECTIONS ACROSS TIME AND PLACE

Peonage and Sharecropping The peonage system that held Latin American farmers in a cycle of poverty was similar in many ways to the sharecropping system in the southern United States. Encourage interested students to do additional research on peonage and to check American history textbooks or the encyclopedia for information about the sharecropping system in the southern United States after the Civil War.

Then have students construct a Venn diagram comparing the two systems. Suggest that they answer questions such as these for each system: Who owned the land? How were the farmers paid?

What caused them to go into debt? Have students share their completed diagrams with the class.

The United States and Latin America

▶ **Key Ideas**
- The United States issues the Monroe Doctrine to prevent recolonization of Latin America.
- The United States joins Cuba's fight for independence from Spain.
- The United States builds the Panama Canal.
- The Roosevelt Corollary gives the United States the right to police Latin American nations.

MORE ABOUT . . .
European Interference in Latin America

European powers interfered many times in Latin America during the 19th century before the United States enforced the Monroe Doctrine: Britain—the Argentinian Falkland Islands (1833); France—Mexico and Uruguay (several times between the 1830s and the 1860s); and Spain—the Chincha Islands (1862–1866).

 IN-DEPTH RESOURCES: UNIT 6
Connections Across Time and Cultures: Responses to Western Pressure, p. 71

HISTORYMAKERS
José Martí

José Martí was a much-admired poet and essayist as well as a revolutionary. One of Martí's poems was set to music in 1961, and the song "Guantanamera" was made famous by U.S. folksinger Pete Seeger. Play a recording of this song for the class and ask students who speak or have studied Spanish to translate it.

---

fund programs that would help them be self-sufficient. Instead, they often borrowed money—at high interest rates—to develop facilities for their export industries. Countries such as Britain, France, the United States, and Germany were willing lenders. The Latin American countries often were unable to pay back their loans, however. In response, foreign lenders either threatened to collect the debt by force or to take over the facility it had funded. Foreigners thus gained control of many industries in Latin America. Thus began a new age of economic colonialism.

The United States and Latin America

Long before the United States had a real economic interest in Latin America, it was aware that its security depended on that of its southern neighbors.

The Monroe Doctrine Most of the Latin American colonies had gained their independence by the early 1800s. But their position was not secure. Many Latin Americans feared that European countries would try to reconquer the new republics. The United States, a young nation itself, feared this too. In 1823, therefore, President James Monroe issued what came to be called the **Monroe Doctrine.** This document stated that "the American continents . . . are henceforth not to be considered as subjects for future colonization by any European powers." Britain was Latin America's largest trading partner. It agreed to back the Monroe Doctrine with its powerful navy. Until 1898, though, the United States did little to enforce the Monroe Doctrine. Cuba provided a real testing ground.

Cuba Declares Independence Cuba was one of Spain's last colonies in the Americas. In 1868, Cuba declared its independence and fought a ten-year war against Spain. In 1878, with the island in ruins, the Cubans gave up the fight.

But some Cubans continued to seek independence. In 1895, **José Martí,** a writer who had been exiled, returned to fight for Cuban independence. Martí was killed early in the war, but the Cubans battled on.

By that time, the United States had developed substantial business holdings in Cuba. Therefore it had an economic stake in the fate of the country. In addition, the Spanish had forced many Cuban civilians into concentration camps. Americans objected to the Spanish brutality. In 1898, the United States joined the Cuban war for independence. This conflict, which came to be known as the **Spanish-American War,** lasted about four months. Years of fighting had exhausted the Spanish soldiers, and they gave up easily.

In 1901, Cuba became an independent nation, at least in name. But the Cubans resented U.S. intervention, the military government the United States had installed, and its preventing Cuba from becoming truly independent. The split that began to develop between the United States and Cuba continues to keep those close neighbors miles apart a century later.

After its defeat in the Spanish-American War, Spain turned over the last of its colonies. Puerto Rico, Guam, and the Philippines became U.S. territories. Having become the dominant imperial power in Latin America, the United States next set its sights on Panama.

The Panama Canal Connects the Oceans Latin Americans were beginning to regard the United States as the political and economic "Colossus of the North." It was also a huge country geographically. By the 1870s, the transcontinental railroad connected its east and west coasts. Land travel was long and difficult, however. And sea travel involved a trip around the tip of South America. This was a

HISTORYMAKERS

José Martí
1853–1895

José Martí was only 15 in 1868 when he first began speaking out for Cuban independence. In 1871, the Spanish colonial government punished Martí's open opposition with exile to Spain.

With only a brief return to his homeland in 1878, Martí remained in exile for about 20 years. He lived most of his life in New York City. There he continued his career as a writer and a revolutionary. "Life on earth is a hand-to-hand combat . . . between the law of love and the law of hate," he proclaimed.

While in New York, Martí helped raise an army to fight for Cuban independence. He died on the battlefield only a month after the war began. But Martí's cry for freedom echoes in his essays and poems and in folk songs that are still sung throughout the world.

THINK THROUGH HISTORY
B. Analyzing Motives Why did the United States join the Cuban war for independence?
B. Possible Answers To protect its economic interests in Cuba and to protest Spain's brutal treatment of Cuban civilians.

Science and Engineering The building of the Panama Canal was one of the greatest feats of modern engineering. Panama was not the only site considered for the canal, however. The United States had also considered building the canal across Nicaragua. Ask students to look at topographical maps of Central

America and identify the pros and cons of each site. Have them discuss why Panama ultimately was chosen.

Have students make a diorama, model, or poster illustrating the building of the Panama Canal. Encourage them to include labels describing technological difficulties workers encountered and how they were overcome.

Literature Not all Americans supported the imperialistic policies of the United States in the late 1800s and early 1900s. One eloquent and outspoken critic was German-American journalist, writer, and politician Carl Schurz.

Ask interested students to read selections from Schurz's autobiography

Autobiography of Carl Schurz or from biographies such as *Carl Schurz: Reformer* by Claude Moore Fuess and *Defender of Human Rights: Carl Schurz* by James P. Terzian. Have them present to the class a short report on Schurz's life, beliefs, and social contributions.

journey of about 13,000 miles. If a canal could be dug across a narrow section of Central America, the coast-to-coast journey would be cut in half. The United States had been thinking about such a project since the early 19th century. In the 1880s, a French company tried—but failed—to build a canal across Panama.

Despite the French failure, Americans remained enthusiastic about the canal. And no one was more enthusiastic than President Theodore Roosevelt, who led the nation from 1901 to 1909. In 1903, Panama was a province of Colombia. Roosevelt offered that country $10 million plus a yearly payment for the right to build a canal. When the Colombian government demanded more money, the United States responded by encouraging a revolution in Panama. The Panamanians had been trying to break away from Colombia for almost a century. In 1903, with help from the U.S. navy, they won their country's independence. In gratitude, Panama gave the United States a ten-mile-wide zone in which to build a canal.

For the next ten years, American engineers battled floods, heat, and disease-carrying insects to build the massive waterway. The United States began a campaign to destroy the mosquitoes that carried yellow fever and malaria, and the rats that carried bubonic plague. The effort to control these diseases was eventually successful. But thousands of workers died during construction of the canal. The **Panama Canal** finally opened in 1914. Ships from both hemispheres soon began to use it. Latin America had become a crossroads of world trade. And the United States controlled the tollgate.

THINK THROUGH HISTORY
C. Making Inferences Why was the United States so interested in building the Panama Canal?
C. Possible Answers Because the canal would provide a water route between the coasts of the United States and give it control over a direct trade link between the Atlantic and Pacific oceans. It would also cut the time it took to ship goods between the Pacific and Atlantic oceans.

Roosevelt Corollary The building of the Panama Canal was only one way that the United States expanded its influence in Latin America in the early 20th century. Its presence in Cuba and large investments in many Central and South American countries strengthened its foothold. To protect those economic interests, in 1904, President Roosevelt issued a corollary, or extension, to the Monroe Doctrine. The **Roosevelt Corollary** gave the United States the right to be "an international police power" in the Western Hemisphere.

The United States used the Roosevelt Corollary many times in the following years to justify American intervention in Latin America. The troops occupied some countries for decades. Many Latin Americans protested this intervention by the United States. But they were powerless to stop their giant neighbor to the north.

The U.S. government turned a deaf ear to these protests. It could not ignore the rumblings of revolution just over its border with Mexico, however. You will learn about this revolution in Section 4.

In the view of this political cartoonist, the Roosevelt Corollary gave the U.S. president so much power, the Caribbean became his wading pool.

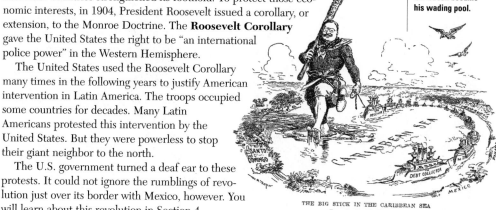

THE BIG STICK IN THE CARIBBEAN SEA
From the *Herald* (New York)

Section 3 Assessment

1. TERMS & NAMES

Identify
- caudillo
- Monroe Doctrine
- José Martí
- Spanish-American War
- Panama Canal
- Roosevelt Corollary

2. TAKING NOTES

Using a time line like the one below, list the major events of U.S. involvement in Latin America.

1823	1898 1903 1904		1914

Which event do you think was most beneficial to Latin America? Why?

3. FORMING OPINIONS

Do you think that U.S. imperialism was more beneficial or harmful to Latin American people? Explain.

THINK ABOUT
- the benefits provided by U.S.-owned companies
- the harmful effects of foreign economic and political influence

4. THEME ACTIVITY

Revolution It is 1898 and you have been fighting for the independence of your country, Cuba, for three years. The United States has just joined the war against Spain. Design a political poster that shows your feelings about U.S. participation in this war.

Transformations Around the Globe **727**

ANSWERS

. TERMS & NAMES
audillo, p. 724
Monroe Doctrine, p. 726
osé Martí, p. 726
panish-American War, p. 726
anama Canal, p. 727
oosevelt Corollary, p. 727

2. TAKING NOTES
1823—Monroe Doctrine; 1898—Spanish-American War; 1903—Panamanian rebellion; 1904—Roosevelt Corollary; 1914—Panama Canal opened. Answers will vary.

3. FORMING OPINIONS
Possible Responses:
Beneficial—The jobs and export income that U.S.-owned companies generated helped poor farmers and working people. Harmful—Foreign intervention prevented Latin American countries from becoming truly independent.

4. THEME ACTIVITY
Posters should include images and text that either support or condemn U.S. intervention in the Cuban war for independence.

MORE ABOUT . . .
The Roosevelt Corollary
The Roosevelt Corollary stated in part, "In the Western Hemisphere the adherence of the United States to the Monroe Doctrine may force the United States, however reluctantly, . . . to the exercise of an international police power." In the first half of the 20th century, the United States used this corollary to justify sending troops into Haiti, Nicaragua, the Dominican Republic, Mexico, Cuba, Honduras, Guatemala, and Costa Rica.

 ELECTRONIC LIBRARY OF PRIMARY SOURCES
from *The Rough Riders*

ASSESS & RETEACH

Section 3 Assessment
Divide the class into three groups and have each group complete one of the first three questions. Ask each group to present its answers to the class. Have pairs of students work on question 4.

Section Quiz
 FORMAL ASSESSMENT
Section Quiz, p. 328

Reteaching Activity
CLASS TIME: 10 MINUTES

Have students review the time line in question 2 and discuss the event they think had the greatest impact on Latin American history. Ask students to support their choice with information from their reading.

 CRITICAL THINKING TRANSPARENCIES
CT28 Patterns of Resistance, 1830–1914

CLOSE ACTIVITY

CLASS TIME: 15 MINUTES

Analyzing Issues
Have student pairs present to the class the posters they made for question 4. Encourage them to discuss why they chose to portray their feelings about U.S. participation in the war the way they did.

The Panama Canal includes an intricate system of locks that raises and lowers ships to the level of the various waterways along the route. The lock mechanisms are so delicate that even the wake from a ship can damage them. Therefore, most large boats are helped through the locks by tugboats and locomotives that run alongside the canal.

IN-DEPTH RESOURCES: UNIT 6
Primary Source: Building the Panama Canal, p. 64
Science and Technology: Technology Revolutionizes Communications, p. 72

CRITICAL THINKING ACTIVITY
CLASS TIME: 15 MINUTES

Interpreting Maps
Ask students to use the elevation chart along the top of the map to identify which part of the canal went through the land with the highest elevation. *the Culebra Cut* What other interesting facts about this part of the canal can they learn from the map and the captions? *It is also the narrowest part.* Why do they think this is so?

Panama Canal

The Panama Canal is considered one of the world's greatest engineering accomplishments. Its completion changed the course of history by opening a worldwide trade route between the Atlantic and Pacific oceans. As shown in the 1914 map below, ships are raised and lowered a total of 170 feet during the 51-mile trip through the canal. It usually takes 15 to 20 hours.

The canal also had a lasting effect on other technologies. Ships are now built to dimensions that will allow them to pass through its locks.

This 1910 engraving shows the excavation of the Gaillard, or Culebra, Cut, at the narrowest part of the canal. Completion of this nine-mile cut took seven years because of frequent landslides. By the time the entire canal was finished, workers had dug up about 211 million cubic yards of earth.

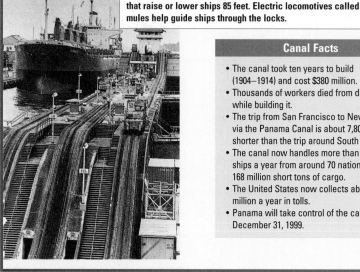

The Gatun Locks include three levels of water-filled chambers that raise or lower ships 85 feet. Electric locomotives called mules help guide ships through the locks.

Canal Facts

- The canal took ten years to build (1904–1914) and cost $380 million.
- Thousands of workers died from diseases while building it.
- The trip from San Francisco to New York City via the Panama Canal is about 7,800 miles shorter than the trip around South America.
- The canal now handles more than 13,000 ships a year from around 70 nations carrying 168 million short tons of cargo.
- The United States now collects about $340 million a year in tolls.
- Panama will take control of the canal on December 31, 1999.

Connect to History

Identifying Problems What difficulties did workers face in constructing the canal?

 SEE SKILLBUILDER HANDBOOK, PAGE 993

Connect to Today

Evaluating Decisions In the more than 80 years since it was built, do you think that the benefits of the Panama Canal to world trade have outweighed the costs in time, money, and human life? Explain your answer.

Connect to History

Identifying Problems
Possible Answers: The workers faced diseases such as malaria, yellow fever, and bubonic plague. As they excavated huge amounts of earth, landslides often occurred, which could bury them alive.

Connect to Today

Evaluating Decisions
Possible Answers: Yes—The canal is one of the world's major trade routes, and the United States collects nearly its cost each year in tolls. No—The money and time could have been better spent in helping Latin American countries develop their economies and become more self-sufficient.

The Mexican Revolution

MAIN IDEA

Political, economic, and social inequalities in Mexico triggered a period of revolution and reform.

WHY IT MATTERS NOW

Mexico has moved toward political democracy and is a strong economic force in the Americas.

SETTING THE STAGE The legacy of Spanish colonialism and long-term political instability that plagued the newly emerging Latin American nations in the 19th century caused problems for Mexico as well. Only Mexico, however, shared a border with the United States. The "Colossus of the North" wanted to extend its territory to the Pacific Ocean. But most of the lands in the American Southwest belonged to Mexico.

Santa Anna and the Mexican War

During the early 19th century, no one dominated Mexican political life more than **Antonio López de Santa Anna.** Santa Anna played a leading role in Mexico's fight for independence from Spain in 1821. In 1829, he fought against Spain again, as the colonial power tried to reconquer Mexico. Then, in 1833, Santa Anna became Mexico's president.

One of Latin America's most powerful caudillos, Santa Anna was a clever politician. He would support a measure one year and oppose it the next if he thought that would keep him in power. His policy apparently worked. Between 1833 and 1855, Santa Anna was Mexico's president four times. He gave up the presidency twice, however, to serve Mexico in a more urgent cause—retaining the territory of Texas.

The Texas Revolt In the 1820s, Mexico encouraged American citizens to move to the Mexican territory of Texas to help populate the country. Thousands of English-speaking colonists, or Anglos, did. In return for inexpensive land, they pledged to follow the laws of Mexico. As the Anglo population grew, though, tensions developed between the colonists and Mexico over several issues, including slavery and religion. As a result, many Texas colonists wanted greater self-government. But when Mexico refused to grant this, Stephen Austin encouraged a revolt against Mexico in 1835.

Santa Anna led Mexican forces north to try to hold the rebellious territory. He won a few early battles, including a bitter fight at the Alamo. However, he was unsuccessful at the Battle of San Jacinto. His troops were defeated, and he was captured. Sam Houston released Santa Anna after he promised to respect the independence of Texas. When he returned to Mexico in 1836, Santa Anna was quickly ousted from power.

War and the Fall of Santa Anna Santa Anna regained power, though, and fought against the United States again. In 1845, the United States annexed Texas.

Mexicans and Americans fought in a blazing, bloody battle at the Alamo, from February 23 to March 6, 1836. Santa Anna's forces had one of their few victories in the attempt to hold the Texas territory.

Transformations Around the Globe **729**

Santa Anna was an opportunist who was true only to his own hunger for power, both inside and outside Mexico. In 1833, for example, he was elected as a liberal. When the country became more conservative, he too shifted to the right. Then in 1845, U.S. president James Polk helped Santa Anna return from exile, with the understanding that Santa Anna would help mediate a peace agreement between the United States and Mexico over the status of Texas. Instead, Santa Anna led the Mexican army in battle against the United States.

OBJECTIVE 2 INSTRUCT

Juárez and La Reforma

Key Ideas
- Benito Juárez leads a reform movement in Mexico.
- During Juárez's rule, Mexico undergoes civil war and invasion from France.
- After the French withdraw, Juárez institutes many reforms.

MORE ABOUT . . .
Benito Juárez

Benito Juárez was a member of the Zapotec, a farming people known for their distinctive pottery and other crafts. As Juárez rose to power, the Zapotec always felt they could count on him. When he was inaugurated governor of Oaxaca, a group of Zapotec gave him a petition that said, "You know what we need and you will give it to us, for you are good and will not forget that you are one of us."

Outraged Mexicans considered this a U.S. act of aggression. In a dispute over the border, the United States invaded Mexico. Santa Anna's army fought valiantly. But U.S. troops defeated them after two years of war. In 1848, the two nations signed the Treaty of Guadalupe Hidalgo. The United States received the northern third of what was then Mexico, including California and the American Southwest. Santa Anna went into exile. He returned as dictator one final time, however, in 1853. After his final fall, in 1855, he remained in exile for almost 20 years. When he returned to Mexico in 1874, he was poor, blind, powerless, and essentially forgotten.

Juárez and *La Reforma*

During the mid-19th century, as Santa Anna's power rose and fell, a liberal reformer, **Benito Juárez,** strongly influenced the politics of Mexico. Juárez was Santa Anna's complete opposite in background as well as in goals. Santa Anna came from a well-off Creole family. Juárez was a poor, orphaned Zapotec Indian. While Santa Anna put his own personal power first, Juárez worked primarily to serve his country.

Benito Juárez Rises to Power Ancestry and racial background were important elements of political power and economic success in 19th-century Mexico. For that reason, the rise of Benito Juárez was clearly due to his personal leadership qualities. Juárez was raised on a small farm in the Mexican state of Oaxaca. When he was 12, he moved to the city of Oaxaca. He started going to school at age 15, and in 1829, he entered a newly opened state-run university. He received his law degree in 1831.

He then returned to the city of Oaxaca, where he opened a law office. Most of his clients were poor people who could not otherwise have afforded legal assistance. Juárez gained a reputation for honesty, integrity, hard work, and good judgment. He was elected to the city legislature and then rose steadily in power. Beginning in 1847, he served as governor of the state of Oaxaca.

Juárez Works for Reform Throughout the late 1840s and early 1850s, Juárez worked to start a liberal reform movement. He called this movement **La Reforma.** Redistribution of land, separation of church and state, and increased educational opportunities were among its goals. In 1853, however, Santa Anna returned to power for the last time. He sent Juárez and other liberals into exile.

Just two years later, rebellion against Santa Anna brought down his government. Benito Juárez and other liberal leaders returned to Mexico to deal with their country's tremendous problems. As in other Latin American nations, rich landowners kept most other Mexicans in a cycle of debt and poverty. Liberal leader Ponciano Arriaga described how these circumstances led to great problems for both poor farmers and the government:

> **A VOICE FROM THE PAST**
> There are Mexican landowners who occupy . . . an extent of land greater than the areas of some of our sovereign states, greater even than that of one of several European states. In this vast area, much of which lies idle, deserted, abandoned . . . live four or five million Mexicans who know no other industry than agriculture, yet are without land or the means to work it, and who cannot emigrate in the hope of bettering their fortunes. . . . How can a hungry, naked, miserable people practice popular government? How can we proclaim the equal rights of men and leave the majority of the nation in [this condition]?
> **PONCIANO ARRIAGA,** speech to the Constitutional Convention, 1856–1857

The French Invade Mexico Not surprisingly, Arriaga's ideas and those of the other liberals in government threatened most conservative upper-class Mexicans. To express their dissatisfaction, these conservative rebels fought against the liberal government. The civil war lasted for three years before the government defeated the rebels. Juárez took over the presidency in 1858. He was officially elected president in 1861.

THINK THROUGH HISTORY
A. Contrasting In what ways did Benito Juárez differ from Santa Anna?
A. Answer Juárez was a poor Indian who was devoted to the cause of the powerless, while Santa Anna was a well-to-do Creole concerned mainly with maintaining his own power.

THINK THROUGH HISTORY
B. Identifying Problems What does Ponciano Arriaga think is Mexico's greatest problem?
B. Answer The unequal distribution of land and extreme poverty of many Mexican peasants.

730 Chapter 28

TEACHING OPTION — BLOCK SCHEDULING

SKILLBUILDER MINI-LESSON: Identifying Problems

CLASS TIME 15 MINUTES

Explaining the Skill Identifying problems in history means finding and summarizing the difficulties faced by a group of people at a certain time. Some problems are stated directly, while others are implied by the ways people acted. For example, the fact that U.S. settlers in Texas rebelled indicates that problems existed in the relations between Mexico and the United States.

Applying the Skill Ask students to identify the problems that Benito Juárez faced in instituting his reform programs in Mexico. Have them decide whether each problem was stated directly or implied in the text. Then have them record it in the correct column of a chart like this one.

Problem Stated Directly	Problem Implied
Santa Anna sent Juárez into exile.	

IN-DEPTH RESOURCES: UNIT 6
Skillbuilder Practice: Identifying Problems, p. 59

The end of the civil war did not end Mexico's troubles, though. The country was deeply in debt. Exiled conservatives plotted with some Europeans to reconquer Mexico. In 1862, France was ruled by Napoleon III, who sent a large army to Mexico. Within 18 months, France had taken over the country. Napoleon appointed Austrian archduke Maximilian to rule Mexico as emperor. Juárez and other Mexicans fought against French rule. After five years under siege, the French decided that the struggle was too costly. They ordered the army to withdraw from Mexico in 1867. Maximilian was captured and executed.

Juárez was reelected Mexico's president in 1867. He returned to the reforms he had proposed more than ten years earlier. He began rebuilding the country, which had been shattered during decades of war. He promoted trade with foreign countries, the opening of new roads, the building of railroads, and the establishment of a telegraph service. He set up a national education system, separate from that run by the Catholic Church. In 1872, Juárez died of a heart attack. But after half a century of civil strife and chaos, he left his country a legacy of relative peace, progress, and reform.

HISTORY THROUGH ART: Political Art

A century after Mexico's long struggle for independence, artist José Clemente Orozco made many paintings dealing with the burdens that prevent people from being free, happy, and creative. Here he depicts the starving, suffering masses protesting their oppression by those in power *(right)*. Benito Juárez emerges as a product of and symbol of hope for his people *(below)*.

Fresco detail at University of Guadalajara (1936–1939), José Clemente Orozco

Fresco detail at Hospicio Cabañas (1948), José Clemente Orozco

Connect *to* History

Making Inferences What conclusions can you draw about Orozco's feeling for his people from these two murals?

 SEE SKILLBUILDER HANDBOOK, PAGE 1005

Connect *to* Today

Comparing What modern countries or peoples face problems similar to those of the 19th-century Mexico that Orozco portrayed?

Transformations Around the Globe **731**

Porfirio Díaz and "Order and Progress"

Key Ideas

- After the death of Benito Juárez, Porfirio Díaz comes to power and rules for 31 years.

- Díaz stabilizes the country's economy, but most Mexicans continue to live in poverty.

 IN-DEPTH RESOURCES: UNIT 6
History Makers: Porfirio Díaz, p. 70

Revolution and Civil War

Key Ideas

- By 1910, many Mexican people want reform.

- Liberal leader Francisco Madero leads an armed revolution.

- Francisco "Pancho" Villa and Emiliano Zapata support the revolution with their armies.

- A progressive Mexican constitution is adopted in 1917 and put into effect in 1920.

 IN-DEPTH RESOURCES: UNIT 6
Primary Source: from The Plan of Ayala, p. 65

HISTORYMAKERS
Francisco "Pancho" Villa

Villa survived the revolution by evading both U.S. and Mexican enemies. When Alvaro Obregón came to power, he granted Villa a ranch in return for his staying out of politics. Villa kept his side of the bargain, but Obregón did not. In 1923, Villa was murdered at his home. Ask interested students to write a poem or folktale about Villa's life.

 IN-DEPTH RESOURCES: UNIT 6
Literature: from *Tom Mix and Pancho Villa*, p. 66

Porfirio Díaz and "Order and Progress"

Juárez's era of reform didn't last long, however. In the mid-1870s, a new caudillo, **Porfirio Díaz,** came to power. Like Juárez, Díaz was an Indian from Oaxaca. He rose through the army and became a noted general in the fight against the French. In 1876, Díaz took control of Mexico by ousting the president. He had the support of the military, whose power had been reduced during and after the Juárez years. Indians and small landholders also supported him, because they thought he would work for land reforms.

During the Díaz years, elections became meaningless. Díaz offered land, power, or political favors to anyone who supported him. He terrorized many who didn't support him, ordering them to be beaten or put in jail. As a political slogan, Díaz adapted a rallying cry from the Juárez era. Juárez's "Liberty, Order, and Progress" became merely "Order and Progress." With this motto and his strong-arm methods, Díaz remained in power until 1911.

Order and progress did come to Mexico under Díaz, in spite of his methods. Railroads expanded, banks were built, the currency stabilized, and foreign investment grew. Mexico seemed to be a stable, prospering country. But appearances were deceiving. The wealthy owned more and more land, which they didn't put to good use. As a result, food costs rose steadily. Most Mexicans remained poor farmers and workers, and they continued to grow poorer.

HISTORYMAKERS

Francisco "Pancho" Villa
1877?–1923

Pancho Villa was famous in Mexico, but infamous in the United States. In 1916, the United States permitted revolutionary politician Venustiano Carranza to use U.S. trains to transport troops who were fighting Villa in northern Mexico. In retaliation, Villa raided the town of Columbus, New Mexico, and killed 16 Americans traveling on a train in northern Mexico.

President Wilson was furious and ordered the U.S. Army to capture Villa. Villa hid out in the desert country he knew so well. The Americans never did find him.

Meanwhile, the Mexican government considered the American pursuit of Villa to be an invasion of its country. The United States and Mexico might well have gone to war over Villa. However, the United States entered World War I in 1917, forcing the withdrawal of its troops from Mexico.

Revolution and Civil War

In the early 1900s, Mexicans from many walks of life began to protest Díaz's harsh rule. Idealistic liberals hungered for liberty. Farm laborers hungered for land. Workers hungered for fairer wages and better working conditions. Even some of Díaz's hand-picked political allies spoke out for reform. A variety of political parties began to form. Among the most powerful was a party led by Francisco Madero.

Madero Begins the Revolution Born into one of Mexico's ten richest families, **Francisco Madero** was educated in the United States and France. He believed in democracy and wanted to strengthen its hold in Mexico. Madero announced his candidacy for president of Mexico early in 1910. Soon afterward, Díaz had him arrested. From exile in the United States, Madero called for an armed revolution against Díaz.

The Mexican Revolution began slowly. Leaders arose in different parts of Mexico and gathered their own armies. In the north, cowboy **Francisco "Pancho" Villa** became immensely popular. He had a bold Robin-Hood policy of taking money from the rich and giving it to the poor. South of Mexico City, another strong, popular leader, **Emiliano Zapata,** raised a powerful revolutionary army. Like Villa, Zapata came from a poor family. He was determined to see that land was returned to peasants and small farmers. He wanted the laws reformed to protect their rights. *"Tierra y Libertad* [Land and Liberty]" was his battle cry. Villa, Zapata, and other armed revolutionaries won important victories against Díaz's army. By the spring of 1911, Díaz agreed to step down. He called for new elections.

Mexican Leaders Struggle for Power Madero was elected president in November 1911. But he had a difficult time holding on to power. He resigned and was murdered shortly afterward. The military leader General Victoriano Huerta then took over the presidency.

THINK THROUGH HISTORY
C. Recognizing Effects What effects did Díaz's rule have on Mexico?
C. Possible Answers Some economic and industrial progress, but increasing poverty for most citizens.

COOPERATIVE ACTIVITY: Making a Mural

Task: Small groups will create poster-size murals depicting aspects of Mexican history and write explanatory paragraphs.

Purpose: To help students understand Mexico's history.

Activity: Tell each group to choose an important event in Mexican history from this chapter for a mural

subject. Supply groups with paper or posterboard and paints or markers. Group members should discuss their ideas and make preliminary sketches before they begin their mural. Each group member should write a paragraph describing the historic event and how he or she helped create the mural. Encourage groups to share their murals with the class.

📁 **Building a Portfolio:** Students should place their paragraph in their portfolio.

📄 **ALTERNATIVE ASSESSMENT BOOK**
Standards for Evaluating a Cooperative Activity

Standards for Evaluation
Murals and paragraphs should . . .

- display an understanding of the important events in Mexican history

- show evidence of teamwork

Huerta was unpopular with many people, including Villa and Zapata. These revolutionary leaders allied themselves with another politician who also wanted to overthrow Huerta. His name was Venustiano Carranza. Their three armies advanced, seizing the Mexican countryside from Huerta's forces and approaching the capital, Mexico City. They overthrew Huerta only 15 months after he took power.

Carranza took over the government. He then turned his army on his former revolutionary allies. Both Villa and Zapata continued to fight. In 1919, however, Carranza lured Zapata into a trap and murdered him. With Zapata's death, the civil war also came to an end. More than a million Mexicans had lost their lives.

The New Mexican Constitution Carranza began a revision of Mexico's constitution. It was adopted in 1917. A revolutionary document, that constitution is still in effect today. As shown in the chart below, it promoted education, land reforms, and workers' rights. Carranza didn't support the final version of the constitution, however, and in 1920, he was overthrown by his former general, Alvaro Obregón.

Reforms of Mexican Constitution of 1917

Land	Religion	Labor	Social Issues
• Breakup of large estates • Restrictions on foreign ownership of land • Government control of resources (oil)	• State takeover of land owned by the Church	• Minimum wage for workers • Right to strike • Institution of labor unions	• Equal pay for equal work • Limited legal rights for women (spending money and bringing lawsuits)

> **SKILLBUILDER: Interpreting Charts**
> 1. Which reforms do you think landowners resented?
> 2. Which reforms benefited workers?

Although Obregón seized power violently, he did not remain a dictator. Instead, he supported the reforms the constitution called for. He also promoted public education. Mexican public schools taught a common language—Spanish—and stressed nationalism. In this way, his policies helped unite the various regions and peoples of the country. Nevertheless, Obregón was assassinated in 1928.

The next year, a new political party that attempted to address the interests of all sectors of the society arose. Although the Institutional Revolutionary Party (PRI) did not tolerate opposition, it initiated an ongoing period of peace and political stability in Mexico. While Mexico was struggling toward peace, however, the rest of the world was on the brink of war.

Section 4 Assessment

1. TERMS & NAMES

Identify
• Antonio López de Santa Anna
• Benito Juárez
• *La Reforma*
• Porfirio Díaz
• Francisco Madero
• Francisco "Pancho" Villa
• Emiliano Zapata

2. TAKING NOTES

In a chart like the one below, list the major accomplishment of each Mexican leader.

Leader	Major Accomplishment

Which leader do you think benefited his country most? Why?

3. ANALYZING ISSUES

Why did Juárez have trouble putting his liberal program *La Reforma* into action?

THINK ABOUT
• the types of reforms Juárez wanted
• how those reforms would affect Mexicans of the upper and lower classes
• the political climate of the country

4. ANALYZING THEMES

Revolution Juárez's motto for change in Mexico was "Liberty, Order, and Progress." Díaz's slogan was "Order and Progress." What did this difference in goals mean for the country?

THINK ABOUT
• Juárez's accomplishments
• Díaz's accomplishments
• the value of order and progress without liberty

Transformations Around the Globe **733**

ANSWERS

TERMS & NAMES

1. Opium War, p. 716
2. Taiping Rebellion, p. 717
3. Boxer Rebellion, p. 719
4. Meiji era, p. 721
5. Russo-Japanese War, p. 723
6. Monroe Doctrine, p. 726
7. Spanish-American War, p. 726
8. Antonio López de Santa Anna, p. 729
9. Benito Juárez, p. 730
10. Francisco "Pancho" Villa, p. 732

REVIEW QUESTIONS

Answers will vary.

11. It had extensive natural resources and industries and was essentially self-sufficient.

12. Population explosion, famine, and government corruption, which led to great suffering for the Chinese people

13. It triggered the Boxer Rebellion and led to a revived sense of Chinese nationalism.

14. The signing of the Treaty of Kanagawa, Japan's granting foreigners permission to trade at treaty ports, and the extension of extraterritorial rights to foreign nations. Because of these actions, the Japanese feared they were losing control of their country and were inspired to westernize in order to maintain control.

15. Invasion of Korea and annexation of Taiwan and the Pescadores Islands in the Sino-Japanese War; defeat of Russia, occupation of Korea following the Russo-Japanese War.

16. Colonialism left many Latin American countries politically and economically unstable and ripe for takeover by the military caudillos. The caudillos were able to maintain power because the upper classes supported them and the people were used to absolute rule.

17. These policies led to ongoing imperialism in Latin America, which kept these countries dependent and unable to deal with their internal problems.

18. The canal provided a short route between the Atlantic and Pacific and between the east and west coasts of the United States. It made worldwide trade easier and made Latin American products more accessible.

19. After accepting Mexico's invitation to move to Texas, colonists ignored Mexican laws and worked to gain independence from Mexico.

TERMS & NAMES

Briefly explain the importance of each of the following to the changes in global power between 1800 and 1914.

1. Opium War
2. Taiping Rebellion
3. Boxer Rebellion
4. Meiji era
5. Russo-Japanese War
6. Monroe Doctrine
7. Spanish-American War
8. Antonio López de Santa Anna
9. Benito Juárez
10. Francisco "Pancho" Villa

Interact *with* History

On page 714, you considered whether or not you would urge your country to trade with foreigners. Now that you've learned how several countries dealt with foreign influence and what the results were, would you change your recommendation? Discuss your ideas in a small group.

REVIEW QUESTIONS

SECTION 1 *(pages 715–719)*

China Responds to Pressure from the West

11. Why was China traditionally not interested in trading with the West?

12. What conditions during the Qing Dynasty gave rise to the Taiping Rebellion?

13. Although Guangxu's Hundred Days of Reform failed, what changes did it finally set in motion?

SECTION 2 *(pages 720–723)*

Japan Modernizes

14. What events caused Japan to end its isolation and begin to westernize?

15. What were the results of Japan's growing imperialism at the end of the 19th century?

SECTION 3 *(pages 724–727)*

U.S. Economic Imperialism in Latin America

16. How were Latin American caudillos able to achieve power and hold on to it?

17. What effects did the Monroe Doctrine and the Roosevelt Corollary have on Latin America?

18. Why was the United States so intent on building the Panama Canal?

SECTION 4 *(pages 729–733)*

The Mexican Revolution

19. What were the major causes of tension between the Mexicans and the American colonists who settled in Texas?

20. What roles did Francisco "Pancho" Villa and Emiliano Zapata play in the Mexican Revolution?

Visual Summary

Transformations Around the Globe

China
- Fails to prevent Britain from pursuing illegal opium trade in 1839 **Opium War**
- Deals with internal unrest during almost two decades of Hong Xiuquan's **Taiping Rebellion**
- Attempts to build self-sufficiency during 1860s in **self-strengthening movement**
- Violently opposes foreigners in 1900 **Boxer Rebellion**
- Begins to establish **constitutional government** in 1908

Japan
- Signs 1854 **Treaty of Kanagawa,** opening Japanese ports to foreign trade
- Modernizes based on Western models during **Meiji era** (1867–1912)
- Fights 1894 **Sino-Japanese War** seeking control of Korea
- Wages 1904 **Russo-Japanese War** seeking control of Manchuria
- Annexes **Korea** in 1910

Foreign Influence

Latin America
- Depends on **exports** to fuel economy
- Receives much **foreign investment**
- Gains U.S. military support in 1898 **Spanish-American War**
- Becomes crossroads of world trade when U.S. completes **Panama Canal** in 1914

Mexico
- Fights to hold **Texas territory** from U.S. colonialism (1835–1845)
- Tries to establish a national identity in the early 1850s under Benito Juárez's *La Reforma*
- Overcomes **French occupation** in 1867
- Stages the **Mexican Revolution** in 1910

20. Both men were leaders of the revolution; they fought to aid and protect poor peasants and small farmers.

Interact *with* History

Possible Responses: Students who originally opted to trade with the foreigners might cite Japan's experience as support for their decision. Those who chose to remain isolated might offer the difficulties Latin American countries and Mexico faced as support. Students might speculate what would have happened if China had refused to trade with the West.

CRITICAL THINKING

1. BYPASSING THE EMPRESS

Do you think that Emperor Guangxu would have been able to put his reforms into practice if the Dowager Empress Cixi had not intervened? Why or why not? Think about China's government, its attitude toward foreign influence, and Guangxu's power.

2. THE SWORD VS. THE PEN

THEME REVOLUTION Consider what you have learned in this and other chapters about Latin American colonial history and about how countries undergo change. What are the pros and cons of both military strategies and peaceful political means of improving a country's economic, social, and political conditions?

3. CHARTING SANTA ANNA'S CAREER

On a time line like the one below, indicate the major events of Santa Anna's military and political career in Mexico. Why do you think he was able to remain in power for so long?

Fights for independence
from Spain

1820s

4. ANALYZING PRIMARY SOURCES

In 1877, the Meiji era of modernization in Japan had been underway for about a decade. The following excerpt from an article in one of Japan's major newspapers, the *Tokyo Times,* comments on the changes that had taken place. Read the selection and answer the questions that follow.

> **A VOICE FROM THE PAST**
> In the second and third years of Meiji, the demand for foreign goods remarkably increased. Those who formerly looked upon them with contempt changed their minds and even dressed in foreign clothes. Our males adopted the European style. They put on fine tall hats instead of wearing large [queues] on their heads, and took to carrying sticks after discarding their swords. They dressed in coats of the English fashion and trousers of the American. They would only eat from tables and nothing would satisfy them but French cookery.

- Do you think this newswriter sees the adoption of foreign ways as a good or a bad thing for Japan? What specific words in the article make you feel that way?

- What dangers might a nation face when its people uncritically take on the behaviors and ways of life of another culture?

CHAPTER ACTIVITIES

1. LIVING HISTORY: Unit Portfolio Project

THEME EMPIRE BUILDING Your unit portfolio project focuses on empire building and colonialism. For Chapter 28, you might use one of the ideas suggested below:

- Stage a debate between a conservative member of the Dowager Empress Cixi's court and an official in Emperor Mutsuhito's Meiji government. Each should defend the leader's position on dealing with foreign intervention.

- Create a poster that dramatically illustrates one of the challenges that Mexico faced from the 1840s to the 1920s.

- Design an action figure based on one of the reformers or leaders you studied in this chapter. Draw a picture of the figure or construct a simple model. Then write a paragraph describing the reformer.

2. CONNECT TO TODAY: Cooperative Learning

THEME CULTURAL INTERACTION On May 5, 1862, badly outnumbered Mexican forces defeated the French at the Battle of Puebla. Mexicans still celebrate their country's triumph on the holiday Cinco de Mayo.

Working with a team, honor Cinco de Mayo by presenting a report to the class about some aspect of Mexican culture.

Use the Internet, books, interviews, and other resources to gather information about topics such as Mexican customs and traditions, music, dance, holidays, food, or art.

- Collect pictures or samples, or decide how you will demonstrate your Mexican custom to make it come alive for the class.

- Consider staging a cultural fair and inviting other students, administrators, parents, and community members to participate.

3. INTERPRETING A TIME LINE

Study the unit time line on pages 628–629. Which events on the Chapter 28 segment were the result of U.S. imperialism? of European imperialism? of Japanese imperialism?

FOCUS ON GEOGRAPHY

The United States wanted the Panama Canal so badly that it both supported a revolution and suffered the deaths of thousands of workers to get it built.

- How many miles did the canal cut from a trip between San Francisco and New Orleans?

- Would a trip from Rio de Janeiro to Valparaíso be shorter via the Panama Canal or the Strait of Magellan?

Connect to History How might the canal have forced Latin American countries to change?

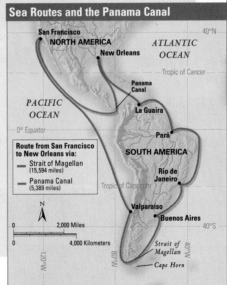

Sea Routes and the Panama Canal

Route from San Francisco to New Orleans via:
— Strait of Magellan (15,594 miles)
— Panama Canal (5,389 miles)

CHAPTER ACTIVITIES

1. LIVING HISTORY

Standards for Evaluation
A debate should meet the following criteria:

- Includes historically correct information about China and Japan.
- Presents persuasive arguments and counter arguments.
- Shows an understanding of each government's point of view.

Standards for Evaluation
A poster should meet the following criteria:

- Illustrates a key challenge between the 1840s and 1920s.
- Illustrates that challenge in an interesting, dramatic way.

Standards for Evaluation
An action figure design should meet the following criteria:

- Is based on a leader or reformer from this chapter.
- Shows an effort to accurately portray the historical figure.
- Includes a paragraph describing the reformer and his actions.

2. CONNECT TO TODAY

Standards for Evaluation
A report should meet the following criteria:

- Uses information from a number of sources.
- Gives indepth information about an aspect of Mexican culture.
- Shows evidence of teamwork.

3. INTERPRETING A TIME LINE

U.S. imperialism—Treaty of Guadalupe Hidalgo, Treaty of Kanagawa, Panama Canal; European imperialism—Opium War, Spanish-American War, Boxer Rebellion; Japanese imperialism—Sino-Japanese War, Russo-Japanese War, Japan annexes Korea

FOCUS ON GEOGRAPHY

- Over 10,000 miles
- Strait of Magellan

Connect to History *Possible Response:* It might have encouraged them to grow more crops for export rather than to feed their own population and to build roads, railroads, and ships to get their products to markets accessible to the canal.

CRITICAL THINKING

1. BYPASSING THE EMPRESS
Possible Responses: Yes—Guangxu had gathered talented advisers and other support. No—The Qing government was too strongly opposed to reform and too powerful.

2. THE SWORD VS. THE PEN
Possible Responses: Military strategies enable leader to seize control of the country and enact his policies, but can cause great suffering for the people. Peaceful political means take longer and are more difficult to achieve than military takeover, but may allow the people more voice in their country.

3. CHARTING SANTA ANNA'S CAREER
Possible Responses: 1833—becomes Mexico's president; 1835—fights to hold Texas; 1836—loses Mexican presidency; 1845—loses Texas to U.S.; 1853—returns as dictator; 1855—exiled

4. ANALYZING PRIMARY SOURCES
Possible Responses: Phrases such as "they would only eat from" and "nothing would satisfy them but" suggest that he thinks these new practices are absurd; when the people of a nation adopt another culture's ways, they run the risk of losing their national pride and identity.

The Menin Road *by Paul Nash*

Nash, a World War I British combat soldier who saw the horrifying human carnage on the Western Front firsthand, found it "utterly indescribable." Instead of depicting this slaughter directly, he implied it by showing the war's savage effects on the landscape.

The Menin Road shows a shell-battered countryside extending into the distance, suggesting endless destruction. The lonely pairs of soldiers in the middle ground seem lost in the chaotic and menacing space.

Nash set the scene in a forward section of the Ypres Salient, a section of Allied-held Belgium projecting into German-held territory. The Salient posed special dangers, exposing Allied soldiers to shellfire from three—and sometimes four—sides. The Menin Road, the main route to the Allied front line, was shelled day and night.

Mud compounded the danger. Rain turned the naturally soggy ground into a soupy morass one could drown in. During one of the bitterest military campaigns in history, the Passchendaele offensive of 1917, tens of thousands of men slogged, hid, fought, died, or disappeared in this treacherous mud.

"How difficult it is," wrote Nash as he was beginning *The Menin Road,* to "brood on those wastes of Flanders, the torments, the cruelty & terror of this war. Well it is on these I brood for it seems the only justification of what I do now—if I can rob the war of the last shred of glory, the last shine of glamour." Nash became one of the most celebrated British artists of the 1900s.

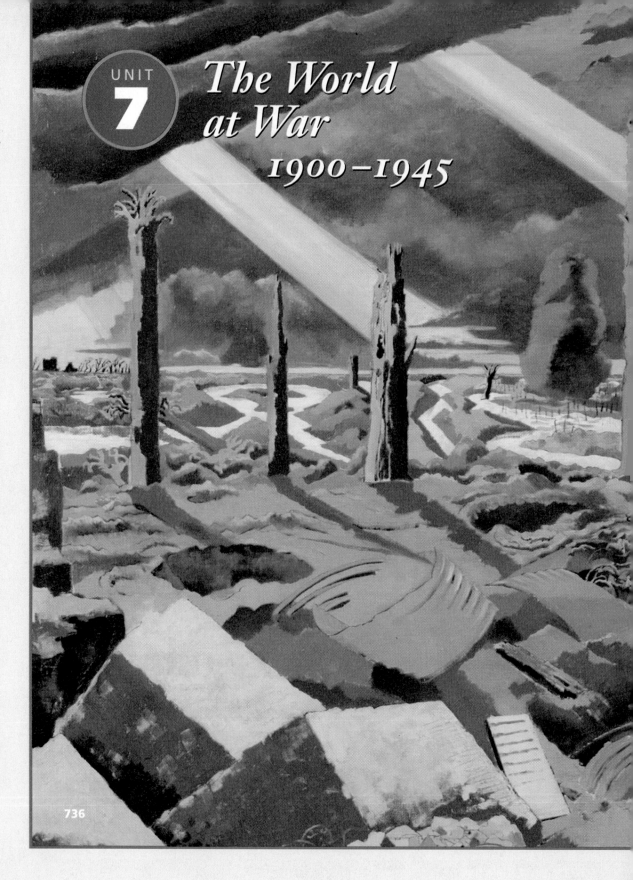

UNIT
7
The World at War
1900–1945

736

This painting, entitled *The Menin Road*, depicts the desolate, bombed-out landscape of World War I through the eyes of artist Paul Nash. Sadly, the war was merely the opening act of a half-century of global violence and bloodshed.

737

Previewing the Unit

This unit covers a period of unprecedented violence and social upheaval—from World War I, to revolution and civil war in Russia and China, to global economic depression and the rise of fascism, to World War II.

Rivalries among European powers lead to a system of military alliances that, sparked by a political assassination, draws Europe and other regions into World War I. The victors dictate harsh peace terms, leaving hard feelings that set the stage for World War II.

World War I helps ignite the Russian Revolutions of 1917, which replace czarist rule with the first communist government, under Lenin. Stalin completes the transformation of the Soviet Union into a totalitarian state. After the fall of the Qing Dynasty in China, nationalists and Communists vie for power. Nationalist movements rise in India and Southwest Asia.

New ideas in science, technology, and the arts emerge in the postwar period. The Great Depression of the 1930s brings new political crises. In response to aggression by Fascist Italy and Nazi Germany, Britain and France pursue a policy of appeasement, while the United States follows a path of isolationism.

The expansionism of Germany and Japan leads to World War II. After initial defeats in Europe and the Pacific, the Allies win the war. The victory costs millions of lives and leaves Europe and Japan economically and socially devastated.

The World at War

Teaching Strategies

Summary Charts Events relevant to a unit sometimes fall outside the range of the Unit Time Line. Also, there may be a large number of important events occurring within the range of a time line, and some events may have had to be omitted due to space limitations. In those cases, summary charts condense such information as an overview.

Because of the large number of events related to World Wars I and II, you will find three summary charts in the time line for Unit 7 *(1915–1919, 1935–1939, 1940–1945)*. You may wish to call students' attention to these charts and point out their usefulness both for synthesizing the major events of these time periods and for review.

	1905	1910	1915	1920	1925

CHAPTER 29 1914–1918
The Great War

1915–1919

1914 *The Balkans* Austria-Hungary's Archduke Franz Ferdinand and his wife are assassinated

1914 *Europe* World War I begins; Russia, France, and Britain against Germany and Austria-Hungary

1915 *Southwest Asia* Allies and Central Powers clash at Gallipoli in the Ottoman Empire

1916 *France* French suffer massive losses at the Battles of Verdun and Somme

1917 *U.S.* U.S. enters the war on the side of the Allies

1918 *Russia* Russia withdraws from the war and signs a peace treaty with Germany

1918 *Europe* The Allies defeat the Central Powers, ending World War I

1919 *France* The Allies and Germany sign the Treaty of Versailles

CHAPTER 30 1900–1939
Revolution and Nationalism

1905 *Russia* Workers revolt in St. Petersburg

1912 *China* Qing Dynasty topples

1917 *Russia* Russian Revolution ushers in a communist government

1918–20 *Russia* Civil war between Bolshevik Red Army and White Army

1919 *India* Gandhi becomes leader of the independence movement

1921 *China* Communist party forms

1922 *Russia* Union of Soviet Socialist Republics (USSR) is formed

1923 *Turkey* Kemal becomes president of the Turkish republic

CHAPTER 31 1919–1939
Years of Crisis

1919 *Germany* Weimar Republic is set up as democratic government

1920 *U.S.* First radio station broadcasts in Pittsburgh

1922 *Italy* Benito Mussolini comes to power

1923 *Germany* Hitler writes *Mein Kampf* while in jail

CHAPTER 32 1939–1945
World War II

◄*1930s Germany*

	1905	1910	1915	1920	192

CONNECTIONS ACROSS TIME AND PLACE

Weapons of War The video for Unit 7, *Arming for War: Modern and Medieval Weapons,* reviews the close relationship that has existed between technological advance and military supremacy. You may wish to discuss examples of this pattern in the video, asking students for additional examples both from history and from today's world. One of the themes developed in the video concerns the constant search for the "ultimate weapon." You might ask students to discuss examples of weapons that were considered "ultimate" in their time. They might also speculate about what the next ultimate weapon might be.

CUSTOMIZING FOR SPECIAL NEEDS

Gifted and Talented Students The first half of the 20th century produced numerous strong leaders who helped shape events in their time. The biographies appearing in *In-Depth Resources: Unit 7* provide accounts of the lives of eight leaders in war, government, diplomacy, and science. You might ask some of your more gifted students to use one of these biographies as a basis for doing further research. They might present the results of their study as a written or oral report with visuals, as a bulletin board, or as a brief dramatic scene highlighting a crucial moment in the person's life.

| 1925 | 1930 | 1935 | 1940 | 1945 |

1915 *Germany* ▶

1925 *China*
Sun Yixian dies;
Jiang Jieshi heads
Kuomintang

1928 *U.S.S.R.*
Stalin becomes
dictator

1930 *China*
Civil war between
Nationalists and
Communists erupts

1930 *India*
Gandhi organizes
the Salt March

1934 *China*
Mao Zedong leads
the Long March

1937 *China*
Japan invades China;
Chinese civil war
suspended

1930s *India* ▶

1927 *U.S.*
Charles Lindbergh
flies solo from
New York to Paris

1929 *U.S.*
Stock market crashes

1931 *China*
Japan invades
Manchuria

1933 *Germany*
Adolf Hitler appointed
chancellor

1935–1939

1935 *Ethiopia*
Italy attacks Ethiopia

1936 *Spain* Civil war erupts

1937 *China* Japan invades China

1938 *Germany* Nazis destroy
Jewish businesses on
Kristallnacht

1938 *Austria* Germany annexes
Austria

1939 *Czechoslovakia* Germany
seizes Czechoslovakia

1939 *Soviet Union* Nazi-Soviet
nonaggression pact signed

1939 *Central Europe*
Germany invades Poland;
World War II begins

1940–1945

1940 *France, Britain*
France surrenders;
Battle of Britain begins

1941 *Eastern Europe*
Germany invades
Soviet Union

1941 *U.S.* Japan bombs
Pearl Harbor; U.S. declares
war on Japan

1943 *Soviet Union* Germans
surrender at Stalingrad

1944 *France* Allies invade
Europe on D-Day

1945 *Germany*
Germany surrenders to Allies

1945 *Japan*
U.S. drops atomic bombs;
Japan surrenders

| 1925 | 1930 | 1935 | 1940 | 1945 |

TIME LINE **739**

Portfolio Project

Science and Technology The projects suggested for Unit 7 deal
with the rapid rate of technological
innovation from the beginning of
the 20th century to the end of
World War II.

Students are asked to consider
both military and civilian advances
during this period, as well as the
uses of technology by totalitarian
states.

The wide-ranging topics suggested for the Portfolio Project in
the unit reflect the multifaceted
developments in science and technology that occurred during the
first half of the 20th century. The
projects should convey a sense of
the rapidity with which these
developments took place.

Visual Learners At least one suggested project per chapter will
appeal to the visual learners in
your classroom. These include:

• a technology display
• a poster about the Trans-Siberian
Railway
• diagrams about oil-drilling techniques in Southwest Asia
• an artwork done in the style of
an architect or artist, and
• a science and technology time
line for World War II

The variety of media and formats
suggested for these projects is
designed to appeal to visual learners of differing interests and
graphic talents. You may wish to
guide students into considering
projects that best utilize their
visual skills.

The Western Civilization Videodisc

SECTION L: World War I and the Russian
Revolution, 1914–1920

Side One:
Frame 38728

SECTION M: Between the Wars, 1920–1939

Side One:
Frame 41521

SECTION N: World War II, 1939–1945

Side One:
Frame 44138

Universal Play
Button

See Master Guide, page 273 for Section L, page
291 for Section M, page 313 for Section N.

	Key Ideas	**COPY MASTERS**	**ASSESSMENT**
SECTION 1 The Stage Is Set for War *pp. 743–746*	*Nationalism unifies countries in Europe but also leads to commercial and territorial rivalries. Bismarck forms the Triple Alliance, while Britain joins with France and Russia to form the Triple Entente. An assassination causes war to break out.*	*In-Depth Resources: Unit 7* • **Guided Reading,** p. 1 • **Skillbuilder Practice:** Summarizing, p. 5 • **Primary Source:** The Murder of Archduke Franz Ferdinand, p. 8 • **History Makers:** Wilhelm II, p. 15	Section 1 Assessment, p. 746 *Formal Assessment* • Section Quiz, p. 338 *Alternative Assessment Book* • Standards for Evaluating a Product or Performance
SECTION 2 War Consumes Europe *pp. 747–752*	*European nations take up frontlines divided between the Central Powers and the Allies. Despite major battles and terrible casualties, neither side advances.*	*In-Depth Resources: Unit 7* • **Guided Reading,** p. 2 • **Geography Application:** The Battle of the Somme, p. 6 • **Primary Source:** Poison Gas, p. 9 • **Literature:** from *All Quiet on the Western Front,* p. 12; "The Soldier" and "Dulce et Decorum Est," p. 14 • **Science and Technology:** Industrial Technology Creates Poison Gas, p. 18	Section 2 Assessment, p. 751 *Formal Assessment* • Section Quiz, p. 339 *Alternative Assessment Book* • Standards for Evaluating a Cooperative Activity
SECTION 3 War Affects the World *pp. 753–759*	*The Allies expand the war beyond Europe. The U.S. enters the conflict. Citizens undergo rationing, and many women go to work in factories. Fresh American troops give the Allies an edge. The Kaiser abdicates, and an armistice is signed.*	*In-Depth Resources: Unit 7* • **Guided Reading,** p. 3 • **Primary Source:** *The Zimmerman Note,* p. 10	Section 3 Assessment, p. 757 *Formal Assessment* • Section Quiz, p. 340 *Alternative Assessment Book* • Standards for Evaluating a Cooperative Activity
SECTION 4 A Flawed Peace *pp. 760–763*	*The Treaty of Versailles ignores Wilson's Fourteen Points, creates new nations in Europe, and is rejected by the U.S. Senate. The war leaves millions dead and wounded and costs hundreds of billions of dollars.*	*In-Depth Resources: Unit 7* • **Guided Reading,** p. 4 • **Primary Source:** Signing the Treaty of Versailles, p. 11 • **History Makers:** Georges Clemenceau, p. 16 • **Connections Across Time and Cultures:** Planning for Peace: Vienna and Versailles, p. 17	Section 4 Assessment, p. 763 *Formal Assessment* • Section Quiz, p. 341 *Alternative Assessment Book* • Standards for Evaluating a Cooperative Activity
CHAPTER RESOURCES	**Chapter Overview** *With a political assassination, a complex system of alliances draws Europe into war. Some colonial subjects support the Allies, while others remain uninvolved. The Treaty of Versailles does little to build a lasting peace.*	*Telescoping the Times* • Chapter Summary, pp. 113–115 *Planning for Block Schedules*	Chapter Assessment, pp. 764–765 *Chapter Activities,* p. 765 *Formal Assessment* • Chapter Test, forms A and B, pp. 342–347 **Test Generator** *Alternative Assessment Book*

1914–1918

TECHNOLOGY

 Warm-Up Transparency 29

 Electronic Library of Primary Sources
- "Death Comes to Sarajevo"

 INTERNET RESOURCES
www.mlworldhistory.com

 Warm-Up Transparency 29

 World Art and Cultures Transparencies
- AT63 *The Fate of the Animals*
- AT64 *L'Assault*

 Electronic Library of Primary Sources
"The German Army Marches through Brussels"

 INTERNET RESOURCES
www.mlworldhistory.com

 Warm-Up Transparency 29

 Battles of the World
- The Battle of Kaiserschlacht

 Electronic Library of Primary Sources
- "A Suffolk Farmhand at Gallipoli"

INTERNET RESOURCES
www.mlworldhistory.com

 Warm-Up Transparency 29

 Geography Transparencies
- GT29 Danzig and the Polish Corridor

 Critical Thinking Transparencies
- CT29 The Human and Financial Costs of World War I
- CT65 Chapter 29 Visual Summary

 Electronic Library of Primary Sources
- The Fourteen Points

INTERNET RESOURCES
www.mlworldhistory.com

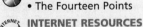 **Chapter Summaries on Audiocassette** in English and Spanish

 INTERNET RESOURCES
www.mlworldhistory.com

Block Scheduling (90 MINUTES)

Day 1
Section 1, pp. 743–746
Section Assessment, p. 746

Day 2
Section 2, pp. 747–752

 COOPERATIVE ACTIVITY
Understanding Life in the Trenches, p. 749 (Teacher's Edition)

Section Assessment, p. 751

Day 3
Section 3, pp. 753–759

 COOPERATIVE ACTIVITY
Making a Propaganda Display, p. 756 (Teacher's Edition)

Section 4, pp. 760–763

 COOPERATIVE ACTIVITY
Debating the Provisions of the Versailles Treaty, p. 761 (Teacher's Edition)

Section Assessments, pp. 757, 763

Chapter Assessments, pp. 764–765

Yearly Pacing *Chapter 29 Total:* 3 days *Yearly Total:* 85 days

Planning for Block Schedules

Customizing for Special Needs

Students Acquiring English

 Access for Students Acquiring English
- **Guided Reading** for Sections 1–4 (Spanish), pp. 291–294
- **Chapter Summary** (Spanish), pp. 288–290
- **Skillbuilder Practice** Summarizing (Spanish), p. 295
- **Geography Application** The Battle of the Somme (Spanish), p. 296

 Chapter Summaries on Audiocassette in English and Spanish

 INTERNET RESOURCES
www.mlworldhistory.com
The Diverse Classroom.

Less Proficient Readers

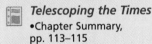 **In-Depth Resources: Unit 7**
- **Guided Reading** for Sections 1–4, pp. 1–4
- **Skillbuilder Practice** Summarizing, p. 5
- **Geography Application** The Battle of the Somme, p. 6

 Telescoping the Times
- Chapter Summary, pp. 113–115

 Chapter Summaries on Audiocassette

Gifted and Talented Students

 In-Depth Resources: Unit 7

Primary Sources
- The Murder of Archduke Franz Ferdinand, p. 8
- Poison Gas, p. 9
- *The Zimmermann Note,* p. 10
- Signing the Treaty of Versailles, p. 11

History Makers
- Wilhelm II, p. 15
- Georges Clemenceau, p. 16

Connections to Literature READINGS FOR STUDENTS

 In-Depth Resources: Unit 7
Literature: from *All Quiet on the Western Front,* p. 12; "The Soldier" and "Dulce et Decorum Est," p. 14

Enrichment Reading

Cummings, E. E.
The Enormous Room
New York: Norton, 1994

The author's experience in the ambulance corps in France during World War I.

Japrisot, Sebastien
A Very Long Engagement
New York: Plume, 1994

This story about five French soldiers in 1917 is part history and part mystery as the fiancée of one soldier later tries to learn how he died.

 PE = Pupil's Edition   = Overhead Transparency   = Software   = Video

 = Copy Master   = CD-ROM   = Audiocassette   = Internet

The Great War, 1914–1918

Accessing Prior Knowledge

• Ask students what other kinds of posters they have seen that encourage people to join a branch of a country's military. What inducements do such posters use?

• Have students note the time frame of the chapter. Perhaps family members can tell them of ancestors who fought in the war or who lived through it on the home front.

Making Predictions

• Ask students to study the war photo on page 741. How might the new weapon shown in the photo have affected the way the war was fought? What might happen if both sides had the same types of weapons?

Geography Connection

Ask students to look at the map on these two pages.

• What neutral country interrupted the line of the Western Front? *Switzerland*

• With what border did the line marking the furthest advance of the Central Powers in the east coincide? *Austria-Hungary and Russia*

CHAPTER
29 The Great War, 1914–1918

Science & Technology

Advances in weaponry, from improvements to the machine gun and airplane, to the invention of the tank, led to mass devastation during World War I.

Economics

The war greatly affected many European economies. The warring governments—desperate for resources—converted many industries to munitions factories. They also took greater control of the production of goods. In addition, they put thousands of unemployed people to work.

Power and Authority

The quest among European nations for greater power played a role in causing World War I. By the turn of the 20th century, the nations of Europe—driven by intense feelings of superiority—competed with each other on many fronts. They also built large armies to display their might.

INTERNET CONNECTION
Visit us at **www.mlworldhistory.com** to learn more about World War I.

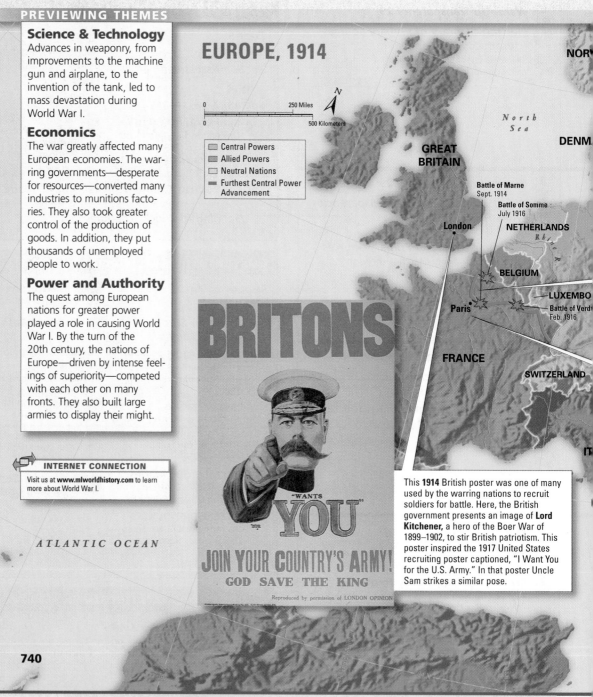

EUROPE, 1914

Central Powers
Allied Powers
Neutral Nations
Furthest Central Power Advancement

0   250 Miles
0   500 Kilometers

North Sea

NOR

GREAT BRITAIN

DENM

Battle of Marne
Sept. 1914

Battle of Somme
July 1916

London

NETHERLANDS

BELGIUM

LUXEMBO

Paris

Battle of Verd
Feb. 1916

FRANCE

SWITZERLAND

IT

ATLANTIC OCEAN

BRITONS

"WANTS" YOU

JOIN YOUR COUNTRY'S ARMY!
GOD SAVE THE KING

Reproduced by permission of LONDON OPINION

This **1914** British poster was one of many used by the warring nations to recruit soldiers for battle. Here, the British government presents an image of **Lord Kitchener,** a hero of the Boer War of 1899–1902, to stir British patriotism. This poster inspired the 1917 United States recruiting poster captioned, "I Want You for the U.S. Army." In that poster Uncle Sam strikes a similar pose.

740

GEOGRAPHY THEMES

Location

Have students examine the map on this page and on page 741 to see the locations of the continents and countries where World War I took place. Tell students that the fighting took place mostly on the continent of Europe but that other areas were also involved because of

ties with an opposing country. Ask students to examine the map here to find names of countries that may be unfamiliar to them (*Bosnia and Herzegovina*), and point out that one of the effects a war has is to rearrange boundaries and rename nations. You might ask students what they know about current unrest in Bosnia.

Movement

Tell students that in this chapter they will read about many battles between opposing armies. Have them consider the vast machinery involved in moving large numbers of soldiers, equipment, weapons, animals, and support systems from one place to another in a short time, and the effects this kind of move-

ment has on the land, the environment, and the people who already live in these areas. Remind students that armies had to seek out tank drivers among people who were wealthy enough to own cars and therefore knew how to drive.

ADDITIONAL RESOURCES

Books for the Teacher

• Dadrian, Vahakn N. *The History of the Armenian Genocide.* Providence, R.I.: Berghahn Books, 1995.

• Tuchman, Barbara. *The Guns of August.* New York: Macmillan, 1962.

Books for the Student

• Masefield, John. *John Masefield's Letters from the Front,* 1915–1917. New York: Watts, 1985.

• Vansittart, Peter. *Voices from the Great War.* New York: Watts, 1984.

Videos

• *The Great War: 1918.* PBS Video, 1989. 800–344–3337. The ordeal of war through the letters and diaries of U.S. soldiers.

• *The Politics of Peacemaking.* Coronet/MTI, 1983. 800–321–3106. Self-interest leads to a failed treaty ending World War I.

• *The Shot That Started the Great War.* Ambrose Video, 1997. 800–526–4663. The murder of Archduke Franz Ferdinand triggers a chain of events.

Software

• *The Causes of World War I.* CD-ROM. Society for Visual Education, 1994. 800–829–1900. Political, economic, and social factors leading to the Great War.

A German machine-gun team engages the enemy along the **Western Front.** The invention of new weapons and the improvement of others led to the killing of people on a scale the world had never before seen. The terrible destruction throughout Europe prompted one French soldier to write, "Humanity is mad! It must be mad to do what it is doing! . . . Hell cannot be so terrible."

This painting by John Christen Johansen depicts the signing of the **Treaty of Versailles** in **1919.** The treaty, failing to resolve many issues that caused the war, left many nations unsatisfied. Particularly bitter was Germany, which was forced to accept full responsibility for the war. "We are required to admit that we alone are war guilty," declared a senior German delegate. "Such an admission on my lips would be a lie."

741

HISTORY THROUGH ART

World War I Recruiting Posters

All of the combatant powers in the Great War used posters as a means to recruit soldiers for the war. In the United States, the government set up the nation's first propaganda agency, the Committee on Public Information, to directly popularize the war. The head of the CPI was a former muckraking journalist named George Creel. He mobilized the nation's artists and advertising people, who created thousands of paintings, cartoons, sculptures, and posters promoting the war.

James Montgomery Flagg's *I Want You,* with its portrayal of Uncle Sam, became the most famous recruiting poster in American history, but there were many others. Some World War I government posters scared Americans into buying Liberty Bonds by portraying the Germans as bloodthirsty barbarians. Some wartime posters encouraged Americans to help the war effort by saving resources such as food.

Interpreting the Art How does this poster make its appeal to potential recruits? To what feelings does it appeal? How might it make a young man feel guilty?

This Interact with History feature motivates students by inviting them to decide whether or not they would come to the support of an ally even if it meant unleashing a destructive war. As they imagine the dilemma, students will analyze the issues, explore their options, and become decision makers.

Purpose

• to set the stage for studying World War I

• to help students understand some of the causes and effects of World War I

• to help students make connections with the people and events they will study in this chapter

Teaching Strategy

Thinking Critically After students have imagined themselves in the situation, have them answer the key question and give reasons for their decision.

EXAMINING *the* ISSUES

Following are suggestions for addressing each bulleted question.

❶ Can students think of situations in today's world in which one nation has been asked to support another in a conflict?

❷ What might happen if countries did not support other countries in their wars?

❸ What might happen if countries that went to war were able to involve lots of other countries in their conflict?

Making Connections Ask students to think about the impact of extensive and destructive wars (such as the Hundred Years' War or the Napoleonic wars) on societies.

Follow Up

A feature on the chapter assessment will ask students to reevaluate their response to the situation presented on this page.

Interact *with* History

It is the summer of 1914 in Europe and tensions are high. The continent has been divided into two rival camps. The countries in each camp have pledged to fight alongside one another in case of war. Suddenly the unthinkable happens. The leader of a country you are allied with is assassinated. The dead leader's country blames a rival nation and declares war. The country calls on you to keep your word and join the war on its side.

As a member of your country's government, you are called to an emergency meeting to discuss your nation's response. On one hand, you have promised to support your ally. However, if you declare war, it probably will set off a chain reaction of war declarations throughout the two camps. As a result, all of Europe could find itself locked in a large, destructive war.

The leader of an allied nation is murdered. His country declares war and asks for your support.

If all nations keep their pledges to go to war, it will force millions of Europeans to fight and die.

Would you support your ally?

Your rival countries also have agreed to help each other in case one goes to war.

742 Chapter 29

EXAMINING *the* ISSUES

❶ • Should you always support a friend, no matter what he or she does?

❷ • What might be the risks of refusing to help an ally?

❸ • What might be the consequences of a war involving all of Europe?

As a class, discuss these questions. In your discussion, consider the various reasons why countries go to war.

As you read about World War I in this chapter, see how the nations reacted to this situation and what factors influenced their decisions.

1 The Stage Is Set for War

TERMS & NAMES
• militarism
• Triple Alliance
• Kaiser Wilhelm II
• Triple Entente

MAIN IDEA

In Europe, military buildup, nationalistic feelings, and rival alliances set the stage for a continental war.

WHY IT MATTERS NOW

Ethnic conflict in the Balkan region, which helped start the war, continued to erupt in that area in the 1990s.

SETTING THE STAGE At the turn of the 20th century, the nations of Europe had been at peace with one another for nearly 30 years. An entire generation had grown up ignorant of the horrors of war. Some Europeans believed that progress had made war a thing of the past. Yet in little more than a decade, a massive war would engulf Europe and spread across the globe.

An Uneasy Peace Grips Europe

Efforts to outlaw war and achieve a permanent peace had been gaining momentum in Europe since the middle of the 19th century. By 1900, hundreds of peace organizations were active. In addition, peace congresses convened regularly between 1843 and 1907. However, below this surface of peace and goodwill, several forces were at work that would help propel Europe into war.

The Steady Rise of Nationalism One such force was nationalism, or a deep devotion to one's nation. Nationalism can serve as a unifying force within a country. However, it also can cause intense competition between nations, with each seeking to overpower the other. By the turn of the 20th century, a fierce rivalry indeed had developed among Europe's Great Powers. Those nations were Germany, Austria-Hungary, Great Britain, Russia, Italy, and France.

This increasing rivalry among European nations stemmed from several sources. Competition for materials and markets was one. Great Britain, home of the Industrial Revolution, had long been Europe's leader in industry, finance, and shipping. After 1850, however, other nations began to challenge Britain's power. One such nation was Germany. Germany's many new industries made its economy the fastest-growing one on the continent. As a result, Germany competed with Great Britain for industrial dominance.

Nationalistic rivalries also grew out of territorial disputes. France, for example, had never gotten over the loss of Alsace-Lorraine to Germany in the Franco-Prussian War (1870). Austria-Hungary and Russia both tried to dominate in the Balkans, a region in southeast Europe. Within the Balkans, the intense nationalism of Serbs, Bulgarians, Romanians, and other ethnic groups led to demands for independence.

Imperialism Another force that helped set the stage for war in Europe was imperialism. As Chapter 27 explained, the nations of Europe competed fiercely for colonies in Africa and Asia. The quest for colonies sometimes pushed European nations to the brink of war. In 1905 and again in 1911, Germany and France nearly fought over who would control Morocco, in northern Africa. With most of Europe supporting France, Germany eventually backed down. As European countries continued to compete for overseas empires, their sense of rivalry and mistrust of one another deepened.

THINK THROUGH HISTORY
A. Analyzing Issues
What helped fuel nationalistic rivalries among the countries of Europe?
A. Possible Answer
Economic competition, territorial disputes, and independence demands.

German chancellor Otto von Bismarck led his nation to victory over France in the Franco-Prussian War in 1870. The war, which earned Germany some French territory, increased tensions between the two nations.

The Great War **743**

SECTION 1 RESOURCES

PRINT RESOURCES
IN-DEPTH RESOURCES: UNIT 7
Guided Reading, p. 1
Skillbuilder Practice: Summarizing, p. 5
Primary Source: The Murder of Archduke Franz Ferdinand, p. 8
History Makers: Wilhelm II, p. 15

ACCESS FOR STUDENTS ACQUIRING ENGLISH
Guided Reading (Spanish), p. 291
Skillbuilder Practice: (Spanish), p. 295

FORMAL ASSESSMENT
Section Quiz, p. 338

ALTERNATIVE ASSESSMENT BOOK

TECHNOLOGY RESOURCES
CD-ROM
Electronic Library of Primary Sources

INTERNET www.mlworldhistory.com

Section 1 Overview

OBJECTIVES

1. To identify the political and military forces that took root in Europe in the late 1800s.

2. To list the countries that composed the Triple Alliance and the Triple Entente.

3. To summarize the events that set World War I in motion.

SKILLBUILDER
• Interpreting maps: region, location, p. 745

CRITICAL THINKING
• Analyzing issues, pp. 743, 746
• Summarizing, p. 745
• Analyzing themes, p. 746

FOCUS

5-Minute Warm-Up

▶ **Interpreting Maps**
To help students understand the situation in Europe on the eve of World War I, have them answer the following questions.

1. Look at the map on page 745. Which landlocked country in the middle of Western Europe was neutral?

2. Which two countries on the North Sea were neutral?

WARM-UP TRANSPARENCY 29

OBJECTIVE 1 INSTRUCT

An Uneasy Peace Grips Europe

▶ **Key Ideas**
• Nationalism unifies countries in Europe but also leads to commercial and territorial rivalries.

• Competition among European nations over colonial holdings in Asia and Africa fuels rivalry.

• The arms race leads to a concentration on large armies and the ability to mobilize quickly for war.

IN-DEPTH RESOURCES: UNIT 7
Guided Reading, p. 1

ACCESS FOR STUDENTS ACQUIRING ENGLISH
Guided Reading (Spanish), p. 291

The Growth of Militarism Beginning in the 1890s, increasing nationalism led to a dangerous European arms race. The nations of Europe believed that to be truly great, they needed to have a powerful military. By 1914, all the Great Powers except Britain had large standing armies. In addition, military experts stressed the importance of being able to quickly mobilize, or organize and move troops in case of a war. Generals in each country developed highly detailed plans for such a mobilization.

The policy of glorifying military power and keeping an army prepared for war was known as **militarism.** Having a large and strong standing army made citizens feel patriotic. However, it also frightened some people. As early as 1895, Frédéric Passy, a peace activist and future Nobel Peace Prize winner, expressed a concern that many shared:

A VOICE FROM THE PAST
The entire able-bodied population are preparing to massacre one another; though no one, it is true, wants to attack, and everybody protests his love of peace and determination to maintain it, yet the whole world feels that it only requires some unforeseen incident, some unpreventable accident, for the spark to fall in a flash . . . and blow all Europe sky-high.

FRÉDÉRIC PASSY, quoted in *Nobel: The Man and His Prizes*

HISTORY MAKERS

**Kaiser Wilhelm II
1859–1941**

Wilhelm II was related to the leaders of two nations he eventually would engage in war. Wilhelm, George V of Great Britain, and Nicholas II of Russia were all cousins.

The Kaiser thought a great deal of himself and his place in history. Once, when a doctor told him he had a small cold, Wilhelm reportedly responded, "No, it is a big cold. Everything about me must be big."

The Kaiser also could be sly and deceitful. After he forced the popular Bismarck to resign, Wilhelm pretended to be upset. "I feel as sorrowful as though I had lost my grandfather all over again," he announced publicly. Most people, however, including Bismarck, were not fooled. In his retirement, the former chancellor grumbled that Wilhelm "thinks he knows better than anyone. He recognizes no authority but himself."

Tangled Alliances

The growing international rivalries had led to the creation of several military alliances among the Great Powers as early as the 1870s. This alliance system had been designed to keep peace in Europe. But it would instead help push the continent into war.

Bismarck Forges Early Pacts Between 1864 and 1871, Prussia's blood-and-iron chancellor, Otto von Bismarck, freely used war to unify Germany. After 1871, however, Bismarck declared Germany to be a "satisfied power." He then turned his energies to maintaining peace in Europe.

Bismarck saw France as the greatest threat to peace. He believed that France still wanted revenge for its defeat in the Franco-Prussian War. Bismarck's first goal, therefore, was to isolate France. "As long as it is without allies," Bismarck stressed, "France poses no danger to us." In 1879, Bismarck formed the Dual Alliance between Germany and Austria-Hungary. Three years later, Italy joined the two countries, forming the **Triple Alliance**. In 1887, Bismarck took yet another possible ally away from France by making a treaty with Russia.

Bismarck knew that his network of alliances was unstable. Two of Germany's allies, Russia and Austria, were themselves bitter rivals for the Balkans. The slightest shift in diplomatic winds could blow apart the fragile web of treaties.

Shifting Alliances Threaten Peace In 1890, Germany's foreign policy changed dramatically. That year, **Kaiser Wilhelm II**—who two years earlier had become ruler of Germany—forced Bismarck to resign. A proud and stubborn man, Wilhelm II did not wish to share power with anyone. Besides wanting to assert his own power, the new Kaiser was eager to show the world just how mighty Germany had become. The army was his greatest pride. "I and the army were born for one another," Wilhelm declared shortly after taking power.

Wilhelm set Germany on a new course. He let his nation's treaty with Russia lapse in 1890. Russia responded by forming a defensive military alliance with France in 1892 and 1894. Such an alliance had been Bismarck's fear. War with either Russia or France would

---

Vocabulary
impulsive: inclined to act on a sudden feeling rather than thought.

make Germany the enemy of both. Germany would then be forced to fight a two-front war, or a war on both its eastern and western borders.

Next, the impulsive Kaiser, envious of Britain's large empire and mighty navy, decided to challenge Britain. During the 1890s, Germany built its own small colonial empire. At the same time, Wilhelm started a tremendous shipbuilding program in an effort to make the German navy equal to Britain's.

Alarmed, Great Britain began to enlarge its own fleet. In 1904, Britain formed an entente, or alliance, with France. In 1907, Britain made another entente, this time with both France and Russia. The **Triple Entente,** as it was called, did not bind Britain to fight with France and Russia. However, it did almost certainly ensure that Britain would not fight against them.

By 1907, two rival camps existed in Europe. On one side was the Triple Alliance—Germany, Austria-Hungary, and Italy. On the other side was the

THINK THROUGH HISTORY
B. Summarizing
Which countries made up the Triple Alliance? the Triple Entente?
B. Answers Triple Alliance: Germany, Austria-Hungary, Italy. Triple Entente: Great Britain, France, Russia.

Triple Entente—Great Britain, France, and Russia. A dispute between two rival powers could draw the entire continent into war.

Crisis in the Balkans

Nowhere was that dispute more likely to occur than on the Balkan Peninsula. This mountainous peninsula in the southeastern corner of Europe was home to an assortment of ethnic groups. With a long history of nationalist uprisings and ethnic clashes, the Balkans were known as the "powder keg" of Europe.

Europe's Powder Keg By the early 1900s, the Ottoman Empire—which included the Balkan region—was in rapid decline. While some Balkan groups struggled to free themselves from Ottoman rule, others already had succeeded in breaking away from their Turkish rulers. These peoples had formed new nations, including Bulgaria, Greece, Montenegro, Romania, and Serbia.

Nationalism was a powerful force in these countries. Each group longed to extend its borders. Serbia, for example, had a large Slavic population. Serbia hoped to absorb all the Slavs on the Balkan Peninsula. On this issue of Serbian nationalism, Russia and Austria-Hungary were in direct conflict. Russia, itself a mostly Slavic nation, supported Serbian nationalism. Austria, which feared rebellion among its small Slavic population, felt threatened by Serbia's growth. In addition, both Russia and Austria-Hungary had hoped to fill the power vacuum created by the Ottoman decline in the Balkans.

In 1908, Austria annexed, or took over, Bosnia and Herzegovina.

Europe on the Eve of World War I, 1914

Triple Alliance
Triple Entente
Non-aligned nations
The Balkans

St. Petersburg
GREAT BRITAIN
North Sea
DENMARK
Baltic Sea
London
NETH.
Berlin
RUSSIA
Elbe R.
BELGIUM
GERMANY
Oder R.
Paris
LUX.
Rhine R.
ALSACE-LORRAINE
Seine R.
Danube R.
Vienna
FRANCE
SWITZ.
AUSTRIA-HUNGARY
Loire R.
BOSNIA AND HERZEGOVINA
ROMANIA
SPAIN
CORSICA (France)
ITALY
Sarajevo
SERBIA
Black Sea
Mediterranean Sea
Rome
MONTENEGRO
BULGARIA
Constantinople
SARDINIA (Italy)
ALBANIA
N
400 Miles
Sea
OTTOMAN EMPIRE
800 Kilometers
SICILY (Italy)
GREECE

GEOGRAPHY SKILLBUILDER:
Interpreting Maps
1. **Region** What countries made up the Balkans?
2. **Location** Based on the map, which alliance might have an advantage if war erupted? Why?

SPOTLIGHT ON

The Armenian Massacre
One group that suffered greatly for its independence efforts was the Armenians. By the 1880s, the roughly 2.5 million Christian Armenians in the Ottoman Empire had begun to demand their freedom. As a result, relations between the group and its Turkish rulers grew strained.

Throughout the 1890s, Turkish troops killed tens of thousands of Armenians. When World War I erupted in 1914, the Armenians pledged their support to the Turks' enemies. In response, the Turkish government deported nearly 2 million Armenians. Along the way, more than 600,000 died of starvation or were killed by Turkish soldiers.

The Great War **745**

History from Visuals

Europe on the Eve of World War I, 1914
Interpreting the Map Tell students to read the map key carefully to help them identify the nations that made up the Triple Alliance and the Triple Entente.

Extension Activity Have students speculate about what advantage Britain might have had in the war because of its geographical setting. *Its island status meant that it could not easily be invaded.*

SKILLBUILDER Answers
1. Serbia, Montenegro, Albania, Greece, Bulgaria, Romania
2. The Triple Entente. It could attack from both sides and make the enemy fight a two-front war.

OBJECTIVE ③ INSTRUCT

Crisis in the Balkans

Key Ideas
• Serbian nationalism forces wedges between Russia and Austria-Hungary.
• A Serbian nationalist assassinates the Austro-Hungarian archduke and duchess in Sarajevo.
• Austria issues an ultimatum to Serbia, rejects Serbia's offer to negotiate, and declares war.

 IN-DEPTH RESOURCES: UNIT 7 Primary Source: The Murder of Archduke Franz Ferdinand, p. 8

 ELECTRONIC LIBRARY OF PRIMARY SOURCES "Death Comes to Sarajevo"

SPOTLIGHT ON
The Armenian Massacre
Ask students to find out more about the massacre of Armenians by the Turks during World War I. Have students share what they discover with the rest of the class.

TEACHING OPTION BLOCK SCHEDULING **SKILLBUILDER MINI-LESSON: Summarizing** **CLASS TIME 15 MINUTES**

Explaining the Skill Restating an idea or a written passage in one's own words can help to clarify the meaning of the material. To summarize means to restate and condense a passage by stating only the main ideas, using words that are different from those in the original version. A summary that used the same words as the original source without giving credit to that source would be seen as plagiarism.

Applying the Skill: *Think Through History Question* To answer the Think Through History question on this page, students will need to review the material on pages 744–745. Have them take note of the boldface terms on these pages as well as the map key on page 745. Then ask the following questions:
1. Which western European nations on this map were non-aligned on the eve of World War I? *the Netherlands,*

Belgium, Luxembourg, Switzerland, Spain
2. Which were the non-aligned nations in eastern Europe and Asia? *the Balkans, the Ottoman Empire*
3. With which side was Corsica allied? *Triple Entente* What about Sardinia? *Triple Alliance*

 IN-DEPTH RESOURCES: UNIT 7 Skillbuilder Practice: Summarizing, p. 5

Teacher's Edition **745**

CONNECT to TODAY
The War in Bosnia

Anna Cataldi, an Italian journalist, was in Sarajevo during much of its long siege by Bosnian Serbs. Because the citizens of the city were forbidden to leave, Cataldi began to collect letters from people to take with her when she left. The letters tell of the horror of the daily bombardments; the stench of death; life without water, electricity, and food. They also reveal a diverse people—Christian, Muslim, and Jewish—who hated what was being done to their multicultural world by those who believed in ethnic cleansing.

Have students read Cataldi's book *Letters from Sarajevo: Voices of a Besieged City* and write about some of the people revealed in the letters. Ask volunteers to read some letters aloud.

ASSESS & RETEACH

Section 1 Assessment
Have students work in pairs to complete the assessment exercises.

Section Quiz

FORMAL ASSESSMENT
Section Quiz, p. 338

Reteaching Activity
CLASS TIME: 15 MINUTES

Go over the students' time lines for item 2 in the section assessment. Mention to students that the lead paragraph they write should answer the questions *who, what, when, why,* and *how.*

CLOSE ACTIVITY

CLASS TIME: 15 MINUTES

Identifying Causes and Effects
Have students make a list of the causes of World War I for review. For each cause, have them give one example of how the cause affected the resolution.

CONNECT to TODAY
The War in Bosnia
Intense nationalism in the Balkans led to bloodshed once again in the 1990s. Beginning in 1991, the different ethnic groups living in the country of Yugoslavia declared their independence. As the Yugoslavian republics of Slovenia, Croatia, and Bosnia and Herzegovina all broke away, the country dissolved into civil war. Serbia—Yugoslavia's largest and most influential republic—fought the independence efforts of other groups.

Eventually, the war took a terrible turn—particularly in Bosnia. With the support of the Serbian republic, Serbs living in Bosnia began a murderous campaign of "ethnic cleansing" to rid Bosnia of its non-Serb peoples. Although a United Nations-enforced agreement ended the fighting in 1996, anger and ethnic hatreds still simmer.

These were two Balkan areas with large Slavic populations. Serbian leaders, who had sought to rule these provinces, were outraged. The possibility of war arose. Russia offered Serbia full support, but the offer meant little. Russia was totally unprepared for war. When Germany stood firmly behind Austria, Russia and Serbia had to back down.

By 1914, tensions in the Balkan region were once again on the rise. Serbia had emerged victorious from several local conflicts. As a result, the nation had gained additional territory and a new confidence. It was more eager than ever to take Bosnia and Herzegovina away from Austria. In response, Austria-Hungary vowed to crush any Serbian effort to undermine its authority in the Balkans.

A Shot Rings Throughout Europe Into this poisoned atmosphere of mutual dislike and mistrust stepped the heir to the Austro-Hungarian throne, Archduke Franz Ferdinand, and his wife, Sophie. On June 28, 1914, the couple paid a state visit to Sarajevo, the capital of Bosnia. It was to be their last. The royal pair were shot at point-blank range as they rode through the streets of Sarajevo in an open car. The killer was Gavrilo Princip, a 19-year-old member of the Black Hand. The Black Hand was a secret society committed to ridding Bosnia of Austrian rule.

Because the assassin was a Serbian, Austria decided to use the murders as an excuse to punish Serbia. An angry Kaiser Wilhelm II urged Austria to be aggressive, and he offered Germany's unconditional support. In effect this gave Austria license to do what it wanted with Serbia. On July 23, Austria presented Serbia with an ultimatum. An ultimatum is a list of demands that if not met, will lead to serious consequences. The ultimatum was deliberately harsh. Demands included an end to all anti-Austrian activity. In addition, Serbian leaders would have had to allow Austrian officials into their country to conduct an investigation into the assassinations. Serbia knew that refusing the ultimatum would lead to war against the more powerful Austria. Therefore, Serbian leaders agreed to most of Austria's demands. They offered to have several others settled by an international conference.

Austria, however, was in no mood to negotiate. The nation's leaders, it seemed, had already settled on war. On July 28, Austria rejected Serbia's offer and declared war. That same day, Serbia's ally, Russia, took action. Russian leaders ordered the mobilization of troops toward the Austrian border.

Leaders all over Europe suddenly took alarm. The fragile European stability seemed about to collapse. The British foreign minister, the Italian government, and even Kaiser Wilhelm himself urged Austria and Russia to negotiate. But it was too late. The machinery of war had been set in motion.

Section 1 Assessment

1. TERMS & NAMES
Identify
- militarism
- Triple Alliance
- Kaiser Wilhelm II
- Triple Entente

2. TAKING NOTES
Create a time line of major events that led to World War I.

Write the lead paragraph of a news story about one event.

3. ANALYZING ISSUES
Why might the "machinery of war," set in motion by the assassination of Archduke Ferdinand, have been difficult to stop?

THINK ABOUT
- nationalism
- militarism
- the alliance system

4. ANALYZING THEMES
Power & Authority With another student, play the roles of Bismarck and Kaiser Wilhelm. In front of the class, debate each other over Germany's foreign policy goals.

THINK ABOUT
- the extent of Germany's "satisfaction" as a world power
- keeping Russia as an ally
- peace in Europe

ANSWERS

1. TERMS & NAMES
militarism, p. 744
Triple Alliance, p. 744
Kaiser Wilhelm II, p. 744
Triple Entente, p. 745

2. TAKING NOTES
Possible Responses: 1882 Triple Alliance formed; 1890 German foreign policy changed; 1890s European arms race; 1907 Triple Entente formed; 1908 Austria annexed Bosnia and Herzegovina; 1914 Archduke Franz Ferdinand & wife killed.

3. ANALYZING ISSUES
Possible Responses: Intense nationalism prompted nations to compete for superiority in all areas; militarism had led to the establishment of large armies, as well as to the glorification of military might; the alliance system required its members to support one another in case of war.

4. ANALYZING THEMES
Students should state clearly and correctly each man's position regarding the mentioned topics.

TERMS & NAMES
• Schlieffen Plan
• Central Powers
• Allies
• Western Front
• trench warfare
• Eastern Front

MAIN IDEA

One European nation after another was drawn into a large and industrialized war that resulted in many casualties.

WHY IT MATTERS NOW

Much of the technology of modern warfare, such as fighter planes and tanks, was introduced in World War I.

SETTING THE STAGE The assassination of Archduke Franz Ferdinand on June 28, 1914, was the spark that ignited a giant blaze. This single terrorist act set off a chain reaction within the alliance system that would result in the largest war Europe—and the world—had ever seen.

The Alliance System Collapses

By 1914, Europe was divided into two rival camps. One alliance, the Triple Entente, included Great Britain, France, and Russia. The other, known as the Triple Alliance, included Germany, Austria-Hungary, and Italy.

Austria-Hungary's declaration of war against Serbia set off a chain reaction within the alliance system. The countries of Europe followed through on their numerous and complex pledges to support one another. As a result, nearly all the nations of Europe soon were drawn into the war.

A Chain Reaction In response to Austria's declaration of war, Russia, Serbia's ally, began moving its army toward the Russian-Austrian border. Expecting Germany to join Austria, Russia also mobilized along the German border. Czar Nicholas II of Russia told the Kaiser that the maneuvers were just a precaution. Yet to Germany, Russia's mobilization amounted to a declaration of war. On August 1, the German government declared war on Russia.

Russia looked to its ally France for help. Germany, however, did not even wait for France to react. Two days after declaring war on Russia, Germany also declared war on France. Much of Europe was now locked in battle.

The Schlieffen Plan Germany quickly put its military plan into effect. The plan was named after its designer, General Alfred Graf von Schlieffen (SHLEE-fuhn). In the event of a two-front war, Schlieffen had called for attacking France and then Russia. The general had reasoned that Russia—with its lack of railroads— would have difficulty mobilizing its troops. Under the **Schlieffen Plan,** a large part of the German army would race west, to defeat France, and then return to fight Russia in the east.

Speed was vital to the German plan. The French had troops all along their border with Germany. Thus, the Germans knew that breaking through would be slow work. There was another route, however: France's northern border with Belgium was unprotected.

Germany demanded that its troops be allowed to pass through Belgium on their way to France. Belgium, a neutral country, refused. Germany then invaded Belgium. This brought Great Britain into the conflict. The British had close

This war poster shows a German soldier dragging off a woman during the invasion of Belgium. The image was intended to stir public outrage over the attack.

REMEMBER BELGIUM

Buy Bonds
Fourth
Liberty
Loan

The Great War **747**

Section 2 Overview

OBJECTIVES

(1) To describe the reaction to Austria's declaration of war.

(2) To summarize the military events on the Western Front.

(3) To explain the progression of the war on the Eastern Front.

SKILLBUILDER

• Interpreting maps: location, p. 748

CRITICAL THINKING

• Making inferences, p. 747
• Recognizing effects, p. 749
• Synthesizing, p. 751
• Comparing and contrasting, p. 751
• Clarifying, p. 752

FOCUS

5-Minute Warm-Up

▶ **Making Inferences**
Have students answer the following questions to help them understand trench warfare.

1. Look at the photograph on page 749. Why would it have been difficult to keep clothes and body clean and dry?

2. What long-term effect would living in such an environment have on people?

 WARM-UP TRANSPARENCY 29

OBJECTIVE ① INSTRUCT

The Alliance System Collapses

▶ **Key Ideas**
• A complex system of alliances and special interests draws continental Europe into war.

• European nations take up frontlines divided between the Central Powers and the Allies.

IN-DEPTH RESOURCES: UNIT 7 Guided Reading, p. 2

ACCESS FOR STUDENTS ACQUIRING ENGLISH Guided Reading (Spanish), p. 292

ELECTRONIC LIBRARY OF PRIMARY SOURCES "The German Army Marches Through Brussels"

SECTION 2 RESOURCES

PRINT RESOURCES

IN-DEPTH RESOURCES: UNIT 7
Guided Reading, p. 2
Geography Application: The Battle of the Somme, p. 6
Primary Source: Poison Gas, p. 9
Literature: from *All Quiet on the Western Front,* p. 12; "The Soldier" and "Dulce et Decorum Est," p. 14
Science and Technology, p. 18

ACCESS FOR STUDENTS ACQUIRING ENGLISH
Guided Reading (Spanish), p. 292
Geography Application Spanish, p. 296

FORMAL ASSESSMENT
Section Quiz, p. 339

TECHNOLOGY RESOURCES

WORLD ART AND CULTURES TRANSPARENCIES
AT63 *The Fate of the Animals*
AT64 *L'Assault*

CD-ROM
Electronic Library of Primary Sources

INTERNET www.mlworldhistory.com

World War I in Europe, 1914–1918

Interpreting the Map Have students examine the map and note the countries in northern Europe that remained neutral. *Norway, Sweden, and Denmark* Also have them note the large country in the west of Europe that remained neutral. *Spain*

Extension Activity Ask students why they think Germany violated Belgium's neutrality but not that of the Netherlands or Switzerland. *Students may suggest that the Netherlands does not border France, and although Switzerland does, the German strategy was to attack France and move quickly to the capital—Paris—which is directly west of Belgium.*

SKILLBUILDER Answers
1. France
2. They were between the Allies. Thus they had to fight a two-front war and could not concentrate all their resources on one front.

A Bloody Stalemate Along the Western Front

▶ **Key Ideas**
- The Allied victory at the Marne breaks the back of the Schlieffen Plan.
- Trench warfare and the failure to capture new ground make life on the Western Front an ongoing horror.
- Despite major battles and horrific casualties, neither side advances.

IN-DEPTH RESOURCES: UNIT 7
Geography Application: The Battle of the Somme, p. 6
Primary Source: Poison Gas, p. 9
Literature: from *All Quiet on the Western Front*, p. 12; "The Soldier" and "Dulce et Decorum Est," p. 14

WORLD ART AND CULTURES TRANSPARENCIES
AT63 *The Fate of the Animals*

World War I in Europe, 1914–1918

GEOGRAPHY SKILLBUILDER: Interpreting Maps
1. **Location** *In which country was almost all of the war in the West fought?*
2. **Location** *What geographic disadvantage did Germany and Austria-Hungary face in fighting the war? How might this have affected their war strategy?*

ties with Belgium, one of their nearest neighbors on the continent. Outraged over the violation of Belgian neutrality, Britain declared war on Germany on August 4.

European Nations Take Sides By mid-August 1914, the battle lines were clearly drawn. On one side were Germany and Austria-Hungary. They were known as the **Central Powers,** because of their location in the heart of Europe. Bulgaria and the Ottoman Empire would later join the Central Powers in the hopes of regaining lost territories.

On the other side were Great Britain, France, and Russia. Together, they were known as the Allied Powers or the **Allies.** Japan joined the Allies within weeks. Italy, which at first was neutral, joined the Allies nine months into the war. Italy claimed that its membership in the Triple Alliance had been a defensive strategy. The Italians felt that the Germans had made an unprovoked attack on Belgium. Therefore, the Italians argued, they were not obligated to stand by their old ally.

In the late summer of 1914, millions of soldiers marched happily off to battle, convinced that the war would be short. Only a few people foresaw the horror ahead. One of them was Britain's foreign minister, Sir Edward Grey. Staring out over London at nightfall, Grey said sadly to a friend, "The lamps are going out all over Europe. We shall not see them lit again in our lifetime."

Background
Before the war, the Central Powers were part of the Triple Alliance, and the Allies were known as the Triple Entente.

A Bloody Stalemate Along the Western Front

It did not take long for Sir Edward Grey's prediction to ring true. As the summer of 1914 turned to fall, Germany's lightning-quick strike instead turned into a long and bloody stalemate, or deadlock, along the battlefields of France. This deadlocked region in northern France became known as the **Western Front.**

748 Chapter 29

Logical-Mathematical Learners The Allied victory in the first Battle of the Marne was due in part to the reinforcement of the Allied lines by troops transported by taxicabs to the battle. Ask students, if 600 taxis were used, each one carrying 5 passengers, how many trips did each taxi make to get 6,000 troops to

the front? *Each of the 600 taxis made two trips, carrying five soldiers each time.* Have students speculate on other ways the troops could have been quickly transported to the front. Have them calculate how many troops were to be transported. How far? In how many trips?

Visual Learners Have students use the map here to aid their understanding of the actions and strategies of the opposing armies throughout the chapter. Help them become familiar with cardinal directions on the map, so that they can comfortably say, "The arrow shows that the Germans moved west across Belgium and into France" and so forth.

Also ask students questions that require their using the map key, such as "Who won the Battle of Tannenberg in August 1914?" or "Who won the Battle of Kovel in June 1916?" Then you might have students trace over the map in order to reinforce their understanding of the geography of the war.

Vocabulary
intelligence: secret information, especially such information about an enemy.

The Conflict Grinds to a Halt Early on, Germany's Schlieffen Plan worked brilliantly. By the end of August, the Germans had overrun Belgium and swept into France. By September 3, German units were on the edge of Paris. A major German victory appeared just days away. The French military then came into possession of intelligence that told them the exact direction the German army was about to take.

On September 5, the Allies attacked the Germans northeast of Paris, in the valley of the Marne River. Every available soldier was hurled into the struggle. When reinforcements were needed, more than 600 taxicabs rushed soldiers from Paris to the front. After four days of fighting, the German generals gave the order to retreat. "It was an inspiring thought," a British officer later wrote, "that the time had now come to chase the German." By September 13, the Germans had been driven back nearly 60 miles.

THINK THROUGH HISTORY
B. Recognizing Effects Why was the Battle of the Marne so significant?
B. Possible Answer It meant the ruin of the Schlieffen Plan and forced Germany to fight a war on two fronts.

Although it was only the first major clash on the Western Front, the First Battle of the Marne was perhaps the single most important event of the war. The defeat of the Germans left the Schlieffen Plan in ruins. A quick victory in the west no longer seemed possible. In the east, Russian forces had already invaded Germany. Germany was going to have to fight a long war on two fronts. Realizing this, the German high command sent thousands of troops from France to aid its forces in the east. Meanwhile, the war on the Western Front settled into a stalemate.

War in the Trenches By early 1915, opposing armies on the Western Front had dug miles of parallel trenches to protect themselves from enemy fire. This set the stage for what became known as **trench warfare.** In this type of warfare, soldiers fought each other from trenches. And armies traded huge losses for pitifully small land gains.

Life in the trenches was pure misery. "The men slept in mud, washed in mud, ate mud, and dreamed mud," wrote one soldier. The trenches swarmed with rats. Fresh food was nonexistent. Sleep was nearly impossible.

The space between the opposing trenches won the grim name "no man's land." When the officers ordered an attack, their men went "over the top" of their trenches into this bombed-out landscape. There, they usually met murderous rounds of machine-gun fire. Staying put in the trench, however, did not ensure one's safety. Artillery fire brought death right into the trenches. "Shells of all calibers kept raining on our sector," wrote one French soldier. "The trenches disappeared, filled with earth

Along the Western Front, soldiers battled one another from trenches dug out of the earth. Here, a British soldier peers out of the trench at "no man's land."

MORE ABOUT . . .
The Battle of the Marne
Finding important information by chance is not just a plot element of war and spy movies. An unfortunate German officer who drove away from his general's camp on the evening of September 1, 1914, took a wrong turn that led him into a French patrol, who killed him. When his bloodstained belongings were examined by the French, they were found to contain a map that showed two important things: the exact location of the German troops and the direction of advancement planned for the next day.

MORE ABOUT . . .
Trench Warfare
When a soldier went "over the top" of the trenches, he was expected to carry the following equipment: a rifle, a bayonet, grenades, 170 rounds of ammunition, a gas mask, a shovel and wire cutters, a full water bottle and food rations, extra clothing and medical supplies, and a portable cooking stove with fuel. Carrying all of this, he had to fight the enemy, assuming he lived while crossing "no man's land." The average kit bag weighed more than 66 pounds.

749

TEACHING OPTION | **BLOCK SCHEDULING** | **COOPERATIVE ACTIVITY: Understanding Life in the Trenches** | **CLASS TIME 30 MINUTES**

Task: Students will learn what soldiers did in the trenches, both when they were fighting and when they were not, and create a classroom display.

Purpose: To understand the mix of boredom and terror that made up life in the trenches.

Activity: Have students find a variety of sources that describe daily life in the trenches: diaries and letters written by soldiers in the war; photographs of trenches,

and narrative descriptions. For the display, some students may draw the design of a trench. Others may prepare short quotes from primary sources describing the weather, rats, bombardment, loneliness, and so forth. Encourage students to mount their writings and illustrations on a large poster display board.

📁 **Building a Portfolio:** Students should add their part of the display to their portfolio.

📖 **ALTERNATIVE ASSESSMENT BOOK**
Standards for Evaluating a Cooperative Activity

Standards for Evaluation
The display should . . .
• present clear graphic examples
• provide detailed written descriptions
• show evidence of research

A Voice from the Past

Valentine Fleming was a member of Parliament and a major in the army. His two sons—Peter, a travel writer, and Ian, the author of the James Bond spy novels—were children during World War I. Fleming ended his letter, "It's going to be a *long* war in spite of the fact that on both sides every single man wants it stopped *at once*." He was killed in 1917, fighting on the Western Front.

Tanks

The first tanks were made in Britain and grew out of a design to put machine guns on motorcycles. When Britain shipped the first of the new vehicles to France, it labeled them "water tanks" to keep the weapon secret. The name stuck. The first tank drivers were from the upper class, because they were the only ones wealthy enough to have cars and therefore know how to drive.

OBJECTIVE 3 INSTRUCT

The Battle on the Eastern Front

Key Ideas

- While Germany gains the upper hand over Russian troops, the Austrian army pushes Russia out of Austria-Hungary.
- Without modern technology, the Russian army hangs on through the sheer strength of its numbers.

The New Weapons of War

Poison Gas
Soldiers wore masks to protect themselves from a horrible new weapon—poison gas. Gas was introduced by the Germans but used by both sides. While some gases caused blinding or severe blisters, others caused death by choking.

Machine Gun
The machine gun, which fires ammunition automatically, was much improved by the time of World War I. As a result, it saw wide use in combat. Because the gun could wipe out waves of attackers and make it difficult for forces to advance, it helped create a stalemate.

Tank
The tank was an armored combat vehicle that moved on chain tracks. It was introduced by the British in 1916 at the Battle of the Somme. The early tanks were slow and clumsy. They eventually improved, and thus aided the Allies in their war effort.

. . . the air was unbreathable. Our blinded, wounded, crawling, and shouting soldiers kept falling on top of us and died splashing us with blood. It was living hell."

The Western Front had become a "terrain of death." It stretched nearly 500 miles from the North Sea to the Swiss border. A British officer described it in a letter:

> **A VOICE FROM THE PAST**
> Imagine a broad belt, ten miles or so in width, stretching from the Channel to the German frontier near Basle, which is positively littered with the bodies of men and scarified with their rude graves; in which farms, villages and cottages are shapeless heaps of blackened masonry; in which fields, roads and trees are pitted and torn and twisted by shells and disfigured by dead horses, cattle, sheep and goats, scattered in every attitude of repulsive distortion and dismemberment.
>
> **VALENTINE FLEMING,** quoted in *The First World War*

Military strategists were at a loss. New tools of war—machine guns, poison gas, armored tanks, larger artillery—had not delivered the fast-moving war they had expected. All this new technology did was kill huge numbers of people more effectively.

The slaughter reached a peak in 1916. In February, the Germans launched a massive attack against the French near Verdun. Each side lost more than 300,000 men.

In July of 1916, the British army tried to relieve the pressure on the French. British forces attacked the Germans northwest of Verdun, in the valley of the Somme River. In the first day of battle alone, more than 20,000 British soldiers were killed. By the time the Battle of the Somme ended in November, each side had suffered over half a million casualties.

What did the warring sides gain? Near Verdun, the Germans advanced about four miles. In the Somme valley, the British gained about five miles.

Background
In war, a casualty is anyone killed, injured, captured, or considered missing in action.

The Battle on the Eastern Front

Even as the war on the Western Front claimed thousands of lives, both sides were sending millions more men to fight on the **Eastern Front.** This area was a stretch of battlefield along the German and Russian border. Here, Russians and Serbs battled Germans, Austrians, and Turks. The war in the east was a more mobile war than that in the west. Here too, however, slaughter and stalemate were common.

Central Powers Gain the Advantage At the very beginning of the war, Russian forces had launched an attack into both Austria and Germany. At the end of August 1914, Germany counterattacked near the town of Tannenberg. During the four-day battle that followed, the Germans crushed the invading Russian army and drove it into full retreat. Germany regained East Prussia and seized numerous guns and horses from the enemy. More than 30,000 Russian soldiers were killed.

750 Chapter 29

TEACHING OPTION | **BLOCK SCHEDULING**

INTERPRETING ART

CLASS TIME 20 MINUTES

Task Students will examine an art transparency to learn the horrors of combat as experienced by the soldiers in World War I. Students should note the look on the face of the soldier in the forefront of the assault.

Materials Needed Use copies of Art Transparency AT64, *L'Assault.* You might also reread

the paragraph in the text on page 750 that describes the Battle of Verdun.

Activity Have students help you make up a factual list of the impact of the battle. Such a list might include the number of troops engaged in the conflict, the number of dead, the number of wounded, the length of the battle, and so forth.

Conclusion Ask students which conditions in battle would have bothered them most. Would it have been the conditions in the trenches? the launching of an assault, when the troops had to storm over the top of the trenches and into "no man's land"?

 WORLD ART AND CULTURES TRANSPARENCIES
AT64 *L'Assault*

Airplane
World War I signaled the first time in history that planes were used in a combat role. At first, nations used planes for taking photographs of enemy lines. Soon, both sides used them to drop bombs. Guns soon were attached to the planes, and pilots fought each other in the air.

Submarine
In 1914, the Germans introduced the submarine as an effective warship. German submarines, known as U-boats, eventually waged unrestricted warfare on Allied ships. The submarine's primary weapon was the torpedo, a self-propelled underwater missile.

Russia fared somewhat better against the Austrians. Russian forces defeated the Austrians twice in September 1914, driving them deep into Austria. Not until December of that year did the Austrian army—with German assistance—manage to turn the tide. In a 17-day battle near Limanowa, Austria defeated the Russians and drove them eastward. Two weeks later, the Austrian army pushed the Russians out of Austria-Hungary.

Russia's War Effort Weakens By 1916, Russia's war effort was near collapse. Unlike the nations of western Europe, Russia had yet to become industrialized. As a result, the Russian army was continually short on food, guns, ammunition, clothes, boots, and blankets. Moreover, the Allies were unable to ship supplies to Russia's ports. In the north, a German naval fleet blocked the Baltic Sea. In the south, the Ottomans still controlled the straits leading from the Mediterranean to the Black Sea.

The Russian army had only one asset—its numbers. Throughout the war the Russian army suffered enormous battlefield losses. More than 2 million Russian soldiers were killed, wounded, or captured in 1915 alone. And yet the army continually rebuilt its ranks from the country's enormous population. For more than three years, the battered Russian army managed to tie up hundreds of thousands of German troops in the east. Thus, Germany could not hurl its full fighting force at the west.

Germany and her allies, however, were concerned with more than just the Eastern or Western Fronts. As the war raged on, fighting spread beyond Europe to Africa, as well as to Southwest and Southeast Asia. In the years after it began, the massive European conflict indeed became a world war.

THINK THROUGH HISTORY
C. Synthesizing
Why was Russia's involvement in the war so important to the other Allies?
C. Possible Answer
Russia's huge army tied up German troops in the east and kept them from fighting in the west.

Section **2** Assessment

1. TERMS & NAMES
Identify
• Schlieffen Plan
• Central Powers
• Allies
• Western Front
• trench warfare
• Eastern Front

2. TAKING NOTES
Using a chart like the one below, write the immediate reason why each nation declared war on the other.

War Declaration	Reason for Declaration
Germany on Russia	
Germany on France	
Britain on Germany	

3. COMPARING AND CONTRASTING
How was war on the Western Front and Eastern Front different? How was it the same?

THINK ABOUT
• trench warfare
• which nations fought on each front
• war casualties

4. THEME ACTIVITY
Science & Technology
Draw a political cartoon showing the effects of the new technology on warfare. Include a caption that expresses the point of the cartoon.

The Great War **751**

MORE ABOUT . . .
The Eastern Front
The Schlieffen Plan was based upon the belief that Russia would take several months to mobilize. Instead, the Russian army was ready within ten days. It quickly defeated the Germans in one early battle and so threatened their army that German general Moltke took three corps from the Western Front and sent them east. The absence of these troops made it possible for the Allies to win the Battle of the Marne, but those same troops in the east helped defeat the Russians at Tannenberg.

ASSESS & RETEACH

Section 2 Assessment
Have students work in small groups to answer the questions. Have each group fill in the chart for item 2 and then compare it with those of other groups.

Section Quiz
FORMAL ASSESSMENT
Section Quiz, p. 339

Reteaching Activity
CLASS TIME: 10 MINUTES

To help students understand why each nation declared war on the others, review the charts they have made for item 2 in the section assessment.

CLOSE ACTIVITY

CLASS TIME: 15 MINUTES

Arranging Events in Sequential Order
Have students list the events in this section. Assign one student to each event. Tell students to arrange themselves in sequential order and then to explain how their event fits into the sequence.

ANSWERS

1. TERMS & NAMES
Schlieffen Plan, p. 747
Central Powers, p. 748
Allies, p. 748
Western Front, p. 748
trench warfare, p. 749
Eastern Front, p. 750

2. TAKING NOTES
Germany on Russia—saw Russia's troops along German border as threat. Germany on France—wanted a quick victory in the west. Britain on Germany—outraged over violation of Belgian neutrality.

3. COMPARING AND CONTRASTING
Possible Responses: Western Front—trench warfare; small land gains; Germany vs. Britain and France. Eastern Front—Germans, Austrians, Turks vs. Russians and Serbs; absence of trenches; more mobile warfare; larger land gains. Both—huge numbers of soldiers killed; mass destruction of land; deplorable conditions; stalemates.

4. THEME ACTIVITY
Students' cartoon should show a specific technology, such as poison gas, and its effect on soldiers, civilians, and/or the environment..

Teacher's Edition 751

The German air force ruled the skies at first. The average air combat time of a new flyer in the British Royal Air Force was 17 hours. When the Allies began to fly Sopwith Camels, they were able to threaten German dominance of the air war. The Sopwiths were so named because they carried guns in a hump behind the engine.

 IN-DEPTH RESOURCES: UNIT 7
Science and Technology: Industrial Technology Creates Poison Gas, p. 18

MORE ABOUT . . .
Pilots

The parachute had been invented by World War I. German pilots carried them, but American pilots did not. The U.S. War Department felt that a pilot would be more likely to try to bring his injured plane to safety if he could not immediately bail out when he was hit.

Aviation

World War I introduced plane warfare. And with it came daring dogfights and legendary pilots. Two such pilots were America's Eddie Rickenbacker and Germany's Baron Manfred von Richthofen, better known as the Red Baron. In a larger sense, however, the war ushered in an era of great progress in the field of aviation. In the warring nations' quest to dominate the skies, they produced thousands of planes and continually worked to improve engine designs. After the war, these nations converted their war planes to commercial use. They also began designing larger, stronger planes for civilian transport. The age of air travel had begun.

By 1926, passenger airlines were operating in Europe, Africa, Australia, and North and South America. Built in 1928, the Ford Tri-motor model, shown below, was one of the better-known American passenger planes of the time.

On the eve of World War I, planes were still considered a novelty. Here, an early plane races an automobile at a track in Columbus, Ohio, in 1914. The finish was so close that no one knew who won.

Designers of the early passenger planes made sure to devote plenty of space for luggage.

The three-motor system gave the plane greater power. It became the prototype for many later models.

Annual Ridership

Riders (in billions)

1930	1960	1990s
Less than 3 million*	100 million*	1.25 billion*

*estimated
Source: *The World Book Encyclopedia*

The Tri-motor carried about 10 passengers. Temperature control, however, was still many years away. Passengers often bundled up in coats to keep warm.

Connect *to* History

Clarifying What role did World War I play in the advancement of aviation technology?

SEE SKILLBUILDER HANDBOOK, PAGE 992.

Connect *to* Today

Investigating Find out about any one of today's more advanced aircraft, such as the Concorde, or the latest military jet or commercial airplane. Write a brief report about the craft's most advanced and interesting features. Present your report to the class.

Connect *to* History

Clarifying
Possible Answer: The desire to win battles in the air led countries to build many planes and develop new designs. These were turned to commercial uses after the war.

Connect *to* Today

Investigating
Have students discuss the different kinds of planes in which they have flown. For example, do they fly only in the big jets, or have some flown in planes with propellors? Have any students flown in gliders or been taken up with friends or relatives who fly their own small planes? Which kinds of plane travel do students prefer? Are there any they dislike?

3 War Affects the World

TERMS & NAMES
- unrestricted submarine warfare
- total war
- rationing
- propaganda
- armistice

MAIN IDEA
World War I spread to several continents and required the full resources of many governments.

WHY IT MATTERS NOW
The war propelled the United States to a new position of international power, which it retains today.

SETTING THE STAGE By early 1915, it was apparent to all the warring nations that swift victory had eluded them. As war on both European fronts promised to be a grim, drawn-out affair, all the Great Powers looked for new allies to tip the balance. They also sought new war fronts on which to achieve victory.

A Truly Global Conflict

Geographical widening of the war actually had begun soon after the conflict started. Japan entered the war on the Allies' side. The Ottoman Turks and later Bulgaria allied themselves with Germany and the Central Powers. That widened the conflict further. By early 1915, the only major neutral power left besides the United States was Italy. And Italy joined the Allies in April. None of these alliances gave an advantage to either side. But they did give military leaders more war zones in which to try to secure victory.

Fighting Rages Beyond Europe As the war dragged on, the Allies desperately searched for a way to end the stalemate. A promising strategy seemed to be to attack a region in the Ottoman Empire known as the Dardanelles. This narrow sea strait was the gateway to the Ottoman capital, Constantinople. By securing the Dardanelles, the Allies believed that they could take Constantinople, defeat the Turks, and establish a supply line to Russia. They might even be able to mount an offensive into the Austrian heartland by way of the Danube River.

The effort to take the Dardanelles strait began in February 1915. It was known as the Gallipoli campaign. British, Australian, New Zealand, and French troops made repeated assaults on the Gallipoli Peninsula on the western side of the strait. Turkish troops, some commanded by German officers, vigorously defended the region. By May, Gallipoli had turned into another bloody stalemate. Both sides dug trenches, from which they battled for the rest of the year. In December, the Allies gave up the campaign and began to evacuate. They had suffered about 250,000 casualties.

Despite the Allies' failure at Gallipoli, they remained determined to topple the Ottoman Empire. In Southwest Asia, the British helped Arab nationalists rise up against their Turkish rulers. Particularly devoted to the Arab cause was a British soldier named T. E. Lawrence. Better known as Lawrence of Arabia, he helped lead daring guerrilla raids against the Turks. With the help of the Arabs, Allied armies took control of Baghdad, Jerusalem, and Damascus.

In various parts of Asia and Africa, Germany's colonial possessions came under assault. The Japanese quickly overran German outposts in China. They also captured Germany's Pacific island colonies.

Background
Although the Ottoman Empire had greatly declined by World War I, it still ruled Arab lands in Southwest Asia.

Arab fighters patrol the desert on camels. The rider in front is believed to be T. E. Lawrence.

753

SECTION 3 RESOURCES

PRINT RESOURCES

IN-DEPTH RESOURCES: UNIT 7
Guided Reading, p. 3
Primary Source: *The Zimmermann Note,* p. 10

ACCESS FOR STUDENTS ACQUIRING ENGLISH
Guided Reading (Spanish), p. 293

FORMAL ASSESSMENT
Section Quiz, p. 340

ALTERNATIVE ASSESSMENT BOOK

TECHNOLOGY RESOURCES

CD-ROM
Battles of the World
Electronic Library of Primary Sources

INTERNET www.mlworldhistory.com

Section 3 Overview

OBJECTIVES

① To describe the escalation of World War I.

② To identify how governments established wartime economies.

③ To summarize how the Allies pushed to victory.

SKILLBUILDERS
- Interpreting maps: region, location, p. 754
- Interpreting graphs, p. 755

CRITICAL THINKING
- Summarizing, pp. 754, 756
- Comparing, p. 757
- Analyzing issues, p. 757
- Analyzing themes, p. 757
- Analyzing motives, p. 759

FOCUS

5-Minute Warm-Up

▶ **Interpreting Maps**
Have students answer the following questions to help them understand the global nature of World War I.

1. Look at the map on page 754. Which colony provided the most soldiers to fight alongside their rulers?

2. Which country that provided troops was farthest away from Europe?

WARM-UP TRANSPARENCY 29

OBJECTIVE ① INSTRUCT

A Truly Global Conflict

▶ **Key Ideas**
- The Allies expand the war, suffering grievous losses.
- Germany's attacks on passenger ships and a German plot bring the U.S. into the conflict.

IN-DEPTH RESOURCES: UNIT 7
Guided Reading, p. 3
Primary Source: *The Zimmermann Note,* p. 10

ACCESS FOR STUDENTS ACQUIRING ENGLISH
Guided Reading (Spanish), p. 293

ELECTRONIC LIBRARY OF PRIMARY SOURCES
"A Suffolk Farmhand at Gallipoli"

Black Sea
Bosporus
Constantinople
Sea of Marmara
GREECE
Gallipoli Peninsula
OTTOMAN EMPIRE
Dardanelles
Aegean Sea
N
0 100 Miles
0 200 Kilometers

English and French troops attacked Germany's four African possessions. They seized control of three.

Elsewhere in Asia and Africa, the British and French recruited subjects in their colonies for the struggle. Fighting troops as well as laborers came from India, South Africa, Senegal, Egypt, Algeria, and Indochina. Many fought and died on the battlefield. Others worked to keep the frontlines supplied. Some colonial subjects wanted nothing to do with their European rulers' conflicts. Others volunteered in the hope that service would lead to their independence. This was the view of Indian political leader Mohandas Gandhi, who supported Indian participation in the war. "If we would improve our status through the help and cooperation of the British," he wrote, "it was our duty to win their help by standing by them in their hour of need."

The United States Enters the War In 1917, the focus of the war shifted to the high seas. That year, the Germans intensified the submarine warfare that had raged in the Atlantic Ocean since shortly after the war began. By 1917, failed crops, as well as a British naval blockade, caused severe food shortages in Germany. Desperate to strike back, Germany decided to establish its own naval blockade around Britain. In January 1917, the Germans announced that their submarines would sink without warning any ship in the waters around Britain. This policy was called **unrestricted submarine warfare.**

The Germans had tried this policy before. On May 7, 1915, a German submarine, or U-boat, had sunk the British passenger ship *Lusitania.* The attack left 1,198 people dead, including 128 U.S. citizens. Germany claimed that the ship had been carrying ammunition—which turned out to be true. Nevertheless, the American public was outraged. President Woodrow Wilson sent a strong protest to Germany. After two further attacks, the Germans finally agreed to stop attacking neutral and passenger ships.

However, the Germans returned to unrestricted submarine warfare in 1917. They knew it might lead to war with the United States. They gambled that their naval

THINK THROUGH HISTORY
A. Summarizing
How did Europe's colonial subjects help in the war effort?

Vocabulary
blockade: the forced closing off of a city or other area to traffic and communication through the use of ships or land forces.

The World at War, 1914–1918

War rages in Southwest Asia as Arab nationalists battle their Turkish rulers.

Main fighting of the war occurs on Western and Eastern Fronts.

Japan declares war on Germany in 1914; seizes German colonies in China and the Pacific.

The United States enters the war on the side of the Allies in 1917.

Brazil is the only South American country to enter the war. It supports the Allies with warships and personnel.

The European colonies throughout Africa become a battlefield as the warring parties strike at one another's colonial possessions.

India provides about 1.3 million men to fight and labor alongside their British rulers throughout Europe.

Both countries fight on the side of the Allies and contribute many troops to the Gallipoli campaign of 1915, in Southwest Asia.

NORTH AMERICA · EUROPE · ASIA · JAPAN · SOUTHWEST ASIA · INDIA · AFRICA · SOUTH AMERICA · AUSTRALIA · ATLANTIC OCEAN · PACIFIC OCEAN

0 4,000 Miles
0 8,000 Kilometers

GEOGRAPHY SKILLBUILDER: Interpreting Maps
1. **Region** Which countries were aligned with the European Allies?
2. **Location** Outside of Europe, where was World War I fought?

754 Chapter 29

blockade would starve Britain into defeat before the United States could mobilize. Ignoring warnings by President Wilson, German U-boats sank three American ships.

In February 1917, another German action pushed the United States closer to war. The British intercepted a telegram from Germany's foreign secretary, Arthur Zimmermann, to the German ambassador in Mexico. The message said that Germany would help Mexico "reconquer" the land it had lost to the United States if Mexico would ally itself with Germany. The British decoded the message and gave it to the U.S. government.

When the Zimmermann note was made public, Americans called for war against Germany. Even before news of the note, many Americans had sided with the Allies. A large part of the American population felt a bond with England. The two nations shared a common ancestry and language, as well as similar democratic institutions and legal systems. In addition, reports—some true and others not—of German war atrocities stirred anti-German sentiment in the United States. More important, America's economic ties with the Allies were far stronger than those with the Central Powers. America traded with Great Britain and France more than twice as much as with Germany.

The Zimmermann note simply proved to be the last straw. On April 2, 1917, President Wilson asked Congress to declare war. The United States entered the war on the side of the Allies.

War Affects the Home Front

By the time the United States joined the Allies, the war had been going on for nearly three years. In those three years, Europe had lost more men in battle than in all the wars of the previous three centuries. The war had claimed the lives of millions and had changed countless lives forever. The Great War, as the conflict came to be known, affected everyone. It touched not only the soldiers in the trenches, but civilians as well. It affected not just military institutions, but also political, economic, and social institutions.

Governments Wage Total War World War I soon became a **total war.** This meant that countries devoted all their resources to the war effort. In Britain, Germany, Austria, Russia, and France, the entire force of government was dedicated to winning the conflict.

In each country, the wartime government took control of the economy. Governments told factories what to produce and how much. Numerous facilities were converted to munitions factories. Nearly every able-bodied civilian was put to work. Unemployment in many European countries nearly disappeared. European governments even enlisted the help of foreign workers. For example, thousands of civilians were deported from German-occupied Belgium and France to work in Germany as farm and factory laborers. Britain and France recruited Chinese, West Indian, Algerian, and Egyptian laborers to work behind their lines at the front.

So many goods were in short supply that governments turned to **rationing.** Under this system, people could buy only small amounts of those items that were also needed for the war effort. Eventually, rationing covered a wide range of goods, from butter to shoe leather.

Governments also suppressed antiwar activity—sometimes forcibly. In addition, they censored news about the war. Many leaders feared

Background
Land Mexico considered "lost" to the United States included New Mexico, Texas, and Arizona.

Vocabulary
atrocity: an act of extreme cruelty or violence.

Global Impact

Influenza Epidemic
In the spring of 1918, a powerful new enemy emerged, threatening nations on each side of World War I. This "enemy" was a deadly strain of influenza. The Spanish flu, as it was popularly known, hit England and India in May. By the fall, it had spread through Europe, Russia, Asia, and to the United States.

The influenza epidemic killed soldiers and civilians alike. In India, at least 12 million people died of influenza. In Berlin, on a single day in October, 1,500 people died. In the end, this global epidemic was more destructive than the war itself, killing 20 million people worldwide.

Unemployment in Germany and Britain

Germany
Great Britain

Source: *European Historical Statistics 1750–1975*

SKILLBUILDER:
Interpreting Graphs
1. *During which year did each country see its lowest unemployment rate?*
2. *Why might unemployment have been lowest during the war years?*

The Great War **755**

Global Impact

Influenza Epidemic
Many epidemiologists now believe that the influenza epidemic started in army camps in the United States. Ask students to find out more about the epidemic and report their findings to the class.

OBJECTIVE 2 INSTRUCT

War Affects the Home Front

▶ *Key Ideas*
• World War I becomes a total war, and governments take control of national economies.
• In the U.S. and Europe, citizens undergo rationing of goods.
• With millions of men at the front, many women go to work in factories and elsewhere.

History from Visuals

Unemployment in Germany and Britain
Interpreting a Graph Help students read the graph by pointing out to them that the unemployment rate in Great Britain in 1914 was about 3.5 percent and in Germany in the same year about 7.25 percent.

Extension Activity Ask students what happened to the unemployment rate at the end of the war. *After dipping during war, the unemployment rate climbed back up at the end of the war.*

SKILLBUILDER Answers
1. Great Britain, 1916; Germany, 1917
2. As part of a total war effort, governments sought to increase production, which meant hiring more workers.

TEACHING OPTIONS

CONNECTIONS ACROSS THE CURRICULUM

Science Antibiotics would not have helped against the virus that causes influenza, because a virus is not a biological agent. Antibiotics work against bacterial infections. However, a growing problem today is that antibiotics are becoming less effective against bacteria, which have developed resistance to them. Just as any organism tries to adapt in order to survive, bacteria have become stronger than the antibiotics used to kill them. Scientists are working hard to develop new antibiotics that will work against these new strains of bacteria.

CUSTOMIZING FOR SPECIAL NEEDS

Gifted and Talented Students
Researching the Influenza Epidemic Influenza was not a new disease in 1918, but it was targeting the young and healthy, including hundreds of thousands of soldiers in the trenches. Drinking fountains were blowtorched every hour, telephones were sterilized with alcohol, and people wore gauze masks. But the flu moved through the countryside and towns despite such precautions. Have students research the flu epidemic of 1918 in order to list some of the treatments that were suggested at the time. *These included chewing snuff, chewing tobacco, removing the patient's tonsils, extracting teeth, and sprinkling sulfur in shoes.*

Teacher's Edition **755**

In total war all citizens were called on to help in the war effort. Thus women were offered new employment opportunities. Pictured here are women workers at a French munitions factory.

that honest reporting of the war would turn people against it. Governments also used **propaganda**—one-sided information designed to persuade—to keep up morale and support for the war. One of the main instruments of propaganda was the war poster. In nations throughout Europe, striking, colorful posters urged support for the war by painting the enemy as monsters and allies as heroes. (See poster on page 747.)

The War's Impact on Women Total war meant that governments turned to help from women as never before. Thousands of women replaced men in factories, offices, and shops. Women built tanks and munitions, plowed fields, paved streets, and ran hospitals. They also kept troops supplied with food, clothing, and weapons. Although most women left the work force when the war ended, they changed many people's views of what women were capable of doing.

The Allies Win the War
With the United States finally in the war, the balance, it seemed, was about to tip in the Allies' favor. Before that happened, however, events in Russia gave Germany a victory on the Eastern Front.

Russia Withdraws from the War By March 1917, civil unrest in Russia—due in part to war-related shortages of food and fuel—had brought the czar's government to the brink of collapse. Czar Nicholas, faced with the prospect of revolution, abdicated his throne on March 15. In his place a provisional government was established. The new government pledged to continue fighting the war. However, by 1917, nearly 5.5 million Russian soldiers had been wounded, killed, or taken prisoner. The war-weary Russian army refused to fight any longer.

Eight months later, a second revolution shook Russia (see Chapter 30). In November 1917, Communist leader Vladimir Ilyich Lenin seized power. Lenin insisted on ending his country's involvement in the war. One of his first acts was to offer Germany a truce. In March 1918, Germany and Russia signed the Treaty of Brest-Litovsk, which ended the war between them.

The treaty was extremely hard on Russia. It required the Russian government to surrender lands to Germany that now include Finland, Poland, Ukraine, Estonia, Latvia, and Lithuania. (See map on page 762.) Even though the treaty became invalid after the war, these nations still gained their independence.

A Failed Final Push Russia's withdrawal from the war at last allowed Germany to send nearly all its forces to the Western Front. In March 1918, the Germans mounted one final, massive attack on the Allies in France. More than 6,000 German cannons opened the offensive with the largest artillery attack of the entire war.

As in the opening weeks of the war, the German forces crushed everything in their path. By late May 1918, the Germans had again reached the Marne River. Paris was less than 40 miles away. Victory seemed within reach.

By this time, however, the German military had weakened. The effort to reach the Marne had exhausted men and supplies alike. Sensing this weakness, the Allies—with the aid of nearly 140,000 fresh American troops—launched a counterattack. Marshal Ferdinand Foch, the French commander of the Allied forces, used Americans to fill the gaps in his ranks. The U.S. soldiers were inexperienced but courageous and eager to

---

1914

June 1914
Archduke Ferdinand and his wife are assassinated.

July 1914
Austria-Hungary declares war on Serbia.

July–August 1914
Russia, France, and Britain go to war against Germany and Austria-Hungary.

1916

1916
Combatants suffer devastating losses at battles of Verdun and the Somme.

1917

1917
United States enters the war.

1918

March 1918
Russia withdraws from the war.

July 1918
Allies defeat Germany at Second Battle of the Marne.

November 1918
Warring nations sign armistice ending the war.

British and German soldiers help one another during a break in the fighting.

fight. A British nurse, Vera Brittain, later recalled her joy in seeing the American reinforcements:

A VOICE FROM THE PAST

They were swinging rapidly toward Camiers, and though the sight of soldiers marching was now too familiar to arouse curiosity, an unusual quality of bold vigor in their swift stride caused me to stare at them with puzzled interest. They looked larger than ordinary men; their tall, straight figures were in vivid contrast to the undersized armies of pale recruits to which we had grown accustomed. . . . Then I heard an excited exclamation from a group of Sisters behind me. "Look! Look! Here are the Americans!"

VERA BRITTAIN, *Testament of Youth*

THINK THROUGH HISTORY
C. Comparing How was the Second Battle of the Marne similar to the first?
C. Possible Answer Both times, the Allies defeated the Germans just as they seemed poised for victory.

In July 1918, the Allies and Germans clashed at the Second Battle of the Marne. Leading the Allied attack were some 350 tanks that rumbled slowly forward, smashing through the German lines. With the arrival of 2 million more American troops, the Allied forces began to advance steadily toward Germany.

Soon, the Central Powers began to crumble. First the Bulgarians and then the Ottoman Turks surrendered. In October, a revolution in Austria-Hungary brought that empire to an end. In Germany, soldiers mutinied, and the public turned on the Kaiser.

On November 9, 1918, Kaiser Wilhelm II was forced to step down. Germany declared itself a republic. A representative of the new German government met with Marshal Foch. In a railway car in a forest near Paris, the two signed an **armistice,** or an agreement to stop fighting. On November 11, World War I came to an end.

After four years of slaughter and destruction, the time had come to forge a peace settlement. Leaders of the victorious nations gathered outside Paris to work out the terms of peace. While these leaders had come with high hopes, the peace settlement they crafted left many feeling bitter and betrayed.

Section 3 Assessment

1. TERMS & NAMES
Identify
• unrestricted submarine warfare
• total war
• rationing
• propaganda
• armistice

2. TAKING NOTES
Using a chart like the one below, list the reasons why the United States entered World War I.

Reasons for U.S. Entry
1.
2.
3.
4.

3. ANALYZING ISSUES
In what ways was World War I truly a global conflict?

THINK ABOUT
• where the war was fought
• who participated in the war effort

4. ANALYZING THEMES
Economics How did the concept of total war affect the warring nations' economies?

THINK ABOUT
• the governments' new role in their economies
• the scarcity of food and other products
• the role of women
• unemployment rates during the war years

The Great War **757**

MORE ABOUT . . .
A Voice from the Past

Vera Brittain lost her fiancé, her brother, and two close friends in the war, not unusual for families in Britain and France, to say nothing of Germany. Her book *Testament of Youth* is well worth reading for an account of the war from an observer on two fronts—at home and as a nurse on the frontlines.

ASSESS & RETEACH

Section 3 Assessment
Have the class divide into two groups to answer the questions, then have one group compare its answers with those of the other.

Section Quiz
FORMAL ASSESSMENT
Section Quiz, p. 340

Reteaching Activity
CLASS TIME: 10 MINUTES

Have students make a list of factors that brought the U.S. into the war and then a second list telling how the war affected people on the home front.

CLOSE ACTIVITY

CLASS TIME: 10 MINUTES

Role-Playing
Have a pair of students play the roles of President Wilson and German foreign secretary Zimmermann. Have them stage a press conference in which they defend their differing views of the telegram sent by the foreign secretary to the German ambassador in Mexico. Other students will play reporters and ask questions of the two.

Honoring War Heroes

Throughout history, people around the world have shared in a somber, healing ritual: honoring their country's soldiers killed in battle. In many nations, people come together to honor those citizens who have fought and died for their country. After World War I, France built a ceremonial grave to honor all of its soldiers killed in the great conflict. From early times to today, other nations have paid their respects to their dead soldiers with medals, monuments, and parades.

France

United States

Italy

China

Tomb of the Unknown Soldier
A woman pays her quiet respects at the Tomb of the Unknown Soldier in Paris. On top of the memorial rests an eternal flame in honor of France's dead soldiers. Each year on Armistice Day, the president of France lays a wreath at the site. Following World War I, similar memorials to unknown dead soldiers were created in the United States, Great Britain, Belgium, and Italy.

a **closer** look WORLD WAR I MONUMENTS

This German war memorial was built in 1926 and placed in the courtyard of the Technical University in Berlin.

The Wall

A man pays tribute at the Vietnam Veterans Memorial in Washington, D.C. The monument, known as the Wall, is a memorial to the men and women who fought and died in the Vietnam War in the 1960s and 1970s. The monument consists of two adjoining black granite walls inscribed with the names of all Americans who either died in the war or were listed as missing in action.

"The People's Heroes"

This monument is a tribute to the Chinese armed forces, officially known as the People's Liberation Army. The monument, which sits in Beijing, is called the Memorial to the People's Heroes. It is a tribute to the soldiers, past and present, who have taken part in the struggle to forge a Communist China, which began around 1946.

Great Britain built its own Tomb of the Unknown Warrior in London to honor those who lost their lives in World War I.

Trajan's Column

The Romans relied greatly on their powerful military to oversee a huge empire. Consequently, they glorified war and soldiers with numerous statues and monuments. Shown here is a detail from Trajan's Column, in Rome. The 100-foot-high column was dedicated in A.D. 113 to the emperor Trajan after he conquered Dacia. The column is a continuous spiral carving of soldiers and battle scenes.

Connect *to* History

Analyzing Motives Why do you think nations honor their dead soldiers?

 SEE SKILLBUILDER HANDBOOK, PAGE 994

Connect *to* Today

Designing Working with one or more students, design a memorial to your country's dead soldiers. Include any words or images that you feel convey your message. Present the memorial to the class.

The Great War **759**

CRITICAL THINKING ACTIVITY
CLASS TIME: 10 MINUTES

Making a Chart
To help students recognize that there are different kinds of memorials, have them make a chart listing the various monuments described on these two pages.

Kind of Monument	Specific Example

MORE ABOUT . . .
Trajan's Column

Trajan's Column stands in Trajan's Forum in Rome. There is a spiral staircase inside the column that leads to the top. According to some sources the ashes of Trajan were sealed inside the column, but they have never been found.

Connect *to* History

Analyzing Motives
Possible Answer: Nations honor their dead for a variety of reasons, including to recognize soldiers' valor in combat, honor their families, encourage the young in martial virtues, and ensure that soldiers' valiant deeds will be remembered.

Connect *to* Today

Designing
Students might work in a variety of mediums to design their memorial. For example, they might draw a design, model one in clay or popsicle sticks, or copy examples of memorials they admire from books and other sources.

OBJECTIVES

 To list the main points of the Treaty of Versailles.

 To describe the effects of World War I on Western society.

SKILLBUILDERS

- Interpreting charts, p. 761
- Interpreting maps: region, location, p. 762

CRITICAL THINKING

- Summarizing, p. 760
- Contrasting, p. 761
- Analyzing issues, p. 762
- Making inferences, p. 763
- Forming opinions, p. 763

FOCUS
5-Minute Warm-Up

▶ **Making Inferences**
To help students understand the importance of individuals in history, have them answer the following questions.

1. Read the History Makers on page 760. Why might Clemenceau have been more concerned with revenge and punishment than was Wilson?

2. What does Lloyd George's comment about the two men seem to imply about them?

 WARM-UP TRANSPARENCY 29

OBJECTIVE ① INSTRUCT

The Allies Meet at Versailles

▶ **Key Ideas**
- Wilson submits 14 points.
- The Treaty of Versailles punishes Germany and makes new nations.
- A League of Nations is created but given little power.

IN-DEPTH RESOURCES: UNIT 7
Guided Reading, p. 4

ACCESS FOR STUDENTS ACQUIRING ENGLISH
Guided Reading (Spanish), p. 294

GEOGRAPHY TRANSPARENCIES
GT29 Danzig and the Polish Corridor, 1919

ELECTRONIC LIBRARY OF PRIMARY SOURCES
The Fourteen Points

---

4 A Flawed Peace

TERMS & NAMES
- Woodrow Wilson
- Georges Clemenceau
- David Lloyd George
- Fourteen Points
- self-determination
- Treaty of Versailles
- League of Nations

MAIN IDEA	WHY IT MATTERS NOW
After winning the war, the Allies dictated a harsh peace settlement that left many nations feeling betrayed.	Hard feelings left by the peace settlement helped cause World War II.

SETTING THE STAGE World War I was over. The killing had stopped. The terms of peace, however, still had to be worked out. On January 18, 1919, a conference to establish those terms began at the Palace of Versailles, outside Paris. For one year this conference would be the scene of vigorous, often bitter debate. The Allied powers struggled to solve their conflicting aims in various peace treaties.

The Allies Meet at Versailles

Attending the talks, known as the Paris Peace Conference, were delegates representing 32 countries. However, the meeting's major decisions were hammered out by a group known as the Big Four: **Woodrow Wilson** of the United States, **Georges Clemenceau** of France, **David Lloyd George** of Great Britain, and Vittorio Orlando of Italy. Russia, in the grip of civil war, was not represented. Neither were Germany and its allies.

Wilson's Plan for Peace In January 1918, while the war was still raging, President Wilson had drawn up a series of proposals. Known as the **Fourteen Points,** they outlined a plan for achieving a just and lasting peace. The first five points included an end to secret treaties, freedom of the seas, free trade, and reduced national armies and navies. The fifth goal was the adjustment of colonial claims with fairness toward colonial peoples. The sixth through thirteenth points were specific suggestions for changing borders and creating new nations. The guiding idea behind these points was **self-determination.** This meant allowing people to decide for themselves under what government they wished to live.

Finally, the fourteenth point proposed a "general association of nations" that would protect "great and small states alike." This reflected Wilson's hope for an organization that could peacefully negotiate solutions to world conflicts.

HISTORY MAKERS

Georges Clemenceau
1841–1929

Woodrow Wilson
1856–1924

The most hostile relationship at the Paris Peace Conference was that between two allies: Wilson and Clemenceau. These two highly intelligent and committed leaders brought very different visions of peace to the negotiating table.

Woodrow Wilson was the son of a Presbyterian minister. He had been a history scholar, professor, and president of Princeton University before becoming president. A morally upright man, he was guided by a deep inner religious faith.

Clemenceau, by contrast, had been a physician, journalist, and sometime playwright before becoming premier of France.

In Paris, the two men clashed. Wilson's idealism, as embodied in the Fourteen Points, stood in stark contrast to Clemenceau's desire to punish Germany.

The stubborn personalities of the two men made reaching agreement even harder. Lloyd George of Britain summed it up nicely when he was asked how he did at the Paris Peace Conference. "Not badly," he replied, "considering I was seated between Jesus Christ and Napoleon."

A. Possible Answer An end to secret treaties, freedom of the seas, free trade, reduced national armies and navies, and the adjustment of colonial claims with fairness toward colonial people.

THINK THROUGH HISTORY
A. Summarizing What were Wilson's general goals for the postwar world?

SECTION 4 RESOURCES

PRINT RESOURCES

IN-DEPTH RESOURCES: UNIT 7
Guided Reading, p. 4
Primary Source: Signing the Treaty of Versailles, p. 11
History Makers: Georges Clemenceau, p. 16

ACCESS FOR STUDENTS ACQUIRING ENGLISH
Guided Reading (Spanish), p. 294

FORMAL ASSESSMENT
Section Quiz, p. 341

ALTERNATIVE ASSESSMENT BOOK

TECHNOLOGY RESOURCES

GEOGRAPHY TRANSPARENCIES
GT29 Danzig and the Polish Corridor, 1919

CRITICAL THINKING TRANSPARENCIES
CT29 The Human and Financial Costs of World War I
CT65 Chapter 29 Visual Summary

CD-ROM
Electronic Library of Primary Sources

 INTERNET www.mlworldhistory.com

THINK THROUGH HISTORY

B. Contrasting
How did Britain and France's aims at Versailles differ from Wilson's?

B. Possible Answer
Britain and France were concerned mainly with punishing Germany and stripping it of its war-making power, while Wilson was more concerned with achieving a just peace.

The Allies Dictate a Harsh Peace As the Paris Peace Conference opened, Britain and France showed little sign of agreeing to Wilson's vision of peace. Both nations were concerned with national security. They also wanted to strip Germany of its war-making power. The French, in particular, were determined to punish Germany. France was where much of the fighting had occurred. The nation had lost more than a million soldiers and had seen large amounts of its land destroyed. Clemenceau wanted Germany to pay for the suffering the war had caused.

The differences between French, British, and U.S. aims led to heated arguments among the nations' leaders. Finally a compromise was reached. The **Treaty of Versailles** between Germany and the Allied powers was signed on June 28, 1919— five years to the day after Franz Ferdinand's assassination in Sarajevo.

Adopting Wilson's fourteenth point, the treaty created a **League of Nations.** The league was to be an international association whose goal would be to keep peace among nations. The five Allied powers—the United States, Great Britain, France, Italy, and Japan—were to be permanent members of the league's Executive Council. Its General Assembly would consist of representatives of 32 Allied and neutral nations. Germany was deliberately excluded. Also left out was Russia. Russia's early withdrawal from the war and its revolutionary leadership had made it an outcast in the eyes of the other Allies.

The treaty also punished Germany. The defeated nation lost substantial territory and had severe restrictions placed on its military operations. As punishing as these provisions were, the harshest was Article 231. It was also known as the "war guilt" clause. It placed sole responsibility for the war on Germany's shoulders. As a result, Germany had to pay reparations to the Allies.

All of Germany's territories in Africa and the Pacific were declared mandates, or territories to be administered by the League of Nations. Under the peace agreement, the Allies would govern the mandates until they were judged ready for independence.

The Treaty of Versailles: Major Provisions

League of Nations	Territorial Losses	Military Restrictions	War Guilt
• International peace organization; membership to include Allied war powers and 32 Allied and neutral nations • Germany and Russia excluded	• Germany returns Alsace-Lorraine to France; French border extended to the west bank of the Rhine River • Germany surrenders all of its overseas colonies in Africa and the Pacific	• Limits set on the size of the German army • Germany prohibited from importing or manufacturing weapons or war materiel • Germany forbidden to build or buy submarines or have an air force	• Sole responsibility for the war placed on Germany's shoulders • Germany forced to pay the Allies $33 billion in reparations over 30 years

SKILLBUILDER: Interpreting Charts
1. *In what ways did the treaty punish Germany?*
2. *What two provinces were returned to France as a result of the treaty?*

The Creation of New Nations The Versailles treaty with Germany was just one of five treaties negotiated by the Allies. The Western powers signed separate peace treaties in 1919 and 1920 with each of the other defeated nations: Austria, Hungary, Bulgaria, and the Ottoman Empire.

These treaties, too, led to huge land losses for the Central Powers. Several new countries were created out of the Austro-Hungarian Empire. Austria, Hungary, Czechoslovakia, and Yugoslavia were all recognized as independent nations.

The Great War **761**

Europe Before World War I
Europe After World War I

Interpreting the Maps Have students examine the maps to see the major changes that occurred from the beginning of the war to the end. Have them note the new nations that were created in the former Austro-Hungarian Empire and in the northern and north-western portions of Russia. Also have them note that on this map color has no political meaning but simply distinguishes one country from another.

Extension Activity Have students note the change in the status of Great Britain by the end of the war. *Ireland had become a dominion in the British Commonwealth.* Have students do some research to find out when and how Ireland achieved its independence.

SKILLBUILDER Answers
1. Austria-Hungary
2. Russia's

MORE ABOUT . . .
The Aftermath

When the German diplomats were called to Versailles to sign the treaty, they were in a terrible position. Britain was blockading Germany, and without regular food deliveries, Germans were close to starvation. The blockade would only be ended if Germany signed the treaty. This situation, added to the provisions of the treaty, increased the Germans' resentment.

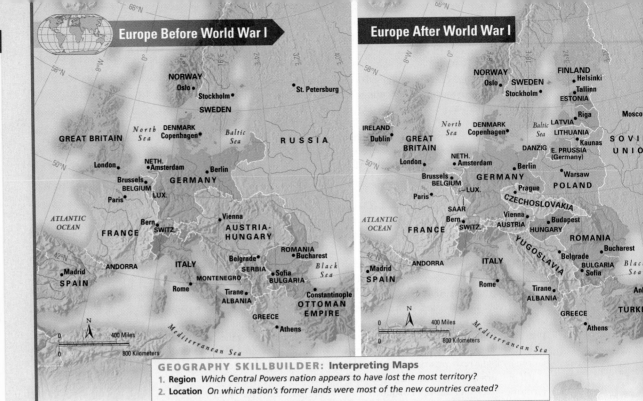

Europe Before World War I

Europe After World War I

GEOGRAPHY SKILLBUILDER: Interpreting Maps
1. **Region** *Which Central Powers nation appears to have lost the most territory?*
2. **Location** *On which nation's former lands were most of the new countries created?*

The Ottoman Turks were forced to give up almost all of their former empire. They retained only the territory that is today the country of Turkey. The Allies carved up the lands that the Ottomans lost in Southwest Asia into mandates rather than independent nations. Palestine, Iraq, and Transjordan came under British control; Syria and Lebanon went to France.

Russia, alienated by the Allies, suffered land losses as well. Romania and Poland both gained Russian territory. Finland, Estonia, Latvia, and Lithuania, formerly part of Russia, became independent nations.

"A Peace Built on Quicksand" In the end, the Treaty of Versailles did little to build a lasting peace. For one thing, the United States—considered after the war to be the dominant nation in the world—ultimately rejected the treaty. Many Americans objected to the settlement and especially to President Wilson's League of Nations. Americans believed that the United States' best hope for peace was to stay out of European affairs. The United States worked out a separate treaty with Germany and its allies several years later.

In addition, the treaty with Germany—in particular the war-guilt clause—left a legacy of bitterness and hatred in the hearts of the German people. Other countries felt cheated and betrayed as well by the peace settlements. Throughout Africa and Asia, people in the mandated territories were angry at the way the Allies disregarded their desire for independence. The European powers, it seemed to them, merely talked about the principle of national self-determination. European colonialism, disguised as the mandate system, continued in Asia and Africa.

Some Allied powers, too, were embittered by the outcome. Both Japan and Italy, which had entered the war to gain territory, had gained less than they wanted.

Lacking the support of the United States, and later other world powers, the League of Nations was in no position to take action on these complaints. The settlements at

762 Chapter 29

C. Possible Answer Germany was embittered by the war-guilt clause, the peoples of Africa and Asia saw the mandate system as a continuation of European colonialism, Japan and Italy had gained less land than they wanted

THINK THROUGH HISTORY
C. Analyzing Issues What complaints did various countries voice about the Treaty of Versailles?

Gifted and Talented Students:
Researching War Poetry Have students find collections of poetry written during World War I, particularly by those who fought. Poets they might investigate include the following: Siegfried Sassoon, Wilfred Owen, Robert Graves, and Alan Seeger. What images

did these poets use to describe their experiences? What feelings did they have about the war and the people who led them into the war? Which poets died in the war? Students may copy out a selection of their favorite poems and mount them in a display, along with biographical information about each poet.

Students Acquiring English:
Developing Vocabulary Have students work with some of the words in this section that denote or describe feelings and emotions. On this page, for example, are *bitterness, hatred, cheated, betrayed, angry,* etc. Have them define each word and give an example of how someone with that

feeling would act. Then have students make lists of related words, such as *bitterness, embittered, bitterly; betrayed, betrayal, traitor;* and so forth, and use each in a sentence. Finally, students might draw pictures of faces showing these emotions or list actions that could result from these feelings.

Versailles represented, as one observer noted, "a peace built on quicksand." Indeed, that quicksand eventually would give way. In a little more than two decades, the treaties' legacy of bitterness would help plunge the world into another catastrophic war.

The Legacy of the War

World War I was, in many ways, a new kind of war. It involved the use of new technologies. It ushered in the notion of war on a grand and global scale. It also left behind a landscape of death and destruction such as was never before seen.

The War's Extreme Cost Both sides in World War I paid a tremendous price in terms of human life. About 8.5 million soldiers died as a result of the war. Another 21 million more were wounded. In addition, the war led to the death of countless civilians by way of starvation, disease, and slaughter. Taken together, these figures spelled tragedy—an entire generation of Europeans wiped out.

The war also had a devastating economic impact on Europe. The great conflict drained the treasuries of Europe. One account put the total cost of the war at $338 billion—a staggering amount for that time. The war also destroyed acres of farmland, as well as homes, villages, and towns.

A Lost Generation The enormous suffering and apparent pointlessness of the Great War left a deep mark on Western society as well. A sense of disillusionment settled over the survivors. The insecurity and despair that many people experienced are reflected in the art and literature of the time. In a poem written in 1919, the Russian poet Anna Akhmatova captured these feelings:

> **A VOICE FROM THE PAST**
> Why is our century worse than any other?
> Is it that in the stupor of fear and grief
> It has plunged its fingers in the blackest ulcer,
> Yet cannot bring relief?
>
> Westward the sun is dropping,
> And the roofs of towns are shining in its light.
> Already death is chalking doors with crosses
> And calling the ravens and the ravens are in flight.
>
> **ANNA AKHMATOVA**, from *You Will Hear Thunder*, translated by D. M. Thomas

The Great War shook European society to its foundations. While the war would continue to haunt future generations, its more immediate impact was to help ignite one of the most significant events of the 20th century. In Chapter 30, you will learn about that event: the Russian Revolution.

Section 4 Assessment

1. TERMS & NAMES

Identify
- Woodrow Wilson
- Georges Clemenceau
- David Lloyd George
- Fourteen Points
- self-determination
- Treaty of Versailles
- League of Nations

2. TAKING NOTES

Using a web diagram like the one below, show the effects of World War I.

Effects of WWI

Which effect do you think was most significant? Why?

3. FORMING OPINIONS

Do you think the peace settlements at Versailles were fair? Why or why not? Consider the warring and nonwarring nations affected.

THINK ABOUT
- Germany's punishment
- the creation of new nations
- the mandate system

4. THEME ACTIVITY

Power and Authority In small groups, create a list of 8-10 interview questions a reporter might ask Wilson, Clemenceau, or Lloyd George about the Paris Peace Conference. Ask about such topics as:

- Wilson's Fourteen Points
- the handling of Germany and Russia
- the numerous demands from different nations and groups

The Great War **763**

TERMS & NAMES

1. Triple Alliance, p. 744
2. Triple Entente, p. 745
3. Central Powers, p. 748
4. Allies, p. 748
5. trench warfare, p. 749
6. total war, p. 755
7. armistice, p. 757
8. Fourteen Points, p. 760
9. Treaty of Versailles, p. 761
10. League of Nations, p. 761

REVIEW QUESTIONS

Answers will vary.

11. Nationalism and imperialism intensified rivalries between nations, while militarism led countries to increase the size of their armies.

12. The Balkans, which are home to many ethnic groups, had a long history of nationalist uprising and ethnic clashes.

13. Germany's defeat there meant that it had to abandon the Schlieffen Plan and fight a two-front war.

14. The Western Front extended across northern France from the North Sea to the Swiss border. The Eastern Front stretched along the German and Russian border.

15. Military stalemate, huge losses on both sides, miserable living conditions, and little territorial gain.

16. The campaign was an attempt to conquer the Dardanelles and Constantinople and eventually establish a supply line to Russia.

17. Unrestricted submarine warfare, the Zimmermann note, a common bond with and sympathy toward the Allies.

18. Governments devoted all their resources to winning the war. They took control of the economy, converted many industries to munitions factories, put numerous citizens to work, used propaganda and censorship, and instituted a policy of rationing.

19. The League of Nations was created to keep peace among nations by settling world conflicts through negotiation.

20. The mandate system was a means by which the Allied countries governed former Central Powers' colonies and territories until they were deemed ready for independence. These groups wanted independence, and they saw the mandate system as just another form of colonialism.

Visual Summary

The Great War

Long-Term Causes

- Nationalism spurs competition among European nations.
- Imperialism deepens national rivalries.
- Militarism leads to large standing armies.
- The alliance system divides Europe into two rival camps.

Immediate Causes

- The assassination of Archduke Franz Ferdinand in June 1914 prompts Austria to declare war on Serbia.
- The alliance system requires nations to support their allies. European countries declare war on one another.

WORLD WAR I

Immediate Effects

- A generation of Europeans are killed or wounded.
- Dynasties fall in Germany, Austria-Hungary, and Russia.
- New countries are created.
- The League of Nations is established to help promote peace.

Long-Term Effects

- Many nations feel bitter and betrayed by the peace settlements.
- Problems that helped cause the war—nationalism, competition—remain.

Chapter **29** Assessment

TERMS & NAMES

Briefly explain the importance of each of the following regarding World War I.

1. Triple Alliance	6. total war
2. Triple Entente	7. armistice
3. Central Powers	8. Fourteen Points
4. Allies	9. Treaty of Versailles
5. trench warfare	10. League of Nations

REVIEW QUESTIONS

SECTION 1 (pages 743–746)
The Stage Is Set for War

11. How did nationalism, imperialism, and militarism help set the stage for World War I?

12. Why were the Balkans known as "the powder keg of Europe"?

SECTION 2 (pages 747–751)
War Consumes Europe

13. Why was the first Battle of the Marne considered so significant?

14. Where was the Western Front? the Eastern Front?

15. What were the characteristics of trench warfare?

SECTION 3 (pages 753–757)
War Affects the World

16. What was the purpose of the Gallipoli campaign?

17. What factors prompted the United States to enter the war?

18. In what ways was World War I a total war?

SECTION 4 (pages 760–763)
A Flawed Peace

19. What was the purpose of the League of Nations?

20. What was the mandate system, and why did it leave many groups feeling betrayed?

Interact *with* History

On page 742, you examined whether you would keep your word and follow your ally into war. Now that you have read the chapter, reevaluate your decision.

If you chose to support your ally, do you still feel it was the right thing to do? Why or why not?

If you decided to break your pledge and stay out of war, what are your feelings now? Discuss your opinions with a small group.

Interact *with* History

Possible Responses: Students who originally wanted to support an ally might feel that the carnage of the war exposed their position as foolish, or they might feel that such loyalty is necessary in international affairs. Those who decided to stay out of the war may feel that the massive number of deaths justified their decision.

CRITICAL THINKING

1. ALLIED LEADERS

THEME POWER AND AUTHORITY Often, it is the people in power who determine events and make history. How did the Treaty of Versailles reflect the different personalities and agendas of the men in power at the end of World War I?

2. THE ALLIANCE SYSTEM

Trace the formation of the two major alliance systems that dominated Europe on the eve of World War I by providing the event that corresponds with each date on the chart.

1879	1887	1892,1894
1882	1890	1907

3. A HOLLOW VICTORY

Winston Churchill, Great Britain's prime minister in the 1940s and 1950s, was under-secretary of the British navy during World War I. He said that the Allied victory in World War I had been "bought so dear [high in price] as to be indistinguishable from defeat." What did he mean by this statement? Use examples from the text to support your answer.

4. ANALYZING PRIMARY SOURCES

The following quotation is from an editorial in the German newspaper *Vossische Zeitung* on May 18, 1915. It is in response to President Wilson's protest to the German government after the sinking of the British passenger ship *Lusitania*. The writer believes that Americans were aboard the ship to deter a possible attack against the ship—and its war cargo.

A VOICE FROM THE PAST

The responsibility for the death of so many American citizens, which is deeply regretted by everyone in Germany, in a large measure falls upon the American government. It could not admit that Americans were being used as shields for English contraband [smuggled goods]. In this regard America had permitted herself to be misused in a disgraceful manner by England. And now, instead of calling England to account, she sends a note to the German government.

- Why does the writer hold the American government responsible for the deaths of the Americans on board?
- How does this paragraph reinforce the idea that history can be based on different points of view?

CHAPTER ACTIVITIES

1. LIVING HISTORY: Unit Portfolio Project

THEME SCIENCE AND TECHNOLOGY Your unit portfolio project focuses on how science and technology have influenced history. (See page 739.) For Chapter 29, you might use one of the following ideas to add to your portfolio:

- Write a piece of historical fiction describing a World War I airplane battle.
- After doing further research, write a brief report describing what life was like aboard a German U-boat.
- Using images from magazines and books, create a display to show how technology affects warfare.

2. CONNECT TO TODAY: Cooperative Learning

THEME ECONOMICS While World War I was extremely costly, staying prepared for the possibility of war today is also expensive.

Work with a small team to present the military and defense budgets of several of the world's nations.

 Use the Internet and other resources to research the topic. Have each group member be responsible for one country.

- Examine how much money each country spends on military and defense, as well as what percentage of the overall budget it represents.
- Combine your research on a large chart and present it to the class.
- Discuss whether the amounts spent for military and defense are justified.

3. INTERPRETING A TIME LINE

Revisit the unit time line on pages 738–739. Examine the Chapter 29 time line. For each event, draw an image or symbol that represents that event.

FOCUS ON GRAPHS

This graph provides the total number of troops mobilized, as well as the number of military deaths each major nation suffered in World War I.

- Which nation suffered the most deaths? Which one suffered the least?
- Which nations had more than a million soldiers killed?

Connect to History

Based on the number of troops each side mobilized, what may be one reason the Allies won?

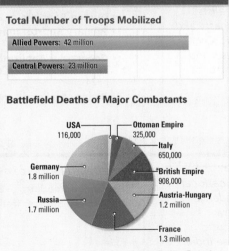

World War I Battlefield Deaths

Total Number of Troops Mobilized

Allied Powers: 42 million
Central Powers: 23 million

Battlefield Deaths of Major Combatants

USA 116,000
Ottoman Empire 325,000
Italy 650,000
*British Empire 908,000
Austria-Hungary 1.2 million
France 1.3 million
Russia 1.7 million
Germany 1.8 million

*Includes troops from Britain, Canada, Australia, New Zealand, India, and South Africa   Source: *Encyclopaedia Britannica*

The Great War **765**

CRITICAL THINKING

Revolution and Nationalism

	Key Ideas	**COPY MASTERS**	**ASSESSMENT**
SECTION 1 Revolutions in Russia *pp. 769–774*	*The Russian Revolutions of 1917 end czarist rule and usher in the first communist government. Lenin seizes power and launches major economic and political reforms.*	*In-Depth Resources: Unit 7* • **Guided Reading,** p. 19 • **Skillbuilder Practice:** Analyzing Causes, p. 23 • **Primary Source:** from Bloody Sunday, p. 26 • **History Makers:** Vladimir Lenin, p. 34	PE *Section 1 Assessment,* p. 774 *Formal Assessment* • Section Quiz, p. 350 *Alternative Assessment Book* • Standards for Evaluating a Cooperative Activity
SECTION 2 Totalitarianism Case Study: Stalinist Russia *pp. 775–780*	*After Lenin's death, Stalin transforms the Soviet Union into a totalitarian state. He revolutionizes the economy and uses terror, propaganda, and censorship to maintain power.*	*In-Depth Resources: Unit 7* • **Guided Reading,** p. 20 • **Primary Source:** The Need for Progress, p. 27 • **Literature:** from *Darkness at Noon,* p. 30; from *1984,* p. 32	PE *Section 2 Assessment,* p. 780 *Formal Assessment* • Section Quiz, p. 351 *Alternative Assessment Book* • Standards for Evaluating a Cooperative Activity
SECTION 3 Collapse of Chinese Imperial Rule *pp. 781–784*	*In 1912, Chinese nationalists overthrow the Qing dynasty and establish a new republic. Civil war erupts as Nationalists and Communists vie for control of China.*	*In-Depth Resources: Unit 7* • **Guided Reading,** p. 21 • **Primary Source:** from *The Peasants of Hunan,* p. 28 • **Geography Application:** Nationalists Battle Warlords and Communists, p. 24 • **History Makers:** Jiang Jieshi, p. 35	PE *Section 3 Assessment,* p. 784 *Formal Assessment* • Section Quiz, p. 352 *Alternative Assessment Book* • Standards for Evaluating a Cooperative Activity
SECTION 4 Nationalism in India and Southwest Asia *pp. 785–789*	*World War I heightens nationalist activity and independence movements to overthrow colonial power. Gandhi uses nonviolent tactics to free India from British rule. Turkey, Persia, and Arabia also seek self-rule.*	*In-Depth Resources: Unit 7* • **Guided Reading,** p. 22 • **Primary Source:** from *Hind Swaraj,* p. 29	PE *Section 4 Assessment,* p. 789 *Formal Assessment* • Section Quiz, p. 353 *Alternative Assessment Book* • Standards for Evaluating a Cooperative Activity
CHAPTER RESOURCES	**Chapter Overview** *Social unrest in Russia erupts in revolution. Under Stalin, the USSR becomes a totalitarian state. After the Qing dynasty falls, Chinese Nationalists and Communists clash. World War II fuels nationalism in India and Southwest Asia.*	*Telescoping the Times* • Chapter Summary, pp. 117–119 *Planning for Block Schedules*	PE *Chapter Assessment,* pp. 790–791 *Chapter Activities,* p. 791 *Formal Assessment* • Chapter Test, forms A and B, pp. 354–359 *Test Generator* *Alternative Assessment Book*

TECHNOLOGY

 Warm-Up Transparency 30

World Art and Cultures Transparencies
• AT65 *Friendship of the People*

 Electronic Library of Primary Sources
• from *Ten Days That Shook the World*
INTERNET RESOURCES
www.mlworldhistory.com

 Warm-Up Transparency 30

Geography Transparencies
• GT30 European Totalitarianism by 1938

Electronic Library of Primary Sources
• from *1984*

INTERNET RESOURCES
www.mlworldhistory.com

 Warm-Up Transparency 30

Electronic Library of Primary Sources
• from *Autobiography of a Chinese Girl*
INTERNET RESOURCES
www.mlworldhistory.com

 Warm-Up Transparency 30

 World Art and Cultures Transparencies
• AT66 *Persian Musicians*

Critical Thinking Transparencies
• CT30 Time Machine: Revolution and Nationalism
• CT66 Chapter 30 Visual Summary

Electronic Library of Primary Sources
• from "*Nonviolence*"

INTERNET RESOURCES
www.mlworldhistory.com

 Chapter Summaries on Audiocassette in English and Spanish

 INTERNET RESOURCES
www.mlworldhistory.com

 ### Block Scheduling (90 MINUTES)

Day 1
Section 1, pp. 769–774

 COOPERATIVE ACTIVITY
Interviewing Key Figures of Revolutionary Russia, p. 772 (Teacher's Edition)

Section 2, pp. 775–780

 COOPERATIVE ACTIVITY
Creating a Fictional

Totalitarian State, p. 776 (Teacher's Edition)

Section Assessments, pp. 774, 780

Day 2
Section 3, pp. 781–784

 COOPERATIVE ACTIVITY
Commemorating the Long March, p. 783 (Teacher's Edition)

Section Assessment, p. 784

Day 3
Section 4, pp. 785–789

 COOPERATIVE ACTIVITY
Investigating Examples of Nonviolent Protests, p. 787 (Teacher's Edition)

Section Assessment, p. 789

Chapter Assessment, pp. 790–791

Yearly Pacing *Chapter 30 Total:* 3 days *Yearly Total:* 85 days

 Planning for Block Schedules

Customizing for Special Needs

Students Acquiring English

 Access for Students Acquiring English
• **Guided Reading** for Sections 1–4 (Spanish), pp. 301–304
• **Chapter Summary** (Spanish), pp. 298–300
• **Skillbuilder Practice:** Analyzing Causes (Spanish), p. 305
• **Geography Application** Nationalists Battle Warlords and Communists (Spanish), p. 306

 Chapter Summaries on Audiocassette in English and Spanish

 INTERNET RESOURCES
www.mlworldhistory.com
The Diverse Classroom.

Less Proficient Readers

 In-Depth Resources: Unit 7
• **Guided Reading** for Sections 1–4, pp. 19–22
• **Skillbuilder Practice:** Analyzing Causes, p. 23
• **Geography Application:** Nationalists Battle Warlords and Communists, p. 24

 Telescoping the Times
• Chapter Summary, pp. 117–119

Chapter Summaries on Audiocassette

Gifted and Talented Students

 In-Depth Resources: Unit 7

Primary Sources
• from Bloody Sunday, p. 26
• The Need for Progress, p. 27
• from *The Peasants of Hunan*, p. 28
• from *Hind Swaraj*, p. 29

History Makers
• Vladimir Lenin, p. 34
• Jiang Jieshi, p. 35

Connections to Literature READINGS FOR STUDENTS

In-Depth Resources: Unit 7
Literature: from *Darkness at Noon*, p. 30; from *1984*, p. 32

 McDougal Littell
Literature Connections
Orwell, George
Animal Farm
(with related readings)
Satirizing the events of the Russian Revolution, this novel uses animals to comment on human society and nature.

 McDougal Littell
Literature Connections
Orwell, George
1984
(with related readings)
This novel presents a chilling vision of a future totalitarian society where the government can control individual thought and even reality itself.

 PE = Pupil's Edition   = Overhead Transparency   = Software   = Video

= Copy Master   = CD-ROM   = Audiocassette   = Internet

Revolution and Nationalism, 1900–1939

Accessing Prior Knowledge

- Ask students to read the captions accompanying each picture and to discuss what they already know about Russia, Turkey, and China.

Predicting and Making Inferences

- Have students examine the poster of an unveiled woman leading Mustafa Kemal on horseback. Then ask them to speculate on the political and social status of Turkish women during Kemal's presidency.

- Ask students what they can tell about the political and social unrest in Russia during the early 1900s from the painting on page 767.

Geography Connection

Ask students to study the political boundaries of the Soviet Union.

- What countries run along the Soviet Union's southern border?

- How might geography influence the relationship between the Soviet Union and these neighboring countries?

CHAPTER
30 *Revolution and Nationalism, 1900–1939*

PREVIEWING THEMES

Revolution
Widespread social unrest in China and Russia during the late 1800s and early 1900s eventually erupted in revolutions. Both countries overthrew autocratic dynasties that had ruled for centuries.

Science and Technology
After World War I, leaders in Russia, China, and Turkey launched new programs to modernize their countries. Advances in technology boosted industrial production. These countries were then able to resist foreign control and to compete in world affairs.

Economics
The gap between rich and poor, especially in Russia and China, was enormous. Growing resentment against economic injustice became a major cause of revolutionary activity.

INTERNET CONNECTION

Visit us at **www.mlworldhistory.com** to learn more about the revolutions in Russia and China, Gandhi's strategy of nonviolent resistance, and related topics.

In **1923**, **Mustafa Kemal,** as president of the new **Republic of Turkey,** favored greater freedom for women. He scorned the Turkish social custom requiring women to wear veils in public. "What is the sense in this behavior?" Kemal asked. "It makes the nation look ridiculous." In this poster, an unveiled woman leads Kemal on horseback.

766

GEOGRAPHY THEMES

Location

Point out that the former Soviet Union was by far the largest country in the world. This vast nation spread across two continents, Europe and Asia. The Soviet Union covered an area of about 8.6 million square miles—roughly two and one half times the size of the United States and almost one-sixth of the Earth's total land surface.

The Soviet Union stretches so far from west to east that it is crossed by eleven standard time zones. Ask students to name the labeled regions that line the Soviet Union's southern border in 1939. *Turkey, Iran, Xinjiang, Outer Mongolia, Manchuria*

Place

Much of the former Soviet Union has long, cold winters because of its northerly location and great distance from the warming effect of the oceans. In addition, the area is cut off from the flow of warm southern air by the large chains of mountains that rim its southern border from the Black Sea to the Pacific Ocean. In fact, the coldest temperatures in the world, besides Antarctica, have been recorded in north central Siberia. Winter temperatures are commonly as low as –60°F (–51°C).

Ask students to discuss why throughout much of Russian history criminals and political prisoners were sent to Siberia.

ADDITIONAL RESOURCES

Books for the Teacher

- Pipes, Richard. *A Concise History of the Russian Revolution.* New York: Knopf, 1995.

- Leone, Bruno. *Nationalism: Opposing Viewpoints.* St. Paul: Greenhaven, 1986.

Books for the Student

- Faber, Doris. *Mahatma Gandhi.* New York: Messner, 1986.

- Vail, John J. *Peace, Land, Bread! A History of the Russian Revolution.* New York: Facts on File, 1995.

Videos

- *Gandhi.* Cambridge Social Studies, 1990. 800-468-4227.

- *The Incredible March.* Ambrose Video, 1997. 800-526-4663.

- *Doctor Zhivago.* Dir. David Lean. MGM/UA Home Videos, 1965.

Software

- *The Russian Revolution.* CD-ROM. Society for Visual Education, 1994. 800-829-1900. Overview of the causes, events, and aftermath of the 1917 revolution.

- *Seeds of Discord (1933–1936).* CD-ROM. AIMS, 1986. 800-367-2467. World political and social changes, including struggles in India and China.

In January **1905**, about 200,000 workers and their families marched to the czar's royal palace in **St. Petersburg.** The marchers demanded reforms. Soldiers fired on the unarmed crowd. An eyewitness described the slaughter, known as "Bloody Sunday": "With shouts and cries, the procession scattered, and the dead and wounded lay upon the snow."

SIBERIA

• Tomsk • Krasnoyarsk

Chita

OUTER MONGOLIA

MANCHURIA

Sea of Okhotsk

PACIFIC OCEAN

Vladivostok

XINJIANG   INNER MONGOLIA

Sea of Japan

40°N

Yellow Sea

CHINA

Bay of Bengal

South China Sea

Philippine Sea

Arctic Circle

Tropic of Cancer

120°E

DIA

0   500 Miles

0   1,000 Kilometers

N

767

In 1911, revolutionaries staged uprisings throughout **China** to overthrow the Qing Dynasty. In February **1912**, they forced **Puyi**, the six-year-old emperor, to give up his throne. Puyi took his place in history as China's last emperor.

HISTORY THROUGH ART

Shooting of the Workers at the Winter Palace in Petersburg, January 1905

N. Vladimirov

The Russian artist N. Vladimirov captures a compelling image from Bloody Sunday—unarmed workers as the victims of senseless violence. Presenting history as an art form has a long tradition. Paintings, like photos, are visual sources that can provide information and opinions about issues or events.

As paintings are artists' interpretations of events and photos show actual events, are photos more historically reliable? Compare Vladimirov's painting of Bloody Sunday to photos of public demonstrations. A close-up of someone being clubbed can give a very different impression than a view of the entire crowd. Publishing the close-up, rather than the broader perspective, affects what people think of the event. Similarly, Vladimirov's choice of painting a close-up view of the victims, rather than the palace guards,

also influences the way people might view this famous event in Russia's past. Both historical paintings and photos are interpretive pictures that typically convey a negative or positive view of an event, person, or group.

Interpreting the Art: What is your emotional response to the painting? In what ways is the painting like a visual editorial?

Interact *with* History

This Interact with History feature motivates students by inviting them to put themselves in a fictional historical setting—a country on the brink of revolution. As students imagine that they are at the center of revolutionary activity, they will analyze the issues surrounding the use of violence and nonviolence to bring about change.

Purpose

• to set the stage for studying revolutionary activity in Russia, China, and India

• to help students understand revolutionary tactics and their impact

• to help students make connections between people and events in the chapter

Teaching Strategy

Thinking Critically After students have imagined themselves in the situation described on this page, have them answer the key questions and give reasons to support their opinion.

EXAMINING *the* ISSUES

Following are suggestions for addressing each bulleted question.

1 Students might cite instances of people using violence in self-defense.

2 Have students describe religious beliefs, such as "turning the other cheek."

3 Have students discuss why nonviolent groups might be perceived as either weak or intimidating.

4 Have students brainstorm possible outcomes resulting from the use of violence in revolutions.

Making Connections Ask students to discuss what they know about Dr. Martin Luther King's nonviolent protests.

Interact *with* History

Y̶ou are living in a country in which the government benefits a small, wealthy class and ignores the demands of the vast majority. Thousands of poor peasants and workers have few rights.

The government has failed to tackle economic, social, and political problems. Various revolutionary groups are all clamoring for change. Some groups call for a violent overthrow of the government. Others believe in battling injustice and achieving change through nonviolent methods, such as peaceful strikes and protests.

In 1920, Mohandas K. Gandhi became the leader of the independence movement to free India of British rule.

In the late 1920s, Communist leader Mao Zedong believed revolution would solve China's problems.

How do you resist oppressive rule— with violent or nonviolent action?

"[Nonviolent] resistance . . . is superior to the force of arms . . . One who is free from hatred requires no sword."

"A revolution is not a dinner party . . . A revolution is an insurrection, an act of violence by which one class overthrows another."

EXAMINING *the* ISSUES

1 • What situations might provoke some people to take violent steps to achieve change?

2 • What strengths would a person need to remain nonviolent in the face of violent attacks?

3 • How might armed and powerful opponents respond to groups committed to nonviolent action?

4 • Which strategy—violence or nonviolence—would prove more successful and bring more long-lasting consequences? Why?

As a class, discuss these questions. In your discussion, consider what you have learned about the strategies revolutionaries used to accomplish change in other countries, such as France, the United States, Brazil, Mexico, Haiti, and so on.

As you read about the revolutions in Russia and China and the independence movement in India, see which strategy was used and rate its effectiveness for achieving change.

Follow Up

A feature on the chapter assessment will ask students to reevaluate their response to the situation presented on this page.

Revolutions in Russia

TERMS & NAMES
- pogrom
- Trans-Siberian Railway
- Bolsheviks
- V. I. Lenin
- Duma
- Rasputin
- provisional government
- soviet

MAIN IDEA	**WHY IT MATTERS NOW**
Long-term social unrest in Russia erupted in revolution, ushering in the first Communist government.	The Communist Party controlled the Soviet Union until the country's breakup in 1991.

SETTING THE STAGE The Russian Revolution was like a firecracker with a very long fuse. The explosion came in 1917. Yet the fuse had been burning for nearly a century. The cruel, oppressive rule of most 19th-century czars caused widespread social unrest for decades. Anger over social inequalities and the ruthless treatment of peasants grew. The czars' unfair governing sparked many violent reactions. Army officers revolted in 1825. Hundreds of peasants rioted. Secret revolutionary groups formed and plotted to overthrow the government. In 1881, student revolutionaries were angry over the slow pace of political change. They assassinated the reform-minded czar, Alexander II. Russia was heading toward a full-scale revolution.

Alexander III Upholds the Autocracy

In 1881, Alexander III succeeded his father, Alexander II, to the throne and halted all reforms in Russia. Like his grandfather, Nicholas I, Alexander III clung to the principles of autocracy, a government in which he had total power. Alexander III was determined to strengthen "autocracy, orthodoxy, and nationality." Anyone who questioned the absolute authority of the czar, worshiped outside the Russian Orthodox Church, or spoke a language other than Russian was tagged as dangerous.

To wipe out revolutionaries, Alexander III used harsh measures. He imposed strict censorship codes on published materials and written documents, including private letters. His secret police carefully watched both secondary schools and universities. Teachers had to send detailed reports on every student. Political prisoners were exiled to Siberia, a region of eastern and central Russia.

To establish a uniform Russian culture, Alexander III oppressed other national groups within Russia. He made Russian the official language of the empire and forbade the use of minority languages, such as Polish, in schools. Alexander made Jews the target of persecution. He subjected them to new laws that encouraged prejudice. Jews could not buy land or live among other Russians. Universities set strict quotas for Jewish students. A wave of **pogroms**—organized violence against Jews—broke out in many parts of Russia. Police and soldiers stood by and watched Russian citizens loot and destroy Jewish homes, stores, and synagogues.

Alexander III turned Russia into a police state, teeming with spies and informers.

THINK THROUGH HISTORY
A. Summarizing
What methods did Alexander III use to maintain his authority over the Russian people?
A. Possible Answers Censorship, secret police, religious persecution, discrimination against minorities

Nicholas II Resists Change

When Nicholas II became czar in 1894, he announced, "The principle of autocracy will be maintained by me as firmly and unswervingly as by my lamented father [Alexander III]." Nicholas stubbornly refused to surrender any of his power. His trust in the tradition of Russian autocracy blinded him to the changing conditions of his times. Yet the sweeping forces of change would override his pledge to preserve the czarist rule of Russia's past.

Revolution and Nationalism **769**

Nicholas II Resists Change

(See page 769.)

▶ **Key Ideas**
- Nicholas II vows to maintain autocratic rule.
- The rapid buildup of Russian industry helps the country prosper.
- Worker exploitation spurs the growth of revolutionary movements.

SPOTLIGHT ON
The Trans-Siberian Railway

The Trans-Siberian Railway crossed huge forests, immense bogs, and open steppes. Railroad workers constructed dozens of tunnels through mountains and countless bridges over rivers. Have students research the difficulties in building the Trans-Siberian Railway.

OBJECTIVE **3** INSTRUCT

Crises at Home and Abroad

▶ **Key Ideas**
- Russia's defeat in the Russo-Japanese War sparks unrest.
- Russia's first parliament is formed after the Revolution of 1905.
- Russia faces defeats and food shortages during World War I.

📖 **IN-DEPTH RESOURCES: UNIT 7**
Primary Source: from Bloody Sunday, p. 26

SPOTLIGHT ON

The Trans-Siberian Railway

The Trans-Siberian Railway ran about 5,800 miles across the vast area of Siberia, from Moscow to the city of Vladivostok on the Sea of Japan. Like the transcontinental railroad in the United States (built from 1863 to 1869), the Trans-Siberian Railway was constructed over difficult terrain and completed in sections.

To celebrate the opening of the Trans-Siberian Railway, Czar Nicholas II had the jewelry firm of Fabergé create a golden Easter egg (shown below) for Czarina Alexandra. The inscription on the silver band encircling the egg reads, "Great Siberian Railway, 1900." Hidden inside the egg is a wonderful surprise—a miniature replica of a train studded with precious gems. The tiny engine is actually a wind-up toy that can pull the cars attached to it.

Economic Growth and Its Impact The number of factories more than doubled between 1863 and 1900. In spite of this, at the beginning of Nicholas II's reign, Russia lagged behind the industrial nations of western Europe. In the 1890s, Sergey Witte (VYEET·tyih), the czar's most capable minister, launched a program to move the country forward. Through higher taxes and foreign investments, Witte helped finance the buildup of Russian industries. Witte's steps also boosted the growth of heavy industry, particularly steel. By around 1900, Russia had become the world's fourth-ranking producer of steel. Only the United States, Germany, and Great Britain produced more steel.

Witte also pushed for the building of the great **Trans-Siberian Railway**—the world's longest continuous rail line. With the help of British and French investors, work began in 1891. The Trans-Siberian Railway was completed in 1904. It connected European Russia in the west with Russian ports on the Pacific Ocean in the east.

The Revolutionary Movement Grows Rapid industrialization also stirred discontent among the people of Russia. The growth of factories brought new problems. Among these problems were grueling working conditions, miserably low wages, and child labor. Trade unions were outlawed. Still, exploited laborers who worked in factories and built the railway lines organized strikes. Workers were unhappy with their low standard of living and lack of political power. The gap between rich and poor was enormous.

Amid the widespread unrest of workers and other members of Russian society, various revolutionary movements began to grow. They also competed for power. The group that would eventually succeed in establishing a new government in Russia followed the views of Karl Marx. These revolutionaries believed that the industrial class of workers would overthrow the czar. The industrial class would then form "a dictatorship of the proletariat." In such a state, the workers would rule.

In 1903, Russian Marxists split into two groups over revolutionary tactics. The Mensheviks (MEHN·shuh·vihks) wanted a broad base of popular support for the revolution. The **Bolsheviks** (BOHL·shuh·vihks) supported a small number of committed revolutionaries willing to sacrifice everything for radical change.

The major leader of the Bolsheviks was Vladimir Ilyich Ulyanov (ool·YAH·nuhf). He adopted the name of **Lenin.** He had an engaging personality and was an excellent organizer. He was also ruthless. These traits would ultimately help him gain command of the Bolsheviks. In the early 1900s, Lenin fled to western Europe to avoid arrest by the czarist regime. He maintained contact with other Bolsheviks. Lenin then waited until he could safely return to Russia.

Crises at Home and Abroad

The revolutionaries would not have to wait long to realize their visions. Between 1904 and 1917, Russia faced a series of crises. These events showed the czar's weakness and paved the way for revolution.

The Russo-Japanese War In the late 1800s, Russia and Japan were imperialist powers. They both competed for control of Korea and Manchuria. The two nations signed a series of agreements over the territories, but Russia broke them. In retaliation, Japan attacked the Russians at Port Arthur, Manchuria, in February 1904.

Though Russian soldiers and sailors went confidently to war, the Japanese defeated them. News of repeated losses sparked unrest at home and led to revolt in the midst of the war.

770 Chapter 30

Vocabulary
minister: person in charge of an area of government, such as finance.

B. Possible Answer
Exploitation of factory workers and the huge gap between the rich and poor caused discontent.

THINK THROUGH HISTORY
B. Analyzing Causes Why did industrialization in Russia lead to unrest?

Background
Karl Marx, a 19th-century German philosopher, argued that the workers of the world would one day overthrow the ruling class and share equally in society's wealth.

| TEACHING OPTION | BLOCK SCHEDULING | SKILLBUILDER MINI-LESSON: Analyzing Causes | CLASS TIME 15 MINUTES |

Explaining the Skill Analyzing causes is the skill historians use to investigate *why* events in the past happened. Historical events, such as social unrest and revolutionary movements, often stem from a number of reasons, or multiple causes. Analyzing causes helps historians see how a series of events are related.

Applying the Skill: *Think Through History Question* To answer the question, suggest that students use the following strategy. Ask them to reread the first two paragraphs under the subheading "The Revolutionary Movement Grows." Then have them create a multiple-causes chart to analyze conditions related to industrialization that created social unrest.

Causes

Causes	Outcome
Exploitation of factory workers • grueling working conditions • miserably low wages • child labor	**Social unrest** • labor strikes • revolutionary activity
Huge gap between rich and poor • low standard of living among factory workers	

📖 **IN-DEPTH RESOURCES: UNIT 7**
Skillbuilder Practice: Analyzing Causes, p. 23

Bloody Sunday: The Revolution of 1905 On January 22, 1905, about 200,000 workers and their families approached the czar's Winter Palace in St. Petersburg. They carried a petition asking for better working conditions, more personal freedom, and an elected national legislature. Nicholas II was not at the palace. His generals and police chiefs were. They ordered the soldiers to fire on the crowd. Between 500 and 1,000 unarmed people were killed. Russians quickly named the event "Bloody Sunday." Lenin called the incident a "dress rehearsal" for the later revolution that would usher in a Communist regime.

Bloody Sunday provoked a wave of strikes and violence that spread across the country. Though Nicholas still opposed reform, in October 1905 he reluctantly promised more freedom. He approved the creation of the **Duma** (DOO·muh)—Russia's first parliament. The first Duma met in May 1906. Its leaders were moderates who wanted Russia to become a constitutional monarchy similar to Britain. Hesitant to share his power, the czar dissolved the Duma after ten weeks. Other Dumas would meet later. Yet none would have real power to make sweeping reforms.

World War I: The Final Blow In 1914, Nicholas II made the fateful decision to drag Russia into World War I. Russia, though, was unprepared to handle the military and economic costs. Russia's weak generals and poorly equipped troops were no match for the German army. Before a year had passed, more than 4 million Russian soldiers had been killed, wounded, or taken prisoner. German machine guns mowed down advancing Russians by the thousands. Defeat followed defeat. As in the Russo-Japanese War, Russia's involvement in World War I revealed the weaknesses of czarist rule and military leadership.

In 1915, Nicholas moved his headquarters to the war front. From there, he hoped to rally his discouraged troops to victory. His wife, Czarina Alexandra, ran the government while he was away. She ignored the czar's chief advisers. Instead, she continued to fall under the influence of the mysterious **Rasputin** (ras·PYOO·tihn)—a self-described "holy man." He claimed to have magical healing powers.

Alexis, Nicholas and Alexandra's son, suffered from hemophilia, a life-threatening disease. Rasputin seemed to ease the boy's symptoms. To show her gratitude, Alexandra allowed Rasputin to make key political decisions. He opposed reform measures and obtained powerful positions for his friends. He spread corruption throughout the royal court. In 1916, a group of nobles murdered Rasputin. They feared his increasing role in government affairs.

Meanwhile, the war was destroying the morale of Russian troops. Soldiers mutinied, deserted, or ignored orders. On the homefront, food and fuel supplies were dwindling. Prices were wildly inflated. People from all classes were clamoring for change and an end to the war. Neither Nicholas nor Alexandra proved capable of tackling these enormous problems.

The March Revolution

In March 1917, women textile workers in Petrograd led a citywide strike. Soon afterward, riots flared up over shortages of bread and fuel. Nearly 200,000 workers swarmed the streets. At first the soldiers obeyed orders to shoot the rioters but later sided with them. The soldiers fired at their commanding officers and joined the rebellion. Large crowds gathered, shouting "Down with the autocracy!" and "Down with the war!"

Revolution and Nationalism **771**

HISTORYMAKERS

**Rasputin
1872–1916**

Born a peasant in Siberia, Rasputin became a religious teacher, although he was never ordained as a priest. The sinister monk seemed to cast a hypnotic spell on people, especially Czarina Alexandra and her ailing son. Rasputin's reputation for having mysterious powers followed him to his grave.

In December 1916, a small group of young aristocrats plotted his assassination because he was reportedly taking control of the government. They lured him to a mansion and fed him poisoned cakes. The poison apparently had no effect on Rasputin's extraordinary strength. The conspirators then shot him several times. Assuming he was finally dead, they threw him in the Neva River. When his body was discovered three days later, doctors confirmed the cause of his death—drowning.

Rasputin's death threw the czarina into shock. His prediction haunted her: "If I die or you desert me, in six months you will lose your son and your throne."

OBJECTIVE 5 INSTRUCT

The Bolshevik Revolution

Key Ideas
• The Bolsheviks overthrow the provisional government, sparking a civil war.

 ELECTRONIC LIBRARY OF PRIMARY SOURCES
from *Ten Days That Shook the World*

WORLD ART AND CULTURES TRANSPARENCIES
AT65 *Friendship of the People*

History from Visuals

Causes and Effects of Two Russian Revolutions

Interpreting the Chart Point out that the middle section of the chart, titled Russian Revolutions of 1917, lists events beginning with the March Revolution and ending with the Bolshevik Revolution.

Extension Activity Ask students to choose one of the causes on the chart and write a paragraph explaining how it helped bring on the revolution.

SKILLBUILDER Answers
1. *Possible Response:* Social inequities, weak government, and military defeats created an overwhelming demand for change.
2. *Possible Response:* In both, violence played a major role, government was ineffective, and the people suffered greatly.

CONNECT to TODAY

DNA Solves the Mystery of Anastasia

For about 65 years after the execution of Czar Nicholas II and his family, a woman named Anna Anderson claimed that she was the Grand Duchess Anastasia, the czar's sole surviving daughter (circled above). According to Anna, she managed to escape her assassins.

Anna's regal manners and detailed knowledge about the Romanov family convinced many that she was telling the truth. Others believed she was a fraud seeking personal gain. Anna held fast to her story until her death in 1984.

In 1993, scientists finally solved the 75-year-old mystery. Prince Philip of Britain is a living descendant of Czarina Alexandra. Scientists compared his DNA to Anna Anderson's. The DNA proved that Anna was not a blood relative of the Romanovs. Instead, she carried the DNA of Polish peasants.

The Czar Steps Down The local protest exploded into a general uprising—the March Revolution. It forced Czar Nicholas II to abdicate his throne. A year later revolutionaries executed Nicholas and his family. The czarist rule of the Romanovs, which spanned over three centuries, had finally collapsed. The March Revolution succeeded in bringing down the czar. Yet it failed to set up a strong government to replace his regime.

Leaders of the Duma established a **provisional government**, or temporary government. It was eventually headed by Alexander Kerensky. His decision to continue fighting the war cost him the support of both soldiers and civilians. As the war dragged on, conditions inside Russia worsened. Angry peasants demanded land. City workers grew more radical. Social revolutionaries, competing for power, formed soviets. **Soviets** were local councils consisting of workers, peasants, and soldiers. In many cities, especially Petrograd, the soviets had more influence than the provisional government.

Lenin Returns to Russia The Germans launched their own "secret weapon" that would erode the provisional government's authority. They arranged Lenin's return to Russia after many years of exile. The Germans believed that Lenin and his Bolshevik supporters would stir unrest in Russia and hurt the Russian war effort. Traveling in a sealed railway boxcar, Lenin reached Petrograd in April 1917.

The Bolshevik Revolution

Lenin and the Bolsheviks recognized their opportunity to seize power. They soon gained control of the Petrograd soviet, as well as the soviets in other major Russian cities. By the fall of 1917, people in the cities were rallying to the call, "All power to the soviets." Lenin's slogan—"Peace, Land, and Bread"—was gaining widespread appeal. Lenin decided to take action.

The Provisional Government Topples In November 1917, without warning, Bolshevik Red Guards made up of armed factory workers stormed the Winter Palace in Petrograd. They took over government offices and arrested the leaders of the provisional government. The Bolshevik Revolution was over in a matter of hours. Kerensky and his colleagues disappeared almost as quickly as the czarist regime they had replaced.

THINK THROUGH HISTORY
C. Making Inferences Why did Kerensky's decision to continue fighting the war cost him the support of the Russian people?
C. Possible Answer Russians lost their faith in the provisional government and felt no better off than when they were under the czar.

Causes and Effects of Two Russian Revolutions

Causes	Russian Revolutions of 1917	Effects
• Widespread discontent among all classes of Russian society	• Abdication of Czar Nicholas	• Civil war (1918–1920)
• Agitation from revolutionaries	• Failure of provisional government	• Czar and his family killed—end of czarist rule
• Weak leadership of Czar Nicholas II	• Growing power of soviets	• Peace with Germany under Treaty of Brest-Litovsk (1918)
• Defeat in Russo-Japanese War (1905)	• Lenin's return to Russia	
• Bloody Sunday (1905)	• Bolshevik takeover under Lenin	• Bolshevik control of government
• Losses in World War I		• Russian economy in ruins
• Strikes and riots		

SKILLBUILDER: Interpreting Charts
1. Based on the chart, form a generalization about why the Russian Revolutions occurred.
2. What similarities exist between the causes of the Revolution and the effects?

Russian Revolution and Civil War, 1905–1922

Legend:
- Western boundaries of Russia, 1905–1917
- ★ Bolshevik uprisings, 1917–1918
- Bolshevik territory, Oct. 1919
- Territories lost (Treaty of Brest-Litovsk, 1918)
- ← White Russian and Allied attacks, 1918–1920
- Bolshevik counterattacks, 1918–1920
- ★ Major civil war battle areas, 1918–1920
- Boundaries of Russia, 1922

Romanov family executed, 1918

Ukraine lost in Treaty of Brest-Litovsk; regained in 1922

GEOGRAPHY SKILLBUILDER: Interpreting Maps
1. **Region** What was the extent (north to south, east to west) of the Bolshevik territory in 1919?
2. **Region** What European countries were no longer within Russian boundaries by 1922 because of the Brest-Litovsk treaty?

Bolsheviks in Power Lenin's next step was tackling the problems he inherited from czarist rule. Within days after the Bolshevik takeover, Lenin ordered that all farmland be distributed among the peasants. Lenin and the Bolsheviks gave control of factories to the workers. The Bolshevik government also signed a truce with Germany to stop all fighting on the eastern war front and began peace talks.

In March 1918, Russia and Germany signed the Treaty of Brest-Litovsk. The price of peace was costly. Russia surrendered a large chunk of its territory to Germany and its allies. The humiliating terms of this treaty triggered widespread anger among many Russians. They objected to the Bolsheviks and their policies.

D. Possible Answer
Russia's involvement in World War I, social unrest, political opponents, civil war, famine

THINK THROUGH HISTORY
D. Identifying Problems What problems did Lenin and the Bolsheviks face after the revolution?

Civil War Rages in Russia Still recovering from their painful losses of land to Germany, the Bolsheviks now faced a new challenge—stamping out their enemies at home. Their opponents formed the White Army. The revolutionary leader Leon Trotsky, who helped negotiate the Treaty of Brest-Litovsk, expertly commanded the Bolshevik Red Army. From 1918 to 1920, civil war raged in Russia. Several Western nations, including the United States, sent military aid and forces to Russia to help the White Army.

Russia's civil war proved far more deadly than the earlier revolutions. Around 15 million Russians died in the three-year struggle and in the famine that followed. The destruction and loss of life from fighting, hunger, and a worldwide flu epidemic left Russia in chaos.

In the end the Red Army triumphed and finally crushed all opposition to Bolshevik rule. The victory showed that the Bolsheviks were able both to seize power and to maintain it. Yet in the aftermath of the civil war, Lenin and the Bolsheviks faced overwhelming problems.

During the Bolshevik Revolution of 1917, these Petrograd workers seized an armored car from the provisional government's forces.

Revolution and Nationalism **773**

Lenin Restores Order

War and revolution destroyed the Russian economy. Trade was at a standstill. Industrial production dropped and many skilled workers fled to other countries. Lenin, who helped mastermind the Bolshevik Revolution, shifted his role. He turned to reviving the economy and restructuring the government.

New Economic Policy In March 1921, Lenin launched the New Economic Policy (NEP). Under the NEP, he temporarily put aside his plan for a state-controlled economy. Instead, he resorted to a small-scale version of capitalism. The reforms under the NEP allowed peasants to sell their surplus crops instead of turning them over to the government. Individuals could buy and sell goods for profit. The government kept control of major industries, banks, and means of communication. However, it did let some small factories, businesses, and farms operate under private ownership. Lenin also tried to encourage foreign investment.

Political Reforms The many different nationalities within Russia had always posed an obstacle to national unity. Lenin began political reform by organizing Russia into several self-governing republics under the central government. In 1922, the country was named the Union of Soviet Socialist Republics (USSR), in honor of the councils that helped launch the Bolshevik Revolution. Each republic was controlled from the new capital—Moscow.

The Bolsheviks also renamed their party the Communist Party. The name came from the writings of Karl Marx. He had used the word *communism* to describe the classless society that would exist after workers had seized power. In 1924, the Communists created a constitution based on socialist and democratic principles. In reality, the Communist Party held all the power. Lenin had established a dictatorship of the Communist Party, not "a dictatorship of the proletariat," as Marx had promoted.

Thanks partly to the new policies and to the peace that followed the civil war, the USSR slowly recovered. By 1928, the country's farms and factories were producing as much as they had before World War I.

Lenin did not live to see this recovery. He had several strokes and spent the last 18 months of his life as a semi-invalid. His death in 1924 opened a power struggle for control of the party and the country. You will learn about the outcome of this struggle in Section 2.

HISTORY MAKERS

V. I. Lenin
1870–1924

A brilliant student, Lenin enrolled in law school as a young man but was expelled for taking part in a student protest meeting. In 1887, when he was 17, his brother, Alexander, was hanged for plotting to kill the czar. Legend has it that this event turned Lenin into a revolutionary.

Though Alexander's execution influenced Lenin, Lenin already harbored feelings against the government. By the early 1900s, he planned to overthrow the czar. After 1917, Russians revered him as the "Father of the Revolution."

Following Lenin's death in 1924, the government placed his tomb in Red Square in Moscow. His preserved body, encased in a bulletproof, glass-topped coffin, is still on display. Many Russians, though, favor moving Lenin's corpse away from public view.

THINK THROUGH HISTORY
E. Making Inferences How did the formation of the USSR benefit both the Communist Party and the many nationalities in Russia?
E. Possible Answer Self-governing republics represented major nationalities; Communist Party controlled the republics.

Section **1** Assessment

1. TERMS & NAMES
Identify
• pogrom
• Trans-Siberian Railway
• Bolsheviks
• V. I. Lenin
• Duma
• Rasputin
• provisional government
• soviet

2. TAKING NOTES
Create a time line like the one below to show significant events during the last phases of czarist rule and the beginning of Communist rule.

1891		1917		1922
	1894		1921	

Write a paragraph explaining one of these events in more detail.

3. EVALUATING DECISIONS
What do you think were Czar Nicholas II's worst errors in judgment during his rule? Why?

THINK ABOUT
• the czar's military decisions
• the political outcome of "Bloody Sunday"

4. ANALYZING THEMES
Revolution Why was Lenin's leadership crucial to the success of the Russian Revolution?

THINK ABOUT
• Lenin's personal traits
• his slogan—"Peace, Land, and Bread"
• his role in organizing the Bolsheviks
• his role after the Revolution

ANSWERS

1. TERMS & NAMES
pogrom, p. 769
Trans-Siberian Railway, p. 770
Bolsheviks, p. 770
V. I. Lenin, p. 770
Duma, p. 771
Rasputin, p. 771
provisional government, p. 772
soviet, p. 772

2. TAKING NOTES
Possible Responses: 1891—Construction of the Trans-Siberian Railway begins. 1894—Nicholas II becomes the last Russian czar. 1917—Russian Revolution ends czarist rule. 1921—Lenin launches New Economic Policy. 1922—Union of Soviet Socialist Republics formed.

2. EVALUATING DECISIONS
Possible Responses: Involvement in the Russo-Japanese War, the czar's refusal to share power with the Duma, Russia's entry into World War I, and the czar's change of headquarters to the war front all paved the way to revolution and the end of czarist rule.

4. ANALYZING THEMES
Possible Responses: Lenin was able to win and maintain power because of his energetic, disciplined leadership; his awareness of the demands of various groups in Russian society; his careful planning; and his ability to tackle difficult problems and crises.

② Totalitarianism

CASE STUDY: Stalinist Russia

TERMS & NAMES
- Joseph Stalin
- totalitarianism
- command economy
- collective farm
- kulak
- Great Purge
- socialist realism

MAIN IDEA	WHY IT MATTERS NOW
After Lenin died, Stalin seized power and transformed the Soviet Union into a totalitarian state.	More recent dictators have used Stalin's tactics for seizing total control over individuals and the state.

SETTING THE STAGE Leon Trotsky and Joseph Stalin were among Lenin's revolutionary supporters. They both helped create the Soviet state. After Lenin died, these two men became bitter rivals for control of the Communist Party. The outcome of this struggle would determine the future course of the Soviet Union. Stalin, Lenin's successor, would aim at dramatically transforming the government and controlling every aspect of citizens' lives.

Stalin Becomes Dictator

Joseph Stalin was a quiet man who rarely received much public notice. During his early days as a Bolshevik, he changed his name from Dzhugashivili (joo·guhsh·VEEL·yih) to Stalin, which means "man of steel" in Russian. The name fit well. Stalin was cold, hard, and impersonal. Lenin, unsure of his successor, began to distrust Stalin. Lenin believed that Stalin was a dangerous man. Shortly before Lenin died, he wrote, "Comrade Stalin has concentrated enormous power in his hands, and I am not sure that he always knows how to use that power with sufficient caution."

From 1922 to 1927, Stalin began his ruthless climb to the head of the government. In 1922, as general secretary of the Communist Party, he worked behind the scenes. He shrewdly moved his followers into strategic government offices. By 1924, he had placed many of his supporters in key positions. By 1928, Stalin was in total command of the Communist Party. Trotsky, forced into exile in 1929, was no longer a threat. Stalin now stood poised to wield absolute power as a dictator.

Background
While in exile, Trotsky published articles and books criticizing Stalin's regime. In 1940, Stalin's agents murdered Trotsky in Mexico.

Stalin Builds a Totalitarian State

Lenin and Trotsky promoted a worldwide Communist revolution. Stalin, however, focused on Russian development. He coined the phrase "socialism in one country" to describe his aims of perfecting a Communist state in Russia. To realize his vision, Stalin would transform the Soviet Union into a totalitarian state.

The term **totalitarianism** describes a government that takes total, centralized state control over every aspect of public and private life. Totalitarian leaders, such as Stalin, appear to provide a sense of security and to give a direction for the future.

Totalitarianism challenges the highest values prized by Western democracies—reason, freedom, human dignity, and the worth of the individual. As the chart on the next page shows, all totalitarian states share basic characteristics.

HISTORY MAKERS

**Joseph Stalin
1879–1953**

Stalin was born in bitter poverty in Georgia, a region in southern Russia. Unlike the well-educated and cultured Lenin, Stalin was rough and crude.

Despite having millions of Russians killed, Stalin tried to create a myth that he was the country's father and savior. Stalin glorified himself as the symbol of the nation. He encouraged people to think of him as "The Greatest Genius of All Times and Peoples."

Many towns, factories, and streets in the Soviet Union were named for Stalin. A new metal was called Stalinite. An orchid was named Stalinchid. Children standing before their desks every morning said, "Thank Comrade Stalin for this happy life."

Section 2 Overview

OBJECTIVES

1. To explain how Stalin gained control of the Communist Party.
2. To describe Stalin's goal of transforming the Soviet Union into a totalitarian state.
3. To summarize Stalin's state-controlled economic programs .
4. To explain the methods of control used in totalitarian states.
5. To describe Soviet daily life.

SKILLBUILDERS
- Interpreting charts, p. 776
- Interpreting graphs, p. 777

CRITICAL THINKING
- Summarizing, p. 777
- Making inferences, p. 778
- Analyzing issues, p. 779
- Comparing, p. 779
- Evaluating, p. 780
- Synthesizing, p. 780

FOCUS
5-Minute Warm-Up

▶ **Interpreting Art**
Answering these questions will help students understand life in the Soviet Union under Stalin.

1. Look at the posters of Soviet workers on page 779. What is most striking about them?
2. What are the slogans written on these posters?

WARM-UP TRANSPARENCY 30

OBJECTIVE ① INSTRUCT

Stalin Becomes Dictator

▶ **Key Ideas**
- Stalin wants to succeed Lenin.
- Stalin ruthlessly climbs to the head of the Soviet government.

IN-DEPTH RESOURCES: UNIT 7
Guided Reading, p. 20

ACCESS FOR STUDENTS ACQUIRING ENGLISH
Guided Reading (Spanish), p. 302

SECTION 2 RESOURCES

PRINT RESOURCES

IN-DEPTH RESOURCES: UNIT 7
Guided Reading, p. 20
Primary Source: The Need for Progress, p. 27
Literature: from *Darkness at Noon*, p. 30; from *1984*, p. 32

ACCESS FOR STUDENTS ACQUIRING ENGLISH
Guided Reading (Spanish), p. 302

FORMAL ASSESSMENT
Section Quiz, p. 351

TECHNOLOGY RESOURCES

GEOGRAPHY TRANSPARENCIES
GT30 European Totalitarianism by 1928

CD-ROM
Electronic Library of Primary Sources

INTERNET www.mlworldhistory.com

Stalin Builds a Totalitarian State

(See page 775.)

▶ **Key Ideas**

- Stalin transforms the Soviet Union into a totalitarian state.
- Totalitarian governments take control over all aspects of life.
- Several totalitarian states emerge during the 20th century.

HISTORY MAKERS
Joseph Stalin

(See page 775.)

President Harry Truman described Stalin as "a little bit of a squirt." Ask students to research other anecdotes about Stalin.

History from Visuals

Patterns of Change: Totalitarianism

Interpreting the Chart
Emphasize that the key traits apply to all totalitarian states, not just the Soviet Union.

Extension Activity Have students cite examples of technology that a totalitarian state today might use to spread propaganda.

SKILLBUILDER Answers
1. Through propaganda and force
2. No individual freedoms, great personal sacrifice, limited privacy

Stalin Seizes Control of the Economy

▶ **Key Ideas**

- Stalin launches Five-Year Plans and ushers in an agricultural revolution.

PATTERNS OF CHANGE: Totalitarianism

Key Traits	Description
Dictatorship and One-Party Rule	• Exercises absolute authority • Dominates the government
Dynamic Leader	• Helps unite people toward meeting shared goals or realizing a common vision • Encourages people to devote their unconditional loyalty and uncritical support to the regime • Becomes a symbol of the government
Ideology (set of beliefs)	• Justifies government actions • Glorifies the aims of the state
State Control Over All Sectors of Society	• business • labor • housing • education • family life • youth groups • religion • the arts
State Control Over the Individual	• Demands total obedience to authority and personal sacrifice for the good of the state • Denies basic liberties
Dependence on Modern Technology	• Relies on mass communication, such as radios, newsreels, and loudspeakers, to spread propaganda • Builds up advanced military weapons
Organized Violence	• Uses force, such as police terror, to crush all opposition • Targets certain groups, such as national minorities and political opponents, as enemies

> **SKILLBUILDER: Interpreting Charts**
> 1. *Based on the chart, how are individuals in a totalitarian state molded into obedient citizens?*
> 2. *How would your life change if you lived in a totalitarian state?*

Other totalitarian governments besides the Soviet Union emerged in the twentieth century. In the 1920s and 1930s, two other European dictators—Hitler in Germany and Mussolini in Italy—were shaping their visions of a totalitarian state. After Communists formed the People's Republic of China in 1949, Mao Zedong used tactics similar to Stalin's to establish totalitarian control. The North Korean dictator Kim Il Sung ruled over a totalitarian Communist state from 1948 to 1994.

By 1928 Stalin began taking great strides to build a totalitarian state. He had achieved personal power and was ready to begin overhauling the economy.

CASE STUDY: Stalinist Russia

Stalin Seizes Control of the Economy

While Lenin's New Economic Policy (NEP) was a mixture of free enterprise and state control, Stalin's economic policies involved total state control. His plans called for a **command economy**—a system in which the government made all economic decisions. Under this system, political leaders identify the country's economic needs and determine how to fulfill them. To modernize the Soviet state, Stalin ushered in revolutions in industry and agriculture.

An Industrial Revolution In 1928, Stalin outlined the first of several Five-Year Plans for the development of the Soviet Union's economy. The government would take drastic steps to promote rapid industrial growth and to strengthen national defense. Stalin announced, "We are fifty or a hundred years behind the advanced countries. We must make good this distance in ten years. Either we do it or we shall be crushed."

The Five-Year Plans set impossibly high quotas, or numerical goals, to increase the output of steel, coal, oil, and electricity. To reach these targets, the government limited production of consumer goods. As a result, people faced severe shortages of housing, food, clothing, and other necessary goods.

The number of tractors in the Soviet Union increased from 25,000 in 1927 to 483,000 in 1938.

   COOPERATIVE ACTIVITY: Creating a Fictional Totalitarian State   **CLASS TIME 30 MINUTES**

Task: Student groups will use the chart on this page to help them create a fictional totalitarian state.

Purpose: To explore the characteristics and costs of totalitarianism.

Activity: Have small groups brainstorm examples for each key trait of totalitarianism listed on the Patterns of Change chart. They should invent a

name for the totalitarian state, identify its location, make up a name for the dictator, and list the effects on individual lives. Ask groups to make charts of their profiles of fictional totalitarian regimes.

Building a Portfolio If the chart is among their best work, students should add it to their portfolio.

ALTERNATIVE ASSESSMENT BOOK
Standards for Evaluating a Cooperative Activity

Standards for Evaluation
Charts should . . .

- include specific examples of each key trait of totalitarianism
- demonstrate a clear understanding of the principles underlying totalitarian regimes
- show how individual lives would be affected

Under Stalin's totalitarian regime, the government controlled every aspect of the worker's life. Officials chose the workers, assigned them jobs, and determined their working hours. Workers needed the police's permission to move. The secret police were ready to imprison or execute those who did not contribute to the Soviet economy. These forceful means of making the Soviet Union a modern industrial nation took a great toll on people's personal lives. Many families and marriages broke up.

Stalin's grim methods, however, also produced fantastic economic results. Although most of the targets of the first Five-Year Plan fell short, the Soviets made impressive gains. A second plan, launched in 1933, proved equally successful. From 1928 to 1937, industrial production increased more than 25 percent.

An Agricultural Revolution Stalin's agricultural revolution was also successful—and far more brutal—than his industrial revolution. In 1928, the government began to seize over 25 million privately owned farms in the USSR. It combined them into large, government-owned farms, called **collective farms**. Hundreds of families worked on these farms, producing food for the state. The government expected that the modern machinery on the collective farms would boost food production and reduce the number of workers.

Peasants resisted fiercely. Many killed livestock and destroyed crops in protest. Stalin used terror and violence to force peasants to work on collective farms. Soviet secret police herded them onto collective farms at the point of a bayonet. Between 5 million and 10 million peasants died as a direct result of Stalin's agricultural revolution. Millions more were shipped to Siberia.

Resistance was especially strong among **kulaks**, a class of wealthy peasants. The Soviet government decided to eliminate them. Thousands were executed or sent to work camps.

By 1938, more than 90 percent of all peasants lived on collective farms. Agricultural production was on the upswing. That year the country produced almost twice the wheat than it had in 1928 before collective farming.

Weapons of Totalitarianism

To dominate an entire nation, Stalin, like other totalitarian leaders, devised methods of control and persuasion.

Police Terror Dictators of totalitarian states use terror and violence to force obedience and to crush opposition. Stalin began building his totalitarian state by destroying his enemies—real and imagined. Stalin's secret police used tanks and armored cars to stop riots. They monitored telephone lines, read mail, and planted informers everywhere. Even children told authorities about disloyal remarks they heard at home. The secret police arrested and executed millions of so-called traitors.

In 1934, Stalin turned against members of the Communist Party. He launched the **Great Purge**—a campaign of terror. It was directed at eliminating anyone who threatened his power. Thousands of old Bolsheviks who helped stage the Revolution in 1917 stood trial. They were executed for "crimes against the Soviet state."

The state had the authority to punish even the most minor acts. The police arrested the director of the Moscow Zoo because his monkeys got tuberculosis. The police

PATTERNS OF CHANGE 777

The Buildup of the Soviet Economy

Source: *European Historical Statistics*

SKILLBUILDER:
Interpreting Graphs
1. *How many more metric tons of coal were produced in 1938 than in 1928?*
2. *What do the graphs show about the contrast between the progress of industry and livestock production under Stalin's first Five-Year Plan?*

CONNECTIONS ACROSS THE CURRICULUM

Economics In a command economic system, a group of central planners have the power to make economic decisions for the entire society. Many of the great cultures of the past, such as Egypt and Rome, were command economies. The leaders of a command system decide what to produce. The rulers of ancient Egypt, for example, built huge pyramids in honor of dead kings and queens. In contrast, Stalin decided to produce what he believed would be good for the Communist state—coal, steel, electrical power.

Often punishments and rewards are used in command economies to support the planner's decisions. Leaders encourage people to work harder by reminding them that their society values their work. The results of hard work will benefit all of society. Punishments for poor production range from wage cuts to imprisonment. Workers sometimes refuse to speak or associate with other workers who are not doing their jobs well.

Command economies are able to act quickly. Central planners can meet emergency situations with prompt action. Economic change can be brought about much faster than in traditional economies.

SPOTLIGHT ON
1984

Rulers of the society depicted in *1984* make widespread use of propaganda. Even a new language—Newspeak—is adopted that will serve the propaganda needs of the state. Ask students to read the appendix to *1984,* which contains a description of Newspeak, and to explain some Newspeak words to the class.

 IN-DEPTH RESOURCES: UNIT 7
Literature: from *1984,* p. 32

 ELECTRONIC LIBRARY OF PRIMARY SOURCES
from *1984*

MORE ABOUT . . .
Artists, Writers, and Propaganda

Art and literature became tools of propaganda, as Stalin ordered intellectuals to become "engineers of human minds." Writers and artists who could successfully create works of propaganda were generously rewarded, often living better than the highest members of government.

MORE ABOUT . . .
Religious Persecution

Under Stalin's totalitarian regime, the chapel of the Iberian Virgin, one of Moscow's most revered religious sites, was destroyed. Religious Soviet citizens were horrified. The gold-domed Church of Christ the Savior, built to commemorate Russia's victory over Napoleon, was blown up to make way for a towering building, the Palace of the Soviets. The Palace, however, was never built.

SPOTLIGHT ON
1984

George Orwell wrote the chilling novel *1984* in response to the threat of two totalitarian regimes. They were Communist Russia under Stalin and Nazi Germany under Adolf Hitler. The novel depicts a frightening world in which personal freedom and privacy have vanished. The sinister slogan "Big Brother Is Watching You" appears everywhere. Even citizens' homes have television cameras that constantly survey their behavior.

Orwell intended his novel, published in 1949, as a warning, not as a prophecy. He sounded an alarm about a world that a totalitarian state could create through modern technology. For millions of people in the Soviet Union and Nazi Germany, the world of totalitarianism was not fiction. It was terrifying fact.

---

themselves were not above suspicion, especially if they did not meet their quotas of "criminals" arrested. Every family came to fear the knock on the door in the early hours of the morning. Such a surprise visit from the secret police usually meant the arrest of a family member.

When the Great Purge ended in 1939, Stalin had gained total control of both the Soviet government and the Communist Party. Historians estimate that Stalin was responsible for the deaths of 8 million to 13 million people.

Indoctrination and Propaganda Totalitarian states rely on indoctrination—instruction in the government's set of beliefs—to mold people's minds. Party leaders in the Soviet Union lectured workers and peasants on the ideals of communism. They also stressed the importance of sacrifice and hard work to build the Communist state. State-supported youth groups served as training grounds for future party members.

Totalitarian states also spread propaganda. Propaganda is biased or incomplete information used to sway people to accept certain beliefs or actions. Soviet newspapers and radio broadcasts glorified the achievements of communism, Stalin, and his economic programs.

Under Stalin, art also became a method of propaganda. In 1930, an editorial in the Communist Party newspaper *Pravda* explained the purpose of art: "Literature, the cinema, the arts are levers in the hands of the proletariat which must be used to show the masses positive models of initiative and heroic labor." **Socialist realism** was an artistic style that praised Soviet life and Communist values. It became a vehicle to rally the workers. Yevgeny Yevtushenko, a Russian poet, described this form of artistic expression:

A VOICE FROM THE PAST

Blankly smiling workers and collective farmers looked out from the covers of books. Almost every novel and short story had a happy ending. Painters more and more often took as their subjects state banquets, weddings, solemn public meetings, and parades.

Poets visited factories and construction sites but wrote more about machines than about the men who worked them. If machines could read, they might have found such poems interesting. Human beings did not.

YEVGENY YEVTUSHENKO, *A Precocious Autobiography*

Censorship Many Soviet writers, composers, and other artists also fell victim to official censorship. Stalin would not tolerate individual creativity that threatened the conformity and obedience required of citizens in a totalitarian state. The government also controlled all newspapers, motion pictures, radio, and other sources of information.

Religious Persecution Communists aimed to replace religious teachings with the ideals of communism. Under Stalin, the government and the League of the Militant Godless, an officially sponsored group of atheists, spread propaganda attacking religion. "Museums of atheism" displayed exhibits to show that religious beliefs were mere superstitions. Yet many people in the Soviet Union still clung to their faiths.

The Russian Orthodox Church was the main target of persecution. Other religious groups, including Roman Catholics and Jews, also suffered greatly under Stalin's totalitarian rule. The police destroyed magnificent churches and synagogues. Many religious leaders of all faiths were killed or sent to labor camps.

THINK THROUGH HISTORY
B. Making Inferences What forms of art did Stalin encourage?
B. Possible Answer Literature, films, and fine art that served a political purpose—glorifying the goals of the Communist state

Vocabulary
atheists: people who do not think there is a god.

---

778 Chapter 30

TEACHING OPTIONS

CUSTOMIZING FOR SPECIAL NEEDS

Less Proficient Readers:
Guided Reading Suggest that students focus their reading by turning each heading and subheading into a question and then reading the material below it to find the answer. For example, the subheadings on pages 777–778 could be turned into these questions:

How did Stalin use police terror to maintain power?

What role did indoctrination and propaganda play in the Soviet Union?

What types of material did the Soviet government censor?

How did Stalin attempt to destroy religious practice in the Soviet Union?

EXPLORING PRIMARY SOURCES

A Voice from the Past In *A Precocious Autobiography,* Yevtushenko recounts a conversation he had with an artist who once produced a movie under Stalin's totalitarian regime. The grand finale showed "thousands of collective farmers having a gargantuan feast against the backdrop of a new power station." When Yevtushenko asked him how he could have made such a film, the producer replied, " 'You know, the strangest thing to me is that I was absolutely sincere. I thought all this was a necessary part of building communism. And then I believed Stalin.' " Ask students to speculate why so many Soviet artists fell under Stalin's spell.

Propaganda Through Art

Low-cost printing techniques made socialist realism posters an important form of propaganda in the Soviet Union. People might not listen to the radio or go to propaganda films. However, if they left their houses, they could not avoid viewing the posters plastered on buildings and walls in every town.

Images of energetic laborers, such as the special groups called "shock brigades," urged Soviets to work harder. Portraits glorifying Stalin were also popular subjects of Soviet posters.

The slogan on this poster reads, "Young Communists [are] the Shock Brigade of the Five-Year Plan."

The slogan on the above poster reads, "Day Laborers and Young Communists—Join the Tractor Shock Brigades for Spring Sowing."

This profile of Stalin is imposed on a shadowy image of Lenin. Miniature portraits of other Communist leaders trail off in the background.

Connect to History

Analyzing Issues What messages do you think these posters communicate?

SEE SKILLBUILDER
HANDBOOK, PAGE 1001

Connect to Today

Comparing How do the Soviet posters portraying workers resemble the billboards that modern-day advertisers use to sell products? Support your answer with examples.

Revolution and Nationalism **779**

Daily Life Under Stalin

Key Ideas

• Soviet women contribute to the prosperity of Stalin's state-controlled economy but also make great sacrifices.

• Soviet state-controlled education indoctrinates citizens and offers them technical training and opportunities for a better life.

ASSESS & RETEACH

Section 2 Assessment

Have students work individually to answer the questions. Then have them check their answers with a partner.

 FORMAL ASSESSMENT
Section Quiz, p. 351

Reteaching Activity

CLASS TIME: 15 MINUTES

For each key trait of totalitarianism described in the chart on page 776, have students cite at least one example from Stalinist Russia.

 GEOGRAPHY TRANSPARENCIES
GT30 European Totalitarianism by 1938

CLOSE ACTIVITY

CLASS TIME: 15 MINUTES

Role-Playing

Write down the following "cast of characters" from Stalinist Russia on 3" × 5" file cards: a member of the secret police, an artist, a journalist, a kulak, a former Bolshevik, a Russian Orthodox priest, a woman doctor, and a college student. Have interested students draw a card. Other students will interview the Soviet characters about how their lives have changed since Stalin came to power.

Daily Life Under Stalin

Stalin's totalitarian rule revolutionized Soviet society. Women's roles greatly expanded. People became better educated and mastered new technical skills. The dramatic changes in people's lives had a downside, though. As servants of a totalitarian state, they would make great sacrifices in exchange for progress.

This Soviet woman worked in a textile factory during Stalin's regime.

Soviet Women With the Bolshevik Revolution of 1917, women won equal rights. After Stalin became dictator, women helped the state-controlled economy prosper. Under his Five-Year Plans, they had no choice but to join the labor force in increasing numbers. Young women performed the same jobs as men. Millions of women worked in factories and built dams and roads.

Given new educational opportunities, women prepared for careers in engineering and science. Medicine, in particular, attracted many women. By 1950, they made up 75 percent of Soviet doctors.

Soviet women paid a heavy price for their rising status in society. Besides their full-time jobs, they were responsible for housework and child care. Motherhood was also considered a patriotic duty in totalitarian regimes. Soviet women were expected to provide the state with future generations of loyal, obedient citizens.

Education Under Stalin, the government controlled all education—from nursery schools through the universities. Schoolchildren learned the virtues of the Communist Party. College professors and students who questioned the Communist Party's interpretations of history or science risked losing their jobs or faced imprisonment.

Education was not merely indoctrination. Stalin's economic plans created a high demand for many skilled workers. University and technical training became the key to a better life. As one young man explained, "If a person does not want to become a collective farmer or just a cleaning woman, the only means you have to get something is through education."

By the mid-1930s, Stalin had forcibly transformed the Soviet Union into a totalitarian regime, as well as an industrial and a political power. He stood unopposed as dictator and maintained his authority over the Communist Party. Stalin also ushered in a period of total social control and rule by terror. His network of laws and regulations guided every aspect of individual behavior.

Like Russia, China would fall under the influence of Karl Marx's theories and Communist beliefs. The dynamic leader Mao Zedong would pave the way for transforming China into a totalitarian Communist state, as you will read in Section 3.

THINK THROUGH HISTORY
C. Evaluating What were the pros and cons of women's new roles in Soviet society under Stalin?
C. Possible Answer Pros—more job and educational opportunities. Cons—motherhood considered a patriotic duty; limited freedom as a worker.

Section 2 Assessment

1. TERMS & NAMES

Identify
• Joseph Stalin
• totalitarianism
• command economy
• collective farm
• kulak
• Great Purge
• socialist realism

2. TAKING NOTES

Create a chart like the one below listing the weapons of totalitarianism. Cite examples from Stalinist Russia for each method shown.

Weapons	Examples
Police Terror	
Propaganda	
Censorship	
Religious Persecution	

Which method do you think was most influential in maintaining Stalin's totalitarian rule? Why?

3. SYNTHESIZING

What kind of person would be considered an ideal citizen under Stalin's totalitarian regime? Support your answer with reasons.

THINK ABOUT

• the chart explaining the key traits of totalitarianism
• personal qualities that are prized under totalitarianism
• people who were persecuted or punished under Stalin

4. THEME ACTIVITY

Economics Role-play an industrial worker in a steel mill, a peasant on a collective farm, or a student at a technical school. Write a secret journal entry describing what your life is like under Stalin's economic plans.

ANSWERS

1. TERMS & NAMES
Identify
Joseph Stalin, p. 775
totalitarianism, p. 775
command economy, p. 776
collective farm, p. 777
kulak, p. 777
Great Purge, p. 777
socialist realism, p. 778

2. TAKING NOTES
Possible Responses: Police Terror—Great Purge, execution of kulaks. Propaganda—socialist realism, training of youth. Censorship—government-controlled media. Religious Persecution—destruction of buildings, elimination of leadership.

3. SYNTHESIZING
Possible Responses: An ideal citizen in Stalinist Russia would be extremely loyal, obedient, uncritical, hard-working, and productive. He or she would embrace Communist beliefs, denounce religion, and willingly make sacrifices for the good of the state.

4. THEME ACTIVITY
Possible Responses: A journal entry might mention the role of the secret police, Stalin's rigid demands under his Five-Year Plans, government control over their jobs and education, and the barrage of propaganda.

3 Collapse of Chinese Imperial Rule

TERMS & NAMES
- Kuomintang
- Sun Yixian
- Mao Zedong
- May Fourth Movement
- Long March

MAIN IDEA

After the fall of the Qing dynasty, nationalist and Communist movements struggled for power.

WHY IT MATTERS NOW

The seeds of China's late-20th-century political thought, communism, were planted at this time.

SETTING THE STAGE In the early 1900s, China was ripe for revolution. China had faced years of humiliation at the hands of outsiders. Foreign countries controlled China's trade and economic resources. Many Chinese believed that modernization and nationalism held the country's keys for survival. They wanted to build up the army and navy, to construct modern factories, and to reform education. Yet others feared change. They believed that China's greatness lay in its traditional ways.

Nationalists Overthrow Qing Dynasty

Among the groups pushing for modernization and nationalization was the **Kuomintang** (KWOH·mihn·TANG), or the Nationalist Party. Its first great leader, **Sun Yixian** (soon yee·shyahn), was a physician who had spent many years in the United States. In 1912, Sun's Revolutionary Alliance, a forerunner of the Kuomintang, succeeded in overthrowing the last emperor of the Qing dynasty. The Qing had ruled China since 1644.

Shaky Start for the New Republic In 1912, Sun became president of the new Republic of China. He held the post for just six weeks. Sun hoped to establish a modern government based on the "Three Principles of the People": (1) nationalism—an end to foreign control, (2) people's rights—democracy, and (3) people's livelihood—economic security for all Chinese. Sun Yixian considered nationalism vital. He said, "The Chinese people . . . do not have national spirit. Therefore even though we have four hundred million people gathered together in one China, in reality, they are just a heap of loose sand." Despite his lasting influence as a revolutionary leader, Sun lacked the authority and the military support to secure national unity.

Sun turned over the presidency to Yuan Shikai (yoo·ahn shee·ky), a powerful general. Yuan quickly betrayed the democratic ideals of the revolution. By 1913, he was ruling as a military dictator. His actions sparked local revolts. Even Yuan's own generals refused to fight the rebels. After Yuan died in 1916, chaos reigned. China remained divided and Sun's Kuomintang powerless. Civil war broke out as one rival group battled another. Sun tried to reorganize his Kuomintang. Real authority, though, fell into the hands of provincial warlords. They ruled territories as large as their armies could conquer.

Vocabulary
warlord: powerful military leader.

As always during times of unrest, the Chinese peasants suffered most. Warlord armies terrorized the countryside. They pillaged and looted everywhere. Roads and bridges fell into disrepair, and crops were destroyed. Famine took the lives of millions. This was the situation in China as World War I was being waged in Europe.

HISTORY MAKERS

Sun Yixian
1866–1925

A traditional Chinese proverb says that knowing what to do is easier than doing it. Sun Yixian disagreed. "Knowledge is difficult," he said. "Action is easy."

Sun led an action-filled life. He traveled, organized, and plotted tirelessly to bring down the Qing dynasty. Aware of Sun's activity and influence, Qing officials tracked him down in London. They kidnapped him and held him prisoner. They planned to ship him back to China, where he faced probable execution.

Sun would meet his death, he said, by "first having my ankles crushed in a vise and broken by a hammer, my eyelids cut off, and finally being chopped up into small fragments so that no one could claim my mortal remains." Sun's British friends helped him escape his captors. The episode made him world-famous as a leader of the revolution in China. Sun Yixian is still known as the "father of modern China."

Revolution and Nationalism **781**

Section 3 Overview

OBJECTIVES

1. To explain the problems facing the Republic of China after the overthrow of the Qing dynasty.

2. To trace the rise of the Communist Party in China.

3. To summarize key events of the civil war between Chinese Communists and Nationalists.

SKILLBUILDERS

- Interpreting maps: region, movement, p. 784

CRITICAL THINKING

- Identifying problems, p. 782
- Contrasting, p. 783
- Recognizing effects, p. 784
- Analyzing themes, p. 784

FOCUS
5-Minute Warm-Up

▶ *Recognizing Facts and Details*

Have students answer these questions to help them gain insight into the leadership of a famous Chinese revolutionary.

- Read the History Makers on page 781. How did Sun Yixian describe his probable execution?

- Who helped Sun escape?

WARM-UP TRANSPARENCY 30

OBJECTIVE ① INSTRUCT

Nationalists Overthrow Qing Dynasty

▶ *Key Ideas*

- Nationalists establish the new Republic of China.

- Sun fails to secure national unity.

- Under the Treaty of Versailles, the Allies give Japan territories previously held by Germany.

- The Treaty of Versailles triggers nationwide protests.

IN-DEPTH RESOURCES: UNIT 7
Guided Reading, p. 21

ACCESS FOR STUDENTS ACQUIRING ENGLISH
Guided Reading (Spanish), p. 303

SECTION 3 RESOURCES

PRINT RESOURCES

IN-DEPTH RESOURCES: UNIT 7
Guided Reading, p. 21
Primary Source: from The Peasants of Hunan, p. 28
Geography Application: Nationalists Battle Warlords and Communists, p. 24
History Makers: Jiang Jieshi, p. 35

ACCESS FOR STUDENTS ACQUIRING ENGLISH
Guided Reading (Spanish), p. 303
Geography Application (Spanish), p. 306

FORMAL ASSESSMENT
Section Quiz, p. 352

ALTERNATIVE ASSESSMENT BOOK

TECHNOLOGY RESOURCES

CD-ROM
Electronic Library of Primary Sources

INTERNET www.mlworldhistory.com

HISTORY MAKERS
Sun Yixian

(See page 781.)

According to his contemporaries, Sun possessed a magnetic personality and a tolerance for others. His experiences as a student in British and American schools left him with a clear understanding of Western ideals. Ask students to discuss how Sun's familiarity with the Western democracies might have influenced his "Three Principles of the People."

OBJECTIVE ② INSTRUCT

The Communist Party in China

▶ **Key Ideas**
- Western democracies' refusal to aid Sun Yixian prompts him to seek the Soviet Union's support.
- Kuomintang leader Jiang Jieshi turns against the Chinese Communists and becomes president of the Nationalist Republic of China in 1928.
- Peasants throw their support to the Chinese Communists led by Mao Zedong.

📖 **IN-DEPTH RESOURCES: UNIT 7**
Primary Source: from *The Peasants of Hunan*, p. 28
History Maker: Jiang Jieshi, p. 35

CRITICAL THINKING ACTIVITY
CLASS TIME: 15 MINUTES

Understanding Sequential Order
To help students track the sequence of events in China, have them create a time line explaining the dates shown below.

| 1920 | 1923 | 1927 |
| 1921 | 1925 | |

World War I Spells More Problems In 1917, the government in Beijing, hoping for an Allied victory, declared war against Germany. For China's participation, some leaders mistakenly believed that the thankful Allies would return control of China to the Chinese. Under the Treaty of Versailles, however, the Allied leaders gave Japan the territories and privileges that had previously belonged to Germany.

The May Fourth Movement When news of the Treaty of Versailles reached China, outrage swept the country. On May 4, 1919, over 3,000 angry students gathered in the center of Beijing. "Down with the European imperialists!" they shouted. "Boycott Japan!" **Mao Zedong** (MOW dzuh·dahng), a young schoolteacher who had studied at Beijing University, supported the student protesters. He would later become China's greatest revolutionary leader, sometimes called "The Great Helmsman."

Student protesters gathered at Tiananmen Square in summer 1919.

Vocabulary
helmsman: person who steers a ship.

The demonstrations spread to other cities and exploded into a national movement. It was called the **May Fourth Movement.** Workers, manufacturers, shopkeepers, and professionals joined the cause. Though not officially a revolution, these demonstrations showed the Chinese people's commitment to the goal of establishing a strong, modern nation. Sun Yixian and members of the Kuomintang also shared the aims of the movement. But they could not strengthen central rule on their own. Many young Chinese intellectuals turned against Sun Yixian's beliefs in Western democracy in favor of Lenin's brand of Soviet communism.

THINK THROUGH HISTORY
A. Identifying Problems What problems did the new Republic of China face?
A. Possible Answer Weak leadership, civil war, terror of warlord armies, famine, outcome of World War I, nationwide protests

The Communist Party in China

In 1920, small groups of young intellectuals were meeting in Shanghai and Beijing University to discuss Marx's revolutionary beliefs. They viewed the Soviet Union under Lenin as a model for political and economic change. In 1921, a group met in Shanghai to organize the Chinese Communist Party. Mao Zedong was among its founders.

Lenin Befriends China While the Communist Party was forming, Sun Yixian and his Nationalist Party set up a government in south China. Like the Communists, Sun became disillusioned with the Western democracies that refused to support his struggling government. Sun decided to ally the Kuomintang with the newly formed Communist Party. Sun used Lenin's blueprint for organizing his party along Bolshevik lines. Sun hoped to unite all the revolutionary groups for common action.

After Western governments failed to aid Sun, he accepted an offer from the Soviets. Lenin preached worldwide revolution. He seized the opportunity to help China's Nationalist government. In 1923, Lenin began sending military advisers and equipment to the Nationalists in return for allowing the Chinese Communists to join the Kuomintang. Several Chinese Nationalist leaders traveled to Moscow for military training.

This portrait of Mao Zedong was taken around 1919, when he was a young revolutionary.

Nationalists and Communists Clash After Sun Yixian died in 1925, Jiang Jieshi (Jee·ahng jee·shee), formerly called Chiang Kai-shek, headed the Kuomintang. Jiang was the son of a middle-class merchant. Many of Jiang's followers were bankers and

Background
Jiang was Sun's brother-in-law and military assistant.

782 Chapter 30

CONNECTIONS ACROSS TIME AND PLACE

Tiananmen Square When the Communists came into power in 1949, they designated the fourth of May as National Youth Day, in honor of the May Fourth Movement of 1919. The 70th anniversary of the May Fourth Movement sparked a new wave of protests. In April 1989, university students in China once again began staging demonstrations at Tiananmen Square. Protesters demanded democracy and political change. On May 29, they constructed a replica of the Statue of Liberty, which they dubbed the "Goddess of Democracy."

China's premier Li Peng took military action. On June 3, 1989, troops in armored tanks entered the square and fired on the crowd. Soldiers killed hundreds of protesters. Government officials ordered the arrest of others, some of whom were executed. Television audiences from the world's democratic countries watched broadcasts of these shocking events. Though the protest was crushed, one student said, "Maybe we'll fail today. Maybe we'll fail tomorrow. But someday we'll succeed. It's a historical inevitability." By 1990, the Chinese government started making economic reforms.

businesspeople. Like Jiang, they feared the Communists' goal of creating a socialist economy modeled after the Soviet Union's.

At first, Jiang put aside his differences with the Communists. Together Jiang's Nationalist forces and the Communists successfully fought the warlords. Soon afterward, though, he turned against the Communists.

In April 1927, Nationalist troops and armed gangs moved into Shanghai. They killed many Communist leaders and trade union members in the city streets. Similar killings took place in other cities. The Nationalists nearly wiped out the Chinese Communist Party. Its few survivors went into hiding.

In 1928, Jiang became president of the Nationalist Republic of China. Great Britain and the United States both formally recognized the new government. The Soviet Union, as a result of the Shanghai massacre, did not. Jiang's treachery also had long-term effects. The Communists' deep-seated rage over the massacre erupted in a civil war that would last until 1949.

Peasants Align Themselves with the Communists Jiang had promised democracy and political rights to all Chinese. Yet his government became steadily less democratic and more corrupt. It launched programs to modernize and develop the cities. However, Jiang did nothing to improve the life of China's rural peasants. As a result, many peasants threw their support to the Chinese Communist Party. To enlist the support of the peasants, Mao divided land that the Communists won among the local farmers.

Communist leader Mao Zedong had survived Jiang's bloody rampage by fleeing to the countryside. He had already begun to develop his own brand of communism. Lenin had shown that a Marxist revolution could take place in a largely rural country, but he had based his organization in Russia's cities. Mao envisioned a different setting. He believed he could bring revolution to a rural country where the peasants could be the true revolutionaries. He argued his point passionately in 1927:

A VOICE FROM THE PAST
The force of the peasantry is like that of the raging winds and driving rain. It is rapidly increasing in violence. No force can stand in its way. The peasantry will tear apart all nets which bind it and hasten along the road to liberation. They will bury beneath them all forces of imperialism, militarism, corrupt officialdom, village bosses and evil gentry.

MAO ZEDONG, quoted in *A History of World Societies*

Civil War Rages in China

By 1930, Nationalists and Communists were fighting a bloody civil war. Mao and other Communist leaders established themselves in the hills of south-central China. Mao referred to this tactic of taking his revolution to the countryside as "swimming in the peasant sea." He recruited the peasants to join his Red Army. He then trained them in guerrilla warfare. Nationalists attacked the Communists repeatedly but failed to drive them out.

The Long March In 1933, Jiang gathered an army of at least 700,000 men. Jiang's army then surrounded the Communists' mountain stronghold. Outnumbered nearly six to one,

Along with the Red Army, Mao (riding on horseback) and his wife He Zizhan (wearing a round hat) made the grueling Long March to safety in western China.

China, 1927–1938

Legend:
- Japanese attacks
- Japanese territory, 1928
- Japanese territory, 1933
- Japanese territory, 1938
- Long March, 1934–35
- Communist bases

Map labels: Sea of Okhotsk, SOVIET UNION, MANCHUKUO (MANCHURIA), CHINA, Beijing, Yan'an, Qin Mts., Huang He (Yellow R.), Chang Jiang (Yangtze R.), Chongqing, Riujan, Guangzhou, Hong Kong (Britain), SIAM, FRENCH INDOCHINA, KOREA, Tokyo, JAPAN, Sea of Japan, Yellow Sea, Nanjing, Shanghai, East China Sea, PACIFIC OCEAN, TAIWAN, South China Sea

500 Miles / 1,000 Kilometers

GEOGRAPHY SKILLBUILDER: Interpreting Maps
1. **Movement** What was the course of the Long March, in terms of direction, beginning in Riujan and ending near Yan'an?
2. **Region** What geographic barriers did Mao's forces face during the Long March?

Communist Party leaders realized that they faced defeat. In 1934, the Communist forces fled. They began a hazardous, 6,000-mile-long journey called the **Long March**. Over the next year, the Communists kept only a step ahead of Jiang's forces.

Mao's Red Army crossed many rivers and climbed over mountain ranges. They fought several major battles and faced minor skirmishes almost every day. They also crossed miles of swampland. They had to sleep sitting up, leaning back-to-back in pairs, to keep from sinking into the mud and drowning.

The chase lasted more than a year. About 100,000 people began the march. From 10,000 to 30,000 reached safety in northwestern China, beyond the reach of Jiang's forces.

Mao and the other Communist survivors settled in caves in northwestern China. Despite the discouraging turn of events, they quickly gained new followers. Meanwhile, as civil war between Nationalists and Communists raged, Japan invaded China.

Japan's Invasion Suspends the Civil War In 1931, as Chinese fought Chinese, the Japanese watched the power struggles with rising interest. Japanese forces took advantage of China's weakening situation. They invaded Manchuria, an industrialized province in the northeast part of China. This attack signaled the onset of World War II in Asia.

In 1937, the Japanese launched an all-out invasion of China. Massive bombings of villages and cities killed thousands of Chinese. The destruction of farms caused many more to die of starvation. By 1938, Japan held control of a large part of China.

The Japanese threat forced an uneasy truce between Jiang's and Mao's forces. The civil war gradually ground to a halt as Nationalists and Communists temporarily united to fight the Japanese. Jiang further agreed to promote changes outlined in Sun Yixian's "Three Principles of the People"—nationalism, democracy, and people's livelihood. As you will learn in Section 4, similar principles were also serving as a guiding force in India and Southwest Asia.

Section 3 Assessment

1. TERMS & NAMES

Identify
- Kuomintang
- Sun Yixian
- Mao Zedong
- May Fourth Movement
- Long March

2. TAKING NOTES

Make a chart like the one below to compare and contrast Jiang Jieshi and Mao Zedong.

	Jiang	Mao
Party		
Key Supporters		
Reforms		
Military Actions		

3. RECOGNIZING EFFECTS

What influence did foreign nations have on China from 1912 to 1938? Support your answer with details from the text.

THINK ABOUT
- the outcome of the Treaty of Versailles
- the role of the Soviet Union
- the temporary truce during the Chinese civil war

4. ANALYZING THEMES

Revolution What caused the Communist revolutionary movement in China to gain strength?

THINK ABOUT
- Jiang's government and policies
- the Soviet Union's influence
- the conditions of rural peasants
- Mao's role and achievements

784 Chapter 30

MAIN IDEA

Nationalism triggered independence movements to overthrow colonial power.

WHY IT MATTERS NOW

These independent nations—India, Turkey, Iran, and Saudi Arabia—are key players on the world stage today.

SETTING THE STAGE The end of World War I stirred nationalist activity in India, Turkey, and some Southwest Asian countries. The British Empire, which controlled India, began to show signs of cracking.

Indian Nationalism Grows

Indian nationalism had been growing since the mid-1800s. Many upper-class Indians who attended British schools learned European views of nationalism and democracy. They began to apply these political ideas to their own country. Well-educated Indians began to resent the two centuries of British rule.

Two groups formed to rid India of foreign rule: the Indian National Congress, or Congress Party, in 1885, and the Muslim League in 1906. Though deep divisions existed between Hindus and Muslims, they found common ground. They shared the heritage of British rule and an understanding of democratic ideals. These two groups both worked toward the goal of national independence.

World War I Heightens Nationalist Activity Until World War I, the vast majority of Indians had little interest in nationalism. The situation changed as over a million Indians enlisted in the British army. In return for their service, the British government promised reforms that would eventually lead to self-government. Indian leaders bided their time. They expected to make gains once the war was over.

Later in the war, Indian demands led to the declaration in Parliament favoring the "increasing association of Indians in every branch of the administration, and the gradual development of self-governing institutions." To many Indians, these political reforms signaled that Indians would gain a greater voice in government and ultimately achieve their goal of self-rule.

In 1918, Indian troops returned home from the war. They expected Britain to fulfill its promise. Instead, they found themselves once again treated as second-class citizens. Radical nationalists carried out acts of violence to show their hatred of British rule. To curb dissent, in 1919 the British passed the Rowlatt Act. This law allowed the government to jail protesters without trial for as long as two years. To Western-educated Indians, denial of a trial by jury violated their individual rights. Violent protests against the act flared in the Punjab, the Indian province with the greatest number of World War I veterans.

Background
Unlike Europeans, Asians, including Indians, viewed World War I as a civil war among the feuding nations of Europe.

Vocabulary
dissent: difference of opinion.

This Indian soldier fought for the British in World War I.

Revolution and Nationalism **785**

Amritsar Massacre To protest the Rowlatt Act, around 10,000 Hindus and Muslims flocked to Amritsar, the capital city of the Punjab, in the spring of 1919. At a huge festival, they intended to fast and pray and to listen to political speeches. A small group of nationalists were also on the scene. The demonstration, especially the alliance of Hindus and Muslims, alarmed the British.

Most people at the gathering were unaware that the British government had banned public meetings. However, General Reginald Dyer, the British commander at Amritsar, believed they were openly defying the ban. He ordered his troops to fire on the crowd without warning. The shooting lasted ten minutes. British troops killed nearly 400 Indians and wounded about 1200.

News of the slaughter sparked an explosion of anger across India. Almost overnight, millions of Indians changed from loyal British subjects into revolutionaries and nationalists. These Indians demanded independence.

Gandhi's Principles of Nonviolence

The massacre at Amritsar set the stage for **Mohandas K. Gandhi** (GAHN·dee) to emerge as the leader of the independence movement. He began to form his social and political ideas during the mid-1880s before he attended law school in England. Gandhi's new strategy for battling injustice evolved from his deeply religious approach to political activity. His teachings blended ideas from all of the major world religions, including Hinduism, Islam, and Christianity. The Indian poet Rabindranath Tagore described him as "this great soul in a beggar's garb." Gandhi attracted millions of followers. Soon they were calling him the Mahatma (muh·HAHT·muh), meaning "Great Soul."

When the British failed to punish the officers responsible for the killings at the Amritsar massacre, Gandhi urged the Indian National Congress to follow a policy of noncooperation with the British government:

> **A VOICE FROM THE PAST**
> This is in essence the principle of nonviolent noncooperation. It follows therefore that it must have its root in love. Its object should not be to punish the opponent or to inflict injury upon him. Even while noncooperating with him, we must make him feel that in us he has a friend and we should try to reach his heart by rendering him humanitarian service wherever possible.
>
> **MOHANDAS K. GANDHI,** quoted in *Gandhi the Man*

Civil Disobedience Gandhi developed the principle of satyagraha (SUH·tyah·grah·ha), or "truth-force." In English, satyagraha is called passive resistance or **civil disobedience**—the deliberate and public refusal to obey an unjust law. Gandhi wrote, "Complete civil disobedience is a rebellion without the element of violence . . . One *perfect* civil resister is enough to win the battle of Right and Wrong." In 1920, under Gandhi's influence, the Congress Party endorsed civil disobedience and nonviolence as the means to achieve independence.

Gandhi launched his campaign of civil disobedience to weaken the British government's authority and economic power. He called on Indians to refuse to do the following: buy British goods, attend government schools, pay British taxes, and vote in elections. Gandhi staged a successful boycott of British cloth, a source of wealth for the

British. He urged all Indians to weave their own cloth. Gandhi himself devoted two hours each day to spinning his own yarn on a simple handwheel. He wore only home-spun cloth and encouraged Indians to follow his example. As a result of the boycott, the sale of British cloth in India dropped sharply.

Throughout 1920, the British arrested thousands of Indians who had participated in strikes and demonstrations. Gandhi's weapon of civil disobedience took an economic toll on the British. They struggled to keep trains running, factories operating, and overcrowded jails from bursting. Despite Gandhi's pleas for nonviolence, protests often led to riots. In 1922, rioters attacked a police station and set several officers on fire.

The Slow March to Independence In 1930, Gandhi organized a demonstration to defy the hated Salt Acts. According to these British laws, Indians could buy salt from no other source but the government. They also had to pay sales tax on salt. To show their opposition, Gandhi and his followers walked about 240 miles to the seacoast. There they began to make their own salt by collecting seawater and letting it evaporate. This peaceful protest was called the Salt March.

Gandhi (standing in the center with his head bowed) led Indians in the Salt March. The demonstrators protested the British government's control of salt sales.

Soon afterward, some demonstrators planned a march to a site where the British government processed salt. They intended to shut this saltworks down. Police officers with steel-tipped clubs attacked the demonstrators. An American journalist was an eyewitness to the event. He described the "sickening whacks of clubs on unprotected skulls" and people "writhing in pain with fractured skulls or broken shoulders." Still the people continued to march peacefully, refusing to defend themselves against their attackers. Newspapers across the globe carried the journalist's story, which won worldwide support for Gandhi's independence movement.

More demonstrations took place throughout India. Eventually, about 60,000 people, including Gandhi, were arrested.

Great Britain Grants India Self-Rule

Gandhi and his followers gradually reaped the rewards of their civil disobedience campaigns and gained greater political power for the Indian people. In 1935, the British Parliament passed the Government of India Act. It provided local self-government and limited democratic elections.

With this act, India began moving toward full independence from Great Britain. However, the Government of India Act also fueled mounting tensions between Muslims and Hindus. These two groups had conflicting visions of India's future as an independent nation. Indian Muslims, outnumbered by Hindus, feared that Hindus would control India if it won independence. In Chapter 34, you will read about the outcome of India's bid for independence.

Revolution and Nationalism **787**

Nationalism Spreads to Southwest Asia

Key Ideas

- Mustafa Kemal leads Turkish nationalists in overthrowing the last Ottoman sultan and helps establish a new republic.
- After a nationalist revolt in Persia, Reza Shah seizes power and in 1935 renames the country Iran.
- Ibn Saud unifies Arabia and in 1932 renames the new kingdom Saudi Arabia.
- High demand for oil transforms the economy of Southwest Asia.

 WORLD ART AND CULTURES TRANSPARENCIES
AT66 *Persian Musicians*

HISTORYMAKERS
Mustafa Kemal

In 1928, Kemal introduced the Latin alphabet, replacing the Arabic letters. He wanted people to forget their history under the Ottomans and to return to the roots of their ancient Turkish language. After his reform, Turkish authors and poets began following the models of Western literature.

CRITICAL THINKING ACTIVITY
CLASS TIME: 15 MINUTES

To help students analyze the similarities and differences among three nationalist leaders in Southwest Asia, have them copy the diagram below and fill it in.

HISTORYMAKERS

Mustafa Kemal
1881-1938

As president of Turkey, Mustafa Kemal campaigned vigorously to mold the new republic into a modern nation. His models were the United States and other European countries.

To reach this goal, Kemal even set rules for clothing:

> A civilized, international dress is worthy and appropriate for our new nation, and we will wear it. Boots or shoes on our feet, trousers on our legs, shirt and tie, jacket and waistcoat—and, of course, to complete these, a . . . hat.

Kemal required government workers to wear Western-style business suits and banned the fez, a brimless red felt hat that was part of traditional Turkish clothing.

Kemal died in 1938. From his leadership, Turkey gained a new sense of its national identity. His influence was so strong that the Turkish people gave him the name Ataturk—"father of the Turks."

Nationalism Spreads to Southwest Asia

Just as the people of India fought to have their own nation after World War I, the people of Southwest Asia also launched independence movements during this time. Each group in Southwest Asia chose a different path toward nation building.

The breakup of the Ottoman Empire and growing Western interest in Southwest Asia spurred the rise of nationalism in this region.

Turkey Becomes a Republic By the end of World War I, Turkey was all that remained of the Ottoman Empire. It included the old Turkish homeland of Anatolia and a small strip of land around Istanbul.

In 1919, Greek soldiers dealt a death blow to the Ottoman Empire. They invaded Turkey and threatened to conquer it. The Turkish sultan, weak and corrupt, was powerless to stop them. In 1922, a brilliant commander, **Mustafa Kemal** (keh·MAHL), led Turkish nationalists in overthrowing the last Ottoman sultan. A young woman who played a major role in the revolution described her strong nationalistic feelings: "I suddenly ceased to exist as an individual. I worked, wrote and lived as a unit of that magnificent national madness."

In 1923, Kemal became the president of the new Republic of Turkey, the first republic in Southwest Asia. He ushered in many sweeping reforms to achieve his goal of transforming Turkey into a modern nation. Kemal separated the laws of Islam from the laws of the nation. He abolished religious courts and created a new legal system based on European law. Under Kemal, women gained more freedom. He granted women the right to vote and to hold public office. Kemal also launched government-funded programs to industrialize Turkey and to spur economic growth.

Persia Becomes Iran Before World War I, both Great Britain and Russia had established spheres of influence in the ancient country of Persia. After the war, when Russia was still reeling from the Bolshevik Revolution, the British tried to take over all of Persia. This maneuver triggered a nationalist revolt in Persia. In 1921, a Persian army officer seized power. In 1925 he deposed the ruling shah.

Persia's new leader, Reza Shah Pahlavi (PAL·uh·vee), like Kemal in Turkey, set out to modernize his country. He established public schools, built roads and railroads, promoted industrial growth, and extended women's rights. Unlike Kemal, Reza Shah kept all power in his own hands. In 1935, he changed the name of his country from Persia to Iran.

Saudi Arabia Keeps Islamic Traditions While Turkey broke with many Islamic traditions, another new country held strictly to Islamic law. In 1902, Abd al-Aziz Ibn Saud (sah·OOD), a member of a once-powerful Arabian family, began a successful campaign to unify Arabia. In 1932, he renamed the new kingdom Saudi Arabia after his family.

Ibn Saud carried on Arab and Islamic traditions. Loyalty to the Saudi government was based on custom, religion, and family ties. Alcoholic drinks were illegal. Like Kemal and Reza Shah, Ibn Saud brought some modern technology, such as telephones and radios, to his country. However, modernization in Saudi Arabia was limited to religiously acceptable areas.

Oil Resources Spur Economic Development While nationalism steadily emerged as a major force in Southwest Asia, the region's economy was also taking a new direction. The rising demand for petroleum products in industrialized countries brought

Background
The Ottoman Empire had ruled in Southwest Asia for about 500 years.

THINK THROUGH HISTORY
C. Comparing How were Kemal's leadership and Reza Shah's leadership similar?
C. Possible Answer Both established policies and launched programs to modernize their countries.

TEACHING OPTIONS

CUSTOMIZING FOR SPECIAL NEEDS

Less Proficient Readers:
Clarifying In reading pages 785–789, less proficient readers might use the SQ3R study method, as follows:

1. Survey the pages by skimming for headings and topic sentences.
2. Jot down any questions about the text, such as what role nationalism played in India, Turkey, Iran, and Saudi Arabia.
3. Read the pages and look for answers to these questions.
4. Recite or record any answers that are found.
5. Review the information to answer any questions that remain.

CONNECTIONS ACROSS THE CURRICULUM

Science The word *petroleum* means "rock oil." Wells are drilled into oil-bearing rock to release the oil. The pressure of the natural gas helps bring the oil to the surface. Unless the drilling is carefully controlled, the high pressure causes wasteful oil gushers. Even with modern technology, only about 40 percent of the oil is pumped out of a given well.

When petroleum is refined, it is separated into many byproducts, such as gasoline for automobiles and kerosene and fuel oil for heating. Other petroleum products are used as lubricants. Both natural gas and petroleum are used as raw materials in making such substances as plastics, fertilizers, medicines, and dyes.

SOVIET UNION

Turkey became a republic in 1923.

Persia was renamed Iran in 1935. Oil was discovered in the early 1900s and continues to be Iran's most important natural resource.

TURKEY

Caspian Sea

LEBANON
SYRIA
Euphrates R. *Tigris R.*
Mediterranean Sea
PALESTINE
IRAQ
IRAN

EGYPT
KUWAIT
TRANS-JORDAN
Neutral Zone
BAHRAIN
Persian Gulf
SAUDI ARABIA
QATAR
Strait of Hormuz
TRUCIAL STATES

The Kingdom of Saudi Arabia was established in 1932. Oil was discovered near the coastline of the Persian Gulf in 1938. Saudi Arabia's oil industry was not developed until after 1941.

Red Sea

MUSCAT AND OMAN

ANGLO-EGYPTIAN SUDAN
YEMEN
FRENCH SOMALILAND
ADEN PROTECTORATE
Gulf of Aden
BRITISH SOMALILAND

N

0   500 Miles
0   1,000 Kilometers

☐ British territory
☐ French territory
⚒ Oil-producing regions

Oil Exports

Oil Production (in thousands of metric tons)

35,000
30,000
25,000
20,000
15,000
10,000
5,000
0

1910 1915 1920 1925 1930 1935 1940 1945 1950

■ Iran   ■ Iraq   ■ Saudi Arabia

GEOGRAPHY SKILLBUILDER: Interpreting Maps
1. **Location** Along what geographical feature are most of the oil-producing regions located?
2. **Region** Based on the graph and map, what country was the leading producer of oil by 1938? Why?

new oil explorations to Southwest Asia. During the 1920s and 1930s, European and American companies discovered huge oil deposits in Iran, Iraq, Saudi Arabia, and Kuwait. Foreign businesses invested huge sums of money to develop these oil fields. Geologists later learned that the land around the Persian Gulf has nearly two-thirds of the world's known supply of oil.

This important resource led to rapid and dramatic economic changes and development. Saudi Arabia, for example, would soon become a nation of wealthy oil exporters. Yet oil proved to be a mixed blessing for Southwest Asia. Though oil brought huge profits, it also encouraged Western nations to try to dominate this region. Meanwhile, Western nations were about to face a more immediate crisis as power-hungry leaders seized control in Italy and Germany.

Section 4 Assessment

1. TERMS & NAMES
Identify
• Mohandas K. Gandhi
• civil disobedience
• Mustafa Kemal

2. TAKING NOTES
Create a web diagram like the one below. Show the different forms of nationalism that developed in the Asian countries shown.

India   Persia
Forms of Nationalism 1900–1939
Turkey   Saudi Arabia

In which of these countries did World War I trigger nationalist movements?

3. HYPOTHESIZING
What do you think a nation might gain and lose by modernizing?

THINK ABOUT
• what positive changes occurred in Turkey and Iran
• why modernization was limited in Saudi Arabia
• why Kemal set rules for clothing
• why Gandhi wore only homespun cloth

4. THEME ACTIVITY
Science and Technology
Work in small groups to research products and consumer goods made from petroleum. Create an illustrated list of items that were in great demand in industrialized countries during the 1930s.

Revolution and Nationalism **789**

ANSWERS

1. TERMS & NAMES
Mohandas K. Gandhi, p. 786
civil disobedience, p. 786
Mustafa Kemal, p. 788

2. TAKING NOTES
Possible Responses: India— Nationalists use nonviolent methods to work for independence from British rule. Turkey— Nationalists overthrow last Ottoman sultan; Kemal seeks Western-style modernization. Persia—Nationalists free Persia from British and Russian rule; Reza Shah changes country's name to Iran. Saudi Arabia—Ibn Saud unifies the nation and creates a state based on Islamic law.

3. HYPOTHESIZING
Possible Responses: Gains— increased economic and political power; greater acceptance and respect from Western nations; equal rights for women. Losses— a unique sense of cultural identity; traditional values and ways of life.

4. THEME ACTIVITY
Possible Responses: Lists should include various plastic products, cosmetics, cleaning products, lubricants, and fuels. Remind students to confine their choice of products to those in demand in the 1930s.

TERMS & NAMES

1. Bolsheviks, p. 770
2. V. I. Lenin, p. 770
3. soviet , p. 772
4. Joseph Stalin, p. 775
5. totalitarianism, p. 775
6. Great Purge, p. 777
7. Mao Zedong, p. 782
8. Long March, p. 784
9. Mohandas K. Gandhi, p. 786
10. civil disobedience, p. 786

REVIEW QUESTIONS

Answers may vary on some questions.

11. Rasputin apparently eased the symptoms of the Romanovs' hemophiliac son. To show their gratitude, the Romanovs allowed Rasputin to make key political decisions.

12. Recurring defeats in battle, the death of many soldiers, the sinking morale of the troops, bread and food shortages led to strikes and riots that forced Nicholas II to abdicate.

13. Causes—opposition in Russia to Communist rule under the Bolsheviks' desire; by Western nations to bring down Bolsheviks. Outcomes— Bolsheviks won, but country faced political chaos; economic crises.

14. Dictatorship and one-party rule; dynamic leader; rigid ideology; state control over all sectors of society; state control over the individual; dependence on modern technology; organized violence to enforce dictator's rule.

15. Stalin's Five-Year Plans—total government control over the economy. NEP— mixture of government control with some free enterprise and some private ownership.

16. Freedom of religion, freedom of speech, artistic freedom, political freedom, freedom to choose professions and locale.

17. Student demonstrations protesting the Treaty of Versailles led to a national movement that included workers, manufacturers, shopkeepers, professionals, Sun Yixian, and members of the Kuomintang.

18. Japan took advantage of China's weakened situation by invading Manchuria.

19. Gandhi called on Indians to refuse to attend government schools or to pay British taxes; staged a successful boycott of British goods, particularly cloth; staged the Salt March and gained international support for his cause.

TERMS & NAMES

Briefly explain the importance of each of the following in Russia, China, or India.

1. Bolsheviks
2. V. I. Lenin
3. soviet
4. Joseph Stalin
5. totalitarianism
6. Great Purge
7. Mao Zedong
8. Long March
9. Mohandas K. Gandhi
10. civil disobedience

Interact *with* History

On page 768, you played the role of a citizen whose country was brimming with revolutionary activity. You evaluated two tactics for change—violence and nonviolence. Now that you have read the chapter, how would you assess the pros and cons of Mao's and Gandhi's strategies? What role did violence play in the Russian and Chinese revolutions? How successful were Gandhi's nonviolent methods in India? Discuss your opinions in a small group.

REVIEW QUESTIONS

SECTION 1 *(pages 769–774)*
Revolutions in Russia

11. How did Rasputin gain political influence over the Romanov family and Russian political affairs?

12. How did World War I lead to the downfall of Czar Nicholas II?

13. Explain the causes of Russia's civil war and its outcome.

SECTION 2 *(pages 775–780)*
PATTERNS OF CHANGE: Totalitarianism
CASE STUDY: Stalinist Russia

14. What are the key traits of totalitarianism?

15. How did Stalin's Five-Year Plans differ from Lenin's New Economic Policy?

16. What individual freedoms are denied in a totalitarian state?

SECTION 3 *(pages 781–784)*
Collapse of Chinese Imperial Rule

17. Briefly describe the May Fourth Movement and its supporters.

18. How did the Japanese react to the civil war in China?

SECTION 4 *(pages 785–789)*
Nationalism in India and Southwest Asia

19. Give examples of Gandhi's campaign of civil disobedience against the British government.

20. What steps did Kemal take to modernize Turkey?

Visual Summary

Revolutionary Leaders: 1900–1939

	Lenin	Stalin	Sun Yixian	Mao Zedong	Gandhi	Kemal
Country	Russia	Russia	China	China	India	Turkey
Political Career	late 1890s–1924	early 1900s–1953	late 1890s–1925	early 1900s–1976	late 1800s–1948	early 1900s–1938
Key Role	Bolshevik revolutionary and first ruler of Communist Russia	Dictator	First president of the new Republic of China	Leader of the Chinese Communist Party	Leader of the Indian independence movement	First president of the new Republic of Turkey
Popular Name	"Father of the Revolution"	"Man of Steel"	"Father of Modern China"	"The Great Helmsman"	"Great Soul"	"Father of the Turks"
Goal	To promote a world-wide Communist revolution led by workers	To perfect a Communist state in Russia through totalitarian rule	To establish a modern government based on nationalism, democracy, and economic security	To stage a Communist revolution in China led by peasants	To achieve Indian self-rule through campaigns of civil disobedience	To transform Turkey into a modern nation

---

20. Kemal abolished religious courts and created a new legal system based on European law; granted women more freedom; launched government-funded programs to industrialize Turkey.

Interact *with* History

Possible Responses: Students who originally advocated violent action may now side with Gandhi's strategy of passive, or nonviolent, resistance, based on the success of his boycotts and demonstrations. Using the aftermath of the Bolshevik Revolution as an example, students may also conclude that violence breeds violence.

CRITICAL THINKING

1. THE SHIFTING ROLES OF WOMEN

Compare and contrast how women's roles changed under Stalin in Russia and Kemal in Turkey.

2. THE SOVIET ECONOMY UNDER STALIN

THEME ECONOMICS Cite evidence that Stalin might have used to disprove this claim: Economic systems that allow private ownership and encourage competition are the most productive.

3. MASSACRES IN RUSSIA AND ASIA

Copy the following chart on your paper to analyze the similarities among the events shown. Fill in the chart and write a paragraph that compares the events.

	Description	Political Outcome
Bloody Sunday (Russia, 1905)		
Amritsar Massacre (India, 1919)		
Shanghai Massacre (China, 1927)		

4. ANALYZING PRIMARY SOURCES

The following quotation from Mohandas K. Gandhi, written in 1922, describes his views of industrialization in India. Read the passage and answer the questions below it.

> **A VOICE FROM THE PAST**
> India does not need to be industrialized in the modern sense of the term. It has 7,500,000 villages scattered over a vast area 1,900 miles long, 1,500 broad. The people are rooted to the soil, and the vast majority are living a hand-to-mouth existence. . . . Agriculture does not need revolutionary changes. The Indian peasant requires a supplementary industry. The most natural is the introduction of the spinning wheel.
> **MOHANDAS K. GANDHI,** *Letter to Sir Daniel Hamilton*

- What picture does Gandhi present of India and its people?
- Gandhi believed that the spinning wheel would make Indians less dependent on the British economy. Based on what you have learned in this chapter, what was the economic impact of the widespread use of the spinning wheel?

CHAPTER ACTIVITIES

1. LIVING HISTORY: Unit Portfolio Project

THEME SCIENCE AND TECHNOLOGY Your unit portfolio project focuses on showing the impact of science and technology during the early 1900s. For Chapter 30, you might use one of these ideas to add to your portfolio.

- After reading more about the Trans-Siberian Railway, create a travel poster for a tourist agency that features interesting facts about the train and its routes.
- Write a science fiction story about a totalitarian state that uses modern technology to spread propaganda and control people. Refer to the section on Stalinist Russia for ideas.
- Draw diagrams that show the technology and methods used to drill oil in Southwest Asia during the 1920s and 1930s. Use encyclopedias or books to research the topic.

2. CONNECT TO TODAY: Cooperative Learning

THEME REVOLUTION You read about the various causes that led to the Russian Revolution of 1917. Work with a team to create a mythical country that is on the brink of revolution today. Write a profile of the conditions in that country that are triggering widespread social unrest.

Use the Internet and other books to find out about more recent revolutions that have occurred in countries around the world. Look for common patterns that countries in political turmoil share. Use the following questions to help you brainstorm ideas for writing a profile of your mythical country.

- What type of government is currently in power?
- Who are the top political leaders, and what are they like?
- What grievances do the citizens have against the government?
- What is the gap between the rich and the poor?
- What revolutionary groups are forming? What are their goals and strategies?

FOCUS ON TIME LINES

The time line below highlights key events discussed in this chapter that fall roughly within the time span of World War I. As you study the time line, note the relationships among events that occurred in Russia, China, and India.

- What two events occurred in 1917?

Connect to History

- Explain the role that the end of World War I played in the following two events: the May Fourth Movement in China and the Amritsar Massacre in India. Support your answer with information from the text.
- How did the Russian Revolutions of 1917 trigger the Treaty of Brest-Litovsk?

Revolution and Nationalism **791**

CHAPTER ACTIVITIES

1. LIVING HISTORY: UNIT PORTFOLIO PROJECT

Standards for Evaluation
A travel poster should meet the following criteria:

- Displays eye-catching graphics.
- Contains anecdotal and historical details about the railway.
- Includes information about stops along the train route.

Standards for Evaluation
A science fiction story should meet the following criteria:

- Re-creates aspects of Stalinist Russia in a futuristic setting.
- Contains a well-constructed plot and interesting characters.
- Features the role of propaganda in a totalitarian state.

Standards for Evaluation
Diagrams of oil-drilling methods and technology should meet the following criteria:

- Be clear and easy to follow.
- Contain well-organized graphic representations.
- Include informative labels for the diagrams.

2. CONNECT TO TODAY: COOPERATIVE LEARNING

Standards for Evaluation
A profile of a mythical country should meet the following criteria:

- Identifies revolutionary groups and their aims.
- Contains information about the oppressive life of ordinary people.
- Analyzes the weaknesses of the political leaders and government in power.
- Shows evidence of research.

FOCUS ON TIME LINES

- Russian Revolution and China's entry into World War I.

Connect to History *Possible Responses:*
- China—Anger over the Treaty of Versailles sparked a student protest that grew into May Fourth Movement. India—End of World War I heightened nationalist activity. The British government failed to keep its promises regarding Indian self-government, then passed the Rowlett Act in 1919 to curb dissent. In protest, demonstrators flocked to Amritsar, where hundreds were gunned down.
- Severe military losses in World War I were one of the causes of the Russian Revolutions. The Bolsheviks fulfilled their promise to obtain peace by signing the Treaty of Brest-Litovsk with the Germans, thus ending Russia's role in the war.

CRITICAL THINKING

1. THE SHIFTING ROLES OF WOMEN

Possible Responses: Under both—equal rights. Under Stalin—new educational and job opportunities but limited freedom. Under Kemal—could vote and hold public office.

2. THE SOVIET ECONOMY UNDER STALIN

Possible Responses: Stalin might cite statistics pointing to the enormous increase in industrial and agricultural production under his state-controlled Five-Year Plans.

3. MASSACRES IN RUSSIA AND ASIA

Possible Responses: Bloody Sunday—The killing of unarmed protesters sparked the Revolution of 1905 and led to the establishment of Russia's first parliament. Amritsar Massacre—The killing of unarmed protesters led to the emergence of Gandhi as the leader of India's independence movement. Shanghai Massacre—The killing of many Communists led to Mao's emergence as a revolutionary leader.

4. ANALYZING PRIMARY SOURCES

Possible Responses: It is largely a rural nation whose people could be self-sufficient. The spinning wheel was key to Gandhi's boycott of British cloth.

Teacher's Edition **791**

	COPY MASTERS	**ASSESSMENT**

SECTION 1
An Age of Uncertainty
pp. 795–800

Key Ideas

New ideas in science, the arts, and technology develop in the postwar period and change the way people look at the world and live their lives.

 In-Depth Resources: Unit 7
- **Guided Reading,** p. 37
- **Primary Source:** from An Interview with Charles Lindbergh, p. 44
- **Literature:** from *This Side of Paradise*, p. 48
- **History Makers:** Sigmund Freud, p. 51

PE *Section 1 Assessment,* p. 800

Formal Assessment
- Section Quiz, p. 362

Alternative Assessment Book
- Standards for Evaluating a Cooperative Activity

SECTION 2
A Global Depression
pp. 801–806

An economic depression begins in the United States in 1929. It spreads throughout the world and lasts for a decade.

 In-Depth Resources: Unit 7
- **Guided Reading,** p. 38
- **Skillbuilder Practice:** Identifying Problems, p 41
- **Primary Source:** German Inflation, p. 45

PE *Section 2 Assessment,* p. 806

Formal Assessment
- Section Quiz, p. 363

Alternative Assessment Book
- Standards for Evaluating a Cooperative Activity

SECTION 3
Fascism Rises in Europe
pp. 807–810

In response to political turmoil and economic crises, many countries in Europe, including Italy and Germany, turn to Fascist dictators.

 In-Depth Resources: Unit 7
- **Guided Reading,** p. 39
- **Primary Source:** Kristallnacht, p. 46
- **Literature:** Poems by Bertolt Brecht, p. 49
- **Connections Across Time and Cultures:** Absolutism and Fascism, p. 53

PE *Section 3 Assessment,* p. 810

Formal Assessment
- Section Quiz, p. 364

Alternative Assessment Book
- Standards for Evaluating a Product or Performance

SECTION 4
Aggressors on the March
pp. 811–815

Germany, Italy, and Japan conquer other countries. The League of Nations and the rest of the world do nothing to stop them, and the specter of another great war haunts Europe.

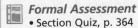 *In-Depth Resources: Unit 7*
- **Guided Reading,** p. 40
- **Geography Application:** Spain During the 1930s, p. 42
- **Primary Source:** The Bombing of Guernica, p. 47
- **History Makers:** Francisco Franco, p. 52

PE *Section 4 Assessment,* p. 815

Formal Assessment
- Section Quiz, p. 365

Alternative Assessment Book
- Standards for Evaluating a Cooperative Activity

CHAPTER RESOURCES

Chapter Overview

The 1920s see great changes in technology, science, and the arts. The Great Depression of the 1930s causes worldwide crisis. In response to aggression by Fascist Italy and Nazi Germany, Britain and France pursue appeasement; the United States, isolationism.

Telescoping the Times
- Chapter Summary, pp. 121–123

Planning for Block Schedules

PE *Chapter Assessment,* pp. 816–817

Chapter Activities, p. 817

Formal Assessment
- Chapter Test, forms A and B, pp. 366–371

Test Generator

Alternative Assessment Book

TECHNOLOGY

 Warm-Up Transparency 31

 World Art and Cultures Transparencies
- AT67 *The Twittering Machine*
- AT68 *Electric Prisms*

 Electronic Library of Primary Sources
- "The Death of God"

INTERNET RESOURCES
www.mlworldhistory.com

 Warm-Up Transparency 31

 Electronic Library of Primary Sources
- "Famine in Russia"

INTERNET RESOURCES
www.mlworldhistory.com

 Warm-Up Transparency 31

 World Art and Cultures Transparencies
- AT69 *Pillars of Society*

 Critical Thinking Transparencies
- CT31 Economic Crisis: Between Two Fires

 Electronic Library of Primary Sources
- from Memos on the Aims of Germany and Japan

INTERNET RESOURCES
www.mlworldhistory.com

 Warm-Up Transparency 31

 Geography Transparencies
- GT31 Expansion of Nazi Germany, 1933–1939

 Critical Thinking Transparencies
- CT67 Chapter 31 Visual Summary

 Electronic Library of Primary Sources
- from Speech in the House of Commons

INTERNET RESOURCES
www.mlworldhistory.com

 Chapter Summaries on Audiocassette in English and Spanish

INTERNET RESOURCES
www.mlworldhistory.com

Block Scheduling (90 MINUTES)

Day 1
Section 1, pp. 795–800

 COOPERATIVE ACTIVITY
Pick a Person of the Decade, p. 797
(Teacher's Edition)

Section 2, pp. 801–806
 COOPERATIVE ACTIVITY
Creating a Political Cartoon, p. 805
(Teacher's Edition)

Section Assessments,
pp. 800, 806

Day 2
Section 3, pp. 807–810
Section 4, pp. 811–815

 COOPERATIVE ACTIVITY
Headlining the News, p. 812 (Teacher's Edition)

Section Assessments,
pp. 810, 815

Chapter Assessment,
pp. 816–817

Yearly Pacing *Chapter 31 Total:* 2 days *Yearly Total:* 85 days

Planning for Block Schedules

Customizing for Special Needs

Students Acquiring English

 Access for Students Acquiring English
- **Guided Reading** for Sections 1–4 (Spanish), pp. 311–314
- **Chapter Summary** (Spanish), pp. 308–310
- **Skillbuilder Practice** Identifying Problems (Spanish), p. 315
- **Geography Application** Spain During the 1930s (Spanish), p. 316

 Chapter Summaries on Audiocassette in English and Spanish

 INTERNET RESOURCES
www.mlworldhistory.com
The Diverse Classroom.

Less Proficient Readers

 In-Depth Resources: Unit 7
- **Guided Reading** for Sections 1–4, pp. 37–40
- **Skillbuilder Practice** Identifying Problems, p. 41
- **Geography Application** Spain During the 1930s, p. 42

 Telescoping the Times
- Chapter Summary, pp. 121–123

 Chapter Summaries on Audiocassette

Gifted and Talented Students

 In-Depth Resources: Unit 7

Primary Sources
- from An Interview with Charles Lindbergh, p. 44
- German Inflation, p. 45
- Kristallnacht, p. 46
- The Bombing of Guernica, p. 47

History Makers
- Sigmund Freud, p. 51
- Francisco Franco, p. 52

Connections to Literature READINGS FOR STUDENTS

 In-Depth Resources: Unit 7
Literature: from *This Side of Paradise*, p. 48; poems by Bertolt Brecht, p. 49

Enrichment Reading

- **Peck, Robert**
Arly
New York: Walker, 1989
The Great Depression doesn't much affect Arly's family because they are already poor field workers. The first schoolteacher in the community has a great impact on Arly's life.

- **Uhlman, Fred**
Reunion
New York: Penguin, 1978
A brief, improbable friendship is shared by two boys in the Germany of 1932. One boy is the son of a Jewish doctor; the other is the son of a Germany aristocrat.

 = Pupil's Edition   = Overhead Transparency   = Software   = Video

 = Copy Master   = CD-ROM   = Audiocassette   = Internet

Years of Crisis, 1919–1939

Accessing Prior Knowledge

- Ask students to read the captions for each of the three pictures and discuss what they already know about Charles Lindbergh and his airplane, the *Spirit of St. Louis,* about the Great Depression, and about the Nazi party.

Drawing Conclusions and Analyzing

- Have students contrast Dorothea Lange's photograph from the Great Depression with the Nazi rally in Nuremberg. Ask them what the mood of each photograph seems to be. Explain how these different feelings are conveyed.

- Ask students to discuss what the people in each picture might be doing. Have them generate a list of questions these pictures raise.

Geography Connection

Ask students to look at the map and inset on these two pages.

- What countries would play major roles in Europe in the period 1919–1939? *Great Britain, Germany, France, Spain, Italy, and the Soviet Union.*

- What island nation in Asia was an aggressor during this time? *Japan.*

CHAPTER
31 *Years of Crisis, 1919–1939*

PREVIEWING THEMES

Science and Technology
The decades of the 1920s and 1930s saw great changes in technology. Transportation was revolutionized by the spread of the automobile and the use of the airplane. Mass communication through radio, telephone, and motion pictures made the world seem smaller.

Economics
Despite signs of prosperity, the world economy of the 1920s suffered from serious flaws. It was too dependent on the economic well-being of the United States. The American stock market crashed in 1929, and the world was plunged into the worst economic depression in history.

Power and Authority
New, and yet untested, democracies rose in Europe from the ashes of World War I. However, the political and economic crises of the post-war period proved fatal for these governments. Many people turned to authoritarian leaders for answers. A new, dangerous form of nationalism—fascism—took hold in Italy and Germany. That fascism led the world to the brink of war in 1939.

THE WORLD BETWEEN THE WARS, 1919–1939

Hudson Bay

0   500 Miles
0   1,000 Kilometers

UNITED STATES OF AMERICA

ATLANTIC OCEAN

Charles Lindbergh flew solo across the Atlantic from New York to Paris in the *Spirit of St. Louis* in **1927**. The flight symbolized the technological advances in the period following World War I.

The Great Depression of the 1930s started in the United States and quickly spread worldwide. It caused unemployment and hardship for millions. Despair is evident in this photo of a jobless man waiting with others for free food in 1933. The photo, taken by photographer Dorothea Lange, is titled *White Angel Breadline, San Francisco.*

INTERNET CONNECTION

Visit us at **www.mlworldhistory.com** to learn more about the world between the wars.

792

GEOGRAPHY THEMES

Movement

Ask students to locate roughly where Lindbergh started his historic 33½-hour solo flight across the Atlantic *(New York)* and where he landed *(Paris, France).* Have them use the scale to find the distance from New York to Paris. Then discuss with them the particular challenges of flying over an ocean rather than over land. *Possible Responses: Could not refuel over the ocean; scarcity of visual landmarks. Also, there was no place to land in an emergency. If a plane did go down, it would be difficult if not impossible to find.*

Human/Environment Interaction

Tell students that in addition to examining the advances in aviation that changed the way humans think about spatial distances and the size of the world, they will also look at how developments in radio and motion pictures have altered the way people communi-cate with one another across the continents. Have students speculate about how the world was connected by transportation and communication during the 1920s and 1930s and how the development of television, computers, and satellites has changed the way we perceive the size of our planet and interact with peoples around the world.

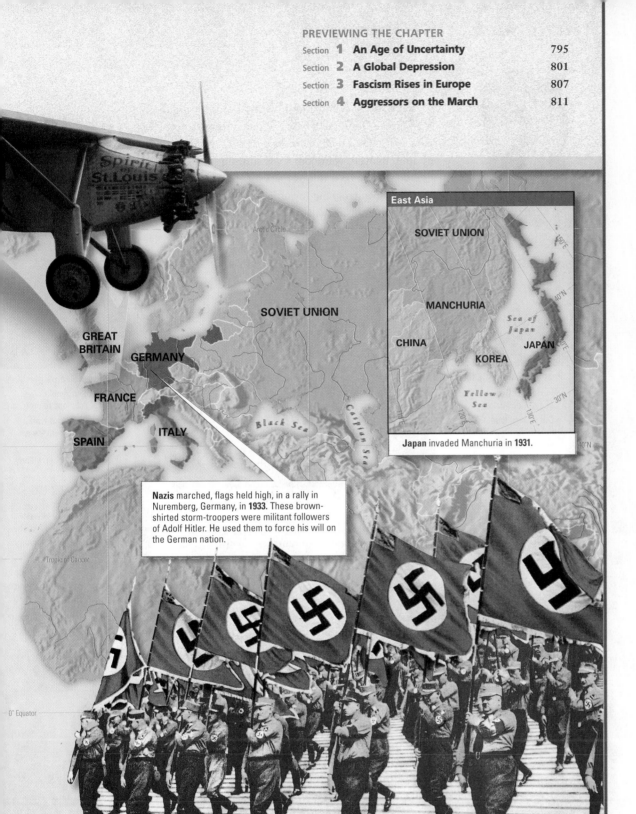

East Asia

SOVIET UNION

MANCHURIA

CHINA

KOREA

JAPAN

Sea of Japan

Yellow Sea

Japan invaded Manchuria in **1931**.

SOVIET UNION

GREAT BRITAIN

GERMANY

FRANCE

SPAIN

ITALY

Black Sea

Caspian Sea

Arctic Circle

Tropic of Cancer

0° Equator

Nazis marched, flags held high, in a rally in Nuremberg, Germany, in **1933**. These brown-shirted storm-troopers were militant followers of Adolf Hitler. He used them to force his will on the German nation.

ADDITIONAL RESOURCES

Books for the Teacher

• Garraty, John Arthur. *The Great Depression.* San Diego: Harcourt, 1986. Causes and consequences.

• Guérin, Daniel. *The Brown Plague: Travels in Late Weimar and Early Nazi Germany.* Durham, NC: Duke UP, 1994. First-person account of the rise of Hitler and the Nazis.

Books for the Student

• Banyard, Peter. *Rise of Dictators, 1919–1939.* New York: Watts, 1986. The rise of Hitler, Mussolini, and Franco.

• Burg, David F. *The Great Depression: An Eyewitness History.* New York: Facts on File, 1996.

Videos

• *Heil Hitler: Confessions of a Hitler Youth.* Ambrose Video, 1991. 800-526-4663. The Third Reich, as viewed through the eyes of a man who joined Hitler's cause at age ten.

• *The World at War: Japan.* Coronet/MTI, 1989. 800-321-3106. Japan's road to war.

• *The World in Conflict: 1929–1945.* Social Studies School Service, 1985. 800-421-4246. Global depression and the rise of fascism.

Software

• *The Causes of World War II.* CD-ROM. Society for Visual Education, 1994. 800-829-1900.

HISTORY THROUGH ART

The Photojournalism of Dorothea Lange

The photo titled *White Angel Breadline, San Francisco,* was taken during the Great Depression in 1933 by American photographer Dorothea Lange (1895–1965). Some have considered it to be one of the most important photographs of the 20th century. This stark, haunting photo of a group of men in a bread line epitomizes in a single image the conflict between dignity and desperation that many people felt during the Great Depression.

Lange's concern for people, her appreciation of the ordinary, and the striking empathy she showed for her subjects made her unique among photographers of her day. Of her work as a photographer, Lange said, "You put your camera around your neck along with putting on your shoes, and there it is, an appendage of the body that shares your life with you. The camera is an instrument that teaches people how to see without a camera."

Many of Lange's photographs of the Great Depression were taken for the Farm Security Administration under a federal government-sponsored photography project to document conditions in the United States during that period.

Interpreting the Photograph What does this photograph tell you about life during the Great Depression? Why do you think only men are waiting in the bread line for food?

This Interact with History feature motivates students by asking them to imagine themselves in a perilous time in history—in Germany in the early 1930s. As they imagine themselves confronted with choosing a leader for their country, students will analyze the issues, explore their options, and become decision makers.

Purpose

• to set the stage for studying the years of crisis, 1919–1939.

• to help students understand some of the critical issues confronting nations, leaders, and citizens.

• to help students make connections with the various people and events that they wiil study in this chapter.

Teaching Strategy

Thinking Critically After students have imagined themselves in the situation described on this page, have them answer the key question and give reasons for their decision.

EXAMINING *the* ISSUES

Following are suggestions for addressing each bulleted question.

❶ Have students explain how the first candidate appeals to German patriotism and bitterness over the Versailles Treaty.

❷ Ask students how they think the crowd will react to the second candidate's statement that there are no simple or quick solutions to Germany's problems and economic recovery will be slow.

❸ Ask students why the strong leadership promised by the first candidate might seem particularly attractive during the Great Depression.

Making Connections Ask students to discuss the issue of choosing leaders in a period of crisis. What qualities are required of an effective leader at such a time?

On a spring evening in the early 1930s during the Great Depression, you are one of thousands of Germans gathered at an outdoor stadium in Munich. You are unemployed; your country is suffering. Like everyone else, you have come to this mass meeting to hear two politicians campaigning for office. Huge speakers blare out patriotic music, while you and the rest of the crowd wait impatiently for the speeches to begin.

Before long you will have to cast your ballot.

First candidate's platform:

• Remember Germany's long and glorious past.

• Our present leadership is indecisive; we need a strong, effective leader.

• Rebuild the army to protect against enemies.

• Regain the lands taken unfairly from us.

• Make sacrifices to return to economic health.

• Put the welfare of the state above all, and our country will be a great power again.

Which candidate will you choose?

Second candidate's platform:

• There are no simple or quick solutions to problems.

• Put people back to work, but economic recovery will be slow.

• Provide for the poor, elderly, and sick.

• Avoid reckless military spending.

• Act responsibly to safeguard democracy.

• Be a good neighbor country; honor our debts and treaty commitments.

EXAMINING *the* ISSUES

❶ • What strategy does each candidate have for solving the nation's problems?

❷ • How does each candidate view the role of the citizen in meeting the challenges facing the nation?

❸ • Which candidate makes the strongest appeal to the listener's emotions?

As a class, discuss these questions. In your discussion, remember what you have read about the defeated nations' bitterness toward the Versailles Treaty following World War I. How might this influence which candidate voters favor?

As you read this chapter, see how dictators were voted into power as people lost faith in democratic government in the 1920s and 1930s. Examine the factors that influenced political decisions in this troubled time.

Follow Up

A question on the chapter assessment will send students back to issues highlighted on this page. Remind students that their opinions may change as they learn more about the solutions offered by democratic leaders and dictators of the period.

1 An Age of Uncertainty

TERMS & NAMES
- Albert Einstein
- theory of relativity
- Sigmund Freud
- existentialism
- Friedrich Nietzsche
- surrealism
- jazz
- Charles Lindbergh

MAIN IDEA

The postwar period was one of loss and uncertainty but also one of invention, creativity, and new ideas.

WHY IT MATTERS NOW

Postwar trends in physics, psychiatry, art, literature, communication, music, and transportation still affect our lives.

SETTING THE STAGE The horrors of World War I shattered the Enlightenment belief that progress would continue and reason would prevail. New ideas and patterns of life developed in the 1920s that changed the way people looked at the world.

Science Challenges Old Ideas

The ideas of two remarkable thinkers became widely known during this "age of uncertainty." They were Albert Einstein and Sigmund Freud. Both had an enormous impact on the 20th century. Einstein and Freud challenged some of the most deeply rooted ideas that people held about themselves and their world. They were part of a scientific revolution as important as that brought about centuries earlier by Copernicus and Galileo.

Impact of Einstein's Theory of Relativity A German-born physicist, **Albert Einstein,** offered startling new ideas on space, time, energy, and matter. He began by tackling a problem that baffled physicists. Scientists had found that light travels at exactly the same speed no matter what direction it moves in relation to earth. Earth moves through space, yet its movement did not affect the speed at which light seemed to travel. This finding seemed to break the laws of motion and gravity discovered by Isaac Newton.

In 1905, Einstein theorized that while the speed of light is constant, other things that seem constant, such as space and time, are not. Space and time can change when measured relative to an object moving near the speed of light—about 186,000 miles per second. Since relative motion is the key to Einstein's idea, it is called the **theory of relativity.** Einstein's ideas had implications not only for science but for how people viewed the world. Now uncertainty and relativity replaced Newton's comforting belief of a world operating according to absolute laws of motion and gravity.

Influence of Freudian Psychology The ideas of **Sigmund Freud,** an Austrian physician, were as revolutionary as Einstein's. Freud treated patients with psychological problems. From his experiences, he constructed a theory about the human mind. He believed that much of human behavior is irrational, or beyond reason. He called the irrational part of the mind the unconscious. In the unconscious, a number of drives existed, especially pleasure-seeking drives, of which the conscious mind was unaware. Freud's theories, first published in *The Interpretation of Dreams* (1900), met with opposition, especially his ideas about the unconscious. His ideas weakened faith in reason. All the same, by the 1920s, Freud's theories had developed widespread influence.

A. Possible Answers They changed the way people thought about the world; they weakened faith in absolute truths and reason.

THINK THROUGH HISTORY
A. Recognizing Effects Why were the ideas of Einstein and Freud revolutionary?

HISTORY MAKERS

Albert Einstein
1879–1955

Albert Einstein was the greatest scientific genius since Isaac Newton. He was thought to be a slow learner as a child because he did not talk at the same age as other children. Later in life, he recalled that at age two or three he wanted to speak in sentences. But he did not want to say sentences aloud until he was sure he had them right.

As a child, Einstein was quiet, serious, and solitary. He was also a daydreamer who did not impress his teachers. In this, he was unlike many geniuses who showed exceptional ability at an early age.

However, it was at this time that Einstein developed a desire to stay with a question until it was answered. He later called this his "flight from wonder."

Years of Crisis **795**

SECTION 1 RESOURCES

PRINT RESOURCES

 IN-DEPTH RESOURCES: UNIT 7
Guided Reading, p. 37
Primary Source: from An Interview with Lindbergh, p. 44
Literature: from *This Side of Paradise*, p. 48
History Makers: Sigmund Freud, p. 51

ACCESS FOR STUDENTS ACQUIRING ENGLISH
Guided Reading (Spanish), p. 311

FORMAL ASSESSMENT
Section Quiz, p. 362

ALTERNATIVE ASSESSMENT BOOK

TECHNOLOGY RESOURCES

WORLD ART AND CULTURES TRANSPARENCIES
AT67 *The Twittering Machine*
AT68 *Electric Prisms*

CD-ROM
Electronic Library of Primary Sources

INTERNET www.mlworldhistory.com

Section 1 Overview

OBJECTIVES

1. To explain how the scientific ideas of Einstein, Freud, and others challenged old beliefs.

2. To describe how the brutality of war led philosophers to question accepted ideas.

3. To summarize new styles in art, architecture, and music.

4. To show how new ideas and ways of life led to a new kind of individual freedom in the 1920s.

5. To explain how technological advances changed daily life.

CRITICAL THINKING
- Recognizing effects, pp. 795, 800
- Making inferences, p. 797
- Summarizing, p. 798
- Analyzing causes, p. 799
- Forming an opinion, p. 800

FOCUS
5-Minute Warm-Up

▶ *Making Inferences*
To help students understand the age of uncertainty, have them answer the following questions.

1. Read "Daily Life in 1927" on page 799. Who were newsmakers that year?

2. Which public figure was the world's newest hero?

WARM-UP TRANSPARENCY 31

OBJECTIVE 1 INSTRUCT

Science Challenges Old Ideas

▶ *Key Ideas*
- Albert Einstein and Sigmund Freud are two important thinkers of the 20th century.
- Einstein's theory of relativity overturns accepted laws of motion and gravity.
- Freud's theories about human behavior weaken faith in reason.

IN-DEPTH RESOURCES: UNIT 7
Guided Reading, p. 37

ACCESS FOR STUDENTS ACQUIRING ENGLISH
Guided Reading (Spanish), p. 311

Literature in an Age of Doubt

The brutality of World War I caused philosophers and writers to question accepted ideas about reason and progress. Disillusioned by the war, many people also feared the future and expressed doubts about traditional religious beliefs. Some artists and writers expressed their anxieties by creating unsettling visions of the present and the future.

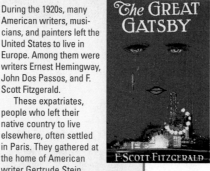

In 1922, T. S. Eliot, an American poet living in England, wrote that Western society had lost its spiritual values. He described the postwar world as a barren "waste land," drained of hope and faith. In 1924, the Irish poet William Butler Yeats conveyed a sense of dark times ahead in the poem "The Second Coming:" "Things fall apart; the centre cannot hold; / Mere anarchy is loosed upon the world . . ."

Thinkers React to Uncertainties In their search for meaning in an uncertain world, some thinkers turned to the philosophy known as **existentialism.** Leaders of this movement included the philosophers Jean Paul Sartre (SAHR·truh) of France and Karl Jaspers of Germany. Existentialists believed that there is no universal meaning to life. Each person gives his or her own meaning to life through choices made and actions taken. The existentialists would have their greatest influence after World War II.

The existentialists had been influenced by the German philosopher **Friedrich Nietzsche** (NEE·chuh). In the 1880s, Nietzsche wrote that Western society had put too much stress on such ideas as reason, democracy, and progress. This stifled actions based on emotion and instinct. As a result, individuality and creativity suffered. Nietzsche urged a return to the ancient heroic values of pride, assertiveness, and strength. He wrote that through willpower and courage, some humans could become supermen. They could rise above and control the common herd. His ideas attracted growing attention in the 20th century and had a great impact on politics in Italy and Germany in the 1920s and 1930s.

Writers Reflect Society's Concerns New attitudes also appeared in literature. The French poet Paul Valéry spoke for many writers of the 1920s when he described how he felt restless and uneasy:

> **A VOICE FROM THE PAST**
> We think of what has disappeared, and we are almost destroyed by what has been destroyed; we do not know what will be born, and we fear the future. . . . Doubt and disorder are in us and with us. There is no thinking man, however shrewd or learned he may be, who can hope to dominate this anxiety, to escape from this impression of darkness.
> **PAUL VALÉRY,** *Variété*

The horror of war made a deep impression on many writers. The Czech-born author Franz Kafka wrote eerie novels like *The Trial* (1925) and *The Castle* (1926). His books featured people crushed in threatening situations they could neither understand nor escape. He started writing before the war, but much of his work was published after his death in 1924. It struck a chord among readers in the uneasy postwar years.

Many novels showed the influence of Freud's theories on the unconscious. The Irish-born author James Joyce caused a stir with his stream-of-consciousness novel *Ulysses* (1922). This lengthy book focused on a single day in the lives of three Dubliners. Joyce broke with normal sentence structure and vocabulary, trying to mirror the workings of the human mind.

Vocabulary
stream of consciousness: a literary technique a writer uses to present a character's thoughts and feelings as they develop.

Rebellion in the Arts

Although many of the new directions in painting, architecture, and music began in the prewar period, they evolved after the war.

Painters Break Away from Tradition Artists rebelled against earlier realistic styles of painting. They wanted to depict the inner world of emotion and imagination rather than show realistic representations of objects. Expressionist painters like Paul Klee and Wassily Kandinsky used bold colors and distorted or exaggerated shapes and forms.

Inspired by traditional African art, Georges Braque of France and Pablo Picasso of Spain founded Cubism in 1907. Cubism transformed natural shapes into geometric forms. Objects were broken down into different parts with sharp angles and edges. Often several views were depicted at the same time.

The Dada movement (1916–1924) was as much a protest as an art movement. Its message was that established values had been made meaningless by the savagery of World War I. The term *Dada*, French for "hobbyhorse," was reportedly picked at random. Sounding like a nonsense word, it fit the spirit of the movement. Dadaist works were meant to be absurd, nonsensical, and meaningless.

Surrealism followed Dada. Inspired by Freud's ideas, **surrealism** was an art movement that sought to link the world of dreams with real life. The term *surreal* means "beyond or above reality."

The Persistence of Memory, a surrealist work by Spanish artist Salvador Dali, 1931, shows watches melting in a desert landscape. Insects feed on the clockwork.

Surrealists tried to call on the unconscious part of their minds. Their paintings frequently had a dream-like quality and depicted objects in unrealistic ways.

Architects Move in New Directions An architectural revolution occurred when architects rejected traditional building styles for completely new forms. Instead of highly ornamented structures, they constructed buildings in which the design reflected the building's function or use. The American architect Frank Lloyd Wright pioneered this new style, known as functionalism. He designed houses featuring clean, low lines and open interiors that blended with the surrounding landscape. Walter Gropius led the functionalist movement in Germany. After the war, he started an art and design school in Weimar called the Bauhaus.

Composers Try New Styles In both classical and popular music, composers moved away from traditional styles. In his ballet masterpiece, *The Rite of Spring,* the Russian composer Igor Stravinsky used irregular rhythms and dissonances, or harsh combinations of sound. The audience booed and walked out of its opening performance. The Austrian composer Arnold Schoenberg rejected traditional harmonies and musical scales. He created his own 12-tone scale in which the notes were unrelated except as mathematical patterns.

A new popular musical style called **jazz** came out of the United States. It was developed by musicians, mainly African Americans, in New Orleans, Memphis, and Chicago. It swept the United States and Europe. The lively, loose beat of jazz seemed to capture the new freedom of the age. Uninhibited, energetic jazz dances, such as the Charleston and the Black Bottom, at first shocked respectable society before becoming widely accepted.

Years of Crisis **797**

Margin notes (left column):

B. Possible Answers Artists broke away from realism, tried to draw on the unconscious part of their mind.

THINK THROUGH HISTORY
B. Making Inferences What was the major trend in art?

Vocabulary
functionalism: doctrine that the function of an object should determine its design and materials.

Background
The 1920s were called the Jazz Age because the music symbolized the freedom and spontaneity of the time.

Society Becomes More Open

► Key Ideas

- In the 1920s, young people are willing to break with the past and experiment with different values.
- Women take on new roles.

MORE ABOUT . . .
Women's Fashions in the 1920s

In the 1920s, women not only shortened their skirts, but shed their petticoats, long cotton stockings, and constricting corsets. The plumply rounded Gibson girl (shown on this page) was replaced by the flapper, with her slim, almost boyish figure. Flappers wore bright lipsticks and other cosmetics that earlier had been considered unacceptable for ladies.

American illustrator John Held, Jr., created the image of the flapper in cartoons he created for such magazines as *Harper's Bazaar, Vanity Fair, Life,* and *The New Yorker.* The flapper with her short hair and skirt, dangling cigarette, beads, and heavy makeup became a symbol for the rebelliousness of young people in the 1920s.

OBJECTIVE **5** INSTRUCT

Technology Changes Life

► Key Ideas

- After World War I ends, the war's technological advances are used to improve transportation and communication.
- The automobile affects where people live and work and increases leisure travel.
- International air travel increases.
- Radio and movies provide new outlets for entertainment.

Society Becomes More Open

Pre-World War I "Gibson girls"

World War I had disrupted traditional social patterns. New ideas and ways of life led to a new kind of individual freedom during the 1920s. Young people especially were willing to break with the past and experiment with values that often differed from those of their parents. Their pleasure-seeking defiance of accepted conventions was the first "youth rebellion" of the 20th century.

The independent spirit of the times showed clearly in the changes women were making in their lives. The war had allowed women to take on new roles. Their work in the war effort was decisive in helping them win the right to vote. After the war, women's suffrage became law in many countries, including the United States, Britain, Germany, Sweden, and Austria.

Women abandoned restrictive clothing and hairstyles. They wore shorter, looser garments and had their hair "bobbed," or cut short. They also wore makeup, drove cars, and drank and smoked in public. Although most women still followed traditional paths of marriage and family, a growing number spoke out for greater freedom in their lives. Wives should not be second-class members of the family, feminists argued, but equal partners with their husbands. Margaret Sanger and Emma Goldman risked arrest by speaking in favor of birth control. As women sought new careers, the numbers of women in medicine, education, journalism, and other professions increased.

Technology Changes Life

World War I quickened the pace of invention. During the war, scientists developed new drugs and medical treatments that helped millions of people in the postwar years. The war's technological advances were put to use to improve transportation and communication after the war.

The Automobile Alters Society The automobile benefited from a host of wartime innovations and improvements—electric starters, air-filled tires, and more powerful engines. Cars no longer looked like boxes on wheels. They were sleek and brightly polished, complete with headlights and chrome-plated bumpers. In prewar Britain, autos were owned exclusively by the rich. British factories produced 34,000 autos in 1913. After the war, prices dropped, and the middle class could afford cars. In 1923 the number of autos built in Britain had almost tripled. By 1937, the British were producing 511,000 autos a year.

From "Gibson girl" to "Flapper," the restrictive clothing styles of the pre-war period depicted in the early 20th-century illustration gave way to the comfortable, casual fashions shown in the 1920s photograph.

Increased auto use by the average family led to lifestyle changes. More people traveled for pleasure. In Europe and the United States, new businesses, from motor hotels to vacation campgrounds, opened to serve the mobile tourist. The auto also affected where people lived and worked. People moved to suburbs and commuted to work.

Airplanes Transform Travel The war also brought spectacular improvements in aircraft. By 1918, planes could fly hundreds of miles. In the postwar era, daring fliers carried the first airmail letters. Wartime aviators became stunt pilots, flying to country fairs to perform aerial acrobatics and take people for their first plane rides.

International air travel became an objective after the war. In 1919, two British pilots made the first successful flight across the Atlantic, from Newfoundland to Ireland. The next major crossing came in 1927, when an American pilot named **Charles Lindbergh** captured world attention with a 33-hour solo flight from New York to Paris. Most of the world's major passenger airlines were established during the

---

Background
"Gibson girl" referred to the idealized type of young woman drawn by illustrator Charles Dana Gibson in the pre-World War I period.

THINK THROUGH HISTORY
C. Summarizing
How did the changes of the post-war years affect women?
C. Answer Women won the right to vote, changed style of dress, sought new careers.

CONNECTIONS ACROSS TIME AND PLACE

The Automobile Help students investigate the many ways the automobile has transformed all aspects of social life. Make a diagram like the one to the right on the chalkboard. Have students work in small groups to complete the diagram, detailing the effects on work, personal life, and travel caused by the automobile. This might include listing businesses that were no longer important, like blacksmithing and harness making, and new businesses, such as auto repair and service stations. Students can also investigate and list the ways the automobile changed dating patterns, where people lived and worked, how they dressed, and how the physical landscape changed through road building.

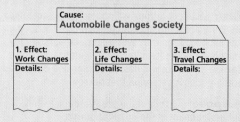

People in the News

Duke Ellington at Cotton Club

NEW YORK CITY, December 4: Featuring jazz pianist and composer Edward Kennedy "Duke" Ellington, Ellington's band opened today at Harlem's Cotton Club for what looks like a long run. Sources say Ellington's nickname Duke comes from the bandleader's expensive taste.

Babe Ruth Slugs Sixtieth Homer

NEW YORK CITY, September 30: Today George Herman "Babe" Ruth thrilled 10,000 fans in Yankee Stadium, swatting his sixtieth home run of the season. He broke his own 1921 record of 59. After hitting the pitch down the right field foul line into the stands, he said, "That's sixty home runs, count 'em. Sixty."

The fast-living, hard-hitting Babe delights the press. They employ many colorful nicknames to refer to him. Among them are the Bambino, the Sultan of Swat, the Mammoth of Maul, and the Colossus of Clout.

Parisians Greet Lindy

PARIS, May 21: Nearly 100,000 Parisians rushed onto the tarmac at Le Bourget Airport this evening. They ran to greet the world's newest hero—Charles Lindbergh. Lindbergh had just touched down safely at 10:24 P.M. in the *Spirit of St. Louis*, after completing the first solo flight across the Atlantic.

Looking pale and worn out, Lindbergh smiled and said, "Well, I made it." He had just flown 33 hours and 39 minutes nonstop from New York to Paris. His flight has great implications for the future of air travel.

Helen Wills Captures Wimbledon Title

WIMBLEDON, England, July 2: Helen Wills won the women's singles title at the All-England Tennis matches here today. She captured the famous tennis trophy for the United States for the first time in 20 years, beating Ella de Alvarez of Spain.

"Little Miss Poker Face," as she is called, is an intense competitor. She took the American Open title at age 17 in 1923 and repeated in 1924 and 1925. Wills also won gold medals in singles and doubles competition at the 1924 Olympics in Paris.

Connect to History

Analyzing Causes What factors contributed to the phenomenon of popular public heroes such as Charles Lindbergh, Babe Ruth, and Helen Wills?

Connect to Today

Researching Using the library or the Internet, compare a recent sporting or popular event to one from the 1920s in terms of audience and effect. Be sure to indicate how today's mass media create popular heroes and fans.

Daily *Life* in 1927

People in the News

The multi-talented Duke Ellington led a jazz band, composed music, and played piano. Born in Washington, D.C., Ellington began playing piano at age 7 and made his professional debut at 17. Ellington did have a long run at the Cotton Club. His band was the house band at this famous Harlem nightclub from 1927 to 1932. Considered one of jazz's greatest composers, Ellington's reputation grew through the many recordings of his compositions, like "Mood Indigo" and "Sophisticated Lady."

MORE ABOUT . . .
Charles Lindbergh

Nicknamed "Lucky Lindy" and "Lone Eagle" by the press, Lindbergh won international fame and became the object of hero worship following his solo, non-stop flight across the Atlantic. He had been a stunt flyer at county fairs and an airmail pilot before competing for the $25,000 prize offered for the first nonstop New York–Paris flight. Several pilots had been killed or injured seeking the prize, which had been offered since 1919.

IN-DEPTH RESOURCES: UNIT 7
Primary Source: from An Interview with Charles Lindbergh, p. 44

MORE ABOUT . . .
Babe Ruth

Babe Ruth was the first great home-run hitter in baseball. His batting skills, coupled with his colorful personality, made him a crowd favorite wherever he went. Babe Ruth started in major-league baseball as a pitcher with the Boston Red Sox and was later an outfielder for the New York Yankees. He hit 714 homers during his career, a record until Henry Aaron hit his 715th home run in 1974. Ruth was one of many larger-than-life celebrities in professional sports in the 1920s and 1930s. Others were Ty Cobb of the Detroit Tigers; Gertrude Ederle, the first woman to swim the English Channel; and heavyweight prizefighters Jack Dempsey and Gene Tunney.

Connect to History

Analyzing Causes
Possible Response: Students might suggest that several factors contributed to the enormous popularity of such public figures as Lindbergh, Ruth, and Wills. They might point out that people in an age of uncertainty were looking for heroes. Certainly the increasing popularity of radio and movies with their newsreels made people more aware than ever before of sporting events and the feats of such men and women as Lindbergh, Ruth, and Wills.

Connect to Today

Researching
Have students make a chart comparing similar events in the two eras.

	1920s	Today
Advance Publicity		
Type of Media Coverage		
Size of Audience		
Impact of event		

Daily *Life*

How Technology Revolutionized Life

The spread of technological innovations in the postwar period changed the way people lived. Autos removed dependence on public transportation. They made travel to work and travel for recreation more convenient and less time-consuming.

The telephone instantly connected family and friends, and buyers and sellers. Radio brought entertainment into the home. The whole family could share listening to sports, comedy, drama, music, and the news.

The drudgery of housework was lightened by labor-saving appliances, including refrigerators, vacuum cleaners, irons, toasters, and washing machines. Convenience foods, such as packaged cereals and quick-frozen vegetables, saved time in the kitchen. The United States was far more advanced than most nations in the use of these technological breakthroughs.

1920s. At first only the rich were able to afford air travel. Still, everyone enjoyed the exploits of the aviation pioneers, including Amelia Earhart. She was an American who, in 1932, became the first woman to fly solo across the Atlantic.

Radio Reaches Millions Guglielmo Marconi conducted his first successful experiments with radio in 1895. However, the real push for radio development came during World War I. The advantages of wireless communication in battle were so great that all countries gave radio research a high priority. Armies developed a wide range of radio equipment that would also have uses in peacetime.

In 1920, the world's first commercial radio station—KDKA in Pittsburgh, Pennsylvania—began broadcasting. Almost overnight, radio mania swept the United States. Soon every major city had stations broadcasting news, plays, and even live sporting events. In many European nations, unlike the United States, radio broadcasting was controlled by the government. In Great Britain, radio was a public monopoly run solely by the British Broadcasting Company, or BBC. Like Americans, however, Europeans eagerly listened to a variety of radio broadcasts. Soon most families owned a radio.

Movies Revolutionize Popular Entertainment In the 1920s, motion pictures were a major industry. Many countries, from Cuba to Japan, produced movies. In Europe, film was a serious art form. Directors like Sergei Eisenstein in Russia and Fritz Lang in Germany created films that explored psychological or political themes. However, in the Los Angeles suburb of Hollywood, where 90 percent of all films were made, movies were entertainment.

From Hollywood in the 1920s came the zany, slapstick comedies of Mack Sennett and his Keystone Kops, and dramas that starred Mary Pickford or Rudolph Valentino. But the king of the silent screen was the English-born Charlie Chaplin, a comic genius best known for his portrayal of the lonely little tramp bewildered by life. In the late 1920s, the addition of sound transformed movies. By the mid-1930s, nearly 90 million Americans escaped from the hardships of life by attending movies each week.

The advances in transportation and communication that followed the war had brought the world in closer touch. Countries had become more interdependent economically. Global prosperity came to depend on the economic well-being of all major nations, especially the United States.

Section ❶ Assessment

1. TERMS & NAMES
Identify
• Albert Einstein
• theory of relativity
• Sigmund Freud
• existentialism
• Friedrich Nietzsche
• surrealism
• jazz
• Charles Lindbergh

2. TAKING NOTES
Draw a chart like the one below. For each category shown, name two people you read about who contributed to that field.

FIELD	CONTRIBUTORS
philosophy	
literature	
art	
architecture	
music	

Write one or two sentences about their beliefs or contributions.

3. FORMING AN OPINION
In your opinion, whose ideas had a bigger impact on the world—Einstein's or Freud's? Give reasons to support your position.

THINK ABOUT
• the state of knowledge before their contributions
• the field in which they worked
• how life would be different without their contributions

4. THEME ACTIVITY
Science and Technology As a class, hold a media event. In small groups, choose a topic from the scientific and technological contributions of the 1920s. Collect pictures, audio tapes, biographies, or literature that represent the people or ideas you have chosen. Present your topic to the class and use your collection to help create a multimedia effect.

ANSWERS

1. TERMS & NAMES
Albert Einstein, p. 795
theory of relativity, p. 795
Sigmund Freud, p. 795
existentialism, p. 796
Friedrich Nietzsche, p. 796
surrealism, p. 797
jazz, p. 797
Charles Lindbergh, p. 798

2. TAKING NOTES
Possible Responses:
Philosophy—Sartre, Jaspers, Nietzsche. Literature—Kafka, Joyce. Art—Klee, Kandinsky, Braque, Picasso, Dali; Architecture—Wright, Gropius. Music—Stravinsky, Schoenberg, Ellington, African-American musicians.

3. FORMING AN OPINION
Possible Responses: Einstein—theory of relativity changed scientific thought, upset absolute laws of science; in contrast, Freud's field was new, unscientific. Freud—developed new theory of human mind; ushered in era of psychoanalysis; created new understanding of human

behavior; Freud's ideas had wide and more personal influence.

4. THEME ACTIVITY
Possible Responses: Students might present photo displays, taped musical selections, speeches, oral interpretations showing or discussing the people or ideas chosen.

TERMS & NAMES
- coalition government
- Weimar Republic
- Great Depression
- Franklin D. Roosevelt
- New Deal

MAIN IDEA

An economic depression in the United States spread throughout the world and lasted for a decade.

WHY IT MATTERS NOW

Many social and economic programs introduced worldwide to combat the Great Depression are still operating.

SETTING THE STAGE By the late 1920s, European nations were rebuilding war-torn economies. They were aided by loans from the more prosperous United States. In the United States, Americans seemed confident that the country would continue on the road to even greater economic prosperity. One sign of this was the booming stock market. Yet the American economy had serious weaknesses that were soon to bring about the most severe economic downturn the world had yet known.

Europe After the War

In both human suffering and economic terms, the cost of World War I was immense. The Great War left every major European country nearly bankrupt. Only the United States and Japan came out of the war in better financial shape than before. Neither had been a wartime battlefield. In fact, both had expanded their trade during the war. In addition, Europe's domination in world affairs had declined since the war. The long and brutal fight had drained the continent's resources.

New Democracies Are Unstable

War's end saw the sudden rise of new democracies. From 1914 to 1918, Europe's last absolute rulers had been overthrown. The dynasties of the Hohenzollerns in Germany, the Hapsburgs in Austria-Hungary, the Romanovs in Russia, and the Ottomans in Turkey all ended. The first of the new governments was formed in Russia in 1917. The Provisional Government, as it was called, hoped to establish constitutional and democratic rule. However, within months it had fallen to a Communist dictatorship. Even so, for the first time, most European nations had democratic governments.

Many citizens of the new democracies had little experience with representative government. For generations, kings and emperors had ruled Germany and the new nations formed from Austria-Hungary. Even in France and Italy, whose parliaments had existed before World War I, the large number of political parties made effective government difficult. Some countries had a dozen or more political groups. In these countries, it was almost impossible for one party to win enough support to govern effectively. When no single party won a majority, a **coalition government,** or temporary alliance of several parties, was needed to form a parliamentary majority. Because the parties disagreed on so many policies, coalitions seldom lasted very long. France,

Demonstrators flee gunfire in the streets of Petrograd in 1917 as the Russian Provisional Government tries to fight off Bolshevik (Communist) revolutionaries.

Years of Crisis **801**

THINK THROUGH HISTORY
A. Drawing Conclusions How did World War I change the balance of economic power in the world?
A. Possible Answers Europe's resources had been drained by World War I. Japan and the U.S. were economically strong.

SECTION 2 RESOURCES

PRINT RESOURCES

 IN-DEPTH RESOURCES: UNIT 7
Guided Reading, p. 38
Skillbuilder Practice: Identifying Problems, p. 41
Primary Source: German Inflation, p. 45

 ACCESS FOR STUDENTS ACQUIRING ENGLISH
Guided Reading (Spanish), p. 312
Skillbuilder Practice: (Spanish), p. 315

 FORMAL ASSESSMENT
Section Quiz, p. 363

ALTERNATIVE ASSESSMENT BOOK

TECHNOLOGY RESOURCES

 CD-ROM
Electronic Library of Primary Sources

INTERNET www.mlworldhistory.com

Section 2 Overview

OBJECTIVES

(1) To describe the impact of World War I on postwar Europe.

(2) To summarize the causes of the Great Depression.

(3) To explain how the United States and Europe reacted to the Depression.

SKILLBUILDER
- Interpreting graphs, pp. 803, 805

CRITICAL THINKING
- Drawing conclusions, p. 801
- Identifying problems, pp. 802, 803
- Synthesizing, p. 805
- Analyzing causes, p. 806
- Analyzing themes, p. 806

FOCUS
5-Minute Warm-Up

▶ *Summarizing*
Having students answer the following will help them understand the Great Depression.

1. Read "Daily Life" on page 804. What kind of aid did the unemployed need?

2. What groups provided relief to the unemployed?

WARM-UP TRANSPARENCY 31

OBJECTIVE ① INSTRUCT

Europe After the War

▶ *Key Ideas*
- The new European democracies formed after the war are weak.
- Frequent changes in government make it hard for democracies to develop strong leadership.
- Many Germans blame the democratic Weimar government for their country's problems.
- Dawes Plan helps Germany curb inflation and build its economy.

ELECTRONIC LIBRARY OF PRIMARY SOURCES
"Famine in Russia"

(continued on next page)

OBJECTIVE ① INSTRUCT

(continued from page 801)

• The Kellogg-Briand peace pact
  raises hopes for world peace.

📋 **IN-DEPTH RESOURCES: UNIT 7**
Guided Reading, p. 38

📋 **ACCESS FOR STUDENTS
ACQUIRING ENGLISH**
Guided Reading (Spanish), p. 312

MORE ABOUT . . .
The Weimar Republic

At the time they signed the Versailles Treaty, the men who became the leaders of the Weimar government recognized that the agreement would cause grave problems for Germany. German Prime Minister Philipp Scheidemann remarked, "What hand would not wither that binds itself and us in these fetters?" Yet the members of the Social Democratic and Catholic Center parties, who later became the leaders of the Weimar government, felt they had no choice but to sign the agreement. The German people never forgave them.

MORE ABOUT . . .
Germany's Money Problems

The German government's printing of large amounts of currency to keep it afloat after the war caused prices in Germany to rise more than 1 trillion percent from August 1922 to November 1923. Economists typically define severe inflation as an annual inflation rate of 10 percent or higher. In 1923, $1 in United States currency was worth over 4 trillion German marks.

📋 **IN-DEPTH RESOURCES: UNIT 7**
Primary Source: German Inflation, p. 45

"Money to burn"— this German woman uses millions of marks made worthless by inflation as heating fuel in the early 1920s.

for example, endured some 40 changes of government from 1919 to 1939.

Frequent changes in government made it hard for democratic countries to develop strong leadership and move toward long-term goals. In peaceful times, a country could get by with weak leadership. However, the weaknesses of a coalition government became a major problem in times of crisis. Voters in several countries were then willing to sacrifice democracy for strong, totalitarian leadership.

Weimar Republic Is Weak Germany's new democratic government was set up in 1919. Known as the **Weimar** (WY·MAHR) **Republic,** it was named after the city where the national assembly met. The Weimar Republic had serious weaknesses from the start. First, Germany lacked a strong democratic tradition. Furthermore, postwar Germany had several major political parties and many minor ones. Worst of all, millions of Germans blamed the Weimar government, not their wartime leaders, for the country's defeat and postwar humiliation. It was, after all, the Weimar government that had signed the Treaty of Versailles.

Inflation Causes Crisis in Germany Germany also faced enormous economic problems that began during the war. Unlike Britain and France, Germany did not greatly increase its wartime taxes. To pay the expenses of the war, the Germans simply printed money. After Germany's defeat, this paper money steadily lost its value. Burdened with heavy reparations payments to the Allies and with other economic problems, Germany printed even more money. The result was the value of the mark, as Germany's currency was called, fell sharply. Severe inflation set in. Germans needed more and more money to buy even the most basic goods. For example, in Berlin a loaf of bread cost less than a mark in 1918, more than 160 marks in 1922, and some 200 billion marks by late 1923. People took wheelbarrows full of money to buy food. The mark had become worthless.

Consequently, people with fixed incomes saw their life savings become worthless. The money people had saved to buy a house now barely covered the cost of a table. Many Germans also questioned the value of their new democratic government.

Attempts at Economic Stability Germany recovered from the 1923 inflation thanks largely to the work of an international committee. The committee was headed by Charles Dawes, an American banker. The Dawes Plan provided for a $200 million loan from American banks to stabilize German currency and strengthen its economy. The plan also set a more realistic schedule for Germany's reparations payments.

Put into effect in 1924, the Dawes Plan helped slow inflation. As the German economy began to recover, it attracted more loans and investments from the United States. By 1929, German factories were producing as much as they had before the war.

Efforts at a Lasting Peace As prosperity returned, Germany's foreign minister, Gustav Stresemann (STRAY·zuh·MAHN), and France's foreign minister, Aristide Briand (bree·AHND), tried to improve relations between their countries. In 1925, they met in Locarno, Switzerland, with officials from Belgium, Italy, and Britain. They signed a treaty promising that France and Germany would never again make war against each other. Germany also agreed to respect the existing borders of France and Belgium. It then was admitted to the League of Nations.

B. Possible Answers lack of democratic tradition, too many political parties, new government bore the blame for defeat.

THINK THROUGH HISTORY
B. Identifying Problems What political problems did the Weimar Republic face?

Background
Germany's reparations payments for damages caused during World War I totaled $33 billion.

802 Chapter 31

CONNECTIONS ACROSS THE CURRICULUM

Economics Crushed by huge war expenses and heavy payments to the Allies, Germany was in the midst of disastrous *hyperinflation* in the early 1920s. From 1918 to 1923, the value of the Germany currency, the *mark,* had fallen sharply and rapidly. By mid-1923, the printing presses at Germany's mints were turning out 400 quadrillion (400,000,000,000,000,000) marks a day!

Hyperinflation is rapid, very high inflation. Left unchecked, it can destroy a nation's economy, because money loses nearly all its value. Hyperinflation occurs when a government spends much more money than it receives in taxes and other revenues. To raise more money, the government simply prints more, further weakening the value of its currency. As money growth increases, inflation rises, driving prices up. The

government is forced to keep printing even more money to pay for its expenditures. A downward spiral begins as the process repeats itself. Have students trace the steps that led to hyperinflation in Germany and then research and report to the class on how the Dawes Plan helped stabilize the currency and break the cycle of rising prices.

In 1928, the hopes raised by the "spirit of Locarno" led to the Kellogg-Briand peace pact. Frank Kellogg, the U.S. Secretary of State, arranged this agreement with France's Briand. Almost every country in the world, including the Soviet Union, signed. They pledged "to renounce war as an instrument of national policy."

Unfortunately, the treaty had no means to enforce its provisions. The League of Nations, the obvious choice as enforcer, had no armed forces. The refusal of the United States to join the League also weakened it. Nonetheless, the peace agreements seemed a good start. In addition, Europeans were enjoying an economic boom based largely on massive American investment.

The Great Depression

In the late 1920s, the world economy was like a delicately balanced house of cards. The key card that held up the rest was American economic prosperity. If the United States economy weakened, the whole world's economic system might collapse. In 1929, it did.

A Flawed U.S. Economy Despite prosperity, three weaknesses in the U.S. economy caused serious problems. These were uneven distribution of wealth, overproduction by business and agriculture, and lessening demand for consumer goods.

By 1929, American factories were turning out nearly half of the world's industrial goods. The rising productivity led to enormous profits. However, this new wealth was not evenly distributed. The richest 5 percent of the population received 33 percent of all personal income in 1929. Yet 60 percent of all American families earned less than $2,000 a year. Thus, most families were too poor to buy the goods being produced. Unable to sell all their goods, store owners eventually cut back their orders from factories. Factories in turn reduced production and laid off workers. A downward economic spiral began. As more workers lost their jobs, families bought even fewer goods. In turn, factories made further cuts in production and laid off more workers.

During the 1920s, overproduction affected American farmers as well. Scientific farming methods and new farm machinery had dramatically increased crop yields. American farmers were producing more food. Meanwhile they faced new competition from farmers in Australia, Latin America, and Europe. As a result, a worldwide surplus of agricultural products drove prices and profits down.

Unable to sell their crops at a profit, many farmers could not pay off the bank loans that kept them in business. Their unpaid debts weakened banks and forced some to close. The danger signs of overproduction by factories and farms should have warned people against gambling on the stock market. Yet no one heeded the warning.

The Stock Market Crashes In 1929, Wall Street, in New York City, was the financial capital of the world. Banks and investment companies lined its sidewalks. At Wall Street's New York Stock Exchange, optimism about the booming U.S. economy showed in soaring prices for stocks. To get in on the boom, many middle-income people began buying stocks on margin. This meant that they paid a small percentage of a stock's price as a down payment and borrowed the rest from a stockbroker. The

THINK THROUGH HISTORY
C. Identifying Problems What major weaknesses had appeared in the American economy by 1929?
C. Possible Answers uneven distribution of wealth, overproduction by business, lessening demand for consumer goods, dropping farm profits from overproduction and foreign competition.

SPOTLIGHT ON
Stocks and the Market

Stocks are shares of ownership in a company. Businesses get money to operate by selling "shares" of stock to investors, or buyers. Companies pay interest on the invested money in the form of dividends to the shareholders. Dividends rise or fall depending on a company's profits.

Investors do not buy stocks directly from the company; stockbrokers transact the business of buying and selling.

Investors hope to make more money on stocks than if they put their money elsewhere, such as in a savings account with a fixed rate of interest. However, if the stock price goes down, investors lose money when they sell their stock at a lower price than when they bought it.

Speculators are investors who are not interested in long-term success. They want to make money quickly and hope for sudden increases in the value of a stock. They try to buy at a lower cost and sell when prices rise.

Stock Prices, 1925–1933

Graph-Source: *Historical Statistics of the United States*

SKILLBUILDER:
Interpreting Graphs
1. What year did stock prices fall lowest before beginning to rise again?
2. What was the average stock price in 1929? in 1932?

Years of Crisis **803**

Daily *Life*

Life in the Depression

During the Great Depression of 1929 to 1939, millions of people worldwide lost their jobs or their farms. They faced a future without hope.

At first the unemployed had to depend on the charity of others to survive. Here unemployed workers in Paris wait in line for free bread. Many jobless and their families begged for food, clothing, and shelter. Some lost their homes and had to live in shanties, or shacks. Others turned to thievery or abandoned their families.

Local governments and charities opened soup kitchens to provide free food. There were long lines of applicants for what work was available, and these jobs usually paid low wages.

Conditions improved when national governments established programs for relief. However, recovery came slowly. The Depression ended only when nations began gearing up for war.

system worked well as long as stock prices were rising. However, if they fell, investors had no money to pay off the loan.

In September 1929, some investors began to feel that stock prices were unnaturally high. They started selling their stocks, believing the rates would soon go down. By Thursday, October 24, the gradual lowering of stock prices had became an all-out slide downward. A panic resulted. Everyone wanted to sell stocks, and no one wanted to buy. Prices sank quickly. The wild shouting of 1,000 brokers and their assistants at the Stock Exchange became what one observer called a "weird roar." Prices plunged to a new low on Tuesday, October 29. A record 16 million stocks were sold. Then the market collapsed.

In the stock market crash, billions of dollars in "paper wealth" simply vanished. People could not pay the money they owed on margin purchases. Stocks they had bought at high prices were now worthless. Within months of the crash, unemployment rates began to rise as industrial production, prices, and wages declined. A long business slump, or depression, followed. The **Great Depression,** as it came to be called, touched every corner of the American economy. By 1932, factory production had been cut in half. Thousands of businesses failed, and banks closed. Around 9 million people lost the money in their savings accounts when banks had no money to pay them. Many farmers lost their lands when they could not make mortgage payments. By 1933 one-fourth of all American workers had no jobs.

A Global Depression The collapse of the American economy sent shock waves around the world. Worried American bankers demanded repayment of their overseas loans, and American investors withdrew their money from Europe. The American market for European goods dropped sharply as the U.S. Congress placed high tariffs on imported goods so that American dollars would stay in the United States and support American workers. The government was trying to force Americans to buy American goods. This policy backfired. Conditions worsened for the United States. Many countries who depended on exporting goods to the United States also suffered. Moreover, when the United States raised tariffs, it set off a chain reaction. Other nations imposed their own higher tariffs. World trade dropped

Background
The day of the stock market crash, Tuesday, October 29, 1929, is called "Black Tuesday."

Vocabulary
tariffs: taxes charged by a government on imported or exported goods.

Unemployment Rate, 1928–1938

Percent of Work Force (y-axis: 0, 5, 10, 15, 20, 25, 30)

- Hitler comes to power
- Roosevelt begins New Deal
- Stock market crashes

(x-axis: 1928, 1930, 1932, 1934, 1936, 1938)

■ Great Britain ■ Germany ■ United States

Sources: *European Historical Statistics: 1750–1970;*
Historical Statistics of the United States: Colonial Times to 1970.

SKILLBUILDER: Interpreting Graphs

1. *What nation had the highest rate of unemployment? How high did it reach?*
2. *When did unemployment begin to decrease in the United States? Germany? Great Britain?*

THINK THROUGH HISTORY
D. Synthesizing
What problems did the collapse of the American economy cause in other countries?
D. Possible Answers Their economies slumped, trade dropped, unemployment soared, and a financial panic started.

by 65 percent. This contributed further to the economic downturn. Unemployment rates soared.

Because of war debts and dependence on American loans and investments, Germany and Austria were particularly hard hit. In 1931, Austria's largest bank failed. This started a financial panic in central European countries and sent their economies plunging.

In Asia, the Japanese economy also slumped. Japanese farmers suffered greatly during the Depression. In the rice-growing areas of the northeast, crop failures in 1931 led to famine. Starving families ate tree bark and the roots of wild plants. City workers suffered, too, as the value of exports fell by half between 1929 and 1931. As many as 3 million workers lost their jobs, forcing many to go back to their rural villages.

The economic crisis fell heavily in Latin America as well. Many of its nations were tied to the global economy by trade in such cash crops or raw materials as sugar, beef, copper, and tin. During the 1920s, world prices and market demand for these products were already dropping. As European and U.S. demand for Latin American products dried up in the 1930s, prices for these goods collapsed. At the same time, the cost of imported goods rose, pushed up by high tariffs. Latin American nations that had borrowed heavily from other nations could not repay their debts. The worldwide crisis spread rapidly.

The World Responds to the Crisis

The Depression confronted democracies with a serious challenge to their economic and political systems. Each country met the crisis in its own way.

Britain Takes Steps to Improve Its Economy Because its economy depended on foreign trade, the Depression hit Britain severely. To meet the emergency, British voters elected a multi-party coalition known as the National Government. This government's policies were designed to rescue the nation from economic calamity. It passed high protective tariffs, increased taxes, and regulated the currency. It also lowered interest rates to encourage industrial growth. These measures brought about a slow but steady recovery. By 1937, unemployment had been cut in half, and production had risen above 1929 levels. Britain avoided political extremes and preserved democracy.

France Responds to Economic Crisis Unlike Britain, France had a more self-sufficient economy. In 1930, it was still heavily agricultural and less dependent on foreign trade. Thus, France was somewhat cushioned against the Depression. Nevertheless, by 1935, one million French workers were unemployed.

The economic crisis contributed to political instability. In 1933, five coalition governments formed and fell. Many political leaders were frightened by the growth of anti-democratic forces both in France and in other parts of Europe. So in 1936, moderates, Socialists, and Communists formed a coalition. The Popular Front, as it was called, passed a series of reforms to help the workers. These reforms included pay increases, holidays with pay, and a 40-hour work week. Unfortunately, price increases quickly offset wage gains. Unemployment remained high. Yet France also preserved democratic government.

Background
Scandinavia, in northern Europe, includes Sweden, Norway, and Denmark. Finland and Iceland are often also included in the region.

Socialist Governments Find Solutions The Socialist governments in the Scandinavian countries of Denmark, Sweden, and Norway also met the challenge of economic crisis successfully. They built their recovery programs on an existing

Years of Crisis **805**

History from Visuals

Unemployment, 1928–1938
Interpreting the Graph Have students read the graph key to identify which color line on the graph indicates each nation. Check comprehension by having students indicate the year in which the stock market crashed *1929,* Roosevelt began the New Deal *1933,* and Hitler came to power *1933.*

Extension Activity Ask students which of the nations on the graph was most effective in responding to the depression, judging solely by the unemployment data shown. *Germany showed the sharpest drop in joblessness.*

SKILLBUILDER Answers
1. Germany—30%
2. United States—after 1933; Germany—after 1932; Great Britain—after 1932

OBJECTIVE 3 INSTRUCT

The World Responds to the Crisis

▶ *Key Ideas*
- The Great Depression challenges democratic political systems in Europe and the United States.
- Britain forms a coalition National Government that preserves democracy.
- In France, the Depression contributes to political instability, but democracy is preserved.
- In Scandinavia, Socialist governments build successful recovery programs based on cooperative community action.
- Franklin Roosevelt's New Deal reform program starts an economic recovery in the U.S.

TEACHING OPTION | BLOCK SCHEDULING

COOPERATIVE ACTIVITY: Creating a Political Cartoon

CLASS TIME
30 MINUTES

Task: Student groups will research the spread of the Great Depression from the United States to other parts of the world and the responses to it. Then they will create political cartoons that comment on the Depression, responses to it, or its spread.

Purpose: To help students understand the impact of the Great Depression worldwide.

Activity: Have groups of three or four students research the impact of the Great Depression on the

United States or on Western European democracies. Within groups, students can brainstorm to create a political cartoon showing either the impact of this event or a specific government's response to it. They might, for example, show how raising tariff barriers hurt world trade and worsened the Depression.

 Building a Portfolio: Students should add their cartoons to their portfolios and attach notes describing their contributions to the cartoons.

ALTERNATIVE ASSESSMENT BOOK
Standards for Evaluating a Cooperative Activity

Standards for Evaluation
Political cartoons should . . .

- express one idea or opinion
- include an appropriate caption
- show clearly an effect or response

Teacher's Edition 805

Unlike Herbert Hoover who had preceded Roosevelt as president, Roosevelt believed that the federal government's role was to revive the economy. His New Deal program began with a package of public works projects to put Americans back to work. By the late 1930s, the government had spent over $10 billion on the construction of 122,000 public buildings, 664,000 miles of roads, 77,000 bridges, and 285 airports.

Although the New Deal improved economic conditions, full recovery did not occur until 1942 after the United States entered World War II. At that time, production of war materials led to almost full employment for Americans.

ASSESS & RETEACH

Section 2 Assessment
Have each student answer the questions and then compare answers with another student. Ask the student pairs to find passages in the text to support their answers.

Section Quiz

FORMAL ASSESSMENT
Section Quiz, p. 363

Reteaching Activity
CLASS TIME: 15 MINUTES

Have students create a concept web to explore what they know about the impact of the Depression on Europe, Latin America, and the United States.

CRITICAL THINKING TRANSPARENCIES
CT78 Concept Web

CLOSE ACTIVITY

CLASS TIME: 20 MINUTES

Analyzing Causes
Have students work in small groups to design their own cause-and-effect flow charts showing the causes and effects of the global depression. Remind students that the effects of the depression had multiple causes.

---

tradition of cooperative community action. In Sweden the government sponsored massive public works projects that kept people employed and producing. All the Scandinavian countries raised pensions for the elderly and increased unemployment insurance, subsidies for housing, and other welfare benefits. To pay for these benefits, the governments taxed all citizens. Under this program, both private and cooperative businesses prospered. Democracy remained intact.

Recovery in the United States In 1932, in the first presidential election after the Depression had begun, U.S. voters elected **Franklin D. Roosevelt.** His confident manner appealed to millions of Americans who felt bewildered by the Depression. On March 4, 1933, the new president sought to restore Americans' faith in their nation.

Governments responded to widespread unemployment by creating jobs. Here is a group of young men employed by the U.S. Civilian Conservation Corps.

A VOICE FROM THE PAST
This great Nation will endure as it has endured, will revive and will prosper. . . . let me assert my firm belief that the only thing we have to fear is fear itself—nameless, unreasoning, unjustified terror which paralyzes needed efforts to convert retreat into advance.
FRANKLIN ROOSEVELT, First Inaugural Address

Roosevelt immediately began a program of reform that he called the **New Deal.** Large public works projects helped to provide jobs for the unemployed. New government agencies gave financial help to businesses and farms. Large amounts of public money were spent on welfare and relief programs. Roosevelt and his advisers believed that government spending would create jobs and start a recovery. Regulations were imposed to reform the stock market and the banking system. Despite these efforts, recovery was slow.

The New Deal did eventually reform the American economic system. Roosevelt's leadership preserved the country's faith in its democratic political system. It also established him as a leader of democracy in a world threatened by ruthless dictators, as you will read about in Section 3.

Section 2 Assessment

1. TERMS & NAMES
- coalition government
- Weimar Republic
- Great Depression
- Franklin D. Roosevelt
- New Deal

2. TAKING NOTES
Using a web diagram like the one below, show the effects of the Great Depression in the United States.

The Great Depression

3. ANALYZING CAUSES
The collapse of the American economy had a devastating effect on the world. List one cause for each of the following effects: American market for European goods dropped; unemployment rates soared; European banks and businesses closed.

THINK ABOUT
- economic conditions in the United States
- the interdependence of the economies of the world

4. ANALYZING THEMES
Economics What actions did the United States, Britain, France, and the Scandinavian countries take to try to recover from the Great Depression? Give specific examples for each country.

THINK ABOUT
- Roosevelt and the New Deal
- coalition governments in Britain and France
- traditional community cooperative action in Scandinavia

ANSWERS

1. TERMS & NAMES
coalition government, p. 801
Weimar Republic, p. 802
Great Depression, p. 804
Franklin D. Roosevelt, p. 806
New Deal, p. 806

2. TAKING NOTES
Possible Responses:
Businesses failed, banks closed, savings were lost, farms were foreclosed, unemployment rose.

3. ANALYZING CAUSES
Possible Responses: High U.S. tariffs; drop in world trade; demand for repayment of American loans and withdrawal of American investment money.

4. ANALYZING THEMES
Possible Responses: United States—New Deal supported public works, financial aid to businesses and farms, money for welfare and relief programs; regulated stock market and banks.

Britain—National Government passed tariffs; increased taxes; regulated currency; decreased interest rates. France—Popular Front enacted worker reforms. Scandinavia—public works projects; raised pensions, unemployment insurance, housing subsidies, welfare benefits.

TERMS & NAMES
- fascism
- Benito Mussolini
- Adolf Hitler
- Nazism
- *Mein Kampf*
- *lebensraum*

Fascism Rises in Europe

MAIN IDEA

In response to political turmoil and economic crises, Italy and Germany turned to totalitarian dictators.

WHY IT MATTERS NOW

These dictators changed the course of history, and the world is still recovering from their abuse of power.

SETTING THE STAGE Many democracies, including the United States, Britain, and France, remained strong despite the economic crisis caused by the Great Depression. However, millions of people lost faith in democratic government. In response, they turned to an extreme system of government called fascism.

Fascist Beliefs and Policies

Background

The term *fascism* was intended to recall memories of ancient Rome. In Latin, *fasces* is the word for a bundle of wooden rods tied around an ax handle—a symbol of authority for Roman officials.

This new, militant political movement called **fascism** (FASH·IHZ·uhm) emphasized loyalty to the state and obedience to its leader. Fascists promised to revive the economy, punish those responsible for hard times, and restore national pride. Their message attracted many people who felt frustrated and angered by the peace treaties that followed World War I and by the Great Depression.

Unlike communism, fascism had no clearly defined theory or program. Nevertheless, most Fascists shared several ideas. They preached an extreme form of nationalism, or loyalty to one's country. Fascists believed that nations must struggle—peaceful states were doomed to be conquered. They pledged loyalty to an authoritarian leader who guided the state. In each nation, Fascists wore uniforms of a certain color, used special salutes, and held mass rallies.

In some ways, fascism was similar to communism. Both systems were ruled by dictators who allowed only their political party (one-party rule). Both denied individual rights. In both, the state was supreme. Neither practiced any kind of democracy. However, unlike Communists, Fascists did not seek a classless society. Rather, they believed that each class had its place and function. Communism claimed to be a dictatorship of the working class. In most cases, fascist parties were made up of aristocrats and industrialists, war veterans, and the lower middle class. Also, Fascists were nationalists, and Communists were internationalists, hoping to unite workers worldwide.

A. Possible Answers Italians felt betrayed by the Paris Peace Conference, faced rising inflation and unemployment and social unrest.

THINK THROUGH HISTORY

A. Analyzing Causes What factors led to the rise of fascism in Italy?

Mussolini Comes to Power in Italy

Fascism's rise in Italy was fueled by bitter disappointment over the failure to win large territorial gains at the 1919 Paris Peace Conference. Rising inflation and unemployment also contributed to widespread social unrest. Italy's upper and middle classes feared a Communist revolution, as in Russia. To growing numbers of Italians, their democratic government seemed helpless to deal with the country's problems. They wanted a leader who would take action.

The Rise of Mussolini A newspaper editor and politician named **Benito Mussolini** boldly promised to rescue Italy by reviving its

OBJECTIVE 2 INSTRUCT

Mussolini Comes to Power in Italy

(See page 807.)

▶ **Key Ideas**

• In Italy, fascism gains followers because of disappointment over the 1919 Paris Peace Conference, inflation, and unemployment.

• Benito Mussolini gains supporters because he is seen as a strong leader.

• In October 1922, after Fascists march on Rome, Mussolini takes charge of Italy's government.

HISTORY MAKERS

Benito Mussolini

(See page 807.)

Have students research Mussolini's rise to power and write a paper describing the way he used symbols of ancient Rome and other propaganda techniques to persuade Italians to support fascism.

OBJECTIVE 3 INSTRUCT

Hitler Takes Control in Germany

▶ **Key Ideas**

• The German brand of fascism is called Nazism.

• Adolf Hitler's skills as an organizer and speaker help him become head of the Nazi party.

• Hitler's book, *Mein Kampf,* sets forth his anti-Semitic beliefs and his plans for conquest.

• Germany's economic problems and fear of the Communist party help Hitler take power legally.

• Hitler uses his power to turn Germany into a totalitarian state.

IN-DEPTH RESOURCES: UNIT 7
Primary Source: Kristallnacht, p. 46
Literature: Poems by Bertolt Brecht, p. 49

economy and rebuilding its armed forces. He vowed to give Italy strong leadership. Mussolini had founded the Fascist Party in 1919. At first, he failed to win widespread support. As economic conditions worsened, however, his popularity rapidly increased. Finally, Mussolini publicly criticized Italy's government. Groups of Fascists wearing black shirts attacked Communists and Socialists on the streets. This campaign of terror weakened his opponents. Because Mussolini played on the fear of a workers' revolt, he began to win support from the middle classes, the aristocracy, and industrial leaders.

In October 1922, about 30,000 Fascists marched on Rome. They demanded that King Victor Emmanuel III put Mussolini in charge of the government. The king decided that Mussolini was the best hope for his dynasty to survive, so he let Mussolini form a government. Thus, after widespread violence and a threat of armed uprising, Mussolini took power "legally." At the time, a foreign diplomat described him as "an actor, a dangerous rascal, and possibly slightly off his head."

Il Duce's Leadership Mussolini was now Il Duce (ihl DOO·chay), or the leader. He abolished democracy and outlawed all political parties except the Fascists. Secret police jailed his opponents. Government censors forced radio stations and publications to broadcast or publish only Fascist doctrines. Mussolini outlawed strikes. He sought to control the economy by allying the Fascists with the industrialists and large landowners. Under his leadership, Italy became the model for Fascists in other countries. However, Mussolini never had the total control achieved by Joseph Stalin in the Soviet Union or Adolf Hitler in Germany.

Hitler Takes Control in Germany

When Mussolini became dictator of Italy in the mid-1920s, **Adolf Hitler** was a little-known political leader whose early life had been marked by disappointment. Born in a small town in Austria in 1889, he dropped out of high school and failed as an artist. When World War I broke out, Hitler found a new beginning. He would fight to defend Germany and crush its opponents. He volunteered for the German army and was twice awarded the Iron Cross, a medal for bravery.

The Rise of the Nazis At the end of the war, Hitler settled in Munich. In early 1920, he joined a tiny right-wing political group. This group shared his belief that Germany had to overturn the Treaty of Versailles and combat communism. The group later named itself the National Socialist German Workers' Party, called Nazi for short. Its policies, supported by people in the middle and lower middle classes, formed the German brand of fascism known as **Nazism.** The party adopted the swastika, or hooked cross, as its symbol. The Nazis also set up a private militia called the storm troopers or Brownshirts.

Within a short time, Hitler's success as an organizer and speaker led him to be chosen *der Führer* (duhr FYUR·uhr), or the leader, of the Nazi

HISTORY MAKERS

Adolf Hitler
1889–1945

Like Mussolini, Hitler could manipulate huge audiences with his fiery oratory. Making speeches was crucial to Hitler. He believed: "All great world-shaking events have been brought about . . . by the spoken word!"

Because he appeared awkward and unimposing, Hitler rehearsed his speeches. Usually he began a speech in a normal voice. Suddenly, he spoke louder as his anger grew. His voice rose to a screech, and his hands flailed the air. Then he would stop, smooth his hair, and look quite calm.

In the 1930s, a foreign diplomat described Hitler: ". . . he was all violence . . . with a fierce energy ready at no provocation to pull down the universe. . . . [His] face was the face of a lunatic."

808 Chapter 31

The swastika, which means "well-being" in Sanskrit, was an ancient good-luck symbol. Forms of it had been used by Hindus, Buddhists, early Christians, and Native Americans.

"Heil Hitler!" Hitler Youth members salute their Führer at a rally in the 1930s. Hitler skillfully used mass rallies to generate enthusiasm.

TEACHING OPTIONS

CUSTOMIZING FOR SPECIAL NEEDS

Gifted and Talented Students
Drawing Conclusions Radically different viewpoints of Nazism were expressed in two highly successful motion pictures of the era. The propaganda film *The Triumph of the Will* (1934) was a documentary made about a Nazi party rally in Nuremberg by a young German female director, Leni Riefenstahl. The comedy *The Great Dictator* (1940) was a satire of Adolf Hitler directed in the United States by actor Charlie Chaplin. Students should view the films and then write a comparison of the political viewpoints in each.

MULTIPLE LEARNING STYLES

Linguistic Learners Have students read the following Hitler quotations. ". . .I, as leader and representative of the German nation, assure the world that now that the Saar issue has been solved, I will make no other territorial request. . . ." "All depends on me . . . because of my political talents. Probably no one will ever again have the confidence of the whole German people as I have . . . [or] more authority. . . ." ". . . [I] would not tolerate a small second-rate country treating the mighty thousand-year-old Reich as something inferior . . .[I] would face any war, even a world war, for this." Then have each student write a paragraph describing what the quotes tell us about Hitler and where he was leading Germany.

Nazi party. These skills also helped make the Nazis a growing political force. Inspired by Mussolini's march on Rome, Hitler and the Nazis plotted to seize power in Munich in 1923. The attempt failed, and Hitler was arrested. He was tried for treason, but sympathetic judges sentenced him to only five years in prison. He served less than nine months.

While in jail, Hitler wrote **Mein Kampf** (*My Struggle*). This book set forth his beliefs and his goals for Germany. It became the blueprint, or plan of action, for the Nazis. Hitler asserted that the Germans, especially those who were blond and blue-eyed—whom he incorrectly called "Aryans"—were a "master race." He declared that non-Aryan "races"—such as Jews, Slavs, and Gypsies—were inferior or subhuman. He called the Versailles Treaty an outrage and vowed to regain the lands taken from Germany. Hitler also declared that Germany was overcrowded and needed more **lebensraum,** or living space. He promised to get that space by conquering eastern Europe and Russia.

After leaving prison in 1924, Hitler revived the Nazi party. Most Germans ignored him and his angry message until the Depression ended the nation's brief postwar recovery. When American loans stopped, the German economy collapsed. Factories ground to a halt and banks closed. Nearly six million people, about 30 percent of Germany's work force, were unemployed in 1932. Civil unrest broke out. Frightened and confused, Germans now turned to Hitler, hoping for security and firm leadership.

Hitler Becomes Chancellor The Nazis had become the largest political party by 1932. Conservative leaders mistakenly believed they could control Hitler and use him for their purposes. In January 1933, they advised President Paul von Hindenburg to name Hitler chancellor. Only Hitler, they said, could stand up to the strong Communist party in Germany. Thus Hitler came to power legally. Soon after, General Erich Ludendorff, a former Hitler ally, wrote to Hindenburg:

> **A VOICE FROM THE PAST**
> By naming Hitler as *Reichschancellor*, you have delivered up our holy Fatherland to one of the greatest [rabblerousers] of all time. I solemnly [predict] that this accursed man will plunge our Reich into the abyss and bring our nation into inconceivable misery.
> ERICH LUDENDORFF, from a letter to President Hindenburg, February 1, 1933

Once in office, Hitler acted quickly to strengthen his position. He called for new elections, hoping to win a parliamentary majority. Six days before the election, a fire destroyed the Reichstag building where parliament met. The Nazis blamed the Communists. By stirring up fear of the Communists, the Nazis and their allies won a slim majority.

With majority control, Hitler demanded dictatorial, or absolute, power for four years. Only one deputy dared to speak against the resulting Enabling Act. Hitler used his new power to turn Germany into a totalitarian state. He banned all other political parties and had opponents arrested. Meanwhile, an elite, black-uniformed unit called the SS (*Schutzstaffel*, or protection squad) was created. It was loyal only to Hitler. In 1934, the SS arrested and murdered hundreds of Hitler's enemies. This brutal action and the terror applied by the Gestapo, the Nazi secret police, shocked most Germans into total obedience.

The Nazis quickly took command of the economy. New laws banned strikes, dissolved independent labor unions, and gave the government authority over business and labor. Hitler put millions of Germans to work. They constructed factories, built highways, manufactured weapons, and served in the military. As a result, unemployment dropped from about 6 to 1.5 million in 1936.

The Führer Is Supreme Hitler wanted more than just economic and political power—he wanted control over every aspect of German life. To shape public opinion and to win

Years of Crisis **809**

THINK THROUGH HISTORY
B. Summarizing
What were the key ideas and goals that Hitler presented in *Mein Kampf*?
B. Answer Germans were a master race, other "races" were inferior, Versailles Treaty was an outrage, Germany needed more living space.

Vocabulary
chancellor: the prime minister in certain countries

C. Possible Answers Because he restored pride in Germany, cut unemployment, repudiated the hated Versailles Treaty, and promised to regain lost German lands

THINK THROUGH HISTORY
C. Making Inferences Why did Germans at first support Hitler?

Global Impact

Fascism to Argentina
Juan Perón served as Argentina's president from 1946 to 1955 and again in 1973 and 1974. The two years he spent in Europe before World War II greatly influenced his strong-man rule.

A career army officer, Perón went to Italy in 1939 for military training. He then served at the Argentine embassy in Rome. A visit to Berlin gave Perón a chance to see Nazi Germany. The ability of Hitler and Mussolini to manipulate their citizens impressed Perón.

When Perón himself gained power, he patterned his military dictatorship on that of the European Fascists. Like them, he restrained his opponents through press censorship and suppression of civil rights. But he never achieved the same total control as his fascist role models.

MORE ABOUT . . .
Mein Kampf
In *Mein Kampf*, or "My Struggle," Hitler blames the Jews and Communists for Germany's problems and urges Germans to seek revenge for the country's defeat in World War I. He also discusses the importance of racial purity and lays out his plan for creation of a racially pure Germany that will dominate the world. The book was highly successful. Around 5.2 million copies had been sold by 1939, and Nazis considered it an excellent wedding present for newly married couples.

MORE ABOUT. . .
Early German Support for Hitler
During the 1920s, Hitler's Nazi party attracted few supporters outside of fanatical anti-Semites, ultra-nationalists, and disgruntled war veterans. However, the 1929 Depression made the ranks of the Nazi party swell.

📖 **WORLD ART AND CULTURES TRANSPARENCIES**
AT69 *Pillars of Society*

Global Impact
Fascism to Argentina
Interested students might research the life of Perón and write a paper comparing and contrasting his leadership style with that of the European Fascist dictators that he admired.

MORE ABOUT . . .
The SS
The *Schutzstaffel*, or SS, was originally formed in 1923 as the personal bodyguard for Hitler. In 1929, Heinrich Himmler became the national leader of the SS. Under Himmler, the SS men became the elite of the Nazi empire. They wore black shirts with the death's head insignia. There were two requirements for membership. The first was unconditional loyalty to Hitler, and the other was "racial purity."

TEACHING OPTIONS

CUSTOMIZING FOR SPECIAL NEEDS

Less Proficient Readers
Sequencing Divide students into small groups. Have each group pick a series of no more than five events from Section 3 and list them in correct sequence. They might include any of these events: Hitler born in Austria, Hitler serves in World War I, Nazi party formed, Hitler becomes Nazi leader, Hitler writes *Mein Kampf,* Hitler

becomes chancellor, Nazis win a majority in the Reichstag, Hitler orders *Kristallnacht*. Once groups have their lists, have students rewrite them in scrambled order and exchange them with other groups. Have each group put the list it receives in chronological order with dates. As a follow-up activity, students can make a time line of the events they have put in sequence.

CONNECTIONS ACROSS THE CURRICULUM

Writing Write the following quote on the chalkboard: "Hungry men are angry men." Have students write a short essay explaining how this statement applies to fascism's rise in Italy and Germany in the 1920s and 1930s.

As an alternative writing activity, students can answer a "What if" question. Have them speculate whether dictatorships

would have emerged in Italy and Germany if a worldwide depression had not occurred. Have them write a scenario for the decade of the 1930s that describes what might have happened to Hitler or Mussolini if prosperity had returned to either country in the postwar period.

Teacher's Edition **809**

Other Countries Fall to Dictators

Key Ideas

- In Hungary and Poland, the new democratic governments formed after World War I fall to dictators.

- In Yugoslavia, Albania, Bulgaria, and Romania, kings suspend constitutions and turn to strong-man rule.

- By 1935, Czechoslovakia is the only democracy in eastern Europe.

- Eastern Europeans turn to dictatorship because they see authoritarian rule as the only way to prevent instability.

 ELECTRONIC LIBRARY OF PRIMARY SOURCES
from Memos on the Aims of Germany and Japan

ASSESS & RETEACH

Section 3 Assessment
Students might work in pairs to respond to the questions. Then have them share with the class their diagrams for item 2.

Section Quiz
 FORMAL ASSESSMENT
Section Quiz, p. 364

Reteaching Activity
CLASS TIME: 10 MINUTES

Use the Guided Reading Worksheet for Section 3 to help review the main ideas of the section.

 IN-DEPTH RESOURCES: UNIT 7
Guided Reading, p. 39

CLOSE ACTIVITY

CLASS TIME: 20 MINUTES

Role-Playing
Assign students the roles of Italian citizens or German citizens. After researching the causes of the rise of Fascism and ideas of Benito Mussolini and Adolf Hitler, have individual students present the views of individual citizens toward these two leaders.

---

praise for his leadership, Hitler turned the press, radio, literature, painting, and film into propaganda tools. Books that did not conform to Nazi beliefs were burned in huge bonfires. Churches were forbidden to criticize the Nazis or the government. Schoolchildren had to join the Hitler Youth (for boys) or the League of German Girls. Hitler was greatly influenced by Social Darwinism. (See page 679.) He believed that a continuous struggle brought victory to the strong. He twisted the philosophy of Friedrich Nietzsche to support his use of brute force to maintain power and his glorification of war.

Hitler Makes War on the Jews Hatred of Jews, or anti-Semitism, was a key part of Nazi ideology. Although Jews were less than one percent of the population, the Nazis used them as scapegoats for all Germany's troubles since the war. This led to a wave of anti-Semitism across Germany. Beginning in 1933, the Nazis passed laws depriving Jews of most of their rights. Violence against Jews mounted. On the night of November 9, 1938, Nazi mobs attacked Jews in their homes and on the streets and destroyed thousands of Jewish-owned buildings. This rampage, called *Kristallnacht* (Night of the Broken Glass), signaled the real start of the process of eliminating the Jews from German life. (See Chapter 32.)

Background
The term *anti-Semitism* is derived from the fact that the earliest Jews were Semites (people who spoke a Semitic language).

SPOTLIGHT On

The 1936 Olympics
The 1936 Summer Olympics were held in Berlin, Nazi Germany's capital. Hitler built a new $30 million stadium for the Games. To hide from the world his persecution of Jews, he took down all anti-Semitic signs in Berlin.

Prior to the Olympics' opening, Hitler announced that the Games would show the world Aryan superiority and the inferiority of Jews and blacks. Hitler's plan failed, however, in part because of the successes of African-American runner Jesse Owens. A sprinter and long jumper, Owens won four gold medals.

When Owens or other black athletes won medals, Hitler left the reviewing stand. He did not want to be seen congratulating them.

Other Countries Fall to Dictators

While Fascists took power in Italy and Germany, the nations formed in eastern Europe after World War I also were falling to dictators. The parliamentary governments that had been set up in these countries rarely lasted. In Hungary in 1919, after a brief Communist regime, military forces and wealthy landowners joined to make Admiral Miklós Horthy the first European postwar dictator. In Poland, Marshal Joseph Pilsudski (pihl·SOOT·skee) seized power in 1926. In Yugoslavia, Albania, Bulgaria, and Romania, kings turned to strong-man rule. They suspended constitutions and silenced foes. In 1935, one democracy, Czechoslovakia, remained in eastern Europe.

Elsewhere in Europe, only in nations with strong democratic traditions—Britain, France, and the Scandinavian countries—did democracy survive. With no democratic experience and severe economic problems, many Europeans saw dictatorship as the only way to prevent instability. Although all of these dictatorships restricted civil rights, none asserted control with the brutality of the Russian Communists or the Nazis.

By the mid-1930s, the powerful nations of the world were split into two antagonistic camps—democratic and totalitarian. And to gain their ends, the Fascist dictatorships had indicated a willingness to use military aggression.

Section **3** Assessment

1. TERMS & NAMES

Identify
- fascism
- Benito Mussolini
- Adolf Hitler
- Nazism
- *Mein Kampf*
- *lebensraum*

2. TAKING NOTES

Draw a chart like the one below. Compare Mussolini and Hitler by completing the chart.

	Hitler	Mussolini
Method of taking power		
Style of leadership		
Handling of economic crisis		
Goals		

Were the two more alike or different? Explain why.

3. DRAWING CONCLUSIONS

Why did a movement like fascism and leaders like Mussolini and Hitler come to power during a period of crisis?

THINK ABOUT
- what problems Italy and Germany faced
- political traditions in each country
- the state of the world at the time

4. THEME ACTIVITY

Power and Authority

Imagine you live in Italy and it is 1933, ten years since Benito Mussolini became dictator. In Germany, President Paul von Hindenburg is considering appointing Adolf Hitler, a Fascist like Mussolini, chancellor of Germany. What would you advise Hindenburg to do? Write him a letter telling him what has happened in your country under a fascist dictatorship.

810 Chapter 31

ANSWERS

1. TERMS & NAMES
fascism, p. 807
Benito Mussolini, p. 807
Adolf Hitler, p. 808
Nazism, p. 808
Mein Kampf, p. 809
lebensraum, p. 809

2. TAKING NOTES
Possible Responses: Hitler—appointed chancellor, then became dictator; revived economy; sought to regain lost lands and take over more. Mussolini—appointed by king then became dictator; took control of economy; wanted Italy to return to its ancient greatness.

3. DRAWING CONCLUSIONS
Possible Responses: During periods of crisis, people often turn to doctrines or leaders who promise to take charge and solve the country's problems. These doctrines or leaders often offer simple solutions to complex problems and blame outsiders, or scapegoats, for the problems.

4. THEME ACTIVITY
Possible Responses: Opposition letters: under Mussolini democracy abolished; all parties except Fascists outlawed; opponents imprisoned; radio and publications censored; strikes banned. Support letters: order restored, economy revived, and national pride awakened.

Aggressors on the March

TERMS & NAMES
• appeasement
• Axis Powers
• Francisco Franco
• isolationism
• Third Reich
• Munich Conference

MAIN IDEA

As Germany, Italy, and Japan conquered other countries, the rest of the world did nothing to stop them.

WHY IT MATTERS NOW

Many nations today take a more active and collective role in world affairs, as in the United Nations.

Section 4 Overview

OBJECTIVES

① To describe Fascist aggression in Asia, Africa, and Europe.

② To summarize why British and French appeasement and American isolationism fail to stop Fascist aggression.

③ To explain why the Soviet Union and Germany sign a peace pact.

SKILLBUILDERS

• Interpreting maps: location, movement, p. 813

CRITICAL THINKING

• Comparing, p. 811
• Making inferences, p. 812
• Analyzing visuals, p. 814
• Summarizing, p. 814
• Recognizing effects, p. 815
• Drawing conclusions, p. 815
• Analyzing themes, p. 815

SETTING THE STAGE By the mid-1930s, Germany and Italy seemed bent on military conquest. The major democracies—Britain, France, and the United States—were distracted by economic problems at home and longed to remain at peace. The Soviet Union was not committed to either camp. With the world moving toward war, many people pinned their hopes for peace on the League of Nations.

World Drifts Toward War

As fascism spread in Europe, a powerful nation in Asia moved toward a similar system. Following a period of reform and progress in the 1920s, Japan fell under military rule.

Democracy Struggles in Japan During the 1920s, the Japanese government became more democratic. In 1922, Japan signed an international treaty agreeing to respect China's borders. In 1928, it signed the Kellogg-Briand Pact renouncing war. Japan's parliamentary system had several weaknesses, however. Its constitution put strict limits on the powers of the prime minister and the cabinet. Most importantly, civilian leaders had little control over the armed forces. Military leaders reported only to the emperor.

A. Possible Answers Both were extremely nationalistic, wanted to solve economic problems by expanding. European fascists wanted a new government; Japanese wanted to return to traditional military control.

Background The control of the government by the military had centuries-old roots in Japanese history. The shoguns had been military leaders.

THINK THROUGH HISTORY
A. Comparing Compare the militarists in Japan with the European Fascists.

Militarists Take Control of Japan As long as Japan remained prosperous, the civilian government kept power. When the Great Depression struck in 1930, the government was blamed. Military leaders gained support and soon won control of the country. Unlike the Fascists in Europe, the militarists did not try to establish a new system of government. They wanted to restore traditional control of the government to the military. Instead of a forceful leader like Mussolini or Hitler, the militarists made the emperor the symbol of state power.

Keeping Emperor Hirohito as head of state won popular support for the army leaders who ruled in his name. Like Hitler and Mussolini, Japan's militarists were extreme nationalists. They wanted to solve the country's economic problems by foreign expansion. They planned a Pacific empire that included a conquered China. The empire would provide Japan with raw materials and markets for its goods. It would also give Japan room for its rising population.

Japan Invades Manchuria Japanese businesses had invested heavily in China's northeast province, Manchuria. It was an area rich in iron and coal. In 1931, the Japanese army seized Manchuria, despite objections from the Japanese parliament. The army then set up a puppet government. Japanese engineers and technicians began arriving in large numbers to build mines and factories.

Victorious Japanese troops march through the streets after occupying Manchuria in 1931.

Years of Crisis **811**

FOCUS

5-Minute Warm-Up

▶ *Interpreting a Time line*
To help students understand aggression in the 1930s, have them answer these questions.

1. Look at the time line on page 812. Who committed the first act of aggression and when?

2. Which country committed more aggressive acts?

WARM-UP TRANSPARENCY 31

OBJECTIVE ① INSTRUCT

World Drifts Toward War

▶ *Key Ideas*
• In the 1930s, military leaders take control of Japan, seize Manchuria, and invade China.
• Mussolini invades Ethiopia.
• Hitler rebuilds armed forces and moves troops into Rhineland.

(continued on next page)

SECTION 4 RESOURCES

PRINT RESOURCES

IN-DEPTH RESOURCES: UNIT 7
Guided Reading, p. 40
Geography Application: Spain During the 1930s, p. 42
Primary Source: The Bombing of Guernica, p. 47
History Makers: Francisco Franco, p. 52

ACCESS FOR STUDENTS ACQUIRING ENGLISH
Guided Reading (Spanish), p. 314
Geography Application: (Spanish), p. 316

FORMAL ASSESSMENT
Section Quiz, p. 365

ALTERNATIVE ASSESSMENT BOOK

TECHNOLOGY RESOURCES

GEOGRAPHY TRANSPARENCIES
GT31 Expansion of Nazi Germany, 1933–1939

CRITICAL THINKING TRANSPARENCIES
CT67 Chapter 31 Visual Summary

CD-ROM
Electronic Library of Primary Sources

INTERNET www.mlworldhistory.com

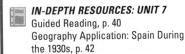
(continued from page 811)

- League of Nations fails to stop aggression.
- Germany, Italy, and Japan become allies as the Axis Powers.
- Civil War in Spain leads to a Fascist dictatorship.

IN-DEPTH RESOURCES: UNIT 7
Guided Reading, p. 40
Geography Application: Spain During the 1930s, p. 42

ACCESS FOR STUDENTS ACQUIRING ENGLISH
Guided Reading (Spanish), p. 314

MORE ABOUT . . .
Ethiopia and the League of Nations

After Italy attacked Ethiopia, the League of Nations called for an embargo restricting loans to and imports from Italy. However, Britain and France feared angering Mussolini, and they refused to place an embargo on oil. Even more important, Britain refused to stop Italian troops and arms from moving through the British-controlled Suez Canal. This inaction fatally weakened the League.

HISTORY MAKERS
Haile Selassie

Discuss Selassie's warning to League members. Ask students why Selassie says: "It is us today. It will be you tomorrow." Have students speculate on how the failure of League members to act affected Mussolini. Have students brainstorm alternate courses of action in Ethiopia and consider what impact they might have had on Italy.

The Japanese attack on Manchuria was the first direct challenge to the League of Nations. In the early 1930s, the League's members included all major democracies except the United States. Also members were the three countries that posed the greatest threat to peace—Germany, Japan, and Italy. When Japan seized Manchuria, many League members vigorously protested. The League condemned Japanese aggression, but it had no power to enforce its decisions. Japan ignored the protests and withdrew from the League in 1933.

Japan Invades China Four years later, a border incident touched off a full-scale war between Japan and China. On July 7, 1937, the Japanese and the Chinese exchanged shots at a railroad bridge near Beijing. Japanese forces then swept into northern China. Despite having a million soldiers, China's army led by Jiang Jieshi was no match for the better equipped and trained Japanese.

Beijing and other northern cities as well as the capital, Nanjing, fell to the Japanese in 1937. Japanese troops killed tens of thousands of captured soldiers and civilians in Nanjing. Forced to retreat westward, Jiang Jieshi set up a new capital at Chongqing. At the same time, Chinese guerrillas led by China's Communist leader, Mao Zedong, continued to fight in the conquered area.

Mussolini Attacks Ethiopia The League's failure to stop the Japanese encouraged Mussolini to plan aggression of his own. Mussolini dreamed of building a colonial empire in Africa like that of Britain and France. He bitterly complained that Britain and France had left only "a collection of deserts" from which to choose.

Ethiopia was one of Africa's four remaining independent nations. The Ethiopians had successfully resisted an Italian attempt at conquest during the 1890s. To avenge that defeat, Mussolini ordered a massive invasion of Ethiopia in October 1935. The spears and swords of the Ethiopians were no match for Italian airplanes, tanks, guns, and poison gas. In May 1936, Mussolini told a cheering crowd that "Italy has at last her empire . . . a Fascist empire."

The Ethiopian emperor Haile Selassie urgently appealed to the League for help. Although the League condemned the attack, its members did nothing. Britain continued to let Italian troops and supplies pass through the British-controlled Suez Canal on their way to Ethiopia. By giving in to Mussolini in Africa, Britain and France hoped to keep peace in Europe.

Hitler Defies Versailles Treaty Hitler had long pledged to undo the Versailles Treaty. Among its provisions, the treaty limited the size of Germany's army. In March 1935, the Führer announced that Germany would not obey these restrictions. In fact, Germany had already begun rebuilding its armed forces. The League issued only a mild condemnation. Banners throughout Germany announced, "Today Germany! Tomorrow the World!"

HISTORY MAKERS

HAILE SELASSIE
1892–1975

Haile Selassie, the emperor of Ethiopia, belonged to a dynasty that traced its roots back to King Solomon and the Queen of Sheba. When he became emperor in 1930, he was hailed as the 111th descendant of Solomon and Sheba to rule.

Five years after he took the throne, his country was invaded by Italy. Selassie was forced into exile. On June 30, 1936, he appeared before the League of Nations to plead for its help.

He warned League members that if they failed to impose military sanctions on Italy, "God and history will remember your judgment. . . . It is us today. It will be you tomorrow." The League did not heed his warning.

THINK THROUGH HISTORY
B. Making Inferences What was the major weakness of the League of Nations? Why?
B. Possible Answers The United States was not a member— League's actions did not have as much authority without the world's largest democracy. League had no enforcement power—could not make nations follow its decrees.

Aggression in Europe and Asia, 1930–1939

	September 1931 Japan invades Manchuria.		**October 1935** Italy attacks Ethiopia.	**March 1938** Germany annexes Austria.	**September 1938** Germany takes Sudetenland.

1930 — 1935 — 1939

	March 1936 Germany occupies Rhineland.	**July 1937** Japan invades China.	**March 1939** Germany seizes Czechoslovakia.	**April 1939** Italy conquers Albania

---

COOPERATIVE ACTIVITY: Headlining the News

CLASS TIME 30 MINUTES

Task: Student groups choose a headline and then write a news article, Internet news piece, or a short news spot for a television or radio news show.

Purpose: To understand the events of the 1930s that led to World War II.

Activity: Before dividing students into small groups, prepare a series of headlines, using the subsections of Section 4 as guides. For example, headlines might include Militarists Take Control of

Japan, Civil War Erupts in Spain, and so on. Write each headline on a slip of paper and have each group draw from a hat. Another option would be to allow each group to write its own headline. Then ask the group to prepare a newspaper article, short skit for a television news show, radio broadcast, or Internet news blurb explaining the headline. Have students present their news pieces for the class.

📁 **Building a Portfolio:** Students may want to put articles or scripts in their portfolios.

 ALTERNATIVE ASSESSMENT BOOK
Standards for Evaluating a Cooperative Activity

Standards for Evaluation
News articles should . . .

- clearly explain the *who, what, when, where,* and if possible, the *why* or *how* of this event
- show an understanding of its significance
- be accurate and factual
- be appropriate in tone and content

The League's failure to stop Germany from rearming convinced Hitler to take even greater risks. The treaty had forbidden German troops to enter a 30-mile-wide zone on either side of the Rhine River. Known as the Rhineland, it formed a buffer zone between Germany and France. It was also an important industrial area. On March 7, 1936, German troops moved into the Rhineland. Stunned, the French were unwilling to risk war. The British urged **appeasement,** giving in to an aggressor to keep peace.

Hitler later admitted that he would have backed down if the French and British had challenged him. The German reoccupation of the Rhineland marked a turning point in the march toward war. First, it strengthened Hitler's power and prestige within Germany. Cautious generals who had urged restraint now agreed to follow him. Second, the balance of power changed in Germany's favor. France and Belgium were now open to attack from German troops. Finally, the weak response by France and Britain encouraged Hitler to speed up his military and territorial expansion.

Hitler's growing strength convinced Mussolini that he should seek an alliance with Germany. In October 1936, the two dictators reached an agreement that became known as the Rome-Berlin Axis. A month later, Germany also made an agreement with Japan. Germany, Italy, and Japan came to be called the **Axis Powers.**

Civil War Erupts in Spain Hitler and Mussolini again tested the will of the democracies of Europe in the Spanish civil war. Spain had been a monarchy until 1931, when a republic was declared. The government, run by liberals and socialists, held office amid many crises. In July 1936, army leaders, favoring a Fascist-style government, joined General **Francisco Franco** in a revolt. Thus began a civil war that dragged on for three years.

Hitler and Mussolini sent troops, tanks, and airplanes to help Franco's forces, which were called the Nationalists. The armed forces of

Vocabulary

axis: a straight line around which an object rotates. Hitler and Mussolini expected their alliance to become the axis around which Europe would rotate.

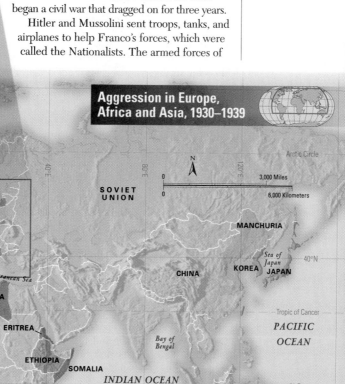

Aggression in Europe, Africa and Asia, 1930–1939

GERMANY
SUDETENLAND
CZECHOSLOVAKIA
AUSTRIA

0   200 Miles
0   400 Kilometers

MEMEL
North Sea
Baltic Sea
E. PRUSSIA (GER.)
UNITED KINGDOM
GERMANY
POLAND
SOVIET UNION
SUDETENLAND
CZECHOSLOVAKIA
RHINELAND
AUSTRIA
ATLANTIC OCEAN
FRANCE
ITALY
Black Sea
SPAIN (Civil War, 1936–1939)
Mediterranean Sea
ALBANIA
40°N

0   500 Miles
0   1,000 Kilometers

■ Italy
■ Italian colony
■ Taken by Italy
■ Germany
■ Taken by Germany
■ Japan
□ Taken by Japan

SOVIET UNION
Arctic Circle
N
0   3,000 Miles
0   6,000 Kilometers
MANCHURIA
CHINA
KOREA
Sea of Japan
JAPAN
40°N
LIBYA
Mediterranean Sea
ERITREA
Bay of Bengal
Tropic of Cancer
PACIFIC OCEAN
ETHIOPIA
SOMALIA
INDIAN OCEAN
0° Equator
ATLANTIC OCEAN

GEOGRAPHY SKILLBUILDER: Interpreting Maps

1. **Location** What countries were aggressors in this period?
2. **Movement** Aggression occurred on what three continents?

CRITICAL THINKING ACTIVITY
CLASS TIME: 20 MINUTES

Recognizing Effects
To help students recognize the effects of each of these peace-treaty violations on relations between Germany, Italy, France, and Britain, have them make a simple cause and effect diagram.

1936: Demilitarized Rhineland occupied by German forces	→ Effect
1938: Austria united with Germany	→ Effect
1938 Sudetenland taken from Czechoslovakia.	→ Effect

MORE ABOUT . . .
Francisco Franco

After the Nationalist victory in the Spanish Civil War, General Francisco Franco declared himself military chief. He ruled Spain until his death in 1975. Initially his reign was quite harsh. He executed 200,000 Spaniards between 1939 and 1943. He sympathized with the Axis Powers but did not enter World War II.

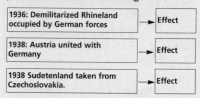 **IN-DEPTH RESOURCES: UNIT 7**
History Makers: Francisco Franco, p. 52
Primary Source: The Bombing of Guernica, p. 47

Learning from Visuals

Aggression in Europe, Africa and Asia, 1930–1939

Interpreting the Map Ask students to explain what the areas in purple *(lands attacked or claimed by Italy)*, pink *(by Germany)*, and gold *(by Japan)* represent.

Extension Have students use the map to name the continents where each Axis Power claimed territory by 1939. *Japan: Asia; Italy: Africa and Europe; Germany: Europe* Ask them why Poland might be a next step for German aggression. *Polish Corridor forms a wedge between Germany and its territory in East Prussia.*

SKILLBUILDER Answers
1. Italy, Germany, Japan.
2. Europe, Africa, and Asia

TEACHING OPTIONS   **CONNECTIONS ACROSS TIME AND PLACE**

Totalitarian Rule A totalitarian government is one that is controlled by a single political group. It suppresses all opposition, often through violent means. It controls all aspects of people's lives, including education, production of goods and services, culture, and travel, both within the country and abroad. A totalitarian state also exercises total

control of the media, particularly newspapers, radio, and television.

Both Nazi Germany under Adolf Hitler and the Soviet Union under Joseph Stalin are examples of totalitarian states. Have students name modern-day dictators such as Saddam Hussein and Fidel Castro and decide whether their rule can be described as totalitarian.

CONNECTIONS ACROSS THE CURRICULUM

Literature Students interested in seeing an insider's perspective on the Spanish Civil War can read the American writer Ernest Hemingway's novel *For Whom the Bell Tolls* (1940). Hemingway was in Spain during the war as a newspaper correspondent. The Englishman George Orwell, best known

for his novels *1984* and *Animal Farm,* wrote a nonfiction work, *Homage to Catalonia* (1938), about his experiences as a soldier. It describes his disillusionment with the Loyalists during the war. Students might contrast the idealism of Hemingway's hero with Orwell's view of war.

Teacher's Edition 813

Western Democracies Fail to Halt Aggression

▶ Key Issues

- In the 1930s, the United States follows an isolationist foreign policy in an effort to keep out of war.
- Germany annexes Austria and takes the Sudetenland from Czechoslovakia.
- Following a policy of appeasement, France and Britain let Hitler have the Sudetenland.
- Appeasement policy convinces Hitler that Britain and France will not stop his seizure of Czechoslovakia.
- Germany and the Soviet Union sign a nonaggression pact.

 GEOGRAPHY TRANSPARENCIES
GT31 Expansion of Nazi Germany, 1933–1939

 ELECTRONIC LIBRARY OF PRIMARY SOURCES
from Speech in the House of Commons

MORE ABOUT . . .
U.S. Isolationism

Many factors contributed to American isolationism. These included fear of war, hatred of profiteers whom many believed had dragged America into World War I, and distrust of presidential power.

MORE ABOUT . . .
Anschluss

Many years before the Anschluss, Hitler had built a strong base of support in Austria. The country had its own Nazi party, which campaigned for union until it was banned in 1934. Working in secret, Austria's Nazi party formed close ties with Germany's Nazi government. After Hitler invaded Austria in March 1938, Austrian Hitler Youth helped to make Austria a solidly pro-Nazi nation almost overnight.

HISTORY THROUGH ART: Fine Art

The Spanish artist Pablo Picasso painted *Guernica* shortly after Nazi planes destroyed the ancient Basque city of Guernica in 1937. The air attacks killed a thousand people, one out of every eight residents. At left, a mother cries over her dead child. In the center, a horse screams and a soldier lies dead. At right, a woman falls from a burning house. The canvas is huge—11 feet high and 25 feet long.

the Republicans, as supporters of Spain's elected government were known, received little help from abroad. The Western democracies remained neutral. Only the Soviet Union sent equipment and advisers. An International Brigade of volunteers fought on the Republican side but had little chance against a professional army. Early in 1939, Republican resistance collapsed. Franco became Spain's Fascist dictator.

Western Democracies Fail to Halt Aggression

Instead of taking a stand against Fascist aggression in the 1930s, Britain and France repeatedly made concessions, hoping to keep peace. Both nations were dealing with serious economic problems as a result of the Great Depression. In addition, the horrors of World War I had created a deep desire to avoid war. Allowing Hitler and Mussolini small territorial gains seemed a small price to pay for peace.

United States Follows an Isolationist Policy Many Americans resisted accepting the nation's new position as a world leader. **Isolationism**—the belief that political ties to other countries should be avoided—won wide support. Isolationists argued that entry into World War I had been a costly error. They were determined to prevent a repeat of this mistake. Beginning in 1935, Congress passed three Neutrality Acts. These laws banned loans and the sale of arms to nations at war. The isolationists believed this action would keep the United States out of another foreign war.

The German Reich Expands On November 5, 1937, Hitler announced to his advisers his plans to absorb Austria and Czechoslovakia into the **Third Reich** (ryk), or German Empire. The Germans would then expand into Poland and Russia. Hitler's first target was Austria. The Treaty of Versailles prohibited Anschluss (AHN·SHLUS), or a union between Austria and Germany. However, many Austrians supported unity with Germany. In March 1938, Hitler sent his army into Austria and annexed it. France and Britain ignored their pledge to protect Austrian independence.

Hitler next turned to Czechoslovakia. After World War I, Czechoslovakia had developed into a prosperous democracy with a strong army and a defense treaty with France. About 3 million German-speaking people lived in the western border regions of Czechoslovakia called the Sudetenland. (See map, page 813.) This heavily fortified area formed the Czechs' main defense against Germany. The Anschluss raised pro-Nazi feelings among Sudeten Germans. In September 1938, Hitler demanded that the Sudetenland be given to Germany. The Czechs refused and asked France for help.

THINK THROUGH HISTORY

C. Summarizing What foreign countries were involved in the Spanish Civil War?

C. Answer Germany and Italy on the side of Franco; the Soviet Union in support of the Spanish government.

Background
According to Hitler, there were three great German empires. They were the Holy Roman Empire; the German Empire of 1871–1918; and the Third Reich, ruled by the Nazis. The Third Reich, Hitler believed, would last 1,000 years.

Britain and France Again Choose Appeasement France and Britain were preparing for war when Mussolini proposed a meeting of Germany, France, Britain, and Italy in Munich, Germany. The **Munich Conference** was held on September 29, 1938. The Czechs were not invited. British Prime Minister Neville Chamberlain believed that he could preserve peace by giving in to Hitler's demand. The next morning, a tense world learned that the crisis was over. Britain and France agreed that Hitler could take the Sudetenland. In exchange, Hitler pledged to respect Czechoslovakia's new borders.

Chamberlain's policy of appeasement seemed to have prevented war. When he returned to London, Chamberlain told cheering crowds, "I believe it is peace for our time." Winston Churchill, then a member of the British Parliament, strongly disagreed. He opposed the appeasement policy and gloomily warned of its consequences.

A VOICE FROM THE PAST

We are in the presence of a disaster of the first magnitude. . . . we have sustained a defeat without a war. . . . And do not suppose that this is the end. . . . This is only the first sip, the first foretaste of a bitter cup which will be proffered to us year by year unless, by a supreme recovery of moral health and martial vigor, we arise again and take our stand for freedom as in the olden time.

WINSTON CHURCHILL, speech before the House of Commons, October 5, 1938

Less than six months after the Munich meeting, Hitler's troops took Czechoslovakia. Soon after, Mussolini seized nearby Albania. Then Hitler demanded that Poland return the former German port of Danzig. The Poles refused and turned to Britain and France for aid. Both countries said they would guarantee Polish independence. But appeasement had convinced Hitler that neither nation would risk war.

Nazis and Soviets Sign Nonaggression Pact Britain and France asked the Soviet Union to join them in stopping Hitler's aggression. Negotiations proceeded slowly. The two democracies distrusted the Communist government, and Stalin resented having been left out of the Munich Conference. As the Soviet leader talked with Britain and France, he also bargained with Hitler. The two dictators reached an agreement. Once bitter enemies, fascist Germany and communist Russia now publicly committed never to attack one another. On August 23, 1939, a nonaggression pact was signed. As the Axis Powers moved unchecked at the end of the decade, the whole world waited to see what would happen next. War appeared inevitable.

THINK THROUGH HISTORY
D. Recognizing Effects What were the effects of isolationism and appeasement?
D. Answer Aggressor nations continued their aggressions unchecked.

CONNECT to TODAY

Aggression in the Persian Gulf
After World War II, the Munich Conference of 1938 became a symbol for surrender. Leaders of democracies vowed never again to appease a ruthless dictator. U.S. President George Bush used Munich as an example when responding to aggression in the Persian Gulf in 1990.

When troops of Iraqi dictator Saddam Hussein invaded nearby Kuwait, the United States responded to Kuwait's call for help by forming a coalition of forces to fight the Persian Gulf War. In explaining why, Bush noted how Britain's Neville Chamberlain failed to help Czechoslovakia after Hitler claimed the Sudetenland. Bush said:

The world cannot turn a blind eye to aggression. You know the tragic consequences when nations, confronted with aggression, choose to tell themselves it is no concern of theirs, "just a quarrel [as Chamberlain said] in a faraway country between people of whom we know nothing."

Section ④ Assessment

1. TERMS & NAMES
Identify
- appeasement
- Axis Powers
- Francisco Franco
- isolationism
- Third Reich
- Munich Conference

2. TAKING NOTES
Trace the movement of Japan from democratic reform in the 1920s to military aggression in the 1930s by supplying the events following the dates shown on the time line below.

```
1922        1930        1936
     1928        1931        1937
```

What event was the most significant? Why?

3. DRAWING CONCLUSIONS
Review Germany's aggressive actions after Hitler defied the Versailles Treaty by rebuilding Germany's armed forces. At what point do you think Hitler concluded that he could take any territory without being stopped? Why?

THINK ABOUT
- Hitler's goals
- responses of the democracies to his statements and actions
- the role of the League of Nations

4. ANALYZING THEMES
Power and Authority After World War I, many Americans became isolationists. Do you recommend that America practice isolationism today? Why or why not?

THINK ABOUT
- America's role as world leader
- the global economy
- America's domestic problems
- the economic and political goals of other countries

Years of Crisis **815**

ANSWERS

1. TERMS & NAMES
appeasement, p. 813
Axis Powers, p. 813
Francisco Franco, p. 813
isolationism, p. 814
Third Reich, p. 814
Munich Conference, p. 815

2. TAKING NOTES
Possible Responses:
1922—Signs treaty agreeing to respect China's borders; 1928—Signs Kellogg-Briand Pact renouncing war; 1930—Great Depression puts military in control; 1931—Invades Manchuria; 1936—Allies with Germany; 1937—Invades China

3. DRAWING CONCLUSIONS
Possible Responses: After Hitler renounced Versailles Treaty—nothing happened; after seizing Rhineland—Britain urged appeasement; after taking Austria—France and Britain ignored pledge to protect Austria; after Munich Conference—Britain and France let Germany take Sudetenland.

4. ANALYZING THEMES
Possible Responses: Yes—world leadership costs in money and respect; global economy costs in jobs and social services; cannot solve other countries' problems. No—power and prestige as a world leader; need to compete in a global economy; benefits from maintaining order.

MORE ABOUT . . .
Winston Churchill
Early in his political career, Winston Churchill's independence of mind often caused him problems. However, this trait made him willing to speak out against the Nazi threat when few others in Britain would do so. Churchill was Britain's most outspoken critic of appeasement. He saw clearly that this policy would only increase Hitler's belief that he would not be stopped in his grab for power and territory.

CONNECT to TODAY
Aggression in the Persian Gulf
Have students research the causes of the Persian Gulf War and the reasons for the decision by the United States to aid Kuwait. Have them decide whether the comparison between Saddam Hussein and Hitler and the United States and Britain is accurate.

ASSESS & RETEACH

Section 4 Assessment
Students might work in pairs to respond to the questions. Then have them share with the class their time line for item 2.

Section Quiz
 FORMAL ASSESSMENT
Section Quiz, p. 365

Reteaching Activity
CLASS TIME: 15 MINUTES

Have students review the time line on page 812, summarizing the significance of each event and adding other events of importance for the 1930–1939 period.

 CRITICAL THINKING TRANSPARENCIES
CT67 Chapter 31 Visual Summary

CLOSE ACTIVITY

CLASS TIME: 20 MINUTES

Summarizing
Using the time line on page 812 as a starting point, have students describe the response of the democracies to each event shown on the time line. Then speculate on whether Axis aggression could have been stopped if the democracies had responded differently and, if so, at what point in the path to war.

Teacher's Edition **815**

TERMS & NAMES

1. Albert Einstein, p. 795
2. Sigmund Freud, p. 795
3. Weimar Republic, p. 802
4. New Deal, p. 806
5. fascism, p. 807
6. Benito Mussolini, p. 807
7. Adolf Hitler, p. 808
8. appeasement, p. 813
9. Francisco Franco, p. 813
10. Munich Conference, p. 815

REVIEW QUESTIONS

Answers will vary.

11. They created a revolution in science and the study of human behavior, disturbing many people and leading them to question their own beliefs.

12. *Possible Responses:* Passenger airlines, improved autos, radio broadcasting widespread, and movies a major industry.

13. Lacked democratic heritage; lacked strong ruling party (had several major parties); criticized for loss of war; humiliation of the Versailles Treaty.

14. Provided for $200 million U.S. loan and better German reparation repayment schedule; increased U.S. investment and industrial production; slowed inflation.

15. Investors bought on margin; investors sold, hoping to reinvest with lower rates; falling prices caused panic selling; stocks lost value.

16. Dissatisfaction with Paris Peace Conference; unemployment; fear of communist revolution; democratic government unable to solve problems.

17. Germans were master race and other "races" inferior; Treaty of Versailles was intolerable and Hitler would reclaim territory; takeover of eastern Europe and Russia would give Germany more *lebensraum*.

18. Through foreign expansion; a Pacific empire on Chinese mainland yielding raw materials; increased living space.

19. The military was convinced Hitler had the power to succeed; with France and Belgium open to attack, the balance of power favored Germany; Hitler pursued military and territorial expansion.

20. From 1936 to 1939 Franco and his Fascist army fought the Spanish Republicans; Franco's forces won, and Franco became the military dictator of Spain.

The Great Depression

Long-Term Causes

- World economies are connected.
- Some countries have huge war debts from World War I.
- Europe relies on American loans and investments.
- Prosperity is built on borrowed money.
- Wealth is unequally distributed.

Immediate Causes

- U.S. stock market crashes.
- Banks demand repayment of loans.
- Farms fail and factories close.
- Americans reduce foreign trade to protect economy.
- Americans stop loans to foreign countries.
- American banking system collapses.

Worldwide Economic Depression

Immediate Effects

- Millions become unemployed worldwide.
- Businesses go bankrupt.
- Governments take emergency measures to protect economies.
- Citizens lose faith in capitalism and democracy.
- Nations turn toward authoritarian leaders.

Long-Term Effects

- Nazis take control in Germany.
- Fascists come to power in other countries.
- Democracies try social welfare programs.
- Japan expands in East Asia.
- World War II breaks out.

TERMS & NAMES

Briefly explain the importance of each of the following during the years 1919 to 1939.

1. Albert Einstein
2. Sigmund Freud
3. Weimar Republic
4. New Deal
5. fascism
6. Benito Mussolini
7. Adolf Hitler
8. appeasement
9. Francisco Franco
10. Munich Conference

REVIEW QUESTIONS

SECTION 1 *(pages 795–800)*
An Age of Uncertainty

11. What effect did Einstein's theory of relativity and Freud's theory of the unconscious have on the public?

12. What advances were made in transportation and communication in the 1920s and 1930s?

SECTION 2 *(pages 801–806)*
A Global Depression

13. List three reasons the Weimar Republic was considered weak.

14. What was the Dawes Plan? How did it affect the German economy?

15. What caused the stock market crash of 1929?

SECTION 3 *(pages 807–810)*
Fascism Rises in Europe

16. List three political and economic reasons the Italians turned to Mussolini.

17. List three of Hitler's beliefs and goals presented in *Mein Kampf*.

SECTION 4 *(pages 811–815)*
Aggressors on the March

18. Explain how Japan planned to solve its economic problems.

19. Why was Germany's reoccupation of the Rhineland a significant turning point toward war?

20. Briefly describe the Spanish Civil War. Include when it occurred, who fought, and who won.

Interact *with* History

On page 794, you chose a candidate to support in German elections in the early 1930s. Now that you have read the chapter, did what you read confirm your decision? Why or why not? Would the candidate you selected have a good or bad effect on the rest of the world? Discuss your opinions with a small group.

Interact *with* History

Possible Responses: Students who selected candidate one may say they made the right choice because their candidate was like Hitler, who made Germany strong again. Or they may rethink their choice, saying that Hitler's kind of nationalistic leadership imposed totalitarian rule to achieve its aims. Those who chose number two may support or reject their choice based on whether they approved of the direction Germany took under Hitler.

CRITICAL THINKING

1. THE STOCK MARKET CRASH

THEME ECONOMICS Your text says that the economy in 1929 was "like a delicately balanced house of cards." Use a sequence graphic like the one below to identify the events that led to the stock market collapse.

2. SUPPORT FOR FASCISM

Millions of people were attracted to fascist principles and leaders following World War I. What conditions made them give their support to these authoritarian doctrines? What were the advantages and disadvantages of being under fascist rule?

3. THE LEAGUE OF NATIONS

What weaknesses made the League of Nations an ineffective force for peace in the 1920s and 1930s? Give specific examples to prove your point.

4. ANALYZING PRIMARY SOURCES

In 1938, France, Britain, Italy, and Germany met to discuss Hitler's demand for the Sudetenland. Columbia Broadcasting System transmitted the following live report on radios around the world.

A VOICE FROM THE PAST
Prague—6:30 p.m.   *September 29*
WILLIAM SHIRER: It took the Big Four just five hours and twenty-five minutes here in Munich today to dispel the clouds of war and come to an agreement over the partition of Czechoslovakia. There is to be no European war. . . the price of that peace is, roughly, the ceding by Czechoslovakia of the Sudeten territory to Herr Hitler's Germany. The German Führer gets what he wanted, only he has to wait a little longer for it. . . .

His waiting ten short days has saved Europe from a world war. . . most of the peoples of Europe are happy that they won't have to be marching off to war on Saturday. Probably only the Czechs. . . are not too happy. But there seems very little that they can do about it in face of all the might and power represented here. . .

WILLIAM SHIRER, quoted in *The Strenuous Decade*

- Summarize the news Shirer is reporting.
- What do you think is Shirer's opinion about it? Give specific examples to support your opinion.

CHAPTER ACTIVITIES

1. LIVING HISTORY: Unit Portfolio Project

THEME SCIENCE AND TECHNOLOGY Your unit portfolio project focuses on the impact of scientific and technological innovation on history. For chapter 31, you might select one of the following ideas to add to your portfolio.

- Study the style of an architect, artist, author, or musician in this chapter. Compose or create your own work imitating this person's style. For example, design a functional building like Wright or a cubist painting like Picasso.
- Give a demonstration speech on an invention, tool, or other device from this time period. While showing the class how it works, explain its social, political, or economic effects.
- With a small group, invent a weapon to be used for peaceful purposes by the League of Nations, and rewrite history. Choose an incident of aggression that you read about and write a fictional account headlined *League's New Weapon Halts Fascists*. Read your version of history to the class.

2. CONNECT TO TODAY: Cooperative Learning

THEME POWER AND AUTHORITY After World War I, authoritarian leaders came to power in many countries during times of crisis. Could a Hitler or Mussolini come to power now in any country? Work with a small group. Select a country to research.

 Using the Internet and library sources, investigate your chosen country's political and economic condition today. Review its history.

- Use information from your research to prepare a scenario, or situation, where a dictator could take power in that country. Present your results.

3. INTERPRETING A TIME LINE

Review the unit time line on page 739. Which three events most seriously defied the peace treaties of this time period? In a short paragraph, explain why. Share your paragraph with another student.

FOCUS ON **CHARTS**

Comparing Fascism/Nazism and Communism Fascism/Nazism and Communism are two different totalitarian political systems with some common characteristics.

	Fascism/Nazism	Communism
Basic principles	Authoritarian; action-oriented; charismatic leader; state more important than individual	Marxist-Leninist ideas; dictatorship of proletariat; state more important than individual
Political	Nationalist; racist (Nazism); one-party rule; supreme leader	Internationalist; one-party rule; supreme leader
Social	Supported by middle class, industrialists, and military	Supported by workers and peasants
Cultural	Censorship; indoctrination; secret police	Censorship; indoctrination; secret police
Economic	Private property control by state corporations or state	Collective ownership; centralized state planning
Examples	Italy, Spain, Germany	U.S.S.R.

- What characteristics do they have in common? How do they differ?

Years of Crisis **817**

CHAPTER ACTIVITIES

1. LIVING HISTORY

Standards for Evaluation
Works of art or architectural designs should meet the following criteria:

- Contain elements of the person's style.
- Show evidence of research

Standards for Evaluation
Demonstration speeches should meet the following criteria:

- Clearly explain the origin and function of the item.
- Discuss the effects of the item on society.

Standards for Evaluation
Student versions of history should meet the following criteria:

- Describe the weapon invented.
- Explain how its use changed history.

2. CONNECT TO TODAY: COOPERATIVE LEARNING

Standards for Evaluation
Takeover scenarios should meet the following criteria:

- Describe the weaknesses and problems in the country.
- Explain how they provide an opportunity for fascist takeover.
- Show how the dictator acquired power.

3. INTERPRETING A TIME LINE

Possible Response: Japan's invasion of Manchuria in 1931, Italy's invasion of Ethiopia in 1935, and Germany's annexation of Austria in 1938. These actions showed the aggressors' willingness to disregard existing treaties and to use force to acquire territory.

FOCUS ON **CHARTS**

Possible Answers: Common characteristics: state more important than individual, one-party rule, supreme leader, censorship, indoctrination, and secret police. Differences: Fascism/Nazism—authoritarian; action-oriented; charismatic leader; nationalist, racist; supported by middle class, industrialists, and military; private property control led by state or state corporations. Communism—Marxist-Leninist ideas, dictatorship of proletariat; internationalist; supported by workers and peasants; collective ownership; and centralized state planning.

CRITICAL THINKING

1. THE STOCK MARKET CRASH
Possible Responses: Stock prices high, investors sold stocks, prices fell, panic resulted, prices plunged further, market crashed.

2. SUPPORT FOR FASCISM
Possible Responses: People were frustrated and angry over problems; wanted strong leaders to restore national pride and provide security and jobs. Advantages—strong leadership, end to social unrest, government put people back to work. Disadvantages—only one political party, no democracy, rights limited, censorship.

3. THE LEAGUE OF NATIONS
Possible Responses: No armed forces to stop aggression. Weakened by the United States not being a member. When it condemned an aggressor, it could not speak for all the world's powers.

4. ANALYZING PRIMARY SOURCES
Possible Responses: Shirer is reporting on the meeting of Germany, France, Britain, and Italy in Munich that allowed Germany to take the Sudetenland from Czechoslovakia. Shirer seems to support the agreement, believing it has saved the world from war. He also appears to sympathize with the Czechs but says they are powerless to resist.

	Key Ideas	COPY MASTERS	ASSESSMENT
SECTION 1 **Hitler's Lightning War** pp. 821–826	Hitler launches a surprise attack on Poland, overruns much of Europe, and invades Russia. Britain survives to fight on alone, aided by arms from the United States.	**In-Depth Resources: Unit 7** • **Guided Reading,** p. 54 • **Primary Source:** from *Berlin Diary,* p. 62 • **History Makers:** Charles de Gaulle, p. 69 Winston Churchill, p. 70	**PE** *Section 1 Assessment,* p. 826 *Formal Assessment* • Section Quiz, p. 374 *Alternative Assessment Book* • Standards for Evaluating a Cooperative Activity
SECTION 2 **Japan Strikes in the Pacific** pp. 827–830	Japan's attack on Pearl Harbor draws the United States into the war. Initial Japanese victories in the Pacific are overturned as U.S. naval forces fight back, gaining the offensive.	**In-Depth Resources: Unit 7** • **Guided Reading,** p. 55 • **Geography Application:** The Fall of Singapore, p. 60	**PE** *Section 2 Assessment,* p. 830 *Formal Assessment* • Section Quiz, p. 375 *Alternative Assessment Book* • Standards for Evaluating a Cooperative Activity
SECTION 3 **The Holocaust** pp. 831–834	Nazi persecution of Jews throughout Germany and the conquered nations leads to Hitler's "Final Solution," the mass extermination of 6 million of Europe's Jews.	**In-Depth Resources: Unit 7** • **Guided Reading,** p. 56 • **Primary Sources:** from *The Diary of a Young Girl,* p. 64 • **Literature:** from *Night,* p. 66	**PE** *Section 3 Assessment,* p. 834 *Formal Assessment* • Section Quiz, p. 376 *Alternative Assessment Book* • Standards for Evaluating a Cooperative Activity
SECTION 4 **The Allies Are Victorious** pp. 835–841	The Allies invade Europe as the Soviet Union drives the Germans westward, leading to Germany's final defeat. Japan surrenders following an atomic bomb attack by the United States.	**In-Depth Resources: Unit 7** • **Guided Reading,** p. 57 • **Skillbuilder Practice:** Following Chronological Order, p. 59 • **Primary Sources:** from *Farewell to Manzanar,* p. 63 from *Hiroshima,* p. 65	**PE** *Section 4 Assessment,* p. 841 *Formal Assessment* • Section Quiz, p. 377 *Alternative Assessment Book* • Standards for Evaluating a Cooperative Activity
SECTION 5 **The Devastation of Europe and Japan** pp. 842–845	A ravaged Europe struggles to survive as the United States occupies Japan and begins to bring political change and stability.	**In-Depth Resources: Unit 7** • **Guided Reading,** p. 58	**PE** *Section 5 Assessment,* p. 845 *Formal Assessment* • Section Quiz, p. 378 *Alternative Assessment Book* • Standards for Evaluating a Cooperative Activity
CHAPTER RESOURCES	**Chapter Overview** The expansionist designs of Germany and Japan lead to worldwide conflict. After initial defeats in Europe and the Pacific, the Allies are victorious but at the cost of millions of lives and the economic and political devastation of Europe and Japan.	*Telescoping the Times* • Chapter Summary, pp. 125–127 *Planning for Block Schedules*	**PE** *Chapter Assessment,* pp. 846–847 *Chapter Activities,* p. 847 *Formal Assessment* • Chapter Test, forms A and B, pp. 379–384 *Test Generator* *Alternative Assessment Book*

1939–1945

 Warm-Up Transparency 32

 Geography Transparencies
- GT32 The Battle of Britain, 1940–1941

 World Art and Cultures Transparencies
- AT70 German and American Propaganda

 Electronic Library of Primary Sources
- from "Blood, Toil, Tears, and Sweat"

INTERNET RESOURCES
www.mlworldhistory.com

 Warm-Up Transparency 32

Electronic Library of Primary Sources
- from "Japanese Attack Sinks HMS *Repulse*"

INTERNET RESOURCES
www.mlworldhistory.com

 Warm-Up Transparency 32

 Electronic Library of Primary Sources
- from Affadavit Given at Nuremberg

INTERNET RESOURCES
www.mlworldhistory.com

 Warm-Up Transparency 32

Battles of the World
- The Battle of Stalingrad

 Electronic Library of Primary Sources
- from Testimony Before the Special Senate Committee on Atomic Energy

Patterns of Interaction: *Arming for War*

Warm-Up Transparency 32

World Art and Cultures Transparencies
- AT71 *Liberation*

Critical Thinking Transparencies
- CT32 The Causes and Effects of World War II
- CT68 Chapter 32 Visual Summary

INTERNET RESOURCES
www.mlworldhistory.com

Chapter Summaries on Audiocassette in English and Spanish

INTERNET RESOURCES
www.mlworldhistory.com

Block Scheduling (90 MINUTES)

Day 1
Section 1, pp. 821–826

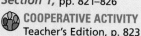 **COOPERATIVE ACTIVITY**
Teacher's Edition, p. 823

Section 2, pp. 827–830

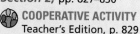 **COOPERATIVE ACTIVITY**
Teacher's Edition, p. 829

Section Assessments,
pp. 826, 830

Day 2
Section 3, pp. 831–834

COOPERATIVE ACTIVITY
Teacher's Edition, p. 833

Section 4, pp. 835–841

COOPERATIVE ACTIVITY
Teacher's Edition, p. 836

Section Assessments,
pp. 834, 841

Day 3
Section 5, pp. 842–845

COOPERATIVE ACTIVITY
Teacher's Edition, p. 843

Section Assessment, p. 845

Chapter Assessment,
pp. 846–847

Yearly Pacing *Chapter 32 Total:* 3 days *Yearly Total:* 85 days

 Planning for Block Schedules

Customizing for Special Needs

Students Acquiring English

 Access for Students Acquiring English
- **Guided Reading** for Sections 1–5 (Spanish), pp. 321–325
- **Chapter Summary** (Spanish), pp. 318–320
- **Skillbuilder Practice** Following Chronological Order (Spanish), p. 326
- **Geography Application** The Fall of Singapore (Spanish), pp. 327–328

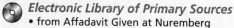 *Chapter Summaries on Audiocassette* in English and Spanish

 Patterns of Interaction: *Arming for War* (Spanish track)

Less Proficient Readers

 In-Depth Resources: Unit 7
- **Guided Reading** for Sections 1–5, pp. 54–58
- **Skillbuilder Practice** Following Chronological Order, p. 59
- **Geography Application** The Fall of Singapore, p. 60

 Telescoping the Times
- Chapter Summary, pp. 125–127

 Chapter Summaries on Audiocassette

Gifted and Talented Students

 In-Depth Resources: Unit 7

Primary Sources
- from *Berlin Diary,* p. 62
- from *The Diary of a Young Girl,* p. 64
- from *Farewell to Manzanar,* p. 63
- from *Hiroshima,* p. 65

History Makers
- Charles de Gaulle, p. 69
- Winston Churchill, p. 70

Connections to Literature READINGS FOR STUDENTS

 In-Depth Resources: Unit 7
Literature: from *Night,* p. 66

McDougal Littell
The Language of Literature, Grade 10
Elie Wiesel, from *Night,* p. 308
Elie Wiesel, from "Nobel Prize Acceptance Speech," p. 314
Jeanne and James Houston, from *Farewell to Manzanar,* p. 330

McDougal Littell
Literature Connections
Houston, Jeanne Wakatsuki
Houston, James
Farewell to Manzanar
(with related readings)

Here is the true story of a Japanese-American confinement in California's Manzanar internment camp during World War II. Ms. Houston's fierce pride and determination shine through this story.

 = Pupil's Edition   = Overhead Transparency   = Software   = Video

= Copy Master   = CD-ROM   = Audiocassette   = Internet

817B

World War II, 1939–1945

Accessing Prior Knowledge

- Have students look at the pictures on these two pages and ask them what they know about World War II. Have they seen stories set during the war in movies or on television? Do they know of any relatives who fought in the war?

Making Inferences

- After students have surveyed the captions and pictures on these pages, ask them what they think it would have been like to have served in the armed forces during this period. What would it have been like to face danger and death? What would it have been like to be away from home, fighting across the ocean?

Geography Connection

Ask students to look at the map on these two pages.

- How might the different locations of the war in Europe and the war in the Pacific have affected tactics and weapons in each area? *In the Pacific, aircraft carriers were likely to have been very important, while in Europe, tanks were of great use because they could move across wide expanses of land (something they could not do in the Pacific war).*

PREVIEWING THEMES

Science and Technology

Far-reaching developments in science and technology changed the course of World War II. Important improvements in aircraft, tanks, and submarines had occurred since World War I. The invention of radar, aircraft carriers, and especially the atomic bomb changed how war was fought.

Empire Building

Germany, Italy, and Japan tried to build empires. They began expanding their own territories by conquering other nations and dominating them politically and economically.

Economics

Fighting the Nazi terror weakened the economies of Great Britain, the Soviet Union, and most other European allies. When the United States entered the war, its economy actually grew sharply after years of depression. With the strength of its economy, the United States strengthened the Allied effort with its resources and products.

INTERNET CONNECTION

Visit us at **www.mlworldhistory.com** to learn more about World War II.

CHAPTER 32
World War II, 1939–1945

THE BATTLES OF WORLD WAR II, 1939–1945

Leningrad (Sept. 1941–Jan. 1944)

Britain (July 1940–May 1941)

Warsaw (Aug. 1944–Jan. 1945)

Minsk (June–Aug. 1944)

Kursk (July 1943)

Normandy (June 1944)

Stalingrad (Aug. 1942–Feb. 1943)

Paris (Aug. 1944)

Berlin (Apr.–May 1945)

Battle of the Bulge (Dec. 1944)

Anzio (Jan.–Mar. 1944)

Sicily (July 1943)

Monte Cassino (May 1944)

Tunis (May 1943)

Tobruk (Nov. 1942)

El Alamein (Oct.–Nov. 1942)

In **1939,** construction began on Nazi concentration camps to kill Jews and members of other groups. Prisoners were to die by hard labor, poor nutrition, and disease. Impatient with the pace of the killing, Adolf Hitler later had death camps built. In the camps, millions were killed by poison gas. Survivors of Hitler's **Holocaust** lived to tell the horrors of Nazi brutality.

☐ Major Allied powers
☐ Major Axis powers
✳ Major battle
☢ Nuclear explosion

ATLANTIC OCEAN

0   1,000 Miles
0   2,000 Kilometers

N

GEOGRAPHY THEMES

Location

Ask students to note the major battles of World War II and identify the areas in which the conflicts occurred. Have students contrast the fighting in Europe with the fighting in the Pacific and ask how the conflicts differ. *Europe was a land war; the Pacific was a sea war.*

Ask students to speculate on the difficulties of fighting a war on two fronts. Discuss with students the different climates that soldiers in these two locations would have encountered. Ask students where they would have preferred to fight—in Europe or in the Pacific. Ask them to explain their choice.

Movement

Point out to students that movement was an important aspect of World War II. The ability to move troops and supplies easily and quickly was crucial to the success of the combatants. Ask students to speculate on what other kinds of movement might be involved in a worldwide conflict. *They may suggest*

the movement of people who are trying to escape the fighting. Ask students in what direction American troops moved to defeat Japan. *westward—from east to west* Ask students in what direction Allied troops moved to defeat Germany. *British and American troops moved eastward; Russian troops moved westward.*

ADDITIONAL RESOURCES

Books for the Teacher

• Miller, Nathan. *War at Sea: A Naval History of World War II.* New York: Scribner's, 1995.

• Shirer, William Lawrence. *The Rise and Fall of the Third Reich: A History of Nazi Germany.* New York: Simon, 1959.

• Toland, John. *The Rising Sun: The Decline and Fall of the Japanese Empire, 1939-1945.* New York: Random, 1970.

• Weinberg, Gerhard L. *A World at Arms: A Global History of World War II.* New York: Cambridge UP, 1994.

Books for the Student

• Sherrow, Victoria. *Hiroshima.* New York: New Discovery, 1994.

• Wigoder, Geoffrey. *The Holocaust.* Danbury, CT: Grolier, 1997.

• Winston, Keith. *Letters of a World War II G.I.* New York: Watts, 1995.

📼 Videos

• *The Atomic Bomb—1945 A.D.* Ambrose Video, 1995. 800-526-4663.

• *Hitler.* Cambridge Social Studies, 1990. 800-468-4227.

• *We Must Never Forget: The Story of the Holocaust.* Society for Visual Education, 1994. 800-829-1900.

💿 Software

• *World War II: 1931-1945.* CD-ROM. Lucerne, 1995. 800-341-2293. Describes events, personalities, and issues related to the war.

On **June 6, 1944**, the Allies launched the greatest naval and land campaign in history against Nazi forces in **Normandy.** Supreme Commander U.S. General Dwight David Eisenhower led the attack against the Nazis with massive air and ground forces. Despite huge losses, the Allies' invasion of Europe spelled the beginning of the end of Adolf Hitler's regime.

Nagasaki (Aug. 9, 1945)

Hiroshima (Aug. 6, 1945)

Okinawa (Apr.–June 1945)

Iwo Jima (Feb.–March 1945)

Midway (June 1942)

Philippine Sea (June 1944)

Wake Island (Dec. 1941)

Pearl Harbor (Dec. 1941)

Bataan

Saipan (June–July 1944)

Guam (July–Aug. 1944)

PACIFIC OCEAN

Leyte Gulf (Oct. 1944)

Singapore (Feb. 1942)

0° Equator

Hollandia (Apr. 1944)

Guadalcanal (Aug. 1942–Feb. 1943)

INDIAN OCEAN

On **April 9, 1942**, the Bataan Peninsula in the Philippines fell to Japan. After their victory, the Japanese led 70,000 American and Filipino prisoners of war on a 60-mile forced march north—the **Bataan Death March.** The prisoners marched under a blazing sun. They were also starved and brutally beaten. Prisoners who showed signs of weakening were often buried alive.

819

HISTORY THROUGH ART

Photography

Photography is both a means of recording important events and an art form. Photographs can both capture dramatic moments in history and preserve them for posterity. The three pictures on these pages capture important events in the history of the Second World War. The Bataan Death March represented a low point in American fortunes early in World War II.

The photograph shows captured American soldiers being marched off to captivity after their defense of Corregidor, the rock fortress of Manila Bay. The D-Day landing on June 6, 1944, marked a dramatic turning point in World War II. The photograph shows troops leaving a landing craft and wading toward a beach in Normandy. The photograph of the prisoner in a concentration camp illustrates the brutality of the Nazi regime. The picture shows an emaciated

survivor drinking from a metal bowl in front of a barracks in Buchenwald.

Interpreting the Art What do these photographs seems to suggest about World War II? What emotions might troops experience while storming a beach? How might captives on a forced march feel? How would a prisoner in a concentration camp feel at the moment of liberation?

Interact *with* History

This Interact with History feature motivates students by inviting them to decide on whether or not to bomb a city during World War II. As they imagine themselves making this difficult decision, students will analyze the issues, explore their options, and become decision makers.

Purpose

- to set the stage for studying World War II
- to help students understand some of the causes and effects of World War II
- to help students make connections with the people and events they will study in this chapter

Teaching Strategy

Thinking Critically After students have imagined themselves in the situation described on this page, have them answer the key questions and give reasons for their decision.

EXAMINING *the* ISSUES

Following are suggestions for addressing each bulleted question.

1 Ask students to suggest arguments for and against shortening a war by taking civilian lives. Does shortening a war by two months justify such actions? Would killing civilians be justified if it shortened a war? Is taking the lives of civilians ever justified?

2 Have students give examples of civilian contributions to a war effort, such as making weapons in factories.

3 Ask students what information a commander would need in order to weigh arguments for lives saved against the percentage of lives lost.

Making Connections Ask students to think about the impact of extensive and destructive wars (such as World War I) on societies and people.

World War II has been going on for several years—at great cost in lives to your side and the enemy's. You are an air force commander who has just received a report from military intelligence. The report identifies a city in enemy territory that is a major weapons manufacturing center. You and other officers know that by destroying the arms factories in the city, the war could be shortened. Thousands of lives could be saved. On the other hand, the bombing will kill hundreds, maybe thousands, of civilians living near the enemy factories. How do you weigh the lives that will be saved against the lives that will be lost?

Would you bomb this city?

One plane-load of bombs will wipe out a vital enemy weapons factory, along with hundreds of civilian homes around it.

Radar tells the pilot where to drop the bombs, but at 10,000 feet, he cannot see the casualties they will cause.

This is a bomb factory in the middle of a residential area.

This raid will probably shorten the war by at least two months.

EXAMINING *the* ISSUES

1 • Does shortening a war to save lives justify killing civilians?

2 • How are civilians sometimes as much a part of a war effort as soldiers?

3 • What percentage of lives saved would justify the deaths caused in the bombing?

As a class, discuss these questions. In your discussion, weigh the arguments for and against both choices.

As you read about World War II, think about the role that civilians play in a situation of total war. Think also about the hard moral choices that people often face in times of war.

820 Chapter 32

Follow Up

A feature on the chapter assessment will ask students to reevaluate their response to the situation presented on this page.

1 Hitler's Lightning War

TERMS & NAMES
- nonaggression pact
- blitzkrieg
- Charles de Gaulle
- Winston Churchill
- Battle of Britain
- Atlantic Charter

MAIN IDEA

Using the sudden, mass attack called the blitzkrieg, Germany overran much of Europe and North Africa.

WHY IT MATTERS NOW

Hitler's actions set off World War II. The results of the war still affect the politics and economics of today's world.

SETTING THE STAGE During the 1930s, Hitler played on the hopes and fears of the Western democracies. Each time the Nazi dictator grabbed new territory, he would declare an end to his demands. Peace seemed guaranteed—until Hitler started expanding again.

Germany Sparks a New War in Europe

After his moves into the Rhineland (March 1936), Austria (March 1938), and Czechoslovakia (September 1938 and March 1939), the Führer turned his eyes to Poland. On April 28, 1939, Hitler spoke before the Reichstag. He demanded that the Polish Corridor, along with its port city of Danzig, be returned to Germany. After World War I, the Allies had cut out the Polish Corridor from German territory to give Poland access to the sea.

This time, Great Britain and France decided to resist this threat of aggression. At this point, as was mentioned in Chapter 31, Soviet dictator Joseph Stalin signed a 10-year **nonaggression pact** with Hitler on August 23. After being excluded from the Munich Conference, Stalin was not eager to join with the West. Also, Hitler was promising him territory. In the public part of the pact, Germany and the Soviet Union promised not to attack each other. Secretly, however, they agreed that they would divide Poland between them. They also secretly agreed that the USSR could take over Finland and the Baltic countries (Lithuania, Latvia, and Estonia).

Background
Hitler hated communism, as Stalin despised fascism. Nonetheless, Hitler did not want to fight both the Allies *and* the Soviet Union. And Stalin wanted to keep his country out of a costly European war.

Germany's Lightning Attack on Poland The new nonaggression pact removed the threat to Germany of a Soviet attack from the east. Hitler then quickly moved ahead with plans to conquer Poland. His surprise attack took place at dawn on September 1, 1939. German warplanes invaded Polish airspace, raining bombs and terror on the Poles. At the same time, German tanks and troop trucks rumbled across the Polish border. The trucks carried more than 1.5 million soldiers into the assault. German aircraft and artillery then began a merciless bombing of Poland's capital, Warsaw. The city crumbled under the assault. A stunned world looked on. No one yet realized that the Polish invasion had unleashed World War II.

France and Great Britain declared war on Germany on September 3. But Poland fell three weeks before those nations could make any military response. After his victory, Hitler annexed the western half of Poland. That region had a large German population.

Ein Volk, ein Reich, ein Führer!

A propaganda poster proclaims to the German nation: "One People, One Reich, One Führer!"

SECTION 1 RESOURCES

PRINT RESOURCES

IN-DEPTH RESOURCES: UNIT 7
Guided Reading, p. 54
Primary Source: from *Berlin Diary*, p. 62
History Makers: Charles de Gaulle, p. 69; Winston Churchill, p. 70

ACCESS FOR STUDENTS ACQUIRING ENGLISH
Guided Reading (Spanish), p. 321

FORMAL ASSESSMENT
Section Quiz, p. 374

TECHNOLOGY RESOURCES

GEOGRAPHY TRANSPARENCIES
GT32 The Battle of Britain, 1940–1941

WORLD ART AND CULTURES TRANSPARENCIES
AT70 German and American Propaganda Posters

CD-ROM
Electronic Library of Primary Sources

INTERNET www.mlworldhistory.com

Section 1 Overview

OBJECTIVES

(1) To summarize events leading to all-out war in Europe.

(2) To describe the fall of France and the Battle of Britain.

(3) To explain the conflict in the Mediterranean and on the Eastern Front.

(4) To explain the importance of United States' aid to the Allies.

SKILLBUILDERS
- Interpreting maps: region, location, p. 822

CRITICAL THINKING
- Analyzing motives, p. 822
- Drawing conclusions, p. 824
- Making inferences, p. 826

FOCUS
5-Minute Warm-Up

▶ **Making Inferences**
To help students understand the nature of dictatorship, have them answer these questions.

1. Look at the German poster on page 821. What do *reich* and *fuhrer* mean?

2. Why do you suppose Hitler is shown looking stern?

WARM-UP TRANSPARENCY 32

OBJECTIVE ① INSTRUCT

Germany Sparks a New War in Europe

▶ **Key Ideas**
- Germany attacks Poland and Britain and France declare war.
- The Soviet Union invades Poland, the Baltic states, and Finland.
- Hitler invades and conquers Denmark and Norway.

IN-DEPTH RESOURCES: UNIT 7
Guided Reading, p. 54
Primary Source: from *Berlin Diary*, p. 62

ACCESS FOR STUDENTS ACQUIRING ENGLISH
Guided Reading (Spanish), p. 321

WORLD ART AND CULTURES TRANSPARENCIES
AT70 German and American Propaganda Posters

World War II: German Advances, 1939–1941

Interpreting the Map Point out to students that the Germans advanced on all fronts and in all directions in these years.

Extension Activity Have students identify one country in each direction of the map into which the Germans advanced. *North—Denmark, Norway, etc.; South—Austria, Yugoslavia, etc.; East—Poland, Soviet Union, etc.; West—Belgium, France, etc.*

SKILLBUILDER Answers

1. Austria, Yugoslavia, Bulgaria, Greece, Romania, Czechoslovakia, Hungary, Poland, Lithuania, Latvia, Estonia, Finland, Norway, Denmark, France, Belgium, the Netherlands.

2. It was centrally located and could strike out in all directions.

MORE ABOUT . . .
Blitzkrieg

The blitzkrieg strategy was developed by General Heinz Guderian, who presented his idea of lightning attacks as early as 1937. Guderian also introduced the idea of the panzer, or "armor," divisions—fast-moving, self-contained forces consisting of two regiments of tanks supported by one infantry and one artillery regiment.

MORE ABOUT . . .
The Maginot Line

Built in the 1930s, the Maginot Line extended along an 87-mile front in northeastern France. Fronted by tank traps, barbed wire, and guns encased in concrete walls ten feet thick, the line was a series of underground forts placed at three- to five-mile intervals. Troops lived underground on three-month tours, manning the observation posts and gun emplacements and enjoying such amenities as sun lamps. But the line was not built for mobile warfare and was useless against the swift, German forces.

World War II: German Advances, 1939–1941

Legend:
- Axis nations, 1938
- Axis-controlled, 1941
- Allies
- Neutral nations
- → German advances

GEOGRAPHY SKILLBUILDER:
Interpreting Maps

1. **Region** Which countries did Germany invade?
2. **Location** In what way was Germany's geographic location an advantage when it was on the offensive in the war?

The German invasion of Poland was the first test of Germany's newest military strategy—the **blitzkrieg** (BLIHTS·kreeg), or "lightning war." It involved using fast-moving airplanes and tanks, followed by massive infantry forces, to take the enemy by surprise. Then, blitzkrieg forces swiftly crushed all opposition with overwhelming force. In the case of Poland, the strategy worked.

The Soviets Make Their Move On September 17, after his secret agreement with Hitler, Stalin sent Soviet troops to occupy the eastern half of Poland. Stalin then began annexing the regions in the second part of the agreement. Lithuania, Latvia, and Estonia fell without a struggle, but Finland resisted.

In November 1939, Stalin sent nearly 1 million Soviet troops into Finland. He thought that his soldiers would win a quick victory. So, Stalin did not worry about the Finnish winter. This was a crucial mistake. The Finns were outnumbered and outgunned, but they fiercely defended their country. In the freezing weather, they attacked on swift skis. Meanwhile, the Soviets struggled through deep snow, crippled by frostbite. Despite their losses, the Soviet invaders finally won through sheer force of numbers. By March 1940, Stalin had forced the Finns to accept his surrender terms.

The Phony War For almost seven months after the fall of Poland, there was a strange calm in the land fighting in Europe. After their declaration of war, the French and British had mobilized their armies. They stationed their troops along the Maginot (MAZH·uh·NOH) Line, a system of fortifications along France's border with Germany. There they waited for Germans to attack—but nothing happened. With little to do, the bored Allied soldiers stared eastward toward the enemy. Equally bored, German soldiers stared back from their Siegfried Line a few miles away. Germans jokingly called it the *sitzkrieg*, or "sitting war." Some newspapers referred to it simply as "the phony war."

Suddenly, on April 9, 1940, the phony war ended. Hitler launched a surprise invasion of Denmark and Norway. He planned to build bases along the Norwegian and Danish coasts to strike at Great Britain. In just four hours after the attack, Denmark fell. Two months later, Norway surrendered as well.

The Battle for France and Great Britain

In May of 1940, Hitler began a dramatic sweep through Holland, Belgium, and Luxembourg. This was part of a strategy to strike at France. Keeping the Allies' attention on those countries, Hitler then sent an even larger force of tanks and troop trucks to slice through the Ardennes (ahr·DEHN). This was a heavily wooded area in northeastern France and Luxembourg. Moving through the forest, the

A. Analyzing Motives What would you say were the political reasons behind Stalin's actions in Europe at the beginning of World War II?

A. Possible Answer Stalin aimed at expanding the Soviet Union's territory and power, while keeping his country out of the war. He seemed ready to make an agreement with anybody, even Hitler, to achieve those goals.

CONNECTIONS ACROSS THE CURRICULUM

Government Germany annexed conquered nations as part of the Third Reich and governed through military commanders. Belgium, the Netherlands, Luxembourg, Norway, and Denmark were occupied by German troops. All the occupied territories were exploited for their material and human resources in order to supply the German war effort.

In France the situation was different. France was divided into two governments. German troops occupied the western coast line and the northern two-thirds of France, which was governed by the German military. The southern third of the nation was "unoccupied" France, headed by a puppet government. Under the leadership of the much admired and respected World War I hero, Marshal Henri Pétain, southern France

was relatively independent until 1942, when German troops took over the entire country.

Have students speculate on Germany's purpose in setting up two different governments in France. What would be the advantage to Germany in allowing southern France to be relatively free? How might the citizens of France have dealt with the occupation?

Germans "squeezed between" the Maginot Line. From there, they moved across France and reached France's northern coast in 10 days.

France Battles Back When the Germans reached the French coast, they swung north again and joined forces with German troops in Belgium. By May 26, 1940, the Germans had trapped the Allied forces around the northern French city of Lille (leel). With a German victory inevitable, Belgium surrendered. Outnumbered, outgunned, and pounded from the air, the Allies escaped to the beaches of Dunkirk, a French port city on the English Channel. They were trapped with their backs to the sea.

In one of the most heroic acts of the war, Great Britain set out to rescue the army. It sent a fleet of some 850 ships across the English Channel to Dunkirk. Along with Royal Navy ships, civilian craft—yachts, lifeboats, motorboats, paddle steamers, and fishing boats—joined the rescue effort. From May 26 to June 4, this amateur armada, under heavy fire from German bombers, sailed back and forth from Britain to Dunkirk. The boats carried an incredible 338,000 battle-weary soldiers to safety.

Hundreds of British soldiers crowd aboard ship during the mass evacuation at Dunkirk.

France Falls Following Dunkirk, France seemed doomed to defeat. On June 10, sensing a quick victory, Italy's Benito Mussolini joined forces with Hitler and declared war on both Great Britain and France. Italy then attacked France from the south. By June 14, Paris had fallen to the Germans. Nazi troops marched triumphantly down the city's main boulevard.

Two days later, seeing defeat approaching, the French parliament asked Marshal Henri Pétain (pay·TAN), an aging hero from World War I, to become prime minister. On June 22, 1940, France surrendered. The Germans took control of the northern part of the country. They left the southern part to a puppet government headed by Pétain. The headquarters of this government was in the city of Vichy (VEESH·ee).

After France fell, a French general named **Charles de Gaulle** (duh GOHL) fled to London. There, he set up a government-in-exile committed to reconquering France. On June 18, 1940, he delivered a broadcast from England. He called on the people of France to resist:

Background
Hitler demanded that the surrender take place in the same railroad car where the French had dictated terms to the Germans in World War I.

A VOICE FROM THE PAST
It is the bounden [obligatory] duty of all Frenchmen who still bear arms to continue the struggle. For them to lay down their arms, to evacuate any position of military importance, or agree to hand over any part of French territory, however small, to enemy control would be a crime against our country. . . .
GENERAL CHARLES DE GAULLE, quoted in *Charles de Gaulle: A Biography*

De Gaulle went on to organize the Free French military forces that battled the Nazis until France was liberated in 1944.

Germany Attacks Great Britain With the fall of France, Great Britain stood alone against the Nazis. **Winston Churchill,** the new British prime minister, had already declared that his nation would never give in. In a speech, he said, "We shall fight on the beaches, we shall fight on the landing grounds, we shall fight in the fields and in the streets . . . we shall never surrender."

World War II **823**

OBJECTIVE ② INSTRUCT

The Battle for France and Great Britain

(See page 822.)

▶ **Key Ideas**
- Sweeping around the Maginot Line, German forces strike into France, pushing Allied troops to the sea.
- Italy enters the war on the German side as France collapses and surrenders.
- Despite devastating German air raids, Britain fights on alone. Its resistance forces Hitler to call off the attacks.

MORE ABOUT . . .
Charles de Gaulle

As a young army officer in the 1930s, Charles de Gaulle had foreseen that future warfare would depend on highly mobile, armored forces, but his proposals that France modernize its army were ignored. When France fell, de Gaulle proclaimed himself leader of the Free French and persistently appealed to his countrymen to liberate France. At 6 feet 4 inches, de Gaulle was an imposing figure, and his manner was aggressive and often arrogant. "I am France," he once declared. De Gaulle's arrogance often put him at odds with Allied leaders. But he prevailed and, when France was liberated, his resistance movement was recognized as the legitimate government of France.

IN-DEPTH RESOURCES: UNIT 7
History Makers: Charles de Gaulle, p. 69

TEACHING OPTION | **BLOCK SCHEDULING** | COOPERATIVE ACTIVITY: Researching War Technology | **CLASS TIME 30 MINUTES**

Task: Student groups will research the technologies developed during World War II and present reports to the class.

Purpose: To learn more about how new technologies affected the course of the war.

Activity: Student groups will divide into four groups each to research one of the following technologies: radar, jet propulsion, decoding devices, rockets. Groups should trace the development of

these technologies, how they were used, and their effectiveness. Student reports should focus on the impact of the technologies on the course of the war for both the Allied and Axis powers. Students groups will present their reports to the class for discussion and evaluation of the impact of the technologies.

 Building a Portfolio If the report is among their best work, students should add it to their portfolio.

ALTERNATIVE ASSESSMENT BOOK
Standards for Evaluating a Cooperative Activity

Standards for Evaluation
Reports should . . .

- convey how technologies affected the war
- compare the impact of these technologies on Axis and Allied powers
- show evidence of thorough research
Teacher's Edition **823**

HISTORYMAKERS

Winston Churchill
1874–1965

Probably the greatest weapon the British had as they stood alone against Hitler's Germany was the nation's prime minister—Winston Churchill. "Big Winnie," Londoners boasted, "was the lad for us. . . ."

Although as a youngster Churchill had a speech defect, he grew to become one of the greatest orators of all time. He used all his gifts as a speaker to rally the people behind the effort to crush Germany. He declared that Britain would

. . . wage war, by sea, land, and air, with all our might and with all the strength that God can give us . . . against monstrous tyranny.

Hitler now turned his mind to an invasion of Great Britain. His plan—*Operation Sea Lion*—was first to knock out the Royal Air Force (RAF) and then to land 250,000 soldiers on England's shores. In the summer of 1940, the Luftwaffe (LOOFT·vahf·uh), Germany's air force, began bombing Great Britain. Badly outnumbered, the RAF had 2,900 planes to the Luftwaffe's 4,500. At first, the Germans targeted British airfields and aircraft factories. Then, on September 7, 1940, they began focusing on the cities, especially London—to break British morale. Bombs exploded daily in city streets. They killed civilians and set buildings ablaze. However, despite the destruction and loss of life, the British fought on.

With the pressure off the airfields, the RAF hit back hard. Two secret weapons helped turn the tide in their favor. One was an electronic tracking system known as radar. Developed in the late 1930s, radar could tell the number, speed, and direction of incoming warplanes. The other was a German code-making machine named Enigma. A complete Enigma machine was smuggled to Great Britain in 1938. With Enigma in their possession, the British had German secret messages open to them. With information gathered by these devices, RAF fliers could quickly get to their airplanes and inflict deadly harm on the enemy.

To avoid the RAF's attacks, the Germans gave up daylight raids in October 1940 in favor of night bombing. At sunset, the wail of sirens filled the air as Londoners flocked to the subways. There they spent the night in air-raid shelters. Some rode out the blasts at home in basements or in smaller air-raid shelters.

The **Battle of Britain** continued until May 10, 1941. Stunned by British resistance, Hitler decided to call off his attacks. Instead, he focused his attention on Eastern Europe and the Mediterranean. The Battle of Britain had ended. And, from it, the Allies had learned a crucial lesson: Hitler's advances could be blocked.

The Eastern Front and the Mediterranean

The stubborn resistance of the British in the Battle of Britain caused a shift in Hitler's strategy in Europe. Although the resistance surprised Hitler, it did not defeat him. He would deal with Great Britain later. Instead, he turned his attention east to the Balkans and the Mediterranean area—and to the ultimate prize, the Soviet Union.

Germany and Italy Attack North Africa Germany's first objective in the Mediterranean region was North Africa—mainly because of Hitler's partner Mussolini. Despite Italy's alliance with Germany, the country had remained neutral at the beginning of the war. With Hitler's conquest of France, however, Mussolini knew he had to take action. Otherwise, Italy would not share in Germany's victories. "I need a few thousand dead," he told a member of his staff. After declaring war on France and Great Britain, Italy became Germany's most important Axis ally. Then, Mussolini moved into France along with the Nazis.

Mussolini took his next step in September 1940. While the Battle of Britain was raging, he ordered Italy's North African army to move east from Libya. His goal was to seize British-controlled Egypt. Egypt's Suez Canal was key to reaching the oil fields of the Middle East. Within a week, Italian troops had pushed 60 miles inside Egypt, forcing British units back. Then both sides dug in and waited.

Great Britain Strikes Back Finally, in December, the British decided to strike back. The result was a disaster for the Italians. By February 1941, the British had swept 500 miles across North Africa. They had taken 130,000 Italian prisoners.

824 Chapter 32

Hitler had to step in to save his Axis partner. In February 1941, he sent General Erwin Rommel, later known as the "Desert Fox," to Libya. His mission was to command a newly formed tank corps, the Afrika Korps. Determined to take control of Egypt and the Suez Canal, Rommel attacked the British at Agheila (uh·GAY·luh) on March 24. Caught by surprise, British forces retreated 500 miles east to Tobruk.

However, by mid-January 1942, after fierce fighting for Tobruk, the British drove Rommel back to where he had started. By June, the tide of battle turned again. Rommel regrouped, pushed the British back across the desert, and seized Tobruk. This was a shattering loss for the Allies. Rommel later wrote, "To every man of us, Tobruk was a symbol of British resistance, and we were now going to finish with it for good."

The War in the Balkans While Rommel campaigned in North Africa, Hitler was active in the Balkans. As early as the summer of 1940, Hitler had begun planning to attack his ally, the USSR, by the following spring. The Balkan countries of southeastern Europe were key to Hitler's invasion plan. Hitler wanted to build bases in southeastern Europe for the attack on the Soviet Union. He also wanted to make sure that the British did not interfere.

To prepare for his invasion, Hitler moved to expand his influence in the Balkans. In the face of overwhelming German strength, Bulgaria, Romania, and Hungary cooperated by joining the Axis powers in early 1941. Yugoslavia and Greece, which had pro-British governments, resisted. On Sunday, April 6, 1941, Hitler invaded both countries. Yugoslavia fell in 11 days. Greece surrendered in 17. In Athens, the Nazis celebrated their victory by raising swastikas on the Acropolis.

Hitler Invades the Soviet Union With the Balkans firmly in control, Hitler could move ahead with his plan to invade the Soviet Union. He called that plan *Operation Barbarossa.* Early on Sunday morning, June 22, 1941, the roar of German tanks and aircraft announced the beginning of the blitzkrieg invasion. The Soviet Union was not prepared for this attack. With its 5 million men, the Red Army was the largest in the world. But it was neither well equipped nor well trained.

The invasion rolled on week after week until the Germans had pushed 500 miles inside the Soviet Union. As the Russians retreated, they burned and destroyed everything in the enemy's path. Russians had used this same strategy against Napoleon.

By September 8, Germans had surrounded Leningrad and isolated the city from the rest of the world. If necessary, Hitler would starve the city's 2.5 million inhabitants. German bombs destroyed warehouses where food was stored. Desperately hungry, people began eating cattle and horse feed, as well as cats and dogs and, finally, crows and rats. More than 1 million people died in Leningrad that terrible winter. Yet the city refused to fall.

Seeing that Leningrad would not surrender, Hitler looked to Moscow, the capital and heart of the Soviet Union. A Nazi drive on the capital began on October 2, 1941.

A Soviet photo taken in 1942 shows the horrors of the war in the Soviet Union. Civilians in the Crimea search over a barren field for their dead loved ones.

825

The United States Aids Its Allies

▶ **Key Ideas**

• The United States gives aid to Britain through the Lend-Lease Act of 1941.

• Roosevelt and Churchill issue the Atlantic Charter declaring free trade among nations and the right of people to choose their own governments.

• The United States draws closer to war when a German submarine attacks a U.S. destroyer.

ASSESS & RETEACH

Section 1 Assessment

Suggest students work in pairs to answer the questions and then exchange answers and compare their responses.

Section Quiz

 FORMAL ASSESSMENT
Section Quiz, p. 374

Reteaching Activity
CLASS TIME: 15 MINUTES

Use the Guided Reading Worksheet for Section 1 to review the key ideas in this section.

 IN-DEPTH RESOURCES: UNIT 7
Guided Reading, p. 54

CLOSE ACTIVITY

CLASS TIME: 10 MINUTES

Arranging Events in Sequential Order

To help students understand the connection between events at the beginning of World War II, have them work in small groups to create a time line of major events from 1939 through 1941. Groups might exchange time lines to compare and comment and add events if necessary.

By December, the Germans had advanced to the outskirts of Moscow. Soviet General Georgi Zhukov (ZHOO·kuhf) counterattacked. He had 100 fresh Siberian divisions and the harsh Soviet winter on his side.

As temperatures fell, the Germans, in summer uniforms, retreated. Their fuel and oil froze. Tanks, trucks, and weapons became useless. Ignoring Napoleon's winter defeat 130 years before, the Führer sent his generals a stunning order: "No retreat!" German troops dug in about 125 miles west of the capital. They held the line against the Soviets until March 1943. Nonetheless, Moscow had been saved and had cost the Germans 500,000 lives.

The United States Aids Its Allies

As disturbing as these events were to Americans, bitter memories of World War I convinced most people in the United States that their country should not get involved. Between 1935 and 1937, Congress passed a series of Neutrality Acts. The laws made it illegal to sell arms or lend money to nations at war. But President Roosevelt knew that if the Allies fell, the United States would be drawn into the war. In September 1939, he persuaded Congress to allow the Allies to buy American arms. According to his plan, they would pay cash and then carry the goods on their own ships.

U.S. industry achieved amazing rates of speed when it began to produce for the war effort. This ship, for example, was produced in a U.S. shipyard in only 10 days.

Under the Lend-Lease Act, passed in March 1941, the president could lend or lease arms and other supplies to any country vital to the United States. By the summer of 1941, the U.S. Navy was escorting British ships carrying U.S. arms. In response, Hitler ordered his submarines to sink any cargo ships they met.

Although the United States had not yet entered the war, Roosevelt and Churchill met secretly on a battleship off Newfoundland on August 9. The two leaders issued a joint declaration called the **Atlantic Charter.** It upheld free trade among nations and the right of people to choose their own government. The charter later served as the Allies' peace plan at the end of World War II.

On September 4, a German U-boat suddenly fired on a U.S. destroyer in the Atlantic. Roosevelt ordered navy commanders to respond. They were to shoot German submarines on sight. The United States was now involved in an undeclared naval war with Hitler. To almost everyone's surprise, however, the attack that actually drew the United States into the war did not come from Germany. It came from Japan.

THINK THROUGH HISTORY
C. Making Inferences What does the fact that German armies were not prepared for the Russian winter indicate about Hitler's expectations for the campaign in the Soviet Union?
C. Possible Answer Hitler expected a quick victory in the Soviet Union and did not think that his fighting men would still be in combat by winter.

Background
Newfoundland is a province of Canada.

Section **1** Assessment

1. TERMS & NAMES

Identify
• nonaggression pact
• blitzkrieg
• Charles de Gaulle
• Winston Churchill
• Battle of Britain
• Atlantic Charter

2. TAKING NOTES

Create a chart like the one below. Identify the effects of each of these early events of World War II.

Cause	Effect
First blitzkrieg	
Allies stranded at Dunkirk	
British radar detects German aircraft	
Lend-Lease Act	

3. MAKING INFERENCES

Great Britain and the Soviet city of Leningrad each fought off a German invasion. Other countries gave in to the Germans without much resistance. What factors do you think a country's leaders consider when deciding whether to surrender or to fight?

THINK ABOUT
• the country's ability to fight
• the costs of resisting
• the costs of surrendering

4. THEME ACTIVITY

Economics In groups of 3 or 4, prepare a dramatic scene for a play or film that focuses on an economic problem that might have been suffered by Europeans during World War II.

ANSWERS

1. TERMS & NAMES
nonaggression pact, p. 821
blitzkrieg, p. 822
Charles de Gaulle, p. 823
Winston Churchill, p. 823
Battle of Britain, p. 824
Atlantic Charter, p. 826

2. TAKING NOTES
Possible Answers: Blitzkrieg: the fall of Poland; Dunkirk: 338,000 soldiers saved, British forces leave Western Europe; Radar: the British able to hold off German occupation; Lend-Lease Act: U.S. supplied Allies with war goods, U.S. decision to favor the Allies.

3. MAKING INFERENCES
Possible Answers: Ability to Fight: army large enough to fight the enemy, sufficient weapons; Costs of Resisting: Major civilian and military deaths, destruction of property, economic chaos; Costs of Surrendering: Enemy control of the government, repression of the population.

4. THEME ACTIVITY
Standards for Evaluation
An effective scene should . . .
• give a sense of time and place
• focus on a war-related economic problem
• convey the human dimension of the economic problem
• show evidence of teamwork

Japan Strikes in the Pacific

TERMS & NAMES
- Isoroku Yamamoto
- Pearl Harbor
- Battle of Midway
- Douglas MacArthur
- Battle of Guadalcanal

MAIN IDEA

Carving out an empire, Japan attacked Pearl Harbor in Hawaii and brought the United States into World War II.

WHY IT MATTERS NOW

World War II established the role of the United States as a leading player in international affairs.

SETTING THE STAGE Like Hitler, Japan's military leaders also had dreams of empire. Japan was overcrowded and faced shortages of raw materials. To solve these problems—and to encourage nationalism—the Japanese began a program of empire building that would lead to war.

Japan Seeks a Pacific Empire

Japan's expansion began in 1931. In that year, Japanese troops took over Manchuria in northeastern China. Six years later, Japanese armies swept into the heartland of China. They expected quick victory. Chinese resistance, however, caused the war to drag on. This caused a strain on Japan's economy. To increase their resources, Japanese leaders looked toward the rich European colonies of Southeast Asia.

The Surprise Attack on Pearl Harbor By August 1940, Americans had cracked a Japanese secret code. They were well aware of Japanese plans for Southeast Asia. If Japan conquered European colonies there, it could also threaten the American-controlled Philippine Islands and Guam. To stop the Japanese advance, the U.S. government sent aid to strengthen Chinese resistance. And when the Japanese overran French Indochina in July 1941, Roosevelt cut off oil shipments to Japan.

Background
French Indochina was an area now made up by Vietnam, Cambodia, and Laos.

Despite an oil shortage, the Japanese continued their conquests. They hoped to catch the United States by surprise. So they planned massive attacks in Southeast Asia and in the Pacific—both at the same time. Japan's greatest naval strategist, Admiral **Isoroku Yamamoto** (ih·soh·ROO·koo YAH·muh·MOH·toh), also argued that the U.S. fleet in Hawaii was "a dagger pointed at our throat" and must be destroyed.

Early in the morning of December 7, 1941, American sailors at **Pearl Harbor** in Hawaii awoke to the roar of explosives. A Japanese attack was underway! The United States had known from a coded Japanese message that an attack might come. But they did not know when or where it would occur. Within two hours, the Japanese had sunk or damaged 18 ships, including 8 battleships—nearly the whole U.S. Pacific fleet. Some 2,400 Americans were killed—with more than 1,000 wounded. News of the attack stunned the American people. The next day, Congress declared war on Japan. In his speech to Congress, President Roosevelt described December 7 as "a date which will live in infamy."

The *U.S.S. West Virginia* in flames after taking a direct hit during the Japanese attack on Pearl Harbor.

World War II **827**

Section 2 Overview

OBJECTIVES

1. To explain how Japanese expansionism led to war with the Allies in Asia.

2. To explain the importance of the Allies' strategy in turning the tide of war against Japan.

SKILLBUILDER
- Interpreting maps: movement, p. 828

CRITICAL THINKING
- Analyzing motives, p. 829
- Identifying problems, p. 830
- Analyzing causes, p. 830
- Evaluating decisions, p. 830
- Analyzing themes, p. 830

FOCUS
5-Minute Warm-Up

▶ *Clarifying*
To help students understand the suffering of soldiers, have them answer these questions.

1. Look at A Voice from the Past on page 830. What were some of the horrors faced by soldiers on Guadalcanal?

2. Why might soldiers have described it as "hell"?

WARM-UP TRANSPARENCY 32

OBJECTIVE ① INSTRUCT

Japan Seeks a Pacific Empire

▶ *Key Ideas*
- Japan attacks the U.S. fleet at Pearl Harbor, and the United States declares war.
- Victories in the Pacific and Asia give Japan a vast empire.

IN-DEPTH RESOURCES: UNIT 7
Guided Reading, p. 55
Geography Application: The Fall of Singapore, p. 60

ELECTRONIC LIBRARY OF PRIMARY SOURCES
from "Japanese Attack Sinks HMS *Repulse*"

ACCESS FOR STUDENTS ACQUIRING ENGLISH
Guided Reading (Spanish), p. 322

SECTION 2 RESOURCES

PRINT RESOURCES

IN-DEPTH RESOURCES: UNIT 7
Guided Reading, p. 55
Geography Application: The Fall of Singapore, p. 60.

ACCESS FOR STUDENTS ACQUIRING ENGLISH
Guided Reading (Spanish), p. 322
Geography Application (Spanish), p. 327

FORMAL ASSESSMENT
Section Quiz, p. 375

ALTERNATIVE ASSESSMENT BOOK

TECHNOLOGY RESOURCES

CD-ROM
Electronic Library of Primary Sources

INTERNET www.mlworldhistory.com

Corregidor

Known as The Rock, the island fortress of Corregidor in Manila Bay was the last U.S. position in the Philippines to surrender. For a month after the fall of Bataan, 13,000 American and Filipino troops held out in a concrete cave called Malinta Tunnel. Bombarded night and day by Japanese guns and suffering from hunger and exhaustion, the defenders finally surrendered on May 6 when Japanese troops swarmed over the rock. The last message sent from Corrigidor said: "Everyone is bawling like a baby. They are piling dead and wounded in our tunnel. The jig is up." The commander, General Jonathan Wainwright, and the survivors joined the Bataan Death March.

History from Visuals

World War II in Asia and the Pacific, 1941-1945

Interpreting the Map Have students note the location of the battle sites on the map and their relation to Japan. Ask what the Allied strategy was in the Pacific. *Possible response: the Allies would take islands close to Japan until they reached the Japanese mainland.*

Extension Activity Using information on the map, have students summarize the Allied advance toward Japan following Pearl Harbor.

SKILLBUILDER Answers
1. Kiska in August 1943.
2. East and south.

The Tide of Japanese Victories The Japanese had planned a series of strikes at the United States in the Pacific. After the bombing at Pearl Harbor, the Japanese seized Guam and Wake Island in the western Pacific. They then launched an attack on the Philippines. In January 1942, the Japanese marched into the Philippine capital of Manila. They overwhelmed American and Filipino defenders on the Bataan Peninsula (buh·TAN) in April—and in May, on the island of Corregidor.

The Japanese also hit the British, seizing Hong Kong and invading Malaya. By February 1942, the Japanese had reached Singapore. After a fierce pounding, the colony surrendered. By March, the Japanese had conquered the resource-rich Dutch East Indies (now Indonesia), including the islands of Java, Sumatra, Borneo, and Celebes (SEHL·uh·BEEZ). After Malaya, the Japanese took Burma, between China and India. China received supplies by way of the Burma Road. The Japanese could now close off the road. Now they might force the Chinese to surrender.

By the time Burma fell, Japan had conquered more than 1 million square miles of land with about 150 million people. Before these conquests, the Japanese had tried to win the support of Asians with the anticolonialist idea of "Asia for the Asians." After victory, however, the Japanese quickly made it clear that they had come as conquerors.

Native peoples often received the same brutal treatment as the 150,000 prisoners of war. On what is called the Bataan Death March, the Japanese subjected prisoners to terrible cruelties. One American soldier reported:

A VOICE FROM THE PAST
I was questioned by a Japanese officer who found out that I had been in a Philippine Scout Battalion. The [Japanese] hated the Scouts. . . . Anyway, they took me outside and I was forced to watch as they buried six of my Scouts alive. They made the men dig their own graves, and then had them kneel down in a pit. The guards hit them over the head with shovels to stun them and piled earth on top.
LIEUTENANT JOHN SPAINHOWER, quoted in *War Diary 1939–1945*

Background
According to the centuries-old warrior code called *Bushido*, a Japanese soldier must commit suicide, or hari-kari, rather than surrender. So Japanese soldiers had contempt for Allied prisoners of war.

World War II in Asia and the Pacific, 1941–1945

GEOGRAPHY SKILLBUILDER: Interpreting Maps
1. **Location** *Which battle was fought in the most northern region?*
2. **Movement** *From what two general directions did Allied forces move in on Japan?*

828

CONNECTIONS ACROSS TIME AND PLACE

Remembering Pearl Harbor The bombing of Pearl Harbor rallied Americans around the cry, "Remember Pearl Harbor!" There was even a popular song that made use of the phrase.

Some three-quarters of the United States' military planes were destroyed at Pearl Harbor and 18 warships were sunk or damaged. However, within weeks many of the ships, with the exception of the *Arizona, Utah,* and *Oklahoma,* were repaired and at sea. But not all of the U.S. fleet was at Pearl Harbor. Most importantly, three aircraft carriers escaped the Japanese surprise attack.

During the remainder of the the war in the Pacific, U.S. naval forces sank all of the Japanese ships involved in the attack on Pearl Harbor. In August 1945, an atomic bomb leveled the city of Nagasaki, which manufactured special torpedoes. And the battleship *West Virginia* was among those gathered in Tokyo Bay when the Japanese signed the surrender on September 2, 1945. Have students do some research on American and Japanese battle fleets, including numbers of ships, kinds of ships, battle tactics, and so forth, and present their findings to the class.

The Allies Strike Back

After a string of victories, the Japanese seemed unbeatable. Nonetheless, the Allies—mainly Americans and Australians—were anxious to strike back in the Pacific. In April 1942, the United States wanted revenge for Pearl Harbor. So the United States sent 16 B-25 bombers under the command of Lieutenant Colonel James H. Doolittle to bomb Tokyo and other major Japanese cities. The bombs did little damage. The attack, however, made an important psychological point: the Japanese could be attacked.

The Allies Turn the Tide of War Doolittle's raid on Japan raised American morale and shook the confidence of some Japanese. As one Japanese citizen described it, "We started to doubt that we were invincible." In addition, Japan had won a vast empire that was becoming difficult to defend and control.

Slowly, the Allies began to turn the tide of war. Early in May 1942, an American fleet with Australian support intercepted a Japanese strike force. The force had been about to attack Port Moresby. The city housed a critical Allied air base in southeastern New Guinea (GIHN·ee). From this base, the Japanese could have easily invaded Australia.

In the battle that followed—the Battle of the Coral Sea—both fleets fought using a new kind of naval warfare. The opposing ships did not fire a single shot. In fact, they often could not see one other. Instead, airplanes taking off from huge aircraft carriers did all the fighting. In the end, the battle was something of a draw. The Allies lost more ships than the Japanese, who claimed victory. But the Allies had stopped Japan's southward expansion for the first time.

The Battle of Midway Japan next targeted Midway Island, west of Hawaii. The island was home to a key American airfield. However, by June 1942, yet another Japanese code had been broken. As a result, the new commander in chief of the U.S. Pacific Fleet, Admiral Chester Nimitz, knew that a force of over 150 ships was heading toward Midway. The Japanese fleet was the largest naval force ever assembled. It could also boast the world's largest battleship, carrying Admiral Yamamoto himself. Yamamoto hoped not only to seize Midway but also to finish off the U.S. Pacific fleet. He hoped the American force would come from Pearl Harbor to defend the island.

Nimitz was outnumbered four to one in ships and planes. Even so, he was preparing an ambush for the Japanese at Midway. On June 4, with American forces hidden beyond the horizon, Nimitz allowed the enemy to launch the first strike. As Japanese planes roared over Midway Island, American carrier planes swooped in to attack Japanese ships. Many Japanese planes were still on the decks of the ships. The strategy was a success. American pilots destroyed 332 Japanese planes, all four aircraft carriers, and one support ship. Yamamoto ordered his crippled fleet to withdraw. By June 6, 1942, the battle was over. One Japanese official commented, "The Americans had avenged Pearl Harbor." The **Battle of Midway** had also turned the tide of war in the Pacific against the Japanese.

The Allies Go on the Offensive With morale high after their Midway victory, the Allies took the offensive. The Pacific war was one of vast distances. Japanese troops had dug in on hundreds of islands across the ocean. General **Douglas MacArthur** was

World War II **829**

Vocabulary
invincible: unconquerable.

A. Possible Answers Midway Island had an important U.S. air base, so defending the island would be vital to the Americans. Midway was located just west of Hawaii, so the Americans would probably do as much as they could to keep the Japanese away from this important American territory.

THINK THROUGH HISTORY
A. Analyzing Motives What reasons might Admiral Yamamoto have had for thinking the Americans would send their entire Pacific fleet to defend Midway Island?

As happened in other battles of the Pacific war, U.S. Marines destroy a cave connected to a Japanese fort on the island of Iwo Jima.

OBJECTIVE ② INSTRUCT

The Allies Strike Back

▶ *Key Ideas*
• Allied bombing of Tokyo shows the Japanese are vulnerable.
• The Allies win significant naval battles by striking with planes from aircraft carriers.
• The Allied strategy of island hopping brings them closer to Japan.

CRITICAL THINKING ACTIVITY
CLASS TIME: 15 MINUTES

Analyzing Effects
Using two subheads on this page, have students analyze the impact of the Allies' strategy in the Pacific on the course of the war by making a chart like this listing Allied actions and their results.

	Actions	Results
Turning the Tide of War		
Going on the Offensive		

MORE ABOUT . . .
Admiral Yamamoto

Although Yamamoto argued for a surprise strike at Pearl Harbor, he had few illusions about the final outcome of the war. In a brief period of study at Harvard and as a naval attaché in Washington, D.C., for two years, Yamamoto was aware of the industrial potential of the United States. In 1940, he advised that Japan could not beat the United States and should not fight it. When the war opened, Yamamoto predicted the future: "In the first six to twelve months of a war with the United States and Britain, I will run wild and win victory after victory. After that, I have no expectation of success."

TEACHING OPTION | **BLOCK SCHEDULING** | **COOPERATIVE ACTIVITY: Charting a Battle Strategy** | **CLASS TIME 30 MINUTES**

Task: Student groups will chart the Allied battle strategy in the Pacific.

Purpose: To explain how the Allied battle strategy in the Pacific turned the tide of war against Japan.

Activity: Student groups will each review a major battle in the Allied offensive against Japan. In their description of the battle, they will identify the opposing forces, the tactics of the battle, and the outcome. They will present their work in a chart of

the battle. Groups should then combine their separate battle charts into a class chart and discuss the overall Allied strategy, explaining how it turned the tide of war against Japan.

📁 *Building a Portfolio* If the chart is among their best work, students should add it to their portfolio.

📓 **ALTERNATIVE ASSESSMENT BOOK**
Standards for Evaluating a Cooperative Activity

Standards for Evaluation
Charts should . . .

• clearly describe the Allied battle strategy
• explain how Japan was defeated
• be visually interesting

Teacher's Edition 829

commander of the Allied land forces in the Pacific. He believed that storming each island would be a long, costly effort. Instead, he wanted to "island-hop" past Japanese strongpoints. He would then seize islands that were not well defended but were closer to Japan. After taking the islands, MacArthur would use air power to cut supply lines and starve enemy troops. "Hit 'em where they ain't, let 'em die on the vine," MacArthur declared.

MacArthur's first target soon presented itself. The U.S. government had learned that the Japanese were building a huge air base on the island of Guadalcanal in the Solomon Islands. The Allies had to strike fast before the base was completed and became another Japanese strongpoint. At dawn on August 7, 1942, about 19,000 U.S. Marines, with Australian support, landed on Guadalcanal and a few nearby islands. Caught unprepared, the Japanese at Guadalcanal radioed, "Enemy forces overwhelming. We will defend our posts to the death."

The marines had easily taken the Japanese airfield. But the battle for control of the island turned into a savage struggle as both sides poured in fresh troops. In February 1943, after six months of fighting on land and at sea, the **Battle of Guadalcanal** finally ended. After losing 23,000 men out of 36,000, the Japanese abandoned the island they came to call "the Island of Death."

To war correspondent Ralph Martin and the soldiers who fought there, Guadalcanal was simply "hell":

HISTORY MAKERS

Douglas MacArthur
1880–1964
Son of a Civil War army officer, Douglas MacArthur said that his first memory was the "sound of bugles." MacArthur yearned, even at an early age, for a life of action and adventure. With a strong will and his mother's encouragement, he grew to become one of the most brilliant military strategists of World War II.

MacArthur believed that destiny had called him to perform great deeds. He once boasted, "All Germany cannot fabricate the shell that will kill me." The general had his critics, but he also inspired deep loyalty among his men. One remarked, "His first thought was always for the soldier."

A VOICE FROM THE PAST
Hell was furry red spiders as big as your fist, giant lizards as long as your leg, leeches falling from trees to suck blood, armies of white ants with bites of fire, scurrying scorpions inflaming any flesh they touched, enormous rats and bats everywhere, and rivers with waiting crocodiles. Hell was the sour, foul smell of the squishy jungle, humidity that rotted a body within hours. . . . Hell was an enemy . . . so fanatic that it used its own dead as booby traps.

RALPH G. MARTIN, quoted in *The GI War*

As Japan worked to establish a new order in Southeast Asia and the Pacific, the Nazis moved ahead with Hitler's plan for a new order in Europe. Hitler's goal was not only the conquest of Europe. He also aimed at enslaving Europe's people and forcing them to work for Germany's prosperity. In particular, the Führer had plans for dealing with those he considered unfit for the Third Reich. You will learn about Hitler's plans in Section 3.

Section 2 Assessment

1. TERMS & NAMES
Identify
- Isoroku Yamamoto
- Pearl Harbor
- Battle of Midway
- Douglas MacArthur
- Battle of Guadalcanal

2. TAKING NOTES
Create a chart like the one below. List four major events of the war in the Pacific between 1941 and 1943.

Event 1:
Event 2:
Event 3:
Event 4:

Which event was most important in turning the tide of the war in the Pacific against the Japanese? Why?

3. EVALUATING DECISIONS
Judging from the effects of the attack on Pearl Harbor, do you think Yamamoto made a wise decision in bombing Pearl Harbor? Why or why not?

THINK ABOUT
- Yamamoto's goals in the bombing
- U.S. involvement in World War II
- the effects of the bombing

4. ANALYZING THEMES
Empire Building What do you think Yamamoto's biggest problems were in building the Japanese empire in the Pacific?

THINK ABOUT
- geographical problems
- European/American interests in the Pacific
- psychological factors

ANSWERS

1. TERMS & NAMES
Isoroku Yamamoto, p. 827
Pearl Harbor, p. 827
Battle of Midway, p. 829
Douglas MacArthur, p. 829
Battle of Guadalcanal, p. 830

2. TAKING NOTES
Possible Answers: Japan bombs Pearl Harbor; United States bombs Tokyo; Battle of Midway; Battle of Guadalcanal.

3. EVALUATING DECISIONS
Wise: If the Japanese did not destroy the U.S. Pacific fleet, it would have been used against them. Unwise: If the Japanese did not bomb Pearl Harbor, the

United States may never have entered the war.

4. ANALYZING THEMES
Possible Answers: Geography: the Pacific region is so huge that it would be difficult to build an empire. European/American Interests: The United States and certain European countries had

military posts in the Pacific. Psychological Factors: After the bombing of Tokyo, Yamamoto had to deal with shaken Japanese confidence.

TERMS & NAMES
- Aryans
- Holocaust
- *Kristallnacht*
- ghettos
- "Final Solution"
- genocide

MAIN IDEA

During the Holocaust, Hitler's Nazis killed 6 million Jews and 5 million other "non-Aryans."

WHY IT MATTERS NOW

The violence against Jews during the Holocaust led to the founding of Israel after World War II.

SETTING THE STAGE As part of their new order for Europe, Nazis proclaimed that **Aryans,** or Germanic peoples, were a "master race." They claimed that Jews and other non-Aryan peoples were inferior. This racist message would eventually lead to the **Holocaust**—the mass slaughter of civilians, especially Jews.

The Holocaust Begins

Nazi propaganda started as an ugly campaign of anti-Semitism. It eventually flared into persecution across Germany. Hitler knowingly tapped into a hatred for Jews that had deep roots in European history. For generations, many Germans, along with other Europeans, had targeted Jews as the cause of their failures. The Nazis even blamed Jews for Germany's defeat in World War I and for its economic problems after that war.

In 1933, the Nazis made persecution a government policy. They first passed laws forbidding Jews to hold public office. Then, in 1935, the Nuremberg Laws deprived Jews of their rights to German citizenship, jobs, and property. To make it easier for the Nazis to identify them, Jews had to wear a bright yellow star attached to their clothing.

THINK THROUGH HISTORY
A. Analyzing Motives Why might the people of a country want to blame a minority group for most of its problems?
A. Possible Answers A minority group may be different culturally, and some people are afraid of differences; targeting a minority for blame takes responsibility away from a country and its leaders, so the majority can feel better about itself.

***Kristallnacht:* "Night of Broken Glass"**
Worse was yet to come. Early in November 1938, 17-year-old Herschel Grynszpan (GRIHN·shpahn), a Jewish youth from Germany, was visiting an uncle in Paris. While Grynszpan was there, he received a postcard. It said that after living in Germany for 27 years, his father had been deported to his native Poland. On November 7, wishing to avenge his father's deportation, Grynszpan shot an employee of the German Embassy in Paris.

When Nazi leaders heard the news, they launched a violent attack on the Jewish community. On November 9, Nazi storm troopers attacked Jewish homes, businesses, and synagogues across Germany and murdered around 100 Jews. An American in Leipzig wrote, "Jewish shop windows by the hundreds were systematically . . . smashed. . . . The main streets of the city were a positive litter of shattered plate glass." It is for this reason that the night of November 9 became known as *Kristallnacht* (krih·STAHL·NAHKT), or "Night of Broken Glass."

Hitler's special troops helped spread the message of the government's anti-Semitic policy. The sign these troops are putting up reads, "Germans! Protect yourselves! Don't buy in Jewish stores!"

World War II **831**

Creating a Summary

Have students use a chart like the one below to summarize the steps the Nazis took against Jews that resulted in the "Final Solution."

```
┌─────────────────────┐
│   Nuremberg Laws    │
└─────────────────────┘
          ▼
┌─────────────────────┐
│                     │
└─────────────────────┘
          ▼
┌─────────────────────┐
│                     │
└─────────────────────┘
          ▼
┌─────────────────────┐
│                     │
└─────────────────────┘
          ▼
┌─────────────────────┐
│                     │
└─────────────────────┘
          ▼
┌─────────────────────┐
│   Final Solution    │
└─────────────────────┘
```

MORE ABOUT . . .
Refugees

France's Vichy government appeared to be indifferent to the fate of Jewish refugees, most of whom the Nazis had forcibly moved to unoccupied France and whom the French detained. One writer reported that when Marshal Henri Pétain was questioned about persecuting Jews, he replied ". . . as for free-masons, I hate them, as for communists I am afraid of them, as for the Jews it is not my fault." The majority of Jewish refugees in Vichy France were housed in camps of window-less barracks surrounded by barbed wire. When in 1941, foreign reporters were allowed to visit some of the camps, one reporter wrote: ". . . these people have been detained for reasons they, in many instances, do not understand and . . . they are without the slightest information about what is to be their future . . . ."

Most of the refugees were kept in the camps until 1942 when the Nazis began transporting them to camps in Eastern Europe.

Young M.I. Libau was only 14 years old when Nazis attacked his family's home. Libau described what the Nazis did:

A VOICE FROM THE PAST
All the things for which my parents had worked for eighteen long years were destroyed in less than ten minutes. Piles of valuable glasses, expensive furniture, linens—in short, everything was destroyed. . . . The Nazis left us, yelling, "Don't try to leave this house! We'll soon be back again and take you to a concentration camp to be shot."

M.I. LIBAU, quoted in *Never to Forget: The Jews of the Holocaust*

Kristallnacht marked a major step-up in the Nazi policy of Jewish persecution. The future for Jews in Germany looked grim.

The Flood of Refugees After Kristallnacht, some Jews realized that violence against them was bound to increase. By the end of 1939, a number of Jews in Germany had fled for safety to other countries. Many of them, however, remained in Germany. Later, there would be millions more in territories conquered by Hitler. At first, Hitler favored emigration as a solution to what he called "the Jewish problem." The Nazis sped up the process. They forced Jews who did not want to leave into emigrating.

Getting other countries to continue admitting Germany's Jews became a problem. France had admitted 25,000 Jewish refugees and wanted no more. The British, who had accepted 80,000 Jews, worried about fueling anti-Semitism if that number increased. Some 40,000 Jews found homes in Latin America, but that region had closed its doors by the end of 1938. The United States took in around 100,000 refugees (including German scientist Albert Einstein). Many Americans, however, wanted U.S. doors closed. Germany's foreign minister observed: "We all want to get rid of our Jews. The difficulty is that no country wishes to receive them."

Isolating the Jews Hitler found that he could not get rid of Jews through emigration. So he put another part of his plan into effect. Hitler ordered Jews in all countries under his control to be moved into certain cities in Poland. In those cities, they were herded into dismal, overcrowded **ghettos,** or segregated Jewish areas. The Nazis then sealed off the ghettos with barbed wire and stone walls. They wanted the Jews inside to starve or die from disease. One survivor wrote, "One sees people dying, lying with arms and legs outstretched in the middle of the road. Their legs are bloated, often frostbitten, and their faces distorted with pain."

Even under these horrible conditions, the Jews hung on. Some formed resistance organizations within the ghettos. They smuggled in food and other needed items. In the midst of chaos, Jews also struggled to keep their traditions. Ghetto theaters produced plays and concerts. Teachers taught lessons in secret schools. Scholars kept records so that one day people would find out the truth.

This pile of shoes taken from Nazi victims represents the murder of thousands of Jews. The inset shows the living inmates at Auschwitz trying to salvage shoes left by the dead.

B. Possible Answers Poland was a weak, con-quered country, so Hitler could do what-ever he wanted there; Hitler considered the Polish subhuman, so he may have felt that he could do whatever he wanted in their country.

THINK THROUGH HISTORY
B. Analyzing Causes Why might Hitler have chosen Poland to put his ghetto policy for "the Jewish problem" into effect?

Task Students will read a primary source and a literature excerpt to examine the horrors of the Holocaust as experienced by two young people during World War II. Students should note that both Anne Frank and Elie Wiesel were teenagers.

Materials Needed Use the Primary Source (Anne Frank) and the Literature selection (Elie Wiesel) for this section from the Teacher's Resources.

Activity Have students compare the experiences of the two young people that are recorded in these excerpts. Have students make up a list of the similarities and differences between their experiences.

Conclusion Ask students to discuss the role of hope in the different lives of these two young people. Why might hope have been easier for Anne Frank to hold on to than for Elie Wiesel?

IN-DEPTH RESOURCES: UNIT 7
Primary Source: from *The Diary of a Young Girl* by Anne Frank, p. 64

Literature: from *Night* by Elie Wiesel, p. 66

Hitler's "Final Solution"

Hitler soon grew impatient waiting for Jews to die from starvation or disease in the ghettos. He decided to take more direct action. His plan was called the **"Final Solution."** It was actually a program of **genocide,** the systematic killing of an entire people.

Hitler believed that his plan of conquest depended on the purity of the Aryan race. To protect racial purity, the Nazis not only had to eliminate the Jews, but also other races, nationalities, or groups they viewed as inferior—as "subhumans." They included gypsies, Poles, Russians, homosexuals, the insane, the disabled, and the incurably ill. But the Nazis focused especially on the Jews.

The Mass Killings Begin After Hitler invaded Poland in 1939, it was still not clear that the Führer meant to eliminate Jews totally. As Nazi armies swept across Eastern Europe, Hitler sent SS units from town to town to hunt Jews down. The SS (Hitler's elite security force) and some thousands of collaborators rounded up Jews—men, women, young children, and even babies—and took them to isolated spots. They then shot their prisoners in pits that became the prisoners' grave.

Jews in communities not reached by the killing squads were rounded up and taken to concentration camps, or slave-labor prisons. These camps were located mainly in Germany and Poland. Later, Nazis built camps in other countries they occupied. (See the map on page 847.) Hitler hoped that the horrible conditions in the camps would speed the total elimination of the Jews.

The prisoners worked seven days a week as slaves for the SS or for German businesses. Guards severely beat or killed their prisoners for not working fast enough. With meals of thin soup, a scrap of bread, and potato peelings, most prisoners lost 50 pounds the first month. "Hunger was so intense," recalled one survivor, "that if a bit of soup spilled over, prisoners would . . . dig their spoons into the mud and stuff the mess into their mouths."

The Final Stage: Mass Extermination The "Final Solution" officially reached its final stage in early 1942. At that time, the Nazis built extermination camps equipped with gas chambers for mass murder. The Nazis built the first six death camps in Poland. The first, Chelmno, actually began operating in late 1941. (See the map on

SPOTLIGHT ON

Nazi Medicine

Nazi doctors, such as the notorious Josef Mengele, used many concentration camp prisoners as guinea pigs for their experiments. To promote "racial purity," doctors tested sterilization methods on some prisoners. Doctors infected other prisoners with typhus and other deadly diseases to see how long they could survive. To practice surgery, student doctors would operate on prisoners without anesthesia. In the hands of the Nazis, even medicine became an instrument of pain and destruction.

Slave workers in the Buchenwald concentration camp in Germany. They were among the lucky to have survived to the end of the war. The prisoner highlighted with a circle is Nobel Prize winning author Elie Wiesel. (See "A Voice from the Past," page 834.)

833

SPOTLIGHT ON
Jewish Resistance

In the ghetto of Kovno in Lithuania, Jews took an oath to resist Nazis in any way they could. "I promise to fight with all my powers against the Nazi occupation; to endanger their encampments; disrupt their transport; burn and blow up bridges; destroy railroads; organize and help carry through acts of sabotage at every opportunity and under all circumstances, without sparing myself—and when necessary, to offer up my life." Ask students to research and identify specific ways in which Jews carried out sabotage from the ghettos and in the labor camps.

ASSESS & RETEACH

Section 3 Assessment
Divide the questions among student groups and have them present their responses orally to the class.

Section Quiz
 FORMAL ASSESSMENT
Section Quiz, p. 376

Reteaching Activity
CLASS TIME: 10 MINUTES

Create a class chart on the board listing the acts against Jews during the Holocaust and their impact. Base the chart on student responses.

CLOSE ACTIVITY

CLASS TIME: 15 MINUTES

Analyzing Events
Ask students to search the Internet for current information about genocide or "ethnic cleansing" in Bosnia, Rwanda, or elsewhere in the world today. Have them report their findings to the class.

834 Chapter 32

In 1941, Hitler's government required all Jews in German-controlled territories to wear a yellow Star of David when appearing in public places.

Jews Killed under Nazi Rule*			
	Original Jewish Population	Jews Killed	Percent Surviving
Poland	3,300,000	3,000,000	10%
Soviet Union	2,850,000	1,252,000	56%
Hungary	650,000	450,000	30%
Romania	600,000	300,000	50%
Germany/Austria	240,000	200,000	16 2/3%

*Estimates

page 847.) The huge gas chambers in the camps could kill as many as 6,000 human beings in a day.

When prisoners arrived at the largest of the death camps, Auschwitz (OUSH·vihts), they paraded before a committee of SS doctors. With a wave of the hand, these doctors separated the strong (mostly men) from the weak, who would die that day. Those chosen to die (mostly women, young children, the elderly, and the sick) were told to undress for a shower. They were led into a chamber with fake showerheads, and the doors closed. The prisoners were then poisoned with cyanide gas that poured from the showerheads. Later, the Nazis installed crematoriums, or ovens, to burn the bodies.

SPOTLIGHT ON

Jewish Resistance

The 700 members of the Jewish Fighting Organization in the Warsaw ghetto were among the Jews who resisted the horrors of Nazism. In April 1943, most of these young people lost their lives battling Nazi tanks and troops who were destroying the ghetto.

Even in the death camps, Jews rose up against the Nazis. In August 1943 at Treblinka, Poland, a small group of Jews revolted. Breaking into the armory, they stole guns and grenades. They then attacked guards and set fire to the gas chambers. Most of these brave fighters died. They had paid the highest price possible to combat Nazi atrocities.

The Survivors Six million Jews died in the death camps and in Nazi massacres. Fewer than 4 million European Jews survived the horrors of the Holocaust. Many had help from non-Jewish people who were against the Nazis' treatment of Jews. Swedish businessman Raoul Wallenberg and Protestant religious thinker Dietrich Bonhoeffer are just two examples of Christians who risked their lives to oppose Hitler's policies. These people risked their lives by hiding Jews or by helping them escape to neutral countries such as Switzerland or Sweden.

Those who survived the camps were changed forever by what they had seen. For Elie Wiesel, 15 years old when he entered Auschwitz, the light had gone out:

A VOICE FROM THE PAST
Never shall I forget the little faces of the children, whose bodies I saw turned into wreaths of smoke beneath a silent blue sky. Never shall I forget those flames which consumed my faith forever. . . . Never shall I forget those moments which murdered my God and my soul and turned my dreams to dust. . . . Never.
ELIE WIESEL, quoted in *Night*

THINK THROUGH HISTORY
C. Analyzing Motives How could concentration camp doctors and guards have justified to themselves the death and suffering they caused other human beings?
C. Possible Answers If they could convince themselves that their prisoners were subhuman, the doctors and guards might tell themselves that they were not actually killing or torturing real human beings; they might claim that they were simply following orders and had no choice.

Section ③ Assessment

1. TERMS & NAMES
Identify
• Aryans
• Holocaust
• *Kristallnacht*
• ghettos
• "Final Solution"
• genocide

2. TAKING NOTES
Using a web diagram like the one below, give examples of Nazi persecutions.

Nazi persecutions

3. MAKING INFERENCES
Why do you think German soldiers and the German people went along with the Nazi policy of persecution of the Jews?

THINK ABOUT
• Nazi treatment of those who disagreed
• Nazi propaganda
• the political and social conditions in Germany at the time

4. THEME ACTIVITY
Science and Technology In groups of three or four students, discuss the ethical dilemmas of German scientists, engineers, and doctors asked to organize and participate in the Holocaust.
How might they have opposed Hitler's policy? In public? In secret? What might have been the consequences of public opposition?

834 Chapter 32

ANSWERS

1. TERMS & NAMES
Aryans, p. 831
Holocaust, p. 831
Kristallnacht, p. 831
ghettos, p. 832
"Final Solution," p. 833
genocide, p. 833

2. TAKING NOTES
Possible Answers: Nuremberg Laws; genocide of Jews; concentration camps; persecution of gypsies, Poles, Russians, homosexuals, the insane, the disabled, the ill; burning of Jewish businesses, homes, and synagogues.

3. MAKING INFERENCES
Possible Answers: Treatment: The people of Germany were afraid for their lives. Propaganda: tried to convince Germans that Jewish people were subhuman. Conditions: A repressive dictatorship.

4. THEME ACTIVITY
Standards for Evaluation
An effective discussion should . .
• give a clear sense of the moral dimension of the Holocaust
• specify options for opposition
• show an awareness of the personal dilemmas and problems that scientists might face

4 The Allies Are Victorious

TERMS & NAMES
- Erwin Rommel
- Bernard Montgomery
- Dwight D. Eisenhower
- Battle of Stalingrad
- D-Day
- Battle of the Bulge
- kamikaze

MAIN IDEA

Led by the United States, Great Britain, and the Soviet Union, the Allies scored key victories and won the war.

WHY IT MATTERS NOW

The Allies' victory in World War II set up conditions for both the Cold War and today's post-Cold War world.

SETTING THE STAGE As 1941 came to an end, Hitler said, "Let's hope 1942 brings me as much good fortune as 1941." Despite the Führer's hopes, Germany's victories slowed considerably during 1942. The United States had entered the war, boosting the Allies' morale and strength.

The Allies Plan for Victory

On December 22, 1941, just after Pearl Harbor, Winston Churchill and President Roosevelt met at the White House to develop a joint war policy. Stalin had asked his allies to relieve German pressure on his armies in the east. He wanted them to open a second front in the west. The second front would split the Germans' strength by forcing them to fight major battles in two regions instead of one. Churchill agreed with Stalin's strategy: The Allies would weaken Germany on two fronts before dealing a deathblow. At first, Roosevelt was torn, but ultimately he agreed.

The Tide Turns on Two Fronts

Churchill urged that Britain and the United States strike first at North Africa and southern Europe. The strategy angered Stalin. He wanted the Allies to open the second front in France. In the meantime, the Soviet Union would have to hold out on its own against the Germans—with the help of some supplies from its partners. Nevertheless, late in 1942, the Allies began to turn the tide of war both in the Mediterranean and on the Eastern Front.

The North African Campaign German forces had been advancing and retreating across the North African desert since early 1941. Finally, General **Erwin Rommel** took the key port city of Tobruk in June 1942. With Tobruk's fall, London sent General **Bernard Montgomery**—"Monty" to his men—to take control of British forces in North Africa. By this time, the Germans had advanced to an Egyptian village called El Alamein (AL-uh-MAYN), west of Alexandria. They were dug in so well that British forces could not go around them. So, Montgomery had to launch the Battle of El Alamein with a massive attack from the front. On the night of October 23, the roar of more than 1,700 British guns took the Axis soldiers totally by surprise. They fought back fiercely, but by November 3, Rommel's army had been beaten. He and his forces retreated westward.

As Rommel retreated west, the Allies launched *Operation Torch*. On November 8, an Allied force of more than 107,000 troops—mostly Americans—landed in Morocco and Algeria. This force was led by American General **Dwight D. Eisenhower.** Caught between the two armies, the Desert Fox's Afrika Korps was finally smashed in May 1943.

Background
Montgomery, like Rommel himself, used dummy regiments built from timber and canvas. They were intended to fool the enemy into thinking that forces were stationed where, in fact, they were not.

HISTORY MAKERS

General Erwin Rommel 1891–1944

On July 20, 1944, a plot to assassinate Hitler by a group of German officers failed. Under torture, one conspirator accused war hero General Erwin Rommel of involvement in the plot. The news shook and enraged Hitler, since Rommel had always been devoted to him.

Was Rommel actually involved? Evidence indicates that he was ready to bypass Hitler and personally negotiate for peace with the Allies. However, many believe that he knew nothing of the plot. Hitler believed that he did. He offered Rommel a choice—a public trial or suicide and a state funeral. On October 14, 1944, Rommel took poison and died.

World War II **835**

Section 4 Overview

OBJECTIVES

(1) To describe the Allied plan for victory.

(2) To show the Allied strategy on two fronts.

(3) To explain how civilians on the Allied home fronts contributed to the war effort.

(4) To summarize events that led to the surrender of Germany.

(5) To explain the importance of the atom bomb in the Allied victory over Japan.

SKILLBUILDER
- Interpreting maps: region, movement, p. 836
- Interpreting maps: human-environment interaction, movement, p. 838

CRITICAL THINKING
- Making inferences, pp. 836, 840
- Analyzing motives, p. 837
- Forming an opinion, p. 841
- Summarizing, p. 841
- Analyzing themes, p. 841

FOCUS

5-Minute Warm-Up

▶ *Interpreting Maps*
Have students answer the following questions to help them understand the D-day invasion.

1. Look at the map on page 838. Which landing area was isolated from the rest?

2. Approximately how many miles is it from Sword Beach in the east to Utah Beach in the west?

 WARM-UP TRANSPARENCY 32

OBJECTIVE (1) INSTRUCT

The Allies Plan for Victory

▶ *Key Idea*
- With the U.S. in the war, the Allies open a second front.

 IN-DEPTH RESOURCES: UNIT 7
Guided Reading, p. 57

ACCESS FOR STUDENTS ACQUIRING ENGLISH
Guided Reading (Spanish), p. 324

SECTION 4 RESOURCES

PRINT RESOURCES

 IN-DEPTH RESOURCES: UNIT 7
Guided Reading, p. 57
Skillbuilder Practice: Following Chronological Order, p. 59
Primary Sources: from *Farewell to Manzanar*, p. 63; from *Hiroshima*, p. 65

 ACCESS FOR STUDENTS ACQUIRING ENGLISH
Guided Reading (Spanish), p. 324
Skillbuilder Practice: (Spanish), p. 326

 FORMAL ASSESSMENT
Section Quiz, p. 377

 ALTERNATIVE ASSESSMENT BOOK

TECHNOLOGY RESOURCES

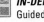 **CD-ROM**
Battles of the World
Electronic Library of Primary Sources

VIDEO *Patterns of Interaction: Arming for War*

INTERNET www.mlworldhistory.com

The Tide Turns on Two Fronts

(See page 835.)

▶ Key Ideas

- The Allied invasion of North Africa smashes Rommel's forces.
- The Soviets defeat Germans at Stalingrad and push the German army westward.
- The Allies attack in southern Europe and push through Italy.

HISTORY MAKERS
General Erwin Rommel

(See page 835.)

Controversy has surrounded the possible role of Rommel in the plot to kill Hitler. He once confided to those he trusted that he believed the war could not be won and that Hitler should be replaced. And he had heard talk from other generals of killing Hitler. On the day of his death, he told his wife the charges were not true. Ask students to research the plot and form an opinion about whether Rommel was involved.

History from Visuals

World War II: Allied Advances, 1942–1945

Interpreting the Map Have students look at the map key to distinguish Axis, Allied, and neutral nations.

Extension Activity Have students note where most of the neutral countries outside of Europe are located on this map and then make a list of them. *Southwest Asia—Turkey, Saudi Arabia*

SKILLBUILDER Answers
1. Ireland, Spain, Portugal, Sweden, Switzerland
2. Germany

World War II: Allied Advances, 1942–1945

- ☐ Axis nations, 1938
- ☐ Axis-controlled, 1942
- ☐ Allies
- ☐ Neutral nations
- → Allied advances

0   500 Miles
0   1,000 Kilometers

GEOGRAPHY SKILLBUILDER: Interpreting Maps
1. **Region** Which European countries remained neutral during World War II?
2. **Movement** What seems to be the destination for most of the Allied advances that took place in Europe during 1943–1944?

Turning Point at Stalingrad As Rommel suffered defeats in North Africa, German armies also met their match in the Soviet Union. They had stalled at Leningrad and Moscow. Germans suffered heavy losses in battle because of the Russian winter. When the summer of 1942 arrived, German tanks were again ready to roll. Hitler sent his Sixth Army south to seize the rich oil fields in the Caucasus Mountains. The army was also to capture Stalingrad (now Volgograd) on the Volga River. With its 500,000 people, Stalingrad was a major industrial center.

The **Battle of Stalingrad** began on August 23, 1942. The Luftwaffe went on nightly bombing raids that set much of the city ablaze and reduced the rest to rubble. The situation looked desperate. Nonetheless, Stalin had already told his commanders to defend the city named after him at all costs. "Not one step backward," he ordered.

By early November 1942, Germans controlled 90 percent of the ruined city. Stalingrad was an "enormous cloud of burning, blinding smoke," as one German officer wrote. Then, another Russian winter set in. On November 19, Soviet troops outside the city launched a counterattack. Closing in around Stalingrad, they trapped the Germans inside and cut off their supplies. Hitler's commander, General Friedrich von Paulus, begged him to order a retreat. But Hitler refused, saying the city was "to be held at all costs."

On February 2, 1943, some 90,000 frostbitten, half-starved German troops surrendered to the Soviets. These pitiful survivors were all that remained of an army of 330,000. Stalingrad's defense had cost the Soviets over 1 million soldiers. The city they defended was 99 percent destroyed. After Stalingrad, however, the Germans were on the defensive, with the Soviets pushing them steadily westward.

The Invasion of Italy As the Battle of Stalingrad raged, Stalin continued to urge the British and the Americans to invade France. In January 1943, Roosevelt and Churchill met at Casablanca, Morocco, and decided to attack Italy first. On July 10, 1943, Allied forces of 180,000 soldiers landed on Sicily and captured it from Italian and German troops by August.

These dazed, freezing, and starved German prisoners were actually lucky to be alive. About 240,000 Germans died during the battle for the city of Stalingrad.

A. Possible Answers The army fighting on its own soil would know the territory better than the invading army; it would have the support of the local population, which the invaders would not; it would have the additional energy that comes with defending one's own home.

THINK THROUGH HISTORY
A. Making Inferences What advantages might a weaker army fighting on its home soil have over a stronger invading army?

Task: Students will represent the Allied leaders (Churchill, Stalin, and Roosevelt) and write letters to one another expressing their points of view about the invasion of Europe and a two-front war.

Purpose: To help students understand the conflict among the Allied leaders.

Activity: Students will work in three groups, each

representing one of the Allied leaders and discuss plans for a war on two fronts. Students should then collaborate to write their letters.

📁 **Building a Portfolio** If the letter is among their best work, students should add it to their portfolio.

📋 **ALTERNATIVE ASSESSMENT BOOK**
Standards for Evaluating a Cooperative Activity

Standards for Evaluation
Letters should . . .

- clearly convey the views of the three leaders
- show an understanding of the views of the other leaders
- show an understanding of the advantages and disadvantages of waging a war on two fronts

The conquest of Sicily toppled Mussolini from power. On July 25, King Victor Emmanuel III fired the dictator and had him arrested. On September 3, Italy surrendered. But the Germans seized control of northern Italy and put Mussolini back in charge. Finally, the Germans retreated northward, and the victorious Allies entered Rome on June 4, 1944. Fighting in Italy, however, continued until Germany fell in May 1945. On April 28, 1945, as the Germans were retreating from northern Italy, the Italian resistance ambushed some trucks. Inside one of them, resistance fighters found Mussolini disguised as a German soldier. The following day, he was shot, and his body was hanged in the Milan town square.

Life on Allied Home Fronts

Wherever Allied forces fought, people on the home fronts rallied to support them. In war-torn countries like the Soviet Union or Great Britain, civilians lost their lives and endured extreme hardships. Except for a few of its territories, such as Hawaii, the United States did not suffer invasion or bombing. Nonetheless, Americans at home made a crucial contribution to the Allied war effort. Americans produced the weapons and equipment that would help win the war.

Mobilizing for Total War Defeating the Axis powers required mobilizing for total war. In the United States, factories converted their peacetime operations to wartime production and made everything from machine guns to boots. Automobile factories produced tanks. A U.S. typewriter company made armor-piercing shells. By 1944, almost 18 million U.S. workers—many of them women—were working in war industries.

In a practice drill in Great Britain, a mock Nazi infiltrator disguised as a nanny "opens fire" on a sentry of the Home Guard after he asked her for identification.

With factories turning out products for the war, a shortage of consumer goods hit the United States. From meat and sugar to tires and gasoline, from nylon stockings to laundry soap, the American government rationed scarce items. Setting the speed limit at 35 miles per hour also helped to save on gasoline and rubber. In European countries directly affected by the war, rationing was even more drastic.

To inspire their people to greater efforts, Allied governments conducted highly effective propaganda campaigns. In the Soviet Union, a Moscow youngster collected enough scrap metal to produce 14,000 artillery shells. Another Russian family, the Shirmanovs, used their life savings to buy a tank for the Red Army. In the United States, youngsters saved their pennies and bought government war stamps and bonds to help finance the war.

Civil Rights Curtailed by the War Government propaganda also had a negative effect. After Pearl Harbor, a wave of prejudice arose in the United States against the 127,000 Japanese Americans. Most lived in Hawaii and on the West Coast. The bombing of Pearl Harbor frightened Americans. This fear, encouraged by government propaganda, was turned against Japanese Americans. They were suddenly seen as "the enemy." On February 19, 1942, President Roosevelt set up a program of internment and loss of property, since Japanese Americans were considered a threat to the country.

In March, the military began rounding up "aliens" and shipping them to relocation camps. Two-thirds of those interned were Nisei, or Japanese Americans who were native-born American citizens. The camps were restricted military areas located away

Allied Victory in Europe

Key Ideas
- Allies invade Normandy and push on toward Germany.
- As Soviet forces invade from the East, Hitler commits suicide and Germany surrenders.

HISTORY MAKERS
General Dwight Eisenhower

Eisenhower once told the poet Carl Sandburg, "When they [soldiers] called me Uncle Ike or . . . just plain Ike, I knew everything was going well." Ask students to identify characteristics Eisenhower had that inspired loyalty.

History from Visuals

The D-Day Invasion, June 6, 1944

Interpreting the Map Have students note the broad front along which Allied forces landed. Have them consider the advantages and disadvantages of invading along such a broad front.

Extension Activity Have students do some research on the various beaches on which the Allied forces landed in the D-Day invasion. They might investigate which beach was invaded by Canadian forces. *Juno Beach*

SKILLBUILDER Answers
1. Flooding.
2. Troops parachuted into France would have moved into the interior more quickly than soldiers who fought their way in from the coast.

---

from the coast. With such a location, it was thought that the Nisei could not participate in an invasion. From 1941 until 1946, the United States imprisoned some 31,275 people it wrongly considered "enemy aliens (foreigners)." Most of those prisoners were American citizens of Japanese descent.

HISTORY MAKERS

General Dwight Eisenhower
1890–1969

In his career, U.S. General Dwight Eisenhower had shown an uncommon ability to work with all kinds of people—even competitive Allies. His Chief of Staff said of Eisenhower, "The sun rises and sets on him for me." He was also wildly popular with the troops, who affectionately called him "Uncle Ike."

So, it was not a surprise when in December 1943, U.S. Army Chief of Staff George Marshall named Eisenhower as supreme commander of the Allied forces in Europe. The new commander's "people skills" enabled him to join American and British forces together to put a permanent end to Nazi aggression.

Allied Victory in Europe

While the Allies were dealing with issues on the home front, they were preparing to push toward victory in Europe. By the end of 1942, the war had begun to turn in favor of the Allies. By 1943, the Allies began secretly building a force in Great Britain. Their plan was to attack the Germans across the English Channel.

The D-Day Invasion By May 1944, the invasion force was ready. Thousands of planes, ships, tanks, landing craft, and 3.5 million troops awaited orders to attack. American General Dwight D. Eisenhower, the commander of this enormous force, planned to strike on the coast of Normandy, in northwestern France. The Germans knew that an attack was coming. But they did not know where it would be launched. To keep Hitler guessing, the Allies set up a huge dummy army with its own headquarters and equipment. They ordered the make-believe army to attack at the French seaport of Calais (ka·LAY).

Code-named *Operation Overlord*, the invasion of Normandy was the greatest land and sea attack in history. The day chosen for the invasion to begin—called **D-Day**—was June 6, 1944.

At dawn on June 6, British, American, French, and Canadian troops fought their way onto a 60-mile stretch of beach in Normandy. The Germans had dug in with machine guns, rocket launchers, and cannons. They protected themselves behind concrete walls three feet thick. Among the Americans alone, 3,000 soldiers died on the beach that day. Captain Joseph Dawson said, "The beach was a total chaos, with men's bodies everywhere, with wounded men crying both in the water and on the shingle [coarse gravel]."

Despite heavy casualties, the Allies held the beachheads. A month later, more than 1 million additional troops had landed. On July 25, the Allies punched a hole in the German defenses near Saint-Lô (san·LOH), and General George Patton's Third Army raced through.

Background
The name *D-Day* came from the words *designated + day*.

Vocabulary
beachheads: enemy shoreline captured just before invading forces move inland.

The D-Day Invasion, June 6, 1944

GEOGRAPHY SKILLBUILDER: Interpreting Maps
1. **Human–Environment Interaction** What environmental problem might have been encountered by 1st Army soldiers landing at Utah Beach?
2. **Movement** Looking at the map, what might have been the Allied strategy behind parachuting troops into France?

The Parachute World War II was the first war in which parachutes were used extensively for a variety of purposes, including landing troops and supplies in isolated or otherwise inaccessible places. On the night before D-Day, some 10,000 American paratroopers were scattered behind the Normandy beaches. The result, writes historian David Howarth, was a "gigantic . . . game of hide-and-seek" in which

"the Americans knew what was happening, but few of them knew where they were; the Germans knew where they were, but none of them knew what was happening."

After World War II, parachuting, or skydiving, emerged as a popular sport. Early parachuting competitions were limited to accuracy in landing.

Later, as skydivers learned to control their bodies in free fall, they added style events that involved performing aerobatic maneuvers before opening their parachutes. In the most popular form of competition, teams of skydivers form geometric patterns, racing to make as many patterns as they can. Today, teams from more than 30 countries participate in world skydiving championships.

Soon, the Germans were retreating. On August 25, the Allies marched triumphantly into Paris. By September, they had liberated France, Belgium, Luxembourg, and much of the Netherlands. They then set their sights on Germany.

The Battle of the Bulge As Allied forces moved toward Germany from the west, the Soviet army was advancing toward Germany from the east. Hitler now faced a war on two fronts. In a desperate gamble, the Führer decided to counterattack in the west. The Führer hoped a victory would split American and British forces and break up Allied supply lines. Explaining the reasoning behind his plan, Hitler said, "This battle is to decide whether we shall live or die. . . . All resistance must be broken in a wave of terror."

On December 16, German tanks broke through weak American defenses along an 85-mile front in the Ardennes. The push into the Allied lines gave the campaign its name—the **Battle of the Bulge.** Although caught off guard, the Allies eventually pushed the Germans back and won. The Nazis could do little but retreat, since Hitler had lost men that he could no longer replace.

Germany's Unconditional Surrender After the Battle of the Bulge, the war in Europe neared its end. In late March 1945, the Allies rolled across the Rhine River into Germany. By the middle of April, a noose was closing around Berlin. Three million Allied soldiers approached Berlin from the southwest. Six million Soviet troops approached from the east—some of them just 40 miles from the capital. By April 25, 1945, the Soviets had surrounded the capital, as their artillery pounded the city.

While Soviet shells burst over Berlin, Hitler prepared for his end in an underground headquarters beneath the crumbling city. On April 29, he married his long-time companion, Eva Braun. He also wrote his final address to the German people. In it, he blamed Jews for starting the war and his generals for losing it. "I myself and my wife choose to die in order to escape the disgrace of . . . capitulation," he said. "I die with a happy heart aware of the immeasurable deeds of our soldiers at the front." Two days later, Hitler shot himself after taking poison. His new wife simply swallowed poison. The bodies were then carried outside and burned.

Vocabulary
capitulation: surrender.

On May 7, 1945, General Eisenhower accepted the unconditional surrender of the Third Reich from the German military. President Roosevelt, however, did not live to witness the long-awaited victory. He had died suddenly on April 12, as Allied armies were advancing toward Berlin. Roosevelt's successor, Harry Truman, received the news of the Nazi surrender. On May 8, the surrender was officially signed in Berlin. The United States and other Allied powers celebrated V-E Day—Victory in Europe Day. The war in Europe had ended at last.

Victory in the Pacific

Although the war in Europe was over, the Allies were still fighting the Japanese in the Pacific. With the Allied victory at Guadalcanal, however, the Japanese advances in the Pacific had been stopped. For the rest of the war, the Japanese retreated before the counterattack of the Allied powers.

The Japanese Retreat By the fall of 1944, the Allies were moving in on Japan. In October, Allied forces landed on the island of Leyte (LAY·tee) in the Philippines. General MacArthur, who had been forced to surrender the islands in February 1942, waded ashore. He then declared, "People of the Philippines, I have returned."

Actually, the takeover would not be quite that easy. The Japanese had decided to destroy the American fleet. The Allies could not then resupply their ground troops. To

World War II **839**

SPOTLIGHT ON
Dresden

On the night of February 13, 1945, 800 British and American bombers launched a massive air attack on Dresden, a German city southeast of Berlin. During the bombing, some 4,000 tons of explosives were dropped, creating raging firestorms. One author described the city as a "furnace fueled by people," as its citizens—mostly women, children, and the elderly—burned to death. Estimates of those killed vary from 35,000 to 135,000.

The firestorm reduced Dresden to rubble, accomplishing no important military goals but killing many civilians. Dresden has come to symbolize the strategy of "total war": massive attacks on both military and civilian targets to break a country's fighting spirit.

SPOTLIGHT ON
Dresden

A young woman named Margret Freyer survived the firestorm in Dresden and described her experience. During the first wave of bombings, she took refuge in a cellar but left for the house of a friend when she thought the bombing was over. She recalled what happened next. "When the sirens sounded again, my friend and I looked at each other, terrified—surely it wasn't possible? Are they coming a second time. . . ? We went down into the cellar. . . . I sat next to [my friend] while a non-stop hail of bombs seemed to last an eternity. . . . We longed for the 'All Clear,' but it never came. . . ."

OBJECTIVE 5 INSTRUCT

Victory in the Pacific

► **Key Ideas**
- As the Japanese retreat, the Allies close in on Japan.
- After heavy fighting, Allied forces are within 500 miles of Japan.
- To avoid an invasion and save lives, the United States drops atom bombs on two Japanese cities, and Japan surrenders.

CRITICAL THINKING ACTIVITY
CLASS TIME: 10 MINUTES

Drawing Conclusions
Have students draw a conclusion about the decision to drop the atom bomb by creating a chart like this one listing the arguments for and against using the weapon.

For	Against
Conclusion	

Explaining the Skill Understanding the relationships between events—causes and effects, problems and solutions—depends on knowing how the events relate in time. Chronological thinking is important in our lives. Using dates provided in the text and clue words about time, students can place events they read about in correct chronological order.

Applying the Skill Help students put the events described on pages 838–839 under the head "Allied Victory in Europe" in chronological order by asking them to identify dates and clue words about time: *By the end of 1942, At dawn on June 6, A month later, Soon, While, Two days later.*

1. Ask students what the word *as* shows at the beginning of the section on "The Battle of the Bulge." *Several things going on at same time.*

2. Ask students what words in the first paragraph under "Germany's Unconditional Surrender" suggest chronological order? *After; In late March 1945; By April 25, 1945.*

 IN-DEPTH RESOURCES: UNIT 7
Skillbuilder Practice: Following Chronological Order, p. 59

The Atomic Bomb

The plane that dropped the atom bomb on Hiroshima was called the *Enola Gay* and was piloted by Colonel Paul W. Tibbets, Jr. He described what he saw after releasing the bomb: ". . . down below [the mushroom cloud] the thing reminded me more of a boiling pot of tar than any other description I can give. It was black and boiling underneath with a steam haze on top of it. . . . We had seen the city when we went in, and there was nothing to see when we came back. It was covered by this boiling, black-looking mass."

IN-DEPTH RESOURCES: UNIT 7
Primary Source: from *Hiroshima*, p. 65

ELECTRONIC LIBRARY OF PRIMARY SOURCES
from Testimony Before the Special Senate Committee on Atomic Energy

Viewing the Video

Show *Arming for War: Modern and Medieval Weapons* to demonstrate that arms races have existed throughout history.

- The first segment of the video chronicles nations' quests for new and more effective weapons during World War I and World War II.

- The second segment shows students that arms races took place in medieval times as well, when the longbow and other weapons changed military history. Using the Teacher's Resource Book as a guide, have students consider how new or enhanced weapons can change warfare; discuss the costs and benefits of weapons development; and enrich the lesson with primary-source and visual-literacy activities included in the resource book.

PATTERNS OF INTERACTION
Arming for War: Modern and Medieval Weapons
Videocassette: Tape 4

The Atomic Bomb

On the eve of World War II, scientists in Germany succeeded in splitting the nucleus of a uranium atom, releasing a huge amount of energy. Albert Einstein wrote to President Franklin Roosevelt and warned him that Nazi Germany might be working to develop atomic weapons. Roosevelt responded by giving his approval for an American program, later code-named the Manhattan Project, to develop an atomic bomb. Roosevelt's decision set off a race to assure that the United States would be the first to develop the bomb.

My body seemed all black, everything seemed dark, dark all over. . . . Then I thought, "The world is ending."
An Atomic Bomb Survivor

A boy carries his brother through the leveled city of Nagasaki. This is one of a series of photos taken by Japanese photographer Yosuke Yamahata soon after the atomic bomb devastated the city on August 9, 1945.

On the morning of August 6, 1945, the B-29 bomber *Enola Gay*, flown by commander Colonel Paul W. Tibbets, Jr., took off from Tinian Island in the Mariana Islands. At precisely 8:16 A.M., the atomic bomb exploded above Hiroshima, a city on the Japanese island of Honshu.

Hiroshima: Day of Fire	
Effects of the bombing	
Ground temperatures	7,000°F
Hurricane force winds	980 miles per hour
Energy released	20,000 tons of TNT
Buildings destroyed	62,000 buildings
Killed immediately	70,000 people
Dead by the end of 1945	140,000 people
Total deaths related to A-bomb	200,000 people

The overwhelming destructive power of the Hiroshima bomb, and of the bomb dropped on Nagasaki three days later, changed the nature of war forever. Nuclear destruction also led to questions about the ethics of scientists and politicians who chose to use the bomb.

Patterns of Interaction

Just as in World War I, the conflicts of World War II spurred the development of ever more powerful weapons. Mightier tanks, more elusive submarines, faster fighter planes—all emerged from this period. From ancient times to the present day, the pattern remains the same: Every new weapon causes other countries to develop others of similar or greater force. This pattern results in a deadly race for an ultimate weapon: for example, the atomic bomb.

VIDEO *Arming for War: Modern and Medieval Weapons*

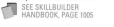
Connect *to* History

Making Inferences What advantages did the United States have over Germany in the race to develop the atomic bomb?
SEE SKILLBUILDER HANDBOOK, PAGE 1005

Connect *to* Today

Contrast If you had to design a memorial to the victims of the Hiroshima and Nagasaki bombings, what symbol would you use? Make a sketch of your memorial.

Nagasaki citizens trudge through the still smoldering ruins of their city in another photo by Yosuke Yamahata.

Connect *to* History

Making Inferences
Possible Answer:
The U.S. mainland was insulated from the war. No bombs were being dropped on the country, so that scientists and technicians were able to pursue their research with less disruption than the Germans had. Also, scientists such as Einstein had fled Germany to work in the United States.

Connect *to* Today

Contrast
You might wish to set aside a special area in the classroom where the students can display their sketches of memorials to the victims of Hiroshima and Nagasaki. Ask students to explain why they chose the symbols that they did to use in their memorials.

carry out this strategy, the Japanese had to risk almost their entire fleet. They gambled everything on October 23, in the Battle of Leyte Gulf. Within three days, the Japanese navy had lost disastrously—eliminating it as a fighting force in the war. Now, only the Japanese army and the feared kamikaze stood between the Allies and Japan. The **kamikaze** were Japanese suicide pilots. They would sink Allied ships by crash-diving into them in their bomb-filled planes.

In March 1945, after a month of bitter fighting and heavy losses, American Marines took Iwo Jima (EE·wuh JEE·muh), an island 660 miles from Tokyo. On April 1, U.S. troops moved to the island of Okinawa, only about 350 miles from southern Japan. The Japanese put up a desperate fight. Nevertheless, on June 22, the bloodiest land battle of the war ended. The Japanese lost 110,000 troops, and the Americans, 12,500.

THINK THROUGH HISTORY
C. Forming an Opinion Was it necessary to drop the second atomic bomb on Nagasaki?

The Atomic Bomb Brings Japanese Surrender After Okinawa, the next stop had to be Japan. President Truman's advisers had informed him that an invasion of the Japanese homeland might cost the Allies half a million lives. Truman had to make a decision whether to use a powerful new weapon called the atomic bomb, or A-bomb. The A-bomb would bring the war to the quickest possible end. It had been developed by the top-secret Manhattan Project, headed by General Leslie Groves and chief scientist J. Robert Oppenheimer. The Manhattan Project became a major spending item in U.S. military budgets. Truman only learned of the new bomb's existence when he became president.

The first atomic bomb was exploded in a desert in New Mexico on July 16, 1945. President Truman then warned the Japanese. He told them that unless they surrendered, they could expect a "rain of ruin from the air." The Japanese did not reply. So, on August 6, 1945, the United States dropped an atomic bomb on Hiroshima, a Japanese city of 365,000 people. Almost 73,000 people died in the attack. Three days later, on August 9, a second bomb was dropped on Nagasaki, a city of 200,000. It killed about 37,500 people. Radiation killed many more. A Japanese journalist described the horror in Hiroshima:

A VOICE FROM THE PAST
Within a few seconds the thousands of people in the streets and the gardens in the center of the town were scorched by a wave of searing heat. Many were killed instantly, others lay writhing on the ground, screaming in agony from the intolerable pain of their burns. Everything standing upright in the way of the blast, walls, houses, factories, and other buildings, was annihilated.
JAPANESE JOURNALIST, quoted in *The American Heritage Picture History of World War II*

The Japanese surrendered to General Douglas MacArthur on September 2. The surrender took place aboard the United States battleship *Missouri* in Tokyo Bay. With Japan's surrender, the war had ended. Now, countries faced the task of rebuilding a war-torn world.

Section 4 Assessment

1. TERMS & NAMES

Identify
- Erwin Rommel
- Bernard Montgomery
- Dwight Eisenhower
- Battle of Stalingrad
- D-Day
- Battle of the Bulge
- kamikaze

2. TAKING NOTES

Create a chart like the one below, listing outcomes of the following World War II battles.

Battle	Outcome
Battle of El Alamein	
Battle of Stalingrad	
D-Day Invasion	
Battle of the Bulge	

Which battle do you think was most important in turning the war in favor of the Allies? Why?

3. SUMMARIZING

Based on what you have read in this section, how do governments gather support for a war effort on the home front?

THINK ABOUT
- the economy
- forms of propaganda
- individual participation in the war effort

4. ANALYZING THEMES

Science and Technology Do you think President Truman made the correct decision by ordering the atomic bomb dropped on Hiroshima and Nagasaki? Why or why not?

THINK ABOUT
- the likely consequences if the atomic bomb had not been dropped
- the destruction caused by the atomic bomb
- World War II after the dropping of the atomic bomb

World War II **841**

ANSWERS

OBJECTIVES

1. To describe the devastation of Europe following the war.

2. To identify some of the political consequences of the Allied victory in postwar Europe.

3. To show how defeat affected political and civic life in Japan.

4. To give examples of ways in which Japan changed under United States' occupation.

SKILLBUILDER
• Interpreting charts, p. 845

CRITICAL THINKING
• Identifying problems, p. 843
• Making inferences, p. 844
• Analyzing causes, p. 845

FOCUS

5-Minute Warm-Up

▶ *Clarifying*
Have students answer these questions to help them understand the human costs of war.

1. Look at the chart on page 845. What was the approximate number of military killed in the war? How many civilians were killed in the war?

2. How many people, both military and civilian, were killed on both sides in the war?

 WARM-UP TRANSPARENCY 32

OBJECTIVE 1 INSTRUCT

Europe in Ruins

▶ *Key Ideas*
• Many European cities lie in ruins.
• Misery in Europe continues for years after the war.

📖 *IN-DEPTH RESOURCES: UNIT 7*
Guided Reading, p. 58

📖 *ACCESS FOR STUDENTS ACQUIRING ENGLISH*
Guided Reading (Spanish), p. 325

🎞 *WORLD ART AND CULTURES TRANSPARENCIES*
AT71 Liberation

🎞 *CRITICAL THINKING TRANSPARENCIES*
CT32 The Causes and Effects of World War II

---

5 The Devastation of Europe and Japan

MAIN IDEA	WHY IT MATTERS NOW
World War II cost millions of human lives and billions of dollars in damages. It left Europe and Japan in ruins.	The United States survived World War II undamaged, allowing it to become a world leader.

SETTING THE STAGE Allied victory in the war had been achieved at a high price. World War II had caused more death and destruction than any other conflict in history. It left 60 million dead, 50 million uprooted from their homes, and property damage that ran into billions of U.S. dollars.

Europe in Ruins

By the end of World War II, Europe lay in ruins. Close to 40 million Europeans had died—two-thirds of them civilians. Constant bombing and shelling had reduced hundreds of cities to rubble. The ground war had destroyed much of the countryside. Displaced persons from many nations were struggling to get home.

A Harvest of Destruction A few of the great cities of Europe—Paris, Rome, Brussels—remained undamaged by war. Many, however, had suffered terrible destruction. The Blitz left blackened ruins in London. Over five years, 60,595 London civilians had died in the German bombings. Eastern Europe and Germany were far worse off. Warsaw, the capital of Poland, was almost wiped from the face of the earth. In 1939, Warsaw had a population of 1,289,000 people. When the Soviets entered the city in January 1945, only 153,000 people remained. In Berlin, 25,000 tons of Allied bombs had demolished 95 percent of the central city. One U.S. officer stationed in Berlin reported, "Wherever we looked we saw desolation. It was like a city of the dead."

Background
Two-thirds of the deaths in the war occurred in Europe, making the war there far bloodier than in Asia.

Winston Churchill looks at Nazi firebomb damage to the British House of Commons.

After the bombings, many civilians stayed where they were and tried to get on with their lives. Some lived in partially destroyed homes or apartments. Others huddled in caves and cellars beneath the rubble. They had no water, no electricity, and very little food. Hunger was a constant companion. With factories destroyed or damaged, most people had no earnings to buy the food that was available.

Although many remained in the cities, a large number of city dwellers fled. They joined the army of displaced persons wandering Europe following the war. These displaced persons included the survivors of concentration camps, prisoners of war, and refugees fleeing the Soviet army. Millions found themselves in the wrong country when the postwar treaties changed national borders. They jammed the roads trying to get home, hoping to find their families or to find a safe place.

SECTION 5 RESOURCES

PRINT RESOURCES

📖 *IN-DEPTH RESOURCES: UNIT 7*
Guided Reading, p. 58

📖 *ACCESS FOR STUDENTS ACQUIRING ENGLISH*
Guided Reading (Spanish), p. 325

📖 *FORMAL ASSESSMENT*
Section Quiz, p. 378

📖 *ALTERNATIVE ASSESSMENT BOOK*

TECHNOLOGY RESOURCES

🎞 *WORLD ART AND CULTURES TRANSPARENCIES*
AT71 Liberation

🎞 *CRITICAL THINKING TRANSPARENCIES*
CT32 The Causes and Effects of World War II
CT68 Chapter 32 Visual Summary

🌐 INTERNET www.mlworldhistory.com

Simon Weisenthal described the search made by survivors of the Holocaust:

A VOICE FROM THE PAST

Across Europe a wild tide of frantic survivors was flowing. . . . Many of them didn't really know where to go. . . . And yet the survivors continued their pilgrimage of despair, sleeping on highways or in railroad stations, waiting for another train, another horse-drawn cart to come along, always driven to hope. "Perhaps someone is still alive. . . ." Someone might tell where to find a wife, a mother, children, a brother—or whether they were dead. . . . The desire to find one's people was stronger than hunger, thirst, fatigue.

SIMON WEISENTHAL, quoted in *Never to Forget: The Jews of the Holocaust*

Vocabulary
barter: to trade goods and services without money.

Misery Continues After the War Although the war had ended, misery in Europe continued for years. Europe lay ravaged by the fighting. Agriculture was disrupted. Most able-bodied men had served in the military and the women had worked in war production. Few remained to plant the fields. With the transportation system destroyed, the meager harvests often did not reach the cities. Thousands died as famine and disease spread through the bombed-out cities. In August 1945, 4,000 citizens of Berlin died every day. To get a few potatoes, people would barter any valuable items they had left. The first post-war winter brought more suffering as people went without shoes and coats.

Postwar Governments and Politics

Despairing Europeans often blamed their leaders for the war and its aftermath. Once the Germans had lost, some prewar governments—like those in Belgium, Holland, Denmark, and Norway—returned quickly. In countries like Germany, Italy, and France, however, a return to the old leadership was not so simple. Hitler's Nazi government had brought Germany to ruins. Mussolini had led Italy to defeat. The Vichy government had collaborated with the Nazis. Much of the old leadership was in disgrace. Besides, in Italy and France, many resistance fighters were Communists.

After the war, the Communist Party promised change, and millions were ready to listen. In both France and Italy, Communist Party membership skyrocketed. The Communists made huge gains in the first postwar elections. Anxious to speed up a political takeover, the Communists staged a series of violent strikes. Alarmed French and Italians reacted by voting for anti-Communist parties. Communist membership and influence then began to decline. And they declined even more so as the economies of France and Italy began to recover.

An Attempt at Justice: The Nuremberg Trials While nations were struggling to recover politically and economically, they also were trying to deal with Germany's guilt in the Holocaust. To make sure that such crimes would never happen again, the Allies put Nazis on trial. In 1946, an International Military Tribunal representing 23 nations put Nazi war criminals on trial in Nuremberg, Germany. In the first of the **Nuremberg Trials,** 22 Nazi leaders were charged with waging a war of aggression. They were also accused of violating the laws of war and of committing "crimes against humanity"—the murder of 11 million people.

Führer Adolf Hitler, SS chief Heinrich Himmler, and Minister of Propaganda Joseph Goebbels had escaped trial by committing suicide. However, Marshal Hermann Göring, Deputy Führer Rudolf Hess, and other high ranking Nazi leaders had to face the charges.

Of the 22 defendants, 12 were sentenced to death. Göring cheated the executioner by killing himself. The rest were hanged on October 16, 1946. Hans Frank, the "Slayer of Poles," was the only convicted Nazi to express remorse: "A thousand years will pass," he said, "and still this guilt of Germany

CONNECT *to* TODAY

Genocide in Rwanda

Genocide is a crime that human beings have committed against one another throughout history. In April 1994, the president of the East African nation of Rwanda died in a suspicious plane crash. The president was a member of the Hutu tribe. In Rwanda, the Hutu and Tutsi tribes have long hated and fought each other.

After the president's death, about 1 million Tutsis were slaughtered by the majority Hutus. In the end, Tutsi rebels ended the worst of the genocide.

The United Nations has set up an international war crimes tribunal to judge the worst acts of genocide. Yet, many criminals are still at large, and ethnic conflict in Rwanda continues.

The Effects of Defeat in Japan

Key Ideas
- U.S. forces occupy Japan under the leadership of General Douglas MacArthur.
- MacArthur begins the process of democratization by drawing up a new constitution.

CRITICAL THINKING ACTIVITY

CLASS TIME: 10 MINUTES

Forming an Opinion
Have students use a chart to list the steps MacArthur took to change Japan's government and economy and the results of those steps and draw a conclusion about the effects of U.S. occupation.

Steps	Results
Conclusion	

U.S. Occupation Brings Deep Changes

Key Ideas
- The power of Japan's emperor as a supreme leader is reduced.
- A new constitution makes Japan a democratic nation.

---

will not have been erased." The bodies of those executed were burned at the concentration camp of Dachau (DAHK·ow). They were cremated in the same ovens that had burned so many of their victims.

The Effects of Defeat in Japan

The defeat suffered by Japan in World War II left the country in ruins. Two million lives had been lost in the war. The country's major cities had been largely destroyed by Allied bombing raids, including the capital, Tokyo. The atomic bomb had left Hiroshima and Nagasaki as blackened wastelands. The Allies had stripped Japan of its colonial empire. They even took away areas that had belonged to the Japanese for centuries.

Emperor Hirohito and U.S. General Douglas MacArthur look distant and uncomfortable as they pose for a photo. The photo was taken in the American Embassy in Tokyo on September 27, 1945.

The United States Occupies Japan Even after these disasters, some Japanese military leaders wanted to continue the fight. In a radio broadcast on August 15, 1945, Emperor Hirohito urged the Japanese people to lay down their arms and work together to rebuild Japan. "Should we continue to fight," he declared, "it would only result in an ultimate collapse . . . of the Japanese nation." Two weeks after that broadcast, General Douglas MacArthur, now supreme commander for the Allied powers, accepted the Japanese surrender. He took charge of the U.S. occupation.

Demilitarization in Japan MacArthur was determined to be fair and not to plant the seeds for a future war. Nevertheless, to ensure that fighting would end, he began a process of **demilitarization**—disbanding the Japanese armed forces. He achieved this quickly, leaving the Japanese with only a small police force. MacArthur also began bringing war criminals to trial. Out of 25 surviving defendants, former Premier Hideki Tojo and six others were condemned to hang.

The general then turned his attention to democratization—the process of creating a government elected by the people. In February 1946, MacArthur and his American political advisers drew up a new constitution. It changed the empire into a parliamentary democracy like that of Great Britain. The Japanese accepted the constitution. It went into effect on May 3, 1947.

MacArthur was not told to revive the Japanese economy. However, he was instructed to broaden land ownership and increase the participation of workers and farmers in the new democracy. Absentee landlords with huge estates had to sell land to tenant farmers at reasonable prices. Workers could now create independent labor unions. Still bitter over Pearl Harbor, Americans did not provide much aid for rebuilding Japan. The United States did send 2 billion dollars in emergency relief. This was a small amount, however, considering the task that lay ahead.

U.S. Occupation Brings Deep Changes

The new constitution was the most important achievement of the occupation. It brought deep changes to Japanese society. In 1945, the Japanese had agreed to surrender. They insisted, however, that "the supreme power of the emperor not be compromised." The Allies agreed, but now things had changed. A long Japanese tradition had viewed the emperor as a god. He was also an absolute ruler whose divine will was law. The emperor now had to declare that he was not a god. That admission was as

B. Possible Answer The reduced military influence of military leaders and increased economic power among the Japanese people might result in a wider sharing of power in Japan.

THINK THROUGH HISTORY
B. Making Inferences How would demilitarization and a revived economy help Japan achieve democracy?

CONNECTIONS ACROSS TIME AND PLACE

Demilitarization One of MacArthur's first acts as head of the U.S. occupation forces was to free about 500 political prisoners and fire 5,000 government people who were known to be "thought police." He also purged the government of those known to be war criminals and dismissed all senior military officials and anyone else who had been actively involved in

promoting aggression since 1931. MacArthur's success as a military leader gave him the authority to impose demilitarization upon the Japanese.

By the time MacArthur was through, a little less than half of 1 percent of the population was barred from public office; in Germany 2.5 percent of the

population was not allowed to take part in public life or hold positions of influence. MacArthur's policies in Japan transformed the nation from a militaristic power to one that since that time has rejected a standing army and resisted attempts over the years to build up a military force.

Costs of World War II: Allies and Axis

	Direct War Costs	Military Killed/Missing	Civilians Killed
United States	$288.0 billion*	292,131**	—
Great Britain	$117.0 billion	271,311	60,595
France	$111.3 billion	205,707***	173,260†
USSR	$93.0 billion	13,600,000	7,720,000
Germany	$212.3 billion	3,300,000	2,893,000††
Japan	$41.3 billion	1,140,429	953,000

*In 1994 dollars.
**An additional 115,187 servicemen died from non-battle causes.
***Before surrender to Nazis.
†Includes 65,000 murdered Jews.
††Includes about 170,000 murdered Jews and 56,000 foreign civilians in Germany.

SKILLBUILDER: Interpreting Charts
1. Which of the nations listed in the chart suffered the greatest human costs?
2. How does U.S. spending on the war compare with the spending of Germany and Japan?

shocking to the Japanese as defeat. His power was also dramatically reduced as he became a constitutional monarch. Like the ruler of Great Britain, the emperor became largely a figurehead—a symbol of Japan.

The new constitution guaranteed that real political power in Japan rested with the people. The people elected a two-house parliament, called the Diet. All citizens over the age of 20, including women, had the right to vote. The government was led by a prime minister chosen by a majority of the Diet. A constitutional bill of rights protected basic freedoms. One more key provision—Article 9—stated that the Japanese could no longer make war. They could only fight if attacked.

In September 1951, the United States and 48 other nations signed a formal peace treaty with Japan. The treaty officially ended the war. With no armed forces, the Japanese also agreed to continuing U.S. military protection for their country. Six months later, the U.S. occupation of Japan was over. Relieved of the burden of paying for the occupation, Japan's economy recovered more quickly. With the official end of the war, the United States and Japan became allies.

In the postwar world, however, enemies not only became allies. Allies also became enemies. World War II had changed the political landscape of Europe. It weakened some nations and strengthened others. The Soviet Union and the United States had come out of the war as allies. Nevertheless, once the fighting was over, the differences in their postwar goals emerged. These differences stirred up conflicts that would shape the modern world for decades.

Section 5 Assessment

1. TERMS & NAMES
Identify
• Nuremberg Trials
• demilitarization

2. TAKING NOTES
Using a Venn diagram like the one below, compare and contrast the aftermath of World War II in Europe and Japan.

3. ANALYZING CAUSES
Why do you think that many Europeans favored communism directly following World War II?

THINK ABOUT
• World War II destruction
• pre-World War II governments
• economic concerns

4. THEME ACTIVITY
Economics Draw a political cartoon from a Japanese absentee landlord's or industrialist's point of view on MacArthur's postwar economic reforms. Remember that MacArthur is an American making important changes in a country that is not his own.

World War II **845**

Costs of World War II: Allies and Axis

Interpreting the Chart Point out to students that these charts help them compare the war costs of individual nations to the total cost of the war.

Extension Activity Ask students what other column they might add to the first chart. *Possible answer: a column on the number of refugees created by the war.*

SKILLBUILDER Answers
1. USSR
2. The United States spent more than Germany and Japan combined.

ASSESS & RETEACH

Section 5 Assessment
Have students answer the questions individually and then meet in small groups to discuss their answers.

Section Quiz
FORMAL ASSESSMENT
Section quiz, p. 378

Reteaching Activity
CLASS TIME: 15 MINUTES
Have students identify the political and economic differences in postwar Japan and Europe and compare and contrast them.

CRITICAL THINKING TRANSPARENCIES
CT68 Chapter 32 Visual Summary

CLOSE ACTIVITY

CLASS TIME: 15 MINUTES

Identifying Problems
Ask students to make a chart listing the problems MacArthur faced in Japan and his solutions to the problems.

Problem	Solution

TERMS & NAMES

1. blitzkrieg, p. 822
2. Atlantic Charter, p. 826
3. Isoroku Yamamoto, p. 827
4. Battle of Midway, p. 829
5. Holocaust, p. 831
6. "Final Solution," p. 833
7. genocide, p. 833
8. D-Day, p. 838
9. Nuremberg Trials, p. 843
10. demilitarization, 844

REVIEW QUESTIONS

Answers may vary for some questions.

11. The German attack on Poland on September 1, 1939.

12. The Suez Canal was the key to getting to the oil fields of Southwest Asia.

13. To destroy the United States fleet.

14. By appealing to their hatred of European colonization, the idea of "Asia for the Asians."

15. *Kristallnacht,* forced emigration, relocation to ghettos in Poland.

16. genocide; concentration camps; death camps; gas chambers.

17. Governments needed to send food and other supplies to armies. Industry began producing war-related products, causing a shortage of consumer goods.

18. *Operation Overlord* was the largest sea, air, and land battle in history. It began on the beaches of Normandy, France, on June 6, 1944. It is also called the D-Day invasion.

19. Many homes and cities were destroyed; so people often had to go searching for a place to live; food was scarce in many areas; people often went in search of lost family members; postwar treaties sometimes forced people to move.

20. Democratization and demilitarization.

Events of World War II

Europe   Pacific

Aug. 1939 Nonaggression pact between Germany and the Soviet Union — **1939**

Sept. 1939 Germany invades Poland; World War II begins

May 1940 Evacuation of British forces at Dunkirk

Jun. 1940 France surrenders; the Battle of Britain begins — **1940**

Jun. 1941 Germany invades the Soviet Union — **1941**

Dec. 1941 Japanese attack Pearl Harbor; U.S. declares war on Japan

Apr. 1942 Allies surrender in Philippines; Bataan Death March begins

Aug. 1942 Hitler orders attack on Stalingrad — **1942**

May 1942 Allies turn back Japanese fleet in Battle of the Coral Sea

Nov. 1942 Allies land in North Africa

Jun. 1942 Allies defeat Japan in Battle of Midway

Feb. 1943 Germans surrender at Stalingrad — **1943**

Feb. 1943 Japanese abandon the island of Guadalcanal

Jun. 1944 Allies invade Europe on D-Day — **1944**

Oct. 1944 Allies defeat Japan in Battle of Leyte Gulf

Dec. 1944 Battle of the Bulge begins

Mar. 1945 Allies capture Iwo Jima

Jun. 1945 Allies capture Okinawa

May 1945 Germany surrenders — **1945**

Aug. 1945 Atomic bombs dropped on Hiroshima and Nagasaki

Sep. 1945 Japan surrenders

TERMS & NAMES

Briefly explain the importance of each of the following during and after World War II.

1. blitzkrieg
2. Atlantic Charter
3. Isoroku Yamamoto
4. Battle of Midway
5. Holocaust
6. Final Solution
7. genocide
8. D-Day
9. Nuremberg Trials
10. demilitarization

REVIEW QUESTIONS

SECTION 1 *(pages 821–826)*
Hitler's Lightning War

11. What event finally unleashed World War II?
12. Why was capturing Egypt's Suez Canal so important to the Axis powers?

SECTION 2 *(pages 827–830)*
Japan Strikes in the Pacific

13. What was Yamamoto's objective at Pearl Harbor?
14. How did Japan try to win support from other Asian countries?

SECTION 3 *(pages 831–834)*
The Holocaust

15. Name two tactics that Hitler used to rid Germany of Jews before creating his "Final Solution."
16. What tactics did Hitler use during the "Final Solution"?

SECTION 4 *(pages 835–841)*
The Allies Are Victorious

17. Why were items rationed during the war?
18. What was *Operation Overlord?*

SECTION 5 *(pages 842–845)*
The Devastation of Europe and Japan

19. Why did Europeans leave their homes following the war?
20. What were two of the most important steps that MacArthur took in Japan following the war?

Interact *with* History

On page 820, you had to decide whether to bomb the civilian population in an enemy city to shorten a war. Now that you have read the chapter, what bombing incidents in World War II seem to reflect a decision to bomb civilians to speed victory? Remember to consider bombings carried out by both sides in the war.

Interact *with* History

Possible Responses: Students might mention the German Luftwaffe's bombing of Great Britain or the Allied bombing of Dresden. Students should consider whether the policy of bombing civilian populations was effective in winning victory.

CRITICAL THINKING

1. WAR LEADERS

Consider the personalities, tactics, and policies of Hitler, Rommel, MacArthur, and Churchill. What qualities do you think make a successful leader in war? Explain your answer.

2. WORLD WAR II BATTLES

Below is a list of World War II battles/conflicts. Copy the chart on your paper and specify for each whether the Axis powers or the Allied powers gained an advantage over their enemies.

Battle/Conflict	Allied or Axis Powers?
Battle of Britain	
War in the Balkans	
Pearl Harbor	
Battle of the Coral Sea	
Battle of Midway	
Battle of Stalingrad	

3. WAR GOALS

THEME EMPIRE BUILDING Compare and contrast Japan's and Germany's goals in World War II.

4. ANALYZING PRIMARY SOURCES

The following quotation comes from the August 29, 1945 edition of *The Christian Century*, a prominent Protestant journal. In this passage, the writer raises questions about the American use of the atomic bomb on the Japanese.

A VOICE FROM THE PAST

Perhaps it was inevitable that the bomb would ultimately be employed to bring Japan to the point of surrender. . . . But there was no military advantage in hurling the bomb upon Japan without warning. The least we might have done was to announce to our foe that we possessed the atomic bomb; that its destructive power was beyond anything known in warfare; and that its terrible effectiveness had been experimentally demonstrated in this country. . . . If she [Japan] doubted the good faith of our representations, it would have been a simple matter to select a demonstration target in the enemy's own country at a place where the loss of human life would be at a minimum. If, despite such warning, Japan had still held out, we would have been in a far less questionable position had we then dropped the bombs on Hiroshima and Nagasaki.

- Does *The Christian Century* oppose all use of the atomic bomb as a weapon of war? Explain.

- What advantages might the alternative proposed by *The Christian Century* have had in ending World War II?

CHAPTER ACTIVITIES

1. LIVING HISTORY: Unit Portfolio Project

THEME SCIENCE AND TECHNOLOGY Your unit portfolio project focuses on how science and technology influence history. For Chapter 32, you might use one of the following ideas to add to your portfolio:

- Do research and create a set of science and technology cards for important inventions developed or perfected during World War II. Include the following categories on your cards: *Name of Invention, Country, Year, Use in the War, Use Today.*

- Write a list of five questions that you would ask Robert Oppenheimer if you were on a committee deciding whether to develop an atomic bomb.

- Do research and create a science and technology time line for 1935–1945. Include major events of the war and five scientific and technological developments.

2. CONNECT TO TODAY: Cooperative Learning

THEME ECONOMICS During World War II, many nations, including the United States, converted their consumer-goods factories to produce vital products for the war effort. Today many of those factories still exist but are back to producing consumer goods.

Work with a team to prepare a short "company history."

Using the Internet, library, magazines, or Chamber of Commerce, do research on a consumer-goods company. (A consumer-goods company makes products for personal use or enjoyment—for example, cars, radios, clothing.) Look for a company that was around before 1945. (Several of today's important car and appliance manufacturers, as well as manufacturers of steel, tires, detergents, etc., existed before 1945.)

As you come up with ideas, try to find answers to questions such as: What products did the company make before World War II? During the war? After? What were working conditions like during the war? After the war? In a two- to three-page paper, write your company history. Include copies of any articles, photographs, or pictures that you find about the company.

3. INTERPRETING A TIME LINE

Revisit the unit time line on pages 738–739. Which two leaders do you think had the largest impact on events between 1939 and 1945? Why?

FOCUS ON GEOGRAPHY

Notice the locations in Europe of German death camps and labor camps.

- Which country had the most labor camps?

- Which country had the most death camps?

Connect to History In what year did most of the death camps begin to operate? Why?

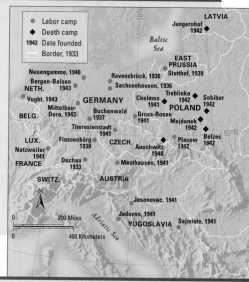

Legend	
●	Labor camp
◆	Death camp
1942	Date founded
	Border, 1933

Baltic Sea

LATVIA
Jungernhof 1942

EAST PRUSSIA
Stutthof, 1939

Neuengamme, 1940
Bergen-Belsen 1943
NETH.
Vught, 1943

Ravensbrück, 1936
Sachsenhausen, 1936

GERMANY
Mittelbau-Dora, 1943
BELG.

Chelmno 1941
Buchenwald 1937

Treblinka 1942
POLAND
Gross-Rosen 1941

Sobibor 1942

Majdanek 1942

Theresienstadt 1941
LUX.
Natzweiler 1941
FRANCE
Flossenbürg 1938
Dachau 1933

CZECH.
Auschwitz 1940

Plasow 1942

Belzec 1942

Mauthausen, 1941

SWITZ.
AUSTRIA

Adriatic Sea

Jasenovac, 1941
Jadovno, 1941
YUGOSLAVIA
Sajmiste, 1941

0 — 200 Miles
0 — 400 Kilometers

UNIT 8

Perspectives on the Present
1945–present

South Africa, April 1994

The long line of voters in this picture is remarkable for the fact that these South Africans are voting in their own country for the first time—and helping elect a black president, Nelson Mandela. The revolution that occurred in South Africa in the early 1990s is part of the ongoing worldwide struggle for democracy that began at the end of World War II. Many nations in Asia, Africa, Latin America, and Eastern Europe are emerging from decades of oppression and are striving to create their own forms of government and to ensure economic security for their people.

Because South Africa's racist policies were so repressive, many people feared that change would come only after armed conflict, as had happened in Angola and Zimbabwe. Instead, the white-controlled government and the black-controlled African National Congress worked together to open the political process to all South Africans.

The call for all races to work together for the future of South Africa was eloquently voiced by President Mandela in his 1994 inauguration speech:

". . . The time for the healing of wounds has come. The moment to bridge the chasms that divide us has come. The time to build is upon us . . . We understand it still that there is no easy road to freedom. We know it well that none of us acting alone can achieve success. We must therefore act together as a unified people, for national reconciliation, for nation building, for the birth of a new world. . . ."

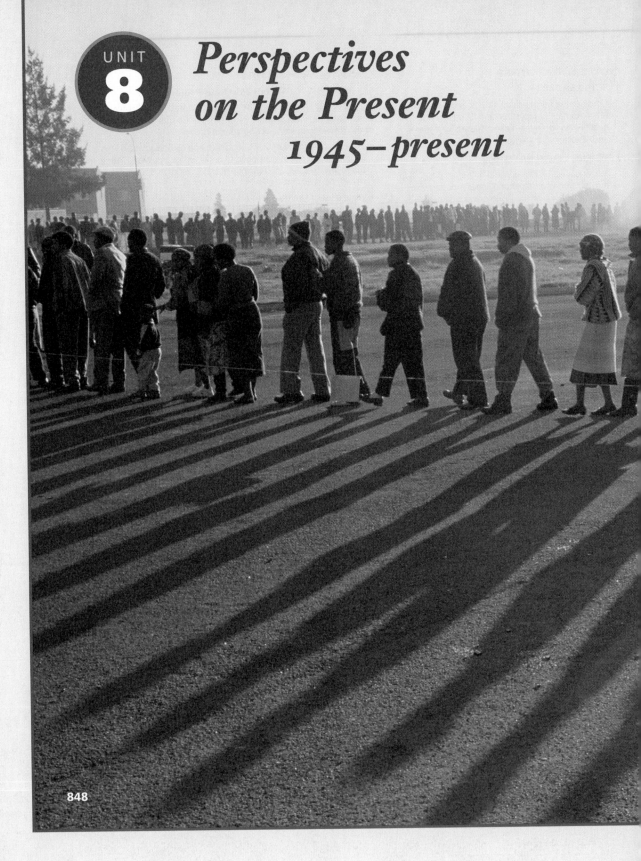

UNIT 8

Perspectives on the Present
1945–present

848

Black South Africans wait to vote during the nation's first "all-races" election in April 1994. While the present era has been one of struggle and strife, it also has produced events that show people's continuing desire to achieve democracy and justice.

849

This unit describes the momentous political, social, and economic changes occurring around the globe after World War II.

With much of Europe and parts of Asia in ruins after World War II, the United States and the Soviet Union emerge as rival superpowers. Their political and military confrontations dominate world affairs for the next 40 years.

The end of World War II also heralds the end of colonialism, as native peoples in Africa, Asia, and the South Pacific demand independence. Although some European nations try to hold onto their colonies, others help native populations prepare for independent rule.

The 1980s and 1990s witness a dramatic shift toward democracy in many areas around the world. The Soviet Union dissolves into 15 separate republics, while military dictatorships fall in Latin America. Nigeria and South Africa pursue democratic goals, and China reforms its economy.

Advances in science, communications, and technology improve life for many people and help create a global economy. Nations around the world must adjust to new patterns of work, ensure the rights of their diverse populations, protect their environments, and achieve peaceful relations with their neighbors.

Perspectives on the Present

Teaching Strategies

Making Generalizations You might ask students to study the time line for Unit 8 to form generalizations about events highlighted there. Ask students to group some time-line events into categories from which they can try to detect general patterns. Categories might include:

- War and Revolution
- Decolonization
- Assassinations
- China
- South Africa
- The Middle East
- India and Pakistan

Generalization Charts You might ask students to create charts with three or four categories and events grouped under them in chronological order. Stress that events may fall into more than one category.

After the charts have been completed, students will examine the events within each category and create one generalization for each of them.

Numerous generalizations can be drawn from the events under these categories—for example, pace of decolonization, the development of the apartheid policy in South Africa, the evolution of China from the postwar era to the present, and many others. Students should be prepared to explain to the rest of the class the process by which they drew their general statements from the information listed in their charts.

UNIT 8 Time Line
Perspectives on the Present

	1945	1955	1965	197
CHAPTER 33 1945–PRESENT Restructuring the Postwar World	**1945 Yalta** Allied leaders meet to plan postwar world **1946 Soviet Union, U.S.** Cold War begins **1946 China** Civil war between Nationalists and Communists resumes **1950-53 Korea** Korean War between North and South Korea **1953 Iran** U.S. restores ousted shah to power	**1958 China** Mao Zedong begins Great Leap Forward **1959 Cuba** Fidel Castro overthrows Batista **1960 Soviet Union** Soviets catch U.S. spy plane in U-2 incident **1961 Cuba** Castro routs U.S.-supported invasion of Bay of Pigs	**1965 Vietnam** U.S. sends troops to Vietnam **1966 China** Red Guards begin Cultural Revolution in China **1969 Vietnam** Nixon begins withdrawal of U.S. troops from Vietnam	
CHAPTER 34 1945–PRESENT The Colonies Become New Nations	**1946 Philippines** Philippines gains independence from U.S. **1947 India** Independent India becomes partitioned into India and Pakistan **1948 Middle East** Israel becomes a nation **1948 India** Gandhi is assassinated	**1957 Ghana** Ghana achieves independence from Great Britain **1962 Algeria** Algeria achieves independence from France **1964 Kenya** Jomo Kenyatta becomes president	**1965 Malaysia** Singapore becomes independent **1967 Indonesia** Suharto becomes president **1971 East Pakistan** East Pakistan becomes independent Bangladesh **1973 Middle East** Arab forces attack Israel in the Yom Kippur War	
CHAPTER 35 1945–PRESENT Struggles for Democracy	**1946 Argentina** Juan Perón is elected president and becomes a dictator **1948 South Africa** National Party sets up apartheid	**1960 South Africa** Police kill 69 demonstrators in Sharpeville Massacre **1964 Brazil** A military government seizes power	**1966 China** Mao Zedong launches Cultural Revolution **1967 Nigeria** Biafra secedes and civil war erupts	
CHAPTER 36 1960–PRESENT Global Interdependence			**1975 Space** U.S. Apollo docks with Soviet Soyuz spacecraft **1975 Finland** Helsinki Accords on Human Rights established	

◄1990s Afghanistan

1945	1955	1965	197

CONNECTIONS ACROSS TIME AND PLACE

Revolutions You might ask students to do research to compare the revolutions mentioned in the time line that occurred from the 1940s to the 1960s with any that are ongoing at the present time.

Students might choose two revolutions (one past and one present) to compare and contrast the objectives, ideologies, and strategies behind each. Ask them to draw conclusions about how revolutions have changed or remained the same in the past 50 or so years.

MULTIPLE LEARNING STYLES

Visual Learners The three photographs included in the time line for Unit 8 are all images drawn from the 1990s. Ask students to go to books, magazines, and the Internet to find five additional images that they feel are characteristic of the 1990s.

After they have chosen their images, they may make a photocopy of the time line and add their new images of the 1990s. They should be prepared to explain to the rest of the class why they made their photo selections.

1979 *Iran* Shah flees Iran; Muslims take over government

1979 *Nicaragua* U.S. and Soviets support Marxist rebels

1979 *Afghanistan* Soviets invade Afghanistan

1981 *Iran* Islamic revolutionaries free U.S. hostages

1950s *China* ▶

Living History
Unit 8 Portfolio Project

THEME Economics

Your portfolio for Unit 8 will show the economic changes within and among nations from World War II to the present. You will trace the growing global interdependence of the economies of all nations of the world.

Living History Project Choices
Each Chapter Assessment offers you choices of ways to show how the economies of the nations grew or shrank and became tied to the economies of others. Activities include the following:

Chapter **33** newscast, poster, skit

Chapter **34** list, chart, magazine article

Chapter **35** action list, poster, interview

Chapter **36** poem or song, map, graphs or charts

1979 *Middle East*
Camp David Accords signed by Egypt's Sadat and Israel's Begin ends war between Egypt and Israel

1981 *Egypt*
Anwar Sadat is assassinated

1984 *India*
Indira Gandhi is assassinated

1987 *Middle East*
Palestinians begin intifada

1993 *Israel*
Israel grants Palestinians self-rule in Gaza Strip and West Bank

1995 *Israel*
Prime Minister Yitzhak Rabin is assassinated

1997 *Congo*
Laurent Kabila becomes president of Democratic Republic of the Congo

---

1978 *China*
Deng Xiaoping begins Four Modernizations

1982 *Argentina*
Britain defeats Argentina in war over Falkland Islands

1989 *Germany* Berlin Wall is knocked down

1989 *China* Student demonstrators killed in Tiananmen Square

1991 *Soviet Union* Soviet Union breaks up into 15 republics

1992 *Bosnia-Herzegovina* Serbs begin war against Muslims and Croats

1994 *South Africa* First all-race election; Nelson Mandela becomes president

1997 *Mexico*
Mexico elects multi-party congress

1997 *Hong Kong*
Britain returns Hong Kong to China

▲ 1990s *South Africa*

1975 *Space*
U.S. *Apollo* docks with Soviet *Soyuz* spacecraft

1975 *Finland*
Helsinki Accords on Human Rights established

1986 *Space*
Soviet space station *Mir* established in space

1990 *Middle East*
Iraq occupies part of Kuwait, provoking Persian Gulf War

1992 *Brazil*
Earth Summit Environmental Conference held in Rio de Janeiro

1995 *China*
International Conference on Women held in Beijing

1995 *Worldwide*
World Trade Organization established

TIME LINE **851**

Portfolio Project

Interaction with Environment The projects suggested for Unit 8 deal with the theme of both economic and environmental interdependence around the globe. Several projects deal with the contrasting characteristics of communism and capitalism—a major element of world events in the 20th century. They may also examine the growth of multinational corporations, the impact of economic conditions on immigration, or the effect of the global economy on the world's ecology.

Logical-Mathematical Learners At least one portfolio project suggestion per chapter in Unit 8 emphasizes the logical skills of listing, categorizing, and contrasting. In Chapter 35, for example, students are asked to create an action list for turning a communist country into a free-market economy. Logical-mathematical learners may want to select these projects to use their skills for organizing information and reducing it to its essentials.

The Western Civilization Videodisc

SECTION O: The Postwar Era: The New Global Civilization, 1945–1990s

Side One:
Frame 46958

Universal Play Button

See Master Guide, page 335 for Section O.

Restructuring the Postwar World

	Key Ideas	**COPY MASTERS**	**ASSESSMENT**
SECTION 1 **Two Superpowers Face Off** *pp. 855–861*	The Soviet Union builds a buffer zone in Eastern Europe, and the United States aids its Western European allies as it struggles to block Communist expansion.	*In-Depth Resources: Unit 8* • **Guided Reading,** p. 1 • **Literature:** from *The Nuclear Age,* p. 13 • **Connections Across Time and Cultures:** Restoring the Peace, p. 18 • **Science and Technology:** Super Spy Plane, p. 19	PE *Section 1 Assessment,* p. 860 *Formal Assessment* • Section Quiz, p. 387 *Alternative Assessment Book* • Standards for Evaluating a Cooperative Activity
SECTION 2 **Communists Triumph in China** *pp. 862–865*	China splits into two nations—one Communist and one not. Mao Zedong expands the Communist state and launches ambitious, but often disastrous, programs to transform its society.	*In-Depth Resources: Unit 8* • **Guided Reading,** p. 2 • **Skillbuilder Practice:** Interpreting Charts, p. 6 • **Primary Source:** from *No Tears for Mao,* p. 9	PE *Section 2 Assessment,* p. 865 *Formal Assessment* • Section Quiz, p. 388 *Alternative Assessment Book* • Standards for Evaluating a Cooperative Activity
SECTION 3 **War in Korea and Vietnam** *pp. 866–870*	The United States fights bloody wars to prevent Communist takeovers in Korea and Vietnam, but Korea remains split into Communist and non-Communist nations and Vietnam becomes Communist.	*In-Depth Resources: Unit 8* • **Guided Reading,** p. 3 • **Primary Source:** from *When Heaven and Earth Changed Places,* p. 10 • **History Makers:** Ho Chi Minh, p. 16	PE *Section 3 Assessment,* p. 870 *Formal Assessment* • Section Quiz, p. 389 *Alternative Assessment Book* • Standards for Evaluating a Cooperative Activity
SECTION 4 **Cold War Around the World** *pp. 871–875*	The United States and the Soviet Union compete for influence throughout the developing world by supporting rival factions in Latin America, Asia, and Africa.	*In-Depth Resources: Unit 8* • **Guided Reading,** p. 4 • **Geography Application:** The Cuban Missile Crisis, p. 7 • **Primary Source:** The Cuban Missile Crisis (Speech by John F. Kennedy), p. 11 • **History Makers:** Ruholla Khomeini, p. 17	PE *Section 4 Assessment,* p. 875 *Formal Assessment* • Section Quiz, p. 390 *Alternative Assessment Book* • Standards for Evaluating a Cooperative Activity
SECTION 5 **The Cold War Thaws** *pp. 876–879*	The Cold War begins to thaw as Khrushchev denounces Stalinism and U.S. leaders adopt a foreign policy of lessened tensions.	*In-Depth Resources: Unit 8* • **Guided Reading,** p. 5 • **Primary Source:** Political Cartoon, p. 12	PE *Section 5 Assessment,* p. 879 *Formal Assessment* • Section Quiz, p. 391 *Alternative Assessment Book* • Standards for Evaluating a Cooperative Activity
CHAPTER RESOURCES	**Chapter Overview** After World War II, the Soviet Union and the United States emerge as rivals. This rivalry is mainly diplomatic and strategic, but also leads both to become involved in military actions around the world. The rivalry dominates world politics for four decades.	*Telescoping the Times* • Chapter Summary, pp. 129–131 *Planning for Block Schedules*	PE *Chapter Assessment,* pp. 880–881 *Chapter Activities,* p. 881 *Formal Assessment* • Chapter Test, forms A and B, pp. 392–397 *Test Generator* *Alternative Assessment Book*

TECHNOLOGY

 Warm-Up Transparency 33

 Geography Transparencies
- GT33 The Berlin Airlift, 1948–1949

 INTERNET RESOURCES
www.mlworldhistory.com

 Warm-Up Transparency 33

 World Art and Cultures Transparencies
- AT72 *Spring Walk to the Chi-Ch'ang Park*

 INTERNET RESOURCES
www.mlworldhistory.com

 Warm-Up Transparency 33

 World Art and Cultures Transparencies
- AT73 *Laying a Road*

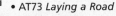 *Battles of the World*
- Tet Offensive

 Electronic Library of Primary Sources
- from *Peace Without Conquest*

 INTERNET RESOURCES
www.mlworldhistory.com

 Warm-Up Transparency 33

 Critical Thinking Transparencies
- CT33 Global Superpowers Face Off

 Electronic Library of Primary Sources
- from *444 Days: The Hostages Remember*

INTERNET RESOURCES
www.mlworldhistory.com

 Warm-Up Transparency 33

Critical Thinking Transparencies
- CT69 Chapter 33 Visual Summary

 Electronic Library of Primary Sources
- Speech on Stalin by Nikita Khrushchev
- from *A Student's Diary*

INTERNET RESOURCES
www.mlworldhistory.com

 Chapter Summaries on Audiocassette in English and Spanish

INTERNET RESOURCES
www.mlworldhistory.com

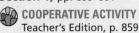 **Block Scheduling** (90 MINUTES)

Day 1
Section 1, pp. 855–861
 COOPERATIVE ACTIVITY
Teacher's Edition, p. 859

Section 2, pp. 862–865
COOPERATIVE ACTIVITY
Teacher's Edition, p. 864

Section Assessments,
pp. 860, 865

Day 2
Section 3, pp. 866–870
COOPERATIVE ACTIVITY
Teacher's Edition, p. 868

Section 4, pp. 871–875
COOPERATIVE ACTIVITY
Teacher's Edition, p. 873

Section Assessments,
pp. 870, 875

Day 3
Section 5, pp. 876–879
COOPERATIVE ACTIVITY
Teacher's Edition, p. 878

Section Assessment, p. 879

Chapter Assessment,
pp. 880–881

Yearly Pacing *Chapter 33 Total:* 3 days *Yearly Total:* 85 days

 Planning for Block Schedules

Customizing for Special Needs

Students Acquiring English

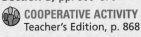 *Access for Students Acquiring English*
- **Guided Reading** for Sections 1–5 (Spanish), pp. 332–336
- **Chapter Summary** (Spanish), pp. 329–331
- **Skillbuilder Practice** : Interpreting Charts (Spanish), p. 337
- **Geography Application** The Cuban Missile Crisis (Spanish), p. 338

 Chapter Summaries on Audiocassette in English and Spanish

INTERNET RESOURCES www.mlworldhistory.com *The Diverse Classroom.*

Less Proficient Readers

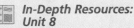 *In-Depth Resources: Unit 8*
- **Guided Reading** for Sections 1–5, pp. 1–5
- **Skillbuilder Practice:** Interpreting Charts, p. 6
- **Geography Application:** The Cuban Missile Crisis, p. 7

 Telescoping the Times
- Chapter Summary, pp. 129–131

 Chapter Summaries on Audiocassette

Gifted and Talented Students

 In-Depth Resources: Unit 8

Primary Sources:
- from *No Tears for Mao,* p. 9
- from *When Heaven and Earth Changed Places,* p. 10
- The Cuban Missile Crisis (Speech by John F. Kennedy), p. 11
- Political Cartoon p. 12

History Makers:
- Ho Chi Minh, p. 16
- Ruholla Khomeini, p. 17

Connections to Literature READINGS FOR STUDENTS

 In-Depth Resources: Unit 8
Literature: from *The Nuclear Age,* p. 13

Enrichment Reading

McDougal Littell
***The Language of LIterature,* Grade 10**
Le Ly Hayslip, from *When Heaven and Earth Changed Places,* p. 140
Tim O'Brien, "On the Rainy River," p. 266
Nguyen Thi Vinh, "Thoughts of Hanoi, p. 754

McDougal Littell
Literature Connections

- Myers, William Dean
Fallen Angels
(with related readings)

In this novel a small group of men come of age during the Vietnam War. Their experiences range from numbingly routine to traumatic and heartbreaking.

 = Pupil's Edition   = Overhead Transparency   = Software   = Video

 = Copy Master   = CD-ROM   = Audiocassette   = Internet

Restructuring the Postwar World, 1945–present

Accessing Prior Knowledge

- Ask students what they already know about the Cold War.

Making Inferences

- After students look at the cartoon and caption about the U.S.-Soviet arms race, ask why they think these countries were hostile to each other.

- What can students infer from the images and captions about the effects of the U.S.-Soviet hostility on the rest of the world?

Geography Connection

Ask students to look at the colored areas of the map.

- Which countries make up the major Communist powers?

- What boundary line divides Europe into Communist and non-Communist areas?

CHAPTER 33

Restructuring the Postwar World, 1945–present

PREVIEWING THEMES

Economics

After World War II, two conflicting economic systems—capitalism and communism—competed for influence and power. The major players in this struggle, the United States and the Soviet Union, each tried to win other nations to its side.

Revolution

In Asia, Latin America, and Eastern Europe, people revolted against repressive governments or rule by foreign powers. These revolutions often became the arenas for conflicts between the United States and the Soviet Union.

Empire Building

The United States and the Soviet Union used military, economic, and humanitarian aid to extend their control over other countries. They also sought to prevent the other superpower from gaining influence.

INTERNET CONNECTION

Visit us at www.mlworldhistory.com to learn more about the Cold War and the wars in Korea and Vietnam.

COLD WAR ENEMIES, 1946

UNITED STATES

ATLANTIC OCEAN

Beginning in the **late 1940s**, the **United States** and the **Soviet Union** faced off in a deadly arms race. Luckily for the world, each side merely stockpiled its weapons, afraid to make the first move.

During the **late 1970s**, **Nicaragua** became the arena for a U.S. stand against communism. These Communist Nicaraguan rebels fought to end the dictatorship of their country's U.S.-supported regime. But they also supported leftist rebels in El Salvador. In response, the United States backed anti-Communist guerrillas in Nicaragua called Contras.

852

GEOGRAPHY THEMES

Place

Tell students that geography played an important role in the development of U.S. and Soviet Cold War strategies. Point out the huge landmass of the Soviet Union and the two oceans that surround the United States. Have them discuss how these factors may have influenced the countries' policies. *The oceans offered the United States natural defense and motivated its leaders to build air and sea power. In contrast, the Soviet Union was vulnerable to land invasion, which led Soviet leaders to build massive armies.*

Location

Ask students to note the caption arrows pointing at Nicaragua and Vietnam. What aspects of their location might have made these countries Cold War hot spots? As they read the chapter, students should verify their predictions and consider why other countries were drawn into Cold War struggles.

Vietnam, located next to China, could have served either as a wall to contain Communism or a funnel through which it would spread. Nicaragua, as part of North America, represented a stronghold against communism that was essential to the United States.

Iron Curtain

SOVIET UNION

Chinese youths waved banners and carried flowers and models of ICBM missiles to celebrate Soviet Premier Nikita Khrushchev's visit to **Beijing**. Despite this enthusiastic welcome, the two Communist giants split in **1959**.

CHINA

PACIFIC OCEAN

Tropic of Cancer

☐ Major Communist powers
☐ Major Non-Communist power
— Iron Curtain

| 0 | 1,000 Miles |
| 0 | 2,000 Kilometers |

N

0° Equator

In **1975,** in the wake of the Vietnam War, this South Vietnamese man fled from his homeland with his family. The war devastated **Vietnam**. It also led to massive popular protests in the United States against U.S. military support for South Vietnam.

Tropic of Capricorn

853

ADDITIONAL RESOURCES

Books for the Teacher

• Kutler, Stanley, ed. *Encyclopedia of the Vietnam War.* New York: Scribner's, 1996.

• Walker, Martin. *The Cold War: A History.* New York: Holt & Co., 1994.

Books for the Student

• Arms, Thomas S. *Encyclopedia of the Cold War.* New York: Facts on File, 1994.

• Denenberg, Barry. *Voices from Vietnam.* New York: Scholastic, 1995.

• Dudman, John. *The Division of Berlin.* Vero Beach, FL: Rourke, 1988.

📼 Videos

• *Berlin Airlift.* Britannica, 1990. 800-554-9862.

• *From Bay of Pigs to the Brink.* Films for the Humanities & Sciences, 1993. 800-257-5126.

• *Vietnam: A Case Study for Critical Thinking.* Society for Visual Education, 1987. 800-829-1900.

💿 Software

• *Decisions, Decisions: The Cold War.* CD-ROM or Diskette. Tom Snyder Productions, 1996. 800-342-0236.

• *Seven Days in August: The Cold War's Defining Moment.* Social Studies School Service, 1995. 800-421-4246. Day-by-day look at the week in 1961 when the Berlin Wall went up.

HISTORY THROUGH ART

South Vietnamese "Convoy of Tears"

This photograph was taken in March 1975, after the South Vietnamese government abandoned the central highlands and as many as 1.5 million people joined what came to be known as a "convoy of tears" in flight from their inland homes to the coast. An estimated 30,000 to 40,000 people died on this 15-day march, harrassed all the way by North Vietnamese army troops.

A Vietnamese participant described this tragic episode in a tragic war:

The evacuees . . . included soldiers, children, very old people. . . . Refugees moving on foot were hit by Communist machine guns, falling down on the road. The blood flowed on the road like a tiny stream. The sound of roaring artillery and small arms, the screams of seriously wounded people at death's door, and children, created a voice out of hell.

Interpreting the Photograph How do you think the photographer of this scene felt? Do you think that photographers are justified in merely recording such human suffering rather than doing what they can to help? Why or why not?

eract with History

his Interact with History feature
motivates students by inviting
them to imagine themselves the
leader of the United States or the
Soviet Union after World War II.
As they consider their country's
goals in the struggle between
superpowers and the importance
of a developing nation in achieving
those goals, they will identify the
issues, weigh their options, and
become decision makers.

Purpose

• to set the stage for studying the
  Cold War

• to help students realize how the
  Cold War influenced world events

• to enable students to experience
  the issues that face powerful
  world leaders

Teaching Strategy

Thinking Critically After students
have imagined themselves in the
situation described on this page,
have them answer the key question and give reasons for their
decision.

EXAMINING the ISSUES

Following are suggestions for
addressing each bulleted item.

1 Ask students when they
have been so angry at or
afraid of someone that they
would do anything to oppose
the person, even if it meant
hurting someone else.

2 Have students consider how
leaders of rival school social
or academic groups enlist
and mobilize their followers.

3 Students may say that such
countries might have to sacrifice either their ideals or
their economic security.

Making Connections Ask students to discuss what they
know about conflicts in countries such as Cuba, Nicaragua,
El Salvador, and Guatemala.

Follow Up

A feature on the chapter assessment will ask students to reevaluate their responses to the
situation presented on this page.

Interact with History

World War II has ended and two superpowers—the United States and
the Soviet Union—dominate the world. You are the leader of one of
those superpowers. Civil war has broken out in a developing country that supplies you with essential raw materials.

For that reason, it is important for you to help restore peace. The ruler of
that country is a brutal dictator who makes life miserable for his people. Rebels
are fighting to topple him, but they are backed by your superpower enemy.

Would you support the country's ruler or the rebels?

Rebel forces are skilled at guerrilla warfare. With weapons
supplied by your superpower enemy and their knowledge of
the land, they are powerful military opponents.

The developing country has rich natural
resources that both superpowers need.

Life is difficult for the
country's people. They
suffer even more as the
civil war continues.

854

EXAMINING the ISSUES

1 • What is most important to you—aiding the people of
the developing nation or preventing your enemy from
gaining influence there?

2 • How might competing superpowers use weaker
countries in their competition?

3 • How might being caught in a struggle between
superpowers affect a developing nation?

As a class, discuss the effects of the conflict between superpowers on the rest of the world. Think about the experiences
of Latin American and other countries under colonialism and
how those lessons might be useful.

As you read about how the two superpowers divided up the
world, notice the part weaker countries played in their conflict.

1 Two Superpowers Face Off

TERMS & NAMES
- United Nations
- iron curtain
- containment
- Truman Doctrine
- Marshall Plan
- Cold War
- NATO
- Warsaw Pact
- brinkmanship
- U-2 incident

MAIN IDEA	WHY IT MATTERS NOW
The conflicting aims between the United States and the Soviet Union led to global competition.	The conflicts between these two superpowers played a major role in reshaping the modern world.

SETTING THE STAGE During World War II, the United States and the Soviet Union joined forces to fight against the Germans. The Soviet army marched west. The Americans marched east to meet them in a defeated Germany. When the Allied soldiers met at the Elbe River, they embraced each other warmly. Their leaders, however, regarded each other much more coolly.

Former Allies Diverge

Even before World War II ended, the U.S. alliance with the Soviet Union had begun to unravel. The United States was upset that Joseph Stalin, the Soviet Union's leader, had signed a nonaggression pact with Adolf Hitler, Germany's leader, in 1939. Later, Stalin blamed the Allies for delaying their invasion of German-occupied Europe until 1944. Driven by these and other conflicts, the two allies began to pursue opposing goals.

A Joint Postwar Plan In February 1945, the war was not yet over. But the leaders of the three Allied nations—the United States, Britain, and the Soviet Union—met in the Soviet Black Sea resort city of Yalta. There, they agreed to divide Germany into zones of occupation controlled by the Allied military forces. Germany also would have to pay the Soviet Union to compensate for its loss of life and property. Stalin promised that Eastern Europeans would have free elections. Skeptical Winston Churchill recognized this as an empty promise. And he predicted that Stalin would keep his pledge only if the Eastern Europeans followed "a policy friendly to Russia." In return, Stalin agreed to join the war against Japan, an ally of Germany.

Creation of the United Nations In June 1945, the United States and the Soviet Union temporarily set aside their differences. They joined 48 other countries in forming the **United Nations.** This international organization was intended to protect the members against aggression. It was to be based in New York. The 50 nations that signed the UN charter pledged "to save succeeding generations from the scourge of war."

The charter for the new peacekeeping organization established a large body called the General Assembly. This was like an international town meeting. Each UN member nation could cast its vote on a broad range of issues, including membership. An 11-member body called the Security Council had the real power to investigate and settle disputes, though. The five permanent members of the Security Council were Britain, China,

SPOTLIGHT ON

Yalta Conference

When the leaders of the United States, the Soviet Union, and Great Britain met at Yalta, their goals were noble ones:

- to promote world peace
- to provide emergency relief
- to help form interim governments based on the will of the people.

Prime Minister Winston Churchill (left) was optimistic about "the broad sunlight of victorious peace."

But "victorious peace" meant very different things to Stalin (right) and Roosevelt (center). The Soviet leader wanted a strong Communist state and protection against renewed invasion from the West. The ailing U.S. president wanted a democratic world led by his country. And those conflicting views made continuing peace impossible.

855

SECTION 1 RESOURCES

PRINT RESOURCES

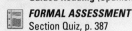 **IN-DEPTH RESOURCES: UNIT 8**
Guided Reading, p. 1
Literature: from *The Nuclear Age*, p. 13
Connections Across Time and Cultures, p. 18
Science and Technology: Super Spy Plane, p. 19

ACCESS FOR STUDENTS ACQUIRING ENGLISH
Guided Reading (Spanish), p. 332

FORMAL ASSESSMENT
Section Quiz, p. 387

TECHNOLOGY RESOURCES

GEOGRAPHY TRANSPARENCIES
GT33 The Berlin Airlift, 1948–1949

INTERNET www.mlworldhistory.com

Section 1 Overview

OBJECTIVES

(1) To explain the U.S.-Soviet postwar split.

(2) To trace how the Soviets came to dominate Eastern Europe.

(3) To describe U. S. containment of Communist expansion.

(4) To define the Cold War.

SKILLBUILDERS

- Interpreting charts, pp. 856, 858
- Interpreting maps: location, place, p. 857

CRITICAL THINKING

- Summarizing, p. 856
- Analyzing causes, p. 857
- Making inferences, pp. 858, 861
- Analyzing issues, p. 859
- Recognizing effects, p. 860
- Analyzing motives, p. 860
- Comparing, p. 861

FOCUS
5-Minute Warm-Up

▶ **Clarifying**
To help students understand the players in the Cold War, have them answer these questions.

1. Look at the chart on page 856. Which country wanted to reunite Germany?

2. Which country wanted to control Eastern Europe?

WARM-UP TRANSPARENCY 33

OBJECTIVE ① INSTRUCT

Former Allies Diverge

▶ **Key Ideas**
- Britain, the Soviet Union, and the United States partition Germany after the war.
- Fifty countries form the United Nations to promote peace.
- The United States and the Soviet Union pursue conflicting goals in Europe.

IN-DEPTH RESOURCES: UNIT 8
Guided Reading, p. 1

ACCESS FOR STUDENTS ACQUIRING ENGLISH
Guided Reading (Spanish), p. 332

SPOTLIGHT On
Yalta Conference

(See page 855.)

Of the "Big Three" leaders who met at Yalta, only Stalin held power seven months later: Roosevelt was dead, and Churchill had been voted out of office.

France, the United States, and the Soviet Union. Each could veto any Security Council action. This provision was intended to prevent any members of the Council from voting as a bloc to override the others.

Differing U.S. and Soviet Goals Despite their agreement at Yalta and their mutual presence on the UN Security Council, the United States and the Soviet Union split sharply after the war ended. The war had affected these two superpowers very differently. The United States, the world's richest and most powerful country at that time, suffered 400,000 deaths. Its cities and factories remained intact, however. The Soviet Union experienced at least 50 times as many fatalities. One in four Soviets was wounded or killed. In addition, many Soviet cities were demolished. These contrasting situations, as well as striking political and economic differences, affected the two countries' postwar goals. As the following chart shows, their aims in postwar Europe were contradictory.

Superpower Aims in Europe	
United States	**Soviet Union**
• Encourage democracy in other countries to help prevent the rise of Communist governments	• Encourage communism in other countries as part of a worldwide workers' revolution
• Gain access to raw materials and markets to fuel booming industries	• Rebuild its war-ravaged economy using Eastern Europe's industrial equipment and raw materials
• Rebuild European governments to promote stability and create new markets for American goods	• Control Eastern Europe to protect Soviet borders and balance the U.S. influence in Western Europe
• Reunite Germany to stabilize it and increase the security of Europe	• Keep Germany divided to prevent its waging war again

SKILLBUILDER: Interpreting Charts
1. *Which Soviet aims involved self-protection?*
2. *Which U.S. and Soviet aims in Europe conflicted?*

The Soviet Union Corrals Eastern Europe

With the end of World War II, a major goal of the Soviet Union was to shield itself from another invasion from the west. Even before the devastation of World War II, centuries of history had taught the Soviets to fear invasion. Because it lacked natural western borders, Russia fell victim to each of its neighbors in turn. In the 17th century, the Poles captured the Kremlin. During the next century, the Swedes attacked. Napoleon overran Moscow in 1812. The Germans invaded Russia during World War I.

Soviets Build a Wall of Satellite Nations As the war drew to a close, the Soviet Union pushed the Nazis back across Eastern Europe. By the end of the war, Soviet troops occupied a strip of countries along the Soviet Union's own western border. The Soviet Union regarded these countries as a necessary buffer, or wall of protection. Stalin ignored the agreement made in Yalta to allow free elections in Eastern Europe. He installed or secured Communist governments in Albania, Bulgaria, Hungary, Czechoslovakia, Romania, Poland, and Yugoslavia.

The Soviet leader's American partner at Yalta, President Franklin D. Roosevelt, had died on April 12, 1945. Roosevelt's successor, President Harry S. Truman, was a tougher adversary for Stalin. To the new president, Stalin's reluctance to allow free elections in Poland and other Eastern European nations represented a clear violation of those countries' rights. Truman, Stalin, and Churchill met at Potsdam, Germany, in July 1945. There, President Truman pressed Stalin to permit free elections in Eastern Europe. The Soviet leader refused. In a speech in early 1946, Stalin declared that

Communist countries
Non-Communist countries

Iron curtain

DENMARK

FINLAND

NETH.
British Zone
Berlin
POLAND

NORWAY

WEST GERMANY
EAST GERMANY

SWEDEN

French Zone

CZECHOSLOVAKIA

50° N

North Sea

DENMARK

Baltic Sea

SOVIET UNION

FRANCE
American Zone

AUSTRIA

SWITZ.

200 Miles

ITALY

400 Kilometers

GREAT BRITAIN

IRELAND

NETH.
E. GER.
POLAND

BEL.
WEST GERMANY
CZECHOSLOVAKIA

LUX.

FRANCE

SWITZ.
AUSTRIA
HUNGARY

ATLANTIC OCEAN

ROMANIA

ITALY
YUGOSLAVIA

BULGARIA
Black Sea

Aral Sea

Caspian Sea

SPAIN

ALBANIA
GREECE
TURKEY

PORTUGAL

Mediterranean Sea

Circle

ELAND

0 500 Miles
0 1,000 Kilometers

GEOGRAPHY SKILLBUILDER: Interpreting Maps
1. **Location** In which part of Germany was Berlin located?
2. **Place** Which countries separated the Soviet Union from Western Europe?

communism and capitalism could not exist in the same world. He said that war between the United States and the Soviet Union was certain.

The Iron Curtain Divides East and West Europe now lay divided between East and West. Germany's postwar fate, which had been decided at Yalta, left the country split into two sections. The Soviets controlled the eastern part, including half of Germany's capital, Berlin. Under a Communist government, East Germany was named the German Democratic Republic. The western zones became the Federal Republic of Germany in 1949. Winston Churchill described the division of Europe:

A VOICE FROM THE PAST
From Stettin in the Baltic to Trieste in the Adriatic, an iron curtain has descended across the continent. Behind that line lie all the capitals of the ancient states of Central and Eastern Europe. . . . All these famous cities and the populations around them lie in the Soviet sphere and all are subject in one form or another, not only to Soviet influence but to a very high and increasing measure of control from Moscow.

WINSTON CHURCHILL, "Iron Curtain" speech, March 5, 1946

THINK THROUGH HISTORY
B. Analyzing Causes What events led to the division of Europe?
B. Answer Soviets surrounding themselves with an "iron curtain" of Communist satellites and refusing to allow free elections.

Churchill's phrase **"iron curtain"** came to represent Europe's division between a mostly democratic Western Europe and a Communist Eastern Europe. From behind the iron curtain, Stalin termed Churchill's words a "call to war."

United States Counters Soviet Expansion

Soviet-American relations continued to worsen in 1946 and 1947. An increasingly worried United States sought to offset the growing Soviet threat in Eastern Europe. President Truman declared that it was time to stop "babying the Soviets." He adopted a foreign policy called **containment**. Containment was a policy directed at blocking Soviet influence and preventing the expansion of communism. Containment policies included creating alliances and helping weak countries resist Soviet advances.

Restructuring the Postwar World **857**

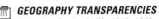

MORE ABOUT . . .
The Truman Doctrine

When Stalin broke his promise to hold free elections in Europe, Truman saw a repetition of Hitler's broken promises to Britain and France before World War II. He was determined not to mimic the British and French indecision that led to such disaster in the war. He therefore took a tough line with Stalin. "A totalitarian state is no different whether you call it Nazi, Fascist, Communist, or Franco's Spain," he wrote in a letter to his daughter. "I went to Potsdam [the final wartime conference of The Big Three in 1945] with the kindliest feeling toward Russia— in a year and a half they cured me of it."

MORE ABOUT . . .
The Marshall Plan

Marshall announced his plan in a quiet 12-minute commencement speech at Harvard University at which he was not even the main speaker. Only one out-of-town reporter covered what was billed as a routine speech. Few who heard it realized its historic importance.

History from Visuals

The Marshall Plan

Interpreting the Chart Ask students how much aid Iceland received. *$29 million.* How many countries received more than $1 billion in aid? *Four.*

Extension Activity Have students use an almanac or statistical abstract to find out which countries listed in the chart currently rank among the top 10 U.S. trading partners. *Germany, Great Britain, France.*

SKILLBUILDER Answers
1. Great Britain.
2. Possible Answer: They were the principal U.S. allies during World War II.

The Truman Doctrine In a speech asking Congress for foreign aid for Turkey and Greece, President Truman contrasted democracy with communism:

A VOICE FROM THE PAST
One way of life is based upon the will of the majority, and is distinguished by free institutions . . . free elections . . . and freedom from political oppression. The second way of life is based upon the will of a minority forcibly imposed upon the majority. It relies upon terror and oppression . . . fixed elections, and the suppression of personal freedoms. I believe it must be the policy of the United States to support free people who are resisting attempted subjugation by armed minorities or by outside pressures.
HARRY S. TRUMAN, speech to Congress, March 12, 1947

Truman's support for countries that rejected communism was called the **Truman Doctrine.** It caused great controversy. Some opponents objected to American interference in other nations' affairs. Others argued that the United States lacked the resources to carry on a global crusade against communism. Still others pointed out that some U.S. support would go to dictators. Congress, however, immediately authorized over $400 million in aid to Turkey and Greece.

The Marshall Plan Much of Western Europe lay in ruins after the war. Europe's problems included record-breaking cold and snow, postwar unemployment, lack of food, and economic turmoil. In June 1947, U.S. Secretary of State George Marshall proposed that America give aid to any European country that needed it. This assistance program, called the **Marshall Plan,** would provide food, machines, and other materials. As Congress debated the $12.5 billion program in February 1948, the Communists seized power in Czechoslovakia. Congress immediately approved the Marshall Plan. The plan achieved spectacular success in Western Europe and in Yugoslavia.

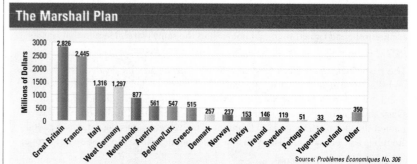

The Marshall Plan

Source: *Problèmes Économiques No. 306*

SKILLBUILDER: Interpreting Charts
1. Which country received the most aid from the United States?
2. Why do you think Great Britain and France received so much aid?

The Berlin Airlift While Europe began rebuilding, the United States and its allies clashed with the Soviet Union over Germany. The Soviets meant to keep their former enemy weak and divided. In 1948, France, Britain, and the United States decided to withdraw their forces from Germany. They would allow their three occupation zones to form one nation. The Soviet Union responded by holding West Berlin hostage.

Although Berlin lay well within the Soviet occupation zone of Germany, it too had been divided into four zones. The Soviet Union cut off highway, water, and rail traffic into Berlin's western zones. Since no supplies could get in, the city faced starvation. Stalin gambled that the threat would frighten Western countries. He hoped it would force them to surrender West Berlin or give up their idea of reunifying Germany.

The Soviet leader lost his gamble. To break the blockade, American and British officials flew food and supplies into West Berlin. For nearly 11 months, planes took

THINK THROUGH HISTORY
C. Making Inferences What was President Truman's major reason for offering aid to other countries?
C. Possible Answers To help European countries rebuild and become strong enough to resist Communist expansion.

TEACHING OPTIONS

CONNECTIONS ACROSS THE CURRICULUM

Economics The Marshall Plan was not just a political, but also a powerful economic, strategy. Rebuilding Europe would create markets for U.S. goods, it was argued, and the benefits would therefore outweigh the costs in the long run. History has proved this argument valid, at least as far as Europe is concerned. Have students discuss whether the same case can be made for President Clinton's 1995 decision to loan billions of dollars to Mexico.

CONNECTIONS ACROSS TIME AND SPACE

Isolationism Remind students of George Washington's "Farewell Address," in which he warned the United States against entanglements in foreign alliances, especially with European nations. This was the traditional underlying principle of American foreign policy which Truman changed by forming NATO.

Ask students to discuss whether Washington's and Truman's policies were justified. If they think both were justified, how had the world changed since Washington's time to make his policy obsolete?

off and landed every three minutes. In 277,000 flights, pilots brought in 2.3 million tons of supplies—food, fuel, medicine, and even Christmas presents. The Soviet Union, admitting defeat, lifted the Berlin blockade in May 1949.

The Cold War and a Divided World

These increasing conflicts were the beginnings of the **Cold War.** This was a state of diplomatic hostility that developed between the two superpowers. Beginning in 1949, the superpowers used spying, propaganda, diplomacy, and secret operations in their dealings with each other. Much of the world allied with one side or the other. In fact, until the Soviet Union finally broke up in 1991, the Cold War dictated not only U.S. and Soviet foreign policy. It influenced world alliances as well.

Rival Alliances The Berlin blockade heightened Western Europe's fears of Soviet aggression. As a result, in 1949, ten Western European nations joined with the United States and Canada to form a defensive military alliance. This alliance was called the North Atlantic Treaty Organization (**NATO).** These nations promised to meet an attack on any NATO member with armed force. For the United States, NATO membership marked the country's first peacetime military commitment.

The Soviet Union viewed NATO as a threat. In response, the Soviets developed an alliance system in 1955 as part of their own containment policy. It was known as the **Warsaw Pact.** This alliance included the Soviet Union, Poland, East Germany, Czechoslovakia, Hungary, Romania, Bulgaria, and Albania.

Not every country joined the new alliances, however. India, for example, chose to remain unallied with either side. And China, the world's largest communist country, came to distrust the Soviet Union. Like India, it remained unallied.

Nuclear Threat As these alliances were forming, the Cold War threatened to heat up enough to destroy the world. The United States already had atomic bombs. As early as 1949, the Soviet Union exploded its own atomic weapon. The superpowers had both become nuclear powers.

President Truman was determined to develop an even more deadly weapon before the Soviets did. He authorized work on a thermonuclear weapon in January 1950. This hydrogen or H-bomb would be thousands of times more powerful than the A-bomb.

Children in West Berlin in 1948 welcome planes that landed every few minutes with supplies to break the Soviet blockade of the city.

Truman's decision to begin developing the H-bomb was highly controversial. Vocal opponents included David Lilienthal, chairman of the Atomic Energy Commission, and J. Robert Oppenheimer, "father" of the A-bomb. Oppenheimer argued that the H-bomb would be too destructive. In fact, the first H-bomb test blasted a hole a mile long and 175 feet deep in the ocean floor and emitted a radioactive cloud 25 miles high.

ASSESS & RETEACH

Section 1 Assessment

Suggest that students review the political cartoon on page 852 and the chart on page 856 before completing question 4.

Section Quiz

FORMAL ASSESSMENT
Section Quiz, p. 387

Reteaching Activity

CLASS TIME: 10 MINUTES

Use the chart on page 856 to review the basis for the U.S.-Soviet split after World War II.

CLOSE ACTIVITY

CLASS TIME: 10 MINUTES

Identifying Main Ideas

Have students work in small groups and write a series of eight to ten newspaper headlines that summarizes the main events of this section.

Its power came from the fusion, or joining together, of atoms, rather than from the splitting of atoms, as in the A-bomb. In November 1952, the United States successfully tested the first H-bomb. By August of the following year, the Soviets had exploded their own thermonuclear weapon.

Dwight D. Eisenhower became the U.S. president in 1953. He appointed the firmly anti-Communist John Foster Dulles as his secretary of state. If the Soviet Union or its supporters attacked U.S. interests, Dulles threatened, the United States would "retaliate instantly, by means and at places of our own choosing." This willingness to go to the brink, or edge, of war became known as **brinkmanship.**

Brinkmanship required a reliable source of nuclear weapons and airplanes to deliver them. So the United States strengthened its air force and began producing stockpiles of nuclear weapons. In response, the Soviet Union made its own collection of nuclear bombs. This arms race would go on for four decades.

The Cold War in the Skies The Cold War also affected the science and education programs of the two countries. In August 1957, the Soviets announced the development of a rocket that could travel great distances. This was a true intercontinental ballistic missile, or ICBM. On October 4, the Soviets used an ICBM to push the first unmanned satellite above the earth's atmosphere.

The Cold War took to the skies as the United States and the Soviet Union raced to produce ICBMs. Missiles like this one were capable of inflicting destruction from great distances.

The launching of this Soviet satellite, *Sputnik I,* made Americans feel as if they had fallen behind in science and technology. In response, the U.S. government poured huge amounts of money into education, especially in science, mathematics, and foreign languages. Within months, by January 1958, the United States had successfully launched its own satellite.

In 1960, the skies provided the arena for an even more serious showdown between the superpowers. Five years earlier, President Eisenhower proposed an "open skies" policy. This policy stated that the United States and the Soviet Union could fly freely over each other's territory to guard against surprise nuclear attacks. The Soviet Union rejected Eisenhower's proposal. In response, the U.S. Central Intelligence Agency (CIA) authorized secret high-altitude spy flights over Soviet territory in planes called U-2s. In May 1960, the Soviets shot down a U-2 plane, and its pilot, Francis Gary Powers, was captured. The Soviets sentenced him to ten years in prison but released him after 19 months. This **U-2 incident** brought mistrust and tensions between the superpowers to a new height.

While Soviet Communists were squaring off against the United States, Communists in China were fighting an internal battle for control of that country.

E. Recognizing Effects How did the U.S. policy of brinkmanship contribute to the arms race?
E. Answer Going to the brink of war required nuclear weapons and a means of delivering them. Neither superpower wanted the other to amass more of these weapons and technology.

Section 1 Assessment

1. TERMS & NAMES

Identify
- United Nations
- iron curtain
- containment
- Truman Doctrine
- Marshall Plan
- Cold War
- NATO
- Warsaw Pact
- brinkmanship
- U-2 incident

860 Chapter 33

2. TAKING NOTES

Using a web diagram like the one below, list the causes of the Cold War between the United States and the Soviet Union.

Which cause was a direct result of World War II? Explain.

3. ANALYZING MOTIVES

What were Stalin's objectives in supporting Communist governments in Eastern Europe?

THINK ABOUT
- the effects of World War II
- the location of the Soviet Union
- U.S. aims in Europe

4. THEME ACTIVITY

Economics Draw a cartoon that shows either capitalism from the Soviet point of view or communism from the U.S. point of view.

ANSWERS

1. TERMS & NAMES
United Nations, p. 855
iron curtain, p. 857
containment, p. 857
Truman Doctrine, p. 858
Marshall Plan, p. 858
Cold War, p. 859
NATO, p. 859
Warsaw Pact, p. 859
brinkmanship, p. 860

U-2 incident, p. 860

2. TAKING NOTES
Incompatible political and economic philosophies; conflicting aims in Europe; desire for world domination; Soviet defiance of Yalta agreement; Berlin blockade. *Possible Responses:* Conflicting aims in Europe,

Soviet defiance of Yalta agreement, Berlin blockade.

3. ANALYZING MOTIVES
To protect borders; to counteract U.S. influence in Europe; to have access to raw materials to help rebuild war-ravaged country; to keep Germany from rebuilding and attacking Russia again.

4. THEME ACTIVITY
Standards for Evaluation
An effective cartoon should meet the following criteria:
- Shows differences between capitalism and communism
- Shows a distinct point of view
- Is clear and consistent

The Space Race

Beginning in the late 1950s, the United States and the Soviet Union competed for influence not only among the nations of the world, but in the skies as well. Once the superpowers had ICBMs to deliver nuclear warheads and aircraft for spying missions, they both began to develop technology that could be used to explore—and ultimately control—space.

The Soviet Union launched *Sputnik*, the first successful artificial space satellite, on October 4, 1957. As it circled the earth every 96 minutes, Premier Nikita Khrushchev boasted that his country would soon be "turning out long-range missiles like sausages." Unable to let this challenge go unanswered, the United States began beefing up its own space program. Its first attempts failed, however, and became known as "Stayputnik" or "Flopnik."

In a major technological triumph, the United States put human beings on the moon on July 20, 1969. In this historic "giant leap for mankind," astronaut Buzz Aldrin plants the U.S. flag and leaves his footprints on the lunar surface.

United States

1961 First American in space (Alan Shepard)

1962 First American orbits the earth (John Glenn, Jr.)

1969 First manned lunar landing

1976 *Viking 1* lands on Mars

1975 U.S. and Soviet Union launch first joint space mission

1977 *Voyager 2* launched to Jupiter, Saturn, Uranus, and Neptune

1981 Space shuttle *Columbia* launched

1992 *Mars Observer* launched

1995 U.S. shuttle *Discovery* links up with Soviet Space Station *Mir*

1997 *Mars Pathfinder* explores surface of Mars

1970 *Venera 7* lands on Venus

1963 First woman in space (Valentina Tereshkova)

1961 First human orbits the earth (Yuri Gagarin)

1959 *Luna 2* probe reaches the moon

1971 First manned space station (*Salyut 1*)

1988 Cosmonauts spend 366 days on space station *Mir*

1997 Two spacecraft land on Mars

Soviet Union

This view of the Soviet spacecraft *Soyuz* taken from the window of the U.S. *Apollo* in 1975 shows the curve of the earth beneath them. It symbolizes the superpowers' realization that they would have to coexist in space as well as on earth.

Connect *to* History

Comparing Which destinations in space did both the United States and the Soviet Union explore?

 SEE SKILLBUILDER HANDBOOK, PAGE 996

Connect *to* Today

Making Inferences What role might space continue to play in achieving world peace?

Restructuring the Postwar World **861**

The space race developed out of the Cold War superpowers' search for military dominance. In reality, however, the skies have provided an opportunity for the United States and the Soviet Union, and now Russia, to learn to cooperate and peacefully coexist.

CRITICAL THINKING ACTIVITY

CLASS TIME: 15 MINUTES

Evaluating

Inform students that the U.S. *Mars Surveyor* is slated to land a spacecraft on Mars every 26 months until 2003. The cost to the American public will be approximately $100 million a year. Discuss whether students think this expenditure is justified. Why or why not?

MORE ABOUT . . .
Current Space Exploration

U.S. astronauts and Russian cosmonauts work together on the Russian space station *Mir*. They took a joint six-hour space walk in September 1997 to repair damage to the space station's exterior. Meanwhile, the United States landed the *Pathfinder* spacecraft on Mars on July 4, 1997. A robot explored the planet's surface and sent images back to earth that were seen by millions of people. The *Pathfinder* mission discovered that Mars may have once had water and supported primitive life.

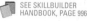 **IN-DEPTH RESOURCES: UNIT 8**
Science & Technology: Super Spy Plane, p. 19

Connect *to* History

Comparing
Both countries have sent missions to explore the moon, Venus, and Mars.

Connect *to* Today

Making Inferences
The United States and Russia continue to cooperate in the exploration of space. The two countries are using space flights to test new metals and industrial materials, to learn more about the structure of the universe, and to research topics such as people's responses to aging and disease. Such joint research projects for peaceful purposes cannot help but contribute to world peace.

OBJECTIVES

1. To analyze the civil war between the Nationalists and the Communists in China.

2. To explain how China split into two nations.

3. To describe how Mao's Marxist regime transformed China.

SKILLBUILDER
- Interpreting charts, p. 863

CRITICAL THINKING
- Recognizing effects, p. 863
- Analyzing issues, p. 864
- Making inferences, p. 865
- Identifying problems, p. 865
- Analyzing themes, p. 865

FOCUS

5-Minute Warm-Up

▶ *Interpreting Charts*
To help students understand the political climate in China after World War II, have them answer these questions.

1. Look at the chart on page 863. Which side did the Soviet Union support?

2. Which side had a weak military organization?

 WARM-UP TRANSPARENCY 33

OBJECTIVE ① INSTRUCT

Civil War in China

▶ *Key Ideas*
- Mao Zedong's Communist guerrillas battle Jiang Jieshi's Nationalists after World War II.
- Despite massive U.S. support, the Communists defeat the unpopular Nationalists.

IN-DEPTH RESOURCES: UNIT 8
Guided Reading, p. 2
Primary Source: from *No Tears for Mao,* p. 9

ACCESS FOR STUDENTS ACQUIRING ENGLISH
Guided Reading (Spanish), p. 333

WORLD ART AND CULTURES TRANSPARENCIES
AT72 *Spring Walk to the Chi-Ch'ang Park*

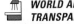
---

2 Communists Triumph in China

TERMS & NAMES
- Mao Zedong
- Jiang Jieshi
- commune
- Red Guards
- Cultural Revolution

MAIN IDEA
After World War II, Chinese Communists defeated Nationalist forces and two separate Chinas emerged.

WHY IT MATTERS NOW
China remains a Communist country and a major player on the world stage.

SETTING THE STAGE In World War II, China fought on the side of the victorious Allies. During the war, however, Japan's occupation armies devastated China's major cities. China's civilian death toll alone was in the millions. This vast country suffered casualties second only to those of the Soviet Union.

Civil War in China

When the Japanese invaded China in 1937, a bitter civil war was raging between the Nationalists and the Communists. During World War II, the political opponents temporarily united to fight the Japanese. With the war's end, however, they resumed their fight for control of the country.

Internal Struggles Under their leader, **Mao Zedong** (mow dzuh-dahng), the Communists held a stronghold in northwestern China. From there, they mobilized Chinese peasants for guerrilla war against the Japanese in the northeast. Thanks to their efforts to teach literacy and improve food production, the Communists won the peasants' loyalty. By 1945, Mao's Red Army controlled much of northern China.

Meanwhile, the Nationalist forces under **Jiang Jieshi** (jee-ahng jee-shee), whose name was formerly spelled Chiang Kai-shek, dominated southwestern China. Protected from the Japanese by rugged mountain ranges, Jiang gathered an army of 2.5 million men. Between 1942 and 1945, the United States sent the Nationalist army at least $1.5 billion in aid to fight the Japanese. Instead of benefiting the army, however, these supplies and money often ended up in the hands of a few corrupt officers. In addition, Jiang's army actually fought few battles against the Japanese. Instead, the Nationalist army saved its strength for the coming battle against Mao's Red Army. As soon as the Japanese surrendered, the Nationalists and Communists resumed their civil war.

Background
The Japanese had controlled Manchuria in northeast China since 1931. In 1937, they launched an all-out attack.

Background
The English spelling of Chinese words has been changed to make the pronunciation as close to Chinese as possible and to standardize it throughout the world.

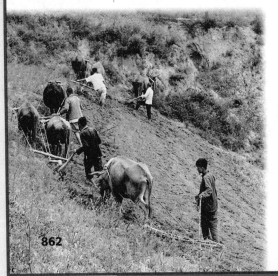

Chinese peasants performed the backbreaking labor that supported the country. After World War II, the Communists worked hard to win their support.

Involvement of the United States That renewed civil war lasted from 1946 to 1949. At first, the Nationalists enjoyed a considerable advantage. Their army outnumbered the Communists' army by as much as three to one. And the United States provided nearly $2 billion more in aid.

The Nationalist forces, however, did little to win popular support. With China's economy collapsing, thousands of Nationalist soldiers deserted to the Communists. In spring 1949, China's major cities fell to the Red forces one by one. Mao's troops were well trained in guerrilla warfare. But they were also enthusiastic about his promised return of land to the peasants. The remnants of Jiang's shattered army fled south. In October 1949, Mao Zedong gained control of the country. He proclaimed it the

862

Chinese Political Opponents—1945

Nationalists		Communists
Jiang Jieshi	**LEADER**	Mao Zedong
Southern China	**AREA RULED**	Northern China
United States	**FOREIGN SUPPORT**	Soviet Union
Defeat of Communists	**DOMESTIC POLICY**	National liberation
Weak due to inflation and failing economy	**PUBLIC SUPPORT**	Strong due to promised land reform
Ineffective, corrupt leadership and poor morale	**MILITARY ORGANIZATION**	Experienced, motivated guerrilla army

SKILLBUILDER: Interpreting Charts
1. *Which party's domestic policy appealed more to Chinese peasants?*
2. *Which aspect of the Communist approach do you think was most responsible for Mao's victory?*

Chinese Political Opponents—1945

Interpreting the Chart Make sure students understand that the middle column identifies the topic of each row. Ask which rows help explain why the Nationalists lost to the Communists. *The last three.*

Extension Activity Have students examine a map and contrast the topography, cities, and resources of northern and southern China. Which area seems to be more developed and economically important? *Southern China.* Ask them to discuss how Mao triumphed given his weaker geographic position.

SKILLBUILDER ANSWERS
1. Communists.
2. Possible Responses: Military organization or public support.

THINK THROUGH HISTORY
A. Recognizing Effects How did the outcome of the Chinese civil war contribute to Cold War tensions?
A. Possible Answer The victory of the Chinese Communists reinforced U.S. belief that the Communists were poised to take over the world.

People's Republic of China. Jiang and other Nationalist leaders retreated to the island of Taiwan, which westerners called Formosa.

Mao Zedong's victory fueled U.S. anti-Communist feelings. Those feelings only grew after the Chinese and Soviets signed a treaty of friendship in February 1950. Many people in the United States viewed the takeover of China as another step in a Communist campaign to conquer the world.

Two Chinas and the Cold War

China had split into two nations. One was the island of Taiwan, or Nationalist China, with an area of 13,000 square miles. The mainland, or People's Republic of China, had an area of more than 3.5 million square miles. The existence of two Chinas, and the conflicting international loyalties they inspired, intensified the Cold War.

The Superpowers React After Jiang Jieshi fled to Taiwan, the United States helped him set up a Nationalist government on that small island. They called it the Republic of China. The Soviets gave financial, military, and technical aid to the Communist People's Republic of China. In addition, the Chinese and the Soviets pledged to come to each other's defense if either country were attacked.

The United States responded by attempting to enlarge its own sphere of influence in Asia. For example, the United States limited the Soviet Union's occupation of Japan to only the few small islands it had gained at the Yalta talks. The two superpowers divided up Korea into a Soviet-supported Communist north and a U.S.-supported south.

Vocabulary
autonomous: self-governing.

Communist China Continues to Expand In the early years of Mao's reign, Chinese troops expanded into southern, or Inner, Mongolia, Tibet, and India. Northern, or Outer, Mongolia, which bordered the Soviet Union, remained in the Soviet sphere. After declaring Inner Mongolia an "Autonomous Area," China challenged that autonomy. It took control of the country.

In a brutal assault in 1950 and 1951, China also took control of Tibet. This was another so-called Autonomous Area. The Chinese promised autonomy to Tibetans, who followed the religious leader, the Dalai Lama. When China's control over Tibet tightened in the late 1950s, however, the Dalai Lama fled to India. Tibetans responded by rioting.

Restructuring the Postwar World **863**

OBJECTIVE ② INSTRUCT

Two Chinas and the Cold War

▶ *Key Ideas*
- China splits into a tiny island nation aided by the United States and a huge mainland nation aided by the Soviet Union.
- Communist China expands into Mongolia and Tibet.

CRITICAL THINKING ACTIVITY
CLASS TIME: 10 MINUTES

Comparing and Contrasting To help students understand the two Chinas, have them complete a Venn diagram such as this.

Nationalists U.S.-supported | Both Dictatorship | Communists Soviet-supported

---

Explaining the Skill Charts offer a visual presentation of information that clarifies the relationships between ideas and makes them easier to grasp. In a chart, information is grouped into categories. Reading down the columns and across the rows of a chart offers a quick summary of the information in a particular category. It also makes the comparison and contrast between entries immediately clear.

Applying the Skill: *Chinese Political Opponents—1945* Have students identify the titles of the rows and columns of this chart. *Rows— Leader, Area ruled, Foreign support, Domestic policy, Public support, Military organization; Columns— Nationalists, Communists.*

1. Based on the information in the chart, which characteristics did the Nationalists and Communists share? *None.*

2. Which category indicates that the conflict in China was part of the Cold War? *Foreign support.*

3. Which category indicates that the Nationalists and the Communists were directly opposed? *Domestic policy.*

 IN-DEPTH RESOURCES: UNIT 8
Skillbuilder Practice: Interpreting Charts, p. 6

Teacher's Edition **863**

Transformation and Revolution

▶ Key Ideas

- Mao Zedong heads both the government and the Communist Party of China.
- Mao redistributes land to peasant collectives and nationalizes China's industries.
- Mao creates huge agricultural communes.
- China splits with the Soviet Union and retreats from Mao's extreme policies.
- In retaliation, Mao launches the Cultural Revolution, which leads to widespread chaos.

HISTORYMAKERS
Mao Zedong

In 1972, when President Nixon told Mao Zedong that his teachings had transformed China and affected the whole world, Mao replied, "All I have done is change Beijing and a few of its suburbs." Considering the size of China's population (a quarter of the world's total), however, Mao may have been the most influential leader of the 20th century. Suggest that students discuss how they would judge the influence of world leaders and create a standard for comparing them.

MORE ABOUT . . .
"The Great Leap Forward"

Mao thought the agricultural communes could make their own steel in "backyard steel furnaces." Though hundreds of these installations were built, they were a dismal failure. Workers sometimes melted down their household implements to make it seem as if they were producing steel. As one critic noted, knives were melted down to make steel which could then be used to make knives.

India welcomed the Dalai Lama and other Tibetan refugees after Tibet's failed revolt in 1959. As a result, resentment between India and China grew. In 1962, when India trespassed across the two countries' unclear border into China's territory, Mao unleashed his forces. China held its border, but resentment continued.

Transformation and Revolution

For decades China had been either at war with or occupied by Japan. Mao and the Communists moved rapidly to strengthen their rule over China's 550 million people. The Communists claimed to have a new "Mandate of Heaven." And they aimed to restore China as a powerful nation.

Transformation Under Mao Zedong After taking power, the Chinese Communists began to tighten their hold on the country. The party's 4.5 million members made up just one percent of the Chinese population. But they were a highly disciplined group. Like the Soviets, the Chinese Communists set up two parallel organizations. These were the Communist party and the national government. Until 1959, Mao ruled as both chairman of the Communist party and head of state.

Mao's Marxist Socialism Mao determined to reshape China's economy based on Marxist socialism. Eighty percent of the population still lived in rural areas. But most Chinese farmers owned no land. Instead, ten percent of the rural population controlled 70 percent of the farmland. Under the Agrarian Reform Law of 1950, Mao seized the holdings of these landlords. He then divided them among the peasants. His forces killed more than a million landlords who resisted this policy.

To further his socialist principles, between 1953 and 1957, Mao's government forced the peasants to join collective farms. These farms each consisted of 200 to 300 households. The Chinese Communists also eagerly embraced Marxist ideas about women and the family. They made women fully equal in the home and in the workplace. They also instituted state-sponsored child care.

Mao's changes also transformed industry and business. Gradually, the government nationalized all private companies, or brought them under government ownership. In 1953, Mao launched a Soviet-style five-year plan that set high production targets for industry. The plan succeeded. By 1957, China's output of coal, cement, and electricity had doubled. Steel production had quadrupled.

Mao's Communes To expand the success of the first five-year plan in industry, Chinese leaders planned another ambitious program. Early in 1958, Mao proclaimed the "Great Leap Forward." This plan called for still larger collective farms, or **communes.** By the end of 1958, the government had created about 26,000 communes. The average commune sprawled over 15,000 acres and supported over 25,000 people.

In the strictly controlled life of the communes, peasants organized into "production battalions." Under the leadership of company and squad leaders, they worked the land together. They ate in communal dining rooms, slept in communal dormitories, and raised children in communal nurseries. And they owned nothing. The peasants had no incentive to work hard when only the state profited from their labor. Most of them hated living in the huge, impersonal communes.

The Great Leap Forward proved to be a great leap backward for China. Poor planning and inefficient "backyard" industries hampered growth. Worst of all, crop failures between 1958 and 1961 unleashed a famine that killed approximately 20 million people. The government officially discontinued the program in 1961.

HISTORYMAKERS

Mao Zedong
1893–1976

Born to a poor, but increasingly wealthy peasant family, Mao embraced Marxist socialism as a young man. Though he began as an urban labor organizer, Mao quickly realized the revolutionary potential of China's peasants. In a 1927 report, Mao predicted:

The force of the peasantry is like that of the raging winds and driving rain. . . . They will bury beneath them all forces of imperialism, militarism, corrupt officialdom, village bosses and evil gentry.

Mao's first attempt to lead the peasants in revolt failed in 1927. But during the Japanese occupation, Mao and his followers won the widespread support of the peasants by reducing rents and promising to redistribute land.

THINK THROUGH HISTORY
B. Analyzing Issues
What aspects of Marxist socialism did Mao try to bring to China?
B. Answer
Collective ownership of land, communal living, government control of industry.

Task: Students will create an edition of a news magazine covering the Communist takeover of China.

Purpose: To explore the significance of Mao's victory from several different perspectives.

Activity: Provide a copy of several issues of *Time* or *Newsweek* for students to use as models. On the board, list magazine components such as a factual

local news report, an analysis of the event's effects on the world, a human-interest story, an editorial, a letter to the editor, and a cartoon. Have each group choose one of these components to develop. Suggest that logical-mathematical learners include charts and graphs in their presentations.

📁 **Building a Portfolio:** Encourage students to include their news stories in their portfolios.

 ALTERNATIVE ASSESSMENT BOOK
Standards for Evaluating a Cooperative Activity

Standards for Evaluation
News magazines should . . .

- include historically accurate information
- present various viewpoints on the Communist victory
- exhibit lively journalistic style

New Policies and Mao's Response China was facing external problems as well as internal ones in the late 1950s. The spirit of cooperation that had bound the Soviet Union and China began to fade. Each sought to lead the worldwide Communist movement. They also shared the longest border in the world. And they faced numerous territorial disputes. In 1960, the Soviets halted economic aid to China.

After the failure of the Great Leap Forward and the split with the Soviet Union, Mao reduced his role in the government. Other leaders moved away from Mao's strict socialist ideas. Under the new leaders, for example, farm families could live in their own homes. They also could sell crops they grew on small private plots. Factory workers could compete for wage increases, bonuses, and promotions.

Mao disapproved of China's new economic policies, believing that they weakened the Communist goal of social equality. Determined to revive the revolution, Mao launched a new campaign in 1966. He urged China's young people to "learn revolution by making revolution." Millions of high school and college students responded to Mao's call. They left their classrooms and formed militia units called **Red Guards.**

The Cultural Revolution The Red Guards led a major uprising known as the **Cultural Revolution.** The goal of the Cultural Revolution was to establish a society of peasants and workers in which all were equal. The new hero was the peasant who worked with his hands. The life of the mind—intellectual and artistic activity—was considered useless and dangerous. To help stamp out this threat, the Red Guards shut down colleges and schools. They lashed out at professors, government officials, factory managers, and even their own parents. They targeted anyone who seemed to have special privileges or who resisted the regime. Exiled intellectuals had to "purify" themselves by doing hard labor in remote villages. Thousands of people were executed or died in jail.

The resulting widespread chaos closed down factories and threatened farm production. Civil war seemed possible. By 1976, even Mao admitted that the Cultural Revolution had to stop. With Mao's approval, the army dissolved the Red Guards. Zhou Enlai (joh ehn·leye), one of the founders of the Chinese Communist party and premier since 1949, began to restore order.

While China was struggling to become stable, the Cold War continued to rage. Between the 1950s and the 1970s, two full-scale wars broke out—in Korea and in Vietnam.

C. Possible Answer The social upheaval it caused brought about economic chaos and threatened civil war.

THINK THROUGH HISTORY
C. Making Inferences Why did the Cultural Revolution fail?

Daily *Life*

The Cultural Revolution
The Cultural Revolution started in 1966, when Chihua Wen was eight years old. For the next decade, his world, and that of every other Chinese child, was turned inside out.

Wen's neighbors were well-known revolutionary writers and loyal members of the Communist Party. Their loyalty became meaningless, however, the night the Red Guards (shown above) stormed into their apartment. There was the sound of breaking glass and a child's scream. Then the teenaged Guards carried a sack of books out to the yard and set them on fire.

They returned to the apartment and emerged carrying two heavy sacks. As they raced off with the sacks in the back of the truck, Wen heard sounds of gagging. "No one ever saw the couple or their child again," he said. And Wen never forgot what he had seen.

Section ② Assessment

1. TERMS & NAMES

Identify
• Mao Zedong
• Jiang Jieshi
• commune
• Red Guards
• Cultural Revolution

2. TAKING NOTES

Using a chart like the one below, summarize the reforms Mao Zedong proposed for China.

Mao Zedong's Reforms

Aspect of Life	Reform
Agriculture	
Industry	
Family	

Create a propaganda poster supporting one of these reforms.

3. IDENTIFYING PROBLEMS

What circumstances prevented Mao's Great Leap Forward from bringing economic prosperity to China?

THINK ABOUT
• Mao's strict socialism
• life in a commune
• environmental problems

4. ANALYZING THEMES

Revolution What policies or actions enabled the Communists to defeat the Nationalists in their long civil war?

THINK ABOUT
• the goals of each group
• the leaders of the Communists and the Nationalists
• foreign support

Restructuring the Postwar World **865**

---

① To trace the course and consequences of the Korean War.

② To summarize the causes and events of the Vietnam War and to describe its aftermath.

SKILLBUILDER

• Interpreting maps: movement, p. 867; human-environment interaction, movement, p. 869

CRITICAL THINKING

• Recognizing effects, pp. 867, 870
• Making inferences, p. 868
• Forming opinions, p. 870

FOCUS
5-Minute Warm-Up

▶ *Making Generalizations*
Have students answer these questions to prepare them to study the wars in Korea and Vietnam.

1. Look at the maps on pages 867 and 869. What similarities do you notice about Korea and Vietnam?

2. Which country shares a border with the Soviet Union?

 WARM-UP TRANSPARENCY 33

OBJECTIVE ① INSTRUCT

War in Korea

Key Ideas
• Communist North Korea invades South Korea but is driven back by UN peacekeeping forces.

• China and the United States pour troops into the war but neither North nor South Korea is victorious.

• South Korea's free-market economy booms after the war, while Communist North Korea's economy declines.

📖 *IN-DEPTH RESOURCES: UNIT 8*
Guided Reading, p. 3

📖 *ACCESS FOR STUDENTS ACQUIRING ENGLISH*
Guided Reading (Spanish), p. 334

Chapter 33

---

3 War in Korea and Vietnam

TERMS & NAMES
• 38th parallel
• Douglas MacArthur
• Ho Chi Minh
• domino theory
• Ngo Dinh Diem
• Vietcong
• Vietnamization
• Khmer Rouge

MAIN IDEA	WHY IT MATTERS NOW
In Asia, the Cold War flared into actual wars supported mainly by the superpowers.	Today, Vietnam is a Communist country and Korea is split into Communist and non-Communist nations.

SETTING THE STAGE When World War II ended, Korea became a divided nation. North of the **38th parallel,** a line that crosses Korea at 38 degrees north latitude, Japanese troops surrendered to the Soviets. South of this line, the Japanese surrendered to the Americans. As in Germany, two nations developed. One was the Communist industrial north. The other was the non-Communist rural south.

War in Korea

By 1949, both the United States and the Soviet Union had withdrawn most of their troops from Korea. The Soviets gambled that the United States would not defend South Korea. So they supplied North Korea with tanks, airplanes, and money in an attempt to take over the peninsula.

Standoff at the 38th Parallel On June 25, 1950, the North Koreans swept across the 38th parallel in a surprise attack on South Korea. Within days, North Korean troops had penetrated deep into the south.

President Truman was convinced that the North Korean aggressors were repeating what Hitler, Mussolini, and the Japanese had done in the 1930s. His policy of containment was being put to the test. And Truman resolved to help South Korea resist Communist influence.

South Korea also asked the United Nations to intervene. When the matter came to a vote in the Security Council, the Soviets were absent. They had boycotted the council to protest the seating of Nationalist China (Taiwan) rather than mainland China. The Soviet Union thus forfeited its chance to veto the UN's plan of action. This plan was to send an international force to Korea to stop the invasion. A total of 15 nations, including Britain and Canada, participated under the leadership of General **Douglas MacArthur.**

Meanwhile, the North Koreans continued to advance. By September 1950, they controlled the entire Korean peninsula except for a tiny area around Pusan in the far southeast. That month, however, MacArthur launched a surprise attack. Troops moving north from Pusan met up with forces that had made an amphibious landing at Inchon. Caught in this pincer action, about half of the North Koreans surrendered. The rest retreated.

Vocabulary
boycotted: refused to take part in.

U.S. infantry troops fire heavy mortar shells at Communist strongholds in North Korea in 1950.

The Fighting Continues The UN army pursued the retreating North Korean troops across the 38th parallel into North Korea. By late November, UN troops had pushed the North Koreans almost to the Yalu River at the border with China. These troops were mostly from the United States.

PRINT RESOURCES

📖 *IN-DEPTH RESOURCES: UNIT 8*
Guided Reading, p. 3
Primary Source: from *When Heaven and Earth Changed Places,* p. 10
History Makers: Ho Chi Minh, p. 16

📖 *ACCESS FOR STUDENTS ACQUIRING ENGLISH*
Guided Reading (Spanish), p. 334

📖 *FORMAL ASSESSMENT*
Section Quiz, p. 389

TECHNOLOGY RESOURCES

 WORLD ART AND CULTURES TRANSPARENCIES
AT73 *Laying a Road*

💿 **CD-ROM**
Electronic Library of Primary Sources
Battles of the World

 INTERNET www.mlworldhistory.com

Then, in October 1950, the Chinese felt threatened by the American fleet off their coast. They sent 300,000 troops to aid North Korea. The fight between North and South Korea had grown into a war between the Chinese and the Americans.

Greatly outnumbering the UN forces, the Chinese drove them southward. By early January 1951, they had pushed all UN and South Korean troops out of North Korea. The Chinese then moved south. They finally captured the South Korean capital, Seoul.

"We face an entirely new war," declared General MacArthur. And he called for a nuclear attack against Chinese cities. President Truman disagreed, viewing MacArthur's proposals as reckless. "We are trying to prevent a world war, not start one," the president explained. MacArthur tried to go over the president's head by taking his case to Congress and to the press. In response, Truman fired him.

Over the next two years, UN forces continued to fight to drive the North Koreans back to the 38th parallel. By 1952, UN troops had recaptured Seoul and regained control of South Korea. Finally, in July 1953, the UN forces and North Korea signed a cease-fire agreement. After three years of fighting, the border between the two Koreas was set near the 38th parallel. This was almost where it had been before the war started. But approximately 5 million soldiers and civilians had died.

War in Korea, 1950–1953

GEOGRAPHY SKILLBUILDER:
Interpreting Maps
1. **Movement** What was the northernmost Korean city UN troops had reached by November 1950?
2. **Movement** Did North or South Korean forces advance further into the other's territory?

Map legend:
- Farthest North Korean advance, September 1950
- Farthest UN advance, November 1950
- Farthest Chinese and North Korean advance, January 1951
- Armistice line, 1953

THINK THROUGH HISTORY
A. Recognizing Effects What effects did the Korean war have on the Korean people and nation?
A. Answer About 5 million Koreans and foreign soldiers died and neither North nor South Korea had gained any territory.

Aftermath and Legacy of the War After the war, Korea remained divided into two countries. In North Korea, the Communist dictator Kim Il Sung established collective farms, developed heavy industry, and built up the country's military power. At Kim's death in 1994, his son Kim Jong Il ascended to power. Under Kim Jong Il's rule, Communist North Korea developed nuclear weapons. Although the country is well-armed, it has serious economic problems. It continues to struggle with shortages of energy and food.

On the other hand, South Korea prospered, thanks to massive aid from the United States and other countries. In the 1960s, South Korea concentrated on developing its industry and boosting foreign trade. A succession of dictatorships ruled the rapidly developing country. With the 1987 adoption of a democratic constitution, however, South Korea established free elections. During the 1980s and early 1990s, South Korea claimed one of the highest economic growth rates in the world.

Political differences keep the two Koreas apart, despite periodic discussions of reuniting the country. In a show of force in 1996, for example, North Korea sent troops into the demilitarized zone that separates the two nations. And the United States still maintains 37,000 troops in South Korea. In 1997, however, South Korea joined several other countries in sending food to North Korea. Although talks continue, the Communist North Koreans remain firmly opposed to reunification.

Restructuring the Postwar World **867**

War in Vietnam

Like America's involvement in the Korean War, its involvement in Vietnam stemmed from its Cold War policy of containment. Beginning after World War II, many Americans and their leaders had one foreign policy goal. They were committed to halting the spread of communism.

By the 1950s, the United States had begun providing financial aid, advisers, and finally, half a million soldiers to a former French colony, Vietnam. America's aim was to keep Southeast Asia from embracing communism as China had done.

The Road to War In the early 1900s, France controlled most of resource-rich Southeast Asia. Nationalist independence movements, however, had begun to develop in the part of French Indochina that is now Vietnam. A young Vietnamese nationalist, **Ho Chi Minh,** turned to the Communists for help in his struggle. During the 1930s, Ho's Indochinese Communist party led revolts and strikes against the French. The French responded by jailing Vietnamese protesters. They also sentenced Ho, the party's leader, to death. Ho fled his death sentence but continued to inspire Vietnam's growing nationalist movement from exile. Ho returned to Vietnam in 1941, a year after the Japanese seized control of his country. He and other nationalists founded the Vietminh (Independence) League.

The Japanese left Vietnam in 1945, after their defeat in World War II. Ho Chi Minh believed that independence would surely follow. France, however, intended to regain its former colony.

War Breaks Out Vietnamese Nationalists and Communists joined to fight the French armies. While the French held most of the major cities, they remained powerless in the countryside. There the Vietminh had widespread peasant support. The Vietminh used hit-and-run tactics to confine the French to the cities.

The French people began to doubt that maintaining their colony in Vietnam was worth the lives and money the struggle cost. In 1954, the French suffered a major military defeat at Dien Bien Phu. They surrendered to Ho.

The United States had supported the French in Vietnam. With the defeat of the French, the United States saw a rising threat to the rest of Asia. U.S. President Eisenhower described this threat in terms of the **domino theory.** The Southeast Asian nations were like a row of dominos, he said. The fall of one to communism would lead to the fall of its neighbors. This theory became a major justification for U.S. foreign policy during the Cold War era.

After France's defeat, an international peace conference met in Geneva to discuss the future of Indochina. Based on these talks, Vietnam was divided at 17° north latitude. North of that line, Ho Chi Minh's Communist forces governed. To the south, the United States and France set up an anti-Communist government under the leadership of **Ngo Dinh Diem** (NOH dihn D'YEM).

Vietnam—A Divided Country Diem, an unpopular leader, ruled the south as a dictator. In contrast, Ho Chi Minh began a popular program of land redistribution in the north. The United States sensed that an election might lead to victory for the Communists. So it supported Diem's cancellation of the elections.

Vietnamese opposition to Diem's corrupt government grew. Communist guerrillas, called **Vietcong,** began to gain strength in the south. While some of the Vietcong were trained soldiers from North Vietnam, most were South Vietnamese who hated Diem. Gradually, the Vietcong won control of large areas of the countryside.

868 Chapter 33

HISTORY MAKERS

Ho Chi Minh
1890–1969

When he was young, the poor Vietnamese Nguyen That (uhng-wihn thaht) Thanh worked as a cook on a French steamship. In visiting American cities where the boat docked, such as Boston and New York, he learned about both American culture and ideals.

He later took a new name—Ho Chi Minh, meaning "He who enlightens." But he held onto those American ideals. Though a Communist, in announcing Vietnam's independence from France in 1945, he declared, "All men are created equal."

His people revered him and fondly called him Uncle Ho. However, Ho Chi Minh did not put his democratic ideals into practice. From 1954 to 1969, he ruled North Vietnam by crushing all opposition.

THINK THROUGH HISTORY
B. Making Inferences What actions might the United States have justified by the domino theory?
B. Possible Answer Intervention in any situation that might result in a gain of Communist territory or power.

In 1963, backed by the United States, a group of South Vietnamese generals planned a coup. Meeting almost no resistance, they overthrew and assassinated Diem. The new leaders, however, were no more popular than Diem had been. A takeover by the Communist Vietcong with the backing of North Vietnam seemed inevitable.

The United States Gets Involved Faced with this possibility, the United States decided to escalate, or increase, its involvement. Americans had been serving as advisers to the South Vietnamese since the late 1950s. But their numbers steadily grew. The United States also sent increasing numbers of planes, tanks, and other military equipment to South Vietnam.

In August 1964, U.S. President Lyndon Johnson told Congress that North Vietnamese patrol boats had attacked two American destroyers in the Gulf of Tonkin. As a result, Congress authorized the president to send American troops into Vietnam. By late 1965, more than 185,000 American soldiers were fighting on Vietnamese soil, although war had not officially been declared. American planes had also begun to bomb North Vietnam. By 1968, more than half a million American soldiers were in combat there.

The United States boasted the best-equipped, most advanced army in the world. Yet the Americans faced two major difficulties. First, they were fighting a guerrilla war in unfamiliar jungle terrain. Second, the South Vietnamese government they were defending was becoming steadily more unpopular. At the same time, popular support for the Vietcong grew. Ho Chi Minh also strongly supported the Vietcong with troops and munitions, as did the Soviet Union and China.

Unable to win a decisive victory on the ground, the United States turned to air power. American forces bombed millions of acres of farmland and forest in an attempt to destroy enemy hideouts. This bombing strengthened peasants' opposition to the South Vietnamese government.

The United States Withdraws During the late 1960s, the war grew increasingly unpopular in the United States. Dissatisfied youth began to protest the tremendous loss of life in an unpopular conflict on the other side of the world. Bowing to intense public pressure, President Richard Nixon began withdrawing U.S. troops from Vietnam in 1969. Nixon's plan was called **Vietnamization.** It allowed for U.S. troops to gradually pull out, while the South Vietnamese increased their combat role. Nixon wanted to pursue Vietnamization while preserving the South Vietnamese government. So he authorized a massive bombing campaign against North Vietnamese bases and supply routes. The president also authorized bombings in neighboring Laos and Cambodia to wipe out Vietcong hiding places.

Restructuring the Postwar World **869**

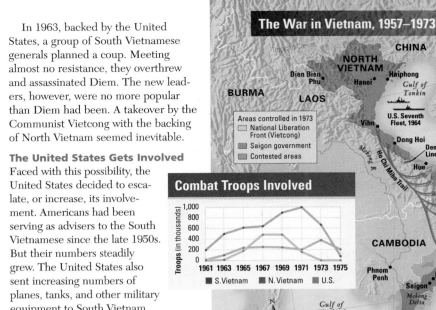

The War in Vietnam, 1957–1973

Areas controlled in 1973
- National Liberation Front (Vietcong)
- Saigon government
- Contested areas

Combat Troops Involved

Troops (in thousands): 1,000 / 800 / 600 / 400 / 200 / 0

1961 1963 1965 1967 1969 1971 1973 1975

■ S.Vietnam ■ N.Vietnam ■ U.S.

GEOGRAPHY SKILLBUILDER:
Interpreting Maps
1. **Human-Environment Interaction** *Did the Saigon government or the Vietcong control more of South Vietnam in 1973?*
2. **Movement** *Which country committed the most troops to the war in Vietnam?*

CONNECT to TODAY
Capitalism in Vietnam

In seeking economic growth through foreign investment, Vietnam is following in the footsteps of China, South Korea, Taiwan, Singapore, Thailand, and several other east Asian countries. One victim of this rapid economic growth has been the environment. The number of elephants in Vietnam's central highlands, for example, has dropped from 2,000 to 300. Ask students what other adverse effects Vietnam's rapid development might have. *Possible Responses: Dependence on foreign countries, pollution, congestion, crime, loss of traditional cultural values.*

ASSESS & RETEACH

Section 3 Assessment

Divide the class in half to work on question 4. Have one group create a propaganda poster for the United States and the other group create a poster for the Soviet Union. Ask the class to discuss the strengths and weaknesses of each poster.

Section Quiz

FORMAL ASSESSMENT
Section Quiz, p. 389

Reteaching Activity

CLASS TIME: 10 MINUTES

Have students compare and discuss the Venn diagrams they created for question 2. Ask them to create a composite class diagram that summarizes their understanding of the wars in Korea and Vietnam.

CLOSE ACTIVITY

CLASS TIME: 15 MINUTES

Making Judgments

Divide the class in half. Ask one group to assume the position of President Truman in 1950 and the other of President Johnson in 1964. Have each group consider whether or not they would commit U.S. troops to the war. Then have them draft a brief presidential address explaining their decision.

The skulls of Cambodian citizens form a haunting memorial to the brutality of the Khmer Rouge during the 1970s.

Under continued popular protest and political pressure at home, President Nixon kept withdrawing U.S. troops. The last forces left in 1973. The North Vietnamese overran South Vietnam two years later because the South Vietnamese could not fend off the North Vietnamese on their own. The Communists renamed Saigon, the former capital of the South, Ho Chi Minh City to honor their dead leader. But more than 1.5 million Vietnamese and 58,000 Americans had also died during the war.

Ongoing Turmoil in Cambodia The end of the war did not put an end to bloodshed and chaos in Southeast Asia, however. Cambodia (also known as Kampuchea) had suffered U.S. bombing during the war. And it remained unstable for years. In 1975, Communist rebels known as the **Khmer Rouge** set up a brutal Communist government under the leadership of Pol Pot. In a ruthless attempt to transform Cambodia into a rural society, Pol Pot's followers slaughtered 2 million people. This was almost one quarter of the nation's population. A Vietnamese invasion in 1978 overthrew the Khmer Rouge. The Vietnamese finally withdrew in 1989. In 1993, under the supervision of UN peacekeepers, Cambodia adopted a democratic constitution and held a free election. Pol Pot was captured and detained in 1997 for the war crimes he had committed.

Postwar Vietnam After 1975, the victorious North Vietnamese imposed strict controls over the South. Officials sent thousands of people to "reeducation camps" for training in Communist thought. They nationalized industries and strictly controlled businesses.

Communist oppression also caused 1.5 million people to flee from Vietnam. Most refugees escaped in dangerously overcrowded ships. More than 200,000 of these "boat people" died at sea. The survivors often spent long months in crowded refugee camps scattered across Southeast Asia. About 70,000 Vietnamese refugees eventually settled in the United States or in Canada.

Though Communists still govern Vietnam, the country now welcomes foreign investment. Much of that investment comes from Vietnam's old enemy, the United States. America lifted its trade embargo against Vietnam in 1994 and is moving toward official recognition of the country.

While the Cold War superpowers were struggling for power in the Korean and Vietnam wars, they also were using economic and diplomatic means to bring other countries under their control.

CONNECT to TODAY

Capitalism in Vietnam

Vietnam is now a Communist country. But its economy is modeled more on that of the Soviets' Cold War enemy, the United States. In 1997, a travel magazine claimed that Hanoi, the capital of Vietnam, "jumps with vitality, its streets and shops jammed with locals and handfuls of Western tourists and businesspeople."

Along Hanoi's shaded boulevards, billboards advertise American and Japanese copiers, motorcycles, video recorders, and soft drinks. On the streets, enterprising Vietnamese businesspeople offer more traditional services. These include bicycle repair, a haircut, a shave, or a tasty snack.

THINK THROUGH HISTORY
C. Recognizing Effects Why did Vietnamization fail?
C. Possible Answer Because the South Vietnamese could not fight the North without U.S. support due to their corrupt, unpopular, and undemocratic leadership.

Section 3 Assessment

1. TERMS & NAMES
Identify
- 38th parallel
- Douglas MacArthur
- Ho Chi Minh
- domino theory
- Ngo Dinh Diem
- Vietcong
- Vietnamization
- Khmer Rouge

2. TAKING NOTES
Using a Venn diagram like the one below, compare and contrast the causes and effects of the wars in Vietnam and Korea.

Korean War | Both | Vietnam War

Do you think the similarities or the differences between the two wars are more striking? Why?

3. FORMING OPINIONS
Do you think U.S. involvement in Vietnam was justified? Why or why not?

THINK ABOUT
- the U.S. policy of containment
- the domino theory
- U.S. public opinion

4. THEME ACTIVITY
Empire Building Create a propaganda poster for either the United States or the Soviet Union supporting its involvement in Asia.

ANSWERS

1. TERMS & NAMES
38th parallel, p. 866
Douglas MacArthur, p. 866
Ho Chi Minh, p. 868
domino theory, p. 868
Ngo Dinh Diem, p. 868
Vietcong, p. 868
Vietnamization, p. 869
Khmer Rouge, p. 870

2. TAKING NOTES
Korean War—neither side gained an advantage; Vietnam War—Soviet-supported North Vietnamese won; Both—American and Soviet involvement stemmed from Cold War; land was destroyed; millions of people died.

3. FORMING OPINIONS
Not justified—It was a civil war that did not involve the United States; war is not justified under any circumstances; Justified—It was the responsibility of a nation founded on democratic ideals to support democracy in other countries, especially those in danger of becoming Communist.

4. THEME ACTIVITY
Standards for Evaluation
An effective poster should meet the following criteria:
- Demonstrates understanding of U.S. or Soviet goals in Asia
- Uses slogans and pictures to convey the message
- Is clear and easy to understand

4 Cold War Around the World

TERMS & NAMES
- Third World
- nonaligned nations
- Fidel Castro
- Anastasio Somoza
- Daniel Ortega
- Shah Mohammed Reza Pahlavi
- Ayatollah Ruholla Khomeini

MAIN IDEA

The Cold War superpowers supported opposing sides in Latin American and Middle Eastern conflicts.

WHY IT MATTERS NOW

Many of these areas today are troubled by political, economic, and military conflict and crisis.

SETTING THE STAGE Vietnam was just one of many countries that attempted to shake off colonial rule after World War II. Local battles for independence provided yet another arena for competition between the Cold War superpowers.

Confrontations over Developing Nations

Background
In the 1970s, the three worlds were redefined in economic terms. The small but prosperous First World was at the top of a pyramid and the large, poverty-stricken Third World was at the bottom.

Following World War II, the world's nations were grouped politically into three "worlds." The First World was the United States and its allies. The Second World included the Soviet Union and its allies. The **Third World** consisted of developing nations, often newly independent, who were not aligned with either superpower.

These Third World countries in Latin America, Asia, and Africa experienced terrible poverty and political instability. This was largely due to a long history of imperialism. They also suffered from ethnic conflicts and lack of technology and education. Each desperately needed a political and economic system around which to build its society. Soviet-style communism and U.S.-style free-market democracy were the countries' main choices.

Cold War Strategies The United States, the Soviet Union, and, in some cases, China, used a variety of techniques to gain influence in the Third World. These competing superpowers sponsored or backed wars of revolution, liberation, or counterrevolution. The U.S. and Soviet spy agencies—the CIA and the KGB—engaged in a variety of covert, or secret, activities. These activities ranged from spying to assassination attempts. The United States also provided military aid, built schools, set up programs to combat poverty, and sent volunteer workers to developing nations in Latin America, Asia, and Africa. The Soviets offered military and technical assistance, mainly to India and Egypt.

A. Possible Answers
Advantages—control over their own politics and economies; ability to accept help from either side; Disadvantages—lack of economic and military support from the strong superpowers, if needed.

THINK THROUGH HISTORY
A. Making Inferences What advantages and disadvantages might being nonaligned have offered a developing nation?

Association of Nonaligned Nations Other developing nations also had pressing needs for assistance. They became important players in the Cold War competition between the United States, the Soviet Union, and also China.

Not all Third World countries wished to play such a role, however. India, for example, vowed to remain neutral in the Cold War. Indonesia, a populous island nation in Southeast Asia, also struggled to stay uninvolved. In 1955, Indonesia hosted the leaders of Asian and African countries in the Bandung Conference. They met to form what they called a "third force" of such independent countries, or **nonaligned nations.**

Nations such as India and Indonesia remained neutral. But other countries took sides with the superpowers or played the competing sides off against each other.

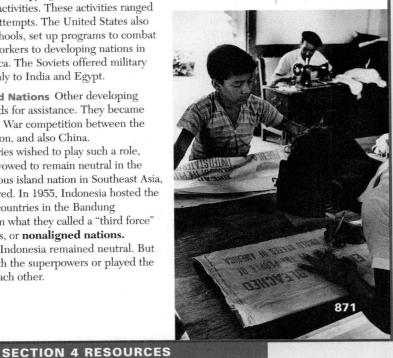

The flour provided by U.S. aid helped keep these Colombian children alive. They also learned to make the flour sacks into clothing in a school run by missionaries.

871

SECTION 4 RESOURCES

PRINT RESOURCES

IN-DEPTH RESOURCES: UNIT 8
Guided Reading, p. 4
Geography Application: The Cuban Missile Crisis, p. 7
Primary Source: The Cuban Missile Crisis (Speech by John F. Kennedy), p. 11
History Makers: Ruholla Khomeini, p. 17

ACCESS FOR STUDENTS ACQUIRING ENGLISH
Guided Reading (Spanish), p. 335
Geography Application (Spanish), p. 338

FORMAL ASSESSMENT
Section Quiz, p. 390

ALTERNATIVE ASSESSMENT BOOK

TECHNOLOGY RESOURCES

CRITICAL THINKING TRANSPARENCIES
CT33 Global Superpowers Face Off

CD-ROM
Electronic Library of Primary Sources

INTERNET www.mlworldhistory.com

Section 4 Overview

OBJECTIVES

1. To explain how the Cold War affected developing nations.
2. To describe superpower confrontations in Latin America after World War II.
3. To identify Cold War conflicts in the Middle East.

SKILLBUILDER
- Interpreting maps: location, region, p. 873

CRITICAL THINKING
- Making inferences, p. 871
- Contrasting, p. 872
- Analyzing motives, pp. 873, 874
- Comparing, p. 875
- Analyzing themes, p. 875

FOCUS
5-Minute Warm-Up

▶ **Analyzing Events**
To give students an appreciation of the worldwide scope of the Cold War, have them answer these questions.

1. Look at the map on page 873. Which countries did the Communists take over?
2. In which Central and South American countries did the United States prevent Communist takeovers?

WARM-UP TRANSPARENCY 33

OBJECTIVE 1 INSTRUCT

Confrontations over Developing Nations

▶ **Key Ideas**
- The superpowers compete for influence among developing nations through covert activities, military force, and economic aid.
- A few nations cling to neutrality.

IN-DEPTH RESOURCES : UNIT 8
Guided Reading, p. 4

ACCESS FOR STUDENTS ACQUIRING ENGLISH
Guided Reading (Spanish), p. 335

Postwar Face-off in Latin America

▶ Key Ideas
- Castro leads a successful Communist revolution in Cuba.
- A face-off over missile sites in Cuba brings the U.S. and the Soviet Union to the brink of nuclear war.
- Communist Sandinistas and U.S.-backed Contras fight a ten-year civil war in Nicaragua.

 IN-DEPTH RESOURCES : UNIT 8
Primary Source: The Cuban Missile Crisis (Speech by John F. Kennedy), p. 11

CRITICAL THINKING ACTIVITY
CLASS TIME: 10 MINUTES

Identifying Main Ideas
As students read this section, have them organize the information they gather about Cold War confrontations in a chart like this.

	Cuba	Nicaragua	Iran	Afghanistan
Leader	Fidel Castro			
Conflict				
Dates				
Superpower involved				
Outcome				

HISTORY MAKERS
Fidel Castro

Since 1959, when he overthrew the Batista regime, Castro has withstood numerous attempts to topple his regime through assassination, invasion, and economic pressure to become the world's longest-surviving Communist ruler.

Postwar Face-off in Latin America

After World War II, rapid industrialization, population growth, and a lingering gap between the rich and the poor led Latin American nations to seek aid from both superpowers. During this period, many Latin American countries alternated between short-lived democracy and harsh military rule.

As described in Chapter 28, U.S. involvement in Latin America began long before World War II. American businesses backed leaders who often oppressed their people, but who protected U.S. interests. After the war, communism and nationalistic feelings inspired a wave of revolutionary movements. These found enthusiastic Soviet support. In response, the United States provided military support and economic assistance to anti-Communist dictators.

Cuban Revolution Throughout the 1950s, U.S. support maintained Cuba's unpopular dictator, Fulgencio Batista. Cuban resentment led to a popular revolution, which overthrew Batista in January 1959. A young lawyer named **Fidel Castro** led that revolution.

At first, many people praised Castro for bringing reforms to Cuba and improving the economy, literacy, health care, and conditions for women. Yet Castro was a harsh dictator. He suspended elections, jailed or executed his opponents, and strangled the press with tight government controls.

When Castro nationalized the Cuban economy, he took over U.S.-owned sugar mills and refineries. In response, President Eisenhower ordered an embargo on all trade with Cuba. As relations with the United States deteriorated, Castro turned to the Soviets for the economic and military aid he needed.

In 1960, the CIA planned an invasion of Cuba and began to train anti-Castro Cuban exiles to carry it out. In April 1961 these exiles landed at the Bay of Pigs in Cuba. The new president, Kennedy, approved the invasion but refused to send U.S. planes to support it. Castro's forces defeated the invaders, humiliating the United States.

The Cuban Missile Crisis The failed Bay of Pigs invasion convinced the Soviet leader, Nikita Khrushchev, that the United States would not resist Soviet expansion in Latin America. Consequently, in July 1962, Khrushchev secretly began to build 42 missile sites in Cuba. In October, an American spy plane discovered the sites. The U.S. President, John F. Kennedy, declared that missiles so close to the U.S. mainland were a threat. He demanded that the Soviets remove the missiles. Kennedy also announced a quarantine, or blockade, of Cuba to prevent the Soviets installing more missiles. Castro protested his country's being used as a tool in the Cold War:

A VOICE FROM THE PAST
Cuba did not and does not intend to be in the middle of a conflict between the East and the West. Our problem is above all one of national sovereignty. Cuba does not mean to get involved in the Cold War.
FIDEL CASTRO, quoted in an interview October 27, 1962

Nevertheless, Cuba was deeply involved. Kennedy's demand for the removal of Soviet missiles put the United States and the Soviet Union on a collision course. U.S. troops assembled in Florida, ready to invade Cuba. People around the world began to fear that

HISTORY MAKERS

Fidel Castro
1927–

The son of a wealthy Spanish-Cuban farmer, Fidel Castro became involved in politics while enrolled at the University of Havana. He first attempted to overthrow the Cuban dictator, Batista, in 1953. He was imprisoned, but vowed not to give up the struggle for independence:

Personally, I am not interested in power nor do I envisage assuming it at any time. All that I will do is to make sure that the sacrifices of so many compatriots should not be in vain. . . .

Despite this declaration, Castro became a staunch Soviet ally and has been dictator of Cuba for over 30 years.

THINK THROUGH HISTORY
B. Contrasting
What differing U.S. and Soviet aims led to the Cuban missile crisis?
B. Answer U.S.—desire to protect itself and prevent the spread of communism; Soviet—desire to support its Communist ally.

EXPLORING PRIMARY SOURCES

A Voice from the Past The same day that Castro insisted on Cuba's desire to stay out of the Cold War, he wrote a letter to Khrushchev asking the Soviet leader to launch a nuclear strike against the United States. He had no idea that Kennedy and Khrushchev were carrying on secret negotiations.

Have interested students read sources such as A.I. Gribkov's *Operation ANADYR: U.S. and Soviet Generals Recount the Cuban Missile Crisis,* and Dino A. Brugioni's *Eyeball to Eyeball: The Inside Story of the Cuban Missile Crisis* to learn more about this period.

CUSTOMIZING FOR SPECIAL NEEDS

Less Proficient Readers:
Recognizing Sequences Pair less proficient readers with more able students. Suggest that each pair create a storyboard that presents the drama of the Cuban missile crisis. Instruct students to work together to decide which events to include in their storyboard and in which order they

should be presented. Then have them plan the pictures and words they will use in each panel and produce the storyboard. Have the pairs present their storyboards to the class.

 IN-DEPTH RESOURCES : UNIT 8
Geography Application: The Cuban Missile Crisis, p. 7

this standoff would lead to World War III and a nuclear disaster. Fortunately, Khrushchev agreed to remove the missiles in return for a U.S. promise not to invade Cuba.

The resolution of the Cuban missile crisis left Castro completely dependent on Soviet support. In exchange for this support, Castro backed Communist revolutions in Latin America and Africa. Approximately 36,000 Cubans fought in Angola's war against colonialism in the 1970s. Soviet aid to Cuba, however, ended abruptly with the breakup of the Soviet Union in 1991. This loss dealt a crippling blow to the Cuban economy. The country still suffers a scarcity of vital supplies. But the aging Castro refuses to adopt economic reforms or to give up power. An equally stubborn United States refuses to lift its trade embargo.

C. Answer Because the Sandinistas were supporting socialist rebels in El Salvador.

THINK THROUGH HISTORY
C. Analyzing Motives Why did the U.S. switch its support from the Sandinistas to the Contras?

Civil War in Nicaragua Just as the United States had supported the unpopular Batista in Cuba, it had funded the Nicaraguan dictatorship of **Anastasio Somoza** and his family since 1933. In 1979, Communist Sandinista rebels toppled the dictatorship of Somoza's son. Both the United States and the Soviet Union initially gave aid to the Sandinistas and their leader, **Daniel Ortega** (awr·TAY·guh).

The Sandinistas, however, had aided other socialist rebels in nearby El Salvador. To help the El Salvadoran government fight those rebels, the United States supported Nicaraguan anti-Communist rebel forces. These rebels were called Contras or *contrarevolucionarios*.

The civil war in Nicaragua lasted over a decade and seriously weakened the country's economy. Finally, in 1990, President Ortega agreed to hold free elections. He was defeated by Violeta Chamorro. In 1997, José Lacayo was elected president.

Cold War Hot Spots, 1948–1975

The United States helps Greece defeat Communist-led rebels (1946–1949) and gives economic and military aid to Turkey (1947–1950).

The Soviets down U.S. U-2 pilot Francis Gary Powers in 1960.

Communists retain or gain control after bloody wars in Korea (1950–1953) and Vietnam (1957–1975) supported by China and the Soviet Union.

The United States and the Soviet Union bring the world to the brink of nuclear war during the Cuban missile crisis in 1962.

The Soviet Union aids anticolonial struggles in Congo (1960) and Mozambique (1971) and, with help from Cuba, in Angola (1974).

Britain helps Indonesian government repress an uprising by Communists in 1965.

The United States prevents Communist takeovers in Guatemala (1954), Bolivia (1956), and Chile (1973).

Communist expansion
Communist expansion prevented by U.S. and allies

NORTH AMERICA · SOUTH AMERICA · EUROPE · GERMANY · ASIA · SOVIET UNION · AFRICA · AUSTRALIA
UNITED STATES · CUBA · GUATEMALA · BOLIVIA · CHILE · GREECE · TURKEY · IRAN · EGYPT · CONGO · ANGOLA · MOZAMBIQUE · CHINA · NORTH KOREA · SOUTH KOREA · VIETNAM · MALAYSIA · INDONESIA

PACIFIC OCEAN · ATLANTIC OCEAN · INDIAN OCEAN · PACIFIC OCEAN
Arctic Circle · Tropic of Cancer · Equator · Tropic of Capricorn
40°N · 0° Equator · 40°S

0   3,000 Miles
0   5,000 Kilometers

GEOGRAPHY SKILLBUILDER: Interpreting Maps
1. **Location** On what continents identified on the map did Cold War conflicts not occur?
2. **Region** About what fraction of the globe did Communists control by 1975?

Restructuring the Postwar World **873**

Confrontations in the Middle East

Key Ideas
- Oil wealth feeds a secular culture in Iran.
- Ayatollah Khomeini leads a religious revolt against the U.S.-backed secular government.
- Khomeini promotes an Islamic state and pursues radical anti-U.S. policies.
- The Soviet Union invades Afghanistan.

 IN-DEPTH RESOURCES : UNIT 8
History Makers: Ruholla Khomeini, p. 17

MORE ABOUT . . .
American Hostages in Iran

Taking diplomats hostage was so unprecedented that no one dreamed how long the Iranian crisis would endure. One of the hostages recalled that he refused to take off his jacket or tie after he was blindfolded and strapped to a chair on the first day because he was due at a dinner party that night. At the time, his most pressing worry was notifying his "very chic Iranian hostess" that he was not going to be able to attend her party.

 ELECTRONIC LIBRARY OF PRIMARY SOURCES
from *444 Days: The Hostages Remember*

Confrontations in the Middle East

As the map on the previous page shows, Cold War confrontations continued to erupt around the globe. (For more information about African conflicts, see Chapter 34.) With its rich supplies of oil, the Middle East lured both the United States and the Soviet Union.

Religious and Secular Values Clash in Iran Throughout the Middle East, wealth from the oil industry fueled a growing conflict between traditional Islamic values and modern Western materialism. In no country did the clash between cultures erupt more dramatically than in the former Persia, or Iran.

After World War II, Iran's leader, **Shah Mohammed Reza Pahlavi** (PAH·luh·vee), embraced Western governments and wealthy Western oil companies. Angry Iranian nationalists resented these foreign alliances. They united under the leadership of Prime Minister Muhammad Mossaddeq (moh·sah·DEHK). They seized and nationalized a British-owned oil company and, in 1953, forced the shah to flee. Fearing that Mossaddeq might turn to the Soviets for support, the United States had him arrested. It then restored the shah to power.

The United States Supports Secular Rule With U.S. support, the shah westernized his country. By the end of the 1950s, Iran's capital, Tehran, featured gleaming skyscrapers, foreign banks, and modern factories. Millions of Iranians, however, still lived in extreme poverty. And the shah's secret police brutally punished anyone who dared to oppose him. The shah also tried to weaken the political influence of religion in the country by limiting the role of Islamic legal and academic experts. Iran's conservative Muslim leaders, known as ayatollahs (eye·uh·TOH·luhz), bitterly opposed this move. They also opposed what they saw as socially and morally corrupting Western influences. They wanted Iran to become a republic ruled strictly by Islamic law.

The leader of this religious opposition, **Ayatollah Ruholla Khomeini** (koh·MAY·nee), was living in exile. Spurred by his tape-recorded messages, Iranian workers went on strike. "Death to the shah!" and "Down with America!" they vowed. In late 1978, riots erupted in every major city in Iran. Faced with overwhelming opposition, the shah fled Iran in January 1979. A triumphant Khomeini returned from exile to establish an Islamic state. He banned the Western influences that the shah had brought to Iran and reinstated traditional Muslim values. Islamic law became the legal code for the country.

Khomeini's Anti-U.S. Policies Adherence to Islam ruled Khomeini's domestic policies. But hatred of the United States was at the heart of his politics. The Americans had long supported the shah. Their admitting him into the United States for medical treatment in 1979, however, was the final insult. That year, with the ayatollah's blessing, a group of young Islamic revolutionaries seized the U.S. embassy in Tehran. They took more than 60 Americans hostage. They also demanded the return of the shah to face trial. Most of the U.S. hostages remained prisoners for 444 days before they were released on January 20, 1981.

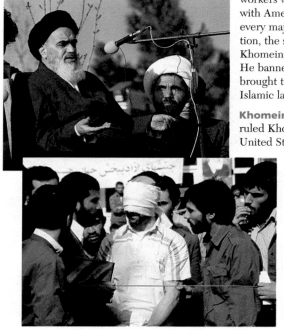

Ayatollah Khomeini (top) supported the taking of U.S. hostages in Tehran in 1979. During their 14-month captivity, the hostages were blindfolded and paraded through the city streets (bottom).

THINK THROUGH HISTORY
D. Analyzing Motives Why did the United States support the Shah of Iran?
D. Answer To maintain the Shah's alliance with the West and prevent the Soviets from gaining influence in Iran.

| TEACHING OPTIONS | MULTIPLE LEARNING STYLES | CONNECTIONS ACROSS TIME AND PLACE |

Logical/Mathematical Learners
Suggest that students create a cause-and-effect graphic to help them understand the sequence of events in the Iranian crisis. They can use a format like this.

Shah Pahlavi welcomes Western oil companies.
↓
Iranian nationalists are angered.
↓
Mossaddeq seizes British oil company.

CRITICAL THINKING TRANSPARENCIES
CT75 Cause and Effect

Worldwide ideological movements In the 1970s, the same time that Islamic fundamentalism was on the rise in Iran under the leadership of Ayatollah Khomeini, Christian fundamentalism was on the rise in the United States.

Similarly, in the 1960s, when U.S. youth were protesting the Vietnam War and authority in general, similar protest movements were sweeping countries from China to France. Encourage students to discuss this phenomenon of worldwide ideological movements. Do they think that these developments are merely coincidental or do they see a broader explanation?

Khomeini also encouraged Muslim fundamentalists, or strict believers, in other countries to overthrow their secular governments. Intended to be a means of unifying Muslims, this policy only heightened tensions between Iran and its neighbor, Iraq. While the Iranians were Shi'a, the Iraqis belonged to the rival Sunni Muslim sect. In addition, a military leader, Saddam Hussein (hoo-SAYN), governed Iraq as a secular state.

War broke out between the two countries in 1980. For eight years, Muslim killed Muslim in a territorial struggle. Caught in the middle, the United States secretly sold weapons to Iran in an effort to get their hostages released. A million Iranians and Iraqis died before a UN ceasefire ended the hostilities in 1988.

The Superpowers Face Off in Afghanistan Iran was not the only country in the Middle East in which Cold War tensions erupted. For several years following World War II, Afghanistan maintained its independence from both the neighboring Soviet Union and the United States. In the 1950s, however, Soviet influence in the country began to increase. In the late 1970s, a Muslim revolt threatened to topple Afghanistan's Communist regime. This revolt triggered a Soviet invasion in December 1979.

The Soviets expected to prop up the Afghan Communists quickly and withdraw. Instead, just as the United States had gotten mired in Vietnam in the 1960s, the Soviets found themselves stuck in Afghanistan. And like the Vietcong in Vietnam, determined Afghan rebel forces outmaneuvered and overpowered a military superpower. Soviet helicopter rocket attacks secured the cities. They failed to dislodge the rebels, called *mujahideen*, from their mountain strongholds, however. Supplied with American weapons, the *mujahideen* fought on.

The United States had armed the rebels because they considered the Soviet invasion a threat to the rich Middle Eastern oil supplies. U.S. President Jimmy Carter sternly warned the Soviets that any attempt to gain control of the Persian Gulf would be "repelled by any means necessary, including military force." No threat developed, though. Therefore, the United States limited its response to an embargo of grain shipments to the Soviet Union. It also boycotted the 1980 summer Olympic games in Moscow.

In the 1980s, a new Soviet regime acknowledged the war's devastating costs to both Afghanistan and the Soviet Union. After a ten-year occupation—as long as U.S. involvement in Vietnam—President Mikhail Gorbachev ordered his forces to withdraw. The last Soviet troops left Afghanistan in February 1989. By then, internal unrest and economic problems were tearing the Soviet Union itself apart.

THINK THROUGH HISTORY
E. Comparing In what ways were U.S. involvement in Vietnam and Soviet involvement in Afghanistan similar?
E. Answer Both superpowers became mired in long, bloody struggles with guerrilla forces who ultimately defeated them.

SPOTLIGHT ON

Boycott of 1980 Olympics

Sixty-two nations, including Japan, West Germany, and Canada, joined the U.S. boycott of the 1980 Moscow Olympics. In sympathy, 16 of the 81 teams who did participate refused to carry their national flags in the opening ceremony.

U.S. athletes had trained for years to compete in the Olympics. They received Congressional Olympic medals as a consolation for their dashed hopes and disappointment.

Disappointed athletes and other critics suggested that future games should be played in a neutral location. This move would help separate international sports competition from politics.

Section 4 Assessment

1. TERMS & NAMES
Identify
- Third World
- nonaligned nations
- Fidel Castro
- Anastasio Somoza
- Daniel Ortega
- Shah Mohammed Reza Pahlavi
- Ayatollah Ruholla Khomeini

2. TAKING NOTES
Using a flow chart like the one below, fill in the main events of U.S. involvement in Cuba.

Castro leads revolution against Batista

Write a newspaper headline for one of the events you listed.

3. COMPARING
What similarities do you see among U.S. actions in Nicaragua, Cuba, and Iran?

THINK ABOUT
- the type of leader the United States supported in each country
- U.S. interests in these countries

4. ANALYZING THEMES
Economics Today, Cuba suffers a severe shortage of vital supplies, largely due to the U.S. trade embargo that has lasted for almost 40 years. Do you think the United States should lift that embargo? Why or why not?

THINK ABOUT
- Castro's leadership
- prior U.S. conflicts with Cuba
- human suffering

Restructuring the Postwar World **875**

ANSWERS

1. TERMS & NAMES
Third World, p. 871
nonaligned nations, p. 871
Fidel Castro, p. 872
Anastasio Somoza, p. 873
Daniel Ortega, p. 873
Shah Mohammed Reza Pahlavi, p. 874
Ayatollah Ruholla Khomeini, p. 874

2. TAKING NOTES
Castro nationalizes U.S.-owned sugar mills; Eisenhower orders embargo on trade; Castro turns to Soviets for aid; Bay of Pigs invasion; Cuban missile crisis.

3. COMPARING
The United States supported dictatorial leaders who were overthrown by popular uprisings. It intervened in all three countries to protect its own interests—a takeover by Communist Sandinistas in Nicaragua and by Castro in Cuba, and loss of vital oil supplies from Iran.

4. ANALYZING THEMES
Lift embargo—Cuba is no longer receiving aid from the Soviets; all Cubans—not only those who agree with Castro—are suffering; Retain embargo—Castro is still a threat to U.S. security; eventually embargo may cause the fall of the Communist regime.

OBJECTIVES

(1) To analyze Soviet domination of Eastern Europe and the Soviet Union–China split.

(2) To trace the origins of détente and its effects on the Cold War.

(3) To describe the renewal of Cold War tensions in the 1980s.

CRITICAL THINKING
• Recognizing effects, p. 876
• Recognizing bias, p. 878
• Analyzing causes, p. 879
• Contrasting, p. 879
• Evaluating decisions, p. 879

FOCUS
5-Minute Warm-Up

▶ **Interpreting Political Cartoons**

To give students a concise idea of the next stages in the Cold War, ask the following questions.

1. Look at the political cartoon on page 878. Which two nations are represented?

2. What does the bomb stand for? What are the two nations trying to do?

 WARM-UP TRANSPARENCY 33

OBJECTIVE (1) INSTRUCT

The Soviets Dominate Eastern Europe

▶ **Key Ideas**
• Khrushchev removes Stalinist influences from the Soviet Union but puts down a revolt in Hungary.

• Brezhnev imposes repressive measures in the Soviet Union and crushes Czechoslovakian reforms.

• China's defiance leads to a split with the Soviet Union.

📄 **IN-DEPTH RESOURCES**
Guided Reading, p. 5
Primary Source: Political Cartoon, p. 12

📄 **ACCESS FOR STUDENTS ACQUIRING ENGLISH**
Guided Reading (Spanish), p. 336

TERMS & NAMES
• Nikita Khrushchev
• destalinization
• Leonid Brezhnev
• John F. Kennedy
• Lyndon Johnson
• détente
• Richard M. Nixon
• SALT
• Ronald Reagan
• Star Wars

5 The Cold War Thaws

MAIN IDEA	WHY IT MATTERS NOW
The Cold War began to thaw as the superpowers entered an era of uneasy diplomacy.	The United States and the countries of the former Soviet Union continue to cooperate and maintain a cautious peace.

SETTING THE STAGE In the postwar years, the Soviet Union kept a firm grip on its satellite countries in Eastern Europe. These countries were Poland, Czechoslovakia, Hungary, Romania, Yugoslavia, Bulgaria, Albania, and East Germany. It did not allow them to direct and develop their own economies. Instead, it insisted that they develop industries to meet Soviet needs. These policies greatly hampered Eastern Europe's economic recovery.

The Soviets Dominate Eastern Europe

After Stalin died, a new, more moderate group of Soviet leaders came to power. These new leaders allowed their satellite countries a taste of independence, as long as they remained firmly Communist and allied with the Soviet Union. During the 1950s and 1960s, however, growing protest movements in Eastern Europe threatened the Soviet Union's grip over the region. Increasing tensions with Communist China also diverted Soviet attention and forces.

Destalinization and Rumblings of Protest Joseph Stalin died on March 5, 1953. Shortly after his death, a loyal member of the Communist party named **Nikita Khrushchev** became the dominant Soviet leader. The shrewd, tough Khrushchev publicly denounced Stalin for jailing and killing loyal Soviet citizens. His speech signaled the beginning of a policy called **destalinization,** or purging the country of Stalin's memory. Workers destroyed monuments of the former dictator and reburied his body outside the Kremlin wall. Khrushchev also called for "peaceful competition" with the capitalist states.

A toppled statue of Stalin lies in Moscow, a stark symbol of Khrushchev's policy of destalinization.

This new Soviet outlook did not change life in the satellite countries, however. Their resentment occasionally turned into active protest. In October 1956, for example, the Hungarian army joined with protesters to overthrow Hungary's Soviet-controlled government. Storming through the capital, Budapest, angry mobs waved Hungarian flags with the Communist hammer-and-sickle emblem cut out. "From the youngest child to the oldest man," one protester declared, "no one wants communism."

A popular and liberal Hungarian Communist leader named Imre Nagy (IHM·ray nahj) formed a new government. Nagy promised free elections and demanded that Soviet troops leave Hungary. In response, in early November, Soviet tanks rolled into Budapest. They were backed by infantry units. Thousands of Hungarian freedom fighters armed themselves with pistols and bottles. The Soviets overpowered them, however. The invaders replaced the Hungarian government with pro-Soviet leaders and eventually executed Nagy.

THINK THROUGH HISTORY
A. Recognizing Effects What effects did destalinization have on Soviet satellite countries?
A. Answer None. Their resentment and protest against Soviet rule continued.

SECTION 5 RESOURCES

PRINT RESOURCES

📄 **IN-DEPTH RESOURCES: UNIT 8**
Guided Reading, p. 5
Primary Source: Political Cartoon, p. 12

📄 **ACCESS FOR STUDENTS ACQUIRING ENGLISH**
Guided Reading (Spanish), p. 336

📄 **FORMAL ASSESSMENT**
Section Quiz, p. 391

📄 **ALTERNATIVE ASSESSMENT BOOK**

TECHNOLOGY RESOURCES

🖥 **CRITICAL THINKING TRANSPARENCIES**
CT69 Chapter 33 Visual Summary

💿 **CD-ROM**
Electronic Library of Primary Sources

🌐 **INTERNET** www.mlworldhistory.com

HISTORY MAKERS

The Victim

HUNGARY

Faces of Protest

Soviet tanks move into Prague in 1968 to stamp out Czech reforms.

Imre Nagy (1896–1958)

Of peasant background, Imre Nagy was captured by the Soviets during World War I and recruited into their army. He became a Communist and lived in Moscow until 1944, when he returned to Soviet-occupied Hungary.

Although he held several posts in his country's Communist government, his loyalty remained with the peasants. Because of his independent approach, he fell in and out of favor with the Soviet regime. He led the anti-Soviet revolt in October 1956.

The Soviets forcefully put down the uprising and deported Nagy. They then brought him back to Hungary, where they tried and executed him. He remained in disgrace until the Hungarian Supreme Court cleared his name in 1989.

The Survivor

CZECHOSLOVAKIA

Alexander Dubček (1921–1992)

Alexander Dubček was the son of a member of the Czech Communist Party and moved rapidly up through the Communist ranks in Czechoslovakia.

In response to the spirit of change in the 1960s, Dubček instituted broad reforms in the 1968 Prague Spring. Not surprisingly, Soviet officials reacted negatively. Tanks rolled into Prague to suppress a feared revolt.

The Soviets expelled Dubček from the Communist Party in 1970. He survived, though. He regained political prominence in 1989, when the Communists agreed to share power in a coalition government. When the new nation of Slovakia was formed in 1992, Dubček became head of its Social Democratic Party.

Brezhnev and the Revolt in Czechoslovakia Despite this show of force in Hungary, Khrushchev lost prestige in his country as a result of the Cuban missile crisis. In 1964, Communist party leaders voted to remove him from power. His replacement, **Leonid Brezhnev,** quickly adopted repressive domestic policies. The Communist party strictly enforced laws to limit such basic human rights as freedom of speech and worship. Government censors carefully controlled what writers could publish. And Brezhnev clamped down on those who dared to protest his government's policies. For example, the secret police arrested many dissidents, including Aleksandr Solzhenitsyn, winner of the 1970 Nobel Prize for literature. They then expelled him from the Soviet Union.

Brezhnev made it clear that he would not tolerate dissent in Eastern Europe either. His policy was put to the test in early 1968. At that time, Czech Communist leader Alexander Dubček (DOOB-chehk) loosened controls on censorship to offer his country socialism with "a human face." This period of reform, when Czechoslovakia's capital bloomed with new ideas, became known as Prague Spring.

Prague Spring, however, did not survive the summer. On August 20, armed forces from the Warsaw Pact nations invaded Czechoslovakia. Brezhnev justified this invasion by claiming the Soviet right to prevent its satellites from rejecting communism.

Split with China While many of the Soviet satellite countries resisted Communist rule, China seemed firmly committed to communism. In fact, to cement the ties between their Communist powers, Mao and Stalin had signed a 30-year treaty of friendship in 1950. Their spirit of cooperation, however, ran out before the treaty did.

Restructuring the Postwar World **877**

HISTORY MAKERS

Faces of Protest: Imre Nagy and Alexander Dubček

Imre Nagy and Alexander Dubček were both unlikely heroes. Nagy seemed to be more of an idealistic bookworm than a man of action. Although some people suspected him of being a Soviet agent, he not only agreed to lead the Hungarian uprising, but defended his country's bid for independence with his life. A Hungarian supporter said, "If his life was a question mark, his death was an answer."

In contrast, Dubček struck many observers as a colorless bureaucrat. He played by Communist rules and rose steadily through the ranks. He revealed his reformist colors, however, in 1967, when he rallied the support of political and economic reformers. He granted greater freedom of expression to the press and, in 1968, proposed a full-blown reform program—"Czechoslovakia's Road to Socialism"—designed to democratize the country.

MORE ABOUT . . .
The Brezhnev Doctrine

Leonid Brezhnev's claim that the Soviet Union had a right to prevent its satellite countries from rejecting Communism came to be known as the Brezhnev Doctrine. This policy was invoked as late as 1979 to justify the Soviet invasion of Afghanistan.

 ELECTRONIC LIBRARY OF PRIMARY SOURCES
Speech on Stalin by Nikita Khrushchev
From *A Student's Diary*

From Brinkmanship to Détente

Key Ideas
- Repeated crises force U.S. and Soviet leaders to seek alternatives to the policy of brinkmanship.
- The U. S. seeks to lessen tensions and avoid confrontations with the Soviet Union.
- President Nixon opens talks with both China and the Soviet Union.

CRITICAL THINKING ACTIVITY

CLASS TIME: 15 MINUTES

Perceiving Causes and Effects
To help students understand the reasons behind and results of détente, have them complete a cause-and-effect diagram as they read.

🏛 **CRITICAL THINKING TRANSPARENCIES**
CT75 Cause and Effect

History from Visuals

Cartoon

Interpreting the Cartoon Make sure students understand that this cartoon depicts the world as a bomb with a lit fuse. Which item in the cartoon represents détente? *The scissors.*

Extension Activity Ask students to discuss ways they might represent the policy of brinkmanship visually. Then have them work in pairs to create a political cartoon about this Cold War strategy.

The Soviets assumed that the Chinese would follow Soviet leadership in world affairs. As the Chinese grew more confident, however, they came to resent being Moscow's junior partner. They began to spread their own brand of communism in Africa and other parts of Asia. In 1959, Khrushchev punished the Chinese for their independence by refusing to share nuclear secrets with them. The following year, the Soviets ended technical economic aid to China. This split eventually grew so wide that fighting broke out along the long Chinese-Soviet border. After repeated incidents, the two neighbors today maintain a fragile peace.

From Brinkmanship to Détente

In the 1970s, the United States and the Soviet Union finally backed away from the aggressive policies of brinkmanship they had followed during the early postwar years. The superpowers slowly moved toward a period of lowered tensions.

Brinkmanship Breaks Down The brinkmanship policy that the United States followed during the Eisenhower, Kennedy, and Johnson administrations resulted in one terrifying crisis after another. Though these crises erupted all over the world, they were united by a common fear. Nuclear war seemed possible.

In 1960, the U-2 incident prevented a meeting between the United States and the Soviet Union to discuss the buildup of arms on both sides. Then, during the presidency of **John F. Kennedy** in the early 1960s, the Cuban missile crisis made the superpowers' use of nuclear weapons a very real possibility. (See pages 872–873.) The crisis ended when the Soviet ships turned back to avoid a confrontation at sea. "We're eyeball to eyeball," the relieved U.S. Secretary of State Dean Rusk said, "and I think the other fellow just blinked." President Kennedy's Secretary of Defense, Robert McNamara, however, admitted just how close the world had come to disaster:

> ### A VOICE FROM THE PAST
> In the face of an air attack [on Cuba] and in the face of the probability of a ground attack, it was certainly possible, and I would say probable, that a Cuban sergeant or Soviet officer in a missile silo, without authority from Moscow, would have launched one or more of those intermediate-range missiles, equipped with a nuclear warhead, against one or more of the cities on the East Coast of the United States.
>
> **ROBERT McNAMARA,** quoted in *Inside the Cold War*

Tensions remained high, and after the assassination of President Kennedy in 1963, **Lyndon Johnson** assumed the U.S. presidency. Committed to stopping the spread of communism, President Johnson escalated U.S. involvement in the war in Vietnam.

The United States Embraces Détente Widespread popular protests wracked the United States during the Vietnam War. And the turmoil did not end with U.S. withdrawal. As it tried to heal its internal wounds, the United States began backing away from its policy of direct confrontation with the Soviet Union. **Détente,** a policy of lessened Cold War tensions, finally replaced brinkmanship during the administration of President **Richard M. Nixon.**

President Nixon's move toward détente grew out of a philosophy known as realpolitik. This term comes from the German word meaning "realistic politics." In practice, realpolitik meant dealing with other nations in a practical and flexible manner. While the United States continued to contain the spread of communism, the two superpowers agreed to pursue détente and to reduce tensions.

Nixon's new policy represented a dramatic personal reversal as well as a political shift for the

In a spirit of cooperation and détente, the U.S. and the Soviet Union try to prevent their conflicts from destroying the world.

(C) J.G. SZABO - ROTHCO CARTOONS   86–6E43

Vocabulary
détente: a French word meaning "a loosening"

THINK THROUGH HISTORY
B. Recognizing Bias Do you think that Robert McNamara's view of the Soviet threat in Cuba was justified or was due to a biased U.S. fear of the Soviet Union? Explain.
B. Possible Answers
Justified—The Soviets had installed missiles in Cuba with the intent to use them against the United States. *Biased*—The Soviets intended their missiles only to be a threat. They knew that using them might start a nuclear war that would destroy the world.

TEACHING OPTION **BLOCK SCHEDULING**   COOPERATIVE ACTIVITY: Honoring Cold War Heroes   **CLASS TIME 30 MINUTES**

Task: Students will write statements and stage a ceremony to honor heroes of the Cold War.

Purpose: To evaluate Cold War issues and personalities.

Activity: Working in small groups, students will choose a Cold War hero, such as Imre Nagy, and write a testimonial statement honoring that person's

contributions to history. Encourage the groups to create visual materials, such as plaques, posters, and collages to accompany their statements. Then have the class stage an awards ceremony in which a volunteer from each group makes a presentation.

📁 **Building a Portfolio:** Students should consider including testimonial statements in their portfolios.

📖 **ALTERNATIVE ASSESSMENT BOOK**
Standards for Evaluating a Cooperative Activity

Standards for Evaluation
Testimonial statements should . . .
- identify the hero
- indicate the person's involvement with the Cold War
- convey the person's personality and achievements

country. His rise in politics in the 1950s was largely due to his strong anti-Communist position. Twenty years later, he became the first American president after World War II to visit Communist China. The visit made sense in a world in which three—rather than just two—superpowers eyed each other suspiciously. "We want the Chinese with us when we sit down and negotiate with the Russians," Nixon explained.

Nixon Visits the Communist Superpowers Three months after visiting Beijing in February 1972, President Nixon made history again by becoming the first American president to visit the Soviet Union. After a series of meetings called the Strategic Arms Limitation Talks (**SALT**), Nixon and Brezhnev signed the SALT I Treaty. This five-year agreement limited to 1972 levels the number of intercontinental ballistic and submarine-launched missiles each country could have. In 1975, 33 nations joined the United States and the Soviet Union in signing a commitment to détente and cooperation, the Helsinki Accords.

Détente Cools

Under Presidents Nixon and Gerald Ford, the United States gradually improved relations with China and the Soviet Union. In the late 1970s, however, President Jimmy Carter's concern over harsh treatment of Soviet protesters threatened to prevent a second round of SALT negotiations. In June 1979, Carter and Brezhnev finally signed the SALT II agreement. When the Soviets invaded Afghanistan in December of that year, however, the U.S. Congress refused to ratify SALT II. Tensions continued to mount as increasing numbers of European and Asian countries began building nuclear arsenals.

Ronald Reagan Abandons Détente The fiercely anti-Communist U.S. president **Ronald Reagan** took office in 1981. He continued his country's retreat from détente. In 1983, he announced a program—the Strategic Defense Initiative (SDI)—to protect America against enemy missiles. The program, called **Star Wars** after a popular movie, was never put into effect. It remained a symbol of U.S. anti-Communist sentiment, however.

Tensions increased as U.S. activities such as arming Nicaragua's Contras pushed the two countries even farther from détente. A transfer of power in the Soviet Union in 1985, however, brought a new policy toward the United States and the beginnings of a final thaw in the Cold War.

The Cold War between the two superpowers ebbed and flowed. Meanwhile, as you will learn in the next chapter, developing countries continued their own struggles for independence from colonialism.

U.S. President Jimmy Carter and Soviet Premier Leonid Brezhnev optimistically mark the signing of the SALT II treaty in Vienna, Austria, in 1979. Carter, however, remained concerned over Soviet violations of its citizens' human rights.

Section 5 Assessment

1. TERMS & NAMES
Identify
• Nikita Khrushchev
• destalinization
• Leonid Brezhnev
• John F. Kennedy
• Lyndon Johnson
• détente
• Richard M. Nixon
• SALT
• Ronald Reagan
• Star Wars

2. TAKING NOTES
In a chart like the one below, indicate each U.S. president's contribution to Cold War tensions by writing his name in the correct column.

Tensions Increased	Tensions Decreased
Eisenhower	

Write a paragraph summarizing the policies and actions of one of these presidents.

3. EVALUATING DECISIONS
Do you think it was a wise political move for Nixon to visit Communist China and the Soviet Union? Why or why not?

THINK ABOUT
• the Cuban missile crisis
• realpolitik
• public sentiment after the Vietnam War

4. THEME ACTIVITY
Revolution Write a poem or song lyrics expressing a Hungarian or Czech citizen's protest against Communist rule.

ANSWERS

Chapter 33 Assessment

TERMS & NAMES

1. containment, p. 857
2. Cold War, p. 859
3. Mao Zedong, p. 862
4. Cultural Revolution, p. 865
5. 38th parallel, p. 866
6. Vietnamization, p. 869
7. Fidel Castro, p. 872
8. Nikita Khrushchev, p. 876
9. détente, p. 878
10. SALT, p. 879

REVIEW QUESTIONS

Answers will vary.

11. They believed the United States should not interfere with other nations' affairs, that it lacked resources to carry out a worldwide war on communism, and that economic aid might support dictators.

12. It proved that it would go to the brink itself by building up a nuclear arsenal and competing aggressively in the arms race.

13. The United States supported the Nationalists in their fight against the Communists. The Soviet Union supported the Communists.

14. Both programs failed to create the powerful socialist nation Mao envisioned and actually weakened it.

15. Five million people died, and North and South Korea remained divided at the 38th parallel, as before the war.

16. Unfamiliar jungle terrain and guerrilla warfare and lack of popular support for the South Vietnamese government they were bolstering.

17. They needed financial aid and investment to help them industrialize as well as a political and economic system on which to model their governments.

18. It secretly built 42 missile sites in Cuba.

19. It did not allow the East Europeans to run their own economies or give them enough money to repair war damages. It also promoted industries necessary to the Soviets, not to the satellite countries.

20. Dealing with nations in a realistic manner, which meant giving up long-held fear and hatred of communism. Pursuit of this policy helped ease Cold War tensions.

TERMS & NAMES

Briefly explain the importance of each of the following in reconstructing the postwar world since 1945.

1. containment
2. Cold War
3. Mao Zedong
4. Cultural Revolution
5. 38th parallel
6. Vietnamization
7. Fidel Castro
8. Nikita Khrushchev
9. détente
10. SALT

Interact with History

On page 854, you considered what action you would take in a civil war in a developing country that both the United States and the Soviet Union were interested in. Now that you have learned more about the Cold War, would your decision change? Discuss your ideas with a small group.

Visual Summary

REVIEW QUESTIONS

SECTION 1 (pages 855–861)
Two Superpowers Face Off

11. Why did some Americans oppose the Truman Doctrine?

12. How did the Soviet Union respond to the U.S. policy of brinkmanship?

SECTION 2 (pages 862–865)
Communists Triumph in China

13. Which sides did the superpowers support in the Chinese internal struggle for control of the country?

14. What were the results of Mao Zedong's Great Leap Forward and Cultural Revolution?

SECTION 3 (pages 866–870)
War in Korea and Vietnam

15. What effects did the Korean War have on Korea's land and people?

16. What major difficulties did the U.S. Army face in fighting the war in Vietnam?

SECTION 4 (pages 871–875)
Cold War Around the World

17. Why did developing nations often align themselves with one or the other superpower?

18. How did the Soviet Union respond to the U.S.-supported Bay of Pigs invasion?

SECTION 5 (pages 876–879)
The Cold War Thaws

19. In what ways did Soviet actions hamper Eastern Europe's economic recovery after World War II?

20. What policies characterized realpolitik and how did they affect the course of the Cold War?

Cold War, 1946–1980

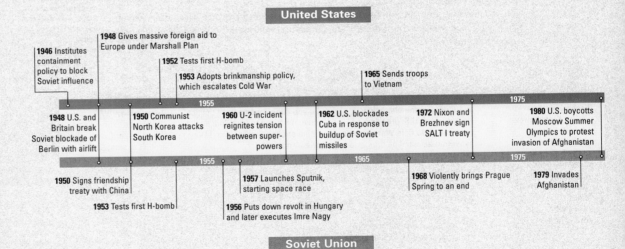

United States

1946 Institutes containment policy to block Soviet influence

1948 Gives massive foreign aid to Europe under Marshall Plan

1952 Tests first H-bomb

1953 Adopts brinkmanship policy, which escalates Cold War

1965 Sends troops to Vietnam

1948 U.S. and Britain break Soviet blockade of Berlin with airlift

1950 Communist North Korea attacks South Korea

1960 U-2 incident reignites tension between superpowers

1962 U.S. blockades Cuba in response to buildup of Soviet missiles

1972 Nixon and Brezhnev sign SALT I treaty

1980 U.S. boycotts Moscow Summer Olympics to protest invasion of Afghanistan

1950 Signs friendship treaty with China

1953 Tests first H-bomb

1957 Launches Sputnik, starting space race

1956 Puts down revolt in Hungary and later executes Imre Nagy

1968 Violently brings Prague Spring to an end

1979 Invades Afghanistan

Soviet Union

Interact with History

Possible Responses: Students who originally wanted to help the rebels may now say that their support by an enemy superpower made them enemies of our vital interests. Others who supported the dictator may now say that his brutality made it difficult for him to ever win the support of the people.

CRITICAL THINKING

1. COLD WAR MANEUVERS

Using a web like the one below, indicate various tactics the Soviet Union and the United States used during the Cold War.

2. RECOGNIZING THE ENEMY

American cartoonist Walt Kelly once said, "We have met the enemy, and he is us." In what sense do you think this saying applies to the Cold War superpowers? In what specific ways were the United States and the Soviet Union more similar than they were different?

3. FROM WORLD WAR TO COLD WAR

THEME EMPIRE BUILDING The Soviet Union emerged from World War II economically and physically devastated. How do you think the development of the Cold War would have proceeded if the United States had been in that position?

4. ANALYZING PRIMARY SOURCES

The following poem by Ho Chi Minh was broadcast over Hanoi Radio on January 1, 1968. Read the poem and answer the questions that follow.

> **A VOICE FROM THE PAST**
> This Spring far outshines the previous Springs,
> Of victories throughout the land come happy tidings.
> South and North, rushing heroically together, shall
> smite the American invaders!
> Go Forward!
> Total victory shall be ours.
> **HO CHI MINH**, quoted in *America and Vietnam*

- In Ho's opinion, who was the enemy in the Vietnam War?
- What purpose might the North Vietnamese have had in broadcasting this poem?

CHAPTER ACTIVITIES

1. LIVING HISTORY: Unit Portfolio Project

THEME ECONOMICS Your unit portfolio project focuses on the ways economic factors influence history. For Chapter 33, you might use one of the following ideas to add to your portfolio.

- Ask classmates to think about what life would be like for peasants in a Communist satellite country. Then stage an interview in which you ask them to discuss their feelings about communism and capitalism. Audiotape your interviews and add a commentary to create an "objective" newscast.
- Create a poster to teach elementary school students about the differences between capitalism and communism.
- Working in a small group, develop and perform a five- to ten-minute skit that pokes fun at communism or capitalism.

2. CONNECT TO TODAY: Cooperative Learning

THEME REVOLUTION During the Cold War, the superpowers played a part in many revolutions or upheavals in developing nations. This unrest continues today as countries struggle to develop suitable political and economic systems.

Working with a team, create an oral presentation about a current political struggle or revolution.

Using the Internet or magazines, research a current political conflict. Investigate the beliefs, programs, tactics, and popular support of the rival factions. Determine which side is in power and what the outcome of the struggle appears to be.

- Collect photographs, charts, artifacts, or other visual aids to illustrate the issues involved in the struggle.
- If possible, interview people from that country who have immigrated to the United States and include their viewpoints in your presentation.

3. INTERPRETING A TIME LINE

Look back at the unit time line on pages 850–851. Which two events during the Cold War do you think had the greatest impact on the U.S. decision to pursue a policy of détente?

FOCUS ON GEOGRAPHY

Cold War tensions between the United States and the Soviet Union were fed by the fear of nuclear war.

- What does this map projection suggest about the distance between the countries?
- Which country had more ICBM bases?

Connect to History
How did the United States and the Soviet Union avoid a nuclear confrontation?

Soviet ICBM base
Soviet radar
U.S. ICBM base
U.S. radar

SOVIET UNION
ARCTIC OCEAN
North Pole
PACIFIC OCEAN
CANADA
UNITED STATES
ATLANTIC OCEAN
1,000 Miles
2,000 Kilometers

1. LIVING HISTORY

Standards for Evaluation
An interview should meet the following criteria:

- Reflects what students have learned about life in a Communist satellite country.
- Includes realistic responses.
- Uses commentary to provide a balanced presentation.

Standards for Evaluation
A poster should meet the following criteria:

- Presents accurate information about communism and capitalism.
- Includes graphs, charts, or other graphic elements.
- Uses language appropriate for elementary school students.

Standards for Evaluation
A skit should meet the following criteria:

- Reflects an understanding of communism or capitalism.
- Makes a clear point.
- Uses exaggeration or other elements to provide humor.

2. CONNECT TO TODAY

Standards for Evaluation
An oral presentation should meet the following criteria:

- Presents a unified picture of a current political struggle.
- Uses graphic materials to identify the major issues in the conflict.
- Includes interviews with immigrants—including students—from the country involved.

3. INTERPRETING A TIME LINE

Students may identify the Bay of Pigs invasion or the withdrawal of troops from the Vietnam War as crucial to the U.S. decision to pursue a policy of détente.

FOCUS ON GEOGRAPHY

- It suggests that the United States and the Soviet Union are very close.
- The Soviet Union.

Connect to History *Possible Responses:*
They maintained a "balance of terror," with each nation increasing its stockpile of weapons so that it could destroy the other no matter who attacked first.

CRITICAL THINKING

1. COLD WAR MANEUVERS

Possible Responses: Backing wars or revolutions; spying; increasing military forces and nuclear arsenals; providing military and economic aid; setting up schools; access to raw materials in developing countries. They both felt that their political and economic systems were the only right ones.

2. RECOGNIZING THE ENEMY

Possible Responses: Both countries became so involved in various conflicts that they defeated themselves. Both wanted to be the dominant world power and to gain

3. FROM WORLD WAR TO COLD WAR

Possible Responses: The Cold War might not have developed, because the Soviet Union might not have felt it necessary to build a wall of satellite nations to protect itself; the United States might not have had the resources to offer aid such as the Marshall Plan.

4. ANALYZING PRIMARY SOURCES

The Americans were the enemy; as propaganda to show that the North and South were fighting together; to pinpoint the Americans as the enemy; to instill confidence in their people and army.

	Key Ideas	COPY MASTERS	ASSESSMENT
SECTION 1 **The Indian Subcontinent Gains Independence** *pp. 885–891*	At the end of World War II, South Asians demand independence. Britain partitions the Indian subcontinent into two new nations, India and Pakistan; a part of Pakistan later becomes Bangladesh. Britain also frees Ceylon.	*In-Depth Resources: Unit 8* • **Guided Reading,** p. 20 • **Primary Source:** from "First Servant of the Indian People," p. 27	P E *Section 1 Assessment,* p. 889 *Formal Assessment* • Section Quiz, p. 400 *Alternative Assessment Book* • Standards for Evaluating a Cooperative Activity
SECTION 2 **Southeast Asian Nations Gain Independence** *pp. 892–895*	Some of the Southeast Asian colonies that become independent after World War II prosper, while others suffer under authoritarian regimes.	*In-Depth Resources: Unit 8* • **Guided Reading,** p. 21 • **Primary Source:** Call to Boycott Presidential Election, p. 28 • **Literature:** from *The Year of Living Dangerously,* p. 31	P E *Section 2 Assessment,* p. 895 *Formal Assessment* • Section Quiz, p. 401 *Alternative Assessment Book* • Standards for Evaluating a Cooperative Activity
SECTION 3 **New Nations in Africa** *pp. 896–900*	Colonizers differ in their willingness to grant independence to their African colonies and in the amount of help they give their colonies in preparing to become modern nations.	*In-Depth Resources: Unit 8* • **Guided Reading,** p. 22 • **Skillbuilder Practice:** Evaluating Decisions, p. 24 • **Geography Application:** The Congo Gains Independence, p. 25 • **Primary Source:** Farewell Without Tears, p. 29 • **Literature:** Négritude poems, p. 32 • **History Makers:** Jomo Kenyatta, p. 34 • **Connections Across Time and Cultures:** p. 36	P E *Section 3 Assessment,* p. 900 *Formal Assessment* • Section Quiz, p. 402 *Alternative Assessment Book* • Standards for Evaluating a Product or Performance
SECTION 4 **Conflicts in the Middle East** *pp. 901–905*	The division of Palestine and the creation of the new nation of Israel after World War II result in conflict between Israeli and Palestinian nationalist movements that continues today.	*In-Depth Resources: Unit 8* • **Guided Reading,** p. 23 • **Primary Source:** The Balfour Declaration, p. 30 • **History Makers:** Golda Meir, p. 35	P E *Section 4 Assessment,* p. 905 *Formal Assessment* • Section Quiz, p. 403 *Alternative Assessment Book* • Standards for Evaluating a Cooperative Activity
CHAPTER RESOURCES	**Chapter Overview** After World War II, imperialist powers rethink the cost of colonies as they demand their independence. The imperialists differ in the speed with which they relinquish control and in the amount of preparation for independence they provide.	*Telescoping the Times* • Chapter Summary, pp. 133–135 *Planning for Block Schedules*	P E *Chapter Assessment,* pp. 906–907 *Chapter Activities,* p. 907 *Formal Assessment* • Chapter Test, forms A and B, pp. 404–409 *Test Generator* *Alternative Assessment Book*

1945–Present

 TECHNOLOGY

 Warm-Up Transparency 34

 World Art and Cultures Transparencies
• AT74 *Vene, Vidi, Vici*

 Electronic Library of Primary Sources
• from Radio Address from New Delhi

 INTERNET RESOURCES
www.mlworldhistory.com

 Warm-Up Transparency 34

Geography Transparencies
• GT34 Indonesia and Malaysia, 1945–1976

Electronic Library of Primary Sources
• "The Fall of President Marcos"

INTERNET RESOURCES
www.mlworldhistory.com

 Warm-Up Transparency 34

INTERNET RESOURCES
www.mlworldhistory.com

  Warm-Up Transparency 34

Critical Thinking Transparencies
• CT34 Time Machine: The Middle East Conflict
• CT70 Chapter 34 Visual Summary

World Art and Cultures Transparencies
• AT76 *After the Storm*

Electronic Library of Primary Sources
• "Enough of Blood and Tears"

INTERNET RESOURCES
www.mlworldhistory.com

 Chapter Summaries on Audiocassette in English and Spanish

 INTERNET RESOURCES
www.mlworldhistory.com

 Block Scheduling (90 MINUTES)

Day 1	**Section 2,** pp. 892–895	**Section 4,** pp. 901–905
Section 1, pp. 885–891	**COOPERATIVE ACTIVITY** Creating a Brochure, p. 894 (Teacher's Edition)	**COOPERATIVE ACTIVITY** Researching West Bank Settlements, p. 903 (Teacher's Edition)
COOPERATIVE ACTIVITY Writing Indian Political Statements, p. 886 (Teacher's Edition)	**Section Assessments,** pp. 889, 895	**Section Assessments,** pp. 900, 905
	Day 2	**Chapter Assessment,** pp. 906–907
	Section 3, pp. 896–900	

Yearly Pacing **Chapter 34 Total:** 2 days **Yearly Total:** 85 days

 Planning for Block Schedules

Customizing for Special Needs

Students Acquiring English

 Access for Students Acquiring English
• **Guided Reading** for Sections 1–4 (Spanish), pp. 343–346
• **Chapter Summary** (Spanish), pp. 340–342
• **Skillbuilder Practice** Evaluating Decisions (Spanish), p. 347
• **Geography Application** The Congo Gains Independence (Spanish), p. 348

 Chapter Summaries on Audiocassette in English and Spanish

 INTERNET RESOURCES www.mlworldhistory.com *The Diverse Classroom.*

Less Proficient Readers

 In-Depth Resources: Unit 8
• **Guided Reading** for Sections 1–4, pp. 20–23
• **Skillbuilder Practice** Evaluating Decisions, p. 24
• **Geography Application** The Congo Gains Independence, p. 25

Telescoping the Times
• Chapter Summary, pp. 133–135

Chapter Summaries on Audiocassette

Gifted and Talented Students

In-Depth Resources: Unit 8

Primary Sources
• from "First Servant of the Indian People," p. 27
• Call to Boycott Presidential Election, p. 28
• Farewell Without Tears, p. 29
• The Balfour Declaration, p. 30

History Makers
• Jomo Kenyatta, p. 34
• Golda Meir, p. 35

Connections to Literature READINGS FOR STUDENTS

 In-Depth Resources: Unit 8
Literature: from *The Year of Living Dangerously*, p. 31; Négritude poems, p. 32

Enrichment Reading
• Head, Bessie
"Snapshots of a Wedding," *African Short Stories*
Oxford: Heinmann, 1987
A bridegroom is forced to choose between

two loves: a traditional girl who would tie him to the past and a modern girl who would take him into an exciting, unknown future.

McDougal Littell
The Language of Literature
Grade 10
Anita Desai, "Games at Twilight," p. 545
Abioseh Nicol, "As the Night the Day," p. 638

 = Pupil's Edition   = Overhead Transparency   = Software   = Video

 = Copy Master   = CD-ROM   = Audiocassette   = Internet

The Colonies Become New Nations, 1945–Present

Accessing Prior Knowledge

- Have students look at the flags displayed in two of the four photographs on this spread. Ask students what a flag represents in the life of a nation. Discuss with them the symbolism of a national flag.

Making Inferences and Predicting

- After students have surveyed the captions and pictures on these pages, ask them what conditions might motivate people to fight for their independence.

- Ask students to predict the possible outcomes of a nationalistic struggle for independence.

Geography Connection

Ask students to look at the map on these two pages.

- On what continents did the struggles for independence that are pictured in the photographs take place? *Africa and Asia.*

- Which of the pictured struggles for independence took place closest to the equator? *Kenya.*

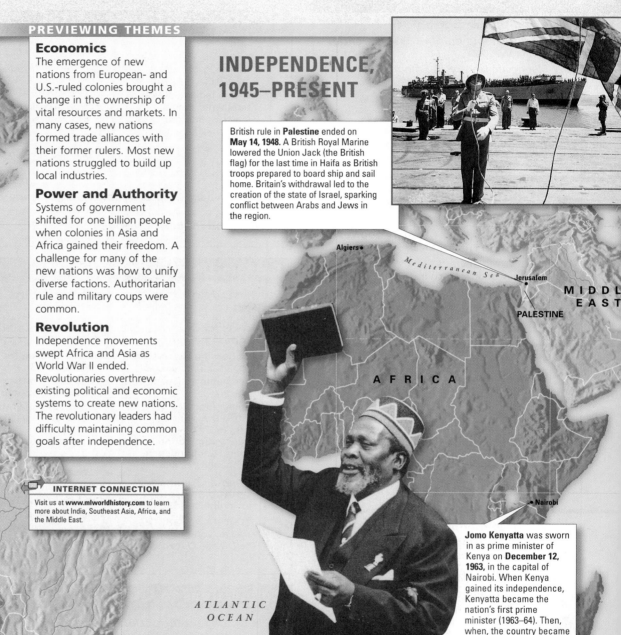

CHAPTER
34 *The Colonies Become New Nations, 1945–Present*

PREVIEWING THEMES

Economics
The emergence of new nations from European- and U.S.-ruled colonies brought a change in the ownership of vital resources and markets. In many cases, new nations formed trade alliances with their former rulers. Most new nations struggled to build up local industries.

Power and Authority
Systems of government shifted for one billion people when colonies in Asia and Africa gained their freedom. A challenge for many of the new nations was how to unify diverse factions. Authoritarian rule and military coups were common.

Revolution
Independence movements swept Africa and Asia as World War II ended. Revolutionaries overthrew existing political and economic systems to create new nations. The revolutionary leaders had difficulty maintaining common goals after independence.

INTERNET CONNECTION
Visit us at **www.mlworldhistory.com** to learn more about India, Southeast Asia, Africa, and the Middle East.

INDEPENDENCE, 1945–PRESENT

British rule in **Palestine** ended on **May 14, 1948**. A British Royal Marine lowered the Union Jack (the British flag) for the last time in Haifa as British troops prepared to board ship and sail home. Britain's withdrawal led to the creation of the state of Israel, sparking conflict between Arabs and Jews in the region.

Algiers

Mediterranean Sea

Jerusalem

MIDDLE EAST

PALESTINE

AFRICA

Nairobi

ATLANTIC OCEAN

882

Jomo Kenyatta was sworn in as prime minister of Kenya on **December 12, 1963**, in the capital of Nairobi. When Kenya gained its independence, Kenyatta became the nation's first prime minister (1963–64). Then, when the country became a republic, he became its first president (1964–78).

GEOGRAPHY THEMES

Place

Tell students that geography played a significant role in the emergence of new nations discussed in this chapter. The natural resources of a colony significantly affected how willing the colonizers were to give up the land. In Kenya, Algeria, and Indonesia, coloniz-ers who had lived there for generations were reluctant to leave. In many places, diverse populations, thrown together by arbitrary boundaries established by the colonizers, made up the new nations. These nations had to create unity among the diverse peoples. Mistakes were made, and old ethnic hostilities sometimes persisted.

Movement

The birth of the new nations was often accompanied by huge migrations of people as Europeans returned to their homelands and ethnic groups sought a more harmonious grouping. The worst of these migrations accompanied the partition of the Indian subcontinent and resulted in the deaths of thousands. Ideas were also on the move as many of the new nations entered the modern world for the first time. New communication technologies broke down barriers between countries and continents and between cities and villages.

ADDITIONAL RESOURCES

Books for the Teacher

- Davidson, Basil. *The Black Man's Burden: Africa and the Curse of the Nation State.* New York: Random, 1993.

- Tessler, Mark A. *A History of the Israeli-Palestinian Conflict.* Bloomington, IN: Indiana UP, 1994.

Books for the Student

- Baynham, Simon. *Africa from 1945.* New York: Watts, 1987.

- De Lee, Nigel. *Rise of the Asian Superpowers from 1945.* New York: Watts, 1987.

Videos

- *The Arab World.* Society for Visual Education, 1988. 800-829-1900.

- *Ghana.* Altschul Group, 1994. 800-323-9084.

- *India Unveiled: Emergence of the State.* Britannica, 1986. 800-554-9862.

- *Raising the Bamboo Curtain: Vietnam, Burma, and Cambodia.* Cambridge Social Studies, 1995. 800-468-4227.

Software

- *Decisions, Decisions: Building a Nation.* CD-ROM or diskette. Tom Snyder Productions, 1996. 800-342-0236.

- *Twentieth-Century Nationalism.* CD-ROM. Society for Visual Education, 1994. 800-829-1900.

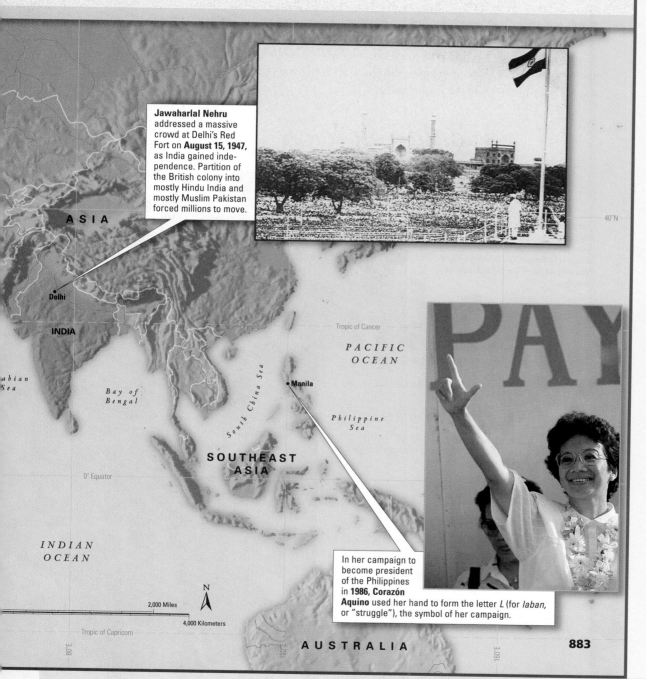

Jawaharlal Nehru addressed a massive crowd at Delhi's Red Fort on **August 15, 1947,** as India gained independence. Partition of the British colony into mostly Hindu India and mostly Muslim Pakistan forced millions to move.

In her campaign to become president of the Philippines in **1986, Corazón Aquino** used her hand to form the letter *L* (for *laban,* or "struggle"), the symbol of her campaign.

883

HISTORY THROUGH ART

Photography

Photography is both a means of recording important events and an art form. Photographs can capture dramatic moments in history and preserve them for posterity. Three of the pictures on these pages show important moments in the history of new nations as they achieve their independence. The British Royal Marine symbolizes a whole empire as he lowers the British flag and prepares to depart from the former British mandate of Palestine. Nehru, who is to become India's first prime minister, addresses a huge crowd on the eve of independence. Jomo Kenyatta jubilantly takes office as Kenya's prime minister when the country gains its independence from Great Britain. All of these pictures capture symbolic moments as British rule is withdrawn from former colonies and protectorates.

Interpreting the Photographs What do these photographs seem to suggest about the end of British rule? What emotions might people in the newly independent nations experience? What emotions and thoughts might they have about their former colonial masters?

Interact *with* History

This Interact with History feature motivates students by inviting them to decide whether or not they would leave their homeland and travel to another country to start a new life. As they imagine themselves deciding whether to stay or go, students will analyze the issues, explore their options, and become decision makers.

Purpose

- to set the stage for studying independence movements in colonies after World War II
- to help students understand some of the causes and effects of the independence movements that swept Asia and Africa
- to help students make connections with the people and events they will study in this chapter

Teaching Strategy

Thinking Critically After students have imagined themselves in the situation described on this page, have them answer the key questions and give reasons for their decision.

EXAMINING *the* ISSUES

Following are suggestions for addressing each bulleted question.

1 Ask students if they have ever moved with their families. What might have been some reasons for the family not to move? Was it difficult to leave friends and familiar places?

2 Ask students who have moved to give the reasons for the move. Was it a job for a parent? A desire to live in a new location?

3 Ask students if they have relatives who live in different cities or states. How often do they see them?

4 Have students brainstorm possible solutions to religious and ethnic conflict.

Making Connections Ask students to discuss the American movement for independence that culminated in the outbreak of the Revolution in 1776.

Interact *with* History

Independence has come to a former British colony, which has been divided into the new nations of India and Pakistan. Serious conflict occurs among the various factions within each country. The Hindu majority in India attacks Muslims, and the Muslim majority in Pakistan attacks Hindus. Some Hindus in Pakistan are choosing to stay in their homeland; others are choosing to flee to India to join the Hindu majority there. Either alternative involves risk.

You are a Hindu whose homeland is Pakistan. Trains are leaving that will carry you through hostile territory to a new homeland, where you will no longer be in a minority. What will you do? Will you leave your homeland behind in order to move to a new land to live among people who share your religious beliefs? Or will you stay where you are and take your chances?

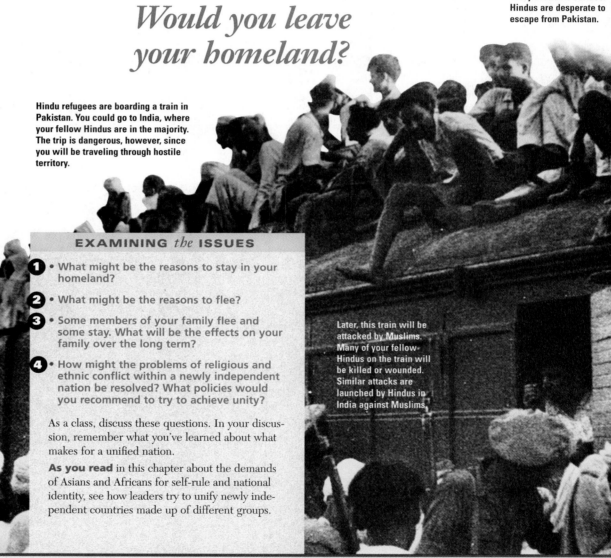

After the passenger cars have been filled, refugees clamber on to every available surface. Hindus are desperate to escape from Pakistan.

Would you leave your homeland?

Hindu refugees are boarding a train in Pakistan. You could go to India, where your fellow Hindus are in the majority. The trip is dangerous, however, since you will be traveling through hostile territory.

EXAMINING *the* ISSUES

1 • What might be the reasons to stay in your homeland?

2 • What might be the reasons to flee?

3 • Some members of your family flee and some stay. What will be the effects on your family over the long term?

4 • How might the problems of religious and ethnic conflict within a newly independent nation be resolved? What policies would you recommend to try to achieve unity?

As a class, discuss these questions. In your discussion, remember what you've learned about what makes for a unified nation.

As you read in this chapter about the demands of Asians and Africans for self-rule and national identity, see how leaders try to unify newly independent countries made up of different groups.

Later, this train will be attacked by Muslims. Many of your fellow Hindus on the train will be killed or wounded. Similar attacks are launched by Hindus in India against Muslims.

Follow Up

A feature on the chapter assessment will ask students to reevaluate their responses to the situation presented on this page.

1 The Indian Subcontinent Gains Independence

TERMS & NAMES
- Congress Party
- Muslim League
- Muhammad Ali Jinnah
- Lord Mountbatten
- partition
- Jawaharlal Nehru
- Indira Gandhi
- Rajiv Gandhi
- Benazir Bhutto

MAIN IDEA

New nations emerged from the British colony of India.

WHY IT MATTERS NOW

India today is the largest democracy in the world.

Section 1 Overview

OBJECTIVES

1. To summarize the effect of World War II on the colonies.
2. To describe the events that led to the partition of India.
3. To summarize the leadership of Nehru and his descendants.
4. To summarize the politics of Pakistan and Sri Lanka.

SKILLBUILDERS
- Interpreting maps: location, p. 887

CRITICAL THINKING
- Recognizing effects, p. 885
- Making inferences, p. 886
- Analyzing causes, p. 887
- Clarifying, p. 889
- Synthesizing, p. 889
- Analyzing themes p. 889

SETTING THE STAGE Britain had ruled India for many years. During this time, some Indians had been pressing for self-rule. In 1939, India was stunned when Britain committed India's armed forces to World War II without first consulting the colony's elected representatives. Indian nationalists felt humiliated. In 1942, the Congress Party launched a "Quit India" campaign. It was intended to drive Great Britain out of India. The end of World War II, in 1945, brought changes to the Indian subcontinent as dramatic as those anywhere in the world.

A Movement Toward Independence

The story was similar throughout the colonial world. When World War II broke out, Africans and Asians answered their colonial rulers' cries for help. These Africans and Asians fought on distant battlefields. They also guarded strategic bases and resources at home. The war brought soldiers from widely separated colonies into contact with one another. Soldiers from the colonies shared their frustrations, dreams for independence, and strategies for achieving it.

"Asia for Asians" During World War II, the Japanese "Asia for Asians" campaign helped to generate nationalism throughout the region. It also sparked independence movements in the various countries Japan occupied in Southeast Asia. The Japanese defeat of European forces was a sign to the nationalists that the Europeans were not as strong as they had thought them to be. Asian nationalists came to realize that their colonial masters were not unbeatable. Sometimes the Europeans suffered defeat at the hands of others—such as the Japanese—who were nonwhite and non-Western, like the nationalists.

THINK THROUGH HISTORY
A. Recognizing Effects What was the effect on Asians of Japanese victories over Europeans?
A. Answer It made Asian nationalists realize the Europeans were vulnerable.

The Colonial Response Britain was recovering from the enormous costs of the war. It began to rethink the expense of maintaining and governing distant colonies. The new government in Britain also called into question the very basis of imperialism. Was it acceptable to take by force the land and resources of another nation in order to enrich the imperial nation?

Independence Brings Partition to India

In 1919, the British massacred unarmed Indians at Amritsar. (See Chapter 30.) This incident, more than any other single event, had marked the beginning of the end of British rule in India. The incident had caused millions of Indians to become strong nationalists overnight. A year later, in 1920, Mohandas Gandhi launched his first nonviolent

This photo shows British soldiers held in a Japanese prisoner-of-war camp at the end of World War II.

The Colonies Become New Nations **885**

FOCUS
5-Minute Warm-Up

▶ *Making Inferences*
To help students understand the changes that swept former colonies, have them answer the following questions.

1. Read Daily Life on page 888. What might Gandhi have thought of Narayanan's election?

2. Why might Narayanan's election suggest that the caste system will be reformed?

WARM-UP TRANSPARENCY 34

OBJECTIVE ① INSTRUCT

A Movement Toward Independence

▶ *Key Ideas*
- Soldiers from the colonies fight in World War II.
- People in the colonies realize their rulers are not unbeatable.
- Britain begins to rethink the cost of maintaining its colonies.

IN-DEPTH RESOURCES: UNIT 8
Guided Reading, p. 20

ACCESS FOR STUDENTS ACQUIRING ENGLISH
Guided Reading (Spanish), p. 343

SECTION 1 RESOURCES

PRINT RESOURCES

IN-DEPTH RESOURCES: UNIT 8
Guided Reading, p. 20
Primary Source: from "First Servant of the Indian People" by Jawaharlal Nehru, p. 27

ACCESS FOR STUDENTS ACQUIRING ENGLISH
Guided Reading (Spanish), p. 343

FORMAL ASSESSMENT
Section Quiz, p. 400

ALTERNATIVE ASSESSMENT BOOK

TECHNOLOGY RESOURCES

WORLD ART AND CULTURES TRANSPARENCIES
AT74 *Vene, Vidi, Vici*

CD-ROM
Electronic Library of Primary Sources

INTERNET www.mlworldhistory.com

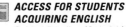

Independence Brings Partition to India

(See page 885.)

▶ *Key Ideas*
- Jinnah proposes partition of India along religious lines.
- Britain supports partition.
- Mass migrations and killings precede independence.

HISTORYMAKERS
Muhammad Ali Jinnah

Have students read the text on page 889 about the breakup of Pakistan. Then have them analyze Jinnah's statement about the distinct culture of Muslims. Ask students how they account for the seeming conflict between Jinnah's view and the subsequent split.

MORE ABOUT . . .
Partition and Religion

A major difference between the two new nations of Pakistan and India was the role religion played in the state. Pakistan established Islam as the official national religion. India's constitution declared India a secular nation with no official religion. The difference influenced each nation's legal system and policies on the family. Pakistan's court system and its marriage and divorce laws, for example, must all be in accordance with Islamic law. India allows Hindus and Muslims to choose to be governed by their own religious codes.

---

campaign for Indian independence. Gandhi was admired as the Mahatma, or "Great Soul," of the Indian independence movement.

The Congress Party and the Muslim League The Indian National Congress, or the **Congress Party,** was a national political party. It claimed to represent all of India. India in the 1940s had approximately 350 million Hindus and about 100 million Muslims. Most members of the Congress Party were Hindus, but the party at times had many Muslim members. A Muslim even served as one of its presidents, from 1940 to 1945.

The **Muslim League** was an organization founded in 1906 in India to protect Muslim interests. The league was concerned that the mainly Hindu Congress Party would look out primarily for Hindu interests. The leader of the Muslim League, **Muhammad Ali Jinnah** (mu·HAM·ihd ah·LEE JIHN·uh), had once been a member of the Congress Party. However, he later insisted that only the league spoke for Muslims. He said that all Muslims ought to resign from the Congress Party. The Muslim League stated that it would never accept Indian independence if it meant rule by the Hindu-dominated Congress Party. Jinnah stated, "The only thing the Muslim has in common with the Hindu is his slavery to the British." The British encouraged the division between Hindus and Muslims in the belief that it would strengthen their authority.

The Muslim League first officially proposed the partition of India into separate Hindu and Muslim nations at its Lahore conference in 1940. Most Muslims lived in the northwest and northeast areas of the subcontinent. Gandhi was deeply hurt. He strongly opposed the two-nation theory on political, cultural, and even moral grounds.

Partition into India and Pakistan When World War II ended, the British government changed from the Conservative Party's Winston Churchill to the Labour Party's Clement Atlee. The stage was set for the British transfer of power. However, the problem persisted of who should receive that power once it was transferred.

Rioting of Hindus and Muslims against one another broke out in Calcutta, East Bengal, Bihar, and Bombay. In August 1946, four days of rioting in Calcutta left more than 5,000 people dead and more than 15,000 hurt. Gandhi walked through the worst areas there. He did his best to reduce the violence between Hindus and Muslims. **Lord Louis Mountbatten** was the last viceroy of India. He feared that the Hindus and Muslims of India would never be able to live together in peace. He began to accept the idea that **partition,** or the dividing up, of India into two nations—mostly Hindu India and mostly Muslim Pakistan—was unavoidable.

The British House of Commons passed an act on July 16, 1947, that granted the two nations independence in one month's time. In that short period, more than 500 independent native princes had to decide which nation they would join—India or Pakistan. The administration of the courts, the military, the railways, and the police—the whole of the civil service—had to be divided down to the last paper clip. Most difficult of all, millions of Hindus, Muslims, and Sikhs would shortly find themselves minorities in a hostile nation. These people had to decide where to go.

During the summer of 1947, 10 million people were on the move in the Indian subcontinent. Whole trainloads of refugees were massacred. Muslims killed Sikhs who were moving into India. Hindus and Sikhs killed Muslims who were headed into Pakistan. In all, an estimated 1 million died. "What is there to celebrate?" Gandhi mourned. "I see nothing but rivers of blood." Gandhi personally went to Delhi to plead for fair treatment of Muslim refugees. While he was there, he himself became

HISTORYMAKERS

**Muhammad Ali Jinnah
1876–1948**

Muhammad Ali Jinnah was born in Karachi, India, which is now part of Pakistan. His Muslim family was wealthy and sent him to England to study. He became a brilliant lawyer and a leader in India's movement for independence.

As the leader of the Muslim League, Jinnah argued for a separate state for Muslims. Called the "great leader," Jinnah was the founder of Pakistan and its first governor-general. He described the Indian Muslims as "a nation with [a] distinct culture and civilization, . . . our own distinctive outlook on . . . life."

Vocabulary
viceroy: a person who governs on behalf of a king.

B. Possible Answer He was hurt that his dream of a unified India was not to be, and he mourned the many lost lives.

THINK THROUGH HISTORY
B. Making Inferences Why did Gandhi mourn as India achieved independence?

Task: Students will write political statements representing different views on the partition of India.

Purpose: To help students understand different perspectives on an issue.

Activity: Divide the class into four groups representing the Indian National Congress, the Muslim League, the British government, and

followers of Gandhi. Have each group research and write a political statement on the partition of India that might have been written by a leader or significant member of the group represented.

📁 **Building a Portfolio:** Students can attach an explanation of the assignment to their statements.

📖 **ALTERNATIVE ASSESSMENT BOOK**
Standards for Evaluating a Cooperative Activity

Standards for Evaluation
Statements should . . .

- use specific details to back up a point of view
- accurately represent the opinions of the group represented
- demonstrate writing skills

a victim. He was shot on January 30, 1948, by a Hindu extremist who thought Gandhi too protective of Muslims.

Modern India

At the stroke of midnight on August 15, 1947, India would become free. It would also become the world's largest democracy. As the hour approached, **Jawaharlal Nehru** (jah·WAH·hahr·lahl NAY·roo), independent India's first prime minister, addressed the Constituent Assembly:

A VOICE FROM THE PAST

Long years ago, we made a tryst [appointment] with destiny, and now the time comes when we shall redeem our pledge, not wholly or in full measure, but very substantially. At the stroke of the midnight hour, when the world sleeps, India will wake to life and freedom.

JAWAHARLAL NEHRU

Nehru Leads India For the first 17 years after independence, India had one prime minister—Jawaharlal Nehru. He had been one of Gandhi's most devoted followers. Educated in Britain, Nehru won popularity among all groups in India. He emphasized democracy, unity, and economic modernization.

Nehru assumed several large challenges along with the office of prime minister. One such challenge was a dispute over the territory of Kashmir. Although its ruler was Hindu, Kashmir had a large Muslim population. The state bordered both India and Pakistan. Pakistan invaded the area shortly after independence, causing Kashmir's ruler to align Kashmir with India. War between India and Pakistan in Kashmir continued until the United Nations arranged a cease-fire in 1949. The cease-fire left a third of Kashmir under Pakistani control and the rest under Indian control. Later, in 1962, China seized part of Kashmir. In 1972, Indian and Pakistani forces fought there again. In that year, a new truce line was set up between the Indian and Pakistani areas of Kashmir. Today, tensions continue to flare along the cease-fire line established by the UN in 1949.

Nehru used his leadership to move India forward. He led other newly independent nations of the world in forming an alliance of countries that were neutral in the dispute between the United States and the Soviet Union. On the home front, Nehru called for a reorganization of the states by language. He also pushed for industrialization and sponsored social reforms. He tried to elevate the status of the lower castes and expand the rights of women.

The Nehru Family Rules Nehru's death in 1964 left the Congress Party with no leader strong enough to hold together its many factions. Then, in 1966, Nehru's daughter, **Indira Gandhi,** was chosen prime minister.

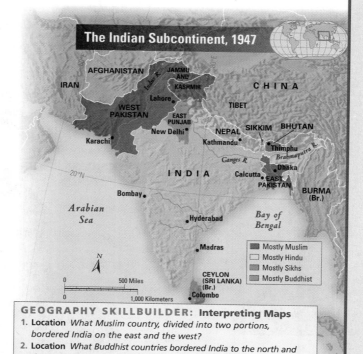

The Indian Subcontinent, 1947

AFGHANISTAN
JAMMU AND KASHMIR
IRAN
CHINA
Indus R.
Lahore
WEST PAKISTAN
TIBET
EAST PUNJAB
New Delhi
Karachi
NEPAL
SIKKIM
BHUTAN
Kathmandu
Thimphu
Brahmaputra R.
Ganges R.
Dhaka
I N D I A
Calcutta
EAST PAKISTAN
Bombay
BURMA (Br.)
Arabian Sea
Hyderabad
Bay of Bengal
Madras

Mostly Muslim
Mostly Hindu
Mostly Sikhs
Mostly Buddhist

CEYLON (SRI LANKA) (Br.)
Colombo

0   500 Miles
0   1,000 Kilometers

GEOGRAPHY SKILLBUILDER: Interpreting Maps
1. **Location** What Muslim country, divided into two portions, bordered India on the east and the west?
2. **Location** What Buddhist countries bordered India to the north and the south?

The Colonies Become New Nations **887**

Daily Life
Voting by Caste

Mohandas Gandhi campaigned tirelessly against the evils of the caste system. He renamed the lowest group *harijans,* or "children of God." Following his lead, the constitution of independent India abolished all practices that discriminated against the untouchables.

Still, analysis of recent election results shows that Indians continue to vote along caste lines. In the past, this practice favored the upper castes. Now it may result in the election to office of more members of the lower castes.

The man who became India's president in July 1997—K. R. Narayanan—is a Dalit. This is the caste formerly known as the untouchables. Narayanan spoke of his election as proof that "the concerns of the common man" will receive attention in the nation's affairs.

After a short spell out of office, she was reelected in 1980. Under Gandhi's leadership, the country substantially increased its production of food grains.

Gandhi soon faced a threat from Sikh extremists, who were agitating for an independent state. Sikh terrorists took refuge in the Golden Temple at Amritsar, the most important Sikh religious center. From there, they ventured out to commit many acts of violence. In June 1984, Indian army troops overran the Golden Temple. They killed about 500 Sikhs and destroyed sacred property. In retaliation, Indira Gandhi was gunned down four months later by two of her Sikh bodyguards. This act set off another murderous frenzy, causing the deaths of thousands of Sikhs.

Gandhi was succeeded by her son, **Rajiv** (rah·jeev) **Gandhi,** in 1984. He immediately called for a new election. He won by the largest majority of any of the Nehru-Gandhi family. His party lost the leadership in 1989, however, because it was accused of corruption. In 1991, while campaigning near Madras, Rajiv was killed by a bomb. It was carried by a female terrorist from Sri Lanka who opposed Gandhi's policies.

Social Issues Challenge India India faces challenges today. Its steadily climbing population is expected to top 1 billion early in the next century. The caste system continues to undermine social equality. India still faces the threat of religious fanaticism. Many separatist movements exist throughout the country. On the plus side, Indian industry has continued to develop. New oil and coal resources have been discovered. Scientific and technical education have expanded.

Background
The Sikhs practiced a monotheistic religion founded in northern India during the 16th century. It combined elements of Hinduism and Islam.

A Turbulent History

Ali Bhutto

1977 Ali Bhutto
Prime Minister Ali Bhutto of Pakistan is deposed in a coup led by General Zia. Bhutto is later hanged for having ordered the assassination of a political opponent.

General Zia

1988 General Zia
General Zia, president of Pakistan, dies in a mysterious plane crash.

Pakistan

| 1950 | 1960 | 1970 | 1980 | 1991 |

India

1948 Mohandas Gandhi
Gandhi is shot to death by a Hindu extremist. The assassin opposes Gandhi's efforts to achieve equal treatment for all Indians, including Muslims.

Mohandas Gandhi

Indira Gandhi

1984 Indira Gandhi
Indira Gandhi is machine-gunned by two of her Sikh bodyguards. Her murder is in retaliation for an attack she ordered on a Sikh temple.

1991 Rajiv Gandhi
Rajiv Gandhi is killed by a bomb while campaigning. The bomb is carried by a woman who belongs to a group of Tamil separatists.

Rajiv Gandhi

888 Chapter 34

Pakistan and Sri Lanka

Pakistan gained its independence in 1947, and Ceylon, an island country southeast of India, in 1948. After independence, both countries suffered from religious and ethnic fighting. In 1972 Ceylon changed its name to Sri Lanka (sree LAHNG·kuh).

Civil War in Pakistan Pakistan began as a divided nation. Its east and west regions were separated by more than 1,000 miles of Indian territory. One region lay to the northeast of India, the other to the northwest. In culture, language, history, geography, economics, and ethnic background, the two regions were very different. Only the Islamic religion united them. East Pakistan had a larger population than the West. It felt neglected by the government in West Pakistan. Rebellion broke out in April 1971. In December 1971, the Indian army lent its support to East Pakistan. The army of West Pakistan, which had occupied East Pakistan, withdrew. A new nation, Bangladesh, was formed from East Pakistan.

Muhammad Ali Jinnah, the first governor-general of Pakistan, died shortly after independence. This left the nation without strong leadership. Pakistan went through a series of military coups, the first in 1958. Ali Bhutto took over leadership of the country following the civil war. A military coup in 1977 led by General Zia removed Bhutto, who was later executed for crimes allegedly committed while in office. After Zia's death, Bhutto's daughter, **Benazir Bhutto,** was twice elected prime minister. After months of disorder, she was removed from office in 1996. Nawaz Sharif became prime minister after the 1997 elections.

Sri Lanka Split by Factions Sri Lanka's recent history has also been one of turmoil. Three-quarters of Sri Lanka's 16 million people are Buddhists. A fifth are Tamils, a Hindu people of southern India and northern Sri Lanka. A militant group of Tamils have called for a separate Tamil nation. Since 1981, when Tamil militants began strong-armed resistance, thousands of lives have been lost. In an effort to end the violence, Rajiv Gandhi and the Sri Lankan president tried to reach an accord in 1983. The agreement called for Indian troops to enter Sri Lanka and help disarm Tamil rebels. This effort was not successful, and the Indian troops left in 1990. A civil war between Tamils and other Sri Lankans continues today.

Pictured here is the emblem of the Liberation Tigers of Tamil Eelam, a militant group based in Sri Lanka. The group has fought for the independence of Tamils.

Section 1 Assessment

1. TERMS & NAMES
Identify
- Congress Party
- Muslim League
- Muhammad Ali Jinnah
- Lord Mountbatten
- partition
- Jawaharlal Nehru
- Indira Gandhi
- Rajiv Gandhi
- Benazir Bhutto

2. TAKING NOTES
Create a time line of prominent Indian prime ministers from independence in 1947 through 1989, using a form like the one below.

```
[first]        [third]
      [second]
```

Note one important accomplishment of each prime minister.

3. SYNTHESIZING
Do you think that India's political and economic success is crucial to the future of democracy in Asia? Why?
THINK ABOUT
- India's influence in Asia
- religious and ethnic differences and conflicts
- social implications of economic failure

4. ANALYZING THEMES
Power and Authority
What were some of the problems shared by leaders of India and Pakistan?
THINK ABOUT
- the factions within these countries
- their thoughts about independence
- how their problems were resolved

ANSWERS

Wedding Rituals

In cultures throughout the world, people get married. They do so for a variety of reasons: to share life with a loved one, to raise a family, to gain social position, to gain independence, to carry on values and customs. In India, an elaborate wedding ritual has evolved within the Hindu tradition. That ritual expresses Hindus' deepest beliefs about the relationship between men and women, the importance of the family, and the role of the spiritual in the significant moments of life. Other cultures have different rituals with which they surround the wedding ceremony.

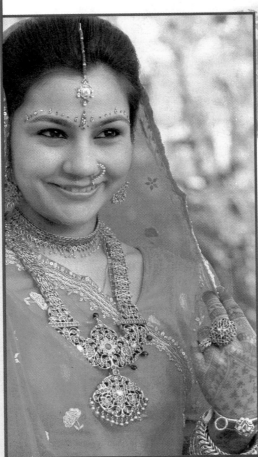

Hindu Wedding in India

Hindus traditionally bestow jewelry on brides. This bride is from West Bengal. She is bedecked with gold, silver, and enamel jewelry inlaid with precious stones. Her sari is from Benares and is made of fine silk and gold brocade. The colors of red and gold symbolize life and good luck. The design on the bride's hands is painted in henna. This traditional pattern is believed to keep away evil spirits.

a closer look HINDU RITUALS

A gold necklace called a thali is placed around the bride's neck. This necklace contains a medallion with the three symbols of the Hindu trinity—a conch shell, a trident, and a ring.

890 Chapter 34

Orthodox Wedding in Russia

The Church of the Transfiguration in St. Petersburg, Russia, is the site of this Russian Orthodox wedding ceremony. Crowns are placed on the heads of the bride and groom, who hold candles. Orthodox churches make lavish use of gold and rich decoration to display religious works of art such as icons.

A Bridal Fair in Morocco

The bridal fair is part of the marriage ritual of some Berbers of Morocco. Marriageable young men and women attend the fair of Imilchil in the Atlas Mountains of North Africa in search of spouses. The women wear capes, headdresses, and veils as they survey the eligible prospects during the fair. Courtship, engagement, and marriage all take place during the three days of the fair. The couples shown are waiting to enter the wedding tent.

Wedding in Guatemala

The Indians shown to the left are of Mayan descent. They live in the highlands of Guatemala. Villagers in Guatemala combine suit jackets and Indian clothing in a wedding ceremony. The clothes worn by the Indians identify their home villages.

In this Hindu wedding ritual, the bride is shrouded in a white sheet and tied to the groom. The couple takes seven steps around the sacred fire, a symbol of purification, to seal the marriage.

Connect *to* History

Comparing What are some elements of the wedding ceremony that seem common from one culture to another?

SEE SKILLBUILDER HANDBOOK, PAGE 996.

Connect *to* Today

Researching Read about wedding rituals in other cultures, and then write a couple of paragraphs describing the ritual that most appeals to you.

The Colonies Become New Nations **891**

Connect *to* History

Comparing
Possible Answer: Most students will note that the bride and groom wear special clothing. Some students might elaborate that although white is worn at Christian marriages in North America and Europe, red is a favored color for weddings in other parts of the world.

Students might also note such common features as a special place for the ceremony; a priest, clergyman, or official who conducts the ceremony; and the attendance of family members and friends, who typically give gifts to the couple.

Connect *to* Today

Researching
To research wedding customs in other cultures, students might look in indexes and databases for the name of the culture, followed by a sub-head (for example, *Sikh weddings*). Back issues of the *National Geographic* are good sources for cross-cultural information.

Southeast Asian Nations Gain Independence

TERMS & NAMES
- Ferdinand Marcos
- Corazón Aquino
- Aung San
- Aung San Suu Kyi
- Sukarno
- Suharto

Section 2 Overview

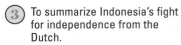

OBJECTIVES

1. To summarize events that led to the Philippines' independence and to describe the political rule of Marcos and his overthrow.

2. To summarize problems facing Burma, Malaysia, and Singapore.

3. To summarize Indonesia's fight for independence from the Dutch.

SKILLBUILDERS

- Interpreting maps: region, p. 893
- Interpreting graphs, p. 895

CRITICAL THINKING

- Making inferences, pp. 892, 894, 895
- Contrasting, p. 895

FOCUS

5-Minute Warm-Up

▶ **Summarizing**

Have students answer the following questions to help them understand the impact that one person can have on history.

1. Read History Makers on page 894. What kind of government is Aung San Suu Kyi struggling to establish in Burma?

2. How does the military government of Burma view her?

 WARM-UP TRANSPARENCY 34

OBJECTIVE 1 INSTRUCT

The United States and the Philippines

▶ **Key Ideas**

- The Philippines gains independence from the United States.

- The continued presence of U.S. military bases in the Philippines causes conflict.

- Ferdinand Marcos imposes authoritarian rule and is eventually forced out of office.

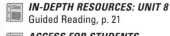 **IN-DEPTH RESOURCES: UNIT 8**
Guided Reading, p. 21

ACCESS FOR STUDENTS ACQUIRING ENGLISH
Guided Reading (Spanish), p. 344

MAIN IDEA

The European colonies in Southeast Asia became independent countries in the postwar period.

WHY IT MATTERS NOW

The power and influence of the Pacific Rim nations are likely to expand during the next century.

SETTING THE STAGE At the end of World War II, colonized people all over the world agitated for independence. As it had in India, Britain gave up control of its Southeast Asian colonies; it gave up Burma quickly and Malaysia after some delay. Some imperialists, the Dutch among them, were reluctant to give up their Southeast Asian possessions. They waged bitter and losing battles to retain control. The United States gave up its Asian colony in the Philippines soon after World War II.

The United States and the Philippines

The Philippines became the first of the world's colonies to achieve independence following World War II. The United States granted the Philippines independence in 1946, on the anniversary of its own Declaration of Independence, the Fourth of July.

The Philippines Achieves Independence The Filipinos' immediate goals were to rebuild the economy and to restore the capital of Manila. The city had been badly damaged in World War II. The United States had promised the Philippines $600 million in war damages. However, the U.S. government insisted that Filipinos approve the Bell Act in order to get the money. This act would establish free trade between the United States and the Philippines for eight years, to be followed by gradually increasing tariffs. Filipinos were worried that American businesses would exploit the resources and environment of the Philippines. In spite of this concern, Filipinos approved the Bell Act and received their money.

The United States wanted to maintain its military presence in the Philippines. With the onset of the Cold War (see Chapter 33), the United States needed to be able to protect its interests in Asia. Both China and the Soviet Union were opponents of the United States at the time. Both were Pacific powers with bases close to allies of the United States as well as to raw materials and resources vital to U.S. interests. Therefore, the United States demanded a 99-year lease on its military and naval bases in the Philippines. The bases—Clark Air Force Base and Subic Bay Naval Base near Manila—proved to be critical to the United States later, in the staging of the Korean and Vietnam wars.

These military bases also became the single greatest source of conflict between the United States and the Philippines. Many Filipinos regarded the bases as proof of American imperialism. Later agreements shortened the terms of the lease, and the United States gave up both bases in 1991.

Vocabulary
Filipino: an inhabitant of the Philippines.

A. Possible Answer To protect its vital economic and political interests. The Philippines were centrally located and therefore within striking distance of many potential hot spots in the region.

THINK THROUGH HISTORY
A. Making Inferences Why might the United States have been interested in maintaining military bases in the Philippines?

Ships of the U.S. Navy docked at Subic Bay in the Philippines from 1901 to 1991.

SECTION 2 RESOURCES

PRINT RESOURCES

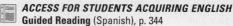 **IN-DEPTH RESOURCES: UNIT 8**
Guided Reading, p. 21
Primary Source: Call to Boycott Presidential Election, p. 28
Literature: from *The Year of Living Dangerously*, p. 31

 ACCESS FOR STUDENTS ACQUIRING ENGLISH
Guided Reading (Spanish), p. 344

 FORMAL ASSESSMENT
Section Quiz, p. 401

ALTERNATIVE ASSESSMENT BOOK

TECHNOLOGY RESOURCES

 GEOGRAPHY TRANSPARENCIES
GT34 Indonesia and Malaysia, 1945–1976

 CD-ROM
Electronic Library of Primary Sources

INTERNET www.mlworldhistory.com

Legend:
Former French colony
Former British colony
Former Dutch colony
Former U.S. colony
Continuously independent
1945 Date of independence

BHUTAN
CHINA
INDIA
20°N
BANGLADESH
BURMA 1948
LAOS 1953
Hanoi
NORTH VIETNAM 1954
Vientiane
Rangoon
THAILAND
Bangkok
CAMBODIA 1953
SOUTH VIETNAM 1954
Phnom Penh
Saigon
PHILIPPINES 1946
Manila
South China Sea
PACIFIC OCEAN
INDIAN OCEAN
BRUNEI (Br.)
MALAYSIA 1957
Kuala Lumpur
Singapore 1965
BORNEO
N
0° Equator
INDONESIA 1949
Jakarta
0   500 Miles
0   1,000 Kilometers
100°E   120°E   140°E

GEOGRAPHY SKILLBUILDER: Interpreting Maps
1. **Region** *Which former Dutch colony is made up of a series of islands spread out from the Indian Ocean to the Pacific Ocean?*
2. **Region** *From what European country did the most colonies shown above gain their independence?*

After World War II, the Philippine government was still almost completely dependent on the United States economically and politically. The Philippine government looked for ways to lessen this dependency. It welcomed Japanese investments. It also broadened its contacts with Southeast Asian neighbors and with nonaligned nations.

The Marcos Regime and Corazón Aquino **Ferdinand Marcos** was elected president of the Philippines in 1965. The country suffered under his rule from 1966 to 1986. Marcos imposed an authoritarian regime and stole millions of dollars from the public treasury. Although the constitution limited Marcos to eight years in office, he got around this restriction by imposing martial law from 1972 to 1981. Two years later, his chief opponent, Benigno Aquino, Jr., was shot when he returned from the United States to the Philippines, lured by the promise of coming elections.

In the elections of 1986, Marcos ran against Aquino's widow, **Corazón Aquino**. Aquino won decisively, but Marcos refused to acknowledge her victory. When he declared himself the official winner, a public outcry resulted. He was forced into exile in Hawaii, where he later died. In 1995, the Philippines succeeded in recovering $475 million Marcos had stolen from his country and deposited in Swiss banks.

During Aquino's presidency, the Philippine government ratified a new constitution. It also negotiated successfully with the United States to end the lease on the U.S. military bases. In 1992, Fidel V. Ramos succeeded Aquino as president. Ramos is restricted by the constitution to a single six-year term. The single-term limit is intended to prevent the abuse of power that occurred during Marcos's 20-year rule.

Background
Before the Philippines belonged to the United States, it was a Spanish colony. This is why many Filipinos, who are mostly Asian, have Spanish names.

The Colonies Become New Nations **893**

British Colonies Gain Independence

Key Ideas

- Burma leaves the British Commonwealth and is later renamed Myanmar.
- Malaysia and Singapore split.
- The city-state of Singapore, dominated by ethnic Chinese, prospers.

MORE ABOUT . . .
Aung San Suu Kyi

Aung San Suu Kyi originally returned to Burma only for a short while, to care for her terminally ill mother. She left her son and husband behind. While under house arrest, she was able to give speeches at her gate to crowds that numbered as many as 5,000 people. She was released from house arrest in 1995 but was forbidden to make speeches.

HISTORY MAKERS
Aung San Suu Kyi

Why did Aung San Suu Kyi not take the government's offer to free her? Students might respond that her having won the Nobel Prize gave her an even greater opportunity than before to be politically effective. She might also have been especially determined to aid Burma because of her father's political assassination.

HISTORY MAKERS

**Aung San Suu Kyi
1945–**

Aung San Suu Kyi won the Nobel Peace Prize in 1991 for her efforts to establish democracy in Burma. She could not accept the award in person, however, because she was still under house arrest. The Nobel Prize committee said that in awarding her the peace prize, it intended

. . . to show its support for the many people throughout the world who are striving to attain democracy, human rights, and ethnic conciliation by peaceful means. Suu Kyi's struggle is one of the most extraordinary examples of civil courage in Asia in recent decades.

The military government had offered to free her if she would leave the country. However, she refused, insisting she would not leave until a civilian government was restored to Burma and all political prisoners were freed.

British Colonies Gain Independence

Britain's timetable for giving its colonies independence depended on local circumstances. Burma had been pressing for independence from Britain for decades. It became a sovereign republic in 1948 and chose not to join the British Commonwealth. In 1989, Burma was officially named Myanmar (myahn·MAH), its name in the Burmese language.

Burma Experiences Turmoil In the postwar years, Burma suffered one political upheaval after another. Its people struggled between repressive military governments and pro-democracy forces. When the Japanese occupied Burma during World War II, they had declared Burma a sovereign state. In fact, the Japanese were in control. Their demands for forced labor were particularly unpopular. The Burmese nationalists' army, led by **Aung San** (owng sahn), at first cooperated with the Japanese in order to drive the British out of Burma. Then the army linked up with British forces to defeat the Japanese. They succeeded in driving out the Japanese and were about to become independent. Then Aung San and most of his cabinet were gunned down on orders of Burmese political rivals.

Conflict among Communists and ethnic minorities disrupted the nation. In 1962, General Ne Win set up a repressive military government, with the goal of making Burma a socialist state. Although Ne Win stepped down in 1988, the military continued to rule Burma repressively. Also in 1988, **Aung San Suu Kyi** (owng sahn soo chee), the daughter of Aung San, returned to Burma after many years abroad. She became active in the newly formed National League for Democracy. For her pro-democracy activities, she was placed under house arrest for six years by the government. In the 1990 election—the country's first multiparty election in 30 years—the National League for Democracy won 80 percent of the seats. The military government refused to recognize the election, and it kept Aung San Suu Kyi under house arrest. She was finally released in 1995 though still kept under surveillance.

Malaysia and Singapore During World War II, the Japanese conquered the Malay Peninsula, formerly ruled by the British. The British returned to the peninsula after the Japanese defeat in 1945. They tried, unsuccessfully, to organize Malaya into one state. They also struggled to put down a Communist uprising. Ethnic groups resisted British efforts to unite their colonies on the peninsula and in the northern part of the island of Borneo. Malays were a slight majority on the peninsula, while Chinese were the largest group in Singapore. In 1957, the Federation of Malaya was created from Singapore, Malaya, Sarawak, and Sabah. The two regions—on the Malay Peninsula and on northern Borneo—were separated by 400 miles of ocean. In 1965, Singapore separated from the federation and became an independent city-state. The Federation of Malaysia—consisting of Malaya, Sarawak, and Sabah—was created. A coalition of many ethnic groups maintained steady economic progress in Malaysia.

Singapore, extremely prosperous, was one of the busiest ports in the world. Lee Kuan Yew ruled Singapore as prime minister from 1959 to 1990. Under his guidance, Singapore emerged as a banking center as well as a trade center. It had a standard of living far higher than any of its Southeast Asian neighbors. In early 1997, the Geneva World Economic Forum listed the world's most competitive economies. Singapore topped the list. It was followed, in order, by Hong Kong, the United States, Canada, New Zealand, Switzerland, and Great Britain.

Vocabulary
repressive government: a government that puts down opposition by force.

Vocabulary
house arrest: confinement to one's quarters, or house, rather than to prison.

B. Possible Answer They are capitalist economies.
THINK THROUGH HISTORY
B. Making Inferences What do these competitive economies all have in common?

Task: Students will create a brochure promoting Singapore.

Purpose: To provide students with an opportunity to learn about one Southeast Asian nation in depth.

Activity: Have students form groups of four. Ask each group to research a different aspect of Singapore, such as the standard of living, business opportunities, cultural life, or government, and then create a section of a brochure promoting the city-state. Before beginning, the class should decide on the intended audience. Each group should name a researcher, a writer-editor, a designer-illustrator, and a producer, who will meet with like members from the other groups to coordinate their efforts.

 Building a Portfolio: Students adding a brochure to their portfolio should attach an explanation of the assignment.

ALTERNATIVE ASSESSMENT BOOK
Standards for Evaluating a Cooperative Activity

Standards for Evaluation
Brochures should . . .

- be tailored to the intended audience
- show evidence of careful research
- demonstrate good writing and visual skills

THINK THROUGH HISTORY
C. Contrasting How did the British and the Dutch differ in their attitudes toward their colonies?

Vocabulary
coup: the sudden overthrow of a government by a small group of people.

Indonesia Gains Independence from the Dutch

The Japanese occupation of Indonesia during World War II destroyed the Dutch colonial order. Waiting in the wings to lead Indonesia was **Sukarno** (soo·KAHR·noh), known only by his one name. He was a leader of the Indonesian independence movement. In August 1945, two days after the Japanese surrendered, Sukarno proclaimed Indonesia's independence and named himself president. The Dutch, however, backed up initially by the British and the United States, attempted to regain control of Indonesia.

The Dutch in Indonesia Unlike British colonialists, who served their term in India and then returned to England, the pre-war Dutch looked upon the East Indies as their permanent home. To keep it that way, the Dutch resisted native Indonesians' attempts to enter the civil service or to acquire higher education. After the war, Indonesians were unwilling to return to their condition of servitude under the Dutch. They therefore put together a successful guerrilla army. After losing the support of the United Nations and the United States, the Dutch agreed to grant Indonesia its independence in 1949.

A Variety of People, Islands, and Religions The new Indonesia became the world's fourth most populous nation. It consisted of more than 13,600 islands, with 300 different ethnic groups, 250 languages, and most of the world's major religions. It contained the world's largest Islamic population. Sukarno, who took the official title of "life-time president," attempted to guide this diverse nation in a parliamentary democracy. Unfortunately, this attempt failed.

In 1965, a group of junior army officers attempted a coup, which was suppressed by a general named **Suharto** (suh·HAHR·toh). He then seized power for himself. He blamed the coup on Indonesian Communists. In the bloodbath that followed, 500,000 to 1 million Indonesians were killed. These included most of the known Communists, Chinese who may or may not have been Communists, and any others who were on a local "hit" list.

Suharto, officially named president in 1967, turned Indonesia into a police state and imposed frequent periods of martial law. Outside observers heavily criticized him for his annexation of East Timor in 1976 and for human rights violations there. The Chinese living in Indonesia met with discrimination but were tolerated because of their financial contributions to the state. Christians were persecuted. Bribery and corruption became commonplace. Although the economy improved, only the rich enjoyed the benefits. President Suharto expects to be appointed to his seventh five-year term in 1998.

Comparing Economies

Gross Domestic Product is the dollar value of all goods and services produced within a country during one year. In this graph, the GDP is divided by the number of productive workers in each country. This results in the GDP per capita, or per person.

- Philippines
- Singapore
- United States

Sources: *World Statistics in Brief* (1978) and *World Statistics Pocketbook* (1995), published by the United Nations.

SKILLBUILDER:
Interpreting Graphs
1. Which country had the highest GDP per capita in both 1965 and 1991? Which had the lowest?
2. Which country showed the biggest increase in GDP per capita from 1985 to 1991?

Section 2 Assessment

1. TERMS & NAMES
Identify
- Ferdinand Marcos
- Corazón Aquino
- Aung San
- Aung San Suu Kyi
- Sukarno
- Suharto

2. TAKING NOTES
Using a chart like the one below, summarize the major challenges the countries faced following independence.

Nation	Colonizer	Challenges Following Independence
The Philippines		
Burma		
Indonesia		

3. MAKING INFERENCES
Why do you think that the United States demanded a 99-year lease on military and naval bases in the Philippines?

THINK ABOUT
- U.S. economic interests in the Philippines
- geographical location
- reasons for military presence

4. THEME ACTIVITY
Power and Authority
Write a two-paragraph essay contrasting a peaceful transfer of authority from a colonial power to a newly independent nation with a transfer that was violent.

The Colonies Become New Nations **895**

OBJECTIVE 3 INSTRUCT

Indonesia Gains Independence from the Dutch

▶ *Key Ideas*
- Japanese occupation of Indonesia during World War II destroys the old colonial order.
- Suharto seizes power and imposes martial law.

History from Visuals

Comparing Economies
Interpreting the Graph The GDP per capita for the Philippines for 1965 is so small that it is hard to see on the graph. Tell students that the blue column representing the Philippines in 1965 is visible at the far left of the graph.

Extension Activity Ask students to find the GDP per capita for these countries for 1997.

SKILLBUILDER Answers
1. The United States; the Philippines.
2. Singapore.

ASSESS & RETEACH

Section 2 Assessment
Have students list pages in the section where answers to the questions can be found.

Section Quiz
FORMAL ASSESSMENT
Section Quiz, p. 401

Reteaching Activity
CLASS TIME: 15 MINUTES

To help students understand the challenges of newly independent countries, review their charts for item 2 in the assessment.

CLOSE ACTIVITY

CLASS TIME: 20 MINUTES

Arranging Events in Sequential Order
Assign one student to each country. Tell students to arrange themselves in the order in which the countries in this section achieved independence. Have each student make a statement telling when, how, and from whom his or her country achieved independence.

Teacher's Edition **895**

1. To identify the Negritude movement.

2. To describe the events surrounding the independence of Ghana and Kenya.

3. To describe the Congo's independence and Mobutu's rule.

4. To summarize Algeria's struggle for independence and conflict with Islamic militants.

5. To identify roles played by world powers in Angola's post-independence civil strife.

SKILLBUILDERS
• Interpreting maps: location, p. 898

CRITICAL THINKING
• Analyzing motives, pp. 896, 900
• Making inferences, p. 898
• Clarifying, p. 899
• Drawing conclusions, p. 900
• Analyzing themes, p. 900

FOCUS
5-Minute Warm-Up

▶ *Clarifying*
Have students answer the following questions to help them understand the motives of those who led Africa to independence.

1. Read History Makers on page 897. Whose ideas influenced Nkrumah?

2. Why does Nkrumah prefer danger to tranquility?

🏛 *WARM-UP TRANSPARENCY 34*

OBJECTIVE ① INSTRUCT

Background to Independence

▶ *Key Ideas*
• W. E. B. Du Bois influences Africans.
• French-speaking Africans form the Negritude movement.

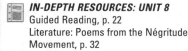
📖 *IN-DEPTH RESOURCES: UNIT 8*
Guided Reading, p. 22
Literature: Poems from the Négritude Movement, p. 32

📖 *ACCESS FOR STUDENTS ACQUIRING ENGLISH*
Guided Reading (Spanish), p. 345

---

3 # New Nations in Africa

TERMS & NAMES
• Negritude movement
• Kwame Nkrumah
• Jomo Kenyatta
• Mau Mau
• Mobutu Sese Seko
• FLN
• Ahmed Ben Bella

MAIN IDEA
After World War II, African leaders threw off colonial rule and created independent countries.

WHY IT MATTERS NOW
Today, many of those independent countries are engaged in building political and economic stability.

SETTING THE STAGE Like the Asian countries, the countries of Africa were unwilling to return to colonial domination after World War II. The problem of building strong, independent nations in Africa, however, was complicated by the way in which European imperialists had divided up the continent, plundered its resources, and left the countries unprepared to deal with independence. The colonialists had imposed borders having little to do with the areas where ethnic groups actually lived. While borders separated culturally similar people, they also enclosed traditional enemies.

Background to Independence

Between the two world wars, an educated middle class had begun to emerge in African cities. Young men went abroad for college and graduate studies. They listened to American jazz musicians and read literature of the Harlem Renaissance. They were influenced by African Americans such as W. E. B. Du Bois as well as by such older Africans as Blaise Diagne, who organized Pan-African (all-African) congresses in 1919 and 1921.

French-speaking Africans and West Indians began to express their growing sense of black consciousness and pride in traditional Africa. They formed the **Negritude movement**—a movement to celebrate African culture, heritage, and values. This movement viewed the black experience as unique. One of the movement's leaders, Leopold Senghor (lay·aw·PAWLD san·GAWR), later became the first president of Senegal.

African soldiers in World War II fought alongside Europeans to "defend freedom." This experience made them unwilling to accept colonial domination when they returned home. The postwar world changed the thinking of Europeans too. They began to question the cost of maintaining their colonies abroad.

Leopold Senghor was a politician and poet. In his poetry, he reaffirmed African traditions and the need for Africa to separate from Europe.

British Colonies Seek Independence

After World War II, many European countries were ready to transfer government to the African people. For the Europeans, the question was when and how to do that.

Ghana Leads the Way to Independence The British colony of the Gold Coast became the first African colony south of the Sahara to achieve independence. Following World War II, the British in the Gold Coast began making preparations. For example, they allowed more Africans to be nominated to the Legislative Council. However, the Africans wanted elected, not nominated, representatives, and they wanted "Freedom Now!" The leader of their largely nonviolent protests was **Kwame Nkrumah** (KWAH·mee uhn·KROO·muh). He was a former teacher who had spent several years studying in the United States. In the 1940s, he worked to liberate the Gold Coast from

A. Possible Answer After World War II, British colonies in Africa were unwilling to be dominated by Britain; Britain began to question the cost of maintaining colonies abroad and coping with rebellion.

THINK THROUGH HISTORY
A. Analyzing Motives Why might the British have been willing to grant the Gold Coast colony its independence?

SECTION 3 RESOURCES

PRINT RESOURCES

📖 *IN-DEPTH RESOURCES: UNIT 8*
Guided Reading, p. 22
Skillbuilder Practice: Evaluating Decisions, p. 24
Geography Application: Congo Gains Independence, p. 25
Primary Source: Farewell Without Tears, p. 29
History Makers: Jomo Kenyatta, p. 34
Literature: Poems from the Négritude Movement, p. 32
Connections Across Time and Cultures: p. 36

📖 *ACCESS FOR STUDENTS ACQUIRING ENGLISH*
Guided Reading (Spanish), p. 345
Skillbuilder Practice (Spanish), p. 347
Geography Application: (Spanish), p. 348

📖 *FORMAL ASSESSMENT*
Section Quiz, p. 402

TECHNOLOGY RESOURCES

 INTERNET www.mlworldhistory.com

the British. Nkrumah organized strikes and boycotts and was often imprisoned by the British government. Ultimately, however, his efforts were successful.

On receiving its independence in 1957, the Gold Coast took the name Ghana. This name honored a famous West African kingdom of the past. Ghana became the first nation governed by black Africans to join the British Commonwealth. During the independence celebrations, Nkrumah addressed the crowds:

A VOICE FROM THE PAST
There is a new African in the world, and that new African is ready to fight his own battle. . . . It is the only way in which we can show the world we are masters of our own destiny.
KWAME NKRUMAH, 1957 speech

Nkrumah became Ghana's first prime minister and later its president-for-life. Nkrumah pushed through expensive development plans and economic projects—new roads, new schools, and expanded health facilities. These costly projects soon crippled the country. His programs for industrialization, health and welfare, and expanded educational facilities showed good intentions. However, the expense of the programs undermined the economy and strengthened his opposition.

In addition, Nkrumah was often criticized for spending too much time on Pan-African efforts and neglecting economic problems in his own country. In his dream of a "United States of Africa," Nkrumah was influenced by the thinking of Marcus Garvey. Garvey was a Jamaican-born black man who in the 1920s called for forcing all Europeans out of Africa and creating a black empire there. Nkrumah, influenced by Garvey (among others), wanted to create an Africa ruled by Africans. Nkrumah helped develop the Pan-African Congress held in Manchester, England, in 1945. Later, in 1958, he hosted the first Pan-African meeting held in Africa. This led to the formation of the Organization of African Unity (OAU) in 1963.

In 1966, while Nkrumah was in China, the army and police in Ghana seized power. Since then, the country has shifted back and forth between civilian and military rule. At the same time, it has struggled for economic stability. Jerry Rawlings, an Air Force pilot, seized power in 1979 and again in 1981, and still rules Ghana today.

Kenya and the Mau Mau Rebellion British settlers had taken over prize farmland in the northern highlands of Kenya. They fiercely resisted independence for Kenya. They were forced to accept black self-government as a result of two developments. One was the strong leadership of Kenyan nationalist **Jomo Kenyatta,** a Kikuyu educated in London. The second was the rise of the **Mau Mau** (MOW mow). This was a secret society made up mostly of Kikuyu farmers forced out of the highlands by the British.

The Mau Mau's aim was primarily to frighten the white farmers into leaving the highlands rather than to engage in outright war. Kenyatta had no connection to the Mau Mau. However, he refused to condemn the organization and was imprisoned by the British for a time for this refusal. By the time the British granted Kenya independence in 1963, more than 10,000 black Kenyans and 100 white Kenyans had been killed.

Kenyatta became president of the new nation. He worked hard to unite the various ethnic and language groups in the country. Nairobi, the capital, grew into a major business center of East Africa. When Kenyatta died in 1978, his successor, Daniel arap Moi, was less successful in governing the country. Moi faced more and more opposition to his one-party rule. Under him, university strikes and protests resulted in the deaths of some students. These demonstrations put pressure on Moi to make the country more democratic.

Background
Many of the leaders of the newly independent nations of Africa developed a pan-African viewpoint. That is, their vision took in the development of all of Africa, not just their own countries.

Vocabulary
Kikuyu: a member of a people of central and southern Kenya.

HISTORY MAKERS

Kwame Nkrumah
1909–1972
Kwame Nkrumah studied at Lincoln University in Pennsylvania from 1935 to 1939. After graduating from Lincoln, he went on to earn a master's degree from the University of Pennsylvania.

Nkrumah studied socialism, especially the writings of Marx and Lenin, and nationalism, especially the thinking of Marcus Garvey. He became president of the African Students' Organization of the United States and Canada.

Nkrumah returned to the Gold Coast in 1947. He helped to stage strikes and riots against the government. He said at the time, "We prefer self-government with danger to servitude in tranquility."

OBJECTIVE 2 INSTRUCT

British Colonies Seek Independence
(See page 896.)

▶ **Key Ideas**
• Kwame Nkrumah leads Ghana to liberation from the British.
• British resist Kenyan independence.
• The Mau Mau fight for Kenya's independence from the British.

IN-DEPTH RESOURCES: UNIT 8
History Makers: Jomo Kenyatta, p. 34
Connections Across Time and Cultures: Becoming a New Nation, p. 36

HISTORY MAKERS
Kwame Nkrumah

Have students paraphrase Nkrumah's statement in the third paragraph. They might add a sentence or two explaining what they think Nkrumah meant.

MORE ABOUT . . .
Elections in Ghana

In 1996, Jerry Rawlings was re-elected to what he announced would be his final four years as president. This was only the second time the country had held elections under a newly installed multiparty system. More than 70 percent of the country's 9.2 million voters turned out. Although Rawlings had ruled the country for most of the past 16 years, the opposition made a healthy showing, racking up 40 percent of the vote. Vote counters, hampered by the hundreds of polling stations and by poor communication, took four days to calculate the results.

Explaining the Skill Historians look at decisions made in the past and evaluate both their short-term and their long-term consequences. For example, historians still debate President Truman's decision to use the atomic bomb to end the war with Japan.

Applying the Skill: Kwame Nkrumah
Ask students to reread the two paragraphs about

Nkrumah that follow "A Voice from the Past" on this page. Then ask them the following questions:

1. For what sorts of expensive programs was Nkrumah criticized in Ghana? *Roads, schools, health facilities.*

2. Why else was he criticized? *For spending too much time on Pan-African efforts and neglecting economic problems.*

3. How else might Nkrumah have handled the economy? *He might have put an emphasis on strengthening the economy rather than on expensive development plans and projects.*

IN-DEPTH RESOURCES: UNIT 8
Skillbuilder Practice: Evaluating Decisions, p. 24

Africa, 1955, and Africa, 1975

Interpreting the Maps What countries were created out of 1955 French West Africa? *Senegal, Mauritania, Mali, Niger, Upper Volta, Guinea, Ivory Coast.*

Extension Activity Have students use an almanac or other reference book to determine the present status of the colonies shown on the 1975 map.

SKILLBUILDER Answers
1. Libya, Egypt, Ethiopia, South Africa, Liberia.
2. 1960s.

OBJECTIVE ③ INSTRUCT

The Congo Gains Independence

Key Ideas
- Belgium leaves the Congo unprepared for independence.
- The first prime minister, Patrice Lumumba, is overthrown and murdered.
- Mobutu Sese Seko rules as a dictator for 32 years.
- Laurent Kabila overthrows Mobutu.

IN-DEPTH RESOURCES: UNIT 8 Primary Source: Farewell Without Tears, p. 29

MORE ABOUT . . .
Ethnic Conflict in the Congo

Within days after the forces of Laurent Kabila took over, rumors began to surface about wholesale massacres in the Congo of Hutu refugees from Rwanda. Kabila was supported by Rwanda, and his army included large numbers of Tutsis. The refugees are ethnic Hutus who fled Rwanda in 1994 after a Tutsi-led government came to power, ending a three-month-long campaign of genocide of Tutsis by Hutus.

Africa, 1955

Africa, 1975

GEOGRAPHY SKILLBUILDER: Interpreting Maps
1. **Location** *Which countries in Africa were already independent in 1955?*
2. **Location** *In what decade did most of the African nations gain their independence?*

In the early 1990s, Kenya's economy suffered a severe reversal. Adding to the nation's woes were corruption in Moi's government and ethnic conflicts that killed hundreds and left thousands homeless.

The Congo Gains Independence

Of all the European possessions in Africa, probably the most exploited was the Belgian Congo. Belgium had ruthlessly plundered the colony's rich resources of rubber and copper. It had employed a system of forced labor. While draining wealth from the colony, Belgium had provided no social services. It also had made no attempt to prepare the people for independence.

Independence Brings Change Belgium's granting of independence in 1960 to the Congo (known as Zaire [zah·IHR] from 1965 to 1997) resulted in upheaval. Patrice Lumumba became the nation's first prime minister. He ruled a divided country. In the mineral-rich southeastern province of Katanga, a local leader named Moise Tshombe (MOH·zee CHUHM·bee) declared that region's independence. This was a serious threat, especially since copper from Katanga's mines was the nation's primary export.

Intervention by outside forces added to the problems. Tshombe was backed by Belgian mining interests. Lumumba, with Communist connections, first appealed to the United Nations for help in putting down Tshombe's rebellion. He then turned to the Soviet Union for aid. At this point, a coup led by an army officer, Colonel Joseph Mobutu, later known as **Mobutu Sese Seko** (moh·BOO·too SAY·say SAY·koh), overthrew Lumumba and turned him over to his enemy, Tshombe. Lumumba was murdered while in Tshombe's custody. Tshombe himself ruled briefly until he was overthrown by Mobutu, who seized power in a bloodless coup in 1965.

B. Possible Answer A lack of preparation by the Belgians, political upheaval, and plotting in the army and among politicians made the Congo vulnerable.

THINK THROUGH HISTORY
B. Making Inferences Why was the Congo vulnerable after independence?

898 Chapter 34

GEOGRAPHY APPLICATION ACTIVITY

CLASS TIME 20 MINUTES

Task Students will examine the map from the Geography Application for this section in order to explore the movement of various groups in the Congo during the years 1960–1965.

Materials Needed Use copies of the Geography Application worksheet for Chapter 34 or make a transparency of the map from that worksheet.

Activity Have the class help you make a list of the participants in the Congo crisis and of the movement of troops during the rebellions of 1960–1965. If you are using a transparency, have individual students point out various points of the rebel advance, railways, centers of rebellion, sites of intervention by Belgian paratroops, and so forth.

Conclusion Ask students to comment on the political situation in the Congo at this time. What must it have been like living in a time of political and social chaos? Why might people have been willing to turn to a dictator?

IN-DEPTH RESOURCES: UNIT 8 Geography Application: The Congo Gains Independence, p. 25

Mobutu Comes to Power For 32 years, Mobutu ruled the country that he renamed Zaire. He used a combination of force, one-party rule, and gifts to supporters. Zaire had the mineral wealth and natural resources to make it one of the richest countries in Africa. It was reduced under Mobutu's rule to one of the continent's poorest. Mobutu and his associates were accused of looting the country of billions of dollars. They opened secret bank accounts abroad and bought real estate in Europe, Africa, and Brazil.

Mobutu successfully withstood several armed rebellions and ethnic clashes. He was finally overthrown in 1997 by Laurent Kabila after a seven-month-long civil war. On becoming president, Kabila banned all political parties. However, he promised a transition to democracy and free elections by April 1999.

Algeria Fights for Its Independence

In 1945, about 1 million French colonists and about 9 million Arab and Berber Muslims were living in the North African country of Algeria, France's principal overseas colony. Some of the colonists had lived there for generations. They were unwilling to give up their land without a fight. France claimed to offer full citizenship rights to its colonial subjects—a policy called assimilation. In reality, assimilation was hard to achieve. The colonists refused to share political power.

The Struggle The post-World War II conflict in Algeria began in 1945 when French troops fired on Algerian nationalists who were demonstrating in the town of Setif. Before peace was restored, thousands of Muslims and about 100 Europeans were killed. Subsequent French reforms did not satisfy the Algerian nationalists.

In 1954, the Algerian National Liberation Front, or **FLN**, announced its intention to fight for independence. The FLN would use guerrilla tactics at home and diplomatic tactics internationally. The French sent over half a million troops into Algeria to fight the FLN. Both sides committed atrocities. European settlers in Algeria began calling for the World War II hero Charles de Gaulle to return as president of France and restore order in the French colony.

De Gaulle Takes Control De Gaulle returned to power in 1958. He soon concluded that Algeria could not be held by force. Fearful that the rebellion might spread, France let go of most of its other possessions in Africa.

In 1962, a referendum setting out the conditions for Algerian independence in cooperation with France passed with overwhelming majorities in Algeria and France. As France planned the transfer of power after the cease-fire in March 1962, 750,000 French settlers fled Algeria. Independence came in July 1962.

Ahmed Ben Bella, a leader of the FLN who had been imprisoned by the French, was named first prime minister (1962–1963) and first president (1963–1965). Ben Bella reestablished national order, began land reforms, and developed new plans for education. In 1965, he was overthrown by his chief of staff.

From 1965 until 1988, Algerians tried to modernize and industrialize. Their efforts were undermined when oil prices plunged in 1985–1986. Unemployment and the unfulfilled promises of the revolution contributed to an Islamic revival. Riots in 1988 against the secular government left hundreds dead. The chief Islamic party, the Islamic Salvation Front (FIS), won local and parliamentary elections in 1990 and 1991. However, the ruling government and army refused to accept the election results. Eventually, a civil war broke out between Islamic militants and the government—a war that continues, on and off, to this day. Efforts to restore democratic government included presidential elections

The Colonies Become New Nations **899**

CONNECT to TODAY

Zaire Again Becomes the Congo

The march of Congo rebels in 1996–1997 from the eastern provinces of Zaire to the capital city of Kinshasa to overthrow Mobutu (pictured above) took only seven months. The rebels met little opposition as they crossed the country. The *New York Times* called the Zaire government "a house that had been eaten by termites. The rebels came along and pushed it over." That is, the corruption of Mobutu's rule had undermined his support among the people.

Laurent Kabila overthrew Mobutu and had himself sworn in as president of the country on May 29, 1997. The name of the country was changed from Zaire to the Congo. Mobutu died in September 1997.

Angola Gains Its Independence

Key Ideas
- Portugal fails to prepare Angola for independence.
- Rebel groups fight for control.
- Portugal leaves without handing over power to anyone.
- The United States helps engineer a cease-fire among warring groups.

GlobalImpact
Cold War Reaches Angola

Was Angola better off or worse off for drawing the attention of world powers? Write a sentence or two to support your view. *Some students will feel foreign powers helped to move Angola toward independence; others will feel that foreign intervention prolonged the chaos and disorder.*

ASSESS & RETEACH

Section 3 Assessment
Assign pairs of students to help each other answer the questions. Then ask selected pairs to share their answers with the rest of the class.

Section Quiz
 FORMAL ASSESSMENT
Section Quiz, p. 402

Reteaching Activity
CLASS TIME: 15 MINUTES

Use the map on page 898 to review the main ideas of the section.

CLOSE ACTIVITY

CLASS TIME: 20 MINUTES

Role Playing
Assign students the roles of various leaders they have read about in this section: Leopold Senghor, Kwame Nkrumah, Jomo Kenyatta, Mobutu Sese Seko, and Ahmed Ben Bella. Have them discuss their views of European colonial rule, independence movements, and other issues. Have the rest of the class, as audience members listening to the discussion, ask questions of the leaders.

---

in 1995 and parliamentary elections in 1997. However, these efforts excluded the FIS. Recently, there have been calls from the FIS for a truce and a national peace conference to end the violence that has claimed the lives of thousands of people.

Angola Gains Its Independence

The Portuguese had been the first Europeans to enter Africa, 400 years ago, and they were the last to leave. Portugal was unwilling to give up any of its colonies. It made no preparations for helping its colony of Angola emerge into the modern world. At the end of World War II, Angola had no education or health facilities and little commerce.

GlobalImpact
Cold War Reaches Angola

Picture the plight of Angola, which had suffered already from the neglect of its colonizer, Portugal. While it struggled to become a nation, Angola became a battleground in the Cold War between the United States and the Soviet Union.

From 1945 until 1991, these two countries competed with one another for economic, political, and cultural dominance around the globe. This rivalry affected their relations with nations around the world. In Africa, even U.S. friendship with Mobutu, the dictator of Zaire, was tied into the Cold War. By urging Mobutu to aid the opposition to the MPLA in Angola, the United States used him as a check against Soviet influence in Angola.

The Movement Towards Independence Still, some Angolans gained an education. Accounts of other African countries that had become independent inspired them. In the 1960s, three revolutionary groups emerged. Foreign powers supported each group.

To put down the rebels in Angola, Portugal sent in 50,000 troops. The cost of the conflict amounted to almost half of Portugal's national budget. Discontent over the colonial wars built up among the Portuguese troops until the Portuguese dictatorship in Lisbon was toppled by the military.

Civil War Follows Independence The Portuguese withdrew from Angola in 1975 without formally handing over power to anyone. The lack of preparation for independence in Angola was complicated by the Communist seizure of power. The MPLA (Popular Movement for the Liberation of Angola) took control of the capital, Luanda. The Communist MPLA declared itself the rightful government. This led to a prolonged civil war among various rebel groups. Each group received help from outside sources. The MPLA was assisted by some 50,000 Cuban troops and by the Soviet Union. The FNLA (National Front for the Liberation of Angola), which eventually faded away, was backed by Zaire and the United States. The major opposition to the MPLA was UNITA (National Union for the Total Independence of Angola), which was assisted by South Africa and the United States.

In 1988, the United States, with a nod from the Soviet Union, pressed for a settlement among the MPLA, UNITA, South Africa, and Cuba and for the evacuation of Cuban troops. A shaky cease-fire went into effect in June 1989. The different groups continued to feel ill at ease with one another. However, in 1995, they began discussions about representation of each group in the government.

Trouble in the Middle East also prompted intervention by the United States and other powers. These efforts, too, met with mixed results, as you will learn in Section 4.

THINK THROUGH HISTORY
D. Drawing Conclusions Why might it have been so important to Portugal to hang on to Angola?
D. Possible Answer As the first European colonial power in Africa, Portugal probably felt tightly bound to its colony: it was also a matter of prestige as well as of economic factors.

Section 3 Assessment

1. TERMS & NAMES
Identify
- Negritude movement
- Kwame Nkrumah
- Jomo Kenyatta
- Mau Mau
- Mobutu Sese Seko
- FLN
- Ahmed Ben Bella

2. TAKING NOTES
Copy the chart below on your paper. Next to each country, list an idea, an event, or a leader important to that country's history.

Ghana	
Kenya	
Zaire	
Algeria	
Angola	

3. ANALYZING MOTIVES
Why do you think that non-African nations supported certain factions that claimed power in the newly independent nations of Africa?

THINK ABOUT
- economic interests of the non-African nations
- Lumumba's request for Soviet aid in the Congo
- U.S. support of the FNLA
- the Cold War

4. ANALYZING THEMES
Revolution Why do you think revolution swept so many African nations following their independence from European rule after World War II?

THINK ABOUT
- how World War II influenced Africans
- the conditions preceding independence
- economic interests of European powers and newly independent nations

---

ANSWERS

1. TERMS & NAMES
Negritude movement, p. 896
Kwame Nkrumah, p. 896
Jomo Kenyatta, p. 897
Mau Mau, p. 897
Mobutu Sese Seko, p. 898
FLN, p. 899
Ahmed Ben Bella, p. 899

2. TAKING NOTES
Possible Responses: Ghana—took its name from African kingdom of the past; Kenya—Nairobi became a major business center; Zaire—renamed the Congo; Algeria—Ben Bella was prime minister and president; Angola—fought Portuguese for independence.

3. ANALYZING MOTIVES
Possible Responses: The factions may have promised non-African nations economic opportunities, such as trading or business privileges, in return for support; the non-African nations may have wanted to preserve economic interests they already had in the region.

4. ANALYZING THEMES
Possible Responses: There were many different religious and ethnic groups with competing interests; Europeans, Americans, and Soviets supported different groups; World War II had given Africans a new confidence.

Conflicts in the Middle East

TERMS & NAMES
- Balfour Declaration
- Suez Crisis
- Six-Day War
- Anwar Sadat
- Golda Meir
- Menachem Begin
- Camp David Accords
- Hosni Mubarak
- PLO

MAIN IDEA

Division of Palestine after World War II made the Middle East a hotbed of competing nationalist movements.

WHY IT MATTERS NOW

The conflict in the Middle East threatens the stability of the region today.

SETTING THE STAGE The division of Palestine after World War II set off bitter disputes in the Middle East. Some of the problems faced by the new nation of Israel were similar to those experienced by new nations in Africa and Asia. These included the writing of a new constitution, the merging of diverse peoples, and involvement in territorial disputes with neighbors. Palestinians who did not remain in Israel faced a disruptive life as refugees.

Palestine and Israel

The conflict between Jews and Arabs (including Palestinians) over a Palestinian homeland is one that has its roots in ancient history. To Jews, their claim to the land goes back 3,000 years, when Jewish kings ruled from Jerusalem. To Palestinians (both Muslim and Christian), the land has belonged to them since the Jews were driven out around A.D. 135. To Arabs, the land has belonged to them since their conquest of the area in the 7th century. Mixed in with the intertwined history of Jews and Arabs in the region have been more modern events. These include the persecution of Jews in Europe, the rising value of oil in the Middle East, and global politics that have influenced decisions half a world away.

Zionists—people who favored a Jewish national homeland in Palestine—had begun to settle in Palestine in the late 19th and early 20th century. At the time, the region was still part of the Ottoman Empire, ruled by Islamic Turks. Zionists at first made up only about 10 percent of the population. After the defeat of the Ottomans in World War I, the League of Nations asked Britain to oversee Palestine until it was ready for independence.

The Early Stages Palestinians feared that the increasing numbers of Jewish immigrants would result in hardships for them. Jews asked that a Jewish nation be carved out of the territory. Engaged in fighting World War I, Britain did not want to lose the support of either side. In a letter from the British foreign secretary to a Zionist supporter, Britain seemed to make promises to both sides.

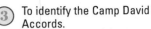

Dear Lord Rothschild,

I have much pleasure in conveying to you, on behalf of His Majesty's Government, the following declaration of sympathy with Jewish Zionist aspirations which has been submitted to, and approved by, the Cabinet

"His Majesty's Government view with favour the establishment in Palestine of a national home for the Jewish people, and will use their best endeavours to facilitate the achievement of this object, it being clearly understood that nothing shall be done which may prejudice the civil and religious rights of existing non-Jewish communities in Palestine, or the rights and political status enjoyed by Jews in any other country"

I should be grateful if you would bring this declaration to the knowledge of the Zionist Federation.

A VOICE FROM THE PAST
His Majesty's Government view with favour the establishment in Palestine of a national home for the Jewish people, and will use their best endeavours to facilitate the achievement of this object, it being clearly understood that nothing shall be done which may prejudice the civil and religious rights of existing non-Jewish communities in Palestine, or the rights and political status enjoyed by Jews in any other country.
ARTHUR JAMES BALFOUR, in a letter to Lord Rothschild, November 2, 1917

The Balfour Declaration is contained in this letter written by Sir Arthur Balfour (pictured above), the British foreign secretary. The letter was addressed to Lord Rothschild, head of the English branch of a banking family and a Zionist leader.

Britain found the terms of the **Balfour Declaration** to be unworkable because the two sides could not live together. Therefore, Britain called for partition of the country. Meanwhile, Nazi Germany's persecution of Jews spurred immigration to Palestine.

The Colonies Become New Nations **901**

A. Answer As long as the civil and religious rights of the non-Jews in Palestine were respected.

THINK THROUGH HISTORY
A. Clarifying Balfour approved the establishment of a home for Jews in Palestine with what qualification?

Section 4 Overview

OBJECTIVES

1. To describe the events that led to the formation of the new nation of Israel.
2. To list the outbreaks of war between Israel and Arab states.
3. To identify the Camp David Accords.
4. To describe the Palestinian struggle for independence.

SKILLBUILDER
- Interpreting maps: location, region, p. 903

CRITICAL THINKING
- Clarifying, p. 901
- Summarizing, pp. 902, 903
- Recognizing effects, p. 903
- Synthesizing, p. 904
- Forming an opinion, p. 905
- Analyzing issues, p. 905

FOCUS
5-Minute Warm-Up

▶ **Interpreting Maps**
Have students answer these questions to help them understand events in the Middle East.

1. Look at the map on page 903. What bodies of water separate the Sinai Peninsula from Egypt?

2. What bodies of water separate the West Bank from Jordan?

 WARM-UP TRANSPARENCY 34

OBJECTIVE ① INSTRUCT

Palestine and Israel

▶ **Key Ideas**
- During WWI, Britain makes promises to Jews and Arabs.
- Germany's persecution of Jews spurs immigration to Palestine.
- Jews accept the UN partition of Palestine, Muslims reject it, and Israel declares its independence.

IN-DEPTH RESOURCES: UNIT 8
Guided Reading, p. 23

ACCESS FOR STUDENTS ACQUIRING ENGLISH
Guided Reading (Spanish), p. 346

SECTION 4 RESOURCES

PRINT RESOURCES

IN-DEPTH RESOURCES: UNIT 8
Guided Reading, p. 23
Primary Source: The Balfour Declaration, p. 30
History Makers: Golda Meir, p. 35

ACCESS FOR STUDENTS ACQUIRING ENGLISH
Guided Reading (Spanish), p. 346

FORMAL ASSESSMENT
Section Quiz, p. 403

ALTERNATIVE ASSESSMENT BOOK

TECHNOLOGY RESOURCES

 WORLD ART AND CULTURES TRANSPARENCIES
AT76 *After the Storm*

 CRITICAL THINKING TRANSPARENCIES
CT34 Time Machine: The Middle East Conflict
CT70 Chapter 34 Visual Summary

 CD-ROM
Electronic Library of Primary Sources

INTERNET www.mlworldhistory.com

Teacher's Edition **901**

Israel and the Arab States in Conflict

▶ Key Ideas

- Israel's Arab neighbors greet the new nation with hostility.
- Full-scale war breaks out four times.
- Israel seizes control of old Jerusalem and other buffer areas, offering citizenship to Palestinians living in Jerusalem.

 CRITICAL THINKING TRANSPARENCIES
CT34 Time Machine: The Middle East Conflict

HISTORY MAKERS
Golda Meir

Have students compare Golda Meir's achievements with those of similarly qualified women of her generation in the United States. Ask how they would explain the differences. *Students might state that reform movements have generally held progressive views of women; also, the small and young nation of Israel could not afford to waste good leadership. Others might say that perhaps Meir was an exception.*

 IN-DEPTH RESOURCES: UNIT 8
History Makers: Golda Meir, p. 35

Israel Becomes a State Britain failed in its many attempts to work out a satisfactory compromise. At the end of World War II, a weary Britain referred the Palestine issue to the United Nations. The UN recommendations, accepted by the General Assembly in 1947, called for a partition of Palestine into a Palestinian state and a Jewish state. Jerusalem was to be an international city owned by neither side.

All of the Islamic countries voted against partition, and the Palestinians rejected it outright. They objected that the UN did not have the right to partition a country without considering the wishes of the majority of its people. However, the Jews welcomed the proposal. The terms of the partition were very favorable to them, giving them 55 percent of the area even though Jews made up only 34 percent of the population. Certain nations, such as the United States and many in Europe, felt sympathy for the Jews because of the Holocaust. Such nations supported the concept of giving Jews their own nation. Finally, the date was set for the formation of Israel—May 14, 1948. On that date, David Ben Gurion, long-time leader of the Jews residing in Palestine, announced the creation of an independent Israel.

Israel and the Arab States in Conflict

The new nation of Israel got a hostile greeting from its neighbors. The day after it proclaimed itself a state, six Arab states—Egypt, Iraq, Jordan, Lebanon, Saudi Arabia, and

HISTORY MAKERS

Golda Meir
1898–1978

Golda Meir, one of the signers of Israel's declaration of independence, was born in Kiev, Russia, and emigrated with her family to Milwaukee, Wisconsin, when she was eight.

In those days, she was known as Goldie Mabovitch. The Mabovitch home was a gathering place for discussions among Zionists. Golda listened excitedly to the talk about Jews working for a Jewish state.

In 1921, after becoming a teacher, Golda and her husband, Morris Myerson, moved to Palestine, where they joined a kibbutz, a collective farm. In 1956, Golda Myerson began using a Hebraic form of her married name, Meir. She served Israel as ambassador to the Soviet Union, minister of labor, foreign minister, and finally prime minister.

Syria—invaded Israel. The first of many Arab-Israeli wars, this one ended within months in a victory for Israel. Israel depended on strong American support in this conflict, as well as in most of its other wars. Full-scale war broke out again in 1956, 1967, and 1973.

The Palestinian state that the UN had set aside for Palestinians never came into being. Israel seized half the land in the 1948–1949 fighting. Egypt took control of the Gaza Strip, and Jordan annexed the West Bank. (See map on page 903.) While the fighting raged, thousands of Palestinians fled, migrating from the areas under Jewish control. They settled in UN-sponsored refugee camps that ringed the borders of their former homeland.

The 1956 Suez Crisis The second Arab-Israeli war followed Egypt's seizure of the Suez Canal in 1956. This seizure was ordered by Egyptian president Gamal Abdel Nasser, who had led the military coup that overthrew King Farouk in 1952. French and British business interests had continued to control the canal after the coup.

In 1956, angered by the loss of U.S. and British financial support for the building of the Aswan Dam, Nasser sent his troops to take the canal. Outraged, the British and the French made an agreement with Israel. With air support provided by their European allies, the Israelis marched on the Suez Canal and quickly defeated the Egyptians. However, pressure from the rest of the world's community, including the United States and the Soviet Union, forced Israel and its European allies to withdraw from Egypt. This left Egypt in charge of the canal and thus ended the **Suez Crisis.**

The 1967 Six-Day War Tensions between Israel and the Arab states began to build again in the years following the resolution of the Suez Crisis. By early 1967, Nasser and his Arab allies, equipped with Soviet tanks and aircraft, felt ready to confront Israel. Nasser announced, "We are eager for battle in order to force the enemy to awake from his dreams, and meet Arab reality face to face." He moved to close off the Gulf of Aqaba, Israel's outlet to the Red Sea. Convinced that the Arabs were about to attack, the Israelis attacked airfields in Egypt, Iran,

THINK THROUGH HISTORY
B. Summarizing
What recommendations did the UN make for Palestine?
B. Possible Answer
The UN recommended the partition of Palestine into a Palestinian state and a Jewish state, with Jerusalem as an international city.

Background
The 1952 overthrow led by Nasser marked the first time that Egypt had been ruled by native Egyptians since the 6th century B.C.

TEACHING OPTIONS

EXPLORING PRIMARY SOURCES

A Voice from the Past Ask students if they think that Jews and non-Jews living in Palestine might have understood the Balfour Declaration (page 901) differently. How might the Jews have interpreted it? How might Muslims and Christians already living there have understood the document?

Could the declaration have been worded differently and still have achieved its purpose of appeasing both sides?

 IN-DEPTH RESOURCES: UNIT 8
Primary Source: The Balfour Declaration, p. 30

CUSTOMIZING FOR SPECIAL NEEDS

Less Proficient Readers Pair less proficient readers with more skilled readers and have them read the text on pages 902–903. Then have them draw a time line of events, beginning with the birth of the new state of Israel. Their time line might look like this:

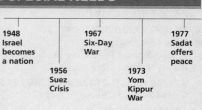

1948 Israel becomes a nation		1967 Six-Day War		1977 Sadat offers peace
	1956 Suez Crisis		1973 Yom Kippur War	

Jordan, and Syria. Safe from air attack, Israeli ground forces struck like lightning on three fronts. The war was over in six days. Israel lost 800 troops in the fighting, while Arab losses exceeded 15,000.

As a consequence of the **Six-Day War,** Israel occupied militarily the old city of Jerusalem, the Sinai Peninsula, the Golan Heights, and the West Bank. This was done to provide a buffer zone and improve security. Palestinians who lived in Jerusalem were given the choice of Israeli or Jordanian citizenship. Most chose the latter. Palestinians who lived in the other areas were not offered Israeli citizenship and became stateless.

The 1973 War A fourth Arab-Israeli conflict erupted in October 1973. Nasser's successor, Egyptian president **Anwar Sadat** (AHN·wahr suh·DAT), planned a joint Arab attack on the date of Yom Kippur, the holiest of Jewish holidays. This time the Israelis were caught by surprise. Arab forces inflicted heavy casualties and recaptured some of the territory lost in 1967. The Israelis, under their prime minister, **Golda Meir** (MY·uhr), launched a counterattack and regained most of the lost territory. An uneasy truce was agreed to after several weeks of fighting, ending the October war.

THINK THROUGH HISTORY
C. Recognizing Effects What were some of the effects of the Arab-Israeli conflicts?
C. Possible Answer Some territory changed hands; hostilities continued; instability threatened the region.

Trading Land for Peace

Since no peace treaty ended the Yom Kippur War, many people feared that another war could start. Four years later, however, in November 1977, Anwar Sadat stunned the world by offering peace to Israel. No Arab country up to this point had recognized Israel's right to exist. In a dramatic gesture, he flew to Jerusalem and told the Knesset, the Israeli parliament, "We used to reject you. . . . Yet, today we agree to live with you in permanent peace and justice." Sadat emphasized that in exchange for peace, Israel would have to recognize the rights of Palestinians. Further, it would have to withdraw from territory seized in 1967 from Egypt, Jordan, and Syria.

President Jimmy Carter recognized that Sadat had created a historic opportunity for peace. In 1978, Carter invited Sadat and Israeli prime minister **Menachem Begin** (mehn·AHK·hehm BAY·gihn) to Camp David, the presidential retreat in rural Maryland. Isolated from the press and from domestic political pressures, Sadat and Begin discussed the issues dividing their two countries. After 13 days of negotiations, Carter triumphantly announced that Egypt recognized Israel as a legitimate state. In exchange, Israel agreed to return the Sinai Peninsula to Egypt. Signed in 1979, the **Camp David Accords,** the first signed agreement between Israel and an Arab country, ended 30 years of hostilities between Egypt and Israel.

D. Answer It was the first signed agreement between Israel and an Arab country.
THINK THROUGH HISTORY
D. Summarizing What was the significance of the Camp David Accords?

While world leaders praised Sadat, his peace initiative enraged many Arab countries. In 1981, a group of Muslim extremists assassinated him. Egypt's new leader, **Hosni Mubarak** (HAHS·nee moo·BAHR·uhk), maintained peace with Israel.

The Colonies Become New Nations **903**

The Middle East, 1947–1997

- Jewish state under 1947 UN partition plan for Palestine
- Acquired by Israel in 1948 War of Independence
- Israeli conquests in the Six-Day War of 1967
- Israeli conquests returned to Egypt, 1967–1982
- Areas of Palestinian self-rule, 1994

Beirut
LEBANON — Damascus
SYRIA
Haifa • Sea of Galilee • Golan Heights
Mediterranean Sea
Tel Aviv • West Bank • Jordan R.
Jerusalem • Amman
Gaza Strip • Bethlehem • Dead Sea
Gaza • Beersheba
ISRAEL
Negev
JORDAN
Nile Delta
Suez Canal
• Cairo
Suez • SINAI PENINSULA
Elat •
EGYPT • *Gulf of Suez* • *Gulf of Aqaba*
SAUDI ARABIA
Nile River
N
0   100 Miles
0   200 Kilometers
Red Sea

30°E 32°E 34°E
32°N
30°N
28°N

GEOGRAPHY SKILLBUILDER: Interpreting Maps
1. **Location** What was the southernmost point in Israel in 1947 and what might have been its strategic value?
2. **Region** What country lies due north of Israel? east? northeast?

History from Visuals

The Middle East, 1947–1997
Interpreting the Map What access do Jews and Palestinians have to the Mediterranean? to the Red Sea? *Jews have seaports on the Mediterranean, and Palestinians have access to it from the Gaza Strip; Jews can reach the Red Sea through the Gulf of Aqaba; Palestinians have no access.*

Extension Activity Compare this map with maps showing the vegetation and resources of the area.

SKILLBUILDER Answers
1. Elat; it gave Israel access, by way of the Gulf of Aqaba, to the Red Sea.
2. Lebanon; Jordan; Syria.

OBJECTIVE 3 INSTRUCT

Trading Land for Peace

▶ *Key Ideas*
- Egypt and Israel sign the Camp David Accords, the first peace treaty between an Arab country and Israel.
- Egypt recognizes the state of Israel, and Israel returns the Sinai Peninsula to Egypt.

MORE ABOUT . . .
Camp David Accords
Some of the most successful peace talks have been held outside of the Middle East, in neutral territory, often in secrecy. This has allowed negotiators to work undistracted by the day-to-day business of running a government. It has also shielded negotiators from groups at home who oppose peace efforts. This was the case at Camp David, in rural Maryland, where Begin of Israel and Sadat of Egypt reached an agreement.

TEACHING OPTION **BLOCK SCHEDULING** **COOPERATIVE ACTIVITY: Researching West Bank Settlements** **CLASS TIME 30 MINUTES**

Task: Students will research various positions on the issue of Israeli settlements on the West Bank.

Purpose: To encourage students to recognize that most issues have many sides to them.

Activity: Ask students to form groups of three or four. Have them do research, using the Internet, newspapers, and current magazines, on the issue of Israeli settlements on the West Bank and their effect on the Palestinian population and the prospects for peace in the region. Have each group research the various positions on the issue and list the arguments for each position.

Building a Portfolio Students may add the list to their portfolio.

ALTERNATIVE ASSESSMENT BOOK Standards for Evaluating a Cooperative Activity

Standards for Evaluation
Lists should . . .
- clearly convey various sides of the issue
- list an equal number of arguments for all sides
- be fair and impartial

Teacher's Edition **903**

Kibbutz Childcare

Children on a kibbutz typically live in special children's houses. That means they eat, sleep, learn, and play with children of similar ages. They go to their family home each day, when school and work are over, to visit with their parents and do their homework. Parents and children eat in separate dining rooms, then the parents go to the children's houses to tuck their children into bed.

MORE ABOUT . . .
Jews Abroad

The surge in immigration to Israel resulted in sudden and drastic changes in Jewish communities elsewhere. For example, the number of Jews in Bulgaria shrank from 45,000 in 1948 to 7,700 in 1951. Almost all Libyan, Yemenite, and Iraqi Jews moved to Israel. Two-thirds of all Polish Jews immigrated to Israel, as did one-third of the Jews in Romania.

Daily *Life* : Israel, 1951

Israeli Independent News

Life on a Kibbutz

On this communal farm, women work right along with men in the fields. Children receive care from trained teachers and nurses. One young girl being raised on a kibbutz wrote her American friend about the freedom and responsibility of kibbutz life: "Among us the children's opinion is very important. We decide when and how to work and when to do a project. I study six hours a day and I work one and a half hours. I am also taking lessons in music and crafts."

Population Doubles in Three Years

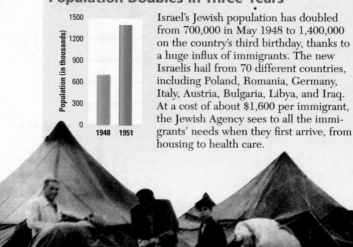

Israel's Jewish population has doubled from 700,000 in May 1948 to 1,400,000 on the country's third birthday, thanks to a huge influx of immigrants. The new Israelis hail from 70 different countries, including Poland, Romania, Germany, Italy, Austria, Bulgaria, Libya, and Iraq. At a cost of about $1,600 per immigrant, the Jewish Agency sees to all the immigrants' needs when they first arrive, from housing to health care.

A tractor driver carries a rifle slung across his back as he works to develop the land on his kibbutz.

From Culture to Agriculture

Many of Israel's eager immigrants are former lawyers, professors, or physicians. They find themselves drawn to the hard work of clearing Israel's swamps and making her deserts bloom. At one collective farm, the professors who work as farmers could probably open their own college. Now, instead of teaching math, philosophy, or psychology, they eagerly pore over the latest publications on scientific farming from the U.S. Department of Agriculture.

Tent cities have sprung up throughout Israel to house new immigrants. Within ten years, these temporary shelters will be replaced by permanent housing.

Temporary Housing Springs Up

Near the large towns and farming areas that offer employment, transit camps called *ma'abarot* offer shelter and food for Israel's refugees. Workers quickly raise tents and canvas huts to house the refugees. Then they build wooden huts to hold kindergartens, nurseries, clinics, and employment centers. Workers can erect a *ma'abarot* within a few weeks. These camps provide welcome shelter for hundreds of thousands of needy immigrants.

Connect *to* History

Synthesizing From the articles in the newsletter, what problems did new immigrants to Israel face in 1951?

SEE SKILLBUILDER HANDBOOK, PAGE 1007.

Connect *to* Today

Researching In the library or on the Internet, research a facet of life in modern-day Israel. You might choose the kibbutzim, Palestinian-Israeli relations, or the current status of Jerusalem.

904 Chapter 34

Connect *to* History

Synthesizing
Students should mention the difficulties in creating a unified population— all speaking Hebrew—out of the great variety of immigrants who flooded Israel immediately after it was created. Students may also point out that many immigrants changed

occupations when they arrived in Israel, requiring them to learn new skills and in some cases to alter their image of who they were. The sudden influx of immigrants required Israel to set up temporary camps in which facilities were at a minimum.

Connect *to* Today

Researching
Suggest to students that they use indexes such as the *Readers' Guide to Periodical Literature* and library computer databases such as the Periodical Abstracts. If students have access to the Internet, they may also look at newspaper and media sites such as CNN or *The New York Times*.

The Palestinians Demand Independence

Peace agreements between Israelis and Palestinians were harder to achieve. Unwilling to give up territories they had seized for security, the Israelis began to build settlements on the West Bank and the Gaza Strip.

The Intifada Palestinians living in Israel resented Israeli rule. As their anger mounted, they turned increasingly to the Palestine Liberation Organization, or **PLO**, led by Yasir Arafat (YAH·sur AR·uh·FAT). During the 1970s and 1980s, the military wing of the PLO conducted a campaign of armed struggle against Israel. Israel turned to strong measures, bombing suspected bases in Palestinian towns. In 1982, the Israeli army invaded Lebanon in an attempt to destroy strongholds in Palestinian villages. The Israelis soon became involved in Lebanon's civil war and were forced to withdraw.

In 1987, Palestinians began to express their frustrations in a widespread campaign of civil disobedience called the intifada, or "uprising." The intifada took the form of boycotts, demonstrations, attacks on Israeli soldiers, and rock throwing by unarmed teenagers. The intifada continued into the 1990s, with little progress made towards a solution. However, the civil disobedience affected world opinion, which, in turn, put pressure on Israel. Finally, in October 1991, Israeli and Palestinian delegates met for the first time in a series of peace talks.

The Declaration of Principles The status of the Israeli-occupied territories proved to be a bitterly divisive issue. In 1993, however, secret talks held in Oslo, Norway, produced a surprise agreement. In a document called the Declaration of Principles, Israel, under the leadership of Prime Minister Yitzhak Rabin (YIHTS·hahk rah·BEEN), agreed to grant the Palestinians self-rule in the Gaza Strip and the West Bank, beginning with the town of Jericho. Rabin and Arafat signed the agreement on the South Lawn of the White House on September 13, 1993.

The difficulty of making an agreement work was demonstrated by the assassination of Rabin in 1995. He was killed by a right-wing Jewish extremist who opposed concessions to the Palestinians. Rabin was succeeded as prime minister by Benjamin Netanyahu (neh·tan·YAH·hoo), who had opposed the plan. Still, Netanyahu made efforts to keep to the agreement. In January 1997, he met with Arafat to work out plans for a partial Israeli withdrawal from Hebron, on the West Bank. The U.S. secretary of state, Madeleine Albright, traveled to the region in September 1997, but peace continued to be difficult to achieve.

E. Possible Answer Most students will probably see that both sides have legitimate claims to the land and have reasonable arguments on their side.

THINK THROUGH HISTORY
E. Forming an Opinion Political commentators have said that the Arab-Israeli conflict represents the struggle not of right against wrong, but of right against right. Do you agree or disagree? Explain.

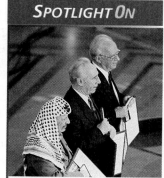

Section 4 Assessment

1. TERMS & NAMES
Identify
- Balfour Declaration
- Suez Crisis
- Six-Day War
- Anwar Sadat
- Golda Meir
- Menachem Begin
- Camp David Accords
- Hosni Mubarak
- PLO

2. TAKING NOTES
Draw a cause-and-effect graphic and fill in some important political and military events that occurred following the Suez Crisis.

Write a paragraph explaining which event is most important.

3. ANALYZING ISSUES
Explain the conflict between Jews and Arabs over a Palestinian homeland. What does each side believe? What other factors influence this issue?

THINK ABOUT
- the Balfour Declaration
- the ancient history of the Middle East
- the economics of oil

4. THEME ACTIVITY
Power and Authority In groups of three or four, come up with a list of ten interview questions for Gamal Abdel Nasser, Anwar Sadat, Yasir Arafat, or Yitzhak Rabin.

The Colonies Become New Nations **905**

OBJECTIVE 4 INSTRUCT

The Palestinians Demand Independence

▶ **Key Ideas**
- Israelis build settlements on the West Bank and the Gaza Strip.
- Palestinians use civil disobedience to resist Israeli rule.
- Secret talks in Oslo, Norway, lead to a peace agreement.
- Prime Minister Yitzhak Rabin is assassinated and is succeeded by Benjamin Netanyahu.

🔘 **ELECTRONIC LIBRARY OF PRIMARY SOURCES**
"Enough of Blood and Tears" by Yitzhak Rabin

SPOTLIGHT ON
Oslo Peace Agreement

Have students compare the Camp David Accords with the Oslo Peace Agreement.

ASSESS & RETEACH

Section 4 Assessment
Have students jot down key points to include in each answer.

Section Quiz
📄 **FORMAL ASSESSMENT**
Section Quiz, p. 403

Reteaching Activity
CLASS TIME: 15 MINUTES

Have pairs of students review the section content by turning heads and subheads into questions that they pose to their partners. For example, the head "Israel and the Arab States in Conflict" might become the question, When and why were Israel and the Arab states in conflict?

CLOSE ACTIVITY

CLASS TIME: 15 MINUTES

Role Playing
Divide the class into groups of four students, and have each student take on the role of either Golda Meir, Benjamin Netanyahu, Hosni Mubarak, or Yasir Arafat. Then have each group hold a mini-debate on the following topic: What is the best way to bring peace to the Middle East?

🏛 **CRITICAL THINKING TRANSPARENCIES**
CT70 Chapter 34 Visual Summary

ANSWERS

1. TERMS & NAMES
Balfour Declaration, p. 901
Suez Crisis, p. 902
Six-Day War, p. 903
Anwar Sadat, p. 903
Golda Meir, p. 903
Menachem Begin, p. 903
Camp David Accords, p. 903
Hosni Mubarak, p. 903
PLO, p. 905

2. TAKING NOTES
Possible Responses: Six-Day War; Yom Kippur War; Sadat peace offer; Camp David Accords

3. ANALYZING ISSUES
Possible Responses: Jews believe their right to a Palestinian homeland is a covenant from God; Palestinian Arabs believe the land has belonged to them since the Jews were driven out in A.D. 135; other Arabs believe it has belonged to them since their 7th-century conquest of the region. Other influences: oil interests; global politics; persecution of Jews in Europe.

4. THEME ACTIVITY
Standards for Evaluation
Interview questions should meet the following criteria:
- present an interesting and stimulating range of issues
- show an understanding of Middle Eastern issues
- show evidence of teamwork

TERMS & NAMES

1. partition, p. 886
2. Jawaharlal Nehru, p. 887
3. Indira Gandhi, p. 887
4. Ferdinand Marcos, p. 893
5. Corazón Aquino, p. 893
6. Negritude movement, p. 896
7. FLN, p. 899
8. Balfour Declaration, p. 901
9. Anwar Sadat, p. 903
10. PLO, p. 905

REVIEW QUESTIONS

Answers to some questions may vary.

11. The massacre of unarmed Indians at Amritsar.

12. India and Pakistan.

13. One-fifth of Sri Lanka's people are Tamils, a Hindu people; some want to set up a separate Tamil nation. Most Sri Lankans are Buddhists, and they oppose the Tamils.

14. The United States got free trading rights; the Filipinos felt U.S. businesses might exploit the Philippines' natural resources and environment.

15. A leader of the Indonesian independence movement, and Indonesia's first president.

16. Some Ghanians felt he spent too much money on programs that the country could not afford and too much time on Pan-African efforts, neglecting Ghana's own problems.

17. Belgium had not prepared the country for independence; the province of Katanga tried to secede.

18. French colonists refused to share political power with the Africans.

19. When Egypt seized the Suez Canal in 1956, Israelis, supported by the British and the French, invaded Egypt and marched toward the canal; they later withdrew because of world pressure, and Egypt regained control of the canal.

20. Most of the world responded favorably; some Arabs were angered by Sadat's peace initiative.

The Struggle for Independence

The time line shows the dates on which various countries in Asia and Africa achieved their independence after World War II. It also shows (in parentheses) the countries from which they achieved independence.

1945

1946
Philippines (United States)

1947
India, Pakistan (Great Britain)

1948
Israel (Great Britain)

1949
Indonesia (The Netherlands)

1955

1957
Federation of Malaya, Ghana (Great Britain)

1960
Zaire (Belgium)

1962
Algeria (France)

1963
Kenya (Great Britain)

1965
Singapore (Great Britain, Malaya)

1971
Bangladesh (Pakistan)

1975
Angola (Portugal)

TERMS & NAMES

Briefly explain the importance of each of the following to colonies becoming new nations after World War II.

1. partition
2. Jawaharlal Nehru
3. Indira Gandhi
4. Ferdinand Marcos
5. Corazón Aquino
6. Negritude movement
7. FLN
8. Balfour Declaration
9. Anwar Sadat
10. PLO

REVIEW QUESTIONS

SECTION 1 *(pages 885–889)*
The Indian Subcontinent Gains Independence

11. What incident marked the beginning of the end of British rule in India?
12. What two nations emerged from the British colony of India in 1947?
13. Briefly explain the reason for the civil disorder in Sri Lanka.

SECTION 2 *(pages 892–895)*
Southeast Asian Nations Gain Independence

14. What were some concerns the Filipinos had regarding the Bell Act?
15. Who was Sukarno?

SECTION 3 *(pages 896–900)*
New Nations in Africa

16. Why were Kwame Nkrumah's politics criticized?
17. Name two problems Zaire faced in gaining independence.
18. Why was the policy of assimilation in Algeria hard to achieve?

SECTION 4 *(pages 901–905)*
Conflicts in the Middle East

19. What was the Suez Crisis?
20. What was the reaction to the Camp David Accords?

Interact *with* History

On page 884, you decided whether to flee your country to take a chance in a new country. Now that you've read the chapter, do you think the separation into different countries of ethnically and religiously similar people was good or bad? List positives and negatives of such splits.

Interact *with* History

Possible Responses: Students who think the separation of ethnically and religiously similar people into different countries was good might cite evidence of the continuing inability of such people to live with people different from them in today's world. Others might cite examples of secular nations in which people of different backgrounds live together peaceably.

CRITICAL THINKING

1. CHALLENGES OF INDEPENDENCE

Using a web diagram like the one below, show some of the challenges that newly independent nations have faced.

Which challenge is the hardest to overcome? Why?

2. REVOLUTIONARY METHODS

THEME REVOLUTION Following independence, many former colonies went through revolutions. They often experienced assassination, rigged elections, and massacres. Keep in mind what you learned about revolutions in this chapter and that revolutions are meant to bring about change. Do you think there should be a limit to the methods revolutionaries employ? Explain your opinion.

3. THE BRITISH COMMONWEALTH

Some new nations, such as Ghana, agreed to become part of the British Commonwealth. Other nations, such as Myanmar (formerly Burma), chose not to join. What factors affected a former colony's decision to join or not to join the British Commonwealth?

4. ANALYZING PRIMARY SOURCES

The following passage comes from an article titled "Reunited Jerusalem Faces Its Problems," published in December 1968. Read the passage and answer the questions below it.

A VOICE FROM THE PAST
Jerusalem nurtured Judaism, Christianity, and Islam, whose adherents have slaughtered each other in its twisted streets throughout centuries of nominal civilization. It has been burned and pillaged, wrecked and razed, always to grow again from its own rubble. Today it remains poor, lovely, and troubled, infinitely greater as a symbol than as a city.

KENNETH MACLEISH, *National Geographic*

- What is the writer trying to point out here?
- What do you think the writer means by "infinitely greater as a symbol than as a city"?

CHAPTER ACTIVITIES

1. LIVING HISTORY: Unit Portfolio Project

THEME ECONOMICS Your unit portfolio project focuses on how economic factors influence history (see page 851). For Chapter 34, you might use one of the following ideas to add to your portfolio:

- List the top four economic issues that newly independent nations face. Read them to your class. Be prepared to answer why you put them in the order you did.
- Choose a country discussed in this chapter and create a chart of major economic events in that country.
- Write a magazine article explaining why the Middle East is historically a hotspot for competing nationalist movements. Be sure to include major economic factors.

2. CONNECT TO TODAY: Cooperative Learning

THEME POWER AND AUTHORITY Following World War II, many newly independent countries were shaped by strong leaders like Indira Gandhi, Anwar Sadat, Jomo Kenyatta, and Suharto. Their actions and policies have continued to affect their countries even up to the present. Work with a team to write a letter to one historical leader mentioned in this chapter.

 Using the Internet or magazines, research current developments in your chosen leader's country.

- Using the library, research the policies of the historic leader you have chosen.
- Write a letter to the historical leader to bring him or her up to date as to the impact that leader's actions and policies have had on the course of development in his or her country.

3. INTERPRETING A TIME LINE

Revisit the unit time line on pages 850–851. Which two events from Chapter 34 do you think were most significant? Explain why.

FOCUS ON GRAPHS

India's population continues to grow very rapidly. Despite the growing population, some headway has been made against poverty, as the graphs below show.

- What percentage of the population was poor in 1951? What percentage was poor in 1994?
- Were there more people living in poverty in India in 1994 or in 1951? Did the percentage of people living in poverty increase or decrease from 1951 to 1994?

Connect to History
What social and economic developments might have contributed to the lower percentage of those living in poverty in India?

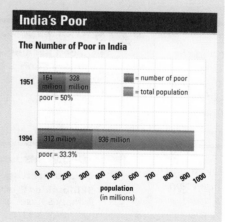

India's Poor

The Number of Poor in India

1951	164 million	328 million	= number of poor
	poor = 50%		= total population
1994	312 million	936 million	
	poor = 33.3%		

population (in millions)
0 100 200 300 400 500 600 700 800 900 1000

The Colonies Become New Nations **907**

CHAPTER ACTIVITIES

1. LIVING HISTORY

Standards for Evaluation
Lists of economic issues should meet the following criteria:

- Use information from the text.
- Show an understanding of basic economic theory.
- Indicate a ranking of issues from most important to least important.
- Include a brief summary of the thinking behind the choices.

Standards for Evaluation
Charts should meet the following criteria:

- Show a graphic arrangement that focuses on the major events.
- Organize information logically.
- Contain clear headings and subheadings.

Standards for Evaluation
Magazine articles should meet the following criteria:

- Be well organized and well developed.
- Contain internal heads to show main ideas.
- Provide explanations for main ideas given.

2. CONNECT TO TODAY

Standards for Evaluation
Letters should meet the following criteria:

- Show an understanding of the importance of the leader chosen.
- Indicate research into the modern history of the country.
- List the effects the leader's policies have had on the country.
- Contain personal opinions about the effects of such policies.

3. INTERPRETING A TIME LINE

Student answers should provide clear reasons and support for choosing two events as most significant.

FOCUS ON GRAPHS

- 50% in 1951; 33.3% in 1993–94.
- In 1993–94; decrease.

Connect to History *Possible Responses:*
Industry in India has developed; new resources, such as oil and coal, have been discovered; scientific and technical education has been expanded.

CRITICAL THINKING

1. CHALLENGES OF INDEPENDENCE

Possible Responses: constant threat of revolution; former colonizers' continued meddling; developing profitable trade relationships with former colonizers; civil wars; random boundaries.

2. REVOLUTIONARY METHODS

Students who think there should be a limit may point out that regardless of whether revolutionaries are fighting for a good or a bad cause, they should go about it peacefully, like Gandhi. Students who think there should be no limit may point out that sometimes it is necessary to use all possible force to get rid of an existing government that is evil.

3. THE BRITISH COMMONWEALTH

Possible Responses: how the colony had been treated by the British during colonization and the struggle for independence; how self-sufficient the economy was; how influenced leaders were by British customs.

4. ANALYZING PRIMARY SOURCES

Possible Responses: Religious groups continue to fight for their rights in the city of Jerusalem. It is not the physical city that is important, but the religious symbolism of the city.

Teacher's Edition 907

Struggles for Democracy

	Key Ideas	COPY MASTERS	ASSESSMENT

SECTION 1
Democracy
Case Study:
Latin American
Democracies

pp. 911–915

Democracy requires key institutions and practices to ensure popular participation. After World War II, Latin American countries struggle to create stable democratic systems.

 In-Depth Resources: Unit 8
- **Guided Reading,** p. 37
- **Geography Application:** Democracy in Central and South America, p. 43
- **Literature:** from *Brazil*, p. 49
- **History Makers:** Juan and Eva Perón, p. 52

PE *Section 1 Assessment,* p. 915

Formal Assessment
- Section Quiz, p. 412

Alternative Assessment Book
- Standards for Evaluating a Cooperative Activity

SECTION 2
Democratic
Challenges
in African
Nations

pp. 916–920

African nations work to build democracy. While Nigeria suffers setbacks, South Africa casts off white rule and lays the foundations for a democratic, multiracial government.

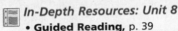 **In-Depth Resources: Unit 8**
- **Guided Reading,** p. 38
- **Primary Sources:** from *Kaffir Boy,* p. 45; Mandela's Inaugural Address, p. 46
- **History Makers:** Nelson Mandela, p. 53

PE *Section 2 Assessment,* p. 920

Formal Assessment
- Section Quiz, p. 413

Alternative Assessment Book
- Standards for Evaluating a Cooperative Activity

SECTION 3
Gorbachev
Moves Toward
Democracy

pp. 921–925

Under Mikhail Gorbachev, the Soviet Union undertakes major reforms to open up the Communist system. Soviet bloc countries in Eastern Europe go a step further and throw off Communist rule completely.

 In-Depth Resources: Unit 8
- **Guided Reading,** p. 39
- **Primary Source:** Political Cartoon, p. 47

PE *Section 3 Assessment,* p. 925

Formal Assessment
- Section Quiz, p. 414

Alternative Assessment Book
- Standards for Evaluating a Cooperative Activity

SECTION 4
Collapse of
the Soviet
Union

pp. 926–930

Reforms lead to unrest and the breakup of the Soviet Union. Yugoslavia, Poland, and Czechoslovakia face problems after becoming free of communism.

 In-Depth Resources: Unit 8
- **Guided Reading,** p. 40
- **Primary Source:** The Road to Marjača, p. 48

PE *Section 4 Assessment,* p. 930

Formal Assessment
- Section Quiz, p. 415

Alternative Assessment Book
- Standards for Evaluating a Cooperative Activity

SECTION 5
China Follows
Its Own Path

pp. 931–935

China opens up to the West and implements reforms while maintaining its Communist system. Questions remain about the prospects for democracy in China, even as China regains Hong Kong.

 In-Depth Resources: Unit 8
- **Guided Reading,** p. 41
- **Skillbuilder Practice:** Analyzing Primary Sources, p. 42

PE *Section 5 Assessment,* p. 935

Formal Assessment
- Section Quiz, p. 416

Alternative Assessment Book
- Standards for Evaluating a Cooperative Activity

CHAPTER RESOURCES

Chapter Overview

The establishment of democracy can be a long, difficult process, as events in Latin America, Africa, the former Soviet bloc, and China show. Democracy appears to be on the rise worldwide as people recognize their common economic and political goals.

Telescoping the Times
- Chapter Summary, pp. 137–139

Planning for Block Schedules

PE *Chapter Assessment,* pp. 936–937

Chapter Activities, p. 937

Formal Assessment
- Chapter Test, forms A and B, pp. 417–422

 Test Generator

 Alternative Assessment Book

TECHNOLOGY

Warm-Up Transparency 35
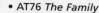
World Art and Cultures Transparencies
• AT76 *The Family*
INTERNET RESOURCES
www.mlworldhistory.com

Warm-Up Transparency 35
World Art and Cultures Transparencies
• AT77 Multiple-Mask Headdress
Electronic Library of Primary Sources
• from "Masakhane—Let Us Build Together"
Patterns of Interaction:
Struggling Toward Democracy
INTERNET RESOURCES
www.mlworldhistory.com

Warm-Up Transparency 35
Geography Transparencies
• GT35 Germany, Post World War I–Present
World Art and Cultures Transparencies
• AT78 *Burning Rods*
Electronic Library of Primary Sources
• "Destruction of the Berlin Wall"
INTERNET RESOURCES
www.mlworldhistory.com

Warm-Up Transparency 35
Electronic Library of Primary Sources
• "Will I Ever Go Home Again?"
INTERNET RESOURCES
www.mlworldhistory.com

Warm-Up Transparency 35
Critical Thinking Transparencies
• CT35 Democratic Struggles Around the Globe
• CT71 Chapter 35 Visual Summary
Electronic Library of Primary Sources
• "The Massacre in Tiananmen Square"

Chapter Summaries on Audiocassette in English and Spanish
INTERNET RESOURCES
www.mlworldhistory.com

Block Scheduling (90 MINUTES)

Day 1
Section 1, pp. 911–915
 COOPERATIVE ACTIVITY
Teacher's Edition, p. 914.
Section 2, pp. 916–920
COOPERATIVE ACTIVITY
Teacher's Edition, p. 919.
Section Assessments,
pp. 915, 920

Day 2
Section 3, pp. 921–925
COOPERATIVE ACTIVITY
Teacher's Edition, p. 923.
Section 4, pp. 926–930
COOPERATIVE ACTIVITY
Teacher's Edition, p. 929.
Section Assessments,
pp. 925, 930

Day 3
Section 5, pp. 931–935
COOPERATIVE ACTIVITY
Teacher's Edition, p. 932.
Section Assessment, p. 935
Chapter Assessment,
pp. 936–937

Yearly Pacing *Chapter 35 Total:* 3 days *Yearly Total:* 85 days

Planning for Block Schedules

Customizing for Special Needs

Students Acquiring English

Access for Students Acquiring English
• **Guided Reading** for Sections 1–5 (Spanish), pp. 353–357
• **Chapter Summary** (Spanish), pp. 350–352
• **Skillbuilder Practice** Analyzing Primary Sources (Spanish), p. 358
• **Geography Application** Democracy in South America (Spanish), p. 359

Chapter Summaries on Audiocassette in English and Spanish

Patterns of Interaction:
Struggling Toward Democracy (Spanish track)

Less Proficient Readers

In-Depth Resources: Unit 8
• **Guided Reading** for Sections 1–5, pp. 37–41
• **Skillbuilder Practice** Analyzing Primary Sources, p. 42
• **Geography Application** Democracy in Central and South America, p. 43

Telescoping the Times
• Chapter Summary, pp. 137–139

Chapter Summaries on Audiocassette

Gifted and Talented Students

In-Depth Resources: Unit 8
Primary Sources:
• from *Kaffir Boy,* p. 45
• Mandela's Inaugural Address, p. 46
• Political Cartoon, p. 47
• The Road to Marjaca, p. 48

History Makers:
• Juan and Eva Perón, p. 52
• Nelson Mandela, p. 53

Connections to Literature READINGS FOR STUDENTS

In-Depth Resources: Unit 8
Literature: from *Brazil,* p. 49

McDougal Littell
Literature Connections
• **Head, Bessie**
When Rain Clouds Gather
(with related readings)
Makhosja flees South Africa in the mid-1960s into Botswana. There he struggles against the bitterness within him as Botswana approaches independence.

McDougal Littell
Literature Connections
• **Mathabane, Mark**
Kaffir Boy
(with related readings)
In this powerful memoir, Mathabane shows how the strength of the human spirit endures even in the face of a crushing system like apartheid.

PE = Pupil's Edition   = Overhead Transparency   = Software   = Video

 = Copy Master   = CD-ROM   = Audiocassette   = Internet

Struggles for Democracy, 1945–Present

Accessing Prior Knowledge

- Have students discuss why Germany was divided and why the Berlin Wall was constructed.

- Ask students what factors in the colonial history of South Africa set the stage for a civil rights movement among its nonwhite citizens.

- Ask students what factors in Brazil's history might have led the government to build a new capital city.

Making Inferences

- Ask students what they can infer about Desmond Tutu from the caption and the photograph.

- Have students consider what the construction of Brasília says about the Brazilian view of government.

Geography Connection

Ask students to study the maps of Europe and Africa.

- Refer to the map of Europe on page 857. In which part of divided Germany was Berlin located?

- Refer to the map of Africa on page 688. Which European country controlled the two areas highlighted in the map of Africa on page 909?

Struggles for Democracy, 1945–Present

PREVIEWING THEMES

Economics

Gorbachev in the Soviet Union and Deng Xiaoping in China allowed reforms that moved their Communist economies toward capitalism. Many nations—such as Brazil and Poland—discovered that economic stability is important for democratic progress.

Revolution

In 1989, democratic revolutions overthrew Communist governments in the Soviet Union and most of Eastern Europe. In China, the Communist government and the army put down a student protest calling for democracy.

Cultural Interaction

Democratic reforms spread from one Eastern European country to another, causing Communist governments to fall like dominoes. In addition, Chinese students brought democratic ideas from the West back to China and tried to change Chinese culture.

INTERNET CONNECTION

Visit us at **www.mlworldhistory.com** to learn more about democratic movements in the 20th century.

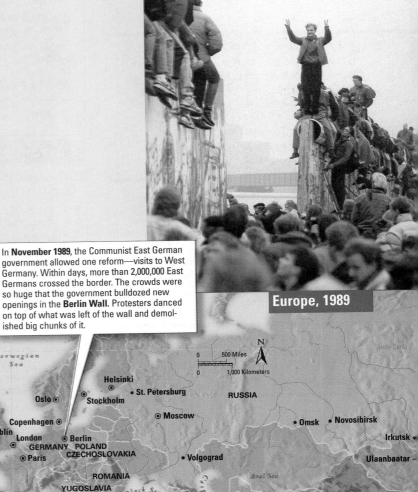

EUROPE, AFRICA, SOUTH AMERICA

In **November 1989**, the Communist East German government allowed one reform—visits to West Germany. Within days, more than 2,000,000 East Germans crossed the border. The crowds were so huge that the government bulldozed new openings in the **Berlin Wall**. Protesters danced on top of what was left of the wall and demolished big chunks of it.

Europe, 1989

GEOGRAPHY THEMES

Place

Point out to students that in 1985 South Africa was the only white-ruled nation left in the southern part of Africa. In the preceding decades, many former colonial governments had given way to black-controlled administrations. In addition, apartheid in South Africa was coming under increasing criticism from the international community. South Africa was more and more isolated from its neighboring states, Europe, and the United States.

Ask students to think about what effect these facts may have had on people in South Africa.

Location

Have students speculate on why Brasília was built in the Brazilian interior. What advantages and disadvantages would this location give the government? Tell students that the Brazilian government wanted the city to be a showcase of architectural design.

On the European map, point out that Germany, which is located in Western Europe, borders the former Soviet satellites. Ask students to consider what impact a reunified Germany might have on Europe in terms of trade and political alliances. Remind them that for decades after World War II, West Germany had the strongest economy in Europe.

ADDITIONAL RESOURCES

Books for the Teacher

- Berry, Ian. *Living Apart: South Africa Under Apartheid.* London: Phaidon, 1996.

- Brown, Archie. *The Gorbachev Factor.* New York: Oxford UP, 1996.

- Miles, James A. R. *The Legacy of Tiananmen: China in Disarray.* Ann Arbor, MI: Michigan UP, 1996.

- Winn, Peter. *Americas: The Changing Face of Latin America and the Caribbean.* New York: Pantheon, 1992.

Books for the Student

- Baynham, Simon. *Africa from 1945.* New York: Watts, 1987.

- Kort, Michael. *China Under Communism.* Brookfield, CT: Millbrook, 1994.

- Symynkywicz, Jeffrey B. *1989: The Year the World Changed.* Parsippany, NJ: Dillon, 1996.

▭▭▭ Videos

- *Project HIP-HOP South Africa,* Cambridge Educational, 800–468–4227.

- *The Revolution in Eastern Europe.* Society for Visual Education, 800–829–1900. Students discuss changes in their countries.

◎ Software

- *The Last Days of Apartheid.* CD-ROM. Society for Visual Education, 800–829–1900.

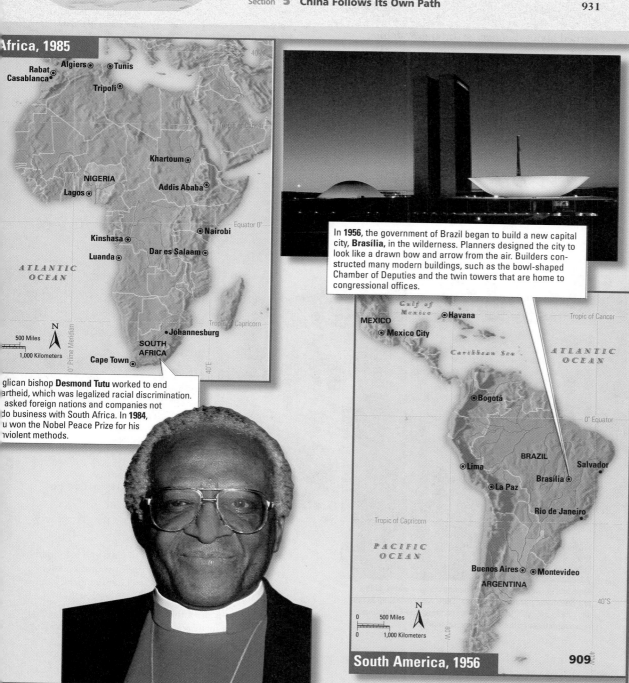

Africa, 1985

Rabat
Casablanca
Algiers
Tunis
Tripoli
Khartoum
NIGERIA
Lagos
Addis Ababa
Equator 0°
Kinshasa
Nairobi
Luanda
Dar es Salaam
ATLANTIC OCEAN
Tropic of Capricorn
Johannesburg
SOUTH AFRICA
Cape Town
500 Miles
1,000 Kilometers

...glican bishop **Desmond Tutu** worked to end ...artheid, which was legalized racial discrimination. ... asked foreign nations and companies not ... do business with South Africa. In **1984**, ...u won the Nobel Peace Prize for his ...violent methods.

In **1956**, the government of Brazil began to build a new capital city, **Brasília**, in the wilderness. Planners designed the city to look like a drawn bow and arrow from the air. Builders constructed many modern buildings, such as the bowl-shaped Chamber of Deputies and the twin towers that are home to congressional offices.

MEXICO
Mexico City
Havana
Tropic of Cancer
Gulf of Mexico
Caribbean Sea
ATLANTIC OCEAN
Bogotá
0° Equator
Lima
BRAZIL
Salvador
Brasília
La Paz
Rio de Janeiro
Tropic of Capricorn
PACIFIC OCEAN
Buenos Aires
Montevideo
ARGENTINA
40°S
0   500 Miles
0   1,000 Kilometers

South America, 1956   909

HISTORY THROUGH ART

Brasília, Brazil

Brasília was completed in 1960, a city of light surrounded by barren wilderness. In building the city, President Juscelino Kubitschek fulfilled a constitutional decree that the capital be placed in the interior of the country. Designed by Brazilian architect Lúcio Costa, the city plan emphasizes efficiency, order, and simplicity. Oscar Niemeyer, architect of the UN headquarters, designed all the government buildings. The twin towers (shown in the picture above) open onto the circle of Three Powers Square. The square contains the legislative, judicial, and executive buildings. Brasília has sectors for hotels, residences, the military, government, leisure activities, conventions and education. The city boasts a population of nearly 2 million people—half of them under the age of 25.

Interpreting the Art What comparisons can you make between Brasília and Washington, D.C.? *Both are designed as seats of national government; both have separate buildings for the executive, judicial, and legislative branches; and both showcase national talent in architecture and the arts.*

This Interact with History feature motivates students by inviting them to think about the foundations of democracy. As they imagine talking with a foreign student, they will consider the factors that make democracy possible and the ways in which living in a democracy affects their lives.

Purpose

- to prepare students to study democratic processes in other countries
- to help students analyze the foundations of democracy
- to help students connect to the people and events they will study in this chapter

Teaching Strategy

Thinking Critically Have students read the page. Then have them answer the key questions and give reasons for their answers.

EXAMINING *the* ISSUES

Following are suggestions for addressing each bulleted question.

1 What rights and institutions did the framers of the U.S. Constitution consider necessary to ensure democratic rule?

2 Ask students to think about ways their parents or other people they know participate in democracy.

3 Have students consider the importance of literacy, economic security, and cultural unity in establishing a successful democracy.

Making Connections If students were drafting a constitution, what rights and guarantees would they rank first, second, and third? Have them explain their answers.

Follow Up

A feature on the chapter assessment will ask students to reevaluate their responses to the situation presented on this page.

Interact *with* History

On the news, you watch stories about protesters who demand more democratic freedom in their countries. Such demonstrations are taking place all over the world. Many times, students lead the protests. These students have learned about democracy through watching television or by attending school in the West.

At school, you meet a foreign exchange student who comes from a country that is controlled by a non-democratic government. At lunch, this student asks you to explain what democracy is and how it works. What would you say?

In Beijing, China, in 1989, students gather in a public square to call for more democracy. For example, they want freedom of speech and the press.

For inspiration, they erect a statue that looks like the Statue of Liberty.

They demand an end to corrupt, authoritarian government.

What makes democracy work?

Students in Czechoslovakia demonstrate in memory of the pro-democracy protests in China. They wear headbands that say "democracy." They also demand more non-Communist representatives in their own government.

EXAMINING *the* ISSUES

1 • What rights and institutions are necessary for a government to be democratic?

2 • How do citizens participate in a democracy? How can participation be encouraged?

3 • What obstacles can prevent a democracy from succeeding?

Discuss these questions in class and list important points on the board. For your discussion, consider what you know about democracy in ancient Greece and in the United States.

As you read this chapter, think about the challenges many countries face in trying to develop democratic systems.

910 Chapter 35

1 Democracy

PATTERNS OF CHANGE

CASE STUDY: Latin American Democracies

TERMS & NAMES
- **Brasília**
- **land reform**
- **standard of living**
- **recession**
- **PRI**

MAIN IDEA

Democracy is not easy to achieve. In Latin America, economic problems and authoritarian rule delayed democracy.

WHY IT MATTERS NOW

By the mid-1990s, almost all Latin American nations had democratic governments.

Background
Indirect democracy is also called representative democracy.

SETTING THE STAGE By definition, democracy is government by the people. Direct democracy, in which all citizens meet to pass laws, is not practical for nations. Therefore, democratic nations such as the United States developed indirect democracy, in which citizens elect representatives to make laws for them.

Making Democracy Work

Democracy is more than a form of government. It is also a way of life and an ideal goal. A democratic way of life includes practices such as free and open elections. The chart on this page lists four basic practices and ideal conditions that help those practices to succeed. Many nations follow these democratic practices to a large degree. However, none does so perfectly. Establishing democracy is a process that takes years.

Even in the United States, the establishment of democracy has taken time. Although the principle of equality is part of the Constitution, many Americans have struggled for equal rights. To cite one example, women did not receive the right to vote until 1920—132 years after the Constitution went into effect. Under the best of circumstances, democracy is always a "work in progress."

Democratic institutions may not ensure stable, civilian government if other conditions are not present. In general, the participation of a nation's citizens in government is essential to democracy. If citizens don't vote or don't contribute to public discussions of important issues, democracy suffers. Education and literacy—the ability to

PATTERNS OF CHANGE: Making Democracy Work

Common Practices	Conditions That Foster Those Practices
Free elections	• Having more than one political party • Universal suffrage — all adult citizens can vote
Citizen participation	• High levels of education and literacy • Economic security • Freedoms of speech, press, and assembly
Majority rule, minority rights	• All citizens equal before the law • Shared national identity • Protection of such individual rights as freedom of religion • Representatives elected by citizens to carry out their will
Constitutional government	• Clear body of traditions and laws on which government is based • Widespread education about how government works • National acceptance of majority decisions • Shared belief that no one is above the law

SKILLBUILDER: Interpreting Charts
1. Which of those conditions that foster democratic practices refer to political institutions?
2. Identify the conditions that increase citizen participation and explain why they would do so.

OBJECTIVES

1. To identify key building blocks of democracy.
2. To describe Brazil's efforts to build democracy.
3. To analyze the struggle for democracy in Mexico.
4. To describe key events in post-war Argentina.

SKILLBUILDER

- Interpreting charts, p. 911
- Interpreting graphs, p. 913

CRITICAL THINKING

- Making inferences, p. 912
- Analyzing motives, p. 912
- Analyzing problems, p. 913
- Recognizing effects, p. 914
- Analyzing causes, p. 915
- Comparing and contrasting, p. 915
- Analyzing themes, p. 915

FOCUS

5-Minute Warm-Up

▶ **Making Inferences**
To help students realize the economic challenges facing Brazil, have them answer the following questions.

1. Read the Daily Life feature on page 912. How did Carolina Maria de Jesus support herself and her children?

2. According to the feature, are favelas disappearing?

 WARM-UP TRANSPARENCY 35

OBJECTIVE 1 INSTRUCT

Making Democracy Work

▶ **Key Ideas**
- Stable democracies require key institutions and practices.

 IN-DEPTH RESOURCES: UNIT 8
Guided Reading, p. 37
Geography Application: Democracy in Central and South America, p. 43

ACCESS FOR STUDENTS ACQUIRING ENGLISH
Guided Reading (Spanish), p. 353

SECTION 1 RESOURCES

PRINT RESOURCES

 IN-DEPTH RESOURCES: UNIT 8
Guided Reading, p. 37
Geography Application, Democracy in Central and South America p. 43
Literature: from *Brazil,* p. 49
History Makers: Juan and Eva Perón, p. 52

ACCESS FOR STUDENTS ACQUIRING ENGLISH
Guided Reading (Spanish), p. 353
Geography Application (Spanish), p. 359

 FORMAL ASSESSMENT
Section Quiz, p. 412

 ALTERNATIVE ASSESSMENT BOOK

TECHNOLOGY RESOURCES

 WORLD ART AND CULTURES TRANSPARENCIES
AT76 *The Family*

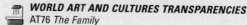 INTERNET www.mlworldhistory.com

THINK THROUGH HISTORY
A. Making Inferences Why would democracy suffer if citizens didn't participate?
A. Possible Answer If a low percentage of the citizens vote, then a minority ends up making decisions—which contradicts majority rule.

read and write—give citizens the tools they need to make political decisions. Also, a stable economy with a strong middle class and opportunities for advancement helps democracy. It does so by giving citizens a stake in the future of their nation.

Other factors advance democracy. First, a firm belief in the rights of the individual promotes the fair and equal treatment of citizens. Second, rule by law helps prevent leaders from abusing power without fear of punishment. Third, a sense of national identity—the idea that members of a society have a shared culture—helps encourage citizens to work together for the good of the nation.

The struggle to establish democracy continued in the 1990s as many nations abandoned authoritarian rule for democratic institutions. Several Latin American countries, such as Brazil, Mexico, and Argentina, were among those making democratic progress.

CASE STUDY: Brazil

From Dictators to Democracy

BRAZIL
SOUTH AMERICA

Many Latin American nations won their independence in the early 1800s. However, three centuries of colonial rule left problems. This included powerful militaries, one-crop economies, and sharp class divisions. These patterns persisted in the modern era. One reason is that Europe and the United States dominated the region economically and politically. In addition, many Latin American leaders seemed more interested in personal power than in democracy.

Like much of Latin America, Brazil struggled to establish democracy. After gaining independence from Portugal in 1822, Brazil became a monarchy. This lasted until 1889, when Brazilians established a republican government—which a wealthy elite actually controlled. Then, in the 1930s, Getulio Vargas became dictator of Brazil. Vargas suppressed political opposition. At the same time, however, he promoted economic growth and helped turn Brazil into a modern industrial nation.

Kubitschek's Ambitious Program After Vargas, three popularly elected presidents tried to steer Brazil toward democracy. Juscelino Kubitschek (zhoo·suh·LEE·nuh KOO·bih·chehk), who governed from 1956 to 1961, continued to develop Brazil's economy. Promising "fifty years of progress in five," Kubitschek encouraged foreign investment to help pay for elaborate development projects. He built a new capital city, **Brasília** (bruh·ZIHL·yuh), in the country's interior. Kubitschek's dream proved expensive. The nation's foreign debt soared and inflation shot up. This caused hardship for most Brazilians.

Kubitschek's successors proposed reforms to lessen economic and social problems. Conservatives resisted this strongly. They especially opposed the plan for **land reform**—breaking up large estates and distributing that land to peasants. In 1964, with the blessing of wealthy Brazilians, the army seized power in a military coup.

Military Dictators For two decades, military dictators ruled Brazil. Emphasizing economic growth at all costs, the generals opened the country to foreign investment. They began huge development projects in the Amazon jungle. The economy boomed, in what many described as Brazil's "economic miracle."

The boom had a downside, though. The government froze wages and cut back on social programs. This caused a decline in the **standard of living**—or quality of life, which is judged by the amount of goods people have. When Brazilians protested, the government imposed censorship. It also jailed and tortured government critics. Nevertheless, opposition to military rule continued to grow.

THINK THROUGH HISTORY
B. Analyzing Motives Why might the wealthy prefer military rule to land reform?
B. Possible Answer They feared that land reform would take away their property and believed the army would protect their property rights.

Daily *Life*

Favelas: The Slums of Brazil

"I am living in a favela (fuh·VEHL·uh). But if God helps me, I'll get out of here," wrote Carolina Maria de Jesus in her diary in the 1950s. A favela was a sprawling slum of flimsy shacks that had no electricity, sewers, or running water. Carolina struggled to provide for herself and her children.

Everything that I find in the garbage I sell. . . . I collected two sacks full of paper. Afterward I went back and gathered up some scrap metal, some cans, and some kindling wood.

In 1960, Carolina published her diary, which was a success. She earned enough money to make a down payment on a home and leave the favela. However, millions of others were not so lucky. In the 1990s, favelas still plagued the cities and had spread to the countryside.

History from Visuals

Patterns of Change: Making Democracy Work

(See page 911.)

Interpreting the Chart Make sure students understand that while the items in the second column are among the most important conditions that foster democracy, they are not the only conditions.

Extension Activity Have students work in small groups to think of other conditions for each common practice. *Examples: Free elections—secret balloting; constitutional government—bill of rights.*

SKILLBUILDER Answers
1. More than one political party, universal suffrage, individual freedoms, equality under the law, protection of rights, elected representatives, body of traditions and law
2. Education and literacy—citizens can understand issues; economic security—citizens feel part of society and country; individual freedoms—citizens can express themselves without fear of repression.

OBJECTIVE ② INSTRUCT

Brazil: From Dictators to Democracy

▶ **Key Ideas**
Brazil strives to overcome economic and political problems to create a stable democracy.

Daily *Life*

Favelas: The Slums of Brazil

Urban slums like the favelas exist in all Latin American countries. In Chile they are known as "mushrooms" while in Peru they are called "young towns." Have students read more about life in these slums.

TEACHING OPTION   BLOCK SCHEDULING

WRITING A PROTEST SONG

CLASS TIME 20 MINUTES

Task: Students will work together to write a protest song about conditions in the Brazilian favelas.

Materials Needed: Textbook, copies of one or two articles on the slums or of an excerpt from Carolina Maria de Jesus's book *Child of the Dark* (New York: Dutton, 1962), and copies of the literature selection by John Updike

Activity: Tell students that in Brazil and other Latin American countries, musicians have challenged censorship laws with their social and political protest songs. Have students read the materials, then write their own song protesting conditions in the Brazilian favelas. Tell them they can use any form—rap, hip-hop, blues, traditional ballad—for their song.

Conclusion: Ask students to think about living in a country where protest music is outlawed. Where

would they perform their song? How would they distribute it to other cities? What role would their music play in the country's political life? Have them contrast such a situation with the situation in the United States, where all types of music can be performed.

 IN-DEPTH RESOURCES: UNIT 8
Literature: from *Brazil* by John Updike, p. 49

Brazilian Economy, 1955-1990

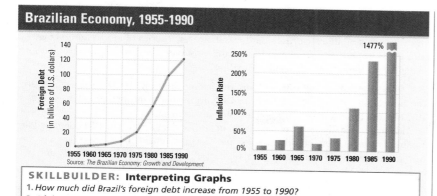

Source: *The Brazilian Economy: Growth and Development*

SKILLBUILDER: Interpreting Graphs
1. How much did Brazil's foreign debt increase from 1955 to 1990?
2. Of the years shown on the bar graph, which was the worst year for inflation?
3. Did Brazil's economy get better or worse from 1955 to 1990? Explain.

Background
Before the change to direct elections, the president was chosen by members of the congress and state legislatures.

THINK THROUGH HISTORY
C. Analyzing Problems In your opinion, what is the worst problem Sarney faced? Explain.
C. Possible Answers The foreign debt because it put Brazil under the power of other nations; inflation because no one could get ahead.

The Road to Democracy By the early 1980s, a **recession**—or slowdown in the economy—gripped Brazil. At that point, the generals decided to open up the political system. They allowed direct elections of local, state, and national officials.

In 1985, a new civilian president, José Sarney (zhoh·ZAY SAHR·nay), took office. Although he was elected indirectly, a 1985 constitutional amendment declared that all future presidents would be elected directly by the people. Sarney inherited a country in crisis:

A VOICE FROM THE PAST
I . . . became the holder of the largest foreign debt on the face of the earth, as well as the greatest internal debt. My inheritance included the deepest recession in our history, the highest rate of unemployment, an unprecedented climate of violence, potential political disintegration and the highest rate of inflation ever recorded in our country's history—250 percent a year, with the prospect of reaching 1,000 percent.
JOSÉ SARNEY, "Brazil: A President's Story"

Though well-intentioned, Sarney failed to solve the country's problems and lost support. The next elected president fared even worse. He resigned because of corruption charges. In 1994, Brazilians elected Fernando Henrique Cardoso, who achieved some success in tackling the nation's economic and political problems. Although Brazil faced many challenges, during the 1990s it continued on the path of democracy. It maintained an elected civilian government.

CASE STUDY: Mexico

One Dominant Party

Unlike Brazil, Mexico enjoyed relative political stability for most of the 20th century. Following the Mexican Revolution, the government passed the Constitution of 1917. It outlined a democracy and promised reforms. This document helped prevent direct military involvement in politics—which has been a common problem in many Latin American countries.

Beginnings of One-Party Domination From 1920 to 1934, Mexico elected several generals as president. However, these men did not rule as military dictators. They did create a ruling party—the National Revolutionary Party, which has dominated Mexico under various names ever since.

From 1934 to 1940, President Lázaro Cárdenas (KAHR·day·nahs) tried to improve life for peasants and workers. He carried out land reform and promoted labor rights.

SPOTLIGHT ON

Liberation Theology
At a 1968 conference, Roman Catholic leaders of Latin America—including several prominent Brazilians—started a movement known as liberation theology. These leaders taught that the Church must become a church of the poor. It must work to ease poverty by becoming involved in political affairs and crying out against injustice.

One of the most outspoken advocates of liberation theology was Archbishop Oscar Romero of El Salvador, shown below. In 1980, a right-wing assassin murdered the Archbishop for speaking out against government oppression of poor Salvadorans.

PATTERNS OF CHANGE 913

He nationalized the Mexican oil industry, kicking out foreign oil companies and creating a state-run oil industry. After Cárdenas, however, a series of more conservative presidents turned away from reform. For the most part, they worked to develop the economy for the benefit of wealthy Mexicans.

The Party Becomes the PRI In 1946, the main political party changed its name to the Institutional Revolutionary Party, or **PRI.** In the half-century that followed, the PRI became the main force for political stability in Mexico.

Although stable, the government was an imperfect democracy. The PRI controlled the congress and won every presidential election. The government allowed opposition parties to compete, but fraud and corruption spoiled elections and blocked opposition gains.

Even as the Mexican economy rapidly developed, Mexico continued to suffer severe economic problems. Lacking land and jobs, millions of Mexicans struggled for survival. In addition, a huge foreign debt forced the government to spend money on interest payments instead of helping the Mexican people. Two episodes highlighted Mexico's growing difficulties. In the late 1960s, students and workers began calling for economic and political change. On October 2, 1968, protesters gathered at the site of an ancient Aztec market in Mexico City. A reporter recalled what happened next:

A VOICE FROM THE PAST
Suddenly one helicopter flew low over the crowd and dropped a flare. Immediately hundreds of soldiers hidden among the Aztec ruins of the square opened fire with automatic weapons. . . . Students who fled . . . were chased and beaten and some were murdered. . . . That night, army vehicles carried away the bodies, while firetrucks washed away the blood.
ALAN RIDING, *Distant Neighbors*

The massacre in the Aztec ruins claimed several hundred lives.

A second critical episode occurred during the early 1980s. By that time huge new oil and natural gas reserves had been discovered in Mexico. The economy had become dependent on oil and gas exports. In 1981, however, world oil prices fell sharply, cutting Mexico's oil and gas revenues in half. Mexico went into an economic decline.

Economic and Political Crises The rest of the 1980s and 1990s saw Mexico facing various crises. In 1988, opposition parties seriously challenged the PRI in national elections. The PRI candidate, Carlos Salinas de Gortari, won the presidency—some argued by fraud. Even so, opposition parties won seats in congress and began to force a gradual opening of the political system.

During his presidency, Salinas signed NAFTA, the North American Free Trade Agreement. NAFTA removed trade barriers between Mexico, the United States, and Canada. In early 1994, just as the agreement was going into effect, peasant rebels in the southern Mexican state of Chiapas (chee·AH·pahs) staged a major uprising. Shortly afterward, a gunman assassinated the PRI presidential candidate.

The PRI Loses Control After these events, Mexicans felt more concerned than ever about the prospects for democratic stability. Nevertheless, the elections of 1994 went ahead as planned. The new PRI candidate, Ernesto Zedillo (zuh·DEE·yoh), won in what appeared to be a fair ballot. At the same time, opposition parties continued to challenge the PRI.

In 1997, two opposition parties each won a large number of congressional seats—denying the PRI control of congress for the first time in its history. At last, Mexico seemed to be on its way to multi-party, democratic rule.

SPOTLIGHT ON
Chiapas Revolt

In January 1994, a rebel army burst out of the jungle and seized several towns in the state of Chiapas. The rebels, one of whom is shown above, called themselves Zapatistas—after the revolutionary hero Emiliano Zapata. Demanding greater democracy, the Zapatistas especially wanted to improve life for Maya Indians, who were among the poorest Mexicans. The Zapatistas demanded better housing, health clinics, and schools.

Although the revolt had little chance of military success, the Mexican president appointed a peace negotiator to discuss the rebels' demands. Negotiations continued for months. Mexico's move toward multi-party rule in 1997 might perhaps provide a way for groups like the Zapatistas to influence the government legally.

Argentina Casts Off Repression

SOUTH AMERICA

ARGENTINA

Mexico and Brazil were not the only Latin American countries where democracy had made progress. By the late 1990s, all of Latin America—except Cuba—was under democratic rule. One notable example of democratic progress was Argentina.

Perón Rules Argentina The second largest country in South America, Argentina had struggled to establish democracy. Argentina was a major exporter of grain and beef. It was also an industrial nation with a large working class. In 1946, Argentine workers supported an army officer, Juan Perón, who won the presidency and then established a dictatorship.

Perón did not rule alone. He received critical support from his wife, Eva—known as "Evita" to the millions of Argentines who idolized her. Together, the Peróns created a welfare state. The state offered social programs with broad popular appeal but limited freedoms. After Eva's death in 1952, Perón's popularity declined and his enemies—the military and the Catholic Church—moved against him. In 1955, the military ousted Perón and drove him into exile.

Repression in Argentina For the next three decades, the military essentially controlled Argentine politics. Perón returned to power once more, in 1973, but ruled for only a year before dying in office. By the mid-1970s, Argentina was in chaos. The economy was in ruins and radical terrorism was on the rise.

In 1976, the generals seized power again. They established a brutal dictatorship and hunted down political opponents. For several years, torture and murder were everyday events. By the early 1980s, several thousand Argentines had simply disappeared— kidnapped by their own government. The government killed at least 10,000 people. Critics charged that some of the victims were pushed out of airplanes over the ocean.

Moving Toward Democracy In 1982, the military government went to war with Britain over the nearby Falkland Islands and suffered a humiliating defeat. Thoroughly disgraced, the generals agreed to step down. In 1983, Argentines elected Raúl Alfonsín (ahl·fohn·SEEN) president in the country's first truly free election in 40 years.

During the 1980s, Alfonsín worked to rebuild democracy and the economy. The next president continued that process. By the late 1990s, democracy seemed established in Argentina, though economic problems continued. In Section 2 you will read how ethnic and racial conflicts slowed democratic progress in parts of Africa.

Vocabulary
welfare state: a government that tries to provide for all its citizens' needs—such as health, education, and employment.

THINK THROUGH HISTORY
E. Analyzing Causes
What finally caused military rule to end in Argentina?
E. Answer The military government lost a humiliating war and had to turn the government over to civilians.

In 1950, President Juan Perón and his wife Eva greet a crowd of hundreds of thousands. The Peróns are standing on the balcony of the government house.

Section 1 Assessment

1. TERMS & NAMES

Identify
- Brasília
- land reform
- standard of living
- recession
- PRI

2. TAKING NOTES

On a chart like the one below, record the steps that Brazil, Mexico, and Argentina have taken toward establishing democracy.

Nation	Steps toward democracy
Brazil	
Mexico	
Argentina	

3. COMPARING AND CONTRASTING

Compare and contrast the roles of the military in the governments of Brazil, Mexico, and Argentina.

THINK ABOUT
- their relationship to civilian governments
- whether they hindered or advanced democracy

4. ANALYZING THEMES

Economics How does the state of a nation's economy affect its democratic progress?

THINK ABOUT
- how economic conditions affect citizens' support for the government
- how economic conditions affect the government's ability to provide for its citizens

PATTERNS OF CHANGE 915

OBJECTIVE 4 INSTRUCT

Argentina Casts Off Repression

Key Ideas
- Juan Perón creates a welfare state with limited freedoms.
- The military takes over and establishes a brutal dictatorship.
- After the generals step down, Argentina moves toward a true democracy.

ASSESS & RETEACH

Section 1 Assessment
Have students work in pairs to answer the questions and then share their answers with other pairs of students.

Section Quiz
FORMAL ASSESSMENT
Section Quiz, p. 412

Reteaching Activity
CLASS TIME: 15 MINUTES

Have students review the section by writing at least three statements about each country's quest for democracy.

CLOSE ACTIVITY

CLASS TIME: 20 MINUTES

Creating a Time Line
Have students work in small groups to create time lines of events in Brazil, Mexico, and Argentina in the postwar period. Students should use information from the section and note instances in which similar events occurred in more than one country. Discuss with them the similarities and differences among the three countries.

Teacher's Edition 915

To explain the legacy of colonialism in Africa.

 To show how ethnic divisions in Nigeria led to war.

 To describe events in Nigeria since 1970.

 To explain the history of white rule in South Africa.

 To describe South Africa's shift toward democracy.

SKILLBUILDER
• Interpreting maps: region, location, p. 917

CRITICAL THINKING
• Recognizing effects, pp. 916, 918
• Clarifying, p. 918
• Making inferences, p. 919
• Analyzing causes, p. 919
• Drawing conclusions, p. 920
• Identifying problems, p. 920

FOCUS
5-Minute Warm-Up

▶ **Interpreting Maps**
Answering the following questions will help students understand the divisions in Nigeria.

1. Study the map on page 917. Into how many regions is Nigeria divided?

2. What Nigerian cities provide access to the Atlantic Ocean?

 WARM-UP TRANSPARENCY 35

OBJECTIVE ① INSTRUCT

Colonial Rule Hampers Democracy

▶ **Key Ideas**
• Colonial rule fails to prepare Africans for democracy.

• African countries face ethnic divisions, weak economies, and political corruption.

 IN-DEPTH RESOURCES: UNIT 8
Guided Reading, p. 38

 ACCESS FOR STUDENTS ACQUIRING ENGLISH
Guided Reading (Spanish), p. 354

---

② # Democratic Challenges in African Nations

TERMS & NAMES
• federal system
• martial law
• dissident
• apartheid
• Nelson Mandela

MAIN IDEA
As the recent histories of Nigeria and South Africa show, ethnic and racial conflicts can hinder democracy.

WHY IT MATTERS NOW
As Nigeria struggled with democracy, in 1996 South Africa adopted a bill of rights that promotes racial equality.

SETTING THE STAGE Beginning in the late 1950s, dozens of European colonies in Africa gained their independence and became nations. As in Latin America, the establishment of democracy in Africa proved difficult. In many cases, the newly independent nations faced a host of problems that slowed their progress toward democracy.

Colonial Rule Hampers Democracy

The main reason for Africa's difficulties was the negative impact of colonial rule. European powers did little to prepare their African colonies for independence. In fact, the lingering effects of colonialism undermined efforts to build stable, democratic states.

European Policies Cause Problems When the Europeans established colonial boundaries, they ignored ethnic or cultural divisions. Borders often divided peoples of the same background or threw different—often rival—groups together. Because of this, a sense of national identity was almost impossible to develop. After independence, the old colonial boundaries became the borders of the newly independent states. As a result, ethnic and cultural conflicts remained, and even increased.

Other problems had an economic basis. European powers had viewed colonies as sources of wealth for the home country. They had no desire to develop the colonies for the benefit of the Africans who lived there. The colonial powers encouraged the export of one or two cash crops—such as coffee or rubber—rather than the production of a range of products to serve local needs. Europeans developed plantations and mines but few factories. Manufactured goods were imported from European countries. They also built few roads, bridges, or communications systems—all necessary for economic development. These policies left new African nations with unbalanced economies and a small middle class. Such economic problems lessened their chances to create democratic society.

European rule also disrupted African family and community life. In some cases, colonial powers moved Africans far from their families and villages to work in mines or on plantations. In addition, colonial governments did little to educate the majority of African people. As a result, most newly independent nations lacked a skilled, literate work force that could take on the task of building a new nation.

This photo shows the 1957 ceremony marking Ghana's independence from Britain. At the ceremony were Britain's Duchess of Kent and Ghana's new President Kwame Nkrumah.

Short-Lived Democracies When Britain and France gave up their colonies, they left new democratic governments in place. Soon problems threatened those governments. Rival ethnic groups often fought each other for power. Strong militaries, left over from colonial rule, became a tool for ambitious leaders. In many cases, a military dictatorship quickly replaced democracy. Since independence, the struggle between democracy and authoritarian rule has torn apart many African nations.

THINK THROUGH HISTORY
A. Recognizing Effects What were the main negative effects of the economic policies of European colonizers?
A. Answer The economy was dependent on one or two products, goods had to be imported to meet local needs, and no structures were built to support industry.

Background
Many colonies had strong militaries because the colonizers created them to control the local people.

SECTION 2 RESOURCES

PRINT RESOURCES

 IN-DEPTH RESOURCES: UNIT 8
Guided Reading, p. 38
Primary Sources: from *Kaffir Boy*, p. 45; Mandela's Inaugural Address, p. 46
History Makers: Nelson Mandela, p. 53

 ACCESS FOR STUDENTS ACQUIRING ENGLISH
Guided Reading (Spanish), p. 354

 FORMAL ASSESSMENT
Section Quiz, p. 413

TECHNOLOGY RESOURCES

 WORLD ART AND CULTURES TRANSPARENCIES
AT77 Multiple-Mask Headdress

 CD-ROM
Electronic Library of Primary Sources

 VIDEO *Patterns of Interaction: Struggling Toward Democracy*

 INTERNET www.mlworldhistory.com

Nigeria Erupts in Civil War

Nigeria provides a good example of the political struggles that have shaken Africa. Nigeria, a former British colony, won its independence peacefully in 1960. Nigeria is Africa's most populous country and one of its richest. Because of that, Nigeria seemed to have good prospects for democratic stability. The country was ethnically divided, however. This soon created problems that led to war.

A Land of Many Peoples Three major ethnic groups and many smaller ones live within Nigeria's borders. In the north are the Hausa-Fulani, who are Muslim. In the south are the Yoruba and the Igbo (also called Ibo), who are mostly either Christians or animists. The Yoruba, a farming people with a tradition of kings, live to the west. The Igbo, a farming people who have a democratic tradition, live to the east.

After independence, Nigeria adopted a **federal system.** In a federal system, power is shared between state governments and a central authority, much like in the United States. The Nigerians set up three states, one for each region and ethnic group, with a corresponding political party in each.

War with Biafra Although one group dominated each state, the states also had other ethnic minorities. In the Western Region—the Yoruba homeland—non-Yoruba minorities began to resent Yoruba control. In 1963, they tried to break away and form their own region. This led to fighting. In January 1966, a group of army officers, most of them Igbo, seized power in the capital city of Lagos. These officers abolished the regional governments and declared **martial law,** or temporary military rule.

The Hausa-Fulani, who had long distrusted the Igbo, launched an attack from the north. They persecuted and killed many Igbo. The survivors fled east to their homeland. In 1967, the Eastern Region seceded from Nigeria, declaring itself the new nation of Biafra (bee·AF·ruh).

Background
In 1995, Nigeria's estimated population was about 95 million. More than 250 ethnic groups live in the country.

During the civil war in Nigeria, Biafra was so desperate for troops that it enlisted boys younger than 18 in its army.

Africa, 1967

Regions of Nigeria, 1967

- Eastern Region
- Midwestern Region
- Western Region
- Northern Region

GEOGRAPHY SKILLBUILDER: Interpreting Maps
1. **Region** Describe the Eastern Region, which seceded as Biafra. Describe its size and location compared to the rest of Nigeria.
2. **Location** In which region is Nigeria's capital city of Lagos?

Struggles for Democracy **917**

OBJECTIVE 2 INSTRUCT

Nigeria Erupts in Civil War

▶ **Key Ideas**
- Nigerians gain independence and have high hopes for democracy.
- The country's ethnic mix soon creates conflict.
- Biafra secedes and war breaks out across Nigeria.

CRITICAL THINKING ACTIVITY
CLASS TIME: 15 MINUTES

Making a Summary Chart
Have students summarize the situation in Nigeria in the 1960s by filling out the following chart.

	Nigeria in the 1960s
Strengths:	
Weaknesses:	
Results:	

History from Visuals

Africa, 1967

Interpreting the Map Have students look at the map and identify Nigeria and its major cities. Point out the inset map and help students understand how it relates to the larger map.

Extension Activity Have students compare this map with the ones in the Atlas, on pages 974 and 975. How does Nigeria's geography and size make it one of the more important nations in Africa? *It is one of the larger countries and has access to the sea.*

SKILLBUILDER Answers
1. Biafra is in the southeastern part of Nigeria and is much smaller than the rest of the country, though comparable in size to the Western Region.
2. Lagos is in the Western Region.

TEACHING OPTIONS

CUSTOMIZING FOR SPECIAL NEEDS

Less Proficient Readers:
Guided Reading Procedure
This procedure helps students recall information, generate their own questions, organize information, and self-correct their reading.

Step 1: Prepare students for the reading assignment. Discuss the material under "Nigeria Erupts in Civil War" to motivate students to read. **Step 2:** Have students read the selection. **Step 3:** Ask students to recall information without looking at the text. **Step 4:** Tell them to read for more facts. **Step 5:** Help students organize the material, using charts, webs, or lists. **Step 6:** Test students to see how much knowledge they have retained.

CONNECTIONS ACROSS TIME AND PLACE

Nigeria Yesterday and Today
Have students create a collage out of images of Nigeria in the 1960s and 1970s and another collage out of images of Nigeria today. The images should illustrate the following: economic conditions in the country, relations among ethnic groups, movement toward democracy, efforts in public health and education, and relations with other nations, particularly Great Britain and other African nations.

Tell students they can find information in magazines, newspapers, and books and on the Internet. Nigeria's struggles have been well documented since the 1960s.

Nigeria's Struggle for Democracy

Key Ideas
- The military governs Nigeria after the war, developing an oil-based economy.
- Democracy returns briefly to Nigeria, but the military again takes over.
- Under military rule, political rights are severely limited.

SPOTLIGHT ON
Silencing Dissidents

Have students use periodicals or the Internet to research the case of Ken Saro-Wiwa and other jailed activists in Nigeria. What were the issues in the case, and what were Saro-Wiwa's objectives as a protester?

South Africa Under White Rule

Key Ideas
- South Africa's rulers create a segregated society.
- After independence, South Africa's white rulers impose apartheid, an even more rigid system of segregation.
- Black South African protests lead to violence and a state of emergency.

 IN-DEPTH RESOURCES: UNIT 8
Primary Source: from *Kaffir Boy*, p. 45

The Nigerian government then went to war to reunite the country. The Nigerian civil war lasted three years. The Igbo fought heroically but were badly outnumbered and outgunned. In 1970, Biafra surrendered. Nigeria was reunited, but the war took a tremendous toll. Although exact numbers are unknown, perhaps several million Igbo died, most from starvation.

Nigeria's Struggle for Democracy

After the war, Nigerians returned to the process of nation-building. "When the war ended," noted one officer, "it was like a referee blowing a whistle in a football game. People just put down their guns and went back to the business of living." The Nigerian government did not punish the Igbo. It used federal money to rebuild the Igbo region.

Federal Government Restored The military governed Nigeria for most of the 1970s. During this time, Nigerian leaders tried to create a more stable federal system, with a strong central government and 19 regional units. The government also tried to build a more modern economy, based on oil income. Nigeria became the world's seventh largest oil producer. For a time, it grew wealthy from oil money.

In 1979, the military handed power back to civilian rulers. Nigerians were cheered by the return to democracy. Some people, like businessman Godfrey Amachree, however, remained concerned about ethnic divisions in the nation:

SPOTLIGHT ON

Silencing Dissidents
On November 10, 1995, Nigeria hanged nine political prisoners—all critics of the military government. Many around the world believed the nine were convicted on false charges just to silence them.

One of the nine was Ken Saro-Wiwa, a noted writer and activist. Saro-Wiwa had protested oil drilling in his native province. He charged oil companies and the government with destroying the environment.

Although Saro-Wiwa died, his protest lived on. Shortly before his death, Saro-Wiwa smuggled several manuscripts out of prison. In one, he wrote:

Injustice stalks the land like a tiger on the prowl. To be at the mercy of buffoons [fools] is the ultimate insult. To find the instruments of state power reducing you to dust is the injury.

A VOICE FROM THE PAST
We've got such great potential in this country if we can truly pull together as one people, one nation. But there are these deep divisions that have torn us apart before. I can only hope we've learned our lesson. Have we? I don't know. I'd only be guessing. It all depends on whether we're ready to start thinking in terms of nation instead of tribe.
GODFREY AMACHREE, from *The Africans* by David Lamb

Nigerian democracy was short-lived. In 1983, the military overthrew the civilian government, charging it with corruption. A new military regime, dominated by the Hausa-Fulani, took charge. It carried out a policy of discrimination against other ethnic groups.

Continued Military Rule Since then, the military has continued to govern Nigeria, while promising to bring back civilian rule. The army held elections in 1993, which resulted in the victory of popular leader Moshood Abiola. However, officers declared the results not valid and handed power to a new dictator, General Sani Abacha.

General Abacha banned political activity and jailed Abiola and numerous other **dissidents,** or opponents of government policy. Although Nigeria's military rulers vowed to move Nigeria gradually toward democracy, they continued to cling to power. Clearly, Nigeria had a long way to go before it became truly democratic.

South Africa Under White Rule

In South Africa, racial conflict was the result of colonial rule. From its beginnings under Dutch and British control, South Africa was racially divided. A small white minority ruled a large black majority. In 1910, South Africa gained self-rule as a dominion of the British Empire. In 1931 it became an independent member of the British Commonwealth. Although South Africa had a constitutional government, the constitution gave whites power and denied the black majority its rights.

Apartheid Segregates Society In 1948, the National Party came to power in South Africa. This party promoted Afrikaner, or Dutch South African, nationalism. It also

THINK THROUGH HISTORY
B. Recognizing Effects What was the effect of the war on the Igbo?
B. Answers They were forced to rejoin Nigeria; millions died.

THINK THROUGH HISTORY
C. Clarifying Review the chart on page 911. Which element of a democratic way of life was Godfrey Amachree discussing?
C. Answer The need for national identity.

Background
South Africa's population is 75.2 percent black, 13.6 percent white, 8.6 percent mixed race, and 2.6 percent Asian.

Civil Rights Struggles Point out that South Africa and the United States have both experienced civil rights struggles. Ask students to construct a chart to compare and contrast the civil rights struggles of the two countries in the following areas: time frames of the civil rights movements, major racial policies established by white rulers, key civil rights organizations and leaders, a few of the key protest events (sit-ins, demonstrations, killings, and so on), important civil rights legislation passed or racial policies eliminated, and current situations in each country.

Geography Have students create a cultural and political map of South Africa as it is today. The map should include the names of ethnic groups, the 11 languages they speak, and where they reside. Students can use a different color to represent each ethnic group, constructing a key to explain the colors.

Ask students to include a 3 × 5 card for each group, giving a brief description of the geography of the area in which the group lives (for example, "semiarid, poor soil, few wild animals"). Display the finished map in class, and have students discuss the difficulties of governing such a diverse population.

instituted a policy of **apartheid,** a complete separation of the races. The minority government banned social contacts between whites and blacks. It established segregated schools, hospitals, and neighborhoods. It provided the best facilities for whites.

In 1959, the minority government set up reserves, called homelands, for the country's major black groups. Blacks were forbidden to live in white areas unless they worked as servants or laborers for whites. The homelands policy was totally unbalanced. Although blacks made up 75 percent of the population, the government set aside only 13 percent of the land for them. Whites kept the best lands.

Blacks Protest Black South Africans resisted the controls imposed by the white minority. In 1912, they formed the African National Congress (ANC) to fight for their rights. The ANC organized strikes and boycotts to protest racist policies. During one demonstration in 1960, police killed 69 people—an incident known as the Sharpeville Massacre. Afterward, the government banned the ANC and imprisoned many of its members. One was ANC leader **Nelson Mandela** (man·DEHL·uh).

The troubles continued. In 1976, riots over school policies broke out in the black township of Soweto, leaving 600 students dead. In 1977, police beat popular protest leader Steve Biko to death while he was in custody. This sparked an international outcry. As protests mounted, the government declared a state of emergency in 1986.

South Africa Moves Toward Democracy

By the late 1980s, South Africa was under enormous pressure to change. For years, a black South African bishop, Desmond Tutu, had led an economic campaign against apartheid. He asked foreign nations not to do business with South Africa. In response, many nations of the world imposed trade restrictions. They also isolated South Africa in other ways. For example, since the 1960s, South Africa had not been allowed to take part in the Olympic Games.

The First Steps In 1989, white South Africans elected a new president, F. W. de Klerk. His goal was to transform South Africa and end its isolation. In February 1990, he legalized the ANC and also released Nelson Mandela from prison.

These dramatic actions marked the beginning of a new era in South Africa. Over the next 18 months, the South African Parliament repealed apartheid laws that had segregated public facilities and restricted land ownership by blacks. World leaders welcomed these changes and began to ease restrictions on South Africa.

Although some legal barriers had fallen, others would remain until a new constitution was in place. First, the country needed to form a multiracial government. After lengthy negotiations, President de Klerk agreed to hold South Africa's first universal elections, in which people of all races could vote, in April 1994.

Majority Rule Among the candidates for president were F. W. de Klerk and Nelson Mandela. During the campaign, the Inkatha Freedom Party—a rival party

GlobalImpact

International Boycott

South Africa's racial policies and violent actions made it an outcast among nations. In 1974, the United Nations forbade South Africa's delegates to attend UN sessions. In 1976, the UN urged its members to stop trading with South Africa and competing against its athletes.

One year later, the UN banned all military sales to the country. In the mid-1980s, many countries imposed trade restrictions on South Africa. For example, in 1985 the U.S. government banned the importing of Krugerrand gold coins, which had been a popular investment item. Eventually, international pressure helped convince South Africa's government that it must end apartheid.

South Africa adopted this flag in 1994.

South Africa 1948–1998

1948	1958		1968		1978		1988		1998
1948 National Party in power; passed apartheid laws	**1959** Black homelands established	**1960** Sharpeville Massacre, 69 protesters killed	**1962** Nelson Mandela jailed	**1976** 600 black students killed during Soweto protest	**1977** Steven Biko killed in police custody	**1989** F.W. de Klerk elected president	**1990** ANC legalized and Mandela released	**1994** ANC won 62.7% of the vote; Mandela elected president	**1996** New constitution adopted

919

OBJECTIVE ⑤ INSTRUCT

South Africa Moves Toward Democracy

▶ **Key Ideas**
• Many nations impose sanctions on South Africa because of its racial policies.
• President F. W. de Klerk moves the country away from apartheid.
• Nelson Mandela wins all-race elections and establishes a democratic, multiracial government.

GlobalImpact
International Boycott

Boycotts have been used against countries before, but rarely with the success of the one against South Africa. Ask students whether they think boycotts are useful tools for imposing international standards of conduct. Why or why not? What other boycotts can they recall from the text or from their own outside research? What made the boycotts succeed or fail?

MORE ABOUT . . .
Nelson Mandela

The *Struggling Toward Democracy* video traces the history of the antiapartheid movement and describes how Nelson Mandela went from prisoner to president. Students might also enjoy reading the biography excerpt for this section.

PATTERNS OF INTERACTION
Struggling Toward Democracy: Revolutions in Latin America and South Africa
Videocassette: Tape 3

IN-DEPTH RESOURCES: UNIT 8
History Makers: Nelson Mandela, p. 53

TEACHING OPTION | **BLOCK SCHEDULING** | **COOPERATIVE ACTIVITY: Comparing Mandela and de Klerk** | **CLASS TIME 15 MINUTES**

Task: Students will write a report comparing Nelson Mandela and F. W. de Klerk.

Purpose: To learn more about the leaders who changed South Africa's history.

Activity: Divide the class into two groups, one researching the life of Nelson Mandela and the other the life of F. W. de Klerk. Then have both groups collaborate to write and present a brief report comparing the two leaders on the following:

motivation for seeking change, personal strengths and characteristics as a leader, position each man held in his community, risks and obstacles overcome, and final results of each one's efforts.

📁 **Building a Portfolio:** Invite students to include their report in their portfolio, along with a description of their role in its preparation.

📋 **ALTERNATIVE ASSESSMENT BOOK**
Standards for Evaluating a Cooperative Activity

Standards for Evaluation
Reports should . . .
• compare the characteristics of the two leaders
• discuss each leader's motivations
• describe the risks and obstacles each overcame
• describe the end results of their efforts

Teacher's Edition **919**

Nelson Mandela and F. W. de Klerk

Both Mandela and de Klerk were called traitors by some members of their own parties. Some whites believed that black rule would destroy South Africa, while some members of the ANC wanted to rid South Africa of all whites. Moderate voices won out, and both races are working together to help the nation.

 IN-DEPTH RESOURCES: UNIT 8
Primary Source: Mandela's Inaugural Address, p. 46

 ELECTRONIC LIBRARY OF PRIMARY SOURCES
from "Masakhane—Let Us Build Together"

ASSESS & RETEACH

Section 2 Assessment
Have students answer the questions and then discuss their answers to items 3 and 4 in class.

Section Quiz
 FORMAL ASSESSMENT
Section Quiz, p. 413

Reteaching Activity
CLASS TIME: 20 MINUTES

Have students make a time line (similar to the one on page 919) showing important events in Nigeria's struggle for democracy. Discuss with students why Nigeria has had a difficult time achieving self-government.

CLOSE ACTIVITY

CLASS TIME: 20 MINUTES

Comparing
Have students make a Venn diagram to compare the struggles for democracy in Nigeria and South Africa. Students should think of ways in which the experiences of the two countries are similar and different, then write these items in the appropriate parts of the diagram.

HISTORY MAKERS

Nelson Mandela
1918–

Nelson Mandela has said that he first grew interested in politics when he heard elders in his village describe how freely his people lived before whites came. Inspired to help his people regain that freedom, Mandela trained as a lawyer and became a top official in the ANC. Convinced that apartheid would never end peacefully, he joined the armed struggle against white rule. For this, he was imprisoned for 27 years.

After his presidential victory, Mandela looked to the future,

We must . . . build a better life for all South Africans. This means creating jobs, building houses, providing education, and bringing peace and security for all.

As president, he continued to work to heal his country.

F.W. de Klerk
1936–

Like Mandela, Frederik W. de Klerk also trained as a lawyer. Born to an Afrikaner family with close links to the National Party, de Klerk was elected to Parliament in 1972.

A firm party loyalist, de Klerk backed apartheid but was also open to reform. Friends say that his flexibility on racial issues stemmed from his relatively liberal religious background. De Klerk explained his willingness to negotiate with black leaders by saying, "Dialogue is God's style."

In 1993, de Klerk and Mandela were jointly awarded the Nobel Peace Prize for their efforts to bring democracy to South Africa. The next year, de Klerk ran for president against Mandela. Coming in second, de Klerk became vice president. The photograph above shows them after one of their campaign debates.

to the ANC—threatened to disrupt the process. Nevertheless, the vote went smoothly. South Africans of all races peacefully waited at the polls in lines that sometimes stretched for up to a kilometer, which is .62 mile. (See pages 848–849.) To no one's surprise, the ANC won 62.7 percent of the vote. They won 252 of 400 seats in the National Assembly (the larger of the two houses in Parliament). Mandela was elected president. In his inaugural address, he looked to the future: "We must therefore act together as a united people, for national reconciliation. . . . Let there be justice for all. Let there be peace for all."

A New Constitution In 1996, after much debate, South African lawmakers passed a new, more democratic constitution. It guaranteed equal rights for all citizens. The constitution included a bill of rights modeled on the U.S. Bill of Rights, but with important differences. The South African document expressly forbids discrimination and protects the rights of minorities and children. It also guarantees the right to travel freely—a right denied blacks in the past. It proclaims social and economic rights, including the right to adequate housing, education, and health care.

As they passed the constitution, South African leaders realized that these sweeping promises would be difficult to fulfill. Many South African blacks wanted instant results. Even so, the political changes that South Africa had achieved gave other peoples around the world great hope for the future of democracy. In Section 3, you will read how democratic ideas changed the Communist Soviet Union.

THINK THROUGH HISTORY
F. Drawing Conclusions How did the memory of apartheid influence the writing of the new bill of rights?
F. Possible Answer The bill of rights guarantees freedoms and rights denied to blacks under apartheid.

Section 2 Assessment

1. TERMS & NAMES
Identify
• federal system
• martial law
• dissident
• apartheid
• Nelson Mandela

2. TAKING NOTES
Compare political events in Nigeria and South Africa using a Venn diagram like the one below.

Nigeria
Both
South Africa

Which is more democratic?

3. IDENTIFYING PROBLEMS
What do you think is the main problem that Nigeria must overcome before it can establish a democratic government?

THINK ABOUT
• the problems that led to the civil war
• the actions of the current military government

4. THEME ACTIVITY
Revolution Working in small teams, write biographies of South African leaders who were instrumental in the revolutionary overturn of apartheid. Include pictures if possible. Use these biographies to create or expand a revolutionaries' "Wall of Fame."

ANSWERS

1. TERMS & NAMES
federal system, p. 917
martial law, p. 917
dissident, p. 918
apartheid, p. 919
Nelson Mandela, p. 919

2. TAKING NOTES
Possible Responses:
Nigeria—civil war when Biafra seceded, reunification of country, continued military rule. Both—former British colonies, conflict among ethnic or racial groups, jailed (and killed) political dissidents. South Africa—passage of apartheid, international protest and boycott, first universal elections, majority rule, first black president, new constitution and bill of rights. South Africa is more democratic.

3. IDENTIFYING PROBLEMS
Possible Responses: The different ethnic groups must learn to accept one another, to prevent future conflicts. The military must give up power and allow civilians to rule.

4. THEME ACTIVITY
Standards for Evaluation
Biographies should meet the following criteria:
• Describe important events in person's life.
• Explain how the person helped overturn apartheid.

3 Gorbachev Moves Toward Democracy

TERMS & NAMES
- Politburo
- Mikhail Gorbachev
- glasnost
- perestroika
- Solidarity
- Lech Walesa
- reunification

MAIN IDEA

Soviet leader Mikhail Gorbachev promoted democratic reforms, which inspired many Eastern Europeans.

WHY IT MATTERS NOW

In the 1990s, most Eastern European nations overthrew communist governments. Germany reunified.

SETTING THE STAGE After World War II, the Soviet Union and the United States engaged in a Cold War. Each tried to increase its worldwide influence. The Soviet Union extended its power over much of Eastern Europe. By the 1960s, it appeared that communism was permanently established in the region.

Gorbachev's Reforms

During the 1960s and 1970s, the Soviet Union's Communist leadership kept tight control over the Soviet people. Leonid Brezhnev and the **Politburo**—the ruling committee of the Communist Party—crushed all political disagreement. Censors decided what writers could publish. The Communist Party restricted such basic rights as freedom of speech and worship.

After Brezhnev's death in 1982, the aging leadership of the Soviet Union tried to hold on to power. Time was against them, however. Each of Brezhnev's two successors died after only about a year in office. Who would succeed them?

A Younger Leader To answer that question, the Politburo debated between two men. One was a conservative named Victor Grishin. The other was **Mikhail Gorbachev** (mih·KYL gawr·buh·CHAWF). Gorbachev's supporters praised his youth, energy, and political skills. With their backing, Gorbachev became the party's new general secretary. In choosing him, Politburo members signalled their support for mild reform in the Soviet Union. They did not realize they were unleashing a second Russian Revolution.

The Soviet people welcomed Gorbachev's election. At 54, he was the youngest Soviet leader since Stalin. Gorbachev was only a child during Stalin's ruthless purge of independent-minded party members. Unlike other Soviet leaders, Gorbachev had not needed to blindly follow Stalin's policies. He could pursue new ideas.

Glasnost Promotes Openness Past Soviet leaders had created a totalitarian state. It rewarded silence and discouraged individuals from acting on their own. As a result, Soviet society rarely changed. Gorbachev realized that economic and social reforms could not occur without a free flow of ideas and information. In 1985, he announced a policy known as **glasnost** (GLAHS·nuhst), or openness. He encouraged Soviet citizens to discuss ways to improve their society.

Glasnost brought remarkable changes. The government allowed churches to open. It released dissidents from prison and allowed the publication of books by previously banned authors. Reporters actively investigated social problems and openly criticized government officials.

Background
Like Nigeria, the Soviet Union jailed dissidents. Aleksandr Solzhenitsyn, a dissident writer who wrote about the Soviet prison system, lived in exile from 1974 to 1994.

THINK THROUGH HISTORY
A. Making Inferences How might Gorbachev's young age have made him more open to reform?
A. Possible Answer Because he had not had to conform to Stalin's policies as older leaders had.

HISTORY MAKERS

Mikhail Gorbachev
1931–

Mikhail Gorbachev's background shaped the role he would play in history. Both of his grandfathers were arrested during Stalin's purges. Both were eventually freed. However, one died at an early age, perhaps because of the torture he had suffered. Gorbachev never forgot his grandfathers' stories.

After working on a state farm, Gorbachev studied law in Moscow and joined the Communist Party. As an official in a farming region, Gorbachev learned much about the Soviet system and its problems.

He advanced quickly in the party. When he became general secretary in 1985, he was the youngest Politburo member and a man who wanted to bring change. He succeeded. Although he pursued reform to save the Soviet Union, ultimately he triggered its breakup.

Struggles for Democracy **921**

Section 3 Overview

OBJECTIVES

1. To list Soviet reforms under Mikhail Gorbachev.
2. To explain reforms in Poland and Hungary.
3. To summarize changes in East Germany.
4. To describe democratic change in Czechoslovakia and Romania.

CRITICAL THINKING
- Making inferences, pp. 921, 922
- Analyzing causes, p. 923
- Clarifying, p. 924
- Contrasting, p. 925
- Synthesizing, p. 925

FOCUS
5-Minute Warm-Up

▶ *Perceiving Cause and Effect*
To help students learn how changes in the Soviet bloc occurred, have them answer the following questions.

1. Read History Makers on page 923. How did Walesa attract world attention to the workers' struggles?
2. What immediate effect did this attention have on the Polish government?

WARM-UP TRANSPARENCY 35

OBJECTIVE 1 INSTRUCT

Gorbachev's Reforms

▶ *Key Ideas*
- Mikhail Gorbachev gains power in the Soviet Union in 1985.
- He promotes reforms to revive the Soviet system.

IN-DEPTH RESOURCES: UNIT 8
Guided Reading, p. 39
Primary Source: Political Cartoon, p. 47

ACCESS FOR STUDENTS ACQUIRING ENGLISH
Guided Reading (Spanish), p. 355

SECTION 3 RESOURCES

PRINT RESOURCES

IN-DEPTH RESOURCES: UNIT 8
Guided Reading, p. 39
Primary Source: Political Cartoon, p. 47

ACCESS FOR STUDENTS ACQUIRING ENGLISH
Guided Reading (Spanish), p. 355

FORMAL ASSESSMENT
Section Quiz, p. 414

ALTERNATIVE ASSESSMENT BOOK

TECHNOLOGY RESOURCES

GEOGRAPHY TRANSPARENCIES
GT35 Germany, Post World War I—Present

WORLD ART AND CULTURES TRANSPARENCIES
AT78 Burning Rods

CD-ROM
Electronic Library of Primary Sources

INTERNET www.mlworldhistory.com

HISTORYMAKERS
Mikhail Gorbachev

(See page 921.)

Gorbachev brought a new sense of energy and style to official life in the Soviet Union. He even walked through crowds, shaking hands like an American politician, a custom unheard of in Soviet politics. Ask students why his gesture might have had such a powerful impact on the Soviet public.

MORE ABOUT . . .
Soviet-U.S. Relations

At first, U.S. officials distrusted Gorbachev and his reforms and argued that the United States, rather than helping, should continue its tough policies toward the Soviet Union. When Gorbachev allowed Eastern Europe to break away from Soviet control, however, the attitude of U.S. officials toward the Soviet leader became more positive.

OBJECTIVE ② INSTRUCT

Reforms in Poland and Hungary

Key Ideas

• Poland and Hungary are among the first Eastern European nations to embrace reform.

• Poland's Solidarity trade union forces change and wins elections.

• Hungary also deposes its Communist regime.

This political cartoon contrasts the old Soviet closed-door system with Gorbachev's new policy. The sign over the open doorway reads "Glasnost," which means openness.

Perestroika Reforms the Economy The new openness allowed Soviet citizens to complain publicly about economic problems. Angry consumers protested that they had to stand in long lines to buy food, soap, and other basics. Gorbachev blamed these problems on the Soviet Union's inefficient system of central planning. Under central planning, party officials told farm and factory managers how much to produce. They also told them what wages to pay, and what prices to charge. Because individuals could not increase their pay by producing more, they had little motive to improve efficiency.

In 1985, Gorbachev introduced the idea of **perestroika** (PEHR·ih·STROY·kuh), or economic restructuring. In 1986, he made changes to revive the Soviet economy. Local managers gained greater authority over their farms and factories, and people were allowed to open small private businesses. Gorbachev's goal was not to throw out communism, but to make the system more efficient and productive.

Democratization Opens the Political System Gorbachev also knew that for the economy to thrive, the Communist Party would have to loosen its grip on Soviet society and politics. In 1987, he unveiled a third new policy called democratization. This would be a gradual opening of the political system.

The plan called for the election of a new legislative body. In the past, voters had merely approved candidates who were hand-picked by the Communist Party. Now, voters could choose from a list of candidates for each office. The election produced many surprises. In several places, voters chose lesser-known candidates over powerful party bosses. Voters also elected a number of outspoken reformers.

Foreign Policy Soviet foreign policy also changed. Gorbachev realized that the troubled Soviet economy could no longer afford the costly arms race. He announced a "new thinking" in foreign affairs that stressed diplomacy over force. Therefore, arms control became one of Gorbachev's top priorities. In December 1987, he and President Reagan signed the Intermediate-Range Nuclear Forces (INF) Treaty. This treaty banned nuclear missiles with ranges of 300 to 3,400 miles.

Gorbachev's new thinking led him to urge Eastern European leaders to open up their economic and political systems. The aging Communist rulers of Eastern Europe resisted reform. However, powerful forces for democracy were building in those countries. In the past, the threat of Soviet intervention had kept those forces in check. Now, Gorbachev was saying that the Soviet Union would not oppose reform. "Each people determines the future of its own country and chooses its own form of society," he announced. "There must be no interference from outside, no matter what the pretext."

Reforms in Poland and Hungary

Poland and Hungary were among the first countries in Eastern Europe to embrace the spirit of change. In fact, the Polish struggle for democracy had begun before Gorbachev's rise to power. In 1978, a Polish archbishop became Pope John Paul II and lent his support to the anti-communist movement. In 1980, workers at the Gdansk shipyard went on strike, demanding government recognition of their union, **Solidarity.** When millions of Poles supported the action, the government gave in to the union's demands. Union leader **Lech Walesa** (lehk vah·WEHN·sah) became a national hero.

THINK THROUGH HISTORY
B. Making Inferences Why would it be inefficient for the central government to decide what should be produced all over the country?
B. Possible Answer Because they would not understand local conditions, needs, or problems.

Background
In 1972, President Nixon and Soviet leader Brezhnev had signed the Strategic Arms Limitation Treaty (SALT), which limited the number of nuclear missiles the superpowers could build.

Background
These striking workers took a great risk. Communist governments often sent the army to attack such protesters.

TEACHING OPTIONS | **CUSTOMIZING FOR SPECIAL NEEDS** | **MULTIPLE LEARNING STYLES**

Gifted and Talented Students:
Discussing Opposing Views
Ask students to consider the following quotations about Gorbachev and his reforms: "Part of his genius is to make what was unthinkable yesterday seem sensible today and inevitable tomorrow" (Strobe Talbott, American journalist).

"Western observers think that glasnost fell from the sky. It's not from the sky. . . . It was society that prepared this glasnost" (Soviet dissident writer). Have students form a panel to discuss the implications of these comments. Ask, Where does change originate—From dynamic leaders or from society?

Visual Learners: *Design a Poster* Invite students to create posters that urge Soviet citizens to support Gorbachev's reforms. Posters may focus on specific reforms, such as glasnost or perestroika, or on the whole reform movement.

Encourage students to find examples of political poster art to serve as models for their designs. Display the posters and have students discuss their different designs and approaches.

Solidarity Defeats Communists The next year, however, the Polish government banned Solidarity again and declared martial law. The Communist Party quickly discovered that military rule could not revive Poland's failing economy. In the 1980s, industrial production declined, while foreign debt rose to more than $40 billion. Frustrated shoppers endured long lines, shortages, and rising prices.

Public discontent deepened as the economic crisis worsened. In August 1988, defiant workers walked off their jobs. They demanded raises and the legalization of Solidarity. Faced with Poland's worst labor unrest since 1980, the military leader, General Jaruzelski (YAH·roo·ZEHL·skee), agreed to hold talks with Solidarity leaders. In April 1989, Jaruzelski legalized Solidarity and agreed to hold Poland's first free election since the Communists took power.

In elections during 1989 and 1990, Polish voters voted against Communists and overwhelmingly chose Solidarity candidates. They elected Lech Walesa president. For the first time, the people of a nation had turned a Communist regime out of office peacefully.

Hungarian Communists Disband Inspired by the changes in Poland, Hungarian leaders also launched a sweeping reform program. To stimulate economic growth, reformers encouraged private enterprise and allowed a small stock market to operate. A new constitution permitted a multiparty system with free parliamentary elections.

The pace of change grew faster when radical reformers took over a Communist Party congress in October 1989. The radicals deposed the party's leaders and then dissolved the party itself. Here was another first: a European Communist Party had voted itself out of existence. A year later, in national elections, the nation's voters put a non-Communist government in power.

In 1994, a socialist party—largely made up of former Communists—won a majority of seats in Hungary's parliament. The socialist party and a democratic party formed a coalition, or alliance, to rule. The following year, the government sought to improve the economy by raising taxes and cutting back on government services.

Vocabulary
deposed: removed from power

Communism Falls in East Germany

THINK THROUGH HISTORY
C. Analyzing Causes How did the fall of communism in Hungary contribute to turmoil in East Germany?
C. Answer The non-Communist government of Hungary gave East Germans more freedom by allowing them to use Hungary as an escape route to Austria and West Germany.

While Poland and Hungary were moving toward reform, conservative leaders in East Germany stubbornly refused to accept change. East Germany's 77-year-old party boss Erich Honecker dismissed reforms as unnecessary. Then in 1989, Hungary allowed vacationing East German tourists to cross the border into Austria. From there they could travel to West Germany. Thousands of East Germans took this new escape route.

Fall of the Berlin Wall In response, the East German government closed its borders entirely. By October 1989, huge demonstrations had broken out in cities across East Germany. The protesters demanded the right to travel freely—and later added the demand for free elections. At one point, Honecker tried to regain control by ordering the police to break up a demonstration in Leipzig. The police refused. Honecker lost his authority with the party and resigned on October 18.

The new East German leader, Egon Krenz, boldly gambled that he could restore stability by allowing people to leave East Germany. On November 9, 1989, he opened the Berlin Wall. Thousands of East Germans poured into West Berlin. The long-divided city of Berlin erupted in joyous celebration. Once-feared border guards smiled as huge crowds climbed on top of the wall to celebrate. The jubilant Berliners danced and chanted, "The wall is gone! The wall is gone!" (See photograph on page 908.)

Struggles for Democracy **923**

Krenz's dramatic gamble to save communism did not work. When the public discovered evidence of widespread corruption among party leaders, Krenz and other top officials were forced to resign in disgrace. By the end of 1989, the East German Communist Party had ceased to exist.

Germany Is Reunified With the fall of Communism in East Germany, many Germans began to speak of **reunification**—the merging of the two Germanys. However, the movement for reunification worried many people. They feared that a united Germany would once again try to dominate Europe.

West German Chancellor Helmut Kohl assured world leaders that Germans had learned from the past. They were now committed to democracy and human rights. Kohl's assurances helped persuade other European nations to accept German reunification. Forty-five years after its crushing defeat in World War II, Germany was officially reunited on October 3, 1990.

Germany's Challenges The newly united Germany faced serious problems. More than 40 years of Communist rule had left eastern Germany in ruins. Its railroads, highways, and telephone system had not been modernized since World War II. Many East German industries produced shoddy goods that could not compete in the global market.

Rebuilding eastern Germany's bankrupt economy was going to be a difficult, costly process. To pay these costs, Kohl raised taxes. As taxpayers tightened their belts, workers in eastern Germany faced a second problem—unemployment. Inefficient factories closed, depriving millions of workers of their jobs.

In spite of these difficulties, German voters returned the ruling coalition of political parties to power in late 1994. Kohl was re-elected chancellor. In early 1995 he met with industry leaders to discuss how to create jobs. In the mid-1990s Germany's economy slowly began to improve.

Reunification forced Germany to rethink its role in international affairs. As central Europe's largest country, Germany had important global responsibilities. For example, in 1993, German troops joined the UN peacekeeping mission in Somalia. As Germany's global responsibilities grew, German leaders began to argue that the country deserved a permanent seat on the UN Security Council. The Security Council is a group of 15 nations with the authority to decide UN actions.

Democracy Spreads

Changes in the Soviet Union, Poland, and Hungary had helped inspire reforms in East Germany. In the same way, changes in East Germany affected other Eastern European countries, including Czechoslovakia and Romania. In those countries, however, repressive governments delayed the movement toward democracy.

Czechoslovakia Reforms While huge crowds were demanding democracy in East Germany, neighboring Czechoslovakia remained quiet. Vivid memories of the violent crackdown against the reforms of 1968 made the Czechs cautious. A conservative

---

government led by Milos Jakes resisted all change. In October 1989, the police arrested several dissidents. Among these was the Czech playwright Vaclav Havel (VAH·tslahv HAH·vehl), a popular critic of the government.

On October 28, 1989, 10,000 people gathered in Wenceslas Square in the center of Prague. They demanded democracy and freedom. Hundreds were arrested. Three weeks later, 25,000 students inspired by the fall of the Berlin Wall gathered in Prague to demand reform. Following orders from the government, the police brutally attacked the demonstrators and injured hundreds.

The government crackdown angered the Czech people. On each of the next eight days, huge crowds gathered in Wenceslas Square. They demanded an end to Communist rule. On November 24, 500,000 protesters crowded into downtown Prague. Within hours, Milos Jakes and his entire Politburo resigned. One month later, a new parliament elected Vaclav Havel president of Czechoslovakia.

Overthrow in Romania By late 1989, only Romania seemed unmoved by the calls of reform. Romania's ruthless Communist dictator Nicolae Ceausescu (chow·SHES·koo) maintained a firm grip on power. His secret police enforced his orders brutally. Nevertheless, Romanians were aware of the reforms in other countries. They began a protest movement of their own. One student explained their anger at the government:

A VOICE FROM THE PAST
We were raised on a mountain of lies. There was a fantastical difference between the things they told us and the things we saw. They published incredible statistics on agricultural production, and in the shops there was nothing to eat. On paper, we had freedom of expression, but any-time anyone said anything, members of the Communist Party told us to keep our mouths shut.

STEFAN GHENCEA, Romanian student

In December, Ceausescu ordered the army to fire on demonstrators in the city of Timisoara (tee·mee·SHWAH·rah). The army killed and wounded scores of people. The massacre in Timisoara ignited a popular uprising against Ceausescu. Within days, the army joined the people. They fought to defeat the secret police and overthrow their ruler. Shocked by the sudden collapse of his power, Ceausescu and his wife attempted to flee. They were captured, however, then hastily tried and executed on Christmas Day, 1989.

Romania held general elections in 1990 and in 1992. The government also made economic reforms to introduce elements of capitalism. At the same time, the slow pace of Gorbachev's economic reforms began to cause unrest in the Soviet Union.

Margin notes (left):

E. Answer In Czechoslovakia, the Communist government resigned without violence. In Romania, the government used violence, and the victorious protesters executed Ceausescu.

THINK THROUGH HISTORY
E. Contrasting Contrast the democratic revolutions in Czechoslovakia and Romania.

SPOTLIGHT ON
Television's Influence
Television played a key role in the movements for democracy. Mikhail Gorbachev used television to spread news of reform programs and bolster his image. In East Germany, people viewed Western programs and saw the contrast between affluence in the West and their own lower standard of living.

In Romania the role of television was more direct. Revolutionaries captured the state television station in Bucharest and broadcast their own views of the struggle. They used television to coordinate revolutionary actions in different parts of the country. When Nicolae Ceausescu and his wife were tried and executed, television carried the news throughout the country—along with pictures of their dead bodies. Ceausescu is shown below.

Section 3 Assessment

1. TERMS & NAMES

Identify
- Politburo
- Mikhail Gorbachev
- glasnost
- perestroika
- Solidarity
- Lech Walesa
- reunification

2. TAKING NOTES

Use a time line like the one below to record significant events in the Soviet Union and Eastern Europe.

1985 — 1995

During which year did most of Eastern Europe turn toward democracy?

3. SYNTHESIZING

Explain how Gorbachev's reforms helped to move the Soviet Union closer toward democracy.

THINK ABOUT
- the democratic practices and conditions listed on the chart on page 911
- how Gorbachev's policies promoted those practices and conditions

4. THEME ACTIVITY

Cultural Interaction With a partner, create a cause-and-effect diagram to show how democratic reform spread through Eastern Europe. The diagram should show the order in which reform happened and which countries influenced others. You may want to look through this textbook for model diagrams.

Struggles for Democracy **925**

MORE ABOUT . . .
Nicolae Ceausescu
Ceausescu exported the bulk of Romania's food, leaving his people near starvation. He also bull-dozed rural villages and forced their residents to move into apartment buildings.

SPOTLIGHT ON
Television's Influence
Ask students what political and economic messages about the United States Eastern Europeans would have received by watching U.S. television.

ASSESS & RETEACH

Section 3 Assessment
Have students work in small groups to discuss the questions and assess one another's responses.

Section Quiz
FORMAL ASSESSMENT
Section Quiz, p. 414

Reteaching Activity
CLASS TIME: 15 MINUTES

Use the Guided Reading worksheet for Section 3 to help students review the main ideas of this section.

IN-DEPTH RESOURCES: UNIT 8
Guided Reading, p. 39

CLOSE ACTIVITY

CLASS TIME: 20 MINUTES

Writing a Journal
Have students think about being citizens of the Soviet Union and living through the changes described in this section. Ask them to choose a country discussed in this section and to write a brief journal entry or two, describing what is happening in their country and how they feel about it.

ANSWERS

1. TERMS & NAMES
Politburo, p. 921
Mikhail Gorbachev, p. 921
glasnost, p. 921
perestroika, p. 922
Solidarity, p. 922
Lech Walesa, p. 922
reunification, p. 924

2. TAKING NOTES
Possible Responses:
1985–1987—Gorbachev introduces glasnost, perestroika, and democratic reforms, signs the INF treaty; 1989—Berlin Wall comes down. Poland, Hungary, Romania, and Czechoslovakia oust Communist leaders; 1990—Germany is reunified; Polish voters choose Solidarity; Romania holds elections; 1993—Neo-Nazis kill Turkish immigrants in Germany; 1994—Socialists win in Hungary. The year 1989.

3. SYNTHESIZING
Possible Responses: Glasnost encouraged freedom of speech and citizen participation. Perestroika promised to improve the economy. Democratic reforms provided more open elections.

4. THEME ACTIVITY
Standards for Evaluation:
Diagrams should meet the following criteria:
- Include only important events.
- Show how each event led to the next.
- Show how various nations influenced one another.

OBJECTIVES

1. To describe the collapse of the Soviet Union.
2. To identify problems facing the Russian government.
3. To summarize the conflict in the former Yugoslavia.
4. To explain problems in Poland and Czechoslovakia.

SKILLBUILDER

- Interpreting maps: place, region, p. 927
- Interpreting maps: region, location, p. 929

CRITICAL THINKING

- Analyzing motives, p. 927
- Evaluating decisions, p. 928
- Identifying problems, p. 929
- Contrasting, p. 930
- Analyzing causes, p. 930
- Analyzing themes, p. 930

FOCUS
5-Minute Warm-Up

▶ *Making Inferences*
Students will understand more about the former Soviet Union by answering the following questions.

1. Study the map on page 927. Where are all the new republics located in relation to Russia?

2. Having been invaded several times, why might Russia have wanted to annex these countries?

🏛 *WARM-UP TRANSPARENCY 35*

OBJECTIVE ① INSTRUCT

Unrest in the Soviet Union

▶ *Key Ideas*
- Soviet republics break away, and the Soviet Union dissolves.

📖 *IN-DEPTH RESOURCES: UNIT 8*
Guided Reading, p. 40

📖 *ACCESS FOR STUDENTS ACQUIRING ENGLISH*
Guided Reading (Spanish), p. 356

---

4 Collapse of the Soviet Union

MAIN IDEA	WHY IT MATTERS NOW
In the early 1990s, the Soviet Union, Yugoslavia, and Czechoslovakia all broke apart.	Many of the new nations created after those breakups continue to struggle to establish democracy.

SETTING THE STAGE The reforms of the late 1980s brought high hopes to the people of the Soviet Union and Eastern Europe. For the first time in decades, they were free to make choices about the economic and political systems governing their lives. They soon discovered that increased freedom sometimes challenges the social order.

Unrest in the Soviet Union

As Eastern Europe gained freedom from Soviet control, various nationalities in the Soviet Union began to call for their own freedom. More than 100 ethnic groups lived in the Soviet Union. Russians were the largest, most powerful group. However, non-Russians formed a majority in the 14 Soviet republics other than Russia.

Ethnic tensions brewed beneath the surface of Soviet society. As reforms loosened central controls, unrest spread across the country. Nationalist groups in Georgia, Ukraine, and Moldavia (now Moldova) demanded self-rule. The Muslim peoples of Soviet Central Asia called for religious freedom.

Lithuania Defies Gorbachev The first challenge came from the Baltic nations of Lithuania, Estonia, and Latvia. These republics had been independent states between the two world wars—until the Soviets annexed them in 1940. Fifty years later, in March 1990, Lithuania declared its independence. To try to force it back into the Soviet Union, Gorbachev ordered a blockade of the republic.

Although Gorbachev was reluctant to use stronger measures, he feared that Lithuania's example might encourage other republics to secede. In January 1991 Soviet troops attacked unarmed civilians in Lithuania's capital. The army killed 14 and wounded more than 150.

Yeltsin Denounces Gorbachev The bloody assault in Lithuania and the lack of real economic progress in the Soviet Union damaged Gorbachev's popularity. More and more people looked for leadership to **Boris Yeltsin.** He was a member of parliament and the former mayor of Moscow. Yeltsin criticized the crackdown in Lithuania and the slow pace of reforms. In June 1991, voters overwhelmingly chose Yeltsin to become the Russian Republic's first directly elected president.

Yeltsin and Gorbachev were now on a collision course. In spite of their rivalry, they faced a common enemy in the old guard of Communist officials. Hard-liners—conservatives who opposed reform—were furious at Gorbachev. They were angry that he had given up the Soviet Union's role as the dominant force in Eastern Europe. They also feared losing their power and privileges. These officials vowed to overthrow Gorbachev and undo his reforms.

HISTORY MAKERS

Boris Yeltsin
1931–

Boris Yeltsin was raised in poverty. For 10 years, his family lived in a single room and slept on the floor next to their goat for warmth.

As a youth, Yeltsin earned good grades but behaved badly. Mikhail Gorbachev named him party boss and mayor of Moscow in 1985. Yeltsin's outspokenness got him into trouble. At one meeting, he launched into a bitter speech criticizing conservatives for working against perestroika. Gorbachev fired him for the sake of party unity.

Yeltsin made a dramatic comeback and won a seat in parliament in 1989. Parliament elected him president of Russia in 1990, and voters re-elected him in 1991. But his health—heart problems—raised doubts about how long he could remain in power.

Background
About three-fourths of the Soviet population were Slavic peoples such as Russians or Ukrainians. Turkic peoples, such as Uzbeks or Azerbaijani, were the second largest group. Most of these were Muslim. Other groups included Georgians and Armenians.

Background
As part of government reform, Gorbachev became president of the Soviet Union—a new office modeled on the U.S. presidency. Each of the 15 republics was also allowed to have a president. For example, Yeltsin was the president of Russia.

PRINT RESOURCES

📖 *IN-DEPTH RESOURCES: UNIT 8*
Guided Reading, p. 40
Primary Source: The Road to Marjača, p. 48

📖 *ACCESS FOR STUDENTS ACQUIRING ENGLISH*
Guided Reading (Spanish), p. 356

📖 *FORMAL ASSESSMENT*
Section Quiz, p. 415

📖 *ALTERNATIVE ASSESSMENT BOOK*

TECHNOLOGY RESOURCES

💿 **CD-ROM**
Electronic Library of Primary Sources

🌐 **INTERNET** www.mlworldhistory.com

Distribution of Territory, 1991

Other Republics (23.3%)

Russian Republic (76.7%)

The Breakup of the Soviet Union, 1991

ARCTIC OCEAN

Arctic Circle

RUSSIA

Sea of Okhotsk

Lake Baikal

ESTONIA
Tallinn
LATVIA
Riga
Moscow
Vilnius
Minsk
BELARUS
...SSIA
LITHUANIA
Kiev
UKRAINE
MOLDOVA
Chisinau
Black Sea
GEORGIA
Tbilisi
ARMENIA
Yerevan
Baku
AZERBAIJAN
Mediterranean Sea
TURKMENISTAN
Ashgabat
UZBEKISTAN
Dushanbe
TAJIKISTAN
KYRGYZSTAN
Bishkek
Tashkent
Almaty
KAZAKHSTAN
Aral Sea
Lake Balkhash
Caspian Sea
Volga R.
Ob R.
Irtysh R.
Yenisey R.
Lena R.
Amur R.

PACIFIC OCEAN
Sea of Japan

N

0   1,000 Miles
0   2,000 Kilometers

— Border of the Soviet Union

GEOGRAPHY SKILLBUILDER: Interpreting Maps
1. **Place** Name the 15 republics of the former Soviet Union.
2. **Region** Which republic received the largest percentage of the former Soviet Union's territory?

The August Coup On August 18, 1991, the hard-liners detained Gorbachev at his vacation home on the Black Sea. They demanded his resignation as Soviet president. Early the next day, hundreds of tanks and armored vehicles rolled into Moscow. The hard-liners—who called themselves the State Committee—assumed that a show of force would ensure obedience. However, the Soviet people had lost their fear of the party. They were willing to defend their freedoms. Protesters gathered at the Russian parliament building, where Yeltsin had his office.

Around midday, Yeltsin emerged and climbed atop one of the tanks. As his supporters cheered, Yeltsin declared, "We proclaim all decisions and decrees of this committee to be illegal. . . . We appeal to the citizens of Russia to . . . demand a return of the country to normal constitutional developments."

On August 20, the State Committee ordered troops to attack the parliament, but they refused. Their refusal turned the tide. On August 21, the military withdrew its forces from Moscow. That night, Gorbachev returned to Moscow.

End of the Soviet Union The coup attempt sparked anger against the Communist party. Gorbachev resigned as general secretary of the party. The Soviet parliament voted to stop all party activities. Having first seized power in 1917 in a coup that succeeded, the all-powerful Communist Party now collapsed because of a coup that failed.

The coup also played a decisive role in accelerating the breakup of the Soviet Union. Estonia and Latvia quickly declared their independence. Other republics soon followed. Although Gorbachev pleaded for unity, no one was listening. By early December, all 15 republics had declared independence.

Struggles for Democracy **927**

THINK THROUGH HISTORY
A. Analyzing Motives Why do you think the Soviet troops refused the order to attack the parliament?
A. Possible Answers They were inspired by Yeltsin's courage, they were sick of Communist rule, or they were unwilling to gun down civilians.

Crowds of citizens surround the tanks in Moscow during the August coup attempt. The soldiers' refusal to fight doomed the coup.

HISTORYMAKERS
Boris Yeltsin
(See page 926.)

A number of political opponents have challenged Yeltsin's power—for example, in the 1996 presidential elections. Have students find out about Yeltsin's recent policies and his record as president.

History from Visuals

The Breakup of the Soviet Union, 1991

Interpreting the Map Have students examine the map and the key and explain what the inset graph shows. *Percentage of former Soviet territory occupied by the various republics.*

Extension Activity Have students use their prior knowledge of Russian history (see Chapters 21 and 30) to debate why Russia would want to conquer and control regions on her eastern and southern borders. What fears did Russia have about its European neighbors?

SKILLBUILDER Answers
1. Russia, Kazakhstan, Ukraine, Turkmenistan, Uzbekistan, Belarus, Kyrgyzstan, Tajikstan, Azerbaijan, Georgia, Lithuania, Latvia, Estonia, Moldova, Armenia.
2. Russia.

MORE ABOUT . . .
The August Coup

The coup attempt hurt Gorbachev politically by making it appear that he had no control over hard-line elements in the Soviet Union. Yeltsin, on the other hand, emerged as a triumphant figure. To many Soviet citizens, Gorbachev seemed to represent the past; Yeltsin, the future.

TEACHING OPTIONS

CUSTOMIZING FOR SPECIAL NEEDS

Gifted and Talented Students:
Conducting an Interview Have interested students interview experts in Eastern European or Soviet history regarding the dramatic events of 1991 in the Soviet Union. An expert might be a professor at a local college, a member of an immigrant group, or even someone in the embassy of a former Soviet republic. Help students plan their interviews and develop their questions. They might ask their interviewees if they can record the interviews on videotape or audiotape. Have students discuss their interviews in class and compare the responses they received.

MULTIPLE LEARNING STYLES

Kinesthetic Learners:
Performing a Drama Invite groups of students to create short plays about the August coup and its political consequences. Students should write scripts based on real events and should take on the roles of both prominent figures and ordinary citizens. Tell them to limit their dramas to significant moments of the coup and not to attempt broad depictions of events. A group might focus on the decision of the military not to fire on the people, for example. Encourage them to try to capture the high drama of these historical events. Have them rehearse their plays and then perform them in class.

Teacher's Edition   927

GlobalImpact
Cuba

Ask students why Cuba came to rely so heavily on Soviet aid. Then ask them to use current periodicals or the Internet to find out what Cuba is doing to cope with its economic problems and what success it is having.

OBJECTIVE 2 INSTRUCT

The Yeltsin Era

Key Ideas
- Boris Yeltsin takes charge of Russia.
- Yeltsin uses "shock therapy" to move Russia toward capitalism.
- Opposition grows to Yeltsin's economic policies and the war in Chechnya.

 IN-DEPTH RESOURCES: UNIT 8
Primary Source: The Road to Marjača, p. 48

OBJECTIVE 3 INSTRUCT

Yugoslavia Falls Apart

Key Ideas
- Yugoslavia, a patchwork quilt of ethnic groups, falls apart in the 1980s.
- War engulfs the region, especially in Bosnia, where Serbs, Croats, and Muslims fight for control.
- A peace agreement is signed in 1995, but unrest continues.

GlobalImpact
Cuba

The Soviet collapse harmed Cuba. Since becoming a Communist state in the early 1960s, Cuba had depended on Soviet assistance. By the late 1980s, Cuba relied on the Soviet Union for more than three-fourths of its imports and all of its oil.

As reform swept the Soviet Union and Eastern Europe, Cuba's leader, Fidel Castro, criticized the reformers. He also vowed that Cuba would remain Communist.

After the August Coup of 1991, Soviet support of Cuba's economy came to an abrupt end. Cut off from Soviet aid and deeply affected by an American trade embargo, Cuba went into severe economic decline. During the 1990s, Cuba struggled to form new trade relationships and mend its tattered economy.

Yeltsin met with the leaders of other republics to chart a new course. They agreed to form the Commonwealth of Independent States, or **CIS,** a loose federation of former Soviet territories. Only the Baltic republics and Georgia refused to join.

The formation of the CIS meant the death of the Soviet Union. On Christmas Day 1991, Gorbachev announced his resignation as president of the Soviet Union, a country that by then had ceased to exist. Although Gorbachev had failed to hold the Soviet Union together, he will be remembered as the man who launched one of the most dramatic revolutions of the 20th century.

The Yeltsin Era

As president of the large Russian Republic, Boris Yeltsin was now the most powerful figure in the CIS. He would face many problems—an ailing economy, tough political opposition, and an unpopular war.

Yeltsin Faces Problems One of Yeltsin's goals was to reform the Russian economy. He adopted a bold plan known as **"shock therapy,"** an abrupt shift to free-market economics. To eliminate government involvement in the economy, Yeltsin lowered trade barriers, removed price controls, and ended subsidies to state-owned industries.

Initially, the plan produced more shock than therapy. Prices soared; from 1992 to 1994, the inflation rate averaged 800 percent. Many factories dependent on government money had to cut production or shut down entirely. This forced thousands of people out of work. By 1993, most Russians were suffering severe economic hardship:

> **A VOICE FROM THE PAST**
> A visitor to Moscow cannot escape the feeling of a society in collapse. Child beggars accost foreigners on the street. . . . Children ask why they should stay in school when educated professionals do not make enough money to survive. . . . A garment worker complains that now her wages do not cover even the food bills, while fear of growing crime makes her dread leaving home.
>
> **DAVID M. KOTZ,** "The Cure That Could Kill"

Economic problems fueled a political crisis. In October 1993, legislators opposed to Yeltsin's policies shut themselves inside the parliament building. Yeltsin ordered troops to bombard the building, forcing hundreds of rebel legislators to surrender. Many were killed. Opponents accused Yeltsin of acting like a dictator.

Chechnya Rebels Yeltsin's troubles included war in Chechnya (CHEHCH·nee·uh), a largely Muslim area in southwestern Russia. In 1991, Chechnya declared its independence, but Yeltsin denied the region's right to secede. In 1994, he ordered 40,000 Russian troops into the breakaway republic. Russian forces pounded the capital city of Grozny (GROHZ·nee) and reduced it to rubble. News of the death and destruction in Chechnya sparked anger throughout Russia. With an election coming, Yeltsin sought to end the war. In August 1996, the two sides signed a peace treaty.

In the presidential elections of mid-1996, Yeltsin faced stiff opposition from former Communists and right-wing nationalists. Although Yeltsin won the election, his future remained unclear. So did the future of Russian democracy.

Yugoslavia Falls Apart

Ethnic conflict also plagued Yugoslavia. This country, formed after World War I, had six major groups of people—Serbs, Croats, Muslims, Slovenes, Macedonians, and Montenegrins. Ethnic and religious differences dating back centuries caused these groups to view each other with suspicion. After World War II, Yugoslavia became a federation of six republics. Each republic had a mixed population.

928 Chapter 35

Background
Georgia did join the CIS later, in 1993, but the Baltic states remained separate.

Vocabulary
subsidies: government funds given to support industries.

THINK THROUGH HISTORY
B. Evaluating Decisions Compare Yeltsin's action here to his actions during the August Coup. Which actions were more supportive of democracy?
B. Possible Answer He was more supportive of democracy during the August coup because he defied a military takeover. Here he used the military to stay in power.

EXPLORING PRIMARY SOURCES

A Voice from the Past Ask students to reread the quotation from David M. Kotz on this page. What details does the writer provide to show that Russia was "a society in collapse"? Tell students that despite the picture of poverty the writer paints, a whole class of Russians became wealthy during this same time. If readers did not know this fact, what impression of Moscow would they get from Kotz's article? Would they think the shift from communism to capitalism had been a mistake? Contrast Kotz's picture of Moscow in 1993 to the picture today. What did he fail to see about economic changes in Russia at that time that might have changed his description?

CONNECTIONS ACROSS TIME AND PLACE

Emerging Republics Ask five or six interested students to role-play a delegation from former Soviet republics who are approaching the United Nations for aid. Students will decide which of the former Soviet republics they will represent and should talk about conditions under former Soviet rule, the problems their country faces today, and the kind of aid the country needs from the United Nations. Each student should also draw or photocopy a picture of the country's flag and national symbol. Students should end their presentations with an evaluation of the Soviet legacy in their countries with regard to language, culture, government, and economics.

Slovenia and Croatia Protest Josip Tito, who led Yugoslavia from 1945 to 1980, held the country together. After Tito's death, however, long-simmering ethnic resentments boiled over. Serbian leader Slobodan Milosevic (mee·LOH·sheh·vihch) asserted Serbian leadership over Yugoslavia. Two republics—Slovenia and Croatia—then declared independence. In June 1991, the Serbian-led Yugoslav army invaded both republics.

The Slovenes quickly repelled the Serbs, but the war in Croatia proved far bloodier. Unlike Slovenia, Croatia had a large Serbian minority, which resented Croatian control. Centuries of Serb-Croat hatred exploded in an all-out war. The fighting claimed thousands of lives and left cities in ruins. By the time the United Nations arranged a cease-fire in January 1992, Serbian forces occupied about 30 percent of Croatia.

The Bosnian Nightmare In February 1992, Bosnia-Herzegovina joined Slovenia and Croatia in declaring independence. (In April, Serbia and Montenegro formed a new Yugoslavia. See the map below.) Bosnia's ethnically mixed population included Muslims (44 percent), Serbs (31 percent), and Croats (17 percent). While Bosnia's Muslims and Croats backed independence, Bosnian Serbs strongly opposed it. Supported by Serbia, the Bosnian Serbs launched a brutal war in March 1992. As many as 200,000 people died over the next three years, while 2 million people—more than half of Bosnia's population—fled their homes.

During the war, the Serbs used murder and other forms of brutality against Bosnian Muslims living in Serb-held lands. Called **ethnic cleansing**, this policy was intended to rid Bosnia of its Muslim population. By 1995, the Serbs controlled 70 percent of Bosnia.

International Response Although Serbia's brutality outraged other nations, they remained anxious to stay out of the fighting. To relieve suffering, a multinational force of 25,000 UN troops was sent to Bosnia to keep peace and to distribute food and medical supplies. UN and U.S.-sponsored negotiations dragged on for several years. In December 1995, the leaders of the three factions involved in the war signed a peace treaty. In September 1996, Bosnians elected a three-person presidency—one leader from each ethnic group. However, the nation continued to experience unrest.

These two women stand in front of a building that has been heavily damaged in the war. The building is in Sarajevo, Bosnia.

Former Yugoslavia, 1989–1997

AUSTRIA HUNGARY
Ljubljana
SLOVENIA Zagreb
CROATIA
Drava River
ROMANIA
Sava River
Danube River
BOSNIA–HERZEGOVINA
Belgrade
Sarajevo
SERBIA
Adriatic Sea
YUGOSLAVIA
MONTENEGRO
Podgorica
ITALY
Skopje
MACEDONIA
ALBANIA

0   100 Miles
0   200 Kilometers

Yugoslavia, 1989
Yugoslavia, 1997

GEOGRAPHY SKILLBUILDER: Interpreting Maps
1. **Region** Which nations now make up what used to be Yugoslavia in 1989?
2. **Location** Where is Serbia located relative to the republics that declared independence from Yugoslavia?

929

Eastern Europe Faces Problems

Key Ideas
- Poland's economy suffers, and the Poles vote Lech Walesa out of office.
- Czechoslovakia's economy also falters, and the country splits into the Czech Republic and Slovakia.

SPOTLIGHT ON
Rising Crime Rates in Poland

Ask students how economic chaos could be a cause of rising crime rates.

ASSESS & RETEACH

Section 4 Assessment
Have students work together to answer the questions. Tell them to note the location of the answers in the text.

Section Quiz
FORMAL ASSESSMENT
Section Quiz, p. 415

Reteaching Activity
CLASS TIME: 20 MINUTES

Arrange small groups of students in the classroom to mimic the geographic locations of the countries discussed in this section. Tell each group which country they represent and have them explain who they are, who the prominent people in their country are, and what is currently going on in their country.

CLOSE ACTIVITY

CLASS TIME: 25 MINUTES

Predicting
Have students predict what will happen in the former Soviet bloc in the next ten years, basing their predictions on what has happened in the past decade. Tell them to write a series of imagined newspaper headlines that convey their predictions.

Eastern Europe Faces Problems

Compared with Yugoslavia, the nations of Eastern Europe were relatively stable in the 1990s and did not experience widespread violence. Nevertheless, countries like Poland faced ongoing challenges.

SPOTLIGHT ON

Rising Crime Rates in Poland
Ruling by fear, the Communist state held down crime rates. After communism fell, crime increased. In Poland, crime was on the rise in the 1990s. Many conditions made the situation worse.

- Criminals tried to make quick money in the open market—for example, by selling stolen goods.
- When Poland turned out the Communists, it replaced the police force with inexperienced officers.
- Police departments didn't have enough money to do their jobs.
- Many Poles ignored the legal system. For example, they paid ransoms for stolen cars instead of calling the police.

It remained to be seen whether rule by law would take root in Poland.

Poland Votes Out Walesa After becoming president in 1991, Lech Walesa tried to revive Poland's bankrupt economy. Like Boris Yeltsin, he adopted a strategy of shock therapy to move Poland toward a free market economy. As in Russia, inflation and unemployment shot up. By the mid-1990s, however, the economy was improving.

Nevertheless, many Poles remained unhappy with the pace of economic progress. In the elections of 1995, they turned Walesa out of office in favor of a former Communist, Aleksandr Kwasniewski (kfahs·N'YEHF·skee). Kwasniewski vowed to combine free market policies with greater social benefits. Despite his Communist background, it appeared that he was committed to democratic rule.

Czechoslovakia Breaks Up In Czechoslovakia, reformers also launched an economic program based on shock therapy. The program caused a sharp rise in unemployment. It especially hurt Slovakia, the republic occupying the eastern third of Czechoslovakia.

Unable to agree on economic policy, the country's two parts—Slovakia and the Czech Republic—drifted apart. In spite of President Havel's pleas for unity, a movement to split the nation gained support. Havel resigned because of this. Czechoslovakia split into two countries on January 1, 1993, just three years after the fall of communism. Havel was elected president of the Czech Republic.

The nations of the former Soviet bloc had made many gains. Even so, they continued to face serious obstacles to democracy. Resolving ethnic conflicts remained crucial, as did economic progress:

A VOICE FROM THE PAST
The clear lesson . . . is that opening up the political process without a corresponding opening up and success in the economy merely gives people more opportunity to gripe about more things. People can handle political processes. You can proclaim a free election and hold it relatively easily. You cannot propose economic success and obtain it easily.
U.S. SENATOR GEORGE MITCHELL, quoted in "Neophyte Democracies Present a Challenge to U.S."

If the nations of Eastern Europe and the former Soviet Union can improve their standard of living, democracy might have a better chance to grow. In the meantime, economic reforms in Communist China sparked demands for democratic reforms.

THINK THROUGH HISTORY
D. Contrasting
Contrast the breakups of Yugoslavia and Czechoslovakia.
D. Answer
Yugoslavia's breakup turned into a violent and prolonged civil war; Czechoslovakia's was peaceful.

Section 4 Assessment

1. TERMS & NAMES
Identify
- Boris Yeltsin
- CIS
- "shock therapy"
- ethnic cleansing

2. TAKING NOTES
Use a chart like the one below to record the main reason or reasons that the Soviet Union, Yugoslavia, and Czechoslovakia each broke apart.

Former nations	Reasons for breakup
Soviet Union	
Yugoslavia	
Czechoslovakia	

3. ANALYZING CAUSES
Why did ethnic tension become such a severe problem in the Soviet Union and Yugoslavia in the early 1990s?

THINK ABOUT
- the role that past Communist leaders had played in holding those countries together
- the democratic reforms demanded by various ethnic groups
- how those demands affected national unity

4. ANALYZING THEMES
Revolution It has been said that Gorbachev's reforms led to a second Russian Revolution. What did this revolution overthrow?

THINK ABOUT
- changes in the Soviet government and in the political process
- who lost and who gained power

ANSWERS

1. TERMS & NAMES
Boris Yeltsin, p. 926
CIS, p. 928
"shock therapy," p. 928
ethnic cleansing, p. 929

2. TAKING NOTES
Possible Responses:
Soviet Union—ethnic tensions, desire for self-rule by various republics, hard-liners' loss of control of people; Yugoslavia—ethnic tensions, loss of Tito's authority, Serbian aggression; Czechoslovakia—economic differences between regions

3. ANALYZING CAUSES
Possible Responses: In the past, Communist leaders had suppressed nationalism and demands for self-rule. With the spread of democratic reforms, many ethnic groups demanded self-rule. This broke apart the Soviet Union. In Yugoslavia, one group—the Serbs—tried to dominate others. This led to civil war.

4. ANALYZING THEMES
Possible Responses: The Soviet Union broke into 15 republics. Authoritarian rule was replaced by more democratic practices. Conservative Communists lost power, and the people gained power.

China Follows Its Own Path

TERMS & NAMES
- Zhou Enlai
- Deng Xiaoping
- Four Modernizations
- Tiananmen Square
- Hong Kong

MAIN IDEA

In recent years, China's government has experimented with capitalism but has rejected calls for democracy.

WHY IT MATTERS NOW

After the 1997 death of Chinese leader Deng Xiaoping, President Jiang Zemin seemed to be continuing those policies.

SETTING THE STAGE The trend toward democracy around the world also affected China to a limited degree. A political reform movement arose in the late 1980s. It built on economic reforms begun earlier in the decade. China's Communist government clamped down on the reformers, however, and maintained a firm grip on power.

Mao's Unexpected Legacy

After the Communists came to power in China in 1949, Mao Zedong set out to transform China. Mao believed that peasant equality, revolutionary spirit, and hard work were all that was needed to improve the Chinese economy. For example, intensive labor could make up for the lack of tractors on the huge agricultural cooperatives that the government had created.

However, lack of modern technology damaged Chinese efforts to increase agricultural and industrial output. In addition, Mao's policies stifled economic growth. He eliminated incentives for higher production. He tried to replace family life with life in the communes. These policies took away the peasants' motive to work for the good of themselves and their families.

Facing economic disaster, some Chinese Communists talked of modernizing the economy. Accusing them of "taking the capitalist road," Mao began the Cultural Revolution to cleanse China of anti-revolutionary influences. The movement proved so destructive, however, that it caused many Chinese to distrust party leadership. Instead of saving radical communism, the Cultural Revolution turned many people against it. In the early 1970s, China entered another moderate period under **Zhou Enlai** (joh ehn·ly). Zhou had been premiere since 1949. During the Cultural Revolution, he had tried to restrain the radicals.

THINK THROUGH HISTORY
A. Recognizing Effects What was the ultimate result of Mao's radical Communist policies? Why?
A. Answer The destructiveness of the Cultural Revolution turned many Chinese people away from radical communism.

Mao's Attempts to Change China

Mao's Programs	Program's Results
First Five-Year Plan 1953–1957	• Industry grew 15 percent a year. • Agricultural output grew very slowly.
Great Leap Forward 1958–1962	• China suffered economic disaster—industrial declines and food shortages. • Mao lost influence.
Cultural Revolution 1966–1976	• Mao regained influence by backing radicals. • Purges and conflicts among leaders created economic, social, and political chaos. • Moderates increasingly opposed radicals in Communist Party.

SKILLBUILDER: Interpreting Charts
1. *Which had more successful results, the first five-year plan or the Great Leap Forward? Explain.*
2. *Did conditions improve or grow worse during the Cultural Revolution? Explain.*

China and the West

Throughout the Cultural Revolution, China played almost no role in world affairs. In the early 1960s, China had split with the Soviet Union over the leadership of world communism. In addition, China displayed hostility toward the United States because of U.S. support for the government on Taiwan and memories of the Korean War.

China Opened Its Doors China's isolation worried Zhou. He began to send out signals that he was willing to form ties to the West. In 1971, Zhou startled the world by

---

SECTION 5 RESOURCES

PRINT RESOURCES

IN-DEPTH RESOURCES: UNIT 8
Guided Reading, p. 41
Skillbuilder Practice: Analyzing Primary Sources, p. 42

ACCESS FOR STUDENTS ACQUIRING ENGLISH
Guided Reading (Spanish), p. 357
Skillbuilder Practice (Spanish), p. 358

FORMAL ASSESSMENT
Section Quiz, p. 416

ALTERNATIVE ASSESSMENT BOOK

TECHNOLOGY RESOURCES

CRITICAL THINKING TRANSPARENCIES
CT35 Democratic Struggles Around the Globe
CT71 Chapter 35 Visual Summary

CD-ROM
Electronic Library of Primary Sources

INTERNET www.mlworldhistory.com

Section 5 Overview

OBJECTIVES

1 To summarize Mao Zedong's rule.

2 To explain changes under Deng Xiaoping.

3 To describe the democracy movement in China.

4 To list China's challenges.

SKILLBUILDER
- Interpreting charts, p. 931

CRITICAL THINKING
- Recognizing effects, p. 931
- Analyzing causes, p. 932
- Contrasting, p. 933
- Drawing conclusions, p. 934
- Comparing, p. 934
- Making inferences, p. 935
- Supporting opinions, p. 935

FOCUS
5-Minute Warm-Up

▶ *Identifying Main Ideas*
Answering the following questions will help students understand life in China.

1. Read Daily Life on page 933. Why did the soldiers accept such harsh training?

2. What was the training designed to do?

🏛 *WARM-UP TRANSPARENCY 35*

OBJECTIVE 1 INSTRUCT

Mao's Unexpected Legacy

▶ *Key Ideas*
- China's economy suffers under Mao Zedong's rule.

📖 *IN-DEPTH RESOURCES: UNIT 8*
Guided Reading, p. 41

📖 *ACCESS FOR STUDENTS ACQUIRING ENGLISH*
Guided Reading (Spanish), p. 357

OBJECTIVE 2 INSTRUCT

China and the West

▶ *Key Ideas*
- China opens to the West and begins to change.

Mao's Attempts to Change China
(See page 931.)

Interpreting the Chart Tell students to notice the increasing amount of political, social, and economic chaos caused by each succeeding plan. What political effects did the plans have on China? *Radicals took over for a while, then moderates came to have more power.*

Extension Activity Ask students to create a cause-and-effect chart about the programs. How did the failures of each program contribute to the failures of the next program? *Example: Agricultural shortages led to food shortages.*

SKILLBUILDER Answers
1. The first five-year plan—both industry and agriculture developed.
2. Conditions grew worse; there was economic, political, and social chaos.

HISTORYMAKERS
Deng Xiaoping

Tell students that Deng was ousted from politics twice and managed to fight his way back each time. Suggest that they read more about Deng's life and values.

OBJECTIVE 3 INSTRUCT

Tiananmen Square

▶ **Key Ideas**
- Economic success creates a demand for political change.
- A democracy movement arises, which the government suppresses.

 ELECTRONIC LIBRARY OF PRIMARY SOURCES
"The Massacre in Tiananmen Square"

---

inviting an American table tennis team to tour China. It was the first visit by an American group to China since 1949.

The visit began a new era in Chinese-American relations. In 1971, the United States reversed its policy and endorsed UN membership for the People's Republic of China. The next year President Nixon made a state visit to China. He met with Mao and Zhou. The three leaders agreed to begin cultural exchanges and a limited amount of trade. In 1979, the United States and China established formal diplomatic relations.

Economic Reform Both Mao and Zhou died in 1976. Shortly afterward, moderates took control of the Communist Party. They jailed several of the radicals who had led the Cultural Revolution. By 1980, **Deng Xiaoping** (duhng show·pihng) had emerged as the most powerful leader in China. Like Mao and Zhou, Deng had survived the Long March. He was the last of the "old revolutionaries" who had ruled China since 1949.

Although a lifelong Communist, Deng boldly supported moderate economic policies. Unlike Mao, he was willing to use capitalist ideas to help China's economy. He embraced a set of goals known as the **Four Modernizations.** These called for progress in agriculture, industry, defense, and science and technology. Deng launched an ambitious program of economic reforms, which he called the "Second Revolution."

First, Deng eliminated Mao's unpopular communes and leased the land to individual farmers. The farmers paid rent by delivering a fixed quota of food to the government. They could then grow any crops they wished and sell them for a profit. Under this system, food production increased by 50 percent in the years 1978 to 1984.

Deng then extended his program to industry. The government permitted small private businesses to operate. It gave the managers of large state-owned industries more freedom to set production goals. Deng also welcomed some foreign technology and investment.

Deng's economic policies produced striking changes in Chinese life. As incomes increased, people began to buy appliances and televisions. Chinese youths now wore stylish clothes and listened to Western music. Gleaming hotels filled with foreign tourists symbolized China's new policy of openness.

Tiananmen Square

Deng's economic reforms produced a number of unexpected problems. As living standards improved, the gap between the rich and poor widened. Increasingly, the public believed that party officials took advantage of their positions by accepting bribes and enjoying privileges denied to others.

Furthermore, the new policies admitted not only Western investments and tourists but also Western political ideas. Increasing numbers of Chinese students studied abroad and learned about the West. Warned by hard-line officials that Communist values were at risk, Deng replied, "If you open the window, some flies naturally get in." In his view, the benefits of opening the economy exceeded the risks. Nevertheless, as Chinese students learned more about democracy, they began to question China's lack of political freedom.

Students Demand Democracy In 1989, students sparked a popular uprising that stunned China's leaders. Beginning in April of that year, more than 100,000 students occupied **Tiananmen** (tyahn·ahn·mehn) **Square.** This square is a huge public space in the heart of Beijing. The students mounted a protest for democracy by chanting, "Down with corruption!" "Down with dictatorship!" and "Long live democracy!"

HISTORY MAKERS

Deng Xiaoping
1904–1997
In his late teens, Deng Xiaoping became a Communist and a close associate of Mao Zedong and Zhou Enlai. In the 1960s, Deng embraced economic pragmatism—he was more interested in what produced results than in Communist theory. He summed up his views by saying, "It doesn't matter whether a cat is black or white, so long as it catches mice."

This flexible attitude caused Deng problems during the Cultural Revolution. Radicals removed him from his position and paraded him through the streets wearing humiliating labels.

Deng re-emerged in the 1970s, however, and became China's chief leader until his death in 1997. A key figure in world history, Deng would be remembered as the man who opened up China's economy while maintaining strict Communist rule.

932 Chapter 35

Background
Table tennis is commonly called Ping-Pong after a brand of the game's equipment.

Background
The moderates jailed Mao's widow and three of her followers—known as the Gang of Four.

B. Answer Western businesses and tourists brought Western ideas into the country, and students went to school overseas for economic reasons but learned about democracy.
THINK THROUGH HISTORY
B. Analyzing Causes How did economic reform introduce new political ideas to China?

TEACHING OPTION · BLOCK SCHEDULING | **COOPERATIVE ACTIVITY: Creating an Eyewitness Account** | **CLASS TIME 20 MINUTES**

Task: Students will research the Tiananmen Square protest and write an eyewitness account.

Purpose: To understand more about events before, during, and after the protest.

Activity: Have students work in small groups to research the protest in Tiananmen Square. Have them write eyewitness accounts, as either participants or

observers, of specific events, such as the creation of the "Goddess of Democracy," the decision of students to remain in the square, or the army's attack on protesters. Students can read A Voice from the Past on page 933 for an example of an eyewitness account. Groups can read their accounts to the class.

 Building a Portfolio: Students can include a copy of their eyewitness account.

ALTERNATIVE ASSESSMENT BOOK
Standards for Evaluating a Cooperative Activity

Standards for Evaluation
Eyewitness accounts should . . .
- clearly describe the events chosen
- reveal the writers' feelings and observations
- demonstrate students' knowledge of the issues

Background
Tiananmen Square had also been used as a staging area for student protests in 1919. (See page 782.)

The student protest won widespread popular support. When several thousand students began a hunger strike to highlight their cause, perhaps a million people poured into Tiananmen Square to support them. Many students now boldly called for Deng Xiaoping to resign.

Deng Orders a Crackdown Instead of considering political reform, Deng declared martial law. He ordered more than 250,000 troops to surround Beijing. One student recalled the mood at the time:

A VOICE FROM THE PAST
It would be a lie to say that we were not afraid, but we were mentally prepared and very determined. Some students could not believe that the army really would use deadly force. But most of all, we were motivated by a powerful sense of purpose. We believed that it would be worth sacrificing our lives for the sake of progress and democracy in China.

ANONYMOUS STUDENT, *San Francisco Examiner*

Although many students left the square after martial law was declared, about 3,000 chose to remain and continue their protest. The students revived their spirits by defiantly erecting a 33-foot statue that they named the "Goddess of Democracy." It resembled the American Statue of Liberty.

THINK THROUGH HISTORY
C. Contrasting
Contrast what the students expected to happen as explained in the quotation with what actually happened at Tiananmen Square.
C. Answer Some believed that the army would not attack them, but the army did attack and kill hundreds. Others were prepared to face anything.

On June 4, 1989, the standoff came to an end. Thousands of heavily armed soldiers stormed Tiananmen Square. Tanks smashed through barricades and crushed the Goddess of Democracy. Soldiers sprayed gunfire into crowds of frightened students. They also attacked protesters elsewhere in Beijing. The assault killed hundreds and wounded thousands.

The attack on Tiananmen Square marked the beginning of a massive government campaign to stamp out protest. Police arrested an estimated 10,000 people. The state used the media to announce that reports of a massacre were untrue. Officials claimed that a small group of criminals had plotted against the government. After showing great restraint, officials said, the army was forced to crush a riot. Television news, however, had already broadcast the truth to the world.

China in the 1990s

The brutal repression of the pro-democracy movement left Deng firmly in control of China. During the final years of his life, Deng continued his program of economic reforms. By the mid-1990s, China's booming economy was producing extraordinary changes:

A VOICE FROM THE PAST
The country today is an endless series of jolting surprises. Streets are clogged with traffic. There is construction everywhere. Indoor malls with glittering new department stores surge with customers for whom shopping is rapidly becoming the recreational pastime of choice. At night, restaurants are packed with China's new urban middle class, raucously eating, drinking, and chain-smoking until the air inside turns gray.

ORVILLE SCHELL, "China—the End of an Era"

Although Deng moved out of the limelight in 1995, he remained China's unquestioned leader. In February 1997, after a long illness, Deng died. Communist Party General Secretary Jiang Zemin (jee·ahng zeh·meen) assumed the presidency.

China After Deng Many questions arose after Deng's death. What kind of leader would Jiang be? Would he be able to hold onto power and ensure political stability? A highly intelligent and educated man, Jiang had served as mayor of Shanghai. He was considered skilled, flexible, and practical. However, he had no military experience.

Struggles for Democracy **933**

Daily *Life*
Training the Chinese Army

Xiao Ye is a former Chinese soldier living in the United States. After Tiananmen Square, he explained how Chinese soldiers are trained to obey orders without complaint:

We usually developed bleeding blisters on our feet after a few days of . . . hiking. Our feet were a mass of soggy peeling flesh and blood, and the pain was almost unbearable. . . . We considered the physical challenge a means of tempering [hardening] ourselves for the sake of the Party. . . . No one wanted to look bad. . . .

And during the days in Tiananmen, once again the soldiers did not complain. They obediently drove forward, aimed, and opened fire on command. In light of their training, how could it have been otherwise?

Daily *Life*
Training the Chinese Army

Ask students whether they think soldiers ever have a right or duty to disobey orders. Have students support their opinions.

MORE ABOUT . . .
Tiananmen Square

For centuries, Tiananmen Square has been an important site and a symbol of power in Beijing. Originally built in 1651, the square was greatly enlarged and finally cemented over in 1958. It covers 100 acres. Each flagstone is numbered, so that it is easy to organize parades in the square.

The square is named after the massive stone gate called Tiananmen ("Gate of Heavenly Peace") at its northern end. In the center of the square is the Monument to the People's Heroes. To the east are two museums dedicated to Chinese history. To the south is the Mao Zedong Memorial Hall, where Mao's body lies in state. To the west is the Great Hall of the People, meeting place for the National People's Congress.

 CRITICAL THINKING TRANSPARENCIES
CT35 Democratic Struggles Around the Globe

OBJECTIVE 4 INSTRUCT

China in the 1990s
▶ **Key Ideas**
• The Chinese economy continues to prosper.
• Deng's death raises questions about China's future.
• China regains Hong Kong, creating fears about the city's future.

TEACHING OPTION **BLOCK SCHEDULING** **SKILLBUILDER MINI-LESSON: Analyzing Primary Sources** **CLASS TIME 25 MINUTES**

Explaining the Skill: Primary sources are written or created by people who were either participants in or observers of historical events. These sources include letters, diaries, journals, speeches, articles, eyewitness accounts, and autobiographies. They contain objective facts and the writers' opinions.

Applying the Skill: Ask students to reread the quotation from Orville Schell on page 933. Have them analyze the passage by listing the facts he provides, by briefly describing his attitude toward the events, and by citing words or phrases that support their description.

Facts: China is changing rapidly; traffic is heavy and construction is everywhere; indoor malls serve more people; the new urban middle class is increasing.

Attitude: The writer feels that China is going through rapid, unsettling changes, which are creating a bustling, noisy, more westernized culture.

Words or Phrases: "jolting surprises," "clogged with traffic," "glittering new department stores," "shopping is . . . the recreational pastime," "raucously eating, drinking, and chain-smoking"

 IN-DEPTH RESOURCES: UNIT 8
Skillbuilder Practice: Analyzing Primary Sources, p. 42

History Through Art

Photojournalism

Tell students that early photojournalists, such as the Civil War photographer Mathew Brady, had only large-format stand-up cameras, which were bulky and hard to use. Brady could not take action pictures, only shots of stationary people, battlefields, and cities. His human subjects had to be posed and remain immobile while the photos were taken.

In the 1920s, the development of easy-to-handle miniature 35-millimeter cameras revolutionized the field, making it easier for photojournalists to capture people and events in action. Now, digital cameras, which produce images that can be computer enhanced and transmitted over telephone lines, allow photojournalists to snap dramatic, split-second action photos as events unfold.

MORE ABOUT. . .
Mao's Image

During Mao Zedong's lifetime, thousands of photos and paintings of his image were prominently displayed in public places and in private homes throughout China. Today his image is less common, but can still be found on tourist items such as T-shirts, key chains, and other mass-marketed products. None of these items would have been allowed in Mao's day.

Capturing Historical Moments

From the earliest days of photography, magazines and newspapers have used photographs to convey the news.

Photojournalists have to respond quickly to recognize the history-making moment and record it before the moment has passed. As the photographs on this page demonstrate, photojournalists have done much to capture the history of Communist China.

Connect *to* History

Drawing Conclusions Which of these photographs seems to have been taken spontaneously when the photojournalist spotted an important historical moment? Which of these photographs seems to have been arranged ahead of time? Explain.

SEE SKILLBUILDER HANDBOOK, PAGE 1006

Connect *to* Today

Compare Look through newspapers or news magazines to find a news photograph that you find interesting. Bring it to class and explain how it compares with the photographs shown here in spontaneity, drama, and historical importance.

Connect *to* History

Drawing Conclusions
The photo of the tanks is spontaneous because it is an action shot. The toast by Zhou Enlai and Richard Nixon seems prearranged because the leaders are posing for other diplomats and the press. The parade is probably prearranged. China was known for staging "spontaneous" demonstrations and parades. In the photo on this page, everyone is carrying the same image of Mao, which would suggest the parade had been organized by officials.

Connect *to* Today

Compare
The photographs that students bring should be news photos, not publicity shots or advertisements. Ask students to discuss the impact of the photos on public awareness of the events. Have them compare their photographs with those in the feature. Do their photos capture significant events in history or more fleeting moments? If there are people in their photos, what do the pictures show about their character?

Therefore, Jiang had few allies among the generals. He also faced challenges from rivals, including hard-line officials who favored a shift away from Deng's economic policies.

Other questions following Deng's death had to do with China's poor human rights record and relations with the United States. During the 1990s, the United States pressured China to release political prisoners and ensure basic rights for political opponents. China remained hostile to such pressure. Its government continued to repress the pro-democracy movement.

Nevertheless, the desire for freedom still ran through Chinese society. If China remained economically open but politically closed, tensions seemed bound to surface. As Chinese writer Liu Binyan observed in 1995, "The government Deng Xiaoping leaves behind will be the weakest in China since Communist rule began in 1949. . . . At the same time, the populace has become more difficult to rule than any other in Chinese history."

In late 1997, Jiang paid a state visit to the United States. During his visit, U.S. protesters demanded more democracy in China. Jiang admitted that China had made some mistakes but refused to promise that China's policies would change.

Transfer of Hong Kong Another major issue for China was the status of **Hong Kong.** Hong Kong was a thriving business center and British colony on the southeastern coast of China. On July 1, 1997, Great Britain handed Hong Kong over to China, ending 155 years of colonial rule.

As part of the negotiated transfer, China promised to respect Hong Kong's economic system and political liberties for 50 years. Many Hong Kong citizens worried about Chinese rule and feared the loss of their freedoms. Others, however, saw the transfer as a way to reconnect with their Chinese heritage.

The case of China demonstrates that the creation of democracy can be a slow, fitful, and incomplete process. Liberal reforms in one area, such as the economy, may not lead immediately to political reforms. Other nations, from Russia and Poland to Nigeria and Brazil, have found the path to democracy equally unpredictable. Even so, people around the world have a desire for more political freedom. As economic and social conditions improve—for example, as the middle class expands and educational opportunities grow—the prospects for democracy also may improve. In addition, as countries are increasingly linked through technology and trade, they will have more opportunity to influence each other politically. This too may promote democratic change.

In 1997, citizens of Hong Kong held their annual candlelight vigil to remember the massacre in Tiananmen Square. Many feared that the Chinese government would ban such memorials now that it controlled Hong Kong.

Section 5 Assessment

1. TERMS & NAMES
Identify
• Zhou Enlai
• Deng Xiaoping
• Four Modernizations
• Tiananmen Square
• Hong Kong

2. TAKING NOTES
Use a diagram like the one below to show the events leading up to the demonstration in Tiananmen Square and the events that followed it.

3. SUPPORTING OPINIONS
Judging from what you have read about the Chinese government, do you think Hong Kong will keep its freedoms under Chinese rule? Explain.

THINK ABOUT
• the economic reforms of Deng Xiaoping
• Tiananmen Square
• the Chinese government's promise to respect Hong Kong's liberties for 50 years

4. THEME ACTIVITY
Cultural Interaction Create a collage showing the different ways that contact with the West led to the call for democratic reform in China. Be sure to include pictures that symbolize all the different types of contact China had with the West.

Struggles for Democracy **935**

ANSWERS

1. TERMS & NAMES
Zhou Enlai, p. 931
Deng Xiaoping, p. 932
Four Modernizations, p. 932
Tiananmen Square, p. 932
Hong Kong, p. 935

2. TAKING NOTES
Possible Responses: China opens doors to U.S.; Deng Xiaoping begins Four Modernizations; Chinese buy Western goods and enjoy Western culture; Western tourists visit China; Chinese students study in West; **Tiananmen Square**; Chinese government massacres protesters; Chinese government represses pro-democracy movement.

3. SUPPORTING OPINIONS
Possible Responses: No—The Chinese government will try to apply its policy of allowing capitalism but repressing democracy in Hong Kong. Yes—The Chinese government will give Hong Kong special treatment, perhaps to keep its economy profitable or to avoid international criticism.

4. THEME ACTIVITY
Standards for Evaluation
Collages should meet the following criteria:
• Show ways that China had contact with the West.
• Illustrate effects of Western influence on Chinese society.

TERMS & NAMES

1. PRI, p. 914
2. apartheid, p. 919
3. Nelson Mandela, p. 919
4. Mikhail Gorbachev, p. 921
5. glasnost, p. 921
6. perestroika, p. 922
7. Lech Walesa, p. 922
8. Boris Yeltsin, p. 926
9. Deng Xiaoping, p. 932
10. Tiananmen Square, p. 932

REVIEW QUESTIONS

11. Free elections, citizen participation, majority rule, and constitutional government.

12. The military.

13. Ethnic conflict between the Igbo on one side and the Hausa-Fulani and Yoruba on the other led the Igbo region to secede. The government went to war to reunify the country.

14. Legalization of the ANC, holding of all-race (universal) elections, and writing of a new constitution and bill of rights.

15. Glasnost, perestroika, democratization, and foreign policy changes, such as pursuit of arms control and reduced interference in other countries.

16. Poland, Hungary, East Germany, Czechoslovakia, and Romania.

17. An attempt in 1991 by hard-line Communists to force Gorbachev to resign and to undo Gorbachev's reforms. It failed because the people would not go along with them.

18. The loss of Tito's leadership allowed ethnic conflicts to rise to the surface; when Serbia tried to dominate the other republics, several of them declared independence. The nation broke apart, and war resulted.

19. Zhou Enlai made overtures to the United States, and Deng Xiaoping initiated economic reforms.

20. It massacred demonstrators in Tiananmen Square, publicly lied about what had happened, and continued to repress the pro-democracy movement.

Chapter **35** Assessment

TERMS & NAMES

Briefly explain the importance of each of the following to the democratic movements that took place from 1945 to the present.

1. PRI
2. apartheid
3. Nelson Mandela
4. Mikhail Gorbachev
5. glasnost
6. perestroika
7. Lech Walesa
8. Boris Yeltsin
9. Deng Xiaoping
10. Tiananmen Square

Interact *with* History

On page 910, you considered what you might tell a foreign exchange student about how U.S. democracy works. Now that you've read the chapter, would your explanation be different? Would you add anything to what you said before? Would you change anything you said before?

REVIEW QUESTIONS

SECTION 1 (*pages 911–915*)
Patterns of Change: Democracy
Case Study: Latin American Democracies

11. Name four common democratic practices.

12. What group held up democratic progress in both Brazil and Argentina until the 1980s?

SECTION 2 (*pages 916–920*)
Democratic Challenges in African Nations

13. What brought about the civil war in Nigeria?

14. Name three significant steps toward democracy taken by South Africa in the 1990s.

SECTION 3 (*pages 921–925*)
Gorbachev Moves Toward Democracy

15. What were the main reforms promoted by Soviet leader Mikhail Gorbachev?

16. Which Eastern European nations overthrew Communist governments in 1989?

SECTION 4 (*pages 926–930*)
Collapse of the Soviet Union

17. What was the August Coup and how did it end?

18. What led to the breakup of Yugoslavia?

SECTION 5 (*pages 931–935*)
China Follows Its Own Path

19. What changes took place in China during the 1970s?

20. How did the Chinese government react to demands for democratic reform?

Visual Summary

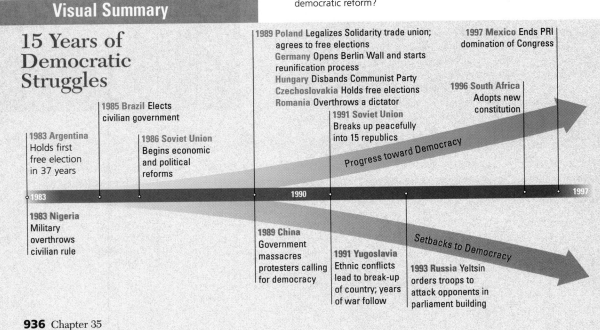

15 Years of Democratic Struggles

1989 Poland Legalizes Solidarity trade union; agrees to free elections
Germany Opens Berlin Wall and starts reunification process
Hungary Disbands Communist Party
Czechoslovakia Holds free elections
Romania Overthrows a dictator

1997 Mexico Ends PRI domination of Congress

1985 Brazil Elects civilian government

1991 Soviet Union Breaks up peacefully into 15 republics

1996 South Africa Adopts new constitution

1983 Argentina Holds first free election in 37 years

1986 Soviet Union Begins economic and political reforms

Progress toward Democracy

1983   1990   1997

1983 Nigeria Military overthrows civilian rule

1989 China Government massacres protesters calling for democracy

1991 Yugoslavia Ethnic conflicts lead to break-up of country; years of war follow

1993 Russia Yeltsin orders troops to attack opponents in parliament building

Setbacks to Democracy

936 Chapter 35

Interact *with* History

Ask students to list the remarks they would add, delete, or change. Students will probably add that building a stable democracy takes time and effort. Without key principles and institutions in place, it is easy for a democracy to be overthrown or torn apart by rival factions who ignore the law. Students may also have been surprised to learn how easily democracy can fall in the face of severe economic crises.

CRITICAL THINKING

1. ROADBLOCKS TO DEMOCRACY

THEME CULTURAL INTERACTION Name some examples from this chapter in which the negative impact of one culture on another blocked democratic progress.

2. DEMOCRATIC LEADERSHIP

Create a chart like the one below. List several leaders who you think helped their nations make democratic progress. For each leader, cite one example of an action that made a positive difference.

Leader	Nation	Positive Action

3. LESSONS OF DEMOCRACY

Think about the democratic movements you have studied in this chapter. Especially consider what conditions helped those movements succeed and what conditions caused difficulties for them. What do you think were the hardest challenges facing democratic movements?

4. ANALYZING PRIMARY SOURCES

The following excerpt comes from an article written about changes in the culture of Hong Kong in the months before it was returned to China. Read the paragraph and then answer the questions below it.

A VOICE FROM THE PAST

Whatever else you can say about the new Hong Kong, it will be more Chinese. Liu Heung-shing, the editor of the new Hong Kong magazine *The Chinese,* says that "for any meaningful art and culture to take off here, Hong Kong must find somewhere to anchor itself. To find that anchor, people will have to go north [to mainland China]." . . . Increasing numbers of Hong Kong's Cantonese speakers are studying mainland Mandarin. . . . At the same time that [Hong Kong] must resist China to retain Britain's legacy of rule of law, it knows that the most logical place for it to turn for commerce and culture is China.

ORVILLE SCHELL, "The Coming of Mao Zedong Chic"

- What is the main change that is taking place in Hong Kong's culture?
- What point of view might a business person have about this change?
- What point of view might a politician have about this change?

CHAPTER ACTIVITIES

1. LIVING HISTORY: Unit Portfolio Project

THEME ECONOMICS Your unit portfolio project focuses on economic changes within nations. For Chapter 35, you might use one of the following ideas to add to your portfolio.

- A government official has asked you for suggestions on how to move a Communist economy to a free market economy. Go through the chapter and compile a "Things to Do" list based on actions that other governments have taken.
- Create a poster with two contrasting lists: "Signs of a Healthy Economy" and "Signs of an Unhealthy Economy."
- Write an interview in which Deng Xiaoping discusses his economic reforms. Have him explain his goals for China.

2. CONNECT TO TODAY: Cooperative Learning

THEME REVOLUTION In this chapter, you read about how the democratic reforms initiated by Gorbachev led to an overturn of the Communist Soviet government. In effect, this was a second Russian Revolution.

Work with a team to create time lines of the first Russian Revolution in 1917 and the revolutionary events of 1985 to 1991. Then write a paragraph about the impact of the second revolution on Russia today.

INTERNET Using the Internet or a library, research Russian politics today. Is there still a Communist party? Is the Communist party still trying to undo the democratic reforms?

- Use this textbook, encyclopedias, or history books to find events for your time lines.
- Illustrate your time lines with photographs, drawings, or political cartoons.
- In your paragraph, evaluate how successful you think the second Russian Revolution was. Do you think the change will be long-lasting? Explain.

3. INTERPRETING A TIME LINE

Revisit the unit time line on pages 850–851. Use the Chapter 35 time line to learn what happened in Argentina in 1946.

FOCUS ON POLITICAL CARTOONS

Look carefully at this political cartoon, dated June 7, 1989.
- Do you recognize any world leaders in this cartoon? If so, who?
- What is the cartoon saying about the state of communism in Poland, China, and the Soviet Union?
- What is the cartoon's point of view—for or against communism? Explain.

Connect to History Judging from what you have read in the chapter, was the cartoon correct in its assessment of the state of communism? Explain your answer by citing specific events for each nation.

937

1. LIVING HISTORY

Standards for Evaluation
"Things to Do" lists should meet the following criteria:

- Contain entries arranged in order of importance.
- Identify governments that have taken each suggested action.
- Explain each suggestion and its ranking.

Standards for Evaluation
Posters should meet the following criteria:

- Contain two distinguishable lists.
- Have related issues arranged in the same order.
- Include explanations of the choices made.

Standards for Evaluation
Interviews should meet the following criteria:

- Include questions by people from both inside and outside China.
- Reasonably reflect Deng Xiaoping's probable answers.
- Show a basic knowledge of events in the relevant period of Chinese history.

2. CONNECT TO TODAY: COOPERATIVE LEARNING

Standards for Evaluation
Time lines should meet the following criteria:

- Show only major events and dates.
- Include graphic information to illuminate specific events.
- Present personal opinions about the relative successes of the two revolutions.

3. INTERPRETING A TIME LINE

In 1946, Juan Perón, a former army officer, was elected president of Argentina. Once in office, he gradually assumed the powers of a dictator, quelling all opposition.

FOCUS ON POLITICAL CARTOONS

- Lech Walesa and Gorbachev.
- The cartoonist is saying that communism is dying in the USSR and Poland and is dead in China.
- Against—The artist depicts communism as dead or dying, and at least one leader is celebrating its demise.

Connect to History Students should justify their answers with examples from the text.

CRITICAL THINKING

1. ROADBLOCKS TO DEMOCRACY

Possible Responses: Legacy of colonialism hindered democratic progress in Africa; ethnic clashes in Eastern Europe led to civil war; economic chaos delayed reforms.

2. DEMOCRATIC LEADERSHIP

Possible Responses: Raúl Alfonsín: Argentina—reformed democracy and economy; *Ken Saro-Wiwa: Nigeria*—fought injustice; *F. W. de Klerk: South Africa*—freed Mandela, helped end apartheid, agreed to open elections; *Nelson Mandela: South Africa*—protested apartheid; called for economic reform and reconciliation; *Mikhail Gorbachev: Soviet Union*—initiated reforms; *Lech Walesa: Poland*—led Solidarity; *Vaclav Havel: Czechoslovakia*—tried to prevent split of nation; *Boris Yeltsin: Russia*—criticized slow pace of reforms, led protest against coup.

3. LESSONS OF DEMOCRACY

Possible Responses: Colonial legacy, ethnic and racial conflict, oppressive governments, centrally controlled economies.

4. ANALYZING PRIMARY SOURCES

Possible responses: Hong Kong is turning to China for cultural inspiration. Business people may view China's markets as opportunities. Politicians may fear that China will curtail the city's freedoms.

CHAPTER 36
Global Interdependence

	Key Ideas	**COPY MASTERS**	**ASSESSMENT**
SECTION 1 **Science and Technology Shape Human Outlook** pp. 941–944	Advances in technology during the second half of the 20th century focus on the exploration of space and also on communications networks and medical and agricultural techniques that improve the quality of people's lives.	*In-Depth Resources: Unit 8* • **Guided Reading,** p. 55 • **Primary Source:** from "Down to Earth," p. 62	*Section 1 Assessment,* p. 944 *Formal Assessment* • Section Quiz, p. 425 *Alternative Assessment Book* • Standards for Evaluating a Cooperative Activity
SECTION 2 **Global Economic Development** pp. 945–951	As the global economy expands, the nations of the world are forced to adjust to new patterns of work and trade and to the necessity of maintaining economic growth while preserving the environment.	*In-Depth Resources: Unit 8* • **Guided Reading,** p. 56 • **Skillbuilder Practice:** Analyzing Assumptions, p. 59 • **Geography Application:** Deforestation in Brazil, p. 60 • **Primary Source:** Recycling Symbol, p. 63 • **Literature:** "Paper," p. 66	*Section 2 Assessment,* p. 950 *Formal Assessment* • Section Quiz, p. 426 *Alternative Assessment Book* • Standards for Evaluating a Cooperative Activity
SECTION 3 **Global Security Issues** pp. 952–956	Nations try to preserve peace and collective security and promote human rights but face many challenges, including ethnic and religious conflicts and the dislocation of peoples through migration.	*In-Depth Resources: Unit 8* • **Guided Reading,** p. 57 • **Primary Source:** The Universal Declaration of Human Rights, p. 64 • **History Makers:** Kofi Annan, p. 69; Rigoberta Menchú, p. 70	*Section 3 Assessment,* p. 956 *Formal Assessment* • Section Quiz, p. 427 *Alternative Assessment Book* • Standards for Evaluating a Cooperative Activity
SECTION 4 **Cultures Blend in a Global Age** pp. 957–961	Expanded communications technology brings peoples of the world closer together, creating conflict as they strive to preserve their uniqueness while respecting and living in harmony with their global neighbors.	*In-Depth Resources: Unit 8* • **Guided Reading,** p. 58 • **Primary Source:** "Cupid's a Korean Computer, Making Wise Matches," p. 65 • **Connections Across Time and Cultures:** Progress and Change, p. 71	*Section 4 Assessment,* p. 961 *Formal Assessment* • Section Quiz, p. 428 *Alternative Assessment Book* • Standards for Evaluating a Cooperative Activity
CHAPTER RESOURCES	**Chapter Overview** Advances in communications technology and increasing economic, cultural, and political interdependence give rise to a global community. People face growing responsibilities for maintaining the environment and working toward world peace.	*Telescoping the Times* • Chapter Summary, pp. 141–143 *Planning for Block Schedules*	*Chapter Assessment,* pp. 962–963 *Chapter Activities,* p. 963 *Formal Assessment* • Chapter Test, forms A and B, pp. 429–434 *Test Generator* *Alternative Assessment Book*

1960–Present

TECHNOLOGY

 Warm-Up Transparency 36

 Patterns of Interaction: Technology Transforms an Age

 INTERNET RESOURCES
www.mlworldhistory.com

 Warm-Up Transparency 36

Geography Transparencies
• GT36 World Per Capita Income, 1990s

World Art and Cultures Transparencies
• AT79 *Time Goes By*

Battles of the World
• The Gulf War

Patterns of Interaction: Trade Connects the World

Electronic Library of Primary Sources
• "Tackling the Menace of Space Junk"

 Warm-Up Transparency 36

Critical Thinking Transparencies
• CT36 Patterns of Refugee Movement

Electronic Library of Primary Sources
• "The Making of a Terrorist"

 INTERNET RESOURCES
www.mlworldhistory.com

 Warm-Up Transparency 36

World Art and Cultures Transparencies
• AT80 *Technology* (Korean video sculpture)

Critical Thinking Transparencies
• CT72 Chapter 36 Visual Summary

Electronic Library of Primary Sources
• "Un-American Ugly Americans"
• "Television Is Defying Borders"

Patterns of Interaction: Cultural Crossroads

 INTERNET RESOURCES
www.mlworldhistory.com

 Chapter Summaries on Audiocassette in English and Spanish

INTERNET RESOURCES
www.mlworldhistory.com

Block Scheduling (90 MINUTES)

Day 1
Section 1, pp. 941–944

 COOPERATIVE ACTIVITY
Dramatizing Space Travel, p. 942 (Teacher's Edition)

Section 2, pp. 945–951

COOPERATIVE ACTIVITY
Drafting a Trade Agreement, p. 948 (Teacher's Edition)

Section Assessments, pp. 944, 950

Day 2
Section 3, pp. 952–956

COOPERATIVE ACTIVITY
Outlining a Nobel Prize Acceptance Speech, p. 954 (Teacher's Edition)

Section 4, pp. 957–961

 COOPERATIVE ACTIVITY
Staging an International Literature Fair, p. 960 (Teacher's Edition)

Section Assessments, pp. 956, 961

Chapter Assessment, pp. 962–963

Yearly Pacing *Chapter 36 Total:* 2 days *Yearly Total:* 85 days

Planning for Block Schedules

Customizing for Special Needs

Students Acquiring English

Access for Students Acquiring English
• **Guided Reading** for Sections 1–4 (Spanish), pp. 364–367
• **Chapter Summary** (Spanish), pp. 361–363
• **Skillbuilder Practice** Analyzing Assumptions (Spanish), p. 368
• **Geography Application** Deforestation in Brazil (Spanish), p. 369

Chapter Summaries on Audiocassette in English and Spanish

Patterns of Interaction Technology Transforms an Age; Trade Connects the World; Cultural Crossroads (Spanish tracks)

Less Proficient Readers

In-Depth Resources: Unit 8
• **Guided Reading** for Sections 1–4, pp. 55–58
• **Skillbuilder Practice** Analyzing Assumptions, p. 59
• **Geography Application** Deforestation in Brazil, p. 60

Telescoping the Times
• Chapter Summary, pp. 141–143

Chapter Summaries on Audiocassette

Gifted and Talented Students

In-Depth Resources: Unit 8

Primary Sources:
• from "Down to Earth," p. 62
• Recycling Symbol, p. 63
• The Universal Declaration of Human Rights, p. 64
• "Cupid's a Korean Computer, Making Wise Matches," p. 65

History Makers
• Kofi Annan, p. 69
• Rigoberta Manchú, p. 70

Connections to Literature READINGS FOR STUDENTS

In-Depth Resources: Unit 8
Literature: "Paper," p. 66

 McDougal Littell *Literature Connections*
• **Foote, Horton** *To Kill a Mockingbird* (the screenplay) *(with related readings)*
Adapted from the Pulitzer Prize–winning novel by Harper Lee, the story examines the consequences of ignorance and hate.

 McDougal Littell *Literature Connections*
• **Potek, Chaim** *The Chosen* *(with related readings)*
In this story, two teenage boys become best friends despite living in different worlds. Reuven, the narrator, slowly comes to understand Danny's sternly Hasidic world.

PE = Pupil's Edition   = Overhead Transparency   = Software   = Video

= Copy Master   = CD-ROM   = Audiocassette   = Internet

Global Interdependence, 1960–present

Accessing Prior Knowledge

- Ask students what picture comes to mind when they hear the phrase *global interdependence*. What does it imply about the peoples, languages, cultures, economies, and politics of the world?

Drawing Conclusions

- What do the pictures of the Arab man and the Huli children suggest about technology and the modern world?

- In what ways are the Tibetan women and the Brazilian Indians trying to influence the future of their world? What ways of the past do they cling to?

GEOGRAPHY CONNECTION

Ask students to examine the position of the continents on this world map.

- How does this presentation differ from a conventional map?

- What does it suggest about the relation of the world's nations and peoples?

CHAPTER 36 — Global Interdependence, 1960–present

PREVIEWING THEMES

Science and Technology
Advances in science and technology have changed the lives of people around the globe. People today eat better, and live longer, healthier, and more comfortable lives. Improved communication and transportation have allowed goods and ideas to move rapidly. Science has even reached out to new horizons in space.

Cultural Interaction
New inventions and innovations have brought the nations of the world closer and exposed people to the ideas and habits of other cultures. Cultures are now blending ideas, customs, and habits. The people of the world have developed a greater sense of being part of a larger global culture.

Economics
Since World War II, nations have worked to expand trade and commerce in world markets. Changes in transportation and technology along with the establishing of multinational companies have blurred national boundaries and created a global market.

INTERNET CONNECTION
Visit us at **www.mlworldhistory.com** to learn more about global interdependence in the modern world.

938

THE WORLD TODAY

Technology has reached into formerly isolated areas across the world to change ways of life. These two children of the **Huli tribe** of **Papua New Guinea** study a Polaroid picture.

Brazilian Indians ride a bus in **Rio de Janeiro, Brazil,** after a meeting during the Earth Summit in **1992.** The Indians discussed issues of the environment, hunger, and land disputes with the Brazilian government.

GEOGRAPHY THEMES

Movement

In the modern world of air travel, the shortest route between places on different continents often involves flying over the North Pole. Ask students to locate the North Pole on the map. *The point in the Arctic Ocean where the lines of longitude converge.* Flights often follow one of the lines of longitude over the pole in what is called a great circle route. Have students trace great circle routes between various sets of points on different continents and compare them with routes that go around the globe. Encourage students to discuss how great circle routes might affect communication in the modern world.

Human–Environment Interaction

The proliferation of modern technology has drastically altered the way people think about and interact with their world. Causes and effects are no longer local and isolated, but act globally. Vastly increased emissions from automobiles and industry, for example, contribute to global warming. A 1997 monetary crisis in the Asian stock market sent the U.S. market plummeting. As technology continues to develop, it will bring new possibilities and opportunities, but also require the commitment of nations to protect the earths environment.

ADDITIONAL RESOURCES

Books for the Teacher

• Kaplan, Robert D. *The Ends of the Earth: A Journey at the Dawn of the 21st Century.* New York: Random, 1996. A pessimistic view of the future.

• Ostry, Sylvia, and Richard R. Nelson. *Techno-Nationalism and Techno-Globalism: Conflict and Cooperation.* Washington, D.C.: Brookings Institution, 1995.

• Rawlins, Gregory J. E. *Moths to the Flame: The Seductions of Computer Technology.* Cambridge: MIT P, 1996.

Books for the Student

• Markley, Oliver W., and Walter R. McCuan, eds. *America Beyond 2001: Opposing Viewpoints.* San Diego: Greenhaven, 1996.

• Yancey, Diane. *Life in War-Torn Bosnia.* San Diego: Lucent, 1996.

▰▰ Videos

• *Exploring the Global Economy.* Social Studies School Service, 1994. 800-421-4246. The fundamental concepts that govern international trade.

• *The Technological Revolution/Toward the Future.* Crystal Productions, 1989. 800-255-8629.

◉ Software

• *Lines in the Sand: The Pursuit of Peace in the Middle East.* CD-ROM. Social Studies School Service, 1995. 800-421-4246.

• *Space: A Visual History.* CD-ROM. Queue, 1994. 800-232-2224.

Tibetan women demonstrate against human rights violations at the Forum on Women in **Huairou, China,** in September **1995.**

New technologies allow an Arab man in **Yemen** using a radio phone to conduct business or contact family and friends.

HISTORY THROUGH ART

Clothing and Personal Adornment

Throughout history, clothing has provided not only protection from the elements, but also a way for people to decorate their bodies and present themselves as works of art. Even in the age of global interdependence, as these images attest, people adorn their bodies in ways that distinguish them from their global neighbors. The Brazilian Indians' headdresses and body paint, the Arab man's head covering and robe,

the Tibetan women's woven aprons, and the Papua New Guineans' face decoration not only identify these people, but also transmit a message about who they are and what they stand for.

Clothing also enables people to exhibit their feelings, such as mourning, and to elicit certain responses in others, such as "dressing for success." A person's mode of dress also places that person in time. Not only do styles of clothing change constantly, but the

materials they are made from reflect the resources and technologies at hand. In today's interdependent world, even an African's loincloth might be fashioned from polyester.

Interpreting the Art Ask students what the clothing of the people pictured here suggests about their geographical locations and ways of life.

Interact *with* History

This Interact with History feature motivates students by inviting them to take a broad view of world events. As they read the headlines of worldwide newspapers, students will consider not only the impact of these events on the people involved, but also the effects on their own and other people's lives.

Purpose
- To introduce students to the concept of a global community
- To give students a broad perspective on world events
- To help students appreciate the many ways in which the world's nations are interdependent

Teaching Strategy
Thinking Critically After students have imagined themselves in the situation described on this page, have them answer the key question and give reasons for their answers.

EXAMINING *the* ISSUES

Following are suggestions for addressing each bulleted question.

❶ Remind students that the Common Market is an economic alliance formed in an attempt to eliminate trade barriers among the member nations.

❷ Over several successive days, bring in the international section of a newspaper or play a radio news broadcast. Have students chart the news stories and discuss the effects of events in one part of the world on people in other parts.

❸ Ask students to list foods, music, books, television shows, and web sites they've experienced in the past week. What international influences do they see?

Making Connections Ask students to discuss how people around the world might respond differently to growing global interdependence.

Interact *with* History

You are walking down a street of our nation's capital on a cloudy summer day. All of a sudden, the sky gets very dark and within minutes a heavy rain begins pouring down. You run for the closest shelter and find yourself at an international newsstand. As you wait for the rain to let up, you scan the headlines of dozens of newspapers from all over the world. They all focus on different events.

What impact do events in different countries have on your life?

Mir Cosmonauts Prepare for U.S. Crew Member

Southeast Asian Common Market Suggested

U.S., Israel, Palestinians to Work on Security

India Flash Floods Kill at Least 110

Brazil's Forests Fading Fastest, Tree Study Says

EXAMINING *the* ISSUES

❶ • What evidence do the headlines give of economic interdependence in today's world?

❷ • How do the headlines illustrate the political interdependence of different nations?

❸ • What do the stories in the newspapers tell you about scientific and cultural interdependence among nations?

As a class, discuss these questions. Remember what you've learned about the recent history of nations in different regions of the world. Try to think of reasons why nations are becoming increasingly dependent on one another.

As you read this chapter, look for more examples of economic, political, and cultural interdependence among the nations of the world.

Follow-Up
A feature on the chapter assessment will ask students to reevaluate their responses to the situation presented on this page.

1 Science and Technology Shape Human Outlook

TERMS & NAMES
- Hubble Space Telescope
- Internet
- genetic engineering
- cloning
- green revolution

MAIN IDEA

Advances in technology after World War II led to increased global interaction and improved quality of life.

WHY IT MATTERS NOW

The lives of all people around the world are affected by advances in science and technology.

SETTING THE STAGE Beginning in the late 1950s, the United States and the Soviet Union competed in the exploration of space. The Soviets launched Earth's first artificial satellite, *Sputnik I,* and put the first human in orbit around the planet. By the late 1960s, however, the United States had surpassed the Soviets. U.S. astronauts landed on the moon in 1969. The heavy emphasis on science and technology spilled over into developing products that improved the ways of life of human beings across the globe.

Probing the Solar System and Beyond

The space race of the 1950s, 1960s, and early 1970s was intensely competitive. Both the United States and the Soviet Union competed to reach the moon and beyond.

Both nations developed manned and unmanned space programs. Although the space race was competitive, it carried the seeds of global cooperation. Orbiting spacecraft beamed back images of a small blue planet, Earth, floating like a jewel in the black void of space. People around the world who saw this view of Earth received a stirring reminder that though they lived in different countries, they all shared the planet. Eventually, space exploration became one of the world's first and most successful arenas for cooperation between U.S. and Soviet scientists.

Space Race Becomes Cooperative In 1972, more than 15 years before the end of the Cold War, the United States and the Soviet Union signed an agreement. Their goal was to work toward docking *Apollo* and *Soyuz* spacecraft in space. Not only did the American and Soviet staffs have to work out engineering problems, they also had to learn each other's language. On July 17, 1975, an American *Apollo* spacecraft docked with the Soviet *Soyuz 19* spacecraft 140 miles above Earth. As the astronauts opened the hatch connecting the space vehicles, TV viewers across the globe watched the crews from Earth's fiercest rival countries greet each other.

This first cooperative venture in space between the United States and the USSR was an isolated event. Over the next 15 years, American and Soviet space programs separately developed space shuttles. Unlike the *Apollo* spacecraft, these shuttles were reusable and could return to Earth under their own power. During the 1980s, shuttle missions put crews in orbit around Earth. The missions were designed to accomplish a variety of scientific and technological experiments. Colonel Frederick Gregory, a

Four U.S. astronauts and one Russian cosmonaut worked together in the Shuttle *Atlantis* cargo bay. They linked with the *Mir* space station.

Global Interdependence **941**

SECTION 1 RESOURCES

PRINT RESOURCES

 IN-DEPTH RESOURCES: UNIT 8
Guided Reading, p. 55
Primary Source: from "Down to Earth," p. 62

 ACCESS FOR STUDENTS ACQUIRING ENGLISH
Guided Reading (Spanish), p. 364

 FORMAL ASSESSMENT
Section Quiz, p. 425

ALTERNATIVE ASSESSMENT BOOK

TECHNOLOGY RESOURCES

VIDEO
Patterns of Interaction: Technology Transforms an Age

INTERNET www.mlworldhistory.com

Section 1 Overview

OBJECTIVES

① To trace exploration of the solar system and to show how it relates to international politics and economics.

② To identify the effects of expanding global communications in the late 20th century.

③ To list advances in health care, medicine, and agriculture, and to evaluate their effects.

CRITICAL THINKING

- Hypothesizing, p. 942
- Summarizing, pp. 943, 944
- Forming and supporting opinions, p. 944
- Analyzing themes, p. 944

FOCUS
5-Minute Warm-Up

▶ **Identifying Main Ideas**
To spark students' interest in the far-reaching effects of science and technology, have them answer these questions.

- Read the Spotlight on Space Junk on page 942. What is space junk?

- What are some hazards it poses for both astronauts in space and people on Earth?

WARM-UP TRANSPARENCY 36

OBJECTIVE ① INSTRUCT

Probing the Solar System and Beyond

▶ **Key Ideas**

- Exploration of space begins as a competition between the United States and the Soviet Union.

- By the 1980s, people from various countries cooperate in exploring the universe.

- Private companies become involved in scientific and commercial ventures in space.

 IN-DEPTH RESOURCES: UNIT 8
Guided Reading, p. 55
Primary Source: from "Down to Earth," p. 62

 ACCESS FOR STUDENTS ACQUIRING ENGLISH
Guided Reading (Spanish), p. 364

SPOTLIGHT ON

Space Junk

Since the late 1950s, thousands of objects have been sent into orbit. Some of these objects have crashed to Earth. For instance, in 1962, a small piece of metal that was part of the Russian satellite *Sputnik IV* fell from the sky and landed on a street in a small town in Wisconsin.

Larger, more dangerous objects have fallen to Earth. Space hazards have included a one-ton tank from the U.S. space station *Skylab* and a nuclear reactor from a failed Soviet satellite.

Space junk is a hazard in space as well. For example, a floating paint chip cracked the outer window of a space shuttle. Scientists try to combat the dangers posed by space junk by tracking debris and designing their spacecraft carefully.

Spacelab 3 astronaut, observed, "I think that science is the stuff that pays for itself on these missions. It's going to improve the quality of life down here [Earth]."

Beginning in the 1970s and increasing in the 1980s, people from different countries worked together to explore space. The Soviets were the first to send an international crew into space. In 1978, they invited Czech astronaut Vladimir Remek to orbit Earth in *Soyuz 28*. In the mid-1980s, the U.S. space agency invited people from Saudi Arabia, France, Germany, and Mexico to fly on the space shuttle.

Both the Soviets and the Americans had launched and lived in space stations since the early 1970s. Since 1986, the Soviet-launched *Mir* space station has been orbiting over 200 miles above Earth. In the mid-1990s, the Russians invited a number of U.S. astronauts to spend time on board *Mir*. Back on Earth, American and Russian scientists worked with scientists from 13 other nations to design and construct the first International Space Station.

Exploring the Universe Helping to study planets of the solar system, unmanned space probes such as *Voyager 2* sent dazzling pictures of Jupiter, Saturn, Uranus, and Neptune back to Earth. The Soviet *Venera* and *Vega* spacecraft and the U.S. *Magellan* spacecraft gathered in-depth information about Venus. In 1997, the U.S. space agency landed the *Pathfinder* probe on Mars. The public was fascinated with pictures sent back to Earth that included the activities of a mechanical rover named *Sojourner*.

In 1986, several nations, including Japan and the Soviet Union, sent spacecraft to study Halley's Comet as it swung by Earth. The U.S. space agency, NASA, and the European space agency, ESA, worked together to make and launch the **Hubble Space Telescope** in 1990. This advanced tool is today observing objects in the most remote regions of the universe.

Space Goes Commercial Meanwhile, private companies have become increasingly involved in space. One company has even contracted to take over much of the U.S. space shuttle program. Some companies launch rockets and satellites that help search for minerals and other resources on Earth. Satellites also follow the weather, aid long-distance learning programs, and even guide cars through cities. In the future, companies may use the zero-gravity environment of space to manufacture perfect crystals. They may eventually send solar collectors into orbit to help generate electricity for Earth. However, the most common commercial use of space today and in the near future will probably remain in the field of communications.

Expanding Global Communications

Since the 1960s, artificial satellites launched into orbit around Earth have aided worldwide communications. With satellite communication, the world was gradually transformed into a global village. Today, political and cultural events occurring in one part of the world often are witnessed live by people in other places. For example, in 1997, more than 2 billion television viewers across the world watched the funeral of Diana, the Princess of Wales. The linking of the globe through worldwide communications was made possible by the miniaturization of the computer.

Smaller, More Powerful Computers In the 1940s, when computers first came into use, they took up a huge room. The computer required fans or an elaborate air-conditioning system to cool the vacuum tubes that powered its operations. In the years since then, however, the circuitry that runs the computer had been miniaturized and made more powerful. This was due in part to the space program, where equipment had to be downsized to fit in tiny space capsules. Silicon chips replaced the bulky vacuum tubes used earlier. Smaller than contact lenses, silicon chips hold millions of microscopic circuits.

Following this development, industries began to use computers and silicon chips to run assembly lines. A variety of consumer products such as microwave ovens, telephones, keyboard instruments, and cars today use computers and chips. Personal computers have become essential in most offices, and millions of people around the globe use personal computers in their homes.

Communications Networks Starting in the 1990s, businesses and individuals began using the Internet. The **Internet** is the voluntary linkage of computer networks around the world. It began in the late 1960s as a method of linking scientists so they could exchange information about research. Through telephone-line links, business and personal computers can be hooked up with computer networks. These networks allow users to communicate with people across the nation and around the world. In the period from 1993 to 1996, the use of the Internet increased by an estimated seven times.

Conducting business on the Internet has become a way of life for many. The Internet, along with fax machines, transmits information electronically to remote locations. Both paved the way for home offices and "telecommuting." Once again, as it has many times in the past, technology has changed how and where people work.

Transforming Human Life

Advances with computers and communications networks have transformed not only the ways people work but lifestyles as well. Technological progress in the sciences, medicine, and agriculture has changed the quality of the lives of millions of people.

Health and Medicine Before World War II, surgeons seldom performed operations on sensitive areas such as the eye, the inner ear, or the brain. Beginning in the 1950s, new technologies employed in advanced surgical techniques developed. More powerful microscopes and innovations such as the laser and ultrasound were among the improvements. For example, by the late 1970s, laser surgery to remove damaged lenses of the eye, such as lenses clouded with cataracts, was common. Such techniques made surgery safer and more accurate and improved patients' chances for quick recovery.

Advances in medical imaging also helped to improve health care. The use of CAT scans and MRI techniques gave doctors three-dimensional views of different organs or regions of the body. Using CAT scans and MRIs, doctors diagnose injuries, detect tumors, or collect other information needed to identify medical conditions.

In the 1980s, genetics, the study of heredity through research on genes, became a fast-growing field of science. Found in the cells of all organisms, genes are hereditary units that cause specific traits, such as eye color, in every living organism. Technology allowed scientists to isolate and examine individual genes that are responsible for different traits. Through **genetic engineering**, scientists were able to introduce new

Global Interdependence **943**

Daily *Life*

Logging On

Each day millions of people across the world "log on"—link their computer with the Internet system, as shown in the diagram above. One study estimates that about 23 percent of people over age 16 in the United States and Canada use the Internet. People use the Internet to share information, to shop for hard-to-find products, and even for "virtual" travel.

The most common usage for the Internet is for sending and receiving electronic mail, or e-mail. With e-mail, people can communicate inexpensively anytime, anywhere in the world. By enabling people from all over the world to share ideas freely, the Internet helps people learn not just about topics of interest but also about each other.

SPOTLIGHT ON

The Human Genome Project
Human genetic material (DNA) contains approximately 50,000 to 100,000 genes. Mapping the thousands of genes contained in human DNA is the goal of the Human Genome Project.

The information led to the development of a new field of medicine called "molecular medicine." This field focuses on how genetic diseases develop and progress. It has resulted in early detection of disease. Eventually, it may lead to individualized treatment based on a person's genetic makeup.

Misuse of this information could drastically alter society. Therefore, a part of the project includes investigation of the ethical, legal, and social issues raised by genetic engineering.

genes into an organism to give that organism new traits. For example, with genetic engineering, scientists removed a gene from an Arctic fish and placed it in a plant. The resulting genetically engineered plant is better able to withstand frost.

Another aspect of genetic engineering is **cloning,** the creation of identical copies of DNA, the chemical chains of genes that determine heredity. Cloning actually allows scientists to reproduce both plants and animals that are identical to existing plants and animals. The applications of genetics research have led to many advances, especially in agriculture.

The Green Revolution In the 1950s, agricultural scientists around the world started a campaign known as the **green revolution.** It was an attempt to increase available food sources worldwide. Scientists promoted the use of fertilizers, pesticides, and high-yield, disease-resistant strains of a variety of crops. The green revolution helped avert famine in Asia and increased yields of crops in many different parts of the world.

However, the green revolution had its negative side, too. Fertilizers and pesticides are dangerous chemicals that cause cancer and pollute the environment. Also, the cost of the chemicals and the equipment to harvest more crops was far too expensive for an average peasant farmer. Consequently, owners of small farms received little benefit from the advances in agriculture. In some cases farmers were forced off the land by larger agricultural businesses.

Advances in genetics research have helped to fulfill some of the goals of the green revolution. In this new "gene revolution," resistance to pests was bred into plant strains, reducing the need for pesticides. Plants bred to tolerate poor soil conditions also reduced the need for fertilizers. The gene revolution involved some risks, including the accidental creation of disease-causing organisms. However, the revolution also brought great promises for increasing food production in a world with an expanding population.

Science and technology has changed the lives of millions of people. In many cases quality of life has improved. What people produce and even their jobs have changed. These changes have altered the economies of nations. Not only have nations become linked through communications networks but they are also linked in a global economic network, as you will see in Section 2.

THINK THROUGH HISTORY
C. Summarizing
What are some of the positive and negative effects of genetic engineering?
C. Possible Answers Positive— more food available, reduced need for fertilizer; negative— accidental creation of disease-causing organisms

---

Section 1 Assessment

1. TERMS & NAMES
Identify
• Hubble Space Telescope
• Internet
• genetic engineering
• cloning
• green revolution

2. TAKING NOTES
Copy the chart below and fill in information on ways science and technology has changed human life.

Science and Technology Changes Lives		
Communications	Health and Medicine	Green Revolution

Which of the three areas do you think has had the greatest global effect?

3. FORMING AND SUPPORTING OPINIONS
What is your opinion about cloning? In your judgment, is there a limit to how far cloning should go? Support your opinion with reasons.

THINK ABOUT
• the Human Genome Project
• positive effects of cloning
• negative effects of cloning

4. ANALYZING THEMES
Science and Technology
Why do you think that space exploration became an arena for cooperation between the Soviet Union and the United States?

THINK ABOUT
• goals of space exploration
• technologies involved
• images of Earth from space

944 Chapter 36

ANSWERS

1. TERMS & NAMES
Hubble Space Telescope, p. 942
Internet, p. 943
genetic engineering, p. 943
cloning, p. 944
green revolution, p. 944

2. TAKING NOTES
Possible Responses:

Communications: television contact across the globe, home offices and telecommuting; *Health and Medicine:* improved diagnoses and surgery; mapping and genetic engineering; *Green Revolution:* increased crop yields; decreased use of pesticides through plant genetics.

3. FORMING AND SUPPORTING OPINIONS
Possible Responses: Cloning has led to many advances in health and agriculture. It can be pushed too far; for example, creating dangerous biological weapons.

4. ANALYZING THEMES
Possible Responses: Both nations saw the advantages of sharing costs and information, pooling technologies, and increasing good will between their countries.

Global Economic Development

TERMS & NAMES
- developed nation
- developing nation
- global economy
- multinational corporation
- free trade
- Gulf War
- ozone layer
- sustainable development

MAIN IDEA

The economies of the world's nations are so tightly linked that the actions of one nation affect others.

WHY IT MATTERS NOW

Every individual is affected by the global economy and the environment.

SETTING THE STAGE At the end of World War II, much of Europe and Asia lay in ruins, with many of the major cities leveled by bombing. The devastation of the war was immense. However, within a decade, with U.S. aid, the economies of western European nations and Japan began expanding rapidly. Their growth continued for half a century, long after the United States ceased supplying aid.

Technology Revolutionizes the World's Economy

Advances in technology caused economic growth in both Asia and the Western world. The explosion in scientific knowledge prompted great progress that quickly led to new industries. A prime example was plastics. In the 1950s, a process to develop plastics at low pressures and low temperatures was perfected. Within a few years, industries made toys, cooking utensils, containers, and a host of other products easily and cheaply out of plastics. The plastics industry boomed. Other technological advances have also changed industrial processes, lowered costs, and increased the quality or the speed of production. For example, robotic arms on automobile assembly lines made possible the fast and safe manufacture of high-quality cars.

Information Industries Change Economies Technological advances in manufacturing reduced the need for factory workers. But in other areas of the economy new demands were emerging. Computerization and communications advances changed the processing of information. By the 1980s, people could transmit information quickly and cheaply. Information industries such as financial services, insurance, market research, and communications services boomed. Those industries depended on what Professor Peter Drucker called "knowledge workers."

Car production has changed a great deal since the production of pre–World War II cars. Today, car assembly plants using efficient robots have eliminated jobs once done by people.

Global Interdependence **945**

SECTION 2 RESOURCES

PRINT RESOURCES

 IN-DEPTH RESOURCES: UNIT 8
Guided Reading, p. 56
Skillbuilder Practice: Analyzing Assumptions, p. 59
Geography Application: Deforestation in Brazil, p. 60
Primary Source: Recycling Symbol, p. 63

 ACCESS FOR STUDENTS ACQUIRING ENGLISH
Guided Reading (Spanish), p. 365
Skillbuilder Practice (Spanish), p. 368
Geography Application (Spanish), p. 369

FORMAL ASSESSMENT
Section Quiz, p. 426

TECHNOLOGY RESOURCES

GEOGRAPHY TRANSPARENCIES
GT36 World Per Capita Income, 1990s

WORLD ART AND CULTURES TRANSPARENCIES
AT79 *Time Goes by*

CD-ROM
Battles of the World: The Gulf War
Electronic Library of Primary Sources

VIDEO
Patterns of Interaction: Trade Connects the World

Section 2 Overview

OBJECTIVES

(1) To discuss the effects of technology on the world economy.

(2) To explain the economic growth of Pacific Rim countries.

(3) To define the global economy.

(4) To identify challenges facing developing nations.

(5) To describe the environmental impact of development.

SKILLBUILDER
- Interpreting graphs, p. 946
- Interpreting maps: location, location, p. 948

CRITICAL THINKING
- Analyzing causes, p. 946
- Recognizing effects, pp. 946, 950
- Summarizing, pp. 947, 949
- Forming an opinion, p. 948
- Clarifying, p. 950
- Drawing conclusions, p. 951

FOCUS

5-Minute Warm-Up

▶ **Making Inferences**
To introduce students to the global economy, have them answer these questions.

- Look at the illustration on the bottom of page 947. Where is the car's engine made?

- What does the car suggest about the reliance of individual countries on each other?

 WARM-UP TRANSPARENCY 36

OBJECTIVE ① INSTRUCT

Technology Revolutionizes the World's Economy

▶ **Key Ideas**
- New technologies spur economic growth.

- A boom in service industries transforms world economies.

IN-DEPTH RESOURCES: UNIT 8
Guided Reading, p. 56

ACCESS FOR STUDENTS ACQUIRING ENGLISH
Guided Reading (Spanish), p. 365

The Growth of Japan and the Pacific Rim

Key Ideas
- Japan achieves rapid economic growth by adapting modern Western technologies.
- Education plays a key role in the economic development of Pacific Rim countries.

IN-DEPTH RESOURCES: UNIT 8
Literature: "Paper," p. 66

History from Visuals

Growth in East Asia

Interpreting the Chart Make sure students understand that per capita gross domestic product (GDP) is the total value of the goods produced in a country divided by its population. Which country had the lowest per capita GDP in 1991? *South Korea.*

Extension Activity Suggest that interested students research current economic information on one of the Pacific Rim countries. Then have them photocopy the chart on this page and add their information to it.

SKILLBUILDER ANSWERS
1. Japan; $27,000
2. Hong Kong, Singapore

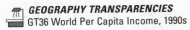**GEOGRAPHY TRANSPARENCIES**
GT36 World Per Capita Income, 1990s

MORE ABOUT . . .
The Pacific Rim

The video *Trade Connects the World: Silk Roads and the Pacific Rim* describes the flourishing economic development in the Pacific Rim and its impact on the rest of the world.

PATTERNS OF INTERACTION
Trade Connects the World: Silk Roads and the Pacific Rim
Videocassette: Tape 1

A VOICE FROM THE PAST
By the end of this century knowledge workers [people whose jobs focus on working with information] will amount to a third or more of the work force in the United States. . . . The majority of knowledge workers will be paid at least as well as blue-collar workers ever were, or better. And the new jobs offer much greater opportunities. . . . The new jobs . . . require a habit of continuous learning.

PETER DRUCKER, *Managing a Time of Great Change*

THINK THROUGH HISTORY
A. Recognizing Effects Why does Peter Drucker think education is the key to the future?
A. Possible Answer Jobs in the future will require continually learning new information.

The Effects of New Economies In the postwar era the expansion of the world's economies led to an increase in the production of goods and services so that many nations benefited. The economic base of some nations shifted. Manufacturing jobs began to move out of **developed nations**—those nations with the industrialization, transportation, and business facilities for advanced production of manufactured goods. The jobs moved to **developing nations,** that is, those in the process of becoming industrialized. Developing countries became prime locations for new manufacturing operations. Some economists believe these areas were chosen because they had many eager workers whose skills fit manufacturing-type jobs. Also, these workers would work for less money than those in developed nations. On the other hand, information industries that required better-educated workers multiplied in the economies of developed nations. The changes brought by technology changed the workplace of both developed and developing nations.

The Growth of Japan and the Pacific Rim

The Japanese began adopting modern technologies from Europe in the mid-1800s, during the Meiji era. After World War II, they continued to import and adapt the best of Western technology. For example, the Sony Corporation of Japan bought the rights to manufacture transistors, which are the basis for all electronic equipment, from an American company. Within 20 years, Sony had built a business empire based on the transistor. The company manufactured radios, stereo equipment, and televisions.

The emphasis that the Japanese and other people from Asia's Pacific Rim have placed on education has made their work force knowledgeable, creative, and flexible. This helped the region enjoy amazing economic growth from the 1950s to the present. Japanese corporations produce high-quality cars, electronic goods, and ships. The success of Japanese corporations fueled the country's high economic growth rate of 10 percent per year from 1955 through 1970. In the 1990s, averaging between 3 and 4 percent annually, Japan's growth was above that of the United States.

Four places in the Pacific Rim—South Korea, Taiwan, Hong Kong, and Singapore—followed Japan's example. In the 1970s, they set out on programs of rapid industrialization designed to make their economies both modern and prosperous. South Korea became a major exporter of automobiles and of electronic goods. Hong Kong became a world financial center. These four newly industrialized countries recorded such impressive economic growth that they became known as the Four Tigers of Asia. In the 1990s, rapidly industrializing China and Malaysia began competing with the other nations of the Pacific Rim. With Japan, the Four Tigers, China, and Malaysia, the Pacific Rim became a key arena of world trade.

Background
Pacific Rim refers to lands of Southeast Asian mainland and islands along the rim of the Pacific Ocean.

B. Answer Japan was a very successful model to copy.
THINK THROUGH HISTORY
B. Analyzing Causes Why would the Four Tigers follow Japan's example in developing their economies?

Growth in East Asia

Per Capita Gross Domestic Product in U.S. Dollars

30,000 / 25,000 / 20,000 / 15,000 / 10,000 / 5,000 / 0

1960 1963 1970 1973 1980 1985 1989 1991

☐ USA ☐ Singapore ☐ S. Korea
☐ Japan ☐ Hong Kong

Source: *United Nations World Statistics in Brief,* 1976, 1986, 1992, 1995.

SKILLBUILDER: Interpreting Graphs
1. *Which country showed the most dramatic growth in the period from 1985 to 1991?*
2. *Which countries in 1985 were at the level of South Korea in 1991?*

946 Chapter 36

TEACHING OPTIONS | **EXPLORING PRIMARY SOURCES** | **CUSTOMIZING FOR SPECIAL NEEDS**

A Voice from the Past Peter Drucker, an economics professor, has written many books on current economic trends. Share with students Drucker's additional thoughts on knowledge and learning.

"Knowledge can be acquired only through schooling. It is not tied to any country. It is portable. It can be created everywhere, fast and cheaply. Finally, it is by definition changing."

Encourage students to discuss whether or not they agree with Drucker's statements. What implications do these statements have for economic growth? for students' futures as members of the workforce?

Gifted and Talented Students
Delving into the Pacific Rim
Ask students to choose a Pacific Rim country that intrigues them. Have them research the history of that country since World War II, focusing on political and cultural events that might help explain the country's explosive economic growth. When students finish their research, ask them to put together a bulletin board display about the country's history, showing political, cultural, and economic trends and suggesting interconnections among them. Have students use the bulletin board as the basis of an oral presentation to the class.

Growth in World Trade

Economies in different parts of the world have been linked for centuries through trade and through national policies, such as colonialism. However, a true global economy didn't take shape until the second half of the 1800s. The **global economy** includes all the financial interactions among people, businesses, and governments that cross international borders. In recent decades, several factors hastened growth in world trade. Huge cargo ships, the length of three football fields, could inexpensively carry enormous supplies of fuels and other goods from one part of the world to another. Telephone and computer linkages made global financial transactions quick and easy. In addition, multinational corporations developed around the world.

Multinational Corporations Companies that operate in a number of different countries are called **multinational corporations** or transnational corporations. U.S. companies such as Ford, IBM, and Exxon; European companies such as Nestlé and Volvo; and Japanese companies such as Honda and Mitsubishi all became multinational giants.

All of these companies have established manufacturing plants in many countries. They select spots where the raw materials or labor are cheapest. This enables them to produce components of their products on different continents. They ship the various components to another location to be assembled. This level of economic integration allows such companies to view the whole world as the market for their goods. Goods or services are distributed throughout the world as if there were no national boundaries.

Expanding Free Trade After World War II, many national leaders felt that economic cooperation among countries across the world would be key to peace and prosperity. The idea of **free trade,** which is the elimination of trade barriers such as tariffs among nations, began to gain acceptance. As early as 1947, nations began discussing ways to open trade. One such agreement was GATT—General Agreement on Tariffs and Trade. Over the years, a general lowering of protective tariffs and an expansion of free trade, region by region, has expanded the global marketplace. By 1995, the World Trade Organization was established to supervise free trade.

A European organization set up in 1951 promoted tariff-free trade among member countries. This experiment in economic cooperation was so successful that seven years later, a new organization, the European Economic Community (EEC), was formed. Over the next 40 years, most of the other Western European countries joined the organization, which now is called the European Union (EU). The European Union began hammering out issues related to the introduction of a common currency and to integrating Eastern European nations as members.

Regional Trade Blocs Through this economic unification, Europe exerted a major force in the world economy. The economic success of the EU inspired countries in other regions to make trade agreements with each other. The North American Free Trade

### Sidebar (left column)

THINK THROUGH HISTORY
C. Summarizing What elements accelerated global trade?
C. Answer Better communication, transportation, financial resources, and multinational companies

Vocabulary
tariff: a tax on goods imported from another country.

Background
The first products to be tariff-free were iron and coal. This helped the countries develop their industries.

### Sidebar (right column)

OBJECTIVE **3** INSTRUCT

Growth in World Trade

Key Ideas
- The global economy grows rapidly with the acceleration of world trade.
- Multinational corporations help the global economy expand.
- Various international trade agreements spur economic growth.
- The success of the European Union inspires other regional trade agreements.

MORE ABOUT . . .
Politics and World Trade

Political influences are arguably as important as economic ones in promoting the growth of world trade. Policy changes in China, for example, have increased the world's workforce, spurred industrialization, and opened up vast new markets. Likewise, the breakup of the Soviet Union and the independence of the former Eastern bloc countries have injected new life into the world economy.

MORE ABOUT . . .
Multinational Corporations

The global economy includes about 37,000 multinational corporations, which control one-third of the world's wealth (excluding governmental assets). Because these corporations carry such weight in the global economy, some policy makers are pushing the World Trade Organization (WTO) to adopt regulatory guidelines to prevent monopolies, deter corruption, and promote occupational and environmental safety. The WTO could then grant accreditation to companies that uphold its standards.

World Car

Glass
China, Brazil, Argentina, Chile, or Poland

Frame
U.S.A.

Instrument panels
Europe

Same design used in cars sold in North and South America, Europe, and Asia, but sold under different company names

Engine
Brazil, Mexico

Transmission
Europe

Seats
U.S.A.

Tires
Canada, Mexico, Argentina, or Brazil

TEACHING OPTION · BLOCK SCHEDULING

SKILLBUILDER MINI-LESSON: Analyzing Assumptions

CLASS TIME 20 MINUTES

Explaining the Skill People and governments make decisions and take action based on many factors, which may be complex and confusing even to the people involved. One of these factors is the assumption, or belief, that people take for granted as true. Examining the background, needs, and goals of a person or government can help historians understand the assumptions that lie behind historical decisions.

Applying the Skill: *Multinational Corporations* Ask students to analyze the assumptions that underlie the establishment of multinational corporations. Have them consider the following questions:

1. What needs or goals might motivate corporations to become multinational?

2. What do corporations gain from operating in worldwide markets?

3. What do consumers gain from buying products made by multinational corporations?

4. What problems might lack of national economic boundaries cause?

 IN-DEPTH RESOURCES: UNIT 8
Skillbuilder Practice: Analyzing Assumptions, p. 59

World Trading Blocs, 1997

Interpreting the Map Have students carefully examine the map key before looking at the map. Which countries are members of the Group of Seven?

Extension Activity Have students identify countries that are not members of any of the trading blocs included in the map. Ask them to research the politics and economics of one of these countries and hypothesize why it does not belong to a trading bloc.

SKILLBUILDER ANSWERS
1. Venezuela, Gabon, Nigeria, Libya, Algeria, Indonesia.
2. NAFTA, G-7

MORE ABOUT . . . NAFTA

The assumptions underlying the formation of NAFTA are the same as those underlying the European Union: lowering or eliminating tariffs and other trade barriers should cause regional trade and economic growth to increase significantly. Some U.S. and Canadian citizens opposed the agreement, however, fearing that their countries would lose jobs to Mexico, where wages tend to be lower.

OBJECTIVE ④ INSTRUCT

Challenges Facing Less-Developed Nations

Key Ideas
- A great chasm exists between life in developed and in less-developed nations.
- Some believe that developed nations should assist less developed nations.
- Long-term economic planning may help less-developed nations grow.

World Trading Blocs, 1997

Legend:
- Organization of Petroleum Exporting Countries (OPEC)
- Asia-Pacific Economic Cooperation (APEC)
- G-7 (Group of Seven)
- Andean Group
- Association of Southeast Asian Nations (ASEAN)
- Central American Common Market (CACM/MCCA)
- Council of Arab Economic Unity (CAEU)
- Caribbean Community and Common Market (CARICOM)
- Commonwealth of Independent States (CIS)
- European Free Trade Association (EFTA)
- European Union (EU)
- Southern Cone Common Market (MERCOSUR)
- North American Free Trade Agreement (NAFTA)
- Southern Africa Development Community (SADC)
- Central African Customs and Economic Union (UDEAC)

GEOGRAPHY SKILLBUILDER: Interpreting Maps
1. **Location** Which countries in OPEC are located outside of Southwest Asia?
2. **Location** To which world trade organizations does the United States belong?

Agreement (NAFTA), put into effect in 1994, called for the rapid elimination of tariffs and trade restrictions among Canada, the United States, and Mexico. This trade-barrier-free zone may eventually extend into other parts of Latin America, which already has its own free trade association, LAFTA. Organizations in Asia, Africa, and the South Pacific are also creating regional trade policies.

Multinational corporations, freer world trade, and regional trading blocs today tie nations together economically. Instead of two nations trading with each other exclusively, trade links many nations. Resources, work forces, and financial support for business and trade come together from many areas of the world. Just how closely linked international economies are was demonstrated in late 1997. In October of that year, the dramatic fall of the Hong Kong stock market caused a ripple effect in markets in Asia, Europe, and North America. Thus, economic and political conditions in one part of the world affect the economies of nations in other parts of the world.

Challenges Facing Less-Developed Nations

Less-developed nations wanting to expand their economies face many challenges. Many people in the less-developed nations live in grinding poverty. On average, people in these nations receive only one-twentieth the income of people in the developed nations. They may lack adequate shelter, a source of clean drinking water, or food for nourishment. Diseases weaken many, and health care is often unavailable. Such poverty can lead to political instability, which affects not only the nation but also the rest of the world.

THINK THROUGH HISTORY
D. Forming an Opinion Which of the elements of global trade do you think was most responsible for expanding world trade?
D. Possible Answer Free trade has helped to expand world trade.

TEACHING OPTION | **BLOCK SCHEDULING** | **COOPERATIVE ACTIVITY: Drafting a Trade Agreement** | **CLASS TIME 30 MINUTES**

Task: Students will research current trade agreements and then draft their own agreement.

Purpose: To enable students to experience the complexities of the world economy.

Activity: Divide students into three groups to research the existing trade agreements—GATT, NAFTA, and LAFTA. Have them share their

information with the class. Have each group then choose either Asia, Africa, or the South Pacific and review the countries in those areas. Ask the groups to draft a trade agreement for their region using appropriate elements of existing agreements and make a presentation to the class.

📁 **Building a Portfolio:** Students might include their trade agreements in their portfolios.

📋 **ALTERNATIVE ASSESSMENT BOOK**
Standards for Evaluating a Cooperative Activity

Standards for Evaluation
Trade agreements should . . .

- be based on existing agreements
- take into account the special needs of the region
- present information clearly and concisely

THINK THROUGH HISTORY
E. Summarizing
What challenges do developing nations face in improving their economies?
E. Answer
Overcoming poverty and unstable political conditions.

Many world leaders believe that the less-developed nations can ease the burden of poverty for their people only by economic development. Some economists have encouraged less-developed nations to assess their resources and to make long-term economic plans. Some also argue that developed nations need to assist the developing nations to climb out of poverty. A report issued by an international commission observed, "Peace, stability, and human justice around the globe depend on how well nations cooperate to help people in all lands share in the earth's resources and wealth."

Impacts of Economic Development

Global development has had a variety of effects, both positive and negative. It brought manufacturing jobs to developing nations. However, as industries moved out, it reduced manufacturing jobs and raised unemployment in developed nations. Global development had an even larger impact on the use of energy and other resources. Worldwide demand for these resources has led to both environmental and political problems.

Political Impacts Manufacturing requires the processing of raw materials; trade requires the transport of finished goods. These activities, essential for development, require the use of much energy. For the past 50 years, one of the main sources of energy used by developed and developing nations has been oil. For nations with little of this resource available in their own land, disruption of the distribution of oil or a large price increase causes economic and political problems. Nations possessing oil reserves have the power to affect economic and political situations in countries all over the world. For example, OPEC declared an oil embargo—a ban on trade—in the 1970s. This caused significant economic decline in developed nations during that decade.

In 1990, Iraq invaded Kuwait and threatened to stop the distribution of Kuwaiti oil. Fears began to mount that Iraq would also invade Saudi Arabia, another major source of oil, and cut off petroleum supplies to the world. When an international economic embargo failed to change Iraq's behavior, countries of the United Nations moved to wage war on Iraq. The war was known as the Persian Gulf War or **Gulf War.** The war served to point out how globally linked the economies of nations are.

Water is another important resource required for many manufacturing processes. It is also essential for agricultural irrigation. In many parts of the world, nations increasingly came into conflict over the use and maintenance of water resources. Poor quality water resources became one of many serious threats to the environment resulting from economic development.

Environmental Impacts Economic development also threatens the environment. The burning of coal and oil as an energy source causes health-damaging air pollution and acid rain. It has led to global warming.

The release of chemicals called chlorofluorocarbons (CFCs), used in refrigerators, air conditioners, and manufacturing processes, has destroyed ozone in the earth's upper atmosphere. The **ozone layer** is our main protection against the sun's damaging ultraviolet rays. With the increase in ultraviolet radiation reaching the earth's surface, the incidence of skin cancer continues to rise in many parts of the world. Increased ultraviolet radiation may damage populations of plants and plankton at the bases of the food chains, which sustain all life on Earth.

Background
The Middle East contains 62 percent of all known oil resources.

Background
Scientists have discovered a hole in the ozone layer in an area above the continent of Antarctica. Ozone in this location has dropped to 33 percent of the 1975 amount.

Global Impact

Allies Protect Oil Supplies
A perfect example of how the nations of the world are dependent on each other was the Gulf War. Iraq threatened to cut off supplies of oil from Kuwait and other parts of the Middle East. This threatened not only the U.S. and European nations but also Japan, which imports almost all of its oil, and other Asian and African countries. Nations worked together against Iraq to stop that threat.

The Gulf War, also known as "Operation Desert Storm," included 700,000 troops from 39 Allies and around 500,000 Iraqi troops. Within three months, the stubborn but out-gunned Iraqis accepted a cease-fire.

While the supplies of oil were made safe, the war resulted in great environmental damage. More than 465 million gallons of oil were dumped into the Persian Gulf.

Global Interdependence **949**

CRITICAL THINKING ACTIVITY
CLASS TIME: 10 MINUTES

Comparing and Contrasting
Ask students to complete a Venn diagram like the one below to help them understand the similarities and differences between developed and less-developed nations.

Developed nations — Both increasing global interdependence — Less-developed nations

OBJECTIVE 5 INSTRUCT

Impacts of Economic Development

Key Ideas
- Economic growth has both positive and negative effects on politics and the environment.
- Political conflict often concerns the allocation and use of energy and water resources.
- Economic development has numerous harmful effects on the environment.
- Nations must decide how to meet economic needs while preserving the environment.

IN-DEPTH RESOURCES: UNIT 8
Geography Application: Deforestation in Brazil, p. 60

Global Impact
Allies Protect Oil Supplies

When Iraqi troops invaded Kuwait and headed toward Saudi Arabia, the world held its breath. If Iraq had managed to conquer both Kuwait and Saudi Arabia, it would have gained control of half the world's oil supplies. Have students discuss why this threat drew together countries from Africa to North America.

 BATTLES OF THE WORLD
The Gulf War

TEACHING OPTIONS | **CONNECTIONS ACROSS THE CURRICULUM** | **MULTIPLE LEARNING STYLES**

Economics Ask students to research one or more of the various proposals that have been made in an attempt to solve the political and environmental problems that have accompanied rapid globalization and economic development. These problems include the overwhelming debt of developing nations and environmental pollution and destruction of habitats. Suggest that students investigate, for example, debt-for-nature deals and the establishment of pollution rights. Have them present their findings to the class.

Kinesthetic Learners Ask students to choose a product such as an item of food or clothing, a piece of recreational or electronic equipment, or an appliance such as a refrigerator. Have them do research in the library or on the Internet to find out all the raw materials, including energy sources, needed to manufacture that product. Encourage them to make a display showing the raw materials and the process by which they are combined and transformed into a finished product. Suggest that students cut pictures from magazines or catalogs or make models to depict their products and collect actual samples of the raw materials, if possible, to include in their displays.

Daily *Life*
Recycling
The children above in Seoul, South Korea, are celebrating Earth Day by promoting recycling. People in many countries recycle paper, glass, metals, and plastics through community recycling programs. One of the most popular items to recycle is cans. Two-thirds of all aluminum cans used in the United States are recycled.

In Great Britain, the government has called for the expanded use of recycled paper. The goal for the near future is that newsprint be made of at least 40 percent recycled paper fibers. One new paper recycling plant may help Britain meet that ambitious goal. This recycling plant is so environmentally friendly that the water it releases from the paper recycling process is cleaner than the river into which the water is discharged.

Economic development has also often involved the deterioration of the land. Large-scale soil erosion is a worldwide problem due to damaging farming techniques. The habitat destruction that comes from land development has also caused the shrinking of numbers of wildlife around the world. In the 1990s the extinction rate of plants and animals is at least a hundred times greater than it ever has been in earth's history. This high extinction rate means that these animals can no longer serve as an economic resource. The loss of so many species also could endanger complex and life-sustaining processes that keep earth in balance.

"Sustainable Growth" Economists and scientists worked together to think of ways to reduce the negative effect development has on the environment. Their goal is to manage development so that growth can occur, but without destroying air, water and land resources. The concept is sometimes called "green growth." Economist Frances Cairncross suggests that completely reducing negative effects on the environment will not happen.

A VOICE FROM THE PAST
Many people hope that economic growth can be made environmentally benign [harmless]. It never truly can. Most economic activity involves using up energy and raw materials; this, in turn, creates waste that the planet has to absorb. Green growth is therefore a chimera [impossible idea]. But greener growth is possible.
FRANCES CAIRNCROSS, *Economic Growth and Sustainable Development*

THINK THROUGH HISTORY
F. Clarifying What does Frances Cairncross mean by "greener growth is possible"?
F. Possible Answer Economic growth with concern about the environment, although not perfect, is possible.

Economic development has frequently led to huge environmental damage. Because of this, people around the world have come together at Earth Summits to try to formulate plans for sustainable development. **Sustainable development** involves two goals: meeting current economic needs, while ensuring the preservation of the environment and the conservation of resources for future generations. Making and putting into practice these plans has proved to be difficult. But meeting both goals is essential for the future of the human population on earth. Because economies of nations are tied to their political climates, such development plans will depend on the efforts of nations in both economic and political areas.

Section ❷ Assessment

1. TERMS & NAMES
Identify
- developed nation
- developing nation
- global economy
- multinational corporation
- free trade
- Gulf War
- ozone layer
- sustainable development

2. TAKING NOTES
Using a diagram like the one below, list examples of forces that have shaped a global economy.

Forces that shape a global economy

3. RECOGNIZING EFFECTS
In what ways has technology changed the workplace of people across the world?

THINK ABOUT
- the kinds of industries people work in
- the location of the workplaces
- the speed at which work is done

4. THEME ACTIVITY
Economics Make a survey of the labels on class members' clothing and shoes. Look for the countries in which clothing or shoes were produced. List all the countries represented. On a world map, shade in each of the countries you listed. What does the information suggest to you about the global economy?

950 Chapter 36

ANSWERS

Economics and the Environment

Is it possible to have economic development while protecting the environment at the same time? To answer this question, the concept of "sustainable development" was created and discussed at Earth Summits. Using this concept, economic development and environmental protection both are considered in producing a long-term development plan for a nation. Sustainable development, though, often involves making difficult choices and trade-offs. And it often highlights differences between developing and developed nations.

LETTER
José A. Lutzenberger

In the following letter written in 1991, the Environmental Secretary of Brazil, José A. Lutzenberger, asks the President of the United States, George Bush, to stop the clear-cutting (removal of all trees in one tract of land at a time) of America's ancient forest, saying it sets a bad example for the world.

Dear Mr. President:

. . . As an ecologist with a holistic view of the world, my concerns and the concerns of our Government go beyond Amazonia. So, we are also very much concerned with the fate of the last remaining old stands of temperate and boreal forests of North America in Alaska, British Columbia, Washington, Oregon and a few remains in California. . . .

At the present rate of clear-cutting practices for pulp and the export of logs, it will all be finished in about fifteen years. An irreparable loss for your country, a shame for Mankind and a very bad example for the Third World. How can we argue against the criminal devastation of tropical forests in Indochina, Malaysia, the Philippines, Indonesia, New Guinea and Africa, as well as here in South America? The powerful and rich U.S. can certainly afford to subsidize a few thousand jobs in a less destructive way.

POLITICAL CARTOON

In the beginning, God created Heaven and earth...

...and He created the seas...

...and then, God made Man...

There goes the neighborhood.

EDITORIAL
Thomas L. Friedman

Thomas L. Friedman, a columnist, discusses the dilemma developing nations find themselves in when trying to consider both the economy and the environment.

Yes, the rich, developed northern nations, who've been polluting for years, have no right to lecture Indonesians, now that they're trying to develop too. Still, it is hard not to feel a sense of tragedy in the making, and those Indonesians who have reached an income and education level where they can afford to think about the environment share this sense of being overwhelmed by global capitalism. For a developing country like Indonesia, plugging into the global market often means a brutal ultimatum: Jobs or trees? You can't have both. This is globalization's dark side.

Connect *to* History

Drawing Conclusions What problems and tradeoffs do the demands of sustainable development create for developing nations and developed nations?

 SEE SKILLBUILDER HANDBOOK, PAGE 1006.

Connect *to* Today

Researching Gather statistics on the ten fastest-growing national economies and the ten most environmentally degraded nations. Create a chart for each. Then, construct a third chart including information from both.

 CD-ROM For another perspective on the environment, see World History: Electronic Library of Primary Sources.

Is Sustainable Development an Attainable Goal?

Discuss with students who the cartoonist holds responsible for the world's environmental problems. Then have students reread A Voice from the Past on page 950. How do they think Cairncross would respond to the ideas stated in each of the documents?

As students discuss these perspectives on economic development and the environment, have them consider whether or not sustainable development is attainable. Suggest that they find articles or editorials in newspapers or magazines that address these questions:
- What is the best way to help the economies of developing nations grow?
- How much does a nation's economy need to grow in order for the nation's people to prosper?
- Who has the right to use a nation's resources?
- Who is responsible for protecting the environment?
- Who is responsible for cleaning up or repairing environmental damage?

Make sure students understand that these questions are extremely complex and that the search for answers shapes the continuing debate on economics and the environment.

 ELECTRONIC LIBRARY OF PRIMARY SOURCES
"Tackling the Menace of Space Junk"

Connect *to* History

Drawing Conclusions
Possible Responses:
Both—a choice of saving jobs or saving the environment, a loss of environmental resources as economic development continues; Developed nations—the responsibility to prevent environmental damage resulting from their extensive use of resources and to serve as a model for developing nations.

Connect *to* Today

Researching
Suggest that students consult sources such as almanacs, encyclopedias, and Internet references for current economic and environmental statistics.

Encourage students to gather data on each nation's economic growth and environmental degradation and to compile this information in their third chart.

OBJECTIVES

① To identify security issues nations face and ways they pursue collective security.

② To cite examples of ongoing ethnic and religious conflicts, and explain how diversity can also lead to world peace.

③ To describe how various organizations and movements have helped support human rights.

④ To explain the increase in migration and discuss its worldwide effects.

CRITICAL THINKING

• Analyzing motives, p. 953
• Clarifying, p. 954
• Making Inferences, p. 955
• Analyzing causes, p. 956
• Identifying problems, p. 956
• Analyzing themes, p. 956

FOCUS

5-Minute Warm-Up

▶ **Identifying Main Ideas**
To introduce students to global security issues, have them answer these questions.

• Read the Spotlight on UN Peacekeepers on page 952. Where are UN peacekeeping forces sent?

• How have UN missions proved to be costly?

 WARM-UP TRANSPARENCY 36

OBJECTIVE ① INSTRUCT

Nations Pursue Collective Security

▶ **Key Ideas**
• Nations seek collective security.
• The UN helps prevent aggression.
• Nations work to limit the spread of armaments.
• Terrorism threatens world security.

📖 **IN-DEPTH RESOURCES: UNIT 8**
Guided Reading, p. 57

📖 **ACCESS FOR STUDENTS ACQUIRING ENGLISH**
Guided Reading (Spanish), p. 366

TERMS & NAMES
• Nuclear Non-Proliferation Treaty
• proliferation
• terrorism
• fundamentalism
• Universal Declaration of Human Rights
• civil rights movement

MAIN IDEA
Since 1945, nations have used collective security efforts to solve problems.

WHY IT MATTERS NOW
Personal security of the people of the world is tied to security within and between nations.

SETTING THE STAGE World War II was one of history's most devastating conflicts. More than 55 million people died as a direct result of bombings, the Holocaust, combat, starvation, and disease. Near the end of the war, one of humankind's most destructive weapons, the atomic bomb, killed more than 100,000 people in Hiroshima and Nagasaki in a matter of minutes. Perhaps because of those horrors, since 1945, powerful nations have repeatedly stepped back from the brink of destruction that could result from another all-out world conflict.

SPOTLIGHT ON

UN Peacekeepers
Soldiers in blue helmets, such as the one pictured above, have been sent on peacekeeping missions all over the world. They come from dozens of different nations, from Finland to Senegal, from Canada to Pakistan. As neutral soldiers they are sent to enforce peace in troubled areas.

Some missions have lasted for decades, such as the 40-year UN mission to monitor the cease-fire agreement between India and Pakistan. Other UN missions are brief. The 1962–1963 UN mission to New Guinea lasted for six months.

Some UN missions are successful in their goal of preventing the continuation of conflict, but others fail. Both kinds of missions have proved costly. More than 1,450 peacekeepers have died in the line of duty.

Nations Pursue Collective Security

In the decades since the end of World War II, the number of limited wars throughout the world increased. Such wars potentially threatened the economic, environmental, and personal security of people in all nations. So nations began to work together to pursue collective security.

Nations Unite and Take Action Many nations consider that having a strong army is important to their security. After World War II, nations banded together to make military alliances. They formed the North Atlantic Treaty Organization (NATO), the Southeast Asian Treaty Organization (SEATO), the Warsaw Pact, and others. The member nations of each of these alliances generally consider an attack on one of them to be an attack on them all. Thus, they each pledged military aid for their common defense.

In addition to military alliances to increase their security, world leaders have recognized that threats of war needed to be reduced. The United Nations (UN), an international agency established in 1945, works in a variety of ways toward increasing collective global security.

Peacekeeping Activities More than 180 nations send representatives to the UN, which has as one of its aims to promote world peace. The UN provides a public forum, private meeting places, and skilled mediators to help nations try to resolve conflicts at any stage of their development.

The UN also provides peacekeeping soldiers at the invitation of the warring parties. These forces try to prevent the outbreak of new fighting or to help enforce a cease-fire. The unarmed or lightly armed soldiers fire their weapons only in self-defense. The presence of neutral UN soldiers helps prevent aggression. In the late 20th century, the UN sent successful peacekeeping forces to such places as El Salvador in Central America, Kuwait in the Middle East, and Namibia in Africa. The UN, however, was only successful when the nations involved in a conflict maintained a commitment to working things out peacefully.

Background
A limited war is one in which only a few nations are involved and nuclear weapons are not used.

SECTION 3 RESOURCES

PRINT RESOURCES

📖 **IN-DEPTH RESOURCES: UNIT 8**
Guided Reading, p. 57
Primary Source: The Declaration of Human Rights, p. 64
History Makers: Kofi Annan, p. 69; Rigoberta Menchú, p. 70

📖 **ACCESS FOR STUDENTS ACQUIRING ENGLISH**
Guided Reading (Spanish), p. 366

📖 **FORMAL ASSESSMENT**
Section Quiz, p. 427

TECHNOLOGY RESOURCES

🖥 **CRITICAL THINKING TRANSPARENCIES**
CT36 Patterns of Refugee Movement

💿 **CD-ROM**
Electronic Library of Primary Sources

🌐 **INTERNET** www.mlworldhistory.com

Controlling Weapons of Mass Destruction Just as nations banded together in the past five decades to try to prevent and contain conflicts, they also forged treaties to limit the manufacture, testing, and trade of weapons. The weapons of most concern are those that cause mass destruction. These include not only nuclear weapons but also chemical weapons, including poison gases and biological weapons that unleash deadly diseases.

In 1968, world nations gathered to work toward reducing their own arsenals of nuclear arms. Some signed a **Nuclear Non-Proliferation Treaty.** In this pact, nations both with and without nuclear power pledged to help prevent the **proliferation,** or spread, of nuclear weapons to other nations. In the 1970s, the United States and Russia signed the Strategic Arms Limitation Treaties. In the 1980s, both countries began to talk about deactivating some of their nuclear weapons. However, at the beginning of the 1990s, ten nations still possessed nuclear weapons.

Many nations also signed treaties promising not to produce biological or chemical weapons. Because these weapons are fairly easy to produce and are so destructive, they are called the "poor countries' nuclear bomb." Use of these weapons is not limited to international situations. Sometimes terrorist groups use them to make their demands known.

Terrorism Threatens Security In March 1995, a Japanese cult member released nerve gas in a Tokyo subway, killing 12 people and injuring thousands. A month later, an American opposed to the power of the U.S. government planted a bomb near the Federal Building in Oklahoma City, Oklahoma, killing more than 160 people. Both tragedies are examples of **terrorism,** the use of force or threats to frighten people or governments to change policies. Terrorism is a tactic used by political or ideological groups to call attention to their demands and to gain major media coverage of their positions. The ease of international travel makes every nation vulnerable to attacks. Because terrorists cross national borders or escape to countries with governments friendly to their cause, terrorism is an international problem.

THINK THROUGH HISTORY
A. Analyzing Motives Of what value would media coverage be to a terrorist group?
A. Possible Answer It allows them to tell thousands what their positions are on issues that concern them.

Two teenage terrorists hold hostages at the Japanese embassy in Lima, Peru. The terrorist group held hostages for over 100 days, in late 1996 and early 1997, before being forced out and killed by the Peruvian military.

Ethnic and Religious Conflicts Disrupt Peace

Conflicts among people of different racial, national, religious, linguistic, or cultural groups are not new. Some ethnic or religious conflicts have roots that reach back for decades and, in some conflicts, for centuries. Such conflicts include the "troubles" between Catholics and Protestants in Northern Ireland and the hostilities between Palestinians and Jews in the Middle East.

Some ethnic conflicts have deep historic causes that simmered under the surface until recently. Examples from the 1990s include the Hutu-Tutsi rivalry in East Africa or the Serb-Bosnian-Croat disputes in the former nation of Yugoslavia. With the removal of authoritarian rule or colonial governments, sometimes these old problems flared into violent confrontations and wars. This created problems for the security of neighboring nations and caused many refugees to seek shelter in the nearby lands.

Religious Conflicts The growth of **fundamentalism**—a strict belief in the basic truths and practice of a particular faith—also contributed to conflict among different peoples. In some countries, fundamentalist groups have worked to gain control of a government in order to impose their ideas upon an entire nation. For example, in 1997, the Taliban movement in Afghanistan gained control of that country after a long civil war. The leaders immediately imposed strict Muslim law on the land. Many opposed the fundamentalist rule even though they also were Muslim.

Global Interdependence **953**

SPOTLIGHT ON
Kurds: A People Without a Country

The Kurds, a nomadic people, follow their herds through the mountains and high plateaus of eastern Turkey, western Iran, and northern Iraq, shown in red on the map. For decades, Kurds have wanted their own separate country. But because their traditional lands cross the borders of three nations, it is a thorny problem.

The Turks have responded to Kurdish nationalism by forbidding Kurds to speak their native language. The Iranians have also persecuted the Kurds, attacking them over religious issues. In the late 1980s, the Iraqis dropped poison gas on the Kurds, killing 5,000.

The Kurds have received support from a number of international organizations, including the United Nations. These groups are working to end the human rights abuses heaped upon the Kurds.

Ethnic and religious conflicts have often been characterized by terrible violence. People caught in these conflicts sometimes suffered torture or massacres of their whole towns or villages. An example of this is violence imposed on the Kurds, a nomadic group in southwest Asia. (See spotlight on Kurds.)

As violence escalates, communication between the conflicting groups shuts down. The Buddhist leader of Tibet, the Dalai Lama, argued that opening communication is the key to understanding differences and resolving conflicts.

A VOICE FROM THE PAST
The various religions must recognize their common responsibility. Therefore it is important that they live together and speak to each other in harmony. Certainly there is a great deal of difference between the religions. But if people openly approach each other wishing sincerely to exchange views and learn from each other they will discover that they are in agreement on many things. A large common basis, I am sure, could be found. The religions could devote this basis to the service of the world's positive development.
DALAI LAMA, quoted in *Global Trends: The World Almanac of Development and Peace*

While some have tried to find common ground through religion to ease conflict, others try to gain wide international guarantees of basic human rights.

Promoting Human Rights Worldwide

After the atrocities of the Holocaust in World War II, the newly formed United Nations resolved to work toward guaranteeing basic human rights for persons of all nations.

UN Issues a Declaration In 1948, to set human rights standards for all nations, the UN drew up and ratified the **Universal Declaration of Human Rights.** The declaration stated, "All human beings are born free and equal in dignity and rights. . . . Everyone has the right to life, liberty, and security of person." It further listed specific rights that all human beings should have. Later, in 1975, the Helsinki Accords addressed the issues of freedom of movement and freedom to publish and exchange information.

Both the declaration and the accords are nonbinding. But many people around the world became committed to ensuring that basic human rights are respected. The UN and other international nonprofit agencies, such as Amnesty International, work to track and publicize human rights violations. They also encourage people to work toward a world in which liberty and justice are available for all.

The American Civil Rights Movement The people of the United States made greater commitments to ensuring basic human rights, especially political rights, to its citizens through the civil rights movement. The **civil rights movement** was a grassroots effort by African Americans to fight discrimination and to make sure all citizens received their rights guaranteed by the U.S. Constitution. During the 1960s, the movement focused on eliminating legal segregation between African Americans and whites. Another goal was to fully empower African Americans with the right to vote and with equal public education.

During the 1950s and 1960s, thousands of Americans, both African Americans and others, organized groups and worked to change the conditions in the United States. One of the best-known leaders of the civil rights movement was Dr. Martin Luther King, Jr. Dr. King patterned his movement after Gandhi's in India, using nonviolent demonstrations to bring attention to serious injustices suffered by African Americans.

After King's assassination in 1968, people of all races and creeds continued to work to eliminate discrimination in employment, housing, and other key areas of life. The civil rights movement fueled the development of other equal rights movements by Native Americans, Hispanics, women, and people with disabilities.

Women's Status Improves
The women's rights movement grew along with the civil rights movement in the late 1950s and early 1960s. When women in Western nations entered the work force, they often met with discrimination in employment and salary. In non-Western countries, many women not only faced discrimination in jobs, they were denied access to education. In regions torn by war or ethnic conflict, they were often victims of violence and abuse. As women suffered, so also did their family members, especially children.

However, in the 1970s, with a heightened awareness of human rights, women in various parts of the world worked to improve their lives through changes in laws and government policies. In 1975, the United Nations held the first of several international conferences on women's status in the world. The fourth conference was held in Beijing, China, in 1995. It addressed such issues as preventing violence against women and empowering women to take leadership roles in politics and in business.

One of the most highly respected activists who attended the Beijing conference was the Albanian missionary Mother Teresa. She devoted her life to caring for the poor and sick. In 1979, Mother Teresa was awarded the Nobel Peace Prize for her efforts on behalf of the homeless on the streets of Calcutta, India. Although she died in 1997, her mission continues to reach more than 25 countries worldwide.

Global Movement of People

Migration is a worldwide phenomenon that has increased in size and scope. Each year poverty, war, drought, famine, and political violence affect millions of people. To escape these life-threatening problems, many people leave their homes and migrate to other countries. Wealthy people sometimes migrate as well. In the late 1980s, some businesspeople left Hong Kong, fearing that after the Chinese regained control of the island from the British in 1997, their rights and opportunities would be limited.

Global Interdependence **955**

THINK THROUGH HISTORY
C. Making Inferences How are civil rights and women's rights related?
C. Possible Answer Both are a part of fundamental human rights.

HISTORY MAKERS

Dr. Martin Luther King, Jr.
1929–1968
Nobel Peace Prize 1964

Dr. Martin Luther King, Jr.'s moving speeches and his commitment to active, nonviolent protest inspired people around the world. He urged them to work to end racial discrimination and toward obtaining full and equal rights for all. In his famous "I Have a Dream" speech, King urged his followers, *"Now* is the time to lift our nation from the quicksands of racial injustice to the solid rock of brotherhood."

King achieved many successes as he led a nationwide movement, organizing marches and sit-ins to demand equal justice before the law. In 1964 and 1965, the U.S. federal government passed laws protecting civil and voting rights.

During the civil rights struggles, Dr. King's home was dynamited and he and his family faced death threats. He was assassinated on April 4, 1968, in Memphis, Tennessee.

Rigoberta Menchú
1959–
Nobel Peace Prize 1992

Violence is no stranger to Guatemala's Rigoberta Menchú. Her brother was burned to death. Her father was killed by hand grenades while leading a peaceful sit-in. Her mother was kidnapped and killed by Guatemalan soldiers.

These wrongs against her family made Rigoberta Menchú more dedicated to preventing human rights abuses of her people, Maya Indians. Beginning in the late 1970s, she helped set up community organizations to speak for Indian rights. She organized marches and protests against unfair government actions.

Francis Sejersted, who presented the Nobel Prize, stated, "By maintaining a disarming humanity in a brutal world, Rigoberta Menchú appeals to the best in us. She stands as a uniquely potent symbol of a just struggle."

Faced with repeated death threats, Menchú now lives in Mexico.

HISTORY MAKERS
Dr. Martin Luther King, Jr.

In 1955, the American South was strictly segregated. Activists in Montgomery, Alabama, asked King, a young Baptist minister, to lead the African-American community in a boycott of the city bus system. King took up the challenge, beginning his leadership role in the civil rights movement. The Montgomery bus boycott ultimately was successful, though it lasted more than a year. Suggest that interested students research this boycott and other actions King led. Encourage them to make a time line of his contributions to civil rights.

Rigoberta Menchú

Rigoberta Menchú has been tireless in seeking to end discrimination and violent attacks against the Mayas. She has advocated a variety of protest methods, however, not just peaceful ones. For this reason, her receiving the Nobel Peace Prize has aroused some controversy. Suggest that students do more in-depth research on Menchú or King, either as a separate project or in conjunction with the Cooperative Activity on page 954.

 IN-DEPTH RESOURCES: UNIT 8
History Makers: Rigoberta Menchú, p. 70

OBJECTIVE ④ INSTRUCT

Global Movement of People

▶ *Key Ideas*
- Worldwide migration increases as people respond to harsh political, economic, or environmental conditions.
- Immigrants include people from every social class.
- Mass migration causes problems, but can also be a positive force for cultural understanding.

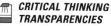 *CRITICAL THINKING TRANSPARENCIES*
CT36 Patterns of Refugee Movement

TEACHING OPTIONS

CUSTOMIZING FOR SPECIAL NEEDS

Less Proficient Readers To help students understand the causes that led to an improvement in the status of women, suggest that they make a concept web such as this. Suggest that they summarize the information in each sentence as they read and enter it in the web. Students should add circles to their webs as necessary and draw lines to connect related concepts.

Women's status improves

CRITICAL THINKING TRANSPARENCIES
CT78 Concept Web

MULTIPLE LEARNING STYLES

Interpersonal Learners Divide students into small groups and encourage them to discuss why people might come to the United States. Ask them to talk about conditions in countries they have visited or heard about, why people they know chose to migrate to the United States, and how those people have adjusted to life in this country. Ask students to indicate how these experiences reinforce or contradict the generalizations mentioned in the text, such as that people often feel pushed out of their homelands or pulled to better opportunities in other countries.

Teacher's Edition **955**

Have students work in pairs to answer question 1. Then have two pairs work together to answer question 2. Ask students to complete questions 3 and 4 as a class.

Section Quiz

📋 **FORMAL ASSESSMENT**
Section Quiz, p. 427

Reteaching Activity

CLASS TIME: 15 MINUTES

List the phrases *collective security, ethnic conflicts, human rights,* and *global migration* on the board. Divide the class into four groups and assign each group to present the main ideas about one of these issues to the class. Then ask students to use their answer to question 3 as a basis for discussing how the four issues are interrelated.

CLOSE ACTIVITY

CLASS TIME: 15 MINUTES

Ask students to stage a debate between the leaders of a developed nation with nuclear weapons and a developing nation. Have them address the benefits and drawbacks of nuclear nonproliferation. Ask the class to vote on the most persuasive ideas presented.

Push-Pull Factors Migration sometimes takes place because people feel pushed out of their homelands. Lack of food due to drought, natural disasters, and political oppression are examples of push factors. Between 1976 and 1996, the number of refugees—people who leave their country to move to another to find safety—grew from under 3 million to almost 20 million yearly.

Not only negative events push people to migrate. Most people have strong connections to their home countries and don't leave unless strong positive attractions pull them away. They hope for a better life for themselves and for their children, and thus migrate to developed nations. For example, hundreds of thousands of people migrate from Africa to Europe and from Latin America to the United States every year. Sometimes the poorest people migrate, but often educated middle-class people migrate.

Effects of Immigration Immigration has both negative and positive effects on the countries receiving new people. Countries generally receive two types of immigrants—political refugees and migrants who come for economic reasons. Although a person has the right to leave a country, the country receiving the migrant does not have to accept that person. The receiving country may have one policy about accepting refugees from political situations, and another about migrants coming for economic reasons. Because of the huge volume of people migrating from war-torn, famine-stricken, and politically unstable regions, millions of immigrants have no place to go. Crowded into refugee camps under squalid conditions, immigrants face a very uncertain future. The cost of supporting these camps may cause political problems and may raise issues of prejudice and discrimination.

On the positive side, immigrants are often a valuable addition to the country where they move. They help offset labor shortages in a variety of industries. They bring experiences and knowledge that can spur the economy. In addition, they contribute to the sharing, shaping, and blending of a newly enriched culture.

Cuban boat people plead for help from a helicopter about 50 miles from Key West, Florida. Some left Cuba because of political differences, while others were looking for a better economic future.

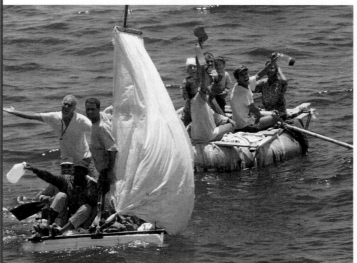

THINK THROUGH HISTORY
D. Analyzing Causes List the push and pull factors that cause people to migrate.
D. Possible Answers Push—natural disasters, political problems, lack of food. Pull—economic reasons, hope for a better life, political freedom.

Section 3 Assessment

1. TERMS & NAMES

Identify
- Nuclear Non-Proliferation Treaty
- proliferation
- terrorism
- fundamentalism
- Universal Declaration of Human Rights
- civil rights movement

2. TAKING NOTES

Using a chart like the one below, list collective methods employed by the nations of the world to increase world security. Give examples.

Method	Examples
1. Form military alliances	NATO, SEATO, Warsaw Pact
2.	
3.	

3. IDENTIFYING PROBLEMS

How are ethnic and religious conflicts related to problems of global security?

THINK ABOUT
- current conflicts
- political/ideological tactics of groups
- immigration

4. ANALYZING THEMES

Science and Technology In what ways have advances in science and technology increased threats to global security?

THINK ABOUT
- the destructive capability of one nuclear weapon
- the ability of less-powerful nations to produce biological or chemical weapons
- the ability to move easily across international borders

956 Chapter 36

ANSWERS

1. TERMS & NAMES
Nuclear Non-Proliferation Treaty, p. 953

proliferation, p. 953

terrorism, p. 953

fundamentalism, p. 953

Universal Declaration of Human Rights, p. 954

civil rights movement, p. 954

2. TAKING NOTES
Possible Responses: Reduce threats of war: UN formed

Promote world peace: UN peacekeeping missions

Control weapons: Nuclear Non-Proliferation Treaty; Strategic Arms Reduction Treaties

3. IDENTIFYING PROBLEMS
Possible Responses: People involved in ethnic and religious conflicts may use terrorist tactics to get attention. These conflicts often endanger the security of neighboring nations. Immigrants from troubled areas can present security problems to their host nations.

4. ANALYZING THEMES
Possible Responses: The technical ease of making biological or chemical weapons makes less-powerful nations able to be more aggressive and threaten security. Rapid transportation allows easy movement of terrorists or armies across international borders.

4 Cultures Blend in a Global Age

TERMS & NAMES
- popular culture
- materialism
- accommodation

MAIN IDEA

Technology has increased contact among the world's people, changing their cultures.

WHY IT MATTERS NOW

Globalization of culture has changed the ways people live, their perceptions, and their interactions.

SETTING THE STAGE Since the beginnings of civilization, people of every culture have blended ideas and ways of doing things from other cultures into their own culture. The same kind of cultural sharing and blending continues today. But it occurs at a much more rapid pace and among people at much wider distances than ever was common in the past.

The Sharing of Cultures Accelerates

The speed and breadth of today's cultural exchanges is due to advances in technology. Twentieth-century technologies allow people from all over the world to have increasing contact with one another. Such contacts promote widespread sharing of cultures.

Cultural elements that reflect a group's common background and changing interests are called popular culture. **Popular culture** involves music, sports, movies, clothing fashions, foods, and hobbies or leisure activities. Popular culture around the world incorporates features originating in many different lands. Of all the technologies that contribute to cultural sharing, television, movies, and other media have been the most powerful.

A family in Afghanistan enjoys watching cartoons on the family TV.

Television and Mass Media More people in the United States have televisions than telephones. In fact, 98 percent of American households have televisions. Eighty-eight percent of the homes have videocassette recorders (VCRs). In Europe, too, the vast majority of households include one or more televisions. The percentages are lower for developing nations. Nevertheless, in many of these countries, the television is a family's most cherished or most wished-for possession.

Television provides a window to the world through daily newscasts and documentaries. The speed at which information about other parts of the world is presented helps create an up-to-the-minute shared experience of global events. For example, in 1991, millions of television viewers across the world watched the waging of the Persian Gulf War. Wars, natural disasters, and political drama in faraway places become a part of everyday life.

Television and other mass media, including radio and movies, are among the world's most popular forms of entertainment. Popular programs not only entertain but also show how people live and what they value in other parts of the world. Mass media is the major way popular culture spreads to all parts of the globe.

Global Interdependence **957**

SECTION 4 RESOURCES

PRINT RESOURCES

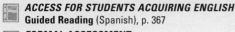 *IN-DEPTH RESOURCES: UNIT 8*
Guided Reading, p. 58
Primary Source: "Cupid's a Korean Computer," p. 65

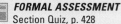 *ACCESS FOR STUDENTS ACQUIRING ENGLISH*
Guided Reading (Spanish), p. 367

 FORMAL ASSESSMENT
Section Quiz, p. 428

 ALTERNATIVE ASSESSMENT BOOK

TECHNOLOGY RESOURCES

 WORLD ART AND CULTURES TRANSPARENCIES
AT80 *Technology* (Korean video sculpture)

 CRITICAL THINKING TRANSPARENCIES
CT72 Chapter 36 Visual Summary

 CD-ROM
Electronic Library of Primary Sources

 VIDEO
Patterns of Interaction: Cultural Crossroads

Section 4 Overview

OBJECTIVES

1 To trace the increase in world-wide cultural interaction.

2 To describe the influences on world culture.

3 To explain cultural bias and to explore possibilities for cultural understanding.

CRITICAL THINKING
- Recognizing effects, pp. 958, 961
- Summarizing, pp. 959, 960
- Making inferences, p. 959
- Analyzing issues, p. 961

FOCUS

5-Minute Warm-Up

▶ *Perceiving Effects*
To help students understand global popular culture, have them answer these questions.

- Look at the Global Impact feature on pages 958 and 959. What types of music influenced the Beatles and the Rolling Stones?

- Which elements of American culture have been influenced by other cultures?

 WARM-UP TRANSPARENCY 36

OBJECTIVE **1** INSTRUCT

The Sharing of Cultures Accelerates

▶ *Key Ideas*
- Advanced technology connects people from all over the world.

- Television and other mass media help spread popular culture.

- Popular culture is now an international phenomenon.

 IN-DEPTH RESOURCES: UNIT 8
Guided Reading, p. 58

 ACCESS FOR STUDENTS ACQUIRING ENGLISH
Guided Reading (Spanish), p. 367

SPOTLIGHT ON
International Baseball

The sport of baseball is an example of global popular culture. When American missionaries and teachers arrived in Japan in the 1870s, they introduced the game of baseball to the Japanese. It gained popularity in the 1930s, when American professional teams toured there. Today, some U.S. teams have Japanese players. However, the Japanese teams limit the number of U.S. players on their teams.

Baseball spread to Mexico, Cuba, Puerto Rico, Panama, and the Dominican Republic in the late 19th and early 20th centuries. The game was taught to local populations by men who learned it in the United States.

Little League Baseball began in the 1930s and expanded rapidly after World War II. Youngsters in the United States and approximately 30 other nations play the sport.

International Elements of Popular Culture The entertainment field, especially television, has a massive influence on popular culture. People from around the world are avid viewers of American TV programs. In India, $M^{\circ}A^{\circ}S^{\circ}H$ reruns are a huge hit. One U.S. business consultant conducted a meeting on cotton plantations in a remote part of northern China. The consultant said the 22 managers attending excused themselves at six o'clock in the evening and returned about an hour later. The American thought the farmers might have had other visitors or another important meeting to attend. When asked, they replied, "No. It was *Dallas* [a rerun of a famous 1980s evening soap opera] on television."

Broadcasts of international sporting events and the popularity of many team sports have found fans of soccer, cycling, and basketball all over the globe. Some figures from these sports attain worldwide fame. For example, a survey of teens in 44 countries of the world revealed that 93 percent recognized the Chicago Bulls logo. Broadcasts of the Olympics attract audiences of over 200 million from around the world.

Music is another aspect of popular culture that has become international. As the equipment for listening to music has become more portable, there are only a few places in the world that do not have access to music from other cultures. People from around the world dance to reggae bands from the Caribbean, chant rap lyrics from the United States, play air guitar to rowdy European bands, and enjoy the fast drumming of Afropop tunes. They might even sing to any of this music using a karaoke machine, which comes from Japan. Recording artists and groups often gain international fame.

A. Answer They have made certain sports, music, and entertainment programs popular internationally.

THINK THROUGH HISTORY
A. Recognizing Effects What effects have television and mass media had on popular culture?

Global Impact: Cultural Crossroads

Rock 'n' Roll

In the middle of the 1950s, a new style of music emerged on the American scene. It was called rock 'n' roll. The music explored social and political themes. Rock music, which seemed to adults to reflect a youth rebellion, soon became the dominant popular music for young people across the world. As the influence of rock music spread, international artists added their own traditions, instruments, and musical styles to the mix called rock.

"Rock and roll music, if you like it and you feel it, you just can't help but move to it. That's what happens to me, I can't help it." —Elvis

During the 1950s and 1960s, Elvis Presley was called the King of American Rock 'n' Roll.

Mick Jagger of the Rolling Stones was part of the "British Invasion." The "British Invasion" was a term for the innovations brought to rock by British bands. The enormously popular Beatles and the enduring Rolling Stones were heavily influenced by American rhythm & blues. For example, the Rolling Stones took their name from a song lyric done by American blues musician, writer, and performer Muddy Waters.

958

World Culture Blends Many Influences

Greater access to the ideas and customs of different cultures often results in cultural blending. As cultural ideas move with people among cultures, some beliefs and habits seem to have a greater effect than others. In the 20th century, ideas from the West have been very dominant in shaping cultures in many parts of the globe.

Westernizing Influences on Different Cultures

Western domination of the worldwide mass media helps explain the huge influence the West has on many different cultures today. However, heavy Western influence on the rest of the world's cultures is rooted in the 19th century. Western domination of areas all over the globe left behind a legacy of Western customs and ideas. Western languages are spoken throughout the world, mainly because of Europe's history of colonization in the Americas, Asia, and Africa.

Background
There are approximately 836 million Mandarin Chinese speakers.

Over the past 50 years, English has emerged as the premier international language. English is spoken by about 500 million people as their first or second language. Although more people speak Mandarin Chinese than English, English speakers are more widely distributed. English is the most common language used on the Internet and at international conferences. The language is used by scientists, diplomats, doctors, and businesspeople around the world. The widespread use of English is responsible, in part, for the emergence of a dynamic global culture.

Western influence can be seen in other aspects of popular culture. For example, blue jeans are the clothes of choice of most of the world's youth. Western business

Little Leaguers celebrate a win. Each year the Little League has a World Series. During the 1970s teams from Taiwan dominated the series.

The multicultural South African band Juluka blends sounds from traditional African instruments along with styles of American rock and sings in English and Zulu.

Patterns of Interaction

The spread of American culture, including sports, fashion, and fast food, has created an international culture recognizable in all corners of the globe. In some cases American culture is simply a powerful influence, as other societies blend American culture with local customs. Cultural blending is evident even in America's past. Symbols of American culture like baseball and hot dogs are themselves the result of cross-cultural influences.

▮ VIDEO *Cultural Crossroads: The United States and the World*

Connect *to* History

Summarizing How have people in other parts of the world changed rock 'n' roll by adopting this American form of popular entertainment?

 SEE SKILLBUILDER HANDBOOK, PAGE 992

Connect *to* Today

Making Inferences How have improvements in technology and global communications aided in the blending of musical styles?

Global Interdependence **959**

Although most countries still favor their own regional cuisines, fast food is now part of world popular culture. The character of this quick cuisine has also expanded far beyond the universal McDonald's hamburger. Asian stir-fry, Mexican tacos, Indian samosas, and French croissants are now available on many international fast-food menus.

SPOTLIGHT On
French Cultural Backlash

Cultural backlash isn't just a French phenomenon. Ask students to think of examples of cultural backlash in the United States and to discuss whether they think it is a constructive response to cultural diversity.

OBJECTIVE 3 INSTRUCT

Future Challenges and Hopes

▶ *Key Ideas*
- Globalization of culture causes many people to fear loss of their unique identities.
- Global interdependence increases the importance and impact of people's ability to live in harmony with each other and the environment.

---

suits are standard uniforms among many people. McDonald's hamburgers and Coca-Cola soft drinks can be purchased in many countries of the world. Mickey Mouse and other Disney characters are almost universally recognized. These examples of common dress, food, and entertainment figures all originated in the West and have been picked up and incorporated by other cultures. But Western influence also has an effect on ways of thinking. The Western mindset of placing a high value on acquiring material possessions—**materialism**—has been adopted by people of many different cultures.

Non-Western Influences Travel to the West Cultural ideas are not confined to moving only from the West to other lands. Non-Western cultures also influence people in Europe and the United States. From music and clothing styles, to ideas about art and architecture, to religious and ethical systems, non-Western ideas are incorporated into Western life. The non-Western mindset of placing value on meditation and contemplation has found a home in the West. The world's fastest-growing religion—Islam—comes from non-Western roots. Cultural blending of Western and non-Western elements opens communications channels for the exchange of ideas throughout the globe.

The Arts Become International Modern art, like popular culture, has become increasingly international. Advances in transportation and technology have facilitated the sharing of ideas about art and the sharing of actual works of art. Shows and museums throughout the world exhibit art of different styles and from different places. It became possible to see art from other cultures that had not previously been available to the public. For example, art from the Forbidden City in China or artifacts from Egyptian tombs can be viewed in museums in Europe and the Americas.

Literature, too, has become internationally appreciated. Well-known writers routinely have their works translated into dozens of languages, resulting in truly international audiences. The list of recent Nobel Prize winners in literature reflects a broad variety of writers' nationalities, including Nigerian, Egyptian, Mexican, West Indian, and Japanese.

THINK THROUGH HISTORY
B. Summarizing
Name three advances that allow a greater sharing of the arts.
B. Answer
Technology, improved transportation, widespread translations

SPOTLIGHT On

French Cultural Backlash

If a French organization to prevent the corruption of the French language by foreign words has its way, the term *le air bag* will officially be replaced with the term *le coussin gonflable de protection.* To a foreigner the substitute must seem awkward. Language purists argue that allowing too many English-language words into the vocabulary will eventually make the French language and culture too foreign.

Since French has no terms to cover new inventions or ideas, language specialists devise terms to help deal with such words as data bank *(banque de données),* microchip *(puce,* which means flea), and software *(logiciel).*

It may be a losing battle, since 80 percent of all French high school students choose to study English as their foreign language.

Future Challenges and Hopes

As the differences between peoples lessen, some worry about losing their group identity. In some lands the leaders have taken measures to preserve the unique elements of their culture.

Cultural Clashes Fear of the loss of a unique identity as a people or nation may create conflict and clashes within groups. For example, in France in the late 1990s, a bureau of the French government was responsible for removing words from the French language that are believed to corrupt the language. A French official told members of the Higher Council of the French Language that keeping language from the excesses of foreign words was "an act of faith in the future of our country." In a similar vein, recently in the United States, debates raged over the question of making English the exclusive official language of the U.S. government. A poll showed that 73 percent of the population agreed with that position.

In other parts of the world, wearing certain kinds of clothing, such as short skirts or jeans, is forbidden because it represents an intrusion of other cultures. Elsewhere, mass media is strictly censored to keep unwanted ideas from entering the land.

Sometimes groups respond to the influence of other cultures by trying to return to traditional ways. Cultural practices and rites of passage may receive even more emphasis as a group tries to preserve its identity. In some countries, native groups take an active role in preserving the traditional ways of life. For example, tribal groups, such as the Maori in New

Background
Twenty-two states have enacted English-only laws.

Task: Students will choose a novel, short story, or poem and write a personal response to present orally in an "international literature fair."

Purpose: To help students appreciate the international character and universal themes of literature.

Activity: Have students survey world literature textbooks or library and Internet sources and choose

a work that interests them. Nonnative English speakers might want to read a work in their native language. Make sure a variety of cultures and literary genres will be represented. Have students write a summary and personal response to their work and present it orally in the class literature fair.

📁 **Building a Portfolio:** Students might add their personal literature responses to their portfolios.

Standards for Evaluation
Personal literary responses should . . .

- give the author, title, genre, and country of origin of the work
- provide a basic summary of the subject matter
- indicate the student's personal response to the work and reasons for that response

THINK THROUGH HISTORY
C. Recognizing Effects How do people react against greater global interdependence?
C. Possible Answer Some people may try harder to stay unique by holding on to parts of their culture such as language and customs.

Zealand, have revived ancestral customs rather than face cultural extinction. Many Maori cultural activities are conducted in a way that preserves Maori ways of thinking and behaving. In 1987, the Maori language was made an official language of New Zealand.

Even when a nation does not have serious concerns about the impact of other cultures, it may struggle with questions of accommodation. **Accommodation** is the level of acceptance of ideas from another culture. Charles Mann, a journalist, describes the feelings of uncertainty that questions of accommodation raise.

A VOICE FROM THE PAST

As human . . . patterns look more and more alike . . . that unique place becomes ever harder to find. Things feel scary; people hunker down. Some retreat into their dialects, others into their national clothes, others into religion or guns. Even as the world unifies, its constituent parts fragment.

CHARLES MANN, *The Material World: A Global Family Portrait*

A Samburu warrior in Kenya uses a cellular phone to stay in contact with others in his group.

Global Interdependence Despite the uncertainty accompanying global interdependence, economic, political, and environmental issues do bring all nations closer together. Nations have begun to recognize that they are dependent on other nations and deeply affected by the actions of others far away. As elements of everyday life and expressions of culture become more international in scope, people across the world gain a sense of oneness with people in other areas of the world. Responses to events such as flooding in Bangladesh were international in scope. Nations from around the world sent assistance. It was as if the flooding had happened in their own country.

Technology has changed the way people, businesses, and nations view the world. Restricting cultural change is now very unlikely except in a few isolated locations.

Throughout history, human beings have faced challenges to survive and to live better. In the 21st century, these challenges will be faced by people who are in increasing contact with one another. They have a greater stake in learning to live in harmony together and with the physical planet. As Dr. Martin Luther King, Jr., stated, "Our loyalties must transcend our race, our tribe, our class, and our nation; and this means we must develop a world perspective."

Section 4 Assessment

1. TERMS & NAMES
Identify
• popular culture
• materialism
• accommodation

2. TAKING NOTES
Draw a diagram like the one below and give details that illustrate the areas of popular culture that have become very international.

International popular culture

Which of the international popular culture aspects has the greatest effect on your life? Write a paragraph to explain why.

3. ANALYZING ISSUES
You have just immigrated to the United States. You are anxious to "fit in" in your new home but don't want to lose aspects of your former culture. What do you accept about the new culture and what do you retain of your birth culture?

THINK ABOUT
• elements of your birth culture you wish to maintain, adapt, or leave behind
• practical and day-to-day concerns
• feelings about your identity

4. THEME ACTIVITY

Cultural Interaction Look at the pictures in this section and those on the opening pages of this chapter. They show types of cultural blending. Study current newspapers and magazines to see if you can find examples similar to the pictures shown. Create a scrapbook of pictures you have found. Write a caption for each picture illustrating cultural blending.

Global Interdependence **961**

ANSWERS

1. TERMS & NAMES
popular culture, p. 957
materialism, p. 960
accommodation, p. 961

2. TAKING NOTES
Possible Responses: Details may include clothing, food, mass media, music. Each circle should have at least one example to illustrate the concept.

3. ANALYZING ISSUES
Possible Responses: Students may want to keep religious and holiday traditions but adapt clothing, food, and social customs to fit in. They would need to learn English, get an education, and acquire practical skills such as how to get a job to survive on a day-to-day basis. Students will vary in how much of their birth culture they would be willing to give up. Some students may feel that giving up too much would threaten their identity. Others may be willing to lose their old identify to be more "American."

4. THEME ACTIVITY
Standards for Evaluation
A scrapbook should meet the following criteria:
• Presents an interesting and stimulating range of pictures.
• Is engagingly written.
• Shows an understanding of global cultural interaction.

Chapter 36 Assessment

TERMS & NAMES

1. genetic engineering, p. 943
2. green revolution, p. 944
3. global economy, p. 947
4. free trade, p. 947
5. Gulf War, p. 949
6. sustainable development, p. 950
7. terrorism, p. 953
8. fundamentalism, p. 953
9. civil rights movement, p. 954
10. popular culture, p. 957

REVIEW QUESTIONS

Answers may vary.

11. Satellites and computers link the globe in a worldwide communications network; they have made it possible for people to work in home offices, improved health diagnoses and treatment, and led to new and better food crops.

12. To increase the available food sources worldwide.

13. A developed nation has all the necessary facilities to produce and manufacture goods. A developing nation is a nation that may have natural and human resources but is still industrializing.

14. South Korea, Taiwan, Hong Kong, Singapore. They are all east Asian nations that grew rapidly after World War II and that have become major trading and economic centers affecting global markets.

15. The World Trade Organization was created to establish standards for and monitor world trade. It was an extension of the GATT agreements.

16. Banded together to form military alliances, supported the United Nations' peacekeeping efforts, controlled the spread of weapons through treaties.

17. Religious and ethnic strife underlie many recent wars and hostilities in the Middle East, Northern Ireland, and the former nation of Yugoslavia. Such conflicts often inspire terrorist activities and create huge numbers of immigrants and refugees.

18. The United Nations issued a Universal Declaration of Human Rights; the American civil rights movement arose to ensure that all citizens, including women and persons with disabilities, received basic rights guaranteed under the U.S. Constitution. In general, the status of women has improved worldwide.

TERMS & NAMES

Briefly explain the importance of each of the following to global interdependence from 1960 to the present.

1. genetic engineering
2. green revolution
3. global economy
4. free trade
5. Gulf War
6. sustainable development
7. terrorism
8. fundamentalism
9. civil rights movement
10. popular culture

Interact *with* History

After reading Chapter 36, do you believe events in other nations affect your life? Which kinds of events are more likely to affect you in a very personal way? Create a survey about global interdependence to ask students in your class or school. Consider asking questions about such things as clothing produced in places outside the United States, international phone calls, or travel to foreign countries.

REVIEW QUESTIONS

SECTION 1 *(pages 941–944)*
Science and Technology Shape Human Outlook

11. In what ways have science and technology changed the lives of people today?

12. What was the goal of the green revolution?

SECTION 2 *(pages 945–950)*
Global Economic Development

13. Explain the difference between a developed nation and a developing nation.

14. Who are the "Four Tigers," and what is significant about their development as major trading nations?

15. Why was the World Trade Organization founded?

SECTION 3 *(pages 952–956)*
Global Security Issues

16. What methods has the world community used to resolve conflicts since World War II?

17. How have religious and ethnic conflicts threatened global security?

18. Describe worldwide efforts to guarantee basic human rights.

SECTION 4 *(pages 957–961)*
Cultures Blend in a Global Age

19. Which technologies have had the most powerful impact on cultural sharing?

20. What explains why Western influences have had a major impact all over the world?

Visual Summary

Global Interdependence

Economics
- Service industries grow in developed nations.
- Free trade expands world markets.
- Environmental challenges continue.

Culture
- Mass media spreads many cultures.
- Pop culture becomes more international.
- Global interdependence awareness develops.

Science and Technology
- Space cooperation stretches horizons.
- Advanced communications allow wider contact.
- Inventions improve life and health.

Politics
- Nations take collective security actions.
- Human rights improve worldwide.
- Immigrants change cultures.

19. TV, movies, the Internet, and other mass media.

20. Western domination and colonization in the 19th century had lasting effects. English continues to serve as an international language. Western popular culture has been widely accepted.

Interact *with* History

Students should recognize the effects of global events on their lives. They should describe the events that most affect them and explain what effect the events have had. For example, have the events changed the music students listen to, the food they eat, the clothes they wear? Or have events changed the way they think, see the world, or look at themselves? Encourage students to recognize the influence of global interdependence in their everyday lives.

CRITICAL THINKING

1. CHANGING LIVES

Using the cause-effect diagram below, show how advances in science and technology created changes in lifestyles.

Cause	Effect
Miniaturization of computer parts	⟶
Expanded global communication	⟶
Genetic research	⟶

2. INTERNATIONAL COOPERATION

THEME CULTURAL INTERACTION Reread the quote at the top of page 949 by the international commission. Do you agree or disagree with this statement? In what ways can developed nations assist developing nations?

3. THE GLOBAL INDIVIDUAL

In what ways are individual persons affected by the global economy and threats to the environment? Be specific.

4. ANALYZING PRIMARY SOURCES

The following passage was written by a German journalist as he reflected on the impact of American culture on the world. Read the passage and answer the questions below it.

> Imagine a roomful of 14-year-olds—from Germany, Japan, Israel, Russia and Argentina. Obviously, they would all be wearing Levi's and baseball caps. But how would they relate to one another? They would communicate in English, though haltingly and with heavy accents. About what? . . . They would debate the merits of Nike versus Converse, of Chameleon versus Netscape. Sure, they would not discuss Herman Melville or George Gershwin, but neither would they compare notes on Dante or Thomas Mann. The point is that they would talk about icons and images "made in the U.S.A."
>
> **JOSEF JOFFE,** in "America the Inescapable"

- Identify the aspects of popular culture mentioned by Mr. Joffe.
- Why would this group of teenagers communicate in English?
- How would these teenagers learn about American culture?

CHAPTER ACTIVITIES

1. LIVING HISTORY: Unit Portfolio Project

THEME ECONOMICS Your unit portfolio project focuses on how economic factors influence history. For Chapter 36, you might use one of the following ideas to add to your portfolio.

- Write a poem or song about the impact the global economy has on the environment.
- With a classmate create a map showing worldwide locations of manufacturing plants controlled by multinational corporations such as IBM, Ford, or Coca-Cola.
- Do some research to find out how the availability of jobs in the developed and developing countries influences the migration of people in various parts of the world. Construct graphs or charts to illustrate your findings.

2. CONNECT TO TODAY: Cooperative Learning

THEME SCIENCE AND TECHNOLOGY Science and technology continue to bring the world new ideas and inventions. These have resulted in greater global interaction and an improved quality of life.

Work with a team to create a 15-minute "special news segment" on the latest advances in science and technology and how they currently (or are expected to) affect everyday life.

 Using the Internet, magazines, or a local museum, research current products, new technologies, and new ideas.

- Divide your group so that each of the following categories has a representative: correspondents, scientists, corporate or government executives.
- Videotape or present the segment in class.

3. INTERPRETING A TIME LINE

Revisit the unit time line on page pages 850–851. Look at the section that relates to Chapter 36. What events have occurred since the development of this time line that you think should be included to bring it up to date? Explain why.

FOCUS ON GRAPHS

Millions of people become refugees each year as the result of poverty, wars, political problems, and environmental disasters.

- Which area has had the largest increase in the number of refugees in the time period shown?
- In which years did Africa experience sharp increases in refugees?
- How many more total refugees were there in 1992 than in 1976?

Connect to History In which year did Europe experience a dramatic increase in refugees? What effect might this have on the nations of Europe?

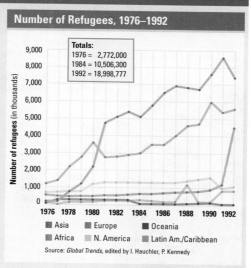

Number of Refugees, 1976–1992

Totals:
1976 = 2,772,000
1984 = 10,506,300
1992 = 18,998,777

Number of refugees (in thousands)

Legend: ■ Asia ■ Europe ● Oceania ■ Africa ■ N. America ● Latin Am./Caribbean

Source: *Global Trends*, edited by I. Hauchler, P. Kennedy

Global Interdependence **963**

The Epilogue provides a review of the eight themes that have been examined and developed throughout the book. Each chapter focuses on three themes that are particularly relevant to the content. Pages 964–965 provide an overview of the eight themes. For each unit, a particular theme is identified and an example or two is cited from the historical period covered in the unit.

Purpose

- to provide a review of the eight themes of the book
- to help students understand how particular themes pervade specific units
- to give an example or two of each theme that is drawn from each unit in order to show the continuity of certain issues in different times, places, and cultures across history

Teaching Strategy

- Refer students to the front of the book, where the World History Themes are defined and explained in detail on pages xxx–xxxi. You might review those pages with students and ask them to give an example of each theme from their study of this book.
- You might use the pictures on these pages as a jumping-off point to discuss the themes.

Epilogue

Themes Through History

Throughout this book, eight themes have been used as frameworks for the comparison of civilizations, cultures, and periods of history. The following pages reexamine the importance of these themes in world history. The pages also look at the themes' continuing significance in today's world and for the future.

Interaction with Environment

Unit 1

3000 B.C. The Nile River Valley Since their earliest days on earth, humans have had to work with and sometimes confront their environment. They do this to survive and to flourish. River valleys, such as those along the Nile, Indus, Tigris, and Euphrates rivers, were the sites of the earliest civilizations. The rich agricultural land that borders these rivers attracted nomads to settle there. Only by interacting with the river were humans able to survive. The river dominated their lives—from supplying basic needs to allowing agriculture and transportation.

Power and Authority

Unit 2

A.D. 1–300 Rome and Aksum The story of history is, as much as anything else, the recording of who has power and what they do with it. In Rome, Augustus became the first emperor. Augustus' title as commander of the Roman army was *imperator,* which came to mean "emperor." He greatly increased the power of the Roman Empire.

In Africa, the kings of Aksum conquered areas along the Red Sea and the Blue Nile. They took control of lands on the Arabian Peninsula, spreading their Aksumite culture to other peoples. Rome and Aksum, two centers of power, eventually came into contact as trading partners.

Religious and Ethical Systems

Unit 3

630 The Rise of Islam Throughout history, religion has played an important role in bringing millions of people together in peace. It has also, at times, driven them apart. It has been the cause behind many wars.

This book has examined history's major religions, including Islam in this unit. Yet many more religions exist throughout the world. And while they are all unique in some way, each one guides the beliefs and behaviors of its members. Whatever emotions it prompts, religion remains one of the most powerful forces in the world.

Cultural Interaction

Unit 4

1492 Columbus Lands in San Salvador Human cultures have generally sought interaction with each other. This interaction has had positive effects, such as the acquiring of new knowledge. However, it also has produced negative effects, such as armed conflict and mass destruction.

One of the most momentous encounters in history took place when Christopher Columbus encountered the Native Americans of the Caribbean, as shown in the painting above.

964

4 Million B.C.	3000 B.C.	2000 B.C.		1500 B.C.	500 B.C.		0		A.D. 500	600
Unit 1										
	Unit 2									
									Unit 3	
									Unit 4	
										550

Task: Pairs of students will choose a theme and do two things. First, they will list other examples from the book that illustrate their chosen theme. Second, they will show how the example(s) cited above for the theme they have chosen might be used to illustrate one of the other eight themes.

Purpose: To learn more about the themes and how

they overlap. Many historical events, personalities, and conflicts illustrate more than one theme.

Activity: Ask each pair of students to choose one of the themes that most interests them. Then have them brainstorm other examples from chapters in the book that they think work well to illustrate the theme. For example, if they choose empire building, students

might mention the Romans, the Persians, or the Chinese. Then, for the second part of their assignment, they might note that the example cited on page 965 of the British in India would also work well to illustrate the theme of Power and Authority.

 ALTERNATIVE ASSESSMENT BOOK
Standards for Evaluating a Cooperative Activity

Revolution

Unit 5

1789 Storming of the Bastille Across the globe, governments and institutions, as well as long-held ideas, often have been overthrown by force.

The painting above shows a mob in Paris storming the Bastille, the fortress looming in the background. The mob attempted to seize the gunpowder stored there. This event ignited the French Revolution, in which the French monarchy was toppled.

Empire Building

Unit 6

1876 The British in India A recurring event in history is the attempt of one group to dominate another. Below left, red-coated British soldiers stand at attention around a royal pavilion. They are participating in a ceremony in India to celebrate Queen Victoria becoming Empress of India in 1876. One British viceroy said of the British role in India: "We are all British gentlemen engaged in the magnificent work of governing an inferior race." Racist attitudes such as this made conflict inevitable and eventually led to independence movements in the colonies.

Science & Technology

Unit 7

1942 The Lockheed P-38 Lightning Whether it's discovering a vaccine or designing a better plane, one of the wonders of history is humankind's ability to continually advance technologically.

Above is the Lockheed P-38 Lightning, a World War II fighter plane. Harley Earl was head of styling at General Motors. He was so taken with the look of the P-38 that he incorporated elements of the plane, including tail fins, into the cars he designed. Fins were first seen on the 1948 Cadillac and then became common on many makes of cars over the next 15 to 20 years.

Economics

Unit 8

1980s Japanese Economic Boom Economics has been a driving force behind countless events in history. Today it is an important measure of a nation's strength.

The Japanese workers below are shown testing computers, manufactured by their company before being shipped out to customers. Japanese dedication to quality control was one of the factors that helped the Japanese economy boom. This was particularly true in the 1980s. This growth helped make Japan an economic powerhouse in the world.

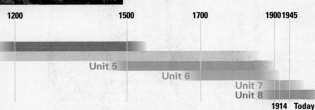

1200	1500	1700	1900	1945

Unit 5
Unit 6
Unit 7
Unit 8

1914 Today

965

TEACHING OPTION

EXPLORING PRIMARY SOURCES

Revolution In Charles Dickens's novel *A Tale of Two Cities,* the narrator describes the storming of the Bastille in Book Two, Chapter 21, "Echoing Footsteps." In this account, Dickens focuses on the character of the wine merchant Defarge and his wife, Madame Defarge, as they lead the storming of the Bastille.

You might read an excerpt from this chapter of the novel to the students. Then you might have them put on a play of this scene, reading their lines from copies of the chapter. Designate one student as the narrator. Assign students to read the lines of Defarge, Madame Defarge, Jacques Three, and the turnkey. The rest of the class can read the lines of the crowd.

Make copies of the chapter, beginning with the paragraph, "Headlong, mad, and dangerous footsteps to force their way into anybody's life, footsteps not easily made clean again if once stained red, the footsteps raging in Saint Antoine afar off, as the little circle sat in the dark London window."

Bombay or Mumbai?

Bombay is the largest city in India. It is located on the Arabian Sea, on an island just off the west coast of the country. The Portuguese founded Bombay as a trading post in the 1500s. It is today the center of trade and finance in India, with many banks and distribution companies. Bombay is the most important port on the west coast of India. Its textile industry, on which its traditional prosperity was founded, is still important but its manufacturing is now very diversified. Bombay is one of the largest and most densely populated cities in the world. There are serious problems of overcrowding and housing shortages. The city has expanded on to the mainland to relieve some of the pressures of overpopulation. The people of Bombay speak Marathi, and they call the city Mumbai.

Mosques in Europe

Istanbul is the largest city in Turkey. Previously, it had been named Constantinople when it was the capital of the Eastern Roman Empire. When the city was captured by the Turks in 1453, it was renamed Istanbul. Its great Christian church, Hagia Sophia (or Holy Wisdom), was turned into a mosque, the largest in Europe.

Connect to Today

THEME Economics — *The Widening Gap*

Gross Domestic Product*

*Per Capita

	India	United States
1965	$105	$3,536
1991	$311	$22,219

(In Dollars)

The gap is widening today between the rich and poor nations of the world. The graph to the left shows the Gross Domestic Product (GDP) of India and the United States. The GDP is the dollar value of all goods, services, and structures produced within a country during one year. In this graph, each country's GDP is divided up per capita, or per person; that is, by the number of productive workers.

Within nations, there is a widening gap between rich people and poor people. The shantytown to the left shows the existence side by side of wealth and poverty in the city of Bombay, India. Slums stand next to luxurious high-rise apartments. Many such striking contrasts exist in cities throughout the world.

THEME Religious and Ethical Systems — *A Return to Tradition*

One growing trend that can be seen around the world is a return to more traditional religious beliefs and rituals. Among Protestant denominations this movement is called fundamentalism. This same development can be observed among Muslims, Jews, Hindus, and others. The picture to the right shows Orthodox Jews in Mea Shearim, an Orthodox community in Jerusalem. The Orthodox men wear the traditional styles of sideburns and heavy black clothes.

The picture below shows Muslims celebrating a tradition of their faith, the end of Ramadan. The celebration here takes place in the Mosque of Rome, the largest modern mosque in Europe.

966 Epilogue

Gifted and Talented Students

Appreciating Architecture Ask students to do some research on the Church of the Holy Wisdom (Hagia Sophia) in Istanbul (formerly Constantinople). The church was captured and plundered twice; first, by the armies of Christian knights embarked on the Fourth Crusade. The church was the focus of Byzantine art and wealth. It contained rare marbles, gold candelabra and mosaics, and precious jewels. Its capture in 1204 by the Crusaders meant the plunder of the ancient church. Then in 1453, the city fell to the Turks. On the orders of the sultan, Mehmet II, Hagia Sophia was converted into a mosque. As part of this process, its mosaics were defaced.

Have students investigate the changes that befell Hagia Sophia at the hands of both Crusaders and Turks. Have students do some research to learn in detail what the Crusaders took from the city and church and where the plunder ended up. *Much of the loot, including priceless works of art, ended up in Saint Mark's Cathedral in Venice.* Then have students investigate the specific changes made by the Muslims as they converted the church into a mosque.

THEME Revolution — *Violent Voices of Change*

Nations throughout the world continue to contend with groups bent on radical and often violent change. This is true from the Basques in Spain, to militia groups in the United States, to Marxist rebels in Central and South America.

This picture shows a car bombing in Madrid, Spain, carried out by Basque terrorists in 1992. Like many such terrorist groups, the Basques have used violent means to achieve their ends. They believe that such acts attract immediate worldwide publicity to their cause. Further, such groups often use violence because they lack faith in the political process.

The Basques in Spain
Recently Princess Sophia, the daughter of King Juan Carlos of Spain, married a Basque soccer player. There was tight security around the wedding ceremony to ensure that there was no violence to mar the occasion. Furthermore, when a new art museum designed by the American architect Frank Gehry opened in the Basque city of Bilbao in northern Spain, tight security was again enforced to prevent any terrorist acts.

EXAMINING THEMES

Economics
Possible responses: Students might explore the potential for social and political turmoil that could result from a large gap between rich and poor.

Religious and Ethical Systems
Possible responses: Students might connect the return to religious belief with the complexity and stress of the modern world. Many people find that religion offers a steadying influence to balance life's turmoils.

Revolution
Possible responses: Students might point out that the American Revolution and the Civil War were both exercises in violence. Many states have been born out of a lack of faith in the political process and a resort to violence. However, many other such efforts have been futile and destructive exercises in terrorism.

Power and Authority
Possible responses: Most people around the world would probably support democracy because it fosters the growth of individual rights. Others, disturbed by the prospect of political chaos, might prefer military rule as a means of preventing the disintegration of the social order.

THEME Power and Authority

A Continuing Struggle for Freedom

As the millennium changes, democracy continues to grow throughout the world. Yet many nations remain in the grip of dictatorship. In Myanmar (formerly Burma), for example, Aung San Suu Kyi leads the struggle for democracy against a repressive military regime. She received the 1991 Nobel Prize for Peace.

Such struggles continue in other parts of the world as well. The enemies of democracy include military rule, ethnic strife, one-party rule, and religious intolerance. Nonetheless, democracy continues to make its appeal to many people around the world.

EXAMINING THEMES

Economics
What might be the long-term consequences of permitting a large gap to develop between rich and poor? How would such a gap affect political stability in the world?

Religious and Ethical Systems
Why might people feel the need to return to basic religious beliefs and rituals? How might such traditional faith enrich their lives?

Revolution
What might cause people to lose faith in the political process to the extent that they would be willing to resort to violence? Is political violence ever justified?

Power and Authority
Why might people support democracy? Why might others prefer military rule?

Epilogue **967**

TEACHING OPTION | BLOCK SCHEDULING — **CONNECTIONS ACROSS THE CURRICULUM**

Foreign Languages The Basque language is something of a mystery to scholars. The Basque people themselves call their language Euskera or Euskara. It is believed to be the only language still spoken in southwestern Europe of those languages spoken before the Romans conquered the region.

Scholars are not sure about the origins of the Basque language. Some believe it is connected to a Hamito-Semitic (Afro-Asiatic) language group. Others believe that it is related to a now-extinct Iberian language. Still others claim a connection to Caucasian, an ancient language spoken in the Caucasus. As of today, Basque remains a language without a family.

The Basque people are believed to have been living in the Pyrenees in prehistoric times, long before such people as the Gauls and the Iberians came to the region and became their neighbors. Have students do some research on the Basques and answer such questions as the number of Basque speakers, the size and location of the area they inhabit, and any other interesting information they come across in their research. *There are approximately 3 million Basque speakers living in an area of approximately 3,900 square miles located in the Pyrenees Mountains on both sides of the border between France and Spain.*

Connect to Today

THEME **Cultural Interaction** *Borderless Issues*

A variety of important issues in the world today bring together people from many different cultures and nations. Prominent among these are women's issues.

This photograph shows the opening ceremony of the United Nations Conference on Women held in Beijing, China, in September 1995. Women from around the world attended this conference. Issues they examined included the role of women, population growth, poverty, education, and health. Both problems and solutions were discussed.

THEME **Science & Technology** *Advancements Spur New Questions*

Dolly is a cloned sheep who was born in July of 1996. She is an identical copy of another adult and has no father. She was cloned by a group of research veterinarians led by Ian Wilmut at the Roslin Institute near Edinburgh, Scotland. Wilmut and his fellow researchers remain opposed to the cloning of humans. Scientific advances in genetic engineering raise ethical controversies about whether scientists should do what they are capable of doing.

968

THEME Interaction with Environment

Challenges and Achievements

A number of serious environmental challenges face the world community, including endangered species and pollution. The image at the center left shows the ozone hole (in the center within the blue boundary) in the Southern Hemisphere. The decline in the ozone layer is caused by the use of certain chemicals on earth. The ozone layer helps to absorb ultraviolet-B radiation. The ozone hole means less radiation will be screened out, which will result in the destruction of plant life and more cases of skin cancer.

On the other hand, the elephants above represent the revival of an endangered species. As forests have been turned into farmland, migration routes have been affected. Some conservation groups are working to restore natural habitats. They have in some cases been successful in establishing migratory trails that elephants have begun using to return to favorite haunts.

THEME Empire Building   *Internet: A New Frontier*

The computer-generated image below shows traffic on the National Science Foundation's computer network. Volume in bytes ranges from zero (purple) to 100 billion (white). The empires of the past were based upon military power; the empires of the future may well be based upon information. The old form of empire building meant the domination by one country of the political, economic, or cultural life of others. The new form of empire might be the domination of information processing and retrieval by a limited number of information corporations in a few powerful nations.

Elephants

The Asian elephant is primarily threatened by the loss of habitat as forests have been cleared and converted into agricultural land. The African elephant is threatened by poachers who kill it for its ivory. This illegal killing is still widespread and is getting even worse in some countries.

EXAMINING THEMES

Cultural Interaction

Possible responses: Some students might argue that women bring a more compassionate viewpoint to issues such as child care, health care, and education. Other students may think compassionate attitudes are not specific to one gender.

Science & Technology

You might use this question to explore with students the practical effects and ethical ramifications of cloning as one example of the power of science and technology. What sorts of constraints, if any, should be placed upon scientific researchers?

Interaction with Environment

Possible responses: Students may cite agreements eliminating the production of chlorofluorocarbons, which damage the ozone layer. However, in some parts of the world, air and water quality remains low because of widespread pollution.

Empire Building

Possible responses: Some students might mention the invasion of privacy and the difficulty of keeping information limited as threats to individuality. Others may think that the Internet is not a threat to the individual or to privacy.

EXAMINING THEMES

Cultural Interaction

What perspective might women bring to problems such as child-care, health care, and education? What special contribution might women make to the solution to such problems?

Science & Technology

Do you think the cloning of human beings would be a good or bad idea? Why?

Interaction with Environment

What is an example of an environmental issue that the world has addressed and begun to solve? What is an example of an environmental issue that remains unsolved?

Empire Building

How might information corporations in a few powerful nations represent a new form of empire? What might be some of the threats to the individual posed by abuses of the Internet?

Epilogue **969**

MULTIPLE LEARNING STYLES

Logical-Mathematical Learners Students whose strength is logical and abstract reasoning may want to devise a game or conceptual model to investigate the ways in which huge information corporations might be able to construct a new form of empire. Students might set up various hypothetical situations, then try to predict the outcomes. For example, is cyberspace more of a cooperative community or a corporate conglomerate?

Some students may feel that the Internet is a force for the spread of ideas—unhampered by bureaucracies, corporations, and governments—and that it will serve as a ballast to the empire-building schemes of giant corporations. Others may feel that the competitive business environment will result in a few corporations, such as Microsoft and Intel, dominating the field.

Have students devise a game in which the individual and information corporations contend in cyberspace. Make sure they balance the rules of the game so that both the individual surfer on the Internet and the conglomerates have certain advantages and disadvantages.

Teacher's Edition   **969**

WORLD HISTORY
PATTERNS OF INTERACTION

Reference Section

970

Atlas

The atlas contains a political map of the world and both political and physical maps of the continents.

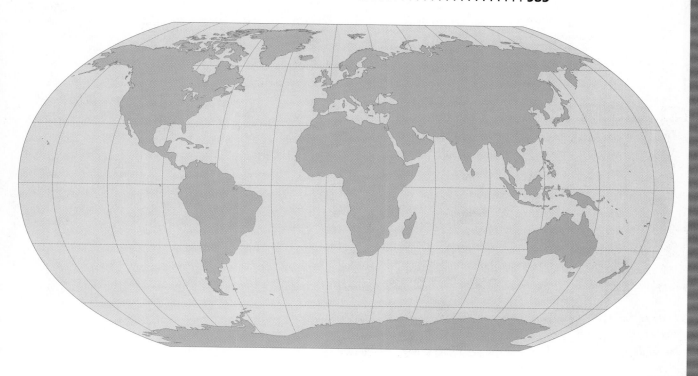

971

ARCTIC OCEAN

GREENLAND

Baffin Bay

RUSSIA

ALASKA (U.S.)

60°N

Bering Sea

Gulf of Alaska

CANADA

Hudson Bay

Labrador Sea

80°N

160°E 180° 160°W 140°W 120°W 100°W 80°W 60°W 40°W

UNITED STATES

40°N

ATLANTIC OCEAN

PACIFIC OCEAN

MEXICO

Gulf of Mexico

20°N

Caribbean Sea

HAWAII (U.S.)

FED. STATES OF MICRONESIA

MARSHALL ISLANDS

GALAPAGOS IS. (Ec.)

VENEZUELA

GUYANA

SURINAME

FRENCH GUIANA

COLOMBIA

ECUADOR

0° Equator

SOLOMON ISLANDS

KIRIBATI

PERU

BRAZIL

WESTERN SAMOA

AMERICAN SAMOA

BOLIVIA

VANUATU

FIJI

TONGA

COOK ISLANDS (N.Z.)

FRENCH POLYNESIA

PARAGUAY

20°S

Coral Sea

NEW CALEDONIA (Fr.)

CHILE

URUGUAY

AUSTRALIA

ARGENTINA

PACIFIC OCEAN

NEW ZEALAND

40°S

FALKLAND ISLANDS (U.K.)

SOUTH GEORGIA (U.K.)

60°S

Alexander Island

Weddell Sea

Ross Sea

Berkner Island

80°S

ANTARCTICA

180° 160°W 140°W 120°W 100°W 80°W 60°W 40°W

Central America and the Caribbean

UNITED STATES

ATLANTIC OCEAN

Gulf of Mexico

BAHAMAS

90°W 80°W 70°W 60°W

Tropic of Cancer

CUBA

20°N

PUERTO RICO

VIRGIN IS. (U.S.) (U.K.)

MEXICO

CAYMAN IS. (U.K.)

HAITI

DOMINICAN REPUBLIC

ANTIGUA & BARBUDA

BELIZE

JAMAICA

ST. KITTS & NEVIS

GUADELOUPE (Fr.)

DOMINICA

GUATEMALA

Caribbean Sea

MARTINIQUE (Fr.)

ST. LUCIA

HONDURAS

ST. VINCENT & THE GRENADINES

EL SALVADOR

NICARAGUA

ARUBA (Neth.)

GRENADA

BARBADOS

10°N

CURACAO (Neth.)

TRINIDAD & TOBAGO

COSTA RICA

PANAMA

VENEZUELA

PACIFIC OCEAN

0 500 Miles

0 1,000 Kilometers

COLOMBIA

GUYANA

972

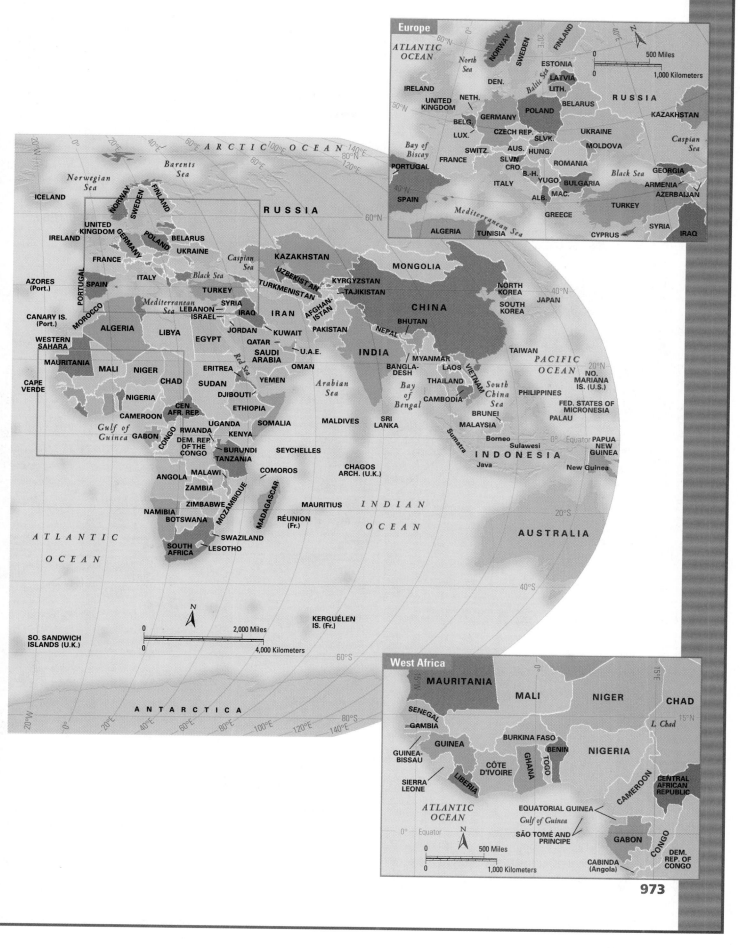

Europe

ATLANTIC OCEAN

NORWAY
SWEDEN
FINLAND
North Sea
IRELAND
DEN.
ESTONIA
LATVIA
LITH.
RUSSIA
UNITED KINGDOM
NETH.
GERMANY
POLAND
BELARUS
KAZAKHSTAN
BELG.
LUX.
CZECH REP.
SLVK.
UKRAINE
Bay of Biscay
FRANCE
SWITZ.
AUS.
HUNG.
SLVN.
CRO.
MOLDOVA
ROMANIA
Caspian Sea
PORTUGAL
ITALY
B.-H.
YUGO.
BULGARIA
Black Sea
GEORGIA
ARMENIA
AZERBAIJAN
SPAIN
ALB.
MAC.
GREECE
TURKEY
Mediterranean Sea
ALGERIA
TUNISIA
CYPRUS
SYRIA
IRAQ

500 Miles
1,000 Kilometers

ARCTIC OCEAN
Barents Sea
Norwegian Sea
ICELAND
NORWAY
SWEDEN
FINLAND
RUSSIA
IRELAND
UNITED KINGDOM
GERMANY
POLAND
BELARUS
UKRAINE
FRANCE
ITALY
Caspian Sea
KAZAKHSTAN
MONGOLIA
AZORES (Port.)
PORTUGAL
SPAIN
Black Sea
TURKEY
UZBEKISTAN
KYRGYZSTAN
TAJIKISTAN
CHINA
NORTH KOREA
SOUTH KOREA
JAPAN
CANARY IS. (Port.)
MOROCCO
Mediterranean Sea
SYRIA
LEBANON
ISRAEL
IRAQ
IRAN
AFGHAN-ISTAN
WESTERN SAHARA
ALGERIA
LIBYA
EGYPT
JORDAN
KUWAIT
QATAR
SAUDI ARABIA
U.A.E.
PAKISTAN
NEPAL
BHUTAN
INDIA
TAIWAN
PACIFIC OCEAN
MAURITANIA
MALI
NIGER
CHAD
SUDAN
ERITREA
YEMEN
OMAN
Arabian Sea
BANGLA-DESH
MYANMAR
LAOS
VIETNAM
South China Sea
NO. MARIANA IS. (U.S.)
CAPE VERDE
NIGERIA
CAMEROON
CEN. AFR. REP.
DJIBOUTI
ETHIOPIA
THAILAND
CAMBODIA
PHILIPPINES
FED. STATES OF MICRONESIA
PALAU
GABON
CONGO
DEM. REP. OF THE CONGO
RWANDA
BURUNDI
UGANDA
KENYA
SOMALIA
MALDIVES
SRI LANKA
Bay of Bengal
BRUNEI
MALAYSIA
Sumatra
Borneo
Sulawesi
Equator
PAPUA NEW GUINEA
Gulf of Guinea
TANZANIA
SEYCHELLES
CHAGOS ARCH. (U.K.)
Java
INDONESIA
New Guinea
ANGOLA
MALAWI
ZAMBIA
ZIMBABWE
COMOROS
MOZAMBIQUE
MADAGASCAR
MAURITIUS
RÉUNION (Fr.)
INDIAN OCEAN
AUSTRALIA
NAMIBIA
BOTSWANA
SWAZILAND
LESOTHO
SOUTH AFRICA
ATLANTIC OCEAN
SO. SANDWICH ISLANDS (U.K.)
KERGUÉLEN IS. (Fr.)
ANTARCTICA

0   2,000 Miles
0   4,000 Kilometers

West Africa

MAURITANIA
MALI
NIGER
CHAD
SENEGAL
GAMBIA
GUINEA
BURKINA FASO
BENIN
NIGERIA
L. Chad
GUINEA-BISSAU
CÔTE D'IVOIRE
GHANA
TOGO
SIERRA LEONE
LIBERIA
CAMEROON
CENTRAL AFRICAN REPUBLIC
ATLANTIC OCEAN
EQUATORIAL GUINEA
Gulf of Guinea
SÃO TOMÉ AND PRINCIPE
GABON
CONGO
Equator
CABINDA (Angola)
DEM. REP. OF CONGO

500 Miles
1,000 Kilometers

973

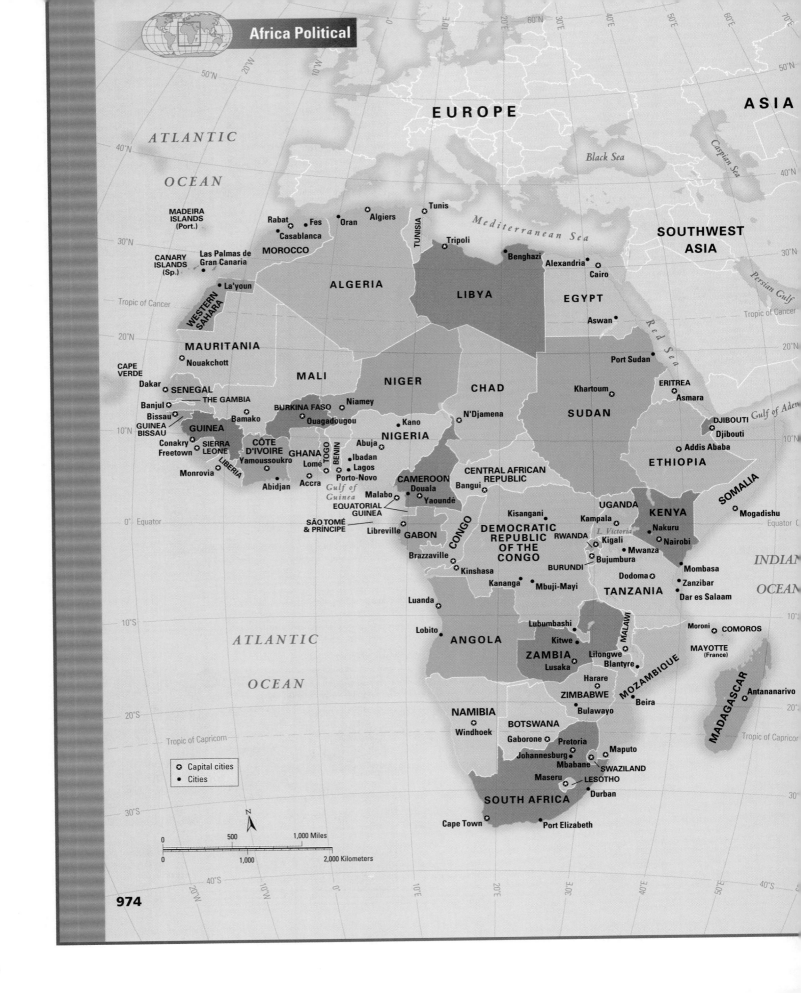

EUROPE

ASIA

ATLANTIC

OCEAN

Black Sea

Caspian Sea

SOUTHWEST
ASIA

Mediterranean Sea

MADEIRA
ISLANDS
(Port.)

Rabat ● Fes ● Oran ✪ Algiers ● Tunis

Casablanca

TUNISIA ● Tripoli

MOROCCO

Benghazi

Persian Gulf

● Alexandria

Cairo

CANARY
ISLANDS
(Sp.)

Las Palmas de
Gran Canaria ●

ALGERIA

LIBYA

EGYPT

Tropic of Cancer

● La'youn

Aswan ●

Red Sea

Tropic of Cancer

WESTERN
SAHARA

MAURITANIA

Port Sudan ●

Gulf of Aden

Nouakchott ✪

MALI

NIGER

CHAD

Khartoum ✪

ERITREA
● Asmara

CAPE
VERDE

Dakar ● ✪ SENEGAL

THE GAMBIA

N'Djamena ●

SUDAN

DJIBOUTI
✪ Djibouti

Banjul ✪

BURKINA FASO ● Niamey

Bissau ✪
GUINEA
BISSAU

Bamako ● ✪ Ouagadougou

● Kano

Addis Ababa ✪

GUINEA

NIGERIA

Conakry ✪ ● SIERRA
Freetown LEONE

CÔTE
D'IVOIRE GHANA

Abuja ✪

● Ibadan

Yamoussoukro ✪ Lomé TOGO BENIN ● Lagos

ETHIOPIA

Monrovia ● LIBERIA

Abidjan ● Accra ✪ Porto-Novo

CAMEROON

CENTRAL AFRICAN
REPUBLIC

Douala ● ✪ Bangui

SOMALIA

*Gulf of
Guinea*

Malabo ✪ Yaoundé ✪

UGANDA

KENYA

EQUATORIAL
GUINEA

Kisangani ●

Kampala ✪

● Mogadishu

Equator

SÃO TOMÉ
& PRÍNCIPE

Libreville ✪ GABON

CONGO

DEMOCRATIC
REPUBLIC
OF THE
CONGO

RWANDA ✪ Kigali

L. Victoria

Nakuru ●

✪ Nairobi

Equator

Brazzaville ✪

BURUNDI ✪ Bujumbura

● Mwanza

● Kinshasa

Dodoma ✪

● Mombasa

INDIAN

Kananga ● ● Mbuji-Mayi

TANZANIA

● Zanzibar

OCEAN

Luanda ✪

Dar es Salaam ●

Lobito ●

Lubumbashi ●

MALAWI

Moroni ● ✪ COMOROS

ATLANTIC

ANGOLA

Kitwe ● Lilongwe ✪

MAYOTTE
(France)

OCEAN

ZAMBIA

Blantyre ●

Lusaka ✪

MOZAMBIQUE

Harare ✪

MADAGASCAR

Antananarivo ✪

NAMIBIA

ZIMBABWE

Beira ●

BOTSWANA

Bulawayo ●

Tropic of Capricorn

Windhoek ✪

Tropic of Capricorn

Gaborone ✪ Pretoria ✪

Maputo ●

Johannesburg ● Mbabane ✪

Maseru ✪ SWAZILAND

✪ Capital cities

● Cities

LESOTHO

Durban ●

SOUTH AFRICA

Cape Town ✪ ● Port Elizabeth

N

0   500   1,000 Miles

0   1,000   2,000 Kilometers

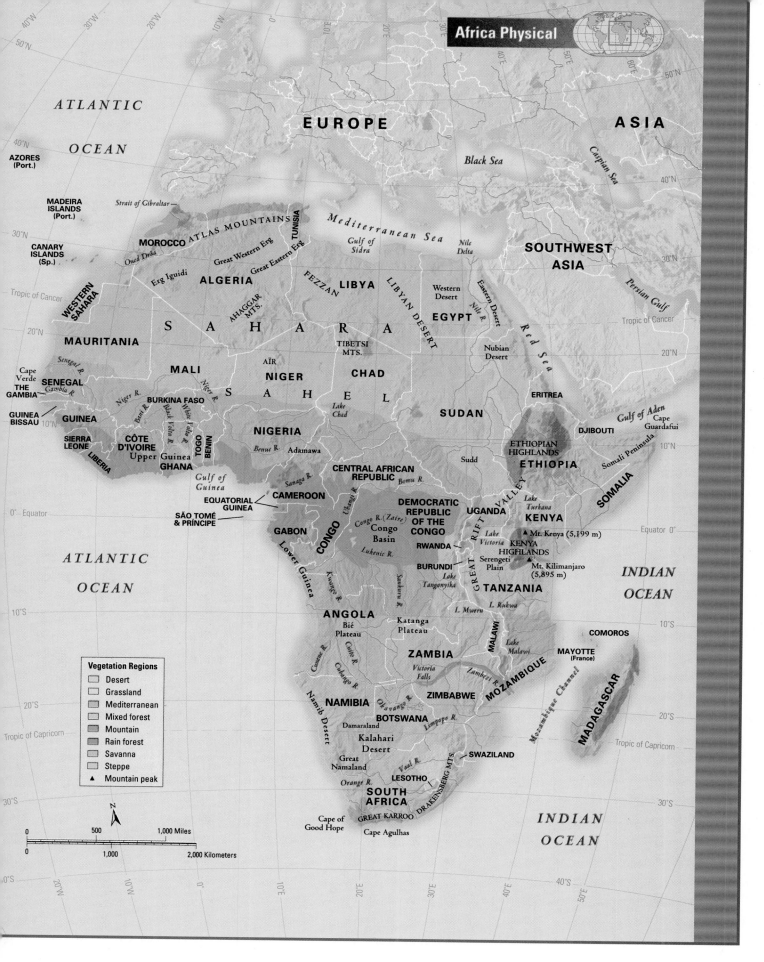

Africa Physical

ATLANTIC OCEAN

AZORES (Port.)

MADEIRA ISLANDS (Port.)

CANARY ISLANDS (Sp.)

EUROPE

ASIA

Black Sea

Caspian Sea

Strait of Gibraltar

Mediterranean Sea

Nile Delta

SOUTHWEST ASIA

Persian Gulf

MOROCCO ATLAS MOUNTAINS TUNISIA

Oued Drâa

Erg Iguidi Great Western Erg Great Eastern Erg

WESTERN SAHARA

ALGERIA FEZZAN LIBYA LIBYAN DESERT

EGYPT

Western Desert

Eastern Desert

Nile R.

Red Sea

Tropic of Cancer

MAURITANIA

S A H A R A

AHAGGAR MTS.

TIBETSI MTS.

AÏR

NIGER CHAD

Nubian Desert

Cape Verde

SENEGAL

THE GAMBIA

Senegal R.

Gambia R.

MALI

S A H E L

ERITREA

GUINEA BISSAU

GUINEA

Niger R.

Bani R.

BURKINA FASO

White Volta R.

Black Volta R.

Niger R.

Lake Chad

SUDAN

Gulf of Aden

Cape Guardafui

DJIBOUTI

SIERRA LEONE

CÔTE D'IVOIRE

Upper Guinea

GHANA

TOGO

BENIN

NIGERIA

Benue R.

Adamawa

Sudd

ETHIOPIAN HIGHLANDS

ETHIOPIA

Somali Peninsula

SOMALIA

LIBERIA

Gulf of Guinea

CENTRAL AFRICAN REPUBLIC

Sanaga R.

Bomu R.

EQUATORIAL GUINEA

CAMEROON

Ubangi R.

DEMOCRATIC REPUBLIC OF THE CONGO

UGANDA

Lake Turkana

KENYA

SÃO TOMÉ & PRÍNCIPE

GABON

CONGO

Congo R. (Zaire)

Congo Basin

RWANDA

Lake Victoria

KENYA HIGHLANDS

Mt. Kenya (5,199 m)

Equator 0°

Lukenie R.

BURUNDI

Serengeti Plain

Mt. Kilimanjaro (5,895 m)

INDIAN OCEAN

Lower Guinea

Kwango R.

Lukenic R.

GREAT RIFT VALLEY

Lake Tanganyika

TANZANIA

L. Rukwa

ATLANTIC OCEAN

ANGOLA

Bié Plateau

Katanga Plateau

L. Mweru

COMOROS

MALAWI

Lake Malawi

MAYOTTE (France)

Vegetation Regions
- Desert
- Grassland
- Mediterranean
- Mixed forest
- Mountain
- Rain forest
- Savanna
- Steppe
- ▲ Mountain peak

Cuanza R.

Cunene R.

Cubango R.

ZAMBIA

Victoria Falls

Zambezi R.

MOZAMBIQUE

Mozambique Channel

MADAGASCAR

NAMIBIA

Okavango R.

ZIMBABWE

Namib Desert

Damaraland

BOTSWANA

Limpopo R.

Tropic of Capricorn

Kalahari Desert

Great Namaland

SWAZILAND

Vaal R.

DRAKENSBERG MTS.

LESOTHO

Orange R.

SOUTH AFRICA

GREAT KARROO

Cape of Good Hope

Cape Agulhas

INDIAN OCEAN

N

0   500   1,000 Miles

0   1,000   2,000 Kilometers

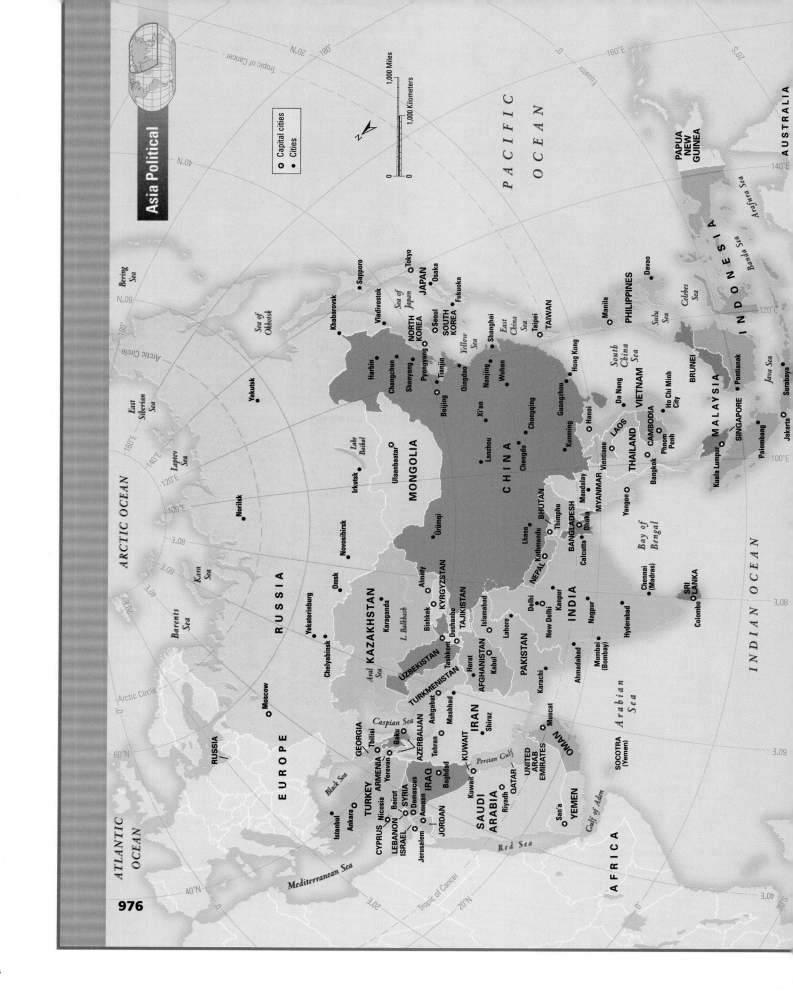

Asia Political

Capital cities
Cities

1,000 Miles
1,000 Kilometers

ARCTIC OCEAN

ATLANTIC OCEAN

PACIFIC OCEAN

INDIAN OCEAN

EUROPE

AFRICA

AUSTRALIA

RUSSIA

Moscow

Barents Sea

Kara Sea

Laptev Sea

East Siberian Sea

Bering Sea

Sea of Okhotsk

Yekaterinburg

Chelyabinsk

Omsk

Novosibirsk

Norilsk

Irkutsk

Yakutsk

Khabarovsk

Vladivostok

Sapporo

Lake Baikal

Ulaanbaatar

MONGOLIA

KAZAKHSTAN

Karaganda

L. Balkhash

Aral Sea

Caspian Sea

Black Sea

TURKEY

Istanbul

Ankara

GEORGIA

Tbilisi

ARMENIA

Yerevan

AZERBAIJAN

Baku

CYPRUS

Nicosia

LEBANON

Beirut

ISRAEL

Jerusalem

SYRIA

Damascus

JORDAN

Amman

IRAQ

Baghdad

Tehran

IRAN

Shiraz

Mashhad

Ashgabat

TURKMENISTAN

UZBEKISTAN

Tashkent

KYRGYZSTAN

Bishkek

TAJIKISTAN

Dushanbe

Almaty

Ürümqi

CHINA

Lanzhou

Xi'an

Chengdu

Chongqing

Kunming

Beijing

Tianjin

Qingdao

Shenyang

Changchun

Harbin

NORTH KOREA

Pyongyang

SOUTH KOREA

Seoul

JAPAN

Tokyo

Osaka

Fukuoka

Sea of Japan

Yellow Sea

East China Sea

Shanghai

Nanjing

Wuhan

Guangzhou

Hong Kong

TAIWAN

Taipei

South China Sea

PHILIPPINES

Manila

Davao

Sulu Sea

Celebes Sea

INDONESIA

MALAYSIA

Kuala Lumpur

SINGAPORE

Pontianak

Palembang

Jakarta

Surabaya

Java Sea

BRUNEI

Banda Sea

Arafura Sea

PAPUA NEW GUINEA

VIETNAM

Hanoi

Da Nang

Ho Chi Minh City

LAOS

Vientiane

THAILAND

Bangkok

CAMBODIA

Phnom Penh

MYANMAR

Yangon

Mandalay

BHUTAN

Thimphu

NEPAL

Kathmandu

Lhasa

BANGLADESH

Dhaka

Calcutta

INDIA

Delhi

New Delhi

Kanpur

Nagpur

Hyderabad

Chennai (Madras)

Mumbai (Bombay)

Ahmadabad

Bay of Bengal

SRI LANKA

Colombo

PAKISTAN

Islamabad

Lahore

Karachi

AFGHANISTAN

Kabul

Herat

SAUDI ARABIA

Riyadh

KUWAIT

Kuwait

QATAR

UNITED ARAB EMIRATES

OMAN

Muscat

YEMEN

San'a

SOCOTRA (Yemen)

Persian Gulf

Arabian Sea

Gulf of Aden

Red Sea

Mediterranean Sea

Tropic of Cancer

Arctic Circle

Equator

ATLANTIC OCEAN

40°N

60°N

20°N

180°

160°E

140°E

120°E

100°E

80°E

60°E

40°E

20°E

20°N

40°N

60°N

20°S

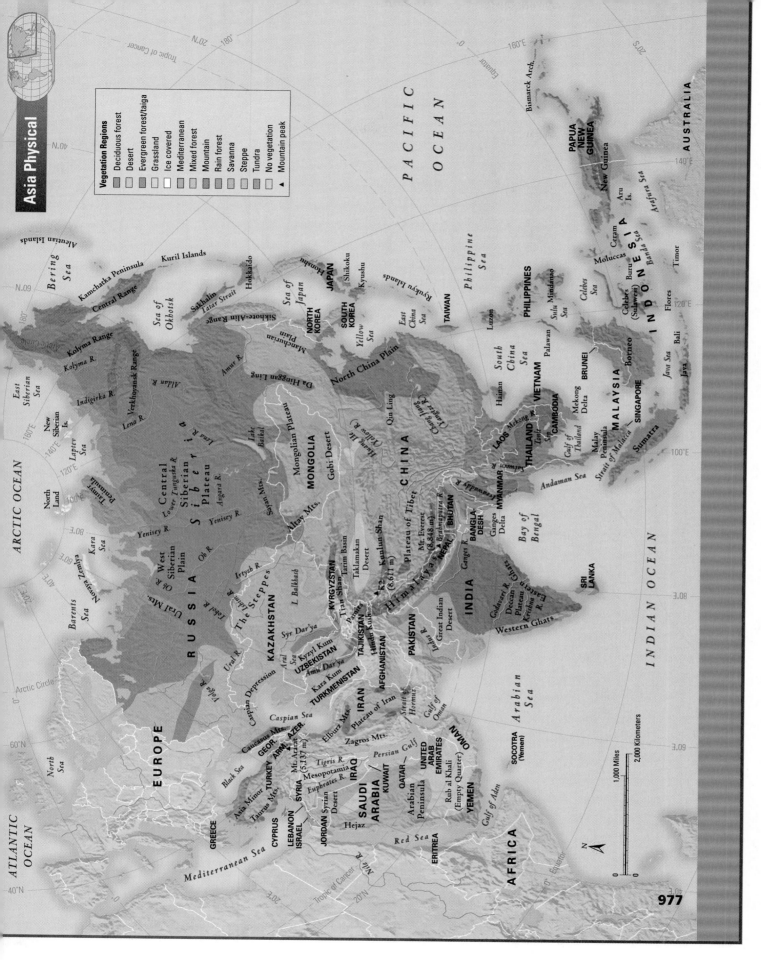

Vegetation Regions

- Deciduous forest
- Desert
- Evergreen forest/taiga
- Grassland
- Ice covered
- Mediterranean
- Mixed forest
- Mountain
- Rain forest
- Savanna
- Steppe
- Tundra
- No vegetation
- ▲ Mountain peak

ARCTIC OCEAN

ATLANTIC OCEAN

PACIFIC OCEAN

INDIAN OCEAN

Aleutian Islands

Bering Sea

Kamchatka Peninsula

Kuril Islands

Central Range

Kolyma Range

Kolyma R.

Sea of Okhotsk

Sakhalin

Tatar Strait

Hokkaido

Sea of Japan

Honshu

JAPAN

Shikoku

Kyushu

East Siberian Sea

New Siberian Is.

Laptev Sea

Verkhoyansk Range

Indigirka R.

Lena R.

Aldan R.

Amur R.

Manchurian Plain

Sikhote-Alin Range

NORTH KOREA

SOUTH KOREA

Yellow Sea

East China Sea

Ryukyu Islands

Philippine Sea

TAIWAN

PHILIPPINES

Luzon

Mindanao

Sulu Sea

Celebes Sea

Moluccas

Buru

Ceram

Banda Sea

Aru Is.

Timor

Arafura Sea

New Guinea

PAPUA NEW GUINEA

Bismarck Arch.

AUSTRALIA

North Land

Taimyr Peninsula

Kara Sea

Novaya Zemlya

Barents Sea

Yenisey R.

Lower Tunguska R.

Central Siberian Plateau

Angara R.

Yenisey R.

Sayan Mts.

Lake Baikal

Da Hinggan Ling

Mongolian Plateau

MONGOLIA

Gobi Desert

North China Plain

Huang He (Yellow R.)

Qin Ling

CHINA

Chang Jiang (Yangtze R.)

Hainan

South China Sea

VIETNAM

LAOS

Mekong Delta

BRUNEI

Borneo

MALAYSIA

SINGAPORE

Sumatra

INDONESIA

Java Sea

Java

Bali

Flores

Celebes (Sulawesi)

Palawan

West Siberian Plain

Ob R.

Irtysh R.

Ural Mts.

RUSSIA

Ishim R.

Tobol R.

The Steppes

KAZAKHSTAN

L. Balkhash

Altay Mts.

Tian Shan

Tarim Basin

Taklamakan Desert

Kunlun Shan

K2 (8,611 m)

Plateau of Tibet

Mt. Everest (8,848 m)

Himalaya

NEPAL

BHUTAN

BANGLA-DESH

Ganges Delta

Bay of Bengal

Brahmaputra R.

Ganges R.

INDIA

Deccan Plateau

Eastern Ghats

Western Ghats

Godavari R.

Krishna R.

Great Indian Desert

MYANMAR

Irrawaddy R.

Salween R.

THAILAND

CAMBODIA

Mekong R.

Tonle Sap

Gulf of Thailand

Malay Peninsula

Strait of Malacca

Andaman Sea

SRI LANKA

EUROPE

Aral Sea

Volga R.

Ural R.

Caspian Depression

Caspian Sea

KYRGYZSTAN

Kyzyl Kum

UZBEKISTAN

Syr Dar'ya

Amu Dar'ya

Kara Kum

TURKMENISTAN

TAJIKISTAN

Pamirs

Hindu Kush

AFGHANISTAN

PAKISTAN

Indus R.

IRAN

Plateau of Iran

Elburz Mts.

Zagros Mts.

Caucasus Mts.

GEOR.

ARM.

AZER.

TURKEY

Mt. Ararat (5,137 m)

Black Sea

Asia Minor

Taurus Mts.

GREECE

CYPRUS

LEBANON

ISRAEL

SYRIA

Syrian Desert

JORDAN

Tigris R.

Euphrates R.

Mesopotamia

IRAQ

KUWAIT

QATAR

UNITED ARAB EMIRATES

OMAN

Gulf of Oman

Strait of Hormuz

Persian Gulf

SAUDI ARABIA

Arabian Peninsula

Rub al Khali (Empty Quarter)

YEMEN

Hejaz

Red Sea

Gulf of Aden

SOCOTRA (Yemen)

Arabian Sea

ERITREA

AFRICA

Nile R.

Mediterranean Sea

North Sea

Arctic Circle

Tropic of Cancer

Equator

Tropic of Cancer

Bay of Bengal

N

1,000 Miles

2,000 Kilometers

Europe Political

Capital cities
Cities

Vegetation Regions
- Deciduous forest
- Desert
- Evergreen forest/taiga
- Grassland
- Ice covered
- Mediterranean
- Mixed forest
- Mountain
- Steppe
- Tundra
- ▲ Mountain peak

500 Miles

1,000 Kilometers

979

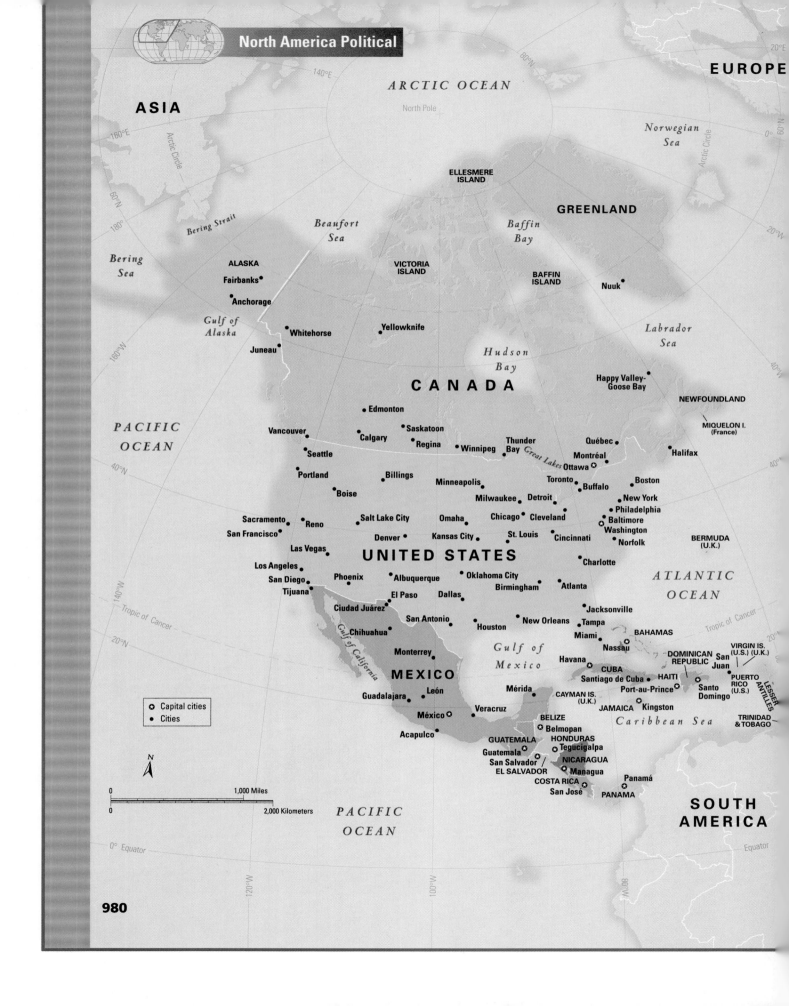

EUROPE

ASIA

ARCTIC OCEAN

North Pole

Norwegian Sea

ELLESMERE ISLAND

GREENLAND

Bering Strait

Beaufort Sea

Baffin Bay

Bering Sea

ALASKA

Fairbanks

Anchorage

VICTORIA ISLAND

BAFFIN ISLAND

Nuuk

Labrador Sea

Gulf of Alaska

Whitehorse

Yellowknife

Hudson Bay

Juneau

CANADA

Happy Valley-Goose Bay

NEWFOUNDLAND

Edmonton

MIQUELON I. (France)

PACIFIC OCEAN

Vancouver

Calgary

Saskatoon

Regina

Winnipeg

Thunder Bay

Great Lakes

Québec

Montréal

Halifax

Seattle

Ottawa

Portland

Billings

Minneapolis

Toronto

Buffalo

Boston

Boise

Milwaukee

Detroit

New York

Sacramento

Reno

Salt Lake City

Omaha

Chicago

Cleveland

Philadelphia

Baltimore

San Francisco

Denver

Kansas City

St. Louis

Cincinnati

Washington

Norfolk

BERMUDA (U.K.)

Las Vegas

UNITED STATES

Charlotte

ATLANTIC OCEAN

Los Angeles

Phoenix

Albuquerque

Oklahoma City

Atlanta

San Diego

El Paso

Dallas

Birmingham

Tijuana

Jacksonville

Ciudad Juárez

San Antonio

Houston

New Orleans

Tampa

Chihuahua

Miami

BAHAMAS

Nassau

Gulf of Mexico

Havana

VIRGIN IS. (U.S.) (U.K.)

Monterrey

DOMINICAN REPUBLIC

San Juan

Gulf of California

MEXICO

CUBA

Santiago de Cuba

HAITI

PUERTO RICO (U.S.)

Guadalajara

León

Mérida

Port-au-Prince

Santo Domingo

CAYMAN IS. (U.K.)

LESSER ANTILLES

México

Veracruz

JAMAICA

Kingston

TRINIDAD & TOBAGO

Acapulco

BELIZE

Caribbean Sea

Belmopan

GUATEMALA

HONDURAS

Tegucigalpa

Guatemala

NICARAGUA

San Salvador

Managua

Panamá

EL SALVADOR

COSTA RICA

PANAMA

San José

SOUTH AMERICA

Tropic of Cancer

Tropic of Cancer

Equator

Equator

PACIFIC OCEAN

N

Capital cities

Cities

0   1,000 Miles

0   2,000 Kilometers

PACIFIC OCEAN

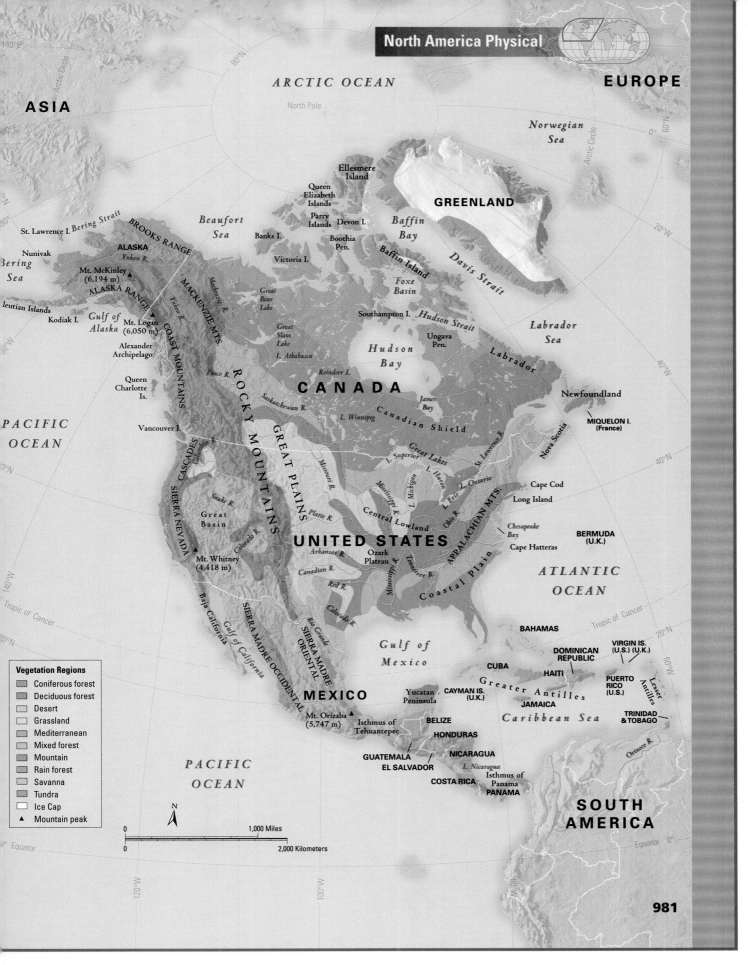

ASIA

EUROPE

ARCTIC OCEAN

North Pole

Norwegian Sea

Ellesmere Island

Queen Elizabeth Islands

Parry Islands

Devon I.

Baffin Bay

GREENLAND

Beaufort Sea

Banks I.

Boothia Pen.

Victoria I.

Baffin Island

St. Lawrence I.

Bering Strait

BROOKS RANGE

Nunivak

ALASKA

Yukon R.

Mt. McKinley (6,194 m) ▲

ALASKA RANGE

Bering Sea

Aleutian Islands

Kodiak I.

Gulf of Alaska

Mt. Logan (6,050 m) ▲

Alexander Archipelago

Mackenzie R.

Yukon R.

MACKENZIE MTS.

COAST MOUNTAINS

Great Bear Lake

Great Slave Lake

L. Athabasca

Foxe Basin

Southampton I.

Hudson Strait

Ungava Pen.

Labrador Sea

Davis Strait

Labrador

PACIFIC OCEAN

Queen Charlotte Is.

Peace R.

ROCKY MOUNTAINS

Saskatchewan R.

Reindeer L.

Hudson Bay

James Bay

CANADA

Canadian Shield

Newfoundland

MIQUELON I. (France)

Vancouver I.

Snake R.

Columbia R.

CASCADES

GREAT PLAINS

L. Winnipeg

L. Superior

Great Lakes

St. Lawrence R.

Nova Scotia

Missouri R.

SIERRA NEVADA

Great Basin

Platte R.

Central Lowland

L. Michigan

L. Huron

L. Erie

L. Ontario

Cape Cod

Long Island

APPALACHIAN MTS.

Chesapeake Bay

BERMUDA (U.K.)

Mt. Whitney (4,418 m) ▲

Colorado R.

Arkansas R.

UNITED STATES

Ozark Plateau

Ohio R.

Tennessee R.

Mississippi R.

Cape Hatteras

ATLANTIC OCEAN

Canadian R.

Red R.

Coastal Plain

Baja California

SIERRA MADRE OCCIDENTAL

Rio Grande

SIERRA MADRE ORIENTAL

Colorado R.

Gulf of California

BAHAMAS

Tropic of Cancer

Tropic of Cancer

Gulf of Mexico

CUBA

DOMINICAN REPUBLIC

HAITI

VIRGIN IS. (U.S.) (U.K.)

PUERTO RICO (U.S.)

Lesser Antilles

MEXICO

Yucatan Peninsula

CAYMAN IS. (U.K.)

Greater Antilles

JAMAICA

TRINIDAD & TOBAGO

Mt. Orizaba (5,747 m) ▲

Isthmus of Tehuantepec

BELIZE

Caribbean Sea

PACIFIC OCEAN

HONDURAS

GUATEMALA

EL SALVADOR

NICARAGUA

L. Nicaragua

COSTA RICA

Isthmus of Panama

PANAMA

Orinoco R.

SOUTH AMERICA

Equator

Equator

Vegetation Regions
- Coniferous forest
- Deciduous forest
- Desert
- Grassland
- Mediterranean
- Mixed forest
- Mountain
- Rain forest
- Savanna
- Tundra
- Ice Cap
- ▲ Mountain peak

N

0   1,000 Miles

0   2,000 Kilometers

981

CENTRAL
AMERICA

Barranquilla
Cartagena
Maracaibo
Caracas
TRINIDAD
& TOBAGO
Barquisimeto
Valencia
Ciudad
Guayana
Cúcuta
VENEZUELA
Georgetown
Paramaribo
Bucaramanga
GUYANA
Cayenne
Medellín
SURINAME
FRENCH
GUIANA
Bogotá
Cali
COLOMBIA

Macapá

0° Equator
Quito
ECUADOR
Guayaquil
Manaus
Belém
0° Equator

Iquitos
Santarém

Piura
Fortaleza

Teresina
Natal
Recife

Trujillo
Rio
Branco
Pôrto
Velho
B R A Z I L
Maceió

PERU
10°S
10°S

Lima
Salvador

Cuzco

Arequipa
La Paz
BOLIVIA
Cuiabá
Brasília

Oruro
Santa Cruz
Goiânia

Sucre
Belo Horizonte

Campo
Grande
20°S
20°S

PARAGUAY
Campinas
Rio de Janeiro

Antofagasta
Curitiba
São Paulo

Tropic of Capricorn
San Miguel
de Tucumán
Asunción
Tropic of Capricorn

Pôrto Alegre

ARGENTINA

CHILE
Córdoba
30°S
30°S

Rosario
URUGUAY

Valparaíso
Buenos Aires
La Plata
Montevideo

Santiago

Concepción
Bahía Blanca
Mar del Plata

| ⊕ Capital cities |
| • Cities |

Puerto Montt
40°S
40°S

N

Stanley
0   500 Miles

50°S
FALKLAND ISLANDS
(U.K.)
0   1,000 Kilometers
SOUTH
GEORGIA
(U.K.)
50°S

Punta Arenas

982

South America Physical

CENTRAL
AMERICA

Caribbean Sea

Cristóbal Colón
(5,775 m)

Pt.
Gallinas

TRINIDAD
& TOBAGO

*Gulf of
Panamá*

L.
Maracaibo

CORD. DE
MERIDA

Orinoco R.

Llanos

VENEZUELA

GUYANA

SURINAME

FRENCH
GUIANA

Guiana Highlands

ATLANTIC
OCEAN

COLOMBIA

Orinoco R.

Branco R.

C. San Francisco

0° Equator

Negro R.

0° Equator

ECUADOR

Putumayo R.

Japurá R.

A m a z o n

Amazon R.

Marajó
Island

*Gulf of
Guayaquil*

Marañón R.

Amazon R.

B a s i n

Madeira R.

Tapajós R.

Xingu R.

Cape
São Roque

Pariñas Pt.

Juruá R.

Purus R.

BRAZIL

Araguaia R.

Tocantins R.

Parnaíba R.

Mt. Huascarán
(6,768 m)

PERU

Ucayali R.

10°S

B r a z i l i a n

São Francisco R.

10°S

Guaporé R.

Mato Grosso
Plateau

H i g h l a n d s

SERRA DO ESPINHAÇO

Mamoré R.

L. Titicaca

BOLIVIA

L.
Poopó

20°S

Atacama Desert

Pantanal

Paraguay R.

20°S

A
N
D
E
S

Gran Chaco

Pilcomayo R.

PARAGUAY

Paraná R.

Campos

Cape São Tomé
Cape Frío

Tropic of Capricorn

Salado R.

SERRA DO MAR

Tropic of Capricorn

CHILE

Paraná R.

Entre Ríos

Uruguay R.

PACIFIC
OCEAN

Mt. Aconcagua
(6,960 m)

Patos
Lagoon

30°S

Salado R.

Pampas

URUGUAY

Río de la Plata

30°S

ARGENTINA

Colorado R.

ATLANTIC
OCEAN

Negro R.

40°S

P a t a g o n i a

San Matías Gulf

40°S

Chiloé I.

Chubut R.

Valdés
Peninsula

Chonos
Arch.

Gulf of
San Jorge

Vegetation Regions

☐ Desert
☐ Grassland
▨ Mediterranean
☐ Mixed forest
▨ Mountain
▨ Rain forest
☐ Savanna
☐ Steppe
▨ Tundra
▲ Mountain peak

Cape Tres Puntas

N

0   500   1,000 Miles
0   1,000   2,000 Kilometers

Wellington I.

FALKLAND ISLANDS
(U.K.)

*Grande
Bay*

50°S

Strait of Magellan

Tierra del
Fuego

Cape Horn

SOUTH
GEORGIA
(U.K.)

50°S

983

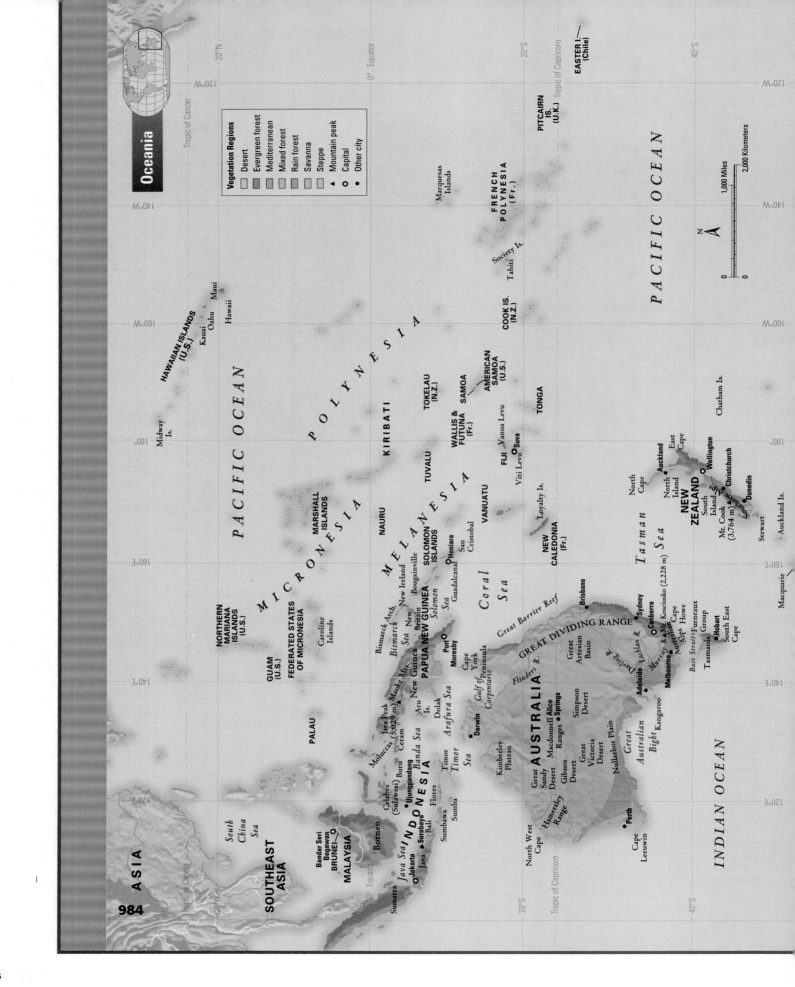

Oceania

Vegetation Regions
Desert
Evergreen forest
Mediterranean
Mixed forest
Rain forest
Savanna
Steppe
▲ Mountain peak
✪ Capital
● Other city

Tropic of Cancer

20°N

Equator

Tropic of Capricorn

20°S

40°S

PACIFIC OCEAN

HAWAIIAN ISLANDS (U.S.)
Midway Is.
Kauai
Oahu
Maui
Hawaii

POLYNESIA

Marquesas Islands

FRENCH POLYNESIA (Fr.)

Society Is.
Tahiti

PITCAIRN IS. (U.K.)

EASTER I. (Chile)

MICRONESIA

NORTHERN MARIANA ISLANDS (U.S.)

GUAM (U.S.)

FEDERATED STATES OF MICRONESIA

PALAU

Caroline Islands

MARSHALL ISLANDS

NAURU

KIRIBATI

TUVALU

TOKELAU (N.Z.)

WALLIS & FUTUNA (Fr.)

SAMOA

AMERICAN SAMOA (U.S.)

COOK IS. (N.Z.)

FIJI
Vanua Levu
Viti Levu ✪ Suva

TONGA

VANUATU

NEW CALEDONIA (Fr.)
Loyalty Is.

SOLOMON ISLANDS
Bougainville
Guadalcanal ✪ Honiara
San Cristobal

MELANESIA

Bismarck Arch.
Bismarck Sea
New Ireland
New Britain
New Guinea

PAPUA NEW GUINEA
Port ✪ Moresby
Maoke Mts.
Java Peak (5029 m) ▲

PACIFIC OCEAN

ASIA

SOUTHEAST ASIA

South China Sea

Borneo

MALAYSIA
BRUNEI ✪ Bandar Seri Begawan

Sumatra

INDONESIA
Java Sea
Jakarta ✪
Java
● Surabaya
Bali
● Ujungpandang
Celebes (Sulawesi)
Banda Sea
Buru
Ceram
Moluccas
Aru Is.
Dolak

Flores
Sumbawa
Sumba
Timor
Timor Sea
Arafura Sea

Darwin ●
Kimberley Plateau
North West Cape
Hamersley Range

Great Sandy Desert
Gibson Desert
Great Victoria Desert

Cape Leeuwin

Perth ●

Nullarbor Plain

Macdonnell Ranges
● Alice Springs

Simpson Desert

AUSTRALIA

GREAT DIVIDING RANGE

Gulf of Carpentaria
Cape York Peninsula

Great Barrier Reef

Flinders R.

Great Artesian Basin

Coral Sea

Brisbane ●

Sydney ●
Lachlan R.
Murray R.
Darling R.
● Canberra ▲ Mt. Kosciusko (2,228 m)

Adelaide ●
Melbourne ●

Great Australian Bight

Kangaroo

Australian Alps

Cape Howe

Furneaux Group

Bass Strait
Tasmania
Hobart ●
South East Cape

Tasman Sea

NEW ZEALAND
North Cape
North Island
● Auckland
East Cape

Wellington ✪
South Island
Christchurch ●
▲ Mt. Cook (3,764 m)
Dunedin ●
Stewart

Chatham Is.

Auckland Is.

Macquarie

INDIAN OCEAN

PACIFIC OCEAN

20°N
Equator
Tropic of Capricorn
20°S
40°S

120°W
140°W
160°W
180°
160°E
140°E
120°E
0°

N

1,000 Miles
2,000 Kilometers

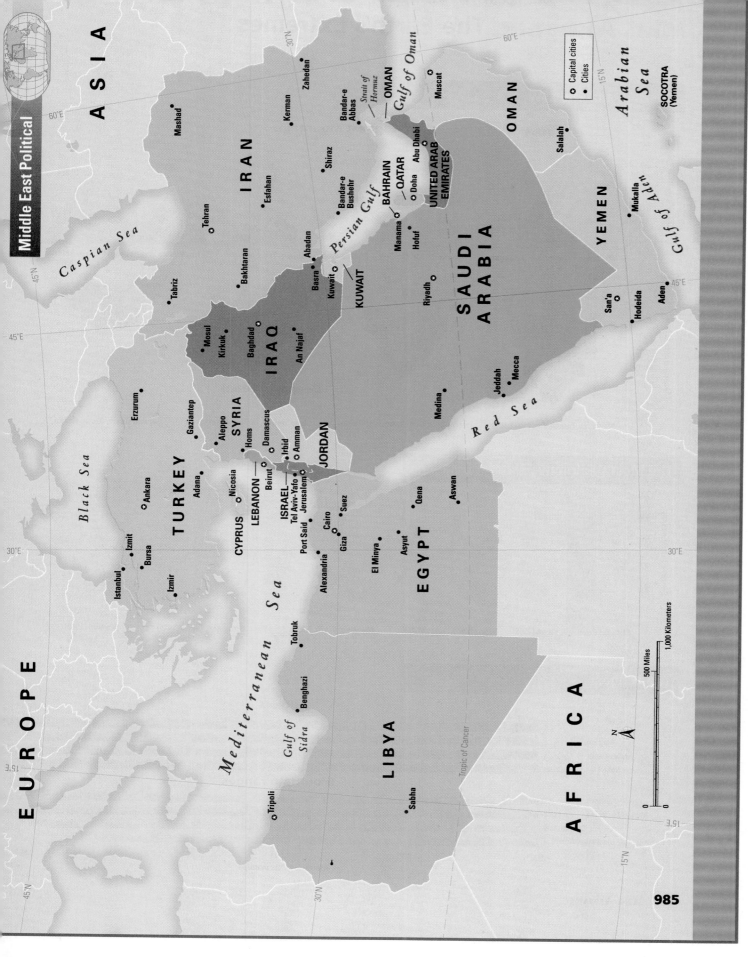

A S I A

E U R O P E

A F R I C A

Caspian Sea

Black Sea

Mediterranean Sea

Red Sea

Persian Gulf

Gulf of Oman

Gulf of Aden

Arabian Sea

Gulf of Sidra

Strait of Hormuz

IRAN

TURKEY

SYRIA

IRAQ

SAUDI ARABIA

EGYPT

LIBYA

OMAN

YEMEN

JORDAN

ISRAEL

LEBANON

CYPRUS

KUWAIT

QATAR

BAHRAIN

UNITED ARAB EMIRATES

Mashad

Zahedan

Kerman

Tehran

Tabriz

Bakhtaran

Esfahan

Shiraz

Bandar-e Abbas

Bandar-e Bushehr

Abadan

Muscat

Salalah

Mukalla

Aden

Hodeida

San'a

OMAN

Abu Dhabi

Doha

Manama

Hofuf

Riyadh

Basra

Kuwait

An Najaf

Baghdad

Mosul

Kirkuk

Erzurum

Gaziantep

Aleppo

Homs

Damascus

Irbid

Amman

Beirut

Nicosia

Adana

Ankara

Izmit

Bursa

Istanbul

Izmir

Tripoli

Benghazi

Tobruk

Sabha

Tel Aviv-Yafo

Jerusalem

Port Said

Suez

Cairo

Giza

Alexandria

El Minya

Asyut

Aswan

Qena

Medina

Mecca

Jeddah

SOCOTRA (Yemen)

Tropic of Cancer

⊕ Capital cities

• Cities

500 Miles

1,000 Kilometers

N

985

Mini Almanac The Earth's Extremes

The High and The Low

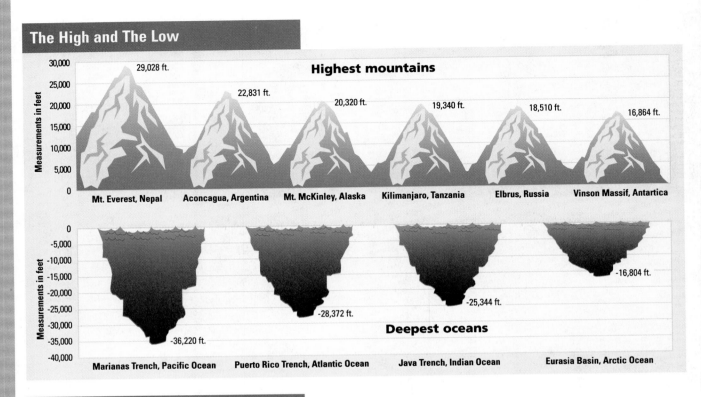

Highest mountains (Measurements in feet)

- Mt. Everest, Nepal — 29,028 ft.
- Aconcagua, Argentina — 22,831 ft.
- Mt. McKinley, Alaska — 20,320 ft.
- Kilimanjaro, Tanzania — 19,340 ft.
- Elbrus, Russia — 18,510 ft.
- Vinson Massif, Antartica — 16,864 ft.

Deepest oceans (Measurements in feet)

- Marianas Trench, Pacific Ocean — -36,220 ft.
- Puerto Rico Trench, Atlantic Ocean — -28,372 ft.
- Java Trench, Indian Ocean — -25,344 ft.
- Eurasia Basin, Arctic Ocean — -16,804 ft.

The Most Destructive Natural Disasters

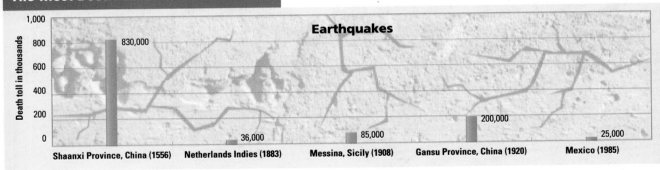

Earthquakes (Death toll in thousands)

- Shaanxi Province, China (1556) — 830,000
- Netherlands Indies (1883) — 36,000
- Messina, Sicily (1908) — 85,000
- Gansu Province, China (1920) — 200,000
- Mexico (1985) — 25,000

The Longest

Rivers

- Nile, Africa
- Amazon, S. America
- Mississippi, N. America
- Chang Jiang (Yangtze), China

Mountain ranges

- Andes, S. America
- Rocky Mountains, N. America
- Himalayas, Central Asia — 2,400 mi.
- Trans-Antartic Mountains, Antartica — 2,200 mi.

Measurements in miles: 500, 1,000, 1,500, 2,000, 2,500

986 MINI ALMANAC

The Wet and Dry

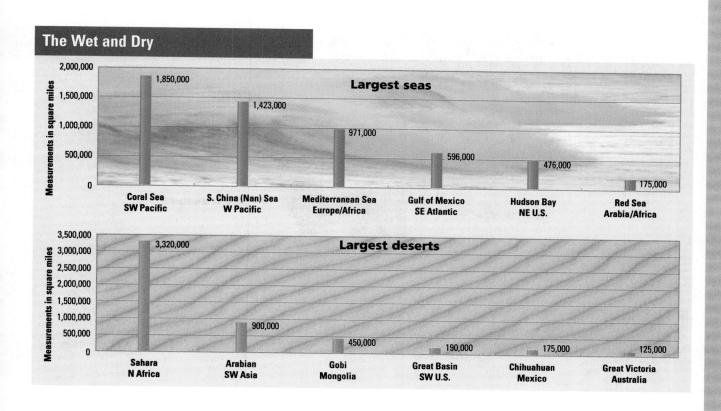

Largest seas

Measurements in square miles

- Coral Sea SW Pacific: 1,850,000
- S. China (Nan) Sea W Pacific: 1,423,000
- Mediterranean Sea Europe/Africa: 971,000
- Gulf of Mexico SE Atlantic: 596,000
- Hudson Bay NE U.S.: 476,000
- Red Sea Arabia/Africa: 175,000

Largest deserts

Measurements in square miles

- Sahara N Africa: 3,320,000
- Arabian SW Asia: 900,000
- Gobi Mongolia: 450,000
- Great Basin SW U.S.: 190,000
- Chihuahuan Mexico: 175,000
- Great Victoria Australia: 125,000

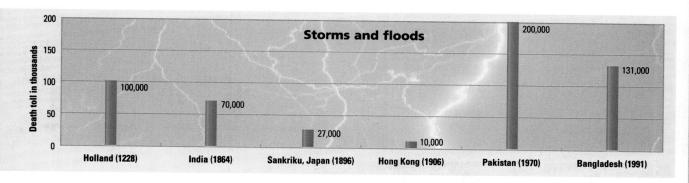

Storms and floods

Death toll in thousands

- Holland (1228): 100,000
- India (1864): 70,000
- Sankriku, Japan (1896): 27,000
- Hong Kong (1906): 10,000
- Pakistan (1970): 200,000
- Bangladesh (1991): 131,000

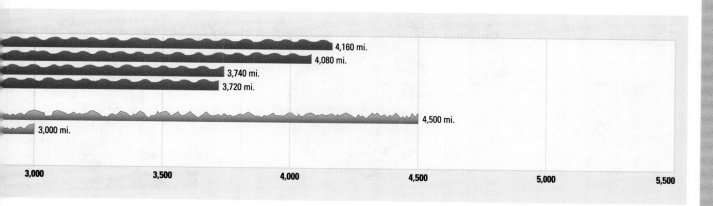

- 4,160 mi.
- 4,080 mi.
- 3,740 mi.
- 3,720 mi.
- 4,500 mi.
- 3,000 mi.

3,000   3,500   4,000   4,500   5,000   5,500

MINI ALMANAC **987**

Population — Projected Growth 1995-2025

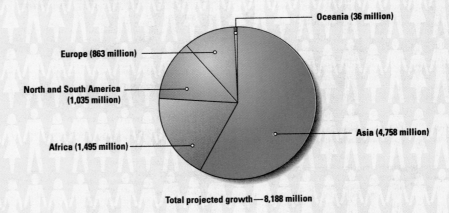

Oceania (36 million)

Europe (863 million)

North and South America (1,035 million)

Asia (4,758 million)

Africa (1,495 million)

Total projected growth — 8,188 million

Communication — Most Widely Spoken Languages

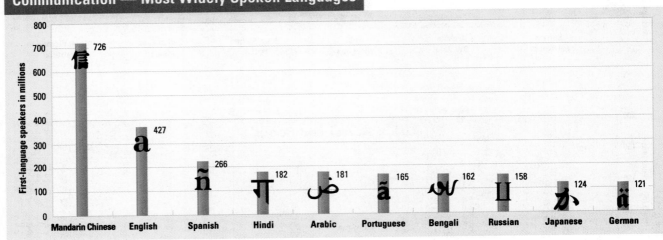

First-language speakers in millions

Mandarin Chinese	English	Spanish	Hindi	Arabic	Portuguese	Bengali	Russian	Japanese	German
726	427	266	182	181	165	162	158	124	121

Important Discoveries and Inventions

5000 B.C.

4400 B.C. loom

4000 B.C. cosmetics

3800 B.C. wheel

3000 B.C. plow

2000 B.C. flush toilet

Technological Milestones

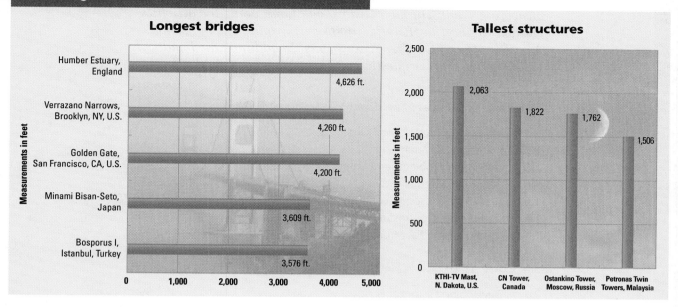

Longest bridges

Measurements in feet

- Humber Estuary, England — 4,626 ft.
- Verrazano Narrows, Brooklyn, NY, U.S. — 4,260 ft.
- Golden Gate, San Francisco, CA, U.S. — 4,200 ft.
- Minami Bisan-Seto, Japan — 3,609 ft.
- Bosporus I, Istanbul, Turkey — 3,576 ft.

(0, 1,000, 2,000, 3,000, 4,000, 5,000)

Tallest structures

Measurements in feet

- KTHI-TV Mast, N. Dakota, U.S. — 2,063
- CN Tower, Canada — 1,822
- Ostankino Tower, Moscow, Russia — 1,762
- Petronas Twin Towers, Malaysia — 1,506

Life Expectancy

Worldwide Longevity

Measurements in years

Japan, United Kingdom, Burundi, Iraq, Mexico, China, Russia, Peru, South Africa, India, United States

■ Male ■ Female

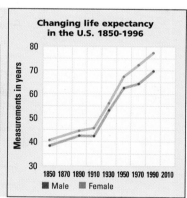

Changing life expectancy in the U.S. 1850-1996

Measurements in years

1850 1870 1890 1910 1930 1950 1970 1990 2010

■ Male ■ Female

Date	Invention
100 B.C.	paper
190	abacus
600	windmill
700	printing
1475	rifle
1590	microscope

1600 to 2000

1608	telescope
1639	steam engine
1656	pendulum clock
1709	piano
1783	parachute
1816	bicycle
1842	anesthetics
1848	chewing gum
1867	dynamite
1876	telephone
1904	radar
1924	frozen food
1926	rocket
1928	computer
1975	home videotape systems

1600 — 1800 — 2000

Mɪɴɪ Aʟᴍᴀɴᴀᴄ **989**

Skillbuilder Handbook

Refer to the Skillbuilder Handbook when you need help in answering Think Through History questions, doing the activities entitled Connect to History, or answering questions in Section Assessments and Chapter Assessments. In addition, the handbook will help you answer questions about maps, charts, and graphs.

1.1 Following Chronological Order

Chronological order is the order in which events happen in time. Historians need to figure out the order in which things happened to get an accurate sense of the relationships among events. As you read history, figure out the sequence, or time order, of events.

UNDERSTANDING THE SKILL

Strategy: Look for time clues. The following paragraph is about the rulers of England after the death of Henry VIII. Notice how the time line that follows puts the events in chronological order.

> **HENRY'S CHILDREN RULE ENGLAND**
>
> After the death of Henry VIII in 1547, each of his three children eventually ruled. This created religious turmoil. Edward VI became king at age nine and ruled only six years. During his reign, the Protestants gained power. Edward's half-sister Mary followed him to the throne. She was a Catholic who returned the English Church to the rule of the pope. Mary had many Protestants killed. England's next ruler was Anne Boleyn's daughter, Elizabeth. After inheriting the throne in 1558, Elizabeth I returned her kingdom to Protestantism. In 1559 Parliament followed Elizabeth's request and set up a national church much like the one under Henry VIII.

Look for clue words about time. These are words like *first, initial, next, then, before, after, finally,* and *by that time.*

Use specific dates provided in the text.

Watch for references to previous historical events that are included in the background.

Strategy: Order events on a time line.

If the events are complex, make a time line of them. Write the dates below the line and the events above the line.

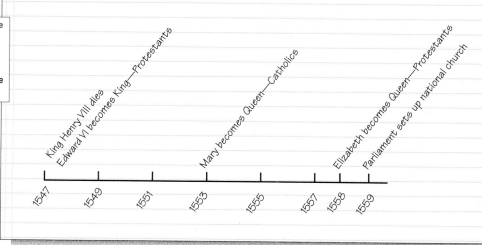

APPLYING THE SKILL

Make your own time line. Skim Chapter 35, Section 3, "Gorbachev Moves Toward Democracy," to find out about the spread of democracy in parts of Europe controlled by the Soviet Union. List the important dates and events. Start with the demonstrations in East Germany in October 1989, include events in Czechoslovakia and Romania, and end with reunification of Germany in October of 1990. Decide on a scale for your time line. Show the important dates below the line and write what happened on each date above the line.

SKILLBUILDER HANDBOOK 991

1.2 Clarifying; Summarizing

Clarifying means making clear and fully understanding what you read. One way to do this is by asking yourself questions about the material. In your answers, restate in your own words what you have read.

Summarizing means condensing what you read into fewer words. You state only the main ideas and the most important details. In your own words, reduce the paragraph or section into a brief report of its general ideas.

UNDERSTANDING THE SKILL

Strategy: Understand and condense the text. The passage below tells about trade in West Africa between 300 and 1600. Following the description is a summary that condenses and also clarifies the key information.

> **Clarify: Look up words or concepts you don't know.**

> **Summarize: Include key facts and statistics.** Watch for numbers, dates, quantities, percentages, and facts.

WEST AFRICAN TRADE

The wealth of the savanna empires was based on trade in two precious commodities, gold and salt. The gold came from a forest region south of the savanna between the Niger and Senegal rivers. Working in utmost secrecy, miners dug gold from shafts as much as 100 feet deep or sifted it from fast-moving streams. Until about 1350, at least two thirds of the world's supply of gold came from West Africa.

Although rich in gold, the savanna and forest areas lacked salt, a material essential to human life. In contrast, the Sahara contained abundant deposits of salt.

Arab traders, eager to obtain West African gold, carried salt across the Sahara by camel caravan. After a long journey, they reached the market towns of the savanna. Meanwhile, the other traders brought gold north from the forest region. The two sets of merchants met in trading centers such as Timbuktu. Royal officials made sure that all traders weighed goods fairly and did business according to law.

> **Summarize: Look for topic sentences stating the main idea.** These are often at the beginning of a section or paragraph. Restate each main idea briefly.

> **Clarify: Make sure you understand.** Ask yourself questions and answer them. For example, who's carrying what?

Strategy: Clarify the main idea.

MAIN IDEA
Gold and salt were traded in West Africa.

Strategy: Write a summary.

> **Clarify and summarize: Write a summary to clarify your understanding of the main ideas.**

SUMMARY
Trade in West Africa was based on gold from the south and salt from the north. Gold was mined in the forest regions. Two thirds of all the world's gold supply came from West Africa. Salt came from the desert. Arab traders met with African traders at trade centers such as Timbuktu.

APPLYING THE SKILL

Clarify and write your own summary. Turn to Chapter 30, pages 777–778, and read "Weapons of Totalitarianism." Note the main ideas. Look up any words you don't recognize. Then write a summary of the section. Condense the section in your own words.

1.3 Identifying Problems and Solutions

Identifying problems means finding and understanding the difficulties faced by a particular group of people at a certain time. Noticing how the people solved their problems is **identifying solutions.** Checking further to see how well those solutions worked is identifying outcomes.

UNDERSTANDING THE SKILL

Strategy: Look for problems and solutions. The passage below summarizes some economic problems facing Latin American nations during the early 20th century.

Look for implied problems. Problems may be suggested indirectly. This sentence suggests that a serious problem in Latin America was the uneven division of wealth.

Look for problems people face.

Look for solutions people tried to deal with each problem.

Check outcomes to the solutions. See how well the solutions worked. Sometimes the solution to one problem caused another problem.

LAND REFORM IN LATIN AMERICA

In Latin America, concentration of productive land in the hands of a few created extremes of wealth and poverty. Poor peasants had no choice but to work large estates owned by a few wealthy families. Landlords had no reason to invest in expensive farm machinery when labor was so cheap. Farming methods were inefficient and economic development was slow.

As Latin American nations began to modernize in the twentieth century, land ownership became a political issue. In response, a handful of countries began land reform programs. These programs divided large estates into smaller plots. Small plots of land were in turn distributed to farm families or granted to villages for communal farming. However, just turning over the land to the landless was not enough. Peasant farmers needed instruction, seeds, equipment, and credit. If the land and the people were to be productive, governments would have to provide assistance to the peasants.

Strategy: Make a chart.

Summarize the problems and solutions in a chart. Identify the problem or problems and the steps taken to solve them. Look for the short- and long-term effects of the solutions.

Problems	Solutions	Outcomes
A few wealthy people owned most of the land.	Land reform programs divided large estates into smaller plots.	Peasants were given land, and communal farms were set up.
Inefficient farming resulted in slow economic development.		
Peasants lacked equipment, resources, skills.	Governments would have to assist with loans and instruction.	Not stated.

APPLYING THE SKILL

Make your own chart. Turn to Chapter 31 and read "Europe After the War" on pages 801–803. Make a chart that lists the problems Germany faced after World War I. List the solutions that were tried and whatever outcomes are mentioned.

1.4 Analyzing Motives

Analyzing motives means examining the reasons why a person, group, or government takes a particular action. To understand those reasons, consider the needs, emotions, prior experiences, and goals of the person or group.

UNDERSTANDING THE SKILL

Strategy: Look for reasons why. On June 28, 1914, Serb terrorists assassinated Austria-Hungary's Archduke Franz Ferdinand and his wife when they visited Sarajevo, the capital of Bosnia. In the following passage, Borijove Jevtic, a Serb terrorist, explains why the assassination occurred. Before this passage, he explains that the terrorists had received a telegram stating that the Archduke would be visiting Sarajevo on June 28. The diagram that follows summarizes the motives of the terrorists for murdering the Archduke.

> **THE ASSASSINATION OF THE ARCHDUKE**
>
> How dared Franz Ferdinand, not only the representative of the oppressor but in his own person an arrogant tyrant, enter Sarajevo on that day? Such an entry was a studied insult.
>
> 28 June is a date engraved deeply in the heart of every Serb, so that the day has a name of its own. It is called the vidovnan. It is the day on which the old Serbian kingdom was conquered by the Turks at the battle of Amselfelde in 1389. It is also the day on which in the second Balkan War the Serbian arms took glorious revenge on the Turk for his old victory and for the years of enslavement.
>
> That was no day for Franz Ferdinand, the new oppressor, to venture to the very doors of Serbia for a display of the force of arms which kept us beneath his heel.
>
> Our decision was taken almost immediately. Death to the tyrant!

Look for motives based on past events or inspiring individuals.

Notice both positive and negative motives.

Look for motives based on basic needs and human emotions. Needs include food, shelter, safety, freedom. Emotions include fear, anger, pride, desire for revenge, patriotism, for example.

Strategy: Make a diagram.

Make a diagram that summarizes motives and actions. List the important action in the middle of the diagram. Then list motives in different categories around the action.

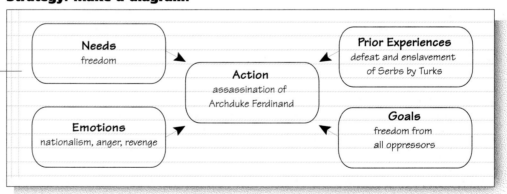

APPLYING THE SKILL

Make your own diagram. Turn to Chapter 27, Section 1, "Imperialists Divide Africa." Read the section and look for motives of European nations in acquiring lands in other parts of the world. Make a diagram like the one above showing the European nations' motives for taking the land.

994 SKILLBUILDER HANDBOOK

1.5 Analyzing Causes; Recognizing Effects

Causes are the events, conditions, and other reasons that lead to an event. Causes happen before the event in time; they explain why it happened. **Effects** are the results or consequences of the event. One effect often becomes the cause of other effects, resulting in a chain of events. Causes and effects can be both short-term and long-term. Examining **cause-and-effect relationships** helps historians see how events are related and why they took place.

UNDERSTANDING THE SKILL

Strategy: Keep track of causes and effects as you read. The passage below describes events leading to the rise of feudalism in Japan. The diagram that follows summarizes the chain of causes and effects.

> ### FEUDALISM COMES TO JAPAN
>
> For most of the Heian period, the rich Fujiwara family held the real power in Japan. Members of this family held many influential posts. By about the middle of the eleventh century, the power of the central government and the Fujiwaras began to slip. This was due in part to court families' greater interest in luxury and artistic pursuits than in governing.
>
> ① Since the central government was weak, large landowners living away from the capital set up private armies. ② As a result, the countryside became lawless and dangerous. Armed soldiers on horseback preyed on farmers and travelers, while pirates took control of the seas. ③ For safety, farmers and small landowners traded parts of their land to strong warlords in exchange for protection. Because the lords had more land, the lords gained more power. This marked the beginning of a feudal system of localized rule like that of ancient China and medieval Europe.

Effects: Look for results or consequences. Sometimes these are indicated by clue words such as *brought about, led to, as a result,* and *consequently.*

Notice that an effect may be the cause of another event. This begins a chain of causes and effects.

Causes: Look for clue words that show cause. These include *because, due to, since,* and *therefore.*

Look for multiple causes and multiple effects. The weakness of the central government caused the three effects shown here.

Strategy: Make a cause-and-effect diagram.

Summarize cause-and-effect relationships in a diagram. Starting with the first cause in a series, fill in the boxes until you reach the end result.

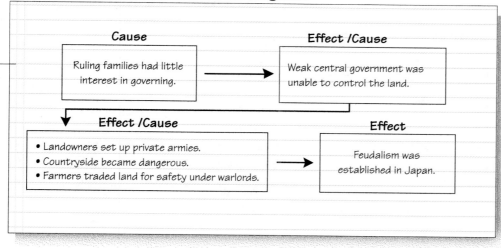

Cause	Effect /Cause
Ruling families had little interest in governing.	Weak central government was unable to control the land.

Effect /Cause	Effect
• Landowners set up private armies. • Countryside became dangerous. • Farmers traded land for safety under warlords.	Feudalism was established in Japan.

APPLYING THE SKILL

Make your own cause-and-effect diagram. Turn to Chapter 28, pages 730–731. Read "Juárez and *La Reforma*" and make notes about the causes and effects of Juárez's reform movement in Mexico. Make a diagram like the one shown above to summarize the information you find.

1.6 Comparing; Contrasting

Historians compare and contrast events, personalities, ideas, behaviors, beliefs, and institutions in order to understand them thoroughly. **Comparing** involves finding both similarities and differences between two or more things. **Contrasting** means examining only the differences between them.

UNDERSTANDING THE SKILL

Strategy: Look for similarities and differences. The following passage describes life in the ancient Greek city-states of Sparta and Athens. The Venn diagram below shows some of the similarities and differences between the two city-states.

> **Compare:** Look for clue words indicating that two things are alike. Clue words include *all, both, like, as, likewise,* and *similarly.*

> **Contrast:** Look for clue words that show how two things differ. Clue words include *unlike, by contrast, however, except, different,* and *on the other hand.*

SPARTA AND ATHENS

The Greek city-states developed separately but shared certain characteristics, including language and religion. Economically, all began as farming economies, and all except Sparta eventually moved to trade. Politically, all city-states, except for Sparta, evolved into early forms of democracies.

The leader in the movement to democracy was Athens. After a series of reforms, every Athenian citizen was considered equal before the law. However, as in the other Greek city-states, only about one fifth of the population were citizens. Slaves did much of the work, so Athenian citizens were free to create works of art, architecture, and literature, including drama.

By contrast, Sparta lived in constant fear of revolts by *helots*, people who were held in slave-like conditions to work the land. The city was set up as a military dictatorship, and Spartan men dedicated their lives to the military. In Sparta, duty, strength, and discipline were valued over beauty, individuality, and creativity. As a result, Spartans created little art, architecture, or literature.

> **Compare:** Look for features that two subjects have in common. Here you learn that both Athens and Sparta started out as farming communities.

> **Contrast:** Look for ways in which two things are different. Here you learn that Athens and Sparta had different values.

Strategy: Make a Venn diagram.

> **Compare and Contrast:** Summarize similarities and differences in a Venn diagram. In the overlapping area, list characteristics shared by both subjects. Then, in one oval list the characteristics of one subject not shared by the other. In the other oval, list unshared characteristics of the second subject.

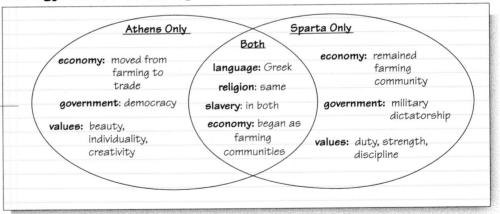

Athens Only
- **economy:** moved from farming to trade
- **government:** democracy
- **values:** beauty, individuality, creativity

Both
- **language:** Greek
- **religion:** same
- **slavery:** in both
- **economy:** began as farming communities

Sparta Only
- **economy:** remained farming community
- **government:** military dictatorship
- **values:** duty, strength, discipline

APPLYING THE SKILL

Make your own Venn diagram. Turn to Chapter 20, pages 493–494, and read the section called "Native American Reaction." Make a Venn diagram comparing and contrasting Dutch and English colonists' relations with Native Americans.

996 SKILLBUILDER HANDBOOK

1.7 Distinguishing Fact from Opinion

Facts are events, dates, statistics, or statements that can be proved to be true. Facts can be checked for accuracy. **Opinions** are judgments, beliefs, and feelings of the writer or speaker.

UNDERSTANDING THE SKILL

Strategy: Find clues in the text. The following excerpt tells about the uprising of Jews in the Warsaw ghetto in 1943. The chart summarizes the facts and opinions.

THE WARSAW GHETTO UPRISING

With orders from Himmler to crush the Jews, the Nazis attacked on April 19, 1943, at the start of the holiday of Passover. Two thousand armed SS troops entered the ghetto, marching with tanks, rifles, machine guns, and trailers full of ammunition. The Jewish fighters were in position—in bunkers, in windows, on rooftops. They had rifles and handguns, hand grenades and bombs that they had made. And they let fly. . . .

Unbelievably, the Jews won the battle that day. The Germans were forced to retreat. . . . The Germans brought in more troops, and the fighting intensified. German pilots dropped bombs on the ghetto. . . .

On May 1, Goebbels [Nazi propaganda minister] wrote in his diary: "Of course this jest will probably not last long." He added a complaint. "But it shows what one can expect of the Jews if they have guns."

Goebbels' tone was mocking. But his forecast was inevitable—and correct. . . . Goebbels did not record in his diary, when the uprising was over, that the starving Jews of the ghetto, with their pathetic supply of arms, had held out against the German army for forty days, longer than Poland or France had held out.

Source: *A Nightmare in History*, by Miriam Chaikin. (New York: Clarion Books, 1987) pp. 77–78

Facts: Look for specific names, dates, statistics, and statements that can be proved. The first two paragraphs provide a factual account of the event.

Opinion: Look for assertions, claims, hypotheses, and judgments. Here Goebbels expresses his opinion of the uprising and of the Jews.

Opinion: Look for judgment words that the writer uses to describe the people and events. Judgment words are often adjectives that are used to arouse a reader's emotions.

Strategy: Make a chart.

Divide facts and opinions in a chart. Summarize and separate the facts from the opinions expressed in a passage.

FACTS	OPINIONS
On April 19, 1943, 2,000 armed SS troops attacked the Warsaw ghetto. Jewish fighters held out for 40 days.	*Goebbels:* The uprising was a jest, but showed the danger of letting Jews get hold of guns. *Author:* It is difficult to believe that Warsaw Jews with their pathetic supply of arms were able to defeat the powerful Nazis. The Jews showed greater courage and determination than did the Poles and French.

APPLYING THE SKILL

Make your own chart. Turn to Chapter 26, page 662, "Democratic Reform and Activism." Find the "Voice from the Past" from the Seneca Falls Convention. Make a chart in which you summarize the facts in your own words, and list the opinions and judgments stated. Look carefully at the language used in order to separate one from the other.

SKILLBUILDER HANDBOOK **997**

2.1 Developing Historical Perspective

Developing historical perspective means understanding events and people in the context of their times. It means not judging the past by current values, but by taking into account the beliefs of the time.

UNDERSTANDING THE SKILL

Strategy: Look for values of the past. The following passage was written by Bartolomé de Las Casas, a Spanish missionary who defended the rights of Native Americans. It challenges an argument presented by a scholar named Sepúlveda, who held that the superior Spaniards had the right to enslave the Native Americans. Following the passage is a chart that summarizes the information from a historical perspective.

> **Identify the historical figure, the occasion, and the date.**

> **Explain how people's actions and words reflected the attitudes, values, and passions of the era.** Las Casas challenges prejudices about Native Americans that were widely held in Europe. His language emphasizes a favorable comparison between Native American and European societies.

IN DEFENSE OF THE INDIANS (1550)
BARTOLOMÉ DE LAS CASAS

Now if we shall have shown that among our Indians of the western and southern shores (granting that we call them barbarians and that they are barbarians) there are important kingdoms, large numbers of people who live settled lives in a society, great cities, kings, judges and laws, persons who engage in commerce, buying, selling, lending, and the other contracts of the law of nations, will it not stand proved that the Reverend Doctor Sepúlveda has spoken wrongly and viciously against peoples like these? . . . From the fact that the Indians are barbarians it does not necessarily follow that they are incapable of government and have to be ruled by others, except to be taught about the Catholic faith and to be admitted to the holy sacraments. They are not ignorant, inhuman, or bestial. Rather, long before they had heard the word Spaniard they had properly organized states, wisely ordered by excellent laws, religion, and custom. They cultivated friendship and, bound together in common fellowship, lived in populous cities in which they wisely administered the affairs of both peace and war justly and equitably, truly governed by laws that at very many points surpass ours, and could have won the admiration of the sages of Athens. . . .

> **Look for clues to the attitudes, customs, and values of people living at the time.** As a Spanish missionary, Las Casas assumes that Europeans are more civilized than Native Americans and that Native Americans need to be converted to Catholicism.

> **Notice words, phrases, and settings that reflect the period.** Las Casas speaks from a time when Europeans looked to classical Greece as a benchmark for civilization.

> **Use historical perspective to understand Las Casas's attitudes.** In a chart, list key words, phrases, and details from the passage. In a short paragraph, summarize the basic values and attitudes of Las Casas.

Strategy: Write a summary.

Key Phrases	Las Casas's *In Defense of the Indians*
• barbarians • Catholic faith • not inhuman, ignorant, or bestial • properly organized states, wisely ordered • sages of Athens	Las Casas argues that Native Americans are not inhuman and do not deserve cruelty and slavery. Rather, they are fully capable of "coming up" to the level of Spanish civilization. Although he makes the statement that Native Americans are barbarians, his language and comparisons seem to suggest that he believes them to be highly civilized in many respects. At the same time, he believes in the importance of converting them to Catholicism.

APPLYING THE SKILL

Write your own summary. Turn to Chapter 11, page 283, and read the excerpt from *The Tale of the Destruction of Riazan*. Read the passage using historical perspective. Then summarize your ideas in a chart like the one above.

998 SKILLBUILDER HANDBOOK

2.2 Formulating Historical Questions

Formulating historical questions is important as you examine primary sources—first-hand accounts, documents, letters, and other records of the past. As you analyze a source, ask questions about what it means and why it is significant. Then, when you are doing research, write questions that you want your research to answer. This step will help to guide your research and organize the information you collect.

UNDERSTANDING THE SKILL

Strategy: Question what you read. The Muslim scholar Ibn Battuta published an account of his journeys in Asia and Africa in the 1300s. Following is part of his description of China. After the passage is a web diagram that organizes historical questions about it.

Ask about the historical record itself. Who produced it? When was it produced?

Ask about the person who created the record. What judgments or opinions does the author express?

IBN BATTUTA IN CHINA, AROUND 1345

The Chinese themselves are infidels, who worship idols and burn their dead like the Hindus. . . . In every Chinese city there is a quarter for Muslims in which they live by themselves, and in which they have mosques both for the Friday services and for other religious purposes. The Muslims are honored and respected. The Chinese infidels eat the flesh of swine and dogs, and sell it in their markets. They are wealthy folk and well-to-do, but they make no display either in their food or their clothes. You will see one of their principal merchants, a man so rich that his wealth cannot be counted, wearing a coarse cotton tunic. But there is one thing that the Chinese take a pride in, that is gold and silver plate. Every one of them carries a stick, on which they lean in walking, and which they call "the third leg." Silk is very plentiful among them, because the silk-worm attaches itself to fruits and feeds on them without requiring much care. For that reason, it is so common as to be worn by even the very poorest there. Were it not for the merchants it would have no value at all, for a single piece of cotton cloth is sold in their country for the price of many pieces of silk.

Ask about the facts presented. Who were the main people? What did they do? What were they like?

Ask about the significance of the record. How would you interpret the information presented? How does it fit in with the history of this time and place? What more do you need to know to answer these questions?

Strategy: Make a web diagram.

Investigate a topic in more depth by asking questions. Ask a large question and then ask smaller questions that explore and develop from the larger question.

What was the historical situation in China at this time?

Why did Ibn Battuta go to China, and who was the audience for his narrative?

What was China like in the 1300s?

How might Ibn Battuta's background have influenced his impressions?

Do other sources agree with Ibn Battuta's description?

APPLYING THE SKILL

Make your own web diagram. Turn to the quotation by Bernal Díaz in Chapter 16, page 403. Use a web diagram to write historical questions about the passage.

SKILLBUILDER HANDBOOK **999**

Section 2: Using Critical Thinking

2.3 Hypothesizing

Hypothesizing means developing a possible explanation for historical events. A hypothesis is an educated guess about what happened in the past or what might happen in the future. A hypothesis takes available information, links it to previous experience and knowledge, and comes up with a possible explanation, conclusion, or prediction.

UNDERSTANDING THE SKILL

Strategy: Find clues in the reading. In studying the Indus Valley civilization, historians do not yet know exactly what caused that culture to decline. They have, however, developed hypotheses about what happened to it. Read this passage and look at the steps that are shown for building a hypothesis. Following the passage is a chart that organizes the information.

> **Identify the event, pattern, or trend you want to explain.**

> **Determine the facts you have about the situation.** These facts support various hypotheses about what happened to the Indus Valley civilization.

MYSTERIOUS END TO INDUS VALLEY CULTURE

Around 1750 B.C., the quality of building in the Indus Valley cities declined. Gradually, the great cities fell into decay. What happened? Some historians think that the Indus River changed course, as it tended to do, so that its floods no longer fertilized the fields near the cities. Other scholars suggest that people wore out the valley's land. They overgrazed it, overfarmed it, and overcut its trees, brush, and grass.

As the Indus Valley civilization neared its end, around 1500 B.C, a sudden catastrophe may have had a hand in the cities' downfall. Archaeologists have found a half-dozen groups of skeletons in the ruins of Mohenjo-Daro, seemingly never buried. Their presence suggests that the city, already weakened by its slow decline, may have been abandoned after a natural disaster or a devastating attack from human enemies. The Aryans, a nomadic people from north of the Hindu Kush mountains, swept into the Indus Valley at about this time. Whether they caused the collapse of the Indus Valley civilization or followed in its wake is not known.

> **Develop a hypothesis that might explain the event.** Historians hypothesize that a combination of ecological change and sudden catastrophe caused the Indus Valley civilization to collapse.

> **Determine what additional information you need to test the hypothesis.** You might refer to a book about India, for example, to learn more about the impact of the Aryan invasions.

Strategy: Make a chart.

> **Use a chart to summarize your hypothesis about events.** Write down your hypothesis and the facts that support it. Then you can see what additional information you need to help prove or disprove it.

Hypothesis	Facts that support the hypothesis	Additional information needed
A combination of ecological change and sudden catastrophe caused the Indus Valley civilization to collapse	• Building quality declined • Indus River tended to change course • Unburied skeletons were found at Mohenjo-Daro • Aryan invasions occurred around same time	• What was Indus Valley culture like? • What were the geographical characteristics of the region? • How did overfarming tend to affect the environment? • What factors affected the decline of other ancient civilizations?

APPLYING THE SKILL

Make your own chart. Turn to Chapter 19, page 476, and read A Voice from the Past. Hypothesize what impact the introduction of firearms might have had on Japan. Then read the surrounding text material. List facts that support your hypothesis and what additional information you might gather to help prove or disprove it.

1000 SKILLBUILDER HANDBOOK

2.4 Analyzing Issues

An issue is a matter of public concern or debate. Issues in history are usually economic, social, political, or moral. Historical issues are often more complicated than they first appear. **Analyzing an issue** means taking a controversy apart to find and describe the different points of view about the issue.

UNDERSTANDING THE SKILL

Strategy: Look for different sides of the issue. The following passage describes working conditions in English factories in the early 1800s. The cluster diagram that follows the passage helps you to analyze the issue of child labor.

> ### CHILDREN AT WORK
>
> Child labor was one of the most serious problems of the early Industrial Revolution. Children as young as 6 years worked exhausting jobs in factories and mines. Because wages were very low, many families in cities could not survive unless all their members, including children, worked.
>
> In most factories, regular work hours were 6 in the morning to 6 in the evening, often with two "over-hours" until 8. It was common for 40 or more children to work together in one room—a room with little light or air. Those who lagged behind in their work were often beaten. Because safety was a low concern for many factory owners, accidents were common.
>
> In 1831, Parliament set up a committee to investigate abuses of child labor. Medical experts reported that long hours of factory work caused young children to become crippled or stunted in their growth. They recommended that children younger than age 14 should work no more than 8 hours. Factory owners responded that they needed children to work longer hours in order to be profitable. As one owner testified, reduced working hours for children would "much reduce the value of my mill and machinery, and consequently of . . . my manufacture." As a result of the committee's findings, Parliament passed the Factory Act of 1833. The act made it illegal to hire children under 9 years old, and it limited the working hours of older children.

Look for a central problem with its causes and effects.

Look for facts and statistics. Factual information helps you understand the issue and evaluate the different sides or arguments.

Look for different sides to the issue. You need to consider all sides of an issue before deciding your position.

Strategy: Make a cluster diagram.

If an issue is complex, make a diagram. A diagram can help you analyze an issue.

APPLYING THE SKILL

Make your own cluster diagram. Chapter 34, page 886, describes the partition of India. Make a cluster diagram to analyze the issue and the positions of the people involved.

SKILLBUILDER HANDBOOK **1001**

2.5 Analyzing Assumptions and Biases

An **assumption** is a belief or an idea that is taken for granted. Some assumptions are based on evidence; some are based on feelings. Whether assumptions are clearly stated or just implied, you can usually figure out what they are.

Bias is a prejudiced point of view. Historical accounts that are biased tend to be one-sided and reflect the personal prejudices of the historian.

UNDERSTANDING THE SKILL

Strategy: Think about the writer as you read. The European explorer Amerigo Vespucci reached the coast of Brazil in 1502, on his second voyage to the Americas. Below are his impressions of the people he met.

Identify the author and information about him or her. Does the author belong to a special-interest group, social class, political party, or movement that might promote a one-sided or slanted viewpoint on the subject?

Search for clues. Are there words, phrases, statements, or images that might convey a positive or negative slant? What might these clues reveal about the author's bias?

Examine the evidence. Is the information that the author presents consistent with other accounts? Is the behavior described consistent with human nature as you have observed it?

AMERIGO VESPUCCI REPORTS ON THE PEOPLE OF BRAZIL

For twenty-seven days I ate and slept among them, and what I learned about them is as follows.

Having no laws and no religious faith, they live according to nature. They understand nothing of the immortality of the soul. There is no possession of private property among them, for everything is in common. They have no boundaries of kingdom or province. They have no king, nor do they obey anyone. Each one is his own master. There is no administration of justice, which is unnecessary to them, because in their code no one rules. . . .

They are also a warlike people and very cruel to their own kind. . . . That which made me . . . astonished at their wars and cruelty was that I could not understand from them why they made war upon each other, considering that they held no private property or sovereignty of empire and kingdoms and did not know any such thing as lust for possession, that is pillaging or a desire to rule, which appear to me to be the causes of wars and every disorderly act. When we requested them to state the cause, they did not know how to give any other cause than that this curse upon them began in ancient times and they sought to avenge the deaths of their forefathers.

Strategy: Make a chart.

Make a chart of your analysis. For each of the heads listed on the left side of the chart, summarize information presented in the passage.

Vespucci's impressions of the native peoples of Brazil	
author, date	Amerigo Vespucci, 1502
occasion	exploration of coast of Brazil on second voyage to Americas
tone	judging, negative, superior
assumptions	Since the native people do not live in organized states and have no private property, they have no system of authority, laws, or moral principles. They have no apparent religious beliefs. They are warlike and cruel and seem to make war on one another for no reason.
bias	The author's comments about the soul seem to show a bias towards his own religious beliefs. He also reveals a prejudice that European customs and practices are superior to all others.

APPLYING THE SKILL

Make your own chart. Look at the quotation by the Qing emperor Kangxi in "A Voice from the Past" in Chapter 19, page 479. Summarize the underlying assumptions and biases using a chart like the one shown.

1002 SKILLBUILDER HANDBOOK

2.6 Evaluating Decisions and Courses of Action

Evaluating decisions means making judgments about the decisions that historical figures made. Historians evaluate decisions on the basis of their moral implications and their costs and benefits from different points of view.

Evaluating various courses of action means carefully judging the choices that historical figures had to make. By doing this, you can better understand why they made some of the decisions they did.

UNDERSTANDING THE SKILL

Strategy: Look for choices and reasons. The following passage describes the decisions U.S. President John Kennedy had to make when he learned of Soviet missile bases in Cuba. As you read it, think of the alternative responses he could have made at each turn of events. Following the passage is a chart that organizes information about the Cuban missile crisis.

THE CUBAN MISSILE CRISIS

During the summer of 1962, the flow of Soviet weapons into Cuba—including nuclear missiles—greatly increased. President Kennedy responded cautiously at first, issuing a warning that the United States would not tolerate the presence of offensive nuclear weapons in Cuba. Then, on October 16, photographs taken by American U-2 planes showed the president that the Soviets were secretly building missile bases on Cuba. Some of the missiles, armed and ready to fire, could reach U.S. cities in minutes.

On the evening of October 22, the president made public the evidence of missiles and stated his ultimatum: any missile attack from Cuba would trigger an all-out attack on the Soviet Union. Soviet ships continued to head toward the island, while the U.S. navy prepared to stop them and U.S. invasion troops massed in Florida. To avoid confrontation, the Soviet ships suddenly halted. Soviet Premier Nikita Khrushchev offered to remove the missiles from Cuba in exchange for a pledge not to invade the island. Kennedy agreed, and the crisis ended.

Some people criticized Kennedy for practicing brinkmanship, when private talks might have resolved the crisis without the threat of nuclear war. Others believed he had been too soft and had passed up a chance to invade Cuba and oust its Communist leader, Fidel Castro.

Look at decisions made by individuals or by groups. Notice the decisions Kennedy made in response to Soviet actions.

Analyze a decision in terms of the choices that were possible. Both Kennedy and Khrushchev faced the same choice. Either could carry out the threat, or either could back down quietly and negotiate.

Look at the outcome of the decisions.

Strategy: Make a chart.

Make a simple chart of your analysis. The problem was that Soviet nuclear missiles were being shipped to Cuba. The decision to be made was how the United States should respond.

Kennedy's choices	pros	cons	your evaluation
Publicly confront Khrushchev with navy and prepare for war.	Show Khrushchev and world the power and strong will of the U.S.; force him to back off.	Nuclear war could occur.	In your opinion, which was the better choice? Why?
Say nothing to U.S. public and negotiate quietly.	Avoid frightening U.S. citizens and avoid threat of nuclear war.	The U.S. would look weak publicly; Khrushchev could carry out plan.	

APPLYING THE SKILL

Make a chart. Chapter 31, page 815, describes the decisions British and French leaders made when Hitler took over the Sudetenland in Czechoslovakia just before World War II. Make a chart like the one shown to summarize the pros and cons of their choice of appeasement and evaluate their decision yourself.

SKILLBUILDER HANDBOOK 1003

2.7 Forming and Supporting Opinions

Historians do more than reconstruct facts about the past. They also **form opinions** about the information they encounter. Historians form opinions as they interpret the past and judge the significance of historical events and people. They **support their opinions** with logical thinking, facts, examples, quotes, and references to events.

UNDERSTANDING THE SKILL

Strategy: Find arguments to support your opinion. In the following passage, journalist Paul Gray summarizes differing opinions about the significance and impact of Columbus's voyages. As you read, develop your own opinion about the issue.

HOW SHOULD HISTORY VIEW THE LEGACY OF COLUMBUS?

In one version of the story, Columbus and the Europeans who followed him brought civilization to two immense, sparsely populated continents, in the process fundamentally enriching and altering the Old World from which they had themselves come.

Among other things, Columbus' journey was the first step in a long process that eventually produced the United States of America, a daring experiment in democracy that in turn became a symbol and a haven of individual liberty for people throughout the world. But the revolution that began with his voyages was far greater than that. It altered science, geography, philosophy, agriculture, law, religion, ethics, government—the sum, in other words, of what passed at the time as Western culture.

Increasingly, however, there is a counterchorus, an opposing rendition of the same events that deems Columbus' first footfall in the New World to be fatal to the world he invaded, and even to the rest of the globe. The indigenous peoples and their cultures were doomed by European arrogance, brutality, and infectious diseases. Columbus' gift was slavery to those who greeted him; his arrival set in motion the ruthless destruction, continuing at this very moment, of the natural world he entered. Genocide, ecocide, exploitation . . . are deemed to be a form of Eurocentric theft of history from [the Native Americans].

Decide what you think about a subject after reading all the information available to you. After reading this passage, you might decide that Columbus's legacy was primarily one of genocide, cruelty, and slavery. On the other hand, you might believe that, despite the negatives, his voyages produced many long-term benefits.

Consider the opinions and interpretations of historians and other experts. Weigh their arguments as you form your own opinion.

Support your opinion with facts, quotes, and examples, including references to similar events from other historical eras.

Strategy: Make a chart.

Summarize your opinion and supporting information in a chart. Write an opinion and then list facts, examples, interpretations, or other information that support it.

Opinion: Voyages of Columbus brought more bad than good to the Americas	
Facts:	**Historical interpretations:**
• Europeans replaced existing cultures with their own	• Europeans were arrogant and brutal
• European diseases killed many Native Americans	• Columbus's arrival set in motion ruthless destruction of environment
• Columbus enslaved Native Americans	• Through conquest and exploitation, Europeans "stole" Native Americans' history and culture

APPLYING THE SKILL

Strategy: Make your own chart. Look at the Different Perspectives on Economics and the Environment in Chapter 36, page 951. Read the selections and form your own opinion about the concept of sustainable development. Summarize your supporting data in a chart like the one shown.

2.8 Making Inferences

Inferences are ideas and meanings not stated in the material. **Making inferences** means reading between the lines to extend the information provided. Your inferences are based on careful study of what is stated in the passage as well as your own common sense and previous knowledge.

UNDERSTANDING THE SKILL

Strategy: Develop inferences from the facts. This passage describes the Nok culture of West Africa. Following the passage is a diagram that organizes the facts and ideas that lead to inferences.

THE NOK CULTURE

Read the stated facts and ideas.

The earliest known culture of West Africa was that of the Nok people. They lived in what is now Nigeria between 900 B.C. and A.D. 200. Their name came from the village where the first artifacts from their culture were discovered by archaeologists. The Nok were farmers. They were also the first West African people known to smelt iron. The Nok began making iron around 500 B.C., using it to make tools for farming and weapons for hunting. These iron implements lasted longer than wood or stone and vastly improved the lives of the Nok.

Use your knowledge, logic, and common sense to draw conclusions. You could infer from these statements that the Nok were a settled people with advanced technology and a rich culture.

Nok artifacts have been found in an area stretching for 300 miles between the Niger and Benue rivers. Many are sculptures made of terra cotta, a reddish-brown clay. Carved in great artistic detail, some depict the heads of animals such as elephants and others depict human heads. The features of some of the heads reveal a great deal about their history. One of the human heads, for example, shows an elaborate hairdo arranged in six buns, a style that is still worn by some people in Nigeria today. This similarity suggests that the Nok may have been the ancestors of modern-day Africans.

Consider what you already know that could apply. Your knowledge of history might lead you to infer the kinds of improvements in life brought about by better farming tools.

Recognize inferences that are already made. Phrases like "the evidence suggests" or "historians believe" indicate inferences and conclusions experts have made from historical records.

Strategy: Make a diagram.

Summarize the facts and inferences you make in a diagram.

Stated Facts and Ideas	Inferences
• iron farming tools • iron harder than wood • tools improved life	iron tools improved agriculture and contributed to cultural development
• Nok artifacts found in 300 mile radius	Nok culture spread across this area
• heads carved in great artistic detail	Nok were skilled potters and sculptors
• sculptures included elephant heads	elephants played a role in people's lives

APPLYING THE SKILL

Make your own diagram. Read the Tamil poem from ancient India quoted in Chapter 7 on page 178. Using a chart like the one above, make inferences from the poem about its author, its subject, and the culture it comes from.

SKILLBUILDER HANDBOOK **1005**

2.9 Drawing Conclusions

Drawing conclusions means analyzing what you have read and forming an opinion about its meaning. To draw conclusions, you look closely at the facts, combine them with inferences you make, and then use your own common sense and experience to decide what the facts mean.

UNDERSTANDING THE SKILL

Strategy: Combine information to draw conclusions. The passage below presents information about the reunification of East and West Germany in 1990. The diagram that follows shows how to organize the information to draw conclusions.

> **GERMANY IS REUNIFIED**
>
> On October 3, 1990, Germany once again became a single nation. After more than 40 years of Communist rule, most East Germans celebrated their new political freedoms. Families that had been separated for years could now visit whenever they chose.
>
> Economically, the newly united Germany faced serious problems. More than 40 years of Communist rule had left East Germany in ruins. Its transportation and telephone systems had not been modernized since World War II. State-run industries in East Germany had to be turned over to private control and operate under free-market rules. However, many produced shoddy goods that could not compete in the global market.
>
> Rebuilding eastern Germany's bankrupt economy was going to be a difficult, costly process. Some experts estimated the price tag for reunification could reach $200 billion. In the short-term, the government had to provide unemployment benefits to some 1.4 million workers from the east who found themselves out of work.
>
> In spite of these problems, Germans had reasons to be optimistic. Unlike other Eastern European countries, who had to transform their Communist economies by their own means, East Germany had the help of a strong West Germany. Many Germans may have shared the outlook expressed by one worker: "Maybe things won't be rosy at first, but the future will be better."

Read carefully to understand all the facts. Fact: Reunification brought social and political freedoms to East Germans.

Read between the lines to make inferences. Inference: After a market economy was introduced, many industries in eastern Germany failed, which put people out of work.

Use the facts to make an inference. Inference: Reunification put a strain on government resources.

Ask questions of the material. What are the long-term economic prospects for eastern Germany? Conclusion: Although it faced challenges, it seemed to have a greater chance for success than other former Communist countries.

Strategy: Make a diagram.

Summarize the facts, inferences, and your conclusion in a diagram.

Facts	Inferences	Conclusion About Passage
East Germans gained freedoms.	East Germans welcomed the end of Communist rule.	Although eastern Germany was in bad shape at the time of reunification, it had the advantage of the strength of western Germany as it made the transition to democracy and capitalism.
Transportation and telephone systems were outmoded.	Rebuilding took time.	
State-run industries produced shoddy goods.	Industries couldn't compete in free-market economy.	
Unemployment skyrocketed.	Reunification put a great financial burden on Germany.	
Cost for reunification could be $200 billion.		

APPLYING THE SKILL

Strategy: Make a diagram. Look at Chapter 6, pages 146–148, on the collapse of the Roman Republic. As you read, draw conclusions based on the facts. Use the diagram above as a model for organizing facts, inferences, and conclusions about the passage.

1006 SKILLBUILDER HANDBOOK

2.10 Synthesizing

Synthesizing is the skill historians use in developing interpretations of the past. Like detective work, synthesizing involves putting together clues, information, and ideas to form an overall picture of a historical event.

UNDERSTANDING THE SKILL

Strategy: Build an interpretation as you read. The following passage describes the first settlement of North and Central America. The call-outs indicate the different kinds of information that lead to a synthesis—an overall picture of Native American life.

Read carefully to understand the facts. Facts such as these enable you to base your interpretations on physical evidence.

Look for explanations that link the facts together. This statement is based on the evidence provided by baskets, bows and arrows, and nets, which are mentioned in the sentences that follow.

Bring together the information you have about a subject. This interpretation brings together different kinds of information to arrive at a new understanding of the subject.

Consider what you already know that could apply. Your general knowledge will probably lead you to accept this statement as reasonable.

THE FIRST AMERICANS

From the discovery of chiseled arrowheads and charred bones at ancient sites, it appears that the earliest Americans lived as big game hunters. The woolly mammoth, their largest prey, provided them with food, clothing, and bones for constructing tools and shelters. People gradually shifted to hunting small game and gathering available plants. They created baskets to collect nuts, wild rice, chokeberries, gooseberries, and currants. Later they invented bows and arrows to hunt small game such as jackrabbits and deer. They wove nets to fish the streams and lakes.

Between 10,000 and 15,000 years ago, a revolution took place in what is now central Mexico. People began to raise plants as food. Maize may have been the first domesticated plant, with pumpkins, peppers, beans, and potatoes following. Agriculture spread to other regions.

The rise of agriculture brought about tremendous changes to the Americas. Agriculture made it possible for people to remain in one place. It also enabled them to accumulate and store surplus food. As their surplus increased, people had the time to develop skills and more complex ideas about the world. From this agricultural base rose larger, more stable societies and increasingly complex societies.

Strategy: Make a cluster diagram.

Summarize your synthesis in a diagram. Use a cluster diagram to organize the facts, opinions, examples, and interpretations that you have brought together to form a synthesis.

- earliest Americans big game hunters
- agriculture allowed people to settle, develop new skills and ideas
- **Synthesis:** The shift from hunting and gathering to agriculture allowed for the development of more complex societies in the Americas.
- shifted to hunting/gathering
- agriculture began in Mexico
- agriculture spread

APPLYING THE SKILL

Make your own cluster diagram. In Chapter 17 on pages 428–429, the beginnings of the Protestant Reformation are discussed. Read the passage and look for information to support a synthesis about its fundamental causes.

SKILLBUILDER HANDBOOK **1007**

3.1 Primary and Secondary Sources

Primary sources are written or created by people who lived during a historical event. The writers might have been participants or observers. Primary sources include letters, diaries, journals, speeches, newspaper articles, magazine articles, eye-witness accounts, and autobiographies.

Secondary sources are derived from primary sources by people who were not present at the original event. They are written after the event. They often combine information from a number of different accounts. Secondary sources include history books, historical essays, and biographies.

UNDERSTANDING THE SKILL

Strategy: Evaluate the information in each type of source. This passage describes political reforms made by Pericles, who led Athens from 461 to 429 B.C. It is mainly a secondary source, but it includes a primary source in the form of a speech.

Secondary source: Look for information collected from several sources. Here the writer presents an overall picture of the reforms made by Pericles and the reasons for them.

Primary source: Analyze the source using historical perspective. Read the source for factual information while also noting the speaker's opinions, biases, assumptions, and point of view.

STRONGER DEMOCRACY IN ATHENS

To strengthen democracy, Pericles increased the number of public officials who were paid salaries. Before, only wealthier citizens could afford to hold public office because most positions were unpaid. Now even the poorest could serve if elected or chosen by lot. This reform made Athens one of the most democratic governments in history. However, political rights were still limited to those with citizenship status—a minority of Athens' total population.

The introduction of direct democracy was an important legacy of Periclean Athens. Few other city-states practiced this style of government. In Athens, male citizens who served in the assembly established all the important policies that affected the polis. In a famous "Funeral Oration" for soldiers killed in the Peloponnesian War, Pericles expressed his great pride in Athenian democracy:

Our constitution is called a democracy because power is in the hands not of a minority but of the whole people. When it is a question of settling private disputes, everyone is equal before the law; when it is a question of putting one person before another in positions of public responsibility, what counts is not membership of a particular class, but the actual ability which the man possesses. No one, as long as he has it in him to be of service to the state, is kept in political obscurity because of poverty.

Secondary source: Look for analysis and interpretation. A secondary source provides details and perspective that are missing in a primary source. It also provides context for the secondary source.

Primary source: Identify the author and evaluate his or her credentials. How is the speaker connected to the event? Here, this speaker is Pericles himself.

Strategy: Make a chart.

Summarize information from primary and secondary sources on a chart.

Primary Source	Secondary Source
Author: Pericles	Author: world history textbook
Qualifications: main figure in the events described	Qualifications: had access to multiple accounts of event
Information: describes his view of Athenian democracy—power in the hands of "the whole people"	Information: puts events in historical perspective—Athens one of most democratic governments in history but limited rights to citizens

APPLYING THE SKILL

Make your own chart. Read the passage "Mehmet II Conquers Constantinople" in Chapter 18, pages 444–445, which includes a quote from the Muslim historian Oruc. Make a chart in which you summarize information from the primary and secondary sources.

3.2 Visual, Audio, Multimedia Sources

In addition to written accounts, historians use many kinds of **visual sources.** These include paintings, photographs, political cartoons, and advertisements. Visual sources are rich with historical details and sometimes reflect the mood and trends of an era better than words can.

Spoken language has always been a primary means of passing on human history. **Audio sources,** such as recorded speeches, interviews, press conferences, and radio programs, continue the oral tradition today.

Movies, CD-ROMs, television, and computer software are the newest kind of historical sources, called **multimedia sources.**

UNDERSTANDING THE SKILL

Strategy: Examine the source carefully. Below are two portraits from the late 1700s, one of Marie Antoinette, the queen of France, and one of a woman who sells vegetables at the market. The chart that follows summarizes historical information gained from interpreting and comparing the two paintings.

A Woman of the Revolution [*La maraîchère*] (1795), Jacques Louis David

Identify the subject and source.

Marie Antoinette, Jacques Gautier d'Agoty

Identify important visual details. Look at the faces, poses, clothing, hairstyles, and other elements.

Use comparisons, information from other sources, and your own knowledge to give support to your interpretation. Royalty usually had their portraits painted in heroic poses. Ordinary people were not usually the subjects of such portraits. David's choice of subject and pose suggests that he sees the common people as the true heroes of France.

Make inferences from the visual details. Marie Antoinette's rich clothing and her hand on the globe symbolize her wealth and power. The contrast between the common woman's ordinary clothing and her defiant pose suggests a different attitude about power.

Strategy: Make a chart.

Summarize your interpretation in a simple chart.

Subject	Visual Details	Inferences	Message
Common woman	Face is worn and clothing is plain, but her head is held high and she wears the red scarf of revolution	Has worked hard for little in life, but strong, proud, and defiant	Although the details are strikingly different, the two paintings convey similar characteristics about their subjects.
Marie Antoinette	Richly dressed and made up; strikes an imperial pose	Lives life of comfort and power; proud, strong, and defiant	

APPLYING THE SKILL

Make your own chart. Turn to the detail from a mural by Diego Rivera in Chapter 16, page 403. The painting is Rivera's historical re-creation of an Aztec festival. Use a chart like the one above to analyze and interpret the painting.

SKILLBUILDER HANDBOOK 1009

3.3 Interpreting Maps

Maps are representations of features on the earth's surface. Historians use maps to locate historical events, to show how geography has influenced history, and to illustrate human interaction with the environment.

Different kinds of maps are used for specific purposes.

Political maps show political units, from countries, states, and provinces, to counties, districts, and towns. Each area is shaded a different color.

Physical maps show mountains, hills, plains, rivers, lakes, and oceans. They may use contour lines to indicate elevations on land and depths under water.

Historical maps illustrate such things as economic activity, political alliances, land claims, battles, population density, and changes over time.

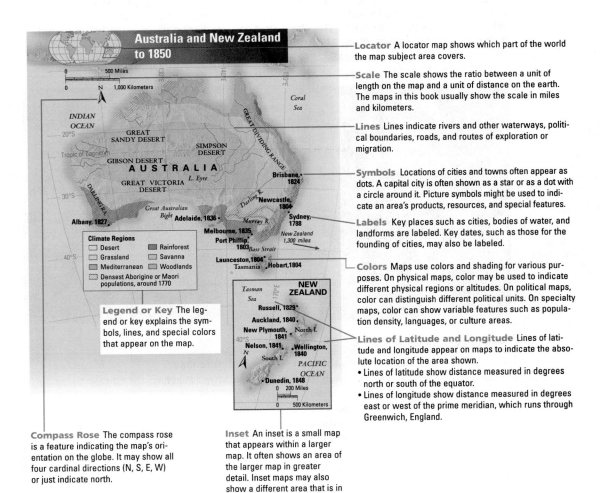

Locator A locator map shows which part of the world the map subject area covers.

Scale The scale shows the ratio between a unit of length on the map and a unit of distance on the earth. The maps in this book usually show the scale in miles and kilometers.

Lines Lines indicate rivers and other waterways, political boundaries, roads, and routes of exploration or migration.

Symbols Locations of cities and towns often appear as dots. A capital city is often shown as a star or as a dot with a circle around it. Picture symbols might be used to indicate an area's products, resources, and special features.

Labels Key places such as cities, bodies of water, and landforms are labeled. Key dates, such as those for the founding of cities, may also be labeled.

Colors Maps use colors and shading for various purposes. On physical maps, color may be used to indicate different physical regions or altitudes. On political maps, color can distinguish different political units. On specialty maps, color can show variable features such as population density, languages, or culture areas.

Lines of Latitude and Longitude Lines of latitude and longitude appear on maps to indicate the absolute location of the area shown.
- Lines of latitude show distance measured in degrees north or south of the equator.
- Lines of longitude show distance measured in degrees east or west of the prime meridian, which runs through Greenwich, England.

Legend or Key The legend or key explains the symbols, lines, and special colors that appear on the map.

Compass Rose The compass rose is a feature indicating the map's orientation on the globe. It may show all four cardinal directions (N, S, E, W) or just indicate north.

Inset An inset is a small map that appears within a larger map. It often shows an area of the larger map in greater detail. Inset maps may also show a different area that is in some way related to the area shown on the larger map.

Strategy: Read all the elements of the map. The historical maps below show European landholdings in North America in 1754 and after 1763. Together they show changes over time.

Europeans in N. America, 1754

Holdings after 1763

Look at the map's title to learn the subject and purpose of the map. What area does the map cover? What does the map tell you about the area? Here the maps show North America in 1754 and after 1763 with the purpose of comparing European claims at two different times.

Legend (1754): Disputed, English, French, Spanish

Legend (1763): English, French, Russian, Spanish

Read the legend. The legend tells you what the symbols and colors on the map mean.

Look at the scale and compass. The scale shows you how many miles or kilometers are represented. Here the scale is 500 actual miles to approximately 5/8 inch on the map. The compass shows you which direction on the map is north.

Find where the map area is located on the earth. These maps show a large area from the Arctic Circle to below latitude 20°N and 50° to 120°W.

Strategy: Make a chart.

Relate the map to the five geographic themes by making a chart. The five themes are described on pages xxxii–xxxiii.

Location	Place	Region	Movement	Human/Environment Interaction
Large area from Arctic Circle to below 20° N, and 50° to 120° W	North American continent	Western Hemisphere	Between 1754 and 1763, land claimed by France was largely taken over by the other two colonialist powers. Spain expanded its territories northward, while Britain took control of almost the entire eastern half of the continent.	Europeans carved out political units in the continent, which already had inhabitants. The land they claimed covered vast areas, with waterways and large mountain ranges to cross.

Make your own chart. Turn to Chapter 12, page 298, and study the map titled "The Mongol Empire, 1294." Make a chart like the one shown above in which you summarize what the map tells you according to the five geography themes.

SKILLBUILDER HANDBOOK **1011**

3.4 Interpreting Charts

Charts are visual presentations of materials. Historians use charts to organize, simplify, and summarize information in a way that makes it more meaningful or easier to remember. Several kinds of charts are commonly used.

Simple charts are used to summarize information or to make comparisons.

Tables are used to organize statistics and other types of information into columns and rows for easy reference.

Diagrams provide visual clues to the meaning of the information they contain. Venn diagrams are used for comparisons. Web diagrams are used to organize supporting information around a central topic. Illustrated diagrams or diagrams that combine different levels of information are sometimes called **infographics.**

UNDERSTANDING THE SKILL

Strategy: Study all the elements of the chart. The infographic below conveys a great deal of information about the three estates, or classes, that existed in 18th-century France. The infographic visually combines a political cartoon, a bulleted chart, a pie graph, and a bar graph.

> Read the title.

The Three Estates

■ **First Estate**
- made up of clergy of Roman Catholic Church
- scorned Enlightenment ideas

■ **Second Estate**
- made up of rich nobles
- held highest offices in government
- disagreed about Enlightenment ideas

■ **Third Estate**
- included bourgeoisie, urban lower class, and peasant farmers
- had no power to influence government
- embraced Enlightenment ideas

Population of France, 1787

98% (Third Estate)

less than 1% (First Estate)

2% (Second Estate)

Percent of Income Paid in Taxes

2% (First Estate)

0% (Second Estate)

50% (Third Estate)

0%   20%   40%   60%   80%   100%

> **Identify the symbols and colors and what they represent.** Here, three colors are used consistently in the infographic to represent the three estates.

> **Survey each of the elements of the infographic and study the information presented.** The political cartoon visually represents the power of the First and Second Estates over the Third Estate. The bulleted chart gives details about the estates. The two graphs give statistics about population and taxes.

> **Look for the main idea.** Make connections among the types of information presented. The infographic shows that the Third Estate made up the vast majority of France's population but had no political power and paid high taxes. The First and Second Estates guarded their power.

Strategy: Write a summary.

> Write a paragraph to summarize what you learned from the chart.

> In 1787, French society was unevenly divided into three estates. Almost all the people, from the bourgeoisie to the peasants, belonged to the Third Estate. They had no political power, paid high taxes, and supported Enlightenment ideas. The First Estate, made up of the clergy, and the Second Estate, made up of rich nobles, held the power and the wealth. Both opposed change, generally rejected Enlightenment ideas, and took advantage of the Third Estate.

APPLYING THE SKILL

Write your own summary. Turn to Chapter 19, page 475, and look at the chart titled "Japanese Society." Study the chart and write a paragraph in which you summarize what you learn from it.

1012 SKILLBUILDER HANDBOOK

Section 3: Exploring Historical Evidence

3.5 Interpreting Graphs

Graphs show statistical information in a visual manner. Historians use graphs to show comparative amounts, ratios, economic trends, and changes over time.

Line graphs are good for showing changes over time, or trends. Usually, the horizontal axis shows a unit of time, such as years or months, and the vertical axis shows numbers or quantities.

Pie graphs are useful for showing relative proportions. The circle represents the whole, such as the entire population, and the slices represent the different groups that make up the whole.

Bar graphs compare numbers or sets of numbers. The length of each bar indicates a quantity. With bar graphs, it is easy to see at a glance how different categories compare.

UNDERSTANDING THE SKILL

Strategy: Study all the elements of the graph. The line graphs below show average global temperatures and world population figures over a period of 25,000 years.

Read the title to identify the main idea of the graph. When two subjects are shown, look for a relationship between them. This set of graphs shows that the agricultural revolution had links to both global temperature and population.

Read the vertical axis. The temperature graph shows degrees Fahrenheit. The other shows population in millions, so that 125 indicates 125,000,000.

Summarize the information shown in each part of the graph. What trends or changes are shown in each line graph?

Look at the legend to understand what colors and certain marks stand for.

Note any information that is highlighted in a box.

Read the horizontal axis. Both graphs cover a period of time from 0 (today) to 25,000 years ago.

Strategy: Write a summary.

Write a paragraph to summarize what you learned from the graphs.

Some 20,000 years ago, after the last Ice Age, temperatures started to rise worldwide. This steady rise in average temperature from 51° to 55° made possible the beginnings of agriculture. As a result of the agricultural revolution, world population grew from about 2 million to about 130 million over a period of 10,000 years.

APPLYING THE SKILL

Write your own summary Turn to Chapter 31, page 805, and look at the graph "Unemployment in Germany and Great Britain." Study the graph and write a paragraph in which you summarize what you learn from it.

3.6 Using the Internet

The **Internet** is a network of computers associated with universities, libraries, news organizations, government agencies, businesses, and private individuals worldwide. Each location on the Internet has a **home page** with its own address, or **URL.**

With a computer connected to the Internet, you can reach the home pages of many organizations and services. You might view your library's home page to find the call number of a book or visit an on-line magazine to read an article. On some sites you can view documents, photographs, and even moving pictures with sound.

The international collection of home pages, known as the **World Wide Web**, is a good source of up-to-the minute information about current events as well as in-depth research on historical subjects. This textbook contains many suggestions for navigating the World Wide Web. Begin by entering **www.mlworldhistory.com** to access the home page for McDougal Littell World History.

UNDERSTANDING THE SKILL

Strategy: Explore the elements on the screen. The computer screen below shows the home page of the history area at PBS, the public television service in Washington, D.C.

Go directly to a Web page. If you know the address of a particular Web page, type the address in the box at the top of the screen and press ENTER (or RETURN). After a few seconds, the Web page will appear on your screen.

Explore the links. Click on any one of the images or topics to find out more about a specific subject. These links take you to another page at this Web site. Some pages include links to related information that can be found at other places on the Internet.

Learn more about the page. Scan the page to learn the types of information contained at this site. This site has information about PBS history programs as well as other historical information and special features.

Explore the features of the page. This page has a feature that lets you find out what happened in history on any given day of the year.

PBS History screen shot courtesy of PBS ONLINE®.

APPLYING THE SKILL

Do your own Internet research. Turn to Chapter 34, Section 4, "Conflicts in the Middle East." Read the section and make a list of topics you would like to research. If you have a computer with Internet access, go to the McDougal Littell World History home page **www.mlworldhistory.com**. Click on "General World History Links" and then click on "Perspectives on the Present" to begin your search.

1014 SKILLBUILDER HANDBOOK

Glossary

The Glossary is an alphabetical listing of many of the key terms from the chapters, along with their meanings. The definitions listed in the Glossary are the ones that apply to the way the words are used in this textbook. The Glossary gives the part of speech of each word. The following abbreviations are used:

adj. adjective   *n.* noun   *v.* verb

Pronunciation Key

Some of the words in this book are followed by respellings that show how the words are pronounced. The following key will help you understand what sounds are represented by the letters used in the respellings.

Symbol	Examples	Symbol	Examples
a	apple [AP·uhl], catch [kach]	oh	road, [rohd], know [noh]
ah	barn [bahrn], pot [paht]	oo	school [skool], glue [gloo]
air	bear [bair], dare [dair]	ow	out [owt], cow [kow]
aw	bought [bawt], horse [hawrs]	oy	coin [koyn], boys [boyz]
ay	ape [ayp], mail [mayl]	p	pig [pihg], top [tahp]
b	bell [behl], table [TAY·buhl]	r	rose [rohz], star [stahr]
ch	chain [chayn], ditch [dihch]	s	soap [sohp], icy [EYE·see]
d	dog [dawg], rained [raynd]	sh	share [shair], nation [NAY·shuhn]
ee	even [EE·vuhn], meal [meel]	t	tired [tyrd], boat [boht]
eh	egg [ehg], ten [tehn]	th	thin [thihn], mother [MUH·thuhr]
eye	iron [EYE·uhrn]	u	pull [pul], look [luk]
f	fall [fawl], laugh [laf]	uh	bump [buhmp], awake [uh·WAYK],
g	gold [gohld], big [bihg]		happen [HAP·uhn], pencil [PEHN·suhl],
h	hot [haht], exhale [ehks·HAYL]		pilot [PY·luht]
hw	white [hwyt]	ur	earth [urth], bird [burd], worm [wurm]
ih	into [IHN·too], sick [sihk]	v	vase [vays], love [luhv]
j	jar [jahr], badge [baj]	w	web [wehb], twin [twihn]
k	cat [kat], luck [luhk]	y	As a consonant: yard [yahrd], mule [myool]
l	load [lohd], ball [bawl]		As a vowel: ice [ys], tried [tryd], sigh [sy]
m	make [mayk], gem [jehm]	z	zone [zohn], reason [REE·zuhn]
n	night [nyt], win [wihn]	zh	treasure [TREHZH·uhr], garage [guh·RAHZH]
ng	song [sawng], anger [ANG·guhr]		

Syllables that are stressed when the words are spoken appear in CAPITAL LETTERS in the respellings. For example, the respelling of *patterns* (PAT·uhrnz) shows that the first syllable of the word is stressed.

Syllables that appear in SMALL CAPITAL LETTERS are also stressed, but not as strongly as those that appear in capital letters. For example, the respelling of *interaction* (IHN·tuhr·AK·shuhn) shows that the third syllable receives the main stress and the first syllable receives a secondary stress.

A

Abbasids [uh·BAS·IHDZ] *n.* a dynasty that ruled much of the Muslim Empire from A.D. 750 to 1258. (p. 240)

Aborigine [AB·uh·RIHJ·uh·nee] *n.* a member of any of the native peoples of Australia. (p. 665)

absolute monarch [MAHN·uhrk] *n.* a king or queen who has unlimited power and seeks to control all aspects of society. (p. 517)

absolute ruler *n.* a ruler who has total power. (p. 147)

accommodation [uh·KAHM·uh·DAY·shuhn] *n.* an acceptance of the ideas and customs of other cultures. (p. 961)

acropolis [uh·KRAHP·uh·lihs] *n.* a fortified hilltop in an ancient Greek city. (p. 115)

Aksum [AHK·soom] *n.* an African kingdom, in what is now Ethiopia and Eritrea, that reached the height of its power in the fourth century A.D. (p. 199)

al-Andalus [al·AN·duh·LUS] *n.* a Muslim-ruled region in what is now Spain, established in the eighth century A.D. (p. 240)

Allah [AL·uh] *n.* God (an Arabic word, used mainly in Islam). (p. 234)

Allies [uh·LYZ] *n.* in World War I, the nations of Great Britain, France, and Russia, along with the other nations that fought on their side; also, the group of nations—including Great Britain, the Soviet Union, and the United States—that opposed the Axis Powers in World War II. (p. 748)

Almohads [AL·moh·HADZ] *n.* a group of Islamic reformers who overthrew the Almoravid Dynasty and established an empire in North Africa and southern Spain in the 12th century A.D. (p. 370)

Almoravids [AL·muh·RAHV·uhdz] *n.* an Islamic religious brotherhood that established an empire in North Africa and southern Spain in the 11th century A.D. (p. 370)

Anabaptists [AN·uh·BAP·tihst] *n.* in the Reformation, a Protestant group that believed in baptizing only those persons who were old enough to decide to be Christian and in separation of church and state. (p. 434)

Anasazi [AH·nuh·SAH·zee] *n.* an early Native American people who lived in the American Southwest. (p. 391)

Anatolia [AN·uh·TOH·lee·uh] *n.* the Southwest Asian peninsula now occupied by the Asian part of Turkey—also called Asia Minor. (p. 58)

Angkor Wat [ANG·kawr WAHT] *n.* a temple complex built in the Khmer Empire and dedicated to the Hindu god Vishnu. (p. 309)

Anglican [ANG·glih·kuhn] *adj.* relating to the Church of England. (p. 432)

animism [AN·uh·MIHZ·uhm] *n.* the belief that spirits are present in animals, plants, and other natural objects. (p. 197)

annexation [AN·ihk·SAY·shuhn] *n.* the adding of a region to the territory of an existing political unit. (pp. 709, 723)

annul [uh·NUHL] *v.* to cancel or put an end to. (p. 431)

anti-Semitism [AN·tee·SEHM·ih·TIHZ·uhm] *n.* prejudice against Jews. (p. 663)

apartheid [uh·PAHRT·HYT] *n.* a South African policy of complete legal separation of the races, including the banning of all social contacts between blacks and whites. (p. 919)

apostle [uh·PAHS·uhl] *n.* one of the followers of Jesus who preached and spread his teachings. (p. 153)

appeasement *n.* the making of concessions to an aggressor in order to avoid war. (p. 813)

aqueduct [AK·wih·DUHKT] *n.* a pipeline or channel built to carry water to populated areas. (p. 167)

aristocracy [AR·ih·STAHK·ruh·see] *n.* a government in which power is in the hands of a hereditary ruling class or nobility. (p. 115)

armistice [AHR·mih·stihs] *n.* an agreement to stop fighting. (p. 757)

artifact *n.* a human-made object, such as a tool, weapon, or piece of jewelry. (p. 7)

artisan [AHR·tih·zuhn] *n.* a skilled worker, such as a weaver or a potter, who makes goods by hand. (p. 18)

Aryans [AIR·ee·uhnz] *n.* **1.** an Indo-European people who, about 1500 B.C., began to migrate into the Indian subcontinent (p. 59). **2.** to the Nazis, the Germanic peoples who formed a "master race." (p. 831)

assembly line *n.* in a factory, an arrangement in which a product is moved from worker to worker, with each person performing a single task in its manufacture. (p. 674)

assimilation [uh·SIHM·uh·LAY·shuhn] *n.* **1.** the adoption of a conqueror's culture by a conquered people (p. 185). **2.** a policy in which a nation forces or encourages a subject people to adopt its institutions and customs. (p. 691)

Assyria [uh·SEER·ee·uh] *n.* a Southwest Asian kingdom that controlled a large empire from about 850 to 612 B.C. (p. 88)

Atlantic Charter *n.* a declaration of principles issued in August 1941 by British prime minister Winston Churchill and U.S. president Franklin Roosevelt, on which the Allied peace plan at the end of World War II was based. (p. 826)

Atlantic slave trade *n.* the buying, transporting, and selling of Africans for work in the Americas. (p. 496)

autocracy [aw·TAHK·ruh·see] *n.* a government in which the ruler has unlimited power and uses it in an arbitrary manner. (p. 100)

Axis Powers *n.* in World War II, the nations of Germany, Italy, and Japan, which had formed an alliance in 1936. (p. 813)

ayllu [EYE·loo] *n.* in Incan society, a small community or clan whose members worked together for the common good. (p. 408)

B

balance of power *n.* a political situation in which no one nation is powerful enough to pose a threat to others. (p. 593)

Balfour Declaration *n.* a statement that the British government supported the establishment of a Jewish national homeland in Palestine, made in a 1917 letter by British foreign secretary Sir Arthur Balfour. (p. 901)

Balkans [BAWL·kuhnz] *n.* the region of southeastern Europe now occupied by Greece, Albania, Bulgaria, Romania, the European part of Turkey, and the former republics of Yugoslavia. (p. 609)

Bantu-speaking peoples *n.* the speakers of a related group of languages who, beginning about 2,000 years ago, migrated from West Africa into most of the southern half of Africa. (p. 204)

baroque [buh·ROHK] *adj.* relating to a grand, ornate style that characterized European painting, music, and architecture in the 1600s and early 1700s. (p. 559)

barter *n.* a form of trade in which people exchange goods and services without the use of money. (p. 21)

Battle of Britain *n.* a series of battles between German and British air forces, fought over Britain in 1940–1941. (p. 824)

Battle of Guadalcanal [GWAHD·uhl·kuh·NAL] *n.* a 1942–1943 battle of World War II, in which Allied troops drove Japanese forces from the Pacific island of Guadalcanal. (p. 830)

Battle of Midway *n.* a 1942 sea and air battle of World War II, in which American forces defeated Japanese forces in the central Pacific. (p. 829)

Battle of Stalingrad [STAH·lihn·GRAD] *n.* a 1942–1943 battle of World War II, in which German forces were defeated in their attempt to capture the city of Stalingrad in the Soviet Union. (p. 836)

Battle of the Bulge *n.* a 1944–1945 battle in which Allied forces turned back the last major German offensive of World War II. (p. 839)

Battle of Trafalgar [truh·FAL·guhr] *n.* an 1805 naval battle in which Napoleon's forces were defeated by a British fleet under the command of Horatio Nelson. (p. 587)

Benin [buh·NIHN] *n.* a kingdom that arose near the Niger River delta in the 1300s and became a major West African state in the 1400s. (p. 377)

Beringia [buh·RIHN·jee·uh] *n.* an ancient land bridge over which the earliest Americans are believed to have migrated from Asia into the Americas. (p. 211)

Berlin Conference of 1884–85 *n.* a meeting at which representatives of European nations agreed upon rules for the European colonization of Africa. (p. 687)

Bill of Rights *n.* the first ten amendments to the U.S. Constitution, which protect citizens' basic rights and freedoms. (p. 567)

bishop *n.* a high-ranking Christian official who supervises a number of local churches. (p. 156)

blitzkrieg [BLIHTS·kreeg] *n.* "lightning war"—a form of warfare in which surprise attacks with fast-moving airplanes are followed by massive attacks with infantry forces. (p. 822)

blockade [blah·KAYD] *n.* the use of troops or ships to prevent commercial traffic from entering or leaving a city or region. (p. 589)

Boer [bohr] *n.* a Dutch colonist in South Africa. (p. 689)

Boer War *n.* a conflict, lasting from 1899 to 1902, in which the Boers and the British fought for control of territory in South Africa. (p. 689)

Bolsheviks [BOHL·shuh·VIHKS] *n.* a group of revolutionary Russian Marxists who took control of Russia's government in November 1917. (p. 770)

Boxer Rebellion *n.* a 1900 rebellion in China, aimed at ending foreign influence in the country. (p. 719)

boyars [boh·YAHRZ] *n.* landowning nobles of Russia. (pp. 275, 531)

Brahma [BRAH·muh] *n.* a Hindu god considered the creator of the world. (p. 178)

Brahmin [BRAH·mihn] *n.* in Aryan society, a member of the social class made up of priests. (p. 59)

brinkmanship *n.* a policy of threatening to go to war in response to any enemy aggression. (p. 860)

Bronze Age *n.* a period in human history, beginning around 3000 B.C. in some areas, during which people began using bronze, rather than copper or stone, to fashion tools and weapons. (p. 19)

bubonic plague [boo·BAHN·ihk PLAYG] *n.* a deadly disease that spread across Asia and Europe in the mid-14th century, killing millions of people. (p. 357)

bureaucracy [byu·RAHK·ruh·see] *n.* a system of departments and agencies formed to carry out the work of government. (p. 98)

burgher [BUR·guhr] *n.* a medieval town dweller. (p. 350)

Bushido [BUSH·ih·DOH] *n.* the strict code of behavior followed by samurai warriors in Japan. (p. 307)

C

cabinet *n.* a group of advisers or ministers chosen by the head of a country to help make government decisions. (p. 539)

caliph [KAY·lihf] *n.* a supreme political and religious leader in a Muslim government. (p. 238)

calligraphy [kuh·LIHG·ruh·fee] *n.* the art of beautiful handwriting. (p. 246)

Calvinism [KAL·vih·NIHZ·uhm] *n.* a body of religious teachings based on the ideas of the reformer John Calvin. (p. 433)

Camp David Accords *n.* the first signed agreement between Israel and an Arab country, in which Egyptian president Anwar Sadat recognized Israel as a legitimate state and Israeli prime minister Menachem Begin agreed to return the Sinai Peninsula to Egypt. (p. 903)

canon law *n.* the body of laws governing the religious practices of a Christian church. (p. 333)

capitalism *n.* an economic system based on private ownership and on the investment of money in business ventures in order to make a profit. (pp. 502, 647)

Carolingian [KAR·uh·LIHN·juhn] **Dynasty** *n.* a dynasty of Frankish rulers, lasting from A.D. 751 to 987. (p. 320)

caste [kast] *n.* one of the four classes of people in the social system of the Aryans who settled in India—priests, warriors, peasants or traders, and non-Aryan laborers or craftsmen. (p. 60)

cataract [KAT·uh·RAKT] *n.* a waterfall or stretch of rapids in a river. (p. 33)

Catholic Reformation [REHF·uhr·MAY·shuhn] *n.* a 16th-century movement in which the Roman Catholic Church sought to reform itself in response to the Protestant Reformation. (p. 435)

caudillo [kaw·DEEL·yoh] *n.* a military dictator of a Latin American country. (p. 724)

centralized government *n.* a government in which power is concentrated in a central authority to which local governments are subject. (p. 181)

Central Powers *n.* in World War I, the nations of Germany and Austria-Hungary, along with the other nations that fought on their side. (p. 748)

Chaldeans [kal·DEE·uhnz] *n.* a Southwest Asian people who helped to destroy the Assyrian Empire. (p. 90)

Chartist movement *n.* a 19th-century British movement in which members of the working class demanded reforms in Parliament and in elections, including suffrage for all men. (p. 660)

Chavín [chah·VEEN] *n.* the first major South American civilization, which flourished in the highlands of what is now Peru from about 900 to 200 B.C. (p. 221)

checks and balances *n.* measures designed to prevent any one branch of government from dominating the others. (pp. 566–567)

chivalry [SHIHV·uhl·ree] *n.* a code of behavior for knights in medieval Europe, stressing ideals such as courage, loyalty, and devotion. (p. 328)

CIS *n.* the Commonwealth of Independent States—a loose association of former Soviet republics that was formed after the breakup of the Soviet Union. (p. 928)

city-state *n.* a city and its surrounding lands functioning as an independent political unit. (p. 29)

civil disobedience *n.* a deliberate and public refusal to obey a law considered unjust. (p. 786)

civilization *n.* a form of culture characterized by cities, specialized workers, complex institutions, record keeping, and advanced technology. (p. 18)

civil rights movement *n.* a grassroots effort to fight discrimination in the United States and to make sure that all U.S. citizens receive the rights guaranteed by the Constitution. (p. 954)

civil service *n.* the administrative departments of a government—especially those in which employees are hired on the basis of their scores on examinations. (p. 183)

civil war *n.* a conflict between two political groups within the same country. (p. 146)

clan *n.* a group of people descended from a common ancestor. (pp. 197, 295)

classical art *n.* the art of ancient Greece and Rome, in which harmony, order, and balance were emphasized. (p. 121)

clergy [KLUR·jee] *n.* a body of officials who perform religious services—such as priests, ministers, or rabbis. (p. 332)

cloning [KLOH·nihng] *n.* the creation of plants or animals that are genetically identical to an existing plant or animal. (p. 944)

coalition [KOH·uh·LIHSH·uhn] **government** *n.* a government controlled by a temporary alliance of several political parties. (p. 801)

codex [KOH·DEHKS] *n.* a book with pages that can be turned, like the one you are reading now. (p. 398)

Cold War *n.* the state of diplomatic hostility between the United States and the Soviet Union in the decades following World War II. (p. 859)

collective bargaining *n.* negotiations between workers and their employers. (p. 650)

collective farm *n.* a large government-controlled farm formed by combining many small farms. (p. 777)

colony *n.* a land controlled by a distant nation. (p. 484)

Colossus of Rhodes [kuh·LAHS·uhs uhv ROHDZ] *n.* an enormous Hellenistic statue that formerly stood near the harbor of Rhodes. (p. 135)

Columbian Exchange *n.* the global transfer of plants, animals, and diseases that occurred during the European colonization of the Americas. (p. 500)

comedy *n.* a humorous form of drama that often includes slapstick and satire. (p. 123)

command economy *n.* an economic system in which the government makes all economic decisions. (p. 776)

Commercial Revolution *n.* the expansion of trade and business that transformed European economies during the 16th and 17th centuries. (p. 500)

Committee of Public Safety *n.* a committee established during the French Revolution to identify "enemies of the republic." (p. 582)

commune [KAHM·YOON] *n.* in Communist China, a collective farm on which a great number of people work and live together. (p. 864)

communism *n.* an economic system in which all means of production—land, mines, factories, railroads, and businesses—are owned by the people, private property does not exist, and all goods and services are shared equally. (p. 649)

Concert [KAHN·SURT] **of Europe** *n.* a series of alliances among European nations in the 19th century, devised by Prince Klemens von Metternich to prevent the outbreak of revolutions. (p. 595)

concordat [kuhn·KAWR·DAT] *n.* a formal agreement—especially one between the pope and a government, dealing with the control of church affairs. (p. 586)

Congress of Vienna [vee·EHN·uh] *n.* a series of meetings in 1814–1815, during which the European leaders sought to establish long-lasting peace and security after the defeat of Napoleon. (p. 593)

Congress Party *n.* a major national political party in India—also known as the Indian National Congress. (p. 886)

conquistadors [kahng·KEE·stuh·DAWRZ] *n.* the Spanish soldiers, explorers, and fortune hunters who took part in the conquest of the Americas in the 16th century. (p. 485)

conservatives *n.* in the first half of the 19th century, those Europeans—mainly wealthy landowners and nobles—who wanted to preserve the traditional monarchies of Europe. (p. 609)

constitutional monarchy [MAHN·uhr·kee] *n.* a monarchy in which the ruler's power is limited by law. (p. 539)

consul [KAHN·suhl] *n.* in the Roman republic, one of the two powerful officials elected each year to command the army and direct the government. (p. 142)

containment *n.* a U.S. foreign policy adopted by President Harry Truman in the late 1940s, in which the United States tried to stop the spread of communism by creating alliances and helping weak countries to resist Soviet advances. (p. 857)

Continental System *n.* Napoleon's policy of preventing trade between Great Britain and continental Europe, intended to destroy Great Britain's economy. (p. 589)

corporation *n.* a business owned by stockholders who share in its profits but are not personally responsible for its debts. (p. 645)

Council of Trent *n.* a meeting of Roman Catholic leaders, called by Pope Paul III to rule on doctrines criticized by the Protestant reformers. (p. 436)

coup d'état [KOO day·TAH] *n.* a sudden seizure of political power in a nation. (p. 585)

covenant [KUHV·uh·nuhnt] *n.* a mutual promise or agreement—especially an agreement between God and the Hebrew people as recorded in the Bible. (p. 73)

creoles [KREE·OHLZ] *n.* in Spanish colonial society, colonists who were born in Latin America to Spanish parents. (p. 604)

Crimean [kry·MEE·uhn] **War** *n.* a conflict, lasting from 1853 to 1856, in which the Ottoman Empire, with the aid of Britain and France, halted Russian expansion in the region of the Black Sea. (p. 698)

crop rotation *n.* the system of growing a different crop in a field each year to preserve the fertility of the land. (p. 633)

Crusade *n.* one of the expeditions in which medieval Christian warriors sought to recover control of the Holy Land from the Muslims. (p. 343)

cultural diffusion *n.* the spreading of ideas or products from one culture to another. (p. 29)

Cultural Revolution *n.* a 1966–1976 uprising in China, led by the Red Guards, with the goal of establishing a society of peasants and workers in which all were equal. (p. 865)

culture *n.* a people's unique way of life, as shown by its tools, customs, arts, and ideas. (p. 7)

cuneiform [KYOO·nee·uh·FAWRM] *n.* a system of writing with wedge-shaped symbols, invented by the Sumerians around 3000 B.C. (p. 18)

Cyrillic [suh·RIHL·ihk] **alphabet** *n.* an alphabet for the writing of Slavic languages, devised in the ninth century A.D. by Saints Cyril and Methodius. (p. 273)

czar [zahr] *n.* a Russian emperor (from the Roman title *Caesar*). (p. 278)

D

daimyo [DY·mee·OH] *n.* a Japanese feudal lord who commanded a private army of samurai. (p. 474)

Daoism [DOW·IHZ·uhm] *n.* a philosophy based on the ideas of the Chinese thinker Laozi, who taught that people should be guided by a universal force called the Dao (Way). (p. 98)

D-Day *n.* June 6, 1944—the day on which the Allies began their invasion of the European mainland during World War II. (p. 838)

Declaration of Independence *n.* a statement of the reasons for the American colonies' break with Britain, approved by the Second Continental Congress in 1776. (p. 564)

Declaration of the Rights of Man *n.* a statement of revolutionary ideals adopted by France's National Assembly in 1789. (p. 577)

delta *n.* a marshy region formed by deposits of silt at the mouth of a river. (p. 34)

demilitarization [dee·MIHL·ih·tuhr·ih·ZAY·shuhn] *n.* a reduction in a country's ability to wage war, achieved by disbanding its armed forces and prohibiting it from acquiring weapons. (p. 844)

democracy *n.* a government controlled by its citizens, either directly or through representatives. (p. 117)

desertification [dih·ZUR·tuh·fih·KAY·shuhn] *n.* a transformation of fertile land into desert. (p. 195)

destalinization [dee·STAH·lih·nih·ZAY·shuhn] *n.* Nikita Khrushchev's policy of eliminating all memory of Joseph Stalin and his programs in the Soviet Union. (p. 876)

détente [day·TAHNT] *n.* a policy of reducing Cold War tensions that was adopted by the United States during the presidency of Richard Nixon. (p. 878)

developed nation *n.* a nation with all the facilities needed for the advanced production of manufactured goods. (p. 946)

developing nation *n.* a nation in which the process of industrialization is not yet complete. (p. 946)

devshirme [dehv·SHEER·meh] *n.* in the Ottoman Empire, the policy of taking children from conquered Christian peoples to be trained as Muslim soldiers. (p. 446)

Diaspora [dy·AS·puhr·uh] *n.* the dispersal of the Jews from their homeland in Palestine—especially during the period of more than 1,800 years that followed the Romans' destruction of the Temple in Jerusalem in A.D. 70. (p. 155)

dictator *n.* in ancient Rome, a political leader given absolute power to make laws and command the army for a limited time. (p. 143)

direct democracy *n.* a government in which citizens rule directly rather than through representatives. (p. 120)

dissident [DIHS·ih·duhnt] *n.* an opponent of a government's policies or actions. (p. 918)

divine right *n.* the idea that monarchs are God's representatives on earth and are therefore answerable only to God. (p. 517)

domestication *n.* the taming of animals for human use. (p. 14)

dominion *n.* in the British Empire, a nation (such as Canada) allowed to govern its own domestic affairs. (p. 665)

domino theory *n.* the idea that if a nation falls under Communist control, nearby nations will also fall under Communist control. (p. 868)

Dorians [DAWR·ee·uhnz] *n.* a Greek-speaking people that, according to tradition, migrated into mainland Greece after the destruction of the Mycenaean civilization. (p. 113)

Dreyfus [DRY·fuhs] **affair** *n.* a controversy in France in the 1890s, centering on the trial and imprisonment of a Jewish army officer, Captain Alfred Dreyfus, who had been falsely accused of selling military secrets to Germany. (p. 663)

Duma [DOO·muh] *n.* a Russian national parliament formed in the early years of the 20th century. (p. 771)

Dutch East India Company *n.* a company founded by the Dutch in the early 17th century to establish and direct trade throughout Asia. (p. 468)

dynastic [dy·NAS·tihk] **cycle** *n.* the historical pattern of the rise, decline, and replacement of dynasties. (p. 50)

dynasty [DY·nuh·stee] *n.* a series of rulers from a single family. (p. 29)

E

Eastern Front *n.* in World War I, the region along the German-Russian border where Russians and Serbs battled Germans, Austrians, and Turks. (p. 750)

Edict of Nantes [EE·DIHKT uhv NAHNT] *n.* a 1598 declaration in which the French king Henry IV promised that Protestants could live in peace in France and could set up houses of worship in some French cities. (p. 518)

Emancipation Proclamation [ih·MAN·suh·PAY·shuhn PRAHK·luh·MAY·shuhn] *n.* a declaration issued by U.S. president Abraham Lincoln in 1863, stating that all slaves in the Confederate states were free. (p. 671)

émigrés [EHM·ih·GRAYZ] *n.* people who leave their native country for political reasons, like the nobles and others who fled France during the peasant uprisings of the French Revolution. (p. 579)

empire *n.* a political unit in which a number of peoples or countries are controlled by a single ruler. (p. 31)

enclosure *n.* one of the fenced-in or hedged-in fields created by wealthy British landowners on land that was formerly worked by village farmers. (p. 633)

encomienda [ehng·kaw·MYEHN·dah] *n.* a grant of land made by Spain to a settler in the Americas, including the right to use Native Americans as laborers on it. (p. 486)

English Civil War *n.* a conflict, lasting from 1642 to 1649, in which Puritan supporters of Parliament battled supporters of England's monarchy. (p. 537)

enlightened despot [DEHS·puht] *n.* one of the 18th-century European monarchs who were inspired by Enlightenment ideas to rule justly and respect the rights of their subjects. (p. 561)

enlightenment [ehn·LYT·uhn·muhnt] *n.* in Buddhism, a state of perfect wisdom in which one understands basic truths about the universe. (p. 64)

Enlightenment *n.* an 18th-century European movement in which thinkers attempted to apply the principles of reason and the scientific method to all aspects of society. (p. 551)

entrepreneur [AHN·truh·pruh·NUR] *n.* a person who organizes, manages, and takes on the risks of a business. (p. 636)

epics *n.* long narrative poems celebrating the deeds of legendary or traditional heroes. (p. 114)

estate [ih·STAYT] *n.* one of the three social classes in France before the French Revolution—the First Estate consisting of the clergy; the Second Estate, of the nobility; and the Third Estate, of the rest of the population. (p. 573)

Estates-General [ih·STAYTS·JEHN·uhr·uhl] *n.* an assembly of representatives from all three of the estates, or social classes, in France. (p. 575)

ethnic cleansing *n.* a policy of murder and other acts of brutality by which Serbs hoped to eliminate Bosnia's Muslim population after the breakup of Yugoslavia. (p. 929)

GLOSSARY 1019

excommunication [EHKS·kuh·MYOO·nih·KAY·shuhn] *n.* the taking away of a person's right of membership in a Christian church. (p. 273)

existentialism [EHG·zih·STEHN·shuh·LIHZ·uhm] *n.* a philosophy based on the idea that people give meaning to their lives through their choices and actions. (p. 796)

extended family *n.* a group that includes a person's parents, children, grandparents, grandchildren, aunts, uncles, and cousins. (p. 197)

extraterritorial [EHK·struh·TEHR·ih·TAWR·ee·uhl] **rights** *n.* an exemption of foreign residents from the laws of a country. (p. 716)

Factors of production *n.* the resources—including land, labor, and capital—that are needed to produce goods and services. (p. 634)

factory *n.* a large building in which machinery is used to manufacture goods. (p. 635)

fascism [FASH·IHZ·uhm] *n.* a political movement that promotes an extreme form of nationalism, a denial of individual rights, and a dictatorial one-party rule. (p. 807)

Fatimid [FAT·uh·MIHD] *n.* a member of a Muslim dynasty that traced its ancestry to Muhammad's daughter Fatima and that built an empire in North Africa, Arabia, and Syria in the 10th–12th centuries. (p. 240)

favorable balance of trade *n.* an economic situation in which a country exports more than it imports—that is, sells more goods abroad than it buys from abroad. (p. 502)

federal system *n.* a system of government in which power is divided between a central authority and a number of individual states. (pp. 567, 917)

Fertile Crescent [FUHR·tuhl KREHS·uhnt] *n.* an arc of rich farmland in Southwest Asia, between the Persian Gulf and the Mediterranean Sea. (p. 27)

feudalism [FYOOD·uhl·IHZ·uhm] *n.* a political system in which nobles are granted the use of lands that legally belong to their king, in exchange for their loyalty, military service, and protection of the people who live on the land. (p. 50)

fief [feef] *n.* an estate granted to a vassal by a lord under the feudal system in medieval Europe. (p. 324)

filial piety [FIHL·ee·uhl PY·ih·tee] *n.* respect shown by children for their parents and elders. (p. 97)

Final Solution *n.* Hitler's program of systematically killing the entire Jewish people. (p. 833)

FLN *n.* the National Liberation Front—an Algerian group that waged a guerrilla struggle for independence from France. (p. 899)

Four Modernizations *n.* a set of goals adopted by the Chinese leader Deng Xiaoping in the late 20th century, involving progress in agriculture, industry, defense, and science and technology. (p. 932)

Fourteen Points *n.* a series of proposals in which U.S. president Woodrow Wilson outlined a plan for achieving a lasting peace after World War I. (p. 760)

Franks *n.* a Germanic people who settled in the Roman province of Gaul (roughly the area now occupied by France) and established a great empire during the Middle Ages. (p. 318)

free trade *n.* commerce between nations without economic restrictions or barriers (such as tariffs). (p. 947)

French and Indian War *n.* a conflict between Britain and France for control of territory in North America, lasting from 1754 to 1763. (p. 493)

fundamentalism [FUHN·duh·MEHN·tuhl·IHZ·uhm] *n.* a strict belief in the basic truths and practices of a particular religion. (p. 953)

Genetic [juh·NEHT·ihk] **engineering** *n.* the transferring of genes from one living thing to another in order to produce an organism with new traits. (pp. 943–944)

genocide [JEHN·uh·SYD] *n.* the systematic killing of an entire people. (p. 833)

gentry *n.* a class of powerful, well-to-do people who enjoy a high social status. (p. 291)

geopolitics [JEE·oh·PAHL·ih·tihks] *n.* a foreign policy based on a consideration of the strategic locations or products of other lands. (p. 698)

Ghana [GAH·nuh] *n.* a West African kingdom that grew rich from taxing and controlling trade and that established an empire in the 9th–11th centuries A.D. (p. 371)

ghazi [GAH·zee] *n.* a warrior for Islam. (p. 443)

ghettos [GEHT·ohz] *n.* city neighborhoods in which European Jews were forced to live. (p. 832)

gladiator [GLAD·ee·AY·tuhr] *n.* in ancient Rome, one of the professional fighters who engaged in battles to the death in public arenas. (p. 151)

glasnost [GLAHS·nuhst] *n.* a Soviet policy of openness to the free flow of ideas and information, introduced in 1985 by Mikhail Gorbachev. (p. 921)

global economy *n.* all the financial interactions—involving people, businesses, and governments—that cross international boundaries. (p. 947)

Glorious Revolution *n.* the bloodless overthrow of the English king James II and his replacement by William and Mary. (p. 539)

glyph [glihf] *n.* a symbolic picture—especially one used as part of a writing system for carving messages in stone. (p. 398)

Gothic [GAHTH·ihk] *adj.* relating to a style of church architecture that developed in medieval Europe, featuring ribbed vaults, stained-glass windows, flying buttresses, pointed arches, and tall spires. (p. 342)

Great Depression *n.* the severe economic slump that followed the collapse of the U.S. stock market in 1929. (p. 804)

Great Fear *n.* a wave of senseless panic that spread through the French countryside after the storming of the Bastille in 1789. (p. 576)

Great Purge *n.* a campaign of terror in the Soviet Union during the 1930s, in which Joseph Stalin sought to eliminate all Communist Party members and other citizens who threatened his power. (p. 777)

Great Schism [SIHZ·uhm] *n.* a division in the medieval Roman Catholic Church, during which rival popes were established in Avignon and in Rome. (p. 357)

Great Trek *n.* a migration of Dutch colonists out of British-controlled territory in South Africa during the 1830s. (p. 689)

Greco-Roman culture *n.* an ancient culture that developed from a blending of Greek, Hellenistic, and Roman cultures. (p. 164)

green revolution *n.* a 20th-century attempt to increase food resources worldwide, involving the use of fertilizers and pesticides and the development of disease-resistant crops. (p. 944)

griot [gree·OH] *n.* a West African storyteller. (p. 197)

guerrilla [guh·RIHL·uh] *n.* a member of a loosely organized fighting force that makes surprise attacks on enemy troops occupying his or her country. (p. 590)

guild [gihld] *n.* a medieval association of people working at the same occupation, which controlled its members' wages and prices. (p. 349)

guillotine [GIHL·uh·teen] *n.* a machine for beheading people, used as a means of execution during the French Revolution. (p. 580)

Gulf War *n.* a 1991 conflict in which UN forces defeated Iraqi forces that had invaded Kuwait and threatened to invade Saudi Arabia. (p. 949)

Gupta [GUP·tuh] **Empire** *n.* the second empire in India, founded by Chandra Gupta I in A.D. 320. (p. 175)

Gutenberg [GOOT·uhn·burg] **Bible** *n.* the first full-sized book printed with movable type and a printing press. (p. 426)

H

habeas corpus [HAY·bee·uhs KAWR·puhs] *n.* a document requiring that a prisoner be brought before a court or judge so that it can be decided whether his or her imprisonment is legal. (p. 538)

Hagia Sophia [HAY·ee·uh soh·FEE·uh] *n.* the Cathedral of Holy Wisdom in Constantinople, built by order of the Byzantine emperor Justinian. (p. 270)

haiku [HY·koo] *n.* a Japanese form of poetry, consisting of three unrhymed lines of five, seven, and five syllables. (p. 476)

hajj [haj] *n.* a pilgrimage to Mecca, performed as a duty by Muslims. (p. 236)

Han [hahn] **Dynasty** *n.* a Chinese dynasty that ruled from 202 B.C. to A.D. 9 and again from A.D. 23 to 220. (p. 181)

Hausa [HOW·suh] *n.* a West African people who lived in several city-states in what is now northern Nigeria. (p. 375)

heliocentric [HEE·lee·oh·SEHN·trihk] **theory** *n.* the idea that the earth and the other planets revolve around the sun. (p. 546)

Hellenistic [HEHL·uh·NIHS·tihk] *adj.* relating to the civilization, language, art, science, and literature of the Greek world from the reign of Alexander the Great to the late second century B.C. (p. 132)

helot [HEHL·uht] *n.* in the society of ancient Sparta, a peasant bound to the land. (p. 116)

heresy [HEHR·ih·see] *n.* religious beliefs or opinions that differ from the official teachings of a Christian church. (p. 157)

hieroglyphics [HY·uhr·uh·GLIHF·ihks] *n.* an ancient Egyptian writing system in which pictures were used to represent ideas and sounds. (p. 38)

Hijrah [HIHJ·ruh] *n.* Muhammad's migration from Mecca to Yathrib (Medina) in A.D. 622. (p. 235)

Hittites [HIHT·yts] *n.* an Indo-European people who settled in Anatolia around 2000 B.C. (p. 58)

Holocaust [HAHL·uh·kawst] *n.* a mass slaughter of Jews and other civilians, carried out by the Nazi government of Germany before and during World War II. (p. 831)

Holy Alliance *n.* a league of European nations formed by the leaders of Russia, Austria, and Prussia after the Congress of Vienna. (p. 595)

Holy Roman Empire *n.* an empire established in Europe in the 10th century A.D., originally consisting mainly of lands in what is now Germany and Italy. (p. 333)

home rule *n.* a control over internal matters granted to the residents of a region by a ruling government. (p. 668)

hominid [HAHM·uh·nihd] *n.* a member of a biological group including human beings and related species that walk upright. (p. 8)

Homo sapiens [HOH·moh SAY·pee·uhnz] *n.* the biological species to which modern human beings belong. (p. 9)

House of Wisdom *n.* a center of learning established in Baghdad in the 800s. (p. 243)

Hubble Space Telescope *n.* a powerful telescope put into orbit around the earth by NASA and the European Space Agency in 1990. (p. 942)

humanism [HYOO·muh·NIHZ·uhm] *n.* a Renaissance intellectual movement in which thinkers studied classical texts and focused on human potential and achievements. (p. 418)

Hundred Days *n.* the brief period during 1815 when Napoleon made his last bid for power, deposing the French king and again becoming emperor of France. (p. 592)

Hundred Years' War *n.* a conflict in which England and France battled on French soil on and off from 1337 to 1453. (p. 359)

hunter-gatherer *n.* a member of a nomadic group whose food supply depends on hunting animals and collecting plant foods. (p. 12)

Hyksos [HIHK·sohs] *n.* a group of nomadic invaders from Southwest Asia who ruled Egypt from 1640 to 1570 B.C. (p. 83)

I

Ice Age *n.* a cold period in which huge ice sheets spread outward from the polar regions, the last one of which lasted from about 1,600,000 to 10,000 B.C. (p. 211)

I Ching [ee jihng] *n.* a Chinese book of oracles, consulted to answer ethical and practical problems. (p. 99)

icon [EYE·kahn] *n.* a religious image used by eastern Christians. (p. 272)

iconoclast [eye·KAHN·uh·klast] *n.* one of the eastern Christians who destroyed religious images in churches during the eighth and ninth centuries. (p. 272)

imperialism [ihm·PEER·ee·uh·LIHZ·uhm] *n.* a policy in which a strong nation seeks to dominate other countries politically, economically, or socially. (p. 686)

impressionism [ihm·PREHSH·uh·NIHZ·uhm] *n.* a movement in 19th-century painting, in which artists reacted against realism by seeking to convey their impressions of subjects or moments in time. (p. 623)

Indo-Europeans [IHN·doh·YUR·uh·PEE·uhnz] *n.* a group of seminomadic peoples who, about 1700 B.C., began to migrate from what is now southern Russia to the Indian subcontinent, Europe, and Southwest Asia. (p. 57)

indulgence [ihn·DUHL·juhns] *n.* a pardon releasing a person from punishments due for a sin. (p. 429)

industrialization [ihn·DUHS·tree·uh·lih·ZAY·shuhn] *n.* the development of industries for the machine production of goods. (p. 634)

Industrial Revolution *n.* the shift, beginning in England during the 18th century, from making goods by hand to making them by machine. (p. 633)

inflation *n.* a decline in the value of money, accompanied by a rise in the prices of goods and services. (p. 158)

Inquisition [IHN·kwih·ZIHSH·uhn] *n.* a Roman Catholic tribunal for investigating and prosecuting charges of heresy—especially the one active in Spain during the 1400s. (p. 346)

institution *n.* a long-lasting pattern of organization in a community. (p. 18)

intendant [ihn·TEHN·duhnt] *n.* a French government official appointed by the monarch to collect taxes and administer justice. (p. 520)

Internet *n.* a linkage of computer networks that allows people around the world to exchange information and communicate with one another. (p. 943)

iron curtain *n.* during the Cold War, the boundary separating the Communist nations of Eastern Europe from the mostly democratic nations of Western Europe. (p. 857)

Iroquois [IHR·uh·KWOY] *n.* a group of Native American peoples who spoke related languages, lived in the eastern Great Lakes region of North America, and formed an alliance in the late 1500s. (p. 393)

irrigation *n.* the bringing of water to crop fields by means of canals and ditches. (p. 28)

Islam [ihs·LAHM] *n.* a monotheistic religion that developed in Arabia in the seventh century A.D. (p. 234)

isolationism *n.* a policy of avoiding political or military involvement with other countries. (p. 814)

Israel [IHZ·ree·uhl] *n.* a kingdom of the united Hebrews in Palestine, lasting from about 1020 to 922 B.C.; later, the northernmost of the two Hebrew kingdoms; now, the Jewish nation that was established in Palestine in 1948. (p. 75)

J

Jainism [JY·NIHZ·uhm] *n.* a religion founded in India in the sixth century B.C., whose members believe that everything in the universe has a soul and therefore should not be harmed. (p. 63)

janissary [JAN·ih·SEHR·ee] *n.* a member of an elite force of soldiers in the Ottoman Empire. (p. 446)

jazz *n.* a 20th-century style of popular music developed mainly by African-American musicians. (p. 797)

Jesuits [JEHZH·oo·ihts] *n.* members of the Society of Jesus, a Roman Catholic religious order founded by Ignatius of Loyola. (p. 435)

"jewel in the crown" *n.* the British colony of India—so called because of its importance in the British Empire, both as a supplier of raw materials and as a market for British trade goods. (p. 701)

joint-stock company *n.* a business in which investors pool their wealth for a common purpose, then share the profits. (p. 502)

Judah [JOO·duh] *n.* a Hebrew kingdom in Palestine, established around 922 B.C. (p. 76)

Justinian [juh·STIHN·ee·uhn] **Code** *n.* the body of Roman civil law collected and organized by order of the Byzantine emperor Justinian around A.D. 534. (p. 270)

K

kabuki [kuh·BOO·kee] *n.* a type of Japanese drama in which music, dance, and mime are used to present stories. (p. 476)

kaiser [KY·zuhr] *n.* a German emperor (from the Roman title *Caesar*). (p. 618)

kamikaze [KAH·mih·KAH·zee] *n.* during World War II, Japanese suicide pilots trained to sink Allied ships by crashing bomb-filled planes into them. (p. 841)

karma [KAHR·muh] *n.* in Hinduism and Buddhism, the totality of the good and bad deeds performed by a person, which is believed to determine his or her fate after rebirth. (p. 63)

Khmer [kmair] **Empire** *n.* a Southeast Asian empire, centered in what is now Cambodia, that reached its peak of power around A.D. 1200. (p. 309)

Khmer Rouge [roozh] *n.* a group of Communist rebels who seized power in Cambodia in 1975. (p. 870)

knight *n.* in medieval Europe, an armored warrior who fought on horseback. (p. 324)

Koryu [KAWR·yoo] **Dynasty** *n.* a dynasty that ruled Korea from A.D. 935 to 1392. (p. 311)

Kristallnacht [krih·STAHL·NAHKT] *n.* "Night of Broken Glass"—the night of November 9, 1938, on which Nazi storm troopers attacked Jewish homes, businesses, and synagogues throughout Germany. (p. 831)

kulak [koo·LAK] *n.* a member of a class of wealthy Russian peasants. (p. 777)

Kuomintang [KWOH·mihn·TANG] *n.* the Chinese Nationalist Party, formed after the fall of the Qing Dynasty in 1912. (p. 781)

Kush [kuhsh] *n.* an ancient Nubian kingdom whose rulers controlled Egypt from 751 to 671 B.C. (p. 85)

L

laissez faire [LEHS·ay·FAIR] *n.* the idea that government should not interfere with or regulate industries and businesses. (p. 647)

land reform *n.* a redistribution of farmland by breaking up large estates and giving the resulting smaller farms to peasants. (p. 912)

La Reforma [lah reh·FAWR·mah] *n.* a liberal reform movement in 19th-century Mexico, founded by Benito Juárez. (p. 730)

lay investiture [ihn·VEHS·tuh·CHUR] *n.* the appointment of religious officials by kings or nobles. (p. 334)

League of Nations *n.* an international association formed after World War I with the goal of keeping peace among nations. (p. 761)

lebensraum [LAY·buhns·ROWM] *n.* "living space"—the additional territory that, according to Adolf Hitler, Germany needed because it was overcrowded. (p. 809)

Legalism *n.* a Chinese political philosophy based on the idea that a highly efficient and powerful government is the key to social order. (p. 99)

legion *n.* a military unit of the ancient Roman army, made up of about 5,000 foot soldiers and a group of soldiers on horseback. (p. 143)

Legislative [LEHJ·ih·SLAY·tihv] **Assembly** *n.* a French congress with the power to create laws and approve declarations of war, established by the Constitution of 1791. (p. 578)

legitimacy [luh·JIHT·uh·muh·see] *n.* the hereditary right of a monarch to rule. (p. 594)

liberals *n.* in the first half of the 19th century, those Europeans—mainly middle-class business leaders and merchants—who wanted to give more political power to elected parliaments. (p. 609)

lineage [LIHN·ee·ihj] *n.* the people—living, dead, and unborn—who are descended from a common ancestor. (p. 368)

loess [LOH·uhs] *n.* a fertile deposit of windblown soil. (p. 46)

Long March *n.* a 6,000-mile journey made in 1934–1935 by Chinese Communists fleeing from Jiang Jieshi's Nationalist forces. (p. 784)

lord *n.* in feudal Europe, a person who controlled land and could therefore grant estates to vassals. (p. 324)

Lutheran [LOO·thuhr·uhn] *n.* a member of a Protestant church founded on the teachings of Martin Luther. (p. 430)

lycée [lee·SAY] *n.* a government-run public school in France. (p. 585)

M

Macedonia [MAS·ih·DOH·nee·uh] *n.* an ancient kingdom north of Greece, whose ruler Philip II conquered Greece in 338 B.C. (p. 128)

Maghrib [MUHG·ruhb] *n.* a region of western North Africa, consisting of the Mediterranean coastlands of what is now Morocco, Tunisia, and Algeria. (p. 369)

Magna Carta [MAG·nuh KAHR·tuh] *n.* "Great Charter"—a document guaranteeing basic political rights in England, drawn up by nobles and approved by King John in A.D. 1215. (p. 353)

Mahabharata [muh·HAH·BAH·ruh·tuh] *n.* a great Indian epic poem, reflecting the struggles of the Aryans as they moved south into India. (p. 60)

Mahayana [MAH·huh·YAH·nuh] *n.* a sect of Buddhism that offers salvation to all and allows popular worship. (p. 177)

maize [mayz] *n.* a cultivated cereal grain that bears its kernels on large ears—usually called corn in the United States. (p. 213)

Mali [MAH·lee] *n.* a West African empire that flourished from 1235 to the 1400s and grew rich from trade. (p. 373)

mamelukes [MAM·uh·LOOKS] *n.* Turkish slaves who served as soldiers and bodyguards in the Abbasid Empire. (p. 279)

Manchus [MAN·chooz] *n.* a people, native to Manchuria, who ruled China during the Qing Dynasty (1644–1912). (p. 471)

Mandate of Heaven *n.* in Chinese history, the divine approval thought to be the basis of royal authority. (p. 50)

manifest destiny *n.* the idea, popular among mid-19th-century Americans, that it was the right and the duty of the United States to rule North America from the Atlantic Ocean to the Pacific Ocean. (p. 670)

manor *n.* a lord's estate in feudal Europe. (p. 325)

Maori [MOW·ree] *n.* a member of a Polynesian people who settled in New Zealand around A.D. 800. (p. 665)

Marshall Plan *n.* a U.S. program of economic aid to European countries to help them rebuild after World War II. (p. 858)

martial [MAHR·shuhl] **law** *n.* a temporary rule by military authorities over a civilian population, usually imposed in times of war or civil unrest. (p. 917)

mass culture *n.* the production of works of art and entertainment designed to appeal to a large audience. (p. 674)

materialism *n.* a placing of high value on acquiring material possessions. (p. 960)

matriarchal [MAY·tree·AHR·kuhl] *adj.* relating to a social system in which the mother is head of the family. (p. 176)

matrilineal [MAT·ruh·LIHN·ee·uhl] *adj.* relating to a social system in which family descent and inheritance rights are traced through the mother. (p. 369)

Mau Mau [MOW MOW] *n.* a secret society of Kikuyu tribesmen that attempted to drive British settlers out of Kenya in the mid-20th century. (p. 897)

Mauryan [MAH·ur·yuhn] **Empire** *n.* the first empire in India, founded by Chandragupta Maurya in 321 B.C. (p. 173)

May Fourth Movement *n.* a national protest in China in 1919, in which people demonstrated against the Treaty of Versailles and foreign interference. (p. 782)

Medes [meedz] *n.* a Southwest Asian people who helped to destroy the Assyrian Empire. (p. 90)

Meiji [MAY·JEE] **era** *n.* the period of Japanese history from 1867 to 1912, during which the country was ruled by Emperor Mutsuhito. (p. 721)

Mein Kampf [MYN KAHMPF] *n.* "My Struggle"—a book written by Adolf Hitler during his imprisonment in 1923–1924, in which he set forth his beliefs and his goals for Germany. (p. 809)

mercantilism [MUR·kuhn·tee·LIHZ·uhm] *n.* an economic policy under which nations sought to increase their wealth and power by obtaining large amounts of gold and silver and by selling more goods than they bought. (p. 502)

mercenary [MUR·suh·NEHR·ee] *n.* a soldier who is paid to fight in a foreign army. (p. 159)

Mesoamerica [MEHZ·oh·uh·MEHR·ih·kuh] *n.* an area extending from central Mexico to Honduras, where several of the ancient complex societies of the Americas developed. (p. 216)

mestizo [mehs·TEE·zoh] *adj.* of mixed Spanish and Native American ancestry. (p. 486)

Middle Ages *n.* the era in European history that followed the fall of the Roman Empire, lasting from about 500 to 1500—also called the medieval period. (p. 317)

middle class *n.* a social class made up of skilled workers, professionals, businesspeople, and wealthy farmers. (p. 639)

middle passage *n.* the voyage that brought captured Africans to the West Indies, and later to North and South America, to be sold as slaves—so called because it was considered the middle leg of the triangular trade. (p. 497)

migration *n.* the act of moving from one place to settle in another. (p. 57)

militarism [MIHL·ih·tuh·RIHZ·uhm] *n.* a policy of glorifying military power and keeping a standing army always prepared for war. (p. 744)

Ming Dynasty *n.* a Chinese dynasty that ruled from 1368 to 1644. (p. 469)

Minoans [mih·NOH·uhnz] *n.* a seafaring and trading people that lived on the island of Crete from about 2000 to 1400 B.C. (p. 67)

Mississippian [MIHS·ih·SIHP·ee·uhn] *adj.* relating to a Mound Builder culture that flourished in North America between A.D. 800 and 1500. (p. 393)

mita [MEE·tuh] *n.* in the Inca Empire, the requirement that all able-bodied subjects work for the state a certain number of days each year. (p. 409)

Moche [MOH·chay] *n.* a civilization that flourished on what is now the northern coast of Peru from about A.D. 100 to 700. (p. 222)

monarchy [MAHN·uhr·kee] *n.* a government in which power is in the hands of a single person. (p. 115)

monastery [MAHN·uh·STEHR·ee] *n.* a religious community of men (called monks) who have given up their possessions to devote themselves to a life of prayer and worship. (p. 318)

monopoly [muh·NAHP·uh·lee] *n.* a group's exclusive control over the production and distribution of certain goods. (p. 185)

monotheism [MAHN·uh·thee·IHZ·uhm] *n.* a belief in a single god. (p. 73)

Monroe Doctrine *n.* a U.S. policy of opposition to European interference in Latin America, announced by President James Monroe in 1823. (p. 726)

monsoon [mahn·SOON] *n.* a wind that shifts in direction at certain times of each year. (p. 42)

mosque [mahsk] *n.* an Islamic place of worship. (p. 236)

movable type *n.* blocks of metal or wood, each bearing a single character, that can be arranged to make up a page for printing. (p. 289)

Mughal [MOO·guhl] *n.* one of the nomads who invaded the Indian subcontinent in the 16th century and established a powerful empire there. (p. 451)

mulattos [mu·LAT·ohz] *n.* persons of mixed European and African ancestry. (p. 604)

multinational corporation *n.* a company that operates in a number of different countries. (p. 947)

mummification [MUHM·uh·fih·KAY·shuhn] *n.* a process of embalming and drying corpses to prevent them from decaying. (p. 37)

Munich [MYOO·nihk] **Conference** *n.* a 1938 meeting of representatives from Britain, France, Italy, and Germany, at which Britain and France agreed to allow Nazi Germany to annex part of Czechoslovakia in return for Adolf Hitler's pledge to respect Czechoslovakia's new borders. (p. 815)

Muslim [MUHZ·luhm] *n.* a follower of Islam. (p. 235)

Muslim League *n.* an organization formed in 1906 to protect the interests of India's Muslims, which later proposed that India be divided into separate Muslim and Hindu nations. (p. 886)

Mutapa [moo·TAHP·uh] *adj.* relating to a southern African empire established by Mutota in the 15th century A.D. (p. 381)

Mycenaeans [MY·suh·NEE·uhnz] *n.* an Indo-European people who settled on the Greek mainland around 2000 B.C. (p. 112)

myths *n.* traditional stories about gods, ancestors, or heroes, told to explain the natural world or the customs and beliefs of a society. (p. 114)

N

Napoleonic [nuh·POH·lee·AHN·ihk] **Code** *n.* a comprehensive and uniform system of laws established for France by Napoleon. (p. 586)

National Assembly *n.* a French congress established by representatives of the Third Estate on June 17, 1789, to enact laws and reforms in the name of the French people. (p. 575)

nationalism *n.* the belief that people should be loyal mainly to their nation—that is, to the people with whom they share a culture and history—rather than to a king or empire. (p. 609)

nation-state *n.* an independent nation of people having a common culture and identity. (p. 609)

NATO [NAY·toh] *n.* the North Atlantic Treaty Organization—a defensive military alliance formed in 1949 by ten Western European nations, the United States, and Canada. (p. 859)

natural rights *n.* the rights that all people are born with—according to John Locke, the rights of life, liberty, and property. (p. 551)

Nazca [NAHS·kah] *n.* a civilization that flourished on what is now the southern coast of Peru from about 200 B.C. to A.D. 600. (p. 222)

Nazism [NAHT·SIHZ·uhm] *n.* the fascist policies of the National Socialist German Workers' party, based on totalitarianism, a belief in racial superiority, and state control of industry. (p. 808)

Negritude [NEE·grih·TOOD] **movement** *n.* a movement in which French-speaking Africans and West Indians celebrated their heritage of traditional African culture and values. (p. 896)

neoclassical [NEE·oh·KLAS·ih·kuhl] *adj.* relating to a simple, elegant style (based on ideas and themes from ancient Greece and Rome) that characterized the arts in Europe during the late 1700s. (p. 559)

Neolithic [NEE·uh·LIHTH·ihk] **Age** *n.* a prehistoric period that began about 8000 B.C. and in some areas ended as early as 3000 B.C., during which people learned to polish stone tools, make pottery, grow crops, and raise animals—also called the New Stone Age. (p. 8)

Neolithic Revolution *n.* the major change in human life caused by the beginnings of farming—that is, by people's shift from food gathering to food producing. (p. 14)

New Deal *n.* U.S. president Franklin Roosevelt's economic reform program designed to solve the problems created by the Great Depression. (p. 806)

New Kingdom *n.* the period of ancient Egyptian history that followed the overthrow of the Hyksos rulers, lasting from about 1570 to 1075 B.C. (p. 83)

nirvana [neer·VAH·nuh] *n.* in Buddhism, the release from pain and suffering achieved after enlightenment. (p. 65)

Nok [nahk] *n.* an African people who lived in what is now Nigeria between 500 B.C. and A.D. 200. (p. 198)

nomad *n.* a member of a group that has no permanent home, wandering from place to place in search of food and water. (p. 12)

nonaggression [NAHN·uh·GREHSH·uhn] **pact** *n.* an agreement in which nations promise not to attack one another. (p. 821)

nonaligned nations *n.* the independent countries that remained neutral in the Cold War competition between the United States and the Soviet Union. (p. 871)

Nuclear Non-Proliferation [NOO·klee·uhr NAHN·pruh·LIHF·uh·RAY·shuhn] **Treaty** *n.* a 1968 agreement intended to reduce the spread of nuclear weapons. (p. 953)

Nuremberg [NUR·uhm·BURG] **Trials** *n.* a series of court proceedings held in Nuremberg, Germany, after World War II, in which Nazi leaders were tried for aggression, violations of the rules of war, and crimes against humanity. (p. 843)

O

obsidian [ahb·SIHD·ee·uhn] *n.* a hard, glassy volcanic rock used by early peoples to make sharp weapons. (p. 400)

Old Regime [ray·ZHEEM] *n.* the political and social system that existed in France before the French Revolution. (p. 573)

oligarchy [AHL·ih·GAHR·kee] *n.* a government in which power is in the hands of a few people—especially one in which rule is based upon wealth. (p. 115)

Olmec [AHL·mehk] *n.* the earliest known Mesoamerican civilization, which flourished around 1200 B.C. and influenced later societies throughout the region. (p. 216)

Open Door Policy *n.* a policy, proposed by the United States in 1899, under which all nations would have equal opportunities to trade in China. (p. 718)

Opium War *n.* a conflict between Britain and China, lasting from 1839 to 1842, over Britain's opium trade in China. (p. 716)

oracle bone *n.* one of the animal bones or tortoise shells used by ancient Chinese priests to communicate with the gods. (p. 48)

ozone layer *n.* a layer of the earth's upper atmosphere, which protects living things from the sun's damaging ultraviolet rays. (p. 949)

P

Pacific Rim *n.* the lands surrounding the Pacific Ocean—especially those in Asia. (p. 706)

Paleolithic [PAY·lee·uh·LIHTH·ihk] **Age** *n.* a prehistoric period that lasted from about 2,500,000 to 8000 B.C., during which people made use of crude stone tools and weapons—also called the Old Stone Age. (p. 8)

Panama Canal *n.* a manmade waterway connecting the Atlantic and Pacific oceans, built in Panama by the United States and opened in 1914. (p. 727)

papyrus [puh·PY·ruhs] *n.* a tall reed that grows in the Nile delta, used by the ancient Egyptians to make a paperlike material for writing on. (p. 38)

parliament [PAHR·luh·muhnt] *n.* a body of representatives that makes laws for a nation. (p. 354)

partition *n.* a division into parts, like the 1947 division of the British colony of India into the two nations of India and Pakistan. (p. 886)

pastoralist [PAS·tuhr·uh·lihst] *n.* a member of a nomadic group that herds domesticated animals. (p. 294)

paternalism [puh·TUR·nuh·LIHZ·uhm] *n.* a policy of treating subject people as if they were children, providing for their needs but not giving them rights. (p. 691)

patriarch [PAY·tree·AHRK] *n.* a principal bishop in the eastern branch of Christianity. (p. 272)

patriarchal [PAY·tree·AHR·kuhl] *adj.* relating to a social system in which the father is head of the family. (p. 176)

patrician [puh·TRIHSH·uhn] *n.* in ancient Rome, a member of the wealthy, privileged upper class. (p. 142)

patrilineal [PAT·ruh·LIHN·ee·uhl] *adj.* relating to a social system in which family descent and inheritance rights are traced through the father. (p. 369)

patron [PAY·truhn] *n.* a person who supports artists, especially financially. (p. 418)

Pax Romana [PAHKS roh·MAH·nah] *n.* a period of peace and prosperity throughout the Roman Empire, lasting from 27 B.C. to A.D. 180. (p. 148)

Peace of Augsburg [AWGZ·BURG] *n.* a 1555 agreement declaring that the religion of each German state would be decided by its ruler. (p. 430)

Peloponnesian [PEHL·uh·puh·NEE·zhuhn] **War** *n.* a war, lasting from 431 to 404 B.C., in which Athens and its allies were defeated by Sparta and its allies. (p. 123)

penal [PEE·nuhl] **colony** *n.* a colony to which convicts are sent as an alternative to prison. (p. 665)

peninsulares [peh·neen·soo·LAH·rehs] *n.* in Spanish colonial society, colonists who were born in Spain. (p. 604)

Peninsular [puh·NIHN·syuh·luhr] **War** *n.* a conflict, lasting from 1808 to 1813, in which Spanish rebels, with the aid of British forces, fought to drive Napoleon's French troops out of Spain. (p. 590)

perestroika [PEHR·ih·STROY·kuh] *n.* a restructuring of the Soviet economy to permit more local decision-making, begun by Mikhail Gorbachev in 1985. (p. 922)

Persian Wars *n.* a series of wars in the fifth century B.C., in which Greek city-states battled the Persian Empire. (p. 118)

perspective [puhr·SPEHK·tihv] *n.* an artistic technique that creates the appearance of three dimensions on a flat surface. (p. 419)

phalanx [FAY·langks] *n.* a military formation of foot soldiers armed with spears and shields. (p. 115)

pharaoh [FAIR·oh] *n.* a king of ancient Egypt, considered a god as well as a political and military leader. (p. 35)

philosophe [FIHL·uh·SAHF] *n.* one of a group of social thinkers in France during the Enlightenment. (p. 552)

philosophers *n.* thinkers who use logic and reason to investigate the nature of the universe, human society, and morality. (p. 124)

Phoenicians [fih·NIHSH·uhnz] *n.* a seafaring people of Southwest Asia, who around 1100 B.C. began to trade and found colonies throughout the Mediterranean region. (p. 68)

Pilgrims *n.* a group of people who, in 1620, founded the colony of Plymouth in Massachusetts to escape religious persecution in England. (p. 491)

plebeian [plih·BEE·uhn] *n.* in ancient Rome, one of the common farmers, artisans, and merchants who made up most of the population. (p. 142)

plebiscite [PLEHB·ih·SYT] *n.* a direct vote in which a country's people have the opportunity to approve or reject a proposal. (p. 585)

PLO *n.* the Palestine Liberation Organization—an organization dedicated to the establishment of an independent state for Palestinians in the Middle East. (p. 905)

pogrom [puh·GRAHM] *n.* one of the organized campaigns of violence against Jewish communities in late-19th-century Russia. (p. 769)

polis [POH·lihs] *n.* a Greek city-state—the fundamental political unit of ancient Greece after about 750 B.C. (p. 115)

Politburo [PAHL·iht·BYOOR·oh] *n.* the ruling committee of the Communist Party in the Soviet Union. (p. 921)

polytheism [PAHL·ee·thee·IHZ·uhm] *n.* a belief in many gods. (p. 29)

pope *n.* the bishop of Rome, head of the Roman Catholic Church. (p. 156)

Popol Vuh [POH·pohl VOO] *n.* a book containing a version of the Mayan story of creation. (p. 398)

popular culture *n.* the cultural elements—sports, music, movies, clothing, and so forth—that reflect a group's common background and changing interests. (p. 957)

potlatch [PAHT·LACH] *n.* a ceremonial feast used to display rank and prosperity in some Northwest Coast tribes of Native Americans. (p. 391)

predestination [pree·DEHS·tuh·NAY·shuhn] *n.* the doctrine that God has decided all things beforehand, including which people will be eternally saved. (p. 433)

Presbyterian [PREHZ·bih·TEER·ee·uhn] *n.* a member of a Protestant church governed by elders (presbyters) and founded on the teachings of John Knox. (p. 433)

PRI *n.* the Institutional Revolutionary Party—the main political party of Mexico. (p. 914)

printing press *n.* a machine for reproducing written material by pressing paper against arrangements of inked type. (p. 426)

proliferation [pruh·LIHF·uh·RAY·shuhn] *n.* a growth or spread—especially the spread of nuclear weapons to nations that do not currently have them. (p. 953)

propaganda [PRAHP·uh·GAN·duh] *n.* information or material spread to advance a cause or to damage an opponent's cause. (p. 756)

Protestant [PRAHT·ih·stuhnt] *n.* a member of a Christian church founded on the principles of the Reformation. (p. 430)

provisional government *n.* a temporary government. (p. 772)

psychology [sy·KAHL·uh·jee] *n.* the study of the human mind and human behavior. (p. 679)

pueblos [PWEHB·lohz] *n.* villages of large apartment-like buildings made of clay and stone, built by the Anasazi and later peoples of the American Southwest. (p. 391)

Puritans *n.* a group of people who sought freedom from religious persecution in England by founding a colony at Massachusetts Bay in the early 1600s. (p. 491)

pyramid [PIHR·uh·mihd] *n.* a massive structure with a rectangular base and four triangular sides, like those that were built in Egypt as burial places for Old Kingdom pharaohs. (p. 35)

Q

Qin [chihn] **Dynasty** *n.* a short-lived Chinese dynasty that replaced the Zhou Dynasty in the third century B.C. (p. 99)

Qing [chihng] **Dynasty** *n.* China's last dynasty, which ruled from 1644 to 1912. (p. 471)

Quetzalcoatl [keht·SAHL·koh·AHT·uhl] *n.* the Feathered Serpent—a god of the Toltecs and other Mesoamerican peoples. (p. 401)

quipu [KEE·poo] *n.* an arrangement of knotted strings on a cord, used by the Inca to record numerical information. (p. 410)

Qur'an [kuh·RAN] *n.* the holy book of Islam. (p. 236)

R

racism [RAY·SIHZ·uhm] *n.* the belief that one race is superior to others. (p. 686)

radicals *n.* in the first half of the 19th century, those Europeans who favored drastic change to extend democracy to all people. (p. 609)

radioactivity *n.* a form of energy released as atoms decay. (p. 678)

Raj [rahj] *n.* the British-controlled portions of India in the years 1757–1947. (p. 704)

rationing [RASH·uh·nihng] *n.* the limiting of the amounts of goods people can buy—often imposed by governments during wartime, when goods are in short supply. (p. 755)

realism *n.* a 19th-century artistic movement in which writers and painters sought to show life as it is rather than life as it should be. (p. 621)

realpolitik [ray·AHL·POH·lih·TEEK] *n.* "the politics of reality"—the practice of tough power politics without room for idealism. (p. 617)

recession *n.* a slowdown in a nation's economy. (p. 913)

Reconquista [reh·kawn·KEES·tah] *n.* the effort by Christian leaders to drive the Muslims out of Spain, lasting from the 1100s until 1492. (p. 346)

Red Guards *n.* militia units formed by young Chinese people in 1966 in response to Mao Zedong's call for a social and cultural revolution. (p. 865)

Red Shirts *n.* the followers of the 19th-century Italian nationalist leader Giuseppe Garibaldi. (p. 616)

Reformation [REHF·uhr·MAY·shuhn] *n.* a 16th-century movement for religious reform, leading to the founding of Christian churches that rejected the pope's authority. (p. 429)

Reign [rayn] **of Terror** *n.* the period, from mid-1793 to mid-1794, when Maximilien Robespierre ruled France nearly as a dictator and thousands of political figures and ordinary citizens were executed. (p. 582)

reincarnation [REE·ihn·kahr·NAY·shuhn] *n.* in Hinduism and Buddhism, the process by which a soul is reborn again and again until it achieves perfect understanding. (p. 63)

religious toleration *n.* a recognition of people's right to hold differing religious beliefs. (p. 174)

Renaissance [REHN·ih·SAHNS] *n.* a period of European history, lasting from about 1300 to 1600, during which renewed interest in classical culture led to far-reaching changes in art, learning, and views of the world. (p. 417)

republic *n.* a form of government in which power is in the hands of representatives and leaders are elected by the people. (p. 142)

Restoration [REHS·tuh·RAY·shuhn] *n.* the period of Charles II's rule over England, after the collapse of Oliver Cromwell's government. (p. 538)

reunification [ree·YOO·nuh·fih·KAY·shuhn] *n.* a bringing together again of things that have been separated, like the reuniting of East Germany and West Germany in 1990. (p. 924)

romanticism [roh·MAN·tih·SIHZ·uhm] *n.* an early-19th-century movement in art and thought, which focused on emotion and nature rather than reason and society. (p. 619)

Roosevelt Corollary [ROH·zuh·VEHLT KAWR·uh·lehr·ee] *n.* President Theodore Roosevelt's 1904 extension of the Monroe Doctrine, in which he declared that the United States had the right to exercise "police power" throughout the Western Hemisphere. (p. 727)

Royal Road *n.* a road in the Persian Empire, stretching over 1,600 miles from Susa in Persia to Sardis in Anatolia. (p. 94)

Russo-Japanese War *n.* a 1904–1905 conflict between Russia and Japan, sparked by the two countries' efforts to dominate Manchuria and Korea. (p. 723)

S

sacrament [SAK·ruh·muhnt] *n.* one of the Christian ceremonies in which God's grace is transmitted to people. (p. 332)

Safavid [suh·FAH·VIHD] *n.* a member of a Shi'a Muslim dynasty that built an empire in Persia in the 16th–18th centuries. (p. 449)

Sahel [suh·HAYL] *n.* the African region along the southern border of the Sahara. (p. 195)

salon [suh·LAHN] *n.* a social gathering of intellectuals and artists, like those held in the homes of wealthy women in Paris and other European cities during the Enlightenment. (p. 558)

SALT *n.* the Strategic Arms Limitation Talks—a series of meetings in the 1970s, in which leaders of the United States and the Soviet Union agreed to limit their nations' stocks of nuclear weapons. (p. 879)

samurai [SAM·uh·RY] *n.* one of the professional warriors who served Japanese feudal lords. (p. 307)

sans-culottes [SANS·kyoo·LAHTS] *n.* in the French Revolution, a radical group made up of Parisian wage-earners and small shopkeepers who wanted a greater voice in government, lower prices, and an end of food shortages. (p. 579)

satrap [SAY·TRAP] *n.* a governor of a province in the Persian Empire. (p. 94)

savanna [suh·VAN·uh] *n.* a flat, grassy plain. (p. 195)

schism [SIHZ·uhm] *n.* a split or division—especially a formal split within a Christian church. (p. 273)

Schlieffen [SHLEE·fuhn] **Plan** *n.* Germany's military plan at the outbreak of World War I, according to which German troops would rapidly defeat France and then move east to attack Russia. (p. 747)

scholastics [skuh·LAS·tihks] *n.* scholars who gathered and taught at medieval European universities. (p. 351)

scientific method *n.* a logical procedure for gathering information about the natural world, in which experimentation and observation are used to test hypotheses. (p. 547)

Scientific Revolution *n.* a major change in European thought, starting in the mid-1500s, in which the study of the natural world began to be characterized by careful observation and the questioning of accepted beliefs. (p. 545)

scorched-earth policy *n.* the practice of burning crops and killing livestock during wartime so that the enemy cannot live off the land. (p. 590)

scribe *n.* one of the professional record keepers in early civilizations. (p. 18)

secede [sih·SEED] *v.* to withdraw formally from an association or alliance. (p. 670)

secular [SEHK·yuh·luhr] *adj.* concerned with worldly rather than spiritual matters. (pp. 319, 418)

segregation [SEHG·rih·GAY·shuhn] *n.* the legal or social separation of people of different races. (p. 672)

self-determination [SEHLF·dih·TUR·muh·NAY·shuhn] *n.* the freedom of a people to decide under what form of government they wish to live. (p. 760)

Seljuks [SEHL·JOOKS] *n.* a Turkish group who migrated into the Abbasid Empire in the 10th century and established their own empire in the 11th century. (p. 279)

senate *n.* in ancient Rome, the supreme governing body, originally made up only of aristocrats. (p. 143)

separation of powers *n.* the assignment of executive, legislative, and judicial powers to different groups of officials in a government. (p. 553)

sepoy [SEE·POY] *n.* an Indian soldier serving under British command. (p. 701)

Sepoy Mutiny [MYOOT·uh·nee] *n.* an 1857 rebellion of Hindu and Muslim soldiers against the British in India. (p. 703)

serf *n.* a medieval peasant legally bound to live on a lord's estate. (p. 324)

Seven Years' War *n.* a conflict in Europe, North America, and India, lasting from 1756 to 1763, in which the forces of Britain and Prussia battled those of Austria, France, Russia, and other countries. (p. 530)

shari'a [shah·REE·ah] *n.* a body of law governing the lives of Muslims. (p. 237)

Shi'a [SHEE·uh] *n.* the branch of Islam whose members acknowledge Ali and his descendants as the rightful successors of Muhammad. (p. 240)

Shinto [SHIHN·toh] *n.* the native religion of Japan. (p. 303)

Shiva [SHEE·vuh] *n.* a Hindu god considered the destroyer of the world. (p. 178)

"shock therapy" *n.* an economic program implemented in Russia by Boris Yeltsin in the 1990s, involving an abrupt shift from a command economy to a free-market economy. (p. 928)

shogun [SHOH·guhn] *n.* in feudal Japan, a supreme military commander who ruled in the name of the emperor. (p. 307)

Sikh [seek] *n.* a member of a nonviolent religious group whose beliefs blend elements of Buddhism, Hinduism, and Sufism. (p. 454)

Silk Roads *n.* a system of ancient caravan routes across Central Asia, along which traders carried silk and other trade goods. (p. 179)

silt *n.* the fine soil carried in the water of rivers. (p. 27)

simony [SY·muh·nee] *n.* the selling or buying of a position in a Christian church. (p. 341)

Six-Day War *n.* a brief 1967 conflict between Israel and several Arab states, during which Israel took control of Jerusalem, the Sinai Peninsula, the Golan Heights, and the West Bank. (p. 903)

skepticism [SKEHP·tih·SIHZ·uhm] *n.* a philosophy based on the idea that nothing can be known for certain. (p. 519)

slash-and-burn farming *n.* a farming method in which people clear fields by cutting and burning trees and grasses, the ashes of which serve to fertilize the soil. (p. 14)

Slavs [slahvz] *n.* a people from the forests north of the Black Sea, ancestors of many peoples in Eastern Europe today. (p. 274)

social contract *n.* the agreement by which people define and limit their individual rights, thus creating an organized society or government. (p. 551)

Social Darwinism [DAHR·wih·NIHZ·uhm] *n.* the application of Charles Darwin's ideas about evolution and "survival of the fittest" to human societies—particularly as justification for imperialist expansion. (p. 686)

socialism *n.* an economic system in which the factors of production are owned by the public and operate for the welfare of all. (p. 648)

socialist realism *n.* a style of art in which Communist values and life under communism are glorified. (p. 778)

Solidarity [SAHL·ih·DAR·ih·tee] *n.* a Polish labor union that during the 1980s became the main force of opposition to Communist rule in Poland. (p. 922)

Songhai [SAWNG·HY] *n.* a West African empire that conquered Mali and controlled trade from the 1400s to 1591. (p. 374)

soviet [SOH·vee·EHT] *n.* one of the local representative councils formed in Russia after the downfall of Czar Nicholas II. (p. 772)

Spanish-American War *n.* an 1898 conflict between the United States and Spain, in which the United States supported Cubans' fight for independence. (p. 726)

specialization *n.* the development of skills in a particular kind of work, such as trading or record keeping. (p. 18)

sphere of influence *n.* a foreign region in which a nation has control over trade and other economic activities. (p. 718)

standard of living *n.* the quality of life of a person or a population, as indicated by the goods, services, and luxuries available to the person or people. (p. 912)

Star Wars *n.* a program to protect the United States against attack by enemy missiles, proposed in 1983 by President Ronald Reagan but never implemented—formally known as the Strategic Defense Initiative. (p. 879)

stateless societies *n.* cultural groups in which authority is shared by lineages of equal power instead of being exercised by a central government. (p. 368)

steppes [stehps] *n.* dry, grass-covered plains. (p. 57)

strike *v.* to refuse to work in order to force an employer to meet certain demands. (p. 650)

subcontinent *n.* a large landmass that forms a distinct part of a continent. (p. 42)

Suez [soo·EHZ] **Canal** *n.* a manmade waterway connecting the Red Sea and the Mediterranean Sea, which was opened in 1869. (p. 699)

Suez Crisis *n.* an international crisis that occurred after Egypt seized control of the Suez Canal in 1956, when Israel, with the support of Britain and France, invaded Egypt and marched toward the canal but withdrew under pressure from the United States and the Soviet Union. (p. 902)

suffrage [SUHF·rihj] *n.* the right to vote. (p. 659)

Sufi [SOO·fee] *n.* a Muslim who seeks to achieve direct contact with God through mystical means. (p. 240)

Sunna [SUN·uh] *n.* an Islamic model for living, based on the life and teachings of Muhammad. (p. 237)

Sunni [SUN·ee] *n.* the branch of Islam whose members acknowledge the first four caliphs as the rightful successors of Muhammad. (p. 240)

surrealism [suh·REE·uh·LIHZ·uhm] *n.* a 20th-century artistic movement that focuses on the workings of the unconscious mind. (p. 797)

sustainable development *n.* economic development that meets people's needs but preserves the environment and conserves resources for future generations. (p. 950)

Swahili [swah·HEE·lee] *n.* an Arabic-influenced Bantu language that is used widely in eastern and central Africa. (p. 378)

T

Taiping [ty·pihng] **Rebellion** *n.* a mid-19th century rebellion against the Qing Dynasty in China, led by Hong Xiuquan. (p. 717)

Taj Mahal [TAHZH muh·HAHL] *n.* a beautiful tomb in Agra, India, built by the Mughal emperor Shah Jahan for his wife Mumtaz Mahal. (p. 454)

Tamil [TAM·uhl] *n.* a language of southern India—also, the people who speak that language. (p. 175)

technology *n.* the ways in which people apply knowledge, tools, and inventions to meet their needs. (p. 9)

Tennis Court Oath *n.* a pledge made by the members of France's National Assembly in 1789, in which they vowed to continue meeting until they had drawn up a new constitution. (p. 576)

terrorism *n.* the use of force or threats to frighten people or governments to change their policies. (p. 953)

theocracy [thee·AHK·ruh·see] *n.* **1.** a government in which the ruler is viewed as a divine figure (p. 35). **2.** a government controlled by religious leaders. (p. 433)

theory of evolution *n.* the idea, proposed by Charles Darwin in 1859, that species of plants and animals arise by means of a process of natural selection. (p. 678)

theory of relativity [REHL·uh·TIHV·ih·tee] *n.* Albert Einstein's ideas about the interrelationships between time and space and between energy and matter. (p. 795)

Theravada [THEHR·uh·VAH·duh] *n.* a sect of Buddhism focusing on the strict spiritual discipline originally advocated by the Buddha. (p. 177)

Third Reich [ryk] *n.* the Third German Empire, established by Adolf Hitler in the 1930s. (p. 814)

Third Republic *n.* the republic that was established in France after the downfall of Napoleon III and ended with the German occupation of France during World War II. (p. 663)

Third World *n.* during the Cold War, the developing nations not allied with either the United States or the Soviet Union. (p. 871)

Thirty Years' War *n.* a European conflict over religion, over territory, and for power among ruling families, lasting from 1618 to 1648. (p. 526)

three-field system *n.* a system of farming developed in medieval Europe, in which farmland was divided into three fields of equal size and each of these was successively planted with a winter crop, planted with a spring crop, and left unplanted. (p. 348)

Tiananmen [tyahn·ahn·mehn] **Square** *n.* a huge public space in Beijing, China—in 1989, the site of a student uprising in support of democratic reforms. (p. 932)

tithe [tyth] *n.* a family's payment of one-tenth of its income to a church. (p. 325)

Tokugawa Shogunate [TOH·koo·GAH·wah SHOH·guh·niht] *n.* a dynasty of shoguns that ruled a unified Japan from 1603 to 1867. (p. 475)

Torah [TAWR·uh] *n.* the first five books of the Hebrew Bible—the most sacred writings in the Jewish tradition. (p. 72)

totalitarianism [toh·TAL·ih·TAIR·ee·uh·NIHZ·uhm] *n.* government control over every aspect of public and private life. (p. 775)

total war *n.* a conflict in which the participating countries devote all their resources to the war effort. (p. 755)

totems [TOH·tuhmz] *n.* animals or other natural objects that serve as symbols of the unity of clans or other groups of people. (p. 394)

tournament *n.* a mock battle between groups of knights. (p. 328)

tragedy *n.* a serious form of drama dealing with the downfall of a heroic or noble character. (p. 123)

Trans-Siberian [TRANS·sy·BEER·ee·uhn] **Railway** *n.* a rail line built between 1891 and 1904 to connect European Russia with Russian ports on the Pacific Ocean. (p. 770)

Treaty of Kanagawa [kah·NAH·gah·wah] *n.* an 1854 agreement between the United States and Japan, which opened two Japanese ports to U.S. ships and allowed the United States to set up an embassy in Japan. (p. 720)

Treaty of Tordesillas [TAWR·day·SEEL·yahs] *n.* a 1494 agreement between Portugal and Spain, declaring that newly discovered lands to the west of an imaginary line in the Atlantic Ocean would belong to Spain and newly discovered lands to the east of the line would belong to Portugal. (p. 466)

Treaty of Versailles [vuhr·SY] *n.* the peace treaty signed by Germany and the Allied powers after World War I. (p. 761)

trench warfare *n.* a form of warfare in which opposing armies fight each other from trenches dug in the battlefield. (p. 749)

triangular trade *n.* the transatlantic trading network along which slaves and other goods were carried between Africa, England, Europe, the West Indies, and the colonies in North America. (p. 497)

tribune [TRIHB·yoon] *n.* in ancient Rome, an official elected by the plebeians to protect their rights. (p. 142)

tribute *n.* a payment made by a weaker power to a stronger power to obtain an assurance of peace and security. (p. 76)

Triple Alliance *n.* **1.** an association of the city-states of Tenochtitlan, Texcoco, and Tlacopan, which led to the formation of the Aztec Empire (p. 402). **2.** a military alliance between Germany, Austria-Hungary, and Italy in the years preceding World War I. (p. 744)

Triple Entente [ahn·TAHNT] *n.* a military alliance between Great Britain, France, and Russia in the years preceding World War I. (p. 745)

triumvirate [try·UHM·vuhr·iht] *n.* in ancient Rome, a group of three leaders sharing control of the government. (p. 147)

Trojan War *n.* a war, fought around 1200 B.C., in which an army led by Mycenaean kings attacked the independent trading city of Troy in Anatolia. (p. 113)

troubadour [TROO·buh·DAWR] *n.* a medieval poet and musician who traveled from place to place, entertaining people with songs of courtly love. (p. 330)

Truman Doctrine *n.* a U.S. policy of giving economic and military aid to free nations threatened by internal or external opponents, announced by President Harry Truman in 1947. (p. 858)

tyrant [TY·ruhnt] *n.* in ancient Greece, a powerful individual who gained control of a city-state's government by appealing to the poor for support. (p. 116)

UV

Umayyads [oo·MY·adz] *n.* a dynasty that ruled the Muslim Empire from A.D. 661 to 750 and later established a kingdom in al-Andalus. (p. 239)

union *n.* an association of workers, formed to bargain for better working conditions and higher wages. (p. 650)

United Nations *n.* an international peacekeeping organization founded in 1945 to provide security to the nations of the world. (p. 855)

Universal Declaration of Human Rights *n.* a 1948 statement in which the United Nations declared that all human beings have rights to life, liberty, and security. (p. 954)

unrestricted submarine warfare *n.* the use of submarines to sink without warning any ship (including neutral ships and unarmed passenger liners) found in an enemy's waters. (p. 754)

urbanization [UR·buh·nih·ZAY·shuhn] *n.* the growth of cities and the migration of people into them. (p. 638)

U.S. Civil War *n.* a conflict between Northern and Southern states of the United States over the issue of slavery, lasting from 1861 to 1865. (p. 671)

utilitarianism [yoo·TIHL·ih·TAIR·ee·uh·NIHZ·uhm] *n.* the theory, proposed by Jeremy Bentham in the late 1700s, that government actions are useful only if they promote the greatest good for the greatest number of people. (p. 648)

Utopia [yoo·TOH·pee·uh] *n.* an imaginary land described by Thomas More in his book *Utopia*—hence, an ideal place. (p. 425)

U-2 incident *n.* the shooting down of a U.S. spy plane and capture of its pilot by the Soviet Union in 1960. (p. 860)

vassal [VAS·uhl] *n.* in feudal Europe, a person who received a grant of land from a lord in exchange for a pledge of loyalty and services. (p. 324)

Vedas [VAY·duhz] *n.* four collections of sacred writings produced by the Aryans during an early stage of their settlement in India. (p. 59)

vernacular [vuhr·NAK·yuh·luhr] *n.* the everyday language of people in a region or country. (pp. 350, 421)

Vietcong [vee·EHT·KAHNG] *n.* a group of Communist guerrillas who, with the help of North Vietnam, fought against the South Vietnamese government in the Vietnam War. (p. 868)

Vietnamization [vee·EHT·nuh·mih·ZAY·shuhn] *n.* President Richard Nixon's strategy for ending U.S. involvement in the Vietnam War, involving a gradual withdrawal of American troops and replacement of them with South Vietnamese forces. (p. 869)

Vishnu [VIHSH·noo] *n.* a Hindu god considered the preserver of the world. (p. 178)

vizier [vih·ZEER] *n.* a prime minister in a Muslim kingdom or empire. (p. 280)

W

War of the Spanish Succession *n.* a conflict, lasting from 1701 to 1713, in which a number of European states fought to prevent the Bourbon family from controlling Spain as well as France. (p. 523)

Warsaw Pact *n.* a military alliance formed in 1955 by the Soviet Union and seven Eastern European countries. (p. 859)

Weimar [WY·MAHR] **Republic** *n.* the republic that was established in Germany in 1919 and ended in 1933. (p. 802)

Western Front *n.* in World War I, the region of northern France where the forces of the Allies and the Central Powers battled each other. (p. 748)

westernization *n.* an adoption of the social, political, or economic institutions of Western—especially European or American—countries. (p. 533)

XYZ

yin and yang *n.* in Chinese thought, the two powers that govern the natural rhythms of life (with yin representing the feminine qualities in the universe, and yang the masculine qualities). (p. 99)

Yoruba [YAWR·uh·buh] *n.* a West African people who formed several kingdoms in what is now Benin and southern Nigeria. (p. 375)

Zapotec [ZAH·puh·TEHK] *n.* an early Mesoamerican civilization that was centered in the Oaxaca Valley of what is now Mexico. (p. 218)

ziggurat [ZIHG·uh·RAT] *n.* a tiered, pyramid-shaped structure that formed part of a Sumerian temple. (p. 21)

Zionism [ZY·uh·NIHZ·uhm] *n.* a movement founded in the 1890s to promote the establishment of a Jewish homeland in Palestine. (p. 663)

Spanish Glossary

A

Abbasids [abasidas] s.dinastía que gobernó gran parte del imperio musulmán entre 750 y 1258 d.C. (pág. 240)

Aborigine [aborigen] s.miembro de cualquiera de los pueblos nativos de Australia. (pág. 665)

absolute monarch [monarca absoluto] s.rey o reina que tiene poder ilimitado y que procura controlar todos los aspectos de la sociedad. (pág. 517)

absolute ruler [gobernante absoluto] s.gobernante que ejerce todo el poder. (pág. 147)

accommodation [acomodación] s.aceptación de las ideas y constumbres de otras culturas. (pág. 961)

acropolis [acrópolis] s.cima fortificada de las antiguas ciudades griegas. (pág. 115)

Aksum s.reino africano en lo que hoy es Etiopía y Eritrea, que alcanzó su mayor auge en el siglo 4. (pág. 199)

al-Andalus s.región gobernada por los musulmanes en lo que hoy es España, establecida en el siglo 8 d.C. (pág. 240)

Allah [Alah] s.Dios (palabra árabe usada en el islamismo). (pág. 234)

Allies [Aliados] s.durante la I Guerra Mundial, las naciones de Gran Bretaña, Francia y Rusia, junto con otras que lucharon a su lado; también, el grupo de naciones —entre ellas Gran Bretaña, la Unión Soviética y Estados Unidos— opuestas a las Potencias del Eje en la II Guerra Mundial. (pág. 748)

Almohads [almohades] s.grupo de reformadores islámicos que tumbaron la dinastía de los almorávides y que establecieron un imperio en el norte de África y en el sur de España en el siglo 12 d.C. (pág. 370)

Almoravids [almorávides] s.hermandad religiosa islámica que estableció un imperio en el norte de África y en el sur de España en el siglo 11 d.C. (pág. 370)

Anabaptist [anabaptista] s.en la Reforma, miembro de un grupo protestante que enseñaba que sólo los adultos podían ser bautizados, y que la Iglesia y el Estado debían estar separados. (pág. 434)

Anasazi [anasazi] s.grupo amerindio que se estableció en el Suroeste de Norteamérica. (pág. 391)

Anatolia s.península del suroeste de Asia actualmente ocupada por la parte asiática de Turquía; también llamada Asia Menor. (pág. 58)

Angkor Wat s.templo construido en el imperio Khmer y dedicado al dios hindú Visnú. (pág. 309)

Anglican [anglicano] adj. relacionado con la Iglesia de Inglaterra. (pág. 432)

animism [animismo] s.creencia de que en los animales, las plantas y otros objetos naturales habitan espíritus. (pág. 197)

annexation [anexión] s.añadir una región al territorio de una unidad política existente. (págs. 709, 723)

annul [anular] v. cancelar o suspender. (pág. 431)

anti-Semitism [antisemitismo] s.prejuicio contra los judíos. (pág. 663)

apartheid s.política de Sudáfrica de separación total y legalizada de las razas; prohibía todo contacto social entre negros y blancos. (pág. 919)

apostle [apóstol] s.uno de los seguidores de Jesús que predicaba y difundía sus enseñanzas. (pág. 153).

appeasement [apaciguamiento] s.otorgar concesiones a un agresor a fin de evitar la guerra. (pág. 813)

aqueduct [acueducto] s.tubería o canal para llevar agua a zonas pobladas. (pág. 167)

aristocracy [aristocracia] s.gobierno en que el poder está en manos de una clase dominante hereditaria o nobleza. (pág. 115)

armistice [armisticio] s.acuerdo de suspender combates. (pág. 757)

artifact [artefacto] s.objeto hecho por el ser humano, como herramientas, armas o joyas. (pág. 7)

artisan [artesano] s.trabajador especializado, como hilandero o ceramista, que hace productos a mano. (pág. 18)

Aryans [arios] s.**1.** pueblo indoeuropeo que, hacia 1500 a.C., comenzó a emigrar al subcontinente de India. (pág. 59). **2.** para los nazis, los pueblos germanos que formaban una "raza maestra". (pág. 831)

assembly line [línea de montaje] s.en una fábrica, correa que lleva un producto de un trabajador a otro, cada uno de los cuales desempeña una sola tarea. (pág. 674)

assimilation [asimilación] s.**1.** adopción de la cultura del conquistador por un pueblo conquistado. (pág. 185). **2.** política de una nación de obligar o alentar a un pueblo subyugado a adoptar sus instituciones y costumbres. (pág. 691)

Assyria [Asiria] s.reino del suroeste de Asia que controló un gran imperio de aproximadamente 850 a 612 a.C. (pág. 88)

Atlantic Charter [Carta del Atlántico] s.declaración de principios emitida en agosto de 1941 por el primer ministro británico Winston Churchill y el presidente de E.U.A. Franklin Roosevelt, en la cual se basó el plan de paz de los Aliados al final de la II Guerra Mundial. (pág. 826)

Atlantic slave trade [trata de esclavos del Atlántico] s.compra, transporte y venta de africanos para trabajar en las Américas. (pág. 496)

autocracy [autocracia] s.gobierno en el cual el gobernante tiene poder ilimitado y lo usa de forma arbitraria. (pág. 100)

Axis Powers [Potencias del Eje] s.en la II Guerra Mundial, las naciones de Alemania, Italia y Japón, que formaron una alianza en 1936. (pág. 813)

ayllu s.en la sociedad inca, pequeña comunidad o clan cuyos miembros trabajaban conjuntamente para el bien común. (pág. 408)

B

balance of power [equilibrio de poder] s.situación política en que ninguna nación tiene suficiente poder para ser una amenaza para las demás. (pág. 593)

Balfour Declaration [Declaración de Balfour] s.declaración de que el gobierno de Gran Bretaña apoyaba el establecimiento de una patria nacional judía en Palestina, expresada en una carta de 1917 del secretario de relaciones exteriores, Sir Arthur Balfour. (pág. 901)

Balkans [Balcanes] s.región del sureste de Europa ocupada actualmente por Grecia, Albania, Bulgaria, Rumania, la parte eureopea de Turquía y las antiguas repúblicas de Yugoslavia. (pág. 609)

Bantu-speaking peoples [pueblos de habla bantú]

s.hablantes de un grupo de lenguas relacionadas, que hace aproximadamente 2,000 años emigraron de África occidental a casi toda la mitad sur del continente. (pág. 204)

baroque [barroco] s.estilo grandioso y ornamentado del arte, la música y la arquitectura a fines del siglo 17 y principios del 18. (pág. 559)

barter [trueque] s.forma de comercio en la cual se intercambian productos y servicios sin dinero. (pág. 21)

Battle of Britain [Batalla Británica] s.batallas entre las fuerzas aéreas de Alemania y Gran Bretaña que se libraron sobre el territorio británico entre 1940–1941. (pág. 824)

Battle of Guadalcanal [Batalla de Guadalcanal] s.batalla de la II Guerra Mundial ocurrida en 1942–1943 en que las fuerzas aliadas expulsaron a las fuerzas japonesas de la isla de Guadalcanal en el Pacífico. (pág. 830)

Battle of Midway [Batalla del Midway] s.batalla aérea y naval de la II Guerra Mundial librada en 1941 en que las fuerzas estadounidenses derrotaron a las japonesas en el Pacífico central. (pág. 829)

Battle of Stalingrad [Batalla de Stalingrado] s.batalla de la II Guerra Mundial ocurrida en 1942–1943 en que las fuerzas alemanas perdieron y no lograron capturar la ciudad de Stalingrado en la Unión Soviética. (pág. 836)

Battle of the Bulge [Batalla del Bolsón] s.batalla de 1944–45 en que las fuerzas aliadas repulsaron la última ofensiva alemana de envergadura en la II Guerra Mundial. (pág. 839)

Battle of Trafalgar [Batalla de Trafalgar] s.batalla naval de 1805 en que las fuerzas de Napoleón fueron derrotadas por una flota inglesa al mando de Horacio Nelson. (pág. 587)

Benin s.reino que surgió en el siglo 14 cerca del delta del río Níger y llegó a ser un gran Estado de África occidental en el siglo 15. (pág. 377)

Beringia s.antiguo puente terrestre por el que se cree que los primeros habitantes de América migraron de Asia. (pág. 211)

Berlin Conference of 1884–85 [Conferencia de Berlín de 1884] s.reunión en la cual representantes de las naciones europeas acordaron reglas para la colonización europea de África. (pág. 687)

Bill of Rights [Carta de Derechos] s.primeras diez enmiendas a la Constitución de E.U.A., que protegen los derechos y libertades básicos de los ciudadanos. (pág. 567)

bishop [obispo] s.autoridad eclesiástica cristiana que supervisa varias iglesias. (pág. 156)

blitzkrieg s."guerra relámpago"; táctica bélica de ataque sorpresa con aviones rápidos, seguidos de numerosas fuerzas de infantería. (pág. 822)

blockade [bloqueo] s.desplazamiento de tropas o barcos para impedir para evitar la entrada o salida de todo tráfico comercial a una ciudad o región. (pág. 589)

Boer [bóer] s.colono holandés que se estableció en Sudáfrica. (pág. 689)

Boer War [Guerra de los Bóers] s.conflicto de 1899 a 1902 entre los bóers y los británicos por el control de territorio en Sudáfrica. (pág. 689)

Bolsheviks [bolcheviques] s.grupo de marxistas revolucionarios rusos que tomó el control del gobierno ruso en noviembre de 1917. (pág. 770)

Boxer Rebellion [Rebelión de los Bóxers] s.rebelión de 1900 en China contra la influencia extranjera en el país. (pág. 719)

boyars [boyardos] s.nobles terratenientes de Rusia. (págs. 275, 531)

Brahma s.dios hindú considerado creador del mundo. (pág. 178)

Brahmin [brahamán] s.en la sociedad aria, miembro de la clase social formada por los sacerdotes. (pág. 59)

brinkmanship [política arriesgada] s.política de amenazar con lanzarse a la guerra en respuesta a una agresión enemiga. (pág. 860)

Bronze Age [Edad del Bronce] s.período de la historia humana, que comenzó aproximadamente en 3000 a.C. en algunas partes, en el cual se comenzó a usar el bronce, en vez del cobre o la piedra, para elaborar herramientas y armas. (pág. 19)

bubonic plague [peste bubónica] s.enfermedad mortal que se extendió por Asia y Europa a mediados del siglo 14 y que cobró millones de víctimas. (pág. 357)

bureaucracy [burocracia] s.sistema de departamentos y dependencias formado para realizar las labores del gobierno. (pág. 98)

burgher [burgués] s.habitante de un pueblo medieval. (pág. 350)

Bushido s.estricto código de conducta de los guerreros samurai en Japón. (pág. 307)

C

cabinet [gabinete] s.grupo de asesores o ministros escogidos por el jefe de gobierno de un país para que participen en la toma de decisiones del gobierno. (pág. 539)

caliph [califa] s.líder político y religioso supremo de un gobierno musulmán. (pág. 238)

calligraphy [caligrafía] s.arte de escritura manuscrita. (pág. 246)

Calvinism [calvinismo] s.conjunto de enseñanzas religiosas basadas en las ideas del reformador Juan Calvino. (pág. 433)

Camp David Accords [Acuerdos de Camp David] s.primer tratado firmado entre Israel y un país árabe, en que el presidente Anwar Sadat de Egipto reconoció el derecho a existir de Israel y el primer ministro israelí Menachem Begin acordó devolver la península del Sinaí a Egipto. (pág. 903)

canon law [derecho canónico] s.conjunto de leyes que gobierna una iglesia cristiana. (pág. 333)

capitalism [capitalismo] s.sistema económico basado en la propiedad privada y en la inversión de dinero en empresas comerciales con el objetivo de obtener ganancias. (págs. 502, 647)

Carolingian Dynasty [dinastía carolingia] s.dinastía de los reyes francos que abarcó del 751 al 887 d.C. (pág. 320)

caste [casta] s.una de las cuatro clases del sistema social de los arios que se establecieron en India: sacerdotes, guerreros, campesinos o comerciantes, y trabajadores o artesanos no arios. (pág. 60)

cataract [catarata] s.cascada de un río. (pág. 33)

Catholic Reformation [Contrarreforma] s.movimiento del siglo 16 en el que la Iglesia Católica intentó reformarse en respuesta a la Reforma protestante. (pág. 435)

caudillo s.dictador militar de un país latinoamericano. (pág. 724)

centralized government [gobierno centralizado] s.gobierno en que el poder se concentra en una autoridad central a la cual se someten los gobiernos locales. (pág. 181)

Central Powers [Potencias Centrales] s.en la I Guerra Mundial, las naciones de Alemania y Austro-Hungría, y las demás que lucharon a su lado. (pág. 748)

Chaldeans [caldeos] *s.* pueblo del suroeste asiático que contribuyó a destruir el imperio asirio. (pág. 90)

Chartist movement [movimiento cartista] *s.* movimiento de reforma inglés del siglo 19 en que miembros de la clase trabajadora pidieron reformas en el Parlamento y en las elecciones, como el voto para todos los hombres. (pág. 660)

Chavín *s.* primera de las grandes civilizaciones de Suramérica, que floreció en las montañas de lo que hoy es Perú, aproximadamente de 900 a 200 a.C. (pág. 221)

checks and balances [control y compensación de poderes] *s.* medidas para evitar que una rama del gobierno domine sobre las otras. (págs. 566–567)

chivalry [caballería] *s.* código de conducta de los caballeros de la Europa medieval que exaltaba ideales como el valor, la lealtad y la dedicación. (pág. 328)

CIS [CEI] *s.* Comunidad de Estados Independientes: asociación de los antiguos territorios soviéticos formada cuando la Unión Soviética se desmembró. (pág. 928)

city-state [ciudad Estado] *s.* ciudad y tierras de los alrededores que funcionaba como una unidad política independiente. (pág. 29)

civil disobedience [desobediencia civil] *s.* negativa pública y deliberada a obedecer una ley considerada injusta. (pág. 786)

civilization [civilización] *s.* forma de cultura que se caracteriza por tener ciudades, trabajadores especializados, instituciones complejas, un sistema de registro y tecnología avanzada. (pág. 18)

civil rights movement [movimiento de derechos civiles] *s.* lucha popular en Estados Unidos contra la discriminación y por lograr que todos los ciudadanos reciban los derechos garantizados en la Constitución. (pág. 954)

civil service [servicio público] *s.* departamentos administrativos del gobierno, especialmente los que requieren a los candidatos a empleo pasar ciertos exámenes. (pág. 183)

civil war [guerra civil] *s.* conflicto entre dos grupos políticos dentro de un mismo país. (pág. 146)

clan *s.* grupo de descendientes de un antepasado común. (págs. 197, 295)

classical art [arte clásico] *s.* arte común de la antigua Grecia y Roma, que subraya la armonía, el orden y el equilibrio. (pág. 121)

clergy [clero] *s.* conjunto de eclesiásticos que celebran servicios religiosos, como sacerdotes, ministros o rabinos. (pág. 332)

cloning [clonación] *s.* creación de plantas o animales genéticamente idénticos a plantas o animales existentes. (pág. 944)

coalition government [gobierno de coalición] *s.* gobierno controlado por una alianza temporal de varios partidos políticos. (pág. 801)

codex [códice] *s.* libro de páginas que se pueden pasar, como éste. (pág. 398)

Cold War [Guerra Fría] *s.* estado de hostilidad diplomática entre Estados Unidos y la Unión Soviética en las décadas siguientes a la II Guerra Mundial. (pág. 859)

collective bargaining [contrato colectivo] *s.* negociaciones entre trabajadores y patrones. (pág. 650)

collective farm [granja colectiva] *s.* granja controlada por el gobierno, formada mediante la unión de muchas pequeñas granjas. (pág. 777)

colony [colonia] *s.* tierra controlada por una nación distante. (pág. 484)

Colossus of Rhodes [Coloso de Rodas] *s.* enorme estatua helénica que se ubicaba cerca del puerto de Rodas. (pág. 135)

Columbian Exchange [trasferencia colombina] *s.* transferencia mundial de plantas, animales y enfermedades durante la colonización europea de América. (pág. 500)

comedy [comedia] *s.* forma humorística de drama con payasadas y sátira. (pág. 123)

command economy [economía de mando] *s.* sistema económico en el que el gobierno toma todas las decisiones económicas. (pág. 776)

Commercial Revolution [Revolución Comercial] *s.* expansión del comercio y los negocios que transformó las economías europeas en los siglos 16 y 17. (pág. 500)

Committee of Public Safety [Comité de Seguridad Pública] *s.* comité establecido durante la Revolución Francesa para identificar a los "enemigos del pueblo". (pág. 582)

commune [comuna] *s.* en la China comunista, granja colectiva en la que mucha gente trabaja y vive junta. (pág. 864)

communism [comunismo] *s.* sistema económico en el que todos los medios de producción —tierras, minas, fábricas, ferrocarriles y negocios— son propiedad del pueblo, en que no existe la propiedad privada, y en que todos los productos y servicios se comparten por igual. (pág. 649)

Concert of Europe [Concierto de Europa] *s.* serie de alianzas entre naciones europeas en el siglo 19, ideadas por el príncipe Klemens von Metternich para impedir revoluciones. (pág. 595)

concordat [concordato] *s.* acuerdo firmado entre Napoleón y el Papa para establecer una nueva relación entre la Iglesia y el Estado. (pág. 586)

Congress of Vienna [Congreso de Viena] *s.* serie de reuniones en 1814 y 1815 en las cuales los dirigentes europeos trataron de establecer una paz y seguridad duraderas tras la derrota de Napoleón. (pág. 593)

Congress Party [Partido del Congreso] *s.* importante partido político nacional de India; también se llama Congreso Nacional de India. (pág. 886)

conquistadors [conquistadores] *s.* soldados, exploradores y aventureros españoles que participaron en la conquista de América en el siglo 16. (pág. 485)

conservatives [conservadores] *s.* en la primera mitad del siglo 19, los europeos —principalmente los terratenientes y nobles acaudalados— que querían preservar las monarquías tradicionales. (pág. 609)

constitutional monarchy [monarquía constitucional] *s.* monarquía en que el poder del gobernante está limitado por la ley. (pág. 539)

consul [cónsul] *s.* en la república romana, uno de los dos poderosos funcionarios elegidos cada año para comandar el ejército y dirigir el gobierno. (pág. 142)

containment [contención] *s.* política exterior estadounidense adoptada por el presidente Harry Truman a fines de la década de 1940 para impedir la expansión del comunismo creando alianzas con países débiles y ayudándolos a contener los avances soviéticos. (pág. 857)

Continental System [Sistema Continental] *s.* política de Napoleón de impedir el comercio de Gran Bretaña con la Europa continental para destruir la economía británica. (pág. 589)

corporation [corporación] *s.* empresa de accionistas que comparten las ganancias pero que no son personalmente responsables de sus deudas. (pág. 645)

Council of Trent [Concilio de Trento] *s.* reunión de líderes de la Iglesia Católica Romana, convocada por el papa Pablo III, para fallar sobre varias doctrinas criticadas por los reformadores protestantes. (pág. 436)

coup d'etat [golpe de Estado] *s.*toma repentina del poder político de una nación. (pág. 585)

covenant [pacto] *s.*promesa o acuerdo mutuo, especialmente un acuerdo entre Dios y el pueblo hebreo, como los que registra la Biblia. (pág. 73)

creoles [criollos] *s.*en la sociedad española colonial, los colonos nacidos en Latinoamérica de padres españoles. (pág. 604)

Crimean War [Guerra de Crimea] *s.*conflicto de 1853 a 1856, en el cual el imperio otomano, con ayuda de Gran Bretaña y Francia, frenó la expansión rusa en la región del mar Negro. (pág. 698)

crop rotation [rotación de cultivos] *s.*sistema que cultiva distintos productos en un campo cada año para conservar la fertilidad de la tierra. (pág. 633)

Crusade [cruzada] *s.*una de las expediciones de guerreros cristianos medievales para quitarle Jerusalén y la Tierra Santa a los musulmanes. (pág. 343)

cultural diffusion [difusión cultural] *s.*proceso de difusión de ideas o productos de una cultura a otra. (pág. 29)

Cultural Revolution [Revolución Cultural] *s.*levantamiento de 1966–1976 en China, encabezado por los Guardias Rojos de Mao Tsetung, con el propósito de establecer una sociedad de campesinos y trabajadores donde todos fueran iguales. (pág. 865)

culture [cultura] *s.*forma distintiva de la vida de un pueblo, representada en sus herramientas, costumbres, artes y pensamiento. (pág. 7)

cuneiform [cuneiforme] *s.*sistema de escritura que usa símbolos en forma de cuña inventado por los sumerios hacia 3000 a.C. (pág. 18)

Cyrillic alphabet [alfabeto cirílico] *s.*alfabeto inventado en el siglo 9 por los santos Cirilo y Metodio para la escritura de los idiomas eslavos. (pág. 273)

czar [zar] *s.*emperador ruso (de la palabra latina *Caesar).* (pág. 278)

D

daimyo *s.*señor feudal de Japón que comandaba un ejército privado de samurais. (pág. 474)

Daoism [taoísmo] *s.*filosofía basada en las ideas del pensador chino Laozi, quien enseñó a guiarse por una fuerza universal llamada Tao. (pág. 98)

D-Day [Día D] *s.*6 de junio de 1944; día elegido para la invasión aliada de Europa continental durante la II Guerra Mundial. (pág. 838)

Declaration of Independence [Declaración de Independencia] *s.*declaración de las razones de la ruptura de las colonias americanas con Gran Bretaña, aprobada por el Segundo Congreso Continental. (pág. 564)

Declaration of the Rights of Man [Declaración de los Derechos del Hombre] *s.*declaración de ideales revolucionarios adoptada por la Asamblea Nacional Francesa en 1789. (pág. 577)

delta *s.*zona pantanosa que se forma con los depósitos de légamo en la desembocadura de un río. (pág. 34)

demilitarization [desmilitarización] *s.*reducción de la capacidad bélica de un país que se logra desbandando sus fuerzas armadas y prohibiéndole que adquiera armas. (pág. 844)

democracy [democracia] *s.*gobierno controlado por sus ciudadanos, bien sea directa o indirectamente, por medio de sus representantes. (pág. 117)

desertification [desertificación] *s.*transformación de tierras fértiles en desiertos. (pág. 195)

destalinization [desestalinización] *s.*política de Nikita Khrushchev para borrar a José Stalin y sus programas de la memoria de la Unión Soviética. (pág. 876)

détente *s.*política de reducir las tensiones de la Guerra Fría, adoptada por Estados Unidos durante la presidencia de Richard Nixon. (pág. 878)

developed nation [país desarrollado] *s.*nación con las instalaciones necesarias para la producción avanzada de productos manufacturados. (pág. 946)

developing nation [país en desarrollo] *s.*nación en vías de industrialización. (pág. 946)

devshirme *s.*en el imperio otomano, política de llevarse a los niños de los pueblos cristianos conquistados para entrenarlos como soldados musulmanes. (pág. 446)

Diaspora [diáspora] *s.*dispersión de los judíos fuera de Palestina, especialmente en los más de 1800 años que siguieron a la destrucción romana del Templo de Jerusalén en 70 d.C. (pág. 155)

dictator [dictador] *s.*en la antigua Roma, líder político con poder absoluto para decretar leyes y dirigir el ejército por un tiempo limitado. (pág. 143)

direct democracy [democracia directa] *s.*gobierno en el cual los ciudadanos gobiernan directamente, no a través de sus representantes. (pág. 120)

dissident [disidente] *s.*opositor a la política oficial de un gobierno. (pág. 918)

divine right [derecho divino] *s.*noción de que los monarcas son representantes de Dios en la Tierra y, por lo tanto, sólo le deben responder a él. (pág. 517)

domestication [domesticación] *s.*entrenamiento de animales para beneficio humano. (pág. 14)

dominion [dominio] *s.*en el imperio británico, una nación (como Canadá) a la que se permitía gobernar sus asuntos internos. (pág. 665)

domino theory [teoría del dominó] *s.*noción de que si una nación cae bajo control comunista, los países vecinos también lo harán. (pág. 868)

Dorians [dorios] *s.*grupo de lengua griega que, según la tradición, emigró a Grecia después de la destrucción de la civilización micénica. (pág. 113)

Dreyfus affair [caso Dreyfus] *s.*controversia surgida en Francia en la década de 1890 por el juicio y encarcelamiento del capitán Alfred Dreyfus, oficial judío falsamente acusado de vender secretos militares a Alemania. (pág. 663)

Duma *s.*parlamento nacional ruso formado a principios del siglo 20. (pág. 771)

Dutch East India Company [Compañía Holandesa de las Indias Orientales] *s.*empresa fundada por holandeses a principios del siglo 17 para establecer y dirigir comercio por todo Asia. (pág. 468)

dynastic cycle [ciclo dinástico] *s.*patrón histórico del surgimiento, caída y sustitución de dinastías. (pág. 50)

dynasty [dinastía] *s.*serie de gobernantes de una sola familia. (pág. 29)

E

Eastern Front [Frente Oriental] *s.*en la I Guerra Mundial, región a lo largo de la frontera ruso-alemana donde rusos y servios pelearon contra alemanes, austriacos y turcos. (pág. 750)

Edict of Nantes [Edicto de Nantes] *s.*declaración en que el rey francés Enrique IV prometió que los protestantes podían vivir en paz en Francia y tener centros de veneración en algunas ciudades. (pág. 518)

Emancipation Proclamation [Proclama de Emancipación] *s.*declaración emitida por el presidente Abraham Lincoln en 1862, asentando la libertad de todos los esclavos de los estados confederados. (pág. 671)

émigrés *s.*quienes abandonan su país de origen por razones políticas, como los nobles y otros que huyeron de Francia durante los levantamientos campesinos de la Revolución Francesa. (pág. 579)

empire [imperio] *s.*unidad política en que un solo gobernante controla varios pueblos o países. (pág. 31)

enclosure [cercado] *s.*uno de los campos rodeados de cercas o de arbustos que crearon terratenientes británicos ricos en tierras que antes trabajaban los campesinos. (pág. 633)

*encomienda s.*tierras otorgadas por España a un colonizador de América, con el derecho de hacer trabajar a los amerindios que vivían en ellas. (pág. 486)

English Civil War [Guerra Civil Inglesa] *s.*conflicto de 1642 a 1649 en que los seguidores puritanos del Parlamento lucharon contra los defensores de la monarquía de Inglaterra. (pág. 537)

enlightened despot [déspota ilustrado] *s.*uno de los monarcas europeos del siglo 18 inspirados por las ideas de la Ilustración a gobernar con justicia y respeto a los derechos de sus súbditos. (pág. 561)

enlightenment [iluminación] *s.*en budismo, estado de perfecta sabiduría en que se entienden las verdades básicas del universo. (pág. 64)

Enlightenment [Ilustración] *s.*movimiento del siglo 18 en Europa que trató de aplicar los principios de la razón y el método científico a todos los aspectos de la sociedad. (pág. 551)

entrepreneur [empresario] *s.*persona que organiza, administra y asume los riesgos de un negocio. (pág. 636)

epics [epopeyas] *s.*poemas narrativos extensos que celebran las hazañas de héroes tradicionales o legendarios. (pág. 114)

estate [estado] *s.*una de las tres clases sociales existentes en Francia antes de la Revolución Francesa; el primer estado era el de la clerecía; el segundo era el de la nobleza; y el tercero era del resto de la población. (pág. 573)

Estates-General [Estados Generales] *s.*asamblea de representantes de los tres estados, o clases sociales, de Francia. (pág. 575)

ethnic cleansing [limpia étnica] *s.*política de asesinatos y otros actos de brutalidad con que los servios quisieron eliminar la población musulmana de Bosnia después de la división de Yugoslavia. (pág. 929)

excommunication [excomunión] *s.*expulsión de una iglesia cristiana. (pág. 273)

existentialism [existencialismo] *s.*filosofía basada en la idea de que el ser humano da significado a su vida con sus decisiones y acciones. (pág. 796)

extended family [familia extensa] *s.*grupo que incluye a los padres, hijos, abuelos, nietos, tíos y primos. (pág. 197)

extraterritorial rights [derechos extraterritoriales] *s.*exención a los extranjeros de las leyes de un país. (pág. 716)

F

factors of production [factores de producción] *s.*recursos —como tierra, mano de obra y capital— necesarios para producir bienes y servicios. (pág. 634)

factory [fábrica] *s.*construcción amplia en que se manufacturan productos con maquinaria. (pág. 635)

fascism [fascismo] *s.*movimiento político que postula una forma extrema de nacionalismo, la supresión de los derechos individuales y un régimen dictatorial de un solo partido. (pág. 807)

Fatimid [fatimitas] *s.*dinastía musulmana cuyos orígenes se remontan a Fátima, hija de Mahoma, y que construyó un imperio en África del Norte, Arabia y Siria en los siglos 9 a 12. (pág. 240)

favorable balance of trade [balanza comercial favorable] *s.*situación económica en la cual un país exporta más de lo que importa, es decir, que vende más productos de los que compra en el extranjero. (pág. 502)

federal system [sistema federal] *s.*sistema de gobierno en el que el poder se divide entre una autoridad central y varios estados. (págs. 567, 917)

Fertile Crescent [Media Luna Fértil] *s.*arco de ricos terrenos de cultivo en el suroeste de Asia, entre el golfo Pérsico y el mar Mediterráneo. (pág. 27)

feudalism [feudalismo] *s.*sistema político en el cual a los nobles se les otorga el uso de tierras de propiedad del rey, a cambio de lealtad, servicio militar y protección de sus habitantes. (pág. 50)

fief [feudo] *s.*dominio concedido a un vasallo por un señor, conforme al sistema feudal de la Europa medieval. (pág. 324)

filial piety [amor filial] *s.*respeto de los hijos a los padres y a sus mayores. (pág. 97)

Final Solution [solución final] *s.*programa de Hitler de asesinar sistemáticamente a todo el pueblo judío. (pág. 833)

FLN *s.*Frente de Liberación Nacional: grupo de Argelia que libró una lucha de guerrillas buscando independizarse de Francia. (pág. 899)

Four Modernizations [cuatro modernizaciones] *s.*serie de objetivos adoptados por el líder chino Deng Xiaoping a finales del siglo 20 con miras al progreso en agricultura, industria, defensa, y ciencia y tecnología. (pág. 932)

Fourteen Points [los catorce puntos] *s.*serie de propuestas en que el presidente estadounidense Woodrow Wilson esbozó un plan para alcanzar una paz duradera después de la I Guerra Mundial. (pág. 760)

Franks [francos] *s.*pueblo germano que se asentó en la provincia romana de Galia (a grandes rasgos, donde está hoy Francia) y que formó un gran imperio durante la Edad Media. (pág. 318)

free trade [libre comercio] *s.*comercio entre naciones sin restricciones o barreras económicas (tales como aranceles). (pág. 947)

French and Indian War [Guerra contra Franceses e Indígenas] *s.*conflicto entre Gran Bretaña y Francia por control de territorio en Norteamérica, de 1754 a 1763. (pág. 493)

fundamentalism [fundamentalismo] *s.*creencia estricta en las verdades básicas y en las prácticas de una religión. (pág. 953)

G

genetic engineering [ingeniería genética] *s.*transferencia de genes de un organismo a otro para producir un organismo con nuevos rasgos. (pág. 944)

genocide [genocidio] *s.*matanza sistemática de todo un pueblo. (pág. 833)

gentry [pequeña nobleza] *s.*clase de ricos y poderosos que gozan de alto nivel social. (pág. 291)

geopolitics [geopolítica] *s.* política exterior basada en una consideración de la ubicación estratégica o de los productos de otras tierras. (pág. 698)

Ghana *s.* reino de África occidental que se enriqueció debido a recaudación de impuestos y al control del comercio, y que estableció un imperio en los siglos 9 a 11. (pág. 371)

ghazi *s.* guerrero del islam. (pág. 443)

ghettos *s.* barrios en que tenían que vivir los judíos europeos. (pág. 832)

gladiator [gladiador] *s.* en la antigua Roma, luchador profesional que luchaba a muerte contra un contrincante en un circo público. (pág. 151)

glasnost *s.* política soviética de "apertura" a la libre circulación de ideas e información introducida en 1985 por Mijail Gorbachev. (pág 921)

global economy [economía global] *s.* todas las interacciones financieras —entre individuos, empresas y gobiernos— que rebasan fronteras internacionales. (pág. 947)

Glorious Revolution [Revolución Gloriosa] *s.* derrocamiento incruento del rey Jacobo II de Inglaterra, quien fue reemplazado por Guillermo y María. (pág. 539)

glyph [glifo] *s.* dibujo simbólico, especialmente el usado como parte de un sistema de escritura para tallar mensajes en piedra. (pág. 398)

Gothic [gótico] *adj.* relacionado con un nuevo estilo de arquitectura religiosa surgido en la Europa medieval, caracterizado por bóvedas de nervadura, vitrales emplomados, contrafuertes volantes, arcos ojivales y altas agujas. (pág. 342)

Great Depression [Gran Depresión] *s.* crisis económica aguda que siguió a la caída del mercado de valores en 1929. (pág. 804)

Great Fear [Gran Miedo] *s.* ola de temor insensato que se extendió por las provincias francesas después de la toma de la Bastilla en 1789. (pág. 576)

Great Purge [Gran Purga] *s.* campaña de terror en la Unión Soviética durante la década de 1930, en la cual José Stalin trató de eliminar a todos los miembros del Partido Comunista y ciudadanos que amenazaban su poder. (pág. 777)

Great Schism [Gran Cisma] *s.* división de la Iglesia Católica Romana medieval, durante la cual había dos Papas rivales, uno en Avignon y el otro en Roma. (pág. 357)

Great Trek [Gran Jornada] *s.* salida de colonos holandeses de territorio controlado por los británicos en Sudáfrica durante la década de 1830. (pág. 689)

Greco-Roman culture [cultura greco-romana] *s.* antigua cultura producto de la mezcla de la cultura griega, helénica y romana. (pág. 164)

green revolution [revolución verde] *s.* esfuerzo en el siglo 20 de aumentar los alimentos en el mundo entero, a través del uso de fertilizantes y pesticidas, y de la creación de cultivos resistentes a enfermedades. (pág. 944)

griot *s.* narrador de África occidental. (pág. 197)

guerrilla [guerrillero] *s.* miembro de una unidad de combate informal que ataca por sorpresa las tropas enemigas que ocupan su país. (pág. 590)

guild [gremio] *s.* asociación medieval de personas que laboraban en lo mismo; controlaba salarios y precios. (pág. 349)

guillotine [guillotina] *s.* máquina para decapitar con que se hicieron ejecuciones durante la Revolución Francesa. (pág. 580)

Gulf War [Guerra del Golfo] *s.* conflicto de 1991 en que fuerzas de la ONU derrotaron las fuerzas de Iraq que invadieron a Kuwait y amenazaban invadir a Arabia Saudita. (pág. 949)

Gupta Empire [imperio gupta] *s.* el segundo imperio en India, fundado por Chandra Gupta I en el 320 d.C. (pág. 175)

Gutenberg Bible [Biblia de Gutenberg] *s.* primer libro completo impreso con tipos móviles y prensa de imprenta. (pág. 426)

H

habeas corpus *s.* documento que requiere que un detenido comparezca ante un tribunal o juez para que se determine si su detención es legal. (pág. 538)

Hagia Sophia [Santa Sofía] *s.* catedral de la Santa Sabiduría en Constantinopla, construida por orden del emperador bizantino Justiniano. (pág. 270)

haiku *s.* poema japonés que tiene tres versos no rimados de cinco, siete y cinco sílabas. (pág. 476)

hajj *s.* peregrinación a la Meca realizada como deber por los musulmanes. (pág. 236)

Han Dynasty [dinastía Han] *s.* dinastía china que gobernó del 202 a.C. al 9 d.C. y nuevamente del 23 al 220 d.C. (pág. 181)

Hausa [hausa] *s.* pueblo de África occidental que vivía en varias ciudades Estado en el actual norte de Nigeria. (pág. 375)

heliocentric theory [teoría heliocéntrica] *s.* idea de que la Tierra y los otros planetas giran en torno al Sol. (pág. 546)

Hellenistic [helénico] *adj.* relacionado con la civilización, el idioma, el arte, la ciencia y la literatura del mundo griego a partir del reino de Alejandro el Magno hasta el siglo 2 a.C. (pág. 132)

helot [ilota] *s.* en la antigua Esparta, campesino atado a la tierra. (pág. 116)

heresy [herejía] *s.* creencia u opinión religiosa que difiere de las enseñanzas oficiales de la Iglesia Católica. (pág. 157)

hieroglyphics [jeroglíficos] *s.* antiguo sistema de escritura egipcia en el cual se usan imágenes para representar ideas y sonidos. (pág. 38)

Hijrah *s.* migración de Mahoma de la Meca a Yathrib (Medina) en el 622 d.C. (pág. 235)

Hittites [hititas] *s.* pueblo indoeuropeo que se estableció en Anatolia hacia 2000 a.C. (pág. 58)

Holocaust [Holocausto] *s.* matanza en masa de judíos y otros civiles, ejecutada por el gobierno de la Alemania nazi, antes y durante la II Guerra Mundial. (pág. 831)

Holy Alliance [Alianza Sagrada] *s.* liga de naciones europeas formada por los dirigentes de Rusia, Austria y Prusia después del Congreso de Viena. (pág. 595)

Holy Roman Empire [Sacro Imperio Romano] *s.* imperio establecido en Europa en el siglo 10, que inicialmente se formó con tierras de lo que hoy es Alemania e Italia. (pág. 333)

home rule [autogobierno] *s.* control sobre asuntos internos que da el gobierno a los residentes de una región. (pág. 668)

hominid [homínido] *s.* miembro del grupo biológico que abarca a los seres humanos y especies relacionadas que caminan erguidas. (pág. 8)

Homo sapiens s. especie biológica de los seres humanos modernos. (pág. 9)

House of Wisdom [Casa de la Sabiduría] *s.* centro de enseñanza en Bagdad en el siglo 9. (pág. 243)

Hubble Space Telescope [telescopio espacial Hubble] s.potente telescopio puesto en órbita alrededor de la Tierra por NASA y la Agencia Europea del Espacio (AEE) en 1990. (pág. 942)

humanism [humanismo] s.movimiento intelectual del Renacimiento que estudió los textos clásicos y se enfocó en el potencial y los logros humanos. (pág. 418)

Hundred Days [Cien Días] s.corto período de 1815 en que Napoleón hizo su último intento de recuperar el poder, depuso al rey francés y de nuevo se proclamó emperador de Francia. (pág. 592)

Hundred Years' War [Guerra de los Cien Años] s.conflicto en el cual Inglaterra y Francia lucharon en territorio francés de 1337 a 1453, con interrupciones. (pág. 359)

hunter-gatherer [cazador-recolector] s.miembro de un grupo nómada que se alimenta de la caza de animales y la recolección de frutos. (pág. 12)

Hyksos [hicsos] s.grupo nómada de invasores del suroeste de Asia que gobernó Egipto de 1640 a 1570 a.C. (pág. 83)

I

Ice Age [Edad de Hielo] s.período de fríos en que enormes capas de hielo se desplazan de las regiones polares; la última fue de aproximadamente 1,600,000 a 10,000 a.C. (pág. 211)

I Ching s.libro chino de oráculos consultado para solucionar problemas éticos y prácticos. (pág. 99)

icon [icono] s.imagen religiosa usada por los cristianos de Oriente. (pág. 272)

iconoclast [iconoclasta] s.uno de los cristianos de Oriente que destruyó imágenes religiosas en iglesias durante los siglos 8 y 9. (pág. 272)

imperialism [imperialismo] s.política en que una nación fuerte buscar dominar la vida política, económica y social de otros países. (pág. 686)

impressionism [impresionismo] s.movimiento de la pintura del siglo 19 en reacción al realismo, que buscaba dar impresiones personales de sujetos o momentos. (pág. 623)

Indo-Europeans [indoeuropeos] s.grupo de pueblos seminómadas que, hacia 1700 a.C., comenzaron a emigrar de lo que es hoy el sur de Rusia al subcontinente hindú, Europa y el suroeste de Asia. (pág. 57)

indulgence [indulgencia] s.perdón que libera al pecador de la penitencia por un pecado. (pág. 429)

industrialization [industrialización] s.desarrollo de industrias para la producción con máquinas. (pág. 634)

Industrial Revolution [Revolución Industrial] s.cambio, que comenzó en Inglaterra durante el siglo 18, de la producción manual a la producción con máquinas. (pág. 633)

inflation [inflación] s.baja del valor de la moneda, acompañada de un alza de precios de bienes y servicios. (pág. 158)

Inquisition [Inquisición] s.tribunal de la Iglesia Católica para investigar y juzgar a los acusados de herejía, especialmente el establecido en España durante el siglo 15. (pág. 346)

institution [institución] s.patrón duradero de organización en una comunidad. (pág. 18)

intendant [intendente] s.funcionario del gobierno francés nombrado por el monarca para recaudar impuestos e impartir justicia. (pág. 520)

Internet s.vinculación de redes de computadora que permite a gente de todo el mundo comunicarse e intercambiar información. (pág. 943)

iron curtain [cortina de hierro] s.durante la Guerra Fría, división que separaba las naciones comunistas de Europa oriental de las naciones democráticas de Europa occidental. (pág. 857)

Iroquois [iroqueses] s.grupo de pueblos amerindios que hablaban lenguas relacionadas, vivían en la parte este de la región de los Grandes Lagos en Norteamérica y formaron una alianza a fines del siglo 16. (pág. 393)

irrigation [irrigación] s.acarreo de agua a campos de cultivo por medio de canales y acequias. (pág. 28)

Islam [islam] s.religión monoteísta que se desarrolló en Arabia en el siglo 7 d.C. (pág. 234)

isolationism [aislacionismo] s.política de evitar lazos políticos o militares con otros países. (pág. 814)

Israel s.reino de los hebreos unidos en Palestina, de aproximadamente 1020 a 922 a.C.; después, el reino norte de los dos reinos hebreos; actualmente, la nación judía establecida en Palestina en 1948. (pág. 75)

J

Jainism [jainismo] s.religión fundada en India durante el siglo 6, cuyos miembros creen que todo en el universo tiene alma y por lo tanto no debe ser lastimado. (pág. 63)

janissary [janísero] s.miembro de una fuerza élite de soldados del imperio otomano. (pág. 446)

jazz s.estilo de música popular del siglo 20 concebido principalmente por músicos afroamericanos. (pág. 797)

Jesuits [jesuitas] s.miembros de la Sociedad de Jesús, orden católica romana fundada por Ignacio de Loyola. (pág. 435)

"jewel in the crown" ["joya de la corona"] s.colonia británica de India, así llamada por su importancia para el imperio británico, tanto como proveedor de materia prima como mercado para sus productos. (pág. 701)

joint-stock company [sociedad de capitales] s.negocio en el que los inversionistas reúnen capital para un propósito común y después comparten las ganancias. (pág. 502)

Judah [Judea] s.reino hebreo establecido en Palestina alrededor del 922 a.C. (pág. 76)

Justinian Code [Código Justiniano] s.cuerpo del derecho civil romano recopilado y organizado por órdenes del emperador bizantino Justiniano hacia el 534 d.C. (pág. 270)

K

kabuki s.forma de teatro japonés en que se representa una historia con música, danza y mímica. (pág. 476)

kaiser s.emperador alemán (del título romano *Caesar*). (pág. 618)

kamikaze s.durante la II Guerra Mundial, pilotos suicidas japoneses entrenados para hundir barcos de los Aliados lanzándose sobre ellos con aviones llenos de bombas. (pág. 841)

karma s.en hinduismo y budismo, la totalidad de actos buenos y malos que comete una persona, que determinan su destino al renacer. (pág. 63)

Khmer Empire [imperio Khmer] s.imperio del sureste asiático, centrado en la actual Camboya, que alcanzó su mayor auge hacia 1200 d.C. (pág. 309)

Khmer Rouge s.grupo de rebeldes comunistas que tomaron el poder en Camboya en 1975. (pág. 870)

knight [caballero] s.en Europa medieval, guerrero con armadura y cabalgadura. (pág. 324)

Koryu Dynasty [dinastía koryu] s.dinastía coreana del 935 a 1392 d.C. (pág. 311)

Kristallnacht *s.* "Noche de cristales rotos": noche del 9 de noviembre de 1938, en que milicianos nazis atacaron hogares, negocios y sinagogas judíos en toda Alemania. (pág. 831)

kulak *s.* miembro de una clase de campesinos ricos en Rusia. (pág. 777)

Kuomintang *s.* Partido Nacionalista de China, formado después de la caída de la dinastía Qing en 1912. (pág. 781)

Kush *s.* antiguo reino nubio cuyos reyes gobernaron a Egipto del 751 a 671 a.C. (pág. 85)

L

laissez faire *s.* idea de que el gobierno no debe regular ni interferir en las industrias y empresas. (pág. 647)

land reform [reforma agraria] *s.* redistribución de tierras agrícolas con división de grandes latifundios y reparto de fincas a campesinos. (pág. 912)

La Reforma *s.* movimiento de reforma liberal en el siglo 19 en México fundado por Benito Juárez. (pág. 730)

lay investiture [investidura seglar] *s.* nombramiento de funcionarios de la Iglesia por reyes y nobles. (pág. 334)

League of Nations [Liga de las Naciones] *s.* organización internacional formada después de la I Guerra Mundial cuyo propósito era mantener la paz entre las naciones. (pág. 761)

lebensraum *s.* "espacio vital": territorio adicional que, según Adolfo Hitler, Alemania necesitaba porque estaba sobrepoblada. (pág. 809)

Legalism [legalismo] *s.* filosofía política china basada en la idea de que un gobierno altamente eficiente y poderoso es la clave del orden social. (pág. 99)

legion [legión] *s.* unidad militar del ejército de la antigua Roma formada por aproximadamente 5,000 soldados de infantería y grupos de soldados de caballería. (pág. 143)

Legislative Assembly [Asamblea Legislativa] *s.* congreso creado por la Constitución francesa de 1791, con poder para emitir leyes y aprobar declaraciones de guerra. (pág. 578)

legitimacy [legitimidad] *s.* derecho hereditario de un monarca a gobernar. (pág. 594)

liberals [liberales] *s.* en la primera mitad del siglo 19, europeos —principalmente empresarios y comerciantes de clase media— que deseaban darle más poder político a los parlamentos elegidos. (pág. 609)

lineage [linaje] *s.* individuos —vivos, muertos y sin nacer— que descienden de un antepasado común. (pág. 368)

loess [loes] *s.* depósito fértil de tierra traída por el viento. (pág. 46)

Long March [Larga Marcha] *s.* viaje de 6,000 millas que realizaron en 1934–35 las fuerzas comunistas de China para escapar de las fuerzas nacionalistas de Jiang Jieshi. (pág. 784)

lord [señor] *s.* en la Europa feudal, persona que controlaba tierras y por lo tanto podía dar feudos a vasallos. (pág. 324)

Lutheran [luterano] *s.* miembro de una iglesia protestante basada en las enseñanzas de Martín Lutero. (pág. 430)

lycée [liceo] *s.* escuela pública en Francia. (pág. 585)

M

Macedonia *s.* antiguo reino del norte de Grecia, cuyo rey Felipe II conquistó a Grecia en 338 a.C. (pág. 128)

Maghrib [Maghreb] *s.* región del norte de África que abarca la costa del Mediterráneo de lo que en la actualidad es Marruecos, Túnez y Argelia. (pág. 369)

Magna Carta [Carta Magna] *s.* "Gran Carta": documento de Inglaterra que garantiza derechos políticos elementales, elaborado por nobles ingleses y aprobado por el rey Juan en 1215 d.C. (pág. 353)

Mahabharata *s.* gran poema épico de India que relata las luchas arias durante su migración al sur de India. (pág. 60)

Mahayana *s.* secta del budismo que ofrece la salvación a todos y permite la veneración popular. (pág. 177)

maize [maíz] *s.* cereal cultivado cuyos granos se encuentran en grandes espigas, o mazorcas. (pág. 213)

Mali *s.* imperio de África occidental que floreció entre 1235 y el siglo 15, y se enriqueció con el comercio. (pág. 373)

mamelukes [mamelucos] *s.* esclavos turcos que sirvieron como soldados y guardaespaldas en el imperio abasida. (pág. 279)

Manchus [manchú] *s.* pueblo originario de Manchuria que gobernó en China durante la dinastía Qing (1644–1912). (pág. 471)

Mandate of Heaven [Mandato del Cielo] *s.* en China, creencia de que la autoridad real era producto de la aprobación divina. (pág. 50)

manifest destiny [destino manifiesto] *s.* idea popular en el siglo 19 en Estados Unidos de que era su derecho y obligación regir Norteamérica, desde el océano Atlántico hasta el Pacífico. (pág. 670)

manor [señorío] *s.* dominios de un señor en la Europa feudal. (pág. 325)

Maori [maorí] *s.* miembro de un pueblo polinesio establecido en Nueva Zelanda hacia 800 d.C. (pág. 665)

Marshall Plan [Plan Marshall] *s.* programa estadounidense de ayuda económica a países europeos para su reconstrucción después de la II Guerra Mundial. (pág. 858)

martial law [ley marcial] *s.* gobierno militar temporal impuesto a la población civil, normalmente en época de guerra o de trastornos civiles. (pág. 917)

mass culture [cultura de masas] *s.* producción de obras de arte y diversión concebidas con el fin de atraer a un amplio público. (pág. 674)

materialism [materialismo] *s.* alto interés en la adquisición de posesiones materiales. (pág. 960)

matriarchal [matriarcal] *adj.* relacionado con un sistema social en el que la madre es jefa de la familia. (pág. 176)

matrilineal *adj.* relacionado con un sistema social en el que la descendencia familiar y los derechos de herencia se trasmiten a través de la madre. (pág. 369)

Mau Mau [Mau-mau] *s.* sociedad secreta de miembros de la tribu kikuyu que trataron de expulsar a los británicos de Kenia a mediados del siglo 20. (pág. 897)

Mauryan Empire [imperio maurio] *s.* primer imperio de India, fundado por Chandragupta Mauria en 321 a.C. (pág. 173)

May Fourth Movement [Movimiento del 4 de Mayo] *s.* protesta nacional china en 1919 con manifestaciones contra el Tratado de Versalles y la interferencia extranjera. (pág. 782)

Medes [medos] *s.* pueblo del suroeste asiático que contribuyó a derrotar al imperio asirio. (pág. 90)

Meiji era [era Meiji] *s.* período de la historia japonesa entre 1867 y 1912, cuando gobernó el emperador Mutshito. (pág. 721)

Mein Kampf [Mi lucha] *s.* libro escrito por Adolfo Hitler en prisión (1923–1924), en el cual expone sus creencias y sus ideales para Alemania. (pág. 809)

1038 SPANISH GLOSSARY

mercantilism [mercantilismo] *s.* política económica de aumentar la riqueza y poder de una nación obteniendo grandes cantidades de oro y plata, y vendiendo más bienes de los que se compran. (pág. 502)

mercenary [mercenario] *s.* soldado que recibe sueldo por pelear en un ejército extranjero. (pág. 159)

Mesoamerica [Mesoamérica] *s.* región que se extiende desde el centro de México hasta Honduras, donde se desarrollaron varias de las antiguas sociedades complejas de América. (pág. 216)

mestizo *s.* mezcla de español y amerindio. (pág. 486)

Middle Ages [Edad Media] *s.* era en la historia europea posterior a la caída del imperio romano, que abarca aproximadamente desde el 500 hasta 1500, también llamada época medieval. (pág. 317)

middle class [clase media] *s.* clase social formada por trabajadores especializados, profesionales, comerciantes y granjeros acaudalados. (pág. 639)

middle passage [travesía intermedia] *s.* viaje que trajo a africanos capturados al Caribe y, posteriormente, a América del Norte y del Sur, para venderlos como esclavos; recibió este nombre porque era considerada la porción media del triángulo comercial trasatlántico. (pág. 497)

migration [migración] *s.* acto de trasladarse de un lugar para establecerse en otro. (pág. 57)

militarism [militarismo] *s.* política de glorificar el poder militar y de mantener un ejército permanente, siempre preparado para luchar. (pág. 744)

Ming Dynasty [dinastía Ming] *s.* dinastía que reinó en China desde 1368 hasta 1644. (pág. 469)

Minoans [minoicos] *s.* pueblo de navegantes y comerciantes que vivió en la isla de Creta de aproximadamente 2000 a 1400 a.C. (pág. 67)

Mississippian [misisipiense] *adj.* relacionado con una cultura constructora de túmulos que floreció en Norteamérica entre el 800 y 1500 d.C. (pág. 393)

mita *s.* en el imperio inca, obligación de todo súbdito de trabajar ciertos días al año para el Estado. (pág. 409)

Moche [moche] *s.* civilización que floreció en la actual costa norte de Perú de aproximadamente 100 a 700 d.C. (pág. 222)

monarchy [monarquía] *s.* gobierno en que el poder está en manos de una sola persona. (pág. 115)

monastery [monasterio] *s.* comunidad religiosa de hombres, llamados monjes, que ceden todas sus posesiones y se dedican a la oración y veneración. (pág. 318)

monopoly [monopolio] *s.* control exclusivo sobre la producción y distribución de ciertos bienes. (pág. 185)

monotheism [monoteísmo] *s.* creencia en un solo dios. (pág. 73)

Monroe Doctrine [doctrina Monroe] *s.* política estadounidense de oposición a la interferencia europea en Latinoamérica, anunciada por el presidente James Monroe en 1823. (pág. 726)

monsoon [monzón] *s.* viento que cambia de dirección en ciertas épocas del año. (pág. 42)

mosque [mezquita] *s.* lugar de veneración islámica. (pág. 236)

movable type [tipo móvil] *s.* bloques de metal o de madera, cada uno con caracteres individuales, que pueden distribuirse para formar una página de impresión. (pág. 289)

Mughal [mogol] *s.* uno de los nómadas que invadieron el subcontinente de India en el siglo 16 y establecieron un poderoso imperio. (pág. 451)

mulattos [mulatos] *s.* personas de ascendencia europea y africana. (pág. 604)

multinational corporation [corporación trasnacional] *s.* empresa que opera en numerosos países. (pág. 947)

mummification [momificación] *s.* proceso de embalsamamiento y secado de cadáveres para evitar su descomposición. (pág. 37)

Munich Conference [Conferencia de Munich] *s.* reunión en 1938 de Inglaterra, Francia, Italia y Alemania, en la cual Gran Bretaña y Francia aceptaron que la Alemania nazi anexara parte de Checoslovaquia, a cambio de la promesa de Adolfo Hitler de respetar las nuevas fronteras checas. (pág. 815)

Muslim [musulmán] *s.* devoto del islam. (pág. 235)

Muslim League [Liga Musulmana] *s.* organización formada en 1906 para proteger los intereses de los musulmanes de India; después propuso la división del país en dos naciones: una musulmana y una hindú. (pág. 886)

Mutapa [mutapa] *adj.* con un imperio de África del sur establecido por Mutota en el siglo 15 a.D. (pág. 381)

Mycenaeans [micénicos] *s.* grupo indoeuropeo que se estableció en Grecia hacia 2000 a.C. (pág. 112)

myths [mitos] *s.* narraciones tradicionales sobre dioses, antepasados o héroes, que explican el mundo natural o las costumbres y creencias de una sociedad. (pág. 114)

N

Napoleonic Code [código napoleónico] *s.* sistema extenso y uniforme de leyes establecido para Francia por Napoleón. (pág. 586)

National Assembly [Asamblea Nacional] *s.* congreso francés establecido el 17 de junio de 1789 por representantes del Tercer Estado para promulgar leyes y reformas en nombre del pueblo. (pág. 575)

nationalism [nacionalismo] *s.* creencia de que la principal lealtad del pueblo debe ser a su nación —es decir, a la gente con quien comparte historia y cultura— y no al rey o al imperio. (pág. 609)

nation-state [nación Estado] *s.* nación independiente de gente que tiene una cultura e identidad común. (pág. 609)

NATO [OTAN] *s.* Organización del Tratado del Atlántico Norte: alianza militar defensiva formada en 1949 por diez naciones de Europa occidental, Estados Unidos y Canadá. (pág. 859)

natural rights [derechos naturales] *s.* derechos con los que nacen todos los individuos, conforme a John Locke: vida, libertad y propiedad. (pág. 551)

Nazca [nazca] *s.* civilización que floreció en la actual costa sur de Perú de 200 a.C. a 600 d.C. (pág. 222)

Nazism [nazismo] *s.* políticas fascistas del Partido Nacional socialista de los Trabajadores de Alemania, basadas en el totalitarismo, la creencia en superioridad racial y el control estatal de la industria. (pág. 808)

Negritude movement [movimiento de negritud] *s.* movimiento de africanos de lengua francesa que celebra el legado de la cultura tradicional africana y sus valores. (pág. 896)

neoclassical [neoclásico] *adj.* relacionado con un estilo sencillo y elegante (inspirado en ideas y temas de la antigua Grecia y Roma) que caracterizó las artes en Europa a fines del siglo 18. (pág. 559)

Neolithic Age [Neolítico] *s.* período prehistórico que comenzó aproximadamente en 8000 a.C. y en algunas partes acabó desde 3000 a.C., durante el cual los grupos humanos aprendieron a pulir herramientas de piedra, hacer cerámica, cultivar alimentos y criar animales; también se llama Nueva Edad de Piedra. (pág. 8)

Neolithic Revolution [Revolución Neolítica] *s.* gran cambio en la vida humana causada por los comienzos de la agricultura; es decir, el cambio de recolectar a producir alimentos. (pág. 14)

New Deal *s.* programa de reformas económicas del presidente Franklin D. Roosevelt ideado para solucionar los problemas creados por la Gran Depresión. (pág. 806)

New Kingdom [Reino Nuevo] *s.* período de la historia del antiguo Egipto tras la caída de los gobernantes hicsos, desde 1570 hasta 1075 a.C. (pág. 83)

nirvana *s.* en budismo, la liberación del dolor y el sufrimiento alcanzada después de la iluminación. (pág. 65)

Nok [nok] *s.* pueblo africano que vivió en lo que es hoy Nigeria entre 500 a.C. y 200 d.C. (pág. 198)

nomad [nómada] *s.* miembro de un grupo que no tiene hogar permanente y que va de un lugar a otro en busca de agua y alimento. (pág. 12)

nonaggression pact [pacto de no agresión] *s.* acuerdo en que dos o más naciones prometen no atacarse. (pág. 821)

nonaligned nations [países no alineados] *s.* naciones independientes que permanecieron neutrales durante la Guerra Fría entre Estados Unidos y la Unión Soviética. (pág. 871)

Nuclear Non-Proliferation Treaty [Tratado de No Proliferación Nuclear] *s.* acuerdo de 1968 ideado para reducir la diseminación de las armas nucleares. (pág. 953)

Nuremberg Trials [juicios de Nuremberg] *s.* serie de juicios realizados en Nuremberg, Alemania, tras la II Guerra Mundial a líderes nazis por agresión, violación a las leyes de guerra y crímenes contra la humanidad. (pág. 843)

O

obsidian [obsidiana] *s.* roca volcánica dura y vítrea con que los primeros seres humanos elaboraban herramientas de piedra. (pág. 400)

Old Regime [antiguo régimen] *s.* sistema político y social que existía en Francia antes de la Revolución Francesa. (pág. 573)

oligarchy [oligarquía] *s.* gobierno en que el poder está en manos de pocas personas, particularmente un gobierno que se basa en la riqueza. (pág. 115)

Olmec [olmeca] *s.* civilización mesoamericana más antigua que se conoce, que floreció hacia 1200 a.C. e influyó sobre las posteriores sociedades de la región. (pág. 216)

Open Door Policy [política de puertas abiertas] *s.* política propuesta por E.U.A. en 1899, que postulaba que todas las naciones tuvieran las mismas oportunidades de comerciar con China. (pág. 718)

Opium War [Guerra del Opio] *s.* conflicto entre Inglaterra y China, de 1839 a 1842, por el comercio inglés de opio en China. (pág. 716)

oracle bone [hueso de oráculo] *s.* hueso de animal o caparazón de tortuga que usaban los antiguos sacerdotes chinos para comunicarse con los dioses. (pág. 48)

ozone layer [capa de ozono] *s.* capa de la atmósfera superior de la Tierra que protege a los seres vivos de los rayos ultravioleta de la luz solar. (pág. 949)

P

Pacific Rim [Cuenca del Pacífico] *s.* tierras que bordean el océano Pacífico, especialmente las de Asia. (pág. 706)

Paleolithic Age [Paleolítico] *s.* período prehistórico que abarcó aproximadamente desde 2.5 millones hasta 8000 a.C., durante el cual los seres humanos hicieron rudi-mentarias herramientas y armas de piedra; también se llama Antigua Edad de Piedra. (pág. 8)

Panama Canal [canal de Panamá] *s.* vía marítima que une al océano Atlántico con el Pacífico, construida en Panamá por Estados Unidos y terminada en 1914. (pág. 727)

papyrus [papiro] *s.* carrizo alto que crece en el delta del Nilo, usado por los antiguos egipcios para hacer hojas de escribir similares al papel. (pág. 38)

parliament [parlamento] *s.* cuerpo de representantes que promulga las leyes de una nación. (pág. 354)

partition [partición] *s.* división en partes, como la división en 1947 de la colonia británica de India en dos naciones: India y Paquistán. (pág. 886)

pastoralist [pastor] *s.* miembro de un grupo nómada que pastorea rebaños de animales domesticados. (pág. 294)

paternalism [paternalismo] *s.* política de tratar a los gobernados como si fueran niños, atendiendo a sus necesidades pero sin darles derechos. (pág. 691)

patriarch [patriarca] *s.* obispo principal de la rama oriental de la cristiandad. (pág. 272)

patriarchal [patriarcal] *adj.* relacionado con un sistema social en el que el padre es jefe de la familia. (pág. 176)

patrician [patricio] *s.* en la antigua Roma, miembro de la clase alta, privilegiada y rica. (pág. 142)

patrilineal [patrilineal] *adj.* relacionado con un sistema social en el que la descendencia y los derechos de herencia se trasmiten a través del padre. (pág. 369)

patron [mecenas] *s.* persona que apoya a los artistas, especialmente, en el aspecto financiero. (pág. 418)

Pax Romana *s.* período de paz y prosperidad por todo el imperio romano, de 27 a.C. a 180 d.C. (pág. 148)

Peace of Augsburg [Paz de Augsburgo] *s.* acuerdo realizado en 1555 que declaró que la religión de cada Estado alemán sería decidida por su gobernante. (pág. 430)

Peloponnesian War [Guerra del Peloponeso] *s.* guerra de 431 a 404 a.C., en la cual Atenas y sus aliados resultaron derrotados por Esparta y sus aliados. (pág. 123)

penal colony [colonia penal] *s.* colonia a donde se mandan convictos como alternativa a una prisión. (pág. 665)

peninsulares *s.* en la sociedad española colonial, colonos nacidos en España. (pág. 604)

Peninsular War [Guerra Peninsular] *s.* conflicto de 1808–1813 en que los rebeldes españoles lucharon con la ayuda de Gran Bretaña para expulsar de España las tropas de Napoleón. (pág. 590)

perestroika *s.* reestructuración de la economía soviética para permitir mayor poder de decisión local, iniciada por Mijail Gorbachev en 1985. (pág. 922)

Persian Wars [Guerras Pérsicas] *s.* guerras del siglo 5 a.C. entre las ciudades Estado de Grecia y el imperio persa. (pág. 118)

perspective [perspectiva] *s.* técnica artística que crea la apariencia de tres dimensiones en una superficie plana. (pág. 419)

phalanx [falange] *s.* formación militar de soldados de infantería armados con lanzas y escudos. (pág. 115)

pharaoh [faraón] *s.* rey del antiguo Egipto, considerado dios, así como líder político y militar. (pág. 35)

philosophe *s.* miembro de un grupo de pensadores sociales de la Ilustración en Francia. (pág. 552)

philosophers [filósofos] *s.* pensadores que investigan la naturaleza del universo, la sociedad humana y la moral a través de la lógica y la razón. (pág. 124)

Phoenicians [fenicios] *s.* pueblo de navegantes del suroeste de Asia, que aproximadamente en 1100 a.C. comenzó a comerciar y a fundar colonias en la región mediterránea. (pág. 68)

Pilgrims [peregrinos] *s.*grupo que en 1620 fundó la colonia de Plymouth en Massachusetts para escapar de persecución religiosa en Inglaterra. (pág. 491)

plebeian [plebeyo] *s.*en la antigua Roma, uno de los agricultores, artesanos o comerciantes comunes que conformaban la mayoría de la población. (pág. 142)

plebiscite [plebiscito] *s.*voto directo mediante el cual la población de un país tiene la oportunidad de aceptar o rechazar una propuesta. (pág. 585)

PLO [OLP] *s.*Organización de Liberación Palestina: organización dedicada a establecer un Estado independiente para los palestinos en el Medio Oriente. (pág. 905)

pogrom *s.*campaña organizada de violencia contra las comunidades judías en Rusia a finales del siglo 19. (pág. 769)

polis *s.*ciudad Estado de Grecia; unidad política fundamental de la antigua Grecia a partir de 750 a.C. (pág. 115)

Politburo [Politburó] *s.*comité dirigente del Partido Comunista en la Unión Soviética. (pág. 921)

polytheism [politeísmo] *s.*creencia en muchos dioses. (pág. 29)

pope [Papa] *s.*obispo de Roma y dirigente de la Iglesia Católica Romana. (pág. 156)

Popol Vuh *s.*libro que narra una versión de la historia maya de la creación. (pág. 398)

popular culture [cultura popular] *s.*elementos culturales —deportes, música, cine, ropa, etc.— que muestran los antecedentes comunes de un grupo y sus intereses cambiantes. (pág. 957)

potlatch *s.*fiesta ceremonial celebrada para mostrar rango y prosperidad en varias tribus del Noroeste de Norteamérica. (pág. 391)

predestination [predestinación] *s.*doctrina que postula que Dios ha decidido todo de antemano, incluso quiénes obtendrán la salvación eterna. (pág. 433)

Presbyterian [presbiteriano] *s.*miembro de una iglesia protestante gobernada por presbíteros conforme a las enseñanzas de John Knox. (pág. 433)

PRI *s.*Partido Revolucionario Institucional: principal partido político en México. (pág. 914)

printing press [prensa de imprenta] *s.*máquina para reproducir material escrito oprimiendo papel contra una bandeja de tipos móviles entintados. (pág. 426)

proliferation [proliferación] *s.*crecimiento o expansión, especialmente la expansión de armas nucleares a naciones que actualmente no las tienen. (pág. 953)

propaganda *s.*información o material distribuido para apoyar una causa o socavar una causa opuesta. (pág. 756)

Protestant [protestante] *s.*miembro de una iglesia cristiana fundada de acuerdo a los principios de la Reforma. (pág. 430)

provisional government [gobierno provisional] *s.*gobierno temporal. (pág. 772)

psychology [psicología] *s.*estudio de la mente y la conducta humanas. (pág. 679)

pueblos *s.*aldeas similares a complejos departamentales hechos de adobe, construidas por los anasazi y pueblos posteriores en el Suroeste de lo que hoy es Estados Unidos. (pág. 391)

Puritans [puritanos] *s.*grupo que, para liberarse de la persecución religiosa en Inglaterra, fundó una colonia en la bahía de Massachusetts a principios del siglo 17. (pág. 491)

pyramid [pirámide] *s.*enorme estructura de base rectangular y cuatro lados triangulares, como las que servían de tumba de los faraones del Reino Antiguo de Egipto. (pág. 35)

Qin Dynasty [dinastía Qin] *s.*dinastía china que reinó brevemente y sustituyó a la dinastía Zhou en el siglo 3 a.C. (pág. 99)

Qing Dynasty [dinastía Qing] *s.*última dinastía china; reinó de 1644 a 1912. (pág. 471)

Quetzalcoatl [Quetzalcóatl] *s.*serpiente emplumada: dios de los toltecas y otros pueblos de Mesoamérica. (pág. 401)

quipu *s.*cuerda con nudos usadas para registrar información numérica por los incas. (pág. 410)

Qur'an [*Corán*] *s.*libro sagrado del islam. (pág. 236)

Racism [racismo] *s.*creencia de que una raza es superior a otras. (pág. 686)

radicals [radicales] *s.*en la primera mitad del siglo 19, los europeos a favor de cambios drásticos para extender la democracia a toda la población. (pág. 609)

radioactivity [radioactividad] *s.*forma de energía liberada mediante la descomposición de átomos. (pág. 678)

Raj *s.*porciones de India controladas por Gran Bretaña de 1757 a 1947. (pág. 704)

rationing [racionamiento] *s.*limitación de la cantidad de bienes que la población puede comprar, generalmente impuesta por un gobierno durante una guerra debido a escasez. (pág. 755)

realism [realismo] *s.*movimiento artístico del siglo 19 en que los escritores y pintores trataron de mostrar la vida como es, no como debiera ser. (pág. 621)

realpolitik *s.*"política de la realidad"; posición política dura que no da lugar al idealismo. (pág. 617)

recession [recesión] *s.*descenso de la economía de una nación. (pág. 913)

Reconquista *s.*campaña de líderes cristianos para expulsar a los musulmanes de España, que empezó en el siglo 12 y terminó en 1492. (pág. 346)

Red Guards [Guardias Rojos] *s.*unidades de milicianos formadas por jóvenes chinos en 1966 en respuesta al llamado de Mao Zedong a llevar a cabo una revolución social y cultural. (pág. 865)

Red Shirts [Camisas Rojas] *s.*seguidores del líder nacionalista italiano del siglo 19 Giuseppe Garibaldi. (pág. 616)

Reformation [Reforma] *s.*movimiento del siglo 16 para realizar cambios religiosos que llevó a la fundación de iglesias cristianas que rechazaron la autoridad del Papa. (pág. 429)

Reign of Terror [Régimen del Terror] *s.*período entre 1793–1794 en que Maximilien Robespierre gobernó a Francia casi como dictador, durante el cual fueron ejecutados miles de personajes políticos y de ciudadanos comunes. (pág. 582)

reincarnation [reencarnación] *s.*en hinduismo y budismo, creencia de que el alma renace una y otra vez hasta alcanzar un conocimiento perfecto. (pág. 63)

religious toleration [tolerancia religiosa] *s.*reconocimiento del derecho de otros a tener creencias religiosas diferentes. (pág. 174)

Renaissance [Renacimiento] *s.*período de la historia europea de aproximadamente 1300 a 1600, durante el cual renació un interés en la cultura clásica que generó

SPANISH GLOSSARY 1041

importantes cambios en el arte, la educación y la visión del mundo. (pág. 417)

republic [república] *s.* forma de gobierno en que el poder está en manos de representantes y líderes elegidos por los ciudadanos. (pág. 142)

Restoration [Restauración] *s.* en Inglaterra, período del reinado de Carlos II, después del colapso del gobierno de Oliver Cromwell. (pág. 538)

reunification [reunificación] *s.* proceso de unir dos elementos que estaban separados, como la reunificación de Alemania oriental y Alemania occidental en 1990. (pág. 924)

romanticism [romanticismo] *s.* movimiento de principios del siglo 19 en el arte y las ideas que recalca la emoción y la naturaleza, más que la razón y la sociedad. (pág. 619)

Roosevelt Corollary [corolario Roosevelt] *s.* ampliación de la doctrina Monroe, emitida por el presidente Theodore Roosevelt en 1904, en que declaró que Estados Unidos tenía el derecho de ejercer "poderes policiales" en el hemisferio occidental. (pág. 727)

Royal Road [Camino Real] *s.* carretera de más de 1,600 millas que cruzaba el imperio persa, desde Susa en Persia hasta Sardes en Anatolia. (pág. 94)

Russo-Japanese War [Guerra Ruso-Japonesa] *s.* conflicto de 1904–1905 entre Rusia y Japón, causada por el interés de los dos países de dominar Manchuria y Corea. (pág. 723)

S

sacrament [sacramento] *s.* una de las ceremonias cristianas en que se trasmite la gracia de Dios a los creyentes. (pág. 332)

Safavid [safávido] *s.* miembro de una dinastía musulmana shi'a que construyó un imperio en Persia del siglo 16 al 18. (pág. 449)

Sahel *s.* región africana a lo largo de la frontera sur del Sahara. (pág. 195)

salon [salón] *s.* reunión social de intelectuales y artistas, como las que celebraban en sus hogares señoras acaudaladas de París y otras ciudades europeas durante la Ilustración. (pág. 558)

SALT *s.* Conversaciones para la Limitación de Armas Estratégicas: serie de reuniones durante la década de 1970 en que líderes de Estados Unidos y la Unión Soviética acordaron limitar el número de armas nucleares de sus países. (pág. 879)

samurai *s.* guerrero profesional que servía a los nobles en el Japón feudal. (pág. 307)

sans-culottes *s.* en la Revolución Francesa, grupo político radical de parisienses asalariados y pequeños comerciantes que anhelaban más voz en el gobierno, bajas de precios y fin a la escasez de alimentos. (pág. 579)

satrap [sátrapa] *s.* gobernador de una provincia en el imperio persa. (pág. 94)

savanna [sabana] *s.* planicie con pastizales. (pág. 195)

schism [cisma] *s.* separación o división, especialmente la división formal de una iglesia cristiana. (pág. 273)

Schlieffen Plan [Plan Schlieffen] *s.* plan militar alemán al comienzo de la I Guerra Mundial, que preveía que Alemania derrotaría rápidamente a Francia y después atacaría a Rusia en el este. (pág. 747)

scholastics [escolásticos] *s.* académicos que se reunían y enseñaban en las universidades medievales de Europa. (pág. 351)

scientific method [método científico] *s.* procedimiento lógico para reunir información sobre el mundo natural, en que se usa experimentación y observación para poner a prueba hipótesis. (pág. 547)

Scientific Revolution [Revolución Científica] *s.* profundo cambio en el pensamiento europeo que comenzó a mediados del siglo 16, en que el estudio del mundo natural se caracterizó por cuidadosa observación y cuestionamiento de teorías aceptadas. (pág. 545)

scorched-earth policy [política de arrasamiento de campos] *s.* práctica de quemar campos de cultivo y de matar ganado durante la guerra para que el enemigo no pueda vivir de las tierras. (pág. 590)

scribe [escriba] *s.* profesional especializado en llevar registros en las civilizaciones tempranas. (pág. 18)

secede [seceder] *v.* retirarse formalmente de una asociación o alianza. (pág. 670)

secular *adj.* relacionado con lo mundano más que con los asuntos espirituales. (págs. 319, 418)

segregation [segregación] *s.* separación legal o social de gente de diferentes razas. (pág. 672)

self-determination [autodeterminación] *s.* libertad de un pueblo para decidir libremente la forma de gobierno que desea. (pág. 760)

Seljuks [seljucs] *s.* grupo turco que emigró al imperio abasida en el siglo 10 y estableció su propio imperio en el siglo 11. (pág. 279)

senate [senado] *s.* en la antigua Roma, organismo supremo de gobierno formado inicialmente sólo por aristócratas. (pág. 143)

separation of powers [separación de poderes] *s.* división de poderes del gobierno en ejecutivo, legislativo y judicial. (pág. 553)

sepoy [cipayo] *s.* soldado hindú bajo el mando británico. (pág. 701)

Sepoy Mutiny [Motín de Cipayos] *s.* rebelión de 1857 de soldados hindúes y musulmanes contra los británicos en India. (pág. 703)

serf [siervo] *s.* campesino medieval legalmente obligado a vivir en los dominios de un señor. (pág. 324)

Seven Years' War [Guerra de los Siete Años] *s.* conflicto en Europa, Norteamérica e India de 1756 a 1763, en que las fuerzas de Inglaterra y Prusia lucharon con las de Austria, Francia, Rusia y otros países. (pág. 530)

shari'a *s.* conjunto de leyes que rigen la vida de los musulmanes. (pág. 237)

Shi'a [shi'a] *s.* rama del islam que reconoce a los primeros cuatro califas como legítimos sucesores de Mahoma. (pág. 240)

Shinto [shintoísmo] *s.* religión oriunda de Japón. (pág. 303)

Shiva *s.* dios hindú considerado destructor del mundo. (pág. 178)

"shock therapy" [terapia de shock] *s.* programa económico implementado en Rusia por Boris Yeltsin en la década de 1990, que implicó un cambio abrupto de una economía de mando a una economía de mercado libre. (pág. 928)

shogun [shogún] *s.* en el Japón feudal, jefe militar supremo que regía en nombre del emperador. (pág. 307)

Sikh [sikh] *s.* miembro de un grupo religioso no violento cuyas creencias combinaban elementos del budismo, el hinduismo y el sufismo. (pág. 454)

Silk Roads [Ruta de la Seda] *s.* sistema de antiguas rutas de las caravanas por Asia central, por las que se transportaban seda y otros productos comerciales. (pág. 179)

silt [légamo] *s.* tierra que arrastran las aguas de los ríos. (pág. 27)

simony [simonía] *s.* venta o compra de una posición en una iglesia cristiana. (pág. 341)

Six-Day War [Guerra de los Seis Días] *s.* breve conflicto en 1967 entre Israel y varios países árabes, durante el cual Israel se apoderó de Jerusalén, la península del Sinaí, la meseta de Golán y Cisjordania. (pág. 903)

skepticism [escepticismo] *s.* filosofía basada en la noción de que nada puede saberse con certeza. (pág. 519)

slash-and-burn farming [agricultura de tala y quema] *s.* método agrícola de desbrozar terrenos talando y quemando árboles y pastos, cuyas cenizas sirven como fertilizante. (pág. 14)

Slavs [eslavos] *s.* pueblo de los bosques al norte del mar Negro, origen de muchos pueblos de la Europa oriental de nuestros días. (pág. 274)

social contract [contrato social] *s.* acuerdo mediante el cual el pueblo define y limita sus derechos individuales, creando así una sociedad o gobierno organizados. (pág. 551)

Social Darwinism [darvinismo social] *s.* aplicación de las teorías de Charles Darwin sobre la evolución y la "sobrevivencia del más apto" a las sociedades humanas, particularmente como justificación para la expansión imperialista. (pág. 686)

socialism [socialismo] *s.* sistema económico en el cual los factores de producción son propiedad del pueblo y se administran para el bienestar de todos. (pág. 648)

socialist realism [realismo socialista] *s.* estilo artístico que exalta los valores comunistas y la vida bajo el comunismo. (pág. 778)

Solidarity [Solidaridad] *s.* sindicato polaco de trabajadores que presentó la principal fuerza de oposición al gobierno comunista en Polonia en la década de 1980. (pág. 922)

Songhai *s.* imperio de África occidental que conquistó Malí y controló el comercio desde el siglo 15 hasta 1591. (pág. 374)

soviet *s.* consejo local de representantes formado en Rusia después de la caída del zar Nicolás II. (pág. 772)

Spanish-American War [Guerra Hispano-Americana] *s.* conflicto de 1898 entre Estados Unidos y España, en que Estados Unidos apoyó la lucha de independencia cubana. (pág. 726)

specialization [especialización] *s.* desarrollo de conocimientos para realizar determinado trabajo, como comerciar o llevar registros. (pág. 18)

sphere of influence [esfera de influencia] *s.* región extranjera en que una nación controla el comercio y otras actividades económicas. (pág. 718)

standard of living [nivel de vida] *s.* calidad de la vida de una persona o población que se mide conforme a los bienes, servicios y lujos que tiene a su disposición. (pág. 912)

Star Wars [Guerra de las Galaxias] *s.* programa para proteger a Estados Unidos de un ataque de misiles enemigos, propuesto en 1983 por el presidente Ronald Reagan pero nunca implementado; su nombre oficial es Iniciativa de Defensa Estratégica. (pág. 879)

stateless societies [sociedades sin Estado] *s.* grupos culturales en los que la autoridad es compartida por linajes de igual poder, en vez de ser ejercida por un gobierno central. (pág. 368)

steppes [estepas] *s.* llanuras secas de pastizales. (pág. 57)

strike [huelga] *s.* paro de trabajo para obligar al patrón a acceder a ciertas demandas. (pág. 650)

subcontinent [subcontinente] *s.* gran masa que forma una parte claramente diferenciada de un continente. (pág. 42)

Suez Canal [canal de Suez] *s.* canal marítimo que une al mar Rojo y al golfo de Suez con el mar Mediterráneo, cuya construcción terminó en 1869. (pág. 699)

Suez Crisis [Crisis de Suez] *s.* crisis internacional ocurrida en 1956 cuando Egipto nacionalizó el canal de Suez e Israel (con ayuda de Gran Bretaña y Francia) tomó el canal por la fuerza, pero se retiró bajo presión de Estados Unidos y la Unión Soviética. (pág. 902)

suffrage [sufragio] *s.* derecho al voto. (pág. 659)

Sufi [sufí] *s.* musulmán que busca contacto directo con Dios por medio del misticismo. (pág. 240)

Sunna [sunna] *s.* modelo islámico de vida que se basa en las enseñanzas y vida de Mahoma. (pág. 237)

Sunni [sunni] *s.* rama del islam que reconoce a Alí y a sus descendientes como sucesores legítimos de Mahoma. (pág. 240)

surrealism [surrealismo] *s.* movimiento artístico del siglo 20 que se concentra en el inconsciente. (pág. 797)

sustainable development [crecimiento sostenido] *s.* desarrollo económico que satisface las necesidades de la población pero preserva el entorno y conserva recursos para futuras generaciones. (pág. 950)

Swahili [suahili] *s.* lengua bantú con influencias árabes que se usa en África oriental y central. (pág. 378)

Taiping Rebellion [Rebelión Taiping] *s.* rebelión a mediados del siglo 19 contra la dinastía Qing en China, encabezada por Hong Xiuquan. (pág. 717)

Taj Mahal *s.* bella tumba en Agra, India, construida por el emperador mogol Shah Jahan para su esposa Mumtaz Mahal. (pág. 454)

Tamil [tamil o tamul] *s.* idioma del sur de India; grupo que habla dicho idioma. (pág. 175)

technology [tecnología] *s.* formas de aplicar conocimientos, herramientas e inventos para satisfacer necesidades. (pág. 9)

Tennis Court Oath [Juramento de la Cancha de Tenis] *s.* promesa hecha por los miembros de la Asamblea Nacional de Francia en 1789 de permanecer reunidos hasta que elaboraran una nueva constitución. (pág. 576)

terrorism [terrorismo] *s.* uso de la fuerza o de amenazas para presionar a personas o gobiernos a que cambien sus políticas. (pág. 953)

theocracy [teocracia] *s.* **1.** gobierno en el cual se ve al gobernante como una figura divina (pág. 35). **2.** gobierno controlado por líderes religiosos. (pág. 433)

theory of evolution [teoría de la evolución] *s.* concepto propuesto por Charles Darwin en 1859 de que las especies de plantas y animales surgen debido a un proceso de selección natural. (pág. 678)

theory of relativity [teoría de la relatividad] *s.* ideas de Albert Einstein acerca de la interrelación entre el tiempo y el espacio, y entre la energía y la materia. (pág. 795)

Theravada *s.* secta del budismo que se adhiere al énfasis original de Buda en la estricta disciplina espiritual. (pág. 177)

Third Reich [Tercer Reich] *s.* Tercer Imperio Alemán establecido por Adolfo Hitler en la década de 1930. (pág. 814)

Third Republic [Tercera República] *s.* república establecida en Francia después de la caída de Napoleón III; acabó con la ocupación alemana de Francia durante la II Guerra Mundial. (pág. 663)

Third World [Tercer Mundo] *s.* durante la Guerra Fría, naciones que no se aliaron ni con Estados Unidos ni con la Unión Soviética. (pág. 871).

Thirty Years' War [Guerra de los Treinta Años] *s.*conflicto europeo de 1618 a 1648 por cuestiones religiosas, territoriales y de poder entre familias reinantes. (pág. 526)

three-field system [sistema de tres campos] *s.*sistema agrícola de la Europa medieval en que las tierras de cultivo se dividían en tres campos de igual tamaño y cada uno se sembraba sucesivamente con un cultivo de invierno, un cultivo de primavera y el tercero se dejaba sin cultivar. (pág. 348)

Tiananmen Square [Plaza Tiananmen] *s.*plaza pública en Beijing, China; sede en 1989 de un enorme levantamiento estudiantil en favor de reformas democráticas. (pág. 932)

tithe [diezmo] *s.*pago de una familia a la Iglesia de la décima parte de sus ingresos. (pág. 325)

Tokugawa Shogunate [shogunato Tokugawa] *s.*dinastía de shogúns que gobernó un Japón unificado de 1603 a 1867. (pág. 475)

Torah *s.*cinco primeros libros de la Biblia hebrea, los más sagrados de la tradición judía. (pág. 72)

totalitarianism [totalitarismo] *s.*gobierno que controla todo aspecto de la vida pública y privada. (pág. 775)

total war [guerra total] *s.*conflicto en el que los países participantes dedican todos sus recursos a la guerra. (pág. 755)

totems [tótemes] *s.*animales u otros objetos naturales que sirven de símbolo de unidad de clanes u otros grupos. (pág. 394)

tournament [torneo] *s.*justa deportiva entre grupos de caballeros. (pág. 328)

tragedy [tragedia] *s.*obra dramática seria profunda acerca de la caída de un personaje heroico o noble. (pág. 123)

Trans-Siberian Railway [Ferrocarril Transiberiano] *s.*vía de ferrocarril construida en Rusia entre 1891 y 1904 para conectar puertos rusos con el océano Pacífico. (pág. 770)

Treaty of Kanagawa [Tratado de Kanagawa] *s.*acuerdo de 1854 entre Estados Unidos y Japón, que abrió dos puertos japoneses a los barcos de Estados Unidos y le permitió abrir una embajada en Japón. (pág. 720)

Treaty of Tordesillas [Tratado de Tordesillas] *s.*acuerdo de 1494 entre Portugal y España que estableció que las tierras descubiertas al oeste de una línea imaginaria en el océano Atlántico pertenecerían a España y las tierras al este pertenecerían a Portugal. (pág. 466)

Treaty of Versailles [Tratado de Versalles] *s.*acuerdo de paz firmado por Alemania y los Aliados después de la I Guerra Mundial. (pág. 761)

trench warfare [guerra de trincheras] *s.*forma de guerra en la que dos ejércitos contrincantes luchan detrás de trincheras cavadas en el campo de batalla. (pág. 749)

triangular trade [triángulo comercial] *s.*red comercial trasatlántica que transportaba esclavos y productos entre África, Inglaterra, Europa continental, el Caribe y las colonias de Norteamérica. (pág. 497)

tribune [tribuno] *s.*en la antigua Roma, funcionario elegido por los plebeyos para proteger sus derechos. (pág. 142)

tribute [tributo] *s.*pago de una potencia más débil a una potencia más fuerte para obtener una garantía de paz y seguridad. (pág. 76)

Triple Alliance [Triple Alianza] *s.***1.** asociación de las ciudades Estado de Tenochtitlan, Texcoco y Tlacopan, que dio origen al imperio azteca (pág. 402). **2.** alianza militar establecida entre Alemania, Austro-Hungría e Italia antes de la I Guerra Mundial. (pág. 744)

Triple Entente [Triple Entente] *s.*alianza militar entre Gran Bretaña, Francia y Rusia establecida antes de la I Guerra Mundial. (pág. 745)

triumvirate [triunvirato] *s.*en la Roma antigua, grupo de tres líderes que compartían el control del gobierno. (pág. 147)

Trojan War [Guerra de Troya] *s.*guerra, aproximadamente en 1200 a.C., en que un ejército al mando de reyes micénicos atacó la ciudad comercial independiente de Troya, ubicada en Anatolia. (pág. 113)

troubadour [trovador] *s.*poeta y músico medieval que viajaba de un lugar a otro para divertir con sus cantos de amor cortesano. (pág. 330)

Truman Doctrine [Doctrina Truman] *s.*política estadounidense de dar ayuda económica y militar a las naciones libres amenazadas por oponentes internos o externos, anunciada por el presidente Harry Truman en 1947. (pág. 858)

tyrant [tirano] *s.*en la antigua Grecia, individuo poderoso que ganaba el control del gobierno de una ciudad Estado apelando al apoyo de los pobres. (pág. 116)

U

Umayyads [omeyas] *s.*dinastía que gobernó el imperio musulmán del 661 al 750 d.C. y después estableció un reino en al-Andalus. (pág. 239)

union [sindicato] *s.*asociación de trabajadores formada para negociar mejores salarios y condiciones de trabajo. (pág. 650)

United Nations [Organización de las Naciones Unidas (ONU)] *s.*organización internacional fundada en 1945 con el propósito de ofrecer seguridad a las naciones del mundo. (pág. 855)

Universal Declaration of Human Rights [Declaración Universal de Derechos Humanos] *s.*declaración en que la ONU proclamó en 1948 que todos los seres humanos tienen derecho a la vida, la libertad y la seguridad. (pág. 954)

unrestricted submarine warfare [guerra submarina irrestricta] *s.*uso de submarinos para hundir sin alerta previa cualquier barco (incluso barcos neutrales y de pasajeros sin armamento) que se encuentre en aguas enemigas. (pág. 754)

urbanization [urbanización] *s.*crecimiento de ciudades y migración hacia ellas. (pág. 638)

U.S. Civil War [Guerra Civil de E.U.A.] *s.*conflicto entre los estados del Norte y el Sur de Estados Unidos desde 1861 a 1865, sobre el asunto de la esclavitud. (pág. 671)

utilitarianism [utilitarismo] *s.*teoría, propuesta por Jeremy Bentham a fines del siglo 18, de que las acciones del gobierno sólo son útiles si promueven el mayor bien para el mayor número de personas. (pág. 648)

Utopia [Utopía] *s.*tierra imaginaria descrita por Tomás Moro en su libro del mismo nombre; lugar ideal. (pág. 425)

U-2 incident [incidente del U-2] *s.*derribamiento en 1960 de un avión estadounidense de espionaje y captura de su piloto por la Unión Soviética. (pág. 860)

V

vassal [vasallo] *s.*en la Europa feudal, persona que recibía un dominio (tierras) de un señor a cambio de su promesa de lealtad y servicios. (pág. 324)

Vedas *s.*cuatro colecciones de escritos sagrados secretos, realizados durante la etapa temprana del asentamiento ario en India. (pág. 59)

vernacular *s.*lenguaje común y corriente de la gente de una región o país. (págs. 350, 421)

Vietcong *s.*grupo de guerrilleros comunistas que, con la ayuda de Vietnam del Norte, pelearon contra el gobierno de Vietnam del Sur durante la Guerra de Vietnam. (pág. 868)

Vietnamization [vietnamización] *s.*estrategia del presidente de E.U.A. Richard Nixon para terminar con la participación en la Guerra de Vietnam, mediante el retiro gradual de tropas estadounidenses y su reemplazo con fuerzas survietnamitas. (pág. 869)

Vishnu [Visnú] *s.*dios hindú considerado responsable de conservar al mundo. (pág. 178)

vizier [visir] *s.*primer ministro de un reino o imperio musulmán. (pág. 280)

W

War of the Spanish Succession [Guerra de Sucesión Española] *s.*conflicto de 1701 a 1713 en que varios Estados europeos lucharon para impedir que la familia Borbón controlara a España, como a Francia. (pág. 523)

Warsaw Pact [Pacto de Varsovia] *s.*alianza militar formada en 1955 por la Unión Soviética y siete países de Europa oriental. (pág. 859)

Weimar Republic [República de Weimar] *s.*república establecida en Alemania en 1919 que acabó en 1933. (pág. 802)

Western Front [Frente Occidental] *s.*en la I Guerra Mundial, región del norte de Francia donde peleaban las fuerzas de los Aliados y de las Potencias Centrales. (pág. 748)

westernization [occidentalización] *s.*adopción de las instituciones sociales, políticas o económicas del Occidente, especialmente de Europa o Estados Unidos. (pág. 533)

YZ

yin and yang [yin y yang] *s.*en China, dos poderes que gobiernan los ritmos naturales de la vida; el yang representa las cualidades masculinas en el universo y el yin las femeninas. (pág. 99)

Yoruba [yoruba] *s.*pueblo del África occidental que formó varios reinos en lo que hoy es Benín y el sur de Nigeria. (pág. 375)

Zapotec [zapoteca] *s.*civilización mesoamericana centrada en el valle de Oaxaca de lo que hoy es México. (pág. 218)

ziggurat [zigurat] *s.*estructura de gradas en forma de pirámide, que formaba parte de un templo sumerio. (pág. 21)

Zionism [sionismo] *s.*movimiento fundado en la década de 1890 para promover el establecimiento de una patria judía en Palestina. (pág. 663)

Index

An *i* preceding a page reference in italics indicates that there is an illustration, and usually text information as well, on that page. An *m* or a *c* preceding an italic page reference indicates a map or a chart, as well as text information on that page.

headhunters, 222
 Moche culture, 222–223
 Nazca culture, 222
 religion, 221
Andhra Dynasty, 175
Angkor Wat, *i 309*
Anglican Church, 432
Anglo-Saxons, 352
Angola, 900, *c 906*
animism, 197
annexation, 709, 723
annul, 431
Anschluss, 814
anthropologists, 7, 204, 217
anti-Semitism, 663, 810, 832
 Kristallnacht, 810
apartheid, 468, 918–919
apostles, 153, 154, 155
appeasement, 813, 815
aqueducts, *i 167,* 199
Aquinas, Thomas, 351
Aquino, Corazón, *i 883,* 893
Arabia, 788. *See* Saudi Arabia.
Arabian Peninsula, 233
Arab scholars, 351
Arafat, Yasir, 905
Arc de Triomphe, *i 601*
arch, 31, 141, 165, *i 246*
archaeological dig, 7, *i 214*
archaeological evidence
 of ancient China, 47–48
 of Aryan culture, 59
 of Aztec civilization, 402
 as clues to prehistory, 7, 11, 15
 of Djenné–Djeno, *i 197,* 198
 of Great Zimbabwe, 380–381
 of Indus Civilization, 45
 at Jarmo, 15
 at La Brea tar pits, Los Angeles, *i 214*
 of Maya society, 396, *i 397*
 of migration to Americas, 212
 of Minoan culture, 67–68
 of Olmec culture, *i 208*
 of Trojan War, 113
archaeologists, *m 5,* 7–10, 15, 20, 113, 211,
 212, *i 214*
Archimedes, 134
architecture
 Akbar period of, 453
 Aksumite, *i 201*
 in Alexandria, *i 132*
 in ancient Egypt, 38
 of Ankgor Wat, *i 309*
 Bauhaus, 797
 cathedral, 342
 church, *i 343*
 Etruscan influence on Roman, 141
 functionalist movement, 797
 Gothic style, 342, *i 343*
 Greek, 121, *i 122,* 135, *c 136*
 Gropius, Walter, 797
 Mayan, 396
 Mughal empire, 453
 Muslim, *i 246,* 247, *c 248*
 Parthenon, *i 122*
 Persian, *c 811, i 441*
 pyramid, *i 36*
 Roman, 135, 165–167
 romanesque style, 342
 Sumerian, 31
 post-World War I, 797
 Wright, Frank Lloyd, 797
 ziggurat, *i 20*

Argentina
 democracy in, 915
 fascism in, 809
 independence of, 605
 Peron, Juan, *i 915*
aristocracy, 115, *c 117,* 142
Aristophanes, 123
Aristotle, *i 125,* 134, 545
arithmetic, 31
Armenian Massacre, 745
armistice (World War I), 757
arms
 control, 922
 race, 860
art. *See also* drama; painting; propaganda;
 sculpture.
 African, 12, *i 198,* 797
 Akkadian, *i 31*
 Algerian, *i 13*
 Andean, *i 221,* 222–223, *c 224*
 Assyrian, *i 80, i 88, i 89, i 103*
 Australian, 12, *i 13*
 Buddhist influence on, 177
 Catholic, 514
 cave painting, *i 13, i 23*
 Chaldean, *i 91*
 Chavín, *i 221*
 Chinese, *i 25, i 49, i 171, i 290, i 472,* 473
 Christian, *i 40, i 153, i 154*
 civic duty to, 123
 as communication, 13
 Dada movement, 797
 Dutch, *i 516*
 Egyptian, *i 24, i 38,* 39, *i 84, i 86*
 Enlightenment values in, *i 560, i 569*
 Ethiopian, *i 202*
 Flemish, 424
 in Florence, *i 415*
 French, *i 13,* 522
 in French Revolution, *i 575*
 in global culture, 960
 Greek (classical), *i 108, i 110, i 117,*
 121–122, 135, *c 136, i 177*
 Hittite, *i 59*
 Impressionism in, *i 622*
 international, 960
 Islamic beliefs in, 246, *i 247*
 jewelry, 87, 195, 223
 magical qualities of, *i 13, i 25*
 Mexican, *i 403*
 Meroë, *i 87*
 Minoan, *i 67,* 113
 mosaic, *i 109, i 124, i 139, i 154, i 164*
 Muslim, 246
 nationalism and, 619
 of Nazca Lines, *i 209*
 Nok, *i 198*
 of Northern Renaissance, *i 423,* 424–425
 Nubian, *i 80, i 85, i 86*
 Olmec, *i 218,* 219
 oracle bones, 48–49
 Ottoman Empire, 447
 Paleolithic, 12
 Persian, *i 93, i 95,* 96
 perspective, 419
 Phoenician, *i 54, i 70*
 photography, 623
 political, 472, *i 557, i 600, i 731*
 pottery, 86, 195, 216, *i 221– c 224, i 287,*
 311, 391, 473
 prehistoric, 12, *i 13*
 as propaganda, 778, *i 779*
 Realism in, *i 622*

 religious, *i 276,* 311
 religious beliefs in, *i 13, i 202,* 221–222,
 i 243, i 247, 342, 414
 Renaissance, *i 416, i 419, i 420,* 421, *i 423,*
 i 425
 revolution in, 619–625
 Roman, *i 150,* 164, *i 169, i 177*
 Romantic movement, 619–621, *i 622*
 Safavid Empire, 449–450
 Shang Dynasty, *i 25, i 49*
 Song Dynasty, 290
 Soviet realism, 778
 Spanish, 514
 Spartan, 116
 Stone Age, *i 23*
 Sumerian, *i 29, i 30,* 31
 surrealism, *i 797*
 Tang Dynasty, 290
 values reflected in, 123, 164, *i 218,* 219,
 246, *i 416,* 424–425
 West Africa, *i 376–377*
 post-World War I, 763, *i 797*
 writing, 49
Arthasastra (Kautilya), 173
artifacts, 7, *i 212*
artisans, 18
artists, 797. *See also* individual names.
Aryans, 45, 59–61, 831
 caste system, 59, 60
 influence on Indian culture, 45
 invasion of India, *m 61*
 Vedas, 59
Asante, 682
Ashurbanipal (Assyrian monarch), *i 80,* 90
Asia, *m 976*
 aggression in (1930–1939), *i 812, m 813*
 "Asia for Asians," 885
 growth of East Asia, *c 946*
 independence in, *c 906*
 physical map, *m 977*
Askia Muhammad (Muslim ruler of
 Songhai), 374–375
Asoka, 174
assembly line, 674
assimilation, 185–186, 691
Assyria, 88
 Ninevah, 90
Assyrian empire, 76, 87–91, *m 90*
 culture, 90
 military power, 88, *c 89*
astrolabe, *i 245,* 464, 465
astrology, 545
astronomy, 219
 Aristarchus, 133
 Daoist effect on, 98
 Greek, *c 133*
 Indian, 178–179
 Mayan, 396–398, *i 397*
 Muslim, 244, *i 245, c 248,* 545
 Ptolomy, 133
 and Scientific Revolution, 546
Athena, *i 108,* 114
Athens, *m 108, i 112,* 117–120, 121
 plague in, 123
 war with Sparta, 123–124
Atlantic Charter, 826
Atlantic slave trade, 495–496, 499. *See also*
 slavery, slaves.
atlas, *m 971, m 972–m 985*
atomic bomb, *i 840,* 952
 in cold War, 859–860
 effects of, in World War II, *c 840*
 Hiroshima, 840–841

communism, 649, c 650, 774, 775, c 817.
    See also Cold War.
    in Cambodia, 870
    in China, 782–784, 862–865, 877–879
    and democratic reforms, 908
    domino theory of, 868
    in eastern Europe, 856–859, 876–877
    economic effects of, 924, 928, 930, 931
    fall of, 923–930
    and fascism, 807
    historic origins of, 649–650, 769–774
    in Latin America, 872–873
    in Middle East, 875
    Politburo of, 921
    in Russia, 775–780
    in Southeast Asia, 866–870
    spread of, 843, c 856–857, 862–865,
        867–870, m 873
compass, 465
    magnetic, c 289
computers, 942–943
concordat, 586
Concordat of Worms, 334
Confucianism, 97–c 99, 183–186, 262–264
    and agriculture, 470, 475
    and commerce, 470, 475
    in China, 97
    Five Relationships, 97
    and government, 98
    in Japan, 475
    in Korea, 310
    Legalists, 99
    social order, 97
    values of, 469
    Yin-Yang, 262
Confucius, 97–99
    Analects, 98
Congo, 898–899
Congress of Vienna, 571, 593–596, c 598
Congress Party, 785, 886
conquistadors, 485
Conservatives, 578, 609
Constantine (Roman emperor), 156, i 157,
    160, 269
    conversion of, 157
Constantinople, 160, 162, 269, 271, m 440
    as capital, 160
    fall of, 278, i 440
    Hagia Sophia, i 267, 270
    Hippodrome, 271
    Nika Rebellion, 271
    Ottoman defeat of, 444–445
    Turkish threat to, 343
Constitution
    first, 537
    of Japan, post-World War II, 844
    Korean, 867
    Mexican, c 733
    Russian, 774
    South African, 920
    United States, c 143, 553, c 566, 671
constitutional monarchy, 771. *See also*
    monarchy.
consuls, 142
containment, 857
    in South Korea, 866
    in Vietnam, 868
Continental System, 589
Contras, i 852, 873
convents, 319
Copernicus, Nicolaus, 546
Coptic Church of Egypt, 201
Coronado, Francisco Vasquez de, 487

corporation, 645
Cortés, Hernando, 402, i 485, 486
cotton
    consumption in Britain, c 636
    in India, 702–703
    in United States, 670
cotton gin, 636
Council of Trent, 436
coup, 895
coup d'état, 585
Court of Nanna, i 20
covenant, 73
    Hebrew, 74
Creoles, 590, 604–605
Crete, 113
criminal justice, 554
Croatia, 928, m 929
Cro-Magnons, 9, 11
Cromwell, Oliver, i 510, 537, 538
cross
    as Christian symbol, i 153
    as political symbol, m 191
crossbow, 51
Crusades (1096–1204), 343–347, m 344,
    c 346
    children in, 346
    economic impact of, 344, 346
    in the Middle Ages, c 362
    Muslim counterattacks, 345
    political impact of, 343–347
    in Seljuk Empire, 281
    social impact of, 346–347
Cuba
    Batista, 872
    Bay of Pigs, 872
    Castro, Fidel, 872
    independence of, 726
    migrations from, i 956
    revolution, 872
Cuban missile crisis, 872, 878
cultural blending. *See also* global culture.
    in the Americas, 480
    in Safavid Empire, c 448–m 450
    in world, 957–961
cultural diffusion, 29
cultural identity, 613, 912, 960
Cultural Revolution (China), 865
culture(s), 7. *See also* Africa; Americas;
    China; Hellenistic culture; India;
    Japan; Roman Empire.
    under Alexander the Great, 131
    mass, i 676–i 677
    means of expanding, 202
    and nationalism, c 613
    popular, 957, 958
cuneiform, 18, c 19, 31, c 52
Curie, Marie, i 678
Cyrillic alphabet, 273
Cyrus the Great (Persian king), 76, 92–93
czar, 278. *See also* individual names of czars.
Czechoslovakia
    in 1990s, 930
    democracy in, 810, 814, 924–925
    falls to Hitler, 814–815
    reforms, 924–925
    Soviet invasion of, i 877

Dada movement, 797
daimyo, 474
Dalai Lama, 863–864, 954

Dali, Salvador, i 797
Dante Alighieri, 350
Danzig, 815
Daoism, 98, c 99
    Laozi, 98
    in Song Dynasty, 290
Darius (Persian king), 93–94, 118
Darius III (Persian king), 129
Darwin, Charles, i 678, 679
David, Jacques Louis, i 109, 571, 575
David (Israeli king), 75
Dawes, Charles, 802
D-Day Invasion (World War II), 838
death rituals, 40–41. *See also* burial rites.
Deborah (Hebrew judge), 74
Decameron (Boccaccio), 422
Deccan Plateau, m 42
decimal system, 179
Declaration of Independence
    Locke's influence on, c 554, 564
    and slavery, 651
Declaration of the Rights of Man, c 554,
    577
De Gaulle, Charles, 823, 899
de Klerk, F. W., 919, i 920
Delian League, 119
Delphi, 122
delta, 34
demilitarization, 844
democracy, i 110, 600, c 911, 912. *See also*
    democratic reforms; government;
    democratic–republican government.
    1945–present, 908–937
    in ancient Greece, 108, 117–118,
        c 120–125, c 136
    in Cambodia, 870
    in China, 784
    Congress of Vienna and, 593
    direct, c 117, 120–121, c 136, 554, 911
    and French Revolution, 595–596
    in Great Britain, 361, 659–662
    in India, 887
    indirect, 911–914
    in industrialized countries, 652
    in Japan, 811
    in Latin America, 911–914
    limited, 117–118
    loss of confidence in, 124, 807
    monarchy and, c 540
    in South Korea, 867
    struggles, c 936
    time line of, c 680
    in United States, c 120, c 539
    Western (1900), m 656
    post-World War I, 792, 801–802
democratic reforms, 651, 659–660,
    c 911–912
    in classical Greece, 108, 117–118,
        c 120–125
    in classical Rome, 142, c 143
    in England, 659–660
    of French Revolution, 577, 585, 593, 597
    in Industrial Revolution, 646
    in Japan, 844
    in Middle Ages, 351
    in modern world, 908–930, 932–933,
        c 936, 967
    in revolutionary China, 781–782
Demosthenes, 128
Deng Xiaoping, i 932, 933, 1065
    Four Modernizations, 932
Depression, the, 803–806, c 816
    causes of, 801–805, c 817

Gibbon, Edward, 163
glaciers, 8
gladiators, 151
glasnost, 921
global communications, 942–943
global culture, c 962
    art of, 960
    English language, 959
    popular culture, 957–959
    Western influences on, 958–959
global economy, 947
global interaction, i 504
global interdependence, 961, i 962
global security, 952–953
    and terrorism, 953
glyphs. See also hieroglyphics.
    Mayan, 398
Gobi Desert, 46, m 47
gold trade, 201, 371, 373
Gonzalez, Rebecca, 217
Gorbachev, Mikhail, i 921, 922
    attempted coup of, 926–927
    glasnost, 921
    INF treaty, 922
    perestroika, 922
Gospels (New Testament), 153
Gothic, 342
Gouges, Olympe de, i 577
government, c 117. See also democracy;
    political systems.
    of Africa, 197
    of ancient China, 50, 183
    aristocracy, 117
    of Assyrian empire, 90
    of Athens, 117–118
    under Augustus, 149
    autocratic, 100
    beginnings of organized, 28
    centralized, 181, 304, 310, 375, 475
    of China, c 52
    coalition, 801
    constitutional, c 911
    democracy, 117
    democratic, c 120, 124, 354, 595–596
    dictators in ancient Rome, 143
    of Egypt, c 52
    of Indus Valley civilization, 45, c 52
    in the Middle Ages, c 362
    military, 310, 918
    monarchy, 117
    natural rights in, 551–552
    oligarchy, 117
    Ottoman, c 446
    papal, 319–320
    in prehistory, 18
    provisional, 772
    representative, 115, 120, c 143, 801
    repressive, 894
    republican, 138, 142, c 143, 515–516,
      537, 565–566, 611
    responsibility of, 32
    Roman influence of, 165
    scholars' influence on, 351
    social contract in, 551
    of Sparta, 116
    of Sumer, c 19, c 52
Goya, Francisco, 557, i 569
gravitas, 150
gravity, law of, 548
Great Depression. See Depression, the.
Great Famine, Irish (1845–1851), c 667
Great Fear, 576
Great Plains, i 656

Great Purge, 777–778
Great Pyramid, i 36, 217. See also pyramids.
Great Schism, 357, 361
Great Trek, 689
Great Wall of China, 80, m 100, i 101, 295
Great War. See World War I.
Great Zimbabwe, 380, 381
Greco, El, 514
Greco-Roman civilization, 164–169. See also
    Greece; Roman empire.
Greece, m 112. See also Hellenistic culture.
    architecture, 122
    arts, 121–123
    city-states, 115
    classical, m 109–m 112, 108–137
    conflict in modern, 610
    Delphi, 122
    democracy in, 120–125
    drama, 121–123
    economy of ancient, 113
    environmental influences on, 111–112
    independence of, 697
    legacy, c 136
    Macedonia's conquest of, 128–129
    Minoan influence, 67
    modern-day, m 108, 109
    nationalism in, 610
    Parthenon, 122
    Peloponnesian War, 123
    Pericles, 120, i 121
    science of, 125
    sculpture, 122
    Sparta, 116, 123
    sports in, i 126
    Sumerian influence, 30
    values, 110, 123
    war in, 115–116, 123, 128–129
    in World War II, 825
Greek fire, 266
green revolution, 944
griots, 197
Gross Domestic Product (GDP), c 895
Guam, 828
Guernica (Picasso), i 814
guerrillas
    in Peninsular War, 590
    Vietcong, 868
guild, 349
guillotine, 580–i 581
Gulf, 949
Gulf War, 949. See Persian Gulf War.
Gullah, 499
gunpowder, 286, c 289, 296, 298, 375, 443
Gupta Empire, 175, i 176, i 188
Gutenberg Bible, 426

H

habeas corpus, 538–539
Hadrian, 151
Hagia Sophia, i 267, 270
haiku, 476
Haile Selassie (Ethiopian emperor), i 812
hajj, 236, 259
Hammurabi, i 26, i 32, 91
    reign of, 31–32
Hammurabi's Code, 26, 32
    compared with Ten Commandments,
      74–75
    similarities to Hittite law, 58–59
Han Dynasty, 101, m 171, 181–189, c 459
Hannibal of Carthage
    Punic Wars, 144–145

    Rome's war with, 144–145
    and war elephants, i 138
Hapsburgs, 513, 526–530
    defeats, 527
    triumphs, 526–527
Harappan civilization. See Indus Valley.
Hatshepsut (pharaoh), i 83, i 525
Hausa, 375
Havel, Vaclav, 925, 930
Hawaii, 709, 827
headhunters, 222
Hebrew Law, 74–75
Hebrews, 72–73. See also Jews; Judaism.
    Abraham, 72
    covenant, 73, 74
    Exodus, 73
    Israel, 75
    judges, 74
    kings, 75
    monotheism, 73
    Moses, i 73
    prophets, 75
    Sumerian influence, 30
    Ten Commandments, 74
    Twelve Tribes, 74
heliocentric theory, 546
Hellenistic culture, 132–137
    in Alexandria, 132
    arts, 134–135
    Epicureanism, 134, 135
    library, 133
    museum, 133
    philosophy, 134–135
    science and technology, 133–134
    stoicism, 134
    trade in, 132–133
helots, 116
Helsinki Accords, 954
hemophilia, 771
Henry II (English king), 353, 354
Henry IV (French king of Bourban
    Dynasty), 518
Henry IV (German emperor), 334
Henry V (English king), 360
Henry VIII (English king), i 431, 432, 667
Henry of Navarre, 518
Henry, Patrick, 542
Hercules, i 110
heresy, 157
Herodotus, 33, 36, 37, 69, 95
Herzl, Theodor, 663
Hidalgo, Miguel, 607
hieroglyphics, 24, i 38, c 52
    Mayan, i 398
Hijrah, 234
Hildegard of Bingen, 342
Himalaya Mountains, 46, m 47
Hinduism, 62, c 78, 256–257, c 264
    central ideas of, 62–64
    gods of, 257
    moksha, 65
    origins of, 55, i 55, 62
    rebirth of, 177–178
    in Southeast Asia, 309
    sacred cows, i 55
    spread of, 64
    in Sri Lanka, 889
    Upanishad, 62–63
    Vedas, 62
Hindus
    burial rites, i 41
    conflict with Muslims, 451, 703, i 704,
      886

Hirohito (Japanese emperor), 811, *i 844*
Hiroshima, Japan, *i 840*–841
history
    beginnings of written, 19
    influence of migration on, *c 203*
    and nationalism, *c 613*
    themes through, 964–965
    writing about, 246
History, Book IV (Herodotus, 5th century B.C.), 69
History of Herodotus, 37
Hitler, Adolph, 776, *i 808*, 809–810, 813, *i 821*. *See also* World War II.
    anti-Semitism, 810
    "Final Solution," 833
    invades Czechoslovakia, 814, 815
    invades Poland, 821–822
    invades Scandinavia, 822
    invades Soviet Union, 825–826
    Mein Kampf, 809
    and Munich Conference, 815
    occupies Rhineland, 813
    SS (*Schutzstaffell*), 809
    suicide of, 839, 843
Hittites, 58–59
    Egyptians' battle with, 84
Hobbes, Thomas, 551
Ho Chi Minh, 649, 868
Holocaust, *i 818*, 831–834, *m 847*, 952
    death camps, 833, *m 847*
    genocide, 833
    Hitler's "Final Solution," 833
    Jewish resistance, 834
    Kristallnacht, 831
    population killed during, *c 834*
Holy Roman Empire, 333–337
    in 1100, *m 334*
    Otto I, 333
    weakening of, 528
Homer, 114
home rule, 668
hominids, 8
    development, *i 8*, 9
Homo erectus, 9, 47
Homo habilis, 8–9
Homo sapiens, 9
Hong Kong, 716, 935, 946–947
    return to China, 935
    and Tiananmen Square, *i 935*
Hongwu, 469
Hong Xiuquan, 717
Hormuz, Straits of, *m 949*
house arrest, 894
House of Commons, 354, *i 659*
House of Lords, 354
House of Wisdom, 231, 243–244
Huang He River, 46, *m 47*, *c 52*
Hubble Space Telescope, 942
Huguenots, 434, 518
Huli tribe, 938
Hull House, 652
Human Genome Project, 944
humanists, 418
    Christian, 425
    Petrarch, Francesco, 422
humanities, 418
Human Rights, Universal Declaration of, 954
human rights violations. *See also* Holocaust; slavery.
    in Argentina, 915
    Bataan Death March, *i 819*, 828
    of British, 786–787

in Bosnia, 929
in China, 783, 932–933, 935
death and labor camps, *m 847*
in India, 787, 888
in Iran, *i 874*
of Japanese, *i 819*, 828
of Khmer Rouge, *i 870*
in Nazi Germany, 809–810
in Nigeria, 918
in Romania, 925
in Soviet Union, 879
under Stalin, 777–778
Hundred Days, 592
Hundred Years' War, 359–361
    effect of, *c 362*
Hungary
    modern reforms in, 923
    Soviet invasion of, 876, 877
hunter–gatherers, 12, *c 22*, 213, 367, 391
    of Africa, 195, 367–368
    modern, 367
hunters, 211–213
Hus, Jan, *i 357*, 428
Hussein, Saddam, 815, 875
Hyksos, 39, 83, 86
Hymn to the Nile, 53

I

Ibn, 244
Ibn Battuta, 374, 379
Ibn al-Haytham, 244
Ibn Khaldun, 246
Ibn Rushd, 244
Ibo. *See* Igbo.
Ice Age, 8, 211
I Ching (Book of Changes), 99
iconoclasts, 272
icons, 272, *i 276*
Igbo (Ibo), 368–369, *c 382*
    democratic tradition of, 917
    stateless society of, 368
Ignatius of Loyola, 435
Iliad, the, 114
immigration. *See* migrations.
imperialism, *m 682*–705
    1850–1914, *c 710*
    American, 892–893
    British, 701–705
    causes of, 686, *c 687*, *c 710*
    economic, 690, 700, 726–727
    economics of, 682
    forms of, *c 690*
    and government, 691
    impact of, 695, *c 710*
    and industrialization, 646
    Japanese, 722–723
    management of, *c 690*, 691
    resistance to, 693, *c 694*
    and Social Darwinism, 679
    technology and, 682
    Third World, 871
    and World War I, 743
impressionism, *i 622*
Inanna (goddess), *i 24*, *i 29*
Inca Civilization (Empire), 407–411, *c 411*, *c 412*
    ayllu, 408
    cultural developments of, 409–410
    Cuzco, 408
    economic developments of, 409
    fall of, *i 480*, *c 502*, *c 504*
    governments of, 408–410

mita, 409
Pachacuti, 407
Pizarro's conquest of, 486
political developments of, 408–411
quipu, 410
religious beliefs of, 407, 410, *c 411*
runner messengers, 409
trade in, 409
India, *m 55*
    2500–1500 B.C., *m 42*
    in 1947, *m 887*
    Alexander's conquest of, 130–131
    Amritsar Massacre, 786, 885
    Aryan invasion of, *m 61*
    British imperialism in, 701–705
    Buddhism in, 66, 177, 180
    caste system, 59-60
    in Cold War, 871
    Congress Party, 886
    empires (250 B.C.–A.D. 400), *m 175*, 173–176
    Gandhi, Mohandas, *i 786*
    geography of, 42
    Government of India Act, 787
    Hinduism, 177
    independence, 785, 787, *i 883*, 885–889, *c 906*
    Kalidasa, 178
    lions as symbol of, *i 174*
    Mahabharata, 60–61
    mathematics of, 179
    modern leaders of, *c 888*
    Mughal Empire, *m 451*–459
    national movements, 705, 785
    natural resources of, 179
    nonviolence, 786
    partitioning of, 886–887
    poverty in, *c 907*
    religion, 177
    Rowlatt Act, 785, 786
    Salt March, *i 787*
    science, 178–179
    self rule in, 785–787
    servants, 703
    Silk Roads, 179
    social issues, 888
    trade in, 179–180
    in World War I, 785
Indian culture
    connection of Indus Valley to, 45
    environmental influence on, 42–43
Indian National Congress, 785, 886
Indian Removal Act, 670
Indians. *See* Native Americans; North America.
Indo-European(s)
    language family, 57
    migrations of, 57–61, *m 58*
Indonesia
    in Cold War, 871
    independence of, 895
Indra, 59
indulgence, 429
Indus River Valley, *m 42*
    central government in, 45
    civilization, 43–45
    geography of, *c 52*
    religious artifacts of, 45
    seals, *i 45*
industrialization, 634, *c 640*. *See also* Industrial Revolution.
    in Belgium, 645
    in Britain, 638–642, 643, 646

in China, 284, 300
decline of, 302, 469
defeat by Vietnam of, 310
Empire of Kublai Khan, 297, 299–302
Genghis Khan, 276–277, i 295–296
Khanate of the Golden Horde (1294),
  m 278
in Korea, 311
period of peace, 297–298
in Russia, 277
overthrow Seljuk Empire, 281
monopoly, 185
monotheism, 72, 73, 138, 234. See also ethical monotheism; polytheism.
in Aksum, 200
Hindu move towards, 178
of Muslims, Jews, and Christians, 237
in teachings of Jesus, 153
Monroe Doctrine, 726
monsoons, c 52, 71
of India, 42–43
Monte Alban, 219
Montesquieu, Baron de, i 553
Montezuma II (Aztec ruler), 406, i 485
Montgomery, General Bernard, 835
More, Thomas, 425, 428
Morelos, Padre Jose, i 607
mosaics, i 109, i 124, i 139, i 154, i 164
Moscow. See also Russia.
Ivan I (prince), 277–278
rise of, 277–278
Moses, 73–74
mosque(s), 236, 237, 267
of Timbuktu, m 372, 373
Mother Goddess, 16, 63, 67
Mother Theresa, 955
Mott, Lucretia, 662
Mound Builders, 392–393
Mountbatten, Lord Louis, 886
mountains, world's highest, c 986
movable type, 289
movies, 675, i 676, 800
Chaplin, Charlie, i 800
Eisenstein, Sergei, 800
Hollywood, California, 800
Lang, Fritz, 800
Mubarak, Hosni, 903
Mughal Empire, 441, m 451–459, c 458
cultural developments of, 453
decline of, 457
economic developments of, 454–457
political developments of, 453–455
Muhammad, 201–202, 230, 234–238, 243,
  258
Hijrah, 235
Medina, 235
Muhammad Ali (Egyptian king), 698–699
mulattos, 604
multinational corporations, 947
Mummar, i 26
mummification, 37, i 40, 41
Incan, 407
Munich Conference, 815
Muses, 132
music
African, 498
in Age of Chivalry, 330
Cajun zydeco, 490
Chinese opera, i 677
classical, 559, 797
in global culture, m 959
jazz, 797
Neanderthal, 11

neoclassical, 559
rock 'n' roll, 958–959
Romanticism and, 620
Stravinsky, Igor, 796
vaudeville, 674–675
post-World War I, 797
Muslim League, 785, 886
Muslims, 235
caliphs, 238, 240
conflict among, 874
conflict with Hindus, 886
and Crusades, 345, 346
influence on sciences of, 545
invasions of, m 323
Ka'aba, 259
in Middle Ages, 351
Mongol conversion to, 297
in North Africa, 368, 369
population, 1990s, c 249
prayer, 237
and Reconquista, 346, 513
shariah, 237
under Soviet rule, 925
Spanish defeat of, 346
Muslim world, m 230, 231, 232–249, i 458.
  See also Islam; Ottoman Empire.
in 1300–1700, m 440, 441–459
al-Andalus, 240
art and architecture, 244, i 246
civil war, 239
Córdoba, 241
Damascus, 239
dynasties, m 230, 231–241, c 248
empires of, c 458
House of Wisdom, 243
imperialism in, 697–700
influence of, 247, 351
mathematics in, 244
population of, c 249
religious tolerance in, 239, 243
science and technology in, 244–245,
  c 248, 545
slavery in, 495
social classes, 242
urban centers, c 242
Mussolini, Benito, 776, i 807, 808
defeat of, 837
in Munich Conference, 815
in World War II, 823
Mutapa empire, 381
Mutsuhito, i 721
Myanmar. See Burma.
Mycenaeans, 112–113, 115
myth
Greek, 114, c 136, 141
of Minotaur, 67
of Quetzalcoatl, i 401
Roman, 141

N

NAFTA (North American Free Trade
  Agreement), 914, 947, 948
Nagasaki, Japan, i 840–841
Nagy, Imre, i 877
Nanna, i 20, 21
Napoleon I (Napoleon Bonaparte, French
  emperor), i 571, i 585, 586–592, c 598
allies of, 587, m 588
exile, 592
restoring order, i 585
Russian campaign, m 591
at Waterloo, 592

Napoleon III (Louis-Napoleon, French
  emperor), 611, 662
Napoleonic Code, 586
National Assembly, 575
nationalism, m 600, 743
and art, 619
Asian, 785, m 789
Balkan, 745–746
Chinese, 718, 781–782
in Europe, 609–610
under fascism, 807
and the French Revolution, 609
ideal of, c 613
and imperialism, 687, c 710
Indian, 705, 785–787, m 789, 885–886
Korean, 472
Kurdish, 954
against Napoleon, 590
and revolution, 595, 766–789
rise of, 361
in southwest Asia, 788, m 789
and World War I, 743
nation-state, 609
Native Americans. See also North America,
  Native.
burial rites of, i 41
in Canada, 664
colonialism and, 486–488, c 504
slavery of, 487
NATO (North Atlantic Treaty
  Organization), 859, 952
natural disasters, c 986–987
natural order, 98
natural resources. See also environmental
  influences.
of Britain, 634
of Congo, 899
natural rights, 551–552
Locke, John, 551
nature. See also environmental influences.
control of, 12–16
Nazca culture, 222
Nazca Lines, i 209
Nazis, i 793, 843
Nazis, Neo–, 924
Nazism, i 793, 808–810, c 817. See also
  Hitler; World War II.
anti-Semitism, 810
Neanderthals, 9–10
musical expression of, 11
Nebuchadnezzar (Chaldean king), 76, 91
Negritude movement, 896
Nehru, Jawaharlal, i 883, 887
neoclassical style, 559
Neolithic Age, 8
Neolithic Revolution, 14–16
Nero, 149, i 150
Netanyahu, Benjamin, 905
Netherlands
in Asian trade, 471, c 478
in European expansion, 468
French invasion of, 522
republic of, 515–516
trade in, 516
trade with Japan, 477
tulips of, 515
United Provinces of, 515–516
Nevsky, Alexander, i 277
New Deal, 806
New England, 491
New France, 490
New Kingdom of Egypt, 83
New Netherland, 491–492

New Stone Age, 8. *See also* Neolithic Age.
New Testament, 153, 157
Newton, Isaac, 548–549
New Zealand, *m 666*
Ngo Dinh Diem, 868
Nicaragua, 852, 879
Nicholas I (Russian czar), 612, 769
Nicholas II (Russian czar), 747, 769,
    770–772
Nietzsche, Friedrich, 796, 810
    and Existentialists, 796
    Hitler's use of, 810
Nigeria
    in 1914, *m 693*
    civil war in, 917–918
    under colonial rule, 690–695
    democracy in, 918
    dissidents, 918
    martial law, 917
Niger River, 198, 377
Nightingale, Florence, 698
Nile River, 33, *i 34*, 52, 964. *See also*
    pyramids.
    Stanley and Livingstone on, 685–686
1984 (book by Orwell), 778
Nineveh, *m 90–91*
nirvana, 65, 177
Nixon, Richard
    in China, 879, 932, *i 934*
    and detente, 878–879
    in Soviet Union, 879
    and Vietnam, 869–870
Nkrumah, Kwame, 896, *i 897*
Noah's ark, 77
Nobel Peace Prize, 894, 905, 909, 920, 923,
    955
Nobunaga, Oda, 474
Nok, 198, *c 206*
nomads, 12, 31, 32, 39, 51. *See also* Mongols.
    of Africa, 195
    Aryan, 170, 181
    of Asian steppe, 294–295
    Aztec, 401
    Bantu, 204
    Bedouins, 233, 235
    conflict of empires with, *c 187*
    Hyksos, 83
    influence on Indian culture of, 45
    in Iran, 92
    Magyar, *m 323*
    modern-day, 195, 295, 954
    Mongol, 161
    of North Africa, 369
    of North America, 392
    pastoral, 14, 195
    Seljuks, 279–280
    on Silk Roads, *i 184*, 185
    transition of Jews from, 74
    warriors, 451
    Xiongnu, 182–183
nonaggression pact, 815, 821
nonaligned nations, 871
nonviolence, 786, 954
Normandy, invasion of, *m 818*
Normans, 352
North Africa
    in World War II, 824–825, 835–836
North America, 391–394, *m 392, m 980.
    See also* North America, Native.
    in 1783, *m 565*
    colonization of, 490–491
    maps, 980–981
North America, Native, *c 412*, 670. *See also*

North America; Native Americans.
    colonization of, 493–494, *c 504*
    cultural developments of, 391, *m 392,*
        393–394
    early societies, 391
    Iroquois league, 393
    Mound Builders, 392–393
    Pacific Northwest, 391
    political developments of, 393
    Pueblo people of, *i 391–392*
    religion in, *i 390*, 391, 393–394
    religious beliefs in, 393–394
    trade in, 393
    Woodlands tribes of, 393
Northern Ireland, 668
Northern Renaissance, 423–427
    art of, *i 423–425*
    technology of, 426–427
    writers of, 425–426
North Korea, 311, 472, 867
    isolation, 472
Nubia, *m 81*, 83–87
Nuclear Non-Proliferation Treaty, 953
nuclear weapons
    in Cold War, 859–860
    reduction of, 953
    in South Korea, 867
number system(s)
    base 20, 398
    base 60, 31
Nunavut Territory, 665
Nuremberg Trials, 843–844
Nur Jahan, 454

O

oases, 180
obsidian, 400
Oceania, *m 984*
oceans, deepest, *c 986*
Octavian, 148. *See* Augustus.
Oda Nobunaga, 474
Odyssey, the, 114
oil, 788–789
    exports, *m 789*
    in India, 888
    in Iran, 92
    in Mexico, 913–914
    in Middle East, 875, 901
    Nigerian conflict over, 918
    as political tool, 949
    in Southwest Asia, 788–789
    supplies, 949
Old Regime, 573, *c 598*
Old Stone Age, *c 8*, 17–18
Old Testament, 157, 255. *See also* Bible.
Olduvai Gorge, 9, 10
oligarchy, 115, *c 117*
Olmec civilization, *i 208*, 216–219, *m 217,*
    395, 400
    decline of, 218
    jaguar worship, 217
    legacy, 218–220
    sculpture, *i 218–i 219*
    trade, 217
Olympic games, *i 126, c 136*
    19th century, 675
    boycott of 1980, 875
    in Nazi Germany, 810
    and politics, 875
    South Africa banned from, 919
OPEC, 949
Open Door Policy, 718

Opium War, 716
opposable thumb, 8
oppression. *See also* Holocaust; human
        rights violations; slavery.
    during Cultural Revolution, 865
    industrialization and, 639–642
    and Nazi rule, 809
    in postwar Vietnam, 870
    in Russia, 769
    in United States during World War II,
        837–838
oracle bones, *i 48*, 49
Oregon Territory, 669
Ortega, Daniel, 873
Orthodox Church, 272
Osiris, 37
Oslo Peace Agreement, 905
Osman, *i 443*
Otto I (Otto the Great, Holy Roman
        Emperor), 333–334
Ottoman Empire, 281, 440, 443, *m 445,*
        c 458, m 697–700
    in the Balkans, 609–610
    cultural developments of, 447, 448–450
    decline of, 447, 528, 614, 698
    government of, 446–447
    nationalism weakens, 697
    social organization, *i 446*
    Spain's resistance to, 513–514
    World War I, *m 753*, 788
    Zionism in, 901
Owens, Jesse, *i 810*
ozone layer, 949

P

Pachacuti (Inca ruler), 407–408
Pacific Rim, 185, 706–709, 946–947
Pahlavi, Mohammed Reza (Iranian shah),
        874
Pahlavi, Reza Shah (Iranian shah), 788
Paine, Thomas, 597
painters. *See* names of painters and
        paintings.
painting, 645. *See also* art.
    American, *i 656*
    of Catal Huyuk, 16
    cave, *i 13, i 23*
    chariot racing in Rome, *i 152*
    Chinese, *i 473*
    of Diego Rivera, *i 403*
    Egyptian tomb, *i 38–39*
    of enlightenment, *i 560*
    Guernica, i 814
    medieval, *i 325*
    Nazi, 810
    perspective in, *i 418, i 419*
    Raphael, *i 414*
    Renaissance, *i 416, i 419, i 420*, 421,
        i 424, 425
    of Richard the Lion–Hearted, *i 363*
    Roman, 165
    Romanticism and, 620
    St. George and the Dragon, *i 314*
    St. Petersburg, *i 535*
    silk, *i 187*
    of Socrates, *i 109*
    of Song Dynasty, *i 290*
    Stone Age, 12
    of van Eyck, *i 416*
    of Velázquez, *i 511*
Pakistan
    civil war in, 889

ACKNOWLEDGMENTS

Text Acknowledgments

Title Page: Quotation from *A History of Civilizations* by Fernand Braudel, translated by Richard Mayne. Copyright © 1987 by Les Editions Arthaud; English translation copyright © 1994 by Richard Mayne. Used by permission of Penguin, a division of Penguin Books USA Inc.

Chapter 1, page 21: Excerpt *From The Poetry of Sumer: Creation, Glorification, Adoration* by Samuel Noah Kramer. Copyright © 1979 The Regents of the University of California Press. Reprinted by permission of the University of California Press.

Chapter 7, page 178: Excerpt from a Tamil poem from *The Wonder That Was India* by A. L. Basham. Published by Sidgwick and Jackson. By permission of Macmillan of London.

Chapter 10, page 243: "Quimis," from *Islam: From The Prophet Muhammad to the Capture of Constantinople,* Vol. l, by Bernard Lewis, ed. and trans. Copyright © 1974 by Bernard Lewis. Reprinted by permission of HarperCollins Publishers, Inc.

Chapter 11, page 280: Four lines from "Rumi Quatrain," from *Unseen Rain,* translated by John Moyne and Coleman Barks. Originally published by Threshold Books, 139 Main Street, Brattleboro, VT 05301. By permission of Threshold Books.

Chapter 12, page 290: "Moonlight Night," from *Tu Fu* by William Hung, Cambridge, Mass.: Harvard University Press. Copyright © 1952 by the President and Fellows of Harvard College.

Chapter 13, page 330: Seven lines from page 84 of *The Song of Roland* by Frederick Goldin, translator. Copyright © 1978 by W. W. Norton & Company, Inc. Reprinted by permission of W. W. Norton & Company, Inc.

page 337: Excerpt from "The Prologue," from *The Canterbury Tales* by Geoffrey Chaucer, translated by Nevill Coghill (Penguin Classics, 1951). Copyright © 1951 Nevill Coghill. Reprinted by permission of Penguin Books Ltd.

Chapter 19, page 476: Haiku poem, from *Matsuo Basho,* translated by Makoto Veda. By permission of Makoto Veda.

Chapter 29, page 763: Excerpt from *You Will Hear Thunder, Akhmatova,* Poems, translated by D. M. Thomas, Martin Secker & Warburg, publisher. By permission of Random House UK Limited.

Chapter 35, page 937: Excerpts from "The Coming of Mao Zedong Chic," from Newsweek, May 19, 1997, Newsweek, Inc. All rights reserved. Reprinted by permission.

Back Cover: Extract from *Millennium: A History of the Last Thousand Years* by Felipe Fernández-Armesto. Copyright © Felipe Fernández-Armesto 1995. Published by Bantam Press, a Division of Transworld Publishers Ltd. All rights reserved.

McDougal Littell Inc. has made every effort to locate the copyright holders for selections used in this book and to make full acknowledgment for their use. Omissions brought to our attention will be corrected in a subsequent edition.

Art and Photography Credits

COVER

front *background* Copyright © 1996 Cosmo & Action/Photonica; *insets, top to bottom* Museo Nazionale, Naples, Italy/Scala/Art Resource, New York; Copyright © Jack Hollingsworth; Copyright © 1995 Archive Photos/PNI; Copyright © SuperStock; Lee Boltin; Copyright © Jack Hollingsworth; **back** *top* Copyright © Index Stock Photography, Inc.; *center* Copyright © 1996 Craig Duncan/DDB Stock Photo; *bottom* Copyright © 1992 Carl Scofield/Index Stock Photography, Inc.

FRONT MATTER

half-title page *background* Copyright © 1996 Cosmo & Action/Photonica; **title spread** *background* Copyright © 1996 Cosmo & Action/Photonica; *top row, left to right* Museo Nazionale, Naples, Italy/Scala/Art Resource, New York; Copyright © SuperStock; Copyright © 1995 Archive Photos/PNI; Lee Boltin; Copyright © 1992 Carl Scofield/Index Stock Photography, Inc.; *second row, left to right* Copyright © 1996 Craig Duncan/DDB Stock Photo; Copyright © Jack Hollingsworth; Copyright © Index Stock Photography, Inc.; *bottom* Copyright © Jack Hollingsworth; **viii** *top* Prehistoric painting, Tassili N'Ajjer, Algeria. Henri Lhote Collection, Musée de l'Homme, Paris/Erich Lessing/Art Resource, New York; *center* Pyramids, Giza, Egypt. Copyright © Robert Caputo/Stock Boston; *bottom* Stone bas-relief from palace of Ashurnasirpal II (9th century B.C.). British Museum, London/Erich Lessing/Art Resource, New York; **ix** *top* Parthenon, Athens, Greece. Copyright © SuperStock; *center, Shiva Nataraja* (13th century). Bronze, 34¼" × 27½" × 13". The Nelson-Atkins Museum of Art, Kansas City, Missouri (Purchase: Nelson Trust); *bottom* Olmec head. Archaeological Museum, Jalapa, Mexico/Art Resource, New York; **x** *top* Map by al-Idrisi (12th century). Copyright © Bodleian Library, Oxford, U.K.; *center* Mosaic portrait of Empress Theodora, S. Vitale, Ravenna, Italy. Copyright © R. Sheridan/Ancient Art & Architecture Collection; *bottom, Lady Tomoe Gozen* (about A.D. 900). E.T. Archive, London; **xi** *top* Saint Gregory and three scribes. Ivory, 20.5 cm × 12.5 cm. Kunsthistorisches Museum, Kunstkammer, Vienna, Austria/Erich Lessing/Art Resource, New York; *bottom* Sculpture of queen mother, Benin. Copyright © British Museum; **xii** *top* Inca jaguar cup. National Museum of the American Indian; *center, Shah Jahan Holding a Turban Jewel* (1617), Abu al-Hasan. Victoria & Albert Museum, London/Art Resource, New York; *bottom, Christopher Columbus,* attributed to Pedro Berruguete. Copyright © Giuliana Traverso/Grazia Neri; **xiii** *top* Detail of *Louis XIV, King of France,* Hyacinthe Rigaud. Louvre, Paris/Scala/Art Resource, New York; *center* Two of Galileo's telescopes. The Granger Collection, New York; *bottom* Painting of Simón Bolívar and Antonio José de Sucre. Mary Evans Picture Library, London; **xiv** *top* View of Sheffield, England, 1879. The Granger Collection, New York; *center* Queen Victoria. Copyright © 1994 Archive Photos/PNI; *bottom, The Siege of the Alamo* (19th-century engraving). The Granger Collection, New York; **xv** *top* British soldiers in World War I. Popperfoto; *center* Mohandas K. Gandhi. Corbis-Bettmann; *bottom* Ships afire at Pearl Harbor. UPI/Corbis-Bettmann; **xvi** *top* Fidel Castro and Nikita Khrushchev. Copyright © 1961 Seymour Raskin/Magnum Photos; *center* Nelson Mandela and F. W. de Klerk. Copyright © Mark Peters/Sipa Press; *bottom* Copyright © Hans Deryk/AP/Wide World Photos; **xviii** *left* Private collection; **xxi** *left* Detail of fresco at University of Guadalajara, Mexico (1936–1939), José Clemente Orozco; *top right* Château, Versailles, France/Giraudon/Art Resource, New York; *bottom right* Copyright © British Museum; **xxii** The Granger Collection, New York; **xxvi** *bottom left* Tony Auth, *Philadelphia Inquirer.* Copyright © 1989. Reprinted with permission of Universal Press Syndicate. All rights reserved; **xxvii** Copyright © R. Sheridan/Ancient Art & Architecture Collection; **xxviii** Palace Museum, Beijing; **xxix** *top left* The Granger Collection, New York; *center right* Copyright © Black Star; **xxx** *top left* Louvre, Paris/Alinari/Art Resource, New York; *bottom right* The Granger Collection, New York; **xxxi** *top left* Copyright © Chad Ehlers/Tony Stone Images; *bottom right* Corbis-Bettmann; **xxxii–xxxiii** Copyright © Pacific Stock/Orion Press; **xxxiii** *center left* FPG International; **xxxvi** Copyright © Stephen Alvarez/National Geographic Image Collection; **xxxvii** *top* Copyright © Kenneth Garrett; *center* Flying machine sketch from Codex Atlanticus, Leonardo da Vinci. Biblioteca Ambrosiana, Milan, Italy/Art Resource, New York; *bottom* Copyright © Warren Morgan/Westlight.

UNIT ONE

xxxviii–1 H. Armstrong Roberts; **2** *top* Sumerian hair ornaments, earrings, and necklace. British Museum, London/Werner Forman Archive/Art Resource, New York; *center* Pyramids, Giza, Egypt. H. Armstrong Roberts; *bottom* Ceramic lion detail from the Ishtar Gate, Babylon. Département des Antiquités Orientales, Louvre, Paris/Erich Lessing/Art Resource, New York; **3** Reclining Buddha, Vientiane, Laos. Copyright © 1986 John Banagan/The Image Bank.

Chapter 1

4 Copyright © Sisse Brimberg/National Geographic Image Collection; **5** *left* British Museum, London/Werner Forman Archive/Art Resource, New York; *right* Frontal articulated view of *Australopithecus afarensis,* "Lucy." Original fossil skeleton found in Hadar, Ethiopia. National Museum of Ethiopia. Copyright © 1985 David L. Brill; **6** *top, center, bottom* Copyright © 1992 W. Neeb, University of Innsbruck, Austria/Stern/Black Star; **7** Boltin Picture Library; **8** UPI/Corbis-Bettmann; **12** Copyright © Paul Hanny/Gamma-Liaison; **13** *top* Copyright © D. Johanson, Institute of Human Origins; *center* Musée de l'Homme, Paris/Erich Lessing/Art Resource, New York; *bottom* Copyright © Colorphoto Hans Hinz, Allschwil-Basel, Switzerland; **16** *left, top right, bottom right* Arlette Mellaart/Ankara Museum of Anatolian Civilizations, Turkey; **17** Copyright © Göran Burenhult Productions; **19** British Museum, London/Bridgeman/Art Resource, New York; **20** *left* Courtesy of University of Pennsylvania Museum, Philadelphia (Neg. #S4-139540); *right* Copyright © British Museum; **22** Copyright © 1992 W. Neeb, University of Innsbruck, Austria/Stern/Black Star; **23** Bruce Coleman, Inc.

Chapter 2

24 *top* Copyright © British Museum; *bottom* Louvre, Paris/Giraudon/Art Resource, New York; **25** *top* Musée Cernuschi, Paris/Giraudon; *bottom* Karachi Museum, Karachi, Pakistan/Scala/Art Resource, New York; **26** Illustration by Tom Jester; **27** Copyright © Desmond Harney/Robert Harding Picture Library; **29** Copyright © British Museum; **30–31** British Museum, London/Erich Lessing/Art Resource, New York; **31** *bottom right* Iraq Museum, Baghdad/Scala/Art Resource, New York; **32** Hirmer Verlag GmbH, Munich, Germany; **33** Copyright © Thierry Borredon/Tony Stone Images; **36** Copyright © Robert Caputo/Stock Boston; **37** Copyright © The Image Works/Topham Picturepoint; **38** *bottom left* The Granger Collection, New York; **38–39** Copyright © Victor R. Boswell, Jr./National Geographic Image Collection; **40** *top left* Corbis-Bettmann; *top right* Copyright © Steve Vidler/Tony Stone Images; *bottom center* The Granger Collection, New York; *bottom right* Louvre, Paris/E.T. Archive, London; **41** *center left* Reproduced from the collections of the Library of Congress (LC-USZ62-48427); *bottom left* Egyptian Museum, Cairo, Egypt/Scala/Art Resource, New York; *top right* Copyright © Michael MacIntyre/The Hutchison Library; **43** Copyright © P. Koch/Robert Harding Picture Library; **44** Illustration by Tom Jester; *inset* From *Civilization of the Indus Valley and Beyond,* Sir M. Wheeler (Thames and Hudson, 1966), Fig. 14.8. Reproduced by permission of Thames and Hudson Ltd.; **45** Copyright © MacQuitty International Collection; **47** Copyright © Keren Su/Tony Stone Images/PNI; **48** Academia Sinica, Taipei. Photo copyright © Wan-go H. C. Weng; **49** Musée Cernuschi, Paris/Giraudon; **51** *top, bottom* Copyright © C. M. Dixon; **52** Illustration by Tom Jester.

Chapter 3

54 Museum, Carthage, Tunisia/Erich Lessing/Art Resource, New York; **55** *top* Copyright © Suzanne Murphy/Tony Stone Images; *bottom, Story of the Cross: The Meeting of Solomon with the Queen of Sheba,* Piero della Francesca. S. Francesco, Arezzo, Italy/Scala/Art Resource, New York; **56** Detail of *Rama and Lakshmana Shooting Arrows at the Demon Ravana* (19th century), Delhi of Jaipur school. Gouache on paper. Victoria & Albert Museum, London/Art Resource, New York; **59** Copyright © R. Sheridan/Ancient Art & Architecture Collection; **60** Victoria & Albert Museum, London/Art Resource, New York; **62** Victoria & Albert Museum, London/E.T. Archive, London; **63** Robert Holmes/Corbis; **64** Copyright © 1984 Grant V. Faint/The Image Bank; **65** Copyright © 1986 John Banagan/The Image Bank; **67** British Museum, London. Photograph copyright © Michael Holford; **68** National Archaeological Museum, Beirut, Lebanon/Erich Lessing/Art Resource, New York; **70** *top left* The Bailey-Matthews Shell Museum. Photo by Sharon Hoogstraten; *top right* Copyright © British Museum; *bottom* Copyright © Nawrocki Stock Photo, Inc.; **73** *Moses with the Tablets of the Law,* Guido Reni. Galleria Borghese, Rome/Scala/Art Resource, New York; **74** Copyright © Zev Radovan, Jerusalem, Israel; **76** British Library, London/Bridgeman/Art Resource, New York; **77** Add. MS 11639, f. 521r. By permission of the British Library; **78** Detail of *Rama*

Art and Photography Credits (Cont.)

and Lakshmana Shooting Arrows at the Demon Ravana (19th century), Delhi of Jaipur school. Gouache on paper. Victoria & Albert Museum, London/Art Resource, New York.

Chapter 4

80 *top* British Museum, London. Photograph copyright © Michael Holford; *bottom* Copyright © 1990 Enrico Ferorelli/National Geographic Image Collection; **81** *top* By permission of the British Library; *bottom* Copyright © SuperStock; **82** Illustration by Patrick Whelan; **83** The Metropolitan Museum of Art, Rogers Fund and Contribution from Edward S. Harkness, 1929 (29.3.2); **84** Copyright © British Museum; **85** Courtesy of University of Pennsylvania Museum, Philadelphia (Neg. #T4-550C.2); **86** *left* Photograph by David Finn, from *Egyptian Sculpture: Cairo and Luxor* by Edna Russman, Copyright © 1989. By permission of the University of Texas Press; *right* Copyright © British Museum; **87** Staatliche Museen zu Berlin/Preussischer Kulturbesitz, Ägyptisches Museum; **88** British Museum, London. Photograph copyright © Michael Holford; **89** British Museum, London/Erich Lessing/Art Resource, New York; **91** Département des Antiquités Orientales, Louvre, Paris/Erich Lessing/Art Resource, New York; **93** *top* Copyright © R. Sheridan/Ancient Art & Architecture Collection; *bottom* SEF/Art Resource, New York; **95** *top* Copyright © British Museum; *bottom* Copyright © MacQuitty International Collection; **96** Copyright © SuperStock; **97** Bibliothèque Nationale, Paris/E.T. Archive, London; **98** *left* Copyright © Bibliothèque Nationale, Paris/Bridgeman Art Library, London/SuperStock; *right* The Granger Collection, New York; **99** Wellcome Institute Library, London; **101** *left* Copyright © 1992 Joe McNally/The Image Bank; *right* Illustration by Patrick Whelan; **102** Illustration by Patrick Whelan; **103** British Museum, London. Photo copyright © Michael Holford.

UNIT TWO

104–105 Palazzo Madama, Rome/Scala/Art Resource, New York; **106** *center left* Portrait of Paquius Proculus with his wife. Fresco from Pompeii. Museo Nazionale, Naples, Italy/Scala/Art Resource, New York; *bottom center* Luba Kifwebe mask, Congo. Copyright © Marc & Evelyn Bernheim/Woodfin Camp & Associates; **106–107** Lid of Chinese vessel, Han Dynasty. Courtesy of the Ontario Science Centre; **107** *top center* Bust of King Philip II of Macedon. Chiaramonti Museum, Vatican State/E.T. Archive, London; *bottom right* Stirrup-spout vessel, Chavín culture, South America. Copyright © R. Sheridan/Ancient Art & Architecture Collection.

Chapter 5

108 Piraeus Museum, Greece; **109** *top, The Death of Socrates* (1787), Jacques Louis David. Oil on canvas, 51" × 77¼". The Metropolitan Museum of Art, Catharine Lorillard Wolfe Collection, Wolfe Fund, 1931 (31.45); *bottom* Museo Nazionale, Naples/Scala/Art Resource, New York; **110** *left* American School of Classical Studies at Athens, Italy, Angora excavations; *center* Copyright © British Museum; *right* Copyright © SuperStock; **111** Copyright © George Grigoriou/Tony Stone Images; **112** Copyright © SuperStock; **113** The Granger Collection, New York; **114** Gift in Honor of Edward W. Forbes from his friends. Courtesy, Museum of Fine Arts, Boston; **115** Museo di Villa Giulia, Rome/Scala/Art Resource, New York; **116** Copyright © British Museum; **117** Rijks Museum van Oudheden, Leiden, The Netherlands; **118** Copyright © Elise Amendola/AP/Wide World Photos; **121** Corbis-Bettmann; **122** *top background* Copyright © SuperStock; *top foreground* National Museum, Athens, Greece/Scala/Art Resource, New York; *bottom* Copyright © SuperStock; *inset left* Copyright © R. Sheridan/Ancient Art & Architecture Collection; *inset right* Copyright © The Lowe Art Museum, the University of Miami, Florida/SuperStock; **124** Museo Archeologico Nazionale, Naples, Italy/Scala/Art Resource, New York; **125** *left* Copyright © Museo Capitolino, Rome/SuperStock; *center* Copyright © Museo Capitolino, Rome/E.T. Archive, London/SuperStock; *right* Copyright © SuperStock; **126** *center left* Museo Nazionale Romano delle Terme, Rome/Scala/Art Resource, New York; *bottom center* Photo by Sharon Hoogstraten; *bottom right* Copyright © British Museum; **127** *top left* Woodblock print by Kunisada. Photo copyright © Michael Holford; *center left* Copyright © SuperStock; *bottom left* National Archaeological Museum, Athens, Greece/Nimatallah/Art Resource, New York; *top right* Copyright © 1996 DUOMO Chris Cole; **128** Chiaramonti Museum, Vatican State/E.T. Archive, London; **129** Copyright © British Library, London/Bridgeman Art Library, London/SuperStock; **130** The Metropolitan Museum of Art, gift of Alexander Smith Cochran, 1913 (13.228.7); **132** The Granger Collection, New York; **133** The Granger Collection, New York; **134** *top* MS D'Orville 301 f. 31v. Copyright © Bodleian Library, Oxford, U.K.; *bottom left* The Granger Collection, New York; *bottom right* Smith Collection, Rare Book and Manuscript Library, Columbia University, New York; **135** Louvre, Paris/Scala/Art Resource, New York; **136** *top* Copyright © British Museum; *bottom* Copyright © SuperStock.

Chapter 6

138 Museo Archeologico Nazionale, Naples, Italy/Scala/Art Resource, New York; **139** *left* Mausoleo Galla Placidia, Ravenna, Italy/Scala/Art Resource, New York; *right* Louvre, Paris/Alinari/Art Resource, New York; **140** Illustration by Patrick Whelan; **142** Copyright © Winfield Parks/National Geographic Image Collection; **143** Copyright © British Museum; **144** Copyright © The Trustees of the British Museum; **146** Uffizi, Florence, Italy/Scala/Art Resource, New York; **147** Museo Pio Clementino, Vatican Museums, Vatican State/Scala/Art Resource, New York; **148** *left* Vatican Museums, Vatican State/Scala/Art Resource, New York; *right* Roger Wood/Corbis; **150** *top left* Charles & Josette Lenars/Corbis; *top right* Copyright © 1992 Archivi Alinari/Art Resource, New York; *bottom right* Museo Nazionale, Naples, Italy/Scala/Art Resource, New York; **151** The Granger Collection, New York; **152** Museo Archeologico Nazionale, Naples, Italy/Art Resource, New York; **153** Oviedo Cathedral/Scala/Art Resource, New York; **154** Mausoleo Galla Placidia, Ravenna, Italy/Scala/Art Resource, New York; **157** Palazzo dei Conservatori, Rome/Erich Lessing/Art Resource, New York; **158** Copyright © Mick Sharp; **159** The Granger Collection, New York; **162** Copyright © Archäologisches Landesmuseum der Christian-Albrechts-Universität, Schloss Gottorf, Schleswig, Germany; **163** *top* The Granger Collection, New York; *bottom* Charles & Josette Lenars/Corbis; **164** Galleria Borghese, Rome/Scala/Art Resource, New York; **165** North Carolina Department of Cultural Resources; **166** Illustration by Phil Colprit/Wood Ronsaville Harlin, Inc.; *top right* John Heseltine/Corbis;

167 Andrew Brown/Ecoscene/Corbis; **168** *top left* Louvre, Paris/Alinari/Art Resource, New York; *bottom right* Illustration by Patrick Whelan; **169** Vittoriano Rastelli/Corbis.

Chapter 7

170 The Nelson-Atkins Museum of Art, Kansas City, Missouri (Purchase: Nelson Trust); **171** *left* Copyright © British Museum; *right* Courtesy of the Chinese Culture Center of San Francisco; **172** Illustration by Patrick Whelan; **174** Copyright © Allan Eaton/Ancient Art & Architecture Collection; **177** National Museum, New Delhi, India/Scala/Art Resource, New York; **181** By permission of the British Library, London; **184** Tomb figures of Bactrian camel and West Asian groom (late 7th–8th century). Earthenware, camel 80 cm high, groom 67 cm high. Royal Ontario Museum, George Crofts Collection, gift of Mrs. H. D. Warren (918.22.11, 918.22.8); **185** *left* Copyright © Viktor I. Sarianidi/National Geographic Image Collection; *right* Copyright © Keren Su/Tony Stone Images; **186** Courtesy of the Ontario Science Centre; **187** *Legend of the Nine Suns*, silk painting from Han Dynasty tomb at Changsha, Hunan, China. British Museum, London/Bridgeman Art Library, London; **188** Illustration by Patrick Whelan; **189** National Museum, Beijing, China/Erich Lessing/Art Resource, New York.

Chapter 8

190 Copyright © Victor Englebert; **191** *left* Copyright © Betty Press/Woodfin Camp & Associates; *right* Copyright © Jane Taylor/Sonia Halliday Photographs; **192** Copyright © Anthony Bannister; *inset* Copyright © T. Magor/Robert Harding Picture Library; **193** Copyright © Martin Dohrn/Photo Researchers, Inc.; **194** *left* Copyright © C. & M. Denis-Huot/Peter Arnold, Inc.; *right* Copyright © Nicholas Parfitt/Tony Stone Images; **196** *center left, bottom left* Copyright © Anthony Bannister; *right* The Hutchison Library; **197** Copyright © M. & A. Kirtley/ANA; **198** Copyright © R. Sheridan/Ancient Art & Architecture Collection; **201** Werner Forman Archive/Art Resource, New York; **202** Photo by Malcolm Varon, N.Y.C. © 1993; **204** Copyright © Marc & Evelyn Bernheim/Woodfin Camp & Associates.

Chapter 9

208 *top* Boltin Picture Library; *bottom* Copyright © Nathan Benn/National Geographic Image Collection; **209** Copyright © 1988 Georg Gerster/Comstock, Inc.; **210** Illustration by Tom Jester; **212** *top* Copyright © Warren Morgan/Westlight; *bottom* Professor Tom D. Dillehay; **213** Copyright © George C. Frison; **214** Copyright © 1997 Georg Gerster/Comstock, Inc.; *bottom left insets* Photo by Sharon Hoogstraten; **216** Copyright © National Museum of Anthropology, Mexico/Explorer, Paris/SuperStock; **217** Copyright © Kenneth Garrett/National Geographic Image Collection; **218** Copyright © 1989 Editoriale Jaca Book spa, Milan, Italy. Photo by Corrado Gavinelli; **219** *bottom left* Archaeological Museum, Jalapa, Mexico/Art Resource, New York; *center* Dumbarton Oaks Research Library and Collections, Washington, D.C.; **220** © SuperStock; **221** Copyright © R. Sheridan/Ancient Art & Architecture Collection; **222** *top* Copyright © Nigel Dickinson/Tony Stone Images; *bottom* Copyright © Gary Milburn/Tom Stack & Associates; **224** Illustration by Tom Jester.

UNIT THREE

226–227 British Library, London. Photo copyright © Michael Holford; **228** *center left* Glazed earthenware horse, China, Tang Dynasty. Victoria & Albert Museum, London/Art Resource, New York; *bottom left, Saint Clare Received by Saint Francis* (13th century). S. Chiara, Assisi, Italy/Scala/Art Resource, New York; *bottom right* Sculpture of queen mother, Benin. Copyright © British Museum; **229** *top* Map by al-Idrisi (12th century). Copyright © Bodleian Library, Oxford, U.K.; *center* Bust of Yaroslav the Wise, prince of Kiev. Sovfoto; *bottom* Detail of manuscript illustration of Joan of Arc. Archives Nationales, Paris/Giraudon/Art Resource, New York.

Chapter 10

230 Bibliothèque Nationale, Paris; **231** *top* Bibliothèque Nationale, Paris; *bottom* Copyright © S. Arb/Camerapix; **232** *center left, bottom left, top right, center right* The Granger Collection, New York; **233** Copyright © Tony Waltham/Robert Harding Picture Library; **235** Copyright © I. Perlman/Stock Boston; **236** *top left* Bojan Brocelj/Corbis; *bottom right* E.T. Archive, London; **237** Copyright © 1993 C. Bruce Forster/Tony Stone Images/PNI; **238–239** By permission of the British Library; **239** *top right* The Granger Collection, New York; **243** MS Elliott, f. 192. Copyright © Bodleian Library, Oxford, U.K.; **244** Copyright © A. Duncan/Middle East Archive; **245** *center left* Copyright © Bodleian Library, Oxford, U.K.; *bottom center* The Granger Collection, New York; *top right* Istanbul University Library; **246** Michael Busselle/Corbis; **247** *left* Copyright © Peter Sanders; **248** *left* The Granger Collection, New York; *right* Copyright © 1993 C. Bruce Forster/Tony Stone Images/PNI.

World Religions

252 Copyright © SuperStock; **253** *top left* Copyright © David Hanson/Tony Stone Images; *bottom left* Oriental Museum, Durham University, England/Bridgeman Art Library, London; *top right* The Hutchison Library; *bottom right* MS Sansk 87r. Copyright © Bodleian Library, Oxford, U.K.; **254** Copyright © Rene Sheret/Tony Stone Images; **255** *top left* Copyright © 1990 Gabe Palmer/The Stock Market; *bottom left* Riverside Book and Bible House, Iowa Falls, Iowa. Style No. 220DN. Photo by Sharon Hoogstraten; *center right* Copyright © Haroldo de Faria Castro/FPG International; **256** Copyright © George Hunter/Tony Stone Images; **257** *top left* Copyright © Anthony Cassidy/Tony Stone Images; *center* Robyn Beeche with permission of Conran Octopus; *bottom left* Copyright © Bipinchandra Mistry; *bottom right* National Museum of India, New Delhi; **258** Copyright © Peter Sanders; **259** *top left* Copyright © Nabeel Turner/Tony Stone Images; *center right* Copyright © Carlos Freire/The Hutchison Library; *bottom left* From *Traditional Textiles of Central Asia* by Janet Harvey. Copyright © 1996 Thames and Hudson Ltd., London. Reproduced by permission of the publishers; *bottom right* By permission of Princeton University Press. Photo by Sharon Hoogstraten; **260** Copyright © Zev Radovan; **261** *center left* Copyright © 1989 Joseph Nettis/Stock Boston; *bottom left* Copyright © Impact Photos; *top right* Copyright © Paul Chesley/Tony Stone Images; *bottom right* Copyright © Zev Radovan; **263** *top left* Copyright © Keren Su/Pacific Stock; *center* Copyright © Orion Press/Pacific Stock; *bottom left* From *The Analects of Confucius*, edited by Chichung Huang. Copyright © 1997 by Chichung Huang. Used by permission of Oxford University Press, Inc.

Art and Photography Credits (Cont.)

Chapter 11

266 Biblioteca Nacional, Madrid, Spain/Arxiu Mas; **267** *top* Sovfoto; *bottom* Copyright © R. Sheridan/Ancient Art & Architecture Collection; **268** Scylitzes Chronicle, f. 217r. Biblioteca Nacional, Madrid, Spain/Werner Forman Archive/Art Resource, New York; **269** *top, bottom* Copyright © British Museum; **271** *left* Museo Civico dell'Età Cristiana, Brescia, Italy/Scala/Art Resource, New York; *right* Copyright © R. Sheridan/Ancient Art & Architecture Collection; **273** Castle Armory, Kreuzenstein, Austria/Erich Lessing/Art Resource, New York; **274** Copyright © Stock Montage; **276** *left, Madonna with Child and Angels* (about 1463), Fra Filippo Lippi. Uffizi, Florence, Italy/Scala/Art Resource, New York; *right* Tass/Sovfoto/Eastfoto; **277** Tass/Sovfoto/Eastfoto; **279** The Granger Collection, New York; **280** *top* Copyright © Roger Wood/Corbis; *bottom* Or. MS 20, f. 124v. By permission of the Edinburgh University Library; **282** Scylitzes Chronicle, f. 217r. Biblioteca Nacional, Madrid, Spain/Werner Forman Archive/Art Resource, New York.

Chapter 12

284 National Palace Museum, Taipei. Copyright © Wan-go H. C. Weng; **285** *top* Denman Waldo Ross Collection. Courtesy, Museum of Fine Arts, Boston; *bottom* Art Resource, New York; **286** *top* Copyright © Science Museum, London/Science & Society Picture Library, London; *bottom* Photo by Sharon Hoogstraten; **287** Victoria & Albert Museum, London/Art Resource, New York; **288** *left* Collection, Palace Museum, Beijing. Photo copyright © Wan-go Weng Archive; *right* Wan-go Weng Archive; **290** *Buddhist Retreat by Stream and Mountains* (Northern Song Dynasty, about 960–980), attributed to Ju Ran. Hanging scroll, ink on silk, 185.4 cm high. Copyright © 1997 The Cleveland Museum of Art, gift of Katherine Holden Thayer (1959.348); **291** The Granger Collection, New York; **292** *center left* Photo by Sharon Hoogstraten; *inset* Copyright © Donna Day/Tony Stone Images; *bottom right* Copyright © James D. Wilson/Gamma-Liaison; **293** *top left* The Egyptian Museum, Cairo/Werner Forman Archive/Art Resource, New York; *top right* Courtesy of the Duckworth Collection, University of Cambridge, England. Photo copyright © G. J. Owen; *center left* Copyright © Peter Menzel/PNI; *bottom center* Copyright © Will & Deni McIntyre/Tony Stone Images; **295** *top left* The Purcell Team/Corbis; *center right* Copyright © James L. Stanfield/National Geographic Image Collection; **296–297** Illustration by Patrick Whelan; **298** Copyright © James L. Stanfield/National Geographic Image Collection; **299** Copyright © James L. Stanfield/National Geographic Image Collection; **300** *top* Copyright © Imperial Collections, Sannomaru Shozo Kan. Photograph by courtesy of the International Society for Educational Information, Inc.; *center left* Copyright © William H. Bond/National Geographic Image Collection; **301** Copyright © 1994 Archive Photos/PNI; **304** Robert Holmes/Corbis; **305** Copyright © Laurie Platt Winfrey, Inc.; **306** *left* The Metropolitan Museum of Art, Rogers Fund, 1904 (04.4.2). Photograph by Schecter Lee; *center* Museo Chiossone, Genoa, Italy/Scala/Art Resource, New York; *right* E.T. Archive, London; **309** *left* Dave Houser/Corbis; *right* Copyright © 1996 Don North/PNI; **310** From *The Warrior Queens* by Antonia Fraser, Vintage Books, a division of Random House, Inc., New York. Copyright © 1988 Antonia Fraser; **312** Photo by Sharon Hoogstraten.

Chapter 13

314 *St. George and the Dragon,* Paolo Uccello. National Gallery, London/Art Resource, New York; **315** *top, Portrait of Charlemagne,* Albrecht Dürer. Copyright © Germanisches Nationalmuseum, Nuremberg, Germany/Lauros-Giraudon, Paris/SuperStock; *bottom* Kunsthistorisches Museum, Kunstkammer, Vienna, Austria/Erich Lessing/Art Resource, New York; **316** Corbis-Bettmann; **318** The Granger Collection, New York; **319** *Saint Benedict,* Hans Memling. Uffizi, Florence, Italy/Scala/Art Resource, New York; **320** Copyright © Cathedral Treasury, Aachen, Germany/E.T. Archive, London/SuperStock; **322** Copyright © University Museum of National Antiquities, Oslo, Norway; **324** Illustration by Karen Barnes/Wood Ronsaville Harlin, Inc.; **325** *March: Two Workmen in a Garden* (about 1515), Simon Bening. Da Costa Hours, MS 399, f. 4v. The Pierpont Morgan Library/Art Resource, New York; **327** Royal Armouries; **328** Illustrations by Karen Barnes/Wood Ronsaville Harlin, Inc.; **329** Illustration by the studio of Wood Ronsaville Harlin, Inc.; **330** Copyright © Archive Photos; **332** Museo Tesoro di San Pietro, Vatican State/Scala/Art Resource, New York; **335** The Granger Collection, New York.

Chapter 14

338 The Granger Collection, New York; **339** *left* Bibliothèque Nationale, Paris/Sonia Halliday Photographs, London; *right* Manuscript illustration of Joan of Arc from Antoine Dufour's *Vie des femmes célèbres* (about 1505). Musée Dobrée, Nantes, France/Giraudon/Art Resource, New York; **340** Illustration by Patrick Whelan; **341** Bibliothèque Nationale, Paris/E.T. Archive, London; **342** S. Chiara, Assisi, Italy/Scala/Art Resource, New York; **343** *left* Copyright © Harry Bliss/National Geographic Image Collection; *center* Copyright © L. Salou/Explorer; *right* Cathedral, Chartres, France/Giraudon/Art Resource, New York; **345** *left* The Granger Collection, New York; *right* MS Roy. 14 C. VII, f. 9. By permission of the British Library; **346** The Granger Collection, New York; **347** *left* The Granger Collection, New York; *center* Copyright © Tony Stone Images; *right* Copyright © Jerry Bauer; **348** Musée Condé, Chantilly, France/Giraudon/Art Resource, New York; **350** Bibliothèque Nationale, Paris/Sonia Halliday Photographs, London; **351** The Granger Collection, New York; **352** MS Cott. Faust. B. VII, f. 72v. By permission of the British Library; **353** Photofest; **354** MS français 6465, f. 212v. Bibliothèque Nationale, Paris/AKG Photo, London; **356** The Granger Collection, New York; **357** University Library, Prague, Czech Republic/E.T. Archive, London; **358** *bottom left* Private collection; *top right, The Plague in Naples on the Piazza Mercatello* (mid-17th century), Micco Spadaro. Museo Nazionale di San Martino, Naples, Italy/G. Westermann/Artothek, Peissenberg, Germany; *inset* Reader's Digest, London; **360** MS Roy. 14 E. IV, f. 14v min. By permission of the British Library; **361** Archives Nationales, Paris/Giraudon/Art Resource, New York; **362** Illustration by Patrick Whelan; **363** By permission of the British Library.

Chapter 15

364 The Granger Collection, New York; **365** *bottom left* St. George, Lalibela, Ethiopia/Werner Forman Archive/Art Resource, New York; *top right* The Walt Disney-Tishman Collection of African Art. Photograph by Jerry Thompson; **366** Illustration by Tom Jester; **367** Copyright © Steven Winn/Anthro Photo File; **368** Copyright © British Museum; **370** Copyright © 1979 Richard Wilkie/Black Star/PNI; **371** Copyright © Lee Foster/PNI; **372** The Granger Collection, New York; **373** The Granger Collection, New York; **374** Copyright © Marc & Evelyn Bernheim/Woodfin Camp & Associates; **375** Copyright © Wendy Watriss/Woodfin Camp & Associates; **376** *center left* Staatliche Museen zu Berlin/Preussischer Kulturbesitz, Museum für Völkerkunde; *top center, right* Copyright © British Museum; **377** Photograph from *Africa: Tribal Art of Forest and Savanna* by Arnold Bamert. Copyright © Arnold Bamert; **378** Photo by Sharon Hoogstraten; **380** Copyright © SuperStock; **381** National Archives of Zimbabwe.

UNIT FOUR

384–385 Copyright © SuperStock; **386** *top* Pyramid of Kukulcan, Chichen Itza, Mexico. Copyright © Cosmo Condina/Tony Stone Images; *center* Detail of portrait of Timur the Lame. Uffizi, Florence, Italy/SEF/Art Resource, New York; *bottom* Building in Forbidden City, Beijing, China. Copyright © Bob Handelman/Tony Stone Images; **387** *top* Portrait of Elizabeth I (1588), George Gower. By courtesy of The National Portrait Gallery, London; *bottom* Engraving of Native Americans attacking a Massachusetts village during King Philip's War. The Granger Collection, New York.

Chapter 16

388 *bottom center* Museo del Templo Mayor, Mexico City/John Bigelow Taylor/Art Resource, New York; *top right* North America, New Mexico, Salado region, Mimbres culture: Cache of ritual figures, stone, wood, cotton, feathers, and pigment (about 1350). Basket 97 cm long, ritual figures 64 cm and 36 cm high, snakes 40 cm and 44 cm long, mountain lion 9 cm high, four throwing sticks each 61.5 cm long, Major Acquisitions Centennial Endowment (1979.17.1–11). Photograph copyright © 1997 The Art Institute of Chicago. All rights reserved; **389** *bottom left* National Museum of the American Indian; *top right* Copyright © 1989 Timothy O'Keefe/Index Stock Photography/PNI; **390** The Seattle Art Museum, gift of John H. Hauberg. Photograph by Paul Macapia; **391** Copyright © 1994 Tom Benoit/Tony Stone Images; **392** Maxwell Museum of Anthropology, Albuquerque, New Mexico/Werner Forman Archive/Art Resource, New York; **394** Copyright © Pat O'Hara/Tony Stone Images; **396** National Museum of Anthropology, Mexico City/Werner Forman Archive/Art Resource, New York; **397** *top right* Danny Lehman/Corbis; *left center* Charles & Josette Lenars/Corbis; *bottom* Copyright © Cosmo Condina/Tony Stone Images; **398** Copyright © British Museum; **399** Jeremy Horner/Corbis; **400** Copyright © SuperStock; **401** Nik Wheeler/Corbis; **403** Detail of *El Tajin Pyramid and Warriors* (1950), Diego Rivera. Mural. National Palace, Mexico/E.T. Archive, London; **404** *left center* National Museum of Anthropology, Mexico City, Mexico/Werner Forman Archive/Art Resource, New York; *bottom right* Copyright © J. P. Courau/Explorer; **405** *bottom left* Andromeda Oxford Ltd.; *top left* Copyright © 1994 Coco McCoy/Rainbow/PNI; *center left* Courtesy of Breitling USA. Breitling is a registered trademark of Breitling Montres S.A.; *top right* The Granger Collection, New York; **406** National Museum of Anthropology, Mexico City/Michael Zabe/Art Resource, New York; **407** The Metropolitan Museum of Art, gift and bequest of Alice K. Bache, 1974 and 1977 (1974.271.35); **409** Courtesy Department of Library Services, American Museum of Natural History (Neg. #K4673); **410** Nick Saunders/Barbara Heller Photo Library, London/Art Resource, New York; **412** *top* North America, New Mexico, Salado region, Mimbres culture: Detail of cache of ritual figures, stone, wood, cotton, feathers, and pigment (about 1350). Basket 97 cm long, ritual figures 64 cm and 36 cm high, snakes 40 cm and 44 cm long, mountain lion 9 cm high, four throwing sticks each 61.5 cm long, Major Acquisitions Centennial Endowment (1979.17.1–11). Photograph copyright © 1997 The Art Institute of Chicago. All rights reserved; *second from top* National Museum of Anthropology, Mexico City/Werner Forman Archive/Art Resource, New York; *second from bottom* National Museum of Anthropology, Mexico City/Michael Zabe/Art Resource, New York; *bottom* The Metropolitan Museum of Art, gift and bequest of Alice K. Bache, 1974 and 1977 (1974.271.35); **413** The Newberry Library, Chicago.

Chapter 17

414 *top* By courtesy of the National Portrait Gallery, London; *bottom, The School of Athens* (1508), Raphael. Stanza della Segnatura, Vatican Palace, Vatican State/Scala/Art Resource, New York; **415** Detail of *The Gates of Paradise,* Lorenzo Ghiberti. Baptistery, Florence, Italy/Scala/Art Resource, New York; **416** *The Madonna of Chancellor Rolin* (about 1434), Jan van Eyck. Louvre, Paris/Scala/Art Resource, New York; **418** *Lorenzo de'Medici* (15th–16th century), unknown artist. Painted terra cotta, 65.8 cm × 59.1 cm × 32.7 cm. National Gallery of Art, Washington, D.C., Samuel H. Kress Collection. Photograph by Philip A. Charles; **419** *top* The Granger Collection, New York; *bottom, Marriage of the Virgin* (1504), Raphael. Brera, Milan, Italy/Scala/Art Resource, New York; **420** *center left* Scala/Art Resource, New York; *bottom center,* David, Michelangelo. Accademia, Florence, Italy/Scala/Art Resource, New York; *top right* Sistine Chapel, Vatican State/Scala/Art Resource, New York; **421** *left* Self-portrait by Leonardo da Vinci. Biblioteca Reale, Turin, Italy/Scala/Art Resource, New York; *right* Detail of *The School of Athens* (1508), Raphael. Stanza della Segnatura, Vatican Palace, Vatican State/Scala/Art Resource, New York; **422** Palazzo Vecchio, Florence, Italy/Scala/Art Resource, New York; **423** *The Adoration of the Trinity* (1511), Albrecht Dürer. Oil on poplar wood, 135 cm × 123.4 cm. Kunsthistorisches Museum, Gemäldegalerie, Vienna, Austria/Erich Lessing/Art Resource, New York; **424** *Peasant Wedding* (1568), Peter Bruegel the Elder. Kunsthistorisches Museum, Vienna, Austria/Saskia/Art Resource, New York; **425** Corbis; **426** Copyright © 1990 Warner Bros., Inc./Photofest; **427** *left, right* The Granger Collection, New York; **428** *Girolamo Savonarola* (early 16th century), Alessandro Bonvicino. E.T. Archive, London; **429** *Portrait of Martin Luther* (1529), Lucas Cranach the Elder. Museo Poldi Pezzoli, Milan, Italy/Bridgeman Art Library, London; **430** The Granger Collection, New York; **431** Corbis; **432** *Elizabeth I* (1588), George Gower. By courtesy of The National Portrait Gallery, London; **433** Bibliothèque Publique et Universitaire, Geneva, Switzerland/Erich Lessing/Art Resource, New York; **434** Musée Condé, Chantilly, France/Giraudon/Art Resource, New York; **436** Louvre, Paris/Giraudon/Bridgeman Art Library, London; **437** Detail of *Portrait of Martin Luther* (1529), Lucas Cranach the Elder. Museo Poldi Pezzoli, Milan, Italy/Bridgeman Art Library, London; **438** Detail of *The Madonna of Chancellor Rolin* (about 1434), Jan van Eyck. Louvre, Paris/Scala/Art Resource, New York.

Art and Photography Credits (Cont.)

Chapter 18

440 *First Attack on Constantinople by the Turks in 1453,* Jacopo Palma Giovane. Oil on canvas. Palazzo Ducale, Venice, Italy/Erich Lessing/Art Resource, New York; **441** *top* SEF/Art Resource, New York; *bottom* Victoria & Albert Museum, London/Art Resource, New York; **442** *The Enthroning of Mehmet II.* MS H. 1523, p. 153b. Topkapi Palace Museum, Istanbul, Turkey. Photo copyright © Sonia Halliday Photographs; **443** Topkapi Palace Museum, Istanbul, Turkey. Photo copyright © Sonia Halliday and Laura Lushington; **444** Uffizi, Florence, Italy/SEF/Art Resource, New York; **446** The Granger Collection, New York; **447** Archives Nationales, Paris/Giraudon/Art Resource, New York; **449** Chihil Sutun, Isfahan, Iran/SEF/Art Resource, New York; **452** MS Add. Or. 1039. Courtesy of the British Library; **453** Victoria & Albert Museum, London/Art Resource, New York; **454** Copyright © M. Khursheed/AP/Wide World Photos; **455** Copyright © Alvaro de Leiva/Liaison International; **456** *bottom left* Copyright © R. Sheridan/Ancient Art & Architecture Collection; *center* Copyright © Norbert Wu; *top right* Victoria & Albert Museum, London/Art Resource, New York; **457** Copyright © British Museum.

Chapter 19

460 By courtesy of the Bibliothèque Nationale, Paris; **461** *top left* The Granger Collection, New York; *inset left* Woodcut of Zheng He from *The Western Sea Cruises of Eunuch San Bao* by Luo Moudeng, 1597; *bottom right* Rijksmuseum, Amsterdam, The Netherlands; **462** The Granger Collection, New York; **463** Globe by Martin Behaim (about 1492). Bibliothèque Nationale, Paris/Giraudon/Art Resource, New York; **464** The Granger Collection, New York; **465** *bottom left, center* Copyright © National Maritime Museum, London; *top right* Museo Naval, Madrid, Spain; **466** Copyright © National Maritime Museum, London; **469** Musée Guimet, Paris/Giraudon/Art Resource, New York; **470** Copyright © Bob Handelman/Tony Stone Images; **471** Palace Museum, Beijing, China; **472** Palace Museum, Beijing, China/Wan-go Weng, Inc.; **473** Copyright © British Museum; **474** Victoria & Albert Museum, London/Art Resource, New York; **476** Bruce Coleman, Inc.; **478** Copyright © National Maritime Museum, London; **479** The Granger Collection, New York.

Chapter 20

480 *top* The Granger Collection, New York; *bottom* Fotomas Index, Kent, England; **481** 1786 C. 9, Pl. IV. By permission of the British Library; **482** Courtesy Department of Library Services, American Museum of Natural History (Neg. #329243). Photo by Logan; **483** Copyright © Giuliana Traverso/Grazia Neri; **485** *left, right* The Granger Collection, New York; **487** The Granger Collection, New York; **488** The John Carter Brown Library at Brown University, Providence, Rhode Island; **489** *left* Copyright © Karsh, Ottawa/Woodfin Camp & Associates; *center* The Granger Collection, New York; *right, Newsweek*/Chris Kleponis. Copyright © 1991, Newsweek, Inc. All rights reserved. Reprinted by permission; **491** The Granger Collection, New York; **492** Illustration from *A General History of the Lives and Adventures of the Most Famous Highwaymen* by Charles Johnson, 1736. Courtesy of the Rare Books Division, The New York Public Library, Astor, Lenox and Tilden Foundations; **494** The Granger Collection, New York; **496** Illustration from *Flore pittoreque et médicale des Antilles* by Michel Étienne Descourtilz. Courtesy of the Botany Libraries, Harvard University, Cambridge, Massachusetts; **498** *top* National Archives; *center left* The Granger Collection, New York; **500** The Granger Collection, New York; **501** *top left, top right inset* Photos by Sharon Hoogstraten; *top right* Copyright © SuperStock; **502** *left, right* The Granger Collection, New York; **503** Library of Congress; **504** Courtesy Department of Library Services, American Museum of Natural History (Neg. #329243). Photo by Logan; **505** The Granger Collection, New York.

UNIT FIVE

506–507 Museo Nacional de Historia, Castillo de Chapultepec, Mexico City/Schalkwijk/Art Resource, New York; **508** *bottom* Detail of *Napoleon Crossing the St. Bernard Pass,* Jacques Louis David. Château de Malmaison, Rueil-Malmaison, France/Giraudon/Art Resource, New York; **509** *top* Portrait of Frederick the Great of Prussia (1740), Antoine Pesne. Schloss Charltenburg, Berlin/Bildarchiv Preussischer Kulturbesitz, Berlin; *bottom* Detail of lithograph by Alexander Isaias, showing Greeks battling Turks during the war for Greek independence. Historical and Ethnological Museum of Greece.

Chapter 21

510 Château, Versailles, France/Giraudon/Art Resource, New York; **511** *top* Copyright © SuperStock; *bottom, Juan de Pareja* (about 1650), Diego Rodríguez de Silva y Velázquez. Oil on canvas, 32" × 27½". The Metropolitan Museum of Art, Fletcher Fund, Rogers Fund, and bequest of Miss Adelaide Milton de Groot (1876–1967), by exchange, supplemented by gifts from friends of the Museum, 1971 (1971.86); **513** Detail of *Philip II on Horseback,* Peter Paul Rubens. Museo del Prado, Madrid, Spain/Scala/Art Resource, New York; **514** The Granger Collection, New York; **515** Photo by Sharon Hoogstraten; **516** *The Syndics,* Rembrandt van Rijn. Oil on canvas, 191.5 cm × 279 cm. Rijksmuseum Foundation, Amsterdam, The Netherlands; **518** *Three Studies of Cardinal Richelieu,* Philippe de Champaigne. National Gallery, London/Art Resource, New York; **519** Corbis; **520** Detail of *Louis XIV in Armor* (about 1674), attributed to Pierre Mignard. Oil on canvas. Columbus Museum of Art, Ohio, bequest of Frederick W. Schumacher; **521** *View of the Chateau of Versailles in 1668,* Pierre Patel the Elder. Versailles and Trianon, France. Copyright © Gérard Blot/Photo RMN; *inset top* Copyright © Tony Craddock/Tony Stone Images; *inset bottom* Corbis; **522** *Siege of Namur in June 1692,* Jean Baptiste Martin the Elder. Oil on canvas. Versailles and Trianon, France. Copyright © Gérard Blot/Photo RMN; **524** *center left* Detail of *Louis XIV, King of France,* Hyacinthe Rigaud. Louvre, Paris/Scala/Art Resource, New York; *bottom center* Detail of *Colbert Presenting to Louis XIV the Members of the Royal Academy of Sciences in 1667,* Henri Testelin. Versailles and Trianon, France. Copyright © Gérard Blot/Photo RMN; *bottom right* Copyright © Louvre, Paris/Photo RMN; **525** *top left* The Granger Collection, New York; *center left* Copyright © 1990 Sandro Tucci/Black Star/*Time* magazine/PNI; *bottom center* The Granger Collection, New York; *top right background, Boki and Liliha,* John Hayter. Oil on fabric. Courtesy of the Kamehameha Schools/Bernice Pauahi Bishop Estate. Copyright © Bishop Museum, Honolulu, Hawaii; *top right foreground* Copyright © Seth Joel/Bishop Museum, Honolulu, Hawaii; **526** The Granger Collection, New York; **529** *left* Kunsthistorisches Museum, Vienna, Austria; *right* Schloss Charltenburg, Berlin/Bildarchiv Preussischer Kulturbesitz, Berlin; **530**

UPI/Corbis-Bettmann; **531** The Granger Collection, New York; **532** Detail of *Peter the Great, Tsar of Russia,* Sir Godfrey Kneller. The Royal Collection, copyright © Her Majesty Queen Elizabeth II; **534** *center left* RIA-Novosti/Sovfoto; *top right* Sovfoto/Eastfoto; *bottom center* Illustration from *The Art and Architecture of Russia* by George Heard Hamilton. Courtesy of Yale University Press, *Pelican History of Art*; **535** The Granger Collection, New York; **536** Title page from the King James Bible (1611). The Pierpont Morgan Library, New York/Art Resource, New York; **538** Guildhall Library, Corporation of London/Bridgeman Art Library, London; **540** Copyright © Tony Craddock/Tony Stone Images.

Chapter 22

542 Detail of *Patrick Henry Before the Virginia House of Burgesses* (1851), Peter F. Rothermel. Red Hill, The Patrick Henry National Memorial, Brookneal, Virginia; **543** *top* The Granger Collection, New York; *bottom, The Anatomy Lesson of Dr. Tulp* (1632), Rembrandt van Rijn. Mauritshuis, The Hague, The Netherlands/Scala/Art Resource, New York; **544** *Galileo Before the Holy Office in the Vatican* (19th century), Joseph Nicolas Robert-Fleury. Louvre, Paris. Copyright © Gérard Blot/Photo RMN; **545** Corbis-Bettmann; **547** The Granger Collection, New York; **548** *top left, top right* The Granger Collection, New York; **549** The Granger Collection, New York; **550** *Edward Jenner Performing the First Vaccination, 1796* (about 1915), Ernest Board. Wellcome Institute Library, London; **551** Copyright © Hulton Getty Picture Collection/Tony Stone Images; **552** The Granger Collection, New York; **553** *top, bottom* The Granger Collection, New York; **555** The Granger Collection, New York; **556** Copyright © 1995 Wood River Gallery/PNI; **557** *top* Michael Nicholson/Corbis; *bottom* "A caza de dientes" [Out hunting for teeth] from *Los caprichos* (1799), Francisco José de Goya y Lucientes. Etching and burnished aquatint, 21.5 cm × 15 cm. Gift of Paul Singer and Henry Lusardi, and the Maria Antoinette Evans Fund by exchange. Courtesy, Museum of Fine Arts, Boston; **558** *First Reading of Voltaire's "L'Orpheline de Chine" at Mme. Geoffrin's in 1755,* Anicet Charles Gabriel Lemonnier. Musée des Beaux-Arts, Rouen, France/Giraudon/Art Resource, New York; **559** *Seated Woman with Book,* Jean Baptiste Chardin. Statens Konstmuseer, Stockholm, Sweden; **560** *center left, Madame Vigée and Her Daughter,* Elisabeth Louise Vigée-Lebrun. Louvre, Paris; *bottom left, A Philosopher Giving a Lecture on the Orrery,* Joseph Wright of Derby. Oil on canvas, 58" × 80". Derby Museum and Art Gallery, England; *top right* The Granger Collection, New York; **562** The Granger Collection, New York; **563** The Metropolitan Museum of Art, gift of William H. Huntington, 1883 (83.2.228); **564** Detail of *Thomas Jefferson* (about 1805), Rembrandt Peale. Oil on canvas. Copyright © Collection of The New-York Historical Society; **566** Copyright © 1992 David Stover/PNI; **569** "El sueño de la razón produce monstruos" [The sleep of reason produces monsters] from *Los caprichos* (1799), Francisco José de Goya y Lucientes. Etching and burnished aquatint, 21.5 cm × 15 cm. Bequest of William P. Babcock. Courtesy, Museum of Fine Arts, Boston.

Chapter 23

570 *top, Portrait of Marie Antoinette,* Jean Baptiste Augustin. Aquarelle on ivory. National Museum of Art, Bucharest, Romania. Copyright © Gérard Blot/Photo RMN; *bottom* Copyright © Labat JM/Explorer, Paris; **571** *top* Mary Evans Picture Library, London; *bottom* Château de Malmaison, Rueil-Malmaison, France/Giraudon/Art Resource, New York; **572** Musée Carnavalet, Paris/Jean-Loup Charmet; **573** *Portrait of Louis XVI,* Antoine François Callet. Versailles and Trianon, France. Copyright © Photo RMN; **574** *Taille: impots et corvées* (late-18th-century engraving). Musée de la Ville de Paris, Musée Carnavalet, Paris/Giraudon/Art Resource, New York; **575** *left, La maraîchère* [Woman of the French Revolution], Jacques Louis David. Musée des Beaux-Arts, Lyon, France/Giraudon/Art Resource, New York; *right, Marie Antoinette,* Jacques Gautier d'Agoty. Château, Versailles, France/Giraudon/Art Resource, New York; **577** Musée de la Ville de Paris, Musée Carnavalet, Paris/Giraudon/Art Resource, New York; **579** *Attaque du palais des Tuileries, le 20 juin 1792: les émeutiers envahissent le palais en présence du roi et de la reine* [Attack on the Tuileries Palace, June 20, 1792: The rioters overrun the palace in the presence of the king and queen], Jean Baptiste Verité. Hand-colored engraving. Versailles and Trianon, France. Copyright © Photo RMN; **580** Musée de la Ville de Paris, Musée Carnavalet, Paris/Giraudon/Art Resource, New York; **581** Illustration by Patrick Whelan; **582** Musée Carnavalet, Paris/Bulloz; **583** Musées Royaux des Beaux-Arts, Brussels, Belgium/Giraudon/Art Resource, New York; **584** Photo by Soalhat/Sipa Press, New York; **586** Musée de l'Armée, Paris/Giraudon/Art Resource, New York; **589** Fotomas Index, Kent, England; **592** Musée de l'Armée, Paris/Giraudon/Art Resource, New York; **593** The Bettmann Archive; **594** Detail of *Masked Ball in the Redoutensaal on Occasion of the Congress of Vienna with Performance of Beethoven's Seventh Symphony and His Composition "Wellington's Victory in the Battle of Vittoria"* (around 1815), Carl Schuetz. Color print. Historisches Museum der Stadt Wien, Austria/Erich Lessing/Art Resource, New York; *inset left* Mary Evans Picture Library, London; **597** *left* Musée des Beaux-Arts, Lille, France/Giraudon/Art Resource, New York; *right* Victoria & Albert Museum, London/Art Resource, New York; **598** *far left center* Parisian sans-culotte (18th century), unknown artist. Musée de la Ville de Paris, Musée Carnavalet, Paris/Giraudon/Art Resource, New York; *left center* Model of a guillotine. Musée de la Ville de Paris, Musée Carnavalet, Paris/Giraudon/Art Resource, New York; *bottom* Musée Carnavalet, Paris/Jean-Loup Charmet.

Chapter 24

600 The Granger Collection, New York; **601** *bottom left* Copyright © 1986 R. van Butselle/Image Bank; **601** *Incontro di Teano* [Encounter at the Teano Bridge], Cesare Maccari. Palazzo Pubblico, Siena, Italy/Scala/Art Resource, New York; **602** *center left, bottom left, center, center right* Courtesy of the Flag Institute; **603** Copyright © 1991 Kathleen Marie Rohr/DDB Stock Photo; **604** The Granger Collection, New York; **605** The Granger Collection, New York; **606** *bottom left* Copyright © D. Donne Bryant; *top right* Corbis-Bettmann; **607** The Granger Collection, New York; **609** Arc de Triomphe de l'Etoile, Paris/Giraudon/Art Resource, New York; **610** *top* Historical and Ethnological Museum of Greece; *center right, George Gordon Byron, 6th Baron Byron* (1813), Thomas Phillips. By courtesy of the National Portrait Gallery, London; **611** The Granger Collection, New York; **612** Victoria & Albert Museum, London/Art Resource, New York; **614** E.T. Archive, London; **616** The Granger Collection, New York; **618** The Granger Collection, New York; **619** Illustration by Arthur Rackham from *Little Brother and Little Sister* by Jakob and Wilhelm Grimm. University of Louisville, Special Collections; **620** Copyright © Photofest; **621** Beethoven House, Bonn, Germany/Erich Lessing/Art Resource, New York; **622** *top left, The Winnowers* (1855), Gustave Courbet. Oil on canvas, 131 cm × 167 cm. Musée des Beaux-Arts, Nantes,

Acknowledgments **1079**

Art and Photography Credits (Cont.)

France/Giraudon/Art Resource, New York; *bottom left, Coquelicots, environs d'Argenteuil* [Poppy field at Argenteuil] (1873), Claude Monet. Oil on canvas, 50 cm × 65 cm. Musée d'Orsay, Paris. Photo copyright © Photo RMN-ADAGP; *top right, Mondaufgang am Meer* [Moonrise over the sea] (1822), Caspar David Friedrich. Oil on canvas, 55 cm × 71 cm. Staatliche Museen zu Berlin/Preussischer Kulturbesitz, Nationalgalerie; **623** *Ships at Low Tide* (about 1844), William Henry Fox Talbot. Salted paper print from calotype negative, 16.5 cm × 21.6 cm. National Museum of American History, Smithsonian Institution, Division of Photographic History; **624** Courtesy of the Flag Institute; **625** Copyright © Stock Montage, Inc.

UNIT SIX

626–627 Copyright © Peabody Essex Museum. Photo by Jeffrey Dykes; **628** *top* Detail of *Kansas Pioneers* (1920), George Melville Stone. Oil on canvas, 72" × 120". Kansas State Historical Society, Topeka. Photo courtesy of the State of Kansas; *bottom* Tea being loaded onto elephants at the Lipton Plantation, India. E.T. Archive, London; **629** *top, Vor dem Streik* [Before the strike], after a painting by Michael Munkacsy. Bildarchiv Preussischer Kulturbesitz, Berlin; *bottom* 19th-century Japanese woman. Mary Evans Picture Library, London.

Chapter 25

631 *left* Detail of *Vor dem Streik* [Before the strike], after a painting by Michael Munkacsy. Bildarchiv Preussischer Kulturbesitz, Berlin; *right* Weidenfeld & Nicolson Archives; **632** Illustration by Patrick Whelan; **633** The Granger Collection, New York; **634** *left, right* The Granger Collection, New York; **634–635** The Granger Collection, New York; **637** The Granger Collection, New York; **638** The Granger Collection, New York; **639** The Granger Collection, New York; **641** The Granger Collection, New York; **643** The Granger Collection, New York; **645** *Das Eisenwalzwerk: Moderne Zyklopen* [The rolling mill: a modern behemoth] (1875), Adolph von Menzel. Staatliche Museen zu Berlin/Preussischer Kulturbesitz, Nationalgalerie; **647** The Granger Collection, New York; **648** Copyright © The College Shop, University College, London; **649** The Granger Collection, New York; **650** *left, right* The Granger Collection, New York; **651** Mansell Collection/Time, Inc.; **652** Jane Addams Memorial Collection, Special Collections, The University Library, The University of Illinois at Chicago; **653** *center* U.S. Steel; *right* Karl Marx Museum, Trier, Germany/E.T. Archive, London; **654** Illustration by Patrick Whelan.

Chapter 26

656 Kansas State Historical Society, Topeka. Photo courtesy of the State of Kansas; **657** *bottom left* Lauros-Giraudon/Art Resource, New York; *top right* Mary Evans Picture Library, London; **658** *bottom left, center* The Granger Collection, New York; *top right* Corbis-Bettmann; **659** National Portrait Gallery, London; **660** *top* Copyright © SuperStock; *bottom* Detail of *Queen Victoria* (1838), Sir George Hayter. National Portrait Gallery, London; **661** *center left* Photo by Sharon Hoogstraten; *top right* Corbis; *center right, The Railway Station* (1862), William Powell Frith. Royal Holloway and Bedford New College, Surrey, England/Bridgeman Art Library, London; **663** *Une rue de Paris en mai 1871, ou La Commune* [A Paris street in May 1871; or, The commune] (1903–1905), Maximilien Luce. Oil on canvas, 150 cm × 225 cm. Musée d'Orsay, Paris/Erich Lessing/Art Resource, New York; **664** Copyright © 1993 Brian Stablyk/Tony Stone Images; **667** Copyright © Hawaii State Archives/Pacific Stock; **668** Photograph reproduced with the kind permission of the Trustees of the Ulster Museum, Belfast, Northern Ireland; **671** *top* Copyright © Hulton Getty Picture Collection; *bottom* Library of Congress; **674** *La chaîne Simpson* (1896), Henri de Toulouse-Lautrec. Poster. Musée Toulouse-Lautrec, Albi, France/Giraudon/Art Resource, New York; **675** Copyright © Hulton Getty Picture Collection/Tony Stone Images; **676** *center left, bottom left* Photofest; *bottom center, bottom right* Copyright © 1994 Archive Photos/PNI; **677** *top left* Copyright © 1988 Itar-Tass/PNI; *center left* Corbis; *bottom left* Copyright © 1994 Archive Photos/PNI; *top right* Copyright © 1979 New China Pictures/Eastfoto/PNI; **678** *top* Corbis-Bettmann; *bottom* Corbis; **680** Corbis-Bettmann; **681** By permission of the British Library.

Chapter 27

682 Copyright © Werner Forman/Corbis; **683** *top left* Copyright © 1994 Archive Photos/PNI; *bottom right* Copyright © Culver Pictures; **684** *top left* The Granger Collection, New York; *center left* Copyright © Hulton Getty Picture Collection/Tony Stone Images; *bottom left* Crown copyright is reproduced with the permission of the Controller of Her Majesty's Stationery Office; *right* Photo by Sharon Hoogstraten; **685** Copyright © British Museum; **686** The Granger Collection, New York; **692** *bottom left* Photo by Sharon Hoogstraten; *top right* Dave Houser/Corbis; **696** Copyright © Culver Pictures; **698** The Granger Collection, New York; **701** E.T. Archive, London; **703** Copyright © Hulton Getty Picture Collection/Tony Stone Images; **704** The Granger Collection, New York; **705** Mary Evans Picture Library, London; **706** Jack Fields/Corbis; **707** Copyright © 1989 Jose Azel/PNI; **708** Corbis-Bettmann; **709** UPI/Corbis-Bettmann.

Chapter 28

712 Photograph from *Historia gráfica de la Revolución mexicana, 1900–1960* by Gustavo Casasola, ed. commemorativa. Copyright © 1960 Editorial F. Trillas, Mexico City; *bottom* Snark International, Paris/Art Resource, New York; **713** *top* Snark International, Paris/Art Resource, New York; *bottom* Carl H. Boehringer Collection/Laurie Platt Winfrey, Inc., New York; **714** Peabody Museum, Salem, Massachusetts/Werner Forman Archive/Art Resource, New York; **715** Laurie Platt Winfrey, Inc.; **716** Copyright © 1989 Jan Halaska/Tony Stone Images/PNI; **719** The Granger Collection, New York; **720** Mary Evans Picture Library, London; **721** *left, right* The Granger Collection, New York; **723** Mary Evans Picture Library, London; **724** Copyright © Loren McIntyre; **726** The Granger Collection, New York; **727** Copyright © Culver Pictures; **728** *bottom left* Copyright © John Lopinot/Black Star; *center, top right* The Granger Collection, New York; **729** The Granger Collection, New York; **731** *top* Detail of fresco at University of Guadalajara, Mexico (1936–1939), José Clemente Orozco; *bottom* The Granger Collection, New York; **732** Copyright © 1994 Archive Photos/PNI.

UNIT SEVEN

736–737 Imperial War Museum, London; **738** Nazi Party parade in Nuremberg, Germany, 1933. Copyright © Hulton Getty Picture Collection/Tony Stone Images; **739** *top* German machine-gun team in